Harris. — CBIAC

Harris. B. L. B.

Dan J. Harris. Savings Cert.

KETTRIDGE'S
FRENCH DICTIONARY

DICTIONARY
OF THE
FRENCH AND ENGLISH LANGUAGES
WITH PHONETIC TRANSCRIPTION
OF EVERY FRENCH VOCABULARY WORD

Spelling based on
the Dictionnaire de l'Académie française (1932–1935)
and on the Oxford English Dictionaries

BY

J. O. KETTRIDGE
OFFICIER D'ACADÉMIE
F.S.A.A., ETC.

LONDON
GEORGE ROUTLEDGE & SONS, LIMITED
BROADWAY HOUSE: 68–74, CARTER LANE, E.C.4
1946

First Edition	.	.	March	1936
Second Impression	.	.	July	1936
Third Impression	.	.	August	1937
Fourth Impression	.	.	September	1938
Fifth Impression	.	.	September	1939
Sixth Impression	.	.	January	1942
Seventh Impression	.	.	January	1943
Eighth Impression	.	.	January	1944
Ninth Impression	.	.	March	1945
Tenth Impression	.	.	April	1946

Printed in Great Britain by Butler & Tanner Ltd., Frome and London

CONTENTS

PREFACE

A dictionary is like a kaleidoscope. The bits of coloured glass are the letters of the alphabet. Together they form words ; and words form sentences, phrases, idioms ; and these reflect images, ideas. The near-in patterns of the kaleidoscope are very plain : these are the literal meanings of words. Farther off they become less distinct : these are the figurative meanings, the extensions of meanings, the analogies, the abuses of the word even. As in a kaleidoscope every turn produces a different pattern, so in a dictionary every paragraph presents another structure. And lastly, as the number of images the kaleidoscope evolves is infinite, so language is boundless and endless.

A wag once said he did not like to read a dictionary as he lost the thread of the story in the great mass of detail. Yet there is a story in words, and a very fascinating one to those who love language : it is called derivation, the word's history and relationships.

And to the lexicographer there is another thread : the love of the thing, the lure of doing something that may live, which, like Ariadne's clew in the Cretan Labyrinth, leads him through a maze of toil into the open sunlight of the finished work.

The Equivalents of

WEIGHTS & MEASURES

will be found in the Dictionary under each separate denomination, French in the French-English section, English in the English-French section.

Comparison of Centimetres with Inches

Note.— In France, the figure 1 is generally written with an upstroke; thus 1 or 1 (this is never done in England).

As a consequence, the figure 7, in France, is crossed; thus, 7 (never in England), as otherwise it might be confused with a 1.

The figure 5, is either written as in England 5, or thus 5 or 5. This is frequently joined on in a flowing style to the preceding figure, thus 25 may be written 25 or 25 or 25 or 25.

ix

KEY TO INTERNATIONAL PHONETIC TRANSCRIPTION

VOWELS

16 symbols to be learnt

a	papa, femme, roi (papa, fam, rwa)
ɑ	passer, bâiller, bas (pɑse, bɑje, bɑ)
ɑ̃	rampant, encan, temps (rɑ̃pɑ̃, ɑ̃kɑ̃, tɑ̃)
e	récréer, fée, chez (rekree, fe, ʃe)
ə	de, que, recevoir (də, kə, rəsəvwaːr)
ɛ	frais, près, rets, bel (frɛ, prɛ, rɛ, bɛl)
ɛ̃	bien, bain, vin, oint (bjɛ̃, bɛ̃, vɛ̃, wɛ̃)
i	civilité, nihiliste, y (sivilite, niilist, i)

o	gros, tôt, peau, aux (gro, to, po, o)
ɔ	colonne, cohorte (kɔlɔn, kɔɔrt)
ɔ̃	componction, mont (kɔ̃pɔ̃ksjɔ̃, mɔ̃)
œ	œuf, cueillir, seul (œf, kœjiːr, sœl)
œ̃	un, parfum, défunt (œ̃, parfœ̃, defœ̃)
ø	bleu, creux, vœu (blø, krø, vø)
u	trou, goût, courroux (tru, gu, kuru)
y	vu, une, murmurer (vy, yn, myrmyre)

1 symbol to be learnt

: indicates that the sound represented by the preceding symbol is long; thus:—

aː	car, bail, soir (kaːr, baːj, swaːr)
ɑː	passe, âme, paille (pɑːs, ɑːm, pɑːj)
ɑ̃ː	ambre, antre, centre (ɑ̃ːbr, ɑ̃ːtr, sɑ̃ːtr)
ɛː	faire, ère, guerre (fɛːr, ɛːr, gɛːr)
ɛ̃ː	sainte, linge, peintre (sɛ̃ːt, lɛ̃ːʒ, pɛ̃ːtr)
iː	fille, lyre, abîme (fiːj, liːr, abiːm)
oː	dôme, rose, haute (doːm, roːz, oːt)

ɔː	fort, bord, corps (fɔːr, bɔːr, kɔːr)
ɔ̃ː	fondre, pompe, onze (fɔ̃ːdr, pɔ̃ːp, ɔ̃ːz)
œː	œil, deuil, beurre (œːj, dœːj, bœːr)
œ̃ː	humble, défunte (œ̃ːbl, defœ̃ːt)
øː	creuse, aqueuse (krøːz, akøːz)
uː	tour, cours, bourre (tuːr, kuːr, buːr)
yː	murmure, usure (myrmyːr, yzyːr)

CONSONANTS

6 symbols to be learnt

g	gangue, gué, exil (gɑ̃ːg, ge, egzil)
j	fiancé, fouille, ayant (fjɑ̃se, fuːj, ɛjɑ̃)
ɲ	cognac, baigner (kɔɲak, bɛɲe)

ʃ	chat, chiche, hache (ʃa, ʃiʃ, aʃ)
ʒ	je, juge, géologie (ʒə, ʒyːʒ, ʒeɔlɔʒi)
ɥ	cuir, huile, fruit (kɥiːr, ɥil, frɥi)

No symbols to be learnt

The following consonants have their usual values:—

b	bonbon, bimbelot (bɔ̃bɔ̃, bɛ̃blo)
d	dedans, demande (dədɑ̃, dəmɑ̃ːd)
f	fifre, graphique (fifr, grafik)
h	= h aspirated about as in English (chiefly French interjections)
k	kaki, caquet, extra (kaki, kakɛ, ɛkstra)
l	lilas, parallèle (lila, paralɛl)
m	momie, minimum (momi, minimɔm)

n	nonne, inanition (nɔn, inanisjɔ̃)
p	papier, obscur (papje, ɔpskyːr)
r	rare, bizarrerie (raːr, bizarri)
s	si, ceci, stoïcisme (si, səsi, stɔisism)
t	quantité, théâtre (kɑ̃tite, teaːtr)
v	vive, verve, wagon (viːv, vɛrv, vagɔ̃)
w	ouest, gloire, allouer (wɛst, glwaːr, alwe)
z	zigzag, magasin (zigzag, magazɛ̃)

The sounds of the symbols to be learnt can only be acquired by hearing them spoken, just as colours must be seen to be appreciated.

NOTE

The author considers himself fortunate in having at his disposal the International Phonetic System, and if the reader will take the trouble to learn it, he will, the author feels sure, hold himself equally blest.

Gone for ever for all practical purposes are the fantastic "imitated" pronunciations. Every language has certain sounds which are peculiar to itself and have no equivalents in another. For this reason, imitated pronunciations, although capable of transcribing French into French phonetically, English into English, and so on, are inherently incapable of transliterating one language into another, and are responsible in large measure for many people's bad pronunciation of foreign languages.

Pronunciation of French is very difficult for the foreigner. Exceptions to rule, silent letters, and other peculiarities, abound. Therefore, every time he refers to a word in the French vocabulary, the English reader is advised to compare, and correct if necessary, his notion of how it should be pronounced.

ARRANGEMENT

As far as is reasonably possible, set or inseparable word groups are entered under the first word of the group.

****

STANDARD

French is a very conservative language and does not lend itself to universality, as English does. Dryden wrote:—"The French have set up purity for a standard of their language; and a masculine vigor is that of ours." Consequently, very few of the multitude of un-French words and derivatives that have been manufactured will ever receive the sanction of good usage. The policy adopted in this dictionary has been to exclude words not conforming to the standard of purity laid down by the highest authorities, especially the French Academy. These considerations, however, do not apply with any great weight to technical words, which by force of circumstances spring into being and multiply indefinitely regardless of academics, though even in this field respect for the genius of the language calls for restraint.

****

ABBREVIATIONS USED IN THIS DICTIONARY

†

ADVERBS

Most French adverbs of manner are formed by adding -ment to the feminine singular of the adjective, corresponding to the English suffix -ly (-le being changed into -ly, -ic into -ically, and -y into -ily); thus,

naturel (natyrɛl), **naturelle** (rɛl); **naturellement** (rɛlmɑ̃), natural; naturally.
correct (kɔrɛkt), **correcte** (rɛkt); **correctement** (təmɑ̃*), correct; correctly.
relatif (rəlatif), **relative** (ti:v); **relativement** (tivmɑ̃‡), relative; relatively.

So also with adjectives ending in e of identical form in both genders; as,

énergique (enɛrʒik); **énergiquement** (ʒikmɑ̃), energetic; energetically.
admirable (admirabl); **admirablement** (bləmɑ̃*), admirable; admirably.
ordinaire (ordinɛ:r); **ordinairement** (nɛrmɑ̃‡), ordinary; ordinarily.

Adjectives whose masculine form ends in -ai (as **vrai**), -é (as **modéré**), -i (as **hardi**), and -u (as **absolu**), add the suffix -ment to the masculine form; thus,

modéré (mɔdere), **modérée** (re); **modérément** (remɑ̃); moderate; moderately.

In order to economize space (most adverbs of manner being long words), French and English adverbs ending regularly as above, and with no appreciable change of meaning, are not given in the dictionary. Instead, the adjectives are marked † (e.g, **naturel**, le†, **modéré†**, e), in reference hereto. Adverbs not formed according to these rules, particularly those presenting peculiarity or difficulty, are given in the ordinary way.

* Note:—When two pronounced consonants immediately precede the ending -ement, the e of ement is pronounced (ə). Otherwise it is silent.
‡ Note that the vowel sound is short here, rəlati:v, tivmɑ̃; ordinɛ:r, nɛrmɑ̃.

It may be observed that most ordinary English adverbs of manner for which no French form ending in -ment exists can be translated by *d'une manière*, plus the corresponding feminine adjective, as **satisfactorily**, d'une manière satisfaisante.

ABBREVIATIONS USED IN THIS DICTIONARY—*continued*

The swing dash (~) signifies repetition in the singular of a leading vocabulary word (word printed in **bold type**). Followed by *s* (~*s*), it signifies the like repetition in the plural.

The paragraph symbol (¶) also signifies repetition of a leading vocabulary word, but indicates the commencement of a different part of speech, or a change of gender. This symbol is used to make the point of transition conspicuous.

An initial letter followed by a period signifies repetition of a translation.

[Brackets] enclose words, or parts of words, which can be used or omitted at will.

' See note under **H** on page 127.

SUBJECT INDICATIONS

Aero.	Aeronautics	*Mach.*	Machinery; Machine
Agric.	Agriculture	*Math.*	Mathematics
Anat.	Anatomy	*Meas.*	Measurement; Measure
Arch.	Architecture	*Mech.*	Mechanics
Arith.	Arithmetic	*Med.*	Medicine; Medical
Artil.	Artillery	*Metall.*	Metallurgy
Astr.	Astronomy	*Meteor.*	Meteorology
Bil.	Billiards	*Mil.*	Military
Biol.	Biology	*Min.*	Mining
Bkkpg	Bookkeeping	*Miner.*	Mineralogy
Boat.	Boating	*Mol.*	Mollusc
Bookb.	Bookbinding	*Motor.*	Motoring; Motor car
Bot.	Botany	*Mus.*	Music
Box.	Boxing	*Myth.*	Mythology
Build.	Building	*Nat. Hist.*	Natural History
Carp.	Carpentry	*Naut.*	Nautical
Chem.	Chemistry	*Nav.*	Navy; Naval
Com.	Commerce	*Need.*	Needlework
Conch.	Conchology, Shell fish, Shells	*Opt.*	Optics
Cook.	Cookery	*Path.*	Pathology
Crust.	Crustacea(n)	*Phar.*	Pharmacy
Cust.	Customs	*Philos.*	Philosophy
Danc.	Dancing	*Phot.*	Photography
Eccl.	Ecclesiastical	*Phys.*	Physics
Elec.	Electricity, Electric	*Phys. Geog.*	Physical Geography
Emb.	Embroidery	*Poet.*	Poetry; Poetic
Engin.	Engineering	*Pol.*	Politics
Fenc.	Fencing	*Post*	Post Office; Postal
Fin.	Finance	*Pros.*	Prosody
Fish.	Fishing	*Radio*	Wireless
Foot.	Football	*Relig.*	Religion
Geog.	Geography	*Rhet.*	Rhetoric
Geol.	Geology	*Rly*	Railway(s)
Geom.	Geometry	*Sch.*	School
Gram.	Grammar	*Ship.*	Shipping
Gym.	Gymnastics	*Shipbldg*	Shipbuilding
Her.	Heraldry	*Stk Ex.*	Stock Exchange
Hist.	History; Historical	*Surg.*	Surgery
Horol.	Horology, Clocks & Watches	*Surv.*	Surveying
Hort.	Horticulture	*Swim.*	Swimming
Hunt.	Hunting	*Teleg.*	Telegraphy
Hyd.	Hydraulics	*Teleph.*	Telephony
Inc. Tax	Income Tax	*Ten.*	Tennis
Insce	Insurance	*Theat.*	Theatre; Theatrical
Join.	Joinery	*Theol.*	Theology
Jump.	Jumping	*Typ.*	Typography; Printing
Knit.	Knitting	*Univ.*	University
Lit.	Liturgy	*Vet.*	Veterinary
Log.	Logic	*Zool.*	Zoology

xiii

Continued on page xiv

a	adjective
abb	abbreviation
abs	absolutely, i.e, (verb) used without its object
ad	adverb or adverbial phrase (See also †ADVERBS, page xii)
a.f	adjective feminine only, i.e, not masculine also
a.m	adjective masculine only, i.e, not feminine also
art	article
att	attributively, i.e, (noun) used as adjective
aux	auxiliary (verb)
c	conjunction or conjunctive phrase
Cf.	Compare
col	collectively, collective noun
comps	compounds; in combination
e.g	for example
Eng.	England; English
&	and, et (The sign & is used in the dictionary only to save space)
&c	et cetera
f	feminine. In the French-English section, *f* = noun feminine
fig.	figuratively
f.pl	feminine plural. In the French-English section, *f.pl* = noun feminine plural
Fr.	France; French
f.s	feminine singular. In the French-English section, *f.s* = noun feminine singular
i	interjection
i.e	that is to say
imp	impersonal
inv	invariable
ir	irregular (verb)
lit.	literally
m	masculine. In the French-English section, *m* = noun masculine
m,f	masculine & feminine (noun)
m.pl	masculine plural. In the French-English section, *m.pl* = noun masculine plural
m.s	masculine singular. In the French-English section, *m.s* = noun masculine singular
n	noun. In the French-English section, *n* = noun masculine & feminine (of persons)
neg.	negative; (used) negatively
oft.	often
opp.	opposed to
p.a	participial adjective
pers.	person(s)
pl	plural
pn	pronoun
p.p	participle past
p.pr	participle present
pr	preposition or prepositional phrase
s	singular
v.i	verb intransitive
v.i. & t	verb intransitive & verb transitive
v.pr	verbe pronominal
v.t	verb transitive
v.t. & i	verb transitive & verb intransitive

FRENCH-ENGLISH DICTIONARY

A

à (a) (à le *is contracted into* au, à les *into* aux) *pr*, to; at; in; within; into; on; by; with; for; of; after; from; under; according to; between; till, until; and. *When coupled with noun, often rendered in English by noun used attributively, as*, canne à sucre, sugar cane. *un homme* ∼ *craindre*, a man to be feared *or* to fear. ∼ *prendre après les repas*, to be taken after meals. ∼ *ne pas confondre avec* . . ., not to be confused with . . . *de 2* ∼ *3 fois par jour*, 2 or 3 times a day.

abaissement (abɛsmã) *m*, lowering; sinking; fall; humiliation. **abaisser** (se) *v.t*, to lower, let down; humble, abase.

abandon (abãdɔ̃) *m*, abandonment, dereliction, desertion; unconstraint. *à l'*∼, in confusion, at random, anyhow; derelict. **abandonnement** (dɔnmã) *m*, profligacy. **abandonner** (ne) *v.t*, to abandon, leave, desert, forsake; disuse; give up, relinquish, surrender; concede.

abaque (abak) *m*, abacus; diagram.

abasourdir (abazurdi:r) *v.t*, to dumbfound, stun.

abâtardir (s') (abatardi:r) *v.pr*, to degenerate.

abat-jour (abaʒu:r) *m*, shade, lampshade. **abats** (ba) *m.pl*. Same as *abattis*. **abat-son** (abasɔ̃) *m*, louvers. **abattage** (bata:ʒ) *m*, felling; slaughtering. **abattant** (tã) *m*, flap. **abattement** (tmã) *m*, prostration, depression, dejection, despondency; relief (*for dependants, Inc. Tax*). **abatteur** (tœ:r) *m*, feller; slaughterman. **abattis** (ti) *m*, demolitions; fell; kill; giblets. **abattoir** (twa:r) *m*, slaughter house, abattoir. **abattre** (tr) *v.t.ir*, to knock down; bring down; cut down; lay; fell; slaughter, kill; mine; deject. **abattu, e** (ty) *a*, depressed, low-spirited, downcast. **abat-vent** (abavã) *m*, wind screen. **abat-voix** (abavwa) *m*, sounding board.

abbaye (abɛi) *f*, abbey. **abbé** (be) *m*, abbot; priest. **abbesse** (bɛs) *f*, abbess.

A b c (abese) *m*, A B C, spelling book, primer.

abcès (apsɛ) *m*, abscess, gathering. ∼ *aux gencives*, gumboil.

abdication (abdikasjɔ̃) *f*, abdication. **abdiquer** (ke) *v.t. & abs*, to abdicate; surrender; waive.

abdomen (abdomɛn) *m*, abdomen.

abécédaire (abesedɛ:r) *m*, A B C, spelling book, primer.

abeille (abɛ:j) *f*, bee. ∼ *ouvrière*, worker b.

aberration (abɛrasjɔ̃) *f*, aberration.

abêtir (abɛti:r) *v.t*, to make dull.

abhorrer (abɔre) *v.t*, to abhor, loathe, detest.

abîme (abi:m) *m*, abyss, gulf, chasm. **abîmer** (bime) *v.t*, to swallow up; ruin, spoil. **s'**∼, to bury (*or* immerse) oneself, welter.

abject, e (abʒɛkt) *a*, abject, mean. **abjection** (sjɔ̃) *f*, abjectness, &c.

abjurer (abʒyre) *v.t*, to abjure, forswear, renounce.

ablatif (ablatif) *m*, ablative [case].

abnégation (abnegasjɔ̃) *f*, abnegation, self-denial.

aboiement (abwamã) *m*, bark[ing], bay[ing]. **aux abois** (bwa), at bay; hard pressed; at one's wits' end.

abolir (abɔli:r) *v.t*, to abolish. **abolition** (lisjɔ̃) *f*, abolition; repeal.

abominable† (abɔminabl) *a*, abominable, nefarious. **abomination** (sjɔ̃) *f*, abomination. **abominer** (ne) *v.t*, to abominate.

abondance (abɔ̃dã:s) *f*, abundance, plenty, galore; fullness. *parler d'*∼, to speak extempore. **abondant, e** (dã, ã:t) *a*, abundant, plentiful, plenteous, profuse. **abondamment** (damã) *ad*, abundantly, &c. **abonder** (de) *v.i*, to abound. ∼ *dans le sens de*, to quite agree with, chime in with.

abonné, e (abɔne) *n*, subscriber; consumer (*gas, elec.*). **abonnement** (nmã) *m*, subscription, season ticket. ∼ *à l'eau*, water-rate. **abonner** (ne) *v.t*, to subscribe for. **s'**∼, to subscribe.

abonnir (abɔni:r) *v.t*, to improve.

abord (abɔ:r) *m*, landing; approach, access. [*tout*] *d'*∼, *au premier* ∼, *de prime* ∼, at first, first of all, to begin with. **abordable** (bɔrdabl) *a*, accessible, approachable. **abordage** (da:ʒ) *m*, landing; collision, fouling. **aborder** (de) *v.i. & t*, to land; approach; broach; board; collide with, foul.

aborigène (abɔriʒɛ:n) *a. & m*, aboriginal; (*m.pl.*) aborigines.

abortif, ive (abɔrtif, i:v) *a*, abortive (*of premature birth*).

aboucher (abuʃe) *v.t*, to bring together; join up.

aboutir (abuti:r) *v.i*, to end, lead; eventuate, materialize; come to a head, culminate.

aboyer (abwaje) *v.i*, to bark, bay; be in full cry; cry out. **aboyeur** (jœ:r) *m*, barker; carriage attendant (*hotel, theatre, &c*).

abrégé (abreʒe) *m*, abridgment, epitome, abstract, summary. *en* ∼, shortly, briefly; abbreviated. **abréger** (ʒe) *v.t*, to abridge, epitomize; abbreviate.

1

B

abreuver (abrœve) v.t, to water; season; soak, steep, drench. s'~, to drink, soak, fill oneself, wallow, bathe. abreuvoir (vwa:r) m, watering place, horse pond, drinking trough.

abréviation (abrevjasjɔ̃) f, abbreviation; contraction.

abri (abri) m, shelter, cover, dug-out; cab (locomotive). à l'~ de, under cover of, sheltered from.

abricot (abriko) m, apricot. abricotier (kɔtje) m, apricot tree.

abriter (abrite) v.t, to shelter, shield, screen.

abrivent (abrivɑ̃) m, shelter, hut; matting, screen.

abrogation (abrɔgasjɔ̃) f, abrogation, repeal. abroger (ʒe) v.t, to abrogate, &c.

abrupt, e (abrypt) a, abrupt, sheer.

abruti, e (abryti) p.a, brutish, besotted, sottish. ¶ m, beast (pers.). abrutir (ti:r) v.t, to brutalize, besot. abrutissement (tismɑ̃) m, brutishness.

absence (apsɑ̃:s) f, absence. ~ [d'esprit], absence of mind. absent, e (sɑ̃, ɑ̃:t) a, absent, away [from home], out, not at home. ~ par congé, away on holiday. ¶ m, absentee. s'absenter (sɑ̃te) v.pr, to absent oneself, keep away.

abside (apsid) f, apse.

absinthe (apsɛ̃:t) f, wormwood; absinth.

absolu†, e (apsɔly) a, absolute; hard & fast; peremptory.

absolution (apsɔlysjɔ̃) f, absolution.

absorbant, e (apsɔrbɑ̃, ɑ̃:t) a, absorbent, bibulous; absorbing, engrossing. absorber (be) v.t. & abs, to absorb, drink in, imbibe; engross. absorption (psjɔ̃) f, absorption.

absoudre (apsudr) v.t.ir, to absolve.

abstème (apstɛːm) a, abstemious. ¶ n, abstainer. s'abstenir (stəni:r) v.pr.ir, to abstain, refrain, forbear. abstention (stɑ̃sjɔ̃) f, abstention. abstinence (stinɑ̃:s) f, abstinence, temperance.

abstraction (apstraksjɔ̃) f, abstraction. ~ faite de, apart from, setting aside. abstraire (strɛːr) v.t.ir, to abstract. abstrait, e (strɛ, ɛːt) a, abstract. l'abstrait, m, the abstract (opp. concrete).

abstrus, e (apstry, yːz) a, abstruse, recondite.

absurde† (apsyrd) a, absurd, preposterous. l'absurde, m, the absurd, an absurdity. absurdité (dite) f, absurdity, nonsense.

abus (aby) m, abuse, misuse; breach. abuser (ze) v.t, to deceive, delude, mislead, misguide. ~ de, to abuse, misuse, trespass on. s'~, to delude oneself. abusif, ive† (zif, iːv) a, abusive, improper.

abysse (abis) m, abyss.

Abyssinie (l') (abisini) f, Abyssinia. abyssinien, ne (njɛ̃, ɛn) a. & A~, n. ou abyssin, e (sɛ̃, in) a. & A~, n, Abyssinian.

acabit (akabi) m, stamp, sort, nature, kidney.

acacia (akasja) m, acacia.

académicien, ne (akademisjɛ̃, ɛn) n, académicien. académie (mi) f, academy, college; academy figure. académique (mik) a, academic(al).

acagnarder (akaɲarde) v.t, to make lazy.

acajou (akaʒu) m, mahogany. ~ des Antilles, Spanish mahogany.

acare (aka:r) m, mite, tick.

acariâtre (akarjɑ:tr) a, peevish, sour[-tempered].

accablement (akɑblømɑ̃) m, despondency, dejection; prostration; great pressure (of business). accabler (ble) v.t, to overwhelm, crush, overcome.

accalmie (akalmi) f, lull.

accaparer (akapare) v.t, to corner, buy up, monopolize. accapareur, euse (rœːr, øːz) n, monopolist.

accéder à (aksede), to accede to, consent to; reach.

accélérateur (akseleratœːr) m, accelerator. accélérer (re) v.t, to accelerate, quicken.

accent (aksɑ̃) m, accent; stress; tone; pronunciation; (pl.) strains. accentuer (tɥe) v.t, to accent, accentuate, emphasize, stress.

acceptable (aksɛptabl) a, acceptable. acceptation (sjɔ̃) f, acceptance. accepter (te) v.t. & abs, to accept, undertake. accepteur (tœːr) m, acceptor. acception (psjɔ̃) f, respect; acceptation (of a word).

accès (aksɛ) m, access, approach; fit, attack, flus... accessible (sɛsibl) a, accessible, approachable.

accession (aksɛsjɔ̃) f, accession; consent.

accessit (aksɛsit) m, honourable mention.

accessoire† (aksɛswa:r) a, accessory. ¶ m, accessory, adjunct; (pl.) fittings, furniture; properties (Theat.).

accident (aksidɑ̃) m, accident; smash; unevenness; hazard (Golf); accidental (Mus.). accidenté, e (te) a, hilly, broken; chequered; eventful. accidentel, le† (tɛl) a, accidental, casual.

acclamation (aklamasjɔ̃) f, acclamation, cheering. acclamer (me) v.t, to acclaim, hail, cheer.

acclimatation (aklimatasjɔ̃) f, acclimatization. acclimater (te) v.t, to acclimatize.

accointance (akwɛ̃tɑ̃:s) f. oft. pl, intimacy; dealings.

accolade (akɔlad) f, embrace, hug; brace, bracket (Typ.). accoler (le) v.t, to brace, bracket.

accommodation (akɔmɔdasjɔ̃) f, accommodation. accommodement (dmɑ̃) m, compromise, arrangement, settlement, terms. accommoder (de) v.t, to suit; please; reconcile; adapt; prepare (food); arrange, settle. s'~ à, to accommodate oneself to.

accompagnateur, trice (akɑ̃paɲatœːr, tris) n, accompan[y]ist. accompagnement (ɲmɑ̃) m, accompaniment; concomitant. accompagner (ɲe) v.t, to accompany, attend, escort.

accompli, e (akɔ̃pli) *a*, accomplished, thorough. **accomplir** (pli:r) *v.t*, to accomplish, achieve, perform, carry out. **accomplissement** (plismɑ̃) *m*, accomplishment, &c.

accord (akɔ:r) *m*, accord, agreement; harmony, concord; consent; chord (*Mus.*); tune; (*pl.*) betrothal. *d'~*, agreed, granted; in tune. *d'un commun ~*, with one accord. **accordage** (kɔrda:ʒ) *m*, tuning. **accordailles** (da:j) *f.pl*, betrothal. **accordéon** (deɔ̃) *m*, accordion. **accorder** (de) *v.t*, to accord, grant, bestow, allow, afford; spare; reconcile; tune; attune. **s'~**, to agree; accord; tune [up]. **accordeur** (dœ:r) *m*, tuner.

accort, e (akɔ:r, ɔrt) *a*, amiable, pleasing.

accoster (akɔste) *v.t*, to accost; come alongside.

accotement (akɔtmɑ̃) *m*, side path, greensward, verge. **accoter** (te) *v.t*, to hold up; lean, rest. **accotoir** (twa:r) *m*, rest, arm.

accouchement (akuʃmɑ̃) *m*, confinement, lying-in, childbirth. **accoucher** (ʃe) *v.i*, to be confined, give birth, deliver, bring forth; speak out. **accoucheur** (ʃœ:r) *m*, maternity doctor.

accouder (s') (akude) *v.pr*, to rest (*or* lean) on one's elbow(s). **accoudoir** (dwa:r) *m*, arm; rail.

accouple (akupl) *f*, leash. **accoupler** (ple) *v.t*, to couple, connect, yoke; pair, mate.

accourcie (akursi) *f*, short cut. **accourcir** (si:r) *v.t*, to shorten.

accourir (akuri:r) *v.i.ir*, to run [up], rush.

accoutrement (akutrəmɑ̃) *m*, trappings, garb, rig. **accoutrer** (tre) *v.t*, to rig out.

accoutumance (akutymɑ̃:s) *f*, habit, use. **accoutumer** (me) *v.t*, to accustom, inure.

accréditer (akredite) *v.t*, to accredit, open a credit for.

accroc (akro) *m*, rent, tear; snag, hitch; stain. **accroche-cœur** (akrɔʃkœ:r) *m*, lovelock, kiss-curl. **accrocher** (ʃe) *v.t*, to hook; grapple; hang [up]; run against; catch. **s'~**, to hang on.

accroire (akrwa:r) *v.t : faire ~ à*, to cause to believe. *en faire ~ à*, to impose [up]on. *s'en faire ~*, to be conceited.

accroître (akrwa:tr) *v.t. & i. ir*, to increase, grow, accrue. **accroissement** (krwasmɑ̃) *m*, increase, &c.

accroupir (s') (akrupi:r) *v.pr*, to squat, crouch, cower.

accueil (akœ:j) *m*, reception, welcome; honour (*bill*). **accueillir** (kœji:r) *v.t.ir*, to receive, welcome, greet; entertain; honour, meet (*bill*).

accul (akyl) *m*, cove, creek; lair.

acculer (akyle) *v.t*, to [drive into a] corner. **s'~**, to stand at bay; jib. *s'~ contre*, to set one's back against.

accumulateur (akymylatœ:r) *m*, accumulator, [storage] battery. **accumulation** (sjɔ̃) *f*,

accumulation. **accumuler** (le) *v.t. & abs. & s'~*, to accumulate; gather.

accusateur, trice (akyzatœ:r, tris) *n*, accuser. *¶ a*, accusing. **accusatif** (tif) *m*, accusative [case]. **accusation** (sjɔ̃) *f*, accusation, charge. **accusé, e** (ze) *n*, accused, prisoner at the bar. **accusé de réception**, *m*, acknowledgement. **accuser** (ze) *v.t*, to accuse, charge; indict; impeach; blame; show, betray; bring out; complain of (*medically*). *~ réception de*, to acknowledge receipt of. **s'~ de**, to avow, acknowledge, confess. *s'~ soi-même*, to plead guilty.

acerbe (asɛrb) *a*, sour, sharp, harsh.

acéré, e (asere) *a*, steeled, sharp, keen, cutting. **acérer** (re) *v.t*, to steel.

acétate (asetat) *m*, acetate.

acétique (asetik) *a*, acetic.

acétylène (asetilɛ:n) *m*, acetylene.

achalandage (aʃalɑ̃da:ʒ) *m*, bringing custom; custom, connection, patronage. **achalandé, e** (de) *p.a*, patronized. **achalander** (de) *v.t*, to bring custom; commercialize. **s'~**, to get custom.

acharné, e (aʃarne) *a*, rabid, furious, fierce, desperate, relentless, ruthless; obstinate, bitter, inveterate, confirmed; intense, eager; fleshed. **acharnement** (nəmɑ̃) *m*, rabidness, &c. **acharner** (ne) *v.t*, to set on, set against; flesh. **s'~**, to attack furiously; be set, be bent, be insatiable, be inveterate.

achat (aʃa) *m*, purchase, buying.

acheminement (aʃminmɑ̃) *m*, step. **acheminer** (ne) *v.t*, to direct; expedite; forward, dispatch, route. **s'~**, to proceed.

acheter (aʃte) *v.t*, to buy, purchase. **acheteur, euse** (tœ:r, øz) *n*, buyer, purchaser.

achevé, e (aʃve) *a*, accomplished, perfect, thorough, out & out, arrant. **achèvement** (ʃɛvmɑ̃) *m*, finishing, completion. **achever** (ʃve) *v.t*, to finish, perfect, end. *achevez donc !* out with it!

achopper (aʃɔpe) *v.i. & s'~*, to stumble.

achromatique (akrɔmatik) *a*, achromatic.

acide (asid) *a*, acid, sour, sharp, tart. *¶ m*, acid. **acidité** (dite) *f*, acidity, &c. **aciduler** (dyle) *v.t*, to acidulate.

acier (asje) *m*, steel. *~ [à coupe] rapide*, high-speed steel. *~ coulé*, cast s. *~ fondu [au creuset]*, [crucible] cast s. **aciérer** (sjere) *v.t*, to steel, caseharden. **aciérie** (ri) *f*, steel works.

acné (akne) *f*, acne.

acolyte (akɔlit) *m*, acolyte.

acompte (akɔ̃:t) *m*, instalment; cover, margin. *~ de dividende*, interim dividend. *~ de préférence*, option money (*on a property*).

aconit (akɔnit) *m*, aconite, monk's-hood, wolf's-bane.

acquinant, e (akɔkinɑ̃, ɑ̃:t) *a*, enticing. **s'acoquiner à, auprès** (ne), to get fond of, become attached to.

Açores (les) (asɔ:r) *f.pl*, the Azores.

à-coup (aku) *m*, jerk, shock.

acoustique (akustik) *a*, acoustic. ¶ *f*, acoustics.

acquéreur (akerœ:r) *m*, purchaser, buyer.

acquérir (ri:r) *v.t.ir*, to acquire, get, win, purchase; (*abs*.) to improve. s'~, to accrue.

acquiescement (akjesmã) *m*, acquiescence.

acquiescer (se) *v.i*, to acquiesce.

acquis, e (aki, i:z) *p.a*, acquired; earned; devoted; vested (*rights*). ¶ *m. s. & pl*, acquirements, attainments, experience.

acquisition (kizisjɔ̃) *f*, acquisition, purchase; haul.

acquit (aki) *m*, receipt, discharge. [*pour*] ~, received [with thanks], paid. à l'~ de, on behalf of, on account of. acquit-à-caution (kitakosjɔ̃) *m*, bond note, transhipment bond. acquitté, e (te) *a*, duty-paid (*Cust.*). à l'acquitté, *ad*, duty paid, ex bond. acquittement (tmã) *m*, discharge, acquittal. acquitter (te) *v.t*, to acquit, discharge; receipt (*bill*). s'~, to acquit oneself, perform; be quits, catch up (*games*).

âcre (a:kr) *a*, acrid, tart, sour, sharp, pungent. âcreté (ukrate) *f*, acridity, &c.

acrimonie (akrimoni) *f*, acrimony. acrimonieux, euse (njø, ø:z) *a*, acrimonious.

acrobate (akrɔbat) *n*, acrobat, tumbler. acrobatie (si) *f*, acrobatics; stunt. acrobatique (tik) *a*, acrobatic.

acrostiche (akrɔstif) *m. & a*, acrostic.

acte (akt) *m*, act, action; deed, indenture, instrument, document, agreement, contract; bond; certificate; licence; (*pl*.) transactions (*of a society*). ~ d'accusation, indictment. ~ de dernière volonté, last will & testament. ~ de naissance, de mariage, de décès, entry in register of births, of marriages, of deaths. ~ dommageable, tort (*Law*). ~ sous seing privé (sẽ), simple contract. [*pièce en un*] ~, one-act play. acteur, trice (tœ:r, tris) *n*, actor, actress, player. ~ à transformations, quick-change artist.

actif, ive (aktif, i:v) *a*, active, brisk; busy. ¶ *m*, active voice; assets.

action (aksjɔ̃) *f*, action, act, deed; effect, agency; share, (*pl*.) stock. ~s au porteur, bearer shares, b. stock. ~[s] de grâce, thanksgiving. ~s de priorité, ~s privilégiées, preference shares, preferred stock. ~s nominatives, registered shares, r. stock. ~s gratuites, bonus shares. ~s [*entièrement*] libérées, fully paid shares. ~s non libérées, partly paid shares. par ~s, joint-stock (*att.*). actionnaire (ɔne:r) *n*, shareholder, stockholder.

actionner (aksjone) *v.t*, to drive, actuate, run, work; bring an action against, sue.

activement (aktivmã) *ad*, actively, briskly.

activer (ve) *v.t*, to quicken, urge, press, rouse, stir up, speed up, hurry. activité (vite) *f*, activity, briskness. en ~ [de service], on active service. en pleine ~, in full operation, in full swing.

actuaire (aktɥe:r) *m*, actuary.

actualité (aktɥalite) *f*, actuality, present state; (*pl*.) passing (*or* current) events, questions of the hour; news (*Cinema*). ~s de la mode, present day fashions.

actuel, le (tɥel) *a*, actual, present, for the time being. actuellement (lmã) *ad*, now, at present.

acuité (akɥite) *f*, sharpness, acuteness, keenness; shrillness.

acutangle (akytɑ̃:gl) *a*, acute-angled.

adage (ada:ʒ) *m*, adage, saying, saw. ~ de droit, legal maxim.

adapter (adapte) *v.t*, to adapt, fit, suit. adapteur (tœ:r) *m*, adapter (*Phot.*).

addition (adisjɔ̃) *f*, addition, cast, tot; bill (*at restaurant*). additionnel, le (ɔnel) *a*, additional. additionner (ne) *v.t*, to add [up], cast, tot up.

adénoïde (adenɔid) *a*, adenoid.

adepte (adept) *n*, adept.

adhérence (aderɑ̃:s) *f*, adherence, adhesion. adhérent, e (rɑ̃, ɑ̃:t) *n*, adherent, supporter, member. adhérer (re) *v.i*, to adhere, cohere, stick. adhésion (zjɔ̃) *f*, adhesion, adhesiveness; membership.

adieu (adjø) *i. & m*, good-bye, tata, farewell, adieu; parting.

adipeux, euse (adipø, ø:z) *a*, adipose, fatty.

adjacent, e (adʒasɑ̃, ɑ̃:t) *a*, adjacent, adjoining.

adjectif (adʒektif) *a.m*, adjectival. ¶ *m*, adjective. ~ attribut, predicative a. ~ épithète, attributive a. ~ verbal, participial a. (*present*). adjectivement (tivmã) *ad*, adjectivally, attributively.

adjoindre (adʒwẽ:dr) *v.t.ir*, to join, associate. adjoint, e (ʒwẽ, ẽ:t) *a. & n*, assistant.

adjudant (adʒydɑ̃) *m*, sergeant major. ~ major, adjutant.

adjudicataire (adʒydikate:r) *n*, purchaser; contractor. adjudication (sjɔ̃) *f*, adjudication; award of contract. adjuger (ʒe) *v.t*, to adjudge, adjudicate; award; award the contract for; knock down.

adjurer (adʒyre) *v.t*, to adjure, beseech.

ad libitum (ad libitɔm), ad libitum (*at pleasure & Mus.*).

admettre (admetr) *v.t.ir*, to admit, allow, grant; pass (*at exam*).

administrateur, trice (administratœ:r, tris) *n*, director; administrator, trix. ~ délégué, ~ directeur, managing director. administration (sjɔ̃) *f*, administration, management, direction; board, directorate; authorities. ~ publique, civil service. administrer (tre) *v.t*, to administer, manage, direct.

admirable† (admirabl) *a*, admirable, wonderful, capital. admirateur, trice (tœ:r, tris) *n*, admirer. admiration (sjɔ̃) *f*, admiration,

5   à-coup — affirmatif

wonder. **admirer** (re) *v.t*, to admire, wonder at.

admissible (admisibl) *a*, admissible. **admission** (sjɔ̃) *f*, admission, admittance; intake; entrance.

admonester (admɔnɛste) *v.t*, to admonish, reprimand. **admonestation** (tasjɔ̃) *f*, **admonition** (nisjɔ̃) *f*, admonition, &c.

adolescence (adɔlɛsɑ̃ːs) *f*, adolescence, youth. **adolescent, e** (sɑ̃, ɑ̃ːt) *a*, adolescent. ¶ *n*, adolescent, youth, girl.

adonis (adɔnis) *m*, Adonis, beau.

adonner (s’) (adɔne) *v.pr*, to give (*or* apply) oneself, addict oneself, take.

adopter (adɔpte) *v.t*, to adopt, carry, pass, confirm. **adoptif, ive** (tif, iːv) *a*, adoptive, adopted. **adoption** (sjɔ̃) *f*, adoption, &c.

adorable (adɔrabl) *a*, adorable, charming, lovely, delightful. **adorateur, trice** (tœːr, tris) *n*, adorer, worshipper, votary. **adoration** (sjɔ̃) *f*, adoration, worship. **adorer** (re) *v.t*, to adore, worship.

adosser (adose) *v.t*, to back, lean. **s’~**, to lean one’s back against.

adoucir (adusiːr) *v.t*, to sweeten; soften; smooth, temper, subdue, allay, alleviate, soothe, ease, appease, assuage, mollify, qualify.

adresse (adrɛs) *f*, address; direction; skill, dexterity, craft, deftness; shrewdness; handiness; clever move. **adresser** (se) *v.t*, to address, direct, send. **s’~ à**, to address, apply to; inquire of; cater for.

Adriatique (adriatik) *a. & f*, Adriatic.

adroit, e† (adrwa, at) *a*, adroit, dext[e]rous, deft, handy, skilful, clever, neat; shrewd.

adulateur, trice (adylatœːr, tris) *a*, adulatory. **adulation** (sjɔ̃) *f*, adulation. **aduler** (le) *v.t*, to adulate.

adulte (adylt) *a. & n*, adult, grown-up.

adultère (adyltɛːr) *n*, adulterer, ess; (*m.*) adultery. ¶ *a*, adulterous.

advenir (advaniːr) *v.i.ir*, to happen, occur, befall, come to pass. *advienne que pourra*, come what may, whate’er betide.

adverbe (advɛrb) *m*, adverb. *~ de quantité*, a. of number. **adverbial, e†** (bjal) *a*, adverbial.

adversaire (advɛrsɛːr) *m*, adversary, opponent, foe. **adverse** (vɛrs) *a*, adverse, opposing. **adversité** (site) *f*, adversity, misfortune.

aérage (aera:ʒ) *m*, **aération** (rasjɔ̃) *f*, ventilation, airing; draught; aeration. **aérer** (re) *v.t*, to ventilate, air; aerate.

aérien, ne (aerjɛ̃, ɛn) *a*, aerial, airy, air (*att.*); overhead.

aérodrome (aerɔdroːm) *m*, aerodrome, aviation ground.

aérodynamique (aerɔdinamik) *a*, aerodynamic; stream-lined. ¶ *f*, aerodynamics. **aérodynamisme** (mism) *m*, stream-lining.

aérolithe (aerɔlit) *m*, aerolite, meteorite.

aéronaute (aerɔnoːt) *n*, aeronaut. **aéro-**

nautique (notik) *a*, aeronautic(al), air (*att.*). ¶ *f*, aeronautics.

aéronef (aerɔnɛf) *m*, aircraft.

aérophare (aerɔfaːr) *m*, air lighthouse.

aéroplane (aerɔplan) *m*, aeroplane, [air]plane.

aéroport (aerɔpoːr) *m*, air station.

aérostat (aerɔsta) *m*, lighter than air machine; balloon. **aérostation** (sjɔ̃) *f*, lighter than air aviation *or* balloon (*Army*); ballooning. **aérostier** (tje) *m*, balloonist.

affabilité (afabilite) *f*, affability. **affable** (bl) *a*, affable.

affadir (afadiːr) *v.t*, to sicken; make insipid, flatten. **affadissement** (dismɑ̃) *m*, loss of flavour; nauseousness.

affaiblir (afɛbliːr) *v.t*, to weaken, enfeeble; reduce (*Phot.*).

affaire (afɛːr) *f*, affair, matter, case, thing, job, proposition, business, piece of business, concern; transaction, dealing, bargain; lawsuit; re (*Law*); engagement (*Mil.*). *~s par correspondance*, mail order business. *~ roulante*, going concern. *ce malade est hors d’~*, this patient is out of danger. **affairé, e** (fɛre) *a*, busy. ¶ *n*, busy man, woman.

affaissement (afɛsmɑ̃) *m*, subsidence, sinking; collapse. **affaisser** (se) *v.t*, to cause to subside; weigh down. **s’~**, to subside, sink, collapse.

affamé, e (afame) *a*, famished, hungry, starving, craving. ¶ *n*, starveling. **affamer** (me) *v.t*, to famish, starve.

affecté, e (afɛkte) *a*, affected; prim. **affecter** (te) *v.t*, to assign, design, charge, apply, set aside; aspire to; assume; affect; move. **affectation** (tasjɔ̃) *f*, assignment, &c.

affection (afɛksjɔ̃) *f*, affection, liking; complaint (*Med.*). **affectionné, e** (ɔne) *a*, **affectueux, euse†** (tɥø, øːz) *a*, affectionate, fond, loving. **affectionner** (ɔne) *v.t*, to be fond of, like.

affermer (afɛrme) *v.t*, to lease, let out, farm [out], rent.

affermir (afɛrmiːr) *v.t*, to strengthen.

affété, e (afete) *a*, affected, mincing. **afféterie** (tri) *f*, affectation.

affiche (afiʃ) *f*, poster, bill, placard; sign. *~ lumineuse*, electric sign. **afficher** (ʃe) *v.t*, to post, bill, placard, stick (*bills*); proclaim, advertise, show up. **afficheur** (ʃœːr) *m*, billposter, billsticker.

affidé, e (afide) *a*, trusty (*bad sense*). ¶ *n*, confederate.

affilé, e (afile) *a*, sharp (*tongue*). **d’affilée**, *ad*, at a stretch. **affiler** (le) *v.t*, to set (*tools*).

affilier (afilje) *v.t*, to affiliate.

affiloir (afilwaːr) *m*, steel; strop.

affinage (afina:ʒ) *m*, refining. **affiner** (ne) *v.t*, to refine. **affinerie** (nri) *f*, refinery. **affineur** (nœːr) *m*, refiner.

affinité (afinite) *f*, affinity.

affiquets (afikɛ) *m.pl*, get-up, finery.

affirmatif, ive† (afirmatif, iːv) *a. & f*, affirmative. **affirmation** (sjɔ̃) *f*, affirmation.

affirmer (me) *v.t*, to affirm, assert, aver, vouch.

affixe (afiks) *m*, affix.

affleurement (aflœrmɑ̃) *m*, levelling; outcrop (*Geol.*). **affleurer** (re) *v.t*, to level, flush; (*v.i.*) to crop out.

affliction (afliksjɔ̃) *f*, affliction. **affliger** (ʒe) *v.t*, to afflict, distress, grieve; mortify; curse.

affluence (aflyɑ̃:s) *f*, affluence; concourse. **affluent** (ɑ̃) *m*, tributary, affluent, feeder. **affluer** (e) *v.i*, to flow; run; abound, flock.

affoler (afɔle) *v.t*, to infatuate; madden; distract.

affouiller (afuje) *v.t*, to undermine, wash away.

affourché, e (afurʃe) *a*, astride, astraddle.

affranchi, e (afrɑ̃ʃi) *n*, emancipated slave. **affranchir** (ʃi:r) *v.t*, to [set] free, liberate; relieve; prepay, stamp (*Post*). **affranchissement** (ʃismɑ̃) *m*, emancipation, enfranchisement; prepayment.

affres (afr) *f.pl*, pangs, throes.

affrètement (afrɛtmɑ̃) *m*, affreightment, chartering. **affréter** (frete) *v.t*, to charter. **affréteur** (tœ:r) *m*, charterer.

affreux, euse† (afrø, ø:z) *a*, frightful, fearful, ghastly.

affriander (afriɑ̃de) & **affrioler** (ɔle) *v.t*, to allure, tempt; make attractive.

affront (afrɔ̃) *m*, affront; slight, cut. **affronter** (afrɔ̃te) *v.t*, to front, confront, face, brave.

affubler (afyble) *v.t*, to dress up.

affût (afy) *m*, hiding place; stand; [gun] carriage. *à l'~*, on the watch, on the lookout. **affûter** (afyte) *v.t*, to sharpen, grind.

afghan, e (afgɑ̃) *a. & A~*, *n*, Afghan.

afin (afɛ̃) *pr*, in order to, so as to, to. **afin que, c**, in order that, so that, that.

africain, e (afrikɛ̃, ɛn) *a. & A~*, *n*, African. **l'Afrique** (frik) *f*, Africa.

agacer (agase) *v.t*, to set on edge, irritate, annoy; provoke, excite. **agacement** (smɑ̃) *m*, setting on edge, &c. **agacerie** (sri) *f*, provocation.

agate (agat) *f*, agate.

âge (ɑ:ʒ) *m*, age. *l'~ de raison*, years of discretion. *l'~ ingrat*, the awkward age. *l'~ viril*, man's estate. *quel ~ a-t-il?* how old is he? *il n'est pas en ~*, he is not of (*or* is under) age. **âgé, e** (aʒe) *a*, aged, old. *~ de*, of age, old.

agence (aʒɑ̃:s) *f*, agency, bureau. *~ d'information*, news agency, press a. *~ de renseignements*, mercantile office, m. agency. *~ immobilière*, estate agency. *~ stockiste*, service station.

agencé, e (aʒɑ̃se) *p.p*, dressed, got up. **agencement** (smɑ̃) *m*, arrangement; fittings & fixtures. **agencer** (se) *v.t*, to arrange, fit [up].

agenda (aʒɛ̃da) *m*, diary.

agenouiller [(s')] (aʒnuje) *v.pr*, to kneel [down]. **agenouilloir** (jwa:r) *m*, hassock.

agent (aʒɑ̃) *m*, agent; broker; officer; medium. *~ comptable*, accountant. *~ de change*, stockbroker (*nominated by the government*). *~ de la douane*, customs officer. *~ de liaison*, liaison officer. *~ de location*, house agent, estate a. *~ [de police]*, policeman, police constable. *~ de police des côtes à terre*, coastguard. *~ de recouvrements*, debt collector, dun. *~ du service sanitaire*, health officer. *~ en douane*, customs agent. *~ maritime*, shipping agent. *~s s'abstenir*, no agents.

aggloméré (aglomere) *m*, briquet[te]. **agglomérer** (re) *v.t*, to agglomerate.

agglutiner (aglytine) *v.t*, to agglutinate.

aggraver (agrave) *v.t*, to aggravate; increase.

agile† (aʒil) *a*, agile, nimble, lithe, active. **agilité** (lite) *f*, agility, &c.

agio (aʒjo) *m*, exchange [premium], agio; discount charges. **agiotage** (ʒjɔta:ʒ) *m*, gambling, jobbery, rigging; exchange business. **agioter** (te) *v.i*, to speculate, gamble. **agioteur** (tœ:r) *m*, speculator, gambler.

agir (aʒi:r) *v.i*, to act, operate, work, do; proceed (*Law*). **s'~**, *v.imp*, to be the matter, be in question. **agissant, e** (ʒisɑ̃, ɑ̃:t) *a*, active. **agissements** (smɑ̃) *m.pl*, goings-on, doings (*underhand*).

agitateur (aʒitatœ:r) *m*, agitator (*Pol.*); stirrer (*rod*). **agiter** (te) *v.t*, to agitate, perturb, shake, stir; wag; wave; debate, discuss. *nuit agitée*, restless night. *mer agitée*, rough sea. **agitation** (tasjɔ̃) *f*, agitation, &c; unrest.

agneau (aɲo) *m*, lamb. *~ femelle*, ewe lamb. **agneler** (nəle) *v.i*, to lamb, yean. **agnelet** (lɛ) *m*, lambkin.

agonie (agɔni) *f*, [death] agony, death struggle. *à l'~*, dying. **agonir** (ni:r) *v.t*, to load (*with abuse*). **agonisant, e** (nizɑ̃, ɑ̃:t) *a*, dying. **agoniser** (ze) *v.i*, to be dying.

agrafe (agraf) *f*, hook, clasp, fastener, snap, staple, cramp. *~ & porte*, hook & eye. **agrafer** (fe) *v.t*, to hook, &c; do up (*dress*); grab, nab.

agraire (agrɛ:r) *a*, agrarian, land (*att.*).

agrandir (agrɑ̃di:r) *v.t*, to enlarge. **agrandisseur** (disœ:r) *m*, enlarger (*Phot.*).

agréable† (agreabl) *a. & m*, agreeable, pleasant, nice, congenial; acceptable, palatable.

agréé (agree) *m*, solicitor (*at tribunal de commerce*). **agréer** (gree) *v.t*, to accept, approve, agree; (*v.i.*) to please, suit. *agréez, monsieur, mes salutations empressées*, yours faithfully.

agrégation (agregasjɔ̃) *f*, admission; aggregation. **agréger** (ʒe) *v.t*, to admit (*as member*).

agrément† (agremɑ̃) *m*, consent, approval; agreeableness, pleasantness, amenity; pleasure, charm; trimming (*dress*). **agrémenter** (te) *v.t*, to adorn, ornament, trim.

agrès (agrɛ) *m.pl*, tackle, gear, rigging.

agresseur (agrɛsœ:r) *m*, aggressor. **agressif, ive** (sif, i:v) *a*, aggressive. **agression** (sjɔ̃) *f*, aggression.

agreste (agrɛst) *a*, rustic; uncouth.

agricole (agrikɔl) *a*, agricultural. **agriculteur** (kyltœ:r) *m*, agricultur[al]ist, farmer. **agriculture** (ty:r) *f*, agriculture, farming, husbandry.

agriffer (s') (agrife) *v.pr*, to claw, cling, lay hold.

agripper (agripe) *v.t*, to lay hold of, clutch, grab, grip.

agronome (agrɔnɔm) *m*, agronomist. **agronomie** (mi) *f*, agronomy, husbandry.

aguerrir (ageri:r) *v.t*, to harden to war; inure, season.

aguets (être aux) (agɛ) to be on the watch *or* lookout.

aheurtement (aœrtəmɑ̃) *m*, obsession. **s'a-heurter** (te) *v.pr*, to cling, be obsessed, be bent.

ahurir (ayri:r) *v.t*, to flurry, fluster, bewilder, daze.

aide (ɛ:d) *f*, aid, help, assistance. *à l'~!* help! ¶ *n*, assistant, helper, mate. *~ de camp*, *m*, aide-de-camp. **aider** (ɛde) *v.t*, to aid, help, assist. **s'~ de**, to make use of.

aide-mémoire (ɛdmemwa:r) *m*, handbook, manual; aide-mémoire (*diplomatic*).

aïe (a:j, oi! or oh! O dear! (*of pain*).

aïeul, e (ajœl) *m*, grandfather, -mother. **aïeux** (ajø) *m.pl*, forefathers.

aigle (ɛgl) *m*, eagle (*male bird*); genius, master mind; (*f.*) eagle (*hen bird & standard*). **aiglon, ne** (glɔ̃, ɔn) *n*, eaglet.

aigre† (ɛ:gr) *a*, sour, tart; bitter; sharp; churlish; shrill. ¶ *m*, sourness, &c; chill (*in the air*). **~-doux, ce** (ɛgrədu, us) *a*, bitter-sweet, sub-acid. **aigrefin** (fɛ̃) *m*, sharper; haddock. **aigrelet, te** (lɛ, ɛt) *a*, sourish, tart. **aigret, te** (grɛ, ɛt) *a*, sourish, tartish.

aigrette (ɛgrɛt) *f*, aigrette, egret, plume. **aigretté, e** (te) *a*, tufted, crested.

aigreur (ɛgrœ:r) *f*, sourness, acerbity. **aigrir** (gri:r) *v.t*, to sour, embitter.

aigu, ë (egy) *a*, acute, sharp, pointed; shrill. ¶ *m*, upper register (*Mus.*).

aigue-marine (ɛgmarin) *f*, aquamarine.

aiguière (ɛgjɛ:r) *f*, ewer.

aiguillade (egɥijad) *f*, goad.

aiguille (egɥi:j) *f*, needle; hand; pointer; point, switch (*Rly*). *~ à coudre*, sewing needle. *~ à passer*, bodkin. *~ à re-priser*, darning needle. *~ à tricoter*, knitting n., k. pin. *~ de glace*, icicle. **aiguillée** (gɥije) *f*, needleful. **aiguillier** (gɥijie) *m*, needle maker; n. case.

aiguillon (egɥijɔ̃) *m*, goad; sting; prickle; spur, stimulus, incentive. **aiguillonner** (jɔne) *v.t*, to goad, spur on, stimulate.

aiguiser (egɥize) *v.t*, to sharpen, grind, whet; stimulate.

ail (a:j) *m*, garlic.

aile (ɛl) *f*, wing; aisle; flange; blade, vane. **ailé, e** (le) *a*, winged. **aileron** (lrɔ̃) *m*, pinion; fin; paddle board; aileron.

ailleurs (ajœ:r) *ad*, elsewhere, somewhere else. **d'~**, *ad*, besides, moreover.

aimable† (ɛmabl) *a*, amiable, pleasant; kind; lovable. **aimant, e** (mɑ̃, ɑ̃:t) *a*, loving, affectionate.

aimant (ɛmɑ̃) *m*, magnet. **aimanter** (te) *v.t*, to magnetize.

aimer (ɛme) *v.t & abs*, to love; be fond of; like.

aine (ɛn) *f*, groin (*Anat.*).

aîné, e (ɛne) *a. & n*, elder; eldest; senior; major (*schoolboy*). **aînesse** (nɛs) *f*, seniority.

ainsi (ɛ̃si) *ad*, so, thus. *~ que*, *c*, [just] as; as also.

air (ɛ:r) *m*, air; look, likeness; manner; way; mien; aria; tune, song. *en l'~*, in the air, airy (*schemes*); idle (*tales*); groundless (*fears*); empty (*threats*). *de plein ~*, out-door (*as games*). *en plein ~*, in the open air, alfresco.

airain (ɛrɛ̃) *m* (*Poet.*), bronze, brass.

aire (ɛ:r) *f*, area, floor; aerie, eyrie. *~ de vent*, point of the compass.

airelle (ɛrɛl) *f*, whortleberry, bilberry.

ais (ɛ) *m*, board, plank.

aisance (ɛzɑ̃:s) *f*, ease; freedom; affluence, sufficiency, competence. **aise** (ɛ:z) *a*, glad, pleased. ¶ *f*, ease, comfort; joy, pleasure; (*pl.*) creature comforts. **aisé, e** (ɛze) *a*, easy; comfortable; well off, affluent. **aisément** (mɑ̃) *ad*, easily; comfortably; readily.

aisselle (ɛsɛl) *f*, armpit.

ajonc (aʒɔ̃) *m*, furze, gorse, whin; (*pl.*) rushes (*Golf*).

ajouré, e (aʒure) *a*, perforated, pierced; open-work (*att.*).

ajourner (aʒurne) *v.t*, to adjourn, postpone, put off; subpoena.

ajouté (aʒute) *m*, rider, addition. **ajouter** (te) *v.t*, to add; implement.

ajustage (aʒysta:ʒ) *m*, fitting, setting up. **ajustement** (təmɑ̃) *m*, adjustment; arrangement, settlement. **ajuster** (te) *v.t*, to adjust, fit [up]; lay out; deck out, array; set straight; aim at (*with gun*). **s'~**, to tidy oneself up. **ajusteur** (tœ:r) *m*, fitter, artificer.

ajutage (aʒuta:ʒ) *m*, nozzle, jet.

alambic (alɑ̃bik) *m*, still. **alambiquer** (ke) *v.t*, to puzzle; spin out, wiredraw (*fig.*).

alanguir (alɑ̃gi:r) *v.t*, to make languid.

alarmant, e (alarmɑ̃, ɑ̃:t) *a*, alarming. **alarme** (larm) *f*, alarm. **alarmer** (me) *v.t*, to alarm; startle.

albâtre (albɑ:tr) *m*, alabaster.

albatros (albatros) *m*, albatross.

albinos (albinos) *n*, albino.

album (albɔm) *m*, album, book. *~ à coller*, paste-on album. *~ à passe-partout*, slip-in album. ~ *d'images pour enfants*, picture book. ~ *de dessin*, sketch book. ~ *de patrons*, fashion book. ~ *pour collections*, scrap book. ~-*tarif*, illustrated price list.

albumen (albymɛn) *m*, albumen.

albumine (albymin) *f*, albumin.

alcali (alkali) *m*, alkali. **alcalin, e** (lɛ̃, in) *a*, alkaline.

alchimie (alʃimi) *f*, alchemy. **alchimiste** (mist) *m*, alchemist.

alcool (alkɔl) *m*, alcohol, spirit[s]. ~ *ammon aromatique*, sal volatile. ~ *dénaturé*, ~ *à brûler*, methylated spirit. **alcoolique** (kɔɔlik) *a. & n*, alcoholic.

alcôve (alko:v) *f*, alcove, recess. ~ *de dortoir*, cubicle.

alcyonien (alsjɔnjɛ̃) *a.m*, halcyon.

aléa (alea) *m*, chance. **aléatoire** (twa:r) *a*, uncertain, contingent, aleatory.

alène (alɛ:n) *f*, awl.

alentour (alɑ̃tu:r) *ad*, around, round about. *d'*~, surrounding. ~**s**, *m.pl*, surroundings.

alerte (alɛrt) *a*, alert, wide-awake. ¶ *i*, up! look out! ¶ *f*, alarm, alert.

aléser (aleze) *v.t*, to ream, broach, bore [out]. **alésage** (za:ʒ) *m*, reaming, &c; bore. **alésoir** (zwa:r) *m*, reamer, broach.

alevin (alvɛ̃) *m*, fry, young fish.

Alexandrie (alɛksɑ̃dri) *f*, Alexandria. **alexandrin, e** (drɛ̃, in) *a*, Alexandrian; Alexandrine.

alfa (alfa) *m*, alfa [grass], esparto [grass].

algarade (algarad) *f*, storm of abuse, blowing up.

algèbre (alʒɛbr) *m*, algebra; Greek (*fig.*).

Alger (alʒe) *m*, Algiers. **l'Algérie** (ʒeri) *f*, Algeria. **algérien, ne** (rjɛ̃, ɛn) *a. & A*~, *n*, Algerian.

algue (alg) *f*, seaweed, alga.

alibi (alibi) *m*, alibi.

aliboron (alibɔrɔ̃) *m*: *un maître* ~, an ass, a blockhead.

aliéné, e (aljene) *n*, mental patient, lunatic. **aliénation *d'esprit*,** ~ *mentale* (nasjɔ̃), insanity, lunacy, madness. **aliéner** (ne) *v.t*, to alienate, estrange; derange, unhinge (*mind*).

aligner (aliɲe) *v.t*, to align, range; dress (*Mil.*); finish off (*phrases*). **alignement** (ɲmɑ̃), *m*, alignment, &c; building line.

aliment (alimɑ̃) *m*, food; nutriment; fuel (*fig.*); (*pl.*) sustenance; (*pl.*) cud. **alimentaire** (tɛ:r) *a*, alimentary, feeding, feed, food (*att.*). **alimentation** (tasjɔ̃) *f*, feeding; feed. **alimenter** (te) *v.t*, to feed, supply.

alinéa (alinea) *m*, [fresh] paragraph, new par[agraph]; subsection.

alité, e (alite) *a*, laid up, bedridden. **aliter** (te) *v.t*, to keep in bed.

alizé (alize) *a*, trade (*wind*).

allaiter (alɛte) *v.t*, to suckle, nurse.

allant, e (alɑ̃, ɑ̃:t) *a*, active. ¶ *m*. activity;

go; initiative. ~**s** *& venants*, passers-by, comers & goers.

allécher (aleʃe) *v.t*, to allure, entice.

allée (ale) *f*, walk, lane, path; drive; passage. ~ *en berceau*, covered walk. ~**s** *& venues*, coming & going, running about.

allégation (alegasjɔ̃) *f*, allegation.

allège (alɛ:ʒ) *f*, lighter, barge, craft. **alléger** (leʒe) *v.t*, to lighten; thin; alleviate. **allégement** (lɛʒmɑ̃) *m*, lightening, &c.

allégorie (allegɔri) *f*, allegory. **allégorique†** (rik) *a*, allegoric(al).

allègre (allɛ:gr) *a*, lively, cheerful, brisk. **allégresse** (allegrɛs) *f*, joy[fulness], cheerfulness.

alléguer (alege) *v.t*, to allege, adduce; plead, urge; quote, cite.

Alléluia (alleluija) *m*, hallelujah.

Allemagne (l' (almaɲ) *f*, Germany. **allemand, e** (mɑ̃, ɑ̃:d) *a. & A*~, *n*, German. **l'allemand**, *m*, German (*language*).

aller (ale) *m*, going, outward journey. ~ *& retour*, there & back, round voyage. *l'*~ *& le venir*, the come-&-go. ¶ *v.i.ir*, to go; run; be (*well, ill, &c*); get; do; fare; fit, suit. ~ *à bicyclette*, to cycle. ~ *à cheval*, to ride. ~ *en auto*, to motor. ~ *en voiture*, to drive. **s'en** ~, to go [away], be off.

alliage (aljaʒ) *m*, alloy. **alliance** (jɑ̃:s) *f*, alliance, union; match; intermarriage; wedding ring. *cousin, &c, par* ~, cousin, &c, by marriage. **allié, e** (je) *n*, ally; relation [by marriage]. **allier** (je) *v.t*, to ally, unite; match; alloy. **s'**~, to unite; marry; intermarry.

alligator (aligatɔ:r) *m*, alligator.

allô (alo) (*Teleph.*) *i*, hello! hullo! are you there?

allocation (allɔkasjɔ̃) *f*, allocation, allowance.

allocution (allɔkysjɔ̃) *f*, speech, address.

allonge (alɔ̃:ʒ) *f*, lengthening piece; rider (*to bill of exchange*). **allonger** (lɔ̃ʒe) *v.t*, to lengthen, elongate; eke out; stretch [out]; deal (*blow*).

allouer (alwe) *v.t*, to allocate, allow, grant.

allumage (alyma:ʒ) *m*, lighting, ignition. **allume-feu** (lymfø) *m*, fire lighter. **allumer** (me) *v.t*, to light, ignite; kindle; fire; stir up. ~ *la lumière*, ~ *l'électricité*, to switch (*or* turn) on the light. **allumette** (mɛt) *f*, match. ~ *bougie*, wax vesta. ~**s** *de sûreté*, safety matches. ~**s** *en carnet*, book matches. **allumeur** (mœ:r) *m*, lighter.

allure (aly:r) *f*, walk, gait, pace; demeanour, carriage; trim; way.

allusion (allyzjɔ̃) *f*, allusion; hint, innuendo.

alluvion (allyvjɔ̃) *f*, alluvion, alluvium.

almanach (almana) *m*, *in liaison*, -nak) *m*, almanac.

aloès (alɔɛs) *m*, aloe. [*suc d'*] ~, aloes.

aloi (alwa) *m*, standard, quality. *de bon* ~, sterling (*fig.*).

alors (alɔ:r) *ad*, then. ~ *que*, *c*, when.

alouette (alwɛt) *f*, lark. ~ *des champs*, skylark.

alourdir (alurdi:r) *v.t*, to make heavy.

aloyau (alwajo) *m*, sirloin (*beef*).

alpaga (alpaga), *m*, alpaca.

Alpes (les) (alp) *f.pl*, the Alps. **alpestre** (pɛstr) *a*, Alpine.

alpha (alfa) *m*, alpha. **alphabet** (bɛ) *m*, alphabet; A B C, primer. **alphabétique†** (betik) *a*, alphabetical.

alpin, e (alpɛ̃, in) *a*, Alpine. **l'alpinisme** (pinism) *m*, mountaineering. **alpiniste** (nist) *n*, Alpinist, mountaineer.

Alsace (l') (alzas) *f*, Alsace. **alsacien, ne** (sjɛ̃, ɛn) *a. & A~, n*, Alsatian.

altérant, e (alterɑ̃, ɑ̃:t) *a*, thirst-creating.

altération (alterasjɔ̃) *f*, alteration, change; adulteration.

altercation (alterkasjɔ̃) *f*, altercation.

altérer (altere) *v.t*, to change; debase, adulterate; garble; weather (*Geol.*); make thirsty. *altéré de sang*, bloodthirsty.

alternatif, ive† (alternatif, i:v) *a*, alternative; alternate; alternating. ¶ *f*, alternative; option. **alterner** (ne) *v.i. & t*, to alternate.

altesse (altɛs) *f*, highness (*title*).

altier, ère (altje, ɛ:r) *a*, haughty, lofty, lordly.

altitude (altityd) *f*, altitude, height, elevation.

alto (alto) *m*, alto; tenor violin, viola; alto saxhorn.

altruiste (altryist) *n*, altruist. ¶ *a*, altruistic.

aluminium (alyminjɔm) *m*, aluminium.

alun (alɛ̃) *m*, alum.

alvéole (alveɔl) *m*, cell; socket (*tooth*).

amabilité (amabilite) *f*, amiability, kindness.

amadou (amadu) *m*, tinder, touchwood. **amadouer** (dwe) *v.t*, to coax, wheedle, cajole, soft-sawder.

amaigrir (amegri:r) *v.t*, to [make] thin, emaciate.

amalgame (amalgam) *m*, amalgam; mixture. **amalgamer** (me) *v.t*, to amalgamate.

amande (amɑ̃:d) *f*, almond; kernel. *des yeux en* ~, almond eyes. **amandier** (mɑ̃dje) *m*, almond [tree].

amant, e (amɑ̃) *m*, paramour; lover.

amariner (amarine) *v.t*, to make a sailor of; man (*prize ship*).

amarre (ama:r) *f*, [mooring] rope, fast, line; hawser. **amarrer** (mare) *v.t*, to make fast, moor; lash, seize; berth; belay.

amas (amɑ) *m*, heap, pile, mass, collection; drift (*snow*); hoard. **amasser** (se) *v.t*, to amass, heap [up], pile up, lay up, hoard.

amateur (amatœ:r) *m*, lover (*devotee*); amateur; fancier. *il est [grand]* ~ *de* . . ., he is [very] fond of . . . (*e.g. art, collecting, gardening*); . . . is his hobby.

amazone (amazo:n) *f*, Amazon; horsewoman. [*habit d'*]~, riding habit. **l'A~**, *m*, le fleuve des A~s, the Amazon (*river*).

ambassade (ɑ̃basad) *f*, embassy; errand. **ambassadeur, drice** (dœ:r, dris) *n*, ambassador, dress; messenger. *l'* ~ *de France*, the French ambassador.

ambiance (ɑ̃bjɑ̃:s) *f*, environment. **ambiant**, e (ɑ̃, ɑ̃:t) *a*, surrounding, ambient.

ambigu†, ë (ɑ̃bigy) *a*, ambiguous. ¶ *m*, mixture. **ambiguïté** (gyite) *f*, ambiguity.

ambitieux, euse† (ɑ̃bisjø, ø:z) *a*, ambitious. **ambition** (sjɔ̃) *f*, ambition. **ambitionner** (one) *v.t*, to be eager for, aspire to.

ambre (ɑ̃:br) *m*, amber. ~ *gris*, ambergris.

ambroisie (ɑ̃brwazi) *f*, ambrosia.

ambulance (ɑ̃bylɑ̃:s) *f*, ambulance. **ambulant**, e (lɑ̃, ɑ̃:t) *a*, itinerant, strolling; travelling.

âme (ɑ:m) *f*, soul, mind, spirit, ghost, life, heart; mainstay; sound post; core; web; bore (*gun*); motto. *dans l'* ~, at heart. ~ *damnée*, [mere] tool (*pers.*).

améliorer (ameljore) *v.t. & s'* ~, to ameliorate, better, improve, mend; appreciate.

amen (amɛn) *i. & m*, amen.

aménager (amenaʒe) *v.t*, to lay out, fit; harness (*waterfall*); reclaim (*submerged land*). **aménagement** (ʒmɑ̃) *m*, lay-out; accommodation, appointments.

amende (amɑ̃:d) *f*, fine.

amender (amɑ̃de) *v.t*, to amend; improve.

amène (amɛ:n) *a*, pleasing, agreeable.

amener (amne) *v.t*, to bring, lead; lead up to; haul down; strike (*colours*). *amené de loin*, far-fetched.

aménité (amenite) *f*, amenity, graciousness.

amenuiser (amənɥize) *v.t*, to thin.

amer, ère† (amɛ:r) *a*, bitter; briny. ¶ *m*, bitter, bitterness; (*pl.*) bitters; gall; sea mark, landmark (*Naut.*).

américain, e (amerikɛ̃, ɛn) *a. & A~, n*, American. **l'Amérique** (rik) *f*, America.

amerrir (ameri:r) *v.i*, to alight [on the water] (*seaplane*).

amertume (amɛrtym) *f*, bitterness.

améthyste (ametist) *f*, amethyst.

ameublement (amœblmɑ̃) *m*, [suite of] furniture.

ameuter (amøte) *v.t*, to pack (*hounds*); stir up (*mob*).

ami, e (ami) *a*, friendly; kindly. ¶ *n*, friend; lover. ~ *de cœur*, bosom friend. *amis & parents*, kith & kin. **amiable†** (mjabl) *a*, amical, e† (mikal) *a*, amicable, friendly, kind. *amiable compositeur*, arbitrator (*Law*). *à l'amiable*, amicably; by private treaty (*sale*).

amidon (amidɔ̃) *m*, starch. **amidonner** (done) *v.t*, to starch.

amincir (amɛ̃si:r) *v.t*, to thin.

amiral (amiral) *m*, admiral; flagship. ~ *commandant d'escadre*, admiral of the fleet. **Amirauté** (rote) *f*, Admiralty (*Eng.*).

amitié (amitje) *f*, friendship, kindness, love, liking; (*pl.*) kind regards.

ammoniaque (amɔnjak) *f*, ammonia.

B *

amnistie (amnisti) f, amnesty, oblivion.
amodier (amɔdje) v.t, to farm out.
amoindrir (amwɛ̃dri:r) v.t, to lessen, decrease.
amollir (amɔli:r) v.t, to soften, mollify; enervate.
amonceler (amɔ̃sle) v.t, to heap [up], pile up, drift.
amont (amɔ̃) m, head waters; upper part. en ∼, ad, up stream, up. en ∼ de, pr, above, up.
amorce (amɔrs) f, bait; allurement; [percussion] cap; priming; beginning, start. **amorcer** (se) v.t, to bait, &c; energize (Elec.).
amorphe (amɔrf) a, amorphous.
amortir (amɔrti:r) v.t, to deaden, damp; redeem, amortize, sink, pay off; write off, depreciate. **amortisseur** (tisœ:r) m, shock absorber (motor); damper (Radio).
amour (amu:r) m, love; passion; idol; (pl.) love affairs, amours. ∼ intéressé, cupboard love. pour l' ∼ de, for the sake (or love) of. **amouracher** (muraʃe) v.t, to enamour. **amoureux, euse**† (rø, ø:z) a, in love, enamoured; loving, amorous; tender, soft. ¶ n, lover, sweetheart. **amourpropre** (amurprɔpr) m, self-respect, pride; self-esteem.
amovible (amɔvibl) a, removable, detachable.
ampère (ɑ̃pɛ:r) m, ampere.
amphibie (ɑ̃fibi) a, amphibious. ¶ m, amphibian.
amphithéâtre (ɑ̃fiteɑ:tr) m, amphitheatre.
ample† (ɑ̃pl) a, ample, full; wide. **ampleur** (ɑ̃plœ:r) f, ampleness, &c. **ampliation** (pliasjɔ̃) f, duplicate, office copy. pour ∼, [certified] a true copy. **amplificateur** (fikatœ:r) m, enlarger (Phot.); amplifier (Radio). **amplifier** (fje) v.t, to amplify. **amplitude** (tyd) f, amplitude.
ampoule (ɑ̃pul) f, phial; blister; bulb (elec. lamp, thermometer). **ampoulé, e** (le) a, inflated, bombastic, high-flown.
amputer (ɑ̃pyte) v.t, to amputate, cut off.
amulette (amylɛt) f, amulet, charm.
amure (amy:r) f, tack (sail).
amuser (amyze) v.t, to amuse, entertain; beguile, fool, trifle with. s'∼, to amuse (or enjoy) oneself; dally, loiter. **amusement** (zmɑ̃) m, amusement, &c. **amusette** (zɛt) f, plaything.
amygdale (amigdal) f, tonsil. **amygdalite** (lit) f, tonsillitis.
an (ɑ̃) m, year. il a 10 ∼s, he is 10 years old.
anachorète (anakɔrɛt) m, anchoret, anchorite.
anachronisme (anakrɔnism) m, anachronism.
anagramme (anagram) f, anagram.
analogie (analɔʒi) f, analogy. **analogue** (lɔg) a, analogous, like.
analyse (anali:z) f, analysis. ∼ grammaticale, parsing. **analyser** (lize) v.t, to analyse; parse. **analyste** (list) m, analyst. **analytique**† (tik) a, analytic(al).

ananas (anana) m, pineapple.
anarchie (anarʃi) f, anarchy. **anarchique**† (ʃik) a, anarchic(al). **anarchiste** (ʃist) n. & a, anarchist.
anatomie (anatɔmi) f, anatomy. **anatomique**† (mik) a, anatomical.
ancestral, e (ɑ̃sɛstral) a, ancestral. **ancêtre** (sɛ:tr) m, ancestor.
anche (ɑ̃:ʃ) f, reed (Mus.).
anchois (ɑ̃ʃwa) m, anchovy.
ancien, ne (ɑ̃sjɛ̃, ɛn) a, ancient, old; of long standing; former; bygone; quondam; late, ex-; senior. ancien combattant, ex-service man. ¶ m, ancient; elder (Eccl.). **anciennement** (ɛnmɑ̃) ad, anciently, of old, formerly. **ancienneté** (nte) f, ancientness, antiquity; seniority. de toute ∼, from time immemorial.
ancolie (ɑ̃kɔli) f, columbine (Bot.).
ancre (ɑ̃:kr) f, anchor. ∼ à jet, kedge [a.]. ∼ de veille (Naut.) & ∼ de salut (fig.), sheet anchor. **ancrer** (ɑ̃kre) (Build.) v.t, to anchor, fix.
andain (ɑ̃dɛ̃) m, swath, wind row.
andouiller (ɑ̃duje) m, tine, antler.
âne (ɑ:n) m, ass, jackass, donkey; dunce, dolt.
anéantir (aneɑ̃ti:r) v.t, to annihilate, crush; prostrate. s'∼, to humble oneself.
anecdote (anɛgdɔt) f, anecdote.
anémie (anemi) f, anaemia. **anémique** (mik) a, anaemic.
anémone (anemɔn) f, anemone.
ânerie (ɑnri) f, gross stupidity.
anéroïde (anerɔid) a, aneroid.
ânesse (ɑnɛs) f, [she] ass, jenny.
anesthésie (anɛstezi) f, anaesthesia. ∼ à la reine, twilight sleep. **anesthésique** (zik) a. & m, anaesthetic.
anfractueux, euse (ɑ̃fraktɥø, ø:z) a, winding, craggy.
ange (ɑ̃:ʒ) m, angel. ∼ déchu, fallen à. être aux ∼s, to be in raptures. **angélique**† (ɑ̃ʒelik) a, angelic(al). ¶ f, angelica. **Angélus** (ly:s) m, angelus [bell].
angine (ɑ̃ʒin) f, angina, quinsy. ∼ de poitrine, angina pectoris.
anglais, e (ɑ̃glɛ, ɛ:z) a, English; British; imperial. **A**∼, n, Englishman, ∼-woman, Briton. l'anglais, m, English (language).
angle (ɑ̃:gl) m, angle, corner.
Angleterre (l') (ɑ̃glətɛ:r) f, England. **anglicisme** (glisism) m, Anglicism. **anglomanie** (glɔmani) f, Anglomania. les îles Anglo-Normandes, the Channel Islands. **anglophile** (fil) a. & n, Anglophil[e], pro-British. **anglophobe** (fɔb) a. & n, Anglophobe, anti-British. **anglo-saxon, ne** (saksɔ̃, ɔn) a. & A∼-S∼, n, Anglo-Saxon.
angoisse (ɑ̃gwas) f, anguish, pang. **angoisser** (se) v.t, to distress, pain.
angora (ɑ̃gɔra) m, Persian [cat].
anguillade (ɑ̃gijad) f, lash, cut.

anguille (ãgi:j) *f*, eel. ~ *de mer*, conger [eel]. *quelque* ~ *sous roche* (*fig.*), something in the wind.

angulaire (ãgylɛːr) *a*, angular, corner (*att.*).

anicroche (anikrɔʃ) *f*, hitch, snag.

ânier, ère (ɑnje, ɛːr) *n*, donkey driver.

aniline (anilin) *f*, aniline.

animal, e (animal) *a*, animal. ¶ *m*, animal, dumb animal, beast, brute; creature. *animaux marins flottants, animaux en caoutchouc*, rubber floating toys. *animaux vivants*, live stock.

animateur, trice (animatœːr, tris) *n*, animator, moving spirit. **animation** (sjɔ̃) *f*, animation, liveliness, bustle, life. **animé, e** (me) *a*, animate; animated, lively, buoyant, spirited, brisk, bustling, agog, astir; instinct. **animer** (me) *v.t*, to animate, quicken, brighten, enliven, inspirit; actuate, impel.

animosité (animozite) *f*, animosity, animus, spite.

anis (ani) *m*, anise. [*graine d'*]~, aniseed.

annales (anal) *f.pl*, annals.

anneau (ano) *m*, ring; coil (*snake*); ringlet; link.

année (ane) *f*, year, twelvemonth. ~ *d millésime*, vintage year.

annexe (anɛks) *f*, annex[e]; dependency (*country*); schedule; enclosure; tender (*boat*). **annexer** (kse) *v.t*, to annex, attach. **annexion** (ksjɔ̃) *f*, annexation.

annihiler (aniile) *v.t*, to annihilate; annul.

anniversaire (anivɛrsɛːr) *a. & m*, anniversary. *l'*~ *de ma naissance*, my birthday.

annonce (anɔ̃:s) *f*, announcement, advertisement. ~*article*, puff paragraph. ~ *de fantaisie*, ~ *courante*, display advertisement. **annoncer** (nɔ̃se) *v.t*, to announce, advertise, proclaim, herald; give out; betoken, foreshadow; inform; state; show in, usher in; preach; foretell. **annonceur** (sœːr) *m*, advertiser. **l'Annonciation** (sjasjɔ̃) *f*, the Annunciation, Lady-day.

annoter (anote) *v.t*, to annotate.

annuaire (anɥɛːr) *m*, annual, year book, directory (*telephone*); list (*Army, Navy, &c*).

annuel, le† (nɥɛl) *a*, annual, yearly. **annuité** (nɥite) *f*, annuity.

annulaire (anylɛːr) *a*, annular. [*doigt*] ~, *m*, ring finger, third f.

annuler (anyle) *v.t*, to annul, nullify, quash, cancel; contra.

anoblir (anɔbliːr) *v.t*, to ennoble.

anode (anɔd) *f*, anode.

anodin, e (anɔdɛ̃, in) *a*, anodyne, soothing; harmless, mild, tame. ¶ *m*, anodyne.

anomal, e (anɔmal) *a*, anomalous. **anomalie** (li) *f*, anomaly.

ânon (anɔ̃) *m*, young ass, foal. **ânonner** (none) *v.i*, to falter, hem, haw, hum & ha.

anonyme (anɔnim) *a*, anonymous; unnamed.

anormal, e (anɔrmal) *a*, abnormal.

anse (ãːs) *f*, handle; bow; cove. *faire le pot à deux* ~*s*, to set one's arms akimbo.

aspect (ãspɛk) *m*, handspike.

antagonisme (ãtagonism) *m*, antagonism. **antagoniste** (nist) *m*, antagonist, opponent.

antan (ãtã) *m*, yester year.

antarctique (ãtar[k]tik) *a*, antarctic.

antécédent, e (ãtesedã, ãːt) *a. & m*, antecedent.

antéchrist (ãtekrist) *m*, antichrist. *l'A*~, the A.

antédiluvien, ne (ãtedilyvjɛ̃, ɛn) *a*, antediluvian.

antenne (ãtɛn) *f*, antenna, feeler, horn; aerial (*Radio*). ~ *d'appartement*, indoor aerial.

antérieur, e† (ãterjœːr) *a*, anterior, prior, previous. **antériorité** (rjorite) *f*, priority.

anthère (ãtɛːr) *f*, anther.

anthologie (ãtɔlɔʒi) *f*, anthology.

anthracite (ãtrasit) *m*, anthracite.

anthrax (ãtraks) *m*, carbuncle (*Med.*).

anthropophage (ãtrɔpɔfaːʒ) *a. & m*, cannibal.

anti-aérien, ne (ãtiaerjɛ̃, ɛn) *a*, anti-aircraft.

antialcoolique (ãtialkɔɔlik) *a*, teetotal.

antichambre (ãtiʃãːbr) *f*, antechamber, anteroom.

anticipation (ãtisipasjɔ̃) *f*, anticipation, advance. **anticiper** (pe) *v.t*, to anticipate, forestall. ~ *sur*, to encroach on.

anticyclone (ãtisiklɔːn) *m*, anticyclone.

antidater (ãtidate) *v.t*, to antedate.

antidérapant, e (ãtiderapã, ãːt) *a*, non-skid.

antidote (ãtidɔt) *m*, antidote.

antienne (ãtjɛn) *f*, anthem.

Antilles (les) (ãti:j) *f.pl*, the West Indies, the Antilles. *la mer des* ~, the Caribbean sea.

antilope (ãtilɔp) *f*, antelope.

antimoine (ãtimwan) *m*, antimony.

antipathie (ãtipati) *f*, antipathy, dislike. **antipathique** (tik) *a*, antipathetic.

antipatriotique (ãtipatriotik) *a*, unpatriotic.

antipodes (ãtipɔd) *m.pl*, antipodes.

antiquailles (ãtika:j) *f.pl*, worthless antiques, lumber. **antiquaire** (kɛːr) *n*, antiquary, -rian. **antique** (tik) *a*, ancient; antique. ¶ *m*, antique (*style*); (*f.*) antique (*relic*). **antiquité** (kite) *f*, antiquity.

antiseptique (ãtisɛptik) *a. & m*, antiseptic; preservative (*for perishable foodstuffs*).

antisocial, e (ãtisɔsjal) *a*, unsocial.

antithèse (ãtitɛːz) *f*, antithesis.

antre (ãːtr) *m*, cave, den, lair.

anus (any:s) *m*, anus.

Anvers (ãvɛːr, -vɛrs) *m*, Antwerp. **anversois, e** (vɛrswa, aːz) *a*, of Antwerp.

anxiété (ãksjete) *f*, anxiety. **anxieux, euse** (ksjø, øːz) *a*, anxious.

aorte (aɔrt) *f*, aorta.

août (u) *m*, August.

apache (apaʃ) *m*, Apache, desperado; hooligan, rough.

apaiser (apɛze) *v.t*, to appease, allay, assuage, quiet, quell, quench. **s'**~, to abate.

aparté (aparte) *m*, aside, stage whisper.

apathie (apati) *f*, apathy. **apathique** (tik) *a*, apathetic, lackadaisical.

apercevoir (apersəvwa:r) *v.t*, to perceive, see, espy. **s'~**, to perceive, find. **aperçu** (sy) *m*, outline, summary; rough estimate.

apéritif (aperitif) *m*, appetizer.

aphorisme (aforism) *m*, aphorism.

apiculture (apikylty:r) *f*, bee keeping.

apitoyer (apitwaje) *v.t*, to move to pity.

aplanir (aplani:r) *v.t*, to level; smooth.

aplatir (aplati:r) *v.t*, to flat[ten]; squash. **aplatissement** (tismã) *m*, flatt[en]ing; flatness.

aplomb (aplɔ̃) *m*, perpendicularity; plumb; self-possession. **d'~**, plumb, upright.

Apocalypse (apɔkalips) *f*, Revelation, Apocalypse.

apogée (apɔʒe) *m*, apogee; height; zenith; acme, high watermark (*fig.*).

apologétique (apɔlɔʒetik) *a*, apologetic. **apologie** (ʒi) *f*, apology, justification.

apoplectique (apɔplɛktik) *a. & m*, apoplectic. **apoplexie** (ksi) *f*, apoplexy.

apostasie (apostazi) *f*, apostasy, defection. **apostat** (ta) *m. & att*, apostate.

aposter (apɔste) *v.t*, to station, post, set.

apostille (apɔsti:j) *f*, marginal note, side note; recommendation. **apostiller** (tije) *v.t*, to make a note on.

apostolat (apɔstɔla) *m*, apostolate, apostleship. **apostolique†** (lik) *a*, apostolic(al).

apostrophe (apɔstrɔf) *f*, apostrophe; reproach. **apostropher** (fe) *v.t*, to apostrophize; upbraid.

apothéose (apɔteo:z) *f*, apotheosis.

apôtre (apo:tr) *m*, apostle.

apparaître (apare:tr) *v.i.ir*, to appear.

apparat (apara) *m*, state, show, pomp.

appareil (apare:j) *m*, array; apparatus, appliance, plant, gear, tackle, rig; attachment (*to machine*); dressing (*on wound*); camera (see *chambre* for varieties). **~ à douche d'air**, hair drier. **~ à sous**, coin machine. **~ avertisseur contre le vol**, burglar alarm. **[~] plus lourd que l'air**, heavier than air machine. **appareiller** (rɛje) *v.t. & i*, to match, pair, mate; fit; get under weigh. **appareilleur** (jœ:r) *m*, fitter.

apparemment (aparamã) *ad*, apparently. **apparence** (rɑ̃:s) *f*, appearance, look; guise; likelihood. **apparent, e** (rã, ã:t) *a*, apparent, seeming.

apparenté, e (aparãte) *a*, related, akin, connected. **apparenter** (te) *v.t*, to connect, ally. **s'~**, to marry (*à* = into); blend.

apparier (aparje) *v.t*, to match, pair.

appariteur (aparitœ:r) *m*, apparitor, beadle.

apparition (aparisjɔ̃) *f*, appearance, advent; apparition.

appartement (apartəmã) *m*, [suite of] rooms, flat.

appartenir (apartəni:r) *v.i.ir*, to belong, [ap]pertain, concern. **s'~**, to be one's own master *or* mistress.

appas (apɑ) *m.pl*, attractions, charms. **appât** (pɑ) *m*, bait, allurement, lure, draw. **appâter** (te) *v.t*, to bait; allure; cram (*poultry*).

appauvrir (apovri:r) *v.t*, to impoverish, beggar.

appeau (apo) *m*, bird call.

appel (apɛl) *m*, call, calling [up]; appeal; invitation; take-off (*Jump.*). **faire l'~**, to take off. **~ d'air**, [in]draught, intake of air. **~ de fonds**, call. **~ [nominal]**, roll call, muster, call over. **appelant** (plã) *m*, decoy bird. **appeler** (ple) *v.t. & i*, to call; term; appeal; invite; call out. **s'~**, to be called. *je m'appelle Adam*, my name is Adam.

appendice (apɛ̃dis) *m*, appendage, appendix. **appendicite** (sit) *f*, appendicitis.

appendre (apɑ̃:dr) *v.t*, to hang up.

appentis (apɑ̃ti) *m*, lean-to, penthouse; outhouse.

appesantir (apəzɑ̃ti:r) *v.t*, to make heavy, dull, weigh down.

appéter (apete) *v.t*, to crave for, long for. **appétissant, e** (apetisã, ɑ̃:t) *a*, appetizing, tempting. **appétit** (ti) *m*, appetite; desire, lust.

applaudir (aplodi:r) *v.t. & i*, to applaud, cheer. **~ à**, to commend. **s'~ de**, to congratulate oneself on. **applaudissement** (dismã) *m. oft. pl*, applause, cheer, plaudit.

application (aplikasjɔ̃) *f*, application; infliction; diligence. [*dentelle d'*]**~**, appliqué lace. **applique** (plik) *f*, appliqué [work] (*metal*); sconce, bracket. **appliqué, e** (ke) *p.a*, applied; close; studious. **appliquer** (ke) *v.t*, to apply, put, lay on; give; charge; inflict.

appoint (apwɛ̃) *m*, small coin, [small] change, odd money; help. **appointements** (tmã) *m.pl*, salary. **appointer** (te) *v.t*, to put on a salary basis (*in p.p*, salaried); point; sew up, stitch together.

appontement (apɔ̃tmã) *m*, wharf.

apport (apo:r) *m*, bringing; transfer, assignment; capital brought in; assets transferred *or* taken over; contribution; collection (*of goods by Rly Co.*); drift (*Geol.*). *valeurs d'*~, vendor's assets. **apporter** (porte) *v.t*, to bring, fetch; transfer, assign; give; waft. *apporte!* fetch it! (*to dog*). **apporteur** (tœ:r) *m*, vendor.

apposer (apoze) *v.t*, to affix, put, append, set. **apposition** (zisjɔ̃) *f*, affixture, &c; apposition. *en* **~** (*Gram.*), in apposition; attributively.

appréciable (apresjabl) *a*, appreciable; measurable. **appréciation** (sjɔ̃) *f*, valuation, estimate; appreciation. **apprécier** (sje) *v.t*, to value, &c.

appréhender (apreãde) *v.t*, to apprehend. **appréhension** (sjɔ̃) *f*, apprehension.

apprendre (aprɑ̃:dr) *v.t. & abs. ir*, to learn, hear, understand; teach; inform, tell. *mal appris*, ill-bred.

apprenti, e (aprɑ̃ti) *n*, apprentice; articled clerk; learner; novice, tyro. **apprentissage** (sa:ʒ) *m*, apprenticeship; articles. **mettre en ~**, to apprentice.

apprêt (aprɛ) *m*, dressing; affectation; (*pl.*) preparations. **apprêté, e** (te) *a*, affected. **apprêter** (te) *v.t*, to prepare; dress.

apprivoiser (aprivwaze) *v.t*, to tame.

approbation (aprɔbasjɔ̃) *f*, approbation, approval, confirmation.

approchant, e (aprɔʃɑ̃, ɑ̃:t) *a*, approximating, like. **approche** (prɔʃ) *f*, approach. **approcher** (ʃe) *v.t. & i*, to approach, draw near; resemble, border on.

approfondi, e (aprɔfɔ̃di) *p.a*, thorough, exhaustive. **approfondir** (di:r) *v.t*, to deepen; dive into.

approprier (aprɔprie) *v.t*, to adapt, suit. **s'~**, to appropriate.

approuver (apruve) *v.t*, to approve, countenance, confirm, pass.

approvisionner (aprɔvizjɔne) *v.t*, to supply, store, stock, provision. **s'~ de**, to lay in [a stock of]. **approvisionnement** (nmɑ̃) *m*, supplying, &c; supply, &c.

approximatif, ive† (aprɔksimatif, i:v) *a*, approximate, rough. **approximation** (sjɔ̃) *f*, approximation.

appui (apɥi) *m*, support, rest; sill; stress (*Gram.*). [*point d'*]**~**, fulcrum. *à hauteur d'*~, elbow-high, breast-high. **~-main**, *m*, maulstick. **appuyer** (pɥije) *v.t. & i*, to support; back; second; hold up; lean, rest; bear; press; lay stress. **s'~**, to rest, lean; rely, depend.

âpre† (ɑ:pr) *a*, rough, harsh; sharp; ruthless; greedy, grasping.

après (aprɛ) *pr*, after. *ap. J.-C.*, A.D. ¶ *ad*, after[wards]. **~ que**, *c*, after, when. **d'~**, *pr*, according to, after, from. **~ coup**, *ad*, too late, after the event, a day after the fair. **~-demain**, *ad. & m*, the day after to-morrow. **d'~-guerre**, *a*, postwar. **~-midi**, *m*, afternoon. *de l'~-midi*, post meridiem, p.m.

âpreté (aprɛte) *f*, roughness, &c, as *âpre*; asperity.

à-propos (aprɔpo) *m*, aptness; opportuneness.

apte (apt) *a*, fit[ted], competent, qualified; apt. **aptitude** (tityd) *f*, aptitude, aptness, &c; faculty, flair.

apurer (apyre) *v.t*, to agree, reconcile; wipe off (*debt*, &c); get discharged, get cancelled.

aquafortiste (akwafɔrtist) *m*, etcher.

aquaplane (akwaplan) *m*, surf board.

aquarelle (akwarɛl) *f*, water colour.

aquarium (akwarjɔm) *m*, aquarium.

aquatique (akwatik) *a*, aquatic, water (*att.*).

aqueduc (akdyk) *m*, aqueduct.

aqueux, euse (akø, ø:z) *a*, aqueous, watery.

à quia (kɥia), nonplussed.

aquilin (akilɛ̃) *a.m*, aquiline, hook[ed], Roman (*nose*).

ara (ara) *m*, macaw, ara.

arabe (arab) *a*, Arab; Arabian; Arabic. ¶ *m*, Arabic (*language*). **A~**, *n*, Arab[ian] (*pers.*). **arabesque** (bɛsk) *f*, arabesque. **l'Arabie** (bi) *f*, Arabia. **Arabique** (bik) *a*, Arabian (*gulf*).

arable (arabl) *a*, arable, tillable.

arachide (araʃid) *f*, groundnut, peanut, monkey nut.

araignée (arɛɲe) *f*, spider.

aratoire (aratwa:r) *a*, agricultural, farming.

arbitrage (arbitra:ʒ) *m*, arbitration†; arbitrament; arbitrage. **arbitraire†** (trɛ:r) *a*, arbitrary; high-handed. **arbitre** (tr) *m*, arbitrator, arbiter; referee, umpire. **~ de lignes**, linesman (*Ten.*). **~ de touche**, linesman (*Association*); touch judge (*Rugby*). **arbitrer** (tre) *v.t*, to arbitrate; arrange; referee, umpire.

arborer (arbɔre) *v.t*, to raise, hoist, set up.

arbre (arbr) *m*, tree; shaft, axle, spindle, mandrel, -il, arbor. **~ de haute futaie**, timber tree. **~ de plein vent**, standard. **~ en espalier**, wall tree. **~ moteur, ~ de couche**, driving shaft. **~ toujours vert**, evergreen. **arbrisseau** (briso) *m*, shrub.

arbuste (arbyst) *m*, bush.

arc (ark) *m*, bow; arc; arch. **arcade** (kad) *f*, archway; arch; (*pl.*) arcade.

arc-boutant (arkbutɑ̃) *m*, [flying] buttress; raking shore; strut, spur, brace. **arc-bouter** (te) *v.t*, to buttress.

arceau (arso) *m*, arch; hoop, wicket (*Croquet*); cradle (*Surg.*).

arc-en-ciel (arkɑ̃sjɛl) *m*, rainbow.

archaïque (arkaik) *a*, archaic.

archange (arkɑ̃:ʒ) *m*, archangel.

arche (arʃ) *f*, arch; ark. *l'~ d'alliance*, the Ark of the Covenant. *l'~ de Noé* (nɔe), Noah's ark.

archéologie (arkeɔlɔʒi) *f*, archaeology. **archéologique** (ʒik) *a*, archaeological(al). **archéologue** (lɔg) *m*, archaeologist.

archer (arʃe) *m*, archer, bowman. **archet** (ʃɛ) *m*, bow, fiddlestick.

archevêché (arʃəvɛʃe) *m*, archbishopric; palace. **archevêque** (vɛ:k) *m*, archbishop.

archidiacre (arʃidjakr) *m*, archdeacon.

archipel (arʃipɛl) *m*, archipelago.

architecte (arʃitɛkt) *m*, architect. **architectural, e** (tyral) *a*, architectural. **architecture** (ty:r) *f*, architecture.

archives (arʃi:v) *f.pl*, archives, records.

arçon (arsɔ̃) *m*, saddle bow; bow.

arctique (arktik) *a*, arctic.

ardent, e (ardɑ̃, ɑ̃:t) *a*, burning, hot, fiery, raging, blazing, live; ardent, keen, fervent, fervid, eager, earnest, spirited; passionate. ¶ *m*, will-o'-the-wisp, jack-o'-lantern. **ardemment** (damɑ̃) *ad*, ardently, &c. **ardeur** (dœ:r) *f*, ardour, heat, &c; zest. *~ d'estomac*, heartburn.

ardoise (ardwa:z) *f*, slate. **ardoisé, e** (dwaze) *a*, s.-coloured. **ardoisière** (zjɛ:r) *f*, s. quarry.

ardu, e (ardy) *a*, steep; arduous, hard, up-hill.

are (a:r) *m*, are = 100 square metres *or* 119·60 sq. yards.

arène (arɛn) *f*, arena, lists, ring; cockpit; sand (*Poet.*).

arête (arɛt) *f*, [fish]bone; ridge, edge, arris; arête; groin, hip (*Arch.*); awn, beard (*Bot.*). ~ **vive**, sharp edge.

argent (arʒɑ̃) *m*, silver; money, cash. ~ *comptant*, ready money, prompt cash, spot cash. ~ *doré*, silver-gilt. *un* ~ *fou*, a mint of money. ~ *mignon*, small savings (*to spend on pleasure*). ~ *sec*, hard cash. ~ *sur table*, cash down. **argenter** (te) *v.t*, to silver[-plate], [electro]plate. **argenterie** (tri) *f*, silver, [s.] plate. **argentin, e** (tɛ̃, in) *a*, argentine, silvery, silvern. ¶ *a. & A~, n*, Argentine (*Geog.*). **l'Argentine,** *f*, the Argentine.

argile (arʒil) *f*, clay. ~ *réfractaire*, fire clay. **argileux, euse** (lø, ø:z) *a*, clayey, argillaceous.

argot (argo) *m*, slang, cant.

arguer (argɥe) *v.t*, to infer, deduce. **argument** (gymɑ̃) *m*, argument; synopsis. **argumenter** (te) *v.i*, to argue.

argutie (argysi) *f*, quibble, cavil, hairsplitting.

aria (arja) *m*, bother, ado, to-do.

aride (arid) *a*, arid, dry, barren. **aridité** (dite) *f*, aridity, &c.

aristocrate (aristokrat) *n*, aristocrat. ¶ *att. &* **aristocratique†** (tik) *a*, aristocratic(al). **aristocratie** (si) *f*, aristocracy.

arithméticien, ne (aritmetisjɛ̃, ɛn) *n*, arithmetician. **arithmétique†** (tik) *a*, arithmetical. ¶ *f*, arithmetic.

arlequin (arlǝkɛ̃) *m*, harlequin; weathercock (*pers.*); scraps, leavings, left-overs, orts, hash. **arlequinade** (kinad) *f*, harlequinade.

armateur (armatœ:r) *m*, [ship]owner, [registered] manager (*ship's*).

armature (armaty:r) *f*, trussing; bracing; fastening, strap; reinforcement; armour, sheathing, plating; gear (*pump*); armature (*Phys.*); key signature (*Mus.*); framework (*fig.*).

arme (arm) *f*, arm, weapon; (*pl.*) arms (*Mil.*); [coat of] arms, [armorial] bearings. ~ *à feu*, firearm. ~ [*à feu*] *portative*, small arm. ~ *blanche*, side arm; cold steel. ~ *de trait*, ~ *de jet*, missile. *sans* ~*s*, unarmed. *faire* (ou *tirer*) *des* ~*s*, to fence. **armée** (arme) *f*, army, force[s]; host. **A~** *du Salut*, Salvation Army.

armeline (armǝlin) *f*, ermine (*fur*).

armement (armǝmɑ̃) *m*, arming; armament; fitting out, equipment; manning; shipping, shipowners.

Arménie (l') (armeni) *f*, Armenia. **arménien, ne** (njɛ̃, ɛn) *a. & A~, n*, Armenian.

armer (arme) *v.t*, to arm; fit out, equip; man; commission (*ship*); truss, brace; reinforce, **armour**, sheathe; set (*Phot. shutter*); cock (*gun*); sign (*clef*); dub (*knight*); (*v.i.*) to arm.

armistice (armistis) *m*, armistice.

armoire (armwa:r) *f*, cupboard, cabinet, wardrobe, press. ~ *à pharmacie*, medicine cabinet. ~ *vitrée*, display cabinet, china cabinet.

armoiries (armwari) *f.pl*, [coat of] arms, [armorial] bearings. **armorial, e** (morjal) *a. & m*, armorial. **armorier** (rje) *v.t*, to [em]blazon.

armure (army:r) *f*, armour, sheathing; armature (*Phys.*). ~ *complète*, suit of armour. **armurier** (myrje) *m*, gunsmith; armourer.

arnica (arnika) *f*, arnica.

aromatique (arɔmatik) *a*, aromatic. **arôme** (ro:m) *m*, aroma.

arpège (arpɛ:ʒ) *m*, arpeggio.

arpentage (arpɑ̃ta:ʒ) *m*, land measuring, surveying. **arpenter** (te) *v.t*, to measure; survey; pace, tramp. **arpenteur** (tœ:r) *m*, [land] surveyor.

arquer (arke) *v.t. & i. & s'~*, to arch, curve, bend.

arrache-clou (araʃklu) *m*, nail extractor. **d'arrache-pied,** *ad*, without intermission; on end, at a stretch. **arracher** (ʃe) *v.t*, to pluck, pull, tear, draw; drag; uproot, dig up; extract; wring; snatch; squeeze, extort, screw out. **arracheur, euse** (ʃœ:r, ø:z) *n*, drawer, puller; (*f.*) grubber.

arraisonner (arɛzɔne) *v.t*, to visit (*Cust.*).

arrangeant, e (arɑ̃ʒɑ̃, ɑ̃:t) *a*, accommodating, obliging. **arrangement** (ʒmɑ̃) *m*, arrangement; settlement. **arranger** (ʒe) *v.t*, to arrange; settle. **s'~**, to agree, come to terms; settle down; get on, manage. *arrangez-vous!* do the best you can! do as you like!

arrenter (arɑ̃te) *v.t*, to lease.

arrérager (areraʒe) *v.i*, to get (*or* fall) into arrear[s]. **arrérages** (ra:ʒ) *m.pl*, interest (*on Government stocks, or the like*); rent, pension, or the like, accrued & due.

arrestation (arɛstasjɔ̃) *f*, arrest, custody. **arrêt** (rɛ) *m*, stoppage, stop; arrest; seizure, detention; standstill; catch; tackle (*Foot.*); judgement, sentence; decree. ~ *en cours de route*, break of journey. ~ *facultatif*, cars stop here if required. ~ *fixe*, all cars stop here. *aux* ~*s*, under arrest (*Mil.*); kept in (*Sch.*). **arrêté, e** (te) *p.a*, decided, settled, preconcerted. ¶ *m*, order, decree; making up, closing, ruling off, rest (*Bkkpg*). **arrêter** (te) *v.t. & i*, to stop; arrest; seize, detain; fix; retain, engage; conclude; make up, close, rule off (*Bkkpg*); fasten off (*Need.*); agree upon; decide on; (*v.t. & abs.*) point, set (*dog*). **s'~**, to stop, stay, call; draw up (*carriage*).

arrhes (a:r) *f.pl*, deposit, earnest [money].

arrière (arjɛ:r) *m*, back [part]; back (*Foot.*); rear; tail; stern. *en* ~, behind; behindhand; back, at the back, in the rear; astern; with one's back to the engine.

Note : **arrière** in *comps* is pronounced arjɛr, thus, **∼-bouche** (arjɛrbuʃ) f, fauces. **∼-boutique**, f, shop parlour. **∼-garde**, f, rear guard. **arrière-grand-mère**, f, **arrière-grand-père**, m, great-grandmother, -father. **∼-main**, m, backhand (*Ten.*). **∼-neveu**, m, **∼-nièce**, f, grand-nephew, -niece. **∼-pensée**, f, ulterior motive, mental reservation. **∼-petite-fille**, f, great-grand-daughter. **∼-petit-fils**, m, g.-grandson. **∼-petits-enfants**, m.pl, g.-grandchildren. **∼-plan**, m, background. **∼-point**, m, backstitch (*Need.*). **∼-port**, m, inner harbour. **∼-saison**, f, late season. **arriéré**, **e** (rjere) a, overdue, in arrear[s]; outstanding, owing; behindhand; backward (*child*); old-fashioned. ¶ m, arrears. **arriérer** (re) v.t, to put off, defer, hold over. **s'∼**, to fall behind; get into arrears.

arrimer (arime) v.t, to stow, trim. **arrimeur** (mœːr) m, stower, trimmer; stevedore.

arrivage (arivaːʒ) m, arrival. **arrivée** (ve) f, arrival, coming; finish[ing] (*Sport*), [winning] post; home (*Running*); inlet. **à l'∼ & d'∼**, incoming; at the finish, finishing. **arriver** (ve) v.i, to arrive, come; get; finish; happen, come about, c. to pass, occur, befall; be due (*train*); succeed. **∼ à égalité**, to tie (*Sport*). **arrive que pourra**, come what may, whate'er betide.

arrogamment (arɔgamɑ̃) ad, arrogantly. **arrogance** (gɑːs) f, arrogance, assumption. **arrogant**, **e** (gɑ̃, ɑ̃ːt) a, arrogant, overbearing. **s'arroger** (ɔʒe) v.pr, to arrogate [to oneself], assume.

arroi (arwa) m, plight, pickle.

arrondir (arɔ̃diːr) v.t, to round [off]. **arrondissement** (dismɑ̃) m, rounding; ward, district.

arroser (aroze) v.t, to water, [be]sprinkle, bedew, wet; baste; stand treat. **arrosoir** (zwaːr) m, watering pot.

arsenal (arsnal) m, arsenal. **∼ maritime**, naval dockyard.

arsenic (arsnik) m, arsenic. **arsenical**, **e** (kal) a, arsenical.

art (aːr) m, art, skill; artfulness, artifice. **∼s d'agrément**, accomplishments. *l'∼ de l'ingénieur*, engineering. *l'∼ de la mécanique*, mechanical engineering. *l'∼ de vendre*, salesmanship. *l'∼ dentaire*, dentistry. **artère** (artɛːr) f, artery; thoroughfare; feeder (*Elec.*). **artériel, le** (terjɛl) a, arterial. **artésien, ne** (artezjɛ̃, ɛn) a, Artesian. **arthrite** (artrit) f, arthritis. **artichaut** (artiʃo) m, artichoke; spikes. **article** (artikl) m, article, subject, matter; section, clause, item, entry; requisite, material, commodity, (*pl.*) wares. **∼ à côté**, side line. **∼ de fond**, leading article, leader. **∼[s] de Paris**, artistic novelties, fancy goods. **∼s dépareillés**, oddments. *faire l'∼*, to puff one's goods.

articulation (artikylasjɔ̃) f, articulation, joint; knuckle; utterance. **articuler** (le) v.t. & i, & **s'∼**, to articulate, joint, link; utter. **artifice** (artifis) m, artifice, artfulness, craft; contrivance; art. **∼s de théâtre**, stage effects. **artificiel, le†** (sjɛl) a, artificial. **artificier** (sje) m, pyrotechnist. **artificieux, euse†** (sjø, øːz) a, artful, cunning, crafty. **artillerie** (artijri) f, artillery, ordnance; gunnery. **∼ de place**, garrison artillery. **artilleur** (jœːr) m, artilleryman, gunner. **artimon** (artimɔ̃) m, mizzen mast; m. sail. **artisan**, **e** (artizɑ̃, an) m, artisan; craftsman; operative; (*fig.*) author, originator, artificer, architect. **∼ en bois**, woodworker. **artison** (artizɔ̃) m, wood worm; clothes moth. **artisonné**, **e** (zɔne) a, worm-eaten; mitheaten. **artiste** (artist) n, artist; artiste, performer. **artiste† & artistique** (tik) a, artistic. **aryen, ne** (arjɛ̃, ɛn) a, Aryan.

as (ɑːs) m, ace. **∼ de l'aviation**, flying ace. **∼ de pique**, ace of spades (*Cards*); rump, parson's nose (*fowl*). **asbeste** (azbɛst) m, asbestos.

ascendant, **e** (asɑ̃dɑ̃, ɑ̃ːt) a, ascending, upward. ¶ m, ascendant, -ent; ascendancy, -ency; (*pl.*) ancestry. **ascenseur** (sœːr) m, [passenger] lift. **ascension** (sjɔ̃) f, ascent, climb, rising, ascension. *l'A∼*, Ascension day. **ascensionniste** (ɔnist) n, climber, mountaineer.

ascète (asɛt) n. & **ascétique** (setik) a, ascetic. **asiatique** (azjatik) a. & **A∼**, n, Asiatic. *l'Asie* (zi) f, Asia. *l'∼ Mineure*, Asia Minor.

asile (azil) m, asylum, shelter; almshouse, home; haven, sanctuary. **∼ d'aliénés**, mental institution.

aspect (aspɛ) m, aspect, sight, appearance, look, bearing; complexion.

asperge (aspɛrʒ) f, asparagus.

asperger (aspɛrʒe) v.t, to [be]sprinkle, asperse.

aspérité (asperite) f, asperity, roughness. **aspersion** (aspɛrsjɔ̃) f, aspersion, sprinkling. **aspersoir** (swaːr) m, holy-water sprinkler.

asphalte (asfalt) m, asphalt.

asphyxie (asfiksi) f, asphyxia, suffocation, gassing. **asphyxier** (sje) v.t, to asphyxiate, &c.

aspic (aspik) m, asp; slanderer, backbiter.

aspirail (aspiraːj) m, air hole, vent, flue. **aspirant**, **e** (aspirɑ̃, ɑ̃ːt) n, aspirant, suitor; candidate. **∼ [de marine]**, midshipman. **aspirateur [de poussières]** (ratœːr) m, vacuum cleaner. **aspiration** (sjɔ̃) f, aspiration; inspiration; yearning. **aspirer** (re) v.t, to inspire, inhale, exhaust, suck, draw; aspirate; (*v.i.*) to aspire. **aspirine** (aspirin) f, aspirin.

assaillant (asajɑ̃) m, assailant. **assaillir** (jiːr) v.t.ir, to assail, assault.

assainir (asɛniːr) v.t, to cleanse, sanitate.

assaisonnement (asɛzɔnmɑ̃) *m*, seasoning, flavouring; dressing (*salad*); condiment, relish. **assaisonner** (ne) *v.t*, to season, &c; leaven (*fig.*).

assassin, e (asasɛ̃, in) *n*, assassin, murderer, ess. *à l'~!* murder! ¶ *a*, bewitching, killing (*looks, eyes*). **assassinat** (sina) *m*, assassination, [wilful] murder. **assassiner** (ne) *v.t*, to assassinate, murder, kill; tire to death, bore, plague.

assaut (aso) *m*, assault, storming, onset, onslaught; match, bout. *~ d'armes*, assault of (*or* at) arms, fencing match. *~ de démonstration*, sparring match.

assèchement (asɛʃmɑ̃) *m*, drainage. **assécher** (sefe) *v.t. & i*, to drain, dry.

assemblage (asɑ̃bla:ʒ) *m*, assemblage, congregation; joint (*in wood, metal, &c*). **assemblée** (ble) *f*, meeting, assembly, conclav congregation; meet (*Hunt.*). **assembler** (ble) *v.t*, to assemble, collect, gather, summon; join. **s'~**, to meet, assemble, congregate, flock.

assener (asəne) *v.t*, to strike, deal (*blow*).

assentiment (asɑ̃timɑ̃) *m*, assent.

asseoir (aswa:r) *v.t.ir*, to seat, set, bed, base, fix, secure, establish; pitch (*camp, tent*). **s'~**, to sit [down].

assermenter (asɛrmɑ̃te) *v.t*, to swear in.

assertion (asɛrsjɔ̃) *f*, assertion.

asservir (asɛrvi:r) *v.t*, to enslave.

assez (ase) *ad*, enough, rather, pretty, fairly.

assidu, e (asidy) *a*, assiduous, sedulous, industrious; regular. **assiduité** (dɥite) *f*, assiduity, &c. **assidûment** (dymɑ̃) *ad*, assiduously, &c.

assiégeant (asjeʒɑ̃) *m*, besieger. **assiéger** (ʒe) *v.t*, to besiege, beleaguer, beset, crowd round, throng; dun.

assiette (asjɛt) *f*, seat, seating, bed, base, foundation; basis; set, firmness, steadiness, stability, security; trim (*ship*); lie (*land, golf ball*); site, position; state; plate; plateful. *~ à dessert*, dessert plate; cheese p. *~ à fromage*, cheese p. *~ creuse*, soup p. *~ plate*, dinner p. *~ pour le pied*, footing, foothold. **assiettée** (te) *f*, plateful.

assignation (asiɲasjɔ̃) *f*, assignation; assignment; charge; summons; writ; subpoena. **assigner** (ne) *v.t*, to assign; charge; summon; cite; subpoena.

assimiler (asimile) *v.t*, to assimilate, liken, compare.

assise (asi:z) *f*, bed, foundation; course (*Build.*); (*pl.*) assize[s] (*Law*).

assistance (asistɑ̃:s) *f*, assistance, aid, help; attendance, audience. *~ judiciaire*, legal aid. *~ privée*, private charity. *~ publique*, public assistance *or* relief. **assistant, e** (tɑ̃, ɑ̃:t) *n*, assistant; bystander, onlooker. **assister** (te) *v.t*, to assist, aid, help. *~ à*, to attend, be present at, witness.

association (asɔsjasjɔ̃) *f*, association; society; g[u]ild; partnership. **associé** *e* (sje) *n*,

associate, member, partner. **associer** (sje) *v.t*, to associate; take into partnership.

assolement (asɔlmɑ̃) *m*, rotation (*crops*).

assombrir (asɔ̃bri:r) *v.t*, to darken, gloom, cloud.

assommant, e (asɔmɑ̃, ɑ̃:t) *a*, killing, oppressive, overwhelming, tiresome, wearisome, boring. **assommer** (me) *v.t*, to knock down, fell, strike dead; beat, thrash, nearly kill; overwhelm, weary to death, bore. **assommoir** (mwa:r) *m*, bludgeon, life preserver, lethal weapon; pole-axe; fall trap, deadfall; dram shop, gin shop.

assomption (asɔ̃psjɔ̃) *f*, Assumption (*Eccl.*).

assortiment (asɔrtimɑ̃) *m*, assortment; set; blend; match. **assortir** (ti:r) *v.t. & i*, to assort, supply; stock; blend; match; suit. **assortissant, e** (tisɑ̃, ɑ̃:t) *a*, suitable, becoming.

assoupir (asupi:r) *v.t*, to make drowsy, send to sleep, lull, deaden; hush up. **s'~**, to doze; die down. **assoupissant, e** (pisɑ̃, ɑ̃:t) *a*, dull, humdrum. **assoupissement** (pismɑ̃) *m*, drowsiness; lethargy.

assouplir (asupli:r) *v.t*, to make supple; make tractable; soften.

assourdir (asurdi:r) *v.t*, to deafen, muffle; tone down.

assouvir (asuvi:r) *v.t*, to satiate, glut.

assujettir (asyʒɛti:r) *v.t*, to subject, subdue; bind, tie down; fix, fasten.

assumer (asyme) *v.t*, to assume.

assurance (asyrɑ̃:s) *f*, assurance; confidence; security; pledge; insurance. *~ contre l'incendie*, fire insurance. *~ contre le chômage*, unemployment i. *~ contre le vol*, burglary i. *~ contre les accidents [corporels]*, [personal] accident i. *~ contre les accidents du travail*, workmen's compensation i. *~ des véhicules automobiles*, motor [car] i. *~ maritime*, marine i., sea i. *~ sur la vie*, life i. **assuré†, e** (re) *a*, assured, sure, safe; confident, bold. *mal ~*, insecure, unsafe. ¶ (*pers.*) *n*, insured, assured. **assurer** (re) *v.t*, to assure, ensure, insure, secure, guarantee; make fast, steady, set, strengthen; affirm; confirm. **s'~**, to make sure; trust; insure (*Insce*). **assureur** (rœ:r) *m*, insurer, underwriter.

Assyrie (l') (asiri) *f*, Assyria. **assyrien, ne** (rjɛ̃, ɛn) *a. & A~, n*, Assyrian.

aster (astɛ:r) *m*, aster.

astérisque (asterisk) *m*, asterisk, star.

astéroïde (asterɔid) *m*, asteroid.

asthmatique (asmatik) *a. & n*, asthmatic. **asthme** (asm) *m*, asthma.

asticot (astiko) *m*, gentle, maggot.

asticoter (astikɔte) *v.t*, to tease.

astigmatique (astigmat) *a*, astigmatic.

astiquer (astike) *v.t*, to polish.

astre (astr) *m*, star, luminary.

astreindre (astrɛ̃:dr) *v.t.ir*, to bind, tie down, compel. **astreinte** (trɛ̃:t) *f*, penalty.

astringent, e (astrɛ̃ʒɑ̃, ɑ̃:t) *a. & m*, astringent.

astrologie (astroloʒi) *f*, astrology. **astrologue** (log) *m*, astrologer.

astronome (astronɔm) *m*, astronomer. **astronomie** (mi) *f*, astronomy. **astronomique†** (mik) *a*, astronomic(al).

astuce (astys) *f*, astuteness, artfulness, craftiness, guile. **astucieux, euse†** (sjø, øːz) *a*, astute, &c.

ataxie locomotrice (ataksi) *f*, locomotor ataxy.

atelier (atəlje) *m*, [work]shop, works, mill, house, workroom, studio; staff; students.

atermoiement (atɛrmwamɑ̃) *m*, delay, procrastination, evasion. **atermoyer** (je) *v.i*, to procrastinate.

athée (ate) *m*, atheist. ¶ *a*, atheistic. **athéisme** (teism) *m*, atheism.

Athènes (atɛn) *f*, Athens. **athénien, ne** (tenjɛ̃, ɛn) *a. & A~, n*, Athenian.

athlète (atlɛt) *m*, athlete; champion (*of the faith*). **athlétique** (letik) *a*, athletic. **athlétisme** (letism) *m*, athletics.

atlantique (atlɑ̃tik) *a*, Atlantic. l'[océan] **A~**, *m*, the A. [ocean].

atlas (atlɑːs) *m*, atlas; [book of] plates.

atmosphère (atmosfɛːr) *f*, atmosphere; medium (*ether*). **atmosphérique** (ferik) *a*, atmospheric(al), air (*att.*).

atome (atoːm) *m*, atom; mote. **atomique** (tomik) *a*, atomic(al).

atone (atoːn) *a*, atonic, toneless, lack-lustre, dull; unstressed (*Gram.*).

atours (atuːr) *m.pl*, finery.

atout (atu) *m*, trump [card], trumps.

âtre (ɑːtr) *m*, hearth, fireplace.

atroce† (atrɔs) *a*, atrocious, heinous, outrageous; excruciating. **atrocité** (site) *f*, atrocity, &c.

atrophie (atrɔfi) *f*, atrophy, wasting away. **attabler (s')** (atable) *v.pr*, to sit down [to table].

attachant, e (ataʃɑ̃, ɑ̃ːt) *a*, interesting; engaging, winning. **attache** (taʃ) *f*, tie, fastening, leash, binder, bond, band, clip, paper fastener; attachment. **attaché** (ʃe) *m*, attaché. **attachement** (ʃmɑ̃) *m*, attachment; fondness; devotion. **attacher** (ʃe) *v.t*, to attach, tie, fasten, bind; rivet (*attention*). **s'~**, to fasten; devote oneself, cling, stick.

attaque (atak) *f*, attack, onset, onslaught; raid; fit, stroke, seizure. **attaquer** (ke) *v.t*, to attack, set on, assault; spur on; impugn. **~ en justice**, to bring an action against. **s'~ à**, to attack; tackle, grapple with.

attarder (s') (atarde) *v.pr*, to loiter, linger.

atteindre (atɛ̃ːdr) *v.t.ir*, to reach, attain; strike; hit; overtake, catch [up]; affect. **atteinte** (tɛ̃t) *f*, reach, &c; blow, stroke, cut; reflection, slur.

attelage (atlaːʒ) *m*, harnessing; coupling; team. **atteler** (tle) *v.t*, to harness, yoke, attach, couple.

attelle (atɛl) *f*, splint; (*pl.*) hames.

attenant, e [à] (atnɑ̃, ɑ̃ːt) *a*, adjoining.

attendant (en) (atɑ̃dɑ̃) *ad*, meanwhile, in the mean time. ¶ *pr*, pending. **en attendant que**, *c*, till, until. **attendre** (tɑ̃ːdr) *v.t. & i*, to wait for, wait, stay, expect, await, bide, look forward to. **s'~ à**, to expect, look for; rely on.

attendrir (atɑ̃driːr) *v.t*, to soften, move, melt, affect.

attendu (atɑ̃dy) *pr*, considering. **~ que**, *c*, seeing that, whereas.

attentat (atɑ̃ta) *m*, (criminal) attempt, assault, outrage. **attentatoire** (twaːr) *a*, prejudicial.

attente (atɑ̃ːt) *f*, waiting, expectation.

attenter à (atɑ̃te), to make an attempt on.

attentif, ive† (atɑ̃tif, iːv) *a*, attentive, careful, mindful. **attention** (sjɔ̃) *f*, attention; notice; care[fulness], heed; kindness. **faire ~**, to pay attention, mind. **~!** mind! look out! caution! by your leave! fore! (*Golf*). **~ au train!** beware of the trains!

atténuer (atenɥe) *v.t*, to attenuate, weaken; minimize; extenuate.

atterrer (atɛre) *v.t*, to overwhelm, dumbfound.

atterrir (atɛriːr) *v.i*, to land, alight.

attestation (atɛstasjɔ̃) *f*, attestation; certificate, testimonial. **attester** (te) *v.t*, to attest, testify, vouch, certify, witness.

attiédir (atjediːr) *v.t*, to cool; warm; make lukewarm.

attifer (atife) *v.t*, to dress up.

attique (atik) *a*, Attic.

attirail (atiraːj) *m*, appliances, apparatus, implements, habiliment; string; baggage, paraphernalia; show, pomp.

attirance (atirɑ̃ːs) *f*, attraction. **attirer** (re) *v.t*, to attract, draw; lure; win. **s'~**, to incur, win.

attiser (atize) *v.t*, to stir, poke; fan (*fig.*).

attitré, e (atitre) *a*, accredited, recognized; by appointment.

attitude (atityd) *f*, attitude, posture.

attouchement (atuʃmɑ̃) *m*, touching, contact.

attractif, ive (ataktif, iːv) *a*, attractive (*Phys.*). **attraction** (ksjɔ̃) *f*, attraction; draw; loadstone; (*pl.*) varieties (*Theat.*); (*pl.*) cabaret [show].

attrait (atrɛ) *m*, attraction; draw; appeal; inclination, bent; (*pl.*) charms.

attrape (atrap) *f*, trap, catch, hoax. **~-nigaud**, *m*, booby trap. **attraper** (pe) *v.t*, to [en]trap, [en]snare, catch, take in, hoax; draw (*in lottery*); hit; hit off. **s'~**, to get caught.

attrayant, e (atrɛjɑ̃, ɑ̃ːt) *a*, attractive, engaging, winning.

attribuer (atribɥe) *v.t*, to attribute, ascribe; predicate; father; allot. **attribuable** (abl) *a*, attributable, &c. **attribut** (by) *m*, attribute; predicate. **attributaire** (tɛːr) *n*, allottee. **attribution** (sjɔ̃) *f*, attribution; allotment.

attrister (atriste) *v.t*, to sadden.

attrition (atrisjɔ̃) *f*, attrition, abrasion.

attroupement (atrupmã) *m*, unlawful assembly to the disturbance of the peace.

aubade (obad) *f*, aubade; catcalling.

aubaine (oben) *f*, windfall, godsend.

aube (o:b) *f*, dawn; alb; blade, vane, paddle, float[board].

aubépine (obepin) *f*, hawthorn, may [bush].

auberge (obɛrʒ) *f*, inn; hostel. **aubergiste** (ʒist) *n*, innkeeper, landlord, -lady.

aubier (obje) *m*, sapwood.

aucun, e (okœ̃, yn) *a*. & *pn*, any; anyone; (*neg.*) no, none; no one. **aucunement** (kynmã) *ad*, in any way; (*neg.*) not at all, by no means, nowise.

audace (odas) *f*, audacity, boldness, daring. **audacieux, euse†** (sjø, ø:z) *a*, audacious, &c.

au-delà, au-dessous, &c. See *delà, dessous, &c.*

audience (odjã:s) *f*, audience, hearing; court. **auditeur, trice** (ditœ:r, tris) *n*, hearer, listener, auditor, tress. **audition** (sjɔ̃) *f*, hearing, audition; concert; recital.

auge (o:ʒ) *f*, **auget** (oʒɛ) *m*, trough, bucket. **augée** (oʒe) *f*, troughful, bucketful.

augmenter (ogmãte) *v.t.* & *i*, to increase, augment, enlarge, enhance; supplement. **augmentation** (tasjɔ̃) *f*, increase, &c; rise (*in salary*).

augure (ogy:r) *m*, augury, omen; prophet, augur. **augurer** (gyre) *v.t*, to augur, make.

auguste (ogyst) *a*, august.

aujourd'hui (oʒurdɥi) *ad*. & *m*, to-day. *d'~ en huit, en quinze*, to-day (*or* this day) week, fortnight.

aumône & l'aumône (omo:n) *f*, alms, charity. **aumônier** (monje) *m*, chaplain.

aune (o:n) *m*, alder.

auparavant (oparavã) *ad*, before[hand].

auprès (oprɛ) *ad*, near, close [by], [near] at hand. ~ **de**, *pr*, near, close to *or* by, bv; [attached] to; with; in.

auréole (oreol) *f*, aureole, halo.

auriculaire (orikylɛ:r) *a*, auricular, ear (*att*). [doigt] ~, *m*, little (*or* fourth) finger.

aurifère (orifɛ:r) *a*, auriferous, gold (*att*).

aurore (oro:r) *f*, dawn, daybreak, morn; aurora. ~ *boréale*, aurora borealis, northern lights.

ausculter (oskylte) *v.t*, to sound (*Med.*).

auspice (ospis) *m*, auspice, omen.

aussi (osi) *ad*, also, too, likewise; so; as. ¶ *c*, therefore, consequently, so. ~ **bien**, besides, moreover. ~ **bien que**, *c*, as well as. **aussitôt** (to) *ad*, directly, at once. ~ *dit*, ~ *fait*, no sooner said than done. ~ **que**, *c*, as soon as.

austère† (ostɛ:r) *a*, austere, stern. **austérité** (terite) *f*, austerity, &c.

austral, e (ostral) *a*, austral, southern. **l'Australasie** (lazi) *f*, Australasia. **l'Australie** (li), Australia. **australien, ne** (ljɛ̃, ɛn) *a*. & *A~*, *n*, Australian.

autan (otã) (*Poet.*) *m*, storm, blast.

autant (otã) *ad*, as (*or* so) much, as many, as far, as well, as good, as often; the like

(*Golf*). ~ **que**, as much as, as far as. *d'~* **que**, *c*, especially as.

autel (otel) *m*, altar.

auteur (otœ:r) *m*, author; authoress; writer; composer; originator; founder (*race*); progenitor; perpetrator (*crime*); party at fault (*accident*); inventor; designer; informant; doer. *les ~s de nos jours*, our progenitors. ~ *dramatique*, playwright.

authentique† (otãtik) *a*, authentic, genuine. **authenticité** (site) *f*, authenticity, &c.

auto (oto, oto) *préfixe*, auto, self-, *e.g. papier ~-vireur*, self-toning paper (*Phot.*).

auto (oto, oto) *f*, motor [car].

autobiographie (otobjografi) *f*, autobiography.

autobus (otoby:s) *m*, motor bus. ~ *à trolley*, trolley bus.

autocar (otoka:r) *m*, motor coach, m. charabanc.

autochenille (otoʃni:j) *f*, caterpillar car.

autocrate, trice (otokrat, tris) *n*, autocrat. **autocratie** (si) *f*, autocracy. **autocratique** (tik) *a*, autocratic(al).

autodidacte (otodidakt) *a*, self-taught.

autogène (otoʒɛ:n) *a*, autogenous.

autographe (otograf) *m*. & *a*, autograph.

automate (otomat) *m*, automaton. **automatique†** (tik) *a*, automatic(al), self-acting, self-.

automnal, e (otomnal) *a*, autumnal. **automne** (ton) *m*, autumn, fall.

automobile (o- *ou* otomobil) *a*, self-propelling, motor (*att.*). ¶ *f*, motor [car]. **automobilisme** (lism) *m*, motoring. **automobiliste** (list) *n*, motorist.

autonome (otonɔm) *a*, autonomous, self-governing. **autonomie** (mi) *f*, autonomy, self-government.

autopsie (otopsi) *f*, post mortem, autopsy.

autorisation (otorizasjɔ̃) *f*, authorization, leave; warrant. **autoriser** (ze) *v.t*, to authorize, empower, allow. **autoritaire** (tɛ:r) *a*, authoritative. **autorité** (te) *f*, authority; power. *faire ~*, to be regarded as an authority.

autoroute (otorut) *f*, motor road.

autour (otu:r) *m*, goshawk.

autour (otu:r) *ad*. & **autour de**, *pr*, round, around, about.

autre (o:tr) *a*. & *pn*, other; another; next (*world*); else. *un ~ soi-même*, one's second self, elsewhere. *à d'~s!* nonsense! **autrefois** (otrəfwa) *ad*, formerly; once [upon a time]. *d'~*, of old, of yore; bygone. **autrement** (otrəmã) *ad*, otherwise; differently; [or] else.

Autriche (l') (otriʃ) *f*, Austria. **autrichien, ne** (ʃjɛ̃, ɛn) *a*. & *A~*, *n*, Austrian.

autruche (otryʃ) *f*, ostrich.

autrui (otrɥi) *pn*, others, other people.

auvent (ovã) *m*, penthouse.

auxiliaire (oksiljɛ:r) *a*. & *m*, auxiliary.

avachi, e (avaʃi) *a*, flabby, baggy; out of shape.

aval (aval) *m*, lower part; tail; guarantee, backing. en ~, *ad*, down stream, down. en ~ de, *pr*, down, below.

avalanche (avalã:ʃ) *f*, avalanche; shower (*fig.*).

avaler (avale) *v.t*, to swallow, devour; stomach; lower; (*v.i.*) to go down stream.

avaliser (avalize) *v.t*, to guarantee, back.

avaloire (avalwa:r) *f*, gullet, throat.

avance (avã:s) *f*, advance, start; lead; projection; fast (*on clock*). à l'~, d'~, en ~, par ~, *ad*, in advance, beforehand. tant de trous d'~, so many holes up (*Golf*). **avancé, e** (vãse) *p.a*, advance[d]; projecting; late (*hour, &c*); high (*meat*). **avancer** (se) *v.t*, to advance, put forward, push, hasten; help; promote, further; put on (*clock*); (*v.i.*) to advance; project, jut out; gain (*of clock*). **avancement** (smã) *m*, advancement, &c; feed (*Mach.*).

avanie (avani) *f*, affront, insult.

avant (avã) *pr*, before; till, until. av. J.-C., B.C. avant terme, premature(ly) (*childbirth*). ~ [que] de, *pr*, ~ que, *c*, before. ¶ ad, forward, before, far, deep[ly]. de l'~ à l'arrière, fore & aft (*Naut.*). en ~, *ad*, forward, on, onward[s], ahead, before. en ~! forward! go ahead! on! en ~, marche! quick march! ¶ *m*, front, forepart; fore; head, bow (*Naut.*); steerage; forward (*Foot.*). ~ [du] centre, centre forward. ~-bras, *m*, forearm. ~-cour, *f*, forecourt. ~-coureur, *m*, forerunner, harbinger, herald; (*att.*) premonitory. ~-dernier, ère, a. & n, last but one. ~-garde, *f*, van[guard]. ~-goût, *m*, foretaste, earnest. d'~-guerre, a, pre-war. ~-hier, ad. & m, the day before yesterday. ~-hier soir, the night before last. ~-mont, *m*, foothill. ~-port, *m*, outer harbour. ~-poste, *m*, outpost. ~-première, *f*, dress rehearsal; private view (*Art*). ~-propos, *m*, foreword, preface. ~-scène, *f*, proscenium; stage box. ~-toit, *m*, eaves. ~-train, *m*, limber (*gun*). l'~-veille, *f*, two days before.

avantage (avãta:ʒ) *m*, advantage, benefit; odds; leverage; upper hand, pull. ~ [de jeu], [ad]vantage [game] (*Ten.*). ~ au servant, advantage in. ~ dehors, ~ au relanceur, A. out. **avantager** (taʒe) *v.t*, to benefit, favour, endow. **avantageux, euse†** (ʒø, ø:z) *a*, advantageous, good, beneficial.

avare† (ava:r) *a*, avaricious; miserly, sparing, chary. ¶ n, miser, screw. **avarice** (varis) *f*, avarice. **avaricieux, euse** (sjø, ø:z) *a*, avaricious.

avarie (avari) *f*, damage; average (*Marine Law*). **avarier** (rje) *v.t*, to damage. s'~, to deteriorate, go bad (*meat, &c*).

avec (avɛk) *pr*, with. d'~, from.

aveline (avlin) *f*, filbert, cob[nut]. **avelinier** (nje) *m*, filbert [tree].

avenant (avnã) *m*, endorsement (*Insce*). à l'~ de, *pr*, in keeping with.

avenant, e (avnã, ã:t) *a*, prepossessing, comely.

avènement (avenmã) *m*, accession; advent, coming (*of Christ*).

avenir (avni:r) *m*, future, prospect; outlook; promise. à l'~, *ad*, in future, hereafter; henceforth.

avent (l') (avã) *m*, advent (*Eccl.*).

aventure (avãty:r) *f*, [ad]venture. dire la bonne ~, to tell fortunes. à l'~, *ad*, haphazard, at random. d'~, par ~, by chance, perchance. **aventurer** (tyre) *v.t*, to [ad]venture. **aventureux, euse** (rø, ø:z) *a*, [ad]venturous. **aventurier, ère** (rje, ɛ:r) *n*, adventurer, ess.

avenue (avny) *f*, avenue; drive.

avéré, e (avere) *p.a*, established, proved.

avers (avɛ:r) *m*, obverse (*coin*).

averse (avɛrs) *f*, shower.

aversion (avɛrsjɔ̃) *f*, aversion, dislike.

avertir (avɛrti:r) *v.t*, to notify, [fore]warn, caution. **avertissement** (tismã) *m*, notification, &c; demand note (*taxes*). **avertisseur** (sœ:r) *m*, call boy; alarm; hooter. ~ d'incendie, fire alarm.

aveu (avø) *m*, avowal, admission, confession; consent.

aveugle (avœ:gl) *a*, blind. ~ de naissance, ~-né, e, born blind. ~ des couleurs, colour blind. ¶ n, blind man, woman. les ~s, *m.pl*, the blind. **aveuglement** (vœgləmã) *m*, blindness (*fig.*). **aveuglément** (glemã) *ad*, blindly. **aveugler** (gle) *v.t*, to blind; stop (*leak*). à l'aveuglette (glɛt), blindly.

aviateur, trice (avjatœr, tris) *a*, flying, flight (*att.*). ¶ n, aviator, airman, -woman, flyer. **aviation** (sjɔ̃) *f*, aviation, flying.

avide† (avid) *a*, greedy, grasping, eager, athirst, avid. **avidité** (dite) *f*, avidity, greed[iness], &c.

avilir (avili:r) *v.t*, to degrade, debase; depreciate.

aviné, e (avine) *a*, intoxicated; smelling of drink; tipsy (*walk*).

avion (avjɔ̃) *m*, aeroplane, [air]plane, heavier than air machine. ~-bombe, fly[ing] bomb. ~ de bombardement, bomber. ~ de chasse, fighter, chaser [plane]. ~ de ligne régulière, air liner. ~ gros porteur, heavy-duty aeroplane. par ~, by air mail (*Post*). **avionnette** (jɔnɛt) *f*, baby plane.

aviron (avirɔ̃) *m*, oar. ~ de couple, scull. ~ de pointe, single oar (opp. *scull*). l'~, rowing.

avis (avi) *m*, opinion; mind; [way of] thinking; judgement; advice; notice, intimation. **avisé, e** (ze) *a*, prudent, circumspect, canny. **aviser** (ze) *v.t*, to advise, notify, warn; espy. s'~ de, to bethink oneself of, dare to. **aviso** (zo) *m*, dispatch boat.

aviver (avive) *v.t*, to revive, brighten.

avocasserie (avɔkasri) *f*, pettifoggery. **avocat** (ka) *m*, counsel, barrister [at law], advocate. ~ *consultant*, ~*-conseil*, chamber counsel. **avocate** (kat) *f*, woman barrister.

avoine (avwan) *f*, oats.

avoir (avwa:r) *m*, possessions, property, holding(s); credit[or], Cr (*Bkkpg*). *tout son* ~, one's all. ¶ *v.t.ir*, to have; hold; keep; get; be; measure; have on; be the matter with, ail. *en* ~, to have some *or* any. *il y a*, there is, there are; it is; ago; for. *il y en a*, there is (are) some. *il n'y en a plus*, there is none left.

avoisinant, e (avwazinɑ̃, ɑ̃:t) *a*, neighbouring, bordering on. **avoisiner** (ne) *v.t*, to border on.

avortement (avɔrtəmɑ̃) *m*, abortion; miscarriage (*fig.*). **avorter** (te) *v.i*, to abort; miscarry.. **avorton** (tɔ̃) *m*, abortion (*creature*).

avoué, e (avwe) *p.a*, acknowledged; ostensible. ¶ *m*, solicitor, lawyer. **avouer** (we) *v.t*, to avow, confess; acknowledge, own. *s'* ~ *coupable*, to plead guilty.

avril (avril) *m*, April. *donner un poisson d'* ~ *à*, to make an April fool of.

axe (aks) *m*, axis; spindle.

axiome (aksjo:m) *m*, axiom.

ayant cause (ɛjɑ̃) *m*, assign. **ayant droit**, *m*, party [entitled].

azalée (azale) *f*, azalea.

azotate (azɔtat) *m*, nitrate. **azote** (zɔt) *m*, nitrogen. **azoteux, euse** (tø, ø:z) *a*, nitrous. **azotique** (tik) *a*, nitric.

azur (azy:r) *m*, azure. **azuré, e** (zyre) *a*, azure.

azyme (azim) *a*, unleavened.

B

babeurre (babœ:r) *m*, butter milk; churn dash[er].

babil (babi) *m*, chatter, tattle, prattle, babble. **babillard, e** (bija:r, ard) *n*, chatterbox. **babiller** (je) *v.i*, to chatter, &c.

babine (babin) *f*, lip, chap, chop.

babiole (babjol) *f*, toy, plaything; trifle, bauble, gewgaw.

bâbord (babo:r) *m*, port [side] (*Naut.*).

babouches (babuʃ) *f.pl*, mules (*slippers*).

babouin (babwɛ̃) *m*, baboon. *petit* ~, *petite babouine* (win), young monkey (*child*).

babylonien, ne (babilɔnjɛ̃, ɛn) *a*, Babylonian.

bac (bak) *m*, ferry[boat]; vat, trough. ~ *d'éléments*, cell jar (*Elec.*). ~ *transbordeur*, train ferry.

bacchanal (bakanal) *m*, row, racket. **bacchanales** (nal) *f.pl*, Bacchanalia.

bâche (bɑ:ʃ) *f*, sheet; cloth; tilt; tank; forcing frame. ~ *goudronnée*, tarpaulin.

bachelier, ère (baʃəlje, ɛ:r) *n*, bachelor (*Science, &c*).

bachique (baʃik) *a*, Bacchic; drinking (*song*).

bachot (baʃo) *m*, wherry; punt.

bacille (basil) *m*, bacillus.

bâcler (bakle) *v.t*, to bar, bolt; scamp.

bactéries (bakteri) *f.pl*, bacteria.

badaud, e (bado, o:d) *n*, saunterer, idler, gaper.

badigeon (badiʒɔ̃) *m*, distemper (*paint*).

badin, e (badɛ̃, in) *a*, playful, jocose. ¶ *n*, wag. **badine** (din) *f*, switch; cane; (*pl.*) tongs. **badiner** (ne) *v.i*, to jest, poke fun, banter, play; flutter.

bafouer (bafwe) *v.t*, to scoff at.

bâfrer (bɑfre) *v.i*, to guzzle, gormandize.

bagage (baga:ʒ) *m. oft. pl*, luggage, baggage, kit, traps.

bagarre (baga:r) *f*, fray, brawl, broil, scuffle, set-to.

bagatelle (bagatɛl) *f*, trifle, bagatelle.

bagne (baɲ) *m*, convict prison.

bagou (bagu) *m*, gift of the gab.

bague (bag) *f*, ring; collar; bush (*Mach.*).

baguenauder (bagnode) *v.i*, to trifle, fiddle, peddle, fool about.

baguer (bage) *v.t*, to tack, baste (*Need.*).

bagues sauves (bag so:v), safe & sound, without a scratch.

baguette (bagɛt) *f*, rod, stick, wand; ramrod; bead (*Arch.*, *&c*). ~*s à jour*, open clocks or clox (*stockings*). ~ *divinatoire* (divinatwa:r), dowsing rod, divining rod.

bah (ba) *i*, bah! pooh! pshaw!

bahut (bay) *m*, chest, trunk.

bai, e (bɛ) *a. & m*, bay (*horse*).

baie (bɛ) *f*, bay (*Geog.*); berry (*Bot.*); opening (*in wall*). ~ *de porte*, doorway.

baignade (bɛɲad) *f*, bathe; dip; bathing place. **baigner** (ne) *v.t. & i. & se* ~, to bathe, dip; bath; wash; steep; suffuse; welter. **baigneur, euse** (nœ:r, ø:z) *n*, bather; bathman, bath attendant. **baignoire** (ɲwa:r) *f*, bath (*tub*); pit box (*Theat.*).

bail (ba:j) *m*, lease.

bâiller (bɑje) *v.i*, to yawn, gape; be ajar.

bailleur, eresse (bajœ:r, jrɛs) *n*, lessor. *bailleur de fonds*, money lender; sleeping partner.

bâillon (bɑjɔ̃) *m*, gag. **bâillonner** (jɔne) *v.t*, to gag.

bain (bɛ̃) *m*, bath; (*pl. & s.*) bathing; (*pl.*) watering place, spa. ~ *de développement*, developing bath (*Phot.*). ~ *de révélateur*, developing bath (*Phot.*). ~ *de siège*, sitz b.; hip b. ~ *de soleil*, sun bath. ~*s de soleil*, sun bathing. ~ *de virage-fixage*, fixing & toning bath (*Phot.*). ~*-marie* (mari) *m*, water bath; double saucepan; boiler (*kitchener*). ~ *mixte*, mixed bathing. ~ *sulfureux*, sulphur bath.

baïonnette (bajɔnɛt) *f*, bayonet.

baisemain (bɛzmɛ̃) *m*, kissing [of] hands.

baiser (ze) *m*, kiss. ¶ *v.t*, to kiss. *Note:* —In sense of "touch with the lips as a sign of affection,'' *baiser* must have a complement, as, *baiser les lèvres, la main,* to kiss the lips, the hand. I kissed my sister, in French, *j'ai embrassé ma sœur.* **baisoter** (zote) *v.t,* to smother with kisses, kiss & cuddle.

baisse (bɛs) *f,* fall, drop. **baisser** (se) *v.t. & i,* to lower, let down, put down; drop; cast down; fall; sink. **se ~,** to stoop, bend. **baissier** (sje) (*Stk Ex.*) *m,* bear, short.

baisure (bɛzy:r) *f,* kissing crust.

bajoue (baʒu) *f,* chop, chap.

bal (bal) *m,* ball, dance; d. hall. **~ costumé, ~ travesti,** fancy dress ball. **~ masqué,** masked ball. **~ par souscription,** subscription dance.

baladeuse (baladø:z) *f,* [coster's] barrow; hanging lamp; trailer.

baladin, e (baladɛ̃, in) *n,* mountebank, clown; buffoon.

balafre (balafr) *f,* gash, slash; scar. **balafrer** (fre) *v.t,* to gash, &c.

balai (balɛ) *m,* broom; brush. **~ à éponger,** mop brush. **~ d'appartement, ~ de soie,** hair broom. **~ d'âtre,** hearth brush. **~ de bouleau,** birch broom, besom. **~ de tapis,** carpet broom. **~ garde-robe,** lavatory brush. **~ mécanique pour tapis,** carpet sweeper.

balance (balɑ̃:s) *f,* balance; poise; scale; [pair of] scales; suspense. **~ de vérification, ~ d'ordre,** trial balance (*Bkkpg*). **balancer** (lɑ̃se) *v.t. & i,* to balance, poise, weigh, offset; swing, sway, rock; hold in suspense, be in suspense, waver, halt. **se ~,** to swing, sway, rock; seesaw; hover. **balancement** (smɑ̃) *m,* balancing, &c. **balancier** (sje) *m,* balancing pole (*tight rope*); beam, bob (*Mach.*); fly press; balance wheel (*Horol.*); pendulum (*Horol.*); scale maker. **~ monétaire,** coining press. **balançoire** (swa:r) *f,* seesaw; swing (*child's*); twaddle.

balayage (balɛja:ʒ) *m,* sweeping. **balayer** (je) *v.t,* to sweep [out, up]; scavenge. **balayette** (jɛt) *f,* whisk [brush, broom], flick. **balayeur, euse** (jœ:r, ø:z) *n,* sweeper, scavenger. **balayeuse,** *f,* street sweeper (*Mach.*). **~ mécanique pour tapis,** carpet sweeper. **balayures** (jy:r) *f.pl,* sweepings.

balbutier (balbysje) *v.t. & i,* to stammer, mumble.

balcon (balkɔ̃) *m,* balcony. [*premier*] **~,** dress circle.

baldaquin (baldakɛ̃) *m,* canopy; tester.

baleine (balɛn) *f,* whale; whalebone; steel (*corset*); rib (*umbrella*). **baleineau** (no) *m,* whale calf. **baleinier** (nje) *m,* whaler (*ship*). **baleinière** (njɛ:r) *f,* whaleboat.

balise (bali:z) *f,* beacon; sea mark; tow path. **baliser** (lize) *v.t,* to beacon; buoy.

baliverne (balivɛrn) *f.* oft. *pl,* twaddle.

Balkans (les) (balkɑ̃) *m.pl,* the Balkans. **balkanique** (kanik) *a,* Balkan.

ballade (balad) *f,* ballad (*poem*).

ballant, e (balɑ̃, ɑ̃:t) *a,* swinging, dangling.

ballast (balast) *m,* ballast (*road, Rly*).

balle (bal) *f,* ball; bullet, shot; bale; pack; husk, chaff; glume; fore ! (*Golf*). **~ à la volée,** trap ball. **~ au but, ~ mise,** hit. **~ au camp,** rounders. **~ au mur,** fives.

ballerine (balrin) *f,* ballet girl. **ballet** (lɛ) *m,* ballet (*Theat.*).

ballon (balɔ̃) *m,* balloon; ball; flask, bulb (*Chem.*). **~ au panier,** basket ball. **~ d'enfant,** toy balloon. **~ d'essai,** pilot balloon; feeler (*fig.*). **~ de boxe,** punching ball. **~ [de football],** [foot]ball. **ballonné, e** (lone) *p.a,* distended; ballooned (*dress*). **ballonner** (ne) *v.t,* to distend (*stomach*).

ballot (balo) *m,* bale; pack; kit bag (*Mil.*). **ballotter** (lɔte) *v.t. & i,* to toss, shake, rattle; bob; send from pillar to post; bandy [about].

balnéaire (balnee:r) *a,* bathing, watering (*place*), seaside (*resort*).

balourd, e (balu:r, urd) *n,* lumpish person, hulking fellow. **balourdise** (lurdi:z) *f,* stupidity; blunder.

balsamier (balzamje) *m,* balsam [tree]. **balsamine** (min) *f,* garden balsam (*plant*). **balsamique** (mik) *a,* balsamic; balmy.

Baltique (la) [mer] (baltik), the Baltic [sea].

balustrade (balystrad) *f,* balustrade; railing. **balustre** (tr) *m,* baluster, banister; railing.

bambin (bɑ̃bɛ̃, in) *m,* little one, kiddy, little chap, sonny, bambino.

bamboche (bɑ̃bɔʃ) *f,* spree, razzle.

bambou (bɑ̃bu) *m,* bamboo.

ban (bɑ̃) *m,* ban. **~s de mariage,** banns.

banal, e (banal) *a,* banal, common[place], trite, hackneyed, humdrum. **banaliser** (lize) *v.t,* to vulgarize.

banane (banan) *f,* banana. **bananier** (nje) *m,* banana [plant, tree].

banc (bɑ̃) *m,* bench, form, seat, settle; box (*jury*); bank, bed, reef, shoal (*sand, fish*); school (*fish*); floe (*ice*). **~ à coulisses,** sliding seat (*rowboat*). **~ [d'église],** pew. **~ [de nage],** thwart. **~ des prévenus,** dock. **sur les ~s,** at school (*fig.*).

bancal, e (bɑ̃kal) *a,* bandy[-legged]; rickety.

bandage (bɑ̃da:ʒ) *m,* bandage; tire; stretching. **~ [herniaire]** (ɛrnjɛ:r), truss. **bande** (bɑ̃:d) *f,* band, strip, slip, tape, belt, strap, bandage; streak; wrapper; heel, list (*Naut.*); cushion (*Bil.*); blurb; troop, company, pack, gang, crew, party, set; ring; flock, flight. **~ molletière,** puttee. **~ noire,** knock-out (*auctions*). **bandeau** (bɑ̃do) *m,* headband, bandeau; bandage (*over eyes*); veil (*fig.*). **bander** (de) *v.t,* to bandage, bind, tie up; stretch, tense, bend, key up, brace; tire (*wheels*). **~ [les yeux à, de],** to blindfold; hoodwink.

banderole (bɑ̃drɔl) *f,* banderol[e], streamer.

bandit (bɑ̃di) *m,* bandit, robber; ruffian.

bandoulière (băduljɛːr) *f*, bandoleer, cross-belt. **en ~,** slung [over shoulder].

banlieue (băljø) *f*, suburbs, outskirts. **de ~,** suburban.

banne (ban) *f*, sheet; tilt; awning; blind (*shop*); hamper.

bannière (banjɛːr) *f*, banner.

bannir (baniːr) *v.t*, to banish; expel.

banque (bɑ̃ːk) *f*, bank; banking.

banqueroute (bɑ̃krut) *f*, bankruptcy. **faire ~,** to go bankrupt. **banqueroutier, ère** (tje, ɛːr) *n*, bankrupt.

banquet (bɑ̃kɛ) *m*, banquet.

banquette (bɑ̃kɛt) *f*, bench, seat; bunker (*Golf*).

banquier (bɑ̃kje) *m*, banker; broker. **~ en valeurs,** stockbroker. **~ marron,** outside broker.

banquise (bɑ̃kiːz) *f*, [ice] pack.

banquiste (bɑ̃kist) *m*, humbug, charlatan.

baptême (batɛːm) *m*, baptism, christening. **~ du tropique, ~ de la ligne,** crossing the line ducking. **baptiser** (tize) *v.t*, to baptize, christen; bless (*bell, &c*); nickname, dub; water, dilute. **baptismal, e** (tismal) *a*, baptismal. **baptistère** (tɛːr) *m*, baptist[e]ry.

baquet (bakɛ) *m*, bucket, tub, trough. **~-baignoire,** bath tub.

bar (baːr) *m*, bar (*drinking*); bass (*fish*).

baragouin (baragwɛ̃) *m*, gibberish, jargon, lingo. **baragouiner** (gwine) *v.i. & t*, to gibber; jabber.

baraque (barak) *f*, hut; booth; hovel.

baraterie (baratri) *f*, barratry.

baratte (barat) *f*, churn. **baratter** (te) *v.t*, to churn.

Barbade (la) (barbad) *f*, Barbado[e]s.

barbare (barbaːr) *a*, barbaric; barbarian; barbarous. ¶ *m*, barbarian. **barbarie** (bari) *f*, barbarism; barbarity. **barbarisme** (rism) *m*, barbarism (*Gram.*).

barbe (barb) *f*, beard; shaving; shave; barb (*feather*); awn; whiskers (*cat*); wattle; (*pl.*) burr; mould (*fungi*). **B~-Bleue,** m, Blue-beard. **~ de bouc,** goatee. **se faire faire la ~,** to get shaved. **barbelé, e** (bəle) *a*, barbed, spiked. **barbiche** (biʃ) *f*, goatee. **barbier** (bje) *m*, barber. **barbifier** (fje) *v.t*, to shave. **barbon** (bɔ̃) *m*, [old] fog[e]y.

barboter (barbote) *v.i*, to dabble, paddle, splash about; flounder; wade; mumble. **barbotage** (taːʒ) *m*, dabbling, &c; mash (*for cattle*). **barboteur** (tœːr) *m*, paddler; mud-lark; muddler; flounderer; duck (*tame*). **barboteuse** (tøːz) *f*, rompers, crawlers (*child's*).

barbouiller (barbuje) *v.t*, to daub, [be]smear; blur; scribble; bungle; mumble.

barbu, e (barby) *a*, bearded. ¶ *f*, brill.

Barcelone (barsəlɔn) *f*, Barcelona.

bardane (bardan) *f*, burdock, bur[r].

barde (bard) *m*, bard (*poet*).

bardot (bardo) *m*, hinny.

barême (barɛːm) *m*, ready reckoner; scale.

barguigner (bargiɲe) *v.t*, to shilly-shally, haggle.

baril (bari) *m*, barrel, cask. **barillet** (rijɛ) *m*, keg; cylinder, barrel, drum.

bariolage (barjɔlaːʒ) *m*, medley, motley. **bariolé, e** (le) *p.a*, motley, particoloured, pied.

baromètre (barɔmɛtr) *m*, barometer, glass. **barométrique** (metrik) *a*, barometric(al).

baron, ne (barɔ̃, ɔn) *n*, baron, ess.

baroque (barɔk) *a*, odd, queer, quaint.

barque (bark) *f*, boat, smack, barque, bark.

barrage (baraːʒ) *m*, barrier; dam; weir; barrage; crossing (*cheque*); closing (*street*); playing off (*tie*). **barre** (baːr) *f*, bar, rod, rail; stroke; stripe; cross (*on letter t*); helm, tiller, wheel (*Naut.*). **~ à sphères,** bar bell. **~ d'eau,** [tidal] bore. **~ de flot, tidal wave. ~ de plage,** surf. **~ fixe,** horizontal bar. **[jeu de] ~s,** prisoners' bars, p—s' base. **barreau** (baro) *m*, bar (*lit. & Law*); rung. **barrer** (re) *v.t*, to bar, rail, fence off; close; dam; cross (*a t, a cheque*); cross out, strike out, blue-pencil. **barrette** (rɛt) *f*, (small) bar; bar brooch; biretta. **barreur** (rœːr) *m*, man at the wheel; coxswain, cox.

barricade (barikad) *f*, barricade. **barricader** (de) *v.t*, to barricade.

barrière (barjɛːr) *f*, barrier, fence; bar; gate; toll gate; starting post; lists (*Hist.*).

barrique (barik) *f*, cask, hogshead.

barrir (bariːr) *v.i*, to trumpet (*elephant*).

baryton (baritɔ̃) *m*, barytone; b. saxhorn.

bas, se (bɑ, ɑːs) *a*, low, lower, nether, down; shallow; cloudy; mean, vile, base, degrading; vulgar; cheap. **bas âge,** infancy. **avoir la vue basse,** to be short-sighted. **bas,** *ad*, low, low down, down; off. ¶ *m*, bottom, foot; lower notes (*Mus.*); stocking; (*pl.*) hose. **~ de casse,** lower case (*Typ.*). **~ de ligne avec émerillons,** trace (*Fish.*). **~ de ligne pour le lancer,** cast. **à ~,** *ad*, down [with] . . . ! **bas les mains!** hands off! **en ~,** *ad*, at the bottom; below; down; downward[s]; downstairs.

basalte (bazalt) *m*, basalt.

basane (bazan) *f*, sheepskin, roan, basan, basil. **basané, e** (ne) *a*, tanned, tawny, swarthy, sunburnt.

bas-bleu (bablø) *m*, bluestocking.

bas-côté (bakote) *m*, aisle.

bascule (baskyl) *f*, balanced lever; rocker; seesaw. **[balance à] ~,** weighing machine, scale[s]. **~ romaine,** platform scales. **basculer** (le) *v.i*, to seesaw, swing, rock, tip [up], tilt. **faire ~,** to dip (*motor head-lights*).

base (bɑːz) *f*, base, bottom, foot; basis, groundwork.

bas-fond (bafɔ̃) *m*, lowland, flat, bottom; shallows (*Naut.*). **~s de la société,** underworld.

basilic (bazilik) *m*, [sweet] basil; basilisk.

basilique (bazilik) *f*, basilica.

basique (bazik) *a*, basic, basal.

basque (bask) *f*, skirt, tail.

bas-relief (bɑrəljɛf) *m*, low relief, bas-relief.

basse (bɑ:s) *f*, bass [voice, singer, string, tuba]; 'cello; reef, flat (*Naut.*).

basse-cour (bɑsku:r) *f*, farmyard, barnyard, poultry yard, stable yard.

bassement (bɑsmɑ̃) *ad*, meanly, basely.

bassesse (sɛs) *f*, meanness, &c; humbleness (*birth*).

basset (basɛ) *m*, basset. ~ **allemand**, dachshund.

bassin (basɛ̃) *m*, basin, bowl, pan; scale (*pan*); [collection] plate; ornamental lake; dock; pelvis. ~ *à flot*, wet dock. ~ *à sec*, dry dock. ~ [*de garde-robe*], *pour malade*, ~ *de lit*, bed pan. ~ *de natation*, swimming bath. **bassine** (sin) *f*, pan, copper. **bassinet** (nɛ) *m*, buttercup. **bassinoire** (nwa:r) *f*, warming pan.

basson (bɑsɔ̃) *m*, bassoon.

baste (bast) *i*, pooh! fudge! bosh!

bastonnade (bɑstɔnad) *f*, cudgelling.

bas-ventre (bɑvɑ̃:tr) *m*, lower part of the abdomen.

bât (bɑ) *m*, packsaddle.

bataclan (bataklɑ̃) *m*, traps, hamper.

bataille (bata:j) *f*, battle, fight, fray. **batailler** (taje) *v.i*, to battle, fight; struggle; wrangle. **batailleur, euse** (jœ:r, ø:z) *a*, combative, pugnacious. **bataillon** (tajɔ̃) *m*, battalion, host; heap. ~ *de travailleurs*, labour battalion.

bâtard, e (bɑta:r, ard) *a. & n*, bastard, mongrel. **bâtardise** (tardi:z) *f*, bastardy.

bateau (bato) *m*, boat, ship, vessel; smack. ~ *à rames*, row[ing] boat. ~ *à roues*, paddle b. ~ *à vapeur*, steamboat. ~ *à voiles*, sailing b. ~ *bouée* [*de virage*], mark b. ~-*citerne*, tanker. ~ *d'habitation*, house boat. ~ *de passage*, ferryboat. ~ *de promenade*, row[ing] b. (*pleasure*). ~ *de sauvetage*, lifeboat. ~-*feu*, lightship. ~ *omnibus*, ~-*mouche*, water [omni]bus. ~-*porte*, *m*, cɑisson (*dock*). ~-*témoin*, stake boat. **batelage** (tla:ʒ) *m*, lighterage; knock-about tricks. **batelée** (tle) *f*, boatload. **bateleur** (tlœ:r) *m*, knock-about comedian. **batelier** (təlje) *m*, bargeman, bargee, lighterman. **batellerie** (tɛlri) *f*, inland navigation; small craft.

bâti (bɑti) *m*, tacking, basting (*Need.*); frame[work], casing. ~ [*d'assise*], bed plate. ~ *de forge*, smith's hearth.

batifoler (batifɔle) *v.i*, to romp, frolic, skylark; dally (*amorously*).

bâtiment (bɑtimɑ̃) *m*, building; house; vessel, ship. ~ *de guerre*, man-of-war. **bâtir** (ti:r) *v.t. & abs*, to build; tack, baste (*Need.*). **bâtisse** (tis) *f*, carcass, carcase (*of a building*); jerry-building.

batiste (batist) *f*, cambric, batiste.

bâton (bɑtɔ̃) *m*, stick; cudgel; singlestick; staff; truncheon; baton; pole; perch; support (*fig.*). ~ *de rouge* [*pour les lèvres*], lipstick. *à* ~*s rompus*, by fits & starts, desultorily. **bâtonner** (tɔne) *v.t*, to beat, cudgel, baste. **bâtonnet** (nɛ) *m*, [tip]cat; chopstick.

battage (bata:ʒ) *m*, beating; threshing; churning. **battant** (tɑ̃) *m*, clapper (*bell*); leaf (*door*). ~ *neuf*, bran[d] new. *pluie battante*, pelting rain. **batte** (bat) *f*, mallet; bat; beater. ~ *à beurre*, churn dash[er]. **battement** (tmɑ̃) *m*, beating, beat, &c, as *battre*. **batterie** (tri) *f*, fight, scuffle; battery; beat[ing]; set; utensils; percussion instruments; (*s. & pl.*) plan(s), tactics. ~ *de tambour*, roll of the drum. **batteur** (tœ:r) *m*, beater; whisk. ~ *de pavé*, lounger, loafer. ~ *en grange*, thresher (*pers.*). **batteuse** (tø:z) *f*, threshing machine. **battoir** (twa:r) *m*, beater; battledore. **battre** (tr) *v.t. & i. ir*, to beat, strike; batter; scour (*country*); thrash; thresh; churn; hammer; ram; coin, mint; raise (*money*); fly (*national flag*); shell (*Mil.*); clap (*hands*); shuffle (*cards*); bang; flap; jar; throb, pulsate, pant; tick (*clock*). ~ *contre-vapeur*, to reverse steam. **se** ~, to fight. **se** ~ *les flancs*, to lash its tail. **battu, e** (ty) *p.a*, beaten. ¶ *f*, drive, battue, beat (*Hunt.*); tramp (*of horse*).

bau (bo) *m*, beam (*ship's timber*).

baudet (bodɛ) *m*, donkey.

baudrier (bodrie) *m*, cross belt.

baudruche (bodryʃ) *f*, gold-beater's skin.

baume (bo:m) *m*, balsam, balm. **baumier** (bomje) *m*, balsam [tree].

bavarder (bavarde) *v.i*, to prate, blab; gossip. **bavarois, e** (bavarwa, a:z) *a. & B*~, *n*, Bavarian.

bave (ba:v) *f*, drivel; slobber; slime. **baver** (bave) *v.i*, to drivel; slobber. **bavette** (vɛt) *f*, **bavoir** (vwa:r) *m*, bib, feeder.

Bavière (la) (bavjɛ:r), Bavaria.

bayer aux corneilles (baje), to star-gaze, gape [at the moon].

bayette (bɛjɛt) *f*, baize.

bazar (baza:r) *m*, bazaar, arcade (*of shops*); (*cheap*) stores.

béant, e (beɑ̃, ɑ̃:t) *a*, gaping, yawning, open.

béat, e† (bea, at) *a*, sanctimonious; blissful; smug, self-satisfied. ¶ *n*, saint. **béatifier** (tifje) *v.t*, to beatify. **béatitude** (tyd) *f*, beatitude, blessedness, bliss.

beau, bel, belle (bo, bɛl) *a*, beautiful, fine, handsome, fair, pretty, comely, lovely, good, nice; graceful; fashionable, smart; bright; palmy (*days*). *le beau monde*, fashionable society. *avoir beau dire*, to speak in vain. *bel esprit*, [man of] wit; witling. *bel & bien*, *ad*, fairly; plainly. *à la belle étoile*, in the open [air]. **beau**, *m*, beautiful; beau, Adonis. *au* ~, *au* ~ *fixe*, at fair, at set fair (*barometer*). *faire le* ~, to beg (*dog*). **beaucoup** (ku) *ad. & m*, a great (*or good*) deal, a good (*or great*) many, very much; much, many, greatly. **de ~,** by far. **beau-fils,** *m*, stepson. **beau-frère,** *m*, brother-in-law. **beau-père,** *m*, father-in-law; stepfather.

beaupré (bopre) *m*, bowsprit.

beauté (bote) *f*, beauty, fairness, loveliness, comeliness; belle.

beaux-arts (boza:r) *m.pl*, fine arts, art.

bébé (bebe) *m*, baby; [baby] doll. **~ dormeur,** sleeping doll.

bec (bɛk) *m*, beak, bill; nose, nozzle, snout; jaw; spout; mouthpiece; mouth; lip, tip; burner, jet; nib; point; cutwater. **~ à incandescence par le gaz,** incandescent gas burner.

bécarre (beka:r) (*Mus.*) *m. & a*, natural, cancel.

bécasse (bekas) *f*, woodcock. **bécasseau** (so) *m*, sandpiper. **bécassine** (sin) *f*, snipe.

bec-de-lièvre (bɛkdəljɛ:vr) *m*, harelip.

bêche (bɛʃ) *f*, spade. **bêcher** (ʃe) *v.t*, to dig, spade.

becqueter (bɛkte) *v.t*, to peck, pick. **se ~,** to bill.

bedeau (bədo) *m*, beadle; verger.

beffroi (befrwa) *m*, belfry; gantry.

bégayer (begɛje) *v.i. & t*, to stutter, stammer, lisp, falter. **bégaiement** (gɛmɑ̃) *m*, stuttering, &c.

bégonia (begɔnja) *m*, begonia.

bègue (bɛ:g) *n*, stutterer, stammerer.

bégueule (begœl) *f*, prude. ¶ *a*, prudish, squeamish, strait-laced. **bégueulerie** (lri) *f*, prudery, &c.

beignet (bɛɲɛ) *m*, fritter (*Cook.*).

bêlement (bɛlmɑ̃) *m*, bleat[ing], baa[ing]. **bêler** (le) *v.t*, to bleat, baa.

belette (bəlɛt) *f*, weasel.

belge (bɛlʒ) *a. & B~, n*, Belgian. **la Belgique** (ʒik), Belgium.

bélier (belje) *m*, ram, tup; battering-ram.

belladone (bɛladɔn) *f*, belladonna, deadly nightshade.

belle (bɛl) *f*, beauty; deciding game, rubber. *la B~ au bois dormant,* the Sleeping Beauty. *la B~ & la Bête,* Beauty & the Beast. **~-de-jour,** *f*, convolvulus. **~-fille,** *f*, stepdaughter; daughter-in-law. **bellement** (lmɑ̃) *ad*, softly, gently. **belle-mère,** *f*, stepmother; mother-in-law. **belles-lettres,** *f.pl*, polite letters *or* literature. **belle-sœur,** *f*, sister-in-law.

belligérant, e (bɛlliʒerɑ̃, ɑ̃:t) *a. & n*, belligerent. **belliqueux, euse** (bɛllikø, ø:z) *a*, warlike, bellicose.

bellot, te (bɛlo, ɔt) *a*, pretty; dapper.

belvédère (bɛlvede:r) *m*, belvedere, lookout.

bémol (bemɔl) *m. & att*, flat (*Mus.*).

bénédicité (benedisite) *m*, grace, blessing (*before meals*). **bénédiction** (ksjɔ̃) *f*, consecration; blessing; benediction. *que c'est une ~,* with a vengeance, & no mistake.

bénéfice (benefis) *m*, advantage, benefit; profit; living, benefice (*Eccl.*). **bénéficiaire** (sjɛ:r) *a*, [showing a] profit; in credit. ¶ *n*, beneficiary, payee. **bénéficier** (sje) *v.i*, to [make a] profit, benefit.

benêt (bənɛ) *a.m*, silly, simple, foolish. ¶ *m*, booby, simpleton, noodle.

bénévole† (benevɔl) *a*, kind; voluntary.

Bengale (le) (bɛ̃gal), Bengal. **bengali** (li) *a.inv. & (bird) m. & B~ (pers.) m*, Bengali, -lee.

béni, e (beni) *p.p*, blessed, blest. **bénin, igne†** (nɛ̃, iɲ) *a*, benign, benignant, kind; mild. **bénir** (ni:r) *v.t*, to consecrate; bless; thank. **bénit, e** (ni, ite) *p.p*, consecrated, holy (*bread, water*). **bénitier** (tje) *m*, holy-water basin, stoup.

benjoin (bɛ̃ʒwɛ̃) *m*, benzoin, benjamin.

benne (bɛn) *f*, hamper, basket; bucket, kibble, tub (*Min.*).

benzine (bɛ̃zin) *f*, benzine, benzoline.

benzol (bɛ̃zɔl) *m*, benzol[e], benzene.

béquille (beki:j) *f*, crutch; crutch handle; crutch key; spud (*Agric.*).

bercail (berka:j) *m*, fold (*Relig.*).

berceau (berso) *m*, cradle; cot; arbour, bower. **bercelonnette** (səlɔnɛt) *f*, bassinet, cot. **bercer** (se) *v.t*, to rock, dandle; lull; bring up; cherish. **berceuse** (sø:z) *f*, rocker (*pers.*); rocking chair; lullaby.

béret (basque) (berɛ) *m*, beret.

bergamote (bergamɔt) *f*, bergamot (*orange, pear*). **bergamotier** (tje) *m*, bergamot [tree] (*orange*).

berge (bɛrʒ) *f*, bank (*river, road*).

berger (bɛrʒe) *m*, shepherd; swain. **bergère** (ʒɛ:r) *f*, shepherdess, nymph; easy chair. **bergerie** (ʒəri) *f*, [sheep]fold, pen. **bergeronnette** (rɔnɛt) *f*, wagtail.

Bermudes (les) (bɛrmyd) *f.pl*, the Bermudas.

bernacle (bernakl) *f*, barnacle (*Crust.*). **bernard-l'ermite** (narlɛrmit) *m*, hermit crab.

berne (bern) *f*, tossing in blanket. *en ~,* at half-mast (*flag*). **berner** (ne) *v.t*, to [toss in] blanket; chaff, quiz.

bernique (bernik) *i*, not a bit of use!

béryl (beril) *m*, beryl.

besace (bəzas) *f*, scrip, wallet (*beggar's*). *réduit à la ~,* reduced to beggary.

besicles (bəzikl) *f.pl*, barnacles (*spectacles*).

besogne (bəzɔɲ) *f*, [piece of] work, task, job. **~ alimentaire,** pot-boiler. **besogneux, euse** (nø, ø:z) *a*, needy, impecunious.

besoin (bəzwɛ̃) *m*, need; requirement; pinch; [referee in] case of need (*Com.*).

bestial, e† (bɛstjal) *a*, bestial; beastly; hoggish. **bestiaux** (tjo) *m.pl*, cattle. **bêta** (beta) *m*, blockhead, noodle. **bétail** (beta:j) *m*, cattle. **bête** (bɛt) *f*, beast, [dumb] animal; creature; fool. **~ à bon Dieu,** ladybird. **~ noire,** pet aversion. **~s à cornes,** horned cattle. **~s fauves,** deer; wild beasts (*big felines*). ¶ †; *a*, stupid, foolish, silly. **bêtise** (beti:z) *f*, stupidity, &c; nonsense.

béton (betɔ̃) *m*, concrete. ~ *armé*, reinforced concrete.

bette (bɛt) *f*, beet. **betterave** (tra:v) *f*, beetroot, beet. ~ *à sucre,* sugar beet. ~ *fourragère*, mangel[-wurzel].

beugler (bøgle) *v.i.* & *t*, to bellow, low, moo; bawl.

beurre (bœ:r) *m*, butter. ~ *d'anchois,* anchovy paste. **beurrée** (bœre) *f*, slice of bread & butter. **beurrer** (re) *v.t*, to butter. **beurrier** (rje) *m*, butter dish. ~ *rafraîchisseur*, butter cooler.

bévue (bevy) *f*, blunder; howler.

biais (bjɛ) *m*, slant; skew; bias; bent; dodge, shift. **biaiser** (ze) *v.i*, to slant; dodge, shuffle, shift.

bibelot (biblo) *m*, curio, [k]nick-[k]nack.

biberon, ne (bibrɔ̃, ɔn) *n*, tippler; (*m.*) feeding bottle.

Bible (bibl) *f*, Bible. **bibliographie** (bliografi) *f*, bibliography. **bibliophile** (fil) *m*, bibliophil[e], book lover. **bibliothécaire** (tekɛ:r) *n*, librarian. **bibliothèque** (tɛk) *f*, library; bookcase; bookstall. ~ *circulante,* circulating library. ~ *de prêt*, lending l. ~ *où les livres se consultent sur place &* ~ *d'ouvrages à consulter*, reference library. ~ *transformable*, unit bookcase. **biblique** (blik) *a*, biblical; Bible (*Society*). **biblorhapte** (blɔrapt) *m*, binder.

biceps (bisɛps) *m*, biceps.

biche (biʃ) *f*, hind (*deer*).

bichon, ne (biʃɔ̃, ɔn) *n*, Maltese [dog, bitch], lap dog. **bichonner** (ʃɔne) *v.t*, to curl; titivate.

bicoque (bikɔk) *f*, shanty.

bicycle (bisikl) *m*, [ordinary *or* high] bicycle. **bicyclette** (klɛt) *f*, [safety] bicycle, cycle. ~ *de course*, racer. ~ *de livraison*, carrier bicycle. ~ *de route*, roadster. ~ *pour les tout petits*, fairy cycle. **bicycliste** (klist) *n*, [bi]cyclist.

bidet (bidɛ) *m*, nag, cob; bidet.

bidon (bidɔ̃) *m*, canteen, water bottle (*Mil.*); tin (*petrol, &c*), can.

bief (bjɛf) *m*, race[way] (*mill*); pond (*canal*).

bielle (bjɛl) *f*, [connecting] rod; strut, brace.

bien (bjɛ̃) *ad*, well; right; proper; nicely; all right; clearly; fully, thoroughly; much; very; far; fast; fain; indeed; duly; really, quite. ~ *de*, much, many. ~ *que, c*, [al]though. ¶ *m*, good; weal; blessing; endowment; mercy; (*oft. pl.*) possessions, property, chattel, estate, substance. ~*s mal acquis*, ill-gotten gains. ~*s [transmissibles par voie de succession]*, hereditament.

bien-aimé, e *ou* **bienaimé, e** (bjɛ̃nɛme) *a*. & *n*, [well-]beloved, darling.

bien-dire (bjɛ̃di:r) *m*, fine speaking. **biendisant, e** (dizɑ̃, ɑ̃:t) *a*, well-spoken, fairspoken.

bien-être (bjɛ̃nɛ:tr) *m*, well-being; welfare.

bienfaisance (bjɛ̃fəzɑ̃:s) *f*, beneficence; benevolence; bounteousness; charity, donations. **bienfaisant, e** (zɑ̃, ɑ̃:t) *a*, beneficent, &c. **bienfait** (fɛ) *m*, kindness, benefaction, benefit, boon; mercy. **bienfaiteur, trice** (tœ:r, tris) *n*, benefactor, tress.

bienheureux, euse (bjɛ̃nœrø, ø:z) *a*, blessed; blissful.

biennal, e (bjɛnal) *a*, biennial.

bienséant, e (bjɛ̃seɑ̃, ɑ̃:t) *a*, proper, becoming, decorous.

biens-fonds (bjɛ̃fɔ̃) *m.pl*, landed property.

bientôt (bjɛ̃to) *ad*, soon, shortly.

bienveillant, e (bjɛ̃vɛjɑ̃, ɑ̃:t) *a*, kind[ly], friendly.

bienvenue (bjɛ̃vny) *f*, welcome; footing.

bière (bjɛ:r) *f*, beer, lager [beer]; coffin. ~ *au tonneau*, ~ *à la pompe*, draught beer. ~ *blonde*, light lager. ~ *brune*, dark lager.

biffer (bife) *v.t*, to strike out, cross out, delete, rule out, cancel.

bifteck (biftɛk) *m*, [beef]steak.

bifurcation (bifyrkasjɔ̃) *f*, bifurcation, fork; junction.

bigame (bigam) *a*, bigamous. ¶ *n*, bigamist. **bigamie** (mi) *f*, bigamy.

bigarade (bigarad) *f*, Seville orange.

bigarré (bigare) *p.a*, variegated, particoloured, pied, motley. **bigarrer** (re) *v.t*, to variegate, medley; [inter]lard.

bigorneau (bigorno) *m*, [peri]winkle (*Crust.*).

bigot, e (bigo, ot) *a*, bigoted. ¶ *n*, bigot. **bigoterie** (gotri) *f*, bigotry.

bigoudi (bigudi) *m*, leather hair curler.

bijou (biʒu) *m*, jewel, gem; darling. **bijouterie** (tri) *f*, jewel[le]ry. **bijoutier, ère** (tje, ɛ:r) *n*, jeweller.

bilan (bilɑ̃) *m*, balance sheet; statement of affairs.

bilboquet (bilbokɛ) *m*, cup & ball.

bile (bil) *f*, bile. **bilieux, euse** (ljø, ø:z) *a*, bilious.

billard (bija:r) *m*, billiards. [*salle de*] ~, billiard room. [*table de*] ~, billiard table. ~ *américain*, pin table. ~ *japonais*, bagatelle; bagatelle board.

bille (bi:j) *f*, ball; billiard ball; marble (*games*); saw-log; bar.

billet (bijɛ) *m*, note, bill; ticket. ~ *à ordre*, note of hand, promissory note. ~ *à prix réduit*, cheap ticket. ~ *d'aller & retour*, return t. ~ *de banque*, bank note. ~ *de complaisance*, accommodation note. ~ *de faveur*, free pass, complimentary ticket. ~ *de quai*, platform ticket. ~ *de logement*, billet (*Mil.*). ~ *de vacances*, tourist ticket. ~ *doux*, love letter. ~ *garde-place*, ~ *de location de place*, reserved seat ticket. ~ *global*, through ticket (*sea-land-sea*). ~ *perdant*, blank (*lottery*).

billevesée (bilvəze) *f*, blether; crotchet, whim.

billion (biljɔ̃) *m*, thousand millions.

billon (bijɔ̃) *m*, ridge (*Agric.*); copper &/or nickel [coin].

billot (bijo) *m*, [chopping] block.
bimbelot (bɛ̃blo) *m*, fancy article. **bimbe-loterie** (blɔtri) *f*, fancy goods.
bimensuel, le (bimɑ̃sɥɛl) *a*, semimonthly, twice monthly. **bimestriel, le** (mɛstriɛl) *a*, bimonthly, [in] alternate months.
biner (bine) *v.t*, to hoe. **binette** (nɛt) *f*, hoe.
binocle (binɔkl) *m*, eyeglasses.
biographe (biograf) *m*, biographer. **bio-graphie** (fi) *f*, biography.
biologie (biɔlɔʒi) *f*, biology. **biologiste** (ʒist) *m*, biologist.
bipède (bipɛd) *a*, biped[al]. ¶ *m*, biped.
biplan (biplɑ̃) *m*, biplane.
bique (bik) *f*, nanny [goat].
birman, e (birmɑ̃, an) *a*. & **B~**, *n*, Burmese. **la Birmanie** (mani), Burma.
bis, e (bi, i:z) *a*, brownish grey; brown (*bread*).
bis (bis) *ad*, bis, repeat (*Mus.*); encore. ¶ *m*, encore. ¶ *a*, ♪, ♪ (*house number*).
bisaïeul, e (bizajœl) *n*, great-grandfather, -mother.
bisannuel, le (bizanɥɛl) *a*, biennial.
bisbille (bisbi:j) *f*, squabble. *en* **~**, at loggerheads.
biscornu, e (biskɔrny) *a*, misshapen; queer, odd.
biscotte (biskɔt) *f*, rusk. **biscuit** (kɥi) *m*, biscuit; biscuit [ware]. **~** *de Savoie*, sponge cake.
bise (bi:z) *f*, cold wind.
biseau (bizo) *m*, bevel. **biseauter** (te) *v.t*, to bevel.
bismuth (bismyt) *m*, bismuth.
bison (bizɔ̃) *m*, bison.
bissac (bisak) *m*, wallet, bag.
bissection (bisɛksjɔ̃) *f*, bisection.
bisser (bise) *v.t*, to encore.
bissextile (bisɛkstil) *a*, leap (*year*).
bistourner (bisturne) *v.t*, to twist, wrench.
bitume (bitym) *m*, bitumen, pitch, asphalt. **bitumineux, euse** (minø, ø:z) *a*, bituminous; tarry.
bivalve (bivalv) *a*. & *m*, bivalve.
bivouac (bivwak) *m*, bivouac. **bivouaquer** (ke) *v.i*, to bivouac, camp out.
bizarre† (biza:r) *a*, odd, queer, peculiar, freakish, outlandish. **bizarrerie** (zarri) *f*, oddness, &c.
blafard, e (blafa:r, ard) *a*, pale, pallid, wan; lurid.
blague (blag) *f*, [tobacco] pouch; gammon, bunkum, rubbish, humbug, blarney, chaff; bounce, brag.
blaireau (blɛro) *m*, badger; shaving brush.
blâme (blɑ:m) *m*, blame, reprimand. **blâmer** (blame) *v.t*, to blame, &c.
blanc, che (blɑ̃, ɑ̃:ʃ) *a*, white; hoary; blank; clean; fair (*skin*). *la mer Blanche*, the White sea. *le mont Blanc*, Mont Blanc. **~** *de lessive*, fresh from the wash. ¶ *m*, white (*colour, man, &c*); blank; margin (*book page*); chalk (*Bil.*); breast (*fowl*). **~** *de baleine*, spermaceti. **~** *de céruse*,

white lead. **~** *de champignon*, mushroom spawn. **~** *de chaux*, whitewash. **~** *de craie*, whiting. **~** *de grand fond*, front margin. **~** *de petit fond*, back margin, (*pl. col.*) gutter. **~** *de pied*, bottom margin. **~** [*de fard*], white face cream. **~** *de terre à pipe*, pipe clay. **~** *de tête*, top margin.
blanc-bec (blɑ̃bɛk) *m*, callow youth.
blanchaille (blɑ̃ʃɑ:j) *f*, fry; whitebait.
blanchâtre (blɑ̃ʃɑ:tr) *a*, whitish. **blanche** (blɑ̃:ʃ) *f*, white (*woman, ball*); minim (*Mus.*).
blancheur (blɑ̃ʃœ:r) *f*, whiteness. **blanchir** (ʃi:r) *v.t*. & *i*, to whiten; blanch; bleach; whitewash; wash; wash for; launder; clean up; scald. **~** *à la chaux*, to whitewash. **blanchisserie** (ʃisri) *f*, laundry; bleachery. **blanchisseuse** (sø:z) *f*, washerwoman. **~** [*de fin*], [fine] laundress.
blanc-manger (blɑ̃mɑ̃ʒe) *m*, blancmange.
blanc-seing (blɑ̃sɛ̃) *m*, blank signature.
blaser (blaze) *v.t*, to blunt, surfeit, pall on.
blason (blazɔ̃) *m*, coat of arms, armorial bearings; blazon[ry], heraldry. **blasonner** (zɔne) *v.t*, to [em]blazon; malign.
blasphémateur, trice (blasfematœ:r, tris) *n*, blasphemer. **blasphématoire** (twa:r) *a*, blasphemous. **blasphème** (fɛ:m) *m*, blasphemy; profanity. **blasphémer** (feme) *v.i*. & *t*, to blaspheme, curse.
blatte (blat) *f*, cockroach, black beetle.
blé (ble) *m*, corn, wheat. [*champ de*] **~**, cornfield. **~** *à moudre*, grist. **~** *de Turquie*, Indian corn, maize. **~** *noir*, buckwheat.
blême (blɛ:m) *a*, pale, pallid, wan, ghastly. **blêmir** (blemi:r) *v.i*, to [turn] pale.
bléser (bleze) *v.i*, to lisp.
blesser (blɛse) *v.t*, to wound, hurt, injure, gall; grate upon (*ear*); shock, offend; pinch (*shoes*). **~** *à mort*, to injure fatally. **~** *quelqu'un au cœur*, to hurt someone's feelings. **blessure** (sy:r) *f*, wound, &c.
blet, te (blɛ, ɛt) *a*, overripe, soft.
bleu, e (blø) *a*, blue. ¶ *m*, blue; blue mark (*bruise*); blue print; recruit (*Mil.*); clouds (*fig.*). **~** *de ciel*, **~** *céleste*, sky blue. **~** *marine*, navy b. **bleuâtre** (a:tr) *a*, bluish. **bleuet** (ɛ) *m*, cornflower. **bleuir** (i:r) *v.t*. & *i*, to blue.
blindage (blɛ̃da:ʒ) *m*, armour-plating; armour; sheeting.
bloc (blɔk) *m*, block, lump; coalition (*Pol.*); guardroom. **~** *journalier*, block calendar.
blocage (blɔka:ʒ) *m*, rubble[work]; clamping, &c, as *bloquer*. **blocaille** (ka:j) *f*, rubble[stone], ballast.
bloc-film (blɔkfilm) *m*, film pack.
blockhaus (blɔko:s) *m*, blockhouse; conning tower.
bloc-mémorandum (blɔkmemɔrɑ̃dɔm) *m*, scribbling block. **bloc-notes** (nɔt) *m*. ou **bloc de correspondance**, [writing] pad. **bloc-sténo** (steno) *m*, shorthand notebook.

blocus (blɔky:s) *m*, blockade.

blond, e (blɔ̃, 5:d) *a*, fair, flaxen, blond, e; light. ¶ *n*, fair-haired person, blond, e. ¶ *m*, blond, e, flaxen (*colour*). ~ *ardent*, auburn. ~*cendré*, ash blonde. ~ *doré*, golden (*hair*). ~ *hasardé*, reddish (*hair*). ~ *platine*, platinum blonde. ~ *roux*, sandy (*hair*).

bloquer (blɔke) *v.t*, to clamp, lock; tie up, lock up (*as shares*); lump; blockade, block.

blottir (se) (blɔti:r) *v.pr*, to squat, crouch, couch, cower; lie hid; cuddle up, nestle, snuggle, nuzzle, huddle.

blouse (blu:z) *f*, smock[frock]; blouse. ~*[-paletot]*, *f*, overalls. **blouser** (bluze) *v.t*, to take in, dupe.

bluette (blyɛt) *f*, literary trifle.

bluter (blyte) *v.t*, to bolt, sift.

boa (bɔa) *m*, boa (*wrap*). ~ *constrictor* (kɔ̃striktɔ:r), boa constrictor.

bobine (bɔbin) *f*, bobbin, reel, spool; coil (*Elec.*). **bobiner** (ne) *v.t*, to wind, coil.

bocage (bɔka:ʒ) *m*, grove, bocager, **ère** (kaʒe, ɛ:r) *a*, sylvan, wood (*nymph*).

bocal (bɔkal) *m*, bottle, jar; globe, fishbowl.

bocard (bɔka:r) *m*, stamp [mill]. **bocarder** (karde) *v.t*, to mill, stamp (*ore*).

bock (bɔk) *m*, glass (*for, or of, beer*).

bœuf (bœf) *m*, ox, bullock; beef.

bogie (bɔʒi) *m*, bogie, truck (*Rly*).

bohème (bɔɛ:m) *n. & a*, Bohemian (*n. & a.*), free & easy. *la* ~, Bohemia (*fig.*). **bohémien, ne** (emjɛ̃, ɛn) *n*, gipsy.

boire (bwa:r) *v.t. & i. ir*, to drink; absorb; imbibe; swallow, pocket (*insult*); drown. ~ *un coup*, to have a drink.

bois (bwa) *m*, wood; park; horns, antlers, head (*stag*); stock (*rifle, plane*); stuff (*one is made of*); (*pl.*) wood[-wind] (*Mus.*). ~ *à brûler*, ~ *de chauffage*, firewood. ~ *contreplaqué*, plywood. ~ [*de charpente*], timber, lumber. ~ *de corps*, quoin (*Typ.*). ~ *de lit*, bedstead. ~ *de placage*, veneer. ~ *de rose*, tulip wood. ~ *de satin*, satin w. ~ *plaqué triplé*, 3-ply w. **boisage** (za:ʒ) *m*, timbering. **boisement** (zmɑ̃) *m*, afforestation. **boiser** (ze) *v.t*, to timber; wainscot; afforest. **boiserie** (zri) *f*, woodwork; wainscoting.

boisseau (bwaso) *m*, bushel.

boisson (bwasɔ̃) *f*, drink, beverage, liquor.

boîte (bwa:t) *f*, box, case, chest, caddy, canister, can. ~ [*à conserves*], [preserving] tin, can. ~ *à musique*, musical box. ~ *à poudre, avec glace & houppe*, vanity case. ~ *à surprise*, jack-in-the-box. ~ *de la poste*, ~ *aux lettres*, posting box, letter b. ~ *de nuit*, all-night resort, night club. ~ [*métallique*] *à couvercle à levier*, lever lid tin. *la* ~ *de Pandore* (pɑ̃dɔ:r), Pandora's box. ~ *de peinture*, box of paints.

boiter (bwate) *v.i*, to limp, halt, hobble. **boiterie** (tri) *f*, lameness. **boiteux, euse** (tø, ø:z) *a*, lame; halting; rickety.

boitier (bwatje) *m*, box with divisions; case (*watch*).

bol (bɔl) *m*, bowl, basin; bolus. ~ *rince-doigts*, finger bowl.

Bolivie (la) (bɔlivi), Bolivia. **bolivien, ne** (vjɛ̃, ɛn) *a. & B~*, *n*, Bolivian.

Bologne (bɔlɔɲ) *f*, Bologna.

bombance (bɔ̃bɑ̃:s) *f*, feasting, junketing.

bombardement (bɔ̃bardəmɑ̃) *m*, bombardment, shelling; bombing. *sinistré des* ~*s*, bombed out. **bombarder** (de) *v.t*, to bombard, &c; pitchfork (*fig.*). **bombe** (bɔ̃:b) *f*, bomb; ball (*signal*); bombshell (*fig.*).

bomber (bɔ̃be) *v.t. & i. & se* ~, to bulge, swell, camber, belly; bend.

bon, ne (bɔ̃, ɔn) *a*, good; sound; kind; nice; fine; boon (*companion*); palatable; fit; right; proper; safe; fast (*colour*). **bon**, *comps* : ~ *enfant*, good-natured. ~ *marché*, *m*, cheapness. [*à*] ~ *marché*, *a*, cheap. *à* ~ *marché*, *ad*, cheap[ly]. ~ *sens* (sɑ̃), [common] sense, [right] senses. **bonne**, *comps*: *la* ~ *année*, a happy new year. ~ *bouche*, titbit. ~ *femme*, simple good-natured woman. ~ *fin*, meeting (*engagement, bills*); protection (*bills*). ~ *maman*, grandmama, granny. **bon**, stet (*Typ.*). **bon à tirer**, [for] press (*Typ.*). ¶ *m*, good; cream (*of story*); order, note; licence; voucher; bond; draft; scrip; profit. (*un*) ~ *à rien*, *m. & a*, (a) good-for-nothing, (a) ne'er-do-well, -weel. ~ *d'ouverture*, inspection order (*Cust.*). ~ *de bord*, mate's receipt.

bonbon (bɔ̃bɔ̃) *m*, sweet[meat]; (*pl.*) confectionery. ~*s de chocolat*, chocolates. **bonbonnière** (bɔnjɛ:r) *f*, confectionery box, chocolate box; sweet bowl; pretty little place (*house*).

bond (bɔ̃) *m*, bound, bounce, spring; rebound; spurt.

bonde (bɔ̃:d) *f*, bung[hole]; bung, plug. **bonder** (bɔ̃de) *v.t*, to fill to the bung, cram.

bondir (bɔ̃di:r) *v.i*, to bound, &c, as *bond*.

bondon (bɔ̃dɔ̃) *m*, bung; bondon. **bondonner** (dɔne) *v.t*, to bung.

bonheur (bɔnœ:r) *m*, happiness, welfare; [good] luck; blessing. *le* ~ *du célibat*, single blessedness.

bonhomie (bɔnɔmi) *f*, good nature, geniality; credulity. **bonhomme** (nɔm) *m*, simple good-natured man. *le* ~ *Noël*, Father Christmas, Santa Claus.

bonification (bɔnifikasjɔ̃) *f*, improvement; allowance. **bonifier** (fje) *v.t*, to improve; allow, credit.

boniment (bɔnimɑ̃) *m*, patter (*showman's*); claptrap.

bonjour (bɔ̃ʒu:r) *m*, good morning, good afternoon, good day.

bonne (bɔn) *f*, [maid]servant; servant[girl]; waitress. ~ *à tout faire*, general servant, maid-of-all-work. ~ [d'enfant], nurse-[maid].

bonnement (bɔnmɑ̃) ad, candidly, plainly.

bonnet (bɔnɛ) m, cap, hat. ~ de police, forage cap. ~ magique, wishing cap.

bonneteau (bɔnto) m, three-card trick.

bonneterie (bɔntri) f, hosiery.

bonneteur (bɔntœ:r) m, card sharper.

bonnetier (bɔntje) m, hosier.

bonsoir (bɔ̃swa:r) m, good evening, good night.

bonté (bɔ̃te) f, goodness, kindness.

bookmaker (bukmɛkɛ:r) m, bookmaker. ~ marron, welsher.

borax (bɔraks) m, borax.

bord (bɔ:r) m, edge, border, brink, verge, fringe, rim, margin; brim; flap; edging, binding, hem; bank, side, shore, coast, strand; board, side (ship); tack (Naut.); ship. à ~, on board, aboard. à grands ~s, broad-brimmed (hat). à pleins ~s, brim-full. par-dessus ~, overboard.

bordé (bɔrde) m, braid; gimp; planking; plating (ship).

bordeaux (bɔrdo) m, Bordeaux, claret.

bordée (bɔrde) f, broadside: volley (fig.); board, tack (ship); watch (Naut.).

border (bɔrde) v.t, to border, edge, hem, bind; flange; tuck in (bed); line; plate (ship); ship (oars); run along, fringe; kerb, curb.

bordereau (bɔrdəro) m, list, schedule, statement, slip, note, contract [note]. ~ de versement, paying-in slip.

bordier (bɔrdje) a.m. & m, lopsided (boat).

bordure (bɔrdy:r) f, border, edge, edging, binding, hem, skirt, rim; kerb, curb; front (sea, river). ~ de fleurs vivaces, herbaceous border.

bore (bɔ:r) m, boron (Chem.).

boréal, e (bɔreal) a, boreal, north[ern].

borgne (bɔrɲ) a. & n, one-eyed (person); blind; dark, dingy; frowsy; low, of ill fame.

borique (bɔrik) a, boric, boracic.

borne (bɔrn) f, bound[ary], landmark, post; spur; terminal (Elec.). ~ kilométrique (Fr.), mile stone (Eng.). ~ postale, pillar box. **borner** (ne) v.t, to bound, confine, mark out; restrict; stint.

bornoyer (bɔrnwaje) v.t, to squint over (an alignment).

Bosphore (le) (bɔsfɔ:r), the Bosphorus.

bosquet (bɔske) m, grove, spinney, thicket, shrubbery.

bosse (bɔs) f, hunch, hump; bump; dent, dint, bruise; boss; mound; painter (boat).

bosseler (sle) v.t, to [em]boss; dent, dint, bruise, batter. **bossoir** (swa:r) m, davit; cathead. **bossu, e** (sy) a, humpbacked, humpbacked. ¶ n, hunchback, humpback. **bossuer** (sɥe) v.t, to dent, dint, bruise, batter.

bot (bo) a.m, club (foot).

botanique (bɔtanik) a, botanic(al). ¶ f, botany. **botaniste** (nist) m, botanist.

botte (bɔt) f, bundle, bunch; truss; coil; clump; thrust, lunge, pass; [high] boot. ~s à genouillère, jack boots. ~s à l'écuyère, riding boots. ~s à revers, top boots. ~s cuissardes (kɥisard), thigh boots; waders. ~s montant aux genoux, Wellingtons. **botteler** (tle) v.t, to bundle, bunch; truss (hay). **botter** (te) v.t, to boot, fit, put boots on. **bottier** (tje) m, bootmaker. **bottine** (tin) f, [half] boot. ~s d'escalade, climbing boots.

bouc (buk) m, he-goat, billy g. ~ émissaire, scapegoat.

boucanier (bukanje) m, buccaneer.

boucaut (buko) m, cask, hogshead.

bouche (buʃ) f, mouth; muzzle (gun); nozzle; hydrant, plug; flue; living. ~ à feu, piece of ordnance. ~ béante, ~ bée, openmouthed. ~ close! not a word! mum['s the word]! **bouchée** (ʃe) f, mouthful, bite; patty, pasty. **boucher** (ʃe) v.t, to stop, obstruct; shut; close; plug, seal; bung; stopper, cork. se ~ le nez, to hold one's nose. bouché à l'émeri, stoppered (bottle).

boucher (buʃe) m, butcher. **boucherie** (ʃri) f, butcher's shop; butchery; slaughter.

bouche-trou (buʃtru) m, stopgap.

bouchon (buʃɔ̃) m, stopper, cork; plug, cap, bung; wisp; bundle; bush (on tavern); tavern; float. ~ à l'émeri, ground stopper. goût de ~, corky taste. **bouchonner** (ʃɔne) v.t, to bundle up; rub down (horse).

boucle (bukl) f, buckle, ring, shackle; loop; sweep; eye, bight; curl, lock, ringlet; handle. ~ d'amarrage, ring bolt. **boucler** (kle) v.t & i, to buckle; ring (bull, &c); curl; loop; bulge; lock up; put away; balance (budget). ~ la boucle, to loop the loop. **bouclier** (klie) m, shield, buckler.

bouddhique (budik) a, buddhist. **bouddhiste** (dist) m, buddhist.

bouder (bude) v.i, to sulk; shirk.

boudin (budɛ̃) m, black pudding; corkscrew curl; saddlebag; flange.

boue (bu) f, mud, dirt, mire; slime, sludge, swarf.

bouée (bue) f, buoy. ~ culotte, breeches b. ~ de sauvetage, life b.

boueux, euse (buø, ø:z) a, muddy, dirty, miry, mud (spring). ¶ m, scavenger, dustman.

bouffe (buf) a, comic, buffo.

bouffée (bufe) f, puff, breath, fume, whiff, gust; fit. **bouffer** (fe) v.i, to puff, swell; rise; bulge. **bouffi, e** (fi) a, puffy, swollen, bloated; turgid, bombastic. **bouffir** (fi:r) v.t, to swell, bloat.

bouffon, ne (bufɔ̃, ɔn) a, comic(al), clownish, farcical. ¶ m, buffoon, jester, clown, merry andrew; laughing-stock, butt. **bouffonnerie** (fɔnri) f, buffoonery, foolery.

bouge (bu:ʒ) m, hole, hovel, den; bulge; bilge (cask).

bougeoir (buʒwa:r) m, [flat] candlestick.

bouger (buʒe) *v.i*, to budge, move, stir.

bougie (buʒi) *f*, candle. ~ *d'allumage*, sparking plug. ~ *de poche*, taper (coiled). ~ *filée*, taper (straight). *une lampe de 60* ~*s*, a 60 candle power lamp.

bougonner (bugɔne) *v.i*, to grumble, grouse.

bougran (bugrɑ̃) *m*, buckram.

bouillant, e (bujɑ̃, ɑ̃:t) *a*, boiling; fiery, hot-headed. **bouillie** (ji) *f*, pap; porridge, gruel; pulp; mush. **bouillir** (ji:r) *v.i.ir*, to boil. *faire* ~, to boil, *v.t*. ~ *à demi*, to parboil. **bouilloire** (jwa:r) *f*, kettle. ~ *à sifflet*, singing k. **bouillon** (jɔ̃) *m*, bubble; gush, spirt, spurt; broth, soup, bouillon, cup of broth, tea (beef, &c); slops (liquid diet); restaurant; blow[hole]; puff; returns (news-paper). **bouillonner** (jɔne) *v.i*, to bubble, boil, seethe. **bouillotte** (jɔt) *f*, kettle; foot warmer. ~ *à eau chaude*, hot-water bottle.

boujaron (buʒarɔ̃) *m*, tot (of rum, &c).

boulanger, ère (bulɑ̃ʒe, ɛ:r) *n*, baker. **boulangerie** (ʒri) *f*, baking; bakery.

boule (bul) *f*, ball; bowl, wood (Bowls). ~ *d'eau chaude*, hot-water bottle. ~ *de neige*, snowball; guelder rose. *[jeu de]* ~*s*, [game of] bowls.

Boule (bul) *m*, buhl[work].

bouleau (bulo) *m*, birch [tree]. ~ *blanc*, silver birch. *[verge de]* ~, birch [rod].

bouledogue (buldɔg) *m*, bulldog.

boulet (bulɛ) *m*, cannon ball; ball. **boulette** (lɛt) *f*, pellet.

boulevard (bulva:r) *m*, boulevard, avenue; bulwark (fig.).

bouleverser (bulvɛrse) *v.t*, to convulse, wreck, upset, overthrow.

boulier (bulje) *m*, ball frame, abacus; scoring board, string (Bil.).

boulin (bulɛ̃) *m*, pigeon hole (in dovecot); putlog.

boulingrin (bulɛ̃grɛ̃) *m*, lawn, grass plot.

boulon (bulɔ̃) *m*, bolt, pin. **boulonner** (lɔne) *v.t*, to bolt.

boulot, te (bulo, ɔt) *a*, dumpy, squat, squab[by], stumpy.

bouquet (bukɛ) *m*, bouquet, nosegay, posy, bunch, cluster, tuft, clump; aroma; crowning piece; climax; prawn, prawns. **bouquetière** (ktjɛ:r) *f*, flower girl.

bouquetin (buktɛ̃) *m*, ibex.

bouquin (bukɛ̃) *m*, old he-goat; buck hare; buck rabbit; [old] book (of little value). **bouquiner** (kinœ:r) *m*, book hunter; lover of old books. **bouquiniste** (nist) *m*, second-hand bookseller.

bourbe (burb) *f*, mud. **bourbeux, euse** (bø, ø:z) *a*, muddy. **bourbier** (bje) *m*, slough, quag[mire]; scrape, fix.

bourde (burd) *f*, fib; blunder. *débiter des* ~*s*, to fib. *donneur* (ou *conteur*) *de* ~*s*, fibber.

bourdon (burdɔ̃) *m*, pilgrim's staff; bumble-bee, humble-bee; great bell; drone (Mus.); drone (bee); out[, see copy] (Typ.). **bour-**

donner (dɔne) *v.i. & t*, to hum, buzz, drone, boom, din, sing (in ears).

bourg (bu:r) *m*, market town, borough. **bourgade** (burgad) *f*, small town, straggling village.

bourgeois, e (burʒwa, a:z) *a*, middle-class; homely, plain (cooking, &c); private (house). *en bourgeois*, in plain clothes, in mufti. ¶ *n*, middle-class man, woman. **bourgeoisie** (ʒwazi) *f*, middle class[es]; bourgeoisie.

bourgeon (burʒɔ̃) *m*, bud; shoot; pimple. **bourgeonner** (ʒɔne) *v.i*, to bud, &c.

bourgogne *ou* **vin de B**~ (burgɔɲ) *m*, burgundy.

bourrade (burad) *f*, blow, thump.

bourrasque (burask) *f*, squall; gust; tantrum.

bourre (bu:r) *f*, hair, flock, waste, down, fluff, floss; padding, stuffing, wad.

bourreau (buro) *m*, executioner, headsman, hangman; tyrant, tormentor. ~ *d'argent*, spendthrift. ~ *des cœurs*, lady-killer. **bourreler** (rle) *v.t*, (of conscience) to torment, prick, sting. *avoir une conscience bourrelée de remords*, to be conscience-stricken.

bourrelet (burlɛ) *m*, cushion; pad; flange. **bourrelier** (rɔlje) *m*, harness maker.

bourrer (bure) *v.t*, to stuff, pad; cram, choke; tamp, ram, pack; snap at; belabour, thrash.

bourriche (buriʃ) *f*, basket, frail.

bourrique (burik) *f*, she-ass; donkey.

bourru, e (bury) *a*, surly, churlish, crusty, grumpy, gruff; rough; downy. ¶ *m*, churl, bear, curmudgeon.

bourse (burs) *f*, purse, bag, pouch; scholar-ship, exhibition; exchange, ['change, market, house; session, business day, working day (on 'change). ~ *à pasteur*, shepherd's-purse (Bot.). ~ *[des valeurs]*, stock exchange. ~ *de marchandises*, ~ *de commerce*, produce exchange, commercial sale rooms. **boursicoter** (sikɔte) *v.i*, to dabble on the stock exchange. **boursier, ère** (sje, ɛ:r) *n*, foundation scholar, exhibitioner; operator (on 'change).

boursouflé, e (bursufle) *p.a*, inflated, turgid, bombastic. **boursoufler** (fle) *v.t. & se* ~, to swell, puff, bloat.

bousculade (buskylad) *f*, scrimmage, hustle, rush. **bousculer** (le) *v.t*, to upset; push about, jostle, hustle; ride out (Polo).

bouse (bu:z) *f*, dung (cattle).

bousillage (buzijaːʒ) *m*, cob, daub, mud; bungle, botch, jerry work.

boussole (busɔl) *f*, [magnetic] compass, dial; (fig.) head, wits; guide. ~ *marine*, mariner's compass.

bout (bu) *m*, end; finish; extremity, tip; cap; bottom; bit, stump; ferrule; button. *[petit]* ~ *d'homme*, midget, chit, manikin. ~ *de lettre*, line or two. ~ *de rôle*, small part (Theat.). *au* ~ *de son rouleau*, at the end of one's tether. *faire un* ~ *de* *toilette*, to tidy oneself up. **~** *de vergue*, yard arm. **~** *du sein*, nipple, teat. *à* **~** *portant*, point-blank. **~** *saigneux* (sɛɲø), scrag end (*mutton*, &c).

boutade (butad) *f*, whim, crotchet, fancy, fit; sally (*wit*). *par* **~s**, in fits & starts.

boute-en-train (butãtrɛ̃) *m*, life [& soul] (*of the party*).

boutefeu (butfø) (*fig.*) *m*, firebrand, mischief maker.

bouteille (butɛ:j) *f*, bottle, flask, jar. **~** *isolante*, vacuum flask.

boutique (butik) *f*, shop, stall, booth, stand; stock (*in shop*); shady concern; concern. **boutiquier, ère** (kje, ɛ:r) *n*, shopkeeper, tradesman, -woman.

boutoir (butwa:r) *m*, snout (*boar*).

bouton (butɔ̃) *m*, bud; pimple; button; stud (*collar*); knob, handle. **~** *à pression*, snap fastener. **~** *d'or*, buttercup. **~s** *de manchettes*, cuff (*or* sleeve) links. **~** *de manivelle*, crank pin. **~** *de sonnette*, bell push. **~** *du sein*, nipple, teat. **boutonner** (tɔne) *v.t*, to button [up]; (*v.i.*) to bud; break out in pimples. **se ~**, to button oneself up. **boutonnière** (njɛr) *f*, buttonhole; cut, gash.

bouture (buty:r) *f*, slip, cutting (*Hort.*).

bouverie (buvri) *f*, cattle pen, ox stall. **bouvier, ère** (vje, ɛ:r) *n*, ox-herd, neatherd, herdsman. **bouvillon** (vijɔ̃) *m*, steer.

bouvreuil (buvrœ:j) *m*, bullfinch.

bovin, e (bovɛ̃, in) *a*, bovine, neat, cattle (*att.*).

box (boks) *m*, loose box (*horse*). **~** *fermé*, lock-up [garage].

boxe (boks) *f*, boxing. **~** *à poings nus*, bare-fist boxing, knuckle fighting. **~** *contre son ombre*, shadow boxing. **boxer** (kse) *v.i. & t*, to box, spar. **boxeur** (ksœ:r) *m*, boxer. **~** *professionnel*, prize fighter.

boyau (bwajo) *m*, gut; hose (*pipe*); tubular [tire] (*bicycle*); passageway. **~** *de tranchée*, communication trench.

bracelet (braslɛ) *m*, bracelet, wristlet, strap, bangle. **~** *de force*, wrist strap. **~** *en caoutchouc*, elastic band, [india]rubber ring.

braconner (brakɔne) *v.i*, to poach. **braconnier** (nje) *m*, poacher.

braguette (bragɛt) *f*, fly (*trousers*).

brahmane (braman) *m*, brahmin.

brai (brɛ) *m*, pitch, tar.

brailler (braje) *v.i*, to bawl, squall.

braiment (bremɑ̃) *m*, bray[ing]. **braire** (brɛ:r) *v.i.ir*, to bray.

braise (brɛ:z) *f*, embers; breeze, cinders. **braiser** (brɛze) *v.t*, to braise. **braisière** (zjɛ:r) *f*, stewpan.

bramer (brame) *v.i*, to bell, troat.

brancard (brɑ̃ka:r) *m*, side sill; shaft, thill; stretcher, litter. **brancardier** (kardje) *m*, shaft horse, wheeler; stretcher bearer.

branchage (brɑ̃ʃa:ʒ) *m*, branches; horns. **branche** (brɑ̃:ʃ) *f*, branch; leg (*compass*, *tripod*); prong, tooth, tine; shank; stick.

~ *de tranchée*, communication trench. **~** *gourmande*, sucker (*Hort.*). **branchement** (brɑ̃ʃmɑ̃) *m*, branch[ing]; branch pipe; branch, tap (*Elec.*); lead (*Elec. service*); turnout (*Rly.*). **brancher** (ʃe) *v.t*, to branch; (*v.i.*) to perch. **branchette** (ʃɛt) *f*, twig. **branchies** (ʃi) *f.pl*, gills (*fish*).

brande (brɑ̃:d) *f*, heather; heath, moor[land].

brandiller (brɑ̃dije) *v.t*, to swing, dangle.

brandir (brɑ̃di:r) *v.t*, to brandish, flourish.

brandon (brɑ̃dɔ̃) *m*, [fire]brand; spark (*from conflagration*).

branlant, e (brɑ̃lɑ̃, ɑ̃:t) *a*, shaky, loose, rocking. **branle** (brɑ̃:l) *m*, swing[ing]; jangle; impulse, impetus; (*fig.*) dance, running, lead, example. **en ~bas** (brɑ̃lbɑ), astir, agog. **branler** (brɑ̃le) *v.t. & i*, to swing, shake, wag[gle], be loose, dance, bob.

braque (brak) *m*, hound; madcap. **braquer** (ke) *v.t*, to traverse (*gun*); point (*telescope*); fix (*eyes*).

bras (brɑ) *m*, arm; flipper; (*pl.*) hands (*workmen*); handle (*oar*, &c); brace (*Naut.*); (*pl.*) jaws (*of death*). **en ~** *de chemise*, in shirt sleeves. **~** *de mer*, arm of sea, sound. **~** *dessus*, **~** *dessous*, arm in arm. *à* [*force de*] **~**, [by] hand[-power], manual.

braser (brɑze) *v.t*, to braze, hard-solder.

brasero (brɑzero) *m*, brazier; fire basket. **brasier** (zje) *m*, bright fire; inferno. **brasiller** (zije) *v.t*, to broil; (*v.i.*) to sparkle.

brassage (brɑsa:ʒ) *m*, brewing; stirring.

brassard (brɑsa:r) *m*, armlet, brassard, badge, band.

brasse (brɑs) *f*, fathom (Fr. *brasse marine* = 1 metre 62; Eng. *fathom* = 6 feet); stroke (*distance covered at one swimming movement*); breast stroke. **brassée** (brɑse) *f*, armful; stroke (*one swimming movement*).

brasser (brɑse) *v.t*, to brew, mash; stir; dispatch, brace (*Naut.*). **brasserie** (sri) *f*, brewery, public house, brasserie. **brasseur** (sœ:r) *m*, brewer. **~** *d'affaires*, man with many irons in the fire; shady financier.

brassiage (brɑsja:ʒ) *m*, fathoming, sounding.

brassière (brɑsjɛ:r) *f*, vest (*baby's*); shoulder strap; (*pl.*) leading strings. **~** *de sauvetage*, life jacket, cork j.

brasure (brɑzy:r) *f*, brazing; braze (*joint*).

bravache (bravaʃ) *m*, blusterer, swaggerer, bully, hector. **bravade** (vad) *f*, bravado, bluster. **brave** (bra:v) *a*, brave, gallant, bold, stout; honest, good, worthy. ¶ *m*, brave man. *mon* **~**, my good man. **bravement** (bravmɑ̃) *ad*, bravely, &c; ably. **braver** (ve) *v.t*, to brave, face; dare, defy. **bravo** (vo) *ad*, bravo! hurrah, -ray! well done! hear! hear! ¶ *m*, cheer. **bravoure** (vu:r) *f*, bravery, gallantry.

brayer (brɛje) *m*, truss (*Surg.*).

break (brɛk) *m*, break, brake, waggonette.

brebis (brɛbi) *f*, ewe, sheep. **~** *galeuse*, plague, nuisance (*pers.*); black sheep (*fig.*).

brèche (brɛʃ) f, breach, gap; nick.

bredouille (brədu:j) a, empty-handed. **bre-douiller** (duje) v.i, to jabber, mumble.

bref, ève (brɛf, ɛ:v) a, brief; curt. [*syllabe*] brève, f, short [syllable]. **bref,** ad, briefly, in short, in fine.

breloque (brələk) f, charm (*seal, &c*).

brème (brɛm) f, bream (*fish*).

Brème (brɛ:m) f, Bremen.

Brésil (le) (brezil), Brazil. **brésilien, ne** (ljɛ̃, ɛn) a. & **B~,** n, Brazilian.

Bretagne (la) (brətaɲ), Brittany.

bretelle (brətɛl) f, brace, suspender, sling; (*pl.*) braces (*men's*); shoulder straps (*women's*).

breuil (brœ:j) m, covert (*game*).

breuvage (brœva:ʒ) m, beverage, drink; draught.

brevet (brəvɛ) m, diploma, certificate; licence; indentures (*apprenticeship*). ~ [*d'invention*], [letters] patent. **breveter** (vte) v.t, to patent; license.

bréviaire (brevjɛ:r) m, breviary; favourite author (*book*).

bribes (brib) f.pl, scraps, leavings; odds & ends; excerpts; snatches.

bric, ad : *de ~ & de broc* (brik, brɔk), here a little & there a little. **bric-à-brac** (kabrak) m, bric-à-brac.

brick (brik) m, brig (*Naut.*).

bricole (brikɔl) f, breast strap; (*pl.*) odd jobs.

bride (brid) f, bridle; rein[s]; curb, check; clamp, cramp; flange; treble (*Crochet*). *à toute ~, à ~ abattue*, at full speed. **brider** (de) v.t. & i, to bridle; check, curb; bind; pinch, be tight; clamp. *des yeux bridés*, slit (*or* almond) eyes.

bridge (bridʒ) m, bridge (*Cards*). ~ *aux enchères*, auction b. ~ *plafond*, ~ *contrat*, contract b.

brièvement (brievmɑ̃) ad, briefly, shortly. **brièveté** (vte) f, brevity, &c.

brigade (brigad) f, brigade; party, posse, gang. **brigadier** (dje) m, colonel commandant; bombardier; corporal (*cavalry*); sergeant (*police*); bowman (*boat*).

brigand (brigɑ̃) m, brigand, highwayman, robber; scamp. **brigandage** (da:ʒ) m, brigandage, highway robbery.

brigue (brig) f, intrigue; faction. **briguer** (ge) v.i. & t, to intrigue; intrigue for; canvass, court, aspire to.

brillamment (brijamɑ̃) ad, brilliantly, brightly. **brillant, e** (jɑ̃, ɑ̃:t) a, brilliant, bright, shining, glittering; blooming; splendid; glossy (*phot. paper*). ¶ m, brilliance, &c; brilliant (*diamond*). **brillantine** (jɑtin) f, brilliantine. **briller** (je) v.i, to shine, brighten; glitter, glisten, glow.

brimade (brimad) f, practical joke (*on new-comer*).

brimbale (brɛ̃bal) f, pump handle. **brim-baler** (le) v.i, to dangle; wobble.

brimborion (brɛ̃bɔrjɔ̃) m, [k]nick-[k]nack, bauble.

brin (brɛ̃) m, blade; slip, sprig; shoot; strand (*rope*); joint (*fishing rod*); bit. ~ *d'osier*, withe, withy. *un beau ~ d'homme, de fille*, a fine well made youth, girl. **brindille** (di:j) f, sprig, twig.

brioche (briɔʃ) f, brioche; blunder.

brique (brik) f, brick; bar (*soap, &c*).

briquet (brikɛ) m, lighter (*petrol, &c*); tinder box, [flint &] steel.

briquetage (brikta:ʒ) m, brickwork. **bri-queterie** (ktri) f, brickfield. **briquetier** (ktje) m, brickmaker. **briquette** (kɛt) f, briquet[te].

bris (bri) m, breaking; wreck[age]. **brisant** (zɑ̃) m, reef; breakwater; groyne; breaker (*wave*); (*pl.*) broken water.

brise (bri:z) f, breeze (*wind*).

brise-bise (brizbi:z) m, draught strip; short curtain, brise-bise. **brisées** (ze) f.pl, footsteps (*fig.*). **brise-jet** (brizʒe) m, anti-splash tap nozzle. **brise-lames** (lam) m, breakwater; groyne. **brisement** (zmɑ̃) m, breaking, &c, as **briser.** ~ *de cœur*, contrition (*Theol.*); heart break. **briser** (ze) v.t. & i, to break, smash, shatter, shiver, dash; knock up (*exhaust*). **se ~,** to break; come to pieces (*be detachable*), fold [up]. **brise-tout** (ztu) m, destructive person. **briseur** (zœ:r) m, breaker (*pers.*). **brisure** (zy:r) f, break; wristband; neck band.

britannique (britanik) a, British, Britannic. *les îles B~s*, the British Isles.

broc (bro) m, jug, pitcher. ~ *de toilette*, water jug, ewer.

brocanter (brokɑ̃te) v.i, to deal in works of art, curios, bargains, used goods.

brocard (broka:r) m, gibe, lampoon.

brocart (broka:r) m, brocade.

brochant sur le tout (broʃɑ̃), to cap all.

broche (broʃ) f, spit, broach; knitting needle; spindle, arbor; spike; pin, pin-tle; tommy [bar]; drift[pin]; brooch; (*pl.*) tusks (*wild boar*). **brochée** (ʃe) f, spitful.

brocher (ʃe) v.t, to brocade; stitch, sew (*books*); paper-cover; drift (*rivets*); scamp (*work*). **brochet** (ʃɛ) m, pike, jack (*fish*). **brochette** (ʃɛt) f, skewer. **brochure** (ʃy:r) f, interwoven pattern (*fabrics*); stitching, sewing; binding in paper wrappers *or* covers; pamphlet, booklet, brochure.

brocoli (brokɔli) m, broccoli.

brodequin (brodkɛ̃) m, lace boot; buskin; sock (*comedy*).

broder (brode) v.t, to embroider. **broderie** (dri) f, embroidery. ~ *à fils couchés*, couching. ~*application*, appliqué (*or* applied) work. **brodeur, euse** (dœ:r, ø:z) n, embroiderer, ess.

brome (bro:m) m, bromine. **bromure** (bromy:r) m, bromide.

broncher (brɔ̃ʃe) v.i, to stumble, trip; flinch, falter.

bronches (brõ:ʃ) *f.pl*, bronchia. **bronchite** (brõʃit) *f*, bronchitis.

bronze (brõ:z) *m*, bronze. ~ [*industriel*], gun metal. **bronzer** (brõze) *v.t*, to bronze; (*fig.*) steel, [case]harden.

broquette (brɔkɛt) *f*, [tin] tack(s).

brosse (brɔs) *f*, brush. ~ *à barbe*, shaving b. ~ *à cheveux*, ~ *à tête*, hairbrush. ~ *à cirer*, ~ *à étendre*, blacking b. ~ *à décrotter*, mud b. (*boots*). ~ *à dents*, tooth b. ~ *à frictions*, flesh b. ~ *à habits*, clothes b. ~ *à laver*, scrubbing b. ~ *à miettes* [*pour la table*], crumb b. ~ *à ongles*, nail b. ~ *à poêles*, stove b. ~ *à reluire*, polishing b. (*boots*). ~ *de garde-robe*, lavatory b. ~ *rude*, *douce*, hard, soft, b. **brossée** (se) *f*, brushing; beating, drubbing. **brosser** (se) *v.t*, to brush; scrub (*floor*); thrash, drub. *se ~ la tête, les dents*, to brush one's hair, teeth. **brosserie** (sri) *f*, brush making; b. works. **brossier, ère** (sje, ɛ:r) *n*, brush maker.

brou (bru) *m*, husk (*walnut, almond*); juice (*of walnut husk*).

brouette (bruɛt) *f*, [wheel]barrow.

brouhaha (bruaa) *m*, hubbub, din, pother.

brouillamini (brujamini) *m*, disorder, muddle.

brouillard (bruja:r) *m*, fog, mist, haze; rough book. **brouillasse** (jas) *f*, [Scotch] mist.

brouille (bru:j) *f*, discord, misunderstanding. **brouiller** (bruje) *v.t*, to jumble, muddle, blur, embroil; shuffle (*cards*); scramble (*eggs*). *se ~*, to break up (*weather*); fall out; fall foul, be at loggerheads. **brouillon, ne** (jõ, ɔn) *n*, muddler; (*m.*) [rough] draft; rough copy; rough book.

brouir (brui:r) *v.t*, to wither, blast, blight. **brouissure** (isy:r) *f*, blight.

broussailles (brusa:j) *f.pl*, brushwood, undergrowth, scrub. **brousse** (brus) *f*, bush (*scrub*).

broussin (brusɛ̃) *m*, gnarl (*on tree*).

brout (bru) *m*, browse. **brouter** (te) *v.t & abs*, to browse (on), nibble; chatter (*tool*). .

broutilles (bruti:j) *f.pl*, twigs; trifles.

broyer (brwaje) *v.t*, to crush, grind, mill.

bruant (bryɑ̃) *m*, bunting (*bird*).

brucelles (brysɛl) *f.pl*, tweezers.

brugnon (brynõ) *m*, nectarine.

bruine (bruin) *f*, drizzle, mizzle. **bruiner** (ne) *v.imp*, to drizzle, mizzle.

bruire (brui:r) *v.i.ir*, to murmur, rustle, sough. **bruissement** (ismɑ̃) *m*, murmur, &c.

bruit (brui) *m*, noise, row, racket, din, clatter, ado, fuss; rumour, report, news. ~ *de pas*, tramp.

brûlant, e (brylɑ̃, ɑ̃:t) *a*, burning, hot, scorching, broiling; afire. **brûle-gueule** (bryl) *m*, cutty (*pipe*). **brûle-parfum** (m), incense burner. **à brûle-pourpoint** (purpwɛ̃) *ad*, point-blank, to one's face. **brûlé** (le) *m*, burning (*smell, taste*). **brûler** (le) *v.t. & i*, to burn, scorch, parch, sear; singe; nip;

roast; mull (*wine*). *je me suis brûlé le bras*, I have burnt my arm. *se ~ la cervelle*, to blow one's brains out. **brûleur** (lœ:r) *m*, burner. ~ *à incandescence par le gaz*, incandescent gas burner. **brûlure** (ly:r) *f*, burn; scald.

brume (brym) *f*, fog, mist, haze. **brumeux, euse** (mø, ø:z) *a*, foggy, &c; wintry.

brun, e (brɛ̃, yn) *a*, brown; dark, dusky. ¶ *m*, brown; (*f.*) dusk, gloaming. **brunâtre** (brynɑ:tr) *a*, brownish. **brunet** (nɛ) *m*, dark man, dark boy. **brunette** (nɛt) *f*, brunette. **brunir** (ni:r) *v.t*, to brown; tan; burnish. **brunissage** (nisa:ʒ) *m*, burnishing.

brusque† (brysk) *a*, blunt, bluff, brusque, offhand, curt, abrupt, gruff. **brusquer** (ke) *v.t*, to treat abruptly; precipitate, rush. ~ *l'aventure*, to chance it. **brusquerie** (kəri) *f*, bluntness, &c.

brut, e (bryt) *a*, raw, crude; uncut (*gem*); unmanufactured; unpolished; unsweetened (*wine*); rough; gross (*Com.*); inorganic; brute (*beast, force*). **brutal, e†** (tal) *a*, brutal; brutish, coarse, rough. ¶ *m*, brute, bully. **brutaliser** (lize) *v.t*, to maltreat; bully. **brutalité** (te) *f*, brutality, &c. **brute** (bryt) *f*, brute.

Bruxelles (brysɛl) *f*, Brussels.

bruyant, e (brɥijɑ̃, ɑ̃:t) *a*, noisy, boisterous, rollicking, clamorous, loud, blatant; hoydenish. **bruyamment** (jamɑ̃) *ad*, noisily, &c.

bruyère (brɥijɛ:r) *f*, heather; heath; moor; brier, briar (*pipe wood*).

buanderie (bɥɑ̃dri) *f*, washhouse, laundry. **buandier, ère** (dje, ɛ:r) *n*, bleacher.

buccin (byksɛ̃) *m*, whelk (*Mol.*).

bûche (by:ʃ) *f*, log, billet, chump; Swiss roll; blockhead. ~ *de Noël*, yule log. **bûcher** (byʃe) *m*, wood shed; pile, stack (*firewood*); pyre; stake (*for burning alive*). ¶ *v.t. & i*, to rough-hew, dress, trim; fag (at); swot. **bûcheron** (frõ) *m*, woodman, lumberman. **bûchette** (ʃet) *f*, stick. **bûcheur, euse** (ʃœ:r, ø:z) *n*, plodder, brain worker.

bucolique (bykɔlik) *a. & f*, bucolic.

budget (bydʒe) *m*, budget; estimates (*parliamentary*).

buée (bɥe) *f*, steam, moisture; fumes.

buffet (byfe) *m*, cupboard; sideboard, buffet; refreshment bar *or* room; running buffet. ~ [*de cuisine*], ~-*étagère*, [kitchen] dresser.

buffle (byfl) *m*, buffalo. [*peau de*] ~, buff [leather].

bugle (bygl) *m*, flügel horn; (*f.*) bugle (*Bot.*).

buire (bɥi:r) *f*, beaker, flagon, jug.

buis (bɥi) *m*, box [tree]; boxwood.

buisson (bɥisõ) *m*, bush. **buissonneux, euse** (sɔnø, ø:z) *a*, bushy. **faire l'école buissonnière** (njɛ:r), to play truant.

bulbe (bylb) *f*, bulb (*Bot.*); (*m.*) bulb (*Anat.*). **bulbeux, euse** (bø, ø:z) *a*, bulbous.

bulgare (bylga:r) *a. & B~*, *n*, Bulgarian. **la Bulgarie** (gari), Bulgaria.

bulle (byl) *f*, bubble; blister, bleb; bull (*Pope's*).

bulletin (byltɛ̃) *m*, paper, note, bulletin; letter; ticket; voucher; form; list; report. ~ *de la cote*, stock exchange daily official list. ~ *de vote*, ballot (*or* voting) paper. ~ *météorologique*, weather forecast.

buraliste (byralist) *n, in France*, keeper of a state-owned tobacco shop (*bureau de tabac*), where also postage stamps are sold, & licences, such as for bicycles, are issued. **bureau** (ro) *m*, writing table; table, desk; bureau; office; counting house; agency; exchange; committee, executive. ~ *américain*, ~ *à rideau*, roll-top desk. ~ [*central téléphonique*], [telephone] exchange. ~ *d'esprit*, coterie of wits. ~ [*de location*], box office. ~ *de garantie*, government assay office. ~ *de placement*, employment agency, registry office. ~ *de police*, police station. ~ *de poste*, post office. ~ *de scrutin*, polling station. ~ *de tabac*, tobacconist's shop. ~ *de ville*, receiving office (*Rly*). ~ *des objets trouvés*, lost property office. ~ *des rebuts*, returned (*or* dead) letter office. ~ *ministre*, pedestal desk, knee-hole d. ~ *municipal de placement gratuit*, labour exchange. *à* ~[*x*] *ouvert*[*s*], on demand, on presentation. ~ *restant*, to be called for. *sur le* ~, (*matter*) under consideration. **bureaucrate** (krat) *m*, bureaucrat. **bureaucratie** (si) *f*, bureaucracy.

burette (byrɛt) *f*, bottle (*oil, vinegar*); cruet (*Eccl.*). ~ [*à huile*], oil can.

burin (byrɛ̃) *m*, graver; chisel. ~ [*à froid*], cold chisel. **buriner** (rine) *v.t*, to engrave; chisel, chip.

burlesque (byrlɛsk) *a. & m*, burlesque, farcical; comic(al).

buse (by:z) *f*, buzzard; air pipe; nozzle; blockhead.

buste (byst) *m*, bust.

but (by; *in liaison*, byt) *m*, butt, mark; target; goal; winning post; aim, object, end, intention, purpose, point. ~ *de transformation*, converted goal. *de* ~ *en blanc*, point-blank, bluntly. ~ *à* ~, even (*Games*).

butée (byte) *f*, abutment (*bridge*); shore (*prop*); thrust (*Mech.*); stop. **buter** (te) *v.i. & t*, to butt; stumble; shore. **se** ~ **à** (*fig.*), to be bent on; be up against.

butin (bytɛ̃) *m*, booty, spoil, loot, plunder. **butiner** (tine) *v.i. & t*, to pillage, plunder, loot.

butoir (bytwa:r) *m*, stop; stop blocks; buffer.

butor (byto:r) *m*, bittern; dolt.

butte (byt) *f*, mound, knoll, hillock; butts (*behind target*). **butter** (te) *v.t*, to ridge; earth, hill.

buvable (byvabl) *a*, drinkable. **buvard** (va:r) *m*, blotter, blotting pad *or* case. **buvette** (vɛt) *f*, refreshment bar *or* room; pump room (*spa*). **buveur, euse** (vœ:r, ø:z) *n*, drinker. ~ *d'eau*, teetotaller. **buvoter** (vote) *v.i*, to sip; tipple.

C

ça (sa) *pn*. Contraction of *cela*.

çà (sa) *ad*: ~ *& là*, here & there, hither & thither, this way & that. **ah!** *çà*, *i,* now then! come now! I say!

cabale (kabal) *f*, cabal; caucus. **cabaler** (le) *v.i*, to plot, intrigue.

cabane (kaban) *f*, cabin, hut; kennel; hutch. ~ *de bois*, log cabin, l. hut. **cabanon** (nɔ̃) *m*, padded cell.

cabaret (kabarɛ) *m*, wine shop *or* cellar; tavern, public house; restaurant; set *or* service (*china, liqueur, &c*). **cabaretier, ère** (bartje, ɛ:r) *n*, publican.

cabas (kaba) *m*, frail; shopping basket.

cabestan (kabɛstɑ̃) *m*, capstan; whim.

cabillaud (kabijo) *m*, cod[fish].

cabine (kabin) *f*, cabin; box; cage, car; call office (*Teleph.*).

cabinet (kabinɛ) *m*, room, closet; chambers; den; practice (*professional*); cabinet (*ministerial*); collection (*curiosities*). ~*s* ou ~ [*d'aisances*], [water] closet. ~ *de consultation*, consulting room, surgery. ~ *de débarras*, lumber room, box r. ~ *de lecture*, reading room, newsroom; lending library. ~ *de toilette*, dressing room, lavatory. ~ *de travail*, study. ~ *de verdure*, arbour, bower. ~ *noir*, dark room (*Phot.*). *vie de* ~, indoor life.

câble (ka:bl) *m*, rope, cable, line, wire, cord. **câbler** (kable) *v.t*, to cable (*Teleg.*).

caboche (kabɔʃ) *f*, pate, noddle, head; hobnail. **cabochon** (ʃɔ̃) *m*, cabochon; gimp nail.

cabosser (kabɔse) *v.t*, to dent, batter.

cabotage (kabota:ʒ) *m*, coasting; coasting trade, home trade. **caboter** (te) *v.i*, to coast. **caboteur** (tœ:r) *m*, coaster.

cabotin, e (kabotɛ̃, in) *n*, strolling player; mummer; theatrical person (*affected*).

cabrer (se) (kabre) *v.pr*, to rear; jib (*fig.*), take offence. **cabri** (kabri) *m*, kid (*goat*). **cabriole** (ɔl) *f*, caper. **cabrioler** (le) *v.i*, to caper. **cabriolet** (lɛ) *m*, gig, cabriolet; handcuffs (*of cord*).

cacahuète (kakawɛt) *f*, peanut, ground nut, monkey nut.

cacao (kakao) *m*, cacao, cocoa. **cacaoyer** (oje) *ou* **cacaotier** (otje) *m*, cacao [tree].

cacatoès (kakatɔɛs) *m*, cockatoo.

cachalot (kaʃalo) *m*, sperm whale, cachalot.

cache (kaʃ) *f*, hiding place; mask (*Phot.*). ~**-ampoule**, *m*, bulb shade (*Elec.*). ~**cache**, *m*, hide-&-seek. ~**-corset**, *m*, camisole, under bodice.

cachemire (kaʃmi:r) *m*, cashmere.

cache-nez (kaʃne) m, muffler, comforter, scarf. cache-pot (po) m, jardinière (pot). cache-poussière (pusjɛːr) m, dust coat. cacher (ʃe) v.t, to hide, conceal, secrete; mask. ~ son jeu, to be a dark horse (fig.). cachet (ʃɛ) m, seal, signet; cachet; ticket, voucher; stamp (fig.); fee, salary. cacheter (ʃte) v.t, to seal, do up. cachette (ʃɛt) f, hiding place. en ~, secretly, stealthily, covertly, on the sly. cachot (ʃo) m, dungeon, cell. cachotter (ʃote) v.t, to make a mystery of. cachottier, ère (tje, ɛːr) n, slyboots; (att.) secretive.
cachou (kaʃu) m, cachou.
cacochyme (kakoʃim) a, sensitive [to illness]; queer.
cacophonie (kakofoni) f, cacophony.
cactus (kaktyːs) m, cactus.
cadastre (kadastr) m, cadastral survey; valuation list (basis for rates & taxes). cadastrer (tre) v.t, to survey [& value]; enter (in valuation list).
cadavéreux, euse (kadaverø, øːz) a, cadaverous, corpse-like. cadavre (daːvr) m, corpse; carcass; skeleton.
cadeau (kado) m, present, gift.
cadenas (kadna) m, padlock. cadenasser (dnase) v.t, to padlock.
cadence (kadɑ̃ːs) f, cadence, rhythm, time, step; tune (fig.). aller en ~, to keep time.
cadet, te (kadɛ, ɛt) a. & n, younger (brother, sister); cadet, junior, minor; caddie (Golf); least (fig.). ~ éclaireur, forecaddie.
Cadix (kadiks) m, Cadiz.
cadran (kadrɑ̃) m, dial [plate], face [plate]. ~ [solaire], [sun] dial.
cadre (kɑːdr) m, frame, framework; frame aerial; limits, scheme, scope, compass. cadrer (kadre) v.i, to square, agree, tally, suit, fit, match.
caduc, uque (kadyk) a, broken, decrepit, declining, frail; lapsed, statute barred. caducité (dysite) f, dilapidated state; decrepitude, senile decay; lapsing, nullity.
cafard, e (kafaːr, ard) n, canter, hypocrite; tell-tale, sneak; (m.) cockroach, black beetle; desert madness.
café (kafe) m, coffee; café. ~ complet, coffee, roll & butter. caféier (feje) m, coffee tree; c. planter. cafetier, ère (ftje, ɛːr) n, café keeper, caterer; (f.) coffee pot.
cage (kaːʒ) f, cage; case, housing; shaft (lift). ~ à poulets, hen coop. ~ d'escalier, stair-case, stairway.
cagnard, e (kaɲaːr, ard) a, lazy, slothful. ¶ n, lazybones. cagnardise (ɲardiːz) f, laziness, sloth.
cagneux, euse (kaɲø, øːz) a, knock-kneed; crooked (legs).
cagnotte (kaɲot) (Cards) f, pool, kitty, pot.
cagot, e (kago, ɔt) n, hypocrite; (att.) sanctimonious.
cagoule (kagul) f, (monk's) hooded cloak; penitent's hood.

cahier (kaje) m, book (of blank forms, &c); exercise book; memorial. ~ d'écriture, copy book. ~ de copie, dit manifold, manifold book. ~ de dessin, sketch book. ~ des charges, specification.
cahin-caha (kaɛ̃kaa) ad, so so, middling. aller ~, to jog on.
cahot (kao) m, jolt, bump; vicissitude. cahoter (ote) v.t. & i, to jolt, bump; toss about.
cahute (kayt) f, hovel; hut.
caille (kaːj) f, quail.
caillé (kaje) m, caillebotte (kajbot) f, curd[s]. cailler (kaje) v.t. & se ~, to curd[le]; clot.
cailletage (kajta:ʒ) m, gossip. caillette (jɛt) f, gossip (pers.).
caillot (kajo) m, clot.
caillou (kaju) m, pebble; flint; stone; boulder (Geol.). caillouteux, euse (tø, øːz) a, pebbly; stony, flinty. cailloutis (ti) m, pebblestone, roadstones.
Caire (le) (kɛːr), Cairo.
caisse (kɛs) f, case, box; tub (for shrub); body (vehicle); drum; cash; cash box, till; coffer, chest; cashier's office or desk or counter, pay office; bank, treasury, fund, association. en ~, in (or on) hand, in the till. ~ à claire-voie, crate. ~ à eau, tank. ~ à médicaments, medicine chest. ~ claire, snare drum. ~ d'amortissement, sinking fund. ~ de dépôts, safe deposit (institution). ~ de prévoyance du personnel, staff provident fund. ~ de retraites pour la vieillesse, old age pension fund. ~ doublée de fer-blanc, tin-lined case. ~ enregistreuse, ~ contrôleuse, cash register. ~ nationale d'épargne [postale], post office savings bank.
caissier, ère (kɛsje, ɛːr) n, cashier; teller (bank). ~-comptable, cashier & book-keeper. ~ des titres, securities clerk.
caisson (kɛsɔ̃) m, caisson, pontoon; bin, bunker, box, locker.
cajoler (kaʒole) v.t, to cajole, wheedle, coax. cajolerie (lri) f, cajolery, &c.
cal (kal) m, callosity, callus.
calaison (kalɛzɔ̃) f, load draught (ship).
calamité (kalamite) f, calamity. calamiteux, euse (tø, øːz) a, calamitous.
calandre (kalɑ̃ːdr) f, calender; mangle; weevil. calandrer (lɑ̃dre) v.t, to calender; mangle.
calcaire (kalkɛːr) m, limestone. ¶ a, calcareous, lime[stone] (att.).
calcédoine (kalsedwan) f, c[h]alcedony.
calciner (kalsine) v.t, to calcine, burn.
calcium (kalsjɔm) m, calcium.
calcul (kalkyl) m, calculation, reckoning; arithmetic; sum; calculus, stone (Med.). calculer (le) v.t. & abs, to calculate, reckon.
cale (kal) f, hold (of ship); wedge, key, scotch. ~ [de construction], stocks, slip[s] (Ship-bldg). ~ de halage, slipway. ~ sèche, ~ de radoub, dry dock, graving d.

calebasse (kalbas) *f*, calabash, gourd.
caleçon (kalsɔ̃) *m*, pants, drawers. ~ *de bain*, bathing drawers. ~ *forme slip*, bathing slip.
calembour (kalɑ̃buːr) *m*, pun. *faire des* ~*s*, to pun. *faiseur de* ~*s*, punster.
calembredaine (kalɑ̃brədɛn) *f. oft. pl*, nonsense, foolery.
calendes (kalɑ̃ːd) *f.pl*, calends. ~ *grecques* (*fig.*), doomsday. **calendrier** (lɑ̃drie) *m*, calendar.
calepin (kalpɛ̃) *m*, notebook; working drawing.
caler (kale) *v.t. & i*, to wedge, key; scotch; draw (*so much water—ship*); strike (*sail*). ~ [*la voile*], to give in, knuckle down, k. under, sing small. *être calé en*, to be well up in (*subject*).
calfater (kalfate) *v.t*, to caulk.
calfeutrer (kalføtre) *v.t*, to list (*door*). **se** ~, to make oneself cosy, shut oneself in.
calibre (kalibr) *m*, calibre, bore; standing (*fig.*); gauge; template, pattern, shape; calliper[s]. **calibrer** (bre) *v.t*, to gauge, calliper, calibrate.
calice (kalis) *m*, chalice, communion cup; cup; calyx.
calicot (kaliko) *m*, calico.
calife (kalif) *m*, caliph.
Californie (la) (kalifɔrni), California. **californien, ne** (njɛ̃, ɛn) *a. & C*~, *n*, Californian.
califourchon (à) (kalifurʃɔ̃) *ad*, astride, astraddle.
câlin, e (kɑlɛ̃, in) *a*, caressing, wheedling. ¶ *n*, pet, darling; wheedler. **câliner** (ine) *v.t*, to fondle, pet, cuddle; wheedle. **câlinerie** (nri) *f*, fondling; wheedling.
calleux, euse (kalø, øːz) *a*, callous, horny.
calligraphie (kaligrafi) *f*, calligraphy, penmanship.
callosité (kalozite) *f*, callosity.
calmant (kalmɑ̃) *a*, sedative, soother.
calmar (kalmaːr) *m*, calamary, squid.
calme (kalm) *a*, calm, quiet, still; composed, collected, cool. ¶ *m*, calm, calmness, &c. ~ *plat*, dead calm. **calmer** (me) *v.t. & i. & se* ~, to calm, &c; soothe, salve; subside, abate.
calomnie (kalɔmni) *f*, calumny, slander. **calomnier** (nje) *v.t*, to calumniate, slander. **calomnieux, euse** (njø, øːz) *a*, calumnious, slanderous.
calorie (kalɔri) *f*, calorie. **calorifère** (rifɛːr) *m*, heater. ~ *à feu continu*, slow-combustion stove. **calorique** (rik) (*Phys.*), *m*, caloric, heat.
calot (kalo) *m*, forage cap. **calotte** (lɔt) *f*, skull cap; cap; calotte; canopy (*heaven*); cuff (*blow*). **calotter** (te) *v.t*, to cuff.
calque (kalk) *m*, tracing; copy (*fig.*). **calquer** (ke) *v.t*, to trace; copy.
calus (kaly:s) *m*, callus, callosity.
Calvaire (kalvɛːr) *m*, Calvary (*place*). **cal-**

vaire, *m*, calvary (*representation*); cross (*fig.*).
calvitie (kalvisi) *f*, baldness.
camarade (kamarad) *n*, comrade, fellow, mate, chum, companion. ~ *d'atelier*, fellow workman. ~ *d'école*, schoolfellow, schoolmate. ~ *de bord*, shipmate. ~ *de bouteille*, boon companion. ~ *de collège*, fellow student. ~ *de jeu*, playfellow, playmate. ~ *de lit*, ~ *de chambrée*, bedfellow, roommate. ~ *de malheur*, fellow sufferer. ~ *de plat*, messmate. ~ *de promotion*, class mate. **camaraderie** (dri) *f*, comradeship, fellowship, friendship.
camard, e (kamaːr, ard) *a*, snub-nosed. *la camarde*, [grim] death (*fig.*).
cambouis (kɑ̃bwi) *m*, cart grease.
cambrer (kɑ̃bre) *v.t. & se* ~, to camber, arch, bend, curve.
cambriolage (kɑ̃briɔlaːʒ) *m*, housebreaking, burglary. **cambrioler** (le) *v.t*, to burgle. **cambrioleur** (lœːr) *m*, burglar, cracksman. ~ *chat*, cat burglar.
cambrure (kɑ̃bryːr) *f*, camber. ~-*support*, *f*, arch support (*for foot in shoe*).
cambuse (kɑ̃byːz) *f*, steward's room (*ship*). **cambusier** (byzje) *m*, steward's mate.
came (kam) *f*, cam, wiper, lifter.
camée (kame) *m*, cameo.
caméléon (kamelɛɔ̃) *m*, chameleon; trimmer; time server.
camélia (kamelja) *m*, camellia.
camelot (kamlo) *m*, camlet; cheap Jack, hawker, street vender (*as news boy*); handbill distributor. **camelote** (lɔt) *f*, rubbish, trash.
camion (kamjɔ̃) *m*, lorry, wag[g]on, truck, troll[e]y; midget pin. ~-*citerne*, *m*, tank wagon. **camionnage** (ɔnaːʒ) *m*, cartage. **camionnette** (nɛt) *f*, light (*motor*) lorry. **camionneur** (nœr) *m*, lorry driver, carter, carman; van horse, vanner.
camisole (kamizɔl) *f*, vest (*woman's*). ~ *de force*, strait waistcoat.
camomille (kamɔmiːj) *f*, c[h]amomile.
camouflage (kamuflaːʒ) *m*, camouflage. **camoufler** (fle) *v.t*, to disguise, camouflage. **camouflet** (kamufle) *m*, snub.
camp (kɑ̃) *m*, camp, field; side. ~ *de concentration* (*civil*), ~ *de prisonniers* (*Mil.*), internment camp. ~ *volant*, flying column; flying visit.
campagnard, e (kɑ̃paɲaːr, ard) *n*, countryman, -woman. **campagne** (paɲ) *f*, country, countryside, fields; field (*Mil.*); campaign; run; cruise (*Nav.*).
campagnol (kɑ̃paɲɔl) *m*, vole.
campanile (kɑ̃panil) *m*, campanile, bell tower.
campanule (kɑ̃panyl) *f*, campanula, bell [flower]. ~ *à grandes fleurs*, Canterbury Bell.
campêche (kɑ̃pɛʃ) *m*, logwood.
campement (kɑ̃pmɑ̃) *m*, encampment; camping [out]. **camper** (pe) *v.i. & t*, to [en]-

camp; lodge, ensconce; put, clap, stick. ~ *là*, to leave in the lurch.

camphre (kã:fr) *m*, camphor. **camphrer** (kãfre) *v.t*, to camphorate.

campos (kãpo) *m*, holiday.

camus, e (kamy, y:z) *a*, flat-nosed, snub-nosed; pug-nosed.

Canada (le) (kanada), Canada. **canadien, ne** (djɛ̃, ɛn) *a. & C~, n*, Canadian.

canaille (kanɑ:j) *f*, rabble, mob, riff-raff, ragtag [& bobtail], tag-rag [& bobtail]; blackguard, cad, scoundrel, rascal.

canal (kanal) *m*, canal, channel, duct, pipe, passage, race[way], ditch, sluice[way]. ~ *de dérivation*, leat. ~ *maritime*, ship canal. **canalisation** (lizasjɔ̃) *f*, canalization, piping, pipe line; mains. **canaliser** (ze) *v.t*, to canalize, pipe; (*fig.*) concentrate, focus, centralize.

canapé (kanape) *m*, sofa, couch, lounge. ~*-divan*, chesterfield. ~*-lit*, lounge bed.

canard (kana:r) *m*, duck, drake; canard, hoax; rag (*worthless newspaper*). *bâtiment* ~, pitching ship. **canarder** (narde) *v.t*, to snipe (*Mil.*); pepper (*with shot*); (*v.i.*) to pitch (*ship*). **canardière** (djɛ:r) *f*, duck pond; decoy (*place*); fowling piece.

canari (kanari) *m*, canary (*bird*). **les [îles] Canaries**, *f.pl*, the Canary Islands, the Canaries.

cancan (kãkã) *m*, cancan (*dance*); tattle, scandal, backbiting.

cancer (kãsɛ:r) *m*, cancer (*Med.*). **cancéreux, euse** (serø, ø:z) *a*, cancerous.

cancre (kã:kr) *m*, crab (*Crust.*); dunce, duffer.

cancrelat (kãkrəla) *m*, cockroach.

candélabre (kãdela:br) *m*, candelabrum; multi-light standard.

candeur (kãdœ:r) *f*, guilelessness, ingenuousness.

candidat, e (kãdida, at) *n*, candidate; examinee. ~ *à la députation*, parliamentary candidate. **candidature** (ty:r) *f*, candidature.

candide† (kãdid) *a*, guileless, ingenuous.

candir (se) (kãdi:r) *v.pr*, to candy. *fruits candis* (di), crystallized fruits. [**sucre**] **candi** (di) *m*, [sugar] candy.

cane (kan) *f*, duck (*female*). **caner** (ne) *v.i*, to funk, run away, show the white feather. **caneton** (ntɔ̃) *m*, duckling (*male*). **canette** (nɛt) *f*, duckling (*female*); [spring-stoppered] bottle (*for, or of, beer*); bobbin.

canevas (kanva) *m*, canvas; sketch, groundwork, outline, skeleton.

caniche (kaniʃ) *n. & a*, poodle.

canicule (kanikyl) *f*, dog days.

canif (kanif) *m*, penknife.

canin, e (kanɛ̃, in) *a*, canine, dog (*att.*).

caniveau (kanivo) *m*, gutter, gully, kennel [stone]; conduit.

canne (kan) *f*, cane; stick; walking stick; singlestick. ~ *à épée*, sword stick. ~ *à lancer*, casting rod (*Fish.*). ~ *à mouche*,

fly rod (*Fish.*). ~ *à pêche*, fishing rod. ~ *à sucre*, sugar cane. ~ *plombée*, loaded stick. ~*-siège*, sportsman's seat, stick s.

canneberge (kanbɛrʒ) *f*, cranberry.

canneler (kanle) *v.t*, to channel, flute, groove, corrugate, rifle.

cannelle (kanɛl) *f*, cinnamon; butt cock.

cannelure (kanly:r) *f*, channel[ling], &c, as *canneler*.

canner (kane) *v.t*, to cane (*chairs*).

cannibale (kanibal) *m*, cannibal, man eater; savage (*fierce man*).

canoë (kanoe) *m*, canoe (*Canadian, &c*).

canon (kanɔ̃) *m*, gun, cannon; cañon, canyon; barrel, pipe, tube; canon (*rule—Eccl.*). ~ *d'amarrage*, bollard. ~ *de campagne à tir rapide*, quick-firing field gun. *droit* ~, canon law. **canonicat** (nɔnika) *m*, canonicate, canonry; sinecure. **canoniser** (ze) *v.t*, to canonize, saint. **canonnade** (nad) *f*, cannonade. **canonnage** (na:ʒ) *m*, gunnery. **canonner** (ne) *v.t*, to cannonade, bombard, shell. **canonnier** (nje) *m*, gunner. **canonnière** (njɛ:r) *f*, gunboat; pop gun (*toy*).

canot (kano) *m*, boat; dingh[e]y; cutter. ~ *à rames*, rowboat. ~ *de sauvetage*, lifeboat. **canotage** (nota:ʒ) *m*, boating, rowing. **canoter** (te) *v.i*, to boat, row. **canotier** (tje) *m*, rower, oarsman; boatman, waterman; boat keeper. [*chapeau*] ~, boater.

cantate (kãtat) *f*, cantata. **cantatrice** (tris) *f*, professional singer (*woman*), vocalist.

cantharide (kãtarid) *f*, Spanish fly.

cantine (kãtin) *f*, canteen. **cantinier, ère** (nje, ɛ:r) *n*, canteen keeper.

cantique (kãtik) *m*, canticle, song, hymn.

canton (kãtɔ̃) *m*, canton, district. **cantonade** (tonad) *f*, wings (*Theat.*). **cantonnement** (nmã) *m*, cantonment, quarters; billets. ~ *de pêche*, stretch of fishing. **cantonner** (ne) *v.t. & i*, to canton, quarter, billet. *se ~ dans*, to withdraw to; keep oneself to. **cantonnier** (nje) *m*, roadman, road mender.

canule (kanyl) *f*, nozzle; butt cock.

caoutchouc (kautʃu) *m*, india[rubber], elastic; [rubber] tire; waterproof, mackintosh; galosh, golosh, overshoe. **caoutchouter** (ʃute) *v.t*, to rubber[ize], waterproof; rubber-tire.

cap (kap) *m*, cape, headland, foreland; head. ~ *à pic*, bluff. *le ~ de Bonne-Espérance*, the Cape of Good Hope. *le ~ Vert*, Cape Verde.

capable (kapabl) *a*, capable; able, fit; efficient, qualified. **capacité** (site) *f*, capacity, capability, &c.

caparaçonner (kaparasɔne) *v.t*, to caparison.

cape (kap) *f*, hooded cape; hood; bowler [hat]. *rire sous* ~, to laugh up one's sleeve, chuckle. **capeline** (plin) *f*, hood.

capharnaüm (kafarnaɔm) *m*, jumble shop.

capiliaire (kapillɛːr) *a*, capillary. ¶ *m*, maidenhair [fern].

capilotade (kapilɔtad) *f*, hash; pulp.

capitaine (kapitɛn) *m*, captain; master, skipper. ~ *au long cours*, deep-sea captain, master of foreign-going vessel. ~ *d'armement*, marine superintendent. ~ *d'entraînement*, coach. ~ *de corvette*, lieutenant commander (*Nav.*). ~ *de frégate*, commander (*Nav.*). ~ *de port*, harbour master. ~ *de vaisseau*, captain (*Nav.*). ~ *marchand*, captain of merchant ship, master mariner.

capital, e (kapital) *a*, capital, principal, main, essential; deadly (*sins*). ¶ *m. oft. pl*, principal, capital, capital sum; capital stock; money; assets. ~*-actions*, *m*, share capital. ~ *de roulement*, working capital. ~ *engagé*, trading capital. *le* ~ *& le travail*, Capital & Labour. ¶ *f*, capital (*town*, *letter*); metropolis. **capitaliser** (lize) *v.t*, to capitalize. **capitaliste** (list) *n*, capitalist.

capitan (kapitã) *m*, blusterer.

capitation (kapitasjɔ̃) *f*, poll tax.

capiteux, euse (kapitø, øːz) *a*, heady.

capitonner (kapitɔne) *v.t*, to upholster; quilt.

capituler (kapityle) *v.i*, to capitulate; compromise (*with conscience*).

capon, ne (kapɔ̃, ɔn) *n*, coward; sneak (*Sch.*).

caporal (kapɔral) *m*, corporal; caporal (*tobacco*).

capot (kapo) *m*, bonnet, hood, cover. *être* ~, to be abashed. *faire* ~, to capsize.

capote (pɔt) *f*, greatcoat, overcoat (*Mil.*); hood, bonnet, cowl. **capoter** (te) *v.i*, to capsize, overturn.

câpre (kɑːpr) *f*, caper (*Bot.*).

caprice (kapris) *m*, caprice, whim, freak; [passing] fancy; vagary. **capricieux, euse†** (sjø, øːz) *a*, capricious, &c; temperamental; wayward.

capsule (kapsyl) *f*, capsule; seal (*bottle*); [percussion] cap.

capter (kapte) *v.t*, to catch, collect, save, recover; obtain by undue influence. *vouloir* ~, to make a bid for.

captieux, euse (kapsjø, øːz) *a*, captious.

captif, ive (kaptif, iːv) *a. & n*, captive. **captiver** (ve) *v.t*, to captivate. **captivité** (vite) *f*, captivity; bondage. **capture** (ty:r) *f*, capture. **capturer** (tyre) *v.t*, to capture, take; catch.

capuce (kapys) *m*, **capuchon** (fɔ̃) *m*, hood, cowl.

capucin, e (kapysɛ̃, in) *n*, Capuchin friar, nun; (*f.*) nasturtium. **capucinade** (sinad) *f*, dull discourse.

caque (kak) *f*, barrel, keg. **caquer** (ke) *v.t*, to cure (*herrings*); barrel.

caquet (kakɛ) *m*, cackle; chatter. **caqueter** (kte) *v.i*, to cackle, &c.

car (kaːr) *c*, for, because.

carabin (karabɛ̃) *m*, medical student; sawbones. **carabine** (bin) *f*, carbine, rifle. **carabiné, e** (ne) *a*, strong, stiff.

caracole (karakɔl) *f*, caracol[e].

caractère (karaktɛːr) *m*, character; characteristic, property, nature; complexion; authority; temper; type, (*pl.*) print. ~ *à jour*, stencil. *écrire en* ~*s d'imprimerie*, to write in block letters. **caractériser** (terize) *v.t*, to characterize. **caractéristique** (ristik) *a*, characteristic. ¶ *f*, characteristic, feature.

carafe (karaf) *f*, water bottle, jug, decanter. **carafon** (fɔ̃) *m*, [small] decanter.

carambolage (karɑ̃bɔlaːʒ) *m*, cannon (*Bil.*).

caramel (karamɛl) *m*, caramel.

carapace (karapas) *f*, carapace, shell.

carat (kara) *m*, carat; carat goods. *sot à vingt-quatre* (ou *à trente-six*) ~*s*, champion idiot, out & out fool.

caravane (karavan) *f*, caravan. **caravansérail** (vãsera:j) *m*, caravanserai.

carbonate (karbɔnat) *m*, carbonate. **carbone** (bɔn) *m*, carbon. **carbonifère** (nifɛːr) *a*, carboniferous, coal[-bearing]. **carbonique** (nik) *a*, carbonic. **carboniser** (ze) *v.t*, to carbonize, char. **carbonnade** (nad) *f*, grill[ed meat]. *à la* ~, grilled.

carburateur (karbyratœːr) *m*, carburettor. **carbure** (by:r) *m*, carbide.

carcan (karkã) *m*, carcan (*Hist.*); yoke.

carcasse (karkas) *f*, carcass, carcase, body, skeleton, shell, frame[work]; shape (*hat*, &c).

cardiaque (kardjak) *a*, cardiac. ¶ *n*, heart case (*pers.*).

cardinal, e (kardinal) *a*, cardinal. ¶ *m*, cardinal (*Eccl.*).

carême (karɛːm) *m*, lent.

carence (karɑ̃ːs) *f*, assets nil; insolvency.

carène (karɛn) *f*, bottom (*of ship*). **caréner** (rene) *v.t*, to careen.

caresse (karɛs) *f*, caress, endearment; blandishment. **caresser** (se) *v.t*, to caress; fondle; stroke; pat; cherish; flatter; indulge.

cargaison (kargɛzɔ̃) *f*, cargo, lading.

cari (kari) *m*, curry.

caricature (karikaty:r) *f*, caricature; cartoon; guy, sight. **caricaturer** (tyre) *v.t*, to caricature. **caricaturiste** (rist) *n*, caricaturist, cartoonist.

carie (kari) *f*, caries, decay; rot. **carier** (rje) *v.t. & se* ~, to rot, decay.

carillon (karijɔ̃) *m*, chime[s]; carillon; peal; racket, row. **carillonner** (jɔne) *v.i & t*, to chime, ring a peal; clatter; noise abroad. **carillonneur** (nœːr) *m*, [bell] ringer.

carlin (karlɛ̃) *m*, pug [dog].

carlingue (karlɛ̃ːg) *f*, ke[e]lson (*Naut.*); cockpit (*Aero.*).

carme (karm) *m*, Carmelite [friar]. **carmélite** (melit) *f*, Carmelite [nun].

carmin (karmɛ̃) *m*, carmine.

carnage (karnaːʒ) *m*, carnage, slaughter, bloodshed. **carnassier, ère** (nasje, ɛːr) *a*, carnivorous. ¶ *m*, carnivore; (*f.*) game-bag.

carnaval (karnaval) *m*, carnival; guy.

carné, e (karne) *a*, flesh-coloured; meaty (*food*); meat (*diet*).

carneau (karno) *m*, flue.

carnet (karnɛ), *m*, notebook, memorandum book; book. ~ *d'alimentation*, ration book. ~ *de bal*, dance programme. ~ *de chèques*, cheque book. ~ *de compte*, ~ *de banque*, [bank] pass book. ~ *de passages en douane*, pass book (*motor car*). ~ *de poche à feuillets mobiles*, loose-leaf pocket-book. ~ *de timbres*, book of stamps. ~ *de voyage*, book of travel coupons.

carnier (karnje) *m*, game bag. carnivore (nivɔ:r) *a*, carnivorous. ~s, *m.pl*, carnivora.

caroncule (karɔ̃kyl) *f*, wattle (*turkey*).

carotte (karɔt) *f*, carrot; bore core; plug, twist (*tobacco*); trick. *des cheveux* [*rouge*] ~, carroty hair, ginger hair.

caroube (karub) *f*, carob [bean], locust [bean].

Carpathes (les) (karpat) *m.pl*, the Carpathians.

carpe (karp) *f*, carp (*fish*).

carpette (karpɛt) *f*, bordered [& seamless] carpet; rug.

carquois (karkwa) *m*, quiver (*for arrows*).

carré, e (kαre) *a*, square. ¶ *m*, square; bed, patch (*Hort.*); landing, floor. ~ *des officiers*, ward room; mess room. ~ *long*, rectangle, oblong. carreau (ro) *m*, tile; floor; squab, cushion; hassock; diamonds (*Cards*); pane, square. carrefour (karfu:r) *m*, cross roads; circus (*in city*). *de* ~, street (*musician*); gutter (*language*). carrelage (rlaːʒ) *m*, tile floor[ing]. ~ *en briques*, brick paving. carrelet (rlɛ) *m*, square ruler; square file; plaice. carrément (remɑ̃) *ad*, square[ly], outright, flat[ly], straightforwardly. carrer (re) *v.t*, to square. se ~, to strut, swagger; settle oneself.

carrier (karje) *m*, quarryman. carrière (ɛːr) *f*, career, course, scope, play, vent; head; walk of life; quarry, pit.

carrosse (karɔs) *m*, coach. carrosserie (sri) *f*, coachbuilding; (*motor*) body; bodywork. carrossier (sje) *m*, coachbuilder; [motor] body builder; coach horse.

carrousel (karuzɛl) *m*, tournament; round-about, merry-go-round, whirligig.

cartable (kartabl) *m*, satchel (*Sch.*).

carte (kart) *f*, card; ticket; map, chart. ~s *à jouer*, playing cards. ~ *à payer* reckoning. ~ *blanche*, free hand, full discretionary power. ~ *céleste*, star map, map of the heavens. ~ *d'abonnement*, season ticket. ~ *d'adresse*, address card, business c. ~ *d'État-major*, ordnance [survey] map. ~ *de résultats*, scoring card (*Golf*). ~ [*de visite*], [visiting] card. ~ *des vins*, wine list. ~ *du jour*, bill of fare, menu. ~ *en courbes de niveau*, contour map. ~-*lettre*, letter card. ~ *peinte*,

court card. ~ *postale illustrée*, picture postcard.

cartel (kartɛl) *m*, challenge; cartel; coalition.

carter (kartɛːr) *m*, gear case.

cartilage (kartilaːʒ) *m*, cartilage, gristle.

cartographe (kartɔgraf) *m*, cartographer, map producer.

cartomancien, ne (kartɔmɑ̃sjɛ̃, ɛn) *n*, fortune teller (*by cards*).

carton (kartɔ̃) *m*, cardboard, pasteboard, millboard; [cardboard] box *or* case, carton; mount (*Phot.*); cartoon; offcut (*Bookb.*); cancel (*Bookb.*). ~ *à chapeau*, hat box. ~ *d'en bas*, inset (*Bookb.*). ~ *d'en haut*, outset (*Bookb.*). ~ *de débarquement*, landing ticket. ~ *de dessins*, portfolio of drawings. ~ *de modiste*, bandbox. ~-*paille*, *m*, strawboard. ~ *pâte*, *m*, papier mâché. ~ *pour coller les épreuves*, paste-on mount. cartonné, e (tɔne) *p.a*, in boards (*book*). cartonnier (nje) *m*, cardboard [box] maker; document cabinet.

cartouche (kartuʃ) *f*, cartridge, round [of ammunition]; case (*firework*); (*m.*) cartouche. ~ *à balle*, ball cartridge. ~ *à blanc*, blank c. cartoucherie (ʃri) *f*, cartridge factory. cartouchière (ʃjɛːr) *f*, cartridge pouch.

carvi (karvi) *m*, caraway.

cas (kα) *m*, case, event, circumstance, instance; matter; cause (*Law*). ~ *limite*, border-line case.

casanier, ère (kazanje, ɛːr) *a. & n*, stay-at-home.

casaque (kazak) *f*, jumper (*woman's*). *tourner* ~, to rat (*Pol.*).

cascade (kaskad) *f*, cascade, waterfall, fall[s]; prank, spree; gag (*actor's*). cascatelle (tɛl) *f*, cascade.

case (kɑːz) *f*, compartment, division, pigeon hole; square (*chessboard*); frame, space (*on printed form*); locker; bin; native hut, cabin.

casemate (kazmat) *f*, casemate.

caser (kaze) *v.t*, to put away; find a situation for, settle.

caserne (kazɛrn) *f*, barrack[s]. caserner (ne) *v.t*, to barrack.

casier (kazje) *m*, cabinet, nest of drawers, [set of] pigeon holes; bin; rack. ~ *judiciaire*, police records.

casino (kazino) *m*, casino, kursaal.

Caspienne (la mer) (kaspjɛn), the Caspian sea.

casque (kask) *m*, helmet; head-phones, ear-phones. ~ *de soleil*, ~ *colonial*, sun helmet. ~ *en moelle*, pith helmet, sola topi, -ee. c. ~ *respiratoire*, smoke helmet, gas mask (*fire*). casquette (kɛt) *f*, (*man's or boy's*) [peak] cap.

cassant, e (kαsα̃, α̃:t) *a*, brittle, crisp, short, hard; blunt, curt. cassation (sαsjɔ̃) *f*, cassation, quashing; reduction to the ranks. **casse** (kɑːs) *f*, breakage, breakages; cassia; case (*Typ.*); ladle, scoop. ¶ (kɑs) *comps*: ~-*cou*, *m*, breakneck [place], death trap; dare-devil; rough-rider; (*i.*) look out! mind! ~-*croûte*, *m*, snack; s. bar. ~ -*noisettes*, *m*, nut-crackers; nuthatch. ~-*noix*, *m*, nut-crackers; nut-cracker (*bird*). ~-*pierres*, *m*, stone breaker (*Mach.*). ~-*tête*, *m*, club, life preserver; puzzle, teaser. **casser** (kɑse) *v.t. & i*, to break, crack, snap; shatter; quash, set aside (*Law*); cashier; reduce to the ranks. ~ *aux gages*, to pay off. *se* ~ *la tête*, to break one's head; puzzle (*or* rack) one's brains.

casserole (kɑsrɔl) *f*, saucepan, stewpan. ~ [*en terre cuite*], casserole.

cassette (kɑset) *f*, casket; case; money box; privy purse.

casseur (kɑsœːr) *m*, breaker. ~ *d'assiettes*, brawler.

cassier (kɑsje) *m*, cassia tree.

cassine (kɑsin) *f*, country cottage.

cassis (kɑsis) *m*, black currant(s); b. c. bush; b. c. cordial; water bar (*across road*).

cassonade (kɑsɔnad) *f*, moist sugar, brown s.

cassure (kɑsyːr) *f*, break, crack, fracture.

castagnette (kɑstaɲet) *f*, castanet.

caste (kɑst) *f*, caste.

castor (kɑstɔːr) *m*, beaver. ~ *du Canada*, musquash (*fur*).

castration (kɑstrasjɔ̃) *f*, castration; gelding.

casuel, le (kɑzɥel) *a*, casual; case (*ending— Gram.*). ¶ *m*, casual profits; perquisites.

casuistique (kɑzɥistik) *f*, casuistry.

cataclysme (kataklism) *m*, cataclysm, disaster.

catacombe (katakɔ̃ːb) *f*, catacomb.

catafalque (katafalk) *m*, catafalque.

catalogue (katalɔg) *m*, catalogue, list. ~ *par ordre de matières*, subject catalogue. ~ *raisonné*, descriptive c. **cataloguer** (ge) *v.t*, to catalogue, list.

cataplasme (kataplasm) *m*, poultice.

catapulte (katapylt) *f*, catapult (*Hist. & Aero.*).

cataracte (katarakt) *f*, cataract (*falls & Med.*); (*pl.*) sluice gates (*of heaven*).

catarrhe (kataːr) *m*, catarrh.

catastrophe (katastrɔf) *f*, catastrophe.

catéchiser (kateʃize) *v.t*, to catechize; reason with, try to persuade. **catéchisme** (ʃism) *m*, catechism.

catégorie (kategɔri) *f*, category, class; predicament (*Log.*). **catégorique**† (rik) *a*, categorical; flat (*refusal*).

cathédrale (katedral) *f*, cathedral, minster.

cathode (katɔd) *f*, cathode.

catholicisme (katolisism) *m*, catholicism, Roman Catholicism. **catholique** (lik) *a*, catholic, Roman Catholic; orthodox. ¶ *n*, catholic, Roman Catholic.

catimini (en) (katimini) *ad*, stealthily, on the sly.

Caucase (le) (kokɑːz), the Caucasus. **caucasien, ne** (kɑzjɛ̃, ɛn) *a. & C~*, *n*, Caucasian.

cauchemar (koʃmaːr) *m*, nightmare, incubus; bugbear.

caudataire (kodatɛːr) *m*, train bearer; toady, toadeater, lickspittle.

cause (koːz) *f*, cause, occasion, ground[s]; case, action (*Law*); brief (*Law*); consideration (*equivalent*, *Law*). ~ *célèbre*, famous case. *à* ~ *de*, on account of, because of, for; for the sake of, through. *en tout état de* ~, in any case. *& pour* ~, & for good reasons, & very properly. *sans* ~, briefless (*barrister*). **causer** (koze) *v.t*, to cause, occasion.

causer (koze) *v.i*, to talk, converse, chat; talk of; sit out (*a dance*). *assez causé!* that'll do! **causerie** (zri) *f*, talk, chat, chit-chat; causerie. **causette** (zet) *f*, little chat. **causeur, euse** (zœːr, øːz) *n*, talker, conversation[al]ist; (*f.*) settee.

caustique (kostik) *a*, caustic, biting, cutting. ¶ *m*, caustic (*Phar.*).

cauteleux, euse (kotlø, øːz) *a*, cunning, crafty.

cautère (kotɛːr) *m*, cautery. **cautériser** (terize) *v.t*, to cauterize, sear.

caution (kosjɔ̃) *f*, surety, security, guarantee, -ty, guarantor, indemnity, bail. ~ *judicatum solvi*, security for costs. *sujet à* ~, unreliable. **cautionnement** (ɔnmã) *m*, security, indemnity, deposit, bail, surety (*or* indemnity) bond, qualification (*in shares*). **cautionner** (ne) *v.t*, to become security for, guarantee, bail; give security for, answer for.

cavalcade (kavalkad) *f*, cavalcade; pageant; ride.

cavalerie (kavalri) *f*, cavalry; horse (*troop*); stable (*horses*). **cavalier, èret** (lje, ɛːr) *a*, offhand, cavalier; free & easy; riding (*track*); bridle (*path*). ¶ *m*, horseman, rider, equestrian; trooper; gentleman, man; cavalier, escort; partner (*at dance*); knight (*Chess*); [wire] staple. ¶ *f*, horsewoman, rider, equestrian.

cave (kaːv) *a*, hollow, sunk[en]. ¶ *f*, cellar, vault; pool (*Cards*). ~ *à liqueurs*, liqueur case *or* set; tantalus. ~ *forte*, strong room. **caveau** (kavo) *m*, [small] cellar; vault (*family grave*). **caver** (ve) *v.t*, to hollow, scoop out, [under]mine, wear away *or* hollow; put up (*money at cards*). **caverne** (vɛrn) *f*, cavern, cave; den. **caverneux, euse** (nø, øːz) *a*, cavernous, hollow.

caviar (kavjaːr) *m*, caviar[e].

cavité (kavite) *f*, cavity, hollow.

cawcher, ère (kauʃe, ɛːr) *a*, kosher.

ce, cet, cette, *pl.* **ces** (sə, sɛt, sɛt, se) *a*, this; that; such [a]; (*pl.*) these; those; such. *cette rue-ci & non cette rue-là*, this street & not that street. *ce soir*, this evening, to-night. *cette nuit*, last night.

ce (sə), **c' ou ç' as in** c'est, ç'a été, *pn*, it; this; that; he, she; they; they; those. *c'est-à-dire* (*abb.* c.-à-d.) that is to say, i.e., viz. *ce que*, what, that which.

ceci (səsi) *pn*, this.

cécité (sesite) *f*, blindness. ∼ *des neiges*, snow b. ∼ *pour les couleurs*, colour b.

cédant, e (sedã, ã:t) *n*, transferor, assignor.

céder (de) *v.t. & i. & abs*, to cede, yield, give up; give in, surrender, cave in; assign, transfer; dispose of, give way. [*le*] ∼ *à*, to yield [the palm] to, be second to.

cédille (sedi:j) *f*, cedilla.

cédrat (sedra) *m*, citron.

cèdre (sɛ:dr) *m*, cedar. ∼ *du Liban* (libã), c. of Lebanon.

cédule (sedyl) *f*, schedule (*Inc. Tax*).

ceindre (sɛ̃:dr) *v.t.ir*, to surround, [en]-compass, [en]circle, gird[le], belt, wreathe. **ceinture** (sɛ̃ty:r), *f*, belt, girdle, sash, waistband; waist, middle; waist lock (*Wrestling*); enclosure. ∼ *cartouchière*, cartridge belt. ∼ *de sauvetage*, life b. ∼ *porte-jarretelles*, suspender b. ∼ *ventrière* (vãtrɛ:r), abdominal b. **ceinturer** (tyre) *v.t*, to grasp round the body. **ceinturon** (rõ) *m*, belt (*sword, &c*).

cela (səla) *pn*, that; it; so. *c'est* ∼, that is it; that's right, just so. **célèbre** (selɛbr) *a*, celebrated, famous, noted. **célébrer** (lebre) *v.t*, to celebrate; solemnize, hold (*funeral*); sing (*praises of*). **célébrité** (brite) *f*, celebrity.

celer (səle) *v.t*, to conceal, hide.

céleri (selri) *m*, celery.

célérité (selerite) *f*, celerity, swiftness, dispatch.

céleste (selɛst) *a*, celestial, heavenly; of the heavens (*map*), star (*map*); sky (*blue*).

célibat (seliba) *m*, celibacy, single life. **célibataire** (tɛ:r) *n*, bachelor, celibate, single man, woman.

cellérier (selerje) *m*, cellarer. **cellier** (lje) *m*, still room.

cellulaire (sɛlylɛ:r) *a*, cellular. **cellule** (lyl) *f*, cell. **celluloïd** (lɔid) *m*, celluloid. **cellulose** (lo:z) *f*, cellulose.

Celte (sɛlt) *n*, Celt, Kelt. **celtique** (tik) *a. & m.* (*language*), Celtic, Keltic.

celui, celle, *pl.* **ceux, celles** (səlɥi, sɛl, sø, sɛl) *pn*, he, she, those; the one. *celui-ci, celle-ci*, this one, this, the latter. *celui-là, celle-là*, that one, that, the former.

cémenter (semãte) *v.t*, to cement (*metal*); caseharden.

cendre (sã:dr) *f. oft. pl*, ash[es]; dust; embers. **cendré, e** (sãdre) *a*, ash[-coloured], ashen, ashy; grey (*brain matter*). ¶ *f*, cinders (*track*). **cendrier** (drie) *m*, ash pan; ash tray. ∼ *sur pied*, smokers' stand.

Cendrillon (sãdrijõ) *f*, Cinderella.

Cène (sɛn) *f*, Last Supper; Lord's supper.

cenelle (sənɛl) *f*, haw; holly berry.

cénotaphe (senotaf) *m*, cenotaph.

censé, e (sãse) *a*, deemed, reputed, supposed. **censément** (mã) *ad*, supposedly, virtually. **censeur** (sœ:r) *m*, censor; critic; auditor; vice principal (*college*); examiner (*plays*). **censure** (sy:r) *f*, censorship; [vote of] censure; [board of] censors. **censurer** (syre) *v.t*, to censure, criticize, find fault with, reprehend.

cent (sã) *a. & m*, hundred. **centaine** (tɛn) *f*, hundred [or so], about a hundred.

centaure (sãto:r) *m*, centaur.

centenaire (sãtnɛ:r) *n*, centenarian; (*m*.) centenary.

centième (sãtjɛm) *a. & m*, hundredth.

centigrade (sãtigrad) *a*, centigrade. Water freezes 0° Cent. = 32 Fahr. Water boils 100° C. = 212 F. *To convert* :—F. = $\frac{9}{5}$ C. + 32 [thus, 100 C. × 9 = 900 ÷ 5 = 180 + 32 = 212 F.] C. = $\frac{5}{9}$ (F. − 32) [thus, 212 F. − 32 = 180 × 5 = 900 ÷ 9 = 100 C.].

centigramme (sãtigram) *m*, centigramme = $\frac{1}{100}$ gramme *or* 0·154 grain. **centilitre** (sãtilitr) *m*, centilitre = $\frac{1}{100}$ litre *or* 0·070 gill.

centime (sãtim) *m*, centime = $\frac{1}{100}$ of franc. **centimètre** (sãtimɛtr) *m*, centimetre = $\frac{1}{100}$ metre *or* 0·3937 inch; tape measure (divided into cms, 1½ metres long). ∼ *carré*, square centimetre = 0·15500 sq. inch. ∼ *cube*, cubic centimetre = 0·0610 cub. inch.

central, e (sãtral) *a*, central. **centraliser** (lize) *v.t*, to centralize. **centre** (sã:tr) *m*, centre, middle; hub (*fig*.). ∼ *de table*, table centre. ∼ *de villégiature*, holiday resort. **centrer** (sãtre) *v.t*, to centre. **centrifuge** (trify:ʒ) *a*, centrifugal. **centripète** (pɛt) *a*, centripetal.

centuple (sãtypl) *m*, centuple, hundredfold.

cep (sɛp) *m*, stock (*vine*); (*pl*.) stocks (*Hist*.). **cépée** (sepe) *f*, head of shoots (*willow, &c*).

cependant (səpãdã) *ad*, in the mean time, meantime, meanwhile. ¶ *c*, yet, nevertheless, though.

céramique (seramik) *f*, ceramics.

cerceau (sɛrso) *m*, hoop; cradle (*Surg*.).

cercle (sɛrkl) *m*, circle; ring, hoop, band; club (*of people*). ∼ *des fées*, fairy ring. *en* ∼*s*, in the wood (*wine*). **cercler** (kle) *v.t*, to hoop (*casks*).

cercueil (sɛrkœ:j) *m*, coffin, shell.

céréale (sereal) *a.f. & f*, cereal.

cérébral, e (serebral) *a*, cerebral, brain (*att*.). **cérémonial** (seremɔnjal) *m*, ceremonial. **cérémonie** (ni) *f*, ceremony, circumstance, fuss, ado, to-do. **cérémonieux, euse** (njø, ø:z) *a*, ceremonious, formal.

cerf (sɛ:r & sɛrf) *m*, stag, hart, deer.

cerfeuil (sɛrfœ:j) *m*, chervil.

cerf-volant (sɛrvɔlã) *m*, stag beetle; kite (*paper*).

cerisaie (sərize) *f*, cherry orchard. **cerise** (ri:z) *f*, cherry. ¶ *a. & m*, cherry-red; cerise. **cerisier** (rizje) *m*, cherry [tree].

cerne (sɛrn) *m*, ring (*tree, eyes, moon*), circle. **cerner** (ne) *v.t*, to surround, [en]circle, [en]compass, ring, hem in; invest (*Mil.*); shell (*nuts*); dig round (*tree*). *les yeux cernés*, rings under the eyes.

certain, e (sɛrtɛ̃, ɛn) *a*, certain; sure; stated; some. *le certain*, *le certain*, fixed (*rate of*) exchange. **certainement** (tɛnmã) *ad*, certainly, of course, by all means. **certes** (sɛrt) *ad*, most certainly, indeed.

certificat (sɛrtifika) *m*, certificate, scrip; testimonial, character. ~ *d'action(s)*, share certificate. ~ *nominatif*, registered (*share*) certificate or scrip. ~ *international de route*, international travelling pass. **certifier** (fje) *v.t*, to certify; witness.

certitude (sɛrtityd) *f*, certainty.

céruse (seryːz) *f*, ceruse, white lead.

cerveau (sɛrvo) *m*, brain; brains, intellect, mind, head. ~ *brûlé*, madcap, hothead. **cervelle** (vɛl) *f*, brain[s], mind, head; pith (*palm tree*); (*s. & pl. Cook.*) brains. *rompre la* ~ *à quelqu'un*, to drive someone crazy.

Cervin (le mont) (sɛrvɛ̃), the Matterhorn.

cessation (sɛsasjɔ̃) *f*, cessation, discontinuance; suspension. *sans cesse* (sɛs), without cease, unceasingly. **cesser** (se) *v.i. & t*, to cease, leave off, break off, stop. *faire* ~, to put a stop to.

cessible (sɛsibl) *a*, transferable. **cession** (sjɔ̃) *f*, transfer, assignment. **cessionnaire** (onɛːr) *n*, transferee.

Ceylan (selã) *m*, Ceylon.

chablis (ʃabli) *m*, windfall (*tree*); Chablis (*wine*).

chabot (ʃabo) *m*, chub (*fish*).

chacal (ʃakal) *m*, jackal.

chacun, e (ʃakœ̃, yn) *pn*, each, each one, every one. ¶ *m*, everybody, everyone, every one.

chafouin, e (ʃafwɛ̃, in) *a. & n*, sorry (*fellow*), poor (*creature*).

chagrin, e (ʃagrɛ̃, in) *a*, sorrowful, glum, moody, grieved, vexed, fretful. ¶ *m*, grief, sorrow, vexation, fret[fulness], chagrin; shagreen, chagreen. ~ *d'amour*, disappointment in love. **chagriner** (grine) *v.t*, to grieve, afflict; vex. *se* ~, to grieve, fret, repine.

chah (ʃa) *m*, shah.

chahut (ʃay) *m*, rag (*Sch.*); shindy.

chaîne (ʃɛːn) *f*, chain; range (*hills*); (*pl.*) fetters, bonds; warp. ~ *de mailles*, chain of stitches, casting off (*Knit.*). *faire une* ~ *de mailles*, to cast off. **chaînette** (ʃɛnɛt) *f*, chain (*small*). **chaînon** (nɔ̃) *m*, link. ~ *manquant*, missing link.

chair (ʃɛːr) *f. sometimes pl*, flesh; meat; pulp (*of fruit*). ~ *à pâté*, mincemeat. ~*s baveuses*, proud flesh. ~ *de poule*, goose flesh (*fig.*). *cela fait venir la* ~ *de poule*, it makes one's flesh creep.

chaire (ʃɛːr) *f*, pulpit; desk; throne (*bishop's*); chair, professorship; mastership; see.

chaise (ʃɛːz) *f*, chair, seat; stall (*choir*); hanger (*Mach.*). ~ *à porteurs*, sedan [chair]. ~ *de pont*, deck chair. ~ *longue*, couch. ~ *paillée*, rush-seat chair. ~ [*percée*], [night] commode. ~ *pliante* [*pour enfant*], folder (*pram*). ~ *roulante* [*pour enfant*], mail cart.

chaland (ʃalã) *m*, barge, lighter, scow. **chaland, e** (ʃalã, ãːd) *n*, customer, patron.

châle (ʃaːl) *m*, shawl, wrap.

chalet (ʃalɛ) *m*, chalet, cottage. ~ *de nécessité*, public convenience.

chaleur (ʃalœːr) *f*, heat, warmth, glow. **chaleureux, euse†** (lœrø, øːz) *a*, warm (*fig.*), cordial.

chaloupe (ʃalup) *f*, launch, longboat. ~ *canonnière*, gunboat.

chalumeau (ʃalymo) *m*, blowpipe; reed; drinking straw; [shepherd's] pipe.

chalut (ʃaly) *m*, trawl [net]. **chalutier** (tje) *m*, trawler.

chamade (ʃamad) *f*, parley, chamade.

chamailler (se) (ʃamɑje) *v.pr*, to bicker, wrangle, squabble, brawl.

chamarrer (ʃamare) *v.t*, to bedizen, bedeck; lard (*fig.*).

chambranle (ʃãbrɑ̃ːl) *m*, jamb lining.

chambre (ʃãːbr) *f*, room, chamber, apartment, lodging; cabin (*ship's*); house; committee; court. ~ *à air*, inner tube (*tire*). ~ [*à coucher*], [bed]room. ~ *à deux lits*, double[-bedded] room. ~ *à un lit*, single r. ~ *d'ami*, guest chamber, spare [bed]room. ~ *d'enfants*, nursery. ~ *d'explosion*, combustion chamber (*motor*). ~ *de chauffe*, stokehole; boiler room. ~ *de compensation*, clearing house. ~ *de* [*mise à*] *mort*, lethal chamber. *C*~ *des communes, des pairs*, House of Commons, of Lords. *C*~ *des députés*, Chamber of Deputies. ~ *des valeurs*, strong room (*ship*). ~*s en enfilade*, suite of rooms. ~ *sur le derrière*, ~ *sur la cour*, back room. ~ *sur le devant*, ~ *sur la rue*, front r. ~ *syndicale des agents de change*, stock exchange committee. ~ *noire*, ~ *obscure*, camera obscura (*Opt.*). ~ [*noire*] *photographique*, photographic camera. ~ *à forme rigide*, box c. ~ *à magasin*, magazine c. ~ *à main à foyer fixe*, fixed-focus hand c. ~ *à mise au point*, focussing c. ~ *à obturateur de plaque*, focal-plane c. ~ *à pellicules en bobines se chargeant en plein jour*, daylight-loading roll-film c. ~ *à pied*, field c., stand c. ~ *d'agrandissement*, enlarging c. ~ *d'atelier*, studio c. ~ *détective*, detective c. ~ *pliante*, folding c. ~ *réflex*, reflex c. ~ *se mettant dans la poche du gilet*, vest-pocket c. **chambrée** (ʃãbre) *f*, roomful; house (*audience*); barrack room. **chambrer** (bre) *v.t*, to confine, closet; chamber, hollow out; take the chill off (*wine*).

chameau (ʃamo) *m*, camel. chamelier (məlje) *m*, c. driver. chamelle (mɛl) *f*, she camel.

chamois (ʃamwa) *m*, chamois. [peau de] ~, wash leather, chamois (or shammy) [leather].

champ (ʃã) *m*, field; ground; scope; range; edge. ~s communs, common [land]. ~ d'aviation, aviation (or flying) ground, aerodrome. ~ de courses, racecourse. ~ de manœuvres, drill ground, parade g. ~ de massacre, shambles. ~ de tir, rifle range, shooting r. ~ du repos, churchyard, God's Acre.

champagne ou vin de C~ (ʃãpaɲ) *m*, champagne. ~ frappé [de glace], iced c.

champêtre (ʃãpɛːtr) *a*, rural, country (att.), rustic, sylvan.

champignon (ʃãpiɲɔ̃) *m*, cowl. ~ [comestible], mushroom. ~ [vénéneux], fungus, toadstool. champignonnière (nɔnjɛːr) *f*, mushroom bed.

champion (ʃãpjɔ̃) *m*, champion. championnat (ɔna) *m*, championship.

chance (ʃãːs) *f*, chance; luck.

chanceler (ʃãsle) *v.i*, to totter, reel, stagger; waver, falter.

chancelier (ʃãsəlje) *m*, chancellor. chancelière (ljɛːr) *f*, foot muff. chancellerie (sɛlri) *f*, chancellery.

chanceux, euse (ʃãsø, øːz) *a*, lucky; hazardous.

chancre (ʃãːkr) *m*, canker; chancre.

chandail (ʃãdaːj) *m*, sweater (Dress).

chandelier (ʃãdəlje) *m*, chandler; candlestick. chandelle (dɛl) *f*, candle; prop, post, shore; lob (Ten.).

chanfrein (ʃãfrɛ̃) *m*, chamfer; forehead (horse).

change (ʃãːʒ) *m*, exchange (Fin.). changeant, e (ʃãʒã, ãːt) *a*, changeable, variable; fitful; fickle; shot (fabrics). changement (ʃmã) *m*, change, alteration; turn (tide); shift (wind, &c); amendment (to document). ~ à vue, transformation scene. ~ de décor[ation], scene shifting. ~ de marche, reversing; r. gear. ~ de vitesse, change [-speed] gear. ~ [de voie], switch, points (Rly). changer (ʒe) *v.t. & abs. & i*, to change, alter; turn; exchange; shift; amend. ~ d'avis, de linge, to change one's mind, one's linen. ~ de pas, to change step. changeur (ʃœːr) *m*, money changer.

chanoine (ʃanwan) *m*, canon (Eccl.).

chanson (ʃãsɔ̃) *f*, song, ballad, ditty; lay; matter, story. ~ [de bord], [sea] chanty, [sea] shanty. ~ de circonstance, topical song. ~ de route, marching song. ~s, [~s]! nonsense! humbug! fiddlesticks! chansonner (sɔne) *v.t*, to lampoon. chansonnette (nɛt) *f*, ditty; comic song. chansonnier, ère (nje, ɛːr) *n*, song writer; (m.) song book.

hant (ʃã) *m*, singing, song, lay, chant; melody; canto; warbling, crowing, chirp.

~ d'allégresse, carol. ~ du coq, cockcrow[ing]. ~ du cygne, swan song. ~ funèbre, ~ de mort, dirge, lament. de ~, edgeways, edgewise, on edge.

chantage (ʃãtaːʒ) *m*, blackmail.

chantant, e (ʃãtã, ãːt) *a*, musical, tuneful; singsong.

chanteau (ʃãto) *m*, [c]hunk, hunch; cutting (snip of cloth).

chanter (ʃãte) *v.i. & t*, to sing, chant, play the air; warble, crow, chirp; talk [about]; say, cry. ~ toujours la même antienne, to be always harping on the same string. ~ victoire sur, to crow over. faire ~ quelqu'un, to blackmail someone. chanterelle (trɛl) *f*, highest string; call bird. chanteur, euse (tœːr, øːz) *n*, singer, vocalist; songster, songstress; (att.) song (bird).

chantier (ʃãtje) *m*, yard; floor (foundry); stocks (Shipbldg); dunnage; gantry, scantling (for cask). ~ de dépôt, dump, tip.

chantonner (ʃãtɔne) *v.i*, to hum (tune).

chantourner (ʃãturne) *v.t*, to jig-saw.

chantre (ʃãːtr) *m*, cantor; Bard.

chanvre (ʃãːvr) *m*, hemp.

chaos (kao) *m*, chaos; [state of] pie. chaotique (ɔtik) *a*, chaotic.

chape (ʃap) *f*, cope; chape; cover, cap, lid; shell; strap; bearings; coating, covering.

chapeau (ʃapo) *m*, hat, bonnet; cap, cover, hood. ~ à cornes, cocked hat. ~ claque, crush h., opera h. ~ [du capitaine], primage. ~ haut de forme, ~ de soie, high hat, silk h. ~ melon, bowler [h.]. ~ rabattu, slouch h. ~ souple, Trilby [h.].

chapechute (ʃapʃyt) *f*, godsend, windfall.

chapelain (ʃaplɛ̃) *m*, chaplain.

chapelet (ʃaplɛ) *m*, chaplet; [string of] beads; string, rope.

chapelier (ʃapəlje) *m*, hatter. [malle] chapelière (ɛːr) *f*, Saratoga [trunk].

chapelle (ʃapɛl) *f*, chapel; meeting house; [church] plate; coterie, set. ~ ardente, chapelle ardente. ~ de la Vierge, Lady chapel. ~ sépulcrale, mortuary chapel.

chapellerie (ʃapɛlri) *f*, hat trade; h. shop.

chapelure (ʃaplyːr) *f*, grated bread crumbs.

chaperon (ʃaprɔ̃) *m*, chaperon; coping. chaperonner (prɔne) *v.t*, to chaperon; cope (wall).

chapiteau (ʃapito) *m*, capital (Arch.); head, cap, top.

chapitre (ʃapitr) *m*, chapter (book, canons); head[ing], item; subject, matter, point. chapitrer (tre) *v.t*, to lecture, reprimand.

chapon (ʃapɔ̃) *m*, capon.

chaque (ʃak) *a*, each, every; either.

char (ʃaːr) *m*, chariot; car. ~ à bancs, charabanc (horse). ~ d'assaut, tank (Mil.). ~ [de deuil], ~ funèbre, hearse.

charade (ʃarad) *f*, charade; conundrum.

charançon (ʃarãsɔ̃) *m*, weevil.

charbon (ʃarbɔ̃) *m*, coal[s]; charcoal; carbon; embers; carbuncle (Med.); anthrax; smut

(*Agric.*).　~ *à dessin*, charcoal [pencil].
~ *à vapeur*, steam coal.　~ *de ménage*,
house c.　~ *de soute*, bunker c.　~ *sans
fumée*, smokeless c. *en* ~, burnt to a
cinder (*meat*, &c.). *faire du* ~, to coal.
sur des ~*s* [*ardents*], on tenterhooks.
charbonnage (bɔna:ʒ) *m*, coal mining; (*pl.*)
collieries. **charbonner** (ne) *v.t*, to black
(*face*, &c). **se** ~, *v.pr. ou* ~, *v.i*, to char,
carbonize; (*v.i.*) to smoke (*lamp*). **charbonnerie** (nri) *f*, coal yard. **charbonnier**
(nje) *m*, charcoal burner; coal merchant;
coalman; coal cellar; collier (*ship*).
charcuter (ʃarkyte) *v.t*, to hack, mangle (*in
carving*). **charcuterie** (tri) *f*, pork butchery; [dressed] pork, pig meat. **charcutier,
ère** (tje, ɛ:r) *n*, pork butcher.
chardon (ʃardɔ̃) *m*, thistle; ·spikes. ~ *à
bonnetier*, ~ *à foulon*, teasel. **chardonneret** (dɔnrɛ) *m*, goldfinch.
charge (ʃarʒ) *f*, load, burden; charge, encumbrance, onus; expense; stress; pressure; head [of water]; loading; shipment;
cargo; trust, care, custody; cure (*of souls*);
duty, office; practice, membership, seat;
instructions, directions; caricature; over-
acting; impersonation (*Theat.*); joke. ~
à la cueillette, general cargo. *à* [*la*] ~ *de*,
on condition that, provided that. *à la*
~ *de*, chargeable to, payable by, at the
expense of; dependent on. *en* ~, live
(*Elec.*); load (*water line*); [now] loading
(*ship*). **chargé, e** (ʒe) *a*, loaded; full; live
(*shell*); furred (*tongue*); overcast, heavy
(*weather*); insured (*Post*). **chargé d'affaires**, *m*, chargé d'affaires. **chargement**
(ʒəmɑ̃) *m*, loading, lading; charging, filling;
shipping, shipment; cargo; consignment;
insurance (*Post*); insured packet. ~ *en
plein jour*, daylight loading (*Phot.*).
charger (ʒe) *v.t*, to load, lade, burden,
charge, fill; stress; inflate (*account*); clog,
saddle; lie heavy on; ship; instruct, order,
direct; entrust; overact; overdo; overdraw;
overcharge; caricature; [in]criminate; insure (*Post*). **se** ~ **de**, to undertake, take
charge of, attend to. **chargeur** (ʒœ:r)
m, charger, loader; shipper; stoker
(*Mach.*).
chariot (ʃarjo) *m*, truck, wag[g]on, wain,
troll[e]y, car; go-cart; carriage, carrier.
charitable† (ʃaritabl) *a*, charitable, benevolent. **charité** (te) *f*, charity; alms; dole.
charivari (ʃarivari) *m*, charivari, hubbub.
charlatan (ʃarlatɑ̃) *m*, charlatan, quack.
charlatanerie (tanri) *f*, quackery.
charmant, e (ʃarmɑ̃, ɑ̃:t) *a*, charming, fascinating, delightful. **charme** (ʃarm) *m*,
charm, spell; attraction, allurement; hornbeam, yoke elm. *sous le* ~, spellbound.
charmer (me) *v.t*, to charm, delight, bewitch; beguile, while away. **charmeur,
euse** (mœ:r, ø:z) *n*, charmer. **charmille**
(mi:j) *f*, hedge *or* bower (*of hornbeam*).

charnel, le† (ʃarnɛl) *a*, carnal, sensual.
charnier (nje) *m*, charnel house, ossuary.
charnière (ʃarnjɛ:r) *f*, hinge. *à* ~, *à* ~*s*,
hinged.
charnu, e (ʃarny) *a*, fleshy, brawny. **charnure**
(ny:r) *f*, flesh (*of pers.*). **charogne** (rɔɲ) *f*,
carrion.
charpente (ʃarpɑ̃:t) *f*, frame[work]. ~ [*en
bois*], timber work. ~ *en fer*, ironwork.
~ *métallique*, iron & steel constructional
work. **charpenter** (pɑ̃te) *v.t*, to carpenter,
frame, put together. **bien charpenté,
well-knit, well-built, of sturdy build.
charpenterie (tri) *f*, carpentry; (*ship's*)
timber yard. **charpentier** (tje) *m*, carpenter. ~ *de vaisseau*, shipwright. ~
en fer, ironworker.
charpie (ʃarpi) *f*, lint; shreds.
charretée (ʃarte) *f*, cartload. **charretier, ère**
(tje, ɛ:r) *n*, carter. **charrette** (rɛt) *f*, cart.
~ *anglaise*, dog cart, trap. **charrier** (rje)
v.t, to cart, carry, convey; drift. **charroi**
(rwa) *m*, cartage. **charroyer** (rwaje) *v.t*,
to cart. **charron** (rɔ̃) *m*, wheelwright.
charrue (ʃary) *f*, plough. ~ *multiple*, gang p.
charte (ʃart) *f*, charter; deed (*ancient*).
~*-partie*, *f*, charter [party]. ~ *de grain*,
grain charter.
chartreuse (ʃartrø:z) *f*, Carthusian monastery;
lone cottage; chartreuse (*liqueur*). **chartreux** (trø) *m*, Carthusian [monk].
chas (ʃa) *m*, eye (*needle*, &c).
chasse (ʃas) *f*, chase, hunt, hunting; shooting;
shoot; pursuit; kill (*of game*); play, clearance (*Mech.*); set (*of saw teeth*); (*pl.*)
squares (*Bookbinding*). ~ *à courre*
(ku:r), hunt[ing] (*riding to hounds*). ~ *à
la grosse bête*, big-game hunting. ~ *au
cerf à l'affût*, deer stalking. ~ *au lévrier*,
coursing. ~ *aux oiseaux*, fowling. ~
d'air, blast (*or* rush) of air. ~ [*d'eau*],
flush, scour. ~ *gardée*, ~ *réservée*,
[game] preserves.
châsse (ʃɑ:s) *f*, reliquary, shrine; frame
(*spectacles*); scales (*lancet*).
chassé (ʃase) *m*, chassé (*Danc.*).
chasse-mouches (ʃasmuʃ) *m*, fly whisk; fly
net. **chasse-neige** (nɛ:ʒ) *m*, snow squall;
snow plough.
chasser (ʃase) *v.t. & abs. & i*, to drive, drive
away *or* out *or* off *or* in; expel; chase;
chevy, chivy; hound out; hunt; shoot;
course; pursue; dismiss; dispel; drift;
drag (*anchor*); chassé (*Danc.*). ~ *à
l'affût*, to stalk. **chasseur, euse** (sœ:r, ø:z)
n, hunter, huntress, huntsman; -catcher
(*butterflies*, &c); messenger, commissionaire, page [boy]; fighter, chaser (*Aero.*).
chassieux, euse (ʃasjø, ø:z) *a*, gummy (*eyes*),
blear-eyed.
châssis (ʃasi) *m*, frame; sash; chassis (*motor*);
panel (*Radio*); chase (*Typ.*); flat (*Theat.*);
stretcher (*for painter's canvas*). ~ *à
fiches*, casement, French sash. ~ *à glace*

dépolie pour la mise au point, ground-glass focussing screen (*Phot.*). ~ *à rouleaux*, spool holder (*Phot.*). ~ *de couche*, forcing frame. ~ *négatif*, ~ *porte-plaque(s)*, dark slide, plate holder. ~-*presse*, printing frame (*Phot.*).

chaste (ʃast) *a*, chaste. **chasteté** (təte) *f*, chastity.

chasuble (ʃazybl) *f*, chasuble.

chat (ʃa) *m*, **chatte** (ʃat) *f*, cat, tom [cat]; he cat, she cat, puss, pussy [cat]; (*m.*) touch [last], tag (*game*). *le Chat botté*, Puss in Boots. ~ *cambrioleur* ~, cat burglar. ~ *d'Espagne*, tortoise-shell cat. ~ *de Siam*, Siamese c. ~ *de gouttières*, stray c. ~ *persan*, ~ *angora*, Persian c.

châtaigne (ʃatɛɲ) *f*, [sweet] chestnut. **châtaignier** (nje) *m*, chestnut [tree]. **châtain, e** (tɛ̃, ɛn) *a*, [chestnut-] brown (*hair*).

château (ʃato) *m*, castle; palace; manor [house], [country] seat, mansion, hall. ~ *d'eau*, water tower. ~ *de cartes*, house of cards. ~ *La Pompe*, Adam's ale. ~*x en Espagne*, castles in the air or in Spain. **châtelain** (tlɛ̃) *m*, lord of the manor, squire. **châtelaine** (tlɛn) *f*, lady of the manor; chatelaine, key chain.

chat-huant (ʃayɑ̃) *m*, tawny owl, brown o.

châtier (ʃatje) *v.t*, to chastise, castigate; chasten. **châtiment** (timɑ̃) *m*, chastisement, &c.

chatoiement (ʃatwamɑ̃) *m*, shimmer; sheen; play of light.

chaton (ʃatɔ̃) *m*, kitten; catkin; bezel, setting (*jewel*).

chatouiller (ʃatuje) *v.t*, to tickle; touch up. **chatouilleux, euse** (tujø, øːz) *a*, ticklish; touchy, sensitive.

chatoyant, e (ʃatwajɑ̃, ɑ̃ːt) *a*, iridescent; shot (*fabrics*). **chatoyer** (je) *v.i*, to shimmer, sparkle.

châtrer (ʃatre) *v.t*, to castrate, geld; prune, thin.

chattemite (ʃatmit) *f*, unctuous hypocrite, Chadband.

chatteries (ʃatri) *f.pl*, blandishments; delicacies, dainties.

chaud, e et (ʃo, oːd) *a*, hot, warm. *à chaud*, [while] hot. *pleurer à chaudes larmes*, to cry bitterly. *avoir chaud*, to be warm (*of pers.*).

chaudière (ʃodjɛːr) *f*, boiler; copper. **chaudron** (drɔ̃) *m*, ca[u]ldron, pot. [**petite**] **chaudronnerie** (drɔnri) *f*, coppersmith's [& brazier's] trade. [**grosse**] **chaudronnerie**, boiler-making *or* works. **chaudronnier** (nje) *m*, coppersmith, brazier; boiler maker. ~ *ambulant*, tinker.

chauffage (ʃofaːʒ) *m*, heating, warming; stoking, firing. ~ *central*, central heating. **chauffard** (faːr) *m*, road hog. **chauffe** (ʃoːf) *f*, fire chamber; stoking; firing; heat, melt; heating. ~-**bain** (ʃof) *m*, geyser.

~-**lit**, *m*, warming pan. ~-**pieds**, *m*, foot warmer. ~-**plats**, *m*, chafing dish. **chauffer** (ʃofe) *v.t*, to heat, warm; air (*linen*); stoke, fire, fuel; push on with; urge on; cram (*exam*); (*v.i.*) to heat, get hot; run hot; get up steam. *se* ~, to warm oneself, bask. *se* ~ *les pieds*, to warm one's feet. **chaufferette** (frɛt) *f*, foot warmer. **chaufferie** (fri) *f*, chafery; stokehole; boiler room. **chauffeur** (fœːr) *m*, stoker, fireman; driver (*motor car*), chauffeur. ~-*mécanicien*, engineman. **chauffeuse** (føːz) *f*, woman driver; fireside chair.

chaufour (ʃofuːr) *m*, lime kiln. **chaufournier** (furnje) *m*, lime burner.

chauler (ʃole) *v.t*, to lime.

chaume (ʃoːm) *m*, culm (*Bot.*); stubble; s. field; thatch; cottage (*fig.*). *couvrir en* ~, to thatch. **chaumière** (ʃomjɛːr) *f*, [thatched] cottage.

chaussée (ʃose) *f*, bank; causeway, carriage-way, road[way].

chausse-pied (ʃospje) *m*, shoehorn. **chausser** (se) *v.t*, to put on (*shoes, stockings*); shoe, boot, make shoes for; suit, fit (*of footwear*); hill, earth up. *se* ~ *d'une opinion*, to get an opinion into one's head. **chaussettes** (set) *f.pl*, socks, half-hose. **chausson** (sɔ̃) *m*, slipper (*list*); shoe; bootee; bed sock; savate; turnover (*Cook.*). **chaussure** (syːr) *f*, footwear; shoe. ~ [*montante*], boot. ~*s à barrette(s)*, bar shoes. ~*s de marche, de ski*, walking, ski, boots. ~*s vernies*, patent leather shoes; dress shoes.

chauve (ʃoːv) *a*, bald. ¶ *m*, baldhead (*pers.*). ~-**souris** (ʃovsuri) *f*, bat.

chauvinisme (ʃovinism) *m*, chauvinism, jingoism.

chaux (ʃo) *f*, lime, Portland cement. ~ *vive*, quicklime.

chavirer (ʃavire) *v.i*, to capsize, overturn, upset; fail. [**faire**] ~, *v.t*, to capsize, &c; tip, dump, shoot.

chef (ʃɛf) *m*, head, chief; chieftain; commander, commanding officer; general (*Mil.*); leader; principal; master; superior; superintendent; manager; foreman; head, heading; authority; right. ~ *d'accusation*, count of indictment. ~ *d'atelier*, shop foreman. ~ *d'attaque*, leader (*violin, chorus*). ~ *d'émeute*, ringleader. ~ *d'équipe*, foreman, ganger, gaffer. ~ *d'orchestre*, conductor. ~ *de bataillon*, major. ~ [*de cuisine*], head cook, chef. ~ *de file*, leader; file leader; fugleman; leading ship. ~ *de gare*, station master. ~ *de maison*, householder. ~ *de musique*, bandmaster (*Mil.*). ~ *de nage*, stroke (*oarsman*). ~ *de pièce*, gun captain. ~ *de salle*, head waiter. ~ *de terrain* marshal (*Sport*). ~ *de théâtre*, musical director. ~ *de train*, head guard. ~ *du jury*, foreman of the jury. ~ *du* *service des ateliers*, works manager. ∼ *éclaireur*, scout master. *de ce* ∼, under this head[ing], hereunder.

chef-d'œuvre (ʃɛdœːvr) *m*, masterpiece; mess.

chef-lieu (ʃɛfljø) *m*, capital (*department, county*), county town, chief town; headquarters, seat.

cheik (ʃɛk) *m*, sheik[h].

chelem (ʃlɛm) *m*, slam (*Cards*).

chemin (ʃəmɛ̃) *m*, way, road, lane, path, track; headway. ∼ *d'escalier*, stair carpet. ∼ *de fer*, railway, railroad. ∼ *de fer à crémaillère*, rack railway. ∼ *de fer à voie de a 1 mètre, à voie étroite, à voie large, à voie normale*, metre-gauge, narrow-gauge, broad-gauge, standard-gauge, railway. ∼ *de fer d'intérêt local*, local line. ∼ *de fer économique*, light railway. ∼ *de halage*, tow[ing] path. ∼ *des écoliers*, longest way round, roundabout way. ∼ *de la croix*, stations of the Cross. ∼ *de table*, table runner. ∼ *de traverse*, cross-road.

chemineau (ʃəmino) *m*, tramp, hobo.

cheminée (ʃəmine) *f*, chimney, smoke stack, shaft, funnel; fireplace, chimney piece, mantelpiece; chimney pot; vent; chute, shoot.

cheminer (ʃəmine) *v.i*, to tramp; walk; trudge; move along, proceed; meander, creep.

cheminot (ʃəmino) *m*, railwayman.

chemise (ʃəmiːz) *f*, shirt (*man's*); vest (*woman's*); jacket (*water, steam*); cover, lining, case, wrapper. ∼*-culotte*, cami-knickers. ∼ *de jour*, chemise (*woman's*); day shirt (*man's*). ∼ *de nuit*, night shirt (*man's*); n. dress, n. gown (*woman's*). ∼ *de soirée*, dress shirt. ∼ *de ville*, tunic s. ∼ [*pour dossier*], folder. **chemiserie** (mizri) *f*, shirt making, hosiery. **chemisier, ère** (zje, ɛːr) *n*, shirt maker, hosier.

chenal (ʃənal) *m*, channel, race, course; fairway; gutter.

chenapan (ʃnapɑ̃) *m*, scamp, rogue.

chêne (ʃɛn) *m*, oak. ∼*-liège*, *m*, cork tree.

chéneau (ʃeno) *m*, gutter (*eaves*).

chenet (ʃənɛ) *m*, [fire]dog, andiron.

chènevis (ʃɛnvi) *m*, hemp seed.

chenil (ʃəni) *m*, kennel (*hounds*); hovel.

chenille (ʃəniːj) *f*, caterpillar; chenille.

chenu, e (ʃəny) *a*, snow-capped; snow-clad; bare at the top (*trees*).

chèque (ʃɛk) *m*, cheque. ∼ *à ordre, au porteur*, order, bearer, c. ∼ *de voyage*, traveller's c. ∼*-dividende*, dividend warrant. ∼ *postal*, in France, a cheque on a *compte courant postal*. ∼ *préscrit*, stale cheque. ∼ *sans provision*, worthless c.

cher, ère† (ʃɛːr) *a*, dear, high[-priced], expensive, costly; precious, scarce (*time*). *ma chère*, my dear. *mon cher*, my dear fellow. **cher**, *ad*, dearly; much.

chercher (ʃɛrʃe) *v.t*, to look for, try to find, search for, hunt for, seek; beg; pick (*quarrel*). *aller* ∼, to go for, [go &] fetch, go to look for. *venir* ∼, to come for, come & fetch, come to look for. **chercheur, euse** (ʃœːr, øːz) *n*, seeker, searcher inquirer, investigator, research worker. ∼ *d'aventures*, adventurer. ∼ *d'or*, gold digger. ¶ *att*, inquiring (*mind*, &c).

chère (ʃɛːr) *f*, living, fare, cheer. *faire bonne* ∼, to fare (*feed*) well. *faire maigre* ∼, to fare badly, be on short commons.

chérir (ʃeriːr) *v.t*, to cherish, hold dear; cling to, hug (*as error*). *mon chéri, ma chérie*, my love, my darling, dearest.

cherté (ʃɛrte) *f*, dearness, costliness.

chérubin (ʃerybɛ̃) *m*, cherub.

chester (ʃɛstɛːr) *m*, *in France*, Cheddar or Cheshire cheese.

chétif, ive† (ʃetif, iːv) *a*, mean, miserable, sorry, paltry, puny, stunted, sickly, wretched.

cheval (ʃəval) *m*, horse. ∼ *à bascule*, rocking h. ∼ *côtier*, ∼ *de renfort*, trace h. ∼ *d'attelage*, carriage h. ∼ *de bât*, pack-horse; drudge. ∼ *de bataille*, war horse, charger; pet argument. ∼ *de bois*, vaulting h.; hobby h. ∼ *de charrette*, cart h. ∼ *de chasse*, hunter. ∼ *de course*, race-horse. ∼ *de louage*, hack. ∼ *de race*, ∼ *pur sang*, thoroughbred [horse]. ∼ *de retour*, old offender, gaol bird, jail bird. ∼ *de trait*, draught horse. ∼ *de volée*, leader (*horse*). *~ favori*, the favourite. ∼ *placé, non placé*, placed, unplaced, horse (*Turf*). ∼ [*vapeur*], horse power (Fr. h.p. = 75 kilogrammetres per second; Eng. h.p. = 550 foot pounds per sec.). *une* [*automobile de*] *10 chevaux*, a 10 horse [power] car. *à* ∼, on horse-back. **chevalement** (lmɑ̃) *m*, trestle shore; [pit-]head frame; derrick. **chevaler** (le) *v.t*, to shore. **chevaleresque** (lrɛsk) *a*, chivalrous, knightly. **chevalerie** (lri) *f*, knighthood, chivalry. ∼ *errante*, knight errantry. **chevalet** (lɛ) *m*, horse, trestle; easel; rest (*Bil.*, &c); bridge (*violin*, &c). **chevalier** (lje) *m*, knight, chevalier. ∼ *d'industrie*, adventurer, swindler. **chevalière** (ljɛːr) *f*, signet ring. **chevalin, e** (lɛ̃, in) *a*, equine, horsy; horse (*species*). **chevauchée** (voʃe) *f*, ride. **chevaucher** (ʃe) *v.i. & t*, to ride; straddle; span; overlap.

chevelu, e (ʃəvly) *a*, long-haired; hairy; bearded. **chevelure** (vlyːr) *f*, [head of] hair, locks; scalp (*trophy*); coma (*Bot. & comet*); foliage.

chevet (ʃəvɛ) *m*, bolster, pillow; bedhead; bedside.

cheveu (ʃəvø) *m*, (*a single human*) hair. *les* ∼*x*, the hair. ∼*x en brosse*, brush head (*of hair*).

cheville (ʃəviːj) *f*, pin, peg; treenail; bolt; pintle; spike; expletive (*in verse*). ∼ [*du pied*], ankle. ∼ *ouvrière*, king bolt, centre pin; mainspring (fig.), master mind, prime mover. **cheviller** (vije) v.t. & i, to pin, peg, bolt; pad (verses).

chèvre (ʃɛ:vr) f, goat (in general); she-goat, nanny [goat]; gin (Mech.); sawhorse; jack. ~ à trois pieds, sheer legs. ~ de carrossier, carriage jack. ~ [verticale], derrick [crane]. **chevreau** (ʃəvro) m, kid; kid [leather]. **chèvrefeuille** (ʃɛvrəfœ:j) m, honeysuckle, woodbine. **chevrette** (ʃəvrɛt) f, kid; she-goat; roe-doe; shrimp, prawn; trivet. **chevreuil** (vrœ:j) m, roebuck; venison. **chevrier, ère** (vrie, ɛ:r) n, goatherd. **chevron** (vrɔ̃) m, rafter; chevron; stripe (long Mil. service). **chevroter** (vrɔte) v.i, to bleat (goat & fig.); quaver, shake; kid. **chevrotin** (tɛ̃) m, fawn; musk deer; kid [leather]. **chevrotine** (tin) f, buckshot.

chez (ʃe) pr, at; at (or to) (or in) the house, &c, of; care of, c/o; of, stocked by; with; among, in. ~ moi, ~ lui, ~ vous, &c, at home. mon ~-moi, my home. ~ soi, [at] home. un ~-soi, a home of one's own.

chiasse (ʃjas) f, speck (fly); cast (worm); scum, dross (metal).

chic (ʃik) a, stylish, chic, natty, smart, swell. ¶ m, stylishness, &c.

chicane (ʃikan) f, chicanery, quibble, pettifoggery, cavil, shuffle; baffle [plate]. **chicaner** (kane) v.i, to chicane, &c; (v.t.) to cavil at, carp at; dispute every inch of (ground); hug (wind, Naut.). **chicanerie** (nri) f, chicanery, &c. **chichet** (ʃiʃ) a, stingy, mean, niggardly, chary, sparing.

chicorée (ʃikɔre) f, chicory.

chicot (ʃiko) m, stump, snag. **chicoter** (kɔte) v.i, to wrangle (about trifles).

chien, ne (ʃjɛ̃, ɛn) n, dog, bitch, hound; (m.) hammer, cock (of gun); dog, pawl, catch. ~ couchant, setter. faire le ~ couchant, to toady, cringe. ~ courant, ~ de chasse, hound. ~ d'arrêt, pointer. ~ de berger, sheep dog. ~ de garde, ~ d'attache, watch d. ~ de luxe, fancy d. ~ de mer, dog fish. ~ de Saint-Bernard, (sɛ̃bɛrna:r), St Bernard dog. ~ de salon, lap d. ~-loup, Alsatian. ~ savant, performing dog. entre chien & loup, at dusk.

chiendent (ʃjɛ̃dɑ̃) m, couch [grass].

chiffe (ʃif) f, rag. **chiffon** (fɔ̃) m, bit of stuff (old or new); rag, clout; scrap; fallal; chiffon; (pl.) dress, finery. **chiffonner** (fɔne) v.t, to [c]rumple; ruffle, annoy, vex, bother; (v.i.) to do needlework, use one's needle. **chiffonnier, ère** (nje, ɛ:r) n, rag picker or merchant, rag [& bone] man; (m.) chiffonier.

chiffre (ʃifr) m, figure, number, numeral, cipher; amount; monogram; colophon. un [seul] ~, a digit (0–9). en ~s connus, in plain figures. ~ d'affaires, turnover. ~-indice, index number. **mot en chiffré** (fre), word in cipher. **chiffrer** (fre) v.i.

to reckon, cipher; figure, appear; (v.t.) to number, figure, cipher. se ~, to figure out, work out, amount.

chignon (ʃiɲɔ̃) m, chignon.

Chili (le) (ʃili), Chile, -li. **chilien, ne** (ljɛ̃, ɛn) a. & C~, n, Chilean, -lian.

chimère (ʃimɛ:r) f, chim[a]era. **chimérique** (merik) a, chimerical; visionary, fanciful. **chimie** (ʃimi) f, chemistry. **chimique†** (mist) a, chemical; actinic (rays). **chimiste** (mist) n, chemist (scientist).

chimpanzé (ʃɛ̃pɑ̃ze) m, chimpanzee.

Chine (la) (ʃin), China. **chinois, e** (nwa, a:z) a. & C~ (pers.), n, Chinese. le chinois, Chinese (language). **chinoiserie** (zri) f, Chinese curio, &c; (pl.) red tape, complicated formalities.

chiper (ʃipe) v.t, to pinch, bag, bone, crib. **chipie** (ʃipi) f, ill-natured woman. **chipoter** (pote) v.i, to nibble; haggle.

chique (ʃik) f, quid, chew (of tobacco). **chiquenaude** (ʃikno:d) f, fillip, flip, flick. **chiquer** (ʃike) v.t.& i, to chew (tobacco).

chirographaire (kirografɛ:r) a, unsecured (creditors, debts); simple, naked (debentures).

chiromancie (kirɔmɑ̃si) f, palmistry, chiromancy. **chiromancien, ne** (sjɛ̃, ɛn) n, palmist, chiromancer.

chirurgical, e (ʃiryrʒikal) a, surgical. **chirurgie** (ʒi) f, surgery. ~ esthétique du visage, face lifting. **chirurgien** (sjɛ̃) m, surgeon.

chiure (ʃjy:r) f, fly speck.

chlorate (klɔrat) m, chlorate. **chlore** (klɔ:r) m, chlorine. **chlorhydrique** (klɔridrik) a, hydrochloric, muriatic (acid). **chloroforme** (rofɔrm) m, chloroform. **chloroformer** (me) v.t, to chloroform. **chlorure** (ry:r) m, chloride. ~ de chaux, c. of lime.

choc (ʃɔk) m, shock, impact, brunt, onset, onslaught, clash; clink (glasses).

chocolat (ʃokola) m, chocolate. ~ au lait, cocoa (drink); milk c. ~s fourrés à la crème, chocolate creams. ~ lacté, milk c. **chocolatier, ère** (latje ɛ:r) n, c. manufacturer; c. seller; (f.) c. pot.

chœur (kœ:r) m, choir, quire; chorus; chancel. faire ~ au refrain, to join in the chorus.

choir (ʃwa:r) v.i.ir, to fall.

choisi, e (ʃwazi) a, select, choice. **choisir** (zi:r) v.t, to choose, select, pick. **choix** (ʃwa) m, choice, selection; pick; option; quality. au ~, all at the same price.

choléra (kolera) m, cholera.

chômage (ʃoma:ʒ) m, closing, idleness, standing [idle], shutting down, unemployment; demurrage (Rly.); lying up (ship). ~ du dimanche, Sunday closing. **chômer** (me) v.i, to close, lie idle; lie fallow; lie up; shut down, stop work, be out [of work]; be short; (v.t.) to keep (une fête = a saint's day). **chômeur, euse** (mœ:r, ø:z) n, unemployed person. les chômeurs, the unemployed.

chope (ʃɔp) f, glass (for, or of, beer). **chopine** (pin) f, pint (about ¼ litre). **chopiner** (ne) v.i, to tipple.

chopper (ʃɔpe) v.i, to stumble; blunder.

choquant, e (ʃɔkã, ã:t) a, shocking; offensive. **choquer** (ke) v.t, to shock, strike, clash with; clink, chink; offend.

choral, e (kɔral) a, choral. [société] chorale, f, choral society.

chorégraphie (kɔregrafi) f, choreography.

choriste (kɔrist) n, chorister; chorus singer (opera). **faire chorus** (ry:s), to [repeat in] chorus.

chose (ʃo:z) f, thing; matter; fact; chattel; property; compliment. la ~ publique, the common weal, the public welfare. ~ qui va sans dire, matter of course.

chott (ʃɔt) m, salt lake (N. Africa).

chou (ʃu) m, cabbage. ~ de Bruxelles, Brussels sprouts. ~ de Milan (milã). savoy. ~-fleur, m, cauliflower. ~ frisé, kale. ~ marin, sea kale. ~-navet, swede. ~-rave, m, kohlrabi. chou[chou], m, darling, ducky, honey. le chouchou, the pet.

choucas (ʃuka) m, jackdaw.

choucroute (ʃukrut) f, sauerkraut.

chouette (ʃwɛt) f, owl.

choyer (ʃwaje) v.t, to pamper, pet, coddle; cherish.

chrétien, ne (kretjɛ̃, ɛn) a. & n, Christian. **chrétiennement** (ɛnmã) ad, christianly. **chrétienté** (ɛte) f, Christendom. **le Christ** (krist), Christ. **christ**, m, crucifix. **christianiser** (tjanize) v.t, to christianize. **christianisme** (nism) m, Christianity.

chromate (krɔmat) m, chromate.

chromatique (krɔmatik) a, chromatic.

chrome (kro:m) m, chromium, chrome. **chromé, e** (krome) a, chrome (steel, leather); chromium (steel); chromium-plated.

chronique (krɔnik) a, chronic. ¶ f, chronicle; gossip; intelligence, notes (in newspaper). **chroniqueur** (kœ:r) m, chronicler; reporter (news).

chronographe (krɔnɔgraf) m, chronograph; stop-watch.

chronologie (krɔnɔlɔʒi) f, chronology. **chronologiquet** (ʒik) a, chronological.

chronométrage (krɔnɔmetra:ʒ) m, timing (race). **chronomètre** (mɛtr) m, chronometer. **chronométrer** (metre) v.t, to time. **chronométreur** (trœ:r) m, timekeeper (Sport).

chrysalide (krizalid) f, chrysalis, pupa.

chrysanthème (krizãtɛ:m) m, chrysanthemum.

chuchoter (ʃyʃɔte) v.i. & t, to whisper. **chuchoterie** (tri) f, whispering. **chuchoteur, euse** (tœ:r, ø:z) n, whisperer.

chuinter (ʃɥɛte) v.i, to hoot (owl).

chut (ʃyt, ʃt) i, hush!

chute (ʃyt) f, fall, drop; downfall, collapse; smash, crash; failure (of a play); spray (flowers, Need.). ~ [d'eau], [water]fall,

falls. la ~ des reins, the small of the back. la ~ du jour, the close of day, nightfall, eventide.

chuter (ʃyte) v.t, to hiss (an actor).

Chypre (ʃipr) f, Cyprus.

ci (si) ad, say (so much money). ~-après, hereinafter, further on, below. ~-contre, opposite. ~-dessous, below, undermentioned, hereunder. ~-dessus, above[-mentioned]. ~-devant, formerly, late. ~-gît, here lies (grave). ~-inclus, e & ci-joint, e, enclosed, herewith, subjoined.

cible (sibl) f, target; butt (fig.).

ciboire (sibwa:r) m, ciborium, pyx.

ciboule (sibul) f, spring onion. **ciboulette** (lɛt) f, c[h]ive.

cicatrice (sikatris) f, scar, mark. **cicatriser** (ze) v.t. & se ~, to scar; mark; heal, skin over.

cicerone (siseron) m, cicerone, guide.

cidre (si:dr) m, cider.

ciel (sjɛl) m, heaven, heavens; sky; air; climate, clime; tester; canopy; roof. à ~ ouvert, in the open air; open-cast, daylight (Min.).

cierge (sjɛrʒ) (Eccl.) m, [wax] candle, taper.

cigale (sigal) f, cicada, grasshopper.

cigare (siga:r) m, cigar. ~ de la Havane, Havana c. **cigarette** (garɛt) f, cigarette. ~s ordinaires, à bouts de liège, à bouts dorés, plain, cork-tipped, gold-tipped, c—s.

cigogne (sigɔɲ) f, stork.

ciguë (sigy) f, hemlock.

cil (sil) m, eyelash; hair (Bot.). **ciller** (sije) v.i, to blink; move an eyelid.

cime (sim) f, top, summit, peak.

ciment (simã) m, cement. **cimenter** (te) v.t, to cement.

cimeterre (simtɛ:r) m, scimitar.

cimetière (simtjɛ:r) m, cemetery, burial ground, graveyard, churchyard.

cimier (simje) m, crest; haunch (venison); buttock (beef).

cinabre (sina:br) m, cinnabar.

cinématographe (sinematɔgraf), **cinéma**, abb, m, cinematograph, cinema, picture palace, pictures. cinéma au ralenti, slow-motion pictures.

cinéraire (sinerɛ:r) a, cinerary. ¶ f, cineraria (Bot.).

cinétique (sinetik) a, kinetic.

cingalais, e (sɛ̃galɛ, ɛ:z) a. & C~, n, Cingalese.

cingler (sɛ̃gle) v.t, to lash, cut, whip; shingle (Metall.).

cinq (sɛ̃[:]k; before a consonant, sɛ̃) a. & m, five; fifth; cinq[ue]. **cinquantaine** (sɛ̃kãten) f, fifty [or so]; golden wedding. **cinquante** (kã:t) a. & m, fifty. **cinquantenaire** (kãtnɛ:r) m, fiftieth anniversary. **cinquantième** (tjɛm) a. & n, fiftieth. **cinquième** (kjɛm) a. & n, fifth.

cintre (sɛ̃:tr) m, arch, curve; centre (for arch); clothes hanger. **cintrer** (sɛtre) v.t, to arch, bend, curve.

cipaye (sipa:j) *m*, sepoy.

cirage (sira:ʒ) *m*, waxing; polishing; blacking (*boots*). ~ *pour chaussures*, [boot] blacking.

circoncire (sirkɔ̃si:r) *v.t.ir*, to circumcise.

circonférence (sirkɔ̃ferɑ̃:s) *f*, circumference, girth.

circonflexe (sirkɔ̃fleks) *a. & m*, circumflex.

circonlocution (sirkɔ̃lɔkysjɔ̃) *f*, circumlocution.

circonscription (sirkɔ̃skripsjɔ̃) *f*, circumscription; area. ~ *électorale*, parliamentary division, constituency. circonscrire (skri:r) *v.t.ir*, to circumscribe; locate.

circonspect, e (sirkɔ̃spe[k], ekt) *a*, circumspect, cautious, wary, guarded.

circonstance (sirkɔ̃stɑ̃:s) *f*, circumstance, occasion; nonce. circonstancié, e (stɑ̃sje) *p.a*, circumstantial, detailed (*account*). circonstancier (sje) *v.t*, to detail.

circonvenir (sirkɔ̃vni:r) *v.t.ir*, to circumvent, outwit, overreach.

circonvoisin, e (sirkɔ̃vwazɛ̃, in) *a*, surrounding.

circuit (sirkɥi) *m*, circuit, round. ~ *de paroles*, circumlocution.

circulaire† (sirkyle:r) *a. & f*, circular. circulant, e (lɑ̃, ɑ̃:t) *a*, circulating; floating. circulation (lasjɔ̃) *f*, circulation, running, travelling, working; traffic; currency; turnover, sales. circuler (le) *v.i*, to circulate, run, travel. circulez! move on! pass along!

cire (si:r) *f*, wax. ~ *à cacheter*, sealing wax. ciré (sire) *m*, oilskin. cirer (re) *v.t*, to wax; polish, black (*boots*). cireur (sirœ:r) *m*, shoeblack. cireuse (rø:z) *f*, floor polisher (*Mach.*). cirier (rje) *m*, wax chandler.

ciron (sirɔ̃) *m*, mite (*insect*).

cirque (sirk) *m*, circus; corrie.

cirrhose (siro:z) *f*, cirrhosis.

cirrus (sir[r]y:s) *m*, cirrus (*Meteor.*).

cisailler (sizaje) *v.t*, to shear, clip. cisailles (za:j) *f.pl*, shears, shearing machine. ciseau (zo) *m*, chisel. ~ *à déballer*, case opener. ~ *à froid*, cold chisel. ~x, *pl*, [pair of] scissors; shears, clippers. ciseler (zle) *v.t*, to chisel; chase. ciselet (zlɛ) *m*, graver. ciselure (zly:r) *f*, chiselling; chasing.

citadelle (sitadɛl) *f*, citadel; stronghold.

citadin, e (sitadɛ̃, in) *n*, townsman, citizen.

citation (sitasjɔ̃) *f*, citation, quotation; summons, subpoena. ~ *à l'ordre de l'armée*, mention in dispatches.

cité (site) *f*, city. ~*jardin*, *f*, garden c. ~ *ouvrière*, workmen's dwellings.

citer (site) *v.t*, to cite, quote; mention; instance; summon; summons; subpoena.

citérieur, e (siterjœ:r) *a*, hither (*Geog.*).

citerne (sitɛrn) *f*, tank, cistern.

cithare (sita:r) *f*, zither.

citoyen, ne (sitwaje, ɛn) *n*, citizen.

citrique (sitrik) *a*, citric. citron (trɔ̃) *m*, lemon; lime. ~ *pressé*, lemon squash.

citronnade (trɔnad) *f*, lemonade. citronnier (nje) *m*, lemon tree; lime tree.

citrouille (sitru:j) *f*, pumpkin.

cive[tte] (siv[ɛt]) *f*, c[h]ive.

civet de lièvre (sive) *m*, jugged hare.

civette (sivet) *f*, civet [cat].

civière (sivjɛ:r) *f*, hand barrow; stretcher, litter, bier.

civil, e† (sivil) *a*, civil; calendar (*month, year*). ¶ *m*, civilian; non-combatant. en ~, in plain clothes, in mufti. civilisateur, trice (lizatœ:r, tris) *a*, civilizing. civilisation (sjɔ̃) *f*, civilization. civiliser (ze) *v.t*, to civilize. civilité (te) *f*, civility; (*pl.*) compliments.

civique (sivik) *a*, civic.

clabauder (klabode) *v.i*, to babble (*of hound*); backbite.

claie (klɛ) *f*, hurdle, wattle; screen. *passer à la* ~, to screen.

clair, e† (klɛ:r) *a*, clear; bright; light; thin; plain, explicit. *sabre au clair*, with drawn sword. *tirer au clair*, *v.t*, to clear up. clair, *ad*, clearly, plainly; thinly. ¶ *m*, light; plain language (*Teleg.*). ~ *de lune*, moonlight. clairet (klɛrɛ) *a.m*, pale (*wine, precious stone*).

claire-voie (klɛrvwa) *f*, grating. *à* ~, openwork, lattice (*att.*).

clairière (klɛrjɛ:r) *f*, glade; clearing; lane.

clair-obscur (klɛrɔpsky:r) *m*, chiaroscuro, light & shade.

clairon (klɛrɔ̃) *m*, bugle; bugler; clarion. claironner (rɔne) *v.t*, to noise abroad.

clairsemé, e (klɛrsəme) *a*, thinly sown; sparse, few & far between.

clairvoyance (klɛrvwajɑ̃:s) *f*, clear-sightedness, shrewdness.

clameur (klamœ:r) *f*, clamour, outcry.

clampin (klɑ̃pɛ̃) *m*, slowcoach.

clan (klɑ̃) *m*, clan; set.

clandestin, e† (klɑ̃dɛstɛ̃, in) *a*, clandestine, underhand.

clapet (klape) *m*, clack [valve], flap.

clapier (klapje) *m*, rabbit burrow, r. hutch.

clapoter (klapɔte) *v.i*, to plash, swash. clapoteux, euse (tø, ø:z) *a*, choppy (*water*).

clapper (klape) *v.i*, to smack (*tongue*).

claque (klak) *f*, slap, smack; claque (*Theat.*). ¶ *m*, crush hat, opera hat.

claquedent (klakdɑ̃) *m*, beggar perished with cold.

claquemurer (klakmyre) *v.t*, to coop up, immure, closet.

claquer (klake) *v.i. & t*, to clap, clatter, slap, snap, smack, crack, chatter, bang, slam. claquet (kɛ) *m*, claquette (kɛt) *f*, clapper; claquoir (kwa:r) *m*, clapper. claquettes, *f.pl*, step dance, tap d.

clarifier (klarifje) *v.t*, to clarify, fine.

clarine (klarin) *f*, cow-bell.

clarinette (klarinɛt) *f*, clari[o]net.

clarté (klarte) *f*, clearness; brightness; light. ~ *des glaces*, iceblink.

classe (klɑːs) *f*, class, order; rate; form, standard (*at school*); school; contingent (*of recruiting year*). ~ *moyenne*, middle class[es]. [*salle de*] ~, class room. **classement** (klasmɑ̃) *m*, classing, classification; rating; filing; order, position (*Running*, &c*). **classer** (se) *v.t*, to class, classify; sort, grade; file (*letters*, &c*); position; marshal. **classeur** (sœːr) *m*, file; filing cabinet; stationery rack. **classification** (klasifikasjɔ̃) *f*, classification. **classique†** (sik) *a*, classic; classical; class, school (*att*.); educational; standard. ¶ *m*, classic.

claudication (klodikasjɔ̃) *f*, lameness.

clause (kloːz) *f*, clause, term, provision, stipulation.

claustral, e (klostral) *a*, claustral, cloistral.

claveau (klavo) *m*, arch-stone, voussoir; sheep pox.

clavecin (klavsɛ̃) *m*, harpsichord.

clavelée (klavle) *f*, sheep pox.

clavette (klavɛt) *f*, key, cotter, pin. ~ *d'essieu*, axle pin, linchpin. ~ *fendue*, split pin.

clavicule (klavikyl) *f*, collar bone.

clavier (klavje) *m*, keyboard; manual; (*musical*) compass, range.

clayonnage (klɛjɔnaːʒ) *m*, wattling; mat[tress].

clef, *sometimes* **clé** (kle) *f*, key; clue (*puzzle*); spanner, wrench; plug, spigot; clef. ~ *à douille*, box spanner. ~ *à marteau*, screw hammer. ~ *à molette*, monkey wrench, adjustable spanner. ~ *anglaise*, coach wrench. ~ *d'ut*, C (*or* tenor) (*or* alto) clef. ~ *de fa*, F (*or* bass) c. ~ *de sol*, G (*or* treble) c. ~ *de voûte*, keystone. *sous* ~, locked up, under lock & key.

clématite (klematit) *f*, clematis.

clémence (klemɑ̃ːs) *f*, clemency, mercy, leniency; mildness. **clément, e** (mɑ̃, ɑ̃ːt) *a*, clement, &c.

cleptomane (klɛptoman) *n*, kleptomaniac. **cleptomanie** (ni) *f*, kleptomania.

clerc (klɛːr) *m*, clerk (*Relig*., *Law*). **clergé** (klɛrʒe) *m*, clergy; priesthood. **clérical, e** (klerikal) *a*. & *n*, clerical.

cliché (kliʃe) *m*, stereotype; block; negative (*Phot*.); stock phrase, hackneyed p., tag. ~ *au trait*, line block. ~ *simili*, ~ *tramé*, half-tone b. **clicher** (ʃe) *v.t*, to stereotype.

client, e (kliɑ̃, ɑ̃ːt) *n*, client, customer; patient. **clientèle** (ɑ̃tɛl) *f*, clientele, public, connection, custom; goodwill, practice.

cligner (kliɲe) *v.i*, to wink; blink; wince. **clignoter** (nɔte) *v.i*, to blink, twinkle; twitch.

climat (klima) *m*, climate. **climatérique** (materik) *a*, climacteric (*Med*.); climatic. **climatique** (tik) *a*, climatic.

clin d'œil (klɛ̃dœːj) *m*, wink; twinkling of an eye, trice.

clinicien (klinisjɛ̃) *m*, clinician. **clinique** (nik) *a*, clinical. ¶ *f*, clinic; nursing home; surgery (*room*).

clinquant (klɛ̃kɑ̃) *m*, tinsel; foil; showiness.

clique (klik) *f*, clique, set, gang; drums & bugles (*Mil*. band).

cliquet (klikɛ) *m*, pawl, click, catch. ~ [*à canon*], engineer's ratchet brace. ~ [*simple*], ratchet spanner. **cliqueter** (kte) *v.i*, to click, clank, clash, rattle, jingle. **cliquetis** (ktI) *m*, click[ing], &c. **cliquettes** (kɛt) *f.pl*, bones, castanets.

clisser (klise) *v.t*, to wicker (*bottles*).

clivage (klivaːʒ) *m*, cleavage (*Miner*.).

cloaque (kloak) *m*, cesspool; sink (*fig*.).

cloche (klɔʃ) *f*, bell; bell glass; bell jar; dish cover; cloche. ~ *à fromage*, cheese cover. ~ *à plongeur*, diving bell.

clochement (klɔʃmɑ̃) *m*, hobble, limp.

cloche-pied (à) (klɔʃpje) *ad*, on one leg. *sauter à* ~, to hop.

clocher (klɔʃe) *m*, belfry. ~ [*pointu*], steeple. *de* ~ (*fig*.), parish (*att*.), parochial.

clocher (klɔʃe) *v.i*, to hobble, limp, halt, be lame.

clocheton (klɔʃtɔ̃) *m*, bell turret.

clochette (klɔʃɛt) *f*, hand bell; bell [flower]. ~ *d'hiver*, snowdrop.

cloison (klwazɔ̃) *f*, partition; bulkhead; septum. [**émail**] **cloisonné** (zɔne) *m*, cloisonné [enamel]. **cloisonner** (ne) *v.t*, to partition [off].

cloître (klwaːtr) *m*, cloister. **cloîtrer** (watre) *v.t*, to cloister, immure.

clopin-clopant (klɔpɛ̃klɔpɑ̃) *ad*, hobbling along. **clopiner** (pine) *v.i*, to hobble.

cloporte (klɔpɔrt) *m*, wood louse.

cloque (klɔk) *f*, blister; rust (*Agric*.).

clore (kloːr) *v.t*. & *i*. *ir*, to close, shut; enclose; conclude. **clos** (klo) *m*, enclosure. **clôture** (kloty:r) *f*, enclosure, fence, fencing; screen (*choir*); closure; closing. ~ *à claire-voie*, paling.

clou (klu) *m*, nail; boil (*Med*.). *les* ~*s*, studded crossing (*pedestrian*). ~ *à crochet*, tenterhook. ~ *à dessin*, drawing pin. ~ *à deux pointes*, [wire] staple. ~ *de girofle*, clove. ~ *de la fête*, chief attraction, star turn. ~ *de Paris*, French nail, wire n. ~ *découpé*, cut n. **clouer** (klue) *v.t*, to nail [up, down]; pin; tie. ~ *la bouche à quelqu'un*, to shut someone up (*silence*). **clouter** (te) *v.t*, to stud. *passage clouté*, stud[de]d crossing (*pedestrian crossing*). **clouterie** (tri) *f*, nail making; n. works. **cloutier** (tje) *m*, nail maker.

clovisse (klɔvis) *f*, cockle (*Mol*.).

clown (klun) *m*, clown. **clownerie** (nri) *f*, clownery.

club (klyb) *m*, club. ~ *de golf*, golf club (*people & stick*).

coaguler (koagyle) *v.t*, to coagulate.

coaliser (se) (koalize) *v.pr*, to combine. **coalition** (sjɔ̃) *f*, coalition; combine, ring.

coaltar (koltaːr) *m*, coal tar.

coasser (koase) *v.i*, to croak (*frog*).

cobalt (kɔbalt) *m*, cobalt.

cobaye (kɔbaːj) *m*, guinea pig.

cobra (kɔbra) *m*, cobra.

cocaine (kokain) *f*, cocaine.

cocarde (kokard) *f*, cockade, rosette.

cocasse (kɔkas) *a*, droll, comical.

coccinelle (kɔksinɛl) *f*, ladybird.

coche (kɔʃ) *f*, sow; notch, score. ¶ *m*, stage coach.

cochenille (kɔʃniːj) *f*, cochineal.

cocher (kɔʃe) *m*, coachman, driver. ~ *de fiacre*, cabman.

cocher (kɔʃe) *v.t*, to notch, score.

cochet (kɔʃɛ) *m*, cockerel.

Cochinchine (la) (kɔʃɛ̃ʃin), Cochin-China. cochinchinois, e (nwa, aːz) *a*. & C~, *n*, Cochin-Chinese.

cochon (kɔʃɔ̃) *m*, hog, pig, porker, swine; dirty pig (*man*). ~ *d'Inde*, guinea pig. ~ *de lait*, sucking pig. cochonnée (ʃɔne) *f*, farrow, litter. cochonner (ɔne) *v.i*, to farrow, pig. cochonnerie (nri) *f*, filthiness, nastiness, muck. cochonnet (nɛ) *m*, jack (*Bowls*).

coco (kɔko) *m*, coco[nut].

coco (kɔko) *m*, cocotte (kɔt) *f*, darling.

cocon (kɔkɔ̃) *m*, cocoon.

cocorico (kɔkɔriko) *m*, cock-a-doodle-doo.

cocotier (kɔkɔtje) *m*, coco[nut] palm.

code (kɔd) *m*, code; statute book; law; canons (*taste*). ~ *de la route*, highway code, road code, code of the road. *mettre en* ~, to dim (*motor lights*). Cf. *phare-code*.

codétenteur, trice (kodetɑ̃tœːr, tris) *n*, joint holder.

codex [pharmaceutique] (kɔdɛks) *m*, pharmacopoeia.

codicille (kɔdisil) *m*, codicil.

codifier (kɔdifje) *v.t*, to codify.

codirecteur, trice (kodirɛktœːr, tris) *n*, joint manager, ess.

coefficient (kɔefisjɑ̃) *m*, coefficient.

cœur (kœːr) *m*, heart; courage; feelings; core; height (*of summer*); depth (*of winter*); hearts (*Cards*).

coffre (kɔfr) *m*, chest, box, trunk, bin, locker, coffer; case. ~-fort (frɔfɔːr) *m*, safe. coffrer (fre) *v.t*, to lock up (*pers.*). coffret (frɛ) *m*, casket, box, chest. ~ *à monnaie*, cash box. ~ *de pharmacie*, medicine chest.

cogérant, e (kɔʒerɑ̃, ɑ̃ːt) *n*, joint manager, ess.

cognac (kɔɲak) *m*, cognac, brandy.

cognassier (kɔɲasje) *m*, quince [tree].

cognée de bûcheron (kɔɲe) *f*, felling axe. cogner (ɲe) *v.t*. & *i*, to drive in; knock, bump, thump.

cohabiter (kɔabite) *v.i*, to cohabit.

cohérence (kɔerɑ̃ːs) *f*, coherence. cohérent, e (rɑ̃, ɑ̃ːt) *a*, coherent, connected; cohesive. cohésion (zjɔ̃) *f*, cohesion.

cohorte (kɔɔrt) *f*, cohort.

cohue (kɔy) *f*, crowd, crush.

coi, te (kwa, at) *a*, still, quiet.

coiffe (kwaf) *f*, head-dress; cap; lining (*hat*). coiffer (fe) *v.t*, to hat; cap; fit, suit (*hat*);

dress (*or* do) [the hair of]. *se* ~ *de* (*fig.*), to be infatuated with. coiffeur, euse (fœːr, øːz) *n*, hairdresser. ¶ *f*, dressing table. ~ *psyché*, cheval d. t. coiffure (fyːr) *f*, head-dress, headgear; style of hairdressing. ~ *à la Ninon* (ninɔ̃), ~ *à la Jeanne d'Arc* (ʒɑ̃ndark), bob[bed hair]. ~ *de cotillon*, paper hat (*Danc.*). ~ *en garçon*, ~ *à la garçonne*, Eton crop.

coin (kwɛ̃) *m*, corner; angle; wedge, key, quoin; die; stamp; mark; plot, patch (*land*). ~ *du feu*, fireside, chimney corner, ingle nook. ~ *intime*, cosy corner. coincer (kwɛ̃se) *v.t*, to wedge, key; jam.

coïncidence (kɔɛ̃sidɑ̃ːs) *f*, coincidence. coïncider (de) *v.i*, to coincide.

coing (kwɛ̃) *m*, quince (*fruit*).

cointéressé, e (kɔɛ̃terɛse) *n*, coadventurer.

coke (kɔk) *m*, coke.

col (kɔl) *m*, collar; neck (*bottle*); pass, col, saddle. ~ *rabattu*, double collar, turndown c. (*attached*). ~ *souple*, soft c. ~ *tenant*, c. attached (*to shirt*). ~ *transformable*, two-way c. *faux* ~, [shirt] collar (*detached*). *faux* ~ *cassé*, wing c. *faux* ~ *montant*, *faux* ~ *droit*, high c., stand-up c. *faux* ~ *rabattu*, double c., turn-down c.

coléoptère (kɔleɔptɛːr) *a*, coleopterous. ¶ *m*, coleopter[an], beetle.

colère (kɔlɛːr) *f*, anger, rage, passion, temper, fume. ~ *bleue*, towering rage. colère & colérique (lerik) *a*, quick-tempered, hasty, peppery, choleric.

colibri (kɔlibri) *m*, humming bird.

colifichet (kɔlifiʃɛ) *m*, [k]nick-[k]nack; (*pl.*) falials; frippery.

colimaçon (kɔlimasɔ̃) *m*, snail. *en* ~, spiral.

colin-maillard (kɔlɛ̃majaːr) *m*, blind-man's buff.

colique (kɔlik) *f*, colic, gripes.

colis (kɔli) *m*, parcel, package; article [of luggage]. ~ *à livrer par exprès*, express parcel (*Post*). ~-*avion*, air p. ~ *contre remboursement*, cash on delivery p. ~ *finances & valeurs*, value p. ~ *messageries à grande vitesse*, express p. (*Rly*). ~ *postal du régime intérieur*, inland p. *par* ~ *postal*, by parcel post.

collaborateur, trice (kɔlabɔratœːr, tris) *n*, collaborator, contributor. collaborer (re) *v.i*, to collaborate. ~ *à*, to contribute to, write for (*journal*).

collage (kɔlaːʒ) *m*, sticking, pasting; gluing; sizing; hanging (*paper*); fining (*wine*). collant, e (lɑ̃, ɑ̃ːt) *a*, sticky; tacky; tight, close-fitting.

collatéral, e (kɔlateral) *a*, collateral, side (*att.*).

collation (kɔlasjɔ̃) *f*, collation; light meal, snack. collationner (one) *v.t*, to collate, compare, read over; repeat; (*v.i.*) to have a snack.

colle (kɔl) *f*, oral test (*exams*); detention (*Sch.*); poser. ~ [*de pâte*], paste. ~ [*de *peaux, &c*], size. ~ [*de poisson*], isinglass; fish glue. ~ **forte**, glue.

collecte (kɔlɛkt) *f*, collection (*money*); collect. **collecteur** (tœ:r) *m*, collector; main (*drain*). ~ **d'impôts**, tax collector. **collectif, ive†** (tif, i:v) *a*, collective, joint. **collection** (sjɔ̃) *f*, collection; file (*newspapers*). **collectionner** (ɔne) *v.t*, to collect. **collectionneur, euse** (nœ:r, ø:z) *n*, collector.

collège (kɔlɛ:ʒ) *m*, college, school. ~ **électoral**, constituency. **collégial, e** (leʒjal) *a*, collegiate. **collégien, ne** (ʒjɛ̃, ɛn) *n*, collegian; schoolboy, -girl.

collègue (kɔlɛg) *m*, colleague.

coller (kɔle) *v.t*, to stick; paste; glue; size; hang (*paper*); fine (*wine*); fix, fasten; cushion (*Bil.*); (*v.i*) to fit tightly, cling. **se ~**, to stick, cling, cleave.

collerette (kɔlrɛt) *f*, collaret[te]; flange.

collet (kɔlɛ) *m*, collar; collet; neck; scrag (*mutton*); scruff of the neck; flange. ~ **monté** (*fig.*), strait-laced; prim. **colleter** (lte) *v.t*, to collar, grapple with.

colleur (kɔlœ:r) *m*, paperhanger; billposter; billsticker; examiner (*Sch.*).

collier (kɔlje) *m*, necklace; collar; strap; ring. ~ **de misère**, drudgery.

colline (kɔlin) *f*, hill.

collision (kɔlizjɔ̃) *f*, collision, clash.

collocation (kɔlɔkasjɔ̃) *f*, settling the list of creditors; dividend (*to creditors*). **bordereau de ~**, list of creditors.

colloque (kɔlɔk) *m*, colloquy, conversation.

colloquer (kɔlɔke) *v.t*, to collocate; foist.

collusion (kɔlysjɔ̃) *f*, collusion.

colombe (kɔlɔ̃:b) *f*, dove.

Colombie (la) (kɔlɔ̃bi), Columbia.

colombier (kɔlɔ̃bje) *m*, dovecot[e].

colon (kɔlɔ̃) *m*, colonist, settler.

colonel (kɔlɔnɛl) *m*, colonel.

colonial, e (kɔlɔnjal) *a*, colonial. **colonie** (ni) *f*, colony, settlement. ~ **de peuplement**, [immigration] settlement. ~ **de vacances**, holiday camp. **la ~ du Cap**, Cape Colony. **coloniser** (nize) *v.t*, to colonize.

colonnade (kɔlɔnad) *f*, colonnade. **colonne** (lɔn) *f*, column, pillar; post.

colophane (kɔlɔfan) *f*, resin (*violin*).

colorer (kɔlɔre) *v.t*, to colour; stain (*glass*). **colorier** (rje) *v.t*, to colour; **coloris** (ri) *m*, colour[ing], hue.

colossal, e† (kɔlɔsal) *a*, colossal. **colosse** (lɔs) *m*, colossus; giant.

colporter (kɔlpɔrte) *v.t*, to hawk, peddle. **colporteur** (tœ:r) *m*, hawker, pedlar.

coltineur (kɔltinœ:r) *m*, porter (*dock*); heaver (*coal*).

colza (kɔlza) *m*, colza.

coma (kɔma) *m*, coma (*Med.*). **comateux, euse** (tø, ø:z) *a*, comatose.

combat (kɔ̃ba) *m*, combat, fight, battle, action; war (*elements*); contest, bout, match. ~ **de boxe**, boxing match. ~ **de boxe professionnel**, prize fight[ing]. ~ **de près**, in-

fighting (*Box.*). **combativité** (tivite) *f*, combativeness. **combattant** (tɑ̃) *m*, combatant, fighter. **combattre** (tr) *v.t. & i. ir*, to fight; oppose; combat; contend with; strive; vie.

combe (kɔ̃:b) *f*, coomb, combe, dale.

combien (kɔ̃bjɛ̃) *ad*, how much; how many; how far; how. ~ **de fois?** how many times? how often? ~ **de temps?** how long?

combinaison (kɔ̃binɛzɔ̃) *f*, combination; plan, contrivance, scheme; combinations (*dress*); creepers, crawlers (*child's*). **combiné** (ne) *m*, compound (*Chem.*). **combiné phono-radio**, *m*, radio-gramophone. **combiner** (ne) *v.t*, to combine; contrive, devise.

comble (kɔ̃:bl) *a*, full, crowded. ¶ *m*, heaping; top; height; highest pitch; acme, summit, sum; last straw; roof. ~ **brisé**, mansard roof. **combler** (kɔ̃ble) *v.t*, to heap, shower, fill, load, overwhelm; make up, make good.

combustible (kɔ̃bystibl) *a*, combustible; fuel (*att.*). ¶ *m*, fuel, firing. **combustion** (tjɔ̃) *f*, combustion; burning; conflagration, fire (*fig.*).

Côme (le lac de) (ko:m), Lake Como.

comédie (kɔmedi) *f*, comedy; theatricals; players; sham. **comédien, ne** (djɛ̃, ɛn) *n*, comedian, enne, actor, tress, player.

comestible (kɔmɛstibl) *a*, edible. ~**s**, *m.pl*, eatables, provisions.

comète (kɔmɛt) *f*, comet; headband (*Bookb.*).

comice agricole (kɔmis) *m*, agricultural show, cattle show.

comique† (kɔmik) *a*, comic; comical; funny, ludicrous. ¶ *m*, comedy; c. writer; comic actor; funny part, joke. ~ **de la troupe** (*fig.*), funny man.

comité (kɔmite) *m*, committee.

commandant (kɔmɑ̃dɑ̃) *m*, commander, commanding officer; commandant; major (*Mil.*). **non**, ~, no, sir (*when addressing officer in command of a ship*). **commande** (mɑ̃:d) *f*, order; indent; driving; drive; driving gear; control. **de ~**, [arranged] to order; feigned. **sur ~**, (*made*) to order, bespoke, commissioned. **commandement** (mɑ̃dmɑ̃) *m*, command, order; commandment; behest; word of command. **commander (de)** *v.t. & i*, to command, order; bespeak; govern; demand; drive (*Mach.*).

commanditaire (kɔmɑ̃ditɛ:r) *m*, sleeping partner. **commandite** (dit) *f*, limited partnership; finance, interest. **commandité (te)** *m*, acting partner. **commanditer** (te) *v.t*, to finance, take an interest in.

comme (kɔm) *ad*, as, like, such as; how. ~ **ci, ~ ça**, so so, middling. ¶ *c*, as, since.

commémorer (kɔmemɔre) *v.t*, to commemorate.

commençant, e (kɔmɑ̃sɑ̃, ɑ̃:t) *n*, beginner, tyro, learner. **commencement** (smɑ̃) *m*, beginning, start, commencement, inception, outset. **commencer** (se) *v.t. & i*, to begin, commence, start.

commensal, e (kɔmɑ̃sal) *n*, messmate, fellow boarder.

comment (kɔmɑ̃) *ad*, how; what! why!

commentaire (kɔmɑ̃tɛːr) *m*, commentary; comment. **commenter** (te) *v.t.* ou ~ **sur**, to comment on.

commérage (komera:ʒ) *m*, gossip, tittle-tattle.

commerçant, e (kɔmɛrsɑ̃, ɑ̃:t) *a*, commercial, trading, business (*att.*). ¶ *n*, trader, merchant. **commerce** (mɛrs) *m*, commerce, trade, trading, business; traders; intercourse, dealings. ~ *à tempérament*, tally trade. *d'un* ~ *agréable*, easy to get on with. **commercer** (mɛrse) *v.i*, to trade, deal; hold intercourse. **commercial, e†** (sjal) *a*, commercial, business, trade, trading (*att.*); produce (*market*).

commère (kɔmɛːr) *f*, fellow sponsor; gossip; busybody; shrewd woman; leading lady (*revue*).

commettant (kɔmɛtɑ̃) *m*, principal (*Law*); (*pl.*) constituents (*Pol.*). **commettre** (mɛtr) *v.t.ir*, to commit; perpetrate; appoint; entrust; compromise. **commis** (mi) *m*, clerk. ~ *aux vivres*, ship's steward. ~ *d'entreprise*, clerk of [the] works. ~ *de course*, clerk of the course (*Turf*). ~ *de magasin*, shop assistant. ~ *voyageur*, commercial traveller. **commissaire** (sɛːr) *m*, commissioner; officer (*emigration*); steward (*fête, race meeting, &c*); purser (*ship*); paymaster (*navy*); superintendent (*police*). ~ *des* (ou *aux*) *comptes*, auditor. ~ *priseur*, auctioneer. **commissariat** (sarja) *m*, status or office (rooms, &c.) of a *commissaire*; thus, ~ *de police*, divisional police station. ~ *des comptes*, auditorship.

commission (kɔmisjɔ̃) *f*, commission; errand; committee. **commissionnaire** (ɔnɛːr) *m*, agent, commission agent, factor; messenger; porter. ~ *chargeur*, shipping agent. ~ *de transport[s]*, forwarding a. ~ *en douane*, customs a. **commissionner** (ne) *v.t*, to commission.

commode (kɔmɔd) *f*, [chest of] drawers. ¶ *a*, convenient, handy; commodious, pleasant; easy, easy-going. **commodément** (demɑ̃) *ad*, conveniently. **commodité** (dite) *f*, convenience; commodiousness; (*pl.*) conveniences (*w.c.*).

commotion (kɔmosjɔ̃) *f*, commotion, upheaval; shock; shell shock. ~ *au cerveau*, concussion of the brain.

commuer (kɔmɥe) *v.t*, to commute.

commun, e (kɔmœ̃, yn) *a*, common; usual; general; ordinary; commonplace; vulgar; average. *peu* ~, uncommon. ¶ *m*, generality, run. *en, hors du*, ~, in, out of the, common. **communal, e** (mynal) *a*, communal; parish (*att.*). ¶ *m*, common [land]. **communauté** (note) *f*, community; commonwealth; sisterhood. *la C~ d'Aus-*

tralie, the Commonwealth of Australia.

commune (myn) *f*, commune, parish (*civil*).

communément (nemɑ̃) *ad*, commonly, generally.

communiant, e (kɔmynjɑ̃, ɑ̃:t) *n*, communicant.

communicatif, ive (kɔmynikatif, iːv) *a*, communicative; copying (*ink*). **communication** (sjɔ̃) *f*, communication; touch; intercourse; interchange; discovery; access (*of, to, documents*); call (*Teleph.*).

communier (kɔmynje) *v.i. & t*, to communicate (*Eccl.*). **communion** (njɔ̃) *f*, communion; sacrament; fellowship; persuasion, faith, denomination.

communiqué (kɔmynike) *m*, official statement (*to press*); communiqué. **communiquer** (ke) *v.t. & i*, to communicate; impart, convey; produce (*documents*).

communisme (kɔmynism) *m*, communism. **communiste** (nist) *n*, communist.

commutateur (kɔmytatœːr) *m*, switch; commutator. **commutation** (sjɔ̃) *f*, commutation.

compacité (kɔ̃pasite) *f*, compactness, closeness. **compact, e** (pakt) *a*, compact, dense; concise, compendious. [*poudre*] *compacte* ou *fard compact*, compact [powder].

compagne (kɔ̃paɲ) *f*, companion; mate; partner (*wife*). ~ *de voyage*, fellow passenger, f. traveller. **compagnie** (ɲi) *f*, company; companionship; bevy; covey. *de bonne* ~, well-bred, gentlemanly, ladylike. *de mauvaise* ~, ill-bred, ungentlemanly, unladylike. *& Cie* (e kɔ̃paɲi), & Co. (*on cheque*). **compagnon** (ɲɔ̃) *m*, companion; mate; journeyman. ~ *de malheur*, fellow sufferer. ~ *de voyage*, fellow passenger, f. traveller.

comparable (kɔ̃parabl) *a*, comparable. **comparaison** (rɛzɔ̃) *f*, comparison; simile.

comparaître (kɔ̃parɛːtr) *v.i.ir*, to appear (*Law*).

comparatif, ive† (kɔ̃paratif, iːv) *a*, comparative. ¶ *m*, comparative (*Gram.*). **comparé, e** (re) *p.a*, comparative (*sciences*). **comparer** (re) *v.t*, to compare, liken.

comparse (kɔ̃pars) *n*, supernumerary (*Theat.*); (*m.*) cipher (*pers.*).

compartiment (kɔ̃partimɑ̃) *m*, compartment.

comparution (kɔ̃parysjɔ̃) *f*, appearance (*Law*).

compas (kɔ̃pɑ) *m*, [pair of] compasses; compass. ~ *à balustre*, bow compasses. ~ *à pointes sèches*, dividers. ~ *à porte-crayon*, *à tire-ligne*, compasses with pencil point, with pen p. ~ *à verge*, beam compasses. ~ [*de calibre*], cal[l]ipers. ~ *de route*, steering compass (*Naut.*). **compasser** (se) *v.t*, to measure.

compassion (kɔ̃pasjɔ̃) *f*, compassion. **compatible** (tibl) *a*, compatible, consistent. **compatir** (tiːr) *v.i*, to sympathize, bear. **compatissant, e** (tisɑ̃, ɑ̃:t) *a*, compassionate.

compatriote (kɔpatriɔt) *n*, compatriot, [fellow] countryman, -woman.

compendieusement (kɔpãdjøzmã) *ad*, briefly. **compendium** (pẽdjɔm) *m*, compendium.

compensateur, trice (kɔpãsatœːr, tris) *a*, compensating; countervailing (*duty*). **compensation** (sjɔ) *f*, compensation; set off, offset; quid pro quo; making up (*Stk Ex.*); clearing (*Banking*). **compenser** (se) *v.t*, to compensate, offset; make up; clear. ~ *les dépens*, to order each party to pay its own costs.

compère (kɔpɛːr) *m*, fellow sponsor; fellow; crony; confederate; leading man (*revue*); compère. ~-**loriot**, *m*, sty[e] (*eye*).

compétence (kɔpetãːs) *f*, competence; jurisdiction; province. **compétent, e** (tã, ã:t) *a*, competent.

compétiteur, trice (kɔpetitœːr, tris) *n*, competitor. **compétition** (sjɔ) *f*, competition.

compiler (kɔpile) *v.t. & abs*, to compile.

complainte (kɔplɛ̃ːt) *f*, ballad, lay.

complaire à (kɔplɛːr) *v.ir*, to gratify, humour. **se complaire**, to take pleasure, [take] delight, fancy oneself, pat oneself on the back. **complaisamment** (plɛzamã) *ad*, complacently; obligingly. **complaisance** (zãːs) *f*, complaisance; deference; kindness; willingness; complacence, -cy; accommodation (*Fin.*). **complaisant, e** (zã, ã:t) *a*, obliging, willing; complaisant, accommodating, compliant; complacent. ¶ *n*, time server.

complément (kɔplemã) *m*, complement. ~ *de poids*, makeweight. **complémentaire** (tɛːr) *a*, complementary, fuller.

complet, ète (kɔplɛ, ɛt) *a*, complete, total, whole, full; all-round; unabridged; utter; wholemeal (*bread*). *wagon complet, charge complète*, truck load. *complet*, house full (*Theat.*). ¶ *m*, complement; suit [of clothes] (*man's*). ~ *jaquette*, morning s. ~ *veston*, lounge s. *au* ~, complete, full. **complètement** (plɛtmã) *ad*, completely, &c; quite; thoroughly. ¶ *m*, completion. **compléter** (plete) *v.t*, to complete.

complexe (kɔplɛks) *a*, complex; many-sided; compound. ¶ *m*, complex. ~ *d'infériorité*, inferiority c.

complexion (kɔplɛksjɔ) *f*, constitution; disposition.

complexité (kɔplɛksite) *f*, complexity.

complication (kɔplikasjɔ) *f*, complication; intricacy.

complice (kɔplis) *a*, accessory, privy, a party (*de* = to). ¶ *n*, accomplice, confederate. ~ *en adultère*, co-respondent. **complicité** (site) *f*, complicity.

complies (kɔpli) *f.pl*, complin[e] (*Eccl.*).

compliment (kɔplimã) *m*, compliment, congratulation; (*pl.*) kind regards. **complimenter** (te) *v.t*, to compliment, &c. **complimenteur, euse** (tœːr, øːz) *a*, overcivil. ¶ *n*, flatterer.

compliquer (kɔplike) *v.t*, to complicate.

complot (kɔplo) *m*, plot. **comploter** (plɔte) *v.t*, to plot.

componction (kɔpɔksjɔ) *f*, compunction.

comporter (kɔpɔrte) *v.t*, to admit of; call for, require. **se** ~, to behave, demean oneself.

composant, e (kɔpozã, ã:t) *a. & m*, component, constituent. **composé, e** (ze) *a*, compound, composite; composed, demure. *bien composée*, select (*company of people*). ¶ *m*, compound. **composer** (ze) *v.t. & i*, to compose; compound; settle; set (*Typ.*); dial (*Teleph.*). **se** ~, to be composed, consist. **compositeur, trice** (pozitœːr, tris) *n*, composer; compositor, [type] setter. **composition** (sjɔ) *f*, composition; settlement; [type] setting; essay; examination (*Sch.*); paper (*Sch.*). **composteur** (pɔstœːr) *m*, composing stick; office printing outfit.

compote (kɔpɔt) *f*, compote, stewed fruit. ~ *de pommes, &c*, stewed apples, &c. *en* ~, done to shreds (*meat*); to a jelly (*face injury*). **compotier** (tje) *m*, fruit bowl.

compréhensif, ive (kɔpreãsif, iːv) *a*, comprehensive. **compréhension** (sjɔ) *f*, comprehension, understanding. **comprendre** (prãːdr) *v.t.ir*, to comprehend, understand, make out; comprise, include, cover. *y compris*, including. *non compris*, not including, exclusive of.

compresse (kɔprɛːs) *f*, compress (*Med.*). **compresseur** (prɛsœːr) *m*, compressor. **compression** (sjɔ) *f*, compression; repression; cut (*in expenditure*). **comprimer** (prime) *v.t*, to compress; repress; restrain.

compromettre (kɔprɔmɛtr) *v.t. & i. ir*, to compromise; impair. **se** ~, to compromise (*or* commit) oneself. **compromis** (mi) *m*, compromise; bond.

comptabilité (kɔtabilite) *f*, bookkeeping; accountancy; accounts. **comptable** (bl) *a*, accountable, responsible; book (*entry, value*); accounting *or* bookkeeping (*machine*). ¶ *n*, accountant, bookkeeper. **comptant** (kɔtã) *m*, cash, prompt (*or* spot) cash, ready money. [*au*] ~, in (*or* for) cash, cash down. **compte** (kɔːt) *m*, counting, count, reckoning; account. ~ *courant & d'intérêts*, account current with interest. ~ *courant postal*, (in Fr.) current account kept with post office acting as bankers. ~ *d'ordre*, suspense account. ~ *de dépôts à terme ou à préavis*, deposit account. ~ *de retour*, notarial charges. ~ *de vente*, account sales. ~ *des points*, score, card. ~-**gouttes** (kɔtgut) *m*, dropper. ~-**pas**, *m*, pedometer. ~ *rendu*, report; review. ~ *rond*, round figures, r. numbers; even money. *à* ~, on account. *tout* ~ *fait*, all told. **compter** (kɔte) *v.t. & i*, to count, reckon, number; rely, depend, calculate; intend, mean. **compteur** (tœːr) *m*, meter, counter; taximeter; clock. ~ *à eau*, water meter. ~ *à gaz*, gas meter. ~ *à paie-*

ment préalable, slot meter. ~ *de bicyclette,* cyclometer. ~ *de sport,* stop watch, recorder. ~ *de tours,* speed (*or* revolution) counter. ~ *de vitesse,* speedometer. **comptoir** (twa:r) *m,* counter; bar; branch, agency; office. ~*-caisse, m,* cash desk.

compulser (kɔ̃pylse) *v.t,* to go through, examine.

comte (kɔ̃:t) *m,* count (*title*). **comté** (kɔ̃te) *m,* (*Eng.*) county, shire. **comtesse** (tɛs) *f,* countess.

concasser (kɔ̃kɑse) *v.t,* to pound, break, crush.

concave (kɔ̃ka:v) *a,* concave. **concavité** (kavite) *f,* concavity.

concéder (kɔ̃sede) *v.t,* to concede, grant.

concentration (kɔ̃sɑ̃trasjɔ̃) *f,* concentration. **concentrer** (tre) *v.t,* to concentrate; centre (*fig.*); repress. **concentrique** (trik) *a,* concentric.

conception (kɔ̃sɛpsjɔ̃) *f,* conception.

concernant (kɔ̃sɛrnɑ̃) *pr,* concerning. **concerner** (ne) *v.t,* to concern, affect.

concert (kɔ̃sɛːr) *m,* concert; chorus (*fig.*). **concertant, e** (sɛrtɑ̃, ɑ̃:t) *n,* concert performer. **concerter** (te) *v.t,* to concert, plan. **concerto** (sɛrto) *m,* concerto.

concession (kɔ̃sɛsjɔ̃) *f,* concession, grant, claim, licence. **concessionnaire** (ɔnɛ:r) *n,* concession[n]aire, grantor claimholder.

concevable (kɔ̃s[ə]vabl) *a,* conceivable. **concevoir** (səvwa:r) *v.t. & abs,* to conceive; entertain; understand; word, couch.

conchyliologie (kɔ̃kiljɔlɔʒi) *f,* conchology.

concierge (kɔ̃sjɛrʒ) *n,* doorkeeper, [hall] porter, portress, caretaker, housekeeper; keeper (*prison*).

concile (kɔ̃sil) *m,* council (*Eccl.*).

concilier (kɔ̃silje) *v.t,* to conciliate, reconcile; win.

concis, e (kɔ̃si, i:z) *a,* concise, terse, crisp, brief. **concision** (sizjɔ̃) *f,* conciseness, &c, brevity.

concitoyen, ne (kɔ̃sitwajɛ̃, ɛn) *n,* fellow citizen.

concluant, e (kɔ̃klyɑ̃, ɑ̃:t) *a,* conclusive. **conclure** (kly:r) *v.t. & i. ir,* to conclude, end; clinch; infer. **conclusion** (klyzjɔ̃) *f,* conclusion, inference; (*pl.*) pleas (*Law.*).

concombre (kɔ̃kɔ̃:br) *m,* cucumber.

concordance (kɔ̃kɔrdɑ̃:s) *f,* agreement, reconciliation; concordance; concord. **concordat** (da) *m,* composition; concordat. **concorde** (kɔrd) *f,* concord, harmony. **concorder** (de) *v.i,* to agree, tally.

concourir (kɔ̃kuri:r) *v.i.ir,* to concur; compete; rank. **concours** (ku:r) *m,* concurrence; assistance, help; concourse; confluence; competition, contest; meeting; show; [competitive] examination; equality. ~ *orthographique,* spelling bee. ~ *par coups,* stroke play, medal p. (*Golf*). ~ *par trous,* match play.

concret, ète (kɔ̃krɛ, ɛt) *a,* concrete. *le concret,* the concrete (opp. *abstract*).

concubine (kɔ̃kybin) *f,* concubine.

concupiscence (kɔ̃kypisɑ̃:s) *f,* concupiscence.

concurrence (kɔ̃kyrɑ̃:s) *f,* competition; equality [of rank]. *à ~ de,* amounting to. *jusqu'à ~ de,* up to, not exceeding. **concurrent, e** (rɑ̃, ɑ̃:t) *a,* concurrent. ¶ *n,* competitor.

concussion (kɔ̃kysjɔ̃) *f,* misappropriation.

condamnation (kɔ̃danasjɔ̃) *f,* condemnation; sentence; judg[e]ment; conviction. **condamné, e** (ne) *n,* convict. ~ *à mort,* condemned man, woman. **condamner** (ne) *v.t,* to condemn; doom; convict; sentence; mulct; give up (*patient*); block up (*door*); board up (*window*); batten down (*Naut.*).

condensateur (kɔ̃dɑ̃satœ:r) *m,* condenser (*Phys., Elec., Opt.*). **condensation** (sjɔ̃) *f,* condensation. **condenser** (dɑ̃se) *v.t,* to condense; boil down. **condenseur** (sœ:r) *m,* condenser (*steam*).

condescendance (kɔ̃desɑ̃dɑ̃:s) *f,* condescension. **condescendre** (dr) *v.i,* to condescend; comply.

condiment (kɔ̃dimɑ̃) *m,* condiment.

condisciple (kɔ̃disipl) *m,* fellow student, schoolfellow.

condition (kɔ̃disjɔ̃) *f,* condition; (*pl.*) terms; position. ~ *provisionnelle,* proviso. *à ~,* on approval. *en ~,* in (*domestic*) service. **conditionnel, le†** (ɔnɛl) *a,* conditional. **conditionner** (ne) *v.t,* to condition; make up.

condoléance (kɔ̃doleɑ̃:s) *f,* condolence.

conducteur, trice (kɔ̃dyktœ:r, tris) *n,* conductor, tress; driver; drover; guard (*Rly*). ~ *des travaux,* foreman of job, works foreman (*Build.*). ~ *principal,* main, lead (*Elec.*). **conduire** (dɥi:r) *v.t. & abs. ir,* to conduct, lead, guide, show; direct, manage, run; drive; steer; take, carry, convey; conduce. *se ~,* to behave. **conduit** (dɥi) *m,* pipe, conduit, duct. **conduite** (dɥit) *f,* conduct, behaviour, bearing; management; lead; care; driving; pipe. ~ [*maîtresse*], main.

cône (ko:n) *m,* cone; taper.

confection (kɔ̃fɛksjɔ̃) *f,* making up; readymade clothes, &c *or* business; outfitting. **confectionner** (one) *v.t,* to make up; concoct. **confectionneur, euse** (nœ:r, øːz) *n,* clothier, outfitter.

confédération (kɔ̃federasjɔ̃) *f,* confederation, confederacy. **se confédérer** (re) *v.pr,* to confederate.

conférence (kɔ̃ferɑ̃:s) *f,* conference; lecture; debating society. **conférencier, ère** (rɑ̃sje, ɛ:r) *n,* lecturer. **conférer** (re) *v.i. & t,* to confer; bestow; compare.

confesse (kɔ̃fɛs) *f,* confession (*to priest*). **confesser** (se) *v.t,* to confess, own. **se ~,** to confess [one's sins]. **confesseur** (sœ:r) *m,* confessor. **confession** (sjɔ̃) *f,* confession. **confessionnal** (ɔnal) *m,* confessional (*box*). **confessionnel, le** (nɛl) *a,* confessional; denominational.

confiance (kɔ̃fjã:s) f, confidence, trust, faith, reliance, dependence. confiant, e (ã, ã:t) a, confident, sanguine, hopeful; confiding. confidemment (fidamã) ad, confidentially. confidence (dã:s) f, confidence, secrecy. confident, e (dã, ã:t) n, confidant, e. confidentiel, le† (sjɛl) a, confidential. confier (fje) v.t, to entrust, confide; trust, commit; vest. se ~, to confide, rely.

configuration (kɔ̃figyrasjɔ̃) f, configuration, lie, lay.

confiner (kɔ̃fine) v.i, to border; (v.t.) to confine. confins (fɛ̃) m.pl, confines; ends.

confire (kɔ̃fi:r) v.t.ir, to preserve; pickle.

confirmer (kɔ̃firme) v.t, to confirm.

confiscation (kɔ̃fiskasjɔ̃) f, confiscation.

confiserie (kɔ̃fizri) f, confectionery; confectioner's shop. confiseur, euse (zœ:r, ø:z) n, confectioner.

confisquer (kɔ̃fiske) v.t, to confiscate; impound.

confiture (kɔ̃fity:r) f. oft. pl, preserve, jam. ~ d'oranges, [orange] marmalade.

conflagration (kɔ̃flagrasjɔ̃) f, conflagration.

conflit (kɔ̃fli) m, conflict, clash, strife.

confluent (kɔ̃flyã) m, confluence, meeting. confluer (flye) v.i, to join, meet.

confondre (kɔ̃fɔ̃:dr) v.t, to confound; mingle; blend; confuse; mistake; discomfit; overwhelm; dash.

conformation (kɔ̃fɔrmasjɔ̃) f, conformation. conforme (fɔrm) a, conformable; according; in harmony; agreeable. pour copie ~, [certified] a true copy. conformé, e (me) p.a, (well, ill) formed. conformément (mã) ad, conformably, according. conformer (me) v.t. & se ~, to conform. conformité (mite) f, conformity, compliance.

confort (kɔ̃fɔ:r) m, comfort(s). confortable† (fɔrtabl) a, comfortable, cosy, snug.

confraternité (kɔ̃fraternite) f, confraternity, brotherhood. confrère (frɛ:r) m, colleague, confrère, brother; contemporary. confrérie (freri) f, brotherhood, sisterhood; confraternity.

confronter (kɔ̃frɔ̃te) v.t, to confront; compare.

confus, e (kɔ̃fy, y:z) a, confused; jumbled; indiscriminate; embarrassed. confusément (fyzemã) ad, confusedly; dimly. confusion (zjɔ̃) f, confusion; embarrassment.

congé (kɔ̃ʒe) m, leave; holiday; furlough; dismissal, discharge; notice [to quit]; permission; clearance (ship); cart note (Cust.); fillet (Arch.). congédier (dje) v.t, to dismiss, discharge; pay off.

congélation (kɔ̃ʒelasjɔ̃) f, congelation, freezing; frostbite. congeler (ʒle) v.t. & se ~, to congeal, freeze.

congénital, e (kɔ̃ʒenital) a, congenital.

congestion (kɔ̃ʒɛstjɔ̃) f, congestion. ~ cérébrale, pulmonaire, sanguine ,c. of the brain,

of the lungs, of the blood. congestionner (one) v.t, to congest (Med.).

conglomérat (kɔ̃glɔmera) m, conglomerate. conglomération (kɔ̃glɔmerasjɔ̃) f, conglomeration. conglomérer (le) v.t, to conglomerate.

congre (kɔ̃:gr) m, conger [eel].

congrégation (kɔ̃gregasjɔ̃) f, congregation (Eccl.).

congrès (kɔ̃grɛ) m, congress. congressiste (sist) n, member of the (or a) congress.

congru, e (kɔ̃gry) a, congruous, fitting. à la portion congrue, on short pay, on a meagre income. congrûment (grymã) ad, congruously.

conifère (konife:r) a, coniferous. ¶ m, conifer.

conique (konik) a, conic(al); taper[ing].

conjectural, e† (kɔ̃ʒɛktyral) a, conjectural. conjecture (ʒɛkty:r) f, conjecture, surmise, guess. conjecturer (tyre) v.t, to conjecture, &c.

conjoindre (kɔ̃ʒwɛ̃:dr) v.t.ir, to [con]join, unite. conjoint, e† (ʒwɛ̃, ɛ̃:t) a, [con]joint. ¶ n, party to a (or the) marriage (Law). conjonction (ʒɔ̃ksjɔ̃) f, conjunction, union. conjoncture (ʒɔ̃kty:r) f, conjuncture.

conjugaison (kɔ̃ʒygɛzɔ̃) f, conjugation.

conjugal, e† (kɔ̃ʒygal) a, conjugal, connubial, matrimonial, marriage (tie), married (life).

conjuguer (kɔ̃ʒyge) v.t, to conjugate. machines conjuguées, twin engines.

conjuration (kɔ̃ʒyrasjɔ̃) f, conspiracy; conjuration. conjuré (re) m, conspirator. conjurer (re) v.t. & i, to conspire; conjure.

connaissance (kɔnɛsã:s) f, knowledge; ken; acquaintance; consciousness, senses; cognizance; (pl.) learning, attainments, acquirements. avoir sa ~, to be conscious (awake). C~ des temps, Nautical Almanac. en ~ de cause, advisedly. figure de ~, familiar face. sans ~, unconscious, insensible, senseless.

connaissement (kɔnɛsmã) m, bill of lading.

connaisseur, euse (kɔnɛsœ:r, ø:z) n, connoisseur, judge. connaître (nɛtr) v.t. & abs. ir, to know, be acquainted with; be aware of; take cognizance. se ~ à (ou en), to be a [good] judge of. se faire ~, to introduce oneself, make oneself known; become known.

connexe (kɔnɛks) a, connected, allied, like. & ~s, & the like. connexion (ksjɔ̃) f, connexion. connexité (ksite) f, connexion.

connivence (kɔnivã:s) f, connivance. être de ~ pour, to connive at.

connu (le) (kɔny), the known.

conque (kɔ̃:k) f, conch.

conquérant, e (kɔ̃kerã, ã:t) n, conqueror, ess. conquérir (ri:r) v.t.ir, to conquer. conquête (kɛ:t) f, conquest.

consacrer (kɔ̃sakre) v.t, to consecrate, hallow; dedicate; devote; appropriate, set apart; sanction. consacré (à la mémoire de), sacred. terme consacré, accepted term.

consanguinité (kõsãginite) *f*, consanguinity, blood relationship.

conscience (kõsjã:s) *f*, conscience; conscientiousness; consciousness; breastplate. *se faire* ~ *de*, to be reluctant to. **consciencieux, euse†** (ãsjø, ø:z) *a*, conscientious. **conscient, e** (sjã, ã:t) *a*, conscious (*aware*); sentient (*being*).

conscription (kõskripsjõ) *f*, conscription. **conscrit** (skri) *m*, conscript; tyro; freshman (*Sch.*).

consécration (kõsekrasjõ) *f*, consecration; dedication; sanction.

consécutif, ive† (kõsekytif, i:v) *a*, consecutive.

conseil (kõse:j) *m*, advice, counsel; board; council; court; counsel (*pers. Law*). ~ *de prud'hommes*, conciliation board. *C* ~ *des ministres, C* ~ *de Cabinet*, cabinet council. ~ *d'administration*, board [of directors]. ~ *de guerre*, council of war; court martial. **conseiller** (seje) *v.t*, to advise, counsel. **conseiller, ère** (je, ε:r) *n*, adviser, counsellor; councillor. **conseilleur, euse** (jœ:r, ø:z) *n*, officious adviser.

consentement (kõsãtmã) *m*, consent; assent. **consentir** (ti:r) *v.i.ir*, to consent, agree.

conséquemment (kõsekamã) *ad*, consequently, accordingly. ~ *à*, consistently with. **conséquence** (kã:s) *f*, consequence; outcome; sequel; inference. **conséquent, e** (kã, ã:t) *a*, consistent, rational; consequent. *par conséquent*, consequently, accordingly, therefore.

conservateur, trice (kõservatœ:r, tris) *n*, conservator, keeper; warden; ranger; curator, trix; conservative (*Pol.*); registrar (*mortgages*). **conservation** (sjõ) *f*, preservation; care; registry. ~ *par le froid*, cold storage. **conservatoire** (twa:r) *m*, school, academy (*music, &c*); museum. **conserve** (serv) *f*, preserve; (*pl.*) tinned (*or* canned) (*or* potted) meats, &c; (*pl.*) preserves (*Opt.*); consort (*Naut.*). ~ *s au vinaigre*, pickles. **conserver** (ve) *v.t. & abs*, to preserve; pickle; conserve, keep. ~ *la composition*, to keep the type standing.

considérable† (kõsiderabl) *a*, considerable; eminent; large. **considérant** (rã) *m*, preamble. **considération** (rasjõ) *f*, consideration; regard. **considérer** (re) *v.t*, to consider; esteem; regard, deem.

consignataire (kõsiɲatε:r) *m*, trustee; consignee. **consignateur** (tœ:r) *m*, consignor. **consignation** (sjõ) *f*, deposit; consignment. **consigne** (siɲ) *f*, orders (*to sentry, &c*); confinement to barracks; cloak room, left luggage office (*Rly*). **consigner** (ɲe) *v.t*, to deposit; consign; record; chronicle; confine [to barracks]. ~ *à la porte*, to refuse admittance.

consistance (kõsistã:s) *f*, consistence, -cy; stability; credit; standing. **consistant, e** (tã, ã:t) *a*, firm, set. **consister** (te) *v.i*, to consist. **consistoire** (twa:r) *m*, consistory.

consolateur, trice (kõsɔlatœ:r, tris) *n*, consoler, comforter. **consolation** (sjõ) *f*, consolation, comfort, solace, cheer. **console** (sɔl) *f*, bracket; console; console table. **consoler** (le) *v.t*, to console, &c.

consolider (kõsɔlide) *v.t*, to consolidate, strengthen; unify, fund (*debt*); exercise, take up (*option*). **consolidation** (dasjõ) *f*, consolidation, &c.

consommateur (kõsɔmatœ:r) *m*, consumer; customer (*at café*). **consommation** (sjõ) *f*, consumption, use; drink; consummation. **consommé, e** (me) *a*, consummate. ¶ *m*, stock (*Cook.*); clear soup. **consommer** (me) *v.t*, to consume; use; drink; spend (*money in café*); consummate. **consomption** (sõpsjõ) *f*, consumption (*destruction & Med.*).

consonance (kõsɔnã:s) *f*, consonance. **consonant, e** (nã, ã:t) *a*, consonant. **consonne** (sɔn) *f*, consonant.

consorts (kõsɔ:r) *m.pl*, confederates. **consortium** (sɔrsjɔm) *m*, syndicate, consortium.

conspirateur, trice (kõspiratœ:r, tris) *n*, conspirator, plotter. **conspiration** (sjõ) *f*, conspiracy, plot. **conspirer** (re) *v.i. & t*, to conspire; plot; tend.

conspuer (kõspɥe) *v.t*, to conspue; hoot, boo, barrack. *conspuez-le!* down with him!

constamment (kõstamã) *ad*, constantly. **constance** (stã:s) *f*, constancy; steadfastness; persistence, perseverance; patience. *avec* ~, steadfastly. **constant, e** (stã, ã:t) *a*, constant; steadfast; enduring; obvious. ¶ *f*, constant.

constater (kõstate) *v.t*, to ascertain; verify, prove, establish; declare; attest; evidence; record; note; show; mention; be of opinion. **constatation** (tasjõ) *f*, ascertainment, &c.

constellation (kõstellasjõ) *f*, constellation; galaxy (*fig.*). **constellé, e** (stelle) *a*, constellated; studded.

consternation (kõsternasjõ) *f*, consternation, dismay. **consterner** (ne) *v.t*, to dismay, stagger.

constipation (kõstipasjõ) *f*, constipation, costiveness. **constiper** (pe) *v.t*, to constipate, bind.

constituant, e (kõstitɥã, ã:t) *a*, constituent, component. **constituer** (tɥe) *v.t*, to constitute; form, incorporate; settle; instruct; brief; appoint. *se* ~ *prisonnier*, to give oneself up [to the police]. **constitution** (tysjõ) *f*, constitution, &c; composition. ~ *de dot*, marriage settlement. **constitutionnel, le†** (ɔnεl) *a*, constitutional; temperamental.

constructeur (kõstryktœ:r) *m*, builder, maker, constructor. **construction** (sjõ) *f*, construction; building; making; build; engineering; erection; structure. **construire** (strɥi:r) *v.t.ir*, to construct; build, erect; make; construe.

consul (kɔ̃syl) *m*, consul. *le ~ britannique*, the British c. *le ~ de France*, the French c. **consulaire** (lɛːr) *a*, consular. **consulat** (la) *m*, consulate; consulship.

consultant, e (kɔ̃syltɑ̃, ɑ̃ːt) *a*, consulting. **consultation** (tasjɔ̃) *f*, consultation; opinion (*legal*), advice. **consulter** (te) *v.t. & i*, to consult; refer to.

consumer (kɔ̃syme) *v.t*, to consume; waste, spend.

contact (kɔ̃takt) *m*, contact; touch; connexion (*Elec.*).

contagieux, euse (kɔ̃taʒjø, øːz) *a*, contagious, infectious, catching. **contagion** (ʒjɔ̃) *f*, contagion; contagiousness.

contamination (kɔ̃taminasjɔ̃) *f*, contamination. **contaminer** (ne) *v.t*, to contaminate.

conte (kɔ̃ːt) *m*, story; tale, yarn; short story; fable. *~ de bonne femme*, *~ de vieille*, *~ à dormir debout*, twaddle. *~ de fées*, *~ bleu*, fairy tale. *~ rimé*, nursery rhyme. *~s en l'air*, cock-&-bull story, moonshine.

contemplatif, ive (kɔ̃tɑ̃platif, iːv) *a*, contemplative. **contemplation** (sjɔ̃) *f*, contemplation; gazing. **contempler** (ple) *v.t*, to contemplate, view; gaze on; meditate upon.

contemporain, e (kɔ̃tɑ̃pɔrɛ̃, ɛn) *a*, contemporaneous, contemporary. ¶ *n*, contemporary.

contempteur, trice (kɔ̃tɑ̃ptœːr, tris) *n*, scorner.

contenance (kɔ̃tnɑ̃ːs) *f*, capacity; content; countenance, demeanour, bearing. **contenant** (nɑ̃) *m*, container. **contenir** (tniːr) *v.t.ir*, to contain, hold; accommodate; comprise; restrain, control.

content, e (kɔ̃tɑ̃, ɑ̃ːt) *a*, content; contentedly; satisfied; pleased; glad. ¶ *m*, fill; heart's content. **contentement** (tɑ̃tmɑ̃) *m*, content[ment]; satisfaction. **contenter** (te) *v.t*, to content, satisfy, gratify.

contentieux, euse (kɔ̃tɑ̃sjø, øːz) *a*, contentious, law (*att.*). ¶ *m*, law (*or* solicitor's) department *or* office; contentious business. **contention** (sjɔ̃) *f*, application, intentness.

contenu (kɔ̃tny) *m*, contents.

conter (kɔ̃te) *v.t*, to tell, relate.

contestable (kɔ̃tɛstabl) *a*, questionable, debatable, moot. **contestation** (sjɔ̃) *f*, dispute, contestation. **sans conteste** (tɛst), indisputably. **contester** (te) *v.t. & abs*, to contest, challenge, question, dispute.

conteur, euse (kɔ̃tœːr, øːz) *n*, narrator; storyteller.

contexte (kɔ̃tɛkst) *m*, context.

contexture (kɔ̃tɛksty:r) *f*, [con]texture.

contigu, ë (kɔ̃tigy) *a*, contiguous, adjoining. **contiguité** (gɥite) *f*, contiguity.

continence (kɔ̃tinɑ̃ːs) *f*, continence. **continent, e** (nɑ̃, ɑ̃ːt) *a*, continent.

continent (kɔ̃tinɑ̃) *m*, continent, mainland. *le c~*, the Continent (*Europe*). **continental, e** (tal) *a*, continental.

contingence (kɔ̃tɛ̃ʒɑ̃ːs) *f*, contingency. **contingent, e** (ʒɑ̃, ɑ̃ːt) *a*, contingent. ¶ *m*, contingent, share; quota. **contingentement** (ʒɑ̃tmɑ̃) *m*, curtailment. **contingenter** (te) *v.t*, to curtail (*output*).

continu, e (kɔ̃tiny) *a*, continuous; direct (*elec. current*). **continuation** (nɥasjɔ̃) *f*, continuation; continuance. **continuel, le** (nɥɛl) *a*, continual, unceasing. **continuer** (nɥe) *v.t. & i*, to continue; carry on; go on; proceed; keep on. **continuité** (nɥite) *f*, continuity; ceaselessness. **continûment** (nymɑ̃) *ad*, continuously.

contondant, e (kɔ̃tɔ̃dɑ̃, ɑ̃ːt) *a*, blunt (*instrument*).

contorsion (kɔ̃tɔrsjɔ̃) *f*, contortion; twist.

contour (kɔ̃tuːr) *m*, contour, outline. *~ de hanches*, *de poitrine*, hip, bust, measurement. **contourner** (turne) *v.t*, to contort, twist; encircle.

contractant, e (kɔ̃traktɑ̃, ɑ̃ːt) *a*, contracting. ¶ *n*, contractant. **contracter** (te), *v.t. & abs*, to contract; enter into; take out, effect (*Insce policy*). **contraction** (sjɔ̃) *f*, contraction, shrinkage. **contractuel, le** (tɥɛl) *a*, contractual.

contradiction (kɔ̃tradiksjɔ̃) *f*, contradiction; discrepancy. **contradictoire** (twaːr) *a*, contradictory; conflicting; after trial; check, control (*att.*), joint.

contraindre (kɔ̃trɛ̃ːdr) *v.t.ir*, to constrain, compel, force, coerce, drive; restrain. *~ par saisie de biens*, to distrain upon (*pers.*). **contrainte** (trɛ̃ːt) *f*, constraint, compulsion, &c.

contraire (kɔ̃trɛːr) *a*, contrary, converse, opposea; unfavourable. ¶ *m*, contrary, reverse, converse, opposite. *au ~*, on the contrary. **contrairement** (trɛrmɑ̃) *ad*, contrarily, contrary, counter.

contralto (kɔ̃tralto) *m*, contralto.

contrariant, e (kɔ̃trarjɑ̃, ɑ̃ːt) *a*, trying, provoking. **contrarier** (rje) *v.t. & abs*, to thwart, interfere with, impede, cross; vex. **contrariété** (rjete) *f*, contrariety; annoyance, nuisance.

contraste (kɔ̃trast) *m*, contrast. **contraster** (te) *v.i. & t*, to contrast.

contrat (kɔ̃tra) *m*, contract; agreement; deed, indenture; articles; letter; bond.

contravention (kɔ̃travɑ̃sjɔ̃) *f*, contravention; breach, infringement; offence.

contre (kɔ̃ːtr) *pr. & ad*, against; contrary to; to (*as* 3 to 1); by, close to; versus. *~ nature*, unnatural.

contre-allée (kɔ̃trale) *f*, side walk.

contre-amiral (kɔ̃tramiral) *m*, rear admiral.

contre-attaque (kɔ̃tratak) *f*, counter attack.

contre-avions (kɔ̃travjɔ̃) *a*, anti-aircraft.

contrebalancer (kɔ̃trəbalɑ̃se) *v.t*, to counterbalance, counterpoise.

contrebande (kɔ̃trəbɑ̃ːd) *f*, smuggling, contraband. *de ~* (*fig.*), counterfeit. **contrebandier, ère** (bɑ̃dje, ɛːr) *n*, smuggler.

contrebas (en) (kɔ̃trəba) *ad*, below, lower down; downwards.

contrebasse (kɔ̃trəbɑːs) *f*, double bass, contra-bass.

contrecarrer (kɔ̃trəkare) *v.t*, to thwart, cross; counteract.

contrecœur (à) (kɔ̃trəkœːr) *ad*, reluctantly.

contrecoup (kɔ̃trəku) *m*, rebound; recoil; reaction.

contredire (kɔ̃trədiːr) *v.t. & abs. ir*, to contradict, gainsay. se ~, to contradict oneself; conflict. **sans contredit** (di), unquestionably.

contrée (kɔ̃tre) *f*, country, region.

contre-écrou (kɔ̃trekru) *m*, lock nut.

contre-expertise (kɔ̃trɛkspertiːz) *f*, resurvey.

contrefaçon (kɔ̃trəfasɔ̃) *f*, counterfeit; forgery; infringement; piracy; [colourable] imitation. ~ *littéraire*, ~ *de librairie*, infringement of copyright. **contrefacteur** (faktœːr) *m*, counterfeiter, &c. **contrefaire** (fɛːr) *v.t.ir*, to counterfeit, &c; mimic, take off; pretend to be; disguise; deform. **contrefaiseur, euse** (fəzœːr, øːz) *n*, mimic.

contre-fiche (kɔ̃trəfiʃ) *f*, strut, brace; raking shore.

contre-fil (à) (kɔ̃trəfil) *ad*, against the grain.

contrefort (kɔ̃trəfɔːr) *m*, buttress; spur.

contre-haut (en) (kɔ̃trəo) *ad*, above, higher up; upwards.

contre-jour (kɔ̃trəʒuːr) *m*, unfavourable light. *à* ~, against the light; with one's back to the light.

contremaître (kɔ̃trəmɛːtr) *m*, foreman.

contremander (kɔ̃trəmɑ̃de) *v.t*, to countermand; call off.

contremarque (kɔ̃trəmark) *f*, countermark; pass-out check (*Theat.*).

contrepartie (kɔ̃trəparti) *f*, counterpart; contra; contrary [opinion]; other side *or* party; another dealer; running stock (*against one's client*).

contrepasser (kɔ̃trəpɑse) *v.t*, to write back, reverse, contra; endorse back.

contre-pédaler (kɔ̃trəpedale) *v.i*, to back-pedal.

contre-petterie (kɔ̃trəpetri) *f*, Spoonerism.

contre-pied (kɔ̃trəpje) *m*, opposite (*course, view*).

contreplaqué (kɔ̃trəplake) *m*, plywood. ~ *en trois*, three-ply [wood].

contrepoids (kɔ̃trəpwa) *m*, counterweight, counterpoise, counterbalance, balance weight.

contre-poil (à) (kɔ̃trəpwal), the wrong way.

contrepoint (kɔ̃trəpwɛ̃) *m*, counterpoint.

contre-pointe (kɔ̃trəpwɛ̃t) *f*, loose headstock, tailstock.

contrepoison (kɔ̃trəpwazɔ̃) *m*, antidote.

contre-porte (kɔ̃trəpɔrt) *f*, screen door.

contreseing (kɔ̃trəsɛ̃) *m*, counter signature.

contresens (kɔ̃trəsɑ̃ːs) *m*, misconstruction; mistranslation; misinterpretation; bull; wrong way *or* sense.

contresigner (kɔ̃trəsiɲe) *v.t*, to countersign.

contretemps (kɔ̃trətɑ̃) *m*, mishap, unfortunate occurrence, awkward incident, hitch. *à* ~, inopportunely.

contre-torpilleur (kɔ̃trətɔrpijœːr) *m*, [torpedo-boat] destroyer.

contrevenir à (kɔ̃trəvəniːr) *v.ir*, to contravene, infringe, transgress.

contrevent (kɔ̃trəvɑ̃) *m*, outside shutter.

contrevérité (kɔ̃trəverite) *f*, untruth.

contribuable (kɔ̃tribɥabl) *n*, taxpayer; rate-payer. **contribuer** (bɥe) *v.i*, to contribute; conduce. **contribution** (bɥsjɔ̃) *f*, contribution; tax; rate.

contrister (kɔ̃triste) *v.t*, to sadden, grieve.

contrit, e (kɔ̃tri, it) *a*, contrite. **contrition** (sjɔ̃) *f*, contrition.

contrôle (kɔ̃troːl) *m*, control; supervision; roster; hall-mark; inspection; check; ticket office; box office. ~ *de présence*, time-keeping. **contrôler** (trole) *v.t*, to control; inspect; supervise; check; hall-mark. **contrôleur** (lœːr) *m*, controller, comptroller; supervisor; examiner; ticket collector; inspector; checker; timekeeper; jumper (*bus*); telltale (*Mach.*). ~ *des tours*, lap scorer.

contrordre (kɔ̃trɔrdr) *m*, counter instructions.

controuvé, e (kɔ̃truve) *p.p*, fabricated, invented.

controverse (kɔ̃trɔvers) *f*, controversy. **controversé, e** (se) *p.p*, debated.

contumace (kɔ̃tymas) *f*, contumacy.

contus, e (kɔ̃ty, yːz) *a*, bruised. **contusion** (tyzjɔ̃) *f*, bruise, contusion. **contusionner** (ɔne) *v.t*, to bruise, contuse.

convaincant, e (kɔ̃vɛ̃kɑ̃, ɑːt) *a*, convincing, cogent. **convaincre** (vɛ̃ːkr) *v.t.ir*, to convince; convict.

convalescence (kɔ̃valesɑ̃ːs) *f*, convalescence. **convalescent, e** (sɑ̃, ɑ̃ːt) *a. & n*, convalescent.

convenable† (kɔ̃vnabl) *a*, proper, fit, [be-]fitting, becoming, decorous; suitable, convenient; expedient. **convenance** (vnɑ̃ːs) *f*, propriety, fitness, congruity; harmony; convenience; expedience, -cy. **convenir** (vniːr) *v.i.ir*, to agree; own; suit; befit; be expedient; become, do. *mot convenu*, code word. *rédiger en langage convenu*, to code.

convention (vɑ̃sjɔ̃) *f*, covenant; agreement; contract; convention. *de* ~ *& conventionnel, le* (ɔnɛl) *a*, conventional.

converger (kɔ̃verʒe) *v.i*, to converge.

convers, e (kɔ̃vɛːr, ɛrs) *a*, lay (*brother, sister*). **converse,** *a.f. & f*, converse.

conversation (kɔ̃versasjɔ̃) *f*, conversation, talk; call (*Teleph.*). **converser** (se) *v.i*, to converse, talk, commune; wheel (*Mil.*).

conversion (sjɔ̃) *f*, conversion; wheel[ing] (*Mil.*). **convertible** (tibl) *a*, convertible.

converti, e (ti) *n*, convert. **convertir** (tiːr) *v.t*, to convert, change, turn. *se* ~, to become converted (*Relig.*). **convertissable** (tisabl) *a*, convertible (*Fin.*). **convertisse-**

ment (smɑ̃) *m*, conversion (*Fin.*). **convertisseur** (sœːr) *m*, converter.

convexe (kɔ̃vɛks) *a*, convex. **convexité** (íte) *f*, convexity.

conviction (kɔ̃viksjɔ̃) *f*, conviction.

convié, e (kɔ̃vje) *n*, guest. **convier** (vje) *v.t*, to invite (*fig.*), urge. **convive** (viːv) *n*, guest; table companion.

convocation (kɔ̃vɔkasjɔ̃) *f*, convocation, calling; notice [of meeting].

convoi (kɔ̃vwa) *m*, convoy; train (*Rly*); funeral [procession].

convoiter (kɔ̃vwate) *v.t*, to covet, lust after. **convoiteux, euse** (tø, øːz) *a*, covetous. **convoitise** (tiːz) *f*, covetousness; lust.

convoler (kɔ̃vɔle) *v.i & abs*, to marry again. ~ *en secondes, en troisièmes, noces*, to marry a second, a third, time.

convolvulus (kɔ̃vɔlvyly:s) *m*, convolvulus.

convoquer (kɔ̃vɔke) *v.t*, to convoke, call, summon, convene; call together.

convoyer (kɔ̃vwaje) *v.t*, to convoy.

convulsif, ive† (kɔ̃vylsif, iːv) *a*, convulsive. **convulsion** (sjɔ̃) *f*, convulsion; upheaval.

coopératif, ive (kɔɔperatif, iːv) *a*, cooperative. [*société*] *coopérative*, cooperative society. **coopération** (sjɔ̃) *f*, cooperation. **coopérer** (re) *v.i*, to cooperate.

coordonner (kɔɔrdɔne) *v.t*, to coordinate.

copain (kɔpɛ̃) *m*, chum.

copeau (kɔpo) *m*, shaving; chip.

Copenhague (kɔpenag) *f*, Copenhagen.

copie (kɔpi) *f*, copy; paper (*Sch.*). ~ *à la presse*, press copy (*letter*). ~ *au papier carbone*, carbon [copy]. ~*lettres*, *m*, [copy] letter book. **copier** (pje) *v.t. & abs*, to copy.

copieux, euse† (kɔpjø, øːz) *a*, copious, full; hearty (*meal*).

copiste (kɔpist) *n*, copyist.

copropriétaire (kɔprɔprietɛːr) *n*, joint owner.

copulation (kɔpylasjɔ̃) *f*, copulation.

coq (kɔk) *m*, cock, rooster; weathercock; bantam (*Box.*); cook (*ship's*). ~ *d-l'âne*, *m*, cock-&-bull story. ~ *d'Inde*, turkey cock. ~ *de bruyère*, heathcock, blackcock, moor cock. ~ *de combat*, game c. ~ *du village*, cock of the walk. [~] *faisan*, cock pheasant.

coque (kɔk) *f*, shell; hull (*ship*); husk; pod; cocoon; cockle (*Mol.*); loop (*of ribbon, hair*).

coquelicot (kɔkliko) *m*, poppy.

coqueluche (kɔklyʃ) *f*, [w]hooping cough; darling.

coquemar (kɔkma:r) *m*, kettle, pot.

coquerico (kɔkɔriko) *m*, cock-a-doodle-doo.

coquet, te† (kɔkɛ, ɛt) *a*, coquettish, skittish; stylish, smart, natty, trim. ¶ *n*, flirt, coquette. **coqueter** (kte) *v.i*, to coquet, flirt.

coquetier (kɔktje) *m*, egg cup; egg merchant.

coquetterie (kɔkɛtri) *f*, coquetry, &c, as *coquet, te*.

coquillage (kɔkija:ʒ) *m*, shellfish; shell conch. **coquille** (kiːj) *f*, shell; bush (*Mach.*); misprint, literal [error]; demy (*paper*). ~ *protectrice*, foul cup (*Box.*).

coquin, e (kɔkɛ̃, in) *n*, rogue, rascal, knave, scamp; (*f.*) hussy, jade, minx. **coquinerie** (kinri) *f*, knavery, roguery, rascality.

cor (kɔːr) *m*, horn (*Mus.*); corn (*on foot*); antler, tine. ~ *d'harmonie*, French horn. *à* ~ *& à cri*, clamorously.

corail (kɔraːj) *m*, coral. **corailleur** (rajœːr) *m*, coral fisher. **banc corallifère** (ralifɛːr), coral reef.

Coran (kɔrɑ̃) *m*, Koran.

corbeau (kɔrbo) *m*, raven; crow; corbel.

corbeille (kɔrbɛːj) *f*, basket. ~ *à papiers*, waste paper b. ~ [*de mariage*], (*bridegroom's*) wedding presents.

corbillard (kɔrbijaːr) *m*, hearse.

cordage (kɔrdaːʒ) *m*, rope; (*pl.*) cordage. **corde** (kɔrd) *f*, rope, cord, line; band; thread; string; halter (*hanging*); chord. *les* ~*s*, the strings (*orchestra*). *à* ~*s*, string[ed] (*Mus.*). ~ *à boyau*, catgut. ~ *à linge*, line rope, clothes line. ~ *à piano*, piano wire. ~ *à sauter*, skipping rope. ~ *de signal d'alarme*, communication cord. ~ *sensible*, sensitive spot. **cordeau** (do) *m*, line, string; chalk line (*cord*); fuse. **cordelette** (dəlɛt) *f*, cord, string. **cordelière** (ljɛːr) *f*, girdle. **corder** (de) *v.t*, to twist; cord, rope. **corderie** (dri) *f*, rope works; r. making.

cordial, e† (kɔrdjal) *a*, cordial, hearty. ¶ *m*, cordial. **cordialité** (lite) *f*, cordiality, &c.

cordier (kɔrdje) *m*, rope maker; drifter (*boat*).

cordon (kɔrdɔ̃) *m*, strand, twist; string; cord; lace (*shoe*); pull (*bell*); border; milled edge; row; cordon, ribbon. **cordonner** (dɔne) *v.t*, to twist, twine. **cordonnerie** (nri) *f*, shoemaker's shop; boot & shoe trade. **cordonnet** (nɛ) *m*, string; milled edge; overcast (*Emb.*). **cordonnier, ère** (nje, ɛːr) *n*, boot & shoe repairer, shoemaker.

Corée (la) (kɔre) *f*, Korea, Corea. **coréen, ne** (reɛ̃, ɛn) *a. & C~*, *n*, Korean.

coriace (kɔrjas) *a*, leathery, tough.

corindon (kɔrɛ̃dɔ̃) *m*, corundum.

Corinthe (kɔrɛ̃:t) *f*, Corinth. **corinthien, ne** (rɛ̃tjɛ̃, ɛn) *a. & C~*, *n*, Corinthian.

cormoran (kɔrmɔrɑ̃) *m*, cormorant.

cornac (kɔrnak) *m*, mahout; keeper; guide.

cornaline (kɔrnalin) *f*, cornelian, carnelian.

corne (kɔrn) *f*, horn; dog['s] ear; gaff (*spar*). ~ *d'abondance*, horn of plenty, cornucopia. ~ *de cerf*, deerhorn. **corné, e** (ne) *a*, horny.

corneille (kɔrnɛːj) *f*, crow; rook.

cornemuse (kɔrnəmyːz) *f*, bagpipe[s].

corner (kɔrne) *v.i*, to sound a horn; hoot (*Motor.*); speak in ear trumpet; din; ring (*ears*); (*v.t.*) to trumpet, din; dog['s] ear, turn down. **cornet** (nɛ) *m*, horn; cornet (*cone*). ~ [*à dés*], dice box. ~ *à pistons*, cornet (*Mus.*). ~ [*acoustique*], ear trumpet. ~ [*avertisseur*], hooter, horn (*motor*).

corniche (kɔrniʃ) *f*, cornice; ledge.

cornichon (kɔrniʃɔ̃) *m*, gherkin.

cornier, ère (kɔrnje, ɛːr) *a*, corner, angle (*att.*). ¶ *f*, angle iron.

Cornouailles (la) (kɔrnwɑ:j), Cornwall.

cornu, e (kɔrny) *a*, horned; absurd. ¶ *f*, retort, still.

corollaire (kɔrɔlɛːr) *m*, corollary.

corolle (kɔrɔl) *f*, corolla (*Bot.*).

coron (kɔrɔ̃) *m*, (coal) miner's dwelling; mining village.

corporation (kɔrpɔrasjɔ̃) *f*, corporation, g[u]ild. corporel, le† (rɛl) *a*, corporeal; corporal, bodily. corps (kɔːr) *m*, body; substance; corps, brigade; bodice; barrel, cylinder; hull (*ship*). ~ 6, 8 ou ~ de 6, de 8, *points*, 6, 8, point [size] (*Typ.*). ~ à ~, hand to hand (*fight*); clinch (*Box.*). ~ composé, compound (*Chem.*). ~ de garde, guard house, g. room. ~ de logis, ~ de bâtiment, main [portion of] building. ~ de métier, g[u]ild. ~ électoral, electorate, country. ~ & biens, crew & cargo, life & property. ~ [mort], [dead] body, corpse. ~ mort, dolphin, moorings (*Naut.*). à ~ perdu, recklessly. ~ simple, element (*Chem.*). faire ~, to corporate. prendre ~, to take shape.

corpulence (kɔrpylɑ̃:s) *f*, stoutness, corpulence, -ency, portliness, burliness. corpulent, e (lɑ̃, ɑ̃:t) *a*, corpulent, &c.

corpuscule (kɔrpyskyl) *m*, corpuscle.

correct, e† (kɔrɛkt) *a*, correct. correcteur, trice (tœːr, tris) *n*, corrector. ~ d'imprimerie, proof reader. correctif (tif) *m*, corrective. correction (sjɔ̃) *f*, correction; correctness; propriety; punishment. ~ des épreuves, proof reading. correctionnel, le† (ɔnɛl) *a*, correctional.

corrélatif, ive (kɔrelatif, iːv) *a*, correlative.

correspondance (kɔrɛspɔ̃dɑ̃:s) *f*, correspondence; letters; [postal] packet; connexion, interchange; transfer (*trams*). ~-avion, *f*, air [mail] packet. correspondant, e (dɑ̃, ɑ̃:t) *a*, corresponding. ¶ *n*, correspondent; friend acting for parents (*to pupil*). correspondre (pɔ̃:dr) *v.i*, to correspond; tally; communicate.

corridor (kɔridɔːr) *m*, corridor, passage.

corrigé (kɔriʒe) *m*, fair copy (*Sch.*); key (*book*). corriger (ʒe) *v.t*, to correct; compensate for; chastise.

corroborer (kɔrɔbɔre) *v.t*, to corroborate.

corroder (kɔrɔde) *v.t*, to corrode.

corroi (kɔrwa) *m*, currying (*leather*); puddle (*clay*).

corrompre (kɔrɔ̃:pr) *v.t*, to corrupt, taint, spoil; bribe.

corrosif, ive (kɔrozif, iːv) *a*. & *m*, corrosive. corrosion (zjɔ̃) *f*, corrosion.

corroyer (kɔrwaje) *v.t*, to curry (*leather*); puddle, pug; weld; trim, dress.

corruptible (kɔryptibl) *a*, corruptible. corruption (sjɔ̃) *f*, corruption; bribery.

corsage (kɔrsa:ʒ) *m*, bust; bodice, corsage.

corsaire (kɔrsɛːr) *m*, corsair, privateer; shark (*Fin.*); rover (*Croquet*).

Corse (la) (kɔrs), Corsica. corse, *a*. & C~, *n*, Corsican.

corsé, e (kɔrse) *p.a*, full-bodied (*wine*); strong, forcible (*language*). corser (se) *v.t*, to fortify, strengthen. se ~, to become serious.

corset (kɔrsɛ) *m*, corset, stays. ~-ceinture, *m*, wrap-round corset. corseter (sete) *v.t*, to corset. corsetier, ère (tje, ɛːr) *n*, corset maker.

cortège (kɔrtɛ:ʒ) *m*, retinue, train; procession; pageant.

corvée (kɔrve) *f*, statute (or forced) labour, corvée; fatigue (*Mil.*); drudgery, fag.

cosaque avec pétard (kɔzak) *m*, [Christmas] cracker.

cosmétique (kɔsmetik) *a*. & *m*, cosmetic.

cosmique (kɔsmik) *a*, cosmic(al).

cosmopolite (kɔsmopɔlit) *m*. & *a*, cosmopolite; cosmopolitan.

cosse (kɔs) *f*, pod, cod, shell, husk, hull; thimble, eye[let] (*Naut.*).

cosser (kɔse) *v.i*, to butt (*rams*).

cossu, e (kɔsy) *a*, well off; rich.

costume (kɔstym) *m*, costume, dress, garb; suit; frock. ~ marin, sailor suit. costumer (me) *v.t*, to dress (*in fancy dress*). costumier, ère (mje, ɛːr) *n*, theatrical & fancy costumier; wardrobe keeper (*Theat.*).

cote (kɔt) *f*, letter, number; quota, share, contribution; assessment, rating; quotation(s), price(s), rates, mark(s), marking, call, list; due dating (*bill*); character, class (*ship*); odds, betting; reading (*survey*). ~ d'amour, favouritism, backstairs influence. ~ de la bourse, stock exchange daily official list. ~ des changes, [foreign] exchange rates. ~ mal taillée, rough & ready settlement, compromise.

côte (kɔt) *f*, rib; slope; hill; [sea]coast, shore, seaboard. à ~s, ribbed, corded. ~ à ~, side by side, alongside. de la ~ de, descended from. faire ~, to run ashore. la C~ d'Azur, the Riviera. la C~ d'Ivoire, the Ivory Coast. la C~ de l'Or, the Gold Coast.

côté (kɔte) *m*, side; way, direction; [broad]side (*Naut.*); beam ends (*Naut.*). ~ des nœuds ou ~ lisse? rough or smooth? (*Ten.*). ~ droit (de la voiture), off side. ~ du montoir, near side (*Riding*). ~ du vent, weather side. ~ faible, weak spot (*fig. of pers.*). ~ gauche (de la voiture), near side. ~ hors du montoir, off side (*Riding*). ~ sous le vent, lee [side]. à ~, ad, near, to one side. à ~ de, pr, by the side of; next to; next door to; beside. de ~, ad, sideways; sidelong; aside, apart, on one side, by. de l'autre ~, on the other side or hand; over the way.

coteau (kɔto) *m*, hill, hillside, slope.

côtelé, e (kotle) *a*, ribbed, corduroy.

côtelette (kotlɛt) *f*, chop, cutlet. ~ *de filet*, loin chop. ~ *de gigot*, chump chop.

coter (kɔte) *v.t*, to letter; number; mark; page; assess, rate; quote; class; rank. *croquis coté*, dimensioned sketch.

coterie (kɔtri) *f*, set, clique, circle.

cothurne (kɔtyrn) *m*, buskin, cothurnus.

côtier, ère (kotje, ɛːr) *a*, coast[ing]; inshore. [*bateau*] *côtier*, coaster. [*cheval*] *côtier*, trace horse.

cotillon (kɔtijɔ̃) *m*, petticoat; cotill[i]on.

cotisation (kɔtizasjɔ̃) *f*, quota, share, contribution; subscription; fee; assessment. **cotiser** (ze) *v.t*, to assess. **se ~**, to club together; subscribe.

coton (kɔtɔ̃) *m*, cotton; c. wool; down, fluff. **~-poudre**, *m*, guncotton. **cotonnade** (tɔnad) *f*, cotton [cloth, goods]. **cotonneux, euse** (nø, øːz) *a*, cottony; downy; fluffy; woolly. **cotonnier, ère** (nje, ɛːr) *a*, cotton (*att.*). ¶ *m*, cotton plant.

côtoyer (kotwaje) *v.t. & abs.*, to run along, hug (*shore*); skirt; coast; border upon.

cotre (kɔtr) *m*, cutter (*boat*). ~ *de la douane*, revenue cutter.

cotret (kɔtrɛ) *m*, fag[g]ot, stick.

cottage (kɔtaʒ) *m*, cottage (*small & elegant country residence*).

cotte (kɔt) *f*, petticoat; overalls. ~ *de mailles*, coat of mail.

cou (ku) *m*, neck. **~-de-pied**, instep.

couard, e (kuaːr, ard) *a*, coward[ly]. ¶ *n*, coward. **couardise** (kuardiːz) *f*, cowardice.

couchant (kuʃɑ̃) *m*, setting; west; wane, decline. **couche** (kuʃ) *f*, bed, couch; hotbed; layer; stratum; seam; sheet; coat[ing]; course; lap[ping]; napkin (*baby's*); ring (*in tree*); (*pl.*) confinement, lying-in, childbed; delivery, birth. **coucher** (kuʃe) *m*, going to bed; setting (*sun, &c*); night's lodging; board; bed[ding]. ~ *de soleil*, sunset. *au ~ du soleil*, at sunset, at sundown. ¶ *v.t*, to lay; lay down; put to bed; lay low; beat down; slope. ~ *en joue*, to aim (at). ~ *par écrit*, to commit to (or put in) (*or* set down in) writing. ¶ *v.i*, to lie, lie down; spend the night, sleep. **se ~**, to lie down, go to bed; couch; set, go down (*sun, moon*). **couchette** (ʃɛt) *f*, crib, cot; berth, bunk, couchette.

couci-couça (kusikusa), **couci-couci**, *ad*, so so, middling.

coucou (kuku) *m*, cuckoo; cowslip. [*pendule à*] ~, cuckoo clock.

coude (kud) *m*, elbow; bend; crank. *jouer des ~s*, to elbow one's way. **coudées franches** (kude) *f.pl*, elbow-room (*fig.*); scope.

cou-de-pied (kudpje) *m*, instep.

couder (kude) *v.t*, to bend, crank. **coudoyer** (dwaje) *v.t*, to elbow, jostle; run up against; come very near to.

coudre (kudr) *v.t. & abs. ir*, to sew; s. up; s. on; stitch; piece, tack (*fig.*).

coudrier (kudrie) *m*, hazel (*bush*).

couenne (kwan) *f*, rind (*bacon*); crackling (*pork*); mole (*Med.*).

couguar (kugwaːr) *m*, cougar, puma.

coulage (kula:ʒ) *m*, running; pouring, casting; leakage. **coulant, e** (lɑ̃, ɑ̃:t) *a*, flowing, easy, liquid, running, loose; accommodating. ¶ *m*, runner (*Hort. & Mech.*); slide. **coulé** (le) *m*, slur (*Mus.*); flow [shot] (*Bil.*); casting. **coulée** (le) *f*, running; flow; cast[ing]; tapping; run (*animal track*); running hand. **couler** (le) *v.t*, to pour, tap, cast; strain; sink, slide; slur (*Mus.*); (*v.i.*) to flow, run; trickle; gutter; leak; glide, slide, slip. ~ *ou* ~ *à fond ou* ~ *à pic ou* ~ *bas*, to sink, founder, go down. *laisser* ~, to spill, shed; slip; turn on water. **se ~**, to slide, slip.

couleur (kulœːr) *f*, colour; colouring; paint; stain (*wood, &c*); suit (*Cards*); (*pl.*) colours (*flag*). *robe de ~*, coloured dress. *ruban ~ de feu*, flame-coloured ribbon. *souliers ~ de rose*, rose-coloured shoes. *sous ~ de*, under colour of (*fig.*).

couleuvre (kulœːvr) *f*, snake; bitter pill (*fig.*). ~ *à collier*, common snake, grass s.

coulis (kuli) *m*, grout[ing].

coulisse (kulis) *f*, slide; slideway; heading, hem (*for tape*); link (*Mach.*); link motion; side scene (*Theat.*); (*pl.*) slips, wings (*Theat.*); coulisse (*unofficial or free market on Paris Bourse*). *dans la ~*, behind the scenes. *à ~*, sliding. *regard en ~*, side-long glance. **coulissier** (sje) *m*, coulissier (*broker on Paris coulisse market*).

couloir (kulwaːr) *m*, passage, corridor; lane (*Running*); lobby; chute, shoot.

couloire (kulwaːr) *f*, strainer.

coup (ku) *m*, blow; stroke; hit; chop; coup; knock; thrust; poke; cut; slash; nip; prick; dig; whack; slap; stab; shock; clap, peal; flap; rap; wave, sweep; touch; shot; report; rush; beat; blast; gust; move (*Chess, &c*); knack; glass, drink; time, moment; try, go; pitch (*angler's*). ~ *au but*, hit. ~ *d'air*, rush of air; chill (*Med.*). ~ *d'amende*, penalty stroke (*Golf*). ~ *d'assommoir*, knock-down blow (*fig.*). ~ *d'envoi*, kick-off (*Foot.*). ~ *d'épaule*, lift. ~ *d'épingle*, pin prick. ~ *d'éponge* (*fig.*), clean slate. ~ *d'essai*, first attempt, trial shot. ~ *d'essai*, practice (*Ten.*). ~ *d'œil*, glance, twinkling; look; judgement; view. ~ *d'ongle*, scratch. *à ~s de*, with (*blows from*). ~ *de balai*, sweep. ~ *de bec*, peck. ~ *de bélier*, water hammer[ing]. ~ *de brosse*, brush. ~ *de but*, goal kick (*Foot.*); g. throw (*Water Polo*). ~ *de chapeau*, salute, bow. ~ *de chiffon*, wipe, rub with a cloth. *à ~s de ciseaux*, with scissors & paste (*fig.*). ~ *de coin*, corner kick; c. throw. ~ *de collier*, tug.

~ *de corne*, butt. ~ *de coude*, nudge. ~ *de dents*, bite. ~ *de deux*, double (*Turf*). *traduire à ~s de dictionnaire*, to translate by looking up every other word in the dictionary. ~ *de feu*, shot. ~ *de filet*, cast; haul; draught; catch. ~ *de fleuret*, pass (*Fenc.*). ~ *de force*, feat of strength. ~ *de foudre*, thunderbolt. ~ *de fouet*, lash; fillip. ~ *de froid*, cold snap; chill (*Med.*). ~ *de grâce*, finishing stroke, quietus. ~ *de griffe*, scratch. *à ~s de hache*, in a rough & ready fashion. ~ *de hasard*, fluke. ~ *de l'étrier*, stirrup cup. ~ *de lumière*, burst of light. ~ *de lunette*, sight. ~ *de main*, surprise attack; swift bold stroke (*action*); lightning move; helping hand. ~ *de marteau*, knock (*at the door*). ~ *de massue*, stunning blow. *un* ~ *de mer*, a great wave, a heavy sea. ~ *de patte*, dig (*fig.*). ~ *de pénalité*, penalty kick; p. throw. ~ [*de pied*], kick. ~ *de poing*, punch; fisticuffs; knuckle-duster. ~ *de réparation*, penalty kick. ~ *de sang*, [apoplectic] stroke. ~ *de sifflet*, [blast of a] whistle. ~ *de soleil*, sun-stroke. ~ *de sonnette*, ring-[of a bell]. ~ *de téléphone*, ring [of the telephone]. ~ *de tête*, butt; rash act. ~ *de théâtre*, stage trick; sensation[al event]. ~ *de tonnerre*, thunder clap, peal of t. ~ *de vent*, squall, gust of wind; flurry; blast; gale. ~ *déloyal*, foul (*Box.*). ~ *écrasé*, smash (*Ten.*). ~*s & blessures*, assault & battery. ~ *franc*, free kick (*Foot.*); f. throw (*Water Polo*). ~ *manqué*, miss, failure. ~ *monté*, put-up job. ~ *placé*, place kick (*Rugby*). ~ *roulé*, putt (*Golf*). ~ *sur* ~, one after another. *à* ~ *sûr*, assuredly, for a certainty. ~ *tiré*, pull (*Golf*). ~ *tombé*, drop kick (*Rugby*).

coupable (kupabl) *a*, guilty, culpable; sinful. ¶ *n*, culprit, offender.

coupage (kupa:ʒ) *m*, blending (*wines*). **coupant, e** (pɑ̃, ɑ̃:t) *a*, cutting, sharp; edge[d]. ¶ *m*, [cutting] edge. **coupe** (kup) *f*, cutting; cutting out (*clothes*); cut; division; section; length (*piece of a stuff*); overarm stroke (*Swim.*); cup, chalice, goblet, glass; bowl, dish; cup (*Sport*); plate (*Turf*). ~ *électrique*, ceiling bowl. **coupé** (pe) *m*, brougham; coupé. **coupe-cigares**, *m*, cigar cutter. **coupe-circuit**, *m*, cut-out (*Elec.*). **coupe-gorge**, *m*, cut-throat place. **coupe-jarret**, *m*, cut-throat (*pers.*). **coupe-verre à molette**, *m*, wheel glass cutter. **coupé-lit**, *m*, sleeping compartment (*Rly*). **coupelle** (pɛl) *f*, cupel. **coupeller** (le) *v.t*, to cupel. **coupe-papier**, *m*, paper knife. **couper** (pe) *v.t. & abs*, to cut; c. off; c. down; c. in (*on road, &c*); c. out; chop off; intersect, cross; slice (*ball*); blend (*wines*); dilute, water; interrupt; switch off. **se** ~, to cut oneself; cut; contradict oneself; intersect. *se faire* ~

les cheveux, to have one's hair cut. **couperet** (prɛ) *m*, cleaver, chopper; knife. **couperose** (kupro:z) *f*, copperas, vitriol; acne. **coupeur, euse** (kupœːr, øːz) *n*, cutter. ~ *de bourses*, pickpocket.

couple (kupl) *f*, couple, two; brace; yoke; leash. ¶ *m*, couple (*pers.*); pair; cell (*Elec.*); timber (*ship*). ~ [*moteur*], torque, couple. **coupler** (ple) *v.t*, to couple, connect. **couplet** (plɛ) *m*, verse; strap hinge. **coupole** (kupɔl) *f*, cupola, dome. **coupon** (kupɔ̃) *m*, remnant; short length; coupon; half (*Rly ticket*). **coupure** (pyːr) *f*, cut; cutting (*newspaper*); denomination.

cour (kuːr) *f*, court; [court]yard; lavatory; courtship, suit. ~ *d'honneur*, quadrangle. ~ *de cassation*, supreme court of appeal. ~ *de l'église*, churchyard. ~ *de récréation*, playground. ~ *martiale*, drum-head court martial. *faire la* ~ *à*, to court, woo, make love to.

courage (kuraːʒ) *m*, courage, fortitude, spirit, pluck, nerve. ~ *arrosé*, Dutch courage. ¶ *i*, courage! cheer up! **courageux, euse†** (raʒø, øːz) *a*, courageous, game.

couramment (kuramɑ̃) *ad*, fluently; usually, commonly. **courant, e** (rɑ̃, ɑ̃:t) *a*, current; running; instant, present; run (*measurement*). ¶ *m*, current; stream; tide; course; current (*or present*) month. ~ *alternatif*, alternating current (*Elec.*) ~ *continu*, direct c., continuous c. ~ *d'affaires*, turnover. ~ *d'air*, air current; blast; draught. ~ *de jusant*, ebb tide. ~ *de palan*, tackle fall. ¶ *f*, diarrhoea.

courbatu, e (kurbaty) *a*, tired out, knocked up. **courbature** (tyːr) *f*, stiffness, tiredness. **courbe** (kurb) *a*, curve[d]. ¶ *f*, curve, bend, sweep. ~ *de niveau*, contour line. **courber** (be) *v.t. & i. & se* ~, to bend, curve, bow. **courbette** (bɛt) *f*, curvet. *faire des* ~*s*, to curvet; bow & scrape. *faire une* ~, to duck. **courbure** (byːr) *f*, curvature, bend.

coureur, euse (kurœːr, øːz) *n*, runner; racer; wanderer, rover; gadabout; frequenter; rake. ~ *cycliste*, racing cyclist. ~ *de bals*, dancing man. ~ *de jetons de présence*, guinea pig (*pers.*). ~ *de prix*, pot hunter. ~ *de spectacles*, playgoer. ~ *de vitesse*, sprinter.

courge (kurʒ) *f*, pumpkin; gourd. ~ *à la moelle*, vegetable marrow.

courir, *v.i. & t. ir*, to run; go; run about; hurry; slip (*or pass*) away; race; sail; circulate, go round; be in fashion; be rife; accrue; tramp up & down; run after; pursue; frequent; hunt; course; hunt after; incur; go through; travel. *le bruit court que . . .*, it is reported (*or rumoured*) that *. . .*, there is a rumour abroad that . . .

courlis (kurli), **courlieu** (ljø) *m*, curlew. **couronne** (kurɔn) *f*, crown; wreath; coronet; corona; circlet; ring; tonsure. ~ [*mortu-*

aire], wreath (*funeral*). **couronnement** (nnᾶ) *m*, coronation; crowning; crowning piece; coping; taffrail. **couronner** (ne) *v.t*, to crown; wreathe; cap; cope; award a prize to; reward; surround.

courrier (kurje) *m*, mail cart, m. coach; mail, post, letters; courier, messenger; news, intelligence. **courriériste** (rjerist) *m*, par writer.

courroie (kurwa) *f*, belt, band; strap. ~s [*de transmission*], belting.

courroucer (kuruse) *v.t*, to incense, anger. **courroux** (ru) *m*, wrath, anger, ire, rage.

cours (ku:r) *m*, course; flow; run; stream; way; class (*Sch.*); currency; tender (*legal*); price, rate, quotation; avenue. ~ *authentique & officiel*, stock exchange daily official list. ~ *d'eau*, stream, watercourse. ~ *de danse*, *pl*, dancing classes, school of dancing. en ~, current; present; instant; in progress.

course (kurs) *f*, run; race; (*pl.*) running, racing; outing, trip; errand; way; course; career; fare; stroke, travel; privateering. **de** ~, racing (*as cycle, ski*); race (*as horse*); speed (*skates*). **en** ~, out [on business]. ~ *à pied*, foot race. ~ *au clocher*, point-to-point r. ~ *d'avions*, air r. ~ *d'élan*, run[-up] (*Jump*.). ~ *d'obstacles*, steeple-chase; obstacle race. ~ *de barrage*, run-off (*from dead heat*). ~ *de chars*, chariot race. ~ *de côte*, hill climb. ~ *de demi-fond*, middle-distance race. ~ *de fond*, long-distance r.; distance swim. ~ *de haies*, hurdle race. ~s *de lévriers*, grey-hound racing, dog r., dogs. ~ *de* (ou *à*) *relais*, relay r. ~ *de taureaux*, bullfight. ~ *de vitesse*, sprint[ing] (*running or swimming*); speed swim. ~ *en sacs*, sack race. ~ *nulle*, ~ *à égalité*, dead heat. ~ *par équipes*, team race. ~ *plate*, flat r. ~ *sur piste*, track r. ~ *sur route*, road race. ~s *sur route*, road racing. **coursier** (sje) *m*, charger (*horse*), steed, courser.

court, e (ku:r, urt) *a*, short; limited. *à courtes vues*, short-sighted (*fig.*). *à court de*, short of; out of stock of. **court**, *ad*, short.

court (kort *ou* ku:r) *m*, court (*Ten.*).

courtage (kurta:ʒ) *m*, broking; brokerage; commission.

courtaud, e (kurto, o:d) *n*, thickset (*or* dumpy) person. **courtauder** (tode) *v.t*, to dock the tail of.

court-circuit (kursirkɥi) *m*, short [circuit].
courte-botte (kurtəbɔt) *m*, shrimp (*pers.*).
courtement (kurtəmᾶ) *ad*, shortly.
courtepointe (kurtəpwɛ̃:t) *f*, [down] quilt.
courtier, ère (kurtje, ɛ:r) *n*, broker. ~ *de marchandises*, produce b. ~ *électoral*, election agent. ~ *maritime*, ship broker. ~ *marron*, outside broker.
courtisan (kurtizᾶ, an) *a*, flattering, obsequious. ¶ *m*, courtier. ¶ *f*, **courtesan.**

courtiser (ze) *v.t*, to court; woo; fawn on. **courtois, e†** (twa, a:z) *a*, courteous; courtly, urbane. **courtoisie** (twazi) *f*, courtesy, &c.

couseur, euse (kuzœ:r, ø:z) *n*, sewer (*Need.*).

cousin, e (kuzɛ̃, in) *n*, cousin; friend. ~ *germain, e*, first cousin, c. german. ~ *issu(e) de germain*, second c. ¶ *m*, gnat, midge. **cousiner** [**ensemble**] (zine) *v.i*, to get on well [together].

coussin (kusɛ̃) *m*, cushion; hassock; bolster; pillow; pad. **coussinet** (sinɛ) *m*, [small] cushion; pad; bearing, brass, bush; [screwing] die; [rail] chair (*Rly*).

coût (ku) *m*, cost.

couteau (kuto) *m*, knife; cutter; knife edge. ~ *à découper*, carving knife, [meat] carver. ~ *à dessert*, cheese knife. ~ *à virole*, *à cran d'arrêt*, clasp k., jack k. ~-*scie à pain*, bread saw. **à** ~, eating (*apples, &c*). **à** ~*x tirés*, at daggers drawn (*fig.*). **le** ~ *à la gorge*, a pistol [held] at one's head (*fig.*). **coutelas** (tlɑ) *m*, big kitchen knife. **coutelier, ère** (təlje, ɛ:r) *n*, cutler. **coutellerie** (tɛlri) *f*, cutlery; c. works *or* shop.

coûter (kute) *v.i*, to cost; (*abs.*) to cost money. *coûte que coûte*, at all costs. **coûteusement** (təzmᾶ) *ad*, expensively. **coûteux, euse** (tø, ø:z) *a*, costly, expensive.

coutil (kuti) *m*, [canvas] tick[ing]; drill; duck.

coutume (kutym) *f*, custom, usage, habit, practice, wont. *de* ~, usual. **coutumier, ère** (mje, ɛ:r) *a*, accustomed to, in the habit; customary; common, unwritten (*law*). ~ *du fait*, in the habit of doing so.

couture (kuty:r) *f*, seam; sewing; needlework; scar; pock, pit. ~ [*à la main*], plain sewing. *battre à plate* ~, to beat hollow (*or* soundly). **couturer** (tyre) *v.t*, to scar, seam (*with wounds*); pock, pit. **couturier** (rje) *m*, costum[i]er, mantle maker. **couturière** (rjɛ:r) *f*, dressmaker, tailoress; seamstress, needlewoman.

couvain (kuvɛ̃) *m*, nest of (*insects*) eggs. **couvaison** (vɛzɔ̃) *f*, brooding time, sitting t. **couvée** (ve) *f*, brood, hatch, clutch; progeny.

couvent (kuvᾶ) *m*, convent, monastery, nunnery; convent school.

couver (kuve) *v.t*, to sit on (*eggs*); hatch; incubate; (*abs.*) to brood, sit; mother (*fig.*); (*v.i.*) to smoulder; brew. ~ *des yeux*, to gaze at; gloat over. *mettre* ~, to set (*hen*).

couvercle (kuvɛrkl) *m*, cover, lid, cap, head.

couvert, e (kuvɛ:r, ɛrt) *p.a*, covered; clad; overgrown; wooded; shady; overcast; covert. ¶ *m*, table [things]; knife, fork, & spoon; spoon & fork; cover; shady retreat. **le** ~, shelter, lodging. *mettre*, *ôter, le* ~, to lay, clear, the table. **à** ~, under cover, sheltered; covered; packed (*consignment*). ¶ *f*, blanket; glaze (*on pottery*). **couverture** (vɛrty:r) *f*, covering; cover; margin; roofing; blanket; counter-

pane; rug (*travelling*); cloth (*horse*). ~
rempliée, paper wrappered, turned over
(*Bookb.*).

couveuse (kuvø:z) *f*, brood hen, sitting hen.
~ *artificielle*, incubator. **couvi** (vi) *a.m*,
addle[d].

couvre-chef (kuvrəʃɛf) *m*, headgear. **couvre-
engrenages** (vrāgrəna:ʒ) *m*, gear case.
couvre-feu (vrø) *m*, lights out (*Mil.*);
curfew. **couvre-joint**, *m*, welt, butt strap.
couvre-lit, *m*, bedspread. **couvre-livre**,
m, jacket, dust cover (*book*). **couvre-
pied**, *m*, down quilt. **couvre-théière**, *m*,
tea cosy. **couvreur** (vrœ:r) *m*, slater;
tiler; thatcher. **couvrir** (vri:r) *v.t.ir*, to
cover; roof; load (*with praise, abuse*);
drown (*sounds*). **se ~**, to cover oneself,
wrap up; put one's hat on; become overcast.

crabe (krab) *m*, crab (*Crust.*).

crac (krak) *m*, crack, snap; (*i.*) before you
could say Jack Robinson *or* knife.

crachat (kraʃa) *m*, spit[tle]; star (*decoration*).
crachement (ʃmā) *m*, spitting. **cracher** (ʃe)
v.i. & t, to spit; spit out; splutter; splash
(*tap*); spout. *tout craché*, to a tee. **crachoir**
(ʃwa:r) *m*, spittoon.

crack (krak) *m*, crack (*racehorse*).

Cracovie (krakɔvi) *f*, Cracow.

craie (krɛ) *f*, chalk.

craindre (krɛ̃:dr) *v.t. & abs. ir*, to fear, be
afraid of, dread; cannot stand. *craint
l'humidité, la chaleur*, to be kept dry, cool
or in a dry, cool, place. **crainte** (krɛ̃:t) *f*,
fear, dread, awe. **craintif, ive†** (krɛ̃tif, i:v)
a, timid, timorous, fearful, afraid.

cramoisi, e (kramwazi) *a. & m*, crimson.

crampe (krā:p) *f*, cramp (*Med.*); staple.
crampon (krāpɔ̃) *m*, cramp [iron], clamp,
holdfast; fastener, catch; staple; [dog]
spike; frost nail; crampon; stud; bore
(*pers.*). **cramponner** (pɔne) *v.t*, to cramp,
clamp, fasten; rough-shoe; pester. **se ~**,
to cling, fasten.

cran (krā) *m*, notch, nick; peg (*fig.*); pluck,
mettle. ~ *d'arrêt*, safety catch.

crâne (krɑ:n) *m*, skull, cranium. ¶ †, *a*,
plucky, jaunty. **crâner** (krɑne) *v.i*, to
swagger; brazen it out.

crapaud (krapo) *m*, toad; low easy chair;
baby grand; cracker (*firework*); flaw. *laid
comme un ~*, [as] ugly as sin. **crapaudière**
(djɛ:r) *f*, toad hole. **crapaudine** (din) *f*,
toadstone; strainer, grating; plug hole;
centre casting.

crapoussin, e (krapusɛ̃, in) *n*, shrimp (*pers.*).

crapule (krapyl) *f*, debauchery; debauchee.
crapuleux, euse† (lø, ø:z) *a*, debauched,
lewd; filthy.

craque (krak) *f*, fib, cram.

craquelin (kraklɛ̃) *m*, cracknel.

craquelure (krakly:r) *f*, crack(s) (*in enamel,
&c*). **craquer** (ke) *v.i*, to crack, crackle,
crunch, creak. **craqueter** (kte) *v.i*, to
crackle.

crasse (kras) *a.f*, crass. ¶ *f*, dirt, filth, grime,
squalor; scum, dross, slag, clinker; scale;
gutter (*fig.*); sordidness. **crasseux, euse**
(sø, ø:z) *a*, dirty, filthy, grimy, grubby,
unwashed, foul, squalid.

cratère (kratɛ:r) *m*, crater.

cravache (kravaʃ) *f*, riding whip, horsewhip.
cravacher (ʃe) *v.t*, to flog; horsewhip.

cravan (kravā) *m*, barnacle (*on ship*).

cravate (kravat) *f*, [neck]tie; bow & tassels
(*of colour staff*). ~ *de soirée*, dress bow.

crayeux, euse (krɛjø, ø:z) *a*, chalky. **crayon**
(jɔ̃) *m*, pencil; sketch, outline. ~ *à mine
de plomb*, lead pencil. ~ *pastel*, crayon.
~ *pour les lèvres*, lipstick. ~ *pour les
yeux*, eyebrow pencil. **crayonner** (jɔne)
v.t, to pencil; sketch, outline.

créance (kreā:s) *f*, credence, belief, trust;
credit; [book] debt; indebtedness; claim.
créancier, ère (āsje, ɛ:r) *n*, creditor. ~
gagiste, lienor, pledgee. ~ *hypothécaire*,
mortgagee.

créateur, trice (kreatœ:r, tris) *n*, creator, tress,
maker; founder, foundress; (*att.*) creative.
création (sjɔ̃) *f*, creation; founding.
créature (ty:r) *f*, creature.

crécelle (kresɛl) *f*, rattle (*toy, &c*).

crécerelle (kresrɛl) *f*, kestrel.

crèche (krɛ:ʃ) *f*, crib, manger; day nursery;
crèche.

crédence (kredā:s) *f*, sideboard; credence
[table].

crédibilité (kredibilite) *f*, credibility. **crédit**
(di) *m*, credit; trust; influence; repute;
creditor; bank; (*pl.*) supplies (*parliamentary*). *au comptant ou à ~*, cash or
terms (*sales*). ~ *municipal*, mortgage
loan office & pawnshop. **créditer** (te) *v.t*,
to credit. **créditeur** (tœ:r) *m. & att*,
creditor.

credo (kredo) *m*, creed, credo; gospel (*fig.*).
crédule (kredyl) *a*, credulous, gullible. **crédulité** (lite) *f*, credulity, &c.

créer (kree) *v.t. & abs*, to create, make;
establish, found; make out, write out
(*cheque*).

crémaillère (kremajɛ:r) *f*, pothook; rack
(*toothed*). *pendre la ~*, to give a house-
warming.

crémation (kremasjɔ̃) *f*, cremation.

crème (krɛm) *f*, cream; custard. ~ *chocolatée*, chocolate cream. ~ *glacée*, ice
cream, cream ice. **crémerie** (mri) *f*, dairy;
creamery; tea shop. **crémeux, euse**
(kremø, ø:z) *a*, creamy. **crémier, ère**
(mje, ɛ:r) *n*, dairyman, -woman; (*m.*) cream
jug.

Crémone (kremɔn) *f*, Cremona. **c~**, *f*,
espagnolette.

créneau (kreno) *m*, battlement; loophole.
créneler (nle) *v.t*, to crenel[l]ate, castellate,
battlement, embattle; tooth, ratchet; mill
(*coin*).

créole (kreɔl) *n. & a*, creole.

créosote (kreɔzɔt) f, creosote.

crêpe (krɛːp) m, crape, crêpe; (f.) pancake. crêper (krɛpe) v.t, to crimp, crisp, frizz[le].

crépi (krepi) m, roughcast (Build.).

crépine (krepin) f, fringe; strainer, rose.

crépins (krepɛ̃) m.pl, grindery.

crépir (krepiːr) v.t, to roughcast; grain (leather).

crépiter (krepite) v.i, to crackle; patter (rain); crepitate.

crépu, e (krepy) a, woolly, fuzzy (hair).

crépuscule (krepyskyl) m, twilight, gloaming, decline.

crescendo (kresēdo) ad. & m, crescendo.

cresson (krɔsɔ̃) m, cress. ~ [de fontaine], watercress. ~ alénois (alenwa), garden cress. cressonnière (sɔnjɛːr) f, watercress bed.

Crésus (krezyːs) m, Croesus.

Crète (la) (krɛːt), Crete.

crête (krɛːt) f, comb; crest; ridge. ~-de-coq, cockscomb (Bot.). crêté, e (krɛte) a, crested.

crétin, e (kretɛ̃, in) n, cretin; idiot; dunce.

cretonne (krɔtɔn) f, cretonne.

creuser (krøze) v.t. & abs, to dig; hollow; excavate; scoop; sink; deepen. se ~, to rack (brains). creusage (za:ʒ), creusement (zmɑ̃) m, digging, &c.

creuset (krøze) m, crucible, [melting] pot.

creux, euse (krø, øːz) a, hollow, deep; sunken; shallow, empty. ¶ m, hollow, cavity; hole; pit; trough (wave); space; hollowness; mould.

crevaison (krəvɛzɔ̃) f, death (animals); bursting; puncture (tire).

crevasse (krəvas) f, crevice, chink, crack, fissure, rift, crevasse; chap (skin). crevasser (se) v.t, to crack; chap.

crève-cœur (krɛvkœːr) m, keen disappointment, wrench (fig.). crever (krəve) v.i. & t, to burst; break; crack; split; puncture; put out (eyes); die. à crevés (ve), slashed, slit (dress).

crevette (krəvɛt) f: ~ [grise], shrimp. ~ [rose], prawn.

cri (kri) m, cry, shout; scream; shriek, screech; squeal; halloo; chirp; outcry; opinion. ~ de guerre, war cry; slogan (Pol.). criailler (aje) v.i, to squeal; scold, nag. criant, e (ɑ̃, ɑ̃:t) a, crying, glaring. criard, e (a:r, ard) a, squealing, squalling, screaming, clamorous; blatant; pressing (debts).

crible (kribl) m, sieve, riddle, screen. cribler (ble) v.t, to sift, riddle, screen; honeycomb. criblure (bly:r) f, siftings, screenings.

cric (kri) m, [lifting] jack. ~ crac! (krikkrak) crack! snap!

cricri (krikri) m, chirp; cricket (insect).

criée (krie) f, auction. crier (e) v.i. & t, to cry, shout; scream, shriek, screech; call out, clamour, protest; halloo; chirp; creak; keep telling. crieur, euse (œːr, øːz) n, crier; hawker. ~ de journaux, news boy.

crime (krim) m, crime; felony; offence; sin. ~ d'État, treason. ~ de faux, forgery. ~ passionnel (pɑsjɔnɛl), love tragedy.

Crimée (la) (krime), the Crimea.

criminel, e† (kriminɛl) a, criminal; felonious; guilty. ¶ n, criminal; felon.

crin (krɛ̃) m, [horse]hair; (vegetable) fibre; (pl.) mane [& tail]. ~ de Florence, d'Espagne, japonais, &c, [silkworm] gut (Fish.). à tous ~s, out & out.

crincrin (krɛ̃krɛ̃) m, (bad) fiddle.

crinière (krinjɛːr) f, mane; horsetail plume; abundant crop (hair).

crique (krik) f, creek, inlet (sea).

criquet (krikɛ) m, locust; cricket.

crise (kriːz) f, crisis; shortage, slump; attack, fit. ~ du logement, housing problem.

crispation (krispasjɔ̃) f, shrivelling; twitching; (pl.) fidgets. crisper (pe) v.t, to clench. se ~, to shrivel [up].

cristal (kristal) m, crystal; [crystal] glass. ~ taillé, cut [crystal] glass. cristaux de soude, [washing] soda. cristallerie (lri) f, crystal glass[ware] making or works. cristallin, e (lɛ̃, in) a, crystalline. ¶ m, crystalline lens (eye). cristalliser (lize) v.t. & i. & se ~, to crystallize. cristallomancie (talɔmɑ̃si) f, crystal gazing.

critère (kritɛːr), criterium (terjɔm) m, criterion, standard; eliminating heat, preliminary trial.

critiquable (kritikabl) a, criticizable, open to criticism, exceptionable. critique (tik) a, critical, censorious; crucial; ticklish. ¶ m, critic; reviewer. ¶ f, criticism, critique; review; critics (pers.); censure, stricture. critiquer (ke) v.t, to criticize, censure.

croasser (krɔase) v.i, to caw, croak.

croc (kro) m, hook; boat hook; fang; tusk (walrus, &c). en ~, curled, turned up (moustache). ¶ (krɔk) i, [s]crunch! ~-en-jambe (krɔkɑ̃ʒɑ̃:b) m, trip [up]; leg lock; dirty trick. croche (krɔʃ) a, crooked. ¶ f, quaver (Mus.). crochet (ʃɛ) m, hook; crook; crank tool; tenterhook; crochet (Need.); c. hook; picklock, skeleton key; sudden turn, swerve; fang; [square] bracket; hook (Box.). ~ à la fourche, hairpin crochet. ~ de suspension, hanger, hook. aux ~s de, at the expense of. crocheter (ʃte) v.t, to pick, force the lock of. crochu, e (ʃy) a, hooked, crooked.

crocodile (krɔkɔdil) m, crocodile.

crocus (krɔky:s) m, crocus (Bot.).

croire (krwaːr) v.t. & abs. ir, to believe; trust; think; take for.

croisade (krwazad) f, crusade. croisé, e (ze) p.a, crossed; cross; double-breasted (coat, &c). ¶ m, crusader; twill. ¶ f, crossing; casement [window]. croisement (zmɑ̃) m, crossing; cross; crossbreeding; frog (Rly). croiser (ze) v.t, to cross; fold; pass; thwart; twill; (v.i.) to lap over; cruise. se ~, to intersect; fold (one's arms). croiseur

D

(zæːr) *m*, cruiser. ~ *cuirassé de combat*, battle c. **croisière** (zjɛːr) *f*, cruise; cruising ground; cruising fleet. **croisillon** (zijɔ̃) *m*, cross [piece]; arm (*of cross*); bar (*window*).

croissance (krwasãːs) *f*, growth. **croissant, e** (sã, ãːt) *a*, growing, increasing. ¶ *m*, crescent; rise; draw out (*days*); wax (*moon*). **croître** (krwɑːtr) *v.i.ir*, to grow; increase; rise; draw out (*days*); wax (*moon*) roll. **croître** (krwɑːtr) *v.i.ir*, to grow; increase; rise; draw out (*days*); wax (*moon*).

croix (krwa) *f*, cross; rood; dagger, obelisk (*Typ.*). ~ *de Malte*, Maltese cross. la **C**~ *Rouge*, the Red Cross.

croquant, e (krokã, ãːt) *a*, crisp.

croque-mitaine (krokmitɛn) *m*, bog[e]y [man]; bugbear. **croque-mort**, *m*, mute.

croquer (kroke) *v.i. & t*, to [s]crunch; munch; gobble up; sketch; croquet. **croquet** (kɛ) *m*, croquet (*Game*). **croquette** (kɛt) *f*, croquette (*Cook.*). **croquis** (ki) *m*, sketch.

crosse (kros) *f*, crosier, crook; butt (*rifle, &c*); crosshead (*piston*); crutch (*or* hook) stick; stick (*Hockey*); club (*Golf*); crosse (*Lacrosse*). la ~ *canadienne*, lacrosse. **crossée** (se) *f*, drive (*Golf, &c*). **crosser** (se) *v.t*, to strike (*ball*); spurn.

crotte (krot) *f*, (*street*) mud, dirt; gutter (*fig.*); dung, droppings. **crotté, e** (te) *p.a*, muddy, dirty. **crotter** (te) *v.t*, to dirty, bespatter. **crottin** (tɛ̃) *m*, dung (*horse, &c*).

crouler (krule) *v.i*, to collapse; sink; crumble.

croup (krup) *m*, croup (*Med.*).

croupe (krup) *f*, croup[e], crupper; rump; ridge (*hill*); hip (*roof*). **croupier** (pje) *m*, croupier (*Gaming*). **croupière** (pjɛːr) *f*, crupper (*harness*); sternfast. **croupion** (pjɔ̃) *m*, rump; parson's nose. **croupir** (piːr) *v.i*, to wallow; stagnate. **croupissant, e** (pisã, ãːt) *a*, stagnant.

croustillant, e (krustijã, ãːt) *a*, crisp, crusty, short. **croustille** (tiːj) *f*, (*bit of*) crust (*bread*). **croustilleux, euse** (tijø, øːz) *a*, spicy, smutty. **croûte** (krut) *f*, crust; rind (*cheese*); scab; daub. **croûton** (tɔ̃) *m*, crust[y] end; sippet; [old] fog[e]y.

croyable (krwajabl) *a*, credible, believable; trustworthy. **croyance** (jãːs) *f*, belief; credit; creed; faith; persuasion. **croyant, e** (jã, ãːt) *a*, believing. ¶ *n*, believer; (*pl.*) the faithful.

cru (kry) *m*, growth; vintage; invention.

cru, e (kry) *a*, raw, crude; garish; indigestible; hard (*water*); blunt; free, broad. **à cru**, next the skin; bareback[ed] (*Riding*).

cruauté (kryote) *f*, cruelty.

cruche (kryʃ) *f*, pitcher, jug; dolt, dunce.

crucifiement (krysifimã) *m*, crucifixion. **crucifier** (fje) *v.t*, to crucify. **crucifix** (fi) *m*, crucifix. **crucifixion** (fiksjɔ̃) *f*, crucifixion.

crudité (krydite) *f*, rawness; raw food; crudity, crudeness; hardness (*water*); belching.

crue (kry) *f*, rising, flood, spate, freshet; advance (*glacier*).

cruel, le† (kryɛl) *a*, cruel; grievous; sore; bitter.

crûment (krymã) *ad*, crudely, bluntly.

crustacé, e (krystase) *a. & m*, crustacean.

crypte (kript) *f*, crypt; follicle.

cubage (kybaːʒ) *m*, cubic content; measurement; yardage.

cubain, e (kybɛ̃, ɛn) *a. & C**~**, *n*, Cuban.

cube (kyb) *m*, cube. ¶ *a*, cubic, cube (*root*). **cuber** (be) *v.t*, to cube; measure, gauge.

cubilot (kybilo) *m*, cupola [furnace].

cubique (kybik) *a*, cubic(al); cube (*root*). **cubisme** (bism) *m*, cubism. **cubiste** (bist) *n*, cubist.

cueillette (kœjɛt) *f*, gathering, picking; crop. **cueilleur, euse** (jœːr, øːz) *n*, picker. **cueillir** (jiːr) *v.t.ir*, to gather, pick, cull, pluck; snatch (*kiss*); buttonhole (*pers.*).

cuiller *ou* **cuillère** (kɥijɛːr) *f*, spoon; ladle; scoop; spoon [bait]. ~ *à café*, ~ *à moka*, coffee spoon. ~ *à dessert*, ~ *à entremets*, dessert s. ~ *à potage*, soup ladle. ~ *à ragoût*, gravy spoon. ~ *à soupe*, ~ *à bouche*, tablespoon. ~ *à thé*, teaspoon. **cuillerée** (jre) *f*, spoonful. ~ *à bouche*, tablespoonful.

cuir (kɥiːr) *m*, leather; hide, skin; strop; incorrect liaison (*in speaking*). ~ *chevelu*, scalp (*Anat.*). ~ *de porc*, pigskin. ~ *de vache*, cowhide. ~ *verni*, patent leather.

cuirasse (kɥiras) *f*, cuirass; armour [plating]; sheathing; saddle (*lathe, &c*). **cuirassé, e** (se) *a*, armoured, ironclad; (*fig.*) steeled; [case]hardened; proof. [*navire*] *cuirassé*, battleship, ironclad. **cuirassier** (sje) *m*, cuirassier.

cuire (kɥiːr) *v.t. & i. ir*, to cook; roast; bake; burn, fire (*bricks, &c*); boil; ripen; smart. **cuisant, e** (kɥizã, ãːt) *a*, smarting, burning; biting (*cold*); bitter. **cuisine** (zin) *f*, kitchen; galley, caboose; cookery, cooking; food; machination. **cuisiner** (ne) *v.i*, to cook; (*v.t.*) to cook; (*fig.*) concoct, fudge; pump (*pers.*). **cuisinier, ère** (nje, ɛːr) *n*, cook. ¶ *m*, cookery book. ¶ *f*, kitchener; cooker, cooking range; Dutch oven.

cuisse (kɥis) *f*, thigh; leg (*fowl*).

cuisson (kɥisɔ̃) *f*, cooking; baking; burning, firing; smarting.

cuissot (kɥiso) *m*, haunch (*venison*).

cuistre (kɥistr) *m*, self-conceited pedant; ill-mannered man.

cuite (kɥit) *f*, burning, firing.

cuivre (kɥiːvr) *m*, copper; copperplate; copper bit (*soldering*). ~ [*jaune*], brass. ~ [*rouge*], copper. *les* ~*s*, the brass (*Mus.*). **cuivré, e** (kɥivre) *a*, copper-coloured; metallic (*voice*); brassy; lurid. **cuivrer** (vre) *v.t*, to copper.

cul (ky) *m*, bottom; tail (*cart*). **culasse** (las) *f*, breech (*gun*). *se chargeant par la* ~, breech-loading. **culbutant** (kylbytã) *m*, tumbler (*pigeon*). **culbute** (byt) *f*, somersault; tumble; fall. **culbuter** (te) *v.i. & t*, to tumble, topple over; tip, tilt, dump, shoot; overthrow; rout. **cul-de-jatte** (kydӡat) m, legless cripple. **cul-de-lampe** (kydlɑ̃:p) m, cul-de-lampe; tailpiece (*Typ.*). **cul-de-sac** (kydsak) m, blind alley, dead end. **culée** (kyle) f, abutment (*bridge*).

culinaire (kylinɛːr) a, culinary.

culminant, e (kylminɑ̃, ɑ̃:t) a, culminating. **culminer** (ne) v.i, to culminate (*Astr.*).

culot (kylo) m, container (*lamp*); base; cap; plug; youngest. **culotte** (lɔt) f, breeches; knee b—s; knickerbockers; knickers; rump (*beef, &c*). ~ **courte**, shorts, trunks. ~ **de cheval**, riding breeches. ~ **de peau**, buckskins. ~ **pour le golf**, plus-fours. **culotté, e** (te) p.p, trousered. **culotter** (te) v.t, to breech; colour (*pipe*).

culpabilité (kylpabilite) f, culpability, guilt.

culte (kylt) m, worship; cult, creed. *le* ~ *des scientistes chrétiens*, Christian science.

cultivateur, trice (kyltivatœːr, tris) n, cultivator, grower, agricultur[al]ist, farmer, husbandman. **cultiver** (ve) v.t, to cultivate, grow; raise; farm, till. **culture** (ty:r) f, culture; cultivation, farming; (*pl.*) land [under cultivation]. ~ *maraîchère*, market gardening.

cumul (kymyl) m, plurality (*of offices*). **cumulatif, ive** (latif, i:v) a, cumulative. **cumulus** (ly:s) m, cumulus.

cunéiforme (kyneiform) a, cuneiform.

cupide (kypid) a, covetous, grasping. **Cupidon** (kypidɔ̃) m, Cupid.

curable (kyrabl) a, curable.

curage (kyra:ӡ) m, cleansing; flushing.

curatelle (kyratɛl) f, guardianship, trusteeship. **curateur, trice** (tœːr, tris) n, guardian, trustee; administrator, trix.

curatif, ive (kyratif, i:v) a. & m, curative.

cure (ky:r) f, cure; vicarship, rectorship; vicarage, rectory. ~ *d'eau, de raisin*, water, grape, cure. **curé** (kyre) m, parish priest; vicar, rector.

cure-dent (kyrdɑ̃) m, toothpick.

curée (kyre) f, quarry (*given to hounds*); scramble.

curer (kyre) v.t, to cleanse, clean; flush; pick (*teeth*). **curette** (rɛt) f, scraper, cleaner. **cureur** (rœːr) m, cleaner; sewerman.

curieux, euse† (kyrjø, øːz) a, curious; interested; odd; quaint; inquisitive, prying. ¶ n, curious (*or* inquisitive) person; sightseer; onlooker; bystander; (m.) curious part *or* thing; collector (*art, books, &c*). **curiosité** (ozite) f, curiosity; quaintness; curio; (*pl.*) sights (*of a city*).

curseur (kyrsœːr) m, runner, slide[r] (*Mech.*). **cursif, ive** (sif, iːv) a, cursive, running.

curviligne (kyrvilin) a, curvilinear.

cuscute (kyskyt) f, dodder (*Bot.*).

cutané, e (kytane) a, cutaneous, skin (*att.*). **cuticule** (tikyl) f, cuticle.

cuve (ky:v) f, vat. ~-*matière*, mash tub. ~ *pour développer en plein jour les pellicules*

en rouleaux, daylight roll-film developing tank. **cuvée** (kyve) f, vatful; vintage. **cuveler** (vle) v.t, to tub, case (*Min.*). **cuvette** (vɛt) f, washbasin; basin; dish; tray; bowl; cup, cistern (*barometer*); pan (*w.c.*). ~ *pour le développement des bobines de pellicules*, roll-film development dish. *à* ~, dished. **cuvier** (vje) m, washtub.

cyanure (sjany:r) m, cyanide.

cyclamen (siklamɛn) m, cyclamen.

cycle (sikl) m, cycle; cycle trade. **cyclecar** (kləka:r) m, cycle car. **cyclisme** (klism) m, cycling. **cycliste** (klist) n, cyclist.

cyclone (siklon) m, cyclone.

cygne (siɲ) m, swan.

cylindre (silɛ̃:dr) m, cylinder; roller; roll; barrel, drum. ~ *compresseur à vapeur*, steam roller. **cylindrer** (lɛ̃dre) v.t, to roll; mangle; calender; round. **cylindrique** (drik) a, cylindrical; parallel (*drill shank, &c*).

cymbales (sɛ̃bal) f.pl, cymbals.

cynique† (sinik) a, cynic, cynical. ¶ m, cynic. **cynisme** (nism) m, cynicism.

cyprès (siprɛ) m, cypress.

cytise (siti:z) m, laburnum.

D

dactylographe (daktilɔgraf) n, typist. **dactylographie** (fi) f, typewriting, typing.

dada (dada) m, gee-gee; hobby horse; pet subject, fad.

dadais (dadɛ) m, booby, ninny.

dague (dag) f, dagger, dirk.

dahlia (dalja) m, dahlia.

daigner (dɛɲe) v.i, to deign to, be pleased to, vouchsafe.

daim (dɛ̃) m, [fallow] deer, buck. [*peau de*] ~, buckskin, doeskin. **daine** (dɛn) f, doe.

dais (dɛ) m, canopy; hood (*car*).

dallage (dala:ӡ) m, flagging, pavement. ~ *rustique*, crazy pavement. **dalle** (dal) f, flag[stone]; slab. **daller** (le) v.t, to pave, flag.

dalmate (dalmat) a, Dalmatian. **la Dalmatie** (si), Dalmatia.

dalot (dalo) m, scupper.

damas (damɑ) m, damask; damson. **D**~, m, Damascus. **damasquiner** (maskine) v.t, to damascene.

dame (dam) f, lady; lady; partner (*Danc.*); queen (*Cards, Chess*); king (*Draughts*); beetle, rammer. *la* ~, Mrs (*Law*). *les* ~*s*, draughts (*game*). ~ *d'onze heures*, star of Bethlehem. ~ *de charité*, district visitor. ~ *de compagnie*, lady companion. ~ [*de nage*], rowlock. ~-*jeanne* (ӡaːn), f, demijohn. ¶ *i*, why! indeed! well! **damer** (me) v.t, to crown (*Draughts*); queen (*Chess*); tamp, ram. **damier** (mje) m, draught board.

damnable† (danabl) *a*, damnable. **damnation** (sjɔ̃) *f*, damnation. **damné, e** (ne) *a. & n*, damned. **damner** (ne) *v.t*, to damn.

damoiseau (damwazo) *m*, galant.

dandiner (se) (dãdine) *v.pr*, to waddle.

dandy (dãdi) *m*, dandy.

Danemark (le) (danmark), Denmark.

danger (dãʒe) *m*, danger, jeopardy; fear. **dangereux, euse†** (ʒrø, ø:z) *a*, dangerous. **danois, e** (danwa, a:z) *a. & (language) m*, Danish. D~ (*pers.*) *n*, Dane.

dans (dã) *pr*, in; into; within; during; among; about; out of; with; hence. ~ **les présentes**, herein (*Law*). ~ **œuvre**, inside, in the clear (*Meas.*).

dansant, e (dãsã, ã:t) *a*, dancing; dance (*tea*). **danse** (dã:s) *f*, dance; dancing. ~ **de Saint-Guy** (sɛ̃gi), St. Vitus's dance. D~ **macabre**, Dance of Death, D. of Macabre. **danser** (dãse) *v.i. & t*, to dance. **danseur, euse** (sœ:r, ø:z) *n*, dancer; partner; ballet dancer. ~ **mondain, e**, ballroom dancer.

dard (da:r) *m*, dart; sting (*insect's*); pistil; dace (*fish*). **darder** (darde) *v.t*, to dart, hurl, fling, shoot; spear.

dare-dare (darda:r) *ad*, post-haste.

dartre (dartr) *f*, dartre, skin disease.

date (dat) *f*, date (*time*). **de longue** ~, of long standing. **dater** (te) *v.t*, to date. **à** ~ **de**, from, on & after.

datif (datif) *m*, dative [case].

datte (dat) *f*, date (*fruit*). **dattier** (tje) *m*, date palm.

dauber (dobe) *v.t*, to drub, thump; jeer at. ~ **sur**, to jeer at.

dauphin (dofɛ̃) *m*, dolphin (*Zool.*).

davantage (davãta:ʒ) *ad*, more, further; longer.

davier (davje) *m*, forceps (*dentist's*).

de (dǝ), d' (d) (de le is contracted into du, de les into des) *pr*, of; from; by; for; in; on; some; any; than; between; with; to. *When coupled with Fr. noun, often rendered in Eng. by noun used attributively, as,* mine de charbon, *coal mine.*

dé (de) *m*, thimble; die (*Gaming & Mach.*); bearing (*Mach.*); tee (*Golf*).

débâcle (deba:kl) *f*, breaking up (*ice*); crash; collapse; landslide (*Pol.*). **débâcler** (bakle) *v.t*, to clear; (*v.i.*) to break up.

déballage (debala:ʒ) *m*, unpacking; show (*of wares*). **déballer** (le) *v.t*, to unpack.

débandade (debãdad) *f*, stampede, rout. **à la** ~, helter-skelter; anyhow. **débander** (de) *v.t*, to relax, unbend; unbandage. **se** ~, to break ranks in disorder.

débaptiser (debatize) *v.t*, to change the name of, rename.

débarbouiller (debarbuje) *v.t*, to wash (*some-one's*) face; extricate.

débarcadère (debarkade:r) *m*, landing [place or stage], wharf; platform (*Rly*).

débarder (debarde) *v.t*, to unload. **débardeur** (dœ:r) *m*, docker; longshoreman.

débarquer (debarke) *v.t. & i*, to land, disembark; detrain; discharge; get rid of; alight. **débarquement** (kǝmã) *m*, landing, &c. **au** ~, ex ship, ex steamer (*sales*).

débarras (debara) *m*, riddance; lumber room; box r. **débarrasser** (rase) *v.t*, to clear, rid, extricate, disburden, relieve. **se** ~ **de**, to get rid of, scrap.

débat (deba) *m*, discussion; debate; (*pl.*) proceedings; (*pl.*) trial, hearing; dispute. **débattre** (tr) *v.t.ir*, to debate, discuss, argue; arrange. **se** ~, to struggle; flounder; wriggle.

débauche (debo:ʃ) *f*, debauch[ery]; carousal; riot (*fig.*); treat. ~ **de boisson**, drunken bout. **débauché, e** (boʃe) *n*, debauchee, rake. **débaucher** (ʃe) *v.t*, to debauch, corrupt; induce to strike; seduce from duty; lead astray; reduce the staff, post notices.

débile† (debil) *a*, weakly; weak; feeble. **débilité** (lite) *f*, debility; weakness. **débiliter** (te) *v.t*, to debilitate, enfeeble.

débit (debi) *m*, sale (*retail*); market; demand; (*government*) licence to sell; (*licensed*) shop; flow, discharge, yield, output, capacity, feed; delivery (*pump, speech*); cutting up, chopping; debit [side], debtor [side]. ~ **de tabac**, licence to sell tobacco; tobacconist's shop. **débitant, e** (tã, ã:t) *n*, dealer, retailer. ~ **de spiritueux**, licensed victualler. ~ **de tabac**, tobacconist. **débiter** (te) *v.t*, to retail, sell; discharge; yield; deliver, utter; spread (*news*); spin (*yarns*); cut up; saw; chop (*firewood*); debit. **débiteur, euse** (tœ:r, ø:z) *n*, utterer (*lies*); -monger (*news, scandal*); (*f.*) gossip. **débitrice** (*In Fr. stores*) girl who conducts customers to cash desk to see that they pay. **débiteur, trice** (tœ:r, tris) *n. & att*, debtor, debit (*att.*). ~ **hypothécaire**, mortgagor.

déblai (deblɛ) *m*, cut[ting], excavation; (*s. & pl.*) waste, rubbish, spoil.

déblatérer contre (deblatere), to abuse.

déblayer (debleje) *v.t*, to clear, c. out, c. away.

déboire (debwa:r) *m*, (*nasty*) after-taste; disappointment.

déboiser (debwaze) *v.t*, to disforest, deforest.

déboîtement (debwatmã) *m*, dislocation (*limb*). **déboîter** (te) *v.t*, to dislocate; disjoint.

débonder (debɔ̃de) *v.t*, to unbung; open the sluice gates of; open, relax (*Med.*). **[se]** ~, to burst forth, break out, escape.

débonnaire† (debɔnɛ:r) *a*, meek; easy-going; accommodating.

débordement (debɔrdǝmã) *m*, overflow; outburst; excess, licentiousness. **déborder** (de) *v.i*, to overflow, brim over, run over; slop [over]; break out; (*v.t.*) to overlap; outflank; untuck; trim the edges of; unship (*oars*).

débotter (debote) *v.t*, to take (*someone's*) boots off. **se** ~, to take one's boots off. **débotté** (te), immediately upon arrival.

débouché (debuʃe) *m*, opening, outlet, issue; outfall; waterway; prospects. **déboucher** (ʃe) *v.t*, to open, unstop, uncork; (*v.i.*) to open, emerge, debouch; run, fall.

déboucler (debukle) *v.t*, to unbuckle; uncurl.

débouler [dans] (debule) *v.i*, to tumble down (*as stairs*).

débourber (deburbe) *v.t*, to clean out, cleanse; extricate.

débourrer (debure) *v.t*, to unhair; unstop; break in (*horse*).

débours (debu:r) & **déboursé** (burse) *m, both mostly pl*, disbursement, out of pocket expense, outgoing, outlay. **débourser** (se) *v.t*, to disburse, lay out, spend.

debout (dǝbu) *ad*, on end, erect; standing; up; head (*wind*). **mourir ~**, to die in harness.

débouter (debute) *v.t*, to nonsuit, dismiss.

déboutonner (debutɔne) *v.t*, to unbutton. **se ~** (*fig.*), to open out, speak one's mind.

débraillé, e (debraje) (*fig.*) *a*, dissolute. **se débrailler** (je) *v.pr*, to unbutton oneself (*unbecomingly*).

débrayer (debreje) (*Mech.*) *v.t*, to throw out of gear, disconnect.

débrider (debride) *v.t*, to unbridle. *sans ~*, without stopping.

débris (debri) *m.pl*, remains, debris, litter; scrap; wreck[age].

débrouiller (debruje) *v.t*, to unravel, disentangle, clear up. **se ~**, to extricate oneself.

débucher (debyʃe) *v.i*, to break cover.

débusquer (debyske) *v.t*, to dislodge, drive out; oust.

début (deby) *m*, beginning, opening, outset, outbreak, start; first appearance; f. work; coming out (*in society*). **débutant, e** (tɑ̃, ɑ̃:t) *n*, beginner; débutant, e. **débuter** (te) *v.i*, to begin, start, make one's first appearance; lead (*Cards, &c*).

deçà (dǝsa) *ad*, on this side. ~, *delà* ou ~ & *delà*, here & there, to & fro. *en ~ de, pr*, on this side of.

décacheter (dekaʃte) *v.t*, to unseal, open.

décade (dekad) *f*, ten days; decad[e] (*books*).

décadence (dekadɑ̃:s) *f*, decadence, decline, decay. **décadent, e** (dɑ̃, ɑ̃:t) *a*, decadent.

décagone (dekagɔn) *m*, decagon.

décaisser (dekɛse) *v.t*, to unpack; withdraw (*money*).

décalage (dekala:ʒ) (*fig.*) *m*, setback.

décalcomanie (dekalkɔmani) *f*, transfer (*for china & as toy*).

décaler (dekale) *v.t*, to unkey; set forward, set back.

décalitre (dekalitr) *m*, decalitre = 10 litres *or* 2·200 gallons.

décalque (dekalk) *m*, transfer (*Emb., &c*).

décamètre (dekamɛ:tr) *m*, decametre = 10 metres *or* 10·936 yards. ~ *d'arpenteur*, measuring tape.

décamper (dekɑ̃pe) *v.i*, to decamp, make off.

décanat (dekana) *m*, deanery (*office*).

décanter (dekɑ̃te) *v.t*, to decant.

décaper (dekape) *v.t*, to scour.

décapiter (dekapite) *v.t*, to behead, decapitate.

décéder (desede) *v.i*, to decease.

déceler (desle) *v.t*, to reveal, betray.

décembre (desɑ̃:br) *m*, December.

décemment (desamɑ̃) *ad*, decently. **décence** (sɑ̃:s) *f*, decency, propriety.

décennal, e (desɛnal) *a*, decennial.

décent, e (desɑ̃, ɑ̃:t) *a*, decent; proper.

décentraliser (desɑ̃tralize) *v.t*, to decentralize.

déception (desɛpsjɔ̃) *f*, disappointment.

décerner (desɛrne) *v.t*, to award.

décès (desɛ) *m*, death, decease, demise.

décevant, e (desvɑ̃, ɑ̃:t) *a*, deceptive, misleading. **décevoir** (s[ǝ]vwa:r) *v.t*, to deceive; disappoint.

déchaîner (deʃɛne) *v.t*, to unchain, let loose. **se ~**, break loose; break out.

déchanter (deʃɑ̃te) *v.i*, to sing small.

décharge (deʃarʒ) *f*, discharge; unloading; outflow; outfall; volley; release; relief; composition (*to creditors*); waste heap. **décharger** (ʒe) *v.t & abs*, to discharge; unload; empty; relieve, disburden, ease; deal (*blow*); come off (*ink, &c*). **déchargeur** (ʒœ:r) *m*, docker; arrester (*Elec., &c*).

décharné, e (deʃarne) *p.a*, emaciated, gaunt, skinny, scraggy.

déchausser (deʃose) *v.t*, to take off (*someone's*) shoes; [lay] bare; dislodge.

déchéance (deʃeɑ̃:s) *f*, [down]fall; loss, forfeiture; lapse, expiration.

déchet (deʃɛ) *m. oft. pl*, waste, loss; scrap, refuse.

déchiffrer (deʃifre) *v.t. & abs*, to decipher, decode, make out; read; read (*or play) at sight.

déchiqueter (deʃikte) *v.t*, to slash; jag; shred.

déchirant, e (deʃirɑ̃, ɑ̃:t) *a*, heart-rending, harrowing. **déchirer** (re) *v.t*, to tear, rend, rip, lacerate; tear up; break up; harrow; split (*ears with noise*). **déchirure** (ry:r) *f*, tear, rent, rip.

déchoir (deʃwa:r) *v.i.ir*, to fall, decline. ~ *de*, to forfeit.

décibel (desibɛl) *m*, decibel (*Phys.*).

décidé (deside) *a*, decided; settled, determined. **décidément** (mɑ̃) *ad*, decidedly; definitely. **décider** (de) *v.t. & abs*, to decide, settle, resolve, determine; induce, persuade, prevail upon. **se ~**, to decide, make up one's mind.

décidu, e (desidy) *a*, deciduous.

décigramme (desigram) *m*, decigramme = ₁/₁₀ gramme *or* 1·543 grains.

décilitre (desilitr) *m*, decilitre = ₁/₁₀ litre *or* 0·176 pint.

décimal, e (desimal) *a. & f*, decimal.

décime (desim) *m*, 10 centimes; 10% surtax. **décimer** (me) *v.t*, to decimate.

décimètre (desimɛtr) *m*, decimetre = ₁/₁₀ metre *or* 3·937 inches; decimetre rule. *double ~*, 2-decimetre rule. ~ *carré*, square d. = 15·500 sq. ins. ~ *cube*, cubic d. = 61·024 cub. ins.

décisif, ive† (desizif, i:v) *a*, decisive; critical; positive. **décision** (zjɔ̃) *f*, decision; conclusion; resolution; ruling, award.

déclamateur (deklamatœ:r) *m*, stump orator, spouter. **déclamation** (sjɔ̃) *f*, declamation, elocution; delivery; rant. **déclamer** (me) *v.t. & abs. & i*, to declaim; recite; spout, rant.

déclaration (deklarasjɔ̃) *f*, declaration; statement; return; proclamation; entry, report (*Cust.*); finding (*jury*). ~ *sous serment*, affidavit. **déclarer** (re) *v.t*, to declare, state, report; proclaim; return; enter; certify; disclose; find (*juries*). **se ~**, to declare oneself; show itself; break out.

déclassé, e (deklɑse) *n*, [social] outcast. **déclasser** (se) *v.t*, to disrate, degrade; displace (*securities*); transfer from one class to another.

déclencher (deklɑ̃ʃe) *v.t*, to trip, release; unlatch. **déclencheur** (ʃœ:r) *m*, [shutter] release (*Phot.*).

déclic (deklik) *m*, trigger, catch, trip, release.

déclin (deklɛ̃) *m*, decline, wane. **déclinaison** (klinɛzɔ̃) *f*, declination; declension (*Gram.*). **décliner** (ne) *v.i. & t*, to decline; wane; give, state (*name*, &c).

déclive (dekli:v) *a*, sloping. **déclivité** (klivite) *f*, declivity, slope.

décocher (dekɔʃe) *v.t*, to let off, let fly.

décoction (dekɔksjɔ̃) *f*, decoction.

décoiffer (dekwafe) *v.t*, to take off the hat of; uncork, crack (*a bottle*); disarrange (*hair*).

décoller (dekɔle) *v.t*, to unstick; (*v.i.*) to go away; take off (*Aero.*). **se ~**, to come unstuck, part.

décolleté, e (dekɔlte) *a*, low-necked; free, licentious. ¶ *m*, low-necked dress; court shoes.

décolorer (dekɔlɔre) *v.t*, to discolour.

décombres (dekɔ̃:br) *m.pl*, demolitions, rubbish.

décommander (dekɔmɑ̃de) *v.t*, to countermand, cancel; call off; ask not to come.

décomposer (dekɔ̃poze) *v.t*, to decompose; distort.

décompte (dekɔ̃:t) *m*, deduction; working out; table, sheet. *éprouver du ~ dans*, to be disappointed in. **décompter** (kɔ̃te) *v.t. & abs*, to deduct; work out; suffer disappointment.

déconcerter (dekɔ̃sɛrte) *v.t*, to disconcert, upset.

déconfire (dekɔ̃fi:r) *v.t.ir*, to nonplus. **déconfiture** (fity:r) *f*, insolvency.

déconseiller (dekɔ̃sɛje) *v.t*, to dissuade.

déconsidérer (dekɔ̃sidere) *v.t*, to discredit.

décontenancer (dekɔ̃tnɑ̃se) *v.t*, to abash.

déconvenue (dekɔ̃vny) *f*, discomfiture.

décor (dekɔ:r) *m*, decoration; set (*Theat.*); (*pl.*) scenery; (*pl.*) regalia (*freemasons'*). **décorateur** (kɔratœ:r) *m*, decorator; scene painter. **décoratif, ive** (tif, i:v) *a*, decora-tive. **décoration** (sjɔ̃) *f*, decoration; order, medal; scenery. **décorer** (re) *v.t*, to decorate; dignify.

décortiquer (dekɔrtike) *v.t*, to bark; peel.

décorum (dekɔrɔm) *m*, decorum; etiquette.

découcher (dekuʃe) *v.i*, to sleep out.

découdre (dekudr) *v.t.ir*, to unstitch; rip.

découler (dekule) *v.i*, to trickle, run down; proceed, issue.

découper (dekupe) *v.t. & abs*, to carve (*meat*); cut up; cut out; fretsaw; punch [out]. **découpeur, euse** (pœ:r, ø:z) *n*, carver (*pers.*).

découpler (dekuple) *v.t*, to slip, uncouple.

découpoir (dekupwa:r) *m*, [hollow] punch.

découpure (py:r) *f*, cutting out; fretwork.

découragement (dekuraʒmɑ̃) *m*, discouragement, despondency. **décourager** (ʒe) *v.t*, to discourage, dishearten, depress, dispirit; daunt; deter. **se ~**, to lose heart, despond.

décousu, e (dekuzy) (*fig.*) *a*, loose, disconnected, disjointed, rambling, desultory. ¶ *m*, looseness.

découvert, e (dekuvɛːr, ɛrt) *a*, uncovered, bare, open, unprotected. **à découvert**, *ad*, uncovered; open; unpacked; unsecured (*loan*); overdrawn. **découvert**, *m*, overdraft; bear account, bears (*Stk Ex.*). **découverte**, *f*, discovery; find; detection; disclosure. *aller à la ~*, to scout. **découvrir** (vri:r) *v.t.ir*, to uncover, bare, open; discover, detect; descry, espy; find; f. out. **se ~**, to expose oneself; take one's hat off; come to light.

décrasser (dekrase) *v.t*, to cleanse, clean, scour.

décréditer (dekredite) *v.t*, to discredit.

décrépit, e (dekrepi, it) *a*, decrepit. **décrépitude** (tyd) *f*, decrepitude, senile decay.

décret (dekrɛ) *m*, decree, fiat, ordinance, order, enactment. **décréter** (krete) *v.t*, to decree, enact, ordain.

décri (dekri) *m*, disrepute. **décrier** (krie) *v.t*, to decry, run down.

décrire (dekri:r) *v.t. & abs. ir*, to describe.

décrocher (dekrɔʃe) *v.t*, to unhook; take down.

décroître (dekrwa:tr) *v.i.ir*, to decrease, shorten, dwindle, wane.

décrotter (dekrɔte) *v.t*, to clean, brush, scrape. **décrotteur** (tœ:r) *m*, shoeblack; boots (*pers.*). **décrottoir** (twa:r) *m*, scraper [mat].

décrue (dekry) *f*, fall (*river*); retreat (*glacier*).

décuple (dekypl) *a. & m*, tenfold. **décupler** (ple) *v.t. & i*, to increase tenfold.

dédaigner (dedɛɲe) *v.t*, to disdain, scorn, despise. **dédaigneux, euse†** (nø, ø:z) *a*, disdainful, scornful, supercilious. **dédain** (dɛ̃) *m*, disdain, disregard, scorn.

dédale (dedal) *m*, maze, labyrinth.

dedans (dədɑ̃) *ad*, inside, in. *de ~*, from within. (*rire*) **en ~**, *ad*, inwardly. **en ~ de**, *pr*, within. ¶ *m*, inside; interior; inside edge (*Skating*).

dédicace (dedikas) *f*, dedication; inscription. **dédier** (dje) *v.t*, to dedicate; devote; inscribe.

dédire (dedi:r) *v.t.ir*, to gainsay. **se ~ de**, to retract, unsay. **dédit** (di) *m*, retractation; penalty, forfeit.

dédommagement (dedɔmaʒmɑ̃) *m*, indemnity, compensation, damages. **dédommager** (ʒe) *v.t*, to compensate, recoup, indemnify.

dédoubler (deduble) *v.t*, to divide into two; duplicate (*train*); unline. **~ les rangs**, to form single file.

déductif, ive (dedyktif, i:v) *a*, deductive, inferential. **déduction** (ksjɔ̃) *f*, deduction; allowance, relief; inference. **déduire** (dɥi:r) *v.t.ir*, to deduct; deduce, infer.

déesse (dess) *f*, goddess.

défaillance (defajɑ̃:s) *f*, swoon, fainting [fit]; lapse; failing; default; eclipse. **défaillant, e** (jɑ̃, ɑ̃:t) *a*, failing; drooping; defaulting. ¶ *n*, defaulter. **défaillir** (ji:r) *v.i.ir*, to faint; fail; flinch; falter.

défaire (defɛ:r) *v.t.ir*, to undo; take off; defeat, rout. **se ~**, to come undone. **se ~ de**, to get rid of; unload (*stocks*); make away with. **défait, e** (fɛ, ɛt) *a*, worn (*look*). **défaite,** *f*, defeat; shuffle, evasion.

défalcation (defalkasjɔ̃) *f*, deduction. **défalquer** (ke) *v.t*, to deduct.

défaut (defo) *m*, defect, fault, flaw, blemish; default, failure, want, lack, deficiency.

défaveur (defavœ:r) *f*, disfavour. **défavorable†** (vɔrabl) *a*, unfavourable, inauspicious.

défectif, ive (defɛktif, i:v) *a*, defective (*Gram.*). **défection** (sjɔ̃) *f*, defection. **défectueux, euse†** (tɥø, ø:z) *a*, defective, faulty, deficient. **défectuosité** (tɥozite) *f*, defect, fault, flaw.

défendable (defɑ̃dabl) *a*, defensible. **défendeur, eresse** (dœ:r, drɛs) *n*, defendant; respondent (*Law*). **défendre** (fɑ̃:dr) *v.t*, to defend; protect, shield; forbid, prohibit. **se ~**, to defend oneself; deny; excuse oneself. **défense** (fɑ̃:s) *f*, defence; (*pl.*) plea; protection; prohibition; tusk; fender (*Naut.*). **~ d'afficher**, stick no bills. **~ d'entrer** [*sans autorisation*], no admittance [except on business], private. **~ d'entrer sous peine d'amende**, trespassers will be prosecuted. **~ d'uriner**, commit no nuisance. **~ de circuler sur l'herbe**, [please] keep off the grass. **~ de fumer**, no smoking. **~ de passer**, no thoroughfare. **~ de toucher**, [please] don't touch. **~ expresse** (ou *absolue*) **de fumer**, smoking strictly prohibited. **défenseur** (fɑ̃sœ:r) *m*, defender; advocate; counsel [for the defence]. **défensif, ive** (sif, i:v) *a. & f*, defensive.

déféquer (defeke) *v.t. & i*, to defecate.

déférence (deferɑ̃:s) *f*, deference, respect. **déférent, e** (rɑ̃, ɑ̃:t) *a*, deferential. **déférer** (re) *v.t*, to confer, bestow; refer (*to court*); hand over (*to justice*); administer (*oath*); (*v.i.*) to defer (*submit*).

déferler (defɛrle) *v.t*, to unfurl; (*v.i.*) to break (*waves*).

déferrer (defɛre) *v.t*, to unshoe (*horse*); disconcert.

défi (defi) *m*, challenge; defiance. **défiance** (fjɑ̃:s) *f*, distrust, mistrust. **~ de soi-même**, diffidence. **défiant, e** (ɑ̃, ɑ̃:t) *a*, distrustful, mistrustful; wary.

déficit (defisi) *m*, deficit, deficiency, short[age], minus quantity. **déficitaire** (tɛ:r) *a*, debit (*att.*), showing a loss, adverse; short.

défier (defje) *v.t*, to challenge; brave; dare; defy, baffle. **se ~ de**, to distrust, mistrust; beware of.

défigurer (defigyre) *v.t*, to disfigure; deface; distort.

défilé (defile) *m*, defile; march past; procession; parade. **défiler** (le) *v.t*, to unthread; (*v.i.*) to defile; file off; march past. **se ~** (*fig.*), to make off.

défini, e (defini) *p.a*, definite; finite (*mood, Gram.*). **définir** (ni:r) *v.t*, to define; describe; determine; decide. **définissable** (nisabl) *a*, definable. **définitif, ive†** (tif, i:v) *a*, definitive; absolute (*decree*); final; ultimate; standard (*edition*). **en définitive, ad**, finally, in short. **définition** (sjɔ̃) *f*, definition; decision.

déflation (deflasjɔ̃) *f*, deflation (*Fin.*).

défléchir (defleʃi:r) *v.t*, to deflect.

défleurir (deflœri:r) *v.i*, to shed its blossoms; (*v.t.*) to deflower, strip of flowers. **défloraison** (flɔrɛzɔ̃) *f*, defloration (*stripping*). **défloration** (rasjɔ̃) *f*, defloration (*ravishment*). **déflorer** (re) *v.t*, to deflower (*strip of flowers & ravish*); take the freshness off (*news*).

défoncer (defɔ̃se) *v.t*, to stave [in]; break up; recess; trench.

déformer (deforme) *v.t*, to deform; distort; strain (*Mech.*).

défourner (defurne) *v.t*, to take out of the oven.

défraîchi, e (defrɛʃi) *p.a*, [shop-]soiled. **défraîchir** (ʃi:r) *v.t. & se ~*, to fade.

défrayer (defrɛje) *v.t*, to defray; entertain; keep up (*conversation*).

défricher (defriʃe) *v.t*, to clear, grub, reclaim.

défriser (defrize) *v.t*, to uncurl; disconcert.

défroncer (defrɔ̃se) *v.t*, to iron out; smooth.

défroque (defrɔk) *f*, cast-off clothing. **défroquer** (ke) *v.t*, to unfrock.

défunt, e (defœ̃, œ̃:t) *a. & n*, deceased, defunct, departed, late (*a.*).

dégagé, e (degaʒe) *a*, free, easy, unconstrained; perky. **dégagement** (ʒmɑ̃) *m*, redemption; clearing; disengagement, evolution; exit. **dégager** (ʒe) *v.t*, to redeem; relieve; extricate; free, disengage, give off, evolve, emit; educe; clear; set off (*figure*).

dégaine (degɛ:n) *f*, awkwardness. **dégainer** (gɛne) *v.t. & abs*, to unsheathe, draw.

déganter (se) (degɑ̃te) *v.pr*, to take off one's gloves.

dégarnir (degarni:r) *v.t*, to strip, dismantle.

dégât (dega) *m. oft. pl*, damage, havoc.

dégauchir (degoʃiːr) v.t, to true, straighten.

dégel (deʒɛl) m, thaw. dégeler (ʒle) v.t. & i. & se ~, to thaw.

dégénérer (deʒenere) v.i, to degenerate. dégénérescence (resɑːs) & dégénération (rasjɔ̃) f, degeneration, degeneracy.

dégingandé, e (deʒɛ̃gɑ̃de) a, ungainly, gawky.

dégoiser (degwaze) v.t, to spout (abuse, &c).

dégommer (degɔme) v.t, to ungum; oust.

dégonfler (degɔ̃fle) v.t, to deflate; relieve.

dégorger (degɔrʒe) v.t, to disgorge; unstop. [se] ~, to discharge; overflow.

dégouliner (deguline) v.i, to trickle, drip.

dégourdi, e (degurdi) p.a, wide-awake, alive. dégourdir (diːr) v.t, to revive. faire ~, to take the chill off (water).

dégoût (degu) m, want of appetite; distaste, dislike, disrelish; disgust, loathing, aversion; disappointment. dégoûtant, e (tɑ̃, ɑ̃ːt) a, disgusting, loathsome; disheartening. dégoûter (te) v.t, to make one sick of; disgust. faire le dégoûté, to be fastidious, be squeamish.

dégoutter (degute) v.i. & abs, to drip, trickle, dribble.

dégradateur (degradatœːr) m, vignetter (Phot.). dégradation (sjɔ̃) f, degradation; defacement; dilapidation. dégrader (de) v.t, to degrade; deface; dilapidate; damage; shade [off], vignette.

dégrafer (degrafe) v.t, to unhook, unfasten.

dégraisser (degrɛse) v.t, to take off the grease (or fat) from; skim; scour.

dégras (degrɑ) m, dubbin[g].

degré (dəgre) m, degree; step, stair; grade; stage; pitch; extent.

dégrèvement (degrɛvmɑ̃) m, relief, reduction, cut (taxes). dégrever (grəve) v.t, to relieve; cancel; disencumber (from mortgage).

dégringolade (degrɛ̃gɔlad) f, tumble; collapse, slump. dégringoler (le) v.t, to rush down. ~ dans, to tumble (or fall) down or into.

dégriser (degrize) v.t, to sober; disillusion.

dégrossir (degrosiːr) v.t, to rough down; rough-hew; sketch out; break in.

déguenillé, e (degnije) a, tattered, ragged.

déguerpir (degɛrpiːr) v.i, to move out; pack off.

déguisement (degizmɑ̃) m, disguise; fancy dress. déguiser (ze) v.t, to disguise; conceal; change (name). se ~, to disguise oneself, masquerade.

dégustateur (degystatœːr) m, taster. dégustation (sjɔ̃) f, tasting. déguster (te) v.t, to taste, sample (alcohol, &c).

déhanchement (deɑ̃ʃmɑ̃) m, waddle.

déharnacher (dearnaʃe) v.t, to unharness.

dehors (dəɔːr) ad, out; outside; out of doors; in the offing. ¶ ! out! (Box., &c). de ~, from without. en ~, ad, outside, outwards; frank. en ~ de, pr, outside, without. ¶ m, outside, exterior; outside edge (Skating); (pl.) outworks (Mil.); (pl.) grounds (of mansion); (pl.) appearances.

déifier (deifje) v.t, to deify. déité (te) f, deity.

déjà (deʒa) ad, already; before.

déjection (deʒɛksjɔ̃) f, evacuation (bowels).

déjeter (deʒte) v.t. & se ~, to warp (wood); buckle.

déjeuner (deʒœne) v.i, to breakfast; lunch. ¶ m, breakfast set, b. service. ~ [du matin], breakfast. ~ [de midi], lunch[eon], midday meal.

déjouer (deʒwe) v.t, to baffle, thwart, frustrate, foil, outwit, outmanœuvre.

déjucher (deʒyʃe) (fig.) v.i, to come down; (v.t.) to bring down.

delà (dəla) pr, beyond. au-~, beyond; more. au-~ de, beyond; more. [plus] en ~, farther [off]. par-~, beyond. l'au-~, m, the beyond (future life).

délabré, e (delabre) p.a, dilapidated; broken-down; tumble-down; ramshackle, gimcrack. délabrement (brəmɑ̃) m, dilapidation; wreck. délabrer (bre) v.t, to dilapidate, shatter.

délacer (delase) v.t, to unlace.

délai (delɛ) m, time, extension [of time]; delay. ~ de congé, [term of] notice.

délaissement (delɛsmɑ̃) m, abandonment, desertion; destitution. délaisser (se) v.t, to forsake; abandon, desert; jilt.

délassement (delasmɑ̃) m, relaxation, recreation. délasser (se) v.t. & abs, to refresh, relax.

délateur, trice (delatœːr, tris) n, informer.

délaver (delave) v.t, to soak; dilute.

délayer (deleje) v.t, to add water to; thin; spin out.

deleatur (deleatyːr) m, dele (sign, Typ.).

délecter (delɛkte) v.t. & se ~, to delight.

délégation (delegasjɔ̃) f, delegation, deputation. délégué, e (ge) n, delegate; deputy. ~ à la presse, press steward. ~ aux concurrents, clerk of the course (Athletic Sports). déléguer (ge) v.t, to delegate, depute.

délester (delɛste) v.t, to unballast; relieve.

délétère (deletɛːr) a, deleterious.

délibération (deliberasjɔ̃) f, deliberation, consideration, proceedings; transaction, business; decision, resolution. délibéré†, e (re) a, deliberate. délibérer (re) v.i, to deliberate, consult; (v.t.) to decide, resolve on. ~ sur, to consider, transact (business at meeting).

délicat, e† (delika, at) a, delicate; nice; refined; dainty, fastidious, squeamish; tender; ticklish, tricky. délicatesse (tɛs) f, delicacy, &c.

délice (delis) m, delight, pleasure, luxury. ~s, f.pl, delight(s), pleasure(s), delectation.

délicieux, euse† (sjø, øːz) a, delicious; delightful; charming.

délié, e (delje) a, thin, slender, slim; glib. ¶ m, thin stroke, up stroke. délier (lje) v.t, to untie; loose[n]; release.

délimiter (delimite) v.t, to delimit[ate].

délinéation (delineasjɔ̃) f, delineation.

délinquant, e (delēkā, ā:t) *n*, delinquent, offender, misdemeanant.

déliquescence (delikψsā:s) *f*, deliquescence; corruption (*fig.*).

délirant, e (delirā, ā:t) *a*, delirious; frenzied. **délire** (li:r) *m*, delirium; frenzy. **délirer** (lire) *v.i*, to be delirious. **delirium tremens** (deliɾjɔm tremē:s) *m*, delirium tremens.

délit (deli) *m*, offence, misdemeanour.

délivrance (delivrā:s) *f*, deliverance; rescue; release; delivery; issue. **délivrer** (vre) *v.t*, to deliver; rescue; release; hand [over]; issue (*tickets*).

déloger (delɔʒe) *v.i*, to [re]move; (*v.t.*) to turn out; dislodge.

déloyal, e† (delwajal) *a*, disloyal; unfair; dishonest. **déloyauté** (jote) *f*, disloyalty.

delta (dɛlta) *m*, delta.

déluge (dely:ʒ) *m*, deluge, flood; [down]pour.

déluré, e (delyre) *a*, wide-awake; knowing.

démagogue (demagɔg) *m*, demagogue.

démailler (demaje) *v.t*, to undo (*knitting*). **se ~**, to ladder (*stocking*, *&c*).

demain (dəmɛ̃) *ad. & m*, to-morrow. **~ matin**, to-morrow morning.

démancher (demāʃe) *v.t*, to unhandle; dislocate.

demande (demā:d) *f*, request, desire; application; inquiry; demand; call; indent; claim; bid; instance; suit; proposal (*marriage*); question. **~ d'emploi**, situation wanted. **demander** (māde) *v.t*, to ask, a. for. request; charge; book; inquire; apply for; demand; claim; want; bid [for]; beg; sue for. **~ par voie d'annonces**, to advertise for. **on demande un . . .**, wanted a . . . **se ~**, to ask oneself, wonder. **demandeur, euse** (dœːr, øːz) *n*, petitioner; applicant. **demandeur, eresse** (dœːr, drɛs) *n*, plaintiff.

démangeaison (demāʒezɔ̃) *f*, itch[ing]; urge, cacoethes; longing. **démanger** (ʒe) *v.i*, to itch; long. *le bras me démange*, my arm itches. *la langue lui démange*, he is itching (*or* longing) to speak.

démanteler (demātle) *v.t*, to dismantle.

démantibuler (demātibyle) *v.t*, to break to pieces.

démarcation (demarkasjɔ̃) *f*, demarcation.

démarche (demarʃ) *f*, gait, walk; bearing; step, measure; (*pl.*) services. **démarcheur** (ʃœːr) *m*, canvasser, runner, share pusher.

démarier (demarje) *v.t*, to unmarry.

démarrage (demara:ʒ) *m*, unmooring; starting. **démarrer** (re) *v.t*, to unmoor; (*v.i.*) to leave her moorings; cast off; start; stir.

démasquer (demaske) *v.t*, to unmask; uncover; show up.

démâter (demate) *v.t*, to dismast.

démêlé (demele) *m*, contention. **démêler** (le) *v.t*, to disentangle, unravel; comb out; quarrel about. **se ~ de**, to get out of. **démêloir** (lwaːr) *m*, dressing comb.

démembrer (demābre) *v.t*, to dismember.

déménagement (demenaʒmā) *m*, removal, moving. **déménager** (ʒe) *v.t. & abs*, to remove, move [out] (*house*); (*v.i.*) to be off; go one's head. **déménageur** (ʒœːr) *m*, removal contractor, [furniture] remover.

démence (demā:s) *f*, insanity, madness, dementia.

démener (se) (demne) *v.pr*, to throw oneself about; strive hard.

dément, e (demā, ā:t) *a. & n*, crazy, mad (person).

démenti (demāti) *m*, denial, contradiction, lie; failure, disappointment. **démentir** (ti:r) *v.t.ir*, to give the lie to; contradict; belie.

démérite (demerit) *m*, demerit, unworthiness. **démériter (te)** *v.i. & abs*, to deserve censure, offend.

démesuré†, e (dem[ə]zyre) *a*, inordinate; enormous, huge.

démettre (demɛtr) *v.t.ir*, to dislocate, put out of joint. **se ~ de**, to resign, throw up.

demeurant (au) (dəmœrā), after all, in other respects. **demeure** (mœːr) *f*, residence, dwelling, abode; delay. *à ~*, fixed, stationary, set. *en ~*, in arrears. **demeurer** (mœre) *v.i*, to reside, live, dwell; stay, remain, stop; lie.

demi, e (dəmi) *a*, half. **demi**, *ad*, half. **¶ m**, half; half-back (*Foot.*). *à ~*, *ad*, half, by halves.

demi (dəmi) *comps*: **~-bas**, *m.pl*, half-hose. **~-cercle**, *m*, semicircle. **~-congé**, *m*, half holiday. **~-dieu**, *m*, demigod. **~-finale**, *f*, semi-final. *de ~-fond*, middle-distance (*Running*, *&c*). **~-frère**, *m*, half-brother. **~-gros**, *m*, small wholesale trade. *une ~-heure*, half an hour. **~-jour**, *m*, half light, twilight. **~-lune**, *f*, crescent (*of buildings*). **~-mot**, *m*, hint. **~-pensionnaire**, *n*, day boarder. **~-place**, *f*, half fare, half price. **~-pose**, *f*, bulb exposure (*Phot.*). **~-relief**, *m*, mezzo-relievo. **~-reliure**, *f*, quarter binding. **~-reliure à petits coins**, half binding. **~-reliure amateur**, three-quarter binding. **~-sœur**, *f*, half-sister, step s. *en ~-solde*, on half pay (*Mil.*). **~-ton**, *m*, semitone. *à ~-voix*, in an undertone.

demie (dəmi) *f*, (a) half; half-hour; half past. *une heure & ~*, an hour & a half; half-past one.

démission (demisjɔ̃) *f*, resignation. **démissionner** (ɔne) *v.i*, to resign.

démobiliser (demɔbilize) *v.t*, to demobilize.

démocrate (demɔkrat) *m*, democrat. **démocratie** (si) *f*, democracy. **démocratique** (tik) *a*, democratic.

démodé, e (demɔde) *a*, old-fashioned; out of date.

demoiselle (dəmwazɛl) *f*, young lady; girl; single woman, maiden [lady], spinster; miss; damsel; dragon fly; beetle, rammer; rowlock. **~ de compagnie**, lady com-

panion. ~ *de magasin, du téléphone*, shop, telephone, girl.
démolir (demolir) *v.t*, to demolish, break up; explode (*fig.*). **démolisseur** (lisœ:r) *m*, breaker (*house, ship*); iconoclast. **démolition** (sj5) *f*, demolition; (*pl.*) demolitions.
démon (dem5) *m*, demon, devil, fiend; daemon; genius; imp. ~ *familier*, familiar [spirit].
démonétiser (demonetize) *v.t*, to demonetize, call in; discredit.
démoniaque (demonjak) *a*, demoniac(al). ¶ *n*, demoniac.
démonstrateur (dem5stratœ:r) *m*, demonstrator (*Sch.*). **démonstratif, ive** (tif, i:v) *a*, conclusive; demonstrative. **démonstration** (sj5) *f*, demonstration; proof. ~ *par l'absurde*, reduction to absurdity, reductio ad absurdum.
démontable (dem5tabl) *a*, sectional. **démonter** (te) *v.t*, to dismount; unhorse, throw; take to pieces; upset, nonplus.
démontrer (dem5tre) *v.t*, to demonstrate, prove; show.
démoraliser (demoralize) *v.t*, to demoralize.
démordre (demordr) *v.i*, to let go; desist.
démunir (se) de (demyni:r), to part with.
démuseler (demyzle) *v.t*, to unmuzzle.
dénaturer (denatyre) *v.t*, to denature; pervert, render unnatural; distort; misrepresent.
dénégation (denegasj5) *f*, denial; disclaimer.
déniaiser (denjeze) *v.t*, to sharpen (*wits*).
dénicher (denife) *v.t*, to take out of the nest; ferret out; (*v.i.*) to fly [away]. **dénicheur** (fœ:r) *m*, birds'-nester; hunter (*curios*).
denier (dənje) *m*: ~ *à Dieu*, earnest money; key money. *le* ~ *de la veuve*, the widow's mite. *le* ~ *de Saint-Pierre*, Peter's pence. ~**s**, *pl*, money, funds.
dénier (denje) *v.t*, to deny; disclaim.
dénigrer (denigre) *v.t*, to disparage, run down, detract from.
dénombrement (den5bromᾶ) *m*, count; census.
dénominateur (denominatœ:r) *m*, denominator. **dénommer** (me) *v.t*, to name, denominate.
dénoncer (den5se) *v.t*, to proclaim, declare; denounce, inform against. **dénonciation** (sjasj5) *f*, denunciation; information.
dénoter (denote) *v.t*, to denote, betoken.
dénouement (denumᾶ) *m*, upshot; ending. **dénouer** (nwe) *v.t*, to untie; undo; loosen; unravel.
denrée (dᾶre) *f. oft. pl*, commodity, produce. ~ *alimentaire*, foodstuff.
dense (dᾶ:s) *a*, dense, close; thick. **densité** (dᾶsite) *f*, density.
dent (dᾶ) *f*, tooth; prong; cog; tusk; serration; [jagged] peak. ~**s** *de dessous, de dessus, de devant, du fond, de lait, de sagesse*, lower, upper, front, back, milk, wisdom, teeth. **dentaire** (tɛ:r) *a*, dental (*Anat.*). **dental, e** (tal) *a*, dental (*Anat. & Gram.*). ¶ *f*, dental (*Gram.*). **denté, e** (te) *a*, toothed, cogged; dentate. ~ *en scie*, serrate.

denteler (tle) *v.t*, to indent, notch, jag, serrate. **dentelle** (tɛl) *f*, lace; laced paper; tracery. ~ *à l'aiguille*, needle-made lace. ~ *au point à l'aiguille*, needle-point l. ~ *aux fuseaux*, pillow l. **dentelure** (tly:r) *f*, indentation, serration. **dentier** (tje) *m*, set of (*artificial*) teeth; denture, [dental] plate. **dentifrice** (tifris) *m*, tooth paste; t. powder; mouth wash. **dentiste** (tist) *m*, dentist; (*att.*) dental (*surgeon*). **dentition** (sj5) *f*, dentition, teething. **denture** (ty:r) *f*, set of (*natural*) teeth; teeth (*cogs*). ~ *artificielle*, denture, [dental] plate.
dénuder (denyde) *v.t*, to denude, bare, strip.
dénué, e (denɥe) *a*, devoid, destitute. **dénuement** (nymᾶ) *m*, destitution, penury. **se dénuer de** (nɥe), to part with.
dépaqueter (depakte) *v.t*, to unpack.
dépareillé, e (depareje) *a*, odd (*pair or set*). **dépareiller** (je) *v.t*, to break (*a set*).
déparer (depare) *v.t*, to strip; spoil, mar; pick out the best.
déparler (deparle) *v.i*, *with neg*, to stop talking.
départ (depa:r) *m*, departure, sailing; start; parting (*Chem.*). *faire le* ~ *entre, de*, to discriminate between. ~ *arrêté*, standing start. ~ *lancé*, flying start. ~ *usines*, ex works, ex mill (*sales*).
départager (departaʒe) *v.t*, to decide between. ~ *les voix*, to give the casting vote.
département (departəmᾶ) *m*, department; ministry, Office (*War, Foreign, Home*); county; province, line. **départemental, e** (tal) *a*, departmental.
départir (departi:r) *v.t.ir*, to divide; part (*metals*); distribute, dispense, endow. *se* ~, to desist; swerve (*fig.*).
dépasser (depase) *v.t*, to go beyond, go over, exceed, be above, top; turn (*a certain age*); pass, leave behind, overshoot, overreach; be longer; project beyond.
dépaver (depave) *v.t*, to unpave.
dépaysé, e (depeize) *p.a*, lost; among strangers; out of one's element. **dépayser** (ze) *v.t*, to send abroad.
dépecer (depose) *v.t*, to cut up; break up.
dépêche (depɛ:ʃ) *f*, dispatch; message; wire. **dépêcher** (peʃe) *v.t*, to dispatch. *se* ~, to make haste, be quick, hurry up; look sharp.
dépeindre (depɛ:dr) *v.t.ir*, to depict, portray, delineate, picture.
dépenaillé, e (depnaje) *a*, in rags; ill-dressed.
dépendance (depᾶdᾶ:s) *f*, dependence; subjection; dependency; outbuilding, outhouse; annex[e]. **dépendant, e** (dᾶ, ᾶ:t) *a*, dependent. **dépendre** (pᾶ:dr) *v.i*, to depend, belong; be a dependency (*de* = of).
dépens (depᾶ) *m.pl*, expense; [law] costs. **dépense** (pᾶ:s) *f*, expense, charge, cost, expenditure; efflux; steward's room. ~ *de bouche*, living expenses. **dépenser** (pᾶse) *v.t*, to spend, expend. **dépensier, ère** (sje, ɛ:r) *a*, extravagant, thriftless. ¶ *n*, spendthrift; bursar.

déperdition (depɛrdisjɔ̃) *f*, waste, loss.

dépérir (deperi:r) *v.i*, to dwindle, pine away, wither, decay.

dépêtrer (depɛtre) *v.t*, to extricate.

dépeupler (depœple) *v.t*, to depopulate; unstock.

dépiler (depile) *v.t*, to depilate, pluck; unhair.

dépiquer (depike) *v.t*, to unquilt; transplant; tread out, thresh (*corn*); cheer up.

dépister (depiste) *v.t*, to track down, run to earth; throw off the scent, foil.

dépit (depi) *m*, spite, spleen, despite. **dépiter** (te) *v.t*, to vex; spite.

déplacé, e (deplase) *a*, out of place, ill-timed; uncalled for. **déplacement** (smɑ̃) *m*, displacement, removal, shift[ing]; travelling. **déplacer** (se) *v.t*, to displace; [re]move, shift.

déplaire (deplɛ:r) *v.i.ir*, to be displeasing, offend. ~ *à*, to displease. **se** ~, to be unhappy; not to thrive. **déplaisant, e** (plɛzɑ̃, ɑ̃:t) *a*, unpleasing, unpleasant. **déplaisir** (zi:r) *m*, displeasure.

déplanter (deplɑ̃te) *v.t*, to take up. **déplantoir** (twa:r) *m*, trowel (*Hort.*).

dépliant (depliɑ̃) *m*, folder. **déplier** (plie) *v.t*, to unfold.

déplisser (deplise) *v.t*, to unpleat, iron out.

déploiement (deplwamɑ̃) *m*, unfolding; deployment.

déplorable† (deplorabl) *a*, deplorable. **déplorer** (re) *v.t*, to deplore, bewail.

déployer (deplwaje) *v.t*, to unfold; unfurl; deploy; spread [out]; expand; display.

déplumer (deplyme) *v.t*, to pluck, deplume. **se** ~, to moult.

dépolir (depɔli:r) *v.t*, to take the surface off. *verre dépoli*, ground glass, frosted glass.

déportements (deportəmɑ̃) *m.pl*, misconduct.

déporter (deporte) *v.t*, to deport; transport (*convict*).

déposant, e (depozɑ̃, ɑ̃:t) *n*, deponent; depositor, customer (*bank*). **dépose** (po:z) *f*, taking up; t. down; t. off. **déposer** (poze) *v.t*, to lay down; t. aside; deposit, place, lodge, hand in; file, lay; depose; register (*trade mark*); prefer; take up, t. down, t. off. **se** ~, to settle. **dépositaire** (pozitɛ:r) *n*, depositary; trustee; storer (*furniture warehouseman*). **déposition** (sjɔ̃) *f*, deposition; evidence.

déposséder (deposede) *v.t*, to dispossess, oust.

dépôt (depo) *m*, deposit; deposition; trust; handing in; filing; depot, store[house], warehouse, repository, depository; shed; yard; cells (*prison*); sediment; scale, fur. *en* ~, on sale [or return]. ~ *de mendicité*, [public assistance] institution, workhouse.

dépoter (depote) *v.t*, to plant out; decant.

dépouille (depu:j) *f*, slough (*serpent, worm*); skin (*wild beast*); spoil; remains (*mortal*). **dépouiller** (puje) *v.t*, to skin; cast (*skin*); strip, divest, despoil; go through; analyse; count (*votes*). **se** ~, to slough, cast its skin; shed its leaves.

dépourvoir (depurwa:r) *v.t.ir*, to deprive. **dépourvu, e** (vy) *p.a*, destitute, bereft, devoid. **au dépourvu**, *ad*, unawares, napping.

dépravation (depravasjɔ̃) *f*, depravation; depravity. **dépraver** (ve) *v.t*, to deprave, vitiate.

dépréciation (depresjasjɔ̃) *f*, depreciation. **déprécier** (sje) *v.t*, to depreciate, underrate, undervalue, disparage.

déprédation (depredasjɔ̃) *f*, depredation.

déprendre (se) (deprɑ̃:dr) *v.pr.ir*, to break away, part.

dépression (depresjɔ̃) *f*, depression. ~ *nerveuse*, nervous breakdown. **déprimer** (prime) *v.t*, to depress; dispirit.

depuis (dəpɥi) *pr. & ad*, since, for, from. ~ *quand?* how long? since when? ~ *que, c,* since.

députation (depytasjɔ̃) *f*, deputation; membership (*parliament*). **député** (te) *m*, deputy (*M.P.*); delegate. **députer** (te) *v.t*, to depute.

déraciné (derasine) (*pers.*) *n*, fish out of water. **déraciner** (ne) *v.t*, to uproot, eradicate.

déraidir (se) (derɛdi:r) (*fig.*) *v.pr*, to unbend, thaw.

dérailler (deraje) *v.i*, to derail; go astray (*fig.*).

déraison (derɛzɔ̃) *f*, unreason[ableness]. **déraisonnable†** (zɔnabl) *a*, unreasonable, preposterous. **déraisonner** (ne) *v.i*, to talk nonsense.

dérangement (derɑ̃ʒmɑ̃) *m*, derangement; disturbance; fault. **déranger** (ʒe) *v.t*, to disarrange; disturb; upset; trouble; put out of order; derange, unsettle.

déraper (derape) *v.t. & i*, to trip (*anchor*); skid; side-slip.

déréglé, e (deregle) *a*, out of order; lawless. **dérèglement** (reglɑ̃mɑ̃) *m*, disordered state; irregularity; derangement; profligacy. **dérégler** (regle) *v.t*, to put out of order; derange; disorder.

dérider (deride) *v.t*, to smooth, unwrinkle; cheer up.

dérision (derizjɔ̃) *f*, derision. **dérisoire** (zwa:r) *a*, derisory, laughable.

dérivation (derivasjɔ̃) *f*, derivation; deflection; loop [line]; flume; shunt (*Elec.*). **dérive** (ri:v) *f*, leeway; drift; breakaway. *en* ~, *à la* ~, adrift. **dérivé** (ve) *m*, derivative. **dériver** (ve) *v.t*, to divert; shunt (*Elec.*); unrivet; (*v.i.*) to be derived; spring, originate; drift, drive (*Naut.*).

dernier, ère (dɛrnje, ɛ:r) *a*, last; hindmost; latter; late; latest; final; closing; junior (*partner*); highest, utmost; extreme; dire; lowest, worst. *dernier cri*, latest [thing out]. *dernier jugement*, crack of doom. *dernières galeries*, gallery (*Theat.*). *dernière heure*, stop press. *dernière main*, finishing touches. **dernièrement** (njɛrmɑ̃) *ad*, lately, latterly, not long ago.

dérobé, e (derɔbe) *a*, secret, hidden, concealed; spare (*time*). **à la dérobée**, *ad*, by stealth, on the sly. **dérober** (be) *v.t*, to steal, rob; snatch; conceal, hide. *se* ~ *à*, to shirk. *se* ~ *de*, to steal away from. *se* ~ *sous*, to give way under.

déroger (derɔʒe) *v.i*, to derogate.

dérouiller (deruje) *v.t*, to rub off the rust from; brush up (*fig.*).

dérouler (derule) *v.t*, to unroll; unwind; unfold.

déroute (derut) *f*, rout; ruin. *mettre en* ~, to rout. **dérouter** (te) *v.t*, to lead astray; baffle, nonplus.

derrière (dɛrjɛːr) *pr. & ad*, behind; aft; astern. ¶ *m*, back; rear; hinder part; tail (*cart*).

derviche (dɛrviʃ) *ou* **dervis** (vi) *m*, dervish.

dès (dɛ) *pr*, from; since. ~ *à présent*, from now onward. ~ *lors*, ever since then; consequently. ~ *que, c,* as soon as.

désabonner (se) (dezabɔne) *v.pr*, to discontinue one's subscription *or* season ticket.

désabuser (dezabyze) *v.t*, to disabuse, undeceive.

désaccord (dezakɔːr) *m*, disagreement; discord (*Mus.*). **désaccorder** (kɔrde) *v.t*, to put out of tune. *se* ~, to break their engagement (*marriage*).

désaccoupler (dezakuple) *v.t*, to uncouple.

désaccoutumer (dezakutyme) *v.t*, to break of the habit.

désaffection (dezafɛksjɔ̃) *f*, disaffection.

désagréable† (dezagreabl) *a*, disagreeable, unpleasant. ~ *au goût*, distasteful; unpalatable.

désagréger (dezagreʒe) *v.t*, to disintegrate, weather.

désagrément (dezagremɑ̃) *m*, source of annoyance; unpleasantness; vexation.

désajuster (dezaʒyste) *v.t*, to derange; disarrange.

désaltérer (dezaltere) *v.t*, to quench (*someone's*) thirst.

désappointement (dezapwɛ̃tmɑ̃) *m*, disappointment. **désappointer** (te) *v.t*, to disappoint.

désapprendre (dezaprɑ̃ːdr) *v.t. & abs. ir*, to forget; unlearn.

désapprobation (dezaprɔbasjɔ̃) *f*, disapprobation, disapproval. **désapprouver** (pruve) *v.t*, to disapprove [of], frown [up]on.

désarçonner (dezarsɔne) *v.t*, to unseat, unhorse, throw; silence, floor.

désarmement (dezarməmɑ̃) *m*, disarmament; laying up (*ship*). **désarmer** (me) *v.t. & i*, to disarm, unarm; uncock (*gun*); lay up.

désarroi (dezarwa) *m*, disarray, disorder.

désassembler (dezasɑ̃ble) *v.t*, to take to pieces, disconnect, disjoint.

désastre (dezastr) *m*, disaster. **désastreux, euse** (trø, øːz) *a*, disastrous.

désavantage (dezavɑ̃taːʒ) *m*, disadvantage, drawback. **désavantager** (taʒe) *v.t*, to place at a disadvantage; handicap.

désavantageux, euse† (ʒø, øːz) *a*, disadvantageous.

désaveu (dezavø) *m*, disavowal, denial, disclaimer. **désavouer** (vwe) *v.t*, to disavow; disown; disclaim; disapprove.

desceller (desɛle) *v.t*, to unseal.

descendance (desɑ̃dɑ̃ːs) *f*, descent, lineage; descendants. **descendant, e** (dɑ̃, ɑ̃ːt) *a*, descending, downward; down (*train, &c*); outgoing (*tide*). ¶ *n*, descendant; (*pl.*) progeny. **descendre** (sɑ̃ːdr) *v.i. & t*, to descend, go down; alight, dismount, get down; stay, stop, put up (*at hotel*); lower; drop; fall; sink; make a descent. ~ [*à terre*], to land. ~ *en vol plané*, to plane down. **descente** (sɑ̃ːt) *f*, descent; fall; lowering; slope, incline; downpipe; raid; run (*of depositors on bank*). ~ *de bain*, bath mat. ~ *de justice*, domiciliary visit. ~ *de lit*, bedside rug.

description (dɛskripsjɔ̃) *f*, description; inventory.

désemparer (dezɑ̃pare) *v.t*, to disable (*ship*). *sans* ~, on the spot, there & then; without intermission, continuous(ly).

désemplir (dezɑ̃pliːr) *v.t*, to partly empty; (*v.i.*) to empty. *ne pas* ~, to be always full.

désenchanter (dezɑ̃ʃɑ̃te) *v.t*, to disenchant; disillusion.

désencombrer (dezɑ̃kɔ̃bre) *v.t*, to disencumber, clear.

désenfiler (dezɑ̃file) *v.t*, to unthread.

désenfler (dezɑ̃fle) *v.t*, to deflate; (*v.i.*) to go down (*swelling*).

désenivrer (dezɑ̃nivre) *v.t*, to sober. *il ne désenivre point*, he is never sober.

désennuyer (dezɑ̃nɥije) *v.t*, to divert, amuse.

désenrhumer (dezɑ̃ryme) *v.t*, to cure of a cold. **désenrouer** (rwe) *v.t*, to cure of hoarseness.

déséquilibré, e (dezekilibre) *a*, unbalanced.

désert, e (dezɛːr, ɛrt) *a*, desert; deserted, empty, desolate. ¶ *m*, desert, wilderness. **déserter** (zɛrte) *v.t. & abs*, to desert, forsake. ~ *de*, to leave. **déserteur** (tœːr) *m*, deserter. **désertion** (sjɔ̃) *f*, desertion. **désertique** (tik) *a*, desert.

désespérance (dezɛsperɑ̃ːs) *f*, despair. **désespérant, e** (rɑ̃, ɑ̃ːt) *a*, heart-breaking. **désespéré†, e** (re) *a*, desperate, hopeless. ¶ *n*, desperate man, woman, madman. **désespérer** (re) *v.i. & abs*, to despair; (*v.t.*) to drive to despair. **désespoir** (pwaːr) *m*, despair; desperation.

déshabillé (dezabije) *m*, undress, dishabille; tea gown; true colours (*fig.*). **déshabiller** (je) *v.t*, to undress, disrobe, strip; lay bare (*fig.*).

déshabituer (dezabitɥe) *v.t*, to break of the habit.

déshérence (dezerɑ̃ːs) *f*, escheat.

déshériter (dezerite) *v.t*, to disinherit.

déshonnête† (dezɔnɛːt) *a*, indecent, immodest.

déshonneur (dezɔnœːr) *m*, dishonour, disgrace. **déshonorant, e** (nɔrɑ̃, ɑ̃ːt) *a*, dishonourable, discreditable. **déshonorer** (re) *v.t*, to dishonour, disgrace.

desiderata (dezidərata) *m.pl*, desiderata, wants.

désigner (deziɲe) *v.t*, to designate; indicate, point out; describe; nominate; appoint. **désignation** (nasjɔ̃) *f*, designation, &c.

désillusionner (dezilyzjɔne) *v.t*, to disillusion, undeceive.

désincorporer (dezɛ̃kɔrpɔre) *v.t*, to disincorporate, disembody.

désinence (dezinɑ̃ːs) *f*, ending (*word*).

désinfectant (dezɛ̃fɛktɑ̃) *m*, disinfectant. **désinfecter** (te) *v.t*, to disinfect, deodorize. **désinfection** (sjɔ̃) *f*, disinfection.

désintéressé, e (dezɛ̃terɛse) *a*, not implicated; disinterested, candid; unselfish. **désintéressement** (smɑ̃) *m*, disinterestedness; unselfishness. **désintéresser** (se) *v.t*, to buy out, satisfy, pay off. *se* ~ *de*, to take no further interest in.

désinviter (dezɛ̃vite) *v.t*, to ask not to come.

désinvolte (dezɛ̃vɔlt) *a*, easy. **désinvolture** (tyːr) *f*, unconstraint; free & easy manner.

désir (deziːr) *m*, desire, wish. **désirable** (zirabl) *a*, desirable. **désirer** (re) *v.t. & abs*, to desire, want, be desirous of, wish, w. for. **désireux, euse** (rø, øːz) *a*, desirous, wishful, anxious.

désistement (dezistəmɑ̃) *m*, waiver (*Law*); withdrawal. **se désister de** (te), to waive; withdraw from; stand down from (*candidature*).

désobéir (dezɔbeiːr) *v.i. & abs*, to disobey. ~ *à*, to disobey (*v.t.*). **désobéissance** (isɑ̃ːs) *f*, disobedience. **désobéissant, e** (sɑ̃, ɑ̃ːt) *a*, disobedient.

désobligeance (dezɔbliʒɑ̃ːs) *f*, disobligingness, unkindness. **désobligeant, e** (ʒɑ̃, ɑ̃ːt) *a*, disobliging, unkind, ungracious. **désobliger** (ʒe) *v.t*, to disoblige.

désobstruer (dezɔpstrye) *v.t*, to clear.

désoccupé, e (dezɔkype) *a*, unoccupied.

désœuvré, e (dezœvre) *a*, idle, at a loose end. ¶ *n*, idler. **désœuvrement** (vrəmɑ̃) *m*, idleness.

désolation (dezɔlasjɔ̃) *f*, desolation. **désolé, e** (le) *p.a*, desolate; disconsolate, forlorn, distressed, extremely sorry. **désoler** (le) *v.t*, to desolate, distress, grieve.

désopilant, e (dezɔpilɑ̃, ɑ̃ːt) *a*, highly amusing.

désordonné, e (dezɔrdɔne) *a*, untidy; disorderly; inordinate. **désordre** (dr) *m*, disorder; disorderliness.

désorganiser (dezɔrganize) *v.t*, to disorganize.

désorienter (dezɔrjɑ̃te) *v.t*, to disconcert, bewilder.

désormais (dezɔrmɛ) *ad*, henceforth; hereafter.

désosser (dezɔse) *v.t*, to bone.

despote (dɛspɔt) *m*, despot. **despotique†** (tik) *a*, despotic. **despotisme** (tism) *m*, despotism.

dessécher (deseʃe) *v.t*, to desiccate; dry up, drain; wither, parch. **dessèchement** (sɛʃmɑ̃) *m*, desiccation, &c.

dessein (desɛ̃) *m*, design, plan, project; purpose. *à* ~, on purpose, designedly.

desseller (desɛle) *v.t*, to unsaddle.

desserrer (desɛre) *v.t*, to loosen, slack[en]; open.

dessert (desɛːr) *m*, dessert (*sweets, cheese, fruit*).

desserte (desɛrt) *f*, duties. [*table de*] ~, service table. ~ *mobile*, service wagon, dinner w. **desservir** (viːr) *v.t.ir*, to serve; minister to (*Eccl.*). ~ [*la table*], to clear the table.

dessiccation (dɛsikasjɔ̃) *f*, desiccation.

dessiller (desije) *v.t*, to open (*eyes*) (*fig.*).

dessin (desɛ̃) *m*, drawing, sketching; design, pattern; sketch; cartoon; plan. ~ *à carreaux*, check [pattern]. ~ *à main levée*, free-hand drawing. ~ *au trait*, outline d. ~ *industriel*, mechanical d. ~ *ombré*, shaded d. **dessinateur, trice** (sinatœːr, tris) *n*, sketcher, drawer; draughtsman; cartoonist; designer. ~ *de jardins*, landscape gardener. **dessiner** (sine) *v.t*, to draw, sketch; design; show; outline. **se** ~, to stand out; show up; loom; take shape.

dessoûler (desule) *v.t*, to sober. *il ne dessoûle jamais*, he is never sober.

dessous (dəsu) *ad. & pr*, under; under it, them; underneath; beneath, below. *au*~ (otsu) *ad*, under[neath], below. *au*~ *de*, *pr*, below, under, beneath. *en* ~, *ad*, underneath; underhand; stealthily; sly. *là*-~, *ad*, under there, under that, underneath. *par*—~, *pr. & ad*, under[neath], beneath. ¶ *m*, under part, underside, bottom; face (*card*); wrong side (*fabric*); worst of it (*fig.*); (*pl.*) underclothing, underwear (*women's*). ~ *de bras*, dress protector. ~ *de plat*, table mat.

dessus (dəsy) *ad*, over, above; on, upon, [up]on it, them. *au*~ (otsy) *ad*, above [it], over it; upwards. *au*~ *de*, *pr*, above, over; beyond. *en* ~, *ad*, on [the] top. *là*-~, *ad*, on that, thereon; thereupon. *par*—~, *pr. & ad*, over; into. *par*— *bord*, overboard. ¶ *m*, upper part; top; back (*hand*); treble (*Mus.*); soprano; right side (*fabric*); upper hand, mastery, whip hand; best of it. ~ *de coussin*, cushion cover. ~ *de fourneau*, top of grate, hob. ~ *de plateau*, tray cloth. ~ *de lit*, bedspread. ~ *du panier*, pick of the basket.

destin (destɛ̃) *m*, destiny, fate, lot, doom. **destinataire** (tinatɛːr) *n*, consignee; receiver, recipient; addressee. *aux risques & périls du* ~, at owner's risk. **destination** (sjɔ̃) *f*, destination; purpose. *à* ~ *de*, [bound] for. **destinée** (ne) *f*, destiny, lot. **destiner** (ne) *v.t*, to destine, design, intend, mean; allot, assign; fate, doom.

destitué, e (dɛstitɥe) *p.a*, devoid, lacking. **destituer** (tɥe) *v.t*, to dismiss, remove, displace. **destitution** (tysjɔ̃) *f*, dismissal, &c.

destructeur (dɛstryktœ:r, tris) *a*, destructive. ¶ *n*, destroyer. **destructif, ive** (tif, i:v) *a*, destructive. **destruction** (sjɔ̃) *f*, destruction.

désuet, te (desɥe, ɛt) *a*, obsolete. **désuétude** (sɥetyd) *f*, disuse.

désunion (dezynjɔ̃) *f*, disunion. **désunir** (ni:r) *v.t*, to disunite.

détachement (detaʃmɑ̃) *m*, detachment; draft (*men*). **détacher** (ʃe) *v.t*, to detach, untie, undo, unfasten; take off, t. down; detail, draft (*Mil.*). **se** ~, to come away; break off; b. away; stand out.

détail (deta:j) *m*, detail, particular; retail. **détaillant, e** (tajɑ̃, ɑ̃:t) *n*, retailer. **détailler** (je) *v.t*, to cut up; retail, peddle; detail.

détaler (detale) *v.i*, to make off, scamper away.

détaxer (detakse) *v.t*, to return (or remit) the duties (*or* charges) on; untax.

détecteur (detɛktœ:r) *m*, detector (*Radio, &c*). **détective** (ti:v) *m*, detective.

déteindre (detɛ̃:dr) *v.t. & i. ir*, to fade. ~ *sur*, to come off on (*dye*); influence.

dételer (detle) *v.t. & abs*, to unharness; unyoke; ease off, stop.

détendre (detɑ̃:dr) *v.t. & abs. & se* ~, to unbend, slack[en], relax, expand; take down. **détenir** (detni:r) *v.t.ir*, to hold; detain. **détente** (detɑ̃:t) *f*, relaxation; expansion; trigger. **détenteur, trice** (detɑ̃tœ:r, tris) *n*, holder (*pers.*). **détention** (sjɔ̃) *f*, holding; detention, detainment. **détenu, e** (tny) *n*, prisoner. *jeune* ~, juvenile offender.

détérioration (deterjorasjɔ̃) *f*, deterioration, impairment, damage, dilapidation. **se détériorer** (re) *v.pr*, to deteriorate.

détermination (detɛrminasjɔ̃) *f*, determination; resolution; resolve. **déterminé, e** (ne) *a*, determinate, definite; determined, resolute; keen; specific. **déterminer** (ne) *v.t*, to determine; fix; decide (upon); resolve; bring about. **se** ~, to resolve, make up one's mind.

déterrer (detere) *v.t*, to unearth, dig up; disinter, exhume.

détestable (detɛstabl) *a*, detestable. **détester** (te) *v.t*, to detest, hate.

détonation (detɔnasjɔ̃) *f*, detonation, report. **détoner** (ne) *v.i*, to detonate.

détonner (detɔne) *v.i*, to be (*or* sing) (*or* play) out of tune; sing flat; jar; be out of keeping; be out of one's element.

détordre (detɔrdr) *v.t*, to untwist. **détors, e** (tɔ:r, ɔrs) *a*, untwisted. **détortiller** (tɔrtije) *v.t*, to untwist; disentangle.

détour (detu:r) *m*, winding; turn[ing]; detour; dodge. *sans* ~, straightforwardly. **détourné, e** (turne) *a*, by (*road*); roundabout, circuitous, devious. **détourner** (ne) *v.t*, to divert, deflect, distract, turn aside, avert;

deter; twist; dissuade; make away with, misappropriate, misapply, embezzle, peculate; abduct. **détournement** (nəmɑ̃) *m*, diversion, &c.

détracteur (detraktœ:r) *m*, detractor.

détraquer (detrake) *v.t*, to derange.

détrempe (detrɑ̃:p) *f*, distemper (*paint*); softening (*steel*). *peindre à la* ~, to distemper. **détremper** (trɑ̃pe) *v.t*, to soak, sodden, dilute; soften.

détresse (detrɛs) *f*, distress; straits.

détriment (detrimɑ̃) *m*, detriment, prejudice.

détritus (detrity:s) *m*, detritus; litter, rubbish.

détroit (detrwa) *m*, strait, straits, sound. *le* ~ *de Gibraltar, du Pas de Calais*, the Straits of Gibraltar, of Dover.

détromper (detrɔ̃pe) *v.t*, to undeceive.

détrôner (detrone) *v.t*, to dethrone.

détrousser (detruse) *v.t*, to rob. **détrousseur** (sœ:r) *m*, footpad.

détruire (detrɥi:r) *v.t. & abs. ir*, to demolish; destroy; ruin.

dette (dɛt) *f*, debt; indebtedness. ~ [*active*], [book] debt, debt [due to the trader]. ~ [*passive*], debt [due by the trader].

deuil (dœ:j) *m*, mourning; bereavement; mourners. *conduire le* ~, to be chief mourner. ~ *de veuve*, widow's weeds.

Deutéronome (døteronom) *m*, Deuteronomy.

deux (dø; *in liaison* døz) *a*, two; second; a (*word, line*); a few (*steps*). ~ *fois*, twice. ~ *fois zéro, cinque, sisse, septe, huite,* double oh, fife, six, sev-en, ate (*Teleph.*). *tous les* ~ *jours*, every other day. ~ *jumeaux, elles*, twins. ~ *n, s, &c*, double n, s, &c (*Spelling*). ¶ *m*, two; deuce (*Cards, Dice*). *à* ~, deuce (*40 all*) (*Ten.*). *à* ~ *de jeux*, five [games] all, games all, deuce [set] (*Ten.*). *tous* [*les*] *deux*, both.

deuxième† (døzjɛm) *a. & n*, second. ~ *de change*, f, second of exchange.

deux-points (døpwɛ̃) *m*, colon.

dévaler (devale) *v.i. & t*, to go down.

dévaliser (devalize) *v.t*, to rifle, strip, rob.

devancer (dəvɑ̃se) *v.t*, to get the start of; precede; forestall; outstrip, outdo, outrival. **devancier, ère** (sje, ɛ:r) *n*, predecessor.

devant (dəvɑ̃) *ad*, before, in front, ahead. ¶ *pr*, before, in front of, ahead of. *aller au-* ~ *de*, to go to meet; anticipate. *par-* ~, *ad. & pr*, in front, before, in the presence of. ¶ *m*, front; fore; frontage; (*pl.*) foreground (*Art*).

devanture (d[ə]vɑ̃ty:r) *f*, front (*shop, &c*); window (*shop show*).

dévastateur, trice (devastatœ:r, tris) *n*, devastator. **dévastation** (sjɔ̃) *f*, devastation. **dévaster** (te) *v.t*, to devastate.

développateur (devlɔpatœ:r) *m*, developer (*proper*) (*Phot.*). **développement** (pmɑ̃) *m*, opening out; spread; growth; development; evolution (*Geom.*); gear (*bicycle*). **développer** (pe) *v.t*, to open out; unwrap; develop.

devenir (dəvni:r) *v.i.ir*, to become; grow; wax; go; get.

dévergondage (devergŏda:ʒ) *m*, licentiousness; extravagance (*fig.*). **dévergondé, e** (de) *a. & n*, licentious, shameless, profligate (person).

déverrouiller (deveruje) *v.t*, to unbolt.

devers (dəve:r): *par-~, pr*, by, before.

dévers, e (deve:r, ers) *a*, out of plumb, out of true. ¶ *m*, cant. **déverser** (verse) *v.t*, to warp; incline; discharge; pour. **déversoir** (swa:r) *m*, weir.

dévêtir (se) (deveti:r) *v.pr.ir*, to strip, undress; leave off some of one's (*warm*) clothes.

déviation (devjasjɔ̃) *f*, deviation; deflection. ~ *de la colonne vertébrale*, curvature of the spine.

dévider (devide) *v.t*, to wind, reel; unwind. **dévidoir** (dwa:r) *m*, reel, spool.

dévier (devje) *v.i*, to deviate, swerve; curve (*spine*); (*v.t.*) to deflect, curve.

devin, ineresse (dəvɛ̃, vinres) *n*, diviner, soothsayer. **deviner** (vine) *v.t. & abs*, to divine; guess. **devinette** (net) *f*, riddle, conundrum.

devis (dəvi) *m*, estimate; specification; manifest (*stowage*).

dévisager (devizaʒe) *v.t*, to stare at.

devise (dəvi:z) *f*, device; motto. ~ [*étrangère*], [foreign] currency, [f.] bill, [f.] exchange. ~ *publicitaire*, slogan.

deviser (dəvize) *v.i*, to chat.

dévisser (devise) *v.t*, to unscrew.

dévoiement (devwamɑ̃) *m*, looseness (*bowels*).

dévoiler (devwale) *v.t*, to unveil; reveal, disclose.

devoir (dəvwa:r) *m*, duty; exercise, task (*Sch.*); (*pl.*) home work; (*pl.*) respects. ¶ *v.t. & abs. ir*, to owe. *Followed by infinitive*: should, ought; must, have to; am to.

dévolu, e (devoly) *a*, devolved, vested.

dévorant, e (devorɑ̃, ɑ̃:t) *a*, ravenous; consuming; wasting; devouring. **dévorer** (re) *v.t*, to devour, lap up; swallow; stifle.

dévot, e† (devo, ɔt) *a*, devout, devotional; religious; sanctimonious. ¶ *n*, devout person; devotee. **dévotion** (vosjɔ̃) *f*, devotion, devoutness.

dévouement (devumɑ̃) *m*, devotion, self-sacrifice. **dévouer** (vwe) *v.t*, to dedicate; devote.

dévoyer (se) (devwaje) *v.pr*. (*Conjugated like envoyer, except Future* je dévoierai), to go astray (*fig.*).

dextérité (dɛksterite) *f*, dexterity, skill.

dextrine (dɛkstrin) *f*, dextrin.

diabète (djabɛt) *m*, diabetes.

diable (dja:bl) *m*, devil; deuce; troll[e]y, truck. ¶ i, the devil! the deuce! the dickens! **diablerie** (djabləri) *f*, devilry, devilment. **diablesse** (blɛs) *f*, she-devil. **diablotin** (blotɛ̃) *m*, little devil, imp. **diabolique†** (bolik) *a*, diabolic(al), devilish; fiendish.

diacre (djakr) *m*, deacon.

diacritique (djakritik) *a*, diacritical.

diadème (djadɛm) *m*, diadem.

diagnostic (djagnostik) *m*, diagnosis. **diagnostiquer** (ke) *v.t*, to diagnose.

diagonal, e† (djagonal) *a. & f*, diagonal.

diagramme (djagram) *m*, diagram, chart.

dialecte (djalɛkt) *m*, dialect.

dialectique (djalɛktik) *f*, dialectics.

dialogue (djalog) *m*, dialogue. **dialoguer** (ge) *v.i*, to converse; write in dialogue.

diamant (djamɑ̃) *m*, diamond.

diamétral, e† (djametral) *a*, diametric. **diamètre** (metr) *m*, diameter.

diane (djan) *f*, reveille (*Mil.*).

diantre (djɑ̃:tr) *m*, the deuce.

diapason (djapazɔ̃) *m*, diapason; pitch; compass, range. ~ *à bouche*, pitch pipe. ~ *à branches*, tuning fork. ~ *normal*, concert pitch.

diaphane (djafan) *a*, diaphanous.

diaphragme (djafragm) *m*, diaphragm; stop.

diaprer (djapre) *v.t*, to diaper, variegate. *étoffe diaprée*, diaper.

diarrhée (djare) *f*, diarrhoea.

diatonique (djatonik) *a*, diatonic.

diatribe (djatrib) *f*, diatribe.

dictateur (diktatœ:r) *m*, dictator. **dictatorial, e** (torjal) *a*, dictatorial. **dictature** (ty:r) *f*, dictatorship.

dictée (dikte) *f*, dictation. **dicter** (te) *v.t. & abs*, to dictate. **diction** (sjɔ̃) *f*, diction, delivery. **dictionnaire** (one:r) *m*, dictionary. ~ *géographique*, gazetteer. **dicton** (tɔ̃) *m*, saying; dictum; saw, byword.

didactique (didaktik) *a*, didactic.

dièse (djɛ:z) *m*, sharp (*Mus.*).

diète (djɛt) *f*, diet. ~ *absolue*, starvation d. mettre à la ~, *v.t*, faire ~, *v.i*, to diet.

Dieu (djø) *m*, God; goodness! *d~*, god.

diffamation (difamasjɔ̃) *f*, defamation, libel, slander. **diffamatoire** (twa:r) *& * **diffamant, e** (mɑ̃, ɑ̃:t) *a*, defamatory, &c. **diffamer** (me) *v.t*, to defame, &c, malign.

différemment (diferamɑ̃) *ad*, differently. **différence** (rɑ̃:s) *f*, difference; odds. **différencier** (rɑ̃sje) *v.t*, to differentiate. **différend** (rɑ̃) *m*, difference, dispute. **différent, e** (rɑ̃, ɑ̃:t) *a*, different, various. **différentiel, le** (rɑ̃sjɛl) *a. & m*, differential. **différer** (re) *v.t. & abs*, to defer, delay, put off; postpone, hold over; tarry; (*v.i.*) to differ; be at variance.

difficile (difisil) *a*, difficult, hard; fastidious; trying. **difficilement** (lmɑ̃) *ad*, with difficulty. **difficulté** (kylte) *f*, difficulty; tiff. **difficultueux, euse** (tɥø, ø:z) *a*, troublesome; fussy.

difforme (diform) *a*, deformed, misshapen, unshapely. **difformité** (mite) *f*, deformity.

diffus, e (dify, y:z) *a*, diffused; diffuse; long-winded, wordy. **diffuser** (fyze) *v.t*, to diffuse; broadcast. **diffusion** (zjɔ̃) *f*, diffusion; broadcasting; long-windedness, wordiness.

digérer (dizere) v.t. & abs, to digest; brook, stomach. je ne digère pas la viande, meat does not agree with me. digestible (zɛstibl) a, digestible. digestif, ive (tif, i:v) a. & m, digestive. digestion (tjɔ̃) f, digestion.

digital, e (dizital) a, digital, finger (att.). ¶ f, foxglove; digitalis (Phar.).

digne (diɲ) a, worthy; deserving; dignified. dignement (nmã) ad, worthily, with dignity; adequately. dignitaire (ɲite:r) m, dignitary. dignité (te) f, dignity; rank.

digression (digrɛsjɔ̃) f, digression.

digue (dig) f, dike, dam; sea wall; barrier (fig.).

dilapider (dilapide) v.t, to squander; misappropriate.

dilater (dilate) v.t, to dilate; expand; swell.

dilemme (dilɛm) m, dilemma.

dilettante (dilɛttã:t) a, dilettante, amateur.

diligemment (diliʒamã) ad, diligently. diligence (ʒã:s) f, diligence; industry; despatch; proceedings, suit (Law); stage coach. diligent, e (ʒã, ã:t) a, diligent; industrious; expeditious.

diluer (dilɥe) v.t, to dilute; water (stock, Fin.).

diluvien, ne (dilyvjɛ̃, ɛn) a, diluvial; torrential (rain).

dimanche (dimã:ʃ) m, Sunday, sabbath. ~ des Rameaux, Palm Sunday.

dîme (di:m) f, tithe.

dimension (dimãsjɔ̃) f, dimension, size, measurement.

diminuer (diminɥe) v.t. & i, to diminish, decrease, reduce, abate, lower; taper; get thin. aller en diminuant, to taper. entièrement diminué, fully fashioned (stocking). diminutif, ive (nytif, i:v) a, diminutive (Gram.). ¶ m, diminutive (Gram.); miniature. diminution (sjɔ̃) f, diminution, &c, as diminuer.

dinanderie (dinãdri) f, brasswares. dinandier (dje) m, brazier.

dînatoire (dinatwa:r) a, substantial (lunch).

dinde (dɛ̃:d) f, turkey [hen]; goose (girl). dindon (dɛ̃dɔ̃) m, turkey [cock]; goose (man); dupe. dindonneau (dono) m, turkey poult.

dîner (dine) m, dinner. ¶ v.i, to dine. dînette (nɛt) f, little dinner; doll's dinner party. dîneur, euse (nœ:r, ø:z) n, diner.

diocésain, e (djosezɛ̃, ɛn) a, diocesan. diocèse (sɛ:z) m, diocese.

dioptrie (dioptri) f, diopter.

diphtérie (difteri) f, diphtheria.

diphtongue (diftɔ̃:g) f, diphthong.

diplomate (diplomat) m, diplomat[ist]; (att.) diplomatic. diplomatie (si) f, diplomacy. diplomatique (tik) a, diplomatic. diplôme (plo:m) m, diploma, certificate. diplômé, e (plome) a. & n, certificated (teacher, &c).

dire (di:r) v.t, saying, assertion; allegation. ¶ v.t.ir, to say; tell; speak; bid (adieu, &c); mean. ~ son fait à quelqu'un, to give

someone a piece of one's mind. dites donc! I say!

direct, e (dirɛkt) a, direct; straight; through (Rly, &c); flat (contradiction). un direct du droit, du gauche, a straight right, left (Box.). directement (təmã) ad, directly, direct; straight; due; through.

directeur, trice (dirɛktœ:r, tris) n, manager, ess; principal, head master, h. mistress; editor; director; warden; leader. [arbitre] directeur de combat, referee (Box.). directeur de conscience, spiritual director. directeur général des postes, télégraphes & téléphones, postmaster general. direction (sjɔ̃) f, direction; strike (lode); way; management; manager's office; guidance; lead[ership]; mastership; steering. Directoire (twa:r) m, Directory; Directoire. dirigeable (riʒabl) a, dirigible. ¶ m, airship, dirigible. diriger (ʒe) v.t, to direct; manage; steer; train (gun). se ~, to make, steer (vers = for).

discernement (disɛrnəmã) m, discrimination; discernment. discerner (ne) v.t, to discern; distinguish; discriminate.

disciple (disipl) m, disciple, follower. disciplinaire (plinɛ:r) a, disciplinary. ¶ m, disciplinarian. discipline (plin) f, discipline. discipliner (ne) v.t, to discipline

discontinuer (diskɔ̃tinɥe) v.t, to discontinue.

disconvenance (diskɔ̃vnã:s) f, dissimilarity, disparity. disconvenir (vni:r) v.i.ir, to deny. ~ de, to gainsay.

discordance (diskɔrdã:s) f, discordance, disagreement; lack of harmony, difference. discorde (kɔrd) f, discord, strife, contention.

discourir (diskuri:r) v.i. & abs. ir, to discourse, descant. discours (ku:r) m, talk; discourse, speech, oration, address. ~ d'apparat, set speech.

discourtois, e (diskurtwa, a:z) a, discourteous. discourtoisie (twazi) f, discourtesy.

discrédit (diskredi) m, discredit, disrepute. discréditer (te) v.t, to discredit.

discret, ète† (diskrɛ, ɛt) a, discreet; unobtrusive; unpretentious; discrete. discrétion (kresjɔ̃) f, discretion; secrecy. à ~, ad libitum, ad lib.

discrimination (diskriminasjɔ̃) f, discrimination.

disculper (diskylpe) v.t, to exculpate.

discursif, ive (diskyrsif, i:v) a, discursive.

discussion (kysjɔ̃) f, discussion; debate; question, dispute. discutable (tabl) a, debatable, arguable, moot. discuter (te) v.t. & abs. & v.i, to discuss, debate, argue; controvert; sell up.

disert, e (dize:r, ɛrt) a, fluent.

disette (dizɛt) f, dearth, scarcity. ~ d'argent, penury. ~ d'eau, drought.

diseur, euse (dizœ:r, ø:z) n, talker; diseur, euse. ~ de bonne aventure, fortune teller. ~ de bons mots, wit. ~ de chansonnettes, entertainer, humorist (at concert).

disgrâce (disgrɑ:s) *f*, disgrace, disfavour; misfortune. **disgracier** (grasje) *v.t*, to dismiss from favour, disgrace. **disgracieux, euse** (sjø, ø:z) *a*, uncouth, ungraceful.

disjoindre (diszwɛ̃:dr) *v.t.ir*, to disjoin.

disloquer (disloke) *v.t*, to dislocate, put out of joint; dismember; break up; dislodge. **dislocation** (kasjɔ̃) *f*, dislocation, &c; breakaway.

dispache (dispaʃ) *f*, average adjustment.

disparaître (dispare:tr) *v.i.ir*, to disappear, vanish.

disparate (disparat) *a*, disparate, ill-assorted. ¶ *f*, incongruity. **disparité** (rite) *f*, disparity.

disparition (disparisjɔ̃) *f*, disappearance. **les disparus** (ry) *m.pl*, the missing (*soldiers*).

dispendieux, euse (dispãdjø, ø:z) *a*, expensive, costly.

dispensaire (dispãse:r) *m*, dispensary. **dispensateur, trice** (satœr, tris) *n*, dispenser. **dispense** (pã:s) *f*, dispensation; exemption. ~ **de bans**, marriage licence. **dispenser** (pãse) *v.t*, to dispense, exempt, excuse, spare.

disperser (disperse) *v.t*, to disperse, scatter. **ordre dispersé**, extended order (*Mil.*). **dispersion** (sjɔ̃) *f*, dispersion, dispersal.

disponibilité (disponibilite) *f*, availability; (*pl.*) available funds, liquid assets. **en** ~, unattached (*Mil.*). **disponible** (bl) *a*, available, spare, disposable; liquid; on hand; unattached; in print. ¶ *m*, spot, ex store, ex warehouse (*sales*).

dispos, e (dispo, o:z) *a*, fit, well, hearty; good (*humour*). **disposer** (poze) *v.t*, to dispose; arrange; lay out; incline; provide; draw (*bill*). **dispositif** (pozitif) *m*, purview (*Law*); device, arrangement, contrivance, gear. ~ **à 3 vitesses**, 3-speed gear. ~ **de fortune**, ~ **de circonstance**, makeshift. ~**s de mines**, preparatory work (*Min.*). **disposition** (sjɔ̃) *f*, disposition, ordering, arrangement; lie; layout; tendency; tone; frame of mind; state; humour; aptitude, flair; disposal; provision (*of a law, &c*); dispensation (*of Providence*); draft (*Fin.*).

disproportion (disproporsjɔ̃) *f*, disproportion. **disproportionné, e** (one) *a*, disproportionate.

disputailler (dispytaje) *v.i*, to wrangle, bicker. **dispute** (pyt) *f*, dispute; contest; contention. **disputer** (te) *v.i. & t*, to dispute; contend; vie; contest. **se** ~, to wrangle.

disqualifier (diskalifje) *v.t*, to disqualify (*Sport*).

disque (disk) *m*, disk, disc; discus; wheel. ~ **de phonographe**, gramophone record.

dissection (discksjɔ̃) *f*, dissection.

dissemblable (disãblabl) *a*, dissimilar. **dissemblance** (blã:s) *f*, dissimilarity.

disséminer (disemine) *v.t*, to disseminate, scatter.

dissension (disãsjɔ̃) *f*, dissension.

dissentiment (disãtimã) *m*, dissent, disagreement.

disséquer (diseke) *v.t*, to dissect.

dissertation (discrtasjɔ̃) *f*, dissertation, disquisition, essay.

dissidence (d016idã:s) *f*, dissidence, dissent. **dissident, e** (dã, ã:t) *a*, dissentient; dissenting. ¶ *n*, dissentient; dissenter.

dissimilaire (disimilɛ:r) *a*, dissimilar.

dissimulé, e (disimyle) *a*, secretive. **dissimuler** (le) *v.t. & abs*, to dissimulate; dissemble; conceal.

dissipateur, trice (disipatœ:r, tris) *n. & a*, spendthrift. **dissipation** (sjɔ̃) *f*, dissipation; extravagance. **dissiper** (pe) *v.t*, to dissipate; dispel; disperse, scatter; fritter away.

dissocier (disosje) *v.t*, to dissociate.

dissolu, e (disoly) *a*, dissolute, profligate. **dissolution** (sjɔ̃) *f*, dissolution; solution; dissoluteness. **dissolvant, e** (vã, ã:t) *a. & m*, [dis]solvent.

dissonance (disonã:s) *f*, dissonance; discord. **dissonant, e** (nã, ã:t) *a*, dissonant, discordant.

dissoudre (disudr) *v.t.ir*, to dissolve.

dissuader (disɥade) *v.t*, to dissuade.

dissyllabe (disilab) *m*, dis[s]yllable.

dissymétrique (disimetrik) *a*, unsymmetrical.

distance (distã:s) *f*, distance; range; way [off]. **garder ses** ~**s** (*fig.*), to keep one's distance. **distancer** (tãse) *v.t*, to [out]distance. **distant, e** (tã, ã:t) *a*, distant; stand-offish, aloof.

distendre (distã:dr) *v.t*, to distend.

distillateur (distilatœ:r) *m*, distiller. **distillation** (sjɔ̃) *f*, distillation; distillate. **distiller** (le) *v.t*, to distil; exude. **distillerie** (lri) *f*, distillery.

distinct, e† (distɛ̃kt) *a*, distinct; clear, plain. **distinctif, ive** (tɛktif, i:v) *a*, distinctive. **distinction** (sjɔ̃) *f*, distinction. **distingué, e** (tɛge) *a*, distinguished; refined; gentlemanly; ladylike. **distinguer** (ge) *v.t*, to distinguish; discriminate; make out; single out.

distique (distik) *m*, distich; couplet.

distorsion (distorsjɔ̃) *f*, distortion.

distraction (distraksjɔ̃) *f*, distraction; absence of mind; appropriation; severance; amusement, hobby. **distraire** (trɛ:r) *v.t.ir*, to distract; appropriate; set aside; take away, t. off; amuse. **distrait, e†** (trɛ, ɛt) *a*, absent-minded; listless, vacant.

distribuer (distribɥe) *v.t*, to distribute, give out; deal out; issue; diss (*type*); deliver (*letters*); arrange; cast (*actors' parts*). **distributeur, trice** (bytœ:r, tris) *n*, distributor. **distributeur automatique**, automatic [delivery] machine, slot machine. **distribution** (sjɔ̃) *f*, distribution; issue; allotment; delivery (*Post*); valve gear; arrangement, layout. ~ **de prix**, prize giving; speech day. ~ **des aumônes**, almsgiving. ~ [des rôles], cast[ing] (Theat.). ~ par coulisse, link motion.

district (distrikt) m, district, field.

dito (dito) (abb. dº) ad, ditto, ‚do.

diva (diva) f, prima donna, diva.

divagation (divagasjɔ̃) f, digression; wandering, rambling. **divaguer** (ge) v.i, to digress, &c.

divan (divɑ̃) m, divan; settee, chesterfield.

divergence (diverʒɑ̃:s) f, divergence. **divergent, e** (ʒɑ̃, ɑ̃:t) a, divergent. **diverger** (ʒe) v.i, to diverge.

divers, e† (divɛr, ɛrs) a, different, diverse; sundry, miscellaneous; various, many. **diversifier** (vɛrsifje) v.t, to diversify, vary. **diversion** (sjɔ̃) f, diversion. **diversité** (site) f, diversity, variety, difference. **divertir** (ti:r) v.t, to divert; amuse, entertain. se ~ aux dépens de, to make fun of, make merry over. **divertissement** (tismɑ̃) m, diversion; amusement, entertainment; divertissement.

divette (divɛt) f, variety actress.

dividende (dividɑ̃:d) m, dividend.

divin, e† (divɛ̃, in) a, divine; godlike. **divination** (vinasjɔ̃) f, divination. **diviniser** (nize) v.t, to deify. **divinité** (te) f, divinity, godhead; deity.

diviser (divize) v.t, to divide; part. **diviseur** (zœ:r) m, divisor. **division** (zjɔ̃) f, division; department; hyphen (end of line).

divorce (divɔrs) m, divorce. **divorcer** (se) v.i, to be divorced. ~ d'avec, to divorce. **divulguer** (divylge) v.t, to divulge, blab.

dix (in liaison, diz; before consonant or ‘h, di) a, ten. ¶ (dis) m, ten; 10th. ~-huit (dizɥit; bef. cons. or ‘h, qi) a. & m, eighteen; 18th. ~-huitième (tjɛm) a. & n, eighteenth. **dixième†** (dizjɛm) a. & n, tenth. **dix-neuf** (diznœf; in liaison, nœv; bef. cons. or ‘h, nœ) a. & m, nineteen; 19th. **dix-neuvième** (vjɛm) a. & n, nineteenth. **dix-sept** (disset; bef. cons. or ‘h, sɛ) a. & m, seventeen; 17th. **dix-septième** (tjɛm) a. & n, seventeenth.

dizain (dizɛ̃) m, ten-line stanza. **dizaine** (zɛn) f, ten [or so], about ten; ten; decad[e].

do (do) (Mus.) m, C.

docile† (dɔsil) a, docile, amenable, ductile. **docilité** (lite) f, docility, &c.

dock (dɔk) m, dock; dock warehouse, warehouse, store. ~ frigorifique, cold store. **docker** (kɛ:r) m, docker.

docte† (dɔkt) a, learned. **docteur** (tœ:r) m, doctor. **doctoral, e†** (tɔral) a, doctoral; pompous; grandiloquent. **doctorat** (ra) m, doctorate.

doctrinaire (dɔktrinɛ:r) m. & a, doctrinaire. **doctrine** (trin) f, doctrine, tenet.

document (dɔkymɑ̃) m, document. **documentaire** (tɛ:r) a, documentary. **documenter** (te) v.t, to document.

dodeliner (dɔdline) v.t, to rock, dandle. ~ de, to wag (head).

dodo (dɔdo) m, bye-bye; cot.

dodu, e (dɔdy) a, plump, rotund.

dogmatique† (dɔgmatik) a, dogmatic(al). **dogmatiser** (ze) v.i, to dogmatize. **dogme** (dɔgm) m, dogma; tenet.

dogue (dɔg) m, big yard dog; bear (fig., pers.).

doigt (dwa) m, finger; digit; thimbleful, nip (liquor). ~ [de pied], toe. à deux ~s de, within an ace of. **doigté** (dwate) m, fingering (Mus.); diplomacy, tact. **doigter** (te) v.i. & t, to finger (Mus.). **doigtier** (tje) m, finger stall.

doit (dwa) m, debit [side], debtor [side].

dol (dɔl) m, wilful misrepresentation.

doléance (dɔleɑ̃:s) f, complaint, grievance. **dolent, e** (lɑ̃, ɑ̃:t) a, doleful; painful; out of sorts.

dollar (dɔla:r) m, dollar.

domaine (dɔmɛn) m, domain, demesne, estate; property; land; province.

dôme (do:m) m, dome; canopy.

domesticité (dɔmɛstisite) f, service; [staff of] servants; household; domesticity. **domestique** (tik) a, domestic, home. ¶ n, servant, domestic; man[servant]; maid[servant]. **domestiquer** (ke) v.t, to domesticate.

domicile (dɔmisil) m, residence, abode, house, premises, domicile. **domicilier** (lje) v.t, to domicile.

dominant, e (dɔminɑ̃, ɑ̃:t) a, dominant, ruling; prevailing. ¶ f, dominant (Mus.). **dominateur, trice** (natœr, tris) n, ruler; (att.) ruling; domineering. **domination** (sjɔ̃) f, domination; dominion; rule, sway. ~ de la lie du peuple, mob law. **dominer** (ne) v.i. & t, to dominate; overlook; tower above; rule; dominate.

dominicain, e (dɔminikɛ̃, ɛn) n, Dominican. **dominical, e** (dɔminikal) a, dominical; Sunday (rest); Lord's (prayer).

domino (dɔmino) m, domino.

dommage (dɔma:ʒ) m, damage, injury, loss; pity (regret). ~s-intérêts, damages (Law).

dompter (dɔte) v.t, to tame; break in; subdue. **dompteur, euse** (tœ:r, ø:z) n, tamer.

don (dɔ̃) m, bestowal; gift; present; donation; dower; knack. **donataire** (dɔnatɛ:r) n, donee. **donateur, trice** (tœ:r, tris) n, donor. **donation** (sjɔ̃) f, donation, gift.

donc (dɔ̃; in liaison or emphatically, dɔ:k) c, therefore, then, hence, so; to be sure.

dondon (dɔ̃dɔ̃) f, bouncing girl; plump woman.

donjon (dɔ̃ʒɔ̃) m, keep (castle).

donnant, e (dɔnɑ̃, ɑ̃:t) a, generous. **donnant donnant**, ad, give & take, tit for tat. **donne** (dɔn) f, deal (Cards). **donnée** (ne) f, datum; fundamental idea, motif. **donner** (ne) v.t, to give, bestow; impart, afford; tender; make; let; yield, give up; show; teach (someone a lesson); set (task, &c); perform (play); deal (Cards); (v.i.) to strike, hit; fall; run; sag. ~ à manger, to cater. ~ *sur*, to face, front, look on, give on, overlook (*street*, &c). **donneur, euse** (nœ:r, ø:z) *n*, giver; donor; dealer (*Cards*), principal.

Don Quichotte (dõkiʃɔt) *m*, Quixote, champion (*of lost causes*).

dont (dõ) *pn*, whose; of whom; of *or* from *or* by whom *or* which; whereof; as per.

donzelle (dõzɛl) *f*, wench.

dorade (dɔrad) *f*, dorado, dolphin; goldfish. **doré, e** (re) *a*, gilt, gilded; golden. ~ *sur tranche*, gilt-edged. **dorée,** *f*, [John] dory.

dorénavant (dɔrenavɑ̃) *ad*, henceforth.

dorer (dɔre) *v.t*, to gild; block (*Bookb.*); glaze (*pastry*). **doreur, euse** (rœ:r, ø:z) *n*, gilder; blocker.

dorique (dɔrik) *a*. & *m*, Doric.

dorloter (dɔrlɔte) *v.t*, to coddle; pamper.

dormant, e (dɔrmɑ̃, ɑ̃:t) *a*, sleeping, dormant, still, standing, stagnant. ¶ *m*, casing, frame. **dormeur, euse** (mœːr, ø:z) *n*, sleeper. ¶ *f*, lounge chair; stud earring; sleeping suit. **dormir** (mi:r) *v.i.ir*, to sleep, be asleep; lie dormant. **dormitif** (mitif) *m*, sleeping draught.

dorsal, e (dɔrsal) *a*, dorsal.

dortoir (dɔrtwa:r) *m*, dormitory.

dorure (dɔry:r) *f*, gilding; blocking (*Bookb.*); gilt; glazing (*pastry*). ~ *à froid*, ~ *sans couleurs*, blind blocking. ~ *en couleurs*, ink blocking. ~ *en or*, gold blocking.

dos (do) *m*, back; back, spine (*book*); bridge (*nose*). *en* ~ *d'âne*, hogbacked.

dose (do:z) *f*, dose, measure. **doser** (doze) *v.t*, to proportion, measure out, dose.

dossier (dɔsje) *m*, back; bundle (*papers*); dossier; brief (*Law*); record.

dot (dɔt) *f*, dowry, dower, [marriage] portion. **dotal, e** (tal) *a*, dowral, dotal. **dotation** (sjõ) *f*, endowment. **doter** (te) *v.t*, to dower, portion; endow.

douairière (dwɛrjɛːr) *f*, dowager.

douane (dwan) *f*, customs; custom house. **douanier, ère** (nje, ɛːr) *a*, customs (*att.*). ¶ *m*, customs officer.

doublage (dubla:ʒ) *m*, doubling; lining; sheathing (*ship*). **double** (bl) *a*, double; twofold; dual; double-dealing. ~ *croche*, *f*, semiquaver. ~ *emploi*, *m*, duplication. *à* ~ *face*, double-faced. ~ *fond, m*, false bottom. ¶ *ad*, double; in duplicate. ¶ *m*, double; duplicate; counterpart. ~ *messieurs, dames, mixte*, men's, women's, mixed, double (*Ten.*). **doublement** (blɔmɑ̃) *ad*, doubly. ¶ *m*, doubling. **doubler** (ble) *v.t*, to double; understudy; overtake; line; sheathe; weather (*cape*); (*v.i.*) to double. *non doublé, e*, unlined. *doublé or*, rolled gold. **doublure** (bly:r) *f*, lining; understudy.

douceâtre (dusɑ:tr) *a*, sweetish. **doucement** (smɑ̃) *ad*, gently; softly; sweetly; slowly; gingerly; quietly; peacefully; smoothly, easily; so-so; pretty well. **doucereux, euse** (srø, ø:z) *a*, mawkish, sickly; mealy-

mouthed, smooth-tongued. **douceur** (sœ:r) *f*, sweetness; softness; gentleness; mildness; meekness; pleasure; (*pl.*) dainties, sweets; sweet nothings. ~*s du farniente* (farnjɛnte), dolce far niente.

douche (duʃ) *f*, douche. ~ [*en pluie*], shower bath. **doucher** (ʃe) *v.t*, to douche.

doucine (dusin) *f*, ogee.

douer (dwe) *v.t*, to endow, endue, gift.

douille (du:j) *f*, socket, holder; case (*cartridge*).

douillet, te† (dujɛ, ɛt) *a*, soft, downy; cosy.

douleur (dulœ:r) *f*, pain, ache; throe; sorrow, grief, woe. **douloureux, euse**† (lurø, ø:z) *a*, painful; sore; mournful, grievous, sad.

doute (dut) *f*, doubt, misgiving. **douter** (te) *v.i. & abs*, to doubt, question. ~ *de*, to doubt, question (*v.t.*). *se* ~ *de*, to suspect. **douteux, euse**† (tø, ø:z) *a*, doubtful, dubious, questionable.

douve (du:v) *f*, stave (*cask*); ditch (*Agric.*); moat (*castle*); water jump (*Turf*); water hazard (*Golf*).

Douvres (du:vr) *m*, Dover.

doux, ouce (du, us) *a*, sweet; soft; dulcet; gentle; mild; meek; quiet (*horse*); smooth; easy; pleasant; fresh (*water*). **le doux,** the sweet (*opp.* the bitter).

douzaine (duzɛn) *f*, dozen. **douze** (du:z) *a*. & *m*, twelve; 12th. **douzième**† (duzjɛm) *a*. & *n*, twelfth.

doyen, ne (dwajɛ̃, ɛn) *n*, dean; doyen; senior. **doyenné** (jene) *m*, deanery.

drachme (drakm) *f*, drachma.

dragage (draga:ʒ) *m*, dredging; dragging; sweeping (*for mines*).

dragée (draʒe) *f*, sugar almond; pill; bird shot.

drageon (draʒõ) *m*, sucker (*Bot.*, *Hort.*).

dragon (dragõ) *m*, dragon; dragoon; termagant, virago.

drague (drag) *f*, dredge[r]; drag; d. net; grains, draff. **draguer** (ge) *v.t*, to dredge, drag, sweep. **dragueur** (gœ:r) *m*, dredger (*pers. & boat*). ~ *de mines*, mine sweeper.

drain (drɛ̃) *m*, drain; d. pipe. **drainage** (drɛna:ʒ) *m*, drainage; drain (*demand*). **drainer** (ne) *v.t*, to drain.

dramatique (dramatik) *a*, dramatic; operatic. **dramatiser** (ze) *v.t*, to dramatize. **dramatiste** (tist) *m*, **dramaturge** (tyrʒ) *n*, dramatist, playwright, dramaturge. **drame** (dram) *m*, drama; tragedy; sensational affair. ~ *pleureur*, sob-stuff.

drap (dra) *m*, cloth; sheet; pickle (*fig.*). ~ *mortuaire*, pall. ~ *vert*, green baize. **drapeau** (po) *m*, flag, colour. **draper** (pe) *v.t*, to drape; pillory (*fig.*). **draperie** (pri) *f*, drapery; cloth trade; bunting. **drapier** (pje) *m*, draper, clothier, cloth merchant; cloth manufacturer.

drastique (drastik) *a*, drastic.

drawback (drobak) *m*, drawback (*Cust.*).

drèche (drɛ:ʃ) *f*, grains, draff.

drelin-drelin (drəlɛ̃) tinkle! tinkle!

drenne (drɛn) f, missel thrush.

Dresde (drɛzd) f, Dresden.

dresser (drɛse) v.t, to erect, raise, set up, rear; prick up (ears); pitch (tent); set (trap); draw up, make out, prepare; make (bed, &c); lay (table); trim; dish up; true, straighten, dress, face; train; drill; break in. **dresseur** (sœ:r) m, trainer (animals). ~ de chevaux, horse breaker. **dressoir** (swa:r) m, sideboard.

drille (dri:j) m, fellow, chap. ¶ f, drill, brace; (pl.) rags (for papermaking).

drisse (dris) f, halyard.

drogman (drɔgmɑ̃) m, dragoman.

drogue (drɔg) f, drug; nostrum; trash; worthless person. **droguer** (ge) v.t, to physic; (v.i.) to wait, cool one's heels. **droguerie** (gri) f, druggist's business; drug store. ~[-épicerie], drysaltery.

droguet (drɔgɛ) m, drugget.

droguiste (drɔgist) m, drysalter; druggist (wholesale).

droit, e (drwa, at) a, straight; upright, erect, plumb; straightforward, honest; right, right-hand[ed]; single-breasted. **droit,** ad, straight; s. on; due (south, &c). **droit,** m, right; due, duty, fee; law; reason. ~s d'adaptation au cinématographe, film rights. ~ d'aînesse, ~ du sang, birthright. ~ d'auteur, copyright; royalty. ~ de cité, citizenship. ~s de reproduction dans les journaux & périodiques, serial rights. ~ de rétention, lien. ~s de succession, estate duty, death duties. ~ de vendre, licence to sell. ~ de vue, ancient lights. ~ des gens, law of nations. de ~, de jure. **droite,** (t) f, right hand, r. side; right. à ~, on (or to) the right. **droitement** (tmɑ̃) ad, uprightly, righteously. **droitier, ère** (tje, ɛ:r) n, right-handed person or player. **droiture** (ty:r) f, uprightness, straightforwardness, rectitude.

drolatique (drɔlatik) a, comic, humorous. **drôle†** (dro:l) a, funny, humorous, droll; queer, odd. un ~ de corps, a queer fellow, an oddity. ¶ m, funny (queer) man; rascal. **drôlerie** (drolri) f, drollery, fun. **drôlesse** (lɛs) f, hussy.

dromadaire (drɔmadɛ:r) m, dromedary.

drome (drɔm) f, raft.

dru, e (dry) a, thick; sturdy. **dru,** ad, thick[ly].

druide (drɥid) m, Druid.

dryade (driad) f, dryad.

dû, due (dy) p.p. & p.a, due; owing; forward (carriage); proper. ¶ m, due (right).

duc (dyk) m, duke. **ducal, e** (kal) a, ducal. **duché** (ʃe) m, duchy; dukedom. **duchesse** (ʃɛs) f, duchess.

ducroire (dykrwa:r) m, del credere.

ductile (dyktil) a, ductile.

duègne (dɥɛɲ) f, duenna.

duel (dɥɛl) m, duel. **duelliste** (list) m, duellist.

dûment (dymɑ̃) ad, duly, properly.

dune (dyn) f, dune, sand hill, down.

dunette (dynɛt) f, poop; poop deck.

Dunkerque (dœ̃kɛrk) m, Dunkirk.

duo (dyo) m, duet.

duodécimal, e (dyodesimal) a, duodecimal.

dupe (dyp) f, dupe, gull. **duper** (pe) v.t, to dupe, gull, take in, fool. **duperie** (pri) f, dupery, trickery, take-in. **dupeur, euse** (pœ:r, ø:z) n, trick[st]er.

duplicata (dyplikata) m, duplicate.

duplicité (dyplisite) f, duplicity; double dealing.

dur, e (dy:r) a, hard; tough; hardened, inured; dire; harsh; hard-boiled (egg).

durable (dyrabl) a, durable, lasting, abiding.

durant (dyrɑ̃) pr, during, for.

durcir (dyrsi:r) v.t. & i. & se ~, to harden. **durcissement** (sismɑ̃) m, hardening.

dure (dy:r) f, bare ground.

durée (dyre) f, duration, length, life.

durement (dyrmɑ̃) ad, hard; harshly.

durer (dyre) v.i. & abs, to last; hang heavy (time); hold out, stand; live.

dureté (dyrte) f, hardness; toughness; harshness. ~ d'oreille, hardness of hearing.

durillon (dyrijɔ̃) m, callus, hard skin.

duvet (dyvɛ) m, down; nap. **duveté, e** (vte) a, downy, fluffy.

dynamique (dinamik) a, dynamic(al). ¶ f, dynamics.

dynamite (dinamit) f, dynamite.

dynamo (dinamo) f, dynamo. ~-électrique (mo) a, dynamo-electric(al).

dynastie (dinasti) f, dynasty.

dysenterie (disɑ̃tri) f, dysentery.

dyspepsie (dispɛpsi) f, dyspepsia.

E

eau (o) f, water; rain. ~ bénite de cour, fair promises, empty words. ~ de boudin (ɔdbudɛ̃), thin air, smoke (fig.). ~ de cale, bilge water. ~ de Cologne (ɔdkɔlɔɲ), eau-de-Cologne. ~ de savon, [soap] suds. ~ de Seltz (ɔdsɛls), seltzer [water]; soda [water]. ~-de-vie (ɔdvi), brandy. ~ dentifrice, mouth wash. ~-forte, aqua fortis; etching. ~ fortuite, casual water (Golf). ~ minérale [artificielle], mineral [water]. ~ minérale [naturelle], mineral w.; table w. ~ régale, aqua regia. de la plus belle, ~ of the finest water (gem); of the deepest dye (fig.). faire ~, to make water, leak. faire de l' ~, to [take in] water.

eaux (o) f.pl, waters; water; fountains; watering place, spa; tide; wake (ship). marcher dans les ~ de, to follow in the wake of (Naut. & fig.). ~ à marée, tidal water. ~ d'égout, sew[er]age. ~ ménagères, slops. ~-vannes, waste water; sewage [water]. ~ vives, spring tide.

ébahir (ebai:r) *v.t*, to dumbfound, amaze.

ébarber (ebarbe) *v.t*, to take the burr off; trim (*edges*); wipe (*joint*).

ébattre (s') (ebatr) *v.pr.ir.* ou **prendre ses ébats** (eba), to frolic, gambol; hop about.

ébaubi, e (ebobi) *a*, dumbfounded.

ébauche (ebo:ʃ) *f*, [rough] sketch, draft, outline. **ébaucher** (boʃe) *v.t*, to sketch [out], draught; rough out; rough down.

ébène (eben) *f*, ebony. **ébénier** (benje) *m*, ebony [tree]. **ébéniste** (nist) *m*, cabinetmaker. **ébénisterie** (tri) *f*, cabinetmaking; cabinetwork.

éblouir (eblui:r) *v.t. & abs*, to dazzle, glare. **ébonite** (ebonit) *f*, ebonite, vulcanite.

éborgner (eborɲe) *v.t*, to blind in one eye; disbud; shut out view from.

ébouillanter (ebujãte) *v.t*, to plunge into boiling water; scald.

éboulement (ebulmã) *m*, falling in, caving in; fall, slip. **ébouler (le)** *v.i*, to fall in; cave in, slip. **éboulis** (li) *m*, fall (*earth*).

ébourgeonner (eburʒɔne) *v.t*, to disbud.

ébouriffer (eburife) *v.t*, to dishevel, ruffle, tousle; stagger.

ébouter (ebute) *v.t*, to cut off the end of.

ébrancher (ebrãʃe) *v.t*, to lop.

ébranlement (ebrãlmã) *m*, shaking; shock, concussion; tottering; jangle. **ébranler (le)** *v.t*, to shake; jangle. **s'~**, to shake, totter; move off.

ébraser (ebraze) *v.t*, to splay.

ébrécher (ebreʃe) *v.t*, to chip, jag; break (*jaw*); make a hole in (*fortune*).

ébriété (ebriete) *f*, drunkenness.

ébrouer (s') (ebrue) *v.pr*, to sneeze (*animals*); snort.

ébruiter (ebrɥite) *v.t*, to noise abroad.

ébullition (ebylisjɔ̃) *f*, boiling, ebullition; turmoil; whirl.

écacher (ekaʃe) *v.t*, to crush; flatten.

écaille (eka:j) *f*, scale; flake; chip; shell. **~ [de tortue]**, tortoise shell. **écailler** (kaje) *v.t*, to scale; open (*oysters*). **s'~**, to scale, flake; peel [off]. **écailler, ère** (je, ɛ:r) *n*, oysterman, -woman. **écailleux, euse** (jø, ø:z) *a*, scaly, flaky.

écale (ekal) *f*, shell; pod. **écaler (le)** *v.t*, to shell.

écarbouiller (ekarbuje) *v.t*, to crush, squash.

écarlate (ekarlat) *f. & a*, scarlet.

écarquiller (ekarkije) *v.t*, to open wide (*eyes*). **~ les yeux**, to stare.

écart (eka:r) *m*, variation, difference; error; digression; flight; straddling; strain (*Vet.*). *faire le grand ~*, to do the splits. *faire un ~*, to side-step; (*horse*) shy. *à l'~*, aside, on one side; aloof. *à l'~ de*, at some distance from. **écarté, e** (karte) *p.a*, out-of-the-way, remote, secluded, lonely. **écarté**, *m*, écarté (*Cards*).

écarteler (ekartəle) *v.t*, to quarter.

écartement (ekartəmã) *m*, spreading; distance apart; d. between; gauge (*Rly*). **~**

des essieux, wheel base. **écarter (te)** *v.t*, to separate, spread, open; turn (*or* push) aside *or* out of the way; avert, ward off; divert; discard (*Cards*). **s'~**, to stand aside; deviate; wander, stray, swerve.

Ecclésiaste (l') (eklezjast) *m*, Ecclesiastes. **ecclésiastique†** (tik) *a*, ecclesiastical, clerical. **¶** *m*, ecclesiastic, clergyman, cleric. **l'E~**, Ecclesiasticus.

écervelé, e (esɛrvəle) *a*, giddy, hare-brained. **¶** *n*, madcap.

échafaud (eʃafo) *m*, scaffold, stage. **échafaudage** (da:ʒ) *m*, scaffolding; structure, fabric (*fig.*). **échafauder (de)** *v.i*, to erect a scaffold; (*v.t.*) to build up (*fig.*).

échalas (eʃala) *m*, pole (*hop, &c*), prop, stick. **échalasser (se)** *v.t*, to pole, prop.

échalier (eʃalje) *m*, stile; hurdle fence.

échalote (eʃalɔt) *f*, shallot, eschalot.

échancrer (eʃãkre) *v.t*, to cut away (*neck of garment*); notch, indent. *col très échancré*, very low neck. **échancrure** (kry:r) *f*, (*neck*) opening; notch; indentation.

échange (eʃã:ʒ) *m*, exchange, barter; interchange. *quelques ~s*, practice (*Ten.*). **échanger** (ʃãʒe) *v.t*, to exchange; barter.

échanson (eʃãsɔ̃) *m*, cup bearer.

échantillon (eʃãtijɔ̃) *m*, sample; dimension, size, section; pattern (*of stuff, &c*), specimen, taste. **échantillonner** (jɔne) *v.t*, to sample; cut off a pattern from; gauge; tram (*tapestry work*).

échappatoire (eʃapatwa:r) *f*, loophole; evasion. **échappé, e** (pe) *n*, runaway. **~ de prison**, escaped prisoner. **échappée** (pe) *f*, prank; snatch; spell; turning space; headroom. **~ [de vue]**, vista; glimpse, peep. **échappement** (pmã) *m*, exhaust, release (*steam*); escape, leak (*gas, &c*) escapement (*Horol.*); turning space, headroom. **échapper** (pe) *v.i. & abs*, to escape, run away; slip; (*v.t.*) to escape. *l'~ belle*, to have a narrow escape. **s'~**, to escape; leak; fly off; vanish; forget oneself.

écharde (eʃard) *f*, splinter, prickle.

écharpe (eʃarp) *f*, scarf; stole; sash; sling. *en ~*, scarfwise; aslant; in a sling. **écharper** (pe) *v.t*, to cut to pieces, hack; lynch.

échasse (eʃa:s) *f*, stilt; pole (*scaffold*). **échassier** (ʃasje) *m*, wader (*bird*).

échauder (eʃode) *v.t*, to scald. **s'~** (*fig.*), to burn one's fingers.

échauffé, e (eʃofe) *n*, hothead (*pers.*). **échauffement** (fmã) *m*, heating; overheating. **échauffer** (fe) *v.t*, to heat; overheat; warm; parboil (*fig.*); excite. **s'~**, to get warm or heated *or* overheated *or* excited. **échauffourée** (fure) *f*, affray, brush.

échéance (eʃeã:s) *f*, due date; date [payable]; maturity; tenor; term; currency; expiration. *le cas échéant* (ʃeã), in that case, should it so happen.

échec (eʃɛk) m, check, failure, repulse; (pl.) chess; chessmen. ¶ i, check! ~ & mat, checkmate. faire quelqu'un ~ & mat, to checkmate someone.

échelle (eʃɛl) f, ladder; scale. ~ à coulisse, extension ladder. ~ de sauvetage, fire escape. ~ double, [pair of] steps. ~ mobile, sliding scale. ~s du Levant, Levantine ports. échelon (ʃlɔ̃) m, rung, round; step, stepping stone (fig.); echelon (Mil.). échelonner (ʃlɔne) v.t, to spread; echelon.

écheniller (eʃnije) v.t, to clear of caterpillars.

écheveau (eʃvo) m, skein, hank.

échevelé, e (eʃəvle) a, dishevelled (hair).

échine (eʃin) f, spine, backbone; chine. échinée (ne) f, chine (Cook.). échiner (ne) v.t, to break (someone's) back; belabour. s'~, to break one's back; knock oneself up; slave.

échiquier (eʃikje) m, chessboard; intricacies; exchequer (Eng.).

écho (eko) m, echo; (pl.) news items (in paper). faire ~, to echo (v.i.). se faire l'~ de, to echo (v.t.).

échoir (eʃwaːr) v.i.ir, to fall, devolve; fall due, mature; expire. intérêts à ~, accruing interest.

échoppe (eʃɔp) f, stall, booth.

échouer (eʃwe) v.i. & t. & s'~, to strand, ground, beach; fail; miscarry, fall through. échoué à sec, high & dry (Naut.).

échu, e (eʃy) p.a, due, outstanding, owing; matured.

éclabousser (eklabuse) v.t, to splash, [be]-spatter. éclaboussure (syːr) f, splash, spatter.

éclair (eklɛːr) m, flash [of light]; [flash of] lightning; flash; glint, gleam. ~ au chocolat, &c, chocolate, &c, éclair. ~[s] de chaleur, heat lightning, summer l. ~ diffus, ~ en nappes, sheet l. ~ ramifié, forked l. ~ sinueux, chain[ed] l. éclairage (klɛraːʒ) m, lighting, illumination; light. ~ au gaz par incandescence, incandescent gas lighting. ~ code, dimmed lights (motor). ~ par projection, flood lighting. éclairant, e (rɑ̃, ɑ̃ːt) a, lighting.

éclaircie (eklɛrsi) f, break, opening, rift; bright interval (Meteor.); clearing, glade; thinning out. éclaircir (siːr) v.t, to clear, c. up; brighten; thin, t. out; elucidate, enlighten.

éclairé, e (eklɛre) p.p, enlightened. éclairer (re) v.t. & abs, to light [up], lighten, illuminate, illumine; throw light upon; clear up; enlighten; reconnoitre (Mil.); (v.i.) to shine (v.imp.) to lighten (emit lightning). éclaireur (rœːr) m, scout; boy scout. éclaireuse (røːz) f, girl guide.

éclanche (eklɑ̃ːʃ) f, shoulder of mutton.

éclat (ekla) m, splinter; chip; fragment; burst, roar; shout; peal, clap; noise, scandal; shake (timber); brilliancy, radi-ancy, brightness, lustre; flash; glare; glamour. éclatant, e (tɑ̃, ɑ̃ːt) a, bright, brilliant, shining; piercing, shrill; splendid; striking, glaring; signal. éclatement (tmɑ̃) m, bursting, explosion. éclater (te) v.i, to burst, explode, blow up; fly; split; splinter; break out; burst out; shine, flash.

éclectique (eklektik) a, eclectic. éclectisme (tism) m, eclecticism.

éclipse (eklips) f, eclipse. éclipser (se) v.t, to eclipse; outshine, overshadow. s'~, to become eclipsed; vanish. écliptique (tik) a. & f, ecliptic.

éclisse (eklis) f, split-wood; splint (Surg.); fish[plate] (Rly). éclisser (se) v.t, to fish[plate].

éclopé, e (eklope) a, footsore, lame, crippled.

éclore (ekloːr) v.i.ir, to hatch; open (flower); come to light. éclosion (klozjɔ̃) f, hatching; opening.

écluse (eklyːz) f, (canal) lock; lock gate; floodgate (fig.). éclusée (klyze) f, (lock) feed; locking, lockage. écluser (ze) v.t, to lock; shut off. éclusier, ère (zje, ɛːr) n, lock keeper.

écœurer (ekœre) v.t, to sicken, nauseate.

école (ekɔl) f, school, college; drill, training; blunder. ~ d'anormaux, school for defective children. ~ de peloton, squad drill. ~ maternelle, infant school. ~ normale, normal school, training college (teachers). ~ pratique, technical school. ~ professionnelle, training centre (trade). écolier, ère (lje, ɛːr) n, schoolboy, -girl, pupil, scholar; tyro.

éconduire (ekɔ̃dɥiːr) v.t.ir, to show out; put off (with excuse).

économat (ekɔnɔma) m, stewardship, bursarship; bursar's office; store. économe (nɔm) a, economical, thrifty, sparing. ¶ n, steward; bursar. économie (mi) f, economy, thrift, saving; management; arrangement. ~ de bouts de chandelle, cheese-paring. ~ domestique, domestic economy, housekeeping. ~ politique, political economy. ~ rurale, husbandry. économique† (mik) a, economical; economic. économiser (ze) v.t. & abs, to economize, save. économiste (mist) m, economist.

écope (ekɔp) f, scoop, bailer. écoper (pe) v.t, to bail (or bale) [out]; (v.i.) to catch it (suffer).

écoperche (ekɔperʃ) f, scaffold pole.

écorce (ekɔrs) f, bark; peel, rind, skin; crust (earth's); surface (fig.). écorcer (se) v.t, to bark; peel.

écorcher (ekɔrʃe) v.t, to flay, skin; abrade, graze, scrape, gall, chafe; murder (language); grate on (ears); fleece (fig.). écorcheur, euse (ʃœːr, øːz) n, shark, extortioner; (m.) knacker. écorchure (ʃyːr) f, abrasion, gall, graze, scrape.

écorner (ekɔrne) v.t, to break off a horn or corner; chip; dog['s] ear; curtail.

écornifler (ekɔrnifle) *v.t,* to cadge; sponge on.

écornure (ekɔrnyːr) *f,* chip.

écossais, e (ekɔsɛ, ɛːz) *a,* Scotch, Scottish. **É~,** *n,* Scotchman, -woman, Scot. **l'Écosse** (kɔs) *f,* Scotland, North Britain.

écosser (ekɔse) *v.t,* to shell, hull.

écot (eko) *m,* share; score; reckoning; lopped tree; stick, faggot.

écoulement (ekulmɑ̃) *m,* flow, outflow; drainage; discharge; gleet; passing; placing, sale. **écouler** (le) *v.t,* to place, sell. **s'~,** to flow out *or* away, run off; disperse; pass (*or* slip) away, elapse; sell.

écourter (ekurte) *v.t,* to cut short; crop, dock; curtail.

écoute (ekut) *f,* sheet (*Naut.*). **aux écoutes,** on the watch *or* lookout. **écouter** (te) *v.t. & abs,* to listen to, listen, hearken; listen in (*Radio*); hear. **~ aux portes,** to eavesdrop. **écouteur, euse** (tœːr, øːz) *n,* listener. **~ aux portes,** eavesdropper. ¶ *m,* receiver, earpiece (*Teleph.*). **écouteux** (tø) *a.m,* skittish (*horse*).

écoutille (ekutiːj) *f,* hatch[way].

écouvillon (ekuvijɔ̃) *m,* mop; sponge (*gun*); swab (*Med.*).

écrabouiller (ekrabuje) *v.t,* to crush, squash.

écran (ekrɑ̃) *m,* screen; filter (*Phot.*); shade. **~ à pied,** fire screen. **~ fumigène** (fymiʒɛn), smoke screen.

écrasé, e (ekraze) *p.a,* squat. **écraser** (ze) *v.t,* to crush; squash; run over; overwhelm. **s'~,** to collapse, crumple up, crash.

écrémer (ekreme) *v.t,* to cream, skim.

écrevisse (ekrəvis) *f,* crayfish, crawfish (*river*).

écrier (s') (ekrie) *v.pr,* to exclaim, cry; c. out.

écrin (ekrɛ̃) *m,* case, jewel case, casket. **~ manucure,** box manicure set.

écrire (ekriːr) *v.t. & abs. ir,* to write; spell. **~ à la machine,** to type[write]. **écrit** (kri) *m,* writing; document. **écrit, e** (kri, it) *p.p,* written; w. on; statute (*law*). **écriteau** (to) *m,* bill, notice; n. board. **écriture** (tyːr) *f,* writing; hand[writing]. **~ à la machine,** typewriting, typing. **~ de pattes de mouche,** crabbed handwriting. **~ moulée,** copperplate [hand]writing. **l'Écriture** [sainte] ou *les* [saintes] *Écritures,* [Holy] Scripture, the Scriptures, Holy Writ. **écrivailler** (vaje) *ou* **écrivasser** (vase) *v.i,* to scribble (*of author*). **écrivailleur, euse** (vajœːr, øːz) *ou* **écrivassier, ère** (vasje, ɛːr) *n,* scribbler, hack-writer, penny-a-liner. **écrivain** (vɛ̃) *m,* writer, author.

écrou (ekru) *m,* nut; entry (*in prison register*). **~ à huit pans,** octagonal nut. **~ à oreilles,** **~ à papillon,** wing n. **~ à six pans,** hexagonal n. **écrouer** (krue) *v.t,* to enter (*in prison register*).

écroulement (ekrulmɑ̃) *m,* collapse. **s'écrouler** (le) *v.pr,* to collapse, give way.

écru, e (ekry) *a,* raw; unbleached.

écu (eky) *m,* shield; escutcheon; (*pl.*) money.

écueil (ekœːj) *m,* reef, rock, shelf; pitfall, cause of downfall.

écuelle (ekɥɛl) *f,* bowl; porringer. **écuellée** (le) *f,* bowlful.

éculer (ekyle) *v.t,* to wear down (*shoe*) at heel.

écume (ekym) *f,* foam; froth; lather; scum, dross, skimmings. **~ de mer,** [sea] wrack; meerschaum. **écumer** (me) *v.i,* to foam, froth; (*v.t.*) to skim [off], scum; scour, rove (*seas*); pick up (*news*). **écumeux, euse** (mø, øːz) *a,* foamy, frothy. **écumoire** (mwaːr) *f,* skimmer.

écurer (ekyre) *v.t,* to scour, cleanse, clean out.

écureuil (ekyrœːj) *m,* squirrel.

écurie (ekyri) *f,* stable; (*pl.*) mews; stud (*racing*).

écusson (ekysɔ̃) *m,* [e]scutcheon, shield, hatchment.

écuyer, ère (ekɥije, ɛːr) *n,* riding master; horseman, -woman; rider; equestrian; equerry; [e]squire (*Hist.*).

eczéma (egzema) *m,* eczema.

édelweiss (edelwɛis ou -vɛs) *m,* edelweiss.

éden (edɛn) *m,* Eden (*fig.*). **l'É~,** [the Garden of] Eden.

édenté, e (edɑ̃te) *a,* toothless.

édicter (edikte) *v.t,* to decree, enact.

édicule (edikyl) *m,* kiosk, shelter; public convenience.

édification (edifikasjɔ̃) *f,* erection; edification. **édifice** (fis) *m,* edifice, building, structure. **édifier** (fje) *v.t,* to erect; build; b. up; edify; enlighten.

édile (edil) *m,* magistrate; aedile (*Hist.*). **édilité** (lite) *f,* magistrature.

Édimbourg (edɛ̃buːr) *m,* Edinburgh.

édit (edi) *m,* edict.

éditer (edite) *v.t,* to publish; edit. **éditeur, trice** (tœːr, tris) *n,* publisher; editor, tress. **édition** (sjɔ̃) *f,* edition; publishing. **~ à tirage restreint,** limited edition.

édredon (edrədɔ̃) *m,* eider down.

éducateur, trice (edykatœːr, tris) *n,* educator. **éducation** (sjɔ̃) *f,* education; training; upbringing; rearing; nurture. **sans ~,** ill-bred. **éduquer** (ke) *v.t,* to bring up, educate; train.

éfaufiler (efofile) *v.t,* to unravel.

effacé, e (efase) *p.a,* unobtrusive. **effacer** (se) *v.t,* to efface, obliterate, delete; erase, rub out, blot out, wipe out, expunge; outshine. **s'~,** to wear away; keep in the background; stand aside. **effaçure** (syːr) *f,* obliteration, deletion; erasure.

effarement (efarmɑ̃) *m,* fright. **effarer** (re) *v.t,* to scare, frighten. **effaroucher** (ruʃe) *v.t,* to startle, frighten away. **s'~,** to take fright.

effectif, ive† (efɛktif, iːv) *a,* effective; real; actual; in cash, in coin; paid up (*capital*). ¶ *m,* effective, strength, complement, force (*men*). **effectuer** (tɥe) *v.t,* to effect, carry out, make, execute.

efféminé, e (efemine) a, effeminate, woman-ish, unmanly, ladylike. ¶ m, effeminate [man], molly. efféminer (ne) v.t, to [make] effeminate.

effervescence (efsrvɛsɑ:s) f, effervescence, -ency; ferment (fig.), unrest. effervescent, e (sɑ̃, ɑ̃:t) a, effervescent.

effet (efɛ) m, effect; action; purpose, avail; impression; screw, break, spin (on ball); negotiable instrument; bill [of exchange], bill or note, draft; (pl.) effects, goods, belongings, things; securities, stock[s & shares]. ~ à payer, à recevoir, bill payable, receivable. à ~, intended for effect. en ~, in fact, indeed.

efficace† (efikas) a, efficacious; effectual; efficient; able; adequate. efficacité (site) f, efficacy; efficiency.

effigie (efiʒi) f, effigy.

effilé (efile) a, slender, slim; tapering, stream-lined. ¶ m, fringe. effiler (le) v.t, to unravel. s'effiloher (lɔfe) v.pr, to fray. effilure (ly:r) f, ravellings.

effilanqué, e (eflɑ̃ke) p.a, emaciated; lank[y]. effleurer (eflœre) v.t, to touch, t. on; graze; glance, skim; scratch.

effleurir (eflœri:r) v.i. & s'~, to effloresce. efflorescence (eflɔrɛsɑ̃:s) f, efflorescence.

effluve (efly:v) m, effluvium.

effondrement (efɔ̃drəmɑ̃) m, fall; subsidence; collapse, downfall; slump. effondrer (dre) v.t, to break open, stave in. s'~, to fall in, cave in; collapse, slump. effondrilles (dri:j) f.pl, grounds, sediment.

efforcer (s') (eforse) v.pr. & abs, to en-deavour, strive, do one's utmost. effort (fo:r) m, effort, exertion, endeavour; force; stress (Mech.); strain, [w]rick (Med.). ~ de traction, pull.

effraction (efraksjɔ̃) f, house breaking.

effraie (efrɛ) f, barn owl, screech owl.

effranger (efrɑ̃ʒe) v.t, to fray.

effrayant, e (efrɛjɑ̃, ɑ̃:t) a, dreadful, fright-ful. effrayer (je) v.t, to frighten, scare.

effréné, e (efrene) a, unbridled, unrestrained; frantic.

effriter (efrite) v.t. & s'~, to crumble.

effroi (efrwa) m, fright, terror.

effronté, e (efrɔ̃te) a, shameless, brazen, impudent, barefaced. effrontément (mɑ̃) ad, shamelessly, &c. effronterie (tri) f, effrontery, &c.

effroyable† (efrwajabl) a, frightful; awful.

effusion (efyzjɔ̃) f, effusion, outpouring; shedding; overflowing; effusiveness. ~ de sang, bloodshed.

égal, e (egal) a, equal; even, level; equable; alike; [all] the same, all one. ¶ n, equal (of pers.). à l'égal de, like. également (lmɑ̃) ad, equally, alike. égaler (le) v.t, to equalize, make equal; equal; match. égaliser (lize) v.t, to equalize; level. égalité (te) f, equality; evens (Betting); evenness; smoothness. ~ à rien, love all

(Ten.). ~ de points, tie (Sport). ~ de voix, tie (Voting). à ~, deuce (40 all) (Ten.); all even (Golf).

égard (ega:r) m, regard, consideration, respect; sake. à l'~ de, with regard (or respect) (or reference) to.

égaré, e (egare) a, lost, stray[ed]; erring; wild (eyes). égarer (re) v.t, to mislead, misguide, lead astray; bewilder; mislay. s'~, to go astray, lose one's way; mis-carry.

égayer (egɛje) v.t, to enliven, cheer [up], exhilarate. s'~, to make merry.

Égée (la mer) (eʒe), the Aegean sea.

égide (eʒid) f, aegis, wing.

églantier (eglɑ̃tje) m, wild (or dog) rose (bush). ~ odorant, sweet briar. églan-tine (tin) f, wild (or dog) rose (flower). ~ odorante, sweet briar, eglantine.

église (egli:z) f, church. l'É~ anglicane (ɑ̃glikan), the Church of England. l'É~ d'État, the established Church. ~ de monastère, ~ abbatiale (abasjal), minster.

égoïsme (egoism) m, egoism, selfishness. égoïste† (ist) a, egoistic(al), selfish. ¶ n, egoist.

égorger (egorʒe) v.t, to cut the throat of; butcher, slaughter; ruin.

égosiller (s') (egozije) v.pr, to shout (or sing) oneself hoarse.

égotisme (egotism) m, egotism. égotiste (tist) a, egotistic(al). ¶ n, egotist.

égout (egu) m, drainage (surplus water); drip[pings]; sewer, drain. égoutier (tje) m, sewerman. égoutter (te) v.t. & i. & s'~, to drain; drip. égouttoir (twa:r) m, drainer, draining rack; plate rack. égout-ture (ty:r) f, drainings; drippings.

égratigner (egratiɲe) v.t, to scratch. égra-tignure (ɲy:r) f, scratch.

égrener (egrəne) v.t, to pick off; shell; gin (cotton); tell (beads). s'~, to seed.

égrillard, e (egrija:r, ard) a, ribald.

Égypte (l') (eʒipt) f, Egypt. égyptien, ne (sjɛ̃, ɛn) a. & É~, n, Egyptian. égypto-logie (tɔlɔʒi) f, Egyptology. égyptologue (lɔg) m, Egyptologist.

eh (e) i, [h]eh! ~ bien! now then! well!

éhonté, e (eɔ̃te) a, shameless, barefaced.

eider (ɛdɛ:r) m, eider [duck].

éjaculation (eʒakylasjɔ̃) f, ejaculation (fluid); fervent prayer. éjaculer (le) v.t. & i, to ejaculate (fluid).

éjecteur (eʒɛktœ:r) m, ejector.

élaborer (elabore) v.t, to elaborate; work out, evolve.

élagage (elaga:ʒ) m, lopping; pruning; prun-ings. élaguer (ge) v.t, to lop; prune.

élan (elɑ̃) m, bound; spring; dash, dart, rush, run[-up] (Jump.); [out]burst; impetus, momentum; flight; glow; elk, moose, eland. avec ~, running (jump, dive). sans ~, standing (j., d.). élancé, e (se) a, slender, slim. **élancements** (smã) *m.pl*, shooting pains, twinges; yearning (*soul*). **élancer** (se) *v.i*, to throb, shoot. **s'~**, to bound, spring, leap, dash, dart.

élargir (elarʒi:r) *v.t*, to enlarge; broaden; widen; let out; extend; release (*prisoner*). **élasticité** (elastisite) *f*, elasticity, spring-[iness], resilience. **élastique** (tik) *a*, elastic, spring[y], resilient; buoyant. ¶ *m*, elastic.

Elbe (l'île d') (ɛlb) *f*, the Island of Elba. l'**Elbe**, *m*, the Elbe (*river*).

eldorado (ɛldorado) *m*, El Dorado.

électeur, trice (elɛktœ:r, tris) *n*, elector, constituent. **élection** (sjɔ̃) *f*, election, polling. ~ *de remplacement*, by-election. **électorat** (tora) *m*, franchise.

électricien (elɛktrisjɛ̃) *m*, electrician. **électricité** (site) *f*, electricity. **électrification** (fikasjɔ̃) *f*, electrification (*of Rly, &c*). **électrifier** (fje) *v.t*, to electrify. **électrique** (trik) *a*, electric(al). **électriser** (ze) *v.t*, to electrify, electrize; thrill. **électro-aimant** (trɔɛmã) *m*, electromagnet. **électrocuter** (kyte) *v.t*, to electrocute. **électrode** (trɔd) *f*, electrode. **électrolyse** (li:z) *f*, electrolysis. **électron** (trɔ̃) *m*, electron. **électrotype** (tip) *m*, electrotype.

élégamment (elegamã) *ad*, elegantly, stylishly. **élégance** (gã:s) *f*, elegance, stylishness. **élégant, e** (gã, ã:t) *a*, elegant, stylish, fashionable. ¶ *n*, man, woman, of fashion, swell.

élégie (eleʒi) *f*, elegy.

élément (elemã) *m*, element; (*pl.*) rudiments (*of a science, an art*); unit; cell (*Phys.*). **élémentaire** (tɛ:r) *a*, elementary.

éléphant (elefã) *m*, elephant.

élevage (elva:ʒ) *m*, breeding, rearing, stock farming. **élévateur** (elevatœ:r) *m*, elevator, lift. **élévation** (sjɔ̃) *f*, elevation; raising; rise; eminence; height; loftiness; altitude. **élévatoire** (twa:r) *m*, elevator (*Surg.*). **élève** (elɛ:v) *n*, pupil, student; rearing (*animal reared*). ~ *de l'école navale*, naval cadet. ¶ *f*, breeding, rearing (*act*). **élevé, e** (elve) *p.a*, high; lofty; bred, brought up. **élever** (ve) *v.t*, to elevate, raise, lift; erect; bring up, rear, breed. **s'~**, to rise; arise. **s'~ à**, to reach, amount to. **éleveur** (lvœ:r) *m*, grazier; breeder.

elfe (ɛlf) *m*, elf, brownie.

élider (elide) *v.t*, to elide.

éligible (eliʒibl) *a*, eligible.

élimer (elime) *v.t*, to wear threadbare.

éliminatoire (eliminatwa:r) *a. & f*, eliminating *or* trial (heat). **éliminer** (ne) *v.t*, to eliminate; weed out.

élingue (elɛ̃:g) *f*, sling.

élire (eli:r) *v.t.ir*, to elect; return.

élision (elizjɔ̃) *f*, elision.

élite (elit) *f*, pick, flower, élite.

élixir (eliksi:r) *m*, elixir.

elle (ɛl) *pn*, she; her; it; herself. **~-même,**

herself; itself. **~s**, *pl*, they; them. **~-mêmes**, themselves.

ellipse (elips) *f*, ellipse; ellipsis. **elliptique†** (tik) *a*, elliptic(al).

élocution (elɔkysjɔ̃) *f*, elocution.

éloge (elɔ:ʒ) *m*, eulogy, praise, encomium. **élogieux, euse†** (lɔʒjø, ø:z) *a*, eulogistic.

éloigné, e (elwaɲe) *p.a*, distant, outlying, far [off *or* away], remote. **éloignement** (ɲmã) *m*, removal; estrangement; distance, remoteness; dislike. **éloigner** (ɲe) *v.t*, to remove; keep away; defer; estrange; disincline. **s'~**, to withdraw, go away; differ; swerve.

éloquemment (elɔkamã) *ad*, eloquently. **éloquence** (kã:s) *f*, eloquence, oratory. **éloquent, e** (kã, ã:t) *a*, eloquent.

Elseneur (ɛlsənœ:r) *f*, Elsinore.

élu, e (ely) *n*, elected member. *les élus*, the elect (*Relig.*).

élucider (elyside) *v.t*, to elucidate.

élucubration (elykybrasjɔ̃) *f*, lucubration.

éluder (elyde) *v.t*, to elude, evade, shirk.

élyme (elim) *m*, lyme-grass.

élysée & (*Myth.*) É~ (elize) *m*, Elysium. l'**É~**, the Élysée (*Paris*). **élyséen, ne** (zeɛ, ɛn) *a*, Elysian.

émacié, e (emasje) *a*, emaciated.

émail (ema:j) *m*, enamel; e. ware; glaze. **émaillage** (maja:ʒ) *m*, enamelling. **émailler** (je) *v.t*, to enamel; glaze; stud; intersperse.

émanation (emanasjɔ̃) *f*, emanation, efflux, effluence.

émanciper (emãsipe) *v.t*, to emancipate. **s'~**, to overstep the mark (*fig.*), forget oneself.

émaner (emane) *v.i*, to emanate, issue.

émarger (emarʒe) *v.t*, to sign [in the margin]; draw (*salary*); trim the margins of.

émasculer (emaskyle) *v.t*, to emasculate.

emballage (ãbala:ʒ) *m*, packing; spurt, burst (*speed*). **emballement** (lmã) *m*, bolting (*horse*); racing (*Mach.*); boom (*Stk Ex.*); excitement. **emballer** (le) *v.t*, to pack [up], wrap [up]; pack off, bundle off; carry away (*fig.*). **s'~**, to bolt; race; be carried away. **emballeur** (lœ:r) *m*, packer.

embarcadère (ãbarkadɛ:r) *m*, landing [place *or* stage]; wharf; platform (*Rly*). **embarcation** (sjɔ̃) *f*, craft, boat, launch.

embardée (ãbarde) *f*, lurch, [sudden] swerve; yaw. *faire une* ~, to yaw; swerve; catch a crab (*Boating*).

embargo (ãbargo) *m*, embargo.

embarquement (ãbarkəmã) *m*, embarkation; shipment; entrainment. **embarquer** (ke) *v.t. & s'~*, to embark; ship; entrain; (*v.i.*) to ship water, ship a sea. *s'~ clandestinement*, to stow away.

embarras (ãbara) *m*, obstruction, block, jam; encumbrance; inconvenience; superfluity; airs (*affectation*); perplexity, fix, nonplus, quandary, embarrassment; straits; difficulty, scrape. ~ *de la langue*, impediment of speech, i. in one's s. **embarrassant, e** (sã, ã:t) *a*, cumbersome; awkward, embarrassing. **embarrasser** (se) *v.t*, to obstruct, block [up]; [en]cumber, hamper; be in the way of; entangle; embarrass, perplex, nonplus.

embâter (ãbate) *v.t*, to saddle.

embatre (ãbatr) *v.t.ir*, to tire (*wheel*).

embaucher (ãboʃe) *v.t*, to engage, take on (*workmen*). **embauchoir** (ʃwa:r) *m*, boot tree.

embaumer (ãbome) *v.t*, to embalm; perfume, scent.

embéguiner (ãbegine) *v.t*, to muffle up; infatuate.

embellie (ãbɛli) *f*, lull. **embellir** (li:r) *v.t*, to embellish, beautify; improve; (*v.i.*) to grow more beautiful.

emberlificoter (ãbɛrlifikɔte) *v.t*, to entangle.

embesogné, e (ãbəzɔɲe) *a*, very busy.

embêter (ãbɛte) *v.t*, to annoy; bore.

emblaver (ãblave) *v.t*, to sow [with corn].

emblée (d') (ãble) *ad*, at the very outset, right away, straight off.

emblématique (ãblematik) *a*, emblematic(al). **emblème** (blɛ:m) *m*, emblem; attribute.

embob[el]iner (ãbɔb[l]ine) *v.t*, to wheedle, coax.

emboîter (ãbwate) *v.t*, to fit in[to], box, nest, house; socket.

embolie (ãbɔli) *f*, embolism.

embonpoint (ãbɔ̃pwɛ̃) *m*, stoutness, plumpness, flesh.

emboucher (ãbuʃe) *v.t*, to put to one's mouth; blow. *mal embouché*, foul-mouthed. **embouchoir** (ʃwa:r) *m*, mouthpiece; boot tree. **embouchure** (ʃy:r) *f*, mouthpiece; mouth.

embouer (ãbwe) *v.t*, to muddy.

embourber (ãburbe) *v.t*, to bog, mire; involve. **s'~**, to stick in the mud.

embourgeoiser (s') (ãburʒwaze) *v.pr*, to marry into (*or* mix with) the middle classes.

embout (ãbu) *m*, ferrule; capping.

embouteiller (ãbutɛje) *v.t*, to bottle; b. up; block (*traffic*).

embouter (ãbute) *v.t*, to ferrule, tip.

emboutir (ãbuti:r) *v.t*, to shape, stamp, press, swage; ferrule.

embranchement (ãbrãʃmã) *m*, branching [off]; junction (*Rly*). ~ *particulier*, private siding (*Rly*). **embrancher** (ʃe) *v.t*, to branch off.

embrasement (ãbrazmã) *m*, conflagration, burning; illumination. **embraser** (ze) *v.t*, to [set on] fire; illuminate (*festively*).

embrassade (ãbrasad) *f*, embrace, hug. **embrasse** (bras) *f*, curtain holder. **embrassement** (smã) *m*, embrace. **embrasser** (se) *v.t*, to embrace, hug; kiss (Cf. *baiser*); take in; take up; espouse. *je vous embrasse* [*de tout cœur*], with [best] love (*letter*).

embrasure (ãbrazy:r) *f*, recess; embrasure.

embrayer (ãbrɛje) *v.t*, to engage (*Mach.*),

throw into gear. **embrayage** (ja:ʒ) *m*, engaging, &c; clutch.

embrever (ãbrəve) *v.t*, to joggle.

embrigader (ãbrigade) *v.t*, to brigade; enroll.

embrocation (ãbrɔkasjɔ̃) *f*, embrocation.

embrocher (ãbrɔʃe) *v.t*, to spit; run through, impale.

embrouillamini (ãbrujamini) *m*, confusion.
embrouiller (je) *v.t*, to ravel, tangle; embroil, muddle, confuse.

embroussaillé, e (ãbrusaje) *a*, brushy; bushy; matted.

embrumer (ãbryme) *v.t*, to fog, shroud, darken. **embrun** (brœ̃) *m*, spray, spindrift.

embryon (ãbriɔ̃) *m*, embryo. **embryonnaire** (ɔnɛ:r) *a*, embryonic.

embûche (ãbyʃ) *f*, trap. **embuscade** (byskad) *f*, ambush, ambuscade. *se tenir en* ~, to lie in wait. **embusqué** (ke) *m*, shirk[er]. **embusquer** (ke) *v.t*, to place in ambush. **s'~**, to ambush, lie in wait; shirk.

émeraude (emro:d) *f*, emerald.

émerger (emɛrʒe) *v.i*, to emerge; loom; peep.

émeri (emri) *m*, emery.

émerillon (emrijɔ̃) *m*, merlin (*bird*); swivel. **émerillonné, e** (jɔne) *a*, bright, sparkling.

émérite (emerit) *a*, experienced; confirmed; emeritus.

émerveiller (emɛrvɛje) *v.t*, to astonish. **s'~**, to marvel.

émétique (emetik) *a. & m*, emetic.

émetteur (emetœ:r) *m*, issuer; (*att.*) transmitting (*Teleg.*). **émettre** (tr) *v.t.ir*, to emit, utter; express; issue.

émeute (emø:t) *f*, riot, disturbance, outbreak. **émeutier** (møtje) *m*, rioter.

émietter (emjete) *v.t. & s'~*, to crumble.

émigrant, e (emigrã, ã:t) *n*, emigrant. **émigration** (grasjɔ̃) *f*, emigration. **émigré, e** (gre) *n*, refugee; émigré (*Hist.*). **émigrer** (gre) *v.i*, to emigrate; migrate.

émincé, e (emɛ̃se) *p.p*, cut into thin slices.

éminemment (eminamã) *ad*, eminently, highly. **éminence** (nã:s) *f*, eminence; height; ball (*thumb*). *Son E~*, *f*, His Eminence (*cardinal*). **éminent, e** (nã, ã:t) *a*, eminent; distinguished; prominent. **éminentissime** (nãtisim) *a*, most eminent.

émir (emi:r) *m*, emir; ameer, amir.

émissaire (emisɛ:r) *m*, emissary. **émission** (sjɔ̃) *f*, emission; issue; uttering.

emmagasiner (ãmagazine) *v.t*, to store, s. up; warehouse.

emmailloter (ãmajɔte) *v.t*, to swathe; bandage.

emmancher (ãmãʃe) *v.t*, to handle; fix; set about. **emmanchure** (ʃy:r) *f*, armhole.

emmêler (ãmɛle) *v.t*, to [en]tangle; muddle.

emménagement (ãmenaʒmã) *m*, moving in (*house*); accommodation, appointments (*ship*). **emménager** (ʒe) *v.t*, to install, settle; move into; (*v.i.*) to move in.

emmener (ãmne) *v.t*, to take away.

emmiellé, e (ãmjɛle) *a*, honeyed.

emmitoufler (ămitufle) *v.t*, to muffle up.

emmortaiser (ămorteze) *v.t*, to mortise.

émoi (emwa) *m*, emotion, agitation, flutter.

émollient, e (emoljɑ̃, ɑ̃:t) *a. & m*, emollient.

émoluments (emolymɑ̃) *m.pl*, emoluments.

émonder (emɔ̃de) *v.t*, to prune. **émondes** (mɔ̃:d) *f.pl*, prunings.

émotion (emosjɔ̃) *f*, emotion; thrill; excitement.

émoucher (emuʃe) *v.t*, to drive away the flies from.

émouchet (emuʃɛ) *m*, kestrel.

émouchette (emuʃɛt) *f*, fly net. **émouchoir** (ʃwa:r) *m*, fly whisk.

émoulu, e (emuly) *a: frais ~ de*, fresh from (*college*); well up in (*subject*).

émousser (emuse) *v.t*, to blunt, dull; remove the moss from.

émoustiller (emustije) *v.t*, to exhilarate.

émouvoir (emuvwa:r) *v.t.ir*, to move; stir [up], rouse.

empailler (ɑ̃paje) *v.t*, to cover (or pack) (or stuff) with straw; stuff (*dead animal*). **empailleur, euse** (jœ:r, ø:z) *n*, chair bottomer; taxidermist.

empanacher (ɑ̃panaʃe) *v.t*, to plume; adorn.

empaqueter (ɑ̃pakte) *v.t*, to pack [up]. **s'~**, to wrap [oneself] up.

emparer (s') de (ɑ̃pare) *v.pr*, to seize, take possession of; monopolize, engross.

empâter (ɑ̃pɑte) *v.t*, to paste; make sticky; cram (*poultry*); impaste.

empattement (ɑ̃patmɑ̃) *m*, footing (*Build.*); wheel base; serif.

empaumer (ɑ̃pome) *v.t*, to strike (*ball*); manipulate (*pers.*).

empêché, e (ɑ̃peʃe) *p.p*, puzzled, at a loss. **empêchement** (ʃmɑ̃) *m*, hindrance, impediment, obstacle, bar; prevention. **empêcher** (ʃe) *v.t*, to prevent, hinder, impede; keep from; preclude. **s'~**, to forbear, refrain, help.

empeigne (ɑ̃pɛɲ) *f*, vamp, upper (*shoe*).

empereur (ɑ̃prœ:r) *m*, emperor.

empesé, e (ɑ̃pəze) *a*, starchy, stiff. **empeser** (ze) *v.t*, to starch.

empester (ɑ̃pɛste) *v.t*, to infect; corrupt; (*abs.*) to stink.

empêtrer (ɑ̃petre) *v.t*, to entangle, hamper; embarrass; involve.

emphase (ɑ̃fa:s) *f*, bombast, pomposity, fustian; magniloquence; emphasis. **emphatique†** (fatik) *a*, bombastic, pompous, magniloquent; emphatic.

empiècement (ɑ̃pjɛsmɑ̃) *m*, yoke (*dress*).

empierrer (ɑ̃pjɛre) *v.t*, to metal (*road*).

empiètement (ɑ̃pjɛtmɑ̃) *m*, encroachment, trespass. **empiéter sur** (pjete) *v.t*, to encroach on; trespass on (*fig.*).

empiffrer (ɑ̃pifre) *v.t*, to stuff, gorge.

empiler (ɑ̃pile) *v.t*, to pile [up]; stack; herd together.

empire (ɑ̃pi:r) *m*, dominion, sway; hold; mastery; rule; empire. *l'~ des Indes*, the Indian Empire. *~ sur soi-même*, self-control.

empirer (ɑ̃pire) *v.t*, to make worse; (*v.i.*) to grow worse.

empirique (ɑ̃pirik) *a*, empiric(al), rule-of-thumb. ¶ *m*, empiric[ist]. **empiriquement** (kmɑ̃) *ad*, empirically, by rule of thumb. **empirisme** (rism) *m*, empiricism.

emplacement (ɑ̃plasmɑ̃) *m*, site, position, location.

emplâtre (ɑ̃plɑ:tr) *m*, plaster (*Phar.*); futile person. *~ adhésif*, sticking plaster.

emplette (ɑ̃plɛt) *f*, purchase, shopping; bargain.

emplir (ɑ̃pli:r) *v.t. & s'~*, to fill; (*v.i.*) to be swamped (*boat*).

emploi (ɑ̃plwa) *m*, employment; job; use; entry (*Bkkpg*); part, line (*of actor*). **employé, e** (je) *n*, employee; clerk. *~ d'administration*, civil servant. *~ du gaz*, gas man. **employer** (je) *v.t*, to employ; use. **s'~**, to occupy (or exert) (or busy) oneself. **employeur, euse** (jœ:r, ø:z) *n*, employer.

emplumé, e (ɑ̃plyme) *p.a*, feathered. **emplumer** (me) *v.t*, to feather; tar & feather.

empocher (ɑ̃pɔʃe) *v.t*, to pocket.

empoignant, e (ɑ̃pwaɲɑ̃, ɑ̃:t) *a*, thrilling, poignant. **empoigner** (ɲe) *v.t*, to grasp; grip; clutch; grab; take to task, abuse; thrill.

empois (ɑ̃pwa) *m*, starch [paste].

empoisonnement (ɑ̃pwazɔnmɑ̃) *m*, poisoning. **empoisonner** (ne) *v.t*, to poison; infect; corrupt; (*abs.*) to be poisonous; stink. **empoisonneur, euse** (nœ:r, ø:z) *n*, poisoner; bad cook.

empoissonner (ɑ̃pwasɔne) *v.t*, to stock (*pond*) with fish.

emporté, e (ɑ̃pɔrte) *a*, hasty, quick-tempered, fiery, passionate. **emportement** (təmɑ̃) *m*, transport (*fig.*); outburst, fit of anger.

emporte-pièce (ɑ̃pɔrtəpjɛs) *m*, [hollow] punch. *à l'~* (*fig.*), trenchant.

emporter (ɑ̃pɔrte) *v.t*, to carry (or take) (or sweep) (or wash) away (or off) (or out); (*Mil.*) carry (*place*). *l'~ sur*, to surpass, outdo; overrule; prevail over; preponderate over. **s'~**, to get angry, fire up; bolt (*horse*).

empoté, e (ɑ̃pɔte) *a*, clumsy. **empoter** (te) *v.t*, to pot.

empourprer (ɑ̃purpre) *v.t*, to purple; crimson.

empreindre (ɑ̃prɛ̃:dr) *v.t.ir*, to imprint, impress, stamp. **empreinte** (prɛ̃:t) *f*, impress[ion], imprint; stamp (*fig.*); mould (*Typ.*). *~ de pas, ~ du pied*, footprint. *~ digitale*, finger print. *~ du doigt*, finger mark.

empressé, e (ɑ̃prɛse) *a*, eager, zealous; attentive. **empressement** (smɑ̃) *m*, eagerness, alacrity, readiness. **s'empresser** (se) *v.pr*, to hasten; be eager. *~ auprès de*, to dance attendance on.

emprise (ãpri:z) *f*, hold, ascendancy.
emprisonnement (ãprizɔnmã) *m*, imprisonment. ~ *cellulaire*, separate cell system.
emprisonner (ne) *v.t*, to imprison, confine.
emprunt (ãprœ̃) *m*, borrowing, loan; [making]
use. ~ *de la Défense nationale*, War loan.
d' ~ (*fig.*), artificial, sham, assumed. emprunté, e (te) *p.a*, borrowed; assumed
(*name*); awkward. emprunter (te) *v.t*, to
borrow; assume (*name*); use, make use of.
emprunteur, euse (tœ:r, ø:z) *n*, borrower.
empuantir (ãpɥãti:r) *v.t*, to infect.
empyrée (ãpire) *m*, empyrean.
émulation (emylasjɔ̃) *f*, emulation. émule
(myl) *n*, emulator, rival.
émulsion (emylsjɔ̃) *f*, emulsion.
en (ã) *pr*, in; into; within; on; to; at; with;
in the; in a; like [a]; as [a]; by; while; of;
under. ~ *classe!* all in! (*Sch.*). ~ *voiture!* take your seats!
en (ã) *pn. & ad*, of it, its, of them, their,
of him, of her; about it, about them, &c;
for (*or* by) (*or* with) (*or* from) it *or* them,
&c; some, any.
enamourer (s') (ãnamure) *v.pr*, to fall in love.
encadrer (ãkadre) *v.t*, to frame; surround;
incorporate; officer.
encager (ãkaʒe) *v.t*, to [en]cage.
encaisse (ãkɛs) *f*, cash [in hand]. ~ *métallique*, cash & bullion in hand. encaisser
(se) *v.t*, to [en]case; [en]cash, collect; put
in the cash [box]; embank (*river*, *road*).
encan (ãkã) *m*, auction.
encanailler (s') (ãkanaje) *v.i*, to contract low
habits.
encaquer (ãkake) *v.t*, to barrel. *encaqués
comme des harengs*, packed like sardines
(*people*).
encart (ãka:r) *m*, insert (*Bookb.*). encarter
(karte) *v.t*, to inset (*Bookb.*); insert (*Bookb.*).
en-cas (ãka) *m*, something (*ready to eat*)
in case of need; umbrella-sunshade.
encastrer (ãkastre) *v.t*, to house; embed;
tail [in].
encaustique (ãkostik) *a. & f*, encaustic.
~ *pour meubles*, furniture polish. encaustiquer (ke) *v.t*, to polish (*furniture*).
encaver (ãkave) *v.t*, to cellar.
enceindre (ãsɛ̃:dr) *v.t.ir*, to enclose, gird,
surround. enceinte (sɛ̃:t) *a.f*, pregnant,
with child, expectant. ¶ *f*, enclosure; precinct; ring (*Box.*); fencing; wall; hall. ~
du pesage, paddock (*Turf*).
encens (ãsã) *m*, incense. ~ *mâle*, frankincense. encenser (se) *v.t*, to [in]cense, burn
i. to; flatter. encensoir (swa:r) *m*, censer.
encercler (ãsɛrkle) *v.t*, to hoop, encircle.
enchaînement (ãʃɛnmã) (*fig.*) *m*, chain, series,
train. enchaîner (ne) *v.t*, to chain [up];
enchain, fetter, manacle; bind; link; enslave; enthrall.
enchantement (ãʃãtmã) *m*, enchantment,
magic, spell; glamour, witchery; delight.
enchanter (te) *v.t*, to enchant, bewitch;

delight, enrapture. enchanteur, eresse
(tœ:r, trɛ:s) *n*, enchanter, tress; (*att.*) en-
chanting, bewitching.
enchâsser (ãʃase) *v.t*, to set, mount; enshrine;
incorporate. enchâssure (sy:r) *f*, setting.
enchère (ãʃɛ:r) *f*, bid[ding]; auction, sale.
~ *au rabais*, Dutch auction. enchérir
(ʃeri:r) *v.t*, to raise the price of; (*v.i.*) to
rise in price; bid. ~ *sur*, to outbid;
outdo. enchérisseur (risœ:r) *m*, bidder.
enchevêtrer (s') (ãʃvetre) *v.pr*, to get [en]-
tangled (*or* confused).
enchifrènement (ãʃifrɛnmã) *m*, cold in the
head, snuffles.
enclave (ãkla:v) *f*, land-locked property
(*Law*); enclave (*international*); recess
(*Build.*). enclaver (klave) *v.t*, to enclose,
shut in, fit in.
enclin, e (ãklɛ̃, in) *a*, inclined, prone, minded,
given.
enclore (ãklɔ:r) *v.t.ir*, to enclose, fence in.
enclos (klo) *m*, enclosure; paddock.
enclouer (ãklue) *v.t*, to spike (*gun*). enclouure (kluy:r) (*fig.*) *f*, rub.
enclume (ãklym) *f*, anvil.
encoche (ãkɔʃ) *f*, notch, nick, slot. encocher
(ʃe) *v.t*, to notch, &c.
encoignure (ãkɔɲy:r) *f*, corner; corner cupboard.
encollage (ãkɔla:ʒ) *m*, sizing; size (*glue*).
encoller (le) *v.t*, to size.
encolure (ãkɔly:r) *f*, neck; neck measurement,
[neck] size; look (*fig.*).
encombrant, e (ãkɔ̃brã, ã:t) *a*, bulky; cumbersome, in the way; embarrassing. sans
encombre (kɔ̃:br), without hindrance.
encombrement (kɔ̃brəmã) *m*, block, congestion, [over]crowding; glut[ting]; litter;
space occupied, floor space; measurement
(*Ship.*). encombrer (bre) *v.t*, to block,
congest, overcrowd; glut, overstock; encumber, litter.
encontre (à l'~ de) (ãkɔ̃:tr), in opposition to.
aller à l'~ de, to run counter to.
encorbellement (ãkɔrbɛlmã) *m*, cantilever.
encore (ãkɔ:r) *ad*, still; yet; again; also;
moreover; too; more; else. ~ *un*, une,
one more, another. ~ *un coup*, once
again, once more. ~ *un peu*, a little
more *or* longer. ~ *que*, *c*, although.
encourager (ãkuraʒe) *v.t*, to encourage,
hearten; foster; promote; countenance,
abet; halloo (*dogs*).
encourir (ãkuri:r) *v.t.ir*, to incur, run.
encrasser (ãkrase) *v.t*, to foul, dirty, grime;
clog.
encre (ã:kr) *f*, ink. ~ *à marquer le linge*,
marking i. ~ *de Chine*, Indian i. ~
stylographique (stilɔgrafik), fountain pen i.
encrer (ãkre) *v.t*, to ink. encrier (krie) *m*,
inkstand, inkpot. ~ *d'écolier*, ink well.
encroûté, e (ãkrute) (*fig.*) *a*, crusted, fogyish.
encuver (ãkyve) *v.t*, to vat; put in the tub.
encyclique (ãsiklik) *a. & f*, encyclic(al).

encyclopédie (äsiklɔpedi) *f*, [en]cyclop[a]edia. **endémique** (ädemik) *a*, endemic.

endenter (ädäte) *v.t*, to tooth, cog.

endetté, e (ädɛte) *p.a*, in debt. **endetter (te)** *v.t*, to involve in debt. **s'~**, to run into d.

endêvé, e (ädɛve) *a*, exasperated. **endêver** (ve) *v.i*, to be furious.

endiablé, e (ädjable) *a*, (*as if*) possessed; wild, frenzied. **endiabler** (ble) *v.i*, to be furious.

endiguer (ädige) *v.t*, to dike; dam.

endimancher (s') (ädimãʃe) *v.pr*, to put on one's Sunday best.

endive (ädi:v) *f*, chicory; endive.

endoctriner (ädɔktrine) *v.t*, to indoctrinate; coach.

endolorir (ädɔlɔri:r) *v.t*, to make ache.

endommager (ädɔmaʒe) *v.t*, to damage, injure.

endormant, e (ädɔrmã, ã:t) *a*, soporific; wearisome. **endormeur** (mœ:r) *m*, bore; luller. **endormi, e** (mi) *p.a*, asleep; sleepy; drowsy. ¶ *n*, sleepyhead. **endormir** (mi:r) *v.t.ir*, to send to sleep; lull. **s'~**, to fall asleep, go to sleep.

endos[sement] (ädo[smã]) *m*, endorsement. **endosser (se)** *v.t*, to put on, don; take on, shoulder; endorse. **endosseur** (sœ:r) *m*, endorser.

endroit (ädrwa) *m*, place, spot, part; right side, face (*fabric*). *à l'~ de*, towards, regarding.

enduire (ädɥi:r) *v.t.ir*, to smear; coat; render. **enduit** (dɥi) *m*, coat[ing]; rendering.

endurance (ädyrã:s) *f*, endurance. **endurant, e** (rã, ã:t) *a*, patient. **rendre ~**, to harden. **endurcir** (si:r) *v.t. & s'~**, to harden. **endurcissement** (sismã) *m*, hardness, callousness, obduracy. **endurer** (re) *v.t*, to endure.

énergétique (enɛrʒetik) *f*, energetics (*Phys.*). **énergie** (ʒi) *f*, energy, power; emphasis; efficacy (*remedy*); backbone. **énergique†** (ʒik) *a*, energetic, powerful, strong; forcible, emphatic; strenuous.

énerver (enɛrve) *v.t*, to enervate; exasperate.

enfance (äfã:s) *f*, childhood; infancy; second childhood, dotage; A B C (*of an art*). **enfant** (fã) *n*, child; infant; boy; girl; fellow, lad. **~ abandonné, e**, waif. **~ de chœur**, choir boy, chorister. **~s perdus**, forlorn hope (*Mil.*). **~ prodige**, infant prodigy. **~ prodigue**, prodigal son. **~ trouvé**, foundling; stowaway. **enfantement** (tmã) *m*, birth (*fig.*). **enfanter** (te) *v.t*, to give birth to (*fig.*). **enfantillage** (tija:ʒ) *m*, childishness. **enfantin, e** (tɛ̃, in) *a*, infantile; childish; infant (*class*); nursery (*language*).

enfariner (äfarine) *v.t*, to [cover with] flour.

enfer (äfɛ:r) *m*, hell, inferno. *les ~s*, the nether regions, the underworld, Hades. *d'~*, infernal; blazing (*fire*).

enfermer (äfɛrme) *v.t*, to shut up; lock up; enclose; impound; contain.

enferrer (äfɛre) *v.t*, to run through (*with sword, &c*). **s'~**, to become involved. *s'~ soi-même*, to give oneself away.

enfieller (äfjɛle) *v.t*, to embitter, sour.

enfilade (äfilad) *f*, suite; series, string; row; enfilade. **enfiler (le)** *v.t*, to thread; string; run (*or* go) through; go along; enfilade, rake; draw in (*person to reckless gaming*).

enfin (äfɛ̃) *ad*, at last, lastly, after all; in short, in fine; in fact; come now!

enflammer (äflame) *v.t*, to [set on] fire, ignite; inflame. **s'~**, to catch (*or* take) fire, ignite, fire up.

enfler (äfle) *v.t. & i. & s~**, to swell, inflate. **enflure** (fly:r) *f*, swelling, &c.

enfoncer (äfõse) *v.t*, to drive [in]; sink, bury, immerse; break open, b. in; b. up; stave in; (*v.i. & abs.*) to sink. **enfoncement** (smã) *m*, driving [in], &c; hollow, depression; recess; background. **enfonçure** (sy:r) *f*, hole; bottom (*cask*).

enfouir (äfwi:r) *v.t*, to bury, hide.

enfourcher (äfurʃe) *v.t*, to bestride; ride to death (*fig.*).

enfourner (äfurne) *v.t*, to put in the oven.

enfreindre (äfrɛ̃:dr) *v.t.ir*, to infringe, break.

enfuir (s') (äfɥi:r) *v.pr*, to flee; escape; run away; elope; leak; fly; vanish.

enfumer (äfyme) *v.t*, to smoke; s. out.

engageant, e (ägaʒã, ã:t) *a*, engaging, winning; inviting. **engagement** (ʒmã) *m*, engagement; booking; entry, fixture (*sporting event*); enlistment; signing on; commitment; liability; undertaking; pledging, pledge, pawning, hypothecation. **engager** (ʒe) *v.t*, to engage; book; enter; enlist; sign [on]; betroth; bind; plight; pledge, pawn; mortgage, hypothecate; invite, urge, induce; foul (*ropes, &c*). **engagé, p.p**, on her beam ends; waterlogged (*boat*). **engagée, p.p**, wired (*of croquet ball*). **s'engager**, to undertake, covenant; enlist; enter; foul.

engainer (ägɛne) *v.t*, to sheathe, case.

engeance (äʒã:s) *f*, brood, lot (*of despicable people*).

engelure (äʒly:r) *f*, chilblain.

engendrer (äʒãdre) *v.t*, to beget; sire; engender; breed; generate.

engerber (äʒɛrbe) *v.t*, to sheaf, bind.

engin (äʒɛ̃) *m*, appliance, contrivance, gear, tackle; engine (*of war*).

englober (äglɔbe) *v.t*, to include, embody.

engloutir (ägluti:r) *v.t*, to swallow; s. up; bolt (*food*); engulf, swamp.

engluer (äglɥe) *v.t*, to [bird]lime; ensnare; take in.

engorger (ägɔrʒe) *v.t*, to choke [up], stop up.

engouer (s') (ägue) *v.pr*, to become infatuated.

engouffrer (ägufre) *v.t*, to engulf, swallow up.

engourdir (ägurdi:r) *v.t*, to [be]numb, dull.

engrais (ägrɛ) *m*, fattening food; manure. **~ fertilisant**, fertilizer. **engraisser** (se) *v.t*, to fatten; manure.

engranger (ãgrãʒe) *v.t*, to garner, get in.

engraver (ãgrave) *v.t*, to strand; (*v.i.*) to ground (*boat*).

engrenage (ãgrəna:ʒ) *m*, gear[ing]; meshes, toils (*fig.*). **engrener** (ne) *v.t*, to [throw into] gear, mesh, engage; feed with corn; set going.

engrumeler (ãgrymle) *v.t*, to clot, curdle.

enguirlander (ãgirlãde) *v.t*, to garland, wreathe; wheedle.

enhardir (ãardi:r) *v.t*, to embolden.

énigmatique† (enigmatik) *a*, enigmatic(al).

énigme (nigm) *f*, riddle, conundrum, puzzle, enigma.

enivrer (ãnivre) *v.t.* to intoxicate, inebriate; elate.

enjambée (ãʒãbe) *f*, stride. **enjamber** (be) *v.t. & abs*, to stride [over *or* along]; (*v.i.*) to encroach, project.

enjeu (ãʒø) *m*, stake (*wager*).

enjoindre (ãʒwɛ̃:dr) *v.t.ir*, to enjoin.

enjôler (ãʒole) *v.t*, to wheedle, inveigle, bamboozle.

enjoliver (ãʒolive) *v.t*, to embellish; set off. **enjoué, e** (ãʒwe) *a*, playful, jocular, vivacious. **enjouement** (ʒumã) *m*, playfulness, &c.

enlacer (ãlase) *v.t*, to [en]lace; entwine; clasp, fold.

enlaidir (ãledi:r) *v.t*, to make ugly; disfigure.

enlevage (ãlva:ʒ) *m*, spurt (*Rowing*). **enlever** (lve) *v.t*, to lift, raise; carry (*or* take) (*or* clear) (*or* sweep) away (*or* off); loft (*Golf*); remove, collect; kidnap; abduct; rape; buy up; take up (*shares*); snap up (*bargain*). *être enlevé par la mer ou par les lames*, to be washed overboard. *se faire ~ par*, to elope with. **enlèvement** (lɛvmã) *m*, lifting, &c; elopement.

enliser (s') (ãlize) *v.pr*, to sink [into the sand *or* mud].

enluminer (ãlymine) *v.t*, to colour, illuminate (*MS.*); flush, redden. **enluminure** (ny:r) *f*, colouring; illumination; high colour.

ennemi, e (ɛnmi) *n*, enemy, foe; hater. ¶ *a*, enemy, inimical, hostile; averse; clashing.

ennoblir (ãnobli:r) *v.t*, to ennoble, uplift, dignify.

ennui (ãnɥi) *m*, wearisomeness, tedium, boredom; bother, nuisance; worry, trouble. **ennuyer** (nɥije) *v.t*, to weary, tire, bore; annoy, worry. **ennuyeux, euse†** (jø, ø:z) *a*, tiresome, tedious, irksome; prosy.

énoncé (enõse) *m*, statement. **énoncer** (se) *v.t*, to state, enunciate, express, specify. **énonciation** (sjasjõ) *f*, stating, enunciation.

enorgueillir (ãnorgœji:r) *v.t*, to make proud, elate. **s'~**, to pride oneself.

énorme (enorm) *a*, enormous, huge, mountainous, tremendous; outrageous. **énormément** (memã) *ad*, enormously, &c. **énormité** (mite) *f*, enormousness, &c; enormity.

enquérir (s') (ãkeri:r) *v.pr.ir*, to inquire, ask. **enquête** (kɛ:t) *f*, inquiry, investigation; inquest.

enraciner (ãrasine) *v.t. & s'~*, to root.

enragé, e (ãraʒe) *p.a*, mad; rabid; enraged, infuriated; raging; wild. ¶ *m*, madman, fiend (*fig.*). **enrageant, e** (ʒã, ã:t) *a*, maddening. **enrager** (ʒe) *v.i*, to fume. *faire ~*, to madden, infuriate.

enrayer (ãrɛje) *v.t*, to drag, skid, lock (*wheel*); spoke (*wheel*); stop, check (*fig.*).

enrégimenter (ãreʒimãte) (*fig.*) *v.t*, to enroll.

enregistrer (ãroʒistre) *v.t*, to register; file; enter [up]; record; book; chronicle. **enregistrement** (trəmã) *m*, registration, &c; registry.

enrhumer (ãryme) *v.t*, to give (*someone*) a cold. **s'~**, to catch [a] cold.

enrichi, e (ãriʃi) *n*, one who has become rich. **enrichir** (ʃi:r) *v.t*, to enrich. **s'~**, to make money.

enrober (ãrobe) *v.t*, to encase.

enrôler (ãrole) *v.t*, to enroll, enlist.

enrouer (ãrwe) *v.t*, to make hoarse *or* husky.

enrouler (ãrule) *v.t*, to wind, coil, wrap, roll [up].

ensablement (ãsabləmã) *m*, sandbank. **ensabler** (ble) *v.t*, to sand [up]; run aground.

ensacher (ãsaʃe) *v.t*, to bag, sack.

ensanglanter (ãsãglãte) *v.t*, to stain with blood.

enseigne (ãsɛɲ) *f*, sign; sign[board]; facia [board]; ensign. *~ lumineuse*, electric sign. *à bonnes ~s*, on sure grounds; on good security. *à telles ~s que*, in proof of which. *~ de vaisseau, m*, sublieutenant (*Nav.*).

enseignement (ãsɛɲmã) *m*, teaching, tuition, training, education; (*pl.*) teachings, lessons. **enseigner** (ɲe) *v.t*, to show; tell of; teach; teach how.

ensellé, e (ãsɛle) *a*, saddle-backed.

ensemble (ãsã:bl) *ad*, together. ¶ *m*, whole; aggregate; general effect; unity, harmony. *~ deux pièces*, two-piece set, two-piece ensemble (*coat & skirt*).

ensemencer (ãsmãse) *v.t*, to sow (*land*).

enserrer (ãsere) *v.t*, to encompass, enclose; tie up (*fig.*); put under glass (*Hort.*).

ensevelir (ãsəvli:r) *v.t*, to bury, entomb; plunge; shroud.

ensoleillé, e (ãsolɛje) *a*, sunny; sunlit. **ensoleiller** (je) *v.t*, to sun; light up; brighten.

ensommeillé, e (ãsomeje) *a*, sleepy, drowsy.

ensorceler (ãsorsəle) *v.t*, to bewitch.

ensuite (ãsɥit) *ad*, afterwards, then, next. **s'ensuivre** (sɥi:vr) *v.pr.ir*, to follow, ensue.

entablement (ãtabləmã) *m*, entablature.

entacher (ãtaʃe) *v.t*, to taint; vitiate.

entaille (ãta:j) *f*, notch, nick, groove, slot; gash, hack. **entailler** (tɑje) *v.t*, to notch, &c.

entame (ãtam) *f*, first cut, outside [cut]. **entamer** (me) *v.t*, to cut [into] (*loaf*, injure; penetrate; break into, broach; shake (*one's faith*); fathom; begin, open, initiate.

entasser (ᾱtɑse) *v.t*, to heap up, pile up, stack; huddle.

ente (ᾱ:t) (*Hort.*) *f*, graft; stock.

entendement (ᾱtᾱdmᾱ) *m*, understanding; intelligence. **entendre** (tᾱ:dr) *v.t. & abs*, to hear; listen to; understand; mean; require. ~ *à*, to consent to. **s'~**, to understand; u. each other; come to an understanding; get on; be subject to. **entendu, e** (tᾱdy) *a*, capable, business-like; versed; arranged; conceived. *bien entendu*, clearly understood; of course. *entendu!* agreed! right [you are]! **entente** (tᾱ:t) *f*, understanding. *mot, phrase, à double ~*, word, phrase, with a double meaning, double entendre.

enter (ᾱte) *v.t*, to [en]graft.

entérique (ᾱterik) *a*, enteric.

enterrement (ᾱtɛrmᾱ) *m*, burial, interment; funeral. **enterrer** (re) *v.t*, to bury, inter; sink (*money, a fortune, en* = in); outlive.

en-tête (ᾱtɛ:t) *m*, head[ing] (*letter, bill, ledger*).

entêté, e (ᾱtɛte) *p.a*, obstinate, headstrong, stubborn. **entêtement** (tmᾱ) *m*, obstinacy, &c. **entêter** (te) *v.t. & abs*, to make giddy; go to the head; infatuate. **s'~**, to become infatuated.

enthousiasme (ᾱtuzjasm) *m*, enthusiasm; rapture. **enthousiasmer** (me) *v.t*, to enrapture, carry away. **s'~**, to go into raptures. **enthousiaste** (ast) *a*, enthusiastic. ¶ *n*, enthusiast.

enticher (ᾱtife) *v.t*, to taint; infatuate.

entier, ère (ᾱtje, ɛ:r) *a*, entire, whole; full; the same, as it was; headstrong, self-willed. ¶ *m*, entirety. [*nombre*] ~, whole number, integer. *en* ~, entirely, in full, right through. **entièrement** (tjɛrmᾱ) *ad*, entirely, wholly; fully; quite; clean (*shaven*).

entité (ᾱtite) *f*, entity.

entoiler (ᾱtwale) *v.t*, to mount [on calico *or* linen]; bind in cloth.

entomologie (ᾱtɔmɔlɔʒi) *f*, entomology. **entomologiste** (ʒist) *m*, entomologist.

entonner (ᾱtɔne) *v.t. & abs*, to intone, intonate; strike up (*tune*); barrel.

entonnoir (ᾱtɔnwa:r) *m*, funnel; hollow; corrie; shell hole; mine crater.

entorse (ᾱtɔrs) *f*, sprain, strain, wrench.

entortiller (tije) *v.t*, to twist, [en]twine, wind, wrap; get round (*someone*).

entour (ᾱtu:r) *m*: *à l'~*, around, round about. **~s**, *pl*, environs, outskirts, purlieus; associates; aspects. **entourage** (tura:ʒ) *m*, setting, surround; environment, associates. **entourer** (re) *v.t*, to surround, beset, hedge.

en-tout-cas (ᾱtuka) *m*, umbrella-sunshade.

entr'acte (ᾱtrakt) *m*, interval, entr'acte; interlude.

entraide (ᾱtrɛ:d) *f*, helpfulness to each other. **s'entraider** (trɛde) *v.pr*, to help one another.

entrailles (ᾱtra:j) *f.pl*, entrails, bowels, inwards; compassion, heart.

entr'aimer (s') (ᾱtrɛme) *v.pr*, to love one another.

entrain (ᾱtrɛ̃) *m*, liveliness, spirit, go, gusto. **entraînant, e** (trɛnᾱ, ᾱ:t) *a*, inspiriting, stirring. **entraînement** (nmᾱ) *m*, impulse; force; enthusiasm; training (*Sport*); sparring; coaching; pacemaking; feed (*Mach.*). **entraîner** (ne) *v.t*, to carry (*or* draw) (*or* wash) away *or* along; drift; involve, entail; lead; train; coach; pace. **s'~** *à la boxe*, to spar. **entraîneur** (nœ:r) *m*, trainer; coach; pacemaker.

entrait (ᾱtrɛ) *m*, tie beam; tie rod.

entrant, e (ᾱtrᾱ, ᾱ:t) *a*, ingoing; insinuating.

entrave (ᾱtra:v) *f*, fetter, shackle, trammel, clog, obstacle; hobble. **entraver** (trave) *v.t*, to fetter, &c; impede, hinder, hamper.

entre (ᾱ:tr) *pr*, between; in, into; among[st]; of. ~ *deux, ad*, in between; middling. ~ *deux âges*, middle-aged. ~ *deux eaux*, under water. ~ *vifs*, inter vivos.

entrebâillé, e (ᾱtrəbaje) *a*, half-open, ajar. **entrebâilleur de fenêtre** (jœ:r) *m*, casement stay.

entrechat (ᾱtrəfa) *m*, entrechat; caper.

entrechoquer (ᾱtrəfɔke) *v.t*, to strike against each other. **s'~**, to clash, collide.

entrecôte (ᾱtrəko:t) *f*, rib steak.

entrecouper (ᾱtrəkupe) *v.t*, to intersect; break.

entrecroiser (s') (ᾱtrəkrwaze) *v.pr*, to intersect; criss-cross.

entre-déchirer (s') (ᾱtrədefire) *v.pr*, to tear one another to pieces.

entre-deux (ᾱtrədø) *m*, space [between]; parting; trough (*sea*); insertion (*Need.*).

entrée (ᾱtre) *f*, entrance, entry; ingress; admittance, admission; [admission] ticket; way in; access; entrée; beginning; mouth; inlet; gate. ~ *dans le monde*, birth; coming out (*in society*). *les ~s de faveur*, the free list (*Theat.*). ~ *de poste*, lead-in (*Radio*). ~ *de serrure*, keyhole. ~ *en douane*, clearance (*or* entry) inwards. ~ *en séance*, opening of the sitting. [*droit d'*]~, import duty.

entrefaite (ᾱtrəfɛt) *f*: *sur ces ~s*, in the midst of all this.

entrefilet (ᾱtrəfilɛ) *m*, [short] paragraph (*newspaper*).

entregent (ᾱtrəʒᾱ) *m*, tact; gumption.

entrelacer (ᾱtrəlase) *v.t*, to interlace, intertwine, interweave.

entrelardé, e (ᾱtrəlarde) *p.a*, streaky (*meat*). **entrelarder** (de) *v.t*, to lard; interlard.

entre-ligne (ᾱtrəliɲ) *m*, interlineation.

entremêler (ᾱtrəmɛle) *v.t*, to [inter]mix, intermingle; intersperse.

entremets (ᾱtrəmɛ) *m*, side dish; sweet (*dinner course*).

entremetteur, euse (ātrəmɛtœːr, øːz) *n*, go-between. **s'entremettre** (tr) *v.pr.ir*, to intervene. **entremise** (miːz) *f*, intervention; agency, medium.

entrepont (ātrəpɔ̃) *m*, between-decks, 'tween-decks.

entreposer (ātrəpoze) *v.t*, to warehouse, store; bond. **entreposeur** (zœːr) *m*, warehouse keeper; bonded storekeeper. **entre-positaire** (zitɛːr) *n*, bonder. **entrepôt** (po) *m*, warehouse, store; emporium, mart. ~ *frigorifique*, cold store. ~ [*légal*], ~ *de douane*, bond[ed warehouse]. *en* ~ ou *à l'* ~ ou *en E.*, in bond[ed warehouse].

entreprenant, e (ātrəprənā, āːt) *a*, enterprising, pushing, go-ahead. **entreprendre** (prāːdr) *v.t.ir*, to undertake; contract for; tackle (*pers.*). ~ *sur*, to encroach on. **entrepreneur** (prənœːr) *m*, contractor. ~ *de monuments funéraires*, monumental mason. ~ *de pompes funèbres*, undertaker. ~ *de transports*, ~ *de roulage*, *cartage* (*or* haulage) contractor, carrier. **entrepreneuse de confection** (øːz) *f*, dressmaker. **entreprise** (priːz) *f*, undertaking; enterprise; concern; business; contract; encroachment.

entrer (ātre) *v.i*, to enter; come in; go in; walk in; march in; step in; get in; go; come. ~ *en déchargement*, to break bulk (*Ship.*). ~ *en vacances*, to break up (*Sch.*). *X. entre* [*en scène*], enter X. (*Theat.*). ¶ *v.t*, to introduce. ~ *en fraude*, to smuggle in.

entresol (ātrəsɔl) *m*, mezzanine [floor].

entre-temps (ātrətā) *ad*, meanwhile. ¶ *m*, interval.

entretenir (ātrətniːr) *v.t.ir*, to maintain; keep in repair; keep up; support, keep; speak to, report to. **s'** ~, to last; hold together; converse. *s'* ~ *la main*, to keep one's hand in. **entretien** (tjɛ̃) *m*, maintenance; upkeep; support, keep; clothes, dress; talk; interview.

entretoile (ātrətwal) *f*, lace insertion.

entretoise (ātrətwaːz) *f*, brace, strut, crosspiece; stay-bolt.

entrevoir (ātrəvwaːr) *v.t.ir*, to catch a glimpse of; see indistinctly; sense. **s'** ~, to see each other, meet. **entrevue** (vy) *f*, interview.

entrouvrir (ātruvriːr) *v.t.ir*, to half-open.

énumérer (enymere) *v.t*, to enumerate, rehearse; recite.

envahir (āvaiːr) *v.t*, to invade, break into; overrun; flood; overgrow; encroach on, trench on. **envahissement** (ismā) *m*, invasion; inrush; encroachment. **envahisseur** (sœːr) *m*, invader.

envaser (s') (āvaze) *v.pr*, to silt up; sink in the mud.

enveloppe (āvlɔp) *f*, envelope; wrapper; cover[ing]; jacket[ing]; sheath[ing]; lagging; casing; skin; outer cover (*tire*); exterior (*fig.*). ~ *à panneau*, ~ *à fenêtre*,

panel envelope, window e. ~ *affranchie pour la réponse*, stamped addressed e. ~ *de lettre chargée ou recommandée*, registered letter e. **envelopper** (vlɔpe) *v.t*, to envelop; wrap [up]; enfold; [en]shroud; cover; case; jacket; lag; involve.

envenimer (āvnime) *v.t*, to poison; envenom, embitter.

envergure (āvɛrgyːr) *f*, spread, span; wing spread, w. span; stretch; expanse; breadth.

envers (āvɛːr) *m*, wrong side, back, reverse; seamy side. *à l'* ~, inside out; topsy-turvy. ¶ *pr*, towards, to. ~ *& contre tous*, through thick & thin.

envi (à l') (āvi), in emulation, vying.

envie (āvi) *f*, envy; wish, desire, mind, longing, fancy; birthmark; agnail, hangnail. **envier** (vje) *v.t*, to envy, begrudge. **envieux, euse** (vjø, øːz) *a*, envious.

environ (āvirɔ̃) *ad*, about, thereabouts. ~ *s*, *m.pl*, environs, outskirts, purlieus, neighbourhood. **environner** (rɔne) *v.t*, to environ, surround; beset.

envisager (āvizaʒe) *v.t*, to look in the face; look on; envisage; contemplate, view.

envoi (āvwa) *m*, sending, forwarding, dispatch; sending in, s. out; remittance; consignment; parcel, package; article (*Post*). ~ *contre remboursement*, cash on delivery.

envol (āvɔl) *m*, flight; taking off (*Aero.*). **envolée (le)** *f*, flight (*fig.*). **s'envoler (le)** *v.pr*, to fly [away].

envoûter (āvute) *v.t*, to bewitch.

envoyé, e (āvwaje) *n*, envoy; messenger. ~ *spécial*, special correspondent. **envoyer** (je) *v.t*, to send, forward, dispatch; send in, s. out; remit; tender. **envoyeur, euse** (jœːr, øːz) *n*, sender.

éolien, ne (eɔljɛ̃, ɛn) *a*, Aeolian, wind (*att.*).

épagneul, e (epaɲœl) *n*, spaniel.

épais, se (epɛ, ɛːs) *a*, thick, dense. ~ *de*, thick (*Meas.*). **épais**, *ad*, thick[ly]. ¶ *m*, thickness. **épaisseur** (pɛsœːr) *f*, thickness; ply; thick; density. **épaissir** (siːr) *v.t*, to thicken. ~, *v.i. & s'* ~, to thicken; get stout.

épanchement (epāʃmā) *m*, effusion, outpouring. ~ *de synovie* (sinɔvi), water on the knee. **épancher** (ʃe) *v.t*, to pour out; vent; open (*heart*).

épandre (epāːdr) *v.t*, to spread; shed.

épanouir (epanwiːr) *v.t. & s'* ~, to open, expand; brighten.

épargne (eparɲ) *f*, saving, economy, thrift. *la petite* ~, the small investor. **épargner** (ɲe) *v.t*, to save [up], lay by, economize, husband; spare, grudge, stint.

éparpiller (eparpije) *v.t*, to scatter; fritter away. **épars, e** (paːr, ars) *a*, scattered, straggling.

épaté, e (epate) *p.a*, with crippled foot; flat (*nose*). **épater** (te) *v.t*, to astonish.

épaulard (epolaːr) *m*, grampus, orc.

épaule (epo:l) *f*, shoulder. **épaulée** (pole) *f*, push with the shoulder. **épaulement** (lmɑ̃) *m*, shoulder (*Carp.*). **épauler** (le) *v.t*, to splay; shoulder; bring (*rifle*) to the shoulder; back up. **épaulette** (let) *f*, yoke (*Dress*); shoulder strap; epaulet[te].

épave (epa:v) *a*, stray[ed]. ¶ *f*, stray; derelict, wreck; (*pl.*) wreckage; jetsam; flotsam; lagan; remnant.

épée (epe) *f*, sword. ~ *de chevet*, fallback; ruling passion; vade-mecum.

épeler (eple) *v.t*, to spell. **épellation** (pɛlasjɔ̃) *f*, spelling.

éperdu† (eperdy) *a*, distracted; desperate.

éperlan (eperlɑ̃) *m*, smelt (*fish*).

éperon (eprɔ̃) *m*, spur; buttress; ram (*battle-ship*). **éperonner** (prɔne) *v.t*, to spur; s. on.

épervier (epervje) *m*, sparrow hawk; sweep net, cast net.

éphélide (efelid) *f*, freckle.

éphémère (efemɛːr) *a*, ephemeral, mushroom. ¶ *m*, ephemera, -ron, May fly. **éphéméride** (merid) *f*, ephemeris; block calendar.

épi (epi) *m*, ear (*grain*); cob (*corn*); spike (*flower*); spray (*jewels*).

épice (epis) *f*, spice. **épicé, e** (se) *a*, spicy. **épicer** (se) *v.t*, to spice. **épicerie** (sri) *f*, grocery; grocer's shop; spices. **épicier, ère** (sje, ɛːr) *n*, grocer, chandler.

épicurien, ne (epikyrjɛ̃, ɛn) *a. & m*, epicurean.

épidémie (epidemi) *f*, epidemic, outbreak (*disease*). **épidémique** (mik) *a*, epidemic(al).

épiderme (epidɛrm) *m*, epidermis. *avoir l'~ sensible*, to be thin-skinned (*fig.*).

épier (epje) *v.i*, to ear (*corn*); (*v.t.*) to spy [on], watch.

épieu (epjø) *m*, boar spear.

épiglotte (epiglɔt) *f*, epiglottis.

épigramme (epigram) *f*, epigram; skit.

épigraphe (epigraf) *f*, epigraph, quotation, motto (*prefixed to book or chapter*).

épilepsie (epilepsi) *f*, epilepsy. **épileptique** (tik) *a. & n*, epileptic.

épiler (epile) *v.t*, to depilate, pluck [out hairs].

épilogue (epilɔg) *m*, epilogue. **épiloguer** (ge) *v.i*, to find fault. **épilogueur, euse** (gœ:r, ø:z) *n*, fault finder.

épinard (*Bot.*) *m. & ~s* (*Cook.*) *pl.* (epina:r), spinach, spinage.

épine (epin) *f*, thorn [bush]; thorn; spine (*Bot.*). ~ *blanche*, hawthorn, white-thorn, may. ~ *noire*, blackthorn. ~ *dorsale*, spine, backbone. **épineux, euse** (nø, ø:z) *a*, thorny, spiny, prickly; knotty. **épine-vinette** (vinɛt) *f*, barberry, berberry.

épingle (epɛ̃:gl) *f*, pin. ~ *à friser*, hair curler. ~ *à linge*, clothes peg. ~ *à onduler*, hair waver. ~ *de sûreté*, ~ *de nourrice*, ~ *anglaise*, safety pin. **épingler** (pɛ̃gle) *v.t*, to pin.

épinoche (epinɔʃ) *f*, stickleback.

Épiphanie (epifani) *f*, Epiphany.

épique (epik) *a*, epic.

épiscopal, e (episkɔpal) *a*, episcopal. **épiscopat** (pa) *m*, episcopate; episcopacy.

épisode (epizɔd) *m*, episode.

épisser (epise) *v.t*, to splice (*rope*). **épissoir** (swa:r) *m*, marline spike, marlinspike. **épissure** (sy:r) *f*, splice.

épistolaire (epistɔlɛ:r) *a*, epistolary. **épistolier, ère** (lje, ɛ:r) *n*, letter writer (*pers.*).

épitaphe (epitaf) *f*, epitaph.

épithète (epitɛt) *f*, epithet.

épitomé (epitɔme) *m*, epitome.

épître (epi:tr) *f*, epistle; letter.

éploré, e (eplɔre) *a*, tearful, in tears, weeping.

éplucher (eplyʃe) *v.t*, to prepare, clean; peel, pare; preen, prink; sift (*fig.*), scan. **s'~**, to plume (*or* preen) (*or* prink) its feathers. **épluchures** (ʃy:r) *f.pl*, parings, peelings.

épointer (epwɛ̃te) *v.t*, to break the point of; point (*sharpen*).

éponge (epɔ̃:ʒ) *f*, sponge. **éponger** (pɔ̃ʒe) *v.t*, to sponge; mop; mop up; dab; blot.

épontille (epɔ̃ti:j) *f*, stanchion (*ship*).

épopée (epɔpe) *f*, epic, epopee, epos.

époque (epɔk) *f*, epoch; era, age; red-letter day; time, date, period.

époumoner (epumone) *v.t*, to puff.

épouse (epu:z) *f*, wife, spouse, consort. **épouser** (puze) *v.t*, to marry, wed; espouse. ~ [*la forme de*], to correspond (*or* conform) in shape to; adapt itself to, fit.

épousseter (epuste) *v.t*, to dust; rub down.

épouvantable† (epuvɑ̃tabl) *a*, frightful, fearful, dreadful. **épouvantail** (ta:j) *m*, scarecrow; bugbear. **épouvante** (vɑ̃:t) *f*, terror, fright. **épouvanter** (vɑ̃te) *v.t*, to terrify, frighten, scare.

époux (epu) *m*, husband, spouse, consort; (*pl.*) husband & wife, [married] couple.

épreindre (eprɛ̃:dr) *v.t.ir*, to press [out], squeeze [out].

éprendre (s') (eprɑ̃:dr) *v.pr.ir*, to be smitten, be enamoured, be taken, fall in love.

épreuve (eprœ:v) *f*, test[ing]; trial; ordeal; proof (*Typ.*); heat (*Sport*); event (*Sport*). ~ *d'endurance*, reliability trial. ~ *d'imprimerie*, printer's proof. ~ *éliminatoire*, eliminating heat. ~ *en placard*, galley proof, slip. [~] *finale*, final [heat]. ~ *négative*, negative (*Phot.*). ~ *nulle*, dead heat. ~ [*positive*], positive (*Phot.*). *à l'~ de*, proof against. *à l'~ du feu, des intempéries, des maladresses*, fire-proof, weather-p., fool-p. *à toute ~*, unflinching; trusty. **éprouver** (pruve) *v.t*, to test, prove, try; experience, meet with, sustain, undergo; suffer; feel. **éprouvette** (vɛt) *f*, test glass; t. tube; t. piece; probe (*Surg.*).

épuisé, e (epɥize) *p.a*, exhausted, spent; effete; out of print; off (*dish in restaurant*). **épuiser** (ze) *v.t*, to exhaust; drain; empty. **épuisette** (zɛt) *f*, landing net; scoop, bailer.

E

épuration (epyrasjɔ̃) *f*, purification; refining; purging, purge. **épure** (py:r) *f*, working drawing; diagram. **épurer** (pyre) *v.t*, to purify; refine; purge, weed out.

équarrir (ekari:r) *v.t*, to square; quarter, cut up (*dead animal*). **équarrisseur** (risœ:r) *m*, knacker.

équateur (ekwatœ:r) *m*, equator. *l'É~* (*Geog.*), Ecuador.

équation (ekwasjɔ̃) *f*, equation.

équatorial, e (ekwatɔrjal) *a*, equatorial. ¶ *m*, equatorial [telescope].

équerre (ekɛ:r) *f*, square (*instrument & at right angles*).

équestre (ekɛstr) *a*, equestrian.

équilibre (ekilibr) *m*, equilibrium; [equi]poise; balance; b. of power (*Pol.*). **équilibrer** (bre) *v.t*, to equilibrate, poise, balance, counterbalance.

équinoxe (ekinɔks) *m*, equinox. **équinoxial, e** (ksjal) *a*, equinoctial.

équipage (ekipa:ʒ) *m*, crew (*ship*); outfit, rig; set; train; equipage, turnout; plight. *~ de chasse*, hunt. **équipe** (kip) *f*, train (*of boats*); shift, gang, corps, squad; crew (*boat*); team, side (*Sport*). **équipée** (pe) *f*, escapade, lark. **équipement** (pmɑ̃) *m*, equipment; outfit. **équiper** (pe) *v.t*, to equip, fit out, rig [out].

équitable† (ekitabl) *a*, equitable, fair, just. **équitation** (ekitasjɔ̃) *f*, riding, horsemanship. **équité** (ekite) *f*, equity, fairness.

équivalent, e (ekivalɑ̃, ɑ̃:t) *a. & m*, equivalent. **équivaloir** (lwa:r) *v.i.ir*, to be equivalent; be tantamount.

équivoque (ekivɔk) *a*, equivocal; ambiguous, dubious, questionable. ¶ *f*, equivocation, ambiguity, prevarication. **équivoquer** (ke) *v.i*, to equivocate, prevaricate.

érable (erabl) *m*, maple. *~ madré*, bird's-eye maple.

éradication (eradikasjɔ̃) *f*, eradication.

érafler (erɑfle) *v.t*, to scratch, graze; scrape (*Golf*). **éraflure** (fly:r) *f*, scratch.

éraillé, e (eraje) *p.a*, frayed; husky, hoarse; bloodshot. **érailler** (je) *v.t*, to fray.

ère (ɛ:r) *f*, era, epoch.

Érèbe (l') (erɛb) *m*, Erebus.

érection (erɛksjɔ̃) *f*, erection; raising.

éreinter (erɛ̃te) *v.t*, to break the back of; tire out, fag, knock up; lash (*fig.*), slate, pull to pieces.

érésipèle (erezipɛl) *m*, erysipelas.

ergot (ɛrgo) *m*, spur (*bird*); snug, lug; pin; ergot (*Bot. & Med.*). **ergoté, e** (gɔte) *a*, spurred (*bird*). **ergoter** (te) *v.i*, to cavil, quibble.

Érié (le lac) (erje), Lake Erie.

ériger (eriʒe) *v.t*, to erect, put up; raise, set up.

ermitage (ɛrmita:ʒ) *m*, hermitage. **ermite** (mit) *m*, hermit.

éroder (erɔde) *v.t*, to erode. **érosion** (zjɔ̃) *f*, erosion.

érotique (erɔtik) *a*, erotic; amatory.

errant, e (ɛrɑ̃, ɑ̃:t) *a*, wandering; roving; stray; errant. **erratique** (ratik) *a*, erratic (*Geol., Med., &c*).

erratum (eratɔm) *m*, erratum.

erre (ɛ:r) *f*, [head]way (*Naut.*); (*pl.*) track, spoor; (*pl.*) footsteps (*fig.*). **errements** (ɛrmɑ̃) *m.pl*, ways, methods. **errer** (ɛre) *v.i*, to wander, roam, rove, stroll, stray; err. **erreur** (rœ:r) *f*, error, mistake; fallacy. *~ de calcul*, miscalculation. *~ de nom*, misnomer. *~ de (ou sur la) personne*, mistaken identity. *~ typographique*, misprint. **erroné, e** (rɔne) *a*, erroneous, wrong, mistaken.

éructation (eryktasjɔ̃) *f*, eructation, belch[ing]. **éructer** (te) *v.i*, to eruct, belch.

érudit, e (erydi, it) *a*, erudite, scholarly, learned. ¶ *m*, scholar, learned man. **érudition** (disjɔ̃) *f*, erudition, learning, scholarship.

éruption (erypsjɔ̃) *f*, eruption; rash. **érysipèle** (erizipɛl) *m*, erysipelas.

ès (ɛs) *pr*, of; in.

escabeau (ɛskabo) *m. & escabelle* (bɛl) *f*, stool.

escadre (ɛska:dr) *f*, squadron (*Nav.*). **escadrille** (kadri:j) *f*, flotilla (*Nav.*); squadron (*air*). **escadron** (drɔ̃) *m*, squadron (*Cavalry*).

escalade (ɛskalad) *f*, scaling. **escalader** (de) *v.t*, to scale, climb [over].

escale (ɛskal) *f*, call (*Ship.*); port of call. *faire ~*, to call.

escalier (ɛskalje) *m*, stair[s], staircase. *~ d'honneur*, grand staircase. *~ roulant*, moving staircase, escalator. *~ tournant*, spiral (*or* winding) stairs.

escamotage (ɛskamɔta:ʒ) *m*, juggling, conjuring. **escamoter** (te) *v.t*, to conjure away, spirit away; filch; (*abs.*) to juggle, conjure. **escamoteur** (tœ:r) *m*, juggler, conjuror, -er; light-fingered gentleman.

escampette (ɛskɑ̃pɛt) *f*: *prendre la poudre d'~*, to bolt, skedaddle. **escapade** (kapad) *f*, escapade, prank, lark.

escarbille (ɛskarbi:j) *f*, [coal] cinder.

escarbot (ɛskarbo) *m*, dung beetle.

escargot (ɛskargo) *m*, (*edible*) snail.

escarmouche (ɛskarmuʃ) *f*, skirmish. **escarmoucher** (ʃe) *v.i*, to skirmish.

escarpe (ɛskarp) *f*, [e]scarp. ¶ *m*, cut-throat, desperado. **escarpé, e** (pe) *a*, precipitous, steep, bluff. **escarpement** (pəmɑ̃) *m*, steepness; escarpment; slope.

escarpin (ɛskarpɛ̃) *m*, pump (*dress shoe*).

escarpolette (ɛskarpɔlɛt) *f*, swing (*child's*).

escarre (ɛska:r) *f*, slough, scab.

Escaut (l') (ɛsko) *m*, the Scheldt.

escient (ɛsjɑ̃) *m*, knowledge. *à bon ~*, knowingly, wittingly.

esclaffer (s') (ɛsklafe) *v.pr*, to burst out laughing.

esclandre (ɛsklɑ̃:dr) *m*, scandal, scene.

esclavage (εsklava:ȝ) *m*, slavery, bondage, thraldom. esclave (kla:v) *n*, slave, thrall.

escobarder (εskɔbarde) *v.i*, to shuffle.

escogriffe (εskɔgrif) *m*, gawk, lout.

escompte (εskɔ̃:t) *m*, discount; discounting. escompter (kɔ̃te) *v.t*,. to discount; cash (*a cheque for someone*); anticipate; bank on.

escorte (εskɔrt) *f*, escort; convoy. escorter (te) *v.t*, to escort; convoy.

escouade (εskwad) *f*, squad; gang.

escrime (εskrim) *f*, fencing, swordsmanship. s'escrimer (me) *v.pr*, to try hard.

escroc (εskro) *m*, swindler, sharper, crook. escroquer (krɔke) *v.t. & abs*, to swindle, swindle out of.

espace (εspas) *m*, space; room; (*f.*) space (*Typ.*). espacer (se) *v.t*, to space.

espadon (εspadɔ̃) *m*, swordfish.

espadrille (εspadri:j) *f*, canvas shoe with hempen sole.

Espagne (l') (εspaɲ) *f*, Spain. espagnol, e (ɲɔl) *a. & (language) m*, Spanish. E~, *n*, Spaniard. espagnolette (lεt) *f*, espagnolette.

espalier (εspalje) *m*, espalier.

espar (εspa:r) *m*, spar (*Naut.*); handspike (*Mil.*).

espèce (εspεs) *f*, kind, sort, species; case in point (*Law*); (*pl.*) cash, coin, specie. *l'~ animale*, the brute creation. *l'~ humaine*, mankind. *~s sonnantes*, hard cash.

espérance (εsperã:s) *f*, hope, expectation; (*pl.*) promise. espérer (re) *v.t. & abs*, to hope for, expect; trust; hope.

espiègle (εspjεgl) *a*, roguish, mischievous, impish, elfish; arch. ¶ *n*, rogue (*playfully*). espièglerie (glǝri) *f*, roguishness, mischief; prank.

espion, ne (εspjɔ̃, ɔn) *n*, spy. espionnage (ɔna:ȝ) *m*, espionage, spying. espionner (ne) *v.t. & abs*, to spy upon; watch; spy.

esplanade (εsplanad) *f*, esplanade, parade.

espoir (εspwa:r) *m*, hope, expectation.

esprit (εspri) *m*, spirit; ghost; mind; nous; feeling; sense; head; wit; temper. *l'~ de caste*, class consciousness. *~ de corps*, esprit de corps; team spirit. *~ fort*, free thinker. *le Saint-Esprit* ou *l'Esprit-Saint*, the Holy Ghost, the Holy Spirit.

esquif (εskif) *m*, skiff.

esquille (εski:j) *f*, splinter (*of bone*).

esquisse (εskis) *f*, sketch; outline. esquisser (se) *v.t*, to sketch, &c.

esquive (εski:v) *f*, slip (*Box.*), dodging. esquiver (kive) *v.t*, to avoid, evade; dodge, slip. s'~, to slip away.

essai (εsε) *m*, test[ing], trial; attempt; try (*Rugby*); assay[ing]; essay.

essaim (εsε̃) *m*, swarm (*bees, &c*). essaimer (εsεme) *v.i*, to swarm; branch out (*fig.*).

essanger (εsãȝe) *v.t*, to soak (*dirty linen*).

essarter (εsarte) *v.t*, to clear; grub up.

essayer (εsεje) *v.t*, to try, essay, endeavour,

attempt; try on (*clothes*); test, assay. s'~ à, to try one's hand (*or* skill) at. essayeur, euse (jœ:r, ø:z) *n*, assayer; fitter (*clothes*). essayiste (jist) *n*, essayist.

esse (εs) *f*, S; S hook; linchpin.

essence (εsã:s) *f*, essence; spirit; [essential] oil; kind *or* species (*of tree or wood*). *~ de bergamote*, bergamot oil. *~ de roses*, otto of roses, attar [of roses]. *~ [minérale]*, petrol, motor spirit. essentiel, le† (sãsjεl) *a*, essential, material. ¶ *m*, essential, main point.

esseulé, e (εsœle) *p.p*, lone[some].

essieu (εsjø) *m*, axle, axletree.

essor (εsɔ:r) *m*, flight, soaring, wing; play; scope; progress, strides.

essorer (εsɔre) *v.t*, to dry; wring (*washing*). essoreuse (rø:z) *f*, wringer.

essoriller (εsɔrije) *v.t*, to crop.

essouffler (εsufle) *v.t*, to blow, wind.

essuie-glace (εsɥiglas) *m*, wind-screen wiper. essuie-main, *m*, [hand] towel. essuieplume, *m*, penwiper. essuie-verres, *m*, glass cloth. essuyer (sɥije) *v.t*, to wipe [up], dry; mop up; endure, go through; experience, meet with.

est (εst) *m*, east.

estacade (εstakad) *f*, wing dam; jetty; boom (*harbour*); coal stage; tip.

estafette (εstafεt) *f*, courier; dispatch rider.

estafilade (εstafilad) *f*, gash; rent.

estame (εstam) *f*, worsted (*fabric*).

estaminet (εstaminε) *m*, small café & public house.

estampe (εstã:p) *f*, print, engraving; swage. estamper (tãpe) *v.t*, to stamp; emboss; swage; drop-forge; rub (*inscription*). estampille (εstãpi:j) *f*, stamp; mark; mark of origin. estampiller (pije) *v.t*, to stamp; mark.

esthétique (εstetik) *a*, aesthetic(al).

estimation (εstimasjɔ̃) *f*, estimate, valuation; dead reckoning (*Naut.*). estime (tim) *f*, esteem, estimation; dead reckoning (*Naut.*). estimer (me) *v.t*, to estimate; value; esteem; deem; reckon.

estival, e (εstival) *a*, summer (*att.*). estiver (ve) *v.t*, to summer (*cattle*).

estoc (εstɔk) *m*, point (*sword*); stock (*tree*). estocade (kad) *f*, thrust (*Fenc.*). estocader (de) *v.t*, to thrust.

estomac (εstɔma) *m*, stomach; pluck. estomaquer (make) *v.t*, to take (*someone's*) breath away; offend.

estompe (εstɔ̃:p) *f*, stump (*Art*). estomper (tɔ̃pe) *v.t*, to stump; tone down (*fig.*).

Estonie (l') (εstoni) *f*, Esthonia.

estouffade (εstufad) *f*, steaming (*Cook.*).

estrade (εstrad) *f*, platform, stage; dais.

estragon (εstragɔ̃) *m*, tarragon.

estropié, e (εstrɔpje) *n*, cripple. estropier (pje) *v.t*, to cripple, lame; maim; murder (*language*).

estuaire (εstɥε:r) *m*, estuary, firth.

esturgeon (ɛstyrʒɔ̃) *m*, sturgeon.
et (e) *c*. (*abb*. &), and, &. ~ . . . ~ . . . , both . . . and . . . . ~ *ainsi de suite*, and so on; and so forth. ~ *patati*, ~ *patata* (patati, ta), and so on, and so forth.
étable (etabl) *f*, (*cow*) shed, house; sty. **établer** (ble) *v.t*, to stable, stall; sty.
établi (etabli) *m*, [work] bench, stand. **établir** (bliːr) *v.t*, to establish; set up; set (*a sail*); lay down; settle; draw [up], make out; strike (*balance*); prove; substantiate. **établissement** (blismã) *m*, establishment, &c; institution; capital expenditure. *É~s des Détroits*, Straits Settlements.
étage (etaːʒ) *m*, floor, stor[e]y; stage, level; step; tier; rank, degree; measures (*Geol.*). **étager** (taʒe) *v.t*, to range; terrace; spread. **étagère** (ʒɛːr) *f*, [set of] shelves; whatnot; dresser. ~ *de cheminée*, overmantel.
étai (etɛ) *m*, shore, prop, post; stay.
étain (etɛ̃) *m*, tin; pewter.
étal (etal) *m*, stall (*butcher's*); butcher's shop.
étalage (laːʒ) *m*, (*shop*) window [show]; window dressing; show; display; stall. **étalagiste** (laʒist) *n*, frontsman; stall holder; window dresser.
étale (etal) *a.inv*, slack (*water*) (*Naut.*).
étaler (etale) *v.t*, to expose for sale; show; show off, flaunt, air; display; lay out; spread [out]; stem (*the tide*). **s'~**, to sprawl.
étalon (etalɔ̃) *m*, stallion, stud horse; standard (*of values*). **étalonner** (lɔne) *v.t*, to stamp (*weights*, &c); rate; standardize.
étambot (etãbo) *m*, sternpost (*ship*).
étamer (etame) *v.t*, to tin; silver (*mirror*).
étamine (etamin) *f*, bolting cloth; filter cloth; stamen (*Bot.*). ~ *à pavillon*, bunting.
étamper (etãpe) *v.t*, to stamp, press; swage; drop-forge.
étanche (etãːʃ) *a*, tight; water-tight; impervious, sta[u]nch. **étancher** (tãʃe) *v.t*, to sta[u]nch, stop; make water-tight; dry; quench, slake.
étançon (etãsɔ̃) *m*, shore; stanchion. **étançonner** (sɔne) *v.t*, to shore [up].
étang (etã) *m*, pond, pool.
étape (etap) *f*, stage, stopping place.
état (eta) *m*, state; condition; frame (*of mind*); plight; repair; order; fettle, trim; status; position, posture; profession, occupation; statement, account, return, list; state (*stage of engraved or etched plate*). *en* [*bon*] ~ *de navigabilité*, seaworthy; airworthy. ~ *de siège*, martial law (*in a town*). ~ *des malades*, sick list. **État**, *m*, State, government. *les ~s des Balkans*, the Balkan States. *l'~ libre d'Irlande*, the Irish Free State. *les ~s malais fédérés*, *non fédérés*, the Federated, Unfederated, Malay States. *l'~ mandchou*, Manchukuo. *les ~s-Unis* [*d'Amérique*], the United States [of America]. **étatisme** (tism) *m*,

State socialism, nationalism. **État-major** (maʒɔːr) *m*, staff (*Mil.*); [staff] headquarters; senior officers, executive.
étau (eto) *m*, vice (*tool*). ~*-limeur* (limœːr), shaping machine.
étayer (etɛje) *v.t*, to shore [up]; prop, support.
et cætera (etsetera) *phrase & m*. (*abb*. etc.), et cetera, etc., &c.
été (ete) *m*, summer; prime [of life].
éteignoir (etɛɲwaːr) *m*, extinguisher (*light*); damper, wet blanket (*fig., pers.*). **éteindre** (tɛ̃ːdr) *v.t.ir*, to extinguish, put out; silence (*enemy's fire*); slake, slack; quench; pay off; soften. ~ *la lumière*, ~ *l'électricité*, to switch off (*or* turn off) the light. **s'~**, to go out (*light*); pass away; die [out]. **éteint**, **e** (tɛ̃, ɛ̃ːt) *p.a*, extinct; out; dull, lack-lustre.
étendage (etãdaːʒ) *m*, hanging out (*washing*); spreading; clothes lines; lying at full length. **étendard** (daːr) *m*, standard, flag, colours. **étendoir** (dwaːr) *m*, clothes line; drying yard. **étendre** (tãːdr) *v.t*, to spread, extend; expand; widen; stretch [out]; reach [out]; lay [out]; hang out; dilute. **s'~**, to extend; spread; stretch; reach; expatiate, enlarge. **étendu**, **e** (tãdy) *a*, extensive, wide, far-reaching; great; outstretched. **étendue** (dy) *f*, extent; area; compass; stretch, expanse, sweep, tract; reach; range; scope; length.
éternel, **le†** (etɛrnɛl) *a*, eternal, everlasting; never-ending. **éterniser** (nize) *v.t*, to etern[al]ize; protract. **s'~**, to last (*or* stay) for ever. **éternité** (te) *f*, eternity.
éternuement (etɛrnymã) *m*, sneezing; sneeze. **éternuer** (nɥe) *v.i*, to sneeze.
étêter (etɛte) *v.t*, to top, poll; take the head off.
éteule (etœl) *f*, stubble.
éther (etɛːr) *m*, ether. **éthéré**, **e** (tere) *a*, ethereal.
Éthiopie (l') (etjɔpi) *f*, Ethiopia. **éthiopien**, **ne** (pjɛ̃, ɛn) *a. & É~**, *n*, Ethiopian.
éthique (etik) *a*, ethical. ¶ *f*, ethics.
ethnographie (ɛtnɔgrafi) *f*, ethnography. **ethnologie** (lɔʒi) *f*, ethnology. **ethnologique** (ʒik) *a*, ethnologic(al). **ethnologue** (lɔg) *m*, ethnologist.
éthyle (etil) *m*, ethyl.
étiage (etjaːʒ) *m*, low water; low water mark (*river*).
étinceler (etɛ̃sle) *v.i*, to sparkle, glitter, glisten, flash. **étincelle** (sɛl) *f*, spark; sparkle, flash.
étioler (etjɔle) *v.t*, to etiolate, blanch. **s'~**, to droop, wilt.
étique (etik) *a*, emaciated, skinny.
étiqueter (etikte) *v.t*, to label; docket; ticket. **étiquette** (kɛt) *f*, label; docket; tally; ticket; etiquette. ~ *volante*, tie-on label, tag label.
étirer (etire) *v.t*, to stretch, draw [out].

étoffe (etɔf) f, stuff; fabric; material; grit (fig.); establishment charges (printer's). ~ à carreaux, ~ en damier, check [material]. **étoffé** (fe) p.a, stuffed; stocky. **étoffer** (fe) v.t, to use sufficient material in; stuff; fill out.

étoile (etwal) f, star; asterisk. ~ de mer, starfish. ~ du matin, ~ matinière (matinjɛːr), morning star. ~ tombante, ~ filante, shooting s., falling s. à la belle ~, in the open. **étoilé, e** (le) a, starry; starli[gh]t; starred.

étole (etɔl) f, stole.

étonnant, e (etɔnɑ̃, ɑ̃ːt) a, astonishing, amazing, surprising; wonderful. **étonnamment** (namɑ̃) ad, astonishingly, &c. **étonnement** (nmɑ̃) m, astonishment, &c. **étonner** (ne) v.t, to astonish, amaze, surprise. **s'~**, to be astonished, wonder, marvel.

étouffant, e (etufɑ̃, ɑ̃ːt) a, stifling, sultry; stuffy.

étouffée (etufe) f, steaming (Cook.).

étouffer (etufe) v.t. & i, to choke, stifle; smother; quell; hush up. **étouffoir** (fwaːr) m, charcoal extinguisher; damper (piano).

étoupe (etup) f, tow, junk, oakum. **étouper** (pe) v.t, to caulk.

étoupille (etupiːj) f, friction tube; fuse.

étourderie (eturdəri) f, thoughtlessness. **étourdi, e** (di) a, thoughtless, heedless; flighty. à l'étourdie & **étourdiment** (dimɑ̃) ad, thoughtlessly. **étourdir** (diːr) v.t, to stun; deafen; din; make dizzy; daze; deaden; parboil. **s'~**, to forget (or drown) one's troubles. **étourdissement** (dismɑ̃) m, dizziness, giddiness; stupefaction.

étourneau (eturno) m, starling (bird); foolish youth.

étrange† (etrɑ̃ːʒ) a, strange, odd, queer; quaint. **étranger, ère** (trɑ̃ʒe, ɛːr) a, foreign; strange; unfamiliar; extraneous; alien, irrelevant. ¶ n, foreigner, alien; stranger. ¶ m, foreign parts. à l'~, ad, abroad. de l'~, from abroad. **étrangeté** (ʒte) f, strangeness, oddness; quaintness.

étranglement (etrɑ̃gləmɑ̃) m, strangulation; narrow. **étrangler** (gle) v.t, to strangle, throttle, choke; narrow; squeeze; strangulate; (v.i.) to choke.

étrave (etraːv) f, stem (ship).

être (ɛːtr) m, being; creature; thing; reality; stock (tree); (pl.) ins & outs (of a house). ¶ v.i.ir, to be; belong; come; have. y ~, to be at home.

étrécir (etresiːr) v.t. & i. & **s'~**, to narrow, shrink, contract.

étreindre (etrɛ̃ːdr) v.t.ir, to clasp, hug, grip; wring; bind. **étreinte** (trɛ̃ːt) f, grip, grasp; hug, embrace.

étrenne (etren) f, first use; (pl.) new year's gift, han[d]sel; Christmas box; C. present. (In Fr. presents are given on or about Jan. 1). **étrenner** (trene) v.t, to be the first customer of; use (or wear) for the first time, han[d]sel.

étrésillon (etrezijɔ̃) m, strut, brace; flying shore.

étrier (etrie) m, stirrup; U bolt; strap.

étrille (etriːj) f, currycomb. **étriller** (trije) v.t, to curry; drub; fleece.

étriper (etripe) v.t, to gut.

étriqué, e (etrike) a, scant[y], narrow; cramped. **étriquer** (ke) v.t, to skimp.

étrivière (etrivjɛːr) f, stirrup leather; (pl.) thrashing.

étroit, e† (etrwa, at) a, narrow; limited; close; tight; strict. **étroitesse** (tɛs) f, narrowness, &c.

étude (etyd) f, study; preparation (Sch.); survey; (lawyer's) office, chambers; practice. **étudiant, e** (djɑ̃, ɑ̃ːt) n, student. **étudier** (dje) v.t & i. & t, to study; read; survey.

étui (etɥi) m, case, box; cover.

étuve (etyːv) f, drying stove; oven (fig.). ~ humide, steam room (bath). ~ sèche, hot room, sweating r. (bath). **étuvée** (tyve) f, steaming (Cook.). **étuver** (ve) v.t, to stove; stew; foment (Med.).

étymologie (etimɔlɔʒi) f, etymology. **étymologique†** (ʒik) a, etymologic(al).

eucalyptus (økalipty:s) m, eucalyptus.

Eucharistie (økaristi) f, Eucharist, holy communion.

eugénie (øʒeni) f, eugenics. **eugénique** (nik) a, eugenic.

euh (ø) i, hem! hum! h'm!

eunuque (ønyk) m, eunuch.

euphémique (øfemik) a, euphemistic. **euphémisme** (mism) m, euphemism.

euphonie (øfɔni) f, euphony. **euphonique** (nik) a, euphonic, euphonious.

Euphrate (l') (øfrat) m, the Euphrates.

Europe (l') (ørɔp) f, Europe. **européen, ne** (peẽ, ɛn) a. & E~, n, European.

eux (ø) pn.m.pl. See lui.

évacuer (evakɥe) v.t & abs, to evacuate, void, clear out.

évader (s') (evade) v.pr, to escape, get away.

évaluation (evalɥasjɔ̃) f, valuation, estimate; casting off (Typ.). **évaluer** (lɥe) v.t, to value, estimate; cast off.

évanescent, e (evansɑ̃, ɑ̃ːt) a, evanescent.

évangélique† (evɑ̃ʒelik) a, evangelic(al). **évangéliste** (list) m, evangelist. **évangile** & **É~** (ʒil) m, gospel.

évanouir (s') (evanwiːr) v.pr, to faint, swoon; vanish, fade away.

évaporation (evapɔrasjɔ̃) f, evaporation. **évaporé, e** (re) n, feather-brained creature. **évaporer** (re) v.t, to evaporate; vent. **s'~**, to evaporate.

évaser (evase) v.t, to flare, bellmouth.

évasif, ive† (evazif, iːv) a, evasive. **évasion** (zjɔ̃) f, escape, flight.

évêché (evɛʃe) m, bishopric; see; bishop's house.

éveil (eve:j) *m*, alert, guard; warning; awakening (*fig.*). **éveillé, e** (veje) *a*, wide-awake; perky. **éveiller** (je) *v.t*, to wake [up]. **s'~**, to awaken (*fig.*).

événement (evenmã) *m*, event, occurrence, incident; emergency; outcome, issue.

évent (evã) *m*, [open] air; vent; air hole; flaw; flatness (*liquor*). **éventail** (ta:j) *m*, fan. **éventaire** (tɛ:r) *m*, flat basket; pavement display (*shop*). **éventé, e** (te) *p.a*, stale, flat, dead; giddy, flighty. **éventer** (te) *v.t*, to fan; air; turn over; flatten; fill (*sail*); open; get wind of; let out.

éventrer (evãtre) *v.t*, to rip open, r. up; disembowel, eviscerate.

éventualité (evãtɥalite) *f*, eventuality, contingency. **éventuel, le†** (tɥɛl) *a*, eventual, contingent.

évêque (evɛ:k) *m*, bishop.

évertuer (s') (evɛrtɥe) *v.pr*, to exert oneself, strive.

éviction (eviksjɔ̃) *f*, eviction.

évidence (evidã:s) *f*, evidence. **en ~**, in e., conspicuous. **évident, e** (dã, ã:t) *a*, evident, obvious, plain. **évidemment** (damã) *ad*, evidently, &c.

évider (evide) *v.t*, to hollow out; cut away; groove, flute.

évier (evje) *m*, sink (*scullery*).

évincer (evɛ̃se) *v.t*, to evict; oust, turn out.

évitable (evitabl) *a*, avoidable. **évitage** (ta:ʒ) *m*. ou **évitée** (te) *f*, sea room; swinging. **évitement** (tmã) *m*. ou *voie d'~* (*Rly*), passing place, turnout, shunting loop. **éviter** (te) *v.t*, to avoid, shun; eschew; evade, dodge, steer clear of; help; (*v.i. & abs.*) to swing (*Naut.*). *~ de la tête*, to duck.

évocation (evɔkasjɔ̃) *f*, evocation, calling up, raising.

évoluer (evɔlɥe) *v.i*, to perform evolutions, manœuvre; evolve. **évolution** (lysjɔ̃) *f*, evolution.

évoquer (evɔke) *v.t*, to evoke, conjure up.

ex- (ɛks) *pr*, ex-; ex; late. *~-dividende*, *~-exercice*, ex dividend. *~-professeur*, ex-professor.

exacerber (ɛgzasɛrbe) *v.t*, to exacerbate.

exact, e† (ɛgzakt) *a*, exact, accurate, correct; punctual. **exaction** (ksjɔ̃) *f*, exaction. **exactitude** (tityd) *f*, exactness, exactitude, accuracy; punctuality.

ex æquo (ɛgzeko) *m*, tie (*Sport*). *être* [*classé*] *~*, to tie; be bracketed (*exams*).

exagération (ɛgzaʒerasjɔ̃) *f*, exaggeration. **exagérer** (re) *v.t. & abs*, to exaggerate; overstate; overdo.

exalter (ɛgzalte) *v.t*, to exalt; extol; excite, inflame.

examen (ɛgzamɛ̃) *m*, examination; scrutiny. **examinateur, trice** (minatœ:r, tris) *n*, examiner. **examiner** (ne) *v.t*, to examine; overhaul; look into.

exaspérer (ɛgzaspere) *v.t*, to exasperate; aggravate (*Med.*).

exaucer (ɛgzose) *v.t*, to hear (*prayer*), grant.

excavateur (ɛkskavatœ:r) *m*, excavator, digger, shovel, navvy. **excavation** (sjɔ̃) *f*, excavation; pot hole.

excédant, e (ɛksedã, ã:t) *a*, surplus; overbearing. **excédent** (dã) *m*, surplus, excess, over[plus]. *~ de bagages*, excess luggage. **excéder** (de) *v.t*, to exceed; weary, tire.

excellemment (ɛksɛlamã) *ad*, excellently. **excellence** (lã:s) *f*, excellence; choiceness. *par ~*, pre-eminently. *Son E~*, *f*, His Excellency. **excellent, e** (lã, ã:t) *a*, excellent. **exceller** (le) *v.i*, to excel.

excentricité (ɛksãtrisite) *f*, eccentricity; throw; remoteness. **excentrique** (trik) *a*, eccentric; outlying. ¶ (*Mech.*) *m*, eccentric, cam.

excepté (ɛksɛpte) *pr*, except[ing], save, but, barring. **excepter** (te) *v.t*, to except. **exception** (sjɔ̃) *f*, exception; plea (*Law*). *~ péremptoire*, demurrer. **exceptionnel, le†** (ɔnɛl) *a*, exceptional.

excès (ɛksɛ) *m*, excess; abuse; violence. *~ de pose*, overexposure (*Phot.*). **excessif, ive†** (sɛsif, i:v) *a*, excessive; fulsome; undue.

excitant (ɛksitã) *m*, stimulant. **excitation** (tasjɔ̃) *f*, excitation; incitement; excitement. **exciter** (te) *v.t*, to excite; incite; stir up; urge; rouse; stimulate, fan.

exclamation (ɛksklamasjɔ̃) *f*, exclamation; ejaculation. **s'exclamer** (me) *v.pr*, to exclaim against.

exclure (ɛkskly:r) *v.t.ir*, to exclude; shut out debar. **exclusif, ive†** (klyzif, i:v) *a*, exclusive; sole. **exclusion** (zjɔ̃) *f*, exclusion. **exclusivité** (zivite) *f*, exclusive (*or* sole) right(s).

excommunier (ɛkskɔmynje) *v.t*, to excommunicate.

excrément (ɛkskremã) *m*, excrement; scum (*fig.*).

excroissance (ɛkskrwasã:s) *f*, excrescence.

excursion (ɛkskyrsjɔ̃) *f*, excursion, trip, tour, outing. *~ à pied*, walking tour, hike. *~ accompagnée*, conducted tour. **excursionniste** (ɔnist) *n*, excursionist; tripper.

excuse (ɛksky:s) *f*, excuse; (*pl.*) apology. **excuser** (kyze) *v.t*, to excuse.

exeat (ɛgzeat) *m*, exeat; dismissal.

exécrable† (ɛgzekrabl) *a*, execrable. **exécrer** (kre) *v.t*, to execrate.

exécutable (ɛgzekytabl) *a*, workable, practicable. **exécutant, e** (tã, ã:t) *n*, performer (*Mus.*). **exécuter** (te) *v.t*, to execute; carry out; perform; fulfil; enforce; expel; buy in against, sell out against (*Stk Ex.*); distrain upon, sell up. **s'~**, to pay up; yield. **exécuteur** [*des hautes œuvres*] (tœ:r) *m*, executioner. **exécuteur (trice)** *testamentaire*, executor, trix. **exécution** (sjɔ̃) *f*, execution, &c. **exécutoire** (twa:r) *a*, executory; enforceable.

exemplaire (ɛgzãplɛ:r) *a*, exemplary. ¶ *m*, copy, specimen. *~ du souffleur*, prompt

book. **exemple** (ɛɑ̃:pl) *m*, example; lead;
illustration; instance; copy.

exempt, e (ɛgzɑ̃, ɑ̃:t) *a*, exempt, free. ¶ *m*,
bye, odd man (*Ten.*, &c). **exempter**
(zɑ̃te) *v.t*, to exempt, free; excuse. *s'~
de*, to abstain from, get out of. **exemption**
(zɑ̃psjɔ̃) *f*, exemption; immunity; freedom.

exercer (ɛgzɛrse) *v.t*, to exercise; train; drill;
practise; ply (*trade*); exert; wield (*power*);
try (*patience*); inspect (*Excise*). **exercice**
(sis) *m*, exercise; drill[ing]; practice; office;
tenure (*of office*); inspection; trading;
[financial] year, [accounting] period. *~
de doigté*, five-finger exercise. *~s de tir*,
musketry (*Mil.*).

exergue (ɛgzɛrg) *m*, exergue.

exfolier (s') (ɛksfɔlje) *v.pr*, to exfoliate.

exhalaison (ɛgzalɛzɔ̃) *f*, exhalation (*mist*).
exhalation (lasjɔ̃) *f*, exhalation (*act*).
exhaler (le) *v.t*, to exhale; vent; reek with,
reek of.

exhausser (ɛgzose) *v.t*, to raise.

exhiber (ɛgzibe) *v.t*, to exhibit, produce,
show. **exhibition** (bisjɔ̃) *f*, exhibition, &c.

exhorter (ɛgzɔrte) *v.t*, to exhort, urge.

exhumer (ɛgzyme) *v.t*, to exhume, disinter;
rake up.

exigeant, e (ɛgziʒɑ̃, ɑ̃:t) *a*, particular, exact-
ing, hard to please. **exigence** (ʒɑ̃:s) *f*,
unreasonableness; requirement; exigence,
-cy. **exiger** (ʒe) *v.t*, to exact, require,
demand; call for. **exigibilité** (ʒibilite) *f*,
[re]payability; demand; current liability.
exigible (bl) *a*, [re]payable; claimable,
exigible.

exigu, ë (ɛgzigy) *a*, exiguous, scanty, jejune,
small, diminutive. **exiguïté** (gɥite) *f*,
exiguity, &c.

exil (ɛgzil) *m*, exile. **exilé, e** (le) *n*, exile.
exiler (le) *v.t*, to exile.

existence (ɛgzistɑ̃:s) *f*, existence; life; stock
(*Com.*). **exister** (te) *v.i*, to exist, be; be
extant.

ex-libris (ɛkslibri:s) *m*, book plate, ex-libris.

exode (ɛgzɔd) *m*, exodus, flight. *l'E~*,
Exodus (*Bible*).

exonérer (ɛgzɔnere) *v.t*, to exonerate, exempt.

exorbitamment (ɛgzɔrbitamɑ̃) *ad*, exorbi-
tantly. **exorbitant, e** (tɑ̃, ɑ̃:t) *a*, exorbitant, extravagant.

exorciser (ɛgzɔrsize) *v.t*, to exorcise.

exorde (ɛgzɔrd) *m*, exordium; beginning.

exotique (ɛgzɔtik) *a*, exotic; foreign.

expansif, ive (ɛkspɑ̃sif, i:v) *a*, expansive;
effusive. **expansion** (sjɔ̃) *f*, expansion.

expatrier (ɛkspatrie) *v.t*, to expatriate.

expectant, e (ɛkspɛktɑ̃, ɑ̃:t) *a*, expectant;
wait-&-see. **expectative** (tati:v) *f*, expectation, expectancy.

expectorer (ɛkspɛktɔre) *v.t. & abs*, to expectorate.

expédient, e (ɛkspedjɑ̃, ɑ̃:t) *a*, expedient.
¶ *m*, expedient, resource, shift.

expédier (ɛkspedje) *v.t*, to expedite; dispose
of; bolt (*food*); dispatch, send, forward,
ship; copy & authenticate (*Law*). *~ [en
douane]*, to clear (*a ship*) [outwards].
expéditeur, trice (ditœ:r, tris) *n*, sender;
(*m.*) shipper; consignor; forwarding agent.
expéditif, ive (tif, i:v) *a*, expeditious.
expédition (sjɔ̃) *f*, expedition; disposal;
dispatch, sending, forwarding; shipment,
consignment; transit; adventure; clearance [outwards]; copy; (*pl.*) [ship's clear-
ance] papers. **expéditionnaire** (onɛ:r) *a*,
expeditionary. ¶ *m*, sender; dispatch
clerk; shipping clerk; copying clerk.

expérience (ɛksperjɑ̃:s) *f*, experiment; experience. **expérimental, et** (rimɑ̃tal) *a*,
experimental. **expérimenter** (te) *v.t*, to
try; (*abs.*) to experiment.

expert, e (ɛkspɛr, ɛrt) *a*, expert, skilled.
¶ *m*, expert; valuer; surveyor. *~-comp-
table*, professional accountant. **expertise**
(pɛrti:z) *f*, survey; examination; report.
expertiser (tize) *v.t*, to survey.

expier (ɛkspje) *v.t*, to expiate, atone for.
expiration (ɛkspirasjɔ̃) *f*, expiration; expiry.
expirer (re) *v.t. & i*, to expire.

explétif, ive (ɛkspletif, i:v) *a*, expletive.

explicatif, ive (ɛksplikatif, i:v) *a*, explanatory.
explication (sjɔ̃) *f*, explanation; construction, rendering. **explicite†** (sit) *a*, explicit.
expliquer (ke) *v.t*, to explain; account for;
construe, render.

exploit (ɛksplwa) *m*, exploit, achievement,
feat; writ. **exploitable** (tabl) *a*, workable;
payable. **exploitant** (tɑ̃) *m*, operator, owner or [his] agent (*mine*, &c). **exploitation**
(tasjɔ̃) *f*, work[ing], operation; mining; exploitation; workings; farming; trading.
~ agricole, farm. **exploiter** (te) *v.t*, to
work, run, operate; farm; mine; exploit;
sweat (*labour*). **exploiteur, euse** (tœ:r, ø:z)
n, exploiter; sweater.

explorateur, trice (ɛksplɔratœ:r, tris) *n*, explorer. **explorer** (re) *v.t*, to explore.

exploser (ɛksploze) *v.i*, to explode. **explosif**
(zif) *m*, explosive. **explosion** (zjɔ̃) *f*, explosion; [out]burst. **explosive** (zi:v) *f*,
explosive (*Gram.*).

exportateur (ɛkspɔrtatœ:r) *m*, exporter.
exportation (sjɔ̃) *f*, export[ation]. **exporter** (te) *v.t*, to export.

exposant, e (ɛkspozɑ̃, ɑ̃:t) *n*, exhibitor;
petitioner (*Law*); (*m.*) exponent, index
(*Math.*). **exposé** (ze) *m*, statement; account. **exposer** (ze) *v.t. & abs*, to expose;
show, display, exhibit; face (*of house*);
open; expound; explain; state. **exposition**
(zisjɔ̃) *f*, exposition; exposure; exhibition;
show; aspect, frontage (*of house*).

exprès, esse (ɛksprɛ, ɛs) *a*, express. **exprès**,
ad, on purpose, purposely. ¶ *m*, express,
e. messenger. [train] **express** (prɛs) *m*,
express [train]. *bateau express*, fast boat.
expressément (prɛsemɑ̃) *ad*, expressly.

expressif, ive (ɛksprɛsif, iːv) a, expressive.
expression (sjɔ̃) f, expression; phrase.
exprimer (prime) v.t, to express; squeeze out; voice.

exproprier (ɛksproprie) v.t, to expropriate.

expulser (ɛkspylse) v.t, to expel, drive out, eject; deport.

expurger (ɛkspyrʒe) v.t, to expurgate, bowdlerize.

exquis, e (ɛkski, iːz) a, exquisite. ¶ m, exquisiteness. exquisément (kizemɑ̃) ad, exquisitely.

exsuder (ɛksyde) v.i, to exude.

extase (ɛkstɑːz) f, ecstasy; trance. s'extasier (tɑzje) v.pr, to go into ecstasies. extatique (tatik) a, ecstatic, rapturous.

extenseur (ɛkstɑ̃sœːr) m, extensor (muscle); chest expander; trouser stretcher. extension (sjɔ̃) f, extension. par ~, in a wider sense.

exténuer (ɛkstenɥe) v.t, to tire out, wear out.

extérieur, e† (ɛksterjœːr) a, exterior, external, outer, outside; outward; foreign. ¶ m, exterior, outside; foreign countries, abroad.

exterminer (ɛkstɛrmine) v.t, to exterminate.

externat (ɛkstɛrna) m, day school. externe (tɛrn) a, external, exterior. pour l'usage ~, for outward application, not to be taken (Med.). ¶ n, day scholar; non-resident assistant to hospital surgeon.

exterritorialité (ɛkstɛritorjalite) f, ex[tra]territoriality.

extincteur [d'incendie] (ɛkstɛ̃ktœːr) m, [fire] extinguisher. extinction (sjɔ̃) f, extinction; slaking; quenching; paying off; loss (of voice). ~ des feux, lights out (Mil.).

extirper (ɛkstirpe) v.t, to extirpate, eradicate.

extorquer (ɛkstorke) v.t, to extort, wring. extorsion (sjɔ̃) f, extortion.

extra (ɛkstra) ad. & m, extra.

extraction (ɛkstraksjɔ̃) f, extraction; winning (Min.); quarrying; birth, parentage.

extrader (ɛkstrade) v.t, to extradite. extradition (disjɔ̃) f, extradition.

extraire (ɛkstrɛːr) v.t.ir, to extract, take out; excerpt; get, win; quarry. extrait (trɛ) m, extract; excerpt. ~s d'auteurs, extracts (or selections) from [the writings or works of] authors. ~ de naissance, birth certificate. ~ mortuaire, death c.

extraordinaire† (ɛkstraordinɛːr) a. & m, extraordinary; special; unusual.

extra-statutaire (ɛkstrastatytɛːr) ad, ultra vires.

extravagance (ɛkstravagɑ̃ːs) f, extravagance; exorbitance; folly. extravagant, e (gɑ̃, ɑ̃ːt) a, extravagant, wild. extravaguer (ge) v.i, to rave.

extrême (ɛkstrɛːm) a & m, extreme (a. & n.); utmost; drastic; dire. ~-onction, f, extreme unction. l'E~-Orient, m, the Far East. extrêmement (trɛmmɑ̃) ad, extremely; exceedingly; intensely. extrémiste (tremist)

n, extremist. extrémité (te) f, extremity; end; tip.

extrinsèque (ɛkstrɛ̃sɛk) a, extrinsic.

exubérance (ɛgzyberɑ̃ːs) f, exuberance; luxuriance. exubérant, e (rɑ̃, ɑ̃ːt) a, exuberant; luxuriant.

exulter (ɛgzylte) v.i, to exult.

ex-voto (ɛksvoto) m, ex voto.

F

fa (fa) m, F (Mus.).

fable (fɑːbl) f, fable; story; byword, laughing stock. fablier (fɑblie) m, fabulist; book of fables.

fabricant (fabrikɑ̃) m, manufacturer, maker. fabricateur, trice (katœːr, tris) n, fabricator; forger. ~ de fausse monnaie, coiner. fabrication (sjɔ̃) f, manufacture; make; work; fabrication. fabrique (brik) f, [manu]factory, works, mill; fabric (edifice); vestry, church council; invention (fig.). fabriquer (ke) v.t, to manufacture, make; coin; fabricate, invent, trump up.

fabuleux, euse† (fabylø, øːz) a, fabulous, fabled. fabuliste (list) m, fabulist.

façade (fasad) f, front, frontage, façade; frontispiece (Arch.).

face (fas) f, face; front; frontage (extent of front); side; obverse, head (coin); aspect. ~ à, facing. en ~, in the face; to one's face. en ~ de, pr, opposite, facing. faire ~ à, to face; keep pace with; front; meet.

face-à-main (fasamɛ̃) m, lorgnette.

facétie (fasesi) f, joke, jest. facétieux, euse (sjø, øːz) a, facetious, waggish, jocular.

facette (fasɛt) f, facet. facetter (te) v.t, to facet.

fâché, e (faʃe) p.a, angry; sorry. fâcher (ʃe) v.t, to make angry, anger; grieve, pain. se ~, to get (or be) angry. fâcherie (ʃri) f, bad feeling; tiff. fâcheux, euse† (ʃø, øːz) a, unfortunate, tiresome, troublesome; sad. ¶ m, unfortunate part; bore, nuisance (pers.).

facial, e (fasjal) a, facial; face (att.). facies (sjeːs) m, facies; cast of features.

facile† (fasil) a, easy; facile; ready; fluent. facilité (lite) f, easiness, ease; facility; fluency; aptitude. faciliter (te) v.t, to facilitate.

façon (fasɔ̃) f, make; workmanship; making; labour; manner, fashion, way, wise, style, pattern; (pl.) manners; (pl.) ceremony, fuss. à ~, jobbing (tailor, &c); own materials made up; (work) given out (materials being supplied), (work, worker). faconde (fakɔːd) f, flow of language.

façonné, e (fasone) p.a, figured (textiles). façonner (ne) v.t, to make; shape, fashion, form, mould; dress. façonnier, ère (nje, ɛːr) a, [over-]ceremonious, fussy.

fac-similé (faksimile) m, facsimile.

factage (fakta:ʒ) *m*, cartage (*parcels*), parcels delivery; porterage. **facteur** (tœːr) *m*, maker (*instruments*); postman; porter (*Rly*); salesman; agent; factor, element. ~ *des télégraphes*, telegraph messenger, t. boy.

factice (faktis) *a*, imitation (*att.*), artificial; factitious; forced; meretricious.

factieux, euse (faksjø, øːz) *a*, factious.

faction (faksjɔ̃) *f*, sentry duty, guard; faction. **factionnaire** (onɛːr) *m*, sentry.

factorerie (faktɔrri) *f*, [foreign *or* colonial] agency.

factotum (faktɔtɔm) *m*, factotum, man Friday.

factrice (faktris) *f*, postwoman.

factum (faktɔm) *m*, diatribe; statement of claim (*Law*).

facture (fakty:r) *f*, invoice, bill; note; treatment (*music, art*); workmanship. ~ *fictive*, pro forma invoice. ~ *générale*, statement [of account]. **facturer** (tyre) *v.t*, to invoice.

facultatif, ive† (fakyltatif, iːv) *a*, optional. **faculté** (te) *f*, faculty; option; right; power; leave; liberty; property; branch [of study]; (*pl.*) means; (*pl.*) cargo, goods (*Marine Insce*).

fadaise[s] (fadɛːz) *f.[pl.]*, twaddle, flummery, rubbish, stuff & nonsense.

fadasse (fadas) *a*, sickly, insipid. **fade** (fad) *a*, insipid, tasteless, flat; mawkish; namby-pamby. **fadeur** (dœːr) *f*, insipidity, &c.

fagot (fago) *m*, faggot; bundle. **fagoter** (gote) *v.t*, to faggot, bundle; dress like a guy.

faiblard, e (fɛbla:r, ard) *a*, weakly. ¶ *n*, weakling. **faible†** (bl) *a*, weak; feeble; low; faint; shallow; slight; thin; light; small; scant[y]; slack; bare. ¶ *m*, weak point; weakness, partiality, sneaking fondness; foible; failing. *les* ~*s*, the weak. **faiblesse** (blɛs) *f*, weakness, &c; swoon. **faiblir** (bliːr) *v.i*, to weaken; slacken; give way; flag, fail.

faïence (fajɑ̃ːs) *f*, earthenware, pottery, crockery, china. **faïencerie** (jɑ̃sri) *f*, pottery [works]; earthenware. **faïencier, ère** (sje, ɛːr) *n*, earthenware, &c, manufacturer *or* dealer.

faille (fa:j) *f*, faille (*fabric*); fault (*Geol.*).

failli (faji) *m*, bankrupt, insolvent. **faillibilité** (bilite) *f*, fallibility. **faillible** (bl) *a*, fallible. **faillir** (jiːr) *v.i.ir*, to fail; to nearly . . .; *to* err. **faillite** (jit) *f*, failure; bankruptcy; insolvency.

faim (fɛ̃) *f*, hunger; starvation. *avoir* ~, *grand-*~, to be hungry, very hungry.

faine (fɛːn) *f*, beechnut; (*pl.*) beechmast.

fainéant, e (feneɑ̃, ɑ̃ːt) *a*, idle, do-nothing. ¶ *n*, idler, lazybones, loafer. **fainéanter** (ɑ̃te) *v.i*, to idle, loaf. **fainéantise** (tiːz) *f*, idleness, &c.

faire (fɛːr) *m*, technique (*Art, &c*). ¶ *v.t. &*

i. ir, to make; do; create; form; perform; effect; write; play; commit; go; run; be; matter; have; get; keep; mind; get ready; lay; put; offer; o. up; give; take; take in (*provisions, &c*); deal (*cards*); cut (*teeth*); make up (*face, the cash*); make out (*pretend*); wage (*war*); pay; ejaculate, say; charge; quote; accustom; call; turn. *se* ~, to be done; be made; happen, take place; be; be getting; become; grow; make oneself; get; gain; turn. **faire-part** (fɛrpa:r) *m*, circular letter (*or* card) announcing betrothal, wedding, birth, death. **faisable** (fəzabl) *a*, feasible, practicable.

faisan, e (fəzɑ̃, an) *n*, pheasant. **faisandé, e** (zɑ̃de) *a*, high, gamy; tainted. **faisandeau** (do) *m*, young pheasant. **se faisander** (de) *v.pr*, to get high. **faisanderie** (dri) *f*, pheasantry.

faisceau (fɛso) *m*, bunch, bundle, cluster, sheaf, nest; beam (*Opt.*); pencil (*Opt.*); pile, stack (*arms*); (*pl.*) fasces (*Hist.*).

faiseur, euse (fəzœ:r, øːz) *n*, maker; doer; -monger; bluffer.

fait (fɛ; *in liaison*, fɛt) *m*, act, deed; feat; fact; point; occurrence, happening. ~*s divers*, news items. ~*s & dits*, sayings & doings. ~*s & gestes*, doings, exploits. *dans* (ou *par*) *le* ~ ou *en* ~, as a matter of fact. *de* ~, de facto, actual.

fait, e (fɛ, ɛt) *p.p. & p.a*: ~ *de boue & de crachat*, jerry-built. ~ *par tailleur*, tailor-made. *un homme fait*, a full-grown man.

faîtage (fɛta:ʒ) *m*, roofing; ridge pole; ridge capping. **faîte** (fɛːt) *m*, top, apex, summit, zenith. **faîtière** (fɛtjɛːr) *a.f*, ridge (*att.*). ¶ *f*, ridge tile; ridge pole (*tent*).

fait-tout (fɛtu) *m*, stewpan.

faix (fɛ) *m*, burden, load, weight, incubus.

fakir (faki:r) *m*, fakir.

falaise (falɛːz) *f*, cliff (*on seashore*).

falbalas (falbala) *m.pl*, furbelows; fallals.

fallacieux, euse† (falasjø, øːz) *a*, fallacious, misleading.

falloir (falwa:r) *v.imp.ir*, to be necessary, must, should, ought, shall, to have to, shall (*or* will) have to; to want; to require; to take. *s'en* ~, to be wanting; be far, fall short.

falot (falo) *m*, lantern.

falot, e (falo, ɔt) *a*, funny little (*pers.*).

falourde (falurd) *f*, bundle of firewood logs. **falsifier** (falsifje) *v.t*, to adulterate; debase; falsify, tamper with; forge.

famé, e (fame) *a*, -famed.

famélique (famelik) *a*, starv[el]ing.

fameux, euse† (famø, øːz) *a*, famous; notorious; capital, first-rate, rare, champion (*att.*).

familial, e (familjal) *a*, family (*att.*). **familiariser** (ljarize) *v.t*, to familiarize, accustom. **familiarité** (te) *f*, familiarity; intimacy; (*pl.*) liberties. **familier, ère** (lje, ɛːr) *a*, familiar; intimate; habitual; collo-

quial; household (*gods*). ¶ *m*, familiar.
familistère (listɛ:r) *m*, community centre;
store[s]. famille (mi:j) *f*, family; people.
en ~, at home.

famine (famin) *f*, famine, starvation.
fanage (fana:ʒ) *m*, tedding; fallen leaves.
fanal (fanal) *m*, light, lamp.
fanatique (fanatik) *a*, fanatic(al); obsessed.
¶ *n*, fanatic; devotee. fanatiser (ze) *v.t*,
to fanaticize. fanatisme (tism) *m*, fanaticism.
fanchon (fɑ̃ʃɔ̃) *f*, kerchief.
fane (fan) *f*, fallen leaf; top (*turnip*, &c).
faner (fane) *v.t*, to ted, toss (*hay*); fade.
faneur, euse (nœ:r, ø:z) (*pers.*) *n*. & (*Mach.*)
f, haymaker, tedder.
fanfare (fɑ̃faːr) *f*, flourish of trumpets, fanfare; brass band. fanfaron, ne (farɔ̃, ɔn)
a, blustering, swaggering, hectoring,
bragging. fanfaronnade (rɔnad) & fanfaronnerie (nri) *f*, bluster, swagger, brag.
fanfreluches (fɑ̃frəlyʃ) *f.pl*, fallals, frills &
furbelows.
fange (fɑ̃:ʒ) *f*, mire, mud, filth, muck; gutter
(*fig.*). fangeux, euse (fɑ̃ʒø, ø:z) *a*, miry, &c.
fanion (fanjɔ̃) *m*, mark flag.
fanon (fanɔ̃) *m*, dewlap; wattle; lappet;
whalebone; fetlock.
fantaisie (fɑ̃tezi) *f*, fancy, notion, whim;
fantasy; fantasia. [*objet de*] ~, fancy
[article]. fantaisiste (zist) *a*, fantastic,
whimsical. fantasmagorie (tasmagori) *f*,
phantasmagoria; fabrication. fantasque
(task) *a*, whimsical, odd; temperamental.
fantassin (fɑ̃tasɛ̃) *m*, infantryman. ~ *de la
flotte*, marine.
fantastique (fɑ̃tastik) *a*. & *m*, fantastic,
fanciful; weird, eerie, uncanny.
fantoche (fɑ̃tɔʃ) *m*, puppet (*pers.*).
fantomatique (fɑ̃tomatik) *a*, ghostly, unearthly. fantôme (to:m) *m*, phantom,
ghost.
faon (fɑ̃) *m*, fawn. faonner (fane) *v.i*, to
fawn (*of deer*).
faquin (fakɛ̃) *m*, scurvy fellow, cad. faquinerie (kinri) *f*, scurvy trick.
faraud, e (faro, o:d) *n*, fop, dandy.
farce (fars) *f*, stuffing, forcemeat; farce;
foolery; joke; practical joke; antic. *faire
ses* ~*s*, to sow one's wild oats. farceur,
euse (sœ:r, ø:z) *n*, joker, humorist; practical joker; comedian. farcir (si:r) *v.t*, to
stuff; cram.
fard (fa:r) *m*, paint, grease p., make-up; disguise, guile. ~ *compact*, compact powder.
fardage (farda:ʒ) *m*, dunnage; top hamper;
hamper.
fardeau (fardo) *m*, burden, load, weight, onus.
farder (farde) *v.t*, to paint, make up (*face*);
gloss, varnish (*fig.*); dunnage (*Ship.*); (*v.i.*)
to weigh [heavy]; sink. se ~, to make
up.
fardier (fardje) *m*, lorry, trolley.
farfadet (farfadε) *m*, goblin, sprite.

farfouiller (farfuje) *v.i*, to rummage [about],
fumble.
faribole[s] (faribol) *f.[pl.]*, twaddle.
farinacé, e (farinase) *a*, farinaceous. farine
(rin) *f*, flour, meal, farina. ~ *de lin*,
linseed meal. ~ *de riz*, ground rice.
farineux, euse (nø, ø:z) *a*, floury, mealy;
farinaceous. farinier, ère (nje, ɛ:r) *n*,
flour dealer; miller.
farouch[e] (faruʃ) *m*, crimson clover.
farouche (faruʃ) *a*, wild, savage, fierce;
grim; surly; unapproachable, shy, coy.
farrago (farago) *m*, mixture (*fodder*); farrago;
hotchpotch.
fascicule (fasikyl) *m*, fascicle; number, part,
instalment (*publication*).
fascinateur, trice (fasinatœ:r, tris) *a*, fascinating. fascination (sjɔ̃) *f*, fascination;
witchery.
fascine (fasin) *f*, fascine; faggot.
fasciner (fasine) *v.t*, to fascinate.
fascisme (fasism) *m*, fascism. fasciste (sist)
m, fascist.
faste (fast) *m*. *no pl*, pomp, pageantry; show,
ostentation; (*m.pl.*) fasti; annals.
fastidieux, euse† (fastidjø, ø:z) *a*, tedious,
wearisome, irksome, dull.
fastueux, euse† (fastɥø, ø:z) *a*, given to
display; ostentatious, showy, gaudy.
fat (fat) *a.m*, foppish. ¶ *m*, fop, coxcomb,
jackanapes.
fatal, e† (fatal) *a*, fatal; fateful; latest, final.
fatalisme (lism) *m*, fatalism. fataliste
(list) *n*, fatalist. fatalité (te) *f*, fate,
fatality; mischance.
fatidique (fatidik) *a*, fatidical, prophetic.
fatigant, e (fatigɑ̃, ɑ̃:t) *a*, fatiguing, tiring;
tiresome; tedious. fatigue (tig) *f*, fatigue,
tiredness, fag; stress, [over]strain. *de* ~,
working (*clothes*). fatiguer (ge) *v.t*, to
fatigue, tire, fag; stress, [over]strain, task,
wear out; (*v.i.*) to labour (*ship*).
fatras (fatra) *m*, jumble, medley. fatrasser
(trase) *v.i*, to potter.
fatuité (fatɥite) *f*, self-conceit.
fauber[t] (fobɛ:r) *m*, swab (*Naut.*).
faubourg (fobu:r) *m*, suburb; quarter (*town*).
faubourien, ne (burjɛ̃, ɛn) *a*. & *n*, working-
class suburban (dweller).
faucard (foka:r) *m*, river weeding shear.
fauchage (foʃa:ʒ) *m*, mowing. faucher (ʃe)
v.t, to mow; m. down. fauchet (ʃε) *m*,
hay rake. faucheur (ʃœ:r) *m*, mower
(*pers.*). ~ *ou* faucheux (ʃø) *m*, harvest-
man (*insect*). faucheuse (ʃo:z) *f*, mower
(*Mach.*). faucille (si:j) *f*, sickle, reaping
hook.
faucon (fokɔ̃) *m*, falcon, hawk. ~ *pèlerin*,
peregrine [falcon]. fauconnerie (kɔnri) *f*,
falconry; hawking. fauconnier (nje) *m*,
falconer. fauconnière (jε:r) *f*, saddle bag.
faufiler (fofile) *v.t*, to tack, baste (*Need.*);
slip in, insinuate. faufilure (ly:r) *f*, tacking, basting.

faune (fo:n) *m*, faun; (*f.*) fauna.

faussaire (fose:r) *n*, forger. **faussement** (smɑ̃) *ad*, falsely; wrongfully. **fausser** (se) *v.t*, to bend; buckle; warp; strain; upset; derange; falsify, pervert. **fausset** (se) *m*, falsetto (*voice*); spigot, vent peg. **fausseté** (ste) *f*, falseness, falsity; falsehood, untruth.

faute (fo:t) *f*, fault; mistake, error; blame; foul (*Foot.*, &c); want, lack. ~ *d'orthographe*, misspelling. ~ *d'impression*, printer's error, misprint. ~ *de copiste*, ~ *de plume*, clerical error. ~ *de pied*, foot fault (*Ten.*). ~ *de*, failing, in default of, for want of. *sans* ~, without fail.

fauteuil (fotœ:j) *m*, armchair, easy chair; chair; seat; stall (*Theat.*). ~ *à bascule*, rocking chair. ~ [*de la présidence*], chair (*at meeting*). ~ *roulant*, Bath chair.

fautif, ive (fotif, i:v) *a*, faulty, at fault, offending.

fauve (fo:v) *a*, fawn[-coloured], fallow; fulvous, tawny; buff; lurid (*light*). ¶ *m*, fawn; buff (*colour*); (*pl.*) deer; wild beasts (*big felines*).

fauvette (fovet) *f*, warbler (*bird*). ~ *à tête noire*, blackcap. ~ *des haies*, hedge sparrow.

faux (fo) *f*, scythe; falx.

faux, fausse (fo, o:s) *a*, false; wrong; untrue; base, counterfeit; forged; spurious; bogus; unjust (*weight*); improper (*navigation*); blank, blind (*window*); attempted (*suicide*). **faux,** *comps:* ~ *bourdon*, drone [bee]. ~ *brillant*, imitation [stone], paste; tinsel (*fig.*). ~ *col*, see col. ~ *coup de queue*, miscue. ~ *ébénier*, laburnum. ~ *frais*, incidental expenses; untaxed costs (*Law*). ~-*fuyant*, *m*, evasion, shift. ~-*monnayeur*, *m*, coiner; forger (*bank notes*). ~ *nom*, alias. ~ *numéro* [*d'appel*], wrong number (*Teleph.*). ~-*pont*, *m*, orlop [deck]. ~-*semblant*, *m*, blind, stalking horse. ~ *témoignage*, false evidence, perjury. ~ *titre*, half-title. **fausse,** *comps:* ~ *boîte*, dummy [box]. ~ *couche*, miscarriage. ~ *déclaration*, misstatement, misrepresentation. ~ *équerre*, bevel [square]. ~ *honte*, false shame; bashfulness. ~ *manche*, sleeve protector. **faux,** *ad*, falsely, wrongly; out of tune. *à* ~, wrongly, unjustly. ¶ *m*, forgery. *le* ~, the false.

faveur (favœ:r) *f*, favour; boon; goodwill. **favorable**† (vorabl) *a*, favourable. **favori, ite** (ri, it) *a. & n*, favourite; pet; minion; (*m.pl.*) [side] whiskers. **favoriser** (ze) *v.t*, to favour, befriend; foster, promote. **favoritisme** (tism) *m*, favouritism.

fébrile† (febril) *a*, febrile, feverish.

fécond, e (fekɔ̃, ɔ̃:d) *a*, fruitful, fecund, fertile; prolific; life-giving; bountiful. **féconder** (kɔ̃de) *v.t*, to fertilize, fecundate, impregnate; milt; fructify. **fécondité** (dite) *f*, fecundity, fertility, fruitfulness.

fécule (fekyl) *f*, starch, farina. **féculent, e** (lɑ̃, ɑ̃:t) *a*, starchy (*food*).

fédéral, e (federal) *a*, federal. **fédération** (sjɔ̃) *f*, federation, union. **fédérer** (re) *v.t*, to federate.

fée (fe) *f*, fairy, pixy, -xie. **féerie** (feri) *f*, fairyhood; Fairyland; fairy scene. **féerique** (ferik) *a*, fairylike.

feindre (fɛ̃:dr) *v.t. & abs. ir*, to feign, pretend, sham; feint. **feint, e** (fɛ̃, ɛ̃:t) *p.a*, feigned, sham; false, blind (*door*, &c). ¶ *f*, feint, pretence, sham.

feldspath (felspat) *m*, fel[d]spar.

fêler (fɛle) *v.t*, to crack.

félicitation (felisitasjɔ̃) *f*, congratulation. **félicité** (te) *f*, happiness, felicity. **féliciter** (te) *v.t*, to congratulate.

félidés (felide) *m.pl*, Felidae. **félin, e** (lɛ̃, in) *a. & m*, feline, cat (*att.*).

félon, e (felɔ̃, ɔn) *a*, disloyal. **félonie** (lɔni) *f*, disloyalty.

fêlure (fɛly:r) *f*, crack, split.

femelle (fəmɛl) *f. & a*, female, she; hen; cow (*elephant*, &c). **féminin, e** (feminɛ̃, in) *a*, feminine; womanish (*voice*); female. ¶ *m*, feminine (*Gram.*). **féminiser** (nize) *v.t*, to feminize. **féminisme** (nism) *m*, feminism. **féministe** (nist) *a. & n*, feminist. **femme** (fam) *f*, woman; female; wife. ~ *auteur*, *f*, authoress. ~ *avocat*, *f*, woman barrister. ~-*caoutchouc*, ~-*serpent*, *f*, contortionist. ~ *de chambre*, lady's maid; housemaid; chambermaid; parlour maid; stewardess (*ship*). ~ *de charge*, housekeeper. ~ *de journée*, cleaner, charwoman; daily help. ~ *de ménage*, cleaner, charwoman; housekeeper (*non resident*). ~ *médecin*, ~ *docteur*, *f*, woman doctor, lady d. ~ *peintre*, *f*, paintress. ~ *poète*, *f*, poetess. ~ *sculpteur*, *f*, sculptress. **femmelette** (mlɛt) *f*, silly little woman; effeminate [man].

fémur (femy:r) *m*, femur.

fenaison (fənɛzɔ̃) *f*, haymaking.

fendant (fɑ̃dɑ̃) *m*, swaggerer.

fendiller (fɑ̃dije) *v.t*, to crack, fissure. **fendre** (fɑ̃:dr) *v.t*, to split; cleave; rend; rive; crack; slot, nick, slit; break (*heart*). ~ *un cheveu en quatre*, to split hairs. **fendu, e** (fɑ̃dy) *a*, split, cleft. *bien fendu*, long-legged (*man*).

fenêtrage (fənɛtra:ʒ) *m*, windows (*col.*). **fenêtre** (nɛ:tr) *f*, window. ~ *à guillotine*, sash w. ~ *à tabatière*, skylight. ~ *en saillie*, bay window. ~ [*ordinaire*], casement [window].

fenil (fəni) *m*, hayloft.

fenouil (fənu:j) *m*, fennel; f. seed.

fente (fɑ̃:t) *f*, crack, cleft, split, slit; fissure, crevice, cranny; slot; nick.

féodal, e (feodal) *a*, feudal. **féodalité** (lite) *f*, feudalism, feudality.

fer (fɛ:r) *m*, iron; bar; section; shoe; bit; head (*lance*, &c); tag (*laces*); tool (*Bookb.*);

sword, weapon; (pl.) irons, chains, shackles; fetters, manacles; obstetrical forceps. ~s à chaud, tooling (Bookb.). ~ à friser, curling tongs. ~s à froid, blind tooling (Bookb.). ~ à repasser, [flat] iron. ~ à souder, soldering iron, soldering bit. ~[s] cavalier[s], horseshoe bars, h. iron, h. sections. ~ de (ou à) cheval, horseshoe. ~ de fonte, cast iron. ~ de lance, spear head. ~s dorés, gilt tooling (Bookb.). ~ en barre[s], bar iron. ~ en lame, sheet i. ~ [forgé], wrought i. ~ moyen, mid iron (Golf).

fer-blanc (fɛrblɑ̃) m, tin [plate]. tinned [sheet] iron. **ferblanterie** (blɑ̃tri) f, tin plate working or trade; tinware. **ferblantier** (tje) m, tinsmith.

férir (fer:r) v.t: sans coup ~, without striking a blow.

ferler (fɛrle) v.t, to furl (sail).

fermage (fɛrma:ʒ) m, rent (farm, land).

fermant, e (fɛrmɑ̃, ɑ̃:t) a, lockup; closing.

ferme† (fɛrm) a, firm, solid, steady, steadfast, staunch. ¶ ad, firmly, firm, fast, hard. ¶ i, steady! ¶ f, lease; farm; farmhouse; homestead; truss, girder (Build.); set piece (Theat.).

ferment (fɛrmɑ̃) m, ferment; leaven. **fermentation** (tasjɔ̃) f, fermentation; ferment (fig.). **fermenter** (te) v.i, to ferment; to [be at] work (fig.).

fermer (fɛrme) v.t. & i, to shut, s. up, s. down, close, c. up, c. down; do up; turn off, shut off; switch off; stop up; enclose. ~ [à clef] v.t. & i, to lock [up]. ~ la marche, to bring up the rear.

fermeté (fɛrməte) f, firmness, steadfastness, steadiness, strength.

fermeture (fɛrməty:r) f, shutting; closing; fastening; fastener. ~ instantanée, zip[p] (or slide) fastener.

fermier, ère (fɛrmje, ɛ:r) n, farmer; tenant (farm); lessee; tenant farmer; (att.) leasing.

fermoir (fɛrmwa:r) m, clasp, fastener, snap; double bevelled chisel. ~ à curseur, zip[p] (or slide) fastener.

féroce (ferɔs) a, ferocious, fierce, savage, wild. **férocité** (site) f, ferocity, &c.

ferrage (fɛra:ʒ) m, shoeing; tiring; tagging.

ferraille (ra:j) f, old iron, scrap iron. **ferrailler** (raje) v.i, to slash about. **ferrailleur** (jœ:r) m, dealer in old iron; sword rattler. **ferré, e** (re) p.a, iron-shod; shod; hobnailed; versed, conversant. ~ à glace, roughshod, frost-nailed. **ferrement** (fɛrmɑ̃) m, ironwork; shoeing; putting in irons. **ferrer** (re) v.t, to iron, bind (with any metal); shoe; tire; tag; metal (road); strike (fish). **ferret** (rɛ) m, tag (lace). **ferreux** (rø) a.m, ferrous. **ferronnerie** (rɔnri) f, ironworks; iron warehouse; ironmongery. **ferronnier, ère** (nje, ɛ:r) n, iron worker; ironmonger. **ferrugineux, euse** (ryʒinø, ø:z) a, ferruginous, chalybeate. **ferrure**

(ry:r) f, ironwork; binding; shoeing; fitting, mounting.

fertile (fɛrtil) a, fertile, fruitful; prolific; fat (land). **fertiliser** (lize) v.t, to fertilize. **fertilité** (te) f, fertility, &c.

féru, e (fery) a, struck; smitten (love).

férule (feryl) f, ferula (Bot.); bondage; cane (Sch.); lash (fig.).

fervent, e (fɛrvɑ̃, ɑ̃:t) a, fervent, earnest. ¶ n, enthusiast, devotee. **ferveur** (vœ:r) f, fervour, earnestness.

fesse (fɛs) f, buttock. **fessée** (se) f, spanking. **fesse-mathieu** (matjø) m, usurer. **fesser** (se) v.t, to spank; birch.

festin (fɛstɛ̃) m, feast, banquet. **festiner** (tine) v.t. & abs, to feast. **festival** (val) m, musical festival.

feston (fɛstɔ̃) m, festoon; scallop (edging). **festonner** (tɔne) v.t, to festoon; scallop. ¶ v.i, to reel about (drunk).

festoyer (fɛstwaje) v.t. & i, to feast.

fête (fɛːt) f, feast, festivity; festival; fête; rollicking; holiday; saint's day; birthday; entertainment, treat. la ~ de [l'anniversaire de] l'Armistice, Armistice Day. la Fête-Dieu, Corpus Christi. ~ foraine, fête (at a fair). ~ légale, public holiday, bank h. **fêter** (fɛte) v.t, to keep [as a holiday], celebrate; fête, entertain.

fétiche (fetiʃ) m, fetish; mascot (as on car); charm. **fétichisme** (ʃism) m, fetishism.

fétide (fetid) a, fetid, foul. **fétidité** (dite) f, fetidness, foulness.

fétu (fety) m, straw; (fig.) straw, rush, rap, fig, pin.

feu (fø) m, fire; flame; flare; flash; light; lamp; firing (Mil.); heat (fig.); home, hearth. ~ à éclipses, intermittent light (Naut.). ~ concentré, group firing (Mil.). ~ d'artifice, firework. ~ de bengale, Bengal light. ~ de bivouac, watch fire. ~ de cheminée, chimney on fire. ~x de circulation, traffic lights, stop & go lights. ~ de joie, bonfire. ~ de paille (fig.), flash in the pan. ~ de peloton, volley firing (Mil.). ~ follet, ignis fatuus, jack-o'-lantern, will-o'-the-wisp. ~ roulant, running fire. ~! fire! (Mil.). au ~! (house, &c, on) fire! faire long ~, to hang fire. ni ~ ni lieu, neither house nor home.

feu, e (fø) a, late, the late (deceased).

feuillage (fœja:ʒ) m, foliage, leafage, leaves. **feuillaison** (jɛzɔ̃) f, leafing, foliation. **feuillard** (ja:r) m, hoop wood. ~ de fer, hoop iron, strap iron, strip iron. **feuille** (fœ:j) f, sheet; leaf; slip; list; roll (pay); [news]paper; blade; flake; foil. ~ d'appel, muster roll. ~ d'audience, cause list. ~ de chou, rag (worthless newspaper). ~ de garde, end paper. ~s de placage, veneer. ~ de présence, time sheet, attendance s. ~ de rose, rose leaf (petal). ~ de route, waybill. ~ de tirée, pull (Typ.). ~ de transfert, transfer deed,

[deed of] transfer. ~ *de versement*, paying-in slip. ~ *de vigne*, fig leaf (*Art*). ~ *mobile*, loose leaf (*book*). ~ *volante*, loose sheet (*paper*). **feuille, e** (fœje) *a*, leafy, foliate. ¶ *f*, greenwood, trees. **feuillet** (jɛ) *m*, leaf (*book*); thin sheet, t. plate; lamina. **feuilleter** (fœjte) *v.t*, to run through, thumb (*book*); roll out (*pastry*); flake. [*gâteau*] *feuilleté, m*, puff. **feuilleton** (tɔ̃) *m*, feuilleton. [*roman*] ~, serial [story]. **feuillu, e** (jy) *a*, leafy. **feuillure** (jy:r) *f*, rabbet, rebate; fillister.

feutre (fø:tr) *m*, felt. ~ *mou*, ~ *souple*, soft felt (*hat*). ~ *velours*, velours. **feutrer** (føtre) *v.t*, to felt, pad. *à pas feutrés*, stealthily.

fève (fɛ:v) *f*, bean. ~ *de marais*, broad bean. **féverole** (fɛvrɔl) *f*, horse bean.

février (fevrie) *m*, February.

fez (fɛ:z) *m*, fez.

fi (fi) *i*, ugh! fie! ~ *donc!* for shame! *faire ~ de*, to pooh-pooh.

fiacre (fjakr) *m*, cab, four-wheeler.

fiançailles (fjɑ̃sa:j) *f.pl*, engagement, betrothal. **fiancé, e** (se) *n*, fiancé, e, betrothed. **fiancer** (se) *v.t*, to betroth, engage, affiance.

fiasco (fjasko) *m*, fiasco, failure, breakdown.

fibre (fibr) *f*, fibre; string (*fig.*). ~ *de coco*, coir. **fibreux, euse** (brø, ø:z) *a*, fibrous, stringy. **fibrille** (bril) *f*, fibril.

ficelé, e (fisle) *p.a*, dressed (*badly*). **ficeler** (sle) *v.t*, to [tie with] string, tie up. **ficelle** (sɛl) *f*, string, twine; packthread; dodge, trick, game.

fiche (fiʃ) *f*, hinge; peg, pin, stake; plug, key; slip (*paper*); card (*loose index*); ticket; counter (*Cards, &c*). ~ *de consolation*, booby prize; some slight consolation. **ficher** (ʃe) *v.t*, to drive in, stick. **fichier** (ʃje) *m*, card index; c. i. cabinet.

fichtre (fiʃtr) *i*, good gracious!

fichu (fiʃy) *m*, neckerchief, fichu.

fictif, ive† (fiktif, i:v) *a*, fictitious, sham. **fiction** (sjɔ̃) *f*, fiction, figment.

fidéicommis (fideikɔmi) *m*, trust (*Law*).

fidèle† (fidɛl) *a*, faithful; loyal; true; reliable, trustworthy; fast; retentive. *les ~s, m.pl*, the faithful. **fidélité** (delite) *f*, fidelity, faithfulness; truthfulness; reliability; retentiveness.

fidibus (fidiby:s) *m*, spill, pipe light.

fiduciaire (fidysjɛ:r) *a*, fiduciary.

fief (fjɛf) *m*, fief, feud, fee (*Hist.*); preserve (*fig.*). **fieffé, e** (fe) *a*, arrant, downright, unmitigated, egregious, regular, outright, rank, out & out, of the deepest dye.

fiel (fjɛl) *m*, gall; rancour. **fielleux, euse** (lø, ø:z) *a*, rancorous.

fiente (fjɑ̃:t) *f*, dung, droppings.

fier (fje) *v.t*, to entrust. **se ~**, to trust, rely.

fier, ère† (fjɛ:r) *a*, proud, haughty; lofty; stately; lordly; rare, fine; arrant. **fier-à-**

bras (fjɛrabra) *m*, swaggerer. **fierté** (fjɛrte) *f*, pride; boldness (*touch*).

fièvre (fjɛ:vr) *f*, fever; heat (*fig.*). ~ *aphteuse* (aftø:z), foot-&-mouth disease. ~ *des foins*, hay fever. ~ *paludéenne*, malaria, marsh fever; ague. **fiévreux, euse†** (evrø, ø:z) *a*, feverish. ¶ *m*, fever case (*pers.*).

fifre (fifr) *m*, fife; fifer.

figé, e (fiʒe) *a*, frozen (*fig.*); set. **figer** (ʒe) *v.t. & se ~*, to congeal, coagulate, set.

fignoler (fiɲɔle) *v.t. & abs*, to overelaborate.

figue (fig) *f*, fig. ~ *de Barbarie*, prickly pear. **figuier** (gje) *m*, fig tree.

figurant, e (figyrɑ̃, ɑ:t) *n*, walker-on, supernumerary; one who takes no prominent part. **figuratif, ive†** (ratif, i:v) *a*, figurative; pictorial (*plan, map*); picture (*writing*). **figure** (gy:r) *f*, figure; form, shape; face (*of pers.*), countenance; show[ing]; (*pl.*) court cards. ~ *de cire*, waxwork. ~ *de mots*, ~ *de rhétorique*, figure of speech. ~ *de proue*, figurehead (*ship*). ~ *en lame de couteau*, hatchet face. **figuré, e** (gyre) *p.a*, pictorial (*plan, map*); figure (*dance, stone*); figurative (*sense*). ¶ *m*, figurative sense. **figurément** (mɑ̃) *ad*, figuratively (*sense*). **figurer** (re) *v.t*, to figure, represent, picture, show; (*v.i.*) to appear, figure, show. **se ~**, to imagine, fancy, picture to oneself. **figurine** (rin) *f*, figurine, statuette; stamp (*postage, &c*).

fil (fil) *m*, thread; yarn; wire; filament; string (*pearls, &c*); [cutting] edge; grain (*wood, &c*); flaw; clew. ~ *à plomb*, plumb line. ~ *carcasse des fleuristes*, flower wire. ~ *de fer barbelé*, barb[ed] wire. ~*s de la Vierge*, gossamer. ~ [*de lin*], linen [thread]. ~ *souple*, flex[ible wire] (*Elec.*). **filage** (la:ʒ) *m*, spinning; pouring (*oil on waves*). **filament** (lamɑ̃) *m*, filament; thread. **filandres** (lɑ̃:dr) *f.pl*, gossamer; strings. **filandreux, euse** (lɑ̃drø, ø:z) *a*, stringy; long-drawn; diffuse. **filant, e** (lɑ̃, ɑ:t) *a*, ropy (*liquid*); falling, shooting (*star*). **filasse** (las) *f*, tow (*flax, hemp*).

filateur, trice (filatœ:r, tris) *n*, spinner (*pers.*); (*m.*) spinner (*owner*). **filature** (ty:r) *f*, spinning mill; spinning; shadowing (*a pers.*).

file (fil) *f*, file, line.

filé (file) *m*, thread. **filer** (le) *v.t*, to spin; draw (*into wire*); pay out (*cable*); pour (*oil on waves*); shadow (*a pers.*); handle (*fig.*); (*v.i.*) to run; be off; make off; file off; flare (*lamp*). ~ *à l'anglaise*, to take French leave. ~ *doux*, to sing small.

filet (file) *m*, thread; string; filament; fillet; fr[a]enum; undercut; loin (*mutton*); worm (*screw*); trickle, stream; dash (*admixture*); rule (*Typ.*); net; netting. ~ *à bagage*, luggage rack (*Rly.*). ~ *à provisions*, string bag, net b. ~*s de sole*, filleted sole. **filetage** (lta:ʒ) *m*, screw cutting. **fileter** (lte) *v.t*, to thread, screw. **fileur, euse** (lœ:r, ø:z) *n*, spinner; net maker.

filial, e† (filjal) *a*, filial. [**société**] **filiale**, *f*, subsidiary [company]. **filiation** (sjɔ̃) *f*, filiation; relationship.

filière (filjɛ:r) *f*, draw plate; die [plate]; screw plate; [screw] stock; wire gauge; purlin; regular channel[s] (*fig.*). ~ *garnie*, stock & dies.

filigrane (filigran) *m*, filigree [work]; watermark (*paper*).

fille (fi:j) *f*, girl; maid; maiden; lass[ie]; daughter. ~ *de ferme*, dairy maid, milkmaid. ~ *de service*, maidservant, housemaid, servant girl. **fillette** (fijɛt) *f*, little girl, lass[ie]. **filleul** (fijœl) *n*, godchild, godson, god-daughter; protégé.

film (film) *m*, film (*Phot. & Cinema*). ~ *d'actualité*, news f. ~ *de reportage*, topical f. ~ *documentaire*, instructional f. ~ *parlé*, ~ *parlant*, talking f. ~ *sonore*, sound f.

filoche (filɔʃ) *f*, netting (*silk, &c*).

filon (filɔ̃) *m*, lode; mine (*fig.*).

filoselle (filozɛl) *f*, floss silk.

filou (filu) *m*, pickpocket; sharper; swindler. **filouter** (te) *v.i*, to rob; filch; cheat. **filouterie** (tri) *f*, robbery; swindle.

fils (fis) *m*, son; junior. ~ *de ses œuvres*, self-made man. ~ *de son père*, chip of the old block.

filtrage (filtra:ʒ) *m. &* **filtration** (trasjɔ̃) *f*, filtration, straining; percolation. **filtre** (tr) *m*, filter; percolator (*coffee*). **filtrer** (tre) *v.t. & i*, to filter, strain; percolate, leach.

fin (fɛ̃) *f*, end, close, finish, last; finis; object, aim, purpose. ~ *d'alerte*, all clear (*Mil.*).

fin (fɛ̃) *m*, fine metal; fine linen. *or à tant de grammes de* ~, gold so many grammes fine.

fin, e (fɛ̃, · in) *a*, fine; delicate; choice; slender; small; keen, sharp; subtle; smart. *fin fond*, farthest end, very depths. *fin matois*, artful dodger. *le fin mot*, the last word; the long & the short of it, the upshot. *fine à l'eau*, brandy & soda. *fine champagne*, liqueur brandy. *fines herbes*, savoury herbs.

final, e† (final) *a*, final; last; ultimate. ¶ *f*, final (*Sport*). **final[e]**, *m*, finale (*Mus.*). **finalité** (lite) *f*, finality.

finance (finɑ̃:s) *f*, finance; (*pl.*) finances, cash, money, exchequer. **financer** (nɑ̃se) *v.i*, to find money, finance. **financier, ère†** (sje, ɛːr) *a*, financial. ¶ *m*, financier.

finasser (finase) *v.i*, to finesse. **finasserie** (sri) *f*, trickery; cunning; (*pl.*) wiles. **finassier, ère** (sje, ɛːr) *n*, trickster.

finaud, e (fino, o:d) *a*, sly, wily. ¶ *n*, artful dodger, slyboots. **finauderie** (odri) *f*, sly dodge.

finement (finmɑ̃) *ad*, finely; shrewdly. **finesse** (nɛs) *f*, fineness, &c, *as fin, e*; finesse.

fini, e (fini) *a*, finished; over; consummate;

finite (*being*). ¶ *m*, finish; (the) finite.

finir (ni:r) *v.t. & abs. & i*, to finish, end. ~ *de parler, &c*, to finish (*or leave off*) speaking, &c. *en* ~, to finish.

Finlande (la) (fɛ̃lɑ̃:d) Finland. **finnois, e** (finwa, a:z) *& finlandais, e* (fɛ̃lɑ̃dɛ, ɛ:z) *a*, Finnish. **Finnois, e** *& Finlandais, e*, *n*, Finn, Finlander. *le finnois*, Finnish (*language*).

fiole (fjɔl) *f*, flask, phial.

fioriture (fjɔrity:r) *f*, grace [note]; flourish.

firmament (firmamɑ̃) *m*, firmament.

fisc (fisk) *m*, Treasury; [Inland] Revenue. **fiscal, e** (kal) *a*, fiscal, [inland] revenue (*att.*). **fiscalité** (lite) *f*, fiscal system; piling up of taxation; methods of [tax] collection.

fissure (fisy:r) *f*, fissure, crack, cleft; hiatus.

fistule (fistyl) *f*, fistula.

fixage (fiksa:ʒ) *m. &* **fixation** (asjɔ̃) *f*, fixing, fixation; fastening. **fixatif** (tif) *m*, fixing [solution] (*Phot.*). **fixe†** (fiks) *a*, fixed, fast, stationary; intent; set. ¶ *i*, eyes front! ¶ *m*, fixed salary. ~*cravate*, *m*, tie clip. **fixer** (kse) *v.t*, to fix, fasten, secure; set; settle; rivet (*fig.*). ~ *dans la mémoire*, to commit to memory, memorize. **fixité** (ksite) *f*, fixity, steadiness.

flaccidité (flaksidite) *f*, flaccidity, flabbiness.

flacon (flakɔ̃) *m*, bottle, flask, flagon. ~ *à couvercle vissé*, screw-capped bottle. ~ *à odeur*, scent b., smelling b.

flageller (flaʒɛle) *v.t*, to scourge, flagellate.

flageoler (flaʒɔle) *v.i*, to tremble, shake.

flageolet (lɛ) *m*, flageolet (*Mus. & bean*).

flagorner (flagɔrne) *v.t*, to fawn [up]on, toady to. **flagornerie** (nɔri) *f*, toadyism, soft sawder, soft soap. **flagorneur, euse** (nœːr, oːz) *n*, toady.

flagrant, e (flagrɑ̃, ɑ̃:t) *a*, flagrant, glaring. *en flagrant délit*, in the [very] act, redhanded.

flair (flɛːr) *m*, scent, smell, nose; acumen; keenness. **flairer** (flɛre) *v.t. & abs*, to scent, smell, scent out, nose [out].

flamand, e (flamɑ̃, ɑ̃:d) *a. & (language)* *m*, Flemish. **F**~, *n*, Fleming (*pers.*).

flamant (flamɑ̃) *m*, flamingo.

flambant, e (flɑ̃bɑ̃, ɑ̃:t) *a*, flaming, blazing; smart. *tout flambant neuf*, *toute flambante neuve*, bran[d] new. **flambeau** (bo) *m*, torch; candlestick. **flambé, e** (be) *p.p*, lost, gone; done for. **flambée** (be) *f*, blaze. **flamber** (be) *v.i*, to flame, blaze, flare; (*v.t.*) to flame (*needle, Surg.*); singe. **flamberge** (bɛrʒ) *f*, sword (*jocularly*). **flamboyer** (bwaje) *v.i*, to blaze; flame, flare, flash.

flamme (flɑ:m) *f*, flame; blaze, flare; light; passion; pennant; pendant, pennon, streamer. ~ *de bengale*, Bengal light. **flammèche** (flamɛʃ) *f*, spark, flake (*ignited matter*).

flan (flɑ̃) *m*, flan; blank (*metal*); mould (*Typ.*); flong.

flanc (flɑ̃) *m*, side, flank; womb.

flancher (flɑ̃ʃe) *v.i*, to give way.

Flandre (la) (flɑ̃:dr), Flanders.

flandrin (flɑ̃drɛ̃) *m*, lanky fellow.

flanelle (flanɛl) *f*, flannel. ~ *de coton*, flannelette.

flâner (flɑne) & **flânocher** (nɔʃe) *v.i*, to saunter; stroll; lounge; loaf. **flânerie** (nri) *f*, sauntering, &c. **flâneur, euse** (nœ:r, ø:z) *n*, saunterer, &c.

flanquer (flɑ̃ke) *v.t*, to flank; fling, throw, chuck; land (*blow*).

flapi, e (flapi) *a*, dead-beat.

flaque (flak) *f*, puddle; pool, plash. ~ *d'eau fortuite*, casual water (*Golf*). **une flaquée d'eau** (ke), some water (*thrown*).

flasque (flask) *a*, flabby, limp, flaccid. ¶ *m*, cheek, side.

flatter (flate) *v.t. & abs*, to flatter; stroke, pat; humour; please. **flatterie** (tri) *f*, flattery. **flatteur, euse** (tœ:r, ø:z) *n*, flatterer. ¶ *a*, flattering.

flatulence (flatylɑ̃:s) *f*, flatulence, -cy. **flatuosité** (tɥozite) *f*, flatus, wind.

fléau (fleo) *m*, flail; scourge, plague, bane, curse; beam (*scale*); bar.

flèche (flɛʃ) *f*, arrow, shaft; spire; jib, boom (*crane*); beam (*plough*); trail (*gun carriage*); flitch (*bacon*); sag, dip. ~ *littorale*, spit (*Phys. Geog.*). **fléchette** (fleʃɛt) *f*, dart.

fléchir (fleʃi:r) *v.t. & i*, to bend, bow, flex; sag; move; flag; yield; give way; relent. **fléchisseur** (fleʃisœ:r) *a.m. & m*, flexor.

flegmatique (flɛgmatik) *a*, phlegmatic; stolid. **flegme** (flɛgm) *m*, coolness, phlegm (*fig.*), stolidity.

Flessingue (flɛsɛ̃:g) *f*, Flushing.

flet (flɛ) *m*, flounder (*fish*). **flétan** (fletɑ̃) *m*, halibut.

flétrir (fletri:r) *v.t*, to fade, wither, wilt, blight; brand. **flétrissure** (trisy:r) *f*, fading, withering; blight; stigma.

fleur (flœ:r) *f*, flower; blossom; bloom; pick; prime, heyday, blush, flush. ~ *de la Passion*, passion flower. ~*s des bois*, ~*s des champs*, ~*s des prés*, wild flowers. *la* ~ *des pois*, the pick of the bunch. *à* ~ *de*, level (*or* even) (*or* flush) with.

fleurer (flœre) *v.i*, to smell.

fleuret (flœrɛ) *m*, foil (*Fenc.*); borer.

fleurette (flœrɛt) *f*, floweret. *conter* ~, to make love. **fleuri** (e (ri) *a*, in bloom; flowery; florid. **fleurir** (ri:r) *v.i*, to flower, blossom, bloom; flourish; (*v.t.*) to deck with flowers. **fleuriste** (rist) *n*, florist; (*att.*) floral, flower. **fleuron** (rɔ̃) *m*, flower work; flower; floret; colophon.

fleuve (flœ:v) *m*, river; river god.

flexible (flɛksibl) *a*, flexible, pliant, pliable. **flexion** (ksjɔ̃) *f*, flexion; deflexion, -ction; inflexion, -ction, ending (*Gram.*).

flibustier (flibystje) *m*, filibuster, freebooter; swindler.

flic flac (flikflak), crack, smack.

flint-glass (flintglas) *m*, flint glass.

flirt (flœrt) *m*, flirtation. **flirter** (te) *v.i*, to flirt.

floc (flɔk) *m*, thud; splash.

flocon (flɔkɔ̃) *m*, flock, tuft; flake. **floconneux, euse** (kɔnø, ø:z) *a*, fleecy; flaky. **flonflon** (flɔ̃flɔ̃) *m*, blare.

floraison (flɔrɛzɔ̃) *f*, flowering, blossoming, blooming. **floral, e** (ral) *a*, floral, flower (*att.*). **flore** (flɔ:r) *f*, flora.

florence (flɔrɑ̃:s) *m*, sarsenet; [silkworm] gut.

florès (flɔrɛ:s): *faire* ~, to make a stir.

Floride (la) (flɔrid), Florida.

florissant, e (flɔrisɑ̃, ɑ̃:t) *a*, flourishing, thriving.

flot (flo) *m. oft. pl*, wave, billow; surge; rush; stream, flood; flood tide. ~ *de la marée*, tidal wave. *à* ~, afloat. *à* ~*s*, in torrents. **flottage** (flota:ʒ) *m*, floating (*lumber*), rafting. **flottant, e** (tɑ̃, ɑ̃:t) *a*, floating; flowing, waving; baggy; wavering; evasive, elusive. **flotte** (flɔt) *f*, fleet; float; floater. **flottement** (tmɑ̃) *m*, swaying; wavering. **flotter** (te) *v.i*, to float; waft; wave; hang; waver, fluctuate. ~ *repassant*, float ironing. **flotteur** (tœ:r) *m*, raftsman; float; floater; ball. **flottille** (ti:j) *f*, flotilla.

flou, e (flu) *a*, fuzzy; woolly; hazy, blurry. **flou**, *ad*, fuzzily, &c. ¶ *m*, fuzziness, &c.

flouer (flue) *v.t*, to swindle.

fluctuation (flyktɥasjɔ̃) *f*, fluctuation.

fluet, te (flyɛ, ɛt) *a*, slender, thin.

fluide (flɥid) *a*, fluid, flowing. ¶ *m*, fluid (*imponderable*). **fluidité** (dite) *f*, fluidity.

fluor (flyɔ:r) *m*, fluorine. **fluorescent, e** (ɔrɛsɑ̃, ɑ̃:t) *a*, fluorescent.

flûte (flyt) *f*, flute; flute [glass]; baton (*bread*). ~ *de Pan*, Pan's pipes. **flûté, e** (te) *a*, fluty. **flûter** (te) *v.i*, to flute, pipe. **flûtiste** (tist) *n*, fl[a]utist.

fluvial, e (flyvjal) *a*, fluvial, river (*att.*). **fluviatile** (atil) *a*, fluviatile.

flux (fly) *m*, flux; flow; flood; flush (*Cards*). **fluxion** (ksjɔ̃) *f*, swelling (*face*).

foc (fɔk) *m*, jib (*sail*).

focal, e (fɔkal) *a*, focal.

fœtus (fety:s) *m*, f[o]etus.

foi (fwa) *f*, faith; troth; belief; reliance, trust; witness. *ajouter* ~ *à*, to credit, believe in. *ma* ~ *non!* O dear no!

foie (fwa) *m*, liver (*Anat.*).

foin (fwɛ̃) *m. oft. pl*, hay.

foire (fwa:r) *f*, fair, market.

fois (fwa) *f*, time. *à la* ~, at a time; at the same t.; both; together. (See also *une, deux, trois*).

foison (fwazɔ̃) *f*, plenty. *à* ~, galore. **foisonner** (zɔne) *v.i*, to abound, be plentiful; swarm; increase.

folâtre (fɔlɑ:tr) *a*, playful, skittish, sportive, wanton. **folâtrer** (lɑtre) *v.i*, to play about, romp, frolic.

foliacé, e (foljase) a, foliaceous. foliation (sjɔ̃) f, foliation; leafing.

folichon, ne (foliʃɔ̃, on) a, wanton, unchaste.

folie (foli) f, madness; folly, foolishness; mania, passion, hobby. à la ~, to distraction.

folio (foljo) m, folio. foliole (ɔl) f, leaflet (Bot.). folioter (ɔte) v.t, to folio.

folk-lore (folklɔːr) m, folklore.

foliement (folmɑ̃) ad, madly; foolishly. follet, te (lɛ, ɛt) a, frolicsome; downy, fluffy (hair). [esprit] follet, m, sprite, [hob]goblin, puck. follette, f, playful creature.

folliculaire (folikylɛːr) m, scribbler, penny-a-liner. follicule (kyl) m, follicle; leaflet.

fomentation (fomɑ̃tasjɔ̃) f, fomentation (Med. & fig.). fomenter (te) v.t, to foment.

foncé, e (fɔ̃se) a, dark, deep (colour). foncer (se) v.t, to bottom (cask, &c); sink (well, &c); (v.i.) to rush; charge.

foncier, ère (fɔ̃sje, ɛːr) a, landed, land, ground, property (att.); deep-seated, fundamental. foncièrement (ɛrmɑ̃) ad, thoroughly.

fonction (fɔ̃ksjɔ̃) f. oft. pl, function, duty, office. faire ~ de, to act as. fonctionnaire (onɛːr) n, official, officer, functionary. ~ public, ique, civil servant. fonctionnarisme (narism) m, officialdom; officialism. fonctionnel, le (nɛl) a, functional. fonctionner (ne) v.i, to function, run, work, act.

fond (fɔ̃) m, bottom; ground; substratum; crown (hat); depth; floor; back; head; groundwork; background; seat (trousers, chair); heart; substance; main issue (Law); undertone; undercurrent; staying power, stamina. ~ de bain, non-slip mat (for bath). ~ de cale, bilge (ship). ~ de plateau, tray cloth. à ~, thoroughly; home. (course, &c) de ~, long-distance (race, &c). de ~ en comble, from top to bottom. faire ~ sur, to rely on.

fondamental, et (fɔ̃damɑ̃tal) a, fundamental, basic; foundation (stone).

fondant, e (fɔ̃dɑ̃, ɑ̃ːt) a, melting (ice); that melts in the mouth, luscious, juicy. ¶ m, flux; fondant.

fondateur, trice (fɔ̃datœːr, tris) n, founder, foundress; promoter. fondation (sjɔ̃) f, foundation; bed; establishment.

fondé de pouvoir(s) (fɔ̃de) m, attorney; proxy; duly authorized representative.

fondement (fɔ̃dmɑ̃) m. oft. pl, foundation, ground, base, basis; fundament. fonder (de) v.t, to found; base, ground. se ~, to take one's stand; be based.

fonderie (fɔ̃dri) f, foundry; [smelting] works; founding. fondeur (dœːr) m, founder.

fondre (fɔ̃ːdr) v.t, to melt, dissolve; smelt; fuse; cast, found; merge; blend; (v.i.) to melt, dissolve, fuse; blow, go (fuse). ~

sur, to fall [up]on, pounce on, swoop down on.

fondrière (fɔ̃drjɛːr) f, pit, hollow, hole (in road); quagmire, morass.

fonds (fɔ̃) m. oft. pl, fund; funds; money; cash; capital; stock; security. ~ d'amortissement, sinking fund. ~ [de commerce], goodwill, business. ~ de prévoyance, contingency fund. ~ de roulement, working capital. ~ [de terre], estate, [piece of] land. ~ perdu, with capital sunk (as in an annuity).

fongueux, euse (fɔ̃gø, øːz) a, fungous. fongus (gy:s) m, fungus.

fontaine (fɔ̃tɛn) f, fountain, spring, well; cistern (house). ~ de Jouvence, fountain of youth. fontainier (nje) m, maker of (or dealer in) domestic water appliances (cisterns, filters, &c); plumber; turncock; well sinker.

fonte (fɔ̃ːt) f, melting; smelting; casting, founding; melt; fo[u]nt (Typ.); holster. ~ d'acier, cast steel. ~ [de fer], [cast] iron. ~ [en gueuses], ~ en saumons, pig [iron].

fonts (fɔ̃) m.pl, font (Eccl.).

football (futbol) m, football (game). ~ association, Association f. [~] rugby, Rugby [f.].

for (fɔːr) m: ~ intérieur, conscience.

forage (foraːʒ) m, boring, drilling.

forain, e (forɛ̃, ɛn) a, non-resident; travelling; itinerant. ¶ m, [travelling] showman. [marchand] forain, market trader.

forban (forbɑ̃) m, [sea] rover; pirate; shark (fig.).

forçage (forsaːʒ) m, forcing (Hort.); overweight (coin).

forçat (forsa) m, convict.

force (fors) f, force; power; strength; potency; might; press (of sail); many, plenty of; (pl.) shears. ~ d'âme, fortitude. ~ d'inertie, inertia. ~ de bras, hand power. ~ de cheval, ~ en chevaux, horse p. ~ de l'âge, prime of life. ~ de levier, leverage. ~ des choses, force of circumstances. ~ du pouls, pulse rate. ~ du sang, call of the blood (fig.). ~ majeure, force majeure, cause beyond control. (travailler) à ~, hard. à ~ de, by dint of. à toute ~, at all costs.

forcé, e (forse) p.a, forced, compulsory; far-fetched; strained. forcément (mɑ̃) ad, perforce, necessarily.

forcené, e (forsəne) n, madman; fury.

forceps (forsɛps) m, obstetrical forceps.

forcer (forse) v.t, to force; wrench open; compel; make; drive; obtrude; strain; constrain; overcome; overwork; crowd; run down (Hunt.). forcerie (səri) f, forcing bed (Hort.).

forclore (forklɔːr) v.t.ir, to debar by time (Law). forclusion (klyzjɔ̃) f, debarment by time.

forer (fore) *v.t*, to bore, drill.

forestier, ère (forɛstje, ɛ:r) *a*, forest (*att.*). ¶ *m*, forester.

foret (fore) *m*, drill; bit. ~ *hélicoïdal*, twist drill.

forêt (fore) *f*, forest; shock (*hair*). *la F~-Noire*, the Black Forest.

foreur (forœ:r) *m*, driller (*pers.*). foreuse (rø:z) *f*, boring machine, drilling m.

forfaire à (forfɛ:r) *v.ir*, to fail in (*duty*); forfeit (*honour*). forfait (fɛ) *m*, crime; contract; fixed price, agreed sum. à ~ *ou forfaitaire* (tɛ:r) *a*, on contract, contractual, at an agreed price; through (*rate*); standard, inclusive (*charge*). forfaiture (ty:r) *f*, breach of trust.

forfanterie (forfɑ̃tri) *f*, bounce, brag.

forge (forʒ) *f*, forge; smithy; blacksmith's shop; ironworks. forger (ʒe) *v.t*, to forge; fabricate; coin (*word*). *se* ~, to conjure up. forgeron (ʒərɔ̃) *m*, [black]smith. forgeur, euse (ʒœ:r, ø:z) *n*, fabricator, coiner (*fig.*); (*m.*) forgeman.

formaliser (se) (formalize) *v.pr*, to take exception, t. offence, t. amiss. formaliste (list) *a*, formal, precise. formalité (te) *f*, formality.

format (forma) *m*, size (*book*), format.

formation (sjɔ̃) *f*, formation; structure.

forme (form) *f*, form, shape; block (*hat*); last (*shoe*); (*pl.*) manners; form[e] (*Typ.*). ~ *de radoub*, graving dock. *rester en* ~, to keep fit, keep in form. formel, le† (mɛl) *a*, formal; express; strict; flat.

former (me) *v.t*, to form, shape, fashion; frame; make; train. ~ *les faisceaux*, to pile arms (*Mil.*). ~ *une liste de jurés*, ~ *un tableau*, to empanel (*or* impanel) a jury.

formidable† (formidabl) *a*, formidable.

Formose (formo:z) *f*, Formosa.

formulaire (formylɛ:r) *m*, formulary. formule (myl) *f*, formula; form; recipe (*Phar.*); prescription (*Med.*). formuler (le) *v.t*, to draw up; write out; formulate.

fornication (fornikasjɔ̃) *f*, fornication.

fort, e (fo:r, ort) *a*, strong; powerful; heavy; stout; stiff; fortified; steep; large; great, big; high; good; bad; full; loud; well up; overweight (*coin*); hard (*solder*). *se faire fort* (*fort* is inv.), to undertake. fort, *ad*, hard; loud[ly]; very. ~ *avant dans la nuit*, far into the night. ¶ *m*, (the) strong (*pers.*); market porter; strongest part; thick[est]; height; depth; strong point, forte; lair; fort, stronghold. forte (fortɛ) *ad*, forte (*Mus.*). fortement (təmɑ̃) *ad*, strongly; highly; hard.

forteresse (fortərɛs) *f*, fortress, stronghold.

fortification (fortifikasjɔ̃) *f*, fortification. fortifier (fje) *v.t*, to strengthen, brace, invigorate; fortify.

fortin (fortɛ̃) *m*, small fort.

fortuit, e† (fortɥi, it) *a*, fortuitous, chance, casual, accidental.

fortune (fortyn) *f*, fortune; luck, chance. ~ *de mer*, perils of the sea. *dîner à la ~ du pot*, to take pot luck. *de* ~, makeshift; chance (*att.*). fortuné, e (ne) *a*, fortunate, lucky; well-to-do, moneyed.

forum (forɔm) *m*, forum.

forure (fory:r) *f*, bore, hole; pipe (*key*).

fosse (fo:s) *f*, pit, hole; den; grave; deep (*ocean*); fosse. ~ *à visiter*, inspection pit. ~ *[d'aisances]*, cesspool. ~ *septique*, septic tank.

fossé (fose) *m*, ditch, trench; moat; rift (*fig.*). *sauter le* ~, to take the plunge (*fig.*). fossette (fosɛt) *f*, dimple; chuck-farthing.

fossile (fosil) *a. & m*, fossil.

fossoyeur (foswajœ:r) *m*, grave digger.

fou, fol, folle (fu, fol) *a*, mad, insane; wild, frantic; foolish; passionately fond; uncontrollable; tremendous; loose, idle (*pulley, &c*). ~ *à lier*, raving mad, stark m. *folle de son corps*, wanton (*woman*). fou, folle, *n*, madman, -woman, lunatic; (*m.*) fool; jester (*court*); bishop (*Chess*). *fou de Bassan* (basɑ̃), common gannet.

fouailler (fwaje) *v.t*, to whip; castigate (*fig.*).

foucade (fukad) *f*, fit; start.

foudre (fudr) *f*, lightning; thunder, [thunder]-bolt; (*m.*) thunderbolt (*fig. & Myth.*); tun. foudroyer (drwaje) *v.t*, to strike with lightning, blast; (*in. p.p.*) thunderstruck; crush.

fouet (fwɛ) *m*, whip; whipcord; whisk (*egg*); tip (*wing*). *le* ~, a flogging. fouetter (te) *v.t. & i*, to whip, flog, lash; beat; whisk; stir (*the blood*).

fougère (fuʒɛ:r) *f*, fern. ~ *[à l'aigle]*, bracken, brake. ~ *arborescente*, tree fern.

fougue (fug) *f*, fire (*fig.*), spirit, mettle. fougueux, euse† (gø, ø:z) *a*, fiery, spirited, mettlesome.

fouille (fu:j) *f*, excavation, cut, trench, pit. fouille-au-pot (fujopo) *m*, cook's boy. fouiller (fuje) *v.t. & abs. & i*, to excavate; dig; mine; burrow in[to]; burrow; nuzzle; root; rummage, ransack; search, dive, peer into; fumble, grope; pry. fouilleur (jœ:r) *m*, searcher. fouillis (ji) *m*, jumble, muddle, litter.

fouine (fwin) *f*, beech marten (*Zool.*); pitchfork; fish spear, grains. fouiner (ne) *v.i*, to slink away; nose about.

foulage (fulaːʒ) *m*, fulling; pressing (*grapes*); impression (*Typ.*).

foulard (fula:r) *m*, foulard.

foule (ful) *f*, crowd, throng; shoal; mob.

fouler (fule) *v.t*, to press; full, mill (*cloth*); give an impression (*Typ.*); tread [on], trample [on]; harass; sprain, wrench; gall. ~ *aux pieds*, to tread under foot; ride roughshod over. foulon (lɔ̃) *m*, fuller.

foulque (fulk) *f*, coot.

foulure (fuly:r) *f*, sprain, wrench.

four (fu:r) *m*, oven; kiln; furnace; failure, fiasco. ~ *à houblon*, oast. ~ *crématoire* (krematwa:r), crematorium.

fourbe (furb) *a*, knavish. ¶ *m*, knave, cheat. ¶ *f.* & **fourberie** (bəri) *f*, knavery, cheating.

fourbir (furbi:r) *v.t*, to furbish, rub up.

fourbu, e (furby) *a*, foundered (*Vet.*); deadbeat.

fourche (furʃ) *f*, fork. ~ *à faner*, pitchfork.

fourcher (ʃe) *v.i*, to fork; branch off. **fourchette** (ʃet) *f*, fork (*table, &c*); trencherman; frog (*horse*); wishing bone, merrythought. *à la* ~, meat (*breakfast*). **fourchon** (ʃɔ̃) *m*, prong; fork (*tree*). **fourchu, e** (ʃy) *a*, forked; cleft; cloven.

fourgon (furgɔ̃) *m*, wag[g]on; truck; van; (*Rly.*) brake [van], guard's van; poker, rake. ~ *de déménagements*, moving van, pantechnicon [van]. ~ *des bagages*, luggage van. **fourgonner** (gɔne) *v.i*, to poke [about].

fourmi (furmi) *f*, ant, emmet; (*pl.*) pins & needles (*fig.*). **fourmilier** (milje) *m*, anteater. **fourmilière** (ljɛ:r) *f*, ant's nest. **fourmi-lion** (ljɔ̃) *m*, ant lion. **fourmiller** (mije) *v.i*, to swarm; teem; abound; tingle.

fournaise (furnɛ:z) *f*, furnace; inferno.

fourneau (no) *m*, stove; furnace; bowl (*pipe*). ~ *à gaz, à pétrole*, gas, oil, stove. ~ *de cuisine*, kitchener, cooking range, cooker. ~ [*de mine*], blast hole. ~ *philanthropique*, soup kitchen. **fournée** (ne) *f*, batch.

fourni, e (furni) *p.a*, stocked; thick, bushy. **fournier, ère** (furnje, ɛ:r) *n*, baker (*for public*). **fournil** (ni) *m*, bakehouse.

fourniment (furnimɑ̃) *m*, equipment (*soldier's*). **fournir** (ni:r) *v.t. & abs*, to furnish, supply, provide; afford, adduce; give; find; lodge, deposit; produce; follow (*Cards*); (*v.i.*) to provide, contribute. ~ *la carrière*, to stay the course. ~ [*à*] *la couleur demandée*, to follow suit. **fournissement** (nismɑ̃) *m*, contribution. **fournisseur, euse** (sœ:r, ø:z) *n*, supplier; dealer; contractor; tradesman. ~ *de l'armée*, army contractor. ~ *de navires*, ship chandler, marine store dealer. **fourniture** (ty:r) *f*, supply, store; requisite; (*pl.*) stationery; material; supplying; trimmings (*tailor's*); seasoning (*for salad, i.e, savoury herbs*).

fourrage (fura:ʒ) *m*, fodder, provender, forage; fur lining. **fourrager** (raʒe) *v.i. & t*, to forage; rummage; ravage. **fourrageur** (ʒœ:r) *m*, forager.

fourré (fure) *m*, thicket, brake; cover (*game*); jungle. **fourré, e** (re) *p.a*, fur-lined; stuffed (*Cook.*); wooded; jungly.

fourreau (furo) *m*, scabbard, sheath; case; cover; sleeve, cylinder.

fourrer (fure) *v.t*, to thrust, poke, shove; stuff, cram; line [with fur]. **fourre-tout**

(rtu) *m*, hold-all. **fourreur,'euse** (rœ:r, ø:z) *n*, furrier.

fourrier (furje) *m*, quartermaster; harbinger.

fourrière (furje:r) *f*, pound, greenyard. *mettre à la* ~, to impound.

fourrure (fury:r) *f*, fur, skin; welt; strap.

fourvoyer (furvwaje) *v.t*, to lead astray; mislead.

fox-terrier (fɔkstɛrje) *m*, fox terrier.

fox-trot (fɔkstrɔt) *m*, fox trot.

foyer (fwaje) *m*, hearth; furnace; fire box; stoker (*mechanical*); fireside; home; seat; hotbed; focus. ~ *d'étudiants*, hostel. ~ *des artistes*, greenroom. ~ [*du public*], foyer, crush room. [*pierre de*] ~, hearthstone.

frac (frak) *m*, dress coat.

fracas (fraka) *m*, crash; roar; din, row, noise, bluster. **fracasser** (kase) *v.t*, to smash, shatter, shiver.

fraction (fraksjɔ̃) *f*, fraction; breaking (*holy bread*). ~ *périodique*, recurring (or circulating) decimal. ~ *ordinaire*, vulgar fraction. **fractionnaire** (ɔnɛ:r) *a*, fractional. **fractionner** (ne) *v.t*, to split.

fracture (frakty:r) *f*, fracture, breaking. **fracturer** (tyre) *v.t*, to fracture, break.

fragile (fraʒil) *a*, fragile; brittle; frail; [glass,] with care. **fragilité** (lite) *f*, fragility, &c.

fragment (fragmɑ̃) *m*, fragment, piece, scrap; snatch. **fragmentaire** (tɛ:r) *a*, fragmentary. **fragmenter** (te) *v.t*, to break [up].

frai (frɛ) *m*, spawning; spawn, fry.

fraîchement (freʃmɑ̃) *ad*, in the cool; coolly; freshly, newly, lately. **fraîcheur** (ʃœ:r) *f*, freshness; cool[ness]; chill; bloom (*fig.*). **fraîchir** (ʃi:r) *v.i*, to freshen. **frais, aîche** (frɛ, ɛ:ʃ) *a*, fresh; cool; chilly; new (*bread, &c*); recent; new-laid; wet (*paint, ink, fish*). *frais & gaillard, frais & dispos*, hale & hearty, fit & fresh. **frais, aîche** (*with p.p.*) *ad*, fresh[ly], newly, *e.g, des roses fraîches cueillies*, fresh[ly] gathered roses. **frais,** *m*, cool. *au* ~ ou *à la fraîche*, in the cool.

frais (frɛ) *m.pl*, expenses; expense; charges; cost; costs (*Law*); efforts, pains. ~ *d'école*, ~ *scolaires*, school fees. ~ *de constitution*, preliminary expenses (*company*). ~ *de contentieux*, legal charges. ~ *divers*, general (or sundry) expenses. ~ *généraux*, standing (or establishment) (or overhead) expenses (or charges).

fraise (frɛ:z) *f*, strawberry; countersink [bit]; [milling] cutter; ruff (*Hist., dress*). ~ *des bois*, wild strawberry. **fraiser** (frɛze) *v.t*, to crimp; countersink; mill. **fraisier** (zje) *m*, strawberry plant.

fraisil (frɛzi) *m*, breeze (*cinders*).

framboise (frɑ̃bwa:z) *f*, raspberry. **framboisier** (bwazje) *m*, raspberry bush.

franc (frɑ̃) *m*, franc = 100 centimes. ~s-*or*, ~s-*argent*, ~s-*papier*, gold, silver, paper, francs.

franc, anche (frɑ̃, ɑ̃:ʃ) *a*, free; frank, candid, outspoken; open, open-hearted; aboveboard; clear (*complete, of days*); clean (*break, jump*); downright, out & out, regular, arrant; volunteer (*corps*); ungrafted (*tree*). **franc arbitre**, free will. **franc (anche) de port** ou **franc de port** (*inv.*), carriage free; post free. **franc, ad**, frankly, candidly.

français, e (frɑ̃sɛ, ɛ:z) *a*, French. **F~, n**, Frenchman, -woman. **les Français**, the French. **le français**, French (*language*).

franc-bord (frɑ̃bɔ:r) *m*, freeboard (*ship*); open space.

France (la) (frɑ̃:s), France.

Francfort (frɑ̃kfɔ:r) *m*, Frankfort.

franchement (frɑ̃ʃmɑ̃) *ad*, frankly, candidly, openly; downright; heartily; boldly.

franchir (frɑ̃ʃi:r) *v.t*, to jump over, leap o., pass o., get o.; pass through; clear; pass; cross; overstep; shoot (*rapids*); bridge; span; turn (*a certain age*); make (*hoop, Croquet*).

franchise (frɑ̃ʃi:z) *f*, exemption; franking (*Post*); frankness, outspokenness; plain dealing; freedom; immunity (*diplomatic*). **~ de poids, ~ de bagages**, weight allowed free, free allowance of luggage.

francisation (frɑ̃sizazjɔ̃) *f*, Frenchification; registration (*ship*).

franciscain (frɑ̃siskɛ̃) *m*, Franciscan, grey friar.

franciser (frɑ̃size) *v.t*, to Frenchify, gallicize.

franc-maçon (frɑ̃masɔ̃) *m*, freemason. **franc-maçonnerie** (sɔnri) *f*, freemasonry.

franco (frɑ̃ko) *ad*, free, f. of charge. **~ [d] bord**, free on board. **~ à quai**, free at wharf, ex wharf. **~ de port**, carriage paid; post p. **~ wagon, ~ gare**, free on rail, f. on truck.

francophile (frɑ̃kɔfil) *a. & n*, Francophil[e], Gallophil[e]. **francophobe** (fɔb) *a. & n*, Francophobe.

franc-tireur (frɑ̃tirœ:r) *m*, sniper; free lance.

frange (frɑ̃:ʒ) *f*, fringe. **franger** (frɑ̃ʒe) *v.t*, to fringe.

franquette (à la bonne) (frɑ̃kɛt) *f*, simply, without ceremony.

frappant, e (frapɑ̃, ɑ̃:t) *a*, striking. **frappe** (frap) *f*, stamp; minting; set of matrices (*Typ.*). **frapper** (pe) *v.t. & abs. & v.i*, to strike; hit; smite; tap; knock; slap; stamp; mint; impose, levy; be secured on. **~ [de glace]**, to ice. **~ de nullité**, to render void. **esprit frappeur** (pœ:r) *m*, rapping spirit.

frasque (frask) *f*, escapade.

frater (frate:r) *m*, lay brother. **fraternel, le†** (ternel) *a*, fraternal, brotherly. **fraterniser** (nize) *v.i*, to fraternize. **fraternité (te)** *f*, fraternity, brotherhood. **fratricide** (trisid) *m*, fratricide; (*att.*) fratricidal.

fraude (fro:d) *f*, fraud; smuggling. **la ~ fiscale, evasion of tax. frauder** (frode)

v.t, to defraud, cheat; evade [payment of]. **fraudeur, euse** (dœ:r, ø:z) *n*, defrauder; smuggler. **~ des droits du fisc**, tax dodger. **frauduleux, euse†** (dylø, ø:z) *a*, fraudulent.

frayer (freje) *v.t. & i*, to open up, clear, blaze; rub; spawn; rub shoulders, associate. **se ~**, to force (*a passage*); fight (*or grope*) (*one's way*).

frayeur (frejœ:r) *f*, fright, fear, dread.

fredaine (frədɛn) *f*, prank.

fredonner (frədɔne) *v.i. & t*, to hum (*tune*).

frégate (fregat) *f*, frigate.

frein (frɛ̃) *m*, brake; curb, check (*fig.*); fr[a]enum (*Anat.*). **~ à ruban, ~ à bande**, band brake. **~ à vide**, vacuum b. **~ sur jantes**, rim b. **~ sur les quatre roues**, four-wheel b. **~ sur moyeux**, hub b. **~ sur pneu**, spoon b. **freiner** (frɛne) *v.i*, ou **serrer les freins**, to [put on (*or* apply)] brake.

frelater (frəlate) *v.t*, to adulterate, doctor.

frêle (frɛ:l) *a*, frail; weak.

frelon (frəlɔ̃) *m*, hornet.

freluche (frəlyʃ) *f*, tassel; tuft. **freluquet** (kɛ) *m*, whipper-snapper, puppy (*man*); coxcomb.

frémir (fremi:r) *v.i*, to rustle; murmur; simmer; vibrate, quiver, shudder.

frêne (frɛ:n) *m*, ash [tree, timber].

frénésie (frenezi) *f*, frenzy. **frénétique†** (tik) *a*, frantic, frenzied.

fréquemment (frekamɑ̃) *ad*, frequently, repeatedly, often. **fréquence** (kɑ̃:s) *f*, frequency; prevalence. **fréquent, e** (kɑ̃, ɑ̃:t) *a*, frequent; rapid (*pulse, &c*). **fréquentation** (kɑ̃tasjɔ̃) *f*, frequentation; (*pl.*) companionship. **fréquenté, e (te)** *p.p*, crowded. **fréquenter (te)** *v.t*, to frequent; resort to; associate with.

frère (frɛ:r) *m*, brother; (*pl.*) brethren (*Eccl.*); friar; sister [ship]. **~ de lait**, foster brother. **frérot** (frero) *m*, [dear] little brother.

fresaie (frəzɛ) *f*, barn owl, screech owl.

fresque (frɛsk) *f*, fresco.

fressure (frɛsy:r) *f*, pluck (*Butchery*).

fret (frɛ) *m*, freight. **prendre à ~, to charter. fréter** (frete) *v.t*, to freight; charter. **fréteur** (tœ:r) *m*, [ship]owner.

frétiller (fretije) *v.i*, to frisk; wriggle; fidget; itch. **~ de la queue**, to wag its tail (*dog*).

fretin (frətɛ̃) *m*, fry (*fish*); small fry (*pers.*); rubbish.

frette (frɛt) *f*, hoop, collar, band, ring, ferrule; fret (*Arch., Her.*). **fretter (te)** *v.t*, to hoop, bind.

freux (frø) *m*, rook (*bird*).

friable (friabl) *a*, friable, crumbly.

friand, e (friɑ̃, ɑ̃:d) *a*, dainty. **~ de**, fond of. **friandise** (ɑ̃di:z) *f*, dainty, delicacy, sweet.

Fribourg (fribu:r) *m*, Fribourg, Freiburg (*Switzerland*). **F~-en-Brisgau** (brizgo) *m*, Freiburg (*Baden*).

fricassée (frikas) *f*, fricassee. **fricasser** (se) *v.t*, to fricassee; fritter away. **fricasseur, euse** (sœːr, øːz) *n*, bad cook; squanderer.

friche (friʃ) *f*, waste land, fallow [land]. **en ~**, fallow; undeveloped.

fricot (friko) *m*, stew. **fricoter** (kote) *v.i*, to stew; cook badly; (*v.t.*) to squander. **fricoteur, euse** (tœːr, øːz) *n*, jobber; shirker.

friction (friksjɔ̃) *f*, friction; rubbing; dry shampoo, scalp massage. **frictionner** (one) *v.t*, to rub, chafe.

frigidité (friʒidite) *f*, frigidity, coldness. **frigorifier** (gorifje) *v.t*, to refrigerate, freeze (*meat, &c*). **frigorifique** (fik) *a*, refrigerating, freezing, cold (*att.*). ¶ *m*, cold store.

frileux, euse (frilø, øːz) *a*, chilly (*pers.*).

frimas (frima) *m*, icy mist, rime.

frime (frim) *f*, sham, pretence.

frimousse (frimus) *f*, phiz, face.

fringale (frɛ̃gal) *f*, hunger; craving. **avoir la ~**, to be peckish, be famishing.

fringant, e (frɛ̃gã, ãːt) *a*, frisky, lively; smart. **fringuer** (ge) *v.i*, to frisk, skip about.

friper (fripe) *v.t*, to [c]rumple, crease. **friperie** (pri) *f*, cast-off clothes, left-off wearing apparel; second-hand furniture; frippery, trumpery; wardrobe dealer's shop. **fripier, ère** (pje, ɛːr) *n*, wardrobe dealer.

fripon, ne (fripɔ̃, ɔn) *n*, knave, rogue, rascal; hussy, minx; thief. ¶ *a*, knavish, roguish, rascally. **friponner** (pone) *v.t. & abs*, to cheat out of; steal from; cheat. **friponnerie** (nri) *f*, knavery, roguery, rascality.

friquet (frikɛ) *m*, tree sparrow.

frire (friːr) *v.t. & i. ir*, to fry.

frise (friːz) *f*, frieze. **la F~**, Friesland.

friser (frize) *v.t. & i*, to curl, frizzle, friz[z], crimp; graze; border on; slur (*Typ.*). **frison** (zɔ̃) *m*, curl.

frison, ne (frizɔ̃, ɔn) *a. & F~, n*, Frisian.

frisotter (frizote) *v.t*, to frizz[le].

frisquet (friskɛ) *a.m. & a.f*, chilly.

frisquette (frisket) *f*, frisket (*Typ.*).

frisson (frisɔ̃) *m*, shiver, shudder, quiver; thrill. **frissonner** (sone) *v.i*, to shiver, &c.

frisure (frizyːr) *f*, curling; curliness; (*pl.*) curls.

friture (frityːr) *f*, frying; frying, crackling (*Teleph.*); fry; frying oil, frying fat; fried fish.

frivole (frivol) *a*, frivolous, flighty; trivial, fiddling, trumpery, flimsy, frothy. **frivolité** (lite) *f*, frivolity, trifle; tatting.

froc (frok) *m*, cowl; frock (*monk's*); monkery, monkhood.

froid, e† (frwa, ad) *a*, cold; frigid; cool, chill[y]. **à froid**, *ad*, cold, when cold; in cold blood. ¶ *m*, cold; c. weather; frost (*degrees of*); coldness; chill[iness]; coolness. **froideur** (dœːr) *f*, coldness, chilliness; cool-

ness; frigidity. **froidure** (dyːr) *f*, coldness, cold.

froisser (frwase) *v.t*, to bruise; crush; [c]rumple; offend, hurt, wound.

frôler (frole) *v.t*, to graze, brush [against]; come very near to (*fig.*).

fromage (fromaːʒ) *m*, cheese; soft job. **~ à la crème**, double-cream cheese. **~ blanc**, cream cheese. **~ de porc**, brawn. **fromager, ère** (maʒe, ɛːr) *n*, cheese maker; cheesemonger; (*att.*) cheese. **fromagerie** (ʒri) *f*, cheese dairy.

froment (fromã) *m*, wheat.

fronce (frɔ̃ːs) *f*, gather; pucker. **~s smock** (smɔk), smocking. **froncer** (frɔ̃se) *v.t*, to wrinkle; purse, pucker (*lips*); gather (*Need.*). **~ le[s] sourcil[s]**, to frown, knit one's brows.

frondaison (frɔ̃dɛzɔ̃) *f*, foliation, leafing; foliage.

fronde (frɔ̃ːd) *f*, sling; catapult (*boy's*); frond (*Bot.*); obstruction (*fig.*). **fronder** (frɔ̃de) *v.i*, to catapult; obstruct; (*v.t.*) to find fault with. **frondeur** (dœːr) *m*, slinger; fault finder; critic. **~, euse** (øːz) *att*, fault-finding.

front (frɔ̃) *m*, front; front [line] (*Mil.*); forehead; brow; face; head; impudence, cheek. **de ~**, abreast; frontal; front.

frontière (frɔ̃tjɛːr) *f. & att*, frontier, border.

frontispice (frɔ̃tispis) *m*, frontispiece (*book*); title page. **fronton** (tɔ̃) *m*, fronton, pediment.

frottage (frotaːʒ) *m*, polishing (*floors*). **frottée** (te) *f*, drubbing, thrashing. **frottement** (tmã) *m*, rubbing; friction; contact, intercourse. **frotter** (te) *v.t. & i*, to rub; polish; scumble; drub, pommel; box (*ears*); strike (*match*). **se ~ à** (*fig.*), to rub shoulders with. **se ~ les mains**, to rub one's hands. **frotteur** (tœːr) *m*, floor polisher (*pers.*); shoe, plough (*Elec.*). **frottis** (ti) *m*, scumble; rubbing (*copy*). **frottoir** (twaːr) *m*, rubber, polisher.

frou-frou (frufru) *m*, rustling, swish.

fructifier (fryktifje) *v.i*, to fructify. **fructueux, euse†** (tɥø, øːz) *a*, fruitful (*fig. & poet.*), profitable.

frugal, e† (frygal) *a*, frugal. **frugalité** (lite) *f*, frugality.

fruit (frɥi) *m*, fruit; profit; benefit; batter (*Build.*). **~ tombé**, windfall. **fruiterie** (tri) *f*, fruit shop; f. trade. **fruitier, ère** (tje, ɛːr) *n*, fruiterer, greengrocer; (*att.*) fruit.

frusques (frysk) *f.pl*, clothes.

frusquin (fryskɛ̃) *m*, worldly goods.

fruste (fryst) *a*, defaced, worn.

frustrer (frystre) *v.t*, to deprive; defraud; frustrate, balk.

fuchsia (fyksja) *m*, fuchsia.

fugace (fygas) *a*, fleeting; unretentive (*memory*). **fugitif, ive** (ʒitif, iːv) *a*, fugitive, fleeting, transitory, short-lived. ¶ *n*, fugitive, runaway.

fugue (fyg) *f*, fugue (*Mus.*); flight; bolt; elopement.

fuir (fɥi:r) *v.i. ir*, to flee, fly, flit, run away; escape; recede; vanish; leak; (*v.t.ir.*) to flee [from], run away from; shun; eschew. **fuite** (fɥit) *f*, flight; escape; leak[age].

fulguration (fylgyrasjɔ̃) *f*, heat (*or* summer) lightning.

fulmicoton (fylmikɔtɔ̃) *m*, guncotton.

fulminer (fylmine) *v.i. & t*, to fulminate, thunder, storm.

fumage (fyma:ʒ) *m*, smoking (*meat, fish*); manuring. **fume-cigarette** *m*, cigarette holder, c. tube. **fumée** (me) *f. oft. pl*, smoke; fume; steam; vapour; reek; phantom, vanity; (*pl.*) dung. **fumer** (me) *v.i. & t*, to smoke; cure; steam; reek; fume; manure. *cheminée qui fume*, smoky chimney. **fumerie** (mri) *f*, opium den. **fumet** (mɛ) *m*, smell; bouquet; scent. **fumeur, euse** (mœ:r, ø:z) *n*, smoker. **fumeux, euse** (mø, ø:z) *a*, smoky; heady; hazy. **fumier** (mje) *m*, litter (*straw & dung*), dung, manure; muck; dunghill. **fumigation** (fymigasjɔ̃) *f*, fumigation.

fumiste (fymist) *m*, heating engineer; practical joker. **fumisterie** (tri) *f*, heating engineering; practical joke. **fumivore** (vɔr) *a*, smoke-consuming. ¶ m. s. consumer, s. preventer. **fumoir** (mwa:r) *m*, smoke house; smoking room.

fumure (fymy:r) *f*, manuring; manure.

funambule (fynɑ̃byl) *n*, funambulist; rope walker. **funambulesque** (lɛsk) *a*, funambulatory; fantastic.

funèbre (fyne:br) *a*, funeral; funereal; dead (*march*); ill-omened (*birds*). **funérailles** (nera:j) *f.pl*, funeral. **funéraire** (rɛ:r) *a*, funeral.

funeste (fynɛst) *a*, deadly, baneful, baleful, fatal.

funiculaire (fynikylɛ:r) *a. & m*, funicular, cable railway.

fur (fy:r) *m: au ~ & à mesure*, in proportion. *au ~ & à mesure des besoins*, as [& when] required. *au ~ & à mesure que*, as [& when].

furet (fyrɛ) *m*, ferret. **fureter** (rte) *v.i. & t*, to ferret, f. about; pry. **fureteur, euse** (rtœ:r, ø:z) *n*, ferreter; rummager; collector; hunter; Paul Pry.

fureur (fyrœ:r) *f*, fury, rage, wrath; passion; distraction; craze; frenzy; furore. **furibond, e** (ribɔ̃, ɔ̃:d) *a*, furious. ¶ n, madman; fury. **furie** (ri) *f*, fury. F~, Fury (*Myth.*). **furieux, euse†** (rjø, ø:z) *a*, furious, raging, mad, raving; tremendous. ¶ n, madman, -woman.

furoncle (fyrɔ̃:kl) *m*, boil (*Med.*).

furtif, ive† (fyrtif, i:v) *a*, furtive, stealthy, sly.

fusain (fyzɛ̃) *m*, spindle tree; charcoal [pencil]; c. drawing.

fuseau (fyzo) *m*, spindle (*Spinning*); pintle.

fusée (fyze) *f*, rocket, fuse; fusee (*Horol.*); (*axle*) journal; [out]burst (*fig.*). ~ *volante*, sky rocket.

fuselage (fyzla:ʒ) *m*, fuselage. **fuselé, e** (zle) *a*, spindle-shaped; taper[ing]; stream-lined.

fusible (fyzibl) *a*, fusible.

fusil (fyzi) *m*, gun, rifle; steel (*sharpener*). ~ *à air comprimé*, ~ *à vent*, air gun. ~ *à deux coups*, double-barrelled g. ~ *mitrailleur*, machine g. ~ *pour le tir à plomb*, shot g. ~ *se chargeant par la culasse*, breech-loader. **fusilier** (zilje) *m: ~ marin*, marine. ~ *mitrailleur*, machine gunner. **fusillade** (zijad) *f*, fusillade. **fusiller** (je) *v.t*, to shoot (*spy, deserter*); bombard (*fig.*).

fusion (fyzjɔ̃) *f*, fusion, melting, smelting. **fusionner** (one) *v.t. & i*, to amalgamate, merge.

fustiger (fystiʒe) *v.t*, to flog; rebuke.

fût (fy) *m*, stock (*rifle, plane*); handle; shank; shaft (*of column*); post; cask; drum. **futaie** (fytɛ) *f*, timber-tree forest. **futaille** (fyta:j) *f*, cask, barrel. **futaine** (fytɛn) *f*, fustian. **futé, e** (fyte) *a*, crafty; sly; sharp. **futile** (fytil) *a*, futile, nugatory; trifling, idle. **futilité** (lite) *f*, futility; (*pl.*) trifles; (*pl.*) trash (*worthless contents of book*).

futur, e (fyty:r) *a*, future. ¶ n, intended (*husband, wife*). ¶ m, future; futurity. ~ *antérieur*, future perfect (*Gram.*). ~ [*simple*], future [tense].

fuyant, e (fɥijɑ̃, ɑ̃:t) *a*, receding, retreating; vanishing (*Perspective*); shifty. **fuyard, e** (fɥija:r, ard) *n*, fugitive, runaway.

G

gabare (gaba:r) *f*, lighter, barge; drag net.

gabarit (gabari) *m*, ga[u]ge, templet; mould (*ship*).

gabegie (gabʒi) *f*, mismanagement & dishonesty.

gabier (gabje) *m*, top[s]man (*Naut.*).

gâche (ga:ʃ) *f*, staple (*lock, wall*). **gâcher** (gaʃe) *v.t*, to temper (*mortar*); spoil, botch, mess up. **gâchis** (ʃi) *m*, (*wet*) mortar; slush, sludge; mess.

gadoue (gadu) *f*, night soil, sewage.

gaffe (gaf) *f*, boat hook; gaff (*Fish.*); blunder, howler. **gaffer** (fe) *v.t*, to hook, gaff; (*v.i.*) to blunder.

gage (ga:ʒ) *m*, pledge, pawn, security, gage; hostage; forfeit (*at play*); token, proof; (*pl.*) wages, pay; forfeits (*game*). *à ~s*, paid, hired. **gager** (ʒaʒe) *v.t*, to pay; bet. **gageure** (ʒy:r) *f*, wager. **gagiste** (ʒist) *m*, employee.

gagnage (gaɲa:ʒ) *m*, pasturage.

gagnant, e (gaɲɑ̃, ɑ̃:t) *n*, winner; (*att.*) winning. **gagne-pain** (ɲpɛ̃) *m*, livelihood. **gagne-petit** (ɲpəti) *m*, knife grinder; one who earns (*or* makes) very little. **gagner** (ɲe) *v.t. & abs. & i,* to gain; be the gainer; get; make; earn; win; gain over; reach, get to; overtake; spread. ~ *à être connu,* to improve on acquaintance. **se** ~, to be catching; spread.

gai, e† (ge) *a,* gay, merry; lively; blithe; bright, cheerful. **gai, i,** merrily!

gaïac (gajak) *m,* lignum vitae.

gaieté (gete) *f,* gaiety; cheerfulness; liveliness; merriment, mirth, glee. *de* ~ *de cœur,* out of sheer wantonness. **gaillard, e**† (gaja:r, ard) *a,* jolly, merry; hearty; free, ribald. ¶ *m,* fellow, fine f., jolly f. ~ *d'arrière,* quarter deck. ~ *d'avant,* fore-castle. ¶ *f,* strapping gay wench. **gaillardise** (jardi:z) *f,* gaiety, jollity; broad humour.

gailletin (gajtɛ̃) *m.* ou **gaillette** (jɛt) *f,* cobbles, nuts (*coal*).

gain (gɛ̃) *m,* gain, profit, lucre; earnings; winning; winnings. ~ *de cause,* decision in one's favour; right, justification. **en** ~, in pocket, to the good.

gaine (gɛ:n) *f,* sheath, case; body belt; pedestal.

gala (gala) *m,* gala.

galamment (galamɑ̃) *ad,* courteously, gallantly; skilfully. **galant, e** (lɑ̃, ɑ̃:t) *a,* gallant (*to women*); amatory; stylish. *galant homme,* gentleman. ¶ *m,* gallant; spark; philanderer; lover; slippery gentleman. **galanterie** (lɑ̃tri) *f,* politeness, gallantry (*to women*); love affair.

galbe (galb) *m,* contour, outline.

gale (gal) *f,* itch; mange; scab.

galée (gale) *f,* composing galley.

galène (galɛn) *f,* galena.

galère (galɛ:r) *f,* galley (*Hist.*).

galerie (galri) *f,* gallery; arcade; level, drive, drift, road[way] (*Min.*); (*pl, Theat.*) circle. ~ *d'écho,* whispering gallery. ~ *d flanc de coteau,* adit. *faire* ~, to sit out.

galérien (galerjɛ̃) *m,* galley slave.

galerne (galɛrn) *f,* north-wester (*wind*).

galet (galɛ) *m,* pebble; (*pl. or s.*) shingle; roller, wheel, runner; castor, caster.

galetas (galta) *m,* garret, attic.

galette (galɛt) *f,* girdle cake; ship biscuit, hard tack.

galeux, euse (galø, ø:z) *a,* itchy; scabby; mangy; scurfy.

galhauban (galobɑ̃) *m,* backstay (*Naut.*).

galimafrée (galimafre) *f,* hash, hotchpotch.

galimatias (galimatja) *m,* balderdash, gibberish.

galion (galjɔ̃) *m,* galleon (*Hist.*).

galle (gal) *f,* gall [nut].

Galles (le **pays** de) (gal), Wales. *la Galles du Nord, du Sud,* North, South. Wales.

gallican, e (galikɑ̃, an) *a. & n,* Gallican. **gallicisme** (sism) *m,* gallicism.

gallinacés (galinase) *m.pl,* Gallinaceae.

gallois, e (galwa, a:z) *a,* Welsh. **G~, n,** Welshman, -woman. *le gallois,* Welsh (*language*).

gallophobe (galɔfɔb) *a. & n,* Gallophobe, anti-French.

galoche (galɔʃ) *f,* clog overshoe.

galon (galɔ̃) *m,* braid, galloon; gimp; stripe (*N.C.O.'s, & Navy*); band (*officer's*). **galonner** (lone) *v.t,* to braid, lace.

galop (galo) *m,* gallop; galop (*dance*); hot haste; scolding. **galoper** (lɔpe) *v.i,* to gallop; run, career. **galopin** (pɛ̃) *m,* urchin.

galuchat (galyʃa) *m,* shagreen.

galvanique (galvanik) *a,* galvanic. **galvaniser** (ze) *v.t,* to galvanize. **galvanisme** (nism) *m,* galvanism. **galvanoplastie** (nɔplasti) *f,* galvanoplasty.

galvauder (galvode) *v.t,* to misuse; botch; (*v.i.*) to loiter. **se** ~, to sully one's name.

gambade (gɑ̃bad) *f,* gambol, frisk; (*pl.*) antics, capers. **gambader** (de) *v.i,* to gambol, &c.

Gambie (la) (gɑ̃bi), Gambia.

gambiller (gɑ̃bije) *v.i,* to skip about.

gambit (gɑ̃bi) *m,* gambit (*Chess*).

gamelle (gamɛl) *f,* mess tin; mess (*Nav.*).

gamin, e (gamɛ̃, in) *n,* urchin; youngster, nipper; (*f.*) hoyden, romp. ~ *des rues,* street child, s. arab. ¶ *a,* saucy. **gaminer** (mine) *v.i,* to play about. **gaminerie** (nri) *f,* child's prank; [tom]foolery.

gamme (gam) *f,* scale; gamut; range; tone, tune (*fig.*).

ganache (ganaʃ) *f,* lower jaw (*horse*); duffer, fogey.

Gand (gɑ̃) *m,* Ghent.

Gange (le) (gɑ̃:ʒ), the Ganges.

ganglion (gɑ̃gliɔ̃) *m,* ganglion.

gangrène (gɑ̃grɛn) *f,* gangrene. **gangrener** (grəne) *v.t,* to gangrene; corrupt, canker.

gangue (gɑ̃:g) *f,* gangue, matrix.

ganse (gɑ̃:s) *f,* cord (*braided*); gimp; loop.

gant (gɑ̃) *m,* glove; gauntlet (*fig.*); (*pl.*) credit. ~*s de peau glacée,* glacé kid gloves. ~*s de Suède,* suède g—s. ~*s de toilette,* bath g—s. **gantelée** (tle) *f,* foxglove. **gantelet** (tlɛ) *m,* gauntlet. **ganter** (te) *v.t,* to glove. **se** ~, to put on one's gloves. **ganterie** (tri) *f,* glove trade. **gantier, ère** (tje, ɛ:r) *n,* glover.

garage (gara:ʒ) *m,* shunting (*Rly*); garage (*motor*); shed (*cycle*); house (*boat*); hangar (*Aero.*).

garance (garɑ̃:s) *f,* madder.

garant, e (garɑ̃, ɑ̃:t) *n,* guarantor, surety (*pers.*); (*m.*) authority; warrant; [tackle] fall (*Naut.*). **garantie** (rɑ̃ti) *f,* guarantee, guaranty, warranty; security, indemnity; safeguard; underwriting (*Fin.*). **garantir** (ti:r) *v.t,* to guarantee; warrant; secure; keep, protect, shield; vouch for; underwrite (*Fin.*).

garcette (garsɛt) *f,* gasket; rope end.

garçon (garsɔ̃) *m*, boy, lad; son; [young] man; fellow, chap; bachelor, single man; [journey]man. ~ *d'écurie*, [h]ostler. ~ *d'étage*, boots (*hotel*). ~ *d'honneur*, best man, groomsman. ~ *de bureau*, messenger, commissionaire. ~ *de cabine*, steward. ~ [*de café*], waiter. ~ *de course*, errand boy. ~ *de magasin*, shopman. ~ *de recette*, walk[s] clerk (*bank*). ~ *manqué*, tomboy, hoyden, romp. **garçonne** (sɔn) *f*, bachelor girl. **garçonnet** (sɔnɛ) *m*, little boy. **garçonnier, ère** (nje, ɛːr) *a*, (*of girl*) mannish, masculine; fond of men's society. ¶ *f*, bachelor flat.

garde (gard) *f*, guardianship; guard; keeping, charge, [safe] custody; watch; heed, care; protection; notice; ward (*lock*); hilt; covering card; end paper. ~ *blanche*, flyleaf. ~ *descendante*, old guard (*Mil.*). ~ *montante*, new guard.

garde (gard) *m*, guard (*pers.*); keeper; watchman; watcher (*Cust.*); warder; ranger. ~*barrière, n*, gate keeper (*level crossing*). ~*cendre, m*, fender. ~*champêtre, m*, rural policeman. ~*chasse, m*, gamekeeper. ~*corps, m*, rail (*ship*). ~*côte, m*, coast-defence ship. ~*crotte, ~boue, m*, mudguard; splash board. ~ [*d'accouchée*], *f*, monthly nurse. ~*feu, m*, fire guard. ~*fou, m*, hand rail, railing. ~*frein, n*, brakesman. ~*jupe, m*, dress guard (*cycle*). ~*magasin, m*, storekeeper. ~*malades, n*, [sick] nurse. ~*manger, m*, pantry, larder; meat safe. ~*meuble, m*, depository; furniture warehouse. ~*robe, f*, wardrobe; motion (*bowels*). ~*vue, m*, eye shade.

gardénia (gardenja) *m*, gardenia.

garder (garde) *v.t*, to keep; retain; harbour; tend, look after, mind; guard, protect. *se ~ de*, to take care not to; beware of; refrain from. **garderie** (dəri) *f*, day nursery. **gardeur, euse** (dœːr, øːz) *n*, keeper, -herd (*cow, swine*). **gardien, ne** (djɛ̃, ɛn) *n*, guardian; keeper, caretaker, custodian, attendant, warder, dress. ~ *de but*, goal keeper. ~ *de la paix*, policeman, constable. ~ *du terrain*, ground man.

gardon (gardɔ̃) *m*, roach (*fish*).

gare (gaːr) *i*, look out! take care! mind. ¶ *f*, station (*Rly.*). ~ *d'embranchement*, ~ *de bifurcation*, junction. ~ *d'évitement*, sidings. ~ *de jonction*, joint station. ~ *maritime*, harbour station. *en ~*, ~ *restante*, [at railway station,] to be called for.

garenne (garɛn) *f*, [rabbit] warren.

garer (gare) *v.t*, to shunt, switch (*train*); garage (*car*). *se ~*, to shunt; pull to one side; get out of the way, take cover.

gargariser (se) (gargarize) *v.pr. & abs*, to gargle; gloat on. **gargarisme** (rism) *m*, gargle.

gargote (gargɔt) *f*, cookshop, eating house.

gargouille (garguːj) *f*, gargoyle; waterspout (*rain*). **gargouiller** (juje) *v.i*, to gurgle; rumble (*bowels*).

gargousse (argus) *f*, cartridge (*cannon*).

garnement (garnəmɑ̃) *m*. ou *mauvais ~*, scapegrace, scamp.

garnir (garniːr) *v.t. & abs*, to furnish; stock; fill; line; lag; stuff; trim; garnish; decorate. **garnison** (nizɔ̃) *f*, garrison. **garniture** (tyːr) *f*, fittings; furniture; trimmings; packing, lagging, gasket; lining; garnish; seasoning (*of salad, i.e. savoury herbs*); set. ~ *de foyer*, fire irons. ~ *de table*, luncheon set.

garrot (garo) *m*, withers; tourniquet; gar[r]otte. **garrotter** (rɔte) *v.t*, to pinion; strangle.

gars (ga) *m*, lad, boy.

gascon, ne (gaskɔ̃, ɔn) *n*, braggart, Gascon. **gasconnade** (kɔnad) *f*, boasting, gasconade.

gaspiller (gaspije) *v.t*, to waste, squander.

gastéropode (gasterɔpɔd) *m*, gast[e]ropod. **gastrique** (trik) *a*, gastric. **gastrite** (trit) *f*, gastritis. **gastronome** (trɔnɔm) *m*, gastronome[r]. **gastronomie** (mi) *f*, gastronomy. **gastronomique** (mik) *a*, gastronomic(al).

gâté, e (gate) *p.a*, spoilt; damaged, rotten. **gâteau** (gato) *m*, cake; comb (*honey*); spoils. ~ *au madère*, tipsy cake.

gâte-métier (gɑtmetje) *m*, [price] cutter; rat. **gâter** (te) *v.t*, to spoil, mar; soil; corrupt; taint; indulge, pamper. **gâterie** (tri) *f*, overindulgence (*to pers.*), spoiling.

gauche (goːʃ) *a*, left; crooked; awkward, clumsy; tactless. ¶ *f*, left. ¶ **le** [**poing**] **gauche**, the left (*Box.*). **gauchement** (goʃmɑ̃) *ad*, awkwardly, clumsily. **gaucher, ère** (ʃe, ɛːr) *a*, left-handed. ¶ *n*, left-hander (*pers. or player*). **gaucherie** (ʃri) *f*, awkwardness. **gauchir** (ʃiːr) *v.i. & t*, to turn aside; shuffle; buckle, bend; warp, wind.

gaudriole (godriɔl) *f*, broad joke.

gaufre (goːfr) *f*, comb (*honey*); waffle; gofer. **gaufrer** (gofre) *v.t*, to gof[f]er; crimp; emboss; figure; tool (*Bookb.*). **gaufrette** (fret) *f*, wafer [biscuit] (*flat*).

gaule (goːl) *f*, pole; fishing rod; switch (*stick*). **gaulois, e** (golwa, aːz) *a*, Gallic; joyous, broad, free. **G~**, *n*, Gaul. **gauloiserie** (lwazri) *f*, broadness; broad humour.

gausser (se) de (gose), to poke fun at.

gavage (gavaːʒ) *m*, cramming; forcible feeding.

gave (gaːv) *m*, mountain torrent.

gaver (gave) *v.t*, to cram (*poultry, pupil for exam*); feed forcibly; stuff.

gavotte (gavɔt) *f*, gavotte.

gaz (gɑːz) *m*, gas; flatus, wind. ~ *lacrymogène* (lakrimɔʒɛn), tear gas. ~ *moutarde*, mustard g. ~ *pauvre*, producer g.

gaze (gɑːz) *f*, gauze.

gazéifier (gazeifje) *v.t*, to gasify; aerate.

gazelle (gazɛl) *f*, gazelle.

gazer (gɑze) v.t, to cover with gauze; veil, tone down; gas (War).

gazette (gazɛt) f, gazette; newsmonger, gossip.

gazeux, euse (gazø, ø:z) a; gaseous; gassy; aerated; effervescing. **gazier** (zje) m, gas worker; gas fitter. **gazogène** (zɔʒɛn) m, gazogene, seltzogene; [gas] producer. **gazomètre** (mɛtr) m, gasometer.

gazon (gɑzɔ̃) m, grass; turf, sod; lawn, [green]sward. **gazonner** (zɔne) v.t, to turf. **gazouiller** (gazuje) v.i, to warble, chirp, twitter; purl, babble; prattle.

geai (ʒɛ) m, jay (bird).

géant, e (ʒeɑ̃, ɑ̃:t) n, giant, ess; (att.) giant.

géhenne (ʒeɛn) f, Gehenna, hell.

geignard, e (ʒɛɲa:r, ard) a, whining, fretful. **geindre** (ʒɛ̃:dr) v.i.ir, to whine, fret.

gélatine (ʒelatin) f, gelatin[e]. **gélatineux, euse** (nø, ø:z) a, gelatinous.

gelé, e (ʒəle) a, frozen; frost-bitten. **gelée** (le) f, frost; jelly. ~ blanche, hoar frost, white f. ~ noire, ~ à glace, black f. **geler** (le) v.t. & i. & imp. & se ~, to freeze.

gémir (ʒemi:r) v.i, to groan, moan; complain. **gémissement** (mismɑ̃) m, groan[ing], &c.

gemme (ʒɛm) f, gem; bud; (att.) gem (stone); rock (salt).

gênant, e (ʒɛnɑ̃, ɑ̃:t) a, in the way; awkward; troublesome.

gencive (ʒɑ̃si:v) f, gum (Anat.).

gendarme (ʒɑ̃darm) m, gendarme (constable); Amazon; martinet; spark; flaw. **se gendarmer** (me) v.pr, to be up in arms, fire up. **gendre** (ʒɑ̃:dr) m, son-in-law.

gêne (ʒɛ:n) f, discomfort; inconvenience; constraint; want; straits, straitened circumstances. sans ~, indifferent (to other people's convenience, &c), unconcerned, cool; unconventional, free & easy.

généalogie (ʒenealɔʒi) f, genealogy; pedigree. **généalogique** (ʒik) a, genealogical, family (tree).

gêner (ʒɛne) v.t, to hinder, hamper, cramp; pinch (shoes, &c); interfere with; inconvenience.

général, e† (ʒeneral) a, general; common; prevailing. le ~, the general (fig.). ~ de brigade, colonel commandant. ~ de corps d'armée, lieutenant general. ~ de division, major general. ~ en chef, (full) general. ¶ f, general's wife; general (roll of the drum). **généralat** (la) m, generalship. **généraliser** (lize) v.t. & abs, to generalize. se ~, to become general. **généralissime** (sim) m, generalissimo, commander-in-chief. **généralité** (te) f, generality.

générateur, trice (ʒeneratœ:r, tris) a, generating. ¶ m, generator. **génération** (sjɔ̃) f, generation.

généreux, euse† (ʒenerø, ø:z) a, generous, bounteous, bountiful.

générique (ʒenerik) a, generic.

générosité (ʒenerozite) f, generosity, bounteousness; (pl.) acts of generosity.

Gênes (ʒɛ:n) f, Genoa.

genèse (ʒənɛ:z) f, genesis. la G~, Genesis (Bible).

genet (ʒənɛ) m, jennet (horse).

genêt (ʒənɛ) m, broom (Bot.). ~ épineux, furze, gorse, whin.

genette (ʒənɛt) f, genet (civet).

gêneur (ʒɛnœ:r) m, nuisance (pers.).

Genève (ʒənɛ:v) f, Geneva.

genévrier (ʒənevrie) m, juniper (genus).

génial, e (ʒenjal) a, [full] of genius. **génie** (ni) m, genius; spirit; Muse; bent; engineering.

genièvre (ʒənjɛ:vr) m, common juniper; geneva, Hollands [gin].

génisse (ʒenis) f, heifer.

génital, e (ʒenital) a, genital.

génitif (ʒenitif) m, genitive [case].

génois, e (ʒenwa, a:z) a. & G~, n, Genoese.

genou (ʒənu) m, knee; (pl.) lap. à ~x, on one's knees, kneeling. **genouillère** (ʒɛ:r) f, knee cap (pad); knuckle [joint] (Mech.).

genre (ʒɑ̃:r) m, kind; sort; line; type; description; genus; manner, way; style; fashion; genre (real life picture); gender (Gram.). le ~ humain, mankind.

gens (ʒɑ̃) m.pl. & f.pl, people, folks, men; servants. ~ d'Église, m.pl, clergy[men]. ~ de guerre, m.pl, military men. ~ de lettres, m.pl, men of letters, literary men, l. people, l. folks. ~ de mer (pl. of homme de mer) m.pl, seamen, seafaring men. ~ de qualité, m.pl, gentlefolk[s]. ~ de robe, m.pl, gentlemen of the robe (lawyers). les ~ du commun, m.pl, [the] common people. **gent** (ʒɑ̃) f, tribe, race, folk.

gentiane (ʒɑ̃sjan) f, gentian.

gentil, le (ʒɑ̃ti) m. & a.m, gentile.

gentil, le (ʒɑ̃ti, i:j) a, nice, pretty, sweet; kind, good. ~ à croquer, perfectly sweet (pers.). **gentilhomme** (tijɔm) m, nobleman; gentleman. ~ campagnard, gentleman farmer. **gentilhommerie** (mri) f, gentility; gentlemanliness. **gentilhommière** (mjɛ:r) f, country seat.

gentilité (ʒɑ̃tilite) f, pagandom; paganism.

gentillâtre (ʒɑ̃tijɑ:tr) m, obscure gentleman.

gentillesse (ʒɑ̃tijɛs) f, prettiness; gracefulness; (pl.) pretty speeches; (pl.) pretty tricks; nasty trick. **gentillet, te** (ʒɛ, ɛt) a, rather nice. **gentiment** (mɑ̃) ad, nicely, prettily.

gentleman (dʒɛntləman) m, gentleman; (att.) gentlemanly.

génuflexion (ʒenyflɛksjɔ̃) f, genuflexion.

géodésie (ʒeɔdezi) f, geodesy. **géognosie** (ɔgnozi) f, geognosy. **géographe** (graf) m, geographer. **géographie** (fi) f, geography. **géographique†** (fik) a, geographic(al).

geôle (ʒo:l) f, gaol, jail; gaoler's lodge. **geôlier, ère** (ʒolje, ɛ:r) n, gaoler; wardress.

géologie (ʒeɔlɔʒi) *f*, geology. ~ *sur le terrain*, field g. **géologique** (ʒik) *a*, geologic(al). **géologue** (lɔg) *m*, geologist.

géométral, e† (ʒeɔmetral) *a*, flat, plane. **géomètre** (mɛtr) *m*, geometer, geometrician; surveyor. ~ *du cadastre*, ordnance surveyor. **géométrie** (metri) *f*, geometry. **géométrique†** (trik) *a*, geometric(al); mathematical (*precise*).

Georgie (la) (ʒɔrʒi), Georgia (*U.S.A.*).
Géorgie (la) (ʒeɔrʒi), Georgia (*Asia*).

gérance (ʒerɑ̃:s) *f*, management.

géranium (ʒeranjɔm) *m*, geranium.

gérant, e (ʒerɑ̃, ɑ̃:t) *n*, manager, ess; (*att.*) managing.

gerbe (ʒɛrb) *f*, sheaf; shower; spray (*flowers*). ~ *d'eau*, spray of water; splash. **gerber** (be) *v.t*, to bind, sheaf, pile.

gerboise (ʒɛrbwa:z) *f*, jerboa.

gerce (ʒɛrs) *f*, crack; clothes moth. **gercer** (se) *v.t*, to chap; crack. **gerçure** (sy:r) *f*, chap; crack; shake (*timber*).

gérer (ʒere) *v.t*, to manage. *mal* ~, to mismanage.

germain, e (ʒɛrmɛ̃, ɛn) *a*, german, own, full (*brother, sister*). Cf. *cousin*.

germandrée (ʒɛrmɑ̃dre) *f*, germander (*Bot.*).

germe (ʒɛrm) *m*, germ; eye (*potato*); tread (*egg*); sprout; bud (*fig.*); seed (*fig.*). **germer** (me) *v.i*, to germinate; shoot, sprout; spring up, germ. **germination** (minasjɔ̃) *f*, germination.

gérondif (ʒerɔ̃dif) *m*, gerund.

géronte (ʒerɔ̃:t) *m*, old man (*in comedy*); old fool.

gésier (ʒezje) *m*, gizzard.

gésir (ʒezi:r) *v.i.ir*, to lie (*sick, dead, &c*).

gesse (ʒɛs) *f*, vetch, pea.

gestation (ʒɛstasjɔ̃) *f*, gestation.

geste (ʒɛst) *m*, gesture; motion, movement; action; wave, flourish, lift (*of the hand*); (*f.*) epic. **gesticuler** (tikyle) *v.i*, to gesticulate.

gestion (ʒɛstjɔ̃) *f*, management, administration; care.

geyser (ʒeze:r) *m*, geyser (*spring*).

ghetto (gɛto) *m*, ghetto.

gibecière (ʒipsjɛ:r) *f*, game bag; pouch; satchel, knapsack. **giberne** (bɛrn) *f*, pouch (*cartridge*); knapsack.

gibet (ʒibɛ) *m*, gibbet, gallows.

gibier (ʒibje) *m*, game (*Hunt.*). ~ *à poil*, ground g. ~ *de potence*, gallows bird.

giboulée (ʒibule) *f*, shower; hail storm.

giboyer (ʒibwaje) *v.i*, to go shooting. **giboyeux, euse** (jø, ø:z) *a*, full of game, gamy.

gicler (ʒikle) *v.i*, to spirt, squirt, splash.

gifle (ʒifl) *f*, slap, smack. **gifler** (fle) *v.t*, to slap, smack.

gigantesque (ʒigɑ̃tɛsk) *a*, gigantic.

gigot (ʒigo) *m*, leg (*of mutton, &c*). **gigoter** (gote) *v.i*, to kick about.

gigue (ʒig) *f*, jig (*Mus., dance*).

gilet (ʒilɛ) *m*, waistcoat, vest; cardigan [jacket]; spencer [coat]; woolly coat.

Gille (ʒil) *m*, clown, fool.

gingembre (ʒɛ̃ʒɑ̃:br) *m*, ginger.

girafe (ʒiraf) *f*, giraffe.

girandole (ʒirɑ̃dɔl) *f*, girandole; epergne.

girasol (ʒirasɔl) *m*, girasol[e] (*opal*).

giration (ʒirasjɔ̃) *f*, gyration. **giratoire** (twa:r) *a*, gyratory; roundabout (*traffic*).

girofle (ʒirɔfl) *m*, clove (*spice*). **giroflée** (fle) *f*, stock (*Bot.*). ~ *jaune*, wallflower. **giroflier** (flie) *m*, clove tree.

giron (ʒirɔ̃) *m*, lap (*of pers.*); bosom, pale (*of the church*); tread (*of stair step*).

girouette (ʒirwɛt) *f*, vane, weathercock (*lit. & fig.*).

gisant, e (ʒizɑ̃, ɑ̃:t) *a*, lying. ¶ *n*, recumbent figure (*statue*). **gisement** (zmɑ̃) *m*, lie, bearing (*Naut.*); bed, seam, deposit, stratum (*Geol.*).

gitane (ʒitan) *f*, gipsy (*woman*).

gîte (ʒit) *m*, home, shelter, lodging; form (*hare*); bed, seam, deposit (*Geol.*); leg of beef. ~ *à la noix*, silver side (*beef*).

givre (ʒi:vr) *m*, hoar frost, rime.

glabre (glɑ:br) *a*, glabrous, hairless; clean-shaven.

glace (glas) *f. sometimes pl. in sense of ice*, ice; (*pl.*) frost, chill (*fig., of age*); glass; [looking] glass, mirror; window (*carriage, &c*); icing (*sugar*); flaw. (thermomètre) *à* ~, at freezing. ~ *d'eau*, water ice. ~ *à crème*, cream ice, ice cream. ~ *de vitrage*, plate glass. ~[*s] flottante*[*s*], floe ice. **glacé, e** (se) *p.a*, frozen; icy; chill; iced; stony (*look*); glacé. **glacer** (se) *v.t*, to freeze, chill; ice; glaze; gloss; scumble. *se* ~, to freeze; glaze. **glaciaire** (sje:r) (*Geol.*) *a*, glacial, glacier, ice (*att.*). **glacial, e** (sjal) *a*, glacial, icy; frozen; frosty; frigid. **glacier** (sje) *m*, ice cream vender; confectioner; glacier. **glacière** (sjɛ:r) *f*, ice house; freezer, ice box. **glacis** (si) *m*, slope; glacis; glaze; scumble. **glaçon** (sɔ̃) *m*, floe; piece of ice; icicle.

gladiateur (gladjatœ:r) *m*, gladiator.

glaïeul (glajœl) *m*, gladiolus.

glaire (glɛ:r) *f*, glair, white of egg.

glaise (glɛ:z) *f*, clay; pug[ging], puddle. **glaiser** (glɛze) *v.t*, to clay, pug, puddle. **glaisière** (zjɛ:r) *f*, clay pit.

glaive (glɛ:v) (*Poet.*) *m*, sword, brand.

glanage (glana:ʒ) *m*, gleaning.

gland (glɑ̃) *m*, acorn; (*pl.*) mast (*oak*); tassel. **glande** (glɑ̃:d) *f*, gland; tumour. *des* ~*s au cou*, swollen glands.

glandée (glɑ̃de) *f*, acorn crop, mast.

glane (glan) *f*, gleaning; rope (*of onions, &c*). **glaner** (ne) *v.t. & abs*, to glean. **glaneur, euse** (nœ:r, ø:z) *n*, gleaner. **glanure** (ny:r) *f*, gleanings.

glapir (glapi:r) *v.i*, to yelp, yap, bark.

glas (glɑ) *m*, knell, passing bell.

glauque (glo:k) *a*, glaucous.

glèbe (glɛ:b) *f*, glebe, soil.

glène (glɛn) *f*, socket (*bone*); coil (*rope*).

glissade (glisad) f, slide, sliding, slip; glissade. glissant, e (sɑ̃, ɑ̃:t) a, slippery. glissé (se) m, glide (Danc.). glissement (smɑ̃) m, sliding, slide, slip[ping]; slump; glide, gliding. glisser (se) v.i. & t, to slide; slip; glide; slur; foist. glisseur, euse (sœ:r, ø:z) n, slider (pers.). ¶ m, hydroplane, speed boat. ~ de course, racing boat. ~ de croisière, fast cruiser (speed boat). glissière (sje:r) f, slide, guide (Mach.). glissoire (swa:r) f, slide (track on ice).

global, e† (global) a, total, inclusive, aggregate (sum); grand, sum (total). globe (glob) m, globe; ball; orb. ~ protecteur en verre, glass shade (clock). ~ de l'œil (bylœ:r) & globuleux, euse (lø, ø:z) a, globular. globule (byl) m, globule.

gloire (glwa:r) f, glory; fame; pride; boast. se faire ~ de, to glory in, pride oneself on. glorieux, euse† (glɔrjø, ø:z) a, glorious; proud; conceited. glorifier (rifje) v.t, to glorify, praise. se ~ de, to glory in, boast of. gloriole (rjɔl) f, vainglory, vanity; kudos.

glose (glo:z) f, gloss, commentary; criticism. gloser [sur] (gloze) v.t. & i, to find fault with. glossaire (glɔsɛ:r) m, glossary. glossateur (satœ:r) m, commentator.

glotte (glɔt) f, glottis.

glouglou (gluglu) m, gurgle, bubbling. glouglouter (te) v.i, to gobble (of turkey).

glousser (gluse) v.i, to cluck; chuckle; giggle; titter.

glouton, ne† (glutɔ̃, ɔn) a, gluttonous. ¶ n, glutton. gloutonnerie (tɔnri) f, gluttony.

glu (gly) f, birdlime; glue (marine). gluant, e (ɑ̃, ɑ̃:t) a, gluey, sticky. gluau (o) m, (bird) lime twig.

glucose (glyko:z) f, glucose.

glume (glym) f, glume; chaff.

gluten (glytɛn) m, gluten. glutineux, euse (tinø, ø:z) a, glutinous.

glycérine (gliserin) f, glycerin[e].

glycine (glisin) f, wistaria.

gnangnan (nɑ̃nɑ̃) n. & a, lackadaisical(person).

gneiss (gnɛs) m, gneiss.

gnome (gno:m) m, gnome.

gnostique (gnɔstik) m, gnostic.

go (tout de) (go) ad, straight off; there & then.

gobelet (gɔblɛ) m, goblet; tumbler; cup (thimblerigger's).

gobelin (gɔblɛ̃) m, [hob]goblin, imp.

gobe-mouches (gɔbmuʃ) m, flycatcher (bird); flytrap (plant); simpleton, gaper. gober (be) v.t, to bolt, gulp down; swallow (fig.).

goberger (se) (gɔbɛrʒe) v.pr, to do oneself well.

godailler (gɔdaje) v.i, to carouse.

godelureau (gɔdlyro) m, young gallant.

goder (gɔde) v.i, to pucker; bag (trousers). godet (dɛ) m, cup; noggin; bucket (elevator); saucer (artist's); pucker, ruck.

godiche (gɔdiʃ) a. & n, awkward (person), hobbledehoy.

godille (gɔdi:j) f, scull (stern oar). godiller (dije) v.t, to scull.

goéland (gɔelɑ̃) m, [sea] gull.

goélette (gɔelɛt) f, schooner.

goémon (gɔemɔ̃) m, seaweed, wrack.

gogo (gogo) m, simpleton, gull. à ~, in plenty; in clover.

goguenarder (gɔgnarde) v.i, to banter, crack jokes; jeer; sneer.

goguette (être en) (gɔgɛt), to be jolly (in drink).

goinfre (gwɛ̃:fr) m, guzzler. goinfrer (gwɛ̃fre) v.i, to guzzle, gorge.

goitre (gwa:tr) m, goitre, wen.

golf (gɔlf) m, golf; golf course, golf links. ~ miniature, ~ réduit, miniature golf.

golfe (gɔlf) m, gulf, bay, bight. ~ Arabique, Arabian Gulf. ~ de Gascogne (gaskɔɲ), Bay of Biscay. ~ du Lion, Gulf of the Lion. ~ Persique (pɛrsik), Persian Gulf.

gommage (gɔma:ʒ) m, gumming. gomme (gɔm) f, gum. ~ [à effacer], eraser. ~ à mâcher, chewing gum. ~ arabique, g. arabic. ~ [élastique], [india]rubber. ~ gutte (gyt), gamboge. ~ pour le crayon, pencil eraser. ~ pour l'encre, ink e. gommer (me) v.t, to gum. gommeux, euse (mø, ø:z) a, gummy. gommier (mje) m, gum tree.

gond (gɔ̃) m, (gate) hook. ~ & penture, hook & hinge.

gondole (gɔ̃dɔl) f, gondola.

gondoler (gɔ̃dɔle) v.i, to swell; warp. gondolier (gɔ̃dɔlje) m, gondolier.

gonfler (gɔ̃fle) v.t. & i. & se ~, to swell, inflate, pump up (tire).

gong (gɔ̃g) m, gong.

gord (gɔ:r) m, weir (Fish.).

goret (gɔrɛ) m, piglet, porker; pig (child).

gorge (gɔrʒ) f, throat, gullet; bosom, bust; neck; mouth (of tunnel); gorge; groove; tumbler (lock); roller (map). gorgée (ʒe) f, mouthful, gulp. gorger (ʒe) v.t, to gorge, cram, load.

gorille (gɔri:j) m, gorilla.

gosier (gozje) m, throat, gullet.

gothique (gɔtik) a, Gothic; old-fashioned.

goton (gɔtɔ̃) f, slut.

gouache (gwaʃ) f, gouache (Art).

gouailler (gwaje) v.t. & i, to chaff, banter.

goudron (gudrɔ̃) m, tar. goudronner (drɔne) v.t, to tar; spray with tar.

gouffre (gufr) m, gulf, abyss, chasm; whirlpool.

gouge (gu:ʒ) f, gouge (tool).

goujat (guʒa) m, cad, blackguard. goujaterie (tri) f, dirty trick.

goujon (guʒɔ̃) m, gudgeon (fish & Mech.); dowel, joggle, stud, pin[tle]. goujonner (ʒɔne) v.t, to dowel, joggle, stud.

goule (gul) f, ghoul.

goulée (gule) f, mouthful, gulp. goulet (lɛ) m, narrows, gut (Naut.). goulot (lo) m, neck (*bottle*). goulotte (lɔt) *f*, spout.

goulu, e (ly) *a*, greedy. goulûment (lymɑ̃) *ad*, greedily.

goupille (gupi:j) *f*, [cotter] pin. ~ *fendue*, split pin. goupillon (pijɔ̃) *m*, holy-water sprinkler; bottle brush.

gourbi (gurbi) *m*, hut; hovel; dug-out.

gourd, e (gu:r, urd) *a*, numb.

gourde (gurd) *f*, gourd; flask; fool.

gourdin (gurdɛ̃) *m*, cudgel.

gourmade (gurmad) *f*, punch, blow.

gourmand, e (gurmɑ̃, ɑ̃:d) *a*, gourmand; greedy. ~ *de*, very fond of. ¶ *n*, gourmand; glutton. gourmander (mɑ̃de) *v.t*, to scold, chide; lard (*Cook.*). gourmandise (di:z) *f*, gluttony.

gourme (gurm) *f*, strangles (*Vet.*); wild oats (*fig.*).

gourmé, e (gurme) *p.a*, stiff, formal. gourmer (me) *v.t*, to curb (*horse*); punch, pommel.

gourmet (gurmɛ) *m*, gourmet, epicure; connoisseur, judge.

gourmette (gurmɛt) *f*, curb (*harness*); free hand (*fig.*).

gousse (gus) *f*, pod, shell. ~ *d'ail*, clove of garlic. ~ *de plomb*, net sinker, n. weight.

gousset (gusɛ) *m*, pocket (*vest*); fob; gusset.

goût (gu) *m*, taste; relish; flavour; tang; liking, fondness; style. goûter (te) *m*, afternoon snack. ¶ *v.t*, to taste; try; relish; like.

goutte (gut) *f*, drop; drip; dram; sip; spot, splash; gout (*Med.*). gouttelette (tlɛt) *f*, tiny drop. goutteux, euse (tø, ø:z) *a*, gouty. gouttière (tjɛ:r) *f*, gutter; (*pl.*) roof, tiles; fore edge, foredge (*book*); splint.

gouvernail (guvɛrna:j) *m*, rudder; helm (*fig.*).

gouvernante (guvɛrnɑ̃:t) *f*, governess; housekeeper. gouvernants (nɑ̃) *m.pl*, government in power. gouverne (vɛrn) *f*, guidance; steering. gouvernement (nəmɑ̃) *m*, government; management, care. gouverner (ne) *v.t. & abs*, to steer (*Naut.*); govern, rule; look after. gouverneur (nœ:r) *m*, governor.

goyave (gɔja:v) *f*, guava. goyavier (javje) *m*, guava [tree].

grabat (graba) *m*, pallet, mean bed. grabataire (tɛ:r) *a. & n*, bedridden (person).

grabuge (graby:ʒ) *m*, row, brawl.

grâce (grɑ:s) *f*, grace; gracefulness; favour; mercy; pardon; thanks; (*pl.*) grace (*after meal*). les [trois] G~s, the Graces. de ~, *ad*, pray, please, for goodness' sake. gracier (grasje) *v.t*, to pardon, reprieve. gracieusement (sjøzmɑ̃) *ad*, graciously; gratuitously, free. gracieuseté (zte) *f*, graciousness; kindness; gratuity. gracieux, euse (sjø, ø:z) *a*, graceful, pleasing; gracious; gratuitous.

gracile (grasil) *a*, slender, slim. gracilité (lite) *f*, slenderness, &c.

gradation (gradasjɔ̃) *f*, gradation. ~ [*ascendante*], climax (*Rhet.*). ~ *descendante*,

anticlimax. grade (grad) *m*, grade; rank; rating; degree (*Univ.*). prendre ses ~s, to graduate. gradé (de) *m*, (*low-grade*) non-commissioned officer. ~s & *soldats*, rank & file. gradin (gradɛ̃) *m*, tier; step; stope (*Min.*). gradué, e (dɥe) *n*, graduate (*Univ.*). graduel, e† (dɥel) *a*, gradual. graduer (dɥe) *v.t*, to graduate; grade.

graillon (grajɔ̃) *m*, burning (*smell, taste, of burnt meat, fat*). graillonner (jɔne) *v.i*, to catch fire (*Cook.*); hawk (*with throat*).

grain (grɛ̃) *m*, grain; corn; seed; berry; bean; bead; speck; dash; spice; modicum; squall (*Naut.*). ~ *de beauté*, beauty spot; mole (*on skin*). ~ *de grêle*, hailstone. ~ *de plomb*, pellet. ~ *de raisin*, grape.

graine (grɛ:n) *f*, seed; silkworms' eggs. ~ *d'anis*, aniseed. ~ *de lin*, linseed. ~ *des canaris*, canary seed. grainetier (grɛntje) *m*, corn chandler. grainier, ère (nje, ɛ:r) *n*, seedsman.

graissage (grɛsa:ʒ) *m*, greasing, lubrication, oiling. graisse (grɛ:s) *f*, fat; grease; blubber; ropiness (*wine*). ~ *de rognon*, suet. ~ *de rôti*, dripping. graisser (grɛse) *v.t*, to grease, lubricate. ~ [*à l'huile*], to oil. graisseur (sœ:r) *m*, greaser; oiler; lubricator. graisseux, euse (sø, ø:z) *a*, greasy, oily; fatty; messy.

gramen (gramɛn) *m*, lawn grass. une graminée (mine), a grass (*plant*).

grammaire (gramɛ:r) *f*, grammar. contre la ~, ungrammatical. grammairien, ne (mɛrjɛ̃, ɛn) *n*, grammarian. grammatical, e† (matikal) *a*, grammatical.

gramme (gram) *m*, gram[me] = 15·432 grains.

gramophone (gramɔfɔn) *m*, gramophone.

grand, e (grɑ̃, ɑ̃:d) *a*, great, large, big; noble; major (*prophet, &c*); high; tall; grown up; long; broad; wide; open (*air*); deep (*mourning*); full (*dress, orchestra, &c*); high-class (*wine*); loud; utter (*regret, &c*); heavy (*rain, &c*); fast (*sailer—ship*); grand; main; trunk (*line*); general (*public*); much, many. grand, *comps:* ~ *canot*, launch, pinnace. ~ *chantre*, precentor. ~ *chemin*, highway, high road, main road. ~ *danois*, great Dane (*dog*). ~ *fond*, front margin (*of a book page*). un ~ *homme manqué*, a might-have-been. au ~ *jour*, in broad daylight; publicly. ~ *jour* [*de la publicité*], limelight. ~ *livre*, ledger; register (*share, stock*). ~ *magasin* [*de nouveautés*], big stores, department[al] store[s]. le ~ *monde*, [high] society, high life, the upper ten. le ~ *nettoyage*, the spring cleaning. ~ *rabbin*, chief rabbi. grande, *comps:* ~s *eaux*, spate, freshet; fountains. à ~s *journées*, by forced marches. ~ *largeur*, double width (*cloth*). ~ *marée*, spring tide. ~ *multiplication*, high gear. ~ *pêche*, deep-sea fishing (*whale & cod*). ~ *pédale*, loud pedal. ~ *personne*, grown-up. à [*la*] ~ *pluie*,

at much rain (*barometer*). ~ **tenue**
& ~ **toilette**, full dress. ~**s vacances**,
summer holidays; long vacation. ~
vitesse, fast train(s), passenger train(s).
grand (grɑ̃) *m*, grandee; (*the*) great; (*pl.*) (*the*)
great ones (*of the earth*). ~ **de l'eau**,
high-water mark. ~**s & petits**, old &
young. **en** ~, on a large scale; life size.
grand-chose (grɑ̃ʃo:z) *pn. usually with neg,*
much.
grand-crosse (grɑ̃krɔs) *f*, driver (*golf club*).
Grande-Bretagne (la) (grɑ̃dbrətaɲ), [Great]
Britain.
grandelet, te (grɑ̃dlɛ, ɛt) *a*, growing (*big*);
rather tall. **grandement** (dmɑ̃) *ad*, grandly;
nobly; greatly; altogether; ample, amply.
grandeur (dœ:r) *f*, size; magnitude; height;
greatness; mightiness; nobility; grandeur.
~ **naturelle**, life size. *Votre G*~, your
Grace; your Lordship.
grand-fer (grɑ̃fɛ:r) *m*, driving iron (*Golf*).
grandiloquence (grɑ̃dilɔkɑ̃:s) *f*, grandiloquence. **grandiloquent, e** (kɑ̃, ɑ̃:t) *a*,
grandiloquent.
grandiose (grɑ̃djo:z) *a*, grandiose, imposing.
grandir (grɑ̃di:r) *v.i*, to grow taller; grow up;
grow; (*v.t.*) to make taller or bigger; magnify.
grandissime (disim) *a*, very great.
grand-maman (grɑ̃mamɑ̃) *f*, grandmamma,
granny. **grand-mère** (grɑ̃mɛ:r) *f*, grand-
mother.
grand-messe (grɑ̃mɛs) *f*, high mass.
grand-oncle (grɑ̃tɔ:kl) *m*, great uncle.
grand-père (grɑ̃pɛ:r) *m*, grandfather.
grand-route (grɑ̃rut) *ou* **grande route** (ɑ̃:d) *f*,
highway, high road, main road.
grand-tante (grɑ̃tɑ̃:t) *f*, great aunt.
grand-voile (grɑ̃vwa:l) *f*, mainsail.
grange (grɑ̃:ʒ) *f*, barn.
granit (grani[t]) *m*, granite.
granule (granyl) *m*, granule. **granuler** (le)
v.t, to granulate.
graphique† (grafik) *a*, graphic. *¶ m*, diagram, chart, graph.
graphite (grafit) *m*, graphite, plumbago,
black lead.
grappe (grap) *f*, bunch, cluster. **grappiller**
(pije) *v.i. & t*, to glean (*grapes*); pick up,
scrape up.
grappin (grapɛ̃) *m*, grapnel; creeper (*well*).
gras, se (grɑ, ɑ:s) *a*, fat; fatty; oily; oil
(*varnish*); ropy (*wine*); plump (*chicken*);
fatted (*calf*); greasy; thick; rich (*food, &c*);
meat (*diet, day, &c*); full-face, bold-faced
(*type*); smutty, ribald, broad (*story*). **gras**,
m, fat. ~ **de la jambe**, calf. ~ **du bras**,
fleshy part of the arm. **grassement**
(grɑsmɑ̃) *ad*, (*to live*) on the fat of the
land; handsomely. **grasset, te** (sɛ, ɛt) *a*,
fattish. **grasseyer** (sɛje) *v.i*, to burr
(*speaking*). **grassouillet, te** (suje, ɛt) *a*,
plump; chubby.
gratification (gratifikasjɔ̃) *f*, bonus, gratuity.
gratifier (fje) *v.t*, to bestow, confer.

gratin (gratɛ̃) *m*, brown crust (*in pot*); gratin.
gratiner (tine) *v.t*, to gratinate (*Cook.*).
gratis (gratis) *ad*, gratis, free.
gratitude (gratityd) *f*, gratitude.
gratte (grat) *f*, scrapings (*savings*); pickings,
graft. **gratte-ciel**, *m*, sky scraper. **gratte-
cul**, *m*, hip (*Bot.*). **gratte-miettes**, *m*,
crumb scoop. **gratte-papier**, *m*, quill
driver. **gratter** (te) *v.t*, to scrape; scratch;
s. out, erase. **grattoir** (twa:r) *m*, knife
eraser; scraper.
gratuit; e† (gratɥi, it) *a*, gratuitous; free;
unpaid (*no salary*); wanton (*insult*). **gratuité** (te) *f*, gratuitousness; free gift (*Relig.*).
grave (gra:v) *a*, grave; solemn; serious;
weighty; severe; grievous; deep (*sound*);
heavy. *¶ m*, lower register (*Mus.*).
graveleux, euse (gravlø, ø:z) *a*, gravelly,
gritty; smutty, ribald. **gravelle** (vɛl) *f*,
gravel (*Med.*). **gravelure** (vly:r) *f*, smut-
tiness, ribaldry.
gravement (gravmɑ̃) *ad*, gravely; seriously;
rather slowly (*Mus.*).
graver (grave) *v.t*, to engrave; grave; cut;
inscribe; impress (*on memory*). ~ **à
l'eau-forte**, to etch. ~ **en creux**, to sink
(*die*). ~ **en relief**, to emboss. **graveur**
(vœ:r) *m*, engraver.
gravier (gravje) *m*, gravel, grit.
gravir (gravi:r) *v.i. & t*, to climb, clamber.
gravitation (gravitasjɔ̃) *f*, gravitation. **gravité** (te) *f*, gravity; weight (*fig.*); depth
(*sound*). **graviter** (te) *v.i*, to gravitate.
gravure (gravy:r) *f*, engraving; cut; print;
illustration. ~ **à l'eau-forte**, etching.
~ **à la manière noire**, mezzotint. ~ **au
trait**, line engraving. ~ **dans le texte**,
illustration in text. ~ **de mode**, fashion
plate. ~ **en creux**, die sinking. ~ **en
pleine page**, full-page illustration. ~
hors texte, illustration outside text. ~
sur bois, wood engraving; woodcut.
gré (gre) *m*, will; free will; wish; pleasure;
liking; taste. **au** ~ **de**, according to; at
the mercy of. **bon** ~, **mal** ~, *willynilly.
de ~ **ou de force**, by fair means or foul.
de ~ **à** ~, by negotiation; by private
treaty.
grèbe (grɛb) *m*, grebe.
grec, ecque (grɛk) *a*, Greek, Grecian. **G**~,
n, Greek (*pers.*). **le grec**, Greek (*language*).
la Grèce (grɛ:s), Greece. **grecque**, *f*, Greek
fret (*Arch.*).
gredin, e (grədɛ̃, in) *n*, villain, scoundrel,
miscreant. **gredinerie** (dinri) *f*, villainy.
gréement (gremɑ̃) (*Naut.*) *m*, rigging; gear.
gréer (gree) *v.t*, to rig.
greffe (grɛf) *m*, registry (*legal*); (*f.*) graft
(*Hort. & Surg.*), scion; grafting. **greffer**
(fe) *v.t*, to graft. **greffier** (fje) *m*, clerk
(*of court*); registrar. **greffon** (fɔ̃) *m*, graft,
scion.
grégaire (gregɛ:r) *a*, gregarious, herd (*att.*).
grège (grɛ:ʒ) *a*, raw (*silk*).

grégorien, ne (gregɔrjɛ̃, ɛn) a, Gregorian.

grêle (grɛːl) a, slender, thin (legs, voice); small (intestine). ¶ f, hail; shower (fig.). grêlé, e (grɛle) p.a, pock-marked, pitted; most unfortunate. grêler (le) v.imp, to hail; (v.t.) to damage by hail.

grelin (grəlɛ̃) m, hawser.

grêlon (grɛlɔ̃) m, (big) hailstone.

grelot (grəlo) m, bell (spherical with ball inside). grelotter (lote) v.i, to shiver (cold).

grenade (grənad) f, pomegranate; grenade. ~ sous-marine, depth charge. G~, f, Granada (Spain). la G~, Grenada (W. Indies). grenadier (dje) m, pomegranate [tree]; bomber; Amazon. grenadille (diːj) f, granadilla (Bot.). grenadin (dɛ̃) m, grenadine (Cook.). grenadine (din) f, grenadine (cordial, fabric).

grenaille (grənɑːj) f, tailings (grain); shot.

grenat (grəna) m, garnet. ~ cabochon, carbuncle.

greneler (grənle) v.t, to grain (leather). grené (ne) m, stipple (Art). grener (ne) v.i, to seed; (v.t.) to granulate; grain. grènetis (grɛnti) m, milling (on coin). grenier (grənje) m, granary; loft; garner; garret; attic; dunnage. en ~, in bulk.

grenouille (grənuːj) f, frog; money box; funds (club, society). grenouillère (nujɛːr) f, froggery; swamp.

grenu, e (grəny) a, grainy, seedy; grained. ¶ m, graining (on leather).

grès (grɛ) m, sandstone; grit; stoneware. ~ meulier (mœlje), millstone grit.

grésil (grezi) m, (tiny hard pellets of) hail. grésiller (je) v.imp, to hail; (v.t.) to shrivel [up].

gresserie (grɛsri) f, sandstone quarry; sandstone (work); stoneware.

grève (grɛːv) f, beach, shore, (poet.) strand; strike. ~ d'agents de chemins de fer, railway strike. ~ de la faim, hunger s. ~ de solidarité (sɔlidarite), sympathetic s. ~ des mineurs [de houille], coal s. ~ des travailleurs des docks, dock s. ~ patronale, lockout. ~ perlée, ca'canny strike, go-slow s. ~ sur le tas, stay-in s. ~ surprise, lightning s. se mettre en ~, faire ~, to [go on] strike.

grever (grəve) v.t, to burden, weight, encumber, saddle, [put] on, [put] upon.

gréviste (grevist) n, striker; (att.) strike.

grianneau (griano) m, young grouse.

gribouiller (gribuje) v.t. & abs, to scrawl; daub.

grief (grief) m, grievance; complaint. grièvement (ɛvmɑ̃) ad, seriously (injured).

griffe (grif) f, claw, talon; clutch; clip; grip; jaw; dog; tendril; facsimile signature; autograph stamp; stamp. griffer (fe) v.t, to claw, scratch; blaze (tree). griffon (fɔ̃) m, griffin; griffon. griffonner (fɔne) v.t. & abs, to scrawl; scribble. griffure (fyːr) f, scratch.

grignon (griɲɔ̃) m, crust[y] end (bread).

grignoter (griɲɔte) v.t. & abs, to nibble; get a few pickings (profit).

gril (gri) m, gridiron; grill; grating. sur le ~, on tenterhooks (fig.). grillade (griJad) f, grilling; broiling; grill (meat). grillage (jaːʒ) m, roasting (ore); grating; [wire] netting; grillage. grille (griːj) f, grating; grill[e]; grid; screen; wire guard; grate; railing[s]. ~-pain (grijpɛ̃) m, toaster. griller (grije) v.t & i, to grill; broil; toast; roast; scorch; burn; long, itch; grate, rail in.

grillon (grijɔ̃) m, cricket (insect).

grimace (grimas) f, grimace, [wry] face, grin; sham. grimacer (se) v.i, to grimace, make faces, grin; pucker, crease. grimacier, ère (sje, ɛːr) a, grinning; mincing; sham.

grime (grim) m, dotard (of comedy). se grimer (me) v.pr, to make up (Theat.).

grimoire (grimwaːr) m, gibberish; scrawl.

grimper (grɛ̃pe) v.i, to climb, clamber; creep.

grincer (grɛ̃se) v.i, to grind, grate, creak. ~ des dents (ou les) dents, to grind (or gnash) one's teeth.

grincheux, euse (grɛ̃ʃø, øːz) a, churlish; crabbed.

gringalet (grɛ̃galɛ) m, shrimp (pers.).

griotte (griɔt) f, morello; griotte.

grippe (grip) f, influenza; dislike. gripper (pe) v.t, to snatch (steal); (v.i.) to seize (Mach.). être grippé, e, to have influenza. se ~, to pucker. grippe-sou, m, money grubber.

gris, e (gri, iːz) a, grey, gray; brown (paper); grizzly; dull; tipsy, fuddled. ¶ m, grey. grisaille (grizɑːj) f, grisaille. grisailler (zaje) v.t, to [paint] grey. grisâtre (zɑːtr) a, greyish. griser (ze) v.t, to fuddle, muddle, intoxicate. grisette (zɛt) f, grisette (girl); white-throat (bird).

grisoller (grizɔle) v.i, to carol (lark).

grison, ne (grizɔ̃, ɔn) a, grey[ish]; grizzled (hair). ¶ m, greybeard; donkey. grisonner (zɔne) v.i, to grey.

grisou (grizu) m, fire damp.

grive (griːv) f, thrush. ~ chanteuse, song t., throstle.

grivois, e (grivwa, aːz) a, broad, ribald.

Groenland (le) (grɔɛlɑ̃[ːd]), Greenland.

grog (grɔg) m, grog.

grogner (grɔɲe) v.i, to grunt; grumble. grognon (nɔ̃) m, grumbler, cross-patch.

groin (grwɛ̃) m, snout (pig).

grommeler (grɔmle) v.i, to grumble at, g. about.

gronder (grɔ̃de) v.i, to growl, snarl; roar; rumble, mutter, peal; howl (wind); grumble; (v.t.) to scold.

groom (grum) m, groom; page [boy]; buttons.

gros, se (gro, oːs) a, big; large; great; broad; stout; loud; strong; hearty; pregnant;

fraught; swollen; coarse; gross; thick; deep; high; heavy; structural (*repairs*). **gros**, *comps*: ~ *bonnet*, bigwig. ~ *boulet*, heavy weight (*Throwing*). ~ *galet*, boulder. ~ *morceau*, lump. ~ *mots*, bad language, foul words; high words. ~ *murs*, main walls. ~ *œuvre*, main structure (*of a building*). ~ *plan*, close-up (*Phot.*). ~ *poisson*, heavy fish. **grosse**, *comps*: ~ *caisse*, bass drum, big drum. ~ *pièce*, heavy casting, heavy fish, &c. **gros**, *ad*, a great deal, much. ¶ *m*, bulk, body, mass; main part; large (*coal*). **en** ~, *ad*, roughly, broadly. [commerce de (*ou* en)] ~, wholesale [trade].

gros-bec (grobɛk) *m*, hawfinch, grosbeak.

groseille (grozɛːj) *f*, currant (*red*, *white*). ~ *verte*, ~ *à maquereau*, gooseberry. **groseillier** (zɛje) *m*, currant bush. ~ *à maquereau*, gooseberry bush.

grosse (groːs) *f*, large hand, text hand (*writing*); engrossment (*Law*); gross (*144*). **grossesse** (grosɛs) *f*, pregnancy. **grosseur** (sœːr) *f*, size; swelling. ~ *de ceinture*, *de poitrine*, waist; chest, measurement.

grossier, **ère†** (grosje, ɛːr) *a*, coarse; rough; gross; rude; rank, crass; glaring; unmannerly, boorish; ribald. **grossièreté** (ɛrte) *f*, coarseness, &c.

grossir (grosiːr) *v.t. & i*, to make bigger, enlarge; magnify; swell, inflate; exaggerate. **grossiste** (grosist) *m*, wholesaler.

grosso-modo (grɔsomodo) *ad*, roughly.

grossoyer (grɔswaje) *v.t*, to engross (*Law*).

grotesque† (grɔtɛsk) *a*, grotesque. ¶ *m*, grotesque[ness]; clown; (*f.*) grotesque (*Art*).

grotte (grɔt) *f*, grotto.

grouiller (gruje) *v.i*, to swarm, be alive (*with vermin*); seethe; move.

groupe (grup) *m*, group, batch, knot, cluster; company; party; set (*Elec.*). **groupement** (pmɑ̃) *m*, grouping; pool (*Fin.*). **grouper** (pe) *v.t*, to group.

grouse (gruːz) *f*, grouse (*bird*).

gruau (gryo) *m*, meal; groats; gruel. ~ *d'avoine*, oatmeal.

grue (gry) *f*, crane (*bird & hoist*).

gruger (gryʒe) *v.t*, to bleed (*fig.*).

grume (grym) *f*, bark (*left on felled tree*). **en** ~, in the log.

grumeau (grymo) *m*, clot, curd. **se grumeler** (mle) *v.pr*, to clot, curdle.

gruyère (gryjɛːr) *m*, gruyère [cheese].

guano (gwano) *m*, guano.

gué (ge) *m*, ford. **guéable** (abl) *a*, fordable. **guéer** (gee) *v.t*, to ford (*river*); water (*horse*); rinse (*linen*).

guelte (gɛlt) *f*, commission (*on shop sales*).

guenille (gəniːj) *f*, rag, tatter.

guenon (gənɔ̃) *& **guenuche** (nyʃ) *f*, she-monkey; fright (*woman*).

guêpe (gɛːp) *f*, wasp. **guêpier** (gɛpje) *m*, wasps' nest; hornets' nest (*fig.*); bee eater.

guère (**ne** . . . .) (nə . . . gɛːr) *ad*, hardly, h.

any; barely; not much; not many; but little; only; hardly ever.

guéret (gerɛ) *m*, ploughed land; fallow land; (*poet.*) field.

guéridon (geridɔ̃) *m*, occasional table; coffee t., cocktail t.

guérilla (gerilla) *f*, guer[r]illa.

guérir (geriːr) *v.t. & abs. & i. & se* ~, to cure; heal; recover; get better. **guérison** (rizɔ̃) *f*, cure, healing, recovery. **guérisseur**, **euse** (sœːr, øːz) *n*, healer; quack doctor, medicine man.

guérite (gerit) *f*, sentry box; signal box; look-out; hooded wicker chair.

Guernesey (gɛrnəzɛ) *f*, Guernsey.

guerre (gɛːr) *f*, war, warfare; strife; feud. ~ *d'usure*, war of attrition. ~ *de mouvement*, open warfare. ~ *de plume*, paper warfare. ~ *de position*, trench warfare. ~ *sociale*, class war. **de bonne** ~ (*fig.*), fair [play]. **guerrier**, **ère** (gɛrje, ɛːr) *a*, warlike, martial, war (*att.*). ¶ *n*, warrior. **guerroyer** (rwaje) *v.i*, to [wage] war.

guet (gɛ) *m*, watch. **~-apens** (gɛtapɑ̃) *m*, ambush; trap; trick.

guêtre (gɛːtr) *f*, gaiter. ~*s de ville*, spats. **guetter** (gɛte) *v.t*, to watch. **guetteur** (tœːr) *m*, look-out [man].

gueule (gœl) *f*, mouth; muzzle. **~-de-loup**, antirrhinum, snapdragon.

gueules (gœl) *m*, gules (*Her.*).

gueuse (gøːz) *f*, pig (*iron*); heavy weight.

gueuser (gøze) *v.i*, to beg. **gueuserie** (zri) *f*, beggary. **gueux**, **euse** (gø, øːz) *n*, beggar; rascal. ¶ *a*, beggarly.

gui (gi) *m*, mistletoe.

guichet (giʃɛ) *m*, wicket [gate]; shutter; counter (*cashier's*). ~ [*de distribution des billets*], booking office; ticket window. **à** ~ **ouvert**, on demand. **guichetier** (ʃtje) *m*, turnkey.

guide (gid) *m*, guide; conductor; guide [book]; (*f.*) [driving] rein. **~-âne**, *m*, manual, handbook. **guider** (de) *v.t*, to guide, conduct; steer. **guiderope** (rɔp) *m*, guide rope, trail r. (*Aero.*). **guidon** (dɔ̃) *m*, mark flag; pennant; handlebar (*cycle*); foresight (*gun*). ~ *de renvoi*, reference [mark].

guigne (giɲ) *f*, heart cherry, gean; bad luck. **guigner** (giɲe) *v.t. & abs*, to peep at; peep; have an eye to.

guignier (giɲje) *m*, heart cherry [tree].

guignol (giɲɔl) *m*, Punch & Judy [show].

guignon (giɲɔ̃) *m*, bad luck.

guillaume (gijoːm) *m*, rabbet plane.

guillemeter (gijmɔte) *v.t*, to put in inverted commas, quote. **guillemets** (mɛ) *m.pl*, quotation marks, inverted commas (*in Fr. printed thus* « »; *written thus* « » *or thus* " ").

guilleret, **te** (gijrɛ, ɛt) *a*, lively, gay; broad (*story*).

guilleri (gijri) *m*, chirp[ing] (*sparrow*).

guillochis (gijoʃi) *m*, guilloche; engine turning; chequering.

guillotine (gijɔtin) *f*, guillotine. **guillotiner** (ne) *v.t*, to guillotine.

guimauve (gimo:v) *f*, marsh-mallow.

guimbarde (gɛbard) *f*, covered wagon; rattle-trap (*vehicle*); Jew's harp.

guimpe (gɛ̃:p) *f*, wimple; blouse front.

guindé, e (gɛ̃de) *p.a*, strained, stiff; stilted. **guinder** (de) *v.t*, to hoist; strain, force (*fig.*).

guinée (gine) *f*, guinea (*21/-*). **la G∼**, Guinea (*Geog.*).

guingan (gɛ̃gɑ̃) *m*, gingham (*fabric*).

guingois (gɛ̃gwa) *m*, crookedness, wryness. *de* ∼, awry, askew, lop-sided.

guinguette (gɛ̃gɛt) *f*, tavern with gardens & dance hall.

guipure (gipy:r) *f*, guipure.

guirlande (girlɑ̃:d) *f*, garland, wreath.

guise (gi:z) *f*, way. *en* ∼ *de*, by way of.

guitare (gita:r) *f*, guitar; repetition, (*same*) old story. ∼ *hawaïenne*, ukulele.

Gulf-Stream (gylfstri:m) *m*, Gulf Stream.

gustation (gystasjɔ̃) *f*, tasting.

gutta-percha (gytaperka) *f*, gutta-percha.

guttural, e (gytyral) *a. & f*, guttural.

Guyane (la) (gɥijan), Guiana.

gymnase (ʒimna:z) *m*, gymnasium. **gymnasiarque** (nazjark) *&* **gymnaste** (nast) *m*, gymnast. **gymnastique** (tik) *a*, gymnastic. ¶ *f*, gymnastics, drill (*Swedish*); gymnastic (*of mind, &c*). **gymnique** (nik) *f*, gymnastics.

gymnote (ʒimnɔt) *m*, electric eel.

gynécologie (ʒinekɔlɔʒi) *f*, gynaecology.

gypaète (ʒipaɛt) *m*, lammergeyer.

gypse (ʒips) *m*, gypsum; plaster of Paris. **gypseux, euse** (sø, ø:z) *a*, gypseous.

gyroscope (ʒirɔskɔp) *m*, gyroscope.

H

The sign ‘ denotes that the **h** *is aspirate in the French sense, i.e, no liaison or elision.*

habile† (abil) *a*, able, clever, skilful, cunning, skilled. **habileté** (lte) *f*, ability, &c, skill.

habilité (abilite) *f*, competency (*Law*). **habiliter** (te) *v.t*, to enable, capacitate.

habillement (abijmɑ̃) *m*, clothing; dress; raiment, habiliments. **habiller** (je) *v.t*, to dress, clothe; suit; abuse. **habilleuse** (jø:z) *f*, dresser (*Theat.*). **habit** (bi) *m*, mostly *pl*, clothes, suit; garb; habit; (*men's evening*) dress; vestment. ∼ *d'arlequin*, motley. ∼*s de tous les jours*, everyday clothes. ∼ *de soirée*, dress coat; (*pl.*) dress [suit], dress clothes.

habitable (abitabl) *a*, [in]habitable.

habitacle (abitakl) *m*, abode; binnacle.

habitant, e (abitɑ̃, ɑ̃:t) *n*, inhabitant, dweller; occupier; resident, occupant, inmate; denizen. **habitat** (ta) *m*, habitat. **habi-**

tation (sjɔ̃) *f*, habitation, dwelling, residence, abode, house. ∼ *à bon marché*, tenement house. ∼ *insalubre*, slum. **habiter** (te) *v.t*, to inhabit, occupy, live in, l. at; (*v.i.*) to live, dwell.

habitude (abityd) *f*, habit; use; practice; wont. **habitué, e** (tɥe) *n*, frequenter. **habituel, le†** (tɥel) *a*, habitual, usual, wonted. **habituer** (tɥe) *v.t*, to habituate, accustom, inure.

‘hâblerie (ɑblɛri) *f*, brag. **‘hâbleur, euse** (blœ:r, ø:z) *n*, braggart.

‘hache (aʃ) *f*, axe. ∼ *à main*, hatchet. ∼ *coupe-gazon*, edging knife. ∼ *d'armes*, battle-axe, pole-axe. ∼*-paille*, *m*, chaff-cutter. **‘hacher** (ʃe) *v.t*, to chop [up]; hack; cut to pieces; hash, mince; hatch (*engrave*). **‘hachis** (ʃi) *m*, hash, mince. **‘hachoir** (ʃwa:r) *m*, mincer; chopping board.

‘hagard, e (agaːr, ard) *a*, haggard, wild; drawn (*face*).

‘haie (ɛ) *f*, hedge[row]; hurdle; line, row (*people*); beam (*plough*). ∼ *vive*, quickset hedge.

‘haillon (ɑjɔ̃) *m*, rag, tatter.

‘haine (ɛːn) *f*, hatred; odium; dudgeon. **‘haineux, euse** (ɛnø, ø:z) *a*, full of hatred.

‘haïr (aiːr) *v.t*, to hate, loathe.

‘haire (ɛːr) *f*, hair shirt.

‘haïssable (aisabl) *a*, hateful.

Haïti (aiti) *f*, Haiti.

‘halage ([h]ala:ʒ) *m*, towing.

‘halbran (albrɑ̃) *m*, young wild duck.

‘hâle (ɑːl) *m*, [heat of the] sun, sunburn. **‘hâlé, e** (ɑle) *p.a*, sunburnt, tanned, weather-beaten.

haleine (alɛn) *f*, breath, wind; training (*fig.*); suspense. *de longue* ∼, (*work, &c*) of time, requiring long persistent effort.

‘haler ([h]ale) *v.t*, to tow, haul, pull, heave; set on (*dog*).

‘hâler (ɑle) *v.t*, to burn, tan. *se* ∼, to get sunburnt.

‘haletant, e (altɑ̃, ɑ̃:t) *a*, panting; breathless. **‘haleter** (te) *v.i*, to pant, gasp [for breath].

‘hall ([h]ɔl) *m*, hall; lounge (*hotel*). ∼ *des guichets*, booking hall.

‘halle (al) *f*, [covered] market; shed (*goods*).

‘hallebarde (albard) *f*, halberd (*Hist.*).

‘hallier (alje) *m*, covert (*game*).

hallucination (alysinasjɔ̃) *f*, hallucination.

‘halo (alo) *m*, halo (*Astr., Anat.*); halation (*Phot.*).

‘halot (alo) *m*, rabbit hole.

‘halte (alt) *f*, halt, stop. ¶ ([h]alt) *&* ∼*-là i*, halt! stop!

haltère (altɛːr) *m*, dumb-bell.

‘hamac (amak) *m*, hammock.

‘Hambourg (ɑ̃buːr) *m*, Hamburg.

‘hameau (amo) *m*, hamlet.

hameçon (amsɔ̃) *m*, [fish] hook; bait (*fig.*).

‘hampe (ɑ̃:p) *f*, staff, shaft, handle; scape (*Bot.*).

ᵗhanche (ɑ̃ːʃ) f, hip; haunch.
ᵗhandicap (ɑ̃dikap) m, handicap (Sport).
 ᵗhandicaper (pe) v.t, to handicap. ᵗhandi-
 capeur (pœːr) m, handicapper.
ᵗhangar (ɑ̃gaːr) m, shed, outhouse. ~
 [d'aviation], hangar.
ᵗhanneton (ɑ̃tɔ̃) m, cockchafer; giddy-head.
ᵗHanovre (anɔːvr) m, Hanover (town). le
 H~, Hanover (province).
ᵗhanter (ɑ̃te) v.t, to frequent, haunt; keep
 (bad company). ᵗhantise (tiːz) f, haunting;
 obsession.
ᵗhappe (ap) f, cramp [iron]; cramp, clamp.
 ᵗhapper (pe) v.t, to snap up; catch.
ᵗhaquet (akε) m, dray.
ᵗharangue (arɑ̃ːg) f, harangue, speech.
 ᵗharanguer (rɑ̃ge) v.t. & i, to harangue.
ᵗharas (arɑ) m, stud farm; stud.
ᵗharasse (aras) f, crate.
ᵗharasser (arase) v.t, to tire out, weary.
ᵗharceler (arsəle) v.t, to harass, harry, bait;
 worry, pepper; heckle.
ᵗharde (ard) f, herd (deer); leash (set of dogs).
 ᵗharder (de) v.t, to leash.
ᵗhardes (ard) f.pl, clothes (worn).
ᵗhardi†, e (ardi) a, bold, daring; hardy; rash;
 forward, pert. ᵗhardiesse (djεs) f, boldness, daring, hardihood; forwardness, pertness; liberty.
ᵗharem (arεm) m, harem.
ᵗhareng (arɑ̃) m, herring. ~ bouffi, bloater.
 ~ salé & fumé, kipper. ~ saur (sɔːr),
 red herring. ᵗharengaison (gεzɔ̃) f, herring season; h. fishery. ᵗharengère (ʒεːr)
 f, fishwife. ᵗharenguier (gje) m, herring
 boat.
ᵗhargneux, euse (arɲø, øːz) a, surly, peevish,
 ill-tempered, nagging, snappy, fractious;
 snarling.
ᵗharicot (ariko) m, kidney bean, French
 bean; haricot. ~ d'Espagne, scarlet
 runner, runner bean. ~s secs, haricot
 beans (dried). ~s verts, French beans
 (unripe).
ᵗharidelle (aridεl) f, jade (horse).
harmonica (armonika) m, harmonica; musical
 glasses. ~ à bouche, mouth organ.
harmonie (ni) f, harmony; (in) keeping;
 band. harmonieux, euse† (njø, øːz) a,
 harmonious, tuneful. harmonique† (nik)
 a. & m, harmonic. harmoniser (ze) v.t,
 to harmonize; attune. s'~, to harmonize, tone. harmonium (njɔm) m, harmonium.
ᵗharnachement (arnaʃmɑ̃) m, harnessing;
 harness; trappings, rig. ᵗharnacher (ʃe)
 v.t, to harness; accoutre, rig out. ᵗharnais
 (nε) m, harness; gear, tackle. blanchir
 sous le harnois (nwa), to grow grey in the
 service.
ᵗharo (aro) m, hue & cry; outcry.
harpagon (arpagɔ̃) m, miser, skinflint.
ᵗharpe (arp) f, harp; toothing (Build.).
ᵗharpie (arpi) f, harpy; hell-cat.

ᵗharpiste (arpist) n, harpist.
ᵗharpon (arpɔ̃) m, harpoon. ᵗharponner
 (pone) v.t, to harpoon.
ᵗhart (aːr) f, withe, withy; halter; hanging.
ᵗhasard (azaːr) m, chance, luck, risk, venture;
 hazard. au ~, at random. ᵗhasarder
 (zarde) v.t, to hazard, risk, venture.
 ᵗhasardeux, euse† (dø, øːz) a, venture-
 some; hazardous, risky.
ᵗhase ([h]aːz) f, doe hare.
ᵗhâte (aːt) f, haste, hurry. ᵗhâter (ɑte) v.t,
 to hasten, hurry; quicken; expedite; force
 (Hort.). se ~, to make haste, hurry.
 ᵗhâtif, ive† (tif, iːv) a, hasty, hurried;
 cursory; forward, early (fruit, &c). ᵗhâti-
 veau (vo) m, early pear, apple, pea, &c.
ᵗhauban (obɑ̃) m, shroud (Naut.); guy, stay.
ᵗhausse (oːs) f, rise; flashboard; wedge (to
 pack up to level); elevator (in shoe); backsight (gun); lead (rifle). ᵗhaussement
 d'épaules (osmɑ̃) m, shrug[ging] [of the
 shoulders]. ᵗhausser (se) v.t, to raise, lift;
 shrug; (v.i.) to rise. ᵗhaussier (sje) m,
 bull (Stk Ex.).
ᵗhaussière (osjεːr) f, hawser.
ᵗhaut, e (o, oːt) a, high; tall; lofty; upper;
 top; up; high-class; loud; deep; remote
 (antiquity); big. le haut commerce, [the]
 big traders, the merchant class. haut
 enseignement, higher education. haut fait
 [d'armes], feat of arms. de hauts faits,
 doughty deeds. haut fourneau, blast
 furnace. haute mer, high seas, open sea.
 haute taille, tallness (pers.). ᵗhaut, ad,
 high; h. up; loudly, aloud. ~ le pied,
 loose (horses); light (Rly engine). ~ les
 mains! hands up! ¶ m, top, head;
 higher notes (Mus.); perch (fig.). ~ de
 casse, upper case, cap c. (Typ.). ~ du
 pavé, wall (side of pavement). de ~, high,
 in height. des ~s & des bas ou ~ & ~
 du bas, ups & downs. en ~, [up] above;
 aloft; upstairs.
ᵗhautain, e (otε̃, εːn) a, haughty, lordly;
 lofty, proud.
ᵗhautbois (obwa) m, oboe, hautboy. ᵗhaut-
 boïste (boist) m, oboist.
ᵗhautement (otmɑ̃) ad, boldly, openly.
 ᵗhauteur (toːr) f, height; elevation; tallness (steeple, &c); loftiness; altitude; level;
 hill; depth; haughtiness. ~ de marche,
 rise (of step). ~ [musicale], pitch (of a
 sound).
ᵗhaut-fond (ofɔ̃) m, shoal.
ᵗhaut-le-cœur (olkœːr) m, heave, retch,
 nausea.
ᵗhaut-le-corps (olkɔːr) m, start, jump.
ᵗhaut-parleur (oparlœːr) m, loud speaker.
ᵗhavane (avan) m, Havana (cigar). ¶ a. inv,
 brown, tan (boots). la H~, Havana
 (Geog.).
ᵗhâve (aːv) a, wan, emaciated.
ᵗhavre (aːvr) m, haven. le H~, Havre
 (Geog.).

'havresac (avrəsak) *m*, knapsack.

Hawaï (avai) *m*, Hawaii. **hawaïen, en** (iĕ, ɛn) *a*. & **H~**, *n*, Hawaiian.

'Haye (la) (ɛ), the Hague.

'**hé** (e) *i*, hi! hoy! hey! hallo[a]! ~ *là-bas!* hallo[a] there!

hebdomadaire (ɛbdɔmadɛːr) *a*, weekly.

héberger (ebɛrʒe) *v.t*, to harbour; lodge, entertain, put up.

hébéter (ebete) *v.t*, to dull; stupefy, daze.

hébraïque (ebraik) *a*, Hebraic, Hebrew. **l'hébreu** (brø) *m*, Hebrew (*language*); Greek (*jargon*).

hécatombe (ekatɔ̃ːb) *f*, hecatomb.

hectare (ɛktaːr) *m*, hectare = 100 ares *or* 2·4711 acres.

hectique (ɛktik) *a*, hectic (*fever*).

hectogramme (ɛktɔgram) *m*, hectogram[me] = 100 gram[me]s *or* 3·527 ozs avoirdupois. **hectolitre** (litr) *m*, hectolitre = 100 litres *or* 2·75 imperial bushels *or* 22·01 imperial gallons. **hectomètre** (mɛtr) *m*, hectometre = 100 metres *or* 109·36 yards.

hégémonie (eʒemɔni) *f*, hegemony.

'**hein** ([h]ɛ̃) *i*, ey! what [do you say]?

hélas (elɑːs) *i*, alas!

héler ([h]ele) *v.t*, to hail, call; speak (*ship*).

hélianthe (eljãːt) *m*, helianthus.

hélice (elis) *f*, helix, spiral; screw, propeller; spinner (*Fish.*). **en ~** & **hélicoïdal, e** (koidal) *a*, spiral, helical, twist (*drill*).

hélicoptère (kɔptɛːr) *m*, helicopter.

héliotrope (eljɔtrɔp) *m*, heliotrope; cherry-pie; bloodstone.

hélium (eljɔm) *m*, helium.

hélix (eliks) *m*, helix (*ear*).

hellénisme (elenism) *m*, Hellenism.

hématite (ematit) *f*, h[a]ematite.

hémisphère (emisfɛːr) *m*, hemisphere.

hémorragie (emɔraʒi) *f*, h[a]emorrhage. **hémorroïdes** (roid) *f.pl*, h[a]emorrhoids, piles.

'**henné** (ɛnne) *m*, henna.

'**hennir** ([h]eniːr) *v.i*, to neigh, whinny.

'**hep** (hɛp) *i*, fore! (*Golf*).

héraldique (eraldik) *a*, heraldic. ¶ *f*, heraldry. '**héraut** (ro) *m*, herald (*Hist.*).

herbacé, e (ɛrbase) *a*, herbaceous. **herbage** (baːʒ) *m*, grass, pasture (*uncut*); herbage; green vegetables, green stuff, greens. **herbe** (ɛrb) *f*, herb; plant; grass; weed; wort (*Bot.*). l'~, grass court (*Ten.*). ~s fines, sweet herbs. l'~ longue, the rough (*Golf*). ~ menue, fine grass. ~s menues, fine herbs (*fine in texture, as savoury herbs*). ~ potagère, pot herb. **en ~**, green; unripe; budding (*fig.*); in embryo (*fig.*). **herbette** (bɛt) (*poet.*) *f*, [green]sward. **herbeux, euse** (bø, øːz) *a*, grassy. **herbier** (bje) *m*, herbal, herbarium. **herbivore** (bivɔːr) *a*. & *m*, herbivorous (*animal*). **herboriser** (bɔrize) *v.i*, to botanize, herborize. **herboriste** (rist) *n*, herbalist. **herbu, e** (by) *a*, grassy.

hercule (ɛrkyl) *m*, Hercules, strong man. **herculéen, ne** (leĕ, ɛn) *a*, Herculean.

'**hère** (ɛːr) *m*, wretch, wight; young stag.

héréditaire† (ereditɛːr) *a*, hereditary. **hérédité** (te) *f*, heirship, inheritance (*right*); heredity.

hérésie (erezi) *f*, heresy. **hérétique** (tik) *a*, heretical. ¶ *n*, heretic.

'**hérissé, e** (erise) *p.a*, bristly; prickly; on end (*hair*); bristling, beset. '**hérisser** (se) *v.i*. & **se ~**, to bristle [up], stand on end; (*v.t.*) to bristle, erect; stud. '**hérisson** (sɔ̃) *m*, hedgehog; (*sea*) urchin; clod crusher; sprocket wheel.

héritage (eritaːʒ) *m*, inheritance; heritage. **hériter** (te) *v.i*. & *t*, to inherit. **héritier, ère** (tje, ɛːr) *n*, heir, heiress.

hermaphrodite (ɛrmafrɔdit) *m*, hermaphrodite.

hermétique† (ɛrmetik) *a*, hermetic.

hermine (ɛrmin) *f*, ermine, stoat. **herminette** (ɛrminɛt) *f*, adze.

'**hernie** (ɛrni) *f*, hernia, rupture.

héroï-comique (erɔikɔmik) *a*, heroicomic, mock-heroic. **héroïne** (in) *f*, heroine. **héroïque†** (ik) *a*, heroic. **héroïsme** (ism) *m*, heroism.

'**héron** (erɔ̃) *m*, heron. '**héronnière** (rɔnjɛːr) *f*, heronry.

'**héros** (ero) *m*, hero. ~ *de la fête*, one in whose honour dinner, &c, is given. ~ *de salon*, carpet knight.

herpès (ɛrpɛs) *m*, herpes.

'**herse** (ɛrs) *f*, harrow; portcullis. '**herser** (se) *v.t*, to harrow.

hésitation (ezitasjɔ̃) *f*, hesitation. **hésiter** (te) *v.i*, to hesitate, waver; falter.

hétaïre (etaiːr) *f*, hetaera, courtesan.

hétéroclite (eterɔklit) *a*, freak[ish], odd, queer; heteroclite. **hétérodoxe** (dɔks) *a*, heterodox, unorthodox. **hétérodoxie** (ksi) *f*, heterodoxy. **hétérogène** (ʒɛn) *a*, heterogeneous; mixed.

'**hêtre** (ɛːtr) *m*, beech [tree, wood]. ~ *rouge*, copper beech.

heure (œːr) *f*, *oft. pl*, hour; time; moment; present; o'clock. l'~ *d'allumer*, lighting-up time. ~ *de la jeunesse*, children's hour (*Radio*). l'~ *du coucher*, bedtime. ~ *du lieu*, local time. l'~ *du repas*, meal t. ~-*limite de dépôt*, latest time for posting. ~s *de bureau*, ~s *d'ouverture*, business hours. ~s *de pointe*, ~s *d'affluence*, peak h—s, rush h—s. ~s *supplémentaires*, overtime. *à la bonne* ~, well & good, all right. *de bonne* ~, *ad*, early, betimes, in good time.

heureux, euse† (œrø, øːz) *a*, happy; pleased; fortunate; prosperous; blissful; blessed; successful; lucky; safe (*arrival*).

'**heurt** (œːr) *m*, shock, knock, bump. '**heurté, e** (œrte) *a*, contrasty. '**heurter** (te) *v.t*. & *i*, to run (against); knock; shock. '**heurtoir** (twaːr) *m*, stop blocks (*Rly*); buffer.

F

hexagone (ɛgzagɔn) m, hexagon. ¶ a, hexagonal. **hexamètre** (mɛtr) m, hexameter.

hiatus (jaty:s) m, hiatus (Gram.).

hiberner (ibɛrne) v.i, to hibernate.

'hibou (ibu) m, owl; recluse; unsociable person.

'hic (ik) m, rub (difficulty).

'hideur (idœ:r) f, hideousness. **'hideux, euse†** (dø, ø:z) a, hideous.

'bie (i) f, beetle, rammer; pile driver.

hiémal, e (jemal) a, winter (att.).

hier (iɛ:r) ad, yesterday. ~ [au] soir, last night.

'hiérarchie (jerarʃi) f, hierarchy.

hiéroglyphe (jeroglif) m, hieroglyph.

hilare (ila:r) a, hilarious, laughing. **hilarité** (larite) f, hilarity, merriment, laughter.

hindou, e (ɛ̃du) a. & H~, n, Hindu, -doo. l'hindoustani (stani) m, Hindustani.

hippique (ippik) a, horse (show, &c), equine. **hippocampe** (ippokɑ̃:p) m, hippocampus, sea horse. **hippodrome** (dro:m) m, hippodrome, circus. **boucherie hippophagique** (faʒik), horse meat (or horse flesh) dealer. **hippopotame** (potam) m, hippopotamus.

hirondelle (irɔ̃dɛl) f, swallow. ~ de fenêtre, [house] martin. ~ de rivage, sand martin.

hirsute (irsyt) a, hirsute, shaggy; fierce.

'hisser ([h]ise) v.t, to hoist; raise.

histoire (istwa:r) f, history; story, tale, yarn; fib; (pl.) fuss. le plus beau de l'~, the best of the story. **historié, e** (tɔrje) p.a, historiated, illuminated, ornamental. **historien** (rjɛ̃) m, historian. **historier** (rje) v.t, to ornament. **historiette** (rjɛt) f, anecdote. **historique†** (rik) a, historical; historic. ¶ m, history, account. ~ du régiment, regimental records.

histrion (istriɔ̃) m, histrion.

hiver (ivɛ:r) m, winter. **hivernage** (vɛrna:ʒ) m, wintering. **hivernal, e** (nal) a, winter (att.), wintry. **hiverner** (ne) v.i. & t, to winter.

'ho (ho) i, hi! ~, du navire! ship ahoy!

'hobereau (obro) m, hobby (bird); petty country gentleman.

'hoche (oʃ) f, notch, nick (on tally).

'hochement (oʃmɑ̃) m, shake; toss (head). **'hochepot** (ʃpo) m, hotchpot[ch]. **'hochequeue** (kø) m, wagtail. **'hocher** (ʃe) v.t. & t, to shake; toss; notch, nick. **'hochet** (ʃɛ) m, rattle, coral; bauble, plaything.

'hockey (ɔkɛ) m, hockey. ~ sur glace, ice h.

hoir (wa:r) m, heir. **hoirie** (wari) f, inheritance.

'holà ([h]ɔla) i, hallo[a]! hi! enough!

'hollandais, e (ɔlɑ̃dɛ, ɛ:z) a, Dutch. **'H~,** n, Dutchman, -woman. le h~, Dutch (language). **la Hollande** (lɑ̃:d), Holland.

holocauste (ɔlɔko:st) m, holocaust, burnt offering; sacrifice.

'hom ([h]ɔm) i, hum! humph!

'homard (ɔma:r) m, lobster.

homélie (ɔmeli) f, homily.

homéopathe (ɔmeɔpat) m, homoeopath[ist]. **homéopathie** (ti) f, homoeopathy. **homéopathique** (tik) a, homoeopathic.

homérique (ɔmerik) a, Homeric.

homicide (ɔmisid) a, homicidal. ¶ n, homicide (pers.); (m.) homicide (act). ~ excusable, justifiable h. ~ involontaire, manslaughter. ~ volontaire, wilful murder.

hommage (ɔma:ʒ) m, homage; (pl.) respects, compliments; token, tribute.

hommasse (ɔmas) a, mannish, masculine (woman). **homme** (ɔm) m, man; (pl.) mankind. ~ à bonnes fortunes, lady-killer. ~ à femmes, ~ galant, ladies' (or lady's) man. ~ à l'heure, casual labourer. ~ à projets, schemer. ~ à tout faire, man of all work, jack of all trades, handy man. ~ calé, man of substance; well-informed man. ~ caoutchouc, ~-serpent, contortionist. ~ d'affaires, business man; business agent; steward. ~ d'État, statesman. ~ d'exécution, man of deeds. ~ dans les affaires, business man. ~ de barre, helmsman, steersman. ~ de bonne volonté, volunteer (for task). ~ de couleur, mulatto. ~ de foyer, family man. l'~ de la rue, the man in the street. ~ de lettres, man of letters, literary m. ~ de métier, craftsman. ~ de mer, seaman, seafaring man. ~ de paille, man of straw. ~ de peine, [common] labourer. ~ de pied, infantryman. ~ de science, scientist. l'~ intérieur, the inner man. ~-orchestre, one-man band. ~-sandwich, sandwich man. ~ sans aveu, vagrant, outcast.

homogène (ɔmɔʒɛ:n) a, homogeneous.

homologuer (ɔmɔlɔge) v.t, to ratify; prove (will); accept (a sport record).

homonyme (ɔmɔnim) m, homonym, namesake.

'hongre (ɔ̃:gr) a.m, gelded. ¶ m, gelding. **'hongrer** (ɔ̃gre) v.t, to geld.

'Hongrie (la) (ɔ̃gri), Hungary. **'hongrois, e** (grwa, a:z) a. & 'H~, n, Hungarian. le hongrois, Hungarian (language).

honnête† (ɔnɛ:t) a, honest, honourable; upright; respectable, straight, decent; well-bred, civil, courteous; fair, reasonable. **honnêteté** (nɛtte) f, honesty; decency, propriety; courtesy; fairness, reasonableness; recompense.

honneur (ɔnœ:r) m, honour; mettle; justice (as to a meal); credit; pleasure (e.g, of seeing you). jouer pour l'~, to play for love. faire ~ à (Com.), to honour, meet.

'honnir (ɔni:r) v.t, to disgrace.

honorable† (ɔnɔrabl) a, honourable; reputable; respectable. **honoraire** (rɛ:r) a, honorary. ~s, m.pl, fee[s], honorarium. **honorariat** (rarja) m, honorary membership. **honorée** (re) (Com.) f, favour (letter). **honorer** (re) v.t, to honour; respect; favour; grace; dignify; do credit to. **honorifique** (rifik) a, honorary.

'honte (ɔ̃:t) *f*, shame, disgrace; reproach, scandal. *avoir ~*, to be ashamed. 'honteux, euse† (ɔ̃tø, ø:z) *a*, ashamed; bashful, shamefaced; sheepish; shameful, disgraceful, inglorious; uncomplaining (*poor*).

hôpital (ɔpital) *m*, hospital. *~ de contagieux*, isolation h. *~ des vénériens*, lock h.

hoquet (ɔkɛ) *m*, hiccup; gasp.

horaire (ɔrɛːr) *m*, time table.

'horde (ɔrd) *f*, horde.

'horion (ɔrjɔ̃) *m*, thump, whack.

horizon (ɔrizɔ̃) *m*, horizon. horizontal, e (tal) *a*, horizontal. horizontalement (lmɑ̃) *ad*, horizontally; across (*cross-word clues*).

horloge (ɔrlɔːʒ) *f*, clock (*big*). *~ à carillon*, chiming c., musical c. *~ à sonnerie*, striking c. *~ de la mort*, death-watch [beetle]. *~ de parquet*, grandfather's clock. horloger (lɔʒe) *m*, clockmaker, watchmaker. horlogerie (ʒri) *f*, horology; clock & watch making; clocks & watches.

hormis (ɔrmi) *pr*, except, but, save.

horoscope (ɔrɔskɔp) *m*, horoscope, nativity; fortune.

horreur (ɔrrœːr) *f*, horror, fright; object. horrible† (ɔrribl) *a*, horrible, frightful; horrid. horripiler (ɔrripile) *v.t*, to exasperate.

'hors (ɔːr) & ~ de, *pr*, out; out of; without; outside; over; beyond; beside; except; save. *~ bord, a. & ad*, outboard. *~-combat, m*, knock-out (*Box.*). *~ concours*, not competing [for prize]. *~ courant*, dead (*wire*). *~ d'œuvre, m*, addition (*to a building*); hors-d'œuvre (*Cook.*); extra, digression. *hors d'œuvre, att*, (*part*) added (*to a building*); outside (*Meas.*); unmounted (*stone*); extra, digressive. *~ de combat*, out of action; disabled. *~ des limites*, out of bounds. *~ jeu*, off-side (*Foot.*). *~ ligne*, out of the common, exceptional. *~ texte*, outside text (*plate, illustration, map, &c*). *~-texte, m*, plate [outside text]. *~ tout*, over all (*Meas.*).

hortensia (ɔrtɑ̃sja) *m*, hydrangea.

horticole (ɔrtikɔl) *a*, horticultural. horticulteur (kyltœːr) *m*, horticulturist. horticulture (ty:r) *f*, horticulture, gardening.

hosanna (ɔzanna) *m*, hosanna; hurrah.

hospice (ɔspis) *m*, asylum; home; almshouse; hostel; hospice. hospitalier, ère (talje, ɛːr) *a*, hospitable; hospital (*att.*). ¶ *f*, sister of mercy, s. of charity. hospitalisé, e (lize) *n*, inmate; in-patient. hospitalité (te) *f*, hospitality.

hostie (ɔsti) *f*, host (*Eccl.*).

hostile† (ɔstil) *a*, hostile, unfriendly, inimical. hostilité (lite) *f*, hostility, &c.

hôte, esse (oːt, otɛs) *n*, host, hostess, guest, visitor; inmate; denizen.

hôtel [*pour voyageurs*] (otɛl) *m*, hotel. *~* [*particulier*], mansion; town house. *~ de la Monnaie, ~ des Monnaies*, mint. *~*

de ville, town hall, guildhall. *~ des postes*, general post office. *~ des ventes*, auction mart, a. rooms. *~-Dieu*, hospital. *~ garni*, lodging house. *~ meublé*, furnished apartments. hôtelier, ère (təlje, ɛːr) *n*, hotel keeper. hôtellerie (tɛlri) *f*, fashionable restaurant; (*archaic*) hostelry.

'hotte (ɔt) *f*, pannier (*on back*); hood.

'houblon (ublɔ̃) *m*, hop [plant]; hops. 'houblonner (blɔne) *v.t*, to hop (*beer*). 'houblonnière (njɛːr) *f*, hop field.

'houe (u) *f*, hoe. 'houer (ue) *v.t*, to hoe.

'houille (uːj) *f*, coal. *~ blanche*, water power. 'houiller, ère (uje, ɛːr) *a*, coal (*att.*), carboniferous. ¶ *f*, colliery, coal mine. 'houilleur (jœːr) *m*, collier, coal miner.

'houle (ul) *f*, swell, surge. *~ de fond*, ground swell. *~ longue*, roller. 'houlette (ulɛt) *f*, shepherd's crook; trowel (*Hort.*). 'houleux, euse (ulø, øːz) *a*, swelling (*sea*); surging, tumultuous.

'houper (upe) *v.t*, to halloo, hollo (*Hunt.*). 'houppe (up) & 'houpette (pɛt) *f*, tuft, tassel; (*powder*) puff.

'hourder (urde) *v.t*, to rough-cast; pug.

'hourra (hurra) *m*, hurrah, hurray.

'hourvari (urvari) *m*, hullabaloo.

'houspiller (uspije) *v.t*, to maul; mob; taunt, abuse.

'housse (us) *f*, horse cloth; hammer cloth; dust sheet; loose cover. 'housser (se) *v.t*, to dust; put loose cover(s) on (*furniture, &c*). 'houssine (sin) *f*, switch. 'houssiner (ne) *v.t*, to switch. 'houssoir (swaːr) *m*, whisk, flick; feather duster.

'houx (u) *m*, holly.

'hoyau (wajo) *m*, mattock.

'hublot (yblo) *m*, scuttle, port [hole].

'huche (yʃ) *f*, trough, bin.

'hue (hy) *i*, gee up! 'huée (ɥe) *f*, whoop; hoot[ing]. 'huer (ɥe) *v.t*, to whoop, halloo; hoot, boo, barrack.

'huette (ɥɛt) *f*, wood owl, tawny owl.

huguenote (ygnɔt) *f*, pipkin, casserole.

huilage (ɥilaːʒ) *m*, oiling. huile (ɥil) *f*, oil. *~ à mécanisme*, machine o. *~ d'éclairage*, lamp o. *~ de coton*, strap o. (*fig.*). *~ de coude*, elbow grease (*fig.*). *~ de foie de morue*, cod liver oil. *~ de [graine de] lin*, linseed o. *~ de paraffine*, liquid paraffin (*Phar.*). *~ de pétrole*, paraffin [oil], kerosene. *~ de spermaceti*, sperm[aceti] oil. *~ de table, ~ comestible*, salad o. huiler (le) *v.t*, to oil. huilerie (lri) *f*, oil mill; oil shop. huileux, euse (lø, øːz) *a*, oily. huilier (lje) *m*, cruet.

huis clos (à) (ɥi), in camera. huissier (sje) *m*, usher; bailiff.

'huit (ɥit; *before a consonant*, ɥi) *a. & m*, eight; eighth. *~* [*jours*] ou 'huitaine [de jours] (ten) *f*, week (*e.g. Friday to Friday*). 'huitième† (tjɛm) *a. & n*, eighth.

huître (qitr) *f*, oyster; booby, muff. ~*s du pays*, natives. ~ *perlière* (pɛrljɛːr), pearl oyster.

'**hulotte** (ylɔt) *f*, wood owl, tawny owl.

humain (ymɛ̃, ɛn) *a*, human; humane. **humaniser** (manize) *v.t*, to humanize. **humanitaire** (tɛːr) *a. & m*, humanitarian. **humanité** (te) *f*, humanity (*all senses*).

humble† (œ̃:bl) *a*, humble, lowly.

humecter (ymɛkte) *v.t*, to moisten, damp, wet.

'**humer** (yme) *v.t*, to suck in; sip; inhale.

humérus (ymery:s) *m*, humerus.

humeur (ymœ:r) *f*, humour, mood; temper; ill-humour, [ill-]temper, petulance.

humide† (ymid) *a*, damp, moist, humid; watery, wet. **humidifier** (difje) *v.t*, to damp, &c. **humidité** (te) *f*, damp[ness], &c.

humilier (ymilje) *v.t*, to humiliate, humble. **humilité** (lite) *f*, humility, lowliness.

humoriste (ymɔrist) *m*, humorist. ¶ ~ *& humoristique* (tik) *a*, humorous. **humour** (mu:r) *m*, humour.

humus (ymy:s) *m*, humus, mould.

'**hune** (yn) *f*, top (*Naut.*). '**hunier** (nje) *m*, topsail.

'**huppe** (yp) *f*, hoopoe; crest. '**huppé, e** (pe) *a*, crested, tufted; smart (*moving in high society*); clever.

'**hure** (y:r) *f*, head (*boar, &c*); jowl (*fish*); brawn.

'**hurler** (yrle) *v.i*, to howl, yell.

hurluberlu (yrlyberly) *m*, harum-scarum.

'**hutte** (yt) *f*, hut, shanty.

hyacinthe (jasɛ̃:t) *f*, hyacinth, jacinth.

hybride (ibrid) *a. & m*, hybrid.

hydrate (idrat) *m*, hydrate.

hydraulique (idrolik) *a*, hydraulic, water (*att.*). ¶ *f*, hydraulics.

hydravion (idravjɔ̃) *m*, sea plane. ~ *à coque*, flying boat. ~ *à flotteurs*, float plane.

hydre (idr) *f*, hydra.

hydrocarbure (idrokarby:r) *m*, hydrocarbon.

hydrogène (ʒɛn) *m. & att*, hydrogen. **hydrophile** (fil) *a*, absorbent (*cotton wool*). **hydrophobie** (fɔbi) *f*, hydrophobia, rabies. **hydropique** (pik) *a*, dropsical. **hydropisie** (pizi) *f*, dropsy. **hydroscope** (skɔp) *m*, water diviner, dowser. **hydroscopie** (pi) *f*, water divining, dowsing. **hydrothérapie** (terapi) *f*, hydropathy. **hydrothérapique** (pik) *a*, hydropathic.

hyène (jɛn) *f*, hy[a]ena.

hygiène (iʒjɛn) *f*, hygiene, hygienics, health, sanitation. **hygiénique†** (ʒjenik) *a*, hygienic(al), healthy, sanitary; toilet (*paper*).

hymen (imɛn) *ou* **hyménée** (mene) *m*, hymen; wedlock. **hyménoptères** (nɔptɛ:r) *m.pl*, hymenoptera.

hymne (imn) *m*, hymn, song, anthem (*national*). ¶ *f*, hymn (*in church*).

hyperbole (ipɛrbɔl) *f*, hyperbole; hyperbola.

hypnotiser (ipnɔtize) *v.t*, to hypnotize. **hypnotisme** (tism) *m*, hypnotism.

hypocondriaque (ipokɔ̃driak) *a. & n*, hypochondriac. **hypocrisie** (krizi) *f*, hypocrisy, cant. **hypocrite†** (krit) *a*, hypocritical. ¶ *n*, hypocrite. **hypodermique** (dɛrmik) *a*, hypodermic. **hyposulfite** (sylfit) *m*, hyposulphite. **hypothécaire** (tekɛ:r) *a*, mortgage (*att.*). **hypothèque** (tɛk) *f*, mortgage. **hypothéquer** (teke) *v.t*, to mortgage. **hypothèse** (tɛ:z) *f*, hypothesis. **hypothétique†** (tetik) *a*, hypothetic(al).

hysope (izɔp) *f*, hyssop.

hystérie (isteri) *f*, hysteria. **hystérique** (rik) *a*, hysteric(al).

I

ïambe (jã:b) *m. & * **ïambique** (jãbik) *a*, iambic. **ibis** (ibis) *m*, ibis.

iceberg (isbɛrg) *m*, iceberg.

ichtyologie (iktyɔlɔʒi) *f*, ichthyology.

ici (isi) *ad*, here; this; now. ~*-bas*, here below. ~ [*poste de*] *Radio-Paris*, Radio-Paris calling. ~ *X.*, X. speaking (*Teleph.*). *d'*~ *là*, between now & then.

icône (ikoːn) *f*, icon. **iconoclaste** (kɔnɔklast) *m*, iconoclast.

ictère (iktɛ:r) *m*, jaundice.

idéal, e† (ideal) *a. & m*, ideal. **idéaliste** (list) *n*, idealist. **idée** (de) *f*, idea, notion; thought; mind; impression; view. ~ *directrice*, guiding principle, loadstar.

idem (idɛm) *ad*, idem, ditto.

identifier (idɑ̃tifje) *v.t*, to identify. **identique†** (tik) *a*, identical. **identité** (te) *f*, identity, sameness.

idiome (idjoːm) *m*, idiom, dialect.

idiosyncrasie (idjosɛ̃krazi) *f*, idiosyncrasy.

idiot, e (idjo, ɔt) *a*, idiotic. ¶ *n*, idiot; imbecile, natural. **idiotie** (josi) *f*, idiocy. **idiotisme** (idjotism) *m*, idiom, locution.

idolâtre (idolɑ:tr) *a*, idolatrous. ¶ *n*, idolater, tress. **idolâtrer** (latre) *v.t*, to idolize. **idolâtrie** (tri) *f*, idolatry. **idolâtrique** (trik) *a*, idolatrous. **idole** (dɔl) *f*, idol.

idylle (idil) *f*, idyll; romance (*love*).

if (if) *m*, yew [tree].

igname (iɲam) *f*, yam.

ignare (iɲa:r) *a*, ignorant. ¶ *n*, ignoramus.

igné, e (igne) *a*, igneous. **ignifuge** (nify:ʒ) *a*, fireproof. **ignifuger** (fyʒe) *v.t*, to fireproof. **ignition** (nisjɔ̃) *f*, ignition.

ignoble† (iɲɔbl) *a*, ignoble, base; filthy.

ignominie (iɲomini) *f*, ignominy. **ignominieux, euse†** (njø, ø:z) *a*, ignominious, inglorious.

ignorance (iɲorɑ̃:s) *f*, ignorance; blunder. **ignorant, e** (rɑ̃, ɑ̃:t) *a*, ignorant; unacquainted. ¶ *n*, ignoramus, dunce. **ignoré, e** (re) *p.a*, unknown. **ignorer** (re) *v.t. & abs*, to be ignorant (*or* unaware) of, not to know.

iguane (igwan) *m*, iguana.

il (il) *pn*, he; it; she (*of ship*); there; (*pl.*) they.

ile (i:l) *f*, island, isle. *les îles Britanniques*, *les îles du Vent*, &c, See under *britannique*, *vent*, &c.

illégal, e† (illegal) *a*, illegal, unlawful. **illégitime†** (ʒitim) *a*, illegitimate; unlawful; spurious. **illégitimité** (mite) *f*, illegitimacy, &c.

illettré, e (illetre) *a. & n*, illiterate.

illicite† (illisit) *a*, illicit, unlawful.

illico (illiko) *ad*, directly, at once.

illimité, e (illimite) *a*, unlimited, unbounded, boundless; indefinite (*leave*).

illisible† (illizibl) *a*, illegible; unreadable.

illogique (illɔʒik) *a*, illogical. **illogisme** (ʒism) *m*, illogicality.

illumination (illyminasjɔ̃) *f*, illumination; inspiration, brain wave. ~ *par projection*, flood lighting. **illuminer** (ne) *v.t*, to illuminate; light up.

illusion (illyzjɔ̃) *f*, illusion; phantasm; delusion. ~ *d'optique*, optical illusion. **illusoire** (zwa:r) *a*, illusory; illusive.

illustration (illystrasjɔ̃) *f*, lustre (*fig.*); celebrity (*pers.*); illustration. **illustre** (tr) *a*, illustrious. **illustrer** (tre) *v.t*, to make illustrious; illustrate. **illustrissime** (trisim) *a*, most illustrious.

ilot (ilo) *m*, islet; island, block (*houses*). ~ *insalubre*, slum area.

ilote (ilot) *m*, helot. **ilotisme** (tism) *m*, helotry.

image (ima:ʒ) *f*, image; reflection; picture; likeness; idea; (*pl.*) imagery. **imagé, e** (maʒe) *p.a*, picturesque, ornate. **imaginaire** (ʒinɛ:r) *a*, imaginary, fancied, fictive. **imagination** (nasjɔ̃) *f*, imagination, fancy. **imaginer** (ne) *v.t*, to imagine; fancy; devise, invent. **s'~**, to imagine, think.

imbécile† (ɛ̃besil) *a*, silly, stupid, imbecile, fatuous. ¶ *n*, fool. **imbécillité** (silite) *f*, stupidity, fatuity.

imberbe (ɛ̃berb) *a*, beardless; raw, callow.

imbiber (ɛ̃bibe) *v.t*, to soak, imbue, wet. **s'~** (de), to imbibe, sink in.

imbriquer (ɛ̃brike) *v.t*, to imbricate, overlap.

imbrisable (ɛ̃brizabl) *a*, unbreakable.

imbroglio (ɛ̃brɔljo) *m*, imbroglio.

imbu, e (ɛ̃by) *a*, imbued.

imbuvable (ɛ̃byvabl) *a*, undrinkable.

imitateur, trice (imitatœ:r, tris) *n*, imitator, mimic. ¶ *a*, imitative, mimic. **imitation** (sjɔ̃) *f*, imitation. **imiter** (te) *v.t*, to imitate; mimic; resemble, be like.

immaculé, e (immakyle) *a*, immaculate.

immanent, e (immanɑ̃, ɑ̃:t) *a*, immanent.

immangeable (imm- *ou* ɛ̃mɑ̃ʒabl) *a*, uneatable.

immanquable† (imm- *ou* ɛ̃mɑ̃kabl) *a*, sure [to happen]; unmistakable.

immatériel, le† (immaterjɛl) *a*, immaterial.

immatriculer (immatrikyle) *v.t*, to register, enter, enrol.

immédiat, e† (immedja, at) *a*, immediate; proximate; direct.

immémorial, e (immemɔrjal) *a*, immemorial.

immense (immɑ̃:s) *a*, immense, huge, vast; boundless. **immensément** (mɑ̃semɑ̃) *ad*, immensely. **immensité** (site) *f*, immensity; vastness; infinitude. **immensurable** (syrabl) *a*, immeasurable.

immerger (immɛrʒe) *v.t*, to immerse, plunge, dip.

immérité, e (immerite) *a*, unmerited, undeserved, unearned.

immersion (immɛrsjɔ̃) *f*, immersion.

immeuble (immœbl) *m. oft. pl*, real property, r. estate, realty; premises. ~ *d appartements*, block of flats, mansions.

immigration (immigrasjɔ̃) *f*, immigration.

imminence (immina:s) *f*, imminence. **imminent, e** (nɑ̃, ɑ̃:t) *a*, imminent, impending.

immiscer (s') (immise) *v.pr*, to [inter]meddle, interfere. **immixtion** (mikstjɔ̃) *f*, interference.

immobile (immɔbil) *a*, immobile, set, immovable, motionless, still; unmoved. **immobilier, ère** (lje, ɛ:r) *a*, real (*estate—Law*); property (*market*); estate (*agency*); building (*society*). **immobilisations** (lizasjɔ̃) *f.pl*, capital expenditure. **immobiliser** (ze) *v.t*, to immobilize; lock up, tie up; capitalize.

immodéré†, e (immɔdere) *a*, immoderate; excessive; unrestrained.

immodeste† (immɔdɛst) *a*, immodest.

immolation (immɔlasjɔ̃) *f*, immolation, sacrifice; holocaust. **immoler** (le) *v.t*, to immolate, sacrifice; slay.

immonde (immɔ̃:d) *a*, unclean, foul. **immondice** (mɔ̃dis) *f. oft. pl*, dirt, refuse, rubbish, litter.

immoral, e (immɔral) *a*, immoral. **immoralité** (lite) *f*, immorality.

immortaliser (immɔrtalize) *v.t*, to immortalize. **immortalité** (te) *f*, immortality. **immortel, le†** (tɛl) *a*, immortal; everlasting, undying. ¶ *m*, immortal; (*f.*) immortelle.

immuable† (immyabl) *a*, immutable, unchangeable; hard-&-fast.

immunité (immynite) *f*, immunity.

impair (ɛ̃pɛ:r) *a*, uneven, odd (*number*). ¶ *m*, blunder.

impalpable (ɛ̃palpabl) *a*, impalpable.

impardonnable (ɛ̃pardɔnabl) *a*, unpardonable, unforgivable.

imparfait, e† (ɛ̃parfɛ, ɛt) *a*, unfinished; imperfect. ¶ *m*, imperfect [tense].

imparité (ɛ̃parite) *f*, unevenness, oddness.

impartial, e† (ɛ̃parsjal) *a*, impartial, unbiassed.

impartir (ɛ̃parti:r) *v.t*, to impart, bestow.

impasse (ɛ̃pɑ:s) *f*, blind alley, dead end; deadlock, cleft stick.

impassible (ɛ̃pasibl) *a*, impassible; impassive.

impatiemment (ɛ̃pasjamɑ̃) *ad*, impatiently. **impatience** (sjɑ:s) *f*, impatience; (*pl.*) fidgets. **impatient, e** (ɑ̃, ɑ̃:t) *a*, impatient; agog. **impatientant, e** (ātā, ā:t) *a*, provoking, tiresome. **impatienter** (te) *v.t*, to put out of patience, provoke. **s'~**, to grow impatient.

impatroniser (s') (ĕpatronize) *v.pr*, to become master (*in a household*).

impayable (ĕpɛjabl) *a*, impayable; invaluable, priceless; highly amusing. **impayé, e** (je) *a*, unpaid; dishonoured (*bill*).

impeccable (ĕpɛkabl) *a*, impeccable; infallible.

impedimenta (ĕpedimɛ̃ta) *m.pl*, impedimenta.

impénétrable† (ĕpenetrabl) *a*, impenetrable; impervious; inscrutable.

impénitence (ĕpenitã:s) *f*, impenitence; obduracy. **impénitent, e** (tā, ā:t) *a*, impenitent; obdurate.

impératif, ive† (ĕperatif, i:v) *a. & m*, imperative.

impératrice (ĕperatris) *f*, empress.

imperceptible† (ĕpɛrsɛptibl) *a*, imperceptible. **~** [*à l'ouïe*], inaudible.

imperfection (ĕpɛrfɛksjɔ̃) *f*, imperfection; incompletion.

impérial, e (ĕperjal) *a*, imperial. **¶** *f*, imperial (*beard*); top, upper deck, outside (*bus*). **impérialiste** (list) *m*, imperialist; (*att.*) imperialistic.

impérieux, euse† (ĕperjø, ø:z) *a*, imperious.

impérissable (ĕperisabl) *a*, imperishable, undying.

impéritie (ĕperisi) *f*, incapacity.

imperméabiliser (ĕpɛrmeabilize) *v.t*, to [water]-proof. **imperméable** (bl) *a*, impermeable, impervious, -proof; -tight (*air, &c*); waterproof. **¶** *m*, waterproof, mackintosh.

impersonnel, le† (ĕpɛrsonɛl) *a*, impersonal.

impertinemment (ĕpɛrtinamã) *ad*, impertinently, pertly. **impertinence** (nã:s) *f*, [piece of] impertinence, pertness. **impertinent, e** (nā, ā:t) *a*, impertinent, pert; irrelevant (*Law*).

imperturbable† (ĕpɛrtyrbabl) *a*, imperturbable, unruffled.

impétrant, e (ĕpetrã, ã:t) *n*, grantee.

impétueux, euse† (ĕpetɥø, ø:z) *a*, impetuous; hot-headed; gusty (*wind*). **impétuosité** (tɥozite) *f*, impetuosity.

impie (ĕpi) *a*, impious, ungodly, godless; unholy. **impiété** (pjete) *f*, impiety, &c.

impitoyable† (ĕpitwajabl) *a*, pitiless, merciless, ruthless, relentless.

implacable† (ĕplakabl) *a*, implacable.

implanter (ĕplãte) *v.t*, to implant.

implicite† (ĕplisit) *a*, implicit; implied. **impliquer** (ke) *v.t*, to implicate; involve; imply.

implorer (ĕplore) *v.t*, to implore, beseech, crave.

impoli†, e (ĕpoli) *a*, impolite. **impolitesse** (tɛs) *f*, impoliteness, rudeness.

impolitique (ĕpolitik) *a*, impolitic.

impondérable (ĕpɔ̃derabl) *a. & m*, imponderable.

impopulaire (ĕpopylɛ:r) *a*, unpopular.

importance (ĕportã:s) *f*, importance, moment; extent, magnitude. **d'~**, *ad*, soundly. **important, e** (tã, ã:t) *a*, important. **faire l'~**, to give oneself airs. **¶** *m*, main thing.

importateur (ĕportatœ:r) *m*, importer. **importation** (sjɔ̃) *f*, import[ation]. **importer** (te) *v.t*, to import; (*v.i.*) to matter, signify. *n'importe*, no matter. *n'importe où*, anywhere.

importun, e (ĕportœ̃, yn) *a*, importunate, tiresome, troublesome. **¶** *n*, intruder; nuisance. **importuner** (tyne) *v.t*, to importune, worry, molest, pester. **importunité** (nite) *f*, importunity, molestation.

imposable (ĕpozabl) *a*, taxable, ratable, assessable, dutiable. **imposé, e** (ze) *n*, taxpayer, ratepayer. **imposer** (ze) *v.t. & abs*, to impose; enforce; lay [on]; thrust; tax, rate, assess; [over]awe. **en ~ à**, to impose [up]on, deceive. **imposition** (zisjɔ̃) *f*, imposition; tax; assessment.

impossibilité (ĕposibilite) *f*, impossibility. **impossible** (bl) *a*, impossible. **l'~**, *m*, impossibilities; one's [very] utmost.

imposte (ĕpost) *f*, impost (*Arch.*).

imposteur (ĕpostœ:r) *m*, impostor, humbug. **imposture** (ty:r) *f*, imposture, imposition.

impôt (ĕpo) *m*, tax; duty; taxes; taxation. **~ du timbre**, stamp duty. **~ foncier**, land tax, property tax. **~ général (ou global) sur le revenu**, surtax. **~ sur le revenu** ou **~[s] cédulaire[s]** (sedylɛ:r), income tax.

impotent, e (ĕpotã, ã:t) *a*, helpless, crippled. **¶** *n*, cripple.

impraticable (ĕpratikabl) *a*, impracticable; impassable.

imprécation (ĕprekasjɔ̃) *f*, imprecation, curse.

imprécis, e (ĕpresi, i:z) *a*, vague. **imprécision** (sizjɔ̃) *f*, vagueness.

imprégner (ĕpreɲe) *v.t*, to impregnate.

imprenable (ĕprənabl) *a*, impregnable.

impresario (ĕprezarjo) *m*, impresario.

impression (ĕpresjɔ̃) *f*, impression; impress; printing, machining, striking off (*Typ.*); print; issue; priming (*paint*); sensation. **impressionnant, e** (onā, ā:t) *a*, impressive. **impressionner** (ne) *v.t*, to impress, affect. **impressionnisme** (nism) *m*, impressionism.

imprévoyance (ĕprevwajã:s) *f*, shortsightedness, improvidence. **imprévu, e** (vy) *a. & m*, unforeseen; unexpected; contingency (*n.*).

imprimé (ĕprime) *m*, printed book, p. form; paper; (*pl.*) p. matter, literature; handbill, leaflet. **imprimer** (me) *v.t*, to imprint; impress; print; prime (*paint*); impart. **imprimerie** (mri) *f*, printing (*art*); p. plant; p. works, p. office. **imprimeur** (mœ:r) *m*, printer.

improbable (ĕprobabl) *a*, improbable.

improbation (ĕprobasjɔ̃) *f*, disapproval.

improbe (ĕprob) *a*, dishonest.

improductif, ive (ĕprodyktif, i:v) *a*, unproductive.

impromptu (ɛprɔ̃[p]ty) *ad*, *a.inv. & m*, impromptu; extempore; offhand.

impropre† (ɛprɔpr) *a*, wrong; inappropriate; unsuitable; unfit.

improuver (ɛpruve) *v.t*, to disapprove [of].

improvisateur, trice (ɛprɔvizatœ:r, tris) *n*, improvisator, trice. **improviser** (ze) *v.t. & abs*, to improvise, extemporize; vamp (*Mus.*). **à l'improviste** (vist) *ad*, unexpectedly, unawares.

imprudemment (ɛprydamɑ̃) *ad*, imprudently. **imprudence** (dɑ̃:s) *f*, imprudence. **imprudent, e** (dɑ̃, ɑ̃:t) *a*, imprudent, incautious.

impubliable (ɛpybliabl) *a*, unprintable.

impudence (ɛpydɑ̃:s) *f*, shamelessness; impudence. **impudent, e** (dɑ̃, ɑ̃:t) *a. & n*, shameless, &c, (person). **impudemment** (damɑ̃) *ad*, impudently, &c.

impudeur (ɛpydœ:r) *f*, immodesty; indecency. **impudicité** (disite) *f*, impudicity, lewdness. **impudique†** (dik) *a*, unchaste, lewd.

impuissance (ɛpɥisɑ̃:s) *f*, powerlessness; inability; impotence, -cy. **impuissant, e** (sɑ̃, ɑ̃:t) *a*, powerless; impotent.

impulsif, ive (ɛpylsif, i:v) *a*, impulsive. **impulsion** (sjɔ̃) *f*, impulse; impetus; impulsion; spur (*of the moment*).

impunément (ɛpynemɑ̃) *ad*, with impunity. **impuni, e** (ni) *a*, unpunished, scot-free. **impunité** (te) *f*, impunity.

impur, e† (ɛpy:r) *a*, impure; unclean. **impureté** (pyrte) *f*, impurity.

imputer (ɛpyte) *v.t*, to impute, ascribe; charge.

inabordable (inabordabl) *a*, inaccessible.

inacceptable (inaksɛptabl) *a*, unacceptable.

inaccessible (inaksesibl) *a*, inaccessible.

inaccordable (inakɔrdabl) *a*, irreconcilable; inadmissible.

inaccoutumé, e (inakutyme) *a*, unaccustomed; unusual.

inachevé, e (inaʃve) *a*, unfinished.

inactif, ive (inaktif, i:v) *a*, inactive; dull, flat. **inaction** (sjɔ̃) *f*, inaction, drift. **inactivité** (tivite) *f*, inactivity, dullness.

inadmissible (inadmisibl) *a*, inadmissible.

inadvertance (inadvɛrtɑ̃:s) *f*, inadvertence, oversight.

inaliénable (inaljenabl) *a*, inalienable.

inaltérable (inalterabl) *a*, unalterable.

inamical, e (inamikal) *a*, unfriendly.

inamovible (inamovibl) *a*, irremovable.

inanimé, e (inanime) *a*, inanimate, lifeless.

inanité (inanite) *f*, inanity, futility.

inanition (inanisjɔ̃) *f*, inanition, starvation.

inaperçu, e (inapersy) *a*, unseen, unnoticed.

inappétence (inapetɑ̃:s) *f*, loss of appetite.

inapplicable (inaplikabl) *a*, inapplicable. **inapplique, e** (ke) *a*, inattentive; unapplied.

inappréciable (inapresjabl) *a*, inappreciable; inestimable, priceless.

inapte (inapt) *a*, inapt, unfit.

inarticulé, e (inartikyle) *a*, inarticulate.

inattaquable (inatakabl) *a*, unassailable.

inattendu, e (inatɑ̃dy) *a*, unexpected.

inattention (inatɑ̃sjɔ̃) *f*, inattention.

inaugurer (inogyre) *v.t*, to inaugurate; unveil, open; usher in (*fig.*).

incalculable (ɛ̃kalkylabl) *a*, incalculable.

incandescence (ɛ̃kɑ̃desɑ̃:s) *f*, incandescence, glow, white heat. **incandescent, e** (sɑ̃, ɑ̃:t) *a*, incandescent, glowing, white-hot.

incantation (ɛ̃kɑ̃tasjɔ̃) *f*, incantation.

incapable (ɛ̃kapabl) *a*, incapable; unfit; unable, unequal; incompetent; inefficient. **les ~s**, *m.pl*, the unemployable. **incapacité** (site) *f*, incapacity, &c; disablement, disability.

incarcérer (ɛ̃karsere) *v.t*, to incarcerate.

incarnadin, e (ɛ̃karnadɛ̃, in) *a*, incarnadine. **incarnat, e** (na, at) *a*, rosy, pink, roseate. **incarnation** (sjɔ̃) *f*, incarnation, embodiment. **incarné, e** (ne) *p.a*, incarnate; ingrowing (*nail*).

incartade (ɛ̃kartad) *f*, prank, indiscretion, lapse; outburst, tirade.

incassable (ɛ̃kasabl) *a*, unbreakable.

incendiaire (ɛ̃sɑ̃djɛ:r) *a. & n*, incendiary. **incendie** (di) *m*, [outbreak of] fire. **~ volontaire**, arson, fire raising, incendiarism. **incendié, e** (dje) *n*, sufferer by a fire. **incendier** (dje) *v.t*, to [set on] fire, set f. to.

incertain, e (ɛ̃sɛrtɛ̃, ɛn) *a*, uncertain; unsettled. **incertitude** (tityd) *f*, uncertainty; suspense.

incessamment (ɛ̃sesamɑ̃) *ad*, incessantly; forthwith. **incessant, e** (sɑ̃, ɑ̃:t) *a*, incessant, unceasing, ceaseless.

incessible (ɛ̃sesibl) *a*, inalienable; not transferable.

inceste (ɛ̃sɛst) *m*, incest. **incestueux, euse†** (tɥø, ø:z) *a*, incestuous.

incidemment (ɛ̃sidamɑ̃) *ad*, incidentally. **incident, e** (dɑ̃, ɑ̃:t) *a*, incidental; incident (*ray*). ¶ *m*, incident; point of law; difficulty.

incinérateur (ɛ̃sineratœ:r) *m*, incinerator, destructor. **incinérer** (re) *v.t*, to incinerate; cremate.

incirconcis, e (ɛ̃sirkɔ̃si, i:z) *a*, uncircumcised.

inciser (ɛ̃size) *v.t*, to incise, cut; lance. **incisif, ive** (zif, i:v) *a*, incisive. **[dent] incisive**, *f*, incisor. **incision** (zjɔ̃) *f*, incision; lancing.

incitation (ɛ̃sitasjɔ̃) *f*, incitement. **inciter** (te) *v.t*, to incite, instigate.

incivil, e† (ɛ̃sivil) *a*, uncivil. **incivilité** (lite) *f*, incivility.

inclément, e (ɛ̃klemɑ̃, ɑ̃:t) *a*, inclement.

inclinaison (ɛ̃klinɛzɔ̃) *f*, inclination; gradient; slope; slant; cant; tilt; dip; pitch; rake. **inclination** (nasjɔ̃) *f*, inclination; leaning, bent; bow, nod; attachment, love, sweetheart. **incliner** (ne) *v.t. & i. & s'~**, to incline; lean; slope; slant; cant; tilt; dip; pitch; rake; bow [down]; nod.

inclure (ɛ̃kly:r) *v.t.ir*, to enclose. **inclusivement** (klyzivmɑ̃) *ad*, inclusively; inclusive (*dates*).

incognito (ĕkɔɲito *ou* ĕkɔgnito) *ad. & m*, incognito.

incohérence (ĕkɔerɑ̃:s) *f*, incoherence. **incohérent, e** (rɑ̃, ɑ̃:t) *a*, incoherent; rambling.

incolore (ĕkɔlɔ:r) *a*, colourless.

incomber (ĕkɔ̃be) *v.i*, to be incumbent, behove, devolve, rest.

incombustible (ĕkɔ̃bystibl) *a*, incombustible, fireproof.

incommensurable (ĕkɔmɑ̃syrabl) *a*, incommensurable.

incommode (ĕkɔmɔd) *a*, inconvenient; uncomfortable; tiresome. **incommodé, e** (de) *p.a*, poorly (*health*); crippled, disabled; embarrassed. **incommodément** (demɑ̃) *ad*, uncomfortably. **incommoder** (de) *v.t*, to inconvenience, incommode. **incommodité** (dite) *f*, inconvenience; nuisance (*Law, &c*); (*ship in*) difficulties (*Navigation*).

incomparable† (ĕkɔ̃parabl) *a*, incomparable.

incompatible (ĕkɔ̃patibl) *a*, incompatible.

incompétent, e (ĕkɔ̃petɑ̃, ɑ̃:t) *a*, incompetent.

incomplet, ète† (ĕkɔ̃plɛ, ɛt) *a*, incomplete.

incompréhensible (ĕkɔ̃preɑ̃sibl) *a*, incomprehensible.

incompris, e (ĕkɔ̃pri, i:z) *a*, misunderstood; unappreciated.

inconcevable (ĕkɔ̃svabl) *a*, inconceivable.

inconciliable (ĕkɔ̃siljabl) *a*, irreconcilable.

inconduite (ĕkɔ̃dɥit) *f*, misconduct, misbehaviour.

incongru, e (ĕkɔ̃gry) *a*, incongruous; uncouth. **incongruité** (gryite) *f*, incongruity; malapropism; impropriety.

inconnu, e (ĕkɔny) *a*, unknown. ¶ *n*, unknown person; stranger; nobody. l'~, *m*, the unknown. [**quantité**] **inconnue** (*f*), unknown [quantity].

inconsciemment (ĕkɔ̃sjamɑ̃) *ad*, unconsciously. **inconscience** (sjɑ̃:s) *f*, unconsciousness. **inconscient, e** (ɑ̃, ɑ̃:t) *a*, unconscious; irresponsible.

inconséquent, e (ĕkɔ̃sekɑ̃, ɑ̃:t) *a*, inconsistent; inconsequent[ial]; flighty.

inconsidéré† *e* (ĕkɔ̃sidere) *a*, inconsiderate; thoughtless.

inconsistant, e (ĕkɔ̃sistɑ̃, ɑ̃:t) *a*, inconsistent.

inconsolable† (ĕkɔ̃sɔlabl) *a*, inconsolable. **inconsolé, e** (le) *a*, unconsoled, forlorn.

inconstant, e (ĕkɔ̃stɑ̃, ɑ̃:t) *a*, inconstant; changeable; fickle.

inconstitutionnel, le† (ĕkɔ̃stitysjɔnɛl) *a*, unconstitutional.

incontestable† (ĕkɔ̃tɛstabl) *a*, undeniable. **incontesté, e** (te) *a*, undisputed.

incontinent, e (ĕkɔ̃tinɑ̃, ɑ̃:t) *a*, incontinent, unchaste.

inconvenance (ĕkɔ̃vnɑ̃:s) *f*, impropriety. **inconvenant, e** (vnɑ̃, ɑ̃:t) *a*, unbecoming, unseemly, indecorous.

inconvénient (ĕkɔ̃venjɑ̃) *m*, inconvenience; drawback.

incorporer (ĕkɔrpɔre) *v.t*, to incorporate; blend.

incorrect, e (ĕkɔrɛkt) *a*, incorrect; inaccurate; unbusinesslike. **incorrectement** (təmɑ̃) *ad*, incorrectly, &c; ungrammatically. **incorrection** (ksjɔ̃) *f*, incorrectness, &c.

incorrigible† (ĕkɔriʒibl) *a*, incorrigible, irreclaimable, hopeless.

incorruptible (ĕkɔryptibl) *a*, incorruptible.

incrédibilité (ĕkredibilite) *f*, incredibility. **incrédule** (dyl) *a*, incredulous. ¶ *n*, unbeliever. **incrédulité** (lite) *f*, incredulity; unbelief.

incréé, e (ĕkree) *a*, uncreated.

incriminer (ĕkrimine) *v.t*, to incriminate; challenge.

incroyable† (ĕkrwajabl) *a*, incredible.

incrustation (ĕkrystasjɔ̃) *f*, incrustation; inlay, inlaid work; fur, scale. **incruster** (te) *v.t*, to incrust; inlay; fur.

incubation (ĕkybasjɔ̃) *f*, incubation.

inculpé, e (ĕkylpe) *n*, accused. **inculper** (pe) *v.t*, to inculpate, charge.

inculquer (ĕkylke) *v.t*, to inculcate, instil[l].

inculte (ĕkylt) *a*, uncultivated, waste; wild; unkempt; uncultured, untutored.

incurable† (ĕkyrabl) *a. & n*, incurable.

incurie (ĕkyri) *f*, carelessness.

incursion (ĕkyrsjɔ̃) *f*, incursion, raid, inroad, foray.

inde (ɛ̃:d) *m. ou* bleu d'~, indigo blue. l'I~, *f*, India. l'I~ anglaise, British I. l'I~ transgangétique (trɑ̃sgɑ̃ʒetik), Further India. I~s occidentales, West Indies. I~s orientales néerlandaises, Dutch East Indies.

indébrouillable (ĕdebrujabl) *a*, inextricable.

indécemment (ĕdesamɑ̃) *ad*, indecently. **indécence** (sɑ̃:s) *f*, indecency. **indécent, e** (sɑ̃, ɑ̃:t) *a*, indecent.

indéchiffrable (ĕdefifrabl) *a*, undecipherable; illegible; unintelligible.

indécis, e (ĕdesi, i:z) *a*, undecided ;unsettled; drawn (*battle, game*). **indécision** (sisjɔ̃) *f*, indecision.

indécrottable (ĕdekrɔtabl) *a*, incorrigible.

indéfendable (ĕdefɑ̃dabl) *a*, indefensible.

indéfini†, e (ĕdefini) *a*, indefinite; undefined. **indéfinissable** (sabl) *a*, indefinable; unaccountable; nondescript.

indélébile (ĕdelebil) *a*, indelible.

indélicat, e† (ĕdelika, at) *a*, indelicate; tactless; unscrupulous, sharp. **indélicatesse** (tɛs) *f*, indelicacy, &c.

indémaillable (ĕdemajabl) *a*, ladderproof.

indemne (ĕdemn) *a*, unscathed, scatheless, unhurt, scot-free. **indemniser** (nize) *v.t*, to indemnify, compensate. **indemnité** (te) *f*, indemnity, compensation; claim, loss (*Insce*); allowance, remuneration, bonus; salary (*M.P's*); consideration [money]. ~ de chômage, unemployment benefit, dole. ~ de vie chère, cost of living bonus.

indéniable (ĕdenjabl) *a*, undeniable.

indépendamment (ĕdepɑ̃damɑ̃) *ad*, independently. ~ de, irrespective of. **indépen-**

dance (dā:s) f, independence. **indépendant, e** (dā, ā:t) a, independent; free; self-contained.

indéracinable (ēderasinabl) a, ineradicable.

indescriptible (ēdɛskriptibl) a, indescribable.

indésirable (ēdezirabl) a, undesirable; objectionable. ¶ n, undesirable.

indestructible (ēdɛstryktibl) a, indestructible.

indéterminé, e (ēdetɛrmine) a, undetermined; indeterminate.

indévot, e (ēdevo, ɔt) a, irreligious.

index (ēdɛks) m, index; pointer; first finger, forefinger; black list. ~ [expurgatoire] (ɛkspyrgatwa:r), index [expurgatorius].

indicateur, trice (ēdikatœ:r, tris) n, informer; (m.) time table, time book; guide [book] (Rly, street, Post); indicator, ga[u]ge. ~ universel des P.T.T. (= Postes, Télégraphes & Téléphones), post office guide. **indicatif, ive** (tif, i:v) a, indicative. [mode] **indicatif,** m, i. [mood]. **indication** (sjɔ̃) f. oft. pl, indication; clue; information; particular; instruction. ~ de nom & de lieu de résidence de l'imprimeur, printer's imprint. ~ de nom (ou de ·firme) de l'éditeur, publisher's imprint. **indice** (dis) m, indication; sign; index; figure; number. ~ du coût de la vie, cost of living figure.

indicible (sibl) a, unspeakable, unutterable.

indien, ne (ēdjē, ɛn) a. & I~, n, Indian. ¶ f, print[ed cotton fabric].

indifféremment (ēdiferamā) ad, indifferently; indiscriminately. **indifférence** (rā:s) f, indifference; unconcern. **indifférent, e** (rā, ā:t) a, indifferent; unconcerned.

indigène (ēdiʒɛ:n) a, native, indigenous. ¶ n, native.

indigent, e (ēdiʒā, ā:t) a. & n, indigent, poor, pauper (n.). ~ de passage, casual.

indigeste (ēdiʒɛst) a, indigestible; undigested (fig.); crude. **indigestion** (tjɔ̃) f, indigestion.

indignation (ēdinasjɔ̃) f, indignation. **indigne†** (diɲ) a, unworthy; undeserving; disqualified (Law); outrageous. **indigné, e** (ɲe) p.a, indignant. **indigner** (ɲe) v.t, to exasperate. **indignité** (ɲite) f, unworthiness; indignity; outrage.

indigo (ēdigo) m, indigo. **indigotier** (gɔtje) m, indigo plant.

indiquer (ēdike) v.t, to indicate, show, point out; mark; mention, state.

indirect, e† (ēdirɛkt) a, indirect; consequential (damages); crooked (fig.).

indiscipliné, e (ēdisipline) a, unruly.

indiscret, ète† (ēdiskrɛ, ɛt) a, indiscreet; forward; prying. **indiscrétion** (kresjɔ̃) f, indiscretion.

indiscutable† (ēdiskytabl) a, indisputable.

indispensable† (ēdispūsabl) a, indispensable. **indisponible** (ēdisponibl) a, inalienable; unavailable; not available.

indisposé, e (ēdispoze) a, indisposed, unwell, poorly, out of sorts. **indisposer** (ze) v.t,

to upset; set against. **indisposition** (zisjɔ̃) f, indisposition.

indissoluble† (ēdisɔlybl) a, indissoluble.

indistinct, e (ēdistē:kt) a, indistinct. **indistinctement** (tēktəmā) ad, indistinctly; indiscriminately.

individu (ēdividy) m, individual; fellow. son ~, oneself, number one. **individualité** (dɥalite) f, individuality. **individuel, le†** (dɥel) a, individual; several (Law).

indivis, e (ēdivi, i:z) a, undivided; joint. par indivis ou indivisément (vizemā) ad, jointly. **indivisible†** (zibl) a, indivisible.

in-dix-huit ou **in-18** (ēdizɥit) a.m. & m, octodecimo, eighteenmo, 18mo.

Indochine (l') (ēdɔʃin) f, Indo-China.

indocile (ēdɔsil) a, intractable.

indolemment (ēdɔlamā) ad, indolently; lazily. **indolence** (lā:s) f, indolence, sloth; apathy, indifference. **indolent, e** (lā, ā:t) a, indolent, slothful; apathetic, indifferent, lackadaisical; painless.

indomptable (ēdɔ̃tabl) a, untamable; indomitable; uncontrollable. **indompté, e** (te) a, untamed; unconquered; unsubdued.

in-douze ou **in-12** (ēdu:z) a.m. & m, duodecimo, twelvemo, 12mo.

indu, e (ēdy) a, untimely (hour).

indubitable† (ēdybitabl) a, indubitable, undoubted.

induction (ēdyksjɔ̃) f, induction; inference. **induire** (dɥi:r) v.t.ir, to lead; infer; induce. ~ en erreur, to mislead. **induit** (dɥi) m, armature (dynamo).

indulgence (ēdylʒā:s) f, indulgence; forbearance, leniency. **indulgent, e** (ʒā, ā:t) a, indulgent; lenient.

indûment (ēdymā) ad, unduly.

industrialiser (ēdystrialize) v.t, to industrialize. **industrialisme** (lism) m, industrialism. **industrie** (tri) f, ingenuity; industry; manufacture, trade. ~-clef, key industry. ~ d'art, handicraft. **industriel, le†** (ɛl) a, industrial; manufacturing. ¶ m, manufacturer; millowner; industrialist. **industrieux, euse†** (ø, ø:z) a, industrious, busy.

inébranlable† (inebrālabl) a, unshakable; immovable; unyielding; steadfast.

inédit, e (inedi, it) a, unpublished (book); novel.

ineffable (inefabl) a, ineffable, unutterable.

ineffaçable (inefasabl) a, ineffaceable.

inefficace† (inefikas) a, inefficacious; ineffectual; ineffective, nugatory.

inégal, e† (inegal) a, unequal; uneven. **inégalité** (lite) f, inequality; unevenness.

inélégant, e (inelegā, ā:t) a, inelegant.

inéligible (ineliʒibl) a, ineligible.

inemployable (inā̃plwajabl) a, unusable (tool, &c). **inemployé, e** (je) a, unemployed (resources, &c).

inénarrable (inenarabl) a, indescribable.

inepte† (inɛpt) a, inept, inane, silly. **ineptie** (si) f, ineptitude, &c.

F *

inépuisable† (inepɥizabl) a, inexhaustible.

inerte (inɛrt) a, inert, sluggish. inertie (si) f, inertia; listlessness.

inespéré†, e (inɛspere) a, unhoped for, unexpected.

inestimable (inɛstimabl) a, inestimable, priceless.

inévitable† (inevitabl) a, inevitable; unavoidable.

inexact, e† (inɛgzakt) a, inexact, inaccurate, incorrect; unpunctual. inexactitude (titɥd) f, inexactitude, &c.

inexcusable (inɛkskyzabl) a, inexcusable.

inexécutable (inɛgzekytabl) a, unworkable; inexecutable. inexécution (sjɔ̃) f, nonperformance.

inexercé, e (inɛgzɛrse) a, unskilled.

inexigible (inɛgziʒibl) a, not due, undue.

inexistant, e (inɛgzistɑ̃, ɑ̃:t) a, non-existent. inexistence (tɑ̃:s) f, non-existence.

inexorable† (inɛgzɔrabl) a, inexorable.

inexpérience (inɛksperjɑ̃:s) f, inexperience. inexpérimenté, e (rimɑ̃te) a, inexperienced, unskilled.

inexplicable (inɛksplikabl) a, inexplicable. inexpliqué, e (ke) a, unexplained.

inexploré, e (inɛksplɔre) a, unexplored.

inexprimable (inɛksprimabl) a, inexpressible.

inexpugnable (inɛkspygnabl) a, impregnable.

in extenso (inɛkstɛ̃so) ad, in extenso, in full.

inextinguible (inɛkstɛ̃gɥibl) a, inextinguishable; unquenchable; irrepressible, uncontrollable.

in extremis (inɛkstremis) ad, in extremis.

inextricable (inɛkstrikabl) a, inextricable.

infaillible† (ɛ̃fajibl) a, infallible; unerring.

infamant, e (ɛ̃famɑ̃, ɑ̃:t) a, defamatory; opprobrious; infamous (Law). infâme (fɑ:m) a, infamous, foul. infamie (fami) f, infamy.

infanterie (ɛ̃fɑ̃tri) f, infantry, foot.

infanticide (ɛ̃fɑ̃tisid) (act) m. & (pers.) n, infanticide. infantile (til) a, infant[ile] (Med.).

infatigable† (ɛ̃fatigabl) a, indefatigable, tireless.

infatuation (ɛ̃fatɥasjɔ̃) f, infatuation. s'infatuer (tɥe) v.pr, to become infatuated.

infécond, e (ɛ̃fekɔ̃, ɔ̃:d) a, barren.

infect, e (ɛ̃fɛkt) a, stinking, foul. infecter (te) v.t, to infect, taint; (v.i.) to stink. infectieux, euse (sjø, ø:z) a, infectious (Med.). infection (sjɔ̃) f, infection; stench.

inférence (ɛ̃ferɑ̃:s) f, inference. inférer (re) v.t, to infer.

inférieur, e (ɛ̃ferjœːr) a, lower, bottom, under, nether; inferior, less. ¶ m, inferior (pers.). infériorité (rjɔrite) f, inferiority.

infernal, e (ɛ̃fɛrnal) a, infernal, hellish.

infertile (ɛ̃fɛrtil) a, infertile, barren.

infester (ɛ̃fɛste) v.t, to infest, overrun.

infidèle† (ɛ̃fidɛl) a, unfaithful; faithless; inaccurate; dishonest; infidel. ¶ n, un-

faithful person; infidel. infidélité (delite) f, infidelity; unfaithfulness; dishonesty; breach of trust.

infiltrer (s') (ɛ̃filtre) v.pr, to infiltrate, percolate.

infime (ɛ̃fim) a, lowest; insignificant; tiny.

infini, e (ɛ̃fini) a, infinite. l'infini, m, the infinite; infinity (Math., Phot.). à l'infini, ad, ad infinitum. infiniment (mɑ̃) ad, infinitely. infinité (te) f, infinity, infinitude. une ~ de, no end of. infinitésimal, e (tezimal) a, infinitesimal. [mode] infinitif (tif) m, infinitive [mood].

infirme (ɛ̃firm) a, infirm, invalid. ¶ n, invalid. infirmer (me) v.t, to invalidate; quash; weaken. infirmerie (mɔri) f, infirmary, sick room (Sch., &c). infirmier, ère (mje, ɛ:r) n, hospital attendant, h. orderly. h. nurse, male n., sick n. infirmière en chef, matron. infirmité (mite) f, infirmity; frailty; weakness.

inflammable (ɛ̃flamabl) a, inflammable. inflammation (sjɔ̃) f, ignition; inflammation.

inflation (ɛ̃flasjɔ̃) f, inflation (Fin.).

infléchir (ɛ̃fleʃiːr) v.t, to inflect, bend. inflexible† (flɛksibl) a, inflexible. inflexion (ksjɔ̃) f, inflexion, -ction.

infliger (ɛ̃fliʒe) v.t, to inflict.

influence (ɛ̃flyɑ̃:s) f, influence, sway. influencer (ɑ̃se) v.t, to influence, sway. influent, e (ɑ̃, ɑ̃:t) a, influential. influer sur (e), to influence.

in-folio (ɛ̃fɔljo) a.m. & m, folio (book).

informateur, trice (ɛ̃fɔrmatœːr, tris) n, informant. information (sjɔ̃) f, mostly pl, in- or enquiry; (pl.) news [bulletin] (Radio). informe (ɛ̃fɔrm) a, shapeless, formless; informal (Law).

informé (ɛ̃fɔrme) m, inquiry (Law). informer (me) v.t, to inform, acquaint. s'~, to in- or enquire.

infortune (ɛ̃fɔrtyn) f, misfortune; adversity; mischance. infortuné, e (ne) a. & n, unfortunate.

infraction (ɛ̃fraksjɔ̃) f, infraction, infringement, breach; offence.

infranchissable (ɛ̃frɑ̃ʃisabl) a, impassable, insuperable.

infréquenté, e (ɛ̃frekɑ̃te) a, unfrequented.

infructueux, euse† (ɛ̃fryktɥø, ø:z) a, fruitless (fig.).

infus, e (ɛ̃fy, y:z) a, inborn, innate. infuser (fyze) v.t, infuse; instil[l]. [s']~, to draw (tea). infusible (zibl) a, infusible. infusion (zjɔ̃) f, infusion; tea. infusoires (zwa:r) m.pl, infusoria.

ingambe (ɛ̃gɑ̃:b) a, nimble.

ingénier (s') (ɛ̃ʒenje) v.pr, to try, contrive. ingénieur (ɛ̃ʒenjœːr) m, engineer. ~-conseil, consulting e. ~ constructeur, engineer (maker). ~ électricien, electrical e. ~ mécanicien, mechanical e.

ingénieux, euse† (ɛ̃ʒenjø, ø:z) a, ingenious. ingéniosité (jozite) f, ingenuity.

ingénu†, e (ɛ̃ʒeny) *a*, ingenuous, artless; unsophisticated. **¶ *f*,** ingénue (*Theat.*). **ingénuité** (nɥite) *f*, ingenuousness, &c.

ingérer (s') (ɛ̃ʒere) *v.pr*, to interfere, meddle.

ingouvernable (ɛ̃guvɛrnabl) *a*, ungovernable; uncontrollable.

ingrat, e (ɛ̃gra, at) *a*, ungrateful; thankless; unpromising; unpleasing. **ingratitude** (tityd) *f*, ingratitude.

ingrédient (ɛ̃gredjɑ̃) *m*, ingredient, constituent.

inguérissable (ɛ̃gerisabl) *a*, incurable; inconsolable.

inhabile† (inabil) *a*, incapable.

inhabitable (inabitabl) *a*, uninhabitable. **inhabité, e** (te) *a*, uninhabited, untenanted.

inhaler (inale) *v.t*, to inhale.

inharmonieux, euse (inarmɔnjø, øːz) *a*, inharmonious; unmusical.

inhérent, e (inerɑ̃, ɑ̃ːt) *a*, inherent.

inhospitalier, ère (inɔspitalje, ɛːr) *a*, inhospitable.

inhumain, e† (inymɛ̃, ɛn) *a*, inhuman. **inhumanité** (manite) *f*, inhumanity.

inhumer (inyme) *v.t*, to inter, bury.

inimaginable (inimaʒinabl) *a*, unimaginable.

inimitable (inimitabl) *a*, inimitable.

inimitié (inimitje) *f*, enmity, ill feeling.

ininflammable (inɛ̃flamabl) *a*, uninflammable.

inintelligent, e (inɛ̃teliʒɑ̃, ɑ̃ːt) *a*, unintelligent. **inintelligible†** (ʒibl) *a*, unintelligible.

ininterrompu, e (inɛ̃tɛrɔ̃py) *a*, uninterrupted, unbroken.

inique† (inik) *a*, iniquitous, nefarious, unrighteous. **iniquité** (kite) *f*, iniquity, sin.

initial, e (inisjal) *a*, initial; opening. **¶ *f*,** initial [letter]. **initiation** (sjɔ̃) *f*, initiation. **initiative** (tiːv) *f*, initiative; push, drive. **initié, e** (sje) *n*, initiate. **initier** (sje) *v.t*, to initiate.

injecté, e (ɛ̃ʒɛkte) *a*, bloodshot; flushed; impregnated (*wood*). **injecter** (te) *v.t*, to inject. **injecteur** (tœːr) *m*, injector. **injection** (ksjɔ̃) *f*, injection.

injonction (ɛ̃ʒɔ̃ksjɔ̃) *f*, injunction.

injure (ɛ̃ʒyːr) *f*, injury, wrong; insult; (*pl.*) abuse; (*s. or pl.*) ravages. **injurier** (ʒyrje) *v.t*, to abuse, insult, revile. **injurieux, euse†** (rjø, øːz) *a*, abusive, insulting, offensive, opprobrious, injurious.

injuste† (ɛ̃ʒyst) *a. & m*, unjust; unrighteous; unfair; inequitable; wrong. **injustice** (tis) *f*, injustice; unrighteousness; unfairness; wrong. **injustifiable** (tifjabl) *a*, unjustifiable.

inné, e (inne) *a*, innate, inborn, inbred. **innéité** (ite) *f*, innateness.

innocemment (inɔsamɑ̃) *ad*, innocently. **innocent, e** (sɑ̃, ɑ̃ːt) *a*, innocent; guiltless, not guilty; sinless, blameless; guileless, artless; harmless. **¶ *n*,** innocent; simpleton. **innocence** (sɑ̃ːs) *f*, innocence, &c. **innocenter** (sɑ̃te) *v.t*, to find not guilty.

innocuité (innɔkɥite) *f*, harmlessness.

innombrable (innɔ̃brabl) *a*, innumerable, numberless, countless, untold.

innomé, e (innɔme) *a*, unnamed. **innommable** (mabl) *a*, unnamable.

innovation (innɔvasjɔ̃) *f*, innovation, [new] departure.

inobservance (inɔpsɛrvɑ̃ːs) *& * **inobservation** (vasjɔ̃) *f*, inobservance, disregard. **inobservé, e** (ve) *a*, not complied with (*rules*).

inoccupé, e (inɔkype) *a*, unoccupied, idle; vacant.

in-octavo *ou* **in-8°** (inɔktavo) *a.m. & m*, octavo, 8vo.

inoculation (inɔkylasjɔ̃) *f*, inoculation. **inoculer** (le) *v.t*, to inoculate.

inodore (inɔdɔːr) *a*, inodorous, odourless.

inoffensif, ive (inɔfɑ̃sif, iːv) *a*, innocuous; innoxious; inoffensive; harmless.

inondation (inɔ̃dasjɔ̃) *f*, inundation, flood. **inonder** (de) *v.t*, to inundate, flood, deluge.

inopérant, e (inɔperɑ̃, ɑ̃ːt) *a*, inoperative.

inopiné, e (inɔpine) *a*, unexpected, sudden.

inopportun, e (inɔpɔrtœ̃, yn) *a*, inopportune.

inorganique (inɔrganik) *a*, inorganic.

inoubliable (inubliabl) *a*, unforgettable.

inouï, e (inwi) *a*, unheard of.

inoxydable (inɔksidabl) *a*, stainless, rustless.

in-quarto *ou* **in-4°** (ɛ̃kwarto) *a.m. & m*, quarto, 4to, 4°.

inquiet, ète (ɛ̃kjɛ, ɛt) *a*, uneasy; troubled; restless, fidgety. **inquiéter** (jete) *v.t*, to make uneasy; disquiet; disturb; trouble; molest. **inquiétude** (tyd) *f*, uneasiness, disquiet[ude]; restlessness.

inquisiteur, trice (ɛ̃kizitœːr, tris) *a*, inquisitive. **inquisition** (sjɔ̃) *f*, inquisition.

insaisissable (ɛ̃sɛzisabl) *a*, not distrainable; difficult to catch; elusive; imperceptible.

insalubre (ɛ̃salybr) *a*, unhealthy; insanitary. **insanité** (ɛ̃sanite) *f*, insanity (*folly*), nonsense.

insatiable† (ɛ̃sasjabl) *a*, insatiable.

insciemment (ɛ̃sjamɑ̃) *ad*, unknowingly.

inscription (ɛ̃skripsjɔ̃) *f*, inscription; writing; epitaph; registration, registry; entry; matriculation; quotation (*in Stk Ex. list*). **~ de (ou en) faux**, pleading of forgery. **~ de rente**, inscribed stock. **prendre des (ses) ~s**, to matriculate. **inscrire** (skriːr) *v.t.ir*, to inscribe; register; enter; write; quote. **s'inscrire en faux**, to plead forgery (*Law*); deny the truth (*contre* = of).

inscrutable (ɛ̃skrytabl) *a*, inscrutable.

insecte (ɛ̃sɛkt) *m*, insect. **insecticide** (tisid) *a*, insect (*powder*). **insectivore** (vɔːr) *a*, insectivorous. **~s**, *m.pl*, insectivora.

insécurité (ɛ̃sekyrite) *f*, insecurity.

in-seize *ou* **in-16** (ɛ̃sɛːz) *a.m. & m*, sextodecimo, sixteenmo, 16mo.

insensé, e (ɛ̃sɑ̃se) *a*, insensate, mad; senseless. **¶ *n*,** madman, -woman. **insensible†** (sibl) *a*, insensible; unfeeling, callous.

inséparable† (ɛ̃separabl) *a*, inseparable. **~s, *n.pl*,** inseparables (*pers.*); love birds.

insérer (ɛsere) v.t, to insert, put in. insertion (sɛrsjɔ̃) f, insertion.

insidieux, euse† (ɛ̃sidjø, ø:z) a, insidious.

insigne (ɛ̃siɲ) a, signal, conspicuous; distinguished; arrant, rank, notorious. ¶ m, badge; (pl.) insignia. ~s de la royauté, regalia.

insignifiant, e (ɛ̃siɲifjã, ã:t) a, insignificant, trifling, trivial, vacuous.

insinuation (ɛ̃sinɥasjɔ̃) f, insinuation; innuendo. insinuer (nɥe) v.t, to insinuate; hint at; introduce.

insipide (ɛ̃sipid) a, insipid; tasteless, vapid.

insistance (ɛ̃sistã:s) f, insistence. insister (te) v.i, to insist.

insociable (ɛ̃sɔsjabl) a, unsociable.

insolation (ɛ̃sɔlasjɔ̃) f, insolation; sun bathing; sunstroke.

insolemment (ɛ̃sɔlamã) ad, insolently. insolence (lã:s) f, insolence. insolent, e (lã, ã:t) a, insolent; overbearing; extraordinary.

insolite (ɛ̃sɔlit) a, unusual, unwonted.

insoluble (ɛ̃sɔlybl) a, insoluble.

insolvabilité (ɛ̃sɔlvabilite) f, insolvency. insolvable (bl) a, insolvent.

insomnie (ɛ̃sɔmni) f. oft. pl, insomnia, sleeplessness.

insondable (ɛ̃sɔ̃dabl) a, unfathomable, fathomless.

insonore (ɛ̃sɔnɔ:r) a, sound-proof.

insouciant, e (ɛ̃susjã, ã:t) a, careless, unconcerned; jaunty. insoucieux, euse (sjø, ø:z) a, heedless, regardless.

insoumis, e (ɛ̃sumi, i:z) a, unsubdued. ¶ m, absentee (Mil.).

insoutenable (ɛ̃sutnabl) a, untenable, indefensible; insufferable.

inspecter (ɛ̃spɛkte) v.t, to inspect, examine. inspecteur, trice (tœ:r, tris) n, inspector; examiner; shop walker. ~ du travail, factory inspector. inspection (ksjɔ̃) f, inspection, examination; inspectorship.

inspiration (ɛ̃spirasjɔ̃) f, inspiration. inspirer (re) v.t, to inspire (air & fig.); prompt.

instabilité (ɛ̃stabilite) f, instability. instable (bl) a, unstable, unsteady.

installation (ɛ̃stalasjɔ̃) f, installation; induction (Eccl.). installer (le) v.t, to install; induct; settle.

instamment (ɛ̃stamã) ad, earnestly; urgently.

instance (stã:s) f, (pl.) entreaties; (Law) instance, suit ¶ a, (stã, ã:t) a, urgent, instant. ¶ m, instant, moment. à l'~, a moment ago; at once. instantané, e (stãtane) a, instantaneous. ¶ m, snap[shot].

instar de (à l') (ɛ̃sta:r) pr, like, as in.

instigation (ɛ̃stigasjɔ̃) f, instigation.

instiller (ɛ̃stille) v.t, to instil[l] (liquid).

instinct (ɛ̃stɛ̃) m, instinct. instinctif, ive† (stɛktif, i:v) a, instinctive.

instituer (ɛ̃stitɥe) v.t, to institute; appoint. institut (ty) m, institute, institution. ~

de beauté, beauty parlour. ~ médico-légal, mortuary. instituteur, trice (tœ:r, tris) n, schoolmaster, -mistress, teacher; governess. institution (sjɔ̃) f, institution; school; hostel.

instructeur (ɛ̃stryktœ:r) m, instructor; drill sergeant. instructif, ive (tif, i:v) a, instructive. instruction (sjɔ̃) f, instruction; education; schooling; tuition; training; lesson; pleading (Law). ~ par écrit, pleadings (Law). sans ~, uneducated. instruire (strɥi:r) v.t.ir, to instruct; teach; educate; train; inform; plead (Law).

instrument (ɛ̃strymã) m, instrument; implement; tool. ~ de paix, pax. instrumental, e (tal) a, instrumental. instrumentiste (tist) n, instrumentalist.

insu de (à l') (ɛ̃sy) pr, unknown to. à mon insu, without my knowledge, unwittingly.

insubmersible (ɛ̃sybmɛrsibl) a, unsinkable.

insubordonné, e (ɛ̃sybɔrdɔne) a, insubordinate.

insuccès (ɛ̃syksɛ) m, failure, miscarriage.

insuffisamment (ɛ̃syfizamã) ad, insufficiently. insuffisance (zã:s) f, insufficiency, shortage. ~ d'imposition, underassessment. insuffisant, e (zã, ã:t) a, insufficient, inadequate; incompetent.

insulaire (ɛ̃syle:r) a, insular. ¶ n, islander.

Insulinde (ɛ̃sylɛ̃:d) f, Indian Archipelago.

insulte (ɛ̃sylt) f, insult. insulter (te) v.t, to insult. ~ à, to jeer at; be an insult to.

insupportable† (ɛ̃sypɔrtabl) a, insupportable; unbearable; insufferable.

insurgé, e (ɛ̃syrʒe) a. & n, insurgent. s'insurger (ʒe) v.pr, to revolt.

insurmontable (ɛ̃syrmɔ̃tabl) a, insurmountable, insuperable.

insurrection (ɛ̃syrɛksjɔ̃) f, insurrection.

intact, e (ɛ̃takt) a, intact; whole; unblemished.

intaille (ɛ̃ta:j) f, intaglio.

intangible (ɛ̃tãʒibl) a, intangible.

intarissable† (ɛ̃tarisabl) a, unfailing, perennial, inexhaustible.

intégral, e† (ɛ̃tegral) a, integral, whole, entire, [in] full; unexpurgated. l'intégralité (lite) f, the whole, the entirety.

intègre (ɛ̃tɛgr) a, upright; honest. intégrité (tegrite) f, integrity.

intellect (ɛ̃tɛlɛkt) m, intellect. intellectuel, le† (tɥel) a. & m, intellectual; brain, att.

intelligemment (ɛ̃teliʒamã) ad, intelligently. intelligence (ʒã:s) f, intelligence, intellect; understanding; knowledge; (on good) terms; (pl.) correspondence; (pl.) dealings. intelligent, e (ʒã, ã:t) a, intelligent. intelligible† (ʒibl) a, intelligible; audible.

intempérance (ɛ̃tãperã:s) f, intemperance; insobriety; excess. intempérant, e (rã, ã:t) a, intemperate. intempérie (ri) f. usually pl, [inclemency of the] weather.

intempestif, ive† (ɛ̃tãpestif, i:v) a, unseasonable, untimely, ill-timed.

intenable (ɛ̃tnabl) a, untenable.

intendance (ɛtɑ̃dɑ̃:s) f, stewardship. ~ *militaire*, commissariat. **intendant** (dɑ̃) m, steward, bailiff.

intense (ɛtɑ̃:s) a, intense; strenuous. **intensif, ive†** (tɑ̃sif, i:v) a, intensive. **intensifier** (fje) v.t, to intensify. **intensité** (te) f, intensity; strength; depth (colour). ~ *lumineuse en bougies*, candle power.

intenter (ɛtɑ̃te) v.t, to enter, bring, institute (action at law).

intention (ɛtɑ̃sjɔ̃) f, intention; intent, purpose; meaning; will. *à l'~ de*, for [the sake of]. **intentionné, e** (ɔne) a, -intentioned, -meaning, -disposed. **intentionnel, le†** (nɛl) a, intentional; wilful.

inter (l') (ɛtɛːr) abb, trunk (Teleph.).

intercaler (ɛtɛrkale) v.t, to intercalate.

intercéder (ɛtɛrsede) v.i, to intercede.

intercepter (ɛtɛrsɛpte) v.t, to intercept.

intercesseur (ɛtɛrsɛsœːr) m, intercessor. **intercession** (sjɔ̃) f, intercession.

interchangeable (ɛtɛrʃɑ̃ʒabl) a, interchangeable.

interdiction (ɛtɛrdiksjɔ̃) f, interdiction; prohibition; ban; deprivation (rights). **interdire** (di:r) v.t.ir, to interdict, prohibit; forbid; ban; taboo; inhibit; deprive (Eccl.); disconcert, nonplus. **interdit** (di) m, person under judicial interdiction; interdict (Eccl.).

intéressé, e (ɛterɛse) n, interested party. ¶ a, selfish. **intéresser** (se) v.t, to interest; concern. **intérêt** (rɛ) m, interest; stake.

interférence (ɛtɛrferɑ̃:s) f, interference (Phys.).

interfolier (ɛtɛrfɔlje) v.t, to interleave.

intérieur, e† (ɛterjœːr) a, interior; internal; inner; inward; inside; inland; home, domestic. ¶ m, interior, inside; home; home life, private life.

intérim (ɛterim) m, interim. *faire l'~*, to deputize. **intérimaire** (mɛːr) a, interim; acting.

interjection (ɛtɛrʒɛksjɔ̃) f, interjection; ejaculation; lodging (appeal). **interjeter** (ʒəte) v.t, to lodge (appeal).

interligne (ɛtɛrliɲ) m, space between lines; space (Mus.); (f.) lead (Typ.). **interligner** (ɲe) v.t, to lead. **interlinéaire** (lineɛːr) a, interlinear.

interlocuteur, trice (ɛtɛrlɔkytœːr, tris) n, interlocutor, tress or trix.

interlope (ɛtɛrlɔp) a, dubious, suspect.

interloquer (ɛtɛrlɔke) v.t, to take aback.

interlude (ɛtɛrlyd) m, interlude (Mus., &c); voluntary (organ).

intermède (ɛtɛrmɛd) m, intermezzo; interlude. **intermédiaire** (medjɛːr) a, intermediate. ¶ m, intermission; intermediary; middleman, go-between; instrumentality; medium.

interminable (ɛtɛrminabl) a, interminable.

intermittent, e (ɛtɛrmitɑ̃, ɑ̃:t) a, intermittent.

internat (ɛtɛrna) m, boarding school; boarding-in, living-in.

international, e (ɛtɛrnasjɔnal) a, international; imperial & foreign (postal system). ¶ f, international (association); internationale (hymn). **internationaliste** (list) n. & a, internationalist.

interne (ɛtɛrn) a, internal; inward. [élève] ~, n, boarder. ¶ (m.) resident assistant surgeon. **interné, e** (ne) n, internee; inmate (asylum). **interner** (ne) v.t, to intern (War, &c); place under restraint (lunatic).

interpeller (ɛtɛrpɛlle) v.t, to interpellate.

interpoler (ɛtɛrpole) v.t, to interpolate.

interposer (ɛtɛrpoze) v.t, to interpose. **s'~**, to interpose, mediate.

interprétation (ɛtɛrpretasjɔ̃) f, interpretation; construction; rendering. **interprète** (prɛt) n, interpreter; exponent. **interpréter** (prete) v.t, to interpret; render.

interrègne (ɛtɛrrɛɲ) m, interregnum.

interrogateur, trice (ɛtɛrrɔgatœːr, tris) n, interrogator, questioner; examiner. **interrogatif, ive†** (tif, i:v) a, interrogative. **interrogation** (sjɔ̃) f, interrogation; question, query. **interrogatoire** (twaːr) m, interrogatory. **interroger** (ʒe) v.t, to interrogate, &c.

interrompre (ɛtɛrrɔ̃:pr) v.t, to interrupt, break, stop. **interrupteur, trice** (ryptœːr, tris) n, interrupter; (m.) switch. **interruption** (sjɔ̃) f, interruption, break.

intersection (ɛtɛrsɛksjɔ̃) f, intersection.

interstice (ɛtɛrstis) m, interstice.

interurbain, e (ɛtɛryrbɛ̃, ɛn) a, interurban; trunk (Teleph.). Cf. *inter* (l').

intervalle (ɛtɛrval) m, interval; space; gap; interlude.

intervenant, e (ɛtɛrvənɑ̃) m, acceptor for honour (Com.). **intervenir** (vəniːr) v.i.ir, to intervene, interfere; happen. **intervention** (vɑ̃sjɔ̃) f, intervention.

interversion (ɛtɛrvɛrsjɔ̃) f, inversion. **intervertir** (tiːr) v.t, to invert.

interview (ɛtɛrvju) f, interview (for news). **interviewer** (vjuve) v.t, to interview.

intestat (ɛtɛsta) a.inv, intestate.

intestin, e (ɛtɛstɛ̃, in) a, intestine; internal. ¶ m, intestine, bowel, gut. **intestinal, e** (tinal) a, intestinal.

intime† (ɛtim) a, intimate; in[ner]most; inward; close, near; private. ¶ m, intimate. **intimer** (me) v.t, to notify.

intimider (ɛtimide) v.t, to intimidate, cow, overawe.

intimité (ɛtimite) f, intimacy, closeness.

intitulé (ɛtityle) m, title, name; premises (deed). **intituler** (le) v.t, to entitle, call, name.

intolérable† (ɛtɔlerabl) a, intolerable, insufferable. **intolérance** (rɑ̃:s) f, intolerance. **intolérant, e** (rɑ̃, ɑ̃:t) a, intolerant.

intonation (ɛtɔnasjɔ̃) f, intonation.

intoxication (ɛtɔksikasjɔ̃) f, poisoning. **intoxiquer** (ke) v.t, to poison.

intrados (ɛ̃trado) *m*, intrados, soffit.

intraduisible (ɛ̃traduizibl) *a*, untranslatable.

intraitable (ɛ̃trɛtabl) *a*, intractable; unreasonable.

intransigeant, e (ɛ̃trɑ̃ziʒɑ̃, ɑ̃:t) *a*, intransigent, uncompromising. ¶ *n*, intransigent, die-hard.

intransitif, ive† (ɛ̃trɑ̃zitif, i:v) *a*, intransitive.

in-trente-deux *ou* in-32 (ɛ̃trɑ̃tdø) *a.m. & m*, thirty-two-mo, 32mo.

intrépide† (ɛ̃trepid) *a*, intrepid, fearless, dauntless. intrépidité (dite) *f*, intrepidity, &c.

intrigant, e (ɛ̃trigɑ̃, ɑ̃:t) *a*, intriguing, designing. ¶ *n*, intriguer, schemer, wirepuller. intrigue (trig) *f*, intrigue; plot. intriguer (ge) *v.t*, to rouse the interest (*or* curiosity) of, intrigue, puzzle; (*v.i.*) to intrigue, plot, scheme, pull the wires.

intrinsèque† (ɛ̃trɛ̃sɛk) *a*, intrinsic.

introducteur, trice (ɛ̃trɔdyktœ:r, tris) *n*, introducer. introduction (ksjɔ̃) *f*, introduction; opening (*law case*). introduire (dɥi:r) *v.t*, to introduce; show in, usher in. s'~, to get in, gain admittance; intrude.

introït (ɛ̃trɔit) *m*, introit.

introniser (ɛ̃trɔnize) *v.t*, to enthrone.

introspection (ɛ̃trɔspɛksjɔ̃) *f*, introspection.

introuvable (ɛ̃truvabl) *a*, undiscoverable; peerless.

intrus, e (ɛ̃try, y:z) *n*, intruder, interloper; trespasser (*Law*). intrusion (tryzjɔ̃) *f*, intrusion; trespass.

intuitif, ive (ɛ̃tɥitif, i:v) *a*, intuitive. intuition (sjɔ̃) *f*, intuition.

inusable (inyzabl) *a*, hard-wearing; for hard wear. inusité, e (zite) *a*, uncustomary; obsolete.

inutile† (inytil) *a*, useless; unprofitable; unnecessary, needless. inutilisable (lizabl) *a*, unusable; unserviceable. inutilisé, e (ze) *a. & p.p*, unutilized. inutilité (te) *f*, uselessness; (*pl.*) useless things.

invalide† (ɛ̃valid) *a*, invalid; invalided. ¶ *m*, old *or* disabled soldier; pensioner. *l'hôtel des I~s ou les I~s* (Paris), Chelsea Royal Hospital (*London*). invalider (de) *v.t*, to invalidate; unseat. invalidité (dite) *f*, invalidity; disablement, disability.

invariable† (ɛ̃varjabl) *a*, invariable, unchangeable.

invasion (ɛ̃vazjɔ̃) *f*, invasion; inrush; influx.

invective (ɛ̃vɛkti:v) *f*, invective. invectiver (tive) *v.i*, to inveigh, rail.

invendable (ɛ̃vɑ̃dabl) *a*, unsalable. invendu, e (dy) *a*, unsold.

inventaire (ɛ̃vɑ̃tɛ:r) *m*, inventory; list; stock taking; valuation; accounts, balance sheet & schedules. inventer (te) *v.t*, to invent; devise; trump up. inventeur, trice (tœ:r, tris) *n*, inventor, tress; discoverer; finder; author (*fig.*). inventif, ive (tif, i:v) *a*,

inventive. invention (sjɔ̃) *f*, invention.

inventorier (tɔrje) *v.t*, to inventory, list; take stock of; value.

inversable (ɛ̃vɛrsabl) *a*, uncapsizable (*boat*); unspillable (*ink bottle*).

inverse† (ɛ̃vɛrs) *a*, inverse; reciprocal; reverse; contrary; contra. ¶ *m*, inverse; reverse; reciprocal. inverser (se) *v.t*, to reverse. inversion (sjɔ̃) *f*, inversion; reversal.

invertébré, e (ɛ̃vɛrtebre) *a. & m*, invertebrate.

invertir (ɛ̃vɛrti:r) *v.t*, to invert; reverse.

investigation (ɛ̃vɛstigasjɔ̃) *f*, investigation.

investir (ɛ̃vɛsti:r) *v.t*, to invest (*all Eng. senses*); vest; dignify. investissement (tismɑ̃) *m*, investment (*Mil.*). investiture (ty:r) *f*, investiture.

invétéré, e (ɛ̃vetere) *p.a*, inveterate, ingrained. s'invétérer (re) *v.pr*, to become inveterate.

invincible† (ɛ̃vɛ̃sibl) *a*, invincible; insurmountable.

inviolable† (ɛ̃vjɔlabl) *a*, inviolable. inviolé, e (le) *a*, inviolate.

invisible† (ɛ̃vizibl) *a*, invisible; never to be seen. devenir ~, to vanish.

invitation (ɛ̃vitasjɔ̃) *f*, invitation. invite (vit) *f*, call (*Cards*). invité, e (te) *n*, guest. inviter (te) *v.t*, to invite, ask; court; request; tempt; call for (*trumps*).

invocation (ɛ̃vɔkasjɔ̃) *f*, invocation.

involontaire† (ɛ̃vɔlɔ̃tɛ:r) *a*, involuntary; unintentional.

invoquer (ɛ̃vɔke) *v.t*, to invoke, call upon.

invraisemblable† (ɛ̃vrɛsɑ̃blabl) *a*, unlikely; improbable. invraisemblablement (bləmɑ̃) *ad*, unlikely, improbably. invraisemblance (blɑ̃:s) *f*, unlikelihood, improbability.

invulnérable (ɛ̃vylnerabl) *a*, invulnerable.

iode (jɔd) *m*, iodine.

ion (iɔ̃) *m*, ion.

ionien, ne (iɔnjɛ̃, ɛn), ionique (nik) *a*, Ionian, Ionic.

iota (jɔta) *m*, iota, jot, tittle, whit.

ipécacuana (ipekakɥana) *m*, ipecacuanha.

irascible (irasibl) *a*, irascible, testy.

iridium (iridjɔm) *m*, iridium.

iris (iris) *m*, iris; rainbow. ~ *des marais*, yellow iris, flag. irisation (zasjɔ̃) *f*, iridescence. irisé, e (ze) *a*, iridescent.

irlandais, e (irlɑ̃dɛ, ɛːz) *a*, Irish. I~, *n*, Irishman, -woman. l'irlandais, *m*, Irish (*language*). l'Irlande (lɑ̃:d) *f*, Ireland. *mer d'Irlande*, Irish Sea.

ironie (irɔni) *f*, irony. ironique† (nik) *a*, ironic(al).

irrachetable (irraʃtabl) *a*, irredeemable (*Fin.*).

irradiation (irradjasjɔ̃) *f*, irradiation.

irraisonnable (irrɛzɔnabl) *a*, irrational, unreasoning. irrationnel, le (irrasjɔnɛl) *a*, irrational.

irréalisable (irrealizabl) *a*, unrealizable.

irréconciliable (irrekɔ̃siljabl) *a*, irreconcilable.

irrécouvrable (irrekuvrabl) *a*, irrecoverable.

irrécusable (irrekyzabl) *a*, unimpeachable, unexceptionable.

irrédentisme (irredãtism) *m*, irredentism.

irréductible (irredyktibl) *a*, irreducible; indomitable (*will*).

irréel, le (irreel) *a*, unreal.

irréfléchi, e (irreflefi) *a*, unconsidered. **irréflexion** (flɛksjɔ̃) *f*, thoughtlessness.

irréfutable† (irrefytabl) *a*, irrefutable. **irréfuté, e** (te) *a*, unrefuted.

irrégularité (irregylarite) *f*, irregularity. **irrégulier, ère†** (lje, ɛːr) *a*, irregular; erratic.

irréligieux, euse† (irrelizjø, øːz) *a*, irreligious.

irrémédiable† (irremedjabl) *a*, irremediable.

irremplaçable (irrãplasabl) *a*, irreplaceable.

irréparable† (irreparabl) *a*, irreparable, irretrievable.

irréprochable† (irreprɔʃabl) *a*, irreproachable.

irrésistible† (irrezistibl) *a*, irresistible.

irrésolu, e (irrezɔly) *a*, irresolute.

irrespectueux, euse† (irrɛspɛktɥø, øːz) *a*, disrespectful.

irresponsable (irrɛspɔsabl) *a*, irresponsible.

irrétrécissable (irretresisabl) *a*, unshrinkable.

irrévérencieux, euse (irreverãsjø, øːz) *a*, disrespectful. **irrévérent, e** (rã, ãːt) *a*, irreverent.

irrévocable† (irrevɔkabl) *a*, irrevocable.

irrigateur (irrigatœːr) *m*, irrigator; garden engine. **irrigation** (sjɔ̃) *f*, irrigation. **irriguer** (ge) *v.t*, to irrigate.

irritable (irritabl) *a*, irritable, testy. **irritation** (sjɔ̃) *f*, irritation. **irriter** (te) *v.t*, to irritate; anger; excite. **s'~**, to grow angry; fret, chafe.

irruption (irrypsjɔ̃) *f*, irruption, inroad, inrush.

Islam (islam) *m*, Islam.

islandais, e (islãdɛ, ɛːz) *a. & (language) m*, Icelandic. **I~**, *n*, Icelander. **l'Islande** (lãːd) *f*, Iceland.

isolateur (izolatœːr) *m*, insulator. **isolé, e** (le) *a*, isolated; detached; unattached (*Mil.*); lonely; alone; aloof. **isolement** (lmã) *m*, isolation; loneliness; insulation. **isolément** (lemã) *ad*, separately; singly. **isoler** (le) *v.t*, to isolate; insulate.

israélite (iz~ *ou* israelit) *n*, Israelite, Jew, Jewess. ¶ *a*, Jewish.

issu, e (isy) *p.p*, descended, born, sprung. **issue** (sy) *f*, issue; end; solution; egress, exit, way out; outlet; outcome, upshot; (*p.*) offal, garbage. **à l'~ de**, *ad*, at the end of, on leaving.

isthme (ism) *m*, isthmus.

Italie (l') (itali) *f*, Italy. **italien, ne** (ljɛ̃, ɛn) *a. & I~*, *n*, Italian. **l'italien**, Italian (*language*).

italique (italik) *a*, italic. ¶ *m*, italics.

item (itɛm) *ad*, item, likewise; ditto.

itinéraire (itinerɛːr) *m*, itinerary, route.

ivoire (ivwaːr) *m*, ivory.

ivraie (ivrɛ) *f*, cockle, darnel; tares (*fig.*).

ivre (iːvr) *a*, drunk[en], intoxicated, inebriate[d], tipsy. **~ à pleurer**, maudlin. **~ mort**, dead drunk. **ivresse** (ivrɛs) *f*, drunkenness, intoxication; frenzy, rapture. **ivrogne** (vrɔɲ) *a*, drunken. ¶ *m*, drunkard, toper, inebriate, sot. **ivrognerie** (ɲri) *f*. drunkenness. **ivrognesse** (ɲɛs) *f*, drunkard, inebriate, sot.

J

jabot (ʒabo) *m*, crop (*bird*); frill. **jaboter** (bote) *& jacasser* (kase) *v.i*, to jabber, chatter.

jachère (ʒaʃɛːr) *f*, fallow [land]. **jachérer** (ʃere) *v.t*, to fallow.

jacinthe (ʒasɛ̃ːt) *f*, hyacinth (*Bot.*); jacinth (*Miner.*). **~ des bois**, wild hyacinth, bluebell.

jacobée (ʒakɔbe) *f*, ragwort.

jacobin (ʒakɔbɛ̃) *m*, jacobin.

Jacques Bonhomme (ʒɑːk) (*Fr.*) *m*, Hodge (*Eng.*).

jactance (ʒaktãːs) *f*, boasting, brag.

jade (ʒad) *m*, jade (*Miner.*).

jadis (ʒadis) *ad*, formerly, once. **au temps ~**, in the olden time.

jaguar (ʒagwaːr) *m*, jaguar.

jaillir (ʒajiːr) *v.i*, to gush, spout, spirt, squirt, jet; fly; splash; spring; well; flash.

jais (ʒɛ) *m*, jet (*lignite*).

jalon (ʒalɔ̃) *m*, peg, stake, picket; range pole; landmark (*fig.*). **jalonner** (lone) *v.t*, to peg, stake [out]; dot. **jalonneur** (nœːr) *m*, marker (*Mil.*).

jalouser (ʒaluze) *v.t*, to be jealous of. **jalousie** (zi) *f*, jealousy; Venetian blind; jalousie. **jaloux, ouse†** (lu, uːz) *a*, jealous; anxious.

Jamaïque (la) (ʒamaik) *f*, Jamaica.

jamais (ʒamɛ) *ad*, ever; never. **à ~ ou pour ~**, for ever. **ne ... ~**, never, ne'er (*Poet.*).

jambage (ʒãbaːʒ) *m*, pier (*Build.*); jamb; down stroke; pothook. **jambe** (ʒãːb) *f*, leg; shank. **~ de force**, strut. **~ deçà, ~ delà**, astride, astraddle. **jambière** (ʒãbjɛːr) *f*, legging; shin guard. **jambon** (bɔ̃) *m*, ham (*hog, boar*).

jante (ʒãːt) *f*, felloe, felly; rim. **jantille** (ʒãtiːj) *f*, paddle [board] (*water wheel*).

janvier (ʒãvje) *m*, January.

Japon (ʒapɔ̃) *m*, Japanese porcelain; J. paper. **le ~**, Japan (*Geog.*). **japonais, e** (pɔnɛ, ɛːz) *a. & J~* (*pers.*) *n*, Japanese. **le japonais**, Japanese (*language*). **japonerie** (nri) *f*, Japanese curio, &c.

japper (ʒape) *v.i*, to yap, yelp.

jaquette (ʒakɛt) *f*, morning coat, tail c. (*man's*); short coat (*woman's*).

jard (ʒaːr) *m*, river gravel.

jardin (ʒardɛ̃) *m*, garden. **~ de rocaille**, **~ alpestre**, rock g. **~ anglais**, landscape g. **~ d'enfants**, kindergarten. **~ de fenêtre**, window box. ~ *de l'église*, churchyard. ~ *des plantes*, botanical gardens. ~ *maraîcher*, market garden. ~ *potager*, kitchen garden. **jardinage** (dina:3) *m*, gardening; garden plots. **jardiner** (ne) *v.i*, to garden. **jardinet** (nɛ) *m*, small garden. **jardinier, ère** (nje, ɛ:r) *n*, gardener; (*f.*) flower stand, jardinière.

jargon (ʒargɔ̃) *m*, jargon; lingo; slang; cant; jargo[o]n (*Miner.*). **jargonner** (ɡɔne) *v.i. & t*, to jabber.

jarre (ʒa:r) *f*, jar (*pot*).

jarret (ʒarɛ) *m*, bend of the knee; ham (*in man*); hock, hough (*horse*); knuckle (*veal*); shin (*beef*). **jarretelles** (rtɛl) *f.pl*, suspenders. **jarretière** (rtjɛ:r) *f*, garter.

jars (ʒa:r) *m*, gander.

jas (ʒɑ) *m*, stock (*anchor*).

jaser (ʒɑze) *v.i*, to chatter; blab. **jaserie** (zri) *f*, chatter. **jaseur, euse** (zœ:r, ø:z) *n*, chatterer.

jasmin (ʒasmɛ̃) *m*, jasmin[e], jessamin[e].

jaspe (ʒasp) *m*, jasper. ~ *sanguin*, bloodstone. **jasper** (pe) *v.t*, to marble; sprinkle (*book edges*); mottle. **jaspure** (py:r) *f*, marbling, &c.

jatte (ʒat) *f*, bowl.

jauge (ʒo:ʒ) *f*, ga[u]ge; gauging rod; register[ed tonnage] (*ship*). **jauger** (ʒoʒe) *v.t*, to ga[u]ge; measure (*ship*); size up (*pers.*).

jaunâtre (ʒonɑ:tr) *a*, yellowish; sallow. **jaune** (ʒo:n) *a*, yellow; sallow; [light] brown (*boots*). *la mer Jaune*, the Yellow sea. ¶ *m*, yellow; yolk (*egg*); anti-red (*Pol.*); (*pl.*) yellow races. **jaunir** (ʒoni:r) *v.t. & i*, to yellow. **jaunisse** (nis) *f*, jaundice.

Java (ʒava) *m*, Java. **javanais, e** (nɛ, ɛ:z) *a. & J~**, *n*, Javan[ese].

javelle (ʒavɛl) *f*, swath (*corn*).

javelot (ʒavlo) *m*, javelin.

je, j' (ʒə, ʒ) *pn*, I.

jérémiade (ʒeremjad) *f*, jeremiad.

jersey (ʒɛrze) *m*, stockinet; jersey. **J~**, *f*, Jersey (*Geog.*). **jersiais, e** (zjɛ, ɛ:z) *a*, Jersey (*cattle*).

Jérusalem (ʒeryzalɛm) *f*, Jerusalem.

jésuite (ʒezɥit) *m*, Jesuit. **jésuitique** (tik) *a*, Jesuitical.

Jésus (ʒezy) *m*, Jesus. **Jésus-Christ** (kri) *m*, Jesus Christ.

jet (ʒɛ) *m*, throw[ing]; cast[ing]; toss[ing]; fling; pouring (*metal*); catch (*fish*); folds (*drapery*); flash (*light*); sprue (*Founding*); spirt, spurt; burst; jet; stream; nozzle, spout; shoot, sprout; attempt, go. ~ *[à la mer]*, jettison. ~ *de sable*, sand blast. **jeté** (ʒɔte) *m*, over (*Knit.*). ~ *de lit*, bedspread, overlay. ~ *de table*, table runner. **jetée** (te) *f*, jetty, pier. ~ *promenade*, pier (*seaside*). **jeter** (te) *v.t. & abs*, to throw; cast; dash; fling; hurl; toss; pitch; splash; put; lay (*foundations*); shed (*light*); heave (*sigh*); utter (*cry*); run,

discharge (*of abscess*); sprout; strike (*root*); pour, run (*metal*). ~ *[à la mer]*, to jettison. **se** ~, to throw oneself; jump; fall, run. **jeton** (tɔ̃) *m*, counter; tally; token. ~*s de présence*, directors' fees; fees.

jeu (ʒø) *m*, play; game; sport; pastime; gaming; gambling; speculation; execution; acting; trick; play (*Mech.*); slack; clearance; lash; stroke (*piston, &c*); blowing [out] (*fuse*); set, assortment; stop (*organ*); pack (*cards*); hand (*Cards*); stake[s]. ~ *d'adresse*, game of skill. ~ *d'anneaux*, ship quoits, ring quoits. ~ *d'esprit*, witticism. ~ *de bague*, tilting at the ring. ~ *de baquet*, tipping (*or* tilting) the bucket. ~ *de barres*, prisoners' bars, p—s' base. ~ *de boules*, [game of] bowls. ~ *de boules couvert*, bowling alley. ~ *de boules découvert*, b. green. ~ *de chat*, touch [last], tag. ~ *de construction en bois*, bricks (*child's game*). ~ *de construction mécanique*, constructional outfit (*for boys*). ~ *de fléchettes*, darts. ~ *de jambes*, foot work (*Sport*). ~ *[bizarre] de la nature*, freak [of nature]. ~ *de la scie*, cat's-cradle. ~*x de main*, horse play, rough & tumble. ~ *de massacre*, Aunt Sally, shooting game; scathing attack, [shattering] broadside. ~ *de mots*, play on words, pun. ~ *de patience*, jig-saw puzzle. ~ *de paume*, real tennis (*ancient game*). ~*x de physionomie*, play of features. ~*x de ping-pong*, game of ping-pong; ping-pong set. ~*x de salon*, ~*x de société*, parlour games, indoor games. ~ *de scène*, stage trick. ~ *de tennis*, game of tennis; t. court. ~ *de volant*, battledore & shuttlecock. ~ *du cochonnet*, [game of] bowls. ~*x innocents*, parlour games, forfeits. ~*, manche, & partie*, game-set-match (*Ten.*). ~ *muet*, dumb show. *pas du* (*ou de*) ~, not fair.

jeudi (ʒødi) *m*, Thursday.

jeun (à) (ʒœ̃) *ad*, fasting; on an empty stomach.

jeune (ʒœn) *a*, young; youthful; juvenile; rising (*generation*); younger; minor. ~ *personne*, *f*, young lady; young person, juvenile. [le] ~, junior, the younger. ¶ *n*, young person.

jeûne (ʒø:n) *m*, fast[ing]; abstinence.

jeunement (ʒœnmɑ̃) *ad*, youthfully. **jeunesse** (nɛs) *f*, youth; youthfulness; boyhood; girlhood; girl. **jeunet, te** (nɛ, ɛt) *a*, [very] young.

jiu-jitsu (ʒyʒitsy) *m*, ju-jutsu, jiu-jitsu, judo.

joaillerie (ʒwajri) *f*, jewel[le]ry. **joaillier, ère** (je, ɛ:r) *n*, jeweller.

jobard, e (ʒɔba:r, ard) *n*, simpleton, muff.

jockey (ʒɔke) *m*, jockey (*Turf*).

jocko (ʒɔko) *m*, orang-outang.

jocrisse (ʒɔkris) *m*, simpleton.

joie (ʒwa) *f*, joy[fulness], glee; mirth, merriment; pleasure; gaiety.

joignant, e [à] (ʒwaɲɑ̃, ɑ̃:t) a, adjoining.
joindre (ʒwɛ̃:dr) v.t. & t. ir. & se ~, to join; unite; fold (hands); combine; adjoin; attach; add; meet. **joint** (ʒwɛ̃) m, joint, join. **jointif, ive** (tif, i:v) a, close. **jointoyer** (twaje) v.t, to point (masonry). **jointure** (ty:r) f, juncture; join[t]; knuckle.
joli, e (ʒɔli) a, pretty; good-looking; nice; fine. **joliment** (mɑ̃) ad, prettily, &c; jolly well.
jonc (ʒɔ̃) m, rush; bulrush; cane; hoop ring. **joncher** (ʃe) v.t, to strew; litter.
jonction (ʒɔ̃ksjɔ̃) f, junction, meeting.
jongler (ʒɔ̃gle) v.i, to juggle. **jonglerie** (gləri) f, juggling; juggle, trick. **jongleur** (glœ:r) m, juggler; trickster.
jonque (ʒɔ̃:k) f, junk (Chinese).
jonquille (ʒɔ̃ki:j) f, jonquil.
jouailler (ʒuaje) v.i, to play [for] low [stakes]; play a little (music).
joubarbe (ʒubarb) f, houseleek.
joue (ʒu) f, cheek; jowl; flange. *mettre (ou coucher)* en ~, to [take] aim at.
jouée (ʒwe) f, reveal (Arch.).
jouer (ʒwe) v.i. & t. & abs, to play; sport; toy; move (Chess, &c); gamble; be on the gamble; speculate; operate; work; perform; act (Theat.); trifle; trick, fool; stake; back (horse); feign; look like; blow [out] (fuse). ~ *dans le trou*, to hole (Golf). ~ *sur les mot(s)*, to play on words, pun. *à qui d ─?* whose move is it? **jouet** (ʒwɛ) m, toy; plaything; sport, butt. **joueur, euse** (ʒwœ:r, ø:z) n, player; performer; gambler; speculator; operator; (good, bad) loser; (att.) fond of play. ~ *un de plus*, odd player (Golf).
joufflu, e (ʒufly) a, chubby.
joug (ʒu[g]) m, yoke.
jouir de (ʒwi:r) v.i, to enjoy; e. the company of; avail oneself of the services of; use; have. **jouissance** (ʒwisɑ̃:s) f, enjoyment; pleasure; delight; use; possession; tenure; fruition; due date of coupon, interest payable (date).
joujou (ʒuʒu) m, plaything, toy.
jour (ʒu:r) m, day; daytime; [day]light; opening, gap; day, surface, grass (Min.); (pl.) openwork (Need.). *le ~ de l'an*, new-year's day. ~ *[de l'escalier]*, well [hole]. ~ *de planche*, lay day (Ship.). *son ~ [de réception]*, her at-home day. *le ~ des Cendres*, Ash Wednesday. *le ~ des morts*, All Souls' Day. *le ~ des propitiations*, the day of atonement. ~ *du terme*, quarter day. ~ *férié* (ferje), [public] holiday, bank h.; holy day. ~ *gras*, meat day (Eccl.). *les ~s gras*, Shrovetide. ~ *maigre*, fast day. *d ~*, open; openwork[ed]; through; up to date. *à ce ~*, to date. *au ~ le ~*, from day to day; from hand to mouth.
Jourdain (le) (ʒurdɛ̃) m, the Jordan.
journal (ʒurnal) m, journal; day book; diary; log [book]; book; register; [news]paper;

gazette. ~ *illustré*, illustrated paper, pictorial. ~ *parlé*, weather & news (Radio). **journalier, ère** (lje, ɛ:r) a, daily; inconstant; fickle. ¶ m, day labourer. **journalisme** (lism) m, journalism; press. **journaliste** (list) m, journalist, pressman. ~ *aux armées*, war correspondent. ~ *d'information*, reporter.
journée (ʒurne) f, day; daytime; day's work; day's pay. ~ *de chemin*, day's journey. **journellement** (nɛlmɑ̃) ad, daily.
joute (ʒut) f, joust; tilt[ing]; contest; fight. ~ *sur l'eau*, water tournament. **jouter** (te) v.i, to joust, &c.
jouvenceau, elle (ʒuvɑ̃so, ɛl) n, youth, damsel.
jovial, e (ʒɔvjal) a, jovial, merry, jolly.
joyau (ʒwajo) m, jewel.
joyeux, euse† (ʒwajø, ø:z) a, joyful, joyous, jolly, genial, convivial, merry, jocund.
jubé (ʒybe) m, rood-screen.
jubilaire (ʒybilɛ:r) a, jubilee, holy (year). **jubilation** (lasjɔ̃) f, jubilation, jollification, jollity. **jubilé** (le) m, jubilee.
jucher (ʒyʃe) v.i. & se ~, to roost, perch. **juchoir** (ʃwa:r) m, roost, perch.
judaïque† (ʒydaik) a, Judaic.
Judas (ʒyda) m, Judas (traitor). **j~**, spy-hole, peephole, judas; window mirror.
judiciaire† (ʒydisjɛ:r) a, judicial; legal.
judicieux, euse† (ʒydisjø, ø:z) a, judicious, discerning.
juge (ʒy:ʒ) m, judge; justice; magistrate; master (taxing); umpire. *les Juges*, Judges (Bible). ~ *d'instruction*, examining magistrate. **jugement** (ʒyʒmɑ̃) m, judg[e]ment; trial; estimation; discernment; sentence; decree. **juger** (ʒe) v.t. & abs, to judge; try (case); pass judgement; think, deem.
jugulaire (ʒygylɛ:r) f, chin strap. [veine] ~, f, jugular [vein]. **juguler** (le) v.t, to strangle.
juif, ive (ʒɥif, i:v) n, Jew, Jewess. *Juif errant*, Wandering Jew. ¶ a, Jewish.
juillet (ʒɥijɛ) m, July.
juin (ʒɥɛ̃) m, June.
juiverie (ʒɥivri) f, Jewry; ghetto.
jujube (ʒyʒyb) m, jujube. **jujubier** (bje) m, jujube [shrub].
julep (ʒylɛp) m, julep.
jumeau, elle (ʒymo, ɛl) a, twin; semi-detached. ¶ n, twin; (f.) binocular [glass], glass[es]; upright, standard, housing. ~[s] *de théâtre*, opera glass[es]. **jumeler** (mle) v.t, to pair.
jument (ʒymɑ̃) f, mare.
jungle (ʒɔ̃:gl) f, jungle.
junior (ʒynjɔ:r) m, junior (Sports).
jupe (ʒyp) f, skirt. ~-*culotte*, divided s. **jupier, ère** (pje, ɛ:r) n, skirt maker. **jupon** (pɔ̃) m, petticoat.
juré, e (ʒyre) a, sworn. ¶ m, juryman, juror. **jurer** (re) v.t. & abs, to swear; s. by; blaspheme; vow; (v.i.) to clash, jar. **jureur** (rœ:r) m, swearer.

juridiction (ʒyridiksjɔ̃) *f*, jurisdiction; province, line. **juridique†** (dik) *a*, juridical, law (*att.*). **jurisconsulte** (riskɔ̃sylt) *m*, jurist. **jurisprudence** (prydɑ̃:s) *f*, jurisprudence, law. **juriste** (rist) *m*, jurist.

juron (ʒyrɔ̃) *m*, (*profane*) oath.

jury (ʒyri) *m*, jury; selection committee. ~ *d'admission*, hanging committee (*Art*). ~ *d'examen*, board of examiners.

jus (ʒy) *m*, juice; gravy; blurb. ~ *de réglisse*, liquorice.

jusant (ʒyzɑ̃) *m*, ebb.

jusque & *poet.* **jusques** (ʒysk) *pr*, to; as (*or* so) far as; till, until; even; up to. *jusqu'à ce que*, till, until. *jusqu'à concurrence de*, up to, not exceeding. *jusqu'à quand?* till when? how long? *jusqu'ici*, so far, thus far; till now, hitherto. *jusqu'où?* how far? *jusque-là*, so far; till then.

juste (ʒyst) *a*, just; right; fair; legitimate; correct; accurate; exact; proper; true; condign; upright; righteous; tight (*fit*). ~ *milieu*, happy medium, golden mean. *à ~ titre*, fairly, rightly. **le ~**, the right. **les ~s**, *m.pl*, the just, the righteous. ¶ *ad*, just; right; barely. **justement** (təmɑ̃) *ad*, justly; exactly, just. **justesse** (tɛs) *f*, accuracy; correctness. **justice** (tis) *f*, justice; equity; right; rights; righteousness; justness fairness; judicature; court of law; law; law officers. **justiciable** (sjabl) *a*, under the jurisdiction; amenable. **justicier** (sje) *m*, justiciary. **justifiable** (fjabl) *a*, justifiable, warrantable. **justificatif, ive** (fikatif, i:v) *a*, justificative; voucher (*att.*). **justifier** (fje) *v.t*, to justify; warrant; vindicate; prove.

jute (ʒyt) *m*, jute.

juter (ʒyte) *v.i*, to be juicy. **juteux, euse** (tø, ø:z) *a*, juicy.

juvénile (ʒyvenil) *a*, juvenile, youthful.

juxtaposer (ʒykstapoze) *v.t*, to juxtapose.

K

kaki (kaki) *a*, khaki.

kaléidoscope (kaleidɔskɔp) *m*, kaleidoscope.

kangourou (kɑ̃guru) *m*, kangaroo.

kaolin (kaolɛ̃) *m*, kaolin, china clay.

Kénia (le) (kenja), Kenya.

képi (kepi) *m*, cap (peaked).

kermesse (kɛrmɛs) *f*, kermis, fête, fair.

khédive (kedi:v) *m*, Khedive.

kilogramme (kilogram) *m*, kilogram[me] = 1000 grammes *or* 2·2046 (about 2¼) lbs.

kilomètre (kilɔmɛtr) *m*, kilometre = 1000 metres *or* 0·62137 (about ⅝) mile. **kilométrique** (metrik) *a*, kilometric(al).

kimono (kimɔno) *m*, kimono.

kiosque (kjɔsk) *m*, kiosk; stall; bookstall; conning tower (*submarine*). ~ *à musique*, bandstand. ~ *de jardin*, summer house.

krach (krak) *m*, crash, smash (*Fin.*).

kyrielle (kirjɛl) *f*, string, rigmarole.

kyste (kist) *m*, cyst (*Med.*).

L

la (la) *m*, A (*Mus.*). *donner le* ~ (*fig.*), to set the fashion.

là (la) *ad*, there; then; that. ~-*bas*, [over] yonder, over there. ~-*dedans*, in there; within. ~-*dehors*, outside, without. ~-*dessous*, under there, underneath. ~-*dessus*, on that; thereon; thereupon. ~-*haut*, up there. *de* ~, away, off; out of there; from then. *par* ~, that way; through there; thereby. ¶ *i*, there [now]! *oh* ~ ~! O dear me!

labeur (labœ:r) *m*, labour, toil; book work (*Typ.*).

labial, e (labjal) *a*, & *f*, labial.

laboratoire (laboratwa:r) *m*, laboratory.

laborieux, euse† (labɔrjø, ø:z) *a*, laborious, hard-working; working (*class*); arduous, toilsome, hard; laboured.

labour (labu:r) *m*, ploughing, tillage. **labourable** (burabl) *a*, arable, plough (*land*). **labourage** (ra:ʒ) *m*, ploughing, tillage. **labourer** (re) *v.t*. & *abs*, to plough, till; plough up; drag (*anchor*); graze (*sea bottom*). **laboureur** (rœ:r) *m*, ploughman.

labyrinthe (labirɛ̃:t) *m*, labyrinth, maze.

lac (lak) *m*, lake, mere. *Note.*—For named lakes, see under proper name, e.g, *le lac Léman*, under *Léman*. ~ *de cirque*, tarn. ~ *salé*, salt lake.

lacer (lase) *v.t*, to lace [up].

lacérer (lasere) *v.t*, to lacerate, tear.

lacet (lasɛ) *m*, lace (*boot*, &c); winding (*road*); nosing (*of locomotive*); snare, noose; (*pl.*) toils.

lâche† (lɑ:ʃ) *a*, loose; slack; lax; faint-hearted, cowardly, unmanly, dastardly, mean. **lâcher** (laʃe) *v.t*, to loose[n]; slacken; let out; relax; let fly; release; liberate; let go; let down; jilt; drop; [let] slip; blurt out; open, turn on (*tap*); utter; fire (*shot*). ~ *pied*, to give way. ~ *prise*, to let go. **lâcheté** (ʃte) *f*, cowardice; meanness.

lacis (lasi) *m*, network, plexus.

laconique† (lakɔnik) *a*, laconic.

lacrymal, e (lakrimal) *a*, lachrymal, tear (*att.*).

lacs (lɑ) *m*, toils (*fig.*). ~ *d'amour*, love-knot, true-love[r's] knot.

lacté, e (lakte) *a*, lacteal; milk (*att.*); milky.

lacune (lakyn) *f*, lacuna; gap; hiatus; blank.

lacustre (lakystr) *a*, lacustrine, lake (*att.*).

lad (lad) *m*, stable boy (*Turf*).

ladre (lɑ:dr) *n*, miser, niggard, skinflint. ¶ *a*, stingy, mean, niggardly. **ladrerie** (ladrəri) *f*, stinginess, &c.

lagune (lagyn) *f*, lagoon.

lai (lɛ) *a.m*, lay (*brother*). ¶ *m*, lay (*poem*).

laiche (lɛʃ) *f*, sedge.

laid, e (lɛ, ɛd) *a*, ugly, plain, ill-favoured, unsightly; naughty. **laideron** (drɔ̃) *m*, plain girl. **laideur** (dœːr) *f*, ugliness, &c.

laie (lɛ) *f*, wild sow.

lainage (lɛnaːʒ) *m*, woollen goods, woollens; teaseling. **laine** (lɛn) *f*, wool. ~ *peignée*, worsted. ~ *renaissance*, shoddy. **lainer** (lɛne) *v.t*, to teasel. **lainerie** (nri) *f*, woollen mill; w. trade; wool shop. **laineux, euse** (nø, øːz) *a*, woolly. **lainier, ère** (nje, ɛːr) *a*, wool[len] (*trade, &c*). ¶ *m*, woollen manufacturer.

laïque (laik) *a. & m*, laic, lay(man); undenominational.

laisse (lɛs) *f*, leash, slip, lead; sea ware; watermark (*tidal*).

laissé pour compte (lɛse) *m*, [goods left] on hand, refused.

laissées (lɛse) *f.pl*, droppings, dung.

laisser (lɛse) *v.t*, to leave; let; allow; let have. ~ *aller & ~ échapper*, to let go. ~ *courre* (kuːr), to slip (*hounds*). ~ *tomber*, to drop; let fall. *laissez donc!* leave off! *laissez passer*, admit bearer. **laisser-aller**, *m*, unconstraint; carelessness. **laisser-faire**, *m*, non-interference, drift. **laissez-passer**, *m*, pass; cart note (*Cust.*).

lait (lɛ) *m*, milk. ~ *condensé*, ~ *concentré*, ~ *conservé*, condensed m. ~ *de beurre*, butter m. ~ *de chaux*, whitewash. **laitage** (taːʒ) *m*, milk food. **laitance** (tɑ̃ːs) *ou* **laite** (lɛt) *f*, soft roe, milt. **laité, e** (te) *a*, soft-roed. **laiterie** (tri) *f*, dairy. **laiteux, euse** (tø, øːz) *a*, milky.

laitier (letje) *m*, slag, scoria[e].

laitier, ère (lɛtje, ɛːr) *m*, milkman, -woman, dairyman. ¶ *f*, milker (*cow*).

laiton (lɛtɔ̃) *m*, brass.

laitue (lɛty) *f*, lettuce. ~ *pommée*, cabbage l. ~ *romaine*, cos, Cos lettuce.

laize (lɛːz) *f*, width (*of cloth*).

lama (lama) *m*, lama (*pers.*); llama (*Zool.*).

lamaneur (lamanœːr) *m*, branch pilot.

lamantin (lamɑ̃tɛ̃) *m*, manatee, sea-cow.

lambeau (lɑ̃bo) *m*, rag, tatter; shred; remnant.

lambin (lɑ̃bɛ̃) *m*, dawdler, slowcoach; (*att.*) dawdling, slow, dilatory, leisurely. **lambiner** (bine) *v.i*, to dawdle, lag.

lambourde (lɑ̃burd) *f*, joist; wall-plate.

lambris (lɑ̃bri) *m*, wainscot; panelling. ~ *d'appui*, dado. ~ *dorés*, gilded apartments. **lambrisser** (se) *v.t*, to wainscot; panel; line.

lame (lam) *f*, [thin] sheet; plate; lamina; flake; blade; cutter; lath, slat (*blind*); spangle; wave, sea, billow; swordsman. **lamé, e** (lame) *a. & m*, lamé. **lamelle** (mɛl) *f*, lamina, flake.

lamentable† (lamɑ̃tabl) *a*, lamentable, deplorable, pitiful, pitiable; woeful. **lamentation** (sjɔ̃) *f*, lament[ation], wail[ing]. **se ~ lamenter** (te) *v.pr*, to lament, wail. *se ~ sur*, to bewail, deplore.

laminer (lamine) *v.t*, to roll (*metal*); laminate. **laminoir** (nwaːr) *m*, rolling mill.

lampadaire (lɑ̃padɛːr) *m*, lamp standard.

lampas (lɑ̃pa) *m*, lampas (*silk & Vet.*).

lampe (lɑ̃ːp) *f*, lamp; valve (*Radio*). ~ *à alcool*, spirit lamp. ~ *à pied*, standard l., floor l. ~ *de poche*, ~ *électrique*, flash l., electric torch. ~ *de travail*, reading lamp. ~-*éclair*, *f*, flash l. (*Phot.*).

lamper (lɑ̃pe) *v.t*, to toss off, swill, swig.

lampion (lɑ̃pjɔ̃) *m*, fairy light, f. lamp. ~ *en papier*, paper lantern. **lampiste** (pist) *m*, lampman. **lampisterie** (təri) *f*, lamp room.

lamproie (lɑ̃prwa) *f*, lamprey.

lampyre (lɑ̃piːr) *m*, glowworm.

lance (lɑ̃ːs) *f*, spear; lance; (hose) branch. ~-*flamme*, *m*, flame thrower. **lancement** (lɑ̃smɑ̃) *m*, throwing; launch[ing]; floating, promotion. ~ *du javelot, du disque, du gros boulet, du marteau*, throwing the javelin, the discus, the heavy weight, the hammer. ~ *du poids*, putting the shot. **lancer** (se) *m*, release (*pigeons*); starting (*Hunt.*). ¶ *v.t*, to throw; cast; put (*the shot*); fling; hurl; shy; drop (*bombs*); dart; shoot; fire; toss; pitch; let off; ejaculate; initiate; launch; catapult (*aeroplane*); float; promote; issue; set (*dog on, fashion, &c*); deliver (*ball, Ten., &c*); fly (*kite*); start (*stag, game, &c*). **lancette** (sɛt) *f*, lancet. **lanciers** (sje) *m.pl*, lancers (*Danc.*). **lancinant, e** (sinɑ̃, ɑ̃ːt) *a*, shooting (*pain*).

landau (lɑ̃do) *m*, landau. ~ [*pour enfant*], baby carriage, perambulator. ~ *pliant*, folding pram. **landaulet** (lɛ) *m*, landaulet.

lande (lɑ̃ːd) *f*, heath, moor[land]; links.

langage (lɑ̃gaːʒ) *m*, language, speech, parlance. ~ *de poissarde*, ~ *des halles*, billingsgate.

lange (lɑ̃ːʒ) *m*, baby square; (*pl, lit. & fig.*) swaddling clothes.

langoureux, euse† (lɑ̃gurø, øːz) *a*, languorous.

langouste (lɑ̃gust) *f*, spiny lobster, (*sea*) crayfish.

langue (lɑ̃ːg) *f*, tongue; language, speech. ~ *verte*, slang. ~ *vulgaire*, vernacular. **languette** (lɑ̃gɛt) *f*, tongue; pointer; feather (*as on a board—Carp., & Mach.*); strip; cleat.

langueur (lɑ̃gœːr) *f*, languor; listlessness; languishment. **languir** (giːr) *v.i*, to languish, pine [away]; mope; long, weary; droop, flag, drag. **languissant, e** (gisɑ̃, ɑ̃ːt) *a*, languishing; languid; lackadaisical; flat, dull.

lanière (lanjɛːr) *f*, thong, lash; strip; lace (*leather*).

lanterne (lɑ̃tɛrn) *f*, lantern; lamp; (*pl.*) nonsense. ~ *avec projecteur à lentille faisant saillie*, bull's-eye [lantern]. ~ *de projection*, ~ *magique*, optical lantern, projection l., slide l., magic l. ~ *sourde*, dark l. ~-*tempête*, hurricane lamp. ~

vénitienne, paper lantern. **lanterner** (ne) *v.i*, to shilly-shally; trifle; (*v.t.*) to humbug. **lanternier** (nje) *m*, lantern maker; lamp-lighter; shilly-shallier.

lapalissade (lapalisad) *f*, truism.

laper (lape) *v.i. & t*, to lap [up], lick up.

lapereau (lapro) *m*, young rabbit.

lapidaire (lapidɛːr) *a. & m*, lapidary. **lapider** (de) *v.t*, to stone; throw stones at; pelt; set on (*someone*).

lapin, e (lapɛ̃, in) *n*, [buck, doe] rabbit, coney. ~ *bélier*, lop-ear[ed r.]. ~ *domestique*, ~ *de clapier*, ~ *de choux*, tame r. ~ *de garenne*, wild r. **lapinière** (pinjɛːr) *f*, rabbitry.

lapis[-lazuli] (lapis[lazyli]) *m*, lapis lazuli.

lapon, one (lapɔ̃, ɔn) *a. & L~, n*, Lapp, Laplander (*n.*). **la Laponie** (pɔni) Lapland.

laps de temps (laps) *m*, lapse of time. **lapsus** (syːs) *m*, lapsus, lapse, slip.

laquais (lakɛ) *m*, lackey, flunkey, menial.

laque (lak) *f*, lac; lake (*paint*). ~ *en écailles*, shellac. ¶ *m*, lacquer, l. work; japan. **laquer** (ke) *v.t*, to lacquer, japan, enamel.

larbin (larbɛ̃) *m*, flunkey.

larcin (larsɛ̃) *m*, larceny; crib, plagiarism.

lard (laːr) *m*, bacon; fat; blubber. **larder** (larde) *v.t*, to lard (*Cook*.); [inter]lard; load; pierce. **lardon** (dɔ̃) *m*, lardo[o]n; gibe.

lares (laːr) *m.pl*, home. [**dieux**] ~, Lares.

large† (larʒ) *a*, broad, wide; large; loose; extensive; sweeping; free; liberal. ¶ *m*, room, space; open sea; offing. *au* ~, in the offing; out at sea; well off. *au* ~! keep off! *de* ~, wide, broad (*Meas.*). **largesse** (ʒɛs) *f*, liberality; bounty, largess[e]. **largeur** (ʒœːr) *f*, breadth; width; beam (*ship*); gauge (*Rly track*).

larguer (large) *v.t*, to let go, cast off, slip.

larix (lariks) *m*, larch [tree].

larme (larm) *f*, tear; drop (*of drink*). **larmier** (mje) *m*, drip[stone]. **larmoiement** (mwamɑ̃) *m*, watering of the eyes. **larmoyant**, e (jɑ̃, ɑ̃ːt) *a*, weeping; in tears; tearful; maudlin. **larmoyer** (je) *v.i*, to water; weep, shed tears.

larron (larɔ̃) *m*, thief.

larve (larv) *f*, larva, grub.

laryngite (larɛ̃ʒit) *f*, laryngitis. **larynx** (rɛ̃ːks) *m*, larynx.

las, asse (lɑ, ɑːs) *a*, tired, weary.

lascif, ive† (lasif, iːv) *a*, lascivious, wanton.

lasser (lɑse) *v.t*, to tire; weary.

lasso (laso) *m*, lasso.

latent, e (latɑ̃, ɑ̃ːt) *a*, latent, hidden.

latéral, e† (lateral) *a*, lateral, side (*att.*).

latex (latɛks) *m*, latex.

latin, e (latɛ̃, in) *a. & m*, Latin. ~ *de cuisine*, dog Latin.

latitude (latityd) *f*, latitude; scope.

latte (lat) *f*, lath. **latter** (te) *v.t*, to lath. **lattis** (ti) *m*, lathing.

laudanum (lodanɔm) *m*, laudanum.

laudatif, ive (lodatif, iːv) *a*, laudatory.

lauréat (lorea) *a.m*, laureate. ¶ *m*, prize-man; prize winner. **laurier** (rje) *m*, laurel, bay; (*pl, fig.*) laurels. ~*-rose*, *m*, oleander.

lavable (lavabl) *a*, washable. **lavabo** (bo) *m*, washstand; lavatory. **lavage** (vaːʒ) *m*, washing, w. out. ~ [*d'intestin*], enema.

lavallière (lavaljɛːr) *f*, Lavallière [neck]tie.

lavande (lavɑ̃ːd) *f*, lavender.

lavasse (lavas) *f*, [wish-]wash, slops.

lave (laːv) *f*, lava.

laver (lave) *v.t*, to wash; w. out; scrub. ~ *la vaisselle*, to wash up. **laverie** (vri) *f*, washhouse. **lavette** (vɛt) *f*, mop; dish cloth. **laveur, euse** (vœːr, øːz) *n*, washer. *laveuse de linge*, washerwoman. **lavis** (vi) *m*, wash (*Art.*); wash drawing. **lavoir** (vwaːr) *m*, washhouse; scullery; washer (*Mach.*).

lawn-tennis (lɔntenis) *m*, lawn tennis.

laxatif, ive (laksatif, iːv) *a. & m*, laxative, aperient, opening (*medicine*).

layetier (lɛjtje) *m*, box maker. ~ *emballeur*, packing case maker. **layette** (jɛt) *f*, baby-linen, layette.

lazaret (lazarɛ) *m*, lazaret[to].

lazzi (lazi) *m*, buffoonery.

le, la, l'; les (lə, l, la, l; le) *art*, the; a, an (*weight, &c*). Often untranslated, as in *le paradis*, paradise. *l'enfer*, hell. *le Japon*, Japan. *la nature*, nature. *l'histoire*, history. *la France*, France. *les enfers*, Hades.

le, l'; la, l'; les (lə, l; la, l; le) *pn*, him; her; it; them; he; she; they; so.

lé (le) *m*, width (*of cloth*).

leader (lidœːr) (*pers.*) *m*, leader (*political*).

lèche (lɛʃ) *f*, thin slice. **lèchefrite** (frit) *f*, dripping pan. **lécher** (leʃe) *v.t*, to lick; overelaborate.

leçon (ləsɔ̃) *f*, lesson; lecture; reading (*text*); story. ~ *de choses*, object lesson.

lecteur, trice (lɛktœːr, tris) *n*, reader. **lecture** (tyːr) *f*, reading; perusal.

ledit, ladite, lesdits, lesdites (lədi, ladit, ledi, ledit) *a*, the said (*Law*).

légal, e† (legal) *a*, legal; statutory; lawful. **légaliser** (lize) *v.t*, to legalize.

légat (lega) *m*, legate. **légataire** (tɛːr) *n*, legatee. ~ *particulier*, specific l. ~ *universel*, residuary l. **légation** (sjɔ̃) *f*, legation.

lège (lɛːʒ) *a*, light (*Naut.*).

légendaire (leʒɑ̃dɛːr) *a*, legendary, fabled. **légende** (ʒɑ̃ːd) *f*, legend; characteristics, reference note, explanatory note, signs & symbols (*on map*).

léger, ère† (leʒe, ɛːr) *a*, light; flighty, frivolous; fast; slight; mild; weak (*tea, &c*). ~ *à la course*, fleet of foot. *à la légère*, lightly, scantily; without due consideration. **légèreté** (ʒɛrte) *f*, lightness, &c; levity.

légion (leʒjɔ̃) f, legion. *ils s'appellent ~,* their name is legion.

législateur, trice (leʒislatœːr, tris) n, legislator, lawgiver. **législatif, ive** (tif, iːv) a, legislative; parliamentary (*election*). **législation** (sjɔ̃) f, legislation. **législature** (tyːr) f, legislature. **légiste** (ʒist) m, legist, lawyer. **légitime†** (ʒitim) a, legitimate; lawful; rightful. ~ *défense,* self-defence. **légitimer** (me) v.t, to legitim[at]ize; legitimate; justify. **légitimité** (mite) f, legitimacy, lawfulness.

legs (lɛg *ou* lɛ) m, legacy, bequest. **léguer** (lege) v.t, to bequeath, will, devise, leave.

légume (legym) m, vegetable. ~*s verts,* greens. **légumier** (mje) m, vegetable dish. **légumineux, euse** (minø, øːz) a, leguminous. ¶ f, legume[n], pulse.

leitmotiv (laitmotif) m, leitmotiv, -if.

Léman (le lac) (lemɑ̃), the Lake of Geneva, Lake Leman.

lendemain (lɑ̃dmɛ̃) m, next day, day after, morrow; future. *sans ~,* short-lived.

Léningrad (leningrad) m, Leningrad.

lent, e† (lɑ̃, ɑ̃ːt) a, slow; dilatory; lingering; low (*fever, speed*). ¶ f, nit. **lenteur** (lɑ̃tœːr) f, slowness, &c.

lenticulaire (lɑ̃tikylɛːr) a, lenticular. **lentille** (tiːj) f, lentil; lens; freckle; bob, ball. ~ *d'eau,* ~ *de marais,* duckweed.

lentisque (lɑ̃tisk) m, lentisk, mastic [tree].

léonin, e (leɔnɛ̃, in) a, leonine; one-sided.

léopard (leɔpaːr) m, leopard. ~ *femelle,* leopardess.

lépas (lepɑs) m, limpet.

lépidoptères (lepidɔptɛːr) m.pl, Lepidoptera.

lèpre (lɛpr) f, leprosy. **lépreux, euse** (leprø, øːz) a, leprous. ¶ n, leper. **léproserie** (prozri) f, leper hospital.

lequel, laquelle, lesquels, lesquelles (ləkɛl, lakɛl, lekɛl) pn, who; whom; which.

lèse-majesté (lɛzmaʒɛste) f, [high] treason; lese-majesty. **léser** (leze) v.t, to injure; wrong.

lésiner (lezine) v.i, to be stingy, higgle. **lésinerie** (nri) f, stinginess, meanness.

lésion (leʒjɔ̃) f, lesion, injury, hurt.

lessive (lɛsiːv) f, washing; wash; lye. **lessiver** (sive) v.t, to wash; scrub, swill; leach. **lessiveuse** (vøːz) f, wash boiler.

lest (lɛst) m, ballast.

leste† (lɛst) a, nimble; smart; flippant; free, indecorous.

lester (lɛste) v.t, to ballast. *se ~ l'estomac,* to line one's stomach.

léthargie (letarʒi) f, lethargy. **léthargique** (ʒik) a, lethargic. **Léthé** (lete) m, Lethe.

léthifère (letifɛːr) a, deadly, lethal.

letton, one (letɔ̃, ɔn) a. & L~, n, Lett; Latvian. **la Lettonie** (tɔni), Latvia.

lettrage (letraːʒ) m, lettering. **lettre** (tr) f, letter; note. ~-*avion,* air [mail] letter. ~ *close* (*fig.*), sealed book. ~ *d'un autre œil,* wrong fount. ~ *de change,* bill of exchange. ~ *de crédit,* ~ *de créance,* letter of credit. ~*s de créance,* credentials. ~ *de [faire] part,* notice announcing a birth, marriage, or death. ~*s de naturalisation,* naturalization papers. ~[*s*] *de service,* commission (*officer's*). ~ *de voiture,* consignment note. ~ *missive,* letter missive. ~ *moulée,* block letter. *la* ~ *moulée,* block writing. *en toutes* ~*s,* in words at length; in full, fully. **lettré, e** (tre) a. & n, lettered, literate, well-read (person). **lettrine** (trin) f, drop letter (*Typ.*); catchword (*at head of dictionary page*).

leur (lœːr) a, their. le ~, la ~, les ~*s,* pn, theirs.

leurre (lœːr) m, lure; catch (*fig.*). **leurrer** (lœre) v.t, to lure.

levain (ləvɛ̃) m, leaven, yeast, barm. *sans ~,* unleavened.

levant (ləvɑ̃) a.m, rising (*sun*). ¶ m, east. *du ~ au couchant,* from east to west. L~, m, Levant. **levantin, e** (tɛ̃, in) a. & L~, n, Levantine.

levé [de plans] (ləve) m, survey[ing]. **levée** (ve) f, raising; lifting; lift; levy; removal; close (*sitting*); collection (*letters*); clearing (*letter box*); trick (*Cards*); embankment; causeway. **lever** (ve) m, rising, getting up (*from bed*); rise (*sun*). ~ [*de plans*], survey[ing]. ~ *de rideau,* curtain raiser. ¶ v.t, to lift; hoist; raise; take up; remove; cut off; levy; clear (*letter box*); close (*sitting*); break up (*camp*); weigh (*anchor*); plot (*plan*); (*v.i*) to rise; shoot (*plant*). *faire ~,* to raise, leaven (*dough*). **se ~,** v.pr. & abs, to rise, get up; stand up.

léviathan (levjatɑ̃) m, leviathan.

levier (ləvje) m, lever; handspike.

lévite (levit) m, Levite; priest; satellite. le **Lévitique** (tik), Leviticus.

levraut (ləvro) m, leveret, young hare.

lèvre (lɛːvr) f, lip.

levrette (ləvrɛt) f, greyhound [bitch]. **lévrier** (levrje) m, greyhound. ~ *de la mer,* ocean greyhound (*fig.*). ~ *russe,* borzoi.

levure (ləvyːr) f, yeast, barm.

lexicographe (lɛksikɔgraf) m, lexicographer. **lexique** (sik) m, lexicon.

Leyde (lɛd) f, Leyden.

lézard (lezaːr) m, lizard.

lézarde (lezard) f, crack, crevice, chink. **lézarder** (de) v.i, to sun oneself. **se ~,** to crack, split.

liais (ljɛ) m, kind of Portland stone.

liaison (ljɛzɔ̃) f, connexion; bond; liaison; slur (*Mus.*); tie (*Mus.*); thickening (*Cook.*). **liaisonner** (zɔne) v.t, to bond (*masonry*).

liane (ljan) f, liana, liane.

liant, e (ljɑ̃, ɑ̃ːt) a, pliant; sociable, responsive. ¶ m, pliancy, &c.

liard (ljaːr) m, farthing (*fig.*), rap. **liarder** (arde) v.i, to higgle.

lias (ljɑ) m, lias (*Geol.*). **liasique** (azik) a, liassic.

liasse (ljas) *f*, bundle; file.
libation (libasjɔ̃) *f*, libation; drinking.
libelle (libɛl) *m*, libel.
libellé (libelle) *m*, drawing [up]; wording; particulars. libeller (le) *v.t*, to draw [up], make; word.
libelliste (libɛllist) *m*, libeller.
libellule (libɛlyl) *f*, dragonfly.
libéral, e† (liberal) *a*, liberal, open-handed; learned (*profession*, in France such as médecin, avocat, notaire, not in the pay of the State, or under its control). ¶ *m*, liberal. libéralisme (lism) *m*, liberalism. libéralité (te) *f*, liberality.
libérateur, trice (liberatœ:r, tris) *n*, liberator, deliverer. libération (sjɔ̃) *f*, liberation; discharge; release; paying up. libérer (re) *v.t*, to liberate, &c. liberté (bɛrte) *f*, liberty, freedom. ~ *[de langage]*, ~ *de parole*, outspokenness. ~ *de parler*, free[dom of] speech.
libertin, e (libɛrtɛ̃, in) *a*, libertine, rakish; wayward. ¶ *m*, libertine, rake. libertinage (tina:ʒ) *m*, licentiousness; waywardness.
libraire (librɛ:r) *m*, bookseller. ~-*éditeur*, b. & publisher. librairie (brɛri) *f*, book trade; book[seller's] shop; publishing house.
libre† (libr) *a*, free; at liberty, disengaged; available; vacant; spare; open; welcome; clear (*way*); unstamped (*paper*). ~ *arbitre*, *m*, free will. ~-*échange*, *m*, f. trade. ~-*échangiste* (eʃɑ̃ʒist) *m*, f. trader. ~ *parole*, f. speech. ~ *penseur*, freethinker. ~ *pratique*, [free] pratique.
librettiste (librɛtist) *m*, librettist.
lice (lis) *f*, lists, arena; bitch hound; warp.
licence (lisɑ̃:s) *f*, licence; licentiate's degree; leave; licentiousness. licencié, e (sɑ̃sje) *n*, licenciate, bachelor (*laws*, *arts*, &c). licencier (sje) *v.t*, to disband (*troops*). licencieux, euse† (sjø, ø:z) *a*, licentious, ribald.
lichen (likɛn) *m*, lichen.
licite† (lisit) *a*, licit, lawful.
licorne (likɔrn) *f*, unicorn.
licou (liku) or *poet*., *before vowel*, licol (kɔl) *m*, halter (*Harness*).
licteur (liktœ:r) *m*, lictor.
lie (li) *f*, lees, dregs; offscourings; scum. faire chère lie, to live well.
lié, e (lje) *p.a*, bound, tied; intimate, thick.
liège (ljɛ:ʒ) *m*, cork.
lien (ljɛ̃) *m*, bond; tie; link; binder; strap. lier (lje) *v.t*, to bind; tie [up]; join; tie; knit; connect; enter into; tie (*Mus*.); slur (*Mus*.); thicken (*sauce*).
lierre (ljɛ:r) *m*, ivy. ~ *terrestre*, ground i.
lieu (ljø) *m*, place; stead; ground[s]; occasion; (*s*. & *pl*.) spot; (*pl*.) premises. ~*x [d'aisance]* ou *petit* ~, water closet, privy, latrine, little place. ~*x communs*, commonplaces (*Rhet*. & *platitudes*). ~*x*

de pêche, where to fish. au ~ de, instead of, in lieu of. au ~ que, whereas. avoir ~, to take place.
lieue (ljø) *f*, league (= 4 kilometres); mile(s) (*long way*). d'une ~, a mile off.
lieur (ljœ:r) (*pers*.) *m*. & lieuse (ø:z) (*Mach*.) *f*, binder (*sheaf*).
lieutenant (ljøtnɑ̃) *m*, lieutenant; mate (*ship*). ~-*colonel*, lieutenant colonel. ~ *de vaisseau*, [naval] lieutenant.
lièvre (ljɛ:vr) *m*, hare.
ligament (ligamɑ̃) *m*, ligament. ligature (ty:r) *f*, ligature.
lige (li:ʒ) *a*. & *vassal* ~, *m*, liege.
ligne (liɲ) *f*, line; rank. ~ *d'autobus*, busway. ~ *de ballon mort*, *d'envoi*, *de renvoi*, dead-ball, half-way, 25-yards, line (*Rugby*). ~ *de but*, *de touche*, goal, touch, l. (*Foot*.). ~ *de charge*, load l. ~ *de départ*, starting l., scratch l. ~ *de faîte*, watershed. ~ *de flottaison* (flɔtɛzɔ̃), water line (*ship*). ~ *de fond*, *de côté*, *de service*, *médiane de service*, base, side, service, centre service, l. (*Ten*.). ~ *de milieu*, half-way l. (*Association*). ~ *du milieu de pénalité*, *de position*, halfdistance, 2-yard penalty, 4-yard penalty, l. (*Water Polo*). ~ *supplémentaire*, le[d]-ger l. (*Mus*.).
lignée (liɲe) *f*, issue, line, stock.
ligneux, euse (liɲø, ø:z) *a*, ligneous, woody. lignite (ɲit) *m*, lignite.
ligoter (ligɔte) *v.t*, to bind, lash.
ligue (lig) *f*, league. liguer (ge) *v.t*, to l.
lilas (lila) *m*. & *att*, lilac.
liliacé, e (liljase) *a*, liliaceous.
lilliputien, ne (lilipysjɛ̃, ɛn) *a*, Lilliputian.
limace (limas) *f*, slug (*Mol*.); Archimedean screw. limaçon (sɔ̃) *m*, snail (*Mol*.). en ~, spiral, winding.
limaille (lima:j) *f*, filings, dust.
limande (limɑ̃:d) *f*, dab (*fish*).
limbe (lɛ̃:b) *m*, limb (*Math*.); (*pl*.) limbo.
lime (lim) *f*, file (*tool*). limer (me) *v.t*, to file; polish (*fig*.).
limier (limje) *m*, bloodhound; sleuth-hound.
liminaire (liminɛ:r) *a*, prefatory.
limitation (limitasjɔ̃) *f*, limitation. ~ *des naissances*, birth control. limite (mit) *f*, limit; bound[ary]. ~ *des neiges éternelles*, snow line. limiter (te) *v.t*, to limit; bound; restrict. limitrophe (trɔf) *a*, bordering.
limon (limɔ̃) *m*, mud, slime, ooze, silt; clay (*fig*.); string (*stairs*); shaft, thill (*cart*); lime (*citrus*). limonade (mɔnad) *f*, lemonade. ~ *gazeuse*, aerated lemonade. ~ *non gazeuse*, still lemonade. limonadier, ère (dje, ɛ:r) *n*, light refreshment caterer, café keeper. limoneux, euse (nø, ø:z) *a*, muddy, slimy. limonier (nje) *m*, lime [tree] (*citrus*).
limousine (limuzin) *f*, limousine.
limpide (lɛ̃pid) *a*, limpid, clear, pellucid.

limure (limy:r) *f*, filing; filings.

lin (lɛ̃) *m*, flax; linen.

linceul (lɛ̃sœl *ou* œ:j) *m*, shroud, winding sheet.

linéaire (linee:r) *a*, linear; lineal. **linéament** (neamɑ̃) *m*, lineament, feature; outline.

linge (lɛ̃:ʒ) *m*, linen; cloth. ~ *à thé*, tea cloth. ~ *de table*, table linen. **linger, ère** (lɛ̃ʒe, ɛ:r) *n*, lingerie maker; fancy draper; (*f.*) wardrobe keeper. **lingerie** (ʒri) *f*, fancy drapery, lingerie; linen room.

lingot (lɛ̃go) *m*, ingot; slug (*bullet & Typ.*).

lingual, e (lɛ̃gwal) *a. & f*, lingual. **linguiste** (gɥist) *n*, linguist. **linguistique** (tik) *f*, linguistics.

linière (linjɛ:r) *a.f*, linen (*industry*). ¶ *f*, flax field.

liniment (linimɑ̃) *m*, liniment.

linoléum (linoleɔm) *m*, linoleum, lino, floor cloth. ~ *imprimé*, printed linoleum, oil-cloth. ~ *incrusté*, inlaid linoleum.

linon (linɔ̃) *m*, linen; lawn.

linot (lino) *m. ou* **linotte** (nɔt) *f*, linnet.

linotype (linɔtip) *a. & f*, linotype.

linteau (lɛ̃to) *m*, lintel, transom.

lion (ljɔ̃) *m*, lion. ~ *marin*, sea l. **lionceau** (so) *m*, l. cub, l. whelp. **lionne** (ɔn) *f*, lioness; fury.

lippe (lip) *f*, thick underlip. *faire la* ~, to pout. **lippu, e** (py) *a*, thick-lipped.

liquéfaction (likefaksjɔ̃) *f*, liquefaction. **liquéfier** (fje) *v.t*, to liquefy. **liqueur** (kœ:r) *f*, liquor, drink; solution (*Chem.*). ~ *d'ammoniaque*, liquid ammonia, hartshorn. ~ [*de dessert*], liqueur. ~ *de ménage*, home-made wine. ~*s fortes*, strong drink. ~*s fraîches*, non-alcoholic drinks. ~ [*spiritueuse*], spirit.

liquidateur (likidatœ:r) *m*, liquidator. **liquidation** (sjɔ̃) *f*, liquidation, winding up; closing; settlement, account (*Stk Ex.*); [liquidation] sale, closing-down sale, selling off.

liquide (likid) *a*, liquid; wet (*goods*). ¶ *m*, liquid; fluid; liquor (*alcoholic*); (*f.*) liquid (*Gram.*).

liquider (likide) *v.t*, to liquidate, wind up; close; settle; pay off; sell off.

liquoreux, euse (likorø, ø:z) *a*, sweet (*wine*). **liquoriste** (rist) *n*, wine & spirit merchant.

lire (li:r) *v.t. & abs. ir*, to read; hear from.

lis (lis) *m*, lily. ~ *tigré*, tiger lily.

Lisbonne (lizbon) *f*, Lisbon.

liséré (lizere) *m*, piping (*braid*); border. **liseron** (lizrɔ̃) *ou* **liset** (ze) *m*, bindweed. **liseur, euse** (lizœ:r, ø:z) *n*, reader. ~ *de pensées*, thought r. ¶ *f*, reading hook; r. stand; bed jacket. **lisible†** (zibl) *a*, legible; readable (*interesting*).

lisière (lizjɛ:r) *f*, selvedge, list; leading-strings; border, edge, skirt.

lisse (lis) *a*, smooth; sleek; plain; flush. ¶ *f*, warp; rail (*ship*). **lisser (se)** *v.t*, to smooth. **lissoir** (swa:r) *m*, smoother.

liste (list) *f*, list; roll; panel (*jury*). ~ *des admis*, pass list (*exams*). ~ *électorale*, register of voters.

lit (li) *m*, bed; bedstead; layer; marriage; set (*of tide, &c*). ~ *à colonnes*, four-poster. ~ *de douleur*, sick bed. *être exposé sur un* ~ *de parade*, to lie in state. ~ *de repos*, bed settee.

litanie (litani) *f*, rigmarole; (*pl.*) litany.

liteau (lito) *m*, stripe (*on cloth*); runner (*for shelf*); haunt (*wolves'*).

litée (lite) *f*, group (*collection of animals in the same den or lair*).

literie (litri) *f*, bedding.

litharge (litarʒ) *f*, litharge.

lithine (litin) *f*, lithia. **lithium** (tiɔm) *m*, lithium.

lithographe (litograf) *m*, lithographer. **lithographie** (fi) *f*, lithography; lithograph. **lithographier** (fje) *v.t*, to lithograph. **lithographique** (fik) *a*, lithographic.

litière (litjɛ:r) *f*, litter (*straw & dung; also palanquin*).

litige (liti:ʒ) *m*, litigation; dispute. **litigieux, euse** (tiʒø, ø:z) *a*, litigious; contentious.

litorne (litorn) *f*, fieldfare.

litre (litr) *m*, litre = 1·75980 (about 1¾) pints; litre measure; litre bottle.

littéraire† (literɛ:r) *a*, literary.

littéral, e† (literal) *a*, literal.

littérateur (literatœ:r) *m*, literary man. **littérature** (ty:r) *f*, literature; learning; empty talk.

littoral, e (litoral) *a*, littoral. ¶ *m*, littoral, seaboard.

Lit[h]uanie (la) (lityani), Lithuania.

liturgie (lityrʒi) *f*, liturgy.

liure (ljy:r) *f*, cart rope.

livide (livid) *a*, livid, ghastly.

Livourne (livurn) *f*, Leghorn.

livrable (livrabl) *a*, deliverable. ¶ (*Com.*) *m*, forward, terminal, [for] shipment; futures, options. **livraison** (vrɛzɔ̃) *f*, delivery; part, number (*publication*).

livre (li:vr) *f*, pound = ½ kilogram; franc. *Note*.—The word *livre* (meaning a present-day French franc) is still sometimes used, but almost exclusively in literature. ~ [*sterling*], pound [sterling]. *la* ~, sterling, the £.

livre (li:vr) *m*, book; journal; register; diary; day book. ~ *à feuille[t]s mobiles*, loose-leaf book. ~ *à succès*, ~ *à grand tirage*, best seller. ~*s d'agrément*, light reading. ~ *d'exemples*, copy book. ~ *d'images*, picture b. ~ *d'office*, ~ *d'église*, ~ *de prières*, prayer b. ~ *de bord* & ~ *de loch*, log [b.]. ~ *de chevet*, favourite b. ~ *de lecture*, reader. ~ *de signatures*, autograph book. ~ *feint*, dummy book (*for bookshelf*). ~ *généalogique*, stud b.; herd b. *à* ~ *ouvert*, at sight. *faire un* ~, to make a book (*Betting*).

livrée (livre) *f*, livery; servants; badge.

livrer (livre) *v.t*, to deliver; d. up; surrender; consign; commit; confide; join, give (*battle*). ~ *par erreur*, to misdeliver.

livret (livrɛ) *m*, book (*small register*); handbook; libretto.

livreur, euse (livrœːr, øːz) *n*, delivery man *or* boy *or* girl, roundsman.

lobe (lɔb) *m*, lobe.

lobélie (lɔbeli) *f*, lobelia.

local, e† (lɔkal) *a*, local. ¶ *m*. oft. pl, premises. **localiser** (lize) *v.t*, to place; localize. **localité** (te) *f*, locality, place.

locataire (tɛːr) *n*, tenant, occupier; leaseholder; lodger; renter; hirer. **locatif, ive** (tif, iːv) *a*, a tenant's (*repairs*); rental, letting (*value*). **location** (sjɔ̃) *f*, letting, renting, hire; reservation, booking; tenancy.

loch (lɔk) *m*, log (*float—ship's*).

loche (lɔʃ) *f*, loach (*fish*); slug (*Mol.*).

lock-out (lɔkaut) *m*, lockout.

locomobile (lɔkomɔbil) *f*, agricultural engine, traction e. **locomoteur, trice** (tœːr, tris) *a*, locomotive. **locomotion** (sjɔ̃) *f*, locomotion. **locomotive** (tiːv) *f*, locomotive, [railway] engine.

locuste (lɔkyst) *f*, locust; shrimp, prawn.

locution (lɔkysjɔ̃) *f*, phrase.

lof (lɔf) *m*, windward side (*ship*); luff. **lofer** (fe) *v.t*, to luff.

logarithme (lɔgaritm) *m*, logarithm.

loge (lɔːʒ) *f*, lodge (*porter's, freemasons'*); loggia; box (*Theat.*); dressing room (*actor's*); cage (*menagerie*); loculus. **logeable** (lɔʒabl) *a*, tenantable, [in]habitable. **logement** (ʒmɑ̃) *m*, lodging, housing, billeting; accommodation, quarters; tenement. **loger** (ʒe) *v.i. & t*, to lodge; live; stay; accommodate; house; billet; stable. **logeur, euse** (ʒœːr, øːz) *n*, landlord, -lady, lodging house keeper.

logicien (lɔʒisjɛ̃) *m*, logician. **logique†** (ʒik) *a*, logical. ¶ *f*, logic.

logis (lɔʒi) *m*, house, home.

loi (lwa) *f*, law; enactment; statute; act; standard (*of coin*).

loin (lwɛ̃) *ad*, far, f. away, f. off; f. back; afar; afield; a long way. ~ *de compte*, out of one's reckoning, wide of the mark. **lointain, e** (tɛ̃, ɛn) *a*, remote, far off, distant. ¶ *m*, distance.

loir (lwaːr) *m*, dormouse.

loisible (lwazibl) *a*, permissible. **loisir** (ziːr) *m*. oft. pl, leisure, [spare] time. **à** ~, *ad*, at leisure.

lombaire (lɔ̃bɛːr) *a*, lumbar.

Lombardie (la) (lɔ̃bardi) *f*, Lombardy.

lombes (lɔ̃ːb) *m.pl*, loins.

londonien, ne (lɔ̃dɔnjɛ̃, ɛn) *a*, London. **L**~, *n*, Londoner. **Londres** (lɔ̃ːdr) *m*, London.

long, ongue (lɔ̃, ɔ̃ːg) *a*, long; lengthy; slow, dilatory. *long échange*, rally (*Ten.*). *à la longue*, in the long run, in the end. ¶ *m*, length. *au* ~, at length, at large.

au ~ *& au large*, far & wide. *de* ~, long (*Meas.*). *de* ~ *en large*, to & fro, up & down. *en* ~, lengthways. *le* ~ *de*, along; alongside. [*syllable*] *longue*, *f*, long [syllable].

longanimité (lɔ̃ganimite) *f*, long-suffering, forbearance.

long-courrier (lɔ̃kurje) *m*, foreign-going ship, ocean-going s. **long cours**, *m*, deep-sea navigation; ocean (*or* foreign) voyage.

longe (lɔ̃ːʒ) *f*, lead rope (*attached to halter*); leading rein; tether; loin (*veal*).

longer (lɔ̃ʒe) *v.t*, to run along, skirt.

longévité (lɔ̃ʒevite) *f*, longevity.

longitude (lɔ̃ʒityd) *f*, longitude. **longitudinal, e†** (dinal) *a*, longitudinal.

longtemps (lɔ̃tɑ̃) *ad*, long; a long while. **longuement** (lɔ̃gmɑ̃) *ad*, long; lengthily. **longuet, te** (gɛ, ɛt) *a*, longish. **longueur** (gœːr) *f*, length; lengthiness; delay. *en* ~, lengthways; slowly. **longue-vue** (lɔ̃gvy) *f*, telescope, spy-glass.

lopin (lɔpɛ̃) *m*, patch, plot (*of ground*), allotment.

loquace (lɔkwas) *a*, loquacious, talkative, garrulous. **loquacité** (site) *f*, loquacity, &c.

loque (lɔk) *f*, rag, tatter.

loquet (lɔkɛ) *m*, latch (*door*). **loqueteau** (kto) *m*, catch (*window*).

loqueteux, euse (lɔktø, øːz) *a. & n*, ragged (person).

lord (lɔːr) *m*, lord (*Eng.*).

lorgner (lɔrɲe) *v.t*, to quiz; eye; ogle, leer at. **lorgnette[s] de spectacle** (nɛt) *f.[pl.]*, opera glass[es]. **lorgnon** (ɲɔ̃) *m*, eyeglasses, pince-nez.

loriot (lɔrjo) *m*, [golden] oriole.

lors (lɔːr) *ad*, then. ~ *de*, at the time of. ~ *même que*, even though. **lorsque** (lɔrskə) *c*, when.

losange (lɔzɑ̃ːʒ) (*Geom.*) *m*, lozenge, rhomb[us], diamond.

lot (lo) *m*, lot; portion; prize (*lottery*). **loterie** (lɔtri) *f*, lottery; sweepstake[s]; raffle, draw; gamble.

lotion (lɔsjɔ̃) *f*, lotion; washing.

lotir (lɔtiːr) *v.t*, to lot [out], parcel out. *bien loti*, lucky; in a fine plight.

loto (lɔto) *m*, lotto (*game*).

lotus (lɔtyːs) *au* **lotos** (tɔs) *m*, lotus.

louable (lwabl) *a*, laudable, praiseworthy; deserving of praise.

louage (lwaːʒ) *m*, letting, renting, hiring; hire. **louange** (lwɑ̃ːʒ) *f*, praise; commendation. **louanger** (ɑ̃ʒe) *v.t*, to laud [to the skies].

louche (luʃ) *a*, cross-eyed, squint[ing]; cloudy; shady, suspicious. ¶ *f*, soup ladle. **loucher** (ʃe) *v.i*, to squint.

louer (lwe) *v.t*, to let [out], rent, hire; reserve, book; praise, laud. *à* ~, to [be] let; for hire. **loueur (euse) de chaises** (lwœːr, øːz), chair attendant. *loueur de chevaux*, jobmaster.

lougre (lu:gr) *m*, lugger (*Naut.*).

louis (lwi) *m*, louis (*old gold coin worth 20 pre-war francs. Nowadays, only as gaming term*, = 20 *present-day francs*).

Louisiane (lwizjan) *f*, Louisiana.

loulou (lulu) *m*, Pomeranian [dog], pom.

loup (lu) *m*, wolf; waster. **loup-cervier** (servje) *m*, [common] lynx (*N. Europe*). ∼ *de mer* (*pers.*), hard-bitten sailor, old salt, [jack] tar.

loupe (lup) *f*, wen (*Med.*); bur[r] (*on tree*); lens, [magnifying] glass. **louper** (pe) *v.i*, to slack; (*v.t.*) to botch.

loup-garou (lugaru) *m*, wer[e]wolf; bugbear; bear (*pers.*).

lourd, e† (lu:r, urd) *a*, heavy; weighty; dull; sluggish; close (*weather*). **lourdaud, e** (lurdo, o:d) *n*, lubber, lout, bumpkin, dolt, numskull, fathead, oaf. **lourdeur** (dœ:r) *f*, heaviness, &c.

loustic (lustik) *m*, wag, funny man.

loutre (lutr) *f*, otter.

louve (lu:v) *f*, [she-]wolf; lewis. **louveteau** (luvto) *m*, wolf cub (*Zool. & Scouting*).

louvoyer (luvwaje) *v.i*, to tack [about].

lover (love) *v.t*, to coil (*rope*).

loyal, e† (lwajal) *a*, honest, straight[forward], fair; true, loyal. **loyalisme** (lism) *m*, loyalty, allegiance (*to sovereign*); loyalism. **loyaliste** (list) *a. & n*, loyalist. **loyauté** (jote) *f*, honesty, &c.

loyer (lwaje) *m*, rent; hire; price; wages.

lubie (lybi) *f*, whim, crotchet, vagary, fad, kink, maggot.

lubricité (lybrisite) *f*, lubricity, lewdness. **lubrifier** (fje) *v.t*, to lubricate, grease. **lubrique** (brik) *a*, lewd, wanton.

lucarne (lykarn) *f*, dormer [window].

lucide (lysid) *a*, lucid, clear. **lucidité** (dite) *f*, lucidity.

luciole (lysjol) *f*, firefly; glowworm.

Lucques (lyk) *f*, Lucca.

lucratif, ive (lykratif, i:v) *a*, lucrative. **lucre** (lykr) *m*, lucre, pelf, gain.

luette (lɥɛt) *f*, uvula.

lueur (lɥœ:r) *f*, glimmer; gleam; glimpse; spark.

luge (ly:ʒ) *f*, luge. **luger** (lyʒe) *v.i*, to luge.

lugubre† (lygy:br) *a*, lugubrious, doleful, gloomy.

lui, leur (lɥi, lœ:r) *pn*, [to] him, her, it, them; at him, &c.

lui, eux (lɥi, ø) *pn.m*, he, it, they; him, it, them. *lui-même, eux-mêmes*, himself, itself, themselves.

luire (lɥi:r) *v.i.ir*, to shine, gleam. **luisant, e** (lɥizɑ̃, ɑ̃:t) *a*, shining, gleaming; bright; glossy. ¶ *m*, shine, gloss, sheen.

lumbago (lɔ̃bago) *m*, lumbago.

lumière (lymjɛ:r) *f*, light; luminary (*pers.*); [port] hole; oil hole; spout hole; vent; mouth; throat; (*pl.*) understanding, insight; (*pl.*) enlightenment. ∼-*éclair*, flash light (*Phot.*). ∼ *magnésique* (maɲezik),

magnesium light. ∼ *oxhydrique*, lime-light. **lumignon** (miɲɔ̃) *m*, snuff (*wick*); candle end; dim light. **luminaire** (nɛ:r) *m*, luminary; light; lights. **lumineux, euse†** (nø, ø:z) *a*, luminous; bright.

lunaire (lynɛ:r) *a*, lunar. ¶ *f*, honesty (*Bot.*). **lunatique** (lynatik) *a. & n*, whimsical (person).

lundi (lœ̃di) *m*, Monday.

lune (lyn) *f*, moon. ∼ *de miel*, honeymoon; threshold (*fig.*).

lunetier (lyntje) *m*, spectacle maker, optician. **lunette** (nɛt) *f*, (*pl.*) spectacles, glasses, goggles; lunette; wishing bone, merrythought; rim (*watch*). ∼ [*d'approche*], [refracting] telescope. ∼ *de repère*, finder. ∼*s en écaille*, horn-rimmed spectacles.

lupin (lypɛ̃) *m*, lupin[e] (*Bot.*).

lupus (lypy:s) *m*, lupus.

lurette (lyrɛt) *f*: *il y a belle* ∼ *que*, it is ages since.

luron (lyrɔ̃) *m*, jolly sturdy fellow. **luronne** (rɔn) *f*, jovial stout-hearted woman.

lusin (lyzɛ̃) *m*, marline.

lustre (lystr) *m*, lustre; gloss; foil (*fig.*); chandelier. ∼ *électrique*, electrolier. **lustrer** (tre) *v.t*, to lustre; gloss; glaze.

lut (lyt) *m*, lute (*cement*). **luter** (te) *v.t*, to lute.

luth (lyt) *m*, lute (*Mus.*). **lutherie** (tri) *f*, musical instrument making.

luthérien, ne (lyterjɛ̃, ɛn) *a. & n*, Lutheran. **luthier** (lytje) *m*, musical instrument maker.

lutin, e (lytɛ̃, in) *a*, roguish, impish. ¶ *m*, [hob]goblin, sprite, elf, imp, puck; pickle (*child*). **lutiner** (tine) *v.t. & i*, to plague, tease.

lutrin (lytrɛ̃) *m*, lectern, reading desk.

lutte (lyt) *f*, wrestling; struggle; fight, contest, tussle, fray. ∼ *à la corde*, tug of war. ∼ *américaine*, all-in wrestling. ∼ *gréco-romaine* (grekorɔmɛn), Gr[a]eco-Roman wrestling. ∼ *libre*, catch-[as-catch-]can. **lutter** (te) *v.i*, to wrestle; struggle, fight, contend; vie. **lutteur** (tœ:r) *m*, wrestler.

luxation (lyksasjɔ̃) *f*, dislocation (*Surg.*).

luxe (lyks) *m*, luxury; sumptuousness; profusion.

Luxembourg (lyksɑ̃bu:r) *m*, Luxemburg.

luxer (lykse) *v.t*, to dislocate.

luxueux, euse (lyksɥø, ø:z) *a*, luxurious. **luxuriant, e** (ksyrjɑ̃, ɑ̃:t) *a*, luxuriant, lush, rank. **luxurieux, euse** (rjø, ø:z) *a*, lustful, lewd.

luzerne (lyzɛrn) *f*, lucern[e].

lycée (lise) *m*, secondary school. **lycéen, ne** (seɛ̃, ɛn) *n*, student (*at a lycée*), schoolboy, -girl.

lymphe (lɛ̃:f) *f*, lymph; sap.

lyncher (lɛ̃ʃe) *v.t*, to lynch.

lynx (lɛ̃:ks) *m*, lynx.

Lyon (ljɔ̃) *m*, Lyons.

lyre (li:r) *f*, lyre. *& toute la* ~, *&* all the rest of it. **lyrique** (lirik) *a*, lyric; lyrical; opera (*house*). ¶ *m*, lyric poet. **lyrisme** (rism) *m*, lyricism.

M

macabre (makɑ:br) *a*, macabre; grim, gruesome, ghastly.

macadam (makadam) *m*, macadam. **macadamiser** (mize) *v.t*, to macadamize.

macaque (makak) *m*, macaco; macaque.

macareux (makarø) *m*, puffin.

macaron (makarɔ̃) *m*, macaroon.

macaroni (makarɔni) *m*, macaroni.

macédoine (masedwan) *f*, macédoine, salad (*fruit*); medley.

macérer (masere) *v.t*, to macerate.

mâchefer (mɑʃfe:r) *m*, clinker.

mâcher (mɑʃe) *v.t*, to chew; masticate; champ (*bit*). *ne pas le* ~, not to mince matters. **mâcheur, euse** (ʃœ:r, ø:z) *n*, chewer.

machiavélique (makjavelik) *a*, Machiavellian.

machinal, e† (maʃinal) *a*, mechanical (*fig.*). **machination** (sjɔ̃) *f*, machination. **machine** (ʃin) *f*, machine; (*pl.*) machinery; engine; gadget. ~ *à coudre*, sewing machine. ~ *à écrire*, typewriter. ~ *à glace*, refrigerator. ~ *à vapeur*, steam engine. ~*-outil*, *f*, machine tool. ~ *routière*, traction engine. **machiner** (ne) *v.t*, to scheme, plot. **machinerie** (nri) *f*, machinery; engine room, e. house. **machinisme** (nism) *m*, mechanization. **machiniste** (nist) *m*, scene shifter.

mâchoire (mɑʃwa:r) *f*, jaw.

mâchonner (mɑʃɔne) *v.t*, to chew; mumble.

mâchurer (mɑʃyre) *v.t*, to black, smudge.

macis (masi) *m*, mace (*spice*).

macle (makl) *f*, twin (*crystal*).

maçon (masɔ̃) *m*, mason; bricklayer. **maçonnage** (sɔna:ʒ) *m*, masonry; brickwork. **maçonner** (ne) *v.t*, to mason; brick up. **maçonnerie** (nri) *f*, masonry; stonework; brickwork. **maçonnique** (nik) *a*, masonic.

macule (makyl) *f*, spot, stain; sun spot, macula. **maculer** (le) *v.t. & i*, to set off, offset (*Typ.*).

madame, *oft.* **M**~ (madam) *f*, madam; Mrs; mistress; lady.

madapolam (madapɔlam) *m*, madapollam.

mademoiselle, *oft.* **M**~ (madmwazɛl) *f*, Miss; lady; waitress!

Madère (madɛ:r) *f*, Madeira.

madone (madɔn) *f*, madonna.

madras (madrɑ[:s]) *m*, madras (*fabric*).

madré, e (madre) *a*, speckled, spotted; bird's-eye (*maple*); crafty, deep.

madrépore (madrepɔ:r) *m*, madrepore.

madrier (madrie) *m*, plank.

madrigal (madrigal) *m*, madrigal.

mafflu, e (mafly) *a*, heavy-cheeked.

magasin (magazɛ̃) *m*, shop; store[s]; warehouse; magazine. ~ *à prix unique*, one-price shop. ~ *à succursales multiples*, multiple shop, chain store. ~ *de nouveautés*, stores. ~ *général*, free warehouse. ~*s généraux-entrepôts*, free & bonded warehouses. *en* ~, in stock. **magasinage** (zina:ʒ) *m*, warehousing, storage. **magasinier** (nje) *m*, storekeeper, warehouseman. **magazine** (zin) *m*, magazine (*periodical*).

mages (ma:ʒ) *m.pl*, Magi.

magicien, ne (maʒisjɛ̃, ɛn) *n*, magician; wizard; sorcerer, ess. **magie** (ʒi) *f*, magic, wizardry; witchery. ~ *noire*, black magic, b. art. **magique** (ʒik) *a*, magic(al).

magister (maʒistɛ:r) *m*, pedagogue. **magistère** (tɛ:r) *m*, dictatorship. **magistral, e†** (tral) *a*, magisterial; masterly; masterful. **magistrat** (tra) *m*, magistrate; judge. **magistrature** (ty:r) *f*, magistracy. ~ *assise*, bench. ~ *debout*, body of public prosecutors.

magnanerie (maɲanri) *f*, silkworm nursery; s. breeding.

magnanime† (maɲanim) *a*, magnanimous. **magnanimité** (mite) *f*, magnanimity.

magnat (magna) *m*, magnate (*Fin., &c*).

magnésie (maɲezi) *f*, magnesia. **magnésium** (zjɔm) *m*, magnesium.

magnétique (maɲetik) *a*, magnetic; mesmeric. **magnétisation** (zasjɔ̃) *f*, magnetization (*Phys.*). **magnétiser** (ze) *v.t*, to mesmerize, magnetize (*fig.*). **magnétiseur** (zœ:r) *m*, mesmerist. **magnétisme** (tism) *m*, magnetism (*Phys. & fig.*); magnetics; mesmerism. **magnéto** (to) *f*, magneto. ~*-électrique*, *a*, magneto-electric.

magnificat (magnifikat) *m*, magnificat. **magnificence** (maɲifisã:s) *f*, magnificence; grandeur; (*pl.*) lavishness; (*pl.*) fine things. **magnifier** (fje) *v.t*, to magnify (*the Lord*). **magnifique†** (fik) *a*, magnificent, splendid, grand, fine; munificent.

magnolia (maɲɔlja) *m*, magnolia.

magot (mago) *m*, magot (*ape & Chinese figure*); Barbary ape; fright (*pers.*); hoard.

mahométan, e (maɔmetã, an) *n. & att*, Mohammedan, Moslem, Muslim. **mahométisme** (tism) *m*, Mohammedanism.

mai (mɛ) *m*, May (*month*); maypole.

maigre (mɛ:gr) *a*, lean; meagre; scanty; thin; skinny; straggling (*beard*); poor; spare; meatless (*meal*); fast (*day*); vegetable (*soup*). ¶ *m*, lean. **maigrelet, te** (mɛgrəlɛ, ɛt) *a*, thinnish, slight. **maigrement** (gromã) *ad*, meagrely, scantily. **maigreur** (grœ:r) *f*, leanness, &c. **maigrir** (gri:r) *v.i*, to grow thin; (*v.t.*) to [make] thin.

maille (mɑ:j) *f*, stitch (*Knit., Crochet, &c*); mesh; speckle; bud; (*pl.*) mail (*armour*). ~ *échappée*, ~ *perdue*, ladder (*stocking*); dropped stitch (*Knit.*). ~ *glissée*, slip stitch (*Knit.*).

maillechort (majʃɔːr) *m*, German silver.
maillet (majɛ) *m*, mallet. **mailloche** (jɔʃ) *f*, mallet, maul.
maillon (majɔ̃) *m*, link (*chain*); shackle.
maillot (majo) *m*, long-clothes (*baby*); tights, *or* any close-fitting woven garment, *as* (*bathing, swimming*) costume, suit, dress; (*football*) jersey; (*running*) zephyr.
main (mɛ̃) *f*, hand; hand[writing]; handle (*drawer*); scoop; tendril; quire (*in Fr. 25 sheets*); trick (*Cards*); lead (*Cards*); deal (*Cards*). ~ *chaude*, hot cockles. ~ *courante*, hand rail; rough book. ~*d'œuvre*, workmanship; labour. ~*s* [*en tissu*] *éponge*, bath gloves. ~*-forte*, assistance (*to police*).
mainmise (mɛ̃miːz) *f*, hold (*influence*).
mainmorte (mɛ̃mɔrt) *f*, mortmain. *biens de* ~, property in mortmain.
maint, e (mɛ̃, ɛ̃ːt) *a*, many a, many.
maintenant (mɛ̃tnɑ̃) *ad*, now. **maintenir** (tniːr) *v.t.ir*, to maintain, keep; uphold. **se** ~, to keep; hold one's own. **maintien** (tjɛ̃) *m*, maintenance, keeping; deportment, bearing.
maiolique (majɔlik) *f*, majolica.
maire (mɛːr) *m*, mayor. **mairie** (mɛri) *f*, mayoralty; town hall, town clerk's office, registry [office].
mais (mɛ) *c. & ad*, but; why. ~ *non!* why no! not at all! ¶ *m*, but, objection.
maïs (mais) *m*, maize, Indian corn.
maison (mɛzɔ̃) *f*, house; home; household; firm; friary; convent. ~ *à succursales multiples*, multiple firm. ~ *d'aliénés*, mental institution. ~ *d'arrêt*, prison, jail, gaol; lockup; guardhouse. ~ *d'éducation*, educational establishment. ~ *d'habitation*, dwelling house. ~ *de commerce*, business house, firm. ~ *de blanc*, linen draper. ~ *de contrepartie*, bucket shop. ~ *de correction*, approved school, reformatory. ~ *de jeu*, gaming house. ~ *de plaisance*, week-end cottage. ~ *de rapport*, revenue-earning house. ~ *de retraite*, home for the aged. ~ *de santé*, nursing home. ~ *de ville*, town hall. ~ *des étudiants*, hostel. ~ *isolée*, detached house. ~ *jumelle*, semi-detached house. ~ *mortuaire*, house of the deceased. ~ *pour fournitures* (de sports, &c), outfitter. *à la* ~, [at] home, indoors.
maisonnée (zɔne) *f*, household, family.
maisonnette (nɛt) *f*, bungalow.
maistrance (mɛstrɑ̃ːs) *f*, petty officers (*Nav.*).
maître (mɛːtr) *m*, master; teacher; Mr (*courtesy title of lawyers*); petty officer. ~*-autel*, high altar. ~ *chanteur*, blackmailer. ~*-coq*, cook (*ship's*). ~ *d'armes*, fencing master. ~ [*d'équipage*], boatswain; master of the hounds. ~ *d'étude*, usher. ~ *d'hôtel*, [house] steward; head waiter; superintendent (*restaurant*). ~ *de chapelle*, choir master. ~ *de conférences*, lecturer.

~ *de forges*, ironmaster. ~ *de timonerie*, quartermaster (*Naut.*). ~ *des cérémonies*, Master of the Ceremonies. ~ *drain*, main drain. ~ *homme*, masterful man. ~ *Jacques*, Jack of all work or trades. ~ *sot*, champion idiot. **maîtresse** (mɛtrɛs) *f*, mistress; paramour. ~ *de piano*, teacher of the pianoforte. ~ *femme*, masterful woman. ~ *poutre*, main beam. **maîtrise** (triːz) *f*, mastery; control; choir. **maîtriser** (e) (mɛtrize) *v.t*, to [over]master; overpower; subdue; control.
majesté (maʒɛste) *f*, majesty; stateliness. *Sa M~*, His (*or* Her) Majesty. **majestueux, euse†** (tɥø, øːz) *a*, majestic; stately.
majeur, e (maʒœːr) *a*, major; greater. *être* ~, to come of [full] age (*Law*). *le lac Majeur*, Lago Maggiore.
majolique (maʒɔlik) *f*, majolica.
major (maʒɔːr) *m* (*Mil.*) *m*, adjutant; medical officer. **majoration** (ʒɔrasjɔ̃) *f*, increase (*price*); overvaluation; overcharge. **majordome** (dɔm) *m*, major-domo; comptroller of the Royal Household. **majorer** (re) *v.t*, to increase (*price*); overvalue; overcharge for *or* in. **majorité** (rite) *f*, majority.
Majorque (maʒɔrk) *f*, Majorca.
majuscule (maʒyskyl) *a. & f*, capital (letter).
mal (mal) *m*, evil; ill; wrong; harm; hurt; mischief; difficulty; damage; pain; ache; sore; ailment; trouble; disease; illness, sickness. *j'ai* ~ *au doigt*, I have a sore finger. ~ *aux yeux*, ~ *d'yeux*, eye trouble, sore eyes. ~ *blanc*, gathering, sore. ~ *d'aventure*, whitlow. ~ *d'enfant*, labour [pains]. ~ *de cœur*, sickness, qualms. ~ *de dents*, ~ *aux dents*, toothache. ~ *de gorge*, sore throat. ~ *de mer*, seasickness. *avoir le* ~ *de mer*, to be seasick. ~ *de montagne*, mountain sickness. ~ *de tête*, headache. ~ *du pays*, homesickness. ¶ *ad*, ill; badly; evil; wrong; amiss. ~ *famé, e*, ill-famed. ~ *gérer*, to mismanage. ~ *réussir*, to fail, turn out badly. *mal venu, e*, stunted; ill-advised. *de* ~ *en pis*, from bad to worse. ¶ *a. inv*, bad.
malachite (malakit) *f*, malachite.
malade (malad) *a*, ill, sick, unwell; diseased; bad, sore; in a bad way. ¶ *n*, sick person; invalid; patient. ~ *du dehors*, out-patient. ~ *interné, e*, in-patient. *faire le* ~ *ou simuler la maladie*, to malinger. **maladie** (di) *f*, illness, sickness, complaint, disease, disorder; obsession. ~ *de langueur*, decline. ~ [*des chiens*], distemper. ~ *du sommeil*, sleeping sickness. ~ *professionnelle*, industrial disease. **maladif, ive** (dif, iːv) *a*, sickly; morbid.
maladresse (maladrɛs) *f*, awkwardness, clumsiness. **maladroit, e†** (drwa, at) *a. & n*, awkward, clumsy (person), maladroit.
malais, e (malɛ, ɛːz) *a. & M~, n*, Malay[an].

malaise (malɛ:z) *m*, indisposition; uneasiness; straits. **malaisé, e** (lɛze) *a*, difficult; not easy; awkward. **malaisément** (mã) *ad*, with difficulty.

Malaisie (la) (malɛzi), Malaysia.

malandrin (malãdrɛ̃) *m*, bandit.

malappris, e (malapri, i:z) *a. & n*, ill-bred (person).

malaria (malarja) *f*, malaria.

malart (mala:r) *m*, mallard.

malavisé, e (malavize) *a*, ill-advised; unwise.

malaxer (malakse) *v.t*, to mix; work up (*butter*).

malbâti, e (malbɑti) *a. & n*, misshapen (person).

malchance (malʃã:s) *f*, ill luck; mischance. **malchanceux, euse** (ʃãsø, ø:z) *a. & n*, unlucky (person).

maldonne (maldɔn) *f*, misdeal (*Cards*).

mâle (mɑ:l) *m. & a*, male; he; cock; buck; bull; dog; man (*child*); masculine; manly; virile.

malédiction (malediksjɔ̃) *f*, malediction, curse.

maléfice (malefis) *m*, [evil] spell.

malencontreux, euse† (malãkɔ̃trø, ø:z) *a*, untoward, unlucky; unfortunate.

mal-en-point (malãpwɛ̃) *ad*, in a bad way, in a sorry plight.

malentendu (malãtãdy) *m*, misunderstanding, misapprehension, misconception.

malfaçon (malfasɔ̃) *f*, bad workmanship.

malfaisant, e (malfəzã, ã:t) *a*, malicious; injurious. **malfaiteur** (fɛtœ:r) *m*, malefactor, evil-doer. ∼ *public*, public menace (*pers.*).

malfamé, e (malfame) *a*, ill-famed.

malformation (malfɔrmasjɔ̃) *f*, malformation.

malgracieux, euse (malgrasjø, ø:z) *a*, ungracious, rude.

malgré (malgre) *pr*, in spite of, notwithstanding. ∼ *tout*, for all that.

malhabile† (malabil) *a*, unskilful; tactless.

malheur (malœ:r) *m*, misfortune; ill luck; unhappiness; evil days; woe. **malheureux, euse**† (lœrø, ø:z) *a*, unlucky; unfortunate; unhappy, miserable; woeful; sad; wretched; pitiful. ¶ *n*, unfortunate [person]; wretch.

malhonnête† (malɔnɛ:t) *a*, dishonest; rude, ill-mannered, unmannerly. **malhonnêteté** (nɛtte) *f*, dishonesty; rudeness.

malice (malis) *f*, malice, spite; artfulness; roguishness; practical joke. **malicieux, euse**† (sjø, ø:z) *a*, malicious, spiteful; roguish, arch.

malignité (maliɲite) *f*, malignity; maliciousness; mischievousness (*playful*). **malin, igne**† (lɛ̃, iɲ) *a. & n*, malicious; malignant; evil (*spirit*); mischievous, wicked, roguish; artful (person). *le malin* [*esprit*], the Evil One.

maline (malin) *f*, spring tide.

malines (malin) *f*, Mechlin [lace].

malingre (malɛ̃:gr) *a*, sickly, puny.

malintentionné, e (malɛ̃tãsjɔne) *a. & n*, evil-disposed (person).

malitorne (malitɔrn) *m*, lout.

mal-jugé (malʒyʒe) *m*, miscarriage of justice.

malle (mal) *f*, trunk; mail (*Post*); mail steamer, m. boat, m. packet. ∼*-armoire*, wardrobe trunk. ∼ *de paquebot*, ∼ *de cabine*, cabin t. ∼[*-poste*], mail [coach] (*stage*).

malléable (malleabl) *a*, malleable.

malléole (malleɔl) *f*, ankle [bone].

malletier (maltje) *m*, trunk & bag manufacturer. **mallette** (lɛt) *f*, case; attaché c. ∼ *garnie*, dressing c., fitted c.

malmener (malməne) *v.t*, to abuse; maul, handle roughly.

malotru (malɔtry) *n*, ill-bred person.

malpeigné (malpeɲe) *m*, unkempt fellow.

malpropre† (malprɔpr) *a*, dirty; indecent. **malpropreté** (prəte) *f*, dirtiness, &c.

malsain, e (malsɛ̃, ɛn) *a*, unhealthy; noisome; unwholesome; insanitary, unsanitary.

malséant, e (malseã, ã:t) *a*, unbecoming, unseemly.

malsonnant, e (malsɔnã, ã:t) *a*, offensive (*words*).

malt (malt) *m*, malt.

maltais, e (maltɛ, ɛ:z) *a. & M∼, n*, Maltese. **Malte** (malt) *f*, Malta.

malterie (maltəri) *f*, malting, malt house. **malteur** (tœ:r) *m*, maltster.

maltôte (malto:t) *f*, extortion (*taxes*).

maltraiter (maltrɛte) *v.t*, to maltreat, illtreat, ill-use, misuse; wrong.

malveillance (malvɛjã:s) *f*, malevolence, ill will, spite. **malveillant, e** (jã, ã:t) *a. & n*, malevolent, ill-disposed (person).

malvenu, e (malvəny) *a*, stunted; ill-advised.

malversation (malvɛrsasjɔ̃) *f*, malpractice, embezzlement, peculation.

mamamouchi (mamamuʃi) *m*, panjandrum.

maman (ma- *ou* mãmã) *f*, mam[m]a, mummy.

mamelle (mamɛl) *f*, breast; udder. **mamelon** (mlɔ̃) *m*, nipple, teat; hummock, mamelon, pap.

mamel[o]uk (mamluk) *m*, Mameluke (*Hist.*); henchman, myrmidon.

mamillaire (mamille:r) *a*, mamillary.

mammifère (mamife:r) *m*, mammal, (*pl.*) mammalia.

mammouth (mamut) *m*, mammoth.

mamours (mamu:r) *m.pl*, caresses, billing & cooing.

manant (manã) *m*, boor, churl.

manche (mã:ʃ) *m*, handle, helve, haft; stick (*umbrella*); neck (*violin*); knuckle [bone] (*mutton*). ∼ *à balai*, broomstick. ¶ *f*, sleeve; hose (*pipe*); channel; game, hand (*Cards*); set (*Ten.*). ∼ *à air*, ∼ *à vent*, ventilator (*ship*). ∼ *de chemise*, shirt sleeve. la **M∼**, the [English] Channel. **manchette** (mãʃɛt) *f*, cuff (*Dress*); ruffle; side note (*Typ.*); headline (*news*). **manchon** (ʃɔ̃) *m*, muff (*ladies'*); coupling

(*Mach.*); sleeve; socket; bush[ing]; mantle (*gas.*). ~ *d'embrayage*, clutch.

manchot, e (mãʃo, ɔt) *a. & n*, one-handed *or* one-armed (person); (*m.*) penguin.

mandant (mãdã) *m*, principal, mandator.

mandarin (mãdarɛ̃) *m*, mandarin. **mandarine** (rin) *f*, mandarin[e] [orange], tangerine [orange].

mandat (mãda) *m*, mandate; order; instructions; trust; procuration; power [of attorney], proxy; order [to pay], cheque, withdrawal notice; writ, warrant (*Law*). ~ *de dépôt*, committal order. ~[-*poste*], money order, post office o.; postal o. **mandataire** (tɛːr) *m*, mandatary, -ory; agent; attorney; proxy. **mandater** (te) *v.t*, to authorize the payment of]; commission.

mandchou, e (mãtʃu) *a. & M~, n*, Manchu[rian]. **la Mandchourie** (ri), Manchuria.

mandement (mãdmã) *m*, charge, pastoral letter. **mander** (de) *v.t*, to tell; inform.

mandibule (mãdibyl) *f*, mandible; jaw.

mandoline (mãdɔlin) *f*, mandolin[e].

mandragore (mãdragɔr) *f*, mandrake.

mandrill (mãdril) *m*, mandrill (*Zool.*).

mandrin (mãdrɛ̃) *m*, mandrel, -il; spindle; arbor; chuck (*lathe*); drift[pin].

manège (manɛːʒ) *m*, training (*horses*); horsemanship, riding; r. school; manège, -ege; horse gear; trick. ~ *de chevaux de bois*, roundabout, merry-go-round.

mânes (mɑːn) *m.pl*, manes, shades.

manette (manɛt) *f*, handle, lever.

manganèse (mãganɛːz) *m*, manganese.

mangeable (mãʒabl) *a*, eatable. **mangeaille** (ʒɑːj) *f*, food, feed. **mangeoire** (ʒwaːr) *f*, manger, crib. **manger** (ʒe) *v.t. & abs*, to eat; feed; have one's meals, mess; eat up; devour; squander; clip (*one's words*). ¶ *m*, food. **mange-tout** (mãʒtu) *m*, spendthrift; skinless pea *or* bean. **mangeur, euse** (ʒœːr, øːz) *n*, eater, feeder. **mangeure** (ʒyːr) *f*, bite (*place bitten by worm, mouse*).

manglier (mãglie) *m*, mangrove.

mangouste (mãgust) *f*, mongoose.

mangue (mãːg) *f*, mango. **manguier** (mãgje) *m*, mango [tree].

maniable (mãnjabl) *a*, supple; manageable; handy.

maniaque (manjak) *a*, maniac(al). ¶ *n*, maniac; faddist, crank. **manie** (ni) *f*, mania; craze; fad.

maniement (manimã) *m*, feeling; handling; management, conduct, care. ~ *des* (ou *d'armes*, manual [exercise], rifle drill. **manier** (nje) *v.t*, to feel; handle; wield; work; ply; manage, conduct. *au* ~, by the feel.

manière (manjɛːr) *f*, manner, way, wise; sort, kind; mannerism; style; (*pl.*) manners (*bearing*). *par d'acquit*, perfunctorily. ~ *noire*, mezzotint[o]. **mani-**

éré, e (jere) *a*, affected, finical; mannered (*style, &c*). **maniérisme** (rism) *m*, mannerism.

manieur (manjœːr) *m*, one who knows how to handle (*money, men*).

manifestant, e (manifɛstã, ã:t) *n*, demonstrator (*Pol., &c*). **manifestation** (tasjɔ̃) *f*, manifestation; demonstration. **manifeste**† (fɛst) *a*, a manifest, obvious, overt. ¶ *m*, manifesto; manifest (*Ship.*). **manifester** (te) *v.t*, to manifest, show; (*v.i.*) to demonstrate.

manigance (manigãs) *f*, intrigue. **manigancer** (gãse) *v.t*, to concoct, plot.

manille (mani:j) *m*, Manil[l]a [cheroot]; (*f.*) shackle; manille (*Cards*). **M~,** *f*, Manil[l]a (*Geog.*).

manioc (manjɔk) *m*, manioc, cassava.

manipuler (manipyle) *v.t*, to manipulate, handle.

manivelle (manivɛl) *f*, crank; handle, winch.

manne (man) *f*, manna; basket, hamper.

mannequin (mankɛ̃) *m*, lay figure, manikin; dress stand; display figure, d. model; dummy; mannequin, model; puppet; basket.

manœuvre (manœːvr) *f*, working, handling, manipulation; shunting (*Rly.*); seamanship; manœuvre; move; (*pl.*) field day; rope (*Naut.*); (*pl.*) rigging (*Naut.*); (*pl.*) scheming. ~*s électorales*, electioneering. ~*s frauduleuses*, swindling (*Law*). ¶ *m*, labourer; hack [writer, *&c*]. **manœuvrer** (nœvre) *v.t. & i*, to work, handle, manipulate; shunt; steer (*ship*); manœuvre. **manœuvrier** (vrie) *m*, (*skilful*) seaman; manœuvrer; tactician.

manoir (manwaːr) *m*, manor [house], country seat.

manomètre (manɔmɛtr) *m*, [pressure] gauge, manometer.

manquant, e (mãkã, ã:t) *a*, missing; absent. ¶ *m*, deficiency, shortage. ~ *à l'appel*, defaulter on parade (*Mil.*). **manque** (mãːk) *m*, want, lack, shortage, deficiency; breach; dropped stitch (*Knit.*), ladder. ~ [*à toucher*], miss. ~ *de pose*, underexposure (*Phot.*). **manqué, e** (mãke) *p.a*, missed; spoiled; misfit (*att.*); unsuccessful; abortive; wasted. *un peintre, &c, manqué*, a failure as a painter, *&c*. Cf. *garçon* ~ *& grand homme* ~. **manquer** (ke) *v.i*, to fail; miss; default; misfire, miss fire; be taken [away] (*die*); be wanting; be missing; be disrespectful; (*v.t.*) to miss; fail in. ~ *de*, to want, lack, run short (*or* out) of; be out of stock of; to nearly ... ~ *de parole*, to break one's word.

mansarde (mãsard) *f*, dormer [window]; attic, garret.

mansuétude (mãsɥetyd) *f*, meekness; forbearance.

mante (mãːt) *f*, mantle. **manteau** (mãto) *m*, coat, cloak, mantle, wrap. ~ *de* *cheminée*, mantelpiece. ~ *de cour*, court train. ~ *de fourrure*, fur coat. ~ *de pluie*, raincoat. *sous* [*le* ~ *de*] *la cheminée*, sub rosa, under the rose. *sous le* ~ *de la religion*, under the cloak of religion. **mantelet** (tle) *m*, tippet; mant[e]let; port lid (*Nav.*). **mantille** (ti:j) *f*, mantilla.

Mantoue (mɑ̃tu) *f*, Mantua.

manucure (manyky:r) *n*, manicurist (*pers.*); (*f.*) manicure (*treatment*); *m.* set.

manuel, le† (manɥɛl) *a*, manual, hand (*as work*). ¶ *m*, manual, [hand] book; text book.

manufacture (manyfakty:r) *f*, manufactory; staff. **manufacturier, ère** (tyrje, ɛːr) *a*, manufacturing. ¶ *m*, manufacturer.

manuscrit, e (manyskri, it) *a*, manuscript, written. ¶ *m*, manuscript.

manutention (manytɑ̃sjɔ̃) *f*, handling; bakehouse (*Mil.*). ~*s maritimes*, stevedoring.

mappemonde (mapmɔ̃:d) *f*, map of the world in hemispheres. ~ *céleste*, map of the heavens in hemispheres.

maquereau (makro) *m*, mackerel.

maquette (makɛt) *f*, model (*of statuary, &c*); dummy (*publisher's blank book*).

maquignon (makiɲɔ̃) *m*, horse dealer; horse chanter; jobber (*shady*). **maquignonnage** (ɲɔna:ʒ) *m*, horse dealing; h. chanting; jobbery. **maquignonner** (ne) *v.t*, to chant (*horses*); manipulate (*bad sense*).

maquillage (makijaːʒ) *m*, making up; makeup. **maquiller** (je) *v.t*, to make up (*face*); camouflage.

marabout (marabu) *m*, marabout; marabou.

maraîcher (marɛʃe) *m*, market gardener.

marais (rɛ) *m*, marsh, swamp, bog, fen, morass. ~ *salant*, saltern.

marasme (marasm) *m*, marasmus; stagnation.

marasquin (maraskɛ̃) *m*, maraschino.

marâtre (maraːtr) *f*, [cruel] stepmother.

maraudage (maroda:ʒ) *m. & maraude* (ro:d) *f*, marauding, foray; pilfering. *en maraude*, cruising (*taxi*). **marauder** (rode) *v.i*, to maraud, raid. **maraudeur** (dœːr) *m*, marauder.

maravédis (maravedi) *m*, [brass] farthing.

marbre (marbr) *m*, marble; [marble] slab *or* top; [imposing] stone; bed (*printing press*); [engineer's] surface plate; overset, overmatter (*Newspaper work*). ~ *de foyer*, hearthstone. **marbrer** (bre) *v.t*, to marble; mottle. **marbrerie** (brəri) *f*, marble work; m. works. **marbreur** (brœːr) *m*, marbler. **marbrier** (brie) *m*, marble mason; monumental mason; marble merchant. **marbrière** (briɛ:r) *f*, marble quarry. **marbrure** (bry:r) *f*, marbling.

marc (ma:r) *m*, marc (*fruit refuse*); grounds (*coffee*); used leaves (*tea*). *au* ~ *le franc*, pro rata, proportionally, in proportion.

marcassin (markasɛ̃) *m*, young wild boar.

marcassite (markasit) *f*, marcasite.

marchand, e (marʃɑ̃, ɑ̃:d) *n*, dealer, trader,

merchant; shopkeeper, -monger, tradesman, -woman, vender; (*att.*) merchant[able], mercantile, commercial, market[able], salable, sale (*att.*). ~ *de journaux*, newsagent. ~ *de nouveautés*, [general] draper. ~ *de volaille*, poulterer. ~ *des quatre saisons*, coster[monger]. ~ *en magasin*, warehouseman. *marchande à la toilette*, wardrobe dealer. **marchandage** (ʃɑ̃da:ʒ) *m*, bargaining, haggling. **marchander** (de) *v.t. & abs*, to haggle (over), bargain, palter; grudge; (*v.i.*) to hesitate. **marchandeur, euse** (dœːr, øːz) *n*, haggler, bargainer. **marchandise** (di:z) *f. oft. pl*, goods, merchandise, wares; commodity; cargo. ~*s d'occasion*, job lot.

marche (marʃ) *f*, walk, walking; march, marching; procession; sailing; steaming; running; run; working; speed; motion; movement, move; journey, course; way, path; progress; step, stair; treadle. ~ *à suivre*, procedure.

marché (marʃe) *m*, market; contract; bargain; dealing. ~ *aux bestiaux*, cattle market. ~ *commercial*, produce m. ~ *des valeurs*, *des titres*, share m., stock m. *par-dessus le* ~, into the bargain.

marchepied (marʃəpje) *m*, [pair of] steps, step ladder; steps; footboard; stepping stone (*fig.*).

marcher (marʃe) *v.i*, to walk; tread; step; travel; tramp; march; be on the march; be driven (*Mach.*); sail; proceed, move on, advance, progress, go, go on; run, ply; work. **marcheur, euse** (ʃœːr, øːz) *n*, walker; (*m.*) (*good, bad, fast*) sailer (*ship*).

marcotte (markot) *f*, layer (*Hort.*). **marcotter** (te) *v.t*, to layer.

mardi (mardi) *m*, Tuesday. *M*~ *gras*, Shrove Tuesday. *m*~ *gras* (*pers.*), guy.

mare (ma:r) *f*, pond, pool. **marécage** (mareka:ʒ) *m*, marsh, swamp, fen, bog. **marécageux, euse** (kaʒø, øːz) *a*, marshy, swampy, boggy.

maréchal (mareʃal) *m*: ~ *de France* (*Fr.*), Field Marshal (*Eng.*). ~ *des logis*, sergeant (*mounted troops*). ~ *des logis chef*, s. major. **maréchalat** (la) *m*, marshalship. **maréchalerie** (lri) *f*, farriery. **maréchal-ferrant** (ferɑ̃) *m*, farrier, shoeing smith.

marée (mare) *f*, tide, water; salt-water fish (*caught & fresh*), fresh sea fish, wet fish.

marelle (marel) *f*, hopscotch.

mareyeur, euse (marejœːr, øːz) *n*, [wet] fish merchant & salesman, -woman.

margarine (margarin) *f*, margarine.

marge (marʒ) *f*, margin. **marger** (ʒe) *v.t*, to lay on, feed (*Typ.*); set a margin (*Typing*). **marginal, e** (ʒinal) *a*, marginal.

margotin (margotɛ̃) *m*, bundle of firewood.

margouillis (marguji) *m*, mess.

marguerite (margərit) *f*, (*petite*) daisy; (*grande*) marguerite, ox-eye daisy. ~ *de la Saint-Michel*, Michaelmas daisy.

mari (mari) *m*, husband. **mariable** (rjabl) *a*, marriageable. **mariage** (rja:ʒ) *m*, marriage, matrimony, wedlock; match; wedding. ~ *d'amour*, ~ *d'inclination*, love match. ~ *d'argent*, money marriage. ~ *de raison*, ~ *de convenance*, marriage of convenience. ~ *par enlèvement*, runaway match. **marié, e** (rje) *n*, bridegroom, bride. **marier** (rje) *v.t. & se* ~, to marry, wed; get married; match, unite. **marieur, euse** (rjœ:r, ø:z) *n*, match maker.

marin, e (marɛ̃, in) *a*, marine; sea (*att.*); nautical (*mile*); sailor (*suit*). ¶ *m*, seaman, mariner, sailor; waterman, boatman. ~ *d'eau douce*, freshwater sailor, landlubber. **marine** (rin) *f*, marine, shipping, maritime navigation; sea piece, sea scape. ~ [*militaire*], ~ *de guerre*, navy. **mariné, e** (rine) *a*, sea-damaged. **mariner** (ne) *v.t*, to pickle; souse.

maringouin (marɛ̃gwɛ̃) *m*, mosquito.

marinier (marinje) *m*, bargeman, bargee.

marionnette (marjɔnɛt) *f*, puppet, marionette.

marital, eⁱ (marital) *a*, marital.

maritime (maritim) *a*, maritime, marine, sea (*att.*); shipping (*att.*); ship (*canal, broker, &c*); naval.

maritorne (maritɔrn) *f*, slut, slattern.

marivauder (marivode) *v.i*, to bandy flirtatious remarks.

marjolaine (marʒɔlɛn) *f*, [sweet] marjoram.

marli (marli) *m*, marli (*gauze & plate rim*).

marmaille (marma:j) *f.col*, children, brats.

Marmara (mer de) (marmara), Sea of Marmora.

marmelade (marmǝlad) *f*, preserve, marmalade. ~ *de pommes, de prunes*, stewed apples, plums. *en* ~, reduced to a pulp (*as cooked meat*); to (*or* in) a jelly (*as face by blow*).

marmenteaux (marmɑ̃to) *m.pl*, ornamental trees.

marmitage (marmita:ʒ) *m*, shelling (*Artil.*).

marmite (marmit) *f*, boiler, pot; pot hole (*Geol.*); heavy shell (*Artil.*). ~ *autoclave*, steamer, steam cooker. **marmiter** (te) *v.t*, to shell. **marmiteux, euse** (tø, ø:z) *a. & n*, miserable (wretch). **marmiton** (tɔ̃) *m*, kitchen boy; scullion.

marmonner (marmɔne) *v.t*, to grumble about.

marmot, te (marmo, ɔt) *n*, youngster, kiddy, chit; (*f.*) marmot (*Zool.*); kerchief. **marmotter** (mɔte) *v.t*, to mutter, mumble.

marmouset (marmuzɛ) *m*, little fellow; firedog.

marne (marn) *f*, marl. **marner** (ne) *v.t*, to marl. **marneux, euse** (nø, ø:z) *a*, marly. **marnière** (njɛːr) *f*, marl pit.

Maroc (le) (marɔk), Morocco. **marocain, e** (kɛ̃, ɛn) *a. & M*~, *n*, Moroccan.

maronner (marɔne) *v.i*, to grumble.

maroquin (marɔkɛ̃) *m*, morocco [leather]. **maroquinerie** (kinri) *f*, fancy leather goods; f. l. shop.

marotique (marɔtik) *a*, archaic, quaint.

marotte (marɔt) *f*, bauble (*Hist.*), cap & bells; milliner's head; hairdresser's head; pet theory, weakness, craze, [mono]mania.

marquant, e (markɑ̃, ɑ̃:t) *p.a*, prominent, outstanding; of note, leading. **marque** (mark) *f*, mark; stamp; brand; pit (*smallpox*); score; book mark[er]; badge; token; tally. ~ *de commerce, de fabrique*, trade mark. ~ *déposée*, registered t. m. ~ *typographique*, colophon. *de* ~, branded, by well known (*or* leading) maker(s); high-class. **marqué, e** (ke) *p.a*, marked; decided. **marquer** (ke) *v.t*, to mark; stamp; brand; score; show; (*v.i.*) to stand out. ~ *le pas*, to mark time. ~ *un but*, to kick (*or* score) a goal (*Foot.*).

marqueter (markǝte) *v.t*, to speckle, spot; inlay. **marqueterie** (kɛtri) *f*, marquet-[e]ry, inlaid work; mosaic; patchwork.

marqueur, euse (markœ:r, ø:z) (*pers.*) *n*, marker; scorer.

marquis (marki) *m*, marquis, -quess. **marquise** (ki:z) *f*, marchioness; marquise; canopy (*Arch.*); awning.

marraine (marɛn) *f*, godmother, sponsor.

marron (marɔ̃) *m*, chestnut; maroon (*firework*); marron (*glacé*); (*att.*) maroon (*colour*). ~ *d'Inde*, horse chestnut.

marron, ne (marɔ̃, ɔn) *a*, [run] wild (*animal*); outside (*broker*); unlicensed; unqualified; pirate (*publisher*). *nègre marron, négresse marronne*, maroon. **marronnage** (rɔna:ʒ) *m*, running away (*slaves*).

marronnier (marɔnje) *m*, chestnut [tree]. ~ *d'Inde*, horse chestnut [tree].

marrube (maryb) *m*, horehound.

mars (mars) *m*, March. **M**~, Mars, warfare.

marseillais, e (marsɛjɛ, ɛ:z) *a. & M*~, *n*, Marseillais, e. *la Marseillaise*, the Marseillaise (*hymn*). **Marseille** (sɛ:j) *f*, Marseilles.

marsouin (marswɛ̃) *m*, porpoise; colonial infantryman.

marsupial (marsypjal) *m*, marsupial.

marteau (marto) *m*, hammer. ~ *d'eau*, water h. ~ *de porte*, door knocker. ~*-pilon*, power hammer. **martel en tête** (tɛl) *m*, uneasiness, worry. **martelé, e** (tǝle) (*fig.*) *p.a*, laboured; strongly stressed. **marteler** (le) *v.t. & abs*, to hammer. *se* ~ [*le cerveau*], to make one uneasy, worry one.

martial, eⁱ (marsjal) *a*, martial, warlike.

martinet (martinɛ) *m*, swift (*bird*); tilt hammer; scourge (*whip*).

martingale (martɛ̃gal) *f*, martingale (*Harness, Betting*); betting system.

martin-pêcheur (martɛ̃pɛʃœ:r) *ou* **martinet-pêcheur** (tinɛ) *m*, kingfisher.

martre (martr) *f*, marten. ~ *zibeline*, sable (*Zool.*).

martyr, eⁱ (marti:r) *n*, martyr; victim. **martyre**, *m*, martyrdom; torment. **martyriser** (tirize) *v.t*, to martyr[ize]; torture.

martyrologe (rɔlɔ:ʒ) *m*, martyrology (*list*).

mascarade (maskarad) f, masquerade.

mascaret (maskarɛ) m, [tidal] bore. *un ~ humain*, shoals of people.

mascaron (maskarɔ̃) m, mascaron, mask.

mascotte (maskɔt) f, mascot, charm.

masculin, e (maskylɛ̃, in) a, male; masculine. ¶ m, masculine [gender]. **masculinité** (linite) f, masculinity; male descent.

masque (mask) m, mask; blind; features; masker, -quer. *à gaz*, gas mask, respirator. ¶ f, hussy, minx. **masquer** (ke) v.t, to mask; cover, conceal. **se ~**, to masquerade.

massacrant, e (masakrɑ̃, ɑ̃:t) a, very bad (*temper*). **massacre** (kr) m, massacre, slaughter. **massacrer** (kre) v.t, to massacre, slaughter; smash; murder; botch. **massacreur, euse** (krœ:r, ø:z) n, slaughterer; smasher; botcher.

massage (masa:ʒ) m, massage.

masse (mas) f, mass, lump; solid; body; bulk; aggregate; funds; fund; sledge [hammer]; mace (*ceremonial*). *~ [d'armes]*, mace (*Hist.*). *~ d'eau*, reed mace, bulrush. *à la ~* (*Elec.*), earthed, connected to frame.

massepain (maspɛ̃) m, marzipan.

masser (mase) v.t, to mass; massage.

massette (masɛt) f, reed mace, bulrush.

masseur, euse (masœ:r, ø:z) n, masseur, euse.

massicot (masiko) m, lead ochre; guillotine (*for paper cutting*).

massier, ère (masje, ɛ:r) n, treasurer; (m.) mace bearer.

massif, ive† (masif, i:v) a, massive; bulky; heavy; solid. ¶ m, [solid] mass; block; body; clump; massif.

massue (masy) f, club, bludgeon.

mastic (mastik) m, mastic; putty.

mastication (mastikasjɔ̃) f, mastication. **mastiquer** (ke) v.t, to masticate; putty.

mastoc (mastɔk) a.inv, lumpish.

mastodonte (mastɔdɔ̃:t) m, mastodon; elephant[ine person].

mastoïde (mastɔid) a, mastoid.

masure (mazy:r) f, hovel, ruin.

mat, e (mat) a, a mat (*colour, &c*), unpolished, lustreless, dead, flat, dull.

mat (mat) a.m, checkmated. *faire ~*, to [check]mate (*Chess*).

mât (mɑ) m, mast; pole. *~ de charge*, derrick (*ship's*). *~ de cocagne* (kɔkaɲ), greasy pole. *~ de fortune*, jury mast. *~ de hune*, topmast. *~ de misaine*, foremast. *~ de pavillon*, flagstaff. *~ de pavoisement* (pavwazmɑ̃), Venetian mast. *~ de signaux*, signal post. *~ de tente*, tent pole.

matador (matadɔ:r) m, matador (*pers. & games*); magnate (*Fin., &c*).

matamore (matamɔ:r) m, swaggerer.

match (matʃ) m, match (*boxing, wrestling, tennis, football, chess, &c*). *~ aller*, first match. *~ nul*, draw[n game]. *~ retour*, return match.

matelas (matlɑ) m, mattress. **matelasser** (lase) v.t, to stuff, pad. **matelassier, ère** (sje, ɛ:r) n, mattress maker.

matelot (matlo) m, sailor, seaman. *~ coq*, cook's mate. *~ de deuxième classe, able[-bodied] seaman. *~ de pont*, deck hand. *~ de première classe*, leading seaman. *~ de troisième classe*, ordinary s. [*vaisseau*] *~*, consort (*Navy*).

mater (mate) v.t, to [check]mate (*Chess*); mortify; humble.

mâter (mɑte) v.t, to mast (*a ship*); toss (*oars*).

matérialiser (materjalize) v.t, to materialize. **matérialisme** (lism) m, materialism. **matérialiste** (list) n, materialist. ¶ a, materialistic. **matériaux** (rjo) m.pl, materials. *~ d'empierrement pour routes*, road metal. **matériel, le†** (rjɛl) a, material, physical, bodily. ¶ m, plant, material, stock. *~ roulant*, rolling stock.

maternel, le† (matɛrnɛl) a, maternal, motherly; mother's (*side*); mother, native (*tongue*). **maternité** (nite) f, maternity, motherhood; maternity hospital, lying-in hospital.

mathématicien, ne (matematisjɛ̃, ɛn) n, mathematician. **mathématique†** (tik) a, mathematical. *~s, f.pl*, mathematics. *~ spéciales*, higher mathematics.

matière (matjɛ:r) f, matter; material, stuff; type metal; subject; grounds; gravamen. *~ à réflexion*, food for thought. *~s d'or & d'argent*, bullion. *~ médicale*, materia medica. *~s premières*, raw material[s] (*used in trade*).

matin (matɛ̃) m, morning. *un de ces ~s*, one of these fine days. ¶ ad, early.

mâtin (mɑtɛ̃) m, mastiff; large watch dog; rascal.

matinal, e (matinal) a, [up] early, early riser (*être = to be an*); morning (*att.*).

mâtiné, e (mɑtine) a, mongrel, cross-bred; mixed.

matinée (matine) f, morning; forenoon; morning performance, matinée; dressing jacket. **matines** (tin) f.pl, mat[t]ins. **matineux, euse** (nø, ø:z) a, [up] early, early riser (*être = to be an*).

matir (mati:r) v.t, to mat, dull. **matité** (tite) f, dullness, deadness.

matois (matwa) a & n, sly (person).

matou (matu) m, tom [cat].

matriarcat (matriarka) m, matriarchy. **matrice** (tris) f, womb; matrix; gangue; die, standard (*weight, measure*). *~ du rôle des contributions*, assessment book (*taxes*). **matricule** (kyl) f, register, roll. [*numéro ~, m*, [regimental] number. **matrimonial, e** (mɔnjal) a, matrimonial. **matrone** (trɔn) f, matron, dame.

maturation (matyrasjɔ̃) f, maturation, ripening.

mâture (mɑty:r) f, masts (*col.*); masting; mast[ing] house.

maturité (matyrite) *f*, maturity, ripeness.

maudire (modi:r) *v.t.ir*, to curse. **maudit, e** (di, it) *p.a*, [ac]cursed, confounded.

maugréer (mogree) *v.i*, to fume, bluster.

Maure (mo:r) *m*, Moor. **m~**, *a*, Moorish. **mauresque** (moresk) *a*, Moresque. ¶ *f*, Morisco, morris [dance].

Maurice [(l'île)] (moris) *f*, Mauritius.

mausolée (mozole) *m*, mausoleum.

maussade (mosad) *a*, sullen, peevish, disgruntled; dull, flat. **maussaderie** (dri) *f*, sullenness, &c; sulks, mumps.

mauvais, e (move, ɛ:z) *a*, bad; ill; evil; nasty; wrong; faulty; broken (*English, French, &c*). **mauvais, comps*: ~ coucheur*, quarrelsome fellow. ~ *œil*, evil eye. ~ *pas*, tight corner; scrape, fix (*fig.*). ~ *plaisant*, sorry jester. ~ *quart d'heure*, bad time [of it], trying time. ~ *service*, disservice. ~ *sujet*, ne'er-do-well, bad lot, scapegrace; bad boy (*Sch.*). ~ *ton*, bad form. **mauvaise, comps*: ~ action*, ill deed. ~ *gestion*, mismanagement, maladministration. ~ *herbe*, weed. ~ *honte*, false shame; bashfulness. ~ *langue*, scandalmonger. **mauvais, ad. & m**, bad.

mauve (mo:v) *f*, mallow. ¶ *m. & att*, mauve.

mauviette (movjɛt) *f*, lark (*bird*); puny creature. **mauvis** (vi) *m*, red wing (*thrush*).

maxillaire (maksillɛ:r) *a*, maxillary, jaw (*bone*).

maxime (maksim) *m*, maxim.

maximum, ma (maksimɔm, ma) *a. & m*, maximum, peak, top (*att.*). ~ *de charge*, burden, burthen (*ship*).

Mayence (majɑ̃:s) *f*, Mayence, Mainz.

mayonnaise (majɔnɛ:z) *f. & att*, mayonnaise.

mazette (mazɛt) *f*, weakling; duffer, rabbit (*at a game*).

mazurka (mazyrka) *f*, mazurka.

me, m' (mə, m) *pn*, me; [to] me; myself. ~ *voici*, here I am.

meâ-culpâ (meakylpa) *m*, peccavi.

méandre (meɑ̃:dr) *m*, meander, winding.

mécanicien (mekanisjɛ̃) *m*, mechanician, mechanist; mechanic; engineman; engine driver; engineer (*ship*); (*att.*) mechanical (*engineer*). ~ *d'avion*, air mechanic. **mécanicienne** (ɛn) *f*, machinist (*sewing*). **mécanique†** (nik) *a*, mechanical; power (*att.*); clockwork (*train, motor car, or other toy*). ¶ *f*, mechanics; mechanism; brake [gear] (*carriage*). *fait à la* ~, machinemade. **mécaniser** (ze) *v.t*, to mechanize, motorize. **mécanisme** (nism) *m*, mechanism, machinery, gear; works (*as of a watch*); technique.

mécène (mesen) *m*, patron (*as of the arts*).

méchant, e (meʃɑ̃, ɑ̃:t) *a*, wicked, evil; ill-natured; unkind; spiteful; mischievous, naughty; wretched, paltry, poor, sorry; unpleasant. ~ *poète*, poetaster. ¶ *n*, wicked, &c, person. **méchamment** (ʃamɑ̃)

ad, wickedly, &c. **méchanceté** (ʃɑ̃te) *f*, wickedness, &c.

mèche (mɛʃ) *f*, wick (*lamp*); tinder; fuse, match; cracker, snapper (*whip*); lock (*hair*); tassel; bit, drill; worm (*corkscrew*); tent (*Surg.*); secret, plot.

mécompte (mekɔ̃:t) *m*, miscalculation, disappointment.

méconnaissable (mekonɛsabl) *a*, unrecognizable. **méconnaître** (nɛ:tr) *v.t.ir*, to fail to recognize *or* diagnose, not to know; disown; disregard, ignore, misunderstand, slight.

mécontent, e (mekɔ̃tɑ̃, ɑ̃:t) *a*, discontent[ed], dissatisfied, disgruntled. ¶ *m*, malcontent. **mécontentement** (tɑ̃tmɑ̃) *m*, discontent[ment], dissatisfaction. **mécontenter** (te) *v.t*, to dissatisfy, displease.

Mecque (la) (mɛk), Mecca.

mécréant, e (mekreɑ̃, ɑ̃:t) *a*, unbelieving. ¶ *n*, unbeliever.

médaille (medɑ:j) *f*, medal; coin (*Greek, Roman*); badge (*porter's*). ~ *d'honneur*, prize medal. **médaillé, e** (daje) *a*, medalled. ¶ *n*, medallist (*recipient*), prize winner. **médailler** (je) *v.t*, to award a medal (to). **médailleur** (jœ:r) *m*, medallist, medal maker. **médaillier** (je) *m*, coin (*or* medal) cabinet; collection of coins *or* medals. **médaillon** (jɔ̃) *m*, medallion; locket.

médecin (medsɛ̃) *m*, medical man, m. officer, physician, surgeon, doctor; (*of time*) healer. ~ *aliéniste* (aljenist), mental specialist. **médecine** (sin) *f*, medicine; surgery; physic. ~ *légale*, medical jurisprudence, forensic medicine.

médiateur, trice (medjatœ:r, tris) *n*, mediator, trix. **médiation** (sjɔ̃) *f*, mediation.

médical, e (medikal) *a*, medical. **médicament** (mɑ̃) *m*, medicament, medicine. **médicamenter** (te) *v.t*, to doctor, physic, dose. **médicamenteux, euse** (tø, ø:z) *a*, medicinal, curative; medicated. **médicastre** (kastr) *m*, medicaster, quack. **médication** (sjɔ̃) *f*, medication. **médicinal, e** (sinal) *a*, medicinal. **médico-légal, e** (kolegal) *a*, medico-judicial.

médiéval, e (medjeval) *a*, medi[a]eval. **médiéviste** (vist) *n*, medi[a]evalist.

médiocre (medjɔkr) *a*, mediocre; poor; middling, moderate. ¶ *m*, mediocrity (*pers. & quality*). **médiocrité** (krite) *f*, mediocrity (*quality*); moderate condition of life.

médire de (medi:r) *v.ir*, to speak ill of, slander. **médisance** (dizɑ̃:s) *f*, slander, backbiting, scandal; scandalmongers. **médisant, e** (zɑ̃, ɑ̃:t) *a*, slanderous. ¶ *n*, slanderer, scandalmonger.

méditatif, ive (meditatif, i:v) *a*, meditative. **méditation** (sjɔ̃) *f*, meditation. **méditer** (te) *v.t. & abs*, to meditate ([up]on), ponder, muse, pore; think; contemplate; plan.

méditerrané, e (mediterane) *a*, mediterranean, land-locked. la [mer] *Méditerranée*, the Mediterranean [sea]. **méditerranéen, ne** (neẽ, ɛn) *a*, Mediterranean.
médium (medjɔm) *m*, middle register (*Mus.*); medium (*Spiritualism*).
médius (medjy:s) *m*, second finger, middle f.
médullaire (medyllɛ:r) *a*, medullary.
méduse (medy:z) *f*, medusa, jelly fish, sea nettle. la tête de M~ (*fig.*), a terrible shock. **méduser** (dyze) *v.t*, to petrify (*fig.*).
meeting (mitiŋ) *m*, meeting (*Pol.*, *Sport*, *social*).
méfait (mefɛ) *m*, misdeed, malpractice.
méfiance (mefjɑ̃:s) *f*, mistrust, distrust. **méfiant, e** (jã, ã:t) *a*, mis- or distrustful. **se méfier de** (fje), to mis- or distrust; beware of.
mégalomanie (megalɔmani) *f*, megalomania.
mégarde (par) (megard) *ad*, inadvertently.
mégère (meʒɛ:r) *f*, termagant, virago, shrew.
mégie (meʒi) & **mégisserie** (sri) *f*, leather dressing, tawing.
meilleur, e (mɛjœ:r) *a*, better. à meilleur marché, cheaper. le ~, la ~, the better, the best. ¶ *m*, best.
Mein (le) (mẽ), the Main (*river*).
mélancolie (melãkɔli) *f*, melancholia; melancholy. **mélancolique†** (lik) *a*, melancholy, melancholic.
Mélanésie (la) (melanezi), Melanesia.
mélange (melã:ʒ) *m*, mixture; blending; medley; mash; (*pl.*) miscellany (*literary*); miscellaneous works. **mélanger** (lãʒe) *v.t*, to mix, mingle, blend. drap mélangé, mixture. laine mélangée, wool mixture.
mélasse (melas) *f*, molasses, treacle. ~ raffinée, golden syrup.
mêlé, e (mele) *p.a*, mixed, miscellaneous, medley. ¶ *f*, fight, mêlée, scrimmage, scrum[mage], scramble. **mêler** (le) *v.t*, to mix, mingle; medley; shuffle (*Cards*); mash. **se** ~, to interfere, meddle.
mélèze (melɛ:z) *m*, larch [tree].
mélodie (melɔdi) *f*, melody. **mélodieux, euse†** (djø, ø:z) *a*, melodious, tuneful.
mélodramatique (melɔdramatik) *a*, melodramatic. **mélodrame** (dram) *m*, melodrama.
melon (məlɔ̃) *m*, melon. [**chapeau**] ~, bowler [hat].
membrane (mãbran) *f*, membrane; web (*bird's foot*). ~ du tympan, ear drum.
membre (mã:br) *m*, member; limb; rib (*ship*). **membré, e** (mãbre) *a*, -limbed. **membrure** (bry:r) *f*, limbs; frame; ribs (*ship*).
même (mɛ:m) *a*. & *pn*, same; like; very; self; itself. ¶ *m*, same [thing]. ¶ *ad*, even, indeed. à ~ de, in a position to, able to. de ~, *ad*, the same, likewise. de ~ que, c, [just] as, like.
mémento (memẽto) *m*, memento, reminder, note; handbook.
mémoire (memwa:r) *f*, memory; recollection;

remembrance; fame. de ~, from memory, by heart. de ~ d'homme, within living memory. pour ~, as a memorandum, no[t] value[d] (*in account*). ¶ *m*, memorandum; paper (*learned*); bill, account; memoir. **mémorable** (mɔrabl) *a*, memorable. **mémorandum** (rãdɔm) *m*, memorandum; memorial (*State paper*). **mémorial** (rjal) *m*, memoirs.
menace (mənas) *f*, threat, menace. **menacer** (se) *v.t. & abs*, to threaten, menace.
ménade (menad) *f*, maenad.
ménage (mena:ʒ) *m*, housekeeping, housewifery; house[hold]; establishment; household goods; home, family; housework. [petit] ~, miniature (*or* dolls') home set. ~ à trois, matrimonial triangle. de ~, household (*bread*); homespun; house *or* domestic (*as coal*); home-made (*as wine*). faire des ~s, to char[e], go out charring. **ménagement** (naʒmã) *m. oft. pl*, care, stint; consideration; deference; tact. **ménager** (ʒe) *v.t*, to husband, manage, economize; save; take care of; look after; make the most of; keep; arrange; make; contrive; bring about; keep in with, humour; handle tactfully; spare. sans ~ les termes, without mincing one's words. **ménager, ère** (ʒe, ɛ:r) *a*, economical, thrifty; careful; sparing; domestic. ¶ *f*, housekeeper, housewife; cruet. **ménagerie** (ʒri) *f*, menagerie.
mendiant, e (mãdjã, ã:t) *n*, beggar; mendicant; (*att.*) mendicant; (*m.pl.*) dessert fruit & nuts. **mendicité** (disite) *f*, begging, mendicancy, mendicity; beggary. **mendier** (dje) *v.i. & t*, to beg; canvass.
meneau (məno) *m*, mullion; transom (*window*).
menée (məne) *f*, (*underhand*) intrigue; track (*Hunt.*). **mener** (ne) *v.t*, to lead, conduct; take, carry; drive; steer; partner (*lady at dance*). mené par sa femme, hen-pecked.
ménestrel (menestrɛl) *m*, minstrel (*Hist.*). **ménétrier** (netrie) *m*, (village) fiddler.
meneur, euse (mənœ:r, ø:z) *n*, leader; ringleader. ~ de train, pacemaker.
menhir (meni:r) *m*, menhir.
méningite (menẽʒit) *f*, meningitis.
menotte (mənɔt) *f*, handy-pandy (*Nursery talk*); (*pl.*) handcuffs, manacles.
mensonge (mãsɔ̃:ʒ) *m*, lie, falsehood, untruth; fiction; vanity. ~ innocent, fib, story. ~ pieux, ~ officieux, white lie. **mensonger, ère†** (sɔʒe, ɛ:r) *a*, lying, mendacious; untrue, false, deceitful.
mensualité (mãsɥalite) *f*, monthly payment, drawing, salary, *or* like. **mensuel, le†** (sɥɛl) *a*, monthly (*a. & ad*).
mensuration (mãsyrasjɔ̃) *f*, mensuration (*of the body*). **mensurer** (re) *v.t*, to measure (*the body*).
mental, e† (mãtal) *a*, mental. **mentalité** (lite) *f*, mentality.

menterie (mɑ̃tri) *f*, story, fib. **menteur, euse** (tœːr, øːz) *n*, liar. ¶ *a*, lying; deceptive.

menthe (mɑ̃ːt) *f*, mint. ~ *poivrée*, peppermint. *pastille de* ~, peppermint [lozenge]. ~ *verte*, spearmint, garden mint. **menthol** (mɑ̃tɔl) *m*, menthol.

mention (mɑ̃sjɔ̃) *f*, mention, reference. **mentionner** (one) *v.t*, to mention, make reference to.

mentir (mɑ̃tiːr) *v.i.ir*, to lie. *sans* ~, to tell the truth (*candidly*).

menton (mɑ̃tɔ̃) *m*, chin. ~ *de* (ou *en*) *galoche*, slipper chin. **M~,** Mentone (Geog.). **mentonnet** (tɔnɛ) *m*, latch catch.

mentor (mɛ̃tɔːr) *m*, mentor.

menu, e (məny) *a*, small; slight; petty; minor (*repairs*); minute; fine. *le menu peuple*, the humbler classes. *menu plomb*, bird shot. *menue paille*, chaff. *menues herbes*, fine herbs (*fine in texture, as savoury herbs*). *menus plaisirs*, occasional expenses. *menus propos*, small talk. **menu,** *ad*, small, fine. ¶ *m*, fare; menu, bill of fare. *par le* ~, in detail. **menuet** (nɥɛ) *m*, minuet. **menuiser** (nɥize) *v.i*, to carpenter. **menuiserie** (zri) *f*, joinery; cabinet making, c. work; woodwork. **menuisier** (zje) *m*, joiner; carpenter; cabinet maker; woodworker.

méphitique (mefitik) *a*, mephitic, noxious, dank.

méplat, e (mepla, at) *a. & m*, flat.

méprendre (se) (meprɑ̃:dr) *v.pr.ir*, to be mistaken. *se* ~ *sur*, to mistake.

mépris (mepri) *m*, contempt, scorn. **méprisable** (zabl) *a*, contemptible, despicable, scurvy; disregardable. **méprisant, e** (zɑ̃, ɑ̃:t) *a*, contemptuous, scornful. **méprise** (priːz) *f*, mistake; oversight. **mépriser** (prize) *v.t*, to despise, scorn; disregard, scoff at.

mer (mɛːr) *f*, sea, ocean. ~ *du Nord*, North sea, German ocean. *Note.*—For other seas, see under proper name, e.g, *la mer Égée*, under *Égée*. *un homme à la* ~! [a] man overboard!

mercanti (mɛrkɑ̃ti) *m*, profiteer. **mercantile** (til) *a*, mercantile, mercenary. **mercantilisme** (lism) *m*, mercantilism, commercialism.

mercenaire (mɛrsənɛːr) *a*, mercenary. ¶ *m*, mercenary, hireling; [paid] worker.

mercerie (mɛrsri) *f*, haberdashery. **mercerisé, e** (ze) *a*, mercerized.

merci (mɛrsi) *f*, mercy; (m.) thanks. ¶ *i*, thanks! thank you!; no, thank you! *Dieu* ~! thank God!

mercier, ère (mɛrsje, ɛːr) *n*, haberdasher.

mercredi (mɛrkrədi) *m*, Wednesday. *le* ~ *des Cendres*, Ash Wednesday.

mercure (mɛrkyːr) *m*, mercury, quicksilver. **mercuriale** (kyrjal) *f*, mercury (*Bot.*); reprimand; official list (*corn, &c*;

prices). **mercuriel, e** (rjɛl) *a*, mercurial, blue (*pill*).

mère (mɛːr) *f*, mother; parent (*lit. & fig.*); dam. *notre* ~ *commune*, mother earth. ~ *abeille*, queen bee. ~ *branche*, bough, limb. *la* ~ *Gigogne* (ʒigɔɲ), the Old Woman who lived in a shoe. *une* ~ *Gigogne*, the mother of many children. ~ *patrie*, parent state. *l'idée* ~, the main idea (*of book*).

méridien, ne (meridjɛ̃, ɛn) *a*, meridian. ¶ *m*, meridian (*as of Greenwich*); (*f.*) siesta; couch. **méridional, e** (djɔnal) *a*, meridional, southern, south. ¶ (*pers.*) *n*, meridional, southerner.

meringue (mərɛ̃ːg) *f*, meringue.

mérinos (merinos) *m*, merino.

merise (məriːz) *f*, wild cherry, merry. **merisier** (rizje) *m*, wild cherry [tree].

méritant, e (meritɑ̃, ɑ̃:t) *a*, deserving, meritorious. **mérite** (rit) *m*, merit, desert, worth. **mériter** (te) *v.t*, to merit, deserve; be worth; earn; require. **méritoire** (twaːr) *a*, meritorious.

merlan (mɛrlɑ̃) *m*, whiting (*fish*).

merle (mɛrl) *m*, blackbird; ouzel, ousel. *c'est le* ~ *blanc*, he is a strange mixture (*of qualities*). *je vous donnerai le* (ou *un*) ~ *blanc*, I'll eat my hat (*if you can do that*). **merlette** (lɛt) *f*, [hen] blackbird.

merlin (mɛrlɛ̃) *m*, cleaving axe (*wood*); pole axe.

merluche (mɛrlyʃ) *f*, dried cod; dried hake. **merlus** (ly) *m*, hake.

merrain (mɛrɛ̃) *m*, stave wood.

merveille (mɛrvɛːj) *f*, marvel, wonder. *à* ~, excellently; wonderfully; capitally. **merveilleux, euse†** (vejø, øːz) *a*, marvellous, wonderful. *le* ~, the marvellous; the wonderful part. ¶ (*pers.*) (*Hist.*) *n*, merveilleux, euse, fop.

mésalliance (mezaljɑ̃:s) *f*, misalliance. **mésallier** (lje) *v.t*, to misally. *se* ~, to make a misalliance.

mésange (mezɑ̃:ʒ) *f*, tit[mouse]. ~ *charbonnière*, great tit, tomtit.

mésaventure (mezavɑ̃ty:r) *f*, misadventure, mishap.

mésestime (mezɛstim) *f*, disrepute. **mésestimer** (me) *v.t*, to undervalue, underestimate, underrate.

mésintelligence (mezɛ̃teliʒɑ̃:s) *f*, variance; misunderstanding.

mesquin, e† (mɛskɛ̃, in) *a*, mean, shabby; poky; stingy, niggardly; paltry; scanty. **mesquinerie** (kinri) *f*, meanness, &c.

mess (mɛs) *m*, mess (*officers', sergeants'*).

message (mɛsa:ʒ) *m*, message; errand. **messager, ère** (saʒe, ɛːr) *n*, messenger; (*m.*) carrier; harbinger. **messagerie** (ʒri) *f. oft. pl*, parcels [service]; mail, passenger & parcels service.

messe (mɛs) *f*, mass (*Eccl.*). ~ *basse*, low m. ~ *chantée*, high m.

messeoir (mɛswaːr) *v.i.ir*, to be unbecoming.
Messie (mɛsi) *m*, Messiah.
messieurs, *oft.* **M~** (mesjø), pl. of *monsieur*, messieurs, Messrs.
Messine (mɛsin) *f*, Messina.
mesurage (məzyraːʒ) *m*, measurement.
mesure (zyːr) *f*, measure; measurement; size; (*pl.*) mensuration; extent; metre (*Poet.*); time (*Mus.*); measure, (*& commonly but wrongly*) bar (*Mus.*); bounds; propriety. *à ~*, in proportion. *à ~ que*, [according] as. *en ~ de*, able to. *sur ~*, to measure, bespoke. **mesuré, e** (zyre) *a*, guarded (*language*). **mesurer** (re) *v.t*, to measure; weigh (*fig.*); proportion.
métairie (metɛri) *f*, farm worked on shares.
métal (metal) *m*, metal. *~ anglais*, Britannia m. **métallifère** (tallifɛːr) *a*, metalliferous. **métallique** (tallik) *a*, metallic; iron &/or steel; wire (*att.*); spring (*att.*). **métallurgie** (tallyrʒi) *f*, metallurgy. **métallurgiste** (ʒist) *m*, metallurgist.
métamorphose (metamɔrfoːz) *f*, metamorphosis. **métamorphoser** (foze) *v.t*, to metamorphose.
métaphore (metafɔːr) *f*, metaphor. *~ incohérente*, mixed m. **métaphorique†** (forik) *a*, metaphorical.
métaphysicien (metafizisjɛ̃) *m*, metaphysician. **métaphysique** (zik) *f*, metaphysics. ¶ *a*, metaphysical.
métayage (meteja:ʒ) *m*, cultivation on shares.
météore (meteoːr) *m*, meteor. **météorique** (ɔrik) *a*, meteoric. **météorologie** (rɔlɔʒi) *f*, meteorology. **météorologique** (ʒik) *a*, meteorologic(al); weather (*forecast, &c*).
méthode (metɔd) *f*, method, way, system. **méthodique†** (dik) *a*, methodical. **méthodisme** (dism) *m*, methodism. **méthodiste** (dist) *n*, methodist.
méthyle (metil) *m*, methyl (*Chem.*).
méticuleux, euse† (metikylø, øːz) *a*, meticulous, punctilious.
métier (metje) *m*, trade; craft; profession, business, calling, line; experience; loom; frame (*Need.*). *~ à broder*, embroidery hoops; tambour frame. *~ de tailleur*, tailoring. *sur le ~* (*fig.*), on the stocks, on hand. *faire son ~*, to mind one's own business.
métis, se (metis) *a*, half-bred; cross-bred; mongrel; hybrid (*Bot.*). ¶ *n*, half-breed; cross; mongrel. **métissage** (tisaːʒ) *m*, cross-breeding.
métonymie (metɔnimi) *f*, metonymy.
métrage (metraːʒ) *m*, measurement, measuring; length (*in metres*); [quantity] surveying. **mètre** (mɛtr) *m*, metre (*verse*); metre = 39·370113 inches; metre measure or tape or stick (1 *metre long*). *~ carré*, square metre = 10·7639 sq. feet. *~ cube*, cubic metre = 35·3148 cub. feet. **métrer** (metre) *v.t*, to measure, survey. **métreur** (trœːr) *m*, [quantity] surveyor. **métrique** (trik) *a*, metrical; metric. ¶ *f*, metrics, prosody.

métronome (metrɔnɔm) *m*, metronome.
métropole (metrɔpɔl) *f*, metropolis; mother country, home c. **métropolitain, e** (litɛ̃, ɛn) *a*, metropolitan; mother (*church*); home, domestic.
mets (mɛ) *m*, dish, food, viand.
mettable (mɛtabl) *a*, wearable. **metteur** (tœːr) *m*: *~ en œuvre*, stone (*gem*) setter; adapter (*pers., fig.*). *~ en pages*, makerup (*Typ.*). *~ en scène*, producer. **mettre** (tr) *v.t.ir*, to put; place; lay; stake; set; poke; draw; make; bring; reduce; put on, wear; tear; take; throw. *~ à l'encre*, to ink in. *~ à la retraite*, to pension. *~ au point*, to focus; adjust; tune up. *~ bas*, to take off (*hat, &c*); drop, foal, whelp. *~ dedans*, to humbug, bamboozle. *~ en accusation*, to arraign, commit for trial. *~ en commun*, to pool. ¶ *les pouces*, to knuckle under. *se ~*, to put oneself; sit [down]; lie [down]; begin; take to; dress; get; go; set. *se ~ en habit pour dîner*, to dress for dinner. *se ~ par quatre*, to form fours. *se ~ sur deux rangs*, to form two deep.
meuble (mœbl) *a*, movable (*property*); light, loose, mellow (*earth*). ¶ *m*, piece of furniture; suite [of f.]; cabinet; (*pl.*) furniture; movables (*Law*). *~-classeur*, filing cabinet. *~ de famille*, heirloom. *~ phonographe*, cabinet gramophone. *~ T.S.F.*, wireless cabinet. **meublé** (ble) *m*, lodgings. **meubler** (ble) *v.t*, to furnish; stock, store (*fig.*).
meugler (møgle) *v.i*, to bellow, low.
meule (møːl) *f*, wheel (*emery, &c*); (*circular*) stack or rick (*hay, &c*); cake (*of gruyère cheese*). *~ [de moulin]*, millstone. *~ de dessous*, *~ gisante*, bedstone. *~ de dessus*, *~ courante*, runner. *~ en grès*, grindstone. **meulière** (møljɛːr) *f*, millstone grit; m. g. quarry. **meulon** (lɔ̃) *m*, cock (*hay*).
meunerie (mønri) *f*, milling (*flour*). **meunier, ère** (nje, ɛːr) *n*, miller; (*m.*) chub (*fish*).
meurt-de-faim (mœrdəfɛ̃) *m*, starveling.
meurtre (mœrtr) *m*, murder; sin, shame (*vandalism*). **meurtrier, ère** (trie, ɛːr) *a*, murderous; internecine; deadly. ¶ *n*, murderer, ess; (*f.*) loophole.
meurtrir (mœrtriːr) *v.t*, to bruise. **meurtrissure** (trisyːr) *f*, bruise.
meute (møːt) *f*, pack (*hounds, enemies*).
mévente (mevã:t) *f*, slump [in trade]; negligible sales (*enabling publisher to close account with author*).
mexicain, e (mɛksikɛ̃, ɛn) *a. & M~*, *n*, Mexican. **Mexico** (ko) *m*, Mexico [City]. **le Mexique** (sik), Mexico (*country*).
mezzo-soprano (mɛdzosoprano) *m*, mezzo-soprano.
mi (mi) *m*, E (*Mus.*). ¶ *word inv*, half, mid. *mi-bas*, *m.pl*, half hose, socks. *la mi-carême*, mid-lent. *à mi-chemin*, midway,

half way. *à mi-corps*, to the waist, waist-high *or* deep. *à mi-côte*, half way up [the hill]. **mi-fil**, *m*, union (*linen & cotton thread*). *la mi-juin*, *&c*, mid June, *&c*. **mi-lourd**, light-heavy (*Box.*). **mi-moyen**, welter (*Box.*). **mi-parti**, *e*, equally divided; half . . . *& half* . . . *la mi-temps*, half time (*Foot.*).

miasmatique (mjasmatik) *a*, malarial. **miasme** (asm) *m*, miasma.

miauler (mjole) *v.i*, to miaow, mew.

mica (mika) *m*, mica.

miche (miʃ) *f*, round loaf (*bread*).

micmac (mikmak) *m*, dirty work (*fig.*).

microbe (mikrɔb) *m*, microbe.

micromètre (mikrɔmɛtr) *m*, micrometer.

microphone (mikrɔfɔn) *m*, microphone.

microscope (mikrɔskɔp) *m*, microscope. *~ d'étude*, students' m. **microscopique** (pik) *a*, microscopic(al).

midi (midi) *m*, noon, midday, noonday, twelve o'clock [in the day]; noontide; heyday (*of life*); south.

mie (mi) *f*, crumb (*bread*, opp. *crust*).

miel (mjɛl) *m*, honey. **mielleux, euse†** (lø, ø:z) *a*, bland; mealy-mouthed; honeyed; mawkish.

mien, ne (*with* le, la, les) (mjɛ̃, ɛn) *pn. & m*, mine; my own.

miette (mjɛt) *f*, crumb (*broken bread, &c*); bit, atom.

mieux (mjø) *ad. & a*, better; rather; more; best; better-looking. **le ~**, *ad*, the best. **le ~**, *m*, [the] best.

mièvre (mjɛ:vr) *a*, [childishly] affected, finical.

mignard, e (miɲar, ard) *a*, mincing; girlish. **mignardise** (nardi:z) *f*, daintiness; affectation; (*pl.*) pretty ways; pink (*Bot.*).

mignon, ne (ɲ5, ɔn) *a*, dainty, petite; sweet; pet. ¶ *n*, pet, darling; (*m.*) minion. **mignonnette** (nɔnɛt) *f*, mignonette (*lace*); pink (*Bot.*); gimp nails; ground pepper; broken pebblestone.

migraine (migrɛn) *f*, migraine, bad headache. **migrateur, trice** (migratœ:r, tris) *a*, migratory; migrant. **migration** (sjɔ̃) *f*, migration.

mijaurée (miʒɔre) *f*, affected woman.

mijoter (miʒɔte) *v.t*, to [let] simmer; (*v.i.*) to simmer. **se ~**, to be brewing.

mil (mil) *m*, mil[le] (*1000*); millet; Indian club. ¶ *a*, thousand (*dates*).

milan (milɑ̃) *m*, kite (*bird*).

Milan (milɑ̃) *m*, Milan. **milanais, e** (lanɛ, ɛ:z) *a. & M~*, *n*, Milanese.

mildiou (mildju) *m*, mildew (*on vines*).

milice (milis) *f*, militia. **milicien** (sjɛ̃) *m*, militiaman.

milieu (miljø) *m*, middle, midst, centre; mean; medium; circle, milieu. *~ de table*, table centre. *au ~ de*, in the midst of, amidst, among. *au ~ des airs*, in mid air. *au ~ du navire*, amidships.

militaire† (milite:r) *a*, military. ¶ *m*, soldier,

military man. *les ~s*, the military. **militant, e** (tɑ̃, ɑ̃:t) *a*, militant. ¶ *m*, fighter. **militariser** (tarize) *v.t*, to militarize. **militer** (te) *v.i*, to militate, tell.

mille (mil) *m. & a. inv*, (a *or* one) thousand; mile. *les M~ & une Nuits*, the Arabian nights. **mille-feuille** *ou* **millefeuille** (fœ:j) *f*, milfoil, yarrow; (*m.*) Genoese pastry. **millénaire** (millenɛ:r) *a. & m*, millenary (*a. & n.*); millennium (*n.*). **mille-pertuis** *ou* **millepertuis** (milpɛrtɥi) *m*, St-John's-wort. **mille-pieds** (pje) *ou* **mille-pattes** (pat) *m*, millepede.

millésime (millezim) *m*, date, year.

millet (mijɛ) *m*, millet grass; millet. *~ des oiseaux*, canary seed.

milliard (milja:r) *m*, milliard, 1,000,000,000 francs. **milliardaire** (jardɛ:r) *n. & a*, multi-millionaire.

milliasse (miljas) *f*, swarm[s].

millième (miljɛm) *a. & m*, thousandth. **millier** (je) *m*, thousand [or so]. **milligramme** (milligram) *m*, milligram[me] = 0·015 grain. **millimètre** (millimɛtr) *m*, millimetre = 0·03937 inch.

million (miljɔ̃) *m*, million; 1,000,000 francs. **millionième** (jɔnjɛm) *a. & m*, millionth. **millionnaire** (nɛ:r) *n*, millionaire.

mime (mim) *m*, mime; mimic. **mimer** (me) *v.t. & abs*, to mime; mimic. **mimétisme** (metism) *m*, mimicry (*Zool.*), mimesis. **mimique** (mik) *a*, mimic. ¶ *f*, mimicry.

mimosa (mimoza) *m*, mimosa.

minable (minabl) *a*, pitiable; wretched.

minauder (minode) *v.i*, to mince, simper, smirk. **minauderie** (dri) *f*, mincing, &c. **minaudier, ère** (dje, ɛ:r) *a*, mincing, &c.

mince (mɛ̃:s) *a*, thin, slender; slight. **minceur** (mɛ̃sœ:r) *f*, thinness, &c.

mine (min) *f*, appearance, countenance, face, mien, look, looks. *de bonne ~*, good-looking.

mine (min) *f*, mine (*lit. & fig.*); mint (*fig.*); lead (*pencil*). *~ de plomb*, black lead. **miner** (ne) *v.t*, to mine; undermine; sap; hollow; wear; prey [up]on (*mind*). **minerai** (nrɛ) *m*, ore. **minéral, e** (neral) *a. & m*, mineral; inorganic (*chemistry*). **minéralogie** (lɔʒi) *f*, mineralogy. **minéralogique** (ʒik) *a*, mineralogical. **minéralogiste** (ʒist) *m*, mineralogist.

minet, te (minɛ, ɛt) *n*, puss[y].

mineur (minœ:r) *m*, miner; sapper (*Mil.*). **mineur, e** (minœ:r) *a*, minor; under age. ¶ *n*, minor (*pers.*); infant (*Law*); (*m.*) minor (*Mus.*); (*f.*) minor premiss (*Log.*).

miniature (minjaty:r) *f*, miniature. **miniaturiste** (tyrist) *n*, miniaturist.

minier, ère (minje, ɛ:r) *a*, mining (*att.*). ¶ *f*, gangue, matrix; surface mine, diggings.

minime (minim) *a*, minute, trifling, trivial.

minimum, ma (minimɔm, ma) *a. & m*, minimum.

ministère (ministɛːr) m, ministry; office; secretaryship; board; agency, services, good offices, ministration. M~ de l'Air, Air Ministry. M~ de Santé publique, M. of Health. M~ de l'Intérieur (Fr.), Home Office (Eng.). M~ de la Guerre, War Office. M~ de la Marine, Admiralty [Office]. M~ des Affaires étrangères, Foreign Office. M~ des Colonies, Colonial Office. M~ des Finances, Treasury Board. M~ des Travaux publics, Office of Works. M~ du Commerce, Board of Trade. ~ public, public prosecutor. ministériel, le (terjɛl) a, ministerial; State nominated (officer); Government (organ). ministre (tr) m, minister; secretary [of state]; clergyman, vicar. ~ de l'Education nationale (Fr.), President of the Board of Education (Eng.). ~ de l'Intérieur, Secretary of State for Home Affairs, Home Secretary. ~ de la Guerre, Secretary of State for War. ~ de la Marine, First Lord of the Admiralty. ~ des Finances, Chancellor of the Exchequer. ~ des Travaux publics, First Commissioner of Works. ~ du Commerce, President of the Board of Trade.

minium (minjom) m, minium; red lead.

minois (minwa) m, face, looks.

minon (minɔ̃) & minou (nu) m, puss[y].

minorité (minorite) f, minority; nonage; infancy (Law).

Minorque (minork) f, Minorca.

minoterie (minɔtri) f, [flour] milling; flour mill. minotier (tje) m, miller; flour merchant.

minuit (minɥi) m, midnight, twelve o'clock [at night].

minuscule (minyskyl) a, minute, tiny. ¶ f, small letter.

minute (minyt) f, minute; small hand (writing); original; draft. minuter (te) v.t, to minute, draw [up], draft.

minutie (minysi) f, trifle, (pl.) minutiae; minuteness, great care. minutieux, euse† (sjø, øːz) a, meticulous; minute, thorough.

mioche (mjɔʃ) m, youngster, kiddy.

mirabelle (mirabɛl) f, mirabelle [plum].

miracle (miraːkl) m, miracle; marvel; miracle [play], mystery [play]. à ~, admirably. miraculeux, euse† (rakylø, øːz) a, miraculous; marvellous.

mirage (miraːʒ) m, mirage; testing, candling (eggs). mire (miːr) f, sight (gun); levelling staff. mirer (mire) v.t. & abs, to aim at, take aim; test, candle (eggs). se ~, to look at oneself; see oneself reflected.

mirifique (mirifik) a, marvellous.

mirliflore (mirliflɔːr) m, spark, dandy.

mirliton (mirlitɔ̃) m, mirliton (musical toy pipe).

mirobolant, e (mirobolɑ̃, ɑ̃ːt) a, wonderful.

miroir (mirwaːr) m, mirror, [looking] glass. ~ d'eau, ornamental lake. ~ défor-

mant, distorting mirror. ~ rétroviseur (retrɔvizøːr), driving mirror. miroiter (rwate) v.i, to flash, gleam, glisten, glint, sparkle. miroiterie (tri) f, mirror trade. miroitier (tje) m, mirror manufacturer or dealer.

misanthrope (mizɑ̃trɔp) m, misanthrope, -pist. ¶ ~ & misanthropique (pik) a, misanthropic(al).

mise (miːz) f, putting, &c, as mettre; stake (gaming); bid (auction); get-up. ~ à prix, reserve [price], upset p. ~ à terre, landing. ~ au point, focussing; adjustment. ~ [de fonds], putting up of money; investment; capital; stake. ~ [de]hors, disbursement. ~ en accusation, indictment. ~ en marche, starting. ~ en œuvre, application. ~ en pages, making up; page proof. ~ en scène, staging; production; setting. ~ en train, starting; making ready (Typ.); practice (Sport). de ~, in fashion; current; admissible; suitable; the thing. miser (mize) v.t. & i, to stake, bid.

misérable† (mizerabl) a, miserable; wretched; unfortunate; worthless. ¶ n, unfortunate, poor wretch; villain, scoundrel. misère (zɛːr) f, misery, wretchedness, distress, destitution; misfortune; trifle; misère (Cards). ~ de santé, ailment. miserere (zerere) m, miserere. miséreux, euse (zerø, øːz) a. & n, poverty-stricken (person).

miséricorde (mizerikɔrd) f, mercy; misericord. ¶ i, mercy on us! good gracious! miséricordieux, euse† (djø, øːz) a, merciful.

misogyne (mizɔʒin) a, misogynic. ¶ m, misogynist, woman hater.

missel (misɛl) m, missal.

mission (misjɔ̃) f, mission. missionnaire (ɔnɛːr) m, missionary. missive (siːv) f, missive.

mistral (mistral) m, mistral (wind).

mitaine (mitɛn) f, mitten; (pl.) caution.

mite (mit) f, mite (insect); moth. miteux, euse (tø, øːz) a, shabby.

mitiger (mitiʒe) v.t, to mitigate, temper.

mitonner (mitone) v.t. & i, to simmer.

mitoyen, ne (mitwajɛ̃, ɛn) a, party (wall, structure). mitoyenneté (jɛnte) f, party rights.

mitraille (mitraːj) f, grape shot; gun firing. mitrailleur (trajœːr) m, machine gunner. mitrailleuse (jøːz) f, machine gun.

mitre (mitr) f, mitre; cowl (chimney). mitré, e (tre) a, mitred. mitron (trɔ̃) m, baker's man.

mixte (mikst) a, mixed; composite; joint; promiscuous. mixtion (tjɔ̃) f, mixture (medicinal). mixture (tyːr) f, mixture; concoction.

mnémonique (mnemɔnik) a, mnemonic. la ~, mnemonics.

mobile (mɔbil) a, movable; portable; flying (column); sliding (scale); adhesive (stamp);

mobile; changeable, fickle. ¶ *m*, moving body (*Mech*.); motive power; prime mover; motive, incentive. **mobilier, ère** (lje, ɛːr) *a*, personal, movable (*Law*); transferable (*securities*). ¶ *m*, furniture, suite [of f.]. **mobilisation** (lizasjɔ̃) *f*, mobilization. **mobiliser** (ze) *v.t. & abs*, to mobilize. **mobilité** (te) *f*. mobility; fickleness.

modalité (modalite) *f*, modality; method. **mode** (mod) *f*, mode, way; fashion, vogue; (*pl*.) millinery. *à la ~ & de ~*, in the fashion, fashionable, modish, stylish. *à la ~*, *ad*, fashionably, modishly, stylishly. ¶ *m*, mode; method; mood (*Gram*.). ~ *d'emploi*, directions for use. ~ *de circulation*, rule of the road.

modelage (modla:ʒ) *m*, modelling; pattern making (*Foundry*). **modèle** (dɛl) *m*, model, pattern; specimen; paragon; (*att*.) model, exemplary. ~ *de broderie*, sampler. **modelé** (dle) *m*, modelling (*relief of forms*). **modeler** (dle) *v.t. & abs*, to model; pattern; mould, shape. **modeleur** (dlœːr) *m*, modeller; pattern maker.

Modène (modɛːn) *f*, Modena.

modération (moderasjɔ̃) *f*, moderation; mitigation. **modéré†**, **e** (re) *a*, moderate. **les modérés**, the moderates (*Pol*.). **modérer** (re) *v.t*, to moderate; check, curb; mitigate.

moderne (modɛrn) *a*, modern; up to date; new (*woman*). **les ~s**, *m.pl*, the moderns. **moderniser** (nize) *v.t*, to modernize.

modeste† (modɛst) *a*, modest; quiet (*dress*). **modestie** (ti) *f*, modesty.

modicité (modisite) *f*, moderateness; lowness.

modification (modifikasjɔ̃) *f*, modification, alteration, variation. **modifier** (fje) *v.t*, to modify, alter, vary.

modique† (modik) *a*, moderate (*price*); small (*sum, &c*).

modiste (modist) *f*, milliner, modiste.

modulation (modylasjɔ̃) *f*, modulation. **module** (dyl) *m*, module; modulus. **moduler** (le) *v.i. & t*, to modulate.

modus vivendi (mody:s vivɛ̃di) *m*, modus vivendi.

moelle (mwal) *f*, marrow; pith. ~ *épinière*, spinal cord. **moelleux, euse†** (lø, øːz) *a*, marrowy; pithy; mellow; soft. ¶ *m*, softness; mellowness.

moellon (mwalɔ̃) *m*, rubble [stone]. ~ *d'appareil*, ashlar.

mœurs (mœrs) *f.pl*, manners, habits; morals, morality.

mohair (mɔɛːr) *m*, mohair.

moi (mwa) *pn*, me; [to] me; I. *à ~! au secours!* help, help! ¶ *m*, self; ego. **~-même**, *pn*, myself; self (*on cheques, &c*).

moignon (mwaɲɔ̃) *m*, stump (*limb, tree*).

moindre (mwɛ̃:dr) *a*, less; lesser; lower; minor. **le, la, ~**, the least; the slightest. **[ne . .] pas le moindrement** (mwɛ̃drəmɑ̃), not in the least.

moine (mwan) *m*, monk, friar; bed warmer. ~ *bourru*, bugaboo, bugbear, goblin, bog[e]y; bear, brute.

moineau (mwano) *m*, sparrow. ~ *franc*, house sparrow.

moinerie (mwanri) *f*, monkhood, monkery.

moins (mwɛ̃) *ad. & pr*, less; not so [much]; fewer; under; minus; to (*of the hour*). [*signe*] ~, *m*, minus [sign]. *à ~ de*, for less than; barring; unless, without. *à ~ que*, unless. *au ~*, at least; however, above all. *le ~*, the least. *pas le ~ du monde*, not in the least. ~ 3, ~ 2, 1 off 3, 1 off 2 (*Golf*). ~ 15 *à rien*, owe 15, love (*Ten*.).

moins-value (mwɛ̃valy) *f*, depreciation; deficit.

moire (mwaːr) *f*, moire, watering. ~ *de soie ou soie moirée* (mware), watered silk, moiré s. **moirer** (re) *v.t*, to water, moiré.

mois (mwa) *m*, month; month's pay, rent, or like. *du ~ dernier*, ultimo. *du ~ prochain*, proximo.

moise (mɔiːz) *m*, wicker cradle.

moise (mwaːz) *f*, brace (*Carp*.); ledger (*Build*.). **moiser** (mwaze) *v.t*, to brace.

moisi, **e** (mwazi) *p.p*, mouldy, mildewy; musty; frowsy. **moisir** (ziːr) *v.t. & i*, & *se ~*, to mildew, turn mouldy. **moisissure** (zisyːr) *f. & moisi* (zi) *m*, mildew, mould, mouldiness, mustiness.

moissine (mwasin) *f*, vine branch with grapes hanging (*as ceiling decoration*).

moisson (mwasɔ̃) *f*, harvest, reaping. **moissonner** (sone) *v.t. & abs*, to reap, harvest; cut off (*fig*.). **moissonneur, euse** (nœːr, øːz) *n*, reaper, harvester (*pers*.); (*f*.) reaping machine, reaper. *moissonneuse-lieuse*, *f*, reaper & binder.

moite (mwat) *a*. moist, damp; clammy. **moiteur** (tœːr) *f*, moistness; clamminess; (*pleasant*) glow (*in the body*).

moitié (mwatje) *f*, half, moiety; better half (*wife*). ¶ *ad*, half, partly. *à ~*, half, by half; on half profits. *à ~ chemin*, half way. *de ~*, by half. *être* (ou *se mettre*) *de ~ avec*, to go halves with.

Moka (moka) *m*, Mocha. *m~ ou café de M~*, mocha, M. coffee; coffee (*ordinary*).

molaire (molɛːr) *a. & f*, molar.

môle (moːl) *m*, mole, breakwater.

moléculaire (molekylɛːr) *a*, molecular. **molécule** (kyl) *f*, molecule.

moleskine (moleskin) *f*, moleskin; oilcloth, American cloth.

molester (moleste) *v.t*, to taunt.

moleter (molte) *v.t*, to mill, knurl. **molette** (lɛt) *f*, rowel; muller; milled nut; knurl; milling tool; cutter wheel.

mollah (molla) *m*, mullah (*pers*.).

mollasse (molas) *a*, flabby; flimsy; spineless (*fig*.). **mollement** (lmɑ̃) *ad*, softly; gracefully; feebly; voluptuously. **mollesse** (lɛs) *f*, softness; mildness; morbidezza; feebleness; flabbiness; overindulgence; voluptuousness. **mollet, te** (lɛ, ɛt) *a*, softish; softboiled (*eggs*); fancy (*roll*). ¶ *m*, calf (*leg*). **molletière** (ltjɛːr) *f*, legging. **molleton** (ltɔ̃) *m*, swan's-down (*cloth*). **mollir** (liːr) *v.i. & t*, to soften; slacken; lull.

mollusque (mɔlysk) *m*, mollusc.

Moluques (les) (mɔlyk) *f.pl*, the Moluccas.

môme (moːm) *n*, youngster.

moment (mɔmɑ̃) *m*, moment; time; momentum. **momentané†, e** (tane) *a*, momentary, temporary.

momerie (mɔmri) *f*, pose (*fig*.); mummery. **momie** (mɔmi) *f*, mummy; sleepyhead. **momifier** (fje) *v.t*, to mummify.

mon, ma, mes (mɔ̃, ma, me) *a*, my. *oui, mon colonel, &c*, yes, sir (*in the army*). **monacal, e†** (mɔnakal) *a*, monastic, monkish. **monarchie** (mɔnarʃi) *f*, monarchy. **monarchique** (ʃik) *a*, monarchic(al). **monarchiste** (ʃist) *m. & att*, monarchist. **monarque** (nark) *m*, monarch.

monastère (mɔnastɛːr) *m*, monastery; convent. **monastique** (tik) *a*, monastic.

monceau (mɔ̃so) *m*, heap, pile.

mondain, e (mɔ̃dɛ̃, ɛn) *a*, worldly, mundane; (*att*.) society. ¶ *n*, society man, woman; worldling. **mondanité** (danite) *f*, worldliness; (*pl*.) social events (*news*). **monde** (mɔ̃ːd) *m*, world; people; company; set; crowd; servants. *le ~ inanimé*, inanimate nature.

monder (mɔ̃de) *v.t*, to hull.

mondial, e (mɔ̃djal) *a*, world[-wide].

monétaire (mɔnetɛːr) *a*, monetary, money (*att*.).

mongol, e (mɔ̃gɔl) *a. & M~, n*, Mongol[ian]. **la Mongolie** (li), Mongolia.

moniteur (mɔnitœːr) *m*, adviser; instructor (*army gymnastics*); gazette.

monnaie (mɔnɛ) *f*, money; currency; coin; coinage; [small] change. *~ de papier*, [convertible] paper money. **la M~**, the mint. **monnayer** (nɛje) *v.t*, to coin, mint; commercialize (*fig*.). **monnayeur** (jœːr) *m*, minter.

monochrome (mɔnɔkroːm) *a*, monochrome. **monocle** (kl) *m*, monocle, eyeglass. **monocorde** (kɔrd) *m*, single-string instrument; monochord; monotonist (*pers*.). **monogamie** (gami) *f*, monogamy. **monogramme** (gram) *m*, monogram. **monographie** (grafi) *f*, monograph. **monolithe** (lit) *a*, monolithic. ¶ *m*, monolith. **monologue** (lɔg) *m*, monologue. **monologuer** (ge) *v.i*, to monologize, soliloquize. **monomanie** (mani) *f*, monomania. **monoplan** (plɑ̃) *m*, monoplane. **monopole** (pɔl) *m*, monopoly. **monopoliser** (lize) *v.t*, to monopolize. **monosyllabe** (silab) *m*, monosyllable. ¶ *~ & monosyllabique* (bik) *a*, monosyllabic. **monotone** (tɔn) *a*, monotonous; humdrum. **monotonie** (ni) *f*, monotony, sameness. **monotype** (tip) *f*, monotype.

mons (mɔ̃ːs) *m*, Master (*so-&-so*) (*jocularly*). **monseigneur**, *oft*. **M~** (mɔ̃sɛɲœːr) *m*, His (*or* Your) Royal Highness; my lord, his (*or* your) lordship, his (*or* your) Grace; jemmy (*burglar's*). **monsieur**, *oft*. **M~** (məsjø) *m*, gentleman; Mr; Esq.; sir; Master (*boy*); my (*or* the) master; man. *~ le juge*, your, his, Worship.

monstre (mɔ̃ːstr) *m. & att*, monster. **monstrueux, euse†** (mɔ̃stryø, øːz) *a*, monstrous, freakish. **monstruosité** (ozite) *f*, monstrosity; freak [of nature].

mont (mɔ̃) *m*, mount, mountain; (*pl*.). *le ~ Blanc, &c*. See under *blanc, &c*. *par ~s & par vaux*, up hill & down dale.

montage (mɔ̃taːʒ) *m*, raising; mounting; setting; erection; fit (*Mech*.). *~ des mailles*, casting on (*Knit*.).

montagnard, e (mɔ̃taɲaːr, ard) *a*, highland, mountain (*att*.). ¶ *n*, highlander, mountaineer. *les Montagnards*, the wild men (*Pol*.). **montagne** (taɲ) *f*, mountain; mountains. *~s russes*, scenic railway, switchback. **montagneux, euse** (nø, øːz) *a*, mountainous.

montant, e (mɔ̃tɑ̃, ɑ̃ːt) *a*, rising, ascending; incoming (*tide*); up-hill; up (*train, &c*); high; high-necked (*dress*); stand-up (*collar*). ¶ *m*, upright; post; stile; amount; total; tang. **monte** (mɔ̃ːt) *f*, covering (*of animals*); mount (*Turf*); riding; jockey. **montecharge** (mɔ̃tʃarʒ) *m*, [goods] lift, hoist. **montée** (mɔ̃te) *f*, ascent, rise, rising.

monténégrin, e (mɔ̃tenegrɛ̃, in) *a. & M~, n*, Montenegrin. **le Monténégro** (gro), Montenegro.

monte-plats (mɔ̃tpla) *m*, service lift, dinner lift. **monter** (te) *v.i. & t*, to go up, ascend; mount; climb; ride; command (*ship*); amount; raise, hoist, elevate; take up, carry up; set up, put up; erect; fit; set; string (*violin, &c*); wind [up] (*spring*); turn up (*wick*); stage (*play*); cast on (*Knit*.); excite. *~ en amazone*, to ride side-saddle. *~ en graine*, to run to seed. *~ en voiture*, to take one's seat in a carriage. *~ sur un vaisseau, en avion*, to [go on] board a ship, an aeroplane. **monteur** (tœːr) *m*, setter, mounter; fitter, erector.

monticule (mɔ̃tikyl) *m*, hillock, mound, knoll, hummock.

montjoie (mɔ̃ʒwa) *f*, cairn.

montoir (mɔ̃twaːr) *m*, horse block.

montrable (mɔ̃trabl) *a*, presentable. **montre** (mɔ̃ːtr) *f*, parade; show; display; [shop] window (*display*); sample; watch. *~ à ancre*, lever watch. *~ à double boîtier*, hunter. *~ à guichet*, half-hunter. *~ à remontoir*, keyless watch. *~ de poignet*, wrist[let] w. *~ jurat* bracelet, strap w. (*man's*). w. on bracelet (*woman's*). *~ sauteuse*, jumping hour w. **montrer** (mɔ̃tre) *v.t*, to show; point [out]; teach. *~ du doigt*, to point at. **montreur** (trœːr) m, showman; exhibitor; operator (*magic lantern*). ~ *d'ours*, bear leader.

montueux, euse (mɔ̃tɥø, øːz) *a*, hilly.

monture (mɔ̃tyːr) *f*, mount (*animal*); mount[ing], setting; hook to gut (*Fish.*). ~ *de rideaux*, cornice pole. *sans* ~, rimless (*glasses*).

monument (mɔnymã) *m*, monument, memorial; building (*public or historic*). ~ *aux morts* [*de la guerre*], war memorial. ~ *historique*, national monument, building, &c, of historic interest. **monumental, e** (tal) *a*, monumental.

moquer (se) de (mɔke), to mock (at), deride, jeer at, laugh at, ridicule, make fun of. **moquerie** (kri) *f*, mockery, jeer[s]. **moquette** (kɛt) *f*, moquette, velvet pile, saddle bag; Brussels carpet. **moqueur, euse** (kœːr, øːz) *n*, mocker, scoffer. ¶ *a*, mocking. [*oiseau*] *moqueur*, mocking bird.

moraillon (mɔrajɔ̃) *m*, hasp.

moraine (mɔrɛːn) *f*, moraine.

moral, e (mɔral) *a*, moral; mental. ¶ *m*, mind; moral[e]. **morale** (ral) *f*, morals (*ethics*); moral (*of story*). **moralement** (lmã) *ad*, morally. **moraliser** (lize) *v.i. & t*, to moralize; lecture. **moraliste** (list) *m*, moralist. **moralité** (te) *f*, morality (*principles*, *drama*); moral (*of fable*).

moratoire (mɔratwaːr) *a*, moratory; on overdue payments (*interest*). ¶ ~ *&* **moratorium** (tɔrjɔm) *m*, moratorium.

Moravie (la) (mɔravi), Moravia.

morbide (mɔrbid) *a*, morbid; unwholesome; **morbidezza** (*att.*). **morbidesse** (dɛs) *f*, morbidezza.

morceau (mɔrso) *m*, piece, bit; morsel; snack; lump, knob; scrap, fragment. ~*x choisis*, selections (*from writings*). ~ *d'ensemble*, part song, p. music. ~ *de concours*, test piece (*music*, &c). *un* ~ *de femme*, a slip of a woman. ~ *de rôti*, cut off the joint. ~ *honteux*, last piece (*left on dish*). **morceler** (sɔle) *v.t*, to parcel [out]; subdivide.

mordant, e (mɔrdã, ãːt) *a*, mordant, biting; pungent. ¶ *m*, mordant; pungency; keenness; shrillness. **mordicus** (dikyːs) *ad*, doggedly. **mordiller** (dije) *v.t*, to nibble.

mordoré, e (mɔrdɔre) *a*, reddish brown; bronze (*shoes*).

mordre (mɔrdr) *v.t. & abs*, to bite, nip; nibble. *ça mord!* I have a bite! (*Fish.*). ~ *à*, to take to (*a study*). ~ *sur* (*fig.*), to find fault with. ~ *sur la latte*, to go over the mark (*Jump.*).

More (mɔːr) *m*, Moor. **m**~, *a*, Moorish.

morelle (mɔrɛl) *f*, nightshade.

moresque (mɔrɛsk) *a*, Moresque. ¶ *f*, Morisco, morris [dance].

morfil (mɔrfil) *m*, wire edge.

morfondre (mɔrfɔ̃ːdr) *v.t*, to chill. *se* ~, to wait in vain, cool one's heels. **morfondu, e** (fɔ̃dy) *p.a*, [as if] frozen stiff.

morganatique† (mɔrganatik) *a*, morganatic.

morgeline (mɔrʒəlin) *f*, chickweed; pimpernel.

morgue (mɔrg) *f*, haughtiness; morgue.

moribond, e (mɔribɔ̃, ɔ̃ːd) *a. & n*, moribund, dying (man, woman).

moricaud, e (mɔriko, oːd) *n*, blackamoor; dark[e]y.

morigéner (mɔriʒene) *v.t*, to take to task.

morne (mɔrn) *a*, gloomy, dismal, dreary, bleak, cheerless.

morose (mɔroːz) *a*, morose, sullen, moody. **morosité** (rozite) *f*, moroseness, &c.

Morphée (mɔrfe) *m*, Morpheus. **morphine** (fin) *f*, morphia, -phine. **morphinomane** (nɔman) *n*, morphinomaniac.

morphologie (mɔrfɔlɔʒi) *f*, morphology; accidence (*Gram.*).

mors (mɔːr) *m*, bit (*bridle*); jaw (*vice*).

morse (mɔrs) *m*, walrus, morse.

morsure (mɔrsyːr) *f*, bite; sting (*fig.*).

mort (mɔːr) *f*, death. *à* ~, to d.; to the d.; mortal (*strife*); mortally; deadly. ~ *& passion*, excruciating pains; agonies (*fig.*). **mort, e** (mɔːr, ɔrt) *a*, dead; still (*water*, *life*); spent (*shot*). *les morts*, the dead. *les morts pour la patrie*, roll of honour. **mort**, *m*, dummy (*Cards*).

mortaise (mɔrtɛːz) *f*, mortise, -ice; slot.

mortalité (mɔrtalite) *f*, mortality; death rate.

mort-aux-rats (mɔrora) *f*, rat poison. **mort-bois** (mɔrbwa) *m*, underwood, brushwood. **morte-eau** (mɔrto) *f*, neap tide. **morte-saison** (təsɛzɔ̃) *f*, dead season, off season.

mortier (mɔrtje) *m*, mortar (*plaster*, *vessel*, *Mil.*). ~ *de tranchée*, trench mortar.

mortifier (mɔrtifje) *v.t*, to mortify; make tender (*meat*, *game*). **mort-né, e** (mɔrne) *a*, still-born. **mortuaire** (mɔrtɥɛːr) *a*, mortuary, [of] death; (*house*) of the deceased; burial (*fees*).

morue (mɔry) *f*, cod[fish]. **morutier** (tje) *m*, cod fisher.

morve (mɔrv) *f*, mucus of the nose; glanders.

mosaïque (mɔzaik) *a*, Mosaic (*law*). ¶ *f*, mosaic, tessellated pavement.

Moscou (mɔsku) *m*, Moscow.

mosquée (mɔske) *f*, mosque.

mot (mo) *m*, word; saying; say; cue. ~ *à* ~ (motamo), *pour* ~, word for word, verbatim. ~*carré*, word square. ~*s croisés* [-*énigmes*], crossword [puzzle]. ~ *d'ordre*, password; watchword, keynote. ~ *de l'énigme*, answer to the riddle. ~ *de passe*, password. ~ *de ralliement*, countersign (*Mil.*). *Note.*—In Fr., the ~ *de ralliement* is given in reply to the ~ *d'ordre*. In Eng., the *countersign* is given in response to the request to give it. ~ *en vedette*, word displayed in bold type, catchword. ~ *piquant*, quip. ~ *pour rire*, joke.

G *

moteur (mɔtœːr) *m*, engine, motor; mover. ~ *à essence*, petrol engine, p. motor. ~ *à gaz*, gas e. ~ *à pétrole*, oil e. **moteur, trice** (tœːr, tris) *att*, motive, driving.

motif (tif) *m*, motive; reason; cause; (*pl.*) grounds; intentions (*matrimonial*); design, motif, traced article, (*pl.*) traced goods; theme, motto (*Mus.*). **motion** (mosjɔ̃) *f*, motion (*proposal at meeting*). **motiver** (mɔtive) *v.t.* to state the reason for; justify.

motoculture (mɔtɔkylty:r) *f*, tractor farming, mechanized f. **motocyclette** (siklɛt), abb. **moto** (mɔto) *f*, motor [bi]cycle. ~ *avec side-car*, motor combination. **motocycliste** (klist) *n*, motor cyclist.

motte (mɔt) *f*, clod; turf, sod; ball (*tan, &c*); roll (*butter*); mound.

motu proprio (mɔty prɔprio), of one's own accord.

motus (mɔtyːs) *i*, mum['s the word]!

mou, mol, molle (mu, mɔl) *a*, soft; lax; slack; inelastic (*Phys.*); limp, flabby; languid; muggy, close; indolent. **mou**, *m*, lights (*animal lungs*).

mouchard (muʃaːr) *m*, spy; police spy. **moucharder** (jarde) *v.t.* to spy.

mouche (muʃ) *f*, fly; patch, beauty spot; spot (*Bil.*); tuft (*on chin*); police spy; bull's-eye (*target*); bull (*shot*). ~ *à feu*, fire fly. ~ *à miel*, honey bee. ~ *à viande*, meat fly, blowfly. ~ *bleue*, bluebottle. ~ *commune*, house fly. ~ *de mai*, May fly. ~ *noyée*, wet fly (*Fish.*). *poids* ~, fly weight (*Box.*). *prendre la* ~, to take huff.

moucher (muʃe) *v.t.* to wipe (*child's, &c*) nose; snuff (*candle*); snub. *se* ~, to blow one's nose.

moucherolle (muʃrɔl) *f*, fly-catcher (*bird*). **moucheron** (frɔ̃) *m*, midge, gnat; whipper-snapper; snuff (*candle*).

moucheté, e (muʃte) *a*, spotted, speckled; tabby (*cat*).

mouchettes (muʃɛt) *f.pl*, snuffers.

moucheture (muʃty:r) *f*, spot, speckle.

mouchoir (muʃwaːr) *m*, handkerchief. ~ *de cou*, silk square.

moudre (mudr) *v.t. & abs. ir*, to grind, mill.

moue (mu) *f*, pout[ing]. *faire la* ~, to pout.

mouette (mwɛt) *f*, [sea] gull, [sea] mew.

mouffette (mufɛt) *f*, skunk (*Zool.*).

moufle (mufl) *f*, pulley block, tackle b.; mitt[en]; (*m.*) pulley block, tackle b.; muffle (*Chem.*).

mouillage (muja:ʒ) *m*, wetting; watering (*wine, &c*); mooring; moorings, anchorage, berth. **mouille-bouche** (mujbuʃ) *f*, bergamot (*pear*). **mouillée** (je) *p.a.*, palat[al]ized (*consonant*). **mouiller** (je) *v.t. & abs. ir*, to wet, moisten, damp; water; anchor, moor, berth. **mouillette** (jɛt) *f*, sippet. **mouilloir** (jwaːr) *m*, damper (*stamps, labels*). **mouillure** (jy:r) *f*, wetting; damp mark (*in books*).

moulage (mula:ʒ) *m*, moulding (*act*); casting. **moule** (mul) *m*, mould; (*f.*) mussel. **mouler** (le) *v.t.* to mould, cast; shape; print (*handwriting*). **mouleur** (lœ:r) *m*, moulder.

moulin (mulɛ̃) *m*, mill; moulin (*glacier*). ~ *à paroles*, chatterbox; windbag. ~ *à prières*, prayer wheel. ~ *à vent*, windmill. **mouliné, e** (line) *p.a. & p.p*, worm-eaten (*wood*); thrown (*silk*). **moulinet** (nɛ) *m*, winch; reel (*Fish.*); turnstile (X *on post*). *faire le* ~, to whirl, twirl. **moulu, e** (ly) *p.a*: ~ *de fatigue*, dead beat. *tout* ~, aching all over.

moulure (muly:r) *f*, moulding (*ornamental strip*).

mourant, e (murɑ̃, ɑ̃:t) *a*, dying; languishing (*eyes*); faint (*voice*). **les mourants**, *m.pl*, the dying. **mourir** (ri:r) *v.i.ir*, to die, be dying; die away; d. out; d. down. *faire* ~, to execute (*criminal*). *se* ~, to be dying; fade out, give out.

mouron (murɔ̃) *m*, pimpernel. ~ [*des oiseaux*], chickweed.

mousquet (muskɛ) *m*, musket. **mousquetaire** (kətɛːr) *m*, musketeer; (*att.*) double (*cuffs*). **mousqueton** (tɔ̃) *m*, carbine; snap hook.

mousse (mus) *m*, ship boy; (*f.*) moss; froth; foam; lather; head (*on glass of beer*); mousse (*cream*).

mousseline (muslin) *f*, muslin; mousseline.

mousser (muse) *v.i*, to froth; foam; lather; effervesce, sparkle. *faire* ~ (*fig.*), to make much of. **mousseux, euse** (sø, øːz) *a*, mossy; moss (*rose*); frothy; foamy; sparkling (*wine*). *non mousseux*, still (*wine*).

mousson (musɔ̃) *f*, monsoon.

moussu, e (musy) *a*, mossy, moss-grown; moss (*rose*).

moustache (mustaʃ) *f*, moustache; whiskers (*animal*). ~ *à la Charlot* (ʃarlo), Charlie Chaplin moustache. ~ *en brosse*, tooth brush m. ~ *en croc*, turned up m. **moustachu, e** (ʃy) *a*, moustached.

moustiquaire (mustikɛːr) *f*, mosquito net, m. curtain. **moustique** (tik) *m*, mosquito.

moût (mu) *m*, must, stum; wort.

moutard (muta:r) *m*, youngster, urchin.

moutarde (mutard) *f. & att*, mustard. *de la* ~ *après dîner*, a day after the fair. **moutardier** (dje) *m*, mustard pot; m. maker.

mouton (mutɔ̃) *m*, sheep; wether; mutton; sheep[skin]; lamb (*pers.*); spy (*on prisoner*); monkey, ram, tup (*pile driving*); yoke, stock (*of bell*); (*pl.*) sheep; (*pl.*) white horses, skipper's daughters (*waves*); (*pl.*) fluff (*under furniture*). **moutonner** (tone) *v.i*, to [break into] foam (*sea*). *nuages moutonnés, ciel moutonné*, fleecy clouds, sky fleeced with clouds. **moutonneux, euse** (nø, ø:z) *a*, foamy; crested (*waves*). **moutonnier, ère** (nje, ɛːr) *a*, sheep-like (*pers.*).

mouture (muty:r) *f*, grinding (*corn*); maslin.

mouvant, e (muvã, ã:t) *a*, moving, shifting, unstable; quick(*sand*). **mouvement** (vmã) *m*, motion; movement; progress; impulse; action, bustle, stir, life; arrangement (*Art*.); conformation (*of ground*); change; changes (*staff*); appointments & promotions; move (*Mil*.); burst (*oratory*); attack (*fever*); fluctuation; traffic; circulation; turnover; statistics (*population*); transaction; works (*Horol*.). ~ *des navires*, shipping intelligence, *s*. news, movements of ships. ~ *populaire*, civil commotion. *dans le* ~ (*fig*.), in the swim. *de son propre* ~, of one's own accord. **mouvementé, e** (te) *a*, lively, bustling, busy; eventful; stirring; broken (*ground*). **mouvoir** (vwa:r) *v.t.ir. & se* ~, to move; actuate, propel.

moyen, ne (mwajɛ̃, ɛn) *a*, middle; mean, average; medium; middling; intermediate (*course*, *Sch*.); doubtful (*virtue*). *d'âge moyen*, middle-aged (*pers*.). *le* ~ *âge*, the middle ages. *du* ~ *âge*, medi[a]eval. ~ *terme*, middle course (*conduct*). ~ [*terme*], middle [term] (*Log*.). **moyen**, *m*, means, way; help; (*pl*.) means (*pecuniary*); grounds (*Law*). ~ *de fortune*, makeshift. **moyenâgeux, euse** (jɛnɑʒø, ø:z) *a*, medi[a]eval. **moyennant** (nã) *pr*, in consideration of; on; at; with the help of. **moyenne** (jɛn) *f*, average, mean. **moyennement** (nmã) *ad*, moderately, fairly.

moyeu (mwajø) *m*, nave; hub; boss. ~ *arrière à roue libre & frein contre-pédalage*, coaster hub.

mucilage (mysila:ʒ) *m*, mucilage.

mucosité (mykozite) *f*. & **mucus** (ky:s) *m*, mucus, phlegm.

mue (my) *f*, moult[ing]; slough[ing]; mew; [hen] coop; breaking (*voice*). **muer** (mɥe) *v.i*, to moult; slough; break; (*v.t*.) to change. **muet, te** (mɥɛ, ɛt) *a. & n*, dumb (*person*); mute; speechless; silent. *à la muette*, without speaking.

muezzin (mɥɛzɛ̃) *m*, muezzin.

mufle (myfl) *m*, muzzle, muffle; cad. **muflier** (flie) *m*, antirrhinum, snapdragon.

muge (my:ʒ) *m*, grey mullet.

mugir (myʒi:r) *v.i*, to low; bellow; roar; whistle (*wind*).

muguet (mygɛ) *m*, lily of the valley.

mulâtre (mylɑ:tr) *a. & m*, **mulâtresse** (lɑtrɛs) *f*, mulatto. **mule** (myl) *f*, [she] mule; mule (*slipper*); slipper *or* toe (*of pope as kissed*). **mulet** (lɛ) *m*, [he] mule; mule (*pers*.); cross, hybrid, mule; grey mullet. **muletier** (ltje) *m*, muleteer; (*att*.) mule (*track*).

mulot (mylo) *m*, field mouse.

multicolore (myltikɔlɔ:r) *a*, multicolour[ed], many-coloured.

multiple (myltipl) *a*, multiple, manifold, multifarious. ¶ *m*, multiple. **multiplicande** (plikɑ̃:d) *m*, multiplicand. **multiplicateur** (katœ:r) *m*, multiplier. **multi-**

plication (sjɔ̃) *f*, multiplication; gear [ratio]. **multiplicité** (site) *f*, multiplicity. **multiplier** (plie) *v.t. & i. & se* ~, to multiply.

multitude (myltityd) *f*, multitude, crowd.

municipal, e (munisipal) *a*, municipal, town (*att*.). **municipalité** (lite) *f*, municipality; [municipal] corporation.

munificence (mynifisã:s) *f*, munificence, bounty.

munir (myni:r) *v.t*, to supply, provide, furnish; fortify. **munitions** (nisjɔ̃) *f.pl*, ammunition. ~ *de bouche*, provisions, food. ~ *de guerre*, war[like] stores, munitions.

muqueux, euse (mykø, ø:z) *a*, mucous. [membrane] **muqueuse**, *f*, m. membrane.

mur (my:r) *m*, wall.

mûr, e (my:r) *a*, ripe, mature; mellow; worn threadbare.

muraille (myrɑ:j) *f*, wall. **mural, e** (ral) *a*, mural, wall (*att*.).

mûre (my:r) *f*, mulberry. ~ *sauvage*, ~ *de ronce*, blackberry.

mûrement (myrmã) *ad*, closely, thoroughly.

murer (myre) *v.t*, to wall; w. up; screen (*fig*.).

mûrier (myrje) *m*, mulberry [tree].

mûrir (myri:r) *v.i. & t*, to ripen; mature; mellow.

murmure (myrmy:r) *m*, murmur; grumbling; mutter; whisper; hum; purl, brawling; gurgle; soughing. **murmurer** (myre) *v.i. & t*, to murmur, &c.

mûron (myrɔ̃) *m*, blackberry; wild raspberry bush.

musaraigne (myzarɛɲ) *f*, shrew [mouse].

musarder (myzarde) *v.i*, to dawdle.

musc (mysk) *m*, musk; m. deer. **[noix] muscade** (kad) *f*, nutmeg. **muscadier** (dje) *m*, nutmeg [tree]. **muscat** (ka) *a. & m*, muscat (grape, wine).

muscle (myskl) *m*, muscle. **musclé, e** (kle) *a*, -muscled. **musculaire** (kylɛ:r) & **musculeux, euse** (lø, ø:z) *a*, muscular.

Muse (my:z) *f*, Muse.

museau (myzo) *m*, muzzle, snout.

musée (myze) *m*, museum.

museler (myzle) *v.t*, to muzzle. **muselière** (zəljɛ:r) *f*, muzzle (*dog*).

muser (myze) *v.i*, to dawdle, moon [about].

musette (myzɛt) *f*, musette (*Mus*.); nosebag; sachel; haversack; bag.

muséum (myzeɔm) *m*, natural history museum.

musical, e† (myzikal) *a*, musical. **music hall** (myzik hɔl) *m*, music hall, variety theatre. **musicien, ne** (sjɛ̃, ɛn) *n*, musician; player; bandsman; (*att*.) musical. **musique** (zik) *f*, music; band; toy musical instrument. ~ *de chats*, caterwauling.

musoir (myzwa:r) *m*, pierhead.

musquer (myske) *v.t*, to[perfume with]musk.

musulman, e (myzylmã, an) *n. & att*, Mussulman.

mutabilité (mytabilite) *f*, mutability. **muta-**

tion (sjɔ̃) f, mutation, change; transfer; conveyance (*Law*).

mutilation (mytilasjɔ̃) f, mutilation, maiming; defacement. mutilé de la guerre (le) m, disabled soldier, disabled sailor. mutiler (le) v.t, to mutilate, &c.

mutin, e (mytɛ̃, in) a. & n, roguish (child), mischievous (child); mutinous; mutineer. se mutiner (tine) v.pr. & mutiner, v.abs, to mutiny, rebel; be unruly. mutinerie (nri) f, mutiny; refractoriness; roguishness.

mutisme (mytism) m, dumbness, muteness.

mutualiste (mytyalist) n, member of a mutual society or association. mutualité (te) f, mutuality; mutual association. ~ de crédit, mutual loan association. mutuel, le† (tɥɛl) a, mutual.

mycélium (miseljɔm) m, mycelium, spawn.

myope (mjɔp) a. & n, short-sighted (person), near-sighted (person). vue ~, short sight, near s. myopie (pi) f, myopia.

myosotis (mjɔzɔtis) m, myosotis, forget-me-not.

myriade (mirjad) f, myriad. myriagramme (gram) m, myriagram[me] = 10000 grammes or 22·046 lbs. myriapode (pɔd) m, myriapod.

myrrhe (mi:r) f, myrrh.

myrte (mirt) m, myrtle. myrtille (til) f, whortleberry, bilberry.

mystère (mistɛ:r) m, mystery; m. [play], miracle [play]. ~ de la Passion, passion play. mystérieux, euse† (terjø, ø:z) a, mysterious. mysticisme (tisism) m, mysticism. mysticité (te) f, mysticalness. mystificateur, trice (fikatœ:r, tris) n, hoaxer, humbug. mystifier (fje) v.t, to mystify; hoax, humbug. mystique† (tik) a, mystic[al]. ¶ n, mystic (*pers.*); (*f.*) mystical theology; mysterious appeal (*as of the olden times*).

mythe (mit) m, myth. mythique (tik) a, mythic[al]. mythologie (tɔlɔʒi) f, mythology. mythologique (ʒik) a, mythological. mythologue (lɔg) n, mythologist.

N

nabab (nabab) m, nabob.

nabot, e (nabo, ɔt) (*pers.*) n, midget, shrimp, manikin.

nacelle (nasɛl) (*Aero.*) f, car, nacelle, gondola; cockpit.

nacre (nakr) f, mother of pearl. nacré, e (kre) a, pearly.

nadir (nadi:r) m, nadir.

nævus (nevy:s) m, naevus, birthmark, mole.

nage (na:ʒ) f, swimming; stroke. ~ [d'aviron], rowing. ~ à la pagaie, paddling. ~ de côté, side stroke. ~ en grenouille, breast s. ~ en couple, sculling. en ~, bathed in perspiration. nageoire (naʒwa:r) f, fin (*fish*); flipper. nager (ʒe) v.i, to

swim, float; welter, revel; row. ~ debout, to tread water; row standing up. ~ en couple, to scull. ~ entre deux eaux, to swim under water. nageur, euse (ʒœ:r, ø:z) n, swimmer; rower, oarsman.

naguère (nagɛ:r) ad, not long since.

naiade (najad) f, naiad, water nymph.

naïf, ïve (naif, i:v) a, artless, naïve, unaffected, ingenuous; unsophisticated; simple-minded, green.

nain, e (nɛ̃, ɛn) n. & att, dwarf.

naissance (nɛsɑ̃:s) f, birth; descent; rise (*river*); spring[ing] (*Arch.*). ~ du jour, dawn, break of day. naissant, e (sɑ̃, ɑ̃:t) a, dawning; budding; nascent. naître (nɛ:tr) v.i.ir, to be born; grow; bud; [a]rise, spring up. à ~, unborn.

naïvement (naivmɑ̃) ad, artlessly, &c, as naïf. naïveté (vte) f, artlessness, &c.

nanan (du) (nanɑ̃) m, sweeties; lovely.

nankin (nɑ̃kɛ̃) m, nankeen.

nanti, e (nɑ̃ti) p.p: ~ de (*fig.*), secured by. homme ~, man who has made his pile. nantissement (smɑ̃) m, hypothecation; collateral security.

napel (napɛl) m, monk's-hood, wolf's-bane. naphtaline (naftalin) f, naphthalene, -ine. naphte (naft) m, naphtha.

napolitain, e (napɔlitɛ̃, ɛn) a. & N~, n, Neapolitan.

nappe (nap) f, table cloth; cloth; sheet (*water, flame*). napperon (prɔ̃) m, cloth (*tea, tray*).

narcisse (narsis) m, narcissus. ~ des prés, daffodil.

narcotique (narkɔtik) a. & m, narcotic, opiate.

narguer (narge) v.t, to flout.

narguilé -ghileh (nargile) m, hookah.

narine (narin) f, nostril.

narquois, e (narkwa, a:z) a, quizzical.

narrateur, trice (narratœ:r, tris) n, narrator, narratress, story teller. narratif, ive (tif, i:v) a, narrative. narration (sjɔ̃) f, narrative, story; narration; essay (*Sch.*). narrer (re) v.t, to narrate, relate, tell.

narval (narval) m, narwhal.

nasal, e (nazal) a. & f, nasal. nasarde (zard) f, fillip; snub. naseau (zo) m, nostril (*horse*). nasiller (zije) v.i, to speak through the nose, snuffle, twang.

nasse (nas) f, eel pot; lobster pot; net; trap.

natal, e (natal) a, native; natal. natalité (lite) f, birth rate, natality.

natation (natasjɔ̃) f, swimming, natation.

natif, ive (natif, i:v) a, native, inborn. les natifs, m.pl, the natives.

nation (nasjɔ̃) f, nation; people. national, e (ɔnal) a, national. nationalisme (lism) m, nationalism. nationaliste (list) n. & a, nationalist. nationalité (te) f, nationality. nationaux (no) m.pl, nationals.

nativité (nativite) f, nativity.

natte (nat) f, mat, matting; pla[i]t. natter (te) v.t, to mat; pla[i]t. se ~, to pla[i]t one's hair. nattier (tje) m, mat maker.

naturalisation (natyralizasjɔ̃) f, naturalization. naturaliser (ze) v.t, to naturalize; stuff (animal); preserve (plant). naturaliste (list) m, naturalist. ~ [fourreur], taxidermist. nature (ty:r) f, nature; life (Art); life size; plain[-boiled]. ~ morte, still life. en ~, in kind. naturel, le† (tyrɛl) a, natural; native; unaffected. ¶ m, naturalness; nature, disposition; native (pers.).

naufrage (nofra:ʒ) m, wreck, shipwreck. faire ~, to be [ship]wrecked. naufragé, e (fraʒe) n, shipwrecked person, castaway.

nauséabond, e (nozeabɔ̃, ɔ̃:d) a, nauseous, sickening, foul. nausée (ze) f, nausea. nauséeux, euse (zeø, ø:z) a, nauseating.

nautile (notil) ou nautilus (ly:s) m, nautilus. nautique (tik) a, nautical; aquatic (sports). nautonier, ère (tonje, ɛ:r) (Poet.) n, mariner; ferryman.

naval, e (naval) a, naval, sea (att.); ship (att.).

navet (navɛ) m, turnip. ~ de Suède, swede.

navette (navɛt) f, rape (oil seed plant); incense box; shuttle. faire la ~, to go to & fro.

navigable (navigabl) a, navigable. navigateur (tœ:r) m, navigator; (att.) seafaring. navigation (sjɔ̃) f, navigation; sailing; shipping. naviguer (ge) v.i, to navigate, sail.

navire (navi:r) m, ship, vessel, boat, bottom. ~ à vapeur, steamship. ~-citerne, m, tank ship. ~ de charge, cargo boat. ~ frère, ~ jumeau, sister ship. ~ de ligne [régulière], liner. ~ pose-mines, mine layer.

navrant, e (navrɑ̃, ɑ̃:t) a, heart-rending, h.-breaking, harrowing. navrer [le cœur] (vre) v.t, to break one's heart, harrow.

ne, n' (nə, n) neg. particle, used mostly with the words pas or point, not, n't. n'importe! no matter!

néanmoins (neɑ̃mwɛ̃) ad, nevertheless, notwithstanding, yet, still.

néant (neɑ̃) m, nothing[ness], nought; nil, none.

nébuleux, euse (nebylø, ø:z) a, nebulous, cloudy; clouded. ¶ f, nebula (Astr.).

nécessaire† (nesesɛ:r) a, necessary, needful. ¶ m, necessary, -ries, needful; busybody; outfit, case. ~ à ouvrage, work box, needlework case. nécessité (site) f, necessity. nécessiter (te) v.t, to necessitate. nécessiteux, euse (tø, ø:z) a, necessitous, needy. les ~, m.pl, the needy, the destitute.

nec plus ultra (nɛkplyzyltra), ne plus ultra, acme, last word.

nécrologe (nekrolɔ:ʒ) m, necrology, obituary (roll, book). nécrologie (loʒi) f, deaths, obituary, necrology (notice). nécromancie (mɑ̃si) f, necromancy. nécromancien, ne (sjɛ̃, ɛn) n, necromancer. nécropole (pol) f, necropolis. nécrose (kro:z) f, necrosis.

nectaire (nɛkte:r) m, nectary. nectar (ta:r) m, nectar.

néerlandais, e (neerlɑ̃dɛ, ɛ:z) a, Netherlandish, Dutch. N~, n, Netherlander, Dutchman, -woman. la Néerlande (lɑ̃:d), the Netherlands.

nef (nɛf) f, nave (church); bark, ship (Poet.).

néfaste (nefast) a, luckless, ill-fated, ill-starred, disastrous.

nèfle (nɛfl) f, medlar. néflier (neflie) m, medlar [tree].

négatif, ive† (negatif, i:v) a, negative. ¶ m, negative (Phot.). la négative, the negative (statement, &c). négation (sjɔ̃) f, negation; negative (Gram.).

négligé, e (negliʒe) p.a, neglected; unheeded; loose; slovenly; slipshod. ¶ m, undress, négligé; tea gown. négligeable (ʒabl) a, negligible. négligemment (ʒamɑ̃) ad, negligently, carelessly. négligence (ʒɑ̃:s) f, negligence, neglect, carelessness; default. négligent, e (ʒɑ̃, ɑ̃:t) a, negligent, careless, neglectful, remiss. négliger (ʒe) v.t, to neglect, slight. se ~, to neglect oneself; slack; be careless.

négoce (negɔs) m, trade; business. négociable (sjabl) a, negotiable; marketable. négociant, e (sjɑ̃, ɑ̃:t) n, trader, merchant. négociateur, trice (atœ:r, tris) n, negociator, tress or trix. négociation (sjɔ̃) f, negotiation; transaction; dealing; bargain. négocier (sje) v.t, to negotiate.

nègre (nɛ:gr) a.m. & a.f, negro. ¶ m, negro, nigger; one who does the donkey work, underling, subordinate. négresse (negrɛs) f, negress. négrier (grie) m, slaver, slave trader; s. driver (hard employer). négrillon, ne (grijɔ̃, ɔn) n, nigger boy, n. girl, piccaninny.

neige (nɛ:ʒ) f. oft. pl, snow. ~s perpétuelles, ~s éternelles, perpetual s. de la ~ fondue, sleet; slush. tomber de la ~ fondue, to sleet. neiger (nɛʒe) v.imp, to snow. neigeux, euse (ʒø, ø:z) a, snowy.

Némésis (nemezi:s) f, Nemesis.

ne m'oubliez pas (nəmubliepɑ) m, forget-me-not.

nénuphar (nenyfa:r) m, water lily.

néologisme (neɔlɔʒism) m, neologism.

néon (neɔ̃) m, neon.

néophyte (neofit) n, neophyte.

néo-zélandais, e (neozelɑ̃dɛ, ɛ:z) a, New Zealand (att.). Néo-Zélandais, e, n, New Zealander.

népotisme (nepotism) m, nepotism.

Néréide (nereid) f, Nereid, sea nymph.

nerf (nɛ:r & nɛrf) m, nerve; band (Bookb.); sinews (of war); (pl.) thews; (pl.) nerves, hysterics; (pl.) tantrums.

nerprun (nɛrprœ̃) m, buckthorn.

nerveux, euse† (nɛrvø, ø:z) a, nervous; highly strung; hysterical; fidgety. nervosité (vozite) f, irritability. nervure (vy:r) f, rib, nerve, nervure, vein (Bot., &c).

net, te (nɛt) *a,* clean; flawless; clear; sharp; empty; free; net. *mettre au net,* to make a clean copy of. **net,** *ad,* clean; plainly, flatly, outright. **nettement** (tmã) *ad,* clearly; frankly, plainly, flatly, downright. **netteté** (nɛtte) *f,* cleanness; clearness. **nettoiement** (nɛtwamã) & **nettoyage** (ja:3) *m,* cleaning, cleansing. **nettoyer** (je) *v.t,* to clean, cleanse; clear. ~ *à sec,* to dry-clean. **nettoyeur, euse** (jœ:r, ø:z) *n,* cleaner.

neuf (nœf & nœ & nœv) *a'. & m,* nine; ninth. ~ *fois sur dix,* nine times out of ten.

neuf, euve (nœf, œ:v) *a,* new; inexperienced, raw.

neurasthénie (nørasteni) *f,* neurasthenia. **neurologiste** (rɔlɔʒist) *ou* **neurologue** (lɔg) *n,* nerve specialist, neurologist.

neutraliser (nøtralize) *v.t,* to neutralize. **neutralité** (te) *f,* neutrality. **neutre** (nø:tr) *a,* neutral; non-committal; neuter; undenominational (*school*). ¶ *m,* neuter; neutral.

neuvième† (nœvjɛm) *a. & n,* ninth.

neveu (nəvø) *m,* nephew. *nos ~x,* posterity.

névralgie (nevralʒi) *f,* neuralgia. **névralgique** (ʒik) *a,* neuralgic; sore (*point*). **névrite** (vrit) *f,* neuritis. **névrose** (vro:z) *f,* neurosis. **névrosé, e** (vroze) *a,* neurotic.

nez (ne) *m,* nose; face; nosing (*stair*); scent (*dogs*). *à vue de ~,* at the first blush.

ni (ni) *c,* nor; or; neither. ~ *fleurs,* ~ *couronnes,* no flowers, by request. ~ *l'un* (*l'une*) *ni l'autre,* pn. & *a,* neither.

niable (njabl) *a,* deniable.

niais, e† (njɛ, ɛ:z) *a. & n,* silly. **niaiser** (ɛze) *v.i,* to play the fool. **niaiserie** (zri) *f,* silliness.

niche (niʃ) *f,* niche; trick, prank, practical joke. ~ *à chien,* dog kennel. **nichée** (ʃe) *f,* nest[ful]; brood. **nicher** (ʃe) *v.i,* to nest; (*v.t.*) to put, ensconce. **nichet** (ʃɛ) *m,* nest egg.

nickel (nikɛl) *m,* nickel. **nickeler** (kle) *v.t,* to nickle.

nicodème (nikɔdɛ:m) *m,* booby.

nicotine (nikɔtin) *f,* nicotine.

nid (ni) *m,* nest; den. ~ *d'hirondelle,* edible bird's nest. ~ *de pie,* crow's-nest (*Naut.*). *il croit avoir trouvé la pie au ~,* he has found a mare's nest.

nièce (njɛs) *f,* niece.

nielle (njɛl) *f,* smut, blight (*Agric.*). ¶ *m,* niello.

nier (nje) *v.t,* to deny; repudiate; (*abs.*) to deny it. ~ *sa culpabilité,* to plead not guilty.

nigaud, e (nigo, o:d) *a,* silly. ¶ *n,* noodle, ninny, booby, nincompoop. **nigauder** (gode) *v.i,* to play the fool. **nigauderie** (dri) *f,* silliness.

nigelle de Damas (niʒɛl) *f,* love-in-a-mist.

nihiliste (niilist) *m,* nihilist.

Nil (le) (nil), the Nile.

nimbe (nɛ:b) *m,* nimbus, halo, glory. **nimbus** (nɛby:s) *m,* nimbus (*Meteor.*).

Ninive (nini:v) *f,* Nineveh.

nippes (nip) *f.pl,* old clothes.

nitouche (sainte) (nituʃ) *f,* [prudish & demure] little hypocrite.

nitrate (nitrat) *m,* nitrate. **nitre** (tr) *m,* nitre, saltpetre. **nitrique** (trik) *a,* nitric. **nitroglycérine** (trɔgliserin) *f,* nitroglycerin[e].

niveau (nivo) *m,* level. ~ *à bulle d'air,* spirit l. ~ *de vie,* standard of living. *de ~,* level, at grade. **niveler** (vle) *v.t,* to level. **niveleur** (vlœ:r) *m,* leveller. **nivellement** (vɛlmã) *m,* levelling.

nobiliaire (nɔbiljɛ:r) *a,* nobiliary. ¶ *m,* peerage (*book*). **noble†** (bl) *a,* noble. ¶ *n,* noble[man], nobleman. **noblesse** (blɛs) *f,* nobility; nobleness; noblesse.

noce (nɔs) *f,* wedding festivities; wedding party; jollification, spree; (*pl.*) wedding, marriage, nuptials. ~*s d'argent, d'or, de diamant,* silver, golden, diamond, wedding. **noceur, euse** (sœ:r, ø:z) *n,* reveller.

nocher (nɔʃe) (*Poet.*) *m,* boatman; ferryman.

nocif, ive (nɔsif, i:v) *a,* noxious.

noctambule (nɔktãby:l) *n,* sleep walker. **nocturne** (tyrn) *a,* nocturnal, night (*att.*). ¶ *m,* nocturne.

Noël (nɔel) *m,* Christmas[tide], yule[tide]. *à la [fête de] ~,* à ~, at Christmas[tide], at yuletide. **n~,** [Christmas] carol.

nœud (nø) *m,* knot; node; cluster; crux; rub; tie, bond (*fig.*). ~ *coulant,* slip knot, running k.; noose. ~ *de ruban,* bow. ~ *gordien* (gɔrdjɛ̃), Gordian knot. ~*[-papillon],* bow (*necktie*). ~ *plat,* reef knot.

noir, e (nwa:r) *a,* black; dark; swarthy; brown (*bread*); black & blue (*bruised*); gloomy. *noir sur blanc,* [down] in black & white (*writing*). *la mer Noire,* the Black sea. ¶ *m,* black; b. mark (*bruise*); b. [man, boy], man of colour; bull's-eye (*target*). ~ *de fumée,* lamp black. ¶ *f,* black [ball] (*Gaming*); crotchet (*Mus.*). **noirâtre** (ra:tr) *a,* blackish; darkish. **noiraud, e** (ro, o:d) *a. & n,* swarthy (man, woman). **noirceur** (sœ:r) *f,* blackness; black spot; smudge, smut. **noircir** (si:r) *v.t. & i,* to blacken; black; blot (*paper with useless writing*). **noircissure** (sisy:r) *f,* smudge.

noise (nwa:z) *f,* quarrel.

noisetier (nwaztje) *m,* hazel (*bush*), nut tree. **noisette** (zɛt) *f,* hazel nut; nut; hazel (*colour, eyes*); nut-brown.

noix (nwa) *f,* walnut; nut. ~ *de coco,* coconut. ~ *de galle,* nut gall. ~ *vomique* (vɔmik), nux vomica.

nolis (nɔli) *m,* freight. **noliser** (ze) *v.t,* to freight, charter.

nom (nɔ̃) *m,* name; style; noun. ~ *à coucher dehors,* crack-jaw name. ~ *de* *baptême*, Christian name. ~ [*de famille*], ~ *patronymique*, surname. ~ *de guerre*, nom de guerre, assumed name, alias; stage name; pen name. ~ *de jeune fille*, maiden name. ~ *de plume*, nom de plume, pen name. ~ *de théâtre*, stage n. ~ *& prénoms*, full n. *sous un* ~ *interposé*, in a nominee's name.

nomade (nɔmad) *a*, nomad(ic). ¶ *m*, nomad, wanderer.

nombre (nɔ̃:br) *m*, number. *les N~s* (*Bible*), Numbers. ~ *des adhérents*, membership. *avoir du* ~, to be well balanced (*phrase*). **nombrer** (nɔ̃bre) *v.t*, to number, count. **nombreux, euse** (brø, ø:z) *a*, numerous; well-balanced (*style, prose*).

nombril (nɔ̃bri) *m*, navel; eye (*fruit*).

nomenclature (nɔmɑ̃klaty:r) *f*, nomenclature. **nominal, e†** (minal) *a*, nominal; face (*value*). **nominatif, ive** (tif, i:v) *a*, nominal, of [the] names; registered (*securities*). ¶ *m*, nominative [case]. **nomination** (sjɔ̃) *f*, nomination; appointment; commissioning (*officer*); gift (*of an office*); award (*at a show*). **nominativement** (tivmɑ̃) *ad*, by name. *un nommé . . .* (me), a man called . . ., one . . . [by name]. **nommément** (memɑ̃) *ad*, namely, to wit, by name. **nommer** (me) *v.t*, to name; call; nominate; appoint; commission; return, elect. *se* ~, to give one's name; be called. *je me nomme Adam*, my name is Adam.

non (nɔ̃) *neg. particle*, no; not. *ni moi* ~ *plus*, nor I either. ¶ *m*, no, nay.

non-activité (en) (nɔnaktivite) *f*, on the unemployed list (*Mil.*).

nonagénaire (nɔnaʒenɛ:r) *a. & n*, nonagenarian.

non avenu, e (nɔnavny) *a*, void, non avenu.

nonce du Pape *ou* **nonce apostolique** (nɔ̃:s) *m*, papal nuncio.

nonchalamment (nɔ̃ʃalamɑ̃) *ad*, nonchalantly, listlessly. **nonchalance** (lɑ̃:s) *f*, nonchalance, listlessness. **nonchalant, e** (lɑ̃, ɑ̃:t) *a*, nonchalant, listless.

nonciature (nɔ̃sjaty:r) *f*, nunciature.

non-combat (nɔ̃kɔ̃ba) *m*, no contest (*Box.*). **non-combattant, e** (batɑ̃, ɑ̃:t) *a. & n*, non-combatant (*Mil.*).

non-conformiste (nɔ̃kɔ̃fɔrmist) *n. & att*, nonconformist.

non-être (nɔnɛ:tr) (*Philos.*) *m*, nonentity, nonexistence.

non-intervention (nɔnɛ̃tɛrvɑ̃sjɔ̃) (*Pol.*) *f*, non-intervention, non-interference.

non-lieu (nɔ̃ljø) *m*, no case to answer (*Law*).

nonne (nɔn) *& nonnain* (nɛ̃) *f*, nun.

nonobstant (nɔnɔpstɑ̃) *pr*, notwithstanding.

non-paiement (nɔ̃pemɑ̃) *m*, non-payment; dishonour (*bill*).

non-sens (nɔ̃sɑ̃:s) *m*, nonsense. *un* ~, all nonsense, meaningless.

non-valeur (nɔ̃valœ:r) *f*, unproductiveness; worthless security; valueless stock; (*pl.*)

irrecoverable arrears (*taxes*); bad debt; non-effective (*Mil.*); useless person.

nord (nɔ:r) *m*, north; (*att.*) north[ern]. *mer du N~*, North sea, German ocean. **nord-est** (nɔr[d]ɛst; *Naut.*, nɔrɛ) *m*, north-east; n.-e. wind; (*att.*) north-east[ern]. **nordique** (dik) *a*, Nordic. **nord-ouest** (nɔr[d]wɛst; *Naut.*, nɔrwa) *m*, north-west, n.-w. wind; (*att.*) north-west[ern].

normal, e† (nɔrmal) *a*, normal; standard; ordinary. *la normale*, bogey, Colonel Bogey (*Golf*). **normalien, ne** (ljɛ̃, ɛn) *n*, student [of a normal school].

normand, e (nɔrmɑ̃, ɑ̃:d) *a*, Norman; non-committal (*fig.*); evasive; feigned. *les îles Normandes*, the Channel Islands. **N~, n**, Norman. *un fin n~*, a shrewd crafty fellow. **la Normandie** (mɑ̃di), Normandy.

norme (nɔrm) *f*, norm.

norois (l'ancien) (nɔrwa) *m*, Old Norse (*language*).

Norvège (la) (nɔrvɛ:ʒ), Norway. **norvégien, ne** (veʒjɛ̃, ɛn) *a. & N~, n*, Norwegian, Norseman. *le norvégien*, Norwegian, Norse (*language*).

nostalgie (nɔstalʒi) *f*, nostalgia, home-sickness; pining. **nostalgique** (ʒik) *a*, nostalgic, home-sick.

nota (*bene*) (nɔta bene) (*abb. N.B.*) *m*, note, nota bene, N.B. **notabilité** (notabilite) *f*, notability. **notable†** (bl) *a*, notable; especial; eminent, distinguished. ¶ *m*, person of distinction, notable.

notaire (nɔtɛ:r) *m*, notary & solicitor.

notamment (notamɑ̃) *ad*, especially, notably.

notation (notasjɔ̃) *f*, notation.

note (nɔt) *f*, note, memorandum; mark (*Sch.*); record (*of service*); bill, account; tune (*fig.*). ~ *d'agrément*, grace note (*Mus.*). ~ *de passage*, passing note (*Mus.*). ~ *naturelle*, natural [note] (*Mus.*). **noter** (te) *v.t*, to note; n. down; write down; mark (*pupil, &c*). **notice** (tis) *f*, notice, account; review (*book*). **notifier** (tifje) *v.t*, to notify.

notion (nosjɔ̃) *f*, notion. *N~s de Physique, &c*, Elementary Physics, &c (*book*).

notoire† (nɔtwa:r) *a*, notorious, well known. **notoriété** (tɔrjete) *f*, notoriety. ~ *publique*, common knowledge.

notre (nɔtr) *a*, our. *Notre-Dame*, Our Lady. *Notre-Seigneur*, Our Lord. **le nôtre, la** ~, **les** ~**s** (no:tr) *pn*, ours; our own. *il est des nôtres*, he is one of us.

noue (nu) *f*, valley (*roof*); water meadow.

nouer (nwe) *v.t*, to tie; knot; knit (*fig.*); form. **noueux, euse** (nuø, ø:z) *a*, knotty, gnarled.

nougat (nuga) *m*, nougat.

nouilles (nu:j) *f.pl*, vermicelli.

nounou (nunu) *f*, nanny, nursy.

nourrain (nurɛ̃) *m*, fry (*fish*).

nourri, e (nuri) *p.p. & a*, fed; (*fig.*) copious; full; steeped; prolonged (*applause*); brisk (*fire, Mil.*). *mal* ~, *pas* ~, underfed, ill-fed. **nourrice** (ris) *f*, [wet] nurse. *être la ~ de*, to nurse, suckle. *mère ~*, nursing mother. **nourrir** (ri:r) *v.t*, to nourish; nurture, rear; suckle, nurse; feed; board, keep; foster, cherish, harbour, entertain. **nourrissage** (risa:ʒ) *m*, rearing (*cattle*). **nourrissant, e** (sɑ̃, ɑ̃:t) *a*, nourishing, nutritious. **nourrisseur** (sœ:r) *m*, cow keeper. **nourrisson** (sɔ̃) *m*, nurseling; suckling; foster child. **nourriture** (ty:r) *f*, food, nourishment, nutriment; sustenance; cud; board; feeding; nurture.

nous (nu) *pn*, we; us, to us, ourselves; each other. *à ~!* help! *~-mêmes*, ourselves.

nouveau, el, le (nuvo, ɛl) *a. & ad*, new; newly; recent; novel; fresh; another, further. *le Nouveau-Brunswick* (brɔ̃zvik), New Brunswick. *nouveau marié, nouvelle mariée*, bridegroom, bride (*about to be married or on marriage day*). *nouveaux mariés*, [newly] married couple; bride & bridegroom. *nouveau-né, e, n. & alt*, new-born (child). *nouveau riche*, upstart. *nouveau venu, nouvelle venue*, new-comer. *la Nouvelle-Écosse*, Nova Scotia. *la Nouvelle-Galles du Sud*, New South Wales. *la Nouvelle-Guinée*, New Guinea. *la Nouvelle-Orléans*, New Orleans. *la Nouvelle-Zélande* (zelɑ̃:d), New Zealand. *la Nouvelle-Zemble* (zɑ̃:bl), Nova Zembla. *le nouveau*, *m*, the new, a novelty, something new. *le nouveau, la nouvelle*, the new boy, man, girl (*Sch., &c*). *à nouveau*, anew, afresh; carried forward. *de nouveau*, again, afresh. **nouveauté** (te) *f*, newness; novelty; new thing, book, play, &c; innovation; (*pl.*) new styles, latest fashions; ladies' & children's wear; drapery.

nouvelle (nuvɛl) *f., oft. pl. in sense of* news, [piece of] news; tidings, intelligence; tale, short story, novelette. *~s à la main* (*Journalism*), to-day's gossip, looking at life.

nouvellement (nuvɛlmɑ̃) *ad*, newly, recently.
nouvelliste (nuvɛlist) *n*, newsmonger, intelligencer, quidnunc.

novateur, trice (nɔvatœ:r, tris) *n*, innovator.
novembre (nɔvɑ̃:br) *m*, November.

novice (nɔvis) *n*, novice; probationer; tiro; apprentice (*Naut.*). ¶ *a*, inexperienced, raw, fresh, green. **noviciat** (sja) *m*, noviciate; apprenticeship.

noyade (nwajad) *f*, drowning (*fatality*); noyade (*Hist.*).

noyau (nwajo) *m*, stone (*fruit*); kernel, core, centre; nucleus; newel. [*eau de*] *~*, noyau.

noyer (nwaje) *m*, walnut [tree, wood].
noyer (nwaje) *v.t*, to drown; flood, deluge; sink; swamp; play (*fish*). *un noyé* (je), a drowned man; a drowning man. *les noyés*, the [apparently] drowned.

nu, e (ny) *a*, naked, nude; bare; barebacked (*horse*); plain. *à l'œil nu*, with the naked

eye. *~ comme un ver*, stark naked. *nu-pieds, inv. ou pieds nus*, barefoot[ed]. *nu-tête, inv. ou tête nue*, bareheaded. ¶ *m*, nakedness, nudity, nude; bareness. *le nu*, the nude. *les nus*, the naked. *à nu*, bare, naked; bareback[ed] (*Riding*).

nuage (nya:ʒ) *m*, cloud; volume (*of smoke, &c*); haze, mist (*fig.*); suspicion. **nuageux, euse** (aʒø, ø:z) *a*, cloudy; hazy.

nuance (nyɑ̃:s) *f*, shade; hue; tinge; nuance; (*pl.*) lights & shades; sign of expression (*Mus.*). **nuancer** (ɑ̃se) *v.t*, to shade; mark (or observe) the signs of expression; execute with feeling.

Nubie (la) (nybi), Nubia. **nubien, ne** (bjɛ̃, ɛn) *a. & N~, n*, Nubian.

nubile (nybil) *a*, nubile, marriageable.

nudité (nydite) *f*, nudity, nakedness; bareness; nude (*Art.*).

nue (ny) (*Poet.*) *f. oft. pl*, cloud, sky. **nuée** (nye) *f*, storm cloud, thunder cloud; cloud (*fig.*), host, swarm; shower.

nuire (nɥi:r) *v.i.ir. & à*, to harm, hurt, injure, wrong, prejudice. **nuisible** (nɥizibl) *a*, harmful, hurtful, injurious, noxious, noisome.

nuit (nɥi) *f*, night; dark[ness]. *cette ~*, to-night; last night. *à [la] ~ close*, after dark. *à la ~ tombante*, at nightfall. **nuitamment** (tamɑ̃) *ad*, by night, in the n.

nul, le (nyl) *a*, no; not any; null, nugatory, nil; of no account; drawn (*game*); dead (*heat*). *nul(le) & non avenu(e)* (avny), null & void. *nulle part, ad*, nowhere. **nul**, *pn*, no one, none. **nulle**, *f*, null (*in cipher*). **nullement** (lmɑ̃) *ad*, in no way, not at all, by no means, nowise. **nullité** (lite) *f*, nullity; emptiness; nonentity, cipher (*pers.*).

nûment (nymɑ̃) *ad*, openly, frankly, nakedly.

numéraire (nymerɛ:r) *a*, numerary. ¶ *m*, coin, cash, specie. **numéral, e** (ral) *a*, numeral. **numérateur** (tœ:r) *m*, numerator (*Arith.*). **numérique†** (rik) *a*, numerical. **numéro** (ro) *m*, number; size; issue (*periodical*). *~ d'ordre*, running number. *~ de circulation*, identification n. (*motor car*). **numérotage** (rɔta:ʒ) *m*, numbering. **numéroter** (te) *v.t*, to number.

numismate (nymismat) *m*, numismatist. **numismatique** (tik) *f*, numismatics.

nuptial, e (nypsjal) *a*, nuptial, bridal, wedding (*att.*); marriage (*att.*).

nuque (nyk) *f*, nape (*of neck*). *~ rasée*, shingle[d hair].

nutritif, ive (nytritif, i:v) *a*, nutritive, nutritious. **nutrition** (sjɔ̃) *f*, nutrition.

nymphe (nɛ̃:f) *f*, nymph.

O

ô (o) *i*, O! oh!
oasis (oazis) *f*, oasis (*lit. & fig.*).

obédience (ɔbedjã:s) *f*, obedience (*Eccl.*). **obéir** (i:r) *v.i*, to obey. ~ **à**, to obey; submit to, yield to; comply with; respond to. **obéissance** (isã:s) *f*, obedience; allegiance; authority. **obéissant, e** (sã, ã:t) *a*, obedient; dutiful; submissive.

obélisque (obelisk) *m*, obelisk.

obérer (obere) *v.t*, to encumber [with debts].

obèse (ɔbɛ:z) *a*, obese, fat. **obésité** (bezite) *f*, obesity, fatness.

obier (ɔbje) *m*, guelder rose.

objecter (ɔbʒɛkte) *v.t*, to object (*que* = that); o. to, o. against; allege. **objectif, ivet** (tif, i:v) *a. & m*, objective (*Philos.*). ¶ *m*, objective, aim. [*verre*] *objectif*, objective, object glass, lens. **objection** (ksjɔ̃) *f*, objection; demur. **objet** (ʒɛ) *m*, object; subject; article. *d'art*, work of art.

objurgation (ɔbʒyrgasjɔ̃) *f*, objurgation.

oblation (ɔblasjɔ̃) *f*, oblation, offering (*Lit.*). **obligataire** (ɔbligatɛ:r) *n*, bondholder, debenture h. **obligation** (sjɔ̃) *f*, obligation; bond; debenture; recognizance. **obligatoire** (twa:r) *a*, obligatory, compulsory, binding. **obligé, e** (ʒe) *a*, usual; obbligato (*Mus.*). ¶ *n*, debtor (*for services*). **obligeamment** (ʒamã) *ad*, obligingly, kindly. **obligeant, e** (ʒã, ã:t) *a*, obliging, kind[ly]; complimentary. **obliger** (ʒe) *v.t*, to oblige, bind, compel; obligate. **s'~**, to bind oneself; undertake.

oblique† (ɔblik) *a*, oblique, slanting, skew; side (*glance*); crooked (*fig.*), underhand. **obliquer** (ke) *v.i*, to slant. **obliquité** (kite) *f*, obliquity; crookedness.

oblitérer (ɔblitere) *v.t*, to obliterate; cancel.

oblong, ongue (ɔblɔ̃, ɔ̃:g) *a*, oblong.

obnubiler (ɔbnybile) *v.t*, to cloud.

obole (ɔbɔl) *f*, [brass] farthing, stiver; mite.

obscène (ɔpsɛ:n) *a*, obscene. **obscénité** (senite) *f*, obscenity.

obscur, e (ɔpsky:r) *a*, dark; dim, murky; obscure. **obscurcir** (skyrsi:r) *v.t*, to darken, &c, overcast, overshadow. **obscurément** (remã) *ad*, darkly, &c. **obscurité** (rite) *f*, dark[ness], &c.

obséder (ɔpsede) *v.t*, to worry; obsess.

obsèques (ɔpsɛk) *f.pl*, obsequies. **obséquieux, euse†** (sekjø, ø:z) *a*, obsequious. **obséquiosité** (kjozite) *f*, obsequiousness.

observance (ɔpsɛrvã:s) *f*, observance (*Theol.*). **observateur, trice** (vatœ:r, tris) *n*, observer; (*att.*) observant. **observation** (sjɔ̃) *f*, observance; observation; remark. **observatoire** (twa:r) *m*, observatory; observation post (*Mil.*). **observer** (ve) *v.t*, to observe; keep; watch; spot.

obsession (ɔpsɛsjɔ̃) *f*, obsession.

obstacle (ɔpstakl) *m*, obstacle. *faire* ~ *à*, to stand in the way of.

obstétrical, e (ɔpstetrikal) *a*, obstetric(al). **obstétrique** (trik) *f*, obstetrics, midwifery.

obstination (ɔpstinasjɔ̃) *f*, obstinacy, stubbornness, wilfulness; doggedness. **obs-**

tinét, e (ne) *a*, obstinate, &c. **s'obstiner** (ne) *v.pr*, to persist.

obstruction (ɔpstryksjɔ̃) *f*, obstruction; stoppage. **obstruer** (strye) *v.t*, to obstruct; block.

obtempérer à (ɔptãpere), to obey, comply with.

obtenir (ɔptəni:r) *v.t.ir*, to obtain, secure, get. *j'ai obtenu de . . .*, I induced . . .; I managed to . . .

obturateur (ɔptyratœ:r) *m*, obturator, plug; shutter (*Phot.*). **obturer** (re) *v.t*, to stop.

obtus, e (ɔpty, y:z) *a*, obtuse.

obus (ɔby:s) *m*, shell. ~ *à balles*, shrapnel. *~-fusée*, rocket shell. **obusier** (byzje) *m*, howitzer.

obvier à (ɔbvje), to obviate, prevent.

ocarina (ɔkarina) *m*, ocarina.

occasion (ɔkazjɔ̃) *f*, opportunity; opening; occasion; bargain. *d'~*, second-hand, used; occasional (*occupation*). **occasionnel, le** (ɔnɛl) *a*, causative; occasional (*Philos.*). **occasionnellement** (lmã) *ad*, occasionally, now & then. **occasionner** (ne) *v.t*, to occasion.

occident (ɔksidã) *m*, west. **occidental, e** (tal) *a*, west[ern].

occiput (ɔksipyt) *m*, occiput.

occire (ɔksi:r) *v.t*, to slay.

occulte (ɔkylt) *a*, occult, hidden.

occupant (ɔkypã) *m*, occupant (*Law*). **occupation** (pasjɔ̃) *f*, occupation; pursuit. **occupé, e** (pe) *p.a*, busy. **occuper** (pe) *v.t*, to occupy; hold. **s'~**, to occupy (*or* busy) oneself, be engaged; attend; see.

occurrence (ɔkyrã:s) *f*, occurrence; emergency; juncture.

océan (ɔseã) *m*, ocean, sea. *l'~ Atlantique, Pacifique, Indien*, the Atlantic, Pacific, Indian, o. *l'~ Glacial arctique, antarctique*, the Arctic, Antarctic, o. **l'Océanie** (ani) *f*, Oceania.

ocre (ɔkr) *f*, ochre.

octave (ɔkta:v) *f*, octave. **octavon, ne** (tavɔ̃, ɔn) *n*, octaroon. **octobre** (tɔbr) *m*, October. **octogénaire** (ʒenɛ:r) *a. & n*, octogenarian. **octogone** (gɔn) *a*, octagonal. ¶ *m*, octagon.

octroi (ɔktrwa) *m*, octroi (*duty on goods entering town*). **octroyer** (trwaje) *v.t*, to grant.

oculaire (ɔkylɛ:r) *a*, ocular, eye (*att.*). [*verre*] *~, m*, eyepiece, ocular. **oculiste** (list) *m*, oculist. *médecin ~*, eye doctor.

ode (ɔd) *f*, ode.

odeur (ɔdœ:r) *f*, odour, smell, scent.

odieux, euse† (ɔdjø, ø:z) *a*, odious, hateful, heinous, outrageous; obnoxious; invidious. ¶ *m*, odium.

odorant, e (ɔdɔrã, ã:t) *a*, fragrant, [sweet-]scented. **odoriférant, e** (riferã, ã:t) *a*, fragrant, [sweet-]scented, odoriferous. **odorat** (ra) *m*, [sense of] smell.

odyssée (ɔdise) *f*, Odyssey (*fig.*).

oé (oe) *i*, wo!, whoa!

œil (œːj) *m*, eye; look; loop; hole; **face** (*Typ.*); lustre; gloss. **~-de-bœuf**, bull's-eye (*window*). **~-de-chat**, cat's-eye (*jewel*). **~-de-perdrix**, soft corn (*foot*). **œillade** (œjad) *f*, glance (*loving*); ogle. **œillère** (jɛːr) *f*, blinker; eye bath. [*dent*] **~**, eye tooth. **œillet** (jɛ) *m*, eyelet; e. hole; pink (*Bot.*). **~** [*des fleuristes*], carnation. **~ de poète**, sweet-william. **œilleton** (jtɔ̃) *m*, sucker, offset (*Hort.*).

œsophage (ezɔfaːʒ) *m*, oesophagus.

œstre (ɛstr) *m*, oestrum, oestrus, gad-fly.

œuf (œf) *m*, egg; (*pl*, *de poisson*) hard roe, spawn. **~** *à la coque*, boiled egg. **~s** *au jambon*, ham & eggs. **~** *clair*, wind egg. **~** *de Pâques*, Easter egg. **œuvé, e** (ve) *a*, hard-roed.

œuvre (œːvr) *f*, work; setting (*jewel*); (*pl.*) charity; (*pl.*) work (*social*). ¶ *m*, carcass, carcase (*of a building*); works (*of an artist*).

offensant, e (ɔfɑ̃sɑ̃, ɑ̃ːt) *a*, offensive, obnoxious, objectionable, insulting. **offense** (fɑ̃ːs) *f*, offence; trespass (*Theol.*). **~** *à la cour*, contempt of court. **offensé, e** (fɑ̃se) *n*, aggrieved party. **offenser** (se) *v.t*, to offend; trespass against; injure. **s'~**, to take offence. **offenseur** (sœːr) *m*, offender. **offensif, ive†** (sif, iːv) *a. & f*, offensive (*attacking*).

offertoire (ɔfɛrtwaːr) *m*, offertory (*Lit.*); voluntary (*organ, between credo & sanctus*).

office (ɔfis) *m*, office; service; worship; department (*Government*). **~** *des morts*, burial service. *d'~*, official[ly]; arbitrary (*assessment*); as a matter of course. ¶ *f*, pantry, servants' hall. **officiel, le†** (sjɛl) *a*, official. ¶ *m*, official (*Sport, &c*). **officier** (sje) *v.i*, to officiate (*Eccl.*). ¶ *m*, officer. **~** *à la suite*, supernumerary o. **~** *de l'état civil*, registrar (*births, &c.*). **~** *de marine*, naval officer. **~** *de service*, orderly o. **~** *du génie*, engineer (*Mil.*). **officieux, euse†** (sjø, øːz), *a*, officious (*Diplomacy*), informal, semi-official, unofficial; white (*lie*). **officine** (sin) *f*, dispensary; hotbed (*fig.*); shady office, thieves' kitchen.

offrande (ɔfrɑ̃ːd) *f*, offering. **le plus offrant** [& dernier enchérisseur] (frɑ̃), the highest bidder. **offre** (fr) *f*, offer; tender. **~** *d'emploi*, situation vacant. *l'~ & la demande*, supply & demand. **offrir** (friːr) *v.t.ir*, to offer, proffer, tender; bid; present; offer up. **~** *sa main*, to propose (*marriage to a man*). **~** *son nom*, to propose (*to a woman*).

offusquer (ɔfyske) *v.t*, to obfuscate, obscure; dazzle; offend.

ogive (ɔʒiːv) *f*, ogive, pointed arch.

ognon (ɔɲɔ̃) *m*, bulb (*Bot.*).

ogre, ogresse (ɔgr, grɛs) *n*, ogre, ogress.

oh (o) *i*, oh! O!

ohé (o[h]e) *i*, hi! hullo[a]!; ahoy!; wo! whoa!

oie (wa) *f*, goose.

oignon (ɔɲɔ̃) *m*, onion; bulb (*Bot.*); bunion. *personne qui se mêle des* **~***s des autres*, meddlesome person, meddler; officious person. **oignonière** (ɔɲɛːr) *f*, onion bed.

oindre (wɛ̃ːdr) *v.t.ir*, to anoint.

oiseau (wazo) *m*, bird, fowl; hod. **~** *de mauvais augure*, bird of ill omen. **~** *de volière*, cage bird. **~-mouche**, *m*, humming bird. **~** *rare*, rare bird, rara avis. *à vol d'~*, as the crow flies. *vue à vol d'~*, bird's-eye view. **oiselet** (zlɛ) *m*, small bird. **oiseleur** (zlœːr) *m*, bird catcher, fowler. **oiselier** (zəlje) *m*, bird fancier. **oisellerie** (zɛlri) *f*, bird fancying; aviary. **oiseux, euse** (wazø, øːz) *a*, idle (*words, &c*). **oisif, ive†** (zif, iːv) *a*, idle (*pers., money*). **oisillon** (wazijɔ̃) *m*, fledgeling. **oisiveté** (wazivte) *f*, idleness. **oison** (wazɔ̃) *m*, gosling. **~** *bridé* (*fig.*), simpleton.

oléagineux, euse (ɔleaʒinø, øːz) *a*, oleaginous, oily; oil (*seed*).

oléandre (ɔleɑ̃ːdr) *m*, oleander.

olfactif, ive (ɔlfaktif, iːv) *a*, olfactory.

olibrius (ɔlibriyːs) *m*, conceited fool.

oligarchie (ɔligarʃi) *f*, oligarchy.

olivaie (vɛ) *f*, o. grove. **olivaison** (vɛzɔ̃) *f*, o. season; o. harvest. **olivâtre** (vaːtr) *a*, olive (*complexion*). **olive** (liːv) *f*, olive. *couleur* [*d'~*], olive[-green]. **olivier** (livje) *m*, o. [tree]; o. [wood].

olympe (ɔlɛ̃ːp) *m*, Olympus (*fig.*). **olympique** (lɛ̃pik) *a*, Olympic.

ombilic (ɔ̃bilik) *m*, umbilicus; navel.

omble[-chevalier] (ɔ̃ːbl) *m*, char (*fish*).

ombrage (ɔ̃braːʒ) *m*, [spread of] foliage; shade; umbrage. **ombragé, e** (braʒe) *p.a*, shady. **ombrager** (ʒe) *v.t*, to shade, overshadow. **ombrageux, euse** (ʒø, øːz) *a*, shy, skittish (*beast*); touchy. **ombre** (ɔ̃ːbr) *f*, shade; shadow; ghost. **~***s chinoises*, galanty show. **~** *portée*, cast shadow. ¶ *m*, grayling. **ombre** [*fish*]. **~-chevalier**, char (*fish*). **ombrelle** (ɔ̃brɛl) *f*, sunshade, parasol. **ombrer** (bre) *v.t*, to shade (*Art*). **ombreux, euse** (brø, øːz) *a*, shady (*Poet.*).

oméga (ɔmega) *m*, omega.

omelette (ɔmlɛt) *f*, omelet[te]. **~** *aux confitures*, sweet o. **~** *aux fines herbes*, savoury o.

omettre (ɔmɛtr) *v.t.ir*, to omit, leave out. **omission** (misjɔ̃) *f*, omission.

omnibus (ɔmnibyːs) *m*, [omni]bus; (*att.*) slow (*train, boat*).

omnipotence (ɔmnipɔtɑ̃ːs) *f*, omnipotence. **omnipotent, e** (tɑ̃, ɑ̃ːt) *a*, omnipotent. **omniscience** (ɔmnisjɑ̃ːs) *f*, omniscience. **omniscient, e** (jɑ̃, ɑ̃ːt) *a*, omniscient.

omnivore (ɔmniːvɔːr) *a*, omnivorous.

omoplate (ɔmɔplat) *f*, shoulder blade.

on (ɔ̃), *oft.* **l'on**, *pn*, one; a man, woman, &c; we; you; they; people; somebody; anybody. ~ *demande . . ., wanted . . .* (*advertisement*). ~ *dit*, it is said, they say. ~*dit* (ɔdi) *m*, hearsay, rumour. *on n'embauche pas*, no hands wanted. *on ne passe pas*, no thoroughfare.

once (ɔ̃:s) *f*, ounce (*Zool.*); snow leopard; grain, particle (*fig.*).

oncle (ɔ̃kl) *m*, uncle.

onction (ɔ̃ksjɔ̃) *f*, unction; rubbing [with oil]. **onctueux, euse†** (tɥø, ø:z) *a*, unctuous; oily; greasy.

onde (ɔ̃:d) *f*, wave, billow; (*Poet.*) sea, main; water; stream. *en* ~*s*, wavy (*hair*). **ondé, e** (ɔ̃de) *a*, waved, wavy; grained (*wood*). **ondée** (de) *f*, heavy shower. **ondoyer** (dwaje) *v.i*, to undulate; wave; billow; surge. **ondulation** (dylasjɔ̃) *f*, undulation; wave. ~ *permanente*, permanent wave (*hair*). **ondulé, e** (le) *a*, undulating; wavy; corrugated (*iron*). **onduler** (le) *v.i*, to undulate; (*v.t.*) to wave (*hair*). *se faire onduler* [*les cheveux*], to have one's hair waved.

onéreux, euse† (ɔnerø, ø:z) *a*, onerous, burdensome.

ongle (ɔ̃:gl) *m*, nail; claw; hoof. **onglée** (ɔ̃gle) *f*, numbness [of the fingers]. **onglet** (glɛ) *m*, guard (*Bookb.*); tab; mitre (*Carp.*). **onglier** (glie) *m*, manicure set. ~ [*en*] *écrin*, box m. s. ~ *suspendu*, m. stand.

onguent (ɔ̃gɑ̃) *m*, ointment, salve.

ongulé, e (ɔ̃gyle) *a*, hoofed.

onomatopée (ɔnɔmatɔpe) *f*, onomatopoeia.

onyx (ɔniks) *m*, onyx.

onze (ɔ̃:z) *a. & m*, eleven; eleventh. **onzième†** (ɔ̃zjɛm) *a. & n*, eleventh. (*Note.*—Say *le onze*, *le onzième*, *not l'onze*, *l'onzième*.)

oolithe (ɔɔlit) *m*, oolite.

opacité (ɔpasite) *f*, opacity.

opale (ɔpal) *f*, opal. **opalin, e** (lɛ̃, in) *a*, opaline.

opaque (ɔpak) *a*, opaque.

opéra (ɔpera) *m*, opera; o. [house]. ~ *bouffe*, comic opera, musical comedy. ~*comique*, opera comique (*spoken dialogue*).

opérateur, trice (ɔperatœːr, tris) *n*, operator; camera man (*film*). **opération** (sjɔ̃) *f*, operation; stage; working; transaction, dealing. **opéré, e** (re) *n*, surgical case (*pers.*). **opérer** (re) *v.t. & abs*, to operate, work, effect; make; do; act; deal; operate on (*Surg.*).

opérette (ɔperɛt) *f*, operetta, light opera, musical play.

ophtalmie (ɔftalmi) *f*, ophthalmia. **ophtalmique** (mik) *a*, ophthalmic.

opiacé, e (ɔpjase) *a*, opiated.

opinant (ɔpinɑ̃) *m*, speaker (*in debate*). **opiner** (ne) *v.i*, to opine; vote. ~ *du bonnet*, to say nothing but ditto to everything. **opiniâtre†** (nja:tr) *a. & n*, [self-] opinionated; self-willed; obstinate, pertinacious, stubborn (person). **s'opiniâtrer** (ɑtre) *v.pr*, to persist. **opiniâtreté** (trəte) *f*,

obstinacy, &c. **opinion** (njɔ̃) *f*, opinion; view; mind; vote.

opiomane (ɔpjɔman) *n*, opium addict. **opium** (jɔm) *m*, opium.

opossum (ɔpɔsɔm) *m*, opossum.

opportun, e (ɔpɔrtœ̃, yn) *a*, opportune, seasonable, timely, well-timed. **opportunément** (tynemɑ̃) *ad*, opportunely, &c. **opportunisme** (nism) *m*, opportunism. **opportuniste** (nist) *n*, opportunist, timeserver, trimmer. **opportunité** (te) *f*, opportuneness; opportunity.

opposant, e (ɔpozɑ̃, ɑ̃:t) *n*, opponent; (*att.*) opposing; opponent. **opposé, e** (ze) *a*, opposed; opposite. ¶ *m*, opposite, reverse, contrary. **opposer** (ze) *v.t. & s'*~ *à*, to oppose. ~ *une exception*, to demur (*Law*). *à l'opposite* (pozit) *ad*, opposite, facing. **opposition** (sjɔ̃) *f*, opposition; contrast; contradistinction; stop; objection.

opprobre (ɔprɔbr) *m*, disgrace, opprobrium.

opter (ɔpte) *v.i*, to choose.

opticien (ɔptisjɛ̃) *m*, optician.

optime (ɔptime) (*Latin word*), very well, all right. **optimisme** (mism) *m*, optimism. **optimiste** (mist) *a*, optimist(ic), hopeful, sanguine. ¶ *n*, optimist.

option (ɔpsjɔ̃) *f*, option.

optique (ɔptik) *a*, optic, optical. ¶ *f*, optics; perspective (*Theat.*).

opulence (ɔpylɑ̃:s) *f*, opulence, affluence, wealth; buxomness. **opulent, e** (lɑ̃, ɑ̃:t) *a*, opulent, &c.

opuscule (ɔpyskyl) *m*, short treatise, tract.

or (ɔːr) *c*, now. ~ *çà*, now then.

or (ɔːr) *m*, gold. ~ *laminé*, rolled g. ~ *moulu*, ormolu. *ni pour* ~ *ni pour argent*, for love or money. *d'*~, gold; golden.

oracle (ɔraːkl) *m*, oracle.

orage (ɔraːʒ) *m*, thunderstorm; storm. **orageux, euse†** (raʒø, ø:z) *a*, stormy; thundery.

oraison (ɔrɛzɔ̃) *f*, prayer. ~ *dominicale*, Lord's prayer. ~ *funèbre*, funeral oration.

oral, e† (ɔral) *a*, oral, viva voce.

orange (ɔrɑ̃:ʒ) *f*, orange. ~ *amère*, Seville o. ~ *sanguine*, blood o. **orange**, *m. & a. & orangé, e* (rɑ̃ʒe) *a. & m*, orange (*colour*). **orangeade** (ʒad) *f*, orangeade. **oranger** (ʒe) *m*, orange [tree]. **orangerie** (ʒri) *f*, orangery.

orang-outang (ɔrɑ̃utɑ̃) *m*, orang-outang.

orateur (ɔratœːr) *m*, orator, speaker. **oratoire** (twaːr) *a*, oratorical; rhetorical, declamatory. *l'art* ~, oratory. ¶ *m*, oratory (*chapel*). **oratorio** (tɔrjo) *m*, oratorio.

orbe (ɔrb) *m*, orb (*heavenly body*). **orbite** (bit) *f*, orbit; socket (*eye*).

Orcades (les) (ɔrkad) *f.pl*, the Orkneys.

orchestral, e (ɔrkɛstral) *a*, orchestral. **orchestre** (tr) *m*, orchestra, band; orchestra stalls (*Theat.*). ~ **noir**, [negro] minstrels. **orchestrer** (tre) *v.t*, to orchestrate, score. **orchidée** (ɔrkide) *f*, orchid. **orchis** (kis) *m*, orchis.

ordalie (ɔrdali) *f*, ordeal (*Hist.*).

ordinaire† (ɔrdinɛ:r) *a*, ordinary; common; customary; usual, everyday. ¶ *m*, wont; ordinary; [company] mess (*Mil.*).

ordinal (ɔrdinal) *a.m*, ordinal.

ordination (ɔrdinasjɔ̃) *f*, ordination (*Eccl.*).

ordonnance (ɔrdɔnɑ̃:s) *f*, ordering (*arrangement*); organization; regulation (*police*); [treasury] warrant; prescription (*Med.*). ¶ *f. or m*, orderly, batman. **ordonnancer** (nɑ̃se) *v.t*, to pass for payment. **ordonnateur, trice** (natœ:r, tris) *n*, director; organizer (*fête*, &c.). **ordonné, e** (ne) *p.a*, tidy, orderly (*pers.*). **ordonner** (ne) *v.t. & abs*, to order; organize; prescribe; ordain. **ordre** (dr) *m*, order; rate. ~ *d'exécution*, death warrant. ~ *du jour*, agenda, business [before the meeting]; order of the day. ~ *public*, law & order, peace; public policy. *à l'*~! order!; chair!

ordure (ɔrdy:r) *f*, filth, dirt, muck; refuse, dust; ordure; smut. **ordurier, ère** (dyrje, ɛ:r) *a*, filthy; scurrilous; smutty.

orée (ɔre) *f*, verge, skirt (*of a wood*).

oreille (ɔrɛ:j) *f*, ear; lug; wing (*nut*). *avoir l'*~ *dure*, to be hard of hearing. *avoir l'*~ *juste*, to have a good ear (*for music*). ~*-d'ours*, bear's-ear, auricula. ~*-de-souris*, forget-me-not. **oreiller** (rɛje) *m*, pillow. **oreillette** (jɛt) *f*, auricle (*heart*); ear (*Bot.*). **oreillon** (jɔ̃) *m*, ear flap; ear (*Bot.*); (*pl.*): mumps.

orémus (ɔremy:s) *m*, prayer.

Orénoque (l') (ɔrenɔk) *m*, the Orinoco.

ores (ɔ:r) *ad*: *d'*~ *& déjà*, now & henceforth.

orfèvre (ɔrfɛ:vr) *m*, goldsmith &/or silversmith. **orfèvrerie** (fɛvrəri) *f*, gold[smith's] &/or silver[smith's] work.

orfraie (ɔrfrɛ) *f*, osprey.

organdi (ɔrgɑ̃di) *m*, organdie; book muslin.

organe (ɔrgan) *m*, organ; spokesman; (*pl, Mach.*) parts, gear. **organique** (nik) *a*, organic. **organisateur, trice** (zatœ:r, tris) *n*, organizer. ~ *du ravitaillement*, food controller. **organisation** (zasjɔ̃) *f*, organization. **organiser** (ze) *v.t*, to organize. *une tête bien organisée, un cerveau organisé*, a level-headed person. **organisme** (nism) *m*, organism. **organiste** (nist) *n*, organist (*Mus.*).

orge (ɔrʒ) *f*, barley. ~ *perlé*, pearl b. **orgeat** (ʒa) *m*, orgeat. **orgelet** (ʒǝlɛ) *m*, sty[e] (*eye*).

orgie (ɔrʒi) *f*, orgy; riot (*fig.*).

orgue (ɔrg) *m*, *the pl. is f*, organ; o. loft. ~ *de Barbarie*, barrel organ.

orgueil (ɔrgœ:j) *m*, pride. **orgueilleux, euse†** (gœjø, ø:z) *a. & n*, proud (person).

orient (ɔrjɑ̃) *m*, orient, east. l'O~ (*Geog.*), the Orient, the East. ~ *moyen*, the Middle East. **oriental, e** (tal) *a*, oriental, eastern. O~, *n*, Oriental, Eastern. **orientation** (tasjɔ̃) *f*, orientation; bearings; direction; aspect; trend; trimming (*sails, yards*). **orienter** (te) *v.t*, to orient[ate]; direct, point; trim (*sails, yards*).

orifice (ɔrifis) *m*, mouth, aperture, port, orifice.

oriflamme (ɔriflɑ:m) *f*, oriflamme; banner.

originaire† (ɔriʒinɛ:r) *a*, original. *être* ~ *de*, to come from, be a native of. **original, e†** (nal) *a*, original; first (*edition*); inventive; odd, queer. ¶ *m*, original; oddity. **originalité** (lite) *f*, originality. **origine** (ʒin) *f*, origin; beginning, outset. **originel, le†** (nɛl) *a*, original.

oripeaux (ɔripo) *m.pl*, tinsel; tawdry finery; rags.

Orléans (ɔrleɑ̃) *m. or f*, Orleans.

ormaie (ɔrmɛ) *ou* **ormoie** (mwa) *f*, elm grove. **orme** (ɔrm) *& ***ormeau** (mo) *m*, elm [tree]. *orme de montagne*, wych-elm. **ormille** (mi:j) *f*, elm row.

orné, e (ɔrne) *p.a*, ornate. **ornemaniste** (nəmanist) *n*, ornamentalist. **ornement** (mɑ̃) *m*, ornament. *sans* ~*s*, unadorned. **ornemental, e** (tal) *a*, ornamental. **ornementation** (tasjɔ̃) *f*, ornamentation. **orner** (ne) *v.t*, to ornament, adorn; grace.

ornière (ɔrnjɛ:r) *f*, rut; groove.

ornithogale (ɔrnitɔgal) *m*, star of Bethlehem. **ornithologie** (lɔʒi) *f*, ornithology. **ornithologiste** (ʒist) *ou* **ornithologue** (lɔg) *n*, ornithologist.

orpailleur (ɔrpɑjœ:r) *m*, gold washer (*pers.*).

orphelin, e (ɔrfǝlɛ̃, in) *n. & att*, orphan. ~ *de père*, fatherless. **orphelinat** (lina) *m*, orphanage.

orphéon (ɔrfeɔ̃) *m*, choral society.

orphie (ɔrfi) *f*, garfish.

orpin (ɔrpɛ̃) *m*, stonecrop.

orque (ɔrk) *f*, orc, grampus.

orteil (ɔrtɛ:j) *m*, toe; great toe.

orthodoxe (ɔrtɔdɔks) *a*, orthodox. **orthodoxie** (ksi) *f*, orthodoxy. **orthographe** (graf) *f*, orthography, spelling. **orthographie** (fi) *f*, orthography (*Arch.*).· **orthographier** (fje) *v.t. & abs*, to spell. *mal* ~, to misspell. **orthographique** (fik) *a*, orthographic(al); spelling (*att.*). **orthopédie** (pedi) *f*, orthopaedy. **orthopédique** (dik) *a*, orthopaedic.

ortie (ɔrti) *f*, nettle. ~ *brûlante*, ~ *grièche* (grjɛʃ), stinging nettle.

ortolan (ɔrtɔlɑ̃) *m*, ortolan.

orvet (ɔrvɛ) *m*, slow-worm, blind-worm.

orviétan (ɔrvjetɑ̃) *m*: *marchand d'*~*s*, quack.

os (os, *pl*. o) *m*, bone. ~ *à moelle*, marrow b. ~ *à ronger*, sop (*fig.*).

osciller (ɔsile) *v.i*, to oscillate, swing, sway about; fluctuate; waver. **oscillation** (lasjɔ̃) *f*, oscillation, &c.

osé, e (oze) *p.a*, daring, bold.

oseille (ozε:j) *f*, sorrel.

oser (oze) *v.t*, to dare, d. to, venture, v. to.

oseraie (ozrε) *f*, osier bed.

oseur, euse (ozœ:r, ø:z) *n*, bold man, woman.

osier (ozje) *m*, osier, wicker.

osmium (ɔsmjɔm) *m*, osmium.

ossature (ɔsaty:r) *f*, frame[work]. osselet (slɛ) *m*, ossicle; (*pl.*) knuckle bones, dibs. ossements (smɑ̃) *m.pl*, bones (*dead*). osseux, euse (so, ø:z) *a*, bony, osseous. ossifier (sifje) *v.t*, to ossify. ossu, e (sy) *a*, big-boned, bony. ossuaire (sɥε:r) *m*, ossuary, charnel house.

Ostende (ɔstɑ̃:d) *m*, Ostend.

ostensible† (ɔstɑ̃sibl) *a*, fit (*or* intended) to be shown; open. ostensoir (swa:r) *m*, ostensory, monstrance. ostentateur, trice (tatœ:r, tris) & ostentatoire (twa:r) *a*, ostentatious, showy. ostentation (sjɔ̃) *f*, ostentation, show.

ostracisme (ɔstrasism) *m*, ostracism.

ostréiculture (ɔstreikylty:r) *f*, oyster culture.

ostrogot[h], e (ɔstrɔgo, ɔt) (*fig.*) *n*, goth, barbarian.

otage (ɔta:ʒ) *m*, hostage. *prendre pour ~*, to kidnap.

otalgie (ɔtalʒi) *f*, earache.

otarie (ɔtari) *f*, otary, sea lion.

ôté (ote) *pr*, barring, except. ôter (te) *v.t*, to remove, take away; t. out; t. off; pull off; doff. *s'~*, to get out (*of way*, &c).

ottoman, e (ɔtɔmɑ̃, an) *a*. & O~, *n*, Ottoman. ottomane, (*f*, ottoman.

ou (u) *c*, or, either. *~ bien*, or [else].

où (u) *ad*, where, whither; whence; how far; which; what; when; in. *d'~*, whence, where from. *par ~*, [by] which way, through which.

ouailles (wɑ:j) *f.pl*, flock (*Christians*).

ouate (wat) *f*, wadding, cotton wool. ouater (te) *v.t*, to wad, pad; quilt.

oubli (ubli) *m*, forgetfulness; oblivion; neglect; oversight; lapse. oublie (bli) *f*, cone, cornet, wafer (*ice cream*). oublier (blie) *v.t*. & *abs*, to forget; neglect; overlook. oubliettes (εt) *f.pl*, oubliette. oublieux, euse (ø, ø:z) *a*, forgetful, oblivious.

Ouessant (wεsɑ̃) *m*, Ushant.

ouest (wεst) *m*, west; (*att.*) west, western.

ouf (uf) *i*, oh! what a relief!

oui (wi) (*particle*), yes; ay; so. ¶ *m*, (*le ~*, *un ~*), yes; ay. *~-da*, *i*, [yes] indeed!

ouï-dire (widi:r) *m*, hearsay. ouïe (wi) *f*, hearing; (*pl.*) sound holes (*Mus.*); (*pl.*) gills (*fish*).

ouiller (uje) *v.t*, to fill up (*ullaged cask*).

ouïr (wi:r) *v.t.ir*, to hear (*witness—Law*).

curagan (uragɑ̃) *m*, hurricane.

Oural (l') (ural) *m*, the Ural. *les monts Ourals*, the Ural Mountains.

ourdir (urdi:r) *v.t*, to warp (*yarn*); hatch (*fig.*); weave (*fig.*).

ourler (urle) *v.t*, to hem. *~ à jour*, to hem-

stitch. ourlet (lɛ) *m*, hem; rim. *~ à jour*, hemstitch. *~ piqué*, stitched hem.

ours (urs) *m*, bear. *~ blanc*, polar b. *~ grizzlé* (grizle), grizzly b. *~ [Martin]*, *~ de peluche*, Teddy b. ourse (urs) *f*, [she-] bear; Bear (*Astr.*). oursin (sɛ̃) *m*, sea urchin; bearskin (*cap*). ourson (sɔ̃) *m*, bear's cub; bearskin (*cap*).

outarde (utard) *f*, bustard.

outil (uti) *m*, tool. outillage (tija:ʒ) *m*, tools; plant, machinery; equipment, outfit. *~ national*, national capital (*Economics*). outiller (je) *v.t*, to equip, fit out.

outrage (utra:ʒ) *m*, outrage; insult; offence; ravages (*time*). outrageant, e (traʒɑ̃, ɑ̃:t) *a*, insulting, scurrilous. outrager (ʒe) *v.t*, to insult; outrage. outrageux, euse† (ʒø, ø:z) *a*, insulting, scurrilous.

outrance (utrɑ̃:s) *f*, excess. *à ~*, to the death; mortal; internecine; desperately, to the bitter end; out & out. outrancier, ère (trɑ̃sje, ε:r) *a*, extremist (*att.*), out & out.

outre (utr) *f*, leather bottle.

outre (utr) *pr*. & *ad*, beyond; further. *d'~ en ~*, through [& through]. *nos voisins d'~-Manche*, our neighbours across the Channel. *en ~*, moreover, besides, further[more]. *~-mer*, *ad*. & *d'~-mer*, *a*, oversea[s].

outré, e (utre) *a*, excessive, far-fetched, overdone, fulsome, outré; carried away; disgusted.

outrecuidance (utrəkɥidɑ̃:s) *f*, presumptuousness. outrecuidant, e (dɑ̃, ɑ̃:t) *a*, overweening.

outremer (utrəmε:r) *m*, ultramarine (*pigment*).

outrepasser (utrəpɑse) *v.t*, to go beyond, overstep.

outrer (utre) *v.t*, to overdo; overstrain; provoke.

ouvert, e† (uvε:r, εrt) *p.a*, open; free; frank. ouverture (vεrty:r) *f*, opening; aperture; orifice; hole; port; gap; spread; overture; openness.

ouvrable (uvrabl) *a*, work[ing], business (*day*). ouvrage (uvra:ʒ) *m*, work; doing (*fig.*). *~s d'agrément*, fancy work. *~s d'art*, permanent works, [p.] structures. *~s de dames*, fancy needlework, art n. *~s de ville*, job work (*Typ.*). ouvragé, e (vraʒe) *a*, [highly] worked, elaborated.

ouvre-boîte (uvrə) *m*, tin opener. ouvre-gants, *m*, glove stretcher.

ouvrer (uvre) *v.i*, to work; (*v.t.*) to work; diaper.

ouvreur, euse (uvrœ:r, ø:z) *n*, opener; (*f.*) box attendant (*Theat.*).

ouvrier, ère (uvrie, ε:r) *n*, workman; workwoman; worker; operative; factory hand; journeyman; labourer (*farm*). *~ d'art*, handicraftsman. ¶ *a*, working, labouring (*class*); workmen's (*train*, &c); labour (*troubles*, &c).

ouvrir (uvri:r) *v.t. & abs. ir*, to open; unlock; disburden; open up; cut; propose; head (*as a list*); turn on, switch on; draw back (*curtains*); sharpen (*appetite*); (*r.i.ir.*) to open. *la maison reste ouverte pendant les travaux*, business as usual during alterations.

ouvroir (uvrwa:r) *m*, workroom (*convent, &c*).

ovaire (ɔvɛ:r) *m*, ovary.

ovale (ɔval) *a. & m*, oval. ~ [*de table*], doily.

ovation (ɔvasjɔ̃) *f*, ovation.

ovine (ɔvin) *a.f*, ovine.

ovipare (ɔvipa:r) *a*, oviparous.

oxhydrique (ɔksidrik) *a*, oxyhydrogen (*blowpipe, &c*); lime(*light*).

oxyde (ɔksid) *m*, oxide. ~ *de carbone*, carbon monoxide. **oxyder** (de) *v.t*, to oxidize. **oxygène** (ɛn) *m*, oxygen.

ozone (ozɔn) *m*, ozone.

P

pacage (paka:ʒ) *m*, grazing; pasturage. **pacager** (kaʒe) *v.t*, to pasture, graze.

pachyderme (paʃidɛrm) *m*, pachyderm.

pacificateur, trice (pasifikatœ:r, tris) *n*, peacemaker. ¶ *a*, pacifying. **pacifier** (fje) *v.t*, to pacify; appease. **pacifique†** (fik) *a*, pacific, peaceable; peaceful. **le P~**, the Pacific. **pacifiste** (fist) *n. & a*, pacificist, pacifist.

pacotille (pakɔti:j) *f*, barter goods; trash.

pacte (pakt) *m*, [com]pact, covenant. **pactiser avec** (tize) *v.t*, to compound with (*condone*); compound (*felony*).

Pactole (le) (paktɔl) (*fig.*), a gold mine.

Padoue (padu) *f*, Padua.

pæan (peã) *m*, paean.

pagaie (pagɛ) *f*, paddle (*canoe*).

paganisme (paganism) *m*, paganism, heathenism.

pagayer (pagɛje) *v.t*, to paddle (*canoe*). **pagayeur, euse** (jœ:r, ø:z) *n*, paddler.

page (pa:ʒ) *f*, page (*book*); chapter (*of one's life*). ¶ (*Hist.*) *m*, page (*noble youth*).

pagel (paʒɛl) *m*, [sea] bream.

paginer (paʒine) *v.t*, to page, paginate.

pagode (pagɔd) *f*, pagoda; mandarin (*toy*).

paie (pɛ) *f*, pay, wages; (*good, bad*) payer. **paiement** (mã) *m*, payment.

païen, ne (pajɛ̃, ɛn) *a. & n*, pagan, heathen.

paillard (pa:ja:r, ard) *a. & n*, lewd (person). **paillasse** (jas) *f*, straw mattress, paillasse, palliasse. ¶ *m*, clown, merry andrew (*pagliaccio*). **paillasson** (sɔ̃) *m*, door mat; matting (*Hort.*). **paille** (pa:j) *f*, straw; flaw; (*fig.*) mote (*in eye*). ~ *de bois*, woodwool. [*couleur*] ~, straw-colour[ed]. **pailler** (paje) (*fig.*) *m*, dunghill. ¶ *v.t*, to mulch; rush (*chair*). **paillet** (jɛ) *a.m*, pale (*red wine*). **paillet d'abordage**, *m*, collision mat. **pailleté, e** (jte) *a*, spangled.

paillette (jɛt) *f*, spangle; flake, scale. ~*s d'or*, float gold. **pailleux** (jo) *a.m*, strawy; flawy. **paillis** (ji) *m*, mulch. **paillon** (jɔ̃) *m*, straw envelope (*bottle*); spangle; foil; grain (*solder*). **paillote** (pajɔt) *f*, straw hut (*native*).

pain (pɛ̃) *m*, bread; loaf (*bread, sugar*); biscuit (*dog*); cake (*soap, fish, &c*); tablet; pat (*butter*). ~ *à cacheter*, signet wafer. ~ *à chanter*, wafer (*Eccl.*). ~ *cornu*, coburg [loaf]. ~ *d'épice*, ginger bread. ~ *de bougie*, taper (*coiled*). ~ *de munition*, ration bread. ~ *de régime*, dietary b. ~ *grillé*, *rôti*, toast. ~ *platine*, tin loaf.

pair (pɛ:r) *a.m*; **paire**, *Arith. only, a.f*, equal, like; even (*number*). ¶ *m*, peer; equal; par, equality; mate (*bird*). *au* ~ (*engagement*) on mutual terms. *marcher de* ~ *avec*, to keep pace with; rank with.

paire (pɛ:r) *f*, pair; brace; yoke (*oxen, &c*).

pairesse (pɛrɛs) (*Eng.*) *f*, peeress. **pairie** (ri) (*Fr. Hist. & Eng.*) *f*, peerage.

paisible† (pɛzibl) *a*, peaceable, peaceful.

paître (pɛ:tr) *v.t. & i. ir*, to graze, pasture, browse; feed; tend.

paix (pɛ) *f*, peace; pax (*Eccl.*). ¶ *i*, hush! be quiet!

pal (pal) *m*, pale, stake.

palabre (pala:br) *f. or m*, palaver. **palabrer** (labre) *v.i*, to palaver.

paladin (paladɛ̃) *m*, paladin; knight errant (*fig.*).

palais (palɛ) *m*, palace; [law] courts; court; law; palate; roof of the mouth. ~ *dur*, hard palate, bony p. ~ *mou*, soft p.

palan (palɑ̃) *m*, pulley block; tackle, purchase. **palanche** (lɑ̃:ʃ) *f*, yoke (*for pails*).

palanque (palɑ̃:k) *f*, stockade.

palatal, e (palatal) *a*, palatal.

palatine (palatin) *f*, fur cape, tippet.

pale (pal) *f*, shut-off; blade (*oar, air propeller*). **pâle** (pɑ:l) *a*, pale, pallid, wan; (*fig.*) colourless.

palée (pale) *f*, sheet piling.

palefrenier (palfrənje) *m*, groom, [h]ostler. **palefroi** (frwa) (*Poet.*) *m*, palfrey.

palémon (palemɔ̃) *m*, prawn.

paléographie (paleɔgrafi) *f*, pal[a]eography. **paléontologie** (ɔ̃tɔlɔʒi) *f*, pal[a]eontology.

Palerme (palɛrm) *f*, Palermo.

paleron (palrɔ̃) *m*, shoulder blade (*horse, ox*).

Palestine (la) (palɛstin), Palestine.

palet (palɛ) *m*, quoit; quoits; puck (*Ice hockey*).

paletot (palto) *m*, covert coat; coatee.

palette (palɛt) *f*, battledore; bat; palette; pallet; paddle.

palétuvier (paletyvje) *m*, mangrove.

pâleur (pɑlœ:r) *f*, pallor, paleness.

palier (palje) *m*, landing (*stairs*); floor; bearings, plummer block; level.

palimpseste (palɛ̃psɛst) *m. & a*, palimpsest.

palinodie (palinɔdi) *f*, recantation.

pâlir (pɑli:r) *v.i. & t*, to pale, blanch; wane; fade.

palis (pali) *m*, pale, paling. **palissade** (sad) *f*, palisade, fence; stockade; hoarding (*street*). **palissader** (de) *v.t*, to palisade, fence.

palissandre (palisɑ̃:dr) *m*, rosewood.

palladium (paladjɔm) *m*, palladium; safeguard.

palliatif, ive (palljatif, i:v) *a. & m*, palliative. **pallier** (pallje) *v.t*, to palliate.

palmarès (palmarɛ:s) *m*, prize list, honours list.

palme (palm) *f*, palm [branch], p. [tree]. **palmé, e** (me) *a*, palmate[d]; webbed.

palmer (palmɛ:r) *m*, micrometer.

palmeraie (palmərɛ) *f*, palm grove. **palmier** (mje) *m*, palm [tree]. **palmipède** (mipɛd) *a*, web-footed. **palmiste** (mist) *m*, cabbage tree.

palombe (palɔ̃:b) *f*, ring dove, wood pigeon.

pâlot, te (pɑlo, ɔt) *a*, palish, wan.

palourde (palurd) *f*, clam (*Mol.*).

palpable (palpabl) *a*, palpable. **palpe** (palp) *f. or* m, palp[us], feeler. **palper** (pe) *v.t*, to feel, finger. **palpitation** (pitasjɔ̃) *f*, palpitation, throbbing, fluttering. **palpiter** (te) *v.i*, to palpitate, &c; go pit-[a-] pat; thrill.

paltoquet (paltɔkɛ) *m*, churl.

paludéen, ne (palydeɛ̃, ɛn) *a*, marshy; malarial. **paludisme** (dism) *m*, malaria.

pâmer (pɑme) *v.i. & se ~*, to swoon, faint; die (*of laughing*, &c).

pampas (pɑ̃pɑs) *f.pl*, pampas.

pamphlet (pɑ̃flɛ) *m*, lampoon. **pamphlétaire** (fletɛ:r) *m*, lampooner.

pamplemousse (pɑ̃pləmus) *f*, grape fruit.

pampre (pɑ̃:pr) *m*, vine branch.

pan (pɑ̃) *m*, skirt, flap; tail (*coat*); face, side; pane, slab; frame. *à 6 ~s*, hexagonal. *à 8 ~s*, octagonal.

pan (pɑ̃) *onomatopoeia*, bang! *~! ~!* rat-tat[-tat]!

panacée (panase) *f*, panacea, nostrum.

panache (panaʃ) *m*, plume, tuft; mettle, go, dash. *faire ~*, to have a spill, turn right over. **panacher** (ʃe) *v.t*, to plume, tuft; streak, variegate, mix.

panais (panɛ) *m*, parsnip.

panama (panama) *m*, panama, Panama hat.

panaris (panari) *m*, whitlow.

pancarte (pɑ̃kart) *f*, placard, bill, show card.

pancréas (pɑ̃kreɑ:s) *m*, pancreas.

pandémonium (pɑ̃demɔnjɔm) *m*, pandemonium.

pandit (pɑ̃di) *m*, pundit.

pandour (pɑ̃du:r) *m*, pandour, bear (*pers.*).

panégyrique (paneʒirik) *m*, panegyric, encomium.

paner (pane) *v.t*, to crumb (*Cook.*).

panerée (panre) *f*, basketful.

panetière (pantjɛ:r) *f*, sideboard.

pangermanisme (pɑ̃ʒermanism) *m*, panGermanism.

panier (panje) *m*, basket, hamper; pottle; pannier; straw hive; lobster basket; governess car[t]; basketful. *~ à ouvrage*, work basket. *~* [*à papiers*], waste paper b. *~ à pêche*, creel. *~ à provisions*, shopping basket; luncheon b. *~-repas*, lunch[eon] b. (*Rly*). *~ roulant*, go-cart.

panique (panik) *a. & f*, panic, scare.

panne (pan) *f*, lard; plush; purlin; pane (*hammer*); breakdown, failure. *avoir une ~ d'essence* ou *une ~ sèche*, to run out of petrol. *laisser en ~*, to leave in the lurch. *mettre en ~*, to heave to (*Naut.*).

panneau (pano) *m*, panel; snare. *~-réclame*, *m*, advertisement hoarding. **panneton** (pɑ̃tɔ̃) *m*, bit, web (*key*).

panonceau (panɔ̃so) *m*, medallion, tablet.

panoplie (panɔpli) *f*, panoply; trophy (*wall*); (*child's*) let's pretend set.

panorama (panɔrama) *m*, panorama.

panse (pɑ̃:s) *f*, belly, paunch.

pansement (pɑ̃smɑ̃) *m*, dressing (*wound*). **panser** (se) *v.t*, to dress; groom (*horse*).

pansu, e (pɑ̃sy) *a*, corpulent.

pantagruélique (pɑ̃tagryelik) *a*, sumptuous (*fare*).

pantalon (pɑ̃talɔ̃) *m*, [pair of] trousers, slacks. **pantalonnade** (lɔnad) *f*, comic turn; clownery; [tom]foolery; masquerade, sham.

pantelant, e (pɑ̃tlɑ̃, ɑ̃:t) *a*, panting; twitching (*flesh*).

panthéisme (pɑ̃teism) *m*, pantheism.

panthéon (pɑ̃teɔ̃) *m*, pantheon.

panthère (pɑ̃tɛ:r) *f*, panther.

pantin (pɑ̃tɛ̃) *m*, (*toy*) jumping jack; (*pers.*) monkey on a stick (*gesticulator*); shallow-brained & fickle person.

pantographe (pɑ̃tɔgraf) *m*, pantograph.

pantois, e (pɑ̃twa, a:z) *a*, flabbergasted.

pantomime (pɑ̃tɔmim) (*pers.*) *n*, pantomimist. ¶ *f*, pantomime, dumb show.

pantoufle (pɑ̃tufl) *f*, slipper. *~s en tapisserie*, carpet s—s. *en ~s*, in a free & easy way.

panure (pany:r) *f*, [grated] bread crumbs.

paon (pɑ̃) *m*, peacock; p. butterfly. **paonne** (pan) *f*, peahen. **paonneau** (pano) *m*, peachick.

papa (papa) *m*, papa, dad[dy].

papal, e (papal) *a*, papal. **papauté** (pote) *f*, papacy. **pape** (pap) *m*, pope.

papegai (papgɛ) *m*, popinjay (*Hist.*); clay bird (*Pigeon Shooting*).

papelard, e (paplar, ard) *a. & n*, sanctimonious (person).

paperasse (papras) *f*, useless old paper. **papeterie** (pap[ɛ]tri) *f*, paper mill; p. making; p. trade; stationer's shop; stationery; s. case, writing case. **papetier, ère** (paptje, ɛ:r) *n*, paper maker; stationer. **papier** (pje) *m*, paper; bills (*Fin.*). *~ à calquer*, *~-calque*, tracing paper. *~ à*

image directe, ~ *à noircissement direct,* printing-out p. (*Phot.*). ~ *à lettres* [in-8o], note p. ~ *à lettres* [in-4o], letter p. ~ *au charbon,* carbon p. (*Phot.*). ~ *auto-vireur* (otɔvirœ:r), self-toning p. ~ *buvard,* ~ *brouillard,* blotting p. ~ *carbone,* carbon [p.] (*duplicating*). ~ *de Chine,* tissue p. ~ *de journal,* newsprint. ~ *de soie,* tissue p. ~ *de verre,* glass p. ~ *hygiénique,* toilet p. ~ *imperméable à la graisse,* ~ *sulfurisé,* grease-proof p. ~ *indien,* India p. ~ *machine,* typewriting p. ~*-monnaie,* m, [inconvertible] paper money. ~ *par développement,* ~ *à image latente,* gaslight p. ~ [*peint*], ~*-tenture,* m, wall p. ~ *pelure,* bank paper, foreign note paper. ~ *quadrillé* (kadrije), squared p., plotting p., section[al] p. ~ *réactif,* test p. ~ *tue-mouches,* fly p. ~ *vélin,* wove p.
papillon (papijɔ̃) m, butterfly; wing nut; bow (*necktie*); slip (*paper*). ~ [*de nuit*], moth. **papillonner** (jone) v.i, to flit about.
papillote (papijɔt) f, curl paper; wrapped sweet, foiled chocolate. **papilloter** (te) v.i, to flicker; blink; dazzle, slur (*Typ.*).
papisme (papism) m, popery. **papiste** (pist) n, papist. ¶ a, popish.
papoter (papɔte) v.i, to gossip.
papule (papyl) f, pimple.
papyrus (papiry:s) m, papyrus.
pâque (pɑ:k) f, passover. **Pâques** (pɑ:k) m.s, Easter. **Pâques fleuries,** f.pl, Palm Sunday.
paquebot (pakbo) m, passenger &/or mail boat, liner, packet [boat]. ~ *à vapeur,* passenger steamer. ~ *aérien,* airship.
pâquerette (pɑkrɛt) f, daisy.
paquet (pakɛ) m, packet, package, bundle, pack; parcel, lot, block; clincher; (*att.*) plump. *un* ~ *de mer,* a [heavy] sea. **paquetage** (kta:ʒ) m, pack (*soldier's*).
par (par) pr, by; through; across; via; out of; per; a; in; into; with; on; about; over; from; for; at; during. ~ *an,* per annum. ~*-ci* ~*-là,* ad, here & there, hither & thither; at odd times. ~*-dessous,* ~*-dessus.* See *dessous, dessus.* ~ *ici,* this way, through here. ~ *là,* that way, through there; by that. *de* ~ *le monde,* somewhere in the world. ~ *les présentes,* hereby (*Law*). ~ *où?* which way? ~ *trop,* far too, too much, unduly.
parabole (parabɔl) f, parable; parabola. **parabolique†** (lik) a, parabolic(al) (*Geom.*).
parachever (paraʃve) v.t, to finish [off], perfect.
parachute (paraʃyt) m, parachute.
parade (parad) f, parade; show; parry[ing]; repartee. **parader** (de) v.i, to parade; show off.
paradis (paradi) m, paradise; gallery, gods (*Theat.*). *le* ~ [*terrestre*], [the earthly] paradise, [the Garden of] Eden.

paradoxal, e (paradɔksal) a, paradoxical. **paradoxe** (dɔks) m, paradox.
parafe (paraf) m, initials; flourish; paraph. **parafer** (fe) v.t, to initial.
paraffine (parafin) f, paraffin [wax].
parage (para:ʒ) m, lineage; (*pl.*) grounds (*fishing, cruising*), waters. *dans ces* ~*s,* in these parts, hereabouts.
paragraphe (paragraf) m, paragraph; section mark (§).
paraître (parɛ:tr) v.i.ir, to appear; show; be published, come out; seem, look. ¶ m, seeming. *l'être & le* ~*,* the seeming & the real.
Paralipomènes (paralipomɛn) m.pl, Chronicles (*Bible*).
parallaxe (paralaks) f, parallax. **parallèle†** (lɛl) a, parallel. ¶ f, parallel (*Geom., Mil.*). ¶ m, parallel (*of latitude; comparison*). **parallélipipède** (lelipipɛd) m, parallelepiped. **parallélogramme** (lɔgram) m, parallelogram.
paralyser (paralize) v.t, to paralyse; cripple (*fig.*). **paralysie** (zi) f, paralysis. ~ *progressive,* creeping paralysis. **paralytique** (tik) a. & n, paralytic.
parangon (parɑ̃gɔ̃) m, paragon.
parapet (parapɛ) m, parapet.
paraphe (paraf) m, initials; flourish; paraph. **parapher** (fe) v.t, to initial.
paraphrase (parafrɑ:z) f, paraphrase; circumlocution. **paraphraser** (fraze) v.t. & abs, to paraphrase; amplify.
parapluie (paraplɥi) m, umbrella. ~ *poucet, petit* ~*,* chubby (*or* Tom Thumb) umbrella.
parasitaire (parazitɛ:r) a, parasitic(al) (*Biol.*). **parasite** (zit) m, parasite; hanger-on; sponger. ~*s atmosphériques,* atmospherics (*Radio*). ¶ a, parasitical; redundant.
parasol (parasɔl) m, sunshade, umbrella (*garden, beach, held over potentate*); tent umbrella.
paratonnerre (paratonɛ:r) m, lightning conductor.
paravent (paravɑ̃) m, screen (*folding & fig.*).
paraverse (paravɛrs) m, rain coat, shower-proof.
parbleu (parblø) i, why, of course! to be sure! rather!
parc (park) m, park; enclosure; yard; paddock; pen; fold; range, run; bed (*oyster*). ~ *à bestiaux* (cattle) & ~ *à matières* (materials), stock yard. ~ *à voitures,* car park. ~ *d'agrément,* pleasure grounds. ~ *d'enfant,* play pen. **parcage** (ka:ʒ) m, parking; penning.
parcelle (parsɛl) f, particle, scrap; drib[b]let; parcel, plot, patch.
parce que (pars[ə]kə) c, because.
parchemin (parʃəmɛ̃) m, parchment; (*fig.*) title; diploma.
parcimonie (parsimɔni) f, parsimony. **parcimonieux, euse†** (njø, ø:z) a, parsimonious, penurious.

parcourir (parkuri:r) *v.t.ir*, to travel over, cover; perambulate; run through. **parcours** (ku:r) *m*, distance, stretch; run; haul; course. ~ *de 18 trous*, 18-hole course (*Golf*). *à travers le* ~, through the green (*Golf*).

pardessus (pardəsy) *m*, overcoat. ~ *raglan* (raglɑ̃), ~ *de demi-saison*, raglan.

pardi (pardi) *i*, of course!

pardon (pardɔ̃) *m*, pardon, forgiveness. **pardonnable** (dɔnabl) *a*, pardonable. **pardonner** (ne) *v.t. & ~ à*, to pardon, forgive; excuse.

pare- (par) *prefix*: ~-*battage*, *m*, fender (*Naut.*). ~-*boue*, *m*, mudguard; dash board. ~-*brise*, *m*, wind screen (*motor*). ~-*chocs*, *m*, bumper (*motor*). ~-*étincelles*, *m*, fire guard.

parégorique (paregorik) *a*, paregoric.

pareil, le (parɛ:j) *a*, like, alike, similar, to match; equal; parallel; such. ¶ *n*, like, equal; parallel; match, fellow. *la* ~, the like (*treatment*). *sans pareil*, unequalled, matchless. **pareillement** (rejmɑ̃) *ad*, in like manner; also, likewise.

parement (parmɑ̃) *m*, facing; face; cuff (*coat*); cloth (*altar*); kerb[stone].

parent, e (parɑ̃, ɑ̃:t) *n*, relative, connexion, kinsman, -woman; relation; (*m.pl.*) parents, kin. **parenté** (rɑ̃te) *f*, relationship, kinship; relations.

parenthèse (parɑ̃tɛ:z) *f*, parenthesis; bracket (,). *par* ~, parenthetically.

parer (pare) *v.t. & i*, to adorn, deck; dress; ward [off]; fend [off]; parry; guard.

paresse (parɛs) *f*, laziness, idleness, sloth; sluggishness. **paresser** (se) *v.i*, to idle; laze; loll, lounge. **paresseux, euse†** (sø, ø:z) *a. & n*, idle, &c (person). ¶ *m*, sloth (*Zool.*).

parfaire (parfɛ:r) *v.t.ir*, to finish [off]; make up. **parfait, e** (fɛ, ɛt) *a*, perfect; thorough; capital. ¶ *m*, perfect [tense]. **parfaitement** (tmɑ̃) *ad*, perfectly; thoroughly; quite; quite so, exactly.

parfiler (parfile) *v.t*, to unravel.

parfois (parfwa) *ad*, sometimes, at times, now & again.

parfum (parfœ̃) *m*, perfume, fragrance; scent. **parfumer** (fyme) *v.t*, to scent, perfume. **parfumerie** (mri) *f*, perfumery. **parfumeur, euse** (mœ:r, ø:z) *n*, perfumer; (*m.*) perfume distiller.

pari (pari) *m*, bet, wager. ~ *à la cote*, betting with bookmakers. ~ *mutuel*, pool betting, betting on the totalizator, pari mutuel.

paria (parja) *m*, outcaste, untouchable; pariah, outcast.

parier (parje) *v.t*, to bet, wager, lay, punt. ~ *sur*, to back (*horse*). *il y a à à* ~ *que* . . ., the odds are that . . . **parieur, euse** (jœ:r, ø:z) *n*, better, -or, punter, backer.

parisien, ne (parizjɛ̃, ɛn) *a. & P~*, *n*, Parisian.

parité (parite) *f*, parity, equality, likeness; equivalent.

parjure (parʒy:r) *m*, perjury; breach of oath. ¶ *n*, perjurer. ¶ *a*, perjured, forsworn. **se parjurer** (ʒyre) *v.pr*, to perjure (*or* forswear) oneself.

parlant, e (parlɑ̃, ɑ̃:t) *a*, speaking, talking (*film, eyes*); life-like; talkative. **parlé (le)** *m*, spoken part (*opera*); patter (*in song*).

parlement (parləmɑ̃) *m*, parliament. **parlementaire** (tɛ:r) *a*, parliamentary; of truce (*flag*). ¶ *m*, member of parliament; bearer of a flag of truce. **parlementer** (te) *v.i*, to parley.

parler (parle) *v.i. & abs. & v.t*, to speak, talk; t. about; tell, mention, say. ~ *du nez*, to speak through the nose. ¶ *m*, way of speaking, speech; dialect. **parleur, euse** (lœ:r, ø:z) *n*, talker; (*att.*) talking (*bird*). **parleur inconnu**, commentator (*Radio*). **parloir** (lwa:r) *m*, parlour (*convent, school*). **parlote** (lɔt) *f*, debating society; gossip.

Parme (parm) *f*, Parma.

parmi (parmi) *pr*, among[st], amid[st].

parodie (parɔdi) *f*, parody. **parodier** (dje) *v.t*, to parody. **parodiste** (dist) *m*, parodist.

paroi (parwa) *f*, wall (*partition, &c*); side; coat[ing] (*stomach, &c*).

paroisse (parwas) *f*, parish; p. church. **paroissial, e** (sjal) *a*, parish (*att.*), parochial. **paroissien, ne** (sjɛ̃, ɛn) *n*, parishioner. ¶ *m*, prayer book.

parole (parɔl) *f*, word; utterance; delivery; speaking; speech; parole. ~ *d'Évangile*, gospel [truth].

paroxysme (parɔksism) *m*, paroxysm.

parpaillot, e (parpajo, ɔt) *n*, heretic.

Parque (park) *f*, Fate (*Myth.*).

parquer (parke) *v.t*, to pen, fold; park.

parquet (parkɛ) *m*, floor, parquet; well (*of court*); central floor of Fr. Bourse reserved for use of *agents de change*. **parqueter** (kəte) *v.t*, to floor, parquet.

parrain (parɛ̃) *m*, godfather, sponsor; proposer, recommender. **parrainage** (rɛna:ʒ) *m*, sponsorship; recommendation.

parricide (parisid) (*pers.*) *n. & (act) m*, parricide; (*att.*) parricidal.

parsemer (parsəme) *v.t*, to strew, intersperse.

parsi (parsi) *m. & parse** (pars) *m. & a*, Parsee.

part (pa:r) (*Law*) *f*, child, birth.

part (pa:r) *f*, share; part; portion; hand, side. ~ *de fondateur*, founder's share (*Fin.*). ~ *du lion*, lion's share. *à* ~, apart, aside; except. *autre* ~, elsewhere, somewhere else. *d'autre* ~, on the other hand or side. *de la* ~ *de*, on the part of, on behalf of, from. *de* ~ *en* ~, right through. *faire* ~, to share; acquaint, inform.

partage (parta:ʒ) *m*, division, sharing; share, lot. ~ *[des voix]*, equality of votes. **partagé, e** (taʒe) *p.a*, reciprocal, mutual (*love*); halved (*hole*) (*Golf*). **partageable** (ʒabl) *a*, divisible. **partager** (ʒe) *v.t*, to divide, share, split.

partance (partɑ:s) *f*, sailing. *en* ~, about to sail, outward bound. **partant** (tɑ̃) *ad*, hence, therefore. ¶ *m*, starter (*horse*, *runner*).

partenaire (partənɛ:r) *n*, partner. ~ *d'entraînement*, sparring partner.

parterre (partɛ:r) *m*, bed (*garden*), plot, parterre; pit (*Theat.*).

parti (parti) *m*, party, side; part; course; decision; match (*marriage*). ~ *pris*, set purpose; prejudice, bias. *faire un mauvais* ~ *à*, to ill-treat. *prendre* ~, to take sides, to side. *tirer* ~ *de*, to make use of, turn to account.

partial, e† (parsjal) *a*, partial, bias[s]ed, unfair. **partialité** (lite) *f*, partiality, &c.

participation (partisipasjɔ̃) *f*, participation, sharing; partaking; share; joint [ad]venture, joint account. **participe** (sip) *m*, participle (*Gram.*). **participer** (pe) *v.i*, to participate, share; partake.

particulariser (partikylarize) *v.t*, to particularize. **particularité** (te) *f*, particularity, peculiarity. **particule** (kyl) *f*, particle; speck. **particulier, ère**† (lje, ɛ:r) *a*, particular; peculiar; [e]special; private. ¶ *n*, [private] individual.

partie (parti) *f*, part; parcel, lot, block; match, round, game; excursion, trip; line (*of business*); party; client (*barrister's*). ~ *de trois*, threesome (*Golf*). ~ *double*, doubles game (*Ten.*); foursome (*Golf*); double entry (*Bkkpg*). ~ *du discours*, part of speech. ~ *en points*, points up game (*Ten.*). *prendre à* ~, to take to task. **partiel, le** (parsjɛl) *a*, partial (*not entire*). **partiellement** (lmɑ̃) *ad*, partially, partly.

partir (parti:r) *v.i.ir*, to depart, set out, start, go; leave; sail; go off; emanate, proceed. *êtes-vous prêts? partez!* are you ready? go! *à* ~ *de*, from; on & after.

partisan (partizɑ̃) *m*, partisan, henchman, follower, believer; supporter; guer[r]illa (*soldier*).

partitif, ive (partitif, i:v) *a*, partitive (*Gram.*). **partition** (sjɔ̃) *f*, score (*Mus.*).

partout (partu) *ad*, everywhere. *2, 3, jeux* ~, 2, 3, all (*Ten.*). ~ *où*, wherever.

parure (pary:r) *f*, adornment; ornament; dress, attire; dressing (*meat*); set (*jewels*, *underclothing*).

parvenir (parvəni:r) *v.i. & abs. ir*, to arrive; succeed. ~ *à*, to arrive at, reach; attain [to]; manage to; succeed in. **parvenu, e** (ny) *n*, upstart, parvenu.

parvis (parvi) *m*, parvis, square; court.

pas (pɑ) *m*, step; pace; stride; gait; walk; march; time (*Mil.*); dance, pas; progress; precedence (*in rank*); foctfall; footprint; threshold; pass (*Phys. Geog.*); strait[s]; pitch, thread (*screw*). ~ *accéléré*, quick march. *P* ~ *de Calais*, Straits of Dover.

~ *de clerc*, blunder. ~ *de la porte*, doorstep. ~ *de porte*, direct access to street (*shop, &c*); premium (*on lease of shop or like*). *à* ~ *de tortue*, at a snail's pace. ~ *seul*, solo dance, pas seul. *au* ~, drive slowly, dead slow (*traffic sign*). *au* ~ *gymnastique*, at the double (*Mil.*).

pas (pɑ) *neg. particle usually coupled with* ne, not; no. ~ *libre*, [I am] sorry, number [is] engaged (*Teleph.*). ~ *possible!* you don't say so!

pascal, e (paskal) *a*, paschal.

pas-d'âne (pɑdɑ:n) *m*, coltsfoot (*Bot.*).

pasquin (paskɛ̃) *m*, lampooner; lampoon. **pasquinade** (kinad) *f*, pasquinade, lampoon, squib.

passable† (pasabl) *a*, passable, tolerable, fair, pretty good. **passade** (sad) *f*, passing fancy (*liaison*); passade. **passage** (sa:ʒ) *m*, passage; passing; crossing; going; transit; transition; pass; passageway, gangway, way, thoroughfare; arcade; ferry; right of way; toll. ~ *à niveau*, level crossing. ~ *clouté*, studded crossing (*pedestrian crossing*). ~ *d'escalier*, stairway. ~ *interdit* [*au public*], no thoroughfare. ~ *souterrain*, subway.

passager, ère (pasaʒe, ɛ:r) *a*, passing, fleeting, transient, fugitive, short-lived, momentary. ¶ *n*, passenger; visitor, sojourner. ~ *clandestin*, stowaway. ~ *d'entrepont*, steerage passenger. **passagèrement** (ʒɛrmɑ̃) *ad*, in passing, for a short time. **passant, e** (pasɑ̃, ɑ̃:t) *n*, passer-by.

passavant (pasavɑ̃) *m*, gangway (*on ship*); transire (*Cust.*).

passe (pɑ:s) *f*, pass; passage; plight; way; thrust; cut; fairway, channel; brim (*hat*). ~ *étroite*, narrow[s] (*Naut.*).

passé, e (pɑse) *p.a*, past, [by]gone, last; over; faded. *passé maître*, a past master. ¶ *m*, past; p. [tense]; satin stitch (*Emb.*). **passé**, *pr*, after.

passe-droit (pɑsdrwa) *m*, injustice, invidious distinction.

passe-lacet (pɑslasɛ) *m*, bodkin.

passement (pɑsmɑ̃) *m*, lace, braid; gimp. **passementerie** (tri) *f*, passementerie, trimmings.

passe-partout (pɑspartu) *m*, master key; latch key; passe-partout; slip-in mount.

passe-plats (pɑspla) *m*, service hatch.

passepoil (pɑspwal) *m*, piping (*braid*).

passeport (pɑspɔ:r) *m*, passport; clearance (*ship*).

passer (pɑse) *v.i. & t*, to pass; p. on; p. by; p. away; go; cross; spend; call, look in; ferry over; slip on; exceed; rank; enter, post; enter into; give, place; file (*a return at a registry*); utter (*coin, &c*). *se* ~ *de*, to do without, dispense with.

passereau (pɑsro) *m*, sparrow.

passerelle (pɑsrɛl) *f*, footbridge; bridge (*ship's*); gangway.

passerose (pɑsro:z) *f*, hollyhock.

passe-temps (pɑstɑ̃) *m*, pastime.

passeur (pɑsœ:r) *m*, ferryman.

passible (pɑsibl) *a*, liable. ~ *de droits*, dutiable.

passif, ive (pɑsif, i:v) *a*, passive. ¶ *m*, passive [voice]; liabilities.

passiflore (pɑsiflɔ:r) *f*, passion flower.

passion (pɑsjɔ̃) *f*, passion. **passionnant, e** (ɔnɑ̃, ɑ̃:t) *a*, thrilling. **passionné†, e** (ne) *a*, passionate; impassioned. *il est ~ pour*, he is passionately fond of; his hobby is. **passionner** (ne) *v.t*, to impassion; enthral[l]. *se ~*, to become impassioned; become enamoured.

passivement (pɑsivmɑ̃) *ad*, passively. **passiveté** (vite) *f*, passivity.

passoire (pɑswa:r) *f*, colander; strainer.

pastel (pastɛl) *m*, crayon; pastel; woad.

pastèque (pastɛk) *f*, water melon.

pasteur (pastœ:r) *m*, shepherd; pastor, minister.

pasteuriser (pastœrize) *v.t*, to Pasteurize.

pastiche (pastiʃ) *m*, pastiche; imitation, copy.

pastille (pasti:j) *f*, lozenge, pastil[le], jujube, drop; patch (*tire*).

pastoral, e (pastɔral) *a*, pastoral. ¶ *f*, pastoral; pastorale.

pastoriser (pastorize) *v.t*, to Pasteurize.

pat (pat) *m*, stalemate (*Chess*); (*att.*) stalemated. *faire ~*, to stalemate.

patache (pataʃ) *f*, rattletrap (*vehicle*).

pataquès (patakɛ:s) *m*, malaprop[ism].

patarafe (pataraf) *f*, scrawl.

patard (pata:r) *m*, [brass] farthing.

patate (patat) *f*, sweet potato; potato.

patatras (patatra) *onomatopoeia*, crash!

pataud, e (pato, o:d) *a. & n*, clumsy (person). ¶ *m*, big-pawed puppy.

patauger (patoʒe) *v.i*, to flounder, squelch; wade.

pâte (pɑ:t) *f*, paste; dough; pulp; impasto; pie (*printers'*). ~ *à polir les métaux*, metal polish. ~ *au bisulfite* (bisylfit), sulphite pulp. ~ *dentifrice*, tooth paste. **pâté** (pate) *m*, pie, pasty; pâté; mud pie; blot; block (*houses*); pie (*printers'*). **pâtée** (te) *f*, mash (*poultry*).

patelin, e (patlɛ̃, in) *a*, wheedling. ¶ *m*, village.

patelle (patɛl) *f*, limpet.

patène (patɛn) *f*, paten.

patent, e (patɑ̃, ɑ̃:t) *a*, patent (*obvious*). ¶ *f*, licence. ~ *de santé*, bill of health.

Pater (pa:tɛr) *m*, paternoster.

patère (patɛ:r) *f*, base, block (*on wall*); hat peg.

paterne (patɛrn) *a*, patronizing. **paternel, le†** (nɛl) *a*, paternal, fatherly; father's (*side*). **paternité** (nite) *f*, paternity, fatherhood; authorship.

pâteux, euse (patø, ø:z) *a*, pasty, clammy, thick.

pathétique† (patetik) *a*, pathetic. ¶ *m*, pathos.

pathologie (patɔlɔʒi) *f*, pathology. **pathologique** (ʒik) *a*, pathological. **pathologiste** (ʒist) *n*, pathologist.

pathos (patɔs) *m*, bathos.

patibulaire (patibylɛ:r) *a*, hang-dog.

patiemment (pasjamɑ̃) *ad*, patiently. **patience** (sjɑ:s) *f*, patience; button stick (*Mil.*); patience (*Cards*); dock (*Bot.*). **patient, e** (sjɑ̃, ɑ̃:t) *a*, patient, enduring. ¶ *n*, patient; sufferer. **patienter** (ɑ̃te) *v.i*, to have patience.

patin (patɛ̃) *m*, patten; skate; runner; skid; shoe; flange. *~s à glace*, (1) *à visser*, (2) *à griffes*, ice skates, (1) screw-on, (2) clamp-on. *~s à roulettes*, roller s—s. *~s de course*, racing s—s. *~s de figure*, figure s—s. *~s de hockey*, hockey s—s. **patinage** (tinaʒ) *m*, skating; skidding, slipping. **patine** (tin) *f*, patina. **patiné, e** (ne) *p.p*, patinated; fumed (*oak*). **patiner** (ne) *v.i*, to skate; skid, slip. **patinette** (nɛt) *f*, scooter. **patineur, euse** (nœ:r, ø:z) *n*, skater.

pâtir (pɑti:r) *v.i*, to suffer. **pâtiras** (tira) *m*, drudge.

pâtis (pɑti) *m*, grazing ground, pasture.

pâtisser (pɑtise) *v.i*, to make pastry. **pâtisserie** (sri) *f*, pastry; confectionery; pastrycook's shop, tea shop. **pâtissier, ère** (sje, ɛr) *n*, pastrycook [&/or confectioner]. **pâtissoire** (swa:r) *f*, pastry board.

patois (patwa) *m*, dialect; jargon.

patouiller (patuje) *v.i*, to flounder.

patraque (patrak) *f. & a*, rattletrap, (machine, &c) the worse for wear.

pâtre (pɑ:tr) *m*, herdsman.

patriarcal, e (patriarkal) *a*, patriarchal. **patriarche** (arʃ) *m*, patriarch.

patrice (patris) *m. & patricien, ne** (sjɛ̃, ɛn) *a. & n*, patrician. **patrie** (tri) *f*, native land, [n.] country, fatherland; home. [*petite*] ~, birthplace. **patrimoine** (trimwan) *m*, patrimony; inheritance, heritage. **patriote** (ɔt) *n*, patriot. ¶ *a. & patriotique* (tik) *a*, patriotic. **patriotisme** (tism) *m*, patriotism. **patron, ne** (trɔ̃, ɔn) *n*, patron, ess; patron saint; employer, principal; master, mistress; governor; skipper; coxswain. ¶ *m*, pattern (*for dress*, &c); templet, template; stencil [plate]. **dès patron-minet**, at peep of day. **patronage** (trɔnaʒ) *m*, patronage; advowson; benevolence; guild, club (*church*). **patronal, e** (nal) *a*, patronal, patron saint's (*day*); employer's, -ers' (*att.*). **patronat** (na) *m*, employers (*col.*). **patronner** (ne) *v.t*, to patronize; stencil. **dame patronnesse** (nɛs) *f*, patroness (*fête*, &c). **nom patronymique** (nimik) *m*, patronymic; surname.

patrouille (patru:j) *f*, patrol. **patrouiller** (truje) *v.i*, to patrol.

patte (pat) *f*, paw; foot; leg; claw; tab; strap; clip; clamp, holdfast; fluke (*anchor*). *d* *quatre* ~*s*, on all fours. ~**-d'oie,** *f*, multiple fork, crowfoot [forking] (*of roads*); crow's-foot (*wrinkle*).

pâturage (patyra:ʒ) *m*, pasturage. **pâture** (ty:r) *f*, pasture; food (*fig.*). **pâturer** (tyre) *v.i*, to pasture, graze.

paturon (patyrɔ̃) *m*, pastern.

paume (po:m) *f*, palm (*hand*); real tennis (*ancient game*).

paupérisme (poperism) *m*, pauperism.

paupière (popjɛːr) *f*, eyelid; eye.

pause (po:z) *f*, pause, stop; rest (*Mus.*).

pauvre† (po:vr) *a. & m*, poor (man); pauper; penurious; scanty, meagre. **pauvresse** (povrɛ:s) *f*, beggar woman. **pauvret, te** (vrɛ, ɛt) *n*, poor little thing (*pers.*). **pauvreté** (vrəte) *f*, poverty; poorness; commonplace.

pavage (pava:ʒ) *m*, pavement; paving.

pavaner (se) (pavane) *v.pr*, to strut [about].

pavé (pave) *m*, paving stone, set[t], pavement; street(s) (*fig.*). **pavement** (vmɑ̃) *m*, paving; pavement. **paver** (ve) *v.t*, to pave. **paveur** (vœːr) *m*, paver, paviour.

pavie (pavi) *f*, clingstone.

Pavie (pavi) *f*, Pavia (*Geog.*).

pavillon (pavijɔ̃) *m*, pavilion; lodge; box (*Hunt.*); summer house; house (*club*); flag, colours (*Naut. & Nav.*); flare; horn; earpiece. ~ **de partance,** Blue Peter. ~ **de poupe,** ensign.

pavois (pavwa) *m*, bulwark (*ship's*); flags (*col.*). **pavoiser** (ze) *v.t*, to dress (*ship*); deck with flags; (*abs.*) to dress ship.

pavot (pavo) *m*, poppy. ~ *somnifère*, opium poppy.

payable (pɛjabl) *a*, payable. ~ *à la commande*, cash with order. ~ *comptant*, pay cash (*cheque crossing*). **payant, e** (jɑ̃, ɑ̃:t) *a*, paying. ¶ *n*, payer. **paye** (pɛ:j) *f*, pay, wages; (*good, bad*) payer. **payement** (pɛjjmɑ̃) *m*, payment. **payer** (je) *v.t. & abs*, to pay; p. for; p. out; cash (*cheque*); stand (*drink, &c*). **payeur, euse** (jœ:r, ø:z) *n*, payer; paymaster; drawee.

pays (pei) *m*, country, land; native place. ~ *de cocagne* (kokaɲ), land of milk & honey, l. of plenty. **les Pays-Bas,** the Netherlands. **paysage** (za:ʒ) *m*, landscape; l. painting; description of scenery; (*pl.*) scenery. **paysagiste** (zaʒist) *m*, landscape painter; (*att.*) landscape (*gardener*).

paysan, ne (peizɑ̃, an) *n. & att*, peasant, rustic. **les paysans,** the peasantry. **paysannerie** (zanri) *f*, portrait of peasant life.

péage (pea:ʒ) *m*, toll; t. house. **péager** (aʒe) *m*, toll collector.

péan (peɑ̃) *m*, paean.

peau (po) *f*, skin, fell, pelt; scruff (*neck*); slough; leather; rind, peel; shell (*nut*); case (*sausage*). ~ *de tambour*, drumhead. *P~ Rouge,* *m*, redskin, red Indian. **peausserie** (sri) *f*, skin dressing; skins,

peltry. **peaussier** (sje) *m*, skin dresser. [*médecin*] *peaussier* ou [*médecin*] *peaucier* (sje) *m*, skin specialist.

pécari (pekari) *m*, peccary.

peccadille (pɛkadi:j) *f*, peccadillo, slip.

pêche (pɛ:ʃ) *f*, peach (*fruit*); fishing (*act & right*); fishery; catch, draught [of fishes]. ~ *à la crevette*, shrimping. ~ *à la dandinette* (dɑ̃dinɛt), sink & draw fishing. ~ *à la ligne*, line fishing, rod f., angling. ~ [*à la ligne*] *flottante*, float fishing. ~ *à la* [*ligne*] *volante*, spinning. ~ *à la mouche*, fly fishing. ~ *à la mouche noyée*, wet fly f. ~ *à la mouche sèche*, dry fly f. ~ *à la truite*, trout f. ~ *à traîner*, trolling. ~ *au bord de la mer*, shore fishing. ~ *au coup*, angling at set pitches. ~ *au lancer*, casting. ~ *au large*, ~ *hauturière* (otyrjɛ:r), offshore fishing, deep-sea f. ~ *au vif*, live-bait f. ~ *chalutière* (ʃalytjɛ:r), trawling. ~ *côtière*, ~ *dans les eaux territoriales*, inshore fishing. ~ *de fond*, ground angling, bottom fishing. ~ *de grand sport*, big-game fishing. ~ *de plage*, surf f., beach f. ~ *du gros poisson*, ~ *des grosses pièces*, heavy f. ~ *du petit poisson*, light f. ~ *du poisson moyen*, medium f. ~ *en bateau*, boat f. ~ *en eaux douces*, ~ *d'eau douce*, freshwater f. ~ *de* (ou *en*) *mer*, sea f., saltwater f. ~ *sportive*, game f.

péché (peʃe) *m*, sin. ~ *d'habitude*, besetting s. ~ *mignon*, pet vice, bosom sin.

pêcher (peʃe) *m*, peach [tree]. ¶ *v.t*, to fish for; fish; f. up; drag (*pond*); pick up, get hold of. ~ *à la ligne*, to angle. ~ *à la traîne*, to troll. **pêcherie** (ʃri) *f*, fishery, fishing ground. **pêcheur, euse** (ʃœ:r, ø:z) *n*, fisherman, angler; fisher (*pearl*).

pécheur, eresse (peʃœ:r, ʃrɛs) *n*, sinner.

péculat (pekyla) *m*, embezzlement (*public funds*). **pécule** (kyl) *m*, savings, nest egg; earnings (*of convict*); gratuity (*on discharge*, *Mil., Navy*).

pécuniaire† (pekynjɛ:r) *a*, pecuniary.

pédagogue (pedagɔg) *m*, pedagogue.

pédale (pedal) *f*, pedal; treadle. ~ *à scies*, rat-trap pedal. ~ *forte*, loud p. ~ *sourde*, soft p. **pédaler** (le) *v.i*, to pedal; cycle. **pédalier** (lje) *m*, pedal [key]board; crank gear (*cycle*).

pédant, e (pedɑ̃, ɑ̃:t) *n*, pedant; prig; wiseacre. ~ *& pédantesque*† (dɑ̃tɛsk) *a*, pedantic, priggish. **pédanterie** (tri) *f. &* **pédantisme** (tism) *m*, pedantry, &c.

pédestre (pedɛstr) *a*, pedestrian (*statue*). **pédestrement** (trəmɑ̃) *ad*, on foot.

pédicure (pediky:r) *n*, chiropodist.

pedigree (pedigri) *m*, pedigree (*beast*).

pégamoïd (pegamɔid) *m*, pegamoid.

Pégase (pega:z) *m*, Pegasus (*fig.*).

pègre (pɛ:gr) *f*, thieves & swindlers (*col.*). *la haute* ~, swell mob[smen].

peignage (pɛɲa:ʒ) *m*, combing, carding (*textiles*). **peigne** (pɛɲ) *m*, comb; card; pecten, scallop. ~ *à décrasser*, ~ *fin*, scurf comb, [small] tooth c. ~ *coiffeur*, hair c. **peignée** (ɲe) *f*, drubbing, thrashing. **peigner** (ɲe) *v.t*, to comb; card; chase (*screws*). **peignier** (ɲje) *m*, comb maker. **peignoir** (ɲwa:r) *m*, dressing gown. ~ *de bain*, bath gown. ~ *éponge*, towelling beach coat. **peignures** (ɲy:r) *f.pl*, combings.

peindre (pɛ̃:dr) *v.t. & abs. ir*, to paint; depict, portray.

peine (pɛn) *f*, punishment, penalty, pain; sorrow; infliction; anxiety; pains, trouble; difficulty. *à* ~, hardly, scarcely, barely. **peiner** (ne) *v.t*, to pain, grieve; (*v.i.*) to labour, [toil &] moil; be difficult. ~. *en lisant un livre*, to wade through a book.

peintre (pɛ̃:tr) *m*, painter; portrayer. ~ *d'enseignes*, sign writer. ~ *en bâtiments*, house painter. ~ *verrier*, stained glass artist. **peinture** (pɛty:r) *f*, painting; picture; paint, colour; portrayal. **peinturlurer** (tyrlyre) *v.t*, to daub.

péjoratif, ive (peʒɔratif, i:v) *a*, pejorative, disparaging, depreciatory.

Pékin (pekɛ̃) *m*, Pekin[g] (*Geog.*). **p~**, *m*, pekin (*fabric*). **pékinois** (kinwa) *m*, Pekinese, peke (*dog*).

pelage (pəla:ʒ) *m*, coat, wool, fur.

pélargonium (pelargɔnjɔm) *m*, pelargonium.

pêle-mêle (pɛlmɛl) *ad. & m*, pell-mell, helter-skelter.

pelé, e (pəle) *p.a*, bare, bald. **peler** (le) *v.t. & i*, to strip, peel, skin.

pèlerin, e (pɛlrɛ̃, in) *n*, pilgrim; fox (*pers.*). ¶ *f*, cape, pelerine. **pèlerinage** (lrina:ʒ) *m*, pilgrimage; place of pilgrimage.

pélican (pelikɑ̃) *m*, pelican.

pelisse (pəlis) *f*, pelisse.

pelle (pɛl) *f*, shovel; scoop. ~ *à poussière*, dust pan. ~ *à sel*, salt spoon. ~ *à tarte*, pastry server. ~*-bêche*, entrencing tool. **pelletée** (lte) *f*, shovelful, spadeful. **pelleterie** (pɛltri) *f*, furriery; peltry. **pelletier, ère** (ltje, ɛ:r) *n*, furrier. **pellicule** (pɛllikyl) *f*, pellicle, skin; film; (*pl.*) dandruff, scurf. ~ *en bobine*, roll film (*Phot.*).

pelote (plɔt) *f*, ball (*wool, string*); pincushion; pile (*money*); pelota. **peloter** (te) *v.i*, to knock the balls about (*Ten., &c*). ~ *en attendant partie*, to fill in time. **peloton** (tɔ̃) *m*, ball; knot; cluster; squad, party, platoon (*Mil.*). ~ *d'exécution*, firing party. **pelotonner** (tɔne) *v.t*, to ball, wind. *se* ~, to curl up, snuggle.

pelouse (plu:z) *f*, lawn, green; public enclosures (*Turf*). ~ *d'arrivée*, putting green (*Golf*).

peluche (plyʃ) *f*, plush. **pelucher** (le) *v.i*, to fluff up. **pelucheux, euse** (ʃø, ø:z) *a*, fluffy.

pelure (ply:r) *f*, peel, skin, rind.

pénal, e (penal) *a*, penal; criminal (*law*); penalty (*clause*). **pénalité** (lite) *f*, penalty.

pénates (penat) *m.pl*, home. *dieux* ~, Penates, household gods.

penaud, e (pəno, o:d) *a*, crestfallen; sheepish.

penchant (pɑ̃ʃɑ̃, ɑ̃:t) *a*, leaning; tottering. ¶ *m*, slope; brink; verge; leaning, inclination, bent, propensity, proclivity, fondness. **penché, e** (ʃe) *p.a*, leaning (*tower*); drooping (*looks*). **penchement** (ʃmɑ̃) *m*, bend[ing]; stoop[ing]. **pencher** (ʃe) *v.t. & i. & se* ~, to bend, incline, tilt; lean; beak; stoop; verge. *faire* ~ *la balance*, to turn the scale.

pendable (pɑ̃dabl) *a*, [deserving of] hanging; outrageous. **pendaison** (dɛzɔ̃) *f*, [death by] hanging. **pendant, e** (dɑ̃, ɑ̃:t) *a*, hanging [down]; dangling; drooping; pendent, -ant; pending. ¶ *m*, drop (*ear*); frog (*sword*); counterpart, fellow, match. *les [deux]* ~*s*, the pair (*pictures, &c*).

pendant (pɑ̃dɑ̃) *pr*, during, for. ~ *que*, while, whilst.

pendard, e (pɑ̃da:r, ard) (*jocular*) *n*, rascal; hussy; gallows-bird. **pendeloque** (pɑ̃dlɔk) *f*, drop (*ear, chandelier*). **pendentif** (dɑ̃tif) *m*, pendentive; pendant, -ent. **penderie** (dri) *f*, hanging cupboard. **pendiller** (dije) *v.i*, to hang, dangle. **pendre** (dr) *v.t. & i*, to hang; h. up, h. out. **pendu** (dy) *m*, pendulum. ¶ ~ *& pendulette* (lɛt) *f*, timepiece, clock. *pendule à sonnerie & à carillon*, striking & chiming clock.

pêne (pɛ:n) *m*, bolt (*lock*).

pénétrant, e (penetrɑ̃, ɑ̃:t) *a*, penetrating, piercing, searching. **pénétration** (trasjɔ̃) *f*, penetration; insight. **pénétrer** (tre) *v.t. & i*, to penetrate, pierce; break into; permeate, pervade, sink in; fathom; see through; imbue.

pénible† (penibl) *a*, laborious, hard; painful.

péniche (peniʃ) *f*, barge, lighter.

péninsulaire (penɛ̃syle:r) *a*, peninsular. **péninsule** (syl) *f*, peninsula.

pénitence (penitɑ̃:s) *f*, penitence; penance; punishment; penalty, forfeit (*at play*). **pénitencier** (tɑ̃sje) *m*, penitentiary, reformatory; convict prison. **pénitent, e** (tɑ̃, ɑ̃:t) *a. & n*, penitent. **pénitentiaire** (tɑ̃sjɛ:r) *a*, penitentiary.

penne (pɛn) *f*, quill (*feather*).

pénombre (penɔ̃:br) *f*, penumbra; twilight; background (*fig.*).

pensant, e (pɑ̃sɑ̃, ɑ̃:t) *a*, thinking; -minded (*bien* = right), -disposed (*mal* = ill). **pensée** (se) *f*, thought; thinking; meditation; mind; idea; pansy, heartsease. **penser** (se) *v.i. & t. & abs*, to think; mean. ¶ *m*, thought (*Poet.*). **penseur** (sœ:r) *m*, thinker. **pensif, ive** (sif, i:v) *a*, pensive, thoughtful.

pension (pɑ̃sjɔ̃) *f*, board [& lodging]; boarding house; b. school; pension; pawn. ~ *ali-*

mentaire, alimony. ~ *pour les chevaux*, livery stables. **pensionnaire** (ɔnɛ:r) *n*, boarder; paying guest; inmate; pensioner. **pensionnat** (na) *m*, boarding school. **pensionner** (ne) *v.t*, to pension.

pensum (pɛ̃sɔm) *m*, imposition (*Sch.*).

Pen[n]sylvanie (la) (pɛ̃silvani), Pennsylvania.

Pentateuque (le) (pɛ̃tatø:k), the Pentateuch.

pente (pɑ̃:t) *f*, slope, incline, [downward] gradient; valance, -ence; bent (*fig.*).

Pentecôte (la) (pɑ̃tko:t), Whitsun[tide]; Pentecost.

penture (pɑ̃ty:r) *f*, hinge (*of hook & hinge*).

pénultième (penyltjɛm) *a*, penultimate.

pénurie (penyri) *f*, penury, scarcity, dearth, lack.

pépie (pepi) *f*, pip (*poultry*); thirst. **pépier** (pje) *v.i*, to peep, chirp.

pépin (pepɛ̃) *m*, pip (*fruit*); stone (*grape*). **pépinière** (pinjɛ:r) *f*, nursery (*Hort. & fig.*). **[jardinier] pépiniériste** (njerist) *m*, nurseryman.

pépite (pepit) *f*, nugget.

perçant, e (pɛrsɑ̃, ɑ̃:t) *a*, piercing; keen, sharp; shrill. **mettre en perce** (pɛrs), to broach, tap (*cask*). **percée (se)** *f*, opening; cutting. **perce-neige**, *f*, snowdrop. **perceoreille**, *m*, earwig.

percepteur (pɛrsɛptœ:r) *m*, collector (*tax*). **perceptible** (tibl) *a*, collectable, -ible; perceptible, discernible, noticeable. ~ *à l'ouïe*, audible. **perception** (sjɔ̃) *f*, collection; collectorship; collector's office; perception.

percer (pɛrse) *v.t. & i*, to pierce; bore; drill; lance; stab; spear; broach; tap; hole; drive; open; penetrate; break through; reveal itself; make one's way. **perceur** (sœ:r) *m*, driller (*pers.*). **perceuse** (sø:z) *f*, dril[ling machine].

percevoir (pɛrsəvwa:r) *v.t*, to collect; charge; perceive.

perche (pɛrʃ) *f*, pole; perch (*fish*). ~ *d'étendoir*, clothes prop. **percher** (ʃe) *v.i*, to perch, roost. **perchoir** (ʃwa:r) *m*, perch, roost.

perclus, e (pɛrkly, y:z) *a*, crippled.

percussion (pɛrkysjɔ̃) *f*, percussion, impact. **percutant, e** (kytɑ̃, ɑ̃:t) *a*, percussive.

perdant, e (pɛrdɑ̃, ɑ̃:t) *n*, loser. ¶ *a*, losing. **perdition** (disjɔ̃) *f*, perdition. *en* ~, in a sinking condition (*ship*). **perdre** (dr) *v.t. & abs*, to lose; waste; ruin.

perdreau (pɛrdro) *m*, young partridge. **perdrix** (dri) *f*, partridge. ~ *des neiges*, ptarmigan.

père (pɛr) *m*, father, parent; sire (*Poet. & beast*); senior. *le* ~ *Noël*, Father Christmas, Santa Claus. *de* ~ *de famille*, safe (*investment*). *en bon* ~ *de famille*, with due & proper care.

pérégrination (peregrinasjɔ̃) *f*, peregrination.

péremptoire† (perɑ̃ptwa:r) *a*, peremptory.

perfection (pɛrfɛksjɔ̃) *f*, perfection. **perfectionner** (ɔne) *v.t*, to perfect; improve.

perfide† (pɛrfid) *a. & n*, treacherous, perfidious (person). **perfidie** (di) *f*, treachery, perfidy.

perforateur (pɛrforatœ:r) *m*, punch (*paper*). **perforatrice** (tris) *f*, drill (*rock, &c*). **perforer** (re) *v.t*, to perforate; drill; punch.

performance (pɛrfɔrmɑ̃:s) *f*, performance (*Sport*). ~ *classée*, winning performance.

pergola (pɛrgola) *f*, pergola.

péricliter (periklite) *v.i*, to be in danger.

péril (peril) *m*, peril. **périlleux, euse†** (rijø, ø:z) *a*, perilous.

périmé, e (perime) *p.p*, out of date (*ticket, &c*); exploded (*theory*). **périmer** (me) *v.i*, to lapse, expire.

périmètre (perimɛtr) *m*, perimeter; limit.

période (perjɔd) *f*, period, stage; spell; repetend; phrase (*Mus.*). ~ *d'interdiction*, close season (*Fishing, &c*). ¶ *m*, pitch; stage. **périodique†** (dik) *a*, periodic; periodical; recurrent, recurring. ¶ *m*, periodical.

péripétie (peripesi) *f*, peripet[e]ia; vicissitude.

périphérie (periferi) *f*, periphery.

périphrase (perifrɑ:z) *f*, periphrasis.

périr (peri:r) *v.i*, to perish, be lost; die; lapse.

périscope (periskɔp) *m*, periscope.

périssable (perisabl) *a*, perishable.

périssoire (periswa:r) *f*, Rob Roy canoe.

péristyle (peristil) *m*, peristyle.

péritonite (peritɔnit) *f*, peritonitis.

perle (pɛrl) *f*, pearl; bead; treasure (*fig.*). ~ *de culture*, cultured pearl. **perlé, e (le)** *a*, pearly; exquisitely done.

permanence (pɛrmanɑ̃:s) *f*, permanence. **permanent, e** (nɑ̃, ɑ̃:t) *a*, permanent, standing; continuous; abiding; perennial.

permanganate (pɛrmɑ̃ganat) *m*, permanganate.

perméable (pɛrmeabl) *a*, permeable, pervious.

permettre (pɛrmɛtr) *v.t.ir*, to permit, to allow; may. *se* ~, to allow oneself, indulge in. *se* ~ *de*, to venture to. **permis** (mi) *m*, permit, licence, order. ~ *[de circulation]*, [free] pass (*Rly.*). ~ *de conduire [les automobiles]*, driver's licence. **permission** (sjɔ̃) *f*, permission; leave, pass (*Mil.*). **permissionnaire** (ɔnɛ:r) *m. & a*, (soldier) on leave.

permutation (pɛrmytasjɔ̃) *f*, exchange (*of posts*); permutation; transposition.

pernicieux, euse† (pɛrnisjø, ø:z) *a*, pernicious, baneful.

péroné (perɔne) *m*, fibula, splint [bone].

péronnelle (perɔnɛl) *f*, pert hussy.

péroraison (perɔrɛzɔ̃) *f*, peroration. **pérorer** (re) *v.i*, to hold forth, speechify.

Pérou (le) (peru), Peru.

Pérouse (peru:z) *f*, Perugia.

peroxyde (perɔksid) *m*, peroxide.

perpendiculaire† (pɛrpɑ̃dikylɛ:r) *a. & f*, perpendicular.

perpétrer (pɛrpetre) v.t, to perpetrate.
perpétuation (pɛrpetɥasjɔ̃) f, perpetuation.
perpétuel, le† (tɥɛl) a, perpetual, permanent; for life. **perpétuer** (tɥe) v.t, to perpetuate. **perpétuité** (tɥite) f, perpetuity. à ~, in perpetuity; for life.
perplexe (pɛrplɛks) a, perplexed, puzzled; perplexing. **perplexité** (ksite) f, perplexity.
perquisition (pɛrkizisjɔ̃) f, search (Law).
perron (pɛrɔ̃) m, steps, perron.
perroquet (pɛrɔkɛ) m, parrot; topgallant. **perruche** (ryʃ) f, parakeet; hen parrot; high-flown random talker (woman).
perruque (pɛryk) f, wig; fog[e]y. **perruquier** (kje) m, wig maker.
pers, e (pɛːr, ɛrs) a, a greenish-blue.
persan, e (pɛrsɑ̃, an) a. & P~, n, Persian (modern). **le persan**, Persian (language). **la Perse** (pɛrs), Persia. **perse, a. & P~**, n, Persian (ancient). **perse, f,** chintz.
persécuter (pɛrsekyte) v.t, to persecute; bait; dun. **persécuteur, trice** (tœːr, tris) n, persecutor. **persécution** (sjɔ̃) f, persecution.
persévérance (pɛrseverɑ̃ːs) f, perseverance. **persévérer** (re) v.i. & abs, to persevere; persist.
persienne (pɛrsjɛn) f, sun shutter, persienne, Persian blind.
persiflage (pɛrsiflaːʒ) m, quizzing, persiflage. **persifler** (fle) v.t, to quiz, chaff.
persil (pɛrsi) m, parsley. **persillé, e** (sije) a, blue-mouldy (cheese).
persistance (pɛrsistɑ̃ːs) f, persistence, -ency. **persistant, e** (tɑ̃, ɑ̃ːt) a, persistent. **persister** (te) v.i, to persist.
personnage (pɛrsɔnaːʒ) m, personage; character; (pl.) dramatis personae. ~ de carton, figurehead. être un ~, to be somebody.
personnalité (nalite) f, personality; (pl.) [well known] people. **personne** (sɔn) f, person; self; (pl.) people. ~ à charge, dependent person; hanger-on. ~ collante, bur[r], sticker. ~ interposée, nominee. ~ morale, ~ juridique, ~ civile, body corporate, legal entity. ¶ pn.m, anybody, anyone; nobody, no one, none. ~? ~? have you finished? (Teleph.). **personnel, le†** (nɛl) a, personal; private; selfish. ¶ m, staff, personnel. **personnifier** (nifje) v.t, to personify; impersonate.
perspective (pɛrspɛktiːv) f, perspective; outlook, view, prospect; vista.
perspicace (pɛrspikas) a, perspicacious. **perspicacité** (site) f, perspicacity.
persuader (pɛrsɥade) v.t. & abs, to persuade; prevail. **persuasif, ive** (zif, iːv) a, persuasive. **persuasion** (zjɔ̃) f, persuasion; belief.
perte (pɛrt) f, loss; leak[age]; waste; casualty (Mil.); ruin; swallow (river); discount (opp. premium). ~ sèche, dead loss. à ~, at a loss. à ~ de vue, as far as the eye can reach. en ~, out of pocket, to

the bad, **a loser**. en pure ~, to no purpose.
pertinent, e (pɛrtinɑ̃, ɑ̃ːt) a, pertinent, apposite, relevant. **pertinemment** (namɑ̃) ad, pertinently, &c.
pertuis (pɛrtɥi) m, sluiceway; strait[s] (Geog.).
perturbateur, trice (pɛrtyrbatœːr, tris) n, disturber. **perturbation** (sjɔ̃) f, disturbance, perturbation.
péruvien, ne (peryvjɛ̃, ɛn) a. & P~, n, Peruvian.
pervenche (pɛrvɑ̃ːʃ) f, periwinkle (Bot.).
pervers, e (pɛrvɛːr, ɛrs) a, perverse. ¶ m, pervert (apostate). **perversion** (vɛrsjɔ̃) f, perversion. **perversité** (site) f, perversity. **pervertir** (tiːr) v.t, to pervert.
pesade (pəzad) f, rearing (horse).
pesage (pəzaːʒ) m, weighing; (Turf) w. in; w. in room; paddock. **pesamment** (zamɑ̃) ad, heavily; ponderously. **pesant, e** (zɑ̃, ɑ̃ːt) a, heavy, weighty; ponderous, unwieldy; ponderable. son pesant d'or, his, its, weight in gold. **pesant, ad,** in weight. **pesanteur** (zɑ̃tœːr) f, heaviness, weight; gravity (Phys.). **pesée** (ze) f, weighing; prize, -se; wrench. **pèse-lettre** (pɛzlɛtr) m, letter scales. **peser** (pəze) v.t, to weigh; ponder; (v.i.) to weigh; lie heavy; bear, press; dwell. **peseur** (zœːr) m, weigher. **peson** (zɔ̃) m, balance (spring, &c).
pessimisme (pɛsimism) m, pessimism. **pessimiste** (mist) n, pessimist. ¶ a, pessimistic.
peste (pɛst) f, plague, pestilence. ~ bovine, cattle plague, rinderpest. ~ (te) v.i, to rail (contre = at). **pestiféré, e** (tifere) a. & n, plague-stricken (person). **pestilentiel, le** (lɑ̃sjɛl) a, pestilential.
pétale (petal) m, petal.
pétarade (petarad) f, sp[l]utter; frisking. **pétarader** (de) v.i, to sp[l]utter. **pétard** (taːr) m, shot, blast; detonator, fog signal; cracker (firework); scandal (news). **pétarder** (tarde) v.t, to blow up, blast.
pétaudière (petodjɛːr) f, bedlam, bear garden.
pétiller (petije) v.i, to crackle; sparkle; fizz[le], bubble [over].
pétiole (pesjɔl) m, petiole, leaf stalk.
petiot, e (pətjo, ɔt) a, tiny, wee. ¶ n, dot, tot, chickabiddy. **petit, e** (ti, it) a, little, small; short; diminutive; young; junior; low; slow; lesser; minor; petty; slight; light; mean; retail. **petit, comps:** au ~ bonheur, I'll risk it, come what may; hit or miss. ~ canot, jolly[boat]. le P~ Chaperon rouge, Little Red Riding Hood. ~ chat, kitten. ~ cheval, donkey engine. ~ chien, pup[py]. ~ comité, select party, informal gathering. le ~ commerce, [the] small traders, tradespeople, the retail trade. ~ commis, office boy. le ~ déjeuner, coffee & rolls, early morning tea.

~ *enfant*, little child, infant. ~*s-enfants*, grandchildren. ~ *équipement*, kit. ~-*fils*, grandson, -child. ~ *fond*, back margin, back edge (*of book page*). ~*s fours*, petits fours. *au* ~ *galop*, at a canter. ~-*gris*, minever, -iver. ~*s jeux*, parlour games, forfeits. *le* ~ *jour*, daybreak. ~ *juif*, funny bone. ~-*lait*, whey. ~ *lieu*, ~ *endroit*, little place, privy. ~-*maître*, fop, coxcomb. ~ *ménage*, miniature (or dolls') home set. *le* ~ *monde*, little people; the lower classes; the child world. ~ *mulet*, hinny. *le* ~ *Noël*, a Christmas present (*to a child*). ~ *nom*, Christian name. ~ *nom d'amitié*, pet name. ~ *pain*, roll. ~ *parapluie*, chubby umbrella, Tom Thumb umbrella. *le* ~ *peuple*, [the] common people. ~*s pois*, green peas. ~ *salé*, pickled pork. ~ *salon*, sitting room, parlour. ~ *trot*, jog-trot. petite, *comps:* ~ *chatte*, kitten. ~ *correspondance*, answers to correspondents. *la* ~ *épargne*, the small investor. ~-*fille*, grand-daughter, grandchild. ~ *gorgée*, sip. ~ *guerre*, mimic war. *à* ~*s journées*, by easy stages. ~ *largeur*, single width (*cloth*). *à* ~ *mentalité*, mentally deficient. ~ *multiplication*, low gear. ~ *noblesse*, gentry. ~ *pédale*, soft pedal. *une* ~ *santé*, poor health. ~*s tables*, separate tables (*meal*). ~ *tenue*, undress (*Mil.*, *Nav.*). ~ *vérole*, smallpox. ~ *vérole volante*, chicken pox. *en* ~ *vitesse* (*Rly*), by slow train; by goods train. petit, e, *n*, little boy, l. girl, l. one. un petit, a young one, cub, pup, whelp. les petits, the small, the little (*people*); little things. petitement (*titmã*) *ad*, meanly; pettily. petitesse (*tɛs*) *f*, littleness, smallness; shortness; pettiness.

pétition (petisjɔ̃) *f*, petition. ~ *de principe*, begging the question, petitio principii. *faire une* ~ *de principe*, to beg the question. **pétitionner** (sjɔne:r) *v.i*, to petition.

péton (petɔ̃) *m*, tootsy[-wootsy].

pétoncle (petɔ̃:kl) *m*, scallop, scollop (*Mol.*).

pétrel (petrɛl) *m*, storm[y] petrel.

pétrification (petrifikasjɔ̃) *f*, petrifaction. **pétrifier** (fje) *v.t*, to petrify.

pétrin (petrɛ̃) *m*, kneading trough; fix, mess. **pétrir** (tri:r) *v.t*, to knead, work, make; shape; steep. **pétrissage** (trisa:ʒ) *m*, kneading, &c.

pétrole (petrɔl) *m*, petroleum, oil. ~ *à brûler*, ~ *lampant* (lɑ̃pɑ̃), paraffin [oil], kerosene. **pétrolier, ère** (lje, ɛ:r) *a*, petroleum, oil (*att.*). [*navire*] *pétrolier*, oil ship.

pétulant, e (petylã, ã:t) *a*, lively, impetuous.

pétunia (petynja) *m*, petunia.

peu (pø) *ad*, little, not much; few, not many; not very. ¶ *m*, little; bit; few; lack; little while. *à* ~ [*de chose*] *près*, about, nearly.

peulven (pølvɛn) *m*, menhir, peulven.

peuplade (pœplad) *f*, tribe. **peuple** (pl) *m*, people, nation; tribe. ¶ *a*, plebeian, common. **peupler** (ple) *v.t*, to people, populate; stock, plant; fill; (*v.i.*) to multiply.

peuplier (pœplie) *m*, poplar.

peur (pœ:r) *f*, fear, fright. *avoir* ~, to be afraid. **peureux, euse**† (pœrø, ø:z) *a*, timid, nervous.

peut-être (pœtɛ:tr) *ad. & m*, perhaps, maybe, perchance, possibly.

phaéton (faetɔ̃) *m*, phaeton.

phalange (falɑ̃:ʒ) *f*, phalanx; host.

phantasme (fɑ̃tasm) *m*, phantasm.

pharaon (faraɔ̃) *m*, Pharaoh; faro (*Cards*).

phare (fa:r) *m*, lighthouse; light; beacon; headlight, headlamp. ~ *anti-éblouissant*, ~-*code*, anti-dazzle lamp or light. ~ *éblouissant*, ~ *de route*, dazzle l.

pharisaïque (farizaik) *a*, Pharisaic(al). **pharisien** (zjɛ̃) *m*, Pharisee.

pharmaceutique (farmasøtik) *a*, pharmaceutical. **pharmacie** (si) *f*, pharmacy; dispensary; chemist's shop; medicine chest. **pharmacien, ne** (sjɛ̃, ɛn) *n*, chemist, druggist; dispenser.

pharyngite (farɛ̃ʒit) *f*, pharyngitis, relaxed throat. **pharynx** (rɛ̃:ks) *m*, pharynx.

phase (fɑ:z) *f*, phase; stage.

phébus (feby:s) *m*, bombast, fustian.

phénacétine (fenasetin) *f*, phenacetin.

phénicien, ne (fenisjɛ̃, ɛn) *a*, Phoenician.

phénix (feniks) *m*, ph[o]enix; paragon.

phénol (fenɔl) *ou* **acide phénique** (nik) *m*, phenol, carbolic acid.

phénoménal, e (fenɔmenal) *a*, phenomenal. **phénomène** (mɛn) *m*, phenomenon; freak [of nature].

Philadelphie (filadɛlfi) *f*, Philadelphia.

philanthrope (filɑ̃trɔp) *n*, philanthropist. **philanthropie** (pi) *f*, philanthropy. **philanthropique** (pik) *a*, philanthropic.

philatélisme (filatelism) *m*, philately. **philatéliste** (list) *n*, philatelist.

philharmonique (filarmɔnik) *a*, philharmonic.

philippique (filipik) *f*, philippic.

philistin (filistɛ̃) *m*, Philistine.

philologie (filɔlɔʒi) *f*, philology. **philologue** (lɔg) *m*, philologist.

philosophe (filɔzɔf) *n*, philosopher; student in philosophy. ¶ *a*, philosophic(al) (*calm*). **philosopher** (fe) *v.i*, to philosophize. **philosophie** (fi) *f*, philosophy. **philosophique**† (fik) *a*, philosophic(al).

philtre (filtr) *m*, philtre, -ter, love potion.

phlébite (flebit) *f*, phlebitis.

phlox (flɔks) *m*, phlox.

phobie (fɔbi) *f*, morbid fear, dread.

phonétique (fɔnetik) *a*, phonetic. ¶ *f*, phonetics. **phonographe** (nɔgraf) *m*, gramophone, phonograph. ~ *coffret*, table gramophone. ~ *meuble*, cabinet g.

phoque (fɔk) *m*, seal (*Zool.*).

phosphate (fɔsfat) *m*, phosphate. **phosphore** (fɔ:r) *m*, phosphorus. **phosphorescence**

(fɔrɛsᾶːs) f, phosphorescence. **phosphorescent, e** (sᾶ, ᾶːt) a, phosphorescent.

photographe (fɔtɔgraf) n, photographer. **photographie** (fi) f, photography; photograph. **photographier** (fje) v.t, to photograph. **photographique** (fik) a, photographic. **photogravure** (vyːr) f, photogravure. **photo-jumelle**, f, binocular camera.

phrase (frɑːz) f, sentence; phrase. ~*s à effet*, claptrap. **phraséologie** (frazeɔlɔʒi) f, phraseology. **phraser** (ze) v.i. & t, to phrase.

phrénologie (frenɔlɔʒi) f, phrenology. **phrénologiste** (ʒist) m, phrenologist.

phtisie (ftizi) f, phthisis, consumption. **phtisique** (zik) a. & n, consumptive.

physicien, ne (fizisjɛ̃, ɛn) n, physicist.

physiologie (fizjɔlɔʒi) f, physiology.

physionomie (fizjɔnɔmi) f, physiognomy, face, countenance; aspect; character.

physique† (fizik) a, physical; bodily. ¶ f, physics. ¶ m, physique.

piaffer (pjafe) v.i, to paw the ground; prance.

piailler (pjaje) v.i, to cheep; squeal.

pianiste (pjanist) n, pianist. **piano** (no) m, piano[forte]. ~ *à cordes droites*, vertically strung piano. ~ *à demi-queue*, baby grand [piano]. ~ *à queue*, [concert] grand piano. ~ *droit*, upright piano. ~ *mécanique*, piano player, player piano; piano organ. ~ *oblique*, overstrung piano.

piauler (pjole) v.i, to cheep; whimper.

pic (pik) m, pick; peak; woodpecker. *à* ~, sheer, precipitous.

piccolo (pikolo) m, piccolo.

picorer (pikɔre) v.i, to forage, peck.

picot (piko) m, splinter; barb; picot. **picoté de petite vérole** (kɔte), pock-marked. **picoter** (te) v.t, to prick; pit; peck; sting, make smart, make tingle; tease.

picotin (pikɔtɛ̃) m, feed of oats.

pictural, e (piktyral) a, pictorial.

pie (pi) f, magpie. ¶ a, piebald; charitable (*works*).

pièce (pjɛs) f, piece; bit; fragment; part; man (*Draughts*); head (*cattle*, *game*); joint (*meat*); document; paper; tip (*gratuity*); cask, barrel; puncheon; gun; room (*house*). [*la*] ~, apiece, each. ~ *à conviction*, exhibit (*Criminal Law*). ~ *à succès*, hit. ~ *à thèse*, problem play. ~ *d'artifice*, firework. ~ *d'eau*, ornamental lake. ~ [*coulée*], casting. ~ [*de monnaie*], coin. ~ *de rechange*, spare [part]. ~ [*de théâtre*], [stage] play. ~ *historique*, costume piece, c. play. ~ *justificative*, ~ *à l'appui*, exhibit (*Civil Law*); voucher (*Com.*, *&c*). ~*s liminaires*, prelim[inarie]s (*book*). ~ *moulée*, moulding; cast.

pied (pje) m, foot; trotter; base, bottom; leg (*chair*, *&c*); stalk; footing; foothold; stand; standard. ~*-à-terre*, m, somewhere to stay, lodging. ~ [*à trois branches*], tripod. ~*-d'alouette*, larkspur, delphinium. ~*-de-*

biche, claw [bar]. ~ *de bœuf*, neat's foot. ~*-droit*, pier (*of arch*). ~ *fumeur*, smoker's stand. *avoir le* ~ *marin*, to have got one's sea legs. *sur* ~, on foot; standing (*crops*). **piédestal** (pjedestal) m, pedestal.

piège (pjɛːʒ) m, trap, snare, pitfall.

pie-grièche (pigrjɛʃ) f, shrike; shrew (*pers.*).

Piémont (le) (pjemɔ̃), Piedmont.

pierraille (pjɛraːj) f, small stones. **pierre** (pjɛːr) f, stone. ~ *à aiguiser*, whetstone, hone. ~ [*à briquet*] & ~ *à fusil*, flint. ~ *à chaux*, ~ *calcaire*, limestone. ~ *à gué*, stepping stone. ~ *blanche*, hearthstone. ~ *d'achoppement* (aʃɔpmᾶ), stumbling block, snag. ~ *d'aimant*, loadstone, lodestone. ~ *de lune*, moonstone. ~ *de touche*, touchstone (*lit.* & *fig.*); test. ~ *philosophale* (filɔzɔfal), philosophers' stone. ~ *précieuse*, precious stone, gem [stone]. ~ *tombale* (tɔ̃bal), ~ *tumulaire* (tymylɛːr), tombstone, gravestone. **pierreries** (pjɛrˈəri) f.pl, precious stones, gems, jewels. **pierreux, euse** (rø, øːz) a, stony; gritty.

pierrot (pjɛro) m, pierrot, clown; sparrow.

piété (pjete) f, piety, godliness; devotion.

piétiner (pjetine) v.t, to trample on, stamp on; tread; (v.i.) to dance (*with rage*). ~ *sur place*, to mark time (*fig.*). **piéton, ne** (tɔ̃, ɔn) n, pedestrian, foot passenger; walker.

piètre† (pjɛtr) a, wretched, poor, shabby.

pieu (pjø) m, stake, post; pile.

pieuvre (pjœːvr) f, octopus.

pieux, euse† (pjø, øːz) a, pious, godly; reverent.

pigeon, ne (piʒɔ̃, ɔn) n, pigeon, dove; greenhorn, gull. ~ *artificiel*, clay bird. ~ *grosse gorge*, pouter. ~ *paon*, fan tail. ~ *ramier*, wood pigeon, ring dove. ~ *voyageur*, carrier pigeon, homing p. **pigeonneau** (ʒɔno) m, young pigeon, squab; gull, dupe. **pigeonnier** (nje) m, dovecot[e].

pigment (pigmᾶ) m, pigment.

pignocher (piɲɔʃe) v.i, to pick at one's food.

pignon (piɲɔ̃) m, gable; pinion. ~ *de chaîne*, sprocket wheel.

pilastre (pilastr) m, pilaster; newel.

pile (pil) f, pile, heap; stack (*of wood*); pier (*bridge*); battery, cell (*Elec.*); reverse (*coin*). ~ *ou face?* heads or tails?

piler (pile) v.t, to pound, pestle, grind.

pilier (pilje) m, pillar, column, post.

pillage (pijaːʒ) m, pillage, looting; pilfering. **piller** (je) v.t, to pillage, plunder, loot, sack, ransack; pilfer; seize, worry (*of dog*).

pilon (pilɔ̃) m, pestle; stamp (*ore*); rammer; hammer (*power*); drumstick (*fowl*).

pilori (pilɔri) m, pillory. **pilorier** (rje) v.t, to pillory, gibbet.

pilotage (pilɔtaːʒ) m, pile work; pilotage, piloting. **pilote** (lɔt) m, pilot. **piloter** (te) *v.t*, to pile; pilot. ~ *dans*, to show (*pers.*) round (*town*). **pilotis** (ti) *m*, pile (*stake*); piling.

pilou (pilu) *m*, flannelette.

pilule (pilyl) *f*, pill.

pimbêche (pɛ̃bɛʃ) *f*, pert conceited woman.

piment (pimɑ̃) *m*, pimento, capsicum, allspice.

pimpant, e (pɛ̃pɑ̃, ɑ̃:t) *a*, smart, spruce, spick & span.

pin (pɛ̃) *m*, pine [tree], fir [tree]. ~ *du Chili*, Chili pine, monkey puzzle.

pinacle (pinakl) *m*, pinnacle.

pince (pɛ̃:s) *f*, grip, hold; (*oft. pl.*) pliers, nippers; forceps; tweezers; tongs; (*s.*) clip; clamp; crowbar; claw, nipper (*crab, &c*); pleat. ~*s à épiler*, eyebrow tweezers. ~*-monseigneur*, *f*, jemmy (*burglar's*). ~*-nez*, *m*, eyeglasses. ~*-sans-rire*, *m*, man of dry humour. **pincé, e** (pɛ̃se) *a*, affected, prim; stiff; wry; pursed (*lips*).

pinceau (pɛ̃so) *m*, paint brush; brush; touch (*fig.*); pencil (*Opt.*). ~ *à barbe*, shaving brush.

pincée (pɛ̃se) *f*, pinch (*snuff, &c*). **pincer** (se) *v.t*, to pinch, nip, squeeze; purse (*lips*); pluck (*strings*); play (*harp, &c*), twang; grip; catch. **pincettes** (sɛt) *f.pl*, tweezers; tongs (*fire*). **pinçon** (pɛ̃sɔ̃) *m*, mark, bruise (*left on the skin by a pinch*).

pineraie (pinrɛ) *f*, pine wood (*forest*).

pingouin (pɛ̃gwɛ̃) *m*, auk.

ping-pong (piŋpɔŋ) *m*, ping-pong, table tennis.

pingre (pɛ̃:gr) *a*, stingy. ¶ *m*, skinflint.

pinnule (pinnyl) *f*, pinnule; sight [vane].

pinson (pɛ̃sɔ̃) *m*, finch; chaffinch.

pintade (pɛ̃tad) *f*, guinea fowl.

pioche (pjɔʃ) *f*, pick; pickaxe; mattock. **piocher** (ʃe) *v.t. & i*, to pick up; work hard, grind.

piolet (pjɔlɛ) *m*, ice axe.

pion (pjɔ̃) *m*, pawn (*Chess*); piece, man (*Draughts*); usher (*Sch.*).

pionnier (pjɔnje) *m*, pioneer.

pipe (pip) *f*, pipe (*cask, tobacco*). **pipeau** (po) *m*, [reed] pipe; lime twig; bird call. **pipée** (pe) *f*, bird catching. **piper** (pe) *v.t*, to lure (*birds*); dupe; load (*dice*); mark (*card*).

pipi[t] (pipi[t]) *m*, pipit, titlark.

piquant, e (pikɑ̃, ɑ̃:t) *a*, prickly; stinging; cutting; pointed; pungent; racy; piquant. ¶ *m*, prickle; sting; quill (*porcupine*); spike; pungency; point, zest, pith. **pique** (pik) *f*, pike (*weapon*); pique, spite; tiff; (*m.*) spade[s] (*Cards*). ~*-assiette*, *m*, sponger. ~*-nique* (nik) *m*, picnic. ~*-notes*, *m*, bill file. **piqué, e** (ke) *a*, quilted; padded; staccato (*notes*); crazy. ~ *des mouches*, fly-blown. ~ *des vers*, worm-eaten, moth-eaten. ¶ *m*, quilting. **piquer** (ke) *v.t*, to prick; sting; bite; spur; goad; prod; nettle; pique; puncture; pit; lard; stitch; quilt; nibble (*fish*); stick; scale

(*boiler*). ~ *du nez*, to nose dive (*Aero.*). **piquet** (kɛ) *m*, peg, stake; picket; piquet (*Cards*). **piqueur** (kœːr) *m*, whipper-in, huntsman; stud groom. **piqueuse** (køːz) *f*, stitcher, sewer (*pers.*). **piqûre** (ky:r) *f*, prick; sting; bite; puncture; pit, hole; spot; speck; quilting.

pirate (pirat) *m*, pirate. **pirater** (te) *v.i*, to pirate. **piraterie** (tri) *f*, piracy.

pire (pi:r) *a*, worse. *le* ~, the worst.

Pirée (le) (pire), Piraeus.

pirogue (pirɔg) *f*, [dug-out] canoe. ~ *de barre*, surf boat. ~ *en écorce*, birch-bark [canoe].

pirouette (pirwɛt) *f*, whirligig; pirouette. **pirouetter** (te) *v.i*, to pirouette, twirl.

pis (pi) *m*, udder, dug.

pis (pi) *ad*, worse. *le* ~, the worst. ~ *aller*, *m*, last resource; makeshift. *au* ~ *aller*, at the worst.

pisciculture (pisikylty:r) *f*, pisciculture. **piscine** (sin) *f*, swimming bath, s. pool.

Pise (pi:z) *f*, Pisa.

pissenlit (pisɑ̃li) *m*, dandelion.

pistache (pistaʃ) *f*, pistachio [nut]. **pistachier** (ʃje) *m*, pistachio tree.

piste (pist) *f*, track (*running, racing*); run (*toboggan*); rink (*skating*); racecourse; track, trail; scent, clue. ~ *de cirque*, ring. ~ *en cendrée*, cinder track; dirt t.

pistil (pistil) *m*, pistil.

pistolet (pistolɛ) *m*, pistol.

piston (pistɔ̃) *m*, piston; cornet (*Mus.*).

pitance (pitɑ̃:s) *f*, livelihood.

pitchpin (pitʃpɛ̃) *m*, pitchpine.

piteux, euse† (pitø, øːz) *a*, piteous, woeful, pitiable; sorry. **pitié** (tje) *f*, pity, mercy.

piton (pitɔ̃) *m*, screw eye; peak (*mountain*).

pitoyable† (pitwajabl) *a*, pitiable, pitiful; wretched, paltry.

pitre (pi:tr) *m*, clown; buffoon.

pittoresque† (pitɔrɛsk) *a*, picturesque, beauty (*spot*); quaint; graphic; pictorial (*magazine*). ¶ *m*, picturesqueness.

pituite (pitɥit) *f*, phlegm; mucus.

pivoine (pivwan) *f*, peony.

pivot (pivo) *m*, pivot, pin; tap root; crux. **pivoter** (vɔte) *v.i*, to pivot, turn, hinge; slew; wheel (*Mil.*).

piz (pi) (*Geog.*) *m*, pap, mamelon.

placage (plaka:ʒ) *m*, veneering; patchwork (*fig.*).

placard (plaka:r) *m*, wall cupboard; placard, poster, bill; galley [proof]; slip (*Typ.*). **placarder** (karde) *v.t*, to post (*bills*) placard.

place (plas) *f*, place; room; way; stead; seat; fare; berth; spot; patch; ground; town market; square (*in town*); churchyard (*public square surrounding a church or cathedral*). ~ *aux dames!* ladies first! ~ *d'armes*, parade ground, drill g. ~ [*de voitures*], [cab] rank. ~*s debout seulement!* standing room only! ~ *face de* *l'arrière*, seat with back to the engine. ~ *face à la machine*, seat facing the engine. ~ *dénudée d'herbes*, bare patch (*Golf.*). ~ *forte*, ~ *de guerre*, fortified place. **placement** (smā) *m*, placing; investment. **placer** (se) *v.t*, to place, put, set; dispose of; deposit; invest (*money*).

placer (plasɛːr) (*Min.*) *m*, placer, diggings.

placide† (plasid) *a*, placid. **placidité** (dite) *f*, placidity.

placier (plasje) *m*, canvasser, traveller.

plafond (plafɔ̃) *m*, ceiling; maximum, peak [figure]. **plafonner** (fɔne) *v.t*, to ceil. **plafonnier** (nje) *m*, ceiling fitting (*light*).

plage (plaːʒ) *f*, beach, shore; seaside resort; sands.

plagiaire (plaʒjɛːr) *m*, plagiarist. **plagiat** (ʒja) *m*, plagiarism. **plagier** (ʒje) *v.t*, to plagiarize.

plaid (plɛd) *m*, plaid; travelling rug.

plaider (plede) *v.i. & t*, to plead, argue. **plaideur, euse** (dœːr, øːz) *n*, litigant; suitor. **plaidoirie** (dwari) *f*, pleading; counsel's speech. **plaidoyer** (dwaje) *m*, speech for the defence.

plaie (plɛ) *f*, wound, sore; evil; plague.

plaignant, e (plɛɲɑ̃, ɑ̃ːt) *n*, plaintiff, prosecutor, trix.

plain, e (plɛ̃, ɛn) *a*, plain; open. *plain-chant*, *m*, plainsong. *de plain-pied*, on one floor, on a level.

plaindre (plɛ̃ːdr) *v.t.ir*, to pity, be sorry for. **se** ~, to complain; moan, groan.

plaine (plɛn) *f*, plain (*Phys. Geog.*).

plainte (plɛ̃ːt) *f*, moan, groan; complaint; action (*Law*). **plaintif, ive†** (plɛtif, iːv) *a*, plaintive, doleful; querulous.

plaire (plɛːr) *v.i.ir*, to please. *s'il vous plaît*, [if you] please. *plût au ciel que . . .*, would to heaven that . . . ~ **à**, to please (*v.t.*). **se** ~, to be pleased; like; thrive. **plaisamment** (plɛzamɑ̃) *ad*, funnily; ludicrously. **de plaisance** (zɑ̃ːs), pleasure (*boat*); week-end (*cottage*). **Plaisance**, *f*, Piacenza. **plaisant, e** (zɑ̃, ɑ̃ːt) *a*, funny, droll, jocular; comical; ludicrous; pleasant. ¶ *m*, wag, joker, fool; comical side. **plaisanter** (zɑ̃te) *v.i*, to joke, jest, trifle; (*v.t.*) to chaff. **plaisanterie** (tri) *f*, joke, jest; fun. **plaisir** (ziːr) *m*, pleasure, delight; treat; convenience; will; sake; amusement; enjoyment; cone, cornet, wafer (*ice cream*).

plan, e (plɑ̃, an) *a*, plane, even, level, flat. ¶ *m*, plane, level; ground (*of painting*); plan; draught; map; table; project, scheme. **planche** (plɑ̃ːʃ) *f*, board; shelf; bed (*Hort.*); plate (*Typ.*). ~ *bouvetée* (buvte), match board. ~ *de salut*, sheet anchor (*fig.*). *faire la* ~, to float (*Swim.*). **planchéier** (plɑ̃ʃeje) *v.t*, to board; floor. **plancher** (ʃe) *m*, floor. *le* ~ *des vaches*, terra firma. **planchette** (ʃɛt) *f*, slat; plane table (*Surv.*). **plancton** (plɑ̃ktɔ̃) *m*, plankton.

plane (plan) *m*, plane [tree]; (*f.*) drawing knife.

planer (plane) *v.t*, to smooth; plane; planish; (*v.i.*) to soar; hover; look down; glide (*Aero.*).

planétaire (planetɛːr) *a*, planetary. ¶ *m*, planetarium, orrery. **planète** (nɛt) *f*, planet. *heureuse* ~, lucky star (*fig.*).

planeur (planœːr) *m*, planisher (*pers.*); glider (*Aero.*).

plant (plɑ̃) *m*, sapling, set, slip; plantation. **plantage** (taːʒ) *m*, planting; plantation. **plantain** (tɛ̃) *m*, plantain (*Plantago*). **plantanier** (tanje) *m*, plantain (*banana*). **plantation** (sjɔ̃) *f*, planting; plantation. **plante** (plɑ̃ːt) *f*, sole (*foot*); plant (*Bot.*). ~ *annuelle*, annual. ~ *marine*, seaweed. ~ *potagère*, vegetable. ~ *vivace*, perennial. **planter** (plɑ̃te) *v.t*, to plant, set. **planteur, euse** (tœːr, øːz) *n*, planter. grower. **plantoir** (twaːr) *m*, dibble. **planton** (tɔ̃) (*Mil.*) *m*, orderly; o. duty.

plantureux, euse† (plɑ̃tyrø, øːz) *a*, copious; fleshy; fertile.

planure (planyːr) *f*, shaving[s].

plaque (plak) *f*, plate; sheet; slab; plaque; tablet; badge. ~ *d'identité*, identity disc. ~ *de cheminée*, fireback, hob. ~ *de gazon*, turf, sod. ~ *de police*, ~ *matricule*, number plate (*Motor.*). ~ *de propreté*, finger plate. ~ *tournante*, turntable (*Rly*). **plaqué** (ke) *m*, electroplate. **plaquer** (ke) *v.t*, to plate; veneer; lay on; cake; lay down (*turf*); tackle (*Rugby*).

plastique (plastik) *a*, plastic.

plastron (plastrɔ̃) *m*, breastplate; front (*shirt, &c*); butt (*pers., fig.*).

plat, e (pla, at) *a*, flat; level; lank, straight (*hair*); smooth (*sea*); dead (*calm*); dull, bald (*fig.*). *à* ~, flat. *à plat* [*ventre*], flat on one's face. ¶ *m*, flat; blade (*oar, &c*); side, board (*book*); pan (*scale*); dish; mess; course (*dinner*). ~ *de quête*, collection plate. ~ *du jour*, special dish for the day. ~ *inférieur*, off side, off board (*book*). ~ *supérieur*, front side, front board.

platane (platan) *m*, plane [tree].

plat-bord (plaboːr) *m*, gunwale, gunnel.

plate (plat) *f*, punt (*boat*).

plateau (plato) *m*, tray; salver; pan (*scale*); dish (*soap*); floor (*Theat.*); plateau, table land; upland; plate, table; face plate, chuck (*lathe*). ~ *roulant*, service wagon.

plate-bande (platbɑ̃ːd) (*Hort.*) *f*, border; bed.

platée (plate) *f*, dishful.

plate-forme (platfɔrm) *f*, platform; stage; flat roof.

platement (platmɑ̃) *ad*, flatly; dully.

platine (platin) *f*, plate, platen; stage (*microscope*); lock (*firearm*). ¶ *m*, platinum.

platitude (platityd) *f*, flatness (*fig.*), dullness; platitude.

platonique (platɔnik) *a*, Platonic.

plâtre (plɑːtr) *m,* plaster; p. cast. ~ *de moulage,* p. of Paris. **plâtrer** (plɑtre) *v.t,* to plaster. **plâtrier** (trie) *m,* plasterer. **plâtrière** (ɛːr) *f,* gypsum quarry.

plausible† (plozibl) *a,* plausible.

plébéien, ne (plebejɛ̃, ɛn) *a,* plebeian. **plébiscite** (bisit) *m,* plebiscite, referendum.

plein, e† (plɛ̃, ɛn) *a,* full; replete; fraught; whole; mid; high (*tide, seas*); solid; open: with young. ~ *comme un œuf,* chokefull. *en plein jour, en plein midi,* in broad daylight. ¶ *m,* plenum; full; height; thick stroke, downstroke. **plénier, ère** (plenje, ɛːr) *a,* full; plenary. **plénipotentiaire** (nipotɑ̃sjɛːr) *m. & att,* plenipotentiary. **plénitude** (tyd) *f,* plenitude, fullness; repletion.

pléonasme (pleonɑsm) *m,* pleonasm.

pléthore (pletoːr) *f,* plethora, glut.

pleur (plœːr) *m. usually pl,* tear. **pleurard, e** (plœrɑːr, ard) *n,* whimperer; (*att.*) whimpering; tearful; maudlin (*voice*). **pleurer** (re) *v.i. & t,* to weep; mourn; bewail; cry; water, run (*eyes*); drip; bleed.

pleurésie (plœrezi) *f,* pleurisy.

pleureur, euse (plœrœːr, øːz) *n,* whimperer; mute; [hired] mourner; (*att.*) weeping. **pleurnicher** (niʃe) *v.i,* to whimper, whine, snivel.

pleutre (pløːtr) *m,* cad.

pleuvoir (plœvwaːr) *v.i.ir,* to rain; pour, shower.

plèvre (plɛːvr) *f,* pleura.

plexus (plɛksyːs) *m,* plexus.

pleyon (plejɔ̃) *m,* withe, withy.

pli (pli) *m,* fold; pleat; wrinkle, pucker, crease; bend; ply; cover, envelope. **pliable** (abl) *a,* pliable. **pliant, e** (plijɑ̃, ɑ̃ːt) *a,* pliant; folding. ¶ *m,* camp stool.

plie (pli) *f,* plaice.

plier (plie) *v.t. & i,* to fold; strike (*tent*); bend; bow. ~ *bagage,* to pack up; decamp; die.

plinthe (plɛ̃ːt) *f,* plinth; skirting [board].

plisser (plise) *v.t. & i,* to pleat, fold; kilt; crease, crumple, wrinkle, pucker.

plomb (plɔ̃) *m,* lead; shot; came; plumb, plummet; plomb (*Cust.*); sink; ballast (*fig.*). ~ [*fusible*], fuse (*Elec.*). **plombage** (baːʒ) *m,* plumbing; stopping (*teeth*). **plombagine** (baʒin) *f,* plumbago, graphite, black lead. **plomber** (be) *v.t,* to lead, plumb; plomb; stop, fill (*tooth*). **plomberie** (bri) *m,* plumbing; lead works. **plombier** (bje) *m,* plumber.

plongeoir (plɔ̃ʒwaːr) *m,* diving board. **plongeon** (ʒɔ̃) *m,* diver (*bird*); dive, plunge. ~ *d'une grande hauteur,* high dive. ~ *sans élan,* plunge (*Swim.*). **plonger** (ʒe) *v.i. & t,* to plunge; dive; submerge; dip; duck; immerse; thrust. **plongeur, euse** (ʒœːr, øːz) *n,* diver (*Swim.*); (*m.*) diver (*in diving dress*); washer-up; plunger (*pump*).

plot (plo) *m,* stud (*Elec. contact*).

ployer (plwaje) *v.t. & i,* to bend, bow; wrap up; give way.

pluie (plɥi) *f,* rain; shower; wet. ~ *d'or,* golden rain (*firework*).

plumage (plymaːʒ) *m,* plumage, feathers. **plumasserie** (masri) *f,* feather trade. **plumassier, ère** (sje, ɛːr) *n,* plumassier. **plume** (plym) *f,* feather (*bird & Box.*); pen. ~ [*à écrire*], nib. ~ *d'oie,* quill [pen]. *sans* ~*s,* unfledged, callow. **plumeau** (mo) *m,* feather duster. **plumée** (me) *f,* penful, dip (*ink*). **plumer** (me) *v.t,* to pluck; fleece (*fig.*); (*v.i.*) to feather (*Rowing*). **plumet** (mɛ) *m,* plume. **plumetis** (mti) *m,* raised satin stitch. **plumeux, euse** (mø, øːz) *a,* feathery, plumose. **plumier** (mje) *m,* pen tray, p. case. **plumitif** (tif) *m,* minute book; quill driver.

plupart (la) (plypaːr) *f,* most, the generality, the majority.

plural, e (plyral) *a,* plural (*vote, &c*). **pluralité** (lite) *f,* plurality; majority. **pluriel, le** (rjɛl) *a. & m,* plural (*Gram.*).

plus (ply) *finally often* plys; *in liaison,* plyz) *ad,* more; -er (*suffix forming comparatives*); longer; any l., any more. *2, 3, de* ~, 2, 3, more (*Golf*). le ~, the ~, the most; -est (*suffix forming superlatives*); the odd (*Golf*). [*signe*] ~ (plys) *m,* plus [sign]. **plusieurs** (zjœːr) *a. & pn,* several. **plus-que-parfait** (plyskəparfɛ) *m,* pluperfect. **plus-value** (plyvaly) *f,* appreciation; surplus; [unearned] increment.

plutôt (plyto) *ad,* rather, sooner, instead.

pluvial, e (plyvjal) *a,* rain (*water*); rainy. **pluvier** (plyvje) *m,* plover. **pluvieux, euse** (plyvjø, øːz) *a,* rainy; wet.

pneumatique (pnømatik) (*abb.* pneu) *m,* [pneumatic] tire. ¶ *a,* pneumatic, air (*att.*).

pneumonie (pnømɔni) *f,* pneumonia.

Pô (le) (po), the Po (*river*).

pochade (pɔʃad) *f,* rapid sketch.

poche (pɔʃ) *f,* pocket; sack; pouch; case; crop (*bird*); ladle; pucker. ~ *rapportée,* patch pocket. ~ *revolver,* hip p. **pocher** (ʃe) *v.t,* to poach (*eggs*); black (*eye*); dash off (*sketch*). **pochette** (ʃɛt) *f,* pocket; pocket case, packet. ~ *en soie, de couleur,* silk coloured handkerchief. **pochoir** (ʃwaːr) *m,* stencil [plate].

poêle (pwɑːl) *f,* frying pan; pan. ¶ *m,* pall; canopy; stove, range. ~ *à pétrole,* oil heater. **poêlier** (pwalje) *m,* stove & range maker. **poêlon** (lɔ̃) *m,* saucepan, pipkin.

poème (pɔɛːm) *m,* poem. **poésie** (ezi) *f,* poetry; poem, piece of poetry. ~ *enfantine,* nursery rhyme. **poète** (ɛt) *m,* poet. **poétereau** (etro) *m,* poetaster. **poétesse** (tɛs) *f,* poetess. **poétique**† (tik) *a,* poetic; poetical.

poids (pwɑ) *m,* weight; shot (*in sport of putting the shot*); heaviness; burden, brunt. ~ *spécifique,* specific gravity.

poignant, e (pwaɲɑ̃, ɑ̃:t) a, poignant.

poignard (pwaɲaːr) m, dagger, dirk, poignard. poignarder (narde) v.t, to stab, knife. poigne (pwaɲ) f, grip; energy. poignée (ɲe) f, handful; handle, grip, hilt; hank. ~ de main, handshake. poignet (ɲɛ) m, wrist; wristband, cuff (soft). ~s mousquetaire, double cuffs.

poil (pwal) m, hair (on animal & body pers.); fur, coat; pile, nap; bristle; down (plant); energy. ~ de chèvre d'Angora, mohair. ~ follet, down (chin, &c). à ~, bareback[ed] (Riding). à ~ ras, short-haired, smooth-haired (dog, &c). au ~ rude, rough-haired, wire-haired (dog). poilu, e (ly) a, hairy, shaggy. ¶ m, French soldier.

poinçon (pwɛ̃sɔ̃) m, punch (solid); awl; point; stamp; king-post; puncheon. ~ de contrôle, hall-mark. poinçonner (sɔne) v.t, to punch; clip (ticket); stamp; hall-mark.

poindre (pwɛ̃:dr) v.i.ir, to dawn, break; come up.

poing (pwɛ̃) m, fist, hand.

point (pwɛ̃) m, point; dot; speck; mark; tick; pip (Cards, Dominoes); score (games); [full] stop, period; note; stitch; point [lace]; degree, extent; verge (fig.); focus. ~ à terre, landmark (Naut.). ~ arrière, back stitch. ~s conducteurs, leader (Typ.). ~ coupé, cut openwork stitch. ~ croisé, herringboning. ~ d'appui, fulcrum. ~ d'appui de la flotte, naval station (foreign). ~ d'éclair, ~ d'inflammabilité, flash[ing] point. ~ d'interrogation, note of interrogation, question mark. ~ d'ourlet, hemming. ~ de chainette, chain stitch. ~ de côté, stitch in the side (Med.). ~ de croix, cross stitch. ~ de fuite, vanishing point. ~ de languette, ~ de feston, blanket stitch, buttonhole s. (Emb.). ~ de marque, marking stitch. ~ de minute, bullion stitch (Crochet). ~ de mire, aim; cynosure (fig.). ~ de piqûre, lock stitch. ~ de réparation, penalty kick mark (Foot.). ~ de repère, reference mark, datum point; bench mark; landmark (fig.). ~ de surjet, oversewing stitch, seam s. ~ de tige, ~ coulé, stem stitch, crewel s. ~ de vue, point of view, standpoint. ~ devant, running stitch. ~ du jour, daybreak, dawn. ~ & virgule ou ~-virgule, m, semicolon. ~ mort, dead centre. ~ noir, blackhead. ~ piqué, stitching. ~ relief, raised stitch (Crochet). ~ roulé, whipping. à ~, [just] in time, to a nicety, to a turn. à ~ nommé, in the nick of time; at the right moment.

point (pwɛ̃) ad, no, not, not at all, [not] any.

pointage (pwɛ̃ta:ʒ) m, ticking [off], checking; timekeeping; timing; scoring; aiming, pointing, laying, training (gun).

pointe (pwɛ̃:t) f, point (sharp end); tip; head;

top; peak; toe (shoe, sock); (pl.) toe dancing; centre (lathe); nail, brad; touch; quip, quirk. ~ de Paris, wire nail, French n., sprig. ~ de terre, headland, foreland. ~ du jour, daybreak, dawn. sur la ~ du pied, on tiptoe.

pointeau (pwɛ̃to) m, centre punch.

pointer (pwɛ̃te) v.t, to tick [off], check, tally; point, aim, level, lay, train; thrust; (v.i.) to soar; appear, sprout. pointeur (tœ:r) m, checker; timekeeper; marker, scorer; gun layer. pointille (ti:j) f, punctilio. pointiller (tije) v.t, to dot; stipple; bait; (v.i.) to cavil; split hairs. pointillerie (jri) f, captiousness, hair splitting. pointilleux, euse (jø, ø:z) a, captious, touchy; fastidious, punctilious.

pointu, e (pwɛ̃ty) a, pointed; sharp; shrill.

pointure (pwɛ̃ty:r) f, size (of shoes, gloves, &c).

poire (pwa:r) f, pear; bulb, ball. poiré (pware) m, perry.

poireau (pwaro) m, leek; wart.

poirier (pwarje) m, pear tree; pear wood.

pois (pwa) m, pea; dot (Emb.); spot (as on tie). ~ carrés, marrowfats. ~ cassés, split peas. ~ chinois, soy[a] bean. ~ de senteur, sweet pea. ~ verts, green peas.

poison (pwazɔ̃) m, poison.

poissard, e (pwasa:r, ard) a, vulgar. ¶ f, fishwife.

poisser (pwase) v.t, to pitch; wax (thread); make sticky. poisseux, euse (sø, ø:z) a, sticky.

poisson (pwasɔ̃) m, fish. faire un ~ d'avril à, to make an April fool of. ~s blancs, coarse fish. ~ de grand sport, big-game fish. ~ de mer, salt-water fish, sea fish. ~ rouge, goldfish. poissonnaille (sɔnɑːj) f, fry. poissonnerie (nri) f, fish market; f. shop. poissonneux, euse (nø, ø:z) a, full of fish. poissonnier, ère (nje, ɛːr) n, fishmonger. ¶ f, fish kettle (Cook.).

poitrail (pwatra:j) m, breast (horse). poitrinaire (trinɛ:r) a. & n, consumptive. poitrine (trin) f, chest, breast; brisket.

poivre (pwa:vr) m, pepper. ~ de Cayenne (kajɛn), ~ rouge, Cayenne p., red p. poivré, e (pwavre) p.a, peppery; spicy (tale). poivrer (vre) v.t, to pepper. poivrier (vrie) m, pepper plant; p. box. poivrière (vriɛ:r) f, pepper box.

poix (pwa) f, pitch; cobbler's wax.

polaire (pɔlɛ:r) a, polar; pole (star). pôle (po:l) m, pole (Astr., Phys., &c).

polémique (pɔlemik) a, polemic(al). ¶ f, polemic; polemics.

poli, e (pɔli) p.a, polished, bright; glossy, sleek; polite, mannerly, refined. ¶ m, polish, gloss.

police (pɔlis) f, policing; police regulations; police [force]; policy (Insce). ~ de la circulation, traffic police. policer (se) v.t, to control, organize, civilize.

polichinelle (pɔliʃinɛl) m, Punch; buffoon.

poliment (pɔlimɑ̃) *ad*, politely. **polir** (li:r) *v.t*, to polish; buff; smooth; refine.

polisson, ne (pɔlisɔ̃, ɔn) *n*, street child; rascal, scamp; immodest person; (*att.*) naughty, precocious, indecent. **polissonner** (sɔne) *v.i*, to run the streets (*child*); be lewd.

politesse (pɔlites) *f*, politeness; compliment.

politicien (pɔlitisjɛ̃) *m*, politician (*as a trade*). **politique†** (tik) *a*, political; politic. ¶ *m*, politician. ¶ *f*, policy; polity; politics. **politiquer** (ke) *v.i*, to talk politics.

polka (pɔlka) *m*, polka.

pollen (pɔllɛn) *m*, pollen.

polluer (pɔllɥe) *v.t*, to pollute; defile; profane. **pollution** (pɔllysjɔ̃) *f*, pollution, &c.

polo (pɔlo) *m*, polo; polo cap.

Pologne (la) (pɔlɔɲ), Poland. **polonais, e** (nɛ, ɛ:z) *a*, Polish. **P~,** *n*, Pole. **le polonais,** Polish (*language*). **polonaise,** *f*, polonaise.

poltron, ne (pɔltrɔ̃, ɔn) *a*, cowardly. ¶ *n*, poltroon, coward. **poltronnerie** (trɔnri) *f*, cowardice.

polygame (pɔligam) *n*, polygamist. ¶ *a*, polygamous. **polygamie** (mi) *f*, polygamy. **polyglotte** (glɔt) *a. & n*, polyglot. **polygone** (gɔn) *m*, polygon. **la Polynésie** (nezi), Polynesia. **polype** (lip) *m*, polyp; polypus. **polysyllabe** (silab) *a*, polysyllabic. ¶ *m*, polysyllable. **polytechnique** (tɛknik) *a*, polytechnic. **polythéisme** *(teism) *m*, polytheism.

pommade (pɔmad) *f*, pomade, pomatum; salve. **pommader** (de) *v.t*, to pomade.

pomme (pɔm) *f*, apple; cone (*fir, pine*); knob; head (*stick, cabbage*); rose (*can*). ~ *d'Adam* (adɑ̃), Adam's apple. ~ *de terre,* potato. ~*s de terre à l'eau,* ~*s de terre nature,* boiled potatoes. ~*s de terre vapeur,* boiled potatoes. ~*s de terre en robe [de chambre],* jacket potatoes. ~ *sauvage,* crab [apple]. **pommé, e** (me) (*fig.*) *p.a,* downright. **pommeau** (mo) *m*, pommel. **pommelé, e** (mle) *p.a,* dapple[d]; mackerel (*sky*). **pommeraie** (mrɛ) *f*, apple orchard. **pommette** (mɛt) *f*, cheek bone. **pommier** (mje) *m*, apple tree. ~ *sauvage,* crab [apple tree].

pompe (pɔ̃:p) *f*, pomp; pump. ~ *à bière,* beer engine. ~ *à incendie,* fire engine. ~ *aspirante,* suction pump. ~ *foulante,* force pump. ~ *funèbre,* funeral; (*pl.*) undertaking.

Pompéi (pɔ̃pei) *f*, Pompeii.

pomper (pɔ̃pe) *v.t. & i*, to pump; suck up.

pompeux, euse† (pɔ̃pø, ø:z) *a*, pompous; stately.

pompier (pɔ̃pje) *m*, pump maker; fireman; conventionalist, formulist; (*att.*) conventional, formulistic.

pompon (pɔ̃pɔ̃) *m*, pompon, tuft, tassel.

ponce (pɔ̃:s) *f*, pumice; pounce (*Art*).

ponceau (pɔ̃so) *m*, culvert; poppy.

poncer (pɔ̃se) *v.t*, to pumice; sand paper;

pounce. poncif (sif) (*fig.*) *m*, conventionalism.

ponction (pɔ̃ksjɔ̃) (*Surg.*) *f*, puncture, tapping.

ponctualité (pɔ̃ktɥalite) *f*, punctuality.

ponctuation (pɔ̃ktɥasjɔ̃) *f*, punctuation.

ponctuel, le† (pɔ̃ktɥɛl) *a*, punctual.

ponctuer (pɔ̃ktɥe) *v.t. & abs*, to punctuate; emphasize.

pondérable (pɔ̃derabl) *a*, ponderable. **pondérer** (re) *v.t*, to balance.

pondre (pɔ̃:dr) *v.t. & abs*, to lay (*eggs*); be delivered of (*fig.*).

poney (pɔnɛ) *m*, pony.

pont (pɔ̃) *m*, bridge; platform; deck (*ship*). ~ *à bascule,* weigh bridge; drawbridge. ~ *abri,* awning deck, hurricane d. ~ *aux ânes,* pons asinorum. ~ *de manœuvre,* hurricane deck. ~ *roulant,* travelling crane. ~ *suspendu,* suspension bridge. ~ *suspendu à chaines,* chain bridge. ~ *tournant,* swing bridge.

ponte (pɔ̃:t) *f*, laying (*eggs*); (*m.*) punt[er] (*Cards, &c*).

ponté, e (pɔ̃te) *a*, decked. **non ~,** open (*boat*).

ponter (pɔ̃te) *v.i*, to punt (*Cards, &c*).

pontife (pɔ̃tif) *m*, pontiff; pundit. **pontifical†** (fikal) *a. & m*, pontifical. **pontificat** (ka) *m*, pontificate.

pont-levis (pɔ̃ləvi) *m*, drawbridge (*castle*).

ponton (pɔ̃tɔ̃) *m*, pontoon; hulk; landing stage.

popeline (pɔplin) *f*, poplin.

populace (pɔpylas) *f*, populace, rabble. **populacier, ère** (sje, ɛ:r) *a*, vulgar. **populaire†** (lɛ:r) *a*, popular. **popularité** (larite) *f*, popularity. **population** (sjɔ̃) *f*, population. **populeux, euse** (lø, ø:z) *a*, populous.

porc (pɔ:r) *m*, pig, swine; pork. ~ *[châtré],* hog.

porcelaine (pɔrsəlɛn) *f*, porcelain, china[ware]; cowrie. ~ *de Saxe,* Dresden china. **porcelainier, ère** (nje, ɛ:r) *n*, china manufacturer; china dealer.

porc-épic (pɔrkepik) *m*, porcupine.

porche (pɔrʃ) *m*, porch.

porcher, ère (pɔrʃe, ɛ:r) *n*, swine herd. **porcherie** (ʃəri) *f*, piggery. **porcine** (sin) *a.f*, porcine, pig (*att.*).

pore (pɔ:r) *m*, pore. **poreux, euse** (pɔrø, ø:z) *a*, porous. **porosité** (rozite) *f*, porousness.

porphyre (pɔrfi:r) *m*, porphyry.

port (pɔ:r) *m*, port, harbour, haven; carrying; wearing; carriage; postage; bearing; burden (*ship*). ~ *d'armes,* gun licence. ~ *d'armement,* home port. ~ *d'attache,* port of registry. ~ *de guerre,* ~ *militaire,* naval port, n. station, n. base. ~ *de toute marée,* deep-water harbour. ~ *à bon ~,* safe[ly]; to a happy issue. **portable** (pɔrtabl) *a*, wearable.

portail (pɔrta:j) *m*, portal.

portant, e (pɔrtɑ̃, ɑ̃:t) *a*, bearing. *bien ~,* in good health. *mal ~,* in bad h. ¶ *m,* chest handle, lifting h.; outrigger (for rowlocks). **portatif, ive** (tatif, i:v) a, portable; small (arms).

porte (pɔrt) f, door, doorway; gate, gateway; arch. ~ **brisée**, folding door. ~ **charretière**, carriage entrance. ~ **cochère** (kɔʃɛːr), built-over carriage entrance. ~ **de service**, back door, tradesmen's entrance. ~-**fenêtre**, French window. ~ **matelassée**, baize door. ~ **va-et-vient**, swing door.

porte- (pɔrt; sometimes **porte** as noted) comps, all m: ~ **à faux**, overhang. ~-**affiches**, notice board. ~-**avions**, aircraft carrier. ~-**bagages**, luggage carrier. ~-**billets**, note case. ~-**bonheur**, mascot. ~-**bouquet**, flower holder. ~-**bouteilles**, bottle rack; bin. ~-**cartes** (tɔkart), card case; map case. ~-**chapeaux**, hat & coat stand. ~-**cigare**, cigar holder. ~-**cigares**, c. case. ~-**clefs** (tɔkle), turnkey; key ring. ~-**couteau**, knife rest. ~-**crayon** (tɔkrɛjɔ̃), pencil case. ~-**en-dehors**, outrigger (for rowlocks). ~-**épée**, frog (sword). ~-**étendard**, standard bearer. ~-**greffe** (tɔgrɛf), stock (Hort.). ~-**habits**, suit case. ~-**livres** (tɔliːvr), book trough. ~-**malheur**, bringer of ill luck; bird of ill omen, Jonah. ~-**menu** (tɔmny), menu holder. ~-**mine** (tɔmin), pencil case (propulsive). ~-**monnaie**, purse. ~-**montre** (tɔmɔ̃:tr), watch stand. ~-**mousqueton**, snap hook. ~-**musc** (tɔmysk), musk deer. ~-**musique**, music case. ~-**outil**, tool holder. ~-**parapluies**, umbrella stand. ~-**parole**, spokesman, mouthpiece (pers.). ~-**pelle** & **pincette** (tɔpɛl), fire[side] companion [set]. ~-**photographie**, photograph frame. ~-**plume** (tɔplym), penholder. ~-**plume [à] réservoir**, fountain pen. ~-**potiche**, pedestal (for vase). ~-**queue** (tɔkø), train bearer. ~-**respect**, person of imposing appearance; weapon. ~-**rôties**, toast rack. ~-**serviettes**, towel horse, t. rail. ~-**trésor**, jewel case (travelling). ~-**vêtements**, clothes hanger. ~-**voix** (tɔvwa), megaphone.

porté, e (pɔrte) p.a, inclined, disposed, prone, apt; fond. ~ **ci-contre**, per contra.

porteballe (pɔrtəbal) m, packman, pedlar.

portée (pɔrte) f, bearing; litter (of pups); span; reach, range, radius, scope, compass, shot; significance, purport; stave, staff (Mus.). **à ~ de la voix**, within call.

portefaix (pɔrtəfɛ) m, porter (street, &c); rough fellow.

portefeuille (pɔrtəfœːj) m, portfolio; letter case, wallet; office (in ministry). ~-**titres**, investments, securities, share holdings, stocks & shares.

portemanteau (pɔrtmɑ̃to) m, hat & coat stand.

porter (pɔrte) v.t. & i, to bear; carry; take; bring; lay; wear, have on; shoulder (arms); drink (health); deal, strike (blow); enter, put, mark; post (Bkkpg); prompt, lead, incline; raise; rest; tell (shot, word); turn

(discussion). ~ **à faux**, to overhang; miss the point (fig.). **se ~**, to go; be; do; stand. **porteur, euse** (tœːr, øːz) n, porter; carrier; (m.) bearer; holder. **porteurs des cordons du poêle**, pall bearers.

portier, ère (pɔrtje, ɛːr) n, porter, doorkeeper, caretaker. ¶ f, door (carriage, car); door curtain.

portion (pɔrsjɔ̃) f, portion, share, part; helping (food).

portique (pɔrtik) m, portico, porch; gantry; gallows (Gym.).

Porto (pɔrto) m, Oporto. **porto ou vin de Porto**, m, port [wine].

portrait (pɔrtrɛ) m, portrait, likeness; image; description. ~ **en buste**, half-length portrait. ~ **en pied**, full-length portrait.

portugais, e (pɔrtygɛ, ɛːz) a. & **P~**, n, Portuguese. **le portugais**, Portuguese (language). **le Portugal** (gal), Portugal.

posage (poza:ʒ) m, laying, fixing. **pose** (poːz) f, laying; pose, posture; lie (golf ball); exposure (Phot.). ~-**plumes**, m, pen rack. **posé, e** (poze) p.a, staid, sedate; steady. **poser** (ze) v.i, to rest, lie; pose, sit (portrait); (v.t.) to place, put; p. down; lay; l. down; set; hang (bells); pose; post (sentry); state; grant. ~ **ses clous**, to down tools. **se ~**, to settle, alight; set up; pose. **poseur, euse** (zœːr, øːz) n, layer; setter; hanger (bells); affected person. **poseur de mines**, mine layer. **poseur de voie**, platelayer.

positif, ive† (pozitif, iːv) a, positive, real; practical, matter-of-fact. ¶ m, real[ity].

position (pozisjɔ̃) f, position; situation; book (Stk Ex.); posture; stance.

possédé, e (pɔsede) p.a, possessed (mad). ¶ n, one possessed. **posséder** (de) v.t, to possess, own, have, hold; be master of. **possesseur** (sɛsœːr) m, possessor, owner. **possession** (sjɔ̃) f, possession; tenure.

possibilité (pɔsibilite) f, possibility. **possible** (bl) a. & m, possible.

postal, e (pɔstal) a, postal, post, mail (att.).

postdater (pɔstdate) v.t, to postdate.

poste (pɔst) f, post, mail; post [office]. ~ **restante**, poste restante, to be called for. **aller un train de ~**, to go post haste.

poste (pɔst) m, post, station; line (Teleph. subscriber's); guard room; berth; set (Radio); head[ing]; item; shift (men). ~ **à galène**, crystal set. ~ **à lampe(s)**, valve set. ~ **central**, exchange (Teleph.). ~ **de l'équipage**, forecastle, foc's'le. ~ **de police**, police station. ~ **supplémentaire**, extension [line] (Teleph.). **poster** (te) v.t, to post, station.

postérieur, e† (pɔsterjœːr) a, posterior, subsequent, later; hind[er], back. ¶ m, posterior.

postérité (pɔsterite) f, posterity, issue.

posthume (pɔstym) a, posthumous.

postiche (pɔstiʃ) a, false, artificial; sham.

postillon (postijɔ̃) *m*, postillion.

post-scriptum (pɔstskriptɔm) (*abb.* P.-S.) *m*, postscript, P.S.

postulant, e (pɔstylɑ̃, ɑ̃:t) *n*, candidate, applicant; postulant. **postuler** (le) *v.t*, to apply for; (*v.i.*) to act for (*client, Law*).

posture (pɔsty:r) *f*, posture; position.

pot (po; *before à, au,* pɔt) *m*, pot, jug, ewer; tankard; can; jar. **~-au-feu**, stock pot; broth; (*att.*) stay-at-home (*pers.*). **~ d'échappement**, silencer. **~-de-vin**, douceur; bribe. **~ pourri**, hotchpotch; medley; musical switch. **dîner à la fortune du ~**, to take pot luck.

potable (potabl) *a*, drinkable, drinking (*water*).

potage (pota:ʒ) *m*, soup. **~ ou consommé?** thick or clear? (*at dinner*). **pour tout ~,** all told. **potager, ère** (taʒe, ɛ:r) *a*, pot (*herb*); kitchen (*garden*). **¶** *m*, kitchen garden; kitchen stove; charcoal-fired cooker.

potasse (potas) *f*, potash. **potassium** (sjɔm) *m*, potassium.

poteau (poto) *m*, post, pole. **~ [d'arrivée],** [winning] post. **~ de départ,** starting p. **~ de signalisation** (siɲalizasjɔ̃), traffic sign. **~ indicateur,** sign post.

potée (pote) *f*, potful, jugful; swarm. **~ d'étain,** putty powder.

potelé, e (potle) *a*, plump; chubby.

potelet (potlɛ) *m*, stud (*scantling in wall*).

potence (potɑ̃:s) *f*, gallows, gibbet; bracket.

potentat (potɑ̃ta) *m*, potentate.

potentiel, le (potɑ̃sjɛl) *a. & m*, potential.

poter (pote) *v.t*, to put[t] (*Golf*).

poterie (potri) *f*, pottery, earthenware; ware. **~ de grès,** stoneware.

poterne (potɛrn) *f*, postern.

poteur (potœ:r) *m*, putter (*golf club*).

potiche (potiʃ) *f*, vase (*Chinese, or like*).

potier (potje) *m*, potter. **~ d'étain,** pewterer.

potin (potɛ̃) *m*, gossip; row, fuss.

potion (posjɔ̃) *f*, potion, draught.

potiron (potirɔ̃) *m*, pumpkin.

pou (pu) *m*, louse.

pouah (pwa) *i*, ugh!

poubelle (pubɛl) *f*, sanitary dustbin.

pouce (pu:s) *m*, thumb.

pouding (pudiŋ) *m*, pudding.

poudre (pu:dr) *f*, powder; dust. **~ à canon,** gunpowder. **~ à lever,** baking powder. **~ d'or,** gold dust. **~ de mine,** blasting powder. **~ de riz,** face powder, toilet powder. **poudrer** (pudre) *v.t*, to powder. **poudrerie** (drəri) *f*, powder mill. **poudreux, euse** (drø, ø:z) *a*, dusty. **poudrier** (drie) *m*, powder box; salt sifter. **poudrière** (ɛ:r) *f*, powder magazine.

pouf (puf) *m*, pouf (*stuffed couch*).

pouffer [de rire] (pufe), to burst out laughing.

pouilleux, euse (pujø, ø:z) *a*, lousy.

poulailler (pulaje) *m*, hen house; poulterer; gallery, gods (*Theat.*).

poulain (pulɛ̃) *m*, colt, foal.

poulaine (pulɛn) *f*, bedroom slipper.

poularde (pulard) *f*, table fowl. **poule** (pul) *f*, hen, fowl; sweepstake[s]; pool (*Cards, Ice Hockey, Fencing, Shooting*). **~ à l'américaine,** American tournament (*Ten.*). **~ d'eau,** moor hen. **~ d'Inde,** turkey [hen]. **~ faisane,** hen pheasant. **~ mouillée,** milksop (*pers.*). **poulet** (lɛ) *m*, chicken, chick. **poulette** (lɛt) *f*, pullet; girl.

pouliche (puliʃ) *f*, filly, foal.

poulie (puli) *f*, pulley, block, sheave.

pouliner (puline) *v.i*, to foal. [**jument**] **poulinière** (njɛ:r) *f*, brood mare; breeder.

pouliot (puljo) *m*, pennyroyal.

poulpe (pulp) *m*, octopus.

pouls (pu) *m*, pulse (*as in wrist*).

poumon (pumɔ̃) *m*, lung.

poupard, e (pupa:r, ard) *a*, chubby; baby (*face*). **¶** *m*, baby; baby doll.

poupe (pup) *f*, stern, poop.

poupée (pupe) *f*, doll; puppet, dummy, block. **poupin, e** (pɛ̃, in) *a*, doll-faced. **poupon, ne** (pɔ̃, ɔn) *n*, baby. **pouponner** (pone) *v.t*, to fondle, dandle, cuddle. **pouponnière** (njɛ:r) *f*, day nursery, crèche.

pour (pu:r) *pr*, for; instead of; per; pro; as; on; to; (*money's*) worth. **~ ainsi dire,** so to speak. **~ cent,** per cent. **~ que,** in order that. **le ~ & le contre,** the pros & cons, for & against.

pourboire (purbwa:r) *m*, tip, gratuity, drink [money].

pourceau (purso) *m*, hog, pig, swine.

pourcentage (pursɑ̃ta:ʒ) *m*, percentage, rate.

pourchasser (purʃase) *v.t*, to pursue; dun.

pourparlers (purparle) *m.pl*, parley; negotiations.

pourpier (purpje) *m*, purslane.

pourpre (purpr) *f*, purple (*robe*); crimson (*colour*); (*m.*) purple (*colour*); (*att.*) crimson (*colour*). **pourpré, e** (pre) *a*, purple (*red-colour*).

pourquoi (purkwa) *ad. & c*, why, wherefore, what. **¶** *m*, why.

pourri, e (puri) *p.a*, rotten. **pourrir** (ri:r) *v.i. & t*, to rot. **pourriture** (rity:r) *f*, rotting; rot; rottenness.

poursuite (pursɥit) *f*, pursuit, chase; (*oft. pl.*) lawsuit, proceedings; prosecution. **poursuivant** (vɑ̃) *m*, plaintiff; prosecutor; suitor, wooer. **poursuivre** (vr) *v.t.ir*, to pursue, chase; haunt; follow up; prosecute, sue.

pourtant (purtɑ̃) *ad*, yet, nevertheless, however.

pourtour (purtu:r) *m*, circumference; surround; precincts, close; gangway.

pourvoi (purvwa) *m*, appeal; petition. **pourvoir** (vwa:r) *v.i. & t. ir*, to provide, supply, furnish. **pourvoyeur** (vwajœ:r) *m*, purveyor, provider, caterer. **pourvu que** (vy) *c*, provided [that].

poussah (pusa) *m*, tumbler (*toy*); tub[by man].

pousse (pus) *f*, growth; cutting (*teeth*); shoot, sprout. **~-pousse**, *m*, ricksha[w]. **poussée** (se) *f*, push, shove; thrust; pressure; outburst; buoyancy. **pousser** (se) *v.t. & i*, to push, shove, thrust; drive; urge; utter, give; grow, shoot, spring up. **~** *à la perche*, **~** *du fond*, to punt (*Boating*). **~** *au large*, to push off (*Naut.*).

poussier (pusje) *m*, dust (*coal, &c*). **poussière** (sjɛːr) *f*, dust. **~** *d'eau*, spray. **poussiéreux, euse** (sjerø, øːz) *a*, dusty.

poussif, ive (pusif, iːv) *a*, broken-winded; wheezy.

poussin (pusɛ̃) *m*, chick; spring chicken. **poussinière** (sinjɛːr) *f*, coop; incubator.

poussoir (puswaːr) *m*, push [button].

poutre (putr) *f*, beam, ba[u]lk; girder.

pouvoir (puvwaːr) *m*, power; authority; power of attorney; proxy; (*pl.*) credentials. ¶ *v.i. & t. ir*, to be able; can; can do; may. **se ~**, to be possible. *cela se peut*, it may be.

prairie (prɛri) *f*, meadow; grassland; prairie.

praline (pralin) *f*, burnt almond; praline.

praticable (pratikabl) *a*, practicable, feasible; passable (*road*). **praticien** (sjɛ̃) *m*, practician; practitioner. **pratique†** (tik) *a*, practical. ¶ *f*, practice; experience; observance; (*pl.*) dealings; practice; custom; customer; squeaker (*Punch's*). **pratiquer** (ke) *v.t*, to practise; make; frequent. **se ~**, to be done; rule (*prices*).

pré (pre) *m*, meadow.

préalable† (prealabl) *a*, previous; preliminary.

préambule (preãbyl) *m*, preamble.

préau (preo) *m*, courtyard, quadrangle; playground (*covered*).

préavis (preavi) *m*, [previous] notice, warning.

prébende (prebãːd) *f*, prebend. **prébendier** (bãdje) *m*, prebendary.

précaire† (prekɛːr) *a*, precarious.

précaution (prekosjɔ̃) *f*, precaution; caution, wariness. **précautionner** (sjone) *v.t*, to caution, warn.

précédemment (presedamã) *ad*, previously. **précédent, e** (dã, ãːt) *a*, preceding, previous, before. ¶ *m*, precedent. **précéder** (de) *v.t*, to precede.

précepte (presɛpt) *m*, precept. **précepteur** (tœːr) *m*, tutor, teacher, preceptor. **préceptorat** (tɔra) *m*, tutorship.

prêche (prɛʃ) *m*, sermon. **prêcher** (ʃe) *v.t. & abs*, to preach; extol; exhort; lecture. **prêcheur** (ʃœːr) *m*, sermonizer.

précieux, euse† (presjø, øːz) *a*, precious; valuable; affected.

précipice (presipis) *m*, precipice.

précipitamment (presipitamã) *a*, precipitately, headlong. **précipitation** (sjɔ̃) *f*, precipitancy, haste; precipitation. **précipité, e** (te) *a*, precipitate, hasty, hurried, headlong. ¶ *m*, precipitate. **précipiter** (te) *v.t*, to precipitate; hasten; plunge. **se ~**, to rush.

précis, e (presi, iːz) *a*, precise, exact; sharp (*hour*); definite. ¶ *m*, abstract, summary, précis. **précisément** (sizemã) *ad*, precisely, exactly. **préciser** (ze) *v.t*, to state precisely, specify. **précision** (zjɔ̃) *f*, precision, accuracy; (*pl.*) particulars.

précité, e (presite) *a*, aforesaid, above.

précoce (prekɔs) *a*, precocious; early, forward. **précocité** (site) *f*, precociousness, &c.

préconçu, e (prekɔ̃sy) *a*, preconceived.

préconiser (prekɔnize) *v.t*, to preconize; [re]commend, advocate.

précurseur (prekyrsœːr) *m*, precursor, forerunner; (*att.*) precursory, premonitory.

prédécès (predesɛ) *m*, predecease. **prédécesseur** (predesɛsœːr) *m*, predecessor.

prédestination (predɛstinasjɔ̃) *f*, predestination.

prédicant (predikã) *m*, preacher.

prédicat (predika) *m*, predicate.

prédicateur (predikatœːr) *m*, preacher. **prédication** (sjɔ̃) *f*, preaching.

prédiction (prediksjɔ̃) *f*, prediction; forecast.

prédilection (predilɛksjɔ̃) *f*, predilection, partiality. **~** *favourite*.

prédire (prediːr) *v.t.ir*, to predict, foretell.

prédisposer (predispoze) *v.t*, to predispose.

prédominer (predɔmine) *v.i*, to predominate, prevail.

prééminent, e (preeminã, ãːt) *a*, pre-eminent.

préemption (preãpsjɔ̃) *f*, pre-emption.

préface (prefas) *f*, preface, foreword; preliminaries; forerunner.

préfecture (prefɛktyːr) *f*, prefecture; headquarters (*of police*).

préférable† (preferabl) *a*, preferable, better. **préférence** (rãːs) *f*, preference. **préférer** (re) *v.t*, to prefer.

préfet (prefɛ) *m*, prefect.

préfixe (prefiks) *m*, prefix. ¶ *a*, prefixed.

préhenseur (preãsœːr) *a.m*, prehensile.

préhistorique (preistɔrik) *a*, prehistoric.

préjudice (preʒydis) *m*, prejudice, detriment; injury. **préjudiciable** (sjabl) *a*, prejudicial, detrimental. **préjudicier** (sje) *v.i*, to be detrimental to. **préjugé** (ʒe) *m*, prejudice; presumption.

prélart (prelaːr) *m*, tarpaulin.

prélasser (se) (prelase) *v.pr*, to strut along; loll. **prélat** (la) *m*, prelate.

prélèvement (prelɛvmã) *m*, deduction, levy. **~** *de sang*, blood test. **prélever** (lve) *v.t*, to deduct, levy.

préliminaire (preliminɛːr) *a. & m*, preliminary.

prélude (prelyd) *m*, prelude; voluntary. **préluder** (de) *v.i*, to prelude (*Mus.*). **~** *à*, to preface, lead up to.

prématuré†, e (prematyre) *a*, premature, untimely.

préméditation (premeditasjɔ̃) *f*, premeditation; malice aforethought, m. prepense. **préméditer** (te) *v.t*, to premeditate.

prémices (premis) *f.pl*, first-fruits; beginning.

premier, ère (prəmje, ɛːr) *a*, first; opening (*price*); maiden; leading; early; earliest; next; prime; primary; premier. **premier, comps**: ~ *choix*, best quality, finest q. ~ *garçon*, head waiter. ~ *ministre*, prime minister, premier. ~**-né**, *m*, first-born. *de* ~ *ordre*, first-class, first-rate; gilt-edged (*securities*). ~ *plan*, foreground; close-up (*Phot.*). ~ *rôle*, leading part; l. man, l. lady. ~*s soins*, first aid. ¶ *m*, first. ¶ *f*, first; f. night; forewoman. ~*de change*, first of exchange. ~*s* (*galeries*), dress circle. **premièrement** (mjɛrmã) *ad*, first[ly].

prémisses (premis) *f.pl*, premis[s]es (*Log.*).

prémonitoire (premɔnitwaːr) *a*, premonitory.

prémunir (premyniːr) *v.t*, to forewarn. *se* ~ *contre*, to provide against.

prenable (prənabl) *a*, pregnable; corruptible. **prenant, e** (nã, ãːt) *a*, taking; prehensile. **prendre** (prãːdr) *v.t.ir*, to take; t. up; t. in; t. over; lay hold of; seize; clasp; catch; pick up; assume; acquire; come to; charge; put on, assume; wreak; (*v.i.ir.*) to set; congeal; curdle; freeze; catch; take root, strike; take, catch on; bear (*to right, left*). ~ *à la* (ou *de*) *volée*, to volley (*Ten. ball*). ~ *un billet, des billets, pour*, to book to. **se** ~, to catch; congeal; cling; clasp. **s'en** ~ *à*, to blame. **s'y** ~, to set about it. **preneur, euse** (prənœːr, øːz) *n*, taker; catcher; buyer; lessee.

prénom (prenɔ̃) *m*, first name, Christian n.

préoccupation (preɔkypasjɔ̃) *f*, preoccupation. **préoccuper** (pe) *v.t*, to preoccupy.

préopinant (preɔpinã) *m*, previous speaker.

préparateur, trice (preparatœːr, tris) *n*, tutor, coach; assistant. **préparatifs** (tif) *m.pl*, preparations. **préparation** (sjɔ̃) *f*, preparation. **préparatoire** (twaːr) *a*, preparatory. **préparer** (re) *v.t*, to prepare, make ready; lay (*fire*); coach (*pupil*); read for (*exam*). **se** ~, to prepare, get ready; brew (*storm*). **prépondérance** (prepɔ̃derãːs) *f*, preponderance. **prépondérant, e** (rã, ãːt) *a*, preponderant; casting (*vote*).

préposé, e (prepoze) *n*, servant; officer; official; clerk. **préposer** (ze) *v.t*, to appoint.

préposition (prepozisjɔ̃) *f*, preposition.

prérogative (prerɔgatiːv) *f*, prerogative; privilege.

près (prɛ) *ad. & pr*, near; by; close to. *à . . .* ~, save on, save in, except for; to a; within. *à peu* ~, nearly, about, pretty much.

présage (prezaːʒ) *m*, presage, omen, portent, foreboding, premonition. **présager** (zaʒe) *v.t*, to presage, portend, [fore]bode; augur.

pré-salé (presale) *m*, salt-meadow sheep; salt-meadow mutton.

presbyte (prɛzbit) *n. & att*, long-sighted (person).

presbytère (prɛzbiteːr) *m*, presbytery; rectory, vicarage, parsonage. **presbytérien, ne** (terjɛ̃, ɛn) *n. & att*, Presbyterian.

prescience (presjãːs) *f*, prescience, foreknowledge.

prescription (prɛskripsjɔ̃) *f*, prescription; bar of the statute of limitations; directions. **prescrire** (skriːr) *v.t.ir*, to prescribe, ordain. **se** ~, to be statute barred.

préséance (preseãːs) *f*, precedence (*in rank*).

présence (prezãːs) *f*, presence; attendance; sight. **présent, e** (zã, ãːt) *a*, present; this (*letter, &c*). ¶ *m*, present; gift. *à* ~, now. **présentable** (zãtabl) *a*, presentable. **présentation** (sjɔ̃) *f*, presentation; introduction. **présentement** (zãtmã) *ad*, at present, now; with immediate possession (*house, &c*). **présenter** (te) *v.t*, to present; offer; pay (*respects*); produce, show; introduce.

préservatif, ive (prezɛrvatif) *m. & a*, preservative, preventive. **préservation** (sjɔ̃) *f*, preservation. **préserver** (ve) *v.t*, to preserve, keep.

présidence (prezidãːs) *f*, presidency; chairmanship. **président, e** (dã, ãːt) *n*, president; chairman; presiding judge. ~ *du conseil* [*des ministres*], premier. **présider** [à] (de) *v.t. & i*, to preside at, over; superintend.

présomptif, ive (prezɔ̃ptif, iːv) *a*, presumptive; (*heir*) apparent. **présomption** (sjɔ̃) *f*, presumption. **présomptueux, euse†** (tɥø, øːz) *a*, presumptuous.

presque (prɛsk) *ad*, almost, nearly, all but; scarcely, hardly (*ever*). **presqu'île** (kil) *f*, peninsula.

pressant, e (presã, ãːt) *a*, pressing, urgent. **presse** (prɛs) *f*, press; clamp, cramp; squeezer; crowd, throng; pressure; congestion; hurry. **presse-citron**, *m*, lemon squeezer.

pressentiment (presãtimã) *m*, presentiment, foreboding, misgiving. **pressentir** (tiːr) *v.t.ir*, to have a presentiment of; sound (*pers.*).

presse-papiers (prɛspapje) *m*, paper weight. **presser** (se) *v.t*, to press; squeeze; clasp; ply; hurry, push. **se** ~, to press, crowd, throng; hurry. **pression** (sjɔ̃) *f*, pressure. **pressoir** (swaːr) *m*, press (*wine, &c*). **pressurer** (syre) *v.t*, to press (*grapes, &c*); grind (*fig.*).

prestance (prɛstãːs) *f*, presence, bearing, portliness.

prestation (prɛstasjɔ̃) *f*, provision; taking (*oath*).

preste† (prɛst) *a*, quick, nimble. **prestesse** (tɛs) *f*, quickness, &c.

prestidigitateur (prɛstidiʒitatœːr) *m*, conjurer, juggler. **prestidigitation** (sjɔ̃) *f*, conjuring, sleight-of-hand, legerdemain.

prestige (prɛstiːʒ) *m*, marvel, magic, glamour; prestige. **prestigieux, euse** (tiʒjø, øːz) *a*, marvellous; influential.

présumer (prezyme) *v.t. & abs*, to presume, suppose.

présupposer (presypoze) *v.t*, to presuppose, take for granted.

présure (prezy:r) *f*, rennet.

prêt, e (prɛ, ɛ:t) *a*, ready, prepared, game.

prêt (prɛ) *m*, loan; advance.

prétendant, e (pretɑ̃dɑ̃, ɑ̃:t) *n*, applicant; claimant; pretender; (*m*.) suitor, wooer. **prétendre** (tɑ̃:dr) *v.t. & i*, to claim, require, pretend; assert; contend; aspire. **prétendu, e** (tɑ̃dy) *p.a*, alleged; would-be; so-called. ¶ *n*, intended (*in marriage*).

prête-nom (prɛtnɔ̃) *m*, dummy (*pers.*).

pretentaine (**courir la**) (prətɑ̃tɛn), to gad about.

prétentieux, euse (pretɑ̃sjø, ø:z) *a*, pretentious. **prétention** (sjɔ̃) *f*, claim, pretension.

prêter (prɛte) *v.t*, to lend; give; take (*oath*); attribute. *un prêté [pour un] rendu*, tit for tat.

prétérit (preterit) *m*, preterite.

prêteur, euse (prɛtœ:r, ø:z) *n*, lender. ~ *sur gages*, lender on security; pawnbroker.

prétexte (pretɛkst) *m*, pretext, pretence, plea, excuse. **prétexter** (te) *v.t*, to plead.

prêtre (prɛ:tr) *m*, priest. **prêtresse** (prɛtrɛs) *f*, priestess. **prêtrise** (tri:z) *f*, priesthood, [holy] orders.

preuve (prœ:v) *f*, proof; evidence; token. ~ *par l'absurde*, reductio ad absurdum. ~ *par présomption*, circumstantial evidence.

preux (prø) *a.m*, doughty, valiant.

prévaloir (prevalwa:r) *v.i.ir*, to prevail. **se** ~ **de**, to presume [up]on.

prévaricateur, trice (prevarikatœ:r, tris) *n*, unjust judge; defaulter. **prévarication** (sjɔ̃) *f*, breach of trust, default. **prévariquer** (ke) *v.i*, to fail in one's duty; betray one's trust.

prévenance (prevnɑ̃:s) *f*, [kind] attention. **prévenant, e** (vnɑ̃, ɑ̃:t) *a*, attentive, kind, considerate, thoughtful; prepossessing. **prévenir** (vni:r) *v.t.ir*, to forestall, prevent; ward off; prepossess; prejudice; bias; [fore]warn, inform. **prévention** (vɑ̃sjɔ̃) *f*, prepossession, prejudice; imprisonment on suspicion, preventive arrest. **prévenu, e** (vny) *n*, accused, prisoner.

prévision (previzjɔ̃) *f*, prevision, forecast, expectation. **prévoir** (vwa:r) *v.t. & abs. ir*, to foresee, forecast; provide for.

prévôt (prevo) *m*, provost.

prévoyance (prevwajɑ̃:s) *f*, foresight, forethought; precaution. ~ *sociale*, state insurance. **prévoyant, e** (jɑ̃, ɑ̃:t) *a*, provident; far-sighted.

prie-Dieu (pridjø) *m*, kneeling desk. **prier** (e) *v.t*, to pray (to); beg, ask, request, beseech, entreat; invite. **prière** (ɛ:r) *f*, prayer; request, entreaty. ~ *de* . . ., please . . . **prieur, e** (œ:r) *n*, prior, ess. **prieuré** (œre) *m*, priory.

primage (prima:ʒ) *m*, primage (*Ship.*).

primaire (primɛ:r) *a*, primary; elementary (*Sch.*).

primat (prima) *m*, primate. **primatie** (si) *f*,

primacy. **primauté** (mote) *f*, primacy; lead (*Cards, &c*).

prime (prim) *a*, first; earliest. ¶ *f*, premium; bounty, bonus; gift (*for coupons*); option (*Stk Ex*.). **primé, e** (me) *p.a*, bounty-fed; prize (*bull, &c*). **primer** (me) *v.t*, to surpass; override; award a prize to; (*v.i.*) to excel; rank before.

primesautier, ère (primsotje, ɛ:r) *a*, impulsive.

primeur (primœ:r) *f*, freshness, newness; early vegetable, early fruit.

primevère (primvɛ:r) *f*, primrose. ~ *des champs*, cowslip. ~ *des jardins*, polyanthus.

primitif, ive† (primitif, i:v) *a*, primitive, original; primeval; pristine; primary; crude.

primo (primo) *ad*, first[ly].

primogéniture (primoʒenity:r) *f*, primogeniture.

primordial, e† (primordjal) *a*, primordial, primary; primeval.

prince (prɛ̃:s) *m*, prince. *bon* ~, a good fellow.

princeps (prɛ̃sɛps) *a.inv*, first (*edition*).

princesse (prɛ̃sɛs) *f*, princess. **princier, ère** (sje, ɛ:r) *a*, princely.

principal, e† (prɛ̃sipal) *a*, principal, chief, head, main; staple (*product*); major (*planet*); senior. ¶ *m*, principal; chief; headmaster; main thing.

principauté (prɛ̃sipote) *f*, principality.

principe (prɛ̃sip) *m*, principle; beginning.

printanier, ère (prɛ̃tanje, ɛ:r) *a*, vernal, spring (*att.*). **printemps** (tɑ̃) *m*, spring-[time].

priorité (priorite) *f*, priority, precedence.

prise (pri:z) *f*, taking; catch; hold, purchase, grip; setting (*cement*); prize (*Naut.*); pinch (*snuff, &c*); dose. ~ *d'eau*, intake of water, tapping; hydrant. ~ *de bec*, altercation, set-to. ~ *de corps*, arrest. ~ *de sang*, blood test. ~ *de tête à terre*, nelson (*Wrestling*).

prisée (prize) *f*, valuation. **priser** (ze) *v.t*, to appraise, value; prize; snuff up; (*abs.*) to take snuff.

prismatique (prismatik) *a*, prismatic. **prisme** (prism) *m*, prism.

prison (prizɔ̃) *f*, prison, gaol, jail; cells; imprisonment (*term*). **prisonnier, ère** (zɔnje, ɛ:r) *n*, prisoner.

privation (privasjɔ̃) *f*, deprivation, loss; privation, hardship.

privauté (privote) *f*, familiarity, liberty.

privé, e (prive) *a*, private. ¶ *m*, privy, water closet.

priver (prive) *v.t*, to deprive, bereave.

privilège (privilɛ:ʒ) *m*, privilege, prerogative; lien, charge. **privilégié, e** (leʒje) *p.a*, privileged; preferential. **privilégier** (ʒje) *v.t*, to privilege; charter.

prix (pri) *m*, price; value, worth, cost; consideration [money]; terms; rate; charge;

fare; prize; stakes (*Turf*). ~ *à réclamer*, selling plate (*Turf*). ~ *d'excellence*, class prize. ~ *de revient* (rəvjɛ̃), *coûtant* (kutɑ̃), cost [price]. ~ *de sagesse*, good conduct prize. ~ *du Jockey-Club*, French Derby.

probabilité (prɔbabilite) *f*, probability, likelihood. **probable†** (bl) *a*, probable, likely.

probant, e (prɔbɑ̃, ɑ̃:t) *a*, convincing, cogent. **probation** (basjɔ̃) *f*, probation (*Eccl.*). **probe** (prɔb) *a*, honest, upright. **probité** (bite) *f*, probity, honesty, &c.

problématique (prɔblematik) *a*, problematic(al). **problème** (blɛm) *m*, problem; puzzle; poser, teaser.

proboscide (prɔbɔsid) *f*, proboscis.

procédé (prɔsede) *m*, proceeding, dealing; behaviour; process; tip (*Bil. cue*). **procéder** (de) *v.i*, to proceed. ~ *à l'impression*, to go to press. **procédure** (dy:r) *f*, procedure; proceedings. **procès** (sɛ) (*Law*) *m*, proceedings, action, case. ~ *civil*, [law]suit. ~ *criminel*, [criminal] trial. **processif, ive** (sɛsif, i:v) *a*, litigious. **procession** (sjɔ̃) *f*, procession. **processus** (sys:s) *m*, process, course. **procès-verbal**, *m*, report; minute(s).

prochain, e (prɔʃɛ̃, ɛn) *a*, nearest; next; near; proximate; forthcoming; coming; neighbouring. ¶ *m*, neighbour, fellow creature. **prochainement** (ʃɛnmɑ̃) *ad*, shortly, soon. **proche** (prɔʃ) *ad*, near, close. ¶ *a*, near, at hand. ~ *Orient*, Near East. ~*s* [*parents*] *m.pl*, near relations, next of kin.

proclamation (prɔklamasjɔ̃) *f*, proclamation. **proclamer** (me) *v.t*, to proclaim, publish; declare.

procrastination (prɔkrastinasjɔ̃) *f*, procrastination.

procréer (prɔkree) *v.t*, to procreate.

procuration (prɔkyrasjɔ̃) *f*, procuration, proxy, power of attorney. **procurer** (re) *v.t*, to procure, obtain, get. **procureur** (rœ:r) *m*, proxy; attorney.

prodigalement (prɔdigalmɑ̃) *a*, lavishly. **prodigalité** (lite) *f*, prodigality, lavishness; wastefulness; (*pl*.) extravagance.

prodige (prɔdi:ʒ) *m*, prodigy, wonder. **prodigieux, euse†** (diʒø, ø:z) *a*, prodigious, stupendous.

prodigue (prɔdig) *a*, prodigal, lavish, unsparing, profuse; wasteful. ¶ *n*, prodigal, spendthrift. **prodiguer** (ge) *v.t*, to lavish; squander.

prodrome (prɔdro:m) *m*, premonitory symptom.

producteur, trice (prɔdyktœ:r, tris) *n*, producer. ¶ ~ *& productif, ive* (tif, i:v) *a*, producing, productive, bearing. **production** (sjɔ̃) *f*, production, output, yield; product. **produire** (dɥi:r) *v.t.ir*, to produce, bring forth, bear, yield; show. ~ *dans le monde*, to introduce into society, bring out. **se** ~, to occur, happen.

produit (dɥi) *m*, product, produce, proceeds, yield; takings, receipts. ~ *chimique*, chemical.

proéminent, e (prɔeminɑ̃, ɑ̃:t) *a*, prominent.

profanation (prɔfanasjɔ̃) *f*, profanation. **profane** (fan) *a*, profane; secular; unconsecrated (*ground*). ¶ *n*, layman; outsider; (the) profane. **profaner** (ne) *v.t*, to profane, desecrate.

proférer (prɔfere) *v.t*, to utter.

profès, esse (prɔfɛ, ɛs) *a*, professed. **professer** (se) *v.t*, to profess; teach. **professeur** (sœ:r) *m*, professor; teacher; master, mistress; lecturer; instructor. **profession** (sjɔ̃) *f*, profession; occupation; calling, business, trade. **professionnel, le** (ɔnel) *a. & n*, professional. ~ *de la boxe*, prize fighter. **professorat** (sora) *m*, professorship.

profil (prɔfil) *m*, profile, side face; contour, outline, section. ~ *de l'horizon*, sky line. **profiler** (le) *v.t*, to profile, stream-line.

profit (prɔfi) *m*, profit, benefit. **profitable** (tabl) *a*, profitable. **profiter** (te) *v.i*, to benefit, profit; avail oneself (*de=* of); thrive. **profiteur, euse** (tœ:r, ø:z) *n*, profiteer.

profond, e (prɔfɔ̃, ɔ̃:d) *a*, deep, profound; low (*bow*); sound (*sleep*). **profondément** (demɑ̃) *ad*, deeply, &c. **profondeur** (dœ:r) *f*, depth; profundity.

profus, e (prɔfy, y:z) *a*, profuse (*perspiration*). **profusément** (fyzemɑ̃) *ad*, profusely, lavishly. **profusion** (zjɔ̃) *f*, profusion, lavishness.

progéniture (prɔʒenity:r) *f*, progeny, offspring.

prognathe (prɔgnat) *a*, prognathous.

programme (prɔgram) *m*, programme; syllabus; platform (*Pol.*). ~ *d'études*, curriculum. ~ *des courses*, race card.

progrès (prɔgrɛ) *m. oft. pl*, progress, [head]-way. **progresser** (grɛse) *v.i*, to progress. **progressif, ive†** (sif, i:v) *a*, progressive, forward. **progression** (sjɔ̃) *f*, progression.

prohiber (prɔibe) *v.t*, to prohibit, forbid. **prohibitif, ive** (bitif, i:v) *a*, prohibitory; prohibitive. **prohibition** (sjɔ̃) *f*, prohibition. **prohibitionniste** (ɔnist) *n*, prohibitionist.

proie (prwa) *f*, prey; quarry.

projecteur (prɔʒɛktœ:r) *m*, projector; search light. ~ *orientable* (ɔrjɑ̃tabl), spot light. **projectile** (til) *a. & m*, projectile, missile. **projection** (sjɔ̃) *f*, projection; lantern slide. **projet** (ʒɛ) *m*, project, scheme, plan; draft. ~ *de loi*, bill, measure. **projeter** (ʒte) *v.t*, to project, throw, cast; plan, contemplate.

prolétaire (prɔletɛ:r) *m*, proletarian. **prolétariat** (tarja) *m*, proletariat[e]. **prolétarien, ne** (rjɛ̃, ɛn) *a*, proletarian.

prolifique (prɔlifik) *a*, prolific.

prolixe (prɔliks) *a*, prolix, long-winded.

prologue (prɔlɔg) *m*, prologue.

prolongation (prɔlɔ̃gasjɔ̃) *f*. **& prolongement** (lɔ̃ʒmɑ̃) *m*, prolongation; extension. **pro-**

longe (lɔ̃:ʒ) f, ammunition wagon. **prolonger** (lɔ̃ʒe) v.t, to prolong, protract, extend, lengthen.

promenade (promnad) f, walking; walk, stroll; ride; drive; trip, outing, ramble; promenade. *sur la* ~ [*de la mer*], on the [sea] front. ~ *en bateau*, row; sail. ~ *militaire*, route march. **promener** (mne) v.t, to take for a walk; pass, run, cast. ~ *par*, ~ *dans*, to show round. **se** ~, to [go for a] walk, stroll. *allez vous* ~! be off with you! **promeneur, euse** (mnœ:r, ø:z) n, walker; tripper. **promenoir** (mnwa:r) m, promenade, walk; lounge.

promesse (promɛs) f, promise. **prometteur, euse** (tœ:r, ø:z) a, promising. **promettre** (mɛtr) v.t. & abs. ir, to promise. *terre promise* (mi:z), *terre de promission* (misjɔ̃), promised land, land of promise.

promiscuité (promiskɥite) f, promiscuity.

promontoire (promɔ̃twa:r) m, promontory.

promoteur, trice (promotœ:r, tris) n, promoter. **promotion** (sjɔ̃) f, promotion, preferment. **promouvoir** (muvwa:r) v.t.ir, to promote, prefer.

prompt, et (prɔ̃, ɔ̃:t) a, prompt, ready, quick. **promptitude** (prɔ̃tityd) f, promptitude, &c, dispatch.

promulguer (promylge) v.t, to promulgate.

prône (pro:n) m, sermon; homily. **prôner** (prone) v.t, to extoll; puff.

pronom (pronɔ̃) m, pronoun. **pronominal, et** (nominal) a, pronominal.

prononcer (pronɔ̃se) v.t. & abs, to pronounce; utter; speak; mention; deliver (*speech*); pass (*sentence*). **se** ~, to declare oneself; be pronounced (*letter, syllable*). **pronunciation** (sjasjɔ̃) f, delivery; passing; pronunciation.

pronostic (pronostik) m, prognostic[ation], forecast; selection (*Betting*); omen. **pronostiquer** (ke) v.t, to prognosticate, forecast.

propagande (propagɑ̃:d) f, propaganda.

propager (propaʒe) v.t, to propagate, spread.

propension (propɑ̃sjɔ̃) f, propensity.

prophète, étesse (profɛt, etɛs) n, prophet, ess, seer. **prophétie** (fesi) f, prophecy. **prophétique†** (tik) a, prophetic(al). **prophétiser** (ze) v.t, to prophesy.

propice (propis) a, propitious, auspicious, lucky.

propitiation (propisjasjɔ̃) f, propitiation. **propitiatoire** (twa:r) m, mercy seat.

proportion (proporsjɔ̃) f, proportion, ratio, percentage. **proportionnel, let** (ɔnɛl) a, proportional; ad valorem. **proportionner** (one) v.t, to proportion.

propos (propo) m, purpose; subject; matter; remark, (*pl.*) talk. ~ *de couloir*, pl, lobbying. **à** ~, a. & ad, to the point, apropos, opportune(ly); seasonable, -bly; apposite(ly); pertinent(ly); apt(ly); by the way. **à** ~ **de**, pr, with regard to, about. *à tout* ~, at every turn. *de* ~ *délibéré*

deliberately, purposely. **proposer** (ze) v.t, to propose; move; propound; offer; put forward; recommend. **se** ~, to offer oneself; purpose, mean. **proposition** (zisjɔ̃) f, proposal, proposition; motion; clause (*Gram.*).

propre† (propr) a, proper; peculiar; inherent; literal; own; appropriate, fit, suited; neat, clean. *un* ~ *à rien*, a good-for-nothing, a ne'er-do-well. ¶ *m*, characteristic, property; literal sense (*word*). **propret, te** (prɛ, ɛt) a, neat, tidy. **propreté** (prəte) f, cleanliness; neatness, tidiness.

propriétaire (propriete:r) n, proprietor, tress, owner; landlord, -lady. **propriété** (te) f, ownership; property, estate, holding; rights; propriety. ~ [*littéraire*], copyright.

propulseur (propylsœ:r) m, propeller. ~ *amovible*, outboard motor. **propulsion** (sjɔ̃) f, propulsion.

prorata (prorata) m: *au* ~ *de*, pr, in proportion to, pro rata to.

proroger (prorɔʒe) v.t, to prorogue; extend.

prosaïque† (prozaik) a, prosaic.

prosateur (prozatœ:r) m, prose writer.

proscrire (proskri:r) v.t.ir, to proscribe, outlaw; banish; do away with. **proscrit, e** (skri, it) n, outlaw.

prose (pro:z) f, prose.

prosélyte (prozelit) n, proselyte.

prosodie (prozodi) f, prosody.

prospecter (prospɛkte) v.t, to prospect (*Min.*). **prospecteur** (tœ:r) m, prospector. **prospection** (sjɔ̃) f, prospecting. **prospectus** (prospɛktys) m, prospectus; handbill.

prospère (prospɛr) a, prosperous, thriving; favourable, kind. **prospérer** (pere) v.i, to prosper, thrive. **prospérité** (rite) f, prosperity.

prostate (prostat) f, prostate [gland].

prosternation (prosternasjɔ̃) f, prostration; (*pl.*) bowing & scraping. **prosterné, e** (ne) p.a, bowing &c, prone. **prosterner** (ne) v.t, to prostrate.

prostituer (prostitɥe) v.t, to prostitute.

prostration (prostrasjɔ̃) f, prostration, breakdown. **prostré, e** (tre) a, prostrate[d].

protagoniste (protagɔnist) m, protagonist.

prote (prot) m, overseer (*Typ.*).

protecteur, trice (protɛktœ:r, tris) n, protector, tress; patron, ess; (*m.*) protector, shield, guard. ¶ a, protective; patronizing. **protection** (sjɔ̃) f, protection; patronage. **protectionniste** (ɔnist) m. & att, protectionist. **protectorat** (tɔra) m, protectorate. **protégé, e** (teʒe) n, protégé, e. **protéger** (ʒe) v.t, to protect, shield, guard; patronize.

protestant, e (protɛstɑ̃, ɑ̃:t) n. & a, protestant. **protestation** (tasjɔ̃) f, protest[ation]. **protester** (te) v.t. & i, to protest; vow. **protêt** (tɛ) m, protest (*bill of exchange*).

protocole (prɔtɔkɔl) *m*, protocol; etiquette.

prototype (prɔtɔtip) *m*, prototype.

protubérance (prɔtybera:s) *f*, protuberance.

proue (pru) *f*, prow.

prouesse (prues) *f*, prowess, valour; feat.

prouver (pruve) *v.t*, to prove; show.

provenance (prɔvnɑ̃:s) *f*, origin, provenance; (*s. & pl.*) produce.

provende (prɔvɑ̃:d) *f*, provender, fodder.

provenir (prɔvni:r) *v.i.ir*, to proceed, come, arise.

proverbe (prɔverb) *m*, proverb. **proverbial, e†** (bjal) *a*, proverbial.

providence (prɔvidɑ̃:s) *f*, providence; godsend; good angel. **providentiel, le†** (dɑ̃sjɛl) *a*, providential.

province (prɔvɛ̃:s) *f*, province; provinces, country. **provincial, e** (vɛ̃sjal) *a*, provincial, country (*att.*).

proviseur (prɔvizœ:r) *m*, head-master. **provision** (zjɔ̃) *f*, provision, store, stock, supply; deposit; funds; cover, margin (*Fin.*); consideration (*Law*); retainer (*Law*). ~s **de bouche**, provisions, food. ~s **de guerre**, munitions. **provisionnel, le** (ɔnɛl) *a*, provisional. **provisoire†** (zwa:r) *a*, provisional, interim, pro tem; nisi (*decree*). **provisorat** (zora) *m*, head-mastership.

provoquer (prɔvɔke) *v.t*, to provoke; challenge; incite, instigate; induce. **provocation** (kasjɔ̃) *f*, provocation, &c.

proximité (prɔksimite) *f*, proximity, nearness, propinquity, vicinity. ~ **du sang**, near relationship.

prude (pryd) *a*, prudish. ¶ *f*, prude.

prudemment (prydamɑ̃) *ad*, prudently. **prudence** (dɑ̃:s) *f*, prudence, discretion; wisdom. **prudent, e** (dɑ̃, ɑ̃:t) *a*, prudent.

pruderie (prydri) *f*, prudery, prudishness.

prud'homme (prydɔm) *m*, member of conciliation board. **prud'hommesque** (mɛsk) *a*, pompous & sententiously dull.

prune (pryn) *f*, plum. **pruneau** (no) *m*, prune. **prunelaie** (nlɛ) *f*, plum orchard. **prunelle** (nɛl) *f*, sloe; pupil, apple (*eye*). [*liqueur de*] ~, sloe gin. **prunellier** (lje) *m*, blackthorn, sloe tree. **prunier** (nje) *m*, plum [tree]. ~ **de damas**, damson [tree].

prurit (pryrit) *m*, pruritus, itching.

Prusse (la) (prys), Prussia. **prussien, ne** (sjɛ̃, ɛn) *a. & P~, n*, Prussian. **prussique** (sik) *a*, prussic.

psalmiste (psalmist) *m*, psalmist. **psalmodie** (mɔdi) *f*, psalmody; singsong. **psalmodier** (dje) *v.i. & t*, to intone, chant; drone. **psaume** (pso:m) *m*, psalm. **psautier** (psotje) *m*, psalter.

pseudonyme (psødɔnim) *m*, pseudonym.

psychanalyse (psikanali:z) *f*, psycho-analysis. **psyché** (ʃe) *f*, cheval glass, full-length mirror. **psychiatre** (kjɑ:tr) *m*, psychiatrist, -trist. **psychique** (ʃik) *a*, psychic(al). **psychologie** (kɔlɔʒi) *f*, psychology. **psychologique** (ʒik) *a*, psychological. **psycho-**

logue (lɔg) *m*, psychologist. **psychose** (ko:z) *f*, psychosis. ~ **traumatique** (tromatik), shell shock.

ptomaïne (ptɔmain) *f*, ptomaine.

puant, e (pyɑ̃, ɑ̃:t) *a*, stinking; foul. **puanteur** (ɑ̃tœ:r) *f*, stink, stench.

puberté (pybɛrte) *f*, puberty.

public, ique† (pyblik) *a*, public; common; national (*debt*); civil (*service*). ¶ *m*, public. **publicain** (kɛ̃) *m*, publican (*Bible*); extortioner. **publication** (kasjɔ̃) *f*, publication; publishing, issue. **publiciste** (sist) *m*, publicist. **publicité** (te) *f*, publicity, advertising. ~ **sur les nuages**, sky writing. **publier** (e) *v.t*, to publish; proclaim; issue.

puce (pys) *f*, flea. ¶ *a*, puce.

pucelle (pysɛl) *f*, maid[en], virgin.

puceron (pysrɔ̃) *m*, green fly.

pudding (pudiŋ) *m*, pudding.

puddler (pydle) *v.t*, to puddle (*iron*).

pudeur (pydœ:r) *f*, modesty, decency, shame. **pudibond, e** (dibɔ̃, ɔ̃:d) *a*, prudish. **pudique†** (dik) *a*, chaste, modest.

puer (pɥe) *v.i*, to stink, smell; (*v.t.*) to stink of, smell of.

puériculture (pɥerikylty:r) *f*, rearing of children. ~ **sociale**, child welfare. **puéril, e†** (ril) *a*, puerile, childish. **puérilité** (lite) *f*, puerility, childishness.

pugilat (pyʒila) *m*, pugilism; set-to. **pugiliste** (list) *m*, pugilist.

pugnace (pygnas) *a*, pugnacious.

puiné, e (pɥine) *a. & n*, younger (brother, sister).

puis (pɥi) *ad*, then, afterwards; next; besides.

puisard (pɥiza:r) *m*, sink, sump. **puisatier** (zatje) *m*, well sinker. **puiser** (ze) *v.t. & i*, to draw, derive.

puisque, puisqu' (pɥisk[ə]) *c*, since, as, seeing that.

puissamment (pɥisamɑ̃) *ad*, powerfully, mightily. **puissance** (sɑ̃:s) *f*, power; might; strength, force; authority, sway. ~ **lumineuse en bougies**, candle power. **puissant, e** (sɑ̃, ɑ̃:t) *a*, powerful; mighty; strong; potent; weighty. **les puissants**, the mighty ones.

puits (pɥi) *m*, well, hole; shaft (*Min.*); fount (*fig.*).

pulluler (pyllyle) *v.i*, to pullulate, swarm.

pulmonaire (pylmɔnɛ:r) *a*, pulmonary.

pulpe (pylp) *f*, pulp. **pulper** (pe) *v.t*, to pulp.

pulsation (pylsasjɔ̃) *f*, pulsation, throb[bing]. **pulvériser** (pylverize) *v.t*, to pulverize, powder; spray. **pulvérulent, e** (rylɑ̃, ɑ̃:t) *a*, powdery.

puma (pyma) *m*, puma, cougar.

punais, e (pynɛ, ɛ:z) *a*, foul-breathed. **punaise** (pynɛ:z) *f*, bug; drawing pin.

punch (pɔ̃:ʃ) *m*, punch (*drink*).

punir (pyni:r) *v.t*, to punish; avenge. **punissable** (nisabl) *a*, punishable. **punition** (sjɔ̃) *f*, punishment.

pupille (pypil) *n*, ward; pupil. ¶ *f*, pupil (*eye*).

pupitre (pypitr) *m*, desk; stand (*music*).

pur, e† (py:r) *a*, pure; unalloyed; plain; mere; sheer; clear; neat (*unwatered*).

purée (pyre) *f*, mash; [thick] soup. ~ *de pommes de terre, de navets*, mashed potatoes, turnips.

pureté (pyrte) *f*, purity; clearness (*sky*).

purgatif, ive (pyrgatif, i:v) *a. & m*, purgative. **purgation** (sjɔ̃) *f*, purging; purge. **purgatoire** (twa:r) *m*, purgatory. **purger** (ʒe) *v.t*, to purge, cleanse, clear; redeem (*mortgage*).

purifier (pyrifje) *v.t*, to purify, cleanse.

puriste (rist) *n*, purist.

puritain, e (pyritɛ̃, ɛn) *n*, Puritan. ¶ *a*, Puritan; puritanic(al).

purpurin, e (pyrpyrɛ̃, in) *a*, purplish.

purulent, e (pyrylɑ̃, ɑ̃:t) *a*, purulent, mattery. **pus** (py) *m*, pus, matter.

pusillanime (pyzilanim) *a*, pusillanimous.

pustule (pystyl) *f*, pustule, pimple.

putatif, ive (pytatif, i:v) *a*, putative, reputed.

putois (pytwa) *m*, polecat.

putréfaction (pytrefaksjɔ̃) *f*, putrefaction. **putréfier** (fje) *v.t*, to putrefy. **putride** (trid) *a*, putrid.

puy (pɥi) *m*, mountain, peak.

pygmée (pigme) *m*, pygmy.

pyjama (piʒama) *m*, pyjamas.

pylône (pilo:n) *m*, pylon, tower.

pyorrhée (pjɔre) *f*, pyorrhea.

pyramide (piramid) *f*, pyramid.

Pyrénées (les) (pirene) *f.pl*, the Pyrenees.

pyrèthre (piretr) *m*, pyrethrum.

pyrite (pirit) *f*, pyrites.

pyrogravure (pirɔgravy:r) *f*, poker work.

pyrotechnie (pirɔtɛkni) *f*, pyrotechnics.

python (pitɔ̃) *m*, python.

Q

quadrangulaire (kwadrɑ̃gylɛ:r) *a*, quadrangular.

quadrant (kwadrɑ̃) *m*, quadrant (*Math.*).

quadrupède (kwadrypɛd) *a*, quadruped(al), four-footed. ¶ *m*, quadruped.

quadruple (kwadrypl) *a. & m*, quadruple, fourfold. ~ *croche*, *f*, semi- or hemidemisemiquaver.

quai (ke) *m*, quay, wharf; embankment (*river*); platform (*Rly*).

quaiche (kɛʃ) *f*, ketch.

qualifier (kalifje) *v.t*, to qualify; call, style; describe. **qualité** (te) *f*, quality; property; qualification, profession; capacity. ~ *d'amateur*, amateur status.

quand (kɑ̃) *c. & ad*, when; [al]though, even if. ~ *même*, all the same, notwithstanding, nevertheless.

quant à (kɑ̃ta) *pr*, as for, as to, as regards,

for. **quant-à-moi, quant-à-soi**, *m*, dignity, reserve, stand-offishness.

quantième (kɑ̃tjɛm) *m*, day of the month, date.

quantité (kɑ̃tite) *f*, quantity; amount; lots, a lot. ~ *de pluie* [*tombée*], rainfall.

quantum (kwɑ̃tɔm) *m*, quantum.

quarantaine (karɑ̃tɛn) *f*, [about] forty; quarantine. *mettre en* ~, to quarantine (*ship*); send (*pers.*) to Coventry. **quarante** (rɑ̃:t) *a*, forty. ¶ *m*, forty; 40th. **quarantième** (rɑ̃tjɛm) *a. & n*, fortieth.

quart (ka:r) *m*, quarter, fourth [part]; ¼ litre; watch (*Naut.*). ~ *d'heure*, quarter of an hour. *un* ~ *ou* & ~, quarter past (*hour*). ~ *de cercle*, quadrant (*Surv. instrument*). ~ [*de vent*], point [of the compass]. **quarte** (kart) *f*, fourth (*Mus.*).

quarteron, ne (kartərɔ̃, ɔn) *n*, quadroon.

quartier (kartje) *m*, quarter; portion, lump; haunch (*meat*); gammon (*bacon*); ward, district; neighbourhood; quarters. ~ *général*, headquarters.

quartz (kwarts) *m*, quartz.

quasi (kazi) *ad*, almost, quasi. ~ *aveugle*, almost blind, purblind. ~-*délit*, *m*, quasi-delict, technical offence. **Quasimodo** (kazimɔdo) *f*, Low Sunday.

quassia (kwasja) *m*, quassia (*bark*). **quassier** (sje) *m*, quassia (*tree*).

quatorze (katorz) *a. & m*, fourteen; 14th. **quatorzième**† (zjɛm) *a. & n*, fourteenth.

quatrain (katrɛ̃) *m*, quatrain.

quatre (katr) *a. & m*, four; 4th. *lac des Q~-Cantons*, Lake of Lucerne. ~ *jumeaux*, quadruplets. *à* ~ *pattes*, on all fours. *Q~-Temps* (trɑ̃tɑ̃) *m.pl*, ember days. ~-*vingt-dix* (trəvɛ̃di[s]) *a. & m*, ninety. ~-*vingt-onze* (vɛ̃ɔ̃:z), 91. ~-*vingt-dixième* (zjɛm) *a. & n*, ninetieth. ~-*vingtième* (tjɛm) *a. & n*, eightieth. ~-*vingts & ~-vingt*, *a. & m*, eighty. ~-*vingt-un* (vɛ̃œ̃), 81. **quatrième**† (triɛm) *a. & n*, fourth.

quatuor (kwatɥɔ:r) *m*, quartet[te].

que, qu' (kə, k) *c. & ad*, that; than; as; whether; how; but, only; lest; let, may. ¶ *pn*, whom; which; that; what. *qu'est-ce que?* (kɛskə) & *qu'est-ce qui* (ki)? what?

quel, le (kɛl) *a*, what; what a; which; who. ~ *que*, whatever; whoever.

quelconque (kɛlkɔ̃:k) *a*, any; some.

quelque (kɛlk[ə]) *a*, some, any; a few. ~ *chose*, *m*, something; anything. ~*fois*, *ad*, sometimes. ~ *part*, *ad*, somewhere.

quelqu'un, quelqu'une (kɛlkœ̃, kyn) *pn*, somebody, someone, one, anybody, anyone. *quelques-uns, unes* (kzœ̃, yn) *pl*, some [people], a few.

quémander (kemɑ̃de) *v.i*, to beg; (*v.t.*) to beg for, solicit.

qu'en-dira-t-on (le) (kɑ̃diratɔ̃) *m*, what people may say.

quenotte (kənɔt) *f*, peggy (*tooth*, *Nursery talk*).

quenouille (kənu:j) *f*, distaff; bed post.
querelle (kərɛl) *f*, quarrel, row. ~ **d'ivrognes**, drunken brawl. **quereller** (le) *v.t*, to quarrel with; scold, nag. **se** ~, to quarrel, wrangle. **querelleur, euse** (lœ:r, ø:z) *n*, quarreller, wrangler. (*att.*) quarrelsome.
question (kɛstjɔ̃) *f*, question; query; point, matter, issue. ~ **d'intérêt secondaire**, side issue. **questionnaire** (ɔnɛ:r) *m*, list of questions. **questionner** (ne) *v.t*, to question.
quête (kɛ:t) *f*, quest, search; collection, offertory. **quêter** (kete) *v.t*, to seek for; collect (*alms*).
queue (kø) *f*, tail; brush (*fox*); pigtail; stem; stalk; handle, shank; cue (*Bil.*); train; rear; queue, file. ~**-d'aronde** (darɔ̃:d) *f*, dovetail. ~**-de-morue** (dmory) ou ~**-de-pie** (dpi) *f*, [swallow] tails (*dress coat*). **queuter** (køte) *v.i*, to push the ball (*Bil.*); spoon (*Croquet*).
qui (ki) *pn*, who; whom; which; that. ~ **vive!** who goes there?
quiconque (kikɔ̃:k) *pn*, who[so]ever.
quiétude (kɥietyd) *f*, quietude.
quignon (kiɲɔ̃) *m*, [c]hunk, hunch.
quille (ki:j) *f*, skittle, ninepin; keel. **quillier** (kije) *m*, skittle alley.
quincaillerie (kɛ̃kajri) *f*, hardware, ironmongery. **quincaillier** (je) *m*, ironmonger.
quinconce (kɛ̃kɔ̃:s) *m*, quincunx.
quinine (kinin) *f*, quinine.
quinquennal, e (kɥɛ̃kɛnnal) *a*, quinquennial; five-year (*plan*).
quinquina (kɛ̃kina) *m*, Peruvian bark.
quintal [métrique] (kɛ̃tal) *m*, [metric] quintal = 100 kilos.
quinte (kɛ̃:t) *f*, quint; fifth (*Mus.*); caprice, crotchet. ~ [**de toux**], fit of coughing.
quintessence (kɛ̃tɛsɑ̃:s) *f*, quintessence.
quintette (kɥɛ̃tɛt) *f*, quintet[te].
quinteux, euse (kɛ̃tø, ø:z) *a*, crotchety; fitful.
quinzaine (kɛ̃zɛn) *f*, [about] fifteen; fortnight. **quinze** (kɛ̃:z) *a. & m*, fifteen; 15th. ~ **jours**, fortnight. **quinzième†** (kɛ̃zjɛm) *a. & n*, fifteenth.
quiproquo (kiprɔko) *m*, mistake, misunderstanding (*mistaking one for another*).
quittance (kitɑ̃:s) *f*, receipt. **quittancer** (tɑ̃se) *v.t*, to r. **quitte** (kit) *a*, quit, rid, free. ~ **à** ~, *ad*, quits. ~ **ou double**, double or quits. **quitter** (te) *v.t. & i*, to leave, quit, vacate; give up; swerve from. **ne quittez pas!** hold on! hold the line! (*Teleph.*). **quitus** (kity:s) *m*, discharge.
qui-vive (kivi:v) *m*, challenge (*sentry's*); qui vive, look-out, alert.
quoi (kwa) *pn. & i*, what; which; that. ~ **qu'il en soit**, be that as it may. **de** ~, something; enough, the wherewithal. **de** ~ **écrire**, writing materials.
quoique, quoiqu' (kwak[ə]) *c*, [al]though.
quolibet (kɔlibɛ) *m*, gibe.
quorum (kɔrɔm) *m*, quorum.

quote-part (kɔtpa:r) *f*, share, quota.
quotidien, ne (kɔtidjɛ̃, ɛn) *a*, daily; everyday. [**journal**] **quotidien**, *m*, daily [paper]. **quotidiennement** (ɛnmɑ̃) *ad*, daily.
quotient (kɔsjɑ̃) *m*, quotient.
quotité (kɔtite) *f*, quota, share.

R

rabâchage (rabɑʃa:ʒ) *m*, endless repetition. *il rabâche toujours les mêmes choses*, he is always harping on the same string.
rabais (rabɛ) *m*, allowance, rebate. *adjudication, &c, au* ~, award, &c, to the lowest tenderer. **rabaisser** (se) *v.t*, to lower; disparage, belittle.
rabat (raba) *m*, beating (*for game*). ~**-joie**, *m*, kill-joy. **rabatteur, euse** (tœ:r, ø:z) *n*, tout; (*m.*) beater. **rabattre** (tr) *v.t.ir*, to beat down, bring d., turn d., press d., lower; bate; take off; beat up (*game, &c*).
rabbin (rabɛ̃) *m*, rabbi.
rabot (rabo) *m*, plane (*tool*). **raboter** (bɔte) *v.t*, to plane; polish (*fig.*). **raboteux, euse** (tø, ø:z) *a*, rough, rugged; knotty.
rabougrir (rabugri:r) *v.t*, to stunt (*growth*).
rabouter (rabute) *ou* **raboutir** (ti:r) *v.t*, to join [up].
rabrouer (rabrue) *v.t*, to rebuff, snub; rebuke.
racaille (rakɑ:j) *f*, rabble, riff-raff.
raccommodage (rakɔmɔda:ʒ) *m*, mending, repairing. **raccommodement** (dmɑ̃) *m*, reconciliation. **raccommoder** (de) *v.t*, to mend, repair; reconcile. **se** ~, to make it up. **raccommodeur, euse** (dœ:r, ø:z) *n*, mender, repairer.
raccord (rakɔ:r) *m*, join; joint; connexion, union, coupling. **raccorder** (kɔrde) *v.t*, to join, connect, couple, link up.
raccourci (rakursi) *m*, abridgement; epitome; short cut; foreshortening. **raccourcir** (si:r) *v.t*, to shorten; abridge, curtail; foreshorten. [**se**] ~, to draw in (*days*).
raccroc (rakro) *m*, fluke, lucky stroke. **raccrocher** (krɔʃe) *v.t*, to hook up, hang up, replace. **se** ~, to clutch, catch; cling.
race (ras) *f*, race, descent, ancestry; strain, blood, breed, stock, tribe, species. **racé, e** (se) *a*, thoroughbred.
rachat (raʃa) *m*, repurchase; redemption; ransom; surrender (*Insce*). **racheter** (ʃte) *v.t*, to repurchase, buy back; redeem; surrender; ransom; atone for.
rachitisme (raʃitism) *m*, rachitis, rickets.
racine (rasin) *f*, root; root, fang (*of tooth*); [silkworm] gut (*Fish.*). ~ **d'iris**, orris root. ~ **pivotante**, tap root.
raclée (rɑkle) *f*, thrashing, hiding. **racler** (kle) *v.t*, to scrape; rake; rasp; strike (*measure*). **racloir** (klwa:r) *m*, scraper; squeegee. **racloire** (klwa:r) *f*, strickle, strike (*grain*). **raclure** (kly:r) *f*, scrapings.
racoler (rakɔle) *v.t*, to recruit; tout for.

racontar (rakõta:r) *m*, gossip, scandal. **raconter** (te) *v.t*, to relate, recount, narrate, tell; (*abs.*) to tell a story (*well, &c*). **en ~**, to draw the long bow, romance.

racornir (rakorni:r) *v.t*, to harden; shrivel.

rade (rad) *f*, roadstead, roads (*Naut.*).

radeau (rado) *m*, raft.

radial, e (radjal) *a*, radial. **radiateur** (tœ:r) *m*, radiator; fire (*gas, elec.*). **~ parabolique**, bowl fire (*elec.*). **radiation** (sjõ) *f*, striking out; s. off; radiation.

radical, e† (radikal) *a. & m*, radical; root.

radier (radje) *v.t*, to strike out; s. off.

radieux, euse (radjø, ø:z) *a*, radiant, beaming.

radioactif, ive (radjoaktif, i:v) *a*, radioactive. **radiodiffuser** (odifyze) *v.t*, to broadcast. **radiodiffusion** (zjõ) *f*, broadcasting. **radiogramme** (gram) *m*, radiogram. **radiographie** (fi) *f*, radiography. **radiotélégraphie** (telegrafi) *f*, radiotelegraphy.

radis (radi) *m*, radish.

radium (radjom) *m*, radium.

radius (radjy:s) *m*, radius (*Anat.*).

radoter (radote) *v.i*, to drivel (*talk*), dote, doat. **radoteur, euse** (tœ:r, ø:z) *n*, dotard.

radouber (radube) *v.t*, to repair (*ship*).

radoucir (radusi:r) *v.t*, to soften; make milder.

rafale (rafal) *f*, squall, gust. **~ de pluie**, cloud burst.

raffermir (rafermi:r) *v.t*, to harden; strengthen.

raffinage (rafina:ʒ) *m*, refining. **raffiné, e** (ne) *p.a*, refined; subtle. **raffinement** (nmã) *m*, refinement, subtlety. **raffiner** (ne) *v.t. & abs*, to refine. **raffinerie** (nri) *f*, refinery.

raffoler de (rafole), to be very fond of, dote on.

rafistoler (rafistole) *v.t*, to patch up.

rafle (ra:fl) *f*, stalk (*grape*); cob (*corn*); clean sweep; raid; round up. **rafler** (rafle) *v.t*, to carry off; round up. **~ le tout**, to sweep the board.

rafraîchir (rafreʃi:r) *v.t. & abs. & i*, to cool, refresh, freshen; revive; trim (*hair, grass*). **rafraîchissements** (ʃismã) *m.pl*, [light] refreshments.

ragaillardir (ragajardi:r) *v.t*, to cheer up.

rage (ra:ʒ) *f*, rage; rabies, madness; mania. **~ de dents**, raging toothache. **rager** (raʒe) *v.i*, to rage. **rageur, euse†** (ʒœ:r, ø:z) *a. & n*, passionate (person), spitfire.

ragot (rago) *m*, gossip, scandal.

ragoût (ragu) *m*, stew. **~ de mouton**, stewed mutton. **ragoûtant, e** (tã, ã:t) *a*, tempting.

ragréer (ragree) *v.t*, to clean up; do up (*repair house, &c*).

rai (rɛ) *m*, ray; spoke.

raid (rɛd) *m*, raid; endurance test.

raide (rɛd) *a*, stiff; stark; tight, taut, tense; steep. **raideur** (dœ:r) *f*, stiffness, &c.

raidir (di:r) *v.t*, to stiffen; tighten.

raie (rɛ) *f*, line, stroke; streak; stripe; ridge (*Agric.*); parting (*hair*); ray, skate (*fish*).

raifort (rɛfo:r) *m*, horse-radish.

rail (ra:j) *m*, rail (*Rly metal or transport*). **~ de courant**, live rail.

railler (raje) *v.t. & abs*, to jeer at, laugh at; joke. **raillerie** (jri) *f*, raillery, banter, joke, jesting.

rainure (rɛny:r) *f*, groove, slot. **~ de clavette**, keyway.

raire (rɛ:r) *v.i.ir*, to troat, bell.

raisin (rɛzɛ̃) *m*, grapes. **~s de Corinthe**, currants (*dried*). **~ de serres**, hothouse grapes. **~s de Smyrne**, sultanas. **~ de treille**, dessert grapes. **~ de vigne**, wine grapes. **~s secs**, raisins. **~s secs muscats**, muscatels.

raison (rɛzõ) *f*, reason, motive, ground; sanity, senses; sense; satisfaction; ratio, rate. **~ (sociale)**, firm [name], style. **avoir ~**, to be right. **raisonnable†** (zonabl) *a*, reasonable; rational; fair, adequate. **raisonnement** (nmã) *m*, reasoning; argument. **raisonner** (ne) *v.i*, to reason; argue; (*v.t.*) to consider; reason with. **raisonneur, euse** (nœ:r, ø:z) *n*, reasoner, arguer; (*att.*) reasoning, argumentative.

rajeunir (raʒœni:r) *v.t*, to rejuvenate; make look younger; renovate.

rajuster (raʒyste) *v.t*, to readjust; put straight; refit.

râle (ra:l) *m*, rail (*bird*); rattle (*in throat*).

ralentir (ralãti:r) *v.t. & i*, to slacken, slow down.

rallier (ralje) *v.t*, to rally; rejoin.

rallonge (ralõ:ʒ) *f*, lengthening piece; leaf (*table*). **rallonger** (lõʒe) *v.t*, to lengthen.

rallumer (ralyme) *v.t*, to relight, rekindle.

rallye (rali) *m*, race meeting, rally. **~-paper** (pepœ:r) *m*, paper chase, hare & hounds.

ramage (rama:ʒ) *m*, floral design; song (*of birds*).

ramas (rama) *m*, heap.

ramasse (ramɑs) *f*, sledge (*Alpine*). **~-couverts**, *m*, plate basket. **~-miettes**, *m*, crumb tray. **~-miettes automatique**, crumb sweeper. **ramassé, e** (se) *p.a*, thick-set, stocky. **ramasser** (se) *v.t*, to gather, collect; pick up. **ramasseur, euse** (sœ:r, ø:z) *n*, collector, gatherer. **ramassis** (si) *m*, heap; set.

rame (ram) *f*, stick (*Hort.*); oar; ream (*500 sheets*); train (*of cars, &c*). **~ directe**, through portion (*Rly*).

rameau (ramo) *m*, branch; bough; palm (*Eccl.*). **ramée** (me) *f*, greenwood, arbour.

ramener (ramne) *v.t*, to bring back; reduce; restore; reset.

ramer (rame) *v.t*, to stick (*Hort.*); (*v.i.*) to row, pull (*oar*). **~ à rebours**, to back water. **~ en couple**, to scull. **rameur, euse** (mœ:r, ø:z) *n*, rower, oarsman, -woman. **~ de couple**, sculler.

ramier (ramje) *m*, ring dove, wood pigeon.

ramification (ramifikasjɔ̃) *f*, ramification. **se ramifier** (fje) *v.pr*, to ramify. **ramilles** (mi:j) *f.pl*, twigs.

ramolli, e (ramɔli) *p.a*, soft-witted. **ramollir** (li:r) *v.t*, to soften; enervate.

ramoner (ramɔne) *v.t*, to sweep (*chimney*). **ramoneur** (nœ:r) *m*, chimney sweep[er].

rampant, e (rɑ̃pɑ̃, ɑ̃:t) *a*, rampant; creeping; crawling; reptile; grovelling. **rampe** (rɑ̃:p) *f*, rise, slope; up grade; rack; banisters, hand rail; footlights. **ramper** (rɑ̃pe) *v.i*, to creep, crawl; cringe, truckle, fawn, grovel. **ramure** (ramy:r) *f*, branches; antlers.

rancart (mettre au) (rɑ̃ka:r) to cast aside.

rance (rɑ̃:s) *a*, rancid, rank. **rancir** (rɑ̃si:r) *v.i*, to become rancid.

rancœur (rɑ̃kœ:r) *f*, rancour, bitterness.

rançon (rɑ̃sɔ̃) *f*, ransom. **rançonner** (sɔne) *v.t*, to ransom; fleece.

rancune (rɑ̃kyn) *f*, rancour, spite; grudge. **rancunier, ère** (nje, ɛ:r) *a*, rancorous, spiteful.

randonnée (rɑ̃dɔne) *f*, circuit; trip, run.

rang (rɑ̃) *m*, row, line; tier; rank, station, place; rate, class. **rangé, e** (ʒe) *p.a*, tidy; steady (*man*); pitched (*battle*). **rangée** (ʒe) *f*, row, line; tier; array. **ranger** (ʒe) *v.t*, to arrange, marshal, array; tidy, put away; rank, range. **se** ∼, to draw up; fall in, side; stand aside; sober down; veer. *rangés comme des harengs en caque*, packed like sardines (*people*).

ranimer (ranime) *v.t*, to revive; stir up; cheer.

rapace (rapas) *a*, rapacious.

rapatrier (rapatrie) *v.t*, to repatriate, send home.

râpe (rɑ:p) *f*, rasp; grater (*nutmeg, &c*). **râpé, e** (rɑpe) *p.a*, grated; threadbare, shabby. **râper** (pe) *v.t*, to rasp; grate; wear threadbare.

rapetasser (raptase) *v.t*, to patch, cobble.

rapetisser (raptise) *v.t. & i*, to shorten; dwarf.

rapide† (rapid) *a*, rapid, fast, swift; speedy; cursory; steep. ¶ *m*, rapid (*river*); fast train, express.

rapiécer (rapjese) *v.t*, to piece, patch.

rapin (rapɛ̃) *m*, art student; dauber.

rapine (rapin) *f*, rapine. **rapiner** (ne) *v.t. & i*, to pillage.

rappareiller (rapareje) & **rapparier** (rje) *v.t*, to match, pair.

rappel (rapɛl) *m*, recall; call[ing]; reminder; repeal. **rappeler** (ple) *v.t*, to recall; call (*to order, &c*); summon; remind; r. of; remember; repeal. **se** ∼, to recollect, remember.

rapport (rapɔ:r) *m*, yield, return; report, account, statement; tale; relation, connexion; regard; (*pl.*) terms; (*pl.*) intercourse; ratio. ∼*s probables*, betting forecast. **rapporter** (pɔrte) *v.t. & abs*, to bring back; retrieve (*game*); yield; get; add;

inset; report, state; tell tales; refer, ascribe; revoke. **se** ∼, to agree, tally; refer, relate. **rapporteur, euse** (tœ:r, ø:z) *m*, talebearer; (*m.*) rapporteur; protractor.

rapprendre (raprɑ̃:dr) *v.t.ir*, to learn again.

rapprocher (raprɔʃe) *v.t*, to bring nearer; b. together; reconcile; compare.

rapt (rapt) *m*, abduction; kidnapping.

raquette (rakɛt) *f*, racket, -quet; battledore. ∼ *à neige*, snow shoe.

rare (rɑ:r) *a*, rare; scarce; uncommon; unusual; sparse, thin. **raréfier** (rarefje) *v.t*, to rarefy. **rarement** (rarmɑ̃) *ad*, rarely, seldom. **rareté** (te) *f*, rarity; scarcity; curiosity.

ras, e (rɑ, ɑ:z) *a*, close-cropped; c.-shaven; bare, naked, open. ∼ (ou au) *ras de*, level with, flush with. *coupé au ras du livre*, cut flush (*book edges*). **rasade** (razad) *f*, bumper (*brim-full glass*).

raser (rɑze) *v.t*, to shave; raze; graze, brush, skim. **rasoir** (zwa:r) *m*, razor.

rassasier (rasaʒje) *v.t*, to satisfy; satiate, sate, surfeit, cloy, glut.

rassembler (rasɑ̃ble) *v.t*, to reassemble; assemble, muster, collect.

rasseoir (raswa:r) *v.t.ir*, to reseat; settle. **se** ∼, to sit down again.

rasséréner (se) (raserene) *v.pr*, to clear [up].

rassis, e (rasi, i:z) *p.a*, settled, calm, staid, sedate, sane; stale (*bread*).

rassortir (rasɔrti:r) *v.t*, to match; restock.

rassurer (rasyre) *v.t*, to reassure, cheer, hearten; strengthen.

rat, e (ra, at) *n*, rat. *un* ∼ *dans la tête*, a bee in one's bonnet. ∼ *de bibliothèque*, bookworm (*pers.*). ∼ *de cave*, exciseman; taper (*coiled*). ∼ *des champs*, field mouse. ∼ *musqué*, musk rat, musquash.

ratatiné, e (ratatine) *p.a*, shrivelled, shrunken; wizened.

rate (rat) *f*, spleen, milt (*Anat.*).

râteau (rɑto) *m*, rake. **râteler** (tle) *v.t*, to rake up. **râtelier** (təlje) *m*, rack; denture.

rater (rate) *v.i*, to miss fire; miscarry, fail; (*v.t.*) to miss; fail in; fail to obtain.

ratier (ratje) *m*, ratter (*dog*). **ratière** (tjɛ:r) *f*, rat trap.

ratifier (ratifje) *v.t*, to ratify, confirm.

ration (rasjɔ̃) *f*, ration, allowance.

rationalisme (rasjɔnalism) *m*, rationalism. **rationnel, le†** (nɛl) *a*, rational; pure (*mechanics*).

rationner (rasjɔne) *v.t*, to ration; stint.

ratisser (ratise) *v.t*, to rake; scrape.

raton (ratɔ̃) *m*, young rat; darling. ∼ *laveur*, rac[c]oon.

rattacher (rataʃe) *v.t*, to refasten; bind; connect.

rattraper (ratrape) *v.t*, to recapture; overtake, catch up; recover.

rature (raty:r) *f*, erasure. **raturer** (tyre) *v.t*, to erase, scratch out.

rauque (ro:k) *a*, hoarse, raucous, harsh.

ravage (rava:ʒ) *m. oft. pl,* ravage, havoc, devastation. **ravager** (vaʒe) *v.t,* to ravage, devastate, lay waste. *ravagé(e)* [*par les intempéries*], weather-beaten.

ravaler (ravale) *v.t,* to swallow again; eat (*one's words*); disparage; rough-cast (*wall*). **se ∼,** to lower oneself, stoop (*fig.*).

ravauder (ravode) *v.t. & abs,* to mend; darn.

rave (ra:v) *f,* [cole] rape.

Ravenne (ravɛn) *f,* Ravenna.

ravigoter (ravigɔte) *v.t,* to revive, enliven.

ravilir (ravili:r) *v.t,* to degrade.

ravin (ravɛ̃) *m,* ravine (vin) *f,* ravine, gully. **raviner** (vine) *v.t,* to gully; furrow.

ravir (ravi:r) *v.t,* to ravish, carry off; delight, enrapture.

raviser (se) (ravize) *v.pr,* to change one's mind.

ravitailler (ravitaje) *v.t,* to [re]victual.

raviver (ravive) *v.t,* to revive.

ravoir (ravwa:r) *v.t,* to get (*something*) back.

rayer (reje) *v.t,* to scratch, score; rule; stripe, streak; rifle; strike out, delete.

ray-grass (rɛgra:s) *m,* rye grass.

rayon (rejɔ̃) *m,* ray, beam; gleam; radius; spoke; comb (*honey*); drill, furrow, row; shelf; department; rayon, artificial silk. **rayonnant, e** (jɔnã, ã:t) *a,* radiant; beaming. **rayonnement** (nmã) *m,* radiation; radiance, effulgence. **rayonner** (ne) *v.i,* to radiate, beam, shine; (*v.t.*) to fit with shelves.

rayure (rɛjy:r) *f,* scratch, &c, as *rayer.*

raz de marée (ra) *m,* tide race, bore; tidal wave.

razzia (razja) *f,* raid, foray. **razzier** (zje) *v.t,* to raid.

ré (re) *m,* D (*Mus.*).

réactif (reaktif) *m,* reagent (*Chem.*). **réaction** (sjɔ̃) *f,* reaction. **réactionnaire** (ɔnɛ:r) *a. & n,* reactionary. **réagir** (ʒi:r) *v.i,* to react.

réaliser (realize) *v.t,* to realize; make (*profit*); close (*bargain*). **réaliste** (list) *a. & n,* realist. **réalité** (te) *f,* reality.

réapparition (reaparisjɔ̃) *f,* reappearance.

réassurer (reasyre) *v.t,* to reinsure.

rébarbatif, ive (rebarbatif, i:v) *a,* grim; surly.

rebâtir (rebati:r) *v.t,* to rebuild; reconstruct.

rebattre (rebatr) *v.t.ir,* to beat again; reshuffle (*cards*); repeat. **rebattu, e** (ty) *p.a,* beaten (*track*); hackneyed.

rebelle (rebɛl) *a,* rebellious; refractory. ¶ *n,* rebel. **se rebeller** (le) *v.pr,* to rebel. **rébellion** (rebeljɔ̃) *f,* rebellion.

rebiffer (se) (rəbife) *v.pr,* to show temper.

rebondi, e (rəbɔ̃di) *a,* rounded; plump. **rebondir** (di:r) *v.i,* to rebound, bounce; crop up again.

rebord (rəbɔ:r) *m,* edge, rim; hem; ledge; flange.

rebours (rəbu:r) *m,* wrong way; contrary, reverse. *à ∼,* the wrong way; backward. *prendre à ∼,* to misconstrue.

rebouteur, euse (rəbutœ:r, ø:z) *n,* bonesetter.

rebrousse-poil (à) (rəbruspwal) *ad,* against the nap, the wrong way. **rebrousser** (se) *v.t,* to rub the wrong way. *∼* [*chemin*], to retrace one's steps.

rebuffade (rəbyfad) *f,* rebuff.

rébus (reby:s) *m,* picture puzzle; riddle.

rebut (rəby) *m,* waste, refuse, rubbish; dead letter (*Post*); scum (*fig.*). **rebutant, e** (tã, ã:t) *a,* disheartening; repellent. **rebuter** (te) *v.t,* to rebuff, repulse; dishearten.

récalcitrant, e (rekalsitrã, ã:t) *a. & n,* recalcitrant; refractory.

récapituler (rekapityle) *v.t,* to recapitulate.

receler (rəsle) *v.t,* to conceal; harbour (*criminal*); receive (*stolen goods*). **receleur, euse** (slœ:r, ø:z) *n,* receiver, fence.

récemment (resamã) *ad,* recently, lately.

recensement (rəsãsmã) *m,* census, return; counting (*votes*); stock taking. **recenser** (se) *v.t,* to take the census of; count.

récent, e (resã, ã:t) *a,* recent, late; fresh.

receper (rəsəpe) *v.t,* to cut back (*Hort.*).

réceptacle (resepise) *m,* receipt. **réceptacle** (sɛptakl) *m,* receptacle; repository. **récepteur** (tœ:r) *m,* receiver (*Teleph., &c*). **réception** (sjɔ̃) *f,* receipt; reception; welcome; acceptance; party, at-home. **recette** (rəsɛt) *f,* receipts, takings; gate money; collectorship; recipe. **recevable** (sɔvabl) *a,* admissible. **receveur, euse** (vœ:r, ø:z) *n,* collector (*taxes, &c*); booking clerk (*Rly*); conductor (*bus, tram*); (*f.*) attendant (*Theat.*). *∼ des postes,* postmaster, -mistress. **recevoir** (vwa:r) *v.t. & abs,* to receive; admit; get; meet with; accept; welcome; take in (*boarders*); be at home (*to visitors*). *être reçu à,* to pass (*exam*).

rechange (rəʃã:ʒ) *m,* change, spare.

réchapper (reʃape) *v.i,* to escape; recover.

recharger (rəʃarʒe) *v.t,* to recharge; reload.

réchaud (reʃo) *m,* stove; ring (*gas*); heater; hot plate. **réchauffer** (ʃofe) *v.t,* to reheat, warm up; revive.

rêche (rɛʃ) *a,* rough, harsh.

recherche (rəʃɛrʃ) *f,* search, quest, pursuit; research, inquiry; prospecting; studied elegance. **recherché, e** (ʃe) *p.a,* sought after, in request; choice; studied; elaborate. **rechercher** (ʃe) *v.t,* to search for, seek.

rechigner (rəʃiɲe) *v.i,* to look sour. *en rechignant* (nã), with a bad grace.

rechute (rəʃyt) *f,* relapse, backsliding.

récidiver (residive) *v.i,* to relapse into crime. **récidiviste** (vist) *n,* person with previous convictions; old offender.

récif (resif) *m,* reef (*of rocks*).

récipiendaire (resipjãdɛ:r) *n,* new member. **récipient** (pjã) *m,* receiver, vessel.

réciproque (resiprɔk) *a,* reciprocal, mutual; inverse; converse. **réciproquement** (kmã) *ad,* reciprocally, &c; vice versa.

récit (resi) *m,* recital, account, narration, narrative; solo (*Mus.*). **récital** (tal) *m.*

recital (*Mus.*). **récitatif** (tatif) *m*, recitative (*Mus.*). **récitation** (sjɔ̃) *f*, recitation. **réciter** (te) *v.t*, to recite; say (*lessons*).

réclamant, e (reklamá, ã:t) *n*, claimant. **réclamation** (masjɔ̃) *f*, claim; complaint, protest. **réclame** (klam) *f*, advertisement, puff. **réclamer** (me) *v.i*, to complain, protest, object; (*v.t.*) to claim; crave; call for. ~ *à grands cris*, to clamour for.

reclus, e (rəkly, y:z) *n*, recluse. **réclusion** (reklyzjɔ̃) *f*, reclusion, seclusion; solitary imprisonment.

recoin (rəkwɛ̃) *m*, nook, recess.

récolte (rekɔlt) *f*, harvest[ing]; crop; vintaging; vintage; collection. **récolter** (te) *v.t*, to harvest; collect.

recommander (rəkɔmɑ̃de) *v.t*, to [re]commend; register (*Post*).

recommencer (rəkɔmɑ̃se) *v.t. & i*, to recommence; begin again.

récompense (rekɔ̃pɑ̃:s) *f*, recompense, reward; retribution, requital. **récompenser** (pɑ̃se) *v.t*, to recompense, &c.

réconcilier (rekɔ̃silje) *v.t*, to reconcile.

reconduire (rəkɔ̃dɥi:r) *v.t.ir*, to escort; see home; show out.

réconfort (rekɔ̃fɔ:r) *m*, comfort, consolation; stimulant. **réconforter** (fɔrte) *v.t*, to strengthen; comfort.

reconnaissable (rəkɔnɛsabl) *a*, recognizable. **reconnaissance** (sɑ̃:s) *f*, recognition; acknowledgement; gratitude, thankfulness; reconnaissance, exploration. **reconnaissant, e** (sɑ̃, ɑ̃:t) *a*, grateful, thankful. **reconnaître** (nɛ:tr) *v.t.ir*, to recognize; tell; sight (*land, &c*); acknowledge; be grateful for; reconnoitre, explore.

reconquérir (rəkɔ̃keri:r) *v.t.ir*, to reconquer; regain.

reconstitution (rəkɔ̃stitysjɔ̃) *f*, reconstruction (*fig.*).

reconstruction (rəkɔ̃stryksjɔ̃) *f*, rebuilding. **reconstruire** (strɥi:r) *v.t.ir*, to rebuild.

reconvention (rəkɔ̃vɑ̃sjɔ̃) *f*, counterclaim.

record (rəkɔ:r) *m*, record (*Sport, &c*). **recorder** (kɔrde) *v.t*, to con, go over; restring. **recors** (kɔ:r) *m*, bailiff's man; minion (*of the law*).

recoupe (rəkup) *f*, middlings (*flour*); chips; clippings.

recourber (rəkurbe) *v.t*, to bend, crook

recourir (rəkuri:r) *v.i.ir*, to run again; have recourse, resort. **recours** (ku:r) *m*, recourse, resort; appeal; remedy (*Law*).

recouvrement (rəkuvrəmɑ̃) *m*, recovery; cover[ing]; [over]lap; (*pl.*) book debts. **recouvrer** (vre) *v.t*, to recover, regain.

recouvrir (rəkuvri:r) *v.t.ir*, to re-cover; cover.

récréation (rekreasjɔ̃) *f*, recreation; playtime.

récréer (rəkree) *v.t*, to re-create.

récréer (rekree) *v.t*, to recreate, divert, entertain; enliven, refresh.

récrier (se) (rekrie) *v.pr*, to cry out, exclaim.

récrimination (rekriminasjɔ̃) *f*, recrimination.

récrire (rekri:r) *v.t.ir*, to rewrite; write again; reply.

recroqueviller (se) (rəkrɔkvije) *v.pr*, to shrivel.

recrudescence (rəkrydɛsɑ̃:s) *f*, recrudescence.

recrue (rəcry) *f*, recruit. **recruter** (te) *v.t*, to recruit.

recta (rɛkta) *ad*, on the nail, punctually.

rectangle (rɛktɑ̃:gl) *a*, right-angled. ¶ *m*, rectangle. ~ [*de table*], doily. **rectangulaire** (tɑ̃gylɛ:r) *a*, rectangular.

recteur (rɛktœ:r) *m*, rector.

rectifier (rɛktifje) *v.t*, to rectify; amend; true, straighten.

rectiligne (rɛktiliɲ) *a*, rectilinear.

rectitude (rɛktityd) *f*, straightness; rectitude, soundness, sanity.

recto (rɛkto) *m*, recto, front, face.

rectum (rɛktɔm) *m*, rectum.

reçu (rəsy) *m*, receipt.

recueil (rəkœ:j) *m*, collection; book. ~ *factice*, miscellany. **recueillement** (kœjmɑ̃) *m*, self-communion. **recueillir** (ji:r) *v.t.ir*, to collect, gather; pick up; reap.

recuire (rəkɥi:r) *v.t.ir*, to rebake; reheat; anneal.

recul (rəkyl) *m*, recoil, kick; setback. **reculade** (lad) *f*, backward movement; retreat. **reculé, e** (le) *p.a*, distant, remote. **reculer** (le) *v.i. & t*, to draw back; move back; recede; retreat; back; recoil; kick; postpone. **à reculons** (lɔ̃) *ad*, backward[s].

récupérer (rekypere) *v.t*, to recover, recoup.

récurer (rekyre) *v.t.*, to scour, clean.

récuser (rekyze) *v.t*, to challenge, object to.

rédacteur, trice (redaktœ:r, tris) *n*, draughtsman; writer (*news*). ~ *en chef*, editor. **rédaction** (sjɔ̃) *f*, drafting, editing; editorial staff.

reddition (rɛddisjɔ̃) *f*, surrender; ¬endering (*of accounts*).

redemander (rədmɑ̃de) *v.t*, to ask for again; ask for more; ask for back.

Rédempteur (redɑ̃[p]tœ:r) *m*, Redeemer. **rédemption** ([p]sjɔ̃) *f*, redemption (*Theol.*).

redescendre (rədɛsɑ̃:dr) *v.i*, to come down again; fall again (*barometer*); back (*wind*).

redevable (rədəvabl) *a*, indebted, beholden; liable. ¶ *n*, debtor. **redevance** (vɑ̃:s) *f*, rent[al]; royalty. **redevoir** (vwa:r) *v.t*, to still owe.

rédiger (rediʒe) *v.t*, to draw up, draft; write; edit.

redingote (rədɛ̃gɔt) *f*, frock coat (*man's*); coat (*woman's*).

redire (rədi:r) *v.t.ir*, to say again; repeat. *trouver à* ~ *à*, to find fault with. **redite** (dit) *f*, repetition.

redondant, e (rədɔ̃dɑ̃, ɑ̃:t) *a*, redundant.

redonner (rədɔne) *v.t*, to give again; restore; (*v.i.*) to fall again; charge again.

redoutable (rədutabl) *a*, redoubtable, formidable.

redoute (rədut) *f*, redoubt; gala night (*at dance hall*).

redouter (rədute) *v.t*, to dread, fear.

redresser (rədrese) *v.t*, to re-erect; straighten; redress; right.

réduction (redyksjɔ̃) *f*, reduction; redueing; cut. **réduire** (dɥi:r) *v.t.ir*, to reduce; boil down. **réduit** (dɥi) *m*, retreat, nook; redoubt.

rééditer (reedite) *v.t*, to republish, re-issue.

réel, **le†** (reɛl) *a*, real; actual. ¶ *m*, real[ity].

réélection (reelɛksjɔ̃) *f*, re-election. **rééligible** (liʒibl) *a*, re-eligible. **réélire** (li:r) *v.t.ir*, to re-elect.

réer (ree) *v.i*, to troat, bell.

réexporter (reɛkspɔrte) *v.t*, to re-export.

refaire (rəfɛːr) *v.t.ir*, to remake, do [over] again; do up, repair; recover. **refait** (fɛ) *m*, draw[n game]; new horns (*stag*). **réfection** (refɛksjɔ̃) *f*, restoration. **réfectoire** (twaːr) *m*, refectory.

refendre (rəfɑ̃ːdr) *v.t*, to split; rip.

référence (referɑ̃:s) *f*, reference. **referendum** (referɛ̃dɔm) *m*, referendum. **référer** (fere) *v.t. & i. & se ~*, to refer; ascribe.

réfléchi, **e** (refleʃi) *p.a*, reflective; thoughtful; considered, deliberate; reflexive (*Gram.*). **réfléchir** (ʃiːr) *v.t. & i*, to reflect; think over, ponder, consider. **réflecteur** (flɛktœːr) *m*, reflector. **reflet** (rəflɛ) *m*, reflection; reflex; shimmer, glint. *~s irisés*, play of colours. **refléter** (flete) *v.t*, to reflect; mirror. **réflexe** (reflɛks) *a. & m*, reflex. **réflexion** (ksjɔ̃) *f*, reflection; reflexion; thought. *~ après coup*, afterthought.

refluer (rəflye) *v.i*, to flow back, ebb; surge. **reflux** (fly) *m*, reflux, ebb.

refondre (rəfɔ̃ːdr) *v.t*, to recast, remodel.

réformateur, **trice** (reformatœːr, tris) *n*, reformer. **réformation** (sjɔ̃) *f*, reformation. **réforme** (form) *f*, reform[ation]; discharge, invaliding (*Mil., Nav.*).

reformer (rəforme) *v.t*, to re-form.

réformer (reforme) *v.t*, to reform, amend; discharge, retire, invalid; reverse (*Law*).

refouler (rəfule) *v.t*, to drive back; stem; compress; ram home; repress; (*v.i.*) to flow back, ebb. **refouloir** (lwaːr) *m*, rammer (*gun*).

réfractaire (refraktɛːr) *a*, refractory; fire [-proof]. ¶ *m*, defaulter (*Mil.*).

réfracter (refrakte) *v.t*, to refract.

refrain (rəfrɛ̃) *m*, refrain, burden; theme. *~ en chœur*, chorus.

refréner (rəfrene) *v.t*, to curb, bridle.

réfrigération (refriʒerasjɔ̃) *f*, refrigeration; freezing; cooling, chilling.

refrogner (se) (rəfroɲe) *v.pr*, to frown, scowl, look sullen.

refroidir (rəfrwadiːr) *v.t. & i. & se ~*, to cool, chill; damp (*fig.*); get cold.

refuge (rəfy:ʒ) *m*, refuge, shelter; [street] refuge. **réfugié**, **e** (refyʒje) *n*, refugee. **se réfugier** (ʒje) *v.pr*, to take refuge.

refus (rəfy) *m*, refusal. *~ d'obéissance*, insubordination; contempt of court **refuser** (ze) *v.t*, to refuse, decline; deny; reject; pluck, plough (*exam*). **se ~**, to object, refuse, decline.

réfuter (refyte) *v.t*, to refute, confute, rebut; disprove.

regagner (rəgaɲe) *v.t*, to regain, win back, recover; make up for; get back to.

regain (rəgɛ̃) *m*, aftermath (*Agric.*); renewal; new lease (*of life*).

régal (regal) *m*, feast; treat. **régaler** (le) *v.t*, to entertain, feast; treat; regale.

regard (rəgaːr) *m*, look, gaze, glance, eye(s); attention, notice; peep hole; manhole. *~ appuyé*, stare. *~ polisson*, leer. *en ~*, opposite, facing. **regardant**, **e** (gardɑ̃, ɑ̃:t) *a*, close-fisted, mean. **regarder** (de) *v.t. & abs*, to look (at, on), see, eye; consider, regard, mind, be one's business; face, front. *~ fixement*, to stare at.

régate (regat) *f*, regatta. [*cravate*] *~*, open-end tie.

régence (reʒɑ̃:s) *f*, regency.

régénérer (reʒenere) *v.t*, to regenerate.

régent, **e** (reʒɑ̃, ɑ̃:t) *n. & a*, regent. **régenter** (ʒɑ̃te) *v.t*, to dictate to; dominate; (*abs.*) to domineer.

régicide (reʒisid) *m*, regicide; (*att.*) regicidal.

régie (reʒi) *f*, administration (*of property*); State (*control*); excise.

regimber (rəʒɛ̃be) *v.i*, to kick, jib.

régime (reʒim) *m*, regime[n], rules, system, conditions; diet; object (*Gram.*); bunch, cluster (*bananas, &c*). *~ de faveur*, preference (*Cust.*). *cas ~*, *m*, objective case.

régiment (reʒimɑ̃) *m*, regiment; swarm. **régimentaire** (tɛːr) *a*, regimental.

région (reʒjɔ̃) *f*, region, district. **régional**, **e** (ɔnal) *a*, regional, district (*att.*); toll (*att.*; *Teleph.*).

régir (reʒiːr) *v.t*, to govern, rule, manage. **régisseur** (ʒisœːr) *m*, manager, agent (*estate*), steward, bailiff (*farm*); stage manager.

registre (rəʒistr) *m*, register, book; record, note; damper (*flue*). *~ des délibérations*, minute book.

règle (rɛgl) *f*, rule; ruler; order. *~ à calcul*, slide rule. **réglé** (regle) *p.a*, regular, steady; set, stated; faint-ruled (*paper*). **règlement** (rɛgləmɑ̃) *m*, settlement, adjustment; regulation, rule. **réglementaire** (tɛːr) *a*, regulation (*att.*), prescribed. **réglementer** (te) *v.t*, to regulate. **régler** (regle) *v.t*, to rule; regulate; order; settle, adjust; set, time.

réglisse (regliːs) *f*, liquorice.

règne (rɛɲ) *m*, reign; sway; kingdom (*Nat. Hist.*). **régner** (ɲe) *v.i*, to reign, rule; obtain; prevail, be prevalent; extend, run.

regorger (rəgɔrʒe) *v.i. & t*, to overflow, brim, abound, teem; burst.

regrattier, **ère** (rəgratje, ɛ:r) *n*, huckster.

regret (rəgrɛ) *m*, regret. **â ~**, reluctantly. **regrettable** (tabl) *a*, regrettable, unfortunate. **le (la) regretté, e . . .** (te), the [late] lamented . . . **regretter** (te) *v.t*, to regret, be sorry (for); miss.

régulariser (regylarize) *v.t*, to regularize. **régularité** (te) *f*, regularity. **régulateur** (tœːr) *m*, regulator, governor. **régulier, ère†** (lje, ɛːr) *a*, regular; orderly, business-like.

réhabiliter (reabilite) *v.t*, to rehabilitate, reinstate; discharge (*bankrupt*).

rehausser (rɔose) *v.t*, to raise; enhance; heighten. **rehauts** (o) *m.pl*, high lights (*Art*).

réimporter (reɛ̃pɔrte) *v.t*, to reimport.

réimposer (reɛ̃poze) *v.t*, to reimpose.

réimpression (reɛ̃presjɔ̃) *f*, reprint[ing]. **réimprimer** (prime) *v.t*, to reprint.

Reims (rɛ̃s) *m*, Rheims.

rein (rɛ̃) *m*, kidney; (*pl.*) loins, back.

reine (rɛn) *f*, queen (*pers. & Chess*); belle (*of ball*). **~-claude** (klo:d), greengage. **~ des abeilles**, queen bee. **~-des-prés**, meadowsweet. **~-marguerite**, China aster.

reinette (rɛnɛt) *f*, pippin, rennet. **~ grise**, russet (*apple*).

réintégrer (reɛ̃tegre) *v.t*, to reinstate.

réitérer (reitere) *v.t*, to reiterate, repeat.

rejaillir (rɔʒajiːr) *v.i*, to gush out; reflect, redound.

rejet (rɔʒɛ) *m*, throwing out; rejection; shoot (*Hort.*). **rejeter** (ʒ[ə]te) *v.t*, to throw back; to out; t. up; reject, set aside, negative; dismiss; disallow. **rejeton** (ʒtɔ̃) *m*, shoot, cane (*raspberry*); scion, offspring.

rejoindre (rɔʒwɛ̃:dr) *v.t. & abs. ir*, to re-join; rejoin (*one's regiment, &c*).

rejouer (rɔʒwe) *v.t. & i*, to replay; play again.

réjoui, e (reʒwi) *p.a*, jolly, joyous, jovial, merry. **réjouir** (ʒwiːr) *v.t. & se ~**, to rejoice, gladden, cheer; be glad; enjoy oneself. **réjouissance** (ʒwisɑ̃:s) *f*, rejoicing; makeweight (*butcher's*).

relâche (rɔlɑ:ʃ) *m*, respite, intermission, breathing space, relaxation; no performance, closed (*Theat.*); (*f.*) call[ing] (*Naut.*); port of call. **relâcher** (lɑʃe) *v.t. & i*, to loosen, slacken; relax; release; put in (*Naut.*).

relais (rɔlɛ) *m*, relay; shift; stage, posting house; sand flats.

relancer (rɔlɑ̃se) *v.t*, to throw back; start again (*Hunt.*); return (*ball, Ten.*); badger. **relanceur, euse** (sœːr, øːz) *n*, striker[-out], receiver (*Ten.*).

relaps, e (rɔlaps) *n*, apostate, backslider.

rélargir (relarʒiːr) *v.t*, to widen; let out.

relater (rɔlate) *v.t*, to relate, state. **relatif, ive†** (tif, iːv) *a*, relative, relating. **relation** (sjɔ̃) *f*, relation, connection, intercourse; acquaintance; narrative.

relaxer (rɔlakse) *v.t*, to relax; release.

reléguer (rɔlege) *v.t*, to relegate, consign; intern (*prisoner in Fr. colony*).

relent (rɔlɑ̃) *m*, bad odour.

relevailles (rɔlva:j) *f.pl*, churching. **relève** (lɛ:v) *f*, relief (*from turn of duty*). **relevé, e** (lve) *p.a*, high, exalted, lofty; strong (*flavour*). ¶ *m*, statement, abstract, return. **~ de potage**, course after soup. ¶ *f*, afternoon. **relever** (lve) *v.t*, to raise, lift [up]; pick up; turn up; take up; restore; make out (*account*); take, read (*meter*); point out, note; set off, enhance, exalt; season; relieve; release; plot (*ground*); (*v.i.*) to depend, rest; recover. **~ le menton â**, to chuck under the chin.

relief (rɔljɛf) *m*, relief, relievo.

relier (rɔlje) *v.t*, to [re]tie; unite; bind (*book*); [re]hoop (*cask*). **relieur, euse** (jœːr, øːz) *n*, [book]binder.

religieux, euse† (rɔliʒjø, øːz) *a*, religious; sacred (*song, &c*); scrupulous. ¶ *m*, monk, friar. ¶ *f*, nun. **religion** (ʒjɔ̃) *f*, religion; vows; bounden duty; sanctity (*oath*).

reliquaire (rɔlikɛːr) *m*, reliquary, shrine.

reliquat (rɔlika) *m*, balance, residue.

relique (rɔlik) *f*, relic.

reliure (rɔljyːr) *f*, [book]binding. **~ amateur**, extra binding. **~ de bibliothèque**, edition b. **~ pleine**, full b., whole b.

relogement (rɔlɔʒmɑ̃) *m*, rehousing.

relouer (rɔlue) *v.t*, to relet; re-rent; sublet.

reluire (rɔlɥiːr) *v.i.ir*, to shine, glitter. **reluisant, e** (lɥizɑ̃, ɑ̃:t) *a*, shining; creditable; brilliant.

reluquer (rɔlyke) *v.t*, to ogle; covet.

remâcher (rɔmɑʃe) *v.t*, to chew again; ruminate on, brood over, chew (*fig.*).

remanier (rɔmanje) *v.t*, to rehandle; relay; recast.

remarquable† (rɔmarkabl) *a*, remarkable; noteworthy; conspicuous. **remarque** (mark) *f*, remark, note. **remarquer** (ke) *v.t*, to re-mark; remark, observe, notice, note, mark.

remballer (rɑ̃bale) *v.t*, to repack.

rembarquer (rɑ̃barke) *v.t. & i*, to re-embark; reship.

remblai (rɑ̃blɛ) *m*, filling up (*with earth*); embankment. **remblayer** (je) *v.t*, to fill [up], [em]bank.

remboîter (rɑ̃bwate) *v.t*, to [re]set; recase.

rembourrer (rɑ̃bure) *v.t*, to stuff, pad, upholster.

rembourser (rɑ̃burse) *v.t*, to repay, pay off, return, refund; redeem; reimburse.

rembrunir (rɑ̃bryni:r) *v.t*, to darken, gloom.

rembucher (se) (rɑ̃byʃe) *v.pr*, to return to cover[t].

remède (rɔmɛd) *m*, remedy, cure. **~ de charlatan**, nostrum. **remédier à** (medje), to remedy, cure.

remémorer (se) (rɔmemɔre) *v.pr*, to remember.

remerciement (rəmɛrsimã) *m. oft. pl,* thanks. **remercier** (sje) *v.t,* to thank; dismiss.

réméré (remere) *m,* repurchase.

remettre (rəmɛtr) *v.t. & abs. ir,* to put back [again]; put on again; restore; remit, send [in]; hand [over]; deliver; commend; put off, postpone; pardon; entrust; remember; calm; set (*bone*). [*coup*] à ~, let (*Ten.*).

remeubler (rəmœble) *v.t,* to refurnish.

réminiscence (reminisã:s) *f,* reminiscence.

remise (rəmi:z) *f,* putting back; restoration; remittance; remission; delivery; postponement; allowance, discount; commission; coach house; shed; cover (*game*). ~ [*sur marchandises*], [trade] discount. *une voiture de* ~ *ou un* ~, a hired carriage. **remiser** (mize) *v.t,* to put up (*vehicle*). **remisier** (zje) *m,* half-commission man.

rémission (remisjɔ̃) *f,* remission.

remmaillage (rãmaja:ʒ) *m,* grafting (*Knit.*).

remmancher (rãmãʃe) *v.t,.* to-rehandle; resume.

remmener (rãmne) *v.t,* to take back.

remontant (rəmɔ̃tã) *m,* stimulant, tonic, pick-me-up. **remonte** (mɔ̃:t) *f,* remount[ing] (*Mil.*). **remonter** (mɔ̃te) *v.i. & t,* to [re]ascend; remount; go back; raise; rise; wind [up] (*spring*); restock, replenish; restage; veer (*wind*). **remontoir** (twa:r) *m,* winder, key; keyless watch. ~ *à heures sautantes,* jumping-hour watch.

remontrance (rəmɔ̃trã:s) *f,* remonstrance, expostulation. **remontrer** (tre) *v.t. & abs,* to show again; point out; remonstrate.

remords (rəmɔ:r) *m,* remorse.

remorque (rəmɔrk) *f,* tow[ing]; trailer. **remorquer** (ke) *v.t,* to tow, haul. **remorqueur** (kœ:r) *m,* tug [boat].

rémouleur (remulœ:r) *m,* [knife] grinder.

remous (rəmu) *m,* eddy, [back]wash, swirl.

rempart (rãpa:r) *m,* rampart; bulwark (*fig.*).

remplaçant, e (rãplasã, ã:t) *n,* substitute; locum tenens. **remplacer** (se) *v.t,* to replace; take the place of; supersede.

rempli (rãpli) *m,* tuck. **remplier** (e) *v.t,* to tuck; turn over (*paper wrapper*—*Bookb.*).

remplir (rãpli:r) *v.t,* to fill up, refill, replenish; fill; swamp (*boat*); fulfil, comply with; perform.

remplumer (se) (rãplyme) *v.pr,* to get new feathers; put on flesh again; pick up again.

remporter (rãpɔrte) *v.t,* to take away; carry off, win, gain.

rempoter (rãpɔte) *v.t,* to repot.

remuant, e (rəmɥã, ã:t) *a,* restless. **remue-ménage** (mymena:ʒ) *m,* bustle, stir, upset. **remuement** (mã) *m,* moving, removal; bustle, stir. **remuer** (mɥe) *v.t. & i,* to move; stir [up], rake up; shake, wag, swish; remove, shift.

rémunérateur, trice (remyneratœ:r, trice) *a,* remunerative, paying. ¶ *m,* rewarder. **rémunération** (sjɔ̃) *f,* remuneration, pay-

ment; consideration; return. **rémunérer** (re) *v.t,* to remunerate, pay for, reward.

renâcler (rənɑkle) *v.i,* to snort; hang back.

renaissance (rənɛsã:s) *f,* rebirth; revival; renaissance. **renaître** (nɛ:tr) *v.i.ir,* to be born again; spring up again; revive.

renard (rəna:r) *m,* fox. ~ *argenté,* silver f. **renarde** (nard) *f,* vixen. **renardeau** (do) *m,* fox cub. **renardière** (djɛ:r) *f,* fox earth, fox's hole.

rencaisser (rãkɛse) *v.t,* to re-box; recash.

renchéri, e (rãʃeri) *n,* fastidious person. **renchérir** (ri:r) *v.i,* to get dearer, go up. ~ *sur,* to outbid; outdo, improve on.

rencogner (rãkɔɲe) *v.t,* to drive into a corner.

rencontre (rãkɔ̃:tr) *f,* meeting, encounter; occurrence; occasion; collision, clash; duel. ~ *de front,* head-on collision. **rencontrer** (kɔ̃tre) *v.t,* to meet, m. with, encounter, come across, strike; run into, collide with.

rendement (rãdmã) *m,* yield, return; output, capacity; efficiency. **rendez-vous** (devu) *m,* appointment; place of meeting; resort; haunt.

rendormir (rãdɔrmi:r) *v.t.ir,* to send to sleep again. **se** ~, to go to sleep again.

rendre (rã:dr) *v.t,* to give back, return; restore; give up; render; give; pay; dispense; repay; yield; deliver; surrender; bring up (*food*); make; drive (*one mad*). **se** ~, to make oneself; go; surrender, yield. **rendu** (rãdy) *m,* rendering (*Art*); return (*article, goods*—*Com.*).

rêne (rɛn) *f,* rein.

renégat, e (rənega, at) *n,* renegade, turncoat.

renfermer (rãfɛrme) *m,* musty smell. **renfermer** (me) *v.t,* to shut up; confine; comprise, contain; restrict.

renflement (rãfləmã) *m,* swell[ing]; bulge, boss. **renfler** (fle) *v.i,* to swell.

renflouer (rãflue) *v.t,* to refloat (*ship*).

renfoncement (rãfɔ̃smã) *m,* driving in; recess; inden[ta]tion (*Typ.*); punch (*blow*). **renfoncer** (se) *v.t,* to drive in; knock in; indent.

renforcé, e (rãfɔrse) *p.a,* stout, strong; out & out; arrant. **renforcer (se)** *v.t,* to reinforce; strengthen, brace; intensify (*Phot.*). **renfort** (fɔ:r) *m,* reinforcement (*Mil.*). *à grand* ~ *de,* with plenty of.

renfrogner (se) (rãfrɔɲe) *v.pr,* to frown, scowl, look sullen.

rengager (rãgaʒe) *v.t,* to re-engage; (*v.i.*) to re-enlist.

rengaine (rãgɛ:n) *f,* tag, story; catchword; hackneyed refrain.

rengainer (rãgene) *v.t,* to sheathe; suppress.

rengorger (se) (rãgɔrʒe) *v.pr,* to bridle [up]; strut, swagger.

renier (rənje) *v.t,* to disown, deny.

renifler (rənifle) *v.i. & t,* to sniff; snuffle; snort.

renne (rɛn) *m,* reindeer.

renom (rənɔ̃) *m,* renown, fame; repute. **renommé, e** (nɔme) *p.a,* renowned, famed, noted. ¶ *f*, fame, renown, name; rumour, report. **renommer** (me) *v.t*, to reappoint.

renonce (rənɔ:s) (*Cards*) *f*, renounce; revoke. **renoncement** (nɔ̃smɑ̃) *m*, renunciation, self-denial. **renoncer** (se) *v.i. & t. & ~ à*, to renounce, give up, forgo; disown, deny; revoke (*Cards*). **renonciation** (sjasjɔ̃) *f*, renunciation, disclaimer.

renoncule (rənɔkyl) *f*, ranunculus, buttercup, crowfoot. ~ *bulbeuse*, kingcup.

renouer (rənwe) *v.t*, to retie; renew, resume.

renouveau (rənuvo) *m*, return of spring. **renouveler** (vle) *v.t*, to renew, renovate; change; revive. **rénover** (renɔve) *v.t*, to renovate, restore.

renseignement (rɑ̃sɛɲmɑ̃) *m. oft. pl*, information, intelligence, particular; inquiry. **renseigner** (ɲe) *v.t*, to inform. **se ~**, to inquire.

rente (rɑ̃:t) *f*, income; annuity; pension; interest; stock; rente. **renter** (rɑ̃te) *v.t*, to endow. **rentier, ère** (tje, ɛ:r) *n*, stockholder, fundholder, investor; annuitant; person of independent means.

rentraire (rɑ̃trɛ:r) *v.t.ir*, to fine-draw.

rentrant, e (rɑ̃trɑ̃, ɑ̃:t) *a*, re-entrant; sunk. **rentré, e** (tre) *p.a*, suppressed (*rage, &c*). ¶ *f*, return; re-entry; reappearance; re-opening; ingathering; collection; receipt. ~ *en touche*, throw-in (*Foot.*). **rentrer** (tre) *v.i*, to re-enter; return; reappear; reopen; (*v.t.*) to bring in; house; indent (*Typ.*). ~ *dans*, to recover; re-enter; return to, rejoin. **rentrez!** all in! (*Sch.*).

renverse (à la) (rɑ̃vɛrs) *ad*, backwards, on one's back. **renverser** (se) *v.t*, to throw down, overthrow, upset; invert, reverse; astound. *se ~ sur sa chaise*, to lean (*or* lie) back (*or* recline) in one's chair.

renvoi (rɑ̃vwa) *m*, return; dismissal; postponement; reference; caret; repeat (*Mus.*); alteration; eructation; countershaft. **renvoyer** (je) *v.t*, to send back, return; dismiss; put off, adjourn; refer. ~ *à une autre audience*, to remand.

réorganiser (reorganize) *v.t*, to reorganize.

réouverture (reuvɛrty:r) *f*, reopening.

repaire (rəpɛ:r) *m*, den, lair; nest; haunt.

repaître (rəpɛ:tr) *v.t.ir*, to feed, feast.

répandre (repɑ̃:dr) *v.t*, to pour out, spill, shed; spread, diffuse, waft, scatter, sprinkle. **répandu, e** (pɑ̃dy) *p.a*, widespread; well known.

réparable (reparabl) *a*, reparable, repairable. **reparaître** (rəparɛ:tr) *v.i.ir*, to reappear. **réparateur, trice** (reparatœ:r, tris) *n*, repairer, mender. **réparation** (sjɔ̃) *f*, repair; reparation; amends, atonement, redress. **réparer** (re) *v.t*, to repair, mend; retrieve; make amends for; make up for; redress, rectify.

repartie (rəparti) *f*, repartee, retort, rejoinder. **repartir** (ti:r) *v.i.ir*, to retort; set out again.

répartir (reparti:r) *v.t*, to distribute, apportion, allot; assess; spread. **répartition** (tisjɔ̃) *f*, distribution, &c.

repas (rəpa) *m*, meal, repast, spread. ~ *de corps*, regimental dinner. ~ *de noce*, wedding breakfast.

repasser (rəpɑse) *v.i. & t*, to repass; recross; come again; re-examine, con, go over, think over; grind, sharpen; set; strop; iron (*linen, &c*). **repasseur** (sœ:r) *m*, grinder; strop (*safety blade*). **repasseuse** (sø:z) *f*, ironer, laundress.

repêcher (rəpeʃe) *v.t*, to fish up, f. out; give a second chance to (*exam*).

repentir (rəpɑ̃ti:r) *m*, repentance. **se ~**, *v.pr.ir*, to repent. **se ~ de**, to repent (*of*), to rue, be sorry for.

repercer (rəpɛrse) *v.t*, to retap (*cask*); pierce (*metal*).

répercussion (repɛrkysjɔ̃) *f*, repercussion. **répercuter** (te) *v.t*, to reverberate.

repère (rəpɛ:r) *m*, reference mark, datum point; bench mark. **repérer** (pere) *v.t*, to mark; locate, spot.

répertoire (repɛrtwa:r) *m*, index, list, register; directory; repertory; repository (*fig.*). ~ *à onglets*, thumb index. **répertorier** (tərje) *v.t*, to index.

répéter (repete) *v.t. & abs*, to repeat; rehearse; claim back (*Law*). **répétiteur, trice** (titœ:r, tris) *n*, assistant teacher; tutor, coach. **répétition** (sjɔ̃) *f*, repetition, recurrence; reproduction, replica, duplicate; rehearsal; private lesson; claiming back. ~ *générale*, dress rehearsal.

repeupler (rəpœple) *v.t*, to repeople; restock; replant.

repiquer (rəpike) *v.t*, to prick again; restitch; plant out.

replacer (rəplase) *v.t*, to replace; reinvest.

replanter (rəplɑ̃te) *v.t*, to replant.

replâtrer (rəplɑtre) *v.t*, to replaster; patch up.

replet, ète (rəplɛ, ɛt) *a*, stout (*pers.*). **réplétion** (replesjɔ̃) *f*, repletion, corpulence.

repli (rəpli) *m*, fold, crease; coil (*snake*); recess (*heart*); falling back (*Mil.*). **replier** (plie) *v.t*, to fold up. **se ~**, to fold up; coil up; fall back.

réplique (replik) *f*, retort, rejoinder, answer; cue (*Theat.*); replica. **répliquer** (ke) *v.t*, to retort, rejoin, answer [back].

répondant, e (repɔ̃dɑ̃, ɑ̃:t) *n*, respondent; surety; sponsor; bail[sman]. **répondre** (pɔ̃:dr) *v.t. & i*, to answer, reply, respond; say in reply; write back (*in reply*); make the responses at; correspond; agree; answer for, guarantee. **répons** (pɔ̃) *m*, response (*Lit.*). **réponse** (pɔ̃:s) *f*, answer, reply; response.

report (rəpo:r) *m*, carry forward; c. over; contango, continuation. **reportage** (pɔrta:ʒ) *m*, reporting; report (*news*). **reporter** (te) *v.t*, to carry forward; c. over; bring

forward; contango, continue (*Stk Ex.*).
reporter (tœːr) *m*, reporter (*news*).

repos (rəpo) *m*, rest, repose; quiet; ease;
peace; pause (*Mus., Pros.*); half-cock (*gun*);
resting place, seat; landing (*stairs*). *de
tout* ~, safe, reliable. **reposant, e** (zɑ̃,
ɑ̃ːt) *a*, restful. **reposé, e** (ze) *p.a*, refreshed;
fresh. ¶ *f*, lair. **reposer** (ze) *v.t*, to replace; re-lay; rest; refresh; order (*arms*);
(*v.i.*) to lie; rest; sleep; be based. **se** ~,
to rest, lie down, recline; rely.

repoussant, e (rəpusɑ̃, ɑ̃ːt) *a*, repulsive,
repellent. **repoussé, e** (se) *p.a*, repoussé;
embossed. **repoussement** (smɑ̃) *m*, rejection; recoil, kick. **repousser** (se) *v.t*,
to push back; repel, repulse, reject; deny;
spurn; (*v.i.*) to recoil; sprout again, grow
again. ~ *avec mépris*, to scout, pooh-
pooh. **repoussoir** (swaːr) *m*, punch (*tool*);
set-off, foil.

répréhensible (repreɑ̃sibl) *a*, reprehensible.

reprendre (rəprɑ̃ːdr) *v.t. & i. ir*, to retake,
recapture; take up [again]; take back;
recover; resume; regain; pick up [again];
reprove, find fault with; reply; rejoin; take
root again; set again; freeze again. ~ *de
volée*, to volley (*Ten.*). ~ *sous œuvre*, to
underpin; reconstruct (*fig.*).

représaille (rəprezaːj) *f*. *oft. pl*, reprisal,
retaliation.

représentant, e (rəprezɑ̃tɑ̃, ɑ̃ːt) *n*, representative; agent; member (*M.P.*). **représentatif, ive** (tatif, iːv) *a*, representative.
représentation (sjɔ̃) *f*, representation; production; [purchase] consideration; performance (*Theat., &c*). ~ *à bénéfice*,
benefit performance. **représenter** (te) *v.t*,
to present again; represent; produce, show;
perform, act; personate; picture; (*abs.*) to
bear oneself; (*abs.*) to entertain.

répression (represjɔ̃) *f*, repression.

réprimande (reprimɑ̃ːd) *f*, reprimand, reproof, rebuke. **réprimander** (mɑ̃de) *v.t*,
to reprimand, reprove, rebuke.

réprimer (reprime) *v.t*, to repress, curb; put
down, quell.

repris de justice (rəpri) *m*, habitual criminal,
old offender, gaol bird, jail bird. **reprisage** (zaːʒ) *m*, darning, mending (*stockings, &c*). **reprise** (priːz) *f*, retaking, recapture; recovery; rally; resumption; renewal; revival; repetition; occasion, time;
premium (*Letting*); round (*Box.*); bout
(*Fenc.*); darn[ing]; repair. ~ *perdue*,
invisible mending. **repriser** (prize) *v.t*,
to darn, mend.

réprobation (reprɔbasjɔ̃) *f*, reprobation.

reproche (rəprɔʃ) *m*, reproach, blame. **reprocher** (ʃe) *v.t*, to reproach, blame, upbraid; taunt, twit. ~ *à*, to grudge.

reproduction (rɔprɔdyksjɔ̃) *f*, reproduction.
reproduire (dɥiːr) *v.t.ir*, to reproduce.
se ~, to recur; reproduce, breed.

réprouvé, e (repruve) *n*, outcast; reprobate.

réprouver (ve) *v.t*, to reprobate; reject,
disapprove of, deprecate.

reps (rɛps) *m*, rep[p], reps.

reptation (rɛptasjɔ̃) *f*, creeping, crawling.
reptile (til) *m*, reptile.

républicain, e (repyblikɛ̃, ɛn) *a. & n*, republi-
can. **république** (lik) *f*, republic; commonwealth; community.

répudier (repydje) *v.t*, to repudiate; renounce.

répugnance (repynɑ̃ːs) *f*, repugnance; reluctance. **répugnant, e** (nɑ̃, ɑ̃ːt) *a*, repugnant.
répugner (ɲe) *v.i*, to feel repugnance, feel
lo[a]th; be repugnant.

répulsif, ive (repylsif, iːv) *a*, repulsive, repellent. **répulsion** (sjɔ̃) *f*, repulsion.

réputation (repytasjɔ̃) *f*, reputation, repute;
name; character. **réputé, e** (te) *p.a*, well
known; of repute. **réputer** (te) *v.t*, to
repute, deem, hold.

requérant, e (rəkerɑ̃, ɑ̃ːt) *n*, applicant, plaintiff.
requérir (riːr) *v.t.ir*, to require; summon.
requête (kɛːt) *f*, request, suit, petition.

requiem (rekɥiɛm) *m*, requiem.

requin (rəkɛ̃) *m*, shark (*fish & preying pers.*).
requinquer (se) (rəkɛ̃ke) *v.pr*, to smarten
oneself up.

réquisition (rekizisjɔ̃) *f*, requisition, levy.
réquisitionner (ɔne) *v.t*, to requisition,
commandeer, impress. **réquisitoire** (twaːr)
m, charge, indictment.

rescapé, e (reskape) *n*, survivor, saved
[person].

rescision (ressizjɔ̃) *f*, rescission.

rescousse (à la) (reskus) *f*, to the rescue.

rescrit (reskri) *m*, rescript.

réseau (rezo) *m*, netting; network; system;
area; plexus; tracery. ~ *de fils de fer*,
wire entanglement (*Mil.*).

réséda (rezeda) *m*, reseda, mignonette.

réservation (rezervasjɔ̃) *f*, reservation. **réserve** (zɛrv) *f*, reservation; booking (*seats*);
reserve; store; exception, qualification;
preserve (*Hunt.*); sanctuary (*animals*).
sous ~ *de*, subject to. *sous* ~ *que*, on
condition that. **réservé, e** (ve) *a*, reserved; cautious, guarded; stand-offish;
shy; coy. **réserviste** (vist) *m*, reservist.
réservoir (vwaːr) *m*, reservoir, tank,
cistern, well.

résidence (rezidɑ̃ːs) *f*, residence, dwelling,
abode. **résident, e** (dɑ̃, ɑ̃ːt) *n. & a*,
resident (*diplomatic*); settler (*colony*).
résider (de) *v.i*, to reside, dwell, live; lie,
rest. **résidu** (dy) *m*, residue.

résignation (rezinasjɔ̃) *f*, resignation; submissiveness. **résigner** (ɲe) *v.t*, to resign.

résiliation (reziljɛ) *v.t*, to cancel, annul.

résille (reziːj) *f*, hair net; cames.

résine (rezin) *f*, resin, rosin. **résineux, euse**
(nø, øːz) *a*, resinous.

résistance (rezistɑ̃ːs) *f*, resistance; opposition;
strength; toughness; endurance, stamina.
résistant, e (tɑ̃, ɑ̃ːt) *a*, resistant, strong,
tough. **résister à** (te) *v.t*, to resist, withstand.

résolut†, e (rezɔly) *p.a*, resolute, determined. **résolution** (sjɔ̃) *f*, resolution; solution; cancellation; resolve.

résonance (rezonɑ̃:s) *f*, resonance. **résonnant, e** (nɑ̃, ɑ̃:t) *a*, resonant. **résonner** (ne) *v.i*, to resound; ring; re-echo; twang.

résoudre (rezu:dr) *v.t.ir*, to resolve, solve; annul.

respect (rɛspɛ) *m*, respect, regard, deference. **respectable** (pɛktabl) *a*, respectable. **respecter** (te) *v.t*, to respect; spare. **respectif, ive†** (tif, i:v) *a*, respective, several. **respectueux, euse†** (tɥø, ø:z) *a*, respectful, dutiful. *~ des lois*, law-abiding.

respiration (rɛspirasjɔ̃) *f*, respiration, breathing. **respirer** (re) *v.i. & t*, to breathe; respire; inhale; exhale.

resplendir (rɛsplɑ̃di:r) *v.i*, to be resplendent, shine, glitter. **resplendissant, e** (disɑ̃, ɑ̃:t) *a*, resplendent; aglow; glorious.

responsabilité (rɛspɔ̃sabilite) *f*, responsibility; liability; care. **responsable** (bl) *a*, responsible, answerable, liable. **responsif, ive** (sif, i:v) *a*, in reply (*Law*).

resquille (rɛski:j) *f*, [gate] crashing. **resquilleur, euse** (kijœ:r, ø:z) *n*, [gate] crasher.

ressac (rəsak) *m*, undertow; surf.

ressaisir (rəsɛzi:r) *v.t*, to recover.

ressasser (rəsase) *v.t*, to resift; repeat.

ressaut (rəso) *m*, projection, set-off.

ressemblance (rəsɑ̃blɑ̃:s) *f*, resemblance, likeness. **ressemblant, e** (blɑ̃, ɑ̃:t) *a*, [a]like. **ressembler à** (ble), to resemble, be like, look like.

ressemeler (rəsəmle) *v.t*, to resole.

ressentiment (rəsɑ̃timɑ̃) *m*, resentment. **ressentir** (ti:r) *v.t.ir*, to feel; resent. **se ~**, to feel.

resserre (rəsɛ:r) *f*, store [room]. **resserrer** (sere) *v.t*, to tighten; close up; bind; put away [again]; contract, narrow, confine, restrict; condense.

ressort (rəso:r) *m*, spring; elasticity; buoyancy; incentive; province; purview; resort, appeal. *~ à boudin*, spiral spring. *à ~*, spring (*balance, &c*); clockwork (*train, &c*). **ressortir** (sorti:r) *v.i*, to be under the jurisdiction of; (*v.i.ir*.) to go out again; stand out (*in relief*); result, appear.

ressource (rəsurs) *f*, resource; expedient, shift, resort.

ressouvenir (rəsuvni:r) *m*, remembrance, memory. **se ~**, *v.pr.ir*, to remember.

ressuer (rəsɥe) *v.i*, to sweat (*walls, &c*).

ressusciter (rəsysite) *v.t*, to resuscitate, revive; raise (*the dead*).

restant, e (rɛstɑ̃, ɑ̃:t) *a*, remaining, left. **restaurant, e** (rɛstɔrɑ̃, ɑ̃:t) *a*, restorative. ¶ *m*, restorative; restaurant, eating house. **restaurateur, trice** (ratœ:r, tris) *n*, restorer; restaurant keeper, caterer. **restauration** (sjɔ̃) *f*, restoration. **restaurer** (re) *v.t*, to restore, re-establish; refresh.

reste (rɛst) *m*, rest, remainder, remains; leavings, remnant. *du ~*, besides, moreover. **rester** (te) *v.i*, to remain, be left; stay, stop, stand, sit, keep, stick; last; live.

restituer (rɛstitɥe) *v.t*, to restore, return. **restitution** (tysjɔ̃) *f*, restitution; restoration. *~ anonyme*, conscience money.

restreindre (rɛstrɛ̃:dr) *v.t.ir*, to restrict, limit. **restriction** (triksjɔ̃) *f*, restriction; reservation.

résultat (rezylta) *m*, result, outcome. **résulter** (te) *v.i*, to result, follow, ensue.

résumé (rezyme) *m*, summary, abstract. *~ des débats*, summing up. **résumer** (me) *v.t*, to summarize; sum up.

résurrection (rezyrɛksjɔ̃) *f*, resurrection.

retable (rətabl) *m*, reredos, altar piece. **rétablir** (retabli:r) *v.t*, to re-establish, restore; retrieve; reinstate.

retaille (rəta:j) *f*, cutting, paring (*snip, bit*). **retaper** (rətape) *v.t*, to do up; recast.

retard (rata:r) *m*, delay. *en ~*, late, behind[hand]; overdue; in arrears; slow (*clock*). **retardataire** (tardatɛ:r) *a*, late, in arrears; overstaying pass (*Mil.*). ¶ *n*, late-comer. **retarder** (de) *v.t*, to retard, delay; hinder; put off; put back (*clock*); (*v.i.*) be slow; lag.

retâter (rətate) *v.t. & i*, to touch again; try again.

retenir (rətni:r) *v.t.ir*, to keep back, retain, withhold, stop; keep; engage; reserve, book, bespeak; detain; hold; h. back, check, restrain; remember; carry (*Arith.*). **se ~**, to refrain; catch hold. **rétention** (retɑ̃sjɔ̃) *f*, retention.

retentir (rətɑ̃ti:r) *v.i*, to [re]sound, echo, ring. **retenu, e** (rətny) *a*, cautious, discreet. ¶ *f*, stoppage (*on pay, &c*); carry (*Arith.*); reserve, discretion. *mettre en ~*, to keep in (*Sch.*).

réticence (retisɑ̃:s) *f*, reticence; concealment.

réticule (retikyl) *m*, reticule; reticle.

rétif, ive (retif, i:v) *a*, a restive; stubborn.

rétine (retin) *f*, retina.

retiré, e (rətire) *p.a*, solitary, secluded. **retirer** (re) *v.t*, to redraw; draw back; withdraw; retire (*bill*); take out; remove; extract; draw, get, derive; recall. **se ~**, to retire, withdraw; stand down; recede; shrink.

retombée (rətɔ̃be) *f*, spring[ing] (*arch.*). **retomber** (be) *v.i*, to fall down [again]; relapse; fall [back]; devolve; hang down.

rétorquer (retɔrke) *v.t*, to retort.

retors, e (rətɔ:r, ɔrs) *a*, twisted; crafty.

retouche (rətuʃ) *f*, retouch[ing]. **retoucher** (ʃe) *v.t. & ~ à*, to retouch, touch up.

retour (rətu:r) *m*, turn; return; recurrence; reversion; reversal; decline (*life*), wane; ruse. *~ de flamme*, back fire. *~ de manivelle*, back fire [kick]. **retourne** (turn) *f*, turn-up (*card*), trumps. **retournement** (nəmɑ̃) *m*, turning, reversal.

~ de bras, hammer lock (*Wrestling*). **retourner** (ne) *v.i. & t.*, to return; revert; turn (*coat, &c*); t. over; t. up; mix (*salad*). se ~, to turn [round], veer (*opinion*).

retracer (rətrase) *v.t*, to retrace; recall. se ~, to recur.

rétracter (retrakte) *v.t*, to retract, recant.

retrait, e (rətrɛ, ɛt) *p.a*, shrunken. ¶ *m*, withdrawal; deprivation; shrinkage; recess. ¶ *f*, retreat; tattoo; withdrawal; retirement; superannuation; pension, retired pay; shelter; seclusion; shrinkage; offset (*Arch.*). ~ aux flambeaux, torchlight tattoo. **retraité, e** (te) *a*, pensioned off, superannuated. [*officier*] *retraité*, officer on the retired list.

retrancher (rətrɑ̃ʃe) *v.t*, to cut off; c. out; take away; deduct; subtract; entrench.

rétrécir (retresi:r) *v.t. & i*, to narrow; shrink.

retremper (rətrɑ̃pe) *v.t*, to retemper; brace.

rétribuer (retribɥe) *v.t*, to remunerate, pay. **rétribution** (bysjɔ̃) *f*, remuneration, salary, reward.

rétroactif, ive (retroaktif, iːv) *a*, retroactive, retrospective (*law*).

rétrograde (retrograd) *a*, retrograde, backward. **rétrograder** (de) *v.i*, to go back[wards] (*Mil.*).

rétrospectif, ive† (retrɔspɛktif, iːv) *a*, retrospective.

retrousser (rətruse) *v.t*, to turn up; tuck up; curl (*lip*).

retrouver (rətruve) *v.t*, to find [again], recover; recognize.

rets (rɛ) *m*, net; (*pl.*) toils (*fig.*).

réunion (reynjɔ̃) *f*, [re]union; assembly, gathering, function, meeting. **réunir** (niːr) *v.t*, to [re]unite; join; combine; lump. se ~, to meet, for[e]gather.

réussi, e (reysi) *p.a*, successful. **réussir** (siːr) *v.i*, to succeed; prosper. **réussite** (sit) *f*, success; patience (*Cards*).

revaloir (rəvalwaːr) *v.t.ir*, to pay (*someone*) out, be even with (*someone*).

revanche (rəvɑ̃:ʃ) *f*, revenge; return; requital, return match.

rêvasser (rɛvase) *v.i*, to have troubled dreams; muse. **rêve** (rɛ:v) *m*, dream; day dream.

revêche (rəvɛʃ) *a*, cantankerous.

réveil (revɛ:j) *m*, waking, awakening; revival (*Relig.*); reveille; alarm clock. **réveille-matin** (vɛj) *m*, alarm clock; awakener. **réveiller** (vɛje) *v.t*, to awake[n], wake[n], call, [a]rouse; revive. se ~, to wake [up]; revive. **réveillon** (jɔ̃) *m*, Christmas eve supper.

révélateur, trice (revelatœːr, tris) *n*, revealer; (*m.*) developer (*Phot.*). **révélation** (sjɔ̃) *f*, revelation; disclosure; eye-opener. **révéler** (le) *v.t*, to reveal, disclose.

revenant (rəvnɑ̃) *m*, ghost.

revenant-bon (rəvnɑ̃bɔ̃) *m*, perquisite.

revendeur, euse (rəvɑ̃dœːr, øːz) *n*, second-hand dealer.

revendiquer (rəvɑ̃dike) *v.t*, to claim, assert.

revendre (rəvɑ̃:dr) *v.t*, to resell. avoir à ~, to have enough & to spare.

revenir (rəvniːr) *v.i.ir*, to come [back], return; come again, recur; revert; recover; cost; amount. ~ sur, to retrace; go back on; reconsider; rake up (*past*).

revente (rəvɑ̃:t) *f*, resale.

revenu (rəvny) *m*, revenue, income. **revenue** (ny) *f*, new growth, young wood.

rêver (rɛve) *v.i. & t*, to dream; d. of; muse; ponder.

réverbère (revɛrbɛːr) *m*, street lamp. **réverbérer** (bere) *v.t*, to reverberate.

reverdir (rəvɛrdiːr) *v.i*, to grow green again; grow young again.

révérence (reverɑ̃:s) *f*, reverence; bow; curts[e]y. **révérenciel, le** (rɑ̃sjɛl) *a*, reverential. **révérencieux, euse†** (sjø, øːz) *a*, obsequious; over-polite. **révérend, e** (rɑ̃, ɑ̃:d) *a*, reverend. **révérendissime** (rɑ̃disim) *a*, most reverend; right r. **révérer** (re) *v.t*, to revere, reverence.

rêverie (rɛvri) *f*, reverie, musing; idle fancy.

revers (rəvɛːr) *m*, reverse; back; backhand [stroke, blow]; facing, lapel; turnover [top] (*stocking, &c*).

reverser (rəvɛrse) *v.t*, to pour out again; pour back; transfer.

réversible (revɛrsibl) *a*, reversible; revertible. **réversion** (sjɔ̃) *f*, reversion.

revêtement (rəvɛtmɑ̃) *m*, facing (*wall, &c*); lining; revetment. **revêtir** (tiːr) *v.t.ir*, to clothe, dress; don, put on; assume; provide; face, line; revet.

rêveur, euse (rɛvœːr, øːz) *a*, dreaming; dreamy. ¶ *n*, dreamer.

revigorer (rəvigɔre) *v.t*, to reinvigorate.

revirement (rəvirmɑ̃) *m*, change, turn; turnover; veering.

reviser (rəvize) *v.t*, to revise; review, reconsider; overhaul. **reviseur** (zœːr) *m*, examiner; proof reader. **revision** (zjɔ̃) *f*, revision; review; proof reading; medical examination (*recruits*).

revivifier (rəvivifje) *v.t*, to revivify, revive. **revivre** (viːvr) *v.i.ir*, to live again, come to life again; revive.

révocation (revɔkasjɔ̃) *f*, revocation; repeal; dismissal, removal.

revoici (rəvwasi) *pr*, here . . . again. le ~, here he is again. **revoilà** (la) *pr*, there . . . again.

revoir (rəvwaːr) *v.t.ir*, to see again, meet again; revise; review. au ~! good-bye!

revoler (rəvɔle) *v.i*, to fly again; fly back.

révoltant, e (revɔltɑ̃, ɑ̃:t) *a*, revolting. **révolte** (vɔlt) *f*, revolt, rebellion, mutiny. **révolté, e** (te) *n*, rebel, insurgent, mutineer. **révolter** (te) *v.t*, to cause to revolt; shock. se ~, to revolt, rebel, mutiny.

révolu, e (revɔly) *a*, completed; plus. *il a 10 ans révolus*, he has completed his 10th year, he is 10 plus. **révolution** (sjɔ̃) *f*, revolution; revulsion. **révolutionnaire** (ɔnɛːr) *a. & n*, revolutionary. **révolutionner** (ne) *v.t*, to revolutionize; upset. **revolver** (revɔlvɛːr) *m*, revolver (*gun*); capstan, turret (*lathe*). ~ *à six coups*, six-chambered revolver.

revomir (rəvɔmiːr) *v.t*, to vomit [up, again].

révoquer (revɔke) *v.t*, to revoke, repeal; dismiss; recall.

revue (rəvy) *f*, review, inspection; magazine; revue.

révulsion (revylsjɔ̃) *f*, revulsion (*Med.*).

rez-de-chaussée (redʃose) *m*, ground floor.

rhabiller (rabije) *v.t*, to repair, mend, overhaul; dress again; reclothe.

rhapsodie (rapsɔdi) *f*, rhapsody (*all Eng. senses*).

rhénan, e (renɑ̃, an) *a*, Rhine (*att.*).

rhétorique (retɔrik) *f*, rhetoric.

Rhin (le) (rɛ̃), the Rhine.

rhinocéros (rinɔserɔs) *m*, rhinoceros.

rhododendron (rɔdɔdɛ̃drɔ̃) *m*, rhododendron.

rhombe (rɔ̃ːb) *m*, rhomb[us].

Rhône (le) (roːn), the Rhone.

rhubarbe (rybarb) *f*, rhubarb.

rhum (rɔm) *m*, rum.

rhumatismal, e (rymatismal) *a*, rheumatic. **rhumatisme** (tism) *m*, rheumatism. **rhume** (*de cerveau, de poitrine*) (rym) *m*, cold (in the head, on the chest).

rhythme (ritm) *m*, rhythm. **rhythmique** (mik) *a*, rhythmic(al).

riant, e (riɑ̃, ɑ̃ːt) *a*, smiling; cheerful.

ribambelle (ribɑ̃bɛl) *f*, string, swarm.

ribote (ribɔt) *f*, drunken bout.

ricaner (rikane) *v.i*, to laugh derisively.

richard (riʃaːr) *m*, [rich] upstart. **riche†** (riʃ) *a*, rich, wealthy; copious; valuable; handsome. **richesse** (ʃɛs) *f*, wealth, riches; richness. **richissime** (ʃisim) *a*, rolling in wealth.

ricin (risɛ̃) *m*, castor oil plant.

ricocher (rikɔʃe) *v.i*, to ricochet. **ricochet** (ʃɛ) *m*, ricochet; (*pl.*) duck & drake.

rictus (riktyːs) *m*, grin.

ride (rid) *f*, wrinkle, line; puckering; ripple; lanyard. **rideau** (do) *m*, curtain; [drop] curtain; screen; veil (*fig.*). ~ *de fer*, safety curtain (*Theat.*). **rider** (de) *v.t*, to wrinkle, line; shrivel; ripple, ruffle.

ridicule† (ridikyl) *a*, ridiculous. ¶ *m*, ridiculousness; ridicule. **ridiculiser** (lize) *v.t*, to ridicule.

rien (rjɛ̃) *pn.m*, anything; (*oft. with ne*) nothing. ~ *à*, love all (*Ten.*). ¶ *m*, trifle, mere nothing; (*pl.*) small talk.

rieur, euse (rjœːr, øːz) *n*, laugher; (*att.*) laughing.

riflard (riflaːr) *m*, jack plane; gamp.

rigide† (riʒid) *a*, rigid; stiff; cast-iron (*fig.*). **rigidité** (dite) *f*, rigidity, stiffness. ~ *cadavérique* (kadaverik), rigor mortis.

rigole (rigɔl) *f*, channel, ditch, trench.

rigoler (rigɔle) *v.i*, to go on the spree; guffaw.

rigoureux, euse† (riguro, øːz) *a*, rigorous, severe; strict. **rigueur** (gœːr) *f*, rigour, severity; hardship; strictness.

rimailler (rimaje) *v.i*, to write bad verse. **rimailleur** (jœːr) *m*, rhym[est]er. **rime** (rim) *f*, rhyme. **rimer** (me) *v.t*, to versify; (*v.i.*) to rhyme. **rimeur** (mœːr) *m*, rhym[est]er.

rincer (rɛ̃se) *v.t*, to rinse; r. out. **rinçure** (syːr) *f*, rinsings, slops.

ringard (rɛ̃gaːr) *m*, poker, rake.

ripaille (ripɑːj) *f*, feasting, carousal.

riper (ripe) *v.t. & i*, to scrape; slide; shift (*cargo*).

ripopée (ripɔpe) *f*, slops; mishmash.

riposte (ripɔst) *f*, riposte, counter[stroke]; retort. **riposter** (te) *v.t*, to riposte, &c.

rire (riːr) *m*, laughter; laugh. ~ *moqueur*, sneer. ¶ *v.i.ir*, to laugh, smile; joke. ~ *en dedans*, ~ *en dessous*, to laugh inwardly, snigger.

ris (ri) *m*, reef (*sail*). ~ *de veau*, sweetbread.

risée (rize) *f*, jeer, mockery; laughing stock, butt. **risible†** (zibl) *a*, ludicrous, laughable.

risque (risk) *m*, risk. ~ *de jeu*, rub of the green (*Golf*). **risquer** (ke) *v.t*, to risk, chance. ~ *le paquet*, to chance it. ~ *le paquet*, to chance it.

rissole (risɔl) *f*, rissole. **rissoler** (le) *v.t*, to brown (*Cook.*).

ristourne (risturn) *f*, return, refund.

rite (rit) *m*, rite. **rituel, le** (tɥel) *a. & m*, ritual.

rivage (rivaːʒ) *m*, shore, foreshore, beach, strand; bank, side.

rival, e (rival) *n. & a*, rival. **rivaliser avec** (lize), to rival, vie with, emulate. **rivalité** (te) *f*, rivalry, emulation.

rive (riːv) *f*, bank, side, shore.

river (rive) *v.t*, to rivet, clinch.

riverain, e (rivrɛ̃, ɛn) *a*, riparian, riverside, waterside; wayside.

rivet (rivɛ) *m*, rivet.

rivière (rivjɛːr) *f*, river; rivière (*gems*); single openwork (*Need.*).- ~ *à truites*, trout stream. *la R~ de Gênes*, the Riviera (*French & Italian*).

rixe (riks) *f*, scuffle, brawl, affray.

riz (ri) *m*, rice. **rizière** (zjɛːr) *f*, rice field.

rob (rɔb) *m*, rubber (*Cards*).

robe (rɔb) *f*, dress, gown, frock; robe (*legal dress*); cloth (*clerical dress*); coat (*animal's*); skin (*onion, bean, &c*); wrapper (*cigar*); colour (*wine*). ~ *de chambre*, dressing gown. ~ *de mariée*, wedding dress. ~ *de ville*, walking [out] dress. ~ *de voyage de noces*, going-away dress.

robin (bɛ̃) *m*, lawyer.

robinet (rɔbinɛ) *m*, cock, tap.

robre (rɔbr) *m*, rubber (*Cards*).

robuste† (rɔbyst) *a*, robust, lusty, sturdy, able-bodied; stout; hardy (*plant*). **robustesse** (tɛs) *f*, robustness, strength.

roc (rɔk) m, rock. rocaille (ka:j) f, rockwork. rocailleux, euse (kajø, ø:z) a, rocky, stony; rugged.

rocambole (rɔkɑ̃bɔl) f, Spanish garlic.

roche (rɔʃ) f, rock, stone, boulder. rocher (ʃe) m, rock, crag, cliff. ~ artificiel, rockery. ~ branlant, rocking stone, logan [stone].

rochet (rɔʃɛ) m, ratchet; rochet (surplice).

rocheux, euse (rɔʃø, ø:z) a, rocky.

rococo (rɔkɔko) m. & att, rococo.

roder (rode) v.t, to grind, lap.

rôder (rode) v.i, to prowl, hang about. rôdeur (dœ:r) m, prowler. ~ de grève, beachcomber.

rodomontade (rɔdɔmɔ̃tad) f, bluster.

rogations (rɔgasjɔ̃) f.pl, rogations.

rogatons (rɔgatɔ̃) m.pl, scraps (food); resurrection pie; odds & ends.

Roger-Bontemps (rɔʒebɔ̃tɑ̃) m, happy-go-lucky fellow.

rogne (rɔɲ) f, itch, mange; scab; [bad] temper.

rogner (rɔɲe) v.t, to clip, trim, pare; cut down; cut (edges of book); (v.i.) to grumble, grouse.

rogneux, euse (rɔɲø, ø:z) a, mangy, scabby.

rognon (rɔɲɔ̃) m, kidney (animal); nodule.

rognonner (rɔɲɔne) v.i, to grumble.

rognure (rɔɲy:r) f, clipping, paring (bit).

rogue (rɔg) a, arrogant, haughty.

roi (rwa) m, king; champion. ~ de la nature, lord of creation.

roide (rɛd & rwad) a, roideur (dœ:r) f, roidir (di:r) v.t. Same as raide, &c.

roitelet (rwatlɛ) m, kinglet; wren.

rôle (ro:l) m, roll, list, roster, rota; cause list (Law); calendar (prisoners for trial); part, rôle. ~ travesti, man's part acted by a woman. à tour de ~, in rotation, in turn.

rollier (rɔlje) m, roller (bird).

romain, e (rɔmɛ̃, ɛn) a. & (pers.) n, Roman. romain, m, roman (Typ.). romaine, f, cos, Cos lettuce; steelyard.

roman, e (rɔmɑ̃, an) a. & m, Romance (language); Romanesque (Arch.). ¶ m, novel; fiction; romance. ~ à deux sous, penny dreadful. ~ policier (polisje), detective story. romance (rɔmɑ̃:s) f, song, ballad; sloppiness, maudlin[ism]. ~ sans paroles, song without words. ¶ a, sloppy, maudlin. romancier, ère (mɑ̃sje, ɛːr) n, novelist. romand, e (mɑ̃, ɑ̃:d) a, French-speaking (Switzerland). romanesque† (manɛsk) a, romantic. romantique (mɑ̃tik) a, romantic (literature).

romarin (rɔmarɛ̃) m, rosemary.

rompre (rɔ̃:pr) v.t. & i, to break; b. up; b. in; b. off; snap; rupture; disrupt; burst; interrupt, cut off; upset; cancel. ~ charge, to tranship (Rly). ~ les chiens, to call off the hounds; change the subject. rompu, e (rɔ̃py) p.a, broken; b. in, used, inured. ~ de fatigue, tired out.

romsteck (rɔmstɛk) m, rump steak.

ronce (rɔ̃:s) f, bramble; blackberry bush; barb[ed] wire; annoyance. ~ de noyer, walnut burr. ~-framboise, loganberry.

rond, e (rɔ̃, ɔ̃:d) a, round; rounded; rotund; even (money). ¶ m, round; circle; ring. ~-de-cuir, quill driver, clerk. ~ de serviette, napkin ring. ~ [de table], doily. ¶ f, round; beat; roundelay; round hand; semibreve. à la ~, [a]round. rondelet, te (rɔ̃dlɛ, ɛt) a, roundish. rondelle (dɛl) f, washer; ring (umbrella); disc. rondement (dmɑ̃) ad, roundly, briskly; bluntly. rondeur (dœ:r) f, roundness, rotundity; fullness; frankness. rondin (dɛ̃) m, billet, log. rond-point (rɔ̃pwɛ̃) m, circus (roads meeting).

ronflant, e (rɔ̃flɑ̃, ɑ̃:t) (fig.) a, sonorous, high-sounding. ronfler (fle) v.i, to snore; boom, roar, hum, whir[r], buzz.

ronger (rɔ̃ʒe) v.t, to gnaw, nibble; pick (bone); eat [away, into], corrode; undermine; fret; prey. rongeur, euse (ʒœ:r, ø:z) a, rodent, gnawing; corroding. ¶ m, rodent.

ronron (rɔ̃rɔ̃) m, purr[ing]; hum; drone.

roquer (rɔke) v.t, to castle (Chess); roquet (Croquet).

roquet (rɔkɛ) m, pug [dog]; cur, mongrel.

roquette (rɔkɛt) f, rocket (Bot.).

rosace (rozas) f, rosette; rose; rose window. rosacé, e (se) a, rosaceous. ¶ f.pl, Rosaceæ. rosaire (zɛ:r) m, rosary (beads).

rosbif (rɔzbif) m, roast beef; roast sirloin.

rose (ro:z) f, rose; rose window; rose diamond. ~ des vents, compass card. ~ moussue, moss rose. ~ muscade, musk r. ~ thé, tea r. ~ trémière (tremjɛ:r), hollyhock. ¶ m. & a, rose [colour]; pink. le mont Rose, Monte Rosa. rosé, e (roze) a, roseate, rosy.

roseau (rozo) m, reed; broken reed (fig.).

rosée (roze) f, dew.

roselet (rɔslɛ) m, ermine (fur).

roseraie (rozrɛ) f, rose garden, rosary, rosery.

rosette (zɛt) f, rosette; bow (ribbon); red ink, r. chalk. rosier (zje) m, rose tree. ~ grimpant, rambler [rose].

rosse (rɔs) f, jade, sorry steed; nasty (or objectionable) person. rosser (se) v.t, to thrash, beat.

rossignol (rɔsiɲɔl) m, nightingale; picklock; whistle; unsalable article, pup.

rot (ro) m, belch.

rôt (ro) m, roast [meat]; roast meat course.

rotation (rɔtasjɔ̃) f, rotation. rotatoire (twa:r) a, rotary.

roter (rɔte) v.i, to belch.

rôti (roti) m, roast [meat]; r. m. course. ~ de porc, r. pork. rôtie (ti) f, [round of] toast. ~ à l'anglaise, Welsh rabbit. ~ au fromage, Welsh rabbit, W. rarebit.

rotin (rɔtɛ̃) m, rat[t]an; r. cane.

rôtir (roti:r) v.t. & i, to roast, broil; toast; scorch. rôtissoire (tiswa:r) f, Dutch oven.

rotocalcographie (rɔtɔkalkɔgrafi) *f*, offset process.

rotonde (rɔtɔ̃:d) *f*, rotunda; cloak. **rotondité** (tɔ̃dite) *f*, rotundity.

rotule (rɔtyl) *f*, knee cap, patella. ~ *sphérique*, ball & socket.

roture (rɔty:r) *f*, commonalty. **roturier, ère** (tyrje, ɛ:r) *n*, commoner.

rouage (rwa:ʒ) *m*, wheels, wheelwork, works; machinery (*fig.*).

rouan, ne (rwɑ̃, an) *a. & n*, roan (*animal*).

roucouler (rukule) *v.i*, to coo; bill & coo; (*v.t.*) to warble.

roue (ru) *f*, wheel. ~ *libre*, free w. *faire la* ~, to spread its tail (*peacock*); turn catherine wheels. **roué** (rwe) *m*, rake, profligate. **rouelle** (rwɛl) *f*, round [slice]; fillet (*veal*).

rouennerie (rwanri) *f*, printed cotton goods.

rouer (rwe) *v.t*, to coil (*rope*); break upon the wheel. ~ *de coups*, to thrash. **rouerie** (ruri) *f*, trickery. **rouet** (rwɛ) *m*, spinning wheel; sheave.

rouflaquette (ruflakɛt) *f*, lovelock, earlock, cowlick.

rouge (ru:ʒ) *m*, red (*colour & pers. in Pol.*); rouge. ¶ *a*, red; red-hot; roan (*shoes*); blushing; glowing. *mer R~*, Red sea. ~ *bord*, bumper. ~*gorge, m*, [robin] redbreast. ~*queue, m*, redstart. **rougeâtre** (ruʒɑ:tr) *a*, reddish. **rougeaud, e** (ʒo, o:d) *a*, red-faced, ruddy. **rougeole** (ʒɔl) *f*, measles. **rouget** (ʒɛ) *m*, red mullet. **rougeur** (ʒœ:r) *f*, redness; blush, flush; red spot (*skin*). **rougir** (ʒi:r) *v.t. & i*, to redden; blush, flush.

rouille (ru:j) *f*, rust; mildew, blight (*Agric.*). **rouillé, e** (ruje) *a*, rusty; mildewed; out of practice. **rouiller** (je) *v.t*, to rust, &c. **rouillure** (jy:r) *f*, rustiness.

roulade (rulad) *f*, roll (*downhill*); roulade, run (*Mus.*). **roulage** (la:ʒ) *m*, haulage. **roulant, e** (lɑ̃, ɑ̃:t) *a*, rolling; travelling; portable; circulating (*capital*). **rouleau** (lo) *m*, roller; roll; spool (*film—Phot.*); scroll; twist (*tobacco*); coil (*rope*). ~ *de couverture*, hold-all. ~ *de pâtissier*, rolling pin. *au bout de son* ~, at the end of one's tether, at one's wits' end. **roulement** (lmɑ̃) *m*, roll[ing]; working; running; r. gear; rumbling (*traffic*); bearings; turn-over (*capital*); rotation. ~ *à billes*, ball bearings. **rouler** (le) *v.t*, to roll; r. up; coil; haul; (*v.i.*) to roll; run, work; turn, rotate; travel, drive; rove, roam; circulate freely; fluctuate. *faire* ~ *la presse*, to machine (*Typ.*). ~ [*sur le sol*], to taxi (*Aero.*). **roulette** (lɛt) *f*, caster, -or; roller; wheel; tape [measure] (*coiled*); roulette. **rouleur** (lœ:r) *m*, haulageman; travelling journeyman. **roulier** (lje) *m*, carter, waggoner. **roulis** (li) *m*, rolling (*ship*). **roulotte** (lɔt) *f*, caravan (*house on wheels*).

roumain, e (rumɛ̃, ɛn) *a. & R~, n. & le

roumain (*language*), R[o]umanian. **la Roumanie** (mani), R[o]umania.

roupiller (rupije) *v.i*, to snooze.

roussâtre (rusɑ:tr) *a*, reddish. **rousseau** (so) *m. & att*, red-haired (person). **rousserolle** (srɔl) *f*, sedge warbler. **rousseur** (sœ:r) *f*, redness. **roussi** (si) *m*, [smell of] burning. **roussir** (si:r) *v.t. & i*, to redden; brown (*meat*); scorch, singe.

route (rut) *f*, road, path, track; route, course, way; transit; journey. ~ *d'évitement*, by-pass [road]. ~ *de priorité*, major road. ~ *nationale de grand itinéraire*, widened main road (= Eng. arterial road). ~ *secondaire*, minor road. ~ *déviée*, loop-way. **routier, ère** (tje, ɛ:r) *a*, road (*att.*). ¶ *m*, campaigner, stager. **routine** (tin) *f*, routine; rote; red tape.

rouvieux (ruvjø) *m*, mange; (*att.*) mangy.

rouvrir (ruvri:r) *v.t.ir*, to reopen.

roux, rousse (ru, ˊrus) *a. & n*, russet; brown[ed]; red (*hair, &c.*); red-haired (person). ¶ *m*, russet (*colour*).

royal, e† (rwajal) *a*, royal, regal, kingly. **royaliste** (list) *a. & n*, royalist. **royaume** (joːm) *m*, kingdom, realm. **royauté** (ote) *f*, royalty; kingship; dominance.

ruade (rɥad) *f*, lashing out; kick (*horse*).

ruban (rybɑ̃) *m*, ribbon; band; tape.

rubéole (rybeɔl) *f*, German measles.

rubicond, e (rybikɔ̃, ɔ̃:d) *a*, rubicund, florid.

rubis (rybi) *m*, ruby; jewel (*Horol.*).

rubrique (rybrik) *f*, red chalk; rubric; heading, section; column (*special subject news*); publisher's imprint (*place of publication*).

ruche (ryʃ) *f*, [bee]hive; ruche. **rucher** (ʃe) *m*, apiary.

rude† (ryd) *a*, rough; rugged; harsh; hard; severe; rude; gruff; stiff; steep. **rudesse** (dɛs) *f*, roughness, &c.

rudiment (rydimɑ̃) *m*, rudiment. **rudimentaire** (tɛːr) *a*, rudimentary.

rudoyer (rydwaje) *v.t*, to use roughly, brow-beat.

rue (ry) *f*, street; rue (*Bot.*). ~ *à sens unique*, one way street. ~ [*passante*], thoroughfare.

ruée (rɥe) *f*, rush, onrush, onslaught.

ruelle (rɥɛl) *f*, lane, alley; ruelle (*bedside*).

ruer (rɥe) *v.t*, to lash out, kick (*horse*). *se* ~ *sur*, to hurl oneself at, rush at.

rugir (ryʒi:r) *v.i*, to roar.

rugueux, euse (rygø, ø:z) *a*, rough, rugged.

ruine (rɥin) *f*, ruin, [down]fall. **ruiner** (ne) *v.t*, to ruin. **ruineux, euse** (nø, ø:z) *a*, ruinous.

ruisseau (rɥiso) *m*, stream[let], brook, rivu-let, rill; gutter (*street & fig.*), kennel. **ruisseler** (sle) *v.i*, to stream, run down, trickle.

rumeur (rymœ:r) *f*, hum (*voices, &c*); uproar; rumour.

ruminant, e (rymɑ̃, ɑ̃:t) *a. & m*, ruminant. **ruminer** (ne) *v.t. & abs*, to ruminate; ponder.

rupture (rypty:r) *f*, breaking; rupture; fracture; breaking off, breach.

rural, e (ryral) *a*, rural, country (*att.*).

ruse (ry:z) *f*, ruse, trick[ery], wile, dodge; stratagem. **rusé, e** (ryze) *a*, artful, crafty, wily. **ruser** (ze) *v.i*, to use cunning.

russe (rys) *a. & R~, n. & le russe* (*language*), Russian. **la Russie** (si), Russia.

rustaud, e (rysto, o:d) *a*, boorish, uncouth. ¶ *n*, boor. **rusticité** (tisite) *f*, rusticity; boorishness. **rustique†** (tik) *a*, rustic; country (*att.*); hardy (*plant*); crazy (*pavement*). **rustre** (str) *m*, boor, churl.

rut (ryt) *m*, rut, heat (*animals*).

rutabaga (rytabaga) *m*, swede (*turnip*).

rythme (ritm) *m*, rhythm. **rythmique** (mik) *a*, rhythmic(al).

S

sabbat (saba) *m*, sabbath (*Jewish, witches'*); row, racket.

sable (sɑ:bl) *m*, sand; gravel (*Med.*); sable (*fur, Her.*). *~ blanc*, silver sand. **sabler** (sɑble) *v.t*, to sand, gravel (*path*); swig, toss off. **sablier** (blie) *m*, hour glass, sand g. **sablière** (ɛ:r) *f*, sand pit, gravel pit; wall plate. **sablon** (blɔ̃) *m*, fine sand. **sablonneux, euse** (blɔnø, ø:z) *a*, sandy. **sablonnière** (njɛ:r) *f*, sand pit.

sabord (sabɔ:r) *m*, port (hole). **saborder** (bɔrde) *v.t*, to scuttle (*ship*).

sabot (sabo) *m*, clog, sabot; shoe; skid; hoof; slipper bath; whipping top; tub (*bad ship*); rubbishy instrument *or* tool. **sabotage** (bɔtaːʒ) *m*, sabotage, foul play. **saboter** (te) *v.t*, to botch; damage wilfully, wreck. **sabotière** (tjɛ:r) *f*, clog dance.

sabouler (sabule) *v.t*, to jostle; rate, scold.

sabre (sɑ:br) *m*, sabre, sword, broadsword, cutlass. **sabrer** (sɑbre) *v.t. & abs*, to sabre; slash; slash about; cut down, blue-pencil.

sac (sak) *m*, sack, bag, pouch, sac; sackcloth (*Theol.*); sacking, pillage. *~ à dépêches*, mail bag. *~ à fermoir articulé*, kit bag (*traveller's*). *~ à main pour dame*, lady's hand bag. *~ à ouvrage*, work b. *~ à provisions*, shopping b. *~ à terre*, sand b. *~ d'ordonnance* (*Mil.*), knapsack; kit bag. *~ de couchage*, sleeping bag. *~ de forme ballon*, brief b. *~ de touriste*, *~ de montagne*, *~ d'alpinisme*, rucksack.

saccade (sakad) *f*, jerk, start. **saccadé, e** (de) *p.a*, jerky; irregular; staccato (*voice*).

saccager (sakaʒe) *v.t*, to sack, pillage; ransack; upset.

saccharin, e (sakarɛ̃, in) *a*, saccharin[e], sugary; sugar (*att.*). ¶ *f*, saccharin[e].

sacerdoce (sasɛrdɔs) *m*, priesthood; ministry. **sacerdotal, e** (tal) *a*, sacerdotal, priestly.

saché, e (saʃe) *f*, sackful, bagful. **sachet** (ʃe) *m*, bag. *~ à parfums*, scent bag, sachet.

sacoche (kɔʃ) *f*, satchel, wallet; saddlebag.

sacramental (sakramɑ̃tal) *m*, sacramental. **sacramentel, le†** (tɛl) *a*, sacramental, binding. **sacre** (kr) *m*, anointing, coronation; consecration (*bishop*). **sacré, e** (kre) *a*, holy, sacred, consecrated. **sacrement** (krəmɑ̃) *m*, sacrament. **sacrer** (kre) *v.t*, to anoint, crown; consecrate. **sacrifice** (krifis) *m*, sacrifice; offering. **sacrifier** (fje) *v.t. & abs*, to sacrifice. **sacrilège** (lɛ:ʒ) *m*, sacrilege; (*att.*) sacrilegious.

sacripant (sakripɑ̃) *m*, rascal, bully.

sacristain (sakristɛ̃) *m*, sacristan. **sacristie** (ti) *f*, vestry, sacristy. **sacro-saint, e** (krosɛ̃, ɛ̃:t) *a*, sacrosanct.

safran (safrɑ̃) *m*, saffron, crocus. *~ des Indes*, turmeric.

sagace (sagas) *a*, sagacious, shrewd. **sagacité** (site) *f*, sagacity, shrewdness.

sage† (sa:ʒ) *a*, wise, sage, sapient; judicious, prudent, sensible; well-behaved, good (*child*); chaste. ¶ *m*, sage, wise man. *~-femme*, *f*, midwife. **sagesse** (3ɛs) *f*, wisdom, &c; good conduct.

sagou (sagu) *m*, sago. **sagou[t]ier** ([t]je) *m*, sago palm.

sagouin (sagwɛ̃) *m*, saguin (*monkey*); sloven.

saignant, e (sɛɲɑ̃, ɑ̃:t) *a*, bleeding; raw; underdone (*meat*). **saignée** (ɲe) *f*, bleeding, blood letting; bend of the arm; trench; holocaust. **saigner** (ɲe) *v.i. & t*, to bleed; stick (*pig*); tap (*tree, &c*); drain; rankle.

saillant, e (sajɑ̃, ɑ̃:t) *a*, salient, projecting prominent; striking, outstanding. **saillie** (ji) *f*, spurt, bound; projection; ledge; protrusion; sally; covering. **saillir** (ji:r) *v.i.ir*, to gush out; project; protrude; sally; (*v.t.ir*) to cover (*of animals*).

sain, e† (sɛ̃, ɛn) *a*, sound; wholesome; healthy, hale; sane. *sain & sauf*, safe & sound.

saindoux (sɛ̃du) *m*, lard.

sainfoin (sɛ̃fwɛ̃) *m*, sainfoin.

saint, e (sɛ̃, ɛ̃:t) *n*, saint, patron s. *le ~ des saints*, the holy of holies, sanctum. ¶ *a*, holy; sainted; saintly, godly; consecrated; hallowed. *saint-frusquin*, worldly goods. *Saint-Siège*, Holy See. *sainte table*, communion table. *la Sainte Vierge*, the Blessed Virgin. **Saint, comps:** *le ~-Esprit* (sɛ̃tɛspri), the Holy Ghost, the Holy Spirit. *la ~-Jean* (ʒɛ̃ʒɑ̃), Midsummer day. *le ~-Laurent* (lorɑ̃), the St Lawrence. *la ~-Martin* (martɛ̃), Martinmas. *la ~-Michel* (miʃɛl), Michaelmas. *la ~-Sylvestre* (silvɛstr), new-year's eve. **Sainte-Hélène** (stelen) *f*, St Helena. **saintement** (tmɑ̃) *ad*, holily, in a godly manner, righteously. **sainteté** (təte) *f*, holiness, saintliness; sanctity.

saisie (sɛzi) *f*, seizure; distraint, execution; distress (*Law*); foreclosure (*mortgage*). **saisir** (zi:r) *v.t*, to seize, lay hold of, grasp; catch; snatch; distrain, attach; foreclose; startle; lay before (*court*). **saisissant, e** (zisɑ̃, ɑ̃:t) *a*, piercing (*cold*); startling, striking; thrilling. **saisissement** (smã) m, shock; thrill.

saison (sɛzõ) f, season, time (*of year*).

salade (salad) f, salad; jumble. **saladier** (dje) m, salad bowl.

salage (sala:ʒ) m, salting, curing.

salaire (salɛ:r) m, wage[s]; pay; hire; reward. ~ *de famine*, starvation wage.

salaison (salɛzõ) f, salting, curing; (*pl.*) salt provisions.

salamalec (salamalɛk) m, salaam.

salamandre (salamã:dr) f, salamander. ~ *aquatique*, newt, eft.

Salamanque (salamã:k) f, Salamanca.

salant (salã) a.m, salt (*marsh*), saline.

salarié, e (salarje) p.a, wage-earning, paid. **salarier** (je) v.t, to pay a wage to.

salet (sal) a, dirty, unclean, filthy; foul; nasty; soiled (*linen*); messy; beastly.

salé, e (sale) p.a, salt, salted; corned (*beef*); briny; keen; broad (*story*); stiff (*price, &c*). [*porc*] *salé*, m, salt pork. **saler** (le) v.t, to salt, pickle, cure, corn; give it (*someone*) hot.

Salerne (salɛrn) f, Salerno.

saleté (salte) f, dirtiness, &c, as *sale*; dirt, filth; mess; rubbish, trash[y goods].

salicole (salikɔl) a, salt (*industry*); saliferous. **salicoque** (kɔk) f, shrimp. **salière** (ljɛ:r) f, salt cellar; salt box. **salin, e** (lɛ̃, in) a, saline, briny, salt[y]. ¶ f, salt works; rock salt mine.

salir (sali:r) v.t, to dirty, soil; foul; sully. **salissure** (lisy:r) f, stain.

salive (sali:v) f, saliva, spittle. **saliver** (live) v.i, to salivate.

salle (sal) f, hall; room; ward (*hospital*); house (*Theat., &c*); auditorium; office. ~ *à manger*, dining room; d. saloon (*ship*); coffee room (*hotel*); mess room (*Mil.*). ~ *commune*, living room. ~ *d'armes*, armoury; fencing school. ~ *d'attente*, waiting room (*Rly*). ~ *de bath*, bath r. ~ *de classe*, schoolroom. ~ *de police*, guardroom (*Mil.*). ~ *des festins*, banqueting hall. ~ *des pas perdus*, booking hall (*Rly*); lobby. ~ *du rapport*, orderly room.

salmigondis (salmigõdi) m, hotchpotch.

salon (salõ) m, reception room; drawing room; parlour; saloon; room; salon, exhibition, show. ~ *d'exposition*, showroom. ~ *de l'automobile*, motor show. ~ *de l'aviation*, aircraft exhibition. ~ *de pose*, studio (*Phot.*). ~ *du cycle*, cycle show.

Salonique (salɔnik) f, Salonica.

salope (salɔp) f, slattern, slut. **saloperie** (pri) f, filth, muck; trash. **salopette** (pɛt) f, overalls.

salpêtre (salpɛ:tr) m, saltpetre, nitre.

salsepareille (salsparɛ:j) f, sarsaparilla.

saltimbanque (saltɛ̃bã:k) m, mountebank.

salubre (salybr) a, salubrious, healthy; wholesome. **salubrité** (brite) f, salubrity, &c; health (*public*).

saluer (salɥe) v.t, to salute, bow to; greet, hail.

salure (saly:r) f, saltness; tang.

salut (saly) m, safety; welfare; salvation; salutation, bow, greeting; salute; evening service (*Eccl.*). ¶ *i*, hail! greeting! **salutairet** (tɛ:r) a, salutary, wholesome, beneficial. **salutation** (tasjõ) f, salutation, greeting, bow.

salve (salv) f, salvo, salute; round (*applause*).

samedi (samdi) m, Saturday.

samovar (samɔva:r) m, urn (*for tea, coffee*).

sanatorium (sanatɔrjɔm) m, sanatorium.

sanctifier (sãktifje) v.t, to sanctify, hallow. **sanction** (sjõ) f, sanction, assent; penalty, punishment. **sanctionner** (ɔne) v.t, to sanction, approve. **sanctuaire** (tɥɛ:r) m, sanctuary; sanctum.

sandale (sãdal) f, sandal, shoe.

sandwich (sãdwitʃ) m, sandwich.

sang (sã) m, blood, gore; race, lineage, kinship. ~-[*de-*]*dragon*, dragon's blood. ~-*froid*, coolness, self-possession, nerve. [*homme de*] ~ *mêlé*, half-caste. **sanglant, e** (glã, ã:t) a, bloody; sanguinary; deadly; cutting, scathing; outrageous.

sangle (sã:gl) f, strap, band, girth, webbing. **sangler** (sãgle) v.t, to strap; girth; lash. se ~, to lace oneself tight[ly].

sanglier (sãglje) m, wild boar.

sanglot (sãglo) m, sob. **sangloter** (glɔte) v.i, to sob.

sangsue (sãsy) f, leech; bloodsucker. **sanguin, e** (gɛ̃, in) a, sanguineous, blood (*att.*); full-blooded, sanguine. ¶ f, red chalk; bloodstone. **sanguinaire** (ginɛ:r) a, sanguinary, bloody; bloodthirsty.

sanitaire (sanitɛ:r) a, sanitary.

sans (sã) pr, without; but for; -less; -lessly; un-; no; non-. ~ *arrêt*, ~ *escale*, non-stop. ~ *cela*, ~ *quoi*, otherwise. ~ *date*, sine die; undated. ~ *empattement*, sanserif. [*perdu*] ~ *nouvelles*, missing (*ship*). ~ *profession*, no occupation, gentleman. ~ *que*, without. ~ *valeur déclarée*, uninsured (*Post*).

sans-cœur (sãkœ:r) n, heartless person.

sans-façon (sãfasõ) m, straightforwardness, bluntness, homeliness.

sans-fil (sãfil) f, wireless [telegraphy]; (*m.*) wireless [telegram].

sans-gêne (sãʒɛn) m, off-handedness, cheek.

sansonnet (sãsɔnɛ) m, starling (*bird*).

sans-souci (sãsusi) n, easy-going person, happy-go-lucky individual; (*m.*) unconcern.

sans-travail (les) (sãtrava:j) m.pl, the workless, the unemployed.

santal (sãtal) m, sandal[wood].

santé (sãte) f, health. ~ *de fer*, iron constitution. *la* ~, quarantine (*station*).

sape (sap) f, sap (*Mil.*); undermining. **saper** (pe) v.t, to sap, &c. **sapeur** (pœ:r) m, sapper. ~-*pompier*, fireman. *les sapeurs-pompiers*, the fire brigade.

saphir (safi:r) *m*, sapphire.

sapin (sapɛ̃) *m*, fir [tree]; spruce [fir]. [*bois de*] ~, deal. **sapinière** (pinjɛ:r) *f*, fir plantation.

Saragosse (saragɔs) *f*, Saragossa.

sarbacane (sarbakan) *f*, pea shooter; blow gun, blowpipe, blow tube (*dart tube*).

sarcasme (sarkasm) *m*, sarcasm, taunt. **sarcastique** (tik) *a*, sarcastic.

sarcler (sarkle) *v.t*, to weed. **sarcleur, euse** (klœ:r, ø:z) *n*, weeder (*pers.*). **sarcloir** (klwa:r) *m*, weeding hoe, weeder.

sarcophage (sarkɔfa:ʒ) *m*, sarcophagus.

Sardaigne (la) (sardɛɲ), Sardinia. **sarde** (sard) *a. & S~*, *n*, Sardinian.

sardine (sardin) *f*, pilchard; sardine.

sardoine (sardwan) *f*, sardonyx.

sardonique (sardɔnik) *a*, sardonic.

sarigue (sarig) *m. & f*, opossum, sarigue.

sarment (sarmã) *m*, vine shoot; bine.

sarrasin (sarazɛ̃) *m*, buckwheat.

sarrau (saro) *m*, smock, overall.

sarriette (sarjet) *f*, savory (*Bot.*).

sas (sɑ) *m*, sieve. **sasser** (se) *v.t*, to sift.

Satan (satɑ̃) *m*, Satan. **satané, e** (tane) *a*, devilish. **satanique** (nik) *a*, satanic.

satellite (satellit) *m*, satellite; henchman.

satiété (sasjete) *f*, satiety, surfeit.

satin (satɛ̃) *m*, satin. **satiner** (tine) *v.t*, to satin; glaze (*paper*, *&c*); burnish (*Phot.*). **satinette** (net) *f*, sateen.

satire (sati:r) *f*, satire. **satirique†** (tirik) *a*, satiric, satirical. ¶ *m*, satirist. **satiriser** (ze) *v.t*, to satirize.

satisfaction (satisfaksjɔ̃) *f*, satisfaction, gratification, comfort; atonement (*Theol.*). **satisfaire** (fɛ:r) *v.t.ir*, to satisfy, please, gratify, answer. ~ **à**, to satisfy; answer, meet; fulfil. **satisfaisant, e** (fəzɑ̃, ɑ̃:t) *a*, satisfactory.

saturer (satyre) *v.t*, to saturate.

saturnales (satyrnal) *f.pl*, saturnalia. **saturnisme** (nism) *m*, lead poisoning.

satyre (sati:r) *m*, satyr.

sauce (so:s) *f*, sauce. **saucer** (sose) *v.t*, to dip in the sauce; drench, souse. **saucière** (sjɛ:r) *f*, sauce boat, gravy b.

saucisse (sosis) *f*, sausage (*fresh*); s. balloon. **saucisson** (sɔ̃) *m*, smoked sausage.

sauf, sauve (sof, so:v) *a*, safe, unhurt, unscathed; saved. **sauf**, *pr*, save, saving, but, except[ed]; unless; subject; under. ~-**conduit**, *m*, safe conduct, pass.

sauge (so:ʒ) *f*, sage (*Bot.*, *Cook.*).

saugrenu, e (sograny) *a*, absurd, preposterous.

saulaie (solɛ) *f*, willow plantation. **saule** (so:l) *m*, willow [tree].

saumâtre (soma:tr) *a*, brackish, briny.

saumon (somɔ̃) *m*, salmon; ingot, pig (*metal*). **saumoneau** (mɔno) *m*, young salmon.

saumure (somy:r) *f*, [pickling] brine.

saunage (sona:ʒ) *m*, salt making; s. trade. **saunerie** (nri) *f*, salt works.

saupoudrer (sopudre) *v.t*, to sprinkle, dredge, dust, powder. **saupoudroir** (drwa:r) *m*, sifter, dredger, castor (*sugar*).

saure (so:r) *a*, sorrel (*horse*). **saurer** (sore) *v.t*, to kipper.

saussaie (sose) *f*, willow plantation.

saut (so) *m*, leap, jump, vault; hop; skip; bound; fall[s] (*water*). ~ **à la perche**, pole vault. ~ **de loup**, ha-ha (*sunk fence*). ~ **de mouton**, buck (*of horse*); leap-frog. ~ **en hauteur**, high jump. ~ **en longueur**, long j. le ~ **périlleux**, a somersault; the plunge (*fig.*). *par* ~*s* & *par bonds*, by fits & starts, spasmodically. **saute** (so:t) *f*, shift, change. ~-**mouton** (sotmutɔ̃) *m*, leap-frog. **sauter** (sote) *v.i*, to leap, jump; skip; hop; bound, spring; vault; fly, fling oneself; explode, blow up; go smash; fall; shift, change (*wind*); (*v.t.*) to leap [over], jump [o.]; skip; leave out; drop (*stitch*); cover (*of animals*). **sauterelle** (trɛl) *f*, grasshopper; locust. **saute-ruisseau** (sotruiso) *m*, errand boy. **sauteur, euse** (tœ:r, ø:z) *n*, jumper, leaper; weathercock (*pers.*); (*f.*) sauté pan; jig saw. **sautiller** (tije) *v.i*, to hop, skip; trip along; jump about. **sautoir** (twa:r) *m*, saltire; kerchief; vaulting standard. *en* ~, crosswise, over the shoulder.

sauvage† (sova:ʒ) *a*, savage, uncivilized; wild; barbarous; unsociable, shy. ¶ *n. & sauvagesse* (vaʒes) *f*, savage; unsociable person. **sauvageon** (ʒɔ̃) *m*, wild stock (*grafting*); wilding, seedling. **sauvagerie** (ʒri) *f*, savagery; unsociability, shyness. **sauvagin, e** (ʒɛ̃, in) *a*, fishy (*taste*, *smell*, *of flesh*).

sauvegarde (sovgard) *f*, safeguard, protection; safe conduct. **sauve-qui-peut** (kipø) *m*, stampede, headlong flight. **sauver** (ve) *v.t*, to save, rescue; salve, salvage. **se** ~, to escape; run away, be off. **sauvetage** (vta:ʒ) *m*, life saving, rescue; salvage. **sauveur** (vœ:r) *m*, saver, deliverer. *le Sauveur*, the Saviour.

savamment (savamã) *ad*, learnedly; knowingly. **savant, e** (vã, ã:t) *a*, learned, scholarly; skilful; performing (*dog*); knowing, precocious (*in vice*), sophisticated. ¶ *n*, scientist, scholar.

savate (savat) *f*, old shoe; boxing with the feet, head, & fists. *en* ~*s*, down at heel, slipshod. **savater** (vte) *v.t*, to botch. **savetier** (vtje) *m*, cobbler; botcher.

saveur (savœ:r) *f*, savour, flavour, taste; relish, zest.

Savoie (la) (savwa), Savoy.

savoir (savwa:r) *v.t.ir*, to know; be aware of, tell; be acquainted with, know of; understand; know how to; be able to; can. ~ [*bon*] *gré à*, to be grateful to. ~ *mauvais gré à*, to be annoyed with. ¶ *m*, knowledge, learning, scholarship. ~-**faire**

I

(vwarfɛ:r) *m*, ability, tact, gumption, nous. **~-vivre**, *m*, good manners.

savon (savɔ̃) *m*, soap. **~ à barbe en bâton**, shaving stick. **savonner** (vone) *v.t*, to soap, wash; lather. **savonnerie** (nri) *f*, soap works; s. trade. **savonnette** (nɛt) *f*, soap ball; hunter (*watch*). **savonneux, euse** (nø, ø:z) *a*, soapy. **savonnier** (nje) *m*, soap maker.

savourer (savure) *v.t*, to taste; relish, enjoy. **savoureux, euse** (rø, ø:z) *a*, savoury, tasty; enjoyable.

saxe (saks) *m*, saxe (*colour*); Dresden china. **la Saxe**, Saxony.

saxhorn (saksɔrn) *m*, saxhorn.

saxifrage (saksifra:ʒ) *f*, saxifrage.

saxon, ne (saksɔ̃, ɔn) *a. & S~, n*, Saxon.

saxophone (saksofɔn) *m*, saxophone.

saynète (sɛnɛt) *f*, playlet, sketch.

sbire (zbi:r) *m*, sbirro; myrmidon.

scabieux, euse (skabjø, ø:z) *a*, scabious, scabby. ¶ *f*, scabious (*Bot.*).

scabreux, euse (skabrø, ø:z) *a*, rough; ticklish; scabrous, improper.

scalpel (skalpɛl) *m*, scalpel.

scalper (skalpe) *v.t*, to scalp.

scandale (skɑ̃dal) *m*, scandal, shame. **scandaleux, euse†** (lø, ø:z) *a*, scandalous, shameful. **scandaliser** (lize) *v.t*, to scandalize, shock.

scander (skɑ̃de) *v.t*, to scan (*verse*); stress (*Mus.*); syllabize (*articulate by syllables*).

scandinave (skɑ̃dina:v) *a. & S~, n*, Scandinavian. **la Scandinavie** (navi), Scandinavia.

scansion (skɑ̃sjɔ̃) *f*, scansion, scanning.

scaphandre (skafɑ̃:dr) *m*, diving dress. **scaphandrier** (fɑ̃drie) *m*, diver (*in diving dress*).

scarabée (skarabe) *m*, beetle; scarab.

scarifier (skarifje) *v.t*, to scarify.

scarlatine (skarlatin) *f*, scarlatina, scarlet fever.

scarole (skarɔl) *f*, endive.

sceau (so) *m*, seal; stamp (*fig.*).

scélérat, e (selera, at) *a*, villainous, wicked. ¶ *n*, villain, scoundrel, miscreant. **scélératesse** (tɛs) *f*, villainy, wickedness.

scellé (sɛle) *m*, seal (*official*). **sceller** (le) *v.t*, to seal; s. up.

scénario (senarjo) *m*, scenario. **scène** (sɛn) *f*, stage; scene; action; local[e]; shindy. **~ militaire à grand spectacle**, military pageant. **scénique** (senik) *a*, scenic, theatrical, stage (*att.*).

scepticisme (sɛptisism) *m*, scepticism. **sceptique** (tik) *a*, sceptical. ¶ *n*, sceptic.

sceptre (sɛptr) *m*, sceptre.

Schaffhouse (ʃafu:z) *f*, Schaffhausen.

schampooing (ʃɑ̃pwɛ̃) *m*, wet shampoo.

schéma (ʃema) *ou* **schème** (ʃɛm) *m*, diagram, plan.

schiedam (skidam) *m*, Hollands [gin].

schisme (ʃism) *m*, schism.

schiste (ʃist) *m*, shale, schist.

schlitte (ʃlit) *f*, lumber sledge.

schooner (ʃunɛ:r) *m*, schooner (*Naut.*).

sciage (sja:ʒ) *m*, sawing.

sciatique (sjatik) *a*, sciatic. ¶ *f*, sciatica.

scie (si) *f*, saw; bore, nuisance; joke; catchword; catch phrase, gag. **~ à chantourner**, jig saw. **~ à métaux**, hack s. **~ de long**, pit s.

sciemment (sjamɑ̃) *ad*, knowingly, wittingly.

science (sjɑ̃:s) *f*, knowledge, learning, lore; science. **~ économique**, economics. **scientifique†** (ɑ̃tifik) *a*, scientific. **scientiste chrétien** (tist) *m*, Christian scientist.

scier (sje) *v.t*, to saw; saw off; reap; bore (*weary*); (*v.i.*) to back water. **scierie** (siri) *f*, saw mill. **scieur** (sjœ:r) *m*, sawyer.

scinder (sɛ̃de) *v.t*, to divide, split (*fig.*).

scintillation (sɛ̃tillasjɔ̃) *f*, scintillation; twinkling. **scintiller** (tije) *v.i*, to scintillate; twinkle.

scion (sjɔ̃) *m*, shoot, scion (*Hort.*); top [joint] (*fishing rod*).

scission (sisjɔ̃) *f*, scission, split, cleavage; secession.

sciure (sjy:r) *f*, sawdust.

sclérose (sklero:z) *f*, sclerosis.

scolaire (skɔlɛ:r) *a*, school (*att.*); academic (*year*); educational. **scolastique** (lastik) *a*, scholastic.

scolopendre (skɔlɔpɑ̃:dr) *f*, centipede.

sconse (skɔ̃:s) *m*, skunk (*fur*).

scorbut (skɔrby) *m*, scurvy.

scorie (skɔri) *f. oft. pl*, slag, scoria; dross, scale.

scorpion (skɔrpjɔ̃) *m*, scorpion.

scribe (skrib) *m*, scribe; copyist.

scrofules (skrɔfyl) *f.pl*, scrofula. **scrofuleux, euse** (lø, ø:z) *a*, scrofulous.

scrupule (skrypyl) *m*, scruple, qualm. **scrupuleux, euse†** (lø, ø:z) *a*, scrupulous.

scrutateur (skrytatœ:r) *m*, scrutinizer; teller; scrutineer. **scruter** (te) *v.t*, to scrutinize; scan; peer into; search. **scrutin** (tɛ̃) *m*, poll, ballot, voting vote.

sculpter (skylte) *v.t*, to sculpture; carve. **sculpteur** (tœ:r) *m*, sculptor; carver. **sculpture** (ty:r) *f*, sculpture. **~ sur bois**, wood carving.

se, s' (sə, s) *pn*, oneself; himself, herself, itself; themselves; each other, one another. *Note:* An English intransitive is often expressed in French by the pronominal form (se, s'); thus, to depreciate, *v*, déprécier, avilir; to depreciate, *v.i*, déprécier, s'avilir. The pronominal for also serves to give to a transitive verb passive meaning; as, lettre qui se prononc letter which is pronounced.

séance (seɑ̃:s) *f*, seat (*at a council*); sitting, session, meeting; performance. **~ spiritisme**, seance. **~ tenante**, sitting; forthwith, there & then, on th spot. **séant, e** (ɑ̃, ɑ̃:t) *p.a*, sitting (ɑ̃ = a in session. ¶ *a*, becoming, seemly, proper. **sur son séant**, in a sitting posture, sitting up.

seau (so) *m*, pail, bucket; pailful. ~ *à biscuits*, biscuit barrel. ~ *à charbon*, coal scuttle. ~ *à ordures*, dustbin. ~ *de toilette*, slop pail. ~ *forme conique*, anthracite vase. ~ *hygiénique pour ordures ménagères*, sanitary dustbin.

sébile (sebil) *f*, wooden bowl.

sec, sèche (sɛk, sɛʃ) *a*, dry; dried; spare, gaunt, lean; curt; bald (*style*, &c). **sec**, *ad*, drily (*answer coldly*); hard (*drinking*); neat (*drinking*). **à sec**, *ad*, [when] dry; dried up. **sec**, *m*, dry; dry place; dry land; dry fodder.

sécateur (sekatœːr) *m*, pruning shears.

sécession (sesesjɔ̃) *f*, secession.

sèchement (sɛʃmɑ̃) *ad*, drily, curtly; baldly. **sécher** (seʃe) *v.t. & i*, to dry; d. up; season (*wood*); wither, pine away. **sécheresse** (ʃrɛs) *f*, dryness; drought; spareness, &c, as *sec*. **séchoir** (ʃwaːr) *m*, drying room; drier; airer; towel horse, t. rail. ~ *à houblon*, oast house. ~ *à linge*, clothes horse.

second, e† (səɡɔ̃, ɔ̃ːd) *a*, second; junior (*partner*). *second plan*, *m*, middle distance; background (*fig*.). *seconde vue*, *f*, second sight, clairvoyance. *un second*, *une seconde*, another (*like*). ¶ *m*, second (*pers*., *floor*); first mate (*Naut*.). ¶ *f*, second (*class*); second, tick (*time*). ~ [*épreuve*], revise (*Typ*.). ~*s* [*galeries*], upper circle (*Theat*.). **secondaire†** (ɡɔ̃dɛːr) *a*, secondary; minor; side (*att*.). **seconder** (ɡɔ̃de) *v.t*, to second, support, back up, further.

secouer (səkwe) *v.t. & abs*, to shake; s. up; s. down; s. off; toss; buffet; jolt; rate, scold. **secourable** (səkurabl) *a*, helpful, helping; relievable. **secourir** (riːr) *v.t.ir*, to succour help, relieve. **secours** (kuːr) *m*, help, succour, relief, aid. ~ *à domicile*, outdoor relief. *au* ~! help! *de* ~, (*att*.) emergency, breakdown, relief, spare.

secousse (səkus) *f*, shake, jerk, jolt, shock.

secret, ète† (səkrɛ, ɛt) *a*, secret. ¶ *m*, secret; s. spring; secrecy, privacy; solitary confinement. **secrétaire** (kretɛːr) *m*, secretary, amanuensis; secretary bird; writing desk. ~ *de la rédaction*, sub-editor. ~ *de mairie*, town clerk. ~ *femme*, lady secretary. ~ *intime*, private s. **secrétariat** (tarja) *m*, secretaryship; secretariat[e]. **sécréter** (sekrete) *v.t*, to secrete (*Physiology*). **sécrétion** (sjɔ̃) *f*, secretion.

sectaire (sɛktɛːr) *m. & att*, secretarian. **sectateur** (tatœːr) *m*, follower, votary. **secte** (sɛkt) *f*, sect.

secteur (sɛktœːr) *m*, sector; quadrant; district. **section** (sjɔ̃) *f*, section; division; [fare] stage (*bus*, &c).

séculaire (sekylɛːr) *a*, secular (*100*); timehonoured. **séculier, ère†** (lje, ɛːr) *a*,

secular (*clergy*, &c); laic; worldly (*life*). ¶ *m*, layman; (*pl*.) laity.

sécurité (sekyrite) *f*, security, reliability; safety. ~ *d'abord*, safety first.

sédatif, ive (sedatif, iːv) *a. & m*, sedative.

sédentaire (sedɑ̃tɛːr) *a*, sedentary, indoor (*staff*).

sédiment (sedimɑ̃) *m*, sediment, deposit.

séditieux, euse† (sedisjø, øːz) *a*, seditious, mutinous. **sédition** (sjɔ̃) *f*, sedition; revolt.

séducteur, trice (sedyktœːr, tris) *n*, tempter; seducer. **séduire** (dɥiːr) *v.t.ir*, to seduce, entice; [al]lure; bribe, suborn. **séduisant, e** (dɥizɑ̃, ɑ̃ːt) *a*, seductive, tempting; fascinating.

segment (sɛɡmɑ̃) *m*, segment; ring (*piston*).

ségrégation (seɡreɡasjɔ̃) *f*, segregation.

seiche (sɛʃ) *f*, cuttle fish.

séide (seid) *m*, blind supporter, henchman.

seigle (sɛɡl) *m*, rye.

seigneur (sɛɲœːr) *m*, lord; squire; noble[man]. **seigneurie** (nœri) *f*, lordship; manor.

sein (sɛ̃) *m*, breast; bosom; lap (*luxury*); bowels (*earth*); members; womb.

seine (sɛn) *f*, seine (*net*).

seize (sɛːz) *a. & m*, sixteen; 16th. **seizième†** (sɛzjɛm) *a. & n*, sixteenth.

séjour (seʒuːr) *m*, stay, sojourn; abode, regions; resort. **séjourner** (ʒurne) *v.i*, to stay, tarry, sojourn; lie.

sel (sɛl) *m*, salt; piquancy, wit. ~ *ammoniac* (amɔnjak), sal-ammoniac. ~ *de Sedlitz* (sɛdlits), Seidlitz powder. ~ *fin*, table salt. ~ *gemme*, rock salt. ~*s pour bains*, bath salts. ~*s* [*volatils*] *anglais*, smelling salts.

sélection (selɛksjɔ̃) *f*, selection, choice. **sélectionner** (ɔne) *v.t*, to select. ~ *les têtes de séries*, to seed the players (*Ten*.).

selle (sɛl) *f*, saddle; seat; stool, motion (*Med*.). **seller** (le) *v.t*, to saddle. **sellerie** (lri) *f*, saddlery; harness room. **sellette** (lɛt) *f*, stool; pedestal (*vase*). *tenir quelqu'un sur la* ~, to cross-examine someone. **sellier** (lje) *m*, saddler, harness maker.

selon (səlɔ̃) *pr*, [according] to. ~ *moi*, in my opinion. *c'est* ~, it all depends.

semailles (səmaːj) *f.pl*, seed time; sowing. **semaine** (səmɛn) *f*, week; week's work, pay, &c. *la* ~ *seulement*, week days only.

sémaphore (semafɔːr) *m*, semaphore.

semblable† (sɑ̃blabl) *a*, [a]like, similar; such. ¶ *m*, fellow [man], like. **semblant** (blɑ̃) *m*, semblance, appearance, show. [*faux*] ~, pretence, sham. *un* ~ *de* . . ., an apology (*bad specimen*) for a . . . **sembler** (ble) *v.i*, to seem, appear, look, strike.

semelle (səmɛl) *f*, sole (*boot*, &c); foot (*stocking*); sock (*cork*, loofa, &c); sill. ~ *débordante*, wide sole.

semence (səmɑ̃ːs) *f*, seed; [tin]tacks. ~ *de perles*, seed pearls. **semer** (me) *v.t*, to sow; scatter, strew, spread; powder (*Emb*.).

semestre (səmɛstr) *m*, half-year; 6 months' pay, duty, leave, &c. **semestriel, le** (triɛl) *a*, half-yearly.

semeur, euse (səmœːr, øːz) *n*, sower; spreader.

semi- (səmi) *prefix*, semi-, half-.

sémillant, e (semijã, ãːt) *a*, sprightly, bright.

séminaire (seminɛːr) *m*, seminary, college.

semis (səmi) *m*, seed plot, seedlings; powdering (*Emb.*).

sémitique (semitik) *a*, Semitic.

semoir (səmwaːr) *m*, sowing machine, drill.

semonce (səmɔ̃ːs) *f*, call (*to a ship*); reprimand, scolding. ~ *conjugale*, curtain lecture. **semoncer** (mɔ̃se) *v.t*, to call upon (*ship*); lecture, scold.

semoule (səmul) *f*, semolina.

sénat (sena) *m*, senate. **sénateur** (tœːr) *m*, senator.

séné (sene) *m*, senna.

seneçon (sənsɔ̃) *m*, groundsel.

Sénégal (le) (senegal) Senegal.

sénestre (senɛstr) *a*, sinister (*Her.*).

sénevé (senve) *m*, mustard (*Bot.*); m. seed.

sénile (senil) *a*, senile. **sénilité** (lite) *f*, senility.

senior (senjoːr) *m*, senior (*Sports*).

sens (sɑ̃ːs, sɑ̃) *m*, sense; judg[e]ment, understanding; opinion; meaning, import; direction, way. ~ *commun* (sɑ̃), [common] sense, senses. ~ *dessus dessous* (sɑ̃), upside down; topsy-turvy. ~ *devant derrière* (sɑ̃), back to front. ~ *giratoire*, roundabout, circus (*traffic*). ~ *interdit*, no [entry], one way [street]. ~ *unique*, entry only[, one way street]. *voyager dans le* ~ *de la machine*, to travel facing the engine. **sensation** (sɑ̃sasjɔ̃) *f*, sensation; feel[ing], sense, *à* ~ & **sensationnel, le** (sjɔnɛl) *a*, sensational, thrilling, exciting. **sensé†, e** (se) *a*, sensible, judicious. **sensibilité** (sibilite) *f*, sensitiveness; feeling. **sensible** (sibl) *a*, sensitive, susceptible, responsive, sensible, alive; sentient; sensitized (*Phot.*); tender, sore; appreciable, palpable, perceptible. **sensiblement** (bləmɑ̃) *a*, appreciably; deeply. **sensiblerie** (ri) *f*, sentimentality. **sensitif, ive** (tif, iːv) *a*, sensitive; sensory. **sensualiste** (sɑ̃sɥalist) *n*, sensualist. **sensualité** (te) *f*, sensuality; voluptuousness. **sensuel, le†** (sɥɛl) *a*, sensual.

sente (sɑ̃ːt) *f*, footpath.

sentence (sɑ̃tɑ̃ːs) *f*, maxim; sentence (*Law*); award. **sentencieux, euse†** (tɑ̃sjø, øːz) *a*, sententious.

senteur (sɑ̃tœːr) *f*, scent, odour, perfume.

senti, e (sɑ̃ti) *p.a*, well expressed, strong. *bien* ~, heartfelt (*words*); home (*truths*).

sentier (sɑ̃tje) *m*, footpath, path, track. ~ *pour cavaliers*, bridle path.

sentiment (sɑ̃timɑ̃) *m*, feeling, sensation; sense; sentiment; opinion. **sentimental, e** (tal) *a*, sentimental. **sentimentalité** (lite) *f*, sentimentality, gush.

sentine (sɑ̃tin) *f*, well (*ship*); sink (*iniquity*).

sentinelle (sɑ̃tinɛl) *f*, sentry, sentinel; guard, watch.

sentir (sɑ̃tiːr) *v.t. & abs. ir*, to feel; be conscious of; smell; scent; taste of; smell of; smack of; be redolent of. *se* ~, to feel.

seoir (swaːr) *v.i.ir*, to sit; be situated.

seoir (swaːr) *v.i.ir*, to suit, become.

séparation (separasjɔ̃) *f*, separation, parting, severance; dispersal; partition (*wall*). ~ *de l'Église & de l'État*, disestablishment [of the Church]. **séparé†, e** (re) *p.a*, separate, distinct; apart. **séparer** (re) *v.t. & se* ~, to separate, part; sever; divide; disband. **séparez!** break! (*Box.*).

sépia (sepja) *f*, sepia; sepia [drawing].

sept (sɛ; *alone & in liaison*, sɛt) *a. & m*, seven; 7th.

septembre (sɛptɑ̃ːbr) *m*, September.

septentrion (sɛptɑ̃triɔ̃) *m*, north. **septentrional, e** (ɔnal) *a*, northern. ¶ *n*, northerner.

septième† (sɛtjɛm) *a. & n*, seventh.

septique (sɛptik) *a*, septic.

septuor (sɛptɥɔːr) *m*, septet[te].

sépulcral, e (sepylkral) *a*, sepulchral. **sépulcre** (kr) *m*, sepulchre. **sépulture** (tyːr) *f*, burial; burial place, resting place; tomb.

séquelle (sekɛl) *f*, crew, gang; string.

séquence (sekɑ̃ːs) *f*, sequence, run (*Cards*, &c).

séquestre (sekɛstr) *m*, sequestration.

sérail (sera:j) *m*, seraglio.

séraphin (serafɛ̃) *m*, seraph. **séraphique** (fik) *a*, seraphic.

serbe (sɛrb) *a. & S~, n*, Serb[ian]. *le serbe* Serb[ian] (*language*). **la Serbie** (bi) Serbia.

serein (sərɛ̃, ɛn) *a*, serene, calm; halcyon. ¶ *m*, evening dew, evening damp.

sérénade (serenad) *f*, serenade.

sérénité (serenite) *f*, serenity; equanimity.

serf, serve (sɛrf, sɛrv) *n*, serf, thrall.

serfouir (sɛrfwiːr) *v.t*, to hoe.

serge (sɛrʒ) *f*, serge.

sergent (sɛrʒɑ̃) *m*, sergeant; cramp (*tool*). ~ *de ville*, policeman. ~ *instructeur* drill sergeant.

sériciculture (serisikyltyːr) *f*, silkworm breeding.

série (seri) *f*, series; range; set; chapter (*accidents*); break (*Bil.*).

sérieux, euse† (serjø, øːz) *a*, serious; grave, sober (*dress*); earnest, genuine, bona fide. ¶ *m*, seriousness, gravity.

serin (sərɛ̃, in) *m*, canary; silly, noodle. **seriner** (rine) *v.t*, to teach (*bird*); din into (*pers.*); drum (*à* = into).

seringa (s[ə]rɛ̃ga) *m*, syringa, seringa.

seringue (s[ə]rɛ̃ːg) *f*, syringe, squirt. ~ [*lavement*], enema. ~ *de Pravaz* (prava) hypodermic syringe. **seringuer** (rɛ̃ge) *v.t* to syringe, squirt, inject.

serment (sɛrmɑ̃) *m*, oath.

sermon (sɛrmɔ̃) m, sermon; lecture (*scolding*).
sermonner (mɔne) v.t. & abs, to sermonize, lecture.

serpe (sɛrp) f, bill hook.

serpent (sɛrpɑ̃) m, serpent, snake. ~ *à sonnettes*, rattlesnake. ~ *caché sous les fleurs*, snake in the grass. **serpentaire** (tɛːr) m, secretary bird. **serpenteau** (to) m, young snake; squib (*firework*). **serpenter** (te) v.i, to wind, meander. **serpentin, e** (tɛ̃, in) a, serpentine. ¶ m, worm (*still, &c*); coil; [paper] streamer. ¶ f, serpentine (*rock*).

serpette (sɛrpɛt) f, pruning knife; bill hook.

serpillière (sɛrpijɛːr) f, sacking; apron.

serpolet (sɛrpɔlɛ) m, wild thyme.

serrage (sɛra:ʒ) m, tightening, application (*brake*). **serre** (sɛːr) f, greenhouse, glasshouse, conservatory; grip; claw, talon. ~ *à palmiers*, palm house. ~ *à vignes*, vinery. ~ *chaude*, hothouse. **serré, e** (sɛre) p.a, tight, close, serried; clenched. **serre-frein** (sɛrfrɛ̃) m, brakesman. **serre-joint**, m, cramp, clamp (*tool*). **serre-livres**, m, book-ends. **serrement** (rmɑ̃) m, pressure; squeeze, shake (*hand*). ~ *de cœur*, pang. **serrer** (re) v.t, to press, squeeze; clasp, hug, wring, grip; clench; shake (*hand*); tighten; put on (*brake*); put away, stow away; furl (*sail*). ~ *sous clef*, to lock up. **serre-tête**, m, headband. **serrure** (ry:r) f, lock. ~ *à demi-tour*, latch. ~ *à entailler*, mortise lock. ~ *encloisonnée* (ɑ̃klwazɔne), rim l. **serrurerie** (ryri) f, locksmithery; metal work, ironwork. ~ *de bâtiment*, builders' hardware, b—s' ironmongery. **serrurier** (rje) m, locksmith; metal worker, ironworker. ~ *charron*, coachsmith.

sertir (sɛrtiːr) v.t, to set (*gem*); crease.

sérum (serɔm) m, serum.

servage (sɛrva:ʒ) m, serfdom, thraldom. **servant** (vɑ̃) a.m, lay (*brother*). ¶ m, gunner; server (*Ten.*). **servante** (vɑ̃:t) f, [maid]-servant; waitress; service table. **serviable** (vjabl) a, obliging. **service** (vis) m, service; serve (*Ten.*); running; booking; supply; department; duty; attendance; waiting (*hotel*, &c); course (*meal*); set (*utensils*, &c). ~ *de table & dessert*, dinner service. ~ *par en bas*, underhand service (*Ten.*). ~ *par en haut*, overhand s. **serviette** (vjɛt) f, dispatch case, document c. ~ [*de table*], [table] napkin, serviette. ~ [*de toilette*], towel. ~ *éponge*, Turkish towel. ~ *hygiénique*, sanitary t. ~ *nid d'abeilles*, huckaback t.

servile† (sɛrvil) a, servile, menial; slavish. **servilité** (lite) f, servility; slavishness.

servir (sɛrviːr) v.i. & t & abs, ir, to serve; be of use; wait (on); attend to; serve up. **se ~ chez**, to deal with (*tradesman*). **se ~ de**, to use. **serviteur** (vitœːr) m, ser-

vant. **servitude** (tyd) f, servitude, slavery; easement (*Law*).

sésame (sezam) m, sesame (*Bot.*). S~, *ouvre-toi*, open sesame.

session (sɛsjɔ̃) f, session, sitting, term.

seuil (sœːj) m, threshold, sill.

seul, e (sœl) a, alone, by oneself, solo; lonely; only; one, single; sole; mere, bare, very. **seulement** (lmɑ̃) ad, only; solely, merely.

sève (sɛːv) f, sap (*plant*); vigour.

sévère† (sevɛːr) a, severe, stern; hard; strict. **sévérité** (verite) f, severity, &c.

sévices (sevis) m.pl, maltreatment, cruelty (*in law*).

Séville (sevil) f, Seville.

sévir (seviːr) v.i, to deal severely (*contre* = with); rage, be rife, be rampant.

sevrage (səvra:ʒ) m, weaning. **sevrer** (vre) v.t, to wean; deprive.

sexe (sɛks) m, sex.

sextant (sɛkstɑ̃) m, sextant.

sextuor (sɛkstɥɔːr) m, sextet[te].

sexuel, le (sɛksɥɛl) a, sexual.

seyant, e (sɛjɑ̃, ɑ̃:t) a, becoming.

si, s' (si, s) c, if, whether; how [much]; what if, suppose. ~ *le temps le permet*, weather permitting. **si**, ad, so; so much; such; however; yes. ¶ m, if; B (*Mus.*).

Siam (le (sjam), Siam. **siamois, e** (mwa, a:z) a. & S~, n, Siamese. **le siamois**, Siamese (*language*).

Sibérie (la) (siberi), Siberia. **sibérien, ne** (rjɛ̃, ɛn) a. & S~, n, Siberian.

sicaire (sikɛːr) m, hired assassin.

siccatif (sikatif) m, drier[s] (*painter's*).

Sicile (la) (sisil), Sicily. **sicilien, ne** (ljɛ̃, ɛn) a. & S~, n, Sicilian.

sicle (sikl) m, shekel (*Bible*).

sidéral, e (sideral) a, sidereal.

siècle (sjɛkl) m, century; age, times; world. *les* ~s *d'ignorance*, the dark ages.

siège (sjɛ:ʒ) m, seat; bench; box (*driver's*); bottom (*chair*); see (*Eccl.*); siege (*Mil.*). ~ *arrière*, back seat; pillion. ~ *social*, registered office, head o. **siéger** (ʒe) v.i, to have its headquarters; sit; be seated.

sien, ne (*with* **le, la, les**) (sjɛ̃, ɛn) pn. & m, his, hers; one's own, his own, her own.

Sienne (sjɛn) f, Sienna.

sieste (sjɛst) f, siesta, nap.

sieur (sjœːr) m, Mr.

siffler (sifle) v.i. & t, to whistle; pipe; hiss; whirr, whizz; wheeze. **sifflet** (flɛ) m, whistle; pipe (*boatswain's*); hiss, catcall. [**canard**] **siffleur** (flœːr) m, widgeon.

signal (siɲal) m, signal. ~ *de manœuvre*, dialling tone (*Teleph.*). ~ *horaire*, time signal (*Radio*). ~ *pas libre*, engaged tone (*Teleph.*). *signaux lumineux de circulation*, traffic lights, stop & go lights. **signalé, e** (le) p.a, signal; conspicuous; well known. **signalement** (lmɑ̃) m, description. **signaler** (le) v.t, to signalize, point out; signal; notify. **signaleur** (lœ:r) m, signaller (Mil.); signalman (Rly).

signataire (sinate:r) n, signatory, signer. **signature** (ty:r) f, signing, signature. **signe** (sin) m, sign, token, mark; motion, wave (hand). ~ *d'omission*, caret. ~ [*de tête*], nod. ~ *des yeux*, wink. **signer** (ne) v.t, to sign. ~ *à*, to witness. se ~, to cross oneself. **signet** (nɛ) m, ribbon book mark[er], tassel, register.

significatif, ive (siɲifikatif, i:v) a, significant, meaning, of deep significance (look). **signification** (sjɔ̃) f, signification, meaning, sense, import; service (writ). **signifier** (fje) v.t, to signify, mean; notify, intimate; serve (a notice).

silence (silɑ̃:s) m, silence, stillness, hush; pause; rest (Mus.). **silencieux, euse†** (lɑ̃sjø, ø:z) a, silent, noiseless, still. ¶ m, silencer.

Silésie (la) (silezi), Silesia. **silésienne** (zjɛn) f, silesia (fabric).

silex (silɛks) m, silex, flint.

silhouette (silwɛt) f, silhouette.

silicate (silikat) m, silicate. **silice** (lis) f, silica.

sillage (sija:3) m, wake, track; headway (ship). **sillet** (jɛ) m, nut (violin, &c.). **sillon** (jɔ̃) m, furrow; drill (furrow); (pl., Poet.) fields; wrinkle; track, trail; streak; groove. **sillonner** (ɔne) v.t, to furrow; plough (seas); wrinkle; streak, groove.

silo (silo) m, silo.

simagrée (simagre) f. oft. pl, pretence; affectation.

simiesque (simjɛsk) a, ape-like, apish.

similaire (simile:r) a, similar, like. **simili-** (li) prefix, imitation (att.), artificial. **simili-gravure** (ligravy:r) f, process engraving, half-tone e. **similitude** (tyd) f, similitude, similarity; simile.

simonie (simɔni) f, simony.

simoun (simun) m, simoom, -oon.

simple† (sɛ̃:pl) a, simple; single; ordinary; private (soldier); plain; homely; mere; simple[-minded]; half-witted. ¶ m, single (Ten.). ~ *messieurs, dames*, men's, women's, single. **simplicité** (sɛ̃plisite) f, simplicity, &c. **simplifier** (fje) v.t, to simplify.

simulacre (simylakr) m, simulacrum, image; dummy (Mil.); show. ~ *de combat*, sham fight, mock f. **simulé, e** (le) p.a, feigned, sham; bogus, fictitious. **simuler** (le) v.t, to simulate, &c. ~ *la maladie*, to malinger.

simulie (simyli) f, sand fly.

simultané†, e (simyltane) a, simultaneous.

Sinaï (le mont) (sinai), Mount Sinai.

sinapisme (sinapism) m, mustard plaster.

sincère† (sɛ̃sɛ:r) a, sincere, candid, unfeigned, genuine. **sincérité** (serite) f, sincerity, candour, &c.

sinécure (sineky:r) f, sinecure.

Singapour (sɛ̃gapu:r) m, Singapore.

singe (sɛ̃:3) m, monkey, ape; copy cat; winch. **singer** (sɛ̃3e) v.t, to ape, mock. **singerie** (3ri) f, monkey house; grimace, monkey trick; grotesque imitation.

singulariser (sɛ̃gylarize) v.t, to make conspicuous. **singulier, ère†** (lje, ɛ:r) a, singular; peculiar; odd, queer, quaint; single (combat). ¶ m, singular (Gram.). **singularité** (larite) f, singularity, &c.

sinistre† (sinistr) a, sinister, ominous; grim; lurid, baleful. ¶ m, disaster, casualty; loss (Insce.).

sinon (sinɔ̃) c, otherwise, else; except, save.

sinueux, euse (sinɥø, ø:z) a, sinuous, winding. **sinuosité** (nɥozite) f, sinuosity, bend.

sinus (siny:s) m, sinus; sine.

siphon (sifɔ̃) m, siphon; trap (drain).

sire (si:r) m, sire (to king).

sirène (sirɛn) f, siren, mermaid; hooter.

sirop (siro) m, syrup. **siroter** (rɔte) v.t, to sip. **sirupeux, euse** (rypø, ø:z) a, syrupy.

sis, e (si, i:z) p.p, situated.

sismique (sismik) a, seismic. **sismographe** (mɔgraf) m, seismograph.

site (sit) m, site. ~ *pittoresque*, beauty spot.

sitôt (sito) ad, as soon, so soon.

situation (sitɥasjɔ̃) f, situation, position; condition, state; statement, return. **situé, e** (tɥe) p.p. & p.a, situated.

six (si; in liaison, siz; at end of phrase, sis) a. & m, six; 6th. ~ *jeux à rien*, love set (Ten.). **sixième†** (sizjɛm) a. & n, sixth. **sixte** (sikst) f, sixth (Mus.).

ski (ski) m, ski. ~ *s de saut*, jumping skis.

slave (sla:v) a. & S~, n, Slav.

slip (slip) m, slip (drawers).

sloughi (slugi) m, saluki.

smilax (smilaks) m, smilax (Bot.).

smoking (smɔkiŋ) m, dinner jacket.

Smyrne (smirn) f, Smyrna.

snob (snɔb) m, genteel (ironical). **snobisme** (bism) m, gentility.

sobre† (sɔbr) a, sober, temperate, abstemious; sparing, chary. **sobriété** (briete) f, sobriety, &c.

sobriquet (sɔbrikɛ) m, nickname.

soc (sɔk) m, ploughshare.

sociable† (sɔsjabl) a, sociable; companionable, genial. **social, e** (sjal) a, social; corporate; registered (capital, offices); of the firm; company's. **socialisme** (lism) m, socialism. **socialiste** (list) n. & a, socialist. **sociétaire** (sjete:r) n, member; shareholder, stockholder. **société** (te) f, society; community; companionship, fellowship; club; company; firm; partnership. ~ *à responsabilité limitée* (Fr.), limited company (private) (Eng.). ~ *anonyme*, limited company (public). ~ *de secours mutuels*, friendly society, benefit s. ~ *de prévoyance*, provident s. S~ *des Nations*, League of Nations. ~ *immobilière*, building society. ~ *par actions*, joint stock company. **sociologie** (sjɔlɔʒi) *f,* sociology.

socle (sɔkl) *m,* pedestal, stand.

socque (sɔk) *m,* clog, patten. **soquettes** (kɛt) *f.pl,* ankle socks.

sodium (sɔdjɔm) *m,* sodium.

sœur (sœ:r) *f,* sister. **sœurette** (sœrɛt) *f,* [dear] little sister.

sofa (sɔfa) *m,* sofa.

soffite (sɔfit) *m,* soffit.

soi (swa) & ~-**même**, *pn,* oneself; himself, herself, itself. ~-**disant** (dizɑ̃) *a.inv,* self-styled, would-be; so-called.

soie (swa) *f,* silk; bristle (*hog*); tang (*of tool*). ~ *floche* (flɔʃ), floss silk. ~ *pour la pêche à la mouche,* fly line. **soierie** (ri) *f,* silk goods, silks; silk mill; silk trade.

soif (swaf) *f,* thirst; craving, hankering. *avoir* ~, to be thirsty, to thirst.

soigné, e (swaɲe) *p.a,* well-finished; trim, neat. **soigner** (ɲe) *v.t,* to take care of, look after; attend to; tend; nurse; manicure. **soigneur** (ɲœ:r) *m,* minder; second (*Box.*). **soigneux, euse†** (ɲø, ø:z) *a,* careful, painstaking; tidy. **soin** (swɛ̃) *m. oft. pl,* care, attention, pains; nursing. ~ *des mains,* manicure. ~ *des pieds,* chiropody. *aux* [*bons*] ~*s de,* care of, c/o.

soir (swa:r) *m,* evening, night; afternoon. **soirée** (sware) *f,* evening; [evening] party. *de* ~, evening (*dress, &c*).

soit (swa) *c,* either; or; whether; suppose, let. ~ *que,* whether. ~! (swat), so be it! agreed!

soixante (swasɑ̃t) *a. & m,* sixty [or so]. **soixante** (sɑ̃:t) *a. & m,* sixty. ~-**dix** (sɑ̃tdis) *a. & m,* seventy. ~-**onze**, ~-**douze**, 71, 72. ~-**dixième** (zjɛm) *a. & n,* seventieth. **soixantième** (tjɛm) *a. & n,* sixtieth.

soja (sɔja) *m,* soy[a] bean.

sol (sɔl) *m,* ground, earth; soil; G (*Mus.*).

solaire (sɔlɛ:r) *a,* solar, sun (*att.*); sunlight (*treatment*).

soldat (sɔlda) *m,* soldier, man. ~ *de plomb,* tin soldier. *le S*~ *inconnu,* the Unknown Warrior *or* Soldier. **soldatesque** (tɛsk) *f,* (*unruly*) soldiery.

solde (sɔld) *f,* pay (*Mil., Nav., &c*). ¶ *m,* balance; settlement; surplus stock, job lot; [clearance] sale. ~ *d'édition,* remainder (*books*). ~ *de dividende,* final dividend. *en* ~, to clear (*shop*). **solder** (de) *v.t,* to balance (*a/c*); pay off, settle; sell off, clear; remainder (*book*). **soldeur** (dœ:r) *m,* remainderman.

sole (sɔl) *f,* sole (*fish, hoof, bed plate*). ~ *limande,* lemon sole.

solécisme (sɔlesism) *m,* solecism.

soleil (sɔlɛ:j) *m,* sun; sunshine; sunflower; catherine wheel (*firework*). ~ *couchant,* setting sun, sunset.

solennel, le† (sɔlanɛl) *a,* solemn; formal;

state (*att.*); impressive. **solenniser** (nize) *v.t,* to solemnize, celebrate. **solennité** (te) *f,* solemnity; celebration.

solfège (sɔlfɛ:ʒ) *m,* sol-fa, solfeggio. ¶ **solfier** (fje) *v.t. & abs,* to sol-fa.

solidaire† (sɔlidɛ:r) *a,* joint & several; solidary. **solide†** (lid) *a,* solid; strong; substantial; hefty; firm; fast (*colour*); sound; sterling (*fig.*). ¶ *m,* solid; s. foundation, s. ground; main chance. **solidifier** (difje) *v.t,* to solidify. **solidité** (te) *f,* solidity; strength; soundness.

soliloque (sɔlilɔk) *m,* soliloquy.

soliste (sɔlist) *n,* soloist; solo (*violin*).

solitaire† (sɔlitɛ:r) *a,* solitary, lonely. ¶ *m,* hermit; solitaire (*gem & game*). **solitude** (tyd) *f,* solitude, loneliness; wilderness, wild.

solive (sɔli:v) *f,* joist, beam, girder.

solliciter (sɔllisite) *v.t,* to solicit, ask for, apply for; canvass; entreat; urge; attract. **sollicitude** (tyd) *f,* solicitude; anxiety.

solo (sɔlo) *m,* solo (*Mus.*).

solstice (sɔlstis) *m,* solstice.

soluble (sɔlybl) *a,* soluble; solvable. **solution** (sjɔ) *f,* solution; break; discharge (*Law*). ~ *fondamentale,* stock solution (*Phot.*).

solvabilité (sɔlvabilite) *f,* solvency (*Fin.*). **solvable** (bl) *a,* solvent.

sombre (sɔ̃:br) *a,* dark, sombre, gloomy; dim. **sombrer** (sɔ̃bre) *v.i,* to founder, sink, go down.

sommaire† (sɔmɛ:r) *a,* summary, compendious; scant. ¶ *m,* summary, synopsis.

sommation (sɔmasjɔ̃) *f,* summons.

somme (sɔm) *f,* sum, amount; burden. ~ *toute ou en* ~, [up]on the whole.

somme (sɔm) *m,* nap, snooze. **sommeil** (mɛ:j) *m,* sleep, slumber; sleepiness. **sommeiller** (mɛje) *v.i,* to slumber, doze, nod.

sommelier (sɔməlje) *m,* butler; wine waiter.

sommer (sɔme) *v.t,* to summon, call on; sum up.

sommet (sɔmɛ) *m,* summit, top; vertex, apex; acme.

sommier (sɔmje) *m,* pack animal; transom; dossier; register. ~ *élastique,* box-spring mattress. ~ *métallique,* wire-spring m.

sommité (sɔmmite) *f,* summit; top; leading man, (*pl.*) leading people.

somnambule (sɔmnɑ̃byl) *n,* somnambulist, sleep walker. **somnambulisme** (lism) *m,* somnambulism. **somnolent, e** (nɔlɑ̃, ɑ̃:t) *a,* somnolent, sleepy.

somptueux, euse† (sɔ̃ptɥø, ø:z) *a,* sumptuous. **somptuosité** (tɥozite) *f,* sumptuousness.

son, sa, ses (sɔ̃, sa, se) *a,* his, her, its, one's.

son (sɔ̃) *m,* sound; clang; tone; bran.

sonate (sɔnat) *f,* sonata.

sonde (sɔ̃:d) *f,* [sounding] lead, plummet; probe; spit; drill (*Min.*); taster (*cheese*). **sonder** (sɔ̃de) *v.t,* to sound; probe; fathom. **sondeur** (dœ:r) *m,* leadsman; driller.

songe (sŏ:ʒ) *m*, dream. **~-creux**, *m*, dreamer, visionary. **songer** (sŏʒe) *v.i*, to dream, muse. ~ *à*, to think of, intend. **songeur, euse** (ʒœ:r, øːz) *a*, dreamy; pensive.

sonnaille (sɔnɑ:j) *f*, cattle bell, cow b. **sonnailler** (naje) *m*, bell-wether. ¶ *v.i*, to keep ringing [the bell]. **sonnant, e** (nɑ̃, ɑ̃:t) *a*, [re]sounding; hard (*cash*). *à l'heure sonnante*, on the stroke of time. **sonné, e** (ne) *p.a*, past, struck (*hour*); turned (*a certain age*). **sonner** (ne) *v.i. & t*, to sound; ring; r. for; toll; strike. **sonnerie** (nri) *f*, ringing; bells; bell; call (*trumpet, bugle*). **sonnet** (nɛ) *m*, sonnet. **sonnette** (nɛt) *f*, bell; pile driver. **sonneur** (nœːr) *m*, bell ringer. **sonore** (nɔ:r) *a*, sonorous; loud (*laugh, cheers*); sound (*att.*). **sonorité** (nɔrite) *f*, sonorousness, volume [of sound].

sophisme (sofism) *m*, sophism; fallacy. **sophistique** (tik) *f*, sophistry. **sophistiquer** (ke) *v.t. & i*, to sophisticate.

soporifique (sɔporifik) *a. & m*, soporific.

soprano (sɔprano) *m*, soprano (*voice & pers.*).

sorbet (sɔrbɛ) *m*, water ice. **sorbetière** (btjɛ:r) *f*, ice cream freezer.

sorbier (sɔrbje) *m*, service tree, sorb. ~ *des oiseaux*, mountain ash.

sorcellerie (sɔrsɛlri) *f*, sorcery, witchcraft. **sorcier, ère** (sje, ɛ:r) *n*, sorcerer, ess, wizard, witch; hag. *sorcier guérisseur*, medicine man, witch doctor.

sordide† (sɔrdid) *a*, sordid; filthy, squalid.

Sorlingues (îles) (sɔrlɛ̃g) *f.pl*, Scilly Islands, Scilly Isles.

sornettes (sɔrnɛt) *f.pl*, nonsense.

sort (sɔ:r) *m*, lot, fate; spell. **sortable** (sɔrtabl) *a*, suitable; eligible. **sortant** (tɑ̃) *a.m*, drawn, winning (*number*); retiring, outgoing (*pers.*).

sorte (sɔrt) *f*, sort, kind; manner, way. *en quelque ~*, in a way, as it were.

sortie (sɔrti) *f*, going out; coming out; exit; leaving, retirement; voluntary (*organ*); issue; export[ation]; sally, sortie; outlet; way out, egress. ~ *de bain*, bath wrap. ~ *de bal*, ~ *de théâtre*, opera cloak, evening wrap.

sortilège (sɔrtilɛ:ʒ) *m*, witchcraft, spell.

sortir (sɔrti:r) *v.i.ir*, to go out; come out; leave; emerge, issue, spring; stand out; (*v.t.ir*.) to bring out; take out; pull out. *X. sort*, exit X. (*Theat.*).

sosie (sozi) *m*, double (*pers.*).

sot, te† (so, ɔt) *a*, silly, foolish; sheepish. ¶ *n*, fool. **sot-l'y-laisse** (sɔliɛs) *f*, parson's nose. **sottise** (sɔti:z) *f*, silliness, foolishness, folly; (*pl*.) nonsense; insult.

sou (su) *m*, sou = 5 centimes; penny (*in sense of very little money*).

soubassement (subɑsmɑ̃) *m*, basement; base.

soubresaut (subrɔso) *m*, start, leap, jolt.

souche (suʃ) *f*, stump, stock, stub; founder (*family*); shaft, stack (*chimney*); counterfoil. *à la ~*, unissued (*stocks, shares*).

souci (susi) *m*, care, concern; worry; marigold. ~ *d'eau*, marsh marigold, kingcup. se **soucier de** (sje), to care for, mind. **soucieux, euse** (sjø, øːz) *a*, anxious.

soucoupe (sukup) *f*, saucer.

soudain, e† (sudɛ̃, ɛn) *a*, sudden. **soudain**, *ad*, suddenly. **soudaineté** (dɛnte) *f*, suddenness.

soude (sud) *f*, soda; saltwort.

souder (sude) *v.t*, to solder; weld.

soudoyer (sudwaje) *v.t*, to hire; bribe.

soudure (sudy:r) *f*, soldering; solder; welding; joint; weld.

souffle (sufl) *m*, breath; puff, waft, blast; inspiration. **souffler** (fle) *v.i. & t*, to blow; b. up; b. out; breathe; prompt; prime; huff (*Draughts*). **soufflerie** (flɛri) *f*, bellows (*organ, &c*). **soufflet** (flɛ) *m*, bellows; hood (*carriage*); box on the ear[s]; slap; snub. **souffleter** (flɛte) *v.t*, to box (*someone's*) ears, slap. **souffleur** (flœ:r) *m*, blower; prompter. **soufflure** (fly:r) *f*, blowhole.

souffrance (sufrɑ̃:s) *f*, sufferance (*Law*); suffering, pain. *en ~*, in suspense, in abeyance, held over; unclaimed, on hand (*goods*); undeliverable (*parcel*). **souffrant, e** (frɑ̃, ɑ̃:t) *a*, suffering; ailing, unwell, poorly. **souffre-douleur** (fradulœ:r) *m*, drudge; butt; scapegoat. **souffreteux, euse** (tø, øːz) *a*, sickly. **souffrir** (frir) *v.t. & i.ir*, to suffer; bear; endure, stand; undergo; allow.

soufre (sufr) *m*, sulphur, brimstone. **soufrière** (frie:r) *f*, sulphur mine.

souhait (swɛ) *m*, wish. ~*s de bonne année*, new-year's wishes, compliments of the season. **souhaitable** (tabl) *a*, desirable. **souhaiter** (te) *v.t*, to wish; w. for. ~ *la* (ou *une bonne*) *fête à quelqu'un*, to wish someone many happy returns [of the day].

souille (su:j) *f*, wallow. **souiller** (suje) *v.t*, to soil, dirty; pollute, taint; stain, sully, besmirch. **souillon** (jɔ̃) *n*, sloven; (*f*.) slut, slattern. **souillure** (jy:r) *f*, spot, stain; blot, blemish.

soûl, e (su, ul) *a*, drunk; gorged. ¶ *m*, fill.

soulager (sulaʒe) *v.t*, to relieve, lighten, ease, alleviate; comfort.

souleur (sulœ:r) *f*, shock (*startling emotion*).

soulèvement (sulɛvmɑ̃) *m*, rising; heaving; upheaval (*Geol.*); revolt. **soulever** (lve) *v.t*, to raise, lift; make heave; moot; rouse. se ~, to rise, heave; revolt.

soulier (sulje) *m*, shoe. ~*s Richelieu* (riʃljø), lace-up shoes.

souligner (suliɲe) *v.t*, to underline; emphasize.

soulte (sult) *f*, balance (*in cash*).

soumettre (sumɛtr) *v.t.ir*, to subdue; submit; subject. se ~, to submit, yield, give in. **soumis, e** (mi, i:z) *p.a*, submissive, dutiful; subject, amenable; liable. **soumission**

(misjɔ̃) *f,* submission; submissiveness; tender; bond. **soumissionner** (ɔne) *v.t,* to tender for.

soupape (supap) *f,* valve; plug (*bath, &c*).

soupçon (supsɔ̃) *m,* suspicion; surmise; dash; touch. **soupçonner** (sɔne) *v.t,* to suspect; surmise. **soupçonneux, euse** (nø, øːz) *a,* suspicious, distrustful.

soupe (sup) *f,* soup; sop.

soupente (supãːt) *f,* loft.

souper (supe) *m,* supper. ~ *assis,* sit-down supper. ~ *debout,* buffet (*at a ball*). ¶ *v.i,* to have supper, sup.

soupeser (supəze) *v.t,* to feel the weight of.

soupière (supjɛːr) *f,* soup tureen.

soupir (supiːr) *m,* sigh; breath; crotchet rest (*Mus.*). **soupirail** (piraːj) *m,* air hole, vent. **soupirant** (rã) *m,* suitor, wooer. **soupirer** (re) *v.i,* to sigh; yearn.

souple (supl) *a,* supple, pliant, pliable; lithe[some], lissom[e]; limp (*binding*); versatile. *feutre* ~, soft felt (*hat*). **souplesse** (plɛs) *f,* suppleness, &c.

source (surs) *f,* source, spring, fountainhead; well; rise; well spring, fount. **sourcier, ère** (sje, ɛːr) *n,* water diviner, dowser.

sourcil (sursi) *m,* eyebrow. **sourciller** (je) *v.i,* to frown; wince. **sourcilleux, euse** (jø, øːz) *a,* beetling; frowning, anxious.

sourd, e (suːr, urd) *a,* deaf; dull; hollow (*voice*); mute[d]; muffled; underhand. ¶ *n,* deaf person. **sourdement** (surdəmã) *ad,* dully; secretly. **sourdine** (din) *f,* mute (*Mus.*); damper. *en* ~, on the sly. **sourd-muet, sourde-muette** (surmɥɛ, dmɥɛt) *a,* deaf & dumb. ¶ *n,* deaf-mute.

sourdre (surdr) *v.i,* to spring, well up.

souriant, e (surjã, ãːt) *a,* smiling.

souriceau (suriso) *m,* young mouse. **souricière** (sjeːr) *f,* mouse trap; trap (*police, &c*).

sourire (suriːr) *m,* smile. ¶ *v.i.ir,* to smile. ~ *à,* to be attractive to, please.

souris (suri) *f,* mouse; knuckle end (*mutton*).

sournois, e† (surnwa, aːz) *a,* sly, underhand.

sous (su; *in liaison,* suz) *pr,* under[neath], beneath, below; in; by; with; within; on. **sous,** *comps:* ~**-affermer,** *v.t,* to sublet, underlet. ~**-bail,** *m,* sublease, under-lease. ~**-cutané, e,** *a,* subcutaneous. ~**-entendre,** *v.t,* to understand, imply. ~**-entendu,** *m,* implication; double en-tendre. **sous-estimer,** *v.t,* to under-esti-mate, undervalue, underrate. ~**-ferme,** *f,* underlease. ~**-gouverneur,** *m,* deputy gov-ernor. **sous-jacent, e** (suʒasã, ãːt) *a,* un-derlying. ~**-lieutenant,** *m,* sublieutenant, second l. ~**-locataire,** *n,* subtenant. ~**-louer,** *v.t,* to sublet, underlet; rent (*as subtenant*). ~**-main,** *m,* blotting pad. ~**-maître,** *m,* assistant master (*Sch.*). ~**-maîtresse,** *f,* a. mistress. ~**-marin, e.a. & m,** submarine. *en* ~**-œuvre,** under-pinned. ~**-officier,** *m,* non-commissioned officer. ~**-ordre,m, subordinate, underling;**

sub-order. *en* ~**-*ordre,*** subordinate(ly). ~**-*produit,*** *m,* by-product. ~**-*secrétaire,*** *m,* under secretary. ~**-*seing*** (sẽ) *m,* simple contract. ~**-*sol,*** *m,* subsoil; base-ment. ~**-*titre,*** *m,* subtitle, caption. ~**-*traitant*** (tretã) *m,* subcontractor. ~**-*traité,*** *m,* subcontract. ~**-*ventrière*** (vãtrieːr) *f,* belly band; [saddle] girth. ~**-*vêtement,*** *m,* undergarment (*man's*); (*pl.*) underwear, underclothing (*men's*).

souscripteur (suskriptœːr) *m,* subscriber; applicant (*shares*); drawer (*bill*); under-writer (*Insce*). **souscription** (sjɔ̃) *f,* execu-tion, signing (*deed*); signature; subscrip-tion; application; underwriting. **sous-crire** (skriːr) *v.t. & i. ir,* to execute, sign; subscribe; draw; apply for; underwrite.

soussigné, e (susiɲe) *a. & n,* undersigned.

soustraction (sustraksjɔ̃) *f,* abstraction; sub-traction. **soustraire** (streːr) *v.t.ir,* to ab-stract (*steal*), purloin; withdraw; screen; subtract (*Arith.*). *se* ~ *à,* to elude, avoid. *se* ~ *à la justice,* to abscond.

soutache (sutaʃ) *f,* braid. **soutacher** (ʃe) *v.t,* to braid.

soutane (sutan) *f,* cassock; cloth (*clergy*).

soute (sut) *f,* [store]room (*Naut.*); magazine, bunker, locker; tank.

soutenable (sutnabl) *a,* bearable; tenable. **soutenir** (tniːr) *v.t.ir,* to sustain, support, hold up; uphold; keep, maintain; back [up]; stand, bear; afford. **soutenu, e** (tny) *p.a,* sustained; unremitting; lofty, rhetori-cal (*style*).

souterrain, e (sutɛrɛ̃, ɛn) *a,* underground, subterranean; underhand. ¶ *m,* tunnel; cavern.

soutien (sutjẽ) *m,* support; mainstay; up-holder. ~ *de famille,* bread winner. ~**-gorge,** *m,* bust bodice, brassière.

soutirer (sutire) *v.t,* to draw off, rack [off] (*wine*); extract (*money*).

souvenance (suvnãːs) *f,* memories. **souvenir** (vniːr) *m,* remembrance, recollection, memory; memento; keepsake. **se** ~, *v.pr.ir,* to remember, recollect.

souvent (suvã) *ad,* often.

souverain, e† (suvrɛ̃, ɛn) *a,* sovereign; su-preme, superlative. ¶ *n,* sovereign. **sou-veraineté** (vrɛnte) *f,* sovereignty.

soviet (sɔvjɛt) *m,* soviet. **soviétique** (etik) *a,* soviet (*att.*).

soya (sɔja) *m,* soy[a] bean.

soyeux, euse (swajø, øːz) *a,* silky.

spacieux, euse† (spasjø, øːz) *a,* spacious, roomy, capacious.

spadassin (spadasẽ) *m,* ruffian.

sparadrap (sparadra) *m,* sticking plaster.

sparte (spart) *m,* esparto [grass].

spartiate (sparsjat) *a. & n,* Spartan.

spasme (spasm) *m,* spasm. **spasmodique** (mɔdik) *a,* spasmodic (*Med.*).

spath (spat) *m,* spar. ~ *fluor,* fluor spar.

spatule (spatyl) *f,* spatula; spoonbill.*

speaker (spikœ:r) *m*, announcer (*Radio*).

spécial, e† (spesjal) *a*, special, particular. se spécialiser dans (lize), to specialize in. spécialiste (list) *n*, specialist. spécialité (te) *f*, speciality. ~ *pharmaceutique*, patent medicine, proprietary medicine.

spécieux, euse† (spesjø, ø:z) *a*, specious.

spécification (spesifikasjɔ̃) *f*, specification. spécifier (fje) *v.t*, to specify. spécifique† (fik) *a. & m*, specific.

spécimen (spesimɛn) *m*, specimen; free copy (*book*).

spectacle (spɛktakl) *m*, spectacle, sight, scene; play, entertainment, show. ~ *forain*, side show (*fair*). ~ *payant*, side show (*exhibition*). ~ *permanent*, continuous performance (*cinema*). spectateur, trice (tœ:r, tris) *n*, spectator, onlooker, bystander; (*m.pl.*) audience (*Theat., &c*).

spectral, e (spɛktral) *a*, spectral; ghostly, unearthly, eerie, -ry, weird. spectre (tr) *m*, spectre, ghost; spectrum. spectroscope (trɔskɔp) *m*, spectroscope.

spéculateur, trice (spekylatœ:r, tris) *n*, speculator. spéculatif, ive (tif, i:v) *a*, speculative. spéculation (sjɔ̃) *f*, speculation. spéculer (le) *v.i*, to speculate.

spermatozoaire (spɛrmatozɔ:r) *m*, spermatozoon. sperme (spɛrm) *m*, sperm.

sphère (sfɛ:r) *f*, sphere, orb, globe. sphérique (sferik) *a*, spherical.

sphincter (sfɛ̃ktɛ:r) *m*, sphincter.

sphinx (sfɛ̃:ks) *m*, sphinx.

spinal, e (spinal) *a*, spinal.

spinelle (spinɛl) *m. & att*, spinel.

spiral, e (spiral) *a*, spiral. ¶ *m*, hair spring; (*f.*) spiral. spire (spi:r) *f*, turn, spire, whorl.

spirite (spirit) *n*, spiritualist (*Psychics*). spiritisme (tism) *m*, spiritualism. spiritualisme (tɥalism) *m*, spiritualism (*Philos.*). spiritualiste (list) *n*, spiritualist. spirituel, le† (tɥel) *a*, spiritual; sacred (*concert*); witty; spirituel[le]. spiritueux, euse (tɥø, ø:z) *a*, spirituous. ¶ *m.pl*, spirits.

Spitzberg (le) (spitsbɛrg), Spitzbergen.

spleen (splin) *m*, spleen, dumps, blues.

splendeur (splɑ̃dœ:r) *f*, splendour. splendide† (did) *a*, splendid, gorgeous.

spolier (spɔlje) *v.t*, to despoil, rob, rifle.

spongieux, euse (spɔ̃ʒjø, ø:z) *a*, spongy.

spontané†, e (spɔ̃tane) *a*, spontaneous; willing.

sporadique (spɔradik) *a*, sporadic.

spore (spɔ:r) *f*, spore.

sport (spɔ:r) *m*, sport, sports. sportif, ive (spɔrtif, i:v) *a*, fond of sport[s]; sporting; sports (*att.*); athletic (*meeting*); game (*fish, fishing, &c*). *un sportif*, a sportsman.

square (skwa:r) *m*, enclosed public garden (*in a town square*).

squelette (skɛlɛt) *m*, skeleton; scrag (*pers.*).

stabat [mater] (stabat [matɛ:r]) *m*, Stabat Mater.

stabilité (stabilite) *f*, stability. stabiliser (ze) *v.t*, to stabilize (*Fin.*). stable (bl) *a*, stable; lasting.

stade (stad) *m*, stadium; stage (*Med.*).

stage (sta:ʒ) *m*, probation; course; articles. stagiaire (staʒjɛ:r) *n*, probationer; articled clerk.

stagnant, e (stagnɑ̃, ɑ̃:t) *a*, stagnant; standing (*water*). stagnation (nasjɔ̃) *f*, stagnation.

stalactite (stalaktit) *f*, stalactite.

stalagmite (stalagmit) *f*, stalagmite.

stalle (stal) *f*, stall; seat (*Theat.*); box (*horse*).

stance (stɑ̃:s) *f*, stanza.

stand (stɑ̃:d) *m*, stand (*racecourse, exhibition*); shooting gallery, rifle range.

station (stasjɔ̃) *f*, station; halt; stop (*bus*); rank (*cab*); resort. ~ *balnéaire*, watering place. ~ *climat[ér]ique*, health resort. ~ *de commerce*, trading station (*Africa, &c*). ~ *de ravitaillement*, filling station. stationnaire (ɔnɛ:r) *a*, stationary. stationnement (nmɑ̃) *m*, stopping, standing, halt; parking. ~ *interdit*, no parking. stationner (ne) *v.i*, to stop, &c.

statique (statik) *a*, static(al). ¶ *f*, statics.

statisticien (statistisjɛ̃) *m*, statistician. statistique (tik) *a*, statistic(al). ¶ *f*, statistics, return[s]. ~ *militaire*, intelligence department.

statuaire (statɥɛ:r) *a*, statuary. ¶ *f*, [art of] statuary. ¶ *m*, statuary (*pers.*). statue (ty) *f*, statue; (*pl. col.*) statuary.

statuer (statɥe) *v.t*, to ordain. ~ *sur*, to decide, resolve on.

statuette (statɥɛt) *f*, statuette.

stature (staty:r) *f*, stature, height (*of pers.*).

statut (staty) *m*, statute; (*pl.*) memorandum & articles [of association]; status. statutaire (tɛ:r) *a*, provided by the articles; appointed by the articles.

stéarine (stearin) *f*, stearin. stéatite (tit) *f*, steatite.

steeple-chase (stiplətʃɛs) *m*, hurdle race (*men's—2000–4000 metres*).

stellaire (stɛllɛ:r) *a*, stellar.

sténodactylographe (stenodaktilɔgraf) *n*, shorthand-typist. sténogramme (gram) *m*, grammalogue. sténographe (graf) *n*, shorthand writer, stenographer, -phist. sténographie (fi) *f*, shorthand, stenography. sténographier (fje) *v.t*, to take down [in shorthand].

stère (stɛ:r) *m*, stere = 1 cub. metre (*firewood*).

stéréoscope (stereɔskɔp) *m*, stereoscope. stéréotyper (stereɔtipe) *v.t*, to stereotype.

stérile† (steril) *a*, sterile, barren; effete; unfruitful; fruitless. stériliser (lize) *v.t*, to sterilize. stérilité (te) *f*, sterility, &c.

sterling (stɛrliŋ) *a.inv*, sterling.

sterne (stɛrn) *m*, tern (*bird*).

sternum (stɛrnɔm) *m*, sternum, breast bone.

stéthoscope (stetɔskɔp) *m*, stethoscope.

tigmate (stigmat) *m*, stigma, brand. **stigmatiser** (tize) *v.t*, to stigmatize, brand.

timulant (stimylɑ̃) *m*, stimulant; whet; stimulus. **stimuler** (le) *v.t*, to stimulate, exhilarate, whet.

tipendiaire (stipɑ̃djɛ:r) *a*, mercenary.

tipuler (stipyle) *v.t*, to stipulate.

tock (stɔk) *m*, stock (*goods, gold*).

tockfisch (stɔkfiʃ) *m*, stockfish.

tockiste (stɔkist) *m*, warehouseman (*trade goods*); accredited dealer.

toïcien, ne (stɔisjɛ̃, ɛn) *a. & m*, Stoic. **stoïcisme** (sism) *m*, stoicism. **stoïque†** (ik) *a*, stoical.

tomacal, e (stɔmakal) *a*, stomachal; stomach (*pump*). **stomachique** (ʃik) *a. & m*, stomachic.

top (stɔp) *i*, stop (*Naut., in telegrams, &c*). **stoppage** (stɔpa:ʒ) *m*, invisible mending. **stopper** (pe) *v.t. & i*, to stop (*ship, &c*); fine-darn.

tore (stɔ:r) *m*, sun blind. **∼-panneau**, store curtain.

trangulation (strɑ̃gylasjɔ̃) *f*, strangulation.

trapontin (strapɔ̃tɛ̃) *m*, tip-up seat.

trasbourg (strazbu:r) *m*, Strasburg.

trasse (stras) *f*, floss silk.

tratagème (strataʒɛm) *m*, stratagem. **stratège** (tɛ:ʒ) *m*, strategist. **stratégie** (teʒi) *f*, strategy; generalship. **stratégique** (ʒik) *a*, strategic(al).

tratification (stratifikasjɔ̃) *f*, stratification.

trict, e† (strikt) *a*, strict.

trident, e (stridɑ̃, ɑ̃:t) *a*, strident, shrill, grating.

trie (stri) *f*, stria, score; ridge. **strié, e** (e) *a*, striate[d]; fluted. **striure** (y:r) *f*, striation.

trophe (strɔf) *f*, stanza, verse.

tructure (strykty:r) *f*, structure, make.

trychnine (striknin) *f*, strychnin[e].

tuc (styk) *m*, stucco.

tudieux, euse† (stydjø, ø:z) *a*, studious.

tupéfiant (stypefjɑ̃) *m*, narcotic, drug. **stupéfier** (fje) *v.t*, to stupefy; amaze. **stupeur** (pœ:r) *f*, stupor; amazement. **stupide†** (pid) *a*, stupid. **stupidité** (dite) *f*, stupidity.

tyle (stil) *m*, style. **styler** (le) *v.t*, to train. **stylet** (lɛ) *m*, stiletto; stylet; probe. **tylographe** (stilɔgraf) *m*, stylograph (*pen*); fountain pen.

u (sy) *m*: *au ∼ de*, to the knowledge of.

uaire (sɥɛ:r) *m*, shroud, winding sheet.

uant, e (sɥɑ̃, ɑ̃:t) *a*, sweating; sweaty.

uave† (sɥa:v) *a*, sweet, soft; suave, bland. **suavité** (avite) *f*, sweetness, &c.

ubalterne (sybaltɛrn) *a*, subordinate, minor. **¶** *m*, underling; subaltern.

ubconscience (sybkɔ̃sjɑ̃:s) *f*, subconsciousness. **subconscient, e** (sjɑ̃, ɑ̃:t) *a. & m*, subconscious.

ubdiviser (sybdivize) *v.t*, to subdivide.

bir (sybi:r) *v.t*, to undergo, submit to, suffer; serve (*a sentence*).

subit, e† (sybi, it) *a*, sudden. **subito** (to) *ad*, all of a sudden.

subjectif, ive† (sybʒɛktif, i:v) *a. & m*, subjective.

subjonctif (sybʒɔ̃ktif) *m*, subjunctive [mood].

subjuguer (sybʒyge) *v.t*, to subjugate, subdue.

sublime† (syblim) *a. & m*, sublime. **sublimité** (mite) *f*, sublimity.

sublunaire (syblynɛ:r) *a*, sublunar[y].

submerger (sybmɛrʒe) *v.t*, to submerge, flood, swamp. **submersion** (sjɔ̃) *f*, submersion; flooding; drowning (*of pers.*).

subodorer (sybɔdɔre) *v.t*, to scent [out], suspect.

subordonné, e (sybɔrdɔne) *a. & n*, subordinate. **subordonner** (ne) *v.t*, to s.

suborner (sybɔrne) *v.t*, to suborn, tamper with.

subrécargue (sybrekarg) *m*, supercargo.

subreptice† (sybrɛptis) *a*, surreptitious.

subroger (sybrɔʒe) *v.t*, to subrogate.

subséquemment (sypsekamɑ̃) *ad*, subsequently. **subséquent, e** (kɑ̃, ɑ̃:t) *a*, subsequent, ensuing.

subside (sypsid) *m*, subsidy.

subsidiaire† (sypsidjɛ:r) *a*, subsidiary.

subsistance (sypsistɑ̃:s) *f*, subsistence, sustenance; (*pl.*) provisions, supplies. **subsister** (te) *v.i*, to subsist.

substance (sypstɑ̃:s) *f*, substance; gist, kernel (*fig.*). **substantiel, le†** (stɑ̃sjɛl) *a*, substantial. **substantif** (tif) *a.m. & m*, substantive.

substituer (sypstitɥe) *v.t*, to substitute; entail (*Law*). **substitut** (ty) *m*, deputy; surrogate.

substruction (sypstryksjɔ̃) *f*, substructure.

subterfuge (syptɛrfy:ʒ) *m*, subterfuge, shift.

subtil, e† (syptil) *a*, subtle; pervasive; keen; fine. **subtiliser** (lize) *v.t*, to filch; (*v.i.*) to subtilize. **subtilité** (te) *f*, subtlety.

suburbain, e (sybyrbɛ̃, ɛn) *a*, suburban.

subvenir à (sybvəni:r) *v.ir*, to come to the aid of; provide for. **subvention** (vɑ̃sjɔ̃) *f*, subsidy, subvention, grant. **subventionner** (ɔne) *v.t*, to subsidize.

subversif, ive (sybvɛrsif, i:v) *a*, subversive. **subversion** (sjɔ̃) *f*, subversion, overthrow.

suc (syk) *m*, juice; pith (*fig.*).

succédané (syksedane) *m*, substitute (*product*). **succéder à** (de), to succeed; s. to; follow; inherit. **succès** (sɛ) *m*, success; issue. **successeur** (sɛsœ:r) *m*, successor. *A, B ∼*, B, successor to A, B, late A (*business*). **successif, ive** (sif, i:v) *a*, successive, running. **succession** (sjɔ̃) *f*, succession, sequence; inheritance, estate. **successivement** (sivmɑ̃) *ad*, successively; seriatim.

succinct, e† (syksɛ̃, ɛ̃:kt) *a*, succinct; meagre.

succion (syksjɔ̃) *f*, suction, sucking.

succomber (sykɔ̃be) *v.i*, to succumb; sink; yield; die.

succulent, e (sykylā, ā:t) *a*, succulent, juicy, luscious, toothsome.

succursale (sykyrsal) *f*, branch (*establishment*). [*église*] ~, chapel of ease.

sucer (syse) *v.t*, to suck; imbibe. **suçoir** (swa:r) *m*, sucker (*of insect*).

sucre (sykr) *m*, sugar. ~ *cristallisé*, granulated s. ~ *d'orge*, barley s. ~ *en morceaux*, ~ *cassé*, lump s., loaf s., cube s. ~ *en pains*, loaf s. (*whole*). ~ *en poudre*, castor s. **sucré, e** (kre) *p.a*, sugared, sweet[ened]; sugary (*fig.*). *elle fait la sucrée*, she is demure. **sucrer** (kre) *v.t*, to sugar, sweeten. **sucrerie** (krəri) *f*, sugar refinery; (*pl.*) sweet[meat]s, confectionery. *aimer les ~s*, to have a sweet tooth. **sucrier, ère** (krie, ɛːr) *a*, sugar (*att.*). ¶ *m*, sugar refiner; sugar basin.

sud (syd) *m*, south; (*att.*) south[ern]. ~-*africain, e*, South African. ~-*américain, e*, South American. ~-*est* (sydɛst; *Naut.*, syɛ) *m*, south east. ~-*ouest* (sydwɛst; *Naut.*, syrwɛ) *m*, south west. *le S~-Ouest africain*, South West Africa.

Suède (la) (sɥɛd), Sweden. **suédois, e** (edwa, a:z) *a. & (language) m*, Swedish. **S~,** *n*, Swede (*pers.*).

suée (sɥe) *f*, sweat (*state*). **suer** (e) *v.i. & t*, to sweat, perspire, ooze; reek of, with. ~ *à grosses gouttes*, to sweat profusely. ~ *d'ahan* (a[h]ā), to toil & moil. **sueur** (œːr) *f*, sweat, perspiration.

suffire (syfiːr) *v.i.ir*, to suffice, be enough, do. ~ *à*, to be equal to, satisfy, cope with. *suffit que*, suffice it to say that. **suffisamment** (fizamā) *ad*, sufficiently, enough, adequately. **suffisance** (zā:s) *f*, sufficiency, adequacy, enough; self-importance, bumptiousness. **suffisant, e** (zā, ā:t) *a*, sufficient, &c.

suffixe (syfiks) *m*, suffix. ¶ *a*, suffixed.

suffocation (syfɔkasjɔ̃) *f*, suffocation, choking. **suffoquer** (ke) *v.t. & i*, to suffocate, stifle, choke.

suffragant (syfragā) *a.m. & m*, suffragan.

suffrage (syfra:ʒ) *m*, suffrage, vote.

suffusion (syfysjɔ̃) *f*, suffusion.

suggérer (syg3ere) *v.t*, to suggest; prompt. **suggestion** (syg3ɛstjɔ̃) *f*, suggestion, hint. **suggestionner** (ɔne) *v.t*, to affect by suggestion (*Psychology*).

suicide (sɥisid) *m. & suicidé (de) (pers.) m*, suicide, felo de se. *suicide du genre humain*, race suicide. **se suicider** (de) *v.pr*, to commit suicide.

suie (sɥi) *f*, soot.

suif (sɥif) *m*, tallow; (*mutton*) fat; candle grease. **suiffer** (fe) *v.t*, to tallow, grease.

suint (sɥɛ̃) *m*, grease (*in wool*). **suinter** (te) *v.i*, to ooze, run; leak.

suisse (sɥis) *a*, Swiss. ¶ *m*, Swiss (*man*); Swiss guard, beadle. **la S~**, Switzerland. **Suissesse** (sɛs) *f*, Swiss (*woman*).

suite (sɥit) *f*, continuation; consequence, result, effect; sequence, series, succession; run; sequel; suite; attendants, retinue, train; set; coherence, consistency. *la ~ au prochain numéro*, to be continued in our next. ~ *& fin*, concluded (*serial*). **suivant, e** (vā, ā:t) *a*, next, following, ensuing. ¶ *n*, follower, attendant; (*f.*) waiting maid (*Theat.*). **suivant**, *pr*, along, according to, pursuant to. ~ *que*, according as. **suivi, e** (vi) *p.a*, coherent, consistent; steady; well-attended. **suivre** (sɥi:vr) *v.t.ir*, to follow; succeed; pursue, watch, observe; attend; practise. ~ *la balle*, to follow through. *à ~*, to be continued (*serial*). *faire ~*, to forward, readdress; run on (*Typ.*).

sujet, te (sy3e, ɛt) *a*, subject, amenable, liable, prone. ¶ *n*, subject (*of a State*). ¶ *m*, subject, topic, matter, theme; cause, grounds; stock (*Hort.*); fellow. **sujétion** (3esjɔ̃) *f*, subjection, subservience; constraint; sedulousness.

sulfate (sylfat) *m*, sulphate. **sulfite** (fit) *m*, sulphite. **sulfure** (fyːr) *m*, sulphide. **sulfuré, e** (fyre) *a*, sulphuretted. **sulfureux, euse** (rø, øːz) *a*, sulphur[ous]. **sulfurique** (rik) *a*, sulphuric.

sultan (syltā) *m*, sultan; silk-lined basket, sachet. **sultane** (tan) *f*, sultana (*pers.*).

superbe (sypɛrb) *a*, superb, stately; vain glorious. ¶ *f*, vainglory.

supercherie (sypɛrʃəri) *f*, fraud, hoax.

superfétation (sypɛrfetasjɔ̃) *f*, redundancy.

superficie (sypɛrfisi) *f*, superficies, surface, area. **superficiel, le†** (sjɛl) *a*, superficial, shallow, skin-deep.

superfin, e (sypɛrfɛ̃, in) *a*, superfine.

superflu, e (sypɛrfly) *a*, superfluous. **super flu, m. & superfluité** (ite) *f*, superfluity.

supérieur, e (syperjœːr) *a*, superior; upper, higher. ¶ *n*, superior, chief; better (*pers.*). **supérieurement** (œrmā) *ad*, superlatively, in a masterly way. ~ *à*, better than. **supériorité** (rjorite) *f*, superiority.

superlatif, ive (sypɛrlatif, iːv) *a*, superlative (*Gram.*); consummate. ¶ (*Gram.*) *m*, superlative.

superposer (sypɛrpoze) *v.t*, to super[im]pose.

superstitieux, euse† (sypɛrstisjø, øːz) *a*, superstitious. **superstition** (sjɔ̃) *f*, superstition.

supplanter (syplāte) *v.t*, to supplant.

suppléance (sypleā:s) *f*, substitution; supply [work] (*Sch.*). **suppléant, e** (ā, ā:t) *n. & a*, substitute, deputy, locum tenens. **suppléer** (ee) *v.t*, to supply, make up for; deputize for; eke out. ~ *à*, to make up for; fill (*vacancy*). **supplément** (mā) *m*, supplement, addition, excess, extra [charge, fare]. **supplémentaire** (tɛːr) *a*, supplementary, additional, extra, further; relief (*train*).

suppliant, e (sypliā, ā:t) *a. & n*, suppliant. **supplication** (kasjɔ̃) *f*, supplication, entreaty. **supplice** (plis) *m*, punishment, torture, torment; (*extreme*) penalty; rack, *(fig.).* **supplier** (plie) *v.t*, to beseech, entreat, implore, supplicate. **supplique** (plik) *f*, petition, prayer.

support (sypo:r) *m*, support, stay; rest, stand, holder. ~ *à chariot*, slide rest *(lathe).* **supportable** (portabl) *a*, supportable, bearable, endurable, tolerable. **supporter** (te) *v.t*, to support; endure, bear, suffer, stand. **supports-chaussettes**, *m.pl*, sock suspenders.

supposé, e (sypoze) *p.a*, suppositious; fictitious. **supposé que**, supposing [that]. **supposer** (ze) *v.t*, to suppose; assume, infer, take; imply; put forward as genuine *(what is false—Law).* **supposition** (zisjɔ̃) *f*, supposition, assumption. ~ *de personne*, impersonation *(Law).*

suppôt (sypo) *m*, tool *(pers.)*, myrmidon.

suppression (sypresjɔ̃) *f*, suppression; discontinuance *(train)*; concealment. **supprimer** (prime) *v.t*, to suppress, do away with, cut out; discontinue; conceal.

suppurer (sypyre) *v.i*, to suppurate.

supputer (sypyte) *v.t*, to compute, reckon.

suprématie (sypremasi) *f*, supremacy. **suprême†** (pre:m) *a*, supreme; highest; crowning; paramount; last *(honours, &c).*

sur (syr) *pr*, on, upon; over, above; by; after; in; about; as to; to; towards; out of. ~ *ce*, thereupon.

sur, e (sy:r) *a*, sour, tart.

sûr, e (sy:r) *a*, sure, safe, secure; reliable; settled *(weather).*

surabondant, e (syrabɔ̃dɑ̃, ɑ̃:t) *a*, superabundant.

suranné, e (syrane) *a*, out of date, antiquated, superannuated.

surcharge (syrʃarʒ) *f*, overload; excess weight *(luggage)*; weight handicap; surcharge; correction, alteration *(M.S.).* **surcharger** (ʒe) *v.t*, to overload; overtax; surcharge; correct, alter *(write over).*

surchauffer (syrʃofe) *v.t*, to overheat; superheat.

surcroît (syrkrwa) *m*, increase. *par* ~, in addition, to boot.

surdité (syrdite) *f*, deafness.

sureau (syro) *m*, elder [tree].

surélever (syrelve) *v.t*, to heighten; raise; tee *(Golf).*

sûrement (syrmɑ̃) *ad*, surely, &c, as *sûr.*

surenchère (syrɑ̃ʃɛ:r) *f*, higher bid. **surenchérir sur** (ʃeri:r) *v.t*, to bid higher than, outbid.

surestaries (syrestari) *f.pl*, demurrage *(ship).*

surestimer (syrestime) *v.t*, to overestimate, overvalue, overrate.

suret, te (syrɛ, ɛt) *a*, sourish.

sûreté (syrte) *f*, safety, security, safe keeping; sureness, reliability. *la S~ Nationale (Fr.)*, the Criminal Investigation Department (Scotland Yard).

surexciter (syrɛksite) *v.t*, to overexcite.

surface (syrfas) *f*, surface; area; standing,

repute. ~ *de but*, goal area *(Foot.).* ~ *de réparation*, penalty a. ~ *des étages*, floor space *(building).*

surfaire (syrfɛ:r) *v.t. & abs. ir*, to overcharge (for); overrate, overestimate.

surfin, e (syrfɛ̃, in) *a*, superfine.

surgeon (syrʒɔ̃) *m*, sucker *(Hort.).*

surgir (syrʒi:r) *v.i*, to rise; arise, loom.

surhausser (syrose) *v.t*, to heighten, raise.

surhomme (syrɔm) *m*, superman.

surhumain, e (syrymɛ̃, ɛn) *a*, superhuman.

surimposer (syrɛ̃poze) *v.t*, to overtax, overassess.

surintendant, e (syrɛ̃tɑ̃dɑ̃, ɑ̃:t) *n*, superintendent, overseer, steward.

surjet (syrʒɛ) *m*, oversewing stitch, seam s.

sur-le-champ (syrləʃɑ̃) *ad*, there & then; out of hand, offhand.

surlendemain (syrlɑ̃dmɛ̃) *m*, day after the morrow.

surmener (syrməne) *v.t*, to overwork; overdrive, override *(horse)*; jade.

surmonter (syrmɔ̃te) *v.t*, to surmount, [over]top; overcome.

surnager (syrnaʒe) *v.i*, to float [on the surface]; survive.

surnaturel, le† (syrnatyrɛl) *a. & m*, supernatural, preternatural.

surnom (syrnɔ̃) *m*, cognomen, appellation, nickname. **surnommer** (nɔme) *v.t*, to [nick]name, call.

surnuméraire (syrnymerɛ:r) *a. & m*, supernumerary.

suroît (syrwa) *m*, sou'wester *(wind, hat).*

surpasser (syrpase) *v.t*, to surpass, overtop, exceed, outdo; astonish.

surpayer (syrpɛje) *v.t*, to overpay.

surplis (syrpli) *m*, surplice.

surplomb (syrplɔ̃) *m*, overhang. **surplomber** (be) *v.i. & t*, to overhang.

surplus (syrply) *m*, surplus, excess; rest.

surprenant, e (syrprənɑ̃, ɑ̃:t) *a*, surprising.

surprendre (prɑ̃:dr) *v.t.ir*, to surprise; catch [unawares]; overtake; intercept; detect; deceive; obtain by fraud. **surprise** (pri:z) *f*, surprise.

surproduction (syrprodyksjɔ̃) *f*, overproduction.

sursaut (syrso) *m*, start, jump; burst *(energy).*

surseoir à (syrswa:r) *(Law) v.ir*, to suspend, delay, stay. ~ *l'exécution de*, to reprieve. **sursis** (si) *m*, stay [of proceedings]; reprieve, respite, postponement, or exemption, in many senses, e.g. *condamné à un an de prison avec* ~, means sentenced to a year's imprisonment but with immediate discharge, akin to Eng. Probation of Offenders.

surtaxe (syrtaks) *f*, surtax; surcharge; overassessment; fee; duty. ~ *de levée exceptionnelle*, late fee *(Post).* **surtaxer** (kse) *v.t*, to surtax; surcharge; overassess.

surtout (syrtu) *ad*, above all, especially. ¶ *m*, centre piece, epergne.

surveillance (syrvɛjɑ:s) f, supervision; watch.
surveillant, e (jɑ̃, ɑ̃:t) n, supervisor, overseer. **surveiller** (je) v.t, to supervise, superintend, watch [over]; look after.

survenir (syrvəni:r) v.i.ir, to arrive unexpectedly; supervene; come upon one; befall.

survie (syrvi) f, survivorship; survival. **survivance** (vɑ̃:s) f, survival, outliving. ~ du plus apte, survival of the fittest. **survivant, e** (vɑ̃, ɑ̃:t) a.t, survivor. **survivre à** (vi:vr) v.ir, to survive, outlive. **se survivre**, to survive; live again.

sus (sy; in liaison, syz) ad, [up]on; come on! en ~, extra, to boot. en ~ de, over & above.

susceptibilité (sysɛptibilite) f, susceptibility; touchiness. **susceptible** (bl) a, susceptible; capable; apt; sensitive; touchy.

susciter (sysite) v.t, to raise up; give rise to; stir up.

suscription (syskripsjɔ̃) f, superscription.

susdit, e (sysdi, it) a. & n, aforesaid, **susmentionné, e** (mɑ̃sjɔne) a, above-mentioned. **susnommé, e** (nɔme) a, above-named.

suspect, e (syspɛkt) a, suspicious, questionable, doubtful, suspect. **suspecter** (te) v.t, to suspect, question.

suspendre (syspɑ̃:dr) v.t, to suspend, hang up; sling; stop; stay. **en suspens** (pɑ̃), in suspense, outstanding. **suspension** (sjɔ̃) f, suspension, hanging; discontinuance. **suspensoir** (swa:r) m, suspensory bandage.

suspicion (syspisjɔ̃) f, suspicion.

sustenter (systɑ̃te) v.t, to sustain, nourish.

susurrer (sysyre) v.i. & t, to murmur, whisper.

suture (syty:r) f, suture; join.

suzerain, e (syzrɛ̃, ɛn) a, paramount. ¶ n, suzerain. **suzeraineté** (rɛnte) f, suzerainty.

svastika (svastika) m, swastika.

svelte (svɛlt) a, slender, slim.

sybarite (sibarit) m, Sybarite.

sycomore (sikomɔ:r) m, sycamore.

sycophante (sikofɑ̃:t) m, sycophant.

syllabaire (silabɛ:r) m, spelling book. **syllabe** (lab) f, syllable.

syllogisme (silɔʒism) m, syllogism.

sylphe (silf) m, **sylphide** (fid) f, sylph.

sylvestre (silvɛstr) a, woodland (att.). **sylviculture** (vikylty:r) f, forestry.

symbole (sɛ̃bɔl) m, symbol. ~ attribué à saint Athanase (atanɑ:z), Athanasian Creed. ~ de Nicée (nise), Nicene Creed. le ~ [des apôtres], the [Apostles'] Creed. **symbolique** (lik) a, symbolic(al). **symboliser** (ze) v.t, to symbolize.

symétrie (simetri) f, symmetry. **symétrique†** (trik) a, symmetric(al).

sympathie (sɛ̃pati) f, sympathy, fellow feeling; (pl.) (one's) likes. **sympathique** (tik) a, sympathetic; congenial; likable; invisible (ink). **sympathiser** (tize) v.i, to sympathize.

symphonie (sɛ̃fɔni) f, symphony.

symptôme (sɛ̃pto:m) m, symptom.

synagogue (sinagɔg) f, synagogue.

synchrone (sɛ̃krɔn) a, synchronous.

syncope (sɛ̃kɔp) f, syncope; syncopation. **syncoper** (pe) v.t, to syncopate.

syndic (sɛ̃dik) m, syndic; trustee, assignee (bankruptcy). **syndicaliste** (kalist) m, trade unionist. **syndicat** (ka) m, trusteeship; syndicate; association, federation. ~ de placement, pool (Fin.). ~ ouvrier, trade union. **syndicataire** (tɛ:r) m, member of a syndicate; underwriter (Fin.). **syndiquer** (ke) v.t, to syndicate.

synode (sinɔd) m, synod.

synonyme (sinɔnim) a, synonymous. ¶ m, synonym.

synovite (sinɔvit) f, synovitis.

syntaxe (sɛ̃taks) f, syntax.

synthèse (sɛ̃tɛ:z) f, synthesis. **synthétique†** (tetik) a, synthetic(al).

Syrie (la) (siri), Syria. **syrien, ne** (rjɛ̃, ɛn) a. & S~, n, Syrian.

systématique† (sistematik) a, systematic; hidebound (fig.). **système** (tɛm) m, system; rowlock.

T

tabac (taba) m, tobacco. ~ à priser, snuff. **tabatière** (batjɛ:r) f, snuff box; skylight.

tabernacle (tabɛrnakl) m, tabernacle.

table (tabl) f, table; board; slab; tablet; list; index. ~ à pied central, pedestal table. ~ à rallonge(s), leaf t. ~ à tirettes, draw-leaf t. ~ alphabétique, alphabetical list; a. table; index (book). ~ d'attente, tablet for inscription; field (Her.). ~ d'harmonie, sound board (Mus.). ~ de jeu, gaming table; card t. ~ de longévité, life t. ~ de nuit, ~ de chevet, bedside t., pedestal cupboard. ~ de salle à manger, dining table. ~ des hors-texte, list of plates. ~ des matières, contents (book). ~ gigogne (ʒigɔɲ), nested table, nest of 3 tables. ~ porte-assiettes, cake stand. ~ rase, tablet for inscription; open mind; clean sweep (fig.). **tableau** (blo) m, board; telegraph board (Sport); picture; view; tableau; curtain!; scene; list, table; roll, rolls; panel; bag (of game). ~ d'autel, altar piece. ~ de distribution, switchboard. **tablette** (blɛt) f, shelf; slab; cake, tablet, lozenge. ~ de cheminée, mantelshelf. **tabletterie** (tri) f, fancy goods (ivory, inlay, &c). **tablier** (blie) m, apron; dashboard; board (Chess, &c); floor, deck (of bridge). ~ [d'enfant], pinafore.

tabou (tabu) m, taboo. il est ~, he, it, is taboo.

tabouret (taburɛ) m, stool; footstool; stocks (Hist.); shepherd's-purse. ~ de piano, music stool.

tache (taʃ) f, stain, spot, speck, blot, blemish, stigma, taint. ~ d'humidité, damp mark (in books). ~ de naissance, birth mark. ~ de rousseur, freckle. ~ de vin, port-wine mark.

tâche (tɑ:ʃ) f, task; job. à la ~, piece, job (work).

tacher (taʃe) v.t, to stain, spot; sully.

tâcher (taʃe) v.i, to try, endeavour; strive. **tâcheron** (ʃrɔ̃) m, jobber.

tacheter (taʃtje) v.t, to spot, speckle.

tacite† (tasit) a, tacit, implied.

taciturne (tasityrn) a, taciturn, silent.

tact (takt) m, touch; tact.

tacticien (taktisjɛ̃) m, tactician.

tactile (taktil) a, tactile, tactual.

tactique (taktik) a, tactical. ¶ f, tactics.

tadorne (tadɔrn) m, sheldrake.

taffetas (tafta) m, taffeta. ~ d'Angleterre, ~ gommé, court-plaster.

tafia (tafja) m, tafia. ~ de laurier, bay rum.

Tage (le) (ta:ʒ), the Tagus.

taïaut (tajo) i, tally-ho!

taie (tɛ) f, case, slip (pillow); cover (cushion).

taillade (tajad) f, cut, slash, gash. **taillader** (de) v.t, to slash, slit, gash; whittle.

taillanderie (tajɑ̃dri) f, edge tools. **taillandier** (dje) m, tool maker. **taillant** (jɑ̃) m, [cutting] edge. **taille** (tɑ:j) f, cutting; cut; pruning; edge (sword); height, stature; size; shape; waist; tally [stick]. ~-crayon, m, pencil sharpener. ~-douce, f, copperplate [engraving]. ~ hors série, outsize. ~-mer, m, cutwater (bow). **tailler** (taje) v.t, to cut; cut out; prune; trim; clip; dress; hew; carve; sharpen, point. **tailleur** (tajœ:r) m, cutter; hewer; tailor; (att.) tailor-made, tailored. **taillis** (ji) m, copse, coppice; brushwood, underwood. **tailloir** (tajwa:r) m, trencher (platter).

tain (tɛ̃) m, silvering (for mirror), foil.

taire (tɛ:r) v.t.ir, to say nothing about; not to mention; leave unsaid; conceal. faire ~, to silence, hush. se ~, to hold one's tongue, be silent.

talc (talk) m, talc; French chalk.

talent (talɑ̃) m, talent; faculty; gift.

talion (taljɔ̃) m, talion, retaliation, eye for eye.

talisman (talismɑ̃) m, talisman.

talle (tal) f, sucker (Hort.).

taloche (talɔʃ) f, cuff, clout.

talon (talɔ̃) m, heel; butt (cue); counterfoil; (pl. fig.) footsteps. ~ rouge (fig.), genteel. **talonner** (lɔne) v.t, to follow on the heels of; dog; dun; spur on; heel out (Rugby). **talonnette** (nɛt) f, heel piece; heel (rubber).

talus (taly) m, slope, batter; bank.

tamarin (tamarɛ̃) m, tamarind.

tambour (tɑ̃bu:r) m, drum; drummer; barrel; tambour, frame. ~ de basque, tambourine. ~-major, drum major. **tambouriner** (bu:rine) v.i, to drum; thrum; (v.t.) to cry (news); cry up.

tamis (tami) m, sieve; sifter; strainer; gauze.

Tamise (la) (tami:z), the Thames.

tamiser (tamize) v.t, to sift; strain; subdue (light).

tampon (tɑ̃pɔ̃) m, plug; bung; tampion, tompion; wad; pad; buffer. **tamponner** (pɔne) v.t, to plug; pad; dab; collide with.

tam-tam (tamtam) m, tomtom; gong.

tan (tɑ̃) m, tan, bark (tanners').

tancer (tɑ̃se) v.t, to rate, scold.

tanche (tɑ̃:ʃ) f, tench.

tandem (tɑ̃dɛm) m, tandem (carriage, cycle).

tandis que (tɑ̃di[s]) c, while, whilst; whereas.

tangage (tɑ̃ga:ʒ) m, pitching (ship).

tangent, e (tɑ̃ʒɑ̃, ɑ̃:t) a, tangent[ial]. ¶ f, tangent.

Tanger (tɑ̃ʒe) m, Tangier.

tangible (tɑ̃ʒibl) a, tangible.

tango (tɑ̃go) m, tango.

tanguer (tɑ̃ge) v.i, to pitch (ship).

tanière (tanjɛ:r) f, den, lair; hole, earth.

tan[n]in (tanɛ̃) m, tannin. **tanne** (tan) f, blackhead. **tanné, e** (ne) p.a, tanned; tan[-coloured]. **tanner** (ne) v.t, to tan; tire, bore. **tannerie** (nri) f, tannery, tan yard. **tanneur** (nœ:r) m, tanner.

tan-sad (tɑ̃sad) m, pillion.

tant (tɑ̃) ad, so much; so many; such; so; as much; as well [as]; as long; as far. ~ soit peu, ever so little, somewhat.

tantale (tɑ̃tal) m, tantalum.

tante (tɑ̃:t) f, aunt.

tantième (tɑ̃tjɛm) m, percentage.

tantinet (tɑ̃tinɛ) m, tiny bit, little bit, dash.

tantôt (tɑ̃to) ad, soon, presently, anon, by & by; in the afternoon; just now; sometimes, now.

taon (tɑ̃) m, gad-fly, horse fly.

tapage (tapa:ʒ) m, noise, uproar, disturbance, row; fuss, ado, stir. **tapageur, euse** (paʒœ:r, ø:z) a, noisy, rowdy, uproarious; loud, flash[y], showy, garish. ¶ n, roisterer, rowdy, brawler.

tape (tap) f, tap, rap, pat, slap. **tapé, e** (pe) p.a, dried (apples, &c, in rings); smart (answer). **tapecul** (pky) m, jigger (sail); rattletrap. **tapée** (pe) f, heaps, swarm. **taper** (pe) v.t. & abs, to tap, smack, slap; beat; pat; type[write]; stamp (foot).

tapinois (en) (tapinwa) ad, stealthily.

tapioca (tapjɔka) m, tapioca.

tapir (se) (tapi:r) v.pr, to squat, crouch, cower; nestle.

tapis (tapi) m, carpet; tapis; cloth; cover. ~-brosse, m, door mat. ~ de gazon, [green]sward. ~ de pied, rug. ~ vert, green baize; gaming table. **tapisser** (se) v.t, to hang with tapestry; paper (wall); cover, line; carpet (with flowers). **tapisserie** (sri) f, tapestry, hangings, arras; tapestry work; rug work. faire ~, to be a wallflower (dance). **tapissier, ère** (sje, ɛ:r) n, tapestry maker; upholsterer. ¶ f, delivery van.

tapon (tapɔ̃) m, knot, tangle.

tapoter (tapote) *v.t.* to tap; strum; thrum.

taquet (take) *m*, stop, block; cleat (*rope*).

taquin *a* (take, in) *n*, tease. **taquiner** (kine) *v.t. & i,* to tease, torment; worry.

taraud (taro) *m*, (*screw*) tap. **taraudage** (da:3) *m*, screw cutting, tapping, threading. **tarauder** (de) *v.t.* to tap, screw, thread.

tard (ta:r) *ad*, late; later. *sur le ~*, late in the day; late in life. **tarder** (tarde) *v.i.* to delay, be long; loiter; (*v.imp.*) to long. **tardif, ive†** (dif, i:v) *a*, tardy, belated; late; slow, sluggish; backward. **tardiveté** (divte) *f*, lateness, backwardness.

tare (ta:r) *f*, defect; taint; tare (*Com.*).

taré, e (tare) *p.a*, damaged, tainted; defective (*child*); depraved.

tarentelle (tarãtɛl) *f*, tarantella. **tarentule** (tyl) *f*, tarantula.

tarer (tare) *v.t.* to spoil, damage; tare (*Com.*).

targuer (se) de (targe), to pride oneself on, plume oneself on.

tarière (tarjɛ:r) *f*, auger.

tarif (tarif) *m*, tariff, rate, rates; scale; price list; fare. *~-album,* *m,* illustrated price list. **tarifer** (fe) *v.t.* to tariff, rate, price.

tarin (tarɛ̃) *m*, siskin.

tarir (tari:r) *v.t. & i,* to dry up; stop.

Tarragone (taragɔn) *f*, Tarragona.

tarse (tars) *m*, tarsus.

tartan (tartɑ̃) *m*, tartan (*cloth, garment*).

tarte (tart) *f*, tart (*Cook.*). **tartine** (tin) *f*, slice of bread & butter; bread & jam; rigmarole; screed.

tartre (tartr) *m*, tartar; scale, fur. **tartrique** (trik) *a*, tartaric.

tartufe (tartyf) *m*, sanctimonious hypocrite.

tas (tɑ) *m*, heap, pile; pack; cock (*hay*); shock, mow; stake [anvil].

Tasmanie (la) (tasmani) *f*, Tasmania.

tasse (tɑ:s) *f*, cup; mug.

tassé, e (tɑse) *p.a*, squat, dumpy.

tasseau (tɑso) *m*, strip, cleat.

tassement (tɑsmɑ̃) *m*, settling, sinking; set-back. **tasser (se)** *v.t.* to press down; squeeze; (*v.i.*) to grow thick. **se ~,** to settle, sink; settle down; have a set-back.

tâter (tɑte) *v.t.* to feel, touch; try; taste.

tatillon, ne (tatijɔ̃, ɔn) *n,* fusser; busybody. **tatillonner** (jɔne) *v.i.* to fuss, meddle.

tâtonnement (tɑtɔnmɑ̃) *m*, groping; tentative effort; (*pl.*) trial & error. **tâtonner** (ne) *v.i.* to grope; fumble. **à tâtons** (tɔ̃) *ad*, gropingly; warily.

tatou (tatu) *m*, armadillo.

tatouage (tatwa:3) *m*, tattooing; tattoo (*on skin*). **tatouer** (twe) *v.t.* to tattoo.

taudis (todi) *m*, hovel; slum.

taupe (to:p) *f*, mole (*Zool.*); moleskin. **taupière** (topjɛ:r) *f*, mole trap. **taupinière** (pinjɛ:r) *f*, mole hill; mean dwelling, hovel.

taureau (tɔro) *m*, bull.

tautologie (totɔlɔʒi) *f*, tautology.

taux (to) *m*, rate, price. *~ officiel [d'escompte],* bank rate.

taverne (tavɛrn) *f*, tavern, public house.

taxation (taksasjɔ̃) *f*, taxation, rating; assessment; charges. **taxe** (taks) *f*, tax, rate, duty, due; charge, fee. *~ de séjour,* visitors' tax. **taxer** (kse) *v.t.* to tax, rate, assess; charge with duty; charge [for]; fix the minimum price of; accuse.

taxi (taksi) *m*, taxi [cab].

tchécoslovaque (tʃekɔslɔvak) *a. & T~, n,* Czecho-Slovak. **Tchécoslovaquie** (ki) *f*, Czecho-Slovakia. **tchèque** (tʃɛk) *a. & (language) m. & T~ (pers.) n*, Czech.

te, t' (tə, t) *pn*, you, yourself, thee, thyself.

té (te) *m*, T, tee. *~ [à dessin],* T square.

technique† (tɛknik) *a*, technical. ¶ *f*, technique. **technologie** (nɔlɔʒi) *f*, technology.

teck (tɛk) *m*, teak.

Te Deum (tedeɔm) *m*, Te Deum.

tégument (tegymɑ̃) *m*, tegument.

teigne (tɛɲ) *f*, moth; ringworm.

teindre (tɛ̃:dr) *v.t.ir,* to dye; stain; tincture. **teint** (tɛ̃) *m*, dye, colour; complexion. **teinte** (tɛ̃:t) *f*, tint, shade, hue; tinge, touch, strain. **teinter** (tɛ̃te) *v.t.* to tint; tone (*paper*); fume (*wood*); tinge. **teinture** (ty:r) *f*, dyeing; dye; tinge; smattering; tincture. **teinturerie** (tyrri) *f*, dyeing; dye works. **teinturier, ère** (tyrje, ɛ:r) *n*, dyer [& cleaner].

tek (tɛk) *m*, teak.

tel, telle (tɛl) *a*, such; like; as; so. ¶ *pn*, such a one, some. *un tel, une telle,* so-&-so.

télégramme (telegram) *m*, telegram, wire. **télégraphe** (graf) *m*, telegraph. **télégraphie** (fi) *f*, telegraphy. *~ sans fil,* (*abb.* T.S.F.), wireless t. **télégraphier** (fje) *v.t. & abs,* to telegraph, wire. **télégraphique†** (fik) *a*, telegraphic, telegraph (*att.*).

télémètre (telemɛtr) *m*, range finder.

télépathie (telepati) *f*, telepathy.

téléphone (telefɔn) *m*, telephone. **téléphoner** (ne) *v.t. & abs,* to telephone. **téléphonie** (ni) *f*, telephony. **téléphonique** (nik) *a*, telephonic, telephone (*att.*).

télescope (telɛskɔp) *m*, [reflecting] telescope. **se télescoper** (pe) *v.pr,* to telescope (*trains*). **télescopique** (pik) *a*, telescopic; minor (*planet*).

télévision (televizjɔ̃) *f*, television. **télévisionniste** (ɔnist) *n*, looker-in.

tellement (tɛlmɑ̃) *ad*, so, in such a way.

téméraire† (temerɛ:r) *a*, rash, reckless, foolhardy. **témérité** (rite) *f*, temerity, rashness, &c.

témoignage (temwaɲa:ʒ) *m*, testimony, evidence, witness; mark, token. **témoigner** (ne) *v.i. & t,* to testify, bear witness, give evidence; evince, show, prove. **témoin** (mwɛ̃) *m*, witness; second (*duel*); telltale, pilot (*lamp, &c*); baton (*relay race*); bore core. *~ à charge,* witness for the prosecution. *~ à décharge,* w. for the defence. *~ muet,* circumstantial evidence.

tempe (tã:p) *f*, temple (*Anat.*).

tempérament (tãperamã) *m*, temperament, constitution. *à* ~, instalment, hire purchase, tally (*att.*).

tempérance (tãperã:s) *f*, temperance. **tempérant, e** (rã, ã:t) *a*, temperate.

température (tãperaty:r) *f*, temperature; (*boiling, &c*) point. **tempéré** (re) *a*, temperate; limited (*monarchy*). **tempérer** (re) *v.t*, to temper, moderate.

tempête (tãpɛ:t) *f*, storm, tempest. *à la* ~, at stormy (*barometer*). **tempêter** (pɛte) *v.i*, to storm, fume. **tempétueux, euse** (petɥø, ø:z) *a*, tempestuous, stormy; boisterous.

temple (tã:pl) *m*, temple; church.

temporaire† (tãporɛ:r) *a*, temporary. **temporel, le** (rɛl) *a*, temporal. **temporiser** (rize) *v.i*, to temporize. **temps** (tã; *in liaison*, tãz) *m*, time; while; times, days, age; season; weather; tense (*Gram.*); beat (*Mus.*); phase. ~ *prohibé*, close season. *au* ~! as you were! *en* ~ *& lieu*, in due course.

tenable (tǝnabl) *a*, tenable; bearable.

tenace (tǝnas) *a*, tenacious; adhesive; tough, stiff; stubborn; retentive. **ténacité** (tenasite) *f*, tenacity, &c.

tenaille (tǝnɑ:j) *f*, tongs; (*pl.*) pincers.

tenancier, ère (tǝnãsje, ɛ:r) *n*, keeper; lessee. **tenant** (nã) *m*, champion, supporter.

tendance (tãdã:s) *f*, tendency, trend. **tendancieux, euse** (dãsjø, ø:z) *a*, tendentious; leading (*question*).

tender (tãdɛ:r) *m*, tender (*locomotive*).

tendeur (tãdœ:r) *m*, layer (*carpets, &c*); setter (*traps, &c*); strainer, stretcher, tightener.

tendon (tãdɔ̃) *m*, tendon, sinew.

tendre (tã:dr) *v.t*, to stretch, tighten, strain; bend (*bow*); crane (*neck*); hold out (*hand, &c*); pitch (*tent*); lay, spread, set; drape; (*v.i.*) to tend, lead, conduce.

tendre† (tã:dr) *a*, tender, soft; sensitive; new (*bread*); early (*youth*); fond. **tendresse** (tãdrɛs) *f*, tenderness, fondness, love; (*pl.*) caresses. **tendreté** (drǝte) *f*, tenderness (*meat, &c*). **tendron** (drɔ̃) *m*, tender shoot; gristle (*veal*); maiden.

tendu, e (tãdy) *p.a*, tense, taut, tight.

ténèbres (tenɛ:br) *f.pl*, dark[ness], gloom. **ténébreux, euse†** (nebrø, ø:z) *a*, dark, murky; gloomy; obscure.

teneur, euse (tǝnœ:r, ø:z) *n*, holder. ~ *de livres*, bookkeeper. **teneur** (r), tenor, purport, terms; content[s], percentage; grade (*ore, &c*).

ténia (tenja) *m*, taenia, tapeworm.

tenir (tǝni:r) *v.t.ir*, to hold; h. on; keep; have; contain; take; t. up (*space*); consider; (*v.i.ir.*) to hold; last; cling; border on; owe; partake, savour, be like; be owing to; rest, lie; be anxious. *se* ~, to keep; stand; sit; stick; contain oneself.

tennis (tɛnis) *m*, [lawn] tennis; t. court.

tenon (tǝnɔ̃) *m*, tenon.

ténor (tenɔ:r) *m*, tenor (*voice, singer*).

tension (tãsjɔ̃) *f*, tension; tightness; strain; pressure; voltage. ~ *artérielle*, blood pressure.

tentacule (tãtakyl) *m*, tentacle, feeler.

tentateur, trice (tãtatœ:r, tris) *n*, tempter, temptress. **tentation** (sjɔ̃) *f*, temptation.

tentative (tãtati:v) *f*, attempt, endeavour. ~ *d'assassinat*, attempted murder.

tente (tã:t) *f*, tent; awning. ~ *conique*, bell tent. ~ *de plage*, bathing t. ~-*pavillon*, *f*, marquee.

tenter (tãte) *v.t*, to attempt, try; tempt.

tenture (tãty:r) *f*, hangings; wall paper.

tenu, e (tǝny) *p.a*, (*well, ill*) kept; neat, trim; (*to be*) bound (*à* = to); firm (*price*). ¶ *m*, hold (*Box., &c*). ¶ *f*, holding; keeping; bearing, carriage, behaviour; seat (*on horse*); dress, clothes, attire; (*review, &c*) order; firmness. ~ *de ville*, morning dress.

ténu, e (teny) *a*, thin, slender, tenuous; fine; watery (*fluid*). **ténuité** (nɥite) *f*, thinness, &c.

tercet (tɛrse) *m*, tercet, triplet (*Pros., Mus.*).

térébenthine (terebãtin) *f*, turpentine.

tergiverser (tɛrʒivɛrse) *v.i*, to shuffle.

terme (tɛrm) *m*, term; end; time; date; account, settlement (*Stk Ex.*); quarter (*year*), q.'s rent, q.'s day; instalment, call; (*pl.*) parlance. **terminaison** (minɛzɔ̃) *f*, termination, ending. **terminer** (ne) *v.t*, to terminate, end, wind up. **terminus** (ny:s) *m*, terminus (*Rly*).

termite (tɛrmit) *m*, termite, white ant.

terne (tɛrn) *a*, dull, lustreless, drab. **ternir** (ni:r) *v.t*, to tarnish, dull; dim; sully.

terrain (tɛrɛ̃) *m*, ground, land; field; site; course, links (*Golf*); court (*Croquet*). ~ *de couverture*, overburden (*Min.*).

terrasse (tɛras) *f*, terrace, bank; flat roof; [pavement] outside (*café*). **terrassement** (smã) *m*, earthwork. **terrasser** (se) *v.t*, to bank up; throw, floor. **terrassier** (sje) *m*, navvy; earthwork contractor.

terre (tɛ:r) *f*, earth; ground; land; soil; estate; loam; clay; shore (*Naut.*); world. ~ *battue*, hard court (*Ten.*). ~ *cuite*, terracotta. ~ *d'ombre*, umber. *la T~ de Feu*, Tierra del Fuego. ~ *de Sienne brûlée*, burnt sienna. *la* ~ *ferme*, the continent, the mainland; terra firma. *T* ~ *Sainte*, Holy Land. **terreau** (tɛro) *m*, [vegetable] mould. ~ *de feuilles*, leaf m. **Terre-Neuve**, *f*, Newfoundland. **terre-neuve**, *m*, N. [dog]. **terre-plein**, *m*, terreplein; open space. **terrer** (tɛre) *v.t*, to earth up; (*v.i.*) to burrow. *se* ~, to burrow; entrench oneself. **terrestre** (rɛstr) *a*, terrestrial; ground (*att.*); land (*att.*); earthly.

terreur (tɛrœ:r) *f*, terror, dread.

terreux, euse (tɛrø, ø:z) *a*, earthy; dull.

terrible† (tɛribl) *a*, terrible, terrific; dreadful.

terrien, ne (tɛrjɛ̃, ɛn) *a. & n*, landed (proprietor); (*m.*) landsman. **terrier** (rje) *m*, burrow, hole; earth (*fox*); terrier (*dog*).

terrifier (tɛrifje) *v.t*, to terrify.

terrine (tɛrin) *f*, [earthenware] pot, pan; (*pl.*) potted meats. **terrinée** (ne) *f*, panful.

territoire (tɛritwa:r) *m*, territory. **territorial, e** (tɔrjal) *a. & m*, territorial. **terroir** (rwa:r) *m*, soil.

terroriser (tɛrɔrize) *v.t*, to terrorize.

tertre (tɛrtr) *m*, hillock, knoll, mound. ~ **de départ**, teeing ground (*Golf*).

Tessin (le) (tɛsɛ̃), the Ticino.

tesson (tɛsɔ̃) *m*, piece of broken glass *or* earthenware, potsherd.

testament (tɛstamɑ̃) *m*, will, testament. **testamentaire** (tɛ:r) *a*, testamentary. **testateur, trice** (tœr, tris) *n*, testator, trix. **tester** (te) *v.i*, to make one's will.

testicule (tɛstikyl) *m*, testicle.

tétanos (tetanos) *m*, tetanus, lockjaw.

têtard (tɛta:r) *m*, tadpole; pollard. **tête** (tɛ:t) *f*, head; top; face; lead; brains; wits. ~-*à*-~, *m*, private interview, p. conversation; 2-cup tea set; sofa. ~ **de linotte**, feather-brained person. ~ **de série**, seeded player (*Ten.*). ~ **forte, forte** ~, good head, strong-minded person.

téter (tete) *v.t. & abs*, to suck (*of child*).

têtière (tɛtjɛ:r) *f*, infant's cap; head stall; chair back.

tétin (tetɛ̃) *m*, nipple, pap, teat (*pers.*). **tétine** (tin) *f*, dug; nipple (*nursing bottle*). **téton** (tɔ̃) *m*, breast (*of woman*).

tétras (tetra) *m*, grouse.

tette (tɛt) *f*, dug, teat (*animal*).

têtu, e (tety) *a*, stubborn, mulish.

teuton, ne (tøtɔ̃, ɔn) *& teutonique* (tɔnik) *a*, Teutonic.

texte (tɛkst) *m*, text. ~ [*composé*], letter-press.

textile (tɛkstil) *a. & m*, textile.

textuel, le† (tɛkstɥɛl) *a*, textual.

texture (tɛksty:r) *f*, texture; arrangement.

thé (te) *m*, tea; t. plant; t. party. ~ **complet**, tea, roll & butter. ~ **de viande**, beef tea.

théâtral, e† (teatral) *a*, theatrical; dramatic. **théâtre** (ɑ:tr) *m*, theatre, playhouse; stage; drama; scene; seat (*as of war*).

théière (teje:r) *f*, teapot.

théisme (teism) *m*, theism.

thème (tɛm) *m*, theme; topic; exercise, composition (*Sch.*); stem (*Gram.*).

théodolite (teɔdɔlit) *m*, theodolite.

théologie (teɔlɔʒi) *f*, theology. **théologien, ne** (ʒjɛ̃, ɛn) *n*, theologian, divine. **théologique†** (ʒik) *a*, theological.

théorème (teɔrɛm) *m*, theorem. **théoricien** (risjɛ̃) *m*, theorist. **théorie** (ri) *f*, theory; procession. ~ **de jeunes filles**, crocodile. **théorique†** (rik) *a*, theoretic(al).

théosophie (teɔzɔfi) *f*, theosophy.

thérapeutique (terapøtik) *a*, therapeutic; apothecaries' (*measure, weight*). ¶ *f*, therapeutics.

thermal, e (tɛrmal) *a*, thermal, hot. **thermes** (tɛrm) *m.pl*, thermal baths.

thermomètre (tɛrmɔmɛtr) *m*, thermometer. ~ **médical**, clinical thermometer.

thésauriser (tezɔrize) *v.t*, to hoard.

thèse (tɛ:z) *f*, thesis, argument.

thon (tɔ̃) *m*, tunny (*fish*).

thorax (tɔraks) *m*, thorax.

thym (tɛ̃) *m*, thyme.

thyroïde (tiroid) *a*, thyroid.

tiare (tja:r) *f*, tiara.

tibia (tibja) *m*, tibia, shin bone; shin.

Tibre (le) (tibr), the Tiber.

tic (tik) *m*, tic; twitching; habit, mannerism, trick.

tic tac (tiktak) *m*, tick[-tack], pit-[a-]pat.

tiède† (tjɛd) *a*, tepid, lukewarm. **tiédeur** (tjedœ:r) *f*, tepidness, &c. **tiédir** (di:r) *v.i*, to become tepid.

tien, ne (*with* le, la, les) (tjɛ̃, ɛn) *pn. & m*, yours, thine, thy own.

tiens (tjɛ̃) *v. abs. imperative*, hullo! well! indeed!

tiers, tierce (tjɛ:r, ɛrs) *a*, third. ¶ *m*, third [part]; third person, third party. ¶ *f*, third. **tiers arbitre**, *m*, referee.

tige (ti:ʒ) *f*, stem, stalk; trunk (*tree*); shaft; shank, leg (*boot, stocking*); rod.

tignasse (tiɲas) *f*, shock, mop (*hair*).

tigre, tigresse (tigr, grɛs) *n*, tiger, tigress. **le Tigre**, the Tigris. **tigré, e** (gre) *a*, striped, tabby.

tillac (tijak) *m*, deck (*ship*).

tille (ti:j) *f*, bast, bass. **tilleul** (tijœl) *m*, lime [tree], linden [tree]; lime blossom.

timbale (tɛ̃bal) *f*, kettledrum; cup (*metal*).

timbrage (tɛ̃bra:ʒ) *m*, stamping. **timbre** (tɛ̃:br) *m*, bell; gong; snare (*drum*); timbre; stamp; s. office; postmark; coupon (*gift goods*). ~ **humide**, pad stamp, rubber s. ~[-*poste*], *m*, [postage] s. ~-*quittance*, *m*, receipt s. ~ **sec**, ~ **fixe**, embossed s., impressed s. **timbré, e** (tɛ̃bre) *p.a*, stamped; cracked, daft. **timbrer** (bre) *v.t*, to stamp; postmark.

timide† (timid) *a*, timid; nervous; shy, bashful, diffident. **timidité** (dite) *f*, timidity, &c.

timon (timɔ̃) *m*, pole (*carriage*); helm (*fig.*). **timonier** (mɔnje) *m*, wheeler (*horse*); signalman (*Navy*); quartermaster (*Naut.*).

timoré, e (timɔre) *a*, timorous.

tinctorial, e (tɛ̃ktɔrjal) *a*, dye (*stuffs, &c*).

tine (tin) *f*, butt, cask; tub.

tintamarre (tɛ̃tama:r) *m*, din, racket, noise.

tinter (tɛ̃te) *v.i. & t*, to ring, toll; tinkle; jingle; clink; chink; tingle, buzz. **tintement** (tmɑ̃) *m*, ringing, &c; singing (*ears*).

tintouin (tɛ̃twɛ̃) *m*, trouble, worry.

tipule (tipyl) *f*, daddy-longlegs, crane fly.

tique (tik) *f*, tick (*insect*). **tiquer** (ke) *v.i*, to twitch; wince.

tiqueté (tikte) *a*, speckled, variegated.

tir (ti:r) *m*, shooting; musketry; gunnery; fire, firing; rifle range; shooting gallery. ~ *à l'arc*, archery. *à* ~ *rapide*, quick-firing.

tirade (tirad) *f*, tirade.

tirage (tira:ʒ) *m*, drawing; pull[ing]; draught; draft; towing; tow[ing] path; extension (*camera*); printing; machining; circulation (*news*).

tiraillement (tirajmɑ̃) *m*, tugging; gnawing (*stomach*); wrangling. **tirailler** (je) *v.t*, to tug, pull; pester; (*v.i.*) to blaze away. **tirailleur** (jœ:r) *m*, skirmisher, sharpshooter, rifleman; free lance.

tirant (tirɑ̃) *m*, string, strap; tie; tag; stay; sinew (*meat*). ~ *d'eau*, draught (*boat*).

tire (ti:r) *comps, all m*: ~*-botte*, bootjack. ~*-bouchon*, corkscrew. ~*-bouton*, button-hook. ~*-feu*, lanyard (*gun*). ~*-fond*, coach screw. ~*-ligne*, drawing pen.

tiré, e (tire) *p.a*, drawn, pinched, haggard. ~ *à quatre épingles*, spick & span, dapper. ~ *par les cheveux*, far-fetched. ¶ *m*, drawee; shoot (*preserve*).

tirelire (tirli:r) *f*, money box.

tirer (tire) *v.t. & i*, to draw; to pull; drag; tug; haul; get, derive; take; wreak; put out (*tongue*); raise, doff (*hat*); milk (*cow*); fire; shoot, let off; print, machine; incline, verge. ~ *[à pile ou face]*, to toss [up]. se ~, to extricate oneself. *se* ~ *d'affaire*, to tide over a difficulty.

tiret (tirɛ) *m*, dash (*line*); hyphen.

tireur, euse (tirœ:r, ø:z) *n*, drawer; marksman, shot. ~ *d'armes*, fencer. ~ *de cartes*, fortune teller. ~ *isolé*, sniper.

tiroir (tirwa:r) *m*, drawer (*table, &c*); slide; slide valve. ~ *de caisse*, till.

tisane (tizan) *f*, infusion, (*herb*) tea.

tison (tizɔ̃) *m*, brand, firebrand. **tisonner** (zɔne) *v.i*, to meddle with the fire. **tisonnier** (nje) *m*, poker.

tissage (tisa:ʒ) *m*, weaving. **tisser** (se) *v.t*, to weave. **tisserand** (srɑ̃) *m*, weaver. **tisseranderie** (dri) *f*, weaving (*trade*). **tissu** (sy) *m*, texture, weave; textile, fabric, cloth, gauze; tissue. ~ *éponge*, sponge cloth; towelling. ~*s pour vêtements*, suitings. **tissure** (sy:r) *f*, texture, tissue. **tistre** (tistr) *v.t.ir*, to weave.

titiller (titille) *v.t*, to titillate, tickle.

titre (titr) *m*, title; [title] deed, muniment, document; proof, evidence; status; title page; heading; certificate, scrip, warrant, bond, security, stock, share; holding; claim; fineness (*coins*); grade; strength (*solution*). *à* ~ *d'office*, ex officio. *à* ~ *de*, by right of, in virtue of, as. *au* ~, standard (*gold*). *en* ~, titular. **titré, e** (tre) *a*, titled; standard (*solution*). **titrer** (tre) *v.t*, to give a title to; titrate; assay.

tituber (titybe) *v.i*, to stagger, lurch.

titulaire (titylɛ:r) *a*, titular. ¶ *n*, holder; occupant; incumbent.

toast (tost) *m*, toast (*health*); buttered toast.

toboggan (tobogɑ̃) *m*, toboggan.

tocsin (toksɛ̃) *m*, alarm bell; tocsin, hue & cry.

toge (to:ʒ) *f*, toga; gown, robe.

tohu-bohu (toyboy) *m*, chaos; hurly-burly.

toi (twa) *pn*, you, thee, thou. ~*-même*, yourself, thyself.

toile (twal) *f*, linen; cloth; canvas; gauze; curtain (*Theat.*); sail (*Naut.*); (*pl.*) toils (*Hunt.*). ~ *à calquer*, tracing cloth. ~ *à matelas*, tick[ing]. ~ *à voiles*, sail cloth, canvas. ~ *cirée*, American cloth, oilcloth. ~ *d'araignée*, spider's web, cobweb. ~ *de matelas*, tick. ~ *de ménage*, homespun [linen]. ~ *de sol*, ground sheet. ~ *écrue*, bise, holland. ~ *huilée*, oilskin. ~ *ouvrée*, huckaback. ~ *peinte*, print[ed fabric].

toilette (twalɛt) *f*, toilet, washing, dressing; dress; dressing table; washstand; lavatory; wrapper; final revision.

toilier, ère (twalje, ɛ:r) *n*, linen draper.

toise (twa:z) *f*, height standard (*apparatus*); standard (*comparison*). **toiser** (twaze) *v.t*, to measure; look (*one*) up & down.

toison (twazɔ̃) *f*, fleece.

toit (twa) *m*, roof; house top; sty. ~ *découvrable* (dekuvrabl), sunshine roof, sliding r. **toiture** (ty:r) *f*, roof[ing].

tôle (to:l) *f*, sheet; [sheet] iron; plate.

Tolède (tolɛd) *f*, Toledo.

tolérable (tolerabl) *a*, tolerable. **tolérance** (rɑ̃:s) *f*, tolerance; toleration; sufferance; margin, limit. **tolérant, e** (rɑ̃, ɑ̃:t) *a*, tolerant. **tolérer** (re) *v.t*, to tolerate, bear, suffer.

toletière (toltjɛ:r) *f*, rowlock.

tollé (tolle) *m*, outcry; hue & cry.

tomate (tomat) *f*, tomato.

tombe (tɔ̃:b) *f*, tomb, grave; death (*fig.*). **tombeau** (tɔ̃bo) *m*, tomb, vault, monument; death.

tombée (tɔ̃be) *f*, fall. ~ *de pluie*, downpour; rainfall. **tomber** (be) *v.i*, to fall, tumble; drop; crash; flag; crumble; lapse; hang [down]; (*v.t.*) to throw (*Wrestling*); damn (*a play*). ~ *d'accord*, to come to an agreement. **tombereau** (bro) *m*, [tip] cart; cartload; tumbrel; -il. **tombola** (bola) *f*, raffle.

Tombouctou (tɔ̃buktu) *m*, Timbuctoo.

tome (to:m) *m*, volume, tome.

ton, ta, tes (tɔ̃, ta, te) *a*, your, thy.

ton (tɔ̃) *m*, tone; tune (*fig.*); style; manners; breeding, form; [whole] tone (*in distinction from a semitone*); key (*Mus.*).

tondeur, euse (tɔ̃dœ:r, ø:z) *n*, shearer. ¶ *f*, shearing machine, shears; clippers; mower (*lawn*). **tondre** (tɔ̃:dr) *v.t*, to shear, clip, crop, mow; fleece (*pers.*).

tonique (tɔnik) *a*, tonic. ¶ *m*, tonic (*Med.*). ¶ *f*, tonic (*Mus.*), keynote.

tonnage (tɔna:ʒ) *m*, tonnage; burden (*ship*); shipping. **tonne** (tɔn) *f*, tun; ton. *Fr. tonne* = 1000 *kilos*. **tonneau** (no) *m*, cask, barrel; tun; butt; tub; bin; drum; governess car[t]; tonneau (*motor*); ton (*Ship.—Fr. tonneau* = 1000 *kilos*). *~ d'arrosage*, water[ing] cart. **tonnelet** (nlɛ) *m*, keg. **tonnelier** (nɔlje) *m*, cooper. **tonnelle** (nɛl) *f*, arbour, bower. **tonnellerie** (lri) *f*, cooperage.

tonner (tɔne) *v.i. & imp*, to thunder; boom; inveigh. **tonnerre** (nɛ:r) *m*, thunder; thunderbolt; breech (*firearm*).

tonsure (tɔ̃sy:r) *f*, tonsure. **tonsurer** (syre) *v.t*, to tonsure.

tonte (tɔ̃:t) *f*, shearing; clipping; mowing.

topaze (tɔpa:z) *f*, topaz.

toper (tɔpe) *v.t*, to agree, consent.

topique (tɔpik) *a*, a topical (*Med.*); local; to the point; in point.

topographie (tɔpɔgrafi) *f*, topography.

toquade (tɔkad) *f*, craze, fancy.

toque (tɔk) *f*, cap; toque.

toqué, e (tɔke) *p.a*, crazy, cracked.

torche (tɔrʃ) *f*, torch; mat, pad. **torcher** (ʃe) *v.t*, to wipe. **torchère** (ʃɛ:r) *f*, cresset; floor lamp. **torchis** (ʃi) *m*, cob (*Build.*). **torchon** (ʃɔ̃) *m*, dish cloth, swab, house flannel, duster; twist of straw.

torcol (tɔrkɔl) *m*, wryneck (*bird*).

tordre (tɔrdr) *v.t*, to twist; distort; wring; wrest. **se** *~*, to writhe; be convulsed (*laughing*).

tore (tɔ:r) *m*, torus; tore.

toréador (tɔreadɔ:r) *m*, toreador.

tornade (tɔrnad) *f*, tornado.

toron (tɔrɔ̃) *m*, strand (*rope*).

torpeur (tɔrpœ:r) *f*, torpor. **torpide** (pid) *a*, torpid.

torpille (tɔrpi:j) *f*, torpedo; mine (*war*). **torpiller** (pije) *v.t*, to torpedo; mine. **torpilleur** (jœ:r) *m*, torpedo boat; t. man.

torréfier (tɔrrefje) *v.t*, to roast.

torrent (tɔrɑ̃) *m*, torrent; flood; flow; stream; rush. **torrentiel, le** (rɑ̃sjɛl) *a*, torrential.

torride (tɔrid) *a*, torrid.

tors, e (tɔ:r, ɔrs) *a*, twisted; contorted; crooked; wry. **torsade** (tɔrsad) *f*, twist, coil; bullion (*fringe*). **torse** (tɔrs) *m*, torso, trunk. **torsion** (sjɔ̃) *f*, torsion.

tort (tɔ:r) *m*, wrong; fault; mistake; injury, harm. *à ~*, wrongly. *à ~ & à travers*, at random.

torticolis (tɔrtikɔli) *m*, crick, stiff neck.

tortillage (tɔrtija:ʒ) *m*, involved language. **tortiller** (je) *v.t*, to twist; twirl; twiddle; kink; (*v.i.*) to shuffle. **se** *~*, to wriggle; writhe. **tortillon** (jɔ̃) *m*, twist; pad (*for carrier's head*); bun (*hair*).

tortionnaire (tɔrsjɔnɛ:r) *a*, torturous. *appareil ~*, instrument of torture. ¶ *m*, torturer.

tortu, e (tɔrty) *a*, crooked; tortuous.

tortue (tɔrty) *f*, tortoise; tortoise shell butterfly. *~ de mer*, turtle.

tortueux, euse† (tɔrtɥø, ø:z) *a*, tortuous; winding; underhand, crooked.

torture (tɔrty:r) *f*, torture; rack. **torturer** (tyre) *v.t*, to torture; strain. **se** *~ l'esprit*, to rack, cudgel, one's brains.

toscan, e (tɔskɑ̃, an) *a. & T~*, *n*, Tuscan. *la* **Toscane**, Tuscany.

tôt (to) *ad*, soon; quickly; early, betimes. *~ ou tard*, sooner or later. *le plus ~ possible*, as soon as possible.

total, e† (tɔtal) *a. & m*, total, whole; utter (*a.*). **totalis[at]eur** (liz[at]œ:r) *m*, totalizer, totalizator. **totalité** (te) *f*, whole, totality.

toton (tɔtɔ̃) *m*, teetotum.

toucan (tukɑ̃) *m*, toucan.

touchant, e (tuʃɑ̃, ɑ̃:t) *a*, touching, moving, affecting. **touchant**, *pr*, concerning, about. **touchau[d]** (ʃo) *m*, touch needle. **touche** (tuʃ) *f*, touch; hit; nibble (*fish*); key (*piano, typewriter, &c*); finger board (*violin*); fret (*guitar, &c*). **touche-à-tout**, *a*, meddlesome, officious. ¶ *m*, meddler, busybody, officious person. **toucher** (ʃe) *m*, touch; feel. ¶ *v.t. & i*, to touch; feel; finger; tap; hit; strike; whip; move, affect; concern; play (*piano, &c*); ink up (*Typ.*); draw, receive, cash; test; touch on, allude to; meddle; adjoin. **toucheur** (ʃœ:r) *m*, drover.

touer (twe) *v.t*, to tow, warp (*Naut.*). **toueur** (twœ:r) *m*, tug.

touffe (tuf) *f*, tuft; wisp; clump; bunch. *~ de gazon*, divot (*Golf*).

touffeur (tufœ:r) *f*, stifling heat (*of room*).

touffu, e (tufy) *a*, bushy, thick; overloaded.

toujours (tuʒu:r) *ad*, always, ever; still; anyhow. *~ vert*, evergreen.

toupet (tupɛ) *m*, tuft of hair, forelock; cheek, impudence.

toupie (tupi) *f*, [peg] top. *~ d'Allemagne*, humming t. **toupiller** (je) *v.i*, to spin round.

tour (tu:r) *f*, tower; castle, rook (*Chess*). ¶ *m*, turn; revolution; round; stroll, walk; trip, tour; spell; bout; row (*stitches*); circumference; size, measurement; lathe; wheel (*potter's*); trick; feat. *~ de Babel* (babɛl), babel (*fig.*). *~ de bâton*, perquisites, pickings. *~ de cartes*, card trick. *~ de col*, collar (*fur, &c*). *~ de cou*, necklet, wrap. *~ de main*, knack; wrinkle. *en un ~ de main*, in a jiffy, in a trice. *~ de nage*, swim. *~ de passepasse*, conjuring trick; juggle; clever trick. *~ [de piste]*, lap. *~ de reins*, strain in the back. *~s & retours*, twists & turns.

tourbe (turb) *f*, peat; rabble, mob. **tourbeux, euse** (bø, ø:z) *a*, peaty, boggy. **tourbière** (bjɛ:r) *f*, peat bog, peatery.

tourbillon (turbijɔ̃) *m*, whirlwind; whirl, swirl; whirlpool; vortex; bustle. **tourbillonner** (jɔne) *v.i*, to whirl, swirl, eddy.

tourelle (turɛl) *f*, turret; capstan (*lathe*).

touret (turɛ) *m*, wheel; reel.

tourie (turi) *f*, carboy.

tourillon (turijɔ̃) *m*, trunnion, gudgeon, journal, pin, pivot.

tourisme (turism) *m*, touring, travel for pleasure. **touriste** (rist) *n*, tourist; tripper.

tourment (turmɑ̃) *m*, torment, torture; pain; pang; worry; plague. **tourmentant, e** (tɑ̃, ɑ̃:t) *a*, tormenting; troublesome. **tourmente** (mɑ̃:t) *f*, storm, gale; turmoil. ~ *de neige*, blizzard. **tourmenté, e** (mɑ̃te) *p.a*, distorted; broken; laboured. **tourmenter** (te) *v.t*, to torment, torture, rack; worry; plague; overelaborate.

tournailler (turnɑje) *v.i*, to wander around.

tournant, e (nɑ̃, ɑ̃:t) *a*, a turning, revolving; swing (*bridge*); winding. ¶ *m*, turning; t. space; t. point; bend; corner (*street*); eddy; shift. **tourné, e** (ne) *p.a*, turned-shaped; disposed; sour (*milk*). **tourne-à-gauche** (nagoʃ) *m*, wrench; saw set. **tournebride** (nəbrid) *m*, road house; roadside inn; somewhere to stay. **tourne-broche** (nəbrɔʃ) *m*, roasting jack. **tournée** (ne) *f*, round, tour; circuit. **tourner** (ne) *v.t. & i*, to turn; t. over; t. out; rotate; revolve; gyrate; swivel; hinge; swing; wind; belay; shoot (*film*). film. **tournesol** (nəsɔl) *m*, sunflower; litmus. **tourneur** (nœ:r) *m*, turner. **tournevis** (nəvis) *m*, screw driver. **tourniquet** (nikɛ) *m*, turnstile; swivel; tourniquet.

tournoi (turnwa) *m*, tournament (*Hist., Chess, &c*); tourney. ~ *par élimination*, knock-out tournament (*Ten., &c*). **tournoyer** (nwaje) *v.i*, to spin, whirl; wheel; swirl.

tournure (turny:r) *f*, turn, course; cast; shape, figure; face.

tourte (turt) *f*, pie, tart. **tourteau** (to) *m*, oil cake.

tourtereau (turtəro) *m*, young turtle dove. **tourterelle** (tərɛl) *f*, turtle dove.

tourtière (turtjɛ:r) *f*, pie dish; baking tin.

Toussaint (la) (tusɛ̃) All Saints' day.

tousser (tuse) *v.i*, to cough.

tout (tu) *pn*, all, everything. le ~, the whole, the lot. **tout, e** (tu, tut) *a.s*, **tous** (tu & tu:s) *a.m.pl*, all, the whole [of], every; any; full; only, sole. *tout le monde*, everybody, every one. *tout le monde descend!* all change! (*Rly*). ¶ *ad*, quite; very; thoroughly; all; right; ready (*made, cooked*); wide; stark (*naked*); bolt (*upright*); just. ~ . . . *que*, however, [al]though. *tout, comps:* ~ *à coup*, suddenly, all at once. ~ *à fait*, quite; altogether; perfectly. ~ *à l'heure*, presently, by & by; just now. ~ *à vous*, yours very truly. ~ *d'un coup*, at one stroke; suddenly. ~ *de suite*, at once, directly. ~ *en parlant*, while speaking. **tout-à-l'égout**, *m*, main drainage. **toute-épice**, *f*, allspice. **toute-**

fois, *ad*, yet, however, nevertheless, still. **toute-puissance**, *f*, omnipotence. **tout-puissant, toute-puissante**, *a*, almighty, omnipotent; all-powerful; overpowering. *le . Tout-Puissant*, the Almighty, the Omnipotent.

toutou (tutu) *m*, bow-wow, doggie.

toux (tu) *f*, cough[ing].

toxine (tɔksin) *f*, toxin. **toxique** (ksik) *a*, toxic, poisonous, poison (*gas*). ¶ *m*, poison.

tracas (trakɑ) *m*, worry, bother. **tracasser** (kase) *v.t*, to worry. **tracasserie** (sri) *f*, wrangling.

trace (tras) *f*, trace; trail; track; spoor; scent; print; footprint; [foot]step; mark; weal. **tracé** (se) *m*, lay-out; outline; graph; traced pattern. **tracer** (se) *v.t*, to trace; lay out; mark out; map out; draw, sketch, outline.

trachée-artère (traʃeartɛ:r) *f*, trachea, windpipe.

tracteur (traktœ:r) *m*, tractor. **traction** (ksjɔ̃) *f*, traction, haulage, draught.

tradition (tradisjɔ̃) *f*, tradition; folklore; delivery (*Law*). **traditionnel, le†** (sjɔnɛl) *a*, traditional.

traducteur, trice (tradyktœ:r, tris) *n*, translator. **traduction** (ksjɔ̃) *f*, translation. **traduire** (dɥi:r) *v.t.ir*, to summon; translate; express, interpret. **se ~**, to show.

trafic (trafik) *m*, traffic; trading; trade. **trafiquant** (kɑ̃) *m*, trader; trafficker. **trafiquer** (ke) *v.i*, to traffic, trade, deal.

tragédie (traʒedi) *f*, tragedy. **tragédien, ne** (djɛ̃, ɛn) *n*, tragedian, tragedienne. **tragi-comédie** (ʒikɔmedi) *f*, tragicomedy. **tragi-comique** (mik) *a*, tragicomic. **tragique†** (ʒik) *a*, tragic(al).

trahir (trai:r) *v.t*, to betray; reveal. **trahison** (izɔ̃) *f*, treachery; treason; betrayal.

train (trɛ̃) *m*, train, string; raft; set; suite; quarters (*horse*); pace, rate; progress; routine; mood. ~ *de paquebot*, boat train. le ~ [*des équipages*], the army service corps. ~ *militaire*, troop train. ~*-poste, m*, mail train.

traînant, e (trenɑ̃, ɑ̃:t) *a*, trailing; shambling; listless, languid; singsong. **traînard** (na:r) *m*, straggler; laggard; slowcoach. **traînasser** (nase) *v.t*, to draw out; drag out; (*v.i.*) to loiter; laze. **traîne** (trɛ:n) *f*, train (*of dress*). *à la* ~, in tow. **traîneau** (treno) *m*, sledge, sleigh; drag net. **traînée** (ne) *f*, trail; train; ground line (*Fish.*). **traîner** (ne) *v.t. & i*, to drag, draw, haul; trail; draggle; drawl; lag; flag, droop; straggle; loiter; loaf. ~ *la jambe*, to shuffle along.

train-train (trɛtrɛ̃) *m*, jog-trot, routine.

traire (trɛ:r) *v.t.ir*, to milk; draw.

trait (trɛ) *m*, pull[ing]; draught; stretch; trace (*Harness*); leash; arrow, dart; shot; beam; thunderbolt; dash (*Teleg.*); stroke; streak; line; flash; sally; gulp; feature;

trait; touch; reference, bearing. ~ d'union, hyphen. ~ de balance, turn of the scale. **traitable** (tabl) a, tractable, manageable. **traite** (trɛt) f, stretch; stage (journey); trade, traffic; transport; trading; draft, bill; milking. la ~ des noirs, la ~ des nègres, the slave trade. **traité** (te) m, treatise; treaty; agreement. **traitement** (tmã) m, treatment; usage; salary, pay, stipend. ~ d'inactivité, retired pay. **traiter** (te) v.t. & i, to treat, use; entertain; deal; negotiate. ~ de, to treat of; call, dub. **traiteur** (tœ:r) m, caterer.

traître, traitresse (trɛ:tr, trɛtrɛs) n, traitor, traitress; betrayer; villain (Theat.). ¶ a, treacherous, traitorous. **traîtreusement** (trøzmã) ad, treacherously. **traîtrise** (tri:z) f, treachery.

trajectoire (traʒɛktwa:r) f, trajectory; path (storm, &c). **trajet** (ʒɛ) m, journey, passage, transit, trip, run, ride, course.

tramail (trama:j) m, trammel [**net**].

trame (tram) f, woof, weft; web, thread (of life); half-tone screen; plot. **tramer** (me) v.t, to weave; hatch (plot).

tramway (tramwɛ) m, tram[car].

tranchant, e (trɑ̃ʃɑ̃, ɑ̃:t) a, cutting, sharp, keen; edge[d]; trenchant; peremptory; glaring. ¶ m, [cutting] edge. **tranche** (trɑ̃:ʃ) f, slice, cut; steak; rasher; slab; block, portion, bit; edge (book, coin). ~ inférieure, tail (book page). ~s non rognées, uncut edges. ~s rognées, cut edges. ~ supérieure, head, top (book page). ~ verticale, fore edge, foredge (book page). **tranché, e** (trɑ̃ʃe) a, well-marked; distinct. **tranchée** (ʃe) f, trench; drain; cutting; (pl.) colic, gripes. **tranche-file** (ʃil) f, headband (Bookb.). **trancher** (ʃe) v.t, to slice; cut; chop off; cut short; settle; contrast. **tranchoir** (ʃwa:r) m, trencher, cutting board.

tranquille† (trɑ̃kil) a, tranquil, quiet, calm, peaceful, still, undisturbed, easy. **tranquilliser** (lize) v.t, to calm, soothe. **tranquillité** (te) f, tranquillity, peace, &c.

transaction (trɑ̃zaksjɔ̃) f, transaction, dealing; compromise.

transatlantique (trɑ̃zatlɑ̃tik) a, transatlantic. [paquebot] ~, m, Atlantic liner.

transborder (trɑ̃sbɔrde) v.t, to tran[s]ship.

transcendant, e (trɑ̃sɑ̃dɑ̃, ɑ̃:t) a, transcendent.

transcription (trɑ̃skripsjɔ̃) f, transcript[ion]; copy; posting (Bkkpg). **transcrire** (skri:r) v.t.ir, to transcribe; post.

transe (trɑ̃:s) f, fright, scare; trance.

transept (trɑ̃sɛpt) m, transept.

transférer (trɑ̃sfere) v.t, to transfer; translate (bishop); alter the date of (function, &c). **transfert** (fɛ:r) m, transfer.

transfiguration (trɑ̃sfigyrasjɔ̃) f, transfiguration. **transfigurer** (re) v.t, to transfigure.

transformateur (trɑ̃sfɔrmatœ:r) m, trans-

former. **transformer** (me) v.t, to transform, change, convert.

transfuge (trɑ̃sfy:ʒ) m, deserter (to enemy); turncoat, rat.

transfuser (trɑ̃sfyze) v.t, to transfuse.

transgresser (trɑ̃sgrɛse) v.t, to transgress.

transiger (trɑ̃ziʒe) v.i, to compound, compromise.

transir (trɑ̃si:r) v.t, to chill; paralyse (fig.).

transit (trɑ̃zit) m, transit (Cust.).

transitif, ive† (trɑ̃zitif, i:v) a, transitive.

transition (trɑ̃zisjɔ̃) f, transition. **transitoire** (twa:r) a, transitory, transient.

translation (trɑ̃slasjɔ̃) f, translation (bishop); transfer, conveyance; alteration of date (function, &c).

translucide (trɑ̃slysid) a, translucent.

transmetteur (trɑ̃smɛtœ:r) m, transmitter. **transmettre** (tr) v.t.ir, to transmit; pass on; hand down; transfer, convey. **transmission** (misjɔ̃) f, transmission, &c; drive, driving, shaft[ing] (Mech.).

transmuer (trɑ̃smɥe) v.t, to transmute.

transparence (trɑ̃sparɑ̃:s) f, transparency. **transparent, e** (rɑ̃, ɑ̃:t) a, transparent. ¶ m, transparency (picture); black lines.

transpercer (trɑ̃spɛrse) v.t, to transfix, pierce.

transpirer (trɑ̃spire) v.i, to perspire; transpire.

transplanter (trɑ̃splɑ̃te) v.t, to transplant.

transport (trɑ̃spɔ:r) m, transport, conveyance, carriage; visit (of experts, &c, Law); transfer (Law); troop ship; rapture. ~ [au cerveau], light-headedness, delirium. **transportation** (portasjɔ̃) f, transportation. **transporter** (te) v.t, to transport, &c.

transposer (trɑ̃spoze) v.t, to transpose.

transsubstantiation (trɑ̃ssypstɑ̃sjasjɔ̃) f, transubstantiation.

transvaser (trɑ̃svaze) v.t, to decant.

transversal, e† (trɑ̃svɛrsal) a, transverse, cross (att.).

trapèze (trapɛ:z) m, trapeze.

trappe (trap) f, trap, pitfall; trap door. **trappeur** (pœ:r) m, trapper.

trapu, e (trapy) a, thick-set, dumpy, squat, stocky.

traque (trak) f, beating (game). **traquenard** (kna:r) m, trap. **traquer** (ke) v.t, to beat (game); surround; track down. **traqueur** (kœ:r) m, beater.

travail (trava:j) m. oft. pl, work; working; labour, toil; piece of work, job; employment; stress (Mech.); travail, childbirth; workmanship. ~ d'artisan, craftsmanship. travaux forcés, transportation with hard labour. **travaillé, e** (vaje) (fig.) p.a, laboured, elaborate. **travailler** (je) v.i, to work, labour, toil; be in stress; (v.t.) to torment; work; w. up; elaborate. **travailleur, euse** (jœ:r, ø:z) n, worker; workman; labourer; toiler. ¶ f, workstand (lady's).

travée (trave) f, bay (Arch.); span (bridge, roof).

travers (travɛːr) *m*, breadth; beam (*ship*), broadside; fault. **à ~**, through. **de ~**, askew, awry, amiss, wrong; askance. **en ~, ad**, across, athwart, cross[wise]. **en ~ de, pr**, across, athwart. **traverse** (vɛrs) *f*, cross bar, c. beam; c. road; transom; sill; sleeper (*rail track*); hitch, setback. **traversée** (se) *f*, crossing, passage. **~ des piétons**, pedestrian crossing. **traverser** (se) *v.t*, to traverse, cross, go through; thwart. **traversin** (sɛ̃) *m*, bolster (*bed*).

travestir (travɛstiːr) *v.t*, to disguise; travesty, burlesque; misrepresent.

trayon (trɛjɔ̃) *m*, dug, teat (*cow, &c*).

trébucher (trebyʃe) *v.i*, to stumble, trip. **trébuchet** (ʃɛ) *m*, trap; balance (*scales*).

tréfiler (trefile) *v.t*, to wiredraw (*metal*).

trèfle (trɛfl) *m*, trefoil; clover; clubs (*Cards*).

tréfonds (trefɔ̃) *m*, subsoil.

treillage (treja:ʒ) *m*, trellis, lattice. **treillis** (ji) *m*, trellis, lattice; netting; sackcloth. **treillisser** (se) *v.t*, to trellis, lattice.

treize (trɛːz) *a. & m*, thirteen; 13th. **~ douze**, 13 as 12. **treizième†** (trɛzjɛm) *a. & n*, thirteenth.

tréma (trema) *m*, diaeresis.

tremblaie (trɑ̃blɛ) *f*, aspen plantation. **tremble** (trɑ̃:bl) *m*, asp[en].

tremblement (trɑ̃bləmɑ̃) *m*, trembling, trepidation, quavering, shaking; tremor. **~ de terre**, earthquake. **tremblé, e** (ble) *p.a*, wavy, waved; shaky. **trembler** (ble) & **trembloter** (blɔte) *v.i*, to tremble, shake, vibrate, quake, quiver, quaver, quail, shiver, flutter, flicker.

trémie (tremi) *f*, hopper (*Mach.*).

tremolo (tremolo) *m*, tremolo (*Mus.*).

trémousser (se) (tremuse) *v.pr*, to fidget; flounce about; bestir oneself. **trémousser de l'aile**, to flutter, flap its wings.

trempe (trɑ̃:p) *f*, damping; tempering, hardening; temper; stamp, kidney (*fig.*). **tremper** (trɑ̃pe) *v.t. & i*, to steep, soak, dip; drench; damp, wet; temper; imbrue. **tremplin** (trɑ̃plɛ̃) *m*, spring board, diving b.; jumping off ground (*fig.*).

trentaine (trɑ̃tɛn) *f*, thirty [or so]. **trente** (trɑ̃:t) *a*, thirty. ¶ *m*, thirty; 30th. **~ et quarante**, rouge et noir. **T~, f**, Trent (*Italy*). **trentième** (trɑ̃tjɛm) *a. & n*, thirtieth. **le Trentin** (tɛ̃) the Trentino.

trépan (trepɑ̃) *m*, trepan; bit, chisel (*boring*). **trépaner** (pane) *v.t*, to trepan.

trépas (trepɑ) *m*, death, decease. **trépasser** (se) *v.i*, to die, pass away. **les trépassés** (se), the dead, the departed.

trépidation (trepidasjɔ̃) *f*, tremor; vibration (*of machinery, car, ship, &c*).

trépied (trepje) *m*, tripod; trivet (*stove*).

trépigner (trepiɲe) *v.i*, to stamp (*rage, &c*).

trépointe (trepwɛ̃:t) *f*, welt (*shoe*).

très (trɛ; *in liaison*, trɛz) *ad*, very, most, [very] much.

trésor (trezɔːr) *m*, treasure; t. trove; treasury.

trésorerie (zɔrri) *f*, treasury; finances. **trésorier, ère** (zɔrje, ɛːr) *n*, treasurer; paymaster, -mistress.

tressaillir (tresajiːr) *v.i.ir*, to start; thrill; wince.

tressauter (tresote) *v.i*, to start, jump.

tresse (trɛs) *f*, plait, tress; braid, tape; gasket. **tresser** (se) *v.t*, to plait; braid; weave (*wicker, &c*).

tréteau (treto) *m*, trestle, horse; (*pl.*) boards, stage.

treuil (trœːj) *m*, winch, windlass, hoist.

trêve (trɛːv) *f*, truce; respite.

Trèves (trɛːv) *f*, Treves, Trier.

trévire (treviːr) *f*, parbuckle.

tri (tri) & **triage** (a:ʒ) *m*, sorting.

triangle (triɑ̃:gl) *m*, triangle (*Geom. & Mus.*). **triangulaire** (ɑ̃gylɛːr) *a*, triangular.

tribord (tribɔːr) *m*, starboard.

tribu (triby) *f*, tribe.

tribulation (tribylasjɔ̃) *f*, tribulation, trial.

tribun (tribœ̃) (*pers.*) *m*, tribune (*Hist.*); demagogue. **tribunal** (bynal) *m*, tribunal; bench; court. **tribune** (byn) *f*, tribune; rostrum; platform; gallery; loft (*organ*); grand stand.

tribut (triby) *m*, tribute. **tributaire** (tɛːr) *a. & m*, tributary (*pers., river*); dependent.

triceps (trisɛps) *a. & m*, triceps.

tricher (triʃe) *v.i. & t*, to cheat; trick; doctor. **tricherie** (ʃri) *f*, cheating; trickery. **tricheur, euse** (ʃœːr, øːz) *n*, cheat; trickster; sharper.

trichromie (trikromi) *f*, three-colour process.

tricot (triko) *m*, knitting (*art*); knitted garment; (*pl.*) knit[ted] wear. **~ à l'endroit, ~ uni**, plain knitting. **~ à l'envers**, purl k., pearl k. **tricotage** (kɔta:ʒ) *m*, knitting (*act*). **tricoter** (te) *v.t. & abs*, to knit. **tricoteur, euse** (tœːr, øːz) *n*, knitter.

trictrac (triktrak) *m*, backgammon; b. board.

tricycle (trisikl) *m*, tricycle.

trident (tridɑ̃) *m*, trident; fish spear.

triennal, e (triɛnnal) *a*, triennial.

trier (trie) *v.t*, to sort; pick. **trieur, euse** (œːr, øːz) *n*, sorter; picker.

trigonométrie (trigɔnɔmetri) *f*, trigonometry.

trille (tri:j) *m*, trill, shake (*Mus.*).

trillion (triljɔ̃) *m*, billion (a million millions).

trimbaler (trɛ̃bale) *v.t*, to drag about.

trimer (trime) *v.i*, to slave, drudge.

trimestre (trimɛstr) *m*, quarter, 3 months; term (*Sch.*); quarter's rent, salary, &c. **trimestriel, le** (triɛl) *a*, quarterly.

tringle (trɛ̃:gl) *f*, rod; chalk line (*mark*).

Trinité (la) (trinite) the Trinity; Trinidad.

trinquer (trɛ̃ke) *v.i*, to clink glasses; hob-nob.

trio (trio) *m*, trio. **triolet** (ɔlɛ) *m*, triolet; triplet (*Mus.*).

triomphal, e† (triɔ̃fal) *a*, triumphal. **triomphe** (ɔ̃:f) *m*, triumph; exultation. **triompher** (ɔ̃fe) *v.i*, to triumph; exult; excel; gloat.

tripaille (tripɑ:j) *f*, garbage, offal.

tripe de velours (trip) *f*, velveteen.

triperie (triːpri) *f*, tripe shop. **tripes** (trip) *f.pl*, tripe. **tripier, ère** (pje, ɛːr) *n*, tripe dresser.

triplet (tripl) *a. & s*, treble, triple, threefold, 3 times; triplicate. ~ **croche**, *f*, demi-semiquaver. ~ **saut**, *m*, hop, step, & jump. **tripler** (ple) *v.t. & i*, to treble, triple. **triplicata** (plikata) *m*, triplicate.

tripoli (tripɔli) *m*, tripoli.

tri-porteur (triportœːr) *m*, carrier tricycle.

tripot (tripo) *m*, gambling den. **tripoter** (pɔte) *v.t. & abs*, to mess about; muddle up; plot; job, rig.

triptyque (triptik) *m*, triptych; pass sheet (*motor car at Cust.*).

trique (trik) *f*, cudgel, bludgeon.

triqueballe (trikbal) *m*, sling cart.

trisaïeul, e (trizajœl) *n*, great-great-grand-father, -mother.

triste† (trist) *a*, sad, sorrowful, woeful; dreary, gloomy, dismal; bleak, depressing; sorry, wretched. **tristesse** (tɛs) *f*, sadness, &c.

triton (tritɔ̃) *m*, triton; merman; newt, eft. **triturer** (trityre) *v.t*, to triturate, grind.

trivial, e† (trivjal) *a*, vulgar, coarse; not in decent use (*expression*); trite, hackneyed. **trivialité** (lite) *f*, vulgarity, &c; vulgarism.

troc (trɔk) *m*, truck, exchange, barter.

trochée (trɔʃe) *m*, head of shoots (*tree stump*).

troène (trɔɛn) *m*, privet (*Bot.*).

troglodyte (trɔglɔdit) *m*, troglodyte, cave dweller.

trognon (trɔɲɔ̃) *m*, core (*apple*); stump (*cabbage*).

trois (trwa) *a. & m. in liaison*, trwaz) *a. & m*, three; third. ~ **fois**, three times, thrice. ~ **jumeaux**, triplets. ~-**mâts**, *m*, three-master. **troisième†** (zjɛm) *a*, third. ¶ *m*, third (*number, pers., floor*). ¶ *f*, third (*class*). ~ **de change**, third of exchange. ~**s** [*galeries*], gallery (*Theat.*).

trolley (trɔlɛ) *m*, troll[e]y (*grooved wheel*).

trombe (trɔ̃ːb) *f*, waterspout. ~ **d'eau**, cloud burst. **entrer en** ~, to burst in.

trombone (trɔ̃bɔn) *m*, trombone.

trompe (trɔ̃ːp) *f*, horn; hooter; trumpet; proboscis; trunk. ~ **d'Eustache** (østaʃ), Eustachian tube.

trompe-l'œil (trɔ̃plœːj) *m*, still-life deception; bluff, window dressing (*fig.*). **tromper** (pe) *v.t*, to deceive, delude; cheat; mislead; disappoint; outwit; while away, beguile. **se** ~, to be mistaken, mistake. **tromperie** (pri) *f*, deceit, deception, imposture; illusion.

trompeter (trɔ̃pəte) *v.t*, to trumpet (*secret*). **trompette** (pɛt) *f*, trumpet, trump (*last, of doom*); whelk. ¶ *m*, trumpeter.

trompeur, euse (trɔ̃pœːr, øːz) *n*, deceiver, cheat. ¶ *a*, deceitful; deceptive.

tronc (trɔ̃) *m*, trunk; parent stock; frustum. ~ **des pauvres**, poor box. **tronçon** (sɔ̃) *m*, (*broken*) piece, stump; section; dock (*of tail*). **tronçonner** (sɔne) *v.t*, to cut up.

trône (troːn) *m*, throne. **trôner** (trone) *v.i*, to sit enthroned, sit in state.

tronquer (trɔ̃ke) *v.t*, to truncate; mutilate.

trop (tro; *in liaison*, trop) *ad. & m*, too; too much; too many; too long; too well; excess. ~ **cuit, e**, overdone. **être de** ~, to be in the way, be unwelcome.

trope (trɔp) *m*, trope.

trophée (trɔfe) *m*, trophy.

tropical, e (trɔpikal) *a*, tropical. **tropique** (pik) *m*, tropic. ~ **du Cancer** (kɑ̃sɛːr), t. of Cancer. ~ **du Capricorne** (kaprikɔrn), t. of Capricorn.

trop-plein (trɔplɛ̃) *m*, overflow.

troquer (trɔke) *v.t*, to barter, exchange.

trot (tro) *m*, trot. **trotte** (trɔt) *f*, distance, step. **trotter** (te) *v.i. & t*, to trot; run (*in one's head*). **trotteur, euse** (tœːr, øːz) *n*, trotter (*horse*). **trottin** (tɛ̃) *m*, errand girl. **trottiner** (tine) *v.i*, to trot; toddle. **trottinette** (nɛt) *f*, scooter. **trottoir** (twaːr) *m*, pavement, footway, footpath.

trou (tru) *m*, hole; eye; blank. ~ **barré**, stimy, stymie (*Golf*). ~ **d'air**, air pocket (*Aero.*). ~ [*d'arrivée*], hole (*Golf*). ~ **d'homme**, manhole. ~ **de sonde**, bore hole.

troubadour (trubaduːr) *m*, troubadour.

trouble (trubl) *a*, troubled, turbid, muddy; cloudy; dim, blurred, misty; overcast; confused. ¶ *m*, disorder; disturbance; trouble. ~-**fête** (blæfɛːt) *m*, spoil-sport, kill-joy. **troubler** (ble) *v.t*, to disturb; muddy; dim; mar; hamper; upset.

trouée (true) *f*, gap. **trouer** (e) *v.t*, to hole (*pierce*).

troupe (trup) *f*, troop, band; host; set, gang; troupe; flock. **troupeau** (po) *m*, herd, drove; flock. **troupier** (pje) *m*, soldier, campaigner.

trousse (trus) *f*, truss; bundle; case; kit; outfit; roll. ~ **manucure**, roll-up mani-cure set. **aux** ~**s de**, at the heels of. **trousseau** (so) *m*, bunch (*keys, &c*); outfit, kit; trousseau. **trousser** (se) to tuck up; turn up; truss; dispatch; polish off. ~ **bagage**, to pack up; decamp; die. **troussis** (si) *m*, tuck.

trouvaille (truvaːj) *f*, [*lucky*] find. **trouver** (ve) *v.t*, to find; discover; get; think; like; spare (*the time*). **se** ~, to be; feel; happen.

truc (tryk) *m*, knack; trick; dodge; gadget; platform car (*Rly*).

truchement (tryʃmɑ̃) *m*, interpreter, spokes-man.

truculent, e (trykylɑ̃, ɑ̃ːt) *a*, truculent.

trudgeon (trydʒɔ̃) *m*, trudgen (*Swim.*).

truelle (tryɛl) *f*, trowel. ~ **à poisson**, fish slice.

truffe (tryf) *f*, truffle.

truie (trɥi) *f*, sow.

truisme (tryism) *m*, truism.

truite (trɥit) *f*, trout. ~ **saumonée** (somone) salmont. **truité, e** (te), speckled, mottled.

trumeau (trymo) *m*, pier (*Arch.*); pier-glass; leg of beef.

truquage (tryka:ʒ) *m*, fake. **truquer** (ke) *v.t*, to fake.

tu (ty) *pn*, you, thou.

tuant, e (tɥɑ̃, ɑ̃:t) *a*, killing; boring.

tuba (tyba) *m*, tuba.

tube (tyb) *m*, tube.

tubercule (tybɛrkyl) *m*, tuber; tubercle. **tuberculeux, euse** (lø, ø:z) *a*, tuberculous. ¶ *n*, consumptive. **tuberculose** (lo:z) *f*, tuberculosis. **tubéreuse** (tybərø:z) *f*, tuberose.

tubulaire (tybylɛ:r) *a*, tubular.

tue-mouches (tymuʃ) *m*, fly swat[ter], fly flap. **tuer** (tɥe) *v.t*, to kill; slay; slaughter; swat (*fly*); bore. *tué à l'ennemi*, killed in action. *les tués*, the killed. *un tué, une tuée*, a fatality (*accident*). **tuerie** (tyri) *f*, slaughter, butchery, carnage. *à tue-tête*, at the top of one's voice. **tueur** (tɥœ:r) *m*, killer, slayer.

tuile (tɥil) *f*, tile. **tuilerie** (lri) *f*, tile works. **tuilier** (lje) *m*, tile maker.

tulipe (tylip) *f*, tulip. **tulipier** (pje) *m*, tulip tree.

tulle (tyl) *m*, tulle, net.

tumeur (tymœ:r) *f*, tumour.

tumulte (tymylt) *m*, tumult, uproar, turmoil; riot. **tumultueux, euse†** (tɥɔ, ø:z) *a*, tumultuous, riotous.

tumulus (tymyly:s) *m*, tumulus, barrow.

tungstène (tœ̃gstɛn) *m*, tungsten.

tunique (tynik) *f*, tunic; coat (*Anat., Bot.*).

Tunis (tynis) *m*, Tunis (*capital*). **la Tunisie** (zi) Tunis (*state*). **tunisien, ne** (zjɛ̃, ɛn) *a. & T~, n*, Tunisian.

tunnel (tynɛl) *m*, tunnel.

turban (tyrbɑ̃) *m*, turban.

turbine (tyrbin) *f*, turbine.

turbot (tyrbo) *m*, turbot.

turbulence (tyrbylɑ̃:s) *f*, turbulence. **turbulent, e** (lɑ̃, ɑ̃:t) *a*, turbulent, unruly, restless; boisterous.

turc, turque (tyrk) *a*, Turkish. **T~,** *n*, Turk. **le turc,** Turkish (*language*). **Turcoman** (kɔmɑ̃) (*pers.*) *m*, Turkoman.

turf (tyrf) *m*, racecourse. *le ~*, the turf.

turgescent, e (tyrʒɛsɑ̃, ɑ̃:t) *a*, turgescent, turgid.

turlupin (tyrlypɛ̃) *m*, buffoon.

turpitude (tyrpityd) *f*, turpitude, baseness.

Turquie (tyrki) *f*, Turkey. *~ d'Asie*, T. in Asia. *~ d'Europe*, T. in Europe.

turquoise (tyrkwa:z) *f. & att*, turquoise.

tussilage (tysila:ʒ) *m*, coltsfoot (*Bot.*).

tutélaire (tytelɛ:r) *a*, tutelar[y], guardian (*att.*). **tutelle** (tɛl) *f*, tutelage, guardianship; protection. **tuteur, trice** (tœ:r, tris) *n*, guardian; (*m.*) prop (*Hort.*).

tutoyer (tytwaje) *v.t*, to thou.

tutu (tyty) *m*, ballet skirt.

tuyau (tɥijo) *m*, pipe; tube; hose; flue; quill; goffer; tip, wrinkle. *~ acoustique*, speak-

ing tube. *~ d'arrosage*, garden hose.

tuyauter (te) *v.t*, to goffer.

tympan (tɛ̃pɑ̃) *m*, tympanum, ear drum; tympan. **tympanon** (panɔ̃) *m*, dulcimer.

type (tip) *m*, type (*model & Typ.*); standard.

typhoïde (tifɔid) *a*, typhoid.

typhon (tifɔ̃) *m*, typhoon.

typhus (tify:s) *m*, typhus.

typique (tipik) *a*, typical.

typographie (tipografi) *f*, typography; printing works. **typographique** (fik) *a*, typographic(al); letterpress (*att.*).

tyran (tirɑ̃) *m*, tyrant. **tyrannie** (rani) *f*, tyranny. **tyrannique†** (nik) *a*, tyrannic(al); high-handed. **tyranniser** (nize) *v.t*, to tyrannize [over].

Tyrol (le) (tirɔl), the Tyrol. **tyrolien, ne** (ljɛ̃, ɛn) *a. & T~, n*, Tyrolese.

tzigane (tsigan) *n. & a*, gipsy, Tzigane.

U

ubiquité (ybikɥite) *f*, ubiquity.

ulcération (ylserasjɔ̃) *f*, ulceration. **ulcère** (sɛ:r) *m*, ulcer. **ulcérer** (sere) *v.t*, to ulcerate; embitter.

ultérieur, e (ylterjœ:r) *a*, ulterior, later, subsequent. **ultérieurement** (œrmɑ̃) *ad*, later [on].

ultimatum (yltimatɔm) *m*, ultimatum.

ultra (yltra) *m*, ultraist, extremist. **~-violet, te** *a*, ultra-violet.

ululer (ylyle) *v.i*, to hoot, ululate.

un (œ̃) *m*, one. **un, une** (œ̃, yn) *a*, one; a, an. *~ à ~*, one by one; one after another. *l'~*, each (*price of articles*). *l'~ l'autre*, *les uns les unes les autres*, one another, each other. *l'~ & l'autre*, both. *l'~ ou l'autre*, either. *ni l'~ ni l'autre*, neither. *une fois*, once. *une fois, deux fois[, trois fois]*; adjugé! going, going; gone! *une fois pour toutes*, once for all. *en une [seule] fois*, in a lump sum, outright (*opp.* by instalments). *il y avait* (*ou il était*) *une fois*, once upon a time.

unanime† (ynanim) *a*, unanimous. **unanimité** (mite) *f*, unanimity, consensus. *à l'~*, unanimously.

uni, e (yni) *p.a*, united; even; level; smooth; plain; uniform.

unième† (ynjɛm) *a*, first (*only after* 20, 30, &c, e.g. *vingt & ~*, 21st; *cent ~*, 101st).

unifier (ynifje) *v.t*, to unify, consolidate; standardize. **uniforme** (fɔrm) *a*, uniform, even. ¶ *m*, uniform; regimentals. **uniformément** (memɑ̃) *ad*, uniformly, evenly. **uniformité** (mite) *f*, uniformity.

unilatéral, e (ynilateral) *a*, unilateral; one-sided.

uniment (ynimɑ̃) *ad*, smoothly, evenly; plainly; simply.

union (ynjɔ̃) *f*, union; unity. *U~ des Républiques soviétiques socialistes*, Union

of Soviet Socialist Republics. U~ Sud-
Africaine, Union of South Africa.
unique (ynik) *a*, only; sole; single; one;
unique. **uniquement** (knã) *ad*, solely,
uniquely; only.
unir (yni:r) *v.t*, to unite, join; level, smooth.
unisson (nisõ) *m*, unison. **unitaire** (te:r) *a*,
unitary; unit (*att.*). **unité** (te) *f*, unit;
unity, one; oneness.
univers (ynivɛ:r) *m*, universe. **universalité**
(vɛrsalite) *f*, universality. **universel, le**†
(sɛl) *a*, universal; world[-wide]. **universitaire** (sitɛ:r) *a*, university (*att.*). **université** (te) *f*, university.
uranium (yranjɔm) *m*, uranium.
urbain, e (yrbɛ̃, ɛn) *a*, urban. **urbanisme**
(banism) *m*, town planning. **urbanité** (te)
f, urbanity.
urètre (yrɛ:tr) *m*, urethra.
urgence (yrʒã:s) *f*, urgency. *d'~*, urgently;
emergency (*as a brake*). **urgent, e** (ʒã, ã:t)
a, urgent.
urinal (yrinal) *m*, urinal (*vessel*). **urine** (rin)
f, urine. **uriner** (ne) *v.i*, to urinate; (*v.t.*)
to pass. **urinoir** (nwa:r) *m*, urinal (*place*).
urique (rik) *a*, uric (*Law*).
urne (yrn) *f*, urn. ~ *électorale*, ballot box.
urticaire (yrtikɛ:r) *f*, nettle rash.
us & coutumes (ys) *m.pl*, use & wont.
usage (za:ʒ) *m*, use; purpose; wear; usage,
custom, practice. ~ [*du monde*], ways of
society. *article d'~*, serviceable article.
valeur d'~, value as a going concern.
usagé, e (za:ʒe) *a*, used, second-hand.
usager (ʒe) *m*, user. **usé, e** (ze) *a*,
worn [out]; shabby. ~ [*jusqu'à la corde*],
threadbare, hackneyed, stale. **user** (ze)
v.t, to use; wear [out, away]; abrade.
~ *de*, to use, exercise. **s'~**, to wear
[away]. *être d'un bon user*, to wear well.
usine (yzin) *f*, works; [manu]factory; mill;
(*power*) station. **usinier** (nje) *m*, mill
owner.
usité, e (yzite) *a*, used, in use. *peu usité*,
rare (*word*).
ustensile (ystãsil) *m*, utensil; implement, tool.
usuel, le† (yzɥɛl) *a*, usual, customary.
usufruit (yzyfrɥi) *m*, usufruct.
usuraire† (yzyrɛ:r) *a*, usurious. **usure** (zy:r)
f, usury; interest; wear [& tear], wearing;
attrition. **usurier, ère** (zyrje, ɛ:r) *n*,
usurer, Shylock, screw.
usurpateur, trice (yzyrpatœ:r, tris) *n*,
usurper. **usurpation** (sjõ) *f*, usurpation;
encroachment. **usurper** (pe) *v.t*, to usurp;
(*v.i.*) to encroach.
ut (yt) *m*, C (*Mus.*).
utérin, e (yterɛ̃, in) *a*, uterine. **utérus** (ry:s)
m, uterus.
utile† (ytil) *a*, useful, serviceable; effective;
due, good (*time*). **utiliser** (lize) *v.t*, to
utilize. **utilitaire** (tɛ:r) *a. & n*, utilitarian.
utilité (te) *f*, utility, use[fulness]; utility
[man] (*Theat.*).

utopie (ytɔpi) *f*, utopia. **utopique** (pik) *a*
*& * **utopiste** (pist) *a. & n*, utopian.
uvule (yvyl) *f*, uvula.

V

vacance (vakɑ:s) *f*, vacancy; (*pl.*) holiday[s];
vacation, recess; abeyance (*Law*). **vacant,
e** (kã, ã:t) *a*, vacant, unoccupied.
vacarme (vakarm) *m*, uproar, din, row.
vacation (vakasjõ) *f*, attendance, sitting
(*experts, &c*); (*pl.*) fees (*lawyer's, &c*);
(*pl.*) vacation (*Law*).
vaccin (vaksɛ̃) *m*, vaccine, lymph. **vaccination** (sinasjõ) *f*, vaccination. **vaccine** (sin)
f, cow-pox. **vacciner** (ne) *v.t*, to vaccinate.
vache (vaf) *f*, cow; cow hide. ~ *à lait*,
~ *laitière*, milch cow. **vacher, ère** (ʃe, ɛ:r)
n, cowherd, neatherd. **vacherie** (fri) *f*,
cow house; dairy [farm].
vaciller (vasile) *v.i*, to be unsteady, wobble;
vacillate, waver; flicker.
vacuité (vakɥite) *f*, vacuity, emptiness.
vade-mecum (vademekɔm) *m*, vade-mecum.
va-et-vient (vaevjɛ̃) *m*, come-&-go; to & fro;
reciprocating motion; swing (*door*); ferry
boat; two-way wiring (*Elec.*).
vagabond, e (vagabõ, ɔ̃:d) *a*, vagabond,
vagrant, roving; truant. ¶ *n*, vagabond,
vagrant, tramp. **vagabondage** (bõda:ʒ)
m, vagrancy; truancy. **vagabonder** (de)
v.i, to rove, wander.
vagir (vaʒi:r) *v.i*, to wail, cry (*of baby*).
vague (va:g) *f*, wave, billow; surge.
vague† (va:g) *a*, vague; hazy; waste (*land*).
¶ *m*, vagueness; void. **vaguer** (vage) *v.i*,
to wander [about].
vaillamment (vajamã) *ad*, valiantly, gallantly. **vaillance** (jã:s) *f*, gallantry,
valour. **vaillant, e** (jã, ã:t) *a*, valiant,
gallant. **vaillantise** (jãti:z) *f*, prowess.
vain, e† (vɛ̃, ɛn) *a*, vain; useless; conceited.
vaine pâture, common [land]. *en vain*, in
vain, fruitlessly.
vaincre (vɛ̃:kr) *v.t.ir*, to vanquish, conquer;
beat; overcome. **les vaincus** (vɛ̃ky) *m.pl*,
the vanquished. **vainqueur** (kœ:r) *m*,
conqueror, victor; winner (*Sport*).
vairon (vɛrõ) *m*, minnow.
vaisseau (vɛso) *m*, vessel; ship; boat; body
(*as nave of church*), main hall. ~ *amiral*,
flagship. ~*-école*, training s. ~*-hôpital*,
hospital s. ~ *rasé*, hulk. ~ *sanguin*,
blood vessel. **vaisselier** (sɔlje) *m*, sideboard; dresser. **vaisselle** (sɛl) *f*, crockery,
plates & dishes. ~ *plaquée*, electroplate.
~ *plate*, plate (*silver, gold, &c*).
val (val) *m*, vale, glen. *par monts & par
vaux*, over hill & dale.
valable† (valabl) *a*, valid, good, available
(*ticket*).
valence (valã:s) *f*, valence, -cy (*Chem.*).
Valence (valã:s) *f*, Valencia (*Spain*).

valet (valɛ) *m*, valet; man[servant]; holdfast; stand; knave, jack (*Cards*). ~ de chambre, valet. ~ de charrue, ploughman. ~ de ferme, farm hand. ~ de pied, footman; flunkey. **valetaille** (ltɑ:j) *f*, menials, flunkeydom. **faire valeter** (lte), to make (*someone*) fetch & carry.

Valette (la) (valɛt), Valetta.

valétudinaire (valetydinɛ:r) *a. & n*, valetudinarian.

valeur (valœ:r) *f*, value; worth; valour, gallantry; value [date], as at (*Com.*); security (*Fin.*); stock; share; investment; holding; asset; bill; paper; money. ~ déclarée: *fr.* —, insured for: — francs. avec ~ déclarée, insured (*parcel*, &c). sans ~ déclarée, uninsured. ~s mobilières, stocks & shares, transferable securities. [objet de] ~, valuable [article], a. of value. **valeureux, euse†** (lœrø, ø:z) *a*, valorous.

valide† (valid) *a*, valid; available; able-bodied, fit for service (*pers.*). **valider** (de) *v.t*, to validate. **validité** (dite) *f*, validity.

valise (vali:z) *f*, portmanteau; bag.

vallée (vale) *f*, valley. **vallon** (lɔ̃) *m*, dale, vale, glen.

valoir (valwa:r) *v.i. & t. ir*, to be worth; win, gain. cela vaut la peine, it is worth while. il vaut mieux, it is better to. autant vaut, one might as well. à ~ sur, on account of. faire ~, to turn to account, make the best of; develop; enforce.

valse (vals) *f*, waltz. **valser** (se) *v.i*, to waltz. **valseur, euse** (sœ:r, ø:z) *n*, waltzer.

valve (valv) *f*, valve.

vampire (vɑ̃pi:r) *m*, vampire.

vanadium (vanadjɔm) *m*, vanadium.

vandale (vɑ̃dal) *m*, vandal. **vandalisme** (lism) *m*, vandalism, wanton destruction.

vandoise (vɑ̃dwa:z) *f*, dace.

vanille (vani:j) *f*, vanilla.

vanité (vanite) *f*, vanity, conceit. **vaniteux, euse** (tø, ø:z) *a*, vain, conceited.

vannage (vana:ʒ) *m*, winnowing; gating. **vanne** (van) *f*, sluice gate, flood gate; gate; shutter. **vanneau** (no) *m*, lapwing, pe[e]wit. œufs de ~, plovers' eggs (*Cook.*). **vanner** (ne) *v.t*, to winnow, fan (*grain*). **vannerie** (nri) *f*, basket making; b. work, wicker work. **vanneur, euse** (nœ:r, ø:z) *n*, winnower. **vannier** (nje) *m*, basket maker.

vantail (vɑ̃ta:j) *m*, leaf (*door, shutter*).

vantard, e (vɑ̃ta:r, ard) *a*, boastful. ¶ *n*, boaster, braggart. **vantardise** (tardi:z) & **vanterie** (tri) *f*, boast[ing], brag[ging]. **vanter** (te) *v.t*, to praise, extol, cry up, vaunt. se ~, to boast, vaunt, brag.

va-nu-pieds (vanypje) *n*, ragamuffin.

vapeur (vapœ:r) *f*, vapour; fume; mist; steam. à ~, steam (*engine, boat*). ¶ *m*, steamer, steamship, steamboat. ~-citerne, tank steamer. ~ de charge, cargo boat. ~ de ligne [régulière], liner. **vaporeux, euse**

(porø, ø:z) *a*, vaporous, -ry; misty; hazy; filmy, gauzy. **vaporisateur** (rizatœ:r) *m*, spray[er], atomizer. **vaporiser** (ze) *v.t*, to vaporize; spray.

vaquer (vake) *v.i*, to be vacant (*employ*); not to sit (*court*). ~ à, to attend to.

varech (varɛk) *m*, seaweed, wrack.

varenne (varɛn) *f*, waste pasturage.

vareuse (varø:z) *f*, guernsey, jumper (*sailor's*); fatigue jacket (*Mil.*); cardigan [jacket] (*woman's*).

variable (varjabl) *a*, variable, changeable, unsettled. au ~, at change (*barometer*). **variante** (rjɑ̃:t) *f*, variant. **variation** (rjasjɔ̃) *f*, variation, change.

varice (varis) *f*, varicose vein.

varicelle (varisɛl) *f*, chicken pox.

varier (varje) *v.t. & i*, to vary, change; variegate, diversify; differ. **variété** (rjete) *f*, variety; diversity; (*pl.*) miscellany.

variole (varjɔl) *f*, smallpox. **varioleux, euse** (lø, ø:z) *n*, smallpox case (*pers.*).

varlet (varlɛ) *m*, varlet (*Hist.*).

varlope (varlɔp) *f*, trying-plane.

Varsovie (varsovi) *f*, Warsaw.

vasculaire (vaskylɛ:r) *a*, vascular.

vase (vɑ:z) *f*, mud, silt, slime, ooze. ¶ *m*, vessel, vase. ~ à filtrations chaudes, beaker. ~ clos, retort. ~ de nuit, chamber [pot].

vaseline (vazlin) *f*, vaseline (*trade name*).

vaseux, euse (vazø, ø:z) *a*, muddy, slimy.

vasistas (vazistɑ:s) *m*, fan light.

vassal, e (vasal) *n*, vassal (*Hist.*).

vaste (vast) *a*, vast, spacious, wide.

va-tout (vatu) *m*, (one's) all.

vaudeville (vodvil) *m*, vaudeville.

vaudoise (vodwa:z) *f*, dace.

vau-l'eau (à) (volo) *ad*, down stream; to rack & ruin.

vaurien, ne (vorjɛ̃, ɛn) *n*, blackguard; rascal.

vautour (votu:r) *m*, vulture.

vautrer (se) (votre) *v.pr*, to wallow; sprawl.

veau (vo) *m*, calf; veal; calf[skin]. ~ d'or, golden calf. ~ gras, fatted c. ~ raciné (rasine), tree calf.

vecteur (vɛktœ:r) *m*, vector.

vécu, e (veky) *p.a*, true to life (*novel, &c*).

vedette (vədɛt) *f*, mounted sentry; scout (*warship*); motor boat; leader; leading counter; star (*Theat., film*). en ~, prominent[ly]. in the limelight; starred; displayed in bold type.

végétal, e (veʒetal) *a*, plant (*life*); vegetable. ¶ *m*, plant. **végétarien, ne** (tarjɛ̃, ɛn) *a. & n*, vegetarian. **végétarisme** (rism) *m*, vegetarianism. **végétation** (sjɔ̃) *f*, vegetation; growth. ~s [adénoïdes], adenoids. **végéter** (te) *v.i*, to vegetate.

véhémence (veemɑ̃:s) *f*, vehemence. **véhément, e†** (mɑ̃, ɑ̃:t), vehement.

véhicule (veikyl) *m*, vehicle; medium. **véhiculer** (le) *v.t*, to cart; convey.

veille (vɛːj) f, watch, vigil, staying up; look-out; wakeful night; eve; day before; brink; point. **veillée** (vɛje) f, evening; vigil; night nursing. **veiller** (je) v.i. & t, to sit up, stay up, lie awake; watch. ~ à, to see that. ~ sur, to look after, take care of. **veilleur, euse** (jœːr, øːz) n, watchman; watcher; (f.) night light; by-pass (gas). veilleuse de nuit, night nurse.

veine (vɛn) f, vein; tricklet (water); luck. **veiner** (ne) v.t, to vein, grain.

vêler (vɛle) v.i, to calve.

vélin (velɛ̃) m, vellum. papier ~, wove paper.

velléité (velleite) f, (irresolute) intention.

vélo (velo) m, bike. **vélocipède** (lɔsipɛd) m, velocipede; cycle. **vélocité** (te) f, swiftness. **vélodrome** (droːm) m, cycle track.

velours (vəluːr) m, velvet. ~ à [grosses] côtes, ~ côtelé, corduroy. ~ de coton, velveteen. sur le ~, dormy, -mie (Golf). **velouté, e** (lute) a, velvet[y].

velu, e (vəly) a, hairy (skin, caterpillar, leaf).

venaison (vənɛzɔ̃) f, venison.

vénal, e† (venal) a, venal; market[able], sale (value). **vénalité** (lite) f, venality.

venant (vənɑ̃) m, comer.

vendable (vɑ̃dabl) a, salable, marketable.

vendange (vɑ̃dɑ̃ʒ) f, grape gathering; vintage. **vendanger** (dɑ̃ʒe) v.t. & abs, to gather. **vendangeur, euse** (ʒœːr, øːz) n, vintager.

vendetta (vɛ̃detta) f, vendetta, feud.

vendeur, euse (vɑ̃dœːr, øːz) n, seller, vendor; salesman, -woman. **vendeur, eresse** (dœːr, drɛs) n, vendor (Law). **vendre** (dr) v.t, to sell, sell at; sell for; sell up. **vendredi** (vɑ̃drədi) m, Friday. le ~ saint, Good Friday.

vénéneux, euse (venenø, øːz) a, poisonous, venomous (plant, food, &c).

vénérable (venerabl) a, venerable. **vénération** (sjɔ̃) f, veneration. **vénérer** (re) v.t, to venerate; worship (saints, relics).

vénerie (venri) f, hunting (science).

vénérien, ne (venerjɛ̃, ɛn) a, venereal.

Vénétie (la) (venesi) f, Venetia.

veneur (vənœːr) m, huntsman.

vengeance (vɑ̃ʒɑ̃s) f, vengeance; revenge. **venger** (ʒe) v.t, to avenge, revenge. **vengeur, eresse** (ʒœːr, ʒrɛs) n, avenger. ¶ a, avenging, vengeful.

véniel, e† (venjel) a, venial.

venimeux, euse (vənimø, øːz) a, venomous, poisonous (bite, animal, & fig.). **venin** (nɛ̃) m, venom, poison.

venir (vəniːr) v.i.ir, to come; strike (idea); occur, happen; hail (de = from); grow. en ~ aux mains, to come to blows. je viens de . . ., I have just . . .

Venise (vəniːz) f, Venice. **vénitien, ne** (venisjɛ̃, ɛn) a. & V~, n, Venetian.

vent (vɑ̃) m, wind; air; blast; draught; scent; inkling; windage; flatus. ~ coulis, draught. en plein ~, in the open air. îles du V~, Windward Islands. îles sous le V~, Leeward Islands.

vente (vɑ̃t) f, sale, selling. ~ à tempérament, ~ par abonnement, hire purchase, hire system, instalment plan. ~ de blanc, white sale. ~ de charité, [charity] bazaar.

venter (vɑ̃te) v.imp, to be windy, blow. **venteux, euse** (tø, øːz) a, windy; breezy. **ventilateur** (tilatœːr) m, fan, ventilator. **ventilation** (sjɔ̃) f, ventilation; airing; apportionment, analysis. **ventiler** (le) v.t, to ventilate, &c.

ventouse (vɑ̃tuːz) f, cupping glass; air hole; sucker (of leech). **ventouser** (tuze) v.t, to cup (Surg.).

ventral, e (vɑ̃tral) a, ventral. **ventre** (vɑ̃tr) m, belly, abdomen; womb; bulge; bilge (cask). faire [le] ~, to bulge, belly. **ventrée** (vɑ̃tre) f, litter (pups, &c).

ventricule (vɑ̃trikyl) m, ventricle. **ventriloque** (ki) f, ventriloquism, -quy.

ventru, e (vɑ̃try) a, corpulent.

venu, e (vəny) n, comer; (f.) coming; appearance; inrush; occurrence; growth.

vêpres (vɛːpr) f.pl, vespers, evensong.

ver (vɛːr) m, worm; grub; maggot; moth. ~ à soie, silkworm. ~ luisant, glowworm. ~ rongeur, canker[worm]. remorse. ~ solitaire, tapeworm.

véracité (verasite) f, veracity, truthfulness.

véranda (verɑ̃da) f, veranda[h].

verbal, e† (vɛrbal) a, verbal. **verbaliser** (lize) v.i, to take particulars; draw up a report. **verbe** (vɛrb) m, verb; [tone of] voice. le Verbe, the Word (Theol.). **verbeux, euse** (bø, øːz) a, verbose, prosy; wordy. **verbiage** (bjaːʒ) m, verbiage. **verbosité** (bozite) f, verbosity, wordiness, prosiness.

verdâl (vɛrdal) m, pavement glass, p. light. **verdâtre** (vɛrdɑːtr) a, greenish. **verdelet, te** (dɛlɛ, ɛt) a, tartish (wine); hale. **verdet** (dɛ) m, verdigris. **verdeur** (dœːr) f, greenness; unripeness; tartness.

verdict (vɛrdikt) m, verdict.

verdier (vɛrdje) m, greenfinch. **verdir** (diːr) v.t. & i, to green. **verdoyant, e** (dwajɑ̃, ɑ̃ːt) a, verdant. **verdoyer** (je) v.i, to green. **verdure** (dyːr) f, verdure, greenery; greenness; greensward; green stuff, greens.

véreux, euse (verø, øːz) a, wormy, maggoty, grubby; shady, bogus, fishy; bad (debt).

verge (vɛrʒ) f, rod; wand, verge; beam (scales); shank (anchor); (pl.) birch [rod]. **vergé** (ʒe) a, laid (paper). ~ blanc, cream-laid. **verger** (ʒe) m, orchard. **vergeture** (ʒəty:r) f, weal.

verglas (vɛrglɑ) m, glazed frost, silver thaw.

vergne (vɛrɲ) m, alder [tree].

vergogne (sans) (vɛrɡɔɲ), shameless.

vergue (vɛrɡ) f, yard (Naut.).

véridique† (veridik) *a*, truthful, veracious.
vérificateur (fikatœ:r) *m*, examiner, inspector. ~ *comptable*, auditor. **vérification** (sjɔ̃) *f*, verification, inspection, examination, checking, vouching, audit[ing]. ~ *de testament*, probate. **vérifier** (fje) *v.t*, to verify, &c.
vérin (verɛ̃) *m*, jack (*Mach.*).
véritable† (veritabl) *a*, true; real, veritable; regular. **vérité** (te) *f*, truth, verity; fact.
vermeil, le (vɛrmɛːj) *a*, vermilion; ruby, rosy. ¶ *m*, silver-gilt.
vermicelle (vɛrmisɛl) *m*, vermicelli; v. soup.
vermillon (vɛrmijɔ̃) *m*, vermilion.
vermine (vɛrmin) *f*, vermin. **vermoulu, e** (muly) *a*, worm-eaten. **vermoulure** (ly:r) *f*, worm hole; dust from worm holes.
vermouth (vɛrmut) *m*, verm[o]uth.
vernal, e (vɛrnal) *a*, vernal, spring (*att.*).
verne (vɛrn) *m*, alder [tree].
verni, e (vɛrni) *a*, varnished, &c, as *vernir*; patent (*leather*), patent leather† (*shoes*). ¶ *m.pl*, patent leather shoes; dress shoes.
vernier (vɛrnje) *m*, vernier.
vernir (vɛrni:r) *v.t*, to varnish; japan; gloss over. ~ *au tampon*, to French-polish. **vernis** (ni) *m*, varnish; japan; glaze; veneer (*fig.*). ~ *à l'alcool*, spirit varnish. ~ *au tampon*, French polish. ~ *gras*, oil varnish. **vernissage** (nisa:ʒ) *m*, varnishing, &c; varnishing day. **vernisser** (se) *v.t*, to glaze (*pottery*).
Vérone (verɔn) *f*, Verona.
véronique (verɔnik) *f*, speedwell, veronica.
verrat (vɛra) *m*, boar.
verre (vɛːr) *m*, glass. ~ *d'illumination*, fairy lamp. ~ *soluble*, water glass. **verrerie** (vɛrri) *f*, glass making; g. works; glass[ware]. **verrier** (rje) *m*, glass maker. **verrière** (rjɛːr) *f*, stained glass window. **verroterie** (rɔtri) *f*, [small] glassware; [glass] beads.
verrou (vɛru) *m*, bolt. *sous les* ~*s*, under lock & key, locked up. **verrouiller** (ruje) *v.t*, to bolt; lock up (*prisoner*).
verrue (vɛry) *f*, wart. **verruqueux, euse** (kø, ø:z) *a*, warty.
vers (vɛːr) *m*, verse, line (*poetry*). ~ *blancs*, blank verse. ¶ *pr*, towards; to; about.
versant (vɛrsã) *m*, side, slope (*hill, &c*).
versatile (vɛrsatil) *a*, fickle. **versatilité** (lite) *f*, fickleness.
verse (vɛrs) *f*, laying, lodging (*corn*). *à* ~, fast, hard (*rain*). **versé(e) dans** (se), versed in, conversant with. **versement** (səmã) *m*, payment, paying in; p. up; remittance; instalment; call; deposit (*Savings Bank*). ~ *de souscription*, application money (*shares*). **verser** (se) *v.t. & i*, to pour [out]; shed, spill; tip; overturn, upset, capsize; lay, lodge (*corn*); pay; p. in, p. up; deposit. **verset** (sɛ) *m*, verse (*Bible*). **versicle** (*Lit.*). **verseuse** (sø:z) *f*, coffee pot.
versificateur (vɛrsifikatœ:r) *m*, versifier.

versifier (fje) *v.i. & t*, to versify. **version** (sjɔ̃) *f*, version; translation. ~ *à livre ouvert*, unseen [translation].
verso (vɛrso) *m*, verso, back. *au* ~, over-leaf.
vert, e (vɛːr, ɛrt) *a*, green; verdant; unripe; unseasoned; callow; raw; sour; sharp; fresh; hale; free, indecorous. ¶ *m*, green; grass. **vert-de-gris** (vɛrdəgri) *m*, verdigris.
vertébral, e (vɛrtebral) *a*, vertebral; spinal (*column*). **vertèbre** (tɛ:br) *f*, vertebra. **vertébré, e** (tebre) *a. & m*, vertebrate; (*m.pl.*) Vertebrata.
vertement (vɛrtəmã) *ad*, sharply, soundly.
vertical, e (vɛrtikal) *a*, vertical, upright. ¶ *f*, vertical. **verticalement** (lmã) *ad*, vertically; down (*cross-word clues*).
verticille (vɛrtisil) *m*, verticil, whorl.
vertige (vɛrti:ʒ) *m*, dizziness; giddiness; vertigo. **vertigineux, euse** (tiʒinø, ø:z) *a*, dizzy, giddy. **vertigo** (go) *m*, staggers (*Vet.*).
vertu (vɛrty) *f*, virtue. *en* ~ *de*, in (or by) v. of; in pursuance of. **vertueux, euse†** (tɥø, ø:z) *a*, virtuous; righteous.
verve (vɛrv) *f*, verve, zest.
vesce (vɛs) *f*, vetch, tare.
vésicatoire (vezikatwa:r) *m*, blister (*plaster*). **vésicule** (kyl) *f*, vesicle, bladder.
vespasienne (vɛspazjɛn) *f*, urinal (*street*).
vessie (vɛsi) *f*, bladder.
vestale (vɛstal) *f*, vestal [virgin].
veste (vɛst) *f*, jacket (*short*). **vestiaire** (tjɛːr) *m*, cloak room; robing room; hall stand; Dorcas.
vestibule (vɛstibyl) *m*, vestibule, [entrance] hall, lobby.
vestige (vɛsti:ʒ) *m*, footprint, track, trace; (*pl.*) vestiges, remains.
veston (vɛstɔ̃) *m*, jacket (*lounge*).
Vésuve (le) (vezy:v) *m*, Vesuvius. **vésuvien, ne** (zyvjɛ̃, ɛn) *a*, Vesuvian.
vêtement (vɛtmã) *m*, garment; vestment; (*pl.*) clothes, clothing. ~ *de dessous*, undergarment (*woman's*); (*pl.*) under-clothing, underwear (*women's*).
vétéran (veterã) *m*, veteran; long service man (*Mil.*). **vétérance** (rã:s) *f*, long service.
vétérinaire (veterinɛːr) *a*, veterinary. [*médecin*] ~, veterinary [surgeon].
vétille (veti:j) *f*, trifle. **vétilleux, euse** (tijø, ø:z) *a*, finical; ticklish.
vêtir (vɛti:r) *v.t.ir*, to clothe, dress.
veto (veto) *m*, veto.
vêture (vɛty:r) *f*, taking the habit, taking the veil (*Eccl.*).
vétusté (vetyste) *f*, decay, [old] age.
veuf, veuve (vœf, vœ:v) *a*, widowed; deprived, bereft. ¶ *m*, widower. ¶ *f*, widow, relict.
veule (vœːl) *a*, slack, flabby.
veuvage (vœva:ʒ) *m*, widowerhood, widowhood.

vexatoire (vɛksatwa:r) a, vexatious. **vexer** (kse) v.t, to vex, provoke.

viabilité (vjabilite) f, good condition (of roads); viability. **viable** (bl) a, viable.

viaduc (vjadyk) m, viaduct.

viager, ère (vjaʒe, ɛːr) a, life (att.), for life. ¶ m, life annuity.

viande (vjɑ̃:d) f, meat. ~ de boucherie, butcher's meat. ~ de cheval, horse flesh, viatique.

viatique (vjatik) m, provision for journey; viaticum.

vibration (vibrasjɔ̃) f, vibration (Phys.). **vibrer** (bre) v.i, to vibrate (Phys. & fig.).

vicaire (vikɛːr) m, vicar; curate. **vicariat** (karja) m, vicariate; curacy.

vice (vis) m, vice; defect, fault, flaw. ~ d'adresse, wrong address. ~ de clerc, clerical error. ~ de conformation, malformation. ~ de construction, constructional defect. ~ de forme, informality. ~ de prononciation, mispronunciation.

vice (vis) prefix, vice: ~-président, e, n, vice- (or deputy) chairman or president. ~-reine, f, vice-reine. ~-roi, m, viceroy.

Vicence (visɑ̃:s) f, Vicenza.

vice versa (viseversa) ad, vice versa.

vicier (visje) v.t, to vitiate, foul. **vicieux, euse†** (sjø, øːz) a, vicious; defective; faulty; unsound.

vicinal, e (visinal) a, parish, local (road).

vicissitude (visisityd) f, vicissitude.

victime (viktim) f, victim; casualty; sufferer.

victoire (viktwaːr) f, victory; win. ~ aux points, win on points (Box.). ~ par hors-combat, knock-out win. **victoria** (tɔrja) f, victoria (carriage). **victorieux, euse†** (rjø, øːz) a, victorious, triumphant.

victuailles (viktɥaːj) f.pl, victuals.

vidange (vidɑ̃:ʒ) f, emptying; clearing; ullage; (pl.) night soil. en ~, ullaged (cask). **vidanger** (dɑ̃ʒe) v.t, to empty. **vidangeur** (ʒœːr) m, nightman. **vide** (vid) a, empty, void; idle. ¶ m, void; vacuum; space; gap; vacancy; empty (case, &c). à ~, [when] empty. ~-poches, m, tidy (receptacle). ~-pomme, f, apple corer. **vider** (de) v.t, to empty, vacate (les lieux = the premises); settle (dispute); thresh out; bore (cannon); draw (fowl); gut (fish); stone (fruit); core (apple, &c).

viduité (vidɥite) f, widowhood.

vie (vi) f, life; lifetime; living, livelihood. la ~ à trois, the eternal triangle. à ~, for life.

vieillard (vjɛjaːr) m, old man. les ~s, the aged (either sex). **vieilleries** (jri) f.pl, old things. **vieillesse** (jɛs) f, [old] age. **vieilli, e** (ji) a, antiquated; obsolete, archaic; aged. **vieillir** (jiːr) v.i, to grow old, age, become obsolete; (v.t.) to age, make [look] old[er]. **vieillissant, e** (jisɑ̃, ɑ̃:t) a, ageing; obsolescent. **vieillot, te** (jo, ɔt) a, oldish, quaint. ¶ n, little old man, little old woman.

Vienne (vjɛn) f, Vienna. **viennois, e** (nwa, aːz) a, & **V~, n,** Viennese.

vierge (vjɛrʒ) f, virgin, maid. ¶ a, virgin; blank (page); free.

vieux, vieil, vieille (vjø, vjɛːj) a, old; stale; obsolete, archaic. **vieux, vieille, n,** old man, old woman. le vieux, the old (opp. the new). les vieux, the old (either sex).

vif, vive (vif, iːv) a, alive; live; living; quick; lively; sprightly; brisk; smart; sharp; vital; keen; crisp, tangy; hasty; spirited; vivid; bright; spring (water, tide). de vive force, by main (or sheer) force. de vive voix, by word of mouth, viva voce. le vif, the quick (flesh, &c); the heart (of a matter); life (Art). **vif-argent,** m, quicksilver.

vigie (viʒi) f, look-out; look-out [man]; vigia.

vigilance (viʒilɑ̃:s) f, vigilance, watchfulness. **vigilant, e** (lɑ̃, ɑ̃:t) a, vigilant, watchful. **vigile** (ʒil) f, vigil, eve (Eccl.).

vigne (viɲ) f, vine; vineyard. ~ vierge, Virginia creeper. **vigneron, ne** (nərɔ̃, ɔn) n, wine grower. **vignette** (nɛt) f, vignette; cut; ornamental border; revenue label. **vignoble** (nɔbl) m, vineyard.

vigogne (vigɔɲ) f, vicugna, vicuña.

vigoureux, euse† (viguɾø, øːz) a, vigorous, strong, forceful; stout, sturdy, robust, lusty; plucky (Phot.). **vigueur** (gœːr) f, vigour, strength. mettre en ~, to put in force, enforce.

vil, e† (vil) a, vile, base, mean. à vil prix, dirt-cheap. **vilain, e†** (lɛ̃, ɛn) a, ugly; wretched; nasty; scurvy; naughty. ¶ n, villain, villein (Hist.); naughty boy, girl, villain; scurvy fellow.

vilebrequin (vilbrəkɛ̃) m, brace, bit stock; crank shaft.

vilenie (vilni) f, meanness; dirty trick; abuse. **vileté** (lte) f, cheapness; worthlessness. **vilipender** (lipɑ̃de) v.t, to vilify.

villa (villa) f, villa. **village** (vilaːʒ) m, village. **villageois, e** (laʒwa, aːz) n, villager; (att.) rustic, country. **ville** (vil) f, town, city. ~ d'eaux, watering place, spa. **villégiature** (leʒjatyːr) f, stay in the country; holiday.

vin (vɛ̃) m, wine. ~ blanc du Rhin, hock. ~ de Bordeaux, claret. ~ de Champagne, champagne. ~ de liqueur, sweet dessert wine. ~ du cru, wine of the country. ~ en cercles, wine in the wood. ~ millésimé (millezime), vintage wine. ~ sans année, ~ non-millésimé, non-vintage wine.

vinage (vina:ʒ) m, fortification (of wine). **vinaigre** (nɛːgr) m, vinegar. **vinaigrer** (nɛgre) v.t, to vinegar. **vinaigrerie** (grəri) f, vinegar works.

vindas (vɛ̃das) m, crab [capstan]; giant['s] stride.

vindicatif, ive (vɛ̃dikatif, iːv) a, vindictive, revengeful; avenging. **vindicte** (dikt) f, (public) prosecution (of crime).

vinée (vine) *f*, vintage (*crop*). **viner** (ne) *v.t*, to fortify (*wine*). **vineux, euse** (nø, ø:z) *a*, vinous; winy; full-bodied (*wine*); rich in vineyards; rich in wines.

vingt (vɛ̃) *a*, twenty. ¶ *m*, twenty; 20th. ~*-deux!* cave!, look out! **vingtaine** (tɛ:n) *f*, score, twenty [or so]. **vingtième** (tjɛm) *a. & n*, twentieth.

vinicole (vinikɔl) *a*, wine-growing. **vinosité** (nozite) *f*, vinosity.

viol (vjɔl) *m*, rape, ravishment.

violacé, e (vjɔlase) *a*, violaceous. **violacées,** *f.pl*, Violaceae.

violariacée (vjɔlarjase) *f*, viola (*Bot.*); (*pl.*) Viola (*génus*).

violateur, trice (vjɔlatœ:r, tris) *a*, violator; transgressor. **violation** (sjɔ̃) *f*, violation, transgression, breach; desecration.

violâtre (vjɔlɑ:tr) *a*, purplish.

violemment (vjɔlamɑ̃) *ad*, violently. **violence** (lɑ̃:s) *f*, violence; duress[e]; stress. **violent e** (lɑ̃, ɑ̃:t) *a*, violent. **violenter** (lɑ̃te) *v.t*, to do violence to. **violer** (le) *v.t*, to violate, transgress, break; rape, ravish; desecrate.

violet, te (vjɔlɛ, ɛt) *a*, violet, purple. **violet,** *m*, violet (*colour*). **violet** *f*, violet (*Bot.*). ~ *de chien*, dog v. ~ *de Parme*, Parma v. ~ *odorante*, sweet v. **violier** (lje) *m*, stock. ~ *jaune*, wallflower.

violon (vjɔlɔ̃) *m*, violin, fiddle; lock-up, clink. **violoncelle** (sɛl) *m*, violoncello, [']cello. **violoncelliste** (list) *n*, [violon]cellist. **violoniste** (lɔnist) *n*, violinist.

vipère (vipɛ:r) *f*, viper, adder.

virage (vira:ʒ) *m*, turning, slewing, swinging; tacking (*Naut.*); turn, bend, corner; toning (*Phot.*).

virago (virago) *f*, Amazon (*forceful woman*).

virement (virmɑ̃) *m*, turning; tacking (*Naut.*); bank transfer; transfer (*Bkkpg*). **virer** (re) *v.i*, to turn; bank (*Aero.*); heave (*Naut.*); (*v.t.*) to transfer; tone (*Phot.*). ~ *de bord*, to tack (*Naut.*).

vireux, euse (virø, ø:z) *a*, noxious.

virginal, e† (virʒinal) *a*, virginal, maiden[ly].

virginie (ni) *m*, Virginia (*tobacco*). la **V~,** Virginia (*Geog.*). **virginité** (te) *f*, virginity, maidenhood.

virgule (virgyl) *f*, comma. ~ *[décimale]* [decimal] point. *Note:* — The decimal point is indicated in French by a comma.

viril, e (viril) *a*, virile, manly. **virilité** (lite) *f*, virility, manliness; manhood.

virole (virɔl) *f*, ferrule.

virtuel, le (virtɥɛl) *a*, virtual. **virtuellement** (lmɑ̃) *ad*, virtually, to all intents & purposes.

virtuose (virtɥo:z) *n*, virtuoso. **virtuosité** (ozite) *f*, virtuosity.

virulence (virylɑ̃:s) *f*, virulence. **virulent, e** (lɑ̃, ɑ̃:t) *a*, virulent. **virus** (ry:s) *m*, virus.

vis (vis) *f*, screw. ~ *ailée*, thumb s., wing s. ~ *d'Archimède* (arʃimɛd) Archimedean s. ~ *sans fin*, worm.

visa (viza) *m*, visa; initials, signature.

visage (viza:ʒ) *m*, face, visage; aspect. *à* ~ *découvert*, barefacedly.

vis-à-vis (vizavi) *& ~ de, pr. & ad*, opposite, o. to; face to face; facing; vis-à-vis; towards. ¶ *m*, person opposite; vis-à-vis.

viscères (visɛ:r) *m.pl*, viscera.

viscose (visko:z) *f*, viscose. **viscosité** (kozite) *f*, viscosity, stickiness.

visée (vize) *f*, sight[ing], observation, aim. **viser** (ze) *v.t*, to aim at; sight; have in view; cater for; visa; initial, sign; mark; certify; address (*golf ball*). ~ *à*, to aim at.

viseur (zœ:r) *m*, [view] finder (*Phot.*); dial (*calculating mach.*). ~ *redresseur*, collapsible view finder. **visibilité** (zibilite) *f*, visibility. **visible†** (bl) *a*, visible; obvious; at home. *pas* ~, engaged; not accessible. **visière** (zjɛ:r) *f*, peak (*cap*); eyeshade; visor (*Hist.*). **vision** (zjɔ̃) *f*, vision, sight; seeing; fantasy, phantasy; hallucination. **visionnaire** (zjɔnɛ:r) *a. & n*, visionary.

visitation (vizitasjɔ̃) *f*, visitation (*Eccl.*). **visite** (zit) *f*, visit, call; attendance; inspection, examination; survey. ~ *à bord*, rummaging (*Cust.*). **visiter** (te) *v.t*, to visit, &c. **visiteur, euse** (tœ:r, ø:z) *n*, visitor, caller; inspector, examiner.

vison (vizɔ̃) *m*, mink (*Zool. & fur*).

visqueux, euse (viskø, ø:z) *a*, viscous, viscid, sticky, tacky.

visser (vise) *v.t*, to screw [on, down, up].

Vistule (la) (vistyl), the Vistula.

visuel, le (vizɥɛl) *a*, visual, (*line, &c*) of sight.

vital, e (vital) *a*, vital; living. **vitalité** (lite) *f*, vitality.

vitamine (min) *f*, vitamin.

vite (vit) *a*, swift, quick, fast. ¶ *ad*, quick[ly], fast.

vitelotte (vitlɔt) *f*, kidney [potato].

vitesse (vitɛs) *f*, speed, velocity, quickness.

viticole (vitikɔl) *a*, viticultural. **viticulteur** (kyltœ:r) *m*, viticultur[al]ist, wine grower. **viticulture** (ty:r) *f*, viticulture.

vitrage (vitra:ʒ) *m*, glazing; windows, glass work; glass door; curtain net, vitrage. **vitrail** (tra:j) *m*, leaded window. *vitraux peints*, stained glass. **vitre** (tr) *f*, [window] pane. **vitrer** (tre) *v.t*, to glaze (*window*). **vitrerie** (trəri) *f*, glaziery. **vitreux, euse** (trø, ø:z) *a*, vitreous, glassy; lack-lustre. **vitrier** (trie) *m*, glazier. **vitrifier** (fje) *v.t*, to vitrify. **vitrine** (trin) *f*, glass case, show case; display cabinet, china cabinet; curio cabinet; shop window.

vitriol (vitriɔl) *m*, vitriol.

vivace (vivas) *a*, long-lived; inveterate; perennial (*Bot.*). **vivacité** (site) *f*, vivacity, liveliness; heat; hastiness; petulance; vividness.

vivandier, ère (vivɑ̃dje, ɛ:r) *n*, sutler.

vivant, e (vivɑ̃, ɑ̃:t) *a*, alive, living; lifelike; live; modern (*language*); lively; vivid.

¶ *m*, living being; lifetime, life. **vivat** (vat) *i. & m*, hurrah, -ray!; cheer. **vive-eau**, *f*, spring tide. **vivement** (vmɑ̃) *ad*, briskly; sharply; keenly; warmly. **viveur** (vœːr) *m*, gay man, fast liver, rake. **vivier** (vje) *m*, fish pond. **vivifier** (vifje) *v.t*, to vivify, quicken; vitalize; invigorate; brace. **vivipare** (paːr) *a*, viviparous. **vivisection** (sɛksjɔ̃) *f*, vivisection. **vivre** (viːvr) *v.i. & t. ir*, to live; be alive; subsist; endure; behave. ¶ *m*, living; food; (*pl.*) provisions, victuals; rations. *le ~ & le couvert*, board & lodging.

vizir (viziːr) *m*, vizi[e]r.

vocable (vɔkabl) *m*, vocable. **vocabulaire** (byleːr) *m*, vocabulary. **vocal, e** (kal) *a*, vocal. **vocaliser** (lize) *v.t*, to vocalize. **vocatif** (katif) *m*, vocative [case]. **vocation** (sjɔ̃) *f*, vocation, calling; call (*divine*).

vociférer (vosifere) *v.i*, to vociferate, shout, bawl, yell.

vœu (vø) *m*, vow; wish; prayer.

vogue (vɔg) *f*, fashion, vogue; request; run. **voguer** (ge) *v.i*, to row; sail.

voici (vwasi) *pr*, here is, here are; here; this is. *me ~!* here I am.

voie (vwa) *f*, way; road; route; track; line; duct; scent; (*wheel*) gauge (*Rly*); set (*saw*). *~ d'eau*, leak; waterway. *~s de fait*, assault [& battery]; blows, violence, force. *~ de garage*, siding. *~ ferrée*, railway. *~ lactée*, Milky Way, galaxy. *~ navigable*, waterway. *~ publique*, public thoroughfare, highway.

voilà (vwala) *pr*, there is, there are; that is.

voile (vwal) *f*, sail, canvas. ¶ *m*, veil; velum; cloth; voile; mist; fog; mask; blind. **voiler** (le) *v.t*, to veil; cloak; muffle; fog; [en]shroud; buckle. **voilerie** (lri) *f*, sail loft; s. making. **voilier** (lje) *m*, sail maker; sailing ship (*good, bad*) sailer (*ship*). **voilure** (lyːr) *f*, sails (*col.*); buckling.

voir (vwaːr) *v.t. & abs. ir*, to see; look [at, on]; behold; sight; understand; examine; visit.

voire (vwaːr) *ad*, nay; even. *~ même*, & even, indeed.

voirie (vwari) *f*, highways committee; refuse dump.

voisin, e (vwazɛ̃, in) *a*, neighbouring; akin; next. ¶ *n*, neighbour. **voisinage** (zinaːʒ) *m*, neighbourhood; vicinity. **voisiner** (ne) *v.i*, to visit one's neighbours.

voiture (vwatyːr) *f*, conveyance; carriage; coach; car; wagon; cart; van. *~ à deux chevaux*, carriage & pair. *~ à deux places*, two seater (*motor*). *~ automotrice*, rail car (*Rly*). *~ cellulaire*, police van. *~ d'enfant*, perambulator. *~ de louage*, hackney carriage. *~ de place*, hackney carriage; cab. **voiturer** (tyre) *v.t*, to convey, carry, cart. **voiturette** (ret) *f*, trap; light car, runabout. **voiturier** (rje) *m*, carter; carrier.

voix (vwa) *f*, voice; register; speech; word;

dictate[s]; opinion; say; vote. *~ de stentor* (stɑ̃tɔːr), stentorian voice.

vol (vɔl) *m*, flying; flight; wing; flock (*birds*). *~ à voile*, gliding (*Aero.*). *à ~ d'oiseau*, as the crow flies. *~ piqué*, dive (*Aero.*). *~ plané*, volplane.

vol (vɔl) *m*, theft, stealing, robbery. *~ à l'américaine*, confidence trick. *~ à l'étalage*, shop lifting. *~ à la tire*, pocket picking; bag snatching. *~ à main armée*, robbery with violence. *~ de grand chemin*, highway robbery. *~ [de nuit avec effraction]*, burglary.

volage (vɔlaːʒ) *a*, fickle, inconstant.

volaille (vɔlaːj) *f*, poultry, fowls; fowl.

volant, e (vɔlɑ̃, ɑ̃ːt) *a*, flying; loose; portable; occasional (*table, &c*). ¶ *m*, shuttlecock; leaf (*opp.* counterfoil); fly wheel; sail (*windmill*); flounce. [*jeu de*] *~*, battledore & shuttlecock. *~ au filet*, badminton. *~ de direction*, steering wheel.

volatil, e (vɔlatil) *a*, volatile. **volatile** (til) *m*, winged creature. **volatiliser** (lize) *v.t*, to volatilize. **se ~**, to volatilize; vanish.

volcan (vɔlkɑ̃) *m*, volcano. **volcanique** (kanik) *a*, volcanic.

volée (vɔle) *f*, flight; wing; flock; volley; peal (*bells*); rank (*class*); splinter bar, swingle-tree; chase (*gun*). *~ de coups*, drubbing. *à la ~*, in the air; on the wing; promptly; broadcast; at random. **voler** (le) *v.i*, to fly; (*v.t.*) to chase, fly at (*Hawking*); steal, rob. **volerie** (lri) *f*, hawking (*Falconry*); thieving.

volet (vɔlɛ) *m*, shutter; volet; sorting board. **voleter** (vɔlte) *v.i*, to flutter; flit; skip.

voleur, euse (vɔlœːr, øːz) *n*, thief, robber; (*att.*) thievish (*pers.*). *~ à la tire*, pick-pocket; bag snatcher. *~ de grand chemin*, footpad.

volière (vɔljeːr) *f*, aviary; run (*pheasants, &c*).

volige (vɔliːʒ) *f*, batten; lath.

volition (vɔlisjɔ̃) *f*, volition.

volontaire (vɔlɔ̃teːr) *a*, voluntary; self-willed; wilful, wayward. ¶ *m*, volunteer (*Mil.*). **volonté** (te) *f*, will; (*pl.*) whims. **volontiers** (tje) *ad*, willingly, gladly; fain; apt, rather.

volt (vɔlt) *m*, volt. **voltage** (taːʒ) *m*, voltage. **voltaïque** (taik) *a*, voltaic.

volte-face (vɔltəfas) *f*, turning about; change of front.

voltige (vɔltiːʒ) *f*, trick riding & similar circus gymnastics. **voltiger** (tiʒe) *v.i*, to fly about, flit, hover; flutter, flap; perform on horseback; perform on the slack rope.

voltmètre (vɔltmɛtr) *m*, voltmeter.

volubile (vɔlybil) *a*, twining (*Bot.*); voluble, glib (*speaker*). **volubilis** (lis) *m*, convolvulus. **volubilité** (lite) *f*, volubility, glibness.

volume (vɔlym) *m*, volume; tome; bulk; measurement. **volumineux, euse** (minø, øːz) *a*, voluminous, bulky.

volupté (vɔlypte) *f*, voluptuousness, pleasure, delight. **voluptueux, euse†** (tɥø, ø:z) *a*, voluptuous. ¶ *n*, voluptuary.

volute (vɔlyt) *f*, volute, scroll.

vomir (vɔmi:r) *v.t. & abs*, to vomit, spew, belch out. **vomissement** (mismɑ̃) *m*, vomiting; vomit.

voracet† (vɔras) *a*, voracious. **voracité** (site) *f*, voracity.

votant (vɔtɑ̃) *m*, voter. **votation** (tasjɔ̃) *f*, voting. **vote** (vɔt) *m*, vote, poll. **voter** (te) *v.i. & t*, to vote; pass, carry. ~ *à main levée*, to vote by a show of hands. **votif, ive** (tif, i:v) *a*, votive.

votre, *pl.* **vos** (vɔtr, vo) *a*, your. ~ *affectionné, e*, yours affectionately. **vôtre** (vo:tr) *a*, yours. *le vôtre, la vôtre, les vôtres*, yours, your own.

vouer (vwe) *v.t*, to vow; dedicate; devote.

vouloir (vulwa:r) *m*, will. ¶ *v.t.ir*, to will; want, wish; like; [be] please[d to]; mean; intend; require, need. *en* ~ *à*, to bear ill will. *s'en* ~ *de*, to be angry with oneself for. **voulu, e** (ly) *p.a*, required, requisite; deliberate, intentional; studied.

vous (vu) *pn*, you; ye; to you; yourself, yourselves; each other. ~-*même*, ~-*mêmes*, yourself, yourselves.

voussoir (vuswa:r) *m*, voussoir, arch stone. **voûte** (vut) *f*, vault, arch; dome; canopy. ~ *palatine*, ~ *du palais*, roof of the mouth. **voûté, e** (te) *p.a*, vaulted; arched; stooping, bent, round-shouldered. **voûter** (te) *v.t*, to vault, arch; bow.

voyage (vwaja:ʒ) *m*, journey, trip, tour; travel; booking. **voyager** (jaʒe) *v.i*, to travel; journey; migrate. **voyageur, euse** (ʒœ:r, ø:z) *n*, traveller; passenger, fare.

voyant, e (vwajɑ̃, ɑ̃:t) *a*, seeing; gaudy, garish; showy; conspicuous. ¶ *n*, clair-voyant.

voyelle (vwajɛl) *f*, vowel.

voyer (vwaje) *m*, surveyor (*roads*).

voyou (vwaju) *m*, gutter snipe; hooligan.

vrac (en) (vrak), in bulk; loose.

vrai, e (vrɛ) *a*, true, truthful; real, genuine; right; downright; thorough, arrant. **vrai & vraiment** (mɑ̃) *ad*, truly, really; indeed. **vrai, m**, truth. **vraisemblable†** (sɑ̃blabl) *a*, probable, likely. **vraisemblance** (blɑ̃:s) *f*, probability, likelihood, verisimilitude.

vrille (vri:j) *f*, tendril; gimlet. **vriller** (vrije) *v.t*, to bore; (*v.i.*) to kink, corkscrew. **vrillette** (jɛt) *f*, death-watch [beetle].

vu (vy) *m*, sight, inspection. ¶ *ad*, considering, seeing. ~ *que*, seeing that; whereas.

vue (vy) *f*, [eye]sight; eyes, eye; view; sight; prospect, outlook, slide; window, light. ~ *cavalière*, ~ *à vol d'oiseau*, bird's-eye view. ~ *de projection*, lantern slide. ~*s fondantes*, dissolving views. *à* ~ *d'œil*, at a rough estimate; visibly.

vulcain (vylkɛ̃) *m*, red admiral (*butterfly*).

vulcaniser (vylkanize) *v.t*, to vulcanize.

vulgaire† (vylgɛ:r) *a*, vulgar; common; low; everyday; vernacular. **le** ~, the common people, the vulgar [herd]. **vulgariser** (garize) *v.t*, to popularize; vulgarize. **vulgarité (te)** *f*, vulgarity. **la Vulgate** (gat), the Vulgate.

vulnérable (vylnerabl) *a*, vulnerable.

W

wagon (vagɔ̃) (*Rly*) *m*, carriage, coach, car; wagon, truck. ~-*bar*, buffet car. ~-*écurie*, horse box. ~ *larguable* (largabl), slip carriage. ~-*lit*, sleeping car. ~-*poste*, mail van. ~-*restaurant*, restaurant car, dining car. ~-*salon*, saloon [car].

warrant (warɑ̃:t) *m*, warrant (*dock, ware-house*).

watt (wat) *m*, watt.

Westphalie (la) (vɛstfali), Westphalia.

whisky (wiski) *m*, whisky.

whist (wist) *m*, whist (*Cards*). ~ *à trois avec un mort*, dummy w. ~ *de Gand*, solo w.

wolfram (vɔlfram) *m*, wolfram.

X

xérès (kerɛs) *m*, sherry.

xylophone (ksilɔfɔn) *m*, xylophone.

Y

y (i) *ad*, there; here; at home. ¶ *pn*, of it, him, &c; to it; about it; at it; by it; in it; it. ~ *compris*, including.

yacht (jɔt) *m*, yacht. *Note*:—le yacht, *not* l'yacht.

yole (jɔl) *f*, gig, skiff, yawl. *Note*:—la yole.

yougoslave (jugɔsla:v) *a. &* **Y**~, *n*, Jugo-Slav. **la Yougoslavie** (slavi), Jugo-Slavia.

ypérite (iperit) *f*, mustard gas.

Z

zèbre (zɛbr) *m*, zebra. **zébré, e** (zebre) *a*, striped.

zélateur, trice (zelatœ:r, tris) *n*, zealot. **zèle** (zɛ:l) *m*, zeal. **zélé, e** (zele) *a*, zealous.

zénith (zenit) *m*, zenith.

zéphyr (zefi:r) *m*, zephyr.

zeppelin (zeplɛ̃) *m*, Zeppelin.

zéro (zero) *m*, cipher, nought, 0; love (*Ten.*); zero (See *centigrade* Fr.-Eng.); nobody. ~ *partout*, love all (*Ten.*).

zeste (zɛst) *m*, woody partitions (*walnut*); peel (*orange, lemon*); straw (*fig.*). ~ *confit*, candied peel.

K

zézayer (zezɛje) *v.i*, to lisp.
zibeline (ziblin) *f*, sable (*Zool.*, *fur*).
zigzag (zigzag) *m*, zigzag.
zinc (zɛ̃:g) *m*, zinc, spelter. zincogravure (zɛ̃kogravy:r) *f*, zincography. zingueur (gœ:r) *m*, zinc worker.
zircon (zirkɔ̃) *m*, zircon.
zizanie (zizani) *f*, discord.
zodiaque (zɔdjak) *m*, zodiac.

zone (zo:n) *f*, zone; belt; area. ~ *des calmes*, doldrums.
zoologie (zɔɔlɔʒi) *f*, zoology. zoologique (ʒik) *a*, zoological. zoologiste (ʒist) *n*, zoologist.
zoulou (zulu) *a*. & Z~, *n*, Zulu.
zut (zyt) *i*, botheration!; go to the devil!
Zuyderzée (le) (zɥidɛrze), the Zuyder Zee.

FRENCH IRREGULAR VERBS

Order of tenses & parts:—
- (1) = Indicative Present
- (2) =   ,,   Imperfect
- (3) =   ,,   Preterite
- (4) =   ,,   Future
- (5) = Conditional Present
- (6) = Imperative
- (7) = Subjunctive Present
- (8) =   ,,   Imperfect
- (9) = Participle Present
- (10) =   ,,   Past

Prefixed verbs not included in the list, such as **abattre, sourire, désapprendre, satisfaire,** follow the second or last element (**battre, rire, prendre, faire**).

absoudre.—(1) j'absous, tu absous, il absout, nous absolvons, vous absolvez, ils absolvent. (2) j'absolvais. (4) j'absoudrai. (5) j'absoudrais. (6) absous, absolvons, absolvez. (7) que j'absolve. (9) absolvant. (10) absous, oute.

abstraire.—like **traire**, *but only used in* (1) (2) *and compound tenses.*

accroitre.—*like* **croitre,** *but* (10) accru, *no circumflex accent.*

acquérir.—(1) j'acquiers, tu acquiers, il acquiert, nous acquérons, vous acquérez, ils acquièrent. (2) j'acquérais. (3) j'acquis. (4) j'acquerrai. (5) j'acquerrais. (6) acquiers, acquérons, acquérez. (7) que j'acquière. (8) que j'acquisse. (9) acquérant. (10) acquis, e.

aller.—(1) je vais, tu vas, il va, nous allons, vous allez, ils vont. (2) j'allais. (3) j'allai. (4) j'irai. (5) j'irais. (6) va (*but* vas-y), allons, allez. (7) que j'aille. (8) que j'allasse. (9) allant. (10) allé, e.

s'en aller.—*like* **aller.** *The auxiliary* être *is used in the compound tenses and is placed between* en *and* allé; *thus,* je m'en suis allé. (6) va-t-en, allons-nous-en, allez-vous-en.

apparaitre.—*like* **connaitre.**

assaillir.—(1) j'assaille, tu assailles, il assaille, nous assaillons, vous assaillez, ils assaillent. (2) j'assaillais. (3) j'assaillis. (4) j'assaillirai. (5) j'assaillirais. (6) assaille, assaillons, assaillez. (7) que j'assaille. (8) que j'assaillisse. (9) assaillant. (10) assailli, e.

asseoir.—(1) j'assieds, tu assieds, il assied, nous asseyons, vous asseyez, ils asseyent. (2) j'asseyais. (3) j'assis. (4) j'assiérai *ou* j'asseyerai. (5) j'assiérais *ou* j'asseyerais. (6) assieds, asseyons, asseyez. (7) que j'asseye. (8) que j'assisse. (9) asseyant. (10) assis, e. *This verb is*

sometimes conjugated in maintaining throughout the oi of the radical; thus, (1) j'assois, nous assoyons. (2) j'assoyais, &c.

astreindre.—*like* **atteindre.**

atteindre.—(1) j'atteins, tu atteins, il atteint, nous atteignons, vous atteignez, ils atteignent. (2) j'atteignais. (3) j'atteignis. (4) j'atteindrai. (5) j'atteindrais. (6) atteins, atteignons, atteignez. (7) que j'atteigne. (8) que j'atteignisse. (9) atteignant. (10) atteint, e.

avoir.—(1) j'ai, tu as, il a, nous avons, vous avez, ils ont. (2) j'avais. (3) j'eus. (4) j'aurai. (5) j'aurais. (6) aie, ayons, ayez. (7) que j'aie. (8) que j'eusse. (9) ayant. (10) eu, e.

battre.—(1) je bats, tu bats, il bat, nous battons, vous battez, ils battent. (2) je battais. (3) je battis. (4) je battrai. (5) je battrais. (6) bats, battons, battez. (7) que je batte. (8) que je battisse. (9) battant. (10) battu, e.

boire.—(1) je bois, tu bois, il boit, nous buvons, vous buvez, ils boivent. (2) je buvais. (3) je bus. (4) je boirai. (5) je boirais. (6) bois, buvons, buvez. (7) que je boive. (8) que je busse. (9) buvant. (10) bu, e.

bouillir.—(1) je bous, tu bous, il bout, nous bouillons, vous bouillez, ils bouillent. (2) je bouillais. (3) je bouillis. (4) je bouillirai. (5) je bouillirais. (6) bous, bouillons, bouillez. (7) que je bouille. (8) que je bouillisse. (9) bouillant. (10) bouilli, e.

braire.—*like* **traire** *but seldom used except in infinitive & in 3rd persons of* (1) (4) & (5).

bruire.—*Seldom used except in infinitive and in 3rd person s. of* (1) il bruit, *and in 3rd persons of* (2) il bruissait, ils bruissaient.

ceindre.—*like* **atteindre.**

choir.—(10) chu, e. *Others not used.*

circoncire.—*like* **confire,** *but* (10) circoncis, e.

circonscrire.—*like* **écrire.**

clore.—(1) je clos, tu clos, il clôt. (4) je clorai, &c. (6) clos. (7) que je close, &c. (10) clos, e. *Other forms not, or very seldom, used.*

comparaitre.—*like* **connaitre,** *but* (10) comparu (*inv.*).

conclure.—(1) je conclus, tu conclus, il conclut, nous concluons, vous concluez, ils concluent. (2) je concluais. (3) je conclus. (4) je conclurai. (5) je conclurais. (6) conclus, concluons, concluez. (7) que je conclue. (8) que je conclusse. (9) concluant. (10) conclu, e.

épreindre.—*like* **atteindre.**

éteindre.—*like* **atteindre.**

être.—(1) je suis, tu es, il est, nous sommes, vous êtes, ils sont. (2) j'étais. (3) je fus. (4) je serai. (5) je serais. (6) sois, soyons, soyez. (7) que je sois. (8) que je fusse. (9) étant. (10) été (*inv.*).

étreindre.—*like* **atteindre.**

exclure.—*like* **conclure.**

faillir.—(1) il faut (*in* s'en faut). (3) je faillis, &c. (10) failli, e. *Seldom used in other forms.*

faire.—(1) je fais, tu fais, il fait, nous faisons, vous faites, ils font. (2) je faisais. (3) je fis. (4) je ferai. (5) je ferais. (6) fais, faisons, faites. (7) que je fasse. (8) que je fisse. (9) faisant. (10) fait, e.

falloir.—(1) il faut. (2) il fallait. (3) il fallut. (4) il faudra. (5) il faudrait. (7) qu'il faille. (8) qu'il fallût. (10) fallu (*inv.*).

feindre.—*like* **atteindre.**

forclore.—(10) forclos, e.

frire.—(1) je fris, tu fris, il frit, nous faisons frire, vous faites frire, ils font frire. (2) je faisais frire. (4) je frirai. (5) je frirais. (6) fris. (10) frit, e.

fuir.—(1) je fuis, tu fuis, il fuit, nous fuyons, vous fuyez, ils fuient. (2) je fuyais. (3) je fuis. (4) je fuirai. (5) je fuirais. (6) fuis, fuyons, fuyez. (7) que je fuie. (8) que je fuisse. (9) fuyant. (10) fui, e.

geindre.—*like* **atteindre.**

gésir.—(1) je gis, tu gis, il gît, nous gisons, vous gisez, ils gisent. (2) je gisais, &c. (9) gisant. *Other forms not used.*

inclure.—*like* **conclure.**

induire.—*like* **conduire.**

inscrire.—*like* **écrire.**

instruire.—*like* **conduire.**

interdire.—*like* **dire,** *except* (1) vous interdisez. (6) interdisez.

introduire.—*like* **conduire.**

joindre.—(1) je joins, tu joins, il joint, nous joignons, vous joignez, ils joignent. (2) je joignais. (3) je joignis. (4) je joindrai. (5) je joindrais. (6) joins, joignons, joignez. (7) que je joigne. (8) que je joignisse. (9) joignant. (10) joint, e.

lire.—(1) je lis, tu lis, il lit, nous lisons, vous lisez, ils lisent. (2) je lisais. (3) je lus. (4) je lirai. (5) je lirais. (6) lis, lisons, lisez. (7) que je lise. (8) que je lusse. (9) lisant. (10) lu, e.

luire.—*like* **conduire,** *except* (10) lui (*inv.*) & no (3) or (8).

maudire.—(1) je maudis, tu maudis, il maudit, nous maudissons, vous maudissez, ils maudissent. (2) je maudissais. (3) je maudis. (4) je maudirai. (5) je maudirais. (6) maudis, maudissons, maudissez. (7) que je maudisse. (8) que je maudisse. (9) maudissant. (10) maudit, e.

méconnaître.—*like* **paraître.**

médire.—*like* **dire,** *except* (1) vous médisez. (6) médisez.

mentir.—*like* **sentir.**

messeoir.—*like* **seoir,** *in sense* to suit.

mettre.—(1) je mets, tu mets, il met, nous mettons, vous mettez, ils mettent. (2) je mettais. (3) je mis. (4) je mettrai. (5) je mettrais. (6) mets, mettons, mettez. (7) que je mette. (8) que je misse. (9) mettant. (10) mis, e.

moudre.—(1) je mouds, tu mouds, il moud, nous moulons, vous moulez, ils moulent. (2) je moulais. (3) je moulus. (4) je moudrai. (5) je moudrais. (6) mouds, moulons, moulez. (7) que je moule. (8) que je moulusse. (9) moulant. (10) moulu, e.

mourir.—(1) je meurs, tu meurs, il meurt, nous mourons, vous mourez, ils meurent. (2) je mourais. (3) je mourus. (4) je mourrai. (5) je mourrais. (6) meurs, mourons, mourez. (7) que je meure. (8) que je mourusse. (9) mourant. (10) mort, e.

mouvoir.—(1) je meus, tu meus, il meut, nous mouvons, vous mouvez, ils meuvent. (2) je mouvais. (3) je mus. (4) je mouvrai. (5) je mouvrais. (6) meus, mouvons, mouvez. (7) que je meuve. (8) que je musse. (9) mouvant. (10) mû, mue (*pl.* mus, mues).

naître.—(1) je nais, tu nais, il naît, nous naissons, vous naissez, ils naissent. (2) je naissais. (3) je naquis. (4) je naîtrai. (5) je naîtrais. (6) nais, naissons, naissez. (7) que je naisse. (8) que je naquisse. (9) naissant. (10) né, e.

nuire.—*like* **conduire,** *except* (10) nui (*inv.*).

offrir.—*like* **ouvrir.**

oindre.—*like* **joindre.**

ouïr.—(10) ouï, ïe.

ouvrir.—(1) j'ouvre, tu ouvres, il ouvre, nous ouvrons, vous ouvrez, ils ouvrent. (2) j'ouvrais. (3) j'ouvris. (4) j'ouvrirai. (5) j'ouvrirais. (6) ouvre, ouvrons, ouvrez. (7) que j'ouvre. (8) que j'ouvrisse. (9) ouvrant. (10) ouvert, e.

paître.—(1) je pais, tu pais, il paît, nous paissons, vous paissez, ils paissent. (2) je paissais. (4) je paîtrai. (5) je paîtrais. (6) pais, paissons, paissez. (7) que je paisse. (9) paissant.

paraître.—*like* **connaître,** *but* (10) paru (*inv.*).

partir.—(1) je pars, tu pars, il part, nous partons, vous partez, ils partent. (2) je partais. (3) je partis. (4) je partirai. (5) je partirais. (6) pars, partons, partez. (7) que je parte. (8) que je partisse. (9) partant. (10) parti, e.

peindre.—*like* **atteindre.**

plaindre.—*like* **craindre.**

plaire.—(1) je plais, tu plais, il plaît, nous plaisons, vous plaisez, ils plaisent. (2) je plaisais. (3) je plus. (4) je plairai.

(5) je plairais. (6) plais, plaisons, plaisez. (7) que je plaise. (8) que je plusse. (9) plaisant. (10) plu (*inv.*).

pleuvoir.—(1) il pleut. (2) il pleuvait. (3) il plut. (4) il pleuvra. (5) il pleuvrait. (7) qu'il pleuve. (8) qu'il plût. (9) pleuvant. (10) plu (*inv.*).

poindre.—*like* **joindre,** *but seldom used except in infinitive &* (4).

pourvoir.—(1) je pourvois, tu pourvois, il pourvoit, nous pourvoyons, vous pourvoyez, ils pourvoient. (2) je pourvoyais. (3) je pourvus. (4) je pourvoirai. (5) je pourvoirais. (6) pourvois, pourvoyons, pourvoyez. (7) que je pourvoie. (8) que je pourvusse. (9) pourvoyant. (10) pourvu, e.

pouvoir.—(1) je peux *ou* je puis, tu peux, il peut, nous pouvons, vous pouvez, ils peuvent. (2) je pouvais. (3) je pus. (4) je pourrai. (5) je pourrais. (7) que je puisse. (8) que je pusse. (9) pouvant. (10) pu (*inv.*).

prédire.—*like* **dire,** *except* (1) vous prédisez. (6) prédisez.

prendre.—(1) je prends, tu prends, il prend, nous prenons, vous prenez, ils prennent. (2) je prenais. (3) je pris. (4) je prendrai. (5) je prendrais. (6) prends, prenons, prenez. (7) que je prenne. (8) que je prisse. (9) prenant. (10) pris, e.

prescrire.—*like* **écrire.**

prévaloir.—*like* **valoir,** *but* (7) que je prévale.

prévoir.—*like* **voir,** *except* (4) je prévoirai. (5) je prévoirais.

produire.—*like* **conduire.**

promouvoir.—*like* **mouvoir,** *but seldom used except in infinitive &* (10) promu, e (*no circumflex accent*).

proscrire.—*like* **écrire.**

raire.—*like* **traire,** *but the only forms in common use are* (1) il rait, ils raient.

reclure.—(10) reclus, e.

reconquérir.—*like* **acquérir.**

reconstruire.—*like* **conduire.**

recouvrir.—*like* **ouvrir.**

récrire.—*like* **écrire.**

recuire.—*like* **conduire.**

réduire.—*like* **conduire.**

réélire.—*like* **lire.**

reluire.—*like* **luire.**

renaître.—*like* **naître,** *but no* (10) *or compound tenses.*

reparaître.—*like* **paraître.**

repentir (se).—*like* **sentir.**

reproduire.—*like* **conduire.**

requérir.—*like* **acquérir.**

résoudre.—(1) je résous, tu résous, il résout, nous résolvons, vous résolvez, ils résolvent. (2) je résolvais. (3) je résolus. (4) je résoudrai. (5) je résoudrais. (6) résous, résolvons, résolvez. (7) que je résolve. (8) que je résolusse. (9) résolvant. (10) résolu, e.

restreindre.—*like* **atteindre.**

rire.—(1) je ris, tu ris, il rit, nous rions, vous riez, ils rient. (2) je riais. (3) je ris. (4) je rirai. (5) je rirais. (6) ris, rions, riez. (7) que je rie. (8) que je risse. (9) riant. (10) ri (*inv.*).

rouvrir.—*like* **ouvrir.**

saillir.—*like* **assaillir.**

savoir.—(1) je sais, tu sais, il sait, nous savons, vous savez, ils savent. (2) je savais. (3) je sus. (4) je saurai. (5) je saurais. (6) sache, sachons, sachez. (7) que je sache. (8) que je susse. (9) sachant. (10) su, e.

séduire.—*like* **conduire.**

sentir.—(1) je sens, tu sens, il sent, nous sentons, vous sentez, ils sentent. (2) je sentais. (3) je sentis. (4) je sentirai. (5) je sentirais. (6) sens, sentons, sentez. (7) que je sente. (8) que je sentisse. (9) sentant. (10) senti, e.

seoir.—*In sense to sit,* (9) séant. (10) sis, e. *In sense to suit,* (1) il sied, ils siéent. (2) il seyait, ils seyaient. (4) il siéra, ils siéront. (7) qu'il siée, qu'ils siéent. (9) séant *ou* seyant. *No other forms.*

servir.—(1) je sers, tu sers, il sert, nous servons, vous servez, ils servent. (2) je servais. (3) je servis. (4) je servirai. (5) je servirais. (6) sers, servons, servez. (7) que je serve. (8) que je servisse. (9) servant. (10) servi, e.

sortir.—(1) je sors, tu sors, il sort, nous sortons, vous sortez, ils sortent. (2) je sortais. (3) je sortis. (4) je sortirai. (5) je sortirais. (6) sors, sortons, sortez. (7) que je sorte. (8) que je sortisse. (9) sortant. (10) sorti, e.

souffrir.—*like* **ouvrir.**

souscrire.—*like* **écrire.**

suffire.—*like* **confire,** *but* (10) suffi (*inv.*).

suivre.—(1) je suis, tu suis, il suit, nous suivons, vous suivez, ils suivent. (2) je suivais. (3) je suivis. (4) je suivrai. (5) je suivrais. (6) suis, suivons, suivez. (7) que je suive. (8) que je suivisse. (9) suivant. (10) suivi, e.

surseoir.—(1) je sursois, tu sursois, il sursoit, nous sursoyons, vous sursoyez, ils sursoient. (2) je sursoyais. (3) je sursis. (4) je surseoirai. (5) je surseoirais. (6) sursois, sursoyons, sursoyez. (7) que je sursoie. (8) que je sursisse. (9) sursoyant. (10) sursis, e.

taire.—*like* **plaire,** *except* (1) il tait (*no circumflex*) & (10) tu, e.

teindre.—*like* **atteindre.**

tenir.—(1) je tiens, tu tiens, il tient, nous tenons, vous tenez, ils tiennent. (2) je tenais. (3) je tins. (4) je tiendrai. (5) je tiendrais. (6) tiens, tenons, tenez. (7) que je tienne. (8) que je tinsse. (9) tenant. (10) tenu, e.

tistre.—*Used only in* (10) tissu, e, *and compound tenses.*

traduire.—*like* **conduire.**

traire.—(1) je trais, tu trais, il trait, nous trayons, vous trayez, ils traient. (2) je trayais. (4) je trairai. (5) je trairais. (6) trais, trayons, trayez. (7) que je traie. (9) trayant. (10) trait, e.

transcrire.—*like* **écrire.**

tressaillir.—*like* **assaillir.**

vaincre.—(1) je vaincs, tu vaincs, il vainc, nous vainquons, vous vainquez, ils vainquent. (2) je vainquais. (3) je vainquis. (4) je vaincrai. (5) je vaincrais. (6) vaincs, vainquons, vainquez. (7) que je vainque. (8) que je vainquisse. (9) vainquant. (10) vaincu, e.

valoir.—(1) je vaux, tu vaux, il vaut, nous valons, vous valez, ils valent. (2) je valais. (3) je valus. (4) je vaudrai. (5) je vaudrais. (6) vaux, valons, valez. (7) que je vaille. (8) que je valusse. (9) valant. (10) valu, e.

venir.—(1) je viens, tu viens, il vient, nous venons, vous venez, ils viennent. (2) je venais. (3) je vins. (4) je viendrai. (5) je viendrais. (6) viens, venons, venez.

(7) que je vienne. (8) que je vinsse. (9) venant. (10) venu, e.

vêtir.—(1) je vêts, tu vêts, il vêt, nous vêtons, vous vêtez, ils vêtent. (2) je vêtais. (3) je vêtis. (4) je vêtirai. (5) je vêtirais. (6) vêts, vêtons, vêtez. (7) que je vête. (8) que je vêtisse. (9) vêtant. (10) vêtu, e.

vivre.—(1) je vis, tu vis, il vit, nous vivons, vous vivez, ils vivent. (2) je vivais. (3) je vécus. (4) je vivrai. (5) je vivrais. (6) vis, vivons, vivez. (7) que je vive. (8) que je vécusse. (9) vivant. (10) vécu (*inv.*).

voir.—(1) je vois, tu vois, il voit, nous voyons, vous voyez, ils voient. (2) je voyais. (3) je vis. (4) je verrai. (5) je verrais. (6) vois, voyons, voyez. (7) que je voie. (8) que je visse. (9) voyant. (10) vu, e.

vouloir.—(1) je veux, tu veux, il veut, nous voulons, vous voulez, ils veulent. (2) je voulais. (3) je voulus. (4) je voudrai. (5) je voudrais. (6) veuille & veux, veuillons & voulons, veuillez & voulez. (7) que je veuille. (8) que je voulusse. (9) voulant. (10) voulu, e.

DIVISION OF FRENCH WORDS INTO SYLLABLES

In French, words are divided into syllables according to the following rules:—

(1) *A consonant between two vowels begins a new syllable:*

ca-pi-tal, ca-pi-ta-li-ser, ca-pi-ta-lis-me, ca-pi-ta-lis-te, li-bé-ra-toi-re, dé-sa-bon-ne-ment, a-rith-mé-ti-que, pri-vi-lè-ge, su-bor-don-né, é-ti-que-ta-ge, e-xa-men, e-xer-ci-ce, i-n-e-xac-te-ment, to-xi-que, i-nu-ti-le, u-ne, u-na-ni-me-ment, vi-gueur, vi-gou-reux, vi-gou-reu-se, paie-ment, em-pla-ce-ment, vé-hi-cu-le, pa-ral-lé-li-pi-pè-de. *Note:*—In order not to misrepresent the pronunciation of certain prefixes, there are a few exceptions to this rule, and collaterally to rule 3 also; such as sub-o-do-rer, sur-é-le-ver, and the like; in-ter-o-cé-a-ni-que, in-ter-ur-bain, and the like.

(2) *Two adjoining consonants (except Rule 4 digraphs) between two vowels separate into two syllables:*

ac-com-mo-der, at-ter-ris-sa-ge, bail-le-res-se, chan-geant, chan-gean-te, cor-res-pon-dan-ce, des-cen-dre, di-a-phrag-me, ex-cep-ti-on-nel-le-ment, ex-pé-di-ti-on-nai-re, in-nom-ma-ble, em-bar-ras-sant, in-ter-val-le, ir-res-pon-sa-bi-li-té, os-cil-ler, fais-ceau, ras-seoir, re-con-nais-san-ce, res-ti-tu-er, sub-di-vi-ser, sur-taux, veil-le, el-les, mal-heur, in-hé-rent, ex-hi-ber, mo-les-ki-ne.

(3) *A vowel can only begin a syllable, other than an initial syllable, when preceded by another vowel:*

ac-cue-il-lir, a-é-ro-pla-ne, po-è-me, a-gré-er, an-ci-en, ar-ri-è-re, bé-né-fi-ci-ai-re, ca-mi-on, ca-out-chouc; co-as-so-ci-é, co-ef-fi-ci-ent, co-in-ci-der, dé-pou-il-le-ment, ex-tra-or-di-nai-re, feu-il-le, li-er, mi-eux, na-ti-on, ou-est, ré-u-ni-on, vic-tu-ail-les, vi-é-il-lir, ré-é-li-re, voi-li-er, pay-a-ble, ba-lay-u-res, en-voy-er, voy-a-ge, roy-au-me, en-nuy-eux.

(4) *The following digraph consonants are inseparable:*

bl, cl, fl, gl, pl: a-bla-tif, pu-bli-que, (*Exception:* sub-lu-nai-re); é-clec-tis-me, ex-clu-sif; ré-fle-xe, ré-fle-xi-on; é-glan-ti-ne, rè-gle-ment; é-plu-cher.

br, cr, dr, fr, gr, pr, tr, vr: a-bri-cot, su-bré-car-gue, (*Exception:* sub-ro-ger & *derivatives*); é-cri-tu-re, ma-nus-crit, pres-cri-re, sous-cri-re, des-crip-ti-ve; a-dres-ser; re-frain; a-gri-co-le; a-près; a-tro-ce; a-vril, ou-vri-er.

ch, dh, ph, rh, th; é-choir, re-cher-che; ré-dhi-bi-toi-re; té-lé-pho-ne, pho-no-gra-phe; en-rhu-mer, ar-rhes; co-thur-ne.

gn: en-sei-gne-ment, si-gnal, es-pa-gnol, i-gna-re (*but* mag-nat, mag-no-li-a, di-ag-nos-ti-que, ig-né, *because here* gn *is not palatalized; in other words, the* g *is hard*).

ng: ving-ti-è-me (*but* sin-gu-li-er, *because here* ng *is not digraph, i.e., expressing one sound*).

pt: lé-pi-do-ptè-res (*but* sculp-ter, &c).

(5) (a) ns, bs, *and* rs *are separable if followed by a vowel:*

con-sa-crer, con-seil-ler, con-si-dé-rer, in-sé-rer, in-sol-va-ble, in-suf-fi-sant, tran-sac-ti-on, tran-sat-lan-ti-que, tran-si-tif; ab-sor-ber, ob-ser-ver; per-su-a-der.

(b) ns, bs, *and* rs *are inseparable if followed by a consonant:*

cons-pi-rer, cons-ta-ter, cons-ti-tu-er, ins-pec-ter, ins-tal-ler, trans-cen-dant, trans-fè-re-ment; trans-port; no-nobs-tant, obs-ta-cles, subs-tan-ce; in-ters-ti-ce, pers-pec-ti-ve.

(c) ns *and* bs *are inseparable if followed by a consonant coupled with* r:

cons-trui-re, ins-cri-re, trans-cri-re, trans-gres-ser; abs-trac-ti-on, obs-truc-ti-on.

(d) ns *and* bs *are separable before* ci:

con-sci-en-ci-eux, in-sci-em-ment; abs-scis-se.

(6) (a) mp *and* nc *followed by* t *are inseparable:*

a-comp-te, comp-ta-ble, es-comp-ter, prémp-emp-ti-on; fonc-ti-on, sanc-ti-on.

(b) *In all other combinations* mp *and* nc *are separable:*

em-ploy-er, em-prun-ter, im-por-tant; a-van-cer, fran-çais, fran-che, fran-co.

(7) *In writing or in print no syllable is separable which does not include a vowel;* thus, trigraph consonants are inseparable initially: scru-tin, but may be separable medially: ins-cru-ta-ble.

ENGLISH-FRENCH DICTIONARY

A

A, *letter*, (*Mus.*) la, *m*; (*house number*) bis. **a**, *indefinite art.* or *a*, un, une. *2 or 3 times* ~ *day*, 2 ou 3 fois par jour.

aback, *ad* taken ~, interloqué, déconcerté.

abacus, *n*, abaque, *m*.

abaft, *ad*, vers l'arrière. ¶ *pr*, sur l'arrière de.

abandon, *v.t*, abandonner, délaisser. ~ment, *n*, abandon, délaissement, *m*.

abase, *v.t*, abaisser, humilier.

abash, *v.t*, décontenancer, confondre.

abate, *v.t*, diminuer, rabattre; (*v.i.*) [se] calmer. **abatement**, *n*, diminution, *f*; rabais, *m*.

abbess, *n*, abbesse, *f*. **abbey**, *n*, abbaye, *f*. **abbot**, *n*, abbé, *m*.

abbreviate, *v.t*, abréger. **abbreviation**, *n*, abréviation, *f*.

A B C, *n*, A b c, abécédaire, alphabet, *m*; enfance, *f*.

abdicate, *v.t. & i*, abdiquer. **abdication**, *n*, abdication, *f*.

abdomen, *n*, abdomen, ventre, *m*. *lower part of the* ~, bas-ventre, *m*. **abdominal**, *a*, abdominal. ~ *belt*, ceinture ventrière, *f*.

abduct, *v.t*, détourner, enlever.

abeam, *ad*, par le travers.

abed, *ad*, au lit, couché.

aberration, *n*, aberration, *f*, égarement, *m*.

abet, *v.t*, soutenir, encourager, exciter.

abeyance, *n*, (*Law*) vacance, *f*. *in* ~, en suspens, en souffrance.

abhor, *v.t*, abhorrer, haïr, avoir en horreur. **abhorrence**, *n*, horreur, haine, *f*. **abhorrent**, *a*, répugnant.

abide, *v.i. & t. ir*, demeurer, rester; souffrir, supporter. *to* ~ *by*, s'en tenir à. **abiding**, *a*, durable, permanent.

ability, *n*, capacité, habileté, *f*, talent, savoir-faire, *m*.

abject, *a*, abject. ~ion, *n*, abjection, *f*.

abjure, *v.t*, abjurer, renoncer.

ablative [*case*], *n*, ablatif, *m*.

ablaze, *ad*, en feu, en flammes.

able, *a*, capable, habile; efficace. ~-*bodied*, robuste, valide. ~-[*bodied*] *seaman*, matelot de deuxième classe, *m*. *to be* ~ *to*, pouvoir, savoir, être en mesure (*ou* à même) de, suffire à. **ably**, *ad*, habilement, bravement.

abnegation, *n*, abnégation, *f*.

abnormal†, *a*, anormal. ~**ity**, *n*, anormal, *m*.

aboard, *ad*, à bord. ¶ *pr*, à bord de.

abode, *n*, domicile, *m*, demeure, habitation, *f*; séjour, *m*.

abolish, *v.t*, abolir, supprimer.

abominable†, *a*, abominable. **abominate**, *v.t*, abominer. **abomination**, *n*, abomination, *f*.

aboriginal, *a. & n*, aborigène, *a. & m*. **aborigines**, *n.pl*, aborigènes, *m.pl*.

abortion, *n*, avortement, *m*; (*creature*) avorton, *m*. **abortive**, *a*, abortif; (*fig.*) avorté, manqué.

abound, *v.i*, abonder, foisonner, fourmiller, affluer.

about, *pr*, autour de; auprès de; pour; dans; en; par; vers; sur; à propos de, touchant. ¶ *ad*, autour, çà & là; environ, à peu [de chose] près. *to be* ~ *to*, être sur le point de, aller. *what is it all* ~? de quoi s'agit-il?

above, *pr*, au-dessus de; sur; plus de; en amont de; en contre-haut. ¶ *ad*, en haut; là-haut; au-dessus; ci-dessus. *from* ~, d'en haut. ~ *all*, surtout, avant tout. ~-*board*, franc, cartes sur table. ~-*mentioned*, susmentionné, ci-dessus. ~-*named*, susnommé.

abrade, *v.t*, user; (*skin*) écorcher. **abrasion**, *n*, (*Phys.*) attrition; (*skin*) écorchure, *f*.

abreast, *ad*, de front; (*Naut.*) par le travers. ~ *of*, à la hauteur de.

abridge, *v.t*, abréger, raccourcir. **abridg[e]ment**, *n*, abrégé, raccourci, *m*.

abroad, *ad*, à l'étranger, à l'extérieur; au large. *from* ~, de l'étranger, de l'extérieur. *there is a rumour* ~ *that* . . ., le bruit court que . . .

abrogate, *v.t*, abroger. **abrogation**, *n*, abrogation, *f*.

abrupt, *a*, abrupt; brusque. *to treat* ~*ly*, brusquer. ~**ness**, *n*, brusquerie, *f*.

abscess, *n*, abcès, *m*.

abscond, *v.i*, s'enfuir, se soustraire à la justice.

absence, *n*, absence, *f*, éloignement; défaut, *m*. ~ *of mind*, absence [d'esprit], distraction, *f*. **absent**, *a*, absent, manquant. ~-*minded*, distrait. *to* ~ *oneself*, s'absenter. **absentee**, *n*, absent; (*Mil.*) insoumis, *m*. **absently**, *ad*, distraitement.

absinth, *n*, absinthe, *f*.

absolute, *a*, absolu. ~*ly*, *ad*, absolument. **absolution**, *n*, absolution, *f*. **absolve**, *v.t*, absoudre.

absorb, *v.t*, absorber. **absorbent**, *a*, absorbant; (*cotton wool*) hydrophile. **absorption**, *n*, absorption, *f*.

abstain, *v.i*, s'abstenir; jeûner. ~**er**, *n*, abstème, *m.f*. **abstemious**, *a*, abstème, sobre. **abstention**, *n*, abstention, *f*. **abstinence**, *n*, abstinence, *f*; jeûne, *m*.

abstract, *a*, abstrait. ¶ *n*, extrait, relevé, résumé, *m*. the ~ (opp. *concrete*), l'abstrait, *m*. ¶ *v.t*, abstraire; relever; (*steal*) distraire, soustraire, détourner. **abstraction**, *n*, abstraction; distraction, soustraction, *f*, détournement, *m*.

abstruse, *a*, abstrus.

absurd†, *a*, absurde. the ~, **an absurdity**, l'absurde, *m*, une absurdité.

abundance, *n*, abondance, *f*, **abundant**, *a*, abondant. ~**ly**, *ad*, abondamment.

abuse, *n*, abus; excès, *m*; injures, insultes *f.pl*. ¶ *v.t*, abuser de; injurier, malmener, maltraiter. **abusive†**, *a*, abusif; injurieux.

abutment (*Arch.*) *n*, culée, butée, *f*.

abyss, *n*, abîme, abysse, gouffre, *m*.

Abyssinia, *n*, l'Abyssinie *f*. **Abyssinian**, *a*, abyssinien, abyssin. ¶ *n*, Abyssinien, ne, Abyssin, e.

acacia, *n*, acacia, *f*.

academic(al†), *a*, académique; (*year*) scolaire. **academician**, *n*, académicien, ne. **academy**, *n*. & ~ *figure*, académie, *f*.

accede, *v.i*, accéder.

accelerate, *v.t*, accélérer. **accelerator**, *n*, accélérateur, *m*.

accent, *n*, accent, *m*. **accent** & **accentuate**, *v.t*, accentuer.

accept, *v.t*, accepter, agréer; (*a sport record*) homologuer. ~**able**, *a*, acceptable; de mise; agréable. ~**ance**, *n*, acceptation; réception, *f*. ~**ation**, *n*, acception, *f*. ~*ed term*, terme consacré, *m*. ~**or**, *n*, accepteur, *m*. ~ *for honour* (Com.), intervenant, *m*.

access, *n*, accès, abord, *m*, entrée, *f*. ~**ible**, *a*, accessible, abordable. ~**ion**, *n*, accession, *f*; avènement, *m*.

accessory†, *a*, accessoire. ¶ *n*, accessoire, *m*; (Law) complice, *m,f*.

accidence (*Gram.*) *n*, morphologie, *f*.

accident, *n*, accident; sinistre, *m*. [*personal*] ~ *insurance*, assurance contre les accidents [corporels] *f*. **accidental†**, *a*, accidentel, fortuit. ¶ (*Mus.*) *n*, accident, *m*.

acclaim, *v.t*, acclamer. **acclamation**, *n*, acclamation, *f*.

acclimatization, *n*, acclimatation, *f*, acclimatement, *m*. **acclimatize**, *v.t*, acclimater.

acclivity, *n*, montée, *f*.

accommodate, *v.t*, arranger; contenir; loger. ~ *oneself to*, s'accommoder à. **accommodating**, *p.a*, accommodant, complaisant, coulant, débonnaire. **accommodation**, *n*, accommodation, *f*; aménagement; logement, *m*. ~ *bill* (Com.), billet de complaisance, *m*.

accompaniment, *n*, accompagnement, *m*. **accompan[y]ist**, *n*, accompagnateur, trice. **accompany**, *v.t*, accompagner.

accomplice, *n*, complice, *m,f*.

accomplish, *v.t*, accomplir. ~**ed**, *a*, accom-

pli, achevé, émérite. ~**ment**, *n*, accomplissement, *m*; (*pl.*) arts d'agrément, *m.pl*.

accord, *n*, accord, *m*. *of one's own* ~, de son propre mouvement, de son plein gré, d'office, motu proprio. *with one* ~, d'un commun accord. ¶ *v.t*, accorder; (*v.i.*) s'a. ~**ance**, *n*, conformité, *f*. **according as**, à mesure que, selon que, suivant que. **according to**, selon, suivant; conforme à, conformément à; conséquemment à; d'après; à. **accordingly**, *ad*, par conséquent; en conséquence; conséquemment.

accordion, *n*, accordéon, *m*.

accost, *v.t*, accoster, aborder.

account, *n*, compte, *m*; (*pl.*) écritures [comptables] *f.pl*; (*pl.*) comptabilité, *f*; (*pl.*) inventaire; exercice; état, exposé, mémoire, *m*, note, *f*; récit, *m*, relation, notice, *f*, historique, *m* (*Stk Ex.*) terme, *m*, liquidation, *f*. *of no* ~, nul. *on* ~ (Com.), à compte, à valoir. *on* ~ *of*, à cause de; (Com.) pour le compte de, à l'acquit de. *on no* ~, en aucune manière, aucunement. ~ *book*, livre de comptabilité, *m*. ~ *current with interest*, compte courant & d'intérêts. ~ *day* (Stk Ex.), jour de la liquidation, *m*. ~ *rendered*, solde à nouveau, *m*. ~ *sales*, compte de vente. ¶ ~ *for*, rendre compte de; expliquer. ~**able**, *a*, comptable; responsable. ~**ancy**, *n*, comptabilité, *f*. ~**ant**, *n*, comptable, *m,f*, agent comptable, *m*. ~**ing**, *n*, comptabilité *f*. ~ *machine*, machine comptable, *f*. ~ *period*, exercice, *m*.

accoutre, *v.t*, équiper; harnacher. ~**ment**, *n*, équipement, *m*.

accredit, *v.t*, accréditer. ~**ed**, *p.a*, accrédité, attitré. ~ *dealer*, stockiste, *m*.

accrue, *v.i*, courir, accroître, s'acquérir. ~*d interest*, intérêt couru, *m*, intérêts accrus, *m.pl*. *accruing interest*, intérêts à échoir.

accumulate, *v.t*, accumuler, amonceler; (*v.i.*) s'accumuler, s'amonceler. **accumulation**, *n*, accumulation, *f*, amoncellement, *m*. **accumulator**, *n*, accumulateur, *m*.

accuracy, *n*, exactitude, justesse, *f*. **accurate†**, *a*, exact, juste.

accursed, *a*, maudit.

accusation, *n*, accusation, *f*. **accusative** [**case**], accusatif, *m*. **accuse**, *v.t*, accuser; taxer. the ~*d*, l'accusé, e, l'inculpé, e. **accuser**, *n*, accusateur, trice. **accusing**, *a*, accusateur.

accustom, *v.t*, accoutumer, habituer, familiariser, faire. ~**ed**, *a*, accoutumé, coutumier, habituel.

ace, *n*, as, *m*. *within an* ~ *of*, à deux doigts de.

acerbity, *n*, âpreté, aigreur, *f*.

acetate, *n*, acétate, *m*. **acetic**, *a*, acétique.

acetylene, *n*, acétylène, *m*. ~ *lamp*, lampe à acétylène, *f*.

ache, *n*, mal, *m*, douleur, *f*. ¶ *v.i*, faire mal; souffrir. *my head aches*, j'ai mal à la tête.

achieve, *v.t*, accomplir, exécuter. ~**ment**, *n*, accomplissement, exploit, *m*.

aching *a*, endolori. ~ *all over*, tout moulu.

achromatic, *a*, achromatique.

acid, *a. & n*, acide, *a. & m*. ~**ity**, *n*, acidité, *f*. **acidulate**, *v.t*, aciduler.

acknowledge, *v.t*, reconnaître, avouer, s'accuser de, confesser. ~ *receipt of*, accuser réception de. **acknowledg[e]ment**, *n*, reconnaissance, *f*; accusé de réception; reçu, *m*; (*pl.*) remerciements, *m.pl*.

acme, *n*, apogée, comble, sommet, *m*.

acne, *n*, acné, couperose, *f*.

acolyte, *n*, acolyte, *m*.

acorn, *n*, gland, *m*. ~ *crop*, glandée, *f*.

acoustic, *a*, acoustique. ~**s**, *n.pl*, acoustique, *f*.

acquaint, *v.t*, faire connaître, faire savoir, faire part, informer. ~**ance**, *n*, connaissance, relation, *f*.

acquiesce, *v.i*, acquiescer. **acquiescence**, *n*, acquiescement, *m*.

acquire, *v.t*, acquérir; prendre. ~**ments**, *n.pl*, acquis, *m.s. & m.pl*, connaissances, *f.pl*. **acquisition**, *n*, acquisition, *f*.

acquit, *v.t*, acquitter. **acquittal**, *n*, acquittement, *m*.

acrid, *a*, âcre. ~**ity**, *n*, âcreté, *f*.

acrimonious, *a*, acrimonieux. **acrimony**, *n*, acrimonie, *f*.

acrobat, *n*, acrobate, *m.f*. **acrobatic**, *a*, acrobatique. ~**s**, *n.pl*, acrobatie, *f*.

across, *ad*, en travers; (*cross-word clues*) horizontalement. ¶ *pr*, en travers de, par. *our neighbours ~ the Channel*, nos voisins d'outre-Manche.

acrostic, *n*, acrostiche, *m*.

act, *n*, acte, *m*, action, *f*, fait, *m*. ~ [*of parliament*], loi [votée] *f*. *in the* [*very*] ~, sur le fait; en flagrant délit. ¶ *v.t*, jouer, représenter; faire; (*v.i.*) agir; fonctionner, opérer. ~ *as*, faire fonction de. ~ *for* (*client*, *Law*), postuler. **acting** (*Theat.*) *n*, jeu, *m*. ~ *manager*, directeur intérimaire, *m*. ~ *partner*, commandité, *m*.

actinic rays, rayons chimiques, *m.pl*.

action, *n*, action, *f*; effet; mouvement; geste, *m*; scène, *f*; combat; procès, *m*, plainte, *f*.

active†, *a*, actif, agissant, agile, allant, énergique. *in ~ service*, en activité [de service]. ~ *voice*, voix active, *f*, actif, *m*. **activity**, *n*, activité, agilité, *f*, allant, *m*.

actor, **tress**, *n*, acteur, trice, comédien, ne.

actual, *a*, actuel, réel, effectif, véritable; de fait. ~**ity**, *n*, actualité, réalité, *f*. ~**ly**, *ad*, réellement, en effet.

actuary, *n*, actuaire, *m*.

actuate, *v.t*, actionner, animer, mouvoir.

acumen, *n*, flair, *m*.

acute, *a*, aigu; vif, poignant. ~**-angled**, acutangle. ~**ly**, *ad*, vivement. ~**ness**, *n*, acuité; finesse, subtilité; vivacité, *f*.

A.D. (*Anno Domini*), ap. J.-C.

adage, *n*, adage, *m*.

adamant (to be), être inflexible.

Adam's ale, château La Pompe, *m*.

Adam's apple, pomme d'Adam, *f*.

adapt, *v.t*, adapter, accommoder, approprier. ~**ation**, *n*, adaptation, *f*. ~**er**, *n*, (*Phot.*) adapteur; (*pers. fig.*) metteur en œuvre, *m*.

add, *v.t*, ajouter; joindre; additionner. (*part*) **added** (*to a building*), hors d'œuvre, *e.g. an added room*, une chambre hors d'œuvre.

adder, *n*, vipère, *f*.

addict oneself to (to), s'adonner à, se livrer à.

addition, *n*, addition, *f*; supplément; (*to a building*) hors-d'œuvre, *m*. ~**al**, *a*, additionnel, supplémentaire.

addled, *a*, couvi; pourri. **addle-headed**, *a*, écervelé.

address, *n*, adresse; allocution, *f*. ¶ *v.t*, adresser; s'adresser à; (*Golf*) viser. ~**ee**, *n*, destinataire, *m.f*.

adduce, *v.t*, alléguer, fournir.

adenoids, *n.pl*, végétations [adénoïdes], *f.pl*.

adept, *a*, habile, versé, expérimenté. ¶ *n*, adepte, *m.f*.

adequate, *a*, suffisant; efficace; raisonnable. ~**ly**, *ad*, suffisamment, raisonnablement; dignement.

adhere, *v.i*, adhérer, s'en tenir. **adherence**, *n*, adhésion, *n*, **adhesiveness**, *n*, adhérence, adhésion, ténacité, *f*. **adhesive**, *a*, adhésif, tenace. ~ *stamp*, timbre mobile, *m*. ~ *tape*, bande gommée, *f*.

adieu, *i. & n*, adieu, *i. & m*.

ad infinitum, *ad*, à l'infini.

adipose, *a*, adipeux.

adit, *n*, galerie à flanc de coteau, *f*.

adjacent, *a*, adjacent, contigu.

adjectival, *a. & adjective**, *n*, adjectif, *a.m. & m*.

adjoin, *v.i*, joindre, être contigu à, toucher. ~**ing**, *a*, contigu, attenant, adjacent, joignant [à].

adjourn, *v.t*, ajourner, renvoyer, remettre. ~**ment**, *n*, ajournement, renvoi, *m*, remise, *f*.

adjudge, **adjudicate**, *v.t*, adjuger. **adjudication**, *n*, adjudication, *f*.

adjunct, *n*, accessoire, *m*.

adjure, *v.t*, adjurer.

adjust, *v.t*, ajuster, régler, mettre au point. ~**able spanner**, clef à molette, *f*. ~**ment**, *n*, ajustement; règlement, réglage, *m*, mise au point, *f*. ~ *of average* (*Insce*), règlement d'avaries, dispache, *f*.

adjutant, *n*, adjudant major, major, *m*.

ad libitum, ad libitum; à volonté, à discrétion.

administer, *v.t*, administrer, gérer; (*oath*) déférer. **administration**, *n*, administration, gestion; régie, *f*. **administrator**, **trix**, *n*, administrateur, trice; curateur, trice.

admirable†, *a*, admirable.

admiral, *n*, amiral, *m*. ~ *of the fleet*, a. commandant d'escadre. **Admiralty**, *n*, (*Eng.*) Amirauté, *f*; (*Fr.*) Conseil supérieur de la Marine, *m*. ~ [*Office*], Ministère de la Marine, *m*.

admiration, *n*, admiration, *f*. **admire**, *v.t*, admirer. **admirer**, *n*, admirateur, trice. **admiringly**, *ad*, avec admiration.

admissible, *a*, admissible; recevable. **admission**, *n*, admission, entrée, *f*; aveu, *m*. **admit**, *v.t*, admettre, reconnaître; (*as member*) recevoir, agréger. ~ *bearer*, laissez passer. **admittance**, *n*, admission, entrée, *f*.

admixture, *n*, dosage, *m*.

admonish, *v.t*, admonester. **admonition**, *n*, admonition, admonestation, *f*.

ado, *n*, façons, *f.pl*, cérémonie, *f*; aria, bruit, tapage, *m*.

adolescence, *n*, adolescence, *f*. **adolescent**, *a. & n*, adolescent, e.

Adonis, *n*, adonis, beau, *m*.

adopt, *v.t*, adopter; prendre. **adopted, adoptive** (*of pers.*) *a*, adoptif. **adoption**, *n*, adoption; prise, *f*.

adorable, *a*, adorable. **adoration**, *n*, adoration, *f*. **adore**, *v.t*, adorer. **adorer**, *n*, adorateur, trice.

adorn, *v.t*, parer, orner, agrémenter, empanacher; (*of pers.*) faire l'ornement de. ~**ment**, *n*, parure, *f*, ornement, *m*.

Adriatic, *a. & n*, Adriatique, *a. & f*.

adrift, *ad*, en (*ou* à la) dérive.

adroit†, *a*, adroit. ~**ness**, *n*, dextérité, *f*.

adulate, *v.t*, aduler. **adulation**, *n*, adulation, *f*. **adulatory**, *a*, adulateur.

adult, *a. & n*, adulte, *a. & m,f*.

adulterate, *v.t*, falsifier, frelater, sophistiquer, altérer. **adulteration**, *n*, falsification, *f*, frelatage, *m*, sophistication, altération, *f*.

adulterer, *ess*, *n*, adultère, *m,f*. **adulterous**, *a*, adultère. **adultery**, *n*, adultère, *m*.

ad valorem, *ad* ad valorem, proportionnel.

advance, *n*, avance; anticipation; (*glacier*) crue; hausse, *f*; prêt, *m*. *in* ~, en avance, d'a., par a., à l'a. ¶ *v.t*, avancer; hausser; (*v.i.*) [s']avancer, cheminer. ~**ment**, *n*, avancement, *m*.

advantage, *n*, avantage, bénéfice, *m*. ~ [*game*] (*Ten.*), avantage [de jeu]. ~ *in*, a. dedans. a. au servant. ~ *out*, a. dehors, a. au relanceur. ~**ous**†, *a*, avantageux.

advent, *n*, venue, apparition, *f*; (*of Christ*) avènement; (*Eccl.*) l'avent, *m*.

adventure, *n*, aventure, expédition, *f*. ¶ *v.t*, aventurer. **adventurer**, *n*, aventurier, chercheur d'aventures, chevalier d'industrie, *m*. **adventuress**, *n*, aventurière, *f*. **adventurous**, *a*, aventureux.

adverb, *n*, adverbe, *m*. ~ *of number*, a. de quantité. **adverbial**†, *a*, adverbial.

adversary, *n*, adversaire, *m*. **adverse**, *a*, adverse; contraire; déficitaire. **adversity**, *n*, adversité, infortune, *f*.

advert, *v.i*, faire allusion.

advertise, *v.t*, annoncer, publier; afficher; (*v.i.*) faire une annonce (des annonces), faire de la publicité. ~ *for*, demander par voie d'annonces. ~**ment**, *n*, annonce; réclame, *f*. ~ *hoarding*, panneau-réclame, *m*. **advertiser**, *n*, annonceur, *m*. **advertising**, *n*, publicité, réclame, *f*.

advice, *n*, avis, conseil, *m*. **advisable**, *a*, à conseiller, expédient, convenable. **advise**, *v.t*, conseiller; engager; aviser. **advisedly**, *ad*, de propos délibéré, en connaissance de cause. **adviser**, *n*, conseiller, ère, moniteur, *m*. **advisory**, *a*, consultatif.

advocate, *n*, avocat, défenseur; partisan, *m*. ¶ *v.t*, préconiser.

advowson, *n*, patronage, *m*.

adze, *n*, herminette, *f*.

Aegean sea (the), la mer Égée.

aegis, *n*, égide, *f*.

Aeolian, *a*, éolien.

aerate, *v.t*, aérer; gazéifier. ~*d drinks*, boissons gazéifiées, *f.pl*. ~*d lemonade*, *water*, limonade, eau, gazeuse, *f*. **aeration**, *n*, aération, *f*.

aerial, *a*, aérien. ¶ (*Radio*) *n*, antenne, *f*.

aerie, aery, *n*, aire, *f*.

aerodrome, *n*, aérodrome, champ d'aviation, *m*.

aerodynamic, *a. & ~s*, *n*, aérodynamique, *a. & f*.

aerolite, *n*, aérolithe, météorite, *m*.

aeronaut, *n*, aéronaute, *m,f*. ~**ic(al)**, *a*, aéronautique. ~**ics**, *n*, aéronautique, *f*.

aeroplane, *n*, aéroplane, avion, *m*.

aesthetic(al), *a*, esthétique.

afar, *ad*, loin, au loin. *from* ~, de loin.

affability, *n*, affabilité, *f*. **affable**, *a*, affable. **affably**, *ad*, avec affabilité.

affair, *n*, affaire, *f*.

affect, *v.t*, affecter, concerner, atteindre, impressionner; toucher, émouvoir, attendrir. ~**ation**, *n*, affectation, afféterie, *f*, apprêt, *m*. ~**ed**, *a*, affecté, affété, précieux, apprêté, maniéré, pincé. ~**edly**, *ad*, avec affectation. ~**ing**, *p.a*, touchant. **affection**, *n*, affection, *f*. ~**ate**†, *a*, affectueux, aimant, affectionné.

affiance, *n*, confiance, foi, *f*; fiançailles, *f.pl*. ¶ *v.t*, fiancer.

affidavit, *n*, déclaration sous serment, *f*.

affiliate, *v.t*, affilier.

affinity, *n*, affinité, *f*.

affirm, *v.t*, affirmer, assurer. ~**ation**, *n*, affirmation, *f*. ~**ative**†, *a*, affirmatif. ¶ *n*, affirmative, *f*.

affix, *n*, affixe, *m*. ¶ *v.t*, apposer. ~**ture**, *n*, apposition, *f*.

afflict, *v.t*, affliger, chagriner. ~**ion**, *n*, affliction, *f*, chagrin, *m*.

affluence, *n*, affluence; opulence, aisance, *f*. **affluent**, *a*, affluent, tributaire; opulent, aisé. ¶ *n*, affluent, *m*.

afford, *v.t*, donner, fournir, accorder. *can* ~ *to*, avoir les moyens de, pouvoir.

afforest, *v.t*, boiser. **~ation**, *n*, boisement, *m.*

affray, *n*, échauffourée, rixe, *f.*

affreightment, *n*, affrètement, *m.*

affront, *n*, affront, *m*, avanie, *f.* ¶ *v.t*, offenser.

Afghan, *a*, afghan. ¶ *n*, Afghan, *e.*

afield, *ad: far* ~, très loin.

afire, *ad*, en feu, embrasé, brûlant.

afloat, *ad. & a*, à flot, sous voile, flottant; *(fig.)* sur pied, en circulation.

aforesaid, *a*, susdit, précité. ¶ *n*, susdit, e.

afraid, *a*, craintif. *to be* ~ *of*, avoir peur de, craindre.

afresh, *ad*, de nouveau, à nouveau.

Africa, *n*, l'Afrique, *f.* **African**, *a*, africain. ¶ *n*, Africain, e.

aft, *a*, arrière. ¶ *ad*, sur l'arrière, derrière.

after, *ad*, après; suivant; passé; à l'issue de. ¶ *c*, après que. ¶ *pr*, après, passé; d'après; à; sur. ~ *all*, après tout, au bout de compte. ~ *the event*, après coup.

aftermath, *n*, regain, *m.*

afternoon, *n*, après-midi, *m.*

after-taste *(nasty) n*, arrière-goût, déboire, *m.*

afterthought, *n*, réflexion après coup, *f.*

afterwards, *ad*, après, ensuite, puis, plus tard.

again, *ad*, encore, de nouveau. ~ *&* ~, mille [& mille] fois. **again** *after a verb is often expressed by the prefix* re- *as, to set out again*, repartir.

against, *pr*, contre, contraire à; sauf. ~ *the grain*, à contre-fil, à rebours. ~ *the light*, à contre-jour.

agate, *n*, agate, *f.*

age, *n*, âge; siècle; temps, *m*; époque; *(old age)* vieillesse; *(decay)* vétusté, *f.* *10 years of age or aged 10*, âgé de 10 ans. *he is not of* (or *is under*) ~, il n'est pas en âge. *to come of* [*full*] ~, être majeur, e. *it is* ~*s since*, il y a belle lurette de.

aged *(of an advanced age) a*, âgé. *he has* ~ *considerably*, il a bien vieilli. *the* ~ *(either sex)*, les vieillards, *m.pl.*

agency, *n*, action; entremise, *f*, ministère, *m*; *(Com.)* agence, *f*, bureau; comptoir, *m*; factorerie; représentation, *f.*

agenda, *n*, ordre du jour, *m.*

agent, *n*, agent, commissionnaire, *m*; représentant, e; stockiste, *m*; mandataire, *m,f*; régisseur, *m.*

agglomerate, *v.t*, agglomérer.

agglutinate, *v.t*, agglutiner.

aggravate, *v.t*, aggraver.

aggregate, *a*, global, d'ensemble. ¶ *n*, total global; ensemble, *m*, masse, *f.* **aggregation**, *n*, agrégation, *f.*

aggression, *n*, agression, *f.* **aggressive**, *a*, agressif. **aggressor**, *n*, agresseur, *m.*

aggrieved party, offensé, e.

aghast, *a*, épouvanté, ébahi.

agile†, *a*, agile. **agility**, *n*, agilité, *f.*

agio, *n*, agio, prix du change, *m.*

agitate, *v.t*, agiter, remuer. **agitation**, *n*, agitation, *f.* **agitator**, *n*, agitateur, *m.*

aglow, *a*, resplendissant.

agnail, *n*, envie, *f.*

ago, *ad*, il y a.

agog, *a*, en branle-bas; animé; impatient.

agonizing, *a*, déchirant, cuisant. **agony**, *n*, douleur déchirante, d. cuisante, *(pl.)* mort & passion; *(death pangs)* agonie, *f.*

agrarian, *a*, agraire.

agree, *v.t*, faire accorder, faire concorder, faire cadrer, apurer; *(v.i.)* s'accorder, s'arranger, s'entendre, cadrer, concorder, convenir. ~ *to*, consentir à, souscrire à, s'engager à. *quite agree with*, abonder dans le sens de. *meat does not* ~ *with me*, je ne digère pas la viande. ~*able†*, *a*, agréable, aimène; conforme. ~*d price*, prix convenu; [prix à] forfait, *m.* ~**ment**, *n*, accord, *m*, entente, convention, concordance, conformité, *f*; acte, contrat, marché, traité, *m.*

agricultural, *a*, agricole, aratoire. ~ *engine*, locomobile, *f.* ~ *implements*, instruments aratoires, *m.pl.* ~ *show*, comice *(ou* comices*)* agricole, *m.* **agricultur[al]ist**, *n*, agriculteur, cultivateur, *m.* **agriculture**, *n*, agriculture, *f.*

agronomist, *n*, agronome, *m.* **agronomy**, *n*, agronomie, *f.*

aground, *ad. & a*, échoué. *to run* ~, *v.i. & t*, [s']échouer.

ague, *n*, fièvre paludéenne, *f.*

ahead, *ad*, en avant, devant. *go* ~! en avant!

ahoy, *i*, ho!, ohé! *ship* ~! ho! du navire!

aid, *n*, aide, assistance, *f*, secours, *m.* ¶ *v.t*, aider, assister, secourir.

aide-de-camp, *n*, aide de camp, *m.*

ail, *v.t. & i*, avoir, souffrir. ~**ing**, *a*, maladif, souffrant. ~**ment**, *n*, mal, *m*, misère de santé, *f.*

aim, *n*, point de mire, *m*, visée, *f*; but, objectif, *m*, fin, *f.* ¶ *v.t*, pointer, coucher en joue. ~ *at*, viser [à]; ajuster, coucher *(ou* mettre*)* en joue. ~**less**, *a*, ~**lessly**, *ad*, sans but.

air, *n*, air; vent; ciel, *m.* *to give oneself* ~*s*, faire l'important, e. ~*craft*, aéronef, *m.* ~*craft carrier*, porte-avions, *m.* ~*craft exhibition*, salon de l'aviation, *m.* ~ *current*, courant d'air, *m.* ~ *cushion*, coussin à air, *m.* ~ *gun*, fusil à air comprimé, f. à vent, *m.* ~ *hole*, aspirail, soupirail, évent, *m*; soufflure, *f.* ~ *lighthouse*, aérophare, *m.* ~ *line*, ligne aérienne, ligne d'avion, *f.* ~ *liner*, avion de ligne régulière, *m.* ~ *mail*, poste aérienne, poste-avion, *f. by* ~ *mail*, par avion. ~ [*mail*] *fee*, surtaxe aérienne, *f.* ~ [*mail*] *letter*, lettre-avion, *f.* ~ [*mail*] *packet*, correspondance-avion, *f.* ~*man*, aviateur, *m.* ~ *mechanic*, mécanicien d'avions, *m.* ~*-minded*, tourné vers l'aviation. *A~ Ministry*, Ministère de l'Air, *m.* ~ *parcel*, colis-avion, *m.* ~ *pilot*, pilote aérien, *m.* ~ *plane*, avion, aéroplane, *m.* ~ *pocket*, trou d'air, *m.* ~ *pump*, pompe à air, *f.*; *(Phys.)* machine pneumatique, *f.* ~ *race*, course d'avions, *f.* ~ *raid*, raid aérien, *m.* ~ *shaft* (*Min.*), puits d'aérage, *m.* ~*ship*, dirigeable, paquebot aérien, *m.* ~ *station*, aéroport, port aérien, *m.* ~*tight*, [à fermeture] hermétique, imperméable à l'air. ~*way*, voie aérienne, voie d'air; (*Min.*) galerie d'aérage, *f.* ~*woman*, aviatrice, *f.* ~*worthiness*, tenue en l'air, *f.* ~*worthy*, en [bon] état de navigabilité. ¶ *v.t*, aérer; ventiler; donner de l'air à; éventer; chauffer; sécher; étaler. ~*ing*, *n*, aérage, *m*, aération, ventilation, *f.* ~*less*, *a*, sans air, privé d'air. ~*y*, *a*, aérien; aéré (*idle*) en l'air.

aisle, *n*, aile, *f*, bas-côté, *m.*

ajar, *a*, entrebâillé, entrouvert. *be ~*, bâiller.

akimbo, *ad*: *to set one's arms ~*, faire le pot à deux anses. *with arms ~*, les mains sur les hanches.

akin, *a*, apparenté, voisin.

alabaster, *n*, albâtre, *m.*

alacrity, *n*, empressement, *m.*

alarm, *n*, alarme, alerte, *f*; avertisseur, *m. alar(u)m clock*, réveille-matin, réveil, *m.* ¶ *v.t*, alarmer. ~*ing*, *a*, alarmant.

alas, *i*, hélas!

alb, *n*, aube, *f.*

albatross, *n*, albatros, *m.*

albino, *n*, albinos, *m,f.*

album, *n*, album, *m.*

albumen, *n*, albumen, *m.* **albumin**, *n*, albumine, *f.*

alchemist, *n*, alchimiste, *m.* **alchemy**, *n*, alchimie, *f.*

alcohol, *n*, alcool, *m.* ~**ic**, *a. & n*, alcoolique, *a. & m,f.*

alcove, *n*, alcôve, *f.*

alder, *n*, aune, ver[g]ne, *m.*

alert, *a*, alerte. *on the ~*, en alerte, en éveil, sur le qui-vive.

Alexandria, *n*, Alexandrie, *f.* **Alexandrian & Alexandrine**, *a*, alexandrin.

alfresco, *a. & ad*, en plein air.

algebra, *n*, algèbre, *f.*

Algeria, *n*, l'Algérie, *f.* **Algerian**, *a*, algérien. ¶ *n*, Algérien, ne. **Algiers**, *n*, Alger, *m.*

alias, *ad*, alias, autrement dit. ¶ *n*, faux nom; nom de guerre, *m.*

alibi, *n*, alibi, *m.*

alien, *a*, étranger. ¶ *n*, étranger, ère.

alienate, *v.t*, aliéner.

alight, *a*, allumé. ¶ *v.i*, descendre, débarquer; atterrir; se poser. ~ [*on the water*] (seaplane) amerrir.

align, *v.t*, aligner. ~**ment**, *n*, alignement, *m.*

alike, *a*, semblable, pareil; ressemblant. ¶ *ad*, également; à la fois. *to be ~*, se ressembler.

alimentary, *a*, alimentaire. **alimony**, *n*, pension alimentaire, *f.*

alive, *a*, en vie, vivant, vif, au monde, animé; sensible; éveillé, dégourdi. *to be ~ with vermin*, grouiller de vermine.

alkali, *n*, alcali, *m.* **alkaline**, *a*, alcalin.

all, *a*, tout. ~ *the year* [*round*], [pendant] toute l'année. ~ [*those*] *who*, tous ceux qui, toutes celles qui. *at ~ hours*, à toute heure. *on ~ occasions*, en toute occasion. ¶ *ad*, tout; entièrement. ~ *at once*, tout à coup. ~ *but*, presque, à peu près. ~ *right!* très bien! c'est bien! à la bonne heure! ~ *the better*, tant mieux. ~ *the same*, tout de même, quand même. ¶ *n*, tous, *m.pl*; tout; avoir, *m.* ~ *of us*, nous tous. *that is* ~, c'est tout, voilà tout. *that is not* ~, il s'en faut de beaucoup. *is that ~?* est-ce là tout? n'est-ce que cela? *one's* ~, tout son avoir, son tout, son va-tout. *2, 3,* ~ (*Ten.*), 2, 3, partout. Cf. *love*. ~ *change!* tout le monde descend! ~ *clear* (*Mil.*), fin d'alerte. ~ *in*, tout compris; (*Sch.*) rentrez!, en classe! ~*-in wrestling*, lutte américaine, *f.* ~ *told* or *in* ~, tout compte fait, pour tout potage.

allay, *v.t*, calmer, apaiser, adoucir.

allegation, *n*, allégation, *f.* **allege**, *v.t*, alléguer, prétendre, objecter.

allegiance, *n*, fidélité, obéissance, *f*, loyalisme, *m.*

allegoric(al†) *a*, allégorique. **allegory**, *n*, allégorie, *f.*

alleviate, *v.t*, alléger, soulager, adoucir. **alleviation**, *n*, allégement, soulagement, adoucissement, *m.*

alley, *n*, ruelle, *f*, passage, *m.*

All Fools' Day, le jour des poissons d'avril.

alliance, *n*, alliance, *f.*

alligator, *n*, alligator, *m.*

all-important, *ad*, de toute importance.

allocate, *v.t*, allouer. **allocation**, *n*, allocation, *f.*

allot, *v.t*, attribuer répartir; destiner. ~**ment**, *n*, attribution, répartition, distribution, *f*; lopin de terre, *m.* **allottee**, *n*, attributaire, *m,f.*

allow, *v.t*, permettre, autoriser; admettre; souffrir; laisser; allouer, accorder, faire, bonifier. ~**ance**, *n*, allouance, allocation; ration; pension; tolérance; bonification, remise, déduction, *f*, rabais, décompte, *m*, ristourne, indemnité, *f.*

alloy, *n*, alliage, *m.* ¶ *v.t*, allier.

all-powerful, *a*, tout-puissant.

all-round, *a*, complet.

All Saints' Day, la Toussaint.

All Souls' Day, le jour des morts.

allspice, *n*, toute-épice, *f*, piment, *m.*

allude to (*to*), toucher.

allure, *v.t*, amorcer, allécher, affrioler, affriander, appâter. ~**ment**, *n*, amorce, *f*, allèchement, appât, *m.*

allusion, *n,* allusion, *f.*

alluvion, alluvium, *n,* alluvion, *f.*

ally, *n,* allié, e. ¶ *v.t,* allier, apparenter.

almanac, *n,* almanach, *m.*

almighty, *a,* tout-puissant. **the Almighty,** le Tout-Puissant.

almond, *n,* amande, *f.* ~ *eyes,* des yeux en amande, des yeux bridés, *m.pl.* ~ [*tree*], amandier, *m.*

almost, *ad,* presque.

alms, *n.s. & pl,* aumône, l'aumône, charité, *f.* ~*giving,* distribution des aumônes, charité, *f.* ~*house,* hospice, asile, *m.*

aloe, *n,* aloès; (*pl.*) [suc d']aloès, *m.*

aloft, *ad,* en haut; dans la mâture.

alone, *a,* seul; isolé. *to let* (or *leave*) ~, laisser tranquille. ¶ *ad,* seulement.

along, *pr. & ad,* le long de; suivant. ~*side of* (*pers.*), côte à côte avec. ~*side* [*the ship*], le long [du bord]. *to come* ~*side,* accoster. *come* ~ *with me,* venez-vous-en avec moi. *all* ~, tout du long; tout le temps.

aloof, *ad,* à l'écart, en dehors, isolé (*from* = de). ¶ *a,* distant.

aloud, *ad,* à haute voix, tout haut.

alpaca, *n,* alpaga, *m.*

alpha, *n,* alpha, *m.* **alphabet,** *n,* alphabet, *m.* ~*ical*†, *a,* alphabétique.

Alpine, *a,* alpin; alpestre. **the Alps,** les Alpes, *f.pl,* les monts, *m.pl.*

already, *ad,* déjà.

Alsace, *n,* l'Alsace, *f.* **Alsatian,** *a,* alsacien. ¶ *n,* (*pers.*) Alsacien, ne; (*dog*) chien-loup, *m.*

also, *ad,* aussi, également, pareillement.

altar, *n,* autel, *m.* ~ *cloth,* nappe d'a., *f.* ~ *piece,* tableau d'a.; retable, *m.*

alter, *v.t,* changer, modifier; surcharger; (*v.i.*) [se] changer. ~ *the date of* (function, &c), transférer. ~*ation,* *n,* changement, *m,* modification; surcharge, *f,* renvoi [en marge], *m.*

altercation, *n,* altercation, prise de bec, *f.*

alternate†, *a,* alternatif. ~ *months* (newspaper appearing), bimensuel. ¶ *v.i. & t,* alterner. **alternating,** *p.a,* alternatif. **alternative,** *a,* alternatif. ¶ *n,* alternative, *f.*

although, *c,* quoique, bien que, encore que, quand, tout . . . que.

altitude, *n,* altitude, élévation, hauteur, *f.*

alto, *n. &* ~ *saxhorn,* alto, *m.* ~ *clef,* clef d'ut, *f.*

altogether, *ad,* tout à fait; en tout; grandement.

altruist, *n. &* ~*ic,* *a,* altruiste, *m,f. & a.*

alum, *n,* alun, *m.*

aluminium, *n,* aluminium, *m.*

always, *ad,* toujours.

amalgam, *n,* amalgame, *m.* ~*ate,* *v.t,* amalgamer, fusionner.

amanuensis, *n,* secrétaire, *m.*

amass, *v.t,* amasser.

amateur, *n,* amateur; dilettante, *m.* ~

status, qualité d'amateur, *f,* statut d'a., *m.*

amatory, *a,* galant, érotique.

amaze, *v.t,* étonner, stupéfier. ~**ment,** *n,* étonnement, *m,* stupeur, *f.*

Amazon (*woman*) *n,* amazone, *f;* grenadier, gendarme, *m,* virago, *f.* **the** ~ (*river*), l'Amazone, *m,* le fleuve des Amazones.

ambassador, dress, *n,* ambassadeur, drice.

amber, *n,* ambre, *m.* ~**gris,** *n,* ambre gris, *m.*

ambiguity, *n,* ambiguïté, équivoque, *f.* **ambiguous**†, *a,* ambigu, équivoque.

ambition, *n,* ambition, *f.* **ambitious**†, *a,* ambitieux.

amble along (to), aller son petit train.

ambrosia, *n,* ambroisie, *f.*

ambulance, *n,* ambulance, *f.*

ambuscade, ambush, *n,* embuscade, *f,* guet-apens, *m.* *to place in ambush,* embusquer. **ambush,** *v.i,* s'embusquer.

ameer, *n,* émir, *m.*

ameliorate, *v.t,* améliorer. **amelioration,** *n,* amélioration, *f.*

amen, *i. & n,* amen, *i. & m.*

amenable, *a,* sujet, soumis; susceptible; justiciable; docile.

amend, *v.t,* amender; réformer; rectifier; changer. ~**s,** *n,* réparation, *f.* *make* ~ *for,* réparer, corriger.

amenity, *n,* aménité, *f;* agrément, *m.*

America, *n,* l'Amérique, *f.* **American,** *a,* américain. ~ *cloth,* toile cirée, moles-kine, *f.* ~ *tournament* (Ten.), poule à l'américaine, *f.* ¶ *n,* Américain, e.

amethyst, *n,* améthyste, *f.*

amiability, *n,* amabilité, *f.* **amiable,** *a,* aimable, accort. **amiably,** *ad,* avec ama-bilité.

amicable†, *a,* amical, amiable.

amid, amidst, *pr,* au milieu de, parmi. **amidships,** *ad,* au milieu du navire.

amiss, *ad. & a,* de travers; mal, en mal, en mauvaise part.

ammonia, *n,* ammoniaque, *f.*

ammunition, *n,* munitions, *f.pl.* ~ *wagon,* prolonge,*f.*

amnesty, *n,* amnistie, *f.*

among, amongst, *pr,* parmi, entre, dans; au milieu de; au nombre de; chez. ~ *strangers,* dépaysé.

amorous†, *a,* amoureux.

amorphous, *a,* amorphe.

amortization, *n,* amortissement, *m.* **amor-tize,** *v.t,* amortir.

amount, *n,* montant, *m,* somme, *f,* chiffre, *m,* quantité, *f.* ¶ *v.i,* monter, se chiffrer, s'élever; revenir. ~*ing to,* à concurrence de.

ampere, *n,* ampère, *m.*

amphibian, *n,* amphibie, *m.* **amphibious,** *a,* amphibie.

amphitheatre, *n,* amphithéâtre, *m.*

ample†, *a,* ample. ~**ness,** *n,* ampleur, *f.* **amplifier** (Radio) *n,* amplificateur, *m.*

amplify, v.t. & i, amplifier; développer; paraphraser. **amplitude**, n, amplitude, f.

amputate, v.t, amputer.

amulet, n, amulette, f.

amuse, v.t, amuser, divertir, distraire. ~ment, n, amusement, plaisir, divertissement, m, distraction, f.

an, indefinite art. or a, un, une.

anachronism, n, anachronisme, m.

anaemia, n, anémie, f. anaemic, a, anémique.

anaesthetic, a. & n, anesthétique, a. & m.

anagram, n, anagramme, f.

analogous, a, analogue. analogy, n, analogie, f.

analyse, v.t, analyser; (Bkkpg) dépouiller, ventiler. analysis, n, analyse; ventilation, f. analyst, n, analyste, m. analytic(al†), a, analytique.

anarchic(al), a, anarchique. anarchist, n, anarchiste, m,f. anarchy, n, anarchie, f.

anatomical†, a, anatomique. anatomy, n, anatomie, f.

ancestor, n, ancêtre, m. ancestral, a, ancestral. ancestry, n, race, f, ascendants, m.pl.

anchor (all senses) n, ancre, f. ¶ (Naut.) v.t. & i, mouiller; (Build. & fig.) v.t, ancrer. ~age (Naut.) n, mouillage, m.

anchoret, anchorite, n, anachorète, m.

anchovy, n, anchois, m. ~ paste, beurre d'anchois, m.

ancient†, a, ancien; antique. ~ lights, droit de vue, m. ¶ n, ancien, m. ~ness, n, ancienneté, antiquité, f.

and, c. (abb. &), et, &. ~ even, voire même. ~ so on or ~ so forth, et ainsi de suite. ~ so on, ~ so forth, et patati, et patata. go ~ see, allez voir. more ~ more, de plus en plus. two ~ two, deux à deux. steak ~ potatoes, bifteck aux pommes.

andiron, n, chenet, m.

anecdote, n, anecdote, historiette, f.

anemone, n, anémone, f.

aneroid [barometer], baromètre anéroïde, m.

anew, ad, à nouveau.

angel, n, ange, m. ~ skin, peau d'ange, f. ~ic(al†), a, angélique. angelica (Bot.) n, angélique, f. angelus [bell], Angélus, m.

anger, n, colère, f, courroux, m. ¶ v.t, mettre en colère, fâcher, courroucer, irriter.

angina, n, angine, f. ~ pectoris, angine de poitrine.

angle, n, angle, m. ~ [iron], fer cornière, m, cornière, f.

angle, v.i, pêcher à la ligne. angler, n, pêcheur à la ligne, m.

Anglicism, n, anglicisme, m.

angling, n, pêche à la ligne, f. ~ at set pitches, pêche au coup.

Anglomania, n, anglomanie, f. Anglophil[e] a. & n, Anglophile, a. & m,f. Anglophobe, n, Anglophobe, m,f. Anglo-

Saxon, a, anglo-saxon. ¶ n, Anglo-Saxon, ne.

angrily, ad, avec colère, en colère. angry, a, en colère, fâché, irrité. to get (or be) ~, se fâcher. to be ~ with oneself for, s'en vouloir de.

anguish, n, angoisse, f.

angular, a, angulaire.

aniline, n, aniline, f. ~ n, dye, teinture d'aniline, f.

animal, a, animal. ¶ n, animal, m.

animate, a, animé, doué de vie. ¶ v.t, animer. animation, n, animation, f.

animosity, animus, n, animosité, f.

aniseed, n, anis, m, graine d'anis, f.

ankle, n, cheville [du pied], malléole, f. ~ socks, socquettes, f.pl.

annals, n.pl, annales, f.pl, fastes, m.pl.

anneal, v.t, recuire. ~ing, n, recuit, m, recuite, f.

annex, v.t, annexer. ~ation, n, annexion, f. annex[e], n, annexe, dépendance, f.

annihilate, v.t, anéantir, annihiler. annihilation, n, anéantissement, m, annihilation, f.

anniversary, a. & n, anniversaire, a. & m.

annotate, v.t, annoter.

announce, v.t, annoncer. ~ment, n, annonce, f. announcer (Radio) n, speaker, m.

annoy, v.t, agacer, tracasser, contrarier, ennuyer. to be ~ed with, savoir mauvais gré à. ~ance, n, agacement, m, tracasserie, contrariété; fâcherie, f. ~ing, a, agaçant, contrariant.

annual†, a, annuel. ¶ n, plante annuelle, f; (book) annuaire, m. annuitant, n, rentier, ère. annuity, n, annuité, rente [à terme], f.

annul, v.t, annuler, annihiler.

annular, a, annulaire.

annum, n: per ~, par an.

Annunciation (the), l'Annonciation, f.

anode, n, anode, f.

anodyne, a, anodin. ¶ n, anodin, m.

anoint, v.t, oindre, sacrer. ~ed, a. & n, oint, a.m. & m.

anomalous, a, anomal. anomaly, n, anomalie, f.

anon, ad, tantôt, tout à l'heure.

anonymous†, a, anonyme.

another, a. & pn, un (une) autre; autre; encore un, e. une; nouveau; un (une) second, e.

answer, n, réponse; réplique, f. ~s to correspondents, petite correspondance, f. ~ to the riddle, mot de l'énigme, m. ¶ v.t, répondre à. ~ [back], répliquer. ~ for, répondre pour, de. ~able, a, responsable.

ant, n, fourmi, f. ~-eater, fourmilier, m. ~-hill, termitière, f. ~-lion, fourmi-lion, m. ~'s nest, fourmilière, f.

antagonism, n, antagonisme, m. antagonist, n, antagoniste, m. antagonize, v.t, rendre hostile.

antarctic, a, antarctique. the A~ ocean, l'océan Glacial antarctique, m.

antecedent, *a. & n,* antécédent, *a. & m.*
antechamber, *n,* antichambre, *f.*
antedate, *v.t,* antidater.
antediluvian, *a,* antédiluvien.
antelope, *n,* antilope, *f.*
ante meridiem (*abb.* a.m.), avant midi; du matin.
antenna, *n,* antenne, *f.*
anterior†, *a,* antérieur.
anteroom, *n,* antichambre, *f.*
anthem, *n,* antienne, *f;* (*national*) hymne, *m.*
anther, *n,* anthère, *f.*
anthology, *n,* anthologie, *f.*
anthracite, *n,* anthracite, *m.* ~ *stove,* poêle à anthracite, *f.* ~ *vase,* seau forme conique, *m.*
anthrax, *n,* charbon, *m.*
anti-aircraft, *a,* anti-aérien, contre-avions.
anti-British, *a,* anglophobe.
antic, *n,* (*pl.*) gambades, *f.pl.*
antichrist, *n,* antéchrist, *m.* the *A~,* l'A.
anticipate, *v.t,* anticiper, prévenir, escompter.
anticipation, *n,* anticipation, prévision, *f.*
anticlimax, *n,* gradation descendante, *f.*
anticyclone, *n,* anticyclone, *m.*
anti-dazzle lamp *or* **light,** phare anti-éblouissant, phare-code, *m.*
antidote, *n,* antidote, contrepoison, *m.*
anti-French, *a,* gallophobe.
antimony, *n,* antimoine, *m.*
antipathetic, *a,* antipathique. **antipathy,** *n,* antipathie, *f.*
antipodes, *n.pl,* antipodes, *m.pl.*
antiquary, antiquarian, *n,* antiquaire, *m,f.*
antiquated, *a,* suranné, vieilli. **antique,** *a,* antique. ¶ *n,* (*style*) antique, *m;* (*relic*) antique, *f.* **antiquity,** *n,* antiquité; ancienneté, *f.*
anti-red (*Pol.*) *n,* jaune, *m.*
antirrhinum, *n,* muflier, *m,* gueule-de-loup, *f.*
antiseptic, *a. & n,* antiseptique, *a. & m.*
anti-splash tap nozzle, brise-jet, *m.*
antithesis, *n,* antithèse, *f.*
antler, *n,* andouiller, *m,* (*pl.*) bois, *m.pl.*
Antwerp, *n,* Anvers, *m.*
anus, *n,* anus, *m.*
anvil, *n,* enclume, *f.*
anxiety, *n,* anxiété, inquiétude; sollicitude, *f.*
anxious, *a,* anxieux, inquiet; soucieux; désireux, jaloux. ~**ly,** *ad,* avec anxiété.
any, *a, ad. & pn,* quelque; quelconque; de; du, de la, des; aucun; tout; plus; quelqu'un. *has he* ~? en a-t-il? ~ *farther,* ~ *further,* plus loin. ~ *more,* encore; (*neg.*) plus.
anybody, anyone, *n. & pn,* quelqu'un; on; personne; aucun; tout le monde; le premier venu.
anyhow, *ad,* de toute façon; en tout cas, toujours; n'importe comment; à l'abandon, à la débandade.
anything, *pn. & n,* quelque chose, *m;* (*neg.*) rien, *m;* quoi que ce soit; n'importe quoi.
anywhere, *ad,* n'importe où; quelque part; (*neg.*) nulle part.

aorta, *n,* aorte, *f.*
apace, *ad,* à grands pas.
apart, *ad,* à part; de côté; séparément. ~ *from,* abstraction faite de.
apartment, *n,* pièce, chambre, *f,* logement, *m.*
apathetic, *a,* apathique, indolent. **apathy,** *n,* apathie, indolence, *f.*
ape, *n,* singe (sans queue), *m.* ¶ *v.t,* singer.
aperient, *n,* laxatif, purgatif, *m.*
aperture, *n,* ouverture, *f,* orifice, *m.*
apex, *n,* sommet, faîte, *m.*
aphorism, *n,* aphorisme, *m.*
apiary, *n,* rucher, *m.*
apiece, *ad,* [la] pièce.
apish, *a,* simiesque.
apogee, *n,* apogée, *f.*
apologetic, *a,* apologétique. **apologize,** *v.i,* faire ses excuses. **apology,** *n,* apologie, *f;* excuses, *f.pl;* semblant, *m.*
apoplectic, *a. & n,* apoplectique, *a. & m.* ~ *fit,* attaque d'apoplexie, *f,* coup de sang, *m.* **apoplexy,** *n,* apoplexie, *f.*
apostasy, *n,* apostasie, *f.* **apostate,** *n. & a,* apostat, *m. & att,* relaps, *a.*
apostle, *n,* apôtre, *m.* the [*A~s'*] *Creed,* le symbole [des apôtres]. **apostolate,** **apostleship,** *n,* apostolat, *m.* **apostolic**(al†), *a,* apostolique.
apostrophe, *n,* apostrophe, *f.* **apostrophize,** *v.t,* apostropher.
apothecaries' measure, mesure pharmaceutique, *f.*
apotheosis, *n,* apothéose, *f.*
appal[l], *v.t,* épouvanter. **appalling,** *a,* épouvantable.
apparatus, *n,* appareil, attirail, *m.*
apparel, *n,* habillement, *m,* vêtements, *m.pl.*
apparent, *a,* apparent; (*heir*) présomptif. ~**ly,** *ad,* apparemment.
apparition, *n,* apparition, *f.*
appeal, *n,* appel; pourvoi; recours; attrait, *m.* ¶ *v.i,* en appeler; faire appel; appeler.
appear, *v.i,* paraître, sembler; apparaître; figurer, ressortir; comparaître. ~**ance,** *n,* apparition; apparence, venue, *f,* semblant, aspect, *m;* mine; comparution, *f;* (*pl.*) apparences, *f.pl,* dehors, *m.pl.*
appease, *v.t,* apaiser, adoucir; pacifier.
appellation, *n,* surnom, *m;* désignation, *f.*
append, *v.t,* apposer. ~**age, appendix,** *n,* appendice, *m.* **appendicitis,** *n,* appendicite, *f.*
appertain, *v.i,* appartenir.
appetite, *n,* appétit, *m.* **appetizer,** *n,* apéritif, *m.* **appetizing,** *a,* appétissant.
applaud, *v.t,* applaudir [à]. **applause,** *n,* applaudissement[s] *m.[pl.].*
apple, *n,* pomme, *f.* (*eye*) prunelle, *f.* ~ *corer,* vide-pomme, *m.* ~ *orchard,* pommeraie, *f.* ~ *tree,* pommier, *m.*
appliance, *n,* engin, appareil, *m;* (*pl.*) attirail, *m.*
applicant, *n,* demandeur, euse; postulant, e; souscripteur, *m.* **application,** *n,* application; contention; affectation; demande,

réclamation; souscription; mise en œuvre, f; (brake) serrage, m. **~ form** (for shares), bulletin de souscription, m. **~ money,** versement de souscription, m. **applied** (of sciences) a, appliqué. **appliqué lace,** [dentelle d']application, f. **appliqué [work]** (metal), applique, f. **appliqué** (or applied) **work** (Emb.), broderie-application, f.

apply, v.t, appliquer, affecter; (brake) serrer. **~ for,** solliciter, postuler, demander, réclamer; souscrire. **~ to,** s'adresser à.

appoint, v.t, nommer, instituer, constituer, désigner, préposer. **~ment,** n, nomination, désignation, constitution, f; rendez-vous; (pl.) aménagement, emménagement, m. **~s & promotions,** mouvement, m. **by ~** (official), attitré.

apportion, v.t, répartir, ventiler.

apposite, a, à propos, pertinent.

apposition, n apposition, f.

appraise, v.t, priser. **~ment,** n, prisée, f. **appraiser,** n, priseur, m.

appreciable, a, appréciable, sensible. **appreciably,** ad, sensiblement. **appreciate,** v.t, apprécier; améliorer; (v.i.) s'améliorer. **appreciation,** n, appréciation; amélioration, plus-value, f.

apprehend, v.t, appréhender; redouter; saisir. **apprehension,** n, appréhension, f.

apprentice, n, apprenti, e; (Naut.) novice, m. ¶ v.t, mettre en apprentissage. **~ship,** n, apprentissage; noviciat, m.

apprise, v.t, prévenir, informer.

approach, n, approche, f; accès, abord, m. ¶ v.t, [s']approcher de, aborder; (v.i.) [s']approcher. **~able,** a, abordable, accessible.

approbation, n, approbation, f.

appropriate†, a, propre, convenable, approprié. ¶ v.t, s'approprier; consacrer, distraire, affecter.

approval, n, approbation, f, agrément, m, sanction, f. **on ~,** à condition. **approve,** v.t., approuver, agréer, sanctionner. **~d school,** maison de correction, f.

approximate†, a, approximatif. **approximation,** n, approximation, f.

apricot, n, abricot, m. **~ tree,** abricotier, m.

April, n, avril, m. **to make an ~ fool of,** donner un poisson d'avril à.

apron, n, tablier, m.

apropos, ad, à propos.

apse, n, abside, f.

apt, a, enclin, sujet, disposé, porté; à propos; apte. **~ly,** ad, à propos. **~ness,** n, à-propos, m. **aptitude,** n, aptitude, facilité, f, dispositions, f.pl.

aqua fortis, eau forte, f. **aquamarine,** n, aigue-marine, f. **aqua regis,** eau régale, f.

aquarium, n, aquarium, m.

aquatic, a, (plant) aquatique; (sport) nautique.

aqueduct, n, aqueduc, m.

aqueous, a, aqueux.

aquiline, a, aquilin.

Arab, a, arabe. ¶ n, Arabe, m,f. **arabesque,** n, arabesque, f. **Arabia,** n, l'Arabie, f. **Arabian,** a, arabe. **~ gulf,** golfe Arabique, m. **the ~ nights,** les Mille & une Nuits. ¶ n, Arabe, m,f. **Arabic** (language) n, l'arabe, m. **Arabic numerals,** chiffres arabes, m.pl.

arable, a, arable, labourable.

arbiter, n, arbitre, m. **arbitrage & arbitrament,** n, arbitrage, m. **arbitrary†,** a, arbitraire; conventionnel; d'office. **arbitrate,** v.t, arbitrer. **arbitration,** n, arbitrage, m. **~ clause,** clause compromissoire, f. **arbitrator,** n, arbitre; (Law) amiable compositeur, m.

arbor, n, arbre, mandrin, m, broche, f.

arbour, n, tonnelle, f, berceau, cabinet de verdure, m.

arc, n, arc, m. **~ lamp,** lampe à arc, f.

arcade, n, arcades, f.pl, galerie, f, passage, bazar, m.

arch, a, espiègle, malicieux. ¶ n, voûte, f, arceau, m, arcade, arche; porte, f; arc, cintre, m. **~ support** (for foot in shoe), cambrure-support, f. ¶ v.t, cintrer, arquer, cambrer, voûter.

archaeologic(al), a, archéologique. **archaeologist,** n, archéologue, m. **archaeology,** n, archéologie, f.

archaic, a, archaïque, vieux, vieilli.

archangel, n, archange, m.

archbishop, n, archevêque, m. **archbishopric,** n, archevêché, m.

archdeacon, n, archidiacre, m.

archer, n, archer, m. **~y,** n, tir à l'arc, m. **Archimedean screw,** vis d'Archimède, limace, f.

archipelago, n, archipel, m.

architect, n, architecte; (fig.) artisan, m. **architectural,** a, architectural. **architecture,** n, architecture, f.

archives, n.pl, archives, f.pl.

archly, ad, malicieusement. **archness,** n, espièglerie, f.

archway, n, arcade, f, passage voûté; portail, m.

arctic, a, arctique. **the A~ ocean,** l'océan Glacial arctique, m.

ardent, a, ardent. **~ly,** ad, ardemment. **ardour,** n, ardeur, f, zèle, m.

arduous, a, ardu, pénible, laborieux.

are. See be. **~ you there!** (Teleph.), allô!

area, n, aire, superficie, surface; zone, étendue, f; réseau, m; cour en sous-sol, f.

arena, n, arène, f.

argentine, a, argentin. **A~** (Geog.) a, argentin. ¶ n (pers.), Argentin, e. **the ~,** l'Argentine, f.

argue, v.i. & t, argumenter, raisonner, discuter, débattre, prétendre, plaider. **argument,** n, argument, m, raisonnement, m, thèse, f. **~ation,** arguing, n, argumentation, f. **~ative,** a, raisonneur.

aria (*Mus.*) *n*, air, *m*.

arid, *a*, aride. ~ity, *n*, aridité, *f*.

aright, *ad*, bien, justement.

arise, *v.i.ir*, s'élever, surgir, naître, survenir.

aristocracy, *n*, aristocratie, *f*. **aristocrat**, *n*, aristocrate, *m,f*. **aristocratic**(al†), *a*, aristocratique.

arithmetic, *n*, arithmétique, *f*, calcul, *m*. ~al†, *a*, arithmétique. ~ian, *n*, arithméticien, ne.

ark, *n*, arche, *f*. the A~ of the Covenant, l'arche d'alliance, *f*.

arm, *n*, (*limb*) bras; (*of cross*) croisillon; *m*; (*weapon*) arme, *f*; (*pl.*, *Her.*) armes, armoiries, *f.pl*, blason, *m*; (*rest*) bras, accotoir, accoudoir, *m*. ~ in ~, bras dessus, bras dessous. to be up in ~s, se gendarmer. ~chair, fauteuil [à bras] *m*. ~hole, emmanchure, *f*. ~pit, aisselle, *f*. ¶ *v.t*, armer; (*v.i.*) [s']armer.

armadillo, *n*, tatou, *m*.

armament, *n*, armement, *m*.

armature, *n*, (*Phys.*) armature, armure, *f*; (*dynamo*) induit, *m*.

Armenia, *n*, l'Arménie, *f*. **Armenian**, *a*, arménien. ¶ *n*, Arménien, ne.

armful, *n*, brassée, *f*.

armistice, *n*, armistice, *m*. A~ Day, la fête [de l'anniversaire] de l'Armistice, le jour anniversaire de l'Armistice.

armlet, *n*, brassard, *m*.

armorial, *a. & n*, armorial, *a. & m*. ~ bearings, armoiries, armes, *f.pl*, blason, *m*.

armour, *n*, armure; (*sheathing*) armature, cuirasse, *f*. ~ plate, plaque de blindage, *f*. ~ plating, blindage, *m*. ~ed, *a*, armé; blindé, cuirassé, protégé. ~ car, automobile blindée, *f*. ~er, *n*, armurier. *m*. ~y, *n*, salle d'armes, *f*.

army, *n*, armée, *f*. ~ contractor, fournisseur de l'armée, *m*. the ~ service corps, le train [des équipages].

arnica, *n*, arnica, *m*.

aroma, *n*, arôme; bouquet, *m*. **aromatic**, *a*, aromatique.

around, *ad*, autour, alentour. ¶ *pr*, autour de.

arouse, *v.t*, réveiller; provoquer.

arpeggio, *n*, arpège, *m*.

arraign, *v.t*, mettre en accusation.

arrange, *v.t*, arranger, disposer, agencer; ménager; distribuer; accommoder; débattre, arbitrer. ~ment, *n*, arrangement, *m*, disposition, *f*, agencement, mouvement, *m*; économie; distribution, *f*; accommodement; dispositif, *m*.

arrant, *a*, franc, insigne, fieffé, achevé, renforcé, fier.

arras, *n*, tapisserie, *f*.

array, *n*, ordre; appareil, *m*; série, rangée, *f*. ¶ *v.t*, ranger; ajuster; revêtir.

arrears, *n.pl*, arriéré, *m*. in arrear[s], en arrière, arriéré, en retard, retardataire; en demeure.

arrest, *n*, arrestation, prise de corps, *f*; arrêt, *m*, under ~, (*Civil*) en état d'arrestation; (*Mil.*) aux arrêts. ¶ *v.t*, arrêter; appréhender. ~er (*Elec.*, *&c*) *n*, déchargeur, *m*.

arris, *n*, arête, *f*.

arrival, *n*, arrivée, *f*; arrivage, *m*. **arrive**, *v.i*, arriver; parvenir. ~ unexpectedly, survenir.

arrogance, *n*, arrogance, *f*. **arrogant**, *a*, arrogant, rogue. ~ly, *ad*, arrogamment. **to arrogate** [to oneself], s'arroger.

arrow, *n*, flèche, *f*, trait, *m*.

arsenal, *n*, arsenal, *m*.

arsenic, *n*, arsenic, *m*. ~al, *a*, arsenical.

arson, *n*, incendie volontaire, *m*.

art, *n*, art; artifice, *m*. ~ metal work, serrurerie d'art, *f*. ~ needlework, ouvrages de dames, *m.pl*. ~ school, école des beaux-arts, *f*.

arterial (*Anat.*) *a*, artériel. ~ road (*Eng.*), route nationale de grand itinéraire, *f*. (= in Fr. *a widened main road*). **artery**, *n*, artère, *f*.

Artesian, *a*, artésien.

artful†, *a*, artificieux, astucieux, rusé. ~ dodger, fin matois, finaud, *m*. ~ness, *n*, artifice, art, *m*, astuce, finauderie, finasserie, ruse, malice, *f*.

arthritis, *n*, arthrite, *f*.

artichoke, *n*, artichaut, *m*.

article, *n*, article, objet, envoi; (*pl.*) stage, apprentissage; (*pl.*) contrat; (*pl.*—*ship's*) rôle d'équipage, rôle d'armement, *m*. ~s [*of association*], statuts, *m.pl*. ~ [*of luggage*], colis, *m*. ~d clerk, stagiaire, *m,f*, apprenti, e.

articulate, *v.t*, articuler; (*v.i.*) [s']articuler. **articulation**, *n*, articulation, *f*.

artifice, *n*, artifice, art, *m*.

artificer, *n*, (*mécanicien*) ajusteur, serrurier mécanicien; (*fig.*) artisan, *m*.

artificial†, *a*, artificiel, factice, simil-, postiche.

artillery, *n*, artillerie, *f*. ~man, *n*, artilleur, *m*.

artisan, *n*, artisan, e.

artist & artiste, *n*, artiste, *m.f*. **artistic**, *a*, artistique; artiste. ~ novelties, articles de Paris, *m.pl*. ~ally, *ad*, artistement.

artless†, *a*, sans art, naturel; innocent; naïf, ingénu.

Aryan, *a*, aryen.

as, *ad. & c*, comme; ainsi que; de même que; parce que; puisque, aussi; que; à titre de; pour. ~ also, ainsi que. ~ [& when] required, au fur & à mesure que. ~ [& when] required, au fur & à mesure des besoins. ~ before, comme par le passé. ~ for, ~ to, ~ regards, quant à. ~ in (like, equal to), à l'instar de. ~ it were, en quelque sorte. ~ per, suivant, dont. ~ well as, aussi bien que, en même temps que. ~ you were! au temps!

asbestos, *n*, asbeste, *m*.

ascend, *v.t. & i*, [re]monter, faire l'ascension de. ~ancy, ~ency & ~ant, ~ent, *n*, ascendant, *m*. ascension, *n*, ascension, *f*. A~ day, l'Ascension. ascent, *n*, ascension; montée, *f*.

ascertain, *v.t*, constater, reconnaître, se rendre compte de.

ascetic, *a*, ascétique. ¶ *n*, ascète, *m.f*.

ascribe, *v.t*, attribuer, imputer, rapporter.

ash, *n*. oft. pl, cendre, *f*. oft. pl. ~ *blonde* (colour), blond cendré, *m*. ~ *pan*, cendrier, *m*. ~ *pit*, fosse aux cendres, *f*. ~ *tray*, cendrier [de fumeur] *m*. ~ *[tree]*, frêne, *m*. A~ *Wednesday*, le mercredi (*ou* le jour) des Cendres.

ashamed, *a*, honteux. to be ~, avoir honte, rougir.

ashen, ashy (*ash-coloured*) *a*, cendré.

ashlar, *n*, moellon d'appareil, *m*.

ashore *ad*, à terre. to run ~, échouer, faire côte.

Asia, *n*, l'Asie, *f*. ~ *Minor*, l'Asie Mineure. Asiatic, *a*, asiatique. ¶ *n*, Asiatique, *m.f*.

aside, *ad*, de côté; à part; à l'écart; en aparté. ¶ *n*, aparté, *m*.

ask, *v.t*, demander, prier, inviter, interroger, solliciter; poser; s'enquérir. ~ *not to come* (guests), désinviter, décommander.

askance, *ad*, de travers, de biais.

askew, *ad*, en biais, de travers, de guingois.

aslant, *ad*, en biais, obliquement.

asleep, *a*, endormi. to fall ~, s'endormir.

asp (*serpent*) aspic; (*tree*) tremble, *m*.

asparagus, *n*, asperge, *f*; asperges, *f.pl*. ~ *tongs*, pince à asperges, *f*.

aspect, *n*, aspect, *m*; face, *f*, visage, *m*; exposition, orientation, *f*.

aspen, *n*, tremble, *m*. ~ *plantation*, tremblaie, *f*.

asperity, *n*, aspérité, âpreté, *f*.

asperse, *v.t*, asperger; diffamer, calomnier, noircir. aspersion, *n*, aspersion, *f*; diffamation, calomnie, *f*.

asphalt, *n*, asphalte, bitume, *m*. ¶ *v.t*, bitumer.

asphyxia, *n*, asphyxie, *f*. asphyxiate, *v.t*, asphyxier.

aspirant, *n*, aspirant, *e*. aspirate, *v.t*, aspirer. aspiration, *n*, aspiration, *f*. to aspire to, aspirer à, prétendre à, affecter, ambitionner, briguer.

aspirin, *n*, aspirine, *f*.

ass, *n*, âne, *m*, (*she*) ânesse, *f*. *ass's foal*, ânon, *m*. *ass's* (or *asses'*) *milk*, lait d'ânesse, *m*.

assail, *v.t*, assaillir. ~ant, *n*, assaillant, *m*.

assassin, *n*, assassin, e. ~ate, *v.t*, assassiner. ~ation, *n*, assassinat, *m*.

assault, *n*, assaut; attentat, *m*. ~ [& *battery*], coups & blessures, *m.pl*, voies de fait, *f.pl*. ¶ *v.t*, assaillir, attaquer.

assay, *n*, essai, *m*. ~ *office* (government), bureau de garantie, *m*. ¶ *v.t*, essayer; (*v.i*.) titrer. ~er, *n*, essayeur, *m*.

assemblage, *n*, assemblage, *m*. assemble, *v.t*, [r]assembler, réunir. assembly, *n*, assemblée, réunion, *f*.

assent, *n*, assentiment; consentement, *m*, sanction, *f*. to ~ to, donner son assentiment à.

assert, *v.t*, soutenir; affirmer; prétendre; revendiquer. assertion, *n*, assertion, *f*; dire, *m*.

assess, *v.t*, coter, imposer, répartir, taxer. ~ment, *n*, cote, cotisation, imposition, répartition, taxation, *f*. ~ *book* (taxes), matrice du rôle des contributions, *f*.

asset, *n*, valeur [active] *f*; (*pl*.) actif, *m*, capitaux, *m.pl*. ~s nil, carence, *f*. ~s transferred or taken over, apport[s] *m.[pl.]*.

assiduity, *n*, assiduité, *f*. assiduous, *a*, assidu. ~ly, *ad*, assidûment.

assign, *n*, ayant cause, *m*. ¶ *v.t*, assigner; céder; apporter; affecter, destiner. ~ation, *n*, assignation, *f*. ~ee, *n*, syndic, *m*. ~ment, *n*, assignation; cession, *f*; apport, *m*.

assimilate, *v.t*, assimiler.

assist, *v.t*, assister, aider, secourir. ~ance, *n*, assistance, aide, *f*, secours; concours, *m*, (*to police*) main-forte, *f*. ~ant, *n*, aide, *m,f*, adjoint, e. ~ *master*, sous-maître, *m*. ~ *mistress*, sous-maîtresse, *f*. ~ *station master*, chef de gare adjoint, *m*.

assize, *n*, assizes, *n.pl*, assises, *f.pl*.

associate, *n*, associé, e. ¶ *v.t*, associer, adjoindre; (*v.i*.) s'associer, frayer. association, *n*, association, *f*; syndicat, *m*; caisse, *f*. A~ *football*, football association, *m*.

assort, *v.t*, assortir. ~ment, *n*, assortiment, jeu, *m*.

assuage, *v.t*, apaiser, adoucir.

assume, *v.t*, prendre, affecter, revêtir; assumer; s'arroger; supposer; (*name*) emprunter. assuming, *a*, prétentieux, arrogant. assumption, *n*, supposition; arrogance, *f*. A~ (*Eccl.*) *n*, assomption, *f*.

assurance, *n*, assurance, *f*. assure, *v.t*, assurer. assuredly, *ad*, assurément, à coup sûr.

Assyria, *n*, l'Assyrie, *f*. Assyrian, *a*, assyrien. ¶ *n*, Assyrien, ne.

aster, *n*, aster, *m*.

asterisk, *n*, astérisque, *m*, étoile, *f*.

astern, *ad*, derrière, en arrière, à (*ou* sur) l'arrière.

asteroid, *n*, astéroïde, *m*.

asthma, *n*, asthme, *m*. asthmatic, *a*, asthmatique.

astigmatic, *a*, astigmate.

astir, *a*, en mouvement, en branle-bas; agité, en émoi.

astonish, *v.t*, étonner, émerveiller, surprendre. ~ingly, *ad*, étonnamment. ~ment, *n*, étonnement, *m*, surprise, *f*.

astound, *v.t*, ébahir.

astray, *ad. & a*, hors du [bon] chemin; égaré.

astride, astraddle, *ad. & a*, à califourchon, à cheval, affourché, jambe deçà, jambe delà.

astringent, *a. & n*, astringent, *a. & m.*

astrologer, *n*, astrologue, *m*. astrology, *n*, astrologie, *f.*

astronomer, *n*, astronome, *m.* astronomic-(al†), *a*, astronomique. astronomy, *n*, astronomie, *f.*

astute, *a*, fin, rusé; astucieux.

asunder, *ad*, en deux; éloigné l'un de l'autre.

asylum, *n*, asile, hospice, *m.*

at, *pr*, à; en; dans; de; par; contre; chez; moyennant. ~ *a loss, profit*, à perte, profit. ~ *all*, du tout. ~ *first*, d'abord. ~ *hand*, à portée [de la main]. ~ *home*, chez soi, chez lui, chez nous, chez vous, &c; y; à la maison; au logis; visible; en famille; à son aise. ~ *last*, ~ *length*, enfin. ~ *least*, au moins. ~ *once*, tout de suite; à la fois, incessamment. ~ *owner's risk*, aux risques & périls du destinataire. ~ *railway station, to be called for*, en gare [restante], bureau restant. ~ *sea*, en mer. ~ *the same time*, en même temps. ~ *war*, en guerre.

Athanasian Creed (the), le symbole attribué à saint Athanase.

atheism, *n*, athéisme, *m*. atheist, *n*, athée, *m.* atheistic, *a*, athée.

Athenian, *a*, athénien. ¶ *n*, Athénien, ne. Athens, *n*, Athènes, *f.*

athirst, *ad*, altéré; avide.

athlete, *n*, athlète, *m*. athletic, *a*, athlétique. ~ *meeting*, ~ *sports*, réunion sportive, *f.* ~ *rules*, règlements d'athlétisme, *m.pl.* athletics, *n.pl*, athlétisme, *m.*

at-home, *n*, réception, *f. her* ~ *day*, son jour [de réception].

athwart, *ad*, en travers. ¶ *pr*, en travers de.

Atlantic, *a*, atlantique. ~ *liner*, [paquebot] transatlantique, *m. the A*~ [*ocean*], l'[océan] Atlantique, *m.*

atlas, *n*, atlas, *m.*

atmosphere, *n*, atmosphère, *f.* atmospheric-(al), *a*, atmosphérique. atmospherics (*Radio*), *n.pl*, parasites atmosphériques, *m.pl.*

atom, *n*, atome, *m*; miette, *f.* ~ic(al), *a*, atomique. *atom*[*ic*] *bomb*, bombe atomique, *f.* ~izer, *n*, vaporisateur, *m.*

atone for (to), expier, racheter. atonement, *n*, expiation, réparation, satisfaction, *f.*

atonic, *a*, atone.

atrocious†, *a*, atroce. atrocity, *n*, atrocité, *f.*

atrophy, *n*, atrophie, *f.*

attach, *v.t*, attacher; atteler; annexer, joindre; (*Law*) saisir. attached, *a*, attaché, *m.* ~ *case*, mallette, *f.* attachment, *n*, attachement, *m*; inclination; attache, *f*; attelage; appareil, *m*; (*Law*) saisie, *f.*

attack, *n*, attaque, *f*; accès, *m*, crise, *f.* ¶ *v.t*, attaquer, s'attaquer à.

attain, *v.t*, atteindre, parvenir à. ~ment, *n*, atteinte, *f*; (*pl.*) acquis, *m.s. & pl*, connaissances, *f.pl.*

attar, *n*, essence de roses, *f.*

attempt, *n*, tentative, *f*, essai, coup, jet;

(*criminal*) attentat, *m. to make an* ~ *on*, attenter à. ¶ *v.t*, tenter, essayer, tâcher. ~*ed murder*, tentative d'assassinat, *f.* ~*ed suicide*, faux suicide, *m.*

attend, *v.t*, accompagner; assister à; suivre; soigner; visiter. ~ *to*, faire attention à, écouter; s'occuper de; soigner, servir. ~ance, *n*, présence; assistance; visite, *f*; service, *m.* ~ant, *n*, suivant, e; (*pl.*) suite, *f*; gardien, *m*; (*Theat.*) receveuse; (*Theat. box*) ouvreuse, *f.* attention, *n*, attention, *f*; soin; regard, *m*; prévenance, *f. to pay* ~, faire attention. attentive†, *a*, attentif, empressé; prévenant.

attenuate, *v.t*, atténuer.

attest, *v.t*, attester, constater. ~ation, *n*, attestation, constatation, *f.*

Attic, *a*, attique.

attic, *n*, mansarde, *f*, grenier, galetas, *m.*

attire, *n*, vêtement, costume, *m*; parure, *f.* ¶ *v.t*, vêtir; parer.

attitude, *n*, attitude, posture, pose, *f.*

attorney, *n*, fondé de pouvoir(s) *m*, mandataire, *m,f*; procureur, *f.*

attract, *v.t*, attirer; solliciter. attraction, *n*, attraction; attirance, *f*; (*pl.*) attraits, appas, charmes, *m.pl.* attractive, *a*, attrayant, attirant; (*Phys.*) attractif.

attributable, *a*, attribuable. attribute, *n*, attribut, emblème, *m.* ¶ *v.t*, attribuer; prêter. attributive adjective, adjectif épithète, *m.* attributively (*Gram.*) *ad*, adjectivement; en apposition.

attrition, *n*, attrition; usure, *f.*

attune, *v.t*, accorder, harmoniser.

auburn hair, cheveux blond ardent, *m.pl.*

auction, *n*, enchère[s] *f.*[*pl.*], encan, *m*, criée, *f.* ~ *bridge*, bridge aux enchères, *m.* ~ *mart*, ~ *rooms*, hôtel des ventes, *m.* ~eer, *n*, commissaire priseur, *m.*

audacious†, *a*, audacieux. audacity, *n*, audace, *f.*

audible, *a*, perceptible à l'ouïe, intelligible.

audience, *n*, (*hearing*) audience; (*pers.*) assistance; *f*; spectateurs, *m.pl.*

audit, *v.t*, vérifier. ~[ing], *n*, vérification [comptable] *f.* audition, *n*, audition, *f.* auditor, *n*, commissaire des (*ou* aux) comptes, censeur, vérificateur comptable, *m*. auditor, tress, *n*, auditeur, trice. auditorium, *n*, salle, *f.*

auger, *n*, tarière, *f*, laceret, *m.*

aught, *n*, quelque chose, rien, *m.*

augment, *v.t*, augmenter.

augur, *n*, augure, *m.* ¶ *v.t*, augurer. ~y, *n*, augure, présage, *m.*

august, *a*, auguste. A~, *n*, août, *m.*

auk, *n*, pingouin, *m.*

aunt, *n*, tante, *f. A*~ *Sally*, jeu de massacre, *m.*

aureole, *n*, auréole, *f.*

auricle (*heart*) *n*, oreillette, *f.* auricula, *n*, oreille-d'ours, *f.* auricular, *a*, auriculaire, *f.*

auriferous, *a*, aurifère.

aurora, n, aurore, f. ~ borealis, a. boréale.

auspice, n, auspice, m. auspicious, a, propice, favorable, de bon augure.

austere†, a, austère, sévère. austerity, n, austérité, f.

austral, a, austral. Australasia, n, l'Australasie, f. Australia, n, l'Australie, f. Australian, a, australien. ¶ n, Australien, ne.

Austria, n, l'Autriche, f. Austrian, a, autrichien. ¶ n, Autrichien, ne.

authentic†, a, authentique. ~ity, n. authenticité, f.

author, n, (lit. & fig.) auteur, m; (fig. only) artisan, inventeur, m. ~ess, n, auteur, m, femme auteur, f.

authoritative, a, autoritaire; d'autorité. ~ly, ad, avec autorité, en maître. authority, n, autorité, puissance, obéissance, f, caractère; garant; chef, m. to be regarded as an ~, faire autorité. the authorities, les autorités, f.pl, l'administration, f.

authorization, n, autorisation, f. authorize, v.t, autoriser; mandater.

authorship, n, métier d'auteur, m; paternité, f.

autobiography, n, autobiographie, f.

autocracy, n, autocratie, f. autocrat, n, autocrate, trice. autocratic(al), a, autocratique.

autogenous, a, autogène.

autograph, n. & a, autographe, m. & a. ~ book, livre de signatures, m. ~ stamp, griffe, f.

automatic(al†), a, automatique. ~ [delivery] machine, distributeur automatique, m. automaton, n, automate, m.

autonomous, a, autonome. autonomy, n, autonomie, f.

autopsy, n, autopsie, f.

autumn, n, automne, m. ~al, a, automnal.

auxiliary, a. & n, auxiliaire, a. & m.

avail, n, effet, m. to ~ oneself of, profiter de. to ~ oneself of the services of, jouir de. ~able, a, disponible; libre; (ticket) valable, valide.

avalanche, n, avalanche, f.

avarice, n, avarice, f. avaricious†, a, avare, avaricieux.

avenge, v.t, venger, punir. avenger, n, vengeur, eresse. avenging, a, vengeur.

avenue, n, avenue, f, boulevard, cours, m.

aver, v.t, soutenir, affirmer.

average, n, moyen; commun. ¶ n, moyenne, f; (Marine Law) avarie[s] f.[pl.]; (Fire Insce) règle proportionnelle, f. ~ adjustment, dispache, f. ¶ v.t, établir la moyenne de.

averse to, from, ennemi de. I am averse to, il me répugne de. aversion, n, aversion, répugnance, f, dégoût, m.

avert, v.t, détourner; écarter.

aviary, n, volière, oisellerie, f.

aviation, n, aviation, f. ~ ground, champ d'aviation, aérodrome, m. aviator, n, aviateur, trice.

avid†, a, avide. ~ity, n, avidité, f.

avocations, n.pl, occupations, f.pl, travaux, m.pl.

avoid, v.t, éviter, se soustraire à, fuir. ~able, a, évitable.

avow, v.t, avouer, s'accuser de. ~al, n, aveu, m.

await, v.t, attendre.

awake, a, réveillé; vigilant. ¶ v.t.ir, réveiller; (v.i.) se réveiller, s'éveiller. awaken, v.t, réveiller. ~er, n, réveille-matin, m. ~ing, n, [r]éveil, m.

award, n, décision, sentence; (at a show) nomination, f. ~ of contract, adjudication, f. ¶ v.t, décerner; adjuger. ~ a medal to, médailler. ~ a prize to, couronner; primer. ~ the contract for, adjuger.

aware, a: to be ~ of, savoir, connaître, ne pas ignorer. not to be ~ of, ignorer.

away, ad, d'ici; de là. ~ [from home], absent. ~ match, away match, m. ~ on holiday, absent par congé. to go ~, s'en aller. ~ with you! allez-vous-en!

awe, n, crainte, f. ~-struck, saisi de crainte ¶ v.t, imposer à. awful†, a, effroyable, terrible; redoutable; solennel.

awhile, ad, un instant, un peu.

awkward, a, incommode, embarrassant, malaisé; gauche, maladroit, emprunté. the ~ age, l'âge ingrat, m. ~ incident, contretemps, m.

awl, n, alène, f, poinçon, m.

awn, n, barbe, arête, f.

awning, n, tente, banne, f, tendelet, m. ~ deck, pont abri, m.

awry, ad. & a, de travers, de guingois.

axe, n, hache, cognée, f.

axis, n, axe, m.

axiom, n, axiome, m.

axle, n, arbre, m. axle[tree], n, essieu, m

ay, i. & n, oui, particle & m.

azalea, n, azalée, f.

Azores (the), les Açores, f.pl.

azure, a, azuré. ¶ n, azur, m.

B

B (Mus.) letter, si, m.

baa, v.i, bêler. baa[ing], n, bêlement, m.

babble, n, babil, m. ¶ v.i, babiller; (stream) gazouiller; (of hound) clabauder.

babel (fig.), n, tour de Babel, f.

baboon, n, babouin, m.

baby, n. & ~ doll, bébé, poupard, m. ~ carriage, landau [pour enfant] m. ~ face physionomie pouparde, f. ~ grand piano à demi-queue, crapaud, m. ~ linen, layette, f. ~ plane, avionnette, f ~ square, lange, m. ~hood, n, première enfance, f. ~ish, a, enfantin.

Babylonian, a, babylonien.

Bacchanalia, n.pl, bacchanales, f.pl. Bacchic a, bachique.

bachelor, *n*, célibataire, garçon, *m*; (*science, &c*) bachelier, ère, licencié, e. ~ *flat*, appartement de garçon *ou* pour célibataire, *m*, garçonnière, *f*. ~ *girl*, garçonne, *f*.

back, *ad*, en arrière; en retour. *Note:—After a verb* **back** *is sometimes expressed by* re- *as, to come* **back**, revenir. ¶ *n*, dos; derrière; arrière; revers; envers; dossier; fond; verso; dessus, *m*; reins, *m.pl*; (*book*) dos; (*Foot.*) arrière, *m*. ~ *to front*, sens devant derrière. *seat with* ~ *to the engine*, place face à l'arrière, *f. to travel with one's* ~ *to the engine*, voyager en arrière. *with one's* ~ *to the light*, à contre-jour. ¶ *v.t*, [faire] reculer; adosser; épauler; appuyer, soutenir, seconder; (*bill of exchange*) avaliser; (*Betting*) parier sur, jouer; (*v.i.*) reculer; (*of wind*) redescendre.

backbite, *v.i*, clabauder. **backbiting**, *n*, médisance, *f*, cancans, *m.pl*.

backbone, *n*, épine dorsale, échine; énergie, *f*.

back door, porte de derrière, p. de service, *f*.

back edge (*book*), petit fond, *m*.

backer, *n*, partisan; (*Betting*) parieur, *m*.

back fire, retour de flamme, *m*. *back fire* [*kick*], retour de manivelle, *m*.

backgammon, *n*. & ~ *board*, trictrac, *m*.

background, *n*, arrière-plan, fond, enfoncement, second plan, *m*; pénombre, *f*.

backhand, *n*, arrière-main, revers, *m*.

backing, *n*, marche arrière, *f*, reculement, *m*.

back margin (*book*), [blanc de] petit fond, *m*.

back-pedal, *v.i*, contre-pédaler.

back room, chambre sur le derrière, c. sur la cour, *f*.

backsight (*gun*) *n*, hausse, *f*.

backslider, *n*, relaps, e. **backsliding**, *n*, rechute, *f*.

backstay (*Naut.*) *n*, galhauban, *m*.

backstitch, *n*, point arrière, arrière-point, *m*.

back tooth, dent du fond, *f*.

backward, *a*, peu avancé, tardif; rétrograde; (*child*) arriéré. ¶ ~, * as*, *ad*, en arrière; à reculons; à la renverse; à rebours. ~**ness**, *n*, tardiveté; répugnance, *f*.

backwash, *n*, remous, *m*.

back water (to), scier, ramer à rebours. **backwater**, *n*, endroit en dehors du courant principal, *m*.

bacon, *n*, lard, *m*.

bacteria, *n.pl*, bactéries, *f.pl*.

bad, *a*, mauvais; mal, malade; grave; fort; irrégulier; véreux. *to go* ~ (*meat, &c*), s'avarier. ~ *form*, mauvais ton, *m*. ~ *language*, gros mots, *m.pl*. ~ *lot*, ~ *boy*, mauvais sujet, *m*. ~ *time* [*of it*], mauvais quart d'heure, *m*. *in a* ~ *way*, mal-en-point, *f*, malade. ~ *workmanship*, malfaçon, *f*. *too* ~! trop fort! ¶ *n*, mauvais, *m*. *from* ~ *to worse*, de mal en pis. *to the* ~ (*out of pocket*), en perte.

badge, *n*, insigne, *m*, marque; plaque, médaille; *f*; brassard; symbole, *m*; livrée, *f*.

badger, *n*, blaireau, *m*. ¶ *v.t*, harceler, relancer.

badly, *ad*, mal; gravement.

badminton, *n*, badminton, volant au filet, *m*.

badness, *n*, mauvais état, *m*; méchanceté, *f*.

baffle, *v.t*, déjouer, déconcerter, frustrer; défier, échapper à. ~ [*plate*] *n*, chicane, *f*.

bag, *n*, sac; sachet; *m*; bourse; valise, *f*; (*of game*) tableau, *m*. ¶ ~ *snatcher*, voleur à la tire, *m*. ¶ *v.t*, ensacher; empocher; chiper; (*v.i. trousers*) goder. ~**ful**, *n*, sachée, *f*.

bagatelle (*trifle*) *n*, bagatelle, *f*. bagatelle (*game*) *n*. & ~ *board*, billard japonais, *m*.

baggage, *n*, bagage; attirail, *m*.

baggy, *a*, avachi, flottant.

bagpipe[**s**], *n*, cornemuse, *f*.

bail, *n*, caution, *f*, cautionnement, *m*. **bail**[**sman**], *n*, caution, *f*, répondant, e. ¶ *v.t*, cautionner. ~ [*out*] (*boat*) *v.t*, écoper, vider. ~*er*, *n*, écope, épuisette, *f*.

bailiff, *n*, huissier; intendant, régisseur, *m*. ~*'s man*, recors, *m*.

bait, *n*, amorce, *f*, appât; hameçon (*fig.*) *m*. ¶ *v.t*, amorcer, appâter; harceler, pointiller, persécuter.

baize, *n*, bayette, *f*, tapis, drap, *m*. ~ *door*, porte matelassée, *f*.

bake, *v.t*, cuire [au four]; (*v.i.*) cuire. ~*house*, *n*, fournil; *m*; (*Mil.*) manutention, *f*. **baker**, *n*, boulanger, ère. ~**y**, *n*, boulangerie, *f*. **baking**, *n*, cuisson; cuite; boulangerie, *f*. ~ *powder*, poudre à lever, *f*. ~ *tin*, tourtière, *f*.

balance, *n*, balance, *f*; peson; équilibre; solde, reliquat, surplus; *m*; soulte, *f*. ~ *of power* (*Pol.*), équilibre, *m*. ~ *sheet*, bilan, *m*. ~ *sheet & schedules*, inventaire, *m*. ~ *weight*, contrepoids, *m*. ~ *wheel* (*Horol.*), balancier, *m*. ¶ *v.t. & i*, balancer, équilibrer, pondérer; solder. ~*d lever*, bascule, *f*. **balancing**, *n*, balancement, *m*. ~ *pole* (*tight rope*), balancier, *m*.

balcony, *n*, balcon, *m*.

bald, *a*, chauve; nu, pelé; plat, sec, décharné. ~*head*, *n*, chauve, *m*.

balderdash, *n*, galimatias, *m*.

baldness, *n*, calvitie; nudité, *f*.

bale, *n*, balle, *f*, ballot, *m*. ¶ *v.t*, emballer. ~ [*out*] (*boat*), *v.t*, écoper, vider.

baleful, *a*, sinistre, funeste.

balk, *n*, tronc d'arbre équarri, *m*, poutre, *f*. ¶ *v.t*, frustrer.

Balkan, *a*, balkanique. *the* ~ *States*, les États des Balkans, *m.pl. the* ~*s*, les Balkans, *m.pl*.

ball, *n*, balle; bille; boule, *f*; boulet; ballon; (*eye, lightning*) globe, *m*; (*thumb*) éminence; (*signal*) bombe; (*pendulum*) lentille; (*wool, string*) pelote, *f*, peloton; (*Danc.*) bal, *m*. ~ & *socket*, rotule sphérique, *m*. ~ *bearings*, roulement à billes, *m*. ~ *cartridge*, cartouche à balle, *f*. ~ *cock*, robinet à flotteur, *m*. ~ *frame*, boulier, *m*. ~*room*, salle de bal, *f*. ¶ *v.t*, pelotonner.

ballad, n, (poem) ballade; (song) chanson, romance, complainte, f.

ballast, n, (road, Rly) ballast, m; (Build.) blocaille, f; (Naut. Aero.) lest; (fig.) plomb, m. ¶ v.t. lester.

ballet, n, ballet, m. ~ dancer, danseur, euse, figurant, e, ballerine, f. ~ skirt, tutu, m.

balloon, n, ballon; aérostat, m. ~ fabric, toile d'avion, f. ~ed (dress) p.a, ballonné. ~ing, n, aérostation, f. ~ist, n, aérostier, m.

ballot, n, [tour de] scrutin, m. ~ box, urne électorale, f. ~ paper, bulletin de vote, m. ¶ v.i, voter au scrutin. ~ for, (pers.) élire par scrutin; (place) tirer au sort; (precedence) tirer au sort pour.

balm, n, baume, m. ~y, a, embaumé, balsamique.

balsam, n, baume, m; (garden plant) balsamine, f. ~ [tree], baumier, balsamier, m. ~ic, a, balsamique.

Baltic [sea] (the), la [mer] Baltique.

baluster, n, balustre, m. **balustrade,** n, balustrade, f.

bamboo, n, bambou, m.

bamboozle, v.t, enjôler, mettre dedans.

ban, n, ban, m; interdiction, f. ¶ v.t, interdire.

banana, n, banane, f. ~ [plant or tree], bananier, m.

band, n, bande; frette; courroie, f; ruban; (Bookb.) nerf, m; musique, f, orchestre, m, harmonie, f. ~box, carton de modiste, m. ~ brake, frein à ruban, f, à bande, m. ~ saw, scie à ruban, f. ~master, chef de musique, m. ~stand, kiosque à musique, m. ¶ v.t, lier, fretter; (v.i.) se liguer.

bandage, n, bandage, bandeau, m, bande, f. ¶ v.t, bander. **bandeau,** n, bandeau, m.

bandit, n, bandit, m.

bandoleer, n, bandoulière, f.

bandsman, n, musicien, m.

bandy, v.t, ballotter, se renvoyer. ~ words with, faire assaut de paroles avec. ~[-legged], a, bancal.

bane, n, fléau, m. ~ful, a, pernicieux, funeste.

bang, n, battement, m; détonation, f. ¶ i, pan! ¶ v.t. & i, frapper, faire battre; battre, cogner.

bangle, n, bracelet; porte-bonheur, m.

banish, v.t, bannir.

banister, n, balustre, m; (pl.) rampe, f.

bank, n, rive, berge, f, bord; talus; banc, m; (Fin.) banque, caisse, f, crédit, m. ~ holiday, fête légale, f. ~ note, billet de banque, m. ~ paper (writing), papier pelure, m. ~ [pass] book, carnet de banque, c. de compte, m. ~ rate, taux officiel [d'escompte] m. ~ transfer, virement, m. ¶ v.t, terrasser, remblayer; verser à la banque; (v.i.) virer, pencher. ~ on, escompter. ~er, n, banquier, m. ~ing, n, banque, f.

bankrupt, n, banqueroutier, ère; failli, m. to go ~, faire banqueroute; faire faillite. ~cy, n, banqueroute; faillite, f.

banner, n, bannière, f; pavillon, m; oriflamme, f.

banns, n.pl, bans de mariage, m.pl.

banquet, n, banquet, festin, m. ~ing hall, salle des festins, f.

bantam weight (Box.), poids coq, m.

banter, n, badinage, m. ¶ v.t, badiner.

baptism, n, baptême, m. ~al, a, baptismal. ~[e]ry, n, baptistère, m. **baptize,** v.t, baptiser.

bar, n, barre, f, barreau, m, barrette; bille, brique; barrière, f; bar, m; (Mus., vertical line) barre; (commonly but incorrectly, portion between two bar lines) mesure, f; (window) croisillon; (counter) comptoir, m, buvette, f, bar, m. ~ bell, barre à sphères, f. ~ of the statute of limitations, prescription, f. ~ iron, fer en barre, m. ~ shoes, chaussures à barrette(s) f.pl. ¶ v.t, barrer.

barb, n, barbe, f; picot, m. ~[ed] wire, fil de fer barbelé, m, ronce, f.

Barbado[es], n, la Barbade.

barbarian, n. & a, barbare, a. & m. **barbaric, barbarous,** a, barbare. **barbarism,** n, barbarie, f; (Gram.) barbarisme, m. **barbarity,** n, barbarie, f.

Barbary ape, magot, m.

barber, n, barbier, m.

barber[r]y, n, épine-vinette, f.

Barcelona, n, Barcelone, f.

bard, n, (poet) barde; chantre, m. the Bard of Avon, le chantre d'Avon.

bare, a, nu; à nu; chenu; découvert; pelé; simple, seul; (majority) faible. ~back[ed] (Riding), à nu, à poil, à cru. ~back horse, cheval nu, m. ~faced, éhonté, effronté. ~facedly, à visage découvert. ~fist boxing, boxe à poings nus, f. ~foot[ed], nu-pieds, pieds nus, déchaussé. ~ ground, dure, f. ~headed, nu-tête, tête nue. ~ patch (Golf), place dénudée d'herbes, f. ¶ v.t, mettre à nu, dénuder, dépouiller, découvrir, déchausser. ~ly, ad, à peine, juste, tout au plus; ne . . . guère. ~ness, n, nudité, f.

bargain, n, marché, m, négociation, affaire; occasion; emplette, f. into the ~, pardessus le marché. ¶ v.i, marchander. ~er, n, marchandeur, euse.

barge, n, chaland, m, gabare, péniche, f. ~ee, bargee, bargeman, n, batelier, marinier, m.

bark, n, (tree) écorce; (left on felled tree) grume, f; (dog) aboiement, m; (boat) barque, f; (Poet.) nef, f. ¶ v.t, écorcer, décortiquer, peler; (v.i.) aboyer. ~ing, n, (tree) décortication, f; (dog) aboiement, m.

barley, n, orge, f. ~ sugar, sucre d'orge, m. ~ water, eau d'orge, f.

barm, n, levure, f, levain, m.

barn, *n*, grange, *f.* ~ *owl*, effraie, fresaie, *f.* ~*yard*, basse-cour, *f.*

barnacle, *n*, (*Crust.*) bernacle, *f*, cravan, *m*; (*pl.—spectacles*) besicles, *f.pl.*

barometer, *n*, baromètre, *m.* **barometric(al)**, *a*, barométrique.

baron, **ess**, *n*, baron, ne.

barque, *n*, barque, *f.*

barrack, *n. oft. pl*, caserne, *f.* ~ *room*, chambrée (militaire) *f.* ¶ *v.t*, caserner; (*boo*) huer, conspuer.

barrage, *n*, barrage, *m.*

barratry, *n*, baraterie, *f.*

barrel, *n*, baril, fût, *m*, futaille, pièce, *f*, tonneau, *m*, caque, *f*; corps, cylindre, tambour, canon, *m.* ~ *organ*, orgue de Barbarie, *m.* ¶ *v.t*, mettre en baril, entonner, [en]caquer.

barren, *a*, stérile, aride. ~**ness**, *n*, stérilité, aridité, *f.*

barricade, *n*, barricade, *f.* ¶ *v.t*, barricader.

barrier, *n*, barrière, *f*; barrage, *m*; digue, *f.*

barring, *pr*, ôté, sauf, à part, hormis, excepté, à moins de.

barrister [**at law**], *n*, avocat, *m.*

barrow, *n*, brouette; (*coster's*) baladeuse, *f*; (*mound*) tumulus, *m.*

barter, *n*, échange, troc, *m.* ~ *goods*, pacotille, *f.* ¶ *v.t*, échanger, troquer.

barytone, *n. & ~ saxhorn*, baryton, *m.*

basal, *a*, basique.

basalt, *n*, basalte, *m.*

bascule bridge, pont à bascule, *m.*

base, *a*, bas, vil, ignoble. ~ *coin*, fausse monnaie, *f.* ~ *metal*, bas métal, métal vil, *m.* pauvre, *m.* ¶ *n*, base, assiette, *f*, fondement[s] *m.*[*pl.*]; soubassement; culot, *m.* ~ *line* (*Ten.*), ligne de fond, *f.* ¶ *v.t*, asseoir, fonder. ~**less**, *a*, sans fondement. ~**ly**, *ad*, bassement, lâchement. ~**ment**, *n*, soubassement, sous-sol, *m.* ~**ness**, *n*, bassesse, *f.*

bashful, *a*, timide, honteux. ~**ness**, *n*, timidité, fausse honte, mauvaise honte, *f.*

basic, *a*, fondamental, (*Chem., &c*) basique.

basil, *n*, (*Bot.*) basilic, *m*; (*hide*) basane, *f.*

basilica, *n*, basilique, *f.*

basilisk, *n*, basilic, *m.*

basin, *n*, bassin; bol, *m*; cuvette, *f.*

basis, *n*, base, assiette, *f*, fondement[s] *m.*[*pl.*].

bask, *v.i*, se chauffer.

basket, *n*, panier, *m*, corbeille; manne; benne; bourriche, *f.* ~ *ball*, basket-ball; ballon au panier, *m.* ~ *maker*, vannier, *m.* ~ *making*, ~ *work*, vannerie, *f.* ~ *ful*, *n*, panier, *m*, panerée, *f.*

bas-relief, *n*, bas-relief, *m.*

bass, *n*, (*fish*) bar, *m*; (*bast*) tille, *f.* ~ [*voice*, *singer*, *string*, *tuba*], basse, *f.* ~ *clef*, clef de fa, *f.* ~ *drum*, grosse caisse, *f.*

bassinet, *n*, bercelonnette, *f.*

bassoon, *n*, basson, *m.*

bast, *n*, tille, *f.*

bastard, *a*, bâtard. ¶ *n*, bâtard, e. ~*y*, *n*, bâtardise, *f.*

baste, *v.t*, (*Need.*) bâtir, baguer, faufiler; (*meat*) arroser; (*beat*) bâtonner.

bat, *n*, bat, *m*; batte; palette, *f*; (*Zool.*) chauve-souris, *f.*

batch, *n*, fournée, *f*; groupe, *m.*

bate, *v.t*, rabattre.

bath, *n*, bain, *m*; (*tub*) baignoire, *f.* ~ *attendant*, baigneur, euse. B~ *chair*, fauteuil roulant, *m.* ~ *gloves*, gants de toilette, *m.pl*, mains [en tissu] éponge, *f.pl.* ~ *gown*, peignoir de bain, *m.* ~*man*, baigneur, *m.* ~ *mat*, tapis de bain, *m.* ~*room*, salle de bain, *f.* ~ *salts*, sel pour bain, *m.* ~ *sheet*, drap de bain, *m.* ~ *tub*, baquet-baignoire, *m.* ~ *wrap*, sortie de bain, *f.* **bathe**, *n*, baignade, *f.* ¶ *v.t*, baigner; (*v.i.*) baigner, se b.; s'abreuver. **bather**, *n*, baigneur, euse. **bathing**, *n*, bains, *m.pl*; bain, *m.* ~ *box*, cabine de bain, *f.* ~ *cap*, bonnet de bain, *m.* ~ *costume*, ~ *suit*, ~ *dress*, maillot (*ou* costume) de bain, *m.* ~ *drawers*, caleçon de b., *m.* ~ *machine*, cabine de bain [sur roues], *f.* ~ *place*, baignade, *f.* ~ *resort*, station balnéaire, *f.* ~ *slip*, caleçon forme slip, *m.* ~ *tent*, tente de plage, *f.*

bathos, *n*, pathos, *m.*

batman, *n*, ordonnance, *f. or m.*

baton, *n*, bâton; (*relay race*) témoin, *m*; (*bread*) flûte, *f.*

battalion, *n*, bataillon, *m.*

batten, *n*, [latte] volige, *f.* ~ *down* (*Naut.*), condamner. ¶ *v.n*, s'engraisser de.

batter (*Build.*) *n*, fruit, talus, *m.* ¶ *v.t*, battre, bossuer, bosseler, cabosser. ~*ing ram*, *n*, bélier, *m.* ~*y*, *n*, batterie, pile, *f.*

battle, *n*, bataille, *f*, combat, *m.* ~*axe*, hache d'armes, *f.* ~ *cruiser*, croiseur cuirassé de combat, *m.* ~*field*, champ de bataille, *m.* ~*ship*, [navire] cuirassé, *m.* ¶ *v.i.*, lutter; batailler.

battledore, *n*, palette, raquette, *f*, battoir, *m.* ~ *& shuttlecock*, [jeu de] volant, *m.*

battlement, *n*, créneau, *m.* ~*ed*, *a*, crénelé.

bauble, *n*, babiole, *f*, brimborion, *m*; (*fool's*) marotte, *f.*

baulk, *n. & v.t.* Same as **balk**.

Bavaria, *n*, la Bavière. **Bavarian**, *a*, bavarois, *f.* ¶ *n*, Bavarois, e.

bawl, *v.i*, brailler, beugler.

bay, *a*, bai. ¶ *n*, (*horse*) bai, *m*; (*Geog.*) baie, *f*; golfe, *m*; (*Arch.*) travée, *f.* B~ *of Biscay*, golfe de Gascogne, *m.* ~ *rum*, tafia de laurier, *m.* ~ [*tree*], laurier, *m.* ~ *window*, fenêtre en saillie, *f. at ~*, aux abois. ¶ *v.i*, aboyer. ~*ing*, *n*, aboiement, *m.*

bayonet, *n*, baïonnette, *f.*

bazaar, *n*, bazar, *m*; vente de charité, *f.*

B.C. (*before Christ*), av. J.-C.

be, *v.i.ir*, être; exister; avoir; faire; se faire; aller, se trouver, se porter; y avoir. ~ *that as it may*, quoi qu'il en soit. *it is . . . since*, il y a . . . que. *there is (are) some*, il y en a. *there is none left*, il n'y en a plus. *I am leaving*, je vais partir, je pars. *a man to be feared*, un homme à craindre. *not to be confused with . . .*, à ne pas confondre avec . . . *to be off*, s'en aller, filer, se sauver. *be off with you!* allez vous promener!

beach, *n*, plage, grève, *f*, rivage, *m*. ~*comber*, rôdeur de grève, *m*. ~ *fishing*, pêche de plage, *f*. ~ *tent*, tente de plage, *f*. ¶ *v.t. & i*, échouer.

beacon, *n*, balise, *f*; phare, *m*. ¶ *v.t*, baliser.

bead, *n*, perle, *f*; grain, *m*; goutte; (*Arch.*) baguette, *f*. [*glass*] ~*s*, verroterie, *f*. [*string of*] ~*s*, fil de perles, chapelet, *m*.

beadle, *n*, appariteur; bedeau; suisse, *m*.

beak, *n*, bec, *m*. ~*er*, *n*, buire, *f*; vase à filtrations chaudes, *m*.

beam, *n*, (*timber, &c*) poutre; (*plough*) flèche, haie, *f*, timon; (*Mach.*) balancier; (*scale*) fléau, *m*, verge, *f*; (*ship's timber*) bau, *m*; (*ship's breadth*) largeur, *f*, travers; (*ray*) rayon, trait; (*rays*) faisceau, *m*. ~ *compasses*, compas à verge, *m*, on her ~ *ends*, sur le côté, engagé. ¶ *v.i*, rayonner.

bean, *n*, fève, *f*; haricot; (*coffee*) grain, *m*.

bear, *n*, ours, e; (B~, *Astr.*) ourse, *f*; (*pers.*) bourru, dogue, *m*; (*Mach.*) poinçonneuse, *f*; (*Stk Ex.*) baissier, *m*. ~ *account or* ~*s* (*Fin.*), découvert, *m*. ~ *garden* (*fig.*), pétaudière, *f*. ~ *leader*, montreur d'ours, *m*. ~*'s cub*, ourson, *m*. ~*s-ear*, oreille-d'ours, *f*. ~*skin* (*cap*), oursin, ourson, *m*. ¶ *v.t. & i. ir*, porter; supporter, souffrir, tolérer, endurer, compatir; appuyer, peser; produire, rapporter; enfanter; (*to right, left*) prendre, (*to*) tendre. ~*able*, *a*, supportable, tenable.

beard, *n*, barbe; (*Bot.*) barbe, arête, *f*. ~*ed*, *a*, barbu, à barbe, chevelu. ~*less*, *a*, imberbe.

bearer, *n*, porteur, euse; (*Fin.*) porteur, *m*. ~ *cheque, shares*, chèque, actions, au porteur. ~ *of a flag of truce*, parlementaire, *m*. **bearing**, *n*, portée, *f*; rapport, trait; aspect; (*Naut.*) gisement, *m*; (*pl. fig.*) orientation, *f*; (*gait*) port, *m*, mine, tenue, démarche, contenance, *f*, maintien, *m*; conduite, *f*; (*Mech.*, *oft. pl*) coussinet, *m. oft. pl*; palier; dé; roulement; *m*; chape, *f*; (*pl. Her.*) armes, armoiries, *f.pl*. ~ *rein*, fausse rêne, *f*. ~ *surface*, surface portante, s. de portée, *f*.

beast, *n*, bête, *f*; animal; abruti, *m*. ~ *of burden*, bête de somme, *f*. ~*ly*, *a*, bestial; dégoûtant.

beat, *n*, battement; coup; temps, *m*; tournée, ronde; (*Hunt.*) battue, *f*. ¶ *v.t. & i. ir*, battre; taper; assommer, bâtonner, brosser;

fourrer; fouetter; (*Hunt.*) rabattre, traquer; vaincre; l'emporter sur, enchérir sur. ~ *back*, ~ *off*, repousser. ~*en path*, chemin [re]battu, c. frayé, *m*. ~*er*, *n*, batteur, battoir, *m*, batte, *f*; (*Hunt.*) rabatteur, traqueur, *m*.

beatify, *v.t*, béatifier.

beating, *n*, battement, battage, *m*; batterie; brossée; défaite, *f*; (*Hunt.*) rabattage, *m*, traque, *f*. ~ *rain*, pluie battante, *f*.

beau, *n*, beau, élégant, adonis, *m*.

beautiful, *a*, beau; magnifique. ¶ *n*, beau, *m*. **beautify**, *v.t*, embellir. **beauty**, *n*, beauté; belle, *f*. B~ & *the Beast*, la Belle & la Bête, *f*. ~ *parlour*, institut de beauté, *m*. ~ *spot*, site pittoresque, *m*; (*patch on face*) mouche, *f*; (*mole*) grain de beauté, *m*.

beaver, *n*, castor, *m*.

becalmed, *a*, encalminé, pris par le calme.

because, *c*, parce que; car. ~ *of*, à cause de.

beck, *n*, signe, *m*; ordres, *m.pl*. **beckon**, *v.t*, faire signe.

become, *v.i.ir*, devenir. *With p.p, often rendered by pronominal form of verb, as*, *to become accustomed*, s'accoutumer; (*v.t.ir.*) venir à. **becoming**, *a*, convenable; [bien]séant, seyant; assortissant, décent.

bed, *n*, lit, *m*, couche, *f*; coucher, *m*; assise, assiette, fondation, plate-forme, *f*; banc, gisement, gîte; (*oyster*) parc; (*Hort.*) carré, *m*, plate-bande, planche, *f*, parterre, *m*. *to go to* ~, [aller] se coucher. ~ *clothes*, draps & couvertures, *m.pl*. ~*fellow*, camarade de lit, c. de chambrée, *m.f*. ~*head*, chevet, *m*. ~ *jacket*, liseuse, *f*. ~ *pan*, bassin [de garde-robe], b. pour malade, b. de lit, *m*. ~ *plate*, plaque d'assise, *f*, bâti d'assise, *m*. ~ *post*, quenouille, *f*. ~*ridden*, alité, grabataire, *m*. ~*room*, chambre [à coucher] *f*. ~*room slippers*, poulaines, *f.pl*. ~ *settee*, lit de repos, *m*. ~*side*, chevet, *m*. ~ *side carpet*, descente de lit, *f*. *a good* ~*side manner*, une bonne manière professionnelle. ~*side table*, table de chevet, t. de nuit, *f*. ~ *socks*, chaussons, *m.pl*. ~*spread*, couvre-lit, dessus de lit, jeté de l., *m*. ~*stead*, bois de lit; lit, *m*. ~*stone*, meule de dessous, m. gisante, *f*. ~ *time*, l'heure du coucher, *f*. ¶ *v.t*, coucher; asseoir; [faire] précipiter. **bedding**, *n*, coucher, *m*, literie, garniture de lit; stratification, *f*.

bedeck, *v.t*, parer, chamarrer.

bedew, *v.t*, arroser, humecter.

bedizen, *v.t*, attifer, chamarrer.

bedlam, *n*, maison de fous; (*fig.*) pétaudière, *f*.

bedraggle, *v.t*, traîner dans la boue.

bee, *n*, abeille, *f*. ~ *eater*, guêpier, *m*. ~*hive*, ruche, *f*. ~ *keeping*, apiculture, *f*. *a* ~ *in one's bonnet*, un rat dans la tête.

beech [*tree*], *n*, hêtre, *m*. ~ *marten*, fouine, *f*. ~*mast*, faînes, *f.pl*. ~*nut*, faîne, *f*.

beef, *n*, bœuf, *m*. ~ *steak*, bifteck, *m*. ~ *tea*, thé de viande, bouillon de bœuf, *m*.

eer, *n*, bière, *f.* ~ *engine*, pompe à b., *f.*

eet, *n*, bette; betterave, *f.* ~ *sugar*, sucre de betterave, *m.* beetroot, *n*, betterave, *f.*

eetle, *n*, coléoptère, scarabée; escarbot, *m*; (*rammer*) dame, demoiselle, hie, *f*, pilon, *m.* beetling brows, sourcils fournis, *m.pl.* beetling crag, rocher qui surplombe, *m.*

efall, *v.i.ir*, arriver, advenir, survenir.

efit, *v.t*, convenir à. befitting, *a*, convenable.

efore, *ad*, devant; avant; auparavant; en avant; déjà; jusqu'ici; précédent. ¶ *c*, avant que. ¶ *pr*, devant; avant; pardevant; avant [que] de. ~ *you could say Jack Robinson* or *say knife*, crac! ~hand, *ad*, à l'avance, d'a., en a., par a.

efriend, *v.t*, favoriser; secourir.

eg, *v.t. & i*, mendier, quémander, chercher, gueuser; demander; prier; (*Com.*) avoir l'honneur de; (*dog*) faire le beau. ~ *for*, solliciter, quémander. ~ *the question*, faire une pétition de principe.

eget, *v.t.ir*, engendrer; faire naître.

eggar, *n*, mendiant, e; gueux, euse; (*fig.*) diable, *m.* ¶ *v.t*, appauvrir, ruiner. ~ly, *a*, gueux; misérable. ~y, *n*, mendicité, gueuserie, misère, *f. reduced to* ~, réduit à la besace.

egin, *v.t. & i. ir*, commencer; débuter; entamer; amorcer; ouvrir; se mettre. ~ *again*, recommencer. beginner, *n*, commençant, e, débutant, e. beginning, *n*, commencement, début, *m*; amorce; ouverture; origine, *f*; prémices, *f.pl.*

egone, *i*, va-t-en! allez-vous-en!

egonia, *n*, bégonia, *m.*

egrudge, *v.t*, envier.

eguile, *v.t*, tromper; séduire; charmer, amuser.

ehalf of (on), de la part de; à l'acquit de; pour le compte de.

ehave, *v.i. & reflexive*, se comporter, se conduire, vivre. ~ [*properly*]! (to child), tiens-toi bien! behaviour, *n*, conduite, *f*, manières, *f.pl*, tenue, *f*, procédé, *m.*

ehead, *v.t*, décapiter. ~ing, *n*, décapitation, *f.*

ehest, *n*, commandement, ordre, *m.*

ehind, *ad*, derrière, en arrière. ¶ *pr*, derrière, en arrière de. ~hand, *ad*, en arrière, arriéré, en retard.

ehold, *v.t. & i. ir*, voir. ¶ *i*, voyez! ~*en to*, à charge à, redevable à. ~er, *n*, spectateur, trice.

ehoof, *n*, profit, *m.* beho[o]ve, *v.t.imp*, incomber.

eing, *n*, être, *m*; existence, *f. for the time* ~, actuel; actuellement.

elabour, *v.t*, charger de coups, bourrer, rosser, échiner.

elated, *a*, attardé; tardif.

elay, *v.t*, tourner, amarrer.

elch[ing], *n*, rot, *m*; crudité, éructation, *f.* belch, *v.i*, roter; éructer; (*v.t, fig.*) vomir.

---

beldam[e], *n*, vieille sorcière, *f.*

beleaguer, *v.t*, assiéger.

belfry, *n*, beffroi, clocher, *m.*

Belgian, *a*, belge. ¶ *n*, Belge, *m,f.* Belgium, *n*, la Belgique.

belie, *v.t*, démentir.

belief, *n*, croyance, foi; persuasion, *f.* believable, *a*, croyable. believe, *v.t. & i*, croire. *to make* . . . ~, faire [ac]croire à . . . believer, *n*, croyant, e; partisan, *m.*

belittle, *v.t*, décrier, rabaisser.

bell, *n*, cloche; clochette, sonnette, sonnerie, *f*, timbre; (*globular*) grelot, *m.* ~ [*flower*], campanule, clochette, *f.* ~ *glass* & ~ *jar*, cloche, *f.* ~ *hanger*, poseur de sonnettes, *m.* ~-*mouth[ed]*, évasé. ~-*push*, bouton de sonnette, *m.* ~ *ringer*, sonneur, carillonneur, *m.* ~ *tent*, tente conique, *f.* ~ *tower*, campanile, *m.* ~ *turret*, clocheton, *m.* ~-*wether*, sonnailler, *m.* ¶ (*of deer*) *v.i*, bramer, raire, réer.

belladonna, *n*, belladone, *f.*

belle, *n*, beauté, reine, *f.*

bellicose, *a*, belliqueux. belligerent, *a. & n* belligérant, e.

bellow, *v.i*, beugler, mugir.

bellows, *n.pl*, soufflet, *m*; soufflerie, *f.*

belly, *n*, ventre, *m*, panse, *f*; bombement, *m.* ~-*band*, sous-ventrière; sangle, *f.* ¶ *v.i*, faire [le] ventre, bomber.

belong, *v.i*, appartenir, dépendre, être. ~ings, *n.pl*, effets, *m.pl.*

beloved, *a. & n*, bien-aimé, e, chéri, e.

below, *ad*, en bas; au-dessous; dessous; ci-dessous; ci-après; là-bas; en contrebas. ¶ *pr*, sous; au-dessous de; en aval de.

belt, *n*, ceinture, *f*; ceinturon, *m*; courroie; bande; zone, *f.* ~ *drive*, ceindre. ~ing, *n*, courroies [de transmission] *f.pl.*

belvedere, *n*, belvédère, *m.*

bemoan, *v.t*, déplorer; pleurer.

bench, *n*, banc, *m*; banquette, *f*; établi; siège, *m*; cour; magistrature assise, *f*, tribunal, *m.* ~ *drill*, foreuse pour établi, *f.* ~ *mark*, [point de] repère, *m.*

bend, *n*, coude, *m*; courbe, courbure, *f*; pli, *m*; inflexion, *f*; tournant, virage; (*knot*) nœud, *m.* ~ *of the arm*, saignée, *f.* ~ *of the knee*, jarret, *m.* ¶ *v.t. & i. ir*, courber, se c., couder; bander, tendre; cintrer; fléchir, plier, ployer; fausser, se f., gauchir. *on* ~*ed knees*, à genoux.

beneath, *ad*, dessous; par-dessous; en bas. ¶ *pr*, au-dessous de, sous.

benediction, *n*, bénédiction, *f.*

benefaction, *n*, bienfait, *m.* benefactor, tress, *n*, bienfaiteur, trice.

benefice, *n*, bénéfice, *m.*

beneficence, *n*, bienfaisance, *f.* beneficent, *a*, bienfaisant.

beneficial, *a*, avantageux, profitable, salutaire. beneficiary, *n*, bénéficiaire, *m,f.*

benefit, *n*, bénéfice, bienfait, avantage, fruit, profit; secours, *m*; (*Theat.*) représentation à bénéfice, *f.* ~ *society*, société de secours mutuels, *f.* ¶ *v.t*, faire du bien à, avantager; (*v.i.*) profiter, bénéficier.

benevolence, *n*, bienfaisance, *f*; patronage, *m.* **benevolent**, *a*, bienfaisant.

Bengal, *n*, le Bengale. ~ *light*, feu de bengale, *m*, flamme de b., *f.* **Bengali**, -**lee**, *a*, bengali, *inv.* ¶ *n*, (*pers.*) Bengali, (*bird*) bengali, *m*.

benighted, *a*, surpris par la nuit; plongé dans les ténèbres.

benign, **benignant**, *a*, bénin. **benignly**, **benignantly**, *ad*, bénignement.

benjamin, *n*, benjoin, *m*.

bent, *a*, courbé, coudé; faussé, gauchi. ~ *lever*, levier coudé, *m*. ~ *wood furniture*, meubles en bois courbé, *m.pl.* ¶ *n*, penchant, *m*, pente, *f*, biais, génie, attrait, *m*. ¶ *to be* ~ *on*, s'acharner à, se buter à, s'acharner à.

benumb, *v.t*, engourdir, morfondre.

benzine, **benzoline**, *n*, benzine, *f*.

benzoin, *n*, benjoin, *m*.

benzol[e], **benzene**, *n*, benzol, *m*.

bequeath, *v.t*, léguer. **bequest**, *n*, legs, *m*.

berber[r]y, *n*, épine-vinette, *f*.

bereave, *v.t.ir*, priver; enlever, ravir. ~**ment**, *n*, deuil, *m*.

beret, *n*, béret [basque] *m*.

bergamot, *n*, (*orange, pear*) bergamote, *f*; (*pear*) mouille-bouche, *f*. ~ *oil*, essence de bergamote, *f*. ~ [*tree*] (orange), bergamotier, *m*.

Bermudas (the), les Bermudes, *f.pl.*

berry, *n*, baie, *f*; (*coffee*) grain, *m*.

berth, *n*, poste de mouillage, mouillage, emplacement, poste, *m*, place; couchette, *f*.

beryl, *n*, béryl, *m*.

beseech, *v.t.ir*, supplier; adjurer, implorer.

beset, *v.t.ir*, entourer, assiéger. *besetting sin*, péché d'habitude, *m*.

beside, *pr*, à côté de; auprès de; hors de; excepté. **besides**, *ad. & pr*, d'ailleurs, du reste, de plus, d'autre part, en outre, puis.

besiege, *v.t*, assiéger. **besieger**, *n*, assiégeant, *m*.

besmear, *v.t*, barbouiller.

besmirch, *v.t*, souiller.

besom, *n*, balai [de bouleau] *m*.

besotted, *a*, abruti.

bespangle, *v.t*, pailleter; parsemer.

bespatter, *v.t*, éclabousser, crotter.

bespeak, *v.t.ir*, retenir; commander; stipuler. **bespoke**, *p.a*, (*suit, &c*) sur commande, sur mesure; (*tailor, bootmaker*) sur mesure.

besprinkle, *v.t*, arroser.

best, *a*, [le] meilleur; le mieux; le plus beau ou grand ou fort. ~ *man* (wedding), garçon d'honneur, *m*. ~ *quality*, premier choix, *m*. ~ *seller*, livre à succès, l. à grand tirage, *m*. ¶ *ad*, mieux, le mieux; plus. ¶ *the* ~, le mieux. *the* ~ *of it*, le meilleur de l'affaire; le plus beau de l'histoire; le dessus. *in one's* [*Sunday*] ~,

endimanché. *do the* ~ *you can!* arrangezvous!

bestial†, *a*, bestial.

bestir oneself (to), se remuer, s'empresser.

bestow, *v.t*, accorder, gratifier, déférer; impartir, donner.

bestride, *v.t.ir*, enjamber, enfourcher.

bet, *n*, pari, *m*. ¶ *v.t*, parier; gager.

betake oneself (to), *v.reflexive ir*, se livrer, recourir; se rendre.

bethink oneself (to), *v.reflexive ir*, s'aviser.

betide, *v.t*, arriver à. *whate'er* ~, arrive (*ou* advienne) que pourra.

betimes, *ad*, de bonne heure, tôt.

betoken, *v.t*, présager; désigner; dénoter; annoncer.

betray, *v.t*, trahir; tromper; révéler, accuser. ~ *one's trust*, prévariquer. ~**al**, *n*, trahison, *f*. ~**er**, *n*, traître, traîtresse.

betroth, *v.t*, fiancer. ~**al**, *n*, fiançailles, *f.pl.* ~**ed**, *n. & a*, fiancé, e.

better, *a*, meilleur; préférable. *my* ~ *half* (wife), ma [chère] moitié. ~*looking*, mieux. *to be* ~ (health), se porter (*ou* aller) mieux. *it is* ~ *to*, il vaut mieux. ¶ *ad*, mieux. *so much the* ~, tant mieux. ¶ (*pers.*) *n*, supérieur, e. ¶ *v.t*, améliorer. ~**ment**, *n*, amélioration, *f*.

better *or* **bettor**, *n*, parieur, euse. **betting**, *n*, pari, *m*; (*odds*) cote, *f*. ~ *forecast*, rapports probables, *m.pl.* ~ *on the totalizator*, pari mutuel. ~ *system*, martingale, *f*. ~ *with bookmakers*, pari à la cote.

between, *pr*, entre; de; à. ~ *now & then*, d'ici là. ~ *this & . . .*, d'ici à . . . . ~ [*times*], dans l'intervalle. ~**-decks**, *n*, entrepont, *m*.

bevel, *n*, biseau, *m*. ~ [*square*], fausse équerre, sauterelle, *f*. ~ *wheel*, roue d'angle, *f*. ¶ *v.t*, biseauter.

beverage, *n*, breuvage, *m*, boisson, *f*.

bevy, *n*, compagnie; volée; troupe, *f*.

bewail, *v.t*, pleurer, déplorer, se lamenter sur.

beware, *v.i*, se garder, se méfier, se défier prendre garde. ~ *of pickpockets!* méfiezvous des voleurs! ~ *of the trains!* attention au train!

bewilder, *v.t*, égarer, désorienter; ahurir.

bewitch, *v.t*, ensorceler, envoûter, enchanter ~**ing**, *a*, ensorcelant, enchanteur. ~**ingly** *ad*, à ravir.

beyond, *ad*, au-delà, plus loin. ¶ *pr* delà de, par-delà, delà; hors; au-dessus de sans; outre. *the* ~ (*future life*), l'au delà, *m*.

bezel, *n*, chaton, *m*.

bias, *n*, biais, *f*; (*fig.*) penchant, parti pris, *m* partialité, *f*. ¶ *v.t*, prévenir. **bias[s]ed** *p.a*, partial.

bib, *n*, bavoir, *m*, bavette, *f*.

Bible, *n*, Bible, *f*. ~ *Society*, Sociét biblique, *f*. **biblical**, *a*, biblique.

bibliography, *n*, bibliographie, *f*. **biblio phil[e]**, *n*, bibliophile, *m*.

bulous, *a*, absorbant; adonné à la boisson.

ceps, *n*, biceps, *m*.

cker, *v.i*, disputailler, se chamailler.

cycle, *n*, (*safety*) bicyclette, *f*; (*high*) bicycle, *m*. bicyclist, *n*, bicycliste, *m,f*.

d, *n*, (*Stk Ex.*) demande; (*auction*) enchère, mise, *f*. ¶ *v.t. & i. ir*, commander, ordonner; (*adieu*) dire; offrir; enchérir, miser; (*Stk Ex.*) demander. ~ *higher than*, surenchérir sur. bidder, *n*, enchérisseur, *m*.

de one's time (to), attendre son heure, se réserver.

ennial, *a*, biennal, bisannuel.

er, *n*, civière, *f*.

furcation, *n*, bifurcation, *f*.

g, *a*, gros; grand; fort; considérable; haut; (*pregnant*) grosse, enceinte, (*animals*) pleine. ~-*boned*, ossu. ~-*game fish*, poisson de grand sport, *m*. ~-*game fishing*, pêche de grand sport, *f*. ~-*game hunting*, chasse à la grosse bête, *f*. ~-*stores*, grand magasin [de nouveautés] *m*. [*the*] ~ *traders*, le haut commerce.

gamist, *n*, bigame, *m,f*. bigamous, *a*, bigame. bigamy, *n*, bigamie, *f*.

ght, *n*, golfe, enfoncement; (*rope*) double, *m*.

gness, *n*, grosseur; grandeur, *f*.

got, *n. & ~ed, a*, bigot, e. ~ry, *n*, bigoterie, *f*.

gwig, *n*, gros bonnet, *m*.

ke, *n*, vélo, *m*.

lberry, *n*, airelle, myrtille, *f*.

le, *n*, bile, *f*.

lge, *n*, (*ship*) fond de cale; (*cask*) bouge, ventre, *m*. ~ *water*, eau de cale, *f*.

lious, *a*, bilieux.

lk, *v.t*, frustrer; flouer.

ll, *n*, (*bird*) bec, *m*; (*notice, &c*) affiche, pancarte, *f*, placard; écriteau; prospectus; programme; (*parliament*) projet de loi, *m*; (*account*) note, *f*, mémoire, *m*; addition; facture, *f*; (*Fin.*) effet, billet, mandat, *m*, échéance, traite, remise, lettre, valeur, *f*; (*pl.*) portefeuille[-effets], papier, *m*. ~ *file*, pique-notes, *m*. ~ *head[ing]*, en-tête de facture, *m*. ~*hook*, croissant, *m*, serpe, serpette, *f*. ~ [*of costs*], mémoire, *m*. ~ *of exchange*, effet de commerce, *m*; lettre de change, traite, *f*. ~ *of fare*, carte de restaurant; carte du jour, *f*, menu, *m*. ~ *of health*, patente de santé, *f*. ~ *of lading*, connaissement, *m*. ~ *payable, receivable*, effet à payer, à recevoir, *m*. ~*poster*, ~*sticker*, afficheur, colleur, *m*. ¶ *v.t*, afficher, placarder; facturer; (*v.i.*) se becqueter. ~ *& coo*, faire des mamours, roucouler.

llet, *n*, (*Mil.*) billet de logement; (*pl.*) cantonnement, *m*; (*log*) bûche, *f*, rondin, *m*. ¶ *v.t*, cantonner; (*on householder*) loger.

illiard: ~ *ball*, bille [de billard] *f*. ~ *room*, salle de billard, *f*, billard, *m*. ~ *table*,

table de billard, *f*, billard, *m*. ~s, *n.pl*, billard, *m*.

billingsgate, *n*, langage de poissarde, l. des halles, *m*.

billion (*a million millions*) *n*, trillion, *m*.

billow, *n*, vague, lame, onde, *f*, flot, *m*. ¶ *v.i*, ondoyer. ~y, *a*, houleux.

billy goat, bouc, *m*.

bimonthly, *a*, (*in alternate months*) bimestriel; (*½ monthly*) semi-mensuel.

bin, *n*, huche, *f*; tonneau, tonnelet, *m*; trémie, case, *f*, casier, caisson, coffre; porte-bouteilles, *m*.

bind, *v.t.ir*, lier, attacher, ligoter; (*sheaf*) [en]gerber; bander; assujettir; serrer; enchaîner; astreindre; border; engager, obliger; (*books*) relier; (*paper covers*) brocher; (*with metal*) ferrer; (*Med.*) resserrer, constiper. *I'll be bound*, j'en réponds. ~er, *n*, (*sheaf, pers.*) lieur, *m*; (*Mach.*) lieuse, *f*; (*book*) relieur, euse; brocheur, euse; (*tie*) lien, *m*, attache, *f*; (*papers*) biblorhapte, *m*. ~ing, *a*, obligatoire. ¶ *n*, reliure, *f*; brochage, *m*, brochure; bordure, *f*, galon, *m*, tresse, *f*.

bindweed, *n*, liseron, liset, *m*.

bine, *n*, sarment, *m*.

binnacle, *n*, habitacle, *m*.

binocular, *n*, jumelle, *f*. ~ *camera*, photo-jumelle, *f*.

biographer, *n*, biographe, *m*. biography, *n*, biographie, *f*.

biologist, *n*, biologiste, biologue, *m*. biology, *n*, biologie, *f*.

biped, *n*, bipède, *m*. ~[al], *a*, bipède.

biplane, *n*, biplan, *m*.

birch, *n*, (*tree*) bouleau, *m*; (*rod*) verges, *f.pl*. ~-*bark* [*canoe*], pirogue en écorce, *f*. ~ *broom*, balai de bouleau, *m*. ¶ *v.t*, frapper de verges. ~ing, *n*, (des) coups de verges, *m.pl*.

bird, *n*, oiseau, (*small*) oiselet, *m*. ~ *call*, appeau, pipeau, *m*. ~ *catcher*, oiseleur, *m*. ~ *catching*, pipée, *f*. ~ *fancier*, oiselier, *m*. ~ *fancying*, oisellerie, *f*. ~*lime*, *m*, glu, *f*; (*v.t.*) engluer. ~ *of ill omen*, oiseau de mauvais augure, porte-malheur, *m*. ~ *of paradise*, oiseau de paradis, *m*. ~-*seed*, graine pour les oiseaux, *f*. ~'*s-eye maple*, érable madré, *m*. ~'*s-eye view*, vue cavalière, vue à vol d'oiseau, *f*. ~ *shot*, menu plomb, *m*, dragée, *f*. ~'*s-nester*, dénicheur, *m*.

birth, *n*, naissance; extraction, *f*; enfantement, *m*; (*childbed*) couches, *f.pl*. ~ *certificate*, extrait de naissance, *m*. ~ *control*, limitation des naissances, *f*. ~*day*, jour de naissance, anniversaire de ma (de sa, &c) naissance, *m*, fête, *f*. ~*mark*, tache de naissance, envie, *f*; nævus, *m*. ~*place*, lieu de naissance, *m*, [petite] patrie, *f*. ~ *rate*, natalité, *f*; pourcentage des naissances, *m*. ~*right*, droit d'aînesse; droit du sang, *m*.

bis, *ad*, bis.
biscuit, *n*, biscuit, *m*. ~ *barrel*, seau à biscuits, *m*. ~[*ware*], biscuit, *m*.
bisect, *v.t*, diviser en deux parties égales.
bisection, *n*, bissection, *f*.
bishop, *n*, évêque, *m*; (*Chess*) fou, *m*. ~'s house & bishopric, *n*, évêché, *m*.
bismuth, *n*, bismuth, *m*.
bison, *n*, bison, *m*.
bit, *n*, morceau, fragment, *m*, pièce, miette, *f*; bout, brin; peu; (*bridle*) mors, frein; (*borer*) foret, *m*, mèche, *f*; (*key*) panneton; (*iron of plane*, &c) fer, *m*. ~ *of stuff* (old or new), chiffon, *m*. ~ *stock*, vilebrequin, *m*.
bitch, *n*, chienne, *f*. ~ *fox*, renarde, *f*. ~ *wolf*, louve, *f*.
bite, *n*, morsure, *f*, coup de dents; mordant, *m*; (*sting*) piqûre; (*to eat*) bouchée; (*place bitten by worm, mouse*) mangeure, *f*. *I have a* ~! (*Fish*.), ça mord! ¶ *v.t. & i. ir*, mordre; piquer. biting, *a*, mordant, piquant; (*cold*) cuisant.
bitter, *a*, amer; aigre; cuisant; cruel; acharné. ~ *pill* (*fig*.), couleuvre, *f*. ~*sweet*, *a*, aigre-doux; (*n. Bot*.) douce-amère, *f*. ~ly, *ad*, amèrement; aigrement; (*cold*) extrêmement. *cry* ~, pleurer à chaudes larmes. ~ness, *n*, amertume, *f*, amer, fiel, *m*. ~s, *n*, amers, *m.pl*.
bittern, *n*, butor, *m*.
bitumen, *n*, bitume, *m*. bituminous, *a*, bitumineux.
bivalve, *a. & n*, bivalve, *a. & m*.
bivouac, *n*, bivouac, *m*. ¶ *v.i*, bivouaquer.
blab, *v.t*, divulguer; (*v.i.*) bavarder, jaser.
black, *a*, noir. ~ & *blue*, meurtri, noir. [*down*] *in* ~ & *white*, noir sur blanc. ~ *ball* (*Voting*), boule noire, *f*. ~*beetle*, blatte, *f*, cafard, *m*. ~*berry*, mûre sauvage, m. de ronce, *f*. ~*berry bush*, ronce, *f*. ~*bird*, merle, m, (hen) merlette, *f*. ~*board*, tableau [noir] *m*. ~*bordered* envelope, enveloppe deuil, *f*. ~*cap*, fauvette à tête noire, *f*. ~*cock*, coq de bruyère, *m*. ~ *currant*(s) & ~ *currant bush* & ~ *currant cordial*, cassis, *m*. ~ *eye*, œil poché, pochon, *m*. *to give someone a* ~ *eye*, pocher l'œil à quelqu'un. *B*~ *Forest*, Forêt-Noire, *f*. ~ *frost*, gelée noire, g. à glace, *f*. ~*guard*, canaille, *f*, goujat, *m*. ~*head*, point noir, *m*, tanne, *f*. ~ *lead*, mine de plomb, plombagine, *f*, graphite, *m*. ~*leg*, renard, *m*. ~ *lines* (under paper), transparent, *m*. ~ *list*, *n*, index, *m*; (*v.t.*) mettre à l'i. ~ *magic*, ~ *art*, magie noire, *f*. ~*mail*, *n*, chantage, *m*; (*v.t.*) faire chanter. ~*mailer*, maître chanteur, *m*. ~ *mark* (bruise), noir, *m*. ~ *pudding*, boudin, *m*. *B*~ *sea*, mer Noire, *f*. ~ *sheep* (*fig*.), brebis galeuse, *f*. ~*smith*, forgeron, *m*. ~*smith's shop*, atelier de forgeron, *m*. ~*thorn*, épine noire, *f*, prunellier, *m*.

¶ *n*, (*colour, man*) noir, *m*; (*ball*—*Gaming*) noire, *f*. ¶ *v.t*, noircir; charbonner; mâchurer; (*boots*) cirer.
blackamoor, *n*, moricaud, e; noir, e.
blacken, *v.t*, noircir. blacking, *n*, noircissement; (*boots*) cirage; cirage pour chaussures, *m*. ~ *brush*, brosse à cirer, b. à étendre, *f*. blackish, *a*, noirâtre. blackness, *n*, noirceur, *f*.
bladder, *n*, vessie; (*Bot*.) vésicule, *f*.
blade, *n*, (*grass*) brin, m; (*knife*, &c) lame, feuille; (*vane*) aile, aube, palette; (*oar*, &c) pale, *f*, plat, *m*.
blame, *n*, blâme, reproche, *m*, faute, *f*. ¶ *v.t*, blâmer, reprocher, accuser, s'en prendre à. ~*less*, *a*, innocent. ~*worthy*, *a*, digne de blâme.
blanch, *v.t. & i*, blanchir, faire pâlir, pâlir.
bland, *a*, doux, suave, douceureux, mielleux. ~*ishment*, *n*, flatterie, chatterie, *f*.
blank, *a*, blanc, vierge. ~ *cartridge*, cartouche à blanc. ~ *signature*, blancseing, *m*. ~ *verse*, vers blancs, *m.p[l]*. ¶ *n*, blanc, *m*; lacune, *f*, trou, m; (*lottery*) billet perdant; (*for coin*) flan, *m*.
blanket, *n*, couverture [en laine], couverte, *f*. ~ *stitch* (*Emb*.), point de languette, p. d[e] feston, *m*.
blare, *n*, flonflon, *m*. ¶ *v.i*, retentir.
blarney, *n*, blague, *f*.
blaspheme, *v.i. & t*, blasphémer, jure[r]. blasphemer, *n*, blasphémateur, trice. blas[phemous], *a*, blasphématoire. blasphem[y], *n*, blasphème, *m*.
blast, *n*, vent, coup de vent, courant d'ai[r] souffle, *m*, chasse d'air, *f*; coup; coup [de mine], pétard, *m*, mine, *f*. ~ *furnac[e]* haut fourneau, *m*. ~ *hole*, fourneau [de mine] *m*. ¶ *v.t*, faire sauter, pétard[er] foudroyer; (*blight*) brouir, flétrir. ~*in[g]* *n*, travail aux explosifs (ou à la poudre), [?] ~ *powder*, poudre de mine, *f*.
blatant, *a*, bruyant, criard.
blaze, *n*, flambée, *f*; éclat, *m*. *in a* ~, [en] flammes. ¶ *v.i*, flamber; flamboyer; (*v[.] tree*) griffer. ~ *a trail*, frayer un chemi[n] ~ *abroad*, claironner. ~ *away*, tiraill[er] blazing, *a*, flambant, flamboyant, arden[t] d'enfer; (*lie*, &c) éclatant.
blazon, *v.t*, blasonner, armorier; proclame[r] ~*ry*, *n*, blason, *m*.
bleach, *v.t*, blanchir. ~*er*, *n*, blanchisse[r] euse, buandier, ère. ~*ery*, *n*, blanchisser[ie] *f*. ~*ing*, *n*, blanchiment, *m*.
bleak, *a*, morne, triste.
blear-eyed, *a*, chassieux.
bleat, *v.i*, bêler; (*goat & fig*.) chevrote[r] bleat[ing], *n*, bêlement, *m*.
bleed, *v.t. & i. ir*, saigner; pleurer. ~*ing*, saignement, *m*; saignée, *f*.
blemish, *n*, tache, tare, défectuosité, *f*[,] défaut, *m*. ¶ *v.t*, tacher; ternir.
blend, *n*, assortiment, *m*. ¶ *v.t.ir*, assort[ir] fondre; confondre; incorporer; (*win[e]*

mélanger, couper; (*v.i.ir.*) [s']assortir, se confondre, s'apparenter. ~ing (*wines*) n, mélange, coupage, m.

ess, *v.t*, bénir; (*bell, &c*) baptiser; favoriser. blessed, blest, a, béni; heureux; bienheureux. *the Blessed Virgin* [*Mary*], la Sainte Vierge. *to be ~ with*, avoir le bonheur d'avoir, de posséder; jouir de. blessedness, n, béatitude; félicité, f. blessing, n, bénédiction, f; bonheur; (*grace*) bénédicité, m.

ight, n, brouissure, nielle, rouille, f. ¶ v.t, brouir, nieller, rouiller; flétrir.

ind, a, aveugle; borgne. ~ *alley*, impasse, f, cul-de-sac, m. ~ *blocking* (*Bookb.*), dorure à froid, d. sans couleurs, f. ~ *man, woman*, aveugle, m,f; *the ~*, les aveugles, m.pl. ~*man's buff*, colin-maillard, m. ~ *tooling* (*Bookb.*), fers à froid, m.pl. ~*worm*, orvet, m. ¶ n, store, m; jalousie; (*shop*) banne, f; (*fig.*) voile, masque, faux-semblant, m. ¶ v.t, aveugler. ~*fold*, v.t, bander [les yeux à, de]. ~*ly*, ad, aveuglément, à l'aveuglette. ~*ness*, n, cécité, f; (*fig.*) aveuglement, m.

ink, n, clign[ot]ement, m. ¶ v.i, clign[ot]er, ciller; vaciller, papilloter; (*v.t.*) se cacher. ~*er*, n, œillère, f.

iss, n, béatitude, félicité, f. ~*ful†*, a, heureux; bienheureux; béat.

ister, n, ampoule, bulle, cloque, f; (*plaster*) vésicatoire, m. ¶ v.t, faire venir des ampoules à. *I ~ easily*, il me vient facilement des ampoules.

ithe, a, gai, joyeux.

izzard, n, tourmente de neige, f.

oat, *v.t*, bouffir. bloater, *n.* or bloated herring, hareng bouffi, m.

ock, n, bloc, massif, m; motte, f; paquet, m; partie, tranche, f, ensemble; (*chopping*) billot, m; (*shape*) forme, poupée, f; (*houses*) pâté, îlot, m; (*pulley*) moufle, poulie, f; (*Typ.*) cliché; (*stoppage*) embarras, encombrement, embouteillage, m. ~ *calendar*, bloc journalier, m, éphéméride, f. ~ *letters* (*e.g.*, *child's writing*) letters moulées, f.pl. *in ~ letters* (as on coupon), en caractères d'imprimerie. ~ *making* (*Typ.*), clichage, m. ~ *of flats*, immeuble à appartements, m. ~ *tin*, étain en saumon, m. ~ *writing*, la lettre moulée. ¶ v.t, obstruer, encombrer; emboutiller; bloquer; (*Bookb.*) dorer. ~ *up* (*door*), condamner.

ockade, n, blocus, m. ¶ v.t, bloquer.

ocker (*Bookb.*) n, doreur, euse.

ockhead, n, bûche, f, imbécile, m,f.

ockhouse, n, blockhaus, m.

ocking (*Bookb.*) n, dorure, f.

ond, *as applied to a woman* blonde, a, blond (blonde, f.). ¶ n, (*colour*) blond, m; (*pers.*) blond, e.

ood, n, sang, m; race, f; (*dandy*) petit-maître, élégant, m. ~ *heat*, température du sang, f. ~*hound*, limier, m. ~ *letting*, saignée, f. ~ *orange*, orange sanguine, f. ~ *poisoning*, empoisonnement du sang, m. ~ *pressure*, tension artérielle, f. ~ *red*, rouge sang, m. ~ *relationship*, consanguinité, f. ~*shed*, effusion de sang, f; carnage, m. ~*shot*, injecté [de sang], éraillé. ~*stone*, jaspe sanguin, héliotrope, m, sanguine, f. ~*sucker*, sangsue, f. ~ *test*, prise de sang, f, prélèvement de s., m. ~*thirsty*, altéré de sang, sanguinaire. ~ *vessel*, vaisseau sanguin, m. ~*less*, a, exsangue; non sanglant. ~*y*, a, ensanglanté, sanglant, en sang; sanguinaire.

bloom, n, fleur; fraîcheur, f. ¶ v.i, fleurir. ~*ing*, a, fleurissant; (*fig.*) florissant. ¶ n, floraison, f.

blossom, n, fleur, f. ¶ v.i, fleurir. ~*ing*, n, floraison, f.

blot, n, pâté, m, tache, f. ¶ v.t, faire un pâté sur, tacher; (*paper with useless writing*) noircir; (*with blotting paper*) éponger. ~ *out*, effacer.

blotch, n, pustule; tache, f.

blotting: ~ *case*, ~ *pad*, blotter, n, buvard, sous-main, m. ~ *paper*, papier buvard, papier brouillard, m.

blouse, n, blouse, f. ~ *front*, guimpe, f.

blow, n, coup, m; bourrade; atteinte, f; (*pl.*) voies de fait, f.pl; échec, m. ~*fly*, mouche à viande, f. ~ *gun*, ~ *pipe*, ~ *tube*, (*dart tube*), sarbacane, f. ~ [*hole*], soufflure, f, bouillon, m. ~*pipe*, chalumeau, m. ¶ v.t.ir, souffler; (*wind instrument*) souffler dans, emboucher; (*to puff, to wind*) essouffler; (*v.i.ir.*) souffler; venter; (*flower*) s'épanouir; (*fuse*) fondre, jouer. ~ *a horn*, corner. ~ *one's brains out*, se brûler la cervelle. ~ *one's nose*, se moucher. ~ *out*, souffler. ~ *up*, v.t, souffler; faire sauter, pétarder; (*v.i.*) sauter. ~*er*, n. souffleur, m.

blubber, n, graisse, f, lard, m. ¶ v.i, sangloter.

bludgeon, n, assommoir, gourdin, m, trique, massue, f.

blue, a, bleu. Bluebeard, Barbe-Bleue, m. ~*bell*, jacinthe des bois, f. ~*bottle*, mouche bleue, f. ~ *devils*, papillons noirs, m.pl. ~-*eyed*, aux yeux bleus. ~*jacket*, marin de l'État, m. ~ *mark* (*bruise*), bleu, m. ~-*mouldy* (*cheese*), persillé. ~*pencil*, v.t, marquer au crayon bleu; sabrer, barrer. B~ *Peter*, pavillon de partance, m. ~ *pill*, pilule mercurielle, f. ~ *print*, bleu, m. ~*stocking*, bas-bleu, m. ~ *tit*, mésange bleue, f. ¶ n, bleu; (*pl.*) spleen, m. ¶ v.t, bleuir.

bluff, a, brusque; franc; escarpé. ¶ n, cap à pic; trompe-l'œil, m. ~*er*, n, faiseur, m.

bluish, a, bleuâtre.

blunder, *n*, bévue, bourde, ignorance, f, impair, m. ¶ v.i faire des bévues, gaffer.

blunt, a, émoussé; contondant; brusque, cru. ¶ v.t, émousser, épointer. ~ly, ad, brusquement, crûment, rondement. ~ness, n, état émoussé; sans-façon, m; brusquerie, f.

blur, n, tache, f; embrouillement, m. ¶ v.t, tacher, barbouiller; [em]brouiller.

blurb, n, jus, m; bande, f.

blurred, p.a, trouble. **blurry**, a, flou.

blurt out, v.t, lâcher, laisser échapper.

blush, n, rougeur; fleur, f. at the first ~, à vue de nez. ¶ v.i, rougir. ~ing, p.a, rougissant, rouge.

bluster, n, fracas, m; fanfaronnade, rodomontade, f. ¶ v.i, tempêter; maugréer. ~er, n, fanfaron, m.

boa (wrap) n, boa, m. ~ constrictor, boa constrictor, m.

boar, n, verrat; (wild) sanglier; (young wild) marcassin, m. ~ hound, vautre, m. ~ hunting, chasse au sanglier, f. ~'s head, hure de sanglier, f. ~ spear, épieu, m.

board, n, planche, f, ais; plat; tableau; tablier; (notice) écriteau, m, enseigne, f; (Naut.) bord, m; bordée, f. in ~s (book), cartonné. on ~, à bord. ~ & lodging, ~-residence, le vivre & le couvert, la table (ou la nourriture) & le logement; pension, f. ~ [of directors], conseil [d'administration] m, administration, f. ~ of examiners, jury d'examen, m. B~ of Trade (England), Ministère du Commerce (France) m. ¶ v.t, planchéier; (ship) monter sur, aborder; (train, car) monter dans; (feed) nourrir. ~ up (window), condamner. ~er, n, pensionnaire; (élève) interne, m,f. ~ing, n, planchéiage, m. ~ house, pension, f. ~-in, internat, m. ~ school, pensionnat, internat, m, pension, f.

boast, n, vanterie; gloire, f. ¶ v.t, vanter; (v.i.) se vanter. ~er, n, vantard e, fanfaron, ne. ~ful, a, vantard e.

boat, n, bateau, canot, m, embarcation, barque, f; navire, bâtiment, vaisseau, m. ~ deck, pont des embarcations, m. ~ fishing, pêche en bateau, f. ~ hook, gaffe [pour l'amarrage des bateaux], f, croc [de batelier] m. ~house, garage [des bateaux] m. ~load, batelée, f. ~man, marin, canotier, m. ~ train, train de paquebot, m. ¶ v.i, canoter. ~ing, n, canotage, m. **boatswain**, n, maître d'[équipage] m.

bob, n, secousse, f; révérence, f; poire, f; plomb; poids, m. ¶ v.i, balloter, branler. bob[bed hair], coiffure à la Ninon, coiffure à la Jeanne d'Arc, f.

bobbin, n, bobine, canette, f.

bobsleigh, n, bobsleigh, m.

bobtail, n, queue écourtée, f.

bode, v.t, présager.

bodice, n, corps, corsage, m. **bodily**, a, corporel; physique; réel; (fear) pour sa personne. ¶ ad, corporellement; en masse.

bodkin, n, passe-lacet, m, aiguille à passer, f.

body, n, corps, m; carcasse, f; vaisseau massif, m; masse, f; gros, m; (water, &) nappe; (vehicle) caisse, f. ~ & ~wo (motor), carrosserie, f. ~ belt, gaine, ~ builder (motor), carrossier, m. ~ co porate, personne morale, p. juridique, civile, f.

bog, n, marais, marécage, m, fondrière, ¶ v.t, embourber.

bogey (Golf) n, la normale.

bog[ey] [man], n, croque-mitaine, m.

boggle, v.i, reculer, hésiter.

boggy, a, marécageux, tourbeux.

bogie (Rly) n, bogie, f.

bogus, a, faux, simulé; véreux.

Bohemia (fig.) n, la bohème. **Bohemian** (fi n. & a, bohème, m,f. & a.

boil (Path.) n, furoncle, clou, m.

boil, v.t, faire bouillir; cuire [à l'eau]; (v. bouillir; bouillonner. ~ down, condense réduire. ~ed, p.a: ~ beef, bœuf boui m. ~ egg, œuf à la coque, m. ~ pot toes, pommes de terre à l'eau, p—s de t nature, p—s de t. vapeur, f.pl. ~er, (steam) chaudière, f; (kitchener) bain marie, m; (pot) marmite, f. ~ make chaudronnier, m. ~ making & ~ work [grosse] chaudronnerie, f. ~ plate, t de chaudière, f. ~ room, chambre chauffe, chaufferie, f. ~ing, n, ébullitio f; bouillonnement, m. ~ point, poi d'ébullition, m. (212° F. or 100° C.).

boisterous†, a, bruyant, turbulent.

bold, a, hardi, osé, audacieux, téméraire assuré; net. ~-faced (type), gras. d played in ~ type, en vedette. ~ ad, hardiment, audacieusement; haut ment, franchement. ~ness, n, hardiess audace; (of touch) facilité, f.

Bolivia, n, la Bolivie. **Bolivian**, a, bolivie ¶ n, Bolivien, ne.

bollard, n, canon d'amarrage, poteau d'a.,

Bologna, n, Bologne, f.

bolster, n, traversin, chevet; coussin, m. up, v.t, étayer.

bolt, n, boulon, m, cheville, f; (door) verro (lock) pêne, m; (thunder) foudre; (fig. fugue, f. ¶ v.t, boulonner; cheviller; ve rouiller; (sift) bluter; (food) expédi gober; (v.i.) (horse) s'emporter, s'emball (pers.) prendre la poudre d'escampette.

bolt upright, tout droit.

bolus, n, bol, m.

bomb, n, bombe, f. ~shell (fig.), bombe, ~ thrower, lance-bombe, m. ¶ v.t, (Aer bombarder; (Mil.) lancer des bombes ~ed out, sinistré des bombardemen **bombard**, v.t, bombarder, canonner; fusill (fig.). ~ier, n, brigadier, m. ~ment, **bombast**, n, emphase, f, phébus. m. ~ic, emphatique, ampoulé, boursouflé, plu **bomber**, n, (Aero.) avion de bombardeme (pers.) grenadier, m.

bona fide, a. & ad, de bonne foi; sérieux.

bond, n, lien, m, attache, f; nœud, m; liaison; chaîne, f; agglutinant; (*Fin.*) bon, m; obligation, f; titre, m, valeur, f; (*Law*) acte, contrat; cautionnement; compromis, m; soumission, f. **bond[ed warehouse]**, entrepôt [légal *ou* de douane] m. *in bond*[*ed warehouse*], en (*ou* à l')entrepôt, en E. **bond note**, acquit-à-caution, m. **bond**, *v.t*, entreposer; (*masonry*) liaisonner. **bondage**, n, captivité, servitude, f, esclavage, m. **bonded storekeeper**, entreposeur, m. **bonder**, n, entrepositaire, m,f. **bondholder**, n, obligataire, m,f.

bone, n, os, m; (*fish*) arête, f; (*pl, dead*) ossements, m.pl; (*castanets*) cliquettes, f.pl. ~ **of contention**, pomme de discorde, f. ~**setter**, rebouteur, euse. ¶ *v.t*, désosser; ôter les arêtes de; (*steal*) chiper.

bonfire, n, feu de joie, m.

bonnet, n, chapeau; (*cover*) capot, m, capote, f.

bonny, a, joli; bien portant; gai.

bonus, n, gratification, prime, indemnité, f. ~ **shares**, actions gratuites, f.pl.

bony, a, osseux; (*big-boned*) ossu. ~ **palate**, palais dur, m.

boo, *v.t*, huer, conspuer.

booby, n, nigaud, e, benêt, dadais, m, huître, f. ~ **prize**, fiche de consolation, f. ~ **trap**, attrape-nigaud, m.

book, n, livre; livret; carnet; registre; journal; cahier; recueil; album; (*old & of little value*) bouquin, m; (*Stk Ex.*) position, f. ~**binder**, relieur, euse. ~**binding**, reliure, f. ~**case**, bibliothèque, f. ~ **debt**, dette active, créance, f, (*pl.*) recouvrements, m.pl. ~**ends**, serre-livres, m. ~ **entry**, écriture comptable, f. ~ **hunter**, bouquineur, m. ~**keeper**, teneur de livres, comptable, m,f. ~**keeping**, tenue de[s] livres, comptabilité, f. ~**keeping machine**, machine comptable, f. ~ **lover**, bibliophile, m. ~**maker**, bookmaker, m. ~**mark[er]**, signet, m, marque, f. ~ **matches**, allumettes en carnet, f.pl. ~ **muslin**, organdi, m. ~ **of certificates**, cahier de certificats. ~ **of stamps**, carnet de timbres. ~ **of travel coupons**, carnet de voyage. ~**plate**, ex-libris, m. ~ **rest**, pupitre, m. ~**seller**, libraire, m. ~**seller & publisher**, libraire-éditeur, m. ~[*seller's*] **shop**, librairie, f. ~**shelf**, rayon, m. ~**stall**, bibliothèque, f; kiosque, m. ~ **trade**, librairie, f. ~**trough**, porte-livres, m. ~ **value**, valeur comptable, f. ~**worm** (*pers.*), rat de bibliothèque, m. ~**work** (*Typ.*), labeur, m. **to make a ~** (*Betting*), faire un livre. ¶ *v.t*, enregistrer; engager, retenir, louer; réserver; demander; (*v.i.*) prendre un billet, des billets. **booking**, n, enregistrement; engagement, m, location; réserve, f; transport, voyage, service, m. ~ **clerk** (*Rly*), receveur, m. ~ **hall** (*Rly*), hall des guichets, m, salle

des pas perdus, f. ~ **office** (*Rly*), guichet [de distribution des billets] m. **booklet**, n, brochure, f, livret, m.

boom, n, (*harbour*) estacade; (*crane*) flèche, f; (*prices*) emballement [à la hausse] m. ¶ *v.i*, gronder, bourdonner, ronfler, tonner.

boon, a, gai, joyeux. ~ **companion**, bon compagnon, camarade de bouteille, m. ¶ n, bienfait, m, faveur, f.

boor, n, rustre, manant, m, rustaud, e. ~**ish**, a, rustaud, grossier. ~**ishness**, n, rusticité, grossièreté, f.

boot, n, chaussure [montante]; bottine; botte, f; brodequin; (*pl., pers.*) décrotteur; garçon d'étage, m. ~ **& shoe repairer**, cordonnier, m. ~ **& shoe trade**, cordonnerie, f. ~**jack**, tire-botte, m. ~**lace**, lacet de chaussure, m. ~**maker**, bottier, m. ~**tree**, embouchoir, embauchoir, m. ¶ *v.t*, chausser; botter. ~**ee**, n, chausson, f.

booth, n, baraque, boutique, échoppe, f.

bootless, a, inutile, vain, futile.

booty, n, butin, m.

booze, *v.i*, riboter, godailler.

boracic, a, borique. **borax**, n, borax, m.

border, n, bord, m, bordure; frontière; lisière, f; cordon, m; (*garden*) plate-bande, f. ~ **land**, pays limitrophe, m. ~**line case**, cas limite, m. ¶ *v.t*, border. ~ [*up*]**on**, avoisiner, côtoyer, friser. ~**ed** [*& seamless*] **carpet**, carpette, f, tapis encadré, m.

bore, n, alésage, calibre; (*Min.*) sondage, forage, m; (*tidal*) barre d'eau, f, mascaret, m; (*nuisance*) scie, f; (*pers.*) raseur, euse, endormeur, m, scie, f, crampon, m. ~ **core**, témoin, m, carotte, f. ~ **hole**, trou de sonde, m. ¶ *v.t*, percer, forer; vriller; aléser; vider; (*fig.*) ennuyer, embêter, scier, assommer, tuer, assassiner. ~**dom**, n, ennui, m.

boric, a, borique.

boring machine, (*Min.*) foreuse; (*Mechanical Engin.*) machine à aléser, f.

born, *p.p. & a*, né; issu; de naissance. ~ **blind**, aveugle de naissance, aveugle-né. **to be ~**, naître.

boron (*Chem.*) n, bore, m.

borrow, *v.t*, emprunter. ~**er**, n, emprunteur, euse. ~**ing**, n, emprunt, m. oft. pl.

borzoi, n, lévrier russe, m.

bosom, n, sein, m; gorge, f; (*church*) sein, giron, m. ~ **friend**, ami de cœur, m. ~ **sin**, péché mignon, m.

Bosphorus (the), le Bosphore.

boss, n, bosse, f; moyeu; (*pers.*) patron, chef, m.

botanic(al), a, botanique. ~ **gardens**, jardin des plantes, m. **botanist**, n, botaniste, m. **botanize**, *v.i*, herboriser. **botany**, n, botanique, f.

botch, n, bousillage, m. ¶ *v.t*, bousiller, gâcher, massacrer.

both, a. & ad, tous [les] deux, deux; l'un(e) & l'autre. ~ . . . **and** . . ., et . . . et . . .;

L

tant . . . que . . .; (*at the same time*) à la
fois . . . et.

bother, *n*, tracas, aria, *m*. ¶ *i*, peste! bigre!
¶ *v.t*, tracasser. ~**ation**, *i*, zut!

botle, *n*, bouteille; canette, *f*; flacon; bocal,
m; burette, *f*. ~ *brush*, goupillon, *m*.
~ *rack*, porte-bouteilles, *m*. ¶ *v.t*, mettre
en bouteille(s), embouteiller. ~ *up*
(*block*), embouteiller.

bottom, *n*, fond, bas, *m*, base, *f*, pied, bout;
dessous; derrière, cul; (*of chair, &c*) siège;
(*lowland*) bas-fond; (*ship*) navire, *m*; (*of
ship*) carène, *f*. ¶ *a*, inférieur; de fond;
de dessous; le plus bas. ~ *fishing*, pêche
de fond, *f*. ~ *margin* (book page), blanc
de pied, *m*. ¶ *v.t*, (*a cask, &c*) foncer;
(*v.i.*) toucher le fond. ~**less**, *a*, sans fond.

bough, *n*, mère branche, *f*; rameau, *m*.

bought book, livre d'achats, *m*.

boulder, *n*, roche, *f*, gros galet, caillou, *m*.

bounce, *n*, bond, *m*; vanterie, blague, *f*.
¶ *v.i*, bondir; se vanter, faire le fanfaron. **bouncing girl**, dondon, *f*.

bound, *n*, borne, limite, *f*; bond, saut, rebond,
m. to exceed all ~*s*, dépasser la mesure.
¶ *v.t*, borner, limiter; (*v.i.*) bondir, sauter.
~ *for* (ship), à destination de. to be ~ *to*,
être tenu(e) de (ou à), être obligé(e) de.
boundary, *n*, limite, borne, *f*. **bounden**
duty, devoir impérieux, *m*, religion, *f*.
boundless, *a*, illimité, sans bornes, immense.

bounteous†, *a*, généreux. **bountiful**†, *a*,
généreux, libéral, bienfaisant; fécond.
bounty, *n*, générosité, munificence, largesse,
f, prime, *f*. ~**fed**, primé.

bouquet, *n*, bouquet, *f*; (*wine*) bouquet, fumet, *m*.

bourn, *n*, ruisseau, *m*.

bourn[e], *n*, borne, limite, *f*.

bout, *n*, tour, assaut, *m*, partie, reprise, *f*.

bovine, *a*, bovin.

bow, *n*, (*knot*) nœud, nœud de ruban;
(*necktie*) nœud[-papillon]; (*curve*) arc;
(*fiddle, &c*) archet; (*saddle*) arçon, *m*;
(*padlock, &c*) anse, *f*. ~ *& tassels* (curtain
staff), cravate, *f*. ~ *compasses*, compas
à balustre, *m*. ~ *window*, bow-window,
m.

bow, *n*, salut, coup de chapeau, *m*, inclination, révérence; *f*; (*ship*) avant, *m*.
¶ *v.t. & i*, courber, incliner, fléchir, plier.
~ *& scrape*, faire des courbettes. ~ *to*,
saluer; s'incliner devant.

bowdlerize, *v.t*, expurger.

bowels, *n.pl*, entrailles, *f.pl*; intestins, *m.pl*;
sein, *m*.

bower, *n*, tonnelle, *f*, berceau, *m*, cabinet de
verdure, *m*.

bowing & scraping, prosternations, *f.pl*.

bowl, *n*, bol, bassin, *m*, écuelle, coupe, cuvette,
jatte, sébile, *f*; plateau; (*pipe*) fourneau,
m; (*game*) boule, *f*. [*game of*] ~*s*, boules,
f.pl; jeu de boules, jeu du cochonnet, *m*.
~**ful**, *n*, écuellée, *f*.

bowler [hat], *n*, [chapeau] melon, *m*, cape, *f*.

bowling: ~ *alley*, jeu de boules couvert, *m*.
~ *green*, jeu de boules découvert.

bowman, *n*, archer; (*boat*) brigadier, *m*.

bowsprit, *n*, beaupré, *m*.

bow-wow, *n*, toutou, *m*.

box, *n*, boîte; caisse, *f*; coffre; coffret; tronc;
boîtier; (*cardboard*) carton; (*driver's*) siège,
m; (*horse*) stalle, *f*; (*jury*) banc, *m*; (*Theat.*)
loge, *f*. ~ *camera*, chambre à forme
rigide, *m*. ~ *maker*, layetier, *m*. ~
manicure set, écrin manucure, onglier [en]
écrin, *m*. ~ *of paints*, boîte de peinture.
~ *office*, bureau [de location], contrôle, *m*.
~ *on the ear[s]*, soufflet, *m*. ~ *room*,
chambre de débarras, *f*, débarras, *m*. ~
spanner, clef à douille, *f*. ~*-spring
mattress*, sommier élastique, *m*. ~ [*tree*] &
~*wood*, buis, *m*. ¶ *v.t*, encaisser; (*someone's ears*) souffleter, frotter; (*fight*) boxer;
(*v.i.*) boxer. ~**er**, *n*, boxeur, *m*. ~**ing**,
n, boxe, *f*. ~ *match*, combat de b.,
assaut de b., match de b., *m*.

boy, *n*, garçon, garçonnet, enfant, gars, *m*.
~ *scout*, boy-scout; éclaireur, scout, *m*.
~**hood**, *n*, jeunesse, *f*. ~**ish**, *a*, enfantin,
puéril.

brace, *n*, (*strut, stay*) entretoise, *f*, étrésillon;
arc-boutant, *m*, contre-fiche; bielle, *f*;
tirant, *m*; moise, *f*; (*tool*) vilebrequin;
cliquet, *m*; (*pair*) couple, paire; (*Typ.*) ~
) accolade, *f*; (*pl. Dress*) bretelles, *f.pl*.
¶ *v.t*, renforcer, armer; moiser; fortifier,
retremper; bander; accolader.

bracelet, *n*, bracelet, *m*.

bracing, *a*, fortifiant, vivifiant.

bracken, *n*, fougère [à l'aigle] *f*.

bracket, *n*, console, potence, applique, *f*;
(*Typ.*) [ ], crochet, *m*; (,), parenthèse;
{ , }, accolade, *f*. ¶ *v.t*, accoler. to be
~*ed* (exams), être [classé] ex æquo.

brackish, *a*, saumâtre.

brad, *n*, pointe, *f*. ~*awl*, *n*, poinçon, *m*.

brag, *n*, vanterie, hâblerie, blague, fanfaronnade, *f*. ¶ *v.i*, se vanter. **braggart**, *n*,
vantard, e, hâbleur, euse, fanfaron, ne.

brahmin, *n*, brahmane, *m*.

braid, *n*, tresse, soutache, *f*, bordé, galon;
passement, *m*. ¶ *v.t*, tresser, soutacher
galonner, passementer.

brain, *n*. & ~*s*, *pl*, cerveau, *m*, cervelle;
tête, *f*; (*pl. Cook.*) cervelle[s], *f*. ~ *fag*,
fatigue cérébrale, *f*. ~ *fever*, fièvre cérébrale, *f*. ~ *wave*, trait de génie, illumination, *f*. ~ *worker*, bûcheur, euse. ~**less**,
a, sans cervelle.

braise, *v.t*, braiser.

brake, *n*, (*on wheel*) frein; (*waggonette*) break,
m; (*bracken*) fougère [à l'aigle] *f*; (*thicket*)
fourré, *m*. ~ [*gear*], timonerie des freins
(*carriage*) mécanique, *f*. ~ [*van*] (*Rly*)
fourgon, *m*. ¶ *v.t*, enrayer. *to put on* (*or*
apply) *the* ~, freiner, serrer les freins.
brakesman, *n*, serre-frein, garde-frein, *m*.

bramble, *n*, ronce, *f*.

bran, n, son, m.

branch, n, branche, f; rameau; embranchement; (*Elec.*) branchement, m. ~ [line] (*Rly*), ligne (*ou* voie) secondaire, f. ~ [office], succursale, f; comptoir, m. ~ pilot, [pilote] lamaneur, m. ~ [pipe], (*Plumbing*) embranchement, m; (*on hose*) lance, f. ¶ v.t, brancher; (v.i.) se ramifier. ~ off, v.t, embrancher; (v.i.) fourcher. ~ out (*fig.*), essaimer.

brand, n, (*fire*) tison, brandon, m; (*fig.*) flétrissure, f, stigmate; (*Poet.*) glaive, m; (*Com. & hot iron*) marque, f. **bran[d] new**, battant (*ou* tout flambant) neuf. ¶ v.t, marquer [à chaud]; flétrir, stigmatiser. **brandish**, v.t, brandir.

brandy, n, eau-de-vie, f, cognac, m. ~ & soda, fine à l'eau, f.

brass, n, laiton, cuivre [jaune]; (*Poet.*) airain, f; (*bearing*) coussinet, m; (*cheek*) effronterie, f, toupet, m. ~ (*Mus.*), les cuivres. ~ band, fanfare, f. ~ farthing, obole, f, maravédis, patard, m. ~ foundry, fonderie de cuivre, robinetterie, f. ~wares, dinanderie, f.

brassière, n, soutien-gorge, m.

brassy, a, cuivré.

brat, n, gamin, e, marmot, m, gosse, m,f, (*pl, col.*) marmaille, f.

bravado, n, bravade, f. **brave†**, a, brave. ~ man, [homme] brave, m. ¶ v.t, braver, affronter, défier. ~ry, n, bravoure, f. **bravo**, i, bravo!

brawl, n, mêlée, bagarre, rixe, querelle, f; tapage, m. ¶ v.i, se chamailler; (*stream*) murmurer. ~er, n, tapageur, euse, f, casseur d'assiettes, m.

brawn, n, hure, f, fromage de porc, m; (*fig.*) force musculaire, f. ~y, a, charnu, musculeux.

bray, v.i, braire. ~[ing], n, braiment, m.

braze, v.t, braser. **braze** (*joint*) & **brazing**, n, brasure, f.

brazen, a, d'airain. ~[-faced], effronté. to ~ it out, crâner, faire le crâne.

brazier, n, (*pers.*) chaudronnier; dinandier; (*pan*) brasero, m.

Brazil, n, le Brésil. **Brazilian**, a, brésilien. ¶ n, Brésilien, ne.

breach, n, brèche; infraction, violation, contravention, f. ~ of faith, manque de foi, m. ~ of promise, violation de promesse de mariage, f. ~ of trust, infidélité, f, prévarication, forfaiture, f, abus de confiance, m.

bread, n, pain, m. ~ crumbs (*Cook.*), panure, chapelure, f. ~ knife, couteau à pain, m. ~ saw, couteau-scie à pain, m. ~ winner, soutien de famille, m.

breadth, n, largeur, envergure, f, travers; (*of stuffs*) largeur, f, lé, m.

break, n, rupture, cassure, brisure; solution; (*gap*) trouée, f; (*day*) point, m; (*voice*) mue; (*prices*) dérobade, f; (*on ball*) effet,

m; (*Bil.*) série, f; (*waggonette*) break, m. ~ of journey, arrêt en cours de route, m, interruption de voyage, f. ¶ v.t.ir, casser, briser; fracturer; fragmenter; rompre; crever; concasser; enfreindre, violer; (*the bank, Gaming*) faire sauter; (*a set*) dépareiller; (*news*) faire part de; (See also *broken*); (v.t.i.ir.) [se] casser, se briser, &c; (*voice*) muer; (*dawn*) poindre; (*waves*) déferler. ¶ (*Box.*), séparez! ~ bulk (*Ship.*), entrer en déchargement. ~ cover (*Hunt.*), débucher. ~ down, v.t, abattre; (v.i.) avoir une panne. ~ into, envahir; pénétrer; entamer. ~ loose, se déchaîner. ~ of the habit, déshabituer, désaccoutumer. ~ one's arm, se casser le bras. ~ one's back, s'échiner. ~ one's word, manquer de parole. ~ open, enfoncer. ~ out, (*fire*) éclater, se déclarer; (*fig.*) déborder se débonder. ~ their engagement (marriage), se désaccorder. ~ through, percer. ~ up, (*school*) entrer en vacances; (*weather*) se brouiller; (*ice*) débâcler. ~ upon the wheel, rouer.

breakable, a, fragile. **breakage**, n, casse, rupture, f, bris, m. **breakaway**, n, dislocation; dérive, f. **breakdown**, n, (*failure*) fiasco, m; (*car, &c*) panne; (*health*) prostration, f. ~ gang, équipe de secours, f. **breaker**, n, (*pers.*) casseur; démolisseur; (*wave*) brisant, m. **breakfast**, n, déjeuner [du matin] m. ~ cup, tasse à déjeuner, f. ~ service, ~ set, déjeuner, m. ¶ v.i, déjeuner. **breaking**, n, rupture, fracture, f, brisement, m; (*holy bread*) fraction; (*voice*) mue, f. **breakneck**, n, casse-cou, m. **breakwater**, n, brise-lames, brisant, môle, m.

bream, n, brème, f; (*sea*) pagel, m.

breast, n, sein, m; poitrine, f; (*horse*) poitrail; (*fowl*) blanc, m. at the ~, à la mamelle. ~bone, sternum, m. ~-high, à hauteur d'appui. ~plate, plastron, m, conscience, f. ~ pocket, poche de poitrine, f. ~ strap, bricole, f. ~ stroke (*Swim.*), brasse, nage en grenouille, f.

breath, n, haleine, f, souffle, soupir, m. **breathe**, v.i. & t, respirer; souffler; soupirer. **breathing**, n, respiration, f. ~ space, temps de respirer, relâche, m. **breathless**, a, inanimé; haletant, essoufflé.

breech, n, derrière, m; (*gun*) culasse, f, tonnerre, m. ~-loading, se chargeant par la culasse. **breeches**, n.pl, culotte, f. ~ buoy, bouée culotte, f.

breed, n, race, f. ¶ v.t.ir, élever; engendrer; (v.t.i.ir.) multiplier, se reproduire. ~er (*stock*) n, éleveur, m. ~ing, n, (*animals*) élevage, m; (*pers.*) éducation, f, ton, m.

breeze, n, (*wind*) brise, f; (*cinders*) fraisil, m, braise, f. **breezy**, a, venteux; frais.

Bremen, n, Brême, f.

brethren, n.pl, frères, m.pl.

breviary, n, bréviaire, m.

brevity, n, concision; brièveté, f.

brew, v.t, brasser; (tea) faire infuser; (v.i.) faire de la bière; (storm) couver, se préparer; (fig.) couver, se tramer, se mijoter. ~er, n, brasseur, m. ~ery, n, brasserie, f. ~ing, n, brassage, m.

briar, n, églantier, m; (pipe wood) bruyère, f.

bribe, n, pot-de-vin, m. ¶ v.t, corrompre, séduire, soudoyer. ~ry, n, corruption, f.

brick, n, brique, f; (pl.—child's game) jeu de construction en bois, m. ~field, briqueterie, f. ~ kiln, four à briques, m. ~layer, maçon, m. ~maker, briquetier, m. ~ paving, carrelage en briques, m. ~work, briquetage, m.

bridal, a, nuptial; de mariée. bride, n, nouvelle mariée; (about to be married or on marriage day) mariée, f. ~ & ~groom, nouveaux mariés, m.pl. ~ cake, gâteau de noce, m. ~groom, nouveau marié; marié, m. bridesmaid, demoiselle d'honneur, f. bridesman, garçon d'honneur, m.

bridge, n, pont, m; (foot & ship's) passerelle, f; (violin) chevalet; (nose) dos; (Cards) bridge, m. ¶ v.t, jeter un pont sur; franchir.

bridle, n, bride, f. ~ path, sentier pour cavaliers, m, piste cavalière, f. ¶ v.t, brider; refréner; (v.i.) se rengorger.

brief, a, bref, concis; de courte durée. ¶ n, cause, f, dossier, m. ~ bag, sac de forme ballon, m. ¶ v.t, confier une cause à, constituer. ~less, a, sans cause. ~ly, ad, brièvement, bref, en abrégé.

brier, n, églantier, m; (pipe wood) bruyère, f.

brig, n, brick, m.

brigade, n, brigade, f; corps, m. ¶ v.t, embrigader.

brigand, n, brigand, m. ~age, n, brigandage, m.

bright, a, brillant, éclatant, luisant; vif; beau; gai; poli; lumineux, clair; encourageant; intelligent. ~ interval (Meteor.), éclaircie, f. ~en, v.t, faire briller; polir; éclaircir; aviver, animer. ~ly, ad, brillamment, clairement. ~ness, n, brillant, éclat, m; bonne orientation, f.

brill, n, barbue, f.

brilliancy, n, éclat, brillant, m. brilliant, a, brillant, éclatant. ¶ n, brillant, m. ~ine, n, brillantine, f. ~ly, ad, brillamment.

brim, n, bord, m. ¶ ~ over, déborder. ~-full or ~ful, a, plein jusqu'aux bords, à pleins bords.

brimstone, n, soufre, m.

brindled, a, tacheté.

brine, n, saumure, f; (Poet.) onde amère, f; larmes, f.pl.

bring, v.t.ir, apporter; amener; conduire; faire; mettre; porter. ~ about, déterminer; ménager. ~ an action against, intenter une action à, actionner, attaquer en justice. ~ back, rapporter; ramener. ~ forth, mettre au monde; produire. ~ forward (Bkkpg), reporter. ~ in (house), rentrer. ~ out (into society), produire dans le monde. ~ up, élever, bercer, nourrir; (food) rendre. ~ up the rear, fermer la marche. ~er of ill luck, porte-malheur, m. ~ing up, éducation, f.

brink, n, bord; penchant, m; veille, f.

briny, a, saumâtre; (Poet.) amer.

briquet[te], n, briquette, f, aggloméré, m.

brisk, a, vif, actif, animé, allègre. ~ fire (Mil.), feu nourri, m.

brisket, n, poitrine, f.

briskness, n, vivacité; activité, f.

bristle, n, soie, f; poil, m. ¶ v.t, hérisser; (v.i.) [se] hérisser. bristling, p.a. & bristly, a, hérissé.

Bristol Channel (the), le canal de Bristol.

Britain, n, la Grande-Bretagne. Britannia metal, métal anglais, m. British, a, britannique; anglais. ~ ambassador, ambassadeur d'Angleterre, m. ~ consul, consul britannique, m. ~ Isles, îles Britanniques, f.pl. ~ India, l'Inde anglaise, f.

Brittany, n, la Bretagne.

brittle, a, cassant, fragile. ~ness, n, fragilité, f.

broach, n, (spit) broche, f; (Mech.) alésoir, m. ¶ v.t, (cask) percer; (bore) aléser; (fig.) entamer, aborder.

broad, a, grand; gros; ample; plein; (accent) prononcé; (ribald) libre, cru, gras; (hint) peu voilé, assez clair. ~ bean, fève de marais, f. ~-brimmed hat, chapeau à grands bords, m. ~cast, a, ad, à la volée; (v.t.) [radio]diffuser. ~casting, [radio]diffusion, f. ~casting station, poste de r. p. d'émission, m. ~ in ~ daylight, au grand jour, en plein jour, en plein midi. ~-minded, à l'esprit large. ~-shouldered, large d'épaules. ~side, (Naut.) flanc de travers, côté, m; (guns, fire) bordée, f; (fig.) jeu de massacre, m. ~sword, sabre, m. ~en, v.t, élargir. ~ly, ad, large ment; ouvertement; en gros. ~ness, n, largeur; grossièreté, f; accent prononcé, m.

brocade, n, brocart, m.

broil, n, bagarre, f; tumulte, m. ¶ v.t, brasiller, griller. broiling, a, brûlant.

broke (hard up), a, aux abois.

broken, a, (country) tourmenté, accidenté, mouvementé; (health) délabrée, caduque, f; (speech, sleep, &c) entrecoupé; (English French, &c) mauvais. to be ~-down (car) être (ou rester) en panne. to be ~-hearted avoir le cœur navré (ou serré de douleur). ~ pebblestone, mignardise, f. ~ reed (fig.), roseau, m. ~ water, brisants, m.pl. ~-winded, poussif.

broker, n, courtier, ère; agent; banquier, m. ~age, n, courtage, m.

bromide, n, bromure, m. bromine, n, brome, m.

ronchia, *n.pl*, bronches, *f.pl.* **bronchitis**, *n*, bronchite, *f*.

ronze, *n*, bronze, *m*. ~ *shoes*, souliers mordorés, *m.pl.* ¶ *v.t.* bronzer.

rooch, *n*, broche; (*bar shaped*) barrette, *f*.

rood, *n*, couvée; nichée, engeance, *f*. ~ *hen*, couveuse, *f*. ¶ *v.i.* couver; ruminer. ~*ing time*, couvaison, *f*.

rook, *n*, ruisseau, *m*. ¶ *v.t.* digérer, tolérer. ~**let**, *n*, ruisselet, *f*.

room, *n*, balai; (*Bot.*) genêt, *m*. ~*stick*, manche à balai, *m*.

roth, *n*, bouillon; pot-au-feu, *m*.

rother, *n*, frère; confrère, *m*. ~*-in-law*, beau-frère. ~*hood*, fraternité, confrérie; confraternité, *f*. ~**ly**, *a*, fraternel.

rougham, *n*, coupé, *m*.

row, *n*, sourcil; (*forehead & cliff*) front; (*hill*) sommet, *m*. ~**beat**, *v.t*, rudoyer.

rown, *a*, brun; (*boots—yellowish*) jaune; (*boots—tan*) havane; (*paper*) gris; (*bread—light*) bis; (*bread—dark*) noir; (*sunburnt*) bruni. ~ *crust* (in pot), gratin, *m*. ~ *hair*, cheveux châtains, *m.pl.* ~ *owl*, chat-huant, *m*. ~ *study*, rêverie, *f*. ~ *sugar*, cassonade, *f*. ¶ *n*, brun, *m*. ¶ *v.t*, brunir; (*meat*) roussir, rissoler. ~*ish*, *a*, brunâtre.

rownie, *n*, elfe, *m*.

rowse, *n*, brout, *m*. ¶ *v.i. & t*, brouter, paître.

ruise, *n*, contusion, meurtrissure, *f*, pinçon, *m*; (*dent*) bosse, *f*. ¶ *v.t*, contusionner, meurtrir, froisser; bossuer, bosseler. ~**d**, *p.a*, meurtri, contus.

runt, *n*, poids; choc, *m*.

rush, *n*, brosse, *f*; pinceau; coup de brosse; (*Elec.*) balai, *m*; (*fox*) queue; (*affray*) échauffourée, *f*. ~ *head* (of hair), cheveux en brosse, *m.pl.* ~ *maker*, brossier, ère. ~ *making*, brosserie, *f*. ~*wood*, broussailles, *f.pl.* [bois] taillis, mort-bois, *m*. ¶ *v.t*, brosser; (*mud off*) décrotter; (*graze*) raser, effleurer, frôler. ~ *one's hair, teeth*, se brosser la tête, les dents. ~ *up* (*fig.*), repolir, dérouiller.

russels, *n*, Bruxelles, *f*. ~ *carpet*, tapis de moquette, *m*, moquette, *f*. ~ *sprouts*, chou de Bruxelles, *m*.

rutal†, *a*, brutal. ~**ity**, *n*, brutalité, *f*. ~**ize**, *v.t*, abrutir. **brute**, *n*, brute, *f*, animal, *m*. ~ *beast*, bête brute, *f*. *the* ~ *creation*, l'espèce animale, *f*. ~ *force*, force brute, *f*. **brutish†**, *a*, brutal, abruti.

ubble, *n*, bulle, *f*; bouillon; projet en l'air, *m*. ¶ *v.i*, bouillonner; pétiller.

uccaneer, *n*, boucanier, *m*.

uck, *n*, (*deer*) daim; (*jump*) saut de mouton; (*pers.*) luron, gaillard, *m*. ~ *rabbit*, lapin mâle, bouquin, *m*. ~*skin*, peau de daim, *f*, daim, *m*; (*pl.*) culotte de peau, *f*. ~*shot*, chevrotine, *f*.

ucket, *n*, seau, *m*, seille, *f*; godet, *m*, auge, *f*,

---

auget; baquet, *m*; benne, *f*. ~ *shop*, maison de contrepartie, *f*. ~**ful**, *n*, seau, *m*; augée, *f*.

buckle, *n*, boucle, *f*. ¶ *v.t*, boucler; fausser, gauchir; (*v.i.*) voiler, gauchir. **buckler**, *n*, bouclier, *m*.

buckram, *n*, bougran, *m*.

buckthorn, *n*, nerprun, *m*.

buckwheat, *n*, [blé-]sarrasin, blé noir, *m*.

bucolic, *a*, bucolique.

bud, *n*, bourgeon, bouton, *m*, gemme, *f*; (*fig.*) germe, *m*. ¶ *v.i*, bourgeonner; naître.

buddhist, *a*, bouddhique. ¶ *n*, bouddhiste, *m*.

budding (*fig.*) *a*, naissant; en herbe.

budget, *n*, budget, *m*. ~ **for**, porter au b.

buff (*colour*) *a. & n*, fauve, *a. & m*. ~ [*leather*], buffle, *m*, peau de buffle, *f*. ¶ *v.t*, polir. **buffalo**, *n*, buffle, *m*.

buffer, *n*, tampon [de choc], heurtoir, butoir, *m*. ~ *state*, état tampon, *m*.

buffet, *n*, (*blow*) soufflet; (*sideboard*) buffet; (*at a ball*) souper debout, *m*. (Cf. *running buffet*). ~ *car*, wagon-bar, *m*. ¶ *v.t*, secouer.

buffoon, *n*, bouffon, ne, pitre, *m*. ~**ery**, *n*, bouffonnerie, *f*.

bug, *n*, punaise, *f*. ~**bear**, *n*, loup-garou, croque-mitaine, épouvantail, cauchemar, *m*.

bugle, *n*, clairon, *m*; (*Bot.*) bugle, *f*. ~ *call*, sonnerie, *f*. **bugler**, *n*, clairon, *m*.

buhl[work] *n*, Boule, *m*.

build, *n*, construction, *f* (*of sturdy* ~ or *well built* (man), bien charpenté. ¶ *v.t.ir*, bâtir, construire. ~ *up*, édifier, échafauder. ~ *er*, *n*, constructeur, entrepreneur [de bâtiments] *m*. ~**ing**, *n*, construction, *f*, bâtiment, édifice; monument, *m*. ~ *line*, alignement, *m*. ~ *materials*, matériaux de construction, *m.pl.* ~ *site*, terrain à bâtir, *m*. ~ *society*, société immobilière, *f*. *built-over carriage entrance*, porte cochère, *f*.

bulb, *n*, (*Bot.*) bulbe, *f*, o[i]gnon, *m*; (*Anat.*) bulbe, *m*; (*elec. lamp, thermometer*) ampoule, *f*; (*Chem.*) ballon, *m*; (*Phot.*) poire, *f*. ~ *exposure*, demi-pose, *f*. ~ *shade* (*Elec.*), cache-ampoule, *m*. ~**ous**, *a*, bulbeux.

Bulgaria, *n*, la Bulgarie. **Bulgarian**, *a*, bulgare. ¶ *n*, Bulgare, *m,f*.

bulge, *n*, bombement, ventre, *m*. ¶ *v.i. & t*, bomber, boucler, bouffer, faire [le] ventre.

bulk, *n*, volume; gros, *m*; masse, *f*. *in* ~ (*Ship.*), en vrac, en grenier. ~**head**, cloison, *f*. ~**y**, *a*, volumineux, massif, encombrant.

bull, *n*, taureau, *m*; (*Pope's*) bulle, *f*; (*incongruity*) prudhommerie, *f*, contresens, *m*; (*Stk Ex.*) haussier, *m*; (*shot*) mouche, *f*. ~ *calf*, veau mâle, taurillon, *m*. ~*dog*, bouledogue, *m*. ~ *elephant*, éléphant mâle, *m*. ~*fight*, course de taureaux, *f*. ~*'s-eye*, (*target*) noir, *m*, mouche, *f*; (*win-*

dow) œil-de-bœuf, *m.* ~*'s-eye (lantern)*, lanterne avec projecteur à lentille faisant saillie, *f.*

bullet, *n*, balle, *f.*

bullfinch, *n*, bouvreuil, *m.*

bullion, *n*, matières d'or & d'argent, *f.pl;* *(fringe)* torsade, *f.* ~ *stitch (Crochet)*, point de minute, *m.*

bullock, *n*, bœuf, *m.*

bully, *n*, bravache, brutal, *m.* ¶ *v.t*, malmener, brutaliser.

bulrush, *n*, jonc, *m;* *(reed mace)* massette, masse d'eau, *f.*

bulwark, *n*, rempart; boulevard; *(ship's)* pavois, *m.*

bumble-bee, *n*, bourdon, *m.*

bump, *n*, bosse, *f; (cahot, heurt, *m.* ¶ *v.t* & *i*, cogner, heurter, se heurter; cahoter.

bumper, *n*, *(brim-full glass)* rasade, *f*, rouge bord; *(motor)* pare-chocs, *m.*

bumpkin, *n*, rustre, lourdaud, *m.*

bumptious, *a*, suffisant. ~**ness**, *n*, suffisance, *f.*

bun *(hair)* *n*, torpillon, *m.*

bunch, *n*, bouquet, *m;* botte, *f;* faisceau, trousseau, *m; (grapes)* grappe, *f; (bananas, &c)* régime, *m.* ¶ *v.t*, botteler.

bundle, *n*, paquet; faisceau, *m;* botte, *f;* fagot, *m;* liasse, *f.* ¶ *v.t*, empaqueter; botteler; fagoter; mettre en liasse.

bung, *n*, bondon, *m*, bonde, *f*, bouchon, tampon, *m.* ~*(hole)*, bonde, *f.* ¶ *v.t*, bondonner, boucher.

bungalow, *n*, maisonnette, *f; (Indian type)* bungalow, *m.*

bungle, *n*, bousillage, *m*, mauvaise besogne, *f.* ¶ *v.t*, bousiller, barbouiller, massacrer. **bungler**, *n*, bousilleur, euse, fagoteur, *m.*

bunion, *n*, oignon, *m.*

bunk, *n*, couchette, *f.*

bunker, *n*, soute, *f;* caisson, *m; (Golf)* banquette, *f.* ~ *coal*, charbon de soute, *m.*

bunkum, *n*, blague, *f.*

bunting, *n*, *(stuff)* étamine à pavillon, *f; (flags)* draperie, *f; (bird)* bruant, *m.*

buoy, *n*, bouée, *f.* ¶ *v.t*, baliser. ~ *up*, soutenir. ~**ancy**, *n*, flottabilité; poussée, *f; (fig.)* ressort, *m.* ~**ant**, *a*, flottant; élastique; vif, animé.

bur[r], *n*, *(Bot.)* capsule hérissée; *(burdock)* bardane, *f; (on tree)* loupe, ronce; personne collante, *f.*

burden, *n*, fardeau, *m*, charge, *f*, poids, faix; *(ship)* port, maximum de charge, tonnage; *(song)* refrain, *m.* ¶ *v.t*, charger; grever. ~**some**, *a*, onéreux.

burdock, *n*, bardane, *f.*

bureaucracy, *n*, bureaucratie, *f.* **bureaucrat**, *n*, bureaucrate, *m.*

burglar, *n*, cambrioleur, *m.* ~ *alarm*, appareil avertisseur contre le vol, *m.* ~**y**, *n*, cambriolage, vol [de nuit avec effraction] *m.* ~ *insurance*, assurance contre le vol, *f.* **burgle**, *v.t*, cambrioler.

burgundy, *n*, bourgogne, vin de B., *m.*

burial, *n*, enterrement, *m*, sépulture, *f.* ~ *fees*, droits mortuaires, *m.pl.* ~ *ground*, cimetière, *m.* ~ *place*, lieu de sépulture, *m.* ~ *service*, office des morts, *m.*

burlesque, *a.* & *n*, burlesque, *a.* & *m.* ¶ *v.t*, travestir.

burly, *a*, solidement bâti; corpulent.

Burma, *n*, la Birmanie. **Burmese**, *a*, birman. ¶ *n*, Birman, e.

burn, *n*, brûlure, *f.* ¶ *v.t.* & *i. ir*, brûler; *(bricks)* cuire; incendier; calciner; *(of sun)* hâler. *I have burnt my arm*, je me suis brûlé le bras. *to burn one's fingers (fig.)*, s'échauder. ~**er**, *n*, brûleur, bec, *m.* ~**ing**, *a*, brûlant, en feu, enflammé; ardent; cuisant. ¶ *n*, combustion; ignition; cuisson, cuite, *f; (smell)* brûlé, roussi, graillon, *m.*

burnish, *v.t*, *(metal, &c)* brunir; *(paper, &c)* satiner. ~**ing**, *n*, brunissage; satinage, *m.*

burnt, *p.a:* ~ *almond*, praline, *f.* ~ *offering*, holocauste, *m.* ~ *Sienna*, terre de Sienne brûlée, *f.*

burr, *n*, barbes, *f.pl.* See also *bur[r]*. ¶ *(speaking) v.i*, grasseyer.

burrow, *n*, terrier, clapier, *m.* ¶ *v.i*, terrer; se terrer; fouiller.

bursar, *n*, économe, *m*, dépensier, ère. ~*'s office* & ~**ship**, *n*, économat, *m.*

burst, *n*, éclat, jet; *(light)* coup; *(speed)* emballement; *(eloquence)* mouvement; *(passion, &c)* transport, élan, *m*, fusée, *f.* ¶ *v.t.ir*, faire éclater, [faire] crever; rompre; *(v.i.ir)* éclater; crever; se précipiter. ~**ing**, *n*, éclatement, *f*, crevaison, *f.*

burthen *(ship)* *n*, port, maximum de charge, tonnage, *m.*

bury, *v.t*, enterrer, ensevelir.

[']bus, *n*, omnibus, *m.* ~*way*, ligne d'autobus, *f.*

bush, *n*, buisson, arbuste, *m; (scrub)* brousse *(Mach.)* coquille, bague, *f*, manchon, *m.*

bushel, *n*, boisseau, *m.* Imperial measure = 8 gallons or 3·637 decalitres.

bushy, *a*, touffu, fourni; embroussaillé, buissonneux.

busily, *a*, activement.

business, *n*, affaires, *f.pl*, commerce, négoce, *m;* affaire, entreprise, *f;* fonds [de commerce] *m;* qualité, *f*, métier, *m;* délibérations, questions [à délibérer] *f.pl*, ordre du jour; *(right)* droit; *(fuss, job)* aria, *m.* ~ *as usual during alterations*, la maison reste ouverte pendant les travaux. ~ *card*, carte d'adresse, *f.* ~ *day*, jour non férié, *m;* bourse, *f.* ~ *hours*, heures d'affaires, heures d'ouverture; *f.pl.* ~ *like*, régulier; pratique, entendu. ~ *man*, homme d' *(ou* dans les) affaires, *m.* ~ *name*, raison de commerce, *f.* ~ *premises*, locaux commerciaux, *m.pl*, immeuble commercial, *m.* ~ *quarter*, quartier commerçant, *m.* ~ *world*, monde des affaires, *m.*

uskin, *n*, brodequin; cothurne, *m*.

ust, *n*, buste, *m*; gorge, *f*, corsage, *m*. ~ *bodice*, soutien-gorge, *m*. ~ *measurement*, [con]tour de poitrine, *m*.

ustard, *n*, outarde, *f*.

ustle, *n*, mouvement; remue-ménage, *m*; animation, *f*, tourbillon, *m*. ¶ *v.i*, se remuer.

usy, *a*, occupé, affairé, embesogné; industrieux; mouvementé; actif; empressé; diligent. ~ *bee*, abeille industrieuse, *f*. ~ *man*, *woman*, affairé, e. ~*body*, touche-à-tout, *m*, commère, *f*, tatillon, ne, nécessaire, *m*.

ut, *c*, mais; que; or. ~ *for*, sans. ¶ *ad.* & *pr*, hormis, excepté, seulement; ne . . . que. ¶ *n*, mais, *m*.

utcher, *n*, boucher, *m*. ~'s *meat*, viande de boucherie, *f*. ~'s *shop*, boucherie, *f*. ¶ *v.t*, égorger, massacrer. ~y, *n*, boucherie, *f*.

utler, *n*, sommelier; maître d'hôtel, *m*.

utt, *n*, (*cask*) tonneau, *m*; (*pl.*, *behind target*) butte; (*rifle*) crosse, *f* (*cue*) talon; (*pers.*) plastron, bouffon, *m*, cible, risée, *f*, souffre-douleur; (*ram, &c*) coup de corne, coup de tête, *m*. ~ *cock*, canule, *f*. ¶ *v.i.* & *t*, cosser; heurter de la tête; buter.

utter, *n*, beurre, *m*. ~ *cooler*, beurrier rafraîchisseur, *m*. ~ *dish*, beurrier, *m*. ~ *milk*, lait de beurre, babeurre, *m*. ¶ *v.t*, beurrer. ~*ed toast*, rôties au beurre, *f.pl*, toast, *m*.

uttercup, *n*, bassinet, bouton d'or, *m*.

utterfly, *n*, papillon [diurne] *m*.

uttock, *n*, fesse, *f*; (*beef*) cimier, *m*.

utton, *n*, bouton; (*pl, boy*) groom, *m*. ~*hole*, boutonnière, *f*. ~*hole scissors*, ciseaux pour b—s, *m.pl*. ~*hole stitch* (*Emb.*), point de languette, p. de feston, *m*. ~*hole* (*detain*), cueillir. ~*hook*, tire-bouton, *m*. ~ *stick* (*Mil.*), patience, *f*. ¶ *v.t*, boutonner. ~ *oneself up*, se b.

uttress, *n*, contrefort, éperon; (*flying*) arc-boutant, *m*. ¶ *v.t*, arc-bouter; soutenir.

uxom, *a*, opulent, plantureux, rondelet & de bonne mine. ~*ness*, *n*, opulence, *f*.

uy, *v.t.ir*, acheter, acquérir. ~ *back*, racheter. ~ *in against* (*Stk Ex.*), exécuter. ~ *out*, désintéresser. ~ *up*, enlever, accaparer. ~*er*, *n*, acheteur, euse, acquéreur, preneur, *m*. ~*ing*, *n*, achat, *m*, acquisition, *f*.

uzz, *v.i*, bourdonner, ronfler, tinter.

y, *pr*, par; à; sur; sous; en; près. ¶ *ad*, près, à part. ~ & ~, tantôt. ~ *the* ~, ~ *the way*, à propos, en passant.

ye (*odd man*) *n*, exempt, *m*.

ye-bye, *n*, dodo, *m*.

y[e]-law, *n*, règlement, *m*.

y-election, *n*, élection de remplacement, *f*.

ygone, *a*, passé, ancien, d'autrefois.

y-pass, *n*, route d'évitement; (*gas*) veilleuse, *f*.

bypath, *n*, chemin écarté, sentier détourné, *m*.

by-product, *n*, sous-produit, *m*.

bystander, *n*, assistant, e, spectateur, trice, curieux, *m*.

byway, *n*, chemin détourné, *m*.

byword, *n*, dicton, *m*; risée, fable, *f*.

C

C (*Mus.*) *letter*, ut, do, *m*. ~ *clef*, clef d'ut, *f*.

cab, *n*, fiacre, *m*, voiture [de place], *f*; (*locomotive*) abri, *m*. ~*man*, cocher de fiacre, *m*. ~ *rank*, place de voitures, station de fiacres, *f*.

cabal, *n*, cabale, *f*.

cabaret [show], *n*, attractions, *f.pl*.

cabbage, *n*, chou, *m*. ~ *lettuce*, laitue pommée, *f*. ~ *tree*, palmiste, *m*.

cabin, *n*, cabine, chambre; cabane, case; guérite, *f*. ~ *boy*, mousse, *m*. ~ *passenger*, passager (ère) de cabine. ~ *trunk*, malle de paquebot, malle de cabine, *f*.

cabinet, *n*, cabinet, *m*; armoire, meuble, *m*. ~ *council*, Conseil des ministres, C. de Cabinet, *m*. ~ *gramophone*, meuble phonographe, *m*. ~*maker*, menuisier, ébéniste, *m*. ~*making* & ~*work*, menuiserie, ébénisterie, *f*. ~ *minister*, ministre d'État, *m*.

cable, *n*, câble, *m*. ~ *railway*, [chemin de fer] funiculaire, *m*. ~ *release* (*Phot.*), déclencheur métallique, *m*. ¶ (*Teleg.*) *v.t*, câbler.

caboose (*Naut.*) *n*, cuisine, *f*.

ca'canny strike, grève perlée, *f*.

cacao, *n*, cacao, *m*. ~ [*tree*], cacaoyer, cacaotier, *m*.

cachet, *n*, cachet, *m*. cachou, *n*, cachou, *m*.

cackle, *n*, caquet, *m*. ¶ *v.i*, caqueter.

cacoethes, *n*, démangeaison, *f*.

cactus, *n*, cactus, *m*.

cad, *n*, canaille, *f*, goujat, pleutre, mufle, *m*.

caddie (*Golf*) *n*, cadet, te.

caddy, *n*, boîte [à thé] *f*.

cadence, *n*, cadence, *f*.

cadet, *n*, cadet; élève (*de l'école navale*), *m*.

cadge, *v.t*, écornifler. cadger, *n*, écornifleur, euse.

Cadiz, *n*, Cadix, *m*.

cage, *n*, cage; cabine; loge, *f*. ~ *bird*, oiseau de volière, *m*. ¶ *v.t*, encager.

cairn, *n*, montjoie, *f*.

Cairo, *n*, le Caire.

caisson, *n*, caisson; (*dock*) bateau-porte, *m*.

cajole, *v.t*, cajoler, amadouer. ~*ry*, *n*, cajolerie, *f*.

cake, *n*, gâteau; pain, *m*; tablette, *f*; (*cattle*) tourteau, *m*. ~ *stand*, table porte-assiettes, *f*. ¶ *v.t*, plaquer.

calabash, *n*, calebasse, *f*.

calamitous, *a*, calamiteux. calamity, *n*, calamité, *f*.

calcareous, *a*, calcaire.

calcine, *v.t*, calciner.

calcium, n, calcium, m.

caiculate, v.t, calculer; (v.i.) compter. ~d to, propre à, de nature à. **calculating machine**, machine à calculer, f. **calculation & calculus** (Med.) n, calcul, m.

caldron, n, chaudron, m.

calendar, n, calendrier; (prisoners for trial) rôle, m. ~ year, année civile, f.

calender, n, calandre, f. ¶ v.t, calandrer, cylindrer.

calf, n, veau; (leg) mollet, gras de la jambe, m. ~[skin], peau de veau, f, [cuir de] veau, m.

calibrate, v.t, calibrer. **calibre, n**, calibre, m.

calico, n, calicot, m.

California, n, la Californie. **Californian, a**, californien. ¶ n, Californien, ne.

caliph, n, calife, m.

call, n, appel; rappel, m; demande; (trumpet, bugle) sonnerie; visite; communication; (Relig.) vocation; (to a ship) semonce; (of a ship) escale; relâche, f; (Fin.) appel [de fonds], versement; terme, m; option, faculté; (Cards) invite, f. ~ bird, chanterelle, f. ~ boy, avertisseur, m. ~ of the blood (fig.), force du sang, f. ~ office, cabine, f. ~ over [of names], appel nominal, m. ~ to arms, appel aux armes. ¶ v.t. & i, appeler; héler; rappeler; convoquer; faire venir; prendre; réveiller; qualifier; traiter de; nommer; surnommer; intituler; passer, s'arrêter; faire; (ship) faire escale; relâcher. ~ back, rappeler. ~ for, demander, réclamer; (trumps) inviter; exiger. ~ off, contremander, décommander; (hounds) rompre. ~ out, appeler, crier. ~ [up]on, sommer, invoquer. **caller, n**, visiteur, euse. **calling, n**, appel, m; convocation; vocation, profession, f; métier, m. Radio-Paris ~, ici [poste de] Radio-Paris.

cal[l]iper, n, calibre; (pl.) compas [de calibre] m. ¶ v.t, calibrer.

callosity & callus, n, callosité, f, cal, durillon, m. callous, a, enduci, insensible; (skin) calleux.

callow, a, sans plumes. ~ youth, la verte jeunesse; jeune homme imberbe, blanc-bec, m.

calm, a, calme. ¶ v.t, calmer. ~ly, ad, tranquillement. ~[ness], n, calme, m, tranquillité, f.

calorie, n, calorie, f.

calumniate, v.t, calomnier. **calumny, n**, calomnie, f.

Calvary (place) n, Calvaire, m. **calvary** (representation) n, calvaire, m.

calve, v.i, vêler.

calyx, n, calice, m.

cam, n, came, f, excentrique, m.

camber, n, bombement, m, cambrure, f.

cambric, n, batiste, f.

came, n, plomb, m, (pl.) résille, f.

camel, n, chameau, m. ~ driver, chamelier, m.

camellia, n, camélia, m.

cameo, n, camée, m.

camera, n, chambre [noire], f, appareil, m. ~ man, opérateur, m. ~ obscura (Opt.), chambre noire, c. obscure, f. in ~, à huit clos.

cami-knickers, n.pl, chemise-culotte, f.

camisole, n, cache-corset, m.

camomile, n, camomille, f.

camouflage, n, camouflage, **m**. ¶ v.t, camoufler, maquiller.

camp, n, camp, m. ~ bed, lit de camp, **m**. ~ stool, [siège] pliant, m. ¶ v.i. & i, camper. ~ out, bivouaquer.

campaign, n, campagne, f. ~er, n, routier, troupier, m.

campanula, n, campanule, f.

camphor, n, camphre, m. ~ate, v.t, camphrer.

camping [out], n, campement, camping, m.

can, n, bidon, m; burette; boîte, f; pot, m. ¶ v.t, mettre en boîte(s), m. en conserve. canned salmon, saumon en boîte(s) m.

can, v.aux.ir, pouvoir; savoir.

Canada, n, le Canada. **Canadian, a**, canadien. ¶ n, Canadien, ne.

canal, n, canal, m. ~ize, v.t, canaliser.

canary, n, serin, e, canari, m. ~ seed, graine des canaris, f, millet des oiseaux, m. the C~ Islands, the Canaries, les [îles] Canaries, f.pl.

cancel, n, (Typ.) carton; (Mus.) bécarre, m. ¶ v.t, biffer, effacer; oblitérer; annuler, résilier, rompre; décommander.

cancer (Med.) n, cancer, m. ~ous, a, cancéreux.

candelabrum, n, candélabre, m.

candid†, a, sincère, franc, désintéressé.

candidate, n, candidat, m, postulant, e, aspirant, e, prétendant, e.

candied peel, zeste confit, m.

candle, n, chandelle, bougie, f; cierge, m ~ grease, suif, m. ~ power, puissance (ou intensité) lumineuse en bougies, f. a 60 c.p. lamp, une lampe de 60 bougies ~stick, bougeoir; chandelier; flambeau, m ¶ (eggs) v.t, mirer. **candling, n**, mirage, m.

candour, n, sincérité, franchise, f.

candy, v.i, se candir. [sugar] ~, [sucre candi, m.

cane, n, canne; badine; (Sch.) férule, f; jonc m. ~ sugar, sucre de canne, m. ¶ v.t donner de la férule à; (chair) canner.

canine, a, canin.

canister, n, boîte [métallique] f.

canker, n, (lit. & fig.) chancre, m. ~worm ver rongeur, m. ¶ v.t, gangrener.

canned goods, conserves [en boîtes] f.pl.

cannibal, n, & a, cannibale, m, anthropophage, m. & a.

cannon, n, canon; (Bil.) carambolage, m. ~ ball, boulet, m. ~ shot, coup de canon m. ~ade, n, canonnade, f. ¶ v.t, canonner.

canny, *a*, fin, sagace; avisé; rusé.

canoe, *n*, (*Canadian*, &c) canoë, *m*; (*Rob Roy*) périssoire; (*dugout*) pirogue, *f*.

canon, *n*, (*Eccl. rule*) canon; (*pl, taste*) code; (*pers.*) chanoine, *m*. ~ *law*, droit canon, *m*. canonicate, canonry, *n*, canonicat, *m*. canonize, *v.t*, canoniser.

canopy, *n*, dais; baldaquin; ciel, *m*; voûte, calotte, *f*, dôme, *m*; (*Arch.*) marquise, *f*.

cant, *n*, argot; jargon, *m*; hypocrisie, *f*; (*slope*) devers, *m*, inclinaison, *f*. ¶ *v.t*, incliner.

cantankerous, *a*, revêche, hargneux. ~ *fellow*, mauvais coucheur, *m*.

cantata, *n*, cantate, *f*.

canteen, *n*, cantine, *f*; (*bottle*) bidon, *m*. ~ *keeper*, cantinier, ère.

canter, *n*, petit galop, *m*; (*pers.*) cafard, e, tartufe, *m*.

Canterbury Bell, campanule à grandes fleurs, *f*.

canticle, *n*, cantique, *m*.

cantilever, *n*, encorbellement, *m*.

canto, *n*, chant, *m*. cantor, *n*, chantre, *m*.

canvas, *n*, canevas, *m*, toile; toile à voiles; voile, *f*. ~ *shoe with hempen sole*, espadrille, *f*.

canvass, *v.t*, débattre; solliciter, mendier, briguer; faire (*the town* = la place). ~er, *n*, solliciteur, euse; placier, démarcheur, *m*.

canyon, cañon, *n*, canon, *m*.

cap, *n*, bonnet, chapeau, *m*; (*peaked*) casquette, *f*, képi, *m*; toque; calotte, *f*; culot, *m*; chape; coiffe, *f*; couvercle; chapiteau, bouchon; bout; détonateur, *m*, capsule, amorce, *f*. ~ & *bells* (*Hist.*), marotte, *f*. ~ *case* (*Typ.*), haut de casse, *m*. ¶ *v.t*, coiffer; couronner. to ~ *all*, brochant sur le tout.

capability, *n*, capacité, *f*. capable, *a*, capable; apte, susceptible. capacious, *a*, spacieux. capacitate, *v.t*, rendre capable; (*Law*) habiliter. capacity, *n*, capacité, *f*; rendement, débit, *m*; qualité; habilité, *f*.

caparison, *v.t*, caparaçonner.

cape, *n*, (*Phys. Geog.*) cap, *m*; (*Dress*) pèlerine, *f*. *C~ Colony*, la colonie du Cap. the *C~ of Good Hope*, le cap de Bonne-Espérance. *C~ Verde*, le cap Vert.

caper, *n*, cabriole, gambade, *f*, entrechat; *m*; (*Bot.*) câpre, *f*. ¶ *v.i*, cabrioler.

capillary, *a*, capillaire.

capital†, *a*, capital; admirable, fameux, parfait, chic; (*letter*) majuscule, capitale. ¶ *n*, (*country*, *province*) [ville] capitale, *f*; (*county*, *department*) chef-lieu, *m*; (*letter*) [lettre] majuscule, [lettre] capitale, *f*; (*Arch.*) chapiteau, *m*; (*Fin.*) capital, *m*, capitaux, *m.pl*; fonds, *m.s.* & *pl*, mise [de fonds] *f*; (*brought in*) apport, *m*. *C~ & Labour*, le capital & le travail. ~ *expenditure*, immobilisations, *f.pl*, établissement, *m*. ~ *stock* & ~ *sum*, capital, *m*. ~ *value*, valeur en capital, *f*. ~ist, *n*,

capitaliste, *m,f.* ~ize, *v.t*, capitaliser, immobiliser.

capitulate, *v.i*, capituler.

capon, *n*, chapon, *m*.

caprice, *n*, caprice, *m*. capricious, *a*, capricieux.

capsicum, *n*, piment, *m*.

capsize, *v.t*, (faire) chavirer; (*v.i.*) chavirer, capoter, faire capot.

capstan, *n*, cabestan, *m*; (*lathe*) revolver, *m*, tourelle, *f*.

capsule, *n*, capsule, *f*.

captain, *n*, (*Mil.*, *Naut.*, *Sport*) capitaine; (*Nav.*) capitaine de vaisseau, *m*. ~ *of merchant ship*, capitaine marchand.

caption, *n*, sous-titre, *m*.

captious, *a*, captieux, difficultueux.

captivate, *v.t*, captiver. captive, *a*, captif. ¶ *n*, captif, ive. captivity, *n*, captivité, *f*.

capture, *n*, capture, prise, *f*. ¶ *v.t*, capturer.

Capuchin friar, nun, capucin, e.

car, *n*, voiture, *f*; wagon; char, chariot, *m*; cabine; (*Aero.*) nacelle, *f*. [*motor*] ~, voiture [automobile], auto[mobile], *f*. ~ *bandit*, bandit en auto, *m*. ~ *park*, parc à voitures, *m*.

caracol[e], *n*, caracole, *f*.

caramel, *n*, caramel, *m*.

carapace, *n*, carapace, *f*.

carat, *n*. & ~ *goods*, carat, *m*.

caravan, *n*, caravane; (*house on wheels*) roulotte, *f*. caravanserai, *n*, caravansérail, *m*.

caraway, *n*, carvi, *m*. ~ *seed*, graine de c., *f*.

carbide, *n*, carbure, *f*.

carbine, *n*, carabine, *f*, mousqueton, *m*.

carbolic acid, acide phénique, phénol, *m*.

carbon, *n*, (*Chem.*) carbone; (*Elec.*) charbon, *m*. ~ [*copy*] copie au papier carbone, *f*. ~ *monoxide*, oxyde de carbone, *m*. ~ [*paper*] (duplicating), papier carbone, *m*. ~ *paper* (*Phot.*), papier au charbon, *m*. carbonate, *n*, carbonate, *m*. carbonic, *a*, carbonique. carboniferous, *a*, carbonifère, houiller. carbonize, *v.t*, carboniser; (*v.i.*) [se] charbonner.

carboy, *n*, tourie, *f*.

carbuncle, *n*, (*jewel*) grenat cabochon; (*Med.*) charbon, anthrax, *m*.

carburettor, *n*, carburateur, *m*.

carcass or carcase, *n*, carcasse, *f*, cadavre, *m*; (*ship*) carcasse; (*building*) bâtisse, *f*, œuvre, *m*.

card, *n*, carte, *f*; (*loose index*) fiche, *f*; (*textiles*) peigne; (*Golf*) compte des points, *m*. ~board, carton, *m*. ~board maker, cartonnier, *m*. ~ *case*, porte-cartes, *m*. ~ *index* & ~ *index* [*cabinet*], fichier, *m*. ~ *sharper*, bonneteur, *m*. ~ *table*, table de jeu, *f*. ~ *trick*, tour de cartes, *m*. ¶ *v.t*, peigner.

cardigan [jacket], *n*, vareuse, *f*, gilet, *m*.

cardinal, *a*, cardinal. ¶ *n*, cardinal, *m*.

care, *n*, soin, *m. oft. pl.* attention; précaution; garde, *f*; souci, *m*; responsabilité; charge; tenue; conservation, *f*; maniement, *m*, manutention, gestion, *f*, gouvernement, *m*. *with due & proper* ~, en bon père de famille. ~ *of, c/o,* chez, aux [bons] soins de. ~*taker,* gardien, ne, concierge, *m*, *f*, portier, ère. ~*worn,* miné (*ou* rongé) par les soucis. ¶ *v.i,* se soucier, s'inquiéter.

careen, *v.t,* caréner.

career, *n*, carrière; course, *f*. ¶ *v.i,* galoper.

careful†, *a*, soigneux, attentif; ménager. ~**ness**, *n*, soin, *m*, attention, *f*. **careless**, *a*, insouciant; négligent. ~**ly**, *ad*, négligemment. ~**ness**, *n*, négligence, inattention, incurie, *f*, laisser-aller, *m*.

caress, *n*, caresse, *f*; (*pl.*) mamours *f.pl. only.* ¶ *v.t,* caresser.

caret, *n*, signe d'omission, renvoi, *m*.

cargo, *n*, cargaison, *f*, chargement, *m*, charge, *f*; marchandises, (*Insce*) facultés, *f.pl.* ~ *boat, steamer,* navire, vapeur, de charge, *m*.

Caribbean sea (the), *n*, la mer des Antilles.

caricature, *n*, caricature, charge, *f*. ¶ *v.t,* caricaturer, charger.

carman, *n*, charretier, voiturier, camionneur, *m*.

Carmelite, *n*, (*friar*) carme, *m*; (*nun*) carmélite, *f*.

carmine, *n*, carmin, *m*.

carnage, *n*, carnage, *m*.

carnal†, *a*, charnel.

carnation (*Bot.*), *n*, œillet [des fleuristes] *m*.

carnelian, *n*, cornaline, *f*.

carnival, *n*, carnaval, *m*.

carnivora, *n.pl,* carnassiers, carnivores, *m.pl.* **carnivorous**, *a. & * **carnivore**, *n*, carnassier, carnivore, *a. & m.*

carob [bean], *n*, caroube, *f*.

carol, *n*, chant d'allégresse, *m*. [*Christmas*] ~, noël, *m*. ¶ *v.i,* chanter; (*lark*) grisoller.

carousal, *n*, orgie, débauche, ripaille, *f*. **carouse**, *v.i,* faire [la] débauche.

carp (*fish*) *n*, carpe, *f*. ¶ ~ *at,* chicaner.

Carpathians (the), les Carpathes, *m.pl.*

carpenter, *n*, charpentier, menuisier, *m*. ¶ *v.t,* charpenter; (*v.i.*) menuiser. **carpentry**, *n*, charpenterie, *f*.

carpet, *n*, tapis, *m*. ~ *broom,* balai de tapis, *m*. ~ *knight,* héros de salon, *m*. ~ *slippers,* pantoufles en tapisserie, *f.pl.* ~ *sweeper,* balai, *m*, (*ou* balayeuse, *f.*) mécanique pour tapis. ¶ *v.t,* recouvrir d'un tapis; (*with flowers, &c*) tapisser.

carriage, *n*, voiture, *f*; wagon; équipage; (*gun*) affût; (*Mach.*) chariot, *m*; démarche, allure, tenue, *f*; transport; port; prix du transport (*ou* de la voiture) *m*. ~ *& pair,* voiture à deux chevaux, *f*. ~ *attendant* (hotel, &c), aboyeur, *m*. ~ *entrance,* porte charretière, *f*. ~ *forward,* port dû, en port dû. ~ *jack,* chèvre de carrossier, *f*. ~ *paid,* ~ *free,* port payé, en port payé, franc de port.

carrier, *n*, porteur; messager, voiturier, transporteur, entrepreneur de transports (*ou* de roulage); (*Mach.*) chariot, *m*; porte-, *e.g,* *luggage* ~, porte-bagage, *m*. ~ *bicycle,* bicyclette de livraison, *f*. ~ *pigeon,* pigeon voyageur, *m*. ~ *tricycle,* triporteur, *m*.

carrion, *n*, charogne, *f*.

carrot, *n*, carotte, *f*. ~**y hair**, des cheveux [rouge] carotte, *m.pl.*

carry (*Arith.*) *n*, retenue, *f*. ¶ *v.t,* porter; emporter; transporter; véhiculer; mener, conduire; charrier, voiturer; (*Arith.*) retenir; adopter, prendre; voter. ~ *away,* enlever, emporter, entraîner; emballer, enthousiasmer. ~ *forward* (*Bkkpg*), reporter. ~ *on,* poursuivre, opérer. ~ *out,* exécuter, effectuer; suivre.

cart, *n*, charrette; voiture; carriole, *f*; tombereau, *m*. ~ *grease,* cambouis, *m*. ~ *horse,* cheval de charrette, *m*. ~*load,* charretée, *f*; tombereau, *m*. ~ *note* (*Cust.*), laissez-passer, congé, *m*. ¶ *v.t,* charrier, charroyer, voiturer, camionner. ~**age**, *n*, charroi, roulage; camionnage; factage; prix du transport, *m*. ~**er**, *n*, charretier, voiturier, camionneur, *m*.

Carthusian [**monk**], *n*, chartreux, *m*. ~ *monastery,* chartreuse, *f*.

cartilage, *n*, cartilage, *m*.

cartoon, *n*, carton; dessin, *m*; caricature, *f*. ~**ist**, *n*, dessinateur, trice; caricaturiste, *m*, *f*.

cartouche, *n*, cartouche, *m*. **cartridge**, *n*, cartouche, *f*; (*cannon*) gargousse, *f*. ~ *belt,* ceinture cartouchière, *f*. ~ *factory,* cartoucherie, *f*. ~ *pouch,* sac à cartouches, *m*, cartouchière, *f*.

carve, *v.t,* sculpter; tailler; (*meat*) découper. **carver** (*pers.*) *n*, sculpteur, *m*; découpeur, euse. **carving**, *n*, sculpture, *f*; découpage, *m*. ~ *knife* or [*meat*] *carver,* couteau à découper, *m*. ~ *tool,* outil de sculpteur, *m*.

cascade, *n*, cascade, cascatelle, *f*.

case, *n*, cas; état, *m*; question, *f*; exemple, *m*; cause, affaire, *f*, procès, *m*; caisse, boîte; mallette, *f*; sac; étui; écrin, *m*; gaine, *f*; porte-, *e.g, suit* ~, porte-habits, *m*; trousse; pochette, poche, cassette, *f*, nécessaire; fourreau; boîtier; portefeuille, *m*; douille; chemise; enveloppe; (*for firework*) cartouche; (*sausage*) peau; (*precision balance*) cage, *f*; (*piano*) coffre, *m*; (*Typ.*) casse, *f*. ~ *ending* (*Gram.*), flexion casuelle, *f*. ~ *of need* (*Com.*), besoin, *m*. ~ *opener,* ciseau à déballer, *m*. ¶ *v.t,* encaisser, envelopper; [en]gainer; (*Min.*) cuveler.

caseharden, *v.t,* aciérer, cémenter. ~**ed** (*fig.*) *p.a,* bronzé, cuirassé.

casemate, *n*, casemate, *f*.

casement, *n*, châssis à fiches, *m*. ~ [*window*], fenêtre [ordinaire], croisée, *f*. ~ *cloth,* tissu pour croisée, *m*. ~ *stay,* entrebâilleur de fenêtre, *m*.

cash, n, espèces, f.pl, numéraire, argent, m, finances, f.pl; comptant, m; caisse, m. encaisse, f, fonds, m.pl. ~ & bullion in hand, encaisse métallique. ~ book, livre de caisse, m. ~ box, coffret à monnaie; m; caisse, f. ~ desk, comptoir-caisse, m; caisse, f. ~ discount, escompte de caisse (ou au comptant) m. ~ down or in ~ & for ~, [au] comptant. ~ in hand, [en]caisse, fonds (ou espèces) en caisse. ~ on delivery, envoi contre remboursement, m. ~ on delivery parcel, colis contre remboursement, m. ~ register, caisse enregistreuse (ou contrôleuse). ~ with order, payable à la commande. ¶ v.t, encaisser, toucher; escompter, payer. ~ier, n, caissier, ère. ~ & bookkeeper, caissier-comptable. ¶ v.t,destituer, casser.

cashmere, n, cachemire, m.

casing, n, enveloppe, f; bâti, dormant, m.

cask, n, tonneau, f, barrique, f, baril, fût, m, futaille, pièce, f.

casket, n, cassette, f, écrin, f.

Caspian sea (the), la mer Caspienne.

casserole, n, casserole [en terre cuite], huguenote, f.

cassia, n, casse, f. ~ tree, cassier, m.

cassock, n, soutane, f.

cast, n, jet, m, coulée; pièce moulée, f; coup de filet; bas de ligne pour le lancer, m; addition; distribution [des rôles] m; (worm) chiasse, f. ~ of features, physionomie, f, facies, m. ~ of mind, tournure d'esprit, mentalité, f. ¶ v.t.ir, jeter, lancer; promener; fondre, couler, mouler; additionner; distribuer. ~ iron, fonte [de fer] f, fer de fonte, m; (att., fig.) rigide. ~ its skin, se dépouiller. ~ net, épervier, m. ~ off, (Typ.) évaluer; (Knit.) faire une chaîne de mailles. ~off clothing, défroque, f. ~ on (Knit.), monter. ~ out, chasser, rejeter. ~ shadow, ombre portée, f. ~ steel, acier coulé, m, fonte d'acier, f. [crucible] ~ steel, acier fondu [au creuset].

castanet, n, castagnette, f.

castaway, n, réprouvé, e; naufragé, e.

caste, n, caste, f.

castellated, a, crénelé.

caster, n, couleur, fondeur, m. (See castor.)

castigate, v.t, châtier. **castigation**, n, châtiment, m.

casting, n, jet, m; coulée, fonte; pièce [coulée], f, moulage, coulé, m; pêche au lancer, f. ~ off, (Typ.) évaluation, f; (Knit.) chaîne de mailles, f. ~ on (Knit.), montage des mailles, m. ~ rod, canne à lancer, f. ~ vote, voix prépondérante, f. to give the ~ vote, départager les voix.

castle, n, château; (Chess) tour, f. ¶ (Chess) v.i, roquer.

castor or caster, n, (bottle) saupoudroir, m; (roller) roulette [pour chaises, &c], f, galet [pivotant] m. **castor oil**, huile de ricin, f.

castor oil plant, ricin, m. **castor (or caster) sugar**, sucre en poudre, m.

castrate, v.t, châtrer. **castration**, n, castration, f.

casual†, a, casuel, accidentel, fortuit; (remark) en passant. ~ labourer, homme à l'heure, m. ~ profit, [fruit] casuel, revenant-bon, m. ~ water (Golf), [flaque d']eau fortuite, f. ¶ n, indigent(e) de passage. ~ty, n, sinistre, m; (pers.) victime; (Mil.) perte, f.

casuistry, n, casuistique, f.

cat, n, chat, te; (tipcat) bâtonnet, m. ~ burglar, cambrioleur chat, m. ~-call, sifflet, m. ~calling, sifflerie, aubade, f. ~'s cradle, jeu de la scie, m. ~'s eye (jewel), œil-de-chat, f. ~'s paw (fig.), patte du chat, f. to be someone's ~'s paw, tirer les marrons du feu pour quelqu'un. ~ tribe, race féline, f.

cataclysm, n, cataclysme, m.

catacomb, n, catacombe, f.

catafalque, n, catafalque, m.

catalogue, n, catalogue, m. ¶ v.t, cataloguer.

catapult, n, (Hist. & Aero.) catapulte; (boy's) fronde, f. ¶ v.t. & abs, fronder; (Aero) lancer.

cataract (falls & Med.) n, cataracte, f.

catarrh, n, catarrhe, m.

catastrophe, n, catastrophe, f.

catch, n, prise; (fish) prise, pêche, f, coup de filet, jet, m; (trick) attrape, f, leurre; (Mech.) arrêt, mentonnet, cran; (window, &c) loqueteau, m. ~phrase, scie, f. ~word, rengaine, scie, f; (displayed in bold type) mot en vedette, m; (at head of dictionary page) lettrine, f. ¶ v.t. & i.ir, attraper; saisir; accrocher; s'engager; gagner; capturer; capter; happer; prendre; se p.; surprendre; frapper. ~-[as-~-]can, lutte libre, f. ~ fire, prendre feu, s'enflammer; (Cook.) graillonner. ~ on, prendre. ~er, n, preneur, chasseur, m. ~ing, a, contagieux; séduisant.

catechism, n, catéchisme, m. **catechize**, v.t, catéchiser.

categorical†, a, catégorique. **category**, n, catégorie, f.

cater, v.i, donner à manger. ~ for, pourvoir à; s'adresser à, viser. **caterer**, n, restaurateur, trice, cafetier, ère, traiteur; pourvoyeur, m.

caterpillar, n, chenille, f. ~ car, autochenille, f.

caterwaul, v.i, miauler. ~ing, n, miaulement, m, musique de chats, f.

catgut, n, corde à boyau, f.

cathead, n, bossoir, m.

cathedral, n, cathédrale, f.

catherine wheel, soleil, m. to turn ~s, faire la roue.

cathode, n, cathode, f.

catholic, a. & n, catholique. a. & m,f. ~ism, n, catholicisme, m.

catkin, n, chaton, m.

cattle, n, bétail, m, bestiaux, m.pl. ~ bell, sonnaille, clarine, f. ~ market, marché aux bestiaux, m. ~ plague, peste bovine, f. ~ show, concours (ou comice) agricole, m. ~ truck, wagon (ou fourgon) à bestiaux (ou à bétail) m.

Caucasian, a, caucasien. ¶ n, Caucasien, ne. the Caucasus, le Caucase.

caucus, n, cabale, f.

cauldron, n, chaudron, m.

cauliflower, n, chou-fleur, m.

caulk, v.t, calfater; matir.

causative, a, occasionnel; (Gram.) causal. cause, n, cause, raison, f, sujet, motif; cas, m. ~ list, rôle, m, feuille d'audience, f. ¶ v.t, causer, occasionner, provoquer, entraîner; faire, e.g, to ~ to vary, faire varier.

causeway, n, chaussée, levée, f.

caustic, a, & n, caustique, a. & m. cauterize, v.t, cautériser. cautery, n, cautère, m.

caution, n, prudence, précaution, f; avertissement, m. ~ ! attention ! ¶ v.t, prémunir, précautionner, avertir. cautious, a, prudent, réservé, retenu, sur ses gardes, en garde. ~ly, ad, avec circonspection. ~ness, n, prudence, f.

cavalcade, n, cavalcade, f.

cavalier†, a, cavalier. ¶ n, cavalier, m.

cavalry, n, cavalerie, f.

cave, n, caverne, f, antre, m. ~ dweller, troglodyte, m. ~ in, v.i, s'effondrer, ébouler; céder.

cavern, n, caverne, f, souterrain, m. ~ous, a, caverneux.

caviar[e], n, caviar, m.

cavil, n, chicane, argutie, f. ¶ v.i, chicaner, ergoter.

cavity, n, cavité, f, creux, m.

caw, v.i, croasser.

Cayenne pepper, poivre de Cayenne, m.

cease, v.i. & t, cesser. without ~, sans cesse. ~less, a, incessant. ~lessness, n, continuité, f.

cedar, n, cèdre, m. ~ of Lebanon, cèdre du Liban.

cede, v.t, céder.

ceil, v.t, plafonner. ~ing, n, plafond, m. ~ bowl, coupe électrique, f. ~ fitting, plafonnier, m.

celebrate, v.t. & i, célébrer; solenniser; fêter. ~d, p.a, célèbre, fameux, renommé. celebrity, n, célébrité; illustration, f.

celery, n, céleri, m.

celestial, a, céleste.

celibacy, n, célibat, m. celibate, n, célibataire, m.f.

cell, n, cellule, f, alvéole; cachot, m; (pl. Mil.) cellule, f; (Phys.) élément, couple, m. ~ jar, bac d'éléments, m.

cellar, n, cave, f, caveau, m. ¶ v.t, encaver. ~er, n, cellérier, m.

cellist, n, violoncelliste, m. [']cello, n, basse, f, violoncelle, m.

cellular, a, cellulaire. celluloid, n, celluloïd, m. cellulose, n, cellulose, f.

Celt, n, Celte, m.f. Celtic, a. & (language) n, celtique, a. & m.

cement, n, ciment, m. ¶ v.t, cimenter; (metal) cémenter.

cemetery, n, cimetière, m.

cenotaph, n, cénotaphe, m.

cense, v.t, encenser. censer, n, encensoir, m.

censor, n, censeur, m. ~ious, a, critique. ~ship & [vote of] censure, n, & [board of] censors, censure, f. ¶ v.t, censurer.

census, n, recensement, dénombrement, m.

centaur, n, centaure, m.

centenarian, n, centenaire, m.f. centenary, n, centenaire, m.

centigrade, a, centigrade. (See note in French-English section.)

centipede, n, scolopendre, f.

central, a, central. C~ America, l'Amérique Centrale, f. ~ heating, chauffage central, m. ~ize, v.t, centraliser; canaliser. centre, n, centre; milieu; noyau; (Arch.) cintre, m; (lathe) pointe, f. ~ bit, mèche à trois pointes, f. ~ casting, crapaudine, f. ~ piece, surtout [de table] m. ~ punch, pointeau, m. ~ service line (Ten.), ligne médiane de service, f. ¶ v.t, centrer; (fig.) concentrer. centrifugal, a, centrifuge. centripetal, a, centripète.

century, n, siècle, m.

ceramics, n, céramique, f.

cereal, a. & n, céréale, a.f. & f.

ceremonial, n, cérémonial, m. ¶ a, de cérémonie. ceremonious†, a, cérémonieux, façonnier. ceremony, n, cérémonie; façon, f. oft. pl.

certain†, a, certain. ~ty, n, certitude, f. for a ~, à coup sûr.

certificate, n, certificat; diplôme; brevet; acte, m; attestation; déclaration, f; extrait; titre, m. ~d, p.a, diplômé. certify, v.t, certifier; viser; attester; déclarer.

cesspool, n, fosse [d'aisances] f; cloaque, m.

Ceylon, n, Ceylan, m.

Chadband, n, chattemite, f.

chafe, v.t, frictionner; écorcher; (v.i.) s'écorcher; s'irriter.

chaff, n, balle; glume; menue paille, f; badinage, m. ~ cutter, hache-paille, m. ¶ v.t, plaisanter, gouailler, berner.

chaffinch, n, pinson, m.

chafing dish, chauffe-plats, m.

chain, n, chaîne; chaînette, f. (Imperial linear meas.) = 22 yards or 20·1168 metres. ~ bridge, pont suspendu à chaînes, m. ~ stitch, point de chaînette, m. ~ store, magasin à succursales multiples, m. ~ & ~ up, v.t, enchaîner.

chair, n, chaise; (Univ.) chaire, f; (at meeting) fauteuil (de la présidence) m; (rail) coussinet, m. ~ attendant, loueur (euse) de chaises.

~ *back* (*Need.*), têtière, *f.* (*loose*) ~ *cover*, housse de fauteuil, *f.* ¶ ~! à l'ordre! ¶ *v.t*, porter en triomphe.

chairman, *n*, président, e. **~ship**, *n*, présidence, *f.*

chalcedony, *n*, calcédoine, *f.*

chalice, *n*, calice, *m*, coupe, *f.*

chalk, *n*, craie, *f*; (*Bil.*) blanc, *m.* ~ *line*, (*cord*) cordeau, *m*; (*mark*) tringle, *f.* ~ *pit*, carrière de craie, *f.* ¶ *v.t*, marquer à la craie. **~y**, *a*, crayeux.

challenge, *n*, défi, cartel, *m*, provocation, *f*; (*Auditing*) sondage; (*Mil.*) qui-vive; (*Sport*) challenge, *m.* ~ *cup*, coupe challenge, *f*, challenge, *m.* ~ *match*, match défi, *m.* ¶ *v.t*, défier, provoquer, contester; récuser; incriminer.

chalybeate, *a*, ferrugineux.

chamber, *n*, chambre, *f*; (*pl.*) cabinet, *m*, étude, *f.* ~ *counsel*, avocat consultant, avocat-conseil, *m.* **~maid**, femme de chambre, *f.* ~ *music*, musique de chambre, *f.* ~ [*pot*], vase de nuit, *m.* *six—ed revolver*, revolver à six coups, *m.*

chameleon, *n*, caméléon, *m.*

chamfer, *n*, chanfrein, *m.*

chamois, *n*, chamois, *m.* ~ [*leather*], peau de chamois, *f*, chamois, *m.*

champ, *v.t*, ronger, mâcher.

champagne, *n*, champagne, vin de Champagne, *m.* ~ *glass*, coupe à c., *f.*

champion, *n*, champion; tenant; Don Quichotte; athlète, *m.* ~ *idiot*, fameux imbécile, maître sot, *m.* ~ *turnip*, roi des navets, *m.* **~ship**, *n*, championnat, *m.*

chance, *a*, de hasard; de fortune; d'occasion, fortuit, aléatoire. ¶ *n*, chance; fortune, *f*; hasard, aléa, *m.* **to ~ it**, risquer le paquet, brusquer l'aventure.

chancel, *n*, chœur, *m.*

chancellery, *n*, chancellerie, *f.* **chancellor**, *n*, chancelier, *m.* C~ *of the Exchequer* (*Eng.*), ministre des Finances (*Fr.*) *m.*

chancre, *n*, chancre, *m.*

chandelier, *n*, lustre, *m.*

chandler, *n*, chandelier, *m*; épicier, ère.

change, *n*, changement; mouvement, *m*; altération; mutation; variation, *f*; revirement, *m*; saute; vicissitude; (*money*) monnaie, *f*; appoint, *m*; (*exchange*) bourse, *f.* at ~ (*barometer*) au variable. ~ *of clothes*, vêtements de rechange, m.pl. ~ *of front*, volte-face, *f.* ~[-*speed*] *gear*, changement de vitesse. ¶ *v.t. & i*, changer; c. de; se c., convertir; altérer; sauter. ~ *here for* . . ., on change de train pour . . . ~ *one's mind, one's linen*, changer d'avis, de linge. ~ *step*, changer de pas. ~ *the subject*, quitter le sujet, rompre les chiens. **~able**, *a*, changeant; mobile; variable, inconstant.

channel, *n*, chenal, *m*, passe, *f*; canal, *m*, rigole, *f*; manche; cannelure; (*fig.*) voie, entremise, *f.* the [*English*] C~, la Manche.

the C ~ *Islands*, les îles [Anglo-]Normandes, *f.pl.* a C~ *tunnel*, un tunnel sous la Manche. ¶ *v.t*, raviner, canneler. **channelling**, *n*, cannelure, *f.*

chant, *n*, chant, *m.* ¶ *v.i. & t*, chanter, psalmodier; (*horses*) maquignonner. **chanty**, *n*, chanson [de bord] *f.*

chaos, *n*, chaos, *m.* **chaotic**, *a*, chaotique.

chap, *n*, garçon; gaillard, *m*; (*pl.*) (*on the skin*) crevasses, gerçures, *f.pl*; (*animal*) babines, bajoues; (*vice*) mâchoires, *f.pl.* ¶ *v.t. & i*, crevasser, gercer, se gercer.

chapel, *n*, chapelle, *f.* ~ *of ease*, (*église*) succursale, *f.*

chaperon, *n*, chaperon, *m.* ¶ *v.t*, chaperonner.

chaplain, *n*, aumônier; chapelain, *m.*

chaplet, *n*, guirlande, *f*; (*beads*) chapelet, *m.*

chapter, *n*, chapitre, *m*; (*fig.*) page; série, *f.*

char (*fish*) *n*, omble[-chevalier], ombre-chevalier, *m.* ¶ *v.t*, carboniser; (*v.i.*) [se] charbonner; faire des ménages.

charabanc, *n*, (*motor*) autocar; (*horse*) char à bancs, *m.*

character, *n*, caractère, *m*; nature, allure; réputation; cote, *f*; rôle; personnage; certificat, *m.* **characteristic**, *a*, caractéristique. ¶ *n*, caractéristique, *f*, caractère, propre, *m*; (*pl. of map*) légende, *f.* **characterize**, *v.t*, caractériser.

charade, *n*, charade, *f.*

charcoal, *n*, charbon [de bois] *m.* ~ *burner* (*pers.*), charbonnier, *m.* ~ *drawing*, [dessin au] fusain; *m.* ~ [*pencil*], fusain, charbon à dessin, *m.*

chare, *v.i*, faire des ménages.

charge, *n*, charge, *f*; soin, *m*, garde; accusation, inculpation, *f*; privilège, *m*; affectation; assignation; imputation, *f*; (*bishop's*) mandement; prix, *m*, taxe, *f*, frais, *m.pl*; dépense; redevance, *f.* ¶ *v.t*, charger; foncer sur; demander; prendre; mettre à [la] charge; taxer; percevoir; imputer; inculper; affecter; appliquer; accuser. **~able**, *a*, à la charge; imputable: affectable; applicable.

charger (*horse*) *n*, cheval de bataille; (*Poet.*) coursier, *m.*

charily, *a*, prudemment; chichement.

chariot, *n*, char, *m.*

charitable†, *a*, charitable, bienfaisant. **charity**, *n*, charité; bienfaisance, assistance, *f*, œuvres [pies] *f.pl*, aumône, l'aumône, *f.*

charlatan, *n*, charlatan, banquiste, *m.*

Charlie Chaplin moustache, moustache à la Charlot, *f.*

charm, *n*, charme, enchantement, agrément, *m*; (*pl.*) appas, attraits, *m.pl*; (*trinket*) breloque, amulette; mascotte, *f*, fétiche, *m.* ¶ *v.t*, charmer, enchanter. **~er**, *n*, charmeur, euse, enchanteur, teresse.

charnel house, charnier, ossuaire, *m.*

chart, *n*, carte, *f*; graphique, diagramme, *m.* ¶ *v.t*, porter sur la carte, le graphique, &c.

charter, *n*, charte, *f*. ~ [*party*], charte-partie, *f*. **grain** ~, c.-p. de grain. ¶ *v.t*, [af]fréter, prendre à fret; privilégier. ~**er**, *n*, affréteur, *m*. ~**ing**, *n*, affrétement, *m*.

charwoman, *n*, femme de ménage, f. de journée, *f*.

chary, *a*, prudent; avare, chiche, sobre.

chase, *n*, chasse, poursuite; (*gun*) volée, *f*; (*Typ*.) châssis, *m*. ¶ *v.t*, chasser, poursuivre; (*Hawking*) voler; (*metals*) ciseler; (*screws*) peigner. **chaser** (*Nav*.) *n*, chasseur, *m*. ~ **plane**, avion de chasse, *m*.

chasm, *n*, abîme, gouffre, *m*.

chassé, *n*, chassé, *m*. ¶ *v.t*, chasser.

chassis, *n*, châssis, *m*.

chaste†, *a*, chaste, pudique.

chasten & **chastise**, *v.t*, châtier. **chastisement**, *n*, châtiment, *m*.

chastity, *n*, chasteté, pudicité, *f*.

chasuble, *n*, chasuble, *f*.

chat, *n*, causerie, causette, *f*. ¶ *v.i*, causer, deviser.

chattel, *n*, chose, *f*; (*pl*.) biens, effets, *m.pl*.

chatter, *n*, babil, *m*, jaserie, *f*. ¶ *v.i*, babiller, jaser; jacasser; (*teeth*) claquer; (*tool*) brouter. ~**box**, moulin à paroles, *m*, babillard, *e*.

chauffeur, *n*, chauffeur, *m*.

cheap, *a*, (*article*, &c) [à] bon marché; (*ticket*, &c) à prix réduit; (*price*) bas. ~ **edition**, édition à bon marché, *f*. ~ **Jack**, camelot, *m*. ~**er**, *a*, [à] meilleur marché, moins cher. ~[**ly**], *ad*, à bon marché, à peu de frais. ~**ness**, *n*, bon marché, *m*, vileté, *f*.

cheat (*pers*.) *n*, fourbe, *m*, *f*; tricheur, euse. ¶ *v.t*. & *i*, tromper; frauder; friponner, tricher, filouter. ~[**ing**], *n*, fourberie; tromperie; tricherie, *f*.

check, *n*, échec, *m*; bride, *f*, frein; contrôle; pointage; bulletin; (*design*) dessin à carreaux, *m*; (*stuff*) étoffe à carreaux, & en damier, *f*; (*att*.) de contrôle, contradictoire, témoin. ¶ *v.t*, brider, enrayer, modérer; contrôler, vérifier; pointer. ¶ (*Chess*) *i*, échec ! ~**mate**, *n*, échec & mat, *m*; (*v.t*.) mater, faire [échec &] mat; (*fig*.) faire échec à.

Cheddar [**cheese**], *n*, chester, *m*.

cheek, *n*, joue, *f*; impudence, *f*, front, toupet, sans-gêne, *m*. ~ **bone**, pommette, *f*. ~**y**, *a*, impudent, hardi, effronté.

cheep, *v.i*, piailler, piauler.

cheer, *n*, (*food*) chère; consolation, *f*; applaudissement, vivat, hourra, bravo, *m*. ¶ *v.t*, réjouir, égayer, rassurer, consoler; applaudir. ~ **up**, ragaillardir. ~ **up !** [du] courage ! ~**ful**†, *a*, gai, joyeux, riant, allègre. ~**fulness**, *n*, gaieté, allégresse, *f*. ~**less**, *a*, triste, morne.

cheese, *n*, fromage, *m*. ~ **cover**, cloche à f., *f*. ~ **dairy**, fromagerie, *f*. ~ **industry**, industrie fromagère, *f*. ~ **knife**, couteau

à dessert, *m*. ~**monger** & ~ **maker**, fromager, ère. ~**paring**, économie de bouts de chandelle, *f*. ~ **plate**, assiette à dessert, assiette à fromage, *m*.

cheetah, *n*, guépard, *m*.

chemical†, *a*, chimique. ¶ *n*, produit chimique, *m*.

chemise, *n*, chemise de jour, *f*.

chemist, *n*, (*scientist*) chimiste, *m*, *f*; (*druggist*) pharmacien, ne. ~**'s shop**, pharmacie, *f*. ~**ry**, *n*, chimie, *f*.

cheque, *n*, chèque, mandat, *m*. ~ **book**, carnet de chèques, *m*.

chequer, *v.t*, guillocher. ~**ed** (*fig*.) *p.a*, accidenté.

cherish, *v.t*, chérir, bercer, caresser, nourrir, choyer.

cherry, *n*, cerise, *f*. ~ **orchard**, cerisaie, *f*. ~**-pie** (*Bot*.), héliotrope [du Pérou] *m*. ~**-red**, *a*. & *n*, cerise, *a*. & *m*. ~ **stone**, noyau de cerise, *m*. ~ [*tree*], cerisier; (*wild*) merisier, *m*.

cherub, *n*, chérubin, *m*.

chervil, *n*, cerfeuil, *m*.

Cheshire cheese, chester, *m*.

chess, *n*, échecs, *m.pl*. ~ **board**, échiquier, *m*. ~**men**, pièces, *f.pl*, échecs, *m.pl*.

chest, *n*, (*Anat*.) poitrine, *f*; (*box*) coffre, *m*, caisse, boite, *f*; bahut, *m*. ~ **expander**, extenseur, *m*. ~ **handle**, portant, *m*. ~ **measurement**, grosseur de poitrine, *f*. ~ **of drawers**, commode, *f*. ~ **register** or **voice**, voix de poitrine, *f*.

chesterfield, *n*, (*overcoat*) pardessus chesterfield; (*couch*) canapé-divan, *m*.

chestnut, *n*, châtaigne, *f*, marron, *m*. ~**-brown**, châtain. ~ [*tree*], châtaignier, marronnier, *m*.

cheval dressing table, coiffeuse psyché, *f*. **cheval glass**, psyché, *f*.

chevy, *v.t*, chasser.

chew, *v.t*. & *i*, mâcher; (*tobacco*) chiquer; (*fig*.) remâcher. ~ **the cud**, ruminer. ~**ing**, *n*, mastication, *f*. ~ **gum**, gomme à mâcher, *f*.

chiaroscuro, *n*, clair-obscur, *m*.

chicane, *v.t*. & *i*, chicaner. ~**ry**, *n*, chicane[rie] *f*.

chick, *n*, poussin, poulet, *m*. **chickabiddy**, *n*, petiot, e. **chicken**, *n*, poulet, te. ~ **heart** (*pers*.) poule mouillée, *f*, poltron, ne. ~**-hearted**, poltron. ~ **pox**, varicelle, petite vérole volante, *f*.

chickweed, *n*, mouron [des oiseaux] *m*, morgeline, *f*.

chicory, *n*, chicorée; endive, *f*.

chide, *v.t*. & *i.ir*, gronder.

chief, *a*, premier, principal; en chef. ~ **attraction**, clou de la fête, *m*. **to be** ~ **mourner**, conduire (*ou* mener) le deuil. ~ **rabbi**, grand rabbin, *m*. ~ **town**, chef-lieu, *m*. ¶ *n*, chef; supérieur, *m*. ~**ly**, *ad*, principalement, surtout. **chieftain**, *n*, chef, *m*.

chiffon, *n*, chiffon, *m*. **chiffonier**, *n*, chiffonnier, *m*.

chilblain, *n*, engelure, *f*.

child, *n*, enfant, *m*, *f*. *from a* ~, dès
l'enfance. *with* ~, enceinte. ~*bed*,
couches, *f.pl*. ~*birth*, travail [d'enfant],
accouchement, *m*. ~'s *play*, un jeu
d'enfant, *m*. ~ *welfare*, puériculture
sociale, *f*. *the* ~ *world*, le petit monde.
~*hood*, *n*, enfance, *f*. ~*ish*, *a*, enfantin;
puéril. ~*ishly*, *ad*, puérilement, ~*ishness*, *n*, enfantillage, *m*, puérilité, *f*.
~*less*, *a*, sans enfant. ~*like*, *a*, comme
un enfant, en enfant. **children**, *n.pl*,
enfants, *m.pl*. ~'s *hour* (*Radio*), heure
de la jeunesse, *f*.

Chile, -li, le Chili. **Chilean**, -lian, *a*,
chilien. ¶ *n*, Chilien, ne.

chill, *a*, froid, glacé. ¶ *n*, froid, frisson,
aigre, *m*, fraîcheur, *f*; coup d'air, c. de
froid, *m*; (*fig., of age*) glaces, *f.pl*. *to take
the* ~ *off*, (*water*) faire dégourdir; (*wine*)
chambrer. ¶ *v.t*, refroidir, glacer, transir,
morfondre. **chilliness**, *n*, froideur, *f*,
froid, *m*. **chilly**, *a*, froid; frisquet; (*pers.*)
frileux.

chime(s), *n.[pl.]*, carillon, *m*. ¶ *v.i*, carillonner. ~ *in with*, abonder dans le sens
de. *chiming clock*, pendule à carillon, *f*.

chim[a]era, *n*, chimère, *f*. **chimerical**, *a*,
chimérique.

chimney, *n*. & ~ *piece*, cheminée, *f*. ~
corner, coin du feu, *m*. ~ *on fire*, feu de
cheminée, *m*. ~ *pot*, cheminée, *f*. ~
sweep[er], ramoneur, *m*.

chimpanzee, *n*, chimpanzé, *m*.

chin, *n*, menton, *m*. ~ *strap*, jugulaire, *f*.

china, *n*. & ~*ware*, *n*, porcelaine, faïence [fine] *f*.
~ *cabinet*, vitrine, armoire vitrée, *f*. ~
clay, terre à porcelaine, *f*, kaolin, *m*.
~ *manufacturer* & ~ *dealer*, porcelainier, ère. ~ *shop*, magasin de porce-
laines, *m*.

China (*Geog.*) *n*, la Chine. ~ *aster*, reine-
marguerite, *f*.

chine, *n*, échine; (*Cook.*) échinée, *f*.

Chinese, *a*, chinois. ~ *curio*, &c, chinoiserie,
f. ~ *lantern*, lanterne vénitienne, *f*,
lampion [en papier] *m*. ~ *puzzle* (*fig.*),
casse-tête chinois, *m*. ¶ *n*, (*language*)
chinois, *m*; (*pers.*) Chinois, e.

chink, *n*, lézarde, fente, crevasse, *f*. ¶ *v.t*,
choquer; (*v.i.*) tinter.

chintz, *n*, perse, *f*.

chip, *n*, copeau, éclat, *m*, écaille, écornure, *f*.
~ *of the old block*, fils de son père, *m*.
¶ *v.t*, tailler par éclats; buriner; écorner;
ébrécher; (*v.i.*) s'écorner.

chiropodist, *n*, pédicure, *m.f*. **chiropody**, *n*,
soin des pieds, *m*.

chirp, *n*, pépiement, guilleri; (*insect*) cri,
cricri, *m*. ¶ *v.i*, pépier; crier.

chisel, *n*, ciseau, burin, *m*. ¶ *v.t*, ciseler,
buriner.

chit, *n*, marmot, te; [petit] bout, *m*. ~ *of a
girl*, petite fille, *f*.

chit-chat, *n*, causerie, *f*; commérage, *m*.

chivalrous, *a*, chevaleresque. **chivalry**, *n*,
chevalerie, *f*.

chive, *n*, cive[tte], ciboulette, *f*.

chivy, *v.t*, chasser.

chlorate, *n*, chlorate, *m*. **chloride**, *n*,
chlorure, *m*. ~ *of lime*, c. de chaux.
chlorine, *n*, chlore, *m*. **chloroform**, *n*,
chloroforme, *m*. ¶ *v.t*, chloroformer.

chocolate, *n*, chocolat, *m*; (*pl.*) bonbons au c.,
m.pl. ~ *box*, bonbonnière, *f*. ~ *cream*,
crème chocolatée, *f*. ~ *creams*, chocolats
fourrés à la crème, *m.pl*. ~ *éclair*, éclair
au chocolat, *m*. ~ *manufacturer* or *seller*,
chocolatier, ère. ~ *pot*, chocolatière, *f*.

choice, *a*, choisi, de [grand] choix; fin;
recherché. ¶ *n*, choix, *m*; élite, fleur, *f*.
~*ness*, *n*, excellence, *f*.

choir, *n*, chœur, *m*. ~ *boy*, enfant de chœur,
m. ~ *master*, maître de chapelle, *m*.

choke, *v.t*, suffoquer, étouffer, étrangler;
engorger, bourrer. ~*-full*, *a*, plein comme
un œuf.

cholera, *n*, choléra, *m*.

choose, *v.t.ir*, choisir; élire; (*v.i.ir.*) opter.

chop, *n*, coup; *m*, côtelette, *f*; (*pl.*) babines,
bajoues, *f.pl*. ¶ *v.t*, (*meat*, &c) hacher;
(*firewood*) débiter. ~ *off*, couper, trancher.

chopper, *n*, couperet, *m*. **chopping block**,
hachoir, billot, *m*. **chopping board**, hachoir, *m*. **choppy** (*water*) *a*, clapoteux.

chopstick, *n*, bâtonnet, *m*.

choral, *a*, choral. ~ *society*, [société]
chorale, *f*, orphéon *m*.

chord, *n*, corde, *f*; (*Mus.*) accord, *m*.

choreography, *n*, chorégraphie, *f*.

chorister, *n*, choriste, *m*, *f*; enfant de chœur,
m. **chorus**, *n*, chœur; refrain en c.;
~ *singer* (*opera*), choriste, *m.f*.
to [*repeat in*] ~, faire chorus. *to join in
the* ~, faire chœur au refrain.

Christ, *n*, le Christ. **christen**, *v.t*, baptiser.
Christendom, *n*, chrétienté, *f*. **christening**,
n, baptême, *m*. **Christian**, *a*, chrétien.
~ *name*, nom de baptême, petit nom,
prénom, *m*. ~ *science*, le culte des
scientistes chrétiens. ¶ *n*, chrétien, ne.
Christianity, *n*, christianisme, *m*. **christianize**, *v.t*, christianiser. **christianly**, *ad*,
chrétiennement.

Christmas & ~*-tide* (*abb.* Xmas) *n*, Noël, *m*.
at ~, à la [fête de] Noël, à Noël. ~ *box*,
~ *present*, *In Fr.*, presents are given on or
about *Jan.* 1 and called étrennes, *f.pl*. *a* ~
present (to child), le petit Noël. ~ *pudding*, pudding de Noël, plum-pudding, *m*.

chromate, *n*, chromate, *m*.

chromatic, *a*, chromatique.

chrome, *n*, chrome, *m*; (*att., steel, leather*)
chromé; (*yellow*) de chrome. **chromium**, *n*,
chrome, *m*; (*att., steel*) chromé. ~*-plated*,
chromé.

chronic, a, chronique.

chronicle, n, chronique, f. C~s (Bible) pl, l'aralipomènes, m.pl. ¶ v.t, enregistrer, consigner. chronicler, n, chroniqueur, m.

chronological†, a, chronologique. chronology, n, chronologie, f.

chronometer, n, chronomètre, m.

chrysalis, n, chrysalide, f.

chrysanthemum, n, chrysanthème, m.

chub (fish) n, chabot, meunier, m.

chubby, a, joufflu, potelé. ~ umbrella, parapluie poucet, petit parapluie, m.

chuck (lathe) n, mandrin, plateau, m. ¶ (throw) v.t, flanquer. ~farthing, fossette, f. ~ out, flanquer à la porte. ~ under the chin, relever le menton à.

chuckle, v.i, glousser, rire sous cape.

chum, n, camarade, m, f, copain, m.

chump, n, bûche, f. ~ chop, côtelette de gigot, f.

chunk, n, quignon, chanteau, m.

church, n, église, f; temple, m. the C~ of England, l'Église anglicane. ~ service, office divin, m. ~warden, marguillier, m. ~yard, cour de l'église, f; jardin de l'église; champ du repos, cimetière, m; (public square surrounding a church, as St Paul's Churchyard) place, f, e.g, la Place de la Madeleine.

churching, n, relevailles, f.pl.

churl, n, manant, bourru, rustre, m. ~ish, a, bourru, aigre.

churn, n, baratte, f. ~ dash[er], batte à beurre, f, babeurre, m. ¶ v.t, baratter, battre.

cider, n, cidre, m.

cigar, n, cigare, m. ~ case, porte-cigares, m. ~ cutter, coupe-cigares, m. ~ holder, porte-cigare, fume-cigare, m.

cigarette, n, cigarette, f. ~ box, coffret à c~s, m. ~ case, étui à c~s, m. ~ holder, ~ tube, porte-cigarette, fume-cigarette, m.

cinder[s], n.[pl.], escarbille[s], f.[pl.], m, braise, f; scorie[s], f.[pl.]; cendrée, f. burnt to a ~ (meat, &c), en charbon. ~ sifter, tamis à escarbilles, m. ~ track, piste en cendrée, f.

Cinderella, n, Cendrillon, f.

cinema, cinematograph, n, cinéma, cinématographe, m. cinema star, vedette de cinéma, v. de l'écran, f.

cineraria (Bot.) n, cinéraire, f.

cinerary, a, cinéraire, f.

Cingalese, a, cingalais. ¶ n, Cingalais, e.

cinnabar, n, cinabre, m.

cinnamon, n, cannelle, f.

cipher, n, chiffre; zéro, m; nullité, f, comparse, m. word in ~, mot en chiffré, m. ¶ v.t. & i, chiffrer.

circle, n, cercle; milieu, m; (Theat.) galeries, f.pl. ¶ v.t, ceindre, cerner. circlet, n, couronne, f. circuit, n, circuit, tour, m. tournée, f. ~ous, a, détourné. circu-

lar†, a. & n, circulaire, a. & f. circulate, v.t, faire circuler, répandre; (v.i.) circuler, rouler. circulating, a, circulant; roulant. ~ decimal, fraction périodique, f. ~ library, bibliothèque circulante, f. circulation, n, circulation, f; mouvement, m; (newspaper) tirage, m.

circumcise, v.t, circoncire.

circumference, n, circonférence, f, tour, m.

circumflex, a. & n, circonflexe, a. & m.

circumlocution, n, circonlocution, f, circuit de paroles, m, paraphrase, f.

circumscribe, v.t, circonscrire.

circumspect, a, circonspect, mesuré, avisé. ~ly, ad, avec circonspection.

circumstance, n, circonstance, f; état; cas, m; cérémonie, f. in easy ~s, à son aise. in straitened (or reduced) ~s, dans la gêne. ~s permitting, sauf imprévu. circumstantial, a: ~ account, relation circonstanciée, f. ~ evidence, témoin muet, m, preuve par présomption, f.

circumvent, v.t, circonvenir.

circus, n, cirque; hippodrome; (in city) rondpoint, carrefour; (traffic) sens giratoire, m, circulation en sens giratoire, f.

cirrhosis, n, cirrhose, f.

cirrus (Meteor.) n, cirrus, m.

cistern, n, fontaine, f; réservoir, m; citerne, f; (barometer) cuvette, f.

citadel, n, citadelle, f.

cite, v.t, citer, alléguer; assigner.

citizen, n, citoyen, ne, citadin, e. ~ship, n, droit de cité, m.

citric, a, citrique. citron, n, cédrat, m.

city, n, ville; cité, f.

civet [cat], n, civette, f.

civic, a, civique.

civil†, a, civil; honnête. ~ commotion, mouvement populaire, m. ~ engineering, génie civil, m. ~ servant, employé(e) d'administration, fonctionnaire public, m. fonctionnaire publique, f. ~ service, administration publique, f. ~ian, n, civil, m. ~ity, n, civilité, f.

civilization, n, civilisation, f. civilize, v.t, civiliser; policer. civilizing, a, civilisateur, trice.

clack, n, claquement; caquet, m. ~ [valve], clapet, m.

claim, n, réclamation, revendication, f, recours; titre, m; prétention, exigence, demande, demande d'indemnité; indemnité, f, sinistre, m; concession; créance, f. ¶ v.t, réclamer, revendiquer, prétendre [à], demander, s'attribuer. ~ back (Law), répéter. ~ant, n, réclamant, e, prétendant, e. ~holder, n, concessionnaire, m, f.

clairvoyance, n, seconde vue, f. clairvoyant, n, voyant, e.

clam (Mol.) n, palourde, f.

clamber [up], v.i. & t, gravir, grimper.

clamminess, n, moiteur, f. clammy, a, moite, pâteux.

clamorous, *a*, bruyant, criard. ~ly, *ad*, à cor & à cri. **clamour**, *n*, clameur, *f*. ¶ *v.i*, crier, vociférer. ~ *for*, réclamer à grands cris.

clamp, *n*, bride [de serrage], presse, happe, *f*, serre-joint[s], crampon, *m*; pince, *f*. ¶ *v.t*, brider, cramponner, bloquer.

clan, *n*, clan, *m*.

clandestine†, *a*, clandestin.

clang, *n*, son, *m*. ¶ *v.i*, retentir.

clank, *n*, cliquetis, *m*. ¶ *v.i*, cliqueter.

clap, *n*, coup; battement, *m*. ~**trap**, phrases à effet, *f.pl*, boniment, *m*. ¶ *v.t. & i*, claquer; battre. **clapper**, *n*, claquet, claquoir, *m*, claquette, *f*; (*bell*) battant, *m*. **clapping**, *n*, battement [de mains] *m*.

claret, *n*, bordeaux [rouge], vin de Bordeaux, *m*.

clarify, *v.t*, clarifier.

clarion, *n*, clairon, *m*. **clari[o]net**, *n*, clarinette, *f*.

clash, *n*, choc, *m*, rencontre, collision, *f*; fracas; cliquetis; conflit, *m*. ¶ *v.i*, s'entrechoquer; être en conflit; jurer.

clasp, *n*, agrafe, *f*, fermoir, *m*; étreinte, *f*, serrement, *m*. ~ *knife*, couteau à virole, c. à cran d'arrêt, *m*. ¶ *v.t*, agrafer; prendre; se prendre; presser, étreindre, serrer.

class, *n*, classe; catégorie; cote, *f*; cours, *m*. ~ *book*, livre de classe, I. classique, *m*. ~ *consciousness*, l'esprit de caste, *m*. ~ *mate*, camarade de classe, c. de promotion, *m,f*. ~ *prize*, prix d'excellence, *m*. ~ *room*, [salle de] classe, *f*. ~ *war*, guerre sociale, *f*. ¶ *v.t*, classer; coter. **classic** & **classical†**, *a*, classique. **classic**, *n*, classique, *m*. **classification**, *n*, classification, *f*. **classify**, *v.t*, classer. **classing**, *n*, classement, *m*.

clatter, *n*, fracas, tapage, *m*. ¶ *v.i*, claquer, carillonner.

clause, *n*, clause, *f*, article, *m*; (*Gram*.) proposition, *f*.

claustral, *a*, claustral.

claw, *n*, griffe, serre, patte, *f*, ongle, *m*; pince, *f*, pied-de-biche, *m*. ¶ *v.t*, griffer, s'agriffer à; égratigner.

clay, *n*, argile; glaise; terre, *f*. ~ *bird*, pigeon artificiel, papegai, *m*. ~ *pipe*, pipe en terre, *f*. ~ *pit*, carrière d'argile, glaisière, *f*. **clayey**, *a*, argileux.

clean, *a*, propre; blanc; net; pur; sain; sans réserves; (*Typ. proof*) peu chargée; (*jump*) franc. ~**shaven**, glabre, entièrement rasé. ~ *slate* (*fig*.), table rase; rafle, *f*. ~ *sweep* (*fig*.), table rase; rafle, *f*. ¶ *v.t*, nettoyer; blanchir; dégraisser; débourber. ~**er**, *n*, nettoyeur, euse; femme de ménage, femme de journée, *f*. ~**ing**, *n*, nettoyage; dégraissage; curage, *f*. **cleanliness**, *n*, propreté, netteté, *f*. **cleanse**, *v.t*, assainir; purger; [é]curer.

clear, *a*, clair; limpide; pur; net; distinct; libre; franc. ~ *soup*, consommé, *m*.

~**sighted**, clairvoyant. ¶ *v.t*, éclaircir; débarrasser; dégager; franchir; évacuer; déblayer; défricher; purger; (*table*) desservir; (*letter box*) [re]lever; (*cheque*) compenser; (*shop goods*) solder; (*Cust.—goods*) dédouaner; (*a ship inwards*) faire l'entrée [en douane]; (*a ship outwards*) expédier [en douane]. to ~ (shop), en solde. ~ *up*, *v.t*, éclaircir, tirer au clair, mettre au net, débrouiller; (*v.i*.) s'éclaircir, se rasséréner. ~**ance**, *n*, (*Mech*.) jeu, *m*, chasse, *f*; (*goods through cust*.) dédouanement, *m*; (*ship through Cust*.) expédition, *f*; (*foreign ship leaving French port*) passeport; (*French ship leaving French port*) congé, *m*. ~ *papers* (ship's), expéditions, *f.pl*. ~ *sale*, solde, *m*. ~**ing** (*glade*) *n*, éclaircie, clairière, *f*. ~ *house* (*Banking*), chambre de compensation, *f*. ~**ly**, *ad*, clair[ement], nettement, bien. ~**ness**, *n*, clarté, netteté; pureté, *f*.

cleat, *n*, tasseau, *m*, languette, *f*; taquet, *m*.

cleavage, *n*, fendage; (*Miner*.) clivage, *m*; (*fig*.) scission, *f*. **cleave**, *v.t.ir*, fendre, refendre; cliver; (*v.i.ir*.) se fendre; se cliver; se coller; s'attacher. **cleaver**, *n*, fendoir, couperet, *m*. *cleaving axe*, merlin, *m*.

clef, *n*, clef, clé, *f*.

cleft, *n*, fente, fissure, *f*. ~ *stick*, piquet fourchu, *m*; (*fig*.) impasse, *f*.

clematis, *n*, clématite, *f*.

clemency, *n*, clémence, *f*. **clement**, *a*, clément.

clench, *v.t*, crisper; serrer.

clergy, *n*, clergé, *m*, gens d'Église, *m.pl*. ~**man**, *n*, ecclésiastique; ministre, *m*. **cleric**, *n*, ecclésiastique, *m*. ~**al**, *a*, d'employé, de commis; (*of clergy*) ecclésiastique, clérical. ~ *error* (*ou* fault) erreur de plume (*ou* de copiste) *f*; (*Law*) vice (*ou* pas) de clerc, *m*. ¶ *n*, clérical, *m*. **clerk**, *n*, employé, e, commis [de bureau], *m*, préposé, e; (*Law & Eccl*.) clerc; (*court*) greffier, *m*. ~ *of the course*, (*Turf*) commis de course; (*Athletic Sports*) délégué aux concurrents, *m*. ~ *of* [the] *works*, commis d'entreprise.

clever†, *a*, habile; adroit. ~ *move*, adresse, *f*. ~**ness**, *n*, dextérité, habileté, *f*.

clew, *n*, fil, *m*.

click, *n*, cliquetis, tic tac (*Mech*.) cliquet, chien, déclic, *m*, détente, *f*. ¶ *v.i*, cliqueter, faire tic tac.

client, *n*, client, e; partie, *f*. **clientele**, *n*, clientèle, *f*.

cliff, *n*, (*coast*) falaise, *f*; (*inland*) rocher [en escarpement] *m*.

climacteric, *a*, critique, climatérique.

climate, *n*, climat; ciel, *m*. **climatic**, *a*, climatérique, climatique.

climax, *n*, (*Rhet*.) gradation [ascendante] *f*; point culminant; bouquet, *m*.

climb, *n*, ascension, montée, *f*. ¶ *v.t. & i*, gravir, monter, faire l'ascension de, grimper. ~ *over*, escalader. ~**er**, *n*, ascensionniste, *m,f*; plante grimpante, *f*. ~**ing** boots, bottines d'escalade, *f.pl.*

clime (*Poet.*) *n*, terre, *f*; ciel, *m*.

clinch (*Box.*) *n*, corps à corps, *m*. ¶ *v.t*, river; (*fig.*) conclure. ~**er**, *n*, paquet, *m*.

cling, *v.i.ir*, se cramponner, s'attacher, s'agripper, se coller, s'aheurter, tenir. ~**stone**, pavie, *f*.

clinic, *n*, clinique, *f*. ~**al**, *a*, clinique; (*thermometer*) médical. ~**ian**, *n*, clinicien, *m*.

clink, *n*, (*glasses*) choc; (*lock-up*) violon, *m*. ¶ *v.t*, choquer, trinquer; (*v.i.*) tinter.

clinker, *n*, mâchefer, *m*.

clip, *n*, pince, serre, griffe, attache, patte [d'attache], virole, *f*, valet, *m*. ¶ *v.t*, cisailler; tailler; tondre; rogner; (*ticket*) poinçonner; (*words*) estropier, manger. ~**pers**, *n.pl*, ciseaux, *m.pl*, tondeuse, *f*. ~**pings**, *n.pl*, rognures, *f.pl*.

clique, *n*, clique, coterie, *f*.

cloak, (*lit. & fig.*) *n*, manteau, *m*. ~ **room**, vestiaire, *m*; (*Rly*) consigne, *f*. ¶ *v.t*, voiler, masquer.

clock, *n*, (*big*) horloge; (*small*) pendule, pendulette, *f*; (*taximeter*) compteur, *m*; (*on stocking*) baguette, *f*. ~ **& watch maker**, horloger, *m*. ~**work** [*movement*], mouvement d'horlogerie, *m*. ~-**work train** (toy), train mécanique, train à ressort, *m*.

clod, *n*, motte, *f*. ~ **crusher**, hérisson, *m*. ~[**hopper**], rustre, rustaud, lourdaud, *m*.

clog, *n*, sabot, socque, *m*, galoche, *f*; (*fig.*) entrave[s] *f[.pl.]*. ~ **dance**, sabotière, *f*. ¶ *v.t*, encrasser; engorger; charger; entraver.

cloister, *n*, cloître, *m*. ¶ *v.t*, cloîtrer. **cloistral**, *a*, claustral.

close, *n*, clos, *m*; fermé; étroit; serré; dense; [r]enfermé; lourd, mou; minutieux; vif; intime; près, proche; appliqué; jointif; soutenu. ~-**fitting garment**, vêtement collant (*woven*) maillot, *m*. ~ **season**, temps prohibé, *m*, période d'interdiction, *f*. ~-**shaven**, rasé de près, ras. ¶ *ad*, près, de près; auprès. ~-**up**, premier plan, gros plan, *m*. ¶ *n*, fin; clôture; levée, *f*; (*precincts*) pourtour, *m*. **the** ~ **of day**, la chute du jour. ¶ *v.t*, fermer; clore; arrêter; régler; lever; liquider, réaliser; serrer; barrer; boucher; (*v.i.*) fermer, se f.; clore; chômer. ~**d** (*Theat.*), relâche. ~**ly**, *ad*, de près; attentivement; strictement; étroitement. ~**ness**, *n*, compacité; intimité; proximité, *f*; manque d'air, *m*; lourdeur, *f*. ~ **closet**, *n*, cabinet, *m*. ¶ *v.t*, chambrer, claquemurer. **closing**, *n*, fermeture, clôture, *f*; chômage, *m*; liquidation, *f*. ~-**down sale**, liquidation, *f*. ~ **price**, dernier cours, c. de clôture, *m*. **closure**, *n*, clôture, *f*.

clot, *n*, caillot, grumeau, *m*. ¶ *v.i*, se cailler, se grumeler.

cloth, *n*, drap, *m*; toile; étoffe, *f*; voile; tissu; linge; tapis, *m*; nappe, *f*; parement, *m*; couverture, *f*; napperon; torchon, *m*; robe, soutane, *f*. ~ **manufacturer & ~ merchant**, drapier, *m*. ~ **trade**, draperie, *f*. **clothe**, *v.t.ir*, habiller, vêtir; revêtir. **clothes**, *n.pl*, habits, vêtements, *m.pl*, tenue, *f*; entretien, *m*; (*worn*) hardes, *f.pl.* ~ **basket**, panier à linge, *m*. ~ **brush**, brosse à habits, *f*. ~ **hanger**, porte-vêtements, cintre, *m*. ~ **horse**, séchoir à linge, *m*. ~ **line**, étendoir, *m*, corde à linge, *f*, (*pl.*) étendage, *m*. ~ **peg**, épingle à linge, *f*. ~ **prop**, perche d'étendoir, *f*. **clothier**, *n*, drapier, *m*; confectionneur, euse. **clothing**, *n*, habillement, vêtement, *m*.

cloud, *n*, nuage, *m*; (*fig.*) nuée; (*Poet.*) nue, *f*. ~ **burst**, trombe d'eau, rafale de pluie, *f*. **in the** ~**s** (*fig.*), dans le bleu. ¶ *v.t*, couvrir de nuages; obscurcir, voiler, obnubiler; assombrir. ~**less**, *a*, sans nuage. ~-**y**, *a*, nuageux, nébuleux; couvert, chargé, bas; terne, trouble, louche.

clout, *n*, torchon; chiffon, *m*; (*blow*) gifle, *f*.

clove, *n*, [clou de] girofle, *m*. ~ **of garlick**, gousse d'ail, *f*. ~ **tree**, giroflier, *m*.

cloven hoof, pied fourchu, *m*.

clover, *n*, trèfle, *m*. **in** ~ (*fig.*), à gogo.

clown, *n*, paillasse, pierrot, clown, Gille, pitre, baladin, bouffon, *m*. ~**ery**, *n*, bouffonnerie, clownerie, pantalonnade, *f*. ~**ish**, *a*, bouffon.

clox, *n.pl*, baguettes, *f.pl*.

cloy, *v.t*, rassasier (*with* = de).

club, *n*, massue, casse-tête, *f*, gourdin, *m*; (*Golf*) crosse, *f*, club, *m*. (Clubs such as brassy, mashie, niblick are named the same in French and are *m*.); (*people*) club, cercle, *m*, société, *f*; (*church*) patronage, *m*; (*Cards, s. & pl.*) trèfle, *m*. ~ **foot**, pied bot, *m*. ~ **together**, se cotiser.

cluck, *n*, gloussement, *m*. ¶ *v.i*, glousser.

clue, *n*, indication; clef, piste, *f*.

clump, *n*, masse; motte; botte; touffe, *f*, massif, bouquet, *m*.

clumsiness, *n*, gaucherie, maladresse, *f*. **clumsy**†, *a*, gauche, maladroit, empoté, pataud; incommode. ~ **fellow**, maladroit, pataud, *m*.

cluster, *n*, faisceau, nœud, bouquet, peloton, groupe, *m*, grappe, *f*, régime, *m*. ¶ *v.i*, se grouper.

clutch, *n*, griffe; (*eggs*) couvée, *f*; (*Mech.*) [manchon d']embrayage, *m*. ~ **it & i**, empoigner, [a]gripper; se raccrocher.

coach, *n*, voiture, *f*, wagon; carrosse, coche; (*tutor*) répétiteur, préparateur; (*Sport*) entraîneur, instructeur; (*Boating*) capitaine d'entraînement, *m*. ~**builder**, carrossier, *m*. ~**building**, carrosserie, *f*. ~ **horse**, carrossier, *m*. ~ **house**, remise, *f*. ~**man**, cocher, *m*. ~**screw**, tirefond, *m*. ~**smith**, serrurier charron, *m*.

~ *wrench*, clef anglaise, *f.* ¶ *v.t*, préparer; entraîner; endoctriner.

coadventurer, *n*, coïntéressé, e.

coagulate, *v.t*, coaguler; (*v.i.*) se coaguler.

coal, *n*, charbon [de terre] *m*, houille, *f.* (*pl.*) charbon[s]. ~ *cellar* & ~ *merchant* or *coalman*, charbonnier, *m.* ~ *field*, terrain carbonifère (*ou* houiller) *m.* ~ *heaver*, coltineur de charbon, *m.* ~ *mine*, mine de charbon (*ou* de houille), houillère, *f.* ~ *miner*, houilleur, mineur de houille, *m.* ~ *mining*, exploitation de la houille *ou* du charbon, *f*, charbonnage, *m.* ~ *scuttle*, seau à charbon, *m.* ~ *stage*, estacade, *f.* ~ *strike*, grève des mineurs [de houille] *f.* ~ *tar*, goudron de houille, coaltar, *m.* ~ *yard*, chantier (*ou parc*) à charbon, *m*, charbonnerie, *f.* ¶ *v.i*, faire du charbon.

coalesce, *v.i*, se confondre. **coalition**, *n*, coalition, *f*, bloc, cartel, *m.*

coarse†, *a*, grossier, gros; rude; brutal. ~ *fish*, poissons blancs, *m.pl.* ~**ness**, *n*, grossièreté, rudesse, *f.*

coast, *n*, côte[s] *f.[pl.]*, littoral, *m*, bord[s] *m.[pl.]*. ~-*defence ship*, [vaisseau] garde-côte, *m.* ~ *station*, station côtière, *f.* ¶ *v.i*, côtoyer. ~**er**, *n*, caboteur, *m*, cabotier, *m.* ~ *hub*, moyeu arrière à roue libre & frein contre-pédalage, *m.* ~**guard**, *n*, agent de police des côtes à terre, *m.* ~**ing**, *n.* & ~ *trade*, cabotage, *m.*

coat, *n*, (*man's*) pardessus; manteau, *m*; (*woman's*) redingote, *f*; (*long*) manteau, *m*; (*short*) jaquette, *f*; (*woolly*) gilet, *m*; (*Mil.*) tunique; (*animal's*) robe, *f*, poil, pelage, *m.* (*Anat., &c*) paroi; tunique; (*layer*) couche, *f*, enduit, *m.* ~ *of arms*, armes, armoiries, *f.pl*, blason, *m.* ~ *of mail*, cotte de mailles, *f.* ¶ *v.t*, enduire, revêtir. ~**ee**, *n*, paletot, *m.*

coax, *v.t*, enjôler, amadouer.

cob, *n*, (*horse*) bidet; (*Build.*) torchis, bousillage; (*corn*) épi, *m*, rafle, *f.* ~[*nut*], grosse noisette, aveline, *f.*

cobalt, *n*, cobalt, *m.*

cobble [*stone*], *n*, galet, pavé, *m.* ~**s** (*coal*) *pl*, gailletin, gaillette, *f.* ¶ *v.t*, saveter, rapetasser. **cobbler**, *n*, savetier, *m.* ~**'s** *wax*, poix, *f.*

cobra, *n*, cobra, *m.*

cobburg [*loaf*], *n*, pain cornu, *m.*

cobweb, *n*, toile d'araignée, *f.*

cocaine, *n*, cocaïne, *f.*

Cochin-China, *n*, la Cochinchine. **Cochin-Chinese**, *a*, cochinchinois. ¶ *n*, Cochinchinois, e.

cochineal, *n*, cochenille, *f.*

cock, *n*, coq; (*tap*) robinet; (*hay*) meulon; (*of gun*) chien, *m.* ~-*a-doodle-doo*, coquerico, cocorico, *m.* ~-*&-bull story*, coq-à-l'âne, *m*, contes en l'air, *m.pl.* ~ *bird*, oiseau mâle, *m.* ~**crow[ing]**, chant du coq, *m.* ~ *of the walk*, coq du village, *m.*

~ *pheasant*, [coq] faisan, *m.* ¶ *v.t*, relever, [re]dresser; (*gun*) armer. ~**ed** *hat*, chapeau à cornes, *m.*

cockade, *n*, cocarde, *f.*

cockatoo, *n*, cacatoès, *m.*

cockchafer, *n*, hanneton, *m.*

cockerel, *n*, cochet, *m.*

cockle, *n*, (*Mol.*) clovisse, coque; (*Bot.*) ivraie, *f.* ¶ *v.t*, recoquiller; (*v.i.*) se r.

cockpit, *n*, arène, *f*; (*Aero.*) poste du pilote, *m*, nacelle, carlingue, *f.*

cockroach, *n*, cafard, cancrelat, *m*, blatte, *f.*

cockscomb, *n*, crête de coq; (*Bot.*) crête-de-coq, *f.*

cocktail (*drink*) *n*, cocktail, *m.* ~ *bar*, bar-cocktail, *m.* ~ *shaker*, shaker, *m.* ~ *table*, guéridon, *m.*

cocoa, *n*, (*bean*) cacao; (*drink*) chocolat, *m.*

coco[nut], *n*, coco, *m*, noix de c., *f.* ~ *palm*, cocotier, *m.*

cocoon, *n*, cocon, *m.*

cod[fish], *n*, morue, *f*, cabillaud, *m*; (*dried*) merluche, *f.* ~ *fisher*, morutier, *m.* ~ *liver oil*, huile de foie de morue, *f.*

coddle, *v.t*, dorloter, câliner, choyer.

code, *n*, code, *m.* ~ *of the road*, c. de la route. ~ *word*, mot convenu, *m.* ¶ *v.t*, rédiger en langage convenu. **codicil**, *n*, codicille, *m.* **codify**, *v.t*, codifier.

coefficient, *n*, coefficient, *m.*

coerce, *v.t*, contraindre.

coffee, *n*, café; moka, *m.* ~ *cup*, tasse à café, *f.* ~ *pot*, cafetière, verseuse, *f.* ~ *room*, salle à manger, *f.* ~ *spoon*, cuiller à café, c. à moka, *f.* ~ *table*, guéridon, *m.* ~ *tree* & ~ *planter*, caféier, *m.*

coffer, *n*, coffre, *m*, caisse, *f.*

coffin, *n*, cercueil, *m*, bière, *f.*

cog, *n*, dent, *f*; alluchon, *m.* ~*wheel*, roue dentée, *f.* ¶ *v.t*, [en]router de dents.

cogency, *n*, force, *f.* **cogent**, *a*, convaincant, probant.

cogitate, *v.i*, méditer, réfléchir.

cognate, *a*, de même origine.

cognizance, *n*, connaissance, *f.* **cognizant of**, instruit de.

cognomen, *n*, surnom, *m.*

cohabit, *v.i*, cohabiter.

cohere, *v.i*, adhérer. **coherence**, *n*, cohérence; suite, *f.* **coherent**, *a*, cohérent; suivi. ~**ly**, *ad*, avec cohérence. **cohesion**, *n*, cohésion, *f.* **cohesive**, *a*, cohérent.

cohort, *n*, cohorte, *f.*

coil, *n*, rouleau, *m*, glène; couronne, botte, torsade, *f*; serpentin; (*snake*) repli, anneau, *m*; (*Elec.*) bobine, *f.* ¶ *v.t*, [en]rouler (*en couronne*], bobiner; (*rope*) lover, rouer. ~ *up*, replier; se replier.

coin, *n*, pièce, [pièce de] monnaie, *f*; numéraire, *m*, espèces [monnayées] *f.pl*; (*ancient*) médaille, *f.* ~ *cabinet*, médaillier, *m.* ~ *machine*, appareil à sous, *m.* ¶ *v.t*, monnayer, frapper, battre; (*fig.*) forger, inventer; fabriquer. ~**age**, *n*,

monnayage, *m*, frappe, *f*; monnaie[s] *f*.[*pl.*], numéraire, *m*.

coincide, *v.i*, coïncider. **coincidence, n,** coïncidence, *f*.

coiner, *n*, faux-monnayeur; fabricateur de fausse monnaie; (*fig.*) forgeur, *m*. **coining press**, balancier monétaire, *m*.

coir, *n*, fibre de coco, *f*.

coke, *n*, coke, *m*.

colander, *n*, passoire, *f*.

cold†, *a*, froid; à froid. *in ~ blood* or *~-blooded*, de sang-froid, à froid. *~-blooded* (animal), à sang froid. *~ chisel*, burin (*ou* ciseau) à froid, *m*. *~ cream*, crème froide, *f*, cold-cream, *m*. *~ snap*, coup de froid, *m*. *~ steel*, arme blanche, *f*. *~ storage*, conservation par le froid, *f*. *~ store*, entrepôt frigorifique, dock frigorifique, frigorifique, *m*. ¶ *n*, froid, *m*; froidure, *f*; (*Path.*) rhume, coup d'air, *m*. *~ on the chest, in the head*, rhume de cerveau, de poitrine. **~ness, n,** froideur, froidure, *f*, froid, *m*, frigidité, *f*.

coleopter[an], n, coléoptère, *m*. **coleopterous, a,** coléoptère.

colic, *n*, colique, *f*, tranchées, *f.pl.*

collaborate, *v.i*, collaborer. **collaborator, n,** collaborateur, trice.

collapse, n, effondrement, écroulement; affaissement, *m*; chute, débâcle, *f*. ¶ *v.i*, s'effondrer, crouler, s'écrouler, s'affaisser. **collapsible, a:** *~ gate*, grille extensible, *f*. *~ view-finder*, viseur redresseur, *m*.

collar, *n*, collier, collet; col; (*fur, &c*) tour de col, *m*; frette, bague, *f*. [*shirt*] *~* (detached), faux col, *m*. *~ (attached)* (to shirt), col tenant, *m*. *~ bone*, clavicule, *f*. *~ stud*, bouton de col, *m*. ¶ *v.t*, colleter.

collate, *v.t*, collationner.

collateral, *a*, collatéral. *~ security*, nantissement, *m*.

collation, *n*, collationnement, *m*; (*snack*) collation, *f*.

colleague, *n*, collègue, *m*.

collect, *n*, collecte, *f*. ¶ *v.t*, recueillir, rassembler, réunir; retirer; enlever; [re]lever; capter; collectionner; recouvrer, récupérer; percevoir; encaisser; quêter. **~ed, p.a,** recueilli, calme. **~ion, n,** rassemblement, recueil, *m*; réunion, *f*; captage; recouvrement, *m*; récupération; perception, rentrée; levée, *f*; relevage; encaissement; enlèvement, apport, *m*; quête, collecte, *f*; cabinet, *m*. *~ of coins or medals*, médaillier, *m*. **~ive†, a,** collectif. **~or, n,** collecteur, receveur, percepteur; collectionneur, fureteur, curieux, *m*, ramasseur, euse. **~orship, n,** perception, recette, *f*.

college, *n*, collège, *m*; école, *f*; séminaire, *m*; académie, *f*; conservatoire, *m*. **collegian, n,** collégien, ne. **collegiate, a,** collégial.

collide, *v.i*, s'aborder, se rencontrer, se tamponner. *~ with*, aborder, rencontrer, tamponner.

collier, *n*, (*pers.*) houilleur; (*ship*) charbonnier, *m*. **~y, n,** houillère, *f*; (*col. pl.*) charbonnage, *m*.

collision, *n*, abordage, *m*, collision, rencontre, *f*, tamponnement, *m*. *~ mat*, paillet d'abordage, *m*.

colloquial†, a, de la conversation; (*words, phrases*) familier. **~ism, n,** expression familière, *f*. **colloquy, n,** colloque, *m*.

collusion, *n*, collusion, *f*.

colon, *n*, deux-points, *m*.

colonel, *n*, colonel, *m*. *C~ Bogey* (*Golf*), la normale [du parcours]. *~ commandant*, général de brigade, brigadier, *m*.

colonial, *a*, colonial. *C~ Office*, Ministère des Colonies, *m*. **colonist, n,** colon, *m*. **colonize**, *v.t*, coloniser.

colonnade, *n*, colonnade, *f*.

colony, *n*, colonie, *f*.

colophon, *n*, marque [typographique] *f*, chiffre, fleuron, *m*.

colossal†, a, colossal. **colossus, n,** colosse, *m*.

colour, *n*, couleur, *f*; teint; coloris, *m*; peinture, *f*; (*pl.*) couleurs, *f.pl*, drapeaux, *m.pl*, pavillon, *m*. *under ~ of* (*fig.*), sous couleur de. *~ bar*, distinction sociale (*ou* légale) entre la race blanche & la race noire, *f*. **~-blind,** aveugle des couleurs. **~ blindness,** cécité pour les c—s, *f*. *~ photography*, photographie en c—s, *f*. ¶ *v.t*, colorer, colorier; enluminer; (*pipe*) culotter. **~able, a,** plausible, spécieux. *~ imitation*, contrefaçon, *f*. **~ed, p.a. &** *p.p*: *~ dress*, robe de couleur, *f*. *flame-~ribbon*, ruban couleur de feu, *m*. *rose-~shoes*, souliers couleur de rose, *m.pl*. *~ sketch*, croquis en couleurs, *m*. **~ing, n,** coloris, *m*. **~less, a,** sans couleur, incolore, pâle.

colt, *n*, poulain, *m*. **coltsfoot** (*Bot.*) *n*, pas d'âne, tussilage, *m*.

Columbia, *n*, la Colombie.

columbine (*Bot.*) *n*, ancolie, *f*.

column, *n*, colonne *f*; pilier, *m*; (*news or special subject*) rubrique, *f*.

colza, *n*, colza, *m*.

coma, *n*, (*Med.*) coma, *m*; (*Bot. & comet*) chevelure, *f*. **comatose, a,** comateux.

comb, *n*, peigne; coup de peigne, *m*; (*crest*) crête, *f*; (*honey*) rayon, gâteau, *m*, gaufre, *~ maker*, peignier, *m*. ¶ *v.t*, peigner. *~ out* (*fig.*), éliminer.

combat, *n*, combat, *m*. ¶ *v.t*, combattre. **~ant, n,** combattant, *m*. **~ive, a,** batailleur. **~iveness, n,** combativité, *f*.

combination, *n*. & **~s** (*dress*) *n.pl*, combinaison, *f*. **combine, n,** coalition, *f*. ¶ *v.t*, combiner, réunir; joindre; (*v.i.*) combiner; se coaliser.

combings, *n.pl*, peignures, *f.pl*.

combustible, *a*, combustible. **combustion, n,** combustion, *f*. *~ chamber* (*motor*), chambre d'explosion, *f*.

come, *v.i.ir*, venir; provenir; arriver; se présenter; se faire; entrer; être. ~*!* ~*!* voyons! ~*!,* ~ *along!,* ~ *on!* allons!, venez!, marchons!, çà! ~ *about,* se faire. ~ *across,* rencontrer. ~ *back,* revenir. ~ *down,* descendre. ~ *for,* venir chercher. ~ *from* (be a native of), être originaire de. ~ *home,* rentrer; revenir; porter coup. ~ *in!* entrez! ~ *now!* enfin!, ah! çà. ~ *off,* se détacher (ink, &c) décharger. ~ *off on* (dye), déteindre sur. ~ *on! sus!* ~ *out,* sortir; débuter (book, &c) paraître. ~ *to,* se monter à; revenir à; (decision) prendre. ~ *to an agreement,* tomber d'accord. ~ *to blows,* en venir aux mains. ~ *to light,* se découvrir. ~ *to pass,* arriver, advenir. ~ *to terms,* s'arranger. ~ *undone, unsewed,* &c, se défaire, se découdre, &c. ~ *up* (sprout), poindre. ~ *upon,* tomber sur. ~ *what may,* arrive (*ou* advienne que) pourra, au petit bonheur.

come-&-go (the), l'aller & le venir, le va-&-vient.

comedian, *n*, comédien, ne; farceur, m. **comedy**, *n*, comédie, *f*, comique, *m*. ~ *writer,* comique, m.

comeliness, *n*, beauté, grâce, bonne mine, *f*. **comely**, *a*, beau, gracieux, avenant.

comer, *n*, venant, *m*; venu, e. ~s *& goers,* allants & venants, m.pl.

comet, *n*, comète, *f*.

comfort, *n*, consolation, satisfaction, aise, *f*, [ré]confort, *m*. ¶ *v.t*, consoler, réconforter, soulager. ~**able†**, *a*, aisé, confortable. ~**er**, *n*, consolateur, trice; (scarf) cache-nez, *m*.

comic & comical, *a*, comique; humoristique, cocasse; plaisant, bouffon, bouffe, burlesque. ~ *actor,* comique, *m*. ~ *opera,* opéra bouffe, *m*. ~ *song,* chanson burlesque, chansonnette, *f*. ~ *turn,* pantalonnade, *f*.

coming, *p.a*, à venir; d'avenir; futur. ¶ *n*, venue, arrivée, *f*, (of Christ) avènement, *m*. [I am] ~*!* j'y vais! on y va! voilà! ~ *& going,* allées & venues, m.pl. ~ *out* (in society), début, *m*, entrée dans le monde, *f*.

comma, *n*, virgule, *f*. *Note:*—Sets of three figures, separated in Eng. by commas, are separated in Fr. either by points or by spaces. (Cf. *decimal point*.)

command, *n*, commandement, *m*; ordre[s] *m.[pl.]*; empire, *m*; facilité, *f*. ¶ *v.t*, commander; monter; ordonner; avoir à sa disposition; (a view of) donner sur. ~**ant**, *n*, commandant, chef, *m*.

commandeer, *v.t*, réquisitionner.

commander, *n*, commandant, chef; (*Nav.*) capitaine de frégate, *m*. ~*-in-chief,* généralissime, *m*. *commanding officer,* commandant, chef, *m*.

commandment, *n*, commandement, *m*.

commemorate, *v.t*, commémorer.

commence, *v.t & i*, commencer, entamer. ~**ment**, *n*, commencement, début, *m*.

commend, *v.t*, recommander; applaudir à, préconiser; remettre. ~**able**, *a*, recommandable, louable. ~**ation**, *n*, éloge, *m*, louange; recommandation, *f*.

commensurate, *a*, proportionné.

comment & commentary, *n*, commentaire, *m*, glose, *f*. ~ *to comment on,* commenter [sur]. **commentator**, *n*, commentateur, glossateur; (*Radio*) parleur inconnu, *m*.

commerce, *n*, commerce, négoce, *m*. **commercial**, *a*, commercial, commerçant, marchand, de commerce, d'affaires. ~ *sale rooms,* bourse de marchandises, b. de commerce, *f*. ~ *traveller,* voyageur de commerce, commis voyageur, *m*. ~**ism**, *n*, mercantilisme, *m*. ~**ize**, *v.t*, achalander, monnayer. ~**ly**, *ad*, commercialement.

commiserate, *v.t*, plaindre.

commissariat, *n*, intendance militaire, *f*.

commission, *n*, commission, remise, *f*; courtage, *m*; (shop) guelte, *f*; (officer's) lettre[s] de service, *f.[pl.]*. ~ *agent,* commissionnaire, *m*. ¶ *v.t*, commissionner, mandater; (officer) nommer; (ship) armer. ~*ed work,* ouvrage de commande, *m*. **commissionaire**, *n*, chasseur; garçon de bureau, *m*. **commissioner**, *n*, commissaire, *m*.

commit, *v.t*, commettre; faire; livrer; confier; renvoyer. ~ *for trial,* mettre en accusation. ~ *no nuisance,* défense d'uriner. ~ *oneself,* s'engager; se compromettre. ~ *to prison,* ordonner l'incarcération de. ~ *to writing,* coucher (*ou* mettre) par écrit. ~**ment** (Com.) *n*, engagement, *m*. *committal order,* mandat de dépôt, *m*.

committee, *n*, comité; bureau, *m*.

commode, *n*, chaise [percée] *f*.

commodious, *a*, commode. ~**ly**, *ad*, commodément. ~**ness**, *n*, commodité, *f*.

commodity, *n*, produit, *m*, denrée, marchandise, matière [première] *f*, article, *m*; ressource, *f*.

common, *a*, commun; général; coutumier; ordinaire; vulgaire; peuple; banal; simple; type; public. ~ *knowledge,* notoriété publique, *f*. ~ [*land*], communal, *m*, champs communs, m.pl, vaine pâture, *f*. ~ *law,* droit coutumier, m. [*the*] ~ *people,* les gens du commun, *m.pl,* le petit peuple, le vulgaire. ~ *sense,* sens commun, bon sens, *m*. ~ *snake,* couleuvre à collier, *f*. *the ~ weal,* la chose publique. *in, out of the,* ~, en, hors du, commun. *to be on short commons,* faire maigre chère. ~**ly**, *ad*, communément, couramment. ~**ness**, *n*, fréquence, *f*. ~**place**, *a*, banal, commun; (*n.*) banalité; pauvreté, *f*, (pl.) lieux communs, m.pl. ~**wealth**, *n*, république, état, *m*, communauté, *f*. *the C~ of Australia,* la Communauté d'Australie.

commonalty, *n*, roture, *f*. **commoner**, *n*, roturier, ère.

commotion, *n*, commotion, *f*, mouvement, *m*.
communal, *a*, communal. **commune**, *v.i*, converser. **communicant**, *n*, communiant, e. **communicate**, *v.t. & i*, communiquer; correspondre; (*Eccl.*) communier. **communication**, *n*, communication, *f*. ~ *cord*, corde de signal d'alarme, *f*. ~ *trench*, branche de tranchée, *f*, boyau de t., *m*. **communicative**, *a*, communicatif. **communion**, *n*, communion, *f*. ~ *cup*, calice, *m*. ~ *service*, office du saint sacrement, *m*. ~ *table*, sainte table, *f*. **communism**, *n*, communisme, *m*. **communist**, *n*, communiste, *m,f*. **community**, *n*, communauté; société, république, *f*. ~ *centre*, familistère, *m*. ~ *singing*, chansons en chœur, *f.pl*.
commutator, *n*, commutateur, *m*.
commute, *v.t*, commuer, *m*.
Como (Lake), le lac de Côme.
compact, *a*, compact. ~ [*powder*], [poudre] compacte, *f*, fard compact, *m*. ¶ *n*, pacte, *m*. ~**ness**, *n*, compacité, *f*.
companion, *n*, compagnon, *m*, compagne, *f*, camarade, *m,f*; (*thing*) pendant, *m*. [*lady*] ~, dame, demoiselle de compagnie. ~**able**, *a*, sociable. ~**ship**, *n*, compagnie, société, *f*, fréquentations, *f.pl*.
company, *n*, compagnie; société; bande; troupe, *f*; groupe; équipage; monde, *m*. *companies act*, loi sur les sociétés, *f*. & *Co*. (on cheque), & Cie.
comparable, *a*, comparable. **comparative†**, *a*, comparatif; (*sciences*) comparé. ¶ (*Gram.*) *n*, comparatif, *m*. **compare**, *v.t*, comparer, assimiler; rapprocher; collationner; conférer. **comparison**, *n*, comparaison, *f*, rapprochement, *m*.
compartment, *n*, compartiment, *m*; case, *f*.
compass, *n*, cadre, *m*, étendue, portée; (*magnetic*) boussole, *f*; compas; (*voice*) diapason; (*musical*) clavier, *m*. ~ *card*, rose des vents, *f*. **compass**[**es**], *n.*[*pl.*], compas, *m*. *compasses with pen point, with pencil point*, compas à tire-ligne, à porte-crayon. **compass**, *v.t*, cerner, ceindre.
compassion, *n*, compassion, *f*. ~**ate**, *a*, compatissant.
compatible, *a*, compatible.
compatriot, *n*, compatriote, *m,f*.
compeer, *n*, égal, e, pair, *m*.
compel, *v.t*, contraindre, astreindre; obliger, forcer.
compendious, *a*, sommaire. **compendium**, *n*, compendium, *m*.
compensate, *v.t*, compenser, indemniser, dédommager. **compensation**, *n*, compensation, indemnité, *f*, dédommagement, *m*.
compete for, concourir pour, à. ~ *with*, faire concurrence à.
competence, **-cy**, *n*, aisance; compétence; aptitude, *f*. **competent**, *a*, compétent, apte.
competition, *n*, concurrence; compétition, *f*;

concours, *m*. **competitor**, *n*, concurrent, e, compétiteur, trice.
compile, *v.t*, compiler.
complacence, **-cy**, *n*, complaisance, *f*. **complacent**, *a*, complaisant. ~**ly**, *ad*, complaisamment.
complain, *v.i*, se plaindre; réclamer; gémir. ~ *of* (medically), accuser. ~**ant**, *n*, plaignant, e. **complaint**, *n*, plainte, doléance, réclamation, *f*, grief; gémissement, *m*; (*Med.*) affection, maladie, *f*.
complaisance, *n*, complaisance, *f*. **complaisant**, *a*, complaisant.
complement, *n*, complément, effectif, *m*. ~**ary**, *a*, complémentaire.
complete†, *a*, complet, au complet. ¶ *v.t*, compléter. ~**d** (*time, age*) *p.p*, révolus. **completion**, *n*, complètement, achèvement, *m*.
complex, *a. & n*, complexe, *a. & m*.
complexion, *n*, (*of face*) teint; (*fig.*) caractère, aspect, *m*.
complexity, *n*, complexité, *f*.
compliance, *n*, conformité, *f*. **compliant**, *a*, facile, complaisant.
complicate, *v.t*, compliquer. **complication**, *n*, complication, *f*.
complicity, *n*, complicité, *f*.
compliment, *n*, compliment, *m*; (*pl.*) compliments, *m.pl*, civilités, politesses, *f.pl*, hommages, *m.pl*, choses, *f.pl*. ~*s of the season*, souhaits de bonne année, *m.pl*. ¶ *v.t*, complimenter. ~**ary**, *a*, de civilité, obligeant; (*dinner, &c*) d'honneur; (*ticket*) de faveur; (*copy*) en hommage.
complin[e] (*Eccl.*) *n*, complies, *f.pl*.
comply, *v.i.abs*, se soumettre. ~ *with*, se conformer à, condescendre à, observer, obéir à, remplir, respecter. *not complied with* (rule), inobservée.
component, *a*, constituant; composant. ¶ *n*, composant, *m*. ~ [*part*], pièce détachée, *f*.
compose, *v.t*, composer. *to be ~d of*, se c. de. ~ *oneself*, se calmer. ~**d**, *p.p*, composé, calme. **composer** (*Mus.*) *n*, compositeur, trice, auteur, *m*. *composing stick* (*Typ.*), composteur, *m*. **composite** *a*, composé, mixte. **composition**, *n*, composition; constitution, *f*; thème, *m*; (*to creditors*) décharge, *f*, concordat, *m*. **compositor** (*Typ.*) *n*, compositeur, trice.
composure, *n*, calme, sang-froid, *m*.
compound, *a*, composé; (*steam*) compound. ~ *interest*, intérêt[s] composé[s], *m.*[*pl.*]. ¶ *n*, composé; combiné, corps composé, camp de concentration, *m*. ¶ *v.t*, composer; pactiser avec (*a felony* = un crime); (*v.i.*) transiger; former.
comprehend, *v.t*, comprendre. **comprehension**, *n*, compréhension, *f*. **comprehensive**, *a*, compréhensif.
compress, *n*, compresse, *f*. ¶ *v.t*, comprimer, refouler. ~**ion**, *n*, compression, *f*. ~**or**, *n*, compresseur, *m*.

omprise, *v.t*, comprendre, renfermer, contenir.

ompromise, *n*, compromis, accommodement, *m*, transaction, *f*. ¶ *v.t. & i*, compromettre, transiger; capituler. ~ *oneself*, se compromettre.

omptroller, *n*, contrôleur, *m*. ~ *of the Royal Household*, majordome, *m*.

ompulsion, *n*, contrainte, *f*. compulsorily, *ad*, forcément. compulsory, *a*, forcé, obligatoire.

ompunction, *n*, componction, *f*.

omputation, *n*, supputation, *f*. compute, *v.t*, supputer, raisonner.

omrade, *n*, camarade, *m,f*. ~ship, *n*, camaraderie, *f*.

on, *v.t*, repasser, recorder.

oncave, *a*, concave. concavity, *n*, concavité, *f*.

onceal, *v.t*, cacher; celer; dérober; dissimuler; supprimer; taire; receler. ~ment, *n*, réticence; dissimulation; suppression, *f*; recèlement, *m*.

oncede, *v.t*, accorder, abandonner; (*grant*) concéder.

onceit, *n*, vanité, suffisance, *f*. ~ed, *a*, vain, vaniteux, suffisant. to be ~, s'en faire accroire.

onceivable, *a*, concevable. conceive, *v.t. & i*, concevoir.

oncentrate, *v.t*, concentrer; canaliser. concentration, *n*, concentration, *f*.

oncentric, *a*, concentrique.

onception, *n*, conception, *f*.

oncern, *n*, affaire, *f*; souci, *m*; sollicitude, inquiétude; entreprise, exploitation; boutique, *f*. ¶ *v.t*, concerner, 'ntéresser, regarder, toucher; appartenir. ~ing, *pr*, concernant, touchant, à l'égard de.

oncert, *n*, concert, *m*; audition, *f*. ~ *grand* [*piano*], piano à queue, *m*. ~ *pitch*, diapason normal, *m*. ¶ *v.t*, concerter.

oncerto, *n*, concerto, *m*.

oncession, *n*, concession, *f*. concession-[n]aire, *n*, concessionnaire, *m,f*.

onch, *n*, conque, *f*; coquillage, *m*. ~ology, *n*, conchyliogie, *f*.

onciliate, *v.t*, concilier. conciliation, *n*, conciliation, *f*. ~ *board*, conseil de prud'hommes, *m*.

oncise, *a*, concis; (*edition*) compacte. ~ness, *n*, concision, *f*.

onclave, *n*, conclave, *m*; assemblée, *f*.

onclude, *v.t. & i*, conclure; arrêter, clore. ~d (*serial*), suite & fin. conclusion, *n*, conclusion; décision, *f*. to try ~s *with*, faire l'essai de ses forces avec. conclusive, *a*, démonstratif; concluant; décisif.

oncoct, *v.t*, confectionner; (*fig*.) cuisiner, machiner, tramer. concoction, *n*, mixture; machination, *f*.

oncomitant, *n*, accompagnement, *m*.

oncord, *n*, concorde, *f*; accord, *m*; concordance, *f*. ~ance, *n*, concordance, *f*.

concourse, *n*, concours, *m*, affluence, *f*.

concrete, *a*, concret. the concrete (opp. *abstract*), le concret. ¶ *n*, béton, *m*.

concubine, *n*, concubine, *f*.

concupiscence, *n*, concupiscence, *f*.

concur, *v.i*, concourir. concurrence, *n*, concours, *m*.

concussion, *n*, ébranlement, *m*. ~ *of the brain*, commotion au cerveau, *f*.

condemn, *v.t*, condamner. ~ed *man, woman*, condamné(e) à mort. condemnation, *n*, condamnation, *f*.

condensation, *n*, condensation, *f*. condense, *v.t*, condenser; resserrer. ~d *milk*, lait condensé, 1. concentré, 1. conservé, *m*. condenser, *n*, (*Phys., Elec., Opt*.) condensateur; (*steam*) condenseur, *m*.

condescend, *v.i*, condescendre. condescension, *n*, condescendance, *f*.

condign, *a*, juste.

condiment, *n*, condiment, assaisonnement, *m*.

condition, *n*, condition, *f*; état, *m*; (*col. pl.*) régime, *m*. on ~ *that*, à condition que, à [la] charge de, sous réserve que. ¶ *v.t*, conditionner. ~alt, *g*, conditionnel.

condole with, exprimer ses condoléances à. condolence, *n*, condoléance, *f*.

condone, *v.t*, passer sur, fermer les yeux sur.

conduce, *v.t*, contribuer, conduire, tendre.

conduct, *n*, conduite, *f*; maniement, *m*. ¶ *v.t*, conduire, guider; gérer, manier, mener. ~ed *tour*, excursion accompagnée, *f*. conductor, tress, *n*, conducteur, trice; guide, *m*; receveur, euse; chef d'orchestre, *m*.

conduit, *n*, conduit; caniveau, *m*.

cone, *n*, (*Geom.*) cône, *m*; (*fir, pine*) pomme; (*ice cream wafer*) oublie, *f*, plaisir, *m*.

confectioner, *n*, confiseur, euse; pâtissier, ère, glacier, *m*. ~'s *shop*, confiserie, pâtisserie, *f*. ~y, *n*, confiserie, *f*, bonbons, *m.pl*. sucreries, *f.pl*; pâtisserie, *f*. ~ *box*, bonbonnière, *f*.

confederacy, *n*, confédération, *f*. confederate, *n*, compère, *m*, complice, *m,f*, (*pl*.) consorts, *m.pl*. ¶ *v.i*, se confédérer. confederation, *n*, confédération, *f*.

confer, *v.t*, conférer; déférer, gratifier; (*v.i.*) conférer. ~ence, *n*, conférence, *f*.

confess, *v.t*, confesser, avouer, s'accuser de; (*v.i.*) se confesser. ~edly, *ad*, de son propre aveu. confession, *n*, confession, *f*, aveu; *m*; confesse, *f*. ~al, *n*, confessionnal, *m*. confessor, *n*, confesseur, *m*.

confidant, e, *n*, confident, e. confide, *v.t*, confier, livrer; (*v.i.*) se confier. confidence, *n*, confiance; assurance; (*secret*) confidence, *f*. ~ *trick*, vol à l'américaine, *m*. confident, *a*, confiant, assuré. confidential, *a*, (*of things*) confidentiel; (*of pers.—in good sense*) de confiance; (*bad sense*) affidé. ~ly, *ad*, confidentiellement, confidemment. confiding, *p.a*, confiant.

confine, *v.t*, confiner, borner; chambrer, enfermer, renfermer, resserrer; retenir, faire garder. ~ *oneself to, within*, se confiner à, dans, se cantonner dans. ~ [*to barracks*], consigner. *to be* ~d (woman), accoucher, faire ses couches. **~ment**, *n*, détention, *f*; (*woman*) couches, *f.pl*, accouchement, *m*. ~ *to barracks*, consigne, *f*. **confines**, *n.pl*, confins, *m.pl*.

confirm, *v.t*, confirmer; ratifier, approuver, adopter. **~ation**, *n*, confirmation; ratification, approbation, adoption, *f*. **~ed**, *p.a*, invétéré, acharné, fieffé, émérite. ~ *invalid*, incurable, *m,f*.

confiscate, *v.t*, confisquer. **confiscation**, *n*, confiscation, *f*.

conflagration, *n*, embrasement, *m*; conflagration, *f*.

conflict, *n*, conflit, *m*. ¶ *v.i. & abs*, se contredire. **~ing**, *p.a*, en conflit; contradictoire.

confluence, *n*, confluent; concours, *m*.

conform, *v.t*, conformer; (*v.i.*) se c. **~able**, *a*, conforme. **~ably**, *ad*, conformément. **~ation**, *n*, conformation, *f*. **~ity**, *n*, conformité, *f*.

confound, *v.t*, confondre. **~ed**, *p.a*, maudit.

confraternity, *n*, confraternité, *f*; (*pers.*) confrérie, *f*.

confront, *v.t*, affronter; confronter.

confuse, *v.t*, confondre, mêler; embrouiller. **confused**, *a*, confus, trouble, enchevêtré. **~ly**, *ad*, confusément. **confusion**, *n*, confusion, *f*, désarroi, *m*.

confute, *v.t*, réfuter.

congeal, *v.t*, congeler, geler, figer; (*v.i.*) se congeler, &c prendre, se prendre.

congenial, *a*, sympathique; agréable.

congenital, *a*, congénital.

conger [eel], *n*, congre, *m*.

congest (*Med.*) *v.t*, congestionner, engorger. **~ion**, *n*, (*Med.*) congestion, *f*, engorgement; (*traffic, &c*) encombrement, *m*, presse, *f*. ~ *of the blood, of the brain, of the lungs*, congestion sanguine, cérébrale, pulmonaire. ~ *of the liver*, encombrement au foie.

conglomerate, *n*, conglomérat, *m*.

congratulate, *v.t*, féliciter, complimenter. ~ *oneself*, se féliciter, s'applaudir. **congratulation**, *n*, félicitation, *f*, compliment, *m*.

congregate, *v.t*, rassembler; (*v.i.*) se r., s'assembler. **congregation**, *n*, assemblage, *m*; (*of pers.*) assemblée, *f*.

congress, *n*, congrès, *m*. **member of the** (*or* **a**) **~**, congressiste, *m,f*.

congruity, *n*, convenance, *f*. **congruous**, *a*, congru. **~ly**, *ad*, congrûment.

conic(al), *a*, conique.

conifer, *n*, conifère, *m*. **~ous**, *a*, conifère, *f*.

conjectural†, *a*, conjectural. **conjecture**, *n*, conjecture, *f*. ¶ *v.t*, conjecturer.

conjoin, *v.t*, conjoindre. **conjoint†**, *a*, conjoint.

conjugal†, *a*, conjugal.

conjugate, *v.t*, conjuguer. **conjugation**, *n* conjugaison, *f*.

conjunction, *n*, conjonction, *f*. **conjuncture** *n*, conjoncture, *f*.

conjure, *v.t*, (*adjure*) conjurer; (*enchant*) en sorceler; (*v.i.*) escamoter. ~ *away*, es camoter. ~ [*up*], évoquer, se forger **conjurer, -or.**, *n*, escamoteur, prestidigita teur, *m*. **conjuring**, *n*, escamotage, *m* prestidigitation, *f*. ~ *trick*, tour d passe-passe, *m*.

connect, *v.t*, relier, raccorder, joindre, ré unir; lier; (*Elec.*) [ac]coupler. **~ed**, *p.a* suivi; apparenté. ~ *to frame* (*Elec.*), à l masse. **connecting rod**, bielle, *f*. **connexion** **-nection**, *n*, connexion; liaison; relation, *f* raccord; contact; rapport, *m*; correspon dance, *f*; parent, e; clientèle, *f*, achalan dage, *m*.

conning tower, blockhaus; (*submarine* kiosque, *m*.

connivance, *n*, connivence, *f*. **connive a** être de connivence pour.

connoisseur, *n*, connaisseur, euse; gourmet, *m*

connubial, *a*, conjugal, matrimonial.

conquer, *v.t*, vaincre, conquérir. **conqueror** **conqueress**, *n*, vainqueur, *m*, conquérant, e *William the Conqueror*, Guillaume le Con quérant. **conquest**, *n*, conquête, *f*.

consanguinity, *n*, consanguinité, *f*.

conscience, *n*, conscience, *f*, for intérieur, *m* ~ *money*, restitution anonyme, *f*. *to b* **~-stricken**, avoir une conscience bou relée de remords. **conscientious†**, *a*, con sciencieux. **~ness**, *n*, conscience, *f*.

conscious, *a*: *to be* ~, avoir sa connaissance *to be* ~ *of*, avoir conscience de, être cons cient de, sentir. **~ly**, *ad*, sciemmen **~ness**, *n*, conscience, connaissance, *f*.

conscript, *n*, conscrit, *m*. **~ion**, *n*, conscri tion, *f*.

consecrate, *v.t*, consacrer; bénir; sacre **~d**, *p.a*, bénit; sacré; saint. **consecratio** *n*, consécration, *f*; bénédiction, *f*; sacre, *m*

consecutive†, *a*, consécutif.

consensus, *n*, unanimité, *f*.

consent, *n*, consentement, accord, agrémer aveu, *m*. ¶ *v.i*, consentir, accéder, s tendre (*to* = à).

consequence, *n*, conséquence, suite; ir portance, *f*. **consequent**, *a*, conséquer *consequential damages*, dommages directs, *m.pl*. **consequently**, *ad*, cons quemment, par conséquent, aussi.

conservative, *a*, conservateur. ¶ *n. & co* **servator**, *n*, conservateur, trice. **conser** **tory**, *n*, serre, *f*.

consider, *v.t*, considérer, regarder, délibérer sur; (*v.i. & abs.*) songer fléchir. **~able†**, *a*, considérable. ~ *a*, prévenant. **~ation**, *n*, considérati *f*; égard, *m*; délibération, *f*; ménagemer *m.pl*; (*Law*) provision, cause, *f*. [*money*], prix, *m*, rémunération, *f*.

sentation, indemnité, f. in ~ of (value received), moyennant. (matter) under ~, sur le bureau. without due ~, à la légère. ~ing, pr, attendu, vu, eu égard à.

consign, v.t, livrer; confier; remettre, expédier; (goods) consigner. ~ee, n, consignataire, destinataire, réceptionnaire, m. ~ment, n, consignation; expédition, f; envoi, chargement, m. ~ note (Rly), lettre de voiture, f. (goods) on ~, en consignation. ~or, n, consignateur, m.

consist, v.i, consister, se composer. ~ence, -cy, n, consistance; suite, f. ~ent, a, conséquent, compatible; qui ne se dément point; suivi. ~ently with, conséquemment à. ~ory, n, consistoire, m.

consolation, n, consolation, f. ~ prize, prix de c., m. console, v.t, consoler. ¶ n. & ~ table, console, f.

consolidate, v.t, consolider; unifier. consolidation, n, consolidation; unification, f. ~ act, loi coordonnée, f.

consonance, n, consonance, f. consonant, a, (Mus., words) consonant. ~ with, en rapport avec. ¶ n, consonne, f.

consort, n, époux, ouse; (Naut.) conserve, f; (Navy) [vaisseau] matelot, m. ¶ v.i, s'associer.

conspicuous, a, voyant, en évidence; insigne, signalé, remarquable. to make oneself ~, se faire remarquer, se singulariser.

conspiracy, n, conspiration, conjuration, f. conspirator, n, conspirateur, trice, conjuré, m. conspire, v.i. & t, conspirer, conjurer.

constable, n, agent [de police] m. constabulary, n, police, f.

constancy, n, constance, f. constant, a, constant. ¶ n, constante, f. ~ly, ad, constamment.

constellation, n, constellation, f.

consternation, n, consternation, f.

constipate, v.t, constiper. constipation, n, constipation, f.

constituency, n, circonscription électorale, f; collège électoral, m; électeurs, m.pl. constituent, a, constituant, composant. ¶ n, composant; ingrédient, m; (pl.) électeurs, commettants, m.pl. constitute, v.t, constituer. constitution, n, constitution, f; tempérament, m. ~alt, a, constitutionnel.

constrain, v.t, contraindre, gêner, forcer. constraint, n, contrainte, gêne, sujétion, f.

construct, v.t, construire, établir. ~ion, n, construction; interprétation; explication, f. ~ional, a, de construction. ~ outfit (boy's), jeu de construction mécanique, f. ~or, n, constructeur, m.

construe, v.t, construire; expliquer.

consul, n, consul, m. ~ar, a, consulaire. ~ate & ~ship, n, consulat, m.

consult, v.t, consulter. ~ation, n, consultation, f. consulting, p.a: ~ engineer, ingénieur-conseil, m. ~ physician, mé-

decin consultant, m. ~ room, cabinet de consultation, salon de c., m.

consume, v.t, consumer, dévorer; (use) consommer. consumer, n, consommateur, m; (town gas, elec.) abonné, e.

consummate, a, consommé, fini, superlatif. ¶ v.t, consommer. consummation, n, consommation, f.

consumption, n, (destruction) consomption; (Med.) consomption, phtisie; (use) consommation, dépense, f. consumptive, a. & n, tuberculeux, euse, poitrinaire, phtisique, a. & m,f.

contact, n, contact; attouchement; frottement, m.

contagion, n, contagion, f. contagious, a, contagieux. ~ness, n, contagion, f.

contain, v.t, contenir, tenir, renfermer. ~er, n, contenant; (lamp) culot, m.

contaminate, v.t, contaminer, souiller. contamination, n, contamination, souillure, f.

contango, n, report, m. ¶ v.t, reporter.

contemplate, v.t, contempler; méditer; projeter; envisager; (v.i.) méditer. contemplation, n, contemplation, f. in ~, en vue. contemplative, a, contemplatif.

contemporaneous & contemporary, a, contemporain. contemporary, n, contemporain, e; (newspaper) confrère, m.

contempt, n, mépris, m. oft. pl, dédain, m. ~ of court, offense à la cour, f; refus d'obéissance, m. ~ible, a, méprisable. contemptuous, a, méprisant, dédaigneux.

contend, v.t. & i: ~ that, prétendre que. ~ with, combattre; lutter contre; disputer.

content, a, content. ¶ n, contentement, m; (holding) contenance; teneur, f; titre; (pl.) contenu, m; table des matières, f. ¶ v.t, contenter. ~ed with, satisfait de. ~edly, ad, content.

contention, n, démêlé, m; dispute, discorde, f. my ~ is that ..., ce que je prétends, c'est que ... contentious, a, litigieux; contentieux.

contentment, n, contentement, m.

contest, n, lutte, f, combat; concours, m, joute, dispute, f. ¶ v.t, contester; disputer.

context, n, contexte, m.

contexture, n, contexture, f.

contiguity, n, contiguïté, f. contiguous, a, contigu.

continence, n, continence, f. continent, a, continent. ¶ n, continent, m; terre ferme, f. the C~ (Europe), le continent. ~al, a, continental.

contingency, n, contingence, éventualité, f, imprévu, m. ~ fund, fonds de prévoyance, m. contingent, a, contingent, aléatoire, éventuel. ¶ n, contingent, m; (of recruiting year) classe, f.

continual†, a, continuel. continuance, n, continuation, f. continuation, n, continuation, suite, f; (Stk Ex.) report, m. continue, v.t. & i, continuer; reporter.

to be ~d (*serial*), à suivre: ~ *in our next*, la suite au prochain numéro. **continuity**, *n*, continuité, *f.* **continuous**, *a*, continu. ~ *performance* (cinema), spectacle permanent, *m.* ~**ly**, *ad*, continûment.

contort, *v.t*, contourner. ~**ed**, *p.a*, tors. **contortion**, *n*, contorsion, *f.* ~**ist**, *n*, homme-caoutchouc, homme-serpent, *m*; femme-caoutchouc, femme-serpent, *f.*

contour, *n*, contour; profil, tracé, galbe, *m.* ~ *line*, courbe de niveau, *f.* ~ *map*, carte en courbes de niveau, *f.*

contra, *n*, contrepartie, *f*; parcontre, *m.* ¶ *v.t*, annuler, contrepasser. ~ *account*, compte contrepartie, *m.* ~ *entry*, article inverse, *m.*

contraband, *n*, contrebande, *f*; (*att.*) de c.

contrabass, *n*, contrebasse, *f.*

contract, *n*, entreprise, *f*, marché, forfait; contrat, *m*, convention, *f*, acte, traité, *m. on* ~ *or by* ~ *or* ~ *att*, à l'entreprise, à forfait, forfaitaire; par contrat. ~ *bridge*, bridge plafond, b. contrat, *m.* ~ [*note*], bordereau, *m.* ¶ *v.t*, (*shrink*) contracter; [r]étrécir, resserrer; (*Law*) contracter; [entre]prendre; (*v.i. or abs.*) contracter; s'étrécir, se rétrécir, se resserrer; (*Law*) contracter. ~**ant** (*pers.*), *n*, contractant, e. ~**ing**, *a*, contractant. ~**ion**, *n*, contraction, *f*, [r]étrécissement, resserrement, *m*; abréviation, *f.* ~**or**, *n*, entrepreneur, euse; fournisseur, euse; adjudicataire, *m,f.* **contractual**, *a*, contractuel, forfaitaire.

contradict, *v.t*, contredire, démentir. ~**ion**, *n*, contradiction, *f*, contredit, démenti, *m.* ~**ory**, *a*, *n*, contradictoire.

contradistinction, *n*, opposition, *f.*

contralto, *n*, contralto, *m.*

contrariety, *n*, contrariété, *f.* **contrarily** & **contrary**, *ad*, contrairement. **contrary**, *a*, contraire; opposé; inverse. ¶ *n*, contraire, opposé, rebours; contre-pied, *m*; contrepartie, *f. on the* ~, au contraire.

contrast, *n*, contraste, *m*, opposition, *f.* ¶ *v.t. & i*, mettre en contraste; contraster; trancher. ~**y**, *a*, heurté.

contravene, *v.t*, contrevenir à, enfreindre. **contravention**, *n*, contravention, infraction, *f.*

contribute, *v t*, contribuer pour; (*v.i.*) contribuer, fournir. ~ *to* (journal), collaborer à. **contribution**, *n*, contribution, *f*; apport, fournissement, *m*, cote, cotisation, *f. to lay under* ~, mettre à contribution. **contributor** (*to journal*) *n*, collaborateur, trice.

contrite, *a*, contrit. **contrition**, *n*, contrition, *f*, brisement de cœur, *m.*

contrivance, *n*, combinaison, *f*, dispositif; artifice, *m.* **contrive**, *v.t*, combiner; ménager. ~ *to*, faire en sorte que, s'ingénier à.

control, *n*, contrôle, *m*; commande, *f*; empire,

m, maîtrise, *f.* ¶ *v.t*, contrôler, contenir; maîtriser; policer. **controller**, *n*, contrôleur, *m.*

controversial, *a*, de controverse. **controversy**, *n*, controverse, *f.* **controvert**, *v.t*, discuter.

contumacy, *n*, contumace, *f.*

contumely, *n*, outrage; opprobre, *m.*

contuse, *v.t*, contusionner. **contusion**, *n*, contusion, *f.*

conundrum, *n*, devinette, charade, énigme, *f.*

convalesce, *v.i*, entrer en convalescence. **convalescence**, *n*, convalescence, *f.* **convalescent**, *a. & n*, convalescent, e.

convene, *v.t*, convoquer.

convenience, *n*, commodité, convenance; aise, *f*; (*w.c.*) commodités, *f.pl.* **convenient**, *a*, commode, convenable. ~**ly**, *ad*, commodément.

convent, *n*, couvent, monastère, *m*, maison, *f.* ~ *school*, couvent, *m.*

convention, *n*, convention, *f.* ~**al**, *a*, conventionnel, de convention; pompier. ~**alism**, *n*, poncif, *m*, le style pompier. ~**alist**, *n*, pompier, *m.*

converge, *v.i*, converger. **convergent**, *a*, convergent.

conversant, *a*, versé, ferré.

conversation, *n*, conversation, *f*; colloque, *m.* ~**al**, *a*, de, de la, de la, conversation. ~[**al**]**ist**, *n*, causeur, euse. **conversazione**, *n*, réunion, *f.*

converse, *a. & n*, contraire, *a. & m*; converse, *a.f. & f*, réciproque, *a. & f.* ¶ *v.i*, converser, causer.

conversion, *n*, conversion, *f*, convertissement (*Fin.*) *m*; transformation, *f.* ~ *loan*, emprunt de conversion, *m.* **convert**, *n*, converti, e. ¶ *v.t*, convertir, transformer. ~*ed goal*, but de transformation, *m. to become* ~*ed* (*Relig.*), se convertir. ~**er**, *n*, convertisseur, *m.* ~**ible**, *a*, convertible; (*stocks*) convertissable.

convex, *a*, convexe. ~**ity**, *n*, convexité, *f.*

convey, *v.t*, [trans]porter, véhiculer, conduire, charrier, voiturer; (*Law*, &c) transmettre; communiquer, exprimer. ~**ance**, *n*, transport, charriage, *m*; voiture; (*Law*) translation, transmission, mutation, *f*; (*deed*) acte de transmission, acte translatif de propriété, *m.*

convict, *n*, condamné, e, forçat, *m.* ~ *prison*, pénitencier, *m.* ¶ *v.t*, convaincre; condamner. ~**ion**, *n*, conviction; condamnation, *f. person with previous* ~, récidiviste, *m,f.*

convince, *v.t*, convaincre. **convincing**, *p.a*, convaincant.

convivial, *a*: ~ *gathering*, joyeuse compagnie, *f.* ~ *person*, joyeux convive, bon c., *m.*

convocation, *n*, convocation, *f.* **convoke**, *v.t*, convoquer.

convolvulus, *n*, convolvulus, volubilis, *m*, belle-de-jour, *f.*

convoy, n, convoi, m; escorte, f. ¶ v.t, convoyer, escorter.

convulse, v.t, bouleverser. 'to be ~d (laughing), se tordre. **convulsion,** n, convulsion, f, bouleversement, m. **convulsive†,** a, convulsif.

cony, -ney, n, lapin, m.

coo, n, roucoulement, m. ¶ v.i, roucouler.

cook, n, cuisinier, ère; (ship's) [maître-]coq, m. ~'s boy, marmiton, fouille-au-pot, m. ~shop, gargote, rôtisserie, f. ~'s mate, matelot coq, m. ¶ v.t, [faire] cuire; (fig.) cuisiner, falsifier; (v.i.) cuisiner. **cooker,** n, cooking range, cuisinière, f, fourneau de cuisine, m. **cookery,** n, cuisine, f. ~ book, livre de cuisine, cuisinier, m. **cooking,** n, cuisine; cuisson, f. ~ apples, pommes à cuire, f.pl.

cool†, a, frais; froid; calme; hardi, sans gêne. ~-headed, a, l'esprit calme. ¶ v.t, rafraîchir, f. in the ~, au frais, à la fraîche, fraîchement. ¶ v.t, attiédir; rafraîchir; refroidir; (v.i.) s'attiédir, se refroidir. ~ down, se calmer, caler (la voile]. ~ one's heels, se morfondre, droguer. ~er, n, rafraîchisseur; refroidisseur, m. ~ness, n, fraîcheur; froideur, f, froid; calme, sang-froid, flegme; sans-gêne, m.

coomb, n, combe, f.

coop, n, cage [à poulets], mue, f. ~ [up], v.t, claquemurer.

cooper, n, tonnelier, m. ~age, n, tonnellerie, f.

cooperate, v.i, coopérer. **cooperation,** n, coopération, f. **cooperative,** a, coopératif. ~ society, [société] coopérative, f.

coordinate, v.t, coordonner.

coot, n, foulque, f.

cope, n, chape, f. ¶ v.t, chaperonner, couronner. ~ with, tenir tête à, suffire à.

Copenhagen, n, Copenhague, f.

coping, n, chaperon, couronnement, m.

copious†, a, copieux, riche, plantureux; nourri.

copper, n, cuivre [rouge] m; chaudière, bassine, f. ~ [coin], cuivre, m, monnaie de cuivre, f, billon, m. ~ beech, hêtre rouge, m. ~ bit (Soldering), cuivre, m. ~-coloured, a, cuivré. ~plate, planche de cuivre, f, cuivre, m. ~plate [engraving], gravure sur cuivre, taille-douce, f. ~plate [hand]writing, écriture moulée, f. ~smith, chaudronnier, m. ~smith's [& brazier's] trade, [petite] chaudronnerie, f. ¶ v.t, cuivrer.

copperas, n, couperose, f.

coppice, copse, n, taillis, m.

copulation, n, copulation, f.

copy, n, copie; transcription; f; calque, exemplaire; exemple; m; (Law) expédition, f. ~ book, cahier d'écriture, livre d'exemples, m. ~ cat, singe, m. ¶ v.t, copier; transcrire; calquer. **copying,** n, transcrip-

tion, f. ~ ink, encre communicative, encre à copier, f. **copyist,** n, copiste, m.f.

copyright, n, droit d'auteur, m, propriété [littéraire] f. ~ by So-&-So, tous droits de reproduction, de traduction, d'adaptation & d'exécution réservés pour tous pays.

coquet, v.i, coqueter. ~ry, n, coquetterie, f. **coquettish,** a, coquet.

coral, n, corail; (baby's) hochet, m. ~ fisher, coralleur, m. ~ reef, banc corallifère, m.

corbel, n, corbeau, m.

cord, n, corde; cordelette; f; cordon; câble; m; (braided) ganse, f. ¶ v.t, corder. ~age, n, cordages, m.pl.

cordial†, a, cordial, chaleureux. ¶ n, cordial, m. ~ity, n, cordialité, f.

corduroy, n, velours à [grosses] côtes, velours côtelé, m.

core, n, cœur, trognon; noyau; m; âme, f. ¶ v.t, vider (une pomme, &c).

Corea, n, la Corée.

co-respondent, n, complice en adultère, m.f.

Corinth, n, Corinthe, f. **Corinthian,** a, corinthien. ¶ n, Corinthien, ne.

cork, n, liège; bouchon [en liège] m. ~ jacket, brassière de sauvetage, f. ~ screw, tire-bouchon, m. ~screw curl, boudin, m. ~screw, v.i, vriller. ~-tipped (cigarettes), à bouts de liège. ~ tree, chêne-liège, m. ¶ v.t, boucher. ~y, a, liégeux. ~ taste, goût de bouchon, m.

cormorant, n, cormoran, m.

corn, n, grain, m; grains, m.pl; blé; (Indian) blé de Turquie, maïs; (on feet) cor, (soft) œil-de-perdrix, m. ~ chandler, grainetier, m. ~ cob, épi de maïs, m, rafle, f. ~ cure, remède contre les cors, m. ~ exchange, bourse des grains, f. ~field, [champ de] blé, m. ~ flour, farine de maïs, de riz, f, &c. ~flower, bleuet, m.

corned beef, bœuf salé, m.

cornelian, n, cornaline, f.

corner, n, coin, angle; tournant, virage, m; encoignure, f; recoin; (Com.) accaparement, m; (att.) cornier, d'angle; d'encoignure, de coin, du coin. ~ cupboard, encoignure, f. ~ free throw (Water Polo), coup franc de coin, m. ~ kick (Foot.), coup de coin, m. ~ stone, pierre angulaire, f. ¶ v.t, acculer, rencogner; (monopolize) accaparer.

cornet, n, (cone) cornet; (Mus.) cornet à pistons, piston; (ice cream wafer) plaisir, m, oublie, f.

cornice, n, corniche, f. ~ pole, monture de rideaux, f.

Cornish, a, de Cornouailles.

cornucopia, n, corne d'abondance, f.

Cornwall, n, la Cornouailles.

corolla, n, corolle, f.

corollary, n, corollaire, m.

corona, n, couronne, f. **coronation,** n, couronnement, sacre, m. **coronet,** n, couronne, f.

corporal† & **corporeal†**, a, corporel. **corporal,** n, caporal; (*cavalry*) brigadier, m. **corporate,** a, social. ¶ *v.i,* faire corps. **corporation,** n, corporation, f. [*municipal*] ~, municipalité, f.

corps, n, corps, m; équipe, f.

corpse, n, cadavre, corps [mort] m. ~-*like,* cadavéreux.

corpulence, -ency, n, corpulence, f, embonpoint, m, réplétion, f. **corpulent,** a, corpulent, ventru.

Corpus Christi, la Fête-Dieu.

corpuscle, n, corpuscule, m.

correct†, a, correct; exact, juste. ¶ *v.t,* corriger; rectifier, redresser; surcharger. ~*ed copy,* corrigé, m. ~*ion,* correction; rectification, f, redressement, m; surcharge, f. ~*ional,* a, correctionnel. ~*ive,* n, correctif, m. ~*ness,* n, correction, exactitude, justesse, f. ~*or,* n, correcteur, trice.

correlative, a, corrélatif.

correspond, *v.i,* correspondre; répondre. ~*ence,* n, correspondance, f; intelligences, *f.pl.* ~*ent,* n, correspondant, e. ~*ing,* *p.a,* correspondant.

corridor, n, couloir, corridor, m. ~ *carriage,* wagon à couloir, m.

corrie (*Geol.*) n, cirque, entonnoir, m.

corroborate, *v.t,* corroborer.

corrode, *v.t,* corroder; ronger, miner. **corrosion,** n, corrosion, f. **corrosive,** a. & n, corrosif, a. & m.

corrugate, *v.t,* canneler, strier; onduler. ~*d* [*sheet*] *iron* & ~*d iron sheet,* tôle ondulée, f.

corrupt, *v.t,* corrompre; débaucher, vicier, gâter, gangrener. ~*ible,* a, corruptible; prenable. ~*ion,* n, corruption, f.

corsair, n, corsaire, m.

corset, n, corset, m. ~ *maker,* corsetier, ère. ¶ *v.t,* corseter.

Corsica, n, la Corse. **Corsican,** a, corse. ¶ n, Corse, m,f.

corundum, n, corindon, m.

coruscate, *v.i,* scintiller.

cos, n. or **Cos lettuce,** [laitue] romaine, f.

cosily, ad, à son aise, confortablement.

cosmetic, a. & n, cosmétique, a. & m.

cosmic(al), a, cosmique.

cosmopolitan & **cosmopolite,** a. & n, cosmopolite, a. & m.

cost, n, coût, prix, m; frais, *m.pl,* dépense, f. *at all* ~*s,* coûte que coûte, à toute force. ~ *of living bonus,* indemnité de vie chère, f. ~ *of living figure,* indice du coût de la vie, m. ~ [*price*], prix de revient, p. coûtant, p. d'acquisition, m. ¶ *v.i.ir,* coûter; revenir.

coster[**monger**], n, marchand des quatre saisons, m.

costive, a, constipé. ~*ness,* n, constipation, f.

costliness, n, cherté; somptuosité, f. **costly,** a, coûteux, dispendieux; somptueux.

costume, n, costume, m. ~ *piece,* ~ *play,* pièce historique, f. **costum**[**i**]**er,** n, costumier, m.

cosy, a, confortable, douillet. ~ *corner,* coin intime, cosy-corner, m. *to make oneself* ~, se calfeutrer.

cot, n, bercelonnette, f; berceau; lit d'enfant; lit, m; couchette, f.

coterie, n, coterie, chapelle, f. ~ *of wits,* bureau d'esprit, m.

cottage, n, chaumière; habitation ouvrière, f; cottage, chalet, m; (*fig.*) chaume, m.

cotter, n, clavette, f; *pin,* goupille, f.

cotton, n, coton, m. ~ [*cloth*], cotonnade, toile de coton, f. ~ *goods,* cotonnade, f. ~ *industry,* industrie cotonnière, f. ~ *mill,* filature de coton, f. ~ *plant,* cotonnier, m. ~ *waste,* bourre de coton, f. ~ *wool,* ouate [de coton] f, coton [en laine] m. ~*y,* a, cotonneux.

couch, n, couche; chaise longue, f; canapé, m. ¶ *v.i,* se coucher; se tapir, se blottir. ~*ed in these terms,* ainsi conçu. ~ [*grass*] n, chiendent, m. ~*ing,* n, broderie à fils couchés, f.

cough, n, toux, f. ~ *mixture,* sirop, m, (*ou* potion, f.) pour la toux. ~ *lozenge,* pastille pour la t., f. ¶ *v.i,* tousser. ~ *up,* expectorer.

council, n, conseil, m; (*Eccl.*) concile, m. **councillor,** n, conseiller, ère.

counsel, n, conseil, m; délibération, f; (*pers.*) avocat, conseil, défenseur, m. ¶ *v.t,* conseiller. **counsellor,** n, conseiller, ère.

count, n, compte, m; (*pers.*) comte, m. ~ *of indictment,* chef d'accusation, m. ¶ *v.t. & i,* compter; nombrer; (*votes*) recenser, dépouiller.

countenance, n, contenance; physionomie, figure, mine, f. ¶ *v.t,* approuver; encourager.

counter, n, riposte, f; (*play*) jeton, m, fiche, f; (*meter*) compteur; (*shop*) comptoir, m; (*cashier's*) caisse, f, guichet, m. ¶ *v.t,* riposter. *to run* ~ *to,* aller à l'encontre de.

counteract, *v.t,* contrecarrer.

counter attack, contre-attaque, f.

counterbalance, n, contrepoids, m. ¶ *v.t,* contrebalancer, équilibrer.

counterclaim, n, reconvention, f.

counterfeit, a, contrefait, faux. ¶ n, contrefaçon, f. ¶ *v.t,* contrefaire. ~*er,* n, contrefacteur, m.

counterfoil, n, souche, f, talon, m.

counter instructions, contrordre, m.

countermand, *v.t,* contremander; (*Com.*) décommander.

counterpane, n, couverture [de lit] f.

counterpart, n, contrepartie, f; (*pers.*) pendant; (*deed*) double, m.

counterpoint, n, contrepoint, m.

counterpoise, n, contrepoids, m. ¶ *v.t,* contrebalancer, équilibrer.

countershaft, *n*, arbre secondaire, a. de renvoi, *m*. ~ [*& accessories*], renvoi [de mouvement] *m*, transmission secondaire, *f*.

countersign (*Mil.*) *n*, mot de ralliement, *m*. ¶ *v.t*, contresigner. *counter signature*, contreseing.*m*.

countersink, *n*, fraisure, *f*. ~ [*bit*], fraise, *f*. ¶ *v.t.ir*, fraiser.

counterstroke, *n*, riposte, *f*.

countervailing duty, droit compensateur, *m*.

counterweight, *n*, contrepoids, *m*.

countess, *n*, comtesse, *f*.

counting, *n*, compte; recensement, *m*. ~ *house*, bureau, *m*. **countless**, *a*, innombrable.

country, *n*, pays, *m*; contrée; campagne; province; patrie, *f*; corps électoral, *m*. ~ *club*, country-club, *m*. ~ *cottage*, cassine, *f*. ~ *dance*, danse rustique, *f*. ~ *house*, maison de campagne, *f*. ~ *life*, vie champêtre, v. rurale, *f*. ~ *man*, *-woman*, campagnard, e. [*fellow*] ~ *man*, *-woman*, compatriote, *m,f*. ~ *seat*, château, manoir, *m*. ~ *side*, campagne, *f*. ~ *town*, ville de province, *f*.

county (*Eng.*) *n*, département (*Fr.*) *m*. ~ *town*, chef-lieu, *m*.

couple, *n*, (*things*) couple, *f*; (*pers.*, *Mech.*) couple, *m*. ¶ *v.t*, coupler, accoupler; atteler. **couplet**, *n*, distique, *m*. **coupling**, *n*, accouplement; manchon; attelage, *m*.

coupon, *n*, coupon, *m*; (*gift goods*) timbre, *m*.

courage, *n*, courage, *m*. ~ **ous†**, *a*, courageux.

courier, *n*, courrier, *m*.

course, *n*, cours; courant, *m*; carrière; route; direction, *f*; chenal; trajet, *m*; marche, *f*; processus; parti; stage; (*meal*) service, plat, *m*; (*Build.*) assise; couche, *f*; (*ground*) champ; terrain; parcours, *m*; (*pl.*, *Med.*) règles, *f.pl. in due* ~, en temps & lieu. *of* ~, naturellement, bien entendu, certainement. *why, of* ~! parbleu! ¶ *v.t. & i*, chasser, courir. **courser** (*Poet.*) *n*, coursier, *m*. **coursing**, *n*, chasse au lévrier, *f*.

court, *n*, cour, *f*; tribunal; conseil, *m*; chambre; audience, *f*; (*Ten.*) court, jeu; tennis; (*Croquet*) terrain, *m*. ~ *card*, carte peinte, *f*, (*pl.*) figures, *f.pl.* ~ *martial*, conseil de guerre, *m*. ~ *s of justice*, palais de justice, *m*. ~ *plaster*, taffetas d'Angleterre, *m*. ~ *shoes*, souliers décolletés, *m.pl*, décolleté, *m*. ~ *train*, manteau de cour, *m*. ~ *yard*, cour, *f*; préau, *m*. ¶ *v.t*, faire sa cour à, courtiser; (*favour*) briguer; (*disaster*) inviter.

courteous†, *a*, courtois, honnête. **courtesan**, *n*, courtisane, hétaïre, *f*. **courtesy**, *n*, courtoisie, honnêteté, *f*. **courtier**, *n*, courtisan, *m*; (*pl.*) gens de cour, *m.pl*.

courtly, *a*, courtois. **courtship**, *n*, cour, *f*.

cousin, *n*, cousin, e.

cove (*bay*) *n*, anse, *f*, accul, *m*.

covenant, *n*, convention, *f*, pacte, *m*. ¶ *v.i*, s'engager.

Coventry (**to send to**) (*fig.*), mettre en quarantaine.

cover, *n*, couverture; enveloppe, *f*; tapis; pli, *m*; gaine, *f*; couvercle; capot, *m*; chape, *f*, chapeau; plateau, *m*; chemise, *f*; étui; fourreau; couvert; abri; fourré, *m*, remise, *f*; masque, voile, *m*; provision, mance, *f*, acompte, *m*; prévision, *f*. ¶ *v.t*, couvrir, recouvrir, envelopper, revêtir, tapisser; masquer; parcourir; comprendre; (*of animals*) saillir, sauter. ~ *ed walk*, allée en berceau, *f*. ~ *ing*, *n*, couverture, *f*; vêtement, *m*; (*of animals*) monte, saillie, *f*. ~ *card*, garde, *f*. ~ *let*, *n*, couverture pour berceau, *f*.

covert, *a*, couvert. ~ *coat*, paletot, *m*. ¶ (*game*) *n*, breuil, hallier, *m*. ~ *ly*, *ad*, en cachette.

covet, *v.t*, convoiter; reluquer. ~ *ous*, *a*, convoiteux, cupide. ~ *ousness*, *n*, convoitise, *f*.

covey, *n*, compagnie, *f*.

cow, *n*, vache, *f*; (*att.*, *of elephants*, *&c*) femelle ~ *bell*, clarine, sonnaille, *f*. ~ *herd*, vacher, ère. ~ *hide*, [peau de] vache, *f*, cuir de v., *m*. ~ *house*, ~ *shed*, étable à vaches, vacherie, *f*. ~ *keeper*, nourrisseur, *m*. ~ *lick*, rouflaquette, *f*. ~ *pox*, vaccine, *f*. ¶ *v.t*, intimider.

coward, *n*, poltron, ne, lâche, couard, *m*. ~ *ice*, *n*, poltronnerie, lâcheté, couardise, *f*. ~ *ly*, *a*, poltron, lâche, couard.

cower, *v.i*, se blottir, se tapir, s'accroupir.

cowl, *n*, capuchon, *m*, capote, *f*, champignon, *m*, mitre, *f*.

cowrie, *n*, porcelaine, *f*.

cowslip, *n*, coucou, *m*, primevère des champs, *f*.

coxcomb, *n*, fat, freluquet, *m*.

coxswain (*abb.* cox) *n*, barreur, patron, *m*.

coy, *a*, réservé, farouche. ~ *ness*, *n*, réserve, *f*.

cozen, *v.t*, duper; séduire.

crab, *n*, (*Crust.*) crabe, cancre; (*Hoisting*) treuil, *m*. ~ [*apple*], pomme sauvage, *f*. ~ [*apple tree*], pommier sauvage, *m*. ~ [*louse*], morpion, *m*. *to catch a* ~ (*Boat.*), faire une embardée. **crabbed**, *a*, acariâtre, revêche, grincheux, bourru. ~ *handwriting*, écriture de pattes de mouche, *f*.

crack, *a*, d'élite, timbré. ~ *brained*, timbré. ~ *jaw name*, nom à coucher dehors, *m*. ¶ *n*, fente, fissure, crevasse, fêlure; craquelure, *f*; (*horse*) crack; (*noise*) craquement; claquement; coup sec, crac, *m*, cric crac, flic flac. ~ *of doom*, dernier jugement, *m*. ¶ *v.t*, fendre; fêler; fendiller; gercer; crever; (*nuts*) casser; (*open a bottle*) décoiffer. ~ *ed* (*daft*) *p.a*, timbré, toqué. **cracker**, *n*, (*firework*) pétard, crapaud, *m*; (*Christmas*) papillote à pétard, *f*, cosaque avec pétard, *m*; (*whip*) mèche, *f*.

crackle, *v.i*, craque[te]r, crépiter, pétiller. **crackling**, *n*, (*Teleph.*) friture; (*pork*) couenne, *f*. **cracknel**, *n*, craquelin, *m*.

cracksman, *n*, cambrioleur, *m*.

Cracow, *n*, Cracovie, *f*.

cradle, *n*, berceau, moïse; (*Surg.*) arceau, cerceau, *m*. ¶ *v.t*, bercer.

craft, *n*, adresse, *f*; artifice, *m*; astuce, *f*; métier, *m*; (*Naut.*) embarcation, allège, *f*. **craftily**, *ad*, artificieusement. **craftsman**, *n*, homme de métier, artisan, *m*. ~**ship**, *n*, travail d'artisan, *m*. **crafty**, *a*, artificieux, rusé, futé, cauteleux, retors.

crag, *n*, rocher [anfractueux] *m*. **craggy**, *a*, anfractueux.

cram, *v.t*, bonder, bourrer, fourrer; farcir; (*poultry*) gaver; (*exam*) gaver, chauffer. ~*full*, bondé.

cramp, *n*, (*Path.*) crampe; (G or C) happe, *f*, serre-joint, *m*, presse à vis, bride de serrage; patte, *f*. ~[*-iron*], crampon, *m*, happe, agrafe, *f*. ¶ *v.t*, resserrer, entraver, gêner; cramponner.

cranberry, *n*, canneberge, *f*.

crane, *n*, (*bird & hoist*) grue, *f*. ~ *fly*, tipule, *f*. ¶ *v.t*, tendre.

cranium, *n*, crâne, *m*.

crank, *n*, (*Mach.*) manivelle, *f*, coude; (*pers.*) excentrique, original, *m*, maniaque, *m,f*; (*whim*) marotte, *f*. ~ *gear* (cycle), pédalier, *m*. ~ *pin*, bouton de manivelle, *m*. ~ *shaft*, arbre à manivelle, arbre coudé, vilebrequin, *m*. ~ *tool*, [outil à] crochet, *m*. ¶ *v.t*, couder.

cranny, *n*, fente, crevasse, *f*.

crape, *n*, crêpe, *m*.

crash, *n*, fracas, écrasement; krach, *m*, débâcle, chute, *f*. ¶ *i*, patatras! ¶ *v.i*, s'abattre; tomber, s'écraser (*sur le sol, la chaussée, &c*). ~**er**, *n*, resquilleur, euse.

crass, *a*, crasse (*a.f.*), grossier.

crate, *n*, caisse à claire-voie, harasse, *f*.

crater, *n*, cratère; (*mine, Mil.*) entonnoir, *m*.

crave, *v.t*, implorer. ~ *for*, appéter.

craven, *a*, poltron, lâche.

craving, *n*, ardent désir, *m*, soif, appétence, fringale, *f*.

crawl, *n*, (*Swim.*) crawl, *m*. ¶ *v.i*, ramper, se traîner. ~**ers** (*child's*) *n.pl*, barboteuse, combinaison, *f*.

crayfish, **crawfish**, *n*, (*river*) écrevisse; (*sea*) langouste, *f*.

crayon, *n*, [crayon] pastel, *m*.

craze, *n*, folie, fureur, toquade, marotte, manie, *f*. **crazy**, *a*, délabré; dément, détraqué, toqué, piqué. *to drive someone* ~, rompre la cervelle à quelqu'un. ~ *pavement*, dallage rustique, *m*.

creak, *v.i*, grincer, crier, craquer.

cream, *n*, crème, *f*; (*of story*) bon, *m*. ~ *cheese*, fromage blanc, *m*. ~*-coloured*, couleur crème. ~ *ice*, glace à la crème, crème glacée, *f*. ~ *jug*, crémier, *m*. ~*-laid*, vergé blanc. ~**ery**, *n*, crémerie, *f*. ~**y**, *a*, crémeux.

crease, *n*, pli, faux pli, godet, *m*. ¶ *v.t*, plisser; (*v.i.*) [se] plisser.

create, *v.t*, créer; faire, produire; provoquer. **creation**, *n*, création, *f*. **creative**, *a*, créateur. **creator**, **tress**, *n*, créateur, trice. **creature**, *n*, créature; *f*, être; animal, *m*, bête, *f*. ~ *comforts*, aises, *f.pl*.

crèche, *n*, crèche, garderie, pouponnière, *f*.

credence, *n*, créance, *f*. **credentials**, *n.pl*, lettres de créance; 1—s d'introduction, *f.pl*; pouvoirs, *m.pl*. **credibility**, *n*, crédibilité, *f*. **credible**, *a*, croyable; digne de foi. **credibly**, *ad*, de bonne source.

credit, *n*, croyance, foi, créance, consistance, *f*; honneur; crédit, avoir, *m*. *do* ~ *to*, honorer. ~ *balance*, solde créditeur, *m*. ~ *note*, note (ou facture) de crédit (ou d'avoir) *f*. ¶ *v.t*, ajouter foi à; créditer, bonifier. ~**able**, *a*, reluisant. ~**or**, *n*, créancier, ère, créditeur, *m*.

credo, *n*, credo, symbole, *m*.

credulity, *n*, crédulité, bonhomie, *f*. **credulous**, *a*, crédule.

creed, *n*, credo, symbole; culte, *m*, croyance, *f*.

creek, *n*, crique, *f*.

creel, *n*, panier à pêche, *m*.

creep, *v.i.ir*, ramper; cheminer. *it makes one's flesh* ~, cela fait venir la chair de poule. ~**er**, *n*, plante grimpante, *f*; (*grapnel*) grappin, *m*. ~**ing paralysis**, paralysie progressive, *f*.

cremate, *v.t*, incinérer. **cremation**, *n*, crémation, incinération, *f*. **crematorium**, *n*, four crématoire, *m*.

Cremona, *n*, Crémone, *f*.

crenel[l]ate, *v.t*, créneler.

creole, *n. & a*, créole, *m,f. & a*.

creosote, *n*, créosote, *f*.

crepitate, *v.i*, crépiter.

crescendo, *ad. & n*, crescendo, *ad. & m*.

crescent, *n*, croissant, *m*; (*of buildings*) demi-lune, *f*.

cress, *n*, cresson, *m*. ~ *bed*, cressonnière, *f*.

cresset, *n*, torchère, *f*.

crest, *n*, crête; huppe, *f*; cimier, *m*. ~*-fallen*, penaud. ~**ed**, *a*, crêté, huppé, aigretté; (*sea*) moutonneuse.

Crete, *n*, la Crète.

cretonne, *n*, cretonne, *f*.

crevasse, *n*, crevasse [glaciaire] *f*. **crevice**, *n*, crevasse, fente, lézarde, *f*.

crew, *n*, (*ship*) équipage, *m*; (*boat*) équipe, *f*; (*set, gang*) bande, *f*.

crewel stitch (*Emb.*), point de tige, point coulé, *m*.

crib, *n*, crèche, mangeoire; cabane; couchette, *f*; larcin, *m*. ¶ *v.t*, chiper.

cribbage, *n*, cribbage, *m*.

crick (*in neck*), *n*, torticolis, *m*.

cricket, *n*, grillon, criquet, cricri; (*game*) cricket, *m*.

crier, *n*, crieur, *m*.

crime, n, crime, forfait, m.

Crimea (the), la Crimée.

criminal†, a, criminel. *the C~ Investigation Department* (abb. C.I.D.), la police secrète, la Sûreté Nationale. ~ *law,* droit pénal, m. ¶ n, criminel, le. **criminate,** v.t, incriminer, charger.

crimp, v.t, friser, crêper; fraiser, gaufrer.

crimson, a, cramoisi, pourpre. ~ *clover,* trèfle incarnat, farouch[e] m. ¶ n, cramoisi, m, pourpre, f. ¶ v.t, empourprer.

cringe, v.i, faire le chien couchant. **cringing,** p.a, servile.

crinkle, n, plissement, m. ¶ v.t. & i, plisser.

cripple, n, impotent, e, estropié, e. ¶ v.t, estropier; (*fig.*) paralyser. **~d,** a, impotent, estropié, éclopé, perclus; (*ship*) incommodé.

crisis, n, crise, f.

crisp, a, cassant, croquant; (*air*) vivifiant, vif; (*hair*) frisé; (*style*) concis. ¶ v.t, crêper.

criss-cross, v.i, s'entrecroiser.

criterion, n, critère, criterium, m.

critic, n, critique; censeur; frondeur, m. **~al,** a, critique; décisif. **criticism,** n, critique, glose, f. **criticizable,** a, critiquable. **criticize,** v.t, critiquer; censurer.

croak, v.i, (*raven*) croasser; (*frog*) coasser.

crochet, n. & ~ *hook,* crochet, m.

crockery, n, faïence, vaisselle, f.

crocodile, n, crocodile, m; théorie de jeunes filles, f. ~ *tears,* larmes de crocodile, f.pl.

crocus, n, crocus, safran, m.

Croesus, n, Crésus, m.

crone, n, vieille femme momifiée, f. **crony,** n, compère, m.

crook, n, crochet, m; houlette, crosse, f; (*pers.*) escroc, m. ¶ v.t, recourber. **~ed,** a, crochu, tortu, tors; gauche; de travers; (*legs*) cagneux; (*fig.*) tortueux, oblique, indirect. **~edly,** ad, de travers; tortueusement. **~edness,** n, guingois, m.

crop, n, récolte; cueillette, f; (*bird*) jabot, m, poche; stick [de chasse] m. ¶ v.t, tondre; bretauder; (*ears*) essoriller, écourter. ~ *up,* surgir. ~ *up again,* rebondir.

croquet, n, croquet, m. ~ *court,* terrain de croquet, m. ¶ v.t, croquer.

crosier, crozier, n, crosse, f.

cross, a, de méchante humeur. ¶ *comps:* **~-bar, ~-beam,** traverse, f. **~-belt,** bandoulière, f; baudrier, m. **~-bred,** métis, mâtiné. **~-breed,** race croisée, f, métis & **~-breeding,** croisement, métissage, m. **~-country running,** race, cross-country, m. **~-examine someone,** faire subir à quelqu'un un interrogatoire; tenir qqn sur la sellette. **~-eyed,** louche. **~-head** (piston), crosse, f. **~-patch,** grognon, m. **~-piece,** entretoise, f. *to be at ~-purposes,* se contrecarrer. **~ reference,** référence croisée, f. **~-road,** chemin de traverse, m, traverse, f; (*pl.*) carrefour, m. ~ *section,* coupe en

travers, f, profil transversal, m. **~-stitch,** point de croix, m. **~-wise,** en travers. **~-word** [*puzzle*], mots croisés[-énigmes], m.pl. ¶ n, croix; (*fig.*) croix, f, calvaire; croisement; croisillon, m; (*on a letter t*) barre, f. ¶ v.t, croiser; traverser, couper, passer, franchir; (*a cheque, a t*) barrer; contrarier, contrecarrer. ~ *oneself,* se signer. ~ *out,* rayer, radier, biffer, barrer.

crosse (*Lacrosse*) n, crosse, f.

crossing, n, croisement, m; traversée, f, passage; (*cheque*) barrement, m. ~ *the line ducking,* baptême du tropique, baptême de la ligne, m.

crotchet, n, (*Mus.*) noire, f; (*whim*) boutade, lubie, quinte, f. ~ *rest* (*Mus.*), soupir, m. **~y,** a, quinteux.

crouch, v.i, se tapir, se blottir, s'accroupir.

croup (*Med.*) n, croup, m.

croup[e] (*rump*) n, croupe, f.

crow, n, corbeau, m, corneille, f; (*cock's*) chant, m; [*bar*], pince [à levier] f. **~-foot** (*Bot.*), renoncule, f. **~-foot** [*forking*] (of roads) & **~'s-foot** (wrinkle), patte-d'oie, f. **~'s-nest** (*Naut.*), nid de pie, m. *as the ~ flies,* à vol d'oiseau. ¶ v.i.ir, chanter. ~ *over,* chanter victoire sur.

crowd, n, foule, presse, f, rassemblement, monde, m, cohue, f. ~ *round,* se presser autour de, assiéger. **~ed,** p.a, fréquenté, comble.

crown, n, couronne, f; (*head, arch*) sommet; (*hat*) fond, m. *C~ Colony,* colonie de la couronne, f. ¶ v.t, couronner; (*Draughts*) damer. **~ing,** n, couronnement, m. ¶ a, suprême. ~ *piece,* couronnement, bouquet, m.

crucial, a, décisif, critique.

crucible, n, creuset, pot, m. ~ *cast steel,* acier fondu au creuset, m.

crucifix, n, crucifix, christ, m. **~ion,** n, crucifiement, m, crucifixion, f. **crucify,** v.t, crucifier.

crude, a, cru, brut; informe; indigeste; primitif. **~ly,** ad, crûment. **~ness,** n, crudité, f.

cruel†, a, cruel. **~ty,** n, cruauté, f; (*in Law*) sévices, m.pl.

cruet, n, ménagère, f, huilier, m; (*Eccl.*) burette, f.

cruise, n, croisière; campagne, f. ¶ v.i, croiser. **cruiser,** n, croiseur, m. **cruising:** ~ *fleet* & ~ *ground,* croisière, f. ~ *taxicab,* taxi en maraude, m.

crumb, n, miette; (*opp. crust*) mie, f. **~-brush,** brosse à miettes [pour la table] f. ~ *scoop,* gratte-miettes, m. **~-sweeper,** ramasse-miettes automatique, m. ~ *tray,* ramasse-miettes, m. ¶ (*Cook.*) v.t, paner.

crumble, v.t, émietter; (*v.i.*) s'émietter; crouler, tomber. **crumbly,** a, friable.

crumple, v.t, chiffonner; (*v.i.*) se c. ~ *up,* s'écraser.

crunch, *v.t. & i*, croquer, craquer. ¶ *i*, croc !

crupper, *n*, croupe; (*harness*) croupière, *f*.

crusade, *n*, croisade, *f*. crusader, *n*, croisé, *m*.

crush (*crowd*) *n*, cohue, *f*. ~ *hat*, [chapeau] claque, *m*. ~ *room*, foyer [du public] *m*. ¶ *v.t*, écraser; froisser; broyer, concasser; foudroyer. ~*ed-strawberry* (colour), fraise écrasée. ~er, *n*, broyeur, concasseur, *m*.

crust, *n*, croûte; croustille; (*earth's*) écorce, croûte, *f*; morceau de pain, *m*.

crustacean, *a. & n*, crustacé, *a. & m*.

crusted, *a*, encroûté. crusty, *a*, (*bread*) croustillant; (*fig.*) irritable, bourru. crust[y] end (bread), croûton, grignon, *m*.

crutch, *n. & ~ handle ~ key*, béquille, *f*. ~ *stick*, crosse, *f*.

crux, *n*, pivot, nœud, *m*.

cry, *n*, cri, *m*. *to be in full ~*, aboyer. ¶ *v.i*, crier, s'écrier; pleurer; (*v.t.*) crier, chanter; tambouriner. ~ *out*, crier; aboyer; s'écrier. ~ *up*, tambouriner. ~ing, *a*, criant. ¶ *n*, cri[s] *m*.[*pl.*]; larmes, *f.pl.*

crypt, *n*, crypte, *f*.

crystal, *n*, cristal, *m*. ¶ *a*, de cristal. ~ *gazing*, cristallomancie, *f*. ~ [*glass*], cristal, *m*. ~ *glass[ware] making* or *works*, cristallerie, *f*. ~ *set* (Radio), poste à galène, *m*. crystalline, *a*, cristallin. ~ *lens* (eye), cristallin, *m*. crystallize, *v.t*, cristalliser; (*v.i.*) [se] cristalliser. *crystallized fruits*, fruits candis, *m.pl.*

cub, *n*, petit, *m*.

Cuban, *a*, cubain. ¶ *n*, Cubain, e.

cube, *n*, cube, *m*. ~ *root*, racine cubique, r. cube, *f*. ~ *sugar*, sucre en morceaux, s. cassé, *m*. ¶ *v.t*, cuber. cubic, *a*, cube; cubique. ~ *foot*, pied cube, *m*. = 0·028317 cubic metre. ~ *inch*, pouce cube, *m*. = 16·387 cubic centimetres. ~ *yard*, yard cube, *m*. = 0·764553 cubic metre. ~al, *a*, cubique.

cubicle, *n*, alcôve de dortoir, *f*.

cubism, *n*, cubisme, *m*. cubist, *n*, cubiste, *m,f*.

cuckoo, *n*, coucou, *m*. ~ *clock*, pendule à coucou, *f*, coucou, *m*.

cucumber, *n*, concombre, *m*.

cud, *n*, substances élaborées dans l'appareil digestif, *f.pl*, nourriture, *f*, aliments, *m.pl.*

cuddle, *v.t*, câliner, pouponner, serrer dans ses bras. ~ *up*, se pelotonner, se blottir.

cudgel, *n*, bâton, gourdin, *m*, trique, *f*. ¶ *v.t*, bâtonner; (*one's brains*) torturer. cudgelling, *n*, bastonnade, *f*.

cue, *n*, mot, *m*; (*Theat.*) réplique; (*Bil.*) queue, *f*.

cuff, *n*, (*blow*) calotte, taloche, *f*; (*shirt*) manchette, *f*; poignet; (*coat*) parement, *m*. ~ *links*, boutons de manchettes, *m.pl.* ¶ *v.t*, calotter.

cuirass, *n*, cuirasse, *f*. ~ier, *n*, cuirassier, *m*.

culinary, *a*, culinaire.

cull, *v.t*, cueillir; recueillir.

cullender, *n*, passoire, *f*.

culm (*Bot.*) *n*, chaume, *m*.

culminate, *v.i*, atteindre sa plus grand hauteur; aboutir; (*Astr.*) culminer. cul minating, *a*, culminant.

culpability, *n*, culpabilité, *f*. culpable, *a* coupable. culprit, *n*, coupable, *m,f*.

cultivate, *v.t*, cultiver. cultivation, *n*, cul ture, *f*. cultivator, *n*, cultivateur, trice culture, *n*, culture, *f*. ~d (*pers.*, *pearl p.a*, de culture.

culvert, *n*, ponceau, *m*.

cum, *pr*, avec; attaché.

cumber, *v.t*, embarrasser, encombrer ~some, cumbrous, *a*, embarrassant, en combrant.

cumulative, *a*, cumulatif.

cumulus, *n*, cumulus, *m*.

cuneiform, *a*, cunéiforme.

cunning, *a*, rusé, artificieux; habile. ¶ *n* finesse, finasserie, ruse, *f*.

cup, *n*, tasse; coupe; timbale, *f*; calice, *m* (*barometer*) cuvette, *f*; (*thimblerigger's* gobelet, *m*. ~ & *ball*, bilboquet, *m*. ~ *bearer*, échanson, *m*. ~board, armoire, buffet; (*wall*) placard, *m*. ~board love amour intéressé, *m*. ¶ (*Surg.*) *v.t*, ven touser.

cupel, *n*, coupelle, *f*. ¶ *v.t*, coupeller.

Cupid, *n*, Cupidon, *m*.

cupidity, *n*, cupidité, *f*.

cupola, *n*, coupole, *f*. ~ [*furnace*], cubilot, *m*

cupping glass, ventouse, *f*.

cur, *n*, roquet, *m*.

curable, *a*, curable.

curacy, *n*, vicariat, *m*. curate, *n*, vicaire, *m*

curative, *a*, curatif, médicamenteux.

curator, trix, *n*, conservateur, trice.

curb, *n*, (*harness*) gourmette; (*street*) bordure (*fig.*) bride, *f*, frein, *m*. ¶ *v.t*, (*horse* gourmer; (*street*) border; (*fig.*) brider modérer.

curd[s], *n.*[*pl.*], caillé, *m*, caillebotte, *f* curdle, *v.t*, cailler; (*fig.*) glacer.

cure, *n*, guérison; cure, *f*; remède, *m*; (*souls* charge, *f*. *water*, *grape*, ~, cure d'eau de raisin. ¶ *v.t*, guérir; remédier à; (*salt* saler; (*smoke*) fumer; (*herrings*) caquer.

curfew, *n*, couvre-feu, *m*.

curiosity & curio, *n*, curiosité, rareté, bibelot, *m*. *curio cabinet*, vitrine, tabl vitrée, *f*. curious†, *a*, curieux. *the ~ part* or *thing*, le curieux. ~ *person* curieux, euse.

curl, *n*, boucle, *f*, frison, *m*, (*pl.*) frisure spirale, *f*. ~ *paper*, papillote, *f*. ¶ *v.t* friser, boucler, bichonner; (*lip*) retrousser ~ *up*, se mettre en boule, se pelotonner curler (*hair*) *n*, épingle [à friser], *f*; (*leathe* bigoudi [à friser] *m*.

curlew, *n*, courlis, courlieu, *m*.

curliness, *n*, frisure, *f*. curling, *n*, frisure, *f* ~ *tongs*, fer à friser, *m*. curly, *a*, fris bouclé.

curmudgeon, *n*, bourru; ladre, pingre, *m*.

currant, *n*, (*red*, *white*) groseille [à grappes] *f*; (*black*) cassis; (*dried*) raisin de Corinthe, *m*. ~ **bush**, groseillier [à grappes]; cassis, *m*.

currency, *n*, cours, *m*, circulation; monnaie, *f*. [*foreign*] ~, devise [étrangère], monnaie étrangère, *f*. **current**, *a*, courant, en cours; de mise. ~ **events**, actualités, *f.pl*. ~ **liabilities**, exigibilités, *f.pl*. ¶ *n*, courant, *m*.

curriculum, *n*, programme d'études, *m*.

curry (*Cook.*), *n*, cari, kari, *m*. ¶ *v.t*, (*leather*) corroyer; (*horse*) étriller. ~ **favour with**, se faufiler dans les bonnes grâces de. ~**comb**, étrille, *f*. ~**ing**, *n*, corroi; étrillage, *m*.

curse, *n*, malédiction, imprécation, *f*; fléau, *m*. ¶ *v.t*, maudire; affliger; (*v.i.*) blasphémer, jurer. **cursed**, *a*, maudit.

cursory, *a*, hâtif, rapide.

curt, *a*, bref, sec, cassant, brusque.

curtail, *v.t*, raccourcir, écourter; (*output*) contingenter.

curtain, *n*, rideau; brise-bise, *m*; toile, *f*; tableau! ¶ *v.t* ~ **holder**, embrasse, *f*. ~ **lecture**, sermon d'alcôve, *m*, semonce conjugale, *f*. ~ **net**, vitrage, *m*. ~ **raiser**, lever de rideau, *m*. ~ **rod**, tringle de rideau; tringle de brise-bise, *f*.

curtly, *ad*, brusquement.

curtsy, -sey, *n*, révérence, *f*.

curvature, *n*, courbure, *f*. ~ **of the spine**, déviation de la colonne vertébrale, *f*.

curve, *n*, courbe, *f*. ¶ *v.t*, courber, cintrer. **curvet**, *n*, courbette, *f*. ¶ *v.i*, faire des courbettes. **curvilinear**, *a*, curviligne.

cushion, *n*, coussin; coussinet; bourrelet; carreau, *m*; (*Bil.*) bande, *f*. ~ **cover**, dessus de coussin, *m*, taie de coussin, *f*.

custard, *n*, crème [culinaire] *f*.

custodian, *n*, gardien, ne. **custody**, *n*, garde, charge; arrestation, *f*.

custom, *n*, usage, *m*, coutume; pratique; clientèle, *f*; achalandage, *m*. ~**ary**, *a*, usuel, d'usage, ordinaire; coutumier. ~**er**, *n*, client, e; chaland, e; (*at café*) consommateur, *m*; (*at bank*) déposant, e. **customs**, *n.pl*, douane[s] *f.[pl.]*. ~ **or custom house**, douane, *f*. ~ [**duty**], douane, *f*, droit[s] de douane, *m.[pl.]*. ~ **agent**, agent en douane, *m*. ~ **officer**, agent de la douane, douanier, *m*.

cut, *n*, coupure, coupe, entaille, saignée; fouille, *f*, déblai, *m*; taille, passe; taillade, balafre, boutonnière, *f*; coup, *m*, atteinte, *f*, affront; morceau, *m*, tranche; réduction, compression, *f*; dégrèvement, *m*; vignette; gravure, *f*. ~ **off the joint**, morceau (*ou* tranche) de rôti. ~**out**, coupe-circuit, *m*. ¶ *v.t.ir*, couper; tailler; entailler; entamer; découper; trancher; rogner; fendre; cingler; (*teeth*) faire; graver. **have one's hair** ~, se faire couper les cheveux. ~ **& dried** *or* **dry**, tout taillé, tout fait. ~ **away** (neck of garment), évider, échancrer. ~

back (*Hort.*), receper. ~ [*crystal*] **glass**, cristal taillé, *m*. ~ **down**, abattre; moissonner; rogner; sabrer. ~ **edge** (book), tranche, *f*. ~ **edges** (book), tranches rognées, *f.pl*. ~ **flush** (book edges), coupé au ras du livre. ~ **in** (on road, &c), couper. ~ **nail**, clou découpé, *m*. ~ **off**, couper; retrancher; amputer; intercepter; isoler; moissonner. ~ **open-work stitch**, point coupé, *m*. ~ **out**, découper, couper, tailler; retrancher; supprimer. ~ **short**, écourter; trancher. ~**throat**, coupe-jarret, escarpe, *m*. ~**throat place**, coupe-gorge, *m*. ~ **up**, découper, dépecer; débiter; tronçonner.

cutaneous, *a*, cutané.

cute, *a*, fin, rusé.

cuticle, *n*, cuticule, *f*.

cutlass, *n*, sabre, *m*.

cutler, *n*, coutelier, ère. **cutlery**, **n.** & ~ **works** & ~ **shop**, coutellerie, *f*.

cutlet, *n*, côtelette, *f*.

cutter, *n*, (*clothes*, &c) coupeur, euse; (*gems*, *stone*, *files*, &c) tailleur; (*price*) gâte-métier, *m*; (*tool*) lame, *f*, couteau, *m*; fraise; molette, *f*; (*boat*) cotre; canot, *m*. ~ **wheel**, molette, *f*. **cutting**, *p.a*, coupant, tranchant; piquant, caustique, acéré. ~ **board**, tranchoir, *m*. ~ **edge**, tranchant, coupant, fil, *m*. ¶ *n*, taille; coupe; (*teeth*) pousse; (*newspaper*) coupure, tranchée, *f*, déblai, *m*; percée; *f*; copeau, *m*; rognure, *f*; (*snip of cloth*) chanteau, *m*, retaille; (*plant*) bouture, *f*. ~ **out** (clothes), coupe, *f*. ~**out scissors**, ciseaux pour coupe, *m.pl*.

cuttle fish, seiche, *f*.

cutty (*pipe*) *n*, brûle-gueule, *m*.

cutwater, *n*, (*bow*) taille-mer; (*bridge*) bec, *m*.

cyanide, *n*, cyanure, *m*.

cyclamen, *n*, cyclamen, *m*.

cycle, *n*, cycle, *m*; bicyclette; *f*; vélocipède, *m*. ~ **car**, cyclecar, *m*. ~ **show**, salon du cycle, *m*. ~ **track**, vélodrome, *m*. ~ **trade**, cycle, *m*. ¶ *v.i*, aller à bicyclette. **cycling**, *n*, cyclisme, *m*. **cyclist**, *n*, [bi]cycliste, *m,f*. **cyclometer**, *n*, compteur de bicyclette, *m*.

cyclone, *n*, cyclone, *m*.

cyclop[a]edia, *n*, encyclopédie, *f*.

cygnet, *n*, jeune cygne, *m*.

cylinder, *n*, cylindre; corps; barillet; fourreau, *m*. **cylindrical**, *a*, cylindrique.

cymbals, *n.pl*, cymbales, *f.pl*.

cynic, *n*, cynique, *m*. ¶ ~ **& cynical†**, *a*, cynique. **cynicism**, *n*, cynisme, *m*.

cynosure (*fig.*) *n*, point de mire, *m*.

cypher, *n*. Same as *cipher*.

cypress, *n*, cyprès, *m*.

Cyprus, *n*, Chypre, *f*.

cyst (*Med.*) *n*, kyste, *m*.

Czech, *a.* & (*language*) *n*, tchèque, *a.* & *m*. ¶ (*pers.*) *n*, Tchèque, *m,f*. **Czecho-Slovak**, *n*, Tchécoslovaque, *m,f*. **Czecho-Slovakia**, *n*, Tchécoslovaquie, *f*.

M

D

D (*Mus.*) *letter*, ré, *m.*

dab, *n*, coup de tampon, d'éponge, de mouchoir, &c, *m*; (*fish*) limande, *f*. ¶ *v.t.* tamponner; éponger. **dabber**, *n*, tampon, *m.*

dabble. *v.i*, barboter, patauger. ~ *on the stock exchange*, boursicoter.

dace, *n*, vandoise, vaudoise, *f*, dard, *m.*

dachshund, *n*, basset allemand, *m.*

dad[dy], *n*, papa, *m.*

daddy-longlegs, *n*, tipule, *f.*

dado, *n*, lambris d'appui, *m.*

daemon, *n*, démon, *m.*

daffodil, *n*, narcisse des prés, *m.*

daft, *a*, timbré.

dagger, *n*, poignard, *m*; (*Typ.*) croix, *f. at* ~*s drawn*, à couteaux tirés.

dahlia, *n*, dahlia, *m.*

daily, *a*, quotidien, journalier. ~ *help*, femme de journée, *f*. ~ [*paper*], [journal] quotidien, *m*. ¶ *ad*, journellement, quotidiennement.

dainties, *n.pl*, friandises, chatteries, douceurs, *f.pl*. **daintily**, *ad*, délicatement. **daintiness**, *n*, délicatesse, chatterie, *f*. **dainty**, *a*, friand, délicat; mignon.

dairy, *n*, laiterie, crémerie, *f*. ~ [*farm*], vacherie, *f*. ~*maid*, fille de ferme, *f*. ~*man*, laitier, crémier, *m.*

dais, *n*, estrade, *f.*

daisy, *n*, marguerite, pâquerette, *f.*

dale, *n*, vallon, val, *m*, combe, *f.*

dally, *v.i*, s'amuser, batifoler; tarder.

Dalmatia, *n*, la Dalmatie. **Dalmatian**, *a*, dalmate.

dam, *n*, barrage, *m*, digue; mère, *f*. ¶ *v.t*, barrer, endiguer.

damage, *n*, dommage, dégât, *m*, avarie, *f*, mal, *m*; (*pl., Law*) dommages-intérêts, *m.pl*. ¶ *v.t*, endommager, avarier. ~ *wilfully*, saboter.

damascene, *v.t*, damasquiner. **Damascus**, *n*, Damas, *m*. **damask**, *n*, damas, *m.*

dame, *n*, dame, matrone, *f.*

damn, *v.t*, damner; (*a play*) tomber. ~**able**, *a*, damnable, maudit. ~**ation**, *n*, damnation, *f*. ~**ed**, *a*, damné, maudit; sacré. *the* ~, les damnés. ~**ing**, *p.a*, accablant, écrasant.

damp, *a*, humide; moite. ~ *mark* (in books), tache d'humidité, mouillure, *f*. ~[-*proof*] *course*, lit isolant, *m*. ¶ *n*, humidité, *f*. ¶ *v.t*, humecter, mouiller, tremper; (*fig.*) refroidir; (*shock*) amortir. ~**er**, *n*, (*piano*) étouffoir; (*furnace*) registre; (*Radio*) amortisseur, *m*, sourdine, *f*; (*stamps, labels*) mouilloir; (*pers.*) éteignoir, *m*. ~**ness**, *n*, humidité, *f.*

damsel, *n*, demoiselle, jeune fille, *f.*

damson, *n*, damas, *m*. ~ [*tree*], prunier de damas, *m.*

dance, *n*, danse, *f*; bal; pas, *m*. ~ *frock*, robe de bal, *f*. ~ *hall*, salle de bal, *f*, bal, *m*. *D*~ *of Death*, *D*~ *of Macabre*, Danse macabre. ~ *partner*, danseur (euse) [de l'établissement]. ~ *tea*, thé dansant, *m*. ¶ *v.i. & t*, danser; branler. ~ *attendance* (on), s'empresser (auprès de).

dancer, *n*, danseur, euse. **dancing**, *n*, la danse. ~ *man*, coureur de bals, *m*. ~ *master*, maître de danse, *m.*

dandelion, *n*, pissenlit, *m.*

dandle, *v.t*, bercer, dodeliner, pouponner.

dandruff, -iff, *n*, pellicules, *f.pl.*

dandy, *n*, dandy, gandin, élégant, *m.*

Dane, *n*, Danois, e.

danger, *n*, danger, *m. this patient is out of* ~, ce malade est hors d'affaire. ~**ous**†, *a*, dangereux.

dangle, *v.i*, pendiller, brimballer; (*v.t.*) brandiller.

Danish, *a*, danois. ¶ (*language*) *n*, le danois.

dank, *a*, méphitique.

dapper, *a*, tiré à quatre épingles; bellot.

dappled, *p.a*, pommelé.

dare, *v.i.ir*, oser, s'aviser; (*v.t.ir*) défier, braver, oser. ~*-devil*, casse-cou, *m*. **daring**†, *a*, audacieux, osé, hardi. ¶ *n*, audace, hardiesse, *f.*

dark, *a*, obscur; sombre; noir; ténébreux; foncé; brun; sourd. *the* ~ *ages*, les siècles d'ignorance, *m.pl*. ~ *horse*, outsider, *m. to be a* ~ *horse*, cacher son jeu. ~ *lager*, bière brune, *f*. ~ *lantern*, lanterne sourde, *f*. ~ *man*, ~ *boy*, brunet, *m*. ~ *room* (Phot.), cabinet noir, *m*. ~ *slide*, châssis négatif, *m*. *c*. porte-plaques, *m*. ~ *woman*, ~ *girl*, brunette, *f*. ¶ *n*, obscurité, nuit, *f*, ténèbres, *f.pl. after* ~, à [la] nuit close. *in the* ~ (fig.), à l'aveuglette. ~**en**, *v.t*, obscurcir; assombrir, embrunir, rembrunir. ~**ish**, *a*, noirâtre. ~**ly**, *ad*, obscurément; sourdement. ~**ness**, *n*, obscurité, nuit, *f*, ténèbres, *f.pl*; teinte foncée, *f*. **dark**[e]**y**, *n*, moricaud, e.

darling, *a*, chéri, bien-aimé, favori. ¶ *n*, chéri, e, bien-aimé, e, bijou, *m*, mignon, ne, câlin, e, chou[chou]; coco, *m*, cocotte, *f*, Benjamin, *m*; favori, ite, coqueluche, *f.*

darn, *n*, reprise, *f*. ¶ *v.t*, repriser. ~**ing**, *n*, reprisage, *m*, reprise, *f*. ~ *needle*, aiguille à repriser, *f.*

darnel, *n*, ivraie, *f.*

dart, *n*, élan; dard, trait, *m*; fléchette, *f*; (*pl.*) jeu de fléchettes, *m*. ¶ *v.t*, darder, lancer; (*v.i.*) s'élancer.

dash, *n*, élan, *m*, fougue, *f*, panache, entrain; grain, tantinet, filet, soupçon, *m*; (*Teleg.*) trait; (*Typ.*) tiret, *m. to make a* ~ *at*, for, s'élancer sur, vers. ~ *board*, garde-crotte, pare-boue, tablier, *m*. ¶ *v.t*, heurter, jeter; briser, abattre; confondre. ~**ing**, *a*, fougueux; pimpant.

dastard, *n*, lâche, *m*. ~**ly**, *a*, lâche.

data, *n.pl*, données, *f.pl*.

date, *n*, date, *f*; quantième; millésime, *m*; échéance, époque; (*fruit*) datte, *f*. to ~, à ce jour. *up* (or *down*) *to* ~, à jour. ~ *palm*, dattier, *m*. ~ *stamp*, timbre à date, *m*. ¶ *v.t*, dater.

dative [case], *n*, datif, *m*.

datum [case], *n*, datif, *m*.

datum, *n*, donnée, *f*; repère, *m*.

daub, *n*, barbouillage, *m*; croûte, *f*; (*for walls*) bousillage, *m*. ¶ *v.t*, barbouiller, peinturlurer; bousiller.

daughter, *n*, fille, *f*. ~-*in-law*, belle-fille, *f*.

daunt, *v.t*, intimider, décourager. ~less†, *a*, intrépide.

davit, *n*, bossoir, *m*.

dawdle, *v.i*, flâner, muser, lambiner, s'amuser.

dawn, *n*, aube, *f*, point du jour, *m*, naissance du jour, (*of day & fig.*) aurore, *f*. ¶ *v.i*, poindre; naître. ~**ing**, *a*, naissant.

day, *n*, jour, *m*; journée. *f. the* ~ *after*, le lendemain. *a* ~ *after the fair*, la moutarde après dîner. *the* ~ *after to-morrow*, le surlendemain. *the* ~ *before*, la veille. *the* ~ *before yesterday*, avant-hier. *one of these fine* ~*s*, un de ces matins. ~ *book*, journal, livre, *m*. ~ *boarder*, demi-pensionnaire, *m,f.* ~*break*, point du jour, *m*, pointe du j., *f*, le petit jour. ~ *dream*, rêve, *m*. ~ *labourer*, journalier, *m*. ~*light*, jour, *m*. ~*light-loading roll-film camera*, chambre pour pellicules en bobines se chargeant en plein jour, *f*. ~ *nursery*, crèche, garderie, pouponnière, *f*. ~ *of atonement*, jour des propitiations. ~ *of the month*, quantième, *m*. ~ *scholar*, [élève] externe, *m,f.* ~ *school*, externat, *m*. ~'*s journey*, journée de chemin, *f*. ~'*s pay* & ~'*s work*, journée, *f*. ~*time*, heures de jour, *f.pl*, jour, *m*, journée, *f*.

daze, *v.t*, ahurir, hébéter; étourdir.

dazzle, *n*, éblouissement, *m*. ~ *lamp*, ~ *light*, phare éblouissant, p. de route, *m*. ¶ *v.t*, éblouir, offusquer; (*v.i.*) papilloter. ~**ling**, *a*, éblouissant.

deacon, *n*, diacre, *m*.

dead, *a. & ad*, mort; mat, terne; (*liquor*) éventé. ~*ball line* (*Rugby*), ligne de ballon mort, *f*. ~*beat*, ~ *tired*, éreinté, fourbu, moulu de fatigue, flapi. ~ *calm*, calme plat, *m*. ~ *centre*, point mort, *m*. ~ *drunk*, ivre mort. ~ *end*, impasse, *f*. ~*fall*, assommoir, *m*. ~ *heat*, épreuve nulle, course nulle, c. à égalité, *f*. ~ *letter*, (*Post*) rebut, *m*; (*fig.*) lettre morte, *f*. ~ *letter office*, bureau des rebuts, *m*. ~*lock*, impasse, *f*. ~ *loss*, perte sèche, *f*. ~*march*, marche funèbre, *f*. ~ *reckoning* (*Naut.*), estime, estimation, *f*. D~ *sea*, mer Morte, *f*. ~ *season*, morte-saison, *f*. ~ *slow* (*traffic sign*), au pas. ~ *wire*, fil hors courant, *m*. **the** ~, les morts, les trépassés, *m.pl*. ~**en**, *v.t*, amortir, étour-

dir. ~**ly**, *a*, mortel, à mort; léthifère; funeste, meurtrier. ~ *nightshade*, belladone, *f*. ~ *sins*, péchés capitaux, *m.pl*.

deaf, *a*, sourd. ~ & *dumb*, sourd-muet. ~ & *dumb alphabet*, alphabet des sourds-muets, *m*. ~-*mute*, sourd-muet, *m*, sourde-muette, *f*. ~**en**, *v.t*, assourdir. ~**ness**, *n*, surdité, *f*.

deal, *n*, (*Cards*) donne, main, *f*; [bois de] sapin, *m*. *a great* ~, *a good* ~, beaucoup, bien. ¶ *v.t.ir*, (*Cards*) donner, faire; (*blow*) porter, assener; (*v.i.ir.*) traiter; faire les cartes. ~ *out*, distribuer. ~ *with* (*shop*), se servir chez. ~**er**, *n*, marchand, e, débitant, e, fournisseur, e; (*Cards*) donneur, euse. ~**ing**, *n*, affaire, opération, négociation, *f*; procédé; (*pl.*) commerce, *m*, pratique, *f*, intelligences, accointances, *f.pl*.

dean, *n*, doyen, ne. ~**ery**, *n*, (*office*) doyenné, décanat; (*house*) doyenné, *m*.

dear, *a. & ad*, cher. *my* ~, ma chère. *my* ~ *fellow*, mon cher. *O* ~*!* aïe!, oh là [là]! *O dear no!* mais foi non! ~**est** (*pers.*), mon chéri, ma chérie, *m,f*. ~**ly**, *ad*, chèrement, cher. ~**ness** (*price*) *n*, cherté, *f*.

dearth, *n*, disette, *f*.

death, *n*, mort, *f*; décès, trépas, *m*; (*pl., obituary*) nécrologie, *f*. ~ *bed*, lit de mort, *m*. ~ *blow*, coup mortel, *m*. ~ *certificate*, extrait mortuaire, *m*. ~ *duties*, droits de succession, *m.pl*. ~ *knell*, glas funèbre, *m*. ~ *rate*, mortalité, *f*, taux de la m., *m*. ~ *trap*, casse-cou, *m*. ~ *warrant*, ordre d'exécution; (*fig.*) arrêt de mort, *m*. ~*watch* [*beetle*], horloge de la mort, vrillette, *f*. ~**less**, *a*, immortel.

debar, *v.t*, exclure, priver. ~ *by time* (*Law*), forclore. ~**ment by time**, forclusion, *f*.

debase, *v.t*, avilir; altérer, falsifier.

debatable, *a*, discutable, contestable, en litige. **debate**, *n*, débat, *m*, discussion, *f*. ¶ *v.t*, débattre, discuter, agiter. *debating society*, conférence, parlote, *f*.

debauch, *v.t*, débaucher. ~**ee**, *n*, débauché, e. ~[**ery**], *n*, débauche, crapule, *f*.

debenture, *n*, obligation, *f*. ~ *holder*, obligataire, *m,f*.

debilitated, *p.a*, débilité. **debility**, *n*, débilité, *f*.

debit, *n*, débit, *m*. ¶ *v.t*, débiter. **debt** [*due by the trader*] *n*, dette [passive] *f*. **debt** [*due to the trader*] *n*, créance, dette [active] *f*. *debt collector*, agent de recouvrements, *m*. *in debt*, endetté. *involve in debt*, endetter. *run into debt*, s'endetter.

debtor, *n*, débiteur, trice; redevable, *m,f*; obligé, e. ~ [*side*], débit, doit, *m*.

decad[e], *n*, dizaine; dizaine d'années; (*books*) décade, *f*.

decadence, *n*, décadence, *f*. **decadent**, *a*, décadent.

decagon, *n*, décagone, *m*.

decamp, *v.i*, décamper, plier bagage.

decant, *v.t*, décanter, transvaser. ~er, *n*, carafe, *f*, (*small*) carafon, *m*.

decapitate, *v.t*, décapiter.

decay, *n*, décadence; carie, *f*. ¶ *v.i*, dépérir; se carier.

decease, *n*, décès, trépas, *m*. ¶ *v.i*, décéder. ~d, *n*, défunt, e.

deceit, *n*, tromperie, *f*. ~ful, *a*, trompeur, mensonger. deceive, *v.t*, tromper, décevoir, abuser. deceiver, *n*, trompeur, euse.

December, *n*, décembre, *m*.

decency, *n*, décence, *f*.

decennial, *a*, décennal.

decent, *a*, décent; honnête. *not in* ~ *use* (words), trivial. ~ly, *ad*, décemment; honnêtement.

decentralize, *v.t*, décentraliser.

deception, *n*, tromperie, *f*. deceptive, *a*, trompeur, décevant, menteur.

decibel (*Phys.*) *n*, décibel, *m*.

decide, *v.t*, décider; statuer sur; (*v.i.*) [se] décider. decided, *a*, décidé, arrêté, marqué. ~ly, *ad*, décidément.

deciduous, *a*, décidu.

decimal, *a*, décimal. ~ *point*, virgule [décimale] *f*. *Note*:—The decimal point is indicated in French by a comma. ¶ *n*, décimale, *f*.

decimate, *v.t*, décimer.

decipher, *v.t*, déchiffrer.

decision, *n*, décision; délibération; *f*; parti, *m*. ~ *in one's favour*, gain de cause, *m*. decisive†, *a*, décisif.

deck, *n*, pont, tillac, *m*; (*of bridge*) tablier, *m*. ~ *cabin, chair*, cabine, chaise, de pont, *f*. ~ *hand*, matelot de p., *m*. ~ *tennis*, deck-tennis, *m*. ¶ *v.t*, parer, orner; (*ship*) ponter. ~ *with flags*, pavoiser. ~ *with flowers*, fleurir.

declaim, *v.i*, déclamer. declamatory, *a*, (*bad sense*) déclamatoire; (*good sense*) oratoire.

declaration, *n*, déclaration, *f*. declare, *v.t*, déclarer; constater; proclamer, dénoncer. *well, I* ~*!* ah! par exemple; ma foi!

declension (*Gram.*) *n*, déclinaison, *f*.

decline, *n*, déclin; retour, *m*; maladie de langueur; baisse, *f*. ¶ *v.i. & t*, décliner; pencher; baisser; refuser.

declivity, *n*, déclivité, pente, *f*.

decoction, *n*, décoction, *f*.

decode, *v.t*, déchiffrer.

decompose, *v.t*, décomposer.

decorate, *v.t*, décorer; garnir; orner. decoration, *n*, décoration, *f*; décor, *m*. decorative, *a*, décoratif. decorator, *n*, décorateur, *m*.

decorous†, *a*, convenable, bienséant. decorum, *n*, décorum, *m*.

decoy, *n*, (*bait*) leurre, *m*; (*place*) canardière, *f*; (*pers.*) mouton, *m*. ~ *bird*, appelant, *m*. ¶ *v.t*, leurrer.

decrease, *n*, décroissement, *m*, décroissance, *f*. ¶ *v.i*, décroître.

decree, *n*, décret, arrêt; jugement, *m*. ~

absolute, jugement définitif. ~ *nisi*, j. provisoire. ¶ *v.t*, décréter, édicter.

decrepit, *a*, décrépit, caduc. decrepitude, *n*, décrépitude, caducité, *f*.

decry, *v.t*, décrier.

dedicate, *v.t*, dédier, [dé]vouer, consacrer. dedication, *n*, consécration, dédicace, *f*, envoi, *m*.

deduce, *v.t*, déduire.

deduct, *v.t*, déduire, retrancher, défalquer, rabattre. ~ion, *n*, déduction, défalcation, *f*.

deed, *n*, action, *f*; acte; fait; exploit; contrat; titre, *m*.

deem, *v.t*, juger, estimer, considérer. ~ed, *p.p*, censé, réputé.

deep, *a*, profond; creux; (*in depth*) de (*ou* en) profondeur; (*colours*) foncé, gros; (*mourning*) grand; (*sound*) grave; rusé, fin, madré. ~-*sea captain*, capitaine au long cours, *m*. ~-*sea fishing*, pêche au large, p. hauturière; (*whale & cod*) grande pêche, *f*. ~-*sea navigation & ~-sea voyage*, long cours, *m*. ~-*seated*, profond, foncier. ~-*water harbour*, port de toute marée, *m*. ¶ *n*, profondeur; fosse, *f*. ~en, *v.t*, approfondir, creuser. ~[ly], *ad*, profondément, avant; sensiblement, fortement.

deer, *n*, bête fauve, *f*; daim; cerf, *m*; (*col.*) bêtes fauves, *f.pl*, fauves, *m.pl*. ~ *stalking*, chasse au cerf à l'affût, *f*.

deface, *v.t*, défigurer, mutiler. ~d, *p.a*, fruste.

de facto, *ad*, de fait.

defalcate, *v.i*, commettre des détournements. defalcation, *n*, détournement, *m*.

defamation, *n*, diffamation, *f*. defamatory, *a*, diffamatoire, diffamant, infamant. defame, *v.t*, diffamer.

default, *n*, défaut, *m*, défaillance, prévarication, négligence, *f*. *in* ~ *of*, à défaut de, faute de. ¶ *v.i*, manquer. ~er, *n*, défaillant, e; prévaricateur; (*Mil.*) réfractaire, *m*. ~ *on parade* (*Mil.*), manquant à l'appel, *m*.

defeat, *n*, défaite, *f*. ¶ *v.t*, défaire; frustrer.

defecate, *v.t. & i*, déféquer.

defect, *n*, défaut, *m*, défectuosité, *f*, vice, *m*, tare, *f*. ~ion, *n*, défection; apostasie, *f*. ~ive†, *a*, défectueux, vicieux; (*child*) taré (Cf. *school*); (*Gram.*) défectif.

defence, *n*, défense, *f*. ~less, *a*, sans défense. defend, *v.t*, défendre. ~ant, *n*, défendeur, eresse. ~er, *n*, défenseur, *m*. defensible, *a*, défendable. defensive, *a*, défensif. ¶ *n*, défensive, *f*.

defer, *v.t. & i*, différer, remettre, arriérer; éloigner; (*submit*) déférer. ~ence, *n*, déférence, *f*, respect, *m*, ménagements, *m.pl*. deferential, *a*, déférent.

defiance, *n*, défi, *m*. defiant, *a*, de défi.

deficiency, *n*, défaut, *m*, insuffisance, *f*, déficit, manquant, *m*. deficient, *a*, défectueux; insuffisant. *to be* ∼ *in*, manquer de. **deficit**, *n*, déficit, *m*, moins-value, *f*.

defile, *n*, défilé, *m*. ¶ *v.i.* défiler; (*v.t.*) souiller. ∼**ment**, *n*, souillure, *f*.

definable, *a*, définissable. **define**, *v.t*, définir. **definite**, *a*, défini; déterminé; précis. ∼**ly**, *ad*, décidément. **definition**, *n*, définition, *f*. **definitive**†, *a*, définitif.

deflate, *v.t*, dégonfler, désenfler. **deflation**, *n*, dégonflement, *m*; (*Fin.*) déflation, *f*.

deflect, *v.t*, défléchir; détourner; dévier. **deflexion, -ction**, *n*, déviation; flexion, *f*.

defloration, *n*, (*ravishment*) défloration; (*stripping of flowers*) défloraison, *f*. **deflower**, *v.t*, (*ravish*) déflorer; (*strip of flowers*) défleurir, déflorer.

deforest, *v.t*, déboiser.

deform, *v.t*, déformer, contrefaire. ∼**ed**, *a*, difforme, contrefait. ∼**ity**, *n*, difformité, *f*.

defraud, *v.t*, frauder, frustrer.

defray, *v.t*, défrayer.

deft†, *a*, adroit. ∼**ness**, *n*, adresse, *f*.

defunct, *a*, défunt. ¶ *n*, défunt, e.

defy, *v.t*, défier, braver.

degeneracy & degeneration, *n*, dégénérescence, dégénération, *f*, abâtardissement, *m*. **degenerate**, *v.i*, dégénérer, s'abâtardir.

degradation, *n*, dégradation, *f*; avilissement, *m*. **degrade**, *v.t*, dégrader; déclasser; [r]avilir.

degree, *n*, degré; point; (*Univ.*) grade, *m*.

deify, *v.t*, déifier, diviniser.

deign to (to), daigner, condescendre à.

deity, *n*, divinité; (*chiefly poet.*) déité, *f*.

deject, *v.t*, abattre. ∼**ion**, *n*, abattement, accablement, *m*.

de jure, *ad*, de droit.

delay, *n*, retard, délai, atermoiement, *f*, longueur, *f*. ¶ *v.t*, différer, retarder, atermoyer; (*v.i.*) tarder.

del credere, *n*, ducroire, *m*.

dele, *printing direction*, deleatur, *m*.

delectation, *n*, délices, *f.pl*.

delegate, *n*, délégué, e, député, *m*. ¶ *v.t*, déléguer. **delegation**, *n*, délégation, *f*.

delete, *v.t*, effacer, biffer, rayer.

deleterious, *a*, délétère.

deliberate, *a*, réfléchi; délibéré; posé; lent. ¶ *v.i*, délibérer. ∼**ly**, *ad*, délibérément; posément. **deliberation**, *n*, délibération, *f*.

delicacy, *n*, délicatesse; friandise, chatterie, *f*. **delicate**†, *a*, délicat; fin.

delicious†, *a*, délicieux. **delight**, *n*, délice, enchantement, *m*; jouissance; volupté, *f*. ¶ *v.t*, délecter, charmer, enchanter, ravir. ∼**ful**, *a*, délicieux, ravissant, charmant. ∼**fully**, *ad*, délicieusement, à ravir.

delimit[ate], *v.t*, délimiter.

delineate, *v.t*, tracer; [dé]peindre. **delineation**, *n*, délinéation; peinture, *f*.

delinquency, *n*, faute; négligence, *f*, méfait, *m*. **delinquent**, *n*, délinquant, e.

deliquescence, *n*, déliquescence, *f*.

delirious, *a*, délirant. *to be* ∼, délirer.

delirium, *n*, délire, *m*. ∼ *tremens*, delirium tremens, *m*.

deliver, *v.t*, délivrer; livrer; remettre; rendre; distribuer; (*Med.*) accoucher; (*ball*, *Ten.*, *&c*) lancer; (*speech*, *&c*) prononcer; (*pump*) refouler. *to be* ∼*ed of*, accoucher de; (*fig.*) pondre. ∼**ance**, *n*, délivrance, *f*. ∼**er**, *n*, libérateur, trice. ∼**y**, *n*, délivrance; livraison; remise; distribution; tradition, *f*; accouchement, *m*; prononciation, déclamation, diction, parole, *f*, débit; refoulement, *m*. ∼ *man*, ∼ *boy*, ∼ *girl*, livreur, euse. ∼ *van*, voiture de livraison, *f*.

dell, *n*, vallon, *m*.

delphinium, *n*, pied-d'alouette, *m*.

delta, *n*, delta, *m*.

delude, *v.t*, tromper, abuser.

deluge, *n*, déluge, *m*. ¶ *v.t*, inonder, noyer.

delusion, *n*, illusion, *f*. **delusive**†, *a*, illusoire.

delve, *v.t*, fouir, sonder.

demagogue, *n*, démagogue, tribun, *m*.

demand, *n*, demande, *f*, débit, *m*; exigence, *f*. ∼ *note* (taxes), avertissement, *m*. *on* ∼, sur demande, à vue; à bureau ouvert, à guichet ouvert, à présentation. ¶ *v.t*, demander; exiger.

demarcation, *n*, démarcation, *f*.

demean oneself (to) (*behave*), se comporter.

demeanour, *n*, allure, *f*, maintien, *m*.

demented, *p.p*, dément. **dementia**, *n*, démence, *f*.

demerit, *n*, démérite, *m*.

demesne, *n*, domaine, *m*.

demigod, *n*, demi-dieu, *m*.

demijohn, *n*, dame-jeanne, *f*.

demise, *n*, mutation, *f*; décès, *m*. ¶ *v.t*, transmettre; léguer.

demisemiquaver, *n*, triple croche, *f*.

demobilize, *v.t*, démobiliser.

democracy, *n*, démocratie, *f*. **democrat**, *n*, démocrate, *m*. ∼**ic**, *a*, démocratique.

demolish, *v.t*, démolir. **demolition**, *n*, démolition, *f*; (*pl.*) démolitions, *f.pl*, abattis, *m*, abats, décombres, *m.pl*.

demon, *n*, démon, *m*.

demonetize, *v.t*, démonétiser.

demoniac, *n*, démoniaque, *m,f*. ∼(al), *a*, démoniaque.

demonstrate, (*v.t.*) démontrer; (*v.i.*) manifester. **demonstration**, *n*, démonstration; (*political*, *&c*) manifestation, *f*. **demonstrative**, *a*, démonstratif. **demonstrator**, *n*, manifestant, e; (*Sch.*) démonstrateur, *m*.

demoralize, *v.t*, démoraliser.

demur, *n*, objection, *f*. ¶ *v.i*, opposer des objections; (*Law*) opposer une exception.

demure, *a*, composé; (*look*) de sainte nitouche; (*woman*) qui fait la sucrée.

demurrage, *n*, surestaries, *f.pl*; chômage, *m*.

demurrer, *n*, exception péremptoire, *f*.

demy, *n*, carré, *m*; coquille, *f*.

den, *n*, antre, repaire, *m*, tanière, caverne, *f*; bouge; nid; cabinet, *m*.

denature, *v.t*, dénaturer.

denial, *n*, dénégation, *f*, démenti; refus; reniement, *m*.

denizen, *n*, habitant, hôte, *m*.

Denmark, *n*, le Danemark.

denominate, *v.t*, dénommer. **denomination**, *n*, dénomination; (*sect*) communion; (*unit*) coupure, *f*. ~**al**, *a*, confessionnel. **denominator**, *n*, dénominateur, *m*.

denote, *v.t*, dénoter.

denounce, *v.t*, dénoncer.

dense†, *a*, dense, compact, épais. **density**, *n*, densité, épaisseur, *f*.

dent, *n*, bosse, *f*. ¶ *v.t*, bossuer, bosseler, cabosser.

dental, *a*, (*Anat.*) dentaire, dental; (*Gram.*) dental. ~ *surgeon*, chirurgien dentiste, *m*. ¶ (*Gram.*) *n*, dentale, *f*. **dentate**, *a*, denté. **dentist**, *n*, dentiste, *m*. ~**ry**, *n*, l'art dentaire, *m*. **dentition**, *n*, dentition, *f*. **denture**, *n*, denture artificielle, *f*.

denude, *v.t*, dénuder, mettre à nu.

denunciation, *n*, dénonciation, *f*.

deny, *v.t*, nier, nier se défendre de; renier; refuser. *to ~ it*, nier.

deodorize, *v.t*, désinfecter.

depart, *v.i*, partir; s'éloigner. ~ *this life*, quitter la vie, q. ce monde, trépasser. ~**ed**, *n*, défunt, e, trépassé, e.

department, *n*, département, *m*; division, *f*; service; rayon; office, *m*. ~**al**, *a*, départemental. ~[*al*] *store*[*s*], grand magasin [de nouveautés] *m*.

departure, *n*, départ, *m*, sortie, *f*; (*lapse*) manquement, *m*; innovation, *f*. ~ *platform*, quai de départ, *m*.

depend, *v.i*, dépendre, s'appuyer, compter. ~**ant**, ~**ent**, *n*, personne à charge, *f*. ~**ence**, *n*, dépendance; confiance, *f*. ~**ency**, *n*, dépendance; (*country*) annexe, *f*. *to be a ~ of*, dépendre de. ~**ent**, *a*, dépendant. *to be ~ on*, être à la charge de; être tributaire de.

depict, *v.t*, dépeindre, peindre.

deplete, *v.t*, amoindrir; épuiser.

deplorable†, *a*, déplorable, lamentable. **deplore**, *v.t*, déplorer, se lamenter sur.

deploy, *v.t*, déployer. ~**ment**, *n*, déploiement, *m*.

deponent (*pers.*) *n*, déposant, e.

depopulate, *v.t*, dépeupler. **depopulation**, *n*, (*action*) dépeuplement, *m*; (*state*) dépopulation, *f*.

deport, *v.t*, expulser. ~**ation**, *n*, expulsion, *f*.

deportment, *n*, maintien, *m*, tenue, *f*, manières, *f.pl*.

depose, *v.t*, déposer.

deposit, *n*, dépôt, *m*; consignation, *f*; versement; cautionnement, *m*; provision [de garantie] *f*; arrhes, *f.pl*, denier à Dieu; (*Geol.*) dépôt, gîte, gisement, *m*. ~ *account* (bank), compte de dépôts à terme ou à préavis, *m*. ~ *book* (savings), livret

[*nominatif*] *m*. ¶ *v.t*, déposer; consigner; verser; placer, mettre; fournir. ~**ary**, *n*, dépositaire, *m,f*. ~**ion**, *n*, déposition, *f*; dépôt, *m*. ~**or**, *n*, déposant, e. ~**ory**, *n*, dépôt; garde-meuble, *m*; (*fig.*) répertoire, *m*. **depot**, *n*, dépôt, *m*.

depravation & depravity, *n*, dépravation, *f*. **deprave**, *v.t*, dépraver. ~**d**, *p.a*, dépravé, taré.

deprecate, *v.t*, réprouver.

depreciate, *v.t*, déprécier, avilir; amortir. **depreciation**, *n*, dépréciation, moins-value, *f*, avilissement; amortissement, *m*. **depreciatory**, *a*, péjoratif.

depredation, *n*, déprédation, *f*.

depress, *v.t*, déprimer. ~**ing**, *p.a*, décourageant; triste. ~**ion**, *n*, dépression, *f*; enfoncement, *m*.

deprivation, *n*, privation, interdiction, *f*; retrait, *m*. **deprive**, *v.t*, priver, dépourvoir, sevrer; (*Eccl.*) interdire.

depth, *n*, profondeur; hauteur, *f*; fond; (*winter*) cœur, fort, *m*; (*colour*) intensité; (*sound*) gravité, *f*. ~ *charge*, grenade sous-marine, *f*.

deputation, *n*, députation, délégation, *f*. **depute**, *v.t*, députer, déléguer. **deputize for**, suppléer, faire l'intérim de. **deputy**, *n*, député, *m*; délégué e; suppléant, e, substitut, *m*. ~ *chairman*, vice-président, e. ~ *governor*, sous-gouverneur, *m*. ~ *professor*, professeur suppléant, *m*.

derail, *v.i*, dérailler. ~**ment**, *n*, déraillement, *m*.

derange, *v.t*, déranger, fausser; aliéner; détraquer.

derelict, *a*, à l'abandon. ¶ *n*, navire abandonné, *m*, épave, *f*. ~**ion**, *n*, abandon; manquement, *m*.

deride, *v.t*, se moquer de. **derision**, *n*, dérision, *f*. **derisive**, *a*, de dérision. **derisory**, *a*, dérisoire.

derivation, *n*, dérivation, *f*. **derivative**, *n*, dérivé, *m*. **derive**, *v.t*, tirer, retirer, puiser. *to be ~d from*, dériver de.

derogate, *v.i*, déroger. **derogatory** (*disparaging*) *a*, dénigrant.

derrick, *n*, chevalement, *m*; (*crane*) chèvre [verticale] *f*; (*ship's*) mât de charge, *m*.

dervish, *n*, derviche, dervis, *m*.

descant, *v.i*, disserter, discourir, s'étendre.

descend, *v.i. & t*, descendre. ~*ed from*, issu de. ~**ant**, *n*, descendant, e. **descent**, *n*, descente; (*lineage*) descendance, naissance, race, *f*.

describe, *v.t*, décrire, définir, qualifier. **description**, *n*, description, *f*, libellé[s] *m.*[*pl.*]; signalement, *m*; qualités, *f.pl*, profession; espèce, *f*, genre, *m*. **descriptive**, *a*, descriptif; (*catalogue*) raisonné.

descry, *v.t*, découvrir, apercevoir.

desecrate, *v.t*, profaner, violer.

desert, *a*, désert, désertique. ¶ *n*, désert, mérite, *m*. ¶ *v.t. & i*, déserter; aban donner, délaisser. ~ed, *a*, abandonné, désert. ~er, *n*, déserteur; transfuge, *m*. ~ion, *n*, désertion, *f*; abandon, délaissement, *m*.

deserve, *v.t*, mériter. deservedly, *ad*, à juste titre. deserving, *a*, méritant; digne (*of* = de). ~ *of praise*, louable.

desiccate, *v.t*, dessécher. desiccation, *n*, dessèchement, *m*, dessiccation, *f*.

desideratum, *n*, desideratum, *m*.

design, *n*, dessein; modèle; dessin; motif, *m*. ¶ *v.t*, destiner, affecter; projeter, se proposer; dessiner.

designate, *v.t*, désigner. designation, *n*, désignation, *f*.

designedly, *ad*, à dessein. designer, *n*, dessinateur, trice; auteur, *m*. designing, *a*, intrigant.

desirable, *a*, désirable, à désirer, souhaitable. desire, *n*, désir; appétit, *m*; envie; demande; prière, *f*. ¶ *v.t*, désirer. desirous, *a*, désireux. *to be* ~ *of*, désirer.

desist, *v.i*, se départir.

desk, *n*, pupitre; bureau, *m*; chaire, *f*; comptoir, *m*, caisse, *f*; lutrin, *m*.

desolate, *a*, désert; désolé. ¶ *v.t*, désoler. desolation, *n*, désolation, *f*.

despair, *n*, désespoir, *m*. *to drive to* ~ & ~, *v.i*, désespérer.

despatch, *n. & v.t*. Same as *dispatch*.

desperado, *n*, apache, escarpe, *m*. desperate, *a*, désespéré; acharné; éperdu. ~ly, *ad*, désespérément; à outrance; éperdument. desperation, *n*, désespoir; acharnement, *m*.

despicable, *a*, méprisable, lâche. despise, *v.t*, mépriser, dédaigner.

despite, *n*, dépit, *m*.

despoil, *v.t*, dépouiller, spolier.

despond, *v.i*, perdre courage, se décourager. ~ency, *n*, abattement, découragement, *m*. ~ent, *a*, abattu, découragé.

despot, *n*, despote, *m*. ~ic†, *a*, despotique. ~ism, *n*, despotisme, *m*.

dessert, *n*, dessert, *m*. ~ *fruit & nuts*, mendiants, *m.pl*. ~ *grapes*, raisin de treille, *m*. ~ *spoon*, cuiller à dessert, c. à entremets, *f*. (*sweet*) ~ *wine*, vin de liqueur, *m*.

destination, *n*, destination, *f*. destine, *v.t*, destiner. destiny, *n*, destin, *m*, destinée, *f*.

destitute, *a*, dans le dénuement; dépourvu, dénué (*of* = de). *the* ~, les nécessiteux, *m.pl*. destitution, *n*, dénuement, délaissement, *m*, misère, *f*.

destroy, *v.t*, détruire. ~er, *n*, destructeur, trice. [*torpedo-boat*] ~, contre-torpilleur, *m*. destruction, *n*, destruction, *f*; ravages, *m.pl*. destructive, *a*, destructif, destructeur, *m*. ~ *person*, brise-tout, *m*. destructor, *n*, incinérateur, *m*.

desultorily, *ad*, à bâtons rompus. desultory, *a*, décousu.

detach, *v.t*, détacher; isoler. ~able, *a*,

amovible, rapporté. ~ed *house*, maison isolée, *f*. ~ment, *n*, détachement, *m*.

detail, *n*, détail, *m*. ¶ *v.t*, détailler; circonstancier; (*Mil.*) détacher.

detain, *v.t*, détenir, retenir, empêcher de partir; arrêter.

detect, *v.t*, découvrir; surprendre. ~ion, *n*, découverte, *f*. ~ive, *n*, détective, *m*. ~ *camera*, chambre détective, *f*. ~ *story*, roman policier, *m*. ~or (*Radio*, *&c*) *n*, détecteur, *m*.

detent, *n*, détente, *f*, chien, *m*. ~ion, *n*, détention, *f*; arrêt, *m*; (*Sch.*) retenue, colle, *f*, arrêt, *m*.

deter, *v.t*, détourner; décourager.

deteriorate, *v.i*, se détériorer.

determinate, *a*, déterminé. determination, *n*, détermination; résolution, *f*. determine, *v.t*, déterminer, décider, définir, résoudre. ~d, *a*, déterminé, résolu.

detest, *v.t*, détester, abhorrer. ~able, *a*, détestable.

dethrone, *v.t*, détrôner.

detonate, *v.i*, détoner; (*v.t.*) faire détoner. detonation, *n*, détonation, *f*. detonator, *n*, détonateur, pétard, *m*.

detract from, rabaisser, dénigrer. detractor, *n*, détracteur, *m*.

detrain, *v.i*, débarquer.

detriment, *n*, détriment, préjudice, *m*. ~al, *a*, préjudiciable. *be* ~ *to*, préjudicier.

detritus, *n*, détritus, *m*.

deuce, *n*, diantre, diable; (*Cards, Dice*) deux, *m*; (*Ten.*) à deux, à égalité. ~ [*set*] (*Ten.*), à deux de jeux.

Deuteronomy, *n*, Deutéronome, *m*.

devastate, *v.t*, dévaster, ravager. devastator, *n*, dévastateur, trice.

develop, *v.t*, développer; faire valoir; (*Min.*) tracer. ~er (*Phot.*) *n*, (*proper*) développateur; (*mixture*) révélateur, *m*. ~ing *bath*, bain de développement, bain révélateur, *m*. ~ment, *n*, développement; traçage, *m*.

deviate, *v.i*, dévier; s'écarter. deviation, *n*, déviation, *f*; écart, *m*.

device, *n*, moyen, expédient; dispositif, *m*; (*emblem*) devise, *f*.

devil, *n*, diable, démon, *m*. *the* ~! diable! ~ish†, *a*, diabolique, diable (*f*, satané). ~ment, *n*, malice; verve endiablée; diablerie, *f*. ~ry, *n*, diablerie, *f*.

devious, *a*, détourné.

devise, *v.t*, combiner, inventer, imaginer; (*Law*) léguer.

devoid, *a*, dépourvu, dénué.

devolve, *v.i*, échoir, incomber, retomber.

devote, *v.t*, dévouer, consacrer, dédier, vouer; livrer. devotee, *n*, dévot, e, fervent, e, fanatique, *m.f*. devotion, *n*, (*Relig.*) dévotion; piété, *f*; (*zeal*) dévouement, attachement, *m*. ~al, *a*, dévot, de dévotion, de piété.

devour, *v.t*, dévorer, avaler, manger.

devout†, *a*, dévot; sincère. **~ness**, *n*, dévotion, *f*.

dew, *n*, rosée, *f*. **~drop**, goutte de r., *f*.

dewlap, *n*, fanon, *m*.

dewy, *a*, couvert de rosée.

dexterity, *n*, dextérité, adresse, *f*. **dextrous†, dexterous†**, *a*, adroit.

dextrin, *n*, dextrine, *f*.

diabetes, *n*, diabète, *m*.

diabolic(al)†, *a*, diabolique.

diacritical, *a*, diacritique.

diadem, *n*, diadème, *m*.

diaeresis, *n*, tréma, *m*.

diagnose, *v.t*, diagnostiquer. **diagnosis**, *n*, diagnostic, *m*.

diagonal†, *a*, diagonal. ¶ *n*, diagonale, *f*.

diagram, *n*, diagramme; graphique; abaque; schéma, *m*; épure, *f*.

dial, *n*, (*plate*) cadran; (*calculating mach.*) viseur; (*Teleph.*) disque [d'appel] *m*; (*compass*) boussole, *f*. ¶ *v.t*, composer [sur son disque d'appel]. **dialling tone**, signal de manœuvre, *m*.

dialect, *n*, dialecte, parler, idiome, patois, *m*.

dialectics, *n*, dialectique, *f*.

dialogue, *n*, dialogue, *m*.

diameter, *n*, diamètre, *m*. **diametric†**, *a*, diamétral.

diamond, *n*, diamant; (*Geom.*) losange, rhombe; (*pl*., *Cards*) carreau, *m*, ~ *wedding*, noces de diamant, *f.pl*.

diaper, *n*, étoffe diaprée, *f*; linge ouvré, *m*. ¶ *v.t*, diaprer, ouvrer.

diaphanous, *a*, diaphane.

diaphragm, *n*, diaphragme, *m*.

diarrhoea, *n*, diarrhée, courante, *f*.

diary, *n*, agenda; livre; (*of one's life*) journal, *m*.

diatonic, *a*, diatonique.

diatribe, *n*, diatribe, *f*, factum, *m*.

dibble, *n*, plantoir, *m*.

dibs (*child's game*) *n.pl*, osselets, *m.pl*.

dice, *n.pl*, dés, *m.pl*. ~ *box*, cornet [à dés] *m*.

dickens (the) *n*, diable, diantre, *m*.

dictate, *v.t. & abs*, dicter. ~ *to*, régenter. ~[s], *n.*[*pl*.], voix, *f*. **dictation**, *n*, dictée, *f*. **dictator**, *n*, dictateur, *m*. **~ial**, *a*, dictatorial. **~ship**, *n*, dictature, *f*; magistère, *m*.

diction, *n*, diction, *f*. **~ary**, *n*, dictionnaire, *m*.

dictum, *n*, dicton, *m*.

didactic, *a*, didactique.

die, *n*, dé [à jouer]; (*Mech.*) dé, *m*; filière, *f*; coussinet, *m*; lunette; matrice, *f*. ~ *sinker*, graveur en creux, *m*.

die, *v.i.i.r*, mourir, trépasser, succomber; périr; s'éteindre; (*animals*) crever; (*of laughing, &c*) mourir, [se] pâmer. ~ *away*, ~ *down*, mourir, s'assoupir. **~hard**, intransigeant, *m*.

diet, *n*, diète, *f*, régime [alimentaire] *m*. ¶ *v.t*, mettre à la diète; (*v.i.*) faire diète. **~ary**, *n*, régime diététique, *m*. ~ *bread*, pain de régime, *m*.

differ, *v.i*, différer, varier, s'éloigner. **~ence**,

n, différence, *f*, écart; différend, *m*. **~ent**, *a*, différent. **differential**, *a*, différentiel. ~ [*gear*], [engrenage] différentiel, *m*. **differentiate**, *v.t*, différencier. **differently**, *ad*, différemment, autrement.

difficult, *a*, difficile, malaisé. ~ *to catch*, insaisissable. **~y**, *n*, difficulté; peine, *f*; embarras, mal, *m. with* ~, difficilement, malaisément. (*ship in*) **difficulties** (*Navigation*), incommodité, *f*.

diffidence, *n*, défiance de soi-même; timidité, *f*. **diffident†**, *a*, timide.

diffuse, *v.t*, diffuser; répandre. ¶ *a*, diffus, filandreux. **~d**, *a*, diffus. **diffusion** *n*, diffusion, *f*.

dig, *n*, coup; (*fig.*) coup de patte, *m*. ¶ *v.t. & i. ir*, creuser; bêcher; fouiller. ~ *down* (*tree*), cerner. ~ *up*, déterrer; arracher.

digest, *v.t. & i*, digérer. **~ible**, *a*, digestible. **~ion**, *n*, digestion, *f*. **~ive**, *a. & n*, digestif, *a. & m*.

digger (*pers.*, *gold*) *n*, chercheur, *m*. **digging**, *n*, creusement, *m*, excavation, fouille, *f*; (*pl*.) placer, *m*, exploitation, minière, *f*.

digit, *n*, doigt, *m. a* ~ (0–9), un [seul] chiffre. **digitalis** (*Phar.*) *n*, digitale, *f*.

dignified, *a*, digne. **dignify**, *v.t*, ennoblir; investir; honorer, décorer. **dignitary**, *n*, dignitaire, *m*. **dignity**, *n*, dignité, *f*; quant-à-moi, quant-à-soi, *m*.

digress, *v.i*, divaguer. **~ion**, *n*, digression, divagation, *f*, écart, hors-d'œuvre, *m*. **digressive**, *a*, hors d'œuvre.

dike, *n*, digue, *f*; (*Geol. & Min.*) filon d'injection, *m*. ¶ *v.t*, endiguer.

dilapidate, *v.t*, dégrader, délabrer, détériorer. **~d state** (*building*), caducité, *f*.

dilate, *v.t*, dilater; (*v.i.*) se d.; s'étendre.

dilatoriness, *n*, lenteur, *f*; (*pers.*) long, lambin; (*policy*) d'attente; (*Law*) dilatoire.

dilemma, *n*, dilemme, *m*.

dilettante, *n*, dilettante, *m*.

diligence, *n*, diligence, *f*. **diligent**, *a*, diligent. **~ly**, *ad*, diligemment.

dilly-dally, *v.i*, lanterner, barguigner.

dilute, *v.t*, étendre, diluer; détremper, délaver; couper, baptiser. **dilution**, *n*, dilution, *f*.

diluvial, *a*, diluvien.

dim, *a*, obscur, sombre; indistinct; vague; trouble. ¶ *v.t*, obscurcir; ternir; offusquer; (*motor lights*) mettre en code. **dimmed lights**, éclairage code, *m*.

dimension, *n*, dimension, *f*; échantillon, *m*. **~ed sketch**, croquis coté, *m*.

diminish, *v.t. & i*, diminuer. **diminution**, *n*, diminution, *f*. **diminutive**, *a*, exigu; fort petit; (*Gram.*) diminutif. ¶ (*Gram.*) *n*, diminutif, *m*.

dimness, *n*, obscurcissement, *m*; obscurité, *f*.

dimple, *n*, fossette, *f*. **~d**, *a*, à fossettes.

din, *n*, bruit, tintamarre, *m*. ¶ *v.t*, corner.

dine, *v.i*, dîner. ~ *out*, dîner en ville.

diner, *n*, dîneur, euse.

ding[e]y, *n*, canot, youyou, *m.*

dingy, *a*, terne; sale; borgne.

dining: ~ *cur*, wagon-restaurant, *m.* ~ *room & ~ saloon*, salle à manger, *f.* ~ *table*, table de salle à manger, *f.* **dinner**, *n*, dîner, *m. at ~*, à table. ~ *jacket*, smoking, *m.* ~ *lift*, monte-plats, *m. give a ~* [*party*], donner à dîner. ~ *plate*, assiette plate, *f.* ~ *service*, service de table & dessert, *m.* ~ *time*, heure du dîner, *f.* ~ *wagon*, plateau roulant, *m*, desserte mobile, *f.*

dint, *n*, bosse, *f. by ~ of*, à force de.

diocesan, *a*, diocésain. **diocese**, *n*, diocèse, *m.*

diopter, *n*, dioptrie, *f.* **dioptric**, *a*, dioptrique.

dip, *n*, plongement, *m*, plongée; baignade; *f*; pendage, *m*, inclinaison; flèche; (*ink*) plumée, *f*. ¶ *v.t*, plonger, tremper, immerger; (*motor headlights*) faire basculer; (*v.i*) plonger; s'incliner.

diphtheria, *n*, diphtérie, *f.*

diphthong, *n*, diphtongue, *f.*

diploma, *n*, diplôme; (*fig.*) parchemin, *m.*

diplomacy, *n*, diplomatie, *f*; doigté, *m.* **diplomatic**, *a*, diplomatique. **diplomat[ist]** *n*, diplomate, *m.*

dire, *a*, (*distress*) dernière, extrême; (*necessity*) dure.

direct, *a*, direct; immédiat. ~ *current* (*Elec.*), courant continu, *m.* ~ *trade*, commerce direct, *m.* ¶ *ad*, directement. ¶ *v.t*, diriger; administrer, conduire; charger; adresser; acheminer; orienter. *to ~ me to . . .*, m'indiquer le chemin pour aller à . . . ~**ion**, *n*, direction; administration; conduite; orientation, *f*; sens, côté, *m*; adresse, *f*; (*pl.*) instructions, *f.pl*, charge, prescription, *f.* ~*s for use*, mode d'emploi, *m.* **directly**, *ad*, directement; immédiatement, à l'instant, aussitôt.

director, *n*, (*of company*) administrateur, trice; (*manager*) directeur, trice; ordonnateur, trice. ~**ate**, *n*, administration, *f.*

directory, *n*, annuaire; répertoire, *m.*

direful, *a*, terrible; sinistre.

dirge, *n*, chant funèbre, chant de mort, *m.*

dirigible, *a. & n*, dirigeable, *a. & m.*

dirk, *n*, dague, *f*, poignard, *m.*

dirt, *n*, saleté, crasse, ordure, immondice, crotte, boue; terre, *f*. ~*cheap*, à vil prix. ~ *track*, piste en cendrée, *f.* **dirtily**, *ad*, salement. **dirtiness**, *n*, saleté, *f.* **dirty**, *a*, sale, malpropre, crasseux; crotté, boueux. ~ *pig*, cochon, *m.* ~ *proof*, épreuve chargée de corrections, *f.* ~ *trick*, vilain tour, croc-en-jambe, *m*, vilenie, goujaterie, saleté, *f.* ~ *work* (*fig.*), sale besogne, *f*, micmac, *m.* ¶ *v.t*, salir, souiller, crotter, barbouiller.

disable, *v.t*, rendre incapable; rendre hors de combat; (*ship*) désemparer. ~*d soldier*, ~*d sailor*, mutilé de la guerre, *m.* ~**ment** & **disability**, *n*, incapacité, invalidité, *f.*

disabuse, *v.t*, désabuser.

disadvantage, *n*, désavantage, *m. place at a ~*, désavantager. ~**ous†**, *a*, désavantageux.

disaffection, *n*, désaffection, *f.*

disagree, *v.i*, n'être pas d'accord, être en désaccord; ne pas convenir. ~**able†**, *a*, désagréable. ~**ment**, *n*, désaccord, *m*, discordance, *f*; dissentiment, *m.*

disallow, *v.t*, rejeter.

disappear, *v.i*, disparaître. ~**ance**, *n*, disparition, *f.*

disappoint, *v.t*, désappointer; tromper, décevoir. *don't ~ me*, ne manquez pas à votre parole, à v. promesse. ~**ment**, *n*, désappointement, *m*, déception, *f*, mécompte, démenti, déboire, *m.* ~ *in love*, déception, *f*, (*ou* chagrin, *m.*) d'amour.

disapprobation & **disapproval**, *n*, désapprobation, improbation, *f.* **disapprove**, *v.t* & ~ *of*, désapprouver, réprouver, improuver.

disarm, *v.t*, désarmer. **disarmament**, *n*, désarmement, *m.*

disarrange, *v.t*, déranger, désajuster. ~ (*someone's*) *hair*, décoiffer.

disarray, *n*, désarroi, *m.*

disaster, *n*, désastre, sinistre; cataclysme, *m.* **disastrous**, *a*, désastreux; néfaste.

disavow, *v.t*, désavouer. ~**al**, *n*, désaveu, *m.*

disband, *v.t*, licencier; (*v.i*) se séparer.

disbelief, *n*, manque de foi, *m.* **disbelieve**, *v.t*, ne pas croire.

disbud, *v.t*, ébourgeonner, éborgner.

disburden, *v.t*, décharger. ~ *oneself*, s'ouvrir.

disburse, *v.t*, débourser. ~**ment**, *n*, déboursement, débours, déboursé, *m*, mise [de]hors, *f.*

disc, *n*, disque, plateau, *m*; rondelle, *f.*

discard, *v.t*, laisser de côté; (*Cards*) écarter.

discern, *v.t*, discerner. ~**ible**, *a*, perceptible. ~**ing**, *a*, judicieux. ~**ment**, *n*, discernement, jugement, *m.*

discharge, *n*, décharge, *f*; déversement, *m*, évacuation, *f*; débit; (*Med.*) écoulement; déchargement, débarquement, *m*; libération, *f*, acquit[tement] *m*, quittance, *f*, quitus; renvoi, congé, *m*; (*Mil., Navy*) réforme; (*bankrupt*) réhabilitation, *f.* ¶ *v.t. & i*, décharger; déverser; débiter; (*abscess*) jeter; débarquer; libérer; [ac]quitter; liquider; renvoyer, congédier; réformer; réhabiliter; apurer. *to get* (obligation) *discharged*, apurer.

disciple, *n*, disciple, *m.* **disciplinarian**, *n*, disciplinaire, *m.* **disciplinary**, *a*, disciplinaire; de discipline. **discipline**, *n*, discipline, *f.* ¶ *v.t*, discipliner.

disclaim, *v.t*, désavouer; dénier. ~**er**, *n*, dénégation, *f*; désaveu, *m*; renonciation, *f.*

disclose, *v.t*, révéler, divulguer, dévoiler. **disclosure**, *n*, révélation, divulgation, *f.*

discoloration, *n*, décoloration, *f.* **discolour**, *v.t*, décolorer.

M *

discomfit, v.t, confondre. ~ure, n, déconvenue, f.

discomfort, n, incommodité, f, malaise, m, gêne, f.

discompose, v.t, troubler. discomposure, n, trouble, m.

disconcert, v.t, déconcerter, interdire, désorienter.

disconnect, v.t, désassembler; (Mech.) débrayer; (Elec.) rompre.

disconsolate, a, désolé.

discontent[ed], a, p.p, mécontent. discontent[ment], n, mécontentement, m.

discontinuance, n, cessation, suspension; suppression, f. discontinue, v.t, discontinuer; (a train) supprimer. ~ one's subscription or season ticket, se désabonner.

discord, n, discorde, f; (Mus.) désaccord, m, dissonance, f. ~ance, n, discordance, f. ~ant, a, discordant, dissonant.

discount, n, escompte, m; remise, f; rabais, m; (opp. premium) perte, f. ~ charges, agio, m. ¶ v.t, escompter.

discountenance, v.t, s'opposer à.

discounter, n, escompteur, m. discounting, n, escompte, m.

discourage, v.t, décourager. ~ment, n, découragement, m.

discourse, n, discours, m. ¶ v.i, discourir.

discourteous, a, discourtois. discourtesy, n, discourtoisie, f.

discover, v.t, découvrir. ~er, n, inventeur, m. ~y, n, découverte, f.

discredit, n, discrédit, m. ¶ v.t, discréditer, déconsidérer, démonétiser. ~able, a, déshonorant.

discreet†, a, discret, retenu.

discrepancy, n, contradiction, f.

discrete, a, discret.

discretion, n, discrétion, retenue, prudence, f. ~ary, a, discrétionnaire. full ~ power, carte blanche, f.

discriminate, v.t, distinguer, discerner, faire le départ. discrimination, n, discernement, m, discrimination, f.

discursive, a, discursif.

discus, n, disque, m.

discuss, v.t, discuter, débattre, agiter. ~ion, n, discussion, f, débat, m.

disdain, n, dédain, m. ¶ v.t, dédaigner. ~ful†, a, dédaigneux.

disease, n, maladie, f; mal, m. ~d, a, malade; (meat) provenant d'animaux malades.

disembark, v.t. & i, débarquer. ~ation, n, débarquement, m.

disembody, v.t, désincorporer.

disembowel, v.t, éventrer.

disenchant, v.t désenchanter.

disencumber, v.t, désencombrer; (Fin.) dégrever.

disengage, v.t, dégager. ~d, a, libre.

disentangle, v.t, démêler, débrouiller.

disestablishment [of the Church] n, séparation de l'Église & de l'État, f.

disfavour, n, défaveur, f.

disfigure, v.t, défigurer, enlaidir. ~ment, n, enlaidissement, m.

disforest, v.t, déboiser.

disgorge, v.t, dégorger.

disgrace, n, disgrâce; honte, f; déshonneur, opprobre, m. ¶ v.t, (dismiss) disgracier; (shame) déshonorer. ~ful†, a, honteux, ignominieux.

disgruntled, a, maussade, mécontent.

disguise, n, déguisement; fard, m. ¶ v.t, déguiser, camoufler; travestir; contrefaire.

disgust, n, dégoût, m. ¶ v.t, dégoûter. ~ing, a, dégoûtant.

dish, n, plat, m; coupe; (Phot.) cuvette, f; (food) mets, m. ~ cloth, torchon [de cuisine] m, lavette, f. ~ cover, cloche [de plat] f. ~ warmer, réchaud, m. ~ washer, laveur de vaisselle, plongeur, m. ~ up, v.t, dresser, servir. ~ed, a, à cuvette. ~ful, n, platée, f.

dishabille, n, déshabillé, m.

dishearten, v.t, décourager, rebuter.

dishevelled, a, échevelé, ébouriffé.

dishonest†, a, malhonnête, infidèle, déloyal. ~y, n, malhonnêteté, infidélité, f.

dishonour, n, déshonneur, m. ¶ v.t, déshonorer. ~able, a, peu honnête, déshonorant. ~ed bill, effet retourné; e. impayé; e. non accepté, m. ~ed cheque, chèque impayé, m.

disillusion, n, désillusion, f. ¶ v.t, désillusionner, dégriser, désenchanter.

disinclination, n, éloignement, m. disincline, v.t, éloigner.

disincorporate, v.t, désincorporer.

disinfect, v.t, désinfecter. ~ant, n, désinfectant, m. ~ion, n, désinfection, f.

disingenuous, a, peu sincère.

disinherit, v.t, déshériter.

disintegrate, v.t, désagréger, effriter.

disinter, v.t, déterrer, exhumer.

disinterested, a, désintéressé. ~ness, n, désintéressement, m.

disinterment, n, exhumation, f.

disjoin, v.t, disjoindre.

disjoint, v.t, désassembler. ~ed, a, décousu.

disk, n, disque, plateau, m; rondelle, f.

dislike, n, dégoût, éloignement, m, aversion, antipathie, grippe, f. ¶ v.t, ne pas aimer, avoir en aversion, avoir de l'aversion pour (ou contre).

dislocate, v.t, disloquer, luxer, démettre, déboîter, démancher. dislocation, n, dislocation, luxation, f.

dislodge, v.t, déchausser, débusquer, disloquer.

disloyal†, a, déloyal, infidèle. ~ty, n, déloyauté, infidélité, f.

dismal†, a, lugubre, morne, sombre.

dismantle, v.t, démanteler, dégarnir.

dismast, v.t, démâter.

dismay, n, consternation, f. ¶ v.t, consterner.

dismember, v.t, démembrer.

ismiss, *v.t*, renvoyer, congédier, remercier, destituer; chasser; rejeter. ~al, *n*, renvoi, congé, *m*, destitution, *f*.

ismount, *v.i*, descendre; (*v.t.*) démonter.

isobedience, *n*, désobéissance, *f*. disobedient, *a*, désobéissant. disobey, *v.t*, désobéir à; (*v.i.*) désobéir.

isoblige, *v.t*, désobliger. disobliging, *a*, désobligeant. ~ness, *n*, désobligeance, *f*.

isorder, *n*, désordre; trouble, *m*; maladie, *f*. ¶ *v.t*, dérégler. ~ly, *a*, désordonné.

isorganize, *v.t*, désorganiser.

isown, *v.t*, désavouer, renier, méconnaître.

isparage, *v.t*, dénigrer, rabaisser, déprécier, ravaler. ~ment, *n*, dénigrement, *m*. disparaging, *a*, dénigrant; péjoratif.

isparate, *a*, disparate. disparity, *n*, disparité, *f*.

ispassionate, *a. & ~ly, ad*, sans passion; sans parti pris.

ispatch, *n*, expédition, *f*, envoi, acheminement, *m*; diligence, célérité, promptitude, rapidité; (*message*) dépêche, *f*. ~ boat, aviso, *m*. ~ case, serviette, *f*. ~ clerk, expéditionnaire, *m*. ~ rider, estafette, *f*. ¶ *v.t*, expédier, envoyer, acheminer; dépêcher, brasser.

ispel, *v.t*, dissiper, chasser.

ispensary, *n*, officine, pharmacie, *f*; (*charitable*) dispensaire, *m*. dispensation, *n*, (*of Providence*) disposition; (*exemption*) dispense, *f*. dispense, *v.t*, dispenser; départir; rendre; (*Med.*) préparer [& débiter]. ~ with, se passer de; supprimer. dispenser, *n*, dispensateur, trice; (*Med.*) pharmacien, ne.

ispersal *& dispersion*, *n*, dispersion, séparation, *f*. disperse, *v.t*, disperser; dissiper.

ispirit, *v.t*, décourager, déprimer.

isplace, *v.t*, déplacer; (*from office*) destituer; (*securities, Fin.*) déclasser. ~ment, *n*, déplacement, *m*; destitution, *f*; déclassement, *m*.

isplay, *n*, montre, parade, *f*; étalage, *m*. ~ advertisement, annonce de fantaisie, a. courante, *f*. ~ cabinet, vitrine, armoire vitrée, *f*. ~ figure, ~ model, mannequin, *m*. ¶ *v.t*, exposer, étaler; faire preuve de. ~ed in bold type, en vedette.

isplease, *v.t*, déplaire à; mécontenter. displeasure, *n*, déplaisir, mécontentement, *m*.

isposable, *a*, disponible. disposal, *n*, disposition; expédition, *f*. dispose, *v.t*, disposer. ~ of, disposer de; placer; expédier. well, ill, ~d towards, bien, mal, disposé pour, envers. disposition, *n*, disposition, *f*; naturel, *m*.

ispossess, *v.t*, déposséder.

isproof, *n*, réfutation, *f*.

isproportion, *n*, disproportion, *f*. ~ate, *a*, disproportionné.

isprove, *v.t*, réfuter.

ispute, *n*, dispute, contestation, *f*, litige, *m*. ¶ *v.t. & i*, disputer, contester. ~ every

inch of the ground (*Mil.*), chicaner le terrain.

disqualification, *n*, disqualification, *f*. disqualified (*Law*) *p.p. & p.a*, indigne. disqualify, *v.t*, disqualifier; (*Law*) frapper d'incapacité.

disquiet, *v.t*, inquiéter. ~[ude], *n*, inquiétude, *f*.

disquisition, *n*, dissertation, *f*.

disrate, *v.t*, déclasser.

disregard, *n*, inobservation, *f*; dédain, *m*. ¶ *v.t*, négliger; mépriser.

disrelish, *n*, dégoût, *m*.

disreputable, *a*, peu honorable; de mauvaise réputation. disrepute, *n*, discrédit, décri, *m*.

disrespect, *n*, manque de respect, *m*, irrévérence, *f*. ~ful†, *a*, irrespectueux, irrévérencieux.

disrobe, *v.t*, déshabiller.

disrupt, *v.t*, rompre.

dissatisfaction, *n*, mécontentement, *m*. dissatisfied, *p.a*, mécontent.

dissect, *v.t*, disséquer. ~ion, *n*, dissection, *f*.

dissemble, *v.t. & i*, dissimuler. dissembler, *n*, dissimulateur, trice.

disseminate, *v.t*, disséminer.

dissension, *n*, dissension, *f*, dissent, *n*, dissentiment, *m*; dissidence, *f*. ¶ *v.i*, s'opposer. ~er *& dissentient*, *n*, dissident, e. ~ing *& dissentient*, *a*, dissident.

dissertation, *n*, dissertation, *f*.

disservice, *n*, mauvais service, *m*.

dissidence, *n*, dissidence, *f*. dissident, *a*, dissident.

dissimilar, *a*, dissemblable, dissimilaire. ~ity, *n*, dissemblance, *f*.

dissimulate, *v.t. & i*, dissimuler.

dissipate, *v.t*, dissiper. dissipation, *n*, dissipation, *f*.

dissociate, *v.t*, dissocier.

dissolute, *a*, dissolu. ~ness, *n*, dissolution, *f*. dissolution, *n*, dissolution, *f*. dissolve, *v.t*, dissoudre, fondre. dissolvent, *a. & n*, dissolvant, *a. & m*. dissolving views, vues fondantes, *f.pl*.

dissonance, *n*, dissonance, *f*. dissonant, *a*, dissonant.

dissuade, *v.t*, dissuader, déconseiller.

dissyllable, *n*, dissyllabe, *m*.

distaff, *n*, quenouille, *f*.

distance, *n*, distance, *f*; éloignement, écart; lointain, *m*; trotte, *f*. keep one's ~, garder ses distances. ~ apart or between, écartement, *m*. ~ swim, course de fond, *f*. ¶ *v.t*, éloigner; distancer. distant, *a*, éloigné, reculé, lointain; distant. ~ signal (*Rly*), signal à distance, *m*.

distaste, *n*, dégoût, *m*. ~ful, *a*, désagréable au goût.

distemper, *n*, maladie [des chiens]; (*paint*) détrempe, *f*, badigeon, *m*. ¶ *v.t*, peindre à la détrempe, badigeonner.

distend, *v.t,* distendre, ballonner. **distension**, *n,* distension, *f,* ballonnement, *m.*

distich, *n,* distique, *m.*

distil, *v.t,* distiller. **distillate** & **distillation**, *n,* distillation, *f.* **distiller**, *n,* distillateur, *m.* ~**y**, *n,* distillerie, *f.*

distinct, *a,* distinct; tranché. ~**ion**, *n,* distinction, *f.* ~**ive**, *a,* distinctif. **distinctness**, *n,* netteté, *f.* **distinguish**, *v.t,* distinguer. *to be* ~**able from,** se distinguer de. ~**ed**, *a,* distingué, de distinction, éminent, notable, insigne.

distort, *v.t,* déformer; défigurer, dénaturer; tordre. ~**ing mirror,** miroir déformant, *m.* ~**ion**, *n,* déformation; distorsion, *f;* *(fig.)* travestissement, *m.*

distract, *v.t,* distraire, détourner; déchirer. ~**ed†**, *p.a,* éperdu, affolé. ~**ion**, *n,* distraction, *f;* affolement, *m;* folie, fureur, *f.*

distrain upon, *(pers.)* exécuter, contraindre par saisie de biens; *(goods)* saisir. ~**able**, *a,* saisissable. *not* ~, insaisissable. **distraint**, *n,* saisie, exécution, *f.*

distress, *n,* détresse; misère; *(Law)* saisie, *f.* ¶ *v.t,* affliger, désoler, angoisser. ~**ing**, *a,* affligeant, désolant, angoissant.

distribute, *v.t,* distribuer, répartir. **distribution**, *n,* distribution, répartition, *f.*

district, *n,* district, *m;* région, *f;* quartier, *m.* ~ **manager,** directeur régional, chef de district, *m.* ~ **visitor,** dame de charité, *f.*

distrust, *n,* défiance; méfiance, *f.* ¶ *v.t,* se défier de; se méfier de. ~**ful**, *a,* défiant; méfiant, soupçonneux.

disturb, *v.t,* troubler, déranger; remuer; inquiéter. ~**ance**, *n,* dérangement, trouble, *m;* perturbation, *f;* tapage, *m;* émeute, *f.*

disunion, *n,* désunion, *f.* **disunite**, *v.t,* désunir.

disuse, *n,* désuétude, *f.* ~**d**, *p.a,* hors d'usage.

ditch, *n,* fossé; canal, *m;* rigole; douve, *f.*

ditto, *n,* dito, idem *(ad.).* *to say nothing but* ~ *to everything,* opiner du bonnet.

ditty, *n,* chanson, chansonnette, *f.*

divan, *n,* divan, *m.*

dive, *n,* plongeon; *(Aero.)* vol piqué, *m.* ¶ *v.i,* plonger; fouiller. **diver**, *n,* *(Swim.)* plongeur, euse; *(in diving dress)* plongeur, scaphandrier; *(bird)* plongeon, *m.*

diverge, *v.i,* diverger. **divergence**, *n,* divergence, *f.* **divergent**, *a,* divergent.

diverse†, *a,* divers, varié. **diversify**, *v.t,* diversifier, varier. **diversion**, *n,* diversion, *f;* divertissement, *m.* **diversity**, *n,* diversité, variété, *f.* **divert**, *v.t,* détourner, dériver, écarter; *(amuse)* divertir.

Dives, *n,* riche; *(Bible)* le mauvais riche, *m.*

divest, *v.t,* dépouiller.

divide, *v.t,* diviser; scinder; partager; répartir. ~**d skirt,** jupe-culotte, *f.* **dividend**, *n,* dividende, *m;* répartition, *f.* ~ **warrant,** chèque-dividende, *m.* **dividers**, *n.pl,* compas à pointes sèches, *m.*

divination, *n,* divination, *f.* **divine†**, *a,* divin. ¶ *n,* théologien, *m.* ¶ *v.t,* deviner. **diviner**, *n,* devin, *m.* **divineresse,** *f.*

diving: ~ **bell,** cloche à plongeur, *f.* ~ **board,** plongeoir, tremplin, *m.* ~ **dress,** scaphandre, *m.*

divining rod, baguette divinatoire, *f.*

divinity, *n,* divinité, *f;* *(science)* théologie, *f.*

divisible, *a,* divisible; partageable. **division**, *n,* division, *f;* partage, *m;* section; coupe; séparation; case, *f.* **divisor**, *n,* diviseur, *m.*

divorce, *n,* divorce, *m.* ¶ *v.t,* divorcer d'avec. *to be* ~**d,** divorcer.

divot *(Golf)* *n,* touffe de gazon, *f.*

divulge, *v.t,* divulguer.

dizziness, *n,* vertige, *m.* **dizzy**, *a,* vertigineux.

do, *v.t.ir,* faire; opérer; *(v.i.ir.)* faire; agir; s'acquitter; aller; se trouver, se porter; convenir, faire l'affaire; suffire. ~ *away with,* supprimer, abolir. *[please] do not touch,* défense de toucher. ~*-nothing,* *a,* fainéant. ~ *one's hair,* se coiffer. ~ *one's utmost to,* s'efforcer de. ~ *over again,* refaire. ~ *up,* fermer, cacheter; empaqueter; *(repair)* refaire, retaper, ragréer. ~ *without,* se passer de. *I have done,* j'ai fini.

docile†, *a,* docile. **docility**, *n,* docilité, *f.*

dock, *n,* *(tail)* tronçon, *m;* *(Bot.)* patience, *f;* *(court)* banc des prévenus, *m.* *(Naut.)* bassin, dock, *m;* forme, cale, *f.* ~ *company,* compagnie des docks, *f.* ~ *strike,* grève des travailleurs des docks, *f.* ~ *warehouse,* dock[-entrepôt] *m.* *naval* ~*yard,* arsenal maritime, *m.* ¶ *v.t,* écourter; rogner; faire entrer en bassin; *(v.i.)* entrer en bassin. ~**er**, *n,* docker, déchargeur, débardeur, *m.*

docket, *n,* étiquette, *f.* ¶ *v.t,* étiqueter.

doctor, *n,* médecin, docteur, *m.* ¶ *v.t,* médicamenter; soigner; *(falsify)* frelater; *(patch up)* tricher. ~**ate**, *n,* doctorat, *m.*

doctrinaire, *n.* & *a,* doctrinaire, *m.* & *a.* **doctrine**, *n,* doctrine, *f.*

document, *n,* document, écrit, *m;* pièce, *f;* acte, titre, *m.* ~ *cabinet,* cartonnier, *m.* ~ *case,* serviette, *f.* ¶ *v.t,* documenter. ~**ary**, *a,* documentaire.

dodder *(Bot.)* *n,* cuscute, *f.* ¶ *v.i,* brandiller [de] la tête.

dodge, *n,* biais; détour; truc, *m;* ruse, *f.* ¶ *v.t,* esquiver, éviter; *(v.i.)* biaiser. **dodger**, *n,* biaiseur, euse. *artful* ~, finassier, ruse compère, *m.*

doe, *n,* *(deer)* daine; *(hare)* hase; *(rabbit)* lapine, *f.* ~**skin**, *n,* peau de daim, *f,* daim, *m.*

doer, *n,* faiseur, euse.

doff, *v.t,* ôter, tirer.

dog, *n,* chien; *(fox, wolf)* mâle; *(fire)* chenet, *m.* ~ *biscuit,* pain de chien, *m.* ~ *cart,* charrette anglaise, *f.* ~ *days,* canicule, *f.* ~ *fish,* chien de mer, *m.* ~ *Latin,* latin de cuisine, *m.* ~ *racing or dogs,* courses de lévriers, *f.pl.* ~ *rose,* rose de chien, églantine, *f;* (*bush*) églantier, rosier sauvage, *m.* ~['s] *ear,* n, corne, *f;* (*v.t.*) [é]corner. ~ *show,* exposition canine, *f.* ~ *violet,* violette de chien, *f.* ¶ *v.t,* talonner. **dogged,** *a,* tenace. ~**ly,** *ad,* mordicus. ~**ness,** n, obstination, *f.*

doggerel, n, méchants vers, *m.pl.*

doggy or **doggie,** n, toutou, m.

dogma, n, dogme. *m.* **dogmatic(al)†,** *a,* dogmatique. **dogmatize,** *v.i,* dogmatiser.

doily, n, rond, ovale, rectangle [de table] m.

doings, *n.pl,* faits & gestes; (*underhand*) agissements, *m.pl.* *your doing* (*fig.*), votre ouvrage.

dolce far niente, douceurs du farniente, *f.pl.*

doldrums (*Naut.*) *n.pl,* calmes, *m.pl,* zone des calmes, *f.* *to be in the* ~ (*fig.*), broyer du noir.

dole, n, charité; indemnité de chômage, *f.* ~ *out,* distribuer parcimonieusement. ~**ful†,** *a,* plaintif, dolent.

doll or **dolly,** n, poupée, *f.* ~-**faced,** poupin. ~'*s dinner party,* dînette, *f.* ~'*s home set,* [petit] ménage, *m.* ~'*s house,* maison de poupée, *f.*

dollar, n, dollar, m.

dolphin, n, (*porpoise*) dauphin, *m;* (*dorado*) dorade, *f;* (*mooring*) corps mort, m.

dolt, n, lourdaud, m.

domain, n, domaine, m.

dome, n, dôme, *m,* coupole, voûte, *f.*

domestic, *a,* domestique; (*coal, or like*) de ménage; (*trade*) intérieur, métropolitain. ~ *training,* éducation domestique, f, enseignement ménager, m. ¶ n, domestique, *m,f.* **domesticate,** *v.t,* domestiquer. **domesticated** (*pers.*) *a,* d'intérieur. **domesticity,** n, domesticité, *f.*

domicile, n, domicile, m. ¶ *v.t,* domicilier. *domiciliary visit,* visite domiciliaire, descente de justice, *f.*

dominant, *a,* dominant. **dominate,** *v.t. & i,* dominer, régenter. **domination,** *f.* **domineer,** *v.i,* dominer; (*domination,* f.) régenter. ~**ing,** *a,* dominateur.

Dominican, n, dominicain, e.

dominion, n, domination, *f,* empire, *m.* *D~ of Canada, of New Zealand,* Dominion du Canada, de la Nouvelle-Zélande, *m.*

domino, n, domino, m.

don, *v.t,* mettre, endosser, revêtir.

donation, n, don, *m,* donation; (*pl.*) bienfaisance, *f.*

done, *p.p,* fait; (*Cook.*) cuit.

donee, n, donataire, *m,f.*

donkey, n, âne, baudet, grison, *m,* bourrique, *f.* ~ *driver,* ânier, ère. ~ *engine,* petit cheval, *m.* ~ *pump,* pompe alimentaire, *f.*

donor, n, donneur, euse; (*Law*) donateur, m, donatrice, *f.*

doom, n, destin; jugement, *m.* ¶ *v.t,* condamner. **doomsday,** n, jour du jugement [dernier], *m;* (*fig.*) calendes grecques, *f.pl.*

door, n, porte; fermeture; (*carriage, car*) portière, *f;* (*peep hole*) regard, m. ~ *curtain,* portière, *f.* ~-*keeper,* concierge, *m,f,* portier, ère, gardien, ne. ~*mat,* paillasson, tapis-brosse, m. ~*step,* pas de la porte, m. ~*way,* [baie de] porte, *f.*

dorado, n, dorade, *f.*

Dorcas, n, vestiaire, m.

Doric, *a. & n,* dorique, *f. & m.*

dormant, *a,* dormant, endormi. ~ *partner,* commanditaire, bailleur de fonds, m. **dormer** [window], n, mansarde, lucarne, *f.* **dormitory,** n, dortoir, m. **dormouse,** n, loir, m.

dormy, -mie (*Golf*) *a,* sur le velours.

dory, n, dorée, *f.*

dose, n, dose, prise, *f.* ¶ *v.t,* médicamenter; doser.

dot, n, point; (*Emb.*) pois, m; (*child*) petiot, e. ¶ *v.t,* marquer d'un point, mettre un p. sur; (*Mus.*) pointer; pointiller; jalonner, parsemer. *dotted line,* ligne pointillée, *f.*

dotage, n, enfance, *f;* radotage, m. **dotard,** n, radoteur, euse; (*of comedy*) grime, m. **dote,** *v.i,* radoter. ~ *on,* être fou, folle, de, raffoler de.

double, *a,* double. ~ *n, s, &c* (*Spelling*) deux n, s, &c. ~ *oh,* fife, six, sev-en, ate, (*Teleph.*), deux fois zéro, cinque, sisse, septe, huite. ~-*acting,* à double effet. ~-*barrelled gun,* fusil à deux coups, m. ~ *bass,* contrebasse, *f.* ~ *bed,* lit à deux places, m. ~-[*bedded*] *room,* chambre à deux lits, *f.* ~-*breasted,* croisé. ~ *collar,* col rabattu; faux col r., m. ~ *cream cheese,* fromage à la crème, m. ~ *cuffs,* poignets mousquetaire, *m.pl.* ~ *dealing,* duplicité, *f;* (*a.*) double. ~-*entry bookkeeping,* tenue des livres en partie double, *f.* ~-*faced,* à double face. ~-*fronted* (*house*), à deux façades. ~ *meaning* or ~ *entendre,* mot à double entente, m, phrase à d. e., *f.* ~ *saucepan,* bain-marie, *f.* ¶ *ad,* double. ~ *width* (*cloth*), grande largeur, *f.* ¶ *ad,* double. ~-*top,* double; (*Turf*) coup de deux; (*counterpart*) pendant, sosie, m. ~ *or quits,* quitte ou double. *at the* ~ (*Mil.*), au pas gymnastique. ~*s game* (*Ten.*), partie double, *f.* ¶ *v.t. & i,* doubler. **doubly,** *ad,* doublement.

doubt, n, doute, m. ¶ *v.i,* douter; (*v.t.*) douter de. ~**ful†,** *a,* douteux; suspect; (*virtue*) moyenne. ~**less,** *a,* sans doute.

douceur, n, pot-de-vin, m.

dough, n, pâte, *f.*

doughty, *a,* preux. ~ *deeds,* hauts faits, *m.pl,* prouesses, *f.pl.*

dour, *a,* froid & sévère; peu démonstratif.

douse, *v.t,* éteindre; tremper.

dove, n, -colombe, *f;* pigeon, m. ~-*cot*[*e*], colombier, pigeonnier, m. ~-*tail,* queue d'aronde, *f.*

dowager, n, douairière, *f.*

dowdy, *a,* [mal] fagoté.

dowel, n, goujon, m. ¶ *v.t,* goujonner.

dower, n, dot, f; don, m. ¶ v.t, doter.
down, a, descendant. ~ **grade**, pente, f. ~ train, train descendant, m.
down, ad, en bas; à bas; bas; à terre; par terre; en aval; (prices) en baisse; (sun, moon) couché, e; (cross word clues) verticalement. to walk with the head ~, the hands ~, marcher la tête basse, les mains basses. ~ at heel, en savates. ~ there, ~ below, là-bas. ~ to, jusqu'à, jusque.
down, comps: ~cast, a, baissé; abattu. ~fall, n, chute, f, effondrement, m, ruine, f. ~hearted, a, découragé, abattu. ~hill, a, en pente; (ad.) en descendant. ~pour, n, tombée de pluie, f, déluge, m. ~right, a, franc, fieffé, pommé, vrai; (ad.), franchement, nettement. ~stairs, ad, en bas. ~-stream, ad, en aval, à vau-l'eau. ~stroke, n, (piston) course descendante, m; (Writing) jambage, plein, m. ~trodden, a, foulé [aux pieds]. ~ward, a, descendant; de baisse, à la baisse. ~ward[s], ad, en bas, en contre-bas.
down, i, à bas! ~ with . . ., à bas . . .! conspuez . . .!
down, n, duvet, poil follet; poil, m; bourre, f; coton, m; (sand hill) dune, f. ~ quilt, couvre-pied, m.
down, pr, en bas de, au bas de; en aval de.
down, v.t, abattre. ~ tools, poser ses clous.
downy, a, duveté, douillet, follet, cotonneux, bourru.
dowral, a, dotal. **dowry**, n, dot, f.
dowser, n, sourcier, m; ère, hydroscope, m. **dowsing**, n, hydroscopie, f. ~ rod, baguette divinatoire, f.
doyley, n, rond, ovale, rectangle [de table] m.
doze, v.i, sommeiller, s'assoupir. to have a ~, faire un somme.
dozen, n, douzaine, f. by the ~, à la d.
drab, a, gris brun; terne.
drachm, n, (apothecaries' measure) = 3·552 millilitres; (a—s' weight) = 3·888 grammes.
drachma, n, drachme, f.
draff (Brewing) n, drèche, drague, f.
draft, n, (men) détachement; (outline) projet, brouillon, m, minute, f; (drawing bill or cheque) tirage, traçage, m; (bill, cheque) traite, disposition, f, effet, mandat, bon, m, échéance, valeur, f. ¶ v.t, détacher; (writings) minuter. **draftsman**, n, dessinateur, traceur; (writings) rédacteur, m.
drag, n, drague, f; sabot [d'enrayage]; tirage, m; résistance, f. ~ net, traîneau, m, drague, f. ¶ v.t, traîner; arracher; (wheel) enrayer; (pond) draguer, pêcher; (anchor) chasser; (v.i.) se traîner; languir; chasser. ~ about, v.t, trimbaler.
draggle, v.t. & i, traîner.
dragoman, n, drogman, m.
dragon, n, dragon, m. ~fly, libellule, demoiselle, f. ~'s blood, sang-[de-] dragon, m.

dragoon, n, dragon, m. ¶ ~ into, forcer à, embrasser.
drain, n, drain, m; tranchée, f; égout; (demand) drainage, m. ~ pipe, tuyau de drainage; drain, m. ¶ v.t, drainer, assécher, dessécher, saigner, épuiser, [faire] égoutter, faire écouler; purger. ~ [away], s'écouler; s'égoutter. ~age, n, drainage, assèchement, dessèchement, épuisement, écoulement, m; purge, f; (surplus water) égout, m. ~er, n. & ~ing rack, égouttoir, m.
drake, n, canard, m.
dram, n, (avoirdupois) = 1·772 grammes; (draught) goutte, f. ~ shop, assommoir, m.
drama, n, drame, m. the ~, le théâtre. **dramatic†**, a, dramatique; théâtral. dramatis personæ, personnages, m.pl, rôle scénique, m. **dramatist**, n, auteur dramatique, dramatiste, m, dramaturge, m.f. **dramatize**, v.t, dramatiser.
drape, v.t, draper; tendre. **draper**, n, (cloth) drapier; (general) marchand de nouveautés, m. ~y, n, draperie, f; nouveautés, f.pl.
drastic, a, drastique, extrême.
draught, n, traction, f; vent, courant d'air; vent coulis; appel d'air; aérage; tirage; tirant d'eau; trait, coup; breuvage, m; potion, f; coup de filet, m, pêche, prise, f; tracé, plan, m, ébauche, f; (pl., game) les dames, f.pl. ~ animal, animal de trait, m. ~ beer, bière au tonneau; b. à la pompe, f. ~ board, damier, m. ~ strip, [bourrelet] dit] brise-bise, m. ¶ v.t, ébaucher, tracer. **draughtsman**, n, dessinateur, traceur; (writings) rédacteur, m. **draughty**, a, exposé aux courants d'air.
draw, n, tirage, m; loterie, f; attrait, m, attraction, f; appât, m; (game) partie nulle, f, match nul, refait, m.
draw, v.t.i.r, tirer; retirer; attirer; traîner; entraîner; remorquer; (Min.) remonter; (metal) étirer; arracher; extraire; puiser; aspirer; (so much water—ship) caler; dessiner; tracer; (wages) toucher; (fowl) vider; (v.i.i.r.) tirer; (tea) [s']infuser. ~ [a game], faire match nul, f. partie nulle. ~ aside, tirer à l'écart. ~ back, reculer; (curtains) ouvrir. ~ down, faire descendre, baisser. ~ in (days), [se] raccourcir. ~ near, approcher. ~ off, tirer; soutirer. ~ on, mettre à contribution. ~ out (days), croître. ~ the long bow, en raconter. ~ up, (writing) dresser, rédiger, formuler; (carriage) s'arrêter.
drawback, n, (Cust.) drawback; (fig.) désavantage, inconvénient, m.
drawbridge, n, pont levant; pont à bascule; (Hist.) pont-levis, m.
drawee, n, tiré, payeur, m. **drawer**, n, tireur, euse, f; (receptacle) tiroir; carton, m; (pl., chest) commode, f; (pl., Dress) caleçon, m.

drawing, *n*, dessin: (*lottery*) tirage, *m*. ~ *board*, planche à dessin, *f*. ~ *knife*, plane, *f*. ~ *pen*, tire-ligne, *m*. ~ *pin*, clou à dessin, *m*, punaise [à d.] *f*. ~ *room*, [grand] salon, *m*.

drawl, *v.t.* traîner.

draw-leaf table, table à tirettes, *f*.

drawn: ~ *battle*, bataille indécise, *f*. ~ *face*, visage tiré, v. hagard, *m*. ~ *game*, partie nulle, p. indécise, p. remise, *f*. ~ *number*, numéro sortant, *m*. *with* ~ *sword*, sabre au clair.

drawplate, *n*, filière [à étirer] *f*.

dray, *n*, haquet, *m*. ~*horse*, cheval de h., *m*. ~*man*, haquetier, *m*.

dread, *a*, redouté. ¶ *n*, terreur, crainte; phobie, *f*. ¶ *v.t*, redouter, craindre. ~**ful†**, *a*, terrible, épouvantable, affreux.

Dreadnought (*Nav.*) *n*, dreadnought, *m*.

dream, *n*, rêve, songe, *m*; rêverie, *f*. ¶ *v.i. & t. ir*, rêver, songer. ~ *of*, rêver. ~**er**, *n*, rêveur, euse; songe-creux, *m*. ~**y**, *a*, rêveur, songeur.

drear[y], *a*, triste, morne. **dreariness**, *n*, tristesse, *f*, aspect morne, *m*.

dredge, *n*, drague, *f*. ¶ *v.t* draguer; (*sprinkle*) saupoudrer. **dredger**, *n*, dragueur; saupoudroir, *m*. **dredging**, *n*, dragage, *m*.

dregs, *n.pl*, lie, *f*.

drench, *v.t*, tremper; saucer; abreuver. ~*ing rain*, pluie battante, *f*.

Dresden, *n*, Dresde, *f*. ~ *china*, porcelaine de Saxe, *f*, saxe, *m*.

dress, *n*, habillement; entretien; costume, *m*; robe; mise; toilette; tenue; parure, *f*; chiffons, *m.pl*. ~ *bow*, cravate de soirée, *f*. ~ *circle*, premières [galeries] *f.pl*, [premier] balcon, *m*. ~ *circle seat*, première, *f*. ~ *coat*, habit de soirée, *m*. ~ *guard* (cycle), garde-jupe, *m*. ~*maker*, couturière; entrepreneuse de confection, *f*. ~*making*, confections pour dames, *f.pl*. ~ *protector*, dessous de bras, *m*. ~ *rehearsal*, avant-première, répétition générale, *f*. ~ *shirt*, chemise de soirée, *f*. ~ *shoes*, chaussures vernies, *f.pl*, vernis, *m.pl*. ~ *stand*, mannequin, *m*. ~ [*suit*], ~ *clothes*, habits de soirée, *m.pl*, habit, *m*. ¶ *v.t*, habiller; [re]vêtir; (*in fancy dress*) costumer; orner, parer; (*ship with flags*) pavoiser; (*wound*) panser; (*food*) apprêter; (*salad*) assaisonner; (*materials*) dresser, tailler, corroyer; (*Mil.*) aligner. ~ [*oneself*], s'habiller, se mettre, se vêtir. ~ *for dinner*, se mettre en habit pour dîner. ~ *like a guy*, fagoter. ~ *ship*, pavoiser. ~ *the window(s)*, faire l'étalage. ~ *up*, ~ *out*, parer; affubler; [en]harnacher, bichonner. **dresser**, *n*, (*Theat.*) habilleuse, *f*; (*kitchen*) buffet, buffet-étagère, *m*, étagère, *f*, vaisselier, *m*. **dressing**, *n*, habillement, *m*; toilette, *f*; (*of wound*) pansement; (*on wound*) appareil, *f*; (*food*) apprêt, *m*; (*meat*) parure, *f*; (*salad*) assaison-

nement, *m*. ~ *case*, mallette garnie, *f*. ~ *comb*, démêloir, *m*. ~ *gown*, robe de chambre, *f*, peignoir, saut de lit, *m*. ~ *jacket*, matinée, *f*. ~ *room*, cabinet de toilette, *m*; (*Theat.*) loge, *f*. ~ *table*, [table de] toilette, coiffeuse, *f*.

dribble, *n*, goutte; (*slaver*) bave, *f*. ¶ *v.i*, dégoutter; baver; (*v.t.*, Foot.) dribbler. **dribbling** (*Foot.*) *n*, dribbling, *m*. *in drib[b]lets*, par parcelles.

dried, *p.a*, séché; (*raisins, fruits, fish, &c*) sec; (*apples, &c, in rings*) tapé. **drier**, *n*, séchoir; (*s. or pl, for paint*) siccatif, *m*.

drift, *n*, direction; vitesse, *f*; but *m*, tendance, portée, *f*; laisser-faire, *m*, inaction; déviation, *f*; (*snow*) amas, *m*; (*Naut. & fig*) dérive; (*Min.*) galerie, *f*; (*Geol.*) apport[s] *m.*[*pl.*]. ~ [*net*], traîne, seine, *f*. ~ [*pin*], broche, *f*, mandrin, *m*. ~*wood*, bois flotté, *m*. ¶ *v.t*, charrier, entraîner, apporter; chasser; amonceler; (*Mech.*) brocher; (*v.i.*) chasser; (*Naut.*) dériver, aller en dérive; s'amonceler. ~*er* (*boat*) *n*, cordier, *m*.

drill, *n*, foret, *m*, mèche; (*Min.*, &c) perforatrice, foreuse, perceuse, sonde, *f*; (*furrow*) sillon, *m*; (*Agric. mach.*) semoir, *m*; (*Mil.*) exercice, *m*, école, *f*; (*fabric*) coutil, *m*. ~ *bow*, archet, *m*. ~ *ground*, champ de manœuvres, *m*, place d'armes, *f*. ~ [*holder*], porte-foret, porte-mèche, *m*. ~ *sergeant*, [sergent] instructeur, *m*. ¶ *v.t*, percer, forer, perforer; (*Mil.*) exercer, faire faire l'exercice à; (*v.i.*) faire l'exercice. **drilling**, *n*, perçage, percement, *m*, perforation, *f*; forage, sondage; (*Mil.*) exercice, *m*. ~ *machine*, machine à percer, perceuse; foreuse, *f*.

drily, *ad*, (*answer coldly*) sèchement, sec; (*with dry sarcasm*) d'un air de pince-sans-rire.

drink, *n*, boisson; consommation, *f*; breuvage, *m*; liqueur, *f*. *to have a* ~, boire un coup. ~ [*money*], pourboire, *m*. ¶ *v.t. & i. ir*, boire; consommer. ~*able*, *a*, buvable, potable. ~**er**, *n*, buveur, euse. ~**ing**, *att*: ~ *fountain*, fontaine publique, *f*. ~ *song*, chanson à boire, c. bachique, *f*, air à boire, *m*. ~ *straw*, chalumeau, *m*. ~ *trough*, abreuvoir, *m*. ~ *water*, eau potable, *f*.

drip, *n*, goutte, *f*. ~ [*stone*], larmier, *m*. ¶ *v.i*, [dé]goutter, découler, pleurer, ruisseler. **dripping**, *n*, graisse de rôti, *f*. ~*pan*, lèchefrite, *f*. ~ *wet*, tout trempé, saucé.

drive, *n*, promenade; avenue, allée; initiative; (*Hunt.*) battue; (*Mach.*) commande, transmission; (*Golf*) crossée, *f*; (*Ten.*) drive, *m*; (*Min.*) galerie, *f*. ¶ *v.t.ir*, chasser, pousser, forcer; (*horse, car, &c*) conduire, mener; (*Golf*) driver; (*Ten.*) chasser; (*screw*) serrer; (*Mach.*) actionner, commander; (*Min.*) chasser, percer [en direction]; enfoncer; forcer, contraindre; faire; (*one mad*) rendre; (*v.i.ir.*) aller (*ou* se promener) en voiture, rouler. ~ *ashore* (ship), dériver à la côte. ~ *away*, chasser. ~ *back*, refouler. ~ *into a corner*, acculer, rencogner. ~ *out*, ~ *off*, chasser, débusquer. ~ *slowly* (traffic sign), au pas.

drivel, *n,* bave, *f.* ¶ *v.i,* baver; (*fig.*) radoter.

driver, *n,* conducteur, *m;* cocher; chauffeur; (*Rly*) mécanicien, *m;* (*Golf*) grand-crosse, *f.* ~*'s licence,* permis de conduire [les automobiles] *m.* **driving,** *n,* conduite; commande, transmission, *f;* serrage; percement; (*nails, piles*) enfoncement; (*piles*) battage, *m.* ~ *iron* (*Golf*), grand-fer, *m.* ~ *mirror,* miroir rétroviseur, *m.* ~ *rain,* pluie battante, *f.* ~ *shaft,* arbre moteur, arbre de couche, *m.*

drizzle, *n,* bruine, *f.* ¶ *v.imp,* bruiner.

droll, *a,* drôle, cocasse, plaisant. ~**ery,** *n,* drôlerie, *f.* **drolly,** *ad,* drôlement.

dromedary, *n,* dromadaire, *m.*

drone, *n,* ronron; (*Mus.*) bourdon, *m.* ~ [*bee*], [faux] bourdon, *m.* ¶ *v.i,* ronronner, bourdonner; (*v.t.*) psalmodier.

droop, *v.i,* pendre, traîner; (*wilt*) s'étioler. ~**ing,** *p.a,* pendant, tombant. ~ *looks,* airs penchés, *m.pl.* ~ *spirits,* forces défaillantes, *f.pl.*

drop, *n,* goutte; larme; chute; baisse; pastille, *f;* pendant, *m;* pendeloque, *f.* ~ *bottle,* flacon compte-gouttes, *m.* ~ *curtain,* rideau, *m.* ~-*forged,* estampé. ~ *kick* (*Rugby*), coup [de pied] tombé, *m.* ~ *letter* (*Typ.*), lettrine, *f.* ¶ *v.t,* laisser tomber goutte à goutte; laisser tomber, lâcher; lancer; (*pers. at door*) descendre; (*letter in post*) jeter; (*a line*) envoyer; (*a stitch*) sauter; (*her young*) mettre bas; (*v.i.*) tomber. **dropped stitch** (*Knit.*), manque, *m,* maille échappée, m. perdue, *f.* **dropper,** *n,* or **dropping tube,** compte-gouttes, *m.* **droppings** (*dung*) n.pl, fiente, crotte, *f.*

dropsical, *a,* hydropique. **dropsy,** *n,* hydropisie, *f.*

dross, *n,* écume, crasse, scorie, chiasse, *f.*

drought, [not *n,* sécheresse; disette d'eau, *f.*

drove, *n,* troupeau, *m.* **drover,** *n,* conducteur [de bestiaux], toucheur, *m.*

drown, *v.t,* noyer; (*sounds*) couvrir; (*v.i.*) boire. ~ *oneself,* se noyer. *the [apparently]* ~*ed,* les noyés. ~**ing,** *n,* submersion; (*fatality*) noyade, *f.* *a* ~ *man,* un noyé.

drowsiness, *n,* assoupissement, *m.* **drowsy,** *a,* endormi, ensommeillé. *to make* ~, assoupir.

drub, *v.t,* [b]rosser, frotter, étriller. **drubbing,** *n,* [b]rossée, frottée, peignée, volée de coups, *f.*

drudge, *n,* souffre-douleur, cheval de bât, pâtiras, *m.* ¶ *v.i,* trimer. ~**ry,** *n,* besognes fastidieuses, *f.pl,* corvée, *f,* collier de misère, *m.*

drug, *n,* drogue, *f;* stupéfiant, narcotique, *m.* ~ *traffic,* trafic des stupéfiants, *m.* ~ *store,* droguerie, *f.* ¶ *v.t,* narcotiser.

drugget, *n,* droguet, *m.*

druggist, *n,* pharmacien; (*wholesale*) droguiste, *m.*

Druid, *n,* druide, *m.*

drum, *n,* tambour, *m,* caisse, *f;* (*ear*) tympan; cylindre, barillet; tonneau, fût, *m.* ~*s & bugles* (*Mil. band*), clique, *f.* ~-*head,* peau de tambour, *f.* ~-*head court martial,* cour martiale, *f.* ~ *major,* tambour-major, *m.* ~-*stick,* baguette de tambour, *f;* (*fowl*) pilon, *m.* ¶ *v.i,* tambouriner. ~ *into,* seriner à. **drummer,** *n,* tambour, *m.*

drunk, *a,* ivre, soûl. *to get* ~, s'enivrer. ~**ard,** *n,* ivrogne, *m.* ~**en,** *a,* ivrogne. ~ *bout,* débauche de boisson, ribote, *f.* ~ *brawl,* querelle d'ivrognes, *f.* ~**enness,** *n,* ébriété, ivresse; (*habitual*) ivrognerie, *f.*

dry, *a,* sec; à sec; desséché; tari. ~-*clean,* nettoyer à sec. ~ *dock,* cale sèche, *f,* bassin [à] sec, *m,* forme de radoub, *f.* ~ *fly fishing,* pêche à la mouche sèche, *f.* ~ *fodder & ~ land* (opp. sea) & ~ *place,* sec, *m.* ~ *goods,* marchandises sèches, *f.pl. man of* ~ *humour,* pince-sans-rire, *m.* ~ *measure,* mesure de capacité pour les matières sèches, *f.* ~ *nurse,* nourrice sèche, *f.* ~ *rot,* carie sèche, *f.* ~*salter,* droguiste, *m.* ~*saltery,* droguerie-épicerie] *f.* ~ *shampoo,* friction, *f.* ~-*shod,* *a.* & *ad,* à pied sec. ~ *wall,* mur en pierre sèche, *f.* ¶ *v.t.* & *i,* sécher; assécher. ~ *up,* tarir, dessécher.

dryad, *n,* dryade, *f.*

dryer[s] (*for paint*) n.[pl.], siccatif, *m.* **drying,** *n,* séchage; assèchement, *m.* ~ *room,* séchoir, *m.* ~ *stove,* étuve, *f.* ~ *yard,* étendoir, *m.* **dryly,** *ad.* Same as *drily.* **dryness,** *n,* sécheresse, aridité, *f.*

dual, *a,* double.

dub, *v.t,* (*knight*) armer; (*nickname*) baptiser.

dubbin[g], *n,* dégras, *m.*

dubious[not, *a,* douteux, incertain; équivoque; interlope.

ducal, *a,* ducal. **duchess,** *n,* duchesse, *f.* **duchy,** *n,* duché, *m.*

duck, *n,* canard, *m,* cane, *f,* barboteur; (*dip*) plongeon; (*cloth*) coutil, *m.* ~ & *drake* (game), ricochets, *m.pl.* ~ *decoy* & ~ *pond,* canardière, *f.* ~*'s egg,* œuf de cane, *m.* ~*weed,* lentille d'eau, l. de marais, *f.* ¶ *v.t,* plonger; (*v.i.*) faire le plongeon, éviter de la tête, faire une courbette. ~**ling,** *n,* caneton, *m,* canette, *f.* ~[**y**] (*pers.*) *n,* poulet, te, chou[chou] *m.*

duct, *n,* canal, conduit, *m,* voie, *f.*

ductile, *a,* (*metals*) ductile; (*pers.*) docile, souple.

dudgeon (in), en haine.

due, *a,* dû; échu; régulier; requis, voulu, utile. *the train is* ~ *at . . .,* le train arrive (*ou* doit arriver) à . . . *in* ~ *course,*

en temps & lieu. ~ *date*, échéance, f.
¶ *ad*, droit; directement. ¶ *n*, dû, *m*;
(*duty*) droit, *m*; taxe, f.

duel, *n*, duel, *m*, rencontre, f. **duellist**, *n*,
duelliste, *m*.

duenna, *n*, duègne, f.

duet[t], *n*, duo, *m*.

duffer, *n*, cancre, *m*, ganache, f. imbécile, *m,f*;
(*at a game*) mazette, f.

dug, *n*, trayon, pis, *m*, tétine, f.

dug-out, *n*, abri [de bombardement] *m*.

duke, *n*, duc, *m*. ~**dom**, *n*, duché, *m*.

dulcet, *a*, doux.

dulcimer, *n*, tympanon, *m*.

dull, *a*, lourd; obtus; assoupissant, assommant, fastidieux; fade; maussade; inactif;
atone; plat; terne; mat; sombre; gris;
sourd; émoussé. ¶ *v.t*, ternir; émousser;
hébéter. ~**ard**, *n*, lourdaud, e. **dul[l]-
ness**, *n*, pesanteur, f, appesantissement;
ennui, *m*; inactivité, atonie, platitude;
ternissure; matité, f.

duly, *ad*, dûment; régulièrement; bien. ~
authorized representative, fondé de pou-
voir(s) *m*.

dumb†, *a*, muet. ~ *animals*, animaux privés
de raison, *m.pl*, bêtes, f.pl. ~**bell**, haltère,
m. ~ *show*, jeu muet, *m*, pantomime, f.

dumbfound, *v.t*, ébahir, atterrer.

dumbness, *n*, mutisme, *m*.

dummy, *a*, feint; faux. ~ *book* (for bookshelf), livre feint, *m*. ¶ *n*, prête-nom;
mannequin, *m*; poupée; fausse boîte;
(*publisher's blank book*) maquette, f; (*Mil.*)
simulacre; (*Cards*) mort, *m*. ~ *whist*,
whist à trois avec un mort, *m*.

dump, *n*, chantier de dépôt, *m*. *to be in the
~s*, avoir le spleen. ¶ *v.t*, culbuter,
chavirer. ~**ing** (*Economy*) *n*, dumping,
m. ~**y**, *a*, trapu, boulot, courtaud.

dun, *a*, fauve gris. ¶ *n*, fauve gris; créancier
importun; agent de recouvrements, *m*.
¶ *v.t*, importuner, pourchasser, assiéger,
persécuter.

dunce, *n*, ignorant, e, cancre, âne, *m*.

dunderhead, *n*, imbécile, *m*.

dune, *n*, dune, f.

dung, *n*, fiente, f; crottin, *m*; bouse; crotte, f.
~ *beetle*, escarbot, *m*. ~**hill**, fumier, *m*;
(*fig.*) pailler, *m*. ¶ *v.t*, fumer.

dungeon, *n*, cachot, *m*.

Dunkirk, *n*, Dunkerque, *m*.

dunnage, *n*, fardage, grenier, chantier [d'ar-
rimage] *m*.

duodecimal, *a*, duodécimal. **duodecimo**,
a. & n, in-douze, in-12, *a.m. & m*.

dupe, *n*, dupe, f. ¶ *v.t*, duper, blouser,
piper. ~**ry**, *n*, duperie, f.

duplicate, *a*, double; (*tools*, *parts*) de rechange. ¶ *n*, double, duplicata, *m*, ampliation; pièce de rechange; répétition, f.
¶ *v.t*, faire le double de; (*train*) dédoubler.
duplication, *n*, double emploi, *m*. **duplicity**, *n*, duplicité, f.

durable, *a*, durable. **duration**, *n*, durée, f.

duress[e], *n*, violence, f.

during, *pr*, pendant, durant, par, dans.

dusk, *n*, la brune. *at ~*, sur (*ou* à) la brune,
entre chien & loup. ~**y**, *a*, brun.

dust, *n*, poussière, f; poussier, *m*; poudre,
f; cendres; ordures, f.pl. ~**bin**, seau
à ordures, *m*. ~ *coat*, cache-poussière, *m*. ~ *cover*, couvre-livre, *m*. ~**man**,
boueux, *m*. ~ *pan*, pelle à poussière, f.
~ *sheet*, housse, f. ¶ *v.t*, épousseter;
housser; (*sprinkle*) saupoudrer. ~**er**,
n, torchon, *m*. ~**y**, *a*, poussiéreux,
poudreux.

Dutch, *a*, hollandais, de Hollande, néerlandais. ~ *auction*, enchère au rabais, f.
~ *cheese*, fromage de Hollande, *m*. ~
courage, courage arrosé, *m*. ~ *East Indies*,
Indes orientales néerlandaises, f.pl. ~**man**,
-*woman*, Hollandais, e, Néerlandais, e.
~ *oven*, rôtissoire, cuisinière, f. ¶ (*language*) *n*, le hollandais.

dutiable, *a*, passible de droits, sujet à des
droits, imposable. **dutiful† & duteous†**,
a, obéissant, soumis, respectueux. **duty**,
n, devoir, *m*; charge, fonction, f, office;
service; droit, *m*, taxe, f, impôt, *m*,
surtaxe, f. *on ~*, de service, de garde.
~*free*, *a*, franc de tout droit; (*ad.*) en
franchise [de droits]. ~*-paid*, *a*, acquitté;
(*ad.*) à l'acquitté.

dwarf, *n. & a*, nain, e. ¶ *v.t*, rapetisser.

dwell, *v.i.ir*, habiter, demeurer; insister,
peser. ~**er**, *n*, habitant, e. ~**ing**, *n*,
habitation, demeure, f, logis, *m*. ~
house, maison d'habitation, f.

dwindle, *v.i*, dépérir. **dwindling**, *n*, dépérissement, *m*.

dye, *n*, teinture, f. ~ *stuffs*, matières tinc-
toriales, f.pl. ~ *works*, teinturerie, f. *of
the deepest ~* (*fig.*), de la plus belle eau,
fieffé. ¶ *v.t*, teindre. ~**ing**, *n*, teinture;
teinturerie, f. **dyer** [& *cleaner*] *n*, teinturier, ère.

dying, *a*, mourant; à l'agonie, agonisant;
moribond. *the ~*, les mourants, *m.pl*.
to be ~, [se] mourir. ~ *words*, dernières
paroles, f.pl.

dyke, *n. & v.t*. Same as *dike*.

dynamic(al), *a*, dynamique. **dynamics**, *n*,
dynamique, f.

dynamite, *n*, dynamite, f.

dynamo, *n*, dynamo, f. ~*-electric(al)*,
dynamo-électrique.

dynasty, *n*, dynastie, f.

dysentery, *n*, dysenterie, f.

dyspepsia, *n*, dyspepsie, f.

E

E (*Mus.*) *letter*, mi, *m*.

each, *a. & pn*, chaque; chacun, e; l'un, l'une,
[la] pièce. ~ *one*, chacun, e. ~ *other*,

l'un (l'une) l'autre, les uns (les unes) les
autres; se, nous, vous.

eager, *a,* ardent, assoiffé, acharné, avide,
empressé. *to be ~ for,* ambitionner.
~ly, *ad,* ardemment, avidement. **~ness,**
n, ardeur, avidité, *f,* empressement, *m.*

eagle, *n, (bird)* aigle, *m,f; (standard)* aigle, *f.*
eaglet, *n,* aiglon, ne.

ear, *n,* oreille, *f; (corn)* épi, *m.* **~ache,**
douleur d'oreille, otalgie, *f.* ~ drum,
membrane du tympan, *f,* tympan, *m.* ~
flap, oreillon, *m.* **~mark,** affecter. **~-
phones,** casque, *m.* **~piece** *(Teleph.),*
écouteur, pavillon, *m.* **~ring,** boucle
[d'oreille] *f.* ~ trumpet, cornet acoustique, *m.*

earliness, *n,* heure peu avancée; précocité, *f.*
early, *a,* peu avancé; prématuré; avancé;
précoce; hâtif; premier; *(youth)* tendre;
ancien. ~ *fruits,* ~ *vegetables,* primeurs,
f,pl. ~ *morning tea,* thé pris au réveil, *m,*
le petit déjeuner. *to be* [up] ~, *to be an*
~ *riser,* être matinal, être matineux.
¶ *ad,* de bonne heure, tôt, matin.

earn, *v.t,* gagner, acquérir; mériter.

earnest, *a,* sérieux; ardent, fervent. ¶ *n,*
gage; *(fig.)* avant-goût, *m.* ~ [*money*],
arrhes, *f,pl,* denier à Dieu, *m.* **~ly,** *ad,*
sérieusement; ardemment; instamment.
~ness, *n,* ardeur, ferveur, instance, *f.*

earning, *n,* acquisition, *f; (pl.)* gain[s] *m,[pl.].*

earth, *n,* terre, *f;* sol; *(of fox)* terrier, *m,*
tanière, *f.* ~ *plate,* prise de terre, *f.*
~quake, tremblement de t., *m.* **~work,**
terrassement, *m.* ¶ *v.t, (Hort.)* butter,
chausser, terrer; *(Elec.)* mettre à la terre;
m. à la masse. **~en,** *a,* de terre. **~en-
ware,** *n,* poterie [de terre], faïence, *f.*
~ly, *a,* terrestre. **~y,** *a,* terreux.

earwig, *n,* perce-oreille, *m.*

ease, *n,* aise, aisance; facilité, *f;* repos;
soulagement, *m.* ¶ *v.t,* adoucir; soulager;
décharger; *(v.i.)* mollir.

easel, *n,* chevalet, *m.*

easement, *n,* servitude, *f.*

easily, *ad,* aisément, facilement; doucement;
not ~, malaisément.

east, *n,* est; *(le)* levant; orient, *m. from ~
to west,* du levant au couchant. *the E~*
(Geog.), l'Orient. ¶ *a,* d'est, de l'est;
oriental. *E~ Africa,* l'Afrique orientale,
f. E~ Indies, Indes orientales, *f,pl.*

Easter, *n,* Pâques, *m.s.* ~ *egg,* œuf de P., *m.*

easterly, *a,* d'est. **eastern,** *a,* de l'est;
oriental; *(question, &c)* d'Orient.

easy, *a,* facile, aisé; doux; commode; coulant;
tranquille; désinvolte. ~ *chair,* fauteuil,
m, bergère, *f,* crapaud, *m.* **~-going person,**
personne commode, *f,* sans-souci, *m. by
~ stages,* à petites journées. ~ *to get on
with (pers.),* d'un commerce agréable.
not ~, malaisé.

eat, *v.t. & i. ir,* manger. ~ *away,* ~ *into,*
ronger. ~ *up,* dévorer. **~able,** *a,* man-

geable. **~ables,** *n,pl,* comestibles, *m,pl.*
~er, *n,* mangeur, euse. **~ing:** ~ *apples,*
pommes à couteau, *f,pl.* ~ *house,* gargote, *f,* restaurant, *m.*

eaves, *n,pl,* avant-toit, *m.* **eavesdrop,** *v.i,*
écouter aux portes. **eavesdropper,** *n,*
écouteur (euse) aux portes.

ebb, *n,* jusant, reflux, *m.* ~ *tide,* courant de
jusant, *m.* ¶ *v.i,* refluer, refouler.

ebonite, *n,* ébonite, vulcanite, *f.*

ebony, *n,* ébène, *f; (tree)* ébénier, *m.*

ebullition, *n,* ébullition, *f.*

eccentric, *a. & (Mech.) n,* excentrique, *a. & m.*
~ity, *n,* excentricité, *f.*

Ecclesiastes, *n,* l'Ecclésiaste, *m.* **ecclesiastic,**
n. & ~al†, a, ecclésiastique, *m. & a.*
Ecclesiasticus, *n,* l'Ecclésiastique, *m.*

echo, *n,* écho, *m.* ¶ *v.i,* faire écho, retentir;
(v.t.) se faire l'écho de.

eclectic, *a,* éclectique, *n.* **eclecticism,** *n,* éclectisme, *m.*

eclipse, *n,* éclipse; défaillance, *f.* ¶ *v.t,*
éclipser. *to become ~d,* s'éclipser. **ecliptic,** *a. & n,* écliptique, *a. & f.*

economic, *a,* économique. **~(al)†,** *a,* économique; économe, ménager. **~s,** *n,pl,*
science économique; situation é., *f.* **economist,** *n,* économiste, *m.* **economize,** *v.t. & i,*
économiser; ménager. **economy,** *n,* économie, *f.*

ecstasy, *n,* extase, *f. to go into ecstasies,*
s'extasier. **ecstatic,** *a,* extatique.

Ecuador, *n,* l'Équateur, *m.*

eczema, *n,* eczéma, *m.*

eddy, *n,* remous, tournant, *m.* ¶ *v.i,* tourbillonner.

edelweiss, *n,* édelweiss, *m.*

Eden *(fig.) n,* éden, *m. [the Garden of]* ~,
l'Éden, le paradis [terrestre].

edge, *n,* bord, rebord, *m,* bordure; lisière;
arête; *f;* chant, champ, *m;* tranche, *f;*
tranchant, coupant, taillant, fil, *m,* taille,
f. ~ *tools,* outils tranchants *(ou* cou-
pants) *m,pl.* taillanderie, *f.* **~ways,**
~wise, *ad. ou* **on** ~, de chant. ¶ *v.t,*
border. **edging,** *n,* bordure, *f,* bord, *m.*
~ *knife,* hache coupe-gazon, *f.*

edible, *a,* comestible. ~ *bird's nest,* nid
d'hirondelle, *m.*

edict, *n,* édit, *m.*

edifice, *n,* édifice, *m.* **edify,** *v.t,* édifier.

Edinburgh, *n,* Édimbourg, *m.*

edit, *v.t,* éditer, rédiger. **~ion,** *n,* édition, *f.*
~ *binding,* reliure de bibliothèque, *f.*
editor, **tress,** *n,* éditeur, trice; rédacteur
(trice) en chef. **editorial,** *a,* de la rédaction; *(n.)* article, *m, (ou* note, *f.)* [émanant]
de la rédaction. ~ *staff,* rédaction, *f.*

educate, *v.t,* élever, instruire, éduquer. **education,** *n,* éducation, *f;* enseignement, *m;*
instruction, *f.* **~al,** *a,* d'éducation; scolaire; *(book)* classique. ~ *establishment,*
maison d'éducation, *f.* **educator,** *n,* éducateur, trice.

educe, *v.t*, tirer; dégager.

eel, *n*, anguille, *f*. ~ *pot*, nasse, *f*.

eerie, -y, *a*, fantastique.

efface, *v.t*, effacer. ~**able**, *a*, effaçable.

effect, *n*, effet, *m*; suite; action, *f*; (*pl.*) effets, *m.pl*. ¶ *v.t*, effectuer, faire, opérer; contracter. ~**ive†**, *a*, effectif; utile. ¶ *n*, effectif, *m*.

effectual†, *a*, efficace.

effeminacy, *n*, caractère efféminé, *m*. **effeminate**, *a*, efféminé. *to* [*make*] ~, efféminer. ~ [**man**], *n*, efféminé, *m*, femmelette, *f*.

effervesce, *v.i*, être en effervescence; faire e.; mousser. **effervescence, -ency**, *n*, effervescence, *f*. **effervescent**, *a*, effervescent. **effervescing** (*drink*) *p.a*, gazeux.

effete, *a*, épuisé.

efficacious†, *a*, efficace.

efficiency, *n*, efficacité, *f*; rendement, *m*. **efficient†**, *a*, efficace; capable.

effigy, *n*, effigie, *f*.

effloresce, *v.i*, [s']effleurir. **efflorescence**, *n*, efflorescence, *f*.

effluence, *n*, émanation, *f*.

effluvium, *n*, effluve, *m*.

efflux, *n*, dépense; émanation, *f*.

effort, *n*, effort, *m*.

effrontery, *n*, effronterie, *f*.

effulgence, *n*, rayonnement, *m*.

effusion, *n*, effusion, *f*; épanchement, *m*. **effusive**, *a*, expansif. ~**ness**, *n*, effusion, *f*.

eft, *n*, triton, *m*, salamandre aquatique, *f*.

egg, *n*, œuf, *m*; (*pl.*, silkworm) graine, *f*. ~ *cup* ~ *merchant*, coquetier, *m*. ~ *shell*, coquille d'œuf, *f*. ~ **on**, *v.t*, pousser.

eglantine, *n*, églantine odorante, *f*.

ego, *n*, moi, *m*. **egoism**, *n*, égoïsme, *m*. **egoist**, *n*, égoïste, *m,f*. **egoistic(al)**, *a*, égoïste. **egotism**, *n*, égotisme, *m*. **egotist**, *n*, égotiste, *m,f*. **egotistic(al)**, *a*, égotiste.

egregious, *a*, grossier; lourd; fieffé.

egress, *n*, sortie, issue, *f*.

egret (*bird & tuft*) *n*, aigrette, *f*.

Egypt, *n*, l'Égypte, *f*. **Egyptian**, *a*, égyptien. ¶ *n*, Égyptien, *m*. **Egyptologist**, *n*, égyptologue, *m*. **Egyptology**, *n*, égyptologie, *f*.

eh, *i*, eh!, hein!

eider [**duck**], *n*, eider, *m*. ~ *down*, édredon, *m*.

eight, *a. & n*, huit, *a. & m*. **eighteen**, *a. & n*, dix-huit, *a. & m*. *18-hole course*, parcours (*ou* golf) de 18 trous, *m*. ~*mo or 18mo*, *a. & n*, in-dix-huit, in-18, *a.m. & m*. **eighteenth**, *a. & n*, dix-huitième, *a. & m,f*; dix-huit, *m*. **eighth**, *a. & n*, huitième, *a. & m,f*; huit, *m*. ~**ly**, *ad*, huitièmement. **eightieth**, *a. & n*, quatre-vingtième, *a. & m,f*. **eighty**, *a. & n*, quatre-vingts, quatre-vingt, *a. & m*. *81*, *a& n*, quatre-vingt-un, *m*.

either, *pn. & a*, l'un (l'une) ou l'autre; l'un d'eux, l'une d'elles; un, une; chaque. ¶ *c*, ou; soit. ¶ *ad*, non plus. *nor I* ~, ni moi n. p.

ejaculate, *v.t. & abs*, lancer, faire; (*fluid*)

éjaculer. **ejaculation**, *n*, interjection, exclamation; (*fluid*) éjaculation, *f*.

eject, *v.t*, expulser. ~**ion**, *n*, expulsion, *f*.

eke out, *v.t*, allonger; suppléer.

elaborate, *a*, travaillé; étudié; recherché. ¶ *v.t*, élaborer; travailler.

elapse, *v.i.s*, s'écouler, [se] passer.

elastic, *a*, élastique. ¶ *n*, élastique, caoutchouc, *m*. ~ *band*, bande en caoutchouc, *f*. ~**ity**, *n*, élasticité, *f*, ressort, *m*.

elate, *v.t*, enivrer; enorgueillir.

Elba (*the Island of*), l'île d'Elbe, *f*.

Elbe (*the*) (*river*), l'Elbe, *m*.

elbow, *n*, coude, *m*. *to rest on one's* ~(*s*), s'accouder. ~ *grease* (*fig.*), huile de coude, *f*. ~ *room*, coudées franches, *f.pl*. ¶ *v.t*, coudoyer. *to* ~ *one's way*, jouer des coudes.

elder, *a*, aîné, plus âgé. ¶ *n*, aîné, e; (*Eccl.*) ancien; (*Bot.*) sureau, *m*. *our* ~*s*, nos aînés. ~ *berry*, baie de sureau, *f*. ~**ly**, *a*, d'un certain âge. **eldest**, *n. & a*, aîné, e.

El Dorado, *n*, eldorado, *m*.

elect, *v.t*, élire, nommer. *the* ~ (*Relig.*), les élus, *m.pl*. ~*ed member*, élu, e. **election**, *n*, élection, *f*. ~ *agent*, agent d'élection, courtier électoral, *m*. **electioneering**, *n*, manœuvres électorales, *f.pl*. **elector**, *n*, électeur, trice. ~**ate**, *n*, corps électoral, *m*.

electric, *a*, électrique ~ *bowl fire*, radiateur électrique parabolique, *m*. ~ *eel*, gymnote, *m*. ~ *sign*, enseigne (*ou* affiche) lumineuse, *f*. ~ *torch*, lampe électrique, l. de poche, *f*. ~**al**, *a*, électrique. ~ *engineer*, ingénieur électricien, *m*. ~ *fitter*, monteur électricien, *m*. ~**ally**, *ad*, par l'électricité. ~**ian**, *n*, électricien, *m*. ~**ity**, *n*, électricité, *f*. **electrify**, *v.t*, électriser; (*Rly, &c*) électrifier. **electrize**, *v.t*, électriser. **electrocute**, *v.t*, électrocuter. **electrode**, *n*, électrode, *f*. **electrolier**, *n*, lustre électrique, *m*. **electrolysis**, *n*, électrolyse, *f*. **electromagnet**, *n*, électro-aimant, *m*. **electron**, *n*, électron, *m*. **electroplate†**, *n*, vaisselle plaquée, *f*, plaqué, *m*. ¶ *v.t*, argenter. **electrotype**, *n*, électrotype, *m*.

elegance, *n*, élégance, *f*. **elegant**, *a*, élégant. ~**ly**, *ad*, élégamment.

elegy, *n*, élégie, *f*.

element, *n*, élément; facteur; (*Chem.*) corps simple; (*voltaic*) couple, *m*. ~**ary**, *a*, élémentaire; (*Sch.*) primaire. *Elementary Physics, &c* (*book*), Notions de Physique, &c, *f.pl*.

elephant, *n*, éléphant, *m*. ~[*ine person*], mastodonte, *m*.

elevate, *v.t*, élever; [re]monter. **elevation**, *n*, élévation; altitude, hauteur, *f*. **elevator**, *n*, élévateur, *m*; monte-charge, ascenseur; (*Surg.*) élévatoire, *m*; (*in shoe*) hausse, *f*.

eleven, *a. & n*, onze, *a. & m*. **eleventh†**, *a. & n*, onzième, *a. & m,f*; onze, *m*.

elf, *n*, elfe, lutin, *m*. **elfin**, *a*, des elfes. **elfish**, *a*, des elfes; lutin, espiègle.

elicit, *v.t*, tirer, soutirer.

elide, *v.t*, élider.

eligible, *a*, éligible; sortable.

eliminate, *v.t*, éliminer. *eliminating heat*, [épreuve] éliminatoire, *f*, critère, criterium, *m*.

elision, *n*, élision, *f*.

elixir, *n*, élixir, *m*.

elk, *n*, élan, *m*.

ellipse & ellipsis, *n*, ellipse, *f*. **elliptic(al)**†, *a*, elliptique.

elm [tree], *n*, orme, ormeau, *m*. ~ *grove*, ormaie, ormoie, *f*. ~ *row*, ormille, *f*.

elocution, *n*, élocution; déclamation, *f*.

elongate, *v.t*, allonger.

elope, *v.i*, se faire enlever (*with* = par); s'enfuir. ~ment, *n*, enlèvement, *m*, fugue, *f*.

eloquence, *n*, éloquence, *f*. **eloquent**, *a*, éloquent. ~ly, *ad*, éloquemment.

else, *a*, autre; autrement, sinon, encore. ~where, *ad*, autre part, ailleurs.

Elsinore, *n*, Elseneur, *f*.

elucidate, *v.t*, élucider, dégager.

elude, *v.t*, éluder, se soustraire à, se dérober à. **elusive**†, *a*, insaisissable; flottant.

Elysian, *a*, élyséen, ne. **Elysium**, *n*, élysée, *f*; (*Myth.*) Élysée, *m*.

emaciated, *p.p*, émacié, décharné, étique, hâve.

emanate, *v.i*, émaner.

emancipate, *v.t*, émanciper, affranchir.

emasculate, *v.t*, émasculer.

embalm, *v.t*, embaumer.

embank, *v.t*, remblayer, terrasser, encaisser. ~ment, *n*, remblai, encaissement; quai, *m*; levée, *f*.

embargo, *n*, embargo, *m*.

embark, *v.t*, embarquer. ~ation, *n*, embarquement, *m*.

embarrass, *v.t*, embarrasser. ~ment, *n*, embarras, *m*.

embassy, *n*, ambassade, *f*.

embattle (*Arch.*) *v.t*, créneler.

embed, *v.t*, encastrer.

embellish, *v.t*, embellir.

ember days, Quatre-Temps, *m.pl*.

embers, *n.pl*, braise, *f*, charbon, *m*; cendre[s] *f*.[*pl*.].

embezzle, *v.t*, détourner. ~ment, *n*, détournement, *m*, malversation, *f*; péculat, *m*.

embitter, *v.t*, envenimer, enfieller, aigrir.

emblazon, *v.t*, blasonner.

emblem, *n*, emblème, *m*. ~atic(al), *a*, emblématique.

embodiment, *n*, incarnation, *f*. **embody**, *v.t*, incarner; englober.

embolden, *v.t*, enhardir.

embolism, *n*, embolie, *f*.

emboss, *v.t*, graver en relief; estamper,

gaufrer; bosseler. ~ed *stamp*, timbre sec, timbre fixe, *m*.

embrace, *v.t*, embrasser, *m*, embrassade, accolade, *f*. ¶ *v.t*, embrasser.

embrasure, *n*, embrasure, *f*.

embrocation, *n*, embrocation, *f*.

embroider, *v.t*, broder. ~er, ~ess, *n*, brodeur, euse. ~y, *n*, broderie, *f*. ~ *cotton*, coton à broder, *m*. ~ *hoops*, métier à broder, *m*.

embroil, *v.t*, [em]brouiller.

embryo, *n*, embryon, *m*. *in* ~ (*fig*.), en herbe. **embryonic**, *a*, embryonnaire.

emend, *v.t*, corriger. ~ation, *n*, correction, *f*.

emerald, *n*, émeraude, *f*.

emerge, *v.i*, émerger, déboucher. **emergence**, *n*, émergence, *f*.

emergency, *n*, urgence, *f*; événement [inattendu] *m*, occurrence, *f*. ~ *brake*, frein d'urgence, *m*. ~ *exit*, sortie de secours, *f*.

emeritus, *a*, émérite.

emery, *n*, émeri, *m*. ~ *cloth*, toile d'é., *f*.

emetic, *a*. & *n*, émétique, *a*. & *m*.

emigrant, *n*, émigrant, e. **emigrate**, *v.i*, émigrer. **emigration**, *n*, émigration, *f*. ~ *officer*, commissaire d'émigration, *m*.

eminence, *n*, éminence, *f*. *His E~* (cardinal), son Éminence, *f*. **eminent**, *a*, éminent; notable, considérable. ~ly, *ad*, éminemment.

emir, *n*, émir, *m*.

emissary, *n*, émissaire, *m*. **emission**, *n*, émission, *f*. **emit**, *v.t*, émettre; dégager.

emollient, *a*. & *n*, émollient, *a*. & *m*.

emoluments, *n.pl*, émoluments, *m.pl*.

emotion, *n*, émotion, *f*, émoi, *m*. ~al, *a*, facile à émouvoir.

empanel a jury, former une liste de jurés, former un tableau.

emperor, *n*, empereur, *m*.

emphasis, *n*, emphase; énergie, *f*. *to lay* ~ *upon* or **emphasize**, *v.t*, appuyer sur, souligner, accentuer, ponctuer. **emphatic**†, *a*, emphatique; énergique.

empire, *n*, empire, *m*.

empiric(al)†, *a*, empirique. **empiricism**, *n*, empirisme, *m*. **empiric[ist]**, *n*, empirique, *m*.

employ, *v.t*, employer; se servir de. *he is in my* ~, je l'emploie. ~ee, *n*, employé, e. ~er, *n*, patron, ne, employeur, euse. ~ment, *n*, emploi, travail, *m*. ~ *agency*, bureau de placement, *m*.

emporium, *n*, entrepôt, *m*.

empower, *v.t*, autoriser, investir du pouvoir.

empress, *n*, impératrice, *f*.

emptiness, *n*, vacuité, *f*; vide, *m*; nullité, *f*. **empty**, *a*, vide; à vide; à blanc; net; désert; creux; vain; en l'air. ~-*handed*, les mains vides. *to be* ~-*headed*, avoir la tête vide. *on an* ~ *stomach*, à jeun. ¶ (*case*, &c) *n*, vide, *m*. ¶ *v.t*, vider, vidanger, épuiser, décharger.

empyrean, *n*, empyrée, *m*.

emulate, *v.t*, rivaliser avec. **emulation**, *n*, émulation, rivalité, *f*. **emulator**, *n*, émule, *m*.

emulsion, *n*, émulsion, *f*.

enable, *v.t*, mettre à même; permettre; (*Law*) habiliter.

enact, *v.t*, décréter, édicter. ~**ment**, *n*, loi, *f*, décret, *m*.

enamel, *n*. & ~ **ware**, émail, *m*. ¶ *v.t*, émailler, laquer. *enamelled iron*, tôle émaillée, *f*. **enamelling**, *n*, émaillage, *m*.

enamoured, *p.p*, épris, amoureux.

encage, *v.t*, encager.

encamp, *v.i*. & *t*, camper. ~**ment**, *n*, campement, *m*.

encase, *v.t*, encaisser, enrober.

encash, *v.t*, encaisser.

encaustic, *a*. & *n*, encaustique, *a*. & *f*.

enchain, *v.t*, enchaîner.

enchant, *v.t*, enchanter. ~**er**, ~**ress**, *n*, enchanteur, eresse, *f*. ~**ing**, *p.a*, enchanteur. ~**ment**, *n*, enchantement, *m*.

encircle, *v.t*, encercler, ceindre, cerner.

enclave, *n*, enclave, *f*.

enclose, *v.t*, enfermer; [en]clore, enceindre; (*in letter*) inclure, joindre. ~**d**, *p.p*, ci-inclus, ci-joint. **enclosure**, *n*, enceinte, clôture, *f*, [en]clos, parc, *m*; (*in letter*) [pièce] annexe, pièce jointe, *f*. *public* ~**s** (*Turf*), pelouse, *f*.

encomium, *n*, panégyrique, éloge, *m*.

encompass, *v.t*, entourer, ceindre.

encore, *i*. & *n*, bis, *ad*. & *m*. ¶ *v.t*, bisser.

encounter, *n*, rencontre, *f*. ¶ *v.t*, rencontrer.

encourage, *v.t*, encourager.

encroach on (to), empiéter sur, envahir; anticiper sur. ~**ment**, *n*, empiètement, envahissement, *m*.

encumber, *v.t*, embarrasser, encombrer; grever, obérer. **encumbrance**, *n*, embarras, *m*; charge, *f*.

encyclic(al), *a*. & *n*, encyclique, *a*. & *f*.

encyclop[a]edia, *n*, encyclopédie, *f*.

end, *n*, fin, *f*, terme, *m*; extrémité; issue, *f*; bout; but, *m*. *no* ~ *of*, une infinité de. *on* ~, debout; (*hair*) hérissés, (*fig*.) d'arrache-pied. ~ *paper*, [feuille de] garde, *f*. ¶ *v.t*, finir, achever, terminer; (*v.i.*) finir, prendre fin; aboutir.

endanger, *v.t*, mettre en danger.

endear, *v.t*, rendre cher. ~**ment**, *n*, caresse, *f*.

endeavour, *n*, effort, *m*, tentative, *f*. ¶ *v.i*, s'efforcer, tâcher, travailler.

ending, *n*, fin, *f*; dénouement; *m*; (*Gram*.) terminaison, désinence, *f*.

endive, *n*, scarole, endive, *f*.

endless, *a*. & ~**ly**, *ad*, sans fin.

endorse, *v.t*, endosser; (*fig*.) souscrire à. ~ *back*, contrepasser. ~ *over*, passer. ~**ment**, *n*, (*bill, cheque*, &c) endos, endossement; (*Insce*) avenant, *m*. **endorser**, *n*, endosseur, *m*.

endow, *v.t*, renter, doter; douer, avantager. ~**ment**, *n*, dotation, *f*.

endue, *v.t*, revêtir; douer.

endurable, *a*, supportable. **endurance**, *n*, endurance; résistance, *f*. ~ *test*, épreuve d'endurance, *f*, raid, *m*. **endure**, *v.t*, endurer, supporter; (*v.i.*) vivre.

enema, *n*, lavage [d'intestin] *m*; seringue [à lavement] *f*.

enemy, *n*. & *a*, ennemi, e.

energetic†, *a*, énergique. ~**s** (*Phys*.) *n.pl*, énergétique, *f*. **energize**, *v.t*, infuser de l'ardeur dans; (*Elec*.) amorcer. **energy**, *n*, énergie; poigne, *f*; travail, *m*.

enervate, *v.t*, énerver, [r]amollir.

enfeeble, *v.t*, affaiblir.

enfilade, *n*, enfilade, *f*. ¶ *v.t*, enfiler.

enfold, *v.t*, envelopper; étreindre.

enforce, *v.t*, imposer; faire valoir; mettre en vigueur, exécuter. ~**able**, *a*, exécutoire.

enfranchise, *v.t*, affranchir; accorder le droit de vote à.

engage, *v.t*, engager, retenir; embaucher; arrêter; prendre; (*Mech*.) engrener; embrayer; (*v.i.*) s'engager, se mettre; engager le combat. ~**d**, *p.p*, occupé, pris, pas visible; fiancé. ~ *tone* (*Teleph*.), signal pas libre, *m*. ~**ment**, *n*, engagement, *m*; fiançailles, *f.pl*. ~ *ring*, bague de fiançailles, *f*. **engaging**, *p.a*, engageant, attrayant, attachant.

engender, *v.t*, engendrer.

engine, *n*, machine, *f*, moteur, *m*; (*Rly*) locomotive, *f*; (*of war*) engin, *m*. ~ *driver*, ~**man**, mécanicien, *m*. ~ *turning*, guillochis, *m*. **engineer**, *n*, ingénieur; (*maker*) ingénieur constructeur; (*ship*) mécanicien; (*Mil*.) officier du génie; soldat du génie, *m*. ¶ *v.t*, provoquer. **engineering**, *n*, l'art (*m*.) (*ou* la science) de l'ingénieur; construction; *f*; génie, *m*. **engineless**, *a*, sans moteur.

England, *n*, l'Angleterre, *f*. **English**, *a*, anglais. *the* ~ *Channel*, la Manche. ~**man**, ~**woman**, Anglais, e. ¶ (*language*) *n*, l'anglais, *m*.

engrave, *v.t*, graver; buriner. **engraver**, *n*, graveur, *m*. **engraving**, *n*, gravure, estampe, *f*.

engross, *v.t*, absorber; s'emparer de; (*Law*) grossoyer. ~**ment** (*Law*) *n*, grosse, *f*.

engulf, *v.t*, engouffrer, engloutir.

enhance, *v.t*, rehausser; augmenter.

enigma, *n*, énigme, *f*. **enigmatic(al)**†, *a*, énigmatique.

enjoin, *v.t*, enjoindre.

enjoy, *v.t*, jouir de, savourer, goûter. ~ *oneself*, s'amuser, se réjouir. ~**able**, *a*, agréable, savoureux. ~**ment**, *n*, jouissance, *f*; plaisir, *m*.

enlarge, *v.t*, agrandir, augmenter, élargir. ~ *upon*, s'étendre sur. ~**ment**, *n*, agrandissement, *m*. **enlarger** (*Phot*.) *n*, agrandisseur, amplificateur, *m*.

enlighten, *v.t*, éclairer, édifier. ~**ment**, *n*, lumières, *f.pl*.

enlist, *v.t*, enrôler, engager. ~**ment**, *n*, enrôlement, engagement, *m*.

enliven, *v.t*, [r]animer, vivifier, égayer.

enmity, *n*, inimitié, *f*.

ennoble, *v.t*, anoblir; (*fig.*) ennoblir.

enormity, *n*, énormité, *f*. **enormous**, *a*, énorme. ~**ly**, *ad*, énormément. ~**ness**, *n*, énormité, *f*.

enough, *a*, assez de; assez; suffisant. ¶ *ad*, assez; suffisamment. ¶ *n*, suffisance, *f*, assez, de quoi. *to have* ~ & *to spare*, avoir à revendre.

enquire, &c. Same as *inquire*, &c.

enrage, *v.t*, rendre furieux, faire enrager.

enrapture, *v.t*, enchanter, ravir, enthousiasmer.

enrich, *v.t*, enrichir.

enrol, **-ll**, *v.t*, enrôler, immatriculer, embrigader, enrégimenter. **enrolment**, *n*, enrôlement, *m*.

ensconce, *v.t*, camper, nicher.

enshrine, *v.t*, enchâsser.

enshroud, *v.t*, envelopper; voiler.

ensign, *n*, (*banner, flag*) enseigne, *f*; (*Naut.*) pavillon de poupe, *m*.

enslave, *v.t*, asservir, enchaîner.

ensnare, *v.t*, attraper.

ensue, *v.i*, s'ensuivre, résulter. **ensuing**, *p.a*, suivant, subséquent.

ensure, *v.t*, assurer.

entablature, *n*, entablement, *m*.

entail, *v.t*, entraîner; (*Law*) substituer.

entangle, *v.t*, empêtrer, emmêler, embarrasser.

enter, *v.t*, entrer dans; pénétrer; engager; inscrire, enregistrer, immatriculer; porter, passer; déclarer; cadastrer; intenter; (*v.i.*) entrer; pénétrer; s'engager. ~ *into* (bargain, contract), faire, passer, souscrire, contracter, intervenir dans. ~ *X.* (*Theat.*), X. entre [en scène].

enteric, *a*, entérique.

enterprise, *n*, entreprise, *f*; esprit entreprenant, *m*. **enterprising**, *a*, entreprenant.

entertain, *v.t*, recevoir, héberger; régaler, fêter; (*abs.*) traiter, représenter; amuser, divertir, défrayer; concevoir, nourrir; accueillir favorablement. ~**er**, *n*, diseur (euse) de chansonnettes. ~**ment**, *n*, hébergement, *m*; fête, *f*; amusement, divertissement; spectacle, *m*. ~ *tax*, taxe sur les spectacles, *f*.

enthral[l], *v.t*, captiver, enchaîner; passionner.

enthrone, *v.t*, introniser. ~**ment**, *n*, intronisation, *f*.

enthusiasm, *n*, enthousiasme, *m*. **enthusiast**, *n*, enthousiaste, *m,f*, fervent, e. ~**ic**, *a*, enthousiaste. ~**ically**, *ad*, avec enthousiasme.

entice, *v.t*, allécher; séduire. ~**ment**, *n*, allèchement, *m*, séduction, *f*. **enticing**, *p.a*, alléchant, acquinant, séduisant.

entire†, *a*, entier, intégral. ~**ty**, *n*, entier, *m*; intégralité, *f*.

entitle, *v.t*, intituler; donner droit à.

entity, *n*, entité, *f*.

entomb, *v.t*, ensevelir.

entomologist, *n*, entomologiste, *m*. **entomology**, *n*, entomologie, *f*.

entr'acte (*Theat.*) *n*, entracte, *m*.

entrails, *n.pl*, entrailles, *f.pl*.

entrain, *v.t*, embarquer.

entrance, *n*, entrée; porte, *f*. ~ [*fee*], cotisation d'admission, *f*; droit d'entrée, *m*.

entrance, *v.t*, jeter en extase; ravir.

entrap, *v.t*, attraper.

entreat, *v.t*, supplier, prier instamment. ~**y**, *n*, supplication, prière, *f*, (*pl.*) instances, *f.pl*.

entrench, *v.t*, retrancher. ~**ing tool**, pelle-bêche, *f*.

entrust, *v.t*, confier, charger, remettre.

entry, *n*, entrée, *f*; engagement, *m*; inscription, *f*, enregistrement, *m*; immatriculation; passation, *f*; article, *.m*; (*Cust.*) déclaration, *f*. ~ *in register of births, of marriages, of deaths*, acte de naissance, de mariage, de décès, *m*. ~ *only*[, *one way street*], sens unique.

entwine, *v.t*, enlacer, entortiller.

enumerate, *v.t*, énumérer.

enunciate, *v.t*, énoncer.

envelope, *n*, enveloppe, *f*, pli, *m*. ¶ *v.t*, envelopper.

envenom, *v.t*, envenimer.

enviable, *a*, enviable. **envious**, *a*, envieux.

environ, *v.t*, environner. ~**ment**, *n*, entourage, milieu, *m*, ambiance, *f*. **environs**, *n.pl*, environs, entours, *m.pl*.

envisage, *v.t*, envisager.

envoy, *n*, envoyé, *m*.

envy, *n*, envie, *f*. ¶ *v.t*, envier.

epaulet[te], *n*, épaulette, *f*.

epergne, *n*, surtout [de table] *m*, girandole, *f*.

ephemera, -ron, *n*, éphémère, *m*. **ephemeral**, *a*, éphémère.

epic, *a*, épique. ¶ *n*, épopée, *f*.

epicure, *n*, gourmet, *m*, friand, e. **epicurean**, *a. & n*, épicurien, *a. & m*.

epidemic, *n*, épidémie, *f*. ~(**al**), *a*, épidémique.

epidermis, *n*, épiderme, *m*.

epiglottis, *n*, épiglotte, *f*.

epigram, *n*, épigramme, *f*.

epigraph, *n*, (*prefixed to book or chapter*) épigraphe; (*on stone*) inscription, *f*.

epilepsy, *n*, épilepsie, *f*. **epileptic**, *a. & n*, épileptique, *a. & m,f*.

epilogue, *n*, épilogue, *m*.

Epiphany, *n*, Épiphanie, *f*.

episcopal, *a*, épiscopal. **episcopate** & **episcopacy**, *n*, épiscopat, *m*.

episode, *n*, épisode, *m*.

epistle, *n*, épître, *f*. **epistolary**, *a*, épistolaire.

epitaph, *n*, épitaphe, *f*.

epithet, *n*, épithète, *f*.

epitome, *n*, épitomé, abrégé, **raccourci**, *m*. **epitomize**, *v.t*, abréger.

epoch, *n*, époque, ère, *f*.

epopee & **epos**, *n*, épopée, *f*.

Epsom salt[s], sel d'Epsom, m.

equable†, a, égal. equal†, a, égal, pareil; pair. ~ to (task), à la hauteur de. ¶ n, égal, e, pareil, le, pair, m. ¶ v.t, égaler. ~ity, n, égalité, f, pair, m; (rights) concurrence, f, concours; (votes) partage, m. ~ize, v.t, égaliser, égaler.

equanimity, n, sérénité, f.

equation, n, équation, f.

equator, n, équateur, m. ~ial, a, equatorial. ~ [telescope], équatorial, m.

equerry, n, écuyer, m.

equestrian, a, équestre. ¶ n, cavalier, ère; écuyer, ère [de cirque].

equilibrate, v.t, équilibrer. equilibrium, n, équilibre, m.

equine, a, chevalin, hippique.

equinoctial, a, équinoxial. equinox, n, équinoxe, m.

equip, v.t, équiper, armer, outiller. ~age, n, équipage, m. ~ment, n, équipement, armement, outillage; fourniment, m.

equipoise, n, équilibre, m.

equitable†, a, équitable. equity, n, équité, f.

equivalent, a. & n, équivalent, a. & m; parité, f. to be ~, équivaloir.

equivocal, a, équivoque. equivocate, v.i, équivoquer. equivocation, n, équivoques, f.pl.

era, n, ère, époque, f.

eradicate, v.t, déraciner, extirper.

erase, v.t, raturer, gratter, effacer. eraser, n, (knife) grattoir, m; (rubber) gomme [à effacer] f. erasure, n, rature, f, grattage, m, effaçure, f.

ere, c, avant que. ~ long, sous peu.

Erebus, n, l'Érèbe, m.

erect, a, droit; debout; ad; dressé. ¶ v.t, ériger; construire; élever; monter; dresser; hérisser. ~ion, n, érection; construction; f; montage; dressage, m. erector (of machinery) n, monteur, m.

Erie (Lake), n, le lac Érié.

ermine, n, hermine; armeline, f, roselet, m.

erode, v.t, éroder. erosion, n, érosion, f.

erotic, a, érotique.

err, v.i, errer, pécher.

errand, n, commission, ambassade, course, f, message, m. ~ boy, garçon de course, saute-ruisseau, m. ~ girl, trottin, m.

errant, a, errant.

erratic, a, irrégulier; (Geol., Med., &c.) erratique.

erratum, n, erratum, m. erroneous, a, erroné, faux. ~ly, ad, par erreur. error, n, erreur, faute, f, mécompte; écart, m.

eructation, n, éructation, f, renvoi, m.

erudite, a, érudit. erudition, n, érudition, f.

eruption, n, éruption, f.

erysipelas, n, érésipèle, érysipèle, m.

escalator, n, escalier roulant, m.

escallop, n, pétoncle, m.

escapade, n, escapade; équipée; frasque, f.

escape, n, fuite; évasion, f; échappement, m; issue, f. ¶ v.i, s'échapper; échapper; fuir;

s'enfuir; se sauver; s'évader; se débonder; (v.t.) échapper à; échapper de; échapper. escaped prisoner, échappé(e) de prison. ~ment, n, échappement, m.

escarpment, n, escarpement, m.

escheat, n, déshérence, f. ¶ v.i, tomber en déshérence; (v.t.) confisquer.

eschew, v.t, éviter, fuir.

escort, n, escorte, f; cavalier, m. ¶ v.t, escorter, reconduire, accompagner.

escutcheon, n, écusson, m.

espagnolette, n, espagnolette, crémone, f.

espalier, n, espalier, m.

esparto [grass], n, sparte, alfa, m.

especial, a, notable, digne d'être signalé, qui mérite une mention particulière; particulier; tout spécial. ~ly, ad, surtout; notamment; particulièrement. ~ as, d'autant que.

espionage, n, espionnage, m.

esplanade, n, esplanade, f.

espousal, n, adoption, adhésion, f. espouse, v.t, épouser; embrasser.

espy, v.t, apercevoir, aviser, découvrir.

esquire (Hist.) n, écuyer, m. Esquire, n. (abb. Esq.), Monsieur, m. (Note.—As a form of address on envelope or in letter, Monsieur should not be abbreviated.)

essay, n, essai, m, composition, dissertation, narration, f. ¶ v.t, essayer. ~ist, n, essayiste, m,f.

essence, n, essence, f. essential†, a, essentiel; capital. ~ oil, huile essentielle, essence, f. ¶ n, essentiel, m.

establish, v.t, établir; créer; asseoir; constater. the ~ed Church, l'Église d'État, f. ~ment, n, établissement, m; création; fondation; constatation, f; ménage, m. ~ charges, frais généraux, m.pl; (printer's) étoffes, f.pl.

estate, n, bien[s] m.[pl.], propriété[s] f.[pl.]; domaine, fonds, m, terre; succession, f. ~agency, agence immobilière, f. ~ agent, (private) régisseur; (public) agent de location, m. ~ duty, droits de succession, m.pl.

esteem, n, estime, f. ¶ v.t, estimer; considérer (ou regarder) comme.

Esthonia, n, l'Estonie, f.

estimate, n, estimation, appréciation, évaluation, prisée, f; état (ou devis) estimatif; (pl.) budget, m. ¶ v.t, estimer, apprécier, évaluer, priser. ~d, p.a, estimatif. estimation, n, jugement, m, estime, f.

estop (Law) v.t, exclure.

estrange, v.t, éloigner, aliéner.

estuary, n, estuaire, m.

et cetera, phrase & n. (abb. etc., &c.), et cætera, etc., phrase & m.

etch, v.t, graver à l'eau-forte. ~er, n, graveur à l'eau-forte, aquafortiste, m. ~ing, n, [gravure à l']eau-forte, f.

eternal†, a, éternel. the ~ triangle, la vie à trois. etern[al]ize, v.t, éterniser. eternity, n, éternité, f.

ether, n, éther, m. ethereal, a, éthéré.

ethical, a, éthique. ethics, n.pl, éthique, f.

Ethiopia, n, l'Éthiopie, f. Ethiopian, a, éthiopien. ¶ n, Éthiopien, ne.

ethnography, n, ethnographie, f. ethnologic(al), a, ethnologique. ethnologist, n, ethnologue, m. ethnology, n, ethnologie, f.

ethyl, n, éthyle, m.

etiolate, v.t, étioler.

etiquette, n, étiquette, f, décorum, protocole, m.

Eton crop, coiffure en garçon, c. à la garçonne, f.

etymologic(al), a, étymologique. etymology, n, étymologie, f.

eucalyptus, n, eucalyptus, m.

Eucharist, n, Eucharistie, f.

eugenic, a, eugénique. ~s, n.pl, eugénie, f.

eulogist†, a, élogieux. eulogize, v.t, faire l'éloge de. eulogy, n, éloge, m.

eunuch, n, eunuque, m.

euphemism, n, euphémisme, m. euphemistic, a, euphémique.

euphonic & euphonious, a, euphonique. euphony, n, euphonie, f.

Euphrates (the), l'Euphrate, m.

Europe, n, l'Europe, f. European, a, européen. ¶ n, Européen, ne.

Eustachian tube, trompe d'Eustache, f.

evacuate, v.t, évacuer.

evade, v.t, éviter, éluder, esquiver; frauder.

evanescent, a, évanescent.

evangelic(al)†, a, évangélique. evangelist, n, évangéliste, m.

evaporate, v.t, [faire] évaporer; (v.i.) s'évaporer. evaporation, n, évaporation, f.

evasion, n, échappatoire, f, faux-fuyant, subterfuge, m, défaite, f, atermoiement, m. ~ of tax, la fraude fiscale. evasive†, a, évasif; flottant; normand.

eve, n, veille, f. even (Poet.) n, soir, m. ~song, vêpres, f.pl. ~tide, chute du jour, f.

even, a, uni; plan; égal; uniforme; pair; (Games) but à but. all ~ (Golf), à égalité. ~ money, compte rond, m. ~ number, nombre pair, m. ~ with (ground, &c.), à fleur de, au ras de. to be ~ with (someone), revaloir. ¶ ad, même; jusque. ~ if, ~ though, même si, quand, lors même que.

evening, n, soir, m; soirée; veillée, f; (fig.) déclin, m. ~ dew, ~ damp, serein, m. ~ dress, (man) tenue de soirée; (woman) toilette de s., f. ~ gown, robe du soir, f.

evenly, ad, uniment; uniformément. evenness, n, égalité; uniformité, f. evens (Betting) n.pl, égalité, f.

event, n, événement; cas, m; (Sport) épreuve, f. ~ful, a, plein d'événements; mouvementé, accidenté.

eventual†, a, éventuel. ~ity, n, éventualité, f. eventuate, v.i, aboutir.

ever, ad, jamais; toujours. for ~, à (ou pour) jamais (ou toujours). ~ so little, tant soit peu.

evergreen, n, arbre toujours vert, m.

everlasting†, a, éternel; immortel.

evermore, ad, toujours. for ~, à tout jamais.

every, a, chaque; tout, e; tous (toutes) les. ~body, everyone, every one (every person), tout le monde, chacun, m. only. ~day, a, quotidien; vulgaire; ordinaire. ~day clothes, vêtements ordinaires, habits de tous les jours, m.pl. ~ one (each), chacun, e. ~thing, n, tout, pn. ~where, ad, partout.

evict, v.t, évincer. ~ion, n, éviction, f.

evidence, n, évidence; preuve, f; témoignage, m; déposition, f; titre, m. to be ~, faire foi. to give ~, témoigner. ¶ v.t, constater. evident, a, évident. ~ly, ad, évidemment.

evil, a, mauvais; méchant; malin, malfaisant. ~ days, malheur, m. ~-disposed (person), a. & n, malintentionné, e. ~ doer, malfaiteur, m. ~ eye, mauvais œil, m. the E~ One, le malin [esprit], l'esprit malin, m. ~ speaking, médisance, f. ~ spirit, esprit malin, malin esprit, m. ¶ ad, mal. ¶ n, mal, m, plaie, f.

evince, v.t, manifester, témoigner.

eviscerate, v.t, éventrer.

evocation, n, évocation, f. evoke, v.t, évoquer.

evolution, n, déroulement, m; (Biol., &c.) évolution, f; (Geom.) développement; (Chem.) dégagement, m. evolve, v.t, élaborer; dégager; (v.i.) évoluer.

ewe, n, brebis, f. ~ lamb, agneau femelle, m.

ewer, n, pot à eau, broc de toilette, m; aiguière, f.

ex-, prefix: ~-professor, ex-professeur, ancien professeur, m. ~-service man, ancien combattant, m.

ex, pr: ~ bond, à l'acquitté. ~ dividend, ex-dividende, ex-exercice. ~ ship, ~ steamer (sales), au débarquement. ~ steamer (transhipment), ex steamer. ~ store, ~ warehouse, disponible. ~ wharf, franco à quai. ~ works, ~ mill, départ usines, prise usine.

exacerbate, v.t, exacerber.

exact, a, exact, précis. ¶ v.t, exiger. ~ing, p.a, exigeant. ~ion, n, exaction, f. ~ly, ad, exactement, au juste, précisément, parfaitement, f. ~ness, exactitude, n, exactitude, f.

exaggerate, v.t. & abs, exagérer, grossir.

exalt, v.t, exalter, relever.

examination, n, examen, m; inspection; visite, f; concours; interrogatoire, m; instruction; expertise, f. ~ paper, composition, f. examine, v.t, examiner; interroger; inspecter; visiter; compulser; instruire.

examinee, n, candidat, e. examiner, n, examinateur, trice; interrogateur, trice;

inspecteur, trice; visiteur; vérificateur; contrôleur; (*plays*) censeur, *m.*

example, *n,* exemple, *m.*

exasperate, *v.t,* exaspérer, énerver, indigner.

excavate, *v.t,* creuser, fouiller. **excavation**, *n,* excavation, fouille, *f,* déblai, *m.* **excavator** (*Mach.*) *n,* excavateur, *m.*

exceed, *v.t,* excéder, [dé]passer, outrepasser. **~ingly**, *ad,* excessivement, extrêmement.

excel, *v.i,* exceller, primer; (*v.t.*) surpasser. **excellence**, *n,* excellence, *f.* ¶ *His Excellency,* Son Excellence, *f.* **excellent**, *a,* excellent. **~ly**, *ad,* excellemment, à merveille.

except, *c,* sinon. **~** *& ~ing*, *pr,* excepté, à l'exception de, hors, hormis, sauf, ôté, à part. **~ion**, *n,* exception; réserve, *f. to take* **~** *to,* se formaliser de. **~ionable**, *a,* récusable; critiquable. **~ional†**, *a,* exceptionnel, hors ligne.

excerpt, *n,* extrait, *m,* bribe, *f.* ¶ *v.t,* extraire.

excess, *n,* excès; excédent; surplus, trop, *m;* outrance, *f;* débordement, *m;* intempérance, *f.* **~** [*fare*], supplément [de taxe] *m.* **~** *profits,* surplus des bénéfices. **~** *weight,* excédent de poids, *m,* surcharge, *f.* **~ive†**, *a,* excessif, immodéré, outré.

exchange, *n,* échange; change; troc, *m;* permutation, *f;* (*Teleph.*) bureau [central], poste central, *m.* **~** *business,* agiotage, *m.* **~** [*premium*], agio, *m.* **~** *rates,* cote des changes, *f.* **~** *station* (*Rly*) gare d'échange, *f.* ¶ *v.t,* échanger; changer; troquer.

exchequer, *n,* trésor, *m,* trésorerie, *f;* (*Eng.*) échiquier, *m;* (*of pers.*) finances, *f.pl.*

excise, *n,* (*Fr.*) régie; (*Eng.*) accise, *f.* **~man**, employé de la régie.

excite, *v.t,* exciter, provoquer; irriter, exalter; agacer. **~ment**, *n,* excitation; exaltation; émotion, *f.*

exclaim, *v.i,* s'écrier, se récrier, s'exclamer. **~** *against, abs,* s'exclamer. **exclamation**, *n,* exclamation, *f.*

exclude, *v.t,* exclure. **exclusion**, *n,* exclusion, *f.* **exclusive†**, *a,* exclusif. **~** *right*(*s*), droit[s] exclusif[s] *m.[pl.]*, exclusivité, *f.*

excommunicate, *v.t,* excommunier.

excrement, *n,* excrément, *m.*

excrescence, *n,* excroissance, *f.*

excruciating†, *p.a,* atroce. **~** *pains,* mort & passion.

exculpate, *v.t,* disculper.

excursion, *n,* excursion; partie; promenade, *f.* **~** *ticket,* billet d'excursion, *m.* **~ist**, *n,* excursionniste, *m,f.*

excuse, *n,* excuse, *f,* prétexte, *m.* ¶ *v.t,* excuser, pardonner; exempter, dispenser de; faire remise de. **~** *me,* excusez-moi; pardon!

execrable†, *a,* exécrable. **execrate**, *v.t,* exécrer.

execute, *v.t,* exécuter; effectuer; (*document*) souscrire; exécuter [à mort], faire mourir.

execution, *n,* exécution, *f;* jeu, *m;* souscription; saisie[-exécution] *f.* **~er**, *n,* exécuteur [des hautes œuvres]; bourreau, *m.*

executive, *n,* bureau; État-major, *m.* **executor**, **trix**, *n,* exécuteur (trice) testamentaire. **executory**, *a,* exécutoire.

exemplary, *a,* exemplaire, modèle. **exemplify**, *v.t,* éclaircir par un exemple, des exemples.

exempt, *a,* exempt. ¶ *v.t,* exempter. **~ion**, *n,* exemption, franchise, *f.*

exercise, *n,* exercice; (*Sch.*) devoir; thème, *m.* **~** *book,* cahier, *m.* ¶ *v.t,* exercer, user de; (*Stk Ex. option*) consolider, lever; (*v.i.*) prendre de l'exercice.

exergue, *n,* exergue, *m.*

exert, *v.t,* exercer. **~** *oneself,* s'évertuer, faire un effort. **~ion**, *n,* effort, *m.*

exfoliate, *v.i,* s'exfolier.

exhalation, *n,* (*act*) exhalation; (*mist*) exhalaison, *f.* **exhale**, *v.t,* exhaler, respirer.

exhaust, *n,* échappement, *m.* ¶ *v.t,* épuiser; aspirer. **~ion**, *n,* épuisement, *f;* aspiration, *f.* **~ive**, *a,* approfondi. **~ively**, *ad,* à fond, mûrement.

exhibit, *n,* objet exposé, produit [à présenter] *m;* (*Law, Civil*) pièce justificative, p. à l'appui; (*Criminal*) p. à conviction, *f.* ¶ *v.t,* exposer; exhiber. **~ion**, *n,* exposition, *f;* salon, *m;* exhibition; (*college*) bourse, *f.* **exhibitioner**, *n,* boursier, ère. **exhibitor**, *n,* exposant, e; montreur, *m.*

exhilarate, *v.t,* émoustiller, égayer, stimuler.

exhort, *v.t,* exhorter, prêcher [à].

exhume, *v.t,* exhumer, déterrer.

exigence, -cy, *n,* exigence, *f.*

exile, *n,* exil, *m;* (*pers.*) exilé, e. ¶ *v.t,* exiler.

exist, *v.i,* exister. **~ence**, *n,* existence, *f.*

exit, *n,* sortie, issue, *f,* dégagement, *m.* **~** *X.* (*Theat.*), X. sort.

ex-libris, *n,* ex-libris, *m.*

exodus, *n,* exode, *m.* *E* **~** (*Bible*), l'Exode, *f.*

ex officio, à titre d'office.

exonerate, *v.t,* exonérer.

exorbitance, *n,* extravagance, *f.* **exorbitant**, *a,* exorbitant. **~ly**, *ad,* exorbitamment.

exorcise, *v.t,* exorciser.

exotic, *a,* exotique. ¶ *n,* plante exotique, *f.*

expand, *v.t,* étendre; déployer; dilater. **expanse**, *n,* étendue; envergure, *f.* **expansion**, *n,* expansion; dilatation; détente, *f.* **expansive**, *a,* expansif.

expatiate, *v.i,* s'étendre.

expatriate, *v.t,* expatrier.

expect, *v.t,* attendre, s'attendre à; espérer. **~ancy**, *n,* expectative, *f.* **~ant**, *a,* expectant. **~** *mother,* femme enceinte, *f.* **~ation**, *n,* attente, expectative; espérance, prévision, *f.*

expectorate, *v.t,n. & abs,* expectorer.

expedience, -cy, *n,* convenance, *f.* **expedient**, *a,* expédient, convenable. ¶ *n,* expédient, *m,* ressource, *f.* **expedite**, *v.t,* expédier; hâter. **expedition**, *n,* expédition, *f.* **~ary**, *a*, expéditionnaire. **expeditious**, *a*, expéditif, diligent.

expel, *v.t*, expulser, chasser, bannir.

expend, *v.t*, dépenser. **expenditure**, *n*, dépense[s] *f*.[*pl*.]. **expense**, *n*, frais, *m.pl*, dépense, charge, *f*, dépens, *m.pl*. *at the ~ of*, aux frais (*ou* dépens) (*ou* crochets) de; à la charge de. **expensive†**, *a*, cher, coûteux, dispendieux.

experience, *n*, expérience, pratique, *f*, métier, *m*, acquis, *m.s. & pl*. ¶ *v.t*, éprouver, essuyer. **experiment**, *n*, expérience, *f*. ¶ *v.i*, expérimenter. *~ on*, faire des expériences sur. *~al†*, *a*, expérimental.

expert, *a*, *& n*, expert, *a. & m*. *~ness*, *n*, habileté, *f*.

expiate, *v.t*, expier.

expiration *& expiry*, *n*, expiration, échéance, déchéance, *f*. **expire**, *v.t & abs*, expirer; (*v.i*.) expirer, échoir, périmer.

explain, *v.t*, expliquer, exposer. *~able*, *a*, explicable. **explanation**, *n*, explication, *f*. **explanatory**, *a*, explicatif. *~ note* (on map), légende, *f*.

expletive (*Gram.*) *a*, explétif. ¶ *n*, mot explétif, *m*, (*in verse*) cheville, *f*; (*oath*) gros mot, juron, *m*.

explicit†, *a*, explicite; clair.

explode, *v.t*, faire exploser, f. éclater: f. sauter; (*fig*.) démolir; (*v.i*.) exploser, éclater, faire explosion. *~d theory*, théorie périmée, *f*.

exploit, *n*, exploit, *m*. ¶ *v.t*, exploiter. *~ation*, *n*, exploitation, *f*.

explore, *v.t*, explorer, reconnaître. **explorer**, *n*, explorateur, trice.

explosion, *n*, explosion, *f*. **explosive**, *n*, explosif, *m*; (*Gram.*) explosive, *f*.

exponent, *n*, interprète, *m,f*; (*Math.*) exposant, *m*.

export, *v.t*, exporter. *~[ation]*, *n*, exportation, sortie, *f*. *~er*, *n*, exportateur, *m*.

expose, *v.t*, exposer, mettre à nu; (*Phot.*) [ex]poser. *~ for sale*, exposer en vente, étaler. **exposition**, *n*, exposition, *f*.

expostulate, *v.i*, faire des remontrances. **expostulation**, *n*, remontrance, *f*.

exposure, *n*, exposition, mise à nu; (*Phot.*) pose, exposition, *f*.

expound, *v.t*, exposer.

express, *a*, exprès, formel. ¶ (*Post, &c*.) *n*, exprès, *m*. *~ letter*, lettre par exprès, *f*. *~ messenger* [porteur-]exprès, *m*. *~ parcel*, (*Post*) colis à livrer par exprès, *m*. (*Rly*) colis messageries à grande vitesse, *m*. *~ [train]*, [train] express, *m*. ¶ *v.t*, exprimer; énoncer; traduire. *~ion*, *n*, expression, *f*. *~ive*, *a*, expressif. **expressly**, *ad*, expressément.†

expropriate, *v.t*, exproprier.

expulsion, *n*, expulsion, *f*.

expunge, *v.t*, rayer, effacer.

expurgate, *v.t*, expurger.

exquisite, *a*, exquis; vif. *~ly*, *ad*, exquisément. *~ness*, *n*, exquis, *m*.

---

extant (to be), exister.

extempore, *a*, improvisé, impromptu. ¶ *ad* d'abondance, impromptu. **extemporize** *v.t. & i*, improviser.

extend, *v.t*, étendre; prolonger. *~ed orde* (*Mil.*), ordre dispersé, *m*. **extension**, *n* extension, *f*, prolongement, *m*; prolongation, *f*; (*camera*) tirage; (*Teleph.*) poste sup plémentaire, *m*. *~ ladder*, échelle à coulisse, *f*. *~ tripod*, trépied extensible *m*. **extensive**, *a*, étendu, large. *~ly*, *ad* largement. **extensor** (*muscle*) *n*, extenseur *m*. **extent**, *n*, étendue; importance, *f* degré, point, *m*, mesure, *f*.

extenuate, *v.t*, atténuer.

exterior†, *a*, extérieur, externe. ¶ *n*, extérieur; dehors, *m*; enveloppe (*fig.*) *f*.

exterminate, *v.t*, exterminer.

external, *a*, externe, extérieur. *~ly*, *ad*, extérieurement.

exterritoriality, *n*, exterritorialité, *f*.

extinct, *a*, éteint. *~ion*, *n*, extinction, *f*. **extinguish**, *v.t*, éteindre. *~er*, *n*, (*light*) éteignoir; (*fire*) extincteur, *m*.

extirpate, *v.t*, extirper.

extol, *v.t*, exalter; vanter; prôner.

extort, *v.t*, extorquer, arracher. *~ion*, *n*, extorsion; maltôte, *f*. *~ionate*, *a*, exorbitant. *~ioner*, *n*, écorcheur, euse, publicain, *m*.

extra, *a*, supplémentaire, supplément de, en sus, hors d'œuvre. *~ binding*, reliure amateur, *f*. *~ fare*, supplément [de taxe] *m*. ¶ *ad*, extra. ¶ *n*, supplément, *m*, plus-value, *f*; hors-d'œuvre, *m*.

extract, *n*, extrait, *m*. ¶ *v.t*, extraire; arracher; [sou]tirer, retirer. *~ion*, *n*, extraction, *f*.

extradite, *v.t*, extrader. **extradition**, *n*, extradition, *f*.

extraneous, *a*, étranger.

extraordinary†, *a*, extraordinaire; insolent. ¶ *n*, extraordinaire, *m*.

extraterritoriality, *n*, exterritorialité, *f*.

extravagance, *n*, extravagance, *f*; dévergondage (*fig*.) *m*; (*money*) folles dépenses, *f.pl*, dissipation[s] *f*.[*pl*.], prodigalités, *f.pl*. **extravagant**, *a*, extravagant; (*of pers.*) dépensier; (*price*) exorbitant. *~ly*, *ad*, follement.

extreme†, *a. & n*, extrême. *a. & m*. *~ penalty*, dernier supplice, *m*. *~ unction*, extrême-onction, *f*. **extremist**, *n*, extrémiste, *m,f*, ultra, *m*; (*att.*) outrancier. **extremity**, *n*, extrémité, *f*, bout, *m*.

extricate, *v.t*, dégager, débarrasser, débarbouiller, dépêtrer, tirer.

extrinsic, *a*, extrinsèque.

exuberance, *n*, exubérance, *f*. **exuberant**, *a*, exubérant.

exude, *v.i*, exsuder; (*v.t*.) distiller.

exult, *v.i*, exulter, triompher.

ex voto, *n*, ex-voto, *m*.

eye, *n*, œil, *m*; paupière; vue, *f*; (*needle, &c*.) œil, chas, trou; (*fruit*) nombril; (*potato*) germe, *m*; boucle, *f*; regard, *m*; porte, *f*. ~*ball*, globe de l'œil, *m*. ~ *bath*, œillère, *f*. ~*bolt*, boulon à œil, *m*. ~*brow*, sourcil, *m*. ~*brow pencil*, crayon pour les yeux, *m*. ~*brow tweezers*, pinces à épiler, *f.pl.* ~ *doctor*, médecin oculiste, *m*. ~*s front!* (*Mil.*), fixe! ~*glass*, monocle, *m*; (*pl.*) binocle, lorgnon, pince-nez, *m*. ~*lash*, cil, *m*. ~*lid*, paupière, *f*. ~*opener*, révélation, *f*. ~*piece*, [verre] oculaire, *m*. ~*shade*, visière, *f*, garde-vue, *m*. ~*sight*, vue, *f*. ~*sore*, objet qui choque la vue, *m*. ~*tooth*, [dent] œillère, *f*. ~ *trouble*, mal aux (*ou* d') yeux, *m*. ~*witness*, témoin oculaire, *m*. ¶ *v.t*, regarder; lorgner. **eyelet**, *n*. & ~ *hole*, œillet, *m*.

eyot, *n*, îlot, *m*.

eyrie, *n*, aire (*de l'aigle*) *f*.

F

F (*Mus.*) letter, fa, *m*. ~ *clef*, clef de fa, *f*. **fable**, *n*, fable. *f*. ~*d*, *p.p*, légendaire, fabuleux.

fabric, *n*, tissu, *m*, étoffe, *f*; (*edifice*) fabrique, *f*; (*fig.*) échafaudage, *m*. ~ *gloves*, gants en tissu, *m.pl.* ~*ate*, *v.t*, fabriquer. ~*ation*, *n*, fabrication; fantasmagorie, *f*. ~*ator*, *n*, fabricateur, trice, forgeur, euse.

fabulist, *n*, fabuliste, *m*. **fabulous†**, *a*, fabuleux.

façade, *n*, façade, *f*.

face, *n*, face, *f*; visage, *m*, figure, *f*; nez; front, *m*; mine; grimace; tournure, *f*; parement; pan; recto; (*cloth*) endroit; (*Cards*) dessous; (*of type*) œil, *m*. ~ *ache*, névralgie faciale, *f*. ~ *cream, white*, blanc [de fard] *m*. ~ *lifting*, chirurgie esthétique du visage, *f*. ~ *massage*, massage facial, *m*. ~ [*plate*] (dial), cadran, *m*. ~ *plate* (lathe), plateau, *m*. ~ *powder*, poudre de riz, *f*. ~ *to* ~, vis-à-vis. ~ *value* (*Fin.*), valeur nominale, *f*. ¶ *v.t*, faire face à; affronter; braver; donner sur, être exposé à; dresser. ~*d with* (silk), à revers de.

facet, *n*, facette, *f*. ¶ *v.t*, facetter.

facetious, *a*, facétieux.

facia [**board**], *n*, enseigne, *f*.

facial, *a*, facial. **facies**, *n*, facies, *m*.

facile, *a*, facile. **facilitate**, *v.t*, faciliter. **facility**, *n*, facilité, *f*.

facing, *n*, revers; parement, revêtement, *m*. ¶ *ad*. & *pr*, en face (de), face à, vis-à-vis (de), à l'opposite (de). ~ *the engine* (to travel) voyager dans le sens de la machine; (*seat*) place face à la machine, *f*.

facsimile, *n*, fac-similé, *m*. ~ *signature & stamp*, griffe, *f*.

fact, *n*, fait, *m*; vérité; chose, *f*.

faction, *n*, faction, brigue, *f*. **factious**, *a*, factieux. **factitious**, *a*, factice.

factor, *n*, facteur; (*pers.*) commissionnaire, *m*. **factory**, *n*, manufacture, fabrique, usine, *f*. ~ *hand*, ouvrier (ère) [de fabrique]. ~ *inspector*, inspecteur du travail, *m*.

factotum, *n*, factotum, *m*.

faculty, *n*, faculté; aptitude, *f*, talent, *m*.

fad, *n*, dada, *m*, marotte, lubie, manie, *f*. **faddist**, *n*, maniaque, *m,f*.

fade, *v.i*, se faner, se défraîchir, déteindre, se flétrir, pâlir. ~ *away*, s'évanouir. ~ *out*, se mourir. ~*d*, *p.a*, fané, défraîchi, passé.

fag, *n*, corvée; fatigue, *f*. ¶ *v.t*, fatiguer, éreinter; (*v.i.*) bûcher. ~ *end*, queue, *f*.

fag[got], *n*, fagot, cotret, *m*. ¶ *v.t*, fagoter.

Fahrenheit, *a*, Fahrenheit. See note under *centigrade* in French-English section.

fail, *v.i*, manquer, faire défaut, défaillir, échouer, mal réussir, rater, chavirer; faiblir; (*Com.*) faire faillite; (*v.t.*) manquer à. ~ *in one's duty*, manquer à son devoir, prévariquer. *without* ~, sans faute. ~*ing*, *n*, faible, *m*; défaillance, *f*. ¶ *pr*, à défaut de, faute de. ~*ure*, *n*, défaut, insuccès, échec, *m*, chute, *f*, coup manqué; four, flasco, *m*; panne; (*Com.*) faillite, *f*. *a* ~ *as a barrister, &c*, un avocat, &c, manqué.

fain, *a*. & *ad*: *to be* ~ *to*, être amené par nécessité à, être réduit à. *I would* ~ *be* . . ., je serais volontiers . . . *I would* ~ *have* . . ., j'aurais bien voulu . . .

faint, *a*, faible; mourant; défaillant. ~*hearted*, lâche. ~ *ruled* (paper), réglé. ¶ *v.i*, s'évanouir, défaillir, [se] pâmer. ~*ing* [**fit**], évanouissement, *m*, défaillance, *f*.

fair, *a*, beau; (*skin*) blanche; (*hair*) blonds; juste, équitable, loyal, honnête; raisonnable; passable. ~ *at* ~ (barometer), au beau. ~ *copy*, copie au net, *f*; (*Sch.*) corrigé, *m*. ~*haired*, aux cheveux blonds. ~*haired person*, blond, e. *by* ~ *means or foul*, de gré ou de force. ~ *play*, bon jeu, *m*, de bonne guerre; traitement honnête, *m*. *not* ~, pas du (*ou* de) jeu. ~ *promises*, eau bénite de cour, *f*. ~ *sex*, beau sexe, *m*. ~*spoken*, bien-disant. ~*way*, chenal, *m*, passe, *f*. ¶ *n*, foire, *f*. ~*ly*, *ad*, à juste titre; bel & bien; loyalement; assez; moyennement. ~*ness*, *n*, beauté, *f*; teint blond, *m*; équité; loyauté, *f*.

fairy, *n*, fée, *f*. ~ *cycle*, bicyclette pour les tout petits, *f*. ~ *lamp*, ~ *light*, verre d'illumination, lampion, *m*. **Fairyland**, féerie, *f*. ~*like*, féerique. ~ *ring*, cercle des fées, *m*. ~ *tale*, conte de fées, conte bleu, *m*.

faith, *n*, foi; confiance; croyance, communion, *f*. ~*ful†*, *a*, fidèle. *the* ~, les fidèles, les croyants, *m.pl.* ~*fulness*, *n*, fidélité, *f*. ~*less*, *a*, sans foi, infidèle. ~*lessness*, *n*, infidélité, *f*.

fake, *n*, truquage, *m*. ¶ *v.t*, truquer.

fakir, *n,* fakir, *m.*

falcon, *n,* faucon, *m.* ~**er,** *n,* fauconnier. **falconry,** *n,* fauconnerie, *f.*

fall, *n,* chute; tombée; descente; baisse, *f;* abaissement, *m;* culbute; ruine, *f;* éboulement; éboulis, *m;* cascade, *f;* saut, *m;* (*pl.*) chute, *f;* (*tackle*) courant, garant; automne, *m.* ~*back,* épée de chevet, *f.* ~ *trap,* assommoir, *m.* ¶ *v.i.ir,* tomber; descendre; baisser; s'abaisser; se jeter; sauter. ~ *back,* se replier. ~ *down,* tomber [par terre]. ~ *due,* échoir. ~ *in,* (*cave in*) ébouler; (*Mil.*) se mettre en rangs; à vos rangs! ~ *in love,* s'enamourer, s'éprendre. ~ *in with* (opinion), se ranger à. ~ *off,* tomber [à bas] de; ralentir. ~ *out with,* ~ *foul of,* se brouiller avec. ~ *through* (fail), échouer.

fallacious, *a,* fallacieux. **fallacy,** *n,* erreur, *f;* (*Log.*) sophisme, *m.*

fallals, *n.pl. &* **fallallery,** *n,* colifichets, falbalas, *m.pl,* fanfreluches, *f.pl.*

fallen angel, ange déchu, *m.* **fallen leaves,** feuilles tombées, fanes, *f.pl,* fanage, *m.*

fallibility, *n,* faillibilité, *f.* **fallible,** *a,* faillible.

falling star, étoile tombante, é. filante, *f.*

fallow, *a,* (*colour of deer*) fauve; (*land*) en jachère, en friche. ~ *deer,* daim, *m.* *to lie* ~, rester en friche, chômer. ¶ *v.t,* jachérer.

false, *a,* faux; mensonger; postiche; feint. ~ *bottom,* double fond, faux f., *m.* ~ *shame,* fausse honte, mauvaise h., *f.* ¶ *ad,* faussement. ~**hood,** *n,* fausseté *f.* ~**ly,** *ad,* faussement. ~**ness,** *n,* fausseté, *f.*

falsetto, *n,* fausset, *m.* **falsify,** *v.t,* falsifier, fausser. **falsity,** *n,* fausseté, *f.*

falter, *v.i,* chanceler, défaillir; hésiter; ânonner; bégayer.

fame, *n,* renommée, *f,* renom, *m,* gloire, mémoire, *f.* ~**d,** *a,* renommé.

familiar†, *a,* familier. ~ *face,* figure de connaissance, *f.* ~ [*spirit*], démon familier, *m.* ¶ *n,* familier, *m.* ~**ity,** *n,* familiarité; privauté, *f.* ~**ize,** *v.t,* familiariser.

family, *n,* famille, *f;* ménage, *m;* maisonnée, *f.* ~ *likeness,* air de famille, *m.* ~ *life,* vie de f., v. familiale, *f.* ~ *man,* père de famille; homme de·foyer, *m.* ~ *tree,* arbre généalogique, *m.*

famine, *n,* famine, *f.* ~ *price,* prix de f., *m.*

famish, *v.t,* affamer. *to be* ~*ing,* avoir la fringale.

famous†, *a,* fameux, célèbre, renommé. ~ *case* (*Law*), cause célèbre, *f.*

fan, *n,* éventail; ventilateur, *m.* ~ *light,* vasistas, *m.* ~ *tail,* pigeon paon, *m.* ¶ *v.t,* éventer; (*corn*) vanner; (*fire, & fig.*) souffler; exciter, attiser.

fanatic, *n,* fanatique, *m,f.* ~(**al**), *a,* fanatique. **fanaticism,** *n,* fanatisme, *m.* **fanaticize,** *v.t,* fanatiser.

fancied, *p.a,* imaginaire. **fancier,** *n,* grand amateur (de . . .) *m.* **fanciful,** *a,* de fantaisie; fantastique, chimérique. **fancy,** *n,* fantaisie; envie; toquade; boutade, *f,* caprice, *m;* imagination; idée, *f.* ~ [*article*], fantaisie, *f,* objet de f., *m.* ~ *bimbelot m.* ~ *bread,* pain de fantaisie, *f.* ~ *dog,* chien de luxe, *m.* ~ *draper,* linger, ère. ~ *drapery,* lingerie, *f.* ~ *dress,* déguisement, *m.* ~ *dress ball,* bal costumé. b. travesti, *m.* ~ *goods,* bimbeloterie tabletterie, *f;* article[s] de Paris, *m.[pl.]* ~ *leather goods or shop,* maroquinerie, *f* ~ *needlework,* ouvrages de dames, *m.pl* ~ *roll,* pain mollet, *m.* ~ *work,* ouvrages d'agrément, *m.pl.* ¶ *v.t,* imaginer; s'imaginer; se figurer. ~ *oneself,* se complaire.

fang, *n,* croc, crochet; *m;* racine, *f.*

fantasia, *n,* fantaisie, *f.* **fantastic,** *a,* fantastique; fantaisiste. **fantasy,** *n,* vision fantaisie, *f.*

far, *ad,* loin, au loin; avant; beaucoup; bien. ~ *from ~,* de loin. *how ~ is it to . . .?* combien y a-t-il d'ici à . . .? ~ *& wide* au long & au large. *as ~ as,* jusqu'à, autant que. *as ~ as the eye can reach,* à perte de vue. ~*-fetched,* tiré par les cheveux, forcé, outré. ~ *into the night* fort avant dans la nuit. ~ *off,* lointain ~*-reaching,* étendu. ~*-sighted,* prévoyant. ~ *too,* par trop. ¶ *a,* éloigné. *the F~ East,* l'Extrême-Orient, *m.*

farce, *n,* farce, *f.* **farcical,** *a,* burlesque, bouffon.

fare, *n,* prix [de la place], prix de passage, tarif, *m,* place; course, *f;* voyageur, euse; chère, *f,* menu, *m.* ~ *stage* (bus, &c) section, *f.* ¶ *v.i,* aller. *to ~* (*to feed*) *well,* faire bonne chère. ~**well,** *i. & n,* adieu, *i. & m.*

farina, *n,* farine; fécule, *f.* **farinaceous,** *a,* farineux, farinacé.

farm, *n,* ferme, exploitation agricole, *f.* ~ *hand,* valet de ferme, *m.* ~**house,** ferme, *f.* ~*yard,* cour de f., basse-cour, *f.* ¶ *v.t,* exploiter, cultiver; (*lease*) affermer. ~ *out,* amodier. ~**er,** *n,* fermier, ère, cultivateur, trice, agriculteur, *m.* ~**ing,** *n,* exploitation [d'une ferme]; agriculture, culture, *f;* (*att.*) aratoire.

faro (*Cards*) *n,* pharaon, *m.*

farrago, *n,* farrago, salmigondis, *m.*

farrier, *n,* maréchal-ferrant, *m.* ~**y,** *n,* maréchalerie, *f.*

farrow, *n,* cochonnée, *f.* ¶ *v.i,* cochonner.

farther, *ad,* plus loin, [plus] en delà. **farthest,** *a,* le plus éloigné. ¶ *ad,* le plus loin.

farthing, *n,* farthing, *m.* = ¼ penny; (*fig.*) liard, *m,* obole, *f.*

fasces (*Hist.*) *n.pl,* faisceaux, *m.pl.*

fascinate, *v.t,* fasciner. **fascinating,** *a,* fascinateur. **fascination,** *n,* fascination, *f.*

fascine, *n,* fascine, *f.*

ascism, n, fascisme, m. **fascist**, n, fasciste, m.
ashion, n, façon; mode, f, genre, m. ~ *book*, album de patrons, m. ~ *plate*, gravure de mode, f. ¶ v.t, façonner. *fully fashioned* (stocking), entièrement diminué. ~**able**, a, à la mode, élégant. ~ *society*, le beau monde. ~**ably**, ad, à la mode.
ast, a, fixe; fidèle; (*dissipated*) léger; rapide, vite; express, de grande vitesse; (*of clock*) en avance; (*on clock*) avance. ~ *asleep*, profondément endormi. ~ *colour*, bon teint, t. solide, m. ~ *cruiser* (speed boat), glisseur de croisière, m. ~ *sailer* (ship), grand marcheur, m. ¶ ad, ferme; bien; vite; (*rain*) à verse. *to hold* ~, tenir bon. *to make* ~, amarrer. ¶ n, jeûne, m; (*Naut.*) amarre, f. ¶ v.i, jeûner. ~**ing**, ad, à jeun. ~[*ing*] *day*, jour de jeûne, j. maigre, m.
asten, v.t, fixer; assujettir; attacher; agrafer. ~ *off* (Need.), arrêter. ~**er** & ~**ing**, n, attache; armature; fermeture; agrafe, f.
asti, n.pl, fastes, m.pl.
astidious (to be), être pointilleux, faire le (*of woman*, la) dégoûté(e), f. le difficile, f. le délicat, f. le (la) renchéri(e).
astness, n, forteresse, f.
at, a, gras; obèse; (*land*) fertile. ~**head**, lourdaud, e. ¶ n, gras, m; graisse, f; lard; suif, m. *to live on the* ~ *of the land*, vivre grassement.
atal†, a, fatal, funeste; mortel. ~**ism**, n, fatalisme, m. ~**ist**, n, fataliste, m,f. ~**ity**, n, fatalité, f; accident mortel, m; tué, e.
ate, n, destin, sort, m, fatalité, f. *the Fates* (Myth.), les Parques, f.pl. *to be* ~*d to*, être destiné à. ~**ful**, a, fatal.
ather, n, père, m. F~ *Christmas*, le père Noël, le bonhomme Noël. ~**-in-law**, beau-père, m. ~**-land**, patrie, f. ~'*s side* (family), côté paternel, m. ¶ v.t, patronner. ~ *upon*, attribuer à. ~**hood**, n, paternité, f. ~**-less**, a, sans père, orphelin de père. ~**ly**, a, paternel, de père.
athom, n, brasse, f. (Eng. *fathom* = 6 feet; Fr. *brasse marine* = 1 metre 62). ¶ v.t, sonder, pénétrer. ~**less**, a, insondable.
atigue, n, fatigue; (*Mil.*) corvée, f. ~ *jacket* (Mil.), vareuse, f. ¶ v.t, fatiguer. **fatiguing**, a, fatigant.
atness, n, obésité; fertilité, f. *fatted calf*, veau gras, m. **fatten**, v.t, engraisser. **fattish**, a, grasset. **fatty**, a, gras, graisseux, adipeux. ~ *degeneration*, dégénérescence graisseuse, f.
atuity, n, imbécillité, f. **fatuous**, a, imbécile.
auces, n.pl, arrière-bouche, f.
ault, n, faute, f; tort; défaut, vice; dérangement, m; (*Geol.*) faille, f. *to find* ~ *with*, trouver à redire à, reprendre, mordre sur; censurer, fronder, gloser [sur]. ~ *finder*, épilogueur, euse, frondeur, euse. ~**less**, a,

sans faute; sans défaut; irréprochable. ~**y**, a, fautif, vicieux, défectueux, mauvais.
faun, n, faune, m. **fauna**, n, faune, f.
favour, n, faveur, grâce, f; plaisir, m; (*Com.*, *letter*) honorée, f. ¶ v.t, favoriser, avantager, honorer. **favourable†**, a, favorable; prospère. **favourite**, a, favori. ~ *author*, auteur de prédilection, m. ~ *book*, livre de chevet, m. ¶ n, favori, ite. *the* ~, le [cheval] favori. **favouritism**, n, favoritisme, m, cote d'amour, f.
fawn, n, faon, chevrotin; (*colour*) fauve, m. ~[*-coloured*], fauve. ¶ (*of deer*) v.i, faonner. ~ [*up*]*on*, flagorner, courtiser, ramper devant.
fear, n, crainte, peur, frayeur, f; danger, m. ¶ v.t. & i, craindre, redouter. ~**ful†**, a, affreux, épouvantable; craintif. ~**less**, a, sans peur, intrépide. ~**lessness**, n, intrépidité, f.
feasibility, n, praticabilité, f. **feasible**, a, faisable, praticable.
feast, n, fête, f; festin, régal, m. ¶ v.i. & v.t, festiner, festoyer, régaler; (*fig.*) repaître. ~**ing**, n, bombance, f.
feat, n, fait, exploit; tour, m, prouesse, f.
feather, n, plume, f; (*pl.*) plumage, m; penne; (*Carp. & Mach.*) languette, f. ~ *bed*, lit de plume, m. ~**-brained** *person*, tête de linotte, f, évaporé, e. ~ *duster*, plumeau, houssoir, m. ~ *stitch*, point de plume, m. ~ *trade*, plumasserie, f. ~ *weight* (Box.), poids plume, m. ¶ (*Rowing*) v.i, plumer. ~**ed**, p.a: ~ *game*, gibier à plume, m. ~ *hat*, chapeau orné de plumes, m. *the* ~ *tribe*, la gent emplumée. ~**y**, a, plumeux.
feature, n, trait, linéament, m; caractéristique, f.
February, n, février, m.
fecund, a, fécond. ~**ate**, v.t, féconder. ~**ity**, n, fécondité, f.
federal, a, fédéral. **federate**, v.t, fédérer. *the Federated Malay States*, les États malais fédérés, m.pl. **federation**, n, fédération, f; syndicat, m.
fee, n. oft. pl, honoraires, m.pl; vacations, f.pl; jeton [de présence]; cachet, m; frais, m.pl; cotisation, f; droit, m; taxe; surtaxe, f.
feeble†, a, faible, débile.
feed, n, nourriture; mangeaille; pâture, f; (*of oats*) picotin, m; alimentation, f; (*Mach.*) avancement, entraînement, m. ~ *pump*, pompe alimentaire, f. ¶ v.t.ir, nourrir; [re]paître; alimenter; (*Typ.*) marger; (v.i.ir) manger. ~ *forcibly*, gaver. ~**er**, n, mangeur, euse; appareil d'alimentation, m; (bib) bavette, f, bavoir; (*stream*, Rly) affluent, m; (*Elec.*) artère, f. ~**ing** *bottle*, biberon, m.
feel, n, manier, toucher, tact, m. ¶ v.t. & i. ir, tâter, palper, manier, toucher; sentir, se s., ressentir, se r., éprouver; se

trouver. ~er, n, antenne, f, palpe, f. or m;
tentacule; (fig.) ballon d'essai, m. **feeling**,
a, sensible, touchant, tendre. ¶ n, maniement, m; sensation; sensibilité, f; (pl.)
cœur; sentiment; esprit, m. ~ly, ad, avec
émotion.

feign, v.t, feindre, simuler, jouer. **feint**, n,
feinte, f. ~-**ruled**, réglé. ¶ v.i, feindre.

felicitous, a, heureux, à propos. **felicity**, n,
félicité, f.

Felidae, n.pl, félidés, m.pl. **feline**, a. & n,
félin, a. & m.

fell, n, peau, f; abat[tis] m. ¶ v.t, abattre;
assommer. ~er, n, abatteur, m. ~ing,
n, abattage, m.

felloe, n, jante, f.

fellow, n, compagnon, m, camarade, m,f;
pareil, pendant; garçon, gaillard, individu,
sujet, diable, m. ~ **boarder**, commensal, e.
~ **citizen**, concitoyen, ne. ~ **countryman**,
-**woman**, compatriote, m,f. ~ **creature**,
~ **man**, semblable, prochain, m. ~
feeling, sympathie, f. ~ **passenger**, ~
traveller, compagnon de voyage, m, compagne de voyage, f. ~ **sponsor**, compère,
m, commère, f. ~ **student**, camarade de
collège, m,f, condisciple, m. ~ **sufferer**,
camarade de malheur, compagnon de
malheur, compagne de malheur. ~ **work-**
man, camarade d'atelier, m. ~**ship**, n,
société; camaraderie, f.

felo de se, n, suicide; (pers.) suicidé, m.
felon, n, criminel, le. ~**ious**, a, criminel.
~**y**, n, crime, m.

fel[d]spar, n, feldspath, m.

felt, n, feutre, m. ~ [hat], [chapeau de]
feutre, m. ¶ v.t, feutrer.

female, a, femelle; de femme; (pers.) féminin.
¶ n, (animal) femelle; (pers.) femme, f.
feminine, a. & n, féminin, a. & m.
feminism, n, féminisme, m. **feminist**,
a. & n, féministe, a. & m,f. **feminize**, v.t,
féminiser.

femur, n, fémur, m.

fen, n, marais, marécage, m.

fence, n, clôture, barrière, palissade, f; (Mach.)
guide, m; (pers.) receleur, euse. ¶ v.t,
palissader; (v.i.) faire (ou tirer) des armes.
~ **in**, enclore. ~ **off**, barrer. **fencer**,
n, tireur d'armes, m; (horse) sauteur,
euse. **fencing**, n, clôture, enceinte; (foils)
escrime, f. ~ **master**, maître d'armes, m.
~ **school**, salle d'armes, s. d'escrime, f.

fend [off], v.t, parer. ~ **for oneself**, se suffire.
~**er**, n, garde-cendre; (Naut.) pare-
battage, m; défense [de canot] f.

fennel, n. & ~ **seed**, fenouil, m.

ferment, n, ferment, m; (fig.) fermentation,
effervescence, f. ¶ v.i, fermenter; (v.t.)
faire f. ~**ation**, n, fermentation, f.

fern, n, fougère, f.

ferocious, a, féroce. **ferocity**, n, férocité, f.

ferret, n, furet, m. ¶ v.i. & t, fureter. ~
about, fureter. ~ **out**, dénicher.

ferrous, a, ferreux.

ferruginous, a, ferrugineux.

ferrule, n, virole, bague, frette, f, [em]bout
m. ¶ v.t, mettre une virole, &c. à.

ferry, n, passage, m. ~[boat], bateau d
passage, bac, m. ~**man**, passeur, m
~ **over**, passer [l'eau].

fertile, a, fertile, fécond, plantureux. **fer**
tility, n, fertilité, fécondité, f. **fertilize**
v.t, fertiliser. **fertilizer**, n, engrais ferti
lisant, m.

fervent & **fervid**, a, fervent, ardent. **fer**-
vently & **fervidly**, ad, avec ferveur, ardem
ment. **fervour** & **fervency**, n, ferveur
ardeur, f.

fester, v.i, s'ulcérer.

festival, n, fête, f; (musical) festival, m
festive, a, de fête. **festivity**, n, fête, f.

festoon, n, feston, m. ¶ v.t, festonner.

fetch, v.t, apporter; aller chercher. ~ it!
(to dog), apporte!

fête, n, fête; kermesse; (at a fair) fête foraine,
f. ¶ v.t, fêter.

fetid, a, fétide. ~**ness**, n, fétidité, f.

fetish, -**ich**[e], n, fétiche. m. **fetishism**, n,
fétichisme, m.

fetlock, n, fanon, m.

fetter, n. oft. pl, entrave, f, fer, m, chaîne, f.
¶ v.t, entraver, enchaîner.

fettle, n, état, m, forme, f.

feud, n, guerre, vendetta, f; (Hist.) fief, m.
~**al**, a, féodal. ~**alism** & ~**ality**, n,
féodalité, f.

fever, n, fièvre, f. ~ **case** (pers.), fiévreux,
euse. ~**ish**†, a, fiévreux; fébrile.

few, a. & n, peu de; peu, m; quelques,
quelques-uns, -unes. ~ & **far between**,
clairsemé. ~**er**, a, moins; moins de.

fez, n, fez, m.

fiasco, n, fiasco, four, m.

fiat, n, décret, m.

fib, n, histoire, bourde, craque, f, mensonge
innocent, m, menterie, f. ¶ v.i, débiter
des bourdes. **fibber**, n, donneur (ou conteur) de bourdes, m.

fibre, n, fibre, f; crin, m. **fibril**, n, fibrille, f.
fibrous, a, fibreux.

fibula, n, péroné, m.

fickle, a, volage, changeant, mobile, versatile, inconstant. ~**ness**, n, inconstance,
mobilité, versatilité, f.

fiction, n, fiction, f, mensonge, m; (prose)
roman, les romans. **fictitious**†, a, fictif,
supposé. **fictive**, a, imaginaire.

fiddle, n, violon, crincrin, m. ~**stick**, archet,
m; (pl., i.) chansons, chansons! ¶ v.i,
jouer du violon; (fig.) baguenauder.
fiddler, n, ménétrier, m. **fiddling**, a,
frivole.

fidelity, n, fidélité, f.

fidget, v.i, remuer, frétiller, se trémousser.
~**s**, n.pl, impatiences, crispations, f.pl.
~**y**, a, inquiet, nerveux.

fiduciary, a, fiduciaire.

e, i, fil

et (*Hist.*) *n*, fief, *m*.

eld, *n*, champ, *m*; (*pl.*) campagne, *f*; (*pl., poet.*) sillons, *m.pl*; terrain, *m*; (*Mil.*) campagne, *f*; (*Turf*) champ; (*Her.*) champ, *m*, table d'attente, *f*. ~ **artillery**, artillerie de campagne, *f*. ~ **camera**, chambre à pied, *f*. ~ **day**, manœuvres, *f.pl*; (*fig.*) grand jour; débat important, *m*. ~**fare**, litorne, *f*. ~ **geology**, géologie sur le terrain, *f*. ~ **glass[es]**, jumelle de campagne, *f*. F~ **Marshal** (*Eng.*), maréchal de France (*Fr.*) *m*. ~ **mouse**, rat des champs, mulot, *m*. ~ **sports**, la chasse, la pêche, & sports analogues.

end, *n*, démon, *m*; enragé, e. ~**ish**, *a*, diabolique.

ierce, *a*, féroce, farouche, acharné, hirsute. ~**ly**, *ad*, avec férocité. ~**ness**, *n*, férocité, *f*.

iery, *a*, de feu; ardent, bouillant, fougueux.

fe & fifer, *n*, fifre, *m*.

fteen, *n*, quinze, *a. & m*. ~**th**†, *a. & n*, quinzième. *a. & m,f*; quinze, *m*. fifth†, *a*, cinquième. ¶ *n*, cinquième, *m,f*; cinq, *m*; (*Mus.*) quinte, *f*. fiftieth, *a. & n*, cinquantième, *a. & m,f*. ~ **anniversary**, cinquantenaire, *m*. fifty, *a. & n*, cinquante, *a. & m*. ~ [*or so*], une cinquantaine.

ig, *n*, figue, *f*; (*fig.*) fétu, *m*. ~ **leaf**, feuille de figuier; (*Art*) feuille de vigne, *f*. ~ **tree**, figuier, *m*.

ight, *n*, combat, *m*; lutte, joute, bataille, mêlée, batterie, *f*. ¶ *v.i.ir*, se battre, combattre, lutter, batailler; (*v.t.ir.*) se battre avec, combattre, lutter contre; (*a battle*) livrer; (*one's way*) se frayer. ~**er**, *n*, combattant; batailleur; militant, *m*. ~[**plane**], chasseur, avion de chasse, *m*.

igment, *n*, fiction, *f*.

igurative, *a*, figuratif. ~ **sense**, [sens] figuré, *m*. ~**ly**, *ad*, figurativement; (*sense*) figurément, au figuré. figure, *n*, figure, *f*; (*bodily shape*) taille, tournure, *f*; (*Arith.*) chiffre, *m*. ~ **dance**, danse figurée, *f*. ~**head**, (*ship*) figure de proue, *f*; personnage de carton, *m*. ~ **of speech**, figure de mots, figure de rhétorique, *f*. ~ **skates**, patins de figure, *m.pl*. ~ **stone**, pierre figurée, *f*. ¶ *v.t. & i*, chiffrer; gaufrer; figurer; (*Mus.*) chiffrer. ~**d** (*textiles*) *p.a*, façonné.

ilament, *n*, filament; fil; filet, *m*.

ilbert, *n*, aveline, *f*. ~ [**tree**], avelinier, *m*.

ilch, *v.t*, escamoter, subtiliser, filouter.

ile, *n*, (*rank*) file; (*of people*) file, queue, *f*; (*for letters*) classeur, *m*; (*bundle*) liasse; collection; (*tool*) lime, *f*. ~ **leader**, chef de file, *m*. ¶ *v.t*, classer; déposer, passer, enregistrer; limer. ~ **off**, filer. ~ **past**, défiler.

ilial†, *a*, filial. filiation, *n*, filiation, *f*.

ilibuster, *n*, flibustier, *m*.

filigree [**work**], *n*, filigrane, *m*. ~**d**, c, façonné en filigrane.

filing, *n*, classement; dépôt; limage, *m*; (*pl.*) limaille, *f*. ~ **cabinet**, [meuble-]classeur, *m*.

fill, *n*, suffisance, *f*, content, soûl, *m*. ¶ *v.t*, [r]emplir; combler; charger; peupler; suppléer à; (*tooth*) plomber. ~ **in**, remplir. ~ **in time**, peloter en attendant partie. ~ **up**, remplir; (*ullaged cask*) ouiller.

fillet, *n*, filet; (*Arch.*) congé, *m*. ~ **of veal**, rouelle de veau, *f*. ~**ed sole**, filets de sole, *m.pl*.

filling, *n*, remplissage, chargement; (*tooth*) plombage, *m*. ~ **station**, station de ravitaillement, *f*.

fillip, *n*, chiquenaude, *f*; (*fig.*) coup de fouet, *m*.

fillister, *n*, feuillure, *f*.

filly, *n*, pouliche, *f*.

film, *n*, pellicule, *f*; film, *m*; (*fig.*) voile, *m*. ~ **camera**, chambre à pellicules, *f*. ~ **pack**, bloc-film, *m*. ~ **rights**, droits d'adaptation au cinématographe, *m.pl*. ~ **star**, vedette de l'écran, v. de cinéma, *f*. ¶ *v.t*, mettre à l'écran, tourner. ~**y**, *a*, vaporeux.

filter, *n*, filtre, *m*; (*Phot.*) écran, *m*. ¶ *v.t. & i*, filtrer.

filth, *n*, immondice, fange, ordure, crasse, saleté, *f*. filthiness, *n*, saleté, *f*. filthy†, *a*, sale, crasseux; crapuleux; fangeux, ignoble.

fin, *n*, nageoire, *f*, aileron, *m*.

final†, *a*, final, dernier, fatal. ~ **dividend**, solde de dividende, *m*. ~ [**heat**], [épreuve] finale, *f*. finale (*Mus.*) *n*, final[e] *m*. finality, *n*, finalité, *f*.

finance, *n*, finance, *f*; commandite, *f*; (*pl.*) finances, *f.pl*, trésorerie, *f*. ¶ *v.i*, financer (*v.t.*) commanditer. financial†, *a*, financier. ~ **year**, exercice [financier] financier, *n*, financier, *m*.

finch, *n*, pinson, *m*.

find, *n*, trouvaille, découverte, *f*. ¶ *v.t.ir*, trouver, retrouver; découvrir; rechercher; s'apercevoir; reconnaître; procurer, se procurer; fournir. ~ **out**, découvrir, se rendre compte. ~**er**, *n*, inventeur; (*camera*) viseur, *m*; (*telescope*) lunette de repère, *f*. ~**ing** (*jury*) *n*, déclaration, *f*.

fine, *a*, beau; fin; délicat; bon; menu; ténu; joli; magnifique. ~ **arts**, beaux-arts, *m.pl*. one of these ~ **days**, one ~ **day**, un de ces matins, un beau matin. ~-**draw**, rentraire. ~ **metal**, fin, *m*. gold 22 carats ~, or à 22 carats de fin. ~ **speaking**, bien-dire, *m*. ~ **things**, objets magnifiques, *m.pl*, magnificences, *f.pl*. ¶ *n*, amende, *f*. in ~, enfin, bref. ¶ *v.t*, mettre (*ou* condamner) à l'amende; (*wine, &c*) coller, clarifier. ~**ly**, *ad*, finement; joliment. ~**ness**, *n*, finesse; ténuité, *f*; (*gold, &c*) titre, *m*. finery, *n*, chiffons colifichets, affiquets, atours, *m.pl.* **finesse,** *n,* finesse, *f.* ¶ *v.t,* finasser. *finest quality,* premier choix, *m.*

finger, *n,* doigt, *m.* ~ *board,* touché, *f.* ~ *bowl,* bol rince-doigts, *m.* ~ *mark,* empreinte du doigt, *f.* ~ *plate,* plaque de propreté, *f.* ~ *post,* poteau indicateur, *m.* ~ *print,* empreinte digitale, *f.* ~ *stall,* doigtier, *m.* ¶ *v.t,* toucher, palper; (*Mus.*) doigter. ~ing (*Mus.*) *n,* doigté, *m.*

finical, finikin[g], *a,* dégoûté, difficile, maniéré, vétilleux, mièvre.

finis, *n,* fin, *f.* **finish,** *n,* fini, *m*; (*end*) fin, *f,* bout, *m.* ¶ *v.t. & abs. & i,* finir; en finir; achever; parachever, parfaire. *to ~ speaking, &c,* finir de parler, &c. ~ing *stroke,* coup de grâce, *m.* ~ing *touches,* dernière main, *f.*

finite, *a,* fini; (*Gram.*) défini.

Finland, *n,* la Finlande. **Fin[n],** **Finlander,** *n,* Finnois, e, Finlandais, e. **Finnish,** *a,* finnois, finlandais. ¶ (*language*) *n,* le finnois.

fir (*tree*), *n,* sapin, pin, *m.* ~ *plantation,* sapinière, *f.*

fire, *n,* feu; incendie; tir, *m*; fougue, *f.* (*house, &c, on*) ~! au feu! ~ *alarm,* avertisseur d'incendie, *m.* ~arms, armes à feu, *f.pl.* ~back (fireplace), plaque de cheminée, *f.* ~box, foyer, *m*; boîte à feu, *f.* ~brand, tison, brandon, boutefeu, *m.* ~ *brick,* brique réfractaire, *f.* ~ *brigade,* sapeurs-pompiers, *m.pl.* ~ *clay,* argile réfractaire, *f.* ~ *damp,* grisou, *m.* ~dog, chenet, *m.* ~ *engine,* pompe à incendie, *f.* ~ *escape,* échelle de sauvetage, *f.* ~ *extinguisher,* extincteur d'incendie, *m.* ~fly, mouche à feu, luciole, *f.* ~guard, garde-feu, pare-étincelles, *m.* ~ *hydrant,* ~ *plug,* bouche d'incendie, *f.* ~ *insurance,* assurance contre l'incendie, *f.* ~ *irons,* garniture de foyer, *f.* ~ *lighter,* allume-feu, *m.* ~man, pompier; sapeur-pompier; (*stoker*) chauffeur, *m.* ~place, cheminée, *f,* âtre, *m.* ~proof, *a,* ignifuge, incombustible, à l'épreuve du feu; (*v.t.*) ignifuger. ~ *raising,* incendie volontaire, *m.* ~ *screen,* écran à pied, *m.* ~side, coin du feu, foyer, *m.* ~side *chair,* chauffeuse, *f.* ~[side] *companion* [*set*], porte-pelle & pincette, *f.* ~ *station,* poste d'incendie, p. de pompiers, *m.* ~wood, bois à brûler, b. de chauffage, *m.* ~work, feu d'artifice, *m,* pièce d'a., *f.* ¶ *v.t,* enflammer, embraser, mettre le feu à; incendier; allumer; chauffer; (*shot*) tirer, lâcher, lancer; (*v.i.*) prendre feu; (*gun*) tirer, faire feu. ~! (*Mil.*), feu! **firing,** *n,* chauffage, *m,* chauffe, *f*; combustible; (*Mil.*) feu, tir, *m.* ~ *party,* peloton d'exécution, *m.*

firkin, *n,* barillet, *m*; *Meas.* = 9 or 8 gallons.

firm†, *a,* ferme; solide; consistant; tenu. ¶ *n,* maison [de commerce]; société [en

nom collectif] *f.* ~ [*name*], rais[.........] [sociale] *f.* ~s *capital,* capital social, [.......]

firmament, *n,* firmament, *m.*

firmness, *n,* fermeté, assiette, solidité; co[.......] sistance; tenue, *f.*

first, *a,* premier; (*after* 20, 30, &c) unièm[.......] (*cousins*) germain. ~ *aid,* premiers soin[.......] *m.pl.* ~ *appearance & ~ work,* or [.......] *book,* début, *m.* to make one's ~ appea[.......] *ance,* débuter. ~ *attempt,* coup d'essai, [.......] ~-born, premier-né, *m.* 1st *class,* [.......] classe, *f.* the ~ *comer,* le premier ven[.......] la première venue. F~ *Commissioner* [.......] *Works* (*Eng.*), ministre des Trava[.......] publics (*Fr.*) *m.* ~ *cut,* entame, [.......] ~ *edition,* édition originale, é. princeps, [.......] ~ *finger,* index, *m.* ~ [*floor*], premi[.......] [étage] *m.* ~-*fruits,* prémices, *f.pl.* F~ *Lord of the Admiralty* (Eng.), ministre [.......] la Marine (*Fr.*) *m.* ~ *match* (opp. retur[.......] *match*), match aller, *m.* ~-*rate,* de pre[.......] mier ordre; fameux. ¶ *ad,* premièremen[.......] primo. ~, *at* ~, *at* ~, [tout] d'abord, [.......] de premier abord, de prime abord. ~ [.......] *foremost,* en premier. *the ~ first,* le premie[.......] la première. *the 1st January,* le 1[.......] janvier. ~ *of exchange,* première d[.......] *change, f.* ~-*ly, ad,* premièrement, prim[.......]

firth, *n,* estuaire, *m.*

fiscal, *a,* fiscal. ~ *system,* fiscalité, *f.*

fish, *n,* poisson, *m.* ~-*bone,* arête, *f.* ~bow[.......] bocal, *m.* ~ *glue,* colle de poisson, [.......] ~hook, hameçon, *m.* ~ *kettle,* poisson[.......] nière, *f.* ~ *market,* halle aux poissons[.......] poissonnerie, *f.* [*wet*] ~ *merchant* [.......] *salesman,* marchand de marée, mareyeu[.......] *m.* ~-*monger,* poissonnier, ère. ~ ou[.......] *of water* (*pers.*), déraciné, e. ~[*plate*[.......] (*Rly*), éclisse, *f.* ~ *pond,* vivier, *m.* [.......] *shop,* poissonnerie, *f.* ~ *slice,* truelle [.......] poisson, *f.* ~ *spear,* fouine, *f,* trident, *m*[.......] ~ *train* (*Rly*), train de marée, *m.* ~wife[.......] poissarde, harengère, *f.* ¶ *v.i. & t. &* [.......] *for,* pêcher. ~ *out,* ~ *up,* [re]pêcher[.......] ~[*plate*], *v.t,* éclisser. ~erman, *n,* pê[.......] cheur, euse. ~ery, *n,* pêche; (*ground*) pêcherie, *f.* ~ing (*act or right*) *n,* pêche, *f*[.......] ~ *boat,* bateau de pêche, *m.* ~ *ground* [.......] parage de pêche, *m,* pêcherie, *f.* ~ *rod*[.......] canne à pêche, gaule, *f.* ~ *tackle,* engins [.......] de pêche, *m,* harnais de p., *m.* ~y, *a*[.......] sauvagin; (*fig.*) véreux.

fissure, *n,* fissure, fente, *f.* ¶ *v.t,* fendiller.

fist, *n,* poing, *m.* **fisticuffs,** *n.pl,* coup[s] de poing, *m.[pl.].*

fistula, *n,* fistule, *f.*

fit, *a,* propre, bon, apte, convenable, approprié, à propos; capable; dispos, frais. ~ *for service,* valide. *to keep* ~ (athletics)[.......] rester en forme. ¶ *n,* accès, *m,* attaque[.......] crise, boutade, bouffée, *f*; (*Mech.*) montage, *m.* ~ *of coughing,* quinte [de toux] *f.* by ~s & starts, par sauts & par bonds[.......] par boutades, à bâtons rompus.

ajuster, adapter, agencer, aménager; cadrer; monter; épouser [la forme de]; chausser; botter; coiffer; (v.i.) s'ajuster, &c; aller. ~ in, emboîter, enclaver. ~ out, équiper, armer, outiller. ~ tightly, coller. ~ up, agencer. **fitful**, a, changeant; agité; saccadé; quinteux. **fitly**, ad, convenablement. **fitness**, n, convenance, aptitude, f. fitted case, mallette garnie, f. **fitter**, n, ajusteur, monteur, appareilleur, m; (clothes) essayeur, euse. **fitting†**, a, convenable. ~s, n.pl, armature, f; garnitures; ferrures, f.pl; appareillage, m. ~ [& fixtures], agencement, m.

ve, a. & n, cinq, a. & m. ~-finger exercise, exercice de doigté, m. ~ [games] all (Ten.), à deux de jeux. ~ year plan, plan quinquennal, m. ~s, n, la balle au mur.

x, n, fixer, assujettir, asseoir; ancrer; arrêter. ~ed†, a, fixe; à demeure. ~ (rate of) exchange, le certain. ~-focus camera, chambre à foyer fixe, f. ~ salary, fixe, m. ~ing, n, fixage, m, fixation, pose, f. ~ & toning bath, bain de virage-fixage, m. ~ [solution] (Phot.), fixateur, m. **fixture**, n, pièce fixe, p. à demeure, f; engagement, m. ~s & fittings, agencement, m.

zz[le], v.i, pétiller. fizzle out, n'aboutir à rien.

abbergast, v.t, atterrer, ébahir.

abbiness & **flaccidity**, n, flaccidité, mollesse, f. **flabby** & **flaccid**, a, flasque, mollasse, avachi, mou, veule.

lag, n, drapeau, pavillon, m; (pl.) pavois, (Bot.) iris des marais, m. ~ of truce, (Mil.) drapeau parlementaire; (Nav.) pavillon p. ~ship, [vaisseau] amiral, m. ~staff, mât de pavillon, m. ~[stone], dalle, f. ¶ v.t, daller; (v.i.) fléchir; faiblir; languir; tomber; traîner.

agellate, v.t, flageller.

ageolet, n, flageolet, m.

agitious, a, scélérat, infâme.

lagon, n, flacon, m, bouteille [lenticulaire] (pour le vin) f.

lagrant, a, flagrant.

lail, n, fléau, m.

lair, n, aptitude, f, dispositions, f.pl.

lake, n, flocon, m; écaille; lame; lamelle; feuille; paillette; flammèche, f. ¶ v.i, floconner; s'écailler. **flaky**, a, floconneux; écailleux; feuilleté; laminé.

lame, n, flamme, feu, m. ~ thrower, lance-flamme, m. ¶ v.i, flamber, flamboyer; s'enflammer; (v.t.) flamber.

lamingo, n, flamant, m.

Flanders, n, la Flandre.

lange, n, bride, f; boudin; rebord; bourrelet; patin, m; aile, f. ¶ v.t, border.

lank, n, flanc, m. ¶ v.t, flanquer.

lannel, n, flanelle, f. ~ette, n, flanelle de coton, f, pilou, m.

flap, n, coup; clapet; bord; pan; abattant, m; trappe; patte; oreille, f. ¶ v.t. & i, battre, voltiger.

flare, n, feu, m, flamme, f; évasement, pavillon, m. ¶ v.i, flamber, flamboyer; (lamp) filer; (bellmouth) s'évaser.

flash, n, tapageur. ¶ n, jet; éclair; éclat; feu; trait, m; saillie, f. ~board, hausse, f. ~ in the pan (fig.), feu de paille. ~ lamp, (elec. torch) lampe de poche, l. électrique; (Phot.) lampe-éclair, f. ~ of light & ~ of lightning, éclair, m. ~[ing] point, point d'éclair, p. d'inflammabilité, m. ¶ v.i, étinceler; miroiter; éclater; jaillir; flamboyer.

flask, n, bouteille; gourde, f; flacon; m; ballon; m; fiole, f.

flat, a, plat; méplat; aplati; (nose) épaté; à plat; plan; géométral; couché; net, formel, catégorique; direct; fade, éventé; maussade; inactif; mat; (Mus.) bémol. ~ iron, fer à repasser, m. ~ race, course plate. ~ roof, toit en terrasse, m. terrasse, plate-forme, f. ¶ ad, à plat. ~ on one's face, à plat [ventre]. to sing ~, détonner. ¶ n, plat; méplat; (rooms) appartement; (plain, shoal) bas-fond, haut-fond, m, basse, f; (Theat.) châssis; (Mus.) bémol, m. ~ly, a, platement; nettement [tout] net, carrément. ~ness, n, aplatissement; (liquor) évent, m; fadeur; platitude, f. **flatten**, v.t, aplatir; éventer; affadir.

flatter, v.t, flatter, caresser. ~er, n, flatteur, euse. ~ing, a, flatteur. ~y, n, flatterie, f.

flatulence, -cy, n, flatulence, f. **flatus**, n, flatuosité, f, gaz, vent, m.

flaunt, v.t, étaler, faire parade de.

flautist, n, flûtiste, m,f.

flavour, n, saveur, f, goût, m. ¶ v.t, assaisonner. ~ing, n, assaisonnement, m.

flaw, n, paille, f, défaut, m, défectuosité; glace, f; crapaud; vice, m. ~less, a, sans défaut, net. ~y, a, pailleux.

flax, n, lin, m. ~ field, linière, f. ~en, a. & n, blond, a. & m.

flay, v.t, écorcher.

flea, n, puce, f. ~ bite, piqûre de puce, f.

fledged (to be), avoir sa plume. **fledg[e]ling**, n, oisillon, m.

flee, v.i. & t. ir, fuir, s'enfuir.

fleece, n, toison, f. ¶ v.t, tondre, plumer, écorcher, étriller. **fleecy**, a, floconneux. ~ clouds, sky fleeced with clouds, nuages moutonnés, m.pl, ciel moutonné, m.

fleet, n, flotte, f. ~ of foot, léger (ère) à la course. ~ing, a, passager, fugitif, fugace.

Fleming, n, Flamand, e. **Flemish**, a. & (language) n, flamand, a. & m.

flesh, n, chair, f; chairs, f.pl; charnure, f; (meat) viande, f; embonpoint, m. ~ brush, brosse à frictions, f. ¶ (Hunt.)

v.t, acharner. ~y, *a,* charnu; plantureux. ~ *part of the arm,* gras du bras, *m.*

flexible, *a,* flexible, souple. *to make* ~, assouplir. **flex[ible wire],** fil souple, *m.*

flexor, *a. & n,* fléchisseur, *a.m. & m.*

flick, *n,* chiquenaude, *f; (sound)* flic flac, *m; (brush)* balayette, *f,* houssoir, *m.*

flicker, *v.i,* papilloter, trembler, vaciller.

flight, *n,* fuite, *f;* vol, envol, *m,* volée; envolée, *f,* essor; élan; exode, *m;* bande, *f;* écart, *m.* ~ *of stairs,* volée d'escalier, *f.* ~ *of steps,* perron, *m.* ~y, *a,* volage, léger, étourdi, frivole.

flimsy, *a,* sans consistance, mollasse; frivole.

finch, *v.i,* défaillir, broncher.

fling, *n,* jet; trait, *m.* ¶ *v.t.ir,* jeter, lancer, darder. ~ *away &* ~ *off,* rejeter.

flint, *n,* silex; caillou, *m;* pierre à fusil; pierre [à briquet] *f.* ~ *& steel,* briquet, *m.* ~ *glass,* flint-glass, *m.* ~y, *a,* siliceux; caillouteux; de pierre.

flippant, *a,* leste.

flipper, *n,* bras, *m,* nageoire, *f.*

flirt *(pers.) n,* coquet, te. ¶ *v.i,* coqueter, flirter. ~**ation,** *n,* coquetterie, *f,* flirt, *m.*

flit, *v.i,* voleter, voltiger; fuir. ~ *about,* papillonner.

flitch, *n,* flèche *(de lard) f.*

float *& * ~**er,** *n,* flotte, *f;* flotteur; bouchon, *m.* ~[**board**], aube, palette, *f,* aileron, *m.* ~ *fishing,* pêche [à la ligne] flottante, *f.* ~ *gold,* or flottant, *m,* paillettes d'or, *f.pl.* ~ *ironing,* flotter repassant. ~ *plane,* hydravion à flotteurs, *m.* ¶ *v.t,* faire flotter; mettre à flot, renflouer; *(Fin.)* lancer; *(v.i.)* flotter; [sur]nager; *(Swim.)* faire la planche. ~**ation** *(Fin.) n,* lancement, *m.* ~**ing,** *a,* flottant.

flock, *n,* troupeau; vol, *m,* bande, troupe, *f;* ouailles, *f.pl; (wool, &c.)* flocon, *m;* bourre, *f.* ¶ *v.i,* s'assembler [en troupe]; affluer.

floe, *n,* glaçon, *m.* ~ *ice,* glace[s] flottante[s] *f.[pl.],* banc de glace, *m.*

flog, *v.t,* fouetter, fustiger, cravacher. *a flogging,* le fouet.

fiong *(Typ.) n,* flan, *m.*

flood, *n,* inondation, *f,* déluge; flot; torrent, *m;* crue, *f; (of the tide)* flux, *m.* ~**gate,** vanne; *(fig.)* écluse, *f.* ~ *lighting,* éclairage par projection, *m,* illumination par p., *f.* ~ *tide,* marée de flot, *f,* flot, *m.* ¶ *v.t,* inonder, noyer, submerger.

floor, *n,* plancher; parquet; carreau; carré, *m;* aire, *f;* plateau; chantier; tablier; *(storey)* étage, palier, *m.* *on one* ~ *(rooms),* de plain-pied. ~ *cloth,* linoléum, *m.* ~ *lamp,* lampe à pied, torchère, *f.* ~ *polisher, (pers.)* frotteur, *m; (Mach.)* cireuse, *f.* ~ *space,* surface des étages, *f;* encombrement, *m.* ¶ *v.t,* planchéier; parqueter; jeter par terre; terrasser, désarçonner.

flora, *n,* flore, *f.* **floral,** *a,* floral; fleuriste. ~ *design,* ramage, *m.* **florid,** *a,* fleuri;

rubicond. **Florida,** *n,* la Floride. **floris[t],** *n,* fleuriste, *m,f.*

floss, *n,* bourre, *f.* ~ *silk,* soie floche, filoselle, strasse, *f.*

flotation *(Fin.) n,* lancement, *m.*

flotilla, *n,* flottille, escadrille, *f.*

flotsam, *n,* épaves [flottantes] *f.pl.*

flounce, *n,* volant, *m.* ¶ *v.t,* garnir de volants. ~ *about,* se trémousser.

flounder *(fish) n,* flet, *m.* ¶ *v.i,* se débattre, barboter, patauger, patouiller.

flour, *n,* farine, *f.* ~ *dealer,* farinier, ère; ~ *merchant,* minotier, *m.* ~ *mill,* moulin à farine, *m,* minoterie, *f.*

flourish, *n,* fioriture, *f;* parafe, *m;* fanfare, *f; (of hand)* geste; *(with stick)* moulinet, *m.* ¶ *v.t,* brandir; *(v.i.)* fleurir; faire le moulinet. ~**ing,** *a,* florissant.

floury, *a,* farineux.

flout, *v.t,* narguer. ~ *at,* se railler de.

flow, *n,* écoulement; cours, *m;* coulée, *f;* flux; torrent, *m.* ~ *of words,* flux de paroles, *m,* faconde, *f.* ¶ *v.i,* couler; s'écouler, affluer.

flower, *n,* fleur, *f.* ~ *garden,* jardin fleuriste, *m.* ~ *girl,* bouquetière, *f.* ~ *holder,* porte-bouquet, *m.* ~ *market,* marché aux fleurs, *m.* ~ *pot,* pot à fleurs, *m.* ~ *show,* exposition de fleurs, e. florale, *f.* ~ *stand,* jardinière, *f.* ~ *wire,* fil carcasse des fleuristes, *m.* ~ *work,* fleurons, *m.pl.* ¶ *v.i,* fleurir. ~**et,** *n,* fleurette, *f.* ~**ing,** *a,* à fleurs. ¶ *n,* floraison, *f.* ~y, *a,* fleuri.

flowing, *a,* coulant, fluide; flottant, tombant.

fluctuate, *v.i,* osciller; flotter. **fluctuation,** *n,* fluctuation, oscillation, *f,* mouvement, *m.*

flue, *n,* tuyau; carneau; aspirail, *m.*

fluency, *n,* facilité, *f.* **fluent,** *a,* facile, disert. ~**ly,** *ad,* couramment.

fluff, *n,* bourre, *f;* coton, *m; (under furniture)* moutons; *(hair)* cheveux follets, *m.pl.* *to* ~ *up,* pelucher. ~y, *a,* duveté; follet; cotonneux; pelucheux.

flügel horn, bugle, *m.*

fluid, *a,* fluide. ¶ *n, (imponderable)* fluide; *(ponderable)* liquide, *m.* ~**ity,** *n,* fluidité, *f.*

fluke, *n, (anchor)* patte, *f;* coup de hasard, raccroc, *m.*

flummery, *n,* fadaises, *f.*

flunkey, *n,* laquais, valet de pied, larbin, *m.* ~**dom,** *n,* valetaille, *f.*

fluorescent, *a,* fluorescent. **fluorine,** *n,* fluor, *m.* *fluor spar,* spath fluor, *m.*

flurry, *n,* ahurissement; coup de vent, *m.* ¶ *v.t,* ahurir.

flush, *a,* à fleur, au ras, de niveau; noyé; lisse; bien pourvu. ¶ *n,* accès, transport; flot de sang, *m;* bouffée; rougeur; fleur; chasse [d'eau] *f; (Cards)* flux, *m.* ¶ *v.t,* affleurer; donner une chasse à, curer; *(v.i.)* rougir. ~**ed face,** face injectée, *f.*

Flushing, *n,* Flessingue, *f.*

...ster, *v.t*, ahurir, troubler; (*with drink*) griser.

...te, *n*, flûte; (*groove*) cannelure, *f.* ~ [*glass*], flûte, *f.* flutist, *n*, flûtiste, *m.f.*

...tter, *n*, battement; émoi, *m.* ¶ *v.i.* & *t*, voleter; voltiger; palpiter.

...ty, *a*, flûté.

...vial, fluviatile, *a*, fluvial, fluviatile.

...ux, *n*, flux; (*Chem. & Metall.*) fondant, *m.* ~', *n*, mouche; (*trouser*) braguette, *f.* ~*-blown*, piqué des mouches. ~*catcher* (*bird*), gobe-mouches, *m*, moucherolle, *f.* ~ *dirt*, chiure de mouche, *f.* ~ *fishing*, pêche à la mouche, *f.* ~*leaf*, garde blanche, *f.* ~ *line*, soie pour la pêche à la mouche, *f.* ~ *net*, chasse-mouches, *m*, émouchette, *f.* ~ *paper*, papier tue-mouches, *m.* ~ *press*, balancier, *m.* ~ *rod* (*Fish.*), canne à mouche, *f.* ~ *speck*, chiure, *f.* ~ *swat*[ter], tue-mouches. ~ *flap*, tue-mouches. ~ *trap* (plant), gobe-mouches, *m.* ~ *weight* (*Box.*), poids mouche, *m.* ~ *wheel*, volant, *m.* ~ *whisk*, chasse-mouches, émouchoir, *m.* ¶ *v.i.ir*, voler, s'envoler; [s'en]fuir; dénicher; éclater; sauter; jaillir; (*v.t.ir*) fuir; (*flag*) battre; (*kite*) lancer. ~ *about*, voltiger. ~ *at*, s'élancer sur; sauter à; s. sur; apostropher; voler. ~ (*spring*) *back*, faire ressort. ~ *open*, s'ouvrir en coup de vent. ~*er*, *n*, aviateur, trice. ~*ing*, *n*, vol, *m*; aviation, *f.* ~ *ace*, as de l'aviation, *m.* ~ *boat*, hydravion à coque, *m.* ~ *bomb*, avion-bombe, *m.* ~ *buttress*, arc-boutant, *m.* ~ *column*, colonne mobile, *f.* ~ *fish*, poisson volant, *m.* ~ *ground*, champ d'aviation, *m.* ~ *squad*, brigade (*Motor Racing*) mille lancé, *m.* ~ *squad*, brigade (*de police*) automobile, *f.* ~ *start*, départ lancé, *m.* ~ *visit*, camp volant, *m.*

...oal, *n*, poulain, *m*, pouliche, *f*; (*ass's*) ânon, *m.* ¶ *v.i.*, pouliner, mettre bas.

...oam, *n*, écume, mousse, *f.* ¶ *v.i.*, écumer, mousser; (*sea*) moutonner. ~*y*, *a*, écumeux, mousseux; (*sea*) moutonneuse.

...ocal, *a*, focal. ~*-plane camera*, chambre à obturateur de plaque, *f.* **focus**, *n*, foyer, *m.* ¶ *v.t.*, mettre au point; canaliser (*fig.*). **focussing**, *p.a:* ~ *camera*, chambre à mise au point, *f.* ~ *screen*, châssis pour la mise au p., *m.*

...odder, *n*, fourrage, *m*, provende, *f.*

...oe, *n*, ennemi, e, adversaire, *m.*

...oetus, *n*, fœtus, *m.*

...og, *n*, brouillard, *m*, brume, *f*; (*Phot.*) voile, *m.* ~ *horn*, trompe de brume, *f.* ~ *signal*, signal de brume; pétard, *m.* ¶ *v.t*, embrumer; (*Phot.*) voiler. **foggy**, *a*, brumeux.

...og[e]y, *n.* or *old* ~, croûton, *m*, [vieille] ganache. [vieille] perruque, *f.* **fogyish**, *a*, encroûté.

...oible, *n*, faible, *m.*

...oil, *n*, (*tinsel*) feuille, *f*, clinquant; paillon; tain; (*Fenc.*) fleuret; (*fig.*) repoussoir, lustre,

m. ¶ *v.t*, déjouer; dépister. ~*ed choco-lates*, papillotes, *f.pl.*

foist, *v.t*, glisser; colloquer; attribuer.

fold, *n*, pli, repli; parc, *m*, bergerie, *f*; (*Relig.*) bercail, *m.* ¶ *v.t*, plier; (*arms*) [se] croiser; (*hands*) joindre; (*sheep*) parquer. ~ *up*, *v.t*, [re]plier; (*v.i.*) se replier. ~*er*, *n*, plieur, euse; chemise [pour dossier] *f*; (*Publicity*) dépliant, *m*; (*child's mail cart*) chaise pliante, *f*; (*pl.*) pince-nez, *m.* ~*ing*, *p.a*: ~ *camera*, chambre pliante, *f.* ~ *door*, porte brisée, *f.* ~ *machine*, machine à plier, plieuse, *f.* ~ *pram*, landau pliant, *m.*

foliaceous, *a*, foliacé. **foliage**, *n*, feuillage, *m*, frondaison, *f*, ombrage, *m*, chevelure, *f.* **foliate**, *a*, feuillé. **foliation**, *n*, foliation, feuillaison, frondaison, *f.*

folio, *n*, folio, *m*; (*book*) *n. & a*, in-folio, *m. & a.* ¶ *v.t*, folioter.

folklore, *n*, folk-lore, *m*, tradition, *f.* **folks**, *n.pl*, gens, *m.pl. & f.pl.*

follicle, *n*, follicule, *m*, crypte, *f.*

follow, *v.t*, suivre; (*Cards*) fournir de; (*v.i.*) s'ensuivre, résulter. ~ *suit*, (*Cards*) fournir [à] la couleur demandée; (*fig.*) faire de même. ~ *through*, suivre la balle. ~ *up*, [pour]suivre. ~ [*shot*] (*Bil.*) *n*, coulé, *m.* ~*er*, *n*, suivant, e; disciple, partisan, sectateur, *m*; suite [de lettre] *f.* ~*ing*, (*day, &c.*) *a*, suivant. *in the* ~ *manner*, & voici comment. *the* ~ [*persons*], les personnes dont les noms suivent. *the* ~ *story*, l'histoire que voici. ¶ *n*, partisans, *m.pl.*

folly, *n*, folie; sottise, bêtise, *f.*

foment, *v.t*, fomenter; étuver. ~*ation*, *n*, fomentation, *f.*

fond†, *a*, tendre, affectueux. *to be* ~ *of*, aimer; affectionner; être friand de, ê. gourmand de; ê. porté pour; ê. amateur de.

fondle, *v.t*, caresser, câliner, pouponner. **fondness**, *n*, affection, tendresse, *f*; penchant, goût, *m.*

font, *n*, (*Eccl.*) fonts, *m.pl*; (*Typ.*) fonte, *f.*

food, *n*, nourriture, *f*, aliment, *m*, vivres, *m.pl*; mangeaille, *f*, mets, *m*; table, cuisine; pâture, *f.* ~ & *drink*, le boire & le manger. ~ *controller*, organisateur du ravitaillement, *m.* ~ *for thought*, matière à réflexion, *f.* ~*stuff*, matière d'alimentation, denrée alimentaire, *f.*

fool, *n*, sot, le; bête, *f*; imbécile, *m.f*, idiot, e; plaisant, *m*; (*Hist., court*) fou, *m.* *to play the* ~, faire l'imbécile, nigauder, niaiser. ~*hardiness*, témérité, *f.* ~*hardy*, téméraire. ~*proof*, à l'épreuve des maladresses. ¶ *v.t*, duper; jouer, amuser. ~ [*about*]. *v.i*, baguenauder. ~*ery*, *n*, farce, *f*, vains propos, *m.pl*, pantalonnade, *f*, calembredaines, *f.pl*, bouffonnerie, *f*; badinage, *m*, gaminerie, *f.* ~*ish*†, *a*, sot, bête, benêt. ~*ishness*, *n*, folie, sottise, *f.*

foot, *n*, pied, *m*; patte; semelle; base, *f*; bas, *m*; infanterie, *f*; (*Meas.*) pied = 0·30480 metre. ~ & *mouth disease*, fièvre aphteuse, *f*. ~*ball*, ballon de football; (*game*) football, *m*. ~ *bath*, bain de pieds, *m*. ~*board*, marchepied, *m*. ~*bridge*, passerelle, *f*. ~*fall*, pas, *m*. ~*fault* (*Ten.*), faute de pied, *f*. ~*hill*, avant-mont, *m*. ~*hold*, assiette pour le pied, *f*, pied, *m*. ~*lights*, rampe, *f*. ~*man*, valet de pied, laquais, *m*. ~*note*, apostille, *f*. ~*pad*, détrousseur, *m*. ~ *passenger*, piéton, *m*. ~*path*, sentier, *m*, sente, *f*; (*street*) trottoir, *m*. ~*print*, empreinte de pas, e. du pied, *f*, pas, vestige, *m*; trace, *f*. ~*race*, course à pied, *f*. ~*sore*, éclopé. ~*step*, pas, *m*, trace, *f*, (*pl.*) brisées (*fig.*), erres (*fig.*) *f.pl.* ~*stool*, tabouret [de pied] *m*. ~ *warmer*, chauffe-pieds, *m*, chaufferette, bouillotte, *f*. ~*wear*, chaussures, *f.pl.* ~ *work*, jeu de jambes, *m*. *on* ~, à pied, pédestrement. ~*ing*, *n*, pied, *m*; assiette pour le pied, *f*; (*Build.*) empattement, *m*; (*to pay for*) bienvenue, *f*.

fop, *n*, fat, petit-maître, *m*. **foppish**, *a*, fat.

for, *pr*, pour; par; à; de; à cause de; pendant; il y a; depuis; malgré. ~ *all that*, malgré cela, malgré tout. ~ *& against*, le pour & le contre. ¶ *c*, car.

forage, *n*, fourrage, *m*. ~ *cap*, bonnet de police, calot, *m*. ¶ *v.i*, fourrager; (*bird*) picorer. **forager**, *n*, fourrageur, *m*.

forasmuch, *c*, étant donné.

foray, *n*, incursion, razzia, maraude, *f*.

forbear, *v.i.ir*, s'abstenir, s'empêcher. ~*ance*, *n*, indulgence, longanimité, mansuétude, *f*.

forbid, *v.t.ir*, défendre, interdire. *God* ~! à Dieu ne plaise! **forbidding**, *a*, rebutant, repoussant.

force, *n*, force, *f*; effort; effectif, *m*; armée, *f*. ~ *of circumstances*, force des choses. *by* ~, à main armée. *in* ~, en vigueur. ~ *pump*, pompe foulante, *f*. ¶ *v.t*, forcer; hâter; se frayer. **forced**, *p.a*, forcé; factice. *by* ~ *marches*, à grandes journées. **forcedly**, *ad*, forcément. **forceful†**, *a*, vigoureux. **forcemeat**, *n*, farce, *f*.

forceps, *n.s. & pl*, (*Surg.*) pince, *f*; (*dental*) dâvier; (*obstetrical*) forceps, *m*, fers, *m.pl.*

forcible, *a*, énergique, corsé. ~ *feeding*, gavage, *m*. **forcibly**, *ad*, énergiquement; de force. *forcing bed*, forcerie, *f*. *forcing frame*, châssis de couche, *m*, bâche, *f*.

ford, *n*, gué, *m*. ¶ *v.t*, guéer. ~*able*, *a*, guéable.

fore, *a*, de devant, *e.g*, ~*paw*, patte de devant, *f*; (*Naut.*) de l'avant. ¶ *ad*, à l'avant. ~ *& aft*, de l'avant à l'arrière. ¶ (*Golf*) *i*, attention!, hep!, balle! ¶ *n*, devant; (*Naut.*) avant, *m*.

forearm, *n*, avant-bras, *m*. ¶ *v.t*, prémunir.

forebode, *v.t*, présager. **foreboding**, *n*, présage, pressentiment, *m*.

forecaddie, *n*, cadet éclaireur, *m*.

forecast, *n*, prévision, *f*. ¶ *v.t.ir*, prévoir.

forecastle *or* **foc's'le**, *n*, gaillard d'avant, poste de l'équipage, *m*.

foreclose, *v.t*, saisir. **foreclosure**, *n*, saisie, *f*.

forecourt, *n*, (*house*) cour de devant; (*castle, palace*) avant-cour, *f*.

fore edge *or* **foredge** (*book*) *n*, tranche vert[ic]ale, gouttière, *f*.

forefathers, *n.pl*, aïeux, *m.pl.*

forefinger, *n*, index, *m*.

foregoing, *p.a*, précédent. *the* ~, ce qui pré[cè]de. *foregone conclusion*, décision pris[e] d'avance, *f*.

foreground, *n*, premier plan, *m*, devant[s] *m.pl.*

forehand [**stroke**] (*Ten.*) *n*, [coup d']avant[-]main, *m*.

forehead, *n*, front, *m*.

foreign, *a*, étranger; extérieur; exotique. ~ *exchange rates* (table), cote des changes, *f*. ~*going ship*, navire au long cours, long-courrier, *m*. ~ *note paper*, papie[r] pelure, *m*. F~ *Office* (Eng.), Ministère (o[u] département) des Affaires étrangères (Fr.) *m*. ~*er*, *n*, étranger, ère.

foreknowledge, *n*, prescience, *f*.

foreland, *n*, cap, *m*, pointe [de terre] *f*.

forelock (*hair*) *n*, toupet, *m*.

foreman, *n*, contremaître, chef d'équipe[,] chef, *m*. ~ *of job* (*Build.*), conducteu[r] des travaux, *m*. ~ *of the jury*, chef d[u] jury.

foremast, *n*, mât de misaine, *m*.

foremost (**the**), le plus avancé; le tout premier[.]

forenoon, *n*, matinée, *f*.

forensic, *a*, de palais; (*medicine*) légale.

forerunner, *n*, avant-coureur, précurseur, *m*[,] préface, *f*.

foresee, *v.t.ir*, prévoir.

foreshadow, *v.t*, annoncer.

foreshore, *n*, rivage, *m*.

foreshorten, *v.t*, raccourcir.

foresight, *n*, prévoyance, *f*; (*gun*) guidon, *m*.

forest, *n*, forêt, *f*; (*att.*) forestier.

forestall, *v.t*, anticiper; prévenir; devancer.

forester, *n*, (*officer*) forestier; habitant de la forêt, *m*. **forestry**, *n*, sylviculture, *f*.

foretaste, *n*, avant-goût, *m*.

foretell, *v.t.ir*, prédire, annoncer.

forethought, *n*, prévoyance; préméditation, *f*[.]

forewarn, *v.t*, prévenir, prémunir, avertir.

forewoman, *n*, première, *f*.

foreword, *n*, avant-propos, *m*, préface, *f*.

forfeit, *n*, dédit, *m*, pénalité, *f*; (*at play*) gage[,] *m*, pénitence, *f*; (*pl.*) gages, jeux innocents[,] petits jeux, *m.pl.* ¶ *v.t*, déchoir de[;] (*honour*) forfaire à. ~*ure*, *n*, déchéance, *f*[.]

forgather, *v.i*, se réunir.

forge, *n*, forge, *f*. ¶ *v.t*, (*metal & fig.*) for[ger]; falsifier, contrefaire. ~*d*, *p.a*, faux.

forgeman, *n*, forgeur, *m*. **forger**, *n*, faus[saire, *m.f*, fabricateur, trice. **forgery**, *n*[,] faux; crime de faux, *m*; contrefaçon, *f*.

rget, *v.t.ir*, oublier; désapprendre. ~*-me-not*, ne m'oubliez pas, myosotis, *m*, oreille-de-souris, *f*. ~ *oneself*, s'échapper, s'émanciper. ~ful, *a*, oublieux. ~ful-ness, *n*, oubli, *m*.

rgive, *v.t.ir*, pardonner; (*pers.*) pardonner à; faire grâce à, remettre. ~ness, *n*, pardon, *m*; rémission; remise, *f*.

rgo, *v.t.ir*, s'abstenir de; renoncer à.

rk, *n*, fourche; (*table, &c.*) fourchette, *f*; (*tree*) fourchon, *m*; (*road, &c.*) bifurcation, *f*. ¶ *v.i*, fourcher, bifurquer. ~ed, *a*, fourchu. ~ *lightning*, éclair ramifié, *m*.

rlorn, *a*, délaissé; désolé, inconsolé. ~ *hope*, vague espoir, *m*; (*Mil.*) enfants perdus, *m.pl*.

rm, *n*, forme, *f*, ton, *m*; (*paper*) formule, *f*, bulletin, *m*; (*school*) classe, *f*; (*seat*) banc; (*hare*) gîte, *m*. ¶ *v.t*, former; façonner; constituer; nouer; faire; se faire, se former. ~ *fours*, se mettre par quatre. ~ *single file*, dédoubler les rangs. ~ *two deep*, se mettre sur deux rangs. ~al†, *a*, formel; de forme; dans les formes; céré-monieux; solennel; formaliste. ~ality, *n*, formalité, *f*. ~ation, *n*, formation; constitution, *f*. form[e] (*Typ.*) *n*, forme, *f*.

rmer, *a*, ancien; passé; précédent. *the* ~, celui-là. ~ly, *ad*, autrefois, jadis, ancienne-ment, ci-devant.

rmidable†, *a*, formidable.

Formosa, *n*, Formose, *f*.

rmula, *n*, formule, *f*. ~ry, *n*, formulaire, *m*. formulate, *v.t*, formuler. formulism, *n*, le style pompier. formulist, *n. & ~ic*, *a*, pompier, *m. & att*.

rnication, *n*, fornication, *f*.

rsake, *v.t.ir*, délaisser; abandonner.

rsooth, *ad*, en vérité, ma foi.

rswear, *v.t.ir*, abjurer. ~ *oneself*, se parjurer.

fort, *n*, fort, (*small*) fortin, *m*. forte (*Mus.*) *ad*, forte. ¶ (*strong point*) *n*, fort, *m*.

forth, *ad*, en avant. ~coming, *a*, [prêt] à paraître; à venir; prochain. ~with, *ad*, in-cessamment, sur-le-champ, séance tenante.

fortieth, *a. & n*, quarantième, *a. & m.f*.

fortification, *n*, fortification, *f*; (*wine*) vinage, *m*. fortify, *v.t*, fortifier; munir; corser; viner. fortified place, place forte, p. de guerre, *f*. fortitude, *n*, force d'âme, *f*, courage, *m*.

fortnight, *n*, quinze jours, *m.pl*, quinzaine, *f*. ~ly, *ad*, tous les quinze jours.

fortress, *n*, forteresse, *f*.

fortuitous†, *a*, fortuit.

fortunate, *a*, heureux, fortuné. ~ly, *ad*, heureusement, par bonheur. fortune, *n*, fortune, *f*; horoscope, *m*. *to tell* ~s, dire la bonne aventure. ~ *teller*, diseur (euse) de bonne aventure; tireur (euse) de cartes, cartomancien, ne.

forty, *a. & n*, quarante, *a. & m*.

forum, *n*, forum, *m*.

forward, *a*, avancé; d'avance; avant; pro-gressif; précoce, hâtif; hardi, indiscret; (*Com.*) à terme, à livrer. ~[s], *ad*, [en] avant. ¶ *n*, (*Com.*) livrable; (*Foot.*) avant, *m*. ¶ *v.t*, avancer; hâter; expédier; acheminer; faire suivre, transmettre. ~ing *agent*, commissionnaire de trans-port[s], expéditeur, *m*. ~ness, *n*, pré-cocité; hardiesse, *f*.

fossil, *a. & n*, fossile, *a. & m*.

foster, *v.t*, encourager; favoriser; nourrir. ~ *brother*, frère de lait, *m*. ~ *child*, nour-risson, *m*.

foul, *a*, sale; crasseux; immonde; mauvais, vilain; infect; vicié; fétide; puant; in-fâme; (*words*) gros. ~-breathed, *a*, punais. ~-mouthed, mal embouché. ~ *play*, vilain tour; sabotage, *m*. ¶ *n*, faute, *f*; coup déloyal, *m*. ~ *cup*, coquille pro-tectrice, *f*. ¶ *v.t*, salir, souiller, encrasser; vicier; fausser; (*Naut., rope, &c.*) engager; (*ship*) aborder. ~ness, *n*, fétidité; noir-ceur, *f*.

found, *v.t*, fonder, créer; (*metal*) fondre, mouler. foundation, *n*, fondation, *f*; fondement; établissement, *m*; assiette, assise, *f*. ~ *scholar*, boursier, ère. ~ *stone*, pierre fondamentale, première p., *f*. founder, *n*, fondateur, créateur; (*race*) au-teur, *m*; (*family*) souche, *f*; (*metal*) fondeur, *m*. ~'s *share*, part de fondateur, *f*. ¶ *v.i*, sombrer, couler, c. à fond, c. à pic, c. bas. foundered (*Vet.*) *p.a*, fourbu.

foundling, *n*, enfant trouvé, *m*.

foundress, *n*, fondatrice, créatrice, *f*.

foundry, *n*, fonderie, *f*.

fount, *n*, fontaine, *f*; puits, *m*; (*Typ.*) fonte, *f*.

fountain, *n*, fontaine, source, *f*; jet d'eau, *m*; (*pl.*) [grandes] eaux, *f.pl*. ~-head, source, *f*. ~ *of youth*, fontaine de Jou-vence. ~ *pen*, stylographe, porte-plume [à] réservoir, *m*. ~ *pen ink*, encre stylo-graphique, *f*.

four, *a. & n*, quatre, *a. & m*. ~fold, qua-druple. ~footed, quadrupède. ~-poster, lit à colonnes, *m*. ~score, *a. & n*, quatre-vingts, quatre-vingt, *a. & m*. ~some (*Golf*), partie double, *f*. ~-wheel brake, frein sur les quatre roues, *m*. ~-wheeled, à quatre roues. ~-wheeler, fiacre, *m*. ~ *yards penalty line* (*Water Polo*), ligne de position, *f*. *on all* ~s, à quatre pattes.

fourteen, *a. & n*, quatorze, *a. & m*. ~th†, *a. & n*, quatorzième, *a. & m.f*; quatorze, *m*.

fourth†, *a*, quatrième. ~ *finger*, petit doigt, [doigt] auriculaire, *m*. ¶ *n*, qua-trième, *m.f*; quatre, *m*; (*part*) quart, *m*; (*Mus.*) quarte, *f*.

fowl, *n*, oiseau; o. de basse-cour, *m*; volaille; poule; poularde, *f*. ~ *house*, poulailler, *m*. ~er, *n*, oiseleur, *m*. ~ing, *n*, chasse aux oiseaux, *f*. ~ *piece*, canardière, *f*.

fox, *n*, renard, *m*. ~ *cub*, renardeau, *m*. ~ *earth*, ~'s *hole*, renardière, *f*. ~glove, gantelée, digitale, *f.* ~*hound*, fox-hound, *m.* ~ *hunting*, chasse au renard, *f.* ~ *terrier*, fox-terrier, *m.* ~ *trot*, fox-trot, *m.* ~**y** (*fig.*) *a*, rusé.

foyer, *n*, foyer [du public] *m.*

fraction, *n*, fraction, *f.* ~**al**, *a*, fractionnaire.

fractious, *a*, hargneux.

fracture, *n*, fracture; cassure, rupture, *f.* ¶ *v.t*, fracturer.

fr[a]enum, *n*, frein, filet, *m.*

fragile, *a*, fragile. **fragility**, *n*, fragilité, *f.*

fragment, *n*, fragment, morceau, éclat, *m.* ~**ary**, *a*, fragmentaire.

fragrance, *n*, bonne odeur, *f*, parfum, *m.* **fragrant**, *a*, odoriférant, odorant.

frail, *a*, frêle; fragile; caduc. ¶ *n*, cabas, *m*; bourriche, *f.* ~**ty**, *f*, fragilité; infirmité, *f.*

frame & ~*work*, *n*, cadre; bâti; châssis; *m*; charpente; membrure; ossature; carcasse; armature; monture; châsse, *f*; pan, *m*; case, *f*; (*Need.*) métier, *m.* ~ *aerial*, cadre, *m.* ~ *of mind*, état d'esprit, *m*, disposition, *f.* *connected to* ~ (*Elec.*), à la masse. ¶ *v.t*, former; charpenter; (*picture*, *&c.*) encadrer. **framing** (*act*) *n*, encadrement, *m.*

France, *n*, la France.

franchise, *n*, droit électoral, électorat, *m.*

Franciscan, *n*, franciscain, *m.*

Francophil[e], *a.* & *n*, francophile, *a.* & *m,f.* Francophobe, *a.* & *n*, francophobe, *a.* & *m,f.*

frank†, *a*, franc, ouvert, en dehors. ~**ness**, *n*, franchise, rondeur, *f.*

Frankfort, *n*, Francfort, *m.*

frankincense, *n*, encens mâle, *m.*

frantic, *a*, frénétique; effréné, fou.

fraternal†, *a*, fraternel. **fraternity**, *n*, fraternité, *f.* **fraternize**, *v.i*, fraterniser. **fratricide**, *n*. & **fratricidal**, *a*, fratricide, *m.* & *a.*

fraud, *n*, fraude; supercherie, *f.* **fraudulent†**, *a*, frauduleux.

fraught with, plein de, gros de.

fray, *n*, lutte, rixe, bagarre; bataille, *f.*

fray, *v.t*, érailler, effranger, effilocher.

freak, *n*, caprice, *m.* ~ [*of nature*], monstruosité, *f*, jeu [bizarre] de la nature, phénomène, *m.* ~**ish†**, *a*, capricieux; bizarre; hétéroclite; monstrueux.

freckle, *n*, tache de rousseur, lentille, éphélide, *f.* ¶ *v.t*, tacheter de rousseurs.

free, *a*, libre; ouvert; large; débarrassé; dépourvu; exempt; vierge; privé; franc; gratuit; net; indépendant; quitte; dégagé; désinvolte; décolleté; cru, vert. ~ *allowance of luggage* or *weight allowed* ~, franchise de bagages, f. de poids, *f.* ~ & *bonded warehouses*, magasins généraux-entrepôts, *m.pl.* ~ & *easy*, sans gêne, bohème, cavalier. ~ & *easy manner*, désinvolture, *f*. *in a* ~ & *easy way*, en pantoufles. ~*board*, franc-bord, *m.* ~*booter*, flibustier, *m.* ~ *copy*, spécimen, *m.* ~ *fight*, mêlée générale, *f.* ~ *gift* (*Relig.*), gratuité, *f.* ~ *hand* (*fig.*), carte blanche, *f.* ~*hand drawing*, dessin à

main levée, *m.* ~ *lance*, franc-tire tirailleur, *m.* *the* ~ *list* (*Theat.*), entrées de faveur, *f.pl.* ~*mason*, fran maçon, *m.* ~*masonry*, franc-maçonner *f.* ~ *pass*, billet de faveur; (*Rly*) pern de circulation, *m.* ~*stone*, pierre franch *f.* ~*thinker*, libre penseur, esprit fort, ~*thinking*, ~ *thought*, libre pensée, *f.* ~ *trade*, libre-échange, *m.* ~ *trader*, libr échangiste, *m.* ~ *verse*, vers libres, m. ~ *warehouse*, magasin général, *m.* ~ *wheel*, roue libre, *f.* ~ *will*, [plein] gr (*Philos.*) libre (*ou* franc) arbitre, *m.* ¶ *gratis*; gracieusement; franco; en franchis ~ *on board*, franco [à] bord. [~] *on ra* franco wagon, f. gare, sur wagon. ¶ *v* libérer, affranchir; dégager; exempte **freedom**, *n*, liberté; exemption; franchis aisance, *f.* ~ [*dom of*] *speech*, lib parole, liberté de parler, *f.* **freely**, *a* librement; franchement; largement.

freeze, *v.t.ir*, geler, glacer, congeler, réfrigére (*v.i.ir*) geler; se g., [se] glacer, prendr **freezer**, *n*, glacière; sorbetière, *f.* *freezi point*, température de congélation, (thermometer) *at freezing*, à glace.

Freiburg (*Baden*) *n*, Fribourg-en-Brisgau, *n*

freight, *n*, fret, m. ¶ *v.t*, fréter.

French, *a*, français. ~ *ambassador*, *consu* ambassadeur, consul, de France, *m.* ~ *beans*, haricots; (*unripe*) haricots vert *m.pl.* ~ *chalk*, talc, *m.* ~ *Derby*, pri du Jockey-Club, *m.* ~ *horn*, cor d'har monie, *m.* *to take* ~ *leave*, filer à l'ar glaise. ~ *lesson*, master, leçon, *f*, pro fesseur, m, de français. ~*man*, ~*woma* Français, e. ~ *nail*, pointe de Paris, clou de P., m. ~ *polish*, n, vernis a tampon, m; (*v.t.*) vernir au t. ~*speakin Switzerland*, la Suisse romande. ~ *window*, porte-fenêtre, *f.* ¶ (*language*) *le français. the* ~, *pl*, les Français *m.pl.* **Frenchify**, *v.t*, franciser.

frenzied, *p.p*, frénétique; délirant. **frenzy**, *r* frénésie, fureur, ivresse, *f.*

frequency, *n*, fréquence, *f.* **frequent**, *a*, fré quent. ¶ *v.t*, fréquenter, pratiquer, han ter, courir. ~**er**, *n*, habitué, e, coureur euse. ~**ly**, *ad*, fréquemment.

fresco, *n*, fresque, *f.*

fresh, *a*, frais; récent, vert; reposé; nouveau novice. ~ *from school*, frais émoulu d collège. ~ *from the wash*, blanc de lessive ~*man*, conscrit, *m.* ~ *paragraph*, alinéa *m.* ~ *water*, eau fraîche; (*not salt*) e douce, *f.* ~*water fishing*, pêche en eaux douces, p. d'eau douce, *f.* ~**en**, *v.t.* & rafraîchir; (*Naut.*) fraîchir. ~**et**, n, crue, *grandes eaux, f.pl.* ~**ly** & ~*ad*, fraîche ment; (*with p.p.*) frais, aîche, e.g, *fresh*[*ly gathered roses*, des roses fraîches cueillies ~**ness**, *n*, fraîcheur; nouveauté; primeur, *f*

fret, *n*, (*on guitar*, *&c.*) touche; (*Arch.*, *Her.* frette, *f.* ~*saw*, *n*, scie à découper, *f.*

(*v.t. & i.*) découper. ~-*work*, découpure, *f.*
¶ *v.i*, s'irriter, se chagriner, geindre; (*v.t.*)
ronger; chagriner, tracasser. ~**ful**, *a*,
chagrin, geignard.

friable, *a*, friable.

friar, *n*, moine, frère, religieux, *m.* ~**y**, *n*,
maison, *f.*

friction, *n*, friction, *f*, frottement, *m.*

Friday, *n*, vendredi, *m.*

fried fish, poisson frit, *m*, friture, *f.*

friend, *n*, ami, e; cousin, e. ~**less**, *a*, sans
ami. ~**liness**, *n*, bienveillance, *f.* ~**ly**,
a, ami, amical, amiable. ~ *society*,
société de secours mutuels, *f.* ~**ship**, *n*,
amitié, camaraderie, *f.*

Friesland, *n*, la Frise.

frieze, *n*, frise, *f.*

frigate, *n*, frégate, *f.*

fright, *n*, frayeur, épouvante, peur, *f*, effroi,
m, transe, *f*; (*pers.*) horreur, *f*, magot, *m*,
guenon, guenuche, *f.* ~**en**, *v.t*, effrayer,
épouvanter. ~**ful†**, *a*, effrayant, épouvantable, affreux.

frigid†, *a*, glacial, froid. ~**ity**, *n*, frigidité,
froideur, *f.*

frill, *n*, ruche, *f*; jabot, *m.* ~*s & furbelows*,
fanfreluches, *f.pl.* ¶ *v.t*, rucher.

fringe, *n*, frange, crépine, *f*, effilé; bord, *m.*
¶ *v.t*, franger; border.

frippery, *n*, friperie, *f*, falbalas, colifichets,
m.pl.

Frisian, *a*, frison. ¶ *n*, Frison, ne.

frisk, *n*, gambade, *f.* ¶ *v.i*, gambader,
fringuer, frétiller.

frisket (*Typ.*) *n*, frisquette, *f.*

frisky, *a*, frétillant, fringant.

fritter (*Cook.*) *n*, beignet, *m.* ~ *away*,
éparpiller, dissiper, fricasser.

frivolity, *n*, frivolité, *f.* **frivolous**, *a*, frivole,
léger.

friz[z], **frizzle**, *v.t*, crêper, friser. **frizzle**
(*bacon*, &c.) *v.t*, faire se recoquiller.

frock, *n*, robe, *f*, costume; *m*; (*smock*) blouse,
f; (*monk's*) froc, *m.* ~ *coat*, redingote, *f.*

frog, *n*, grenouille; (*horse*) fourchette, *f*; (*Rly*)
croisement; (*sword*) porte-épée, pendant, *m.*
froggery, *n*, grenouillère, *f.*

frolic, *v.i*, folâtrer. ~*some*, *a*, follet.

from, *pr*, de; d'avec; de chez; depuis; dès; à;
d'après; à partir de, à dater de; de la part
de; par.

frond, *n*, fronde, *f.*

front, *a*, de devant; d'avant; de front; de tête;
de face; premier. ~ [*line*] (*Mil.*), front, *m*,
première ligne, *f.* ~ *margin* (book page),
[blanc de] grand fond, *m.* ~ *room*,
chambre sur le devant, *f*, ou sur la rue, *f.*
~ *side*, ~ *board* (book), plat supérieur, *m.*
¶ *n*, devant; avant, *m*, tête; devanture;
face; façade, *f*; front; recto, *m*; (*shirt*)
plastron, *m.* *in* ~ *& in* ~ *of*, devant. *on
the* [*sea*] ~, en bordure de la mer; sur la
promenade [de la mer]; (*hotel*) sur la mer.
¶ *v.t*, affronter, faire face à; donner sur;

~**age**, *n*, devant, *m*; (*extent*) face; façade;
exposition, *f.* ~**al**, *a*, de front; (*Anat.*)
frontal.

frontier, *n. & att*, frontière, *f. & att.*

frontispiece, *n*, (*book*) frontispice, *m*; (*Arch.*)
façade, *f.*

frontsman, *n*, étalagiste, *m.*

frost, *n*, gelée, *f*; (*degrees of*) froid, *m*; (*fig., of
age*) glaces, *f.pl.* ~-*bite*, gelée, congélation, *f.*
~-*bitten*, gelé. ~-*ed glass*, verre dépoli, *m.*
~**y**, *a*, glacial, de glace.

froth, *n*, écume; mousse, *f.* ¶ *v.i*, écumer;
mousser. ~**y**, *a*, écumant; mousseux;
frivole.

frown, *n*, froncement des sourcils, *m.* ¶ *v.i*,
froncer le[s] sourcil[s], sourciller, se
re[n]frogner. ~ [*up*]*on*, regarder d'un
mauvais œil, désapprouver.

frowzy, *a*, moisi; borgne.

frozen, *p.a*, gelé, glacé; glacial; (*meat*, &c.)
frigorifié; (*credit*) gelé. [*as if*] ~ *stiff*,
morfondu.

fructify, *v.i*, fructifier; (*v.t.*) féconder.

frugal†, *a*, frugal. ~**ity**, *n*, frugalité, *f.*

fruit, *n*, fruit, *m.* ~ *bowl*, coupe à fruits, *f*,
compotier, *m.* ~ *press*, presse à fruits, *f.*
~ *salad*, macédoine de fruits, salade de
f—s, *f.* ~ *shop & ~ trade*, fruiterie, *f.*
~ *tree*, arbre fruitier, *m*. à fruit, *m.* **fruiterer**,
n, fruitier, ère. **fruitful†**, *a*, fertile, fécond;
fructueux (*fig. & poet.*). ~**ness**, *n*, fertilité, fécondité, *f.* **fruition**, *n*, jouissance;
réalisation, *f.* **fruitless**, *a*, sans fruit; (*fig.*)
infructueux; vain. ~**ly**, *ad*, en vain.

frump, *n*, femme mal fagotée, *f.*

frustrate, *v.t*, frustrer, déjouer. **frustration**,
n, insuccès, renversement, *m.*

frustum, *n*, tronc, *m.*

fry, *n*, (*fish*) fretin, frai, alevin, nourrain, *m*,
poissonnaille, blanchaille; (*Cook.*) friture, *f.*
¶ *v.t*, [faire] frire; (*v.i.*) frire. ~**ing**, *n*,
& ~ *oil or fat*, friture, *f.* ~ *pan*, poêle [à
frire] *f.*

fuchsia, *n*, fuchsia, *m.*

fuddle, *v.t*, griser. ~**d**, *p.a*, gris.

fudge, *i*, baste! ¶ *v.t*, rapetasser; cuisiner.

fuel, *n*, combustible; (*fig.*) aliment, *m.* ~ *oil*,
pétrole combustible, *m.* ¶ *v.t*, chauffer.

fugitive, *a*, fugitif, passager. ¶ *n*, fugitif, ive,
fuyard, e.

fugleman, *n*, chef de file; meneur; porte-
parole, *m.*

fugue, *n*, fugue, *f.*

fulcrum, *n*, [point d']appui, *m.*

fulfil, *v.t*, remplir, accomplir; satisfaire à,
exécuter. ~**ment**, *n*, accomplissement, *m*,
exécution, *f.*

full, *a*, plein; comble; rempli; complet; au
complet; entier; plénier; tout; copieux;
nourri; intégral; germain. ~ *binding*,
reliure pleine, *f.* ~-*blooded*, sanguin.
~-*bodied* (*wine*), vineux, corsé. *in* ~ *discharge*, libératoire. ~ *dress*, grande tenue,
tenue de cérémonie; grande toilette, *f.*

~-face (type), gras. ~-grown, fait. ~-length mirror, psyché, f. ~-length portrait, portrait en pied, m. ~ name, (pers.) nom & prénoms; (stock, &c.) désignation détaillée, f. ~ of fish (river, lake), poissonneux. ~ orchestra, grand orchestre, m. ~-page illustration, gravure en pleine page, f. ~ point, ~ stop, point [final] m. ~ price, prix fort, m. ~ size, grandeur naturelle, f. in ~, in extenso. Also = fully. ¶ n, plein, m.

full, v.t, fouler. ~er, n, foulon, m. ~'s earth, terre à foulon, f.

fully, ad, pleinement; complètement; entièrement; intégralement; bien; en toutes lettres. ~ paid share, action [entièrement] libérée, f.

fulminate, v.i. & t, fulminer.

ful[l]ness, n, plénitude; ampleur; rondeur; abondance, f. **fulsome**, a, outré, excessif, exagéré, écœurant.

fumble, n, v.i, [far]fouiller, tâtonner.

fume, n, fumée, vapeur, bouffée, buée; colère, f. ¶ v.i. & t, fumer; enrager, maugréer. ~d (oak), a, patiné, teinté.

fumigate, v.t, faire des fumigations dans.

fun, n, amusement, m; plaisanterie, drôlerie, f. in ~, pour rire. to make ~ of, se moquer de, se divertir aux dépens de.

function, n, fonction, f; office, m; réunion, f. ~al, a, fonctionnel. ~ary, n, fonctionnaire, m, f.

fund, n, fonds, m, caisse, masse, f; (pl.) fonds, deniers, m.pl; fonds, m, masse, provision, f. ~holder, rentier, ère, f. ¶ v.t, consolider.

fundament, n, fondement, m. ~al†, a, fondamental, foncier.

funeral, n, enterrement, m, (elaborate) funérailles, f.pl; convoi, m, pompe funèbre, f. ¶ a, funéraire; funèbre. ~ oration, oraison funèbre, f. **funereal**, a, funèbre, d'enterrement.

fungous, a, fongueux; transitoire. **fungus**, n, fongus; champignon [vénéneux] m.

funicular, a. & n, funiculaire, a. & m.

funnel, n, entonnoir, m; cheminée, f.

funny, a, comique, drôle, plaisant. ~ bone, petit juif, m. ~ little (pers.), falot, a. ~ man, comique de la troupe, loustic, m. a ~ (queer) man, un drôle. the ~ part, le comique.

fur, n, fourrure, f, poil; pelage; dépôt, tartre, m, incrustation, f. ~ coat, manteau de fourrure, m. ~-lined, fourré. ~ lining, fourrage, m. ~ trade, pelleterie, f.

furbelows, n.pl, falbalas, m.pl.

furbish, v.t, fourbir.

furious†, a, furieux, acharné.

furl, v.t, serrer, ferler.

furlong, n, furlong, m. = ⅛ mile or 201·168 mètres.

furlough, n, congé, m.

furnace, n, four; fourneau; foyer, m; fournaise, f.

furnish, v.t, fournir; pourvoir; garnir; meubler. ~ed apartments or rooms, [appartement] meublé, hôtel meublé, m. ~ing fabrics, tissus d'ameublement, m.pl. **furniture**, n, meubles, m.pl; ameublement, mobilier, m; garniture, f, accessoires, m.pl. ~ polish, encaustique pour meubles, f. ~ remover, déménageur, m. ~ van, voiture de déménagements, tapissière, f. ~ warehouse, garde-meuble, m.

furore, n, fureur, f.

furred (tongue) p.a, chargée.

furrier, n, fourreur, pelletier, m. ~y, n, pelleterie, f.

furrow, n, sillon, m. ¶ v.t, sillonner; raviner.

furry, a, (tongue) chargée.

further, a, supplémentaire, nouveau; plus éloigné. F~India, l'Inde transgangétique, f. ¶ ad, plus loin; au-delà; [plus] en delà; [en] outre; de plus; encore, davantage. ¶ v.t, avancer, seconder. ~ance, n, avancement, m. ~more, ad, de plus, d'ailleurs, en outre. **furthest**, a, le plus éloigné. ¶ ad, le plus loin.

furtive†, a, furtif.

fury, n, furie, fureur, f, acharnement, m; (pers.) furie, forcenée, lionne, f. F~ (Myth.), Furie, f.

furze, n, ajonc, genêt épineux, m.

fuse, n, fusée; mèche; étoupille, f; (Elec.) plomb [fusible] m. ¶ v.t. & i, fondre.

fusee (Horol.), n, fusée, f.

fuselage, n, fuselage, m.

fusible, a, fusible.

fusillade, n, fusillade, f.

fusion, n, fusion, f.

fuss, n, bruit, tapage, m, cérémonies, façons, histoires, f.pl. ¶ v.i, tatillonner. ~y, a, façonnier, difficultueux.

fustian, n, futaine; (fig.) emphase, f, phébus, m.

fusty, a, qui sent le renfermé; moisi.

futile, a, futile. **futility**, n, futilité, f.

future, a, futur; d'avenir; à venir; (Ccm.) à terme. ¶ n, avenir, futur; (pl., Com.) livrable, m. ~ [tense], futur [simple] m. ~ perfect, futur antérieur. **futurity**, n, futur, m.

fuzzy, a, (hair) crépus; (image) flou.

G

G (Mus.) letter, sol, m. ~ clef, clef de sol, f.

gabble, v.t, débiter trop vite; (v.i.) caqueter.

gable, n, pignon, m. ~ roof, comble sur pignon(s), m.

gad about, courir çà & là, c. la pretentaine. **gadabout**, n, coureur, euse.

gad-fly, n, œstre, taon, m.

gadget, n, machine, f, truc, m.

gaff, n, (spear) gaffe; (spar) corne, f.

gaffer, n, vieux paysan; chef d'équipe, m.

gag, n, bâillon, m; (actor's) scie, cascade, f. ¶ v.t, bâillonner.

gage, n, gage; gant, m.   See also ga[u]ge.

gaiety, n, gaieté, joie; gaillardise, f. **gaily,** ad, gaiement.

gain, n, gain, m.   ¶ v.t, gagner; remporter; valoir; (v.i.) profiter; (Clock) avancer. ~ admittance, s'introduire. to be the gainer (by), gagner (à).

gainsay, v.t, contredire, disconvenir de.

gait, n, démarche, allure, f, pas, m.

gaiter, n, guêtre, f.

gala, n, gala, m; (att., day, night, dress, performance) de gala. ~ night (at dance hall), redoute, f.

galanty show, ombres chinoises, f.pl.

galaxy, n, (Astr.) voie lactée; (fig.) constellation, f.

gale, n, grand vent, m, tourmente, f, coup de vent, m.

galena, n, galène, f.

gall, n, fiel; amer, m; écorchure, f. ~ [nut] [noix de] galle, f.   ¶ v.t, écorcher, blesser.

gallant, a, vaillant, brave; (to women) galant. ¶ n, galant, m.   ~ly, ad, vaillamment; galamment.   ~ry, n, valeur, vaillance; galanterie, f.

galleon, (Hist.) n, galion, m.

gallery, n, galerie; tribune, f; (Theat.) troisièmes [galeries], dernières galeries, f.pl, poulailler, paradis, m.

galley, n, (boat) galère; (cook's) cuisine; (Typ.) galée, f.   ~ [proof], épreuve en placard, f, placard, m.   ~ slave, galérien, m.

Gallic, a, gaulois. **Gallican,** a. & n, gallican, e. **gallicism,** n, gallicisme, m. **gallicize,** v.t, franciser.

Gallinaceae, n.pl, gallinacés, m.pl.

gallipot, n, pot de faïence, m.

gallon, (imperial) n, gallon, m. = 4 quarts or 4·5459631 litres.

galloon, n, galon, m.

gallop, n, galop, m.   ¶ v.i, galoper.   ~ing consumption, phtisie galopante, f.

Gallophil[e], a. & n, francophile, a. & m.f. **Gallophobe,** a. & n, gallophobe, a. & m.f.

gallows, n.pl. & s, potence, f, gibet; (Gym.) portique, m.   ~-bird, gibier de potence, m, pendard, m.

galop (dance) n, galop, m.

galore, ad, à foison.

galosh, n, caoutchouc, m.

galvanic, a, galvanique. **galvanism,** n, galvanisme, m. **galvanize,** v.t, galvaniser. **galvanoplasty,** n, galvanoplastie, f.

Gambia, n, la Gambie.

gambit, n, gambit, m.

gamble, n, loterie, f. be on the ~, jouer, être au jeu. have a ~, aller jouer.   ¶ v.i, jouer, agioter.   ~ away, perdre au jeu. **gambler,** n, joueur, euse; agioteur, m. **gambling,** n, jeu[x], m.[pl.]; agiotage, m. ~ den, tripot, m.

gamboge, n, gomme-gutte, f.

gambol, n, gambade, f.   ¶ v.i, gambader.

game, n, jeu, m; partie; manche; (dodge)

ficelle, f; (Hunt.) gibier, m.   ~s all (Ten.), à deux de jeux.   ~ bag, carnassière, f, carnier, m, gibecière, f.   ~ cock, coq de combat, m.   ~-keeper, garde-chasse, m.   ~ licence (to kill), permis de chasse, m.   ~ of skill, jeu d'adresse, m.   ~-set-match (Ten.), jeu, manche, & partie.   ¶ a, courageux; prêt; sportif.   ~ fish, poisson sportif, m.   ~ fishing, pêche sportive, f. to have a ~ leg, être estropié de la jambe.   ¶ v.i, jouer.   ~ster, n, joueur, euse.

gaming, n, jeu, m.   ~ house, maison de j., f.   ~ table, table de j., f, tapis vert, m.

gammon, n, (bacon) quartier, m; (fig.) blague, f.

gamp, n, riflard, m.

gamut, n, gamme, f.

gamy, a, giboyeux; (Cook.) faisandé.

gander, n, jars, m.

gang, n, bande; brigade, équipe, f.   ~ plough, charrue multiple, f.   ~er, n, chef d'équipe, m.

Ganges (the), le Gange.

gauglion, n, ganglion, m.

gangrene, n, gangrène, f.   ¶ v.t, gangrener.

gangue, n, gangue, matrice, f.

gangway, n, passage; pourtour; (on ship) passavant, m; (to shore) passerelle, f.

gannet, n, fou [de Bassan], m.

gantry, n, portique; beffroi; (for cask) chantier, m.

gaol, n, maison d'arrêt, prison, geôle, f.   ~-bird, repris de justice, cheval de retour, m. **gaoler, gaoleress,** n, geôlier, ère.

gap, n, brèche, trouée, ouverture, f, intervalle, vide, m, lacune, f.

gape, v.i, bâiller.   ~ [at the moon], bayer aux corneilles. **gaper,** n, gobe-mouches, m, badaud, m.

garage, n, garage, m.   ¶ v.t, garer.

garb, n, costume, habit, accoutrement, m.

garbage, n, issues, f.pl, tripaille; saleté, f.

garble, v.t, altérer, tronquer.

garden, n, jardin; (small) jardinet, m.   ~ city, cité-jardin, f.   ~ cress, cresson alénois, m.   ~ engine, irrigateur, m.   ~ flower, fleur de jardin, f.   ~ hose, tuyau d'arrosage, m.   ~ mint, menthe verte, f. the G~ of Eden, Éden, m, le paradis [terrestre].   ~ party, garden-party, f.   ~ plant, plante jardinière, f.   ~ plots, jardinage, m.   ~ stuff, produits du jardinage, m.pl.   ~ tools, outils de jardinage, m.pl.   ¶ v.i, jardiner.   ~er, n, jardinier, ère.

gardenia, n, gardénia, m.

gardening, n, jardinage, m, horticulture, f.

garfish, n, orphie, f.

gargle, n, gargarisme, m.   ¶ v.i, se gargariser.

gargoyle, n, gargouille, f.

garish, a, éblouissant; voyant, tapageur, cru.

garland, n, guirlande, f.

garlic, n, ail, m.

garment, n, vêtement, m.

N *

garner, *n*, grenier, *m*. ¶ *v.t*, engranger; rassembler.

garnet, *n*, grenat, *m*.

garnish, *n*, garniture, *f*. ¶ *v.t*, garnir.

garret, *n*, mansarde, *f*, galetas, grenier, *m*.

garrison, *n*, garnison, *f*. ~ *artillery*, artillerie de place, *f*.

garrulous, *a*, bavard, loquace.

garter, *n*, jarretière, *f*.

gas, *n*, gaz, *m*. ~ *bracket*, applique à g., *f*. ~ *company*, compagnie du g., *f*. ~ *cooker*, ~ *oven*, ~ *stove*, cuisinière à g., *f*, fourneau à g., *m*. ~ *engine*, ~ *motor*, machine à g., *f*, moteur à g., *m*. ~ *fire*, radiateur à g., *m*. ~ *fitter*, gazier, *m*. ~ *fittings*, appareils de distribution du gaz, *m.pl*. ~*light*, lumière du g., *f*. ~*light paper* (*Phot*.), papier par développement, p. à image latente, *m*. ~ *lighting*, éclairage au gaz, *m*. ~ *main*, employé du gaz, *m*. ~ *mask*, (*war*) masque à g.; (*fire*) casque respiratoire, *m*. ~ *meter*, compteur à gaz, *m*. ~ *pipe*, tuyau de g., *m*. ~ *producer*, gazogène, *m*. ~ *ring*, réchaud à gaz, *m*. ~ *shell*, obus à g., *m*. ~ *worker*, gazier, *m*. ~ *works*, usine à gaz, *f* ¶ *v.t*, asphyxier; (*War*) gazer. ~*eous*, *a*, gazeux.

gash, *n*, balafre, estafilade, *f*. ¶ *v.t*, balafrer.

gasify, *v.t*, gazéifier.

gasket, *n*, garcette, *f*, raban, *m*; tresse; garniture, *f*.

gasogene, *n*, gazogène, *m*. gasometer, *n*, gazomètre, *m*.

gasp, *n*, effort pour respirer; souffle coupé; hoquet, *m*. to ~ *for breath*, haleter.

gassy, *a*, gazeux; verbeux.

gast[e]ropod, *n*, gastéropode, *m*. gastric, *a*, gastrique. gastritis, *n*, gastrite, *f*. gastronome[r], *n*, gastronome, *m*. gastronomic(al), *a*, gastronomique. gastronomy, *n*, gastronomie, *f*.

gate, *n*, porte; barrière; (*sluice*) vanne, *f*. ~ *crasher*, resquilleur, euse. ~ *crashing*, resquille, *f*. ~ *keeper*, portier, ère; (*level crossing*) garde-barrière, *m,f*. ~ *money*, recette, *f*. ~*way*, porte, *f*.

gather, *v.t*, froncer, *f*. ¶ *v.t*, [r]assembler; [r]amasser; [re]cueillir; récolter; vendanger; inférer; (*Need*.) froncer. ~*er*, *n*, ramasseur, euse. ~*ing*, *n*, rassemblement, *m*; accumulation; cueillette; réunion, *f*; (*Med*.) mal blanc, abcès, *m*.

gating (*Hyd*.) *n*, vannage, *m*.

gaudy, *a*, fastueux, voyant, tapageur.

ga[u]ge, *n*, calibre, *m*; jauge, *f*; gabarit (*Rly track*) écartement, *m*, voie, largeur, *f*; manomètre; indicateur, *m*. ¶ *v.t*, calibrer; jauger; cuber. *gauging rod*, jauge, *f*.

gaunt, *a*, décharné, sec.

gauntlet, *n*, gantelet; (*fig*.) gant, *m*.

gauze, *n*, gaze; toile, *f*, tissu, tamis, *m*. gauzy, *a*, vaporeux.

gavotte, *n*, gavotte, *f*.

gawky, *a*, dégingandé.

gay, *a*, gai. ~ *man*, viveur, *m*.

gaze, *n*, regard, *m*. to ~ *at*, contempler, couver des yeux.

gazelle, *n*, gazelle, *f*.

gazette, *n*, gazette, *f*, journal, *m*; journal officiel; moniteur, *m*.

gazetteer, *n*, dictionnaire géographique, *m*.

gear, *n*, appareil[s] *m.*[*pl*.]; engins; organes; agrès, *m.pl*; mécanisme; dispositif; harnais, *m*; armature, *f*; gréement, *m*; (*toothed*) engrenage[s] *m.*[*pl*.]; (*ratio*) multiplication, *f*; (*bicycle*) développement, *m*. ~ *box*, boîte à engrenages; boîte de changement de vitesse, *f*. ~ *case*, carter; couvre-engrenages, *m*. ~ *ratio*, multiplication, *f*. ~ *wheel*, roue d'engrenage, *f*. ¶ *v.t*.

gee-gee, *n*, dada, *m*. gee up, *i*, hue!

gehenna, *n*, géhenne, *f*.

gelatin[e], *n*, gélatine, *f*. gelatinous, *a*, gélatineux.

geld, *v.t*, châtrer, hongrer. ~*ing*, *n*, castration, *f*; [cheval] hongre, *m*.

gem, *n*, pierre précieuse, [pierre] gemme, *f*; bijou, *m*; (*pl*.) pierreries, *f.pl*.

gender, *n*, genre, *m*.

genealogical, *a*, généalogique. genealogy, *n*, généalogie, *f*.

general, *a*, général, d'ensemble; commun; collectif. ~ *cargo*, charge à la cueillette, *f*. ~ *effect*, ensemble, *m*. ~ *expenses*, frais divers, *m.pl*. ~ *post office*, hôtel des postes, *m*. *the* ~ *public*, le grand public. ~ *servant*, bonne à tout faire, *f*. *to become* ~, se généraliser. ¶ *n*, général en chef, chef, *m*; (*roll of the drum*) générale, *f*. *the* ~ (*fig*.), le général. ~*issimo*, *n*, généralissime, *m*. ~*ity*, *n*, généralité; plupart, *f*. ~*ize*, *v.t*. & *i*, généraliser. ~*ly*, *ad*, généralement; communément. ~*ship*, *n*, généralat, *m*; stratégie, *f*.

generate, *v.t*, engendrer; produire. generating, *p.a*, générateur. generation, *n*, génération, *f*. generator, *n*, générateur, *m*.

generic, *a*, générique.

generosity, *n*, générosité, *f*. generous†, *a*, généreux, donnant.

genesis, *n*, genèse, *f*. G~ (*Bible*), la Genèse.

genet (*civet*) *n*, genette, *f*.

geneva (*gin*) *n*, genièvre, *m*. G~ (*Geog*.), Genève, *f*. *Lake of G~*, lac de Genève, lac Léman, *m*.

genial, *a*, bienfaisant; chaleureux; joyeux; sociable. ~*ity*, *n*, bonhomie, *f*.

genital, *a*, génital.

genitive [*case*], *n*, génitif, *m*.

genius, *n*, génie; démon, *m*.

Genoa, *n*, Gênes, *f*. Genoese, *a*, génois. ¶ *n*, Génois, *m*.

genteel (*ironical*) *a*, snob, talon rouge.

gentian, *n*, gentiane, *f*.

gentile, *n*, gentil, *m*.

gentility, *n*, gentilhommerie, *f*; snobisme, *m*.

gentle, *a*, doux. *of* ~ *birth*, de qualité.
~*folk*[s], gens de qualité, *m.pl.* ~*man*,
monsieur; galant homme; homme de
qualité, gentilhomme, gentleman; cavalier, *m*; sans profession. ~*man farmer*,
gentilhomme campagnard, *m.* ~*manliness*, savoir-vivre, *m*, gentilhommerie, *f.*
~*manly*, comme il faut; distingué; gentleman. ~*men of the robe* (lawyers), gens
de robe, *m.pl.* ~*woman*, femme de
qualité, *f.* ¶ *n*, asticot, *m.* ~**ness**, *n*,
douceur, *f.* **gently**, *ad*, doucement, bellement. **gentry**, *n*, petite noblesse, *f.*

genuflexion, *n*, génuflexion, *f.*

genuine, *a*, vrai; authentique; sincère; sérieux.
~**ness**, *n*, authenticité; sincérité, *f.*

genus, *n*, genre, *m.*

geodesy, *n*, géodésie, *f.* **geognosy**, *n*, géognosie, *f.* **geographer**, *n*, géographe, *m.*
geographic(al)†, *a*, géographique. **geography**, *n*, géographie, *f.* **geologic(al)**, *a*,
géologique. **geologist**, *n*, géologue, *m.*
geology, *n*, géologie, *f.* **geometer** *& geometrician**, *n*, géomètre, *m.* **geometric(al)**†,
a, géométrique. **geometry**, *n*, géométrie, *f.*

Georgia, *n*, (*U.S.A.*) la Georgie; (*Asia*) la
Géorgie.

geranium, *n*, géranium, *m.*

germ, *n*, germe, *m.*

German, *a*, allemand; d'Allemagne. ~
measles, rubéole, *f.* ~ *ocean*, mer du Nord,
f. ~ *silver*, maillechort, *m.* ¶ *n*, (*pers.*)
Allemand, e; (*language*) l'allemand, *m.*

germander (*Bot.*) *n*, germandrée, *f.*

germane to, se rapportant à.

Germany, *n*, l'Allemagne, *f.*

germinate, *v.i*, germer. **germination**, *n*, germination, *f.*

gerund, *n*, gérondif, *m.*

gestation, *n*, gestation, *f.*

gesticulate, *v.i*, gesticuler. **gesture**, *n*, geste, *m.*

get, *v.t.ir*, obtenir; gagner; acquérir; procurer; se p.; se faire; se mettre; tirer;
recevoir; retirer; trouver; avoir; (*v.i.ir.*)
aller; arriver; parvenir; devenir; se faire; se
trouver. *Often rendered by* se, *e.g.* ~ *an
opinion into one's head*, se chausser d'une
opinion. ~ *away*, s'échapper; se sauver.
~ *back*, *v.t*, ravoir; (*v.i.*) revenir. ~ *down*,
descendre. ~ *hold of*, s'emparer de; saisir.
~ *in*, entrer; s'introduire; (*corn*) engranger.
~ *married*, se marier. ~ *on*, s'arranger;
s'entendre; réussir. ~ *out*, sortir. ~ *out
of the way*, s'ôter de là; se garer. ~ *over*,
franchir, surmonter. ~ *ready*, préparer; se
préparer. ~ *round* (someone), entortiller.
~ *up*, se lever. ~ *up steam*, chauffer.

get-up, *n*, mise, *f*; affiquets, *m.pl.*

gewgaw, *n*, colifichet, *m.*

geyser, *n*, (*spring*) geyser; chauffe-bain, *m.*

ghastly, *a*, de spectre, de déterré; macabre;
blême, livide; affreux.

Ghent, *n*, Gand, *m.*

gherkin, *n*, cornichon, *m.*

ghetto, *n*, ghetto, *m*, juiverie, *f.*

ghost, *n*, esprit, *m*; âme, *f*; fantôme, spectre,
revenant, *m*, ombre, *f.* ~ *story*, histoire
de revenants, *f.* ~**ly**, *a*, spectral, fantomatique.

ghoul, *n*, goule, *f.*

giant, *a*, géant. **giant, ess**, *n*, géant, e, colosse, *m.* *giant*['s] *stride*, pas de géant,
vindas, *m.*

gibber, *v.i*, baragouiner. ~**ish**, *n*, baragouin,
galimatias, *m.*

gibbet, *n*, gibet, *m*, potence, *f.* ¶ (*fig.*) *v.t*,
pilorier.

gibe, *n*, brocard, quolibet, lardon, *m.* ¶ *v.i*,
lancer des brocards *ou* des lardons (*at* = à).

giblets, *n.pl*, abattis, *m. & m.pl.*

giddiness, *n*, vertige, étourdissement, *m.*
giddy, *a*, (*height*) vertigineux; (*flighty*)
écervelé. *it makes me feel* ~, cela me
donne le vertige. ~-*head*, hanneton, *m.*

gift, *n*, don; cadeau, *m*; donation; (*for coupons*) prime; (*of an office*) nomination, *f*,
talent, *m.* *the* ~ *of the gab*, du bagou.
~**ed**, *a*, doué, de talent.

gig, *n*, cabriolet, *m*; (*boat*) yole, *f.*

gigantic, *a*, gigantesque.

giggle, *v.i*, rire bêtement, glousser.

gild, *v.t.ir*. See *g[u]ild*, dorer. ~**er**,
n, doreur, euse. ~**ing**, *n*, dorure, *f.*

gill, *n*, (*fish*) ouïe, branchie, *f*; (*imperial meas.*)
¼ pint *ou* 0·142 litre.

gilt, *n*, dorure, *f.* ¶ *p.a*, doré. ~-*edged*,
(*book, bill of exchange*) doré sur tranche;
(*investment, security*) de premier ordre. ~
tooling, fers dorés, *m.pl.* ~ *top*, tête
dorée, *f.*

gimcrack, *n*, bibelot, *m*; patraque, *f.* ¶ *a*,
de camelote; délabré.

gimlet, *n*, vrille, *f.*

gimp, *n*, ganse, *f*; galon, bordé, passement, *m.*
~ *nail*, cabochon, *m*, (*pl.*) mignonnette, *f.*

gin, *n*, (*snare*) trébuchet, *m*; (*hoist*) chèvre,
f; treuil, *m*; (*cotton*) égreneuse, *f*; (*spirit*)
gin, *m.* ~ *shop*, assommoir, *m.* ¶ *v.t*,
égrener.

ginger, *n*, gingembre, *m.* ~ *bread*, pain
d'épice, *m.* ~ *hair*, des cheveux [rouge]
carotte, *m.pl.* ~ *nut*, nonnette, *f.* ~**ly**,
ad, en tâtonnant.

gingham (*fabric*) *n*, guingan, *f.*

gipsy, *n*, bohémien, ne, gitane, *f*, tzigane, *m,f.*

giraffe, *n*, girafe, *f.*

girandole, *n*, girandole, *f.*

girasol[e] (*opal*) *n*, girasol, *m.*

gird, *v.t.ir*, [en]ceindre. ~**er**, *n*, poutre;
solive; ferme, *f.* ~, *n*, ceinture, cordelière, *f.* ~ *cake*, galette, *f.* ¶ *v.t*,
ceindre.

girl, *n*, fille, jeune fille, fillette, enfant, demoiselle, *f.* ~ *guide*, éclaireuse, *f.*
~-**hood**, *n*, jeunesse, *f.* ~**ish**, *a*, de jeune
fille; mignard.

girth, *n*, sangle; sous-ventrière; circonférence, *f.*

gist, *n*, substance, *f.*

give, *v.t. & i. ir*, donner; accorder; prêter; apporter; passer; rendre; fournir; faire; pousser. ~ *& take*, donnant donnant. ~ *one's name*, décliner son nom, se nommer. ~ *in*, céder. ~ *oneself away*, s'enferrer soi-même. ~ *out*, annoncer, distribuer; *(lamp, &c.)* se mourir. ~ *someone a piece of one's mind*, dire son fait à quelqu'un. ~ *up*, renoncer à; livrer; abandonner, quitter; céder. *(patient)* condamner. ~ *way*, céder; fléchir; s'effondrer. **given to**, adonné à; enclin à. **giver**, *n*, donneur, euse.

gizzard, *n*, gésier, *m.*

glacé kid gloves, gants de peau glacée, *m.pl.*

glacial, *a*, glacial; *(Geol.)* glaciaire. **glacier**, *n*, glacier, *m.* ~ *snow*, névé, *m.*

glad, *a*, [bien] aise; content; heureux; joyeux. **gladden**, *v.t*, réjouir.

glade, *n*, clairière, *f.*

gladiator, *n*, gladiateur, *m.*

gladiolus, *n*, glaïeul, *m.*

gladly, *ad*, volontiers. **gladness**, *n*, joie, *f.*

glamour, *n*, enchantement; éclat; prestige, *m.*

glance, *n*, coup d'œil, regard, *m*; *(loving)* œillade, *f.* ¶ *v.i*, effleurer. ~ *at*, jeter un coup d'œil sur.

gland, *n*, glande, *f.*

glanders, *n.pl*, morve, *f.*

glare, *n*, éclat; éblouissement; regard perçant; r. furieux, *m.* ¶ *v.i*, éblouir. ~ *at (pers.)* lancer un regard furieux à. **glaring**, *a*, éclatant, éblouissant; grossier; flagrant; criant; tranchant; *(eyes)* furibonds.

glass, *n*, verre; cristal, *m*; vitre; glace; coupe, *f*; bock, *m*; chope, *f*; miroir, *m*; lunette, *f*; *(pl.)* lunettes, *f.pl*; jumelle, *f*; baromètre, *m.* ~[*, with care*], fragile. ~ *beads*, verroterie, *f.* ~ *case*, vitrine, *f.* ~ *cloth*, essuie-verres, *m*; toile verrée, *f*; tissu de verre, *m.* ~ *cutter*, diamant de vitrier; *(wheel)* coupe-verre à molette, *m.* ~ *door*, porte vitrée, *f*, vitrage, *m.* ~ *house*, serre, *f.* ~ *maker*, verrier, *m.* ~ *making* & ~ *works*, verrerie, *f.* ~ *of beer*, bock, *m*, chope, *f.* ~ *paper*, papier de verre, *m.* ~ *shade*, globe protecteur en verre, *m.* ~[*ware*], verrerie, *f*; *(small)* verroterie, *f.* ~ *y*, *a*, vitreux.

glaucous, *a*, glauque.

glaze, *n*, émail, vernis, *m*, couverte, *f*; lustre, *m.* ¶ *v.t*, *(window)* vitrer; émailler, vernir, vernisser; lustrer; satiner; glacer; dorer; *(v.i.)* se glacer. ~*d frost*, verglas, *m.* **glazier**, *n*, vitrier, *m.* ~ *y*, *n*, vitrerie, *f.*

gleam, *n*, lueur, *f*, rayon, *m.* ¶ *v.i*, luire, miroiter.

glean, *v.t*, glaner; *(grapes)* grappiller. ~ *er*, *n*, glaneur, euse. ~ *ing*, *n*, glanage, *m*, glane; *(pl.)* glanure, *f.*

glebe, *n*, glèbe; terre d'église, *f.*

glee, *n*, joie, gaieté; chanson à plusieurs voix, *f.*

gleet, *n*, écoulement, *m.*

glen, *n*, vallon, val, *m.*

glib, *a*, *(pers.)* volubile; *(tongue)* déliée.

glide, *n*, glissement; *(Danc.)* glissé, *m.* ¶ *v.i*, glisser; couler. **glider** *(Aero.)* *n*, planeur, *m.* **gliding** *(Aero.)* *n*, vol à voile, *m.*

glimmer, *n*, lueur, *f.* ¶ *v.i*, jeter une faible lueur.

glimpse, *n*,'lueur, *f*; coup d'œil, *m*; échappée [de vue] *f.* ~ *catch a* ~ *of*, entrevoir.

glint, *n*, reflet, *m.* ¶ *v.i*, étinceler, miroiter.

glisten, **glitter**, *v.i*, briller, reluire, miroiter. **glitter**, *n*, brillant, *m.*

gloaming, *n*, crépuscule, *m*, brune, *f.*

gloat over, triompher de; couver des yeux.

globe, *n*, globe, *m*, sphère, *f*; *(fish bowl)* bocal, *m.* **globular**, *a*, globulaire, globuleux. **globule**, *n*, globule, *m.*

gloom, *v.t*, rembrunir. ~[*iness*], *n*, obscurité, *f*, ténèbres, *f.pl*; air sombre, *m*, tristesse, *f.* ~ *y*, *a*, sombre, ténébreux; triste, morne, noir, lugubre.

glorify, *v.t*, glorifier. **glorious†**, *a*, glorieux; resplendissant. **glory**, *n*, gloire, *f*; nimbe, *m.* ~ *in*, se glorifier de, se faire gloire de.

gloss, *n*, luisant, lustre, poli, œil, *m*; *(comment)* glose, *f.* ¶ *v.t*, lustrer; glacer; *(text)* gloser. ~ [*over*], vernir, farder. ~ *ary*, *n*, glossaire, *m.* ~ *y*, *a*, luisant; lustré; poli; *(phot. paper)* brillant.

glottis, *n*, glotte, *f.*

glove, *n*, gant, *m.* ~ *stretcher*, ouvre-gants, *m.* ~ *trade*, ganterie, *f.* ¶ *v.t*, ganter. *to put on one's* ~*s*, se ganter. **glover**, *n*, gantier, ère.

glow, *n*, incandescence, *f*; embrasement, *m*; chaleur, *f*; élan, *m*; *(pleasant, in the body)* moiteur, *f.* ~ *lamp*, lampe à incandescence, *f.* ~*worm*, ver luisant, lampyre, *m*, luciole, *f.* ¶ *v.i*, briller d'un vif éclat. ~*ing with health*, rouge de santé.

glower at, regarder d'un air féroce.

gloze over, vernir.

glucose, *n*, glucose, *f.*

glue, *n*, colle forte; colle; *(marine)* glu, *f.* ~ *pot*, pot à colle, *m.* ¶ *v.t*, coller. ~*y*, *a*, gluant.

glum, *a*, morose, chagrin.

glume, *n*, glume, balle, *f.*

glut, *n*, pléthore, *f*; encombrement, *m.* ¶ *v.t*, gorger, rassasier; encombrer.

gluten, *n*, gluten, *m.* **glutinous**, *a*, glutineux.

glutton, *n*, glouton, ne, gourmand, e. ~*ous†*, *a*, glouton, gourmand. ~*y*, *n*, gloutonnerie, gourmandise, *f.*

glycerin[e], *n*, glycérine, *f.*

gnarl, *n*, broussin, *m.* ~*ed*, *a*, noueux.

gnash one's teeth, grincer des *(ou* les*)* dents.

gnat, *n*, moucheron, cousin, *m.*

gnaw, *v.i*, ronger. ~*ing*, *n*, rongement; tiraillement, *m.*

gneiss, *n*, gneiss, *m.*

gnome, n, gnome, m.

gnostic, n, gnostique, m.

go, n, entrain, allant, panache, m; mode, vogue, f; jet, m. ¶ v.i. & t. ir, aller; se rendre, se porter; se mettre; marcher; passer; partir; s'en aller; faire; tourner; devenir. are you ready? go! êtes-vous prêts? partez! who goes there? qui vive? ~-ahead, entreprenant. ~ astray, s'égarer; se dévoyer. ~ away, s'en aller; partir. ~ back, retourner. ~-between, intermédiaire, m; entremetteur, euse. ~ by, passer. ~-cart, chariot, panier roulant, m. ~ down, descendre; baisser; (sun, moon) se coucher; (ship) sombrer, couler; (swelling) désenfler. ~ for, aller chercher; a. faire; a. prendre. ~ in, entrer; monter. ~ off, partir. ~ on, aller; avancer; continuer. ~ on! allons donc! ~ on board a ship, an aeroplane, monter sur un navire, en avion. ~ out, sortir; (light) s'éteindre. ~ over, passer sur; traverser; parcourir (Jump.) dépasser, mordre sur (the mark = la latte). ~-slow strike, grève perlée, f. ~ through, passer par, traverser, parcourir; dépouiller. ~ to press, procéder à l'impression. ~ to sleep, s'endormir. ~ to sleep again, se rendormir. ~ up, monter; remonter; renchérir. ~ with, accompagner. ~ without, se passer de.

goad, n, aiguillon, m. ¶ v.t, aiguillonner, piquer.

goal, n, but, m. ~ area, line, surface, ligne, de b., f. ~ free throw (Water Polo), coup franc de b., m. ~ keeper, kick, post, gardien, coup [de pied] (Water Polo), poteau de b., m.

goat, n, chèvre, f; (he) bouc, m; ~-herd, chevrier, ère. ~ee, n, barbe de bouc, barbiche, f.

gobble, v.t, manger goulûment; (v.i, of turkey) glouglouter.

goblet, n, gobelet, m; coupe, f.

goblin, n, lutin, follet, farfadet, gobelin, m.

God, n, Dieu, m. God's acre, champ du repos, m. god, n, dieu; (pl, Theat.) poulailler, paradis, m. ~-child, filleul, e. ~-daughter, filleule, f. ~-father, parrain, m. ~-head, divinité, f. ~-mother, marraine, f. ~-send, providence, aubaine, chapecute, f. ~-son, filleul, m. goddess, n, déesse, f. godless, a, sans Dieu; impie. godlike, a, divin. godliness, n, piété, f. godly, a, pieux, saint, de Dieu.

goffer, n, tuyau, m. ¶ v.t, gaufrer, tuyauter.

goggles, n.pl, lunettes, f.pl.

going, n, aller, m. ~ & coming, allées & venues, f.pl. ~ back to school, rentrée des classes, f.pl. ~ concern, affaire roulante, f. value as a ~ concern, valeur d'usage, f. ~, ~; gone! une fois, deux fois, [trois fois]; adjugé! ~-s-on, procédés, agissements, m.pl.

goitre, n, goitre, m.

gold, n, or, m. ~-beater's skin, baudruche, f. the G~ Coast, la Côte de l'Or. ~-digger, chercheur d'or, m. ~-field, champ aurifère, m. ~-finch, chardonneret, m. ~-fish, poisson rouge, m; dorade, f. ~ mine, mine d'or, f. ~-smith & or silversmith, orfèvre, m. ~-[smith's] & or silver[smith's] work, orfèvrerie, f. ~-tipped (cigarettes), à bouts dorés. ~ washer (pers.), orpailleur, m. ¶ a, d'or, en or. ~ blocking (Bookb.), dorure en or, f. ~-francs, francs-or, m.pl. ~-en, a, d'or; doré; (hair) blond doré. ~ calf, veau d'or, m. ~ mean, juste milieu, m. ~ rain, pluie d'or, f. ~ syrup, mélasse raffinée, f. ~ wedding, noces d'or, f.pl, cinquantaine, f.

golf, n, golf, m. ~ club (pers. & stick) club de g, m. ~ course, links (terrain de] golf, m. ~-er, n, joueur (euse) de golf.

golosh, n, caoutchouc, m.

gondola, n, gondole, f; (Aero.) nacelle, f. gondolier, m.

gong, n, gong, tam-tam; timbre, m.

good, a, bon; beau; de bien; brave; (of a child) sage; avantageux; utile. ~ angel, bon ange, m; providence, f. ~ breeding, politesse, f; savoir-vivre, m. ~-bye, i. & n, adieu; i. & m; au revoir! ~ conduct prize, prix de sagesse, m. a ~ deal, a ~ many, beaucoup. a ~ ear (for music), l'oreille juste. ~ evening! ~ night bonsoir! bonne nuit! (a) ~-for-nothing, n. & a, (un) propre à rien. G~ Friday, le vendredi saint. ~ gracious! miséricorde! ~-looking, joli, de bonne mine. my ~ man, mon brave. ~ morning! ~ afternoon! ~ day! bonjour! ~ nature, bonhomie, f, bon naturel, m. ~-natured, (pers.) bon enfant; (laugh) jovial. ~ offices, ministère, m. the ~ old days, le bon vieux temps. a ~ way, un bon bout de chemin. ~ will, bienveillance, bonne volonté, faveur, f; fonds [de commerce] m, clientèle, f. ¶ i, bon! bien! ~ n, bien, m. for ~, pour de bon. it's no ~ . . ., inutile de . . . to the ~, en gain. goodies, n.pl, [du] nanan, m. goodness, n, bonté, f. for ~' sake, de grâce.

goods, n.pl, marchandises, f.pl; biens; effets, m.pl. ~ train, train de marchandises, m, petite vitesse, f.

goose, n, oie, f. ~ flesh (fig.), chair de poule, f. ~ step, pas de l'oie, m.

gooseberry, n, groseille verte, g. à maquereau, f. ~ bush, groseillier à maquereau, m.

Gordian knot, nœud gordien, m.

gore, n, sang [caillé] m. ¶ v.t, percer de coups de corne.

gorge, n, gorge, f. ¶ v.t, gorger.

gorgeous†, a, magnifique, splendide.

gorilla, n, gorille, m.

gormandize, v.i, goinfrer, bâfrer.

gorse, n, ajonc, genêt épineux, m.

gory, a, sanglant, ensanglanté.

goshawk, *n*, autour, *m.*

gosling, *n*, oison, *m.*

gospel, *n*, Évangile; credo, *m.* ~ [*truth*], parole d'Évangile, *f.*

gossamer, *n*, fils de la Vierge, *m.pl*, filandres, *f.pl.*

gossip, *n*, commérage, bavardage de commères, racontar, *m*; (*pers.*) commère, *f.* ¶ *v.i*, commérer, bavarder.

goth (*fig.*) *n*), ostrogot[h], e. Gothic, *a*, gothique.

gouache (*Art*) *n*, gouache, *f.*

gouge, *n*, gouge, *f.*

gourd, *n*, courge, calebasse, *f.*

gourmand, *a. & n*, gourmand, e.

gourmet, *n*, gourmet, *m.*

gout, *n*, goutte, *f.* ~y, *a*, goutteux.

govern, *v.t*, gouverner, régir; (*Gram.*) régir. ~ess, *n*, institutrice, gouvernante, *f.* ~ car[t], tonneau, *m.* ~ment, *n*, gouvernement; État, *m.* ~ *in power*, gouvernants, *m.pl.* ~ *organ*, journal ministériel, *m.* ~or, *n*, gouverneur; patron; (*Mach.*) régulateur, *m.*

gown, *n*, robe; toge, *f.*

grab, *v.t*, empoigner, agripper.

grace, *n*, grâce, *f*; (*before meal*) le bénédicité; (*after*) les grâces, *f.pl.* ~ *note*, note d'agrément, *f. the G~s*, les [trois] Grâces. *his G~*, monseigneur, *m. your G~*, Votre Grandeur, *f.* ¶ *v.t*, orner; honorer. ~ful†, *a*, gracieux.

gracious†, *a*, gracieux. ~ness, *n*, gracieuseté, *f.*

gradation, *n*, gradation, *f.* grade, *n*, grade, degré, *m*; teneur, *f*, titre, *m.* ¶ *v.t*, classer; graduer; régulariser. gradient, *n*, (*up*) rampe; (*down*) pente; (*up or down*) inclinaison, *f.* gradual†, *a*, graduel. graduate, *v.t*, graduer; (*v.i.*) prendre ses grades. ¶ *n*, gradué, e.

Gr[a]eco-Roman wrestling, lutte gréco-romaine, *f.*

graft, *n*, (*Hort.*) greffe, ente; (*Surg.*) greffe; (*spoils*) gratte, *f.* ¶ *v.t*, greffer; enter. ~ing (*Knit.*) *n*, remmaillage, *m.*

grain, *n*, grain, *m*; grains, *m.pl*; (*wood, &c*) fil; (*weight*) grain, *m.* = 0·0648 gramme; (*pl. brewer's*) drêche, drague, *f.* ¶ *v.t*, grener, greneler; veiner. ~ed, *p.a*, (*leather, &c*) grenu; (*wood*) ondé. ~ing, *n*, grenu, *m.*

grains (*fish spear*) *n*, fouïne, *f.*

grammalogue, *n*, sténogramme, *m.*

grammar, *n*, grammaire, *f.* ~ian, *n*, grammairien, ne. grammatical†, *a*, grammatical.

gramophone, *n*, phonographe, gramophone, *m.* ~ *needle*, aiguille de phonographe, *f.* ~ *record*, disque de phonographe, *m.*

grampus, *n*, épaulard, *m*, orque, *f.*

Granada (*Spain*) *n*, Grenade, *f.*

granadilla (*Bot.*) *n*, grenadille, *f.*

granary, *n*, grenier, *m.*

grand†, *a*, grand; magnifique. ~child' ~son, ~-daughter, petit-fils, *m*, petite-fille, *f.* ~children, petits-enfants, *m.pl.* ~father, grand-père, aïeul, *m.* ~father's clock, horloge de parquet, *f.* ~mamma, grand-maman, bonne maman, *f.* ~mother, grand-mère, aïeule, *f.* ~ piano, piano à queue, *m.* ~ staircase, escalier d'honneur, *m.* ~ stand, tribune, *f.* ~ total, somme globale, somme toute, *f.* grandee, *n*, grand, *m.* grandeur, *n*, grandeur, majesté; splendeur, *f.*

grandiloquence, *n*, grandiloquence, *f.* grandiloquent, *a*, grandiloquent, doctoral.

grandiose, *a*, grandiose.

granite, *n*, granit, *m.*

granny, *n*, grand-maman, bonne maman, *f.*

grant, *n*, concession; allocation; subvention, *f.* ¶ *v.t*, accorder; concéder; octroyer; admettre; poser. *to take for ~ed*, présupposer. ~ee, *n*, concessionnaire, *f*, impétrant, e. ~or, *n*, cédant, e.

granulate, *v.t*, grener; granuler. ~d sugar, sucre cristallisé, *m.* granule, *n*, granule, *m.*

grape, *n*, grain de raisin, *m*; (*pl.*) raisin[s] *m.[pl.].* ~ fruit, pamplemousse, *f.* ~ shot, mitraille, *f.* ~ stone, pépin de raisin, *m.*

graph, *n*, graphique, tracé, *m.* ~ic†, *a*, graphique; pittoresque.

graphite, *n*, graphite, *m*, plombagine, *f.*

grapnel, *n*, grappin, *m.* grapple, *v.t*, accrocher. ~ *with*, s'attaquer à; colleter.

grasp, *n*, prise; étreinte; poigne; poignée; portée, *f.* ¶ *v.t*, saisir, empoigner; serrer. ~ *round the body*, ceinturer. ~ing†, *p.a*, avide, cupide, âpre [au gain].

grass, *n*, herbe, *f*, herbage; gazon, *m*; verdure, *f*; vert, *m*; (*Min.*) surface, *f*, jour, *m. a* ~ (*plant*), une graminée. ~ court (*Ten.*), l'herbe, *f.* ~hopper, sauterelle; cigale, *f.* ~land, prairie, *f.* ~ plot, boulingrin, *m*, pelouse, *f.* ~ snake, couleuvre à collier, *f.* ~ widow, veuve à titre temporaire, *f.* ~y, *a*, herbeux, herbu.

grate, *n*, grille, *f.* ¶ *v.t*, griller; râper; (*teeth*) grincer des ou les; (*ears*) écorcher, blesser. ~d bread crumbs, panure, chapelure, *f.*

grateful, *a*, reconnaissant; agréable. *to be ~ to*, savoir [bon] gré à. ~ness, *n*, reconnaissance, *f.*

grater, *n*, râpe, *f.*

gratification, *n*, satisfaction, *f*, plaisir, *m.* gratify, *v.t*, satisfaire, contenter.

gratin, *n*, gratin, *m.* ~ate, *v.t*, gratiner.

grating, *n*, grille, *f*; grillage; gril, *m*; claire-voie; crapaudine, *f.* ¶ *p.a*, strident.

gratis, *ad*, gratis, gratuitement.

gratitude, *n*, reconnaissance, gratitude, *f.*

gratuitous†, *a*, gratuit, gracieux; sans motif. ~ness, *n*, gratuité, *f.* gratuity, *n*, gratification, gracieuseté, *f*; (*on discharge*) pécule, *m.*

gravamen, *n*, matière, *f*.

grave†, *a*, grave, sérieux. ¶ *n*, fosse; tombe, *f*, tombeau, *m*. ~ *clothes*, linceul, suaire, *m*. ~*digger*, fossoyeur, *m*. ~*stone*, pierre tombale, tombe, *f*. ~*yard*, cimetière, *m*. ¶ *v.t.* (*ship*) radouber; (*v.t.ir.*) (*fig.*) graver.

gravel, *n*, gravier[s] *m.*[*pl.*]; (*Med.*) graviers, *m.pl*, gravelle, *f*, sable, *m*. ~ *path*, ~ *walk*, allée sablée, *f*. ~ *pit*, gravière, *f*. ~ly, *a*, graveleux.

graver, *n*, burin, ciselet, *m*.

graving dock, forme de radoub, *f*.

gravitate, *v.i*, graviter. gravitation, *n*, gravitation, *f*. gravity, *n*, (*Phys.*) gravité, pesanteur, *f*, poids, *m*; (*fig.*) gravité, *f*; sérieux, *m*.

gravy, *n*, jus, *m*. ~ *boat*, saucière, *f*. ~ *spoon*, cuiller à ragoût, *f*.

gray. See grey. grayling, *n*, ombre, *m*.

graze, *n*, écorchure, *f*. ¶ *v.t.* & *i*, effleurer, raser, friser, frôler; écorcher; (*sea bottom*) labourer; (*cattle*) paître, pâturer, pacager.

grazier, *n*, éleveur, *m*. grazing farm, exploitation d'élevage, *f*.

grease, *n*, graisse, *f*; (*in wool*) suint, *m*. ~ *box*, boîte à graisse, *f*. ~ *paint*, fard, *m*. ~*-proof paper*, papier imperméable à la graisse, p. sulfurisé, *m*. ¶ *v.t*: graisser; suiffer. greasiness, *n*, onctuosité, *f*. ~ *pole*, mât de cocagne, *m*.

greasy, *a*, graisseux, gras, onctueux.

great, *a*, grand; gros; fort. ~ *aunt*, grandtante, *f*. ~ *bell*, bourdon, *m*. G~ *Britain*, la Grande-Bretagne. ~*coat*, pardessus, *m*; (*Mil.*) capote, *f*. ~ *Dane*, grand danois, *m*. *a* ~ *deal*, *a* ~*many*, beaucoup. ~*grandchildren*, arrière-petits-enfants, *m.pl*. ~*granddaughter*, ~*son*, arrière-petite-fille, *f*, a.-petit-fils, *m*. ~*grandfather* *-mother*, arrière-grand-père, *m*, a.-grand-mère, *f*, bisaïeul, e. ~*grandfather*, *-mother*, trisaïeul, e. ~ *toe*, gros doit du pied, orteil, *m*. ~ *uncle*, grandoncle, *m*. the ~ (*de la terre*), le grand. the ~ *ones*, les grands (*de la terre*). ~ly, *ad*, grandement; fort. ~ness, *n*, grandeur, *f*.

grebe, *n*, grèbe, *m*.

Grecian, *a*, grec. Greece, *n*, la Grèce.

greed[iness], *n*, avidité, âpreté; gourmandise, *f*. greedy†, *a*, avide; gourmand, goulu.

Greek, *a*, grec. ~ *fret* (*Arch.*), grecque, *f*. ¶ *n*, (*pers.*) Grec, ecque; (*language*) le grec; (*fig.*) du grec, de l'hébreu (*to me* = pour moi).

green, *a*, vert; en herbe; novice; naïf. ~ *baize*, tapis vert, drap v., *m*. ~*finch*, verdier, *m*. ~*fly*, puceron, *m*. ~*gage*, [prune de] reine-claude, *f*. ~*grocer*, marchand de légumes, *m*, fruitier, ère. ~*horn*, novice, conscrit, pigeon, *m*. ~*house*, serre, *f*. ~ *peas*, petits pois, pois verts, *m.pl*. ~*room*, foyer des artistes, *m*. ~ *stuff* or greens, *n.pl*, herbages, légumes

verts, *m.pl*, verdure, *f*. ~*sward*, tapis de gazon, *m*, herbette, verdure, *f*; (*roadside*) accotement, *m*. ~*wood*, feuillée, ramée, *f*. ~*yard*, fourrière, *f*. ¶ *n*, vert, *m*; (*grass plot & Golf*) pelouse, *f*. *through the* ~ (*Golf*), à travers le parcours. ¶ *v.t.* & *i*, verdir, verdoyer. ~ery, *n*, verdure, *f*. ~ish, *a*, verdâtre.

Greenland, *n*, le Groenland.

greenness, *n*, verdure; verdeur; naïveté, *f*.

greet, *v.t*, saluer; accueillir. ~ing, *n*, salutation, *f*, salut, *m*.

gregarious, *a*, grégaire.

Gregorian, *a*, grégorien.

Grenada (*W. Indies*) *n*, la Grenade. grenade, *n*, grenade, *f*. grenadine, *n*, (*cordial, fabric*) grenadine, *f*; (*Cook.*) grenadin, *m*.

grey, grey, *a*, *&* *n*, gris, *a*, *&* *m*. ~ *friar*, franciscain, *m*. ~ *matter of the brain*, substance grise (*ou* cendrée) du cerveau, *f*. ~ *mullet*, mulet, muge, *m*. ~ily, grisailler. ~ish, *a*, grisâtre. ~ness, *n*, couleur grise, *f*.

greyhound, *n*, lévrier, *m*, levrette, *f*. ~ *racing*, courses de lévriers, *f.pl*.

grid, *n*, grille, *f*. ~*iron*, gril, *m*.

grief, *n*, chagrin, *m*, douleur, peine, affliction, *f*. grievance, *n*, grief, *m*. grieve, *v.t*, chagriner, affliger, peiner, fâcher. grievous†, *a*, grave; cruel.

griffin, griffon, *n*, griffon, *m*.

grill, *n*, gril, *m*; (*meat*) grillade, *f*. ¶ *v.t*, [faire] griller.

grill[e], *n*, grille, *f*.

grim, *a*, farouche, rébarbatif; macabre. ~ *death*, la camarde.

grimace, *n*, grimace, *f*, rictus, *m*. ¶ *v.i*, grimacer.

grime, *n*, crasse, *f*. ¶ *v.t*, encrasser, noircir. grimy, *a*, crasseux, noir.

grin, *n*, grimace, *f*. ¶ *v.i*, grimacer.

grind, *v.t.ir*, moudre; broyer; aiguiser, affûter, repasser; roder; grincer [de]; pressurer, opprimer; jouer. ~ *at*, piocher. ~*stone*, meule en grès, *f*. ~ery, *n*, crépins, *m.pl*. ~ing (*corn*) *n*, mouture, *f*.

grip, *n*, prise, pince, serre; poigne; étreinte; poignée; griffe, *f*. ¶ *v.t*, saisir, empoigner, serrer, étreindre; pincer, agripper.

gripes, *n.pl*, tranchées, *f.pl*; colique, *f*.

grisly, *a*, effrayant, horrible, affreux.

grist, *n*, blé à moudre, *m*.

gristle, *n*, cartilage, *m*. gristly, *a*, cartilagineux.

grit, *n*, graviers, *m.pl*, sable; grès, *m*; (*fig.*) de l'étoffe. gritty, *a*, graveleux; pierreux.

grizzled, *a*, grison. grizzly bear, ours grizzly, ours grizzlé, *m*.

groan, *n*, gémissement, *m*. ¶ *v.i*, gémir.

groats, *n.pl*, gruau; gruau d'avoine, *m*.

grocer, *n*, épicier, ère. ~'s *shop* & grocery, *n*, épicerie, *f*.

grog, *n*, grog, *m*. groggy, *a*, ivre; aviné; chancelant.

groin, *n*, aine; (*Arch.*) arête, *f*.

groom, *n*, palefrenier, *m*. ¶ *v.t*, panser.

groomsman, *n*, garçon d'honneur, *m*.

groove, *n*, rainure; cannelure, *f*; sillon, *m*; gorge; ornière, *f*. ¶ *v.t*, canneler; sillonner.

grope, *v.t. & i*, fouiller, tâtonner.

grosbeak, *n*, gros-bec, *m*.

gross†, *a*, grossier; gros; (*Com.*) brut. ¶ (*144*) *n*, grosse, *f*. ~ness, *n*, grossièreté, *f*.

grotesque†, *a. & *~[ness] *n*, grotesque, *a. & m*. ¶ (*Art*), *n*, grotesque, *f*.

grotto, *n*, grotte, *f*.

ground, *n*, terre, *f*; sol; terrain; champ, *m*; place, *f*; fond; plan; sujet, lieu, *m*, raison, (*pl.*) cause, *f*, lieu, *m*, matière, *f*; (*pl, Law*) motifs, moyens, *m.pl*; (*pl, dregs*) marc, *m*; effondrilles, *f.pl*; sédiment; *m*; (*of mansion*) dehors, *m.pl*, parc, *m*; (*fishing, cruising*) parages, *m.pl*. ~ *angling*, pêche de fond, *f*. ~ *floor*, rez-de-chaussée, *m*. ~ *game*, gibier à poil, *m*. ~ *ivy*, lierre terrestre, *m*. ~ *landlord*, propriétaire foncier, *m*. ~ *line* (*Fish.*), ligne de fond, traînée, *f*. ~ *man*, gardien du terrain, *m*. ~nut, arachide, cacahuète, *f*. ~ *rent*, redevance foncière, *f*. ~ *sheet*, toile de sol, *f*. ~ *swell*, houle de fond, *f*. ~*work*, base, *f*; canevas, *m*. ¶ *p.p*, en poudre; moulu; (*rice, &c*) farine de . . .; (*glass*) dépoli; (*stopper*) à l'émeri. ¶ *v.t. & i*, mettre à terre; (*Elec.*) m. à la terre; fonder; (*ship*) échouer, engraver. ~less, *a. & ~*lessly, *ad*, sans fondement; en l'air.

groundsel, *n*, seneçon, *m*.

group, *n*, groupe, *m*. ~ *firing* (*Artil.*), feu concentré, *m*, mitraille, *f*. ¶ *v.t*, grouper.

grouse, *n*, petit coq de bruyère, tétras, *m*, grouse, *f*; (*young*) grianneau, *m*. ¶ *v.i*, rogner, bougonner.

grout[ing] (*Build.*) *n*, coulis, *m*.

grove, *n*, bocage, bosquet, *m*.

grovel, *v.i*, ramper.

grow, *v.i.ir*, croître; pousser; venir; grandir; [s']accroître; devenir, se faire; *often expressed by se, e.g.* ~ *cold*, se refroidir; (*v.t.ir.*) cultiver. ~ *green again & ~ young again*, reverdir. ~er, *n*, cultivateur, trice, planteur, euse. ~*ing crops*, récoltes sur pied, *f.pl*.

growl, *n*, grondement, *m*. ¶ *v.i*, gronder.

grown up, grand. grown-up, *a. & n*, adulte, *a. & m.f*, grande personne, *f*. growth, *n*, croissance; venue; pousse; végétation, *f*; (*vintage*) cru; développement, *m*.

groyne, *n*, brise-lames, brisant, *m*.

grub, *n*, larve, *f*, ver, *m*. ~ [up], *v.t*, défricher, essarter. grubber, *n*, arracheuse, *f*.

grubby, *a*, (*wormy*) véreux; (*dirty*) crasseux.

grudge, *n*, rancune, *f*. ¶ *v.t*, marchander, reprocher à.

gruel, *n*, gruau, *m*, bouillie, *f*.

gruesome, *a*, macabre.

gruff, *a*, rude, brusque, bourru.

grumble, *v.i*, murmurer, gronder, grogner.

~ *at*, ~ *about*, grommeler, marmonner. grumpy, *a*, bourru.

grunt, *n*, grognement, *m*. ¶ *v.i*, grogner.

guano, *n*, guano, *m*.

guarantee, -ty, *n*, garantie; caution, *f*; aval, *m*. ¶ *v.t*, garantir; cautionner; avaliser. guarantor, *n*, garant, e, caution, *f*.

guard, *n*, garde; sentinelle, *f*; protecteur, *m*; (*pers.*) garde; (*train*) conducteur; (*Bookb.*) onglet, *m*. on ~, en faction. ~ *house*, ~ *room*, corps de garde, poste, *m*, salle de police, *f*. ~'s *van*, fourgon, *m*. ¶ *v.t. & i*, [se] garder; se prémunir; parer. ~ed, *p.a*, mesuré; réservé. guardian, *n*, gardien, ne; curateur, trice, tuteur, trice, correspondant, e; (*att.*) gardien, tutélaire. ~ship, *n*, garde; (*Law*) tutelle, curatelle, *f*.

guava, *n*, goyave, *f*; (*tree*) goyavier, *m*.

gudgeon, *n*, goujon; tourillon, *m*.

guelder rose, boule de neige, *f*, obier, *m*.

guer[r]illa, *n*, guérilla, *f*, partisan, *m*. ~ *war[fare]*, guerre de guérillas, g. de partisan, *f*.

Guernsey, *n*, Guernesey, *f*. g~, *n*, vareuse, *f*.

guess, *n*, conjecture, *f*. ¶ *v.t. & i*, deviner, conjecturer.

guest, *n*, convive, *m.f*, convié, e; hôte, esse, invité, e. ~ *chamber*, chambre d'ami, *f*. ~ *of honour*, invité(e) d'honneur.

guffaw, *v.i*, rigoler.

Guiana, *n*, la Guyane.

guidance, *n*, direction; gouverne, *f*. guide, *n*, guide; cicerone, *m*. ~ [*book*], guide, indicateur, *m*. ~ *post*, poteau indicateur, *m*. ~ *rope*, câble-guide, *f*. (*Aero.*) guiderope, *m*. ¶ *v.t*, guider, conduire. guiding principle, idée directrice, *f*.

g[u]ild, *n*, corps de métier, *m*, corporation; association, *f*; (*church*) patronage, *m*. guildhall, *n*, hôtel de ville, *m*.

guile, *n*, ruse, astuce, *f*, artifice, fard, *m*. ~less, *a*, innocent, candide; naïf.

guillotine, *n*, guillotine, *f*; (*for paper cutting*) massicot, *m*. ¶ *v.t*, guillotiner.

guilt, *n*, culpabilité, *f*. ~less, *a*, innocent. ~y, *a*, coupable, criminel.

guinea (21/-) *n*, guinée, *f*. ~ *fowl*, pintade, *f*. ~ *pig*, cochon d'Inde, cobaye; (*pers.*) coureur de jetons de présence, *m*. G~ (*Geog.*), la Guinée.

guise, *n*, apparence, *f*.

guitar, *n*, guitare, *f*.

gules (*Her.*) *n*, gueules, *m*.

gulf, *n*, golfe; gouffre, abîme, *m*. G~ *of the Lion*, golfe du Lion, *m*. G~ *Stream*, Gulf-Stream, *m*.

gull, *n*, (*sea*) mouette, *f*, goéland, *m*; (*pers.*) dupe, *f*. ¶ *v.t*, duper.

gullet, *n*, gosier, *m*, gorge, *f*.

gullible, *a*, crédule.

gully, *n*, ravine, *f*, ravin; (*gutter*) caniveau, *m*. ~ *hole*, bouche d'égout, *m*.

gulp, *n*, goulée, gorgée, *f*, trait, *m*. to ~ *down*, gober.

gum, *n*, gomme; (*Anat.*) gencive, *f*. ~ *arabic*, gomme arabique. ~*boil*, abcès aux gencives, *m*. ~ *tree*, gommier, *m*. ¶ *v.t*, gommer. **gummy**, *a*, gommeux.

gumption, *n*, entregent, savoir-faire, *m*.

gun, *n*, fusil; canon, *m*, pièce, *f*. ~*boat*, [chaloupe] canonnière, *f*. ~ *captain*, chef de pièce, *m*. ~ *carriage*, affût, *m*. ~*cotton*, coton-poudre, fulmicoton, *m*. ~ *licence*, port d'armes, *m*. ~ *layer*, pointeur, *m*. ~ *metal*, bronze [industriel] *m*. ~*powder*, poudre à canon, *f*. ~*shot*, portée de fusil, p. de canon, *f*. ~*shot wound*, blessure d'arme à feu, *f*. ~*smith*, armurier, *m*. **gunner**, *n*, artilleur, canonnier, servant, *m*. ~**y**, *n*, tir, *m*, artillerie, *f*, canonnage, *m*.

gunwale, **gunnel**, *n*, plat-bord, *m*.

gurgle, *n*, glouglou, *m*. ¶ *v.i*, faire glouglou; gargouiller.

gurnard, **gurnet**, *n*, trigle, grondin, rouget, *m*.

gush, *n*, jaillissement, bouillon, *m*; sentimentalité, *f*. ¶ *v.i*, jaillir.

gusset, *n*, gousset, *m*.

gust, *n*, coup, *m*, bourrasque, rafale, bouffée, *f*.

gusto, *n*, entrain, *m*.

gusty, *a*, (*wind*) impétueux; (*day*) de grand vent.

gut, *n*, boyau; intestin; (*Fish.*) crin, florence, *m*, racine, *f*; (*Naut.*) goulet, *m*. ¶ *v.t*, vider, étriper.

gutta-percha, *n*, gutta-percha, *f*.

gutter, *n*, (roof) gouttière, *f*, chéneau; (*street*) ruisseau; (*conduit*) caniveau; chenal, *m*; rigole, *f*; (*book*) blancs de petit fond, *m.pl*; (*fig.*) ruisseau; carrefour, *m*, crasse, fange, crotte, *f*. ~ *language*, langage de carrefour, *m*. ~*snipe*, voyou, *m*. ¶ *v.i*, couler.

guttural, *a*, guttural. ¶ *n*, gutturale, *f*.

guy, *n*, (rope) hauban, *m*; (*pers.*) caricature, *f*, mardi gras, *m*.

guzzle, *v.i*, bâfrer, goinfrer.

gymnasium, *n*, gymnase, *m*. **gymnast**, *n*, gymnaste, gymnasiarque, *m*. ~**ic**, *a. & n*, gymnastique, *a. & f*. ~**ics**, *n.pl*, gymnastique, gymnique, *f*.

gynaecology, *n*, gynécologie, *f*.

gypseous, *a*, gypseux. **gypsum**, *n*, gypse, *m*. ~ *quarry*, plâtrière, *f*.

gyrate, *v.i*, tourner. **gyration**, *n*, giration, *f*. **gyratory**, *a*, giratoire. **gyroscope**, *n*, gyroscope, *m*.

H

haberdasher, *n*, mercier, ère. ~**y**, *n*, mercerie, *f*.

habiliment, *n*, attirail; (*pl.*) habillement, *m*.

habit, *n*, habitude, coutume, *f*; (*pl.*) mœurs, *f.pl*; tic; (*dress*) habit, *m*. *to be in the ~ of doing so*, être coutumier (ère) du fait. ~**able**, *a*, habitable. **habitat**, *n*, habitat,

m. **habitation**, *n*, habitation, *f*. **habitual**†, *a*, habituel, familier. ~ *criminal*, repris de justice, *m*. **habituate**, *v.t*, habituer.

hack, *n*, entaille, *f*; cheval de louage; c. de selle, *m*; (jade) rosse, *f*. ~ *saw*, scie à métaux, *f*. ~ [writer], écrivailleur, euse, manœuvre, *m*. ¶ *v.t*, écharper, hacher, charcuter.

hackney carriage, voiture de place; v. de louage, *f*. **hackneyed**, *p.p*, banal, rebattu, usé jusqu'à la corde. ~ *phrase*, cliché, *m*. ~ *refrain*, rengaine, *f*.

haddock, *n*, aigrefin, *m*.

Hades, *n*, les enfers, *m.pl*.

haematite, *n*, hématite, *f*.

haemorrhage, *n*, hémorragie, *f*. **haemorrhoids**, *n.pl*, hémorroïdes, *f.pl*.

haft, *n*, manche, *m*, poignée, *f*.

hag, *n*, sorcière, *f*.

haggard, *a*, hagard, tiré.

haggle, *v.i*, marchander, barguigner, chipoter.

Hague (the), la Haye.

ha-ha (*sunk fence*) *n*, saut de loup, *m*.

hail, *n*, grêle, *f*, grésil, *m*. *to damage by* ~, grêler. ~*stone*, grain de grêle, (big) grêlon, *m*. ~ *storm*, orage [accompagné] de grêle, *m*, giboulée, *f*. ¶ *i*, salut! ~ *fellow well met*, de pair à compagnon. ¶ *v.i.imp*, grêler, grésiller; (*v.t*.) faire pleuvoir; saluer; héler; acclamer. ~ *from*, venir de. *within* ~, à portée de la voix.

hair, *n*, (un) cheveu, *m*; (des) cheveux, *m.pl*; chevelure, *f*; poil; crin, *m*; soie; bourre, *f*. ~ *broom*, balai d'appartement, b. de soie, *m*. ~*brush*, brosse à cheveux, b. à tête, *f*. ~ *comb*, peigne coiffeur, *m*. ~ *curler*, épingle à friser, *f*; (leather) bigoudi à f., *m*. ~ *cutting*, coupe de cheveux, *f*. ~*dresser*, coiffeur, euse. ~*dresser's head*, marotte, *f*. ~ *drier*, appareil à douche d'air, *m*. ~ *mattress*, matelas de crin, *m*. ~ *net*, filet à cheveux, *m*, résille, *f*. ~ *oil*, huile pour les cheveux, *f*. ~*pin*, épingle à cheveux, *f*. ~*pin bend*, virage en é. à c., *m*. ~*pin crochet*, crochet à la fourche, *m*. ~*shirt*, haire, *f*. ~*splitting*, pointillerie, argutie, *f*. ~ *spring*, spiral, *m*. ~ *waver*, épingle à onduler, *f*. ~**less**, *a*, sans poils; glabre. ~**y**, *a*, velu; poilu; chevelu.

hake, *n*, merlus, *m*; (dried) merluche, *f*.

halation (*Phot.*) *n*, halo, *m*.

halberd (*Hist.*) *n*, hallebarde, *f*.

halcyon days, jours alcyoniens; (*fig.*) jours sereins, *m.pl*.

hale, *a*, sain, vert, verdelet, frais. ~ *& hearty*, frais & gaillard, frais & dispos.

half, *n*, moitié; demie, *f*; demi; (Rly ticket) coupon, *m*. *by* ~, à moitié; de moitié. *to go halves with*, être (ou se mettre) de moitié avec. *No* 29½ (house), No 29 bis. ¶ *a*, demi-. *on* ~ *profits*, à moitié. ¶ *ad*, moitié; à moitié; à mi-; à demi. ~ *a crown*, une demi-couronne. ~ *a cup*, la moitié d'une tasse, une demi-tasse.

~ *an hour*, une demi-heure. ~*-back* (*Foot.*), demi, *m.* ~ *binding*, demi-reliure à petits coins, *f.* ~*-bred*, métis. ~*-breed*, métis, métisse. ~*-brother*, demi-frère, *m.* ~*-caste*, [homme de] sang mêlé, *m.* ~*-cock*, repos, *m.* ~*-commission man*, remisier, *m.* ~*-distance line* (*Water Polo*), ligne du milieu, *f.* ~ *fare*, ~ *price*, demi-place, *f.* ~ *holiday*, demi-congé, *m.* ~*-hose*, [de]mi-bas, *m.pl,* chaussettes, *f.pl.* ~*-hunter*, montre à guichet, *f.* ~*-length portrait*, portrait en buste, *m.* ~ *light*, demi-jour, *m.* at ~*-mast* (flag), en berne. ~*-open*, a, entrouvert, entrebâillé; (*v.t.*) entrouvrir. ~ *past twelve*, midi & demi; minuit & demi. ~ *past two*, deux heures & demie. on ~ *pay*, en demi-solde. ~*penny*, demi-penny, *m.* ~*-sister*, demi-sœur, *f.* ~ *time* (*Foot.*), la mi-temps. ~*-title*, faux titre, *m.* ~*-tone block*, cliché simili, *m.* ~*-tone engraving*, simili-gravure, *f.* ~*-tone screen*, trame, *f.* ~ *way*, à mi-chemin, à moitié chemin. ~*-way house*, maison à mi-chemin, *f.* ~*-way line*, (*Association*) ligne de milieu; (*Rugby*) ligne d'envoi, *f.* ~ *way up* [*the hill*], à mi-côte. ~*-witted*, simple. ~*-year*, semestre, *m.* ~*-yearly*, a, semestriel; (*ad.*) par semestre.

halibut, *n*, flétan, *m.*

hall, *n*, vestibule; hall, *m*; salle: enceinte, *f*; château, *m.* ~*-mark*, *n*, [poinçon de] contrôle, *m*; (*v.t.*) contrôler, poinçonner. ~ *porter*, concierge, *m.* ~ *stand*, vestiaire, *m.*

hallelujah, *n*, Alléluia, *m.*

hallo[**a**], *i*, holà!, hé! ~ *there!* hé là-bas!

halloo, *n*, cri [d'appel] *m.* ¶ *v.i*, crier, huer; (*v.t, dogs*) houper, encourager. ~ *to*, appeler à grands cris.

hallow, *v.t*, sanctifier, consacrer. ~*ed*, *p.a*, saint.

hallucination, *n*, hallucination, vision, *f.*

halo, *n*, halo, *m*, auréole, *f*, nimbe, *m.*

halt, *n*, halte, station, *f*; stationnement, *m.* ¶ *i*, halte[-là]! ¶ *v.i*, faire halte; stationner; (*waver*) balancer; (*limp*) boiter.

halter, *n*, (*Harness*) licou, *m*; (*hanging*) corde, *f.*

halting, *a*, boiteux.

halve, *v.t*, partager en deux, p. par la moitié. ~*d hole* (*Golf*), trou partagé, *m.*

halyard, *n*, drisse, *f.*

ham, *n*, (*in man*) jarret; (*hog, boar*) jambon, *m.* ~ *& eggs*, œufs au jambon, *m.pl.*

Hamburg, *n*, Hambourg, *m.*

hames, *n.pl*, attelles, *f.pl.*

hamlet, *n*, hameau, *m.*

hammer, *n*, marteau; (*power*) pilon; (*gun*) chien, *m.* ~ *cloth*, housse, *f.* ~ *lock* (*Wrestling*), retournement de bras, *m.* ¶ *v.t*, marteler, battre.

hammock, *n*, hamac, *m.*

hamper, *n*, [gros] panier, *m*, manne; maile en osier, *f*; (*impedimenta*) bataclan; (*Naut.*) fardage, *m.* ¶ *v.t*, empêtrer; troubler.

hand, *n*, main, *f*; poing, *m*; (*pointer*) aiguille; écriture; signature, *f*; (*side*) côté, *m*, part; (*Cards*) main, *f*, jeu, *m*; (*horse*) = 4 inches or 10-16 centimetres; (*pl, men*) bras, hommes, *m.pl*; (*att.*) à main, à bras; à la main; manuel. *on* ~. See under *on*. *on the other* ~, de l'autre côté, d'autre part. ~ *bag* (lady's, &c), sac à main, *m.* ~*bill*, prospectus, imprimé; (*political, &c*) tract, *m.* ~*book*, manuel, livret, aide-mémoire, guide-âne, mémento, *m.* ~*cuff*, *v.t* mettre les menottes à; (*n.pl.*) menottes, *f.pl.* ~*kerchief*, mouchoir, *m*; (*silk*) pochette, *f.* ~*s off!* bas les mains! ~ *rail*, main courante, rampe, *f*, garde-fou, *m.* ~*shake*, poignée de main, *f.* ~*spike*, levier; anspect; espar, *m.* ~ *to* ~ (fight), corps à corps. *from* ~ *to mouth*, au jour le jour. ~*s up!* haut les mains! ~*writing*, écriture, *f.* ¶ *v.t*, passer. ~ *down* (*fig.*), transmettre. ~ *in*, déposer. ~ [*over*], remettre, délivrer. ~ *over* (to justice), remettre, déférer. ~*ful*, *n*, poignée, *f.*

handicap, *n*, (*Sport*) handicap; (*fig.*) désavantage, *m.* ¶ *v.t*, handicaper; désavantager. **handicapper**, *n*, handicapeur, *m.*

handicraft, *n*, industrie d'art, *f.* *handicraftsman*, ouvrier d'art, *m.*

handle, *n*, manche, *m*; poignée; (*umbrella*) poignée; main; manivelle; manette, *f*; bras; fût, *m*; anse; queue; branche; boucle, *f*; bouton, *m.* ~*bar* (cycle), guidon, *m.* ¶ *v.t*, manier; manipuler; traiter; filer; emmancher. *one who knows how to handle* (money, men), manieur, *m.* *to* ~ *roughly*, malmener. **handling**, *n*, manutention, *f*, maniement, *m*, manipulation, *f.*

handsel, *n*, étrennes, *f.pl.* ¶ *v.t*, étrenner.

handsome, *a*, beau; riche. ~*ly*, *ad*, grassement. ~*ness*, *n*, beauté, *f.*

handy, *a*, sous la main; commode; maniable; adroit; (*man*) à tout faire. ~*-pandy* (hand, *Nursery talk*), menotte, *f.*

hang, *v.t. & i. ir*, pendre; suspendre; [r]accrocher; tomber; tapisser, tendre; poser. ~ *about*, rôder. ~ *heavy* (time), durer. ~ *out* (washing), étendre. ~*-dog*, *a*, patibulaire. ~*man*, bourreau, *m.* ~*nail*, envie, *f.*

hangar, *n*, hangar [d'aviation], garage [d'aéroplane] *m.*

hanger, *n*, crochet de suspension, *m*; (*Mach.*) chaise, *f.* ~*-on*, suivant, e; personne à charge, *f*; parasite, *m.* **hanging**, *p.a*, suspendu. ~ *committee* (Art), jury d'admission, *m.* ~ *cupboard*, penderie, *f.* ~ *garden*, jardin suspendu, *m.* ~ *lamp*, baladeuse, *f.* ~ *matter*, cas pendable, *m.* [*death by*] ~, pendaison, mort par suspension, *f.* **hangings**, *n.pl*, tapisserie, *f.*

hank, *n*, écheveau, *m*, poignée, *f*.

hanker after, soupirer après, avoir soif de.

Hanover, *n*, Hanovre, *m*; (*province*) le H.

haphazard, *ad*, au hasard, à l'aventure.

hapless, *a*, infortuné.

happen, *v.i*, arriver; advenir, venir, se passer, se trouver. ∼ing, *n*, fait, *m*.

happiness, *n*, bonheur, *m*; félicité, *f*. happy†, *a*, heureux. ∼-*go-lucky person*, sanssouci, *m.f. to a* ∼ *issue*, à bon port. ∼ *medium*, juste milieu, *m. a* ∼ *new year*, la bonne année.

harangue, *n*, harangue, *f*. ¶ *v.t. & i*, haranguer.

harass, *v.t*, harceler, fouler.

harbinger, *n*, avant-coureur, messager, fourrier, *m*.

harbour, *n*, port; refuge, *m*. ∼ *master*, capitaine de port, *m*. ∼ *station*, gare maritime, *f*. ¶ *v.t*, héberger; nourrir; garder; (*criminal*) receler.

hard, *a*, dur; rude; rigoureux; ardu, laborieux, pénible; (*water*) crue. ∼ & *fast*, absolu, immuable. ∼-*bitten sailor*, loup de mer, *m*. ∼-*boiled* (egg), dur. ∼ *brush*, brosse rude, *f*. ∼ *cash*, espèces sonnantes, *f.pl*. ∼ *court* (*Ten.*), terre battue, *f*. ∼ *labour*, travail disciplinaire, *m*. ∼ *palate*, palais dur, *m*. ∼ *roe*, œufs, *m.pl*. ∼-*roed*, œuvé. ∼ *solder*, soudure forte, *f*. ∼ *tack*, galette, *f*. ∼ *to please*, exigeant. ∼*ware*, quincaillerie; (*builder's*) serrurerie, *f*. ∼-*wearing & for* ∼ *wear*, inusable. ∼-*working*, laborieux. ¶ *ad*, dur; durement; fort; fortement; (*drink*) sec; (*look*) fixement; (*raining*) à verse. ∼ *up*, à sec, aux abois. harden, *v.t*, durcir, endurcir; (*to temper metal*) tremper. hardihood, *n*, hardiesse, *f*. hardly, *ad*, durement; à peine; ne . . . guère; presque. hardness, *n*, dureté; rigueur; (*water*) crudité, *f*. ∼ *of hearing*, dureté d'oreille. hardship, *n*, privation; rigueur, *f*. hardy, *a*, hardi; (*plant*) robuste, rustique.

hare, *n*, lièvre, *m*; (*young*) levraut, *m*. ∼ & *hounds*, rallye-paper, *m*. ∼-*bell*, campanule, clochette, *f*. ∼-*brained*, écervelé. ∼-*lip*, bec-de-lièvre, *m*.

harem, *n*, harem, *m*.

haricot beans (*dried*), haricots secs, *m.pl*.

hark, *i*, écoute!, écoutez!

harlequin, *n*, arlequin, *m*. ∼ade, *n*, arlequinade, *f*.

harm, *n*, mal; tort, *m*. ¶ *v.t*, faire du mal à; nuire à. ∼ful, *a*, nuisible, pernicieux. ∼less, *a*, inoffensif, innocent, anodin. ∼lessness, *n*, innocuité; innocence, *f*.

harmonic†, *a. & n*, harmonique, *a. f*. harmonica, *n*, harmonica, *m*. harmonious†, *a*, harmonieux. harmonium, *n*, harmonium, *m*. harmonize, *v.t*, harmoniser. harmony, *n*, harmonie, *f*; ensemble, *m*.

harness, *n*, harnais; harnachement, *m*. *die in* ∼, mourir debout. ∼ *maker*, bour-

relier; sellier, *m*. ∼ *room*, sellerie, *f*. ¶ *v.t*, harnacher; (*waterfall*) aménager.

harp, *n*, harpe, *f. to be always* ∼*ing on the same string*, chanter toujours la même antienne, rabâcher toujours les mêmes choses. ∼ist, *n*, harpiste, *m.f*.

harpoon, *n*, harpon, *m*. ¶ *v.t*, harponner.

harpsichord, *n*, clavecin, *m*.

harpy, *n*, harpie, *f*.

harrow, *n*, herse, *f*. ¶ *v.t*, herser; (*fig.*) déchirer, navrer.

harry, *v.t*, harceler; dévaster.

harsh†, *a*, dur; rude; âpre; aigre. ∼ness, *n*, dureté; rudesse; âpreté; aigreur, *f*.

hart, *n*, cerf, *m*. hartshorn, *n*, liqueur d'ammoniaque, *f*.

harum-scarum, *n*, hurluberlu, *m*.

harvest, *n*, moisson; récolte, *f*. ∼ *festival*, fête de la moisson, *f*. ∼-*man* (insect), faucheur, faucheux, *m*. ¶ *v.t*, moissonner; récolter. ∼er, *n*, moissonneur, euse; (*Mach.*) moissonneuse, *f*.

hash, *n*, hachis, *m*, capilotade, *f*. ¶ *v.t*, hacher.

hasp, *n*, moraillon, *m*.

hassock, *n*, agenouilloir; carreau, coussin, *m*.

haste, *n*, hâte; précipitation, *f*. *to [make]* ∼ & hasten, *v.i*, se dépêcher, se hâter, s'empresser. hasten, *v.t*, hâter, presser, précipiter. hasty†, *a*, hâtif, à la hâte, précipité; vif, emporté.

hat, *n*, chapeau, *m*. ∼ & *coat stand*, portechapeaux, portemanteau, *m*. ∼ *box*, boîte à chapeau(x), *f*. ∼ *brush*, brosse à chapeaux, *f*. ∼ *peg*, patère, *f*. ∼ *shop & ∼ trade*, chapellerie, *f*.

hatch (brood) *n*, couvée, *f*. ∼[*way*], *n*, panneau, *m*, écoutille, *f*. ¶ *v.i*, (*eggs*) éclore; (*v.t.*) faire éclore; (*fig.*) couver, ourdir, tramer; (*engrave*) hacher.

hatchet, *n*, hache à main, *f*. ∼ *face*, figure en lame de couteau, *f*.

hatching, *n*, éclosion; (*engraving*) hachure, *f*.

hatchment, *n*, écusson; blason funèbre, *m*.

hate, *n*, haine, *f*. ¶ *v.t*, haïr; détester. ∼ful†, *a*, haïssable; odieux. hater, *n*, ennemi, e (*of* = de). hatred, *n*, haine, *f*. *full of* ∼, haineux.

hatter, *n*, chapelier, *m*.

haughtily, *ad*, avec hauteur, d'une manière hautaine. haughtiness, *n*, hauteur, morgue, *f*. haughty, *a*, hautain, altier, rogue.

haul, *n*, coup de filet; parcours, trajet, *m*; acquisition, *f*. ¶ *v.t*, haler; traîner, tirer; remorquer; rouler. ∼ *down*, amener. ∼*age contractor*, entrepreneur de roulage, e, de transports, *m*.

haunch, *n*, hanche, *f*; (*meat*) quartier, cuissot, cimier; (*Arch.*) rein, *m*.

haunt, *n*, rendez-vous, lieu fréquenté (*of* = par); repaire, *m*, caverne, *f*, liteau, *m*. ¶ *v.t*, hanter, fréquenter; poursuivre.

hautboy (*Mus.*) *n*, hautbois, *m*.

Havana, *n*, la Havane. ∼ [*cigar*], cigare de la Havane, havane, *m*.

have, *v.t.ir*, avoir; posséder; jouir de; tenir; prendre; faire. ~ *on* (wear), porter, avoir. ~ *you finished?* (*Teleph.*), personne? personne?

haven, *n*, havre, port; (*fig.*) asile, *m*.

haversack, *n*, musette, f, sac, *m*.

havoc, *n*, ravage[s] *m.*[*pl.*], dégâts, *m.pl.*

Havre, *n*, le Havre.

haw (*Bot.*) *n*, cenelle, f. ~*finch*, gros-bec, *m*. ~*thorn*, aubépine, épine blanche, f. ¶ *v.i*, ânonner.

Hawaii, *n*, Hawaï, *m*. ~*an*, *a*, hawaïen.

hawk, *n*, faucon, *m*. ¶ *v.i*, chasser au faucon; (*throat*) graillonner; (*v.t.*) colporter. ~*er*, *n*, colporteur, *m*; crieur, euse; camelot, *m*. ~*ing* (*Falconry*) *n*, volerie, f.

hawser, *n*, haussière, amarre, f, grelin, *m*.

hay, *n*, foin, *m. oft. pl*. ~ *cock*, tas de foin, *m*. ~ *fever*, fièvre des foins, f. ~*loft*, fenil, *m*. ~*maker*, faneur, euse. ~*making*, fenaison, f. ~*rick*, ~*stack*, meule de foin, f.

Hayti, *n*, Haïti, *m*.

hazard, *n*, hasard, *m*; (*Golf*) hasard, accident, *m*. ¶ *v.t*, hasarder. ~*ous*†, *a*, hasardeux, chanceux.

haze, *n*, brume, f, brouillard; nuage, *m*.

hazel, *n*, noisetier, coudrier, *m*; (*att., colour, eyes*) [de] noisette, *m*. ~ *nut*, noisette, f.

hazy, *a*, brumeux; nuageux; vaporeux; vague; flou.

he, *pn*, il; lui; celui; ce, c'. ¶ *n. & att*, mâle, *m*. ~*goat*, bouc, *m*.

head, *n*, tête, f; cerveau, *m*; [*of hair*] chevelure, f; chef; titre; haut; fond; chapiteau; cap, *m*; pointe; pomme, f, poste, f, chapitre; en-tête; (*bed*) chevet, *m*; (*on glass of beer*) mousse, f; (*coin*) face; (*book page*) tête, tranche supérieure, f; (*deer*) bois, *m*; (*game*) pièce; (*boar, &c*) hure, f; (*ship*) avant, cap, *m*; (*lathe*) poupée, f; (*spear, &c*) fer, *m*. ~*s or tails?* pile ou face? ~*ache*, mal de tête, *m*. ~*band*, bandeau, serre-tête, *m*; (*Bookb.*) tranchefile, comète, f. ~ *clerk*, chef de bureau, *m*. ~ *cook*, chef [de cuisine] *m*. ~*dress*, ~*gear*, coiffure, coiffe, f, couvre-chef, *m*. ~*land*, pointe de terre, f, cap, *m*. ~*light*, feu d'avant, fanal de tête; (*motor*) phare, *m*. ~*line*, (*book*) titre courant, *m*; (*news*) manchette, f. ~*long*, *a*, précipité; (*ad.*) précipitamment. ~ *master*, directeur, principal; proviseur, *m*. ~*mastership*, direction, f; provisorat, *m*. ~*mistress*, directrice, f. ~ *of shoots*, cépée, trochée, f. ~ *office*, siège [principal], siège social, *m*. ~*-on collision*, rencontre de front, f. ~*phones*, casque, *m*. ~ *quarters*, quartier général; (*staff*) État-major; chef-lieu, *m*; préfecture, f. ~ *register* or *voice*, voix de tête, f. ~*room*, échappée, f. ~*sman*, bourreau, *m*. ~ *stall*, têtière, f. ~*stone*, pierre tombale, tombe, f. ~*strong*, entêté,

entier. ~ *waiter*, maître d'hôtel, premier garçon, chef de salle, *m*. ~ *waters*, amont, *m*. ~*way*, chemin, progrès, *m*; (*Naut.*) erre, f. ~ *wind*, vent debout, *m*. ¶ *v.t*, être (ou se mettre) à la tête de. ~ *the procession*, ouvrir la marche. ~*ed* (*paper*) *p.a*, à en-tête. ~*ing*, *n*, titre; en-tête, *m*; rubrique, f, poste, *m*; (*for tape*) coulisse, f. ~*y* (*liquor*) *a*, capiteux.

heal, *v.t*, guérir; (*v.i.*) [se] g. ~*er*, *n*, guérisseur, euse; (*of time*) médecin, *m*. ~*ing*, *n*, guérison, f.

health, *n*, santé, f; salubrité; hygiène, f. ~ *officer*, agent du service sanitaire, *m*. ~ *resort*, station climat[ér]ique, f. ~*y*†, *a*, sain; salubre; hygiénique.

heap, *n*, tas, amas, monceau, *m*. ¶ *v.t*, entasser, amonceler, amasser.

hear, *v.t. & i. ir*, entendre; écouter; (*witness —Law*) ouïr; (*learn*) apprendre; (*prayer*) exaucer. ~ *from*, lire. ~*er*, *n*, auditeur, trice. ~*ing*, *n*, ouïe; oreille; audition; audience, f; débats, *m.pl. to be hard of ~*, avoir l'ouïe (ou l'oreille) dure. ~*say*, on-dit, ouï-dire, *m*.

hearken, *v.i*, écouter.

hearse, *n*, corbillard, char [funèbre], char de deuil, *m*.

heart, *n*, cœur, *m*; âme, f; entrailles, f.pl; fond, vif, *m*. *by ~*, par cœur, de mémoire. ~ *& soul* (*fig.*), tout son cœur. ~*break*, brisement de cœur, *m*. ~*breaking*, ~*rending*, désespérant, navrant, déchirant. ~*burn*, ardeur d'estomac, f. ~ *case* (*pers.*), cardiaque, *m,f*. ~ *cherry*, guigne, f; (*tree*) guignier, *m*. ~ *disease*, maladie de cœur, f. *in one's ~ of ~s*, au fond du cœur. ~, *en*, *v.t*, encourager, rassurer. ~*felt*, *a*, bien senti. *to be ~less*, n'avoir point de cœur. ~*less person*, sans-cœur, *m,f*. **heartsease** (*Bot.*) *n*, pensée, f.

hearth, *n*, âtre; foyer; feu; (*smith's*) bâti, *m*. ~ *brush*, balai d'âtre, *m*. ~ *rug*, tapis de foyer, t. de cheminée, *m*. ~*stone*, pierre de foyer, f, [marbre de] foyer, *m*; (*whitening*) pierre blanche, f.

heartily, *ad*, cordialement; franchement.

hearty, *a*, cordial; (*fit*) dispos; (*laugh*) gros; (*meal*) solide, copieux.

heat, *n*, chaleur, f; calorique, *m*; température; chauffe; fièvre; vivacité, ardeur, f, feu, *m*; (*Sport*) épreuve, f, tour, *m*. ~ (*animals*) rut, *m*. ~ *lightning*, éclair[s] de chaleur, *m.*[*pl.*], fulguration, f. ~ *stroke*, coup de chaleur, *m*. ~ *wave*, vague de c., f. ¶ *v.t*, chauffer, échauffer. ~*er*, *n*, calorifère; réchaud; fer à chauffer, *m*.

heath, *n*, (*land*) bruyère, brande, lande; (*shrub*) bruyère, brande, f. ~*cock*, coq de bruyère, *m*.

heathen, *n*, païen, ne. ~[*ish*], *a*, païen. ~*ism*, *n*, paganisme, *m*.

heather, *n*, bruyère, brande, f.

heating, *n,* chauffage; échauffement, *m.* ~ *engineer,* fumiste, *m.* ~ *engineering,* fumisterie, *f.* ~ *surface,* surface de chauffe, *f.*

heave, *v.t.ir,* soulever; pousser; jeter; lancer; haler; virer; (*v.i.ir.*) palpiter; (*retch*) faire des haut-le-cœur. ~ *to* (*Naut.*), mettre en panne.

heaven, *n,* ciel, *m,* cieux, *m.pl.* ~**ly,** *a,* céleste.

heavier than air machine, [appareil] plus lourd que l'air, avion, *m.* **heavily,** *ad,* lourdement, pesamment. **heaviness,** *n,* pesanteur, *f,* poids, *m;* lourdeur, *f.* **heavy,** *a,* lourd; pesant; massif; fort; chargé; grave; gros; grand. ~*-checked,* maffiu. ~*-duty aeroplane,* avion gros porteur, *m.* ~ *fish,* gros poisson, *m,* grosse pièce, *f.* ~ *fishing,* pêche du gros poisson, p. des grosses pièces, *f.* ~ *shell* (*Artil.*), marmite, *f.* ~ *weight,* (*for lifting*) gueuse [d'athlétisme] *f;* (*for throwing*) gros boulet; (*Box.*) poids lourd, *m.*

Hebraic & **Hebrew,** *a,* hébraïque. **Hebrew** (*language*) *n,* l'hébreu, *m.*

hecatomb, *n,* hécatombe, *f.*

heckle, *v.t,* harceler [de questions].

hectic (*fever*) *a,* hectique.

hector, *n,* bravache, fanfaron, *m.*

hedge, *n,* haie, *f.* ~*hog,* hérisson, *m.* ~*row,* haie, *f.* ~ *sparrow,* fauvette des haies, *f,* mouchet, *m.* ¶ *v.t,* entourer [de haies]; (*v.i.*) chercher des échappatoires; (*Fin.*) faire un arbitrage, se couvrir. ~ *in,* [r]enfermer.

heed, *n,* attention; garde, *f.* ¶ *v.t,* faire attention à. ~**less,** *a,* insoucieux.

heel, *n,* talon, *m;* (*rubber*) talonnette; (*Naut.*) bande, *f.* *at the* ~*s,* aux trousses de. *to* ~ *out* (*Rugby*), talonner.

hefty, *a,* solide.

hegemony, *n,* hégémonie, *f.*

heifer, *n,* génisse, *f.*

height, *n,* hauteur, élévation, altitude, *f;* comble, plein, apogée, *m;* (*stature*) taille, *f;* (*of summer*) cœur, fort, *m.* ~ *standard* (apparatus), toise, *f.* ~**en,** *v.t,* rehausser; surélever.

heinous, *a,* odieux; atroce.

heir, ess, *n,* héritier, ère, hoir, *m.* ~*loom,* meuble de famille, *m.* ~*ship,* hérédité, *f.*

helianthus, *n,* hélianthe, *m.*

helical, *a,* en hélice, hélicoïdal.

helicopter, *n,* hélicoptère, *m.*

heliotrope, *n,* héliotrope, *m.*

helium, *n,* hélium, *m.*

helix, *n,* hélice, *f;* (*ear*) hélix, *m.*

hell, *n,* enfer, *m;* géhenne, *f;* (*gambling*) tripot, *m.* ~*-cat,* harpie, *f.*

Hellenism, *n,* hellénisme, *m.*

hellish, *a,* infernal.

hello (*Teleph.*) *i,* allô!

helm, *n,* barre, *f;* (*fig.*) gouvernail, timon, *m.* **helmsman,** homme de barre, *m.*

helmet, *n,* casque, *m.*

helot, *n,* ilote, *m.* ~**ism,** *n,* ilotisme, *m.*

help, *n,* aide, assistance, *f,* moyen, secours; remède, *m.* ¶ *v.t,* & *i,* aider, assister, secourir; s'empêcher; éviter. ~ *one another,* s'entraider. ~! au secours! à l'aide! à moi! à nous! ~**er,** *n,* aide, *m,f.* ~**ful,** *a,* secourable. ~**ing** (*food*) *n,* portion, *f.* ~**less,** *a,* impuissant; impotent.

helter-skelter, *ad.* & *n,* pêle-mêle, *ad.* & *m.*

helve, *n,* manche, *m.*

hem, *n,* ourlet; [re]bord, *m,* bordure; (*for tape*) coulisse, *f.* ¶ *v.t,* ourler; border; (*v.i.*) ânonner. ~ *in,* cerner.

hematite, *n,* hématite, *f.*

hemidemisemiquaver, *n,* quadruple croche, *f.*

hemisphere, *n,* hémisphère, *f.*

hemlock, *n,* ciguë, *f.*

hemorrhage, *n,* hémorragie, *f.* **hemorrhoids,** *n.pl,* hémorroïdes, *f.pl.*

hemming, *n,* point d'ourlet, *m.*

hemp, *n,* chanvre, *m.* ~ *seed,* chènevis, *m.* ~[**en**], *a,* de chanvre.

hemstitch, *n,* ourlet à jour, *m.* ¶ *v.t,* ourler à jour.

hen, *n,* poule; femelle, *f.* ~ *coop,* cage à poulets, mue, *f.* ~ *house,* poulailler, *m.* ~ *partridge,* perdrix femelle, *f.* ~*-pecked,* mené par sa femme. ~ *pheasant,* [poule] faisane, *f.* ~ *roost,* juchoir, *m.*

hence, *ad,* d'ici; de là; dans; partant; donc. ~**forth,** ~**forward,** *ad,* désormais, dorénavant, dès maintenant.

henchman, *n,* partisan, satellite, séide, *m.* mamel[o]uk, *m.*

henna, *n,* henné, *m.*

her, *pn* & *a,* la; le; lui; son, sa, ses.

herald, *n,* (*Hist.*) héraut; (*fig.*) avant-coureur, *m.* ¶ *v.t,* annoncer. ~**ic,** *a,* héraldique. ~**ry,** *n,* blason, *m,* héraldique, *f.*

herb, *n,* herbe, *f.* ~**aceous,** *a,* herbacé. ~ *border,* bordure de fleurs vivaces, *f.* ~**age,** *n,* herbage, *m.* ~**al,** *n,* herbier, *m.* ~**alist,** *n,* herboriste, *m,f.* ~**arium,** *n,* herbier, *m.* ~**ivorous,** *a.* & ~ *animal,* herbivore, *a.* & *m.* **herborize,** *v.i,* herboriser.

Herculean, *a,* herculéen. *a Hercules,* un hercule.

herd, *n,* troupeau, *m;* (*deer*) harde, *f.* ~ *book,* livre généalogique, herd-book, *m.* *the* [*common*] ~, le vulgaire. *the* ~ *instinct,* le sentiment grégaire. ~ *together,* vivre en troupe. ~*ed together,* empilé. **herdsman,** *n,* bouvier, pâtre, *m.*

here, *ad,* ici; que voici; y; présent! ~ *a little* & *there a little,* de bric & de broc. ~ & *there,* ici & là; de[çà] & [de]là; par-ci, par-là. ~ *below,* ici-bas. ~ *I am,* me voici. ~ *is,* ~ *are,* voici. ~ *lies* (*grave*), ci-gît, ici repose. [*look*] ~! tenez!

hereabout[**s**], *ad,* ici près, dans ces parages.

hereafter, *ad,* désormais, à l'avenir; dans la vie future. **hereby** (*Law*) *ad,* par les présentes.

hereditament, n, biens [transmissibles par voie de succession] m.pl. **hereditary†**, a, héréditaire. **heredity**, n, hérédité, f.

herein (Law) ad, dans les présentes. **hereinafter**, ad, ci-après.

heresy, n, hérésie, f. **heretic**, n, hérétique, m,f. **~al**, a, hérétique.

hereunder, ad, ci-dessous; de ce chef. **hereupon**, ad, sur ces entrefaites. **herewith**, ad, ci-joint, ci-inclus.

heritage, n, héritage, patrimoine, m.

hermaphrodite, n, hermaphrodite, m.

hermetic†, a, hermétique.

hermit, n, ermite, solitaire, m. ~ **crab**, bernard-l'ermite, m. **~age**, n, ermitage, m.

hernia, n, hernie, f.

hero, n, héros, m. ~ **worship**, culte des héros, m. **~ic†**, a, héroïque. **~icomic**, a, héroï-comique. **~ine**, n, héroïne, f. **~ism**, n, héroïsme, m.

heron, n, héron, m. **~ry**, n, héronnière, f.

herpes, n, herpès, f.

herring, n, hareng, m. ~ **boat**, harenguier, m. ~ **boning** (Need.), point croisé, m. ~ **fishery** & ~ **season**, harengaison, f.

hers, pn, le sien, la sienne, les siens, les siennes; ses; à elle. **herself**, pn, elle-même; elle; soi, soi-même; se.

hesitate, v.i, hésiter, balancer, marchander. **hesitation**, n, hésitation, f.

heterodox, a, hétérodoxe. **~y**, n, hétérodoxie, f.

heterogeneous, a, hétérogène.

hew, v.t.ir, (tree) abattre, couper; (stone) tailler.

hexagon, n, hexagone, m. **~al**, a, hexagone. ~ **nut**, écrou à 6 pans, m. **hexameter**, n, hexamètre, m.

heyday of life, midi de la vie, m, fleur de l'âge, f.

hi, i, ohé!

hiatus, n, fissure; lacune, f; (Gram.) hiatus, m.

hibernate (Zool.) v.i, hiberner.

hiccup, n, hoquet, m. ¶ v.i, avoir le h.

hidden, p.p, caché; dérobé; occulte; latent.

hide, v.t.ir, cacher. ~ [oneself], se cacher. **~-&-seek**, cache-cache, m. **~bound** (fig.), systématique.

hide, n, peau, f, cuir, m.

hideous†, a, hideux.

hiding (thrashing) n, raclée, f.

hiding place, cache[tte] f, affût, m.

hierarchy, n, hiérarchie, f.

hieroglyph, n, hiéroglyphe, m.

higgle, v.i, marchander, lésiner, liarder.

higgledy-piggledy, ad, pêle-mêle.

high, a, haut; plein; élevé; grand; gros; fort; (dear) cher; (meat) avancé; (game) faisandé; (in height) de haut, haut de. ~ **altar**, maître-autel, grand autel, m. ~ **& dry** (Naut.), échoué à sec. **~-born**, de haute naissance. ~ **bicycle**, bicycle, m. **~-class**, de marque; (wine) grand; haut; perfec-

tionné. ~ **collar**, faux col montant, m. ~ **dive**, plongeon d'une grande hauteur, m. **~-flown**, ampoulé. ~ **gear**, grande multiplication, f. **~-handed**, arbitraire; tyrannique. ~ **hat**, chapeau haut de forme, m. ~ **jump**, saut en hauteur, m. ~ **lights** (Art), rehauts, m.pl. ~ **mass**, grand-messe, messe chantée, f. **~-necked dress**, robe montante, f. ~ **priest**, grand prêtre, m. ~ **society**, ~ **life**, le grand monde. **~-speed steel**, acier [à coupe] rapide, m. ~ **tide**, ~ **water**, marée haute, pleine mer, f. **to be ~-waisted** (dress), avoir la taille haute. **~-water mark**, grand de l'eau, m, laisse de haute mer, f; (fig.)apogée, m. **~-way**, grand chemin, m, grand-route, grande route; voie publique, f. **~-way code**, code de la route, m. **~-wayman**, voleur de grand chemin, m. **~-way robbery**, vol de grand chemin, brigandage, m. **~-ways committee**, voirie, f. **~-words**, gros mots, m.pl, injures, f.pl. ¶ ad, haut. **~-er**, a, plus haut; supérieur. **~-bid**, surenchère, f. **~-education**, haut enseignement, m. ~ **mathematics**, mathématiques spéciales, f.pl. **~-notes** (Mus.), haut, m. **the ~-est bidder**, le plus offrant [& dernier enchérisseur]. **~-ly**, ad, hautement; fortement, éminemment. ~ **amusing**, désopilant, impayable. ~ **strung**, nerveux. **~-ness**, n, hauteur; (title) altesse, f.

hiker, n, excursionniste à pied, m,f.

hilarious, a, hilare. **hilarity**, n, hilarité, f.

hill, n, colline, f, coteau, m, côte, hauteur, f. ~ **climb**, course de côte, f. ~ **up** ~ **& down dale**, par monts & par vaux. ¶ (Hort.) v.t, butter, chausser. **hillock**, n, monticule, tertre, m, butte, f. **hilly**, a, montueux; accidenté.

hilt, n, poignée; garde, f.

him, pn, le; lui. **himself**, pn, lui-même; lui; soi, soi-même; se.

hind (deer) n, biche, f.

hind[er], a, de derrière; [d']arrière.

hinder, v.t, empêcher, gêner, entraver.

hindmost, a, dernier.

hindrance, n, empêchement, m. **without ~**, sans encombre.

Hindu, **-doo**, a, hindou. ¶ n, Hindou, m. **Hindustani**, n, l'hindoustani, m.

hinge, n, charnière; fiche; penture, f; (fig.) pivot, m. ¶ v.i, tourner, pivoter. **~d**, p.a, à charnière(s).

hinny, n, petit mulet, bardot, m.

hint, n, allusion; suggestion, f; mot [couvert] m. ¶ v.t, laisser entendre. ~ **at**, insinuer.

hip, n, hanche; (Arch.) arête, croupe, f. ~ **bath**, bain de siège, m. ~ **pocket**, poche revolver, f. ~ **measurement**, [con]tour de hanches, m.

hippodrome, n, hippodrome, m.

hippopotamus, n, hippopotame, m.

hire, *n*, louage, *m*, location, *f*; loyer, *m*.
~ *purchase*, ~ *system*, vente à tempérament, *v*. par abonnement, *f*. ¶ *v.t*, louer; (*assassin*, &c) soudoyer. ~**d**, *p.p*, de louage; à gages; mercenaire. ~ *carriage*, voiture de remise, *f*, remise, *m*. ~**ling**, *n*, mercenaire, *m,f*. **hirer**, *n*, loueur, euse.

hirsute, *a*, hirsute.

his, *pn & a*, le sien, la sienne, les siens, les siennes; son, sa, ses; à lui; de lui.

hiss, *v.t. & i*, siffler; chuter. ~[**ing**], *n*, sifflement; sifflet, *m*.

historian, *n*, historien, *m*. **historiated**, *a*, historié. **historic** & ~**al**, *a*, historique; d'histoire. **history**, *n*, histoire, *f*; historique, *m*.

histrion, *n*, histrion, *m*. ~**ic**, *a*, du théâtre.

hit, *n*, coup, *m*; pièce à succès; touche; balle au but, balle mise, *f*, coup au but, *m*. ~ *or miss*, au petit bonheur. ¶ *v.t.ir*, frapper; toucher; atteindre; attraper.

hitch, *n*, accroc, contretemps, *m*. ¶ *v.t*, accrocher.

hither (*Geog.*) *a*, citérieur. ~ & *thither*, çà & là; par-ci, par-là. ~**to**, *ad*, jusqu'à présent, jusqu'ici.

hive, *n*, ruche, *f*.

hoard, *n*, amas; magot, *m*. ¶ *v.t*, amasser; (*v.i.*) thésauriser.

hoarding, *n*, clôture en planches, *f*, palissade, *f*; panneau-réclame, *f*.

hoar frost, gelée blanche, *f*, givre, *m*.

hoarhound, *n*, marrube, *m*.

hoarse, *a*, enroué, éraillé; rauque. ~**ness**, *n*, enrouement, *m*.

hoary, *a*, blanc; blanchi.

hoax, *n*, mystification; attrape, *f*, canard, *m*; supercherie, *f*. ¶ *v.t*, mystifier; attraper. ~**er**, *n*, mystificateur, trice.

hob, *n*, plaque de cheminée, *f*; dessus [de fourneau] *m*.

hobble, *v.i*, clocher, clopiner, boiter; (*v.t.*) entraver. **hobbledehoy**, *n*, [garçon] godiche, *m*. **hobbling along**, clopin-clopant.

hobby, *n*, (*bird*) hobereau, *m*. (*an art, collecting, gardening*) *is his* ~, il est [grand] amateur de . . . . . . est sa folie, . . . est sa distraction. (*a sport*) *is his* ~, il est passionné pour le . . . ~ *horse*, cheval de bois, dada, *m*.

hobgoblin, *n*, esprit follet, *m*.

hobnail, *n*, caboche, *f*, gros clou, *m*. ~**ed**, *p.a*, ferré.

hob-nob with, être à tu & à toi avec; trinquer avec.

Hobson's choice (*it is*), c'est à prendre ou à laisser.

hock, *n*, vin blanc du Rhin; (*horse*) jarret, *m*.

hockey, *n*, hockey, *m*. ~ *skates*, patins de h., *m.pl*. ~ *stick*, crosse de h., canne de h., *f*, bâton de h., *m*.

hocus, *v.t*, mystifier, attraper. ~-**pocus**, *n*, jeu de passe-passe, *m*.

hod, *n*, oiseau [de maçon] *m*.

Hodge (*Eng.*) *n*, Jacques Bonhomme (*Fr.*) *m*.

hoe, *n*, houe; binette, *f*; sarcloir, *m*. ¶ *v.t*, houer; biner; serfouir.

hog, *n*, cochon, pourceau, porc [châtré] *m*. ~**backed**, en dos d'âne. **hoggish**, *a*, bestial.

hogshead, *n*, barrique, *f*, boucaut, *m*.

hoist, *n*, treuil; monte-charge, *m*. ¶ *v.t*, [re]monter; lever; hisser; guinder; (*flag*) arborer.

hold, *n*, prise, pince; emprise, mainmise, *f*; (*Box.*) tenu; empire, *m*; (*ship*) cale, *f*. ¶ *v.t.ir*, tenir; retenir; détenir; occuper; contenir; posséder, avoir; réputer; célébrer. ~-*all*, rouleau de couverture, fourre-tout, *m*. ~ *back*, ~ *in*, retenir. ~**fast**, crampon, *m*; patte, *f*; valet, *m*. ~ *forth*, pérorer. ~ *on*, tenir [bon]. t. sa position. ~ *on! the line!* (*Teleph.*), ne quittez pas! ~ *one's own*, se maintenir. ~ *one's nose*, se boucher le nez. ~ *one's tongue*, se taire. ~ *out*, tendre; présenter; durer. ~ *up*, soutenir. ~**er**, *n*, support, *m*; porte- *always m, e.g. tool* ~, porte-outil, *m*, douille, *f*; (*pers.*) détenteur, trice; titulaire, *m,f*; porteur, *m*. ~**ing**, *n*, tenue; détention; possession; propriété, *f*; avoir, *m*; valeur, *f*, portefeuille, *m*.

hole, *n*, trou; orifice, *m*; ouverture; (*fox's*) tanière; fosse, *f*, puits; œil, *m*; lumière, *f*; creux, *m*; piqûre, *f*; (*Golf*) trou [d'arrivée] *m*. ~-&-*corner*, négocié sous main. ¶ *v.t*, trouer, percer; (*Golf*) jouer dans le trou.

holiday, *n*, jour de fête; jour férié, *m*; fête, *f*; vacances, *f.pl*; [jour de] congé; campos, *m*; villégiature, *f*. ~ *camp*, colonie de vacances, *f*. ~ *resort*, centre de villégiature, *m*.

holily, *ad*, saintement. **holiness**, *n*, sainteté, *f*.

Holland (*Geog.*) *n*, la Hollande. ~**s** [**gin**], *n*, genièvre, schiedam, *m*. **h**~, *n*, toile écrue, toile bise, *f*.

hollo, *v.t*, houper.

hollow, *a*, creux; cave; caverneux; (*voice*) sourde. ~-*ground*, évidé, creusé. *to beat* ~, battre à plate couture. ¶ *n*, creux; enfoncement; entonnoir, *m*; cavité, *f*. ~ [*out*], *v.t*, creuser; évider; caver; miner; chambrer.

holly, *n*, houx, *m*. ~ *berry*, cenelle, *f*. **hollyhock**, *n*, rose trémière, passerose, *f*.

holocaust, *n*, holocauste, *m*; (*fig.*) immolation, saignée, *f*.

holster, *n*, fonte, *f*.

holy, *a*, saint; sacré; (*bread, water*) bénit, e; (*day*) férié. *Holy Ghost*, *Holy Spirit*, Saint-Esprit, *m*. *H*~ *Land*, Terre Sainte, *f*. ~ *orders*, ordres sacrés, *m.pl*, prêtrise, *f*. *H*~ *See*, Saint-Siège, *m*. ~-*water basin*, bénitier, *m*. ~-*water sprinkler*, aspersoir, goupillon, *m*. *H*~ *Writ*, l'Écriture sainte, *f*. ~ *year*, année jubilaire, *f*.

homage, n, hommage[s] m.[pl.].

home, n, foyer familial, foyer [domestique]; feu; chez-moi; chez-soi; intérieur; logis, m; maison, f; gîte, m; lares, pénates, m.pl; ménage, m; famille, f; pays, m; patrie, f; asile; hospice, m; (Running) l'arrivée, f. ~ for the aged, maison de retraite. at ~. See under at. ¶ a, chez soi; à la maison; juste; à fond; à bloc. ¶ a, domestique; de famille; indigène; intérieur; métropolitain. ~ country, métropole, f. ~ life, vie d'intérieur, f. ~-made wine, liqueur de ménage, f. ~ match, home match, m. H~ Office (Eng.), Ministère (ou département) de l'Intérieur & Ministère de la Justice (Fr.) m. ~ port, port d'armement, m. H~ Rule, indépendance législative, f. H~ Secretary, ministre de l'Intérieur, m. ~sick, nostalgique. ~-sickness, mal du pays, m, nostalgie, f. ~ trade, commerce intérieur, c. métropolitain; (Ship.) cabotage, m. ~ truths, vérités bien senties, bonnes vérités, f.pl. ~ work, (Sch.) devoirs [à faire à la maison] m.pl; (trade) travail à façon, m. ~less, a, sans foyer, sans asile. **homeliness**, n, sans-façon, m. **homely**, a, simple, sans façon, bourgeois.

homeopath, &c. Same as homoeopath, &c.

Homeric, a, homérique.

homespun, n, toile de ménage, f. **homestead**, n, ferme, f. **homeward**, a. & ad, de retour; en r. ~ bound, en retour, effectuant son voyage de retour. ~s, ad, en retour.

homicidal, a, homicide. **homicide**, n, (pers.) homicide, m,f; (act) homicide, m.

homily, n, homélie, f, prône, m.

homing pigeon, pigeon voyageur, m.

homoeopath[ist], n, homéopathe, m. **homoeopathic**, a, homéopathique. **homoeopathy**, n, homéopathie, f.

homogeneous, a, homogène.

homonym, n, homonyme, m.

hone, n, pierre à aiguiser, f.

honest†, a, honnête, probe, droit, intègre; brave, de bien. ~y, n, honnêteté, probité, intégrité; (Bot.) lunaire, f.

honey, n, miel; (pers.) chou[chou] m. ~ bee, mouche à miel, f. ~comb, s, gâteau de miel; rayon de m., m; (v.t.) cribler. ~moon, lune de miel, f. ~suckle, chèvrefeuille, m. ~ed, a, [em]miellé; mielleux.

honorarium, n, honoraires, m.pl. **honorary**, a, honoraire; honorifique; sans rétribution. ~ membership, honorariat, m. **honour**, n, honneur; (Com.) accueil, m; (Com.) intervention, f. ~s list, palmarès, m. ¶ v.t, honorer; faire honneur à, accueillir. ~able†, a, honorable. ~ mention, accessit, m. ~ed, p.a, honoré; respecté.

hood, n, capuchon; chapeau; capot, m; capote; cape; capeline, f; dais; soufflet, m; hotte, f. ~wink, bander [les yeux à, de].

hoof, n, sabot, ongle, m. ~ed, a, ongulé.

hook, n, crochet; croc; gond, m; agrafe, f;

(Fish.) hameçon; (Box.) crochet, m. ~ & eye, agrafe & porte. ~ & hinge, gond & penture. ~ stick, crosse, f. ~ to gut (Fish.), monture, f. by ~ or by crook, de façon ou d'autre. ¶ v.t, accrocher; agrafer. ~[ed] (nose) a, aquilin.

hookah, n, narguilé, narghileh, m.

hooligan, n, apache, voyou, m.

hoop, n, cercle; cerceau, m; frette, f; arceau, m. ~ iron, feuillard de fer, m. ~ ring, jonc, m. ¶ v.t, [en]cercler; relier; fretter.

hooping cough, coqueluche, f.

hoopoe, n, huppe, f.

hoot, v.t, huer, conspuer; (v.i.) (owl) chuinter; (Motor.) corner. ~er, n, sirène; trompe, f; cornet [avertisseur] m. ~[ing] (hoot[ing]) n, huée[s] f.[pl.].

hop, n, saut; (pl.) houblon, m. ~ [plant], houblon, m. ~ field, houblonnière, f. ~ picking, cueillette du houblon, f. ~ pole, perche à houblon, f, échalas, m. ~scotch, marelle, f. ~, step, & jump, triple saut, m. ¶ v.t, houblonner; (v.i.) sauter à cloche-pied; (like a sparrow) sautiller. ~ about, s'ébattre.

hope, n, espérance, f; espoir, m. ¶ v.t. & i, espérer. ~ful, a, plein d'espoir; encouragé; confiant; optimiste; (lad) de grandes espérances. ~less, a, sans espoir, désespéré; incorrigible.

hopper, n, (insect) sauteur, m; (Mach.) trémie, f.

horde, n, horde, f.

horehound, n, marrube, m.

horizon, n, horizon, m. **horizontal†**, a, horizontal.

horn, n, corne, f; (pl. deer) bois, m.pl; (insect) antenne, f; cor; cornet, m; trompe, f; (gramophone) pavillon, m. ~beam, charme, m. ~ of plenty, corne d'abondance, f. ~-rimmed spectacles, lunettes en écaille, f.pl. horned cattle, bêtes à cornes, bêtes cornues, f.pl.

hornet, n, frelon, m. ~'s nest (fig.), guêpier, m.

horny, a, corné; (hands) calleuses.

horology, n, horlogerie, f.

horoscope, n, horoscope, m.

horrible† & **horrid†**, a, horrible. **horror**, n, horreur, f.

horse, n, cheval, m; (pl.) cavalerie, f; (trestle) chevalet, m, chèvre, f. ~ artillery, artillerie à cheval, f. on ~back, à cheval. ~ bean, féverole, f. ~ block, montoir, m. ~ box, wagon-écurie, m. ~ breaker, dresseur de chevaux, m. ~ chanter, maquignon, m. ~ chanting, maquignonnage, m. ~-chestnut, marron d'Inde (tree) marronnier d'I., m. ~ dealer, marchand de chevaux, maquignon, m. ~flesh, viande de cheval, f. ~flesh (or ~meat) dealer, boucherie hippophagique, f. ~fly, taon, m. ~ gear, manège, m. ~hair, crin, m. ~man, cavalier, écuyer, m. ~manship, équitation, manège, m.

~ *play*, jeux de main, *m.pl.* ~*pond*, abreuvoir, *m.* ~ *power* [vapeur] *m*, force de cheval, *f.* en chevaux, *f.* (Eng. h.p. = 550 foot pounds per second; Fr. h.p. = 75 kilogrammetres per sec.) *a* 10 ~ [*power*] *car*, une [automobile de] 10 chevaux. ~ *race*, course de chevaux, *f.* ~ *racing*, les courses, *f.pl.* ~*radish*, raifort, *m.* ~ *shoe*, fer à cheval, *m.* ~*shoe roll*, croissant, *m.* ~ *show*, concours hippique, *m.* ~ *species*, race chevaline, *f.* ~*tail plume*, crinière, *f.* ~*whip*, *n*, cravache, *f*; (*v.t.*) cravacher. ~*woman*, cavalière, écuyère, amazone, *f.* **horsy**, *a*, de cheval, chevalin.

horticultural, *a*, horticole. **horticulture**, *n*, horticulture, *f.* **horticulturist**, *n*, horticulteur, *m.*

hosanna, *n*, hosanna, *m.*

hose, *n*, (*Dress, col. as pl.*) bas, *m.pl* (*pipe*) tuyau, boyau, *m*, manche, *f.* ~ *branch*, lance, *f.* **hosier**, *n*, chemisier, bonnetier, *m.* ~**y**, *n*, chemiserie, bonneterie, *f.*

hospitable, *a*, hospitalier. **hospital**, *n*, hôpital, *m.* *Chelsea Royal* H~ (*London*), l'hôtel des Invalides, *m*, les Invalides (*Paris*). ~ *attendant*, ~ *nurse*, infirmier, ère. ~ *service*, service hospitalier, *m.* ~ *ship*, vaisseau-hôpital, *m.* **hospitality**, *n*, hospitalité, *f.*

host, *n*, (*pers.*) hôte, *m*; armée, *f*, bataillon, *m*, troupe, nuée, phalange, *f*; (*Eccl.*) hostie, *f.* ~**ess**, *n*, hôtesse, *f.*

hostage, *n*, otage, *m*; (*fig.*) gage, *m.*

hostel, *n*, auberge, *f*, foyer d'étudiants, *m*, maison des étudiants, *f*; hospice, *m*, institution, *f.* ~**ry** (*archaic*) *n*, hôtellerie, *f.*

hostile†, *a*, hostile. **hostility**, *n*, hostilité, *f.*

hostler, *n*, garçon d'écurie, palefrenier, *m.*

hot, *a*, chaud; à chaud; ardent; brûlant. *to get* ~ *& to run* ~, chauffer. *I gave it him* ~, je l'ai salé de la belle manière. ~*bed*, (*Hort.*) couche [de fumier] *f*; (*fig.*) foyer, *m*, officine, *f.* ~ *cockles*, main chaude, *f.* *in* ~ *haste*, en toute hâte, au [grand] galop. ~*head*, cerveau brûlé, *m*, échauffé, e. ~*headed*, bouillant, impétueux. ~*house*, serre chaude, *f.* ~*house grapes*, raisin de serres, *m.* ~ *plate*, réchaud, *m.* ~ *room* (bath), étuve sèche, *f.* ~ *spring*, source thermale, *f.* ~*water bottle*, boule d'eau chaude, *f.*

hotchpotch, *n*, (*Cook.*) hochepot, (*Cook. & fig.*) salmigondis, pot pourri, *m.*

hotel, *n*, hôtel, *m.* ~ *keeper*, hôtelier, ère.

hotly, *ad*, chaleureusement.

hough, *n*, jarret, *m.*

hound, *n*, chien courant, c. de chasse, chien, *m*; (*bitch*) lice, *f.* ~ *out*, chasser.

hour, *n*, heure, *f.* ~ *glass*, sablier, *m.* ~ *hand*, petite aiguille, *f.* ~**ly**, *a*, par heure; (*ad.*) d'heure en heure.

house, *n*, maison, *f*; logis, *m*; habitation, *f*; hôtel; pavillon, *m*; bourse, *f*; bâtiment; atelier; ménage, *m*; (*Theat.*) salle: chambrée, *f.* *neither* ~ *nor home*, ni feu ni lieu. ~ *agent*, agent de location, *m.* ~ *boat*, bateau d'habitation, *m.* ~*breaking*, effraction, *f*, cambriolage, *m.* ~ *coal*, charbon de ménage, *m.* ~ *dog*, chien de garde, c. d'attache, *m.* ~ *flannel*, torchon, *m.* ~ *fly*, mouche commune, *f.* ~ *full* (*Theat.*), complet. ~*hold*, ménage, *m*; (*staff*) maison, domesticité, *f.* ~*hold bread*, pain de ménage, *m.* ~*hold gods*, dieux familiers, dieux pénates, *m.pl.* ~*hold goods*, ménage, *m.* ~*hold linen*, linge de maison, *m.* ~*holder*, chef de famille, *m.* ~*keeper*, femme de charge; f. de ménage; gouvernante; ménagère, *f*; concierge, *m,f.* ~*keeping*, ménage, *m*; économie domestique, *f.* ~ *leek*, joubarbe, *f.* ~*maid*, fille de service, servante, *f.* ~ *martin*, hirondelle de fenêtre, *f.* ~ *number*, numéro d'habitation, *m.* H~ *of Commons, of Lords*, Chambre des communes, des pairs, *f.* ~ *of the deceased*, maison mortuaire, *f.* ~ *painter*, peintre en bâtiments, *m.* ~ *properly*, biens-fonds, *m.pl.* ~ *sparrow*, moineau franc, pierrot, *m.* ~ *top*, toit, *m.* *to give a* ~ *warming*, pendre la crémaillère. ~*wife*, maîtresse de maison, *f.* ~*wifery*, ménage, *m.* ~*work*, ménage, *m.* ¶ *v.t*, loger; mettre à l'abri; (*Carp., &c*) encastrer, emboîter; (*harvest*) rentrer, engranger; (*carriage*) remiser. **housing**, *n*, logement, *m*; rentrée, *f*; remisage, *m.* ~ *problem*, crise du logement, *f.*

hovel, *n*, taudis, bouge, *m*, baraque, *f.*

hover, *v.i*, planer, voltiger; se balancer.

how, *ad*, comment; comme; que. ~ *long*? combien de temps? ~ *much*, ~ *many*, combien.

however, *ad*, de quelque manière que; quelque . . . que, si . . . que; tout . . . que; pourtant.

howitzer, *n*, obusier, *m.*

howl, *n*, hurlement, *m.* ¶ *v.i*, hurler; (*wind*) gronder. ~**er**, *n*, bévue, gaffe, *f.*

hoyden, *n*, gamine bruyante, *f*, garçon manqué, *m.*

hub, *n*, moyeu, *m*; (*fig.*) centre, *m.* ~ *brake*, frein sur moyeux, *m.*

hubbub, *n*, brouhaha, charivari, *m.*

huckaback, *n*, toile ouvrée, *f.* ~ *towel*, serviette nid d'abeilles, *f.*

huckster, *n*, regrattier, ère.

huddle, *v.t*, entasser; (*v.i.*) se blottir.

hue, *n*, teinte; nuance, *f.*

hue & cry, *n*, haro, tocsin, tollé, *m.*

huff (*Draughts*) *v.t*, souffler. *to take* ~, prendre la mouche. *he is in a* ~, il a pris la mouche.

hug, *n*, étreinte, *f*, embrassement, *m*, accolade, *f.* ¶ *v.t*, serrer, étreindre, embrasser;

(the wind, Naut.) chicaner; *(the shore)* côtoyer; *(an error)* chérir.

huge, *a*, énorme, immense, démesuré. ~**ly**, *ad*, énormément, immensément, démesurément.

hulk, *n*, vaisseau rasé; ponton, *m*. ~**ing**, *a*, balourd.

hull, *n*, *(husk)* cosse; *(ship)* coque, *f*, corps, *m*. ¶ *v.t*, monder.

hullabaloo, *n*, hourvari, *m*.

hullo[a], *i*, hé! ohé! tiens! *(Teleph.)* allô!

hum, *v.i. & t*, *(bee, &c.)* bourdonner; *(top)* ronfler; *(tune)* fredonner, chantonner. ¶ *i*, hem! hom! ~ *& ha*, ânonner.

human†, *a*, humain. **humane**†, *a*, humain. **humanitarian**, *a. & n*, humanitaire, *a. & m*. **humanity**, *n*, humanité, *f*. **humanize**, *v.t*, humaniser.

humble†, *a*, humble. ¶ *v.t*, humilier, abaisser, mater. ~ *bee*, bourdon, *m*. ~**ness**, *n*, humilité; *(birth)* bassesse, *f*. *the humbler classes*, le menu peuple.

humbug, *n*, blague; mystification; *f*; *(pers.)* blagueur, euse; mystificateur, trice; imposteur, *m*. ¶ *i*, chansons! chansons! ¶ *v.t*, mystifier; lanterner, enjôler; mettre dedans.

humdrum, *a*, monotone; banal; assoupissant.

humerus, *n*, humérus, *m*.

humid, *a*, humide. ~**ity**, *n*, humidité, *f*.

humiliate, *v.t*, humilier. **humility**, *n*, humilité, *f*.

humming bird, oiseau-mouche, colibri, *m*.

humming top, toupie d'Allemagne, *f*.

hummock, *n*, mamelon; monticule, *m*.

humorist, *n*, humoriste; farceur, euse; *(entertainer)* diseur (euse) de chansonnettes. **humorous**, *a*, humoriste; humoristique; drôle, drolatique. ~**ly**, *ad*, avec humour; par facétie. **humour**, *n*, *(mood)* humeur, disposition, *f*; *(jocosity)* humour, *m*. ¶ *v.t*, complaire à, flatter; ménager.

hump, *n*, bosse, *f*. ~**back**, *n. & ~backed*, *a*, bossu, e.

humph, *i*, hem! hom!

hunch, *n*. bosse, *f*; *(chunk)* chanteau, *m*. ~**back**, *n. & ~backed*, *a*, bossu, e.

hundred, *a. & n*, cent, *a. & m*. ~ *[or so]*, centaine, *f*. ~**weight**, *n*, *(imperial measure)* = 112 pounds or 50·80 kilogrammes. ~**fold**, *n*, centuple, *m*. ~**th**, *a. & n*, centième, *a. & m*.

Hungarian, *a*, hongrois. ¶ *n*, Hongrois, e; *(language)* le hongrois. **Hungary**, *n*, la Hongrie.

hunger, *n*, faim, fringale, *f*. ~ *strike*, grève de la faim, *f*. ~ *striker*, gréviste de la faim, *m,f*. ~ *after*, être affamé de, avoir une fringale de. **hungrily**, *ad*, d'un œil affamé; avidement. **hungry**, *a*, affamé. *to be* ~, *very* ~, avoir faim, grand-faim.

hunk, *n*, chanteau, *m*; *(pl, miser)* grigou, *m*.

hunt, *n*, chasse; *(riding to hounds)* chasse à courre, *f*; équipage de chasse, *m*. ¶ *v.t. & i*,

chasser, courir. ~ *for*, chercher. ~**er**, *n*, chasseur; cheval de chasse; *(curios)* dénicheur, *m*; *(watch)* savonnette, montre à double boîtier, *f*. **hunting**, *n*, chasse; c. à courre; *(science)* vénerie, *f*. ~ *box*, pavillon de chasse, *m*. **huntress**, *n*, chasseuse, *f*. **huntsman**, *n*, chasseur; *(man in charge)* veneur, piqueur, *m*.

hurdle, *n*, claie; haie, *f*. ~ *fence*, échalier, *m*. ~ *race*, course de haies, *f*; *(2000–1000 metres)* steeple-chase, *m*.

hurl, *v.t*, lancer, darder, projeter.

hurly-burly, *n*, tohu-bohu, *m*.

hurrah, **-ray**, *n*, hourra, hosanna, *m*. ¶ *i*, bravo! vivat!

hurricane, *n*, ouragan, *m*. ~ *deck*, pont de manœuvre; pont abri, *m*. ~ *lamp*, lanterne-tempête, *f*.

hurry, *n*, précipitation, hâte; presse, *f*. ¶ *v.t*, presser, hâter, précipiter; *(v.i.)* se hâter. ~ *up*, se dépêcher.

hurt, *n*, mal, *m*; blessure; lésion, *f*; tort, *m*. ¶ *v.t.ir*, faire [du] mal à; blesser; nuire à.

husband, *n*, mari, époux, *m*. ¶ *v.t*, ménager. **husbandman**, *n*, cultivateur, *m*. **husbandry**, *n*, économie rurale, agronomie, *f*.

hush, *n*, silence, *m*. ~ *money*, prix du silence, *m*. ¶ *i*, silence!; chut! motus!; paix! ¶ *v.t*, faire taire. ~ *up*, étouffer.

husk, *n*, cosse, *f*; *(walnut)* brou, *m*; *(grain)* balle, *f*. ~**y**, *(hoarse)* a, enroué, éraillé.

hussy, **-zzy**, *n*, coquine, friponne, drôlesse, masque, *f*.

hustle, *v.t*, bousculer.

hut, *n*, hutte, cabane, baraque, *f*.

hutch, *n*, cabane, *f*, clapier, *m*.

hyacinth, *n*, jacinthe, hyacinthe, *f*.

hyaena, *n*, hyène, *f*.

hybrid, *a*, hybride, métis. ¶ *n*, hybride, mulet, *m*.

hydra, *n*, hydre, *f*.

hydrangea, *n*, hortensia, *m*.

hydrant, *n*, bouche [d'eau]; prise d'eau, *f*.

hydrate, *n*, hydrate, *m*.

hydraulic, *a. & ~s*, *n.pl*, hydraulique, *a. & f*.

hydrocarbon, *n*, hydrocarbure, *m*. **hydrochloric**, *a*, chlorhydrique. **hydrogen**, *n*, hydrogène, *m*. **hydropathic**, *a*, hydrothérapique. ¶ *n*, établissement hydrothérapique, *m*. **hydropathy**, *n*, hydrothérapie, *f*. **hydrophobia**, *n*, hydrophobie, *f*. **hydroplane**, *n*, glisseur, *m*.

hyena, *n*, hyène, *f*.

hygiene *& hygienics*, *n*, hygiène, *f*. **hygienic(al)**†, *a*, hygiénique.

hymen, *n*, hymen, hyménée, *m*.

hymenoptera, *n.pl*, hyménoptères, *m.pl*.

hymn, *n*, hymne, *m*; *(in church)* hymne, *f*, cantique, *m*. ~ *book*, recueil d'hymnes, *m*.

hyperbola *& hyperbole*, *n*, hyperbole, *f*.

hyphen, *n*, trait d'union, tiret, *m*; *(end of line)* division, *f*.

hypnotism, *n*, hypnotisme, *m*. **hypnotize**, *v.t*, hypnotiser.

hypochondriac, *a. & n,* hypochondriaque. *a. & m,f.* **hypocrisy,** *n,* hypocrisie, *f.* **hypocrite,** *n,* hypocrite, *m,f.* **hypocritical†,** *a,* hypocrite. **hypodermic,** *a,* hypodermique. ~ *syringe,* seringue de Pravaz, *f.* **hyposulphite,** *n,* hyposulfite, *m.* **hypothecation,** *n,* nantissement, *m.* **hypothesis,** *n,* hypothèse, *f.* **hypothetic(al)†,** *a,* hypothétique.

hyssop, *n,* hysope, *f.*

hysteria, *n,* hystérie, *f.* **hysteric(al),** *a,* hystérique; nerveux. **hysterics,** *n.pl,* crise de nerfs, *f,* nerfs, *m.pl.*

I

I, *pn,* je; moi.

iambic, *a,* ïambique. ¶ *n,* ïambe, *m.*

ibex, *n,* bouquetin, *m.*

ibis, *n,* ibis, *m.*

ice, *n,* glace, *f. oft. pl.* ~ **age,** période glaciaire, *f.* ~ **axe,** piolet, *m.* ~ **berg,** iceberg, *m.* ~ **blink,** clarté des glaces, *f.* ~ **box** & ~ **house,** glacière, *f.* ~ **cream,** crème glacée, glace à la crème, *f.* ~ **cream freezer,** sorbetière, *f.* ~ **cream vender,** glacier, *m.* ~ **hockey,** hockey sur glace, *m.* ~ **pack,** banquise, *f.* ~ **pail,** seau à glace, *m.* ~ **skates,** (1) screw-on, (2) clamp-on, patins à glace, (1) à visser, (2) à griffes, *m.pl.* ¶ *v.t,* glacer; (*wine, &c*) frapper [de glace].

Iceland, *n,* l'Islande, *f.* ~ **er,** *n,* Islandais, e. ~ **ic,** *a. & (language) n,* islandais, *a. & m.*

ichthyology, *n,* ichtyologie, *f.*

icicle, *n,* aiguille de glace, *f,* glaçon, *m.* **icing** (*sugar*) *n,* glace, *f.*

icon, *n,* icône, *f.* **iconoclast,** *n,* iconoclaste, démolisseur, *m.*

icy, *a,* glacé, glacial.

idea, *n,* idée, pensée; image, *f.* **ideal†,** *a. & n,* idéal, *a. & m.* ~ **ist,** *n,* idéaliste, *m,f.*

identical†, *a,* identique. **identification,** *n,* identification, *f.* ~ **number** (motor car), numéro de circulation, *m.* **identify,** *v.t,* identifier. **identity,** *n,* identité, *f.* ~ **disc,** plaque d'identité, *f.*

idiocy, *n,* idiotie, *f.*

idiom, *n,* (*dialect*) idiome; (*phrase*) idiotisme, *m.*

idiosyncrasy, *n,* idiosyncrasie, *f.*

idiot, *n. &* ~ **ic,** *a,* idiot, e.

idle, *a,* oisif; paresseux; fainéant; inoccupé; désœuvré; de loisir; sans affaires; futile; oiseux, en l'air. ~ *fancy,* rêverie, *f.* ¶ *v.i,* paresser, fainéanter. ~ **ness,** *n,* oisiveté; paresse, *f;* chômage, *m.* **idler,** *n,* oisif, ive, paresseux, euse, fainéant, e; badaud, e. **idly,** *ad,* dans l'oisiveté.

idol, *n,* idole, *f;* amour, *m.* **idolater, tress,** *n,* idolâtre, *m,f.* **idolatrous,** *a,* idolâtre, idolâtrique. **idolatry,** *n,* idolâtrie, *f.* **idolize,** *v.t,* idolâtrer.

---

idyl[1], *n,* idylle, *f.* **idyllic,** *a,* idyllique.

if, *c,* si, s'. ~ *not,* sinon.

igneous, *a,* igné. **ignis fatuus,** *n,* feu follet, *m.* **ignite,** *v.t,* enflammer; allumer. **ignition,** *n,* ignition; inflammation, *f;* allumage, *m.*

ignoble†, *a,* ignoble.

ignominious†, *a,* ignominieux. **ignominy,** *n,* ignominie, *f.*

ignoramus, *n,* ignorant, e, ignare, *m,f.* **ignorance,** *n,* ignorance, *f.* **ignorant,** *a,* ignorant, ignare. *to be* ~ *of,* ignorer. **ignore,** *v.t,* méconnaître; ne faire aucune attention à.

iguana, *n,* iguane, *m.*

ill, *n,* mal, *m.* *speak* ~ *of,* médire de. ¶ *a,* malade, souffrant; mauvais; méchant. ¶ *ad,* mal; peu. ~ **advised,** malavisé; malvenu, mal venu. ~ **assorted,** disparate. ~ **bred,** mal élevé, malappris, sans éducation. ~ **famed,** malfamé, mal famé. ~ **fated,** néfaste. ~ **favoured,** laid. ~ **feeling,** inimitié, *f.* ~ **gotten gains,** biens mal acquis, *m.pl.* ~ **humour,** humeur, *f.* ~ **luck,** mauvaise chance, malchance, *f,* malheur, *m.* ~ **mannered,** malhonnête. ~ **natured** (*person*), méchant, e. ~ **omened,** de mauvais augure, funèbre. ~ **temper,** humeur [chagrine] *f.* ~ **tempered,** d'h. c., revêche, hargneux. ~ **timed,** intempestif, déplacé. ~ **treat,** ~ **use,** maltraiter, faire un mauvais parti à. ~ **will,** malveillance, *f. to bear* ~ *will,* en vouloir à.

illegal†, *a,* illégal.

illegible†, *a,* illisible.

illegitimacy, *n,* illégitimité, *f.* **illegitimate†,** *a,* illégitime.

illicit†, *a,* illicite.

illiterate, *a,* illettré.

illness, *n,* maladie, *f,* mal, *m.*

illogical, *a,* illogique. ~ **ity,** *n,* illogisme, *m.*

illuminate, *v.t,* éclairer; (*festively*) illuminer, embraser; (*MS.*) enluminer, historier. **illumination,** *n,* éclairage, *m;* illumination, *f,* embrasement, *m;* enluminure, *f.* **illumine,** *v.t,* éclairer.

illusion, *n,* illusion, tromperie, *f.* **illusive,** **illusory,** *a,* illusoire.

illustrate, *v.t,* illustrer. ~ *d price list,* tarif-album, *m.* **illustration,** *n,* illustration, *f;* exemple, *m.* ~ *in text,* gravure dans le texte. ~ *outside text,* gravure hors texte. **illustrious,** *a,* illustre. *to make* ~, illustrer.

image, *n,* image, *f.* ~ **ry,** *n,* images, *f.pl.*

imaginary, *a,* imaginaire. **imagination,** *n,* imagination, *f.* **imagine,** *v.t. & i,* imaginer; s'imaginer; se figurer.

imbecile, *a,* imbécile. ¶ *n,* idiot, e.

imbibe, *v.t,* absorber; s'imbiber de; boire, sucer.

imbricate, *v.t,* imbriquer.

imbroglio, *n,* imbroglio, *m.*

imbrue, *v.t,* tremper.

imbue, *v.t*, imbiber; pénétrer. ~d, *p.p*, imbu, inspiré.

imitate, *v.t.i*, imiter; contrefaire. imitation, *n*, imitation; contrefaçon, *f*; (*att*.) [d']imitation, simili-; faux. imitator, *n*, imitateur, trice.

immaculate, *a*, immaculé. the I~ Conception, l'Immaculée Conception, *f*.

immanent, *a*, immanent.

immaterial, *a*, immatériel; sans importance.

immature, *a*, qui n'est pas mûr.

immeasurable, *a*, immensurable.

immediate†, *a*, immédiat.

immemorial, *a*, immémorial.

immense, *a*, immense. ~ly, *ad*, immensément. immensity, *n*, immensité, *f*.

immerse, *v.t*, immerger, plonger. immersion, *n*, immersion, *f*.

immigrate, *v.i*, immigrer.

imminence, *n*, imminence, *f*. imminent, *a*, imminent.

immoderate†, *a*, immodéré.

immodest†, *a*, immodeste.

immolate, *v.t*, immoler.

immoral, *a*, immoral. ~ity, *n*, immoralité, *f*.

immortal†, *a*. & *n*, immortel, *a*. & *m*. ~ity, *n*, immortalité, *f*. ~ize, *v.t*, immortaliser. immortelle, *n*, immortelle, *f*.

immovable†, *a*, inébranlable.

immunity, *n*, immunité, *f*; exemption; franchise, *f*.

immure, *v.t*, claquemurer, cloîtrer.

immutable†, *a*, immuable.

imp, *n*, diablotin, lutin, démon, *m*.

impact, *n*, choc, *m*; percussion, *f*.

impair, *v.t*, détériorer; compromettre.

impale, *v.t*, embrocher; (*Hist*.) empaler.

impalpable, *a*, impalpable.

impanel a jury, former une liste de jurés, former un tableau.

impart, *v.t*, impartir; imprimer; faire part de.

impartial†, *a*, impartial. ~ity, *n*, impartialité, *f*.

impassable, *a*, impraticable, infranchissable.

impassible & impassive, *a*, impassible.

impassioned, *p.p*, passionné.

impasto, *n*, pâte, *f*, empâtement de couleurs, *m*.

impatience, *n*, impatience, *f*. impatient, *a*, impatient. to grow ~, s'impatienter. ~ly, *ad*, impatiemment.

impeach, *v.t*, accuser.

impecunious, *a*, besogneux.

impede, *v.t*, entraver, empêcher. impediment, *n*, empêchement, obstacle, *m*. ~ of speech, ~ in one's speech, empêchement (ou embarras) de la langue, *m*. impedimenta, *n.pl*, impedimenta, *m.pl*.

impel, *v.t*, pousser, animer.

impending, *p.a*, imminent.

impenetrable, *a*, impénétrable.

impenitence, *n*, impénitence, *f*. impenitent, *a*, impénitent.

imperative†, *a*. & *n*, impératif, *a*. & *m*.

imperceptible†, *a*, imperceptible, insaisissable.

imperfect†, *a*. & ~ [tense], *n*, imparfait, *a*. & *m*. ~ion, *n*, imperfection, *f*.

imperial, *a*, impérial; (*weights & measures*) anglais; ~ & *foreign*, (*postal system*) international; (*mails*) maritime. ¶ (*beard*) *n*, impériale, *f*. ~ist, *n*. & ~istic, *a*, impérialiste, *m*. & *a*.

imperil, *v.t*, mettre en danger.

imperious†, *a*, impérieux.

imperishable, *a*, impérissable.

impermeable, *a*, imperméable.

impersonal†, *a*, impersonnel.

impersonate, *v.t*, personnifier. impersonation, *n*, personnification; (*Theat*.) charge; (*Law*) supposition de personne, *f*.

impertinence, *n*, impertinence, *f*. impertinent, *a*, impertinent. ~ly, *ad*, impertinemment.

imperturbable†, *a*, imperturbable.

impervious, *a*, imperméable, impénétrable.

impetuous†, *a*, impétueux, pétulant.

impetus, *n*, impulsion, *f*, élan, branle, *m*.

impiety, *n*, impiété, *f*.

impinge [up]on, venir en contact avec.

impious, *a*, impie.

impish, *a*, lutin, espiègle.

implacable†, *a*, implacable.

implant, *v.t*, implanter.

implement, *n*, instrument, ustensile, *m*. ¶ *v.t*, rendre effectif; ajouter.

implicate, *v.t*, impliquer. not ~d, désintéressé. implication, *n*, implication, *f*; sous-entendu, *m*. implicit†, *a*. & implied, *p.a*, implicite, tacite.

implore, *v.t*, implorer, supplier.

imply, *v.t*, impliquer; [pré]supposer; sous-entendre.

impolite†, *a*, impoli. ~ness, *n*, impolitesse, *f*.

impolitic, *a*, impolitique.

imponderable, *a*. & *n*, impondérable, *a*. & *m*.

import, *n*, (*meaning*) portée, signification, *f*, sens, *m*; (*Com*., &c) importation, *f*. ~ duty, droit d'entrée, *m*, entrée, *f*. ¶ *v.t*, signifier; (*Com*., &c) importer.

importance, *n*, importance, *f*. important, *a*, important.

importation, *n*, importation, *f*. importer, *n*, importateur, *m*.

importunate, *a*, importun. importune, *v.t*, importuner. importunity, *n*, importunité, *f*.

impose, *v.t*, imposer; frapper. ~ [up]on someone, en faire accroire à (ou en imposer à) quelqu'un. person of imposing appearance, porte-respect, *m*. imposing stone, marbre, *m*. imposition, *n*, imposition; imposture, *f*; (*Sch*.) pensum, *m*.

impossibility, *n*, impossibilité, *f*, l'impossible, *m*. impossible, *a*, impossible.

impost (*Arch*.) *n*, imposte, *f*.

impostor, *n*, imposteur, *m*. imposture, *n*, imposture, *f*.

impotence, -cy, *n*, impuissance, *f*. impotent, *a*, impuissant.

impound, *v.t,* mettre à la fourrière; enfermer; confisquer.

impoverish, *v.t,* appauvrir.

impracticable, *a,* impraticable.

imprecation, *n,* imprécation, *f.*

impregnable, *a,* inprenable, inexpugnable.

impregnate, *v.t,* imprégner; féconder. **~d** (*wood*) *p.a,* injecté.

impresario, *n,* impresario, *m.*

impress, *n,* empreinte, impression, *f.* ¶ *v.t,* imprimer, empreindre; graver; impressionner; réquisitionner. **~ed stamp,** timbre sec, t. fixe, *m.* **~ion,** *n,* impression; empreinte, *f;* (*Typ.*) foulage, *m. to be under the ~,* avoir dans l'idée. **~ionism,** *n,* impressionnisme, *m.* **impressive,** *a,* impressionnant; solennel.

imprint, *n,* empreinte, *f.* See also *printer's & publisher's ~.* ¶ *v.t,* imprimer, empreindre.

imprison, *v.t,* emprisonner. **~ment,** *n,* emprisonnement, *m;* prison, *f.*

improbability, *n,* improbabilité, invraisemblance, *f.* **improbable,** *a,* improbable, invraisemblable. **improbably,** *ad,* invraisemblablement.

impromptu, *ad. a. & n,* impromptu, *ad. a. & m.*

improper, *a,* inconvenant, incongru; impropre, abusif; vice de . . .; faux. **~ly,** *ad,* improprement; abusivement. **impropriety,** *n,* inconvenance, incongruité; impropriété, *f.*

improve, *v.t,* améliorer; perfectionner; bonifier; amender. **~ on,** renchérir sur. **~ on acquaintance,** gagner à être connu. **~ment,** *n,* amélioration, *f;* perfectionnement, *m;* bonification, *f;* embellissement, *m.*

improvidence, *n,* imprévoyance, *f.* **improvident,** *a,* imprévoyant.

improvise, *v.t,* improviser.

imprudence, *n,* imprudence, *f.* **imprudent,** *a,* imprudent. **~ly,** *ad,* imprudemment.

impudence, *n,* impudence, *f,* toupet, *m.* **impudent,** *a,* impudent. **~ly,** *ad,* impudemment. **impudicity,** *n,* impudicité, *f.*

impugn, *v.t,* attaquer.

impulse & impulsion, *n,* impulsion, *f;* mouvement; branle, *m.* **impulsive,** *a,* impulsif; primesautier.

impunity, *n,* impunité, *f. with ~,* impunément.

impure†, *a,* impur. **impurity,** *n,* impureté, *f.*

imputation, *n,* imputation, *f.* **impute,** *v.t,* imputer.

in, *pr,* dans; en; à; au; entre; chez; auprès de; sur; sous; par; de; pour; à la. ¶ *ad,* dedans; chez lui; y; arrivé. **~ between,** entre deux. **~ demand,** demandé. **~ fashion,** à la mode, de mode, de mise. **~ print,** imprimé, disponible. **~ the press,** sous presse. **~ there,** là-dedans.

ins & outs, détours; êtres, *m.pl.*

inability, *n,* impuissance, *f.*

inaccessible, *a,* inaccessible, inabordable.

inaccuracy, *n,* inexactitude, infidélité, *f.* **inaccurate†,** *a,* inexact, infidèle.

inaction, *n,* inaction, *f.* **inactive,** *a,* inactif.

inadequate, *a,* insuffisant. **~ly,** *ad,* insuffisamment.

inadmissible, *a,* inadmissible.

inadvertently, *ad,* par inadvertance, par mégarde.

inalienable, *a,* inaliénable, incessible.

inane, *a,* inepte.

inanimate, *a,* inanimé. **~ nature,** le monde inanimé. **inanition,** *n,* inanition, *f.*

inanity, *n,* inanité, ineptie, *f.*

inapplicable, *a,* inapplicable.

inapposite, *a,* hors de propos.

inappreciable, *a,* inappréciable.

inappropriate†, *a,* impropre, qui ne convient pas, peu en situation.

inapt, *a,* inapte. **inaptitude,** *n,* inaptitude, *f.*

inarticulate, *a,* inarticulé.

inasmuch, *a,* étant donné.

inattentive, *a,* inattentif.

inaudible†, *a,* imperceptible [à l'ouïe].

inaugurate, *v.t,* inaugurer.

inauspicious, *a,* défavorable.

inborn & inbred, *a,* inné, infus, naturel, natif.

incalculable, *a,* incalculable.

incandescence, *n,* incandescence, *f.* **incandescent,** *a,* incandescent; (*lamp, &c*) à incandescence.

incantation, *n,* incantation, *f.*

incapable, *a,* incapable; inhabile; non-susceptible. **incapably,** *ad,* inhabilement. **incapacitate,** *v.t,* rendre incapable. **incapacity,** *n,* incapacité; impéritie, *f.*

incarcerate, *v.t,* incarcérer.

incarnate, *a,* incarné. **incarnation,** *n,* incarnation, *f.*

incautious, *a,* imprudent.

incendiarism, *n,* incendie volontaire, *m.* **incendiary,** *a. & n,* incendiaire, *a. & m,f.*

incense, *n,* encens, *m.* **~ box,** navette, *f.* **~ burner,** brûle-parfum, *m.* ¶ *v.t,* (*perfume*) encenser; (*enrage*) courroucer.

incentive, *n,* aiguillon; mobile, ressort, *m.*

inception, *n,* commencement, *m.*

incessant, *a,* incessant. **~ly,** *ad,* incessamment.

incest, *n,* inceste, *m.* **incestuous,** *a,* incestueux.

inch, *n,* pouce, *m. = 2·54 (about 2½)* centimetres.

incidence, *n,* incidence, *f.* **incident,** *n,* incident, événement, *m.* ¶ *a,* incident. **~al,** *a,* incident. **~ expenses,** faux frais, *m.pl.* **~ally,** *ad,* incidemment.

incinerate, *v.t,* incinérer. **incinerator,** *n,* incinérateur, *m.*

incipient, *a,* naissant.

incise, *v.t,* inciser. **incision,** *n,* incision, *f.* **incisive,** *a,* incisif. **incisor,** *n,* [dent] incisive, *f.*

incite, *v.t.*, inciter, provoquer; exciter. ~ment, *n*, incitation; excitation, *f*.

incivility, *n*, incivilité, *f*.

inclemency, *n*, inclémence, *f*. inclement, *a*, inclément.

inclination, *n*, inclination, *f*; penchant; attrait, *m*; inclinaison, *f*. incline, *n*, plan incliné, *m*; (*down*) pente; (*up*) rampe, *f*. ¶ *v.t. & i*, incliner; pencher; porter; (*colour*) tirer. inclined, *p.a. & p.p*, (*plane*) incliné; (*fig.*) enclin, porté.

include, *v.t*, comprendre, englober, renfermer. including, *participle*, y compris. not ~, non compris. inclusive, *a*, tout compris; (*sum*) globale; (*dates*) inclusivement. *our terms are* ~, notre tarif s'entend tous frais compris. ~ *charge*, prix à forfait, *m*. ~ *of*, y compris. ~ly, *ad*, inclusivement.

incognito, *ad. & n*, incognito, *ad. & m*.

incoherence, *n*, incohérence, *f*. incoherent, *a*, incohérent.

incombustible, *a*, incombustible.

income, *n*, revenu, *m*. oft. *pl*; rapport; *m*; rente, *f*. oft. *pl*. ~ *tax*, impôt sur le revenu, *m*, impôt[s] cédulaire[s], *m.[pl.]*. ~ *tax return*, déclaration de revenu, *f*.

incoming, *a*, à l'arrivée; d'arrivée; d'entrée; à échoir; (*tide*) montante.

incommensurable, *a*, incommensurable. incommensurate with, hors de proportion avec.

incommode, *v.t*, incommoder.

incomparable†, *a*, incomparable.

incompatibility, *n*, incompatibilité, *f*. ~ *of temper*, incompatibilité d'humeurs. incompatible, *a*, incompatible.

incompetence, -cy, *n*, incompétence, incapacité, *f*. incompetent, *a*, incompétent, incapable, insuffisant.

incomplete†, *a*, incomplet. incompletion, *n*, imperfection, *f*.

incomprehensible, *a*, incompréhensible.

inconceivable, *a*, inconcevable.

inconclusive, *a*, non concluant.

incongruity, *n*, incongruité, disparate, *f*. incongruous, *a*, incongru, disparate. ~ly, *ad*, incongrûment.

inconsequent[ial], *a*, inconséquent.

inconsiderable, *a*, sans importance.

inconsiderate†, *a*, inconsidéré.

inconsistency, *n*, inconséquence; inconsistance, *f*. inconsistent, *a*, inconséquent; inconsistant.

inconsolable†, *a*, inconsolable, inguérissable.

inconspicuous, *a*, peu (*ou* pas) en évidence.

inconstancy, *n*, inconstance, *f*. inconstant, *a*, inconstant, volage, journalier.

incontinent, *a*, incontinent.

incontrovertible, *a*, incontestable.

inconvenience, *n*, incommodité, *f*; inconvénient, *m*. ¶ *v.t*, incommoder. inconvenient, *a*, incommode.

incorporate, *v.t*, incorporer; encadrer; enchâsser; (*a limited company*) constituer.

incorrect†, *a*, incorrect; inexact. ~ness, *n*, incorrection; inexactitude, *f*.

incorrigible†, *a*, incorrigible, indécrottable.

incorruptible, *a*, incorruptible.

increase, *n*, augmentation, *f*, accroissement, *m*, majoration, *f*. ¶ *v.t*, augmenter, accroître; aggraver, majorer. increasing, *p.a*, croissant.

incredibility, *n*, incrédibilité, *f*. incredible†, *a*, incroyable. incredulity, *n*, incrédulité, *f*. incredulous, *a*, incrédule.

increment, *n*, accroissement, *m*; plus-value, *f*.

incriminate, *v.t*, incriminer, charger.

incrust, *v.t*, incruster.

incubate, *v.t. & i*, couver. incubation, *n*, incubation, *f*. incubator, *n*, couveuse artificielle, poussinière, *f*.

incubus, *n*, cauchemar; faix, *m*.

inculcate, *v.t*, inculquer.

inculpate, *v.t*, inculper.

incumbent, *n*, bénéficier, titulaire, *m*. *to be* ~ *on*, incomber à.

incur, *v.t*, encourir; courir; s'attirer.

incurable†, *a. & n*, incurable, *a. & m,f*.

incursion, *n*, incursion, *f*.

indebted, *a*, redevable. ~ness, *n*, dette; créance, *f*; dettes & créances, *f.pl*.

indecency, *n*, indécence, malpropreté, *f*. indecent, *a*, indécent, malpropre. ~ly, *ad*, indécemment, malproprement.

indecision, *n*, indécision, *f*.

indecorous, *a*, inconvenant.

indeed, *ad*, vraiment, en effet; certes; bien, voire même, même. ¶ *i*, vraiment!, tiens!

indefatigable†, *a*, infatigable.

indefensible, *a*, indéfendable.

indefinable, *a*, indéfinissable. indefinite†, *a*, indéfini; (*leave*) illimité.

indelible, *a*, indélébile.

indelicacy, *n*, indélicatesse, *f*. indelicate†, *a*, indélicat.

indemnify, *v.t*, indemniser, dédommager. indemnity, *n*, indemnité; caution, *f*.

indent, *n*, demande; commande [reçue de l'étranger] *f*. ¶ *v.t*, denteler, échancrer; (*Typ.*) renfoncer, [faire] rentrer. ~ *for*, faire une demande de. indentation, *n*, denteure, échancrure, *f*. indention, *n*, renfoncement, *m*. indenture, *n*, acte, contrat; (*pl.*) brevet, *m*.

independence, *n*, indépendance, *f*. independent, *a*, indépendant. *to be* ~, avoir une fortune indépendante. *person of* ~ *means*, rentier, ère. ~ly, *ad*, indépendamment.

indescribable, *a*, indescriptible, inénarrable.

indestructible, *a*, indestructible.

indeterminate, *a*, indéterminé.

index, *n*, indice, *m*; table; table alphabétique, *f*; index; répertoire, *m*. ~ *expurgatorius*, index expurgatoire. ¶ *v.t*, dresser la table [alphabétique] de; répertorier.

India, *n*, l'Inde, *f*. ~ *paper*, papier indien, *m*. Indian, *a*, indien. ~ *Archipelago*,

archipel Indien, *m*, Insulinde, *f*. ~ *club*,
massue en bois, *f*, mil, *m*. ~ *corn*, blé
de Turquie, maïs, *m*. ~ *Empire*, empire
des Indes, *m*. ~ *ink*, encre de Chine, *f*.
~ *Ocean*, océan Indien, *m*, mer des Indes,
f. ¶ *n*, Indien, ne.

indiarubber, *n*, caoutchouc, *m*, gomme
[élastique] *f*. ~ *stamp*, timbre en caoutchouc, timbre humide, *m*.

indicate, *v.t*, indiquer, désigner. **indication**,
n, indication, *f*; indice, *m*. **indicative**, *a*,
indicatif. ~ [*mood*], *m*, [mode] indicatif,
m. **indicator**, *n*, indicateur, *m*.

indict, *v.t*, accuser. ~**ment**, *n*, acte d'accusation, réquisitoire, *m*.

Indies (the) *n.pl*, les Indes, *f.pl*.

indifference, *n*, indifférence; indolence, *f*.
indifferent, *a*, indifférent; indolent; sans
gêne. ~**ly**, *ad*, indifféremment.

indigence. ~**n**, indigence, *f*.

indigenous, *a*, indigène.

indigent, *a*, indigent.

indigestible, *a*, indigeste, cru [à l'estomac].
indigestion, *n*, indigestion, *f*.

indignant, *a*, indigné. ~**ly**, *ad*, avec indignation. **indignation**, *n*, indignation, *f*.
indignity, *n*, indignité, *f*.

indigo, *n*, indigo, *m*. ~ *blue*, [bleu d']inde,
m. ~ *plant*, indigotier, *m*.

indirect†, *a*, indirect.

indiscreet†, *a*, indiscret. **indiscretion**, *n*,
indiscrétion; incartade, *f*.

indiscriminate, *a*, sans aucun discernement;
confus. ~**ly**, *ad*, indistinctement, sans
distinction.

indispensable†, *a*, indispensable.

indisposed, *p.p*, indisposé. **indisposition**, *n*,
indisposition, *f*, malaise, *m*; disposition peu
favorable, *f*.

indisputable†, *a*, indiscutable.

indissoluble†, *a*, indissoluble.

indistinct†, *a*, indistinct.

indite, *v.t*, rédiger; composer.

individual†, *a*, individuel. ¶ *n*, individu;
particulier, *m*. ~**ity**, *n*, individualité, *f*.

indivisible†, *a*, indivisible.

Indo-China, *n*, l'Indochine, *f*.

indolence, *n*, indolence, *f*. **indolent**, *a*, indolent, mou. ~**ly**, *ad*, indolemment.

indomitable, *a*, indomptable. (*will*) irréductible.

indoor, *a*, d'intérieur; de cabinet; (*staff*)
sédentaire; (*games*) de société; (*plants*,
aerial) d'appartement; (*Phot.*) en chambre;
à l'atelier. ~**s**, *ad*, à la maison; à l'abri.

indubitable†, *a*, indubitable.

induce, *v.t*, porter; décider; engager; induire; provoquer. ~ *to strike*, débaucher.
~**ment**, *n*, stimulant, *m*.

induct, *v.t*, installer. ~**ion**, *n*, induction;
(*Eccl.*) installation, *f*.

indulge, *v.t*, gâter; caresser. ~ *in*, se permettre. **indulgence**, *n*, indulgence, *f*.
indulgent, *a*, indulgent.

indurate, *v.t*, [en]durcir.

industrial†, *a*, industriel. ~ *disease*, maladie
professionnelle, *f*. ~**ism**, *n*, industrialisme, *m*. ~**ize**, *v.t*, industrialiser. **in-
dustrious†**, *a*, industrieux, diligent, travailleur, assidu. ~**ly**, *ad*, industrieusement,
diligemment. **industry**, *n*, industrie; diligence, *f*.

inebriate, *a*, ivre. ¶ *n*, ivrogne, *m*, ivrognesse, *f*. ¶ *v.t*, enivrer.

ineffable, *a*, ineffable.

ineffaceable, *a*, ineffaçable.

ineffective† & **ineffectual†** & **inefficacious†**,
a, inefficace.

inefficient, *a*, incapable.

inelastic (*Phys.*) *a*, mou.

inelegant, *a*, inélégant.

ineligible, *a*, inéligible.

inept, *a*, inepte. **ineptitude**, *n*, ineptie, *f*.

inequality, *n*, inégalité, *f*.

inequitable†, *a*, injuste.

ineradicable, *a*, indéracinable.

inert, *a*, inerte. **inertia**, *n*, inertie, *f*.

inestimable, *a*, inestimable.

inevitable†, *a*, inévitable.

inexact†, *a*, inexact. **inexactitude**, *n*, inexactitude, *f*.

inexcusable, *a*, inexcusable.

inexecutable, *a*, inexécutable.

inexhaustible†, *a*, inépuisable, intarissable.

inexorable†, *a*, inexorable.

inexpedient, *a*, pas expédient.

inexpensive, *a*, peu coûteux.

inexperience, *n*, inexpérience, *f*. ~**d**, *a*,
inexpérimenté, novice, neuf.

inexplicable, *a*, inexplicable.

inexplicit, *a*, pas explicite.

inexpressible, *a*, inexprimable.

in extenso, *ad*, in extenso.

inextinguishable, *a*, inextinguible.

in extremis, *ad*, in extremis.

inextricable, *a*, inextricable.

infallible†, *a*, infaillible, impeccable.

infamous, *a*, infâme; (*Law*) infamant. **infamy**, *n*, infamie, *f*.

infancy, *n*, enfance, *f*; bas âge, *m*; (*Law*)
minorité, *f*. **infant**, *n*, [petit, e] enfant,
m,f; (*Law*) mineur, e. ~ *colony*, colonie
naissante, *f*. ~ *mortality*, mortalité infantile, *f*. ~ *prodigy*, enfant prodige.
~ *school*, école maternelle, *f*. **infanticide**,
n, infanticide (*act*) *m*; (*pers.*) *m,f*. **infantile**, *a*, enfantin; (*Med.*) infantile.

infantry, *n*, infanterie, *f*. ~ *man*, fantassin,
homme de pied, *m*.

infatuate, *v.t*, affoler, embéguiner. *to become
~d*, s'infatuer, s'engouer. **infatuation**, *n*,
infatuation, *f*, engouement, *m*.

infect, *v.t*, infecter, empester. ~**ion**, *n*, infection, *f*. ~**ious**, *a*, infectieux; contagieux.

infer, *v.t*, inférer, conclure, supposer, déduire.
~**ence**, *n*, inférence, conclusion, déduction, *f*. **inferential**, *a*, déductif. ~**ly**, *ad*,
par déduction.

inferior†, *a. & n*, inférieur, *a. & m*. ~ity, *n*, infériorité, *f*. ~ *complex*, complexe d'i., *m*.

infernal, *a*, infernal. **inferno, *n***, enfer; brasier, *m*, fournaise, *f*.

infertile, *a*, infertile.

infest, *v.t*, infester.

infidel, *a. & n*, infidèle. *a. & m,f*. ~ity, *n*, infidélité, *f*.

in-fighting (*Box.*) *n*, combat de près, *m*.

infiltrate, *v.i*, s'infiltrer.

infinite†, *a*, infini. the ~, l'infini, *m*. in-finitesimal, *a*, infinitésimal. **infinitive** [mood], *n*, [mode] infinitif, *m*. **infinitude** & **infinity**, *n*, infinité; immensité, *f*. **infinity** (*Math., Phot.*) *n*, l'infini, *m*.

infirm, *a*, infirme. ~ary, *n*, infirmerie, *f*. ~ity, *n*, infirmité, *f*.

inflame, *v.t*, enflammer; exalter. **inflammable**, *a*, inflammable. **inflammation**, *n*, inflammation, *f*.

inflate, *v.t*, gonfler; (*fig.*) enfler; grossir; charger. ~d (*fig.*) *p.p*, enflé, ampoulé, boursouflé. **inflation**, *n*, gonflement, *m*; enflure; (*Fin.*) inflation, *f*.

inflect, *v.t*, infléchir. **inflexible†**, *a*, inflexible. **inflexion, -ction**, *n*, inflexion; flexion, *f*.

inflict, *v.t*, infliger, appliquer. ~ion, *n*, application; châtiment, *m*; peine, *f*.

inflow, *n*, venue, *f*.

influence, *n*, influence, *f*; crédit, *m*; cote d'amour, *f*. ¶ *v.t*, influer sur; influencer. **influential**, *a*, influent, prestigieux.

influenza, *n*, grippe, *f*.

influx, *n*, venue; invasion, *f*.

inform, *v.t*, informer, instruire, renseigner, faire part, mander, prévenir. ~al, *a*, officieux; (*Law*) informe. ~ *gathering*, petit comité, *m*. ~ality, *n*, vice de forme, *m*. ~ant, *n*, informateur, trice, auteur, *m*. ~ation, *n*, renseignement[s], *m*.[pl.], indication[s] *f*.[pl.]; (*Law*) dénonciation, *f*. ~er, *n*, délateur, trice, indicateur, trice.

infraction, *n*, infraction, *f*.

infrequent, *a*, peu fréquent, rare.

infringe, *v.t*, enfreindre, contrevenir à; contre-faire. ~ment, *n*, infraction, contraven-tion; contrefaçon, *f*. ~ *of copyright*, contrefaçon littéraire, c. de librairie.

infuriate, *v.t*, faire enrager.

infuse, *v.t*, infuser. **infusible**, *a*, infusible. **infusion**, *n*, infusion; tisane, *f*. **infusoria**, *n.pl*, infusoires, *m.pl*.

ingathering, *n*, rentrée, *f*.

ingenious†, *a*, ingénieux. **ingenuity**, *n*, in-géniosité, industrie, *f*.

ingenuous†, *a*, ingénu, naïf, candide.

ingle nook, coin du feu, *m*.

inglorious†, *a*, honteux, ignominieux; obscur.

ingoing, *a*, entrant.

ingot, *n*, lingot, saumon, *m*.

ingrained, *a*, enraciné, invétéré.

ingratiate oneself with, s'insinuer dans les bonnes grâces de.

ingratitude, *n*, ingratitude, *f*.

ingredient, *n*, ingrédient, *m*.

ingress, *n*, entrée, *f*.

ingrowing (*nail*) *a*, incarné.

inhabit, *v.t*, habiter. ~able, *a*, habitable. ~ant, *n*, habitant, e.

inhale, *v.t*, inhaler, aspirer, respirer, humer.

inherent, *a*, inhérent; propre.

inherit, *v.t. & abs*, hériter, succéder à. ~ance, *n*, héritage, patrimoine, *m*, hoirie, succession; (*right*) hérédité, *f*.

inhibit, *v.t*, interdire.

inhospitable, *a*, inhospitalier.

inhuman†, *a*, inhumain. ~ity, *n*, inhuma-nité, *f*.

inimical, *a*, ennemi, hostile.

inimitable, *a*, inimitable.

iniquitous†, *a*, inique. **iniquity**, *n*, ini-quité, *f*.

initial, *a*, initial. ¶ *n*, initiale, *f*; (*pl.*) paraphe, parafe, *m*, initiales, *f.pl*, visa, *m*. ¶ *v.t*, parapher, parafer, viser.

initiate, *n*, initié, e. ¶ *v.t*, prendre l'initiative de; (*pers.*) initier; entamer, lancer. **initia-tion**, *n*, initiation, *f*. **initiative**, *n*, initia-tive, *f*, allant, *m*.

inject, *v.t*, injecter; seringuer. ~ion, *n*, in-jection, *f*. ~or, *n*, injecteur, *m*.

injudicious, *a*, peu judicieux.

injunction, *n*, injonction, *f*.

injure, *v.t*, léser; nuire à; offenser; endom-mager; blesser. ~ *fatally*, blesser à mort. **injurious†**, *a*, nuisible; malfaisant; pré-judiciable; injurieux. **injury**, *n*, injure, *f*; préjudice, tort, *m*; lésion, blessure, *f*.

injustice, *n*, injustice, *f*; passe-droit, *m*.

ink, *n*, encre, *f*. ~ *blocking* (*Bookb.*), dorure en couleurs, *f*. ~ *eraser*, gomme pour l'encre, *f*. ~*stand*, ~*pot*, ~*bottle*, encrier, *m*. ~ *well*, encrier d'écolier, *m*. ¶ *v.t*, encrer; tacher d'encre. ~ *in*, mettre à l'encre. ~ *up* (*Typ.*), toucher.

inkling, *n*, vent, *m*.

inlaid, *p.a*: ~ *linoleum*, linoléum incrusté, *m*. ~ *work*, incrustation; marqueterie, *f*.

inland, *a*, intérieur; (*Post*) du régime in-térieur. ~ *revenue*, recettes fiscales, *f.pl*; fisc, *m*. ¶ *ad*, dans l'intérieur [du pays].

inlay, *v.t.ir*, incruster; marqueter.

inlet, *n*, crique; entrée; arrivée, *f*.

inmate, *n*, habitant, e; hôte, esse; (*paying*) pensionnaire, *m,f*; (*asylum*) interné, e; hospitalisé, e.

inmost, *a*, le plus intime.

inn, *n*, auberge, *f*. ~*keeper*, aubergiste, *m,f*.

innate, *a*, inné, infus. ~ness, *n*, innéité, *f*.

inner, *a*, intérieur, interne. ~ *harbour*, arrière-port, *m*. the ~ *man*, l'homme intérieur. ~ *tube* (tire), chambre à air, *f*.

innermost, *a*, le plus intime.

innings, *n*, tour, *m*.

innocence, *n*, innocence, *f*. **innocent**, *a. & n*, innocent, *a. & m*. ~ly, *ad*, innocemment.

innocuous, innoxious, *a*, inoffensif.

innovation, *n,* innovation, nouveauté, *f.*
innovator, *n,* novateur, trice.
innuendo, *n,* insinuation, allusion, *f.*
innumerable, *a,* innombrable.
inobservance, *n,* inobservance, inobservation, *f.*
inoculate, *v.t,* inoculer. **inoculation,** *n,* inoculation, *f.*
inodorous, *a,* inodore.
inoffensive, *a,* inoffensif.
inoperative, *a,* inopérant.
inopportune, *a,* inopportun. ~**ly,** *ad,* mal à propos, à contretemps.
inordinate†, *a,* démesuré.
inorganic, *a,* (*matter*) inorganique; (*body*) brut; (*chemistry*) minérale.
in-patient, *n,* malade interné, e, hospitalisé, e.
inquest, *n,* enquête, *f.*
inquire, *v.t. & i,* demander; s'informer (de); s'enquérir (de); se renseigner; s'adresser; enquêter. **inquirer,** *n,* chercheur, euse; demandeur de renseignements, *m.* *inquiring mind,* [esprit] chercheur, *m.* **inquiry,** *n,* demande, *f;* renseignements, *m.pl;* informations, *f.pl;* recherche; enquête, *f;* informé, *m.* ~ *office,* bureau de renseignements, *m.* ~ *operator* (*Teleph.*), opératrice des renseignements, *f.*
inquisition, *n,* inquisition, *f.* **inquisitive,** *a,* inquisiteur; curieux.
inroad & **inrush,** *n,* incursion; irruption, venue, *f.*
insane, *a,* fou; insensé. **insanity,** *n,* démence, aliénation d'esprit; (*folly*) insanité, *f.*
insanitary, *a,* insalubre, malsain.
insatiable†, *a,* insatiable.
inscribe, *v.t,* inscrire; graver; dédier. ~*d stock,* inscription de rente, *f.* **inscription,** *n,* inscription; dédicace, *f.*
inscrutable, *a,* inscrutable, impénétrable.
insect, *n,* insecte, *m.* ~ *powder,* poudre insecticide, *f.* **insectivora,** *n.pl,* insectivores, *m.pl.* **insectivorous,** *a,* insectivore.
insecure, *a,* mal assuré. **insecurity,** *n,* insécurité, *f.*
insensate, *a,* insensé. **insensible†,** *a,* insensible; sans connaissance.
inseparable†, *a. & n,* inséparable, *a. & m,f.*
insert (*Bookb.*) *n,* encart, *m.* ¶ *v.t,* insérer (*Bookb.*) encarter. ~**ion,** *n,* insertion, *f;* (*Need.*) entre-deux, *m.*
inset, *n,* pièce rapportée, *f;* (*Bookb.*) carton d'en bas, *m.* ¶ *v.t.ir,* rapporter; (*Bookb.*) encarter.
inshore, *a,* côtier. ~ *fishing,* pêche côtière, pêche dans les eaux territoriales, *f.*
inside, *n,* dedans; intérieur, *m.* ¶ *a,* intérieur; d'i. ~ *edge* (*Skating*) dedans, *m.* ¶ *ad,* [en] dedans, à l'intérieur; (*Meas.*) dans œuvre. ~ *out,* à l'envers.
insidious†, *a,* insidieux.
insight, *n,* pénétration, *f,* lumières, *f.pl.*
insignia, *n.pl,* insignes, *m.pl.*

insignificant, *a,* insignifiant,, infime.
insincere, *a,* qui n'est pas sincère. **insincerity,** *n,* absence de sincérité, *f.*
insinuate, *v.t,* insinuer, faufiler.
insipid, *a,* insipide, fade, fadasse.
insist, *v.i,* insister. ~**ence,** *n,* insistance, *f.*
insobriety, *n,* intempérance, *f.*
insolation, *n,* insolation, *f.*
insolence, *n,* insolence, *f.* **insolent,** *a,* insolent. ~**ly,** *ad,* insolemment.
insoluble, *a,* insoluble.
insolvency, *n,* insolvabilité, carence, faillite; déconfiture, *f.* **insolvent,** *a,* insolvable. ¶ *n,* failli, *m.*
insomnia, *n,* insomnie[s] *f.*[*pl.*].
insomuch, *ad,* à tel point.
inspect, *v.t,* inspecter, visiter, contrôler; (*Excise*) exercer. ~**ion,** *n,* inspection, visite, *f,* contrôle; exercice, *m;* revue, *f.* ~ *committee,* comité de surveillance, *m.* ~ *order* (*Cust.*), bon d'ouverture, *m.* ~**pit,** fosse à visiter, *f.* ~**or,** *n,* inspecteur, trice; visiteur; contrôleur; (*weights, &c*) vérificateur, *m.* ~**orship,** *n,* inspection, *f.*
inspiration, *n,* inspiration;' aspiration; illumination, *f,* souffle, *m.* **inspire,** *v.t,* inspirer; aspirer.
inspirit, *v.t,* animer. ~**ing,** *a,* entraînant.
instability, *n,* instabilité, *f.*
install, *v.t,* installer, emménager. ~**ation,** *n,* installation, *f.*
instalment, *n,* acompte, paiement à compte; versement; terme; fascicule, *m.* ~ *plan,* vente à tempérament, vente par abonnement, *f.*
instance, *n,* cas, *m;* demande; (*Law*) instance, *f. for* ~, par exemple. ¶ *v.t,* citer. **instant,** *a,* instant; (*month*) courant. ¶ *n,* instant, *m.* **instantaneous,** *a,* instantané. ~**ly,** *ad,* instantanément.
instead, *ad,* plutôt. ~ *of,* au lieu de, à la place de, pour.
instep, *n,* cou-de-pied, *m.*
instigate, *v.t,* provoquer, inciter. **instigation,** *n,* instigation, *f.*
instil[l], *v.t,* instiller; (*fig.*) inculquer, infuser, faire pénétrer.
instinct, *n,* instinct, *m.* ¶ *a,* doué, animé. ~**ive†,** *a,* instinctif.
institute, *v.t,* instituer; intenter. **institution,** *n,* institution, *f;* institut, établissement, *m.*
instruct, *v.t,* instruire; charger; (*counsel*) constituer. ~**ion,** *n,* instruction, *f;* (*pl.*) instructions, indications, *f.pl;* charge, *f,* mandat, *m.* ~**ional film,** film documentaire, *m.* ~**ive,** *a,* instructif. **instructor,** *n,* professeur; (*Mil.*) instructeur; (*Mil. gym.*) moniteur, *m.* **instructress,** *n,* professeur, *m.*
instrument, *n,* instrument; (*Law*) instrument, acte, *m.* ~**al,** *a,* instrumental. ~**alist,** *n,* instrumentiste, *m,f.* ~**ality,** *n,* intermédiaire, *m.*

insubordinate, *a*, insubordonné.
insufferable†, *a*, insupportable.
insufficiency, *n*, insuffisance, *f*. insufficient, *a*, insuffisant. ~ly, *ad*, insuffisamment.
insular, *a*, insulaire. ~ity, *n*, insularité, *f*.
insulate, *v.t*, isoler. insulation, *n*, isolement, *m*. insulator, *n*, isolateur, *m*.
insult, *n*, insulte, injure, sottie, *f*, outrage, *m*. ¶ *v.t*, insulter, outrager. ~ingt, *a*, injurieux, offensant, outrageant, outrageux.
insuperable, *a*, insurmontable.
insupportable†, *a*, insupportable.
insurance, *n*, assurance, *f*; (*Post*) chargement, *m*. ~ card, carte d'assuré, *f*. ~ company, compagnie d'assurance[s] *f*.
insure, *v.t*, assurer, faire a.; (*Post*) charger; (*v.i.*) s'assurer, se faire assurer. ~d (*pers.*) *n*, assuré, e. ~d for: £—— (*Post*), valeur déclarée: ——£. ~d parcel, colis avec valeur déclarée, colis chargé, *m*. insurer, *n*, assureur, *m*.
insurgent, *n. & a*, insurgé, e, révolté, e.
insurmountable, *a*, insurmontable.
insurrection, *n*, insurrection, *f*.
intact, *a*, intact.
intaglio, *n*, intaille, *f*.
intake, *n*, prise, admission, *f*, appel, *m*.
intangible, *a*, intangible.
integer, *n*, [nombre] entier, *m*. integral†, *a*, intégral. integrity, *n*, intégrité, *f*.
intellect, *n*, intellect, *m*, intelligence, *f*, cerveau, *m*. intellectual†, *a. & n*, intellectuel, *a. & m*.
intelligence, *n*, intelligence, *f*, entendement, *m*; nouvelles, *f.pl*; chronique, *f*, courrier, *m*. ~ department, service des renseignements, *m*, statistique militaire, *f*. intelligencer, *n*, nouvelliste, *m,f*. intelligent, *a*, intelligent. ~ly, *ad*, intelligemment. intelligible†, *a*, intelligible.
intemperance, *n*, intempérance, *f*. intemperate, *a*, intempérant.
intend, *v.t*, se proposer, avoir l'intention, compter; vouloir; destiner. ~ed, *n*, prétendu, e, futur, e.
intense, *a*, intense. ~ly, *ad*, extrêmement. intensifier (*Phot.*) *n*, renforçateur, *m*. intensify, *v.t*, intensifier; (*Phot.*) renforcer. intensity, *n*, intensité, *f*.
intent, *a*, fixe. ~ on, tout entier à. ¶ *n*, intention, *f*, but, *m*. to all ~s & purposes, virtuellement. ~ion, *n*, intention, *f*, but; (*pl, matrimonial*) motif, *m*. ~ional†, *a*, intentionnel, voulu. -intentioned, *a*, intentionné. intentness, *n*, contention, *f*.
inter, *v.t*, enterrer, inhumer.
intercalate, *v.t*, intercaler.
intercede, *v.i*, intercéder.
intercept, *v.t*, intercepter, surprendre.
intercession, *n*, intercession, *f*. intercessor, *n*, intercesseur, *m*.
interchange, *n*, communication, *f*, échange, *m*. ~able, *a*, interchangeable.

intercourse, *n*, commerce; frottement, *m*; rapports, *m.pl*.
interdict, *n*, interdit, *m*. ¶ *v.t*, interdire. ~ion, *n*, interdiction, *f*.
interest, *n*, intérêt, *m*; intérêts, *m.pl*; arrérages, *m.pl*; usure; commandite, *f*. *to take no further ~ in*, se désintéresser de. ~ *on overdue payments*, intérêts moratoires. ~ *payable* (date), jouissance. ¶ *v.t*, intéresser. ~ed, *p.a*, intéressé; curieux. ~ *party*, intéressé, e. ~ing, *p.a*, intéressant; attachant. *in an ~ condition* (pregnant), dans une situation intéressante.
interfere, *v.i*, intervenir, s'immiscer, s'ingérer. ~ *with* (hinder), contrarier, gêner. interference, *n*, intervention, immixtion, ingérence; (*Phys.*) interférence, *f*.
interim, *n*, intérim, *m*. ~ *dividend*, acompte de dividende, dividende intérimaire, dividende provisoire, *m*.
interior†, *n. & a*, intérieur, *a. & m*.
interject, *v.t*, placer. ~ion, *n*, interjection, *f*.
interlace, *v.t*, entrelacer.
interlard, *v.t*, entrelarder.
interleave, *v.t*, interfolier.
interline, *v.t*, écrire dans l' (*ou* en) interligne. interlinear, *a*, interlinéaire. interlineation, *n*, entre-ligne, *m*.
interlocutor, tress *or* trix, *n*, interlocuteur, trice.
interloper, *n*, intrus, e.
interlude, *n*, intervalle, intermède; (*Mus., &c*) interlude, *m*.
intermarriage, *n*, mariage entre individus de tribus diverses (*ou* de races différentes), *m*, alliance, *f*. intermarry, *v.i*, se marier entre eux, s'allier.
intermeddle, *v.i*, se mêler, s'immiscer.
intermediary, *n. & a*, intermédiaire, *m. & a*. intermediate, *a*, intermédiaire. ~ *course*, (*Sch.*), cours moyen, *m*.
interment, *n*, enterrement, *m*, inhumation, *f*.
intermezzo, *n*, intermède, *m*.
interminable, *a*, interminable.
intermingle, *v.t*, entremêler.
intermission, *n*, relâche, intermédiaire, *m*.
intermittent, *a*, intermittent. ~ *light* (*Naut.*), feu à éclipses, *m*.
intermix, *v.t*, entremêler.
intern, *v.t*, interner.
internal, *a*, interne; intérieur; intestin. ~ly, *ad*, intérieurement.
international, *a*, international. ~ *travelling pass*, certificat international de route, *m*. ~ (*association*) ~e (*hymn*) *n*, internationale, *f*. ~ist, *n. & a*, internationaliste, *m,f. & a*.
internecine, *a*, meurtrier, à outrance.
internment, *n*, internement, *m*. ~ *camp*, (*Civil*) camp de concentration; (*Mil.*) camp de prisonniers, *m*.
interpolate, *v.t*, interpoler.
interpose, *v.t*, interposer; (*v.i.*) s'interposer.

interpret, *v.t*, interpréter; traduire. **~ation**, *n*, interprétation, *f*. **~er**, *n*, interprète, *m*, *f*, truchement, *m*.

interregnum, *n*, interrègne, *m*.

interrogate, *v.t*, interroger. **interrogation**, *n*, interrogation, *f*. **interrogative†**, *a*, interrogatif. **interrogatory**, *n*, interrogatoire, *m*.

interrupt, *v.t*, interrompre; couper. **~er**, *n*, (*pers.*) interrupteur, trice; (*switch*) interrupteur, *m*. **interruption**, *n*, interruption, *f*.

intersect, *v.t*, couper; entrecouper. **~ion**, *n*, intersection, *f*.

intersperse, *v.t*, entremêler; émailler.

interstice, *n*, interstice, *m*.

intertwine, *v.t*, entrelacer.

interval, *n*, intervalle, entre-temps, *m*; (*Theat.*) entracte, *m*.

intervene, *v.i*, intervenir. **intervention**, *n*, intervention, *f*.

interview, *n*, entretien, *m*, entrevue, *f*; (*for news*) interview, *m*. **¶** *v.t*, interviewer.

inter vivos, entre vifs.

interweave, *v.t.ir*, entrelacer. **interwoven** *pattern* (fabrics), brochure, *f*.

intestate, *a*, intestat (*inv.*).

intestinal, *a*, intestinal. **intestine**, *a. & n*, intestin, *a. & m*.

intimacy, *n*, intimité, familiarité, accointance, *f*. **intimate†**, *a. & n*, intime, *a. & m*, lié, *a*, familier, *a. & m*. **¶** *v.t*, faire entendre, signifier. **intimation**, *n*, avis; mot, *m*.

intimidate, *v.t*, intimider.

into, *pr*, dans; en; à; entre; par; par-dessus.

intolerable†, *a*, intolérable. **intolerance**, *n*, intolérance, *f*. **intolerant**, *a*, intolérant.

intonation, *n*, intonation, *f*. **intonate**, **intone**, *v.t*, entonner.

intoxicate, *v.t*, enivrer. **~d**, *a*, ivre, enivré. **intoxication**, *n*, ivresse, *f*.

intractable, *a*, intraitable, indocile.

intrados, *n*, intrados, *m*.

intransitive†, *a*, intransitif. (See Note under *se*, *s'* in French-English section.)

intrench, *v.t*, retrancher.

intrepid†, *a*, intrépide. **~ity**, *n*, intrépidité, *f*.

intricacy, *n*, complication, *f*; embrouillement, *m*. **intricate**, *a*, compliqué, embrouillé.

intrigue, *n*, intrigue, brigue, *f*. **¶** *v.i*, intriguer, briguer, cabaler; (*v.t.*) intriguer. **intriguer**, *n. & intriguing*, *a*, intrigant, e.

intrinsic†, *a*, intrinsèque.

introduce, *v.t*, introduire; insinuer; présenter. **~** *into society*, produire dans le monde. **~** *oneself*, se présenter, se faire connaître. **introducer**, *n*, introducteur, trice. **introduction**, *n*, introduction; présentation, *f*.

introit, *n*, introït, *m*.

introspection, *n*, introspection, *f*.

intrude, *v.i*, s'introduire [contre le droit *ou* la forme]. **intruder**, *n*, intrus, e, importun, e. **intrusion**, *n*, intrusion, *f*.

intuition, *n*, intuition, *f*. **intuitive**, *a*, intuitif. **~ly**, *ad*, par intuition.

inundate, *v.t*, inonder. **inundation**, *n*, inondation, *f*.

inure, *v.t*, aguerrir, rompre, habituer.

invade, *v.t*, envahir. **invader**, *n*, envahisseur, *n*.

invalid, *a*, malade, infirme, invalide; (*Law*) invalide. **¶** *n*, malade, infirme, *m*, *f*, invalide, *m*. **¶** *v.t*, réformer. **~ate**, *v.t*, invalider, infirmer. **invalided**, *p.a*, invalide, réformé. **invalidity**, *n*, invalidité, *f*.

invaluable, *a*, inestimable, impayable.

invariable†, *a*, invariable.

invasion, *n*, invasion, *f*, envahissement, *m*.

invective, *n*, invective, *f*. **inveigh**, *v.i*, invectiver, tonner.

inveigle, *v.t*, enjôler.

invent, *v.t*, inventer, imaginer. **~ion**, *n*, invention, *f*; (*fiction*) cru, *m*, fabrique, *f*. **~ive**, *a*, inventif, original. **inventor**, **tress**, *n*, inventeur, trice, auteur, *m*.

inventory, *n*, inventaire, *m*, description, *f*. **¶** *v.t*, inventorier.

inverse†, *a*, inverse, réciproque. **inversion**, *n*, renversement, *m*; interversion; inversion, *f*. **invert**, *v.t*, renverser; invertir. **~ed commas**, guillemets, *m.pl*. *to put in* **~ed commas**, guillemeter.

invertebrate, *a. & n*, invertébré, *a. & m*.

invest, *v.t*, revêtir; investir; cerner; (*money*) placer, investir.

investigate, *v.t*, rechercher, examiner. **investigation**, *n*, investigation, enquête, *f*. **investigator**, *n*, chercheur, euse.

investiture, *n*, investiture, *f*.

investment, *n*, placement, *m*; valeur, *f*; portefeuille, *m*; mise [de fonds] *f*; (*Mil.*) investissement, *m*. **investor**, *n*, rentier, ère. *the small* **~**, la petite épargne.

inveterate, *a*, invétéré, acharné, vivace.

invidious, *a*, méchant; odieux. **~** *distinction*, distinction contre le droit & l'usage ordinaire, *f*, passe-droit, *m*.

invigorate, *v.t*, fortifier, vivifier.

invincible†, *a*, invincible.

inviolable†, *a*, inviolable. **inviolate**, *a*, inviolé.

invisible†, *a*, invisible. **~** *ink*, encre sympathique, *f*. **~** *mending*, reprise perdue, *f*, stoppage, *m*.

invitation, *n*, invitation, *f*; appel, *m*. **invite**, *v.t*, inviter, prier; convier; appeler, faire appel à. **inviting**, *p.a*, engageant.

invocation, *n*, invocation, *f*.

invoice, *n*, facture, *f*. **¶** *v.t*, facturer.

invoke, *v.t*, invoquer.

involuntary†, *a*, involontaire.

involve, *v.t*, envelopper; entraîner; impliquer; empêtrer. **~d**, *p.a*, compliqué, embrouillé. **~** *language*, tortillage, *m*.

invulnerable, *a*, invulnérable.

inward, *a*, intérieur; interne; intime; d'entrée. **~** *bound*, en retour; effectuant son voyage de retour. **~[s]** & **~ly**, *ad*, intérieurement, en dedans. **~s**, *n.pl*, entrailles, *f.pl*.

iodine, *n*, iode, *m*.

ion, *n*, ion, *m*.

Ionian, Ionic, *a*, ionien, ionique.

iota, *n*, iota, *m*.

ipecacuanha, *n*, ipécacuana, *m*.

irascible, *a*, irascible. irate, *a*, irrité, en colère. ire, *n*, courroux, *m*.

Ireland, *n*, l'Irlande, *f*.

iridescence, *n*, irisation, *f*. iridescent, *a*, irisé, chatoyant.

iridium, *n*, iridium, *m*.

iris, *n*, iris, *m*.

Irish, *a*, irlandais. *the ~ Free State*, l'État libre d'Irlande. *~man*, *~woman*, Irlandais, e. *~ Sea*, mer d'Irlande, *f*. ¶ (*language*) *n*, l'irlandais, *m*.

irksome, *a*, ennuyeux, fastidieux.

iron, *n*, (*metal*, *wrought*, *for linen*, *Golf*, *&c*) fer, *m*; (*cast*, *pig*) fonte; (*sheet*) tôle, *f*. ¶ *a*, en fer, de fer; en (*ou* de) fonte. *~* [*& steel*] *constructional work*, charpenterie métallique, *f*. *~* [*or steel*] *bridge*, pont métallique, *m*. *~ & steel shares*, valeurs sidérurgiques, v--s du groupe forges & fonderies, *f.pl*. *~clad*, [navire] cuirassé, *m*. *~ constitution*, santé de fer, *f*. *~master*, maître de forges, *m*. *~monger* (*small*) quincaillier; (*big*) ferronnier; (*builders*') serrurier, *m*. *~mongery*, quincaillerie; ferronnerie; serrurerie, *f*. *~-shod*, ferré. *~work*, ferrement, *m*; ferrure; serrurerie; (*girders*, *&c*) charpente en fer, *f*. *~worker*, ferronnier; serrurier; charpentier en fer, *m*. *~works*, ferronnerie, *f*; forge[s] *f*.[*pl*.]; usine sidérurgique, *f*. ¶ *v.t*, ferrer; (*linen*) repasser. *~ out*, défroncer, déplisser. *~er*, *n*, repasseuse, *f*. *~ing*, *n*, repassage, *m*.

ironic(al)†, *a*, ironique. irony, *n*, ironie, *f*.

irradiation, *n*, irradiation, *f*.

irrational, *a*, irrationnel, irraisonnable.

irreclaimable†, *a*, (*pers*.) incorrigible; (*land*) indéfrichable.

irreconcilable, *a*, irréconciliable; inconciliable.

irrecoverable, *a*, irrécouvrable. *~ arrears* (taxes), non-valeurs, *f.pl*.

irredeemable, *a*, non amortissable, irrachetable.

irredentism, *n*, irrédentisme, *m*.

irreducible, *a*, irréductible.

irrefutable†, *a*, irréfutable.

irregular†, *a*, irrégulier; saccadé. *~ity*, *n*, irrégularité, *f*; dérèglement, *m*.

irrelevant, *a*, hors de propos, non pertinent, étranger; (*Law*) impertinent.

irreligious†, *a*, irréligieux, indévot.

irremediable†, *a*, irrémédiable.

irremovable, *a*, inamovible.

irreparable†, *a*, irréparable.

irrepressible, *a*, irrépressible; (*laughter*) inextinguible.

irreproachable†, *a*, irréprochable

irresistible†, *a*, irrésistible.

irresolute, *a*, irrésolu.

irrespective of, indépendamment de, sans égard à.

irresponsible, *a*, irresponsable; inconscient.

irretrievable†, *a*, irréparable.

irreverent, *a*, irrévérent.

irrevocable†, *a*, irrévocable.

irrigate, *v.t*, irriguer. irrigation, *n*, irrigation, *f*. irrigator, *n*, irrigateur, *m*.

irritable, *a*, irritable. irritate, *v.t*, irriter; agacer. irritation, *n*, irritation, *f*; agacement, *m*.

irruption, *n*, irruption, *f*.

isinglass, *n*, colle de poisson, *f*.

Islam, *n*, Islam, *m*.

island, *n*, île, *f*; (*houses*) îlot, *m*. *~er*, *n*, insulaire, *m,f*. isle, *n*, île, *f*. islet, *n*, îlot, *m*.

isolate, *v.t*, isoler. isolation, *n*, isolement, *m*. *~ hospital*, hôpital de contagieux, *m*.

Israelite, *n*, israélite, *m,f*.

issue, *n*, issue, *f*; événement, *m*; distribution; délivrance; sortie, *f*; succès, *m*; émission; impression; publication, *f*; numéro, *m*; lignée, postérité; question, *f*. ¶ *v.i*, sortir; découler; émaner; (*v.t*.) lancer; émettre; publier; distribuer; délivrer.

isthmus, *n*, isthme, *m*.

it, *pn*, il, elle; le, la; lui, elle; ce, c', ç'; cela; y. *~ is said that . .*, on dit que . . *about ~*, en; y. *at ~*, y. *by ~*, y; en. *for ~*, en; pour cela. *from ~*, en. *of ~*, en; y. *to ~*, y; lui.

Italian, *a*, italien. ¶ *n*, (*pers*.) Italien, ne; (*language*) l'italien, *m*.

italic, *a*. & *~s*, *n.pl*, italique, *a*. & *m*. italicize, *v.t*, mettre en italique.

Italy, *n*, l'Italie, *f*.

itch, *v.i*, démanger; (*fig*.) frétiller, griller. *my arm itches*, le bras me démange. *~[ing]*, *n*, démangeaison, *f*, prurit, *m*; gale, *f*; *~y*, *a*, galeux.

item, *n*, article, poste, chapitre, *m*. ¶ *ad*, item.

itinerant, *a*, ambulant. itinerary, *n*, itinéraire, *m*.

its, *a*, son, sa, ses; en.

itself, *pn*, lui[-même], elle[-même], soi[-même]; même; se.

ivory, *n*, ivoire, *m*. *the I~ Coast*, la Côte d'Ivoire.

ivy, *n*, lierre, *m*.

J

jabber, *v.i*. & *t*, jaboter, bredouiller, jargonner.

jacinth, *n*, jacinthe, *f*.

jack, *n*, (*Mach*.) vérin; cric, *m*; chèvre, *f*; (*spit*) tournebroche; (*fish*) brochet; (*Cards*) valet; (*Bowls*) cochonnet, *m*. *~ass*, âne, baudet, *m*. *~ boots*, bottes à genouillère, *f.pl*. *~daw*, choucas, *m*. *J~ in office*, fonctionnaire plein de son importance, *m*. *~-in-the-box*, boîte à surprise, *f*. *~ knife*,

couteau à virole, c. à cran d'arrêt, *m.*
J ~ *of all trades* or *work*, homme à tout
faire, maître Jacques, *m.* ~*-o'-lantern*,
feu follet, ardent, *m.* ~ *plane*, riflard, *m.
before you could say* J ~ *Robinson*, crac!; en
moins d'un instant. ~ *tar*, loup de mer,
m. ~ *towel*, touaille, *f.*

jackal, *n*, chacal, *m.*

jackanapes, *n*, fat, *m.*

jacket, *n*, (*lounge*) veston, *m*; (*short*) veste, *f*;
(*cardigan*) gilet; (*book*) couvre-livre, *m*;
(*steam, water*) chemise, *f.* ~ *potatoes*,
pommes de terre en robe [de chambre] *f.pl.*

jacobin, *n*, jacobin, *m.*

jade, *n*, (*horse*) rosse, haridelle; (*woman*)
coquine, *f*; (*Miner.*) jade, *m.* ~**d**, *p.p,*
surmené.

jag, *v.t* ébrécher, denteler, déchiqueter.

jaguar, *n*, jaguar, *m.*

jail, *&c.* Same as *gaol, &c.*

jam, *n*, (*fruit*) confiture, *f. oft. pl*; (*squeeze*)
coincement; (*traffic*) embarras, *m.* ~ *pot*,
pot à confitures, *m.* ¶ *v.t.* coincer.

Jamaica, *n*, la Jamaïque.

jamb, *n*, jambage, *m.* ~ *lining*, chambranle, *m.*

jangle, *n*, ébranlement, *m.* ¶ *v.t.* ébranler.

January, *n*, janvier, *m.*

japan, *n*, laque [de Chine], vernis [japonais]
m. ¶ *v.t.* laquer, vernir. **Japan**, *n*, le
Japon. **Japanese**, *a*, japonais. ~ *curio,
&c*, japonerie, *f.* ~ *gut*, crin japonais, *m.*
~ *paper* & ~ *porcelain*, Japon, *m.* ¶ *n*,
(*pers.*) Japonais, *e*; (*language*) le japonais.

jar, *n*, secousse, *f*, battement; pot, *m*, jarre,
bouteille, *f*, bocal, *m.* ¶ *v.i.* détoner, jurer.
~ *upon*, agacer.

jardinière, *n*, (*stand*) jardinière, *f*; (*pot*) cache-
pot, *m.*

jargon, *n*, jargon, baragouin, patois, *m.*

jarring, *a*, discordant.

jasmin[e], *n*, jasmin, *m.*

jasper, *n*, jaspe, *m.*

jaundice, *n*, jaunisse, *f*, ictère, *m.*

jaunt, *n*, course, promenade, *f.* ~**y†**, *a,*
insoucieux, crâne.

Java, *n*, Java, *m.* **Javan[ese]**, *a*, javanais.
¶ *n*, Javanais,'e.

javelin, *n*, javelot, *m.*

jaw, *n*, mâchoire; mandibule, *f*; mors, bec,
m; (*pl* *of death*) bras, *m.pl.* ~ *bone*, [os]
maxillaire, *m.*

jay (*bird*) *n*, geai, *m.* ~ *walker*, piéton
étourdi, *m.*

jealous†, *a*, jaloux. ~**y**, *n*, jalousie, *f.*

jeer, *n*, risée, moquerie, *f.* ¶ *v.i,* goguenarder. ~ *at*, insulter à, se moquer de;
(*pers.*) railler, se moquer de, dauber [sur].

jejune, *a*, maigre; exigu.

jelly, *n*, gelée, *f.* *to* (or *in*) *a* ~ (as face by
blow), en marmelade, en compote. ~*fish*,
méduse, *f.*

jemmy, *n*, monseigneur, *m*, pince-monsei-
gneur, *f.*

jennet, *n*, genet, *m.*

jeopardize, *v.t.* mettre en danger. **jeopardy,**
n, danger, *m.*

jerboa, *n*, gerboise, *f.*

jeremiad, *n*, jérémiade, *f.*

jerk, *n*, à-coup, *m*, saccade, secousse, *f.*
¶ *v.t*, donner un à-coup, des secousses, à.
~**y**, *a*, saccadé.

jerry-build, *v.t.* bousiller. ~**er**, *n*, bousilleur, *m.* ~**ing**, *n*, bâtisse, *f.* **jerry-built,**
a, de carton, fait de boue & de crachat.
jerry-work, *n*, bousillage, *m.*

jersey, *n*, maillot; jersey, *m.* **J~** (*Geog.*), *n,*
Jersey, *f.* **J~** *cow*, vache jersiaise, *f.*

Jerusalem, *n*, Jérusalem, *f.*

jessamin[e], *n*, jasmin, *m.*

jest, *n*, plaisanterie, facétie, *f.* ¶ *v.i,* plaisanter, badiner. ~**er**, *n*, plaisant, *m,*
bouffon, fou; (*court*) fou, *m.*

Jesuit, *n*, jésuite, *m.* ~**ical**, *a*, jésuitique.

Jesus, *n*, Jésus, *m.* **Jesus Christ**, Jésus-
Christ, *m.*

jet, *n*, jet; bec; ajutage; (*lignite*) jais, *m.*
~[-*black*], noir comme [du] jais.

jetsam, *n*, épaves [rejetées] *f.pl.* **jettison,**
n, jet [à la mer] *m.* ¶ *v.t.* jeter [à la
mer].

jetty, *n*, jetée, estacade, *f.*

Jew, *n*, juif, israélite, *m.* ~'*s harp*, guimbarde, *f.*

jewel, *n*, bijou, joyau; (*Horol.*) rubis, *m.* ~
case, écrin [à bijoux]; (*travelling*) porte-
trésor, *m.* **jeweller**, *n*, bijoutier, ère,
joaillier, ère. **jewel[le]ry**, *n*, bijouterie,
joaillerie, *f.*

Jewess, *n*, juive, israélite, *f.* **Jewish**, *a*, juif,
israélite. **Jewry**, *n*, juiverie, *f.*

jib, *n*, (*sail*) foc, *m*; (*crane*) volée, flèche, *f.*
¶ *v.i*, regimber, se cabrer, s'acculer.

jibe, *n. & v.i.* Same as *gibe.*

jiffy, *n*, tour de main, instant, *m.*

jig, *n*, (*Mus., dance*) gigue, *f.* ~*-saw,*
sauteuse, scie à chantourner, *f.* ~*-saw*
puzzle, jeu de patience, *m.*

jilt, *v.t.* délaisser, lâcher.

jingle, *n*, tintement; cliquetis, *m.* ¶ *v.i. & t,*
tinter.

jingoism, *n*, chauvinisme, *m.*

jinricksha, *n*, pousse-pousse, *m.*

jiu-jitsu, *n*, jiu-jitsu, *m.*

job, *n*, tâche; besogne, *f*; travail; emploi; *m*;
affaire, *f.* ~ *line* or ~ *lot*, marchandises
d'occasion, *f.pl*, solde, *m.* ~*-master,*
loueur de chevaux, *m.* ~ *work*, travail à
la tâche, *m*; (*Typ.*) ouvrages de ville, *m.pl.*
jobber (*shady*) *n*, maquignon, *m.* **jobbery,**
n, tripotage; agiotage, maquignonnage, *m.*
jobbing (*tailor, &c*) *p.a*, à façon.

jockey (*Turf*) *n*, jockey, *m.* **J~** *Club,*
Jockey-Club, *m.*

jocose, *a*, badin.

jocular, *a*, enjoué, facétieux, plaisant. ~**ly,**
ad, en plaisantant.

jocund, *a*, joyeux.

jog, *v.t*, secouer, pousser. ~ *along*, aller son chemin. ~ *on*, aller cahin-caha. ~-*trot*, petit trot; (*fig.*) train-train, *m*.

joggle, *n*, secousse, *f*; (*Carp.*) embrèvement; goujon,, *m*. ¶ *v.t*, embrever.

John dory, *n*, dorée, *f*.

join, *v.t*, joindre; assembler; [ré]unir; raccorder; rabouter, raboutir; relier; rejoindre. ~ *in*, faire chorus. ~**er**, *n*, menuisier, *m*. ~**ery**, *n*, menuiserie, *f*. **joint**, *n*, joint, *m*; jointure; articulation,*f*; assemblage; (*fishing rod*) brin, *m*; (*meat*) pièce, *f*. *to put out of* ~, démettre, disloquer. ¶ *v.t*, articuler; assembler. ¶†, *a*, conjoint; indivis; co-; (*survey*) contradictoire; (*commission*) mixte. *on* ~ *account*, en participation. ~ & *several*, solidaire. ~ & *several liability*, solidarité, *f*. ~ *manager*, codirecteur, cogérant, *m*. ~ *station*, gare de jonction, *f*. ~-*stock bank*, banque par actions, société de crédit, *f*. ~-*stock company*, société par actions, *f*.

joist, *n*, solive, *f*; soliveau, *m*, poutrelle; lambourde, *f*.

joke, *n*, plaisanterie, facétie, *f*, mot pour rire, *m*; (le) comique de l'histoire. ¶ *v.i*, plaisanter, rire, railler. **joker**, *n*, farceur, euse, plaisant, *m*.

jollification & **jollity**, *n*, jubilation, noce, gaillardise, gaieté, *f*. **jolly**†, *a*, gaillard, jovial, gai. ~ *well*, joliment. *to be* ~ (in drink), être en goguette.

jolt, *n*, cahot, *m*. ¶ *v.i*. & *t*, cahoter.

Jonah (*fig.*) *n*, porte-malheur, *m*.

jonquil, *n*, jonquille, *f*.

Jordan (the), le Jourdain.

jostle, *v.t*, coudoyer, bousculer.

jot, *n*, iota, *m*. ~ *down*, tenir note (*ou* registre) *m*.

journal, *n*, journal; livre; (*shaft*) tourillon, *m*; (*axle*) fusée, *f*. ~**ism**, *n*, journalisme, *m*. ~**ist**, *n*, journaliste, *m*.

journey, *n*, voyage, *m*; marche; route, *f*; trajet; parcours, *m*. ~**man**, compagnon, garçon, ouvrier, *m*.

joust, *n*, joute, *f*. ¶ *v.i*, jouter.

jovial†, *a*, jovial, réjoui. ~**ity**, *n*, jovialité, *f*.

jowl, *n*, joue; (*fish*) hure, *f*.

joy, *n*, joie, *f*. ~**ful** & ~**ous**†, *a*, joyeux. ~**fulness**, *n*, allégresse, *f*.

jubilation, *n*, jubilation, *f*. **jubilee**, *n*, jubilé, *m*. ~ *year*, année jubilaire, *f*.

Judaic, *a*, judaïque.

Judas (*traitor*) *n*, Judas, *m*.

judo, *n*, jiu-jitsu, *m*.

judge, *n*, juge; magistrat, *m*; connaisseur, euse; gourmet, *m*. ¶ *v.t*. & *i*, juger. **judg[e]ment**, *n*, jugement; arrêt; avis; sens; coup d'œil, *m*. **Judges** (*Bible*) *n.pl*, les Juges, *m.pl*.

judicature, *n*, justice, *f*. **judicial**†, *a*, judiciaire.

judicious†, *a*, judicieux, sage, sensé.

jug, *n*, cruche, *f*, broc, pot, *m*; carafe, *f*. ~**ful**, *n*, potée, *f*. *jugged hare*, civet de lièvre, *m*.

juggle, *v.i*, jongler, escamoter. ¶ ~ & ~**ry**, *n*, tour de passe-passe, *m*, jonglerie, *f*, escamotage, *m*. **juggler**, *n*, jongleur, escamoteur, *m*.

Jugo-Slav, *a*, yougoslave. ¶ *n*, Yougoslave, *m*,*f*. **Jugo-Slavia**, *n*, la Yougoslavie.

jugular [vein], *n*, [veine] jugulaire, *f*.

juice, *n*, jus; suc, *m*. **juicy**, *a*, juteux; succulent; fondant.

jujube, *n*, jujube, *m*; pastille, *f*. ~ [*shrub*], jujubier, *m*.

ju-jutsu, *n*, jiu-jitsu, *m*.

julep, *n*, julep, *m*.

July, *n*, juillet, *m*.

jumble, *n*, pêle-mêle, fouillis, fatras, *m*, salade, *f*. ~ *sale*, vente d'objets dépareillés, *f*. ~ *shop*, capharnaüm, *m*. ¶ *v.t*, brouiller.

jump, *n*, saut; sursaut; haut-le-corps, *m*. ¶ *v.i*. & *t*, sauter; se jeter. ~ *over*, sauter, franchir. ¶ *n*, (*pers.*) sauteur, euse; (*sailor's*) vareuse; (*woman's*) casaque, *f*, pull-over; (*bus*) contrôleur, *m*. ~**ing**: ~-*hour watch*, montre sauteuse, *f*, remontoir à heures sautantes, *m*. ~ *jack*, pantin, *m*. ~-*off ground* (*fig.*), tremplin, *m*. ~ *skis*, skis de saut, *m.pl*.

junction, *n*, jonction; (*Rly line*, &c) bifurcation, *f*, embranchement, *m*; (*Rly station*) gare de bifurcation, gare d'embranchement, *f*. **juncture**, *n*, jonction; occurrence, *f*.

June, *n*, juin, *m*.

jungle, *n*, jungle, *f*, fourré, *m*. **jungly**, *a*, fourré.

junior, *a*, cadet; (*partner*) second, dernier; (*clerk*) petit. ¶ *n*, cadet, te; [le] jeune; (*son*) fils; (*Sports*) junior, *m*. ~ *event*, épreuve pour juniors, *f*.

juniper, *n*, (*genus*) genévrier; (*common*) genièvre, *m*.

junk, *n*, (*Chinese*) jonque; (*tow*) étoupe, *f*; (*refuse*) rebut, *m*.

junket, *v.i*, faire bombance.

juridical†, *a*, juridique. **jurisdiction**, *n*, juridiction; compétence, *f*. **jurist**, *n*, juriste, jurisconsulte, *m*.

juror, **juryman**, *n*, juré, *m*. **jury**, *n*, jury, *m*. ~ *mast*, mât de fortune, *m*.

just, *a*, juste; équitable. ¶ *ad*, juste; justement; ne . . . que; tout. ~ *as*, de même que. *I have* ~ . . . , je viens de . . . ~-*ice*, *n*, justice, *f*; (*as to a meal*) honneur; (*pers.*) juge, *m*.

justifiable, *a*, justifiable; (*homicide*) excusable. **justification**, *n*, justification, *f*; gain de cause, *m*. **justify**, *v.t*, justifier; motiver.

justly, *ad*, justement, équitablement. **justness**, *n*, justice, *f*.

jut [**out**], *v.i*, faire saillie, [s']avancer.

jute, *n*, jute, *m*.

juvenile, *a*, juvénile; jeune; (*books*) pour la jeunesse. ¶ *n*, jeune personne, *f*.

juxtapose, *v.t*, juxtaposer.

K

kale, *n*, chou frisé, *m*.

kaleidoscope, *n*, kaléidoscope, **m**.

kangaroo, *n*, kangourou, *m*.

kaolin, *n*, kaolin, *m*.

kedge [anchor], *n*, ancre à jet, *f*.

keel, *n*, quille, *f*. **ke**[e]**lson**, *n*, carlingue, *f*.

keen, *a*, acéré; tranchant; vif; fin; mordant; (*sportsman*, &c) ardent, déterminé. *a* ∼ *disappointment*, un crève-cœur. ∼**ly**, *ad*, vivement. ∼**ness**, *n*, acuité, finesse, *f*; mordant; flair, *m*.

keep, *n*, entretien; (*castle*) donjon, *m*. ¶ *v.t.ir*, tenir; maintenir; garder; retenir; ménager; entretenir; hanter; nourrir; conserver; garantir; préserver; avoir; faire; observer; (*v.i.ir*) se tenir; se conserver; rester. ∼ *a saint's day*, chômer une fête. ∼ *away*, s'absenter. ∼ *back*, retenir. ∼ *in* (*Sch.*), mettre en retenue. ∼ *in with*, ménager. ∼ *off*, s'éloigner; au large! [*please*] ∼ *off the grass*, ne marchez pas sur les pelouses, défense de circuler sur l'herbe. ∼ [*on*], continuer. ∼ *one's hand in*, s'entretenir la main. ∼ *oneself to*, se cantonner dans. ∼ *the type standing*, conserver la composition. ∼**er**, *n*, garde, *m*; gardien, ne; concierge, *m,f*; cornac; conservateur, *m*; tenancier, ère. ∼**ing**, *n*, garde; conservation; tenue, *f*. ∼ *apples*, pommes à conserver, *f.pl. in* ∼ *with*, en harmonie avec, à l'avenant de.

keepsake, *n*, souvenir, *m*.

keg, *n*, caque, *f*; baril[let], tonnelet, *m*.

ken, *n*, connaissance, *f*.

kennel, *n*, Kénia, cabane, *f*; (*hounds*) chenil; (*street gutter*) caniveau, ruisseau, *m*.

Kenya, *n*, Kénia, *m*. ∼ *Colony & Protectorate*, la colonie & le protectorat de Kénia.

kerb, *n*, bordure, *f*, parement, *m*. ¶ *v.t*, border.

kerchief, *n*, fanchon, marmotte, *f*.

kernel, *n*, (of *nut*, *stone fruit*, *seed*) amande, *f*; (*nucleus*) noyau, *m*; (*gist*) substance, *f*.

kerosene, *n*, pétrole à brûler, p. lampant, *m*, huile de pétrole, *f*.

kestrel, *n*, crécerelle, *f*, émouchet, *m*.

ketch, *n*, quaiche, *f*.

kettle, *n*, bouilloire, bouillotte, *f*, coquemar, *m*. ∼*drum*, timbale, *f*. ∼*drummer*, timbalier, *m*.

key, *n*, clef, clé, *f*; (*winder*) remontoir, *m*; (*piano*, &c) touche, *f*; (*to school book*) corrigé; (*Mus.*) ton, *m*; (*Mech.*) clavette; cale, *f*. ∼*board*, clavier, *m*. ∼*chain*, châtelaine, *f*. ∼*hole*, trou de serrure, *m*. ∼*hole saw*, scie à guichet, *f*. ∼*industry*, industrie-clef, *f*. ∼*money*, denier à Dieu,

m. ∼*note*, [note] tonique, *f*; (*fig.*) mot d'ordre, *m*. ∼*ring*, [anneau] porte-clefs, *m*. ∼ *signature* (*Mus.*), armature, *f*. ∼*stone*, clef de voûte, *f*. ∼*way*, rainure de clavette, *f*. ¶ *v.t*, caler; coincer. ∼**ed**, *p.a*, à clef. ∼**less**, *a*, sans clef; (*watch*) à remontoir.

khaki, *n*, kaki, *m*.

Khedive, *n*, khédive, *m*.

kibble, *n*, benne, *f*.

kick, *n*, coup de pied, *m*; (*horse*) ruade, *f*; (*gun*) recul, *m*. ∼*off* (*Foot.*), coup [de pied] d'envoi, *m*. ¶ *v.t*, donner un coup (des coups) de pied à; (*a goal*) marquer; (*v.i.*) (*horse*) ruer, regimber; (*gun*) reculer. ∼ *about*, gigoter. ∼ *at* (*fig.*), regimber contre. ∼**er**, *n*, rueur, euse.

kid, *n*, chevreau, *m*, chevrette, *f*, cabri, *m*. ∼ *gloves*, gants de [peau de] chevreau, g∼s de chevrotin, *m.pl*. **kiddy**, *n*, bambin, e, marmot, te, mioche, *m*.

kidnap, *v.t*, enlever, prendre pour otage.

kidney, *n*, (*Anat.*) rein; (*meat*) rognon; (*fig.*) acabit, *m*, trempe, *f*. ∼ *bean*, haricot, *m*. ∼ [*potato*], vitelotte, *f*.

kill, *n*, chasse, *f*; abattis, *m*. ¶ *v.t*, tuer; assassiner; abattre. *to nearly* ∼, assommer. *killed in action*, tué à l'ennemi. *the killed*, les tués, *m.pl*. ∼*joy*, rabat-joie, trouble-fête, *m*. ∼**er**, *n*, tueur, *m*. ∼**ing**, *n*, tuerie, *f*; abattage, *m*. ¶ *a*, tuant, assommant; (*bewitching*) assassin.

kiln, *n*, four, *m*. ∼*dry*, sécher au four.

kilometric(al), *a*, kilométrique.

kilt, *v.t*, plisser.

kimono, *n*, kimono, saut de lit, *m*.

kin, *n*, parents, *m.pl*; parenté, *f*.

kind, *a*, bon; aimable; gentil; bienveillant, obligeant; prospère. ∼ *regards*, amitiés, *f.pl*; compliments, *m.pl*. ¶ *n*, genre, *m*; espèce; sorte; manière; (*of wood*) essence, *f*. *in* ∼, en nature.

kindergarten, *n*, jardin d'enfants, *m*.

kindle, *v.t*, allumer.

kindliness, *n*, bienveillance; bénignité, *f*. **kindly**, *a*, bienveillant, obligeant; ami. ¶ *ad*, obligeamment. **kindness**, *n*, bonté; amabilité; attention, *f*.

kindred, *n*, parenté, *f*. ¶ *a*, de la même famille.

king, *n*, roi, *m*; (*Draughts*) dame, *f*. ∼*bolt*, cheville ouvrière, *f*. ∼*cup*, renoncule bulbeuse, *f*; souci d'eau, *m*. ∼*post*, poinçon, *m*. ∼*fisher*, martin-pêcheur, *m*. *oil*, *steel*, ∼, roi des pétroles, de l'acier. ∼*dom*, *n*, royaume; (*Nat. Hist.*) règne, *m*. ∼*let*, roitelet, *m*. ∼**ly**, *a*, royal.

kink, *n*, tortillement, *m*; (*fig.*) lubie, *f*. ¶ *v.t*, tortiller; (*v.i.*) vriller.

kinship, *n*, parenté, *f*, sang, *m*. **kinsman**, **-woman**, *n*, parent, e.

kiosk, *n*, kiosque; édicule, *m*.

kipper, *n*, hareng salé & fumé, *m*. ¶ *v.t*, saler & fumer, saurer.

kiss, *n*, baiser, *m*. ¶ *v.t*, embrasser; baiser (*see note under this word*). ~ & *cuddle*, baisoter. ~*ing.crust*, baisure *f*.

kit, *n*, petit équipement; trousseau, *m*; trousse, *f*. ~ *bag*, sac à fermoir articulé; (*Mil*.) ballot, sac d'ordonnance, *m*.

kitchen, *n*, cuisine, *f*. ~ *boy*, marmiton, *m*. ~ *garden*, [jardin] potager, *m*. ~ *maid*, fille de cuisine, *f*. ~**er**, *n*, cuisinière, *f*, fourneau de cuisine, *m*.

kite, *n*, (*bird*) milan; (*toy & Com*.) cerf-volant, *m*.

kith & kin, amis & parents, *m.pl*.

kitten, *n*, chaton, chat, *m*, petite chatte, *f*.

kleptomania, *n*, cleptomanie, *f*. **kleptomaniac**, *n*, cleptomane, *m,f*.

knack, *n*, don, coup; truc, tour de main, *m*.

knacker, *n*, équarrisseur, écorcheur, *m*.

knapsack, *n*, sac; havresac, *m*.

knave, *n*, fripon, coquin, fourbe; (*Cards*) valet, *m*. ~**ry**, *n*, friponnerie, coquinerie, fourberie, fourbe, *f*. **knavish**, *a*, fourbe.

knead, *v.t*, pétrir. ~*ing trough*, pétrin, *m*.

knee, *n*, genou, *m*. ~ *breeches*, culotte, *f*. ~ *cap*, (*Anat*.) rotule; (*pad*) genouillère, *f*. ~*hole desk*, bureau ministre, *m*.

kneel [**down**], *v.i.ir*, [s']agenouiller. *kneeling desk*, prie-Dieu, *m*.

knell, *n*, glas, *m*.

knickerbockers & knickers, *n.pl*, culotte, *f*.

knick-knack, *n*, colifichet, brimborion, *m*.

knife, *n*, couteau, *m*. ~ *board*, planche à couteaux, *f*. ~ *cleaner*, nettoyeur les c—x, *f*. ~*edge*, couteau, *m*. ~, *fork, & spoon*, couvert, *m*. ~ *grinder*, rémouleur, *m*. ~ *rest*, porte-couteau, *m*. *before you can say* ~, crac!; en moins d'un instant. *to the* ~ (*war*), à outrance. ¶ *v.t*, poignarder.

knight, *n*, chevalier; (*Chess*) cavalier, *m*. ~ *errant*, chevalier errant; (*fig*.) paladin, *m*. ~ *errantry*, chevalerie errante, *f*. ~*hood*, *n*, chevalerie, *f*. ~**ly**, *a*, chevaleresque.

knit, *v.t. & i. ir*, tricoter; (*brow*) froncer; (*fig*.) lier, nouer. **knitted** (*vest, &c*) *p.a*, de tricot. ~ *garment*, tricot, *m*. **knitter**, *n*, tricoteur, euse. **knitting**, *n*, tricotage; tricot, *m*. ~ *needle*, ~ *pin*, aiguille à tricoter, broche, *f*. **knitwear**, *n*, tricots, *m.pl*.

knob, *n*, bouton, *m*; pomme, *f*; morceau, *m*.

knock, *n*, coup; (*at the door*) coup de marteau, *m*. ¶ *v.t. & i*, frapper; heurter; cogner; taper. ~*about comedian*, bateleur, *m*. ~ *down*, assommer; terrasser; abattre; (*auction*) adjuger. ~*kneed*, cagneux. ~*out* (*Box*.) hors-combat, *m*; (*auctions*) bande noire, *f*. ~*out tournament* (*Ten., &c*), tournoi par élimination, *m*. ~*out win*, victoire par hors-combat, *f*. ~ *the balls about* (*Ten., &c*), peloter. ~**ed up**, éreinté, brisé, courbatu. ~**er** (*door*), *n*, marteau, *m*.

knoll, *n*, monticule, tertre, *m*, butte, *f*.

knot, *n*, nœud; (*cluster*) peloton; (*tangle*) tapon, *m*. ¶ *v.t*, nouer. **knotty**, *a*, noueux; raboteux; (*fig*.) épineux.

know, *v.t. & i. ir*, connaître; savoir. ~ [*again*], reconnaître. ~ *how to*, savoir. *not to* ~, ignorer. ~*ing*, *a*, savant, déluré. ~**ingly**, *ad*, savamment, sciemment, à bon escient. **knowledge**, *n*, connaissance; intelligence; science, *f*; savoir, *m*; notoriété, *f*. *to my* ~, à mon su. *without my* ~, à mon insu. **known**, *n*, connu, *m*.

knuckle, *n*, jointure, articulation, *f*; (*veal*) jarret, *m*. ~ [*bone*] (mutton), manche, *m*. ~ *bones* (game), osselets, *m.pl*. ~ *duster*, coup de poing, *m*. ~ *end* (mutton), souris, *f*. ~ *fighting*, boxe à poings nus, *f*. ~ [*joint*] (*Mech*.), genouillère, *f*. *knuckle under* or *down*, mettre les pouces, caler [la voile].

knurl, *n*, molette, *f*. ¶ *v.t*, moleter.

kohlrabi, *n*, chou-rave, *m*.

Koran, *n*, Coran, *m*.

Korea, *n*, la Corée.

kosher, *a*, cawcher.

kudos, *n*, glorioie, *f*.

kursaal, *n*, casino, *m*.

L

label, *n*, étiquette, *f*. ¶ *v.t*, étiqueter.

labial, *a*, labial. ~ *n*, labiale, *f*.

laboratory, *n*, laboratoire, *m*.

laborious†, *a*, pénible; laborieux. **labour**, *n*, main-d'œuvre, *f*; travail; labeur, *m*; peine; façon, *f*. ~ *battalion*, bataillon de travailleurs, *m*. ~ *exchange*, bureau municipal de placement gratuit, *m*. ~ *market*, marché du travail, *m*. ~ [*pains*], mal d'enfant, *m*. ~ *party*, parti du travail, *m*. ~*saving*, *a*, économisant la main-d'œuvre. ~ *troubles*, troubles ouvriers, *m.pl*. ¶ *v.i. & t*, travailler, peiner; (*ship*) fatiguer. ~**ed** (*fig*.) *p.a*, travaillé, martelé, tourmenté, laborieux. ~**er**, *n*, manœuvre, homme de peine; (*farm*) ouvrier, *m*.

laburnum, *n*, faux ébénier, cytise, *m*.

labyrinth, *n*, labyrinthe, dédale, *m*.

lac, *n*, [gomme] laque, *f*.

lace, *n*, dentelle, *f*; point; passement; (*boot, &c*) lacet, cordon, *m*; (*leather*) lanière, *f*. ~ *boots*, bottines (*or if high*, bottes) à lacets (*ou* à lacer), *f.pl*, brodequins, *m.pl*. ~ *insertion*, entredeux, *f*. ~*up shoes*, souliers Richelieu, *m.pl*. ¶ *v.t*, galonner; (*fasten*) lacer. ~ *oneself tight*[*ly*], se sangler. ~*d paper*, dentelle, *f*.

lacerate, *v.t*, déchirer, lacérer.

lack, *n*, manque, défaut, *m*, pénurie, disette, *f*, peu, *m*. ¶ *v.t*, manquer de. ~*ing in*, destitué de. ~*lustre*, *a*, atone; vitreux.

lackadaisical, *a*, languissant; indolent, apathique, gnangnan.

lackey, *n*, laquais, *m*.

laconic†, *a*, laconique.

lacquer, *n*. & *~ work*, laque, *m*. ¶ *v.t*, laquer.

lacrosse, *n*, la crosse canadienne.

lacteal, *a*, lacté.

lacuna, *n*, lacune, *f*.

lacustrine, *a*, lacustre.

lad, *n*, garçon; enfant, gars, *m*.

ladder, *n*, échelle; (*stocking, &c*) échelle, maille échappée, maille perdue, *f*, manque, *m*. *~proof*, indémaillable. ¶ *v.i*, se démailler.

lade, *v.t.ir*, charger.

ladle, *n*, cuiller; louche; casse; poche, *f*. *~ful*, *n*, cuillerée, *f*.

lady, *n*, dame; madame; mademoiselle, *f*, *ladies' & children's wear*, nouveautés, *f.pl. Ladies & Gentlemen!* Mesdames, Messieurs! *ladies first!* place aux dames! *~bird*, coccinelle, bête à bon Dieu, *f*. *~ book-keeper*, teneuse de livres, *f*. *~ cashier*, caissière, *f*. L*~ chapel*, chapelle de la Vierge, *f*. *~ clerk*, employée, *f*. *~ companion*, dame de compagnie, demoiselle de c., *f*. L*~ Day*, fête de l'Annonciation, *f*; le 25 mars. *~ doctor*, femme médecin, *f*, docteur, *f*. *~-killer*, bourreau des cœurs, homme à bonnes fortunes, *m*. *his* (*my*) *~-love*, la dame de ses (de mes) pensées. *~ of the manor*, châtelaine, *f*. *~ secretary*, secrétaire femme, *m*. *~'s hand bag*, sac à main pour dame, *m*. *~'s maid*, femme de chambre, *f*. *~'s* (*or ladies'*) *man*, homme galant, h. à femmes, *m*. *~like*, comme il faut, distingué; efféminé.

lag, *v.i*, traîner; lambiner; (*v.t*.) garnir.

lager [beer], *n*, bière, *f*.

lagoon, *n*, lagune, *f*.

laic, *n*, & **laic**(al), *a*, laïque, séculier, *m*. & *a*.

laid paper, papier vergé, *m*. **laid up** (*in bed*) alité; (*ship*) désarmé.

lair, *n*, tanière, reposée, *f*, repaire, antre, fort, *m*.

laity, *n*, laïques, *m.pl*.

lake, *n*, lac, *m*; (*paint*) laque, *f*. *~ dwelling*, habitation lacustre, *f*.

lama, *n*, lama, *m*.

lamb, *n*, agneau; (*pers.*) agneau, mouton, *m*. ¶ *v.i*, agneler. *~kin*, *n*, agnelet, *m*.

lambent, *a*, [doucement] radieux, lumineux.

lame, *a*, boiteux, éclopé, estropié; (*fig.*) qui cloche. ¶ *v.t*, estropier.

lamé, *a. & n*, lamé, *a. & m*.

lameness, *n*, claudication; boiterie, *f*.

lament, *n*, lamentation, *f*; chant funèbre, *m*. ¶ *v.i*, se lamenter. *~ablet*, *a*, lamentable. *~ation*, *n*, lamentation, *f*. **the** [*late*] *~ed . . .*, le (la) regretté, e . . .

lamina, *n*, lamelle, lame, *f*, feuillet, *m*. **laminate**, *v.t*, laminer.

lammergeyer, *n*, gypaète, *m*.

lamp, *n*, lampe; lanterne, *f*; fanal; feu; (*street*) réverbère, *m*. *~ black*, noir de fumée, *m*. *~ lighter*, allumeur de réverbères, *m*.

~man, lampiste, *m*. *~ oil*, huile d'éclairage, h. de lampe, *f*. *~ post*, *~ standard*, poteau de réverbère; lampadaire, *m*. *~ room*, lampisterie, *f*. *~shade*, abat-jour, *m*.

lampas (*silk & Vet.*) *n*, lampas, *m*.

lampoon, *n*, pasquinade, *f*, pasquin, pamphlet, brocard, *m*. ¶ *v.t*, chansonner. *~er*, *n*, faiseur de pasquinades, pamphlétaire, *m*.

lamprey, *n*, lamproie, *f*.

lance, *n*, lance, *f*. ¶ (*Surg.*) *v.t*, inciser, percer, ouvrir. **lancers** (*Danc.*) *n.pl*, lanciers, *m.pl*. **lancet**, *n*, lancette, *f*.

land, *n*, terre, *f*; terrain; pays, *m*. *~ bank*, banque territoriale, b. agraire, b. hypothécaire, *f*. *~ carriage*, transport terrestre, *m*. *~-locked*, (*sea, &c*) méditerrané; (*Law*) enclavé. *~-locked property*, enclave, *f*. *~-lord*, *~-lady*, propriétaire, *m,f*; logeur, euse; aubergiste, *m,f*. *~lubber*, marin d'eau douce, *m*. *~mark*, borne, *f*; point à terre, amer; point de repère, *m*. *~ of milk & honey*, *~ of plenty*, pays de cocagne. *~owner*, propriétaire foncier, *m,f*, terrien, ne. *~scape & ~scape painting*, paysage, *m*. *~scape garden*, jardin anglais, *m*. *~scape gardener*, dessinateur de jardins, architecte (*ou* jardinier) paysagiste, *m*. *~scape painter*, [peintre] paysagiste, *m*. *~slide*, *~slip*, éboulement de terres, *m*. *~slide* (*Pol.*), débâcle, *f*. *~ tax*, impôt foncier, *m*. ¶ *v.t*, mettre à terre, débarquer; (*blow*) flanquer; (*v.i.*) débarquer; aborder; atterrir.

landau, *n*, landau, *m*. *~ let*, *n*, landaulet, *m*.

landed property, propriété foncière, *f*, biens-fonds, *m.pl*. **landing**, *n*, mise à terre, *f*, débarquement; atterrissage; (*stairs*) palier, repos, *m*. *~ gear* (*Aero.*), train d'atterrissage, *m*. *~ net*, épuisette, *f*. *~ place*, *~ stage*, embarcadère, débarcadère, ponton, *m*. *~ ticket*, carton de débarquement, *m*. **landsman**, *n*, terrien, *m*.

lane, *n*, chemin, *m*; allée; ruelle; clairière, *f*; (*Running*) couloir, *m*.

language, *n*, langage, *m*; langue, *f*.

languid, *a*, mou; languissant; traînant. **languish**, *v.i*, languir. *~ing*, *a*, languissant, mourant. **languor**, *n*, langueur, *f*. *~ous*, *a*, langoureux.

lank, *a*, efflanqué; (*hair*) plats. *~y*, *a*, efflanqué.

lantern, *n*, lanterne, *f*; falot, *m*. *~-jawed*, aux joues en lanterne. *~ slide*, [vue de] projection, *f*.

lanyard, *n*, (*Naut.*) ride, *f*; (*gun*) tire-feu, *m*.

lap, *n*, (*of pers.*) giron, *m*, genoux, *m.pl*; (*of luxury*) sein; (*of dress*) pan; (*overlap*) recouvrement, *m*; (*layer*) couche, *f*; (*Sport*) tour (de piste); (*polisher*) rodoir, *m*. *~-dog*, chien de salon, *m*, bichon, ne. *~ scorer*, contrôleur des tours, *m*. ¶ *v.t*, envelopper; (*grind*) roder. *~ over*, *v.i*, chevaucher, croiser. *~ [up]*, *v.t*, laper.

lapel, *n*, revers, *m*.

lapidary, *a. & n*, lapidaire, *a. & m*.

lapis lazuli, *n*, lapis[-lazuli] *m*.

Lapland, *n*, la Laponie. **Lapp**, *a*, lapon. **Lapp, Laplander**, *n*, Lapon, one.

lappet, *n*, fanon, *m*.

lapse, *n*, lapsus; oubli, *m*; *(moral)* défaillance, incartade; *(expiration)* déchéance, *f*; *(time)* laps, *m*. ¶ *v.i*, périmer, périr, devenir caduc; s'écouler; tomber.

lapwing, *n*, vanneau, *m*.

larceny, *n*, larcin, *m*.

larch, *n*, mélèze, larix, *m*.

lard, *n*, saindoux, *m*, panne, *f*. ¶ *v.t*, *(Cook.)* larder, piquer; *(fig.)* larder, chamarrer. ~**er**, *n*, garde-manger, *m*.

Lares, *n.pl*, [dieux] lares, *m.pl*.

large, *a*, gros; grand; fort; considérable; large. ~ *hand (Writing)*, grosse, *f*. at ~, en liberté; [tout] au long; en général. ~**ly**, *ad*, grandement; en grande partie. ~**ness**, *n*, grandeur, *f*.

largess[e], *n*, largesse, *f*.

lark, *n*, *(bird)* alouette; *(frolic)* mauviette; équipée, escapade, *f*. ~**spur**, pied-d'alouette, *m*.

larva, *n*, larve, *f*.

laryngitis, *n*, laryngite, *f*. **larynx**, *n*, larynx, *m*.

lascivious†, *a*, lascif.

lash, *n*, *(of whip)* lanière, *f*; *(cut with a whip)* coup de fouet; *(eye)* cil; *(Mech.)* jeu, *m*; *(fig.)* férule, *f*. ¶ *v.t*, cingler, sangler, fouetter; ligoter; *(Naut.)* amarrer. ~ *its tail*, se battre les flancs. ~ *out*, ruer.

lass[ie], *n*, [jeune] fille, fillette, *f*.

lassitude, *n*, lassitude, *f*.

lasso, *n*, lasso, *m*. ¶ *v.t*, prendre au lasso.

last, *a*, dernier; final; *(honours)* suprêmes. ~ *but one*, *a. & n*, avant-dernier, ère. ~ *night*, cette nuit; hier [au] soir. ~ *piece* (left on dish), morceau honteux, *m*. ~ *resource*, pis aller, *m*. ~ *straw*, comble [de nos maux] *m*. ~ *week*, la semaine dernière, la s. passée. ~ *will & testament*, acte de dernière volonté, *m*. *the* ~ *word*, le dernier [mot], le fin mot. *the* ~ *word in* (as elegance), le nec plus ultra de. ¶ *ad*, pour la dernière fois; en dernier lieu. ¶ *n*, dernier, ère; fin; *(shoe)* forme, *f*. at ~, enfin. ¶ *v.i*, durer, tenir. ~**ing**, *a*, durable, stable. ~**ly**, *ad*, en dernier lieu, enfin.

latch, *n*, *(gate)* loquet, *m*; *(door)* serrure à demi-tour, *f*. ~ *catch*, mentonnet, *m*. ~ *key*, clé de maison, *f*, passe-partout, *m*.

late, *a*, tardif; en retard, retardataire; avancé; récent; dernier; ancien, ex-; *(deceased)* feu; défunt. ~*comer*, retardataire, *m,f*. ~ *fee*, surtaxe de levée exceptionnelle, *f*. ~ *season*, arrière-saison, *f*. ¶ *ad*, tard; en retard. ~ *in the day &* ~ *in life*, sur le tard. *B, late A,* A, B successeur, B, ci-devant A. ~**ly**, *ad*, dernièrement; récemment. ~**ness**, *n*, tardiveté, *f*. *the* ~ *of the hour*, l'heure tardive, *f*.

latent, *a*, latent; caché.

later, *a*, postérieur, ultérieur. ~ [on], *ad*, plus tard, ultérieurement.

lateral†, *a*, latéral.

latest, *a*, dernier; fatal. ~ *style* (in dress), dernière mode; [haute] nouveauté, *f*. ~ [thing out], dernier cri, *m*. ~ *time for posting*, heure-limite de dépôt, *f*.

latex, *n*, latex, *m*.

lath, *n*, latte; volige; *(blind)* lame, *f*. ¶ *v.t*, latter; voliger.

lathe, *n*, tour, *m*.

lather, *n*, mousse; écume; *f*; *(v.t.)* savonner.

lathing, *n*, lattis, *m*.

Latin, *a. & n*, latin, *a. & m*.

latitude, *n*, latitude, *f*.

latrine, *n*, lieux [d'aisance] *m.pl*.

latter (the), ce dernier, cette dernière; celui-ci, celle-ci, ceux-ci, celles-ci. ~**ly**, *ad*, dernièrement.

lattice, *n*, treillis, treillage, *m*. ¶ *v.t*, treillisser.

Latvia, *n*, la Lettonie. **Latvian**, *a*, letton. ¶ *n*, Letton, one.

laud, *v.t*, louer. ~ [*to the skies*], louanger. ~**able**, *a*, louable. **laudatory**, *a*, laudatif.

laugh, *n*, rire, *m*. ¶ *v.i*, rire; se r., se moquer. ~ *derisively*, ricaner. ~**able†**, *a*, risible; dérisoire. *it is no* ~*ing matter*, il n'y a pas [là] de quoi rire. ~*ing stock*, risée, fable, *f*. ~**laughter**, *n*, rire[s] *m.[pl.]*, hilarité, *f*.

launch, *n*, embarcation; chaloupe, *f*; grand canot, *m*. ¶ *v.t*, lancer. ~[**ing**], *n*, lancement, *m*.

launder, *v.t*, blanchir. **laundress**, *n*, blanchisseuse [de fin], repasseuse [de linge fin] *f*. **laundry**, *n*, blanchisserie; buanderie, *f*.

laureate, *a*, lauréat. *a.m*.

laurel, *n*, laurier, *m*; *(pl, fig.)* lauriers, *m.pl*.

lava, *n*, lave, *f*.

Lavallière [neck]tie, lavallière, *f*.

lavatory, *n*, cabinet de toilette, *m*, toilette, *f*, lavabo, *m*. ~ *brush*, balai garde-robe,*m*, brosse de garde-robe, *f*.

lavender, *n*, lavande, *f*.

lavish, *a*, prodigue. ¶ *v.t*, prodiguer. ~**ly**, *ad*, prodigalement. ~**ness**, *n*, prodigalité, magnificences, *f.pl*.

law, *n*, loi, *f*; droit, *m*; justice; jurisprudence, *f*; palais, *m*. ~*abiding*, respectueux des lois. ~ *& order*, ordre public, *m*. ~ *case*, affaire contentieuse, *f*. ~ *costs*, frais de justice, dépens, *m.pl*. ~ *courts*, cours de justice, *f.pl*, tribunaux, *m.pl*; palais [de justice] *m*. ~ *department*, [service du] contentieux, *m*. ~*giver*, législateur, *m*. ~ *of nations*, droit des gens. ~ *officers*, justice, *f*. ~*suit*, procès civil, *m*, affaire, *f*. ~ *term*, terme de palais, *m*. ~**ful†**, *a*, légale; légitime; licite. ~**fulness**, *n*, légalité, légitimité, *f*. ~**less**, *a*, sans loi; déréglé.

lawn, n, pelouse, f, gazon, boulingrin; (linen) linon, m. ~ **grass**, gramen, m. ~ **mower**, tondeuse à gazon, f. ~ **tennis**, le [lawn-] tennis.

lawyer, n, homme de loi; avoué; légiste, juriste, jurisconsulte, m.

lax†, a, lâche; relâché; mou. ~**ative**, a. & n, laxatif, a. & m. ~**ity**, n, relâchement, m.

lay, a: ~ **brother**, frère lai, f. convers, f. servant, frater, m. ~**man**, laïque, séculier; profane, m. ~ **sister**, sœur converse, f. ¶ n, chanson, f; chant, m; complainte; (of ground) configuration, f. ¶ v.t.ir, mettre; poser; dresser; porter; déposer; abattre; coucher; imposer; [é]tendre; (fire) préparer; (gun) pointer; (eggs) pondre; (a wager) faire; (to stake) parier. ~ **bare**, mettre à nu, déshabiller. ~ **before** (court), saisir. ~ **down**, [dé]poser; plaquer. ~ **hold of**, saisir, s'agriffer à, agripper. ~ **in** [a stock of], s'approvisionner de. ~ **on**, appliquer; plaquer; étendre; imposer; (Typ.) marger. ~ **out**, disposer; aménager; ajuster; tracer; débourser. ~ **up**, amasser; (ship) désarmer.

lay day (Ship.) n, jour de planche, m.

layer, n, (pipes, rails, &c) poseur, euse; (carpets, &c) tendeur, m; (stratum, bed) couche, f, lit, m; (Hort.) marcotte, f.

lay figure, n, mannequin, m.

laying, n, mise; pose; (eggs) ponte, f.

layout, n, disposition, f; tracé, m.

lazaretto, lazaret, n, lazaret, m.

laze, v.i, paresser, traînasser. **lazily**, ad, paresseusement; indolemment. **laziness**, n, paresse, f. **lazy**, a, paresseux. ~**bones**, paresseux, euse, fainéant, e, cagnard, e.

lea (Poet.) n, pré, m, prairie, f.

leach, v.t. & i, lessiver; filtrer.

lead, n, plomb, m; (for pencils) mine [de plomb]; (Typ.) interligne, f; (Naut.) plomb [de sonde] m, sonde, f. ~ **pencil**, crayon à mine de plomb, m. ~ **poisoning**, intoxication par le plomb, f, saturnisme, m. ~ **work** & ~ **works**, plomberie, f. ¶ v.t, plomber; (Typ.) interligner.

lead, n, direction; conduite; avance; tête, f; exemple, m; (Cards) main, primauté, f; (Elec.) conducteur principal; (Elec. service) branchement, m; (leash) laisse, f. ~**in** (Radio), entrée de poste, m. ~ **rope** (attached to halter), longe, f. ¶ v.t. & i. ir, mener; conduire; diriger; amener; aboutir; induire; porter; tendre; (Cards, &c) débuter. ~ **astray**, égarer, dérouter; fourvoyer; débaucher. ~ **back**, reconduire. ~ **up to** (fig.), amener; préluder à.

leaden, a, de plomb; (sky) de plomb, plombé.

leader, n, directeur; meneur; chef de file, m; vedette, f; (political) leader; (violin, chorus) chef d'attaque; (horse) cheval de volée; (news) article de fond; (Anat.) tendon, m; (Typ.) points conducteurs, m.pl. ~**ship**,

n, direction, tête, f. **leading**, a, principal; premier; marquant. ~ **article**, article de fond, m. ~ **counter**, vedette, f. ~ **lady**, (Theat.) premier rôle, m; (Revue) commère, f. ~ **man**, premier rôle; compère, m. ~ **part** (Theat.), premier rôle, m. ~ **people**, sommités, f.pl. ~ **rein**, longe, f. ~ **question**, question tendancieuse, f. ~ **seaman**, matelot de première classe, m. ~ **strings**, lisière, f. brassières, f.pl.

leadsman, n, sondeur, m.

leaf, n, feuille, f; feuillet; volant; (door) battant, vantail, m; (table) rallonge; tirette; (rifle) hausse, f. ~ **mould**, terreau de feuilles, m. ~ **stalk**, pétiole, m. ~ **table**, table à rallonge(s) f. ~**age**, n, feuillage, m. ~**let**, n, follicule, imprimé, m; (Bot.) foliole, f. ~**y**, a, feuillu, feuillé.

league, n, ligue; (of Nations) société; (Meas.) lieue, f. ¶ v.t, liguer.

leak, n, ~**age**, n, fuite, perte, f, échappement, coulage, m; voie d'eau, f. ¶ v.i, fuir, perdre, s'échapper; couler, faire eau. ~**y**, a, qui perd, qui fuit; qui fait eau.

lean, a, maigre; sec. ¶ n, maigre, m. ¶ v.t.ir, appuyer, accoter, adosser; (v.i.ir) (rest) s'appuyer; (slope) pencher. ~ **back in**, se renverser sur. ~ **on one's elbow**(s), s'accouder. ~**ing** (fig.), n, penchant, m. ~ **tower** (Pisa), tour penchée, f. ~**ness**, n, maigreur, f. ~**to**, n, appentis, m.

leap, n, saut, bond; soubresaut, m. **by** ~**s** & **bounds**, par sauts & par bonds. ¶ v.t. & i. ir, sauter, bondir. ~**frog**, saute-mouton, saut de mouton, m. ~ **year**, année bissextile, f. **leaper**, n, sauteur, euse.

learn, v.t. & i.ir, apprendre. ~**ed**, a, savant, érudit, docte, instruit; (profession) libérale. ~**edly**, ad, savamment, doctement. ~**er**, n, apprenti; et commençant, e. ~**ing**, n, connaissance, f.pl, savoir, m, science, littérature, f.

lease, n, bail, m; ferme, f. ¶ v.t, (grant) donner à bail, affermer, arrenter; (take) prendre à bail. ~**holder**, locataire, m,f.

leash, n, laisse, [ac]couple, attache, f, trait, m; (set of dogs) harde, f. ¶ v.t, harder.

least (the), a, le moindre; le plus petit. ¶ ad. & n, le moins. **at** ~, au moins; du moins. **not in the** ~, pas le moins du monde, [ne . . .] pas le moindrement.

leat, n, canal de dérivation, m.

leather, n, cuir, m, peau, f. ~ **bottle**, outre, f. ~ **dressing**, mégie, mégisserie, f. ~**ette**, n, similicuir, m. ~**y**, a, coriace.

leave, n, permission; autorisation; faculté; liberté, f; congé, m. **by your** ~! attention! **on** ~, en permission, permissionnaire. ¶ v.t.ir, laisser, abandonner; partir de, sortir de, quitter; léguer; (v.i.ir) partir; déloger. ~ **off**, cesser; laissez donc! ~ **out**, omettre. **on leaving**, à l'issue de.

leaven, n, levain; ferment, m. ¶ v.t, faire lever; (fig.) assaisonner.

leavings, *n.pl*, restes, *m.pl*, bribes, *f.pl.*

lecherous†, *a*, lascif.

lectern, *n*, lutrin, *m.*

lecture, *n*, leçon; conférence; (*scolding*) semonce, mercuriale, *f*, sermon, *m.* ¶ *v.t*, sermonner, chapitrer, moraliser. ~ *on*, faire une leçon, une conférence, sur. lec-turer, *n*, professeur, *m*; conférencier, ère, maître de conférences, *m.*

ledge, *n*, corniche, *f*; rebord; appui, *m*; saillie, *f.*

ledger, *n*, grand livre, *m*; (*Build.*) moise, *f.* ~ *line* (*Mus.*), ligne supplémentaire, *f.*

lee [side], *n*, côté sous le vent, *m.*

leech, *n*, sangsue, *f.*

leek, *n*, poireau, *m.*

leer, *n*, regard polisson, *m. to* ~ *at*, lorgner.

lees, *n.pl*, lie, *f.*

leeward, *a*, sous le vent. L~ *Islands*, îles sous le Vent, *f.pl*. leeway, *n*, dérive, *f.*

left, *a*. & *n*, gauche, *a*. & *f. the* ~ (*Box.*), le [poing] gauche. ¶ *ad*, à gauche. ~-*hand page*, verso, *m*. ~-*handed*, *a*. & ~-*hander* (pers. or player) *m*, gaucher, ère.

left (to be), rester. *left luggage office*, con-signe [des bagages] *f. left-off wearing apparel*, friperie, *f. left-overs*, *n.pl*, bribes, *f.pl.*

leg, *n*, jambe; (*birds, insects, &c*) patte; (*fowl*) cuisse, *f*; (*mutton*) gigot; (*table, &c*) pied, *m*; (*compass, &c*) branche; (*boot, stocking*) tige, *f.* ~ *lock* (*Wrestling*), croc-en-jambe, *m.* ~ *of beef*, trumeau, gîte, *m. on one* ~, à cloche-pied.

legacy, *n*, legs, *m.*

legal†, *a*, légal; judiciaire. ~ *aid*, assis-tance judiciaire, *f.* ~ *charges*, frais de con-tentieux, *m.pl.* ~ *entity*, personne morale, p. juridique, p. civile, *f.* ~ *maxim*, adage de droit, *m.* ~ *tender* [*currency*], (*value*) pouvoir libératoire, *m*; (*money*) monnaie légale, *f.* ~ *ize*, *v.t*, légaliser.

legate, *n*, légat, *m.* legatee, *n*, légataire, *m,f.*

legation, *n*, légation, *f.*

legend, *n*, légende, *f.* ~ary, *a*, légendaire.

legerdemain, *n*, prestidigitation, *f.*

leger line, ligne supplémentaire, *f.*

leggings, *n.pl*, molletières; jambières, *f.pl.*

Leghorn, *n*, Livourne, *f.*

legible†, *a*, lisible.

legion, *n*, légion, *f. their name is* ~, ils s'appellent légion.

legislate, *v.i*, faire les lois. legislation, *n*, législation, *f.* legislator, *n*, législateur, *m.* legislature, *n*, législature, *f.* legist, *n*, légiste, *m.*

legitimacy, *n*, légitimité, *f.* legitimate†, *a*, légitime. legitim[at]ize, *v.t*, légitimer.

legume[n], *n*, légumineuse, *f.* leguminous, *a*, légumineux.

leisure, *n*, loisir[s] *m.*[*pl.*]. *at* ~, à loisir. *a* ~*ly man*, un homme lambin. [*in a*] ~*ly* [*way*], *ad*, sans se presser, sans hâte, avec lenteur.

leitmotiv, -if, *n*, leitmotiv, *m.*

lemon, *n*, citron, *m.* ~ *squash*, citron pressé, *m.* ~ *squeezer*, presse-citron, *m.* ~ *tree*, citronnier, *m.* ~ade, *n*, limonade, citronnade, *f.*

lemon sole, sole limande, *f.*

lend, *v.t.ir*, prêter. ~er, *n*, prêteur, euse. ~ing, *n*, prêt, *m*, prestation, *f.* ~ *library*, bibliothèque de prêt, *f*, cabinet de lec-ture, *m.*

length, *n*, longueur, *f*, long, *m*; étendue; durée; (*piece of a stuff*) coupe, *f. at* ~, au long; à la fin. ~en, *v.t*, [r]allonger; pro-longer. ~ening *piece*, [r]allonge, *f.* ~ways, ~wise, *ad*, en long. ~y, *a*, long.

lenient, *a*, indulgent, clément; de douceur.

lens, *n*, lentille; loupe, *f*; (*camera, microscope, &c*) objectif, *m.*

lent, *n*, carême, *m.* ~en, *a*, de carême.

lenticular, *a*, lenticulaire.

lentil, *n*, lentille, *f.*

leonine, *a*, léonin.

leopard, *n*, léopard, *m.* ~ess, *n*, l. femelle, *m.*

leper, *n*, lépreux, euse. ~ *hospital*, lépro-serie, *f.*

Lepidoptera, *n.pl*, lépidoptères, *m.pl.*

leprosy, *n*, lèpre, *f.* leprous, *a*, lépreux.

lesion, *n*, lésion, *f.*

less, *a*, moindre; inférieur. ~-~, *suffix*, sans; in-. ¶ *ad*, moins, m. de. ¶ *n*, moins, *m.*

lessee, *n*, preneur, euse; fermier, ère; tenan-cier, ère.

lesser, *a*, plus petit; moindre; petit.

lesson, *n*, leçon, *f.*

lessor, *n*, bailleur, eresse.

lest, *c*, de peur que . . . [ne].

let (*Ten.*), *n*, [coup] à remettre, *m.* ¶ *v.t*. *aux. ir*, laisser; permettre; faire; louer. *to* [*be*] ~, à louer. ~ *down*, [a]baisser; (*fail pers. at need*) lâcher, laisser en panne. ~ *go* (*hold*), lâcher prise, démordre; lar-guer. ~ *have*, donner. ~ *loose*, déchaîner. ~ *in*, faire entrer. ~ *off*, faire grâce à; (*gun*) tirer; (*epigram*) décocher. ~ *out*, laisser sortir; l. échapper, lâcher; (*clothes*) [r]élargir.

lethal, *a*, léthifère, mortel. ~ *chamber*, chambre de [mise à] mort, *f.* ~ *weapon*, assommoir, *m.*

lethargic, *a*, léthargique. lethargy, *n*, lé-thargie, *f.* Lethe, *n*, Léthé, *m.*

let's pretend set (*child's*), panoplie, *f.*

letter, *n*, lettre; épître; cote, *f.* ~ *book*, copie-lettres, *m.* ~ *box*, boîte aux lettres, *f.* ~ *card*, carte-lettre, *f.* ~ *case*, porte-feuille, *m.* ~ *missive*, lettre missive, *f.* ~ *opener*, ouvre-lettre[s] *m.* ~ *paper*, papier à lettres [in-4°] *m.* ~ *post*, poste aux lettres, *f.* ~*press*, texte [composé] *m.* ~*press printing*, impression typo-graphique, *f.* ~ *scales*, pèse-lettre, *m.* ~ *writer*, (*pers.*) épistolier, ère; manuel de correspondance, *m.* ¶ *v.t*, coter; (*book cover*) marquer par des lettres. ~*ed* (*man, woman*), lettré, e, *a. & m,f.* ~*ing, n,* lettrage, *m.*

letting, *n,* location, *f.* ~ *value,* valeur locative, *f.*

lettuce, *n,* laitue, *f.*

Levant, *n,* Levant, *m.* **Levantine,** *a,* levantin; (*ports*) du Levant. ¶ *n,* Levantin, e.

level, *a,* de niveau; en palier; plat; plan; uni; égal. ¶ ~ *crossing,* passage à niveau, *m.* *a ~-headed person,* une tête bien organisée, un cerveau organisé. ~ *with,* à fleur de, à ras de. ¶ *n,* niveau; plan, *m;* hauteur, *f;* palier, *m;* (*Min.*) galerie, *f.* ¶ *v.t,* niveler; aplanir; égaliser; unir; (*gun, &c*) pointer. **levelling,** *n,* nivellement, *m.* ~ *screw,* vis de calage, *f.* ~ *staff,* mire, *f.*

lever, *n,* levier, *m;* manette, *f.* ~ *lid tin,* boîte à couvercle à levier, *f.* ~ *watch,* montre à ancre, *f.* ~ [*up*] *v.t,* soulever au moyen d'un levier, s. avec la pince. ~**age,** *n,* force de levier, *f;* (*fig.*) avantage, *m.*

leveret, *n,* levraut, *m.*

leviathan, *n,* léviathan, *m.*

Levite, *n,* lévite, *m.* **Leviticus,** *n,* le Lévitique.

levity, *n,* légèreté, *f.*

levy, *n,* levée, réquisition, *f;* prélèvement, *m.* ¶ *v.t,* [pré]lever, frapper.

lewd†, *a,* impudique, crapuleux. ~**ness,** *n,* impudicité, *f.*

lewis, *n,* louve, *f.*

lexicographer, *n,* lexicographe, *m.*

lexicon, *n,* lexique, *m.*

Leyden, *n,* Leyde, *f.*

liability, *n,* obligation, *f;* engagement, *m;* responsabilité, *f;* (*pl, Fin.*) passif, *m.* **liable,** *a,* tenu; soumis; sujet; passible; responsable; solidaire.

liaison officer, *n,* agent de liaison, *m.*

liana, liane, *n,* liane, *f.*

liar, *n,* menteur, euse.

lias, *n,* lias, *m.* **liassic,** *a,* liasique.

libation, *n,* libation, *f.*

libel, *n,* libelle, *m;* diffamation, *f.* ~ *action,* action en diffamation, *f.* ¶ *v.t,* diffamer. **libellous,** *a,* diffamatoire.

liberal†, *a,* libéral; large. ¶ *n,* libéral, *m.* ~**ism,** *n,* libéralisme, *m.* ~**ity,** *n,* libéralité, *f.*

liberate, *v.t,* libérer; affranchir; lâcher.

libertine, *a. & n,* libertin, *a. & m.*

liberty, *n,* liberté; faculté; privauté, *f.* *at* ~*,* libre.

librarian, *n,* bibliothécaire, *m,f.* **library,** *n,* bibliothèque, *f.*

librettist, *n,* librettiste, *m.* **libretto,** *n,* livret, *m.*

licence, *n,* licence, *f;* permis, *m;* dispense, *f;* brevet; bon; acte, *m;* concession, *f.* ~ *to sell,* droit de vendre; (*tobacco, spirits, &c*) débit, *m.* **license,** *v.t,* accorder un permis à; breveter. ~*d victualler,* débitant(e) de spiritueux. **licentiate,** *n,* licencié, e. ~*'s degree,* licence, *f.* **licentious†,** *a,*

licencieux, dévergondé, décolleté. ~**ness,** *n,* licence, *f,* dévergondage, *m.*

lichen, *n,* lichen, *m.*

licit†, *a,* licite.

lick, *v.t,* lécher. ~ *up,* laper.

lictor, *n,* licteur, *m.*

lid, *n,* couvercle, *m;* (*eye*) paupière, *f.* *give the* ~ *to,* démentir. ¶ *v.i,* mentir.

lie, *n,* mensonge; démenti, *m.* *give the* ~ *to,* démentir. ¶ *v.i,* mentir.

lie, *n,* (*of ground*) disposition, configuration; (*Golf, &c*) assiette, pose, *f;* (*Naut.*) gisement, *m.* ¶ *v.i.ir,* coucher, reposer; gésir; séjourner, stationner; résider, tenir. ~ *back in,* se renverser sur. ~ *dormant,* dormir. ~ *down,* se coucher. ~ *idle,* chômer. ~ *in wait,* se tenir en embuscade, s'embusquer.

liege, *a,* lige. ¶ *n,* vassal lige, *m.*

lien, *n,* privilège; droit de rétention, d. de gage, *m.* ~*or,* *n,* créancier gagiste, *m.*

lieu of (in), au lieu de.

lieutenant, *n,* lieutenant; (*naval*) l. de vaisseau, *m.* ~ *colonel,* lieutenant-colonel, *m.* ~ *commander,* capitaine de corvette, *m.* ~ *general,* général de corps d'armée, *m.*

life, *n,* vie; existence, *f;* vivant, *m;* durée, *f;* mouvement, *m.* *for* ~*,* à vie, viager; perpétuel, à perpétuité. *from* ~ (*Art*), d'après nature, au vif, sur le vif. *to the* ~*,* au naturel. *2 lives lost,* 2 personnes ont péri. ~ *& property* (*Law*), corps & biens. ~ (*& soul*) (*of the party*), boute-entrain, *m.* ~ *annuity,* rente viagère, *f;* viager, *m.* ~ *belt,* ceinture de sauvetage, *f.* ~ *boat,* bateau de s., *m.* ~ *buoy,* bouée de s., *f.* ~*-giving,* fécond. ~ *insurance,* assurance sur la vie, *f.* ~ *jacket,* brassière de sauvetage, *f.* ~ *preserver,* casse-tête, assommoir, *m.* ~*-saving,* sauvetage, *m.* ~ *size,* en grand, grandeur naturelle, nature, *f.* ~ *table,* table de longévité, *f.* ~*-time,* vivant, *m.* ~**less,** *a,* sans vie; inanimé. ~**like,** *a,* vivant; parlant. ~**long,** *a,* de toute la vie.

lift, *n,* coup d'épaule; (*of the hand*) geste; ascenseur; monte-charge, *m.* ~*man,* garçon de l'ascenseur, liftman, *m.* ¶ *v.t,* lever; soulever; élever; enlever; relever.

ligament, *n,* ligament, *m.* **ligature,** *n,* ligature, *f.*

light, *a,* léger; faible; petit; (*ship unladen*) lège; (*Rly engine*) haut le pied; (*colour*) clair; (*earth*) meuble. ~ *car,* voiturette, *f.* ~*-fingered gentleman,* escamoteur, *m.* ~ *fishing,* pêche du petit poisson, *f.* ~*-headed,* délirant. ~*-headedness,* transport, *m.* ~*-heavy weight* (*Box.*), poids mi-lourd, *m.* ~ *lager,* bière blanche, b. blonde, *f.* ~ *lorry,* camionnette, *f.* ~ *meal,* collation, *f.* ~ *opera,* opérette, *f.* ~ *railway,* chemin de fer économique, *m.* ~ *reading,* livres d'agrément, *m.pl.* ~ *refreshments,* rafraîchissements, *m.pl.* ~ *weight* (*Box.*), poids léger, m. ¶ n, lumière, f; jour; éclairage, m; vue; clarté, f, clair; feu, fanal, phare, m; flamme, f. against the ~, à contre-jour. ~s out (Mil.), extinction des feux, f, couvre-feu, m. ~ & shade, (Art) clair-obscur, m; (pl, Mus., &c) nuances, f.pl. ~house, phare, m. ~ship, bateau-feu, m. ¶ v.t.ir, allumer; éclairer. ~ up, illuminer. ~ [up]on, tomber sur.

lighten, v.t, alléger; soulager; éclairer; (v.imp.) éclairer, faire des éclairs.

lighter, a, plus léger. ~ than air aviation or branch (army), aérostation, f. ~ than air machine, (appareil) plus léger que l'air, aérostat, m.

lighter, n, (pers.) allumeur; (petrol) briquet, m; (boat) allège, gabare, f, chaland, m. ~man, batelier, marinier, m. ~age, n, batelage, m. **lighting**, n, éclairage, m. ~ up time, l'heure d'allumer, f.

lightly, ad, légèrement; à la légère. **lightness**, n, légèreté, f.

lightning, n, éclair, m. oft. pl, foudre, f. ~ conductor, paratonnerre, m. ~ strike, grève surprise, f.

lights (animal lungs) n.pl, mou, m.

ligneous, a, ligneux. **lignite**, n, lignite, m. lignum vitae, [bois de] gaïac, m.

likable, a, sympathique. **like**, a, pareil; pair; semblable; analogue; approchant; ressemblant; même; tel; à l'égal de. to be ~, ressembler, approcher de, imiter. to look ~, avoir l'air de, ressembler. ¶ n, pareil, le; semblable, m. the ~, (treatment, &c) la pareille; (Golf) autant. & the ~, & connexes, &... analogues. ~s & dislikes, sympathies & antipathies, f.pl. ¶ pr, ad, comme; de même que; tel que; à l'instar de; en. ¶ v.t. & i, aimer; affectionner; vouloir; se plaire à; trouver; goûter. to look ~, avoir l'air de, ressembler. ¶ n, pareil.

likelihood, n, probabilité; apparence; vraisemblance, f. **likely**, a, probable, vraisemblable. very ~, vraisemblablement.

liken, v.t, comparer, assimiler.

likeness, n, ressemblance; parité, f; air, m; image, f; portrait, m.

likewise, ad, pareillement, également, aussi, de même.

liking, n, goût; gré, m; affection, f.

lilac, n. & a, lilas, m. & att.

liliaceous, a, liliacé.

Lilliputian, a, lilliputien.

lily, n, lis, m. ~ of the valley, muguet, m.

limb, n, membre, m; (tree) mère branche, f; (Math., &c) limbe, m. -limbed, a, membré.

limber, a, souple. ¶ n, avant-train, m. ~ up, mettre l'avant-train.

limbo, n, les limbes, m.pl.

lime, n, chaux, f; citron [des Antilles], m. ~ burner, chaufournier, m. ~ juice, jus de citron, m. ~ kiln, four à chaux, chaufour, m. ~light, lumière oxhydrique, f. to be in the ~light, être sous les feux de la rampe. (fig.) être en vedette. ~stone,

pierre à chaux, p. calcaire, f, calcaire, m. ~ [tree], (citrus) citronnier; (linden) tilleul, m. ~ twig, gluau, pipeau, m. ¶ v.t. (Agric.) chauler; (twig) engluer.

limit, n, limite, borne, f; périmètre, m. ¶ v.t, limiter, borner. ~ation, n, limitation, f. limited, p.p. & p.a, limité, borné, étroit; (monarchy) tempérée; (edition) à tirage restreint. ~ company (Eng.), (public, Fr.) société anonyme; (private, Fr.) société à responsabilité limitée, f. ~ partnership, [société en] commandite, f.

limousine, n, limousine, f.

limp, a, flasque, mou; (binding) souple. ¶ n, boitement, clochement, m. ¶ v.i, boiter, clocher.

limpet, n, lépas, m, patelle, f.

limpid, a, limpide. ~ity, n, limpidité, f.

linchpin, n, clavette d'essieu, esse, f.

linden, n, tilleul, m.

line, n, ligne; file; haie; voie, f, trait, m; raie; ride; (Teleph. subscriber's) ligne, f, poste; (Poet.) vers; câble, m; corde, f; cordeau, m; amarre, f; genre; métier; emploi; département; ressort, m; partie; juridiction, f. ~ block, cliché au trait, m. ~ engraving, taille-douce; gravure au trait, f. ~ rope, corde à linge, f. ¶ v.t, doubler; tapisser; garnir; revêtir; rider, sillonner; border. ~ one's stomach, se lester l'estomac.

lineage, n, descendance, f, parage, m.

lineal, a, linéaire; (pers.) en ligne directe.

lineament, n, linéament, trait, m. **linear**, a, linéaire.

linen, n, toile [de lin] f; [tissu de] lin; (made up) linge, m; ~ draper, toilier, ère, maison de blanc, f. ~ embroidery, broderie sur toile, f. ~ room, lingerie-f. ~ [thread], fil [de lin] m. ~ trade, industrie linière, toilerie, f.

liner, n, vapeur de ligne [régulière], paquebot, m.

linesman, n, (Mil.) soldat de ligne; (Teleg., Teleph.) poseur de lignes; (Ten.) arbitre de lignes; (Association) arbitre de touche, m.

ling, n, (fish) grande morue barbue; (Bot.) bruyère, brande, f.

linger, v.i, s'attarder; traîner. ~ing death, mort lente, f.

lingerie, n, lingerie [fine] f. ~ maker, ~ dealer, linger, ère.

lingo, n, jargon, baragouin, m. **lingual**, a, lingual. ¶ n, linguale, f. **linguist**, n, linguiste, m. ~ics, n, linguistique, f.

liniment, n, liniment, m.

lining, n, doublure; garniture; chemise; (hat) coiffe, f; revêtement, m.

link, n, chaînon, maillon, anneau, m; (Mach.) coulisse, f; (fig.) lien, m. ~ motion, [distribution par] coulisse, f. ¶ v.t, articuler; enchaîner. ~ up, raccorder.

links, n.pl. & s, lande, f; (Golf) terrain, m.

linnet, n, linotte, f, linot, m.

linoleum, n., also lino, abb, linoléum, m.

linotype, *n. & att.* linotype, *f. & a.*

linseed, *n,* graine de lin, *f.* ~ *oil,* huile de [graine de] lin, *f.*

lint, *n,* charpie, *f.*

lintel, *n,* linteau, sommier, *m,* traverse, *f.*

lion, **ess**, *n,* lion, ne. ~ *cub,* ~ *whelp,* lionceau, *m.* ~*'s share,* part du lion, *f.*

lip, *n,* lèvre; babine, *f;* bec, *m.* ~ *stick,* crayon (*ou* bâton de rouge) pour les lèvres, *m.*

liquefaction, *n,* liquéfaction, *f.* **liquefy**, *v.t,* liquéfier.

liqueur, *n,* liqueur [de dessert] *f.* ~ *brandy,* fine champagne, *f.* ~ *case,* ~ *set,* cave à liqueurs, *f;* cabaret à liqueurs, *m.*

liquid, *a,* liquide; (*Com., Fin.*) liquide, disponible; (*fig.*) coulant, doux. ~ *ammonia,* liqueur d'ammoniaque, *f.* ~ *assets,* disponibilités, *f.pl.* ~ *paraffin* (*Phar.*), huile de paraffine, *f.* ¶ *n,* liquide, *m;* (*Gram.*) liquide, *f.*

liquidate, *v.t,* liquider. **liquidation**, *n,* liquidation, *f.* **liquidator**, *n,* liquidateur, *m.*

liquor, *n,* liquide, *m,* boisson; liqueur, *f.*

liquorice, *n,* réglisse, *f;* jus de réglisse, *m.*

Lisbon, *n,* Lisbonne, *f.*

lisp, *v.i,* zézayer, bléser; bégayer.

lissom[e], *a,* souple.

list, *n,* liste, *f;* bordereau, *m;* feuille, *f;* rôle; tableau, *m;* table, *f;* inventaire; bulletin; catalogue, *m;* cote, *f;* (*Army, Navy, &c*) annuaire, *m;* (*Naut.*) bande; (*selvage*) lisière, *f;* (*pl.*) lice, arène, barrière, *f.* ~ *of plates,* table des hors-texte. ~ *slipper,* chausson de lisière, *m.* ¶ *v.t,* cataloguer; inventorier; (*door*) calfeutrer; (*v.i,* Naut.) donner [de] la bande.

listen, *v.i.* & ~ *in* (*Radio*) écouter. ~**er,** *n,* (*hearer & Radio*) auditeur, *m;* (*spy*) écouteur, euse.

listless†, *a,* nonchalant, distrait, traînant.

litany, *n,* litanies, *f.pl.*

literal, *a,* littéral. ~ [*error,*] coquille, *f.* ~ *sense,* (*passage*) sens littéral; (*word*) [sens] propre, *m.*

literary, *a,* littéraire. ~ *man,* homme de lettres, littérateur, *m.* **literate**, *a,* qui sait lire; lettré. **literature**, *n,* littérature, *f.*

litharge, *n,* litharge, *f.*

lithe, *a,* souple, agile.

lithia, *n,* lithine, *f.* **lithium**, *n,* lithium, *m.*

lithograph & ~**y**, *n,* lithographie, *f.* ¶ *v.t,* lithographier. ~**er,** *n,* lithographe, *m.* ~**ic**, *a,* lithographique.

Lithuania, *n,* la Lit[h]uanie.

litigant, *n,* plaideur, euse. **litigation**, *n,* litige, *m.* **litigious**, *a,* litigieux, processif.

litmus, *n,* tournesol, *f.*

litter, *n,* (*palanquin*) litière, civière, *f,* brancard, *m;* (*straw & dung*) litière, *f,* fumier, *m;* (*young*) portée, ventrée; (*pigs*) cochonnée, *f;* encombrement, fouillis, *m;* immondices, *f.pl,* détritus, débris, *m.pl.* ¶ *v.t,* encombrer; joncher.

little, *a,* petit. [*dear*] ~ *brother,* frérot, *m.* ~ *chap,* bambin, *m.* ~ *devil,* diablotin, *m.* ~ *dinner,* dînette, *f.* ~ *finger,* petit doigt, [doigt] auriculaire, *m.* ~ *ones,* petits enfants; (*cubs*) petits, *m.pl.* ~ *place* (w.c.), petit endroit, *m.* L~ *Red Riding Hood,* le Petit Chaperon Rouge. [*dear*] ~ *sister,* sœurette, *f.* *a* ~ [*while*] *longer,* un peu. ¶ *ad,* peu; ne . . . guère. ¶ *n,* peu, *m.* ~**ness,** *n,* petitesse, *f.*

live, *a,* vif; vivant; (*coal*) ardent; (*axle*) tournant; (*Elec.*) en charge; (*shell*) chargé. ~*bait fishing,* pêche au vif, *f.* ~ *stock,* animaux vivants, *m.pl.* ~ *rail,* rail de courant, *m.*

live, *v.i.* & *t* vivre; durer; se nourrir (*on, milk, &c* = de); demeurer, résider, habiter, rester. ~ *again in,* survivre dans.

livelihood, *n,* vie, *f,* gagne-pain, *m,* pitance, *f.*

liveliness, *n,* vivacité, animation, *f,* entrain, *m.* **lively**, *a,* vif, vivant, animé, mouvementé; allègre, fringant, émerillonné.

liver (*Anat.*) *n,* foie, *m.*

livery, *n,* livrée, *f.* ~ *stables,* pension pour les chevaux, *f.*

livid, *a,* livide. ~**ity**, *n,* lividité, *f.*

living, *a,* vivant; en vie; (*force*) vive. ~ *being,* vivant, *m.* *within* ~ *memory,* de mémoire d'homme. ¶ *n,* vie, *f,* vivre, *m;* (*fare*) chère, *f;* (*Eccl.*) bénéfice, *m.* ~ *expenses,* dépense de bouche, *f.* ~*in,* internat, *m.* ~ *room,* salle commune, *f;* l'espace vital. the ~, les vivants, *m.pl.*

lizard, *n,* lézard, *m.*

llama, *n,* lama, *m.*

Lloyd's, *n,* le Lloyd. ~ *agent,* agent du Lloyd, *m.*

loach, *n,* loche, *f.*

load, *n,* charge, *f;* fardeau, *m.* ~ *draught* (ship), calaison, *f.* ~*star,* étoile polaire; (*fig.*) idée directrice, *f;* but de ses efforts, *m.* ~*stone,* pierre d'aimant, *f;* (*fig.*) attrait, *m.* ~ [*water*] *line,* ligne de [flottaison en] charge, *f.* ¶ *v.t,* charger; combler; couvrir; (*dice*) piper; (*v.i.*) prendre charge. ~**ed,** *p.p,* chargé. ~ *stick,* canne plombée, *f.* ~**er,** *n,* chargeur, *m.* ~**ing,** *n,* charge, *f;* chargement, *m.* [*now*] ~ (ship), en charge.

loaf, *n. & ~ of bread,* pain, *m;* (*round loaf*) miche, *f.* ~ *sugar,* sucre en pains; s. en morceaux, s. cassé, *m.*

loaf, *v.i,* fainéanter, battre le pavé. ~**er,** *n,* fainéant, batteur de pavé, *m.*

loam, *n,* terre grasse; terre, *f.*

loan, *n,* prêt; emprunt, *m.*

loath (to be), ne vouloir pas, répugner. **loathe**, *v.t,* haïr, abhorrer. **loathing**, *n,* dégoût, *m.* **loathsome**, *a,* dégoûtant.

lob (*Ten.*) *n,* chandelle, *f.*

lobby, *n,* vestibule; couloir, *m;* salle des pas perdus, *f.* ~**ing,** *n,* propos de couloir, *m.pl.*

lobe, *n,* lobe, *m.*

lobelia, *n,* lobélie, *f.*

lobster, *n,* homard, *m.* ~ *pot,* ~ *basket,* nasse, *f,* panier, *m.*

local, *a,* local; topique; de clocher; (*custom*) de place, des lieux; (*on letter*) en ville. ~ *line,* chemin de fer d'intérêt local, *m.* ~ *time,* heure du lieu, *f.* ~[e], *n,* scène, *f.* ~**ity,** *n,* localité, *f.* ~**ize,** *v.t,* localiser. ~**ly,** *ad,* localement; sur place.

locate, *v.t,* fixer [l'emplacement de]; repérer; rechercher.

lock, *n,* serrure; (*canal*) écluse; (*hair*) boucle, mèche; (*pl.*) chevelure; (*gun*) platine, *f.* ~ *under* ~ *& key,* sous clef. ~ *hospital,* hôpital des vénériens, *m.* ~*jaw,* tétanos, *m.* ~ *nut,* contre-écrou, *m.* ~*out,* lock-out, *m,* grève patronale, *f.* ~*smith,* serrurier, *m.* ~ *stitch,* point de piqûre, *m.* ~*up,* (*police*) violon; (*garage*) box fermé, *m*; (*att.*) fermant à clef. ¶ *v.t,* bloquer; (*boat*) écluser. ~ *out,* fermer la porte à clef sur; (*men*) renvoyer en masse. ~ *up,* fermer à clef; mettre (*ou* serrer) sous clef; verrouiller, enfermer, coffrer, boucler; (*Fin.*) immobiliser, bloquer.

locker, *n,* case, *f*; caisson, *m*; soute, *f.*

locket, *n,* médaillon, *m.*

locomotion, *n,* locomotion, *f.* **locomotive,** *a,* locomoteur. ¶ *n,* locomotive, *f.* *loco-motor ataxy,* ataxie locomotrice, *f.*

loculus, *n,* loge, *f.*

locum tenens, *n,* remplaçant, e, suppléant, e.

locust, *n,* sauterelle, locuste, *f,* criquet, *m.* ~ [*bean*], caroube, *f.*

locution, *n,* façon de s'exprimer, *f,* tour de langage, idiotisme, *m.*

lode, *n,* filon, *m.* ~*star,* ~*stone.* Same as *loadstar, loadstone.*

lodge, *n,* loge, *f*; pavillon, *m.* ¶ *v.t,* loger; déposer; [re]mettre, fournir; (*appeal*) interjeter; (*v.i.*) loger, camper. **lodger,** *n,* locataire, *m.f.* **lodging,** *n,* logement, *f,* chambre, *f,* le couvert; (*pl.*) meublé, *m.* ~ *house,* hôtel garni, *m.* ~*house keeper,* logeur, euse.

loft, *n,* grenier, *m*; soupente; (*organ*) tribune, *f.* ¶ (*Golf*) *v.t,* enlever. **loftiness,** *n,* élévation, hauteur, *f.* **lofty,** *a,* élevé; relevé; fier; hautain, altier; (*style*) soutenu.

log, *n,* bûche, *f*; (*Naut.*) loch, *m.* (wood) *in the* ~, en grume. ¶ [*book*], livre de loch; l. de bord, *m.* ~ *cabin,* ~ *hut,* cabane de bois, *f.* ~*wood,* [bois de] campêche, *m.*

loganberry, *n,* ronce-framboise, *f.*

logan [*stone*], *n,* rocher branlant, *m.*

logarithm, *n,* logarithme, *m.*

loggerheads (**at**), en bisbille.

logic, *n,* logique, *f.* ~**al**†, *a,* logique. ~**ian,** *n,* logicien, *m.*

loin, *n,* (*veal*) longe, *f*; (*mutton*) filet, *m*; (*pl.*) reins, lombes, *m.pl.* ~ *chop,* côtelette de filet, *f.* ~ *cloth,* pagne, *m.*

loiter, *v.i,* s'attarder, traîner, s'amuser. ~**er,** *n,* traînard, *m.*

loll, *v.i,* se prélasser; (*tongue*) pendre.

Lombardy, *n,* la Lombardie.

London, *n,* Londres, *m*; (*att.*) londonien. ~**er,** *n,* Londonien, ne.

loneliness, *n,* solitude, *f,* isolement, *m.* **lonely** & **lone**[**some**], *a,* solitaire, isolé, esseulé. *lone cottage,* chartreuse, *f.*

long, *a,* long; grand; allongé; (*Meas.*) de long. ~*boat,* chaloupe, *f.* ~*clothes,* maillot, *m.* ~*distance race,* course de fond, *f.* ~*drawn,* filandreux. ~*haired,* chevelu. ~ *jump,* saut en longueur, *m.* ~*legged* (*man*), bien fendu. ~*lived,* vivace. ~ *service,* vétérance, *f.* ~*shoreman,* débardeur, *m.* ~ *sighted* (*person*), presbyte, *a. & m.f.* ~ [*syllable*], [syllable] longue, *f.* ~ *vacation,* grandes vacances, *f.pl.* ~ *a while,* un long temps, long-temps, *ad.* ~*winded,* prolixe, diffus. ¶ *ad,* longtemps; le long de. ~ *ago,* il y a longtemps. *not* ~ *since,* naguère. ~*suffering,* longanimité, *f.* ¶ *n: the* ~ *& the short of it,* le fin mot. ¶ *v.i: I* ~ *to,* il me tarde de, je brûle de, je grille de. ~ *for,* languir pour, soupirer après. *to be* ~ (delay), tarder. *longest way round,* chemin des écoliers, *m.*

longevity, *n,* longévité, *f.*

longing, *n,* [grande] envie, démangeaison, *f.*

longish, *a,* longuet.

longitude, *n,* longitude, *f.* **longitudinal**†, *a,* longitudinal.

look, *n,* regard, *m*; coup d'œil; œil; air, *m*; mine; apparence, *f,* aspect, *m.* ~*out,* veille, vigie, *f,* qui-vive, *m*; (*box*) guérite, *f*; (*man*) guetteur, *m*; affaire, *f.* ¶ *v.i,* regarder; avoir l'air; sembler; paraître. ~ *after,* veiller à, soigner, ménager, gouverner. ~ *at,* regarder. ~ *down* (from on high), planer. ~ *down* [*up*]*on,* mépriser. ~ *for,* chercher; s'attendre à. ~ *into,* examiner. ~ *like,* ressembler à, jouer. ~ *on,* regarder; envisager; (*front*) donner sur. ~*out* (post, man, Rly car), vigie, *f.* ~ *out!* attention!, gare!, alerte!, casse-cou! (*cave*) vingt-deux! ~ *out for,* chercher; s'attendre à. ~ *out of the window,* regarder par la fenêtre. ~ *over,* parcourir; repasser. ~ *up a word in the dictionary,* chercher un mot dans le dictionnaire. *to translate by looking up every other word in the dictionary,* traduire à coups de dictionnaire. ~**er-in,** *n,* télévisionniste, *m.f.* ~**ing glass,** glace, *f,* miroir, *m.*

loom, *n,* métier [à tisser] *m.*

loom, *v.i,* se dessiner, émerger, surgir.

loop, *n,* boucle; coque, *f*; œil, *m*; ganse, *f.* ~*hole,* meurtrière, *f,* créneau, *m*; (*fig.*) échappatoire, *f.* ~ [*line*], [voie de] dérivation, *f.* ~*way,* route déviée, *f.* ¶ *v.t,* boucler. ~ *the* ~, boucler la boucle.

loose, *a,* mobile; volant; branlant; flottant; coulant; large; lâche; (*pulley*) folle; libre;

négligé; desserré; décousu; (*horses*) haut le pied; (*in bulk*) en vrac. ~ *box* (horse), box, *m*. ~ *cover*, housse, *f*. *at a* ~ *end*, désœuvré. ~ *headstock*, contre-pointe, *f*. ~ *piece*, pièce rapportée, *f*. **loose**[n], *v.t*, [re]lâcher; délier; desserrer.

loot, *n*, butin, *m*. ¶ *v.t. & i*, piller.

lop, *v.t*, élaguer, ébrancher. ~*ear*[*ed rabbit*], lapin bélier, *m*. ~*sided*, de guingois; (*boat*) bordier. *lopped tree*, écot, *m*.

loquacious, *a*, loquace. **loquacity**, *n*, loquacité, *f*.

lord, *n*, seigneur; (*Eng*.) lord, *m*. L~ *Mayor* (*Eng*.), lord-maire, *m*. ~ *of creation*, roi de la nature, *m*. ~ *of the manor*, châtelain, *m*. *the Lord* (God), le Seigneur. *Lord's prayer*, oraison dominicale, *f*; *Lord's supper*, communion, Cène, *f*. ~ *it over*, faire le maître avec. ~*ly*, *a*, hautain, altier, fier. ~*ship*, *n*, seigneurie, *f*. *Your L*~, Votre Grandeur, *f*.

lore, *n*, science, *f*.

lorgnette, *n*, face à main, *f*.

lorry, *n*, camion; binard, *m*. ~ *driver*, camionneur, *m*.

lose, *v.t. & i. ir*, perdre; (*train*) manquer; (*clock*) retarder. ~ *heart*, se décourager. **loser**, *n*, perdant, e; (*good, bad*) joueur, euse. *be a* ~, être en perte. **loss**, *n*, perte; déperdition, *f*; déchet[s] *m*.[*pl*.]; sinistre, *m*. ~ *of appetite*, inappétence, *f*. ~ *of voice*, extinction de voix, *f*. *at a* ~, à perte; (*fig*.) empêché. **lost**, *p.p. & p.a*, perdu; égaré; dépaysé; (*in thought*) absorbé, abîmé; (*motion*) rejetée. ~ *property office*, bureau des objets trouvés, *m*.

lot, *n*, lot, *m*; partie, *f*; paquet; partage; sort; destin, *m*, destinée, *f*. *a* ~, ~*s*, quantité, *f*. *the* ~, le tout. *to draw* ~*s*, tirer au sort. ~ [*out*] *v.t*, lotir.

loth (**to be**), ne vouloir pas, répugner.

lotion, *n*, lotion, *f*.

lottery, *n*, loterie, *f*.

lotto, *n*, loto, *m*.

lotus, *n*, lotus, lotos, *m*.

loud, *a*, haut; fort; grand; gros; sonore; bruyant; tapageur. ~ *cheers*, vivats sonores, *m.pl*. ~ *pedal*, grande pédale, p. forte, *f*. ~ *speaker*, haut-parleur, *m*. ~[*ly*], *ad*, [tout] haut; fort.

Louisiana, *n*, la Louisiane.

lounge, *n*, (*hotel, &c*) hall; (*music hall, &c*) promenoir; canapé, *m*. ~ *bed*, canapé-lit, *m*. ~ *chair*, dormeuse, *f*. ~ *suit*, complet veston, *m*. ¶ *v.i*, flâner, paresser. **lounger**, *n*, flâneur, batteur de pavé, *m*.

louse, *n*, pou, *m*. **lousy**, *a*, pouilleux.

lout, *n. & ~ish*, *a*, rustre, rustaud, *m. & a*.

louvers, *n.pl*, abat-son, *m*.

lovable, *a*, aimable. **love**, *n*, amour, *m*; inclination; tendresse, *f*; chéri, e, bijou, *m*. *for ~ or money*, ni pour or ni pour argent. *in* ~, amoureux, épris. *fall in* ~, s'enamourer, s'éprendre. *make* ~ *to*, faire la cour à. *play for* ~, jouer pour l'honneur. [*with*] [*best*] ~ (letter), je vous embrasse [de tout cœur], amitiés. ~ *all* (*Ten*.), zéro partout, égalité à rien, rien à rien. ~ *bird*, inséparable, *m. ou f*. ~*-in-a-mist*, nigelle de Damas, *f*. ~ *knot*, lacs d'amour, *m*. ~ *letter*, billet doux, *m*. ~*-knot*, lacs d'amour, *m*. ~*-lock*, (*on man*) rouflaquette, *f*; (*on woman*) accroche-cœur, *m*. ~ *match*, mariage d'amour, m. d'inclination, *m*. ~ *potion*, philtre, *m*. ~ *set* (*Ten*.), 6 jeux à rien. ~*-sick*, qui languit d'amour. ~ *story*, roman d'amour, *m*. ~ *tragedy*, crime passionnel, *m*. ~ *one another*, s'entr'aimer.

loveliness, *n*, beauté, *f*. **lovely**, *a*, beau; adorable; du nanan.

lover, *n*, amant; amoureux; galant, *m*; ami, e; amateur, *m*. ~ *of old books*, bouquineur, *m*. **loving†**, *a*, affectueux, aimant.

low, *a*, bas; petit; faible; (*fever, speed*) lente; (*bow*) profonde; vulgaire. L~ *Countries*, Pays-Bas, *m.pl*. ~ *gear*, petite multiplication, *f*. ~ *mass*, messe basse, petite m., *f*. ~ *very* ~*neck*, col très échancré, *m*. ~ *relief*, bas-relief, *m*. L~ *Sunday*, Quasimodo, *f*. ~*-water mark*, (sea) laisse de basse mer, *f*; (*river*) étiage, *m*. ¶ *ad*, bas; profondément. ~*-bred*, mal élevé. ~*-necked* (*dress*), décolletée, *a. & m*. ~*-spirited*, abattu. *to be* ~*-waisted* (dress), avoir la taille basse.

low, *v.i*, mugir, beugler.

lower, *a*, plus bas; inférieur; bas; moindre. ~ *case* (*Typ*.), bas de casse, *m*. ~ *register* (*Mus*.), grave, *m*. ~ *tooth*, dent de dessous, *f*. ¶ *v.t*, [a]baisser; rabattre; descendre, avaler. ~ *oneself* (*fig*.), se ravaler. *award, &c, to the lowest tenderer*, adjudication, &c, au rabais, *f*.

lowlands, *n.pl*, basses terres, *f.pl*.

lowliness, *n*, humilité, *f*. **lowly**, *a*, humble.

lowness, *n*, peu de hauteur, *m*; (*price, &c*) modicité; (*vileness*) bassesse, *f*.

loyal†, *a*, loyal, fidèle. ~**ism**, *n*, loyalisme, *m*. ~**ist**, *n. & att*, loyaliste, *m.f. & a*. ~**ty**, *n*, loyauté, *f*; (*to sovereign*) loyalisme, *m*.

lozenge, *n*, pastille, tablette, *f*; (*Geom*.) losange, *m*.

lubber, *n*, lourdaud, mastoc, *m*.

lubricate, *v.t*, graisser, lubrifier. *lubricating oil*, huile à graisser, *f*. **lubricator**, *n*, graisseur, *m*.

Lucca, *n*, Lucques, *f*.

lucern[e], *n*, luzerne, *f*.

Lucerne (**Lake of**), lac des Quatre-Cantons, *m*.

lucid, *a*, lucide. ~**ity**, *n*, lucidité, *f*.

luck, *n*, chance, *f*, hasard, *m*; veine; fortune, *f*; bonheur, *m*. ~**less**, *a*, malheureux, néfaste. ~**y†**, *a*, heureux, chanceux, fortuné, bien loti; propice. ~ *star*, bonne étoile, heureuse planète, *f*.

lucrative, *a*, lucratif. **lucre**, *n*, lucre, gain, *m*.

lucubration, *n*, élucubration, *f*.

ludicrous†, a, risible, comique; plaisant.

luff, n, lof, m. ¶ v.t, lofer.

lug, n, oreille, f, ergot, m. ¶ v.t, traîner.

luge, n, luge, f. ¶ v.i, luger.

luggage, n, bagage[s] m.[pl.]. ~ carrier, porte-b—s, m. ~ van, fourgon à b—s, m.

lugger, n, lougre, m.

lugubrious†, a, lugubre.

lukewarm, a, tiède. ~ness, n, tiédeur, f.

lull, n, accalmie, embellie, f. ¶ v.t, bercer; mollir; assoupir. lullaby, n, berceuse, f.

lumbago, n, lumbago, m. lumbar, a, lombaire.

lumber, n, vieilleries, antiquailles, f.pl; bois [de charpente] m. ~man, bûcheron, m. ~ room, [cabinet de] débarras, m.

luminary, n, luminaire, astre, m; (pers.) lumière, f. luminous†, a, lumineux. ~ dial (watch), cadran lumineux, m.

lump, n, [gros] morceau, m, masse, f, bloc, m, motte, f. ~ sugar, sucre en morceaux, s. cassé, m. ~ sum, somme grosse, f. in a ~ sum (opp. by instalments), en une [seule] fois. ¶ v.t, bloquer, réunir. ~ish, a, balourd, mastoc (inv.).

lunacy, n, aliénation d'esprit, aliénation mentale, démence, f.

lunar, a, lunaire.

lunatic, n, aliéné, e. ~ asylum, hospice (ou asile) d'aliénés, m.

lunch & luncheon, n, déjeuner [de midi] m. lunch[eon] basket, panier à provisions; (Rly) panier-repas, m. luncheon set, garniture de table, f. lunch, v.i, déjeuner.

lung, n, poumon, m.

lunge, n, botte, f.

lupin[e] (Bot.) n, lupin, m.

lupus (Med.) n, lupus, m.

lurch, n, embardée, f. leave in the ~, camper là, planter là, laisser en panne. ¶ v.i, tituber.

lure, n, leurre, m. ¶ v.t, leurrer; (birds) piper.

lurid, a, blafard; cuivré, fauve; sinistre.

lurk, v.i, se cacher; se dissimuler.

luscious, a, succulent; fondant.

lush, a, luxuriant.

lust, n, luxure, f, appétit, m; convoitise, f. ~ after, convoiter. ~ful, a, luxurieux.

lustre, n, lustre, œil, m; (fig.) illustration, f. ¶ v.t, lustrer. ~less, a, terne.

lusty†, a, vigoureux, robuste.

lute, n, (Mus.) luth; (cement) lut, m. ¶ v.t, luter.

Lutheran, a. & n, luthérien, ne.

Luxemburg, n, Luxembourg, m.

luxuriance, n, exubérance, f. luxuriant, a, luxuriant, exubérant. luxurious, a, luxueux; voluptueux. luxury, n, luxe; délice, m.

lye, n, lessive, f.

lying, a, mensonger, menteur. ¶ n, mensonge, m.

lying-in, n, couches, f.pl. ~ hospital, maternité, f.

lyme-grass, n, élyme, m.

lymph, n, lymphe, f; vaccin, m.

lynch, v.t, écharper, lyncher.

lynx, n, lynx; (common) loup-cervier, m.

Lyons, n, Lyon, m.

lyre, n, lyre, f. ~-bird, oiseau-lyre, m.

lyric & ~al, a, lyrique. lyricism, n, lyrisme, m.

M

macaco or macaque, n, macaque, m.

macadam, n, macadam, m. ~ize, v.t, macadamiser.

macaroni, n, macaroni, m.

macaroon, n, macaron, m.

macaw, n, ara, m.

mace, n, masse, f; (spice) macis, m. ~ bearer, massier, m.

macerate, v.t, macérer.

Machiavellian, a, machiavélique.

machination, n, machination, cuisine, f.

machine, n, machine, f. ~-cut, taillé à la machine. ~ gun, fusil mitrailleur, m, mitrailleuse, f. ~ gunner, [fusilier] mitrailleur, m. ~-made, fait à la mécanique. ~ oil, huile pour machine, f. ~ tool, machine-outil, f. ¶ v.t, travailler à la machine; (Typ.) tirer; (v.i.) faire rouler la presse. machinery, n, machinerie, f, machines, f.pl, outillage; (fig.) rouage, m.

machining (Typ.) n, tirage, m, impression, f. machinist (Sewing) n, mécanicienne, f.

mackerel, n, maquereau, m. ~ sky, ciel pommelé, m.

mackintosh, n, imperméable, caoutchouc, m.

mad, a, fou; insensé; furieux (pers. & bull); enragé (pers. & dog). ~cap, écervelé, e, cerveau brûlé, m. ~man, -woman, fou, m, folle, f, insensé, e, forcené, e, désespéré, e, enragé, e.

madam, n, madame, f.

madapollam, n, madapolam, m.

madden, v.t, rendre fou; affoler; faire enrager. ~ing, p.a, enrageant.

madder, n, garance, f.

Madeira, n, Madère, f.

madly, ad, follement, en fou. madness, n, folie; démence; (dog's) rage, f.

madonna, n, madone, f.

madras (fabric) n, madras, m.

madrepore, n, madrépore, m.

madrigal, n, madrigal, m.

magazine, n, magasin, m; soute; revue, f, magazine, m. ~ camera, chambre à magasin, f. ~ gun, fusil à répétition, m.

Maggiore (Lago), le lac Majeur, m.

maggot, n, ver; asticot, m; (fig.) lubie, f. ~y, a, véreux.

Magi, n.pl, mages, m.pl.

magic, a, magique. ~ lantern, lanterne magique, l. de projection, f. ¶ n, magie, f; enchantement; prestige, m. ~al, a, magique. ∼**ally**, *a*, d'une façon magique. ∼**ian**, *n*, magicien, ne.

magisterial, *a*, de magistrat; (*fig.*) magistral. ∼**ly**, *ad*, en magistrat; magistralement.

magistracy, *n*, magistrature, *f.* **magistrate**, *n*, magistrat; juge, *m.*

magnanimity, *n*, magnanimité, *f.* **magnanimous†**, *a*, magnanime.

magnate, *n*, magnat, matador, *m.*

magnesia, *n*, magnésie, *f.* **magnesium**, *n*, magnésium, *m.* ∼ **light**, lumière magnésique, *f.*

magnet, *n*, aimant, *m.* ∼**ic**, *a*, magnétique; (*bar*, *needle*) aimanté, e; (*fig.*) attirant. ∼**ics**, *n.* & ∼**ism**, *n*, magnétisme, *m.* ∼**ize**, *v.t*, aimanter; (*fig.*) magnétiser.

magneto, *n*, magnéto, *f.* ∼**-electric**, *a*, magnéto-électrique.

magnificat, *n*, magnificat, *m.*

magnificence, *n*, magnificence, *f.* **magnificent†**, *a*, magnifique.

magnify, *v.t*, gressir, grandir; (*the Lord*) magnifier. *magnifying glass*, verre grossissant, *m*, loupe, *f.*

magniloquence, *n*, emphase, *f.* **magniloquent**, *a*, emphatique.

magnitude, *n*, grandeur; importance, *f.*

magnolia, *n*, magnolia, *m.*

magot (*Chinese figure & ape*), *n*, magot, *m.*

magpie, *n*, pie, *f.*

mahogany, *n*, acajou, *m.*

mahout, *n*, cornac, *m.*

maid, *n*, fille; vierge, pucelle, *f.* ∼[*servant*], fille [de service], bonne, domestique, servante, *f. maid of all work*, bonne à tout faire. *maid's room*, chambre de domestique, *f.* **maiden**, *n*, vierge, fille; pucelle, *f.* ∼ [*lady*], demoiselle, *f.* ¶ *a*, virginal; (*speech*) de début, premier; (*trip*) premier. ∼*hair* [*fern*], capillaire, *m.* ∼ *name*, nom de jeune fille, *m.* ∼**hood**, *n*, virginité, *f.* ∼**ly**, *a*, de jeune fille, virginal.

mail, *n*, (*armour*) mailles, *f.pl*; (*Post*) malle, poste, *f*, courrier, *m.* ∼ *bag*, sac à dépêches, *m.* ∼ *boat*, ∼ *steamer*, paquebot-poste, *m.* ∼ *carriage* (*Rly*), wagonposte, *m.* ∼ *cart* (*child's*, chaise roulante, *f.* ∼ *cart* ∼ *coach* (*Post*), courrier, *m.* ∼ *coach* (*stage*), malle[-poste] *f.* ∼ *order business*, affaires par correspondance, *f.pl.* ∼ *train*, train-poste, *m.*

maim, *v.t*, estropier, mutiler.

main, *a*, principal; grand; maître, esse. ∼ [*portion of*] *building*, corps de logis, c. de bâtiment, *m.* *the* ∼ *chance*, le solide. ∼ *deck*, pont principal, *m.* ∼ *drain*, maître drain, d. collecteur, *m.* ∼ *drainage*, le tout-à-l'égout. *by* ∼ *force*, de vive force. ∼ *hall* (*body of building*), vaisseau, *m. the* ∼ *idea* (*of a book*), l'idée mère. ∼ *issue* (*Law*), fond, *m.* ∼**land**, continent, *m*, terre ferme, *f.* ∼ *line* (*Rly*), ligne principale, grande l., *f.* ∼*mast*, grand mât, *m. the* ∼ *point*, le

point principal, l'essentiel, *m.* ∼ *road*, grand chemin, *m*, grand-route, *f.* ∼**sail**, grand-voile, *f.* ∼*spring*, grand ressort, *m*; (*fig.*) cheville ouvrière, *f*, mobile, *m.* ∼*stay* (*fig.*), âme, *f*; soutien, *m.* ∼ *structure* (*of a building*), gros œuvre, *m. the* ∼ *thing*, le principal, l'important, *m.* ∼ *walls*, gros murs, *m.pl.* ¶ *n*, (*pipe*) conduite [maîtresse]; (*pl.*) canalisation, *f*; (*Elec.*) conducteur principal, *m*; (*sea*, *Poet.*) onde, *f. in the* ∼, en général. **the M**∼ (*river*), le Mein. ∼**ly**, *ad*, principalement.

maintain, *v.t*, maintenir; soutenir; entretenir. **maintenance**, *n*, maintien, soutien; entretien, *m.*

Mainz, *n*, Mayence, *f.*

maisonette, *n*, appartement (*dans une maison à deux appartements*) *m.*

maize, *n*, maïs, blé de Turquie, *m.*

majestic†, *a*, majestueux. **majesty**, *n*, majesté, *f. His*, *Her*, *My* ∼, Sa Majesté.

majolica, *n*, majolique, maïolique, *f.*

major, *a*, majeur (*prophet*, *&c*) grand; (*pers.*) aîné. ∼ *planet*, planète principale, *f.* ∼ *road*, route de priorité, *f.* ¶ (*Mil.*) commandant, chef de bataillon, *m.* ∼ *general*, général de division, *m.*

Majorca, *n*, Majorque, *f.*

majority, *n*, majorité, *f*; pluralité, (la) plupart, *f.*

make, *n*, façon; fabrication, *f.* ∼*believe*, feinte, frime, *f.* ∼*shift*, moyen de fortune, dispositif de circonstance, pis aller, *m.* ∼*up*, maquillage, fard, *m.* ∼*weight*, complément de poids, *m*; (*butcher's*) réjouissance, *f*; (*fig.*) remplissage, *m.* ¶ *v.t.ir*, faire; dresser; pratiquer; fabriquer; confectionner; créer; rendre; forcer; réaliser; mettre; (*inquiries*) prendre; (*v.i.ir.*) se diriger; contribuer. ∼ *a hoop* (*Croquet*), franchir un arceau. ∼ *away with*, se défaire de; détourner. ∼ *faces*, grimacer. ∼ *hay*, faire les foins. ∼ *it up*, se raccommoder. ∼ *light of*, faire peu de cas de. ∼ *money*, s'enrichir. ∼ *much of*, faire mousser. ∼ *off*, filer, décamper. ∼ *one's will*, tester. ∼ *out*, distinguer; déchiffrer; comprendre; dresser. ∼ *the most of*, ménager. ∼ *up*, faire; conditionner; confectionner; combler; (*a/c*) arrêter; (*face*) se farder, se maquiller; (*Theat.*) se grimer; (*Typ.*) mettre en pages. ∼ *up for*, suppléer [à]. ∼ *up one's mind*, se décider, se déterminer. **maker**, *n*, créateur, trice; faiseur, euse; fabricant; constructeur, *m.* ∼*up* (*Typ.*), metteur en pages, *m.* **making**, *n*, création; fabrication; construction; confection, *f.* ∼*ready* (*Typ.*), mise en train, *f.* ∼*up price* (*Stk Ex.*), cours de compensation, *m.*

malachite, *n*, malachite, *f.*

maladministration, *n*, mauvaise gestion, *f.*

maladroit†, *a*, maladroit.

malady, *n*, maladie, *f.*

Malagasy, *a*, malgache. ¶ *n*, Malgache, *m*,*f.*

malaprop[ism], *n*, incongruité, *f*, pataquès, *m*.

malar, *a*, malaire. ¶ *n*, os malaire, *m*.

malaria, *n*, paludisme, *n*, malaria, *f*. malarial, *a*, paludéen; miasmatique.

Malay[an], *a*, malais. ¶ *n*, (*pers.*) Malais, e; (*language*) le malais. **Malaysia**, *n*, la Malaisie.

malcontent, *a. & n*, mécontent, *a. & m*.

male, *n*, mâle, *m*. ¶ *a*, mâle; masculin. ~ *descent*, masculinité, *f*. ~ *nurse*, infirmier, *m*.

malediction, *n*, malédiction, *f*.

malefactor, *n*, malfaiteur, *m*.

malevolent, *a*, malveillant.

malformation, *n*, malformation, *f*, vice de conformation, *m*.

malice, *n*, malice, rancune, *f*. ~ *aforethought*, ~ *prepense*, préméditation, *f*. malicious†, *a*, malicieux, malfaisant.

malign, *v.t*, diffamer, blasonner. malign†, malignant†, *a*, malin.

malinger, *v.i*, faire le malade, simuler la maladie.

mallard, *n*, malart, *m*.

malleable, *a*, malléable.

mallet, *n*, maillet, *m*, mailloche, batte, *f*.

mallow, *n*, mauve, *f*.

malt, *n*, malt, *m*. ~ *house*, malterie, *f*. ¶ *v.t*, convertir en malt. ~ing, *n*, malterie, *f*. ~ster, *n*, malteur, *m*.

Malta, *n*, Malte, *f*. **Maltese**, *a*, maltais. ~ *cross*, croix de Malte, *f*. ~ [*dog, bitch*], chien(ne) de Malte, bichon, ne. ¶ *n*, (*pers.*) Maltais, e; (*language*) le maltais.

maltreat, *v.t*, maltraiter, brutaliser. ~ment, *n*, mauvais traitements; sévices, *m.pl*.

mamillary, *a*, mamillaire.

mam[m]a, *n*, maman, *f*.

mammal, *n*, mammifère, *m*. mammalia, *n.pl*, mammifères, *m.pl*.

mammoth, *n*, mammouth, *m*.

man, *n*, homme; monsieur; cavalier; garçon; employé; ouvrier; valet, *m*; (*Draughts*) pièce, *f*, pion, *m*. ~ & *wife*, mari & femme. ~ *at the wheel*, barreur, *m*. ~ *child*, enfant mâle, *m*. ~-*eater*, mangeur d'hommes, *m*. ~ *Friday*, factotum, *m*. ~ *hole*, (*Mach.*) trou d'homme; (*sewer, &c*) regard, *m*. *the* ~ *in the street*, l'homme de la rue. ~ *of all work*, homme à tout faire. ~ *of colour*, noir, *m*. ~ *of deeds*, homme d'exécution. ~ *of fashion*, élégant, *m*. ~ *of straw*, homme de paille. ~ *of substance*, homme calé. ~-*of-war*, bâtiment de guerre, *m*. ~'s *estate*, l'âge viril, *m*. ~'s *part acted by a woman*, rôle travesti, *m*. ~[*servant*], domestique, valet, *m*. ~*slaughter*, homicide involontaire, *m*. *men's single, double* (*Ten.*), simple, double, messieurs, *m*. ¶ *v.t*, (*boat, &c*) armer; (*prize ship*) amariner. ~hood, ~kind, ~ly, &c. See below.

manacle, *v.t*, mettre des menottes à; (*fig.*) enchaîner. ~s, *n.pl*, menottes, *f.pl*, fers, *m.pl*.

manage, *v.t*, diriger, administrer; gérer; conduire; manier; ménager; (*v.i.*) s'arranger; savoir. ~ *to*, parvenir à; obtenir de. ~ment, *n*, direction, administration; gérance, gestion; conduite; économie, *f*; gouvernement; maniement, *m*. manager, ess, *n*, directeur, trice, gérant, e; chef; (*ship's*) armateur, *m*. *managing director*, administrateur délégué, *a*. directeur, *a*. gérant, *m*.

manatee, *n*, lamantin, *m*.

Manchukuo, *n*, l'État mandchou, *m*. **Manchuria**, *n*, la Mandchourie. **Manchu[rian]**, *a*, mandchou. ¶ *n*, Mandchou, e.

mandarin, *n*, mandarin, *m*; (*toy*) pagode, *f*. mandarin[e] [*orange*], *n*, mandarine, *f*.

mandatary, -ory, *n*, mandataire, *m*. mandate, *n*, mandat, *m*. ~*d territory*, pays sous mandat, *m*. mandator, *n*, mandant, *m*.

mandible, *n*, mandibule, *f*.

mandolin[e], *n*, mandoline, *f*.

mandrake, *n*, mandragore, *f*.

mandrel, -il (*lathe*), *n*, mandrin, arbre, **m**.

mandrill (*baboon*), *n*, mandrill, *m*.

mane, *n*, crinière, *f*, crins, *m.pl*.

manège, -ege, *n*, manège, *m*.

manes, *n.pl*, mânes, *m.pl*.

manfully, *ad*, en homme, courageusement.

manganese, *n*, manganèse, *m*.

mange, *n*, gale, rogne, *f*, rouvieux, *m*.

mangel[-wurzel] or mangold[-wurzel], *n*, betterave fourragère, *f*.

manger, *n*, mangeoire, crèche, *f*.

mangle, *n*, calandre, *f*. ¶ *v.t*, mutiler; (*in carving*) charcuter; (*linen*) calandrer.

mango, *n*, mangue, *f*. ~ [*tree*], manguier, *m*.

mangrove, *n*, manglier, palétuvier, *m*.

mangy, *a*, galeux, rogneux, rouvieux.

manhood, *n*, virilité, *f*; âge viril, *m*. ~ *suffrage*, suffrage masculin, *m*.

mania, *n*, manie; folie; rage; marotte, *f*. maniac, *n. & ~(al)*, *a*, maniaque, *m, f. & a*.

manicure, *n*, soin des mains, *m*, manucure, *f*. ~ *set*, onglier, *m*, manucure, *f*. ~ *stand*, onglier suspendu, *m*. ~ *the hands*, soigner les mains, faire de la manucure. manicurist, *n*, manucure, *f,m*.

manifest†, *a*, manifeste. ¶ *n*, (*Ship.*) *n*, manifeste, *m*. ¶ *v.t*, manifester.

manifesto, *n*, manifeste, *m*.

manifold, *a*, multiple. ~-*book*, carnet genre manifold, cahier de copie, *dit* manifold, *m*.

manikin, *n*, [petit] bout d'homme; (*lay figure*) mannequin, *m*.

Manil[l]a, *n*, (*Geog.*) Manille, *f*; (*cheroot*) manille, *m*.

manioc, *n*, manioc, *m*.

manipulate, *v.t*, manœuvrer, manipuler; (*pers.*) empaumer.

mankind, *n*, le genre humain, l'espèce humaine; les hommes. manliness, *n*, virilité, *f*. manly, *a*, mâle, viril; (*woman*) hommasse.

manna, *n*, manne, *f.*

mannequin (*pers.*) *n*, mannequin, *m.*

manner, *n*, manière; façon, *f*; air; genre, *m*; (*pl.*) manières, formes, mœurs, *f.pl*, ton, *m.* ~ed (*style*, &*c*) *a*, maniéré. ~ism, *n*, maniérisme, *m*, manière, *f*, tic, *m.* ~ly, *a*, poli.

mannish, *a*, garçonnier, hommasse.

manœuvre, *n*, manœuvre, *f.* ¶ *v.i.* & *t*, manœuvrer, évoluer.

manometer, *n*, manomètre, *m.*

manor, *n*, manoir, château, *m*, seigneurie, *f.*

mansard roof, comble brisé, *f.*

mansion, *n*, hôtel [particulier]; château, *m*; (*pl.*) immeuble à appartements, *m.*

mant[e]let, *n*, mantelet, *m.*

mantelpiece, *n*, manteau de cheminée, *m*, cheminée, *f.* mantelshelf, *n*, tablette de cheminée, *f.*

mantilla, *n*, mantille, *f.*

mantle, *n*, manteau; (*gas*) manchon, *m.* ~ maker, couturier, *m.*

Mantua, *n*, Mantoue, *f.*

manual†, *a*, manuel, à bras. ~ [*exercise*] (*Mil.*), maniement des (*ou* d') armes, *m.* ¶ *n*, manuel, aide-mémoire, guide-âne; (*organ*) clavier, *m.*

manufactory, *n*, fabrique, manufacture, usine, *f.* manufacture, *n*, fabrication, industrie, *f.* manufacturer, *n*, industriel, fabricant, manufacturier, *m.* ~'s price, prix de fabrique, *m.* manufacturing, *p.a*, manufacturier.

manure, *n*, engrais; fumier, *m.* ¶ *v.t*, engraisser; fumer.

manuscript. *n.* & *a*, manuscrit, *m*. & *a.*

Manx, *a*, de l'île de Man.

many, *a*, beaucoup; bien des; force; grand; maint, divers. ~ *a*, plus d'un, maint. ~coloured, multicolore. ~sided, complexe. a great ~, un grand nombre (de). as ~, autant. so ~, tant. the ~, la multitude. too ~, trop.

map, *n*, carte, *f*; plan, *m.* ~ case, portecartes, *m.* ~ of the heavens, carte céleste, *f.* ~ of the heavens in hemispheres, mappemonde céleste, *f.* ~ of the world in hemispheres, mappemonde, *f.* ~ producer, cartographe, *m.* ¶ *v.t*, dresser (*ou* faire) la carte de. ~ out, tracer.

maple, *n*, érable, *m.*

mar, *v.t*, gâter; troubler.

marabou & marabout, *n*, marabout, *m.*

maraschino, *n*, marasquin, *m.*

marasmus, *n*, marasme, *m.*

Marathon [race], *n*, course de Marathon, *f.*

maraud, *v.t*, marauder. ~er, *n*, maraudeur, *m.* ~ing, *n*, maraudage, *m*, maraude, *f.*

marble, *n*, marbre, *m*; (*games*) bille, *f.* ~ mason & ~ merchant, marbrier, *m.* ~ quarry, marbrière, *f.* ~ work & ~ works, marbrerie, *f.* ¶ *v.t*, marbrer. marbler, *n*, marbreur, *m.* marbling, *n*, marbrure, *f.*

marc (*fruit refuse*) *n*, marc, *m.*

---

marcasite, *n*, marcassite, *f.*

March, *n*, mars, *m.*

march, *n*, marche, *f*; pas, *m.* ~ past, défilé, *m.* ¶ *v.i*, marcher. ~ in, entrer. ~ off, se mettre en marche. ~ out, sortir. ~ past, défiler. ~ing, *n*, marche, *f.* ~ song, chanson de route, *f.*

marchioness, *n*, marquise, *f.*

mare, *n*, jument, *f.* he has found a ~'s nest, il croit avoir trouvé la pie au nid.

margarine, *n*, margarine, *f.*

margin, *n*, marge; (*book page*) marge, *f*, blanc; bord, *m*; provision; tolérance, *f.* ~al, *a*, marginal.

marguerite, *n*, grande marguerite, *f.*

marigold, *n*, souci, *m.*

marine, *a*, maritime; marin. ~ glue, glu marine, *f.* ~ stores, fournitures pour navires, f—s maritimes, *f.pl.* ~ superintendent, capitaine d'armement, *m.* ¶ *n*, (*shipping*) marine, *f*; (*pers.*) soldat d'infanterie de marine, fantassin de la flotte, fusilier marin, *m.* mariner, *n*, marin, *m.* ~'s compass, boussole marine, *f.*

marionette, *n*, marionnette, *f.*

marital, *a*, marital.

maritime, *a*, maritime.

marjoram, *n*, marjolaine, *f.*

mark, *n*, marque, *f*; point; signe; repère, *m*; trace, *f*; but, *m*; estampille; cote, *f*; témoignage; (*Sch.*) point, *m*, note, *f.* ~ boat, bateau bouée [de virage] *m.* ~ flag, fanion, guidon, *m.* ~ of origin, estampille, *f.* ¶ *v.t*, marquer; indiquer; porter [la mention]; noter; estampiller; coter; remarquer; faire attention à; (*card*) piper. ~ out, tracer; borner. ~ time, marquer le pas; piétiner sur place. ~ed, *p.a*, marqué, prononcé, sensible; (*man*) noté; (*cheque*) visé; (*cards*) biseautées. ~er, *n*, marqueur, euse; pointeur; (*Mil.*) jalonneur, *m*; (*book*) marque, *f*, signet, *m.*

market, *n*, marché, *m*; place; bourse; (*covered*) halle, *f*; débouché; débit, *m.* ~ garden, jardin maraîcher, *m.* ~ gardener, maraîcher, *m.* ~ gardening, culture maraîchère, *f.* ~ porter, fort [de la halle] *m.* ~ town, ville à marché, *f*, bourg, *m.* ~ trader, [marchand] forain, *m.* ~ value, valeur marchande, v. vénale, *f.* ¶ *v.t*, mettre en vente. ~able, *a*, marchand; de vente; vénal; négociable. ~ing, *n*, mise en vente, *f.*

marking, *n*, marquage, *m*; cote, *f.* ~ ink, encre à marquer le linge, *f.* ~ stitch, point de marque, *m.*

marksman, *n*, [bon] tireur, *m.*

marl, *n*, marne, *f.* ~ pit, marnière, *f.* ¶ *v.t*, marner.

marline, *n*, lusin, *m.* ~ spike, marlinspike, épissoir, *m.*

marly, *a*, marneux.

marmalade, *n*, confitures (*d'oranges*) *f.pl*; marmelade, *f.*

Marmora (Sea of), mer de Marmara, *f.*

marmot (*Zool.*) *n*, marmotte, *f.*

maroon, *a*, marron. ¶ *n*, couleur marron, *f*; (*firework*) marron, *m*; (*pers.*) nègre marron, *m*, négresse marronne, *f.*

marquee, *n*, tente-pavillon, *f.*

marquet[e]ry, *n*, marqueterie, *f.*

marquis, -quess, *n*, marquis, *m.*

marriage, *n*, mariage, *m*; noces, *f.pl.* ∼ *articles*, contrat de mariage, *m.* ∼ *licence*, dispense de bans, *f.* ∼ *of convenience*, mariage de raison, m. de convenance. ∼ *portion*, dot, *f.* ∼ *settlement*, constitution de dot, *f.* ∼ *tie*, lien conjugal, *m. cousin*, *&c, by* ∼, cousin, &c, par alliance. ∼*able*, *a*, mariable, nubile. ∼ *daughter*, fille à marier, *f.* **married**, *p.a*, marié. [*newly*] ∼ *couple*, nouveaux mariés, *m.pl.* ∼ *life*, vie conjugale, *f. get* ∼, se marier.

marrow, *n*, moelle; (*vegetable*) courge à la moelle, *f.* ∼*bone*, os à moelle, *m.* ∼*fats*, pois carrés, *m.pl.* ∼**y**, *a*, moelleux.

marry, *v.t*, marier; épouser; (*v.i.*) se marier; s'allier. ∼ *a second, a third, time*, convoler en secondes, en troisièmes, noces. ∼ *again*, se remarier, convoler. ∼ *into*, s'apparenter à.

Marseillais, e, *a*, marseillais, e. ¶ *n*, Marseillais, e. *the Marseillaise* (hymn), la Marseillaise. **Marseilles**, *n*, Marseille, *f.*

marsh, *n*, marais, marécage, m. ∼ *mallow*, guimauve, *f.* ∼ *marigold*, souci d'eau, *m.*

marshal, *n*, (*Mil.*) maréchal; (*Sport*) chef de terrain, m. ¶ *v.t*, classer, ranger; trier. ∼*ship*, *n*, maréchalat, *m.*

marshy, *a*, marécageux, paludéen.

marsupial, *n*, marsupial, *m.*

mart, *n*, centre des affaires; (*Poet.*) marché, *m.*

marten, *n*, martre; fouine, *f.*

martial, *a*, martial; (*pers.*) guerrier. ∼ *law* (in a town), état de siège, *m.*

martin, *n*, hirondelle de fenêtre, *f.*

martinet, *n*, gendarme, *m.*

martingale (*Harness, Betting*) *n*, martingale, *f.*

Martinmas, *n*, la Saint-Martin.

martyr, *n*, martyr, e. ∼*dom*, *n*, martyre, *m.* ∼*[ize]*, *v.t*, martyriser. ∼*ology* (*list*) *n*, martyrologe, *m.*

marvel, *n*, merveille, *f*; prestige, miracle, *m.* ¶ *v.i*, s'émerveiller, s'étonner. **marvellous**†, *a*, merveilleux, prestigieux.

marzipan, *n*, massepain, *m.*

mascot, *n*, mascotte, *f*, porte-bonheur, fétiche, *m.*

masculine, *a*, masculin, mâle; (*woman*) hommasse, garçonnier. ∼ [*gender*], [genre] masculin, *m.* **masculinity**, *n*, masculinité, *f.*

mash, *n*, mélange; (*cattle*) barbotage, *m*; (*poultry*) pâtée; (*Cook.*) purée, *f.* ∼ *tub*, cuve-matière, *f.* ¶ *v.t*, mélanger, brasser; réduire en purée. ∼*ed potatoes, turnips*, purée de pommes de terre, de navets, *f.*

mask, *n*, masque, *m*; (*Arch.*) mascaron, *m*;

(*Phot.*) cache, *f.* ¶ *v.t*, masquer, cacher. ∼*ed ball*, bal masqué, *m.* **masker, -quer** (*pers.*) *n*, masque, *m.*

maslin, *n*, mouture, *f.*

mason, *n*, maçon, *m.* ¶ *v.t*, maçonner. ∼*ic*, *a*, maçonnique. ∼*ry*, *n*, maçonnerie, *f*; maçonnage, *m.*

masquerade, *n*, mascarade; (*fig.*) mascarade, pantalonnade, *f.* ¶ *v.i*, se masquer, se déguiser.

mass, *n*, masse, *f*; amas, *m*; (*Relig.*) messe, *f.* ∼ *production*, production en masse, fabrication en série, *f.* ¶ *v.t*, masser.

massacre, *n*, massacre, *m.* ¶ *v.t*, massacrer.

massage, *n*, massage, *m.* ¶ *v.t*, masser. **masseur, euse**, *n*, masseur, euse.

massive†, *a*, massif; en amas; en masses.

mast, *n*, mât, *m*; (*pl.*) mâture, *f*; (*beech*) faînes, *f.pl*; (*oak*) glands, *m.pl*, glandée, *f.* ∼ *house*, mâture, *f.* ¶ *v.t*, mâter.

master, *n*, maître; professeur; directeur; chef; patron; capitaine, m. *be* ∼ *of*, posséder. *be one's own* ∼, s'appartenir. *M* ∼ *A.* (boy), Monsieur A. ∼ *card*, carte maîtresse, *f.* ∼ *key*, clef de maître, *f*, passepartout, m. ∼ *mariner*, capitaine marchand. ∼ *mind*, cheville ouvrière, *f*, aigle, *m. M* ∼ *of the Ceremonies*, maître des cérémonies. *f.* ∼ *of foreign-going vessel*, capitaine au long cours. *f.* ∼ *of the hounds*, maître d'équipage. ∼*piece*, chef-d'œuvre, m. ∼ *stroke*, coup de maître, m. ¶ *v.t*, maîtriser. ∼*ful*, *a*, (*tone, &c*) magistral. ∼ *man* ∼ *woman*, maître homme, maîtresse femme. ∼*ly*, *a*, de maître, magistral. *in a* ∼ *way*, magistralement, supérieurement. ∼**ship**, *n*, maîtrise; direction; chaire, *f.* ∼**y**, *n*, maîtrise, *f*, empire; dessus, *m.*

mastic, *n*, mastic, *m.* ∼ [*tree*], lentisque, *m.*

masticate, *v.t*, mâcher, mastiquer. **mastication**, *n*, mastication, *f.*

mastiff, *n*, mâtin, *m.*

masting, *n*. & ∼ *house*, mâture, *f.*

mastodon, *n*, mastodonte, *m.*

mastoid, *a*, mastoïde.

mat, *a*, mat. ¶ *n*, natte, *f*; paillasson; tapis; (*plate*) dessous, m. ∼ *maker*, nattier, m. ¶ *v.t*, natter. *matted hair*, cheveux embroussaillés, *m.pl.*

matador (*pers. & games*) *n*, matador, *m.*

match, *n*, (*light*) allumette; (*fuse*) mèche; alliance, *f*, parti, m; assortiment; pendant; (*pers.*) pareil, le; (*Ten., &c*) partie, *f*, match; (*Box., Wrestling*) combat, match, m. ∼ *board*, planche bouvetée, *f.* ∼ *box*, boîte à allumettes, *f.* ∼ *maker*, marieur, euse. ∼ *play* (*Golf*), concours par trous, m. ¶ *v.t*, allier; marier; égaler; assortir; [r]appareiller; [r]apparier. **to** ∼, pareil. ∼*less*, *a*, sans pareil.

mate, *n*, camarade, m.*f*, compagnon, *m*, compagne, *f*; aide, m.*f*; (*bird*) pair; (*Naut.*) second, lieutenant; (*Chess*) mat, m. ∼*'s* *receipt,* bon de bord, *m.* ¶ *v.t,* appareiller, accoupler; (*Chess*) faire mat, mater.

material†, *a,* matériel; essentiel. ¶ *n,* matière, *f;* matériel, *m;* étoffe, *f;* (*pl.*) matières, *f.pl;* matériaux, *m.pl;* fournitures, *f.pl;* articles, *m.pl.* **~ism,** *n,* matérialisme, *m.* **~ist,** *n. & ~istic,* *a,* matérialiste. **~ize,** *v.t,* matérialiser; (*v.i.*) se m.; aboutir. *materia medica,* matière médicale, *f.*

maternal†, *a,* maternel. **maternity,** *n. & ~ hospital,* maternité, *f.* **~ doctor,** accoucheur, *m.*

mathematical†, *a,* mathématique; (*precise*) géométrique; (*instruments*) de mathématiques. **mathematician,** *n,* mathématicien, ne. **mathematics,** *n.pl,* mathématiques, *f.pl.*

matinée, *n,* matinée, *f.* **matins,** *n.pl,* matines, *f.pl.*

matriarchy, *n,* matriarcat, *m.*

matriculate, *v.i,* prendre des (ses) inscriptions. **matriculation,** *n,* inscription, *f.*

matrimonial†, *a,* conjugal; (*Law, agent, &c*) matrimonial. **~ triangle,** ménage à trois, *m.* **matrimony,** *n,* mariage, *m,* vie conjugale, *f.*

matrix, *n,* matrice; gangue, *f.*

matron, *n,* matrone; (*hospital, &c*) infirmière en chef, *f.* **~ly,** *a,* de matrone.

matter, *n,* matière; affaire; chose; question, *f;* propos; cas; sujet; article; chapitre; (*Med.*) pus, *m.* *as a ~ of course,* comme une chose toute naturelle *ou* qui va de soi. *as a ~ of fact,* dans (*ou* par) le fait, en fait. **~-of-fact,** positif. *~ of history,* fait historique, *m. be the ~,* s'agir. *be the ~ with,* avoir. ¶ *v.i,* importer, faire. *no ~!* n'importe!

Matterhorn (the), le mont Cervin.

mattery, *a,* purulent.

matting, *n,* natte[s] *f.[pl.],* paillasson; abrivent, *m.*

mattins, *n.pl,* matines, *f.pl.*

mattock, *n,* pioche-hache, *f;* hoyau, *m.*

mattress, *n,* matelas; sommier, *m.* **~ maker,** matelassier, ère.

mature†, *a,* mûr. ¶ *v.i. & t,* mûrir; (*Com.*) échoir. **maturity,** *n,* maturité; échéance, *f.*

maudlin, *a,* romance; bêtement sentimental; ivre à pleurer; pleurard, larmoyant. **~[ism],** *n,* romance, *f.*

maul, *v.t,* malmener. **~stick,** appui-main, *m.*

Mauritius, *n,* [l'île] Maurice, *f.*

mausoleum, *n,* mausolée, *m.*

mauve, *n. & a,* mauve, *f. & att.*

mawkish†, *a,* mielleux, doucereux, fade.

maxim, *n,* maxime, sentence, *f;* adage, *m.*

maximum, *n,* maximum; plafond, *m.* ¶ *a,* maximum.

May (month) *n,* mai, *m. May day,* le premier mai. *May fly,* mouche de mai, *f,* éphémère, *m. maypole,* mai, *m.*

may (Bot.) *n,* fleurs d'aubépine, *f.pl.* **~ [bush],** aubépine, épine blanche, *f.*

may, *v. aux. ir,* pouvoir; permettre; que. *it ~ be,* cela se peut. **~be,** *ad,* peut-être.

mayonnaise, *n. & att,* mayonnaise, *f. & att.*

mayor, *n,* maire, *m.* **~alty,** *n,* mairie, *f.* **~ess,** *n,* femme du maire, *f.*

maze, *n,* labyrinthe, dédale, *m.*

mazurka, *n,* mazurka, *f.*

me, *pn,* me; moi.

meadow & (Poet.) mead, *n,* pré, *m,* prairie, *f. meadow-sweet,* reine des prés, *f.*

meagre†, *a,* maigre, pauvre; succinct. **~ness,** *n,* maigreur, pauvreté, *f.*

meal, *n,* repas, *m;* farine, *f,* gruau, *m.* **~ time,** l'heure du repas, *f. at ~ times,* aux heures de repas. **~y,** *a,* farineux. **~-mouthed,** mielleux, doucereux.

mean†, *a,* bas; vil; abject; chétif; mesquin; ladre; chiche; petit; (*average*) moyen. *in the ~ time (or while) or ~time,* **~while,** *ad,* en attendant; entretemps, cependant. ¶ *n,* milieu, *m;* (*Math.*) moyenne, *f;* (*pl.*) moyen, *m;* moyens, *m.pl,* facultés, *f.pl. by no ~s,* nullement. ¶ *v.t. & i. ir,* se proposer; avoir l'intention de; vouloir; compter; penser; vouloir dire; signifier; entendre; destiner; faire exprès.

meander, *n,* méandre, *m.* ¶ *v.i,* cheminer, serpenter.

meaning, *n,* signification, *f,* sens, *m;* intention, *f.* **-meaning,** *a,* intentionné. **~less,** *a,* sans aucun sens, un non-sens.

meanness, *n,* bassesse, abjection, ladrerie, vilenie, *f.*

measles, *n.pl,* rougeole, *f.*

measurable, *a,* mesurable, appréciable. **measure,** *n,* mesure; dose; démarche; (*tape, &c*) mesure, *f;* mètre; centimètre, *m;* (*bill*) projet de loi, *m;* (*pl,* Geol.) étage, *m,* série, *f,* terrain, *m. to ~* (clothes, &c), sur mesure. ¶ *v.t. & i,* mesurer; métrer; arpenter; jauger; cuber; toiser; (*the body*) mensurer; (*for fitting*) prendre mesure à; avoir. **~ out,** doser. **~ment,** *n,* mesurage, *m;* mesure; grosseur, *f;* tour; cubage; encombrement, *m;* volume; arpentage; jaugeage, *m.*

meat, *n,* viande; chair, *f.* **~ breakfast,** déjeuner à la fourchette, *m.* **~ day (Eccl.),** jour gras, *m.* **~ diet,** alimentation carnée, *f,* régime gras, *m.* **~ safe,** garde-manger, *m.* **~y,** *a,* charnu; (*food*) carné.

Mecca, *n,* la Mecque.

mechanic, *n,* [ouvrier] mécanicien, serrurier mécanicien, *m.* **~al†,** *a,* mécanique; (*fig.*) machinal. **~ dentistry,** prothèse dentaire, *f.* **~ drawing,** dessin industriel, *m.* **~ engineer,** ingénieur mécanicien, *m.* **~ engineering,** l'art de la mécanique, *m;* construction mécanique, *f.* **mechanician & mechanist,** *n,* mécanicien, m. **mechanics,** *n.pl,* mécanique, *f.* **mechanism,** *n,* mécanisme, *m,* mécanique, *f,* organes, *m.pl.* **mechanization,** *n,* machinisme, *m.* **mech-**

anize, *v.t*, mécaniser. ~*d farming*, moto-culture, *f*.

Mechlin (*lace*), *n*, malines, *f*.

medal, *n*, médaille, *f*. ~ *cabinet & collection of* ~*s*, médailler, *m*. ~ *maker or* **medallist**, *n*, médailleur, *m*. ~ *play* (*Golf*), concours par coups, *m*. *award a* ~ *to*, médailler. **medalled**, *a*, médaillé. **medallion**, *n*, médaillon, *m*. **medallist** (*recipient*), *n*, médaillé, e.

meddle, *v.i*, se mêler, s'immiscer, s'ingérer; toucher. **meddler**, *n*, or **meddlesome person**, touche-à-tout, *m*, personne qui se mêle des oignons des autres, *f*. **meddling**, *n*, immixtion, ingérence, *f*.

mediaeval, *a*, médiéval, du moyen âge, moyenâgeux. ~**ist**, *n*, médiéviste, *m,f*.

mediate, *v.i*, s'interposer. **mediation**, *n*, médiation; pensée, *f*. **mediator**, **trix**, *n*, médiateur, trice.

medical, *a*, médical; (*school, &c*) de médecine; (*student*) en médecine. ~ *examination* (*recruits*), revision, *f*. ~ *jurisprudence*, médecine légale, *f*. ~ *man*, *&* *officer*, médecin, *m*. **medicament**, *n*, médicament, *m*. **medicated**, *p.a*, médicamenteux. **medicinal**, *a*, médicinal; médicamenteux. **medicine**, *n*, médecine, *f*; médicament, *m*. ~ *ball* (*Box.*), medicine ball, *m*. ~ *cabinet*, armoire à pharmacie, *f*. ~ *chest*, coffret de pharmacie, *m*, pharmacie; caisse à médicaments, *f*. ~ *man* [sorcier] guérisseur, *m*. **medico-judicial**, *a*, médico-légal.

medieval, *&c*. Same as *mediaeval*, *&c*.

mediocre, *a*, médiocre. **mediocrity**, *n*, (*quality*) médiocrité, *f*, médiocre, *m*; (*pers.*) médiocre, *m*.

meditate ([up]on), *v.t. & i*, méditer (sur); contempler. **meditation**, *n*, méditation, *f*. **meditative**, *a*, méditatif.

mediterranean, *a*, méditerrané. **M**~, *a*, méditerranéen. **the M**~ [**sea**], la [mer] Méditerranée.

medium, *a*, moyen. ~ *fishing*, pêche du poisson moyen, *f*. ¶ *n*, milieu; agent; véhicule, *m*; (*ether*) atmosphère; (*agency*) entremise, *f*, intermédiaire; (*Spiritualism*) médium, *m*.

medlar, *n*, nèfle, *f*. ~ [*tree*], néflier, *m*.

medley, *n*, mélange, *m*, macédoine, *f*, fatras; bariolage, pot pourri, *m*. ¶ *a*, mêlé. ¶ *v.t*, mêler; bigarrer.

medullary, *a*, médullaire.

medusa (*jelly fish*) *n*, méduse, *f*.

meek, *a*, doux; débonnaire. ~**ly**, *ad*, avec douceur. ~**ness**, *n*, douceur, mansuétude, *f*.

meerschaum, *n*, écume de mer, *f*.

meet (*Hunt.*) *n*, assemblée, *f*. ¶ *v.t.ir*, rencontrer; trouver; faire face à; accueillir; honorer; (*v.i.ir.*) se rencontrer; confluer; s'assembler; se réunir. ~ *with*, éprouver, essuyer. ~**ing**, *n*, rencontre; jonction, *f*; confluent, *m*; entrevue; assemblée; ré-

union, *f*; meeting; concours, *m*; séance; (*of engagements, bills of exchange*) bonne fin, *f*. ~ *house*, chapelle, *f*.

megaphone, *n*, porte-voix, *m*.

melancholia *&* **melancholy**, *n*, mélancolie, *f*. **melancholic** *&* **melancholy**, *a*, mélancolique.

Melanesia, *n*, la Mélanésie.

mellow, *a*, mûr; moelleux; (*earth*) meuble. ¶ *v.t*, mûrir.

melodious*, *a*, mélodieux. **melody**, *n*, mélodie, *f*, chant, *m*.

melon, *n*, melon, *m*.

melt (*Foundry*) *n*, fonte, chauffe, *f*. ¶ *v.t. & i. ir*, fondre; attendrir; s'a. *that* ~*s in the mouth* (*as a pear*), fondant. ~**er**, *n*, fondeur, *m*. ~**ing**, *n*, fonte, fusion, *f*. ~ *point*, point de fusion, *m*. ~ *pot*, creuset, *m*.

member, *n*, membre, *m*, adhérent, e, associé, e; représentant, *m*. ~ *of a conciliation board*, prud'homme, *m*. ~ *of a* (or *the*) *congress*, congressiste, *m,f*. ~ *of a mutual society or association*, mutualiste, *m,f*. ~ *of parliament*, membre du parlement, parlementaire; représentant à la Chambre, *m*. ~**ship**, *n*, qualité [de membre]; adhésion; charge; (*parliament*) députation, *f*; nombre des adhérents, *m*.

membrane, *n*, membrane, *f*.

memento, *n*, mémento; souvenir, *m*.

memoir, *n*, mémoire, *m*; (*pl, book*) mémorial, *m*.

memorable, *a*, mémorable. **memorandum**, *n*, mémorandum, *m*, note, *f*, mémoire, *m*. *as a* ~, pour mémoire. ~ *book*, carnet, calepin, *m*. ~ [*of association*], statuts, *m.pl*. **memorial**, *n*, mémorandum; cahier; monument, *m*. **memorize**, *v.t*, fixer dans la mémoire. **memory**, *n*, mémoire, *f*; souvenir, *m*; (*pl.*) souvenances, *f.pl. from* ~, de mémoire, de tête.

menace, *n*, menace, *f*. *public* ~ (*pers.*), malfaiteur public, *m*. ¶ *v.t*, menacer.

menagerie, *n*, ménagerie, *f*.

mend, *v.t*, raccommoder; réparer; repriser; améliorer; réformer.

mendacious, *a*, mensonger. **mendacity**, *n*, l'habitude du mensonge, *f*.

mender, *n*, raccommodeur, euse, réparateur, trice.

mendicancy *&* **mendicity**, *n*, mendicité, *f*. **mendicant**, *a. & n*, mendiant, e.

mending, *n*, raccommodage, *m*, réparation; reprise, *f*.

menhir, *n*, menhir, peulven, *m*.

menial, *a*, servile. ¶ *n*, laquais, *m*.

meningitis, *n*, méningite, *f*.

mensuration, *n*, mesure, *f*; (*science*) mesures, *f.pl*; (*of the body*) mensuration, *f*.

mental, *a*, mental; moral. ~ *arithmetic*, calcul mental, *m*. ~ *institution*, maison d'aliénés, *f*, asile d'a~s, *m*. ~ *patient*, aliéné, e. ~ *reservation*, restriction mentale, arrière-pensée, *f.* ~ *specialist*, médecin aliéniste, *m.* ~**ity**, *n*, mentalité, *f.* ~**ly**, *ad.* mentalement. ~ *deficient*, à petite mentalité.

menthol, *n*, menthol, *m*.

mention, *n*, mention; constatation, *f.* ~ *in dispatches*, citation à l'ordre de l'armée, *f.* ¶ *v.t*, mentionner, parler de, prononcer; indiquer; citer; constater. *don't* ~ *it!* il n'y a pas de quoi!, du tout!

Mentone, *n*, Menton, *m*.

menu, *n*, menu, *m*; carte du jour, *f.* ~ *holder*, porte-menu, *m*.

mercantile, *a*, marchand, commercial, de commerce; (*mercenary*) mercantile. ~ *marine*, marine marchande, *f.* ~ *office*, ~ *agency*, agence de renseignements.

Mercator's projection, projection de Mercator, *f.*

mercenary, *a*, mercenaire, stipendiaire, vénal, mercantile. ¶ *n*, mercenaire, *m*.

mercer, *n*, marchand de soieries, *m*. ~**ized**, *a*, mercerisé.

merchandise, *n*, marchandise, *f.* oft. *pl*.

merchant, *n*, négociant, e, commerçant, e; marchand, e. *the* ~ *class*, le haut commerce. ~**man**, navire marchand, *m*. ~ *service*, marine marchande, *f.*

merciful†, *a*, miséricordieux, clément. **merciless†**, *a*, impitoyable.

mercurial, *a*, (*Chem.*) mercuriel; (*barometer*, *&c*) à mercure; (*fig.*) vif. **mercury**, *n*, (*metal*) mercure, *m*; (*Bot.*) mercuriale, *f.*

mercy, *n*, miséricorde, merci, clémence, grâce, *f*, bienfait, bien, *m*; pitié, *f.* *at the* ~ *of*, à la merci de; au gré de. ~ *on us!* miséricorde! ~ *seat*, propitiatoire, *m*.

mere†, *a*, simple, pur, seul. ~ *nothing*, un rien. ¶ *n*, lac, *m*.

meretricious, *a*, de courtisane; factice.

merge, *v.t*, fondre; fusionner.

meridian, *n. & a* méridien, *m*. & *a*. **meridional**, *a. & n*, méridional, e.

meringue, *n*, meringue, *f.*

merino, *n*, mérinos, *m*.

merit, *n*, mérite, *m*. ¶ *v.t*, mériter. **meritorious**, *a*, méritoire; (*of pers.*) méritant.

merlin (*bird*) *n*, émerillon, *m*.

mermaid, *n*, sirène, *f.* **merman**, *n*, triton, *m*.

merrily, *ad*, gaiement, joyeusement; gai! **merriment**, *n*, gaieté, joie, hilarité, *f.* **merry**, *a*, gai, joyeux; jovial. *a* ~ *Christmas!* joyeux Noël! *make* ~, se réjouir, s'égayer. *make* ~ *over*, se divertir [aux dépens] de. ~ *andrew*, bouffon, paillasse, *m*. ~**-go-round**, manège de chevaux de bois, carrousel, *m*. ~ *making*, réjouissances, *f.pl.* ~**thought**, lunette, fourchette, *f.*

merry (*wild cherry*) *n*, merise, *f.*

mesh, *n*, maille, *f.* *in* ~ (*Mech.*), en prise. ¶ *v.t*, engrener.

mesmeric, *a*, magnétique. **mesmerism**, *n*,

magnétisme, *m*. **mesmerist**, *n*, magnétiseur, *m*. **mesmerize**, *v.t*, magnétiser.

mess, *n*, mets, plat, *m*; (*Mil.*, *Nav.*) table, *f*, mess, *m*; gamelle, *f*; ordinaire; plat; (*fig.*) gâchis, margouillis, pétrin, chef-d'œuvre, *m*; saleté, *f.* ~**mate**, camarade de plat, *m,f*, commensal, e. ~ *room*, salle à manger, *f.* ~ *tin*, gamelle, *f.* ¶ *v.t*, salir; (*v.i.*) manger. ~ *about*, tripoter. ~ *up*, gâcher.

message, *n*, message, *m*; dépêche, *f.* **messenger**, *n*, messager, ère; envoyé, e; ambassadeur, drice; courrier; commissionnaire; porteur; chasseur; garçon de bureau, *m*.

Messiah, *n*, Messie, *m*.

Messina, *n*, Messine, *f.*

messuage, *n*, maison et ses dépendances.

messy, *a*, sale, graisseux.

metal, *n*, métal, *m*; (*for roads*) matériaux d'empierrement; (*pl*, *Rly*) rails, *m.pl.* ~ *saw*, *screw*, scie, vis, à métaux, *f.* ~ *worker*, (*ouvrier*) serrurier, *m*. ¶ (*road*) *v.t*, empierrer, ferrer. **metallic**, *a*, métallique; (*voice*) cuivrée. **metalliferous**, *a*, métallifère. **metallurgist**, *n*, métallurgiste, *m*. **metallurgy**, *n*, métallurgie, *f.*

metamorphose, *v.t*, métamorphoser. **metamorphosis**, *n*, métamorphose, *f.*

metaphor, *n*, métaphore, *f.* ~**ical†**, *a*, métaphorique.

metaphysical, *a*, métaphysique. **metaphysician**, *n*, métaphysicien, *m*. **metaphysics**, *n.pl*, métaphysique, *f.*

mete [**out**], *v.t*, mesurer, doser.

meteor, *n*, météore, *m*. ~**ic**, *a*, météorique. ~**ite**, *n*, aérolithe, *m*. ~**ologic(al)**, *a*, météorologique. ~**ology**, *n*, météorologie, *f.*

meter, *n*, compteur, *m*.

method, *n*, méthode, *f*, mode, *m*, modalité, *f.* ~**ical†**, *a*, méthodique. ~**ism**, *n*, méthodisme, *m*. ~**ist**, *n*, méthodiste, *m,f.*

methyl (*Chem.*) *n*, méthyle, *m*. ~**ated** *spirit*, alcool dénaturé, alcool à brûler, *m*.

meticulous†, *a*, méticuleux.

metonymy, *n*, métonymie, *f.*

metre (*Poet.*) *n*, mesure, *f*, mètre, *m*. ~**-gauge** *railway*, chemin de fer à voie de 1 mètre, *m*. **metric & metrical**, *a*, métrique. **metrics** (*Poet.*) *n*, métrique, *f.*

metronome, *n*, métronome, *m*.

metropolis, *n*, capitale; métropole, *f.* **metropolitan**, *a*, de la capitale; métropolitain.

mettle, *n*, fougue, *f*, panache, cran; honneur, *m*. ~**some**, *a*, fougueux.

mew, *n*, (*sea gull*) mouette, *f*; (*cage for hawks*) mue, *f.* ¶ *v.i*, miauler. ~[**ing**], *n*, miaulement, *m*. **mews**, *n*, écuries, *f.pl.*

Mexican, *a*, mexicain. ¶ *n*, Mexicain, e. **Mexico** (*country*) *n*, le Mexique. ~ [**City**], Mexico, *m*.

mezzanine [**floor**], *n*, entresol, *m*. **mezzorelievo**, *n*, demi-relief, *m*. **mezzo-soprano**, *n*, mezzo-soprano, *m.* **mezzotint,** *n*, manière noire; gravure à la m. n., *f.*

miaow, *n*, miaulement, *m.* ¶ *v.i.* miauler.

miasma, *n*, miasme, *m.*

mica, *n*, mica, *m.*

Michaelmas, *n*, la Saint-Michel. ~ *daisy*, marguerite de la Saint-Michel, *f.*

microbe, *n*, microbe, *m.*

micrometer, *n*, micromètre, palmer, *m.*

microphone, *n*, microphone, *m.*

microscope, *n*, microscope, *m.* **microscopic(al),** *a*, microscopique.

mid, *a: in ~ air, Channel*, au milieu de l'air, de la Manche. ~*day*, midi, *m.* ~*iron* (*Golf*), fer moyen, *m.* ~ *lent*, la mi-carême. ~*night*, minuit, *m.* ~*shipman*, aspirant [de marine] *m.* ~*summer*, milieu de l'été, *m. Midsummer day*, la Saint-Jean; le 24 juin. ~*way*, *adj*, à moitié chemin, à mi-chemin. ~*wife*, sage-femme, *f.* ~*wifery*, l'obstétrique, *f. in ~ winter*, en plein hiver.

middle, *a*, du milieu; moyen. ~*-aged*, d'âge moyen, entre deux âges. ~ *ages*, moyen âge, *m.* ~ *class[es]*, classe moyenne, bourgeoisie, *f.* ~*class house*, maison bourgeoise, *f.* ~*class man*, *woman*, bourgeois, e. ~ *course* (*conduct*), moyen terme, *m.* ~ *distance*, second plan, *m.* ~*-distance race*, course de demi-fond, *f. the M ~ East*, l'Orient moyen, *m.* ~*finger*, doigt du milieu, médius, *m.* ~*man*, intermédiaire, *m.* ~ *register* (*Mus.*), médium, *m.* ~ [*term*] (*Log.*), moyen [terme] *m.* ~ *weight* (*Box.*), poids moyen, *m.* ¶ *n*, milieu; centre, *m;* (*waist*) ceinture, *f.*

middling†, *a*, moyen; médiocre. ¶ *ad*, assez bien, entre deux, comme ci, comme ça, cahin-caha. ~**s** (*flour*) *n.pl*, recoupe, *f.*

midge, *n*, moucheron, cousin, *m.*

midget, *n*, nabot, e, [petit] bout d'homme, *m.* ~ *pin*, camion, *m.*

midnight, midshipman, &*c.* See under **mid.**

midst, *n*, milieu, sein, *m.*

mien, *n*, mine, *f*, air, *m.*

might, *n*, puissance; force, *f. with ~ & main*, de toutes ses forces. *one ~ as well*, autant vaut. *a ~-have-been*, un grand homme manqué. **mightiness,** *n*, puissance; grandeur, *f.* **mighty†,** *a*, puissant. *the ~ ones*, les puissants, *m.pl.*

mignonette, *n*, (*Bot.*) réséda, *m;* (*lace*) mignon-nette, *f.*

migrant, *a*, migrateur. **migrate,** *v.i*, émigrer, voyager. **migration,** *n*, migration, *f.* **migratory,** *a*, migrateur, voyageur, de passage.

Milan, *n*, Milan, *m.* ~**ese,** *a*, milanais. ¶ *n*, Milanais, e.

milch cow, vache à lait, vache laitière; (*fig.*) vache à lait, *f.*

mild†, *a*, doux; bénin; anodin. **mildew,** *n*, moisi, *m*, moisissure; (*blight on*

plants) rouille, *f;* (*on vines*) mildiou, *m.* ¶ *v.t*, moisir; (*v.i.*) [se] moisir.

mildness, *n*, douceur, *f.*

mile, *n*, mille [anglais] *m.* = 1·6093 kilo-metres (*Note:—To convert miles to kilo-metres, approximately, multiply miles by 8 and divide by 5*); (*long way*) lieue, *f. a ~ off*, d'une lieue. ~ *stone*, pierre milliaire; (*Fr.*) borne kilométrique, *f.*

milfoil, *n*, mille-feuille, millefeuille, *f.*

militant, *a. & n*, militant, *a. & m.* **militarize,** *v.t*, militariser. **military†,** *a. & ~ man*, militaire, *a. & m. the ~*, les militaires, *m.pl. ~ pageant*, scène militaire à grand spectacle, *f.* **militate,** *v.i*, militer. **militia,** *n*, milice, *f.* ~*man*, milicien, *m.*

milk, *n*, lait, *m.* ~ *& water*, lait coupé. ~ *chocolate*, chocolat lacté, c. au lait, *m.* ~ *diet*, régime lacté, *m*, diète lactée, *f.* ~ *fever*, fièvre de lait, *f.* ~ *food*, laitage *m.* ~ *jug*, pot à lait, *m.* ~*maid*, fille de ferme, *f.* ~*man*, ~*woman*, laitier, ère. ~*sop* (*pers.*), poule mouillée, *f.* ~ *tooth*, dent de lait, *f.* ~ *van* (*Rly*), wagon-laitière, *m.* ¶ *v.t*, traire, tirer. ~*er*, *n*, trayeur, euse; (*cow*) laitière, *f.* ~*ing*, *n*, traite, mulsion, *f.* **milky,** *a*, laiteux *M~ Way*, voie lactée, *f.*

mill, *n*, moulin, *f*, fabrique; usine, *f;* atelier *m.* ~*board*, carton [épais] *m.* ~*hand*, ouvrier (ère) d'usine. ~*owner*, industriel usinier, *m.* ~*stone*, meule de moulin, *f.* ~*stone grit* & ~*stone grit quarry*, meulière *f.* ¶ *v.t*, moudre; (*ore*, &*c*) bocarder broyer; (*cloth*) fouler; (*to knurl*) moleter (*to slot*) fraiser; (*a coin*) créneler. ~*ed edge*, cordon[net], crénelage, *m.*

millenary, *n*, millénaire, *a. & m* **millennium,** *n*, millénaire; (*fig.*) bonheur sans mélange, paradis terrestre, *m.*

millepede, *n*, mille-pieds, mille-pattes, *m.*

miller, *n*, meunier, ère, minotier, *m;* farinier, ère.

millet, *n*, millet, mil, *m.* ~ *grass*, millet, *m*

milliard (*1,000,000,000*) *n*, milliard, *m.*

milliner, *n*, modiste, *f;* marchand(e) de modes. ~*'s head*, marotte, *f.* ~*y*, *n* modes, *f.pl*, articles de modes, *m.pl.*

milling, *n*, (*flour*) meunerie, minoterie, *f;* (*ore*) broyage; (*cloth*) foulage; (*metal*) fraisage (*coins*) crénelage, grènetis, *m.* ~ *cutter* fraise, *f.* ~ *machine*, machine à fraiser, *f.*

million, *n*, million, *m. the ~*, la multitude la masse du peuple. **millionaire,** *n*, mil lionnaire, *m,f.* **millionth,** *a. & n*, millio nième, *a. & m.*

milt, *n*, (*in mammals*) rate; (*in fish*) laitance laite, *f.* ¶ *v.t*, féconder.

mime, *n*, mime, *m.* ¶ *v.i*, mimer. **mimic** *a*, mimique, imitateur. ~ *war*, petit guerre, *f.* ¶ *n*, mime, *m*, imitateur, trice ¶ *v.t*, mimer, imiter, contrefaire. **mimicry** *n*, mimique, *f.* **mimicry or mimesi** (*Zool.*) *n*, mimétisme, *m.*

nimosa, *n*, mimosa, *m*.

nince, *n*, hachis, *m*. ~meat, chair à pâté, *i.* ¶ *v.t*, (*meat*) hacher [menu]; (*v.i.*) minauder. ~ one's words, ménager les termes; parler avec affectation. not to ~ matters, ne pas le mâcher. **mincer**, *n*, hachoir, *m*. **mincing** (*fig.*) *n*, minauderie, *f*. ¶ *a*, minaudier, mignard, affété, grimacier.

nind, *n*, esprit, *m*; âme, *f*; moral; cerveau, *m*, cervelle, *f*; envie; idée, pensée, *f*; avis, *m*, opinion, *f*. go out of one's ~, perdre la raison. ¶ *v.t*, faire attention à; se soucier de; regarder à; attention. ~! attention!, casse-cou! ~ your own business! mêlez-vous de vos affaires! faites votre métier! -~ed, *a*, disposé, porté, pensant, enclin. ~er, *n*, soigneur, *m*. ~ful, *a*, attentif.

aine, *pn*, le mien, la mienne, les miens, les miennes; à moi. a friend of ~, un de mes amis, un ami à moi.

aine, *n*, mine; (*fig.*) mine, *f*, filon, *m*; (*War*) mine, torpille, *f*. ~ crater, entonnoir, *m*. ~ layer, poseur de mines, *m*. ~ sweeper, dragueur de mines, *m*. ¶ *v.t. & i*, exploiter; abattre; fouiller; miner; caver; torpiller. **miner**, *n*, mineur, *m*. **mineral**, *a. & n*, minéral, *a. & m*. ~ water, eau minérale (naturelle) *f*. ~ [water], eau minérale [artificielle] *f*. **mineralogical**, *a*, minéralogique. **mineralogist**, *n*, minéralogiste, *m*. **mineralogy**, *n*, minéralogie, *f*.

ainever, -iver, *n*, petit-gris, *m*.

aingle, *v.t*, mélanger, mêler, confondre.

iniature, *n*, miniature, *f*; diminutif, *m*. ~ golf, golf miniature, g. réduit, *m*. ~ home set, [petit] ménage, *m*. **miniaturist**, *n*, miniaturiste, *m*.

inim, *n*, (*Mus.*) blanche, *f*; (*apothecaries' measure*) = 0·059 millilitre.

inimize, *v.t*, atténuer. **minimum**, *n. & a*, minimum, *m. & a*.

aining, *n*, exploitation [de mines] *f*; (*att.*) minier. ~ engineer, ingénieur [civil] des mines, *m*.

inion, *n*, mignon, favori, *m*. ~s of the law, recors de la justice, *m.pl*.

inister, *n*, ministre; pasteur, *m*. ~ to, pourvoir à; servir; (*Eccl.*) desservir. ~ial, *a*, ministériel. ~ing angel, ange de bonté, ange; sœur de charité, *f*. **ministration**, *n*, ministère, *m*. **ministry**, *n*, ministère; département; sacerdoce, *m*. ~ *M*—of Health, of Labour, Ministère de Santé publique, du Travail.

ink (*Zool. & fur*), *n*, vison, *m*.

innow, *n*, vairon, *m*.

inor, *a*, petit; secondaire, subalterne; moindre; peu important; peu grave; mineur; (*repairs*) menues; (*planet*) télescopique; (*pers.*) jeune, cadet; (*poet*) de second ordre. ~ road, route secondaire, *f*. ¶ *n*, (*pers.*) mineur, e; (*Mus.*) mineur, *m*.

norca, *n*, Minorque, *f*.

minority, *n*, minorité, *f*.

minster, *n*, église de monastère, é. abbatiale; cathédrale, *f*.

minstrel, *n*, (*Hist.*) ménestrel; chanteur, musicien, *m*. [*negro*] ~s, orchestre noir, *m*.

mint, *n*, Monnaie, *f*, hôtel de la Monnaie, h. des Monnaies, *m*; (*fig.*) mine; (*Bot.*) menthe, *f*. a ~ of money, un argent fou. ¶ *v.t*, monnayer, frapper. ~er, *n*, monnayeur, *m*.

minuet, *n*, menuet, *m*.

minus, *pr*, moins. ~ quantity, déficit, *m*. ~ [sign], *n*, [signe] moins, *m*.

minute, *a*, menu, minime, minuscule; minutieux. ¶ *n*, minute, *f*; procès-verbal, *m*. ~ book, registre des délibérations, r. des procès-verbaux, plumitif, *m*. ~ gun, coups de canon tirés de minute en minute, *m.pl*. ~ hand, aiguille des minutes, *f*. ¶ *v.t*, minuter; constater par procès-verbal. ~ly, *ad*, minutieusement. ~ness & minutia, *n*, minutie, *f*.

minx, *n*, coquine, friponne, masque, *f*.

miracle, *n*, miracle, *m*. ~ [play], miracle, mystère, *m*. **miraculous†**, *a*, miraculeux.

mirage, *n*, mirage, *m*.

mire, *n*, fange, boue, *f*. ¶ *v.t*, embourber.

mirror, *n*, miroir, *m*, glace, *f*. ¶ *v.t*, refléter.

mirth, *n*, joie, gaieté, *f*. ~ful†, *a*, joyeux, gai.

miry, *a*, fangeux, boueux.

misadventure, *n*, mésaventure, *f*.

misalliance, *n*, mésalliance, *f*. make a ~, se mésallier. **misally**, *v.t*, mésallier.

misanthrope, -pist, *n*, misanthrope, *m*. **misanthropic(al)**, *a*, misanthropique, misanthrope.

misapply, *v.t*, mal appliquer; détourner.

misapprehend, *v.t*, mal comprendre. **misapprehension**, *n*, malentendu, *m*.

misappropriate, *v.t*, détourner, dilapider.

misbehave [oneself], se comporter mal. **misbehaviour**, *n*, mauvaise conduite, inconduite, *f*.

miscalculate, *v.i*, se tromper. **miscalculation**, *n*, erreur de calcul, *f*, mécompte, *m*.

miscarriage, *n*, (*letter, &c*) égarement, *m*; (*Med.*) fausse couche, *f*; (*failure*) avortement, insuccès, *m*. ~ of justice, mal-jugé, *m*. **miscarry**, *v.i*, s'égarer; (*Med.*) faire une fausse couche; (*fail*) avorter, échouer, rater.

miscellaneous, *a*, divers; mêlé. ~ works or **miscellany** or **miscellanea**, *n*, mélanges, *m.pl*, variétés, *f.pl*; recueil factice, *m*.

mischance, *n*, infortune, fatalité, *f*.

mischief, *n*, mal, *m*; (*playful*) espièglerie, *f*. ~ maker, boutefeu, *m*. **mischievous†**, *a*, méchant; espiègle.

misconceive, *v.i*, mal concevoir. **misconception**, *n*, malentendu, *m*.

misconduct, *n*, déportements, *m.pl*; inconduite, *f*. ~ oneself, se conduire mal.

misconstruction, *n*, contresens, *m*. **misconstrue**, *v.t*, prendre à rebours.

miscreant, *n*, gredin, scélérat, *m*.

miscue, *n*, faux coup de queue, *m*.

misdeal (*Cards*) *n*, maldonne, *f*.

misdeed, *n*, méfait, *m*.

misdeliver, *v.t*, livrer par erreur.

misdemeanant, *n*, délinquant, e. **misdemeanour**, *n*, délit, *m*.

misdirect, *v.t*, mal diriger; (*a letter*) se tromper d'adresse sur.

miser, *n*, avare, *m,f*, harpagon, *m*.

miserable†, *a*, misérable, malheureux; chétif.

misère (*Cards*) *n*, misère, *f*.

miserere, *n*, miserere, *m*.

misericord, *n*, miséricorde, *f*.

miserly, *a*, avare.

misery, *n*, misère, *f*; souffrances, *f.pl*.

misfire, *n*, raté [d'allumage] *m*. ¶ *v.i*, rater, manquer.

misfit, *n*, vêtement mal ajusté, v. manqué, *m*; chaussure manquée, *f*.

misfortune, *n*, malheur, *m*, infortune, adversité, disgrâce, misère, *f*.

misgiving, *n*, doute, *f*; pressentiment, *m*.

misgovern, *v.t*, mal gouverner. **~ment**, *n*, mauvais gouvernement, *m*.

misguide, *v.t*, égarer; abuser. **misguided**, *p.p*, mal dirigé, dévoyé.

mishap, *n*, contretemps, *m*, mésaventure, *f*.

misinform, *v.t*, mal renseigner.

misinterpretation, *n*, contresens, *m*.

misjudge, *v.t*, mal juger.

mislay, *v.t*, égarer.

mislead, *v.t*, égarer, fourvoyer, abuser; induire en erreur; tromper. **~ing**, *p.a*, décevant, fallacieux.

mismanage, *v.t*, mal faire, mal gérer. **~ment**, *n*, mauvaise gestion, *f*.

misnamed, *p.p*, mal nommé.

misnomer, *n*, erreur de nom, *f*.

misogynist, *n*, misogyne, *m*.

misplace, *v.t*, mal placer.

misprint, *n*, faute d'impression, erreur typographique, coquille, *f*.

mispronounce, *v.t*, mal prononcer. **mispronunciation**, *n*, vice de prononciation, *m*.

misquotation, *n*, citation inexacte, *f*. **misquote**, *v.t*, citer à faux.

misrepresent, *v.t*, travestir, dénaturer. **~ation**, *n*, travestissement, *m*; déclaration inexacte, *f*.

misrule, *n*, mauvaise administration, *f*.

miss, *n*, manque [à toucher] *m*; demoiselle, *f*. *M~*, mademoiselle; Mademoiselle, *f*. ¶ *v.t. & i*, manquer; rater; regretter; sauter. *~ fire*, rater, manquer. *~ the point*, porter à faux.

missal, *n*, missel, *m*.

missel thrush, *n*, drenne, *f*.

misshapen, *a*, contrefait, biscornu, difforme, malbâti.

missile, *n*, arme de trait, arme de jet, *f*; projectile, *m*.

missing, *a*, manquant; (*ship*) [perdu] sans nouvelles. *~ link*, chaînon manquant, *m*. *the ~* (*Mil*.), les disparus, *m.pl*. *be ~*, manquer.

mission, *n*, mission, *f*. **~ary**, *n*, missionnaire, *m*. **missive**, *n*, missive, *f*.

misspell, *v.t*, mal orthographier. **~ing**, *n*, faute d'orthographe, *f*.

misstatement, *n*, déclaration inexacte, *f*.

mist, *n*, brouillard, *m*, brume; brouillasse; vapeur, *f*, nuage, voile, *m*.

mistake, *n*, erreur, faute, bévue; méprise, *f*, quiproquo, tort, *m*. ¶ *v.t.ir*, se méprendre sur, se tromper de, confondre. **mistaken**, *a*, erroné. *~ identity*, erreur de (*ou* sur la) personne, *f*. *~ kindness*, indulgence mal comprise, *f*. *be ~*, se tromper.

mister, *n*, monsieur, *m*.

mistletoe, *n*, gui, *m*.

mistranslation, *n*, contresens, *m*.

mistress, *n*, maîtresse; patronne; institutrice, *f*; professeur, *m*; madame, *f*. *be one's own ~*, s'appartenir.

mistrust, *n*, méfiance, défiance, *f*. ¶ *v.t*, se méfier de, se défier de. **~ful**, *a*, méfiant, défiant.

misty, *a*, brumeux; vaporeux; trouble.

misunderstand, *v.t.ir*, mal comprendre, méconnaître. **~ing**, *n*, malentendu, *m*, mésintelligence, brouille, *f*; quiproquo, *m*. **misunderstood** (*pers*.) *p.a*, incompris.

misuse, *n*, abus, *m*. ¶ *v.t*, abuser de, galvauder; maltraiter.

mite, *n*, (*farthing*) obole, *f*, denier, *m*; (*child*) petit, e; (*insect*) mite, *f*, acare, ciron, *m*.

mitigate, *v.t*, atténuer; mitiger; modérer.

mitre, *n*, (*bishop's*) mitre, *f*; (*Carp*.) onglet, *m*. **~d**, *a*, mitré (*Carp*.) à onglet.

mitt[en], *n*, moufle, mitaine, *f*.

mix, *v.t*, mêler, mélanger, malaxer; (*salad*) retourner. **mixed**, *a*, mêlé, &c; mixte; hétérogène. *~ bathing*, bain mixte, *m*. *~ double* (*Ten*.), double mixte, *m*. *~ ice*, glace panachée, *f*. *~ metaphor*, métaphore incohérente, *f*. *~ school*, école mixte, *f*. **mixture**, *n*, mélange, *m*; mixture, *f*; ambigu, *m*; (*Med*.) mixtion, *f*; (*fodder*) farrago; (*cloth*) drap mélangé, *m*, *wool ~*, laine mélangée, *f*.

miz[z]en [sail], *n. & miz*[z]*en mast*, artimon, *m*.

mizzle, *n*, bruine, *f*. ¶ *v.imp*, bruiner.

mnemonic, *a*, mnémonique. **~s**, *n.pl*, mnémonique, *f*.

moan, *n*, gémissement, *m*, plainte, *f*. ¶ *v.i*, gémir, se plaindre.

moat, *n*, fossé, *m*, douve, *f*.

mob, *n*, foule; canaille, populace, *f*. *~ law*, domination de la lie du peuple, *f*. ¶ *v.t*, houspiller.

mobile, *a*, mobile. **mobility**, *n*, mobilité, *f*.

Mocha, *n*, Moka, *m*. *Mocha coffee* or *mocha*, *n*, café de Moka, moka, *m*.

mock, *v.t*, se moquer de; singer. ~ *fight*, simulacre de combat, *m*. ~*-heroic*, héroï-comique. ~**er**, *n*, moqueur, euse. ~**ery**, *n*, moquerie, *f*. ~*ing bird*, [oiseau] moqueur, *m*.

mode, *n*, (*way, fashion*) mode, *f*; (*form, method*) mode, *m*.

model, *n*, modèle, *m*; maquette, *f*; mannequin, *m*; (*att*.) modèle. ¶ *v.t*, modeler. **modeller**, *n*, modeleur, *m*. **modelling**, *n*, modelage; modelé, *m*.

moderate, *a*, modéré; (*price*) modique. ¶ *v.t*, modérer, tempérer. ~**ly**, *ad*, modérément, moyennement. ~**ness**, *n*, modicité, *f*. **moderation**, *n*, modération, *f*.

modern, *a. & n*, moderne, *a. & m*. ~ *language*, langue vivante, *f*. ~**ize**, *v.t*, moderniser.

modest†, *a*, modeste. ~**y**, *n*, modestie, *f*.

modicum, *n*, petite quantité; légère dose, *f*, grain, *m*.

modification, *n*, modification, *f*. **modify**, *v.t*, modifier.

modish, *a*, à la mode, de mode. ~**ly**, *ad*, à la mode.

modulate, *v.t*, moduler. **modulation**, *n*, modulation, *f*. **module & modulus**, *n*, module, *m*.

modus operandi, mode d'opération, *m*.

modus vivendi, modus vivendi, *m*.

mohair, *n*, poil de chèvre d'Angora, mohair, *m*.

Mohammedan, *n. & a*, mahométan, e. ~**ism**, *n*, mahométisme, *m*.

moiety, *n*, moitié, *f*.

moil, *v.i*, peiner.

moire, *n*, moire, *f*. **moiré**, *v.t*, moirer. ~ *silk*, moire de soie, soie moirée, *f*.

moist, *a*, humide; moite. ~ *sugar*, cassonade, *f*. ~**en**, *v.t*, humecter; mouiller. ~**ness & ~ure**, *n*, humidité; moiteur; buée, *f*.

molar, *a. & n*, molaire, *a. & f*.

molasses, *n*, mélasse, *f*.

mole, *n*, nævus, *m*, couenne, *f*, grain de beauté; (*jetty*) môle, *m*; (*Zool*.) taupe, *f*. ~ *hill*, taupinière, *f*. ~**skin**, [fourrure de] taupe; moleskine, *f*. ~ *trap*, taupière, *f*.

molecular, *a*, moléculaire. **molecule**, *n*, molécule, *f*.

molest, *v.t*, tourmenter, inquiéter, importuner. ~**ation**, *n*, importunité, *f*.

mollify, *v.t*, amollir; adoucir.

mollusc, *n*, mollusque, *m*.

molly, *n*, efféminé, *m*. ~*-coddle*, poule mouillée, *f*.

molten, *p.p*, fondu, en fusion, en bain.

Moluccas (the), les Moluques, *f.pl*.

moment, *n*, moment; instant, *m*; importance, *f*. *a* ~ *ago*, à l'instant. ~**ary**†, *a*, momentané, passager. ~**ous**, *a*, de la dernière importance. **momentum**, *n*, (*Mech*.) moment; (*impetus*) élan, *m*.

monarch, *n*, monarque, *m*. ~**ic(al)**, *a*,

monarchique. ~**ist**, *n*, monarchiste, *m*. ~**y**, *n*, monarchie, *f*.

monastery, *n*, monastère, couvent, *m*. **monastic**, *a*, monastique, monacal. **monastically**, *ad*, monacalement.

Monday, *n*, lundi, *m*.

monetary, *a*, monétaire. **monetize**, *v.t*, transformer en monnaie. **money**, *n*, argent, *m*; monnaie, *f*; numéraire, *m*; fonds, *m.pl*; capital, *m*, capitaux, *m.pl*; valeurs; finances, *f.pl*; deniers, *m.pl*. ~ *changer*, changeur, *m*. ~ *box*, tirelire; cassette, grenouillère, *f*. ~ *grubber*, grippe-sou, *m*. ~ *lender*, bailleur de fonds, *m*. ~ *market*, marché de l'argent, *m*. ~ *order*, mandat [de poste] *m*. ~**ed**, *a*, fortuné.

-monger, *n*, marchand, e; faiseur, euse.

Mongolia, *n*, la Mongolie. **Mongol[ian]**, *a*, mongol. ¶ *n*, Mongol, e.

mongoose, *n*, mangouste, *f*.

mongrel, *a*, métis, bâtard, mâtiné. ¶ *n*, métis, se, bâtard, e; (*cur*) roquet, *m*.

monk, *n*, moine, religieux, *m*. ~*'s-hood* (*Bot*.), aconit, napel, *m*. ~**ery & ~hood**, *n*, moinerie, *f*. ~**ish**, *a*, monacal.

monkey, *n*, singe, *m*, (*she*) guenon, guenuche, *f*; (*pile driving*) mouton, *m*. ~ *young* ~ (*child*), petit(e) babouin(e). ~ *house*, singerie, *f*. ~ *nut*, arachide, cacahuète, *f*. ~ *puzzle*, pin du Chili, *m*. ~ *trick*, singerie, *f*. ~ *wrench*, clef à molette, *f*.

monochord, *n*, monocorde, *m*. **monochrome**, *a*, monochrome. **monocle**, *n*, monocle, *m*. **monogamy**, *n*, monogamie, *f*. **monogram**, *n*, monogramme, chiffre, *m*. **monograph**, *n*, monographie, *f*. **monolith**, *n. & ~ic**, *a*, monolithe, *m. & a*. **monologize**, *v.i*, monologuer. **monologue**, *n*, monologue, *m*. **monomania**, *n*, monomanie, *f*. **monoplane**, *n*, monoplan, *m*. **monopolist**, *n*, accapareur, euse. **monopolize**, *v.t*, monopoliser, accaparer, s'emparer de. **monopoly**, *n*, monopole, *m*. **monosyllabic**, *a*, monosyllabique. **monosyllable**. **monosyllable**, *n*, monosyllabe, *m*. **monotonist** (*pers*.), *n*, monocorde, *m*. **monotonous**, *a*, monotone. **monotony**, *n*, monotonie, *f*. **monotype**, *n*, monotype, *f*.

monster, *n. & a*, monstre, *m. & att*.

monstrance, *n*, ostensoir, *m*.

monstrosity, *n*, monstruosité, *f*. **monstrous**†, *a*, monstrueux.

Mont Blanc, le mont Blanc. **Montenegrin**, *a*, monténégrin. ¶ *n*, Monténégrin, e. **Montenegro**, *n*, le Monténégro. **Monte Rosa**, le mont Rose.

month, *n*, mois, *m*. ~*'s pay, rent, or like*, mois, *m*. **monthly**, *a*, mensuel; au mois. ~ *nurse*, garde [d'accouchée] *f*. ~ *payment, drawing, salary, or like*, mensualité, *f*. ~ *statement* (*Com*.), relevé de fin de mois, *m*. ¶ *ad*, mensuellement, par mois. ¶ *n*, revue mensuelle, *f*.

monument, *n*, monument; tombeau, *m*. ~al, *a*, monumental. ~ *mason*, entrepreneur de monuments funéraires, marbrier, *m*.

moo, *v.i*, beugler. ¶ *n*, beuglement, *m*.

mood, *n*, humeur, *f*, train; (*Gram.*) mode, *m*. ~y, *a*, morose, chagrin.

moon, *n*, lune, *f*. ~*beam*, rayon de l., *m*. ~*light*, clair de l., *m*. ~*lit*, éclairé par la l. ~*shine*, contes en l'air, *m.pl*. ~*stone*, pierre de lune, *f*. ~*struck*, toqué. ~ [about], muser.

moor & ~*land*, *n*, lande, brande, bruyère, *f*. ~ *cock*, coq de bruyère, *m*. ~ *hen*, poule d'eau, *f*.

Moor (*pers.*) *n*, More, Maure, *m*.

moor, *v.t*, amarrer, mouiller. ~ing, *n*, amarrage, mouillage; (*pl.*) mouillage; (*dolphin*) corps mort, *m*.

Moorish, *a*, more, maure.

moose, *n*, élan, *m*.

moot, *a*, discutable, contestable. ¶ *v.t*, soulever.

mop, *n*, lavette, *f*; écouvillon, *m*; (*of hair*) tignasse, *f*. ~ *broom*, balai à éponger, *m*. ¶ *v.t*, éponger. ~ *up*, essuyer, éponger.

mope, *v.i*, languir. *in the* ~*s*, dans une grande dépression.

moraine, *n*, moraine, *f*.

moral†, *a*, moral. ¶ *n*, (*of story, of fable*) morale, moralité, *f*; (*pl, manners*) mœurs, *f.pl*; (*pl, ethics*) morale, *f*. ~[e], *n*, moral, *m*. ~ist, *n*, moraliste, *m*. ~ity, *n*, moralité, *f*; [bonnes] mœurs, *f.pl*. ~ize, *v.i*. & *t*, moraliser.

morass, *n*, fondrière, *f*, marais, marécage, *m*.

moratorium, *n*, moratorium, moratoire, *m*.

Moravia, *n*, la Moravie.

morbid, *a*, morbide, maladif. **morbidezza**, *n*, morbidesse, mollesse, *f*.

mordant, *a*. & *m*, mordant, *a*. & *m*.

more, *a*, plus de; plus. ¶ *ad*, plus; davantage; encore; de plus. *2, 3*, ~ (*Golf*), *2, 3*, de plus. ~*over*, *ad*, d'ailleurs, aussi bien, en outre, du reste, encore.

Moresque, *a*, moresque, mauresque.

morganatic†, *a*, morganatique.

moribund, *a*, moribond.

morning & (*Poet.*) **morn**, *n*, matin, *m*; matinée; aurore, *f*. ~ *coat*, jaquette, *f*. ~ *dress*, tenue de ville, *f*. ~ *performance*, matinée, *f*. ~ *star*, étoile du matin, é. matinière, *f*. ~ *suit*, complet jaquette, *m*.

Moroccan, *a*, marocain. ¶ *n*, Marocain, e. **Morocco**, *n*, le Maroc. **morocco** [*leather*], maroquin, *m*.

morose, *a*, morose. ~ness, *n*, morosité, *f*.

Morpheus, *n*, Morphée, *m*. **morphia**, **-phine**, *n*, morphine, *f*. **morphinomaniac**, *n*, morphinomane, *m,f*.

morris [dance] (*Moorish*) *n*, [danse] moresque, [danse] mauresque, *f*.

morrow (the) & on the ~, le lendemain.

morsel, *n*, morceau, *m*.

mortal†, *a*, mortel; (*strife*) à mort, à outranc ¶ *n*, mortel, le. ~ity, *n*, mortalité, *f*.

mortar (*plaster, vessel, Mil.*) *n*, mortier, m

mortgage, *n*, hypothèque, *f*. ~ *deed*, co trat d'h., c. hypothécaire, *m*. ¶ *v.t*, hyp théquer; engager. **mortgagee**, *n*, créa cier hypothécaire, *m*. **mortgagor**, *n*, dét teur h., *m*.

mortification, *n*, mortification, *f*. **mortif** *v.t*, mortifier, affliger, mater.

mortise, -ice, *n*, mortaise, *f*. ~ *lock*, serru à entailler, *f*. ¶ *v.t*, emmortaiser.

mortmain, *n*, mainmorte, *f*. *property in* ~ biens de mainmorte, *m.pl*.

mortuary, *a*, mortuaire. ~ *chapel*, chapel sépulcrale, *f*. ¶ *n*, institut médico-légal, *n*

Mosaic (*of Moses*) *a*, mosaïque.

mosaic, *n*, mosaïque, marqueterie, *f*.

Moscow, *n*, Moscou, *m*.

Moslem, *n*. & *a*, mahométan, e.

mosque, *n*, mosquée, *f*.

mosquito, *n*, moustique; maringouin, *m*. ~ *net*, ~ *curtain*, moustiquaire, *f*.

moss, *n*, mousse, *f*. ~*-grown*, moussu. ~ *rose*, rose moussue, rose mousseuse, *f*. ~ *a*, mousseux; moussu.

most, *a*, le plus de; la plupart de. ~ *eminer* éminentissime. ~ *illustrious*, illustrissim ~ *reverend*, révérendissime. ¶ *ad*, le plu plus; très. ~ly, *ad*, pour la plupart.

mote, *n*, (*dust*) atome, *m*; (*in eye, fig.*) paille,

moth, *n*, papillon [de nuit] *m*; teigne, gerce, artison; ver, *m*, mite, *f*. ~*-eaten*, mang aux mites, artisonné.

mother, *n*, mère, *f*. ~ *church*, église métr politaine, *f*. ~ *country*, métropole, *f*. ~ *earth*, notre mère commune. ~*-in-la* belle-mère, *f*. ~ *of pearl*, nacre, *f*. ~ *side* (family), côté maternel, *m*. ~ *superio* mère supérieure, *f*. ~ *tongue*, (*nativ* langue maternelle; (*original*) l. mère, *f*. ~ *wit*, esprit naturel, *m*. ¶ *v.t*, servir d mère à; (*fig.*) couver. ~less, *a*, sa mère. ~ly, *a*, maternel, de mère.

motif, *n*, (*Art, Need.*) motif, *m*; (*literar* donnée, *f*. **motion**, *n*, mouvement, *m* marche, *f*; signe, *m*; (*proposal*) motion; pr position; (*Med.*) selle, garde-robe, *f*. ¶ *v* faire signe. ~less, *a*, sans mouvemen immobile. **motive**, *a*, moteur. ~ *powe* force motrice, *f*, mobile, *m*. ¶ *n*, raison, motif; mobile, *m*.

motley, *a*, bariolé, bigarré; mêlé. ¶ bariolage; habit d'arlequin, *m*.

motor, *n*, moteur, *m*. ~ [*bi*]*cycle*, mot cyclette, bicyclette à moteur, moto, *f*. ~ *boat*, canot automobile, *m*, vedette, *f*. ~ *body builder*, carrossier, *m*. ~ *bus*, aut bus, *m*. ~ [*car*], automobile, auto, *f*. ~ [*car*] *insurance*, assurance des véhicul automobiles, *f*. ~ *coach*, autocar, *m*. ~ *combination*, motocyclette avec side-car, ~ *cyclist*, motocycliste, *m,f*. ~ *lorr* camion automobile, *m*. ~*man*, wattma *m.* ~ *road,* autoroute, *f.* ~ *ship,* navire à moteur, *m.* ~ *show,* salon de l'automobile, *m.* ¶ *v.i,* aller en auto. ~**ing,** *n,* automobilisme, *m.* ~**ist,** *n,* automobiliste, *m,f.* ~**ize,** *v.t,* motoriser.

mottled soap, savon marbré, *m.*

motto, *n,* devise; (*of a device*) âme; (*prefixed to book or chapter*) épigraphe, *f;* (*Mus.*) motif, *m.*

mould, *n,* moule, creux, *m;* (*Typ.*) empreinte, *f,* flan; (*vegetable*) terreau, humus; (*ship*) gabarit; (*decay*) moisi, *m,* moisissure, *f.* ¶ *v.t,* mouler; modeler; (*Typ.*) prendre l'empreinte de. ~**er,** *n,* mouleur, *m.* ~**er [away],** *v.i,* tomber en poussière. **mouldiness,** *n,* moisissure, *f,* moisi, *m.* **moulding,** *n,* (*act*) moulage, *m;* (*ornamental strip*) moulure, *f.* **mouldy,** *a,* moisi. *turn* ~, [se] moisir.

moult, *v.i,* muer, se déplumer. ~**[ing],** *n,* mue, *f.*

mound, *n,* monticule, *m,* butte, *f,* tertre, *m,* bosse, motte, *f.*

mount, *n,* (*as Etna*) le mont; carton [pour montage photographique] *m;* (*horse, &c*) monture; (*Horse Racing*) monte, *f.* ¶ *v.i. & t,* monter. ~ [*on calico* or *linen*], entoiler.

mountain, *n,* montagne, *f.* ~ *ash,* sorbier des oiseaux, *m.* ~ *sickness,* mal de montagne, *e;* (*climber*) alpiniste, ascensionniste, *m,f.* ~**eering,** *n,* l'alpinisme, *m.* ~**ous,** *a,* montagneux; énorme.

mountebank, *n,* saltimbanque, baladin, *m.*

mounted, *p.a,* à cheval; monté. **mounter,** *n,* monteur, *m.* **mounting,** *n,* montage, *m;* monture; ferrure, *f.*

mourn, *v.t. & i,* pleurer. **the** ~**ers,** le deuil. [*hired*] ~**er,** pleureur, euse. ~**ful†,** *a,* douloureux. ~**ing,** *n,* deuil, *m.* ~ *band,* brassard de d., *m.* ~ *coach,* voiture de d., *f.* ~ *paper,* papier à lettres deuil, *m.*

mouse, *n,* souris, *f;* (*young*) souriceau, *m.* ~ *trap,* souricière, *f.*

moustache, *n,* moustache, *f.* ~**d,** *a,* moustachu.

mouth, *n,* bouche; embouchure; gueule, *f;* bec; orifice; trou, *m;* entrée; lumière, *f.* ~ *organ,* harmonica à bouche, *m.* ~ *piece,* embouchure, *f;* bec; (*pers.*) organe, porteparole, *m.* ~ *wash,* eau dentifrice, *f.* ~**ful,** *n,* bouchée, goulée, gorgée, *f.*

movable, *a,* mobile; (*Law*) meuble, mobilier. **move,** *n,* mouvement, *m;* manœuvre, *f;* (*Chess, &c*) coup, *m. whose* ~ *is it?* à qui à jouer? ¶ *v.t,* [faire] mouvoir; remuer; déplacer; jouer; affecter, toucher, émouvoir, attendrir; proposer; (*v.i.*) se mouvoir; bouger; déloger. ~ *along,* cheminer. ~ *back,* reculer. ~ *in* (house), emménager. ~ *off,* s'éloigner, s'ébranler. ~ *on!* circulez! ~ [*out*] (house), déménager. ~**ment,** *n,* mouvement, *m,* marche, *f;*

geste, *m.* **moving,** *p.a:* ~ *body* (Mech.), mobile, *m.* ~ *picture,* tableau mouvant, *m.* ~ *spirit,* animateur, *m.* ~ *staircase,* escalier roulant, *m.* ~ *moving van,* fourgon de déménagements, *m.*

mow, *n,* tas, *m.* ¶ *v.t.ir,* faucher; (*turf*) tondre. ~ *down,* faucher. ~**er,** *n,* (*pers.*) faucheur, *m;* (*Mach.*) faucheuse; (*lawn*) tondeuse, *f.*

Mr, Monsieur, M.; (*partner in firm*) sieur; (*courtesy title of lawyers*) maître, *m.* **Mrs,** Madame, Mme; (*Law*) la dame. *Note.— As a form of address on envelope or in letter* Monsieur *or* Madame *should not be abbreviated.*

much, *n. & ad,* beaucoup (de); grand-chose (*usually with neg.*); bien (de); très; cher. *as* ~, autant (de). *as* ~ *as,* autant que. *at* ~ *rain* (barometer), à [la] grande pluie. *so* ~, [au]tant (de). *very* ~, beaucoup; bien; très.

mucilage, *n,* mucilage, *m.*

muck, *n,* fumier, *m;* fange; cochonnerie, *saloperie, f.*

mucous, *a,* muqueux. ~ *membrane,* [membrane] muqueuse, *f.* **mucus,** *n,* mucosité, *f,* mucus, *m,* pituite, morve, *f.*

mud, *n,* boue, *f. oft. pl,* crotte, bourbe, fange; (*river*) vase, *f,* limon, *m.* ~ *bath,* bain de boue[s minérales] *m.* ~ *brush* (boots), brosse à décrotter, *f.* ~ *guard,* garde-crotte, garde-boue, pare-boue, *m.* ~ *lark,* barboteur, *m.* ~ *pie,* pâté, *m.* ~ *spring,* source boueuse, *f.*

muddle, *n,* [em]brouillamini; fouillis, *m.* ¶ *v.t,* [em]brouiller, emmêler; (*with drink*) griser. ~ *up,* tripoter. **muddler,** *n,* barboteur, euse, fatrassier, ère, brouillon, *m.*

muddy, *a,* boueux, crotté, bourbeux, fangeux; vaseux, limoneux; trouble. ¶ *v.t,* embouer.

muezzin, *n,* muezzin, *m.*

muff, *n,* manchon; (*pers.*) serin, *m,* jobard, *e,* huître, *f.* **muffle** (Chem.) *n,* moufle, *m.* ¶ *v.t,* assourdir; (*drum*) voiler. ~ *up,* embéguiner, emmitoufler. ~**d,** *p.a,* sourd. **muffler,** *n,* cache-nez, *m.*

mufti (in), en civil, en bourgeois.

mug, *n,* timbale, tasse, *f.*

muggy, *a,* mou.

mulatto, *n,* mulâtre, homme de couleur, *m,* mulâtresse, *f.* ¶ *a,* mulâtre.

mulberry, *n,* mûre, *f.* ~ (*tree*) mûrier, *m.*

mulch, *n,* paillis, *m.* ¶ *v.t,* pailler.

mulct, *v.t,* condamner (*in* = à).

mule, *n,* (*he & pers.*) mulet, *m,* (*she*) mule, *f;* (*pl, slippers*) mules, babouches, *f.pl.* ~ *track,* piste muletière, *f.* **muleteer,** *n,* muletier, *m.* **mulish,** *a,* têtu.

mulled wine, vin brûlé, *m.*

muller (*grinding*), *n,* molette, *f.*

mullet, *n,* (*grey*) mulet, muge; (*red*) rouget, *m.*

mullion, *n,* meneau, *m.*

multicolour[ed], *a,* multicolore.

multifarious, *a*, multiple.
multi-light standard, candélabre, *m*.
multi-millionaire, *n*. *& a*, milliardaire, *m, f. & a*.
multiple, *n. & a*, multiple, *m. & a*. ~ *firm*, maison à succursales multiples, *f*. ~ *fork* (of roads), patte d'oie, *f*. ~ *shop*, magasin à succursales multiples, *m*. **multiplicand**, *n*, multiplicande, *m*. **multiplication**, *n*, multiplication, *f*. **multiplicity**, *n*, multiplicité, *f*. **multiplier**, *n*, multiplicateur, *m*. **multiply**, *v.t*, multiplier; (*v.i*.) [se] m.; peupler.
multitude, *n*, multitude, *f*.
mum['s the word], motus!, bouche close!
mumble, *v.i*, marmotter, balbutier, barboter.
mummer, *n*, cabotin, e. ~y, *n*, momerie, *f*.
mummify, *v.t*, momifier. **mummy**, *n*, momie, *f*. (*mother*) maman, *f*.
mumps. *n*, (*Med*.) oreillons, *m.pl*; (*sulks*) bouderie, *f*.
munch, *v.t. & i*, croquer.
mundane, *a*, du monde, de ce m.; mondain.
municipal, *a*, municipal. ~ity, *n*, municipalité, *f*.
munificence, *n*, munificence, *f*. **munificent**, *a*, magnifique.
muniment, *n*, acte, titre, *m*.
munitions, *n.pl*, provisions de guerre, munitions de guerre, *f.pl*.
mural, *a*, mural.
murder, *n*, meurtre, assassinat, *m*. ~! à l'assassin! ¶ *v.i*, assassiner; (*fig*.) massacrer; (*language*) estropier, écorcher. ~er, ~ess, *n*, meurtrier, ère, assassin, e. ~ous, *a*, meurtrier.
muriatic, *a*, chlorhydrique.
murky, *a*, sombre, obscur, ténébreux.
murmur, *n*, murmure, *m*. ¶ *v.i. & t*, murmurer; bruire.
murrain, *n*, peste, *f*.
muscat (grape, wine), *n*, [raisin, vin] muscat, *m*. **muscatels**, *n.pl*, raisins secs muscats, *m.pl*.
muscle, *n*, muscle, *m*. **-muscled**, *a*, musclé. **muscular**, *a*, (*force*) musculaire; (*pers*.) musculeux.
Muse, *n*, Muse, *f*; génie, *m*.
muse, *v.i*, méditer; rêver, rêvasser.
museum, *n*, musée; (*natural history*) muséum, *m*.
mush, *n*, bouillie, *f*.
mushroom, *n*, champignon [comestible] *m*; (*pers*.) parvenu, e; (*att*.) éphémère, d'un jour. ~ *bed*, champignonnière, *f*. ~ *spawn*, blanc de champignon, *m*.
music, *n*, musique, *f*. ~ *cabinet*, casier à m., *m*. ~ *case*, porte-musique, *m*. ~ *hall*, music-hall, *m*. ~ *master*, professeur de musique, *m*. ~ *stand*, pupitre à m., *m*. ~ *stool*, tabouret de piano, *m*. **musical**, *a*, musical; chantant; (*pers*.) musicien. ~ *box*, boîte à musique, *f*. ~ *chairs*, chaises musicales, *f.pl*. ~ *clock*, horloge à carillon, *f*. ~ *comedy*, opéra bouffe, *f*. ~

director, directeur musical, chef de théâtre *m*. ~ *ear*, oreille pour la musique, *f*. ~ *evening*, soirée musicale, s. chantante, *f*. ~ *glasses*, harmonica, *m*. ~ *instrument*, instrument de musique, *m*; (*toy*) musique *f*. ~ *instrument maker*, luthier, *m*. ~ *instrument making*, lutherie, *f*. ~ *interlude*, entracte de musique, *m*. ~ *play*, opérette, *f*. ~ *switch*, pot pourri, *m*. **musician**, *n*, musicien, ne.
musing, *n*, rêverie, *f*.
musk, *n*, musc, *m*. ~ *deer*, [porte-]musc chevrotin, *m*. ~ *rat*, rat musqué, *m*. ~ *rose*, rose muscade, *f*. *to* [*perfume with*] ~ musquer.
musket, *n*, mousquet, *m*. ~**eer** (*Hist*.) *n* mousquetaire, *m*. ~**ry** (*Mil*.) *n*, tir, *m*; exercices de tir, *m.pl*.
Muslim, *n. & a*, mahométan, e.
muslin, *n*, mousseline, *f*.
musquash, *n*, rat musqué; (*fur*) castor du Canada, *m*.
mussel, *n*, moule, *f*.
Mussulman, *n. & a*, musulman, e, *m, f. & att*.
must, *v.aux.ir*, falloir; devoir.
must, *n*, moût, *m*.
mustard, *n*, moutarde; (*Bot*.) moutarde, *f*, sénevé, *m*. ~ *gas*, gaz moutarde, *m*, ypérite, *f*. ~ *maker & pot*, moutardier *m*. ~ *plaster*, sinapisme, *m*. ~ *sauce*, sauce moutarde, *f*. ~ *seed*, graine de m. *f*, sénevé, *m*. ~ *spoon*, cuiller à m., pelle à m., *f*.
muster, *n*, appel [nominal] *m*. ~ *roll*, feuille d'appel, *f*. ¶ *v.t*, faire l'appel de, rassembler.
musty, *a*, moisi; (*smell*) de renfermé.
mutability, *n*, mutabilité, *f*. **mutation**, *n*, mutation, *f*.
mute, *a*, muet; sourd. ¶ *n*, muet, te; pleureur; croque-mort, *m*; (*Mus*.) sourdine *f*. ~**d**, *p.a*, sourd; en sourdine. ~**ly**, *ad*, en silence.
mutilate, *v.t*, mutiler. **mutilation**, *n*, mutilation, *f*.
mutineer, *n*, mutin, révolté, *m*. **mutinous**, *a*, mutin. **mutiny**, *n*, mutinerie, révolte *f*. ¶ *v.i*, [se] mutiner, se révolter.
mutter, *v.i*, murmurer [entre ses dents] marmotter; (*of thunder*) gronder.
mutton, *n*, mouton, *m*. ~ *cutlet*, côtelette de mouton, *f*.
mutual†, *a*, mutuel; réciproque, partagé. ~ *association*, mutualité, *f*. ~ *loan association*, mutualité de crédit. *on* ~ *term* (engagement), au pair. ~**ity**, *n*, mutualité réciprocité, *f*.
muzzle, *n*, (*animal*) museau, *m*; (*gun*) bouche gueule; (*for dog*) muselière, *f*. ~*loading*, se chargeant par la bouche. ¶ *v.t*, museler.
my, *a*, mon, ma, mes.
myopia, *n*, myopie, *f*. **myopic**, *a*, myope.
myriad, *n*, myriade, *f*.
myriapod, *n*, myriapode, *m*.

myrmidon, *n*, suppôt, sbire, mamel[o]uk, *m*.
myrrh, *n*, myrrhe, *f*.
myrtle, *n*, myrte, *m*. ~ *berry*, baie de m., *f*.
myself, *pn*, moi-même; moi; me.
mysterious†, *a*, mystérieux. ~ *appeal* (as of
the olden times), mystique, *f*. **mystery**, *n*,
mystère, *m*. ~ [*play*], mystère, miracle,
m. **mystic** (*pers.*) *n*, mystique, *m,f*.
~(**al**)†, *a*, mystique. **mysticalness**, *n*,
mysticité, *f*. **mysticism**, *n*, mysticisme, *m*.
mystify, *v.t*, mystifier.
myth, *n*, mythe, *m*. ~**ic**(**al**), *a*, mythique.
~**ologic**(**al**), *a*, mythologique. ~**ologist**,
n, mythologue, *m,f*. ~**ology**, *n*, mythologie, *f*.

N

nabob, *n*, nabab, *m*.
nadir, *n*, nadir, *m*.
naevus, *n*, nævus, *m*, tache de naissance, *f*.
nag, *n*, bidet, *m*. ~ (**at**), *v.t. & i*. criailler
(après), quereller. **nagging**, *p.a*, hargneux.
naiad, *n*, naïade, *f*.
nail, *n*, (*finger*, *toe*) ongle; (*metal*) clou, *m*;
pointe, *f*. ~ *brush*, brosse à ongles, *f*. ~
extractor, arrache-clou, *m*. ~ *file*, lime à
ongles, *f*. ~ *maker*, cloutier, *m*. ~
making & works, clouterie, *f*. ~ *scissors*, ciseaux à ongles, *m.pl*. on the ~,
recta. ~ [**up**], *v.t*, clouer.
naive†, *a*, naïf. **naivety**, *n*, naïveté, *f*.
naked, *a*, nu; à nu; ras. *with the* ~ *eye*, à
l'œil nu. ~**ly** (*fig.*) *ad*, nûment. ~**ness**,
n, nudité, *f*.
namby-pamby, *a*, fade.
name, *n*, nom, *m*; dénomination; raison, *f*;
intitulé, *m*; renommée; réputation, *f*. *by*
~, (*to mention*) nommément; (*be called on*)
nominativement. *my* ~ *is Adam*, je
m'appelle Adam, je me nomme A. ~
plate, plaque de porte, *f*. ~**sake**, homonyme, *m*. ¶ *v.t*, nommer; dénommer;
intituler. ~**less**, *a*, sans nom. ~**ly**, *ad*,
[à] savoir; (*of pers.*) nommément.
nankeen, *n*, nankin, *m*.
nanny, *n*, nounou, *f*. ~ [*goat*], chèvre,
bique, *f*.
nap, *n*, (*sleep*) somme, *m*, sieste, *f*; (*pile*) poil;
duvet, *m*. *to catch napping*, prendre au
dépourvu.
nape [**of the neck**], *n*, nuque, *f*.
naphtha, *n*, naphte, *m*. **naphthalene, -ine**, *n*,
naphtaline, *f*.
napkin, *n*, serviette [de table]; (*baby's*)
couche, *f*. ~ *ring*, rond de serviette, *m*.
narcissus, *n*, narcisse, *m*.
narcotic, *a*, narcotique. ¶ *n*, narcotique,
stupéfiant, *m*.
narrate, *v.t*, narrer, raconter. **narration &
narrative**, *n*, narration, *f*, récit, *m*, relation,
f. **narrative**, *a*, narratif. **narrator, tress**,
n, narrateur, trice, conteur, euse.

narrow†, *a*, étroit, resserré. *to have a* ~
escape, l'échapper belle. ~*gauge railway*,
chemin de fer à voie étroite, *m*. ~*minded*,
à esprit étroit. ¶ *n*, (*Naut.*) passe étroite,
f, goulet; étranglement, *m*. ¶ *v.t*, [r]étré-
cir, resserrer, étrangler. ~**ness**, *n*, étroitesse, *f*.
narwhal, *n*, narval, *m*.
nasal, *a*, nasal. ¶ (*Gram.*) *n*, nasale, *f*.
nascent, *a*, naissant.
nastiness, *n*, saleté; méchanceté, *f*; goût, &c,
désagréable, *m*.
nasturtium, *n*, capucine, *f*.
nasty†, *a*, sale; désagréable; vilain; rosse.
natal, *a*, natal.
natation, *n*, natation, *f*.
nation, *n*, nation, *f*, peuple, *m*. ~**al**, *a*,
national; public. ~ *capital* (*Economics*)
outillage national, *m*. ~ *monument*,
monument historique, *m*. **nationalism**, *n*,
nationalisme; étatisme, *m*. **nationalist**, *n*.
& att, nationaliste, *m,f. & a*. **nationality**,
n, nationalité, *f*. **nationals**, *n.pl*, nationaux, *m.pl*.
native, *a*, naturel; natif; natal; originaire;
indigène; maternel. ~ *land*, ~ *coun-
try*, patrie, *f*. ¶ *n*, natif, ive; indigène,
m,f; naturel, *m*; (*pl, oysters*) huîtres du pays,
f.pl. **nativity**, *n*, nativité, *f*; horoscope, *m*.
natty, *a*, chic, coquet, propret.
natural†, *a*, naturel. ¶ *n*, idiot, e; (*Mus.*)
(*note*) note naturelle, *f*; (*cancel sign*)
bécarre, *m*. ~ *history museum*, muséum
[d'histoire naturelle] *m*. ~**ist**, *n*, naturaliste, *m*. ~**ization**, *n*, naturalisation, *f*.
~ *papers*, lettres de n., *f.pl*. ~**ize**, *v.t*,
naturaliser. ~**ness**, *n*, naturel, *m*.
nature, *n*, nature, *f*; naturel, caractère,
acabit, *m*. ~ **-natured**, *a*, d'un (*bon*, *mauvais*) naturel.
naughtiness, *n*, méchanceté, *f*. **naughty†**, *a*,
méchant, vilain, laid; (*indecent*) polisson,
croustilleux, graveleux, gras.
nausea, *n*, nausée, *f*. **nauseate**, *v.t*, écœurer.
nauseating, *a*, nauséeux. **nauseous**, *a*,
nauséabond.
nautical, *a*, (*science*, *almanac*) nautique;
(*mile*) marin.
nautilus, *n*, nautile, nautilus, *m*.
naval, *a*, naval; maritime; de marine; de la m.
~ *cadet*, élève de l'école navale, *m*. ~
dockyard, arsenal maritime, *m*. ~ *officer*,
officier de marine, *m*. ~ *port*, ~ *base*,
~ *station*, port de guerre, p. militaire;
point d'appui de la flotte, *m*.
nave, *n*, (*wheel*) moyeu, *m*; (*church*) nef, *f*.
navel, *n*, nombril, *m*.
navigable, *a*, navigable. **navigate**, *v.i*,
naviguer; (*v.t.*) naviguer sur, faire naviguer. **navigation**, *n*, navigation, *f*. **navigator**, *n*, navigateur, *m*.
navvy, *n*, terrassier, *m*.
navy, *n*, marine [militaire]. *m*. de guerre, *f*.
~ *blue*, bleu marine, *m*.

P

nay, *neg. particle*, & qui plus est, voire. ¶ *n*, non, *m*.

Neapolitan, *a*, napolitain. ¶ *n*, Napolitain, e.

neap tide, morte-eau, *f*.

near, *a*, proche; près de; rapproché; intime. *the N∼ East*, le proche Orient. ∼ *relations*, proches [parents] *m.pl*. ∼ *relationship*, proximité du sang; *f*. ∼ *side*, côté gauche (de la voiture); (*Riding*) côté du montoir, *m*. ∼ *sight*, vue myope, *f*. ∼*sighted* (*person*), myope, *a*. & *m,f*. ¶ *ad*, près; proche; auprès; de près. ¶ *pr*, près de; auprès de. ¶ *v.i*, s'approcher de. ∼*ly*, *ad*, de près; à peu [de chose] près; presque. *he ∼ fell*, il a manqué de tomber. *I ∼ missed the train*, j'ai failli manquer le train. ∼**ness**, *n*, proximité, *f*.

neat†, *a*, propre; soigné; bien tenu; pur, sec; adroit. ∼ [*cattle*], bêtes bovines, *f.pl*. ∼**herd**, bouvier, ère, vacher, ère, pâtre, *m*. ∼*'s foot*, pied de bœuf, *m*. ∼*'s foot oil*, huile de p. de b., *f*. ∼*'s leather*, cuir de vache, *m*. ∼**ness**, *n*, propreté, *f*.

nebula (*Astr.*) *n*, nébuleuse, *f*. **nebulous**, *a*, nébuleux.

necessarily, *ad*, nécessairement, forcément. **necessary**, *a*, nécessaire. *if ∼*, s'il est n., au besoin. ¶ *n. & necessaries*, *n.pl*, le nécessaire. **necessitate**, *v.t*, nécessiter. **necessitous**, *a*, nécessiteux. **necessity**, *n*, nécessité, *f*.

neck, *n*, cou, *m*; gorge; encolure, *f*; col; collet; goulot; (*violin*) manche, *m*. ∼ *band*, bande de fer, brisure, *f*. ∼*lace*, collier, *m*. ∼ *measurement*, *f*, size, encolure, *f*. ∼*tie*, cravate, *f*. *to win by a ∼*, gagner par une encolure. **neckerchief**, *n*, fichu, *m*. **necklet**, *n*, tour de cou, *m*.

necrology, *n*, (*notice*) nécrologie, *f*; (*roll, book*) nécrologe, *m*. **necromancer**, *n*, nécromancien, *m*. **necromancy**, *n*, nécromancie, *f*. **necropolis**, *n*, nécropole, *f*. **necrosis**, *n*, nécrose, *f*.

nectar, *n*, nectar, *m*. ∼**ine**, *n*, brugnon, *m*. ∼**y**, *n*, nectaire, *m*.

need, *n*, besoin, *m*. ¶ *v.i. & t*, avoir b. (de); vouloir. ∼**ful**, *a. & n*, nécessaire, *a*. & *m*.

needle, *n*, aiguille, *f*. ∼ *case*, étui à aiguilles, aiguillier, *m*. ∼*-made lace*, dentelle à l'aiguille, *f*. ∼ *maker*, aiguillier, *m*. ∼*-point lace*, dentelle au point à l'aiguille, *f*. ∼*woman*, couturière, *f*. ∼*work*, travail à l'aiguille, *m*, couture, *f*. *to do ∼work*, travailler à l'a., chiffonner. ∼*work case*, trousse de couture, *f*, nécessaire à ouvrage, *m*. ∼**ful**, *n*, aiguillée, *f*.

needless†, *a*, inutile. **needs**, *ad*, nécessairement. **needy**, *a*, nécessiteux, besogneux.

ne'er (*Poet.*) *ad*, ne . . . jamais. ∼*-do-well, -weel*, *a*, propre à rien. *a ∼-do-well, -weel*, un mauvais sujet, un propre à rien.

nefarious†, *a*, inique, abominable.

negation, *n*, négation, *f*. **negative†**, *a*, négatif. ¶ *n*, (la) négative; (*Gram.*) néga-

tion, *f*; (*Phot.*) cliché, négatif, *m*, épreuve négative, *f*. ¶ *v.t*, rejeter.

neglect, *v.t*, négliger, oublier. **neglect** & **negligence**, *n*, négligence, *f*, oubli, *m*. **neglectful†** & **negligent†**, *a*, négligent. **negligible**, *a*, négligeable.

negotiable, *a*, négociable. ∼ *instrument*, effet de commerce, *m*. **negotiate**, *v.t. & i*, négocier, traiter, trafiquer. **negotiation**, *n*, négociation, *f*; (*pl.*) pourparlers, *m.pl*. *by ∼*, de gré à gré. **negotiator, tress** or **trix**, *n*, négociateur, trice.

negress, *n*, négresse, *f*. **negro**, *n*, nègre, *m*. ¶ *a*, nègre, *a.m.* & *a.f*.

neigh, *v.i*, hennir. ∼[**ing**], *n*, hennissement, *m*.

neighbour, *n*, voisin, e; prochain, *m*. ∼**hood**, *n*, voisinage, *m*, environs, *m.pl*; quartier, *m*. ∼**ing**, *a*, voisin, avoisinant, prochain. *in a ∼ly way*, en bon voisin.

neither, *pn. & a*, ni l'un (l'une) ni l'autre. ¶ *c*, ni; ne . . . pas non plus. ¶ *ad*, non plus.

nelson (*Wrestling*) *n*, prise de tête à terre, *f*.

Nemesis, *n*, Némésis, *f*.

nemine contradicente (abb. *nem. con.*), à l'unanimité.

neologism, *n*, néologisme, *m*.

neon, *n*, néon, *m*. ∼ *light*, lumière néon, *f*.

neophyte, *n*, néophyte, *m,f*.

nephew, *n*, neveu, *m*.

ne plus ultra, nec plus ultra.

nepotism, *n*, népotisme, *m*.

Nereid, *n*, néréide, *f*.

nerve, *n*, nerf, *m*; (*Bot.*) nervure, *f*; courage, sang-froid, *m*. ∼ *specialist*, neurologiste, neurologue, *m,f*. ∼**less**, *a*, énervé. ∼ *breakdown*, prostration nerveuse, *f*. ∼**ness**, *n*, timidité, *f*.

nervous†, *a*, nerveux; peureux, timide.

nest, *n*, nid; (*tubes*, &c) faisceau; (*fig.*) repaire, *m*. ∼ *egg*, nichet; (*savings*) pécule, *m*. ∼ *of drawers*, casier, *m*. ∼ *of* (insect's) *eggs*, couvain, *m*. ¶ *v.i*, nicher. ∼*ed table* or ∼ *of 3 tables*, table gigogne, *f*. ∼[**ful**], *n*, nichée, *f*. **nestle**, *v.i*, se blottir, se tapir. **nestling**, *n*, petit oiseau au nid, *m*.

net, *n*, filet; rets; tulle, *m*; résille; *f*. ∼ *bag*, filet à provisions, *m*. ∼ *maker*, fileur, euse. ∼ *sinker*, ∼ *weight* (*Fish.*), gousse de plomb, *f*. ∼*work*, réseau; lacis, *m*. ¶ (*Com.*) *a*, net. ¶ (*catch*) *v.t*, prendre au filet.

nether, *a*, inférieur, bas. ∼ *millstone* (*fig.*), cœur de meule, *m*. ∼ *regions*, enfers, *m.pl*. **Netherlander**, *n*, Néerlandais, e. **Netherlandish**, *a*, néerlandais. **the Netherlands**, les Pays-Bas, *m.pl*, la Néerlande. **nethermost**, *a*, (le) plus bas.

netting, *n*, filet, *m*, filoche, *f*; (*wire*) treillis, treillage, grillage, réseau, *m*.

nettle, *n*, ortie, *f*. ∼ *rash*, urticaire, *f*. ¶ *v.t*, piquer.

neuralgia, *n*, névralgie, *f*. **neuralgic**, *a*, névralgique. **neurasthenia**, *n*, neurasthénie.

f. **neuritis**, *n,* névrite, *f.* **neurologist**, *n,* neurologiste, *-logue, m,f.* **neurosis**, *n,* névrose, *f.* **neurotic**, *a,* névrosé.

neuter, *a. & n,* neutre, *a. & m.* neutral, *a. & n,* neutre, *a. & m.* ~**ity**, *n,* neutralité, *f.* ~**ize**, *v.t,* neutraliser.

never, *ad,* jamais; ne ... jamais; ne ... pas. ~**-ending**, éternel. **nevertheless**, *ad. & c,* néanmoins; cependant; toutefois; pourtant, quand même.

new, *a,* neuf; nouveau; récent; frais, tendre. ~**-born** *(child)*, nouveau-né, e. ~ *comer*, nouveau venu, *m,* nouvelle venue, *f.* *Newfoundland [dog]*, terre-neuve, *m.* ~ *growth* (*Forestry*), revenue, *f.* ~ *guard* (*Mil.*), garde montante, *f.* ~ *horns* (stag), refait, *m.* ~**-laid**, frais [pondu]. ~ *lease of life*, regain de vie, *m.* ~ *member* (of a society), récipiendaire, *m.* ~ *par[agraph]*, alinéa, *m.* N~ *Testament*, Nouveau Testament. *N~ the woman*, la femme moderne. ~**-year card**, carte de nouvel an, *f.* ~**-year's day**, le jour de l'an. ~**-year's eve**, veille du j. de l'a., *f,* la Saint-Sylvestre. ~**-year's gift**, étrennes, *f.pl.* ~**-year's wishes**, souhaits (*ou* vœux) de bonne année, *m.pl.*

New (*Geog.*) *a:* ~ *Brunswick*, le Nouveau-Brunswick. ~*foundland*, Terre-Neuve, *f.* ~ *Guinea*, la Nouvelle-Guinée. ~ *Orleans*, la Nouvelle-Orléans. ~ *South Wales*, la Nouvelle-Galles du Sud. ~ *York*, New-York, *m.* ~ *Zealand*, la Nouvelle-Zélande; (*att.*) néo-zélandais. ~ *Zealander*, Néo-zélandais.

newel, *n,* noyau; pilastre, *m.*

newly, *ad,* nouvellement, fraîchement. **newness**, *n,* nouveauté; primeur, *f.*

news, *n,* nouvelle, *f. oft. pl;* courrier; bruit, *m;* (*Cinema*) actualités, *f.pl.* ~ *agency*, agence d'information, *f.* ~ *agent*, marchand de journaux, *m.* ~ *boy*, crieur de journaux, *m,* camelot, *m.* ~ *[bulletin]* (*Radio*), informations, *f.pl.* ~ *film*, film d'actualité, *m.* ~ *items* (in paper), faits divers, échos, *m.pl.* ~*monger*, nouvelliste, *m,* gazette, *f.* ~*paper*, journal, *m,* feuille, *f.* ~*paper rate*, tarif des [imprimés] périodiques, *m.* ~*print*, papier de journal, *m.* ~*room*, cabinet de lecture, *m.*

newt, *n,* triton, *m,* salamandre aquatique, *f.*

next, *a,* voisin; d'à côté; prochain; plus prochain; suivant; (*world*) autre. *the ~ day*, le lendemain. *the ~ day but one*, le surlendemain. ~ *door to*, à côté de. ¶ *ad,* après; ensuite; puis. ~ *the skin*, à cru. ~ *to*, [au]près de; à côté de; presque. ¶ ~ *of kin*, plus proche parent; *v,* proches [parents] *m.pl.*

nib, *n,* plume [à écrire], *f,* bec, *m.*

nibble (*Fish.*) *n,* touche, *f.* ¶ *v.t. & i,* grignoter, chipoter, mordiller; (*grass*) brouter; (*fish*) piquer, mordre.

nice, *a,* bon; agréable; friand; délicat; beau; joli; gentil. ~**ly**, *ad,* bien; joliment; gentiment.

Nicene Creed (the), le symbole de Nicée.

nicety, *n,* précision; subtilité, *f. to a ~,* à point.

niche, *n,* niche, *f.*

nick, *n,* [en]coche, hoche, entaille, *f,* cran, *m,* saignée, fente, *f. in the ~ of time,* à point nommé. ¶ *v.t,* encocher, entailler, hocher, fendre.

nickel, *n,* nickel, *m.* ¶ *v.t,* nickeler.

nick-nack, *n,* colifichet, brimborion, *m.*

nickname, *n,* sobriquet, surnom, *m.* ¶ *v.t,* baptiser; surnommer.

nicotine, *n,* nicotine, *f.*

niece, *n,* nièce, *f.*

niello, *n,* nielle, *m.*

niggard, *n,* ladre, *m,f.* ~**ly**, *a,* ladre, mesquin, chiche.

nigger, *n,* nègre, *m,* négresse, *f.* ~ *boy, girl,* négrillon, ne.

nigh, *a,* proche. ¶ *ad,* près; presque.

night, *n,* nuit, *f;* soir, *m. at ~,* la nuit, le soir; (*hour*) du soir. *by ~,* de nuit, nuitamment. *the ~ before last,* avant-hier soir. ~ *cap,* bonnet de nuit, *m.* ~ *club,* boîte de n., *f.* ~ *commode,* chaise [percée] *f.* ~ *dress,* ~ *gown,* chemise de nuit, *f.* ~*fall,* la tombée de la nuit, la chute du jour. *at ~fall,* à la nuit tombante. ~ *lamp* & ~ *light,* veilleuse, *f.* ~*man,* vidangeur, *m.* ~*mare,* cauchemar, *m.* ~ *nurse,* veilleuse de nuit, *f.* ~ *nursing,* veillée, *f.* ~*shade,* morelle, *f.* ~ *shirt,* chemise de nuit, *f.* ~*'s lodging,* coucher, *m.* ~ *soil,* vidanges, *f.pl,* gadoue, *f.*

nightingale, *n,* rossignol, *m.*

nightly, *a,* de nuit. ¶ *ad,* toutes les nuits; tous les soirs.

nihilist, *n,* nihiliste, *m.*

nil, *n,* rien, néant, *m,* nul, *a.*

Nile (the), le Nil.

nimble†, *a,* agile, leste, preste, ingambe. ~**ness**, *n,* agilité, prestesse, *f.*

nimbus, *n,* nimbe; (*Meteor.*) nimbus, *m.*

nincompoop, *n,* nigaud, *m.*

nine, *a. & n,* neuf, *a. & m.* 9-*hole course,* parcours (*ou* golf) de 9 trous, *m.* ~*pins,* quilles, *f.pl.* ~ *times out of ten,* neuf fois sur dix. **nineteen**, *a. & n,* dix-neuf, *a. & m.* **nineteenth**, *a. & n,* dix-neuvième, *a. & m,f;* dix-neuf, *m.* **ninetieth**, *a. & n,* quatre-vingt-dixième, *a. & m,f.* **ninety**, *a. & n,* quatre-vingt-dix, *a. & m.* 91, 92, &c, quatre-vingt-onze, -douze, &c.

Nineveh, *n,* Ninive, *f.*

ninny, *n,* nigaud, *m,* dadais, *m.*

ninth, *a. & n,* neuvième, *a. & m,f;* neuf, *m.* ~**ly**, *ad,* neuvièmement.

nip, *n,* (*liquor*) doigt, *m.* ¶ *v.t,* pincer; serrer; mordre; brûler. **nipper**, *n,* (*boy*) gamin, *m;* (*of crustacean, &c*) pince, *f;* (*pl.*) pinces [de serrage], tenailles, *f.pl.*

nipple, *n*, mamelon, bout du sein, *m*; (*nursing bottle*) tétine, *f*.

nit, *n*, lente, *f*.

nitrate, *n*, nitrate, azotate, *m*. **nitre**, *n*, nitre, salpêtre, *m*. **nitric**, *a*, azotique, nitrique. **nitrogen**, *n*, azote, *m*. **nitroglycerin[e]**, *n*, nitroglycérine, *f*. **nitrous**, *a*, azoteux.

no, *ad*; non; pas. ¶ *n*, non, *m*. ¶ *a*, aucun; nul; ne . . . pas de; pas de; pas moyen de. ~ *admittance* [*except on business*], entrée interdite, défense d'entrer [sans autorisation]. ~ *agents*, agents s'abstenir. ~ *case to answer* (*Law*), non-lieu, *m*. ~ *contest* (*Box.*), non-combat. ~ *doubt*, sans doute. ~ *entry* [, *one way street*], sens interdit. ~ *flowers, by request*, ni fleurs, ni couronnes. ~ *hands wanted*, on n'embauche pas. ~ *matter!* n'importe! ~ *occupation*, sans profession. ~ *one*, personne, *m*, aucun, e. ~ *parking*, stationnement interdit. ~ *performance*, relâche. ~ *reply* (*Teleph.*), [ne] répond pas. ~ *smoking*, défense de fumer. ~ *thoroughfare*, défense de passer, on ne passe pas, passage interdit [au public]. ~ *value* (in account), pour mémoire.

Noah's ark, l'arche de Noé, *f*.

nobiliary, *a*, nobiliaire. **nobility**, *n*, noblesse; grandeur, *f*. **noble**, *a*, *n*, noble; grand. ~[*man*], noble, seigneur, gentilhomme, *m*. ~*woman*, noble, *f*. ~**ness**, *n*, noblesse, *f*.

nobody, *n*, personne, *pn.m*. *a* ~, un zéro; un (une) inconnu, e.

nocturnal, *a*. & **nocturne**, *n*, nocturne, *a*. & *m*.

nod, *n*, signe [de tête] *m*, inclination de t., *f*. ¶ *v.i*, s'incliner; s'assoupir.

node, *n*, nœud, *m*. **nodule**, *n*, rognon, *m*.

noggin, *n*, gode, *m*; (*Meas.*) ¼ pint.

noise, *n*, bruit; fracas, tapage, vacarme; (*in ears*) tintement; (*fig.*) éclat, retentissement, *m*. ~ *abroad*, *v.t*, ébruiter, carillonner, claironner. ~**less†**, *a*, silencieux.

noisome, *a*, nuisible; malsain.

noisy†, *a*, bruyant; tapageur.

nolens volens, bon gré, mal gré; de gré ou de force.

nomad, *n*. & ~ (**ic**), *a*, nomade, *m*. & *a*.

nomenclature, *n*, nomenclature, *f*.

nominal†, *a*, nominal; (*of* [*the*] *names, as a list*) nominatif. **nominate**, *v.t*, nommer, désigner. **nomination**, *n*, nomination, désignation, *f*. **nominative** [*case*], nominatif, *m*. **nominee**, *n*, personne nommée; personne interposée, *f*. *in a* ~'*s name*, sous un nom interposé.

non, *prefix*: ~-*alcoholic drinks*, liqueurs fraîches, *f.pl*. ~-*combatant*, *n*. & *att*, non-combattant; civil, *m*. & *a*. ~-*commissioned officer*, sous-officier, gradé, *m*. ~-*committal*, qui n'engage à rien, normand. *to be* ~-*committal*, rester neutre. ~-*copying ribbon* (*Typewriter*), ruban fixe, *m*. ~-*effective* (*Mil.*), non-valeur, *f*. ~-*exist-*

ence, inexistence, *f*; (*Philos.*) non-être, *m*. ~-*existent*, inexistant. ~-*interference*, *n*, ~-*intervention*, non-intervention, *f*, laissez-faire, *m*. ~-*payment*, non-paiement, *m*. ~-*performance*, inexécution, *f*. ~-*skid*, *a*, antidérapant. ~-*slip mat*, paillasson non glissant; (*for bath*) fond de bain, *m*. ~-*stop*, *a*, sans arrêt; s. escale. ~-*vintage wine*, vin sans année, v. non-millésimé, *m*.

nonage, *n*, minorité, *f*.

nonagenarian, *a*. & *n*, nonagénaire, *a*. & *m,f*.

nonce, *n*, circonstance, *f*; (*att.*) de c.

nonchalance, *n*, nonchalance, *f*. **nonchalant**, *a*, nonchalant. ~**ly**, *ad*, nonchalamment.

nonconformist, *n*. & *att*, non-conformiste, *m,f*. & *att*.

nondescript, *a*, indéfinissable.

none, *a*. & *pn*, aucun; nul; pas un; pas; personne, *pn.m*.

nonentity, *n*, (*Philos.*) non-être, *m*; (*pers.*) nullité, *f*, homme nul, *m*.

nonplus, *n*, embarras, *m*. ¶ *v.t*, embarrasser, dérouter, démonter.

nonsense, *n*, non-sens, *m*, absurdité, insanité, *f*, sottises, bêtises, lanternes, sornettes; chinoiseries, *f.pl*. *all* ~, un non-sens. ¶ *i*, allons donc!; chansons, chansons!

nonsuit, *v.t*, débouter.

noodle, *n*, nigaud, e, bêta, *m*.

nook, *n*, recoin, réduit, *m*.

noon & **noonday** & **noontide**, *n*, midi, *m*.

noose, *n*, nœud coulant; lacet, *m*.

nor, *c*, ni; ne . . . pas non plus.

Nordic, *a*, nordique.

norm, *n*, norme, *f*. **normal†**, *a*, normal.

Norman, *a*, normand. ¶ *n*, Normand, e. **Normandy**, *n*, la Normandie.

Norse, *a*. & *n*. & ~-*man*, *n*, norvégien, *a*. & *m*. *Old Norse* (language), l'ancien norois, *m*.

north, *n*, nord; septentrion, *m*. ¶ *ad*, au nord. ¶ *a*, [du] nord; septentrional. *N*~ *Africa*, l'Afrique septentrionale, *f*. *N*~ *America*, l'Amérique du Nord, *f*. *N*~ *Britain*, Écosse, *f*. ~-*east*, *n*, nord-est, *m*. *N*~ *pole*, pôle nord, *m*. *N*~ *sea*, mer du Nord, *f*. *N*~ *Wales*, la Galles du Nord. ~-*west*, *n*, nord-ouest, *m*. ~-*wester* (wind) *n*, galerne, *f*. **northerly**, *a*, du nord. **northern**, *a*, [du] nord, boréal. ~ *lights*, aurore boréale, *f*. **northerner**, *n*, septentrional, e. **northward[s]**, *ad*, vers le nord.

Norway, *n*, la Norvège. **Norwegian**, *a*, norvégien; (*pers.*) Norvégien, ne; (*language*) le norvégien.

nose, *n*, nez; (*beast*) museau; (*tool*) bec; (*scent*) flair, *m*. *to blow one's* ~, se moucher. ~ *bag*, musette, *f*. ~ *band*, muserolle, *f*. ~-*dive*, *v.i*, piquer du nez. ~*gay*, bouquet, *m*. ~ *about*, fouiner. ~ [*out*], *v.t*, flairer. **nosing**, *n*, (*of step*) nez; (*of locomotive*) lacet, *m*.

nostalgia, *n*, nostalgie, *f*. **nostalgic**, *a*, nostalgique.

nostril, *n*, narine, *f*; (*horse*) naseau, *m*.

nostrum, *n,* remède de charlatan, *m,* drogue; panacée, *f.*

not, n't, *ad,* ne . . . pas, ne . . . point, ne, n'; non; pas; non pas. ~ *at all,* pas du tout, point du tout, nullement, mais non, aucunement. ~ *at home,* absent. *not competing* [*for prize*], hors concours. ~ *exceeding,* jusqu'à concurrence de, ne dépassant pas. ~ *guilty,* innocent. *to find* ~ *guilty,* innocenter. ~ *negotiable* (cheque), non négociable. ~ *to be confused with* . . ., à ne pas confondre avec . . . ~ *to be taken* (*Med.*), pour l'usage externe. ~ *transferable,* incessible, rigoureusement personnel. ~ *valued* (in account), pour mémoire.

nota bene (*abb.* N.B.), nota [bene] *m.*

notability, *n,* notabilité, *f.* **notable†,** *a,* notable.

notarial charges (*on bill*), compte de retour, *m.* **notary,** *n,* notaire, *m.*

notation, *n,* notation, *f.*

notch, *n,* [en]coche, entaille, hoche, *f,* cran, *m.* ¶ *v.t,* [en]cocher, entailler, hocher.

note, *n,* note, *f,* mémento, *m;* remarque, *f;* billet, *m;* lettre, *f;* bulletin; bordereau, *m;* facture, *f;* bon; permis; (*!!*) point, *m;* (*Mus.*) note, *f;* (*please observe*) nota [bene]. (pers.) *of* ~, de marque. ~*book,* carnet, calepin, *m.* ~ *case,* porte-billets, *m.* ~ *of hand,* billet à ordre. ~ *paper,* papier à lettres, *m.* ~*worthy,* digne de remarque, remarquable. ¶ *v.t,* noter; relever; constater; remarquer. **noted,** *p.p,* renommé, célèbre.

nothing, *n,* rien; rien de; néant; zéro, *m.* ~ *at all,* rien du tout. ~*ness,* *n,* néant, *m.*

notice, *n,* observation, *f;* regard, *m;* attention, garde, *f;* avis; préavis; avertissement, *m;* notice, *f;* écriteau, *m.* *at short* ~, à bref délai; (*loan*) à court terme. [*term of*] ~, délai de congé, *m.* ~ *board,* écriteau, *m,* porte-affiches, *m.* ~ *of meeting,* avis de convocation, *m,* convocation d'assemblée, *f.* ~ [*to quit*], congé, *m.* ¶ *v.t,* observer, remarquer, faire attention à. ~**able,** *a,* digne d'attention; perceptible. **notify,** *v.t,* notifier, avertir, signaler, aviser, intimer.

notion, *n,* notion, idée, *f.*

notoriety, *n,* notoriété, *f.* **notorious†,** *a,* notoire; insigne, fameux.

notwithstanding, *pr,* malgré, nonobstant. ¶ *ad,* néanmoins, quand même.

nought, *n,* rien, néant; (*Arith.*) zéro, *m.*

noun, *n,* nom, substantif, *m.*

nourish, *v.t,* nourrir. ~**ing,** *a,* nourrissant. ~**ment,** *n,* nourriture, *f.*

nous, *n,* esprit, *m;* savoir-faire, *m.*

Nova Scotia, la Nouvelle-Écosse.

Nova Zembla, la Nouvelle-Zemble.

novel, *a,* nouveau, inédit. ¶ *n,* roman, *m.* ~ *with a sex interest,* roman intime. ~**ette,** *n,* nouvelle, *f.* ~**ist,** *n,* romancier, ère. ~**ty,** *n,* nouveauté, *f.*

November, *n,* novembre, *m.*

novice, *n,* novice, *m,f,* apprenti, e. **noviciate,** *n,* noviciat, *m.*

now, *ad,* maintenant, à présent, actuellement; tantôt. ¶ *c,* or. ¶ *n,* [moment] présent, *m.* ¶ *i,* voyons! ~ *then!* eh bien!, ah! çà, or çà! ~ *& again,* de temps à autre, à diverses reprises, parfois, occasionnellement. ~ *& henceforth,* d'ores & déjà. *between* ~ *& then,* d'ici là. [*every*] ~ *& then,* de temps en temps. *from* ~, d'ici. *from* ~ *onward,* dorénavant. **nowadays,** *ad,* de nos jours, aujourd'hui; par le temps qui court.

nowhere, *ad,* nulle part, en aucun lieu. **nowise,** *ad,* nullement, aucunement.

noxious, *a,* nuisible, nocif, vireux.

noyau, *n,* noyau, *m,* eau de noyau, *f.*

nozzle, *n,* ajutage bec, jet, *m;* tuyère, buse, *f.*

Nubia, *n,* la Nubie. **Nubian,** *a,* nubien. ¶ *n,* Nubien, ne.

nubile, *a,* nubile.

nucleus, *n,* noyau, *m.*

nude, *a. & n,* nu, *a. & m.*

nudge, *n,* coup de coude, *m.* ¶ *v.t,* donner un coup de coude à, pousser du coude.

nudity, *n,* nudité, *f;* nu, *m.*

nugatory, *a,* futile; inefficace; nul.

nugget, *n,* pépite, *f.*

nuisance, *n,* ennui, embêtement, *m,* contrariété, scie; (*Law, &c*) incommodité, *f;* (*pers.*) gêneur, *m,* importun, e, brebis galeuse, *f;* (*child*) tourment, *m.*

null, *a,* nul. ~ *& void,* nul(le) & non avenu(e). ¶ *n,* nulle, *f.* **nullify,** *v.t,* annuler. **nullity,** *n,* nullité, caducité, *f.*

numb, *a,* engourdi, gourd, transi. ¶ *v.t,* engourdir, transir.

number, *n,* nombre; numéro, chiffre, *m,* cote, *f;* (*publication*) livraison, *f.* **N~s** (*Bible*), les Nombres. ~ *one,* son individu. ~ *plate* (motor car), plaque de police, p. matricule, *f.* ¶ *v.t,* compter; numéroter; chiffrer; coter. ~**ing,** *n,* numérotage, *m.* ~**less,** *a,* innombrable.

numbness, *n,* engourdissement, *m;* (*of fingers*) onglée, *f.*

numeral, *a,* numéral. ¶ *n,* chiffre, *m.* **numerary,** *a,* numéraire. **numerator** (*Arith.*) *n,* numérateur, *m.* **numerical,** *a,* numérique. **numerous,** *a,* nombreux.

numismatics, *n,* numismatique, *f.* **numismatist,** *n,* numismate, *m.*

numskull, *n,* lourdaud, e.

nun, *n,* religieuse, nonne, nonnain, *f.*

nunciature, *n,* nonciature, *f.* **nuncio,** *n,* nonce, *m.*

nunnery, *n,* couvent, *m.*

nuptial, *a,* nuptial. ~**s,** *n.pl,* noces, *f.pl.*

nurse, *n,* nourrice, *f;* infirmier, ère; garde-malades, *m,f.* ~ [*maid*], bonne [d'enfant] *f.* ¶ *v.t,* nourrir, allaiter; soigner; dorloter. **nursery,** *n,* chambre d'enfants; (*Hort. & fig.*) pépinière, *f.* ~ *language,* langage enfantin, *m.* ~**man**, [jardinier] pépiniériste, *m.* ~ *rhyme*, poésie enfantine, *f*, conte rimé, *m.* ~ *tale*, conte de nourrice, conte de fées, *m.* **nursing**, *n*, allaitement *m*; soins, *m.pl.* ~ *home*, maison de santé, clinique, *f.* ~ *mother*, mère nourrice, *f.* **nurs[e]ling**, *n*, nourrisson, *m.* **nursy**, *n*, nounou, *f*.

nurture, *n*, éducation; nourriture, *f.* ¶ *v.t*, nourrir.

nut, *n*, noix; noisette, *f*; (*violin, &c*) sillet; (*for bolt*) écrou, *m*; (*pl, coal*) gaillette, *f*, gailletin, *m.* ~*-brown*, noisette. ~*cracker* (bird), casse-noix, *m.* ~**cracker face**, figure en casse-noisettes, *f.* ~**crackers**, casse-noisettes, casse-noix, *m.* ~ **gall**, noix de galle, *f.* ~*hatch*, sittelle, *f*, casse-noisettes, *m.* ~*shell*, coquille de noix, *f.* ~ *tree*, noisetier, *m*.

nutmeg, *n*, [noix] muscade, *f.* ~ [*tree*], muscadier, *m*.

nutriment, *n*, aliment, *m.* **nutrition**, *n*, nutrition, *f.* **nutritious** & **nutritive**, *a*, nourrissant, nutritif.

nutting, *n*, cueillette des noisettes, *f.* **nutty**, *a*, qui sent la noisette.

nux vomica, noix vomique, *f*.

nuzzle, *v.i. & t*, fouiller; se blottir.

nymph, *n*, nymphe; bergère, *f*.

O

O, *i*, ô! ~ *dear!* (of pain), aïe!

oaf, *n*, enfant disgracié par la nature; lourdaud, *m*.

oak [*tree*], *n*, chêne, *m.* ~ [*wood or timber*], [bois de] chêne, *m.* ~ *apple*, pomme de chêne, *f.* ¶ *att.* & ~**en**, *a*, de chêne.

oakum, *n*, étoupe, *f*.

oar, *n*, rame, *f*, aviron, *m.* **oarsman**, *n*, rameur, nageur, canotier, *m.* **oarswoman**, *n*, rameuse, *f*.

oasis (*lit. & fig.*) *n*, oasis, *f*.

oast, *n*, four à houblon, *m.* ~ *house*, séchoir à houblon, *m*.

oat, *n*, (*pl.*) avoine, *f.* ~*meal*, farine d'avoine, *f*; gruau d'avoine, *m*.

oath, *n*, serment; (*profane*) juron, *m*.

obbligato, *a*, obligé. ¶ *n*, partie obligée, *f*.

obdurate, *a*, endurci; impénitent.

obedience, *n*, obéissance, soumission; (*Eccl.*) obédience, *f.* **obedient**, *a*, obéissant, soumis. ~**ly**, *ad*, avec obéissance, avec soumission. **obeisance**, *n*, révérence, *f*.

obelisk, *n*, obélisque, *m*; (*Typ.*) croix, *f*.

obese, *a*, obèse. **obesity**, *n*, obésité, *f*.

obey, *v.t*, obéir à; (*v.i.*) obéir.

obfuscate, *v.t*, offusquer, obscurcir.

obituary, *n*, nécrologie, *f*.

object, *n*, objet; but, *m*; (*fright*) horreur, *f*; (*Gram.*) régime, *m.* ~ *lesson*, leçon de choses; (*fig.*) application pratique, *f.* ¶ *v.t. & i*,

objecter; réclamer. **objection**, *n*, objection, *f*; mais, *m*; opposition, *f.* ~**able**, *a*, susceptible d'objections; indésirable; offensant, rosse. **objective†**, *a*, objectif. ¶ (*aim, Opt.*) *n*, objectif, *m.* ~ [*case*], cas régime, *m. the* ~ (*Philos.*), l'objectif, *m*.

objurgation, *n*, objurgation, *f*.

oblation, *n*, oblation, offrande, *f*.

obligate, *v.t*, obliger. **obligation**, *n*, obligation, *f.* **obligatory**, *a*, obligatoire. **oblige**, *v.t*, obliger. **obliging**, *a*, obligeant, serviable, arrangeant. ~**ly**, *ad*, obligeamment.

oblique, *a*, oblique. ~**ly**, *ad*, en biais. **obliquity**, *n*, obliquité, *f*.

obliterate, *v.t*, oblitérer, effacer.

oblivion, *n*, oubli, *m*; (*Pol.*) amnistie, *f.* **oblivious**, *a*, oublieux.

oblong, *a*, oblong. ¶ *n*, figure oblongue, *f*, carré long, *m*.

obloquy, *n*, reproche; dénigrement, *m*.

obnoxious, *a*, offensant, odieux.

oboe, *n*, hautbois, *m.* **oboist**, *n*, hautboïste, *m*.

obscene, *a*, obscène. **obscenity**, *n*, obscénité, *f*.

obscure, *a*, obscur, ténébreux, fumeux. ¶ *v.t*, obscurcir, offusquer. ~**ly**, *ad*, obscurément. **obscurity**, *n*, obscurité, *f*.

obsequies, *n.pl*, obsèques, *f.pl.* **obsequious†**, *a*, obséquieux. ~**ness**, *n*, obséquiosité, *f*.

observance, *n*, observation; (*Theol.*) observance; (*religious*) pratique, *f.* **observant**, *a*, observateur. **observation**, *n*, observation, *f.* ~ *post* (*Mil.*) & **observatory**, *n*, observatoire, *m.* **observe**, *v.t*, observer; remarquer; suivre. **observer**, *n*, observateur, trice.

obsess, *v.t*, obséder. *to be* ~*ed by, with*, être obsédé par, être fanatique de, s'aheurter à. ~**ion**, *n*, obsession, aheurtement, dada, *m*, hantise, maladie, *f*.

obsolescent, *a*, vieillissant. **obsolete**, *a*, vieux, vieilli, inusité, désuet.

obstacle, *n*, obstacle, *m.* ~ *race*, course d'obstacles, *f*.

obstetric(al), *a*, obstétrical. **obstetrics**, *n.pl*, obstétrique, *f*.

obstinacy, *n*, obstination, opiniâtreté, *f*, entêtement; acharnement, *m.* **obstinate**, *a*, obstiné, opiniâtre, entêté; acharné; rebelle. ~**ly**, *ad*, obstinément, opiniâtrement.

obstreperous, *a*, turbulent.

obstruct, *v.t*, obstruer, boucher; (*v.i.*) fronder. ~**ion**, *n*, obstruction; (*fig.*) obstruction, fronde, *f*.

obtain, *v.t*, obtenir, procurer; (*v.i.*) régner.

obtrude, *v.t*, forcer.

obturator, *n*, obturateur, *m*.

obtuse, *a*, obtus.

obverse (*coin*) *n*, avers, *m*, face, *f*.

obviate, *v.t*, obvier à.

obvious†, *a*, évident, manifeste, constant, visible.

ocarina, n, ocarina, m.

occasion, n, occasion; circonstance; cause, f, lieu, m; reprise, f. ¶ v.t, occasionner, donner lieu à; causer. **~al**, a, par occasion; (occupation) d'occasion; de circonstance; de temps en temps; (cause, Philos.) occasionnelle. **~ expenses**, menus plaisirs, m.pl. **~ table**, table volante, f, guéridon, m. **~ally**, aa, occasionnellement, parfois.

occiput, n, occiput, m.

occult, a, occulte. **~ing light**, feu à éclipses, m. **~ism**, n, occultisme, m.

occupant, n, habitant, e; occupant, m; titulaire, m,f. **occupation**, n, occupation; profession, f, état, m, qualités, f.pl. **occupier**, n, habitant, e, locataire, m,f. **occupy**, v.t, occuper; habiter.

occur, v.i, [sur]venir, se présenter, s'offrir; arriver, advenir. **occurrence**, n, occurrence, venue, f, fait, événement, m, rencontre, f.

ocean, n, océan, m, mer, f. **~[-going]**, a, au long cours. **~ greyhound** (fig.), lévrier de la mer, m. **Oceania**, n, l'Océanie, f.

ochre, n, ocre, f.

o'clock, heure(s).

octagon, n. & **~al**, a, octogone, m. & a. **~al nut**, écrou à 8 pans, m. **octave**, n, octave, f. **octavo**, a. & n. (abb. 8vo), in-octavo, in-8o, a.m. & m. **October**, n, octobre, m. **octodecimo**, a. & n, in-dix-huit, in-18, a.m. & m. **octogenarian**, a. & n, octogénaire, a. & m.f. **octopus**, n, poulpe, m, pieuvre, f. **octoroon**, n, octavon, m.

ocular, a. & n, oculaire, a. & m. **oculist**, n, oculiste, m.

odd, a, (number) impair; & quelques; & quelque chose; (pair or set) dépareillé; singulier, étrange, bizarre, baroque, original, drôle. **~ jobs**, bricoles, f.pl. **~ money**, appoint, m, passe, f. **~ player** (Golf), joueur de plus, m. **at ~ times**, par-ci, par-là. **the ~** (Golf), le plus. **~ity**, n, singularité, bizarrerie, f; (pers.) original, drôle de corps, m. **~ly**, ad, étrangement, bizarrement. **~ments**, n.pl, articles dépareillés, m.pl. **~ness**, n, imparité; singularité, f. **odds**, n,pl, chances; forces supérieures, f.pl; avantage, m; (Turf) cote, f. **to lay ~ of 3 to 1**, parier 3 contre 1. **the ~ are that . . .**, il y a à parier que . . . **~ & ends**, bribes, f.pl, rogatons, m.pl.

ode, n, ode, f.

odious†, a, odieux. **odium**, n, haine, f; odieux, m.

odoriferous, a, odoriférant, odorant. **odour**, n, odeur, f. **~less**, a, inodore.

Odyssey (fig.) n, odyssée, f.

oesophagus, n, œsophage, m.

oestrus or **oestrum**, n, œstre, m.

of, pr, de; en; parmi; entre; d'entre; à; chez.

off, pr, éloigné de; au large de; de dessus; de là. **1 ~ 3, 1 ~ 2** (Golf), moins 3, m. 2.

~ colour, indisposé. **~hand**, a. & ad, impromptu; sur-le-champ; sans cérémonie; cavalier; brusque. **~handedness**, sans-gêne, m. **~ season**, morte-saison, f. **~shore fishing**, pêche au large, p. hauturière, f. **~ side**, côté droit (de la voiture); (Riding) côté hors montoir, m. **~ side**, **~ board** (book), plat inférieur, m. ¶ ad, de distance; d'ici. **to be ~**, s'en aller; partir; (dish at restaurant) être épuisé. **~ side** (Foot.), hors jeu.

offal, n, issues, f.pl, tripaille, f.

offcut (Bookb.) n, carton, m.

offence, n, offense, blessure, f, outrage; délit; crime; infraction, contravention, f. **to take ~**, s'offenser, se formaliser. **offend**, v.t, offenser, blesser, choquer, offusquer; (v.i.) pécher. **~er**, n, offenseur, m; coupable, m,f; délinquant, e. **offensive**, a, offensant, blessant, choquant; malsonnant; (attacking) offensif.

offer, n, offre, f. ¶ v.t, offrir; proposer; présenter. **~ up**, offrir. **~ing**, n, offrande; oblation; f; sacrifice, m. **~tory**, n, (Lit.) offertoire, m; (collection) quête, f.

office, n, charge, f, office, exercice, m, fonction, f. oft. pl, place, f, ministère; portefeuille; bureau; cabinet, m, étude; salle, f; siège; comptoir, m; caisse, recette, f. **~ boy**, petit commis, m. **~ copy**, ampliation, f. **O~ of Works**, Ministère des Travaux publics. **~ printing outfit**, composteur, m. **officer**, n, officier, m; fonctionnaire, m,f; agent, m, préposé, e. ¶ v.t, encadrer. **official†**, a, officiel; d'office. **~ statement** (to press), communiqué, m. ¶ n, fonctionnaire, m,f, préposé, e; (Sport, &c) officiel, m. **~dom** & **~ism**, n, fonctionnarisme, m. **officiate**, v.i, (Eccl.) officier; exercer les fonctions (as = de). **officious**, a, touche-à-tout; (Diplomacy) officieux. **~ adviser**, conseilleur, euse. **~ person**, touche-à-tout, m, personne qui se mêle des oignons des autres, f.

offing, n, large, m. **in the ~**, au l., dehors.

offscourings (fig.) n.pl, lie, f, bas-fonds, m.pl.

offset, n, compensation, f; (Hort.) rejeton, œilleton; (Arch.) ressaut, m; retraite; (Typ.) maculature, f. **~ process**, impression rotocalcographique, rotocalcographie, f.

offshoot, n, rejeton, m.

offspring, n, rejeton, m; progéniture, f.

often & (Poet.) **oft**, ad, souvent. **how often?** combien de fois?

ogee, n, doucine, f. **ogive**, n, ogive, f.

ogle, n, œillade, f. ¶ v.t, lorgner, reluquer.

ogre, ogress, n, ogre, m, ogresse, f.

oh, i, oh! ô! ah!

oil, n, huile, f; pétrole, m; essence, f. **~ cake**, tourteau, m. **~ can**, (storage) bidon à huile, m; (nozzled) burette à h., f. **~cloth**, (table, &c) toile cirée, moleskine, f; (floor) linoléum imprimé, *m.* ~ *colour*, ~ *paint*, couleur à l'huile, *f.* ~ *engine*, moteur à pétrole, *m.* ~ *field*, champ de pétrole, *m.* ~ *fuel*, pétrole combustible, *m.* ~ *heater*, poêle à pétrole, *m.* ~ *hole*, trou de graissage, *m.* ~ *man*, marchand d'huile, *m.* ~ *mill*, huilerie, *f.* ~ *painting*, peinture à l'huile, *f.* ~ *seed*, graine oléagineuse, *f.* ~ *shares*, valeurs de pétrole, *f.pl.* ~ *ship*, [navire] pétrolier, *m.* ~ *shop*, magasin d'huile, *m.* huilerie, *f.* ~*skin*, toile huilée, *f*; (*garment*) ciré, *m.* ~ *stone*, pierre à huile, *f.* ~ *stove*, fourneau à pétrole, *m.* ~ *varnish*, vernis gras, *m.* ~ *well*, puits à pétrole, *m.* ¶ *v.t*, graisser [à l'huile], huiler. ~y, *a,* huileux; onctueux; oléagineux.

ointment, *n,* onguent, *m.*

old, *a,* vieux; ancien. *how ~ is he? he is 10 years ~,* quel âge a-t-il? il a 10 ans, il est âgé de 10 ans. *the ~,* (opp. *new*) le vieux; (*people*) les vieux, *m.pl.* ~ & *young,* grands & petits. *of ~,* jadis, anciennement. ~ *age,* la vieillesse; (*decay*) vétusté, *f.* ~ *age pension fund,* caisse de retraites pour la vieillesse, *f.* ~ *clothes,* vieilles hardes, nippes, *f.pl.* ~*established,* fort ancien. ~*-fashioned,* à l'ancienne mode; passé de mode, démodé; arriéré; gothique. ~ *fellow,* ~ *boy* ~ *chap* (as form of address), mon vieux. ~ *gold,* vieil or, *m.* ~ *guard* (*Mil.*), garde descendante, *f.* ~ *iron,* vieux fer[s] *m.[pl.],* ferraille, *f.* ~ *maid,* vieille fille, *f.* ~ *man,* vieillard, vieux; (*in comedy*) géronte, *m.* ~ *master* (*Art*), ancien maître, *m.* ~ *offender,* récidiviste, *m,f,* repris de justice, cheval de retour, *m.* ~ *paper[s]* (accumulation), paperasse, *f.* ~ *salt* (sailor), loup de mer, *m. the same ~ story,* la même histoire, la même guitare. O~ *Testament,* Ancien Testament, *m.* ~ *things,* vieilleries, *f.pl. the good ~ times,* le bon vieux temps. ~ *woman,* vieille [femme] *f*; *the* O~ *Woman who lived in a shoe,* la mère Gigogne. **in the ~en time,** au temps jadis. ~*ish,* *a,* vieillot.

oleaginous, *a,* oléagineux.

oleander, *n,* laurier-rose, oléandre, *m.*

olfactory, *a,* olfactif.

oligarchy, *n,* oligarchie, *f.*

olive, *n,* olive, *f.* ~ [*tree, wood*], olivier, *m.* ~ (*complexion, &c) a,* olivâtre. ~*-[green*], vert olive, couleur [d']olive. ~ *grove,* olivaie, *f.* ~ *oil,* huile d'olive, *f.*

Olympic games, jeux olympiques, *m.pl.* **Olympus** (*fig.*) *n,* olympe, *m.*

omega, *n,* oméga, *m.*

omelet[te], *n,* omelette, *f.*

omen, *n,* augure, présage, auspice, pronostic, *m.* **ominous,** *a,* de mauvais augure; sinistre; menaçant.

omission, *n,* omission, *f.* **omit,** *v.t,* omettre.

omnibus, *n,* omnibus, *m.*

omnipotence, *n,* omnipotence, toute-puissance, *f.* **omnipotent,** *a,* omnipotent, tout-puissant. *the Omnipotent,* le Tout-Puissant. **omniscience,** *n,* omniscience, *f.* **omniscient,** *a,* omniscient.

omnivorous, *a,* omnivore.

on, *pr,* sur; à; de; en; après; par; pour; sous. ~ & *after,* à partir de, à dater de. ~ *hand,* (*work*) sur le métier; (*orders*) en carnet, en portefeuille; (*cash*) en caisse, disponible; (*goods uncollected*) en souffrance. [*goods left*] ~ *hand, refused,* laissé pour compte, *m.* ¶ *ad,* dessus; en avant. *on that,* là-dessus.

once, *ad,* une fois; une seule fois. ~ *again,* ~ *more,* encore une fois, encore un coup. ~ *for all,* une fois pour toutes. ~ *upon a time,* il y avait (*ou* il était) une fois, autrefois.

one, *a,* un; seul; unique. ~*act play,* pièce en un acte, *f,* acte, *m.* ~*armed* & ~*handed* (*person*), manchot, ote. ~*class liner,* paquebot à classe unique, *m.* ~*eyed,* borgne. ~*horse* (carriage), à un cheval. ~*man band,* homme-orchestre, *m.* ~*price shop,* magasin à prix unique, *m.* ~*sided,* unilatéral; (*fig.*) léonin. ~*way street,* rue à sens unique, *f.* ~*way traffic,* circulation à s. u., *f.* ¶ *n, m*; unité, *f.* ¶ *pn,* celui, celle; quelqu'un, e; on; un(e) nombre(e), un(e) certain(e). ~ & *all,* tous sans exception. ~ *another,* l'un(e) l'autre; les uns (les unes) les autres; se. ~ *by* ~ *or* ~ *after another,* un à un, une à une. *he is ~ of us,* il est des nôtres. ~*ness,* *n,* unité, *f.*

onerous, *a,* onéreux.

one's, *pn,* son, sa, ses. **oneself,** *pn,* même; soi; le; son individu.

onion, *n,* oignon, *m.* ~ *bed,* oignonière, *f.* ~ *sauce,* sauce à l'oignon, *f.* ~ *skin,* ~ *peel,* pelure d'oignon, *f.*

onlooker, *n,* assistant, e, spectateur, trice, curieux, *m.*

only, *a,* seul, unique, tout. ¶ *ad,* seulement, rien que, ne . . . guère; uniquement.

onomatopoeia, *n,* onomatopée, *f.*

onset, onrush, onslaught, *n,* attaque, ruée, *f,* assaut, choc, *m.*

onus, *n,* charge, *f.* ~ *of proof,* charge de la preuve.

onward, *a,* progressif. ~[s], *ad,* en avant; plus loin.

onyx, *n,* onyx, *m.*

ooze, *n,* vase, *f,* limon; suintement, *m.* ¶ *v.i,* suinter, suer. ~ *out,* transpirer.

opacity, *n,* opacité, *f.*

opal, *n,* opale, *f.* ~*ine,* *a,* opalin.

opaque, *a,* opaque. ~*ness,* *n,* opacité, *f.*

open, *v.t,* ouvrir; percer; entamer; écarter; découvrir; exposer; inaugurer; (*bottle*) déboucher; (*oysters*) écailler; (*Med.*) débonder; (*v.i.*) ouvrir; s'o.; (*flowers*) s'épanouir. ~ *out* (*pers., fig.*), se déboutonner.

~ *sesame*, Sésame, ouvre-toi. ¶ *a*, ouvert; découvert, à découvert; exposé; ostensible; libre; franc; (*boat*) non ponté. *in the* ~ [*air*], en plein air, au grand air, à ciel ouvert. *the* ~ [*country*], la pleine campagne, la rase c. *in the open* (publicly), au grand jour. ~ *clocks or clox*, baguettes à jour, *f.pl.* ~*-end tie*, [*cravate*] régate, *f.* ~*-handed*, libéral. ~*-hearted*, franc. ~ *house*, table ouverte, *f.* ~ *mind*, table rase, *f.* ~*-mouthed*, bouche béante, b. bée. *in the* ~ *sea*, en pleine (*ou* haute) mer, au large. ~ *space*, terre-plein, franc-bord, *m.* ~ *warfare*, guerre de mouvement, *f.* ~[*work*], *att.* à jour, ajouré, à claire-voie. ~*work* (*Need.*) *n*, (les) jours, *m.pl.* ~*er*, *n*, ouvreur, euse. ~*ing*, *n*, ouverture; percée; éclaircie; (*neck*) échancrure; introduction, *f*; débouché, *m*; occasion, *f.* ¶ *a*, initial; d'ouverture; de début; préliminaire; premier; (*Med.*) laxatif. ~*ly*, *ad*, ouvertement; ostensiblement; hautement; franchement. ~**ness**, *n*, franchise, candeur, *f.*

opera, *n*. & ~ *house*, opéra, *m.* ~ *cloak*, sortie de bal, s. de théâtre, *f.* ~ *glass*[*es*], jumelle[s] de théâtre, lorgnette[s] de spectacle, *f.*[*pl.*]. ~ *hat*, [chapeau] claque, *m.* **operate**, *v.t.* ouvrir; exploiter; (*v.i.*) opérer, agir; jouer. ~ *on* (*Surg.*), opérer. **operatic**, *a*, d'opéra; lyrique, dramatique. **operating room** *or* **theatre**, salle d'opération, *f.* **operation**, *n*, opération; exploitation, *f.* **operative**, *n*, ouvrier, ère, artisan, e. **operator**, *n*, opérateur, trice; exploitant; montreur, *m*; joueur, euse, boursier, ère. **operetta**, *n*, opérette, *f.*

ophthalmia, *n*, ophtalmie, *f.* **ophthalmic**, *a*, ophtalmique.

opiate, *n*, narcotique, *m.* ~**d**, *a*, opiacé. **opine**, *v.i.* opiner. **opinion**, *n*, opinion, voix, *f*; cri; sentiment, avis, sens, *m*; (*legal*) consultation, *f.* ~**ated**, *a*, opiniâtre, entier. **opium**, *n*, opium, *m.* ~ *addict*, opiomane, *m,f.* ~ *den*, fumerie, *f.* ~ *poppy*, pavot somnifère, *m.*

Oporto, *n*, Porto, Oporto, *m.*

opossum, *n*, opossum, *m*; sarigue, *m,f.*

opponent, *n*, opposant, e, adversaire, antagoniste, *m.* ¶ *a*, opposant.

opportune, *a*, opportun, à propos. ~**ly**, *ad*, opportunément, à propos. ~**ness**, *n*, opportunité, *f*, à-propos, *m.* **opportunism**, *n*, opportunisme, *m.* **opportunist**, *n*, opportuniste, *m,f.* **opportunity**, *n*, occasion; opportunité, *f.*

oppose, *v.t.* opposer, s'opposer à; combattre. ~**d**, *p.p*, contraire. **opposing**, *a*, opposant, adverse. **opposite**, *n*, opposé, contraire, contre-pied, *m.* ~ (**to**), *a*, *pr*, *ad*, opposé; en face (de), vis-à-vis (de); en regard (de), contraire (à); (*sex*) opposé. **opposition** *n*, opposition; résistance, *f.*

oppress, *v.t*, opprimer; oppresser (*Med. &*

fig.). ~**ion**, *n*, oppression, *f.* ~**ive**, *a*, oppressif, assommant. ~**or**, *n*, oppresseur, *m.*

opprobrious, *a*, infamant, injurieux. **opprobrium**, *n*, opprobre, *m.*

optic, *n*, optique. ~**al**, *a*, optique; (*glass*, *instruments*, *illusion*) d'optique. ~ *lantern*, lanterne de projection, *f.* **optician**, *n*, opticien; lunetier, *m.* **optics**, *n*, optique, *f.*

optimism, *n*, optimisme, *m.* **optimist**, *n*. & ~ (**ic**), *a*, optimiste, *m,f. & a.*

option, *n*, faculté; option; alternative, *f*, choix, *m*; (*Stk Ex.*) prime, *f.* ~**al**†, *a*, facultatif.

opulence, *n*, opulence, *f.* **opulent**, *a*, opulent.

or, *c*, ou; soit; (*neg.*) ni. ~ *else*, ou bien, autrement. *2 ~ 3 times a day*, de 2 à 3 fois par jour.

oracle, *n*, oracle, *m.*

oral†, *a*, oral. ~ *examination*, examen oral, *m*; (*preparatory test*) colle, *f.*

orange, *n*, orange, *f*; (*colour*) orange, *m*, orangé, *m.* ¶ *a*, orange, orangé. ~ [*tree*], oranger, *m.* ~ *blossom*, fleurs d'oranger, *f.pl.* ~ *marmalade*, confitures d'oranges, *f.pl.* ~ *peel*, pelure d'orange, écorce d'o., *f.* ~**ade**, *n*, orangeade, *f.* ~**ry**, *n*, orangerie, *f.*

orang-outang, *n*, orang-outang, jocko, *m.*

oration, *n*, discours, *m*; (*funeral*) oraison, *f.* **orator**, *n*, orateur, *m.* ~**ical**, *a*, oratoire. **oratorio**, *n*, oratorio, *m.* **oratory**, *n*, l'art oratoire, *m*, éloquence, *f*; (*chapel*) oratoire, *m.*

orb, *n*, globe, *m*, sphère, *f*, orbe, *m.* **orbit**, *n*, orbite, *f.*

orc, *n*, orque, *f*, épaulard, *m.*

orchard, *n*, verger, *m.*

orchestra, *n*, orchestre, *m.* ~ *stall*, fauteuil d'orchestre, *m.* **orchestral**, *a*, orchestral. **orchestrate**, *v.t*, orchestrer.

orchid, *n*, orchidée, *f.* **orchis**, *n*, orchis, *m.*

ordain, *v.t*, ordonner; décréter, prescrire.

ordeal, *n*, épreuve; (*Hist.*) ordalie, *f.*

order, *n*, ordre, *m*; règle, *f*; état, *m*; classe, *f*; classement, *m*; commande, *f*; mandat, bon, permis; arrêté, *m*; décoration, *f*; (*Mil.*) tenue, *f*; (*pl, Mil.*) ordres, *m.pl*, consigne, *f.* ~*!* à l'ordre! *in* ~ *that*, afin que, pour que. *in* ~ *to*, afin de. ~ *book*, livre (*ou* carnet) de commandes, *m.* ~ *cheque*, chèque à ordre, *m.* ~ *form*, bon (*ou* bulletin) de commande, *m.* ¶ *v.t*, ordonner; statuer; régler; charger; (*goods*) commander; (*arms*, *Mil.*) reposer. ~**ing**, *n*, ordonnance, disposition, *f.* ~**ly**, *a*, ordonné, rangé, régulier. ¶ *n*, (*Mil.*) ordonnance, *f. or* ~ *m*, planton, *m*; (*hospital*) infirmier, *m.* *on* ~ *duty*, de planton. ~ *officer*, officier de service, *m.* ~ *room*, salle du rapport, *f.*

ordinal [*number*], *n*, nombre ordinal, *m.*

ordinance, *n*, décret, *m.*

P *

ordinary†, *a*, ordinaire; commun; normal.
~ [*bicycle*], bicycle, *m*. ~ *seaman*, simple
matelot, matelot de troisième classe, *m*.
¶ *n*, ordinaire, *m*; table d'hôte, *f*.

ordination, *n*, ordination, *f*.

ordnance, *n*, artillerie, *f*. ~ [*survey*] *map*,
carte d'État-major, *f*. ~ *surveyor*, géomètre du cadastre, *m*.

ore, *n*, minerai, *m*.

organ, *n*, organe; (*Mus.*) orgue, *m*. ~
grinder, joueur d'orgue de Barbarie, *m*.
~ *loft*, tribune d'orgues, *f*. ~ *pipe*,
tuyau d'orgue, *m*.

organdie, *n*, organdi, *m*.

organic, *a*, organique. **organization**, *n*,
organisation; (*fête, &c*) ordonnance, *f*.
organize, *v.t*, organiser; ordonner; policer.
organizer, *n*, organisateur; trice; ordonnateur, trice.

oriel [*window*], *n*, fenêtre en encorbellement, *f*.

orient, *n*, orient, *m*. *the O~* (*Geog.*), l'O.
~**al**, *a*, oriental. **O~**, *n*, Oriental, e.
~[**ate**], *v.t*, orienter.

orifice, *n*, orifice, *m*, ouverture, *f*.

oriflamme, *n*, oriflamme, *f*.

origin, *n*, origine; provenance, *f*. ~**al†**, *a*,
(*not copied*) original; (*primitive*) originaire,
originel. ¶ *n*, original, *m*. ~**ality**, *n*,
originalité, *f*. ~**ate**, *v.t*, prendre l'initiative de; (*v.i.*) tirer son origine, dériver.
originator, *n*, auteur, *m*.

Orinoco (**the**), l'Orénoque, *m*.

oriole (*bird*), *n*, loriot, *m*.

Orkneys (**the**), les Orcades, *f.pl*.

Orleans, *n*, Orléans, *m. or f*.

orlop [*deck*], *n*, faux-pont, *m*.

ormolu, *n*, or moulu, *m*.

ornament, *n*, ornement, *m*; parure, *f*. ¶ *v.t*,
orner, agrémenter, historier. ~**al**, *a*,
ornemental; d'ornement; historié; d'agrément. ~ *border*, vignette, *f*. ~ *lake*,
bassin, miroir d'eau, *m*, pièce d'eau, *f*.
~ *trees*, arbres d'ornement, marmenteaux, *m.pl*. **ornamentalist**, *n*, ornemaniste, *m.f*. **ornamentation**, *n*, ornementation, *f*. **ornate**, *a*, orné; imagé.

ornithologist, *n*, ornithologiste, ornithologue, *m.f*. **ornithology**, *n*, ornithologie, *f*.

orphan, *n. & a*, orphelin, e. ~**age** (*asylum*)
n, orphelinat, *m*.

orrery, *n*, planétaire, *m*.

orris root, racine d'iris, *f*.

orthodox, *a*, orthodoxe, catholique. ~**y**,
n, orthodoxie, *f*. **orthographic**, *a*, orthographic; (*Arch.*) orthographie, *f*. **orthopaedic**, *a*, orthopédique. **orthopaedy**, *n*,
orthopédie, *f*.

ortolan, *n*, ortolan, *m*.

orts, *n.pl*, restes, *m.pl*, bribes, *f.pl*, arlequin, *m*.

oscillate, *v.i*, osciller; (*v.t.*) faire osciller,
osciller. **oscillation**, *n*, oscillation, *f*.

osier, *n*, osier, *m*. ~ *bed*, oseraie, *f*.

osmium, *n*, osmium, *m*.

osprey, *n*, orfraie, *f*.

osseus, *a*, osseux. **ossicle**, *n*, osselet, *m*.
ossify, *v.t*, ossifier. **ossuary**, *n*, ossuaire, *f*,
charnier, *m*.

Ostend, *n*, Ostende, *f*.

ostensible, *a*, avoué. **ostensibly**, *ad*, en
apparence, sous prétexte. **ostensory**, *n*,
ostensoir, *m*. **ostentation**, *n*, ostentation,
f, faste, *m*. **ostentatious**, *a*, ostentateur,
ostentatoire; fastueux.

ostler, *n*, garçon d'écurie, palefrenier, *m*.

ostracism, *n*, ostracisme, *m*. **ostracize**, *v.t*,
frapper d'ostracisme, mettre au ban.

ostrich, *n*, autruche, *f*. ~ *feather*, plume
d'autruche, *f*.

otary, *n*, otarie, *f*.

other, *a. & pn*, autre. *every ~ day*, tous les
deux jours. *the ~ side* (opinion, pers.),
la contrepartie. *on the ~ side or hand*,
de l'autre côté. ~*s*, ~ *people*, les autres,
d'autres, autrui. ~**wise**, *ad*, autrement,
sinon, sans quoi, sans cela.

otter, *n*, loutre, *f*.

Ottoman, *a*, ottoman. ¶ *n*, Ottoman, e.
o~, *n*, ottomane, *f*.

otto of roses, essence de roses, *f*.

oubliette, *n*, oubliettes, *f.pl*.

ought, *n*, quelque chose, rien, *m*. ¶ *v.aux.ir*,
devoir; falloir.

ounce, *n*, (*Zool.*) once; (*Meas.*) once, *f*:
(*avoirdupois*) = 28·350 grammes; (*troy
& apothecaries' weight*) = 31·1035 grammes;
(*apothecaries' measure*) = 2·84123 centi-
litres.

our, *a*, notre, nos, *pl. Our Lady*, Notre-
Dame, *f. our Lord*, Notre-Seigneur, *m*.
~**s**, *pn*, le nôtre, la nôtre, les nôtres; nos;
à nous; de nous. **ourselves**, *pn*, nous-
mêmes; nous.

ousel, *n*, merle, *m*.

oust, *v.t*, débusquer, dégommer; évincer,
déposséder.

out, *ad. & pr*, dehors; hors; sorti, absent, en
course; en fleur; paru; éteint. ~ *& out*,
franc, fieffé, achevé, renforcé, à tous crins,
à outrance, outrancier. ~ *loud*, tout
haut. ~[, *see copy*] (*Typ.*), bourdon, *m*.
~ *there*, là-dehors. **out of**, *comps*: ~
action, hors de combat. ~ *bounds*, hors
des limites. ~ *date*, suranné, démodé;
(*ticket, &c*) périmé. ~ *doors*, dehors, au
grand air. ~ *fashion*, passé de mode,
démodé. ~ *hand*, sur-le-champ; échappé
à tout contrôle. ~ *one's element*, hors de
son élément, dépaysé. ~ *one's reckoning*,
loin de compte. ~ *order*, déréglé, dé-
rangé. ~ *place* (*fig.*), déplacé, hors de
propos. ~ *pocket*, en perte. ~ *pocket
expenses*, débours[és] *m.pl*. ~ *practice*,
rouillé. ~ *print*, épuisé. ~ *shape*,
avachi. ~ *sight*, hors de vue. ~ *sorts*,
indisposé, dolent. *to be ~ stock of*, être
à court de, manquer de. ~ *the common*,
hors ligne. *out-of-the-way*, *a*, écarté, re-

tiré, isolé. ~ *true*, gauchi, dévié, faussé, dévers. ~ *tune*, faux. *to be out* [*of work*], être sans travail, chômer. **out**, *i*, dehors! hors d'ici! (*Box.*) dehors! ~ *with him!* à la porte! ~ *with it!* achevez donc!

outbid, *v.t.ir*, [r]enchérir sur, surenchérir sur.

outboard, *ad*, hors bord. ~ *motor*, propulseur amovible, *m*.

outbreak, *n*, début, *m*; (*riot*) émeute; (*disease*) épidémie, *f*. ~ *of fire*, incendie, *m. at the* ~ *of war*, quand la guerre éclata.

outbuilding, *n*, dépendance, *f*.

outburst, *n*, débordement, emportement, déchaînement, élan, accès, *m*, poussée, explosion; incartade, *f*.

outcast, *n*, déclassé, e, réprouvé, e, paria, homme sans aveu, *m*.

outcaste, *n*, paria, *m*.

outcome, *n*, conséquence, issue, *f*, résultat, *m*.

outcrop (*Geol.*) *n*, affleurement, *m*.

outcry, *n*, cri, clameur, *f*, haro; tollé, *m*.

outdistance, *v.t*, distancer.

outdo, *v.t.ir*, surpasser; l'emporter sur; devancer.

outdoor, *a*, en plein air, au grand air, de plein air. ~ *relief*, secours à domicile, *m*.

outer, *a*, extérieur. ~ *cover* (tire), enveloppe, *f*. ~ *harbour*, avant-port, *m*.

outfall, *n*, décharge, *f*; (*mouth*) débouché, *m*.

outfit, *n*, équipement, équipage, nécessaire, trousseau, *m*, trousse, *f*. **outfitter**, *n*, maison pour fournitures (*de sports*, &*c*) *f*; confectionneur, euse.

outflank, *v.t*, déborder.

outflow, *n*, écoulement, *m*, décharge, *f*.

outgoing, *a*, sortant, de sortie, de départ, au départ; (*tide*) descendante. ~**s**, *n.pl*, débours, déboursés, *m.pl*.

outgrow, *v.t.ir*, devenir trop grand pour; se guérir de.

outhouse, *n*, dépendance, *f*; appentis, *m*.

outing, *n*, course, excursion, promenade, *f*.

outlandish, *a*, bizarre.

outlast, *v.t*, durer plus longtemps que.

outlaw, *n*, proscrit, e. ¶ *v.t*, proscrire, mettre hors la loi. ~**ry**, *n*, proscription, *f*.

outlay, *n*, débours, déboursés, *m.pl*.

outlet, *n*, issue, sortie, *f*; débouché, *m*.

outline, *n*, contour, tracé, crayon, galbe, canevas, aperçu, *m*, esquisse, ébauche, *f*. ~ *drawing*, dessin au trait, *m*. ¶ *v.t*, établir les grandes lignes de, tracer, dessiner, crayonner, esquisser.

outlive, *v.t*, survivre à, enterrer.

outlook, *n*, perspective, vue, *f*; avenir, *m*.

outlying, *a*, éloigné; avancé; excentrique.

outmanœuvre, *v.t*, déjouer.

outnumber, *v.t*, surpasser en nombre.

out-patient, *n*, malade du dehors, *m.f*.

outport, *n*, port de mer, port maritime, *m*.

outpost, *n*, avant-poste, *m*.

outpouring, *n*, épanchement, *m*, effusion, *f*.

output, *n*, rendement, *m*, production, *f*, débit, *m*.

outrage, *n*, outrage, *m*, indignité, *f*; attentat, *m*. ¶ *v.t*, outrager, faire outrage à; violer. ~**ous**†, *a*, indigne; odieux; pendable; sanglant; énorme.

outrider, *n*, piqueur, *m*.

outrigger, *n*, (*boat*) outrigger; (*for rowlocks*) porte-en-dehors, *m*.

outright, *a*, fieffé. ¶ *ad*, net, carrément; (*opp. by instalments*) en une [seule] fois.

outrival, *v.t*, devancer.

outset, *n*, début, *m*, origine, *f*; (*Bookb.*) carton d'en haut, *m*.

outshine, *v.t.ir*, éclipser.

outside, *a*, extérieur. ~ *broker*, banquier marron, courtier m., *m*. ~ [*cut*], entame, *f*. ~ *edge* (*Skating*), dehors, *m*. ~ *margins* (book), marges extérieures, *f.pl*, grand fond, *m*. ~ *shutter*, contrevent, *m*. ¶ *ad*, [en] dehors, là-dehors, à l'extérieur. ~ *text* (plate, map, &c), hors texte. ¶ *n*, extérieur, dehors, *m*; (*bus*) impériale; (*café*) terrasse, *f. at the* ~, tout au plus. **outsider**, *n*, (*pers.*) profane, *m,f*; (*horse*) outsider, *m*.

outsize, *n*, taille hors série, *f*.

outskirts, *n.pl*, environs, entours, *m.pl*; banlieue, *f*.

outspoken, *a*, franc. ~**ness**, *n*, franchise, liberté [de langage], liberté de parole, *f*.

outspread, *a*, étendu.

outstanding, *a*, échu, à payer; arriéré; en suspens; marquant, saillant.

outstretched, *a*, étendu.

outstrip, *v.t*, devancer.

out-turn, *n*, rendement, *m*.

outward†, *a*, extérieur; d'aller; de sortie. *for* ~ *application* (*Med.*), pour l'usage externe. ~ *bound*, en partance; effectuant son voyage d'aller. ~[**s**], *ad*, en dehors.

outwit, *v.t*, déjouer, circonvenir, tromper.

outwork, *n*, travail à façon, *m*; (*pl*, *Mil.*) dehors, *m.pl*. ~**er**, *n*, travailleur à façon, *m*.

ouzel, *n*, merle, *m*.

oval, *a. & n*, ovale, *a. & m*.

ovary, *n*, ovaire, *m*.

ovation, *n*, ovation, *f*.

oven, *n*, four, *m*; (*fig.*) étuve, *f*.

over, *ad*, dessus; par-dessus; au-dessus; davantage, en sus; trop; fini; passé. ~ *again*, de nouveau, encore une fois. ~ *& above*, en sus de. ~ *there*, là-bas. ¶ *pr*, sur; par-dessus; au-dessus de; plus de; en sus de; de l'autre côté de; par. ~ *all* (*Meas.*), hors tout. ¶ *n*, excédent; (*Knit.*) jeté, *m*.

overact, *v.t*, charger.

overall, *n*, sarrau, *m*; (*pl.*) blouse[-paletot], cotte, salopette, *f*.

overarm stroke, coupe, *f*.

overassess, *v.t*, surimposer, surtaxer. **overassessment**, *n*, surimposition, surtaxe, *f*.

overawe, *v.t*, intimider.

overbalance, v.i, perdre l'équilibre.

overbearing, a, insolent, arrogant, excédant.

overboard (Naut.) ad, par-dessus bord. [a] man ~ ! un homme à la mer!

overburden (Min.), n, terrains de couverture, m.pl. ¶ v.t, surcharger.

overcast, a, couvert, chargé, trouble. ¶v.t.ir, obscurcir. ¶ (Emb.) n, cordonnet, m.

overcautious, a, prudent à l'excès.

overcharge, n, majoration, f. ¶ v.t. & i, surfaire; trop taxer; charger.

overcoat, n, pardessus m; (Mil.) capote, f.

overcome, v.t.ir, surmonter, vaincre; accabler.

overcrowd, v.t, encombrer.

overdo, v.t.ir, outrer, charger. overdone, a, exagéré, outré; (Cook.) trop cuit.

overdose, n, trop forte dose, f.

overdraft, n, découvert, m, avance à découvert, f. overdraw, v.t.ir, (an a/c) mettre à découvert; (fig.) charger.

overdrive, v.t.ir, surmener.

overdue, a, arriéré, en retard.

overelaborate, v.t, tourmenter, fignoler, lécher.

overestimate, v.t, surestimer, surfaire, majorer.

overexcite, v.t, surexciter.

overexposure (Phot.) n, excès de pose, m.

overfeed, v.t.ir, trop nourrir.

overflow, n, débordement; trop-plein, m. ¶ v.i, [se] déborder; surabonder.

overgrow, v.t.ir, envahir. overgrown, p.a, couvert, encombré; trop grand. overgrowth, n, surcroissance, f.

overhand service (Ten.), service par en haut, m.

overhang, n, surplomb, porte à faux, m. ¶ v.i. & t.ir, surplomber.

overhaul, v.t, reviser; visiter; examiner; remettre à point.

overhead, a, aérien; de plafond. ~ charges, frais généraux, m.pl. ¶ ad, au-dessus de la tête; en haut, en l'air, au ciel.

overhear, v.t.ir, entendre [par hasard].

overheat, v.t, échauffer; surchauffer.

overindulgence, n, excès d'indulgence, m, mollesse; gâterie, f.

overjoyed, p.p, comblé de joie, ravi.

overladen, p.p, surchargé.

overland, ad. & a, par terre, de terre.

overlap, v.t. & i, chevaucher, recouvrir, déborder, imbriquer.

overlay, n, jeté de lit, m.

overleaf, ad, au verso.

overload, v.t, surcharger.

overlock, v.t, donner sur; dominer; laisser échapper; oublier; négliger.

overmantel, n, étagère de cheminée, f.

overmatter (Newspaper work) n, marbre, m.

overmuch, ad, [par] trop, à l'excès.

overnight, ad, pendant la nuit; la veille au soir.

overpay, v.t.ir, surpayer, trop payer.

overplus, n, excédent, m.

over-polite, a, révérencieux.

overpower, v.t, maîtriser; accabler. ~ing, a, accablant; tout-puissant.

overproduction, n, surproduction, f.

overrate, v.t, surestimer, surfaire.

overreach, v.t, dépasser; circonvenir.

override, v.t.ir, surmener; primer.

overripe, a, trop mûr, blet.

overrule, v.t, écarter; l'emporter sur; gouverner.

overrun, v.t.ir, envahir; infester; (Typ.) remanier.

oversea[s], a, d'outre-mer. ¶ ad, outre-mer.

overseer, n, surveillant; (Typ.) prote, m.

overset (Newspaper work) n, marbre, m. ¶ v.t.ir, [ren]verser, [faire] chavirer.

oversewing stitch, [point de] surjet, m.

overshadow, v.t, ombrager; obscurcir; éclipser.

overshoe, n, caoutchouc, m.

overshoot, v.t.ir, dépasser.

oversight, n, inadvertance, f, oubli, m, méprise; surveillance, f.

oversleep oneself (to), v. reflexive ir, dormir trop longtemps.

overspread, v.t.ir, se répandre sur.

overstate, v.t, exagérer.

overstaying pass (Mil.), retardataire, a.

overstep, v.t, outrepasser, franchir.

overstock, v.t, encombrer.

overstrain, v.t, outrer; surmener.

overstrung piano, piano oblique, m.

overtraining, n, surentraînement, m.

oversubscribed, p.p, surpassé.

overt†, a, manifeste

overtake, v.t.ir, rattraper, surprendre, atteindre, gagner; (Motor.) doubler.

overtax, v.t, surtaxer, surimposer; surcharger.

overthrow, v.t.ir, renverser, bouleverser, subvertir.

overtime, n, heures supplémentaires, f.pl.

overtop, v.t, surpasser, surmonter.

overture, n, ouverture, f.

overturn, v.t, [ren]verser, [faire] chavirer.

overvalue, v.t, surestimer, surfaire, majorer.

overweening, a, outrecuidant.

overweight, n, poids fort, m.

overwhelm, v.t, accabler, atterrer, assommer; combler.

overwork, v.t, surmener, forcer.

ovine, a, ovine, a.f.

oviparous, a, ovipare.

owe, v.t, devoir, être redevable de. ~ 15 love (Ten.), moins 15 à rien. owing, a, dû, échu; arriéré.

owl, n, hibou, m, chouette, f.

own, a, propre; (brother, sister) germain, e. not my ~, pas à moi, pas le mien. one's ~, son [propre]; à soi. ¶ v.t, posséder; reconnaître; avouer. owner, n, propriétaire, m,f, possesseur; (ship's manager) armateur, (ship's proprietor) propriétaire, m. ~-driver, propriétaire-conducteur, m. ~ or [his] agent (mine, &c), exploitant, m.

at ~'s *risk*, aux risques & périls du destinataire. ~**ship**, *n*, propriété, *f*.

ox, *n*, bœuf, *m*. ~-**eye daisy**, grande marguerite, *f*.

oxide, *n*, oxyde, *m*. **oxidize**, *v.t*, oxyder.

oxygen, *n*, oxygène, *m*. **oxyhydrogen** (*blowpipe*, &c) att, oxhydrique.

oyster, *n*, huître, *f*. ~ *bed*, banc d'h~s; parc à h~s, *m*. ~ *culture*, ostréiculture, *f*. ~**man**, ~**woman**, écailler, ère.

ozone, *n*, ozone, *m*.

P

pace, *n*, pas, *m*; allure, *f*; train, *m*. *to keep* ~ *with*, marcher du même pas que; (*fig.*) marcher de pair avec. ~**maker**, meneur de train, entraîneur, *m*. ¶ *v.t*, arpenter; entraîner.

pachyderm, *n*, pachydermе, *m*.

pacific, *a*, pacifique. P~ [*ocean*], [océan] Pacifique, *m*. **pacificist**, **pacifist**, *n. & att*, pacifiste, *m,f. & a*. **pacify**, *v.t*, pacifier. **pacifying**, *p.a*, pacificateur.

pack, *n*, ballot, *m*, balle, *f*, paquet; (*soldier's*) paquetage, *m*; bande, *f*, tas, *m*; (*hounds*) meute, *f*; (*Cards*) jeu, *m*; (*ice*) banquise, *f*. ~**horse**, cheval de bât, sommier, *m*. ~**man**, porteballe, *m*. ~**saddle**, bât, *m*. ~**thread**, ficelle, *f*. ¶ *v.t*, emballer, empaqueter; (*hounds*) ameuter. ~ [*up*], plier (*ou* trousser) bagage, faire ses malles. ~**age**, *n*, colis; envoi, *m*. ~ed, *p.a*, à couvert. ~ *like sardines* (*people*), rangés comme des harengs en caque. ~**er**, *n*, emballeur. ~**et**, *n*, paquet; envoi, *m*; pochette, *f*. ~ [*boat*], paquebot, *m*. ~**ing**, *n*, emballage, *m*; garniture, *f*. ~ *case*, caisse d'emballage, *f*. ~ *case maker*, layetier emballeur, *m*.

pad, *n*, coussinet, bourrelet; (*for carrier's head*) tortillon; (*stamp*) tampon; (*blotting*) sous-main; (*writing*) bloc-notes, bloc de correspondance, *m*. ¶ *v.t*, [rem]bourrer, matelasser, feutrer, ouater; tamponner; (*verses*) cheviller. *padded cell*, cabanon, *m*. **padding**, *n*, [rem]bourrage, *m*; bourre, *f*.

paddle (*canoe*) *n*, pagaie, *f*. ~ [*board*], aube, *f*, aileron, *m*; (*water wheel*) jantille, *f*. ~ *boat*, bateau à roues, *m*. ~ *box*, tambour, *m*. ~ *wheel*, roue à aubes, *f*. ¶ *v.i*, pagayer; (*splash about*) barboter. **paddler**, *n*, pagayeur, *m*, barboteur, *m*. **paddling**, *n*, nage à la pagaie, *f*; barbotage, *m*.

paddock, *n*, enclos, parc [pour chevaux] *m*; (*Turf*) enceinte du pesage, *f*, pesage, *m*.

padlock, *n*, cadenas, *m*. ¶ *v.t*, cadenasser.

Padua, *n*, Padoue, *f*.

paean, *n*, péan, pæan, *m*.

pagan, *a. & n*, païen, ne. ~**ism** & ~**dom**, *n*, paganisme, *m*, gentilité, *f*.

page, *n*, (*book*) page, *f*; (*Hist.*, *noble youth*)

page, *m*. ~ [*boy*], groom, chasseur, *m*. ~ *proof*, mise en pages, *f*. **page** *or* **paginate**, *v.t*, paginer.

pageant, *n*, scène à grand spectacle, *f*; cortège [à spectacle] *m*, cavalcade, *f*. ~**ry**, *n*, faste, *m*.

paid, *p.p*, payé; versé; [pour] acquit; salarié, à gages. ~ *up*, (*capital*) versé, effectif, réel; (*shares*) libérées.

pail, *n*, seau, *m*. ~[**ful**], *n*, seau, *m*.

paillasse, *n*, paillasse, *f*.

pain, *n*, douleur, souffrance, *f*, mal, *m*; peine, *f*. *in* ~, souffrant. ¶ *v.t*, faire mal à; angoisser, peiner, fâcher. ~**ful**†, *a*, douloureux; dolent; pénible; cruel. ~**less**, *a*, sans douleur, indolent. **pains**, *n.pl*, peine, *f*, soin, *m*, frais, *m.pl*. ~**taking**, *a*, soigneux.

paint, *n*, peinture, couleur, *f*; (*face*) fard, *m*. ~ *brush*, brosse à peindre, *f*; pinceau, *m*. ¶ *v.t*, peindre; (*face*) farder. ~**er**, *n*, peintre, *m*; (*boat*) bosse, *f*. ~**ing**, *n*, peinture, *f*. **paintress**, *n*, femme peintre, *f*.

pair, *n*, paire, *f*; couple, *m*. ~ *of compasses*, compas, *m*. ~ *of scales*, balance, *f*. ~ *of scissors*, ciseaux, *m.pl*. ~ *of steps*, marchepied, *m*, échelle double, *f*. ~ *of trousers*, pantalon, *m*. ~ (*pictures*, &c), les [deux] pendants, *m.pl*. ¶ *v.t*, apparier, appareiller, accoupler, jumeler.

palace, *n*, palais; château, *m*.

paladin, *n*, paladin, *m*.

palaeo-. Same as *paleo-*.

palatable, *a*, agréable [au goût], bon. **palatal**, *a*, palatal. *palat[al]ized consonant*, consonne mouillée, *f*. **palate**, *n*, palais, *m*. **palatial**, *a*, vaste & somptueux.

palaver, *n*, palabre, *f. or m*. ¶ *v.i*, palabrer.

pale, *a*, pâle; blafard, blême; clairet, paillet. ¶ *n*, palis; pal, *m*. ¶ *v.i*, pâlir, blêmir. ~**ness**, *n*, pâleur, *f*.

paleography, *n*, paléographie, *f*.

paleontology, *n*, paléontologie, *f*.

Palermo, *n*, Palerme, *f*.

Palestine, *n*, la Palestine.

palette, *n*, palette, *f*. ~ *knife*, couteau à palette, *f*.

palfrey (*Poet.*) *n*, palefroi, *m*.

palimpsest, *n. & a*, palimpseste, *m. & a*.

paling, *n*, palis, *m*; clôture à claire-voie, *f*.

palisade, *n*, palissade, *f*. ¶ *v.t*, palissader.

palish, *a*, pâlot.

pall, *n*, poêle, drap mortuaire, *m*. ~ *bearers*, porteurs des cordons du poêle, *m.pl*. ~ *on*, blaser, rassasier.

pallet, *n*, palette, *f*; (*bed*) grabat, *m*.

palliasse, *n*, paillasse, *f*.

palliate, *v.t*, pallier. **palliative**, *a. & n*, palliatif, *a. & m*.

pallid, *a*, pâle, blafard, blême. **pallor**, *n*, pâleur, *f*.

palm (*hand*) *n*, paume, *f*. ~ [*branch*], palme, *f*; (*tree*) palmier, *m*, palme, *f*. ~ *grove*, palmeraie, *f*. ~ *house*, serre à

palmiers, *f.* ~ *oil*, huile de palme, *f.*
P~ *Sunday*, dimanche des Rameaux, *m*,
Pâques fleuries, *f.pl.* ~ *off*, faire passer.
~ate[d], *a*, palmé. ~ist, *n*, chiromancien,
ne. ~istry, *n*, chiromancie, *f.* ~*y days*,
beaux jours, *m.pl.*

palp[us], *n*, palpe, *f.* or *m*. palpable, *a*,
palpable, sensible. palpitate, *v.i*, palpiter.
palpitation, *n*, palpitation, *f.*

palter, *v.i*, tergiverser; marchander; se jouer.
paltry, *a*, mesquin, méchant, chétif, pitoyable.

pampas, *n.pl*, pampas, *f.pl.*

pamper, *v.t*, gâter; dorloter.

pamphlet, *n*, brochure, *f.*

pan, *n*, poêle; terrine; casserole; bassine, *f*;
(*scale*) bassin, plateau, plat, *m*; (*w.c.*)
cuvette, *f.*

panacea, *n*, panacée, *f.*

panama, *n*. or *Panama hat*, panama, *m*.

pancake, *n*, crêpe, *f.*

pancreas, *n*, pancréas, *m.*

pandemonium, *n*, pandémonium; tumulte, *m.*

pander to, se faire le ministre complaisant de.

Pandora's box, la boîte de Pandore.

pane, *n*, (*glass*) carreau, *m*, vitre, *f*; (*side or face*) pan, *m*; (*hammer*) panne, *f.*

panegyric, *n*, panégyrique, *m.*

panel, *n*, panneau; (*Radio*) châssis; tableau,
m, liste, *f.* ~ *envelope*, enveloppe à
panneau, e. à fenêtre, *f.* ¶ *v.t*, lambrisser.

pang, *n*, serrement de cœur, tourment, *m*,
angoisse, *f*; (*pl.*) affres, *f.pl.*

pan-Germanism, *n*, pangermanisme, *m.*

panic, *n*, [terreur] panique, *f.* ¶ *a*, de
panique.

panjandrum, *n*, mamamouchi, *m.*

pannier, *n*, panier, *m*; (*on back*) hotte, *f.*

pannikin, *n*, petit pot, *m.*

panoply, *n*, panoplie, *f.*

panorama, *n*, panorama, *m.*

pansy, *n*, pensée, *f.*

pant, *v.i*, haleter; battre; soupirer.

pantechnicon [van], *n*, fourgon de déménagements, *m.*

pantheism, *n*, panthéisme, *m.*

pantheon, *n*, panthéon, *m.*

panther, *n*, panthère, *f.*

panting, *p.a*, haletant, pantelant.

pantograph, *n*, pantographe, *m.*

pantomime (*dumb show*) *n*, pantomime, *f.*
pantomimist, *n*, pantomime, *m.f.*

pantry, *n*, office, *f*, garde-manger, *m.*

pants, *n.pl*, caleçon, *m.*

pap, *n*, bouillie; pulpe, *f*; mamelon, piz, *m.*

papa, *n*, papa, *m.*

papacy, *n*, papauté, *f.* papal, *a*, papal. ~
nuncio, nonce du Pape, n. apostolique.

paper, *n*, papier, *m*; pièce, *f*; bulletin; (*news*)
journal, *m*, feuille, *f*; (*learned*) mémoire, *m*;
(*Sch.*) composition, copie, *f.* ~ *case*,
papeterie, *f.* ~ *chase*, rallye-papier, *m.*
in ~ *covers*, broché. ~ *clip*, ~ *fastener*,
attache [de bureau] *f.* ~*hanger*, colleur,

m. ~ *hat* (*Danc.*), coiffure de cotillon, *f.*
~ *knife*, coupe-papier, *m.* ~ *lantern*
(Chinese, Japanese), lampion en papier, *m*,
lanterne vénitienne, *f.* ~ *maker*, papetier, ère. ~ *making* & ~ *trade*, papeterie, *f.* ~ *money*, (*convertible*) monnaie de papier, *f*; (*inconvertible*) papiermonnaie, *m.* ~ *streamer*, serpentin, *m.*
~ *warfare*, guerre de plume, *f.* ~ *weight*,
presse-papiers, *m.* ~ *wrappered*, broché.
~ *wrappered, turned over*, couverture rempliée. ¶ *v.t*, tapisser.

papier mâché, carton-pâte, *m.*

papist, *n*, papiste, *m.f.*

papyrus, *n*, papyrus, *m.*

par, *n*, pair, *m.* (See also *paragraph*).

parable & parabola, *n*, parabole, *f.* parabolic(al)†, *a*, en paraboles; (*Geom.*) parabolique.

parachute, *n*, parachute, *m.*

parade, *n*, parade, *f*; (*of mannequins*) défilé, *m*;
esplanade, *f.* ~ *ground*, place d'armes, *f*,
champ de manœuvres, *m.*

paradise, *n*, paradis, *m*; (*Eden*) le paradis
[terrestre]

paradox, *n*, paradoxe, *m.* ~ical, *a*, paradoxal.

paraffin [oil], *n*, huile de pétrole, *f*, pétrole à
brûler, pétrole lampant, *m.* ~ [wax],
n, paraffine, *f.*

paragon, *n*, parangon, modèle, phénix, *m.*

paragraph (*abb.* par) *n*, paragraphe; alinéa;
entrefilet, *m.* *par writer*, courriériste, *m.*

parakeet, *n*, perruche, *f.*

parallax, *n*, parallaxe, *f.*

parallel†, *a*, parallèle; (*drill shank*, &c)
cylindrique; (*fig.*) pareil. ~ *bars*, barres
parallèles, *f.pl.* ~ *ruler*, règle à tracer
des parallèles, *f.* ¶ *n*, (*Geom.*, *Mil.*)
parallèle, *f*; (*of latitude*) parallèle, *m*;
(*comparison*) parallèle, pareil, *m.* parallelepiped, *n*, parallélipipède, *m.* parallelogram,
n, parallélogramme, *m.*

paralyse, *v.t*, paralyser; transir. paralysis, *n*,
paralysie, *f.* paralytic, *a.* & *n*, paralytique,
a. & *m.f.* ~ *stroke*, attaque de paralysie, *f.*

paramount, *a*, suprême; suzerain.

paramour, *n*, amant, *m*, maîtresse, *f.*

parapet, *n*, parapet, *m.*

paraphernalia, *n.pl*, attirail, bataclan, *m.*

paraphrase, *n*, paraphrase, *f.* ¶ *v.t.* & *i*,
paraphraser.

parasite, *n*, parasite, *m.* parasitic(al), *a*,
parasite; parasitaire.

parasol, *n*, ombrelle, *f.*

parboil, *v.t*, faire bouillir à demi, étourdir;
(*fig.*) échauffer.

parbuckle, *n*, trévire, *f.* ¶ *v.t*, trévirer.

parcel, *n*, colis; envoi, *m*; partie, *f*, lot,
paquet, *m*, parcelle, *f.* ~ *post*, service
des colis postaux, *m.* *by* ~ *post*, par colis
postal. ~*s delivery*, factage, *m.* ~ [s]
office, bureau de messageries, *m.* ~ [out],
v.t, morceler, lotir.

parch, *v.t,* brûler; dessécher.

parchment, *n,* parchemin, *m.*

pardon, *n,* pardon, *m;* grâce, *f.* ¶ *v.t,* pardonner, pardonner à; gracier. ~able, *a,* pardonnable, excusable.

pare, *v.t,* rogner; éplucher.

paregoric, *a,* parégorique.

parent, *n,* père, *m,* mère; *(fig.)* mère; *(pl.)* parents, *m.pl; (att.)* mère. ~ state, mère patrie, *f.* ~ stock, tronc, *m.* ~age, *n,* extraction, *f.* ~al, *a,* de père, de mère, des parents.

parenthesis, *n,* parenthèse, *f.* parenthetic(al), *a,* entre parenthèses. parenthetically, *ad,* par parenthèse.

pariah, *n,* paria, *m.*

paring, *n,* rognure; retaille; épluchure, *f.*

pari passu, *ad,* pari passu. to *rank* ~, prendre le même rang.

parish, *n, (civil)* commune; *(Eccl.)* paroisse, *f; (att.)* communal; paroissial. ~ church, église paroissiale, paroisse, *f.* parishioner, *n,* habitant(e) de la commune; paroissien, ne.

Parisian, *a,* parisien. ¶ *n,* Parisien, ne.

parity, *n,* parité, *f.*

park, *n,* parc; bois, *m.* ¶ *v.t,* parquer; *(v.i.)* stationner. ~ing, *n,* stationnement, parcage, *m.* ~ place, parc de stationnement, *m.*

parlance, *n,* langage, *m,* termes, *m.pl.*

parley, *n,* pourparlers, *m.pl,* chamade, *f.* ¶ *v.i,* parlementer.

parliament, *n,* parlement, *m.* ~ary, *a, (government, &c)* parlementaire; *(election)* législative; *(candidate)* à la députation. ~ division, circonscription électorale, *f.*

parlour, *n, [petit]* salon; *(convent, school)* parloir, *m.* ~ games, jeux de salon; jeux innocents, petits jeux, *m.pl.* ~ maid, femme de chambre *(servant à table) f.*

Parma, *n,* Parme, *f.* ~ violet, violette de Parme, *f.*

parochial, *a, (civil)* communal; *(Eccl.)* paroissial; *(fig.)* de clocher.

parodist, *n,* parodiste, *f.* parody, *n,* parodie, *f.* ¶ *v.t,* parodier.

parole, *n,* parole, *f.*

paroxysm, *n,* paroxysme, *m.*

parquet, *n,* parquet, *m.* ¶ *v.t,* parqueter.

parricidal, *a,* parricide. parricide, *n, (pers.)* parricide, *m,f; (act)* parricide, *m.*

parrot, *n,* perroquet, *m; (hen)* perruche, *f.*

parry, *v.t,* parer. ~[ing], *n,* parade, *f.*

parse, *v.t,* analyser.

Parsee, *n,* parsi, parse, *m.* ¶ *a,* parse.

parsimonious†, *a,* parcimonieux. parsimony, *n,* parcimonie, *f.*

parsing, *n,* analyse grammaticale, *f.*

parsley, *n,* persil, *m.*

parsnip, *n,* panais, *m.*

parson, *n,* curé; ecclésiastique, *m.* ~'s nose, croupion, as de pique, sot-l'y-laisse, *m.* ~age, *n,* presbytère, *m.*

part, *n,* partie, part, portion, *f;* endroit, parage, *m;* pièce, *f,* organe; *(side)* parti; *(Theat.)* rôle, emploi; *(book)* fascicule, *m,* livraison, *f.* ¶ *v.t,* diviser; séparer; *(metals)* départir; *(v.i.)* se séparer; se décoller ~ with, se défaire de; céder.

partake, *v.i.ir,* participer.

partial†, *a, (biased)* partial; *(not entire)* partiel. to be ~ to, avoir un faible pour. ~ity, *n,* partialité; prédilection, *f,* faible, *m.*

participate, *v.i,* participer.

participial adjective, *(present)* adjectif verbal; *(past)* participe passé employé *(ou pris)* adjectivement, *m.* participle, *n,* participe, *m.*

particle, *n,* particule, parcelle; *(Gram.)* particule, *f.*

particoloured, *a,* bigarré, bariolé.

particular†, *a,* particulier; spécial; exigeant; méticuleux. ¶ *n,* particularité, *f,* point, détail, *m; (pl.)* détails, *m.pl,* indications, *f.pl,* libellé, *m,* renseignements, *m.pl,* précisions, *f.pl.* ~ity, *n,* particularité, *f.* ~ize, *v.t,* particulariser.

parting, *n,* séparation, *f;* décollement; entredeux, *m; (hair)* raie, *f;* adieu, *m.*

partisan, *n,* partisan, *m.*

partition, *n,* séparation; cloison, *f.* ~ off, cloisonner. partitive *(Gram.) a,* partitif.

partly, *ad,* [en] partie; moitié; partiellement; ~ paid share, action non libérée, *f.*

partner, *n, (Com.)* associé, e; *(Sports, Games, Danc., & husband)* partenaire, *f; (wife)* compagne, *f; (Danc.)* danseur, euse, cavalier, *m,* dame, *f.* ¶ *(a lady, Danc.) v.t,* mener. ~ship, *n,* société, association, *f.* to enter into ~ with, s'associer avec.

partridge, *n,* perdrix, *f, (young)* perdreau, *m.*

party, *n, (body united in cause)* parti, *m; (united in pleasure)* partie, *f;* complice *(to =* de); groupe, *m,* bande; brigade; réception; soirée, *f.* ~ at fault *(accident),* auteur, *m.* ~coloured, bigarré, bariolé. ~ *[entitled] (Law),* ayant droit, *m.* ~ to a *(or the) marriage (Law),* conjoint, e. ~ rights *(Law),* mitoyenneté, *f.* ~ spirit, esprit de parti, *m.* ~ wall, mur mitoyen, *m.*

paschal, *a,* pascal.

pass, *n,* passage, *m;* passe, *f;* col, pas; laissezpasser, sauf-conduit; permis, *m; (Mil.)* permission, *f.* ~ book, carnet de compte, c. de banque; *(motors)* c. de passages en douane, *m.* ~ list *(exams),* liste des admis, *f.* ~ sheet *(motors at Cust.),* triptyque, *m.* ~word, mot de passe; *(Mil.)* mot d'ordre, *m.* ¶ *v.i. & t,* passer; admettre, être reçu à; prononcer; faire; adopter, prendre, approuver; voter; dépasser; franchir; croiser; uriner. ~ along! circulez! ~ away, passer; s'écouler; trépasser. ~ by, passer. ~ for payment, ordonnancer. ~ on, transmettre; passer [son chemin]; p. outre. ~out check *(Theat.),* contremarque, *f.* ~able†, *a,* passable;

(*road*, &c) praticable. ~**age**, *n*, passage, *m*; traversée, *f*; trajet; canal; couloir, corridor, *m*. ~ *money*, prix de passage, p. de voyage, *m*.

passenger, *n*, (*land, sea, or air*) voyageur, euse; (*sea or air*) passager, ère. ~ *lift*, ascenseur, *m*. ~ *ship*, paquebot, *m*. ~ *steamer*, paquebot à vapeur, *m*. ~ *train*, train de voyageurs, *m*, grande vitesse, *f*.

passer-by, *n*, passant, e, (*pl.*) allants & venants, *m.pl.* **passing**, *n*, passage, *m*; adoption, *f. in* ~, en passant, passagèrement. ~ *bell*, glas, *m.* ~ *events*, actualités, *f.pl.* ~ *fancy*, caprice, *m*; (*liaison*) passade, *f.* ~ *note* (*Mus.*), note de passage, *f.*

passion, *n*, passion; flamme; fureur; colère, *f.* ~ *flower*, fleur de la Passion, passiflore, *f.* ~ *play*, mystère de la Passion, *m.* ~**ate**, *a*, emporté; rageur; passionné, ardent. ~**ately**, *ad*, rageusement; passionnément, ardemment, à la folie. ~ *fond of*, fou de.

passive†, *a*, passif. ~ [*voice*], *n*, passif, *m*. **passivity**, *n*, passivité, *f*.

passover, *n*, pâque, *f.*

passport, *n*, passeport, *m.*

past, *n*, passé, *m.* ¶ *a. & p.p.* passé. *a master*, passé maître, *m.* ~ [*tense*] [temps] passé, *m. it is* ~ *ten*, il est dix heures sonnées.

paste, *n*, pâte; colle [de pâte]; pierre d'imitation, p. factice, *f*, faux brillant, *m.* ~*board*, carton [de collage] *m.* ¶ *v.t*, coller. ~*on album*, album à coller, *m.* ~*on mount*, carton pour coller les épreuves, *m.*

pastel, *n*, pastel, *m.* ~**ist**, *n*, pastelliste, *m,f.*

pastern, *n*, paturon, *m.*

Pasteurize, *v.t*, pasteuriser, pastoriser.

pastil[le], *n*, pastille, *f.*

pastime, *n*, passe-temps, jeu, *m.*

pastor, *n*, pasteur, *m.* ~**al**, *a*, pastoral. ~*al & ~ale*, *n*, pastorale, *f.*

pastry, *n*, pâtisserie, *f.* ~ *board*, pâtissoire, *f.* ~*cook* [& *confectioner*], pâtissier, ère. ~*cook's shop*, pâtisserie, *f.* ~ *server*, pelle à tarte, *f.*

pasturage, *n*, pâturage, pacage, gagnage, *m.* **pasture**, *n*, pâture, *f*, pâtis; (*uncut*) herbage, *m.* ¶ *v.t*, faire paître, pacager.

pasty, *a*, pâteux. ¶ *n*, pâté, *m*, bouchée, *f.*

pat, *a. & ad*, à propos, tout juste. ¶ *n*, tape, *f*; (*butter*) pain, *m.* ¶ *v.t*, taper, tapoter; (*an animal*) flatter, caresser. ~ *oneself on the back*, se complaire.

patch, *n*, (*ground*) lopin, coin; (*cabbages* &c) carré, *m*; (*face*) mouche; (*tire*) pastille, *f.* ~ *pocket*, poche rapportée, *f.* ~*work*, rapiéçage, *m*; marqueterie, *f*, placage, *m.* ¶ *v.t*, rapiécer. ~ *up*, replâtrer, rafistoler.

pate, *n*, caboche, *f.*

paten, *n*, patène, *f.*

patent, *a*, breveté; (*obvious*) patent. ~ *leather*, cuir verni, *m*; (*att.*) verni.

medicine, spécialité pharmaceutique, *f.* ¶ *n*, brevet [d'invention] *m.* ¶ *v.t*, [faire] breveter.

paternal†, *a*, paternel. **paternity**, *n*, paternité, *f.* **paternoster**, *n*, Pater, *m.*

path, *n*, sentier, chemin, *m*; allée; (*storm*, &c) trajectoire, *f.*

pathetic†, *a*, pathétique.

pathological, *a*, pathologique. **pathologist**, *n*, pathologiste, *m,f.* **pathology**, *n*, pathologie, *f.*

pathos, *n*, pathétique, *m.*

patience, *n*, patience; constance; (*Cards*) réussite, patience, *f. to put out of* ~, impatienter. **patient†**, *a*, patient, endurant. ¶ *n*, malade, *m,f*, patient, e, client, e.

patina, *n*, patine, *f.* **patinated**, *a*, patiné.

patriarch, *n*, patriarche, *m.* ~**al**, *a*, patriarcal.

patrician, *a. & n*, patricien, ne.

patrimony, *n*, patrimoine, *m.*

patriot, *n*, patriote, *m,f.* ~**ic**, *a*, patriotique; patriote. ~**ism**, *n*, patriotisme, *m.*

patrol, *n*, patrouille, *f.* ¶ *v.i*, patrouiller; (*v.t.*) patrouiller sur.

patron, *n*, patron, protecteur, mécène, *m*; (*shop*) chaland, e. ~ [*saint*], patron, ne, saint, e. ~ *saint's day*, fête patronale, *f.* ~**age**, *n*, patronage, *m*, protection, *f*; (*shop*) achalandage, *m.* ~**ess**, *n*, patronne, protectrice; (*fête*, &c) dame patronnesse, *f.* **patronize**, *v.t*, patronner, protéger. ~**d** (*shop*) *p.p*, achalandé. **patronizing**, *a*, paterne, protecteur.

patronymic, *n*, nom patronymique, *m.*

patten, *n*, socque, patin, *m.*

patter, *n*, bruit [des pas, des sabots, &c]; (*in song*) parlé; (*showman's*) boniment, *m.* ¶ *v.i*, trotter à petits pas; (*rain*) crépiter. *a ~ing of feet*, un bruit de pas précipités.

pattern, *n*, modèle; échantillon; calibre, gabarit; patron; dessin, *m.* ~ *maker* (*Foundry*), modeleur, *m.* ~ *making*, modelage, *m.* ¶ *v.t*, modeler.

patty, *n*, bouchée, *f.*

Paul Pry, *n*, fureteur, *m.*

paunch, *n*, panse, *f.*

pauper, *n*, indigent, e, pauvre, *m.* ~**ism**, *n*, paupérisme, *m.*

pause, *n*, pause, *f*; silence; repos, *m.* ¶ *v.i*, faire une pause.

pave, *v.t*, paver; (*fig.*) frayer. ~**ment**, *n*, pavage, pavement; pavé; dallage; trottoir, *m*; (*outside café*) terrasse, *f.* ~ *display* (*shop*), éventaire, *m.* ~ *light*, ~ *glass*, verdal, *m.* **paver, paviour**, *n*, paveur, *m.*

Pavia, *n*, Pavie, *f.*

pavilion, *n*, pavillon, *m.*

paving, *n*, pavage, pavement, *m.* ~ *stone*, pavé; grès à paver, *m.*

paw, *n*, patte, *f. to* ~ *the ground*, piaffer.

pawl, *n*, cliquet, chien, *m.*

pawn, *n*, gage, *m*; pension (*Fin.*) *f*; (*Chess*)

pion, *m.* ~*broker*, prêteur sur gages, *m.* ~*shop*, crédit municipal, *m.* ¶ *v.t*, engager.

pax, *n*, paix, *f*, instrument de paix, *m.*

pay, *n*, paie, paye, *f*, salaire, traitement, *m*, gages, *m.pl*; solde, *f.* ~*master*, payeur, trésorier; commissaire, *m.* ~ *office*, caisse, *f.* ¶ *v.t. & i. ir*, payer; verser; solder, gager; rémunérer; rapporter; (*visit*, &c) faire; (*respects*) présenter; (*homage*) rendre. ~ *back*, rembourser, rendre. ~ *cash* (cheque crossing), payable comptant. ~ *for*, payer, rémunérer. ~ *in*, verser, ~ *off*, solder; désintéresser; casser aux gages, congédier; (*mortgage*) purger. ~ *out*, payer, verser; (*cable*) filer; (*someone*) revaloir. ~ *up*, (*v.t.*) libérer; (*v.i.*) se libérer, s'exécuter. ~**able**, *a*, payable; exigible; à payer; à la charge; exploitable. ~**ee**, *n*, bénéficiaire, *m.f.* ~**er**, *n*, payeur, euse, payant, e; (*good, bad*) paie, paye, *f.* ~**ing**, *a*, payant, rémunérateur. ~ *guest*, pensionnaire, *m.f.* ~*in slip*, bordereau de versement, *m.* ~**ment**, *n*, paiement, *f*, payement; versement, *m*; rémunération, *f.*

pea, *n*, pois, *m.* ~*chick*, paonneau, *m.* ~*cock & ~cock butterfly*, paon, *m.* ~**hen**, paonne, *f.* ~*nut*, arachide, cacahuète, *f.* ~*shooter*, sarbacane, *f.* ~ *soup*, purée de pois, *f.* ~ *stick*, rame à pois, *f.*

peace, *n*, paix; tranquillité, *f*, repos; ordre public, *m.* ~*maker*, pacificateur, trice. ~**able**† & ~**ful**†, *a*, paisible; pacifique; tranquille.

peach, *n*, pêche, *f.* ~ [*tree*], pêcher, *m.*

peak, *n*, cime, *f*, sommet; piton, pic, *m*, dent; (*cap*) visière; pointe, *f*, maximum, plafond, *m.* ~ *hours*, heures de pointe, *f.pl.*

peal, *n*, carillon, *f*, volée, *f*; éclat, coup, *m.*

pear, *n*, poire, *f.* ~ *tree & ~wood*, poirier, *m.*

pearl, *n*, perle, *f.* ~ *button*, bouton de nacre, *m.* ~ *barley*, orge perlé, *m.* ~ *knitting*, tricot à l'envers, *m.* ~ *oyster*, huître perlière, *f.* ~**y**, *a*, de perle, perlé, nacré.

peasant. *n. & att*, paysan, ne. ~**ry**, *n*, les paysans, *m.pl.*

peat, *n*, tourbe, *f.* ~ *bog*, ~**ery**, *n*, tourbière, *f.* ~**y**, *a*, tourbeux.

pebble, *n*, caillou; galet, *m.*

peccadillo, *n*, peccadille, *f.*

peccary, *n*, pécari, *m.*

peccavi, *n*, meâ-culpâ, *m.*

peck, *n*, coup de bec, *m*; *Meas.* = 9·092 litres. ¶ *v.t*, becqueter, picoter; (*v.i.*) picorer. *to be ~ish*, avoir la fringale.

pecten (*Mol.*) *n*, peigne, *m.*

peculate, *v.t*, détourner. **peculation,** *n*, détournement, *m*, malversation, *f.*

peculiar†, *a*, particulier; propre; singulier, bizarre. ~**ity**, *n*, particularité, singularité, *f.*

pecuniary†, *a*, pécuniaire.

pedagogue, *n*, pédagogue, magister, *m.*

pedal, *n*, pédale, *f.* ~ [*key*]*board*, pédalier, *m.* ¶ *v.i*, pédaler.

pedant, *n*, pédant, e. ~**ic**†, *a*, pédant; pédantesque. ~**ry**, *n*, pédanterie, *f*, pédantisme, *m.*

peddle, *v.i. & t*, baguenauder; détailler; colporter.

pedestal, *n*, piédestal, pied, socle, *m*, gaine; sellette, *f*, porte-potiche, *m.* ~ *cupboard*, table de nuit, *f.* ~ *desk*, bureau-ministre, *m.* ~ *table*, table à pied central, *f.*

pedestrian, *n*, piéton, *m.* ~ *crossing*, traversée des piétons, *f.* ¶ *a*, à pied; (*statue*) pédestre.

pedigree, *n*, généalogie, *f*; pedigree, *m.*

pediment, *n*, fronton, *m.*

pedlar, *n*, colporteur, porteballe, *m.*

pedometer, *n*, podomètre, compte-pas, *m.*

peel, *n*, peau, pelure, écorce, *f*; zeste, *m.* ¶ *v.t*, peler, éplucher, écorcer, décortiquer. ~ [*off*], *v.i*, se peler, s'écailler. ~**ings**, *n.pl*, épluchures, *f.pl.*

peep, *n*, regard [furtif] *m*; échappée [de vue] *f.* ~ *at*, ~ *of day*, dès patron-minet. ~*hole*, regard, judas, *m.* ¶ *v.i*, regarder; regarder sans faire semblant, guigner; émerger; (*chirp*) pépier. ~ *at*, guigner.

peer, *n*, pair, *m.* ~ *into*, scruter; fouiller. ~**age**, *n*, pairie, *f*; (*book*) nobiliaire, *m.* ~**ess**, *n*, pairesse, *f.* ~**less**, *a*, sans pair; introuvable.

peevish, *a*, maussade.

peewit, *n*, vanneau, *m.*

peg, *n*, cheville; fiche, *f*; jalon; (*degree*) cran, *m.* ~ *top*, toupie, *f.* ¶ *v.t*, cheviller; jalonner. ~ [*away*], persister.

pegamoid, *n*, pégamoïd, *m.*

Pegasus (*fig.*) *n*, Pégase, *m.*

peggy (*tooth, Nursery talk*) *n*, quenotte, *f.*

pekin (*fabric*) *n*, pékin, *m.* **Pekinese or peke** (*dog*) *n*, pékinois, *m.* **Pekin[g]** (*Geog.*) *n*, Pékin, *m.*

pelargonium, *n*, pélargonium, *m.*

pelf, *n*, lucre, gain, *m.*

pelican, *n*, pélican, *m.*

pelisse, *n*, pelisse, *f.*

pellet, *n*, boulette, *f*; grain de plomb, *m.*

pellicle, *n*, pellicule, *f.*

pell-mell, *ad. & n*, pêle-mêle, *ad. & m.*

pellucid, *a*, limpide.

pelt, *n*, peau, *f.* ¶ *v.t*, lapider, assaillir à coups (*with* = de). ~*ing rain*, pluie battante, *f.* ~**ry**, *n*, peausserie, *f*; pelleterie, *f.*

pelvis, *n*, bassin, *m.*

pen, *n*, plume, *f*; parc, *m*; bergerie, *f.* ~ *& ink drawing*, dessin à la plume, *m.* ~*holder*, porte-plume, *m.* ~*knife*, canif, *m.* ~*manship*, calligraphie, *f.* ~ *name*, nom de plume, n. de guerre, pseudonyme, *m.* ~ *rack*, pose-plumes, *m.* ~ *tray*, plumier, *m.* ~*wiper*, essuie-plume, *m.* ¶ *v.t*, écrire, composer; parquer.

penal, *a*, pénal. ~**ty**, *n*, pénalité, peine, sanction; pénitence, *f*, dédit, *m.* ~ *area*

(*Foot.*), surface de réparation, *f.* ~ *clause*, clause pénale, *f.* ~ *kick*, coup de réparation, c. de pénalité, *m.* ~ *kick mark*, point de réparation, *m.* ~ *stroke* (*Golf*), coup d'amende, *m.* ¶ **penance**, *n*, pénitence, *f.*

Penates, *n.pl*, dieux pénates, *m.pl.*

pencil, *n*, crayon; (*Opt.*) faisceau, pinceau, *m.* ~ *case*, porte-crayon; (*propulsive lead*) porte-mine, *m.* ~ *sharpener*, taille-crayon, *m.* ¶ *v.t*, crayonner.

pendant, -ent, *n*, pendentif, *m*; (*Nav.*) flamme, *f.* ¶ **pendent, -ant**, *a*, pendant. **pendentive** (*Arch.*) *n*, pendentif, *m.* **pending**, *a*, pendant. ¶ *pr*, en attendant. **pendulum**, *n*, pendule; (*Horol.*) balancier, *m.*

penetrate, *v.t. & i*, pénétrer; percer.

penguin, *n*, manchot, *m.*

peninsula, *n*, péninsule, presqu'île, *f.* **peninsular**, *a*, péninsulaire.

penitence, *n*, pénitence, *f.* ¶ **penitent**, *a. & n*, pénitent, *a.* **penitentiary**, *a*, pénitentiaire. ¶ *n*, pénitencier, *m*; maison de correction, *f.*

pennant, *n*, flamme, *f.*

penniless, *a*, sans le sou.

pennon, *n*, flamme, *f*; guidon, *m.*

Pennsylvania, *n*, la Pen[n]sylvanie.

penny, *n*, penny, = $\frac{1}{12}$ of a shilling: (*very little money*) sou, *m.* ~*a-liner*, folliculaire, *m*, écrivailleur, euse. ~ *dreadful*, roman à deux sous, *m.* ~*royal*, pouliot, *m.* ~*weight*, Meas. = 1·5552 grammes.

pension, *n*, pension, rente, *f.* ¶ *v.t*, pensionner. ~ *off*, retraiter. ~**er**, *n*, pensionnaire, *m,f*; (*Mil.*) invalide, *m.*

pensive, *a*, pensif, songeur.

Pentateuch (the), le Pentateuque.

Pentecost, *n*, la Pentecôte.

penthouse, *n*, appentis, auvent, *m.*

penultimate, *a*, pénultième.

penumbra, *n*, pénombre, *f.*

penurious†, *a*, pauvre. **penury**, *n*, pénurie, disette d'argent, *f.*

peony, *n*, pivoine, *f.*

people, *n*, peuple, *m*; nation, *f*; gens, *m.pl. & f.pl*; personnes; personnalités, *f.pl*; population, *f*; monde, *m*; famille, *f.* ~ *say*, on dit. ¶ *v.t*, peupler.

pepper, *n*, poivre, *m.* ~ *box*, poivrière, *f*, poivrier, *m.* ~*corn*, grain de poivre, *m.* ~*mint*, menthe poivrée, *f.* ~*mint* [*lozenge*], pastille de menthe, *f.* ~ *plant*, poivrier, *m.* ¶ *v.t*, poivrer; (*shot*) canarder; (*questions*) harceler. ~**y**, *a*, poivré; irascible, colérique.

per, *pr*, par; pour. ~ *annum*, par an, l'an. ~ *cent*, pour cent. ~ *contra*, en contrepartie, porté ci-contre.

perambulate, *v.t*, parcourir. **perambulator**, *n*, voiture d'enfant, *f*, landau [pour e.] *m.*

perceive, *v.t*, apercevoir; s'apercevoir de; (*Philos.*) percevoir.

percentage, *n*, pourcentage, tant pour cent, tantième, *m*; proportion, teneur, *f.*

perceptible, *a*, perceptible. **perception**, *n*, perception, *f.*

perch, *n*, (*bird's*) perchoir, bâton; (*fig.*) haut, *m*; (*fish*) perche, *f*; Meas. = 25·293 sq. metres. ¶ *v.i*, percher, jucher, brancher.

perchance, *ad*, peut-être.

percolate, *v.i. & t*, filtrer.

percussion, *n*, percussion, *f.* ~ *cap*, capsule, amorce, *f.* ~ *instruments*, instruments de percussion, *m.pl*; batterie, *f.* **percussive**, *a*, percutant.

perdition, *n*, perdition, *f.*

peregrination, *n*, pérégrination, *f.* **peregrine** [*falcon*], *n*, faucon pèlerin, *m.*

peremptory†, *a*, péremptoire; tranchant, absolu.

perennial, *a*, permanent, intarissable; vivace. ¶ *n*, plante vivace, *f.*

perfect†, *a*, parfait; achevé; vrai. ¶ *v.t*, [par]achever; perfectionner. ~**ion**, *n*, perfection, *f.* ~*ly sweet* (*pers.*), gentil à croquer.

perfidious†, *a*, perfide. **perfidy**, *n*, perfidie, *f.*

perforate, *v.t*, perforer.

perforce, *ad*, forcément.

perform, *v.t. & i*, faire; exécuter, accomplir; jouer, donner, représenter. ~**ance**, *n*, exécution, *f*, accomplissement, *m*; (*Sport*) performance; (*Theat.*) représentation; (*Cinema, &c*) séance, *f.* ~**er**, *n*, exécutant, e; jouer, euse; concertant, e; artiste, *m,f.* ~*ing dog*, chien savant, *m.*

perfume, *n*, parfum, *m.* ~ *distiller*, parfumeur, *m.* ¶ *v.t*, parfumer; embaumer. **perfumer**, *n*, parfumeur, euse. ~**y**, *n*, parfumerie, *f.*

perfunctory, *a*, fait par manière d'acquit.

pergola, *n*, pergola, *f.*

perhaps, *ad*, peut-être.

peril, *n*, péril, *m.* ~*ous†*, *a*, périlleux.

perimeter, *n*, périmètre, *m.*

period, *n*, période; époque; *f*; terme; exercice; (*stop*) point, *m.* ~**ic** *& ~ical†*, *a*, périodique. ~**ical**, *n*, périodique, *m.*

periphery, *n*, périphérie, *f.*

periphrasis, *n*, périphrase, *f.*

periscope, *n*, périscope, *m.*

perish, *v.i*, périr. ~**able**, *a*, périssable.

peristyle, *n*, péristyle, *m.*

peritonitis, *n*, péritonite, *f.*

periwinkle, *n*, (*Mol.*) bigorneau, *m*; (*Bot.*) pervenche, *f.*

perjure oneself, se parjurer. ~**d**, *p.a*, parjure. **perjurer**, *n*, parjure, *m,f*; (*Law*) faux témoin, *m.* **perjury**, *n*, faux témoignage; parjure, *m.*

perky, *a*, éveillé; dégagé.

permanence, *n*, permanence, *f.* **permanent**, *a*, permanent; perpétuel. ~ *wave*, ondulation permanente, *f.* ~ *way* (*Rly*), voie [fixe] *f.* ~ *works*, ~ *structures*, ouvrages d'art, *m.pl.* ~**ly**, *ad*, de façon permanente.

permanganate, *n*, permanganate, *m.*

permeable, *a*, perméable. **permeate**, *v.t*, pénétrer; saturer.

permissible, *a*, loisible. **permission**, *n*, permission, *f*. **permit**, *n*, permis, *m*. ¶ *v.t*, permettre.

pernicious†, *a*, pernicieux.

peroration, *n*, péroraison, *f*.

peroxide, *n*, peroxyde, *m*.

perpendicular†, *a. & n*, perpendiculaire, *a. & f*.

perpetrate, *v.t*, perpétrer, commettre; faire. **perpetrator** (*crime*) *n*, auteur, *m*.

perpetual†, *a*, perpétuel. **perpetuate**, *v.t*, perpétuer. **perpetuity**, *n*, perpétuité, *f*.

perplex, *v.t*, embarrasser. ~ed & ~ing, *a*, perplexe. ~ity, *n*, perplexité, *f*, embarras, *m*.

perquisite, *n*, revenant-bon, *m*, (*pl.*) casuel, *m*.

perry, *n*, poiré, *m*.

persecute, *v.t*, persécuter. **persecution**, *n*, persécution, *f*. **persecutor**, *n*, persécuteur, trice.

perseverance, *n*, persévérance, constance, *f*. **persevere**, *v.i*, persévérer. ~ence, ~ency, *n*, persistance, constance, *f*. ~ent, *a*, persistant.

Persia, *n*, la Perse. **Persian** (*modern*) *a*, persan. ~ blind, persienne, *f*. ~ carpet, tapis de Perse, *m*. ~ cat, chat persan, [c.] angora, *m*. ~ Gulf, golfe Persique, *m*. ¶ *n*, (*pers.*) Persan, e; (*language*) le persan. **Persian** (*ancient*) *a*, perse. ¶ *n*, Perse. *m,f*.

persist, *v.i*, persister, s'obstiner, s'opiniâtrer; persévérer. ~ence, ~ency, *n*, persistance, constance, *f*. ~ent, *a*, persistant.

person, *n*, personne, *f*. ~ of independent means, rentier, ère. ~ opposite, vis-à-vis, *m*. ~age, *n*, personnage, *m*. ~al†, *a*, personnel; mobilier, meuble. ~ality, *n*, personnalité, *f*. ~alty, *n*, biens meubles, *m.pl*. ~ate, *v.t*, représenter; se faire passer pour. **personify**, *v.t*, personnifier.

perspective, *n*, perspective; (*Theat.*) optique, *f*.

perspicacious, *a*, perspicace. **perspicacity**, *n*, perspicacité, *f*. **perspicuous†**, *a*, clair, net.

perspiration, *n*, transpiration, sueur, *f*. *bathed in* ~, en nage. **perspire**, *v.i*, transpirer, suer.

persuade, *v.t*, persuader; décider. **persuasion**, *n*, persuasion; croyance, communion, *f*. **persuasive**, *a*, persuasif.

pert†, *a*, hardi; impertinent.

pertain, *v.i*, appartenir; avoir rapport.

pertinacious†, *a*, opiniâtre. **pertinacity**, *n*, opiniâtreté, *f*.

pertinent, *a*, pertinent, à propos. ~ly, *ad*, à propos.

pertness, *n*, hardiesse; impertinence, *f*.

perturb, *v.t*, troubler, agiter. ~ation, *n*, perturbation, agitation, *f*.

Peru, *n*, le Pérou.

Perugia, *n*, Pérouse, *f*.

perusal, *n*, lecture, *f*. **peruse**, *v.t*, lire attentivement.

Peruvian, *a*, péruvien. ~ bark, quinquina, *m*. ¶ *n*, Péruvien, ne.

pervade, *v.t*, pénétrer. **pervasive**, *a*, pénétrant, subtil.

perverse, *a*, pervers. **perversion**, *n*, perversion, *f*. **perversity**, *n*, perversité, *f*. **pervert** (*apostate*) *n*, pervers, *m*. ¶ *v.t*, pervertir; dénaturer; fausser.

pervious, *a*, perméable.

pessimism, *n*, pessimisme, *m*. **pessimist**, *n*. & ~ic, *a*, pessimiste, *m*. & *a*.

pest, *n*, peste, *f*.

pester, *v.t*, tourmenter, importuner.

pestilence, *n*, peste, *f*. **pestilential**, *a*, pestilentiel.

pestle, *n*, pilon, *m*. ¶ *v.t*, piler.

pet, *n*, accès de mauvaise humeur; animal favori, *m*; favori, ite, mignon, ne, câlin, e, chéri, e, chouchou, *m*. ~ argument, cheval de bataille, *m*. ~ aversion, bête noire, *f*. ~ dog, chien favori, *m*. ~ name, petit nom d'amitié, *m*. ~ scheme, plan favori, *m*. ~ subject, sujet favori, dada, *m*. ~ theory, marotte, *f*. ~ vice, péché mignon, *m*. ¶ *v.t*, câliner, choyer.

petal, *n*, pétale, *m*.

Peter's pence, le denier de Saint-Pierre.

petiole, *n*, pétiole, *m*.

petite, *a*, mignonne.

petition, *n*, pétition, supplique; requête, *f*. ¶ *v.t*, adresser une requête à; (*v.i.*) pétitionner. ~er, *n*, pétitionnaire, *m,f*; requérant, e, demandeur, euse.

petitio principii, pétition de principe, *f*.

petrel, *n*, pétrel, *m*.

petrifaction, *n*, pétrification, *f*. **petrify**, *v.t*, pétrifier; méduser.

petrol, *n*, essence [minérale] *f*. ~ tank, réservoir d'e., *m*. ~ tin, bidon à e., *m*. **petroleum**, *n*, pétrole, *m*.

petticoat, *n*, jupon, cotillon, *m*, cotte, *f*.

pettifoggery, *n*, avocasserie; chicane[rie] *f*.

pettiness, *n*, petitesse, *f*.

pettish, *a*, maussade.

petty, *a*, petit; menu. ~ officer, maître, *m*; (*pl. col.*) maistrance, *f*.

petulance, *n*, vivacité [de caractère], humeur, *f*.

petunia, *n*, pétunia, *m*.

pew, *n*, banc [d'église] *m*.

pewit, *n*, vanneau, *m*.

pewter, *n*, étain, *m*. ~er, *n*, potier d'é., *m*.

phaeton, *n*, phaéton, *m*.

phalanx, *n*, phalange, *f*.

phantasm, *n*, phantasme, *m*, illusion, *f*. **phantasy**, *n*, vision, *f*. **phantasmagoria**, *n*, fantasmagorie, *f*. **phantom**, *n*, fantôme, *m*.

Pharaoh, *n*, pharaon, *m*.

Pharisaic(al), *a*, pharisaïque. **Pharisee**, *n*, pharisien, *m*.

pharmaceutical, *a*, pharmaceutique. **pharmacy**, *n*, pharmacie, *f*.

pharyngitis, *n*, pharyngite, *f*. **pharynx**, *n*, pharynx, *m*.

phase, *n*, phase, *f*; temps, *m*.

pheasant, *n*, faisan, e, (*young*) faisandeau, *m*. ~**ry**, *n*, faisanderie, *f*.

phenacetin, *n*, phénacétine, *f*.

phenomenal, *a*, phénoménal. **phenomenon**, *n*, phénomène, *m*.

phial, *n*, fiole; ampoule, *f*.

Philadelphia, *n*, Philadelphie, *f*.

philander, *v.i*, faire le galant. ~**er**, *n*, galant, *m*.

philanthropic, *a*, philanthropique. **philanthropist**, *n*, philanthrope, *m,f*. **philanthropy**, *n*, philanthropie, *f*.

philatelist, *n*, philatéliste, *m,f*. **philately**, *n*, philatélisme, *m*.

philharmonic, *a*, philharmonique.

philippic, *n*, philippique, *f*.

Philistine, *n*, philistin, *m*.

philologist, *n*, philologue, *m*. **philology**, *n*, philologie, *f*.

philosopher, *n*, philosophe, *m*. ~**s' stone**, pierre philosophale, *f*. **philosophic(al)**†, *a*, philosophique; (*calm*) philosophe. **philosophize**, *v.i*, philosopher. **philosophy**, *n*, philosophie, *f*.

philtre, -ter, *n*, philtre, *m*.

phlebitis, *n*, phlébite, *f*.

phlegm, *n*, mucosité, pituite, *f*; (*fig.*) flegme, *m*. ~**atic**, *a*, flegmatique.

phlox, *n*, phlox, *m*.

ph[o]enix, *n*, phénix, *m*.

phonetic, *a*, phonétique. ~**s**, *n.pl*, phonétique, *f*.

phonograph, *n*, phonographe, *m*.

phosphate, *n*, phosphate, *m*. **phosphorescence**, *n*, phosphorescence, *f*. **phosphorescent**, *a*, phosphorescent. **phosphorus**, *n*, phosphore, *m*.

photograph, *n*, photographie, *f*. ~ **frame**, porte-photographie, *m*. ¶ *v.t*, photographier. ~**er**, *n*, photographe, *m,f*. ~**ic**, *a*, photographique. ~**y**, *n*, photographie, *f*. **photogravure**, *n*, photogravure, *f*.

phrase, *n*, locution, expression, phrase; (*Mus.*) phrase, période, *f*. ¶ *v.t*, phraser. **phraseology**, *n*, phraséologie, *f*.

phrenologist, *n*, phrénologiste, *m*. **phrenology**, *n*, phrénologie, *f*.

phthisis, *n*, phtisie, *f*.

physic, *n*, médecine, *f*. ¶ *v.t*, médicamenter. ~**al**†, *a*, physique; matériel. ~**ian**, *n*, médecin, *m*. ~**ist**, *n*, physicien, ne. ~**s**, *n.pl*, physique, *f*.

physiognomy, *n*, physionomie, *f*.

physiology, *n*, physiologie, *f*.

physique, *n*, physique, *m*.

Piacenza, *n*, Plaisance, *f*.

pianist, *n*, pianiste, *m,f*. **piano[forte]**, *n*, piano, *m*. *piano organ* ou ~ *player*, piano mécanique, *m*. ~ *wire*, corde à piano, *f*.

piccaninny, *n*, négrillon, ne.

piccolo, *n*, piccolo, *m*.

pick, *n*, pic, *m*, pioche, *f*; choix, *m*; élite, fleur, *f*; (*of the basket*) dessus, *m*. ~**axe**,

---

pioche, *f*. ~**lock**, crochet [de serrurier] rossignol, *m*. ~**-me-up**, remontant, *m*. **the** ~ **of the bunch**, la fleur des pois. ~**pocket**, filou, voleur à la tire, pickpocket, coupeur de bourses, *m*. ¶ *v.t*, cueillir; trier; choisir; (*bone*) ronger; (*lock*) crocheter; (*teeth*) curer; (*quarrel*) chercher; (*peck*) becqueter. ~ *at one's food*, pignocher. ~ *up*, relever; ramasser; (*passengers*) prendre; (*news*) écumer.

pickaback, *ad*, sur le dos.

picked, *p.a*, choisi, de choix; d'élite. **picker**, *n*, cueilleur, euse; trieur, euse.

picket, *n*, piquet; jalon, *m*. ¶ *v.t*, piqueter.

picking, *n*, cueillette, *f*; triage, *m*; (*pl. pilferings*) gratte, *f*, tour de bâton, *m*.

pickle, *n*, (*brine*) saumure, *f*; (*plight*) arroi; (*child*) lutin, *m*; (*pl.*) conserves au vinaigre, *f.pl*. ¶ *v.t*, mariner, saler; conserver [au vinaigre]. ~**d**, *a*, (*vegetables*) au vinaigre; (*meat*) salé.

picnic, *n*, pique-nique, *m*, partie de plaisir, *f*. ~ *basket*, panier pique-nique, *m*. ¶ *v.i*, faire un pique-nique.

pictorial, *a*, pictural; en images; (*journal*) illustré, pittoresque; (*plan, map*) figuratif, figuré. ¶ *n*, journal illustré, *m*. **picture**, *n*, tableau, *m*, peinture; image, *f*. ~ *book*, livre d'images, album d'images pour enfants, *m*. ~ *gallery*, galerie de tableaux, *f*. ~ *palace* ou ~**s**, cinéma[tographe] *m*. ~ *postcard*, carte postale illustrée, *f*. ~ *puzzle*, rébus, *m*. ~ *writing*, écriture figurative, *f*. ¶ *v.t*, dépeindre, figurer, représenter. ~ *to oneself*, se figurer. **picturesque**†, *a*, pittoresque, imagé. ~**ness**, *n*, pittoresque, *m*.

pie, *n*, (*meat*) pâté, *m*; (*fruit*) tourte, *f*; (*printers'*) pâté, *m*, pâte, *f*. [*state of*] (*fig.*), chaos, *m*. ~ *dish*, tourtière, *f*.

piebald, *a*, pie.

piece, *n*, morceau; fragment; tronçon, *m*; pièce, *f*. ~ *of business*, affaire, *f*. ~ *of furniture*, meuble, *m*. ~ *of ice*, glaçon, *m*. ~ *of impertinence*, impertinence, *f*. ~ *of news*, nouvelle, *f*. ~ *of ordnance*, bouche à feu, *f*. ~ *of poetry*, poésie, *f*. ~ *of work*, travail, *m*; besogne, *f*. ~ *work*, travail à la tâche, *m*. ¶ *v.t*, rapiécer. ~ *together* (*fig.*), coudre ensemble. **piecemeal**, *ad*, en morceaux; par degrés.

pied, *a*, bigarré, bariolé.

Piedmont, *n*, le Piémont.

pier, *n*, jetée; jetée promenade; pile, *f*; pied-droit; jambage, trumeau, *m*. ~**head**, musoir, *m*.

pierce, *v.t. & i*, percer; repercer; pénétrer. **piercing**, *p.a*, perçant; (*cold*) saisissant.

piety, *n*, piété, *f*.

pig, *n*, cochon, porc, pourceau; (*child*) goret, *m*; (*Founding*) gueuse, *f*, saumon, *m*. ~ *breeding*, l'industrie porcine, *f*. ~**headed**, têtu comme un mulet. ~ [*iron*], fonte en gueuses, *f*. en saumons, [gueuse de] fonte, f. ~ meat, charcuterie, f. ~skin, peau de porc, f, cuir de p., m. ~sty or piggery, n, étable à pourceaux, m, porcherie, f. ~tail (hair), queue, f.

pigeon, n, pigeon, ne; (young) pigeonneau, m. ~ hole, boulin, m; (in desk) case, f. [set of] ~ holes, casier, m. ~ry, n, pigeonnier, m.

piglet, n, goret, m.

pigment, n, pigment, m.

pigmy, n, pygmée, f.

pike, n, pique, f; (fish) brochet, m.

pilaster, n, pilastre, m.

pilchard, n, sardine, f.

pile, n, pile, f, monceau, amas, tas, m; pelote, f; (mass of buildings) amas; (wood) bûcher, m; (arms) faisceau; (stake) pieu, pilotis; (nap) poil, m. ~ driver, sonnette, hie, f. man who has made his ~, homme nanti, m. ~ [up], v.t, empiler, entasser, amonceler, amasser. pile arms, former les faisceaux.

piles (Med.) n.pl, hémorroïdes, f.pl.

pilfer, v.t, piller.

pilgrim, n, pèlerin, n.e. ~age, n. & place of pilgrimage, pèlerinage, m.

piling (pile work) n, pilotis, m. ~ up of taxation, fiscalité, f.

pill, n, pilule; dragée, f.

pillage, n, pillage, m. ¶ v.t, piller.

pillar, n, pilier, m, colonne, f. ~ box, borne postale, f.

pillion (Motor.) n, siège arrière, tan-sad, m. ~ rider, passager (ère) de tan-sad.

pillory, n, pilori, m. ¶ v.t, pilorier, draper.

pillow, n, oreiller; chevet; (Lace making) coussin, m. ~ case, ~ slip, taie d'oreiller, f. ~ lace, dentelle aux fuseaux, f.

pilot, n, pilote, m. ~ balloon, ballon d'essai, m. ~ boat, bateau-pilote, m. ~ lamp, lampe témoin, f. ¶ v.t, piloter.

pimpernel, n, mouron, m, morgeline, f.

pimple, n, bouton, bourgeon, m, pustule, papule, f. to break out in ~s, boutonner, bourgeonner.

pin, n, épingle; (peg) cheville, f, boulon, m; goupille, clavette; broche; fiche, f; (fig.) épingle, f, fétu, m. ~s & needles (fig.), fourmis, f.pl. ~cushion, pelote [à épingles] f. ~ money, argent de poche, m. ~ prick, piqûre d'épingle, f, coup d'é., m. ~ table, billard américain, m. ¶ v.t, épingler; cheviller; clouer.

pinafore, n, tablier [d'enfant] m.

pincers, n.pl, tenailles, f; (smith's) tricoises, f.pl.

pinch, n, (of salt) pincée; (snuff) prise, f. at a ~, au besoin. ¶ v.t, pincer; blesser, brider, gêner. ~ed, p.a, tiré.

pine [apple], n, ananas, m. pine [tree], n, pin, m. pine wood (forest), pineraie, f.

pine, v.i, languir; dépérir, sécher.

ping-pong, n, ping-pong, tennis de table, m. ~ set, jeu de p.-p., jeu de t. de t., m.

pining, n, dépérissement, m; nostalgie, f.

pinion, n, aileron; (Mech.) pignon, m. ¶ v.t, couper les ailes à; (pers.) garrotter.

pink, a, rose, incarnat. ¶ n, rose; (Bot.) œillet, m, mignardise, f.

pinnace, n, grand canot, m.

pinnacle, n, pinacle, m.

pint, n, Imperial Meas. = 0·568 litre.

pintle, n, cheville, broche, f.

pioneer, n, pionnier, m.

pioust†, a, pieux.

pip, n, (seed) pépin; (cards, dominoes) point, m; (disease) pépie, f.

pipe, n, tuyau, conduit, m, conduite, f; canal; (key) canon, m, forure; (tobacco) pipe, f; (flute) pipeau, chalumeau; (boatswain's) sifflet, m. ~ clay, terre de pipe, f; blanc de terre à pipe, m; (v.t.) passer à la t. de p. ~ light, fidibus, m. ~ line, canalisation, f. ¶ v.i. & t, siffler. piping (braid) n, passepoil, liséré, m.

pipit, n, pipi[t] m.

pipkin, n, poêlon, m, huguenote, f.

pippin, n, reinette, f.

piquancy, n, goût piquant; (fig.) piquant, sel, m. piquant, a, piquant. pique, n, pique, f. ¶ v.t, piquer. piquet, n, piquet, m.

piracy, n, piraterie; contrefaçon, f. pirate, n, pirate; forban, m. ~ publisher, éditeur marron, m. ¶ v.t, contrefaire; (v.i.) pirater.

Piraeus, n, le Pirée.

pirouette, n, pirouette, f. ¶ v.i, pirouetter.

Pisa, n, Pise, f.

pisciculture, n, pisciculture, f.

pistachio, n, (nut) pistache, f; (tree) pistachier, m.

pistil, n, pistil, dard, m.

pistol, n, pistolet, m. a ~ [held] at one's head (fig.), un couteau à la gorge.

piston, n, piston, m.

pit, n, fosse, fouille, f, creux, puits, m; carrière; (in metal, &c) piqûre; (pock) marque, couture, f; (Theat.) parterre, m. ~fall, trappe, f, piège; (fig.) écueil, m. ~ saw, scie de long, f. ¶ v.t, marquer, couturer; piquer; mettre aux prises.

pit-[a-]pat (to go), faire tic tac, palpiter.

pitch, n, poix, f; brai, bitume; point, degré, m, période; inclinaison, pente, f; (Mus.) diapason, m, hauteur [musicale] f; (Mech.) pas; (Naut.) coup de tangage; (angler's) coup, m. ~ dark, noir comme poix. ~fork, fourche à faner, fouine, f. ~fork someone into an office, bombarder quelqu'un à une place. ~pine, pitchpin, m. ~ pipe, diapason à bouche, m. ¶ v.t, poisser; jeter, lancer; dresser, tendre, asseoir; (v.i.) plonger; (ship) tanguer, canarder. ~ed battle, bataille rangée, f.

pitcher, n, cruche, f, broc, m.

piteous†, a, piteux, pitoyable.

pith, n, moelle; (palm tree) cervelle; (fig.) moelle, f, suc; (of a story) piquant, m.

~ **helmet**, casque en moelle, *m.* **~y**, *a*, moelleux; (*fig.*) plein de moelle.

pitiable† & **pitiful†**, *a*, piteux, à faire pitié; pitoyable, lamentable. **pitiless†**, *a*, impitoyable, sans pitié.

pittance, *n*, maigre revenu, revenu dérisoire, *m*; faible portion, *f*.

pity, *n*, pitié, *f*; (*regret*) dommage, *m*. to move to ~, apitoyer. ¶ *v.t*, plaindre, avoir pitié de.

pivot, *n*, pivot, *m*. ¶ *v.i*, pivoter.

pixy, -xie, *n*, fée, *f*.

placard, *n*, placard, *m*, affiche, pancarte, *f*. ¶ *v.t*, placarder, afficher.

place, *n*, place, *f*; endroit; lieu, *m*; localité, *f*. ~ kick (*Rugby*), coup placé, *m*. to take ~, avoir lieu, se passer. ¶ *v.t*, placer; mettre; déposer; poser. ~*d horse*, cheval placé, *m*.

placer (*Min.*) *n*, placer, *m*.

placid†, *a*, placide. **~ity**, *n*, placidité, *f*.

plagiarism, *n*, plagiat, larcin, *m*. **plagiarist**, *n*, plagiaire, *m*. **plagiarize**, *v.t*, plagier.

plague, *n*, peste; plaie, *f*, fléau; tourment, *m*, brebis galeuse, *f*. ~*-stricken* (*person*), pestiféré, e, *a*. & *n*. ¶ (*fig.*) *v.t*, tourmenter, assassiner; (*tease*) lutiner.

plaice, *n*, plie, *f*, carrelet, *m*.

plain, *a*, uni; lisse; plat; simple; (*cigarettes*) ordinaires; clair, évident; distinct; nu; au naturel; laid. ~[*-boiled*], nature. in ~ *clothes*, en civil, en bourgeois. ~ *cooking*, cuisine bourgeoise, *f*. ~ *dealing*, franchise, *f*. in ~ *figures*, en chiffres connus. ~ *girl*, jeune fille laide, *f*, laideron, *m*. ~ *knitting*, tricot à l'endroit, t. uni, *m*. ~ *language* (*Teleg.*), [langage] clair, *m*. ~ *sewing*, couture [à la main] *f*. ~*-song*, plain-chant, *m*. ¶ *n*, plaine, *f*. ~**ly**, *ad*, simplement; clairement; distinctement; nettement, net, bonnement. **~ness**, *n*, simplicité; clarté; netteté; laideur, *f*.

plaintiff, *n*, demandeur, eresse, plaignant, e. **plaintive†**, *a*, plaintif.

plait, *n*, natte, tresse, *f*. ¶ *v.t*, natter, tresser. to ~ one's hair, se natter.

plan, *n*, plan; projet, dessein, *m*, batterie, *f*. ¶ *v.t*, dresser le plan de; projeter, méditer, concerter.

plane, *a*, plan. ¶ *n*, plan, *m*, surface plane, *f*; (*tool*) rabot; avion, aéroplane, *m*. ~ *table*, planchette, *f*. ~ [*tree*], platane, plane, *m*. ¶ *v.t*, raboter; planer. ~ *down*, descendre en vol plané.

planet, *n*, planète, *f*. **planetarium**, *n*, planétaire, *m*. **planetary**, *a*, planétaire.

planing machine, machine à raboter, *f*.

planish, *v.t*, planer.

plank, *n*, madrier, ais, *m*.

plankton, *n*, plancton, *m*.

plant, *n*, plante, herbe, *f*, végétal; matériel, outillage, appareil, *m*. ~ *life*, vie végétale, *f*. ¶ *v.t*, planter; poser. ~ *out*, repiquer, dépoter.

plantain, *n*, plantain; (*banana*) plantanier, *m*.

plantation, *n*, plantation, *f*, plantage, plant, *m*. **planter**, *n*, planteur, euse.

plaque, *n*, plaque, *f*.

plash, *n*, flaque, *f*. ¶ *v.i*, clapoter.

plaster, *n*, plâtre; (*Med.*) emplâtre, *m*. ~ *cast*, plâtre, *m*. ~ *of Paris*, plâtre de moulage, gypse, *m*. ¶ *v.t*, plâtrer. **~er**, *n*, plâtrier, *m*.

plastic, *a*, plastique. **~ity**, *n*, plasticité, *f*.

plat, *n*, natte, tresse, *f*. ¶ *v.t*, natter, tresser.

plate, *n*, plaque; lame, *f*, plateau, *m*; tôle; vaisselle plate; (*church*) chapelle; (*eating*) assiette, *f*; (*collection*) plat, bassin, *m*; (*Phot.*) plaque; (*book*) planche, *f*, horstexte, *m*; (*Turf*) coupe, *f*. [*book of*] ~*s*, atlas, *m*. ~*s & dishes*, vaisselle, *f*. ~ *basket*, ramasse-couverts, *m*. ~ *glass*, glace de vitrage, *f*. ~ *glass insurance*, assurance contre le bris de glaces, *f*. ~ *holder* (*Phot.*), châssis négatif, c. porte-plaque(s) *m*. ~ *layer*, poseur [de voie] *m*. ~ *rack*, égouttoir, *m*. ¶ *v.t*, plaquer; argenter; (*ship*) border. ~[*ful*], *n*, assiettée, assiette, *f*.

plateau, *n*, plateau, *m*.

platen (*Typ.*) *n*, platine, *f*.

platform, *n*, plate-forme; estrade; tribune, *f*; pont; (*Rly*) quai, débarcadère, embarcadère; (*Pol.*) programme, *m*. ~ *car* (*Rly*), truc, *m*. ~ *scales*, bascule romaine, *f*. ~ *ticket*, billet de quai, *m*.

platinotype, *n*, platinotypie, *f*. **platinum**, *n*, platine, *m*. ~ *blonde* (*colour*), blond platine, *m*.

platitude, *n*, platitude, *f*.

Platonic, *a*, platonique.

platoon, *n*, peloton, *m*.

plaudit, *n*, applaudissement, *m*.

plausible†, *a*, plausible.

play, *n*, jeu, *m*; récréation, *f*; essor, *m*, carrière; pièce [de théâtre] *f*; spectacle; (*pl.*) théâtre; (*Mech.*) jeu, *m*, chasse, *f*. ~ *bill*, affiche de théâtre, *f*. ~*fellow, -mate*, camarade de jeu, *m,f*. ~*goer*, coureur (euse) de spectacles. ~*ground*, cour de récréation, *f*, (*covered*) préau, *m*. ~*house*, salle de spectacle, *f*, théâtre, *m*. ~ *of colours*, reflets irisés, *m.pl*. ~ *of features*, jeux de physionomie, *m.pl*. ~ *of light*, jeu de lumière, chatoiement, *m*. ~ *on words*, jeu de mots, *m*. ~ *pen*, parc d'enfant, *m*. ~*thing*, jouet, joujou, *m*, amusette, babiole, *f*. ~*time*, récréation, *f*. ~*wright*, auteur dramatique, dramatiste, *m*, dramaturge, *m,f*. ¶ *v.i*, jouer; (*v.t.*) jouer; j. de; faire; (*harp*, &c) pincer; (*a fish*) noyer. ~ *about*, folâtrer, badiner, gaminer. ~ [*for*] *low* [*stakes*] & ~ *a little* (music), jouailler. ~**er**, *n*, joueur, euse; musicien, ne; acteur, trice, comédien, ne. ~ *piano*, piano mécanique, *m*. **~ful**, *a*, folâtre, enjoué, badin.

~fulness, n, enjouement, m. *playing cards*, cartes à jouer, f.pl. *playing off (tie)*, barrage, m.

plea, n, prétexte, m; (*Law*) défenses, f.pl. exception, f; (*pl.*) conclusions, f.pl. **plead**, v.t. & i, plaider, alléguer, prétexter; (*draw pleadings*) instruire. ~ *forgery*, s'inscrire en faux. ~ *guilty*, s'avouer coupable, s'accuser soi-même. ~ *not guilty*, nier sa culpabilité. ~ing (*Law*) n, (*oral advocacy*) plaidoirie; (*preparatory formalities*) instruction; (*pl, statement*) instruction par écrit, f. ~ *of forgery*, inscription de (*ou* en) faux, f.

pleasant†, a, agréable, aimable; commode. ~ness, n, agrément, m. ~ry, n, plaisanterie, f. **please**, v.t, plaire à, agréer à; sourire à; flatter; accommoder; (*abs.*) plaire. ¶ *imperative*, s'il vous plaît; veuillez; prière de . . .; de grâce! ~d, p.a, content, heureux, aise. **pleasing†**, a, agréable, amène; gracieux. **pleasurable†**, a, agréable. **pleasure**, n, plaisir; agrément, m; douceur; jouissance; volupté, f; honneur; gré, m. ~ *boat*, bateau de plaisance, m. ~ *grounds*, parc d'agrément, m. ~ *resort*, ville où les distractions abondent, v. gaie, f; endroit où l'on s'amuse, m. ~ *trip*, ~ *party*, partie de plaisir, f.

pleat, n, pli, m, pince, f. ¶ v.t, plisser.

plebeian, a, plébéien, peuple. **plebiscite**, n, plébiscite, m.

pledge, a, gage, engagement, m, assurance, f. ¶ v.t, engager; boire à la santé de.

plenary, a, plénier. **plenipotentiary**, a. & n, plénipotentiaire, a. & m. **plenitude**, f, plénitude, f. **plenteous†** & **plentiful†**, a, abondant. *to be plentiful*, foisonner. **plenty**, n, abondance; foison, f. ~ *of*, force. *with* ~ *of*, à grand renfort de. **plenum**, n, plein, m.

pleonasm, n, pléonasme, m.

plethora, n, pléthore, f.

pleura, n, plèvre, f. **pleurisy**, n, pleurésie, f.

plexus, n, plexus, réseau, lacis, m.

pliable, **pliant**, a, pliable, pliant, flexible, souple. **pliancy**, n, flexibilité, souplesse, f.

pliers, n.pl, pince, f, pinces, f.pl.

plight, n, état, m, passe, f, arroi, équipage, m. ¶ v.t, engager.

plinth, n, plinthe, f.

plod on, **along**, v.i, avancer péniblement. **plodder**, n, bûcheur, euse.

plomb (*Cust.*), n, plomb, m. ¶ v.t, plomber.

plot, n, parcelle, f, lopin, coin; parterre; complot, m, conspiration, trame, intrigue; (*novel, play*) intrigue, f. ¶ v.t. & i, rapporter; (*reliever*) tracer; comploter, conspirer, machiner. **plotter**, n, conspirateur, trice. *plotting paper*, papier quadrillé, m.

plough, n, charrue, f; (*Elec.*) frotteur, m. ~ *land*, terre labourable, f. ~*man*, laboureur, valet de charrue, m. ~*share*, soc, m. ¶ v.t. & i, labourer; (*fig.*) sillon-

ner; (*exam*) refuser. ~ing, n, labourage, labour, m.

plover, n, pluvier, m. ~*s' eggs* (*Cook.*), œufs de vanneau, m.pl.

pluck, n, courage, estomac, cran, m; (*Butchery*) fressure, f. ¶ v.t, arracher; [dé]plumer, dépiler; cueillir; (*Mus. strings*) pincer; (*exam*) refuser. ~y†, a, courageux, crâne; (*Phot.*) vigoureux.

plug, n, tampon, bouchon, obturateur, m, bonde; bouche; (*bath*) soupape; (*Elec.*) fiche, f; (*dottle left in pipe*) culot, m; (*twist of tobacco*) carotte, f. ~ *hole*, crapaudine, f. ¶ v.t, tamponner, boucher.

plum, n, prune, f; (*dried*) pruneau, m. ~ *orchard*, prunelaie, f. ~ *pudding*, plum-pudding, m. ~ [*tree*], prunier, m.

plumage, n, plumage, m. **plumassier**, n, plumassier, ère.

plumb, a, droit. ¶ *ad*, à plomb, d'aplomb. ¶ n, plomb, m. ~ *line*, fil à plomb, m. ¶ v.t, plomber. **plumbago**, n, plombagine, f, graphite, m. **plumber**, n, plombier, fontainier, m. **plumbing**, n, plombage, m; plomberie, f.

plume, n, plumet, panache, m, aigrette, f. ¶ v.t, empanacher. ~ *its feathers*, s'éplucher. ~ *oneself on*, se piquer de, se targuer de.

plummer block, palier, m.

plummet, n, plomb; fil à plomb, m; sonde, f.

plump, a, rebondi, dodu, potelé, en chair, paquet; (*chicken*) gras. ~ness, n, embonpoint, m.

plunder, n, pillage; butin, m. ¶ v.t, piller, butiner. ~er, n, pillard, e.

plunge, n, plongeon; (*Swim.*) plongeon sans élan, m. *to take the* ~ (*fig.*), faire le saut périlleux, sauter le fossé. ¶ v.t, plonger, immerger; ensevelir; (*v.i.*) [se] plonger. **plunger**, n, plongeur, m.

pluperfect, n, plus-que-parfait, m.

plural, a, plural; (*Gram.*) pluriel. ¶ n, pluriel, m. ~ity, n, pluralité, f; (*of offices*) cumul, m.

plus, pr, plus. *he is 10, 12*, ~, il a 10, 12, ans révolus. ~*fours*, culotte pour le golf, f. ~ [*sign*], [signe] plus, m.

plush, n, peluche, panne, f.

ply, n, pli, m, épaisseur, f. ~*wood*, [bois] contreplaqué, m. ¶ v.t, (*tool*) manier; (*questions*) presser (*with* = de); (*trade*) exercer; (*v.i.*) faire le service, marcher.

pneumatic, a, pneumatique; à air comprimé. ~ [*tire*], [bandage] pneumatique, pneu, m.

pneumonia, n, pneumonie, f.

Po (the), le Pô.

poach, v.t, pocher; (*v.i.*) braconner. ~er, n, braconnier, m.

pocket, n, poche, f; (*vest*) gousset, m; (*Bil.*) blouse, f. ~ *book*, carnet de poche, m. ~ *money*, argent de p., m. ~ *in* ~, en gain. *in one's* ~ (*fig.*), en poche. ¶ v.t, empocher. ~ful, n, pleine poche, f.

pock-marked, *a*, marqué (*ou* picoté) de petite vérole, grêlé.

pod, *n*, cosse, gousse, *f*.

poem, *n*, poème, *m*, poésie, *f*. **poet**, *n*, poète, *m*. ~**aster**, *n*, poétereau, *m*. ~**ess**, *n*, poétesse, femme poète, *f*. ~**ic**, ~**ical**†, *a*, poétique. ~**ry**, *n*, poésie, *f*.

poignant, *a*, poignant, empoignant.

point, *n*, point; fait, *m*; pointe, *f*; poinçon; bec, *m*; (*Rly*) aiguille, *f*; piquant, *m*; température; question, *f*. ~**-blank**, *ad*, de but en blanc, à bout portant, à brûle-pourpoint. ~ *lace*, point, *m*. ~ *of law*, incident, *m*. ~ *of the compass*, aire de vent, *f*, quart de v., *m*. ~**s up game** (*Ten.*), partie en points, *f*. ~**-to**~ *race*, course au clocher, *f*. 6, 8, ~ [*size*] (*Typ.*), corps 6, 8; corps de 6, de 8, points, *m*. *to the* ~, à propos. ¶ *v.t*, pointer; appointer, épointer, tailler [en pointe]; (*masonry*) jointoyer; (*v.t. & abs.*, *of dog*) arrêter. ~ *at*, montrer du doigt. ~ *out*, signaler, indiquer, désigner. ~**ed**, *a*, pointu; piquant; peu voilé, peu équivoque. ~ *arch*, ogive, *f*. ~**er**, *n*, aiguille, *f*, index; chien d'arrêt, *m*.

poise, *n*, balance, *f*, équilibre, *m*. ¶ *v.t*, balancer, équilibrer.

poison, *n*, poison, toxique, *m*. ~ *gas*, gaz toxique, *m*. ¶ *v.t*, empoisonner, intoxiquer. ~**er**, *n*, empoisonneur,euse. ~**ing**, *n*, empoisonnement, *m*, intoxication, *f*. ~**ous**, *a*, toxique; vénéneux; venimeux. *substance which is* ~, substance qui empoisonne.

poke, *n*, coup, *m*. ¶ *v.t*, fourrer; mettre; (*fire*) attiser, fourgonner. ~ *about*, fourgonner. **poker**, *n*, tisonnier, fourgon; (*Cards*) poker, *m*. ~ *work*, pyrogravure, *f*. **poky**, *a*, resserré, étroit, mesquin.

Poland, *n*, la Pologne.

polar, *a*, polaire. ~ *bear*, ours blanc, *m*. **pole**, *n*, poteau, *m*, perche, gaule, *f*, mât; bâton; (*hop, &c*) échalas; (*carriage*) timon; (*Astr.*, *Phys.*, *&c*) pôle, *m*; *Meas.* = 25·293 sq. metres. **P**~, *n*, Polonais, e. ~**axe**, *n*, merlin, assommoir, *m*; (*Hist.*) hache d'armes, *f*. ~**cat**, putois, *m*. ~ *jump*, saut à la perche, *m*. ~ *star*, étoile polaire, *f*. ¶ *v.t*, échalasser.

polemic(al), *a*, polémique. **polemic**, *n. &* ~**s**, *n.pl*, polémique, *f*.

police, *n*, police, *f*. ~ *court*, tribunal de simple police, *m*. ~**man**, agent de police, gardien de la paix, sergent de ville, *m*. ~ *records*, casier judiciaire, *m*. ~ *station*, bureau de police, poste de p.; (*divisional*) commissariat de p., *m*. ~ *van*, voiture cellulaire, *f*.

policy, *n*, politique, *f*; (*public*) ordre, *m*; (*Insce*) police, *f*.

Polish, *a*, polonais. ¶ *n*, le polonais.

polish, *n*, poli; vernis; *m*; pâte à polir, *f*. ¶ *v.t*, polir; vernir; cirer; faire reluire;

frotter; encaustiquer. ~ *off*, trousser. ~**ing brush** (boots), brosse à reluire, *f*.

polite, *a*, poli. **politely**, *ad*, poliment. ~**ness**, *n*, politesse; (*to women*) galanterie, *f*.

politic & ~**al**†, *a*, politique. ~**ian**, *n*, [homme] politique; (*as a trade*) politicien, *m*. ~**s**, *n.pl. &* **polity**, *n*, politique, *f*. *to talk politics*, politiquer.

polka, *n*, polka, *f*.

poll, *n*, scrutin, vote, *m*. ~ *tax*, capitation, *f*. ~**ing station**, bureau de scrutin, *m*.

pollard, *n*, têtard, *m*. ¶ *v.t*, étêter.

pollen, *n*, pollen, *m*.

pollute, *v.t*, polluer, souiller.

polo, *n. &* ~ *cap*, polo, *m*.

polonaise, *n*, polonaise, *f*.

poltroon, *n*, poltron, ne.

polyanthus, *n*, primevère des jardins, *f*. **polygamist**, *n. &* **polygamous**, *a*, polygame, *m,f. & a*. **polygamy**, *n*, polygamie, *f*. **polyglot**, *a. &* n, polyglotte, *a. & m,f*. **polygon**, *n*, polygone, *m*. **Polynesia**, *n*, la Polynésie. **polyp & polypus**, *n*, polype, *m*. **polysyllabic**, *a. &* **polysyllable**, *a*, polysyllabe, *a. & m*. **polytechnic**, *a*, polytechnique. **polytheism**, *n*, polythéisme, *m*.

pomade, **-atum**, *n*, pommade, *f*. ¶ *v.t*, pommader.

pomegranate, *n*, grenade, *f*. ~ [*tree*], grenadier, *m*.

Pomeranian [dog], *n.* or **pom**, *abb*, loulou [de Poméranie] *m*.

pommel, *n*, pommeau, *m*. ¶ *v.t*, rosser, frotter, gourmer.

pomp, *n*, pompe, *f*, faste, apparat, attirail, *m*. **Pompeii**, *n*, Pompéi, *f*. **pomposity**, *n*, emphase, *f*. **pompous**†, *a*, pompeux; emphatique; doctoral.

pond, *n*, étang, *m*, mare, *f*; (*of canal*) bief, *m*.

ponder, *v.i*, réfléchir, méditer, rêver; (*v.t*.) peser, ruminer. ~**able**, *a*, pondérable, pesant. ~**ous**†, *a*, pondéreux.

pons asinorum, pont aux ânes, *m*.

pontiff, *n*, pontife, *m*. **pontifical**†, *a. & n*, pontifical, *a. & m*. **pontificate**, *n*, pontificat, *m*.

pontoon, *n*, ponton, caisson, *m*. ~ *bridge*, pont de bateaux, *m*.

pony, *n*, poney, *m*.

poodle, *n*, caniche, *m,f*.

pooh, *i*, bah!, baste! **pooh-pooh**, *v.t*, faire fi de, repousser avec mépris.

pool, *n*, mare, *f*, étang, *m*; (*Cards*) poule, cagnotte, *f*; (*Fencing, Shooting, Ice Hockey*) poule, *f*; (*Com.*) pool; (*Fin.*) syndicat de placement, groupement, *m*. ~ *betting*, pari mutuel, *m*. ¶ *v.t*, mettre en commun.

poop, *n. &* ~ *deck*, dunette, *f*.

poor, *a*, pauvre; indigent; maigre; méchant. ~ *box*, tronc des pauvres, *m*. ~ *health*, une santé médiocre, une petite santé. ~ *little thing* (*pers.*), pauvret, te. ~ *rate*, taxe des pauvres, *f*. *the* ~, les pauvres,

les indigents, *m.pl.* **~ly**, *ad*, pauvrement.
¶ *a*, indisposé, incommodé, souffrant.
~ness, *n*, pauvreté, *f*.

pope, *n*, pape, *m*. **~ry**, **n**, papisme, *m*.

pop gun, canonnière, *f*.

popinjay (*Hist.*) *n*, papegai, *m*.

popish, *a*, papiste.

poplar, *n*, peuplier, *m*.

poplin, *n*, popeline, *f*.

poppy, *n*, pavot; coquelicot, ponceau, *m*.

populace, *n*, populace, *f*. **popular†**, *a*, populaire; (*treatise*) de vulgarisation. **~** *edition*, édition populaire, *f*. **~ity**, *n*, popularité, *f*. **~ize**, *v.t.* vulgariser. **populate**, *v.t*, peupler. **population**, *n*, population, *f*. **populous**, *a*, populeux.

porcelain, *n*, porcelaine, *f*.

porch, *n*, porche, portique, *m*.

porcupine, *n*, porc-épic, *m*.

pore, *n*, pore, *m*. **~** *over*, s'absorber dans la lecture de; méditer sur.

pork, *n*, porc, *m*; charcuterie, *f*. **~** *butcher*, charcutier, *m*. **~er**, *n*, cochon; goret, *m*.

porosity, *n*, porosité, *f*. **porous**, *a*, poreux.

porphyry, *n*, porphyre, *m*.

porpoise, *n*, marsouin, *m*.

porridge, *n*, bouillie, *f*. **porringer**, *n*, écuelle, *f*.

port, *n*, port; (*side*) bâbord, *m*. **~** (*hole*), sabord, hublot, *m*. **~** *lid*, mantelet, *m*. **~** *of call*, escale; relâche, *f*. **~** *of registry*, port d'attache. **~** [*wine*], porto, vin de Porto, *m*. **~-*wine mark***, tache de vin, *f*.

portable, *a*, portatif, mobile, roulant.

portal, *n*, portail, *m*.

portcullis, *n*, herse, *f*.

portend, *v.t*, présager. **portent**, *n*, présage, *m*. **portentous**, *a*, de mauvais présage.

porter, *n*, concierge, portier; porteur; portefaix; commissionnaire; facteur, *m*. **~age**, *n*, portage, factage, *m*.

portfolio, *n*, portefeuille; carton, *m*.

portico, *n*, portique, *m*.

portion, *n*, portion, part, *f*, quartier, *m*; (*of Rly train*) rame; (*marriage*) dot, *f*. ¶ *v.t*, partager; doter.

Portland cement, chaux-limite, *f*.

portliness, *n*, corpulence; prestance, *f*. **portly**, *a*, corpulent, gros; d'un port noble.

portmanteau, *n*, valise, *f*.

portrait, *n*, portrait, *m*. **portray**, *v.t*, [dé]peindre. **portrayal**, *n*, peinture, *f*.

portress, *n*, concierge, portière, *f*.

Portugal, *n*, le Portugal. **Portuguese**, *a*, portugais. ¶ *n*, (*pers.*) Portugais, e; (*language*) le portugais.

pose, *n*, pose; momerie, *f*. ¶ *v.i. & t*, poser. **poser**, *n*, problème, *m*, colle, *f*. **position**, *n*, position, situation; posture; condition; assiette, *f*; emplacement; classement, *m*. ¶ *v.t*, classer.

positive†, *a*, positif; absolu.

posse, *n*, brigade, *f*.

possess, *v.t*, posséder. **~ed**, *p.p*, possédé; (*as if* **~**) endiablé. *one* **~**, possédé, e.

~ion, *n*, possession; jouissance, *f*; (*pl.*) possessions, *f.pl*, avoir, bien, *m*. *with immediate* **~**, présentement. **~ive**, *a*, possessif. **~or**, *n*, possesseur, *m*.

possibility, *n*, possibilité, *f*. **possible**, *a. & n*, possible, *a. & m. to be* **~**, se pouvoir. **possibly**, *ad*, peut-être. *he cannot* **~** . . ., il est impossible qu'il . . .

post, *n*, (*upright*) poteau; montant; pieu; étai, *m*; chandelle; colonne; borne, *f*; (*place*) poste, *m*; (*P.O.*) poste, *f*; (*letters*) courrier, *m*. **~card**, carte postale, *f*. **~** *free*, franc[o] de port. *to go* **~-haste**, aller un train de poste, accourir dare-dare. **~man**, facteur [des postes] *m*. **~mark**, **n**, timbre, *m*; (*v.t.*) timbrer. **~master, mistress**, maître (maîtresse) de poste, receveur (euse) des postes. **~master general**, directeur général des postes, télégraphes & téléphones, *m*. **~** *office*, bureau de poste, *m*, poste, *f*. **~** *office guide*, indicateur universel des P.T.T., *m*. **~** *office order*, mandat[-poste] *m*. **~** *office savings bank*, caisse nationale d'épargne [postale] *f*. **~woman**, factrice [des postes] *f*. ¶ *v.t*, mettre à la poste; afficher; placarder; mettre au courant; (*Bkkpg*) [re]porter; (*men*) [a]poster, poser. **~** *notices* (reduction of staff), débaucher. **~age**, *n*, port, *m*. **~** *stamp*, timbre-poste, *m*. **~al**, *a*, postal. **~** *order*, mandat[-poste] *m*.

postdate, *n*, postdate, *f*. ¶ *v.t*, postdater.

poster, *n*, affiche, placard, *m*.

posterior†, *a. & n*, postérieur, *a. & m*.

posterity, *n*, postérité, *f*, nos neveux, *m.pl*.

postern, *n*, poterne, *f*.

posthumous, *a*, posthume.

postillion, *n*, postillon, *m*.

posting, *n*, mise à la poste, *f*; affichage; (*Bkkpg*) report, *m*; (*sentry*) pose, *f*. **~** *box*, boîte de la poste, b. aux lettres, *f*.

post meridiem (*abb.* p.m.), après midi; de l'après-midi, du soir.

post mortem, *n*, autopsie, *f*.

postpone, *v.t*, remettre, renvoyer, différer, ajourner.

postscript (*abb.* P.S.) *n*, post-scriptum, P.-S., *m*.

postulant, *n*, postulant, e.

posture, *n*, posture, pose, attitude, *f*; état, *m*. **~er**, *n*, pantin, *m*.

post-war, *a*, d'après-guerre.

posy, *n*, bouquet, *m*.

pot, *n*, pot, *m*; marmite, *f*; chaudron, *m*; terrine, *f*; creuset, *m*; (*Sport*) coupe; (*Cards*) cagnotte, *f*. **~** *boiler*, besogne alimentaire, *f*. **~** *boy*, **~** *man*, garçon de cabaret, *m*. **~herb**, herbe potagère, *f*. **~** *hole*, excavation, marmite, *f*. **~hook**, crémaillère, *f*; (*Writing*) jambage, *m*. **~house**, cabaret, *m*. **~** *hunter*, coureur de prix, *m*. *to take* **~** *luck*, dîner à la fortune du pot. ¶ *v.t*, empoter. **~ful**, *n*, potée, *f*.

potable, *a*, potable.

potash, n, potasse, f. **potassium**, n, potassium, m.

potato, n, pomme de terre, f.

potency, n, force, f. **potent†**, a, puissant; fort. **potentate**, n, potentat, m. **potential**, a. & n, potentiel, a. & m.

pother, n, brouhaha, m.

potion, n, potion, f.

potted, p.a, en pot, en terrine. ~ **meats**, conserves en vases, terrines, f.pl.

potter, n, potier, m. ~'s **wheel**, tour de potier, m. ¶ v.i, fatrasser. ~**y**, n, poterie; faïence; faïencerie, f.

pottle, n, panier, m.

pouch, n, poche, f, sac, m, bourse; cartouchière, giberne; gibecière; (tobacco) blague, f.

pouf, n, pouf, m.

poulterer, n, marchand de volaille, m.

poultice, n, cataplasme, m.

poultry, n, volaille, f. ~ **yard**, basse-cour, f.

pounce, n, ponce, f. ¶ v.t, poncer. ~ **on**, fondre sur.

pound, n, (for cattle) fourrière, (£) livre; (avoirdupois weight) livre [poids] f. = 0·45359243 kilogramme. ¶ v.t, piler. ~**age**, n, droit de commission, m.

pour, n, déluge, m. ~ [out], v.t, verser; couler, jeter; répandre; épancher; (oil on waves) filer. it is ~ing, il pleut à verse. ~ing rain, pluie battante, f.

pout, v.i, faire la moue, faire la lippe. ~**er**, n, pigeon grosse gorge, m.

poverty, n, pauvreté, f. ~-**stricken** (person), miséreux, euse.

powder, n, poudre, f. ~ **bowl** & ~ **box**, boîte à poudre, f, poudrier, m. ~ **magazine**, poudrière, f. ~ **mill**, poudrerie, f. ~ **puff**, houppe à poudrer, f. ¶ v.t, pulvériser; poudrer; saupoudrer; (Emb.) semer. ~**ing** (Emb.) n, semis, semé, m. ~**y**, a, pulvérulent.

power, n, puissance, f; pouvoir, m; énergie; force; faculté; autorité, f; (att.) mécanique, marchant au moteur. ~ **hammer**, marteau-pilon, m. ~ **house**, ~ **station**, usine de force motrice, f. ~**ful†**, a, puissant; fort; énergique. ~**less**, a, impuissant.

practicable, a, praticable, faisable, exécutable. **practical†**, a, pratique; (pers.) positif. ~ **joke**, farce, malice, niche, fumisterie; brimade, f. ~ **joker**, farceur, euse, fumiste, m. **practice**, n, pratique; habitude, f; usage, m; coutume, f; exercice; tir, m; (Sport) mise en train, f; quelques coups d'essai, quelques échanges, m.pl; clientèle; charge; étude, f, cabinet, m. **practician**, n, praticien, m. **practise**, v.t, pratiquer; exercer; suivre; s'exercer à; user de. **practitioner**, n, praticien, m.

prairie, n, prairie, f.

praise, n, louange, f; éloge, m. ¶ v.t, louer; glorifier; prôner, vanter. ~**worthy**, digne d'éloges, louable.

prance, v.i, piaffer.

prank, n, escapade, fredaine, cascade, équipée, incartade, espièglerie, niche, f.

prate, v.i, bavarder.

pratique, n, [libre] pratique, f.

prattle, n, babil, gazouillement, m. ¶ v.i, babiller, gazouiller.

prawn, n, crevette rose, chevrette, locuste, f, palémon, bouquet, m.

pray, v.t. & i, prier. ¶ (form of address), je vous prie, veuillez; de grâce; je vous le demande? **prayer**, n, prière; supplique, f, orémus, m. ~ **book**, livre d'église, l. de prières, l. d'office, paroissien, m. ~ **wheel**, moulin à prières, m.

preach, v.t. & i, prêcher, annoncer. ~**er**, n, prédicateur; (protestant) prédicant, m. ~**ing**, n, prédication, f.

preamble, n, préambule, considérant, m.

prebend, n, prébende, f. ~**ary**, n, prébendier, m.

precarious†, a, précaire.

precaution, n, précaution, prévoyance, f. ~**ary**, a, de précaution, de prévoyance.

precede, v.t, précéder, devancer. **precedence**, n, priorité; préséance, f, pas, m. **precedent**, n. & **preceding**, a, précédent, m. & a.

precentor, n, grand chantre, m.

precept, n, précepte, m. ~**or**, n, précepteur, m.

precinct, n, enceinte, f; (pl.) pourtour, m.

precious†, a, précieux.

precipice, n, précipice, m. **precipitancy** & **precipitation**, n, précipitation, f. **precipitate**, v.t. & i, précipiter; brusquer. ¶ a. & n, précipité, a. & m. ~**ly**, ad, précipitamment. **precipitous**, a, escarpé, à pic.

precise, a, précis; formaliste. ~**ly**, ad, précisément. to state ~, préciser. **precision**, n, précision, f.

preclude, v.t, empêcher.

precocious, a, précoce; (too knowing) savant; (in vice) polisson. ~**ness**, n, précocité, f.

preconceived, **preconcerted**, a, préconçu, arrêté.

precursor, n. & ~**y**, a, précurseur, m. & a.m.

predatory, a, rapace; de proie.

predecease, n, prédécès, m. ¶ v.i, prédécéder.

predecessor, n, prédécesseur, m, devancier, ère.

predestination, n, prédestination, f.

predicament, n, [mauvaise] passe, situation difficile; (Log.) catégorie, f.

predicate (Log. & Gram.) n, attribut, prédicat, m. ¶ v.t, attribuer; affirmer (ou énoncer) un rapport (of = entre). **predicative adjective**, adjectif attribut, m.

predict, v.t, prédire. ~**ion**, n, prédiction, f.

predilection, n, prédilection, f.

predispose, v.t, prédisposer.

predominance, n, prédominance, f. **predominate**, v.i, prédominer.

pre-eminent, a, prééminent. ~**ly**, ad, par excellence.

pre-emption, n, préemption, f.

preen, *v.t,* éplucher. ~ *its feathers,* s'éplucher.

preface, *n,* préface, *f,* avant-propos, *m.* ¶ *v.t,* préluder à. **prefatory,** *a,* liminaire; à titre de préface.

prefect, *n,* préfet, *m.* ~**ure,** *n,* préfecture, *f.*

prefer, *v.t,* préférer, aimer mieux; promouvoir; déposer. ~**able†,** *a,* préférable. ~**ence,** *n,* préférence, *f;* (*Cust.*) régime de faveur, *m,* préférence, *f.* ~ *shares* or **preferred stock,** actions de priorité, *a—s* privilégiées, *f.pl.* **preferential,** *a,* de préférence, privilégié. **preferment,** *n,* promotion, *f.*

prefix, *n,* préfixe, *m.* ¶ *v.t,* joindre à titre de préface; joindre comme préfixe. ~**ed** (*Gram.*) *p.a,* préfixe.

pregnable, *a,* prenable.

pregnancy, *n,* grossesse, *f.* **pregnant,** *a,* enceinte, grosse; (*animal*) pleine; (*fig.*) gros, plein.

prehensile, *a,* préhenseur, *a.m.* ~ *tail,* queue prenante, *f.*

prehistoric, *a,* préhistorique.

prejudge, *v.t,* préjuger. **prejudice,** *n,* préjudice, détriment; préjugé, *m,* prévention, *f,* parti pris, *m. without* ~ *to,* sans préjudice de. ¶ *v.t,* prévenir; nuire à. **prejudicial,** *a,* préjudiciable; attentatoire.

prelacy, *n,* prélature, *f.* **prelate,** *n,* prélat, *m.*

preliminary, *a,* préliminaire, préalable. ~ *expenses* (company), frais de constitution, *m.pl.* ~ *trial* (*Racing*), critère, criterium, *m.* **preliminaries,** *n.pl,* préliminaires, *m.pl,* préface, *f;* (*book, abb.* **prelims**) pièces liminaires, *f.pl.*

prelude, *n,* prélude, *m.* ¶ *v.i,* préluder.

premature†, *a,* prématuré; (*childbirth*) avant terme.

premeditate, *v.t,* préméditer. **premeditation,** *n,* préméditation, *f.*

premier, *a,* premier. ¶ *n,* président du conseil [des ministres], premier ministre, *m.* ~**ship,** *n,* présidence du conseil, *f.*

premise, *v.t,* faire remarquer d'avance. ~**s,** *n.pl,* immeuble, *m,* locaux, lieux, *m.pl;* (*deed*) intitulé, *m.* **premis[s]es** (*Log.*) *n.pl,* prémisses, *f.*

premium, *n,* prime; (*Letting*) reprise, *f;* (*on lease of shop or like*) pas de porte, *m.*

premonition, *n,* présage, *m.* **premonitory,** *a,* prémonitoire, avant-coureur, précurseur. ~ *symptom,* prodrome, *m.*

preoccupation, *n,* préoccupation, *f.* **preoccupy,** *v.t,* préoccuper.

preparation, *n,* préparation; (*Sch.*) étude, *f;* (*pl.*) préparatifs, apprêts, *m.pl.* **preparatory,** *a,* préparatoire. ~ *work* (*Min.*), dispositifs de mines, *m.pl.* **prepare,** *v.t,* préparer; apprêter. ~**d** (*ready*) *p.a,* prêt.

prepay, *v.t,* payer d'avance; affranchir.

preponderance, *n,* prépondérance, *f.* **to preponderate over,** l'emporter sur.

preposition, *n,* préposition, *f.*

prepossess, *v.t,* prévenir. ~**ing,** *a,* prévenant, avenant. ~**ion,** *n,* prévention, *f.*

preposterous†, *a,* déraisonnable, absurde, saugrenu.

prerogative, *n,* prérogative, *f,* privilège, *m.*

presage, *n,* présage, *m.* ¶ *v.t,* présager.

Presbyterian. *n. & a,* presbytérien, ne.

prescience, *n,* prescience, *f.*

prescribe, *v.t,* prescrire; (*Med.*) ordonner. **prescription,** *n,* prescription; (*Med.*) ordonnance, prescription, formule, *f.*

presence, *n,* présence, *f;* prestance, *f.* **present,** *a,* présent; actuel; courant. ~ *day fashions,* actualités de la mode, *f.pl.* ¶ *n,* présent; (*gift*) cadeau, présent, *m. at* ~, présentement. ¶ *v.t,* présenter; offrir. ~**able,** *a,* présentable; montrable. **presentation,** *n,* présentation, *f.* ~ *copy,* exemplaire en hommage, *m.*

presentiment, *n,* pressentiment, *m. to have a* ~ *of,* pressentir.

presently, *ad,* tantôt, tout à l'heure.

preservation, *n,* conservation; préservation, *f.* **preserve,** *n,* conserve, *f,* confiture, *f. oft. pl,* marmelade; réserve, (*pl.*) chasse gardée, chasse réservée, *f;* (*fig.*) fief, *m;* (*pl, Opt.*) conserves, *f.pl.* ¶ *v.t,* préserver; conserver; confire; (*plant*) naturaliser. ~**d** *ginger,* gingembre confit, *m.*

preside, *v.i,* présider. ~ *at, over,* présider [à]. **presidency,** *n,* présidence, *f.* **president,** *n,* président, *m. P~ of the Board of Education* (Eng.), ministre de l'Éducation nationale (*Fr.*) *m. P~ of the Board of Trade,* ministre du Commerce. **presiding** *judge,* président, *m.*

press, *n,* presser, *m;* pressoir, *m;* armoire, *f;* journalisme, *m;* (*of sail*) force, *f. the* ~ (newspapers), la presse. [*for*] ~, bon à tirer. *in the* ~, sous presse. ~ *agency,* agence d'information, *f.* ~ *copy,* (letter) copie à la presse, *f;* (*book*) exemplaire de presse, e. de publicité, *m.* ~ *cutting,* coupure de journal, *f.* ~**man,** journaliste, (*Typ.*) pressier, *m.* ¶ *v.t. & i,* presser; serrer; pressurer; fouler; activer; appuyer; peser. ~ *out,* exprimer. ~**ing,** *a,* pressant, pressé, urgent; (*debt*) criarde. **pressure,** *n,* pression, *f;* serrement, *m;* presse, *f;* accablement, *m;* charge, poussée; tension, *f.* ~ *gauge,* manomètre, *m.*

prestige, *n,* prestige, *m.*

presume, *v.t. & i,* présumer. ~ [*up*]*on,* se prévaloir de. **presumption,** *n,* présomption, *f;* préjugé, *m.* **presumptuous,** *a,* présomptueux. ~**ness,** *n,* outrecuidance, *f.*

presuppose, *v.t,* présupposer.

pretence, *n,* [faux] semblant, *m,* feinte, *f;* prétexte, *m.* **pretend,** *v.t. & i,* faire semblant; prétexter; feindre; prétendre. ~**er,** *n,* prétendant, *m.* **pretension,** *n,* prétention, *f.* **pretentious,** *a,* prétentieux.

preterite, *n,* prétérit, *m.*

preternatural†, *a,* surnaturel.

pretext, n, prétexte, m.

prettiness, n, gentillesse, f. **pretty†**, a, joli, gentil, bellot. ¶ ad, assez. ~ *good*, passable, passablement bon. ~ *much*, à peu près.

prevail over, prévaloir sur, l'emporter sur. *prevail* [*up*]*on*, décider, persuader à. **prevailing**, p.a, dominant, régnant; général. **prevalence**, n, fréquence, prédominance, f. **prevalent**, a, régnant, prédominant. *to be* ~, régner.

prevaricate, v.i, tergiverser, équivoquer. **prevarication**, n, tergiversation, équivoque, f.

prevent, v.t, empêcher, obvier à, prévenir. ~**ion**, n, empêchement, m; défense préventive, f. *society for the* ~ *of cruelty to animals*, société protectrice des animaux, f. ~**ive**, n, préservatif, m.

previous†, a, précédent, antérieur, préalable. ~ *speaker*, préopinant, m.

prevision, n, prévision, f.

pre-war, a, d'avant-guerre.

prey, n, proie, f. ~ [*up*]*on*, faire sa proie de; (*the mind*) miner, ronger.

price, n, prix; cours; taux, m; cote, f. *all at the same* ~ (shop), au choix. ~ *list*, prix courant, tarif, m. ¶ v.t, tarifer. ~**less**, a, sans prix, inappréciable, inestimable, impayable.

prick, n, piqûre, f; coup; (*conscience*) reproche, m. ¶ v.t, piquer; (*conscience*) bourreler. ~ *up* (ears), dresser. **prickle**, n, aiguillon, piquant, m. **prickly**, a, épineux, piquant. ~ *pear*, figue de Barbarie, f.

pride, n, orgueil, m, fierté, gloire, f; amour-propre, m; (*collection of animals*) troupe, f. ~ *oneself* [*up*]*on*, s'enorgueillir de, se faire gloire de, se piquer de, se targuer de.

priest, n, prêtre, abbé, m. ~**ess**, n, prêtresse, f. ~**hood**, n, prêtrise, f, sacerdoce; clergé, m. ~**ly**, a, sacerdotal.

prig, n, pédant, e. **priggish**, a, pédant.

prim, a, pincé, affecté, collet monté.

primacy, n, primatie, primauté, f.

prima donna, prima donna, diva, f.

prima facie, prima facie, de prime face.

primage, n, chapeau [du capitaine], primage, m.

primary†, a, primitif; premier; primordial; primaire. **primate**, n, primat, m. **prime**, a, premier; primordial; de première qualité. ~ *cost*, prix de revient, m. ~ *minister*, président du conseil [des ministres], premier ministre, m. ~ *mover*, mobile, m; cheville ouvrière, f. ~ *of life*, fleur de l'âge, force de l'âge, f, été, m. ¶ v.t, (*pump, Blasting*) amorcer; (*with paint*) imprimer; (*pers.*) souffler. **primer**, n, premier livre de lecture, alphabet, A b c, abécédaire, m. **primeval**, a, primitif. **priming**, n, amorce; (*paint*) impression, f. **primitive†**, a, primitif; primordial. **primogeniture**, n, primogéniture, f. **primordial**, a, primordial. **primrose**, n, primevère, f.

prince, n, prince, m. ~**ly**, a, princier. **princess**, n, princesse, f.

principal†, a, principal; capital. ¶ n, principal; chef, m; directeur, trice; proviseur; patron, ne; mandant, commettant, donneur d'ordre; (*of debt*) capital, principal, m. ~**ity**, n, principauté, f.

principle, n, principe, m.

prink, v.t, éplucher.

print, n, empreinte; impression; (*Phot.*) épreuve [positive]; gravure; estampe, f; (*type*) caractères, m.pl. ¶ v.t, imprimer; tirer; (*with pen*) mouler. ~ [*ed cotton fabric*], indienne, f. ~ [*ed fabric*], toile peinte, f. ~**ed paper** & ~**ed book** & ~**ed form**, imprimé, m. ~**er**, n, imprimeur, m. ~**'s error**, faute d'impression, erreur typographique, f. ~**'s imprint**, indication de nom & de lieu de résidence de l'imprimeur, f. ~**ing**, n, impression, f; tirage, m; (*art*) imprimerie, f. ~ *frame* (Phot.), châssis-presse, m. ~ *ink*, encre d'imprimerie, f. ~ *office*, ~ *works*, imprimerie, typographie, f. ~**out paper** (*Phot.*), papier à image directe, papier à noircissement direct, m.

prior, a, antérieur. ¶ n, prieur, m. ~**ess**, n, prieure, f. ~**ity**, n, priorité, antériorité, f. **priory**, n, prieuré, m.

prise, n, levier, m, pesée, f. ¶ v.t, forcer.

prism, n, prisme, m. ~**atic**, a, prismatique.

prison, n, prison, f. ~ *breaking*, bris de p., m. ~**er**, n, prisonnier, ère, détenu, e; prévenu, e. ~ *at the bar*, accusé, e. ~**s' bars**, ~**s' base**, jeu de barres, m, barres, f.pl.

pristine, a, primitif.

privacy, n, secret, m. **private**, a, privé; particulier; personnel; intime; bourgeois; simple; (*on door*) défense d'entrer. ~ [*soldier*], [simple] soldat, m. *by* ~ *treaty*, à l'amiable, de gré à gré. ~ *view* (Art), avant-première, f. **privateer**, n, corsaire, m. **privateering**, n, course, f. **privately**, ad, en particulier; dans le privé; privément; en bourgeois.

privation, n, privation, f. **privative** (*Gram.*) a. & n, privatif, a. & n.

privet, n, troène, m.

privilege, n, privilège, m; prérogative, f. ¶ v.t, privilégier.

privily, ad, en secret. **privy**, a, privé. ~ *purse*, cassette, f. ~ *to*, instruit de. ¶ n, privé, m, lieux [d'aisance] m.pl.

prize, n, prix, m; (*Nav.*) prise, f; (*lottery*) lot, m; (*leverage*) levier, m, pesée, f. ~ *bull*, taureau primé, m. ~ *court*, conseil des prises, m. ~ *fight*[*ing*], combat de boxe professionnel, m. ~ *fighter*, boxeur professionnel, professionnel de la boxe, m. ~ *giving*, distribution de prix, f. ~ *list*, palmarès, m. ~**man**, lauréat, m. ~ *medal*, médaille d'honneur, f. ~ *winner*, médaillé, e, lauréat, e. ¶ v.t, (*value*) priser; (*lever*) forcer.

pro, *pr*, pour. *the ~s & cons*, le pour & le contre.

probability, *n*, probabilité, vraisemblance, *f*. **probable†**, *a*, probable, vraisemblable.

probate, *n*, vérification de testament, *f*.

probation, *n*, stage, *m*; (*Eccl.*) probation, *f*. ~**er**, *n*, stagiaire, novice, *m*,*f*.

probe, *n*, sonde, *f*, stylet, *m*. ¶ *v.t*, sonder.

probity, *n*, probité, *f*.

problem, *n*, problème, *m*. ~ *play*, pièce à thèse, *f*. ~**atic(al)**, *a*, problématique.

proboscis, *n*, trompe; proboscide, *f*.

pro-British, *a*, anglophile.

procedure, *n*, marche à suivre; (*Law*) procédure, *f*. **proceed**, *v.i*, procéder; provenir; découler; partir; cheminer; s'acheminer; se rendre; marcher; continuer. ~ *against* (*Law*) & ~ *on* & ~ *with*, poursuivre. ~**ing**, *n*, procédé, *m*; (*pl.*) actes, *m.pl* démarches; délibérations, *f.pl*; débats, *m.pl*; procédure, *f*; poursuites, *f.pl*. **proceeds**, *n.pl*, produit, *m*.

process, *n*, cours; procédé; processus, *m*. *in* ~ *of time*, dans la suite. ~ *engraving*, simili-gravure, *f*.

procession, *n*, procession, *f*, défilé, *m*, marche, *f*, cortège, convoi, *m*.

proclaim, *v.t*, proclamer; publier; annoncer; déclarer; dénoncer; afficher. **proclamation**, *n*, proclamation; déclaration, *f*.

proclivity, *n*, penchant, *m*.

procrastinate, *v.i*, aller de délai en délai, atermoyer. **procrastination**, *n*, procrastination, *f*, atermoiement, *m*.

procreate, *v.t*, procréer.

proctor (*Univ.*) *n*, censeur, *m*.

procuration, *n*, procuration, *f*, mandat, *m*. **procure**, *v.t*, procurer.

prod, *v.t*, piquer.

prodigal, *a. & n*, prodigue, *a. & m*,*f*. ~ *son*, enfant p., *m*. ~**ity**, *n*, prodigalité, *f*.

prodigious†, *a*, prodigieux, **prodigy**, *n*, prodige, *m*.

produce, *n*, produit[s] *m.*[*pl.*]; provenances, denrées, *f.pl*. ~ *broker*, courtier de marchandises, *m*. ~ *exchange*, bourse de m—s, *f*. b. de commerce, *f*. ~ *market*, marché commercial, *m*. ¶ *v.t*, produire; rapporter; fournir; exhiber; [re]présenter; communiquer. **producer**, *n*, producteur, trice; metteur en scène, *m*. ~ *gas*, gaz pauvre, *m*. **product**, *n*, produit, *m*, **production**, *f*. ~**ion**, *n*, production; exhibition, [re]présentation, communication; mise en scène, *f*. ~**ive**, *a*, productif.

profanation, *n*, profanation, *f*. **profane**, *a*, profane; blasphémateur. ¶ *v.t*, profaner. **profanity**, *n*, irrévérence, *f*; blasphème, *m*.

profess, *v.t*, professer. ~**ed**, *a*, profès, déclaré. ~**ion**, *n*, profession, *f*; état, métier, *m*. ~**ional**, *a. & n*, professionnel, le. ~ *accountant*, expert-comptable, *m*. ~ *jealousy*, jalousie de métier, *f*. ~**or**, *n*,

professeur, *m*. ~**orship**, *n*, professorat, *m*, chaire, *f*.

proficient, *a*, versé, expert.

profile, *n*, profil, *m*. ¶ *v.t*, profiler.

profit, *n*, profit, bénéfice, gain, *m*. ¶ *v.i*, profiter, bénéficier. ~**able**, *a*, rémunérateur, profitable, fructueux. ~**ably**, *ad*, fructueusement. ~**eer**, *n*, profiteur, euse, mercanti, *m*.

profligacy, *n*, dérèglement, *m*. **profligate**, *a*, dissolu, débauché. ¶ *n*, dévergondé, e.

pro forma (*invoice*), fictive, simulée.

profound, *a*, profond, approfondi. ~**ly**, *ad*, profondément. **profundity**, *n*, profondeur, *f*.

profuse, *a*, abondant; prodigue; profus. ~**ly**, *ad*, abondamment; profusément. **profusion**, *n*, profusion, *f*, luxe, *m*.

progenitor, *n*, auteur, *m*. *our* ~s, les auteurs de nos jours. **progeny**, *n*, descendants, *m.pl*; progéniture, couvée, *f*.

prognathous, *a*, prognathe.

prognosticate, *v.t*, pronostiquer. **prognostic[ation]**, *n*, pronostic, *m*.

programme, *n*, programme; carnet [de bal] *m*.

progress, *n*, progrès, *m*. *oft. pl*, essor, *m*, marche, *f*, mouvement, train, *m*. *in* ~, en cours. ¶ *v.i*, s'avancer, progresser, faire des progrès. ~**ion**, *n*, progression, *f*. ~**ive†**, *a*, progressif.

prohibit, *v.t*, défendre, interdire, prohiber. ~**ion**, *n*, défense, interdiction, prohibition, *f*. ~**ionist**, *n*, prohibitionniste, *m*. ~**ive** & ~**ory**, *a*, prohibitif.

project, *n*, projet, plan, dessein, *m*. ¶ *v.t*, projeter; (*v.i.*) se p., faire saillie, saillir, avancer. ~ *beyond*, dépasser. ~**ile**, *n*. & *a*, projectile, *m*. & *a*. ~**ing**, *p.a*, en saillie, saillant, avancé. ~**ion**, *n*, projection; (*protruding*) saillie, avance, *f*; ressaut, *m*. ~ *lantern*, lanterne de projection, *f*. ~**or** (*Opt.*) *n*, projecteur, *m*.

proletarian, *a*, prolétarien. ¶ *n*, prolétaire, *m*. **proletariat[e]**, *n*, prolétariat, *m*.

prolific, *a*, prolifique; fécond, fertile.

prolix, *a*, prolixe. ~**ity**, *n*, prolixité, *f*.

prologue, *n*, prologue, *m*.

prolong, *v.t*, prolonger. ~**ation**, *n*, prolongation, *f*; prolongement. *m*. *prolonged applause*, applaudissements nourris, *m.pl*.

promenade, *n*, promenade, *f*; promenoir, *m*. ~ *deck*, pont-promenade, *m*.

prominence, *n*, proéminence; saillie, *f*. **prominent**, *a*, proéminent; saillant; éminent; en vedette.

promiscuity, *n*, promiscuité, *f*. **promiscuous**, *a*, mixte. ~**ly**, *ad*, pêle-mêle.

promise, *n*, promesse, *f*; espérances, *f.pl*; avenir, *m*. ¶ *v.t. & i*, promettre; s'engager. ~*d land, land of* ~, terre promise, t. de promission, *f*. **promising**, *a*, prometteur. *promissory note*, billet à ordre, *m*.

promontory, *n*, promontoire, *m*.

promote, *v.t*, encourager, favoriser; avancer, promouvoir; lancer. **promoter**, *n*, promoteur, trice; lanceur, *m*, fondateur, trice.
promotion, *n*, promotion, *f*; avancement; (*of a public company, &c*) lancement, *m*.
prompt†, *a*, prompt. ~ *cash*, [argent] comptant, *m*. ¶ *v.t*, porter; suggérer; inspirer; (*Theat., &c*) souffler. ~ *book*, exemplaire du souffleur, *m*. ~**er**, *n*, souffleur, *m*. ~**itude**, *n*, promptitude, *f*.
promulgate, *v.t*, promulguer.
prone, *a*, couché sur le ventre; prosterné; sujet, enclin, porté. ~**ness**, *n*, inclination, *f*, penchant, *m*.
prong, *n*, dent, branche, *f*, fourchon, *m*.
pronominal†, *a*, pronominal. **pronoun**, *n*, pronom, *m*.
pronounce, *v.t. & i*, prononcer. **pronunciation**, *n*, prononciation, *f*; accent, *m*.
proof, *n*, preuve, *f*; titre; gage, *m*; épreuve, *f*. *in ~ of which*, à titre enseignes que. ~ *against*, à l'épreuve de; cuirassé contre. ~ *reader*, correcteur d'imprimerie, reviseur, *m*. ~ *reading*, correction des épreuves, revision, *f*. ~ *spirit*, esprit preuve, *m*. ¶ *v.t*, imperméabiliser.
prop, *n*, étai, *m*; chandelle, *f*; échalas; tuteur, *m*. ¶ *v.t*, étayer; échalasser.
propaganda, *n*, propagande, *f*.
propagate, *v.t*, propager.
propel, *v.t*, donner l'impulsion à, mouvoir. **propeller**, *n*, propulseur, *m*.
propensity, *n*, propension, *f*, penchant, *m*.
proper†, *a*, propre; bon; bien; convenable; [bien]séant, décent. ~**ty**, *n*, propriété, *f*, bien, *m. oft. pl*, avoir; domaine, *m*; chose; faculté, qualité, *f*, caractère, propre, *m*; (*pl. Theat.*) accessoires, *m.pl.* ~ *market*, marché immobilier, *m*. ~ *tax*, impôt foncier, *m*.
prophecy, *n*, prophétie, *f*. **prophesy**, *v.t & i*, prophétiser. **prophet**, *n*, prophète; augure, *m*. ~**ess**, *n*, prophétesse, *f*. ~**ic(al)†**, *a*, prophétique.
propinquity, *n*, proximité, *f*.
propitiate, *v.t*, rendre propice. **propitious**, *a*, propice.
proportion, *n*, proportion, *f*. ¶ *v.t*, proportionner, mesurer. ~**al†**, *a*, proportionnel.
proposal, *n*, proposition; demande, *f*. **propose**, *v.t. & i*, proposer; (*toast*) porter; (*marriage to woman*) offrir son nom, (*to man*) offrir sa main. **proposer**, *n*, parrain, *m*. **proposition**, *n*, proposition, affaire, *f*.
propound, *v.t*, proposer.
proprietary, *a*, (*rights*) de propriété. ~ *medicine*, spécialité pharmaceutique, *f*. **proprietor, tress**, *n*, propriétaire, *m,f*. **propriety**, *n*, décence, bienséance, convenance, mesure; correction, propriété, *f*.
propulsion, *n*, propulsion, *f*.
pro rata, *ad*, au marc le franc. ~ *to*, au prorata de.
prorogue, *v.t*, proroger.

prosaic†, *a*, prosaïque.
proscenium, *n*, avant-scène, *f*.
proscribe, *v.t*, proscrire.
prose, *n*, prose, *f*. ~ *writer*, prosateur, *m*.
prosecute, *v.t*, poursuivre. **prosecution**, *n*, poursuites, *f.pl*, vindicte, *f*. **prosecutor, trix**, *n*, poursuivant, e, plaignant, e.
proselyte, *n*, prosélyte, *m,f*. **prosiness**, *n*, verbosité, *f*.
prosody, *n*, prosodie, *f*.
prospect, *n*, vue; perspective, *f*, avenir, débouché, *m*. ¶ *v.t*, prospecter. ~**ing**, *n*, prospection, *f*, recherches, *f.pl*. ~**ive**, *a*, en perspective. ~**or**, *n*, prospecteur, *m*.
prospectus, *n*, prospectus, *m*.
prosper, *v.i*, prospérer, réussir. ~**ity**, *n*, prospérité, *f*. ~**ous†**, *a*, prospère, fortuné, florissant, heureux.
prostate (gland), *n*, prostate, *f*.
prostitute, *v.t*, prostituer.
prostrate, *a*, prosterné; prostré, anéanti. ¶ *v.t*, prosterner; anéantir. ~ *oneself*, se prosterner. **prostration**, *n*, prosternation; (*Med.*) prostration, *f*.
prosy, *a*, verbeux, ennuyeux.
protagonist, *n*, protagoniste, *m*.
protect, *v.t*, protéger, garder, défendre, préserver. ~**ion**, *n*, protection, garde, défense, préservation, sauvegarde, tutelle; (*bills of exchange*) bonne fin, *f*. ~**ionist**, *n. & att*, protectionniste, *m. & att*. ~**ive**, *a*, protecteur. **protector, tress**, *n*, protecteur, trice. ~**ate**, *n*, protectorat, *m*.
pro tempore (*abb*. pro tem.) *ad*, à titre provisoire.
protest, *n*, protestation, réclamation, *f*; (*bill*) protêt, *m*. ¶ *v.t. & i*, protester; crier. ~**ant**, *n. & a*, protestant, e.
protocol, *n*, protocole, *m*.
prototype, *n*, prototype, *m*.
protract, *v.t*, prolonger. ~**or**, *n*, rapporteur, *m*.
protrude, *v.i*, faire saillie.
protuberance, *n*, protubérance, *f*.
proud†, *a*, fier; orgueilleux; glorieux. ~ *flesh*, chairs baveuses, *f.pl*.
prove, *v.t*, prouver, faire la preuve de, vérifier, justifier [de]; démontrer; constater; éprouver; (*will*) homologuer.
provender, *n*, fourrage, *m*, provende, *f*.
proverb, *n*, proverbe, *m*. ~**ial†**, *a*, proverbial.
provide, *v.t*, pourvoir, fournir, prescrire, stipuler, prévoir. ~ *against*, se prémunir contre. ~*d* [*that*], pourvu que, à [la] charge de. **providence**, *n*, prévoyance; providence; (*God*) Providence, *f*. **provident**, *a*, prévoyant. ~ *fund*, caisse de prévoyance, *f*. ~**ial†**, *a*, providentiel. **provider**, *n*, pourvoyeur, *m*.
province, *n*, province; (*pl.*) province; (*sphere*) compétence, *f*, ressort, domaine, département, *m*, juridiction, *f*. **provincial**, *a*, provincial; de province.

provision, *n*, provision; prestation; disposition; (*pl.*) provisions de bouche, munitions de b., *f.pl.* vivres, comestibles, *m.pl.* subsistances, *f.pl.* ¶ *v.t.* approvisionner. **~al†**, *a*, provisoire; provisionnel.

proviso, *n*, condition provisionnelle, *f.*

provocation, *n*, provocation; agacerie, *f.* **provoke**, *v.t.* provoquer, agacer, contrarier, vexer, impatienter.

provost, *n*, prévôt; recteur, *m.*

prow, *n*, proue, *f.*

prowess, *n*, prouesse, vaillantise, *f.*

prowl, *v.i*, rôder. **~er**, *n*, rôdeur, *m.*

proximate†, *a*, prochain; immédiat. **proximity**, *n*, proximité, *f.* **proximo**, *ad*, du mois prochain.

proxy, *n*, pouvoir, mandat, *m*, procuration, *f*; mandataire, *m*, fondé de pouvoir(s), *m.*

prude, *n*, prude, bégueule, *f.*

prudence, *n*, prudence, sagesse, *f.* **prudent†**, *a*, prudent, sage, avisé. **~ial**, *a*, de prudence.

prudery, *n*, pruderie, bégueulerie, *f.* **prudish**, *a*, prude, pudibond, bégueule.

prune, *n*, pruneau, *m.* ¶ *v.t*, tailler, émonder, élaguer. **pruning**, *n*, taille, *f*, émondage, élagage, *m*; (*pl.*) élagage, *m*, émondes, *f.pl.* **~ hook**, serpe, *f*, croissant, *m.* **~ knife**, serpette, *f.* **~ shears**, sécateur, *m.*

pruriency, *n*, sensualité, *f.* **prurient**, *a*, sensuel, lascif. **pruritus**, *n*, prurit, *m.*

Prussia, *n*, la Prusse. **Prussian**, *a*, prussien. **~ blue**, bleu de Prusse, *m.* ¶ *n*, Prussien, ne. **prussic**, *a*, prussique.

pry, *v.i*, fureter, fouiller. **~ing**, *a*, indiscret, curieux.

psalm, *n*, psaume, *m.* **~ist**, *n*, psalmiste, *m.* **psalter**, *n*, psautier, *m.*

pseudonym, *n*, pseudonyme, *m.*

pshaw, *i*, bah!, allons donc!

psychiater, **psychiatrist**, *n*, psychiatre, *m.* **psychic(al)**, *a*, psychique. **psycho-analysis**, *n*, psychanalyse, *f.* **psychological**, *a*, psychologique. **psychologist**, *n*, psychologue, *m.* **psychology**, *n*, psychologie, *f.*

ptarmigan, *n*, perdrix des neiges, *f.*

ptomaine, *n*, ptomaïne, *f.* **~ poisoning**, empoisonnement par les ptomaïnes, *f.*

puberty, *n*, puberté, *f.*

public†, *a*, public. **~ assistance**, **~ relief**, assistance publique, *f.* **~ assistance institution**, dépôt de mendicité, *m.* **~ convenience**, chalet de nécessité, *m.* **~ holiday**, fête légale, *f.* **~ house**, cabaret, estaminet, *m*, taverne, brasserie, *f.* **~ prosecutor**, ministère public, *m.* ¶ *n*, public, *m*; clientèle, *f.* **~an**, *n*, cabaretier, ère; (*Bible*) publicain, *m.* **~ation**, *n*, publication, *f.* **~ist**, *n*, publiciste, *m.* **~ity**, *n*, publicité, *f.* **publish**, *v.t*, publier; éditer; faire paraître; proclamer. *to be ~ed* (book), paraître. **~er**, *n*, éditeur, *m.* **~'s imprint**, indication de nom (ou de firme) de l'éditeur; (*place only*) rubrique, *f.*

~ing, *n*, publication, édition, *f.* **~ house**, maison d'édition, librairie, *f.*

puce, *a*, puce.

puck, *n*, lutin, [esprit] follet; (*Ice hockey*) palet, puck, *m.*

pucker, *n*, poche, fronce, *f*, godet, pli, *m.* ¶ *v.t*, froncer, plisser; (*v.i.*) goder, [se] plisser.

pudding, *n*, pudding, pouding, *m.*

puddle, *n*, flaque, *f.* ¶ *v.t*, (clay) corroyer; (*Metall.*) puddler.

puerile†, *a*, puéril.

puff, *n*, souffle, *m*; bouffée; réclame, *f*; (dress) bouillon, *m*; (powder) houppe, *f*; [gâteau] feuilleté, *m.* **~ paragraph**, annonce-article, *f.* ¶ *v.t. & i*, souffler; bouffer; époumoner; plisser; prôner. **~ one's goods**, faire l'article.

puffin, *n*, macareux, *m.*

puffy, *a*, bouffi, soufflé.

pug (clay), *n*, corroi, *m.* **~** [dog], carlin, roquet, *m.* **~ nose**, nez camus, *m.* ¶ *v.t*, corroyer; hourder.

pugilism, *n*, pugilat, *m.* **pugilist**, *n*, pugiliste, *m.* **pugnacious**, *a*, pugnace, batailleur.

pule, *v.i*, piauler.

pull, *n*, tirage, trait, *m*, traction, *f*; effort [de traction] *m*; (drink) lampée; (*Typ.*) feuille de tirée, *f*; (bell) cordon; (*Golf*) coup tiré; (fig.) avantage, *m.* **~-over**, pull-over, *m.* ¶ *v.t. & i*, tirer; arracher; ramer. **~ the wires for** (fig.), intriguer pour. **~ to one side** (traffic), se garer. **~ to pieces**, mettre en pièces; (fig.) éreinter.

pullet, *n*, poulette, *f.*

pulley, *n*, poulie, *f.* **~ block**, moufle, *f. or m.*

Pullman [car], *n*, voiture Pullman, *f.*

pullulate, *v.i*, pulluler.

pulmonary, *a*, pulmonaire.

pulp, *n*, pulpe; chair; (*Paper making*) pâte; bouillie, *f.* ¶ *v.t*, pulper.

pulpit, *n*, chaire [du prédicateur] *f.*

pulsate, *v.i*, battre. **pulsation**, *n*, pulsation, *f*, battement, *m.* **pulse**, *n*, (*Anat.*) pouls, *m*; légumineuse, *f.* **~ rate**, force du pouls, *f.*

pulverize, *v.t*, pulvériser.

puma, *n*, puma, couguar, *m.*

pumice [stone], *n*, [pierre] ponce, *f.* ¶ *v.t*, poncer.

pump, *n*, pompe, *f*; (dress shoe) escarpin, *m.* **~ handle**, levier de pompe, *m*, brimbale, *f.* **~ maker**, pompier, *m.* **~ room** (at spa), buvette, *f.* ¶ *v.t. & i*, pomper; (fig.) sonder, cuisiner. **~ up** (tire), gonfler.

pumpkin, *n*, citrouille, courge, *f*, potiron, *m.*

pun, *n*, calembour, jeu de mots, *m.* ¶ *v.i*, faire des calembours, jouer sur le(s) mot(s).

punch, *n*, coup de poing, renfoncement, *m*, gourmade, *f*; (tool) poinçon; emporte-pièce; (drink) punch, *m.* **~ bowl**, bol à punch, *m.* **P~**, *n*, polichinelle, *m.* **~ & Judy** [show], guignol, *m.* ¶ *v.t*, gourmer; poinçonner; découper.

puncheon, *n*, poinçon, *m*; pièce, *f.*

punching ball, ballon de boxe, *m.*

punctilio, n, pointille, f. **punctilious**, a, pointilleux, méticuleux.

punctual†, a, ponctuel, exact. ~ity, n, ponctualité, exactitude, f. **punctuate**, v.t. & abs, ponctuer. **punctuation**, n, ponctuation, f. **puncture**, n, piqûre; (Surg.) ponction; (tire) crevaison, f. ¶ v.t. & i, piquer; ponctionner; crever.

pundit, n, pandit, pontife, m.

pungency, n, piquant, m; âcreté, f; mordant, m. **pungent**, a, piquant; âcre; mordant.

punish, v.t, punir. ~able, a, punissable. ~ment, n, punition; peine, sanction, pénitence, f; supplice, m.

punster, n, faiseur de calembours, m.

punt (boat) n, bachot, m, plate, f. ¶ v.i, (Cards) ponter; (Betting) parier; (Boating) pousser du fond; (v.t.) pousser (un bateau) à la perche. ~er, n, (Cards) ponte; m; (Betting) parieur, euse.

puny, a, chétif, malingre.

pup, n, petit chien, m. sell a ~ (fig.), repasser un rossignol. ¶ v.i, mettre bas.

pupa, n, chrysalide, f.

pupil, n, (eye) pupille, prunelle, f; (scholar) élève, m,f, écolier, ère; pupille, m,f.

puppet, n, marionnette, poupée, f, mannequin, fantoche, m.

puppy, n, petit chien; (pers.) freluquet, m.

purblind, a, quasi aveugle.

purchase, n, achat, m, acquisition; (shopping) emplette; (hold) prise, f; (tackle) palan, m. ¶ v.t, acheter, acquérir. **purchaser**, n, acheteur, euse, acquéreur, m.

pure†, a, pur. ~ mechanics, mécanique rationnelle, f. ~ness, n, pureté, f.

purgative, a. & n, purgatif, a. & m. **purgatory**, n, purgatoire, m. **purge**, n, purge, épuration, f. ¶ v.t, purger, épurer.

purify, v.t, purifier; épurer. **purist**, n, puriste, m,f. **Puritan**, n. & a. & puritanic(al), a, puritain, e. **purity**, n, pureté, f.

purl, v.i, murmurer, gazouiller. ~ knitting, tricot à l'envers, m.

purlieus, n.pl, environs, entours, m.pl.

purlin, n, panne, f.

purloin, v.t, soustraire.

purple, n, pourpre, m; (robe) pourpre, f. ¶ a, violet. ~ red, rouge pourpré, m. ¶ (fig.) v.t, empourprer. **purplish**, a, pourpurin, violâtre.

purport, n, teneur, portée, f. ¶ v.t, signifier, vouloir dire; sembler, paraître.

purpose, n, but, m, fin; intention, f; propos; dessein; effet; usage, m. to no ~, en pure perte. ¶ v.t, se proposer. ~ly, ad, à dessein, exprès.

purr, n, ronron, m. ¶ v.i, faire ronron.

purse, n, porte-monnaie, m, bourse, f. ¶ (lips) v.t, pincer. **purser**, n, commissaire [de la marine marchande] m.

purslane, n, pourpier, m.

pursuant to, in pursuance of, en vertu de, suivant. **pursue**, v.t, [pour]suivre, chasser.

pursuit, n, poursuite, chasse; recherche; occupation, f.

purulent, a, purulent.

purvey, v.t, pourvoir. ~or, n, pourvoyeur, m.

purview, n, ressort; (Law) dispositif, m.

pus, n, pus, m.

push, n, poussée; initiative, f. ~-ball, pushball, m ~ [button], poussoir, m. ¶ v.t, pousser; presser; avancer. ~ about, bousculer. ~ back, repousser, reculer. ~ off (Naut.), pousser au large. ~ing, a, entreprenant.

pusillanimous, a, pusillanime.

puss[y], n, minet, te, minon, minou, m. Puss in Boots, le Chat botté.

pustule, n, pustule, f.

put, v.t.ir, mettre; placer; porter; poser; apposer; appliquer; faire. ~ (things) away, ranger, serrer. ~ down, réprimer; baisser. ~ forward, avancer; proposer. ~ in, insérer; (Naut.) relâcher. ~ off, remettre; différer. ~ on, mettre; revêtir; prendre; avancer; (brake) serrer. ~ out, éteindre; (tongue) tirer. ~ out of joint, démettre, disloquer. ~ out of order, dérégler, déranger. ~ out of tune, désaccorder. ~ the shot, lancer le poids. ~ up, (money) faire mise de; (money at cards) caver [de]; (vehicle) remiser; (at hotel) descendre. ~-up job, coup monté, m. ~ up with, supporter.

put[t] (Golf.) n, coup [roulé] m. ¶ v.t, poter.

putlog, n, boulin, m.

putrefaction, n, putréfaction, f. **putrefy**, v.t, putréfier; (v.i.) se p. ~ putrid, a, putride.

puttee, n, bande molletière, f.

putter (club) n, poteur, m. **putting green**, pelouse d'arrivée, f. **putting the shot**, lancement du poids, m.

putty, n, mastic, m. ~ powder, potée d'étain, f. ¶ v.t, mastiquer.

puzzle, n, casse-tête; problème, m; énigme, f. ¶ v.t, intriguer, alambiquer. ~d, p.a, perplexe.

pygmy, n, pygmée, m.

pyjamas, n.pl, pyjama, m.

pylon, n, pylône, m.

pyorrhoea, n, pyorrhée, f.

pyramid, n, pyramide, f.

pyre, n, bûcher, m.

Pyrenees (the), les Pyrénées, f.pl.

pyrethrum, n, pyrèthre, m.

pyrites, n, pyrite, f.

pyrotechnics, n.pl, pyrotechnie, f. **pyrotechnist**, n, artificier, m.

python, n, python, m.

pyx, n, ciboire, m.

Q

qua, c, en tant que.

quack [doctor], n, charlatan, médicastre, m, guérisseur, euse. ~ery, n, charlatanisme,m.

quadrangle, *n*, figure quadrangulaire, *f*; préau, *m*; cour d'honneur, *f*.

quadrant, *n*, quadrant; quart de cercle; secteur, *m*.

quadroon, *n*, quarteron, ne.

quadruped, *n*. & *a*, quadrupède, *m*. & *a*.

quadruple, *a*. & *n*, quadruple, *a*. & *m*. **quadruplets**, *n.pl*, quatre jumeaux, *m.pl*.

quaff, *v.t*, boire.

quag[mire], *n*, fondrière, *f*, bourbier, *m*.

quail, *n*, caille, *f*. ¶ *v.i*, trembler.

quaint, *a*, vieillot; pittoresque; baroque; étrange; curieux. **~ness**, *n*, étrangeté, *f*, curiosité, *f*.

quake, *v.i*, trembler.

qualification, *n*, qualité; capacité; aptitude; réserve, *f*; (*in shares*) cautionnement, *m*. **qualified**, *p.a*, qualifié; capable, apte; sous réserve. **qualify**, *v.t*, qualifier; adoucir. **quality**, *n*, qualité, *f*; choix; aloi, *m*.

qualms, *n.pl*, mal de cœur, *m*; scrupules, *m.pl*.

quandary, *n*, embarras, *m*.

quantity, *n*, quantité, *f*. **~ surveying**, métrage, *m*. **~ surveyor**, métreur, *m*.

quantum, *n*, quantum, *m*.

quarantine, *n*, quarantaine, *f*; (*station*) la santé. ¶ *v.t*, mettre en quarantaine.

quarrel, *n*, querelle, *f*. ¶ *v.i*, se quereller. **~some**, *a*, querelleur.

quarry, *n*, carrière; proie, *f*. **~man**, carrier, *m*. ¶ *v.t*, extraire.

quart, *n*, *Imperial Meas*. = 1·136 litres.

quarter, *n*, quartier; (*¼th*) quart; (*3 months*) trimestre; terme, *m*; (*28 lbs*) = 12·70 kilos; (*8 bushels*) = 2·909 hectolitres; (*pl.*) logement; cantonnement, *m*; quartiers, *m.pl*; (*horse*) train, *m*. **a ~ of an hour**, un quart d'heure. **~ binding**, demi-reliure, *f*. **~ day**, [jour du] terme, *m*. **~ deck**, gaillard d'arrière, *m*. **~master**, (*Mil.*) fourrier; (*Naut.*) maître de timonerie, *m*. **~ past**, un quart, et quart. ¶ *v.t*, diviser en quatre parties; écarteler; loger; cantonner. **~ly**, *a*, trimestriel; (*ad.*) par trimestre.

quartet[te], *n*, quatuor, *m*.

quarto *or* **4to** *or* **4o**, *n*. & *att*, in-quarto, in-4o, *m*. & *a.m*.

quartz, *n*, quartz, *m*.

quash, *v.t*, casser, annuler, infirmer.

quasi, *c*. & **quasi-**, *prefix*, quasi (*ad.*), quasi-.

quassia, *n*, (*tree*) quassier; (*bark*) quassia, *m*.

quatrain, *n*, quatrain, *m*.

quaver (*Mus.*) *n*, croche, *f*. ¶ *v.i*, chevroter, trembler.

quay, *n*, quai, *m*.

queen, *n*, reine; (*Cards*, *Chess*) dame, reine, *f*. **~ bee**, reine des abeilles, mère abeille, *f*. ¶ (*Chess*) *v.t*, damer. **~ly**, *a*, de reine.

queer, *a*, étrange, bizarre, singulier, original, drôle; indisposé. **a ~ fellow**, un drôle de corps.

quell, *v.t*, réprimer, étouffer; apaiser.

quench, *v.t*, éteindre; (*thirst*) étancher, apaiser.

querulous†, *a*, plaintif.

query, *n*, question, interrogation, *f*. **quest**, *n*, quête, recherche, *f*. **question**, *n*, question; demande; interrogation, *f*. ¶ *v.t*, questionner, interroger; contester, mettre en question, suspecter. **questionable**, *a*, contestable; suspect; équivoque.

queue, *n*, queue, *f*. **~ to up**, faire queue.

quibble, *n*, chicane, argutie, *f*. ¶ *v.i*, chicaner, ergoter.

quick, *a*, vif; rapide; prompt; preste. **~-change artist**, acteur à transformations, *m*. **~-firing**, à tir rapide. **~lime**, chaux vive, *f*. **~ march**, pas accéléré, *m*; en avant, marche! **~sand**, sable mouvant, *m*. **~set hedge**, haie vive, *f*. **~silver**, vif-argent, mercure, *m*. **~-tempered**, emporté, vif. ¶ *ad*, vite, prestement. **be ~!** vite!; dépêchez-vous! ¶ *n*, vif, *m*. **~en**, *v.t*, vivifier, animer; accélérer, activer. **~ly**, *ad*, vite, tôt, promptement. **~ness**, *n*, promptitude, prestesse, *f*.

quid (*tobacco*) *n*, chique, *f*.

quidnunc, *n*, nouvelliste, *m,f*.

quid pro quo, *n*, compensation, *f*.

quiescent, *a*, en repos. **quiet†**, *a*, tranquille; calme; doux; modeste. **be ~!** paix! ¶ *v.t*, calmer, apaiser. **~[ness]** & **~ude**, *n*, tranquillité, *f*, repos, calme, *m*, quiétude, *f*. **quietus**, *n*, coup de grâce, *m*.

quill, *n*, tuyau; (*porcupine*) piquant, *m*. **~ driver**, gratte-papier, rond-de-cuir, plumitif, *m*. **~ [feather]**, penne, *f*. **~ [pen]**, plume d'oie, *f*.

quilt, *n*, couvre-pied, *m*. ¶ *v.t*, ouater, piquer, capitonner. **~ing**, *n*, piqué, *m*.

quince, *n*, coing, *m*. **~ [tree]**, cognassier, *m*.

quincunx, *n*, quinconce, *m*.

quinine, *n*, quinine, *f*.

quinquennial, *a*, quinquennal, *f*.

quinsy, *n*, angine, *f*.

quint, *n*, quinte, *f*.

quintessence, *n*, quintessence, *f*.

quintet[te], *n*, quintette, *m*.

quip, *n*, pointe, *f*, mot piquant, *m*.

quire, *n*, main, *f*, (*in Fr.* 25 *sheets*); chœur, *m*.

quirk, *n*, (*quip*) pointe, *f*; caprice; (*Join.*) carré, *m*.

quit, *a*, quitte. ¶ *v.t*, quitter.

quite, *ad*, tout à fait; tout, e; bien; complètement; parfaitement. **~ so**, parfaitement.

quits, *a*, quitte à quitte; quittes.

quiver (*for arrows*) *n*, carquois, *m*. ¶ *v.i*, trembler, frémir, frissonner. **~[ing]**, *n*, tremblement, frisson[nement] *m*.

Quixote, *n*, Don Quichotte, *m*. **quixotic**, *a*, de D. Q. **~ally**, *ad*, en D. Q.

quiz, *v.t*, persifler, berner; lorgner. **quizzical**, *a*, narquois.

quoin, *n*, coin; (*Typ.*) bois de corps, *m*.

quoit, *n*. & **~s**, *n.pl*, palet, *m*.

Q

quondam, *a*, ancien.

quorum, *n*, quorum, *m*.

quota, *n*, quote-part, quotité, cote, cotisation, *f*, contingent, *m*.

quotation, *n*, citation; épigraphe; (*Com., Fin.*) cote, *f*, cours, prix, *m*; (*in Stk Ex. list*) inscription, *f*. ~ marks, guillemets, *m.pl*. quote, *v.t*, citer; alléguer; guillemeter; coter, faire; inscrire.

quoth he, dit-il, fit-il.

quotient, *n*, quotient, *m*.

R

rabbet, *n*, feuillure, *f*. ~ plane, guillaume, *m*.

rabbi, *n*, rabbin, *m*.

rabbit, *n*, lapin, e, (*young*) lapereau, *m*; (*pers. at game*) mazette, *f*. ~ burrow, ~ hole, terrier de lapin, clapier, halot, *m*. ~ hutch, cabane à lapins, *f*, clapier, *m*. ~ry, *n*, lapinière, *f*.

rabble, *n*, canaille, populace, *f*.

rabid, *a*, acharné, enragé. rabies, *n*, la rage, hydrophobie, *f*.

rac[c]oon, *n*, raton laveur, *m*.

race, *n*, (*tribe*) race, *f*; sang, *m*; (*contest, &c*) course, *f*; (*sea*) raz, *m*. ~ card, programme des courses, *m*. ~course, champ de courses, terrain de courses, turf, *m*, piste, *f*. ~horse, cheval de course, *m*. ~ meeting, réunion de courses, *f*; rallye, *m*. ~ suicide, suicide du genre humain, *m*. ~[way], bief, canal, chenal, *m*. ¶ *v.i*, courir; (*v.t*) (*horses*) faire courir. racer, *n*, coureur, euse; cheval de course, *m*; bicyclette de course, *f*. racial, *a*, de race. racing, *n*, courses; (*horse*) les courses, *f.pl*. ~ boat, glisseur de course, *m*. ~ calendar, calendrier des courses, *m*. ~ cyclist, coureur cycliste, *m*.

rack, *n*, râtelier, *m*; rampe, *f*; casier, *m*; (*cogged*) crémaillère, *f*; (*luggage, Rly*) filet; supplice, *m*, torture, *f*. ~ railway, chemin de fer à crémaillère, *m*. to ~ & ruin, à vau-l'eau. ~ [off], *v.t*, soutirer. to ~ one's brains, se torturer l'esprit, se casser la tête, se creuser le cerveau.

racket, *n*, tapage; bacchanal, *m*. racket *or* racquet, *n*, raquette, *f*. ~ press, presse à raquette, *f*.

racy (*fig.*) *a*, piquant.

radial, *a*, radial. radiance & radiation, *n*, rayonnement, *m*. radiancy, *n*, éclat, *m*. radiant, *a*, rayonnant; radieux. radiate, *v.i*, rayonner. radiator, *n*, radiateur, *m*.

radical, *a*. & *n*, radical, *a*. & *m*.

radioactive, *a*, radioactif. radiogram, *n*, radiogramme, *m*. radio-gramophone, *n*, combiné phono-radio, *m*. radiography, *n*, radiographie, *f*. radiotelegraphy, *n*, radio-télégraphie, *f*.

radish, *n*, radis, *m*.

radium, *n*, radium, *m*.

radius, *n*, rayon, *m*; portée, *f*; (*Anat.*) radius, *m*.

raffle, *n*, loterie, tombola, *f*. ¶ *v.t*, mettre en loterie.

raft, *n*, radeau, *m*, drome, *f*; train [de bois] *m*.

rafter, *n*, chevron, *m*.

rafting, *n*, flottage, *m*. raftsman, *n*, flotteur, *m*.

rag, *n*, chiffon; lambeau, *m*, loque, guenille; (*pl, for paper making*) drille; (*newspaper*) feuille de chou, *f*, canard; (*Sch.*) chahut, *m*. ~ picker, ~ merchant, ~ [& bone] man, chiffonnier, ère. ~tag [& bobtail], canaille, *f*. ~wort, jacobée, *f*.

ragamuffin, *n*, petit va-nu-pieds, *m*.

rage, *n*, rage, fureur; colère, *f*, courroux, *m*. ¶ *v.i*, faire rage; (*of war, &c*) sévir.

ragged, *a*, déguenillé, loqueteux.

raging, *a*, furieux. ~ fever, fièvre ardente, *f*. ~ toothache, rage de dents, *f*.

raglan, *n*, pardessus raglan, pardessus de demi-saison, *m*.

ragout, *n*, ragoût, *m*.

raid, *n*, incursion, descente, razzia, *f*, raid, *m*; rafle; attaque, *f*. ¶ *v.t*, razzier; marauder; faire une descente dans.

rail, *n*, barre, *f*; barreau, *m*; traverse; rampe, *f*, garde-fou, accoudoir, *m*; (*ship's*) lisse, *f*, garde-corps, *m*; (*Rly*) rail; (*bird*) râle, *m*. ~ car, voiture automotrice, *f*. ¶ *v.t*, barrer. ~ at, invectiver contre, pester contre. ~ in, griller. ~ing, *n*, grille, balustrade, *f*, balustre, garde-fou, *m*.

raillery, *n*, raillerie, *f*.

railway & railroad, *n*, chemin de fer, *m*, voie ferrée, *f*. ~man, employé de chemin de fer, cheminot, *m*. ~ strike, grève d'agents de chemins de fer, *f*.

raiment, *n*, vêtement, habillement, *m*.

rain, *n*, pluie, eau, *f*. ~bow, arc-en-ciel; (*halo*) iris, *m*. ~ coat, manteau de pluie, *m*. ~fall, quantité de pluie [tombée] *f*. ~ gauge, pluviomètre, *m*. ~ water, eau de pluie, *f*, eaux pluviales, *f.pl*. ¶ *v.i*, pleuvoir; (*v.t.*) faire pleuvoir. ~y, *a*, pluvieux, pluvial; (*day*) de pluie.

raise, *v.t*, lever; soulever; relever; remonter; [sur]élever; hausser; exhausser; augmenter; porter; (*hat*) tirer; (*flag*) arborer; cultiver; faire naître; produire; (*money for some purpose*) procurer; (*money for oneself*) se procurer; (*the dead*) ressusciter. raised, *p.a*, en relief; saillant. ~ satin stitch, plumetis, *m*. ~ stitch, point relief, *m*.

raisin, *n*, raisin sec, *m*.

rake, *n*, râteau, *m*; (*fire*) fourgon, ringard, *m*; inclinaison, *f*; libertin, débauché, roué, coureur, *m*. ¶ *v.t*, ratisser, râteler; enfiler. ~ up, remuer; revenir sur. raking fire, feu d'enfilade, *m*. raking shore, arc-boutant, *m*, contre-fiche, *f*. rakish, *a*, libertin.

rally, *n*, ralliement, *m*; reprise, *f*; (*Ten.*) long échange, *m*; (*race meeting*) rallye, *m*. ¶ *v.t*, rallier; (*v.i.*) se rallier; [se] reprendre.

ram, n, bélier; (*pile driving*) mouton, pilon; piston; (*battleship*) éperon, m. ¶ *v.t*, damer, battre; bourrer; refouler.

ramble, n, excursion, promenade, f. ¶ *v.i*, errer; (*rave*) divaguer. **rambler**, n, rosier grimpant, m. **rambling**, a, errant; (*discourse*) décousu, incohérent.

ramification, n, ramification, f. **ramify**, v.i, se ramifier.

rammer, n, pilon, m, dame, demoiselle, hie, f; (*cannon*) refouloir, m.

rampant (*Her.*) a, rampant. **to be ~**, sévir, courir.

rampart, n, rempart, m.

ramrod, n, baguette, f.

ramshackle, a, délabré.

ranch, n, prairie d'élevage, f, ranch, m.

rancid, a, rance. **~ness**, n, rancidité, f.

rancorous, a, rancunier, fielleux. **rancour**, n, rancune, rancœur, f, fiel, m.

random, a. & at ~, au hasard, à l'aventure, à l'abandon, à la volée, à coup perdu.

range, n, étendue; portée; distance; f; champ, m; série; gamme, f; (*voice*) diapason; (*musical*) clavier, m; (*hills*) chaîne, f; fourneau; parc, m. ~ *finder*, télémètre, m. ~ *pole*, jalon, m. ¶ *v.t*, étager; aligner; parcourir; ranger; (*v.i.*) s'aligner; varier. **ranger**, n, conservateur; garde, m.

Rangoon, n, Rangoun, Rangoon, m.

rank, n, rang; grade, m; dignité; (*cab*) station, place, f. ~ & *file*, gradés & soldats. ¶ *v.t*, ranger; (*v.i.*) prendre rang; marcher de pair. ¶, a, luxuriant; rance; grossier; insigne, fieffé.

rankle, v.i, saigner.

ransack, v.t, saccager, piller; fouiller.

ransom, n, rançon, f, rachat, m. ¶ *v.t*, rançonner, racheter.

rant, n, déclamation, f. ¶ *v.i*, déclamer.

ranunculus, n, renoncule, f.

rap, n, coup, m, tape, f; (*fig.*) fétu, m. ¶ *v.t.* & *i*, taper.

rapacious, a, rapace. **rape**, n, enlèvement; (*Law*) viol, m; (*oil seed plant*) navette; (*colerape*) rave, f.

rapid†, a, rapide; (*pulse, &c*) fréquent. ¶ n, rapide, m. **~ity**, n, rapidité, f.

rapier, n, rapière, f.

rapine, n, rapine, f.

rapping spirit, esprit frappeur, m.

rapt, a, ravi, en extase. **rapture**, n, ravissement, enthousiasme, m, ivresse, f. **rapturous**, a, extatique.

rara avis, rara avis, oiseau rare, m. **rare†**, a, rare; (*word*) peu usité; fameux. **rarefy**, v.t, raréfier. **rareness**, n, rareté, f.

rascal, n, coquin, e, fripon, ne; canaille, f. **~ity**, n, coquinerie, friponnerie, f. **~ly**, a, canaille.

rash†, a, téméraire, hardi. ¶ n, éruption, f. **~ness**, n, témérité, f.

rasher, n, tranche, f.

rasp, n, râpe, f. ¶ *v.t*, râper; racler.

raspberry, n, framboise, f. ~ *bush*, framboisier, m. ~ *cane*, rejeton de framboisier, m.

rat, n, rat, e, (*young*) raton; (*pers.*) gâte-métier; (*Pol.*) transfuge, m. ~ *catcher*, preneur de rats, m. ~ *poison*, mort aux rats, f. ~ *trap*, ratière, f. ~ *-trap pedal*, pédale à scies, f. ¶ *v.i*, tuer des rats; (*Pol.*) tourner casaque.

ratable, a, imposable.

ratchet, n, rochet, m. ~ *brace*, vilebrequin à cliquet; cliquet [à canon] m. ~ *spanner*, cliquet [simple] m. ¶ *v.t*, créneler.

rate, n, taux; pourcentage; cours; prix; tarif; ordre, rang, m, classe; raison, f; train, m; taxe, contribution, f, impôt, m. *at any ~*, quoi qu'il en soit. ¶ *v.t*, tarifer; imposer; taxer; coter; (*scold*) tancer.

rather, ad, un peu; assez; plutôt; mieux. ~ *nice*, gentillet. ~ *slowly* (*Mus.*), gravement. ~*! pour sûr!, parbleu!

ratification, n, ratification, f. **ratify**, v.t, ratifier.

rating, n, classement; (*Naut.*) grade, m; réprimande, f.

ratio, n, rapport, m, raison, proportion, f.

ration, n, ration, f, (*pl.*) vivres, m.pl. ~ *book*, carnet d'alimentation, m. ¶ *v.t*, rationner.

rational†, a, rationnel, raisonnable; conséquent; raisonné. **rationalism**, n, rationalisme, m. **rationalization**, n, organisation rationnelle, f.

rat[t]an, n. & ~ *cane*, rotin, m.

rat-tat[-tat], n, pan! pan!

ratter, n, [chien] ratier, m.

rattle, n, crécelle, f; (*baby's*) hochet; ballottement, claquement, m; (*throat*) râle, m. ~*snake*, serpent à sonnettes, m. ~*trap*, patraque, f; (*vehicle*) guimbarde, patache, f, tapecul, m. ¶ *v.i.* & *t*, ballotter; cliqueter.

raucous, a, rauque.

ravage, v.t, ravager. **~s**, n.pl, ravages, m.pl; (*of time*) injure[s], f.[pl.], outrage, m.

rave, v.i, être en délire; extravaguer.

ravel, v.t, embrouiller. **ravellings**, n.pl, effilure, f.

raven, n, corbeau, m.

Ravenna, n, Ravenne, f.

ravenous†, a, vorace; dévorant.

ravine, n, ravin, m, ravine, f.

raving, n, délire, m. ~ *mad*, fou à lier.

ravish, v.t, ravir; violer. **ravishing**, a, ravissant. **ravishingly**, ad, à ravir.

raw, a, cru; brut; (*silk*) grège; (*meat, wound*) saignante; (*Sienna*) naturelle; (*material*) première; (*fig.*) vert; novice; imberbe; (*weather*) humide & froid. **~ness**, n, crudité, f.

ray, n, rayon, m; (*fish*) raie, f.

rayon, n, rayon, m, soie artificielle, f.

raze, v.t, raser. **razor**, n, rasoir, m.

re, pr, affaire.

reach, n, portée; atteinte; étendue, f. ¶ v.t, atteindre [à]; arriver à, parvenir à; s'élever à. ~ [*out*], étendre.

react, v.i, réagir. **~ion**, n, réaction, f; contrecoup, m. **~ionary**, a. & n, réactionnaire, a. & m.f.

read, v.t. & i. ir, lire; (*report*) donner lecture de; (*law, &c*) étudier; (*meter*) relever. ~ **for** (exam), préparer. ~ **over**, collationner. **~able†**, a, lisible.

readdress, v.t, faire suivre.

reader, n, lecteur, trice; liseur, euse; (*Typ.*) correcteur, reviseur; livre de lecture, m.

readiness, n, promptitude, f; empressement, m; facilité, f.

reading, n, lecture; leçon; cote, f. ~ **desk**, pupitre; (*church*) lutrin, m. ~ **glass**, loupe à lire, f. ~ **hook** & **stand**, liseuse, f. ~ **lamp**, lampe de travail, f. ~ **room**, salle de lecture, f; cabinet de l., m.

ready†, a, prêt; prompt; facile. **~-made**, tout fait (f. toute faite), confectionné. ~ **money**, [argent] comptant, m. ~ **reckoner**, barème, m.

reagent, n, réactif, m.

real†, a, réel; positif; véritable; vrai; effectif; (*Law*) immeuble, immobilier. ~ **tennis** (ancient game), jeu de paume, m, paume, f. **~ist**, n. & a, réaliste, m.f. & a. **~ity**, n, réalité, f; le réel; positif, m. **~ize**, v.t, réaliser.

realm, n, royaume, m.

realty, n, biens immeubles, m.pl.

ream, n, rame, f. (*In Fr. 500 sheets*). ¶ v.t, aléser. **~er**, n, alésoir, m.

reap, v.t, moissonner; recueillir (fig.). **reaper**, n, moissonneur, euse, aoûteron, m. ~ & **binder**, moissonneuse-lieuse, f. **reaping**, n, moisson, f. ~ **hook**, faucille, f. ~ **machine** or **reaper**, n, moissonneuse, f.

reappear, v.i, reparaître, réapparaître. **~ance**, n, réapparition, f.

reappoint, v.t, renommer.

rear, n, arrière, m; queue, f. ~ **admiral**, contre-amiral, m. ~ **guard**, arrière-garde, f. ~ **lamp**, lanterne arrière, f. ~ **rank**, dernier rang, m. ¶ v.t, élever, nourrir; (v.i.) se cabrer, se dresser. **~ing of children**, puériculture, f.

reason, n, raison; cause, f; motif, m. **to state the ~ for**, motiver. ¶ v.i, raisonner. ~ **with**, raisonner, catéchiser. **~able†**, a, raisonnable; honnête. **~er**, n, raisonneur, euse. **~ing**, n, raisonnement, m.

reassure, v.t, rassurer.

rebate, n, rabais, m, ristourne; (*Join.*) feuillure, f.

rebel, n, rebelle, m.f, révolté, e. ¶ v.i, se rebeller, se révolter. **rebellion**, n, rébellion, révolte, f. **rebellious**, a, rebelle.

rebind, v.t.ir, relier de nouveau.

rebirth, n, renaissance, f.

rebound, n, [second] bond; contrecoup, m. ¶ v.i, rebondir.

rebuff, n, rebuffade, f. ¶ v.t, rebuter.

rebuild, v.t.ir, rebâtir, reconstruire.

rebuke, n, réprimande, f. ¶ v.t, réprimander.

rebut, v.t, réfuter.

recalcitrant, a. & n, récalcitrant, e.

recall, n, rappel, m. ¶ v.t, rappeler, retracer; révoquer; (*recollect*) se rappeler.

recant, v.t, rétracter. **~ation**, n, rétractation, palinodie, f.

recapitulate, v.t, récapituler.

recapture, n, reprise, f. ¶ v.t, reprendre.

recast, v.t.ir, refondre; remanier.

recede, v.i, reculer; se retirer; fuir. **receding** (*forehead, chin*) p.a, fuyant.

receipt, n, réception; reçu, m, quittance, f, acquit, m; récépissé, m; (*pl.*) recette, f. oft. pl. ~ **stamp**, timbre-quittance, m. ¶ v.t, acquitter, quittancer. **receive**, v.t, recevoir; accueillir; (*money*) toucher; (*stolen goods*) receler. **receiver**, n, destinataire, m.f; receleur, euse; (*Ten.*) relanceur, euse; (*Teleph.*) récepteur, écouteur; (*vessel*) récipient, m. **receiving office** (*Rly*) bureau de ville, m.

recent†, a, récent, nouveau, frais.

receptacle, n, réceptacle, m. **reception**, n, réception, f; accueil, m. ~ **room**, salon, m.

recess, n, [r]enfoncement, retrait, m, retraite, enclave; embrasure, f, recoin, m; (*pl. heart*) replis, m.pl; (*holidays*) vacances, f.pl. ¶ v.t, défoncer.

recipe, n, recette, f; (*Phar.*) formule, f.

recipient, n, destinataire, m.f.

reciprocal, a, réciproque; inverse; partagé. **reciprocate**, v.t, payer de retour. **reciprocating**, p.a, alternatif, de va-et-vient. **reciprocity**, n, réciprocité, f.

recital, n, récit, m; énumération, f; (*Mus.*) récital, m; audition, f. **recitation**, n, récitation, f. **recitative**, n, récitatif, m. **recite**, v.t, réciter; déclamer; énumérer.

reckless, a, téméraire; insouciant. ~ **driving**, conduite à tombeau ouvert, conduite en chauffard, f. **~ly**, ad, témérairement; à corps perdu.

reckon, v.t. & i, compter, calculer, chiffrer; estimer. **~ing**, n, compte, calcul, m; carte à payer; addition, f, écot, m.

reclaim, v.t, ramener dans la bonne voie; (*uncultivated land*) défricher; (*submerged land*) aménager.

recline, v.i, se renverser, se reposer.

recluse, n, reclus, e. **reclusion**, n, réclusion, f.

recognition, n, reconnaissance, f. **recognizable**, a, reconnaissable. **recognizance**, n, obligation, f. **recognize**, v.t, reconnaître.

recoil, n, recul, repoussement, m. ¶ v.i, reculer, repousser.

recoin, v.t, refondre, refrapper.

recollect, v.t, se rappeler. **~ion**, n, souvenir, m, mémoire, f.

recommence, v.t. & i, recommencer.

recommend, v.t, recommander; préconiser; proposer. **~ation**, n, recommandation;

proposition, *f*; (*for election*) parrainage, *m*.
~**er**, *n*, parrain, *m*.

recompense, *n*, récompense, *f*. ¶ *v.t*, récompenser.

reconcile, *v.t*, réconcilier, [r]accommoder; concilier.

recondite, *a*, abstrus, obscur.

reconnoitre, *v.t*, reconnaître.

reconsider, *v.t*, revenir sur, reviser.

reconstruct, *v.t*, reconstruire; (*fig.*) constituer de nouveau, reprendre sous œuvre. ~**ion**, *n*, reconstruction; (*fig.*) reconstitution, *f*.

record, *n*, registre, *m*; note, *f*; dossier, *m*; (*pl.*) archives, *f.pl*; (*pl.*) historique; (*Sport, &c*) record; (*gramophone*) disque, *m*. ~ **ribbon** (typewriter), ruban fixe, *m*. ¶ *v.t*, enregistrer; consigner; constater. ~**er**, *n*, enregistreur; compteur de sport, *m*.

re-count, *v.t*, recompter.

recount, *v.t*, raconter.

recoup, *v.t*, récupérer; dédommager.

recourse, *n*, recours, *m*.

re-cover, *v.t*, recouvrir.

recover, *v.t*, recouvrer; rattraper; (*v.i.*) se rétablir; [se] reprendre, se relever. ~**y**, *n*, recouvrement, *m*; reprise, *f*.

recreant, *a. & n*, lâche; apostat, *a. & m*.

re-create, *v.t*, recréer.

recreate, *v.t*, récréer. **recreation**, *n*, récréation, *f*; délassement, *m*.

recrimination, *n*, récrimination, *f*.

recrudescence, *n*, recrudescence, *f*.

recruit, *n*, recrue, *f*. ¶ *v.t*, recruter, racoler; (*v.i.*) se rétablir. ~**ing sergeant**, sergent recruteur, *m*.

rectangle, *n*, rectangle, carré long, *m*. **rectangular**, *a*, rectangulaire.

rectify, *v.t*, rectifier; redresser.

rectilinear, *a*, rectiligne.

rectitude, *n*, rectitude; droiture, *f*.

recto, *n*, recto, *m*.

rector, *n*, recteur; curé, *m*. ~**ship**, *n*, cure, *f*. ~**y**, *n*, presbytère, *m*, cure, *f*.

rectum, *n*, rectum, *m*.

recumbent, *a*, couché. ~ *figure* (statue), gisant, e.

recuperate, *v.i*, se récupérer.

recur, *v.i*, revenir, se reproduire, se retracer. **recurrence**, *n*, retour, *m*, répétition, *f*. *recurring decimal*, fraction périodique, *f*.

red, *a. & n*, rouge, *a. & m*; (*hair, &c*) roux, *a*. *the* ~**s** (*Pol.*), les rouges, *m.pl*. ~ *admiral* (butterfly), vulcain, *m*. ~**breast**, rougegorge, *m*. *the R*~ *Cross*, la Croix Rouge. ~*-faced* (*person*), rougeaud, e. ~*-haired* (*person*), roux, rousse, rousseau, *m. & att*. ~*-handed*, sur le fait, en flagrant délit. ~ *herring*, hareng saur, *m*. ~*-hot*, [chauffé au] rouge; tout chaud. ~ *Indian* or ~*skin*, Peau Rouge, *m*. ~ *lead*, minium, *m*. *to be a* ~*-letter day*, faire époque. ~ *mullet*, rouget, *m*. ~ *pepper*, poivre rouge, p. de Cayenne, *m*. *R*~ *sea*,

mer Rouge, *f*. ~ *spot* (skin), rougeur, *f*. ~*start*, rouge-queue, *m*. ~ *tape*, chinoiseries, *f.pl*; routine, *f*. ~*wing*, mauvis, *m*. **redden**, *v.t & i*, rougir; roussir. **reddish**, *a*, rougeâtre; roussâtre; (*hair*) blond hasardé.

redeem, *v.t*, racheter; rembourser; amortir; dégager; purger; s'acquitter de. **Redeemer**, *n*, Rédempteur, *m*. **redemption**, *n*, rachat; remboursement; amortissement; dégagement, *m*; (*mortgage*) purge, *f*; (*Relig.*) rachat, *m*, rédemption, *f*.

redness, *n*, rougeur; rousseur, *f*.

redolent of, qui sent le, la.

redoubt, *n*, redoute, *f*, réduit, *m*.

redoubtable, *a*, redoutable.

redound, *v.i*, rejaillir.

redress, *n*, redressement, *m*, réparation, *f*. ¶ *v.t*, redresser, réparer.

reduce, *v.t*, réduire; diminuer; ramener; affaiblir. ~ *the staff*, débaucher. ~ *to lower rank* (*Mil.*), rétrograder. ~ *to the ranks*, casser, réduire à la condition de simple soldat. **reduction**, *n*, réduction; diminution, *f*; (*tax*) dégrèvement, *m*. ~ *to the absurd* or *reductio ad absurdum*, démonstration (*ou* preuve) par l'absurde, *f*. ~ *to the ranks*, cassation, *f*.

redundant, *a*, redondant, parasite.

re-echo, *v.i*, résonner.

reed, *n*, roseau; (*pipe*) chalumeau, *m*; (*Mus.*) anche; (*Arch.*) baguette, *f*. ~ *mace*, massette, masse d'eau, *f*.

reef, *n*, récif, écueil, banc, brisant; (*in sail*) ris, *m*. ~ *knot*, nœud plat, *m*.

reek, *n*, odeur fétide; exhalaison pestilentielle, *f*. ~ *with*, of, exhaler; suer. ~*ing with*, fumant de.

reel, *n*, dévidoir, *m*, bobine, *f*; touret, (*Fish.*) moulinet, *m*. ¶ *v.t*, dévider, bobiner; (*v.i.*) chanceler. (*when drunk*) festonner.

re-elect, *v.t*, réélire. ~**ion**, *n*, réélection, *f*. **re-eligible**, *a*, rééligible.

re-embark, *v.t*, rembarquer; (*v.i.*) [se] r.

re-engage, *v.t*, rengager.

re-enlist, *v.i*, [se] rengager.

re-enter, *v.i*, rentrer; (*v.t.*) rentrer dans. **re-entrant**, *a*, rentrant. **re-entry**, *n*, rentrée, *f*.

re-establish, *v.t*, rétablir, restaurer.

reeve (*Naut.*), *v.t.ir*, passer.

re-examine, *v.t*, repasser, revoir.

re-export, *v.t*, réexporter.

refectory, *n*, réfectoire, *m*.

refer, *v.t*, référer; renvoyer; déférer. ~ *to*, se référer à, se reporter à; renvoyer à, consulter. ~**ee**, *n*, arbitre; tiers arbitre; (*Box.*) [arbitre] directeur de combat, *m*. ¶ *v.t*, arbitrer. **reference**, *n*, renvoi; *m*; référence; mention, *f*; trait, *m*. ~ *library*, bibliothèque où les livres se consultent sur place; b. d'ouvrages à consulter, *f*. ~ [*mark*], [guidon de] renvoi, *m*. ~ *note* (on map), légende, *f*. *with* ~ *to*, à l'égard de. **referendum**, *n*, referendum, plébiscite, *m*.

refine, *v.t*, affiner; raffiner; épurer; polir; (*v.i.*) raffiner. ~**d**, *p.a*, raffiné, distingué; poli; délicat. ~**ment** (*fig.*) *n*, raffinement, *m*. **refiner**, *n*, affineur; raffineur, *m*. **refinery**, *n*, affinerie; raffinerie, *f*.

reflect, *v.t. & i*, réfléchir; refléter; rejaillir. ~**ion**, *n*, réflexion; image, *f*; reflet, *m*; atteinte, *f*. ~**ive**, *a*, réfléchi. ~**or**, *n*, réflecteur, *m*. **reflex**, *a*, réflexe. ~ *camera*, chambre reflex, *f*. ¶ *n*, reflet; réflexe, *m*. **reflexion**, *n*, réflexion, *f*. **reflexive** (*Gram.*) *a*, réfléchi.

refloat (*ship*) *v.t*, renflouer.

reflux, *n*, reflux, *m*.

re-form, *v.t*, reformer.

reform, *n*, réforme, *f*. ¶ *v.t*, réformer. ~**ation**, *n*, réformation; réforme, *f*. ~**atory**, *n*, maison de correction, *f*, pénitencier, *m*. ~**er**, *n*, réformateur, trice.

refract, *v.t*, réfracter. ~**ing telescope**, lunette [d'approche] *f*. **refractoriness**, *f*, mutinerie, *f*. **refractory**, *a*, réfractaire.

refrain, *n*, refrain, *m*. ¶ *v.i*, se retenir; s'abstenir.

refresh, *v.t*, rafraîchir; restaurer; délasser; reposer, récréer. **refreshment**, *n*, rafraîchissement, *m*. ~ *bar*, ~ *room*, buvette, *f*, buffet, *m*.

refrigerate, *v.t*, frigorifier. **refrigeration**, *n*, réfrigération, *f*. **refrigerator**, *n*, machine frigorifique; glacière, *f*.

refuge, *n*, refuge, *m*. *to take* ~, se réfugier. **refugee**, *n*, réfugié, e, émigré, e.

refulgent, *a*, éclatant.

refund, *v.t*, rembourser.

refurnish, *v.t*, remeubler.

refusal, *n*, refus, *m*. **refuse**, *n*, rebut, déchet, *m*. *oft. pl*; immondices, *f.pl*, ordure, *f*. ~ *dump*, voirie, *f*. ¶ *v.t. & i*, refuser; se r. ~ *admittance*, consigner à la porte.

refute, *v.t*, réfuter.

regain, *v.t*, regagner; reconquérir.

regal†, *a*, royal.

regale, *v.t*, régaler.

regalia, *n*, insignes de la royauté; décors, *m.pl*.

regard, *n*, égard, *m*; considération, *f*; respect; rapport, *m*. *with* ~ *to*, ~*ing*, à l'égard de, à propos de, quant à, à l'endroit de. ¶ *v.t*, regarder; considérer. ~**less**, *a*, insoucieux, sans se soucier.

regatta, *n*, régate, *f*. *oft. pl*.

regency, *n*, régence, *f*.

regenerate, *v.t*, régénérer. **regeneration**, *n*, régénération, *f*.

regent, *n. & a*, régent, e.

regicidal, *a. & regicide**, *n*, régicide, *a. & n*.

regild, *v.t.ir*, redorer.

regimen, *n*, régime, *m*. **regiment**, *n*, régiment, *m*. **regimental**, *a*, régimentaire. ~ *number*, dépas de corps, *m*. ~ *number*, [numéro] matricule, *m*. ~ *records*, historique du régiment, *m*.

region, *n*, région, contrée, *f*. ~**al**, *a*, régional.

register, *n*, registre, livre, journal; grand livre; répertoire, *m*; matricule; voix, *f*; (*book mark*) signet, *m*. ~ *of voters*, liste électorale, *f*. ¶ *v.t*, enregistrer, inscrire, immatriculer; (*design, &c*) déposer; (*Post*) recommander. ~**ed**, *p.a*, (*capital, office*) social; (*shares*) nominatives. ~ *letter envelope*, enveloppe de lettre chargée ou recommandée, *f*. *register[ed manager* (*of a ship*), armateur, *m*. *register[ed tonnage]*, tonnage [de jauge] *m*, jauge, *f*. *registered trade mark*, marque déposée, *f*. **registrar**, *n*, greffier; conservateur; (*births, &c*) officier de l'état civil, *m*. **registry** [**office**], *n*, (*marriage*) mairie, *f*; (*servants*) bureau de placement, *m*.

regret, *n*, regret, *m*. ¶ *v.t*, regretter.

regular†, *a*, régulier; réglé; assidu; véritable; franc, fieffé. ~ *channel[s]* (*fig.*), filière, *f*. ~**ity**, *n*, régularité, *f*. ~**ize**, *v.t*, régulariser. **regulate**, *v.t*, régler; réglementer. **regulation**, *n*, réglementation, *f*; règlement, *m*, ordonnance, *f*; (*att.*) réglementaire. **regulator**, *n*, régulateur, *m*.

rehabilitate, *v.t*, réhabiliter.

rehandle, *v.t*, remmancher.

rehearsal, *n*, répétition, *f*. **rehearse**, *v.t*, répéter; énumérer.

rehousing, *n*, relogement, *m*.

reign, *n*, règne, *m*. ¶ *v.i*, régner. ~**ing**, *a*, régnant.

reimburse, *v.t*, rembourser.

reimport, *v.t*, réimporter.

reimpose, *v.t*, réimposer.

rein, *n*, rêne, guide, bride, *f*.

reindeer, *n*, renne, *m*.

reinforce, *v.t*, renforcer; (*concrete*) armer. ~**ment**, *n*, renforcement, *m*; armature, *f*; (*men*) renfort, *m*.

reinstate, *v.t*, réintégrer, rétablir, réhabiliter.

reinsure, *v.t*, réassurer.

reinvest (*Fin.*) *v.t*, replacer.

reinvigorate, *v.t*, redonner de la vigueur à, revigorer.

reissue (*book*) *n*, réédition, *f*.

reiterate, *v.t*, réitérer.

reject, *v.t*, rejeter; repousser; refuser. ~**ion**, *n*, rejet; repoussement, *m*.

rejoice, *v.t*, réjouir; (*v.i.*) se r. **rejoicing**, *n*, réjouissance, *f*.

re-join, *v.t*, rejoindre.

rejoin, *v.t*, répliquer; (*one's regiment, &c*) rejoindre, rallier. **rejoinder**, *n*, réplique, repartie, *f*.

rejuvenate, *v.t*, rajeunir.

rekindle, *v.t*, rallumer.

relapse, *n*, (*Med., &c*) rechute, *f*; (*Fin.*) recul, *m*; (*crime*) récidive, *f*. ¶ *v.i*, retomber; reculer. ~ *into crime*, récidiver.

relate, *v.t*, raconter, narrer, relater; (*v.i.*) se rapporter, avoir rapport. ~*d to*, ayant rapport avec, apparenté à. **relation** *n*, relation, *f*; rapport, *m*; parent, e; allié, e; (*pl.*) parenté, *f.* ~**ship**, *n,* parenté; filiation, *f.* **rela-tive**†, *a,* relatif. ¶ *n,* parent, e.

relax, *v.t,* relâcher; détendre, débander; délasser; (*Med.*) [re]lâcher. ~**ed throat,** pharyngite, *f.* ~**ation,** *n,* relâchement; relâche, délassement, *m.* ~**ing** (*climate*) *a,* énervant.

re-lay, *v.t,* reposer.

relay, *n,* relais, *m.* ~ **race,** course de (*ou* à) relais, *f.* ¶ *v.t,* relayer.

release, *n,* relaxation, *f,* élargissement; (*pigeons*) lancer, *m;* libération; délivrance, *f;* (*Mech.*) déclic; (*Phot.*) déclencheur, *m.* ¶ *v.t,* relaxer, élargir; lancer; libérer; lâcher; délivrer; délier.

relegate, *v.t,* reléguer.

relent, *v.i,* fléchir. ~**less**†, *a,* impitoyable, acharné.

relet, *v.t.ir,* relouer. **reletting,** *n,* relocation, *f.*

relevant, *a,* pertinent; qui se rapporte à.

reliability, *n,* sûreté, sécurité; fidélité, *f.* ~ *trial,* épreuve d'endurance, *f.* **re-liable**†, *a,* sûr; de tout repos; de confiance. **reliance,** *n,* confiance, foi, *f.*

relic, *n,* relique, *f;* reste, *m.*

relict, *n,* veuve, *f.*

relief, *n,* soulagement; secours, *m,* assistance, *f;* (*tax*) dégrèvement; (*for dependants, Inc. Tax*) abattement; (*Art*) relief, *m;* (*Mil.*) relève, *f.* ~ *fund,* caisse de secours, *f.* ~ *train,* train supplémentaire, *m.* **relieve,** *v.t,* soulager, secourir, assister; dégrever; relever; débarrasser.

relight, *v.t,* rallumer.

religion, *n,* religion, *f.* **religious**†, *a,* religieux; (*book, &c*) dévot, de dévotion. ~**ness,** *n,* religiosité, *f.*

relinquish, *v.t,* abandonner.

reliquary, *n,* reliquaire, *m,* châsse, *f.*

relish, *n,* goût, *m;* saveur, *f;* assaisonnement, *m.* ¶ *v.t,* goûter; savourer.

reluctance, *n,* répugnance, *f. I am reluctant to,* il me répugne de, je me fais conscience de. **reluctantly,** *ad,* à contrecœur, à regret.

rely, *v.i,* compter, se reposer, faire fond.

remain, *v.i,* rester; demeurer. **remainder,** *n,* reste, restant; solde d'édition, *m.* ¶ *v.t,* solder. **remaindersman,** *n,* soldeur, *m.* **remains,** *n.pl,* restes, vestiges, débris, *m.pl;* dépouille, *f.*

remake, *v.t.ir,* refaire.

remand, *v.t,* renvoyer à une autre audience.

remark, *n,* remarque, observation, *f,* propos, *m.* **remark** *&* **re-mark,** *v.t,* remarquer. ~**able**†, *a,* remarquable.

remedy, *n,* remède, *f;* (*Law*) recours, *m.* ¶ *v.t,* remédier à.

remember, *v.t,* se [res]souvenir de; se rappeler; retenir. **remembrance,** *n,* [res]souvenir, *m;* mémoire, *f.*

remind of, faire penser à, rappeler à. *you* ~ *me of someone,* vous me rappelez quelqu'un. ~**er,** *n,* mémento; rappel, *m.*

reminiscence, *n,* réminiscence, *f.*

remiss† *a,* négligent. ~**ion,** *n,* rémission; remise, *f.* **remit,** *v.t,* remettre; envoyer. **remittance,** *n,* remise, *f;* envoi, *m.*

remnant, *n,* reste; coupon; lambeau, *m;* épave, *f.*

remodel, *v.t,* remodeler; refondre.

remonstrance, *n,* remontrance, *f.* **remonstrate,** *v.i,* faire des remontrances, [en] remontrer (*with* = à).

remorse, *n,* remords, *m.* ~**less,** *a. &* ~**lessly,** *ad,* sans remords.

remote, *a,* éloigné, écarté; (*antiquity*) reculée, haute. ~**ness,** *n,* éloignement, *m.*

remount, *n,* remonte, *f.* ¶ *v.t,* remonter.

removable, *a,* amovible. **removal,** *n,* déplacement; éloignement; déménagement; enlèvement, *m;* (*of officer*) destitution, *f.* ~ *contractor,* [*furniture*] *remover,* déménageur, *m.* **remove,** *n,* déplacer; éloigner; déménager; enlever; lever; destituer.

remunerate, *v.t,* rémunérer, rétribuer. **remuneration,** *n,* rémunération, rétribution, *f.*

renaissance, *n,* renaissance, *f.*

rename, *v.t,* débaptiser.

rend, *v.t.ir,* déchirer; (*the air*) fendre.

render, *v.t,* rendre; expliquer; interpréter; (*plaster*) enduire. ~ *void,* frapper de nullité. ~**ing,** *n,* (*accounts*) reddition, *f;* (*Art*) rendu, *m;* explication; interprétation, *f;* (*plaster*) enduit, *m.*

renegade, *n,* renégat, e.

renew, *v.t,* renouveler. ~**al,** *n,* renouvellement, *m;* rénovation; reprise, *f.*

rennet, *n,* présure, *f;* (*apple*) reinette, *f.*

renounce, *v.t,* renoncer à, répudier, abjurer.

renovate, *v.t,* renouveler, rénover, rajeunir.

renown, *n,* renommée, *f,* renom, *m.* ~**ed,** *a,* renommé.

rent, *n,* (*tear*) déchirure, *f;* accroc; (*periodical payment*) loyer; fermage, *m;* rente; redevance, *f.* ¶ *v.t,* louer; sous-louer. ~**al,** *n,* prix de location, *m;* redevance; valeur locative, *f.* ~**er,** *n,* locataire, *m,f.*

renunciation, *n,* renonciation, répudiation, *f,* renoncement, *m.*

reopen, *v.t,* rouvrir; (*v.i.*) se r.; rentrer. ~**ing,** *n,* réouverture; rentrée, *f.*

reorganize, *v.t,* réorganiser.

rep *or* **repp** *or* **reps,** *n,* reps, *m.*

repack, *v.t,* remballer.

repair, *n,* état, *m;* réparation, *f.* ¶ *v.t,* réparer; raccommoder; (*v.i.*) se rendre. ~**able** *&* **reparable,** *a,* réparable. **reparation,** *n,* réparation, *f.*

repartee, *n,* repartie, parade, *f.*

repast, *n,* repas, *m.*

repatriate, *v.t,* rapatrier.

repay, *v.t.ir,* rembourser; rendre.

repeal, *n,* rappel, *m,* révocation, *f.* ¶ *v.t,* rappeler, révoquer.

repeat (*Mus.*) *ad,* bis. ¶ (*Mus.*) *n,* renvoi, *m.* ¶ *v.t,* répéter, redire. ~**edly,** *ad,* fréquemment, à plusieurs reprises. ~**ing** (*rifle, watch*) *p.a,* à répétition.

repel, v.t, repousser. repellent, a, rebutant, repoussant; (Phys.) répulsif.

repent, v.i, se repentir; (v.t.) se repentir de. ~ance, n, repentir, m.

repeople, v.t, repeupler.

repercussion, n, répercussion, f.

repertory, n, répertoire, m.

repetend, n, période, f. repetition, n, répétition; redite; reprise, f.

repine, v.i, se chagriner.

replace, v.t, replacer; reposer; remplacer.

replant, v.t, replanter, repeupler.

replay, v.t, rejouer.

replenish, v.t, remplir; remonter. replete, a, plein. repletion, n, plénitude; réplétion, f.

replica, n, réplique, répétition, f.

reply, n, réponse, f. ~ paid, avec réponse payée. in ~ (Law), responsif. ¶ v.t. & i, répondre.

report, n, rapport; reportage; bulletin; compte rendu; procès-verbal, m; expertise, f; bruit, m, renommée; détonation, f. ¶ v.t, rendre compte de, rapporter. ~er (news) n, reporter, chroniqueur, journaliste d'information, m. ~ing, n, reportage, m.

repose, n, repos, m. ¶ v.i, se reposer.

repository, n, dépôt, magasin; réceptacle; (fig.) répertoire, m.

repot, v.t, rempoter.

repoussé work, travail de repoussé, m.

reprehend, v.t, reprendre, censurer. reprehensible, a, répréhensible.

represent, v.t, représenter. ~ation, n, représentation, f. ~ative, a, représentatif. ¶ n, représentant, e.

repress, v.t, réprimer, refouler, comprimer, concentrer. ~ion, n, répression, compression, f.

reprieve, n, sursis, m. ¶ v.t, surseoir à l'exécution de, gracier.

reprimand, n, réprimande, semonce, mercuriale, f; blâme, m. ¶ v.t, réprimander, chapitrer; blâmer.

reprint, n, réimpression, f. ¶ v.t, réimprimer.

reprisal, n, représaille, f.

reproach, n, reproche, m; honte, f. ¶ v.t, faire des reproches à; reprocher. ~ful, a, de reproche. ~fully, ad, d'un ton de reproche.

reprobate, n, réprouvé, m. ¶ v.t, réprouver. reprobation, n, réprobation, f.

reproduce, v.t, reproduire. reproduction, n, reproduction; répétition, f.

reproof, n, réprimande, f. reprove, v.t, reprendre.

reptile, n, reptile, m. ¶ a, rampant.

republic, n, république, f. ~an, a. & n, républicain, e.

republish, v.t, publier de nouveau.

repudiate, v.t, répudier, [re]nier.

repugnance, n, répugnance, f. repugnant, a, répugnant. to be ~ to, répugner à.

repulse, n, échec, m. ¶ v.t, repousser, rebuter. repulsion, n, répulsion, f. repulsive, a, repoussant; (Phys.) répulsif.

repurchase, n, rachat, m. ¶ v.t, racheter.

reputable, a, honorable. reputation & repute, n, réputation, renommée, f; renom, crédit, m. of repute, réputé. reputed, p.p, réputé; censé; putatif.

request, n, demande, prière, requête, instance; vogue, f. by ~, on ~, sur demande. in ~, en vogue; recherché, demandé. ¶ v.t, demander, prier, inviter.

requiem, n, requiem, m.

require, v.t, exiger; requérir; demander; réclamer; vouloir; avoir besoin de; falloir. ~ment, n, exigence, f; besoin, m. requisite, a, requis, voulu. ¶ n, article, m; fourniture, f. requisition, n, réquisition, f. ¶ v.t, réquisitionner.

requital, n, récompense; revanche, f. requite, v.t, récompenser.

reredos, n, retable, m.

resale, n, revente, f.

rescind, v.t, annuler. rescission, n, rescision, f.

rescript, n, rescrit, m.

rescue, n, délivrance, f; sauvetage, m. to the ~, à la rescousse. ¶ v.t, délivrer; sauver.

research, n, recherche, f. ~ worker, chercheur, euse.

reseat, v.t, rasseoir; remettre un fond à.

resemblance, n, ressemblance, f. resemble, v.t, ressembler à, approcher de, imiter.

resent, v.t, s'indigner contre, ressentir. ~ment, n, ressentiment, m.

reservation, n, réserve, réservation; (mental) restriction, arrière-pensée; (seats) location, f. reserve, n, réserve, provision; retenue, f. ~ [price], mise à prix, f. ¶ v.t, réserver; retenir, louer. ~d seat ticket, billet garde-place, billet de location de place, m. reservist, n, réserviste, m. reservoir, n, réservoir, m.

reset, v.t.ir, remonter; remettre; (Typ.) recomposer. resetting (Typ.) n, recomposition, f.

reship, v.t, rembarquer.

reshuffle, v.t, rebattre.

reside, v.i, résider, demeurer. residence, n, résidence, f; séjour, m; demeure, f, domicile, m, habitation, f. resident, n, habitant, e; (diplomatic) résident, m.

residuary legatee, légataire universel, m. residue, n, résidu; reliquat, m.

resign, v.t, résigner, se démettre de; (v.i.) démissionner. resignation, n, résignation, démission; (submission) résignation, f.

resilient, a, élastique.

resin, n, résine; (for violin) colophane, f. ~ous, a, résineux.

resist, v.t, résister à; (v.i.) résister. ~ance, n, résistance, f.

resole, v.t, ressemeler.

resolute†, a, résolu, déterminé. resolution, n, résolution; détermination; délibération, décision; proposition, *f.* **resolve**, *n*, détermination, *f.* ¶ *v.t*, résoudre, déterminer. ~ **on**, statuer sur, décider.

resonance, *n*, résonance, *f.* **resonant**, *a*, résonnant.

resort, *n*, recours; ressort, *m*, ressource, *f*; rendez-vous; séjour, *m*; station, *f*, centre, *m*. ~ **to**, recourir à; se rendre à; fréquenter.

resound, *v.i*, résonner, retentir.

resource, *n*, ressource, *f*; expédient, *m*. ~**ful**, *a*, de ressources.

respect, *n*, respect; rapport, égard, *m*; acception, *f.* ¶ *v.t.* respecter. ~**able**, *a*, respectable, honorable, honnête; ~**ably**, *ad*, honorablement. ~**ful†**, *a*, respectueux. ~**ing**, *pr*, concernant. ~**ive†**, *a*, respectif.

respiration, *n*, respiration, *f.* **respirator**, *n*, masque à gaz, *m*.

respite, *n*, répit, relâche, *m*, trêve, *f*; sursis, *m*.

resplendent, *a*, resplendissant.

respond, *v.i*, répondre; obéir. ~**ent**, *n*, répondant, e; (*Law*) défendeur, eresse.

response, *n*, réponse, *f*; (*Eccl.*) répons *m*. **responsibility**, *n*, responsabilité, *f.* **responsible**, *a*, responsable; solidaire. **responsive**, *a*, sensible, liant.

rest, *n*, repos; (*Mus.*) silence, *m*, pause, *f*; support; appui; (*Bil., &c*) chevalet; (*remainder*) reste, *m*. *& all the* ~ *of it, &* toute la lyre. ¶ *v.i*, se reposer; reposer; poser; s'appuyer; porter; tenir; résider; incomber; (*v.t.*) reposer, appuyer.

re-stage, *v.t*, remonter.

restaurant, *n*, restaurant; cabaret, *m*. ~ **keeper**, restaurateur, trice.

restful, *a*, reposant. **resting place**, repos, *m*; sépulture, *f.*

restitch, *v.t*, repiquer.

restitution, *n*, restitution, *f.*

restive, *a*, rétif.

restless, *a*, inquiet; agité; remuant; turbulent.

restock, *v.t*, rassortir, remonter.

restoration, *n*, restauration; réfection, *f*; rétablissement, *m*; restitution, *f.* **restorative**, *a. & n*, restaurant, *a. & m.* **restore**, *v.t*, restaurer; rénover; rétablir; ramener; rendre; restituer. **restorer**, *n*, restaurateur, trice.

restrain, *v.t*, retenir, contenir, comprimer, contraindre. **restraint**, *n*, contrainte, *f. to place* (lunatic) *under* ~, interner.

restrict, *v.t*, restreindre, borner, renfermer. ~**ion**, *n*, restriction, *f.*

restring, *v.t.ir*, recorder.

result, *n*, résultat, *m*; suite, *f.* ¶ *v.i*, résulter.

resume, *v.t*, reprendre; renouer. **resumption**, *n*, reprise, *f.*

resurrection, *n*, résurrection, *f.* ~ *pie*, rogatons, *m.pl.*

resurvey, *v.t.ir*, contre-expertise, *f.*

resuscitate, *v.t*, ressusciter.

retail, *n*, [commerce de] détail; petit commerce, *m.* ¶ *v.t*, détailler, débiter. ~**er**, *n*, détaillant, e.

retain, *v.t*, retenir; arrêter. ~**er**, *n*, (*fee*) provision, *f*; (*pl.*) gens, *m.pl.*

retake, *v.t.ir*, reprendre.

retaliate, *v.i*, user de représailles (*upon* = envers). **retaliation**, *n*, représailles, *f.pl*, talion, *m.* **retaliatory**, *a*, de représailles.

retard, *v.t*, retarder.

retch, *v.i*, avoir des haut-le-cœur.

retention, *n*, rétention, *f.* **retentive**, *a*, tenace, fidèle.

reticence, *n*, réticence, *f. to be reticent*, se taire à dessein.

reticle, *n*, réticule, *m.* **reticule**, *n*, réticule, sac, *m.*

retina, *n*, rétine, *f.*

retinue, *n*, suite, *f*, cortège, *m.*

retire, *v.t*, retirer; mettre à la retraite; (*officer*) réformer; (*v.i.*) se retirer. ~**d**, *p.p*, en retraite. *officer on the* ~ *list*, [officier] retraité, *m.* ~ *pay*, traitement d'inactivité, *m*, [pension de] retraite, *f.* ~**ment**, *n*, retraite, *f.* **retiring**, *p.a*, (*director, &c*) sortant; (*pension*) de retraite.

retort, *n*, réplique, riposte; (*Chem.*) cornue, *f*, vase clos, *m.* ¶ *v.t. & i*, rétorquer, répliquer, riposter.

retouch, *v.t*, retoucher, retoucher à. ~[**ing**], *n*, retouche, *f.*

retrace, *v.t*, retracer; revenir sur, rebrousser.

retract, *v.t*, rétracter; (*v.i.*) se rétracter.

retreat, *n*, retraite; reculade; (*glacier*) décrue, *f.* ¶ *v.i*, se retirer, reculer.

retrench, *v.t*, retrancher, restreindre.

retribution, *n*, récompense, *f.*

retrieve, *v.t*, rétablir, réparer; (*game*) rapporter. **retriever** (*dog*) *n*, retriever, *m. a good* ~, un chien qui rapporte bien.

retroactive, *a*, rétroactif.

retrograde, *a*, rétrograde.

retrospect, *n*, revue rétrospective, *f.* ~**ive†**, *a*, rétrospectif; (*effect of a law*) rétroactif.

return, *n*, retour, *m*; rentrée; restitution; revanche, *f*; remboursement; renvoi; rendu; état, relevé, *m*; déclaration; statistique; rémunération, *f*; rapport, rendement; (*pl.—books, newspapers*) bouillon, *m.* ~ *match*, revanche, *f.* ~ *ticket*, billet d'aller & retour. ¶ *v.t*, rendre; restituer; renvoyer; retourner; rembourser; déclarer; élire, nommer; (*Ten.*) relever (*le service*); (*v.i.*) retourner; revenir; rentrer. ~**able**, *a*, restituable; (*packings*) à rendre. ~*ed letter*, lettre renvoyée, *f.* ~*ed letter office*, bureau des rebuts, *m.*

reunion, *n*, réunion, *f.* **reunite**, *v.t*, réunir; (*v.i.*) se réunir.

reveal (*Arch.*) *n*, jouée, *f.* ¶ *v.t*, révéler.

reveille, *n*, réveil, *m*, diane, *f.*

revel, *n. oft. pl*, réjouissance, *f. oft. pl*; ripaille, *f.* ¶ *v.i*, ripailler. ~ *in*, nager dans.

Q *

revelation, n, révélation, f. R~ (Bible), Apocalypse, f.

reveller, n, noceur, euse. revelry, n, ripaille, f.

revenge, n, vengeance; revanche, f. ~ oneself, se venger. ~ful, a, vindicatif.

revenue, n, revenu; rapport; fisc, m. ~cutter, cotre de la douane, m. ~-earning house, maison de rapport, f. ~ stamp, timbre fiscal, m.

reverberate, v.t, réverbérer; répercuter. reverberatory furnace, four à réverbère, m.

revere, v.t, révérer. reverence, n, révérence, f. ¶ v.t, révérer. reverend, a, révérend. reverent†, a, pieux. reverential, a, révérenciel. reverentially, ad, avec révérence.

reverie, n, rêverie, f.

reversal, n, retournement; retour, m, inversion, f. reverse, n, revers; envers; inverse; contraire, opposé; rebours; (of coin, of medal) revers, m, pile, f. ¶ v.t, renverser; inverser, invertir; (Law) réformer.

reversing, n. & ~ gear, changement de marche, m. reversion, n, réversion, f; retour, m. revert, v.i, revenir, retourner.

revet, v.t, revêtir. ~ment, n, revêtement, m.

revictual, v.t, ravitailler.

review, n, revue; revision, f; (book) compte rendu, m, notice, critique [littéraire] f. ¶ v.t, revoir, reviser; (Mil.) passer en revue; (book) faire le compte rendu de. ~er, n, critique [littéraire] m.

revile, v.t, injurier.

revise (Typ.) n, seconde [épreuve] f. ¶ v.t, revoir, reviser. revision, n, revision, f.

revival, n, reprise; renaissance, f; rétablissement; (Relig.) réveil, m. revive, v.t, ranimer; raviver; réveiller.

revoke, v.t, révoquer; (v.i, Cards) renoncer.

revolt, n, révolte, f; soulèvement, m. ¶ v.i, se révolter, se soulever. ~ing, a, révoltant.

revolution, n, révolution, f; tour, m. ~ary, a. & n, révolutionnaire, a. & m,f. ~ize, v.t, révolutionner; modifier entièrement. revolve, v.t & i, tourner.

revolver, n, revolver, m.

revue, n, revue, f.

revulsion, n, révolution; (Med.) révulsion, f.

reward, n, récompense, f. ¶ v.t, récompenser; couronner.

rewrite, v.t.ir, récrire.

rhapsody, n, rhapsodie, f.

Rheims, n, Reims, m.

rhetoric, n, rhétorique, f. ~al, a, oratoire; soutenu.

rheumatic, a, rhumatismal. rheumatism, n, rhumatisme, m.

Rhine, n (the), le Rhin. ¶ att, rhénan; (wine) du Rhin. the ~land, les pays rhénans.

rhinoceros, n, rhinocéros, m.

rhododendron, n, rhododendron, m.

rhomb[us], n, rhombe, losange, m.

Rhone (the), le Rhône.

rhubarb, n, rhubarbe, f.

rhyme, n, rime, f. ¶ v.i, rimer. rhym[est]er, n, rim[aill]eur, m. rhythm, n, r[h]ythme, m, cadence, f. ~ic(al), a, r[h]ythmique.

rib, n, côte; nervure; (ship) côte, f, membre, m; (umbrella) baleine, f. ~ steak, entre-côte, f.

ribald, a, gaillard, égrillard, licencieux.

ribbed, a, côtelé, à côtes; à nervure(s).

ribbon or riband, n, ruban; cordon, m. ~ book mark[er], signet, m. ~ maker, rubanier, ère. ~ trade, rubanerie, f.

rice, n, riz, m. ~ field, rizière, f. ~ paper, papier de Chine, m.

rich†, a, riche; (food) gras. the ~, les riches, m.pl. richen, n.pl, richesse, f. oft. pl. richness, n, richesse, f.

rick, n, (hay) meule, f; (strain) effort, m. ~ cloth, bâche de meule, f.

rickets, n, rachitisme, m. rickety, a, rachitique; boiteux, bancal.

ricksha[w], n, pousse-pousse, m.

ricochet, n, ricochet, m. ¶ v.i, ricocher.

rid, v.t.ir, débarrasser. riddance, n, débarras, m.

riddle, n, énigme, devinette, f, rébus; (sieve) crible, m. ¶ v.t, cribler.

ride, n, promenade; chevauchée; cavalcade, f; trajet, m. ¶ v.t & i. ir, monter; chevaucher; aller. ~ out (Polo), bousculer. ~ side-saddle, monter en amazone. ~ to death (fig.), enfourcher; revenir sans cesse à.

rider, n, cavalier, ère; écuyer, ère; (P.S.) ajouté, m; (to bill of exchange) allonge, f.

ridge, n, arête; strie; (roof) crête; (hill) croupe; (Agric.) raie, f; (left by plough) billon, m. ~ capping, faîtage, m. ~ pole, faîtage, m; (tent) faîtière, f. ~ tile, [tuile] faîtière, f. ¶ v.t (Agric.) v.t, butter.

ridicule, n, ridicule, m. ¶ v.t, ridiculiser. ridiculous†, a, ridicule. ~ness, n, ridicule, m.

riding, n, équitation, f; manège; chevauchement, m; (Turf) monte, f. ~ boots, bottes à l'écuyère, f.pl. ~ breeches, culotte de cheval, f. ~ habit, amazone, f. ~ school, école d'équitation, f, manège, m. ~ whip, cravache, f.

rife (to be), régner, sévir, courir [les rues].

riff-raff, n, canaille, racaille, f.

rifle, n, fusil, m; carabine, f. ~ drill, maniement des (ou d') armes, m. ~ man, tirailleur, m. ~ range, [champ de] tir (gallery) tir, stand, m. ¶ v.t, (rob) dévaliser, spolier; (groove) rayer, canneler.

rift, n, crevasse; éclaircie, f; (fig.) fossé, m.

rig, v.t, équiper; accoutrer; harnacher; (ship) gréer. rigging, n, gréement, m, agrès, m.pl. ~ the market, tripotage de bourse, m.

right, a, droit; bon; bien; juste; vrai; qu'il faut. ~-angled, rectangle. ~-handed person or player, droitier, ère. ~-minded, bien pensant. at the ~ moment, à point nommé. ~ side (fabric), endroit, dessus, *m. to be* ~, avoir raison. ¶ *ad*, tout droit; bien; tout. ~ *honourable*, très honorable. ~ *reverend*, révérendissime. ~ *& left, ad*, à droite & à gauche. ~ *through*, de part en part; en entier. ¶ *n*, droit, *m*; faculté; raison, *f*; chef; gain de cause, *m*; (*side*) droite; (*pl.*) justice, *f*. ~ *of way*, [droit de] passage, *m. by* ~*s*, en toute justice. ¶ *v.t*, redresser.

righteous, *a*, vertueux; juste. ~*ly*, *ad*, droitement. ~*ness, n*, justice, *f*.

rightful†, *a*, légitime. **rightly**, *ad*, justement; bien; à juste titre.

rigid†, *a*, rigide. ~*ity, n*, rigidité, *f*.

rigmarole, *n*, litanie, kyrielle, tartine, *f*.

rigor mortis, rigidité cadavérique, *f*.

rigorous†, *a*, rigoureux. **rigour**, *n*, rigueur, *f*.

rill, *n*, ruisseau, *m*.

rim, *n*, [re]bord, *m*, bordure, *f*, ourlet, *m*; (*wheel*) jante, *f*; (*watch*) lunette, *f*. ~ *brake*, frein sur jantes, *m*. ~ *lock*, serrure encloisonnée, *f*. ¶ *v.t*, border. ~*less* (*glasses*) *a*, sans monture.

rime, *n*, givre, frimas, *m*.

rind, *n*, écorce, peau; (*cheese*) pelure, croûte; (*bacon*) couenne, *f*.

rinderpest, *n*, peste bovine, *f*.

ring, *n*, cercle; anneau, *m*; bague; boucle; frette, *f*; rond; segment; collier; cerne, *m*; couche; enceinte; arène; piste de cirque; coalition; bande, *f*; coup de sonnette; coup de téléphone, *m*. ~ *bolt*, boucle d'amarrage, *f*. ~ *dove*, palombe, *f*, [pigeon] ramier, *m*. ~ *finger*, [doigt] annulaire, *m*. ~*leader*, meneur; chef d'émeute, *m*. ~*quoits*, jeu d'anneaux, *m*. ~*s under the eyes*, les yeux cernés. ~*worm*, teigne, *f*. ¶ *v.t. & i. ir*, sonner; corner; tinter; résonner; retentir; cerner; (*bull, &c*) boucler. ~ *a peal*, carillonner. ~ *for*, sonner. ~ *up*, sonner au téléphone.

ringlet, *n*, boucle, *f*.

rink, *n*, piste, *f*.

rinse & ~ *out*, *v.t*, rincer. **rinsings**, *n.pl*, rinçure, *f*.

riot, *n*, émeute, *f*; tumulte, *m*; (*fig.*) orgie, débauche, *f*.' ¶ *v.i*, prendre part à une émeute; ripailler. ~*er*, *n*, émeutier, *m*. ~*ous†*, *a*, tumultueux.

rip, *n*, déchirure, *f*. ¶ *v.t*, fendre, déchirer; refendre; découdre; éventrer. ~ *saw*, scie à refendre, *f*.

riparian, *a*, riverain.

ripe, *a*, mûr. **ripen**, *v.t. & i*, mûrir. **ripeness**, *n*, maturité, *f*. **ripening**, *n*, maturation, *f*.

ripple, *n*, ride, *f*. ¶ *v.t*, rider; (*v.i.*) se r.

riposte, *n*, riposte, *f*. ¶ *v.t*, riposter.

rise, *n*, élévation; montée; rampe, *f*; lever, *m*; crue; naissance; source; hausse; augmentation; (*of a step*) hauteur de marche, *f*. ¶ *v.i.ir*, se lever; se relever; se soulever; s'élever; monter; naître; croître; bouffer; augmenter; hausser; (*dead*) ressusciter.

rising, *n*, lever, *m*; ascension, *f*; soulèvement, *m*. ¶ *p.a*: ~ *generation*, jeune génération, *f*. ~ *sun*, soleil levant, *m*. ~ *tide*, marée montante, *f*.

risk, *n*, risque; hasard, *m*. ¶ *v.t*, risquer; hasarder. *I'll* ~ *it*, au petit bonheur. ~*y*, *a*, hasardeux, chanceux.

rissole, *n*, rissole, *f*.

rite, *n*, rite, *m*. **ritual**, *a. & n*, rituel, *a. & m*.

rival, *a*, rival. ~, *n*, rival, e, émule, *m,f*. ¶ *v.t*, rivaliser avec. ~*ry*, *n*, rivalité, *f*.

rive, *v.t.ir*, fendre; (*v.i.ir*.) se fendre.

river, *n*, rivière, *f*; fleuve, *m*; (*att.*) de rivière, fluvial. ~ *god*, fleuve, *m*. ~*side*, bord de l'eau, *m*; (*att.*) riverain.

rivet, *n*, rivet, *m*. ¶ *v.t*, river; enchaîner, attacher.

Riviera (the), la Rivière de Gênes, la Côte d'Azur.

rivulet, *n*, ruisseau, *m*.

roach (*fish*) *n*, gardon, *m*.

road, *n*, route; voie, *f*; chemin, *m*. ~ *code*, code de la route, *m*. ~ *hog*, chauffard, *m*. ~*man or* ~*mender*, cantonnier, *m*. ~ *map*, carte routière, *f*. ~ *race*, course sur route, *f*. ~*side*, bord de la route, *m*; (*att.*) sur le b. de la r. ~*side inn & road house*, tournebride, *m*. ~*side station*, gare de passage, g. d'escale, *f*. ~ [*stead*] rade, *f*. ~ *stones*, cailloutis, *m*. ~ [*way*] chaussée, *f*. **roadster**, *n*, bicyclette de route, *f*.

roam, *v.i*, rouler, errer.

roan, *a*, (*animal*) rouan; (*shoes*) rouges. ¶ *n*, (*animal*) rouan, e; (*sheepskin*) basane, *f*.

roar, *v.i. & t*, rugir; mugir; gronder; ronfler; éclater.

roast, *v.t. & i*, rôtir; cuire [au four]; brûler; griller; torréfier. ~ *beef*, bœuf rôti, rosbif, *m*. ~ [*meat*] & ~ *meat course*, rôti, *m*. ~ *mutton*, rôti de mouton, *m*. ~*ing jack*, tournebroche, *m*.

rob, *v.t*, voler, dérober, dévaliser, filouter. **robber**, *n*, voleur, euse, brigand, *m*. ~*y*, *n*, vol, *m*; filouterie, *f*. ~ *with violence*, vol à main armée.

robe, *n*, robe; toge, *f*.

robin [**redbreast**], *n*, rouge-gorge, *m*.

robing room, vestiaire, *m*.

Rob Roy canoe, périssoire, *f*.

robust, *a*, robuste, vigoureux.

rock, *n*, rocher; roc, *m*; roche, *f*. ~ *crystal*, cristal de roche, *m*. ~ *drill*, perforatrice [au rocher] *f*. ~ *garden*, jardin de rocaille, jardin alpestre, *m*. ~ *salt*, sel gemme, *m*. ~*work*, rocaille, *f*. ¶ *v.t*, balancer; bercer. ~*er*, *n*, bascule; (*pers.*) berceuse, *f*. ~*ery*, *n*, rocher artificiel, *m*. ~*et*, *n*, fusée; (*Bot.*) roquette, *f*. ~ *shell*, obus-fusée, *m*. ~*ing*, *n*, balancement, bercement, *m*. ~ *chair, horse*, fauteuil, cheval, à bascule, *m*. ~ *stone*, rocher branlant, *m*. ~*y*, *a*, rocailleux; rocheux.

R~ Mountains, montagnes Rocheuses, *f.pl.*

rococo, *n. & a,* rococo, *m. & att.*

rod, *n,* baguette; verge; barre; tige; tringle; bielle; canne; *f; Meas.* = 25·293 sq. metres.

rodent. *n. & a,* rongeur, *m. & a.*

roe, *n,* (*fish*) See *hard, soft.* ~**buck,** chevreuil, *m.* ~**-doe,** chevrette, *f.*

rogations, *n.pl,* rogations, *f.pl.*

rogue, *n,* coquin, e, fripon, ne; espiègle, *m.f.* **roguish,** *a,* fripon; espiègle, mutin, malicieux. **roguishness & roguery,** *n,* friponnerie; espièglerie, malice, *f.*

roisterer, *n,* tapageur, euse.

roll, *n,* rouleau; cylindre, *m;* (*downhill*) roulade; (*package*) trousse; (*butter*) motte, *f;* petit pain; rôle, *m;* matricule, *f,* tableau; (*pl.*) tableau, *m.* ~ *call,* appel [nominal] *m.* ~ *of honour,* les morts pour la patrie. ~ *of the drum,* batterie de tambour, *f.* ¶ *v.t. & i,* rouler; cylindrer; laminer. ~*-top desk,* bureau américain, b. à rideau, *m.* ~*-film camera,* chambre à pellicules en bobines, *f.* ~*-film developing tank,* cuve pour développer les pellicules en rouleaux, *f.* ~ *up,* rouler. ~*-up manicure set,* trousse manucure, *f.* ~*-ed gold,* or laminé, *m,* doublé or. **roller,** *n,* rouleau; cylindre, *m;* roulette, *f;* galet, *m;* (*map*) gorge, *f;* (*bird*) rollier, *m;* (*wave*) houle longue, *f.* ~ *skates,* patins à roulettes, *m.pl.* ~ *skating,* patinage à r—s, *m.* ~ *towel,* essuie-main à rouleau, *m.*

rollick, *v.i,* faire la fête. ~**ing,** *a,* bruyant.

rolling, *n,* roulement; laminage; (*ship*) roulis, *m.* ~ *in wealth,* richissime. ~ *mill,* laminoir, *m.* ~ *pin,* rouleau de pâtissier, *m.* ~ *stock,* matériel roulant, *m.*

Roman, *a,* romain; (*nose*) aquilin. ~ *candle,* chandelle romaine, *f.* ~ *Catholic, a. & n,* catholique, *a. & m.f.* ~ *Catholicism,* catholicisme, *m.* ¶ *n,* (*pers.*) Romain, e; (*Typ.*) romain, *m.*

romance, *n,* roman, *m;* idylle, *f.* R~, *a. & n,* roman, *a. & m.* ¶ *v.i,* en raconter.

Romanesque, *a,* roman.

romantic, *a,* romanesque; (*literature*) romantique.

romp, *n,* jeu bruyant, *m;* gamine bruyante, *f,* garçon manqué, *m.* ¶ *v.i,* folâtrer, batifoler. ~**ers** (*child's*) *n.pl,* barboteuse, combinaison, *f.*

rood, *n,* croix, *f; Meas.* = 10·117 ares. ~ *screen,* jubé, *m.*

roof, *n,* toit; comble, faîte; ciel, *m;* voûte, *f.* ~ *garden,* jardin sur le toit, *m.* ~ *of the mouth,* voûte palatine, voûte du palais, *f,* palais, *m.* ¶ *v.t,* couvrir. ~**ing,** *n,* toiture, couverture, *f,* faîtage, *m.*

rook, *n,* freux, *m,* corneille; (*Chess*) tour, *f.* ~**ery,** *n,* colonie de freux; c. de miséreux, *f.*

room, *n,* pièce; chambre, *f;* cabinet; (*pl.*) appartement; salon, *m;* salle; soute; place, *f;* large, espace, *m.* ~**mate,** camarade

de lit, camarade de chambrée, *m.f.* ~**ful,** *n,* chambrée, *f.* ~**y,** *a,* spacieux.

roost, *n,* juchoir, perchoir, *m.* ¶ *v.i,* [se] jucher, percher. ~**er,** *n,* coq, *m.*

root, *n,* racine, *f;* radical, *m.* ¶ *v.i,* s'enraciner; fouiller.

rope, *n,* corde, *f,* cordage; câble; *m;* manœuvre, *f;* chapelet, *m,* glane, *f.* ~ *dancer,* danseur (euse) de corde. ~ *end,* garcette, *f.* ~ *maker,* cordier, *m.* ~ *making & ~ works,* corderie, *f.* ~ *walker,* funambule, *m.f.* ¶ *v.t,* corder. ~**iness** (*wine*) *n,* graisse, *f.* ~**y,** *a,* (*liquid*) filant; (*wine*) gras.

roquet (*Croquet*) *v.t,* roquer.

rosary, *n,* rosaire, *m;* (*rose garden*) roseraie, *f.*

rose, *n,* rose, *f;* (*colour*) rose, *m;* (*ceiling*) rosace; (*can*) pomme; (*pipe*) crépine, *f.* ~ *bud,* bouton de rose, *m.* ~ *diamond,* rose, *f.* ~ *grower,* rosiériste, *m.* ~ *tree,* rosier, *m.* ~ *window,* rose, rosace, *f.* ~*wood,* palissandre, *m.* ~ *under the ~,* sous [le manteau de] la cheminée. **roseate,** *a,* rosé, incarnat. **rosemary,** *n,* romarin, *m.* **rosery,** *n,* roseraie, *f.* **rosette,** *n,* rosette; cocarde; (*Arch.*) rosace, *f.*

rosin, *n,* résine, *f;* (*for violin*) colophane, *f.*

roster, *n,* contrôle, rôle, *m.*

rostrum, *n,* tribune, *f.*

rosy, *a,* [de] rose, rosé, incarnat, vermeil.

rot, *n,* pourriture; carie, *f.* ¶ *v.i,* pourrir; se carier; (*v.t.*) faire pourrir; carier.

rota, *n,* rôle, *m.* **rotary,** *a,* rotatoire, tournant. **rotate,** *v.t. & i,* tourner; rouler. **rotation,** *n,* rotation, *f;* (*in office*) roulement; (*crops*) assolement, *m.* in ~, à tour de rôle, par roulement.

rote, *n,* routine, *f.*

rotten, *a,* pourri; carié; (*egg, &c*) gâté. ~**ness,** *n,* pourriture; carie, *f.*

rotund, *a,* rond, arrondi; pompeux. **rotunda,** *n,* rotonde, *f.* **rotundity,** *n,* rondeur, rotondité, *f.*

rouge, *n,* rouge, *m.* ~ *et noir,* trente et quarante. ¶ *v.i,* mettre du rouge.

rough, *a,* grossier; brut; rude; brutal; bourru; raboteux; rugueux; âpre; (*sea*) agitée. ~ *account,* arrêté de compte en gros, *m.* in *a ~ & ready fashion,* à coups de hache, à la serpe, à coups de serpe. ~ *& tumble,* jeux de main, *m.pl.* ~*cast* (*walls*) *n,* crépi, *m;* (*v.t.*) crépir; hourder; ravaler. ~ *draft,* brouillon, *m.* ~ *estimate,* aperçu, *m.* at (or on) *a ~ estimate,* à vue d'œil, par aperçu. ~*haired,* au poil rude. ~*-rider,* casse-cou, *m.* ~*shod* (*horse*), ferré à glace. *to ride* ~*shod over,* fouler aux pieds, traiter avec rudesse. ¶ *n,* apache, m. *the* ~ (*Golf*), l'herbe longue, *f.* ~ *or smooth?* (*Ten.*), côté des nœuds ou côté lisse? ¶ ~, ~ *down,* ~ *out,* ~**hew,** *v.t,* dégrossir, ébaucher. ~**ness,** *n,* aspérité; rudesse; grossièreté; âpreté, *f.*

Roumania, *n*, la Roumanie. **Roumanian**, *a*, roumain. ¶ *n*, (*pers.*) Roumain, e; (*language*) le roumain.
round, *a*, rond. ~ **hand** (Writing), ronde, *f*. ~-*shouldered*, voûté. ~ *voyage*, aller & retour. ¶ *n*, rond, *m*; (*slice*) rouelle, *f*; (*rung*) échelon, *m*; (*tour*) ronde, tournée; (*applause*) salve, *f*; (*lap*) circuit, *m*; (*Sport*) partie; (*Box.*) reprise, *f*. ~ [of ammunition], cartouche, *f*. ~ *of toast*, rôtie, *f*. ¶ *ad*, autour. ~ *about*, alentour. ¶ *pr*, autour de, alentour de. ¶ *v.t*, arrondir. ~ *up*, rafler. **roundabout**, *a*, détourné; (*traffic*) giratoire. ¶ *n*, manège de chevaux de bois, carrousel; (*traffic*) sens giratoire, *m*, circulation en s. g., *f*. **roundelay**, *n*, ronde, *f*. **rounders**, *n.pl*, balle au camp, *f*. **roundish**, *a*, rondelet. **roundly**, *ad*, rondement. **roundness**, *n*, rondeur, *f*. **roundsman**, *n*, livreur, *m*.
rouse, *v.t*, [r]éveiller; exciter.
rout, *n*, déroute, débandade, *f*. ¶ *v.t*, mettre en déroute, défaire, culbuter.
route, *n*, route, voie, *f*. ~ *march*, promenade militaire, *f*. ¶ *v.t*, acheminer.
routine, *n*, routine, *f*, train, *m*.
rove, *v.i*, rouler, errer, vagabonder; (*v.t.*) écumer. **rover**, *n*, coureur; (*sea*) forban; (*Croquet*) corsaire, *m*. **roving**, *a*, vagabond.
row, *n*, rang, *m*, rangée, *f*; (*of stitches, Knit., &c*) tour, *m*; haie, *f*; cordon; bruit; tapage, fracas, potin, *m*; promenade en bateau, *f*. **a** ~ *of houses*, une rangée de maisons, des maisons en enfilade, *f.pl*. ¶ *v.i*, ramer, aller à la rame, canoter, nager, voguer. ~[*ing*] *boat*, bateau à rames; bateau de promenade, *m*.
rowdy, *n. & a*, tapageur, *m. & a*.
rowel, *n*, molette, *f*.
rower, *n*, rameur, euse, nageur, canotier, *m*.
rowing, *n*, canotage, *m*, nage [d'aviron] *f*, l'aviron, *m*. ~ *club*, cercle de l'aviron, club nautique, *m*. **rowlock**, *n*, dame de nage, demoiselle, toletière, *f*, système, *m*.
royal†, *a*, royal. *His, Your, R*~ *Highness*, monseigneur, son, votre, altesse royale. ~**ist**, *n. & att*, royaliste, *m.f. & a*. ~**ty**, *n*, royauté (*rent*) redevance, *f*; (*author's*) droit d'auteur, *m*.
rub, *n*, (*with a cloth*) coup de chiffon; (*fig.*) hic, nœud, *m*, enclouure, *f*. ~ (*of the green* (Golf), risque de jeu, *m*. ¶ *v.t. & i*, frotter; frictionner; (*inscription*) estamper. ~ *down* (horse), épousseter, bouchonner. ~ *one's hands*, se frotter les mains. ~ *out*, effacer. ~ *shoulders with*, se frotter à, frayer avec. ~ *up*, fourbir. **rubber**, *n*, frottoir; (*Cards*) rob[re] *m*; (*3rd game*) belle, *f*; caoutchouc, *m*; gomme [élastique] *f*. ~ *floating toys*, animaux marins flottants, animaux en caoutchouc, *m.pl*. ~ *shares*, valeurs de caoutchouc, *f.pl*. ~ *stamp*, timbre en c., t. humide, *m*. ~ *tire*, [bandage en] caoutchouc, *m*. ~-*tire*

& ~[*ize*], *v.t*, caoutchouter. **rubbing**, *n*, frottement, *m*; friction, *f*. oft. *pl*; (*with oil*) onction, *f*; (*copy*) frottis, *m*.
rubbish, *n*, décombres, *m.pl*, détritus, *m*; (*dirt*) immondice; (*trash*) camelote, saleté; (*nonsense*) blague, *f*, fadaises, *f.pl*.
rubble[**stone**], *n*, blocaille, *f*, moellon, *m*. ~[*work*], *n*, blocage, *m*.
rubicund, *a*, rubicond.
rubric, *n*, rubrique, *f*.
ruby, *n*, rubis, *m*. ¶ (*lips*) *a*, vermeilles.
ruck, *n*, pli, godet, *m*.
rucksack, *n*, sac de touriste, s. de montagne, s. d'alpinisme, *m*.
rudder, *n*, gouvernail, *m*.
ruddy, *a*, coloré, rougeaud, rubicond.
rude†, *a*, grossier, malhonnête, malgracieux; rude. ~**ness**, *n*, grossièreté, malhonnêteté, *f*.
rudiment, *n*, rudiment, *m*; (*pl, of a science, an art*) éléments, *m.pl*. ~**ary**, *a*, rudimentaire.
rue (*Bot.*), *n*, rue, *f*. ¶ *v.t*, se repentir de. ~**ful**†, *a*, triste.
ruff (*Hist., dress*) *n*, fraise, *f*.
ruffian, *n*, bandit, *m*. ~**ly**, *a*, de brigand.
ruffle, *n*, manchette, *f*. ¶ *v.t*, rider; froisser, chiffonner; (*hair*) ébouriffer.
rug, *n*, tapis de pied, *m*; carpette; descente de lit; (*travelling*) couverture, *f*, **plaid**, *m*. ~ *work*, tapisserie, *f*.
Rugby [**football**], *n*, [football] rugby, *m*.
rugged, *a*, raboteux; rugueux; rocailleux; rude. ~**ness**, *n*, aspérité; rudesse, *f*.
ruin, *n*, ruine, perte, *f*. ¶ *v.t*, ruiner, perdre, abîmer. ~**ous**, *a*, ruineux.
rule, *n*, règle; domination, *f*; empire; (*Typ.*) filet, *m*. ~ *of the road*, mode de circulation, *m*. ~ *of thumb*, procédé empirique, *m*; (*att.*) empirique. *by* ~ *of thumb*, empiriquement. ¶ *v.t*, régler; rayer; gouverner; régir; (*v.i.*) gouverner; régner; (*prices*) se pratiquer. **ruler**, *n*, gouvernant; dominateur, *m*; (*for lines*) règle, *f*. **ruling**, *p.a*, dominant; (*price*) pratiqué. ~ *passion*, passion dominante, épée de chevet, *f*. ¶ *n*, réglage, *m*, réglure; décision, *f*.
rum, *n*, rhum, *m*.
Rumania, *&c*. Same as *Roumania, &c*.
rumble, *v.i*, gronder; rouler; (*bowels*) gargouiller.
ruminant, *n. & a*, ruminant, *m. & a*. **ruminate**, *v.i. & t*, ruminer.
rummage, *v.t. & i*, fouiller, farfouiller.
rumour, *n*, rumeur, renommée, *f*, bruit, on-dit, *m*. *it is* ~*ed that*, le bruit court que.
rump, *n*, croupe, *f*; (*bird*) croupion, *m*; (*beef*) culotte, *f*. ~*steak*, romsteck, *m*.
rumple, *v.t*, chiffonner, froisser.
run, *n*, course; marche; campagne, *f*; cours; parcours, trajet, *m*; roulade; coulée; suite; séquence; vogue, *f*; commun, *m*; descente;

ruée; volière, f; parc, m. *in the long ~*, à la longue. ~*-off (from dead heat)*, course de barrage, f. ¶ ~*[-up] (Jump.)*, course d'élan, f, élan, m. ¶ *v.i.ir*, courir; **accourir**; affluer; fonctionner; marcher; circuler; trotter; couler; pleurer, suinter; tourner; rouler; aller; être; (*b.t.ir.*) faire; faire courir; faire marcher; actionner; conduire; [en]courir. ~ *about*, faire des allées & venues. ~ *against*, heurter. ~ *aground*, échouer. ~ *along*, longer, border, côtoyer. ~ *away*, s'enfuir, se **sauver**. ~ *into*, rencontrer. ~ *on (Typ.)*, [faire] suivre. ~ *out of (stock)*, manquer de, être à court de. ~ *out of petrol*, avoir une panne d'essence *ou* une p. sèche. ~ *over*, parcourir; déborder. *to be ~ over*, être écrasé. ~ *stock [against one's client]*, faire la contrepartie. ~ *the streets*, polissonner. ~ *through*, parcourir; feuilleter; transpercer, enferrer, embrocher. ~ *to earth*, dépister. ~ *to seed*, monter en graine. ~ *up against (pers.)*, coudoyer.

runabout, n, coureur, euse; voiturette, f.
runaway, n. & a, fugitif, ive, fuyard, e, échappé, e. ~ *match*, mariage par enlèvement, m.
rung, n, échelon; barreau, m.
runner, n, coureur, euse; (*tout*) démarcheur; (*slide*) curseur, m; (*millstone*) meule de dessus, meule courante, f; (*for shelf*) liteau; (*Hort., Bot.*) coulant; (*slider of sledge*) patin, m. ~ *bean*, haricot d'Espagne, m.
running, n, courses, f.pl; marche, f; roulement; service, m. ~ *stock (against one's client)*, contrepartie, f. ¶ *p.a.*, courant; coulant; cursif; successif, de suite. ~ *buffet*, buffet, m. ~ *dive*, plongeon avec élan, m. ~ *fire*, feu roulant, m. ~ *gear*, roulement, m. ~ *hand*, coulée, f. ~ *number*, numéro d'ordre, m. ~ *stitch*, point devant, m.
rupee, n, roupie, f.
rupture, n, rupture; (*Med.*) hernie, f. ¶ *v.t*, rompre. *to be ~d*, avoir une hernie.
rural, a, rural, champêtre.
ruse, n, ruse, f.
rush, n, jonc, m; (*pl. Golf*) ajoncs, m.pl; (*fig.*) fétu; élan, m; ruée, bousculade; presse; chasse, f; flot, torrent, m. ~ *chair*, chaise paillée, f. ~ *hours*, heures d'affluence, f.pl. ¶ *v.t*, brusquer; (*v.i.*) se précipiter, se ruer, accourir, foncer. ~ *down*, dégringoler, dévaler.
rusk, n, biscotte, f.
russet, a, roux. ¶ n, roux, m; (*apple*) reinette grise, f.
Russia, n, la Russie. **Russian**, a, russe. ¶ n (*pers.*) Russe, m,f; (*language*) le russe.
rust, n, rouille, f. *to rub off the ~ from*, dérouiller. ¶ *v.t*, rouiller; (*v.i.*) se r.

rustiness, n, rouillure, f. **rustless**, a, inoxydable.
rustic, a, rustique, agreste, paysan. ¶ n, rustre, paysan, m. **rusticate**, *v.i*, être en villégiature.
rustle, *v.i*, frémir, bruire; (*dress*) faire froufrou.
rusty, a, rouillé.
rut, n, (*groove*) ornière, f; (*of animals*) rut, m.
ruthless, a, impitoyable, acharné, âpre.
rye, n, seigle, m. ~ *grass*, ray-grass, m.

S

S, n. & *S hook*, esse, f, S, m.
sabbath, n, sabbat; dimanche, m.
sable, n, (*Zool.*) [martre] zibeline; (*fur*) zibeline, f, sable; (*Her.*) sable, m.
sabre, n, sabre, m. ¶ *v.t*, sabrer.
sac, n, sac, m, bourse, f.
saccharin[e], n, saccharine, f.
sacerdotal, a, sacerdotal.
sachet, n, sachet à parfums, sultan, m.
sack, n, sac, m. ~ *cloth, sacking*, toile à sacs, f, treillis, m, serpillière, f; (*Theol.*) sac, m. *in ~cloth & ashes*, sous le sac & la cendre. ~ *race*, course en sacs, f. ¶ *v.t*, ensacher; saccager, mettre à sac. ~**ful**, n, sachée, f.
sacrament, n, sacrement, m, communion, f. ~**al†**, a, sacramental. ~**al**, n, sacramental, m. **sacred**, a, sacré; saint; inviolable; (*song, &c*) religieux; (*concert*) spirituel; (*to the memory of*) consacré. **sacrifice**, n, sacrifice, m. ¶ *v.t. & i*, sacrifier, immoler. **sacrificial**, a, du sacrifice. **sacrilege**, n & **sacrilegious**, a, sacrilège, m. & a. **sacristy**, n, sacristie, f. **sacrosanct**, a, sacro-saint.
sad, a, triste, douloureux, fâcheux. **sadden**, *v.t*, attrister, contrister.
saddle, n, selle; (*lathe*) cuirasse, f; (*mountain*) col, m. ~**-backed**, ensellé. ~ *bag*, sacoche; fauconnière; (*stuff*) moquette, f. ~ *bow*, arçon, m. ~ *horse*, cheval de selle, m. ¶ *v.t*, seller; (*pack animal*) embâter; (*fig.*) grever, charger. **saddler**, n, sellier, m. **saddlery**, n, sellerie, f.
sadly, ad, tristement; cruellement. **sadness**, n, tristesse, f.
safe, a, sauf; sûr; sans danger; assuré; de sécurité; (*investment*) sûr, de tout repos, de père de famille; (*arrival*) bonne, heureuse. ~ *& sound*, sain & sauf, bagues sauves. ~ *conduct*, sauf-conduit, m, sauvegarde, f. ~ *custody*, garde [en dépôt] f. ~ *keeping*, sûreté, f. ¶ n, coffre-fort, m. ~ *deposit*, service de coffres-forts, m; (*institution*) caisse de dépôts, f. ~*guard*, n, sauvegarde, garantie, f, palladium; m; (*v.t.*) garantir. ~**ly**, ad, en sûreté; sûrement; sans danger; sans accident; (*arrival*) à bon port. ~**ty**, n, sûreté; sécurité, f; salut, m. ~ *bicycle*,

bicyclette, f. ~ **catch**, cran d'arrêt, m. ~ **curtain**, rideau de fer, m. ~ **first**, sécurité d'abord. ~ **pin**, épingle de sûreté, é. de nourrice, é. anglaise, f. ~ **razor**, rasoir de sûreté, r. mécanique, f. ~ **valve** (*lit. & fig.*), soupape de sûreté, f.

saffron, n, safran, m.

sag, n, flèche, f. ¶ v.i, fléchir, donner.

sagacious, a, sagace. **sagacity**, n, sagacité, f.

sage, n, (*pers.*) sage, m; (*herb*) sauge, f. ¶ a, sage.

sago, n, sagou, m. ~ **palm**, sagou[t]ier, m.

said (the) (*Law*) p.a, ledit.

sail, n, voile, toile, (*pl.*) voilure, f; (*windmill*) volant, m; promenade en bateau, f. ~ **cloth**, toile à voiles, f. ~ **loft & ~ making**, voilerie, f. ~ **maker**, voilier, m. ¶ v.i, faire voile; naviguer; voguer; marcher; courir; partir; (*v.t.*) faire naviguer; naviguer sur. ~**er**, n, voilier, marcheur, m. ~**ing**, n, navigation [à voile] f; départ, m; partance; marche, f. ~ **ship**, navire à voiles, voilier, m. ~**or**, n, marin; matelot, m. ~ **suit**, costume marin, m.

sainfoin, n, sainfoin, m.

saint, a, saint. ¶ n, saint, e. ~'s **day**, fête, f. St Bernard **dog**, chien de Saint-Bernard, m. Saint Helena, Sainte-Hélène, f. St-John's-**wort**, mille-pertuis, m. Saint Lawrence, Saint-Laurent, m. St Vitus's **dance**, danse de Saint-Guy, chorée, f. ¶ v.t, canoniser. ~**ed**, p.p, saint, canonisé. **saintliness**, n, sainteté, f. **saintly**, a, saint.

sake, n, cause, f; amour; plaisir; égard, m.

sal, n, sel, m. ~-**ammoniac**, sel ammoniac. ~ **volatile**, alcool ammon aromatique, spiritus aromaticus.

salaam, n, salamalec, m.

salable, a, vendable, de vente; marchand, vénal.

salacious, a, lascif, lubrique.

salad, n, salade, f. ~ **bowl**, saladier, m. ~ **oil**, huile de table, h. comestible, f.

Salamanca, n, Salamanque, f.

salamander, n, salamandre, f.

salaried, p.a, appointé. **salary**, n, appointements, m.pl, traitement; (*cinema star's*) cachet, m; (*M.P.'s*) indemnité, f. *to put on a ~ basis*, appointer.

sale, n, vente, f; débit; solde, m; liquidation; enchère, f. ~ *by private treaty*, vente à l'amiable. *on ~* [*or return*], en dépôt.

Salerno, n, Salerne, f.

salesman, -woman, n, vendeur, euse; (*market*) facteur (de la halle) m. ~**ship**, l'art de vendre, m.

Salic law, loi salique, f.

salient, a. & n, saillant, a. & m.

saline, a, salin.

saliva, n, salive, f. **salivate**, v.i, saliver.

sallow, a, jaunâtre.

sally, n, (*Mil.*) sortie, saillie; (*wit*) saillie, f, trait d'esprit, m, boutade, f.

salmon, n, saumon, (*young*) saumoneau, m. ~ **pink**, rose saumon, m. ~ **trout**, truite saumonée, f.

Salonica, n, Salonique, f.

saloon, n, salon, m. ~ **car**, wagon-salon, m.

salt, n, sel, m. ~ **cellar**, salière, f. ~ **industry**, industrie salicole, f, saunage, m. ~ **lake**, lac salé, m. ~-**meadow sheep & ~-meadow mutton**, pré-salé, m. ~ **pork**, [porc] salé, m. ~ **provisions**, salaisons, f.pl. ~ **sifter**, salière de table, *dite* poudrier, f. ~ **spoon**, pelle à sel, f. ~ **water**, eau salée, e. saline, f. ~-**water fish**, poisson de mer, m; (*caught & fresh*) marée, f. ~-**water fishing**, pêche en mer, f. ~ **works**, saunerie, saline, f. ¶ v.t, saler. ~**ing**, n, salage, m; salaison, f. ~**ness**, n, salure, f. **saltern**, n, marais salant, m.

saltpetre, n, salpêtre, nitre, m.

salubrious, a, salubre.

saluki, n, sloughi, m.

salutary†, a, salutaire. **salutation**, n, salutation, f, salut, m. **salute**, n, salut; (*guns*) salut, m, salve, f. ¶ v.t, saluer.

salvage, n, sauvetage, m. ¶ v.t, sauver. **salvation**, n, salut, m. S~ *Army*, Armée du Salut, f. **salve**, n, onguent, m; pommade, f. ¶ (*fig.*) v.t, calmer.

salver, n, plateau, f.

salvo, n, salve, f.

salvor, n, sauveteur, m.

Salzburg, n, Salzbourg, m.

same, a, même. ~**ness**, n, identité; monotonie, f.

sample, n, échantillon, m, montre, f. ¶ v.t, échantillonner; (*taste wines, &c*) déguster. **sampler**, n, modèle de broderie, m.

sanatorium, n, sanatorium, m.

sanctify, v.t, sanctifier. **sanctimonious†**, a, béat, cagot, papelard, dévot. **sanction**, n, sanction; consécration, f. ¶ v.t, sanctionner; consacrer. **sanctity**, n, sainteté; religion, f. **sanctuary**, n, sanctuaire; asile, m; réserve, f. **sanctum**, n, le saint des saints; sanctuaire, m.

sand, n, sable; sablon, m; (*pl.*) plage, f. ~ **bag**, sac à terre, m. ~ **bank**, banc de sable, ensablement, m. ~ **blast**, jet de sable, m. ~ **flats**, relais, m. ~ **fly**, simulie, f. ~ **glass**, sablier, m, horloge de sable, f. ~ **hill**, dune, f. ~ **martin**, hirondelle de rivage, f. ~ **paper**, n, papier de verre, m; (*v.t.*) poncer. ~**piper**, bécasseau, f. ~ **pit**, sablière; sablonnière, f. ~**stone**, grès, m. ~**stone quarry**, gresserie, f. ¶ v.t, sabler. ~ [**up**], ensabler.

sandal, n, sandale, f. ~ [*wood*], [bois de] santal, m.

sandwich, n, sandwich, m. ~ **man**, homme-sandwich, m.

sandy, a, sablonneux. ~ **hair**, chevelure blond roux, f.

sane, a, sain, rassis.

sanguinary, *a*, sanguinaire. **sanguine**, *a*, optimiste; plein d'espérance; (*full-blooded, Hist.*) sanguin.

sanitary, *a*, sanitaire; hygiénique. ~ *dustbin*, seau hygiénique pour ordures ménagères, *m*, poubelle, *f*. ~ *inspector*, inspecteur sanitaire, *m*. ~ *towel*, serviette hygiénique, *f*. **sanitate**, *v.t*, assainir. **sanitation**, *n*, assainissement, *m*; hygiène, *f*.

sanity, *n*, raison, *f*; bon sens, *m*; rectitude, *f*.

sanserif, *a*, sans empattement.

Santa Claus, le père Noël, le bonhomme Noël.

sap, *n*, sève; lymphe; (*Mil.*) sape, *f*. ~ *wood*, aubier, *m*. ¶ *v.t*, saper. **sapling**, *n*, plant, *m*. **sapper**, *n*, [sapeur] mineur, *m*.

sapphire, *n*, saphir, *m*.

sappy, *a*, plein de sève.

Saragossa, *n*, Saragosse, *f*.

Saratoga [trunk], *n*, [malle] chapelière, *f*.

sarcasm, *n*, sarcasme, *m*. **sarcastic**, *a*, sarcastique.

sarcophagus, *n*, sarcophage, *m*.

sardine, *n*, sardine, *f*.

Sardinia, *n*, la Sardaigne. **Sardinian**, *a*, sarde. ¶ *n*, Sarde, *m,f*.

sardonic, *a*, sardonique.

sardonyx, *n*, sardoine, *f*.

sarsaparilla, *n*, salsepareille, *f*.

sarsenet, *n*, florence, *f*.

sash, *n*, ceinture; écharpe, *f*; `(*window*) châssis, *m*. ~ *window*, fenêtre à guillotine, *f*.

Satan, *n*, Satan, *m*. ~**ic**, *a*, satanique.

satchel, *n*, cartable, *m*; gibecière, sacoche, *f*.

sate, *v.t*, rassasier.

sateen *or* satinet[te], *n*, satinette, *f*.

satellite, *n*, satellite; lévite, *m*.

satiate, *v.t*, rassasier. **satiety**, *n*, satiété, *f*.

satin, *n*, satin, *m*. ~ *stitch* (*Emb.*), passé, *m*. ~ *wood*, bois satiné, *m*. ~**y**, *a*, satiné.

satire, *n*, satire, *f*. **satiric** *&* ~**al**, *a*, satirique. **satirist**, *n*, satirique, *m*. **satirize**, *v.t*, satiriser.

satisfaction, *n*, satisfaction; raison, *f*. **satisfactorily**, *ad*, d'une manière satisfaisante. **satisfactory**, *a*, satisfaisant. **satisfy**, *v.t*, satisfaire, satisfaire à; contenter.

saturate, *v.t*, saturer.

Saturday, *n*, samedi, *m*.

saturnalia, *n.pl*, saturnales, *f.pl*.

saturnine, *a*, sombre; (*Chem.*) saturnin.

satyr, *n*, satyre, *m*.

sauce, *n*, sauce; impertinence, *f*. ~ *boat*, saucière, *f*. ~ *ladle*, cuiller à sauce, *f*. ~ *pan*, casserole, *f*; poêlon, *m*. **saucer**, *n*, soucoupe, *f*; (*artist's*) godet, *m*. **saucy**, *a*, gamin; impertinent.

sauerkraut, *n*, choucroute, *f*.

saunter, *v.i*, flâner. ~**ing**, *n*, flânerie, *f*.

sausage, *n*, (*fresh*) saucisse, *f*; (*smoked*) saucisson, *m*. ~ *balloon*, saucisse, *f*. ~ *skin*, ~ *case*, peau à saucisses, *f*.

sauté potatoes, pommes de terre sautées, *f.pl*.

savage†, *a*, sauvage; féroce, farouche. ¶ *n*,

sauvage, *m,f*, sauvagesse, *f*, cannibale, *m*. ~**ry**, *n*, sauvagerie; férocité, *f*.

savant, *n*, savant, *m*.

save, *v.t*, sauver; épargner; ménager; économiser; gagner; capter; (*v.i.*) économiser. ¶ *pr*, sauf, sinon, hormis, près. **saving**, *n*, épargne; économie, *f*. ~ *clause*, clause de sauvegarde, *f*. ~*s bank*, caisse d'épargne, *f*. **the Saviour**, le Sauveur.

savory (*Bot.*) *n*, sarriette, *f*. **savour**, *n*, saveur, *f*. **to** ~ **of**, tenir de, sentir le, la. **savoury**, *a*, savoureux. ~ *herbs*, fines herbes, *f.pl*. ~ *omelet*, omelette aux fines herbes, *f*.

Savoy, *n*, la Savoie. **s**~, chou de Milan, *m*.

saw, *n*, scie, *f*; dicton, adage, *m*. ~*bones*, carabin, *m*. ~*dust*, sciure, *f*. ~*mill*, scierie, *f*. ¶ *v.t.ir*, scier; débiter. ~ *off*, scier. ~**ing**, *n*, sciage, *m*. ~**yer**, *n*, scieur, *m*.

saxe (*colour*) *n*, saxe, *m*.

saxhorn, *n*, saxhorn, *m*.

saxifrage, *n*, saxifrage, *f*.

Saxon, *a*, saxon. ¶ *n*, Saxon, ne. **Saxony**, *n*, la Saxe.

saxophone, *n*, saxophone, *m*.

say, *n*, mot, *m*; voix, *f*. ¶ *v.t.ir*, dire; réciter; parler. ¶ (*so much*), disons; ci. *I* ~! dites donc!; écoutez!; ah! çà. *you don't* ~ *so!* pas possible! ~ *again*, redire, répéter. **saying**, *n*, mot, dire; dicton, adage, *m*. ~*s & doings*, faits & dits, *m.pl*.

scab, *n*, croûte; (*Vet.*) gale; (*Hort.*) rogne, *f*.

scabbard, *n*, fourreau, *m*.

scabby *&* scabious, *a*, scabieux, galeux, rogneux. **scabious** (*Bot.*) *n*, scabieuse, *f*.

scaffold, *n*, échafaud, *m*. ~ *pole*, écorperche, *f*. **scald**, *n*, brûlure, *f*. ¶ *v.t*, échauder, ébouillanter; blanchir.

scale, *n*, échelle; (*Mus.*) gamme, *f*; barème; tarif; (*pan*) plateau, bassin, *m*; (*pl, lancet*) châsse; écaille, paillette; incrustation; (*s. or pl.*) balance; bascule, *f*. ~ *maker*, balancier, *m*. ¶ *v.t*, (*wall*) escalader; (*boiler*) piquer; (*v.i.*) s'écailler.

scallop, *n*, (*Mol.*) pétoncle, peigne; (*edging*) feston, *m*. ¶ *v.t*, festonner.

scalp, *n*, cuir chevelu, *m*; (*trophy*) chevelure, *f*. ~ *massage*, friction, *f*. ¶ *v.t*, scalper.

scalpel, *n*, scalpel, *m*.

scaly, *a*, écailleux.

scamp, *n*, chenapan, vaurien, polisson, [mauvais] garnement, *m*. ¶ *v.t*, brocher, bâcler.

scamper away, s'enfuir en courant, détaler.

scan, *v.t*, scruter, éplucher; (*verse*) scander.

scandal, *n*, scandale, éclat, *m*; honte; médisance, *f*, cancan, racontar; pétard, *m*. ~*monger*, médisant, e; mauvaise langue, *f*. ~**ize**, *v.t*, scandaliser. ~**ous†**, *a*, scandaleux.

Scandinavia, *n*, la Scandinavie. **Scandinavian**, *a*, scandinave. ¶ *n*, Scandinave, *m,f*.

scansion, *n*, scansion, *f*.

scant[y], *a*, exigu; étriqué; maigre; faible; pauvre; mesquin; (*attire*) sommaire.

scape (*Bot.*) *n*, hampe, *f*. ~*goat*, bouc émissaire, *m*, souffre-douleur, *m*. ~*grace*, [mauvais] garnement, mauvais sujet, *m*.

scar, *n*, cicatrice, couture, balafre, *f*. ¶ *v.t*, cicatriser, couturer, balafrer.

scarab, *n*, scarabée, *m*.

scarce, *a*, rare; (*time*) cher. ~*ly, ad*, à peine; presque. scarcity, *n*, rareté; disette, *f*.

scare, *n*, panique, transe, *f*. ¶ *v.t*, épouvanter, effrayer, effarer. ~*crow*, *n*, épouvantail, *m*.

scarf, *n*, écharpe, *f*, cache-nez, *m*.

scarify, *v.t*, scarifier.

scarlatina, *n*. or scarlet fever, [fièvre] scarlatine, *f*. ~ scarlet, *a*, écarlate, *f. & a*. ~ runner, haricot d'Espagne, *m*.

scarp, *n*, escarpe, *f*.

scatheless, *a*, indemne. scathing, *a*, cinglant, sanglant. ~ attack (*fig.*), jeu de massacre, *m*.

scatter, *v.t*, disperser, éparpiller; semer.

scavenge, *v.t*, balayer. scavenger, *n*, boueux, balayeur; animal qui se nourrit de charogne, *m*.

scenario, *n*, scénario, *m*. scene, *n*, scène, *f*; spectacle; tableau; théâtre, *m*. *behind the* ~*s*, dans la coulisse. ~ *painter*, peintre de décors, décorateur, *m*. ~ *shifter*, machiniste, *m*. ~ *shifting*, changement de décor[ation] *m*. ~*ry*, *n*, paysages, *m.pl*; (*Theat.*) décors, *m.pl*, décoration, *f*. scenic, *a*, scénique. ~ *railway*, montagnes russes, *f.pl*.

scent, *n*, parfum, *m*; odeur; senteur, *f*; flair, fumet, nez; vent, *m*, piste, voie, *f*. ~ *bag*, sachet à parfums, *m*. ~ *bottle*, flacon à odeur, *m*. *to throw off the* ~, dépister. ¶ *v.t*, parfumer, embaumer; flairer, subodorer. ~*ed, a*, parfumé, odorant.

sceptic, *n. & ~al, a*, sceptique, *m,f. & a*. scepticism, *n*, scepticisme, *m*.

sceptre, *n*, sceptre, *m*.

Schaffhausen, *n*, Schaffhouse, *f*.

Scheldt (the), l'Escaut, *m*.

schedule, *n*, annexe, *f*, bordereau, *m*; (*Inc. Tax*) cédule, *f*.

scheme, *n*, projet, plan; cadre, *m*, combinaison, *f*. ¶ *v.t*, projeter; machiner; (*v.i*) former des projets; intriguer. schemer, *n*, homme à projets, *m*; intrigant, e. scheming, *n*, manœuvres, *f.pl*.

schism, *n*, schisme, *m*.

schist, *n*, schiste, *m*. ~ose, *a*, schisteux.

scholar, *n*, écolier, ère; savant, érudit, *m*. ~*ly*, *a*, savant, érudit. ~*ship*, *n*, savoir, *m*, érudition; bourse, *f*. scholastic, *a*, scolastique. school, *n*, école; classe, *f*; collège; conservatoire; (*of fish*) banc, *m*. ~ *book*, livre de classe, l. classique, l. scolaire, *m*. ~*boy*, *~girl*, écolier, ère, lycéen, ne, collégien, ne. ~ *fees*, frais d'école, *f*. scolaires, *m.pl*. ~*fellow*, camarade d'école, *m,f*, condisciple, *m*. ~ *for defective children*, école d'anormaux. ~*master*, ~*mistress*, instituteur, trice. ~ *of dancing*, académie de danse, *f*; cours de danse, *m.pl*. ~ *room*, [salle de] classe, *f*. schooling, *n*, instruction, *f*.

schooner, *n*, schooner, *m*, goélette, *f*.

sciatic, *a. & sciatica, n*, sciatique, *a. & f*.

science, *n*, science, *f*. scientific, *a*, scientifique; (*instruments*) de précision. scientist, *n*, savant, homme de science, *m*.

Scilly Islands or Isles, îles Scilly, îles Sorlingues, *f.pl*.

scimitar, *n*, cimeterre, *m*.

scintillate, *v.i*, scintiller.

scion, *n*, (*Hort.*) scion; (*pers.*) rejeton, *m*.

scissors, *n.pl*, ciseaux, *m.pl*. *with* ~ *& paste* (*fig.*), à coups de ciseaux.

sclerosis, *n*, sclérose, *f*.

scoff at, se moquer de; mépriser. scoffer, *n*, moqueur, euse, railleur, euse. scoffing, *n*, moquerie, *f*.

scold, *n*, grondeuse, mégère, *f*. ¶ *v.t*, gronder, tancer, semoncer, quereller; (*v.i.*) criailler.

scollop, *n. & v.t*. Same as scallop.

sconce, *n*, applique, *f*.

scoop, *n*, pelle; main; cuiller; casse; écope, *f*. ~ *out*, caver.

scooter, *n*, patinette, trottinette, *f*.

scope, *n*, étendue, *f*, champ, *m*; latitude, *f*; cadre, *m*, portée; carrière, *f*; essor, *m*.

scorch, *v.t*, brûler, rôtir, roussir.

score, *n*, coche; strie, *f*; écot; point, *m*, marque, *f*; compte des points; c. des coups, *m*; (*Mus.*) partition; vingtaine, *f*. ¶ *v.t*, cocher; rayer; marquer; (*Mus.*) orchestrer. scorer, *n*, marqueur, euse; pointeur, *m*.

scoria, *n*, scorie, *f*.

scoring, *n*, pointage, *m*; orchestration, *f*. ~ *board* (*Bil.*), bouilier, *m*. ~ *card* (*Golf*), carte de résultats, *f*.

scorn, *n*, mépris, dédain, *m*. ¶ *v.t*, mépriser, dédaigner. ~*er*, *n*, contempteur, trice. ~*ful*, *a*, dédaigneux.

scorpion, *n*, scorpion, *m*.

scotch, *n*, cale, *f*. ¶ *v.t*, caler.

Scotch, *a*, écossais; d'Écosse. ~*man, -woman*, Écossais, e. *the* ~, les Écossais, *m.pl*. ~ *mist*, brouillasse, *f*.

scot-free, *a*, indemne, impuni.

Scotland, *n*, l'Écosse, *f*. ~ *yard* (London), la Préfecture de Police (*Paris*); (*C.I.D.* =) la Sûreté Nationale. Scottish, *a*, écossais.

scoundrel, *n*, scélérat, e, gredin, e.

scour, *n*, chasse [d'eau] *f*. ¶ *v.t*, donner une chasse à; dégraisser, décaper; (*seas*) écumer; (*country*) battre.

scourge, *n*, (*whip*) martinet; (*plague*) fléau, *m*. ¶ *v.t*, flageller.

scout, *n*, éclaireur, *f*. (*warship*) vedette, *f*. ~ *master*, chef éclaireur, *m*. ¶ *v.i*, aller à la découverte; (v.t.) repousser avec mépris.

scowl, v.i, se re[n]frogner.

scrag, n, (mutton) collet; (pers.) squelette. m. ~ end, bout saigneux, m. **scraggy,** a, décharné.

scramble, n, mêlée; (for place, &c) curée, f. ~d eggs, œufs brouillés, m.pl.

scrap, n, bout, morceau; chiffon, m; (metal) déchets, plombs, m.pl; (pl.) restes, m.pl; bribes, f.pl. ~ book, album pour collections, m. ~ iron, ferraille, f. ¶ v.t, mettre au rebut; se débarrasser de.

scrape, v.t, gratter; racler; décrotter; (Golf) érafler. ¶ n, embarras, m. **scraper,** n, grattoir; racloir, m; curette, f; (mat) décrottoir, m. **scrapings,** n.pl, raclure; (savings) gratte, f.

scratch, n, égratignure, f; coup de griffe, m; rayure, f; (Sport) scratch, m. ~ line, ligne de départ, f. ~ race, course scratch, f. ¶ v.t, gratter; rayer; effleurer; (Sport) rayer de l'épreuve. ~ out, gratter; raturer.

scrawl, n, griffonnage, m, patarafe, f. ¶ v.t. & i, griffonner.

scream & screech, n, cri, m. ¶ v.i. & t, crier. screech owl, effraie, fresaie, f.

screed, n, tartine, f.

screen, n, écran; paravent; rideau, m; (choir) clôture; grille, f; crible, m, claie, f. ~ door, contre-porte, f. ¶ v.t, abriter; murer; soustraire; cribler; (Cinema) présenter à l'écran. ~ings, n.pl, criblure, f.

screw, n, vis; hélice, f; (on ball) effet, m; (pers.) avare; usurier, m. ~-capped bottle, flacon à couvercle vissé, m. ~ cutting, filetage, m. ~ driver, tournevis, m. ~ eye, piton, m. ~ hammer, clef à marteau, f. ~ plate, filière, f. ~ steamer, vapeur à hélice, f. ¶ v.t, visser.

scribble, n, griffonnage, m. ¶ v.t, griffonner; (v.i, of author) écrivailler. **scribbler,** n, griffonneur, euse; écrivassier, ère, folliculaire, m. scribbling block, bloc-mémorandum, m. **scribe,** n, scribe, m.

scrimmage, n, mêlée; bousculade, f.

scrip, n, titre provisoire; titre, m.

Scripture, n. oft. pl, l'Écriture, f. oft. pl.

scrofula, n, scrofules, f.pl. **scrofulous,** a, scrofuleux.

scroll, n, rouleau, m; volute, f.

scrub (bush) n, broussailles, f.pl. ¶ v.t, brosser; laver; lessiver. scrubbing brush, brosse à laver, f.

scruff of the neck, peau du cou, f, collet, m.

scrum[mage], n, mêlée; bousculade, f.

scrunch, v.t, croquer. ¶ i, croc!

scruple, n, scrupule, m; (apothecaries' measure) = 1·184 millilitres; (apothecaries' weight) = 1·296 grammes. ~ to, se faire scrupule de. **scrupulous†,** a, scrupuleux, religieux.

scrutineer, n, scrutateur, m. **scrutinize,** v.t, scruter. **scrutiny,** n, examen, m.

scuffle, n, rixe, bagarre, batterie, f.

scull, n, aviron de couple, m; (stern oar) godille, f. ¶ v.t, godiller; (v.i.) ramer en couple, nager en couple. ~er, n, rameur de couple, m.

scullery, n, lavoir [de cuisine] m.

scullion, n, marmiton, fouille-au-pot, m.

sculptor, n, sculpteur, m. **sculptress,** n, femme sculpteur, f. **sculpture,** n, sculpture, f. ¶ v.t, sculpter.

scum, n, écume, crasse; (fig.) écume, lie, f.

scumble, n, frottis, glacis, m. ¶ v.t, frotter, glacer.

scupper, n, dalot, m.

scurf, n, pellicules [du cuir chevelu] f.pl. ~ comb, peigne à décrasser, p. fin, m.

scurrilous, a, outrageant, ordurier.

scurvy, n, scorbut, m. ¶ a, vilain; méprisable.

scutcheon, n, écusson, m.

scuttle, n, (coal) seau; (Naut.) hublot, m. ¶ v.t, saborder; (v.i.) se sauver.

scythe, n, faux, f.

sea, n, mer, f, lame, f, paquet de mer, m. ~board, littoral, m. ~ bream, pagel, m. ~coast, côte de la mer, f. ~ cow, lamantin, m. ~-damaged, mariné. ~farer or ~faring man, homme de mer, m. ~faring people, peuple navigateur, m. ~ fishing, pêche en mer, f. ~going (ship), de mer, f. ~ gull, mouette, f, goéland, m. ~ horse, cheval marin, hippocampe, m. ~ kale, chou marin, m. to have got one's ~ legs, avoir le pied marin. ~ level, niveau de la mer, m. ~ lion, lion marin, m, otarie, f. ~man, marin, homme de mer, matelot; (skilful) manœuvrier, m. in a ~manlike manner, en bon marin. ~manship, manœuvre, f. ~ mark, balise, f, amer, m. ~men, gens de mer, m.pl. ~ nymph, nymphe de la mer, Néréide, f. ~ plane, hydravion, m. ~ scape, f, piece, marine, f. ~ shore, rivage de la mer, m. ~ sickness, mal de mer, m. to be ~sick, avoir le m. de m. ~side, bord de la mer, m. ~side resort, plage, station balnéaire, f. ~ urchin, oursin, hérisson de mer, m. ~ wall, digue, f. ~ ware, laisse, f. ~weed, plante marine, algue, f, varech, goémon, m. ~worthy, en [bon] état de navigabilité.

seal, n, sceau; cachet, m; (bottle) capsule, f; (Zool.) phoque, m. ~skin, peau de phoque, f. ¶ v.t, sceller; cacheter; boucher. ~ed book (fig.), lettre close, f. ~ing wax, cire à cacheter, f.

seam, n, couture; (Geol.) couche, f, gisement, m. ~ stitch (Need.), [point de] surjet, m. ¶ v.t, couturer. ~less, a, sans couture. **seamstress,** n, couturière, f. seamy side (lit. & fig.), envers, m.

seance, n, séance de spiritisme, f.

sear, a, desséché, fané. ¶ v.t, brûler; cautériser.

search, n, recherche, f. oft. pl; (Law) perquisition, f. ~ light, projecteur, m. ~ warrant, mandat de perquisition, m. ¶ v.t, scruter. ~ for, [re]chercher. ~er, n, chercheur, euse, fouilleur, m. ~ing, a, pénétrant; scrutateur.

season, n, saison, f, temps, m. ~ ticket, carte d'abonnement, f. ¶ v.t, assaisonner, relever; (wood) sécher; (fig.) aguerrir. ~able, a, de saison; opportun. ~ably, ad, à propos. ~ing (Cook.) n, assaisonnement, m; (of a salad) garniture, fourniture, f.

seat, n, siège, m; place, m; place assise; stalle, f; chef-lieu, m; charge; séance, f; office; théâtre; foyer; château; banc, m; banquette; chaise, f; repos, (trousers, chair) fond, m; assiette; (on horse) tenue, f. ¶ v.t, asseoir. 2-, 3-seater, voiture à 2, à 3, places, f.

secede, v.i, faire scission, faire sécession.

secluded, p.a, retiré. **seclusion**, n, retraite; réclusion, f.

second†, a, second; deuxième; deux; (cousin) issu(e) de germain. ~ childhood, enfance, f. ~ finger, doigt du milieu, médius, m. ~-hand, d'occasion; de seconde main. ~-hand bookseller, bouquiniste, m. ~-hand dealer, revendeur, euse, brocanteur, euse. ~ lieutenant, sous-lieutenant, m. one's ~ self, un autre soi-même. on ~ thoughts, réflexion faite. Charles the S~, Charles Deux. [on] the ~ of September, le deux septembre. ¶ n, second, m; deuxième, m,f; (Box.) second, soigneur; (duel) témoin, m; (time) seconde, f. ~ hand, aiguille des secondes, f. ~ of exchange, deuxième de change, f. ¶ v.t, seconder; appuyer. ~ary, a, secondaire. ~ school école secondaire, f, lycée, m.

secrecy, n, secret, m; discrétion, f. **secret**, a, secret; caché; dérobé. ~ spring, secret, m. ¶ n, secret, m. **secretary**, n, secrétaire, m. ~ bird, serpentaire, secrétaire, m. S~ of State for Home Affairs (Eng.), ministre de l'Intérieur (Fr.) m. S~ of State for War, ministre de la Guerre. ~ship & secretariat[e], n, secrétariat; ministère, m. **secrete**, v.t, cacher; (Physiology) sécréter. **secretion**, n, sécrétion, f. **secretive**, a, dissimulé, cachottier. **secretly**, ad, secrètement, en cachette; sourdement.

sect, n, secte, f. ~arian, n. & a, sectaire, m. & att.

section, n, section; coupe, f; profil; fer; tronçon; article, m, rubrique, f. ~ mark (§), paragraphe, m. ~al, a, démontable; (iron) profilé; (paper) quadrillé; (view) en coupe. **sector**, n, secteur, m.

secular†, a, séculier; profane; (100) séculaire. **secure**†, a, sûr; à l'abri. ¶ v.t, mettre à l'abri; assurer; garantir; asseoir; fixer; obtenir. **security**, n, sécurité; sûreté; assiette; garantie; assurance; caution, f;

cautionnement; titre, m; valeur, f. **securities clerk**, caissier (ère) des titres.

sedan [chair], n, chaise à porteurs, f.

sedate†, a, posé, rassis. **sedative**. n. & a, sédatif, calmant, m. & a. **sedentary**, a, sédentaire.

sedge, n, laîche, f. ~ warbler, rousserolle, f.

sediment, n, sédiment, dépôt, m.

sedition, n, sédition, f. **seditious**†, a, séditieux.

seduce, v.t, séduire. ~ from duty, débaucher. **seducer**, n, séducteur, trice. **seduction**, n, séduction, f. **seductive**, a, séduisant.

sedulous, a, assidu. ~ly, ad, assidûment.

see, n, siège [épiscopal] m, chaire, f, évêché, m.

see, v.t. & i. ir, voir; regarder; reconduire; s'occuper; veiller. ~ home, reconduire. ~ through, pénétrer. ¶ (vide) v.imperative, voir, voyez.

seed, n, semence; graine, f; grain; (fig.) germe, m. ~ corn, blé de semence, m. ~ pearls, semence de perles. ~ time, semailles, f.pl. ¶ v.i, grener, s'égrener. ~ the players (Ten.), sélectionner les têtes de séries. ~ed player, tête de série, f. ~ling, n, jeune plant, sauvageon, (pl.) semis, m. **seedsman**, n, grainier, ère.

seeing, n, vision, f. ~ that, vu que, attendu que, puisque.

seek, v.t. & i. ir, chercher, rechercher. ~er, n, chercheur, euse.

seem, v.i, sembler, paraître. **seeming**, n, paraître, m. the ~ & the real, l'être & le paraître. ¶ p.a, apparent. ~ly, ad, en apparence. **seemly**, a, [bien]séant.

seer, n, prophète, m.

seesaw, n, bascule, balançoire, f. ¶ v.i, basculer, se balancer.

seethe, v.i, bouillonner; grouiller.

segment, n, segment, m.

segregate, v.t, séparer. **segregation**, n, ségrégation, f.

Seidlitz powder, sel de Sedlitz, m.

seine (net) n, seine, f.

seismic, a, sismique. **seismograph**, n, sismographe, m.

seize, v.t, saisir, arrêter, prendre, s'emparer de; (of dog) piller; (Naut.) amarrer; (v.i, Mach.) gripper. **seizure**, n, saisie, f; arrêt, m; attaque de paralysie, f.

seldom, ad, rarement.

select, a, choisi; bien composé. ~ party, petit comité, m. ¶ v.t, choisir; (Sport) sélectionner. ~ion, n, choix, m; sélection, f; recueil, m; (pl, from writings) morceaux choisis, m.pl; (Betting) pronostic, m. ~ committee, jury, m.

self, n, personne, f; moi-même; moi, m; -même. ~-acting, automatique. ~-communion, recueillement, m. ~-conceit, fatuité, f. ~-contained, indépendant. ~-control, empire sur soi-même, m, maîtrise de soi, f. ~-defence, légitime défense, f. ~-denial, abnégation, f, renoncement, m.

~-esteem, amour-propre, *m.* ~-govern-ment, autonomie, *f.* ~-importance, suffi-sance, *f.* ~-made man, fils de ses œuvres; parvenu, *m.* ~-opinionated, opiniâtre. ~-possession, sang-froid, aplomb, *m.* ~-reliance, confiance en soi, *f.* ~-respect, amour-propre, *m.* ~-sacrifice, dévoue-ment, *m.* ~-satisfied, béat. ~-styled, soi-disant, *a.inv.* ~-taught, autodidacte. ~-toning (*Phot.*), auto-vireur. ~-willed, entier, opiniâtre, volontaire.

selfish†, *a,* égoïste, intéressé, personnel. ~ness, *n,* égoïsme, *m.*

sell, *v.t.ir,* vendre; débiter; (*v.i.ir.*) se vendre, s'écouler. ~ off, liquider, solder. ~ out against (*Stk Ex.*), exécuter. ~ up, vendre, exécuter, discuter. **seller**, *n,* vendeur, euse. *selling plate* (*Turf*), prix à ré-clamer, *m.*

seltzer [water], *n,* eau de Seltz, *f.*

selvage -edge, *n,* lisière, *f.*

semaphore, *n,* sémaphore, *m.*

semblance, *n,* semblant, *m,* apparence, *f.*

semi, *prefix:* ~breve, ronde, *f.* ~circle, demi-cercle, *m.* ~colon, point & virgule, point-virgule, *m.* ~demisemiquaver, qua-druple croche, *f.* ~-detached, jumelle. ~-final, demi-finale, *f.* ~-official, semi-officiel; officieux. ~quaver, double croche, *f.* ~tone, demi-ton, *m.*

seminary, *n,* séminaire, *m.*

Semitic, *a,* sémitique.

semolina, *n,* semoule, *f.*

sempstress, *n,* couturière, *f.*

senate, *n,* sénat, *m.* **senator**, *n,* sénateur, *m.*

send, *v.t. & i. ir,* envoyer; expédier; remettre. ~ away & ~ back, renvoyer. ~ for, en-voyer chercher, faire appeler. ~ to sleep, endormir. ~ to sleep again, rendormir. ~**er**, *n,* envoyeur, euse, expéditeur, trice.

Senegal, *n,* le Sénégal.

senile, *a,* sénile. ~ decay, décrépitude, caducité, *f.* **senility**, *n,* sénilité, *f.*

senior, *a,* aîné; ancien; principal; chef. ~ officers (liner), état-major, *m.* ¶ *n,* aîné, e; père, *m;* doyen, ne; (*Sports*) senior, *m.* ~ity, *n,* aînesse, ancienneté, *f.*

senna, *n,* séné, *m.*

sensation, *n,* sensation; impression, *f.* ~al, *a,* sensationnel. ~ affair, drame, *m.*

sense, *n,* sens; sentiment, *m;* sensation, *f;* esprit, *m;* raison, *f;* bon sens, sens commun, *m;* acception, part, *f.* ¶ *v.t,* entrevoir. ~less, *a,* insensé; sans connaissance. **sensibility**, *n,* sensibilité, *f.* **sensible**, *a,* sensé, sage; sensible. **sensibly**, *ad,* sensé-ment. **sensitive**, *a,* sensible; sensitif; tendre; susceptible; chatouilleux. **sensi-tized** (*Phot.*) *a,* sensible.

sensual†, *a,* sensuel, charnel. ~ist, *n,* sen-sualiste, *m.f.* ~ity *n,* sensualité, *f.*

sentence, *n,* sentence, *f,* jugement, *m;* (*Gram.*) phrase, *f.* ¶ *v.t,* condamner. **sententious†**, *a,* sentencieux.

sentient, *a,* sensible; conscient. **sentiment**, *n,* sentiment, *m.* ~al†, *a,* sentimental. ~ality, *n,* sentimentalité, sensiblerie, *f.*

sentinel, *n,* sentinelle, *f.* **sentry**, *n,* senti-nelle, *f,* factionnaire, *m;* (*mounted*) vedette, *f.* ~ box, guérite, *f.* ~ duty, faction, *f.*

separate†, *a,* séparé; distinct; à part. ~ cell system, emprisonnement cellulaire, *m.* at ~ tables (meal), par petites tables. ¶ *v.t,* séparer. **separation**, *n,* séparation, *f.*

sepia, *n,* sépia, *f.*

sepoy, *n,* cipaye, *m.*

September, *n,* septembre, *m.*

septet[te], *n,* septuor, *m.*

septic, *a,* septique. ~ tank, fosse s., *f.*

septum, *n,* cloison, *f.*

sepulchral, *a,* sépulcral. **sepulchre**, *n,* sé-pulcre, *m.*

sequel, *n,* suite; conséquence, *f.* **sequence**, *n,* suite, succession; (*Cards*) séquence, *f.*

sequestered, *p.p,* retiré, écarté. **sequestra-tion** (*Law*), *n,* séquestre, *m.*

seraglio, *n,* sérail, *m.*

seraph, *n,* séraphin, *m.* ~ic, *a,* séraphi-que.

Serbia, *n,* la Serbie. **Serb**[ian], *a,* serbe. ¶ *n.* (*pers.*) Serbe, *m,f;* (*language*) le serbe.

sere, *a,* desséché, fané.

serenade, *n,* sérénade, *f.* ¶ *v.t,* donner une sérénade à.

serene, *a,* serein. **serenity**, *n,* sérénité, *f.*

serf, *n,* serf, *m,* serve, *f.* ~dom, *n,* ser-vage, *m.*

serge, *n,* serge, *f.*

sergeant, *n,* sergent; (*Cavalry*) maréchal des logis; (*Police*) brigadier, *m.* ~ major, adjudant; maréchal des logis chef, *m.*

serial, *a,* en série. ~ rights, droits de re-production dans les journaux & périodi-ques, *m.pl.* ~ [story], [roman] feuilleton, *m.* **seriatim**, *ad,* successivement. **series**, *n,* série, suite, *f.*

serif, *n,* empattement, *m.*

seringa, *n,* seringa, *m.*

serious†, *a,* sérieux; grave. ~ness, *n,* sé-rieux, *m;* gravité, *f.*

sermon, *n,* sermon; prône; prêche, *m.* ~ize, *v.t,* sermonner. ~izer, *n,* prêcheur, *m.*

serosity, *n,* sérosité, *f.* **serous**, *a,* séreux.

serpent, *n,* serpent, *m.* **serpentine**, *a,* ser-pentin. ¶ *n,* serpentine, *f.*

serration, *n,* denture; dent, *f.* **serrate**[d], *a,* denté en scie, dentelé, en dents de scie.

serried, *a,* serré.

serum, *n,* sérum, *m.*

servant, *n,* employé, e, préposé, e; serviteur, *m;* domestique, *m,f;* bonne; (*pl.*) domesti-cité, livrée, maison, *f,* gens, *m.pl.* ~ girl, fille de service, *f.* ~s' hall, office, *f.*

serve, *v.t. & i. ir,* servir; desservir; (*a sentence*) subir; (*a notice*) signifier. ~ up, servir. ¶ (*Ten.*) *n,* service, *m.* **server** (*Ten.*) *n,* servant, *m.* **service**, *n,* service, *m;* des-serte; démarche, *f;* ministère; office, *m;*

(*domestic*) domesticité, condition, *f*; (*china, &c*) service, cabaret, *m*; (*of writ*) signification, *f. to grow grey in the ~*, blanchir sous le harnois. **~ hatch**, passe-plats, *m*. **~ lift**, monte-plats, *m*. **~ line** (*Ten.*), ligne de service, *f*. **~ station**, agence stockiste, *f*. **~ table**, [table de] desserte, [table] servante, *f*. **~ tree**, sorbier, *m*. **~ wagon**, plateau roulant, *m*, desserte mobile, *f*. **~able**, *a*, d'usage; utile.

serviette, *n*, serviette, *f*. **~ ring**, rond de serviette, *m*.

servile†, *a*, servile. **servility**, *n*, servilité, *f*. **servitude**, *n*, servitude, *f*.

sesame, *n*, sésame, *m*.

session, *n*, session; séance; bourse, *f*.

set, *n*, série, *f*; jeu; assortiment; train, *m*; batterie; suite; garniture; trousse; tranche; parure, *f*; ensemble; service, *m*; (*matrices, Typ.*) frappe, *f*; (*Elec.*) groupement; (*Radio*) poste; monde, *m*; coterie; bande, *f*; (*paving stone*) pavé, *m*; (*fixity*) assiette, *f*; (*of saw*) voie, chasse, *f*; (*of current*) lit; (*sapling*) plant; (*Theat.*) décor, *m*; (*Ten.*) manche, *f*, set, *m. 1 set all*, 1 set partout. **~ of** (*artificial*) *teeth*, dentier, *m*. **~-back**, recul, tassement; décalage, *m*, traverse, *f*. **~-off**, compensation, *f*; (*foil*) repoussoir; (*Arch.*) ressaut, *m*; (*Typ.*) maculature; (*Law*) reconvention, *f*. **~-out**, début; étalage, *m*. **~-to**, prise de bec; bagarre, *f*; pugilat, *m*. ¶ *v.t.ir*, mettre; poser; placer; aposter; fixer; planter; asseoir; assurer; (*bone*) remettre, remboîter; (*dog on, fashion, &c*) lancer; (*of dog*) arrêter; (*gem*) sertir, enchâsser, monter; (*hen*) mettre couver; (*a sail*) établir; (*saw*) donner la voie à; (*seal*) apposer; (*shutter—Phot.*) armer; (*task, example, &c*) donner; (*tools*) affiler, repasser; (*trap*) tendre, dresser; (*type*) composer; (*watch*) régler; (*v.i.ir*.) se figer, prendre; (*sun*) se coucher. **~ about it**, s'y prendre. **~** (*pers.*) *against* (pers.), indisposer. **~ down in writing**, coucher par écrit. **~ off**, (*figure*) dégager; (*Typ.*) maculer. **~ on** (pers.), lapider. **~ out**, partir. **~ out again**, repartir. **~ up**, monter; ériger; établir. ¶ *p.a*: **~ face**, visage immobile, *m*. **~ fair**, beau fixe. **~ phrase**, expression figée, *f*. **~ piece** (*Theat.*), ferme, *f*. **~ purpose**, parti pris, *m*. **~ screw**, vis de pression, *f*. **~ smile**, sourire figé, *m*. **~ speech**, discours d'apparat, *m*.

settee, *n*, divan, *m*, causeuse, *f*.

setter, *n*, poseur, euse; tendeur; monteur; metteur; compositeur; chien couchant, *m*. **setting**, *n*, entourage, encadrement, *f*; (*cement*) prise; (*gem*) enchâssure, œuvre, *f*; chaton; (*sun*) coucher, *m*; (*type*) composition, *f*. **~ aside**, abstraction faite de. **~ sun**, soleil couchant, *m*.

settle, *n*, banc, *m*. ¶ *v.t*, régler; arranger; accommoder; trancher; liquider; établir;

installer; emménager; (*property*) constituer; (*v.i.*) se fixer; s'établir; (*alight*) se poser; (*matter*) se déposer; (*ground*) [se] tasser. **~d**, *p.a*, décidé, arrêté; (*weather*) sûr. **~ment**, *n*, règlement, *m*; constitution, *f*; (*Stk Ex.*) terme, *m*, liquidation; colonie, colonie de peuplement, *f*. **settler**, *n*, colon, *m*; résident, e.

seven, *a. & n*, sept, *a. & m*. **seventeen**, *a. & n*, dix-sept, *a. & m*. **seventeenth**, *a. & n*, dix-septième, *a. & m.f*; dix-sept, *m*. **~ly**, *ad*, en dix-septième lieu. **seventh**, *a. & n*, septième, *a. & m.f*; sept, *m*. **~ly**, *ad*, septièmement. **seventieth**, *a. & n*, soixante-dixième, *a. & m.f*. **seventy**, *a. & n*, soixante-dix, *a. & m*. 71, 72, soixante et onze, soixante-douze.

sever, *v.t*, séparer. **~al†**, *a*, respectif; individuel; plusieurs. **~ance**, *n*, séparation, distraction, *f*.

severe†, *a*, sévère; rigoureux; rude; grave. **severity**, *n*, sévérité; rigueur; gravité, *f*.

Seville, *n*, Séville, *f*. **~ orange**, bigarade, orange amère, *f*.

sew, *v.t.ir*, coudre. **~er**, *n*, couseur, euse, piqueuse, *f*.

sewer, *n*, égout, *m*. **~man**, égoutier, cureur, *m*. **sew[er]age**, *n*, eaux d'égout, eaux-vannes, *f.pl*.

sewing, *n*, couture, *f*. **~ machine**, machine à coudre, *f*.

sex, *n*, sexe, *m*. **~ appeal**, sex-appeal, *m*, attirance du sexe, *f*.

sextant, *n*, sextant, *m*.

sextet[te], *n*, sextuor, *m*.

sexton, *n*, sacristain, *m*.

sexual, *a*, sexuel.

shabby, *a*, usé, râpé, miteux; mesquin.

shackle, *n*, boucle; manille, *f*; maillon, *m*; (*fig.*) entrave, *f*. ¶ *v.t.ir*, entraver.

shade, *n*, ombre, *f*; ombrage, *m*; (*pl, spirits*) mânes, *m.pl*; nuance, *f*; abat-jour; écran; globe protecteur, *m*. ¶ *v.t*, ombrager; (*Art*) ombrer; (*v.i.*) passer. **~ off**, dégrader. **shadow**, *n*, ombre, *f*. **~ boxing**, boxe contre son ombre, *f*. ¶ *v.t*, filer. **shady**, *a*, ombragé; (*Poet.*) ombreux; (*disreputable*) louche, véreux. *to be on the ~ side of* 40, avoir dépassé la quarantaine.

shaft, *n*, flèche, *f*, trait, *m*; (*spear, &c*) hampe; (*smoke*) cheminée; (*of chimney*) souche, *f*; (*cart*) limon, brancard, *f*; (*Arch.*) fût, *m*, tige, *f*; (*Mech.*) arbre, *m*, transmission, *f*; (*Min.*) puits, *m*; (*lift*) cage, *f*. **~ horse**, brancardier, timonier, *m*.

shaggy, *a*, poilu, hirsute.

shagreen, *n*, chagrin; galuchat, *m*.

shah, *n*, schah, shah, chah, *m*.

shake, *n*, secousse, *f*; (*head*) hochement; (*hand*) serrement, *m*, poignée; (*timber*) gerçure, *f*, éclat; (*Mus.*) trille, *m*. ¶ *v.t.ir*, secouer; agiter; [é]branler; hocher; serrer; (*Mus.*) orner de trilles; (*v.i.ir*.) trembler; s'ébranler; ballotter; flageoler; chevroter.

shaky, *a*, branlant; chancelant; chevrotant; tremblé.

shale, *n*, schiste, *m*. ~ **oil**, huile de s., *f*.

shall, *v.aux.ir*, is expressed in Fr. by future tense. Also by falloir.

shallot, *n*, échalote, *f*.

shallow, *a*, peu profond, bas; faible; creux; frivole; superficiel. ~**s**, *n.pl*, bas-fond, *m*.

sham, *n*, feinte, *f*, [faux-]semblant, *m*. ¶ *a*, feint; simulé; fictif. ~ **fight**, simulacre de combat, *m*. ¶ *v.t. & i*, feindre, simuler.

shambles, *n*, champ de massacre, *m*.

shambling, *p.a*, traînant.

shame, *n*, honte; pudeur, *f*; scandale, *m*. **for** ~! fi donc! ¶ *v.t*, faire honte à. ~**faced**, *a*, honteux, penaud. ~**full**, *a*, honteux; scandaleux. ~**less**, *a*, éhonté, dévergondé, impudent. ~**lessly**, *ad*, sans vergogne, impudemment.

shammy [leather], *n*, peau de chamois, *f*, chamois, *m*.

shampoo, *n*, (*wet*) schampooing, *m*; (*dry*) friction, *f*. ¶ *v.t*, faire un schampooing à; faire une friction à.

shamrock, *n*, petit trèfle blanc, *m*.

shank, *n*, jambe; queue; tige, *f*.

shanty, *n*, baraque; chanson (de bord) *f*.

shape, *n*, forme; figure; taille, tournure; carcasse, *f*; profil, *m*. ¶ *v.t*, former; façonner; mouler, modeler; pétrir. ~**less**, *a*, informe. *shaping machine*, étau-limeur, *m*.

share, *n*, part; quote-part, quotité, *f*; écot, *m*; (*Fin.*) action, valeur, *f*; titre; (*plough*) soc, *m*. ~ **capital**, capital-actions, *m*. ~**holder**, actionnaire; sociétaire, *m,f*. ~ **pusher**, démarcheur, *m*. ¶ *v.t. & i*, partager, participer (à).

shark (*fish & rapacious pers.*), *n*, requin, *m*.

sharp, *a*, tranchant; aigu; acéré; fin; net; vif; perçant; (*acid*) aigre; (*rebuke*) vert. ~ **practices**, procédés indélicats, *m.pl*. ~**shooter**, tirailleur, *m*. ¶ *ad.* (*hour*), précise. **look** ~! dépêchez-vous! vite! ¶ (*Mus.*) *n*, dièse, *m*. ~**en**, *v.t*, aiguiser; affûter; repasser; tailler [en pointe]; (*wits*) déniaiser. ~**er**, *n*, escroc, filou, tricheur, *m*. ~**ly**, *ad*, vertement; vivement; nettement. ~**ness**, *n*, acuité; finesse; âcreté; netteté, *f*.

shatter, *v.t*, briser, fracasser.

shave, *v.t*, raser; (*v.i*) se raser, se faire la barbe. **shaving**, *n*, la barbe; (*chip*) copeau, *m*; rognure, planure, *f*. ~ **brush**, pinceau à barbe, blaireau, *m*. ~ **stick**, savon à barbe en bâton, *m*.

shawl, *n*, châle, *m*.

she, *pn*, elle; celle; ce, e; (*of ship*) il. ¶ *n*, femelle, *f*. ~**ass**, ânesse, bourrique, *f*. ~**bear**, ourse, *f*. ~**camel**, chamelle, *f*. ~**devil**, diablesse, *f*. ~**goat**, chèvre, chevrette, *f*. ~**monkey**, guenon, guenuche, *f*. ~**wolf**, louve, *f*.

sheaf, *n*, gerbe, *f*; faisceau, *m*. ¶ *v.t*, [en]gerber.

shear, *v.t.ir*, tondre; cisailler. ~**er**, *n*, ton-

deur, euse. ~**ing**, *n*, tonte, *f*. ~ **machine**, tondeuse, *f*. **shears**, *n.pl*, cisailles, forces, *f.pl*; ciseaux, *m.pl*, tondeuse, *f*.

sheath, *n*, gaine, *f*; fourreau, *m*. **sheathe**, *v.t*, [r]engainer; armer; doubler.

sheave, *n*, poulie, *f*, rouet, *f*.

shed, *n*, hangar, *m*; baraque; halle; remise; étable, *f*. ¶ *v.t.ir*, verser; répandre; se dépouiller de. **shedding** (*blood*) *n*, effusion, *f*.

sheen, *n*, luisant, chatoiement, *m*.

sheep, *n*, mouton, *m*; brebis, *f*. ~ **dog**, chien de berger, *m*. ~**fold**, bergerie, *f*; parc à moutons, *m*. ~**like** (*pers.*), moutonnier. ~ **pox**, claveau, *m*, clavelée, *f*. ~[**skin**], peau de mouton, *f*, mouton, *m*, basane, *f*. ~**ish**, *a*, penaud, sot, honteux.

sheer, *a*, pur; (*force*) vive; abrupt, à pic. ~ **legs**, chèvre à trois pieds, *f*. ~ **off**, prendre le large.

sheet, *n*, feuille; lame; nappe; couche; bâche; tôle, plaque; (*Naut.*) écoute, *f*; (*bed*) drap, *m*. ~ **anchor**, ancre de veille; (*fig.*) a. de salut, planche de s., *f*. ~ **glass**, verre à vitres, *m*. ~ **iron**, tôle [de fer] *f*. ~ **lead**, plomb en feuilles, *m*. ~ **lightning**, éclair diffus, é. en nappes, *m*. ~ **piling**, palée, *f*. ~**ing**, *n*, toile pour draps de lit, *f*; (*Civil Engin.*) blindage, *m*.

sheik[**h**], *n*, cheik, *m*.

shekel (*Bible*) *n*, sicle, *m*.

sheldrake, *n*, tadorne, *m*.

shelf, *n*, planche, tablette, *f*, rayon; (*Naut.*) écueil, *m*. [*set of*] **shelves**, étagère, *f*.

shell, *n*, coquille; coque; carapace; cosse; écale; peau, *f*; coquillage, *m*; écaille; chape, *f*; (*coffin*) cercueil; (*Artil.*) obus, *m*. ~ **fish**, coquillage, *m*. ~ **hole**, entonnoir, *m*. ~ **shock**, commotion, psychose traumatique, *f*. ¶ *v.t*, écaler, écosser, égrener, cerner; bombarder, canonner, battre.

shellac, *n*, laque en écailles, *f*.

shelter, *n*, abri, *m*, le couvert, asile, refuge; édicule, *m*. ¶ *v.t*, abriter.

shelve, *v.t*, aller en pente.

shepherd, *n*, berger, pasteur, *m*. ~'**s crook**, houlette, *f*. ~'**s-purse**, bourse à pasteur, *f*, tabouret, *m*. ~**ess**, *n*, bergère, *f*.

sherry, *n*, xérès, vin de Xérès, *m*.

shew, *n. & v.ir*. Same as **show**.

shield, *n*, bouclier; protecteur; (*armour*) bouclier, écu; (*Her.*) écusson, *m*. ¶ *v.t*, abriter; défendre; protéger; garantir.

shift, *n*, déplacement; changement, *m*; (*Naut., of wind*) saute; équipe, *f*, poste; expédient, tournant, *m*, ressource, *f*; subterfuge, biais, *m*. ¶ *v.t. & i*, déplacer; se d.; changer; changer de place; sauter; (*cargo*) riper; biaiser. ~**ing**, *p.a*, changeant; (*sand*) mouvant. ~**y**, *a*, fuyant.

shilling ($\frac{1}{20}$ *of a £*) *n*, shilling, *m*. (*In Fr. pronounced* [ʃəlɛ̃].)

shilly-shally, *v.i*, lanterner, barguigner.

shimmer, *v.i*, chatoyer.

shin, *n*, tibia; (*beef*) jarret, *m*. ~ *bone*, tibia, *m*. ~ *guard*, jambière, *f*.

shindy, *n*, chahut, *m*, scène, *f*.

shine, *n*, brillant; luisant, *m*. ¶ *v.i.ir*, luire; briller; rayonner, reluire.

shingle, *n*, galets, *m.pl*, galet; (*Build.*) bardeau, *m*. ¶ (*Metall.*) *v.t*, cingler. ~[*d hair*], nuque rasée, *f*.

shining & **shiny**, *a*, [re]luisant; brillant.

ship, *n*, navire; vaisseau; bâtiment, bateau; bord, *m*. ~ *biscuit*, galette, *f*. ~ *broker*, courtier maritime, *m*. ~ *building*, construction navale, *f*. ~ *canal*, canal maritime, *m*. ~ *chandler*, fournisseur de navires, *m*. ~ *mate*, camarade de bord, *m*. ~*owner*, armateur, *m*. ~ *quoits*, jeu d'anneaux, *m*. ~*shape*, à sa place. ~*wreck*, naufrage, *m*. *to be* ~*wrecked*, faire naufrage. ~*wright*, constructeur de navires; charpentier de vaisseau, *m*. ~*yard*, chantier naval, *m*. ¶ *v.t*, charger; embarquer; expédier; (*oars*) border. ~ *water*, ~ *a sea*, embarquer. **shipment**, *n*, chargement; embarquement, *m*; expédition, *f*. **shipper**, *n*, chargeur, expéditeur, *m*. **shipping**, *n*, navigation, *f*; transport maritime, *m*; marine, *f*; tonnage; armement, *m*. ~ *agent*, agent maritime, commissionnaire chargeur, *m*. ~ *charges*, frais d'expédition, *m.pl*. ~ *clerk*, expéditionnaire, *m*.

shire, *n*, comté, *m*.

shirk, *v.t*, éluder, se soustraire à; (*v.i.*) s'embusquer. ~[*er*], *n*, embusqué, fricoteur, *m*.

shirt, *n*, chemise, *f*. ~ *collar*, col de chemise; faux col, *m*. ~ *maker*, chemisier, ère. ~*ing*, *n*, toile à chemises, *f*, shirting, *m*.

shiver, *v.t*, briser, fracasser; (*v.i.*) frissonner, grelotter.

shoal, *n*, (*sand, fish*) banc; (*shallow*) haut-fond, *m*. ~*s of people*, un mascaret humain.

shock, *n*, choc; coup; saisissement; ébranlement, à-coup, *m*, secousse; (*hair*) tignasse, forêt, *f*; (*corn*) tas, *m*. ~ *absorber*, amortisseur, *m*. ~*headed*, ébouriffé. ¶ *v.t*, heurter, choquer; (*fig.*) choquer, scandaliser, révolter, blesser.

shoddy, *n*, laine renaissance; camelote, *f*.

shoe, *n*, soulier, *m*, chaussure, *f*; chausson; (*horse*) fer; sabot; patin, *m*. ~*black*, décrotteur, *m*. ~ *brush*, brosse à souliers, *f*. ~ *horn*, chausse-pied, *m*. ~ *maker*, cordonnier, *m*. ¶ *v.t.ir*, chausser; ferrer; saboter. **shoeing**, *n*, ferrage, *m*. ~ *smith*, maréchal-ferrant, *m*.

shoot, *n*, chasse, *f*, tiré, *m*; rejeton; couloir, *m*. ¶ *v.t.ir*, tirer; lancer; darder; chasser; blesser [d'un coup de fusil, d'une flèche]; tuer [d'un coup de fusil, &c]; (*spy, deserter*) fusiller; (*tip*) culbuter; (*rapids*) franchir; (*v.i.ir.*) tirer; chasser [au fusil]; (*grow*) pousser, germer; (*Foot.*) shooter; (*pain*) élancer. **shooting**, *n*, tir, *m*; chasse [au

tir] *f*. ~ *box*, rendez-vous de chasse, *m*. ~ *gallery*, tir, stand, *m*. ~ *game*, jeu de massacre, *m*. ~ *pains*, douleur lancinante, *f*, élancements, *m.pl*. ~ *star*, étoile filante, *f*.

shop, *n*, magasin, *m*, boutique, *f*; débit; (*works*) atelier, *m*. ~ *assistant*, commis de magasin, *m*, demoiselle de m., *f*. ~ *foreman*, chef d'atelier, *m*. ~ *front*, devanture de magasin, *f*. ~*keeper*, marchand, e, boutiquier, ère. ~ *lifting*, vol à l'étalage, *m*. ~*soiled*, défraîchi. ~ *parlour*, arrière-boutique, *f*. ~ *walker*, inspecteur, *m*. ~ *window*, vitrine, montre, *f*. ¶ *v.i*, faire des emplettes. *shopping basket*, panier à provisions, *m*.

shore, *n*, rivage, bord; étai; accore, *m*. ~ *fishing*, pêche au bord de la mer, *f*. *on* ~, à terre. ¶ *v.t*, étayer; chevaler; accorer.

short, *a*, court; petit; bref; déficitaire; (*pastry*) croustillant; cassant. ~ *circuit*, *m*, court-circuit, *m*. ~*coming*, manquement, *m*. ~ *curtain* (for window), brise-bise, *m*. ~ *cut*, raccourci, *m*. ~*haired* (dog, &c), à poil ras. ~*hand*, sténographie, *f*. ~*hand-typist*, sténodactylographe, *m.f*. ~*hand writer*, sténographe, *m.f*. ~ *length* (stuff), coupon, *m*. ~*lived*, passager, fugitif, sans lendemain. . . . *are* ~*lived*, . . . ne vivent pas longtemps. ~*sighted*, myope; à courtes vues; imprévoyant. ~ *story*, conte, *m*, nouvelle, *f*. ~ [*syllable*], [syllabe] brève, *f*. ¶ *ad*, [tout] court. *in* ~, bref, enfin. ~*age*, *n*, manque; déficit, *m*, crise, *f*. ~*en*, *v.t*, [r]accourcir. ~*ly*, *ad*, bientôt, prochainement, sous peu; peu de temps (*avant*, *après*); brièvement. ~*ness*, *n*, brièveté; courte durée; petitesse, *f*. ~ *of breath*, courte haleine, *f*.

shot, *n*, coup de feu; coup; trait; boulet, *m*; balle, *f*; plomb, *m*; grenaille, *f*; (*putting the shot*) poids, *m*; portée, *f*; tireur, *m*. ~ *gun*, fusil pour le tir à plomb, *m*.

shot (fabrics) *p.p*, changeant, chatoyant.

should, *v.aux*, *is expressed in Fr. by conditional mood. Also by* devoir, falloir.

shoulder, *n*, épaule, *f*; (*Carp.*) épaulement, *m*. ~ *blade*, plat de l'épaule, *m*, omoplate, *f*; (*horse*, *ox*) paleron, *m*. ~ *of mutton*, épaule de mouton, éclanche, *f*. ~ *strap*, bretelle; épaulette, *f*. ¶ *v.t*, pousser de l'épaule; prendre sur ses épaules; (*arms*) porter; (*fig.*) endosser.

shout, *n*, cri; éclat, *m*. ¶ *v.t*. & *i*, crier; vociférer.

shove, *n*, poussée, *f*. ¶ *v.t*. & *i*, pousser. ~ *off*, pousser au large.

shovel, *n*, pelle, *f*. ¶ *v.t*, remuer à la pelle. ~*ful*, *n*, pelletée, *f*.

show, *n*, semblant; simulacre; étalage; déballage, *m*; montre; parade; représentation, *f*, spectacle, *m*; exposition, *f*, concours, salon, *m*. ~ *card*, pancarte, *f*. ~ *case*, vitrine, *f*. ~*man*, forain; mon-

treur, m. ~ *room*, salon d'exposition, m.
¶ *v.t.ir*, montrer; manifester; enseigner;
accuser; [re]présenter; constater; prouver;
(*v.i.ir*) se montrer; paraître. ~ *in*, faire
entrer, introduire. ~ *off*, faire parade
(de); (*abs.*) parader. ~ *out*, reconduire.
~ *round*, piloter dans, promener par,
promener dans. ~ *the white feather*,
caner. ~ *up*, démasquer, afficher.

shower, n, ondée; averse; giboulée; pluie;
grêle; nuée; avalanche, f. ~ *bath*,
douche (en pluie) f. ~*proof*, paraverse,
m. ¶ *v.t*, faire pleuvoir; combler. **showery**
weather, temps à ondées, m.

showy, a, ostentateur, ostentatoire, fastueux,
voyant.

shrapnel, n, obus à balles, m.

shred, n, lambeau, m; (*pl.*) charpie, f. ¶ *v.t*,
déchiqueter.

shrew, n, mégère, f. ~ [*mouse*], musaraigne, f.

shrewd, a, sagace, clairvoyant; adroit.
~*ness*, n, sagacité, clairvoyance; adresse, f.

shriek, n, cri, m. ¶ *v.i*, crier.

shrike, n, pie-grièche, f.

shrill, a, aigu, perçant, strident. ~*ness*, n,
acuité, f; (*voice*) mordant, m.

shrimp, n, crevette [grise], locuste, salicoque,
f; (*pers.*) gringalet, m. ~*ing*, n, pêche à
la crevette, f.

shrine, n, châsse, f, reliquaire; sanctuaire, m.

shrink, v.i.ir, [se] rétrécir; se retirer; (*v.t.ir*)
rétrécir. ~*age*, n, rétrécissement; retrait,
m, retraite, f.

shrivel, v.t, rider, grésiller, ratatiner, racornir.

shroud, n, linceul, suaire, f; (*Naut.*) hauban, m.
¶ *v.t*, envelopper; embrumer.

Shrovetide, n, les jours gras, m.pl. *Shrove
Tuesday*, mardi gras, m.

shrub, n, arbrisseau, m. **shrubbery**, n, plantation d'arbrisseaux, f; bosquet, m.

shrug, n, haussement d'épaules, m. ¶ *v.t*,
hausser.

shudder, v.i, frissonner, frémir.

shuffle, v.t, mêler, battre; (*v.i.*) biaiser, tortiller, tergiverser. ~ *along*, traîner la
jambe. ¶ (*excuse*) n, défaite, f. *shuffling
gait*, pas traînant, m.

shun, v.t, éviter, fuir.

shunt (*Elec.*) n, dérivation, f. ¶ *v.t*, (*Rly*)
garer, manœuvrer; (*Elec.*) dériver.

shut, v.t.ir, fermer; (*v.i.*) [se] f. ~ *in*, enfermer. ~ *out*, fermer la porte à; exclure.
~ *up*, fermer; enfermer; clouer la bouche à.
shutter, n, volet; contrevent; (*Phot.*) obturateur, m.

shuttle, n, navette, f. ~*cock*, volant, m.

shy†, a, timide, sauvage, réservé, farouche,
ombrageux. ¶ *v.i*, faire un écart; (*v.t.*)
lancer. ~*ness*, n, timidité, sauvagerie, f.

Shylock, n, usurier, m.

Siam, n, le Siam. **Siamese**, a, siamois.
~ *cat*, chat de Siam, m. ¶ n, (*pers.*)
Siamois, e; (*language*) le siamois.

Siberia, n, la Sibérie. **Siberian**, a, sibérien.
¶ n, Sibérien, ne.

Sicilian, a, sicilien. ¶ n, Sicilien, ne.
Sicily, n, la Sicile.

sick, a, malade; dégoûté. *to be* ~, être
malade; (*stomach*) avoir mal au cœur.
the ~, les malades, m,f.pl. ~ *& tired*,
excédé. ~ *bed*, lit de douleur, m. ~
headache, mal de tête accompagné de
nausées, m. ~ *leave*, congé de maladie,
c. de convalescence, m. ~ *list*, état des
malades, m. ~ *room*, chambre de malade; (*Sch.*, *&c*) infirmerie, f. ~*en*, v.i,
tomber malade; (*v.t.*) écœurer.

sickle, n, faucille, f.

sickly, a, maladif, souffreteux, malingre;
chétif; doucereux, fadasse. **sickness**, n,
maladie, f; (*stomach*) mal de cœur, m.

side, n, côté; flanc; bord, m, rive, f; versant;
plat, m; face; part, f; parti; camp, m. ~
by ~, côte à côte. ~ *arm*, arme blanche,
f. ~*board*, buffet, dressoir, m, panetière,
crédence, f. ~ *car*, side-car, m. ~ *dish*,
entremets, m. ~ *door*, porte latérale, f.
~ *face*, profil, m. ~ *glance*, regard
oblique, m. ~ *issue*, question d'intérêt
secondaire, f. ~ *line*, article à côté, m;
(*Ten.*) ligne de côté, f. ~*long*, de côté;
(*glance*) en coulisse. ~ *note*, note mar-
ginale; (*Typ.*) manchette, f. ~ *path*,
accotement, m. ~ *saddle*, selle de dame,
f. ~ *scene*, coulisse, f. ~ *show*, spectacle
payant; (*fair*) spectacle forain, m. ~*slip*,
déraper. ~*step*, faire un écart. ~
stroke, nage de côté, f. ~ *walk*, contre-
allée, f. ~*ways*, de côté. ~ *whiskers*,
favoris, m.pl. ~ *with*, se ranger du
côté de.

sidereal, a, sidéral.

siding, n, voie de garage, f; (*private*) embranchement, m.

sidle in, entrer de guingois.

siege, n, siège, m. ~ *gun*, pièce de s., f.

Sienna, n, Sienne, f. *s*~, n, terre de S., f.

siesta, n, sieste, méridienne, f.

sieve, n, tamis, sas, crible, m. **sift**, v.t,
tamiser, sasser, cribler; bluter; (*question*)
éplucher. **siftings**, n.pl, criblure, f.

sigh, n, soupir, m. ¶ *v.i*, soupirer.

sight, n, vue; vision, f; aspect, m; présence;
(*Surv.*) visée, f, coup [de lunette] m; (*gun*)
mire, f; spectacle, m; curiosité; caricature,
f. *at* ~, à première vue; (*reading*) à
livre ouvert; (*Com.*) à vue. ~*seer*,
curieux, euse. ~ [*vane*], pinnule, f.
¶ *v.t*, viser; voir; (*land*) reconnaître.

sign, n, signe, m; enseigne, f. ~ [*board*], enseigne, f. ~ *of expression* (*Mus.*), nuance,
f. ~ *post*, poteau indicateur, m. ~
writer, peintre d'enseignes, m. ¶ *v.t. & i*,
signer; (*in the margin*) émarger; faire signe.
~ [*on*], engager.

signal, n, signal, m. ~ *box*, cabine à
signaux, f. ~*man* (*Rly.*), signaleur, m.

(*Navy*) timonier, *m.* ¶ *a*, signalé, insigne. ¶ ~ *&* ~*ize*, *v.t*, signaler. **signaller**, *n*, (*Mil.*) signaleur. **signatory** or **signer**, *n*, signataire, *m,f.* **signature**, *n*, signature; souscription; (*Mus.*) armature; (*Typ.*) signature, *f.* **signet**, *n*, cachet, *m.* ~ *ring*, [bague à la] chevalière, *f.* ~ *wafer*, pain à cacheter, *m.*

significance, *n*, portée, *f. look of deep* ~, regard [fort] significatif, r. d'intelligence, *m.* **significant**, *a*, significatif. **signify**, *v.t. & i*, signifier; importer.

silence, *n*, silence, *m.* ¶ *v.t*, faire taire; (*enemy's fire*) éteindre. **silencer**, *n*, silencieux, pot d'échappement, *m.* **silent**†, *a*, silencieux, taciturne; (*Gram., &c*) muet. ~ *partner*, commanditaire, *m. to be* ~, se taire.

Silesia, *n*, la Silésie. **s**~, *n*, silésienne, *f.*

silhouette, *n*, silhouette, *f.*

silica, *n*, silice, *f.* **silicate**, *n*, silicate, *m.*

silk, *n*, soie, *f.* ~ *coloured handkerchief*, pochette en soie, de couleur, *f.* ~ *goods* or *silks*, soierie, *f.* ~ *hat*, chapeau de soie, *m.* ~ *square*, mouchoir de cou, *m.* **silkworm**, *n*, ver à soie, *m.* ~ *breeding*, magnanerie, sériciculture, *f.* ~ *gut*, crin de Florence, d'Espagne, japonais, *&c;* florence, *m*, racine anglaise, *&c, f.* ~*s' eggs*, graine, *f.* **silky**, *a*, soyeux.

sill, *n*, seuil; appui, *m*, traverse, semelle, *f.*

silliness, *n*, niaiserie, bêtise, *f.* **silly**, *a*, niais, sot, bête. ¶ *n*, niais, e, sot, te, serin, *m.*

silo, *n*, silo, *m.* ¶ *v.t*, ensiler.

silt, *n*, vase, *f*, limon, *m.* ~ *up*, s'envaser.

silver, *n*, argent, *m.* ~ *birch*, bouleau blanc, *m.* ~ *fox*, renard argenté, *m.* ~*gilt*, vermeil, argent doré. ~ *mine*, mine d'argent, *f.* ~*plate*, *n*, argenterie, *f;* (*v.t.*) argenter. ~ *sand*, sable blanc, *m.* ~ *side*, gîte à la noix, *m.* ~*smith*, orfèvre, *m.* ~ [*smith's*] *work*, orfèvrerie, *f.* ~ *thaw*, verglas, *m.* ~ *wedding*, noces d'argent, *f.pl.* ¶ *v.t*, argenter; (*mirror*) étamer. ~*ing* (*for mirror*) *n*, tain, *m.* ~*y*, *a*, argenté; argentin.

simian, *a*, qui appartient au singe.

similar, *a*, semblable, pareil, similaire. ~*ity & similitude*, *n*, similitude, *f.* ~*ly*, *ad*, semblablement. **simile**, *n*, comparaison, similitude, *f.*

simmer, *v.i. & t*, mijoter, mitonner.

simony, *n*, simonie, *f.*

simoom, **simoon**, *n*, simoun, *m.*

simper, *n*, sourire affecté, *m.* ¶ *v.i*, minauder.

simple†, *a. & n*, simple, *a. & m.* ~ *contract*, acte sous seing privé, sous-seing, *m.* ~ *good-natured man, woman*, bonhomme, *m*, bonne femme, *f.* ~*hearted*, au cœur simple. ~*minded*, simple, naïf. **simpleton**, *n*, niais, e, gogo, *m*, innocent, e. **simplicity**, *n*, simplicité; bonhomie, *f.* **simplify**, *v.t*, simplifier.

simulacrum, *n*, simulacre, *m.* **simulate**, *v.t*, simuler, feindre.

simultaneous†, *a*, simultané.

sin, *n*, péché, *m;* iniquité, *f;* (*shame*) meurtre, *m.* ¶ *v.i*, pécher.

Sinai (**Mount**), le mont Sinaï.

since, *ad. & pr*, depuis. ¶ *c*, depuis que; que; puisque, comme.

sincere†, *a*, sincère. **sincerity**, *n*, sincérité, *f.*

sine, *n*, sinus, *m.*

sinecure, *n*, sinécure, *f.*

sine die, sine die, sans date.

sine qua non, sine qua non, *m.*

sinew, *n*, tendon; (*in meat*) tirant; (*pl. of war*) nerf, *m.*

sinful, *a*, coupable.

sing, *v.t. & i. ir*, chanter. ~ *small*, déchanter, filer doux. ~ *to sleep*, endormir en chantant.

Singapore, *n*, Singapour, *m.*

singe, *v.t*, flamber, brûler; roussir.

singer, *n*, chanteur, euse; cantatrice, *f.* **singing**, *n*, chant; (*ears*) tintement, *m;* (*att.*) de chant; (*kettle*) à sifflet.

single, *a*, unique; seul; simple. ~ *bed*, lit à une place, *m.* ~ *blessedness*, le bonheur du célibat. ~*breasted*, droit. ~ *combat*, combat singulier, *m.* ~*handed*, tout seul, à moi seul. *a* ~ *life*, le célibat. ~ *man*, célibataire, garçon, *m.* ~ *oar* (*opp. scull*), aviron de pointe, *m.* ~ *openwork* (*Need.*), rivière, *f.* ~ *room*, chambre à un lit, *f.* ~*stick*, la canne, le bâton. *single-string instrument*, [instrument] monocorde, *m.* ~ *ticket*, billet simple. ~ *width* (*cloth*), petite largeur, *f.* ~ *woman*, demoiselle, *f.* ¶ (*Sport*) *n*, simple, *m.* ~ *out*, distinguer. **singly**, *ad*, isolément; un(e) à un(e).

singsong, *a*, chantant, traînant. ¶ *n*, psalmodie, *f.*

singular†, *a. & n*, singulier, *a. & m.*

sinister, *a*, sinistre; (*Her.*) sénestre.

sink, *n*, évier; plomb; puisard; (*fig.*) cloaque, *m*, sentine, *f.* ¶ *v.i.ir*, [s']enfoncer; s'affaisser; se tasser; crouler; s'abaisser; baisser; descendre; succomber; (*ship*) couler [à fond], c. bas; (*v.t.ir.*) enfoncer; noyer; foncer, creuser; couler; (*die*) graver en creux; (*money, a fortune*) enterrer (*in* = en); (*loan, national debt*) amortir. ~ *& draw fishing*, pêche à la dandinette, *f.* ~*in*[*to*], pénétrer; s'imbiber. *in a sinking condition* (*ship*), en perdition. *sinking fund*, fonds d'amortissement, *m*, caisse d'amortissement, *f.*

sinless, *a*, innocent. **sinner**, *n*, pécheur, *m*, pécheresse, *f.*

sinuous, *a*, sinueux.

sinus, *n*, sinus, *m.*

sip, *n*, petite gorgée; goutte, *f.* ¶ *v.t. & i*, siroter, humer, buvoter.

siphon, *n*, siphon, *m.*

sippet, *n*, mouillette, *f;* croûton, *m.*

sir, *n*, monsieur, *m*; (*title*) sir. **no**, ~, (*Army*) non, mon colonel, &c; (*Navy*) non, amiral, &c; (*but to any officer in command of a ship*) non, commandant. **sire**, *n*, père; (*to kings*) sire, *m*. ¶ *v.t*, engendrer.

siren (*Myth. & hooter*) *n*, sirène, *f*.

sirloin, *n*, aloyau, *m*. **a roast ~**, un rosbif.

siskin, *n*, tarin, *m*.

sister, *n*, sœur, *f*. **~-in-law**, belle-sœur, *f*. **~** [*ship*], (navire) frère, *n*. jumeau, *m*. **~hood**, confrérie; communauté, *f*. **~ly**, *a*, de sœur.

sit, *v.i.ir*, s'asseoir; rester; [se] tenir; (*portrait*) poser; (*court, &c*) siéger; (*hen*) couver. **~ down**, s'asseoir. **~ down again**, se rasseoir. **~-down supper** (ball), souper assis, *m*. **~ for**, (*portrait*) poser pour; (*Pol.*) représenter. **~ enthroned &** ~ **in state**, trôner. **~ on** (eggs), couver. **~ out**, faire galerie. **~ out a dance**, causer une danse. **~ up**, se tenir droit; veiller.

site, *n*, emplacement; terrain; site, *m*; assiette, *f*.

sitting, *n*, séance; audience; pose, *f*. **~ hen**, couveuse, *f*. **~-posture**, séant, *m*. **~-room**, petit salon, *m*. **~ time**, couvaison, *f*.

situated, *a*, situé; sis; placé; dans une position. **situation**, *n*, situation, assiette, position; place, *f*. **~ vacant**, offre d'emploi, *f*. **~ wanted**, demande d'emploi, *f*.

sitz bath, bain de siège, *m*.

six, *a. & n*, six, *a. & m*. **sixteen**, *a. & n*, seize, *a. & m*. **~mo or 16mo**, *a. & n*, in-seize, in-16, *a.m. & f*. **sixteenth†**, *a. & n*, seizième, *a. & m,f*; seize, *m*. **sixth†**, *a. & n*, sixième, *a. & m,f*; six, *m*; (*Mus.*) sixte, *f*. **sixtieth**, *a. & n*, soixantième, *a. & m,f*. **sixty**, *a. & n*, soixante, *a. & m*.

size, *n*, dimension, *f*. oft. *pl*; grandeur; grosseur; mesure, *f*; échantillon, *m*; taille; pointure, *f*; numéro; format; calibre, *m*; (*glue, &c*) colle, *f*, encollage, *m*. ¶ *v.t*, classer en grosseur; [en]coller. **~ up** (*pers.*), jauger.

skate, *n*, patin, *m*. (See *ice skates*); (*fish*) raie, *f*. ¶ *v.i*, patiner. **skater**, *n*, patineur, euse. **skating rink**, piste de patinage, *f*.

skedaddle, *v.i*, prendre la poudre d'escampette.

skein, *n*, écheveau, *m*.

skeleton, *n*, squelette, *m*; carcasse, *f*; canevas, *m*. **~ in the cupboard**, secret de la famille, *m*. **~ key**, crochet [de serrurier] *m*.

sketch, *n*, esquisse, *f*, croquis, dessin, crayon, canevas, *m*; (*playlet*) saynète, *f*. **~ book**, album de dessin, cahier de dessin, *m*. ¶ *v.t*, esquisser, croquer, crayonner, dessiner, tracer.

skew, *a*, biais, oblique. ¶ *n*, biais, *m*.

skewer, *n*, brochette, *f*.

ski, *n*, ski, *m*. **~ stick**, bâton de ski, *m*. ¶ *v.i*, faire du ski. **skiing**, *n*, courses en ski, *f.pl*.

skid, *n*, enrayure, *f*, sabot, patin; (*slip*) dérapage, *m*. ¶ *v.t*, enrayer; (*v.i.*) patiner, déraper.

skiff, *n*, skiff, esquif, *m*, yole, *f*.

skilful†, *a*, habile, adroit. **skill**, *n*, habileté, adresse, *f*. **~ed**, *a*, expérimenté, expert.

skim, *v.t*, écumer, dégraisser, écrémer; effleurer, raser. **~ milk**, lait écrémé, *m*. **skimmer**, *n*, écumoire; écrémoire, *f*. **skimmings**, *n.pl*, écume, *f*.

skimp, *v.t*, étriquer.

skin, *n*, peau; (*pl.*) peausserie; fourrure; dépouille, *f*; cuir, *m*; pelure; écorce; enveloppe, *f*. **~-deep**, superficiel. **~ disease**, maladie cutanée, *f*. **~ dresser**, peaussier, *m*. **~ dressing**, peausserie, *f*. **~ mat**, tapis de fourrure, *m*. **~ specialist**, spécialiste des maladies de peau, [médecin] peaussier [médecin] peaucier, *m*. ¶ *v.t*, écorcher; dépouiller; peler. **~-flint**, *n*, ladre, *m,f*, pingre, *m*. **~ over**, se cicatriser. **~less**, **pea** or **bean**, mange-tout, *m*. **skinny**, *a*, décharné, maigre.

skip, *n*, saut, *m*. ¶ *v.t. & i*, sauter; voleter. **~ about**, gambiller, fringuer. **skipper**, *n*, patron; capitaine, *m*. **~'s daughters** (waves), moutons, *m.pl*. **skipping rope**, corde à sauter, *f*.

skirmish, *n*, escarmouche, *f*. ¶ *v.i*, escarmoucher. **~er**, *n*, tirailleur, *m*.

skirt, *n*, jupe; basque, *f*, pan, *m*; (*of a wood*) lisière, orée, *f*. ¶ *v.t*, longer. **~ing** [board], *n*, plinthe, *f*.

skit, *n*, épigramme, *f*. **skittish**, *a*, (*horse*) ombrageux, écouteux; folâtre; coquet.

skittle, *n*, quille, *f*. **~ alley**, quillier, *m*.

skulk, *v.i*, se dissimuler.

skull, *n*, crâne, *m*. **~ cap**, calotte, *f*.

skunk, *n*, mouffette, *f*; (*fur*) sconse; (*pers.*) ladre, *m*.

sky, *n*, ciel, *m*; (*pl*, *Poet.*) nues, *f.pl*. **~ blue**, bleu de ciel, b. céleste, *m*. **~ lark**, alouette des champs, *f*. **~light**, [fenêtre à] tabatière, *f*. **~ line**, profil de l'horizon, *m*. **~ rocket**, fusée volante, *f*. **~ scraper**, gratte-ciel, *m*. **~ writing**, publicité sur les nuages, *f*.

slab, *n*, dalle, plaque, table, tranche, *f*, pan, *m*; tablette, *f*; (*Typ.*) marbre, *m*.

slack†, *a*, lâche; mou; faible. **~ water** (*Naut.*), mer étale, *f*, l'étale de la marée, *m*. ¶ **~ &** **~en**, *v.t. & i*, détendre; se d.; relâcher; se r.; ralentir; (*lime*) éteindre. **~er**, *n*, fricoteur, euse. **~s**, *n.pl*, pantalon, *m*.

slag, *n*, scorie, *f*, laitier, *m*.

slake, *v.t*, éteindre.

slam (*Cards*), *n*, chelem, *m*. ¶ (*bang*) *v.i. & t*, claquer.

slander, *v.t*, médire de, calomnier; diffamer. **~ous**, *a*, médisant.

slang, *n*, argot, *m*; langue verte, *f*, jargon, *m*.

slant, *n*, inclinaison, *f*. ¶ *v.i. & t*, incliner.

slap, *n*, tape, claque, *f*, soufflet, *m*. ¶ *v.t*, frapper, taper, claquer, souffleter.

slash, *v.t,* tailler, balafrer. ~ *about,* ferrailler. ~ed (*dress*) *p.a,* à crevés, taillardé.

slat, *n,* planchette; (*blind*) lame, *f.*

slate, *n,* ardoise, *f.* ~*-coloured,* ardoisé. ~ *pencil,* crayon d'ardoise, *m.* ~ *quarry,* ardoisière, *f.* ¶ *v.t,* couvrir d'ardoises; (*fig.*) éreinter.

slattern, *n,* souillon, salope maritorne, *f.*

slaughter, *n,* tuerie, *f,* massacre, carnage, *m.* ~ *house,* abattoir, *m.* ~ *man,* abatteur, *m.* ¶ *v.t,* massacrer, égorger; (*cattle*) abattre.

Slav, *a,* slave. ¶ *n,* Slave, *m,f.*

slave, *n,* esclave, *m,f.* ~ *bangle,* bracelet esclave, *m.* ~ *driver* & ~ *trader* & **slaver,** *n,* négrier, *m.* ~ *trade,* traite des noirs, *f.* **slave,** *v.i,* s'échiner, trimer.

slaver, *n,* bave, *f.* ¶ *v.i,* baver.

slavery, *n,* esclavage, *m.* **slavish†,** *a,* servile. ~ness, *n,* servilité, *f.*

slay, *v.t.ir,* immoler. ~er, *n,* tueur, *m.*

sledge, *n,* traîneau, *m;* (*man-guided, in the Alps*) ramasse, *f.* ~ [*hammer*], masse, *f.* **sledging,** *n,* traînage, *m.*

sleek, *a,* lisse, poli.

sleep, *n,* sommeil, *m.* ~ *walker,* somnambule, noctambule, *m,f.* ¶ *v.i. & t. ir,* dormir; reposer; coucher. ~ *out,* découcher. ~er, *n,* dormeur, euse; traverse, *f;* wagon-lit, *m.* **sleepiness,** *n,* envie de dormir, somnolence, *f,* sommeil, *m.* **sleeping,** *p.a,* endormi. ~ *bag,* sac de couchage, *m. the S~ Beauty,* la Belle au bois dormant. ~ *car,* wagon-lit, *m.* ~ *doll,* bébé dormeur, *m.* ~ *compartment,* coupé-lit, *m.* ~ *draught,* dormitif, *m.* ~ *partner,* commanditaire, bailleur de fonds, *m.* ~ *sickness,* maladie du sommeil, *f.* ~ *suit,* dormeuse, *f.* **sleepless,** *a,* sans dormir. ~ness, *n,* insomnie, *f.* **sleepy,** *a,* ensommeillé, somnolent. ~head, endormi, e, momie, *f.*

sleet, *n,* de la neige fondue, pluie mêlée de neige, *f.* ¶ *v.i,* tomber de la neige fondue.

sleeve, *n,* manche, *f;* (*Mach.*) manchon, *m.* ~ *link,* bouton de manchette, *m. to laugh up one's* ~, rire sous cape. ~less, *a,* sans manches.

sleigh, *n,* traîneau, *m.* ~ing, *n,* traînage, *m.*

sleight-of-hand, *n,* prestidigitation, *f.*

slender, *a,* mince; délié; fluet; grêle; gracile, svelte; faible.

sleuth hound, *n,* limier, *m.*

slew, *v.t,* faire pivoter.

slice, *n,* tranche; tartine, *f.* ~ *of bread & butter,* beurrée, tartine, *f.* ¶ *v.t,* trancher; (*ball*) couper.

slide, *n,* glissade; glissoire; débâcle; coulisse, *f;* tiroir; coulant; curseur; (*microscope*) porte-objet, *m;* (*lantern*) vue, projection, *f.* ~ *fastener* (zip), fermoir à curseur, *m.* ~ *lantern,* lanterne de projection, *f.* ~ *rest,* support à chariot, *m.* ~ *rule,* règle à calcul, *f.* ¶ *v.i.ir,*

glisser; couler. **sliding,** *p.a:* ~ *roof,* toit découvrable, *m.* ~ *scale,* échelle mobile, *f.* ~ *seat* (boat), banc à coulisse, *m.*

slight†, *a,* léger; mince; faible; petit; menu, maigrelet. ¶ *n,* affront, *m.* ¶ *v.t,* méconnaître; négliger; faire un affront à. *the* ~*est,* le moindre, la moindre.

slim, *a,* svelte, gracile, élancé.

slime, *n,* bave; vase, *f,* limon, *m,* boue, *f.* **slimy,** *a,* baveux; visqueux; vaseux.

sling, *n,* fronde; écharpe; bretelle; élingue, *f.* ~ *cart,* triqueballe, *m.* ¶ *v.t.ir,* jeter, lancer; suspendre. **slung** [*over the shoulders*], en bandoulière.

slink away, *v.i.ir,* se dérober.

slip, *n,* glissement, *m,* glissade, *f;* faux pas; lapsus, *m,* erreur; peccadille; bande; fiche; feuille, *f;* papillon; (*Typ.*) placard, *m,* épreuve en placard; (*lead*) laisse, *f;* (*drawers*) slip, *m;* (*pillow*) taie, *f;* (*twig*) brin, *m,* brindille, *f;* (*Hort.*) plant, *m,* bouture; (*Naut.*) cale; (*Box.*) esquive, *f;* (*pl, Theat.*) coulisses, *f.pl.* ~ *carriage,* wagon larguable, *m.* ~ *in album,* album à passe-partout, *m.* ~ *in mount,* passe-partout, *m.* ~ *knot,* nœud coulant, *m. a slip of a woman,* un morceau de femme. ~shod, en savates; négligé. ~ *stitch,* maille glissée, *f.* ¶ *v.i. & t,* glisser; couler; patiner; échapper; (*dog*) lâcher, laisser courre; (*rope*) larguer. ~ *in, v.t,* faufiler. ~ *on* (garment) *v.t,* passer. **slipper,** *n,* pantoufle, *f;* chausson, *m;* mule, *f.* ~ *bath,* baignoire à sabot, *f,* sabot, *m.* ~ *chin,* menton de (ou en) galoche, *m.* **slippery,** *a,* glissant.

slit, *n,* fente, *f.* ¶ (*dress*) *p.a,* taillardé, à crevés. ¶ *v.t.ir,* fendre.

slobber, *n,* bave, *f.* ¶ *v.i,* baver.

sloe, *n,* prunelle, *f.* ~ *gin,* [liqueur de] prunelle, *f.* ~ [*tree*], prunellier, *m.*

slogan, *n,* cri de guerre, *m;* devise publicitaire, *f.*

sloop, *n,* sloop, *m.*

slop [over], *v.i,* déborder. *slop pail,* seau de toilette, *m.*

slope, *n,* pente; rampe, *f;* talus, *m.* ¶ *v.i,* s'incliner, aller en pente.

sloppiness (*fig.*) *n,* romance, *f.* **sloppy,** *a,* plein de flaques; (*fig.*) romance. **slops,** *n.pl,* rinçure, *f;* eaux ménagères, *f.pl;* (*thin soup*) lavasse, *f;* (*liquid diet*) bouillon, *m.*

slot, *n,* mortaise, rainure; (*of a slot machine, &c*) fente, *f.* ~ *machine,* distributeur automatique, *m.* ~ *meter,* compteur à paiement préalable, *m.*

sloth, *n,* paresse, indolence, *f;* (*Zool.*) paresseux, *m.* ~ful, *a,* paresseux, indolent.

slouch, *v.i,* donner un air disloqué à sa taille, à son attitude, à sa marche. ~ *hat,* chapeau rabattu, *m.*

slough, *n,* bourbier, *m;* (*snake*) dépouille, peau, mue, *f;* (*Med.*) escarre, *f.* ¶ *v.i,* se dépouiller, muer.

sloven, *n,* sagouin, e, souillon, *m.f.* ∼ly, *a,* négligent; négligé, lâché.

slow†, *a,* lent; tardif; lambin; (*train*) omnibus, de petite vitesse; (*clock*) en retard. *to be* ∼ (tedious), manquer d'entrain. ∼*coach,* lambin, e, traînard, clampin, *m.* ∼*-combustion stove,* calorifère à feu continu, *m.* ∼*-motion picture,* cinéma au ralenti, *m.* ¶ *ad,* lentement. ∼ **down,** ralentir. **slowness,** *n,* lenteur, *f.*

slow-worm, *n,* orvet, *m.*

sludge, *n,* gâchis, *m;* vase, boue, *f.*

slug, *n,* limace, loche, *f;* (*bullet & Typ.*) lingot, *m.*

sluggard, *n,* paresseux, euse. **sluggish†,** *a,* paresseux; inerte; tardif.

sluice, *n,* canal, *m.* ∼ *gate,* vanne, *f.* ∼ *gates of heaven,* cataractes du ciel, *f.pl.*

slum, *n,* taudis, *m,* habitation insalubre, *f.* ∼ *area,* îlot insalubre, *m.*

slumber, *n,* sommeil, *m.* ¶ *v.i,* sommeiller.

slump, *n,* (*in prices*) effondrement, *m,* dégringolade; (*in trade*) mévente, crise, *f.* ¶ *v.i,* s'effondrer.

slur, *n,* atteinte; (*Mus.*) liaison, *f.* ¶ *v.t,* (*Mus.*) lier; (*v.i, Typ.*) friser. ∼ *over,* glisser sur.

slush, *n,* gâchis, *m,* de la neige fondue, *f.*

slut, *n,* souillon, salope, maritorne, *f.*

sly†, *a,* sournois; rusé. ∼*boots,* cachottier, ère, finaud, e. ∼ *ly, a,* à la dérobée.

smack, *n,* claque; barque, *f,* bateau, *m;* teinture, *f.* ¶ *v.t,* claquer; taper; (*tongue*) clapper. *to* ∼ *of,* sentir le, la.

small, *a,* petit; faible; modique; menu; fin; (*intestine*) grêle; (*arms, Mil.*) portatives. ∼ *craft,* batellerie, *f.* ∼ *fry* (*fig.*), fretin, *m.* ∼ *hand* (writing), minute, *f.* ∼ *part* (*Theat.*), bout de rôle, *m.* ∼*pox,* petite vérole, variole, *f.* ∼*pox case* (*pers.*), varioleux, euse. ∼ *stones,* pierraille, *f.* ∼ *talk,* menus propos, *m.pl,* conversation banale, *f,* choses indifférentes, *f.pl,* (dire) des riens. ¶ ∼ *of the back,* chute des reins, *f.* ∼*ness,* *n,* petitesse, *f,* peu d'importance, *m.*

smart, *n,* cuisson, *f.* ¶ *v.i,* cuire. ¶ *a†,* vif; fin; beau, chic, pimpant, coquet, huppé. *the* ∼ *set,* les gens huppés. ∼*en oneself up,* se requinquer. ∼*ing, n,* cuisson, *m.* ¶ *p.a,* cuisant. ∼*ness, n,* finesse, *f;* chic, *m.*

smash, *n,* accident; (*Fin.*) krach; (*Ten.*) coup écrasé, *m. to go* ∼ (bank, &c), sauter. ¶ *v.t,* briser, fracasser, massacrer; (*Ten.*) écraser, tuer.

smattering, *n,* teinture, *f.*

smear, *v.t,* enduire; barbouiller.

smell, *n,* odorat, *m;* odeur, *f.* ¶ *v.t. & i. ir,* sentir; fleurer; flairer; puer. *smelling bottle,* flacon à odeur, *m.* ∼ *salts,* sels [volatils] anglais, *m.pl.*

smelt, *n,* éperlan, *m.*

smelt, *v.t,* fondre. ∼*ing works,* fonderie, *f.*

smilax, *n,* smilax, *m.*

smile, *n,* sourire, *m.* ¶ *v.i,* sourire. **smiling,** *a,* [sou]riant.

smirch, *v.t,* salir.

smirk, *n,* sourire affecté, *m.* ¶ *v.i,* minauder.

smite, *v.t.ir,* frapper. (Cf. *smitten.*)

smith, *n,* forgeron, *m.* ∼*'s hearth,* bâti de forge, *m.* ∼*y,* *m,* forge, *f.*

smitten, *p.p,* (*remorse*) pris; (*love*) épris, féru.

smock [**frock**], *n,* blouse, *f,* sarrau, *m.* **smocking,** *n,* fronces smock, *f.pl.*

smoke, *n,* fumée; (*fig.*) fumée, eau de boudin, *f.* ∼*-consuming,* fumivore. ∼ *helmet,* casque respiratoire, *m.* ∼ *house,* fumoir, *m.* ∼ *screen,* écran de fumée, *m.* ∼ *stack,* cheminée, *f.* ¶ *v.i. & t,* fumer; enfumer; (*lamp*) charbonner. ∼*d sausage,* saucisson, *m.* ∼*less, a,* ∼ sans fumée.

smoker, *n,* fumeur, euse, *m.* ∼*'s stand,* pied fumeur, cendrier sur pied, *m.* **smoking,** *n,* l'habitude de fumer, *f.* ∼ *compartment,* compartiment pour fumeurs, *m.* ∼ *room,* fumoir, *m.* ∼ *strictly prohibited,* défense expresse de fumer. **smoky,** *a,* qui fume, fumeux.

smooth, *a,* lisse; uni; doux; (*sea*) unie, plate. ∼*bore,* à canon lisse. ∼*haired* (dog), à poil ras. ∼*tongued,* mielleux, doucereux. ¶ *v.t,* lisser; polir; unir; planer; aplanir; adoucir; défroncer. ∼*ing plane,* rabot de menuisier, *m.* ∼*ly, ad,* uniment; doucement. ∼*ness, n,* égalité; douceur, *f.*

smother, *v.t,* étouffer.

smoulder, *v.i,* couver.

smudge, *n,* noirceur, *f.* ¶ *v.t,* barbouiller, mâchurer.

smug, *a,* béat.

smuggle, *v.t,* passer en contrebande; (*v.i.*) faire la contrebande. ∼ *in, v.t,* entrer en fraude. **smuggler,** *n,* contrebandier, ère, fraudeur, euse.

smut, *n,* noirceur; (*Agric.*) nielle, *f.* **smutty,** *a,* noirci; niellé; (*obscene*) graveleux.

Smyrna, *n,* Smyrne, *f.*

snack, *n,* morceau [sur le pouce], casse-croûte, *m,* collation, *f. to have a* ∼, collationner. ∼ *bar,* casse-croûte, *m.*

snag, *n,* chicot; (*fig.*) accroc, *m.*

snail, *n,* [co]limaçon; (*edible*) escargot, *m. at a* ∼*'s pace,* à pas de tortue.

snake, *n,* couleuvre, *f;* serpent, (*young*) serpenteau, *m. there is a* ∼ *in the grass,* le serpent est caché sous les fleurs.

snap, *n,* crac; cric crac!; coup sec, *m;* agrafe, *f,* fermoir, *m.* ∼*dragon,* muflier, *m,* gueule-de-loup, *f.* ∼ *fastener,* bouton à pression, *m.* ∼ *hook,* [porte-]mousqueton, *m.* ∼[*shot*], instantané, *m.* ¶ *v.t,* casser, rompre; faire claquer. ∼ *at,* bourrer. ∼ *up,* happer; enlever. **snapper** (*whip*) *n,* mèche, *f.* **snappy,** *a,* hargneux.

snare, *n,* piège, *f;* (*drum*) timbre, *m.* ∼ *drum,* caisse claire, *f.* ¶ *v.t,* attraper.

snarl, *v.i,* gronder. ∼*ing, p.a,* hargneux.

snatch (*scrap*) *n*, fragment, *m*, bribe, *f*. ¶ *v.t*, gripper; arracher; dérober; (*kiss*) cueillir.

sneak, *n*, sournois, e; (*Sch*.) capon, ne. ~ **away**, s'en aller à la dérobée. *a* ~*ing fondness for*, du (*ou* un) faible pour.

sneer, *n*, rire moqueur, *m*. ¶ *v.i*, goguenarder. ~ *at*, railler.

sneeze, *v.i*, éternuer; (*animals*) s'ébrouer.

sniff, *v.i. & t*, renifler.

snigger, *v.i*, rire en dedans, rire en dessous.

snip, *n*, coup de ciseaux; bout, *m*. ¶ *v.t*, cisailler.

snipe, *n*, bécassine, *f*. ¶ *v.t*, canarder.

sniper, *n*, tireur isolé, franc-tireur, *m*.

snivel, *v.i*, pleurnicher.

snooze, *n*, somme, *m*. ¶ *v.i*, roupiller, pioncer.

snore, *v.i*, ronfler.

snort, *v.i*, renifler, renâcler, s'ébrouer.

snout, *n*, museau; (*pig*) groin; (*boar*) boutoir, *m*.

snow, *n*, neige, *f. ôft. pl.* ~ **ball**, boule de neige, *f*. ~ **blindness**, cécité des neiges, *f*. ~ **boots**, chaussures pour la n., *f.pl*. ~**capped**, chenu. ~ **drift**, amas de n., *m*. ~**drop**, perce-neige, clochette d'hiver, *f*. ~ **leopard**, once, *f*. ~ **line**, limite des neiges éternelles, *f*. ~ **plough**, chasseneige, *m*. ~ **shoes**, raquettes à n., *f.pl*. ~ **squall**, chasse-neige, *m*. ~ **storm**, tempête de n., *f*. ¶ *v.i*, neiger. ~**y**, *a*, neigeux.

snub, *n*, camouflet, soufflet, *m*, nasarde, *f*. ~**nosed**, camus, camard. ¶ *v.t*, rabrouer, moucher.

snuff, *n*, tabac à priser, *m. to take* ~, prendre du tabac, priser. ~ *box*, tabatière, *f*. ~ *taker*, priseur, euse. ¶ *v.t*, moucher. ~ *up*, priser.

snuffle, *v.i*, renifler, nasiller. ~**s**, *n.pl*, enchifrènement, *m*.

snug†, *a*, confortable.

snuggle, *v.i*, se pelotonner, se blottir.

so, *ad. c. & pn*, ainsi; aussi; donc; si; oui; tellement; tel, telle; tant; le. ~*-&-*~, un tel, une telle. ~*-called*, soi-disant, *a.inv*. prétendu. ~ *as to*, de manière à: afin de. ~ ~, comme ci, comme ça; couci-couça. ~ *soon as*, sitôt que. ~ *that*, de sorte que; afin que. ~ *to speak*, pour ainsi dire.

soak, *v.t*, imbiber, [dé]tremper; (*dirty linen*) essanger.

soap, *n*, savon, *m*. ~ *dish*, plateau à s., *m*. ~ *maker*, savonnier, *m*. ~ *making & works*, savonnerie, *f*. ~*stone*, pierre de savon, *f*. ~ *suds*, eau de s., *f*. ¶ *v.t*, savonner. ~**y**, *a*, savonneux.

soar, *v.i*, pointer, planer, prendre son essor.

sob, *n*, sanglot, *m*. ~*stuff*, drame pleureur, *m*. ¶ *v.i*, sangloter.

sober†, *a*, sobre; sérieux; pas en état d'ébriété. *he is never* ~, il ne désenivre point, il ne

dessoule jamais. ¶ *v.t*, désenivrer, dégriser. ~**ness**, *n*, sobriété, *f*.

sociable†, *a*, sociable, liant. **social**, *a*, social. ~ *events* (news), mondanités, *f.pl*. ~**ism**, *n*, socialisme, *m*. ~**ist**, *n. & a*, socialiste, *m,f. & a*. **society**, *n*, société, association; (*fashionable world*) société, *f*, le monde, le grand monde; (*att.*) mondain. ~ *man*, *woman*, mondain, e. **sociology**, *n*, sociologie, *f*.

sock, *n*, chaussette; semelle [pour chaussures] (*en liège, lofa, &c*), *f*. ~ *suspenders*, supports-chaussettes, *m.pl*.

socket, *n*, douille, *f*, manchon, *m*; (*eye*) orbite, *f*; (*tooth, &c*) alvéole, *m*; (*bone*) glène, *f*. ¶ *v.t*, emboîter.

sod, *n*, gazon, *m*; plaque de gazon, motte, *f*.

soda, *n*, soude, *f*; (*washing*) cristaux de soude, *m.pl*. ~ [*water*], soda, *m*, eau de Seltz, *f*.

sodden, *a*, détrempé.

sodium, *n*, sodium, *m*.

sofa, *n*, canapé, sofa, *m*.

soffit, *n*, soffite; intrados, *m*.

soft†, *a*, mou; doux; tendre; moelleux; (*fruit*) blet. ~*-boiled* (eggs), mollet. ~ *brush*, brosse douce, *f*. ~ *collar*, col souple, *m*. ~ *corn*, œil-de-perdrix, *m*. ~ *felt* (hat), feutre souple, feutre mou, *m*. ~ *furnishings*, tissus d'ameublement, *m.pl*. ~ *job*, un fromage. ~ *nothings*, douceurs, *f.pl*. ~ *palate*, palais mou, *m*. ~ *pedal*, petite pédale, p./sourde, *f*. ~ *roe*, laitance, laite, *f*. ~*-roed*, laité. ~ *sawder & ~ soap* (fig.), flagornerie, *f*; (*v.t*.) amadouer. ~ *solder*, soudure tendre, *f*. ~ *soap*, savon mou, *m*. ~*-witted*, ramolli. ~**en**, *v.t*, [r]amollir; adoucir; attendrir. ~*ening of the brain*, ramollissement du cerveau, *m*. ~**ish**, *a*, mollet. ~**ness**, *n*, mollesse, *f*; moelleux, *m*; douceur; tendresse, *f*.

soil, *n*, sol, *m*, terre, *f*, terroir, *m*, glèbe, *f*. ¶ *v.t*, salir, souiller. ~**ed**, *p.a*, (*linen*) sale; (*shop goods*) défraîchi.

sojourn, *n*, séjour, *m*. ¶ *v.i*, séjourner.

solace, *n*, consolation, *f*. ¶ *v.t*, consoler.

solar, *a*, solaire. ~ *plexus*, plexus s., *m*.

sola topi, -ee (*India*), casque en moelle de millet (*Fr.*), *m*.

solder *& ~ing*, *n*, soudure, *f*. ¶ *v.t*, souder. ~*ing iron*, fer à souder, *m*.

soldier, *n*, soldat, militaire, troupier, *m*. ~**y**, *n*, militaires, *m.pl*; (*unruly*) soldatesque, *f*.

sole†, *a*, seul; unique; tout; exclusif. ¶ *n*, (*foot*) plante; (*shoe*) semelle; (*hoof, plate, fish*) sole, *f*. ¶ *v.t*, (*shoes*) ressemeler.

solecism, *n*, solécisme, *m*.

solemn†, *a*, solennel; grave. ~**ity**, *n*, solennité; gravité, *f*. ~**ize**, *v.t*, solenniser; (*wedding, &c*) célébrer.

sol-fa, *n*, solfège, *m*. ¶ *v.t. & i*, solfier.

solicit, *v.t*, solliciter, quémander; briguer. ~**or**, *n*, *in Fr.* avoué; agréé; notaire, *m*.

~ous, *a*, désireux; inquiet; jaloux. ~ude, *n*, sollicitude, *f*.

solid†, *a*, solide; ferme; massif; plein. ~ rock, roc vif, *m*. ¶ *n*, solide, *m*. ~ify, *v.t*, solidifier. ~ity, *n*, solidité, *f*.

soliloquize, *v.i*, monologuer. soliloquy, *n*, soliloque, *m*.

soling, *n*, ressemelage, *m*.

solitaire (*gem*, *game*) *n*, solitaire, *m*. solitary†, *a*, solitaire; retiré. ~ confinement, secret, *m*. ~ imprisonment, réclusion, *f*. solitude, *n*, solitude, *f*.

solo, *n*, solo; récit, *m*. ~ dance, pas seul, *m*. ~ violin, violon solo, *m*. ~ whist, whist de Gand, *m*. ~ist, *n*, soliste, *m,f*.

solstice, *n*, solstice, *m*.

soluble, *a*, soluble. solution, *n*, solution; résolution; issue; dissolution; liqueur, *f*. solve, *v.t*, résoudre. solvency, *n*, solvabilité, *f*. solvent, *a*, dissolvant; (*Com.*) solvable. ¶ *n*, dissolvant, *m*.

sombre, *a*, sombre.

some, *a*, quelque, quelques; du, de la, des; certain. ¶ *pn*, quelques-uns, -unes; certains, certaines; les uns, les unes; en. somebody & someone, *n*, quelqu'un, *m*; on, *pn*. ~ else, quelqu'un d'autre. to be somebody, être un personnage. somehow [or other], *ad*, d'une manière ou d'une autre; tant bien que mal.

somersault, *n*, culbute, *f*, (le) saut périlleux.

something, *n*, quelque chose, *m*; q. c. de; de quoi. ~ in the wind, quelque anguille sous roche. sometimes, *ad*, quelquefois; parfois; tantôt. somewhat, *ad*, quelque peu, un peu, tant soit peu. somewhere, *ad*, quelque part. ~ else, ailleurs, autre part. ~ in the world, de par le monde. ~ to stay, pied-à-terre, tournebride, *m*.

somnambulism, *n*, somnambulisme, *m*. somnambulist, *n*, somnambule, *m.f*. somnolent, *a*, somnolent.

son, *n*, fils; garçon, *m*. ~-in-law, gendre, *m*.

sonata, *n*, sonate, *f*.

song, *n*, chant, *m*; chanson; romance, *f*; air; cantique; (*of birds*) chant, ramage; (*mere trifle*) morceau de pain, *m*. ~ bird, oiseau chanteur, *m*. ~ book, chansonnier, *m*. ~ thrush, grive chanteuse, *f*. ~ without words, romance sans paroles. ~ writer, chansonnier, ère. ~ster, ~stress, *n*, chanteur, euse.

sonnet, *n*, sonnet, *m*.

sonorous, *a*, sonore; ronflant.

soon, *ad*, bientôt; tôt. as ~ as, [aus]sitôt que, dès que. as ~ as possible, le plus tôt possible. ~er, *ad*, plus tôt; (*rather*) plutôt. ~ or later, tôt ou tard. no ~ said than done, aussitôt dit, aussitôt fait.

soot, *n*, suie, *f*. ~y, *a*, noir de suie.

soothe, *v.t*, adoucir, calmer.

soothsayer, *n*, devin, *m*, devineresse, *f*.

sop, *n*, soupe, *f*; (*fig.*) os à ronger, *m*.

sophism, *n*, sophisme, *m*. sophisticate, *v.t*,

sophistiquer. ~d, *p.a*, savant. sophistry, *n*, sophistique, *f*.

soporific, *a*. & *n*, soporifique, *a*. & *m*.

soprano (*voice & pers.*) *n*, soprano, *m*.

sorcerer, ess, *n*, sorcier, ère, magicien, ne. sorcery, *n*, sorcellerie, *f*.

sordid†, *a*, sordide. ~ness, *n*, vilenie, *f*.

sore†, *a*, douloureux, meurtri; malade; sensible; endolori; affligé; cruel. I have a ~ finger, j'ai mal au doigt. ~ eyes, mal aux (*ou* d') yeux. ~ point, endroit sensible, point névralgique, *m*. ~ throat, mal à la gorge. ¶ *n*, plaie, *f*; (*gathering*) mal blanc, *m*.

sorrel, *n*, oseille, *f*. ¶ *a*, saure.

sorrily, *ad*, tristement. sorrow, *n*, chagrin, *m*, douleur, peine, *f*. ¶ *v.i*, s'affliger. ~ful, *a*, chagrin; triste. ~fully, *ad*, tristement. sorry, *a*, fâché; triste; méchant, mauvais, pauvre, piteux. to be ~ for, être fâché de; plaindre; se repentir de. in a ~ plight, mal-en-point.

sort, *n*, sorte, *f*, genre, *m*, espèce, nature; manière, *f*; (*pl*, *Typ.*) assortiment, *m*. ¶ *v.t*, trier; classer. ~er, *n*, trieur, euse.

sortie, *n*, sortie, *f*.

sot, *n*, ivrogne, *m*, ivrognesse, *f*. sottish, *a*, abruti.

sough, *v.i*, bruire, murmurer.

sought after, recherché.

soul, *n*, âme, *f*. ~less, *a*, sans âme.

sound†, *a*, sain; bon; solide; (*sleep*) profond. ¶ *n*, son; (*Geog.*) bras de mer, détroit, *m*; (*probe*) sonde, *f*. ~[ing] board, abat-voix, *m*; (*Mus.*) table d'harmonie, *f*. ~ film, film sonore, *m*. ~ hole, ouïe, *f*. ~ post, âme, *f*. ~-proof, insonore. ¶ *v.t*, faire sonner; sonner; sonder; pressentir; (*Med.*) ausculter; (*v.i.*) sonner, résonner. ~ness, *n*, solidité; rectitude, *f*.

soup, *n*, potage, bouillon, *m*; soupe, purée, *f*. ~ kitchen, fourneau philanthropique, *m*. ~ ladle, cuiller à potage, louche, *f*. ~ plate, assiette creuse, *f*. ~ tureen, soupière, *f*.

sour, *a*, aigre, sur, acide, vert; (*milk, &c*) tourné. ¶ *v.t*, aigrir, enfieller. ~ish, *a*, aigrelet, suret. ~ly, *ad*, aigrement. ~ness, *n*, aigreur, acidité, *f*.

source, *n*, source, *f*.

souse, *n*, marinade, *f*. ¶ *v.t*, mariner; saucer.

south, *n*, sud; midi, *m*. ¶ *ad*, au sud. ¶ *a*, du sud; méridional; austral. S~ Africa, l'Afrique du Sud *ou* australe *ou* méridionale, *f*. S~ African, sud-africain. S~ America, l'Amérique du Sud, *f*. S~ American, sud-américain. S~ Australia, l'Australie méridionale, *f*. ~-east, sud-est, *m*. S~ pole, pôle sud, *m*. S~ Sea Islands, îles du Pacifique, *f.pl*. S~ Wales, la Galles du Sud. ~-west, sud-ouest, *m*. S~ West Africa, le Sud-Ouest africain, *m*. ~ern, *a*, [du] sud; méridional; austral. ~er, *n*, méridional, e. southward[s], *ad*, vers le sud.

souvenir, *n,* souvenir, *m.*

sou'wester (*wind, hat*) *n,* suroît, *m.*

sovereign, *a. &* (*pers.*) *n,* souverain, e; (£) souverain, *m.* ~ty, *n,* souveraineté, *f.*

soviet, *n,* soviet, *m;* (*att.*) soviétique.

sow, *n,* truie, coche; (*wild*) laie, *f.*

sow, *v.t. & i. ir,* semer; ensemencer. ~er, *n,* semeur, euse. **sowing,** *n,* ensemencement, *m,* semailles, *f.pl.* ~ *machine,* semoir, *m,* semeuse, *f.* ~ *time,* temps des semailles, *m,* semailles, *f.pl.*

soy[a] bean, soya, soja, pois chinois, *m.*

spa, *n,* ville d'eaux, *f,* eaux, *f.pl,* bains, *m.pl.*

space, *n,* espace; intervalle; entre-deux; vide, creux; (*Mus.*) interligne, *m;* (*on printed form*) case; (*Typ.*) espace, *f.* ~ *between lines,* interligne, *m.* ¶ *v.t,* espacer. **spacious,** *a,* spacieux.

spade, *n,* bêche, *f;* (*pl, Cards*) pique, *m.* ¶ *v.t,* bêcher. ~ful, *n,* pelletée, *f.*

Spain, *n,* l'Espagne, *f.*

span, *n,* envergure; portée, travée, ouverture, *f.* ¶ *v.t,* franchir, chevaucher.

spandrel, *n,* tympan, *m.*

spangle, *n,* paillette, *f.* ~d, *p.p,* pailleté.

Spaniard, *n,* Espagnol, e. **spaniel,** *n,* épagneul, e. **Spanish,** *a,* espagnol; d'Espagne. ~ *fly,* cantharide, *f.* ~ *mahogany,* acajou des Antilles, *m.* ~ *onion,* oignon doux d'Espagne, *m.* ¶ *n,* l'espagnol, *m.*

spank, *v.t,* fesser. ~ing, *n,* fessée, *f.*

spanner, *n,* clef, clé, *f.*

spar, *n,* (*Naut.*) espar; (*Miner.*) spath, *m.* ~ *deck,* spardeck, *m.* ¶ *v.i,* boxer; s'entraîner à la boxe.

spare, *a,* maigre, sec; disponible; libre; de rechange. ~ [*bed*]*room,* chambre d'ami, *f.* ~ [*part*], pièce de rechange, *f.* ~ *time,* loisir, *m. oft. pl,* heures dérobées, *f.pl.* ~ *wheel,* roue de secours, *f.* ¶ *v.t,* épargner; ménager; accorder; se passer de; respecter; faire grâce de; trouver. *to have enough & to* ~, avoir à revendre. **sparing,** *p.a,* économe, ménager; chiche, avare.

spark, *n,* étincelle; flammèche, *f;* brandon; gendarme, *m;* lueur, *f;* (*pers.*) mirliflore, galant, *m.* ~ing *plug,* bougie d'allumage, *f.* **sparkle,** *v.i,* étinceler, briller, miroiter; pétiller; mousser. **sparkling,** *a,* étincelant; émerillonné; (*wine*) mousseux.

sparring, *n,* entraînement, *m.* ~ *match,* assaut de démonstration, *m.* ~ *partner,* partenaire d'entraînement, *m.*

sparrow, *n,* moineau, passereau, pierrot, *m.* ~ *hawk,* épervier, *m.*

sparse, *a,* peu dense, clairsemé, rare.

Spartan, *a. & n,* spartiate, *a. & m.f.*

spasm, *n,* spasme, *m.* **spasmodic,** *a,* saccadé; (*Med.*) spasmodique. ~ally, *ad,* par saccades, par sauts & par bonds.

spate, *n,* grandes eaux, *f.pl,* crue, *f.*

spats, *n.pl,* guêtres de ville, *f.pl.*

spatter, *v.t,* éclabousser.

spatula, *n,* spatule, *f.*

spawn, *n,* (*fish*) frai; (*mushroom*) blanc, mycélium, *m.* ¶ *v.i,* frayer.

speak, *v.i. & t. ir,* parler; dire; prononcer; prendre la parole; (*ship*) héler. ~ *one's mind,* se déboutonner. ~er, *n,* opinant; orateur, *m.* ~ X. ~ (*Teleph.*), ici X. *without* ~, à la muette. ~ *likeness,* portrait parlant, *m. we are not on* ~ *terms,* nous ne nous parlons pas. ~ *trumpet,* porte-voix, *m.* ~ *tube,* tuyau acoustique, *m.*

spear, *n,* lance, *f.* ~ *head,* fer de lance, *m.* ~mint, menthe verte, *f.* ¶ *v.t,* percer; darder.

special†, *a,* spécial; particulier; extraordinaire. ~ *correspondent,* envoyé spécial, *m.* ~ *dish for the day,* plat du jour, *m.* ~ist, *n,* spécialiste, *m.f.* ~ity, *n,* spécialité, *f.* ~ize *in,* se spécialiser dans.

specie, *n,* espèces, *f.pl,* numéraire, *m.*

species, *n,* espèce, *f.*

specific†, *a,* spécifique; déterminé. ~ *gravity,* poids spécifique, *m.* ~ *legatee,* légataire particulier, *m.* ¶ *n,* spécifique, *m.* ~ation, *n,* spécification; énonciation, *f;* devis; cahier des charges, *m.* **specify,** *v.t,* spécifier; énoncer; préciser. **specimen,** *n,* spécimen; échantillon; modèle; exemplaire, *m.* **specious†,** *a,* spécieux.

speck, *n,* point, *m;* petite tache, *f;* grain, *m,* particule; piqûre, *f.* ~le, *v.t,* tacheter, moucheter.

spectacle, *n,* spectacle, *m;* (*pl.*) lunettes, *f.pl.* ~ *case,* étui à l—s, *m.* ~ *maker,* lunetier, *m.* **spectacular,** *a,* à [grand] spectacle. **spectator,** *n,* spectateur, trice.

spectral, *a,* spectral. **spectre,** *n,* spectre, *m.* **spectroscope,** *n,* spectroscope, *m.* **spectrum,** *n,* spectre, *m.*

speculate, *v.i,* spéculer; jouer, agioter. **speculation,** *n,* spéculation, *f;* jeu, *m.* **speculative,** *a,* spéculatif, de spéculation. **speculator,** *n,* spéculateur, trice; agioteur, *m,* joueur, euse.

speech, *n,* parole, *f;* langage, *m;* langue, *f;* parler; discours, *m,* allocution, harangue, *f.* ~ *day* (*Sch.*), distribution de prix, *f.* ~ *for the defence,* plaidoyer, *m.* ~ify, *v.i,* pérorer. ~less, *a,* sans voix, muet.

speed, *n,* vitesse; célérité; rapidité, *f.* ~ *boat,* [canot] glisseur, *m.* ~ *counter,* compteur de tours, *m.* *3-speed gear,* dispositif à 3 vitesses, *m.* ~ *swim,* course de vitesse, *f.* ¶ *v.i.ir,* voler. ~ *up,* activer. **speedometer,** *n,* compteur de vitesse, *m.* **speedwell** (*Bot.*) *n,* véronique, *f.* **speedy,** *a,* rapide.

spell, *n,* charme, enchantement; sort; maléfice; tour, *m;* période, échappée, *f.* ~bound, sous le charme, *f.* ¶ *v.t. & i. ir,* épeler; écrire; orthographier. **spelling,** *n,* orthographe; épellation, *f.* ~ *bee,* concours orthographique, *m.* ~ *book,* abécédaire, syllabaire, *m.*

spelter, *n*, zinc, *m*.

spencer, *n*, gilet, spencer, *m*.

spend, *v.t. & i. ir*, dépenser; passer. ~*thrift*, *n. & att*, dépensier, ère, prodigue, *m,f. & a*. **spent bullet**, balle morte, *f*.

sperm, *n*, sperme, *m*. ~ *oil*, huile de spermaceti, *f*. ~ *whale*, cachalot, *m*. **spermaceti**, *n*, blanc de baleine, *m*. **spermatozoon**, *n*, spermatozoaire, *m*.

spew, *v.t. & i*, vomir.

sphere, *n*, sphère, *f*. **spherical**, *a*, sphérique.

sphincter, *n*, sphincter, *m*

sphinx, *n*, sphinx, *m*.

spice, *n*, épice, *f*; (*fig*.) grain, *m*.

spick & span, tiré à quatre épingles, pimpant.

spicy, *a*, épicé, poivré.

spider, *n*, araignée, *f*. ~['*s*] **web**, toile d'a., *f*.

spigot, *n*, fausset, *m*.

spike, *n*, broche; cheville, *f*, crampon; (*pl, on wall*) chardon, artichaut; piquant; (*of flower*) épi, *m*. ¶ (*gun*) *v.t*, enclouer.

spill (*pipe light*) *n*, fidibus, *m*. *to have a* ~, faire panache. ¶ *v.t.ir*, répandre, renverser; verser.

spin (*on ball*) *n*, effet, *m*. ¶ *v.t.ir*, filer; (*top*) faire tourner, faire aller; (*v.i*.) tournoyer, toupiller. ~ *out*, délayer. ~ *yarns*, débiter des histoires.

spinach, -age, *n*, épinard, *m*; (*Cook*.) épinards, *m.pl*.

spinal, *a*, spinal; (*column*) vertébrale. ~ *cord*, moelle épinière, *f*. ~ *complaint*, maladie de la moelle épinière, *f*.

spindle, *n*, fuseau, *m*; broche, *f*; mandrin; arbre, *m*. ~ *tree*, fusain, *m*.

spindrift, *n*, embrun, *m*.

spine, *n*, (*Bot*.) épine; (*Anat*.) é. dorsale, *f*; (*of book*) dos, *m*. ~**less** (*fig*.) *a*, mollasse.

spinel, *n. & att*, spinelle, *m. & a*.

spinner, *n*, fileu❘r, euse, filateur, trice; (*owner*) filateur, *m*; (*Fish*.) hélice, *f*.

spinney, *n*, bosquet, *m*.

spinning, *n*, filature; pêche à la [ligne] volante, *f*. ~ *mill*, filature, *f*. ~ *wheel*, rouet, *m*.

spinster, *n*, demoiselle, *f*.

spiny, *a*, épineux. ~ *lobster*, langouste, *f*.

spiral, *a*, spiral; hélicoïdal; (*spring*) à boudin; (*stairs*) tournant. ¶ *n*, spirale, *f*.

spire, *n*, flèche; (*whorl*) spire, *f*.

spirit, *n*, esprit, *m*; âme, *f*; génie; entrain, *m*; fougue; essence, *f*; alcool, *m*; liqueur [spiritueuse] *f*, (*pl*.) spiritueux, *m.pl*. ~ *lamp*, lampe à alcool, *f*. ~ *level*, niveau à bulle d'air, *m*. ~[*s*] *of salt, of wine*, esprit de sel, de vin. ~ *stove*, réchaud à alcool, *m*. ~ *varnish*, vernis à l'a., *m*. ~ *away*, faire disparaître comme par enchantement, escamoter. ~**ed**, *a*, vif, animé; ardent, fougueux; courageux. ~**less**, *a*, sans courage. **spiritual†**, *a*, spirituel. **spiritualism**, *n*, (*Psychics*) spiri-

tisme; (*Philos*.) spiritualisme, *m*. **spiritualist**, *n* (*Psychics*) spirite; (*Philos*.) spiritualiste, *m,f*. **spirituous**, *a*, spiritueux.

spirt, *n*, jet, *m*. ¶ *v.i*, jaillir, gicler.

spit, *n*, (*roasting*) broche; (*Geog*.) flèche littorale; (*Cust*.) sonde, *f*. ¶ *v.t*, embrocher; sonder.

spit, *v.i. & t. ir*, cracher.

spite, *n*, dépit, *m*, malveillance, rancune, pique, *f*. *in* ~ *of*, en dépit de, malgré. ¶ *v.t*, dépiter. ~**ful†**, *a*, malicieux, malveillant, rancunier, méchant.

spitfire, *n*, rageu❘r, euse.

spittle, *n*, salive, *f*. **spittoon**, *n*, crachoir, *m*.

Spitzbergen, *n*, le Spitzberg.

splash, *n*, (*of water*) gerbe d'eau, *f*; (*into water*) floc, *m*; (*mud, &c*) éclaboussure; (*colour, &c*) goutte, *f*. ~ *board*, garde-crotte, *m*. ¶ *v.t*, jeter; faire jaillir; éclabousser; (*v.i*.) gicler; (*tap*) cracher. ~ *about*, s'agiter.

splay, *v.t*, couper en sifflet, ébraser; (*dislocate*) épauler.

spleen, *n*, (*Anat*.) rate, *f*; (*dumps*) spleen; (*spite*) dépit, *m*.

splendid†, *a*, splendide, magnifique; brillant. **splendour**, *n*, splendeur, magnificence, *f*.

splice, *n*, épissure, *f*. ¶ *v.t*, épisser.

splint, *n*, éclisse, attelle, *f*. ~ [*bone*], péroné, *m*.

splinter, *n*, éclat, *m*, écharde; (*bone*) esquille, *f*. ~ *bar*, volée, *f*. ¶ *v.t*, faire éclater; (*v.i*.) éclater.

split, *n*, fente; fêlure; (*fig*.) scission, *f*. *to do the* ~*s*, faire le grand écart. ¶ *v.t.ir*, fendre; refendre; fractionner; (*ears with noise*) déchirer; (*v.i*.) se fendre, éclater; crever. ~ *hairs*, fendre un cheveu en quatre, pointiller. ~ *peas*[*e*], pois cassés, *m.pl*. ~ *pin*, goupille fendue, *f*. ~*wood*, bois de fente, *m*, éclisse, *f*. *splitting headache*, mal de tête affreux, *m*.

splutter, *n*, pétarade, *f*. ¶ *v.i*, cracher, pétarader.

spoil, *n*, dépouille, *f*, butin, gâteau, *m*. ¶ *v.t*, gâter, gâcher, abîmer; corrompre. ~*sport*, trouble-fête, *m*.

spoke, *n*, rayon, *m*. ~ *shave*, vastringue, *f*. ¶ *v.t*, enrayer.

spoken part (*opera*), parlé, *m*.

spokesman, *n*, porte-parole, organe, *m*.

spoliation, *n*, spoliation, *f*.

sponge, *n*, éponge, *f*; (*gun*) écouvillon, *m*. ~ *bag*, sac à éponge, *m*. ~ *cake*, biscuit de Savoie, *m*. ~ *cloth*, tissu éponge, *m*. ¶ *v.t*, éponger. **sponger**, *n*, pique-assiette, parasite, *m*. **spongy**, *a*, spongieux.

sponsor, *n*, répondant, e; (*Eccl*.) parrain, *m*, marraine, *f*.

spontaneous†, *a*, spontané.

spook, *n*, fantôme, spectre, *m*.

spool, *n*, bobine, *f*; rouleau, *m*. ¶ *v.t*, bobiner.

spoon, *n* & ~ [*bait*], cuiller, cuillère, *f.* ~*bill,* spatule, *f.* ~ *brake,* frein sur pneu, *m.* ¶ (*Croquet*) *v.i,* queuter.

Spoonerism, *n,* contre-petterie, *f.*

spoor, *n,* trace, *f.* erres, *f.pl.*

sporadic, *a,* sporadique.

spore, *n,* spore, *f.*

sport, *n,* badinage; jeu; (*s.* & *pl.*) sport, *m.* ~s *editor,* rédacteur sportif, *m.* ~s *ground,* terrain de jeux, *m.* ~s *suit,* complet de sport, *m.* ¶ *v.i,* jouer. ~ing, *a,* (*dog, gun, &c*) de chasse; (*editor, spirit, &c*) sportif. **sportsman,** *n,* sportif, amateur de sports, *m.*

spot, *n,* tache; macule; piqûre, *f;* pois, *m;* goutte; place, *f,* endroit, site, lieu, *m,* lieux, *m.pl;* (*Bil.*) mouche, *f;* (*Com.*) disponible; comptant, *m.* on the ~, sur [la] place; séance tenante. ~ *light,* projecteur orientable, *m.* ¶ *v.t,* tacher; observer, repérer. **spotted,** *p.p,* tacheté, moucheté. **spotless,** *a,* sans tache.

spouse, *n,* époux, *m,* épouse, *f.*

spout, *n,* goulotte, *f;* bec; jet, *m.* ¶ *v.i.* & *t,* jaillir; déclamer, dégoiser.

sprain, *n,* entorse, foulure, *f.* to ~ one's ..., se fouler le, la ...

sprat, *n,* sprat, *m.*

sprawl, *v.i,* s'étaler, se vautrer.

spray, *n,* poussière [d'eau], gerbe [d'eau] *f;* (*sea*) embrun; (*jewels*) épi, *m;* (*flowers*) gerbe, chute, *f.* (*Need.*) chute, *f;* (*squirt*) vaporisateur, *m.* ¶ *v.t,* pulvériser, vaporiser.

spread, *n,* développement, *m;* envergure; ouverture; propagation, *f;* repas, *m.* ¶ *v.t.ir,* (é)tendre; déployer; répandre; semer; propager; échelonner, répartir, étager.

spree, *n,* noce, bamboche, *f.*

sprig, *n,* brin, *m,* brindille; pointe, *f.*

sprightly, *a,* vif, sémillant, éveillé; gai.

spring, *n,* élan, bond; ressort, *m;* élasticité; source, fontaine; (*arch*) naissance, retombée, *f;* (*season*) printemps, *m;* (*att.*) printanier. ~ *balance,* peson à ressort, *m.* ~ *board,* tremplin, *m.* ~ *chicken,* poussin, *m.* ~ *cleaning,* grand nettoyage, *m.* ~ *mattress.* See box-spring & wire-spring. ~ *onion,* petit oignon, *m,* ciboule, *f.* ~*stoppered bottle,* canette, *f.* ~ *tide,* grande marée, vive-eau, maline, *f.* ¶ *v.i.ir,* s'élancer, bondir; sourdre; dériver. ~ *up,* naître. ~y, *a,* élastique.

sprinkle, *v.t,* répandre; arroser; asperger; saupoudrer; (*book edges*) jasper. **sprinkler,** *n,* arrosoir, *m.*

sprint, *n,* course de vitesse, *f.* ~er, *n,* coureur de vitesse, *m.*

sprite, *n,* [esprit] follet, farfadet, *m.*

sprocket wheel, pignon de chaîne, *m.*

sprout, *n,* pousse, *f,* germe, *m.* ¶ *v.i,* pointer, germer.

spruce, *a,* pimpant. ¶ *n,* sapin, *m.*

sprue, *n,* jet [de coulée] *m.*

sprung (*provided with springs*) *p.a,* à ressorts.

spud (*Agric.*) *n,* béquille, *f.*

spur, *n,* éperon, *m;* (*bird*) ergot; (*mountain*) contrefort; (*Build.*) arc-boutant, *m;* (*fig.*) aiguillon, *m.* on the ~ of the moment, sous l'impulsion du moment. ~ [*post*], borne, *f.* ¶ *v.t,* éperonner, talonner, piquer; aiguillonner. **spurred** (*bird*) *p.a,* ergoté.

spurious, *a,* faux, falsifié, contrefait, illégitime.

spurn, *v.t,* repousser, repousser du pied.

spurt, *v.i,* jaillir, gicler; (*price*) bondir, sauter. ¶ *n,* jet; bond, saut; (*Running*) emballage; (*Rowing*) enlevage, *m.*

sputter, *n,* pétarade, *f.* ¶ *v.i,* pétarader.

spy, *n,* espion, ne; (*police*) mouchard, *m.* ~*glass,* longue-vue, *f.* ~*hole,* judas, *m.* ¶ *v.t.* & *i,* espionner; moucharder; épier.

squab, *n,* pigeonneau, *m.*

squabble, *n,* querelle, *f.* ¶ *v.i,* se chamailler.

squab[by], *a,* boulot.

squad, *n,* escouade, *f;* (*Mil.*) peloton, *m.* ~ *drill,* école de peloton, *f.* **squadron,** *n,* (*Cavalry*) escadron, *m;* (*Navy*) escadre, *f.* (*Air*) escadrille, *f.*

squalid, *a,* crasseux, sordide.

squall, *n,* grain, *m,* rafale, bourrasque, *f.* ¶ *v.i,* brailler. ~y, à grains, à rafales.

squalor, *n,* crasse, *f.*

squander, *v.t,* prodiguer, gaspiller, manger.

square, *a,* carré. ~ *foot,* pied carré, *m.* = 9·2903 sq. decimetres. ~ *inch,* pouce carré, *m.* = 6·4516 sq. centimetres. ~ *meal,* ample repas, *m.* ~ *measure,* mesure de surface, *f.* ~ *mile,* mille carré, *m.* = 259·00 hectares. ~ *root,* racine carrée, *f.* ~ *ruler* & ~ *file,* carrelet, *m.* ~*shouldered,* carré des épaules. ~ *yard,* yard carré, *m.* = 0·836126 sq. metre. ¶ *n,* carré, *m;* (*instrument* & *at right angles*) équerre; (*town*) place, *f;* (*parvis*) parvis, *m;* (*chessboard*) case, *f;* (*pl.*, Bookb.) chasses, *f.pl.* ~ *of glass,* carreau de vitre, *m.* ¶ *v.t,* carrer; équarrir; régler. ~*d paper,* papier quadrillé, *m.* ~[ly], *ad,* carrément.

squash, *v.t,* écraser, écrabouiller; aplatir.

squat, *v.i,* s'accroupir; se blottir, se tapir. ¶ *a,* ragot, boulot, tassé, écrasé.

squeak, *n,* cri, *m.* ¶ *v.i,* crier, piailler. ~er (*Punch's*) *n,* pratique, *f.*

squeal, *n,* cri [perçant] *m.* ¶ *v.i,* crier, piailler.

squeamish, *a,* dégoûté.

squeegee, *n,* racloir, *m.*

squeeze, *n,* compression, *f;* serrement, *m.* ¶ *v.t,* presser; serrer; pincer. ~ *out,* exprimer; (*fig.*) arracher de.

squelch, *v.i,* patauger.

squib, *n,* serpenteau, *m;* (*fig.*) pasquinade, *f.*

squid, *n,* calmar, *m.*

squint, *v.i,* loucher. ~ *over,* bornoyer.

squire, *n,* châtelain, seigneur, *m.*

squirrel, *n,* écureuil, *m.*

squirt, n, seringue, f. ¶ v.t, seringuer; (v.i.) jaillir.

stab, n, coup (de poignard, &c) m. ¶ v.t, percer; poignarder.

Stabat Mater, n, stabat [mater], m.

stability, n, stabilité; consistance, f. stabilize, v.t, rendre stable; (Fin.) stabiliser. stable, a, stable. ¶ n, écurie; cavalerie, f. ~ boy (Turf), lad, m. ¶ v.t, loger; établer.

staccato, a, (note) piquée; (voice) saccadée.

stack, n, (Agric.) meule; (heap) pile, f; (arms) faisceau, m; (chimney) souche, f. ¶ v.t, empiler; mettre en meule.

stadium, n, stade, m.

staff, n, bâton; (pilgrim's) bourdon, m; (Mus.) portée, f; personnel, atelier; (Mil.) État-major, m. ~ officer, officier d'É.-m., m.

stag, n, cerf, (young) hère, m. ~ beetle, cerf-volant, m.

stage, n, estrade, f; échafaud, m; scène, f; théâtre, m; tréteaux, m.pl; platine, f; degré; stade, m, période, f. & m; phase; opération, f; relais, m; étape, traite; section, f. ~ box, [loge d'avant-scène, f. ~ coach, diligence, f; coche, m. ~ effect, effet scénique, artifice de théâtre, m. ~ manager, régisseur, m. ~ name, nom de théâtre, n. de guerre, m. ~ trick, jeu de scène, coup de théâtre, m. ~ whisper, aparté, m. ¶ v.t, mettre en scène, monter. old stager, vieux routier, m.

stagger, v.i, chanceler, tituber; (v.t.) consterner, ébouriffer. ~s (Vet.) n.pl, vertigo, m.

stagnant, a, stagnant; (foul) croupissant. stagnation, n, stagnation, f, marasme, m.

staid, a, posé, rassis.

stain, n, tache; macule; souillure; couleur, f. ¶ v.t, tacher, souiller; colorer; mettre en couleur, teindre. stained glass, verre coloré, m; (church, &c) vitraux peints, m.pl. stained glass artist, peintre verrier, m. stained glass window, verrière, f. stainless, a, sans tache; (steel) inoxydable.

stair, n, marche, f, degré, m. ~ carpet, tapis d'escalier, m. ~case & ~[s], escalier, m. ~ rail, rampe d'e., f. ~ rod, tringle d'e., f. ~way, cage d'escalier, f.

stake, n, pieu, poteau, piquet, jalon; bûcher; intérêt; enjeu, m; mise, f; (pl, Turf) prix, m. ~ boat, bateau-témoin, m. ¶ v.t, jouer; mettre.

stalactite, n, stalactite, f.

stalagmite, n, stalagmite, f.

stale, a, vieux; rassis; éventé; usé; (cheque) prescrit.

stalemate (Chess) n, pat, m. ¶ v.t, faire pat. ~d, p.a, pat.

stalk, n, tige, queue, f; pied, m. ¶ v.t, chasser à l'affût. ~ing horse (fig.), faux-semblant, m.

stall, n, stalle; chaise, f; kiosque; étalage, étal,

m, échope, boutique, f; (Theat.) fauteuil, m. ~ holder, étalagiste, m,f. ¶ v.t, établer.

stallion, n, étalon, m.

stalwart, a, robuste, vigoureux.

stamen, n, étamine, f.

stamina, n, résistance, f, fond, m.

stammer, v.i. & t, bégayer. ~er, n, bègue, m,f.

stamp, n, poinçon; coin; pilon; bocard, m; marque; estampille, f; timbre, m; griffe; trempe, empreinte, f, cachet, sceau, m. ~ duty, droit de timbre, m. ~ office, [bureau du] timbre, m. ¶ v.t. & i, frapper; piétiner, taper, trépigner; poinçonner; bocarder; marquer; étamper; estamper; estampiller; timbrer; affranchir. ~ed addressed envelope, enveloppe affranchie pour la réponse, f.

stampede, n, sauve-qui-peut, m.

stance, n, position, f.

stanch, a. & v.t. Same as staunch.

stanchion, n, étançon, m; (ship) épontille, f.

stand, n, place; station, f; support; établi; pied; socle; affût; (music) pupitre; (exhibition) stand, m; (stall) boutique, f. ~ camera, chambre à pied, f. ~ point, point de vue, m. ~ still, arrêt, m. ¶ v.i.ir, se tenir; se tenir debout; rester debout; se soutenir; stationner; se placer; se mettre; s'arrêter; se porter; tenir; durer; rester; reposer; (v.t.ir.) supporter, soutenir; subir; résister à; souffrir; (drink, &c) payer. ~ aside, se ranger. ~ back! rangez-vous! ~ down, (from witness box) se retirer; (from candidature) se désister. ~ idle, chômer. ~ in the way of, faire obstacle à. ~ on end (hair), [se] hérisser. ~ out, [res]sortir; se détacher, marquer. ~ up, se tenir debout; se lever; se dresser. ~ up collar, faux col montant, faux col droit, m.

standard, n, étendard; (values) étalon, m; (weight, measure) matrice, f; (gold) titre, m; (of coin) loi, f; critère, criterium; niveau, m; toise; classe, f; pied; arbre de plein vent; (Vaulting) sautoir, m. ~ bearer, porte-étendard, m. ¶ att, étalon; type; classique; (gauge) normale; (edition) définitive; (charge) forfaitaire; (gold) au titre; (solution) titrée; (lamp) à pied. ~ize, v.t, unifier; (Chem.) titrer.

standing, n, position; consistance; surface, f. of long ~, de longue date, ancien. ¶ a, debout; (crops) sur pied; (Naut.) dormant; (water) stagnante; (orders, army, &c) permanent, e; (expenses) généraux; (jump, dive) sans élan; (start) arrêté. ~ room only! places debout seulement! ~ start mile, mille, départ arrêté, m. ~ type, conservation, f.

stand-offish, a, distant, réservé. ~ness, n, quant-à-moi, quant-à-soi, m.

stanza, n, stance, strophe, f.

staple, n, (wall) crampon; (wire) cavalier, m; (lock) gâche; (to fasten papers) agrafe, f.

~ [*product*], produit principal, *m*, production principale, *f*.

star, *n*, étoile, *f*; astre, *m*; (*lucky*) étoile, planète; (*Theat*) étoile,. vedette, *f* (*Typ.*) astérisque, *m*. ~**fish**, étoile de mer, *f*. ~**gaze**, bayer aux corneilles. ~ *map*, carte céleste, *f*. ~ *of Bethlehem*, ornithogale, *m*. ~ *shell*, obus à étoiles, *m*. ~ *turn*, clou de la fête, *m*.

starboard, *n*, tribord, *m*.

starch, *n*, amidon, *m*; fécule, *f*; (*paste*) empois, *m*. ¶ *v.t*, empeser, amidonner. ~**y** (*food*), *a*, féculent.

stare, *n*, regard appuyé, *m*. ¶ *v.i*, écarquiller les yeux. ~ *at*, regarder fixement, dévisager.

stark, *a*, raide. ~ *mad*, fou à lier. ~ *naked*, tout nu, nu comme un ver.

starling (*bird*), *n*, sansonnet, étourneau, *m*.

starry, *a*, étoilé.

start, *n*, tressaillement, sursaut, soubresaut, haut-le-corps; commencement, début; départ, *m*; avance, *f*. ¶ *v.i*, tressaillir; partir; commencer, débuter; démarrer; (*v.t*) commencer; amorcer; mettre en marche; lancer; (*quarry*) lancer, débûcher. ~**er**, *n*, (*signal giver*) starter; (*horse, runner*) partant, *m*. ~**ing line**, ligne de départ, *f*. ~**ing post**, poteau de départ, *m*, barrière, *f*.

startle, *v.t*, faire tressaillir, effrayer, effaroucher, alarmer. **startling**, *p.a*, alarmant, saisissant.

starvation, *n*, inanition, faim, famine, *f*. ~ *diet*, diète absolue, *f*. ~ *wage*, salaire de famine, *m*. **starve**, *v.t*, priver de nourriture, affamer; (*v.i.*) mourir de faim. ~**ling**, *n*, affamé, *e*, meurt-de-faim, *m*. **starving**, *p.a*, affamé.

state, *n*, état, *m*; disposition, *f*; apparat, *m* (*stage of engraved or etched plate*) état, *m*. *to lie in* ~ (*of body*), être exposé sur un lit de parade. ~ *controlled*, ~ *managed*, en régie. ~ *insurance*, prévoyance sociale, *f*. ~ *nominated officer*, officier ministériel, *m*. ~ *railway*, chemin de fer de l'État, *m*. ~ *reception*, réception solennelle, *f*. ~ *rooms*, ~ *apartments*, (*palace*) grands appartements [d'apparat]; (*ship*) appartements de luxe, *m.pl*. *S*~ *socialism*, étatisme, *m*. ¶ *v.t*, énoncer; déclarer; relater; annoncer; poser. ~**d**, *p.a*, réglé; certain. ~**liness**, *n*, majesté, *f*. ~**ly**, *a*, majestueux, pompeux, superbe; fier. **statement**, *n*, énoncé, *m*, déclaration, *f*; relevé, état, exposé; bordereau, *m*. ~ *of affairs*, bilan, *m*. ~ *of claim* (*Law*), factum, *m*. **statesman**, *n*, homme d'État, *m*.

static(al), *a. & statics*, *n*, statique, *a. & f*.

station, *n*, station, *f*; poste, *m*; gare, *f*; rang, *m*. ~*s of the Cross*, chemin de la croix, *m*. ~ *master*, chef de gare, *m*. ¶ *v.t*, [a]poster. ~**ary**, *a*, stationnaire; fixe, à demeure.

stationer, *n*, papetier, ère. ~**y**, *n*, papeterie, *f*, fournitures, *f.pl*. ~ *case*, papeterie, *f*. ~ *rack*, classeur, *m*.

statistic(al), *a*, statistique. **statistician**, *n*, statisticien, *m*. **statistics**, *n*, statistique, *f*; mouvement, *m*.

statuary, *a*, statuaire. ¶ *n*, statues, *f.pl*; (*art*) statuaire, *f*; (*pers.*) statuaire, *m*. **statue**, *n*, statue, *f*. **statuette**, *n*, statuette, figurine, *f*.

stature, *n*, stature, taille, *f*.

status, *n*, statut, titre, état, *m*, qualité, *f*.

statute, *n*, loi, *f*; statut, *m*. ~**-barred**, caduc. *to be* ~*-barred*, se prescrire. ~ *book*, code, *m*. ~ *law*, droit écrit, *m*. **statutory**, *a*, légal.

staunch, *a*, étanche; ferme; dévoué. ¶ *v.t*, étancher.

stave, *n*, douve; (*Mus.*) portée, *f*. ~ *wood*, merrain, *m*. ~ *in*, *v.t.ir*, enfoncer, défoncer. ~ *off*, parer.

stay, *n*, séjour; support; étai; tirant; hauban; (*pl.*) corset; (*Law*) sursis, *m*. ~ *in the country*, villégiature, *f*. ¶ *v.i*, rester; demeurer; séjourner; attendre; s'arrêter; (*v.t.*) suspendre; (*Law*) surseoir à; étayer. ~*-at-home*, *a. & n*, casanier, ère, pot-au-feu, *a*. ~ *away*, s'absenter. ~*in strike*, grève sur le tas, *f*. ~ *the course*, fournir la carrière. ~ *up*, veiller. ~**ing power**, fond, *m*.

stead, *n*, lieu, *m*, place, *f*.

steadfast, *a*, constant, ferme. ~**ly**, *ad*, avec constance. ~**ness**, *n*, constance, *f*.

steady†, *a*, ferme; stable; rangé; posé; réglé; suivi. ¶ *i*, fermel

steak, *n*, tranche, *f*; (*beef*) bifteck, *m*.

steal, *v.t. & i. ir*, voler, dérober. ~ *away*, se dérober. ~ *in*, se glisser dans. ~**ing**, *n*, vol, *m*. *by stealth*, à la dérobée. **stealthy**†, *a*, furtif.

steam, *n*, vapeur, *m*; fumée; buée, *f*; (*att.*) à vapeur. ~ *room* (*bath*), étuve humide, *f*. ¶ *v.t*, (*Cook.*) mettre à l'étuvée; (*v.i.*) marcher [à la vapeur]; fumer. ~**er** or ~*boat* or ~*ship*, *n*, vapeur, *m*, bateau à v., navire à v., steamer, *m*. ~**er** or ~*cooker*, *n*, marmite autoclave, *f*. ~**ing** (*Cook.*) *n*, étuvée, étouffée, estouffade, *f*.

stearin, *n*, stéarine, *f*. **steatite**, *n*, stéatite, *f*.

steed, *n*, coursier, *m*.

steel, *n*, acier, *m*; (*of tinder box*) briquet; (*sharpener*) fusil, *m*; (*corset*) baleine, *f*; (*att.*) d'acier, en acier; métallique. ~ *works*, aciérie, *f*. ~*yard*, [balance] romaine, *f*. ¶ *v.t*, acérer; aciérer; (*fig.*) cuirasser.

steep, *a*, raide, escarpé, ardu, fort, rapide. ¶ *v.t*, tremper, baigner. ~*ed in* (*fig.*), pétri de. **steeple**, *n*, clocher [pointu] *m*. ~*chase*, course d'obstacles, *f*. **steepness**, *n*, raideur, *f*, escarpement, *m*.

steer, *n*, bouvillon, *m*. ¶ *v.t. & i*, diriger, conduire, guider; gouverner. ~ *clear of*, éviter. **steerage**, *n*, avant, *m*. ~ *pas-*

senger, passager de l'a., p. d'entrepont, *m.*
steering, *n*, direction; (*Naut.*) gouverne, *f.*
~ *compass*, compas de route, *m.* ~ *wheel* (*Motor.*) volant de direction, *m.*
steersman, *n*, homme de barre, *m.*
stellar, *a*, stellaire.
stem, *n*, tige; queue; *f*; (*ship*) étrave, *f*; (*Gram.*) thème, *m.* ~ *stitch*, point de tige, p. coulé, *m.* ¶ *v.t*, refouler; étaler.
stench, *n*, puanteur, infection, *f.*
stencil, *n*, patron, pochoir; caractère à jour; (*Typing*) stencil, *m.* ¶ *v.t*, patronner.
stenographer, -phist, *n*, sténographe, *m,f.*
stenography, *n*, sténographie, *f.*
stentorian, *a*, de stentor.
step, *n*, pas, *m*; trotte; marche, *f*; degré; gradin; échelon; *m*; démarche, mesure, *f*; acheminement; (*pl.*) marchepied, *m*; échelle double, *f.* ~ *brother*, demi-frère, *m.* ~ *dance*, claquettes, *f.pl.* ~*daughter*, belle-fille, *f.* ~*father*, beau-père, *m.* ~*mother*, belle-mère; (*cruel*) marâtre, *f.* ~ *sister*, demi-sœur, *f.* ~*son*, beau-fils, *m.* ¶ *v.i*, faire un pas; marcher; aller; venir; monter. ~ *in*, entrer. *stepping stone*, pierre à gué, *f*; (*fig.*) marchepied, échelon, *m.*
stereoscope, *n*, stéréoscope, *m.*
stereotype, *n*, cliché, *m.* ¶ *v.t*, clicher, stéréotyper.
sterile, *a*, stérile. **sterility**, *n*, stérilité, *f.* **sterilize**, *v.t*, stériliser.
sterling, *a*, (*Eng. money*) sterling, *a.inv.*; (*fig.*) de bon aloi; solide. ¶ *n*, la livre.
stern†, *a*, sévère; austère. ¶ *n*, arrière, *m*; poupe, *f.* ~*fast*, croupière, *f.* ~*post*, étambot, *m.* ~*sheets*, chambre, *f.* **sternness**, *n*, sévérité; austérité, *f.*
sternum, *n*, sternum, *m.*
stet (*Typ.*), bon. ¶ *v.t*, donner son bon à.
stethoscope, *n*, stéthoscope, *m.*
stevedore, *n*, arrimeur, *m.* **stevedoring**, *n*, manutentions maritimes, *f.pl.*
stew, *n*, ragoût, *m.* ~*pan*, casserole, braisière, *f*; fait-tout, *m.* ¶ *v.t*, étuver; (*abs.*) fricoter. ~*ed*, *p.p*, ragoût de (*mouton, &c*) *m*; compote de (*pommes*, &c) *f.*
steward, *n*, maître d'hôtel; intendant; régisseur; commissaire; homme d'affaires; économe; garçon de cabine; commis aux vivres; délégué, *m.* ~*'s mate* (ship), cambusier, *m.* ~*'s room*, dépense; (*ship*) cambuse, *f.* ~**ess**, *n*, femme de chambre, *f.*
stick, *n*, bâton, *m*; canne, *f*; (*umbrella*) manche, *m*; baguette, *f*; cotret, *m*, (*pl.*) du bois. ~ *seat*, canne-siège, *f.* ¶ *v.t.ir*, piquer; ficher; coller; (*bills*) afficher; (*Hort.*) ramer; (*pig*) saigner; (*v.i.ir.*) s'attacher; [se] coller; adhérer; rester, tenir. ~ *in the mud*, s'embourber. ~ *no bills*, défense d'afficher. ~**er**, *n*, personne collante, *f.* **stickiness**, *n*, viscosité, *f.* *sticking plaster*, emplâtre adhésif, *m.*
stickleback, *n*, épinoche, *f.*

sticky, *a*, collant, gluant, visqueux.
stiff, *a*, raide; fort; rigide; tenace; (*strained*) empesé, guindé; (*price*) salé. ~ *collar*, faux col rigide, *m.* ~ *neck*, torticolis, *m.* ~**en**, *v.t*, raidir. ~**ness**, *n*, raideur; (*in the joints of the body*) courbature, *f.*
stifle, *v.t*, étouffer, suffoquer.
stigma, *n*, stigmate, *m*, flétrissure, tache, *f.* **stigmatize**, *v.t*, stigmatiser.
stile, *n*, échalier, *f.* (*door*) montant, *m.*
stiletto, *n*, stylet, *m.*
still, *a*, calme, tranquille; silencieux; immobile, en repos; (*water*) dormante, morte; (*wine*) non mousseux; (*lemonade*) non gazeuse. ~*born*, mort-né. ~ *life* (*Art*) nature morte, *f.* ¶ *ad*, encore, toujours; cependant; néanmoins, toutefois. ¶ *n*, calme; alambic, *m*, cornue, *f.* ~ *room*, cellier, *m.* ¶ *v.t*, calmer, apaiser, tranquilliser. ~**ness**, *n*, calme, *m*, tranquillité, *f*, silence, *m.*
stilt, *n*, échasse, *f.* ~**ed**, *a*, guindé.
stimulant, *n*, stimulant, remontant, réconfort, *m.* **stimulate**, *v.t*, stimuler. **stimulus**, *n*, stimulant, aiguillon, *m.*
stimy (*Golf*), *n*, trou barré, *m.*
sting, *n*, aiguillon, dard, *m*, piqûre; (*fig.*) morsure, *f.* ¶ *v.t. & i. ir*, piquer; (*of conscience*) bourreler. **stinging**, *p.a*, piquant. ~ *nettle*, ortie brûlante, ortie grièche, *f.*
stingy, *a*, avare, pingre, mesquin, chiche.
stink, *n*, puanteur, *f.* ¶ *v.i.ir*, puer.
stint, *n*, ménagement, *m.* ¶ *v.t*, épargner; rationner. ~ *oneself*, se priver; se rationner.
stipend, *n*, traitement, *m.*
stipple, *n*, pointillé, grené, *m.* ¶ *v.t*, pointiller.
stipulate, *v.t*, stipuler.
stir, *n*, remue-ménage, tapage; mouvement, *m.* *make a* ~, faire florès. ¶ *v.t*, remuer; agiter; (*fire*) attiser; (*the blood*) fouetter; (*v.i.*) remuer, bouger. ~ *up*, exciter, susciter, émouvoir. **stirring**, *p.a*, émouvant; vibrant.
stirrup, *n*, étrier, *f.* ~ *cup*, coup de l'étrier, *m.* ~ *leather*, étrivière, *f.*
stitch, *n*, point [de couture] *m*; (*Knit., Crochet*, &c) maille, *f.* ~ *in the side* (*Med.*), point de côté. ¶ *v.t*, coudre; (*leather*) piquer; (*books*) brocher. ~ *together*, appointer. ~*ed hem*, ourlet piqué, *m.* ~**er**, *n*, piqueuse, *f.* ~**ing**, *n*, point piqué, *m.*
stiver (*fig.*) (*n*) obole, *f.*
stoat, *n*, hermine, *f.*
stock, *n*, (*descent*) race, lignée; (*tree*, *&c*) souche, *f*, estoc; (*rifle, plane*, &c) fût, bois; (*anchor*) jas; (*bell*) mouton; (*bit*) vilebrequin, *m*; (*die*) filière, *f.* (*Hort.*) sujet, portegreffe, (*wild*) sauvageon; (*vine*) cep, *m*; (*flower*) giroflée, *f*, violier, *m*; (*Com.*) existence, *f*, stock, *m*, boutique; provision; ap-

provisionnement; matériel, m; (Fin.) valeur, f. oft. pl, titre, m. oft. pl; effets, fonds, m.pl; actions, f.pl; (Cook.) consommé, m; (pl, Naut.) chantier, m, cale [de construction] f; (pl, Hist.) ceps, m.pl, tabouret, m. in ~, en magasin. ~ & dies, filière garnie. ~s & shares, valeurs mobilières, f.pl, portefeuille[-titres] m. ~broker, agent de change; banquier en valeurs, m. ~ exchange, bourse [des valeurs] f. ~ exchange committee, chambre syndicale des agents de change, f. ~ exchange daily official list, bulletin de la cote, m. ~ farming, élevage, m. ~fish, stockfisch, m. ~holder, détenteur de titres, m; actionnaire, sociétaire, m,f, rentier, ère. ~ in trade, existence en magasin. ~jobbing, affaires de placement & de spéculation, f.pl. ~ phrase, cliché, m. ~ pot, pot-au-feu, m. ~ solution (Phot.), solution fondamentale, f. ~-still, sans mouvement. ~ taking, inventaire; recensement, m. ~ yard, (cattle) parc à bestiaux; (materials) parc à matières, m. ¶ v.t, approvisionner; assortir; peupler; meubler; empoissonner. ~ed by, chez.

stockade, n, palissade, palanque, f.

stockinet, n, jersey, m. **stocking**, n, bas, m.

stocky, a, trapu, ramassé, étoffé.

Stoic, n. & at, stoïcien, m. & a. **stoical†**, a, stoïque. **stoicism**, n, stoïcisme, m.

stoke, v.t, chauffer. ~hole, ~hold, chaufferie, chambre de chauffe, f. **stoker**, n, chauffeur; (mechanical) chargeur, m.

stole, n, étole; écharpe, f.

stolid, a, flegmatique. ~ity, n, flegme, m.

stomach, n, estomac; (fig.) cœur, m. ~ ache, mal d'estomac, m. ~ pump, pompe stomacale, f. ¶ v.t, digérer, avaler. ~ic, a. & m, stomachique, a. & m.

stone, n, pierre; roche, f; caillou, m; (fruit) noyau; (grape) pépin, m; (Meas.) (14 lbs =) 6·350 kilos. ~ breaker (Mach.), casse-pierres, m. ~crop, orpin, m. ~ dead, raide mort. ~ fruit, fruit à noyau, m. ~ jar, pot de grès, m. ~ (gem) setter, metteur en œuvre, m. ~'s throw, jet de pierre, m. ~ware, poterie de grès, f; grès, m, gresserie, f. ~work, maçonnerie, f. ¶ v.t, (to death) lapider; (fruit) vider. **stony**, a, pierreux; cailouteux; (heart, &c) de pierre, de roche[r]; (look) glacé.

stool, n, tabouret; escabeau, m; sellette (Med.) selle, f.

stoop, v.i, se pencher; s'abaisser.

stop, n, arrêt, m; halte; station; pause; opposition, f; (buffer) butoir, m; (Mech.) butée, f; (organ) jeu; (Phot.) diaphragme; (Typ.) point, m. to put a ~ to, faire cesser. ~ & go lights, signaux lumineux de circulation, feux de c., m.pl. ~ blocks (Rly), heurtoir, m. ~ cock, robinet [d'arrêt] m. ~gap, bouche-trou, m. ~ press [news], [informations de la] dernière heure. ~ watch, chronographe; compteur de sport, m. ¶ v.t, arrêter (Naut., &c) stopper; interrompre; suspendre; mettre opposition sur; cesser; (wages) retenir; (leak) boucher, aveugler; (teeth) plomber; (v.i.) s'arrêter; stationner; rester; cesser. ¶ i, halte[-là]!; (Naut., in telegrams, &c) stop.

stope (Min.), n, gradin, m.

stoppage, n, arrêt; chômage, m; retenue; obstruction, f. **stopper**, n, bouchon, m. ¶ v.t, boucher.

storage, n, [em]magasinage, m. **store**, n, approvisionnement, m, provision, fourniture; réserve; resserre, f, magasin, dépôt; entrepôt; économat; (pl.) magasin de nouveautés; bazar, m. ~ curtain, store-panneau, m. ~keeper, garde-magasin; (fig.) meubler; emmagasiner. **storer**, n, dépositaire, m.

storey, n, étage, m. **3-storied** à 3 étages.

stork, n, cigogne, f.

storm, n, orage, m; tempête, tourmente, f. ~ cloud, nuée, f. ~ of abuse, algarade, f. ¶ v.t, donner l'assaut à; (v.i.) tempêter. **stormy**, a, orageux, tempétueux. ~ petrel, pétrel, m. at ~ (barometer), à la tempête.

story, n, histoire, f; conte, m; narration; fable; menterie, f; (floor) étage, m. ~ book, livre de contes, d'histoires, m. ~ teller, conteur, euse; narrateur, trice.

stoup, n, bénitier, m.

stout†, a, fort, vigoureux; robuste; renforcé; brave; gros, corpulent, replet. ¶ (beer) n, stout, m. ~ness (of body) n, embonpoint, m.

stove, n, poêle; fourneau; réchaud, m; étuve, f. ~ & range maker, poêlier, m. ~ brush, brosse à poêles, f.

stow (Naut.) v.t, arrimer. ~ away, v.t, serrer; (v.i.) s'embarquer clandestinement. ~away, n, passager (ère) clandestin(e), enfant trouvé, m.

straddle, v.t. & i, chevaucher.

straggle, v.i, traîner. **straggler**, n, traînard, m. **straggling**, a, (houses) éparses (village) aux maisons éparses; (beard) maigre.

straight, a, droit; (hair) plats; (respectable) honnête. a ~ left, right (Box.), un direct du gauche, du droit. ¶ ad, [tout] droit; directement. ¶ n, ligne droite, f. ~en, v.t, [re]dresser, rectifier. **straightforward**, a, droit. **straightforwardly**, ad, sans détour; carrément. **straightforwardness**, n, droiture, f; sans-façon, m. **straightness**, n, rectitude, f.

strain, n, (molecular) tension; (Mech.) déformation; (overstrain) fatigue, f; (Med.) effort, (Vet.) écart, m; (descent) race; (dash) teinte, f; (pl.) accents, m.pl. ~ in the back, tour de reins, m. ¶ v.t, tendre;

déformer; fatiguer; torturer; (*Med.*, *&c*) forcer; (*filter*) passer, filtrer, tamiser. ~ed (*fig.*) *p.a.* guindé; ~er, *n*, passoire, couloire, *f*, tamis, *m*; crépine, *f*.

strait, *n*, (*s. & pl.*) détroit, pertuis, *m*; (*pl.*) gêne, détresse, *f*, malaise, embarras, *m*. S~s of Dover, [détroit du] Pas de Calais, *m*. S~s of Gibraltar, détroit de Gibraltar. S~s Settlements, Établissements des Détroits, *m.pl.* **strait-laced**, *a*, collet monté, bégueule. **strait waistcoat**, camisole de force, *f*. **in straitened circumstances**, dans la gêne.

strand, *n*, rivage; (*rope*) cordon, toron, brin, *m*. ¶ *v.t. & i*, échouer, engraver.

strange†, *a*, étrange; étranger; bizarre. *he is a ~ mixture*, c'est le merle blanc. **stranger**, *n*, étranger, ère; inconnu, e. **strangeness**, *n*, étrangeté; bizarrerie, *f*.

strangle, *v.t*, étrangler, juguler. ~s (*Vet.*) *n.pl*, gourme; (*fig.*) étranglement, *m*, strangulation, *f*.

strap, *n*, courroie; sangle; bande, *f*, bracelet; tirant; lien, *m*. ~ oil (*fig.*), huile de cotret, *f*. ~ watch, montre [sur] bracelet, *f*. ¶ *v.t*, sangler.

Strasburg, *n*, Strasbourg, *m*.

stratagem†, *n*, stratagème, *m*, ruse, *f*. **strategic(al)†**, *a*, stratégique. **strategist**, *n*, stratège, *m*. **strategy**, *n*, stratégie, *f*.

stratified, *p.p.* stratifié. **stratum**, *n*, couche, *f*, gisement, *m*.

straw, *n*, paille, *f*; fétu; (*drinking*) chalumeau; (*fig.*) fétu, *m*. *the last ~*, le comble [de nos maux]. ~board, carton-paille, *m*. ~-colour[ed], [couleur] paille. ~ envelope (bottle), paillon, *m*. ~ hat, chapeau de paille, *m*. ~ hive (bees), panier, *m*. ~ hut (native), paillote, *f*. ~ mattress, paillasse, *f*.

strawberry, *n*, fraise, *f*. ~ ice, glace aux fraises, *f*. ~ plant, fraisier, *m*.

stray, *v.i*, errer; s'écarter. ¶ *a*, égaré; errant; épave. ~ cat, chat de gouttières, *m*. ¶ *n*, épave, *f*.

streak, *n*, trait, sillon, *m*, raie, bande, *f*. ¶ *v.t*, rayer, sillonner. ~y (*meat*) *a*, entrelardée.

stream, *n*, cours d'eau; ruisseau; flot; jet; filet; cours; torrent, *m*. ~-lined, profilé, fuselé, effilé, [à profil] aérodynamique. ~-lining, aérodynamisme, *m*. ¶ *v.i*, ruisseler. ~er, *n*, flamme, *f*; (*paper*) serpentin, *m*.

street, *n*, rue, *f*; (*s. & pl, fig.*) pavé, *m*. ~ child, ~ arab, gamin(e) des rues, polisson, ne. ~ lamp, réverbère, *m*. ~ musician, musicien de carrefour, *m*.

strength, *n*, force; puissance; résistance; robustesse; intensité, *f*; (*of a solution*) titre; (*men*) effectif, *m*. ~en, *v.t*, renforcer; consolider; fortifier.

strenuous†, *a*, énergique; (*life*) intense.

stress, *n*, effort; travail, *m*; charge; fatigue;

(*weather*) violence, *f*; accent, appui, *m*. *to be in* ~ (*Mech.*), travailler. ¶ *v.t*, charger; fatiguer; appuyer sur; accentuer; (*Mus.*) scander.

stretch, *n*, trait, *m*; étendue, traite; (*of person's arms*) envergure, *f*; parcours; (*Mech.*) allongement, *m*. ~ of fishing, cantonnement de pêche, *m*. ¶ *v.t*, étendre, étirer; allonger; tendre. ~ oneself, s'étirer.

stretcher, *n*, brancard, *m*, civière, *f*; raidisseur; (*for painter's canvas*) châssis, *m*. ~ bearer, brancardier, *m*.

strew, *v.t.ir*, répandre; joncher; [par]semer.

stria, *n*, strie, *f*. **striate[d]**, *a*, strié. **striation**, *n*, striure, *f*.

strickle, *n*, racloire, *f*.

strict†, *a*, strict; formel; rigoureux; sévère; exact. ~ness, *n*, rigueur; sévérité, *f*. ~ure, *n*, critique, *f*; (*Med.*) rétrécissement, *m*.

stride, *n*, enjambée, *f*, pas, *m*; (*pl.*) essor, *m*. ~ along, *v.i.ir*, marcher à grands pas.

strident†, *a*, strident.

strife, *n*, guerre, *f*, conflit, *m*.

strike, *n*, direction; rencontre; (*strickle*) racloire, *f*; (*of pers.*) grève, *f*; (*att.*) gréviste. ¶ *v.t.ir*, frapper; assener, porter; choquer; (*match*) frotter; rencontrer; atteindre; battre; sonner; (*root, v.t. & abs.*) jeter, prendre; (*tent*) plier; (*sail*) caler; (*colours*) amener; (*measure*) racler; (*a balance*) établir, faire; (*fish*) ferrer; (*v.i.ir.*) frapper; sonner; se mettre en grève, faire g. *it ~s me*, il me semble, il me vient l'idée. *without striking a blow*, sans coup férir. ~ down, abattre. ~ off, radier. ~ out, effacer, rayer, radier, biffer. ~ up (tune), entonner. ~er, *n*, gréviste, *m,f*. ~er [-out]† (*Ten.*), relanceur, euse. ~ing, *p.a*, frappant, saisissant; marquant; saillant. ~ clock, pendule à strike, *f*.

string, *n*, ficelle; corde; cordelette, *f*; cordon; tirant; filet, *m*; fibre; filandre, *f*; chapelet; attirail; train, *m*; enfilade, *f*; (*subject*) See under *harp*; (*stairs*) limon; (*Bil.*) bouilier, *m*. *the ~s* (*Mus.*), les cordes. ~ bag, filet à provisions, *m*. ~ band, orchestre à cordes, *m*. ¶ *v.t.ir*, corder; enfiler; (*violin*, *&c*) monter. ~ed, *p.a*, à cordes.

stringent, *a*, rigoureux.

stringy, *a*, fibreux; filandreux.

strip, *n*, bande, *f*; ruban, *m*. ¶ *v.t*, dépouiller; dégarnir; (*v.i.*) se déshabiller.

stripe, *n*, raie, barre, *f*, liteau; (*N.C.O.'s, Navy*) galon, *m*. ~d, *a*, rayé, à raies; tigré, zébré.

strive, *v.i.ir*, s'efforcer, tâcher; combattre.

stroke, *n*, coup, *m*; atteinte, *f*; battement, *m*; course, *f*; trait, *m*; raie, barre; attaque, *f*; coup de sang, *m*; (*Swim.*) nage; brassée, brasse, *f*; (*Rowing*) chef de nage, *m*. ~ play (*Golf*), concours par coups, *m*. *on the ~ of time*, à l'heure sonnante, *f*. ¶ *v.t*, caresser, flatter.

stroll, *n*, tour, *m*, promenade, *f*. ¶ *v.i*, se promener; errer; flâner. **strolling**, *p.a*, ambulant.

strong†, *a*, fort; puissant; vigoureux; énergique; renforcé; résistant; solide; (*flavour*) relevé; (*wind*, *&c*) carabiné; (*language*) corsé; (*well up in*) calé. ~ *box*, coffrefort, *m*. ~ *drink*, liqueurs fortes, *f.pl*. ~*hold*, forteresse, citadelle, *f*, fort, *m*. ~ *man* (professional), hercule, *m*. ~*-minded person*, tête forte, forte tête, *f*. ~*-minded woman*, apôtre des revendications féminines, *m*. ~ *point*, fort, *m*. ~ *room*, cave forte; (*ship*) chambre des valeurs, *f*.

strop, *n*, cuir [à rasoir], affiloir; (*safety blade*) repasseur, *m*. ¶ *v.t*, repasser [sur le cuir, &c].

structural, *a*, · (*steel*, *&c*) de construction; (*repairs*) grosses. **structure**, *n*, structure; construction; formation, *f*; édifice; ouvrage d'art; (*fig*.) échafaudage, *m*.

struggle, *n*, lutte, *f*. ¶ *v.i*, lutter, batailler.

strum, *v.t*, tapoter.

strut, *n*, entretoise; contre-fiche; bielle, *f*. ¶ *v.i*, se pavaner; se rengorger, se carrer.

strychnin[e], *n*, strychnine, *f*.

stub, *n*, souche, *f*, chicot; bout, *m*.

stubble, *n*, chaume, *m*, éteule, *f*.

stubborn†, *a*, obstiné, entêté, têtu; tenace. ~*ness*, *n*, obstination, opiniâtreté; ténacité, *f*.

stucco, *n*, stuc, *m*.

stuck-up, *a*, fier.

stud, *n*, clou; crampon, *m*; pointe, *f*; goujon; bouton; plot [de contact]; (*scantling in wall*) potelet, *m*; (*horses*) écurie, *f*; (*breeding*) haras, *m*. ~ *book*, livre généalogique, stud-book, *m*. ~ *earring*, dormeuse, *f*. ~ *farm*, haras, *m*. ~ *groom*, piqueur, *m*. ~ *horse*, étalon, *m*. ¶ *v.t*, clouter; parsemer, émailler; hérisser. *studded crossing* (street), passage clouté, *m*, les clous, *m.pl*.

student, *n*, élève, *m,f*; étudiant, e; normalien, ne. ~'*s microscope*, microscope d'étude, *m*. **studied**, *p.p*, étudié; recherché; (*deliberate*) voulu. ~ *elegance*, recherche, *f*.

studio, *n*, atelier; théâtre; studio; salon de pose, *m*. **studious**†, *a*, studieux, appliqué.

study, *n*, matière; étoffe, *f*; (*fig*.) bois, *m*. ~ *& nonsense*, fadaises, *f.pl*. ¶ *v.t*, rembourrer; fourrer; bourrer; (*dead animal*) empailler; (*Cook*.) farcir. ~*ing*, *n*, bourre, *f*; (*Cook*.) farce, *f*. ~*y*, *a*, étouffant.

stultify, *v.t*, neutraliser.

stumble, *v.i*, broncher, trébucher, [s']achopper. *stumbling block*, pierre d'achoppement, *f*.

stump, *n*, tronçon; moignon; chicot, *m*; souche, *f*; trognon; bout, *m*; (*Art*) estompe, *f*. ~ *orator*, déclamateur, *m*. ~*y*, *a*, trapu, boulot.

stun, *v.t*, étourdir. *stunning blow*, coup de massue, *m*.

stunt (*Aero*.) *n*, acrobatie, *f*.

stunted, *p.p*, rabougri, avorté, malvenu, chétif.

stupefy, *v.t*, hébéter; (*narcotize*) stupéfier.

stupendous†, *a*, prodigieux.

stupid†, *a*, stupide; bête. ~*ity*, *n*, stupidité; bêtise, *f*. **stupor**, *n*, stupeur, *f*.

sturdy†, *a*, vigoureux, robuste.

sturgeon, *n*, esturgeon, *m*.

stutter, *v.i. & t*, bégayer. ~*er*, *n*, bègue, *m,f*. **sty**, *n*, étable, *f*, toit, *m*. ¶ *v.t*, établer.

sty[e] (*on the eye*) *n*, orgelet, compère-loriot, *m*.

style, *n*, style,· *m*; manière, *f*, genre, goût, chic; nom, *m*; (*firm name*) raison [sociale] *f*. ~ *of hair-dressing*, coiffure, *f*. ¶ *v.t*, qualifier; donner le titre de.

stylet, *n*, stylet, *m*.

stymie (*Golf*) *n*, trou barré, *m*.

stylish†, *a*, élégant, galant, à la mode; chic; coquet.

stylograph, *n*, stylographe, *m*.

suave†, *a*, suave. **suavity**, *n*, suavité, *f*.

sub-acid, *a*, aigre-doux.

subaltern, *n*, [officier] subalterne, *m*.

subconscious, *a. & n*, subconscient, *a. & m*. ~*ness*, *n*, subconscience, *f*.

subcontract, *n*, sous-traité, *m*. ~*or*, *n*, sous-traitant, *m*.

subcutaneous, *a*, sous-cutané.

subdivide, *v.t*, subdiviser, morceler.

subdue, *v.t*, subjuguer, soumettre, assujettir; maîtriser; adoucir; (*light*) adoucir, tamiser.

sub-editor, *n*, secrétaire de la rédaction, *m*.

subject, *n*, sujet; propos, *m*; (*pers*.) sujet, te. ~ *catalogue*, catalogue par ordre de matières, *m*. ¶ *v.t*, soumettre, assujettir. ¶ ~ *to*, sujet(te) à; soumis(e) à; sous [le] bénéfice de; sous réserve de; sauf à. ~*ion*, *n*, sujétion, *f*, assujettissement, *m*; dépendance, *f*. ~*ive*†, *a. & n*, subjectif, *a. & m*.

subjoined, *p.p*, ci-joint.

subjugate, *v.t*, subjuguer.

subjunctive [mood], *n*, subjonctif, *m*.

sublet, *v.t.ir*, sous-louer, relouer.

sublieutenant, *n*, sous-lieutenant; enseigne de vaisseau, *m*.

sublime†, *a. & n*, sublime, *a. & m*. **sublimity**, *n*, sublimité, *f*.

sublunar[y], *a*, sublunaire.

submarine, *a. & n*, sous-marin, *a. & m*.

submerge, *v.t*, submerger; (*v.i.*) plonger.

submission, *n*, soumission, *f*. **submissive**, *a*, soumis, obéissant. ~*ness*, *n*, soumission, résignation, *f*. **submit**, *v.t*, soumettre. ~ *to*, se soumettre à, obéir à; subir.

sub-order, *n*, sous-ordre, *m*.

subordinate, *a*, subordonné, subalterne, en sous-ordre. ¶ *n*, subordonné, e, sous-ordre, *m*. ¶ *v.t*, subordonner.

suborn, *v.t*, suborner, séduire. ~*er*, *n*, suborneur, euse.

subpoena, n, citation, assignation, f. ¶ v.t, citer, assigner, ajourner.

subrogate, v.t, subroger.

sub rosa, sous [le manteau de] la cheminée.

subscribe, v.t. & i, souscrire; s'abonner; se cotiser. subscriber, n, souscripteur, m; abonné, e. subscription, n, souscription; cotisation, f; abonnement, m. ~ dance, bal par souscription, m.

subsection, n, alinéa, m.

subsequent†, a, subséquent, postérieur.

subservience, n, sujétion, f. subservient, a, auxiliaire, subalterne; servile.

subside, v.i, baisser; s'affaisser; [se] calmer. subsidence, n, baisse, f; affaissement, effondrement, m.

subsidiary†, a, subsidiaire; auxiliaire. ~ [company], [société] filiale, f.

subsidize, v.t, subventionner. subsidy, n, subvention, f; subside, m.

subsist, v.i, subsister; vivre. ~ence, n, subsistance, f.

subsoil, n, sous-sol; (Law) tréfonds, m.

substance, n, substance, f; fond; corps; bien, m. substantial, a, substantiel; solide; (lunch) dînatoire. ~ly, ad, substantiellement, en substance. substantiate, v.t, établir.

substantive, a. & n, substantif, a. & m.

substitute, n, succédané, m; (pers.) remplaçant, e; suppléant, e. ¶ v.t, substituer.

substratum, n, fond, m.

substructure, n, substruction, f.

subtenant, n, sous-locataire, m,f.

subterfuge, n, subterfuge, m.

subterranean, a, souterrain.

subtilize, v.t. & i, subtiliser.

subtitle, n, sous-titre, m.

subtle†, a, subtil, raffiné, fin. ~ty, n, subtilité, f, raffinement, m.

subtract, v.t, soustraire, retrancher. ~ion, n, soustraction, f.

suburb, n, faubourg, m, (pl.) banlieue, f. ~an, a, suburbain; de banlieue.

subvention, n, subvention, f.

subversive, a, subversif. subvert, v.t, renverser.

subway, n, passage souterrain, m.

succeed, v.t, succéder à; suivre; (v.i.) succéder; (prosper) réussir, succéder; arriver; parvenir. ~ing, p.a, suivant. success, n, succès, m, réussite, f. ~ful†, a, heureux; réussi. succession, n, succession; suite, f. successive†, a, successif. successor, n, successeur, m.

succinct†, a, succinct. ~ness, n, concision, f.

succour, n, secours, m. ¶ v.t, secourir.

succulent, a, succulent.

succumb, v.i, succomber.

such, a, tel; pareil; semblable. ~ as, tel que; comme.

suck, v.t. & i, sucer; téter; aspirer. ~ in, humer. ~ up, pomper. ~er, n, (of insect) suçoir, m; (of leech) ventouse, f;

(Hort.) drageon, surgeon, m, talle, f, œilleton, m; branche gourmande, f. ~ing pig, cochon de lait, m. ~le, v.t, allaiter, nourrir. ~ling, n, enfant à la mamelle; nourrisson, m. suction, n, succion; aspiration, f. ~ pump, pompe aspirante, f.

sudden†, a, soudain, subit; brusque. ~ turn (road), crochet, m. all of a ~, soudain, subito. ~ness, n, soudaineté, f.

suds, n.pl, eau de savon, f.

sue, v.t, poursuivre, actionner. ~ for, demander.

suède gloves, gants de Suède, m.pl.

suet, n, graisse de rognon, f.

suffer, v.t, supporter; subir; éprouver; tolérer; (v.i.) souffrir; pâtir. ~able†, a, supportable. ~ance, n, souffrance; tolérance, f. ~er, n, victime; f; patient, e. ~ing, n, souffrance, f. ~ing, p.a, souffrant.

suffice, v.i, suffire. ~ it to say that, suffit que. ~iency, n, suffisance; aisance, f. sufficient†, a, suffisant.

suffix, n, suffixe, m. ~ed, p.a, suffixe.

suffocate, v.t, suffoquer; asphyxier. suffocation, n, suffocation; asphyxie, f.

suffragan, a. & n, suffragant, a.m. & m.

suffrage, n, suffrage, m. suffragette, n, suffragette, f.

suffuse, v.t, se répandre sur; baigner. suffusion, n, suffusion, f.

sugar, n, sucre, m. ~ almond, dragée, f. ~ basin, sucrier, bol à sucre, m. ~ beet, betterave à s., f. ~ candy, sucre candi, m. ~ cane, canne à s., f. ~ refiner, sucrier, m. ~ industry, industrie sucrière, i. saccharine, f. ~ refinery, sucrerie, f. ~ sifter, saupoudroir à sucre, m. ~ tongs, pinces à s., f.pl. ¶ v.t, sucrer. ~s, a, sucré; saccharin.

suggest, v.t, suggérer, dicter. ~ion, n, suggestion, f. ~ive, a, suggestif.

suicide, n, suicide, m; (pers.) suicidé, m. to commit ~, se suicider.

suit, n, diligence; requête; instance; cour, f; procès civil; complet; habit; costume, m; (Cards) couleur, f. ~ case, porte-habits, m. ~ of armour, armure complète, f. ~ of clothes, complet, m. ~ to measure, complet sur mesure. ¶ v.t, adapter; approprier; assortir; aller à; convenir à; accommoder; (v.i.) cadrer; convenir. ~ability, n, convenance; adaptation, f. ~able†, a. & ~ed, p.p, convenable, sortable, adapté, approprié, assortissant; propre.

suite, n, suite, f, train, m; enfilade, f. ~ [of furniture], ameublement; mobilier, m. ~ [of rooms], appartement, m, chambres en enfilade, f.pl.

suitings, n.pl, tissus pour vêtements, m.pl.

suitor, n, (Law) plaideur; (wooer) aspirant, prétendant, soupirant, poursuivant, m.

sulk, v.i, bouder. ~y, a, boudeur.

sullen, *a,* renfrogné, maussade, morose. **~ness,** *n,* maussaderie, *f.*

sully, *v.t,* souiller, tacher, ternir.

sulphate, *n,* sulfate, *m.* **sulphide,** *n,* sulfure, *m.* **sulphite,** *n,* sulfite, *m.* ~ *pulp,* pâte au bisulfite, *f.* **sulphur,** *n,* soufre, *m.* ~ *bath,* bain sulfureux, *m.* ~ *mine,* soufrière, *f.* **sulphuretted,** *a,* sulfuré. **sulphuric,** *a,* sulfurique. **sulphurous,** *a,* sulfureux.

sultan, *n,* sultan, *m.* **sultana,** *n,* sultane, *f;* *(pl.)* raisins de Smyrne, *m.pl.*

sultry, *a,* étouffant, lourd, caniculaire.

sum, *n,* somme, *f;* calcul; comble, *m.* ~ *total,* somme totale, *f,* montant global, *m.* ~ **up,** résumer; résumer les débats. **summarize,** *v.t,* résumer. **summary†,** *a,* sommaire. ¶ *n,* sommaire, résumé, *m.*

summer, *n,* été, *m.* ~ *holidays,* grandes vacances, *f.pl.* ~ *house,* pavillon [de jardin], kiosque de j., *m.* ~ *lightning,* éclair[s] de chaleur, *m.[pl.].* ~ *resort,* station estivale, *f.* ~ *time,* heure d'été, *f.* ¶ *v.i,* passer l'été; *(v.t.)* estiver.

summing up, résumé des débats, *m.*

summit, *n,* sommet, *m,* cime, *f,* faîte, comble, *m.*

summon, *v.t,* citer, assigner; sommer; convoquer. ~ *back* & ~ *up,* rappeler. **summons,** *n,* sommation; citation, *f.* ¶ *v.t,* citer.

sump, *n,* puisard, *m.*

sumptuous†, *a,* somptueux; *(fare)* pantagruélique. **~ness,** *n,* somptuosité, *f,* luxe, *m.*

sun, *n,* soleil, *m.* ~ *bath,* bain de s., *m.* ~ *bathing,* bains de s., *m.pl,* insolation, *f.* ~*beam,* rayon de s., *m.* ~ *blind,* store, *m.* ~ *bonnet,* bavolet, *m.* **~burn,** hâle, *m.* **~burnt,** hâlé, basané. *to get* ~*burnt,* se hâler. ~ *dial,* cadran solaire, *m.* ~*flower,* soleil, tournesol, *m.* ~ *helmet,* casque de soleil, *m.* ~*light,* lumière du s., *f.* ~*light treatment,* traitement solaire, *m.* ~*lit,* ensoleillé. ~*rise,* lever du s., *m.* ~*set,* coucher de s., s. couchant, *m.* *at* ~*set* or *at* ~*down,* au coucher du s. ~*shade,* ombrelle; *f,* parasol, *m.* ~*shine,* soleil, *m.* ~*shine roof,* toit découvrable, *m.* ~*shiny day,* jour de s., *m.* ~ *shutter,* persienne, *f.* ~ *spot,* tache du s., *t.* solaire, macule, *f.* ~*stroke,* insolation *f,* coup de s., *m.* ¶ *v.t,* ensoleiller. ~ *oneself,* se chauffer au soleil, lézarder.

Sunday, *n,* dimanche, *m.* *to put on one's* ~ *best,* s'endimancher. ~ *closing,* chômage du dimanche, *m.* ~ *rest,* repos dominical, *m.*

sunder, *v.t,* séparer.

sundries, *n.pl,* [articles] divers, *m.pl.* **sundry,** *a,* divers.

sunken, *p.a,* creux; cave; noyé.

sunless, *a,* sans soleil. **sunny,** *a,* ensoleillé.

sup, *v.i,* souper.

superabundant†, *a,* surabondant.

superannuated, *p.p,* suranné; retraité. *superannuation fund,* caisse des retraites, *f.*

superb†, *a,* superbe.

supercargo, *n,* subrécargue, *m.*

supercilious†, *a,* dédaigneux.

superficial†, *a,* superficiel. **superficies,** *n,* superficie, *f.*

superfine, *a,* superfin, surfin.

superfluity, *n,* superfluité, *f,* superflu, embarras, *m.* **superfluous,** *a,* superflu.

superheat, *v.t,* surchauffer.

superhuman, *a,* surhumain.

super[im]pose, *v.t,* superposer.

superintend, *v.t,* surveiller; présider à. **~ence,** *n,* surveillance, *f.* **~ent,** *n,* surveillant, e; surintendant, e; chef; *(police)* commissaire; *(restaurant)* maître d'hôtel, *m.*

superior†, *a.* & *n,* supérieur, e. **~ity,** *n,* supériorité, *f.*

superlative†, *a,* souverain; *(Gram.)* superlatif. ¶ *n,* superlatif, *m.*

superman, *n,* surhomme, *m.*

supernatural†, *a.* & *n,* surnaturel, *a.* & *m.*

supernumerary *a.* & *n,* surnuméraire, *a.* & *m.* ~ *officer,* officier à la suite, *m.* ¶ *(Theat.)* *n,* figurant, e, comparse, *m,f.*

superscription, *n,* suscription, *f.*

supersede, *v.t,* remplacer.

superstition, *n,* superstition, *f.* **superstitious†,** *a,* superstitieux.

supertax, *n,* impôt de superposition, *m.*

supervene, *v.i,* survenir.

supervise, *v.t,* surveiller, contrôler. **supervision,** *n,* surveillance, *f,* contrôle, *m.* **supervisor,** *n,* surveillant, e, contrôleur, *m.*

supine, *a,* couché sur le dos; indolent; léthargique.

supper, *n,* souper, *m.* *to have* ~, souper. ~ *time,* heure du s., *f.* ~*less,* *a,* sans s.

supplant, *v.t,* supplanter.

supple, *a,* souple. *to make* ~, assouplir.

supplement, *n,* supplément, *m.* ¶ *v.t,* augmenter. **~ary,** *a,* supplémentaire.

suppleness, *n,* souplesse, *f.*

suppliant, *a.* & *n,* suppliant, e. **supplicate,** *v.t,* supplier. **supplication,** *n,* supplication, *f.*

supplier, *n,* fournisseur, euse. **supply,** *n,* provision, fourniture, *f,* approvisionnement, *m;* *(pl.)* subsistances, *f.pl;* crédits, *m.pl;* service, *m.* ~ & *demand,* l'offre & la demande. ~ *[work],* suppléance, *f.* ¶ *v.t,* fournir, approvisionner; pourvoir; assortir de; alimenter; suppléer.

support, *n,* support; soutien; appui; entretien, *m.* ¶ *v.t,* supporter; soutenir; appuyer; entretenir. **~er,** *n,* partisan, tenant, *m,* adhérent, e.

suppose, *v.t,* supposer; présumer. *supposing [that],* suppose que. **supposition,** *n,* supposition, *f.* **supposititious,** *a,* supposé.

suppress, *v.t,* supprimer. ~*ed rage,* rage rentrée, *f.* ~**ion,** *n,* suppression, *f.*

suppurate, *v.i,* suppurer.

supremacy, *n,* suprématie, *f.* **supreme†,** *a,* suprême; souverain.

surcharge, *v.t,* surcharger, surtaxer.

sure†, *a,* sûr; certain; assuré, immanquable. *to make* ∼ *of,* s'assurer de. ∼**ness,** *n,* sûreté, *f.* ∼**ty,** *n,* sûreté; caution, *f.*

surf, *n* barre de plage, *f,* ressac, *m.* ∼ *board,* aquaplane, *m.* ∼ *boat,* pirogue de barre, *f.* ∼ *fishing,* pêche de plage, *f.* ∼ *riding,* sport de l'aquaplane, *m.*

surface, *n,* surface; superficie, *f.* ∼ *mine,* mine à ciel ouvert, minière, *f.* ∼ *plate,* marbre, *m.*

surfeit, *n,* satiété, *f.* ¶ *v.t,* rassasier; blaser.

surge, *n,* houle, *f.* ¶ *v.i,* refluer, ondoyer.

surgeon, *n,* chirurgien; médecin, *m.* **surgery,** *n,* chirurgie; médecine, *f;* cabinet de consultation, *m,* clinique, *f.* **surgical,** *a,* chirurgical. ∼ *case* (*pers.*), opéré, e.

surging, *p.a,* houleux.

surly, *a,* rébarbatif, bourru, maussade.

surmise, *n,* soupçon, *m.* ¶ *v.t,* soupçonner.

surmount, *v.t,* surmonter.

surname, *n,* nom [de famille] *m.*

surpass, *v.t,* surpasser. ∼**ing,** *a,* supérieur; suprême.

surplice, *n,* surplis, *m.*

surplus, *n,* surplus, excédent, *m.* ∼ *stock,* solde, *m.*

surprise, *n,* surprise, *f;* étonnement, *m.* ∼ *attack,* attaque faite à l'improviste, *f,* coup de main, *m.* ¶ *v.t,* surprendre; étonner. **surprising,** *a,* surprenant, étonnant. ∼**ly,** *ad,* étonnamment.

surrender, *n,* reddition, *f;* abandon; (*Insce*) rachat, *m.* ¶ *v.t,* rendre, livrer; abandonner, abdiquer, céder; (*insurance policy*) racheter; (*v.i.*) se rendre.

surreptitious†, *a,* subreptice.

surrogate, *n,* substitut, *m.*

surround, *v.t,* entourer, enceindre, encadrer. ¶ *n,* pourtour, *m.* ∼**ing,** *p.a,* environnant; ambiant. ∼**ings,** *n.pl,* alentours, *m.pl.*

surtax, *n,* surtaxe, *f;* impôt général (*ou* global) sur le revenu, *m.* ¶ *v.t,* surtaxer.

survey, *n,* étude; visite; expertise, *f;* levé [de plans]; arpentage; cadastre; métrage, *m.* ¶ *v.t,* étudier; visiter; expertiser; arpenter; cadastrer; métrer. ∼**or,** *n,* inspecteur; expert; (*land*) arpenteur, géomètre; (*quantity*) métreur; (*roads*) [agent] voyer, *m.*

survival, *n,* survivance, survie, *f.* ∼ *of the fittest,* survivance du plus apte. **survive,** *v.t,* survivre à; (*v.i.*) se survivre. **survivor,** *n,* survivant, e; rescapé, e. ∼**ship,** *n,* survie, *f.*

susceptible, *a,* susceptible, sensible.

suspect, *a,* suspect, interlope. ¶ *n,* suspect, *m.* ¶ *v.t,* suspecter; se douter de.

suspend, *v.t,* suspendre. ∼**er,** *n,* jarretelle; bretelle, *f.* ∼ *belt,* ceinture porte-jarretelles, *f.* **suspense,** *n,* incertitude, *f.* *in* ∼, en suspens, en souffrance. ∼ *account,* compte d'ordre, *m.* **suspension,** *n,*

suspension, *f.* ∼ *bridge,* pont suspendu, *m.* *suspensory bandage,* suspensoir, *m.*

suspicion, *n,* soupçon; nuage, *m;* (*Law*) suspicion, *f.* **suspicious†,** *a,* soupçonneux; suspect; louche.

sustain, *v.t,* soutenir; sustenter; éprouver. ∼**ing,** *p.a,* (*power*) soutenant; (*food*) qui soutient. **sustenance,** *n,* subsistance, nourriture, *f.*

sutler, *n,* vivandier, ère.

suture, *n,* suture, *f.*

suzerain, *n,* suzerain, e. ∼**ty,** *n,* suzeraineté, *f.*

swab, *n,* torchon; (*Naut.*) fauber[t]; (*Med.*) écouvillon, *m.*

swaddling clothes (*lit. & fig.*), langes, *m.pl.*

swage, *n,* étampe, *f.* ¶ *v.t,* étamper.

swagger, *v.i,* se rengorger, se carrer; faire le fanfaron. ∼**er,** *n,* fanfaron, bravache, *m.*

swain, *n,* berger, *m.*

swallow, *n,* hirondelle, *f;* gosier, *m;* (*river*) perte, *f.* ∼*-tail* (*coat*), queue-de-morue, queue-de-pie, *f.* ¶ *v.t,* avaler; engloutir.

swamp, *n,* marais, marécage, *m,* grenouillère, *f.* ¶ *v.t,* inonder, faire submerger; engloutir, noyer. *be* ∼*ed* (*boat*), s'emplir. ∼**y,** *a,* marécageux.

swan, *n,* cygne, *m.* ∼*'s-down,* duvet de cygne; (*cloth*) molleton, *m.* ∼ *song,* chant du cygne, *m.*

sward, *n,* [tapis de] gazon, *m,* herbette, *f.*

swarm, *n,* (*bees*) essaim; (*multitude*) essaim, *m,* nuée, milliasse, potée, *f.* ¶ *v.i,* (*bees*) essaimer; pulluler, fourmiller, foisonner.

swarthy, *a,* noir; noiraud, basané.

swash, *v.i,* clapoter.

swastika, *n,* svastika, *m.*

swat (*fly*) *v.t,* tuer. (*Cf. fly swat*[*ter*].)

swath, *n,* javelle, *f;* (*path cut*) andain, *m.*

swathe, *v.t,* emmailloter.

sway, *n,* balancement; empire, *m;* domination, puissance, *f.* ¶ *v.t,* balancer; influencer.

swear, *v.i. & t. ir,* jurer; prêter serment; (*witness, &c*) assermenter.

sweat, *n,* sueur; suée, *f.* ¶ *v.i. & t,* suer; ressuer; exploiter. ∼ *profusely,* suer à grosses gouttes. ∼**er,** *n,* exploiteur, euse; (*vest*) chandail, *m.* ∼**ing room** (*bath*), étuve sèche, *f.* ∼**y,** *a,* suant.

Swede, *n,* Suédois, e. *s*∼, *n,* navet de Suède, chou-navet, rutabaga, *m.* **Sweden,** *n,* la Suède, *f.* **Swedish,** *a,* suédois. ∼ *drill,* gymnastique suédoise, *f.* ¶ *n,* le suédois.

sweep, *n,* coup de balai; coup, mouvement; (*pers.*) ramoneur, *m;* boucle, courbe; étendue, *f.* ¶ *v.t. & i. ir,* balayer; (*chimney*) ramoner; (*Naut.*) draguer. ∼ *away,* enlever. ∼ *the board,* rafler le tout. ∼**er,** *n,* balayeur, euse; (*Mach.*) balayeuse, *f.* ∼**ing gesture,** geste large, *m.* ∼**ings,** *n.pl,* balayures, *f.pl.* ∼**stake**[*s*], *n,* poule, *f;* sweepstake, *m,* loterie, *f.*

sweet†, *a*, doux; sucré; (*wine*) liquoreux; suave; charmant; gentil, mignon. **~bread**, ris de veau, *m*. **~ briar**, églantine odorante, *f*; (*bush*) églantier odorant, *m*. **~heart**, amoureux, euse, inclination, *f*. **~ herbs**, herbes fines, *f.pl.* **~ omelet[te]**, omelette aux confitures, *f*. **~meat**, sucrerie, *f*, bonbon, *m*. **~ oil**, huile douce, *f*. **~ pea**, pois de senteur, *m*. **~ potato**, patate, *f*. **~[-scented]**, odorant, odoriférant. *to have a ~ tooth*, aimer les sucreries. **~william**, œillet de poète, *m*. **the ~** (*opp.* the bitter), le doux. ¶ *n*, entremets [sucré], plat sucré; bonbon, sucrerie, *f*; (*pl.*) douceurs, *f.pl.* **~en**, *v.t*, sucrer; adoucir. **~ies**, *n.pl*, du nanan. **~ish**, *a*, douceâtre. **~ness**, *n*, douceur; suavité, *f*; charme, *m*.

swell, *n*, bombement; renflement, *m*; (*sea*) houle, *f*; (*pers.*) élégant, e. ¶ *a*, chic. **~ mob[smen]**, la haute pègre. ¶ *v.t & i. ir*, enfler, s'e.; gonfler; se g.; renfler; grossir; dilater; bouffer, gondoler. **swelling**, *n*, enflure, grosseur, fluxion, *f*; gonflement, renflement, *m*.

swelter, *v.i*, étouffer de chaleur.

swerve, *n*, crochet, *m*, embardée, *f*. ¶ *v.i*, faire une embardée; s'écarter, se départir.

swift†, *a*, rapide, vite. **~-footed**, au pied léger. ¶ *n*, martinet, *m*. **~ness**, *n*, rapidité, célérité, vélocité, *f*.

swig, *v.t*, lamper, sabler.

swill, *v.t*, laver à grande eau, lessiver; (*drink*) lamper.

swim, *n*, tour de nage, *m*. *in the ~*, dans le mouvement. ¶ *v.i. & t. ir*, nager. **~ across**, passer à la nage. **~ under water**, nager entre deux eaux. **swimming**, *n*, natation, *f*. **~ bath**, **~ pool**, bassin de n., *m*, école de n., piscine, *f*. **~ costume**, *swim suit*, maillot de bain, *m*.

swindle, *n*, escroquerie, *f*. ¶ *v.t*, escroquer. **swindler**, *n*, escroc, filou, *m*.

swine, *n*, pourceau, porc, cochon, *m*. **~ herd†**, porcher, ère.

swing, *n*, oscillation, *f*, balancement; branle, *m*; balançoire, escarpolette, *f*. *in full ~*, en pleine activité. **~ bridge**, pont tournant, *m*. **~ door**, porte va-et-vient, *f*. ¶ *v.t. & i. ir*, balancer; se b.; osciller; branler; basculer; tourner.

swingletree, *n*, volée, *f*.

swirl, *n*, tourbillon; remous, *m*. ¶ *v.i*, tourbillonner, tournoyer.

swish, *n*, sifflement; frou-frou, *m*. ¶ *v.t*, remuer.

Swiss, *a*, suisse. **~ guard**, suisse, *m*. **~ roll**, bûche, *f*. ¶ *n*, Suisse, *m*, Suissesse, *f*.

switch, *n*, badine, houssine; (*Rly*) aiguille, *f*; (*Elec.*) interrupteur, *m*. **~back**, montagnes russes, *f.pl.* **~ board**, tableau de distribution, *m*. ¶ *v.t*. **~ off**, couper, mettre hors circuit; (*light*) éteindre. **~ on**, mettre en circuit; (*light*) allumer.

Switzerland, *n*, la Suisse.

swivel, *n*, émerillon; tourniquet, *m*. ¶ *v.i*, pivoter, tourner.

swollen glands, des glandes au cou, *f.pl.*

swoon, *n*, évanouissement, *m*, défaillance, *f*. ¶ *v.i*, s'évanouir, [s'] pâmer.

swoop down on, fondre sur.

sword, *n*, épée, *f*; sabre; (*Poet.*) glaive, *m*; (*in fun*) flamberge, *f*. **~ belt**, ceinturon, *m*. **~fish**, espadon, *m*. **~ rattler**, ferrailleur, *m*. **~ stick**, canne à épée, *f*. **swordsman**, *n*, lame, *f*. **swordsmanship**, *n*, escrime, *f*.

Sybarite, *n*, sybarite, *m*.

sycamore, *n*, sycomore, *m*.

sycophant, *n*, sycophante, *m*.

syllabize, *v.t*, scander. **syllable**, *n*, syllabe, *f*.

syllabus, *n*, programme; (*Eccl.*) syllabus, *m*.

syllogism, *n*, syllogisme, *m*.

sylph, *n*, sylphe, *m*, sylphide, *f*.

sylvan, *a*, champêtre, bocager.

symbol, *n*, symbole, *m*. **~ic(al)**, *a*, symbolique. **~ize**, *v.t*, symboliser.

symmetric(al)†, *a*, symétrique. **symmetry**, *n*, symétrie, *f*.

sympathetic, *a*, sympathique. **~ strike**, grève de solidarité, *f*. **sympathize**, *v.i*, sympathiser, compatir. **sympathy**, *n*, sympathie, *f*.

symphony, *n*, symphonie, *f*.

symptom, *n*, symptôme, *m*.

synagogue, *n*, synagogue, *f*.

synchronous, *a*, synchrone.

syncopate, *v.t*, syncoper. **syncopation &** **syncope**, *n*, syncope, *f*.

syndicate, *n*, syndicat, *m*. ¶ *v.t*, syndiquer.

synod, *n*, synode, *m*. **~ic(al)**, *a*, synodique.

synonym, *n*. **& synonymous**, *a*, synonyme, *m. & a.*

synopsis, *n*, argument, sommaire, *m*.

synovitis, *n*, synovite, *f*.

syntax, *n*, syntaxe, *f*.

synthesis, *n*, synthèse, *f*. **synthetic(al)†**, *a*, synthétique.

Syria, *n*, la Syrie, *f*. **Syrian**, *a*, syrien. ¶ *n*, Syrien, ne.

syringa, *n*, seringa, *m*.

syringe, *n*, seringue, *f*. ¶ *v.t*, seringuer.

syrup, *n*, sirop, *m*. **~y**, *a*, sirupeux.

system, *n*, système; régime; réseau, *m*. **~atic†**, *a*, systématique.

T

T, *n*, T, té, *m*. **~ square**, té [à dessin] *m*. *to a ~*, tout craché.

tab, *n*, patte, *f*; onglet, *m*.

tabby cat, chat moucheté, chat tigré, *m*.

tabernacle, *n*, tabernacle, *m*.

table, *n*, table; tablette, *f*; bureau; plateau; tableau; plan; décompte, *m*. **~ centre**, centre de table, milieu de t., *m*. **~ cloth**, nappe [de t.] *f*. **~ companion**, convive,

m.f. ~ *cover*, tapis de t., *m.* ~-*cut*
(gem), en table. ~ *fowl*, poularde, *f.*
~ *fruit*, fruit de t., f. à couteau, *m.*
~ *gramophone*, phonographe coffret, *m.*
~ *knife*, couteau de t., *m.* ~ *land*, plateau,
m. ~ *mat*, dessous de plat, *m.* ~
napkin, serviette de t., *f.* ~ *salt*, sel fin,
m. ~ *runner*, chemin de t., jeté de t., *m.*
~*spoon*, cuiller à bouche, c. à soupe, *f.*
~*spoonful*, cuillerée à bouche, *f.* ~ *talk*,
propos de t., *m.pl.* ~ *water*, eau minérale
[naturelle] *f.* ¶ *v.t.* déposer sur le bureau.
tableau, *n. & i.* tableau, *m. & i.* **tablet**, *n.*
table, tablette, plaque; *f.* pain, *m.* ~ *for
inscription*, table d'attente, table rase.
taboo, *n,* tabou, *m.* *he, it, is* ~, il est
tabou. ¶ *v.t.* déclarer tabou.
tabular, *a,* en forme de tableau. **tabulate**,
v.t. dresser en forme de tableau.
tacit, *a,* tacite. **taciturn**, *a,* taciturne.
~**ity**, *n,* taciturnité, *f.*
tack, *n,* (*s. & pl.*) broquette, (*pl.*) semence;
(*Naut.*) bordée, f, bord, *m;* (*of sail*) amure,
f. ¶ *v.t.* clouer avec de la broquette, de
la **semence**; (*Need.*) bâtir; (*fig.*) coudre;
(*v.i.*) virer de bord, louvoyer. ~*ing
cotton*, coton à bâtir, *m.*
tackle, *n,* engin, *m.* oft. *pl;* appareil, *m.* oft. *pl;*
harnais, *m;* agrès, *m.pl;* treuil; palan;
(*Foot.*) arrêt, *m.* ~ *block*, moufle, *f.* or *m.*
~ *fall*, courant de palan; garant, *m.*
¶ *v.t.* s'attaquer à; (*Foot.*) plaquer; (*pers.,
fig.*) entreprendre.
tacky, *a,* collant, visqueux.
tact, *n,* tact, doigté, savoir-faire, *m,* ménagements, *m.pl.* ~**ful**, *a,* [plein] de tact.
~**less**, *a,* dépourvu de tact, malhabile.
tactical, *a,* tactique. **tactician**, *n,* tacticien,
manœuvrier, *m.* **tactics**, *n.pl,* tactique, *f.*
tactile, tactual, *a,* tactile.
tadpole, *n,* têtard, *m.*
taffeta, *n,* taffetas, *m.*
taffrail, *n,* couronnement, *m.*
tag, *n,* (*lace, &c*) ferret; (*boot*) tirant; (*stock
phrase*) cliché, *m;* (*old story*) rengaine, *f;*
[jeu du] chat, *m.* ~ *label*, étiquette
volante, *f.* ~*rag* [*& bobtail*], canaille, *f.*
¶ *v.t.* ferrer.
Tagus (the), le Tage.
Tahiti, *n,* Taïti, Tahiti, *m.*
tail, *n,* queue, *f;* arrière; aval; derrière; (*coat,
&c*) pan, *m,* basque; (*coin*) pile; (*book page*)
queue, tranche inférieure, *f.* ~ *coat or
tails*, (*evening*) queue-de-morue, queue-de-
pie; (*morning*) jaquette, *f.* ~*piece*, cul-de-
lampe, *m.* ~ *stock* (lathe), contre-pointe,
f. ~**ings**, *n.pl,* résidus, *m.pl;* (*grain*)
grenaille, *f.*
tailor, *n,* tailleur, *m.* ~*made or* ~*ed*, [fait
par] tailleur. ~**ess**, *n,* couturière, *f.*
~**ing**, *n,* métier de tailleur, *m.*
taint, *n,* infection; tache, tare, *f.* ¶ *v.t.*
corrompre, infecter; souiller. ~**ed** (*meat,
&c*) *p.a,* gâté, faisandé.

take, *v.t.ir,* prendre; porter; conduire; mener; faire; mettre; relever; tirer; tenir;
supposer; falloir; (*v.i.*) prendre. ~ *away*,
emmener, ôter; [r]emporter. ~ *back*,
ramener; reprendre. ~ *cover*, se garer.
~ *down*, descendre; décrocher; démonter.
~ *down* [*in shorthand*], sténographier.
~ *in*, prendre; recevoir; faire; embrasser;
attraper; (*Aero.*) décoller, prendre son
vol; (*Jump.*) faire l'appel. ~-*off* (*Jump.*),
appel, *m.* ~ *on* (hands), embaucher.
~ *out*, ôter; retirer; arracher; sortir;
(*Insce policy*) contracter. ~ *over*, prendre.
~ *shape*, se dessiner. ~ *to*, s'appliquer à; s'adonner à, mordre à. ~ *to
pieces*, désassembler, démonter. ~ *to
task*, prendre à partie, morigéner. ~
up, relever; lever; monter; s'occuper de;
occuper, tenir; prendre; (*shares*) enlever;
(*option*) lever, consolider. ~ *your seats!*
(in carriage), en voiture! **taker**, *n,* preneur,
euse. **taking**, *a,* séduisant, avenant. ¶ *n,*
prise, *f;* (*pl.*) recette, *f.* oft. *pl,* produit, *m.*
~ *off* (*Aero.*), décollage, envol, *m.*
talc, *n,* talc, *m.*
tale, *n,* conte, *m,* histoire, nouvelle, *f.*
~*bearer*, rapporteur, euse.
talent, *n,* talent, *m.* ~**ed**, *a,* de talent.
talisman, *n,* talisman, *m.*
talk, *n,* conversation, causerie, *f,* entretien;
discours, *m;* propos, *m.pl;* bavardage, *m.*
¶ *v.i. & t,* parler; causer; converser;
bavarder. ~**ative**, *a,* parlant, causeur,
loquace. ~**er**, *n,* parleur, euse, causeur,
euse; bavard, e. ~**ing**, *a,* parlant; (*film*)
parlé, parlant; (*bird*) parleur.
tall, *a,* grand; haut. ~**ness**, *n,* (*pers.*)
haute taille; (*steeple, &c*) hauteur, *f.*
tallow, *n,* suif, *m.* ¶ *v.t.* suifer.
tally, *n,* (*stick*) taille; marque, *f;* (*check*)
pointage, *m;* (*label*) étiquette, *f.* ~ *trade*,
commerce à tempérament, *m.* ¶ *v.i,*
concorder, correspondre, cadrer, se rapporter. ~-**ho**, *i,* taïaut!
talon, *n,* serre, *f;* (*counterfoil*) talon, *m.*
talus, *n,* talus, *m.*
tamarind, *n,* tamarin, *m.*
tambour, *n,* tambour, métier [à broder] *m.*
~**ine**, *n,* tambour de basque, *m.*
tame, *a,* apprivoisé; (*fig.*) anodin. ~ *rabbit*,
lapin(e) domestique, l. de clapier, l. de
choux. ¶ *v.t,* apprivoiser, dompter. **tamer**,
n, dompteur, euse.
tam-o'-shanter, *n,* béret écossais, *m.*
tamp, *v.t,* bourrer; damer, pilonner.
tamper with, falsifier; (*witness*) suborner.
tampion, *n,* tampon, *m.*
tan, *n,* tan, *m.* ~ *yard*, tannerie, *f.* ¶ *v.t,*
tanner; brunir, hâler, basaner. ¶ *a,* tanné.
tandem, *n,* tandem, *m.* ¶ *a. & ad,* en tandem.
tang, *n,* goût; montant, *m;* salure; (*shank*)
soie, queue, *f. there is a* ~ *in the air,*
l'air est vif.

tangent, n, tangente, f. ~[ial], a, tangent.

tangerine, n, mandarine, f.

tangible, a, tangible, palpable.

Tangier, n, Tanger, m.

tangle, n, enchevêtrement, m. ¶ v.t, enchevêtrer, emmêler.

tango, n, tango, m.

tank, n, réservoir, m, citerne; bâche; cuve; caisse à eau, soute, f; (Mil.) char d'assaut, tank, m. ~ steamer, bateau-citerne à vapeur, m.

tankard, n, pot (d'étain) m.

tanner, n, tanneur, m. ~y, n, tannerie, f.

tannin, n, tanin, tannin, m.

tantalize, v.t, mettre au supplice. tantalum, n, tantale, m. tantalus, n, cave à liqueurs, f.

tantamount to (to be), équivaloir à.

tantrums, n.pl, nerfs, m.pl; bourrasques, f.pl.

tap, n, tape, f, coup; (water, &c) robinet; (screw) taraud, m. ~ dance, claquettes, f.pl. ~ root, racine pivotante, f, pivot, m. ¶ v.t. & i, taper; toucher; frapper; (screw) tarauder; (cask) mettre en perce; (tree, &c) saigner; (Surg.) faire une ponction à.

tape, n, ruban, m; tresse; bande, f. ~ machine, télégraphe imprimeur, m. ~ measure, mesure à ruban, f; mètre à r.; centimètre, m; roulette, f. ~worm, ver solitaire, ténia, m.

taper, n, bougie filée; (coiled) bougie de poche, f, pain de bougie, rat de cave; (church) cierge; cône, m. ¶ v.t, fuseler, fuseler; (v.i.) aller en diminuant; se terminer en pointe. ~[ing], a, conique, fuselé.

tapestry, n. & ~ work, tapisserie, f.

tapioca, n, tapioca, m.

tapir, n, tapir, m.

tapis (to be on the), être sur le tapis.

tar, n, goudron; brai; (pers.) loup de mer, m. ~ macadam, macadam au goudron, m. ~ spraying, goudronnage, m. ¶ v.t, goudronner. ~ & feather, emplumer.

tarantella, n, tarentelle, f. tarantula, n, tarentule, f.

tardy†, a, tardif.

tare, n, vesce, (pl, fig.) ivraie; (Com.) tare, f.

target, n, cible, f, but, m. ~ practice, tir à la cible, m.

tariff, n, tarif, m. ¶ v.t, tarifer.

tarn, n, lac de cirque, m.

tarnish, v.t, ternir; (v.i.) se ternir.

tarpaulin, n, bâche goudronnée, f, prélart, m.

tarragon, n, estragon, m.

Tarragona, n, Tarragone, f.

tarry, a, bitumineux.

tarry, v.i, séjourner; tarder; attendre.

tarsus, n, tarse, m.

tart†, a, aigre, âcre, acide. ¶ n, (open) tarte, f; (covered) tourte, f.

tartan, n, tartan, m.

tartar, n, tartre, m. ~ic, a, tartrique.

tartness, n, aigreur, âcreté, acidité, f.

task, n, tâche, besogne, f; devoir, m. to

take to ~, prendre à partie, morigéner. ¶ v.t, mettre à l'épreuve; fatiguer.

Tasmania, n, la Tasmanie.

tassel, n, gland, m, houppe, f; (book) signet, m.

taste, n, goût; gré; échantillon, m. ¶ v.t. & i, goûter; g. de; (tea, wine, &c) déguster. ~ of, sentir le, la, les. ~ful, a, de bon goût. ~less, a, sans goût, fade, insipide. taster, n, dégustateur, m; (cheese) sonde, f. tasting, n, gustation; dégustation, f. tasty, a, savoureux.

tata, i, adieu!; au revoir!

tatter, n, haillon, lambeau, m. ~ed, a, déguenillé; en lambeaux.

tatting, n, frivolité, f.

tattle, n, babil[lage] m. ¶ v.i, babiller. tattler, n. & tattling, a, babillard, e.

tattoo, n, tatouage, m; (Mil.) retraite, f. ¶ v.t, tatouer; (v.i.) tambouriner.

taunt, n, sarcasme, m. ¶ v.t, houspiller, molester. ~ with, reprocher à.

taut, a, raide, tendu. ~en, v.t, raidir.

tautologic(al), a, tautologique. tautology, n, tautologie, f.

tavern, n, taverne, f, cabaret, m. ~ with gardens & dance hall, guinguette, f.

taw, v.t, mégisser.

tawdriness, n, faux éclat, m. tawdry, a, qui a un faux éclat. ~ finery, oripeaux, m.pl.

tawny, a, fauve; basané. ~ owl, chat-huant, m, hulotte, f.

tax, n, impôt, m, taxe, contribution, imposition, f. ~ collector, percepteur, collecteur d'impôts, m. ~ dodger, fraudeur (euse) des droits du fisc, m.f. ~ free, net d'impôts. ~payer, imposé, e, contribuable, m.f. ¶ v.t, imposer; taxer. ~able, a, imposable. ~ation, n, taxation, f, impôts, m.pl.

taxi (Aero.) v.i, rouler [sur le sol]. ~ [cab], taxi, m. ~ driver, ~ man, chauffeur de taxi, conducteur de taxi, m. ~meter, compteur, m.

taxidermist, n, naturaliste [fourreur] m, empailleur, euse. taxidermy, n, empaillage, empaillement, m.

tea, n, thé, m; infusion, tisane, f. ~ caddy, boîte à thé, f. ~ cloth, linge à thé, m. ~ cosy, couvre-théière, m. ~ cup, tasse à thé, f. ~ gown, négligé, déshabillé, m. ~ party, thé, m. ~ plant, thé, m. ~ pot, théière, f. ~ roll, & butter, thé complet. ~ room(s), salon de thé, m, pâtisserie, f. ~ rose, rose thé, f. ~ spoon, cuiller à thé, f. ~ time, l'heure du thé, f.

teach, v.t. & i, ir, enseigner, instruire; apprendre; professer; montrer à; (bird) seriner. ~ someone a lesson, donner une leçon à quelqu'un. ~ someone manners, donner à quelqu'un une leçon de politesse. ~er, n, instituteur, trice; professeur; précepteur, m; maître, esse. ~ing, n, enseignement, m; instruction, f.

teak, n, teck, tek, m.

teal, n, sarcelle, f.

team, n, attelage, m; équipe, f. ~ *race,* course par équipes, f. ~ *spirit,* esprit de corps, m. ~ *work,* travail d'équipe, m.

tear, n, déchirure, f; accroc, m. ¶ v.t.ir, déchirer; arracher. ~ *one another to pieces,* s'entre-déchirer.

tear, n, larme, f, pleur, m. ~ *gas,* gaz lacrymogène, m. ~ful, a, éploré, larmoyant.

tease, v.t, taquiner; lutiner; tourmenter. ¶ (pers.) m, taquin, e.

teasel, n, chardon à bonnetier, c. à foulon, m. ¶ v.t, lainer.

teaser, n, (pers.) taquin, e; problème, casse-tête, m. **teasing,** n, taquinerie, f.

teat, n, bout du sein, mamelon, tétin, m.

technical†, a, technique; d'ordre t. ~ *offence,* quasi-délit, m. ~ *school,* école pratique, f. **technique,** n, technique, f, faire, mécanisme, m. **technology,** n, technologie, f.

ted, v.t, faner. **tedder,** n, faneuse, f.

Teddy bear, ours [martin], o. de peluche, m.

Te Deum, n, Te Deum, m.

tedious†, a, ennuyeux, fastidieux, fatigant. ~ness & tedium, n, ennui, m.

tee, n, té, T; (Golf) dé, m. to a ~, tout craché. ¶ (Golf) v.t, surélever. ~ing ground (Golf), tertre de départ, m.

teem with, fourmiller de, regorger de.

teens (in one's), adolescent.

teethe, v.i, faire ses dents. **teething,** n, dentition, f.

teetotal, a, antialcoolique. ~ism, n, antialcoolisme, m. **teetotaller,** n, buveur d'eau, m.

teetotum, n, toton, m.

tegument, n, tégument, m.

telegram, n, télégramme, m, dépêche, f. **telegraph,** n, télégraphe, m. ~ *board* (Sport), tableau, m. ~ *boy,* ~ *messenger,* petit télégraphiste, facteur des télégraphes, m. ~ *office,* [bureau du] télégraphe, m. ¶ v.t. & i, télégraphier. ~ese, n, style télégraphique, m. ~ic†, a, télégraphique. ~y, n, télégraphie, f.

telepathy, n, télépathie, f.

telephone, n, téléphone, m. ¶ v.t. & i, téléphoner. ¶ att. & telephonic, a, téléphonique. **telephony,** n, téléphonie, f.

telescope, n, (reflecting) télescope, m; (refracting) lunette, f; (spy-glass) longue-vue, f. ¶ v.i, se télescoper. **telescopic,** a, télescopique; (sliding) à coulisse.

televise, v.t, envoyer par télévision. **television,** n, télévision, f.

tell, v.t. & i. ir, dire; [ra]conter; narrer; apprendre; savoir; reconnaître; (of remark, &c) porter; (in one's favour) militer. ~er, n, (voting) scrutateur; (bank) caissier, m. ~ing, a, qui porte. ~tale, n, (pers.) rapporteur, euse; (Mach.) contrôleur, témoin, m.

temerity, n, témérité, f.

temper, n, caractère, m; humeur; trempe; colère, f. ¶ v.t, (metal) tremper; (mortar) gâcher; (fig.) tempérer, mitiger. **temperament,** n, tempérament, m. ~al, a, constitutionnel; capricieux, fantasque. **temperance,** n, tempérance, f. **temperate,** a, tempérant, sobre; (climate, speech) tempéré. **temperature,** n, température, f.

tempest, n, tempête, f. **tempestuous,** a, tempétueux.

template, -plet, n, gabarit, calibre, m.

temple, n, temple, m; (Anat.) tempe, f.

temporal†, a, temporel. **temporary†,** a, temporaire, momentané. **temporize,** v.i, temporiser.

tempt, v.t, tenter; inviter; affriander. ~ation, n, tentation, f. **tempter, tress,** n, tentateur, trice, séducteur, trice. **tempting,** a, tentant, séduisant; (food) appétissant, ragoûtant.

ten, a, dix. ¶ n, dix, m; dizaine, f. ~fold, a. & ad, décuple, a. & m. to increase ~, décupler.

tenable, a, tenable; soutenable. **tenacious,** a, tenace. ~ly, ad, avec ténacité.

tenancy, n, location, f. **tenant,** n, locataire, m,f; (farm) fermier, ère. ~ *farmer,* fermier, ère. ~'s *repairs,* réparations locatives, f.pl. ~able, a, logeable.

tench, n, tanche, f.

tend, v.t, garder; soigner; (v.i.) tendre; conspirer. ~ency, n, tendance; disposition, f. **tendentious,** a, tendancieux. **tender,** n, soumission; offre; (boat) annexe, f; (Rly) tender, m. ¶ v.t, offrir; donner. ~ *for,* soumissionner.

tender†, a, tendre; sensible; délicat. ~ness, n, tendresse; délicatesse; (eatables) tendreté, f.

tendon, n, tendon, m.

tendril, n, vrille, main, f.

tenement, n, habitation, f, logement, m. ~ *house,* habitation à bon marché, m.

Teneriffe, n, Ténériffe, f.

tenet, n, dogme, m, doctrine, f.

tennis, n, tennis, m. ~ *court,* jeu de tennis [court de] tennis, m.

tenon, n, tenon, m. ~ *saw,* scie à t., f.

tenor, n, teneur; (bill) échéance, f; (voice, singer) ténor, m. ~ *clef,* clef d'ut, f.

tense, a, tendu, raide. ¶ n, temps, m. **tension,** n, tension, f.

tent, n, tente; (Surg.) mèche, f. ~ *pole,* mât de t., m. ~ *umbrella,* parasol, m.

tentacle, n, tentacule, m.

tentative [effort], tâtonnement, m.

tenterhook, n, crochet [du fabricant de drap]; clou à crochet, m. on ~s, sur des charbons [ardents], sur le gril, au supplice.

tenth†, a, dixième. ¶ n, dixième, m,f; dix, m.

tenuity, n, ténuité, f. **tenuous,** a, ténu.

tenure, n, possession; jouissance, f; mode de possession; exercice, m. during his ~ of office, pendant l'exercice de ses fonctions.

tepid†, *a*, tiède. **~ness**, *n*, tiédeur, *f*.

term, *n*, terme, *m*; clause; durée; session, *f*; trimestre, *m*; (*pl.*) conditions, *f.pl*; pied; prix, *m*; (*pl.*, opp. [*for*] *cash*) à crédit; (*pl.*) rapports, *m.pl*, intelligence; teneur, *f*; accommodement, *m*. ¶ *v.t*, appeler.

termagant, *n*, mégère, *f*, dragon, *m*.

terminable, *a*, résoluble. **terminal**, *a*, terminal; de tête de ligne. ¶ *n*, borne, *f*; (*Com.*) livrable, *m*. **terminate**, *v.t*, terminer; résoudre. **termination**, *n*, terminaison; fin, *f*. **terminus**, *n*, terminus, *m*.

termite, *n*, termite, *m*, fourmi blanche, *f*.

tern, *n*, sterne, *m*.

terrace, *n*, terrasse, *f*. ¶ *v.t*, étager.

terracotta, *n*, terre cuite, *f*. *a* ~, une terre cuite.

terra firma, la terre ferme, le plancher des vaches.

terrestrial, *a*, terrestre.

terrible†, *a*, terrible.

terrier, *n*, [chien] terrier, *m*.

terrific†, *a*, terrible. **terrify**, *v.t*, terrifier.

territorial, *a. & n*, territorial, *a. & m*. **territory**, *n*, territoire, *m*.

terror, *n*, terreur, *f*. **~ize**, *v.t*, terroriser.

terse, *a*, concis. **~ness**, *n*, concision, *f*.

tessellated pavement, mosaïque, *f*.

test, *n*, épreuve, *f*, essai, *m*; pierre de touche, *f*. ~ *glass & ~ tube & ~ piece*, éprouvette, *f*. ~ *paper*, papier réactif, *m*. ~ *piece* (*Mus., &c*), morceau de concours, *m*. ¶ *v.t*, essayer, éprouver; (*eggs*) mirer.

testament, *n*, testament, *m*. **~ary**, *a*, testamentaire. **testator**, **trix**, *n*, testateur, trice. **testicle**, *n*, testicule, *m*. **testify**, *v.t. & i*, témoigner. **testimonial**, *n*, attestation, *f*; certificat, *m*. **testimony**, *n*, témoignage, *m*.

testy, *a*, irritable, irascible.

tetanus, *n*, tétanos, *m*.

tether, *n*, longe, *f*. *at the end of one's* ~, au bout de son rouleau. ¶ *v.t*, mettre au piquet.

Teutonic, *a*, teutonique, teuton.

text, *n*, texte, *m*. ~ *book*, manuel, *m*. ~ *hand*, grosse, *f*.

textile, *n*, textile, tissu, *m*. ¶ *a*, textile.

textual†, *a*, textuel; (*error*) de texte.

texture, *n*, texture, tissure, *f*, tissu, *m*, contexture, *f*.

Thames (the), la Tamise.

than, *c. & pr*, que; de.

thank, *v.t*, remercier; bénir. ~ *God!* Dieu merci! ~ *Heaven!* grâce au ciel! ~ *oneself*, s'en prendre à soi-même. ~ *you!* & *no* ~ *you!* merci! **~ful**, *a*, reconnaissant. **~fully**, *ad*, avec reconnaissance. **~fulness**, *n*, reconnaissance, gratitude, *f*. **~less**, *a*, ingrat. thanks, *n.pl*, remerciements, *m.pl*.; ¶ *i*, merci! ~ *to*, grâce à. **thanksgiving**, *n*, action[s] de grâce, *f.*[*pl.*].

that, *a. & pn*, ce, cet, cette; ce . . ., & *c*, -là; celui, celle; cela, ça; ce, c', ç'; qui; que;

là. ~ *is all*, c'est tout; voilà tout. ~ *is to say*, c'est-à-dire. ¶ *c*, que; afin que; pour que.

thatch, *n*, chaume, *m*. ¶ *v.t*, couvrir en c. *~ed cottage*, chaumière, *f*. **~er**, *n*, couvreur en chaume, *m*.

thaw, *n*, dégel, *m*. ¶ *v.t. & i*, dégeler; se d.; (*fig.*) dégeler; se dégeler; se déraidir.

the, *art*, le, l', m, la, l', *f*, les, m,f.pl; *from* ~, of ~, du, de l', de la, des. *to* ~, *at* ~, au, à l', à la, aux.

theatre, *n*, théâtre, *m*. **theatrical†**, *a*, de théâtre, du théâtre; théâtral, scénique. ~ & *fancy costumier*, costumier, *m*. **theatricals**, *n.pl*, comédie, *f*.

thee, *pn*, te; toi.

theft, *n*, vol, *m*.

their, *a*, leur, leurs (*pl.*). **theirs**, *pn*, le leur, la leur, les leurs; à eux, à elles.

theism, *n*, théisme, *m*. **theistic(al)**, *a*, théiste.

them, *pn*, eux, elles; les; leur; ceux, celles. **~selves**, eux[-mêmes], elles[-mêmes]; se.

theme, *n*, thème; sujet; (*Mus.*) motif, *m*.

then, *ad*, alors; ensuite; puis; donc; lors. **thence**, *ad*, de là. **thenceforth**, **thenceforward**, *ad*, dès lors.

theodolite, *n*, théodolite, *m*.

theologian, *n*, théologien, *m*. **theological†**, *a*, théologique. **theology**, *n*, théologie, *f*.

theorem, *n*, théorème, *m*. **theoretic(al†)**, *a*, théorique. **theorist**, *n*, théoricien, *m*. **theory**, *n*, théorie, *f*.

theosophy, *n*, théosophie, *f*.

therapeutic, *a. & ~s*, *n.pl*, thérapeutique, *a. & f*.

there, *ad*, là; y; là-bas; il. ~ & *back*, aller & retour. ~ & *then*, séance tenante, sur-le-champ, tout de go. ~ *is* ~ *are*, il y a. *~about*[*s*], par là; environ. **~by**, par là; de cette manière. **~fore**, c'est pourquoi; donc, aussi, par conséquent. **~on**, là-dessus. **~upon**, sur ce, là-dessus. **~withal**, en outre.

thermal, *a*, thermal. **thermometer**, *n*, thermomètre, *m*.

these, *a. & pn*, ces; ces . . . -ci; ceux-ci; celles-ci.

thesis, *n*, thèse, *f*.

thews, *n.pl*, nerfs, *m.pl*.

they, *pn*, ils, elles; eux, elles; ceux, celles; il; ce, c'; on.

thick, *a*, épais; dense; puissant; gros; gras; dru; fourni; touffu; (*with someone*) lié. ~ *or clear* (soup)? potage ou consommé? **~lipped**, lippu. **~set**, trapu, ramassé; dru. ~ *stroke*, plein, *m*. **~[ly]**, *ad*, épais; dru. *in the* ~ *of*, au fort de. *through* ~ & *thin*, envers & contre tous. **~en**, *v.t*, épaissir; (*sauce*) lier. **~ening**, *n*, épaississement, *m*; (*for sauce*) liaison, *f*. **~et**, *n*, fourré, bosquet, *m*. **~ness**, *n*, épaisseur; puissance, *f*.

thief, *n*, voleur, euse, larron, *m*. **thieve**, *v.t*, voler. **thieves' kitchen**, officine, *f*. **thievish**, *a*, de voleur; (*pers.*) voleur.

thigh, n, cuisse, f. ~ *bone*, os de la c., m.
~ *boots*, bottes cuissardes, f.pl.

thill, n, limon, brancard, m.

thimble, n, dé [à coudre] m; (*Naut.*) cosse, f.
~*rigger*, joueur de gobelets, m. ~ful, n,
doigt, m.

thin, a, mince; maigre; délié, ténu; faible;
clair; (*hair, grass, &c*) rare; (*legs, voice*)
grêle. ~ *air* (*fig.*), eau de boudin, f.
to be ~*-skinned* (*fig.*), avoir l'épiderme
sensible. ~ *slice*, mince tranche, lèche, f.
~ *stroke*, délié, m. ¶ *v.t.*, amincir, amenuiser; éclaircir; amaigrir.

thine, pn, le tien, la tienne, les tiens, les
tiennes; à toi.

thing, n, chose; affaire, f; (*pers.*) être, m; (*pl.*)
effets, m.pl. *the* ~ (in fashion), de mise.

think, v.t. & i. ir, penser; songer; juger;
réfléchir; croire; trouver; s'imaginer. ~er,
n, penseur, m. thinking, a, pensant.
¶ n, pensée; réflexion, f; avis, m.

thinly, ad, clair. ~ *sown*, semé clair,
clairsemé. thinness, n, minceur, ténuité;
maigreur; rareté, f. thinnish, a, maigrelet.

third†, a, troisième; tiers. ~ *finger*, [doigt]
annulaire, m. ~ *person*, tiers, m; tierce
personne, f; (*Gram.*) troisième personne, f.
¶ n, tiers, m; tierce, f; troisième, m,f;
trois, m. ~ *of exchange*, troisième de
change, f.

thirst, n, soif, f. ~*-creating*, altérant. ~
for, avoir soif de. thirsty, a, altéré;
(*country*) de la soif. *to be* ~, avoir soif.

thirteen, a. & n, treize. a. & m. ~ *as*
twelve, treize douze. ~th†, a. & n,
treizième. a. & m,f; treize, m.

thirtieth, a. & n, trentième. a. & m,f; trente,
m. thirty, a. & n, trente. a. & m.
~*-two-mo* or 32mo, a. & n, in-trente-
deux, in-32, a.m. & m.

this, a. & pn, ce, cet, cette; ce . . , &c, -ci;
celui-ci, celle-ci; ceci; présent. ~ *day*
week, d'aujourd'hui en huit. ~ *way!*
par ici! ~ *way & that*, çà & là.

thistle, n, chardon, m. ~ *down*, duvet
du chardon, m.

thong, n, lanière, f.

thorax, n, thorax, m.

thorn, n, ~ [*bush*] n, épine, f. ~y, a,
épineux.

thorough, a, achevé; accompli; approfondi;
minutieux; parfait. ~*bred* [*horse*], cheval
pur sang, c. de race, c. racé, m. ~*fare*,
voie, f, passage, m; rue [passante]; artère, f.
~ly, ad, à fond, foncièrement; mûrement;
complètement; parfaitement.

those, a. & pn, ces; ces . . . -là; ceux, celles;
ceux-là; celles-là, f.

thou, pn, tu; toi. ¶ v.t, tutoyer.

though, c, quoique, bien que, quand; cependant, tout . . . que. as ~, comme si.

thought, n, pensée; réflexion; idée, f. ~
reader, liseur (euse) de pensées. ~ful, a,
pensif, réfléchi. ~less†, a, étourdi; irré-

fléchi. ~lessness, n, étourderie; irréflexion, f.

thousand, a, mille; mil. ¶ n, mille; millier,
m. ~th, a. & n, millième, a. & m.

thraldom, n, servage; esclavage, m. thrall,
n, serf, m, serve, f; esclave, m,f.

thrash, v.t, battre, rosser. ~ing, n, peignée, f.

thread, n, fil, m; corde, f; filament, filé
(*screw*) filet; (*screw pitch*) pas, m; (*of life*)
trame, f. ~*bare*, usé jusqu'à la corde,
râpé; usé. ¶ v.t, enfiler; (*screw*) fileter.

threat, n, menace, f. ~en, v.t, menacer.

three, a. & n, trois, a. & m. ~*-colour*
process, trichromie, f. ~*-master*, trois-
mâts, m. ~*-ply* [*wood*], contreplaqué en
trois, bois plaqué triplé, m. ~*-quarter*
binding, demi-reliure amateur, f. ~*-*
score [*years*] & *ten*, soixante-dix ans, m.pl.
~*-some*, partie de trois, f. ~*-speed gear*,
dispositif à 3 vitesses, m. ~fold, a, triple.

thresh, v.t, battre, dépiquer. ~ *out*, vider.
~er (*pers.*) n, batteur en grange, m.
~ing machine, batteuse, f.

threshold, n, seuil, pas, m.

thrice, ad, trois fois.

thrift, n, économie, épargne, f. ~less, a,
prodigue, dépensier. ~y, a, économe,
ménager.

thrill, n, tressaillement, saisissement, frisson,
m, vive émotion, f. ¶ v.t, électriser; empoigner; (*v.i.*) tressaillir, palpiter. ~ing,
a, passionnant, palpitant, empoignant.

thrive, v.i.ir, prospérer; (*plant*) se plaire.
not to ~, se déplaire. thriving, a, florissant, prospère.

throat, n, gorge, f; gosier, m. ~ *register*,
voix de gorge, f.

throb, v.i, battre, palpiter; (*Med.*) élancer.

throe, n, douleur, f; (*pl.*) affres, f.pl.

throne, n, trône, m; (*bishop's*) chaire, f.

throng, n, foule, presse, f. ¶ v.t, accourir
en foule à; assiéger; (*v.i.*) se presser.

throstle, n, grive chanteuse, f.

throttle, n, gosier; régulateur; étrangleur, m.
¶ v.t, étrangler.

through, pr, à travers; au t. de; par; à
cause de. ~ *thick & thin*, envers & contre
tous. ¶ ad, à travers; au t.; de part en
part, à jour; jusqu'au bout; d'un bout à
l'autre; directement. ¶ a, direct; à forfait, forfaitaire. ~ *portion* (*Rly*), rame
directe, f. ~ *rate*, taux à forfait, t. forfaitaire, m. ~ *ticket* (*to final destination*)
billet direct; (*sea-land-sea*) billet global, m.
~out, pr, par tout; pendant tout; (*ad.*)
complètement, jusqu'au bout.

throw, n, jet, m; (*Mech.*) excentricité, f.
~*in*, rentrée en touche, f. ¶ *v.t.ir*, jeter;
lancer; démonter; terrasser; tomber;
mettre. ~ *away*, jeter. ~ *back*, rejeter.
~ *down*, ~ *over*, renverser. ~ *open*,
ouvrir. ~ *out*, chasser; rejeter. ~ *up*,
jeter en l'air; se démettre de. ~ing, n,
lancement, m.

thrum, *v.t*, tapoter (*on* = sur); (*v.i.*) tambouriner.

thrush, *n*, grive, *f*.

thrust, *n*, coup, *m*; (*Fenc.*) botte, estocade; (*Mech.*) poussée, butée, *f*. ¶ *v.t.ir*, pousser; plonger; (*sword*) pointer; (*Fenc.*) estocader; imposer. ~ *aside*, repousser. ~ *at* (*Fenc.*), porter une botte à.

thud, *n*, coup sourd, son mat; floc, *m*.

thug, *n*, étrangleur, *m*.

thumb, *n*, pouce, *m*. ~ *index*, répertoire à onglets, *m*. ~ *nut*, écrou à oreilles, papillon, *m*. ¶ *v.t*, feuilleter.

thump, *n*, coup sourd, *m*; bourrade, *f*, horion, *m*. ¶ *v.t*, cogner, dauber.

thunder, *n*, tonnerre, *m*, foudre, *f*. ~*bolt*, foudre, *f*, coup de foudre, tonnerre, *m*; (*pl, Jove's*) foudres, traits, *m.pl*. ~ *clap*, coup de tonnerre, *m*. ~*cloud*, nuée, *f*. ~*storm*, orage, *m*. ~*struck*, foudroyé. ¶ *v.i. & t*, tonner; fulminer. ~**y**, *a*, orageux.

Thursday, *n*, jeudi, *m*.

thus, *ad*, ainsi, de cette façon. ~ *far*, jusqu'ici.

thwack, *n*, coup, *m*. ¶ *v.t*, frapper.

thwart, *n*, banc [de nage] *m*. ¶ *v.t*, croiser, contrecarrer, traverser.

thy, *a*, ton, ta, tes.

thyme, *n*, thym (*m*); (*wild*) serpolet, *m*.

thyroid, *a*, thyroïde.

thyself, *pn*, toi-même; toi; te.

tiara, *n*, tiare, *f*.

Tiber (the), le Tibre.

tibia, *n*, tibia, *m*.

tic, *n*, tic, *m*.

Ticino (the), le Tessin.

tick, *n*, toile de matelas; *f*; coutil, *m*, toile à matelas; (*insect*) tique, *f*, acare; tic tac; point, *m*; seconde, *f*. ~*tack*, tic tac, *m*. ¶ *v.i*, battre; (*v.t.*) pointer.

ticket, *n*, billet; bulletin; cachet, *m*; entrée; carte; étiquette, *f*. ~ *collector*, contrôleur, *m*. ~ *window*, guichet [de distribution des billets] *m*. ¶ *v.t*, étiqueter.

tickle, *v.t. & i*, chatouiller. **ticklish**, *a*, chatouilleux; critique, délicat, scabreux.

tidal, *a*: ~ *basin*, bassin de marée, *m*. ~ *water*, eaux à m., *f.pl*. ~ *wave*, flot de la marée, raz de m., *m*, barre de flot, *f*.

tide, *n*, marée, *f*; courant, *m*. ~*way*, lit de la marée, *m*. *to tide over a difficulty*, tirer d'affaire.

tidiness, *n*, propreté, *f*, bon ordre, *m*.

tidings, *n.pl*, nouvelles, *f.pl*.

tidy, *a*, bien tenu, rangé; (*pers.*) ordonné. ¶ *n*, vide-poches, *m*. ¶ *v.t*, ranger. ~ *oneself up*, s'ajuster, faire un bout de toilette.

tie, *n*, lien, *m*; attache, *f*; tirant, *m*; cravate, *f*; nœud, *m*; (*Mus.*) liaison; (*Voting*) égalité de voix; (*Sport*) égalité de points, *f*, ex æquo, *m*. ~ *clip*, fixe-cravate, *m*. ~*pin*, épingle de cravate, *f*. ¶ *v.t.ir*, lier;

attacher; clouer; (*knot*) faire; (*v.i.*) (*Sport*) arriver à égalité; (*exams*) être [classé] ex æquo. ~ *down*, lier; astreindre. ~ *up*, lier; bander; mettre à l'attache.

tier, *n*, rangée, *f*, rang, étage, gradin, *m*.

tierce, *n*, tierce, *f*.

Tierra del Fuego, la Terre de Feu.

tiff, *n*, fâcherie, pique, difficulté, *f*.

tiger, *n*, tigre, *m*. ~ *cat*, chat-tigre, *m*. ~ *lily*, lis tigré, *m*.

tight, *a*, serré; tendu; raide; étroit, juste; collant; étanche. ~ *corner*, coin étranglé; mauvais pas, *m*. ~**en**, *v.t*, [res]serrer, tendre; raidir. ~[**ly**], *ad*, serré; étroitement. ~**ness**, *n*, tension, raideur; étroitesse; étanchéité, *f*. **tights**, *n.pl*, maillot, *m*.

tigress, *n*, tigresse, *f*.

Tigris (the), le Tigre.

tile, *n*, tuile, *f*; carreau, *m*; (*pl, roof*) gouttières, *f.pl*. ~ *floor[ing]*, carrelage, *m*. ~ *maker*, tuilier, *m*. ~ *works*, tuilerie, *f*. ¶ *v.t*, couvrir de tuiles; carreler.

till, *n*, caisse, *f*, tiroir de c., *m*. ¶ *v.t*, labourer. ¶ *pr*, jusqu'à; jusque; avant; à. ¶ *c*, jusqu'à ce que; en attendant que. **tillage**, *n*, labourage, *m*. **tiller**, *n*, laboureur, *m*; barre [du gouvernail] *f*.

tilt, *n*, bâche; joute; inclinaison, *f*. ¶ *v.t*, incliner; culbuter; (*v.i.*) s'incliner; jouter. **tilting** (*Hist.*) *n*, joute, *f*. ~ *at the ring*, jeu de bague, *m*. ~ *the bucket*, jeu de baquet, *m*.

timber, *n*, bois [de charpente] (*m*); (*ship*) couple, *m*. ~ *tree*, arbre de haute futaie, *m*. ~*tree forest*, futaie, *f*. ~ *work*, charpente [en bois] *f*. ~ *yard*, chantier de bois, *m*. ¶ *v.t*, boiser. ~**ing**, *n*, boisage, *m*.

timbre, *n*, timbre, *m*.

Timbuctoo, *n*, Tombouctou, *m*.

time, *n*, temps; moment, *m*; époque; saison, *f*; siècle, *m*; heure; fois, reprise, *f*; terme, *m*; mesure; cadence, *f*; pas, *m*. *at* ~*s*, parfois. [*just*] *in* ~, à point. (*work, &c*) *of* ~, de longue haleine. ~ *bargain*, marché à terme, *m*. ~ *fuse*, fusée à temps, *f*. ~*honoured*, séculaire. ~*keeper* (*pers.*), pointeur, contrôleur; (*Sport*) chronométreur, *m*. ~*piece*, pendule, pendulette, *f*. ~*server*, opportuniste, *m,f*, caméléon, *m*, complaisant, e. ~ *sheet*, feuille de présence, *f*. ~ *signal*, signal horaire, *m*. ~ *table*, (*book*) indicateur; (*placard & scheme of work*) horaire, *m*. ¶ *v.t*, (*watch*) régler; (*Sport*) chronométrer. ~**ing**, *n*, pointage, *m*. **timeliness**, *n*, opportunité, *f*. **timely**, *a*, opportun.

timid†, *a*, timide, peureux. ~**ity**, *n*, timidité, *f*. ~ **timorous**, *a*, timoré.

tin, *n*, étain (*m*); (*can*) bidon, *m*; boîte [métallique] *f*. ~ *foil*, feuille d'étain, *f*. ~ *loaf*, pain platine, *m*. ~ *opener*, ouvre-boîte, *m*. ~ [*plate*], fer-blanc, *m*. ~*soldier*, soldat de plomb, *m*. ~*smith*, ferblantier, *m*. ~ *tack*, (*s. & pl*.) broquette, (pl.) semence, f. ~ware, ferblanterie, f. ¶ v.t. étamer; mettre en boîte(s), m. en conserve. tinned foods, conserves, f.pl. tinned salmon, saumon en boîte(s) m.

tincture, n, teinture, f. ¶ v.t. teindre.

tinder, n, mèche, f; (German) amadou, m. ~ box, briquet, m.

tine, n, dent, branche, f; (deer) andouiller, m.

tinge, n, teinte, nuance, f. ¶ v.t. teinter.

tingle, v.i, picoter; fourmiller; (ears) tinter.

tinker, n, chaudronnier ambulant, m.

tinkle, v.i, tinter. ~! ~! drelin-drelin!

tinsel, n, clinquant, m, oripeaux, m.pl; (fig.) faux brillant, m.

tint, n, teinte, f, ton, m. ¶ v.t. teinter.

tiny, a, minuscule, petiot, infime. ~ bit, tantinet, tout petit peu, m. ~ drop, gouttelette, f.

tip, n, bout; bec, m; pointe; extrémité, f; (wing) fouet; (Bil. cue) procédé; (gratuity) pourboire, m, pièce, f; (information) tuyau; (dump) chantier de dépôt, m. ¶ v.t. embouter; basculer; culbuter; verser; donner un pourboire à; donner un tuyau à. ~ cart, tombereau, m. ~-up seat, strapontin, m.

tipcat, n, bâtonnet, m.

tippet, n, palatine, f, mantelet, m.

tipping the bucket, jeu de baquet, m.

tipple, v.i, buvoter, chopiner. tippler, n, biberon, ne.

tipster, n, donneur de tuyaux, m.

tipsy, a, ivre. a ~ gait or walk, une démarche avinée. ~ cake, gâteau au madère, m.

tiptoe (on), sur la pointe du pied.

tiptop, n, comble, m. ¶ a, excellent, parfait.

tirade, n, tirade, incartade, f.

tire, n, bandage; pneu[matique], caoutchouc, m. ¶ v.t. embattre, bander, ferrer.

tire, v.t, fatiguer, lasser, excéder; (v.i.) se fatiguer, se lasser. ~d out, rompu [de fatigue]. ~less, a, infatigable. ~some, a, fatigant; ennuyeux, fâcheux.

tiro, n, commençant, e, novice, m,f, écolier, ère.

tissue, n, tissu, m; tissure, f. ~ paper, papier de soie, m.

tit (bird) n, mésange, f. ~ for tat, donnant donnant; un prêté [pour un] rendu.

titbit, n, bonne bouche, f.

tithe, n, dîme, f. not a ~, pas un dixième.

titillate, v.t, titiller, chatouiller.

titivate, v.t, bichonner.

titlark, n, pipi[t], m.

title, n, titre; intitulé; parchemin, m. ~ [deed], titre, m. ~ page, page du titre, f, titre, frontispice, m. ~d, a, titré.

titmouse, n, mésange, f.

titter, v.i, rire bêtement, glousser.

tittle, n, iota, m. ~tattle, n, commérage, m.

titular, a, titulaire, en titre.

to, pr, à; de; pour; afin de; en; dans; envers; vers; jusqu'à; chez; auprès de, près de; sur;

contre; (of the hour) moins. to go ~ & fro, aller de long en large, aller deçà, delà; aller & venir, faire la navette. ~ be called for, bureau restant, poste restante; télégraphe restant; gare restante, en gare. ~ be kept cool, dry or in a cool, dry, place, craint la chaleur, l'humidité. ~ be taken after meals, à prendre après les repas. ~ boot, en sus, par surcroît, avec ça. ~ match, pareil. ~ measure, sur mesure. ~ wit, savoir; (of pers.) nommément.

toad, n, crapaud, m. ~ hole, crapaudière, f. ~stone, crapaudine, f. ~stool, champignon [vénéneux] m. toady, n, flagorneur, euse, chien couchant, m. ~ to, flagorner. ~ism, n, flagornerie, f.

toast, n, pain grillé, m, rôtie, f; (buttered) toast; (health) toast, m. ~ rack, porte-rôties, m. ¶ v.t, griller, rôtir; (health) porter un toast à. ~er, m, grille-pain, f. ~ing fork, fourchette à griller le pain, f.

tobacco, n, tabac, m. ~ pouch, blague à t., f. tobacconist, n, débitant de t., m. ~'s shop, débit de t., bureau de t., m.

toboggan, n, toboggan, m. ~ run, piste de toboggan, f.

to-day, ad. & n, aujourd'hui, ad. & m. ~'s gossip, nouvelles à la main, f.pl. ~ week, fortnight, d'aujourd'hui en huit, en quinze.

toddle, v.i, trottiner.

to-do, n, cérémonies, f.pl; aria, m.

toe, n, doigt [de pied], orteil, m; (shoe, sock) pointe, f. ~ dancing, pointes, f.pl. ~ nail, ongle d'orteil, m.

toga, n, toge, f.

together, ad, ensemble; à la fois. ~ with, avec, en compagnie de, ainsi que.

toil, n, travail, labeur, m; (pl.) lacets, lacs, rets, m.pl, toiles, f.pl. ¶ v.i, peiner. ~ & moil, suer d'ahan, peiner. ~er, n, travailleur, euse.

toilet, n, toilette, f. ~ paper, papier hygiénique, m. ~ powder, poudre de riz, f. ~ roll, rouleau hygiénique, m.

toilsome, a, pénible, laborieux.

token, n, signe, témoignage, m, preuve, marque, f; gage, hommage; jeton, m.

Toledo, n, Tolède, f.

tolerable, a, tolérable; passable. tolerably, ad, passablement. tolerance & toleration, n, tolérance, f. tolerate, v.t, tolérer.

toll, n, péage, passage, m. ~ call (Teleph.), communication régionale, f. ¶ v.t. & i, tinter, sonner. ~ing, n, tintement funèbre, m.

tom: ~boy, garçon manqué, m. ~ [cat], matou, chat, m. ~foolery, farce, pantalonnade, gaminerie, f. T ~ Thumb umbrella, parapluie poucet, petit p., m. ~tit, mésange charbonnière, f.

tomato, n, tomate, f. ~ sauce, sauce t., f.

tomb, n, tombe, f, tombeau, m, sépulture, f. ~stone, pierre tombale, f.

tome, *n*, tome, volume, *m*.

tommy [bar], *n*, broche, *f*.

to-morrow, *ad. & n*, demain, *ad. & m*. ~ *morning*, demain matin. ~ *night*, ~ *evening*, demain soir.

tompion, *n*, tampon, *m*.

tomtom, *n*, tam-tam, *m*.

ton, *n*, tonne, *f*; tonneau, *m*. Eng. ton (2240 lbs) = 1016 kilos.

tone, *n*, ton; son; accent, *m*; gamme, *f*; dispositions, *f.pl*. ¶ (*v.t*, *Phot.*) virer; (*v.i*) s'harmoniser. ~ *down*, adoucir, assourdir, estomper. ~**d** (*paper*) *p.p*, teinté.

tongs, *n.pl*, pince, tenaille, *f*; pincettes, *f.pl*.

tongue, *n*, langue; (*strip, slip*) languette, *f*.

tonic, *a*, tonique; remontant. ~ *sol-fa*, tonic-sol-fa, *m*. ¶ *n*, (*Med. & drink*) tonique, remontant, *m*; (*Mus.*) tonique, *f*.

to-night, *ad. & n*, ce soir, cette nuit.

toning (*Phot.*) *n*, virage, *m*.

tonnage, *n*, tonnage, *m*; jauge, *f*.

Tonquin, *n*, le Tonkin.

tonsil, *n*, amygdale, *f*. **tonsillitis**, *n*, amygdalite, *f*

tonsure, *n*, tonsure, couronne, *f*. ¶ *v.t*, tonsurer.

too, *ad*, trop; aussi; également; de même; encore. ~ *long*, (*length*) trop long; (*time*) trop [longtemps]. ~ *much*, ~ *many & ~ well*, trop.

tool, *n*, outil; instrument; ustensile; (*Bookb.*) fer; (*pers.*) suppôt, *m*, âme damnée, *f*. ~ *box*, boîte à outils, *f*. ~ *maker*, fabricant d'outils, taillandier, *m*. ¶ *v.t*, (*Mach.*) travailler; (*Bookb.*) gaufrer. ~**ing** (*Bookb.*) *n*, fers à chaud, *m.pl*, gaufrage, *m*.

tooth, *n*, dent, *f*. ~ *ache*, mal de dents, *m*, (*violent*) rage de dents, *f*. ~ *brush*, brosse à dents, *f*. ~ *brush moustache*, moustache en brosse, *f*. ~ *paste*, pâte dentifrice, *f*, dentifrice, *m*. ~ *pick*, cure-dents, *m*. ~ *powder*, poudre dentifrice, *f*, dentifrice, *m*. ¶ *v.t*, [en]denter, créneler. ~**some**, *a*, succulent.

tootsy[-**wootsy**] (*Nursery talk*) *n*, peton, *f*.

top, *n*, haut; sommet, *m*; cime, *f*; faîte; comble; dessus, *m*; tête, pointe, *f*; (*bus*) impériale; (*Naut.*) hune; (*turnip, &c*) fane; (*book page*) tête, tranche supérieure; (*toys*) toupie, *f*, sabot, *m*. *at the ~ of one's voice*, à tue-tête. ~ *boots*, bottes à revers, *f.pl*. ~ *coat*, pardessus, *m*. ~ *figure*, chiffre maximum, *m*. ~ *gallant*, perroquet, *m*. ~ *hamper*, fardage, *m*. ~ *hat*, chapeau haut de forme, *m*. ~ *heavy*, trop lourd du haut. ~ [*joint*] (*fishing rod*) scion, *m*. ~**man** (*Naut.*), gabier, *m*. ~ *margin* (*book*), blanc de tête, *m*. ~ *mast*, mât de hune, *m*. ~ *sail*, hunier, *m*. ¶ *v.t*, couronner; surpasser; dépasser; être à la tête de; (*tree*) étêter.

topaz, *n*, topaze, *f*.

toper, *n*, ivrogne, *m*.

topic, *n*, sujet, thème, *m*. ~ *al film*, film de reportage, *m*. ~ *al song*, chanson de circonstance, *f*.

topographic(**al**), *a*, topographique. **topography**, *n*, topographie, *f*.

topple over, culbuter.

topsyturvy, *ad*, sens dessus dessous.

torch, *n*, flambeau, *m*, torche, *f*. ~ *bearer*, porte-flambeau, *m*. *by ~light*, à la lueur des flambeaux, aux flambeaux. ~*light tattoo*, retraite aux flambeaux, *f*.

toreador, *n*, toréador, *m*.

torment, *n*, tourment, supplice, *m*. ¶ *v.t*, tourmenter; travailler; taquiner. **tormentor**, *n*, bourreau, *m*.

tornado, *n*, tornade, *f*.

torpedo, *n*, torpille, *f*. ~ *boat*, [bateau] torpilleur, *m*. ¶ *v.t*, torpiller.

torpid, *a*, torpide. **torpor**, *n*, torpeur, *f*.

torrent, *n*, torrent, *m*. *in ~s*, à torrents, à flots. ~**ial**, *a*, torrentiel, diluvien.

torrid, *a*, torride.

torsion, *n*, torsion, *f*.

torso, *n*, torse, *m*.

tort (*Law*) *n*, acte dommageable, *m*.

tortoise, *n*, tortue, *f*. ~ *shell*, écaille [de t.] *f*. ~ *shell butterfly*, tortue, *f*. ~ *shell cat*, chat d'Espagne, *m*.

tortuous†, *a*, tortueux, tortu. **torture**, *n*, torture, *f*, tourment, supplice, *m*. *instrument of ~*, instrument de torture, appareil tortionnaire, *m*. ¶ *v.t*, torturer; tourmenter. **torturer**, *n*, tortionnaire, bourreau, *m*. **torturous**, *a*, tortionnaire.

torus *de* **tore**, *n*, tore, *m*.

toss, *v.t. & i*, jeter; ballotter; cahoter; secouer; (*head*) hocher; (*oars*) mâter. ~ *in blanket*, berner. ~ *off* (*drink*), lamper, sabler. ~ [*up*] (coin), tirer [à pile ou face].

tot, *n*, (*child*) petiot, e; (*rum, &c*) boujaron, *m*; (*Arith.*) addition, *f*.

total†, *a*, total; global; complet. ¶ *n*, total; montant, *m*. **totalizer**, **totalizator**, *n*, totaliseur, totalisateur, *m*.

totter, *v.i*, chanceler; s'ébranler.

toucan, *n*, toucan, *m*.

touch, *n*, toucher; tact, *m*; touche, *f*; contact, *m*; communication, *f*; coup, *m*; (*Art*) pinceau; soupçon, *m*; pointe, *f*. ~ *judge*, arbitre de touche, *m*. ~ [*last*], [jeu du] chat, *m*. ~ *line*, ligne de touche, *f*. ~ *needle*, touchau[d] *m*. ~ *stone*, pierre de touche, *f*. ~*wood*, amadou, *m*. ¶ *v.t. & i*, toucher; t. à; se t.; tâter; effleurer. ~ *up*, retoucher; chatouiller. ~**ed** (*crazy*), *p.p*, toqué, timbré. ~**iness**, *n*, susceptibilité, *f*. ~**ing**, *a. & pr*, touchant. ~**y**, *a*, susceptible, chatouilleux.

tough†, *a*, dur; résistant; tenace; coriace. ~**en**, *v.t*, durcir. ~**ness**, *n*, dureté; ténacité, résistance, *f*.

tour, *n*, tour, voyage, *m*, tournée, *f*. ~**ing**, *n*, tourisme, *m*. ~ *car*, voiture de tourisme, *f*. ~**ist**, *n*, touriste, *m,f*. ~

agency, agence de tourisme, *f.* ~ *ticket*, billet de vacances, *m.*

tournament, *n*, tournoi; carrousel, *m.* **tourney**, *n*, tournoi, *m.*

tourniquet, *n*, tourniquet, garrot, *m.*

tousle, *v.t*, ébouriffer.

tout, *n*, rabatteur, euse. ~ *for*, racoler.

tow, *n*, filasse, étoupe, *f*; (*boat*) remorqué, *m. in* ~, à la remorque, à la traîne. ¶ *v.t*, remorquer; haler; touer. ~[*ing*] *path*, chemin de halage, tirage, *m.*

toward[s], *pr*, vers; envers; vis-à-vis de, à l'endroit de; sur.

towel, *n*, serviette [de toilette] *f*, essuie-mains, *m.* ~ *horse*, ~ *rail*, porte-serviettes, séchoir, *m.* **towelling**, *n*, tissu éponge, *m.* ~ *beach coat*, peignoir éponge, *m.*

tower, *n*, tour, *f*; pylône, *m.* ~ *above*, dominer. ~*ing rage*, colère bleue, *f.*

town, *n*, ville; place, *f.* ~ *clerk*, secrétaire de mairie, *m.* ~ *clerk's office*, mairie, *f.* ~ *council*, conseil municipal, *m.* ~ *crier*, crieur public, *m.* ~ *hall*, hôtel de ville, *m*, maison de ville, mairie, *f.* ~ *house*, hôtel, *m.* ~ *planning*, urbanisme, *m.* **townsman**, *n*, citadin, *m.*

toxic, *a*, toxique. **toxin**, *n*, toxine, *f.*

toy, *n*, jouet, joujou, *m*, babiole, *f.* ~ *balloon*, ballon d'enfant, *m.* ¶ *v.i*, jouer, badiner.

trace, *n*, trace, *f*; (*Harness*) trait; (*Fish.*) bas de ligne avec émerillons, *m.* ~ *horse*, [cheval] côtier, cheval de renfort, *m.* ¶ *v.t*, tracer; calquer; suivre la trace de; suivre à la trace. ~ *back*, faire remonter. ~*d article*, motif, *m.* ~*d goods*, motifs, *m.pl.* ~*d pattern*, tracé, *m.* ~**ry**, *n*, réseau, *m*, dentelle, *f.*

trachea, *n*, trachée-artère, *f.*

tracing, *n*, calque, *m.* ~ *cloth*, toile à calquer, *f.*

track, *n*, trace; piste; voie, *f*; chemin, sentier, *m*; route, *f*; sillage; sillon, *m.* ~ *race*, course sur piste, *f.* ¶ *v.t*, suivre à la piste. ~ *down*, (*game*) dépister; (*criminal*) traquer.

tract, *n*, étendue, *f*; (*paper*) opuscule, *m.* ~**able**, *a*, traitable. **traction**, *n*, traction, *f.* ~ *engine*, machine routière; locomobile, *f.* **tractor**, *n*, tracteur, *m.* ~ *farming*, motoculture, *f.*

trade, *n*, commerce; négoce; trafic, *m*, traite, *f*; métier, *m*; industrie, *f.* ~ *discount*, remise [sur marchandises] *f.* ~ *mark*, marque de commerce, *m.* de fabrique, *f.* ~ *price*, prix de gros, *m.* ~ *reference*, référence de fournisseur, *f.* ~ *route*, route commerciale, *f.* ~ *union*, syndicat ouvrier, *m.* ~ *unionist*, syndicaliste, syndiqué, *m.* ~ *winds*, vents alizés, *m.pl.* ¶ *v.i*, trafiquer (*in* = en), faire [le] commerce (*in* = de). **trader**, *n*, commerçant, e; trafiquant, *m*; (*col. pl.*) le commerce. **trading**, *n*, commerce, *m*;

traite, *f*; exercice, *m.* ~ *account*, compte d'exploitation, *m.* ~ *capital*, capital engagé, *m.* ~ *concern*, entreprise commerciale, *f.* ~ *station*, station de commerce, *f.* **tradesman**, *n*, marchand; boutiquier; fournisseur, *m.* *tradesmen's entrance*, porte de service, *f.*

tradition, *n*, tradition, *f.* ~**al†**, *a*, traditionnel.

traduce, *v.t*, calomnier. ~**er**, *n*, diffamateur, *m.*

traffic, *n*, trafic, *m*, traite, *f*; mouvement, *m*; circulation, *f.* ~ *block*, encombrement de voitures, *m.* ~ *lights*, signaux lumineux de circulation, feux de c., *m.pl.* ~ *police*, police de la circulation, *f.* ~ *roundabout*, ~ *circus*, circulation en sens giratoire, *f.* ~ *sign*, poteau de signalisation, *m.* **trafficker**, *n*, trafiquant, *m.*

tragedian, *n*, [auteur] tragique, *m.* ~ *tragedienne*, tragédien, ne. **tragedy**, *n*, tragédie, *f*; drame, *m.* **tragic(al†)**, *a*, tragique. **tragicomedy**, *n*, tragi-comédie, *f.* **tragicomic**, *a*, tragi-comique.

trail, *n*, piste, trace; traînée, *f*, sillon, *m*; (*gun carriage*) flèche, *f.* ~ *rope* (*Aero.*), guiderope, *m.* ¶ *v.t*, suivre à la piste; traîner. ~**er**, *n*, remorque, baladeuse, *f.*

train, *n*, train; convoi, *m*; suite, *f*; cortège, *m*; (*dress*) traîne, queue; (*comet*) queue; (*powder*) traînée, *f*; (*events*) enchaînement, *m.* ~ *bearer*, caudataire, *m.* ~ *ferry*, bac transbordeur, *m.* ~ *oil*, huile de baleine, *f.* ¶ *v.t*, former, styler; instruire; dresser; éduquer; entraîner; (*gun, &c*) diriger, pointer. ~**er**, *n*, dresseur; entraîneur, *m.* **training**, *n*, éducation; école; instruction, *f*; enseignement; dressage, manège; entraînement, *m*, haleine, *f.* ~ *centre*, école professionnelle, *f.* ~ *college*, école normale, *f.* ~ *ship*, vaisseau-école, *m.*

trait, *n*, trait, *m.*

traitor, tress, *n*, traître, *m*, traîtresse, *f.* ~**ous**, *a*, traître. ~**ously**, *ad*, en traître.

trajectory, *n*, trajectoire, *f.*

tram (*Tapestry work*) *v.t*, échantillonner.

tram [**car**], *n*, tramway, *m.* ~ *tramway* [*line*], ligne de tramways, *f.*

trammel, *n*, (*net*) tramail, *m*; (*pl.*) entraves, *f.pl.* ¶ *v.t*, entraver.

tramp, *n*, bruit de pas, *m*; (*horses*) battue; promenade [à pied] *f*; (*pers.*) chemineau, *m*, vagabond, e. ~ [*steamer*], tramp[-steamer], navire vagabond, *m.* ¶ *v.i*, marcher pesamment; cheminer; marcher; (*v.t.*) arpenter. ~ *up & down*, courir.

trample [**on**] [**down**], *v.t*, fouler, piétiner.

trance, *n*, extase; (*hypnotic*) transe, *f.*

tranquil†, *a*, tranquille. **tranquillity**, *n*, tranquillité, *f.*

transact, *v.t*, traiter; faire; délibérer sur. ~**ion**, *n*, négociation; affaire, transaction; délibération; *f*; (*pl.*) actes, *m.pl.*

transatlantic, *a*, transatlantique.

transcend, *v.t*, dépasser; surpasser. ~**ent**, *a*, transcendant.

transcribe, *v.t*, transcrire. **transcript** & **transcription**, *n*, transcription, *f*.

transept, *n*, transept, *m*.

transfer, *n*, transmission; cession, *f*; apport; transfert; transport; virement; (*Emb.*, &c) décalque, *m*; (*for china & as toy*) décalcomanie; (*tram, bus*) correspondance, *f*. ~ [*deed*], transfert, *m*, feuille de t., *f*. ¶ *v.t*, transmettre; céder; apporter; transférer; transporter; virer; décalquer. ~**able**, *a*, cessible; mobilier. ~**ee**, *n*, cessionnaire, *m,f*. ~**or**, *n*, cédant, e.

transfiguration, *n*, transfiguration, *f*.

transfix, *v.t*, transpercer.

transform, *v.t*, transformer. ~**ation**, *n*, transformation, *f*. ~ *scene*, changement à vue, *m*. ~**er**, *n*, transformateur, *m*.

transfuse, *v.t*, transfuser.

transgress, *v.t*, transgresser, contrevenir à. ~**or**, *n*, violateur, trice; pécheur, eresse.

tran[s]ship, *v.t*, transborder; (*v.i.*) rompre charge. ~**ment**, *n*, transbordement, *m*; rupture de charge, *f*. ~ *bond*, acquit-à-caution, *m*.

transient†, *a*, transitoire, passager.

transire (*Cust.*) *n*, passavant, *m*.

transit, *n*, (*Cust.*) transit; passage; transport, *m*. *in* ~, en transit; en cours de route. ~**ion**, *n*, transition, *f*, passage, *m*. ~**ive**†, *a*, transitif. ~**ory**†, *a*, transitoire.

translate, *v.t*, traduire; (*bishop*) transférer.

translation, *n*, traduction; version; (*bishop*) translation, *f*. ¶ **translator**, *n*, traducteur, trice.

translucent, *a*, translucide.

transmigration, *n*, transmigration, *f*.

transmission, *n*, transmission, *f*. **transmit**, *v.t*, transmettre. **transmitter**, *n*, transmetteur, *m*.

transmute, *v.t*, transmuer.

transom, *n*, traverse, *f*, sommier; meneau, *m*.

transparency, *n*, transparence, *f*; (*picture*) transparent, *m*. **transparent**, *a*, transparent.

transpire, *v.i*, transpirer.

transplant, *v.t*, transplanter, dépiquer.

transport, *n*, transport, *m*. ¶ *v.t*, transporter.

transpose, *v.t*, transposer.

transubstantiation, *n*, transsubstantiation, *f*.

transverse†, *a*, transversal.

trap, *n*, trappe, *f*, traquenard, piège; guet-apens; (*drain*) siphon, *m*; charrette anglaise, voiturette, *f*; (*pl.*) bagages, *m.pl*. ~ *ball*, balle à la volée, *f*. ~ *door*, trappe, *f*. ¶ *v.t*, prendre au piège, attraper.

trapeze, *n*, trapèze, *m*.

trapper, *n*, trappeur, *m*.

trappings, *n.pl*, harnachement, *m*.

trash, *n*, camelote, drogue, pacotille, salo-
perie, saleté, *f*; (*worthless contents of book*) futilités, *f.pl*.

travail, *n*, travail [d'enfant] *m*.

travel, *n*, voyage, *m*. ¶ *v.i*, voyager; marcher; rouler. ~ *over*, parcourir. **traveller**, *n*, voyageur, euse; placier, *m*. ~'s *cheque*, chèque de voyage, *m*. **travelling**, *p.a*, ambulant. ~ *crane*, pont roulant, *m*. ~ *dress*, costume de voyage, *m*. ~ *journeyman*, rouleur, *m*. ~ *rug*, couverture de voyage, *f*, plaid, *m*.

traverse, *v.t*, traverser.

travesty, *n*, travestissement, *m*. ¶ *v.t*, travestir.

trawl [*net*], *n*, chalut, *m*, traille, *f*. ¶ *v.i*, pêcher au chalut, p. à la traille. ~**er**, *n*, [*bateau*] chalutier, *m*. ~**ing**, *n*, pêche chalutière, *f*.

tray, *n*, plateau, *m*. ~ *cloth*, dessus de p., *m*.

treacherous†, *a*, perfide, traître. **treachery**, *n*, traîtrise, perfidie, trahison, *f*.

treacle, *n*, mélasse, *f*.

tread, *n*, pas; (*of stair step*) giron; (*egg*) germe, *m*. ¶ *v.i.ir*, marcher; (*v.t.ir*.) fouler. ~ *water*, nager debout. ~**le**, *n*, marche, pédale, *f*.

treason, *n*, trahison, *f*, crime d'État, *m*.

treasure, *n*. & ~ *trove*, trésor, *m*. ¶ *v.t*, garder précieusement. **treasurer**, *n*, trésorier, ère, massier, ère. **treasury**, *n*, trésor, *m*, trésorerie, caisse, *f*; fisc, *m*. *T* ~ *Board* (*Eng.*), Ministère des Finances (Fr.) *m*.

treat, *n*, régal; plaisir, *m*; débauche, *f*. ¶ *v.t*. & *i*, traiter; régaler. **treatise**, *n*, traité, *m*. **treatment**, *n*, traitement, *m*; (*music, art*) facture, *f*. **treaty**, *n*, traité, *m*. *by private* ~, à l'amiable.

treble†, *a*, triple. ¶ *n*, triple; (*Mus.*) dessus, *m*; (*Crochet*) bride, *f*. ~ *clef*, clef de sol, *f*. ¶ *v.t*, tripler.

tree, *n*, arbre, *m*. ~ *calf*, veau raciné, *m*. ~ *fern*, fougère arborescente, *f*. ~**nail**, cheville de bois, *f*. ~ *sparrow*, moineau des bois, friquet, *m*. ~**less**, *a*, dépourvu d'arbres.

trefoil, *n*, trèfle, *m*.

trellis, *n*, treillis, treillage, *m*. ¶ *v.t*, treillisser.

tremble,*v.i*, trembler. **trembling**,*n*,tremblement, *m*.

tremendous, *a*, énorme, formidable, effroyable, furieux, fou.

tremolo, *n*, tremolo, *m*. **tremor**, *n*, tremblement, *m*, trépidation, *f*. **tremulous**, *a*, tremblant.

trench, *n*, tranchée, *f*, fossé, *m*, saignée, rigole, *f*. ~ *coat*, trench-coat, *m*. ~ *mortar*, mortier de tranchée, *m*. ~ *warfare*, guerre de tranchées, g. de position, *f*. ¶ *v.t*, défoncer. ~ *upon*, envahir; friser. ~**ant**, *a*, tranchant, à l'emporte-pièce. **trencher**, *n*, tranchoir, tailloir, *m*. **trencherman**, *n*, mangeur, *m*, fourchett

trend, n, direction; tendance, f. ¶ v.i, se diriger.

Trent, n, Trente, f. **the Trentino**, le Trentin.

trepan, n, trépan, m. ¶ v.t, trépaner.

trepidation, n, tremblement, m.

trespass, n, intrusion; offense, f. ~ against, offenser. ~ on, s'introduire sans droit dans; (fig.) empiéter sur, abuser de. ~er, n, intrus, e. ~s will be prosecuted, défense d'entrer sous peine d'amende.

tress, n, tresse, f.

trestle, n, tréteau, chevalet, m. ~ shore, chevalement, m.

Treves, n, Trèves, f.

trial, n, essai, m, épreuve; tribulation, f; procès; jugement, m; débats, m.pl. ~ & error, tâtonnements, m.pl. ~ balance, balance de vérification, b. d'ordre, f. ~ trip, voyage d'essai, m.

triangle (Geom. & Mus.) n, triangle, m.

triangular, a, triangulaire.

tribe, n, tribu; peuplade; race, f.

tribulation, n, tribulation, f.

tribunal, n, tribunal, m. **tribune**, n, tribune, f; (Hist. pers.) tribun, m.

tributary, a, tributaire. ¶ n, tributaire; affluent, m. **tribute**, n, tribut; hommage, m.

trice, n, clin d'œil, m.

triceps, æ. & n, triceps, a. & m.

trick, n, tour, jeu, m; ruse; ficelle; (Cards) levée, f; truc, m; (habit) tic, m. ~ riding, voltige, f. ¶ v.t, tricher. ~ery, n, tricherie, finasserie, f.

trickle, n, filet, m. ¶ v.i, [dé]couler, ruisseler.

trickster, n, tricheur, euse, finassier, ère, jongleur, m. **tricky**, a, adroit à s'évader; délicat.

tricycle, n, tricycle, m.

trident, n, trident, m.

triennial, a, triennal.

trifle, n, bagatelle, vétille, f, rien, m; misère; futilité, f. ¶ v.i, s'amuser à des riens; baguenauder. ~ with, se jouer de. **trifler**, n, baguenaudier, homme futile, m. **trifling**, a, insignifiant, minime; futile.

triforium, n, triforium, m.

trigger, n, détente, f; déclic, m.

trigonometry, n, trigonométrie, f.

Trilby [hat], n, chapeau souple, m.

trill, n, trille, m. ¶ v.t, orner de trilles.

trim, a, soigné, bien tenu; coquet. ¶ n, état, m; assiette, allure, f; arrimage, m. ¶ v.t, parer; agrémenter; garnir; (edges) rogner; (book edges, &c) ébarber; (hair, &c) tailler, rafraîchir; (wood) dresser; (ship) arrimer; (sails) orienter. **trimmer**, n, opportuniste, m,f; (Fish.) trimmer (pêchant seul & avertissant le pêcheur); (Naut.) arrimeur, m. **trimmings**, n.pl, passementerie; garniture, f, fourniture, f. oft. pl; (Cook.) garniture, f.

Trinidad, n. & **the Trinity**, la Trinité.

trinket, n, colifichet, bibelot, m.

trio, n, trio, m.

trip, n, croc-en-jambe; tour, voyage, m, excursion, f. ~ [up], v.t, faire trébucher, donner un croc-en-jambe à; (Mech.) déclencher; (anchor) déraper; (v.i.) trébucher. ~ along, sautiller.

tripe, n, tripes, f.pl. ~ dresser, tripier, ère. ~ shop, triperie, f.

triplet, a, triple. ¶ v.t. & i, tripler. **triplet**, n, triolet, tercet, m; (pl.) trois jumeaux, m.pl. **triplicate**, n, triplicata, triple, m.

tripod, n, pied [à trois branches], trépied, m.

tripoli, n, tripoli, m.

tripper, n, excursionniste, m,f, promeneur, euse.

triptych, n, triptyque, m.

trite, a, banal. ~ness, n, banalité, f.

triton, n, triton, m.

triumph, n, triomphe, m. ¶ v.i, triompher. ~al, a, triomphal, de triomphe. ~ant, a, triomphant, victorieux. ~antly, ad, triomphalement.

trivet, n, trépied, m, chevrette, f.

trivial, a, insignifiant, minime; frivole.

troat, v.i, bramer, réer, raire.

troglodyte, n, troglodyte, m.

Trojan, a, troyen; (war) de Troie.

troll (Fish.) v.i, pêcher à la traîne.

troll[e]y, n, chariot, camion, fardier, diable; trolley, m. ~ bus, autobus à trolley, m.

trolling, n, pêche à traîner, f.

trombone, n, trombone, m.

troop, n, troupe; bande, f. ~ ship, transport, m. ~ train, train militaire, m. ~er, n, cavalier, m.

trope, n, trope, m.

trophy, n, trophée, m; panoplie, f.

tropic, n, tropique, m. ~ of Cancer, of Capricorn, tropique du Cancer, du Capricorne. ~al, a, tropical.

trot, n, trot, m. ¶ v.i. & t, trotter.

troth, n, foi, f.

trotter, n, trotteur, euse; (pl.) pieds, m.pl.

troubadour, n, troubadour, m.

trouble, n, peine, f; chagrin; ennui; mal; trouble, m. ¶ v.t, inquiéter, tourmenter, chagriner; déranger. ~d, p.a, agité, inquiet. ~ waters (fig.), eau trouble, f. ~some, a, fâcheux; difficultueux; gênant; (child) tourmentant.

trough, n, bac, baquet, m, auge; huche, f; (of wave, &c) creux; (sea) entre-deux, m.

trounce, v.t, rosser, étriller.

troupe, n, troupe, f.

trouser, n, (pl.) pantalon, m. ~ stretcher, extenseur [pour pantalons] m. ~ed, p.p, culotté.

trousseau, n, trousseau, m.

trout, n, truite, f. ~ fishing, pêche à la t., f. ~ stream, rivière à truites, f.

trowel, n, truelle, f; (Hort.) houlette, f, déplantoir, m.

truancy, n, vagabondage, m. **truant**, a, vagabond. **to play** ~, faire l'école buissonnière.

truce, *n*, trêve, *f*.

truck, *n*, (*barter*) troc; (*Rly*) wagon; (*lorry*) chariot, camion; (*hand*) diable; (*engine*) bogie, *m*. ~ *load*, wagon complet. ¶ *v.t*, rouler.

truckle, *v.i*, ramper.

truculent, *a*, truculent.

trudge, *v.i*, cheminer.

trudgen (*Swim*.) *n*, trudgeon, *m*.

true, *a*, vrai; véritable; loyal; fidèle; juste; conforme; rectiligne. *in one's* ~ *colours*, en déshabillé. [*certified*] *a* ~ *copy*, pour copie conforme, pour ampliation. ~*love[r's] knot*, lacs d'amour, *m*. ~ *to life*, vécu. ¶ *v.t*, dégauchir, rectifier, [re]dresser.

truffle, *n*, truffe, *f*.

truism, *n*, truisme, *m*. truly, *ad*, vraiment, véritablement; fidèlement.

trump, *n*, trompette, *f*. ~ [*card*], *n. & ~s, n.pl*, atout, *m*, retourne, *f*. ~ *up*, fabriquer, inventer.

trumpery, *n*, friperie; camelote; blague, *f*. ¶ *a*, de pacotille; frivole.

trumpet, *n*, trompette, *f*. ~ *call*, sonnerie de t., *f*. ¶ *v.t. & i*, (*fig*.) trompeter, corner; (*elephant*) barrir; (*Mus*.) sonner de la trompette. ~er, *n*, trompette, *m*.

truncate, *v.t*, tronquer.

truncheon, *n*, bâton, *m*.

trundle, *n*, roulette, *f*. ¶ *v.t*, rouler.

trunk, *n*, tronc, *m*; tige, *f*; torse, *m*; (*elephant*) trompe; malle, *f*, coffre; bahut, *m*; (*pl*.) culotte, *f*; (*pl*, *Teleph*.) l'inter, *m*. ~ & *bag manufacturer*, malletier, *m*. ~ *call*, communication interurbaine, *f*. ~ *line*, grande artère, *f*.

trunnion, *n*, tourillon, *m*.

truss, *n*, trousse, botte, *f*; bandage [herniaire], brayer, *m*; (*Build*.) ferme, *f*. ¶ *v.t*, (*fowl*) trousser; (*hay*) botteler; (*Build*.) armer.

trust, *n*, confiance; créance, foi, *f*, crédit; fidéicommis; dépôt, *m*; charge, *f*; mandat; (*oil, steel*) trust, *m*. ~ *deed*, acte de fidéicommis, *m*. ¶ *v.t. & i*, se fier à; croire; faire crédit à; espérer. ~ed, *p.a*, de confiance. ~ee, *n*, curateur, trice; dépositaire, *m,f*, consignataire; syndic, *m*. ~ful, *a*, confiant. ~worthy, *a*, digne de confiance, croyable, fidèle. ~y, *a*, à toute épreuve; (*bad sense*) affidé.

truth, *n*, vérité, *f*. ~ful, *a*, vrai, véridique. ~fulness, *n*, véracité, *f*.

try, *n*, essai, coup, *m*. ¶ *v.t. & i*, essayer; éprouver; expérimenter; goûter; tenter; tâter; chercher; (*law case*) juger; (*patience*) exercer. ~ *on*, essayer. ~ing, *a*, difficile; contrariant. ~ *time*, mauvais quart d'heure, *m*.

tub, *n*, cuve, *f*, baquet, tub; tonneau, *m*; caisse, *f*; (*bad ship*) sabot, *m*. *tub[by man*], poussah, *m*.

tuba, *n*, tuba, *m*.

tube, *n*, tube; canon, *m*.

tuber & tubercle, *n*, tubercule, *m*.   tuber-
culosis, *n*, tuberculose, *f*. tuberculous, *a*, tuberculeux. tuberose, *n*, tubéreuse, *f*.

tubular, *a*, tubulaire. ~ [*tire*], boyau, *m*.

tuck, *n*, rempli, troussis, *m*. ¶ *v.t*, remplier. ~ *in*, border. ~ *up*, [re]trousser.

Tuesday, *n*, mardi, *m*.

tuft, *n*, touffe, *f*; bouquet; panache, *m*; huppe; houppe; (*on chin*) mouche, *f*. ~ed, *a*, touffu; aigretté, huppé, houppé.

tug, *n*, tiraillement; coup de collier; (*boat*) remorqueur, toueur, *m*. ~ *of war*, lutte à la corde, *f*; (*fig*.) effort suprême, *m*. ¶ *v.t*, tirer.

tuition, *n*, enseignement, *m*.

tulip, *n*, tulipe, *f*. ~ *tree*, tulipier, *m*. ~ *wood*, bois de rose, *m*.

tulle, *n*, tulle, *m*.

tumble, *n*, chute, dégringolade, culbute, *f*. ~ *down*, tomber, dégringoler, culbuter, débouler. ~*down*, *a*, délabré. tumbler, *n*, (*pers*.) acrobate; (*pigeon*) culbutant; (*toy*) poussah; (*glass*) [verre] gobelet, *m*.

tumbrel, -il, *n*, tombereau, *m*.

tumour, *n*, tumeur, glande, *f*.

tumult, *n*, tumulte, *m*. tumultuous†, *a*, tumultueux, houleux.

tumulus, *n*, tumulus, *m*.

tun, *n*, tonne, *f*, tonneau, foudre, *m*.

tune, *n*, air; accord, *m*; (*fig*.) cadence; (*fig*.) note, *f*, ton, *m*, gamme, *f*. ¶ *v.t*, accorder; mettre d'accord. tuner, *n*, accordeur, *m*. tuneful†, *a*, harmonieux, mélodieux.

tungsten, *n*, tungstène, *m*.

tunic, *n*, tunique, *f*. ~ *shirt*, chemise de ville, *f*.

tuning, *n*, accordage, *m*. ~ *fork*, diapason à branches, *m*.

Tunis, *n*, (*state*) la Tunisie; (*capital*) Tunis, *m*. Tunisian, *a*, tunisien. ¶ *n*, Tunisien, ne.

tunnel, *n*, tunnel, souterrain, *m*. ¶ *v.t*, percer un tunnel sous.

tunny, *n*, thon, *m*.

tup, *n*, bélier; (*pile driving*) mouton, *m*.

turban, *n*, turban, *m*.

turbid, *a*, trouble.

turbine, *n*, turbine, *f*.

turbot, *n*, turbot, (*young*) turbotin, *m*.

turbulence, *n*, turbulence, *f*. turbulent, *a*, turbulent.

tureen, *n*, soupière, *f*.

turf, *n*, gazon, *m*; plaque de g., motte, *f*. *the* ~ (*Racing*), le turf. ¶ *v.t*, gazonner.

turgid, *a*, turgescent, boursouflé.

Turk, *n*, Turc, *m*, Turque, *f*. Turkey, *n*, la Turquie. ~ *in Asia*, T. d'Asie. ~ *in Europe*, T. d'Europe. ~ *carpet*, tapis de T., *m*. *t*~ [*cock*], dindon, coq d'Inde, *m*. *t*~ [*hen*], dinde, poule d'Inde, *f*. *t*~ *poult*, dindonneau, *m*. Turkish, *a*, turc. ~ *bath*, bain turc, *m*. ~ *towel*, serviette-éponge, *f*. ¶ (*language*) *n*, le turc.

Turkoman (*pers*.) *n*, Turcoman, *m*.

turmeric, *n*, safran des Indes, *m*.

uncomely, *a*, peu avenant.
uncomfortable, *a*, incommode; (*of pers.*) mal à son aise.
uncommon†, *a*, rare; singulier.
uncommunicative, *a*, taciturne.
uncomplaining, *a*, résigné. *the ~ poor*, les pauvres honteux, *m.pl.*
uncompleted, *a*, inachevé.
uncompromising, *a*, intransigeant.
unconcern, *n*, indifférence, *f*, sans-souci, *m*.
unconditional, *a*. & *~ly*, *ad*, sans condition.
unconfirmed, *a*, non confirmé.
unconnected (*desultory*) *a*, décousu.
unconquerable†, *a*, invincible.
unconscious†, *a*, inconscient; (*dead faint*) sans connaissance. *~ness, n*, inconscience, *f*; une perte de connaissance.
unconsecrated ground, terre profane, *f*.
unconstitutional†, *a*, inconstitutionnel.
unconstrained, *a*, dégagé. unconstraint, *n*, désinvolture, *f*, abandon, laisser-aller, *m*.
uncontested, *a*, incontesté.
uncontrollable, *a*, ingouvernable; indomptable; inextinguible.
unconventional, *a*, sans gêne.
unconvincing, *a*, peu vraisemblable.
uncork, *v.t*, déboucher.
uncorrected, *a*, non corrigé.
uncouple, *v.t*, découpler.
uncouth, *a*, disgracieux, grossier, rude, rustaud.
uncover, *v.t*, découvrir; (*v.i.*) se découvrir.
uncreated, *a*, incréé.
uncrossed (*cheque*) *a*, non barré.
unction, *n*, onction, *f*. unctuous†, *a*, onctueux.
uncultivated & uncultured, *a*, inculte.
uncurbed, *a*, indompté.
uncurl, *v.t*, défriser; dérouler.
uncustomary, *a*, inusité. uncustomed, *a*, (*not liable to duty*) franc de tout droit, libre à l'entrée; (*having paid no duty*) non acquitté.
uncut, *a*, (*gem*) brut; (*cake*) non entamé. *~ edges* (book), tranches non rognées, *f.pl.*
undamaged, *a*, non endommagé; non avarié.
undated, *a*, sans date, non daté.
undaunted, *a*, intrépide.
undeceive, *v.t*, détromper; désillusionner.
undecided, *a*, indécis; incertain.
undecipherable, *a*, indéchiffrable.
undefended, *a*, sans défense; sans défenseur; (*law case*) non contestée; (*heard ex parte*) jugée par défaut.
undefiled, *a*, sans souillure.
undefined, *a*, indéfini.
undeliverable, *a*, en souffrance. undelivered, *a*, non livré; non distribué.
undeniable, *a*, indéniable, incontestable.
undenominational, *a*, laïque, neutre.
under, *pr*, sous; dessous; au-dessous de; en; à; sauf. *~ there*, là-dessous. *~ water*,

entre deux eaux. ¶ *ad*, dessous; au-dessous.
underassessment, *n*, insuffisance d'imposition, *f*.
underclothing, *n*, (*women's*) [vêtements de] dessous; (*men's*) sous-vêtements, *m.pl.*
undercurrent, *n*, courant de fond; courant sous-marin; (*in air*) courant inférieur; (*fig.*) courant secret, fond, *m*.
undercut (*meat*) *n*, filet, *m*.
under-developed, *a*, trop peu développé.
underdone, *a*, pas [assez] cuit; peu cuit, saignant.
under-estimate, *v.t*, sous-estimer, mésestimer.
under-exposure (*Phot.*) *n*, manque de pose, *m*.
undergarment, *n*, (*men's*) sous-vêtement; (*women's*) vêtement de dessous, *m*.
undergo, *v.t.ir*, subir, souffrir.
underground, *a*, souterrain. ¶ *ad*, en souterrain.
undergrowth, *n*, broussailles, *f.pl.*
underhand, *a*, clandestin, souterrain, sournois, sourd; (*Ten. service*) par en bas. ¶ *ad*, sous main, clandestinement.
underlease, *n*, sous-bail, *m*; sous-ferme, *f*. underlet, *v.t.ir*, sous-louer; sous-affermer.
underline, *v.t*, souligner.
underling, *n*, employé subalterne, nègre, *m*.
underlying, *a*, sous-jacent.
undermentioned, *a*, ci-dessous.
undermine, *v.t*, miner, affouiller, caver.
undermost, *a*, le plus bas.
underneath, *ad*, dessous; au-dessous. ¶ *pr*, sous.
underpay, *v.t.ir*, payer trop peu.
underpin, *v.t*, reprendre en sous-œuvre.
underrate, *v.t*, mésestimer, déprécier.
underscore, *v.t*, souligner.
under-sea, *a*, sous-marin.
under-secretary, *n*, sous-secrétaire, *m*.
undersell, *v.t.ir*, vendre moins cher que.
underside, *n*, dessous, *m*.
undersigned, *a*. & *n*, soussigné, *a*.
understand, *v.t*. & *i. ir*, comprendre, voir; entendre; s'e. à; apprendre; sous-entendre. *~ing, n*, intelligence, *f*; entendement, sens, *m*; compréhension; entente, *f*.
understrapper, *n*, employé subalterne, *m*.
understudy, *n*, doublure, *f*. ¶ *v.t*, doubler.
undertake, *v.t.ir*, entreprendre; se charger de; s'engager, se faire fort. undertaker, *n*, entrepreneur de pompes funèbres, *m*. undertaking, *n*, engagement, *m*; entreprise, *f*; pompes funèbres, *f.pl.*
undertone (in an), à demi-voix.
undertow, *n*, ressac, *m*.
undervalue, *v.t*, mésestimer, déprécier.
underwear, *n*. Same as *underclothing*.
underwood, *n*, [bois] taillis, mort-bois, *m*, broussailles, *f.pl.*
underworld, *n*, enfers; bas-fonds de la société, *m.pl.*
underwrite, *v.t.ir*, (*Assce*) souscrire, s. pour; (*Fin.*) garantir. underwriter, *n*, sous-

cripteur, assureur; (*Fin.*) syndicataire, *m.*
underwriting, *n*, souscription; garantie, *f.*
undeserved, *a*, immérité. **undeserving**, *a*,
peu méritant; indigne (*of* = de).
undesirable, *a. & n*, indésirable, *a. & m,f.*
undetermined, *a*, indéterminé.
undeveloped, *a*, en friche.
undigested, *a*, non digéré; (*fig.*) indigeste.
undignified, *a*, sans dignité.
undisciplined, *a*, indiscipliné.
undiscoverable, *a*, introuvable. **undiscovered**,
a, non découvert.
undismayed, *a*, sans être découragé.
undisputed, *a*, incontesté.
undisturbed, *a*, tranquille.
undo, *v.t.ir*, défaire, détacher; (*knitting*) démailler. ~**ing**, *n*, ruine, *f.* **come undone**,
se défaire.
undoubted†, *a*, indubitable.
undress, *n*, déshabillé, négligé, *m*; (*Mil.,
Nav.*) petite tenue, *f.* ¶ *v.t*, déshabiller;
(*v.i.*) se déshabiller.
undrinkable, *a*, imbuvable.
undue, *a*, exagéré, excessif; inexigible.
undulate, *v.i*, onduler, ondoyer. **undulating**,
a, ondulé. **undulation**, *n*, ondulation, *f.*
unduly, *ad*, indûment; par trop.
undutiful, *a*, qui manque à ses devoirs.
undying, *a*, impérissable, immortel.
unearned, *a*, non acquis; immérité. ~
increment, plus-value, *f.*
unearth, *v.t*, déterrer. ~**ly**, *a*, spectral,
fantomatique.
uneasiness, *n*, malaise, *m*, inquiétude, *f*, mar-
†el en tête, *m.* **uneasy**†, *a*, inquiet.
uneatable, *a*, immangeable.
uneducated, *a*, sans instruction.
unemployable (**the**), les incapables, *m.pl.*
unemployed, *a*, inemployé; (*pers.*) sans
travail, en chômage. **on the** ~ **list** (*Mil.*),
en non-activité. **the** ~, les sans-travail,
les chômeurs, *m.pl.* **unemployment**, *n*,
manque de travail; chômage [involon-
taire] *m.* ~ **benefit**, indemnité de chômage, *f.* ~ **insurance**, assurance contre
le chômage, *f.*
unending, *a*, sans fin.
unenterprising, *a*, sans initiative.
unenviable, *a*, peu enviable.
unequal†, *a*, inégal. ~ **to** (task), pas à la
hauteur de, incapable de. **unequalled**, *a*,
sans égal, sans pareil.
unequivocal, *a*, non équivoque.
unerring†, *a*, infaillible; sûr.
uneven†, *a*, inégal; (*number*) impair. ~**ness**,
n, inégalité; (*number*) imparité, *f.*
unexceptionable, *a*, irrécusable.
unexpected, *a*, inattendu; inespéré.
unexpired, *a*, non expiré; non couru; non
échu; non périmé.
unexplained, *a*, inexpliqué.
unexplored, *a*, inexploré.
unexpurgated, *a*, intégral.
unfailing, *a*, infaillible; (*spring*) intarissable.

unfair†, *a*, injuste; déloyal; partial. ~**ness**,
n, injustice; déloyauté; partialité, *f.*
unfaithful†, *a*, infidèle. ~**ness**, *n*, infidélité, *f.*
unfamiliar, *a*, étranger.
unfasten, *v.t*, dégrafer, défaire.
unfathomable, *a*, insondable, abyssal.
unfavourable†, *a*, défavorable, contraire. ~
light, contre-jour, *m.*
Unfederated Malay States (**the**), les États
malais non fédérés, *m.pl.*
unfeeling, *a*, insensible.
unfeigned†, *a*, sincère.
unfenced, *a*, sans clôture.
unfettered, *a*, sans entraves.
unfinished, *a*, inachevé, imparfait.
unfit, *a*, impropre; hors d'état; inapte;
incapable. *the* ~, les inaptes, *m.pl.*
~**ness**, *n*, inaptitude; incapacité, *f.* **un-
fitting**, *a*, inconvenant.
unflagging, *a*, soutenu.
unfledged, *a*, sans plumes.
unflinching, *a*, à toute épreuve.
unfold, *v.t*, déployer; dérouler.
unforeseen, *a*, imprévu.
unforgettable, *a*, inoubliable.
unforgivable, *a*, impardonnable.
unfortified, *a*, non fortifié; (*town*) ouverte.
unfortunate†, *a*, malheureux, infortuné;
regrettable. *the* ~, les malheureux, les
infortunés, *m.pl.*
unfounded, *a*, sans fondement.
unfrequented, *a*, infréquenté.
unfriendly, *a*, inamical; hostile.
unfrock, *v.t*, défroquer.
unfruitful, *a*, stérile. ~**ness**, *n*, stérilité, *f.*
unfulfilled, *a*, non accompli.
unfurl, *v.t*, déferler, déployer.
unfurnished, *a*, non meublé.
ungainly, *a*, dégingandé.
ungathered, *a*, non cueilli.
ungenerous, *a*, peu généreux.
ungodliness, *n*, impiété, *f.* **ungodly**, *a*, impie.
ungovernable, *a*, ingouvernable; indomptable.
ungraceful, *a*, disgracieux.
ungracious, *a*, malgracieux, disgracieux.
ungrafted, *a*, franc.
ungrammatical, *a*, contre la grammaire.
~**ly**, *ad*, incorrectement.
ungrateful, *a*, ingrat. ~**ness**, *n*, ingratitude, *f.*
ungrudgingly, *ad*, de bon cœur.
unguarded, *a*, sans défense; indiscret.
unhair (*skins*) *v.t*, dépiler, débourrer.
unhallowed, *a*, profane.
unhappiness, *n*, malheur, *m.* **unhappy**†, *a*,
malheureux.
unharmed, *a*, indemne.
unharness, *v.t*, déharnacher.
unhatched, *a*, non éclos.
unhealthiness, *n*, insalubrité, *f.* **unhealthy**,
a, insalubre; malsain.
unheard of, inouï.
unheeded, *a*, négligé.
unhesitatingly, *ad*, sans hésitation.

unhewn, *a,* non taillé.

unhindered, *a,* sans empêchement.

unhinge, *v.t,* démonter; troubler, aliéner.

unholiness, *n,* impiété, *f.* **unholy,** *a,* impie.

unhonoured, *p.a,* méconnu.

unhook, *v.t,* décrocher.

unhoped for, inespéré.

unhorse, *v.t,* démonter, désarçonner.

unhurt, *a,* indemne, sauf.

unicorn, *n,* licorne, *f.*

uniform, *a,* uniforme; uni. ¶ *n,* uniforme, *m,* tenue, *f.* ~**ity,** *n,* uniformité, *f.* ~**ly,** *ad,* uniformément. **unify,** *v.t,* unifier.

unilateral, *a,* unilatéral.

unimaginable, *a,* inimaginable.

unimpeachable, *a,* irrécusable.

unimpeded, *a,* sans entraves.

unimportant, *a,* insignifiant.

uninflammable, *a,* ininflammable.

uninhabitable, *a,* inhabitable. **uninhabited,** *a,* inhabité.

uninitiated person, profane, *m,f.*

uninjured, *a,* indemne.

uninstructed, *a,* ignorant.

uninsured, *a,* non assuré; (*Post*) sans valeur déclarée, non chargé.

unintelligent, *a,* inintelligent. **unintelligible,** *a,* inintelligible.

unintentional†, *a,* involontaire.

uninterested, *a,* indifférent. **uninteresting,** *a,* sans intérêt.

uninterrupted, *a,* ininterrompu. ~**ly,** *ad,* sans interruption.

uninvited (*stocks, shares*) *a,* à la souche.

uninvited, *a,* sans invitation. **uninviting,** *a,* peu attrayant; peu appétissant.

union, *n,* union; alliance, *f;* (*Mech.*) raccord; (*thread*) mi-fil, *m.* U~ *of South Africa,* Union Sud-Africaine. U~ *of Soviet Socialist Republics,* Union des Républiques soviétiques socialistes.

unique†, *a,* unique.

unison, *n,* unisson, *m.*

unissued (*stocks, shares*) *a,* à la souche.

unit, *n,* unité, *f;* élément, *m.* ~ *bookcase,* bibliothèque transformable, *f.* ~ *price,* prix unitaire, *m.* **unite,** *v.t,* unir; joindre; réunir; allier; marier. **united,** *a,* uni; joint; réuni. U~ *Kingdom* [*of Great Britain and Northern Ireland*], Royaume-Uni [de Grande-Bretagne et Irlande du Nord] *m.* U~ *States* [*of America*], États-Unis [d'Amérique] *m.pl.* **unity,** *n,* unité; union, *f;* ensemble, *m.*

universal†, *a,* universel. ~**ity,** *n,* universalité, *f.* **universe,** *n,* univers, *m.* **university,** *n,* université, *f;* (*att.*) universitaire.

unjust†, *a,* injuste. ~ *judge,* [juge] prévaricateur, *m.* **unjustifiable,** *a,* injustifiable.

unkempt, *a,* mal peigné, inculte.

unkind, *a,* désobligeant; méchant. ~**ness,** *n,* désobligeance; méchanceté, *f.*

unknown, *a,* inconnu; ignoré. ~ *person,* inconnu, **e.** ~ [*quantity*], [quantité] in-connue, *f.* ~ *to,* à l'insu de. *the* ~, l'inconnu, *m. the* U~ *Warrior* or *Soldier,* le Soldat inconnu.

unlace, *v.t,* délacer.

unlawful†, *a,* illégal, illicite. ~ *assembly to the disturbance of the peace,* attroupement, *m.* ~**ness,** *n,* illégalité, *f.*

unlearn, *v.t,* désapprendre. ~**ed,** *a,* illettré.

unleavened, *a,* sans levain; (*Jewish*) azyme.

unless, *c,* à moins que . . .[ne]; à moins de; si . . . ne . . . pas; sauf.

unlettered, *a,* illettré.

unlicensed, *a,* marron.

unlicked cub, ours mal léché, *m.*

unlike, *a,* dissemblable. ¶ *pr,* dissemblable à. **unlikelihood,** *n,* invraisemblance; improbabilité, *f.* **unlikely,** *a,* invraisemblable; improbable.

unlimber, *v.i,* décrocher l'avant-train.

unlimited, *a,* illimité.

unlined, *a,* non doublé.

unload, *v.t,* décharger; (*Fin.*) se défaire de.

unlock, *v.t,* ouvrir; (*Typ.*) desserrer.

unlooked for, *a,* inattendu.

unloose, *v.t,* lâcher.

unlovely, *a,* disgracieux.

unlucky†, *a,* malheureux, malchanceux, malencontreux.

unmake, *v.t.ir,* défaire.

unman, *v.t,* ôter tout courage de.

unmanageable, *a,* intraitable; impossible à conduire.

unmanly, *a,* lâche; efféminé.

unmannerly, *a,* grossier.

unmanufactured, *a,* brut.

unmarketable, *a,* invendable.

unmarried, *a,* non marié; célibataire. **unmarry,** *v.t,* démarier.

unmask, *v.t,* démasquer.

unmentionable, *a,* dont on ne parle pas.

unmerciful†, *a,* impitoyable.

unmerited, *a,* immérité.

unmethodical, *a,* non méthodique, incorrect.

unmindful, *a,* inattentif, oublieux.

unmingled, *a,* sans mélange, pur.

unmistakable†, *a,* évident, manifeste; immanquable.

unmitigated, *a,* fieffé, insigne.

unmixed, *a,* sans mélange, pur.

unmolested, *a,* en paix.

unmoor, *v.t,* démarrer.

unmounted, *a,* non monté; (*gem*) hors d'œuvre; (*pers.*) à pied.

unmoved, *a,* immobile; impassible.

unmusical, *a,* inharmonieux.

unmuzzle, *v.t,* démuseler.

unnamable, *a,* innommable. **unnamed,** *a,* innomé; anonyme.

unnatural, *a,* dénaturé; contre nature.

unnavigable, *a,* non navigable, impropre à la navigation.

unnecessary†, *a,* inutile.

unneighbourly way (in an), en mauvais voisin.

unnerve, v.t, ôter tout courage de.

unnoticed, unobserved, a, inaperçu, **unobservant,** a, inattentif.

unobstructed, a, non obstrué; (*view*) dégagée.

unobtainable, a, impossible à se procurer.

unobtrusive, a, effacé; discret. **~ly,** ad, discrètement.

unoccupied, a, inoccupé; libre, disponible.

unoffending, a, inoffensif.

unofficial, a, non officiel; (*information*) officieux.

unopened, a, non ouvert.

unopposed, a, sans opposition.

unorganized, a, non organisé.

unorthodox, a, hétérodoxe.

unostentatious, a. & **~ly,** ad, sans ostentation.

unpack, v.t, dépaqueter, déballer, décaisser. **~ed,** a, à découvert.

unpaid, a, (*bill, &c*) impayé; (*capital, &c*) non versé; (*carriage, &c*) non affranchi; (*no salary*) gratuit.

unpalatable, a, désagréable au goût.

unparalleled, a, sans pareil.

unpardonable, a, impardonnable.

unparliamentary, a, peu parlementaire.

unpatriotic, a, antipatriotique.

unpave, v.t, dépaver. **~d,** a, non pavé.

unperceived, a, inaperçu.

unphilosophical, a, peu philosophique.

unpin, v.t, enlever les épingles de.

unplaced horse, cheval non placé, m.

unpleasant†, a, désagréable, méchant. **~ness,** n, désagrément, m.

unpleasing, a, déplaisant, ingrat.

unpoetic(al), a, peu poétique.

unpolished, a, non poli; mat; brut; rude.

unpolluted, a, non souillé.

unpopular, a, impopulaire. **~ity,** n, impopularité, f.

unpractical, a, peu pratique.

unpractised, a, inexercé; novice.

unprecedented, a, sans précédent(s).

unprejudiced, a, sans préjugés, impartial.

unpremeditated, a, sans préméditation.

unprepared, a, sans être préparé, au dépourvu.

unprepossessing, a, peu engageant.

unpretentious, a, sans prétentions; modeste, discret.

unprincipled, a, sans principes.

unprintable, a, impubliable.

unprocurable, a, impossible à se procurer.

unproductive, a, improductif.

unprofessional, a, contraire aux usages de sa profession.

unprofitable, a, peu lucratif; inutile; ingrat. **unprofitably,** ad, sans profit; inutilement.

unpromising, a, qui ne promet guère; ingrat.

unpronounceable, a, non prononçable. **~ name,** nom à coucher dehors, m.

unpropitious, a, peu propice.

unprotected, a, découvert, à découvert.

unprovided, a, dépourvu (*with* = de).

unprovoked, a, sans provocation, gratuit.

unpublished (*book*) a, inédit.

unpunctual†, a, inexact. **~ity,** n, inexactitude, f.

unpunished, a, impuni.

unqualified, a, sans les qualités requises; marron; formel; sans réserve.

unquenchable, a, inextinguible.

unquestionable†, a, indiscutable.

unravel, v.t, démêler, débrouiller, parfiler; dénouer.

unread, a, illettré; sans être lu. **~able** (*writing, insupportable book*) a, illisible.

unreal, a, irréel. **~ity,** n, irréalité, f.

unrealizable, a, irréalisable.

unreasonable†, a, déraisonnable, intraitable. **~ness,** n, déraison, f. **unreasoning,** a, irraisonnable.

unrecognizable, a, méconnaissable.

unredeemable, a, irrachetable. **unredeemed,** a, (*stock*) non amorti; (*pledge*) non dégagé.

unrefined, a, non épuré; brut.

unrefuted, a, irréfuté.

unregistered, a, non enregistré; (*Post*) non recommandé; (*trade mark*) non déposée.

unrelenting†, a, inexorable.

unreliable, a, peu sûr; inexact; sujet à caution.

unremitting†, a, incessant, soutenu.

unremunerative, a, peu lucratif.

unrepealed, a, non abrogé.

unrepentant, a, impénitent.

unreservedly, ad, sans réserve.

unrest, n, agitation, effervescence, f.

unrestrained, a, immodéré; effréné.

unrestricted, a, sans restriction.

unretentive (*memory*) a, fugace.

unrewarded, a, sans récompense.

unrighteous†, a, injuste. **~ness,** n, injustice, f.

unripe, a, vert; en herbe. **~ness,** n, verdeur, f.

unrivalled, a, sans rival.

unrivet, v.t, dériver.

unroll, v.t, dérouler.

unruffled, a, imperturbable; calme, tranquille.

unruly, a, indiscipliné; turbulent.

unsaddle, v.t, desseller; (*pack animal*) débâter.

unsafe, a, peu sûr, mal assuré.

unsalable, a, invendable.

unsalaried, a, sans rétribution.

unsalted, a, non salé.

unsanitary, a, malsain, insalubre.

unsatisfactorily, ad, d'une manière peu satisfaisante. **unsatisfactory,** a, peu satisfaisant.

unsavoury, a, peu savoureux.

unsay, v.t.ir, se dédire de. **to leave unsaid,** taire.

unscathed, a, indemne, sauf.

unscientific, a, peu scientifique.

unscrew, v.t, dévisser. **to come ~ed,** se d.

unscrupulous, *a*, peu scrupuleux, indélicat. ~ly, *ad*, sans scrupule.

unseal, *v.t*, desceller; (*letter*) décacheter.

unseasonable, *a*, hors de saison; hors de propos, inopportun. unseasonably, *ad*, mal à propos, inopportunément. unseasoned (*wood*) *a*, vert.

unseat, *v.t*, invalider; (*rider*) désarçonner.

unseaworthy, *a*, en mauvais état de navigabilité.

unsecured, *a*, à découvert; chirographaire.

unseemly, *a*, malséant, inconvenant, folichon.

unseen, *a*, inaperçu. ~ [*translation*], version à livre ouvert, *f*.

unselfish, *a*, désintéressé.

unserviceable, *a*, inutilisable.

unsettle, *v.t*, déranger; (*pers.*) bouleverser. ~d, *a*, (*weather*) incertain, variable; (*question*) indécise.

unshakable†, *a*, inébranlable.

unshapely, *a*, difforme.

unshaven, *a*, non rasé.

unsheltered, *a*, sans abri; non protégé.

unsheathe, *v.t*, dégainer.

unship, *v.t*, débarquer; (*oars*) déborder.

unshoe (*horse*) *v.t.ir*, déferrer.

unshrinkable, *a*, irrétrécissable.

unsightliness, *n*, laideur, *f*. unsightly, *a*, laid.

unsigned, *a*, non signé.

unsinkable, *a*, insubmersible.

unskilful, *a*, malhabile, maladroit. ~ness, *n*, maladresse, *f*. unskilled, *a*, inexpérimenté.

unsla[c]ked lime, chaux vive, *f*.

unsociable, *a*, insociable.

unsocial, *a*, antisocial.

unsold, *a*, invendu.

unsolicited, *a*, non sollicité, spontané.

unsolved, *a*, non résolu.

unsophisticated, *a*, non frelaté; naïf, ingénu.

unsought, *a*, sans qu'on le cherche.

unsound, *a*, vicieux; défectueux. of ~ mind, ne ... pas sain d'esprit.

unsparing, *a*, prodigue; impitoyable.

unspeakable, *a*, indicible; ineffable.

unspent, *a*, non dépensé; non épuisé.

unspillable (*ink bottle*) *a*, inversable.

unspotted, *a*, sans tache.

unstable, *a*, instable; mouvant.

unstained, *a*, non teint; sans tache.

unstamped, *a*, non timbré; (*paper with no revenue stamps on*) libre; (*letter*) non affranchie.

unsteadiness, *n*, instabilité; vacillation, *f*. unsteady, *a*, instable; chancelant; vacillant.

unstitch, *v.t*, découdre.

unstop, *v.t*, déboucher.

unstressed (*Gram.*) *a*, atone.

unstudied, *a*, naturel.

unsubdued, *a*, insoumis, indompté.

unsubstantial, *a*, sans substance; immatériel.

unsuccessful, *a*, sans succès; manqué; infructueux. ~ly, *ad*, sans succès.

unsuitable†, *a*, impropre. unsuited, *a*, mal adapté; peu fait.

unsullied, *a*, sans tache.

unsupported, *a*, en porte à faux; sans appui.

unsurpassed, *a*, non surpassé.

unsuspected, *a*, non soupçonné. unsuspecting & unsuspicious, *a*, peu soupçonneux; exempt de soupçon. unsuspectingly, *ad*, sans défiance.

unsweetened, *a*, non sucré; (*wine*) brut.

unswerving, *a*, inébranlable.

unsymmetrical, *a*, dissymétrique.

untack (*Need.*) *v.t*, débâtir.

untainted, *a*, non corrompu, non gâté; sans tache.

untamable, *a*, indomptable. untamed, *a*, indompté.

untarnished, *a*, non terni.

untaught, *a*, ignorant; inculte.

untenable, *a*, (*position, &c*) intenable; (*assertion, &c*) insoutenable.

untenanted, *a*, inhabité.

unthinkable, *a*, inimaginable. unthinking, *a*, irréfléchi.

unthread, *v.t*, désenfiler.

untidiness, *n*, désordre, *m*. untidy†, *a*, malpropre, désordonné, mal tenu.

untie, *v.t*, délier, délacer; dénouer.

until, *pr*, jusqu'à; jusque; avant; à. ¶ *c*, jusqu'à ce que; en attendant que. not ~, ne ... pas avant de, ne ... pas avant que.

untimely, *a*, intempestif, prématuré; (*hour*) indue.

untiring†, *a*, infatigable.

untold, *a*, indicible; inimaginable; innombrable. ~ gold, des monceaux d'or.

untouchable, *n*, paria, *m*. untouched, *a*, intact; sans y toucher; non ému.

untoward, *a*, malencontreux, fâcheux.

untrained, *a*, inexercé; (*animal*) non dressé.

untranslatable, *a*, intraduisible.

untravelled, *a*, (*country*) non parcouru; (*pers.*) qui n'a jamais voyagé.

untried, *a*, non essayé, non éprouvé.

untrimmed, *a*, sans garniture; non rogné.

untrodden, *a*, non frayé, non battu.

untroubled, *a*, calme, paisible, tranquille.

untrue, *a*, faux; mensonger; infidèle. untruly, *ad*, faussement.

untrustworthy, *a*, indigne de confiance.

untruth, *n*, contrevérité; fausseté, *f*, mensonge, *m*. ~ful, *a*, peu véridique, menteur.

untuck, *v.t*, déborder.

untutored, *a*, inculte.

untwist, *v.t*, détordre, détortiller.

unused, *a*, non employé; non utilisé; peu habitué. unusual, *a*, peu commun, inaccoutumé, insolite, rare. ~ly, *ad*, extraordinairement.

unutterable, *a*, indicible, ineffable.

unvarnished, *a*, non verni; pur & simple.

unvarying, *a*, uniforme, invariable.

unveil, *v.t*, dévoiler; inaugurer.

unventilated, *a,* non aéré; mal aéré.

unversed in, peu versé dans.

unwarily, *ad,* sans précaution.

unwarlike, *a,* peu belliqueux.

unwarrantable, *a,* inexcusable, injustifiable.

unwary, *a,* peu circonspect.

unwashed, *a,* non lavé; crasseux.

unwavering, *a,* inébranlable.

unweaned, *a,* non sevré.

unwearied, *a,* infatigable.

unwelcome, *a,* de trop; désagréable.

unwell, *a,* indisposé, souffrant.

unwholesome, *a,* malsain; morbide.

unwieldy, *a,* lourd, pesant; incommode.

unwilling, *a,* peu disposé, mal disposé. **~ly,** *ad,* à contre-cœur. **~ness,** *n,* mauvaise volonté; répugnance, *f.*

unwind, *v.t.ir,* dévider, dérouler.

unwisdom, *n,* manque de sagesse, *m.* **unwise,** *a,* peu sage, malavisé. **~ly,** *ad,* follement.

unwittingly, *ad,* sans y penser.

unwonted, *a,* inaccoutumé, insolite.

unworkable, *a,* inexécutable, impraticable. **unworked,** *a,* inexploité. *in an unworkmanlike manner,* en mauvais ouvrier.

unworn, *a,* non usé.

unworthiness, *n,* indignité, *f.* **unworthy,** *a,* indigne.

unwounded, *a,* non blessé.

unwrap, *v.t,* développer.

unwrinkled, *a,* sans rides.

unwritten, *a,* non écrit. **~ law,** droit coutumier, *m.*

unwrought, *a,* non travaillé, non ouvré.

unyielding, *a,* inflexible, inébranlable.

unyoke, *v.t,* dételer.

up, *a,* montant. **~ grade,** rampe, *f.* **~ stroke** (writing), délié, *m.* **~ train,** train montant, *m.* ¶ *ad,* en haut; au haut; haut; en amont; debout; sur pied; fini; (*prices*) en hausse; (*risen*) levé, e. **~ & down,** en haut & en bas; de long en large. **~stairs,** en haut. **~-stream,** *ad,* en amont. **~ there,** là-haut. **~ to,** jusqu'à [concurrence de]. **~ to date,** à jour; (*att.*) moderne. *so many holes* **~** (*Golf*), tant de trous d'avance. *well up in* (subject), fort en, calé en. ¶ *ups & downs,* hauts & bas, *m.pl.* ¶ *up!* debout! alerte! levez-vous!

upbraid, *v.t,* reprocher.

upheaval, *n,* (*Geol.*) soulèvement; (*fig.*) bouleversement, *m,* convulsion, *f.*

uphill, *a,* montant; ardu. ¶ *ad,* en montant.

uphold, *v.t,* soutenir, maintenir. **~er,** *n,* soutien, *m.*

upholster, *v.t,* capitonner, rembourrer. **~er,** *n,* tapissier, ère.

upkeep, *n,* entretien, *m.*

upland, *n,* [haut] plateau, *m.*

uplift, *v.t,* ennoblir.

upon, *pr,* sur; dessus.

upper, *a,* supérieur; haut; de dessus. **~ case**

(*Typ.*), haut de casse, *m.* **~ circle, seconde** [galeries] *f.pl.* *the* **~ classes,** les hautes classes, *f.pl.* **~ deck,** pont supérieur, *m;* (*bus*) impériale, *f.* **U ~ Egypt,** la Haute-Égypte. *the* **~ hand** (*fig.*), le dessus; l'avantage, *m.* **~ register** (*Mus.*), aigu, *m.* *the* **~ ten,** le grand monde. **~ tooth,** dent de dessus, *f.* ¶ (*shoe*) *n,* empeigne, *f.* **~most,** *a,* le plus haut, le plus élevé; le plus fort.

upright, *a. & ad,* droit; debout; vertical; d'aplomb; intègre, honnête. **~ piano,** piano droit, *m.* **~ness,** *n,* perpendicularité; droiture, intégrité, *f.*

uprising, *n,* soulèvement, *m.*

uproar, *n,* tumulte, vacarme, tapage, bacchanal, *m.* **~ous†,** *a,* bruyant, tapageur.

uproot, *v.t,* déraciner, arracher.

upset, *n,* remue-ménage, *m.* ¶ *v.t,* renverser; verser; chavirer; déranger; bouleverser, rompre. **~ price,** mise à prix, *f.*

upshot, *n,* issue, *f,* fin mot; dénouement, *m.*

upside down, *ad,* sens dessus dessous.

upstart, *n,* parvenu, e.

upstroke, *n,* (*piston*) course montante, *f;* (*Writing*) délié, *m.*

upward, *a,* ascendant; ascensionnel; jeté vers le haut. **~[s],** *ad,* en haut, en contre-haut; en montant; au-dessus, **~s** *of,* plus de.

Ural (the), l'Oural, *m. the* **~ Mountains,** les monts Ourals, *m.pl.*

uranium, *n,* uranium, *m.*

urban, *a,* urbain. **urbane,** *a,* courtois, poli. **~ly,** *ad,* avec urbanité.

urchin, *n,* gamin, galopin, moutard, *m.*

urethra, *n,* urètre, *m.*

urge, *n,* démangeaison, *f.* ¶ *v.t,* pousser, presser, solliciter; exhorter; alléguer. **urgency,** *n,* urgence, *f.* **urgent,** *a,* urgent, pressant, instant. **~ly,** *ad,* instamment.

uric, *a,* urique. **urinal,** *n,* urinoir, *m,* vespasienne, *f;* (*vessel*) urinal, *m.* **urinate,** *v.i,* uriner. **urine,** *n,* urine, *f.*

urn, *n,* urne, *f;* (*tea, &c*) samovar, *m.*

us, *pn,* nous.

usage, *n,* usage; traitement, *m.* **usance,** *n,* usance, *f.* **use,** *n,* usage; emploi; emprunt, *m;* jouissance; utilité; habitude; consommation, *f.* **~ & wont,** us & coutumes, *m.pl. to be of* **~,** servir. ¶ *v.t,* se servir de, employer, emprunter; consommer; user de; traiter. **~ no hooks,** ne pas se servir de crochets. **~d,** *p.a,* usité; accoutumé, rompu; ayant déjà servi; usagé, d'occasion. **~** *tea leaves,* marc de thé, *m.* **~ful†,** *a,* utile. **~fulness,** *n,* utilité, *f.* **~less†,** *a,* inutile; vain. **~ person,** non-valeur, *f.* **~ things,** inutilités, *f.pl.* **~lessness,** *n,* inutilité, *f.* **user,** *n,* usager, *m.*

Ushant, *n,* Ouessant, *m.*

usher, *n,* huissier; maître d'étude, pion, *m.* **~ in,** introduire, annoncer; (*fig.*) inaugurer.

usual†, *a,* usuel; habituel; obligé; ordinaire.

usufruct, *n*, usufruit, *m*.

usurer, *n*, usurier, ère, fesse-mathieu, *m*. usurious†, *a*, usuraire.

usurp, *v.t.* usurper. ~ation, *n*, usurpation, *f*. ~er, *n*, usurpateur, trice.

usury, *n*, usure, *f*.

utensil, *n*, ustensile; vase, *m*.

uterine, *a*, utérin. uterus, *n*, utérus, *m*.

utilitarian, *a. & n*, utilitaire, *a. & m.f*.

utility, *n. & ~ man*, utilité, *f*. utilize, *v.t*, utiliser.

utmost, *a*, extrême, dernier. *one's* [*very*] ~, [tout] son possible, l'impossible, *m*. *to the* ~, à outrance.

utopia, *n*, utopie, *f*. utopian, *a*, utopique, utopiste. ¶ *n*, utopiste, *m.f*.

utter†, *a*, complet; total; extrême; grand. ¶ *v.t*, proférer, prononcer, dire, débiter; (*cry*) pousser; (*money*) passer. ~ance, *n*, articulation; parole, *f*; débit, *m*. ~most, *a*, extrême; le plus reculé.

uvula, *n*, luette, uvule, *f*.

V

vacancy, *n*, vacance, *f*; vide, *m*. vacant, *a*, vacant; libre, inoccupé; distrait. vacate, *v.t*, (*office*) quitter; (*premises*) vider. vacation, *n*, vacances; (*Law*) vacations, *f.pl*.

vaccinate, *v.t*, vacciner. vaccination, *n*, vaccination, *f*. vaccine, *n*, vaccin, *m*.

vacillate, *v.i*, vaciller. vacillation, *n*, vacillation, *f*.

vacuity, *n*, vacuité, *f*.. vacuous, *a*, insignifiant. vacuum, *n*, vide, *m*. ~ *brake*, frein à vide, *m*. ~ *cleaner*, aspirateur [de poussières] *m*. ~ *cleaning*, nettoyage par le vide, *m*. ~ *flask*, bouteille isolante, *f*.

vade-mecum, *n*, vade-mecum, *m*, épée de chevet, *f*.

vagabond, *n. & a*, vagabond, e.

vagary, *n*, caprice, *m*, lubie, *f*.

vagrancy, *n*, vagabondage, *m*. vagrant, *n*, vagabond, e, homme sans aveu, *m*. ¶ *a*, vagabond.

vague†, *a*, vague, imprécis. ~ness, *n*, vague, *m*, imprécision, *f*.

vain†, *a*, vain, vaniteux. ~glorious, *a*, vaniteux, glorieux, superbe. ~glory, *n*, gloriole, superbe, *f*.

valance, *n*, pente, *f*.

vale, *n*, vallon, val, *m*.

valedictory, *a*, d'adieu.

valence, -cy (*Chem.*) *n*, valence, *f*.

Valencia, *n*, Valence, *f*.

valet, *n*, valet [de chambre] *m*. ¶ *v.t*, faire office de valet à.

Valetta, *n*, la Valette.

valetudinarian, *a. & n*, valétudinaire, *a. & m.f*.

valiant†, *a*, vaillant, brave.

valid†, *a*, valide; (*ticket*) valable. ~ate, *v.t*, valider. ~ity, *n*, validité, *f*.

valise, *n*, valise, *f*.

valley, *n*, vallée, *f*; (*of roof*) noue, *f*.

valorous†, *a*, valeureux. valour, *n*, valeur, vaillance, bravoure, *f*.

valuable, *a*, de valeur, de prix, riche; précieux. ~s, *n.pl*, valeurs, *f.pl*, objets de valeur, *m.pl*. valuation, *n*, évaluation, *f*. ~ *list*, cadastre, *m*. value, *n*, valeur, *f*; prix, *m*. ~ *parcel*, colis finances & valeurs, *m*. ¶ *v.t*, évaluer; apprécier; faire cas de. ~less, *a*, sans valeur. valuer, *n*, priseur, expert, *m*.

valve, *n*, soupape, *f*, clapet; tiroir, *m*; valve; lampe, *f*. ~ *set*, poste à lampe(s) *m*.

vamp (*shoe*) *n*, empeigne, *f*. ¶ *v.t. & i*, improviser.

vampire, *n*, vampire, *m*.

van, *n*, voiture; tapissière, *f*; wagon; fourgon, *m*. ~[*guard*], avant-garde, *f*.

vanadium, *n*, vanadium, *m*.

vandal, *n*, vandale, *m*. ¶ *a*, de vandale. ~ism, *n*, vandalisme, *m*.

vane, *n*, girouette; aube; aile; pinnule, *f*.

vanilla, *n*, vanille, *f*. ~ *ice*, glace à la v., *f*.

vanish, *v.i*, s'évanouir, disparaître, devenir invisible; s'éclipser, se volatiliser, fuir. ~ing point, point de fuite, *m*.

vanity, *n*, vanité, *f*; mensonge, *m*. ~ *case*, boîte à poudre, avec glace & houppe, *f*.

vanner (*horse*) *n*, camionneur, *m*.

vanquish, *v.t*, vaincre. *the* ~ed, les vaincus, *m.pl*.

vantage (*Ten.*) *n*, avantage [du jeu] *m*. ~ ground, position avantagée, *f*.

vapid, *a*, insipide, fade, plat.

vaporize, *v.t*, vaporiser. vaporizer, *n*, vaporisateur, *m*. vaporous, -ry, *a*, vaporeux. vapour, *n*, vapeur, *f*. ~ *bath*, bain de vapeur, *m*.

variable, *a*, variable; changeant. *at variance*, en désaccord, en mésintelligence. variant, *n*, variante, *f*. variation, *n*, variation, *f*; changement, *m*; modification, *f*.

varicose vein, varice, *f*.

variegate, *v.t*, varier, bigarrer, panacher, diaprer. varieties (*Theat.*) *n.pl*, attractions, *f.pl*. variety, *n*, variété, *f*. ~ *actress*, divette, *f*. ~ *theatre*, music hall, *m*.

various†, *a*, différent, divers.

varlet (*Hist.*) *n*, varlet, *m*.

varnish, *n*, vernis, *m*. ¶ *v.t*, vernir. ~ing, *n. & ~ day*, vernissage, *m*.

vary, *v.t. & i*, varier; diversifier; modifier.

vascular, *a*, vasculaire.

vase, *n*, vase, *m*; (*Chinese, &c*) potiche, *f*.

vaseline (*proprietary term*), *n*, vaseline, *f*.

vassal (*Hist.*), *n*, vassal, e.

vast, *a*, vaste, immense. ~ly, *ad*, grandement. ~ness, *n*, immensité, *f*.

vat, *n*, cuve, *f*, bac, *m*. ¶ *v.t*, encuver.

vaudeville, *n*, vaudeville, *m*.

vault, *n*, voûte; cave, *f*; caveau; tombeau; (*leap*) saut, *m*. ¶ *v.t*, voûter; (*v.i.*) sauter.

~*ing horse*, cheval de bois, *m.* ~*ing standard*, sautoir, *m.*

vaunt, *n*, vanterie, *f.* ¶ *v.t*, vanter; (*v.i.*) se vanter.

veal, *n*, veau, *m.* ~ *cutlet*, côtelette de v., *f.*

vector, *n*, vecteur, *m.*

veer, *v.i.* (*wind*) se ranger, remonter; (*opinion*) se retourner. ~ *out*, filer. ~*ing* (*opinion*) *n*, revirement, *m.*

vegetable, *n*, légume, *m*, plante potagère, *f.* ¶ *a*, végétal. ~ *dish*, légumier, *m.* ~ *marrow*, courge à la moelle, *f.* ~ *soup*, soupe maigre, *f.* **vegetarian**, *a. & n*, végétarien, ne. **vegetarianism**, *n*, végétarisme, *m.* **vegetate**, *v.i*, végéter. **vegetation**, *n*, végétation, *f.*

vehemence, *n*, véhémence, *f.* **vehement**†, *a*, véhément.

vehicle, *n*, (*carriage*) véhicule, *m*, voiture, *f*; (*medium*) véhicule, *m.* *vehicular traffic*, circulation des voitures, *f.*

veil, *n*, voile, *m*; voilette, *f*; (*fig.*) voile, rideau, bandeau, *m.* ¶ *v.t*, voiler.

vein, *n*, veine, *f*; (*leaf*) nervure, *f.* ¶ *v.t*, veiner.

vellum, *n*, vélin, *m.*

velocipede, *n*, vélocipède, *m.*

velocity, *n*, vitesse, *f.*

velours, *n*, feutre velours, *m.*

velum (*Anat.*) *n*, voile, *m.*

velvet, *n*, velours, *m.* ~ *pile*, moquette, *f.* **velveteen**, *n*, velours de coton, *m*, tripe de velours, *f.* **velvet**[**y**], *a*, velouté.

venal†, *a*, vénal. ~*ity*, *n*, vénalité, *f.*

vender, *n*, marchand, e. **vendor**, *n*, vendeur, euse; (*Law*) vendeur, eresse; (*Law*) apporteur, *m.* ~ *company*, société apporteuse, *f.* ~*'s assets*, valeurs d'apport, *f.pl.*

veneer, *n*, bois de placage, *m*, feuilles de p., *f.pl*; (*fig.*) vernis, *m.* ¶ *v.t*, plaquer; (*fig.*) donner du vernis à.

venerable, *a*, vénérable. **venerate**, *v.t*, vénérer. **veneration**, *n*, vénération, *f.*

venereal, *a*, vénérien.

Venetia, *n*, la Vénétie. **Venetian**, *a*, vénitien. ~ *blind*, jalousie, *f.* ~ *mast*, mât de pavoisement, *m.* ¶ *n*, Vénitien, ne.

vengeance, *n*, vengeance, *f.* **vengeful**, *a*, vengeur.

venial†, *a*, véniel.

Venice, *n*, Venise, *f.*

venison, *n*, venaison, *f*, chevreuil, *m.*

venom, *n*, venin, *m.* ~**ous**, *a*, venimeux; vénéneux.

vent, *n*, évent, aspirail, soupirail, *m*; lumière; cheminée, *f*; libre cours, *m*, carrière, *f.* ~ *hole* (cask), trou de fausset, *m.* ~ *peg*, fausset, *m.* ¶ *v.t*, exhaler; donner libre cours à, évaporer. **ventilate**, *v.t*, aérer, donner de l'air à, ventiler. **ventilation**, *n*, aérage, *m*, aération, ventilation, *f.* **ventilator**, *n*, ventilateur, *m*; (*ship*) manche à air, manche à vent, *f.*

ventral, *a*, ventral.

ventricle, *n*, ventricule, *m.*

ventriloquism, -**quy**, *n*, ventriloquie, *f.* **ventriloquist**, *n*, ventriloque, *m,f.*

venture, *n*, aventure; entreprise; spéculation, *f*, hasard, *m.* ¶ *v.t*, aventurer, hasarder. ~ *to*, oser, se permettre de. ~**some**, *a*, aventureux; hasardeux.

veracious†, *a*, véridique. **veracity**, *n*, véracité, *f.*

veranda[**h**], *n*, véranda, *f.*

verb, *n*, verbe, *m.* **verbal**†, *a*, verbal. **verbatim**, *ad. & a*, mot à mot, *m*. pour m. **verbiage**, *n*, verbiage, *m.* **verbose**, *a*, verbeux. **verbosity**, *n*, verbosité, *f.*

verdant, *a*, verdoyant; naïf.

verdict, *n*, verdict, *m.*

verdigris, *n*, vert-de-gris, verdet, *m.*

verdure, *n*, verdure, *f.*

verge, *n*, bord, *m*; orée, *f*; (*road*) accotement, *f*; (*fig.*) penchant, point, *m*; (*rod*) verge, *f.* ¶ ~ *on*, tirer à; (*ruin*) pencher vers. **verger**, *n*, bedeau, *m.*

verification, *n*, vérification, *f.* **verify**, *v.t*, vérifier. **verisimilitude**, *n*, vraisemblance, *f.* **veritable**†, *a*, véritable. **verity**, *n*, vérité, *f.*

vermicelli, *n*, vermicelle, *m*, nouilles, *f.pl.*

vermilion, *n*, vermillon, *m.* ¶ *a*, vermeil.

vermin, *n*, vermine, *f*; animaux nuisibles, *m.pl.* ~**ous**, *a*, couvert de vermine.

vermouth, *n*, vermouth, *m.*

vernacular, *a*, vulgaire. ¶ *n*, langue vulgaire, *f.*

vernal, *a*, printanier; (*equinox*) de printemps.

vernier, *n*, vernier, *m.*

Verona, *n*, Vérone, *f.*

veronica, *n*, véronique, *f.*

versatile, *a*, souple. **versatility**, *n*, souplesse d'esprit, *f.*

verse, *n*, vers, *m*; vers, *m.pl*; verset; couplet, *m*, strophe, *f.* **versed in**, versé dans, ferré en. **versicle** (*Lit.*) *n*, verset, *m.* **versifier**, *n*, versificateur, *m.* **versify**, *v.t*, versifier, rimer. **version**, *n*, version, *f.*

verso, *n*, verso, *m.*

versus, *pr*, contre.

vertebra, *n*, vertèbre, *f.* **vertebral**, *a*, vertébral. **Vertebrata**, *n.pl*, vertébrés, *m.pl.* **vertebrate**, *a. & n*, vertébré, e. & *m.*

vertex, *n*, sommet, *m.* **vertical**, *a*, vertical. ¶ *n*, verticale, *f.* ~**ity**, *n*, verticalité, *f.* ~**ly**, *ad*, verticalement. ~ *strung piano*, piano à cordes droites, *m.*

vertiginous, *a*, vertigineux. **vertigo**, *n*, vertige, *m.*

verve, *n*, verve, *f.*

very, *a*, même; seul. ¶ *ad*, très; fort; bien; tout. ~ *much*, beaucoup.

vesicle, *n*, vésicule, *f.*

vespers, *n.pl*, vêpres, *f.pl.*

vessel, *n*, vase, récipient; (*blood*, &*c*) vaisseau; (*ship*) vaisseau, bâtiment, navire, *m.*

vest, *n*, (*man's*) gilet, *m*; (*woman's*) chemise, camisole; (*baby's*) brassière, *f.* ~~*pocket* *camera*, chambre se mettant dans la poche du gilet, *f.* ¶ *v.t,* investir; confier. ~*ed rights,* droits acquis, *m.pl.*

vesta, *n,* allumette, *f.*

vestal [virgin], *n,* vestale, *f.*

vestibule, *n,* vestibule, *m.*

vestige, *n,* vestige, *m,* trace, *f.*

vestment, *n,* vêtement, *m.*

vestry, *n,* sacristie; (*council*) fabrique, *f.*

Vesuvian, *a,* vésuvien. **Vesuvius,** *n,* le Vésuve.

vetch, *n,* gesse; (*tare*) vesce, *f.*

veteran, *n,* vétéran, *m.* ¶ *a,* qui a vieilli dans sa profession; de longue date; depuis longtemps sous les drapeaux.

veterinary, *a,* vétérinaire. ~ [*surgeon*], [médecin] vétérinaire *m.*

veto, *n,* veto, *m.* ¶ *v.t,* mettre le (son) v. à.

vex, *v.t,* contrarier, chagriner, vexer. ~**ation,** *n,* contrariété, *f;* désagrément, *m;* vexation, *f.* **vexatious,** *a,* contrariant, vexatoire. **vexed** (*question*) *p.a,* controversée, longuement débattue.

via, *pr,* par la voie [de], par.

viability, *n,* viabilité, *f.* **viable,** *a,* viable.

viaduct, *n,* viaduc, *m.*

vial, *n,* fiole, *f.*

viand, *n,* mets, *m.*

vibrate, *v.i,* (*Phys. & fig.*) vibrer; (*machinery, car, &c*) trembler. **vibration,** *n,* (*Phys.*) vibration; (*mach., &c*) trépidation, *f.*

vicar, *n,* vicaire; curé; ministre, *m.* ~**age,** *n,* cure, *f;* presbytère, *m.* ~**ship,** *n,* cure, *f.*

vice, *n,* (*depravity*) vice; (*tool*) étau, *m.*

vice-, *prefix,* vice-. ~**chairman,** ~**president,** vice-président, e. ~**principal** (college), censeur, *m.* ~**reine,** vice-reine, *f.* ~**roy,** vice-roi, *f.*

Vicenza, *n,* Vicence, *f.*

vice versa, *ad,* vice versa, réciproquement.

vicinity, *n,* voisinage, *m,* proximité, *f.*

vicious†, *a,* vicieux. ~ *circle,* cercle vicieux, *m.* ~**ness,** *n,* nature vicieuse, *f.*

vicissitude, *n,* vicissitude, péripétie, *f;* cahot, *m.*

victim, *n,* victime, *f.* ~**ize,** *v.t,* rendre victime.

victor, *n,* vainqueur, *m.* **victoria** (*carriage*) *n,* victoria, *f.* **victorious†,** *a,* victorieux. **victory,** *n,* victoire, *f.*

victual, *v.t,* ravitailler. ~**s,** *n.pl,* vivres, *m.pl,* victuailles, *f.pl.*

vicugna, -uña, *n,* vigogne, *f.*

vide, *v. imperative,* voir, voyez.

vie, *v.i,* rivaliser; lutter; faire assaut.

Vienna, *n,* Vienne, *f.* **Viennese,** *a,* viennois. *n,* Viennois, e.

view, *n,* vue; perspective, *f,* coup d'œil; tableau, *m;* idée, opinion, *f.* *to have in* ~, viser. ~*finder,* viseur, *m.* ¶ *v.t,* contempler; envisager.

vigil, *n,* veille, *f.* veillée, *f.* (*Eccl.*) vigile, *f.* ~**ance,** *n,* vigilance, *f.* ~**ant,** *a,* vigilant. ~**antly,** *ad,* avec vigilance.

vignette, *n,* vignette, *f.* ¶ *v.t,* dégrader. **vignetter,** *n,* dégradateur, *m.*

vigorous†, *a,* vigoureux. **vigour,** *n,* vigueur; sève, *f.*

vile, *a,* vil; abject. ~**ness,** *n,* bassesse; abjection, *f.* **vilify,** *v.t,* vilipender.

villa, *n,* villa, *f.* **village,** *n,* village, *m;* bourgade, *f;* (*att.*) villageois, de village, de clocher. **villager,** *n,* villageois, e.

villain, *n,* scélérat, e, misérable, *m,f,* bandit; (*Theat.*) traître, *m;* (*Hist.*) vilain, e. ~**ous†,** *a,* scélérat. ~**y,** *n,* scélératesse, *f.* **villein,** *n,* vilain, e.

vindicate, *v.t,* justifier. **vindication,** *n,* justification, *f.*

vindictive, *a,* vindicatif.

vine, *n,* vigne, *f.* ~ *shoot,* sarment, *m.* **vinegar,** *n,* vinaigre, *m.* ~ *works,* vinaigrerie, *f.* ¶ *v.t,* vinaigrer. **vinery,** *n,* serre à vignes, *f.* **vineyard,** *n,* vigne, *f;* vignoble, *m.* **vinosity,** *n,* vinosité, *f.* **vinous,** *a,* vineux. **vintage,** *n,* (*growth*) cru, *m,* cuvée; (*season*) vendange; (*crop*) récolte, *f.* ~ *wine,* vin millésimé, *m.* ~ *year,* année à millésime, *f.* **vintager,** *n,* vendangeur, euse.

viola, *n,* (*Mus.*) alto, *m;* (*Bot.*) violariacée, *f.* **Violaceae,** *n.pl,* violacées, *f.pl.* **violaceous,** *a,* violacé.

violate, *v.t,* violer. **violation,** *n,* violation, *f;* (*rape*) viol, *m.* **violator,** *n,* violateur, trice. **violence,** *n,* violence, *f.* *do* ~ *to,* violenter. **violent†,** *a,* violent; carabiné.

violet, *n,* (*Bot.*) violette, *f;* (*colour*) violet, *m.* ¶ *a,* violet.

violin, *n,* violon, *m.* ~**ist,** *n,* violoniste, *m,f.* **violoncellist,** *n,* violoncelliste, *m,f.* **violoncello,** *n,* violoncelle, *m.*

viper, *n,* vipère, *f.*

virago, *n,* dragon, *m,* mégère, *f.*

virgin, *n,* vierge; pucelle, *f.* ¶ *a,* vierge. ~**al†,** *a,* virginal. **Virginia** (*Geog.*) *n,* la Virginie, *f.* ~ *creeper,* vigne vierge, *f.* ~ [*tobacco*], virginie, *m.* **virginity,** *n,* virginité, *f.*

virile, *a,* viril, mâle. **virility,** *n,* virilité, *f.*

virtual†, *a,* virtuel. **virtue,** *n,* vertu, *f.* **virtuosity,** *n,* virtuosité, *f.* **virtuoso,** *n,* virtuose, *m,f.* **virtuous†,** *a,* vertueux.

virulence, *n,* virulence, *f.* **virulent,** *a,* virulent. **virus,** *n,* virus, *m.*

visa, *n,* visa, *m.* ¶ *v.t,* viser.

visage, *n,* visage, *m,* figure, *f.*

viscera, *n.pl,* viscères, *m.pl.*

viscid *&* **viscous,** *a,* visqueux. **viscose,** *n,* viscose, *f.* **viscosity,** *n,* viscosité, *f.*

viscount, *n,* vicomte, *m.* ~**ess,** *n,* vicomtesse, *f.*

visibility, *n,* visibilité, *f.* **visible,** *a,* visible. **visibly,** *ad,* visiblement; à vue d'œil.

vision, *n,* vision, *f.* ~**ary,** *a,* visionnaire; chimérique. ¶ *n,* visionnaire, *m,f.*

visit, *n,* visite, *f.* ¶ *v.t,* visiter; voir; (*Cust.*) arraisonner. ~**ation,** *n,* visite; (*Eccl.*)

visitation, *f.* ~ing card, carte de visite, *f.*
~or, *n,* visiteur, euse; hôte, esse; passager,
ère. ~s' *tax,* taxe de séjour, *f.*
visor, *n,* visière, *f.*
vista, *n,* échappée [de vue]; perspective, *f.*
Vistula (the), la Vistule.
visual, *a,* visuel.
vital, *a,* vital; (*fig.*) vif. ~ity, *n,* vitalité, *f.*
~ize, *v.t,* vivifier. ~s, *n.pl,* parties
vitales, *f.pl.* **vitamin,** *n,* vitamine, *f.*
vitiate, *v.t,* vicier. **vitiation,** *n,* viciation, *f.*
viticultural, *a,* viticole. **viticultur[al]ist,** *n,*
viticulteur, *m.* **viticulture,** *n,* viticulture, *f.*
vitreous, *a,* vitreux; (*humour*) vitrée. **vit-**
rify, *v.t,* vitrifier. **vitriol,** *n,* vitriol, *m.*
~ic, *a,* vitriolique.
vituperate, *v.t,* injurier, vilipender. **vitupera-**
tion, *n,* injures, *f.pl.*
vivacious, *a,* enjoué. to be ~, avoir de la
vivacité. ~ly, *ad,* avec vivacité. **viva**
voce, *ad,* de vive voix. ¶ *a,* oral. ¶ *n,*
examen oral, *m.* **vivid,** *a,* vif, vivant.
vividness, *n,* vivacité, *f.* **vivify,** *v.t,* vivifier.
viviparous, *a,* vivipare. **vivisection,** *n,*
vivisection, *f.*
vixen, *n,* renarde; (*woman*) mégère, *f.*
viz, *ad, abb,* c'est-à-dire, [à] savoir.
vizi[e]r, *n,* vizir, *m.*
vocable, *n,* vocable, *m.* **vocabulary,** *n,* vocabulaire, *m.* **vocal,** *a,* vocal. ~ist, *n,*
chanteur, euse, cantatrice, *f.* ~ize, *v.t,*
vocaliser. **vocation,** *n,* vocation, *f.* **vo-**
cative [case], *n,* vocatif, *m.*
vociferate, *v.i,* vociférer. **vociferous,** *a,*
bruyant. ~ly, *ad,* bruyamment.
vogue, *n,* vogue, mode, *f.*
voice, *n,* voix, *f.* ¶ *v.t,* exprimer.
void, *a,* vide; nul. ¶ *n,* vide; vague, *m.*
¶ *v.t,* évacuer; annuler.
voile (*textile*) *n,* voile, *m.*
volatile, *a,* volatil. **volatilize,** *v.t,* volatiliser.
volcanic, *a,* volcanique. **volcano,** *n,* volcan, *m.*
vole (*Zool.*) *n,* campagnol, *m.*
volition, *n,* volition, *f.*
volley, *n,* volée; décharge, *f.* ~ ball, volley-
ball, *m.* ~ firing, feu de peloton, *m.*
¶ (*Ten.*) *v.t,* [re]prendre à là (*ou* de) volée;
(*abs.*) jouer à là (*ou* de) volée.
volplane, *n,* vol plané, *m.* ¶ *v.i,* descendre
en vol plané.
volt, *n,* volt, *m.* ~age, *n,* voltage, *m.*,
tension, *f.* **voltaic,** *a,* voltaïque. **volt-**
meter, *n,* voltmètre, *m.*
volubility, *n,* volubilité, *f.* **voluble,** *a,* volubile, fécond en paroles.
volume, *n,* volume; tome; (*of smoke, &c*)
nuage, *m.* **voluminous,** *a,* volumineux.
voluntary†, *a,* volontaire; bénévole. ¶ (*organ*)
n, (*before service*) prélude; (*during*) interlude, *m;* (*after*) sortie, *f;* (*between credo &
sanctus*) offertoire, *m.* **volunteer,** *n,* (*Mil.*)
volontaire; (*for task*) homme de bonne
volonté, *m.* ~ *corps,* corps franc, *m.*

voluptuary, *n,* voluptueux, euse. **voluptu-**
ous†, *a,* voluptueux. ~ness, *n,* volupté,
sensualité, mollesse, *f.*
volute, *n,* volute, *f.*
vomit, *n,* vomissement, *m.* ¶ *v.t. & i,*
vomir, revomir.
voracious, *a,* vorace. ~ly, *ad,* avec voracité. ~ness, **voracity,** *n,* voracité, *f.*
vortex, *n,* tourbillon, *m.*
votary, *n,* adorateur, trice; sectateur, *m.*
vote, *n,* vote, scrutin, suffrage, *m,* voix,
opinion, *f.* ~s *for women,* suffrage des
femmes; la Française doit voter! ¶ *v.t. &
i,* voter, donner sa voix, opiner. ~ *by a
show of hands,* voter à main levée. **voter,**
n, votant, *m.* **voting,** *n,* votation, *f.* ~
paper, bulletin de vote, *m.* **votive,** *a,* votif.
vouch, *v.t,* attester; vérifier. ~ *for,* répondre de, garantir. ~ *for* juste justificative, p. à l'appui, *f;* bon, bulletin, *m.*
~safe, *v.t,* accorder; daigner.
voussoir, *n,* voussoir, *m.*
vow, *n,* vœu, *m.* ¶ *v.t,* vouer; (*v.i.*) faire
vœu; jurer.
vowel, *n,* voyelle, *f.*
voyage, *n,* voyage, *m.* ¶ *v.i,* voyager.
vulcanite, *n,* caoutchouc vulcanisé, *m,*
ébonite, *f.* **vulcanize,** *v.t,* vulcaniser.
vulgar†, *a,* vulgaire; populacier; trivial,
commun, bas; (*fraction*) ordinaire. the ~
[*herd*], le vulgaire. ~ism, *n,* expression
vulgaire, trivialité, *f.* ~ity, *n,* vulgarité,
trivialité, *f.* ~ize, *v.t,* vulgariser; banaliser. the *Vulgate,* la Vulgate.
vulnerable, *a,* vulnérable.
vulture, *n,* vautour, *m.*

W

wad, *n,* bourre, *f;* tampon, *m.* ¶ *v.t,* ouater.
wadding, *n,* ouate, *f.*
waddle, *n,* dandinement, déhanchement, *m.*
¶ *v.i,* marcher comme une cane, se dandiner.
wade, *v.i,* se mettre à l'eau sans nager;
patauger, barboter. ~ *through* (ford),
passer à gué. ~ *through a book,* peiner
en lisant un livre. **wader,** *n,* (*bird*) échassier, *m;* (*pl.*) bottes cuissardes, *f.pl.*
wafer, *n,* (*flat biscuit*) gaufrette; (*cornet
biscuit*) oublie, *f,* plaisir; (*signet*) pain [à
cacheter]; (*Eccl.*) pain à chanter, *m.*
waffle, *n,* gaufre, *f.* ~ *irons,* gaufrier, *m.*
waft, *n,* souffle, *m.* ¶ *v.t,* apporter, répandre.
wag, *n,* plaisant, loustic, farceur, *m.* ¶ *v.t,*
(*tail*) agiter, frétiller de; (*head*) branler,
dodeliner de (*la tête*).
wage, *n. oft. pl,* salaire, *m,* paie, *f,* gages,
loyers, *m.pl.* ~ *earner,* salarié, e. to
pay a ~ *to,* salarier. **to** ~ **war,** faire la
guerre, guerroyer.
wager, *n,* pari, *m,* gageure, *f.* ¶ *v.t,* parier.
waggish, *a,* facétieux, badin.
waggle, *v.t. & i,* branler.

wag[g]on, *n*, chariot, *m*; voiture, *f*, wagon; fourgon, *m*. **~load**, charretée, *f*. **~er**, *n*, charretier, roulier. *m*. **~ette**, *n*, break, *m*.

wagtail, *n*, hochequeue, *m*, bergeronnette, *f*.

waif, *n*, enfant abandonné, e, *m,f*.

wail, *n*, lamentation, *f*. ¶ *v.i*, se lamenter; (*of baby*) vagir.

wain, *n*, chariot, *m*.

wainscot, *n*, lambris, *m*. ¶ *v.t*, lambrisser.

waist, *n*, ceinture, taille, *f*. **~ band**, ceinture, *f*. **~coat**, gilet, *m*. **~ lock** (*Wrestling*), ceinture, *f*. **~ measurement**, tour de taille, *m*, grosseur de ceinture, *f*.

wait, *n*, attente, *f*. *to lie in* **~**, se tenir en embuscade, s'embusquer. ¶ *v.t. & i*, attendre. **~-&-see**, *a*, expectant. **~** [*up*]*on*, servir; se présenter chez. **waiter**, *n*, garçon [de café, &c] *m*. **~!** garçon! **waiting**, *n*, attente, *f*. **~ maid** (*Theat*.), suivante, *f*. **~ room**, salon d'attente, *m*; (*Rly*, &c) salle d'a., *f*. **waitress**, *n*, servante, bonne, *f*. **~!** mademoiselle!

waive, *v.t*, renoncer à, se désister de.

wake, *n*, sillage, *m*, eaux, *f.pl*. *follow in the* **~** *of* (*Naut. & fig*.), marcher dans les eaux de. ¶ *v.t.ir. & waken*, *v.t*, [r]éveiller. (*v.i*.) s'éveiller. **~ful**, *a*, privé de sommeil; vigilant. **~fulness**, *n*, insomnie, *f*.

Wales, *n*, le pays de Galles.

walk, *n*, marche; promenade [à pied] *f*, tour; pas, *m*; allure, démarche; allée, *f*; promenoir, *m*. **~** *of life*, carrière, profession, *f*. **~** *over*, (*Sport*) walk-over, *m*; (*fig*.) victoire facile, marche triomphale, *f*. **~**[*s*] *clerk* (bank), garçon de recette, *m*. ¶ *v.t. & i*, marcher; cheminer; aller à pied; aller au pas. **~** *about*, se promener. **~** *in*, entrer. **~** *off*, s'en aller. **~** *out*, sortir. **walker**, *n*, marcheur, euse; piéton, ne; promeneur, euse. **~-on**, figurant, e. **walking**, *n*, marche; promenade [à pied] *f*. ¶ *p.a. or att*, ambulant; (*dress*) trotteur, de ville; (*boots*) de marche. **~-on part**, rôle de figurant, e, rôle de comparse, *m*. **~** *stick*, canne, *f*. **~** *tour*, excursion à pied, *f*.

wall, *n*, mur, *m*, muraille; paroi, *f*; haut du pavé, *m*. **~** *cupboard*, placard, *m*. **~flower**, giroflée jaune, *f*, violier jaune, *m*. *to be a* **~flower**, faire tapisserie. **~** *map*, carte murale, *f*. **~** *paper*, papier peint, papier-tenture, *m*, tenture, *f*. **~** *plate*, sablière; lambourde, *f*. **~** *tree*, arbre en espalier, *m*. ¶ *v.t*, murer.

wallet, *n*, sacoche, *f*; portefeuille, *m*.

wallow, *n*, souille, *f*. ¶ *v.i*, se vautrer; croupir.

walnut, *n*, noix, *f*; (*tree*, *wood*) noyer, *m*. **~ burr**, ronce de noyer, *f*.

walrus, *n*, morse, *m*.

waltz, *n*, valse, *f*. ¶ *v.i*, valser. **~er**, *n*, valseur, euse.

wan, *a*, blême, blafard; (*face*) hâve.

wand, *n*, baguette, *f*.

wander, *v.i*, errer, vagabonder, vaguer; s'écarter; divaguer. **~** *around*, tournailler. **~er**, *n*, coureur, nomade, *m*. *the Wandering Jew*, le Juif errant.

wane, *n*, déclin, retour, *m*. ¶ *v.i*, décroître, décliner.

want, *n*, besoin; manque, défaut, *m*; gêne, *f*. ¶ *v.t*, avoir besoin de; manquer de; désirer; falloir; vouloir. **~ed** (*advt*), on demande.

wanton, *a*, folâtre; folichon, folle de son corps, lascif; gratuit, sans motif. **~** *destruction*, vandalisme, *m*. *out of sheer* **~ness**, de gaieté de cœur.

war, warfare, *n*, guerre, *f*; combat, *m*. *war correspondent*, journaliste aux armées, *m*. **~** *dance*, danse guerrière, *f*. **~** *horse*, cheval de bataille, *m*. **W~** *loan*, emprunt de la Défense nationale, *m*. **~** *memorial*, monument aux morts [de la guerre] *m*. **~** *of attrition*, guerre d'usure. **W~** *Office*, Ministère (*ou* département) de la Guerre, *m*. **~ship**, vaisseau de guerre, *m*. ¶ *v.i*, faire la guerre, guerroyer.

warble, *v.i*, gazouiller; (*v.t*.) roucouler. **warbler** (*bird*) *n*, fauvette, *f*.

ward, *n*, pupille, *m,f*; quartier; arrondissement, *m*; (*hospital*) salle; (*lock*) garde, *f*. **~** *room*, carré des officiers, *m*. **~** [*off*], *v.t*, parer. **~en**, *n*, conservateur; directeur, *m*. **warder**, **dress**, *n*, gardien, ne. **wardrobe**, *n*, armoire; garde-robe, *f*. **~** *dealer*, fripier, ère, marchande à la toilette, *f*. **~** *keeper*, lingère, *f*; (*Theat*.) costumier, ère. **~** *trunk*, malle-armoire, *f*.

warehouse, *n*, magasin; dépôt; entrepôt; dock, *m*. **~** *keeper* (bonded), entreposeur, *m*. **~man**, magasinier; marchand en magasin, stockiste, *m*. ¶ *v.t*, emmagasiner; entreposer.

wares, *n.pl*, marchandise, *f*, articles, *m.pl*.

warily, *ad*, avec circonspection, à tâtons.

wariness, *n*, précaution, défiance, *f*.

warlike, *a*, guerrier, belliqueux; martial. **~** *stores*, munitions de guerre, *f.pl*.

warm†, *a*, chaud; (*fig*.) chaleureux. *to be* **~** (of pers.), avoir chaud. ¶ *v.t*, chauffer; réchauffer; échauffer. **~ing pan**, bassinoire, *f*, chauffe-lit, *m*. **~th**, *n*, chaleur, *f*.

warn, *v.t*, avertir, prévenir. **~ing**, *n*, avertissement, préavis, *m*.

warp, *n*, chaîne, lice, lisse, *f*. ¶ *v.t*, déjeter; (*yarn*) ourdir; (*Naut*.) touer; (*v.i*.) se déjeter, gauchir, gondoler.

warrant, *n*, autorisation, *f*; garant; mandat; warrant, bulletin de gage; titre, *m*. ¶ *v.t*, garantir; justifier. **~able**, *a*, justifiable. **~y**, *n*, garantie, *f*.

warren, *n*, garenne, *f*.

warrior, *n*, guerrier, ère.

Warsaw, *n*, Varsovie, *f*.

wart, *n*, verrue, *f*, poireau, *m*. **~y**, *a*, verruqueux.

wary, *a*, circonspect; défiant.

wash, *n,* (*linen*) lessive, *f;* (*Art*) lavis, *m;* (*mouth*) eau, *f;* (*ship*) remous, *m;* (*slops*) lavasse, *f.* ~ *to have a* ~, se laver. ~ *&* *brush up,* brin (*ou* bout) de toilette, *m;* toilette *&* coup de brosse. ~*basin,* cuvette, *f.* ~ *boiler,* lessiveuse, *f.* ~ *drawing,* [dessin au] lavis, *m.* ~*house,* lavoir, *m,* laverie, buanderie, *f.* ~*leather,* peau de chamois, *f,* chamois, *m.* ~*stand,* toilette, *f;* lavabo, *m.* ~*tub,* cuvier, *m.* ¶ *v.t.* & *i,* laver; se l.; blanchir; baigner. ~ *away,* emporter, entraîner; affouiller. ~ *out,* laver. ~ *up,* laver la vaisselle. ~*able,* *a,* lavable. *washed overboard,* enlevé par la mer. **washer,** *n,* (*pers.*) laveur, euse; (*Mach.*) lavoir, *m;* (*ring*) rondelle, *f.* ~*woman,* laveuse de linge, blanchisseuse, *f.* **washing,** *n,* lavage; blanchissage, *m;* lessive; toilette; ablution; lotion, *f.* ~*board,* planche de lavage, *f.* ~ *day,* jour de lessive, *m.*

wasp, *n,* guêpe, *f.* ~*s' nest,* guêpier, *m.*

waste, *a,* inculte, vague; (*gas, heat*) perdu; (*matter*) de rebut. *to lay* ~, dévaster, ravager. ¶ *n,* gaspillage, *m;* perte, *f;* déchet; rebut, *m.* ¶ *comps:* ~ *book,* brouillard, *m.* ~ *heap,* décharge, *f.* ~ *paper,* papier de rebut, *m;* papiers inutiles, *m.pl.* ~ *paper basket,* corbeille à papiers, *f,* panier [à papiers] *m.* ~ *pipe,* trop-plein, *m.* ~ *water,* eaux-vannes, *f.pl.* ¶ *v.t,* gaspiller; perdre; consumer. ~ *away,* se consumer; s'atrophier. ~*d life,* vie manquée, *f.* **waster,** *n,* gaspilleur, euse; rebut, loup, *m,* pièce manquée, *f.* **wasteful,** *a,* dissipateur, prodigue. **wastefulness,** *n,* prodigalité, *f.*

watch, *n,* veille; garde, sentinelle, *f;* (*Naut.*) quart, *m,* bordée, *f;* (*Horol.*) montre, *f. on the* ~, aux aguets, à l'affût. ~ *chain,* chaîne de montre, *f.* ~ *dog,* chien de garde, c. d'attache, *m.* ~ *fire,* feu de bivouac, *m.* ~*maker,* horloger, *m.* ~*man,* veilleur, garde, *m.* ~ *on bracelet,* montre [sur] bracelet, *f.* ~ *stand,* porte-montre, *m.* ~*word,* mot d'ordre, *m.* ¶ *v.t.* & *i,* veiller; surveiller; observer; guetter; suivre. ~*er,* *n,* veilleur, euse. ~*ful†,* *a,* vigilant. ~*fulness,* *n,* vigilance, *f.*

water, *n,* eau, *f;* eaux, *f.pl;* (*tide*) marée, *f,* eaux, *f.pl;* (*pl.*) eaux, *f.pl,* parages, *m.pl.* ~ *bar* (*across road*), cassis, *m.* ~ *bath,* bain-marie, *m.* ~ *bed,* matelas à eau, *m.* ~ *bottle,* carafe, *f;* (*Mil.*) bidon, *m.* ~ *butt,* tonneau à eau, *m.* ~ *cart,* tonneau d'arrosage, *m.* ~ *closet,* cabinets, *m.pl.* cabinet [d'aisance] *m.* ~ *colour,* aquarelle, *f.* ~ *company,* compagnie des eaux, *f.* ~ *course,* cours d'eau, *m.* ~*cress,* cresson [de fontaine] *m.* ~*cress bed,* cressonnière, *f.* ~ *diviner,* hydroscope, *m,* sourcier, ère. ~ *divining,* hydroscopie, *f.* ~*fall,* chute d'eau; cascade, *f.* ~*fowl,* oiseau aquatique, *m.* ~*glass,* verre soluble, *m.* ~ *hammer[ing],* coup de bélier, *m.* ~ *hazard* (*Golf*), douve, *f.* ~ *ice,* glace à l'eau, *f,* sorbet, *m.* ~ *jacket,* chemise d'eau, *f.* ~ *jug,* pot à eau, *m.* ~ *jump* (*Turf*), douve, *f.* ~ *level,* niveau d'eau, *m.* ~ *lily,* nénuphar, *m.* ~ *line,* ligne de flottaison, *f.* ~*logged,* imbibé d'eau; (*boat*) engagé. ~*man,* batelier; marin, canotier, *m.* ~*mark,* (*tidal*) laisse, *f;* (*paper*) filigrane, *m.* ~ *meadow,* noue, *f.* ~ *melon,* melon d'eau, *m,* pastèque, *f.* ~ *meter,* compteur à eau, *m.* ~ *mill,* moulin à eau, *m.* ~ *nymph,* naïade, *f.* ~ [*omni*]*bus,* bateau omnibus, bateau-mouche, *m.* ~ *on the brain,* hydrocéphalie, *f.* ~ *on the knee,* épanchement de synovie, *m.* ~ *pipe,* tuyau d'eau, *m,* conduite d'eau, *f.* ~ *power,* force hydraulique, houille blanche, *f.* ~*proof,* *a,* imperméable (à l'eau); (*n.*) imperméable, caoutchouc, *m;* (*v.t.*) imperméabiliser. ~ *polo,* waterpolo, *m.* ~ *rat,* rat d'eau, *m.* ~ *rate,* abonnement à l'eau, *m.* ~*shed,* ligne de faîte, *m.* ~*side,* bord de l'eau, *m;* (*att.*) riverain. ~*spout,* (*rain*) gargouille, *f;* (*Meteor.*) trombe, *f.* ~ *tight,* étanche [à l'eau]. ~ *tournament,* joute sur l'eau, *f.* ~ *tower,* château d'eau, *m.* ~*way,* voie navigable, v. d'eau; (*bridge*) débouché, *m.* ~ *wheel,* roue hydraulique, *f.* ~*works,* usine hydraulique, *f.* ¶ *v.t,* (*garden,* &c) arroser; (*horse,* &c) abreuver; (*drink*) couper, baptiser; (*stock, Fin.*) diluer; (*silk*) moirer; (*v.i.*) (*eyes*) pleurer, larmoyer; (*take in water*) faire de l'eau. ~ *it makes one's mouth* ~, cela fait venir l'eau à la bouche. ~*ed silk,* moire de soie, soie moirée, *f.* ~*ing,* *n,* arrosement; arrosage; abreuvage, *m;* moire, *f.* ~ *place,* abreuvoir, *m;* ville d'eaux, *f,* eaux, *f.pl;* bains, *m.pl,* station balnéaire, *f.* ~ *pot,* arrosoir, *m.* ~*less,* *a,* dépourvu d'eau. ~*y,* *a,* aqueux; humide; (*fluid*) ténu.

watt, *n,* watt, *m.*

wattle, *n,* (*rods & twigs*) claie; (*bird*) barbe, caroncule, *f,* fanon, *m;* (*fish*) barbe, *f.* ¶ *v.t,* clayonner.

wave, *n,* vague, *f;* flot, *m;* lame, *f;* coup de mer, *m;* onde; ondulation, *f;* (*hand*) signe, geste; (*wand*) coup, *m.* ¶ *v.i,* flotter; ondoyer; (*v.t.*) agiter; faire signe de; onduler. *to have one's hair* ~*d,* se faire onduler [les cheveux]. **waver,** *v.i,* hésiter, vaciller, flotter, chanceler. **wavy,** *a,* onduleux, ondé, en ondes; (*line*) tremblée.

wax, *n,* cire, *f;* (*cobbler's*) poix, *f.* ~ *chandler,* cirier, *m.* ~ *vesta,* allumette bougie, *f.* ~*works,* figures de cire, *f.pl.* ¶ *v.t,* cirer; (*v.i.*) croître; devenir. ~*ed thread,* fil poissé, *m.* ~*y,* *a,* comme cire.

way, *n,* chemin, *m,* route; voie; distance, *f;* passage, *m;* place, *f;* progrès, *m;* marche; direction, *f;* côté; sens, *m;* manière, **façon,**

sorte, *f*; genre; moyen, *m*; allure, *f*, air; usage, *m*; guise, *f*; cours, *m*; passe; (*Naut.*) erre, *f*. *by the* ~, chemin faisant; (*fig.*) à propos. *in the* ~, encombrant, gênant. *over the* ~, de l'autre côté. ~*bill*, feuille de route, *f*. ~*farer*, voyageur, euse. ~ *in*, entrée, *f*. ~*lay*, tendre une embûche à. ~ *out*, sortie; issue; *f*. ~*side*, bord de la route, *m*; (*att.*) sur le b. de la r.; riverain; (*Rly station*) de passage, d'escale.

wayward†, *a*, capricieux, volontaire, libertin. ~**ness**, *n*, libertinage, *m*.

we, *pn*, nous; on.

weak†, *a*, faible; débile; (*tea*) léger. ~ *spot* (*fig. of pers.*), côté faible, *m*. ~**en**, *v.t*, affaiblir; atténuer; (*v.i.*) faiblir. ~**ling**, *n*, faible, *e*. ~**ly**, *a*, débile, faiblard. ~**ness**, *n*, faiblesse, *f*; faible, *m*.

weal, *n*, bien, *m*. (Cf. *the common* ~); vergeture, trace d'un coup, *f*.

wealth, *n*, richesses, *f.pl*, opulence, *f*, biens, *m.pl*. ~**y**, *a*, riche, opulent.

wean, *v.t*, sevrer. ~**ing**, *n*, sevrage, *m*.

weapon, *n*, arme, *f*; porte-respect, *m*. ~**less**, *a*, sans armes.

wear, *n*, usage, *m*; usure, *f*. *the worse for* ~, patraque. ¶ *v.t. & i. ir*, user; s'u.; miner; porter; mettre. ~ *out*, user; épuiser; exténuer. ~ *well*, être d'un bon user. ~**able**, *a*, mettable, portable.

weariness, *n*, fatigue, lassitude, *f*.

wearing, *n*, usure, *f*; port, *m*.

wearisome, *a*, endormant, assommant; fastidieux. ~**ness**, *n*, ennui, *m*. **weary**, *a*, fatigué, las. ¶ *v.t*, fatiguer, lasser; ennuyer. ~ *for*, languir après.

weasel, *n*, belette, *f*.

weather, *n*, temps, *m*; intempéries, *f.pl*. ~ *& news* (*Radio*), journal parlé, *m*. ~*-beaten*, ravagé [par les intempéries]; hâlé. ~*cock*, girouette, *f*, coq, *m*; (*fig.*) girouette, *f*, sauteur, arlequin, *m*. ~ *forecast*, bulletin météorologique, *m*. ~ *permitting*, si le temps le permet. ~ *side*, côté du vent, *m*. ~ *strip*, brise-bise, *f*. ¶ *v.t*, résister à; (*cape*) doubler; (*Geol.*) altérer, désagréger.

weave, *n*, tissu, *m*. ¶ *v.t.ir*, tisser; (*basket*) tresser; (*fig.*) ourdir, tramer. **weaver**, *n*, tisserand, *m*. **weaving**, *n*, tissage, *m*; tisseranderie, *f*.

web, *n*, toile, *f*; (*bird's foot*) membrane; (*girder, &c*) âme, *f*; (*key*) panneton, *m*; (*of life*) trame, *f*. ~*-footed*, palmipède. **webbed**, *a*, palmé. **webbing**, *n*, sangle, *f*.

wed, *v.t*, épouser; marier; (*v.i.*) se m. **wedded**, *a*, conjugal; (*to opinion*) attaché. **wedding**, *n*, noces, *f.pl*, mariage, *m*. ~ *breakfast*, repas de noce, *m*. ~ *cake*, gâteau de noce, *m*. ~ *day*, jour de mariage, *m*. ~ *dress*, robe de mariée, *f*. ~ *festivities & ~ party*, noce, *f*. ~ *march*, marche nuptiale, *f*. ~ *present*, cadeau de noce, *m*;

(*bridegroom's*) corbeille [de mariage] *f*. ~ *ring*, alliance, *f*, anneau nuptial, *m*.

wedge, *n*, coin, *m*; cale; hausse, *f*. ¶ *v.t*, coincer; caler.

wedlock, *n*, mariage, *m*.

Wednesday, *n*, mercredi, *m*.

wee, *a*, petiot, tout petit.

weed, *n*, [mauvaise] herbe, *f*. ¶ *v.t*, sarcler. ~ *out*, éliminer, épurer. ~**er**, *n*, (*pers.*) sarcleur, euse; (*hoe*) sarcloir, *m*. ~**ing shear** (*river*), faucard, *m*.

week, *n*, semaine; (*e.g. Friday to Friday*) semaine, huitaine, *f*, huit jours, *m.pl*. ~ *day*, jour de semaine, *m*. ~ *days only*, la semaine seulement. ~*-end cottage*, maison de plaisance, *f*. ~*-end ticket*, billet de fin de semaine, *m*. ~**ly**, *a*, hebdomadaire.

weep, *v.i. & t. ir. & ~ for*, pleurer. ~**er**, *n*, pleureur, euse. **weeping**, *n*, pleurs, *m.pl*, larmes, *f.pl*. ¶ *a*, qui pleure, éploré; (*tree*) pleureur.

weevil, *n*, charançon, *m*. ~**y**, *a*, charançonné.

weft, *n*, trame, *f*.

weigh, *v.t*, peser; mesurer; (*anchor*) lever; (*v.i.*) peser; farder. ~ *bridge*, pont à bascule, *m*. ~ *down*, appesantir, affaisser. *to get under* ~, appareiller. ~**er**, *n*, peseur, *m*. ~**ing**, *n*, pesage, *m*; pesée, *f*. ~ *in & ~ in room*, pesage, *m*. ~ *machine*, [balance à] bascule, *f*. **weight**, *n*, poids, *m*; pesanteur; gravité; importance, *f*. ~ *allowed free*, franchise de poids, *f*. de bagages, *f*. *his, its, ~ in gold*, son pesant d'or. *in* ~, pesant. ~ *handicap*, surcharge, *f*. ~**y**†, *a*, pesant; puissant; grave.

weir, *n*, barrage; déversoir, *f*; (*Fish.*) gord, *m*.

weird, *a*, fantastique.

welcome, *a*, bienvenu; libre. ¶ *n*, bienvenue, *f*, [bon] accueil, *m*, réception, *f*. ¶ *v.t*, bien accueillir, recevoir.

weld, *n*, soudure, *f*. ¶ *v.t*, souder; corroyer.

welfare, *n*, bien-être, bonheur; (*public*) salut, *m*, chose, *f*.

well, *n*, puits, *m*; source, fontaine, *f*; réservoir, *m*; (*of ship*) sentine, *f*; (*of court*) parquet, *m*. ~ *sinker*, puisatier, fontainier, *m*. ~ *spring*, source, *f*. ¶ *v.i*, sourdre, jaillir.

well, *a*, bien; dispos, bien portant, en bonne santé. ¶ *ad*, bien. *to do oneself* ~, se goberger. *to live* ~, faire chère lie. ~*-advised*, bien conseillé. ~ *& good*, à la bonne heure. ~*-attended*, suivi. ~*-balanced*, bien équilibré; (*style, prose*) nombreux. *to be* ~ *balanced* (phrase), avoir du nombre. ~*-behaved*, sage. ~*-being*, bien-être, *m*. ~ *beloved*, *a. & n*, bien-aimé, e, bienaimé, e. ~*-bred*, bien élevé, bien appris, de bonne compagnie, honnête. ~*-built*, bien charpenté. ~*-knit*, bien charpenté. ~*-disposed & ~-meaning*, bien intentionné. ~ *done*, bien cuit. ~ *done!* bravo! ~*-finished*, soigné. ~*-informed* calé. ~ *known*, bien connu, réputé, signalé, répandu. ~ *marked*, tranché. ~ *off & ~-to-do*, à son aise, aisé, au large, fortuné, calé, cossu. ~*read*, instruit, lettré. ~*spoken*, bien-disant. ~*timed*, opportun.

Wellingtons, *n.pl*, bottes montant aux genoux, *f.pl*.

Welsh, a, gallois; du pays de Galles. ¶ *n*, le gallois. ~*man*, ~*woman*, Gallois, e. ~ *rabbit*, ~ *rarebit*, rôtie à l'anglaise, r. au fromage, *f.* ~*er*, *n*, bookmaker marron, *m.*

welt, *n*, (shoe) trépointe, f; (strap) couvrejoint, *m*, fourrure, *f.* *wide* ~ (shoe), semelle débordante, f.

welter, *v.i*, nager, se baigner, s'abîmer. ~ *weight* (*Box.*), poids mi-moyen, *m.*

wen, *n*, loupe, *f*, goitre, *m.*

wench, *n*, donzelle, *f.*

wend, *v.i*, poursuivre.

wer[e]wolf, *n*, loup-garou, *m.*

west, *n*, ouest; (le) couchant; occident, *m.* ¶ *a*, de l'ouest, d'ouest, occidental. *W~ Africa*, l'Afrique occidentale, *f.* *the W~ Indies*, les Indes occidentales, les Antilles, *f.pl.* **westerly**, *a*, d'ouest. **western**, *a*, de l'ouest; occidental; d'Occident. *W~ Australia*, l'Australie occidentale, *f.*

Westphalia, *n*, la Westphalie.

wet, *a*, mouillé; humide; pluvieux; (goods) liquide; (paint, ink) fraîche. ~ *blanket*, éteignoir, rabat-joie, *m.* ~ *dock*, bassin à flot, *m.* ~ *fish*, poisson frais, *m*, marée, *f.* ~ *fly fishing*, pêche à la mouche noyée, *f.* ~ *nurse*, nourrice, *f.* ~ *through*, trempé. *wet & ~ness*, *n*, humidité, *f.* ¶ *out in the wet*, dans la pluie. ¶ *v.t*, mouiller; imbiber; humecter; arroser.

wether, *n*, mouton, *m.*

whack, *n*, coup, horion, *m.* ¶ *v.t*, battre.

whale, *n*, baleine, *f.* ~ *boat*, baleinière, *f.* ~*bone*, fanon de baleine, m, baleine, *f.* ~ *calf*, baleineau, *m.* **whaler**, *n*, baleinier, *m.*

wharf, *n*, quai, appontement, débarcadère, embarcadère, *m.* **wharfinger**, *n*, propriétaire de quai, *m.*

what, *pn*, *a*, *& ad*, quoi; qu'est-ce qui; qu'est-ce que; que; quel, quelle; ce qui; ce que, tant; comment. ~ *a*, quel, quelle. ~ *a relief! ouf!* ~ *for?* pourquoi? ~ *people may say*, le qu'en-dira-t-on. *whatever & whatsoever*, *pn. & a*, tout ce qui; tout ce que; quelque . . . qui; quelque . . . que; quelconque; quoi que; quel(le) que.

whatnot, *n*, étagère, *f.*

wheat, *n*, froment, blé, *m.* ~*en*, *a*, de froment.

wheedle, *v.t*, cajoler, enjôler.

wheel, *n*, roue, *f*; volant; disque; galet, *m*; roulette; (emery, &c) meule; (helm) barre; (*Mil.*) conversion, *f.* ~*barrow*, brouette, *f.* ~ *base*, écartement des essieux, empattement, *m.* ~*work*, wheels, rouage,

m. ~*wright*, chairon, *m.* ¶ *v.t*, rouler; (v.i.) (birds, &c) tournoyer; (*Mil.*) converser, pivoter. -*wheeled*, a, à . . . roues. **wheeler**, *n*, timonier, brancardier, *m.*

wheeze, *v.i*, siffler. **wheezy**, *a*, sifflant; (pers) poussif.

whelk, *n*, buccin, *m.*

when, *ad*, quand, lorsque; alors que, après que. **whence**, *ad*, d'où. **whenever**, *ad*, toutes les fois que.

where, *ad*, où; là où; à l'endroit où. ~ *to fish*, lieux de pêche. **whereabouts**, *ad*, où. *one's* ~, où on est. **whereas**, *ad*, tandis que, au lieu que; attendu que, vu que. **whereat**, *ad*, sur quoi. **whereby**, *ad*, par où, par lequel. **wherefore**, *ad*, pourquoi. **wherein**, *ad*, en quoi. **whereof**, *ad*, dont. **where[up]on**, *ad*, sur quoi. **wherever**, *ad*, partout où, où que. *the wherewithal*, de quoi, les moyens, *m.pl.*

wherry, *n*, bachot, *m.* ~*man*, bachoteur, *m.*

whet, *n*, stimulant, *m.* ~ (*tools*) repasser, aiguiser; (appetite) aiguiser, stimuler. ~*stone*, pierre à aiguiser, *f.*

whether, *c*, soit; soit que; que; si.

whey, *n*, petit-lait, *m.*

which, *pn. & a*, qui; que; lequel, laquelle; ce qui; ce que; ce dont; quel, quelle. ~ *way?* par où? **whichever**, *pn*, n'importe quel, n'importe quelle.

whiff, *n*, bouffée, *f.*

while, *n*, temps, *m.* *it is worth* ~, cela vaut la peine. *while & whilst*, *c*, tandis que, pendant que; [tout] en. *while away*, [faire] passer; charmer, tromper.

whim, *n*, caprice, *m*, fantaisie; boutade, *f*; (*Mach.*) treuil, cabestan, *m.*

whimper, *v.i*, pleurnicher, piauler, geindre. ~*er*, *n*, pleureur, euse, pleurard, e.

whimsical†, *a*, capricieux, fantasque, lunatique.

whin, *n*, ajonc, genêt épineux, *m.*

whine, *v.i*, pleurnicher, piauler, geindre.

whinny, *n*, hennissement, *m.* ¶ *v.i*, hennir.

whip, *n*, fouet, *m.* ~*cord*, [fil de] fouet, *m.* ~ *hand* (fig.), dessus, *m.* ¶ *v.t. & i*, fouetter; toucher. **whipper-in**, *n*, piqueur, *m.* **whipper-snapper**, *n*, moucheron; freluquet, *m.* **whipping**, *n*, le fouet; (*Need.*) point roulé, *m.* ~ *top*, sabot, *m.*

whir[r], *v.i*, siffler, ronfler.

whirl, *n*, ébullition, *f*; tourbillon, *m.* ¶ *v.i*, tournoyer, tourbillonner. ~*pool*, tourbillon, gouffre, *m.* ~*wind*, tourbillon, *m.* **whirligig**, *n*, pirouette, *f*; carrousel, *m.*

whisk, *n*, (brush, broom) balayette, *f*, houssoir, *m*; (egg) fouet, *m.* ¶ *v.t.* (dust) épousseter; (eggs) fouetter.

whiskers, *n.pl*, favoris, *m.pl*; (cat) moustache, *f.*

whisky, *n*, whisky, *m.*

whisper, *n*, chuchotement; murmure, *m.* ¶ *v.i. & t*, chuchoter; murmurer. ~*er*, *n*, chuchoteur, euse. ~ing, n, chuchoterie, f. ~ gallery, galerie à écho, f.

whist (Cards) n, whist, m.

whistle, n, sifflet; coup de sifflet, m. ¶ v.t. & i, siffler; (wind) mugir. whistler, n, siffleur, euse.

whit, n, iota, m.

white, a, blanc. ~ ant, fourmi blanche, f, termite, m. ~bait, blanchaille, f. show the ~ feather, caner. ~ horses (sea), moutons, m.pl. ~ heat, incandescence, f. ~-hot, chauffé à blanc, incandescent. ~ lead, blanc de céruse, m, céruse, f. ~ lie, mensonge pieux, m. officieux, m. W~ sea, mer Blanche, f. ~-throat, grisette, f. ~wash, n, blanc de chaux, m; (v.t.) blanchir à la chaux; (fig.) blanchir. ¶ n, (colour, man) blanc, m; (ball, woman) blanche, f. ~ of egg, blanc d'œuf, m, glaire, f. ~ sale, vente de blanc, f. white[n], v.t, blanchir. whiteness, n, blancheur, f.

whither, ad, où.

whiting, n, blanc de craie; (fish) merlan, m.

whitish, a, blanchâtre.

whitlow, n, panaris, mal d'aventure, m.

Whitsuntide, n, la Pentecôte. Whit Sunday, dimanche de la Pentecôte, m.

whittle, v.t, taillader.

whiz[z], n, sifflement, m. ¶ v.i, siffler.

who, pn, qui. ~ goes there? qui vive?

whoa, i, oé! ohé!

whoever, pn, quiconque.

whole, a, tout; entier; intégral; intact; complet; total; plein. ~ binding, reliure pleine, f. ~-length (portrait), en pied. ~meal bread, pain complet, m. ¶ n, tout, m, totalité, intégralité, f. [up]on the ~, à tout prendre, en somme. wholesale, a, en masse. ~ [trade], [commerce de (ou en)] gros; (small) demi-gros, m. wholesome†, a, sain; salubre; salutaire. wholly, ad, entièrement; intégralement; complètement; en totalité.

whom, pn, que; qui; lequel, laquelle, lesquels, lesquelles. whomsoever, pn, quiconque.

whoop, n, huée, f, cri, m. ¶ v.i, huer, crier. ~ing cough, coqueluche, f.

whorl, n, verticille, m, spire, f.

whortleberry, n, airelle, myrtille, f.

whose, pn, dont; de qui; à qui? whosoever, pn, quiconque.

why, ad. & m, pourquoi, ad, c, & m. ¶ i, mais! comment!

wick, n, mèche, f.

wicked†, a, méchant, mauvais. ~ness, n, méchanceté, f.

wicker, n, osier, m. ~ cradle, moïse, m. ~work, vannerie, f. ¶ v.t, clisser.

wicket, n, guichet, m. (Croquet) arceau, m.

wide, a, large; vaste; grand; ample; étendu; (Meas.) large de, de largeur. to be ~ awake, être tout(e) éveillé(e). ~-awake, éveillé, dégourdi, déluré, en éveil. ~ of

the mark, loin de compte. ~-spread, [largement] répandu. ~ welt (shoe), semelle débordante, f. ~ly, ad, largement. widen, v.t, [r]élargir; étendre. in a wider sense, par extension.

widgeon, n, [canard] siffleur, m.

widow, n, veuve, f. the ~'s mite, le denier de la v. ~'s weeds, deuil de v., m. ~ed, p.p, veuf. ~er, n, veuf, m. ~hood, n, veuvage, m, viduité, f.

width, n, largeur; (cloth) largeur, laize, f, lé, m.

wield, v.t, manier; (power) exercer.

wife, n, femme; épouse, f.

wig, n, perruque, f. ~ maker, perruquier, m.

wight, n, hère, m.

wild, a, sauvage; farouche; inculte; fou; endiablé; égaré, hagard. ~ beast, bête féroce, b. sauvage, f, (pl.) bêtes fauves, f.pl, fauves, m.pl. ~ boar, sanglier, (young) marcassin, m. ~ cherry, merise, f; (tree) merisier, m. ~ flowers, fleurs des bois, f—s des champs, f—s des prés, f—s sauvages, f.pl. ~ goose chase, folle entreprise, f. the wild men (Pol.), les Montagnards, m.pl. to sow one's ~ oats, jeter sa gourme, faire ses farces. ~ rabbit, lapin de garenne, m. ~ raspberry bush, framboisier sauvage, mûron, m. ~ rose, églantine, rose de chien, f; (bush) rosier sauvage, églantier, m. ~ sow, laie, f. wild & wilderness, n, lieu sauvage, m, solitude, f, désert, m. ~ing, n, sauvageon, m. ~ly, ad, d'un air effaré follement. ~ness, n, état sauvage; égarement, m.

wile & wiliness, n, ruse, astuce, (pl.) finasserie, f.

wilful, a, volontaire, intentionnel. ~ misrepresentation, dol, m. ~ murder, homicide volontaire, assassinat, m. ~ly, ad, volontairement; avec préméditation. ~ness, n, obstination, f.

will, n, volonté; intention, f; vouloir; gré; plaisir; testament, m. ¶ v.t, regular & ir, vouloir; léguer par [son] testament; v.aux, is expressed in Fr. by future tense. Also by vouloir. willing, a, volontaire, spontané; (hands) de volontaires; complaisant. to be ~, vouloir [bien]. ~ly, ad, volontiers. ~ness, n, bonne volonté, complaisance, f.

will-o'-the-wisp, n, feu follet, ardent, m.

willow, n, saule, m. ~ plantation, saulaie, saussaie, f.

willynilly, ad, bon gré, mal gré.

wilt, v.t, flétrir; (v.i.) se f., se faner, s'étioler.

wily, a, rusé, finaud, astucieux.

wimple, n, guimpe, f.

win, n, victoire, f. ~ on points, v. aux points. ¶ v.t.ir, gagner; concilier; acquérir; remporter; valoir.

wince, v.i, sourciller; cligner; tiquer; tressaillir.

winch, n, moulinet; treuil, m; manivelle, f.

wind, n, vent, m; haleine; flatuosité, f. ~*bag,* moulin à paroles, m. ~ *egg,* œuf clair, m. ~ *erosion,* érosion éolienne, f. ~*fall,* fruit tombé, m; [bonne] aubaine, chapechute, f. ~*mill,* moulin à vent, m. ~*pipe,* trachée-artère, f. ~ *row,* andain, m. ~ *screen,* pare-brise; (Hort.) abat-vent, m. ~ *screen wiper,* essuie-glace, m. *to get* ~ *of,* éventer. ¶ v.t. essouffler.

wind, v.t.ir, enrouler, dévider, bobiner, pelotonner; (Min.) [re]monter; (v.i.ir.) serpenter, tourner. ~ *up,* [re]monter; terminer; liquider. ~*ing,* a, tournant; sinueux, anfractueux, tortueux. ¶ n, détour, m, sinuosité, f, lacet, méandre, m. ~ *sheet,* linceul, suaire, m. **windlass,** n, treuil, m.

window, n, fenêtre; vue, f; (pl. col.) fenêtrage, vitrage, m; (casement) croisée, f; (leaded) vitrail; m; (carriage) glace; (shop) vitrine, devanture, montre, f, étalage, m. ~ *box,* jardin de fenêtre, m. ~ *dresser,* étalagiste, m,f. ~ *dressing* (fig.), trompe-l'œil, m. ~ *envelope,* enveloppe à fenêtre, e. à panneau, f. ~ *glass,* verre à vitres, m. ~ *ledge,* ~ *sill,* appui de fenêtre, m. ~ *mirror,* judas, m. ~ *pane,* vitre, f.

windward, n, côté du vent, m; (a.) au vent. W ~ *Islands,* îles du Vent, f.pl. **windy,** a, venteux; (day) de grand vent. *to be* ~, venter.

wine, n, vin, m; liqueur, f. ~ *& spirit merchant,* liquoriste, m,f. ~ *glass,* verre à vin, m. ~ *grapes,* raisin de vigne, m. ~ *grower,* vigneron, ne, viticulteur, m. ~*growing,* a, vinicole, viticole. ~ *list,* carte des vins, f. ~ *of the country,* vin du cru, m. ~ *trade,* commerce des vins, m. ~ *waiter,* sommelier, m.

wing, n, aile, f; vol, essor, m; (pl, Theat.) coulisses, f.pl, cantonade, f. ~ *collar,* faux col cassé, m. ~ *dam,* estacade, f. ~ *nut,* écrou à oreilles, [é.] papillon, m. ~ *spread,* ~ *span,* envergure, f. ~*ed,* a, ailé. ~ *creature,* oiseau, m.

wink, n, clin d'œil, signe des yeux, clignement, m. ¶ v.i, cligner.

winkle (Crust.) n, bigorneau, m.

winner, n, gagnant, e; vainqueur, m. **winning,** a, gagnant; (number) sortant; attrayant, attachant. ~ *performance,* 'performance classée, f. ~ *post,* poteau d'arrivée, m, arrivée, f, but, m. **winning,** n. & ~**s,** n.pl, gain, m.

winnow, v.t, vanner. ~*ing,* n, vannage, m.

winsome, a, agréable.

winter, n, hiver, m. ¶ v.i. & t, hiverner. ¶ ~, att. & **wintry,** a, d'hiver, hivernal, hiémal.

wipe, n, coup de chiffon, de mouchoir, &c, m. ~ [up], v.t, essuyer; torcher; (joint) ébarber. ~ *off* (debt, &c) apurer. ~ *out,* effacer.

wire, n, fil; câble, m; dépêche [télégraphique]

~ *draw,* tréfiler; (fig.) alambiquer. ~ *edge,* morfil, m. ~ *entanglement,* réseau de fils de fer, m. ~ *fence,* clôture en fil de fer, f. ~ *gauge,* jauge pour fils métalliques, filière, f. ~*haired* (dog), au poil rude. ~ *nail,* pointe de Paris, f, clou de Paris, m. ~ *netting,* treillis métallique, grillage, m. ~*puller,* intrigant, m. ~ *rope,* câble métallique, m. ~*spring mattress,* sommier métallique, m. ¶ v.t, (house, Elec.) poser des fils dans; télégraphier. ~**d** (of croquet ball) p.p, engagée.

wireless, a: ~ (telegram), sans-fil, m, télégramme sans fil, m. ~ [telegraphy], sans-fil, f, télégraphie sans fil, T.S.F., f. ~ *cabinet,* meuble T.S.F., m.

wisdom, n, sagesse; prudence, f. ~ *tooth,* dent de sagesse, f. **wise,** a, sage. ~*acre,* pédant, e; sot qui se donne un air de sage, m. ¶ n, manière, façon, f.

wish, n, désir; gré; souhait; vœu, m. ¶ v.t. & i, désirer; vouloir; souhaiter. ~ *someone many happy returns [of the day],* souhaiter la [ou une bonne] fête à quelqu'un. ~**ful,** a, désireux. ~*ing bone,* lunette, fourchette, f. ~*ing cap,* bonnet magique, m.

wish-wash, n, lavasse, f.

wisp, n, bouchon, m, touffe, f.

wistaria, n, glycine, f.

wistful, a, désenchanté, privé de ses illusions. ~*ly,* ad, avec envie.

wit, n, esprit; sel; (pers.) bel esprit, diseur de bons mots, m; (pl.) intelligence, f, esprit, m; tête, f. *at one's* ~*'s end,* au bout de son rouleau, aux abois.

witch, n, sorcière, f. ~*craft,* sorcellerie, f, sortilège, m. ~ *doctor,* sorcier guérisseur, m. ~*ery,* n, magie, fascination, f.

with, pr, avec; à coups de; à; par; de; chez; en; dans; sous; auprès de.

withdraw, v.t.ir, retirer; se désister de, (v.i.ir.) se retirer; se cantonner; (candidature) se désister. ~*al,* n, retrait, m; retraite, f; désistement, m.

withe, n, brin d'osier, pleyon, m, hart, f.

wither, v.t, dessécher; (v.i.) se dessécher, dépérir. ~*ing* (look) a, foudroyant.

withers, n.pl, garrot, m.

withhold, v.t.ir, retenir.

within, pr, dans; en; en dedans de; là-dedans; à; sous. ~ *call,* à portée de la voix. *from* ~, de dedans.

without, pr, sans; sans que; en dehors de; là-dehors. *from* ~, de dehors. *to do* ~, se passer de.

withstand, v.t.ir, résister à.

withy, n, brin d'osier, pleyon, m, hart, f.

witless, a, sans esprit. **witling,** n, bel esprit, m.

witness, n, témoin; témoignage, m; foi, f. ~ *box,* barre des témoins, f. ~ *for the defence,* témoin à décharge. ~ *for the prosecution,* t. à charge. ¶ v.t, être témoin de; assister à; attester; signer à; certifier.

witticism, *n,* trait d'esprit, jeu d'esprit, *m.*

wittingly, *ad,* sciemment, à bon escient.

witty†, *a,* plein d'esprit; spirituel.

wizard, *n,* sorcier, magicien, *m.* ~ry, *n,* magie, *f.*

wizened, *a,* ratatiné.

wo, i, oé!, ohé!

woad, *n,* pastel, *m.*

wobble, *v.i,* brimbaler; vaciller.

woe, *n,* douleur, *f;* malheur, *m.* ~begone *& ~*ful†, *a,* triste; malheureux; lamentable.

wolf, *n,* loup, *m,* louve, *f.* ~ cub (*Zool. & Scouting*), louveteau, *m.* ~'s-bane, napel, *m.*

wolfram, *n,* wolfram, *m.*

woman, *n,* femme, *f.* ~ barrister, femme avocat, avocate, *f.* ~ doctor, femme médecin, f. docteur, *f.* ~ driver, chauffeuse, *f.* ~ hater, misogyne, *m.* ~ of fashion, élégante, *f.* ~ suffrage, suffrage des femmes, s. féminin, *m.* women's single, double (*Ten.*), simple, double, dames, *m.* ~ish, *a,* efféminé; (*voice*) féminine. ~ly, *a,* de femme.

womb, *n,* matrice, *f,* ventre, sein, flanc, *m.*

wonder, *n,* étonnement, *m;* merveille, *f;* prodige, *m.* ¶ *v.i,* s'étonner (*at* = de); se demander (*why* = pourquoi). ~ful†, *a,* étonnant; merveilleux; admirable.

wont, *n,* coutume, *f,* ordinaire, *m.* ~ed, *a,* habituel.

woo, *v.t,* faire la cour à.

wood, *n,* bois, *m;* (*Bowls*) boule, *f. in the ~* (wine), en cercles. ~bine, chèvrefeuille, *m.* ~ carver, sculpteur sur bois, *m.* ~cock, bécasse, *f.* ~cut, gravure sur bois, *f.* ~land, pays de bois, *m;* (*att.*) des bois; sylvestre. ~louse, cloporte, *m.* ~man, bûcheron, *m.* ~ nymph, nymphe bocagère, *f.* ~ owl, chat-huant, *m,* hulotte, *f.* ~pecker, pic, *m.* ~ pigeon, [pigeon] ramier, *m,* palombe, *f.* ~ screw, vis à bois, *f.* ~ shed, bûcher, *m.* the ~[-wind], les bois, *m.pl.* ~wool, paille de bois, *f.* ~work, menuiserie; boiserie, *f.* ~worker, artisan en bois, *m.* ~ed, *a,* boisé, fourré. ~en, *a,* de bois, en b. ~y, *a,* ligneux.

wooer, *n,* prétendant, soupirant, poursuivant, *m.*

woof, *n,* trame, *f.*

wool, *n,* laine, *f;* (*animal's coat*) pelage, *m.* ~ shop, lainerie, *f.* **woollen,** *a,* de laine; lainier. ~ goods or ~s, *n.pl,* lainage, *m.* oft. pl. ~ manufacturer, lainier, *m.* ~ mill, lainerie, *f.* ~ trade, industrie lainière, lainerie, *f.* **woolly,** *a,* laineux; (*fruit, style*) cotonneux; (*hair*) crépus; (*outline, sound*) flou.

word, *n,* mot, *m;* parole, *f;* terme, *m.* ~ square, mot carré. by ~ of mouth, de

vive voix. the Word (*Theol.*), le Verbe. ¶ *v.t,* libeller, concevoir. **wordiness,** *n,* verbosité, *f.* **wording,** *n,* libellé, *m,* termes, *m.pl.* **wordy,** *a,* verbeux.

work, *n,* travail, *m.* oft. pl; fonctionnement; ouvrage, *m.* besogne; œuvre, *f;* (*social*) œuvres, *f.pl;* (*of art*) œuvre, *f,* objet; (*col. pl, of an artist*) œuvre, *m;* (*pl.*) rouage, *m.* oft. pl, mécanisme, mouvement, *m;* (*pl. & s.*) usine, fabrique, *f;* atelier, *m.* ~ bag, sac à ouvrage, *m.* ~ box, nécessaire à o., *m.* ~man, -woman, ouvrier ère. ~manlike, en bon ouvrier. ~manship, main-d'œuvre, façon, facture, *f,* travail, *m.* ~men's compensation insurance, assurance contre les accidents du travail, *f.* ~room, atelier, *m;* (*convent*) ouvroir, *m.* ~s manager, chef du service des ateliers, *m.* ~ shop, atelier, *m.* ~stand, travailleuse, *f.* ¶ *v.t,* travailler; faire t.; manœuvrer; opérer; actionner; exploiter; ouvrer; faire; se f.; (*v.i.*) travailler; fonctionner; jouer; marcher; aller; rouler; agir; fermenter. ~ hard, travailler à force, piocher. ~ loose, prendre du jeu. ~ out, *v.t,* élaborer; épuiser; décompter; (*v.i.*) se chiffrer. ~ up, travailler; malaxer. ~able, *a,* exécutable; exploitable. ~er, *n,* travailleur, euse; ouvrier, ère. ~ bee, abeille ouvrière, *f.* ~ing, *n,* travail, *m;* exploitation, *f;* fonctionnement, *m;* manœuvre; marche, *f;* jeu, *m.* ~ capital, capital de roulement, fonds de r., *m.* ~ class, classe ouvrière, c. laborieuse, *f.* ~ clothes, habits de fatigue, *m.pl.* ~ day, jour ouvrable, *m;* journée de travail, *f.* ~ drawing, épure, *f;* (*Build.*) calepin, *m.* ~ expenses, frais d'exploitation, *m.pl.* the ~less, les sans-travail, *m.pl.*

world, *n,* monde, *m;* siècle, *m.* ~[-wide] *a,* mondial, universel. **worldliness,** *n,* mondanité, *f.* **worldling,** *n. & worldly,** *a,* mondain, e. all one's worldly goods, tout son [saint-]frusquin.

worm, *n,* ver; (*screw*) filet, *m;* (*corkscrew*) mèche, *f;* (*Mach.*) vis sans fin, *f;* (*still*) serpentin, *m.* ~-eaten, rongé des vers, vermoulu. ~ fishing, pêche au ver, *f.* ~wood, *n,* [armoise] absinthe, *f.* ~ oneself into, s'insinuer dans. ~y, *a,* véreux.

worry, *n,* ennui, tourment, tracas, souci, *m.* ¶ *v.t,* ennuyer, tourmenter, tracasser, harceler; (*of dog*) piller.

worse, *a,* pire, plus mauvais; plus mal. (*machine, &c,*) the ~ for wear, patraque, f. & a. ¶ *ad,* pis. grow ~, s'empirer. make ~, empirer.

worship, *n,* culte, *m;* adoration, *f;* office, *m.* your, his, W~, monsieur le juge. ¶ *v.t. & i,* (*God, gods*) adorer; (*saints, relics*) vénérer. **worshipper,** *n,* adorateur, trice.

worst, *a,* pire, plus mauvais, &c. ¶ *ad,* pis. ¶ *n,* pis, pire, *m.* at the ~, au pis aller.

worsted, *n,* laine peignée, estame, *f.*

wort, n, (of beer) moût, m; (plant) herbe, f.

worth, n, valeur, f; prix, m; mérite, m; (money's) pour. ¶ a, qui mérite; digne de. to be ~, valoir; mériter. **~less,** a, sans valeur; misérable; (cheque) sans provision. **~lessness,** n, vileté, f. **~y†,** a, digne.

would, v.aux, is expressed in Fr. by conditional mood. Also by vouloir. ~ to heaven that . . ., plût au ciel que . . . **~-be,** a, soi-disant, inv, prétendu.

wound, n, blessure; plaie, f. ¶ v.t, blesser. the ~ed, les blessés, m.pl.

wove paper, papier vélin, m.

wrack, n, varech, goémon, m.

wrangle, n, querelle, f. ¶ v.i, se quereller, se disputer. **wrangling,** n, tiraillement, m.

wrap, n, sortie (de bal, de bain) f; manteau; tour de cou; châle, m. ~ [up], v.t, envelopper; enrouler; entortiller; ployer. ~ [oneself] up, s'empaqueter, se couvrir. **~-round corset,** corset-ceinture, m. **wrapped sweets,** papillotes, f.pl. **wrapper,** n, enveloppe; chemise; toilette; (newspaper) bande; (cigar) robe, f.

wrath, n, courroux, m, fureur, f. **~ful,** a, courroucé.

wreak, v.t, tirer, prendre (vengeance).

wreath, n, guirlande, couronne; couronne mortuaire, f; (smoke) panache, m. **wreathe,** v.t, enguirlander; ceindre.

wreck, n, naufrage; sinistre; délabrement, m. **~[age],** n, débris, m.pl, épave, f, bris, m. **wreck,** v.t, causer le naufrage de; saboter (a train = la voie ferrée); bouleverser. to be ~ed, faire naufrage.

wren, n, roitelet, m.

wrench, n, (Med.) entorse, foulure; (twist) pesée; (tool) clef, f, tourne-à-gauche; (fig.) crève-cœur, m. ¶ v.t, fouler, bistourner. ~ open, forcer.

wrest, v.t, tordre; arracher.

wrestle, v.i, lutter. **wrestler,** n, lutteur, m. **wrestling,** n, lutte, f. ~ match, match de lutte, m.

wretch, n, malheureux, euse, misérable, m,f, hère, m. **~ed,** a, malheureux, misérable; pitoyable, méchant, piètre; **~edness,** n, misère, f.

wrick, v.t, effort, m. to ~ one's back, se donner un effort.

wriggle, v.i, s'agiter, frétiller, se débattre.

wring, v.t.ir, tordre; étreindre, serrer; arracher; extorquer; (linen) essorer. **~er,** n, essoreuse, f. ~ing wet, mouillé à tordre.

wrinkle, n, ride, f, pli, sillon; (tip) tuyau; (how to do something) tour de main, m. ¶ v.t, rider, sillonner, plisser.

wrist, n, poignet, m. **~band,** poignet, m, brisure, f. ~ strap, bracelet de force, m. **~[let] watch,** montre de poignet, f. **~let,** n, bracelet, m.

writ, n, exploit; mandat, m; assignation, f.

write, v.t. & i. ir, écrire; inscrire; rédiger. ~ back, répondre; (Bkkpg) contrepasser.

~ for (journal), écrire dans, collaborer à. ~ off, amortir. ~ out, tracer; rédiger; formuler. **writer,** n, écrivain; auteur, m.

writhe, v.i, se tordre, se tortiller.

writing, n, écriture, f; écrit, m; inscription, f. ~ case, papeterie, f. ~ desk, table, bureau, secrétaire, m. ~ ink, encre à écrire, f. ~ materials, de quoi écrire. ~ pad, bloc-notes, bloc de correspondance, m. **written,** p.p, par écrit, manuscrit.

wrong, a, faux; mauvais; mal; erroné; inexact. **~ fount,** lettre d'un autre œil, f. ~ side (fabric), envers, dessous, m. ~ side up, sens dessus dessous. the ~ way, ad, à rebours; à contresens; à contre-poil, à rebrousse-poil. ¶ ad, mal; de travers. ¶ n, mal; tort, préjudice, m. ¶ v.t, faire [du] tort à, léser, maltraiter, nuire à. **~ful†,** a, injuste. **~ly,** ad, à tort; à faux.

wrought iron, fer [forgé] m.

wry, a, (neck) tors; (smile) pincé. ~ face, grimace, f. **~neck** (bird), torcol, m. **~ness,** n, guingois, m.

wych-elm, n, orme de montagne, m.

X

Xmas, abb. See Christmas.

X-rays, n.pl, rayons X, m.pl.

xylonite, n, celluloïd, m.

xylophone, n, xylophone, m.

Y

yacht, n, yacht, m. **~ing,** n, promenade en yacht, f.

yam, n, igname, f.

yap, v.i, glapir, japper.

yard, n, cour, f; parc, chantier, m; (Naut.) vergue, f; Meas. = 0·914399 metre. ~ arm, bout de vergue, m.

yarn, n, (thread) fil, m; (tale) histoire, f.

yarrow, n, mille-feuille, millefeuille, f.

yaw, n, embardée, f. ¶ v.i, faire une e.

yawl, n, yole, f.

yawn, v.i, bâiller. **~ing,** a, béant.

ye, pn, vous.

yean, v.i, agneler.

year, n, année, f; an; (Fin.) exercice, m. ~ book, annuaire, m. ~s of discretion, l'âge de raison, m. **~ly,** a, annuel; (ad.) annuellement.

yearn for, soupirer après. **yearning,** n, aspiration, f; élancements, m.pl.

yeast, n, levure, f, levain, m.

yell, n, hurlement, m. ¶ v.i, hurler.

yellow, a. & n, jaune, a. & m. the ~ races, les races jaunes, f.pl, les jaunes, m.pl. Y~ sea, mer Jaune, f. ¶ v.t. & i, jaunir. **~ish,** a, jaunâtre.

yelp, v.i, glapir, japper.

yes, particle, oui; si. ¶ n, oui, m.

yesterday, n, hier, m. *yester year,* antan, m.
yet, c, cependant, toutefois, pourtant. ¶ ad,
encore.
yew [tree], n, if, m.
yield, n, rendement, rapport, m. ¶ v.t, rendre,
rapporter; (v.i.) céder; obéir; succomber.
yoke, n, joug, m; paire, couple, f, attelage, m;
(for pail) palanche, f; (of bell) mouton;
(dress) empiècement, m, épaulette, f. ~
elm, charmille, f. ¶ v.t, atteler.
yokel, n, rustre, m.
yolk, n, jaune (d'œuf) m.
yonder, a, ce . . . -là. ¶ ad, là-bas.
yore (of), d'autrefois, jadis.
you, pn, vous, tu; on.
young, a, jeune; petit. ~ lady, demoiselle,
jeune personne, f. ~ one, petit, e.
¶ (animals) n, petits, m.pl. ~er, a, [plus]
jeune, cadet. ~ brother, sister, puîné, e.
to make look ~, rajeunir. ~ster, n,
gamin, moutard, m, môme, m,f.
your, a, votre, vos; ton, ta, tes. **yours,** pn.
& **your own,** le vôtre, la vôtre, les vôtres;
à vous; de vous. ~ affectionately, votre
affectionné, e. ~ faithfully, ~ truly,
agréez (ou recevez), monsieur, mes salutations empressées. ~ very truly, tout à
vous, bien à vous. **yourself, yourselves,**
pn, vous-même, vous-mêmes; vous.
youth, n, jeunesse; adolescence, f; jeune

homme, adolescent, m. ~ful†, a, jeune;
juvénile; de jeunesse.
yule[tide], n, Noël, m, la [fête de] Noël.
yule log, bûche de Noël, f.

Z

zeal, n, zèle, m. **zealot,** n, zélateur, trice.
zealous, a, zélé, empressé. ~ly, ad, avec
zèle.
zebra, n, zèbre, m.
zenith, n, zénith; (fig.) zénith, faîte, apogée, m.
zephyr, n, zéphyr; (vest) maillot, m.
Zeppelin, n, zeppelin, m.
zero, n, zéro, m. See centigrade Fr.-Eng.
zest, n, piquant, m; ardeur, f.
zigzag, n, zigzag, m. ¶ v.i, aller en zigzag.
zinc, n, zinc, m. ~ worker, zingueur, m.
zincography, n, zincogravure, f.
zip[p] fastener, fermeture instantanée, f,
fermoir à curseur, m.
zircon, n, zircon, m.
zither, n, cithare, f.
zodiac, n, zodiaque, m. ~al, a, zodiacal.
zone, n, zone, f.
zoological, a, zoologique. **zoologist,** n,
zoologiste, m,f. **zoology,** n, zoologie, f.
Zulu, a, zoulou. ¶ n, Zoulou, m,f.
Zuyder Zee (the), le Zuyderzée.

ENGLISH IRREGULAR VERBS

Except as otherwise stated, order of parts is
   (1) Infinitive (*i.*) & Present (*pr.*);
   (2) Past (*p.*);
   (3) Past Participle (*p.p.*).

Prefixed verbs not included in the list, such as **arise, regild**, follow the second or last element (**rise, gild**).

abide; *p. & p.p.* abode *sometimes* abided.
awake; awoke; awoke, awaked.
i. **be;** *pr. indicative* am, art, is, *pl.* are; *pr. ind.* was, wast *or* wert, was, *pl.* were; *pr. subjunctive* be; *p. subj.* were *except 2 sing.* wert; *imperative* be; *p.pr.* being; *p.p.* been. *Contractions:* 'm = am, 's = is, 're = are.
bear; bore; borne. *When referring to birth* born & borne, *e.g.* born 19—; has borne a child; born of, borne by, woman.
beat; beat; beaten *sometimes* beat.
beget; begot; begotten.
begin; began; begun.
bend; bent; bent.
bereave; *p. & p.p.* bereaved *or* bereft.
beseech; besought; besought.
bespeak; bespoke; bespoke, -spoken.
bestride; bestrode; bestridden, bestrid, bestrode.
bid; bad, bade, bid; bidden, bid.
bind; bound; bound.
bite; bit; bitten *sometimes* bit.
bleed; bled; bled.
blend; *p. & p.p.* blended *or* blent.
blow; blew; blown.
break; broke; broken *sometimes* broke.
breed; bred; bred.
bring; brought; brought.
build; built; built.
burn; *p. & p.p.* burnt *sometimes* burned.
burst; burst; burst.
buy; bought; bought.
can.—*pr.* I, he, &c, can, thou canst. *neg.* cannot, can't. *p. & conditional,* I, he, &c, could, thou could[e]st. *i., p.pr. & p.p.* wanting; *defective parts supplied from* be able to.
cast; cast; cast.
catch; caught; caught.
chide; chid; chidden *or* chid.
choose; chose; chosen.
cleave; clove *or* cleft; cloven *or* cleft.
cling; clung; clung.
clothe; *p. & p.p.* clothed *or* clad.
come; came; come.
cost; cost; cost.
could. See **can.**

creep; crept; crept.
crow; crew *or* crowed; crowed.
cut; cut; cut.
dare; dared & durst; dared.
deal; dealt; dealt.
die; died; *p.pr.* dying; *p.p.* died.
dig; dug; dug.
i. **do;** *pr. indicative* do, doest (*as auxiliary* dost), does, *pl.* do; *p.* did, didst, did, *pl.* did; *p.p.* done. *Contractions:* don't = do not. doesn't = does not. didn't = did not.
draw; drew; drawn.
dream; *p. & p.p.* dreamt *or* dreamed.
drink; drank; drunk.
drive; drove; driven.
dwell; dwelt; dwelt.
eat; ate *or* eat; eaten.
fall; fell; fallen.
feed; fed; fed.
feel; felt; felt.
fight; fought; fought.
find; found; found.
flee; fled; fled.
fling; flung; flung.
fly; flew; flown.
forbear; forbore; forborne.
forbid; forbad *or* -bade; forbidden.
forget; forgot; forgotten.
forsake; forsook; forsaken.
freeze; froze; frozen.
get; got; got, *also* -gotten *in combination as* ill-gotten.
gild; *p. & p.p.* gilded & gilt.
gird; *p. & p.p.* girt & *poet.* girded.
give; gave; given.
go; *pr.* I go, thou goest, he goes, we, &c, go; *p.* went; *p.p.* gone.
grave; graved; graven & graved.
grind; ground; ground.
grow; grew; grown.
hang; *p. & p.p.* hung & hanged.
i. **have;** *pr.* I have, *archaic* thou hast, he has, we, you, they, have; *p.* had, *archaic* thou hadst; *p.p.* had; *abb.* I've, we've, &c; I'd, we'd, &c; 's = has; *colloquially neg.* haven't, hasn't; hadn't.
hear; heard; heard.
heave; *p. & p.p.* heaved *or* hove.
hew; hewed; hewn *or* hewed.
hide; hid; hidden & hid.
hit; hit; hit.
hold; held; held.
hurt; hurt; hurt.
inset; *p. & p.p.* inset *or* insetted.
keep; kept; kept.
kneel; knelt; knelt.
knit; *p. & p.p.* knitted *or* knit.

know; knew; known.
lade; laded; laden.
lay; laid; laid.
lead; led; led.
lean; *p. & p.p.* leaned *or* leant.
leap; *p. & p.p.* leapt *or* leaped.
learn; *p. & p.p.* learnt, learned.
leave; left; left.
lend; lent; lent.
let; let; let.
lie; lay; *p.pr.* lying; *p.p.* lain.
light; *p. & p.p.* lit *or* lighted.
lose; lost; lost.
make; made; made.
pr. I may, he may; *p.* might.
mean; meant; meant.
meet; met; met.
melt; melted; melted, molten.
mow; mowed; mown.
pr. I must, he must; *p.* must.
pr. ought; *p.* ought.
outbid; outbid *or* -bade; outbid *or* -bidden.
overhang; overhung; overhung.
pay; paid; paid.
put; put; put.
read; read; read.
reeve; *p. & p.p.* rove *or* reeved.
rend; rent; rent.
rid; ridded, rid; rid.
ride; rode; ridden.
ring; rang; rung.
rise; rose; risen.
rive; rived; riven.
run; ran; run.
saw; sawed; sawn.
say; said; said.
see; saw; seen.
seek; sought; sought.
sell; sold; sold.
send; sent; sent.
set; set; set.
sew; sewed; sewed *or* sewn.
shake; shook; shaken.
pr. I shall, thou shalt, he, &c, shall; *p. & conditional* I should, thou should[e]st, he, &c, should; *neg.* shall not *or* shan't; should not *or* shouldn't.
shear; sheared; shorn.
shed; shed; shed.
shew; shewed; shewn.
shine; shone; shone.
shoe; shod; shod.
shoot; shot; shot.
should. See *shall.*
show; showed; shown.
shrink; shrank; shrunk.
shut; shut; shut.
sing; sang; sung.
sink; sank; sunk.

sit; sat; sat.
slay; slew; slain.
sleep; slept; slept.
slide; slid; slid.
sling; slung; slung.
slink; slunk; slunk.
slit; slit; slit.
smell; smelt; smelt.
smite; smote; smitten.
sow; sowed; sown *or* sowed.
speak; spoke; spoken.
speed; sped; sped.
spell; *p. & p.p.* spelt *or* spelled.
spend; spent; spent.
spill; *p. & p.p.* spilt *or* spilled.
spin; spun *or* span; spun.
spit; spat; spat.
split; split; split.
spread; spread; spread.
spring; sprang; sprung.
stand; stood; stood.
stave; *p. & p.p.* staved *or* stove.
steal; stole; stolen.
stick; stuck; stuck.
sting; stung; stung.
stink; stank *or* stunk; stunk.
strew; strewed; strewn, strewed.
stride; strode; (*rare*) stridden *or* strid.
strike; struck; struck & stricken.
string; strung; strung.
strive; strove; striven.
swear; swore; sworn.
sweep; swept; swept.
swell; swelled; swollen.
swim; swam; swum.
swing; swung; swung.
take; took; taken.
teach; taught; taught.
tear; tore; torn.
tell; told; told.
think; thought; thought.
thrive; throve; thriven.
throw; threw; thrown.
thrust; thrust; thrust.
tie; tied; *p.pr.* tying; *p.p.* tied.
tread; trod; trodden.
wake; woke, waked; waked, woken, woke.
wear; wore; worn.
weave; wove; woven & wove.
weep; wept; wept.
pr. I, he, &c, will *or* 'll, thou wilt *or* 'lt; *p. & conditional* I, he, &c, would *or* 'd, thou would[e]st *or* 'dst; *neg.* will not *or* won't; would not *or* wouldn't *or* 'd not.
win; won; won.
wind; wound; wound.
would. See *will.*
wring; wrung; wrung.
write; wrote; written.

PHONETICS OF CERTAIN PLACE NAMES
WHOSE PRONUNCIATION IN FRENCH PRESENTS SOME PECULIARITY OR DIFFICULTY

The English spelling is added in [brackets] where it differs from the French.

Abruzzes (abry:z).
Aden (adɛn).
Ain (ɛ̃).
Aisne (ɛn).
Aix (ɛks).
Alger (alʒe) [Algiers].
Allier (alje).
Alsace (alzas).
Amiens (amjɛ̃).
Amsterdam (amstɛrdam).
Andes (ã:d).
Angers (ãʒe).
Annam (annam).
Anvers (ãvɛ:r ou ãvɛrs) [Antwerp].
Arras (ara:s).
Asnières (anjɛ:r).
Assam (asam).
Atlas (atla:s).
Aurillac (ɔrijak).
Auxerre (osɛ:r).
Auxonne (osɔn).
Avesnes (avɛn).
Bassam (basam).
Bazas (bazas).
Beaumesnil (bomenil).
Belley (bɛlɛ).
Bénarès (benarɛ:s) [Benares].
Bengale (bɛ̃gal) [Bengal].
Berber (bɛrbɛ:r).
Bergen (bɛrgɛn).
Be[h]ring (berɛ̃g).
Béziers (bezje).
Billom (bijɔ̃).
Bitche (bitʃ).
Bois-d'Oingt (bwɑdwɛ̃).
Bombay (bɔ̃bɛ).
Boom (bo:m).
Boos (bo:s).
Borgerhout (bɔrʒerut).
Bourg (bu:r ou burk).
Braine-l'Alleud (brɛnlalø).
Braisne (brɛn).
Brécey (brɛse).
Breil (brɛ:j).
Brenner (brɛnɛ:r).
Breslau (brɛslo).
Bresle (brɛl).
Brest (brɛst).
Briec (briɛk).
Briey (briji ou brie).
Broons (brɔ̃).
Bruxelles (brysɛl) [Brussels].
Bucarest (bykarɛst).
Budapest (bydapɛst).

Buenos-Ayres (byɛnozɛ:r ou buɛnosa:jrɛs) [Buenos Ayres].
Buxy (bysi).
Cadix (kadiks) [Cadiz].
Caen (kɑ̃).
Calvados (kalvadɔs).
Cenis (sɛni).
Ceuta (søta).
Ceylan (sɛlɑ̃) [Ceylon].
Chablis (ʃabli).
Chamonix (ʃamoni).
Château-Yquem (ʃatoikɛm).
Chemnitz (kɛmnits).
Cher (ʃɛr).
Cherbourg (ʃɛrbu:r).
Chiers (ʃjɛ:r).
Condom (kɔ̃dɔ̃).
Cos (kɔs).
Coutras (kutra).
Craon (krɑ̃).
Craonne (krɑ:n).
Creusot (krøzo).
Croatie (kroasi) [Croatia].
Curaçao (kyraso).
Dahomey (daɔmɛ).
Dalmatie (dalmasi) [Dalmatia].
Damas (damɑ) [Damascus].
Davos (davɔs).
Doubs (du).
Eecloo (eklo).
Elven (ɛlvɛ).
Emden (ɛmdɛn).
Enghien (ãgɛ̃).
Essen (ɛsɛn).
Étaples (etapl).
Eupen (øpɛn).
Euphrate (øfrat) [Euphrates].
Fès (fɛ:s).
Finlande (fɛ̃lã:d) [Finland].
Flers (flɛ:r).
Francfort (frãkfɔ:r) [Frankfort].
Fréjus (freʒy:s).
Fribourg (fribu:r) [See p. 115].
Gambie (gãbi) [Gambia].
Gap (gap).
Ger (ʒɛr).
Gers (ʒɛ:r).
Gex (ʒɛks).
Gisors (ʒizɔ:r).
Groenland (grɔɛlã[:d]) [Greenland].

Guiers (gje).
Guil (gil).
Guise (gɥi:z ou gi:z).
Hainaut (ɛno).
Ham (am).
Hambourg (ãbu:r) [Hamburg].
Hawaï (avai) [Hawaii].
Haye (ɛ) [Hague].
Hazebrouck (azbruk).
Hendaye (ãdaj).
Hérault (ero).
Hesdin (edɛ̃).
Hilversum (ilvɛrsɔm).
Hombourg (ɔ̃bu:r) [Homburg].
Honduras (ɔ̃dyra:s).
Hong-Kong (ɔ̃kɔ̃).
Huisne (ɥin).
Huy (ɥi).
Iéna (jena) [Jena].
Indus (ɛ̃dy:s).
Inn (in).
Innsbruck (insbryk).
Interlaken (ɛ̃tɛrlakɛn).
Islande (islã:d) [Iceland].
Jérusalem (ʒeryzalɛm) [Jerusalem].
Jutland (ʒytlã).
Laeken (lakɛn).
Lagos (lagɔs).
Laon (lã).
Léman (lemã) [Leman].
Lemnos (lɛmnɔs).
Lens (lã:s).
Leyde (lɛd) [Leyden].
Liban (libã) [Lebanon].
Lons-le-Saunier (lɔ̃sləsonje).
Loos (los).
Lot (lɔt).
Louhans (luã).
Luxembourg (grand-duché) (lyksãbu:r) [Luxemburg].
Luz (lyz).
Madras (madra:s).
Magenta (maʒɛ̃ta).
Mamers (mamɛ:r).
Mandchourie (mãtʃuri) [Manchuria].
Mans (mã).
Marans (marã).
Marengo (marɛ̃go).
Maurice (mɔris) [Mauritius].
Mein ou Main (mɛ̃) [Main].
Memphis (mɛ̃fis).

Mens (mã:s).
Metz (mɛs).
Milan (milã).
Millau *ou* Milhau (mijo).
Mons (mõ:s).
Montargis (mõtarʒi).
Montauban (mõtobã).
Montivilliers (mõtivilje).
Montpellier (mõpɛlje).
Montréal (mõreal) [Montreal].
Montserrat (mõsera).
Morcenx (mɔrsɛ̃:s).
Mozambique (mɔzãbik).
Mulhouse (mylu:z) [Mulhouse *or* Mülhausen].
Munich (mynik).
Mysore (miso:r).
Nangis (nãʒi).
Nankin (nãkɛ̃).
Naples (napl).
Neuchâtel (nøʃatɛl).
Neufchâteau (nøʃato).
Neufchâtel (nøʃatɛl).
Neuilly (nœji).
Nevers (nəvɛ:r).
New-York (nœjɔrk) [New York].
Niger (niʒe:r).
Niort (njɔ:r).
Nuremberg (nyrɛ̃bɛ:r).
Oder (ɔde:r).
Oran (ɔrã).
Orléans (ɔrleã) [Orleans].
Ostende (ɔstã:d) [Ostend].
Ouessant (wesã) [Ushant].
Ourcq (urk).
Palestine (palɛstin).
Palmas (palma:s).
Pamiers (pamje).
Paraguay (parag[w]ɛ).
Paris (pari).
Paros (parɔs).
Patras (patra:s).
Pau (po).
Pékin (pekɛ̃) [Pekin].
Pendjab (pɛ̃dʒab) [Punjab].
Périers (perje).
Périm (perim) [Perim].
Pézenas (pezəna:s).
Pilsen (pilsɛn).
Pleyben (plɛbɛ̃).
Plouescat (pluɛska).
Plougastel-Daoulas (plugastɛldaula:s).
Plouguenast (plugənast).
Poitiers (pwatje).
Pompéi (põpei) [Pompeii].
Pons (põ:s).
Pontarlier (põtarlje).
Pont-Audemer (põtodmɛ:r).

Pont-Aven (põtavɛn).
Port-Arthur (pɔrarty:r) [Port Arthur].
Posen (pozɛn).
Potsdam (pɔtsdam).
Privas (priva).
Provins (provɛ̃).
Puy (pɥi).
Quesnoy (kenwa).
Questembert (kɛstãbɛ:r).
Quimper (kɛ̃pɛ:r).
Rabastens (rabastɛ̃:s).
Raismes (rɛ:m).
Rambervillers (rãbɛrvile).
Rambouillet (rãbuje).
Reims (rɛ̃:s) [Rheims].
Renwez (rãve).
Retiers (rətje).
Rhodes (rɔd).
Riez (rjɛ:z).
Riom (rjõ).
Rive-de-Gier (rivdəʒje).
Roanne (rwan).
Rochefoucauld (rɔʃfuko).
Rombas (rõba).
Rome (rɔm).
Rotterdam (rɔtɛrdam).
Rouen (rwã).
Roulers (rulɛrs).
Royan (rwajã).
Saigon (saigõ) [Saigon].
Saint-Brieuc (sɛ̃brjø).
Saint-Cloud (sɛ̃klu).
Saint-Cyr (sɛ̃si:r).
Saint-Denis (sɛ̃dəni).
Saint-Gall (sɛ̃gal).
Saint-Gilles (sɛ̃ʒil).
Saint-Nicolas (sɛ̃nikɔla).
Saint-Omer (sɛ̃tɔmɛ:r).
Saint-Ouen (sɛ̃twɛ̃).
Saint-Saëns (sɛ̃sã:s).
Saint-Thomas (sɛ̃tɔma).
Salzbourg (salzbu:r) [Salzburg].
Samarang (samarã).
Samos (samɔs).
Santander (sãtãdɛ:r).
Santos (sãtɔs).
Saône (so:n).
Sarrebruck (sarbryk) [Saarbruck *or* Saarbrücken].
Sault (so).
Schaffhouse (ʃafu:z) [Schaffhausen].
Schiedam (skiɛdam).
Schwy[t]z (ʃvits).
Sedan (sədã).
Senlis (sãlis).
Sens (sã:s).
Seraing (sərɛ̃).
Shanghaï (ʃãgai) [Shanghai].

Siam (sjam).
Sillery (sijri).
Simplon (sɛ̃plõ).
Singapour (sɛ̃gapu:r) [Singapore].
Sorrente (sɔrã:t) [Sorrento].
Soudan (sudã).
Stavanger (stavãʒe:r).
Stenay (stəne).
Stettin (stetɛ̃).
Stockholm (stɔkɔlm).
Strasbourg (strazbu:r) [Strasburg].
Suez (sɥɛ:z).
Suresnes (syrɛn).
Tanger (tãʒe) [Tangier *or* Tangiers].
Taunus (tony:s).
Taurus (tory:s).
Ténédos (tenedɔs) [Tenedos].
Tessin (tɛsɛ̃) [Ticino].
Thiers (tjɛ:r).
Thuringe (tyrɛ̃:ʒ) [Thuringia].
Tibet (tibɛ).
Tiflis (tiflis).
Timgad (tɛ̃gad).
Tlemcen (tlɛmsɛn).
Tombouctou (tõbuktu) [Timbuktu *or* Timbuctoo].
Tonkin (tõkɛ̃).
Touggourt (tugurt).
Toul (tul).
Tourcoing (turkwɛ̃).
Tours (tu:r).
Tunis (tynis).
Tunisie (tynizi) [Tunis *or* Tunisia].
Turin (tyrɛ̃).
Turkestan (tyrkɛstã).
Turnhout (tyrnut).
Uruguay (yryg[w]ɛ).
Uzès (yzɛ:s).
Valparaiso (valparezo).
Verviers (vɛrvje).
Vésuve (vezy:v) [Vesuvius].
Vevey (vəvɛ).
Viborg (vibɔ:r).
Vierzon (vjɛrzõ).
Villach (vilak).
Wagram (vagram).
Waterloo (vatɛrlo).
Weser (vezɛ:r).
Wiesbaden (visbadɛn).
Wurtemberg (vyrtɛ̃bɛ:r).
Ypres (ipr).
Yser (ize:r).
Zeebrugge (zebryg).
Zug (zyg).
Zurich (zyrik).
Zuyderzée (zɥidɛrze) [Zuyder Zee].

The phonetics of many other geographical names whose pronunciation presents no peculiarity will be found in their alphabetical places in the dictionary.

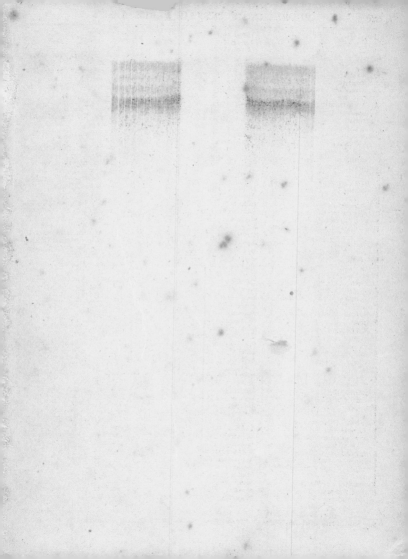